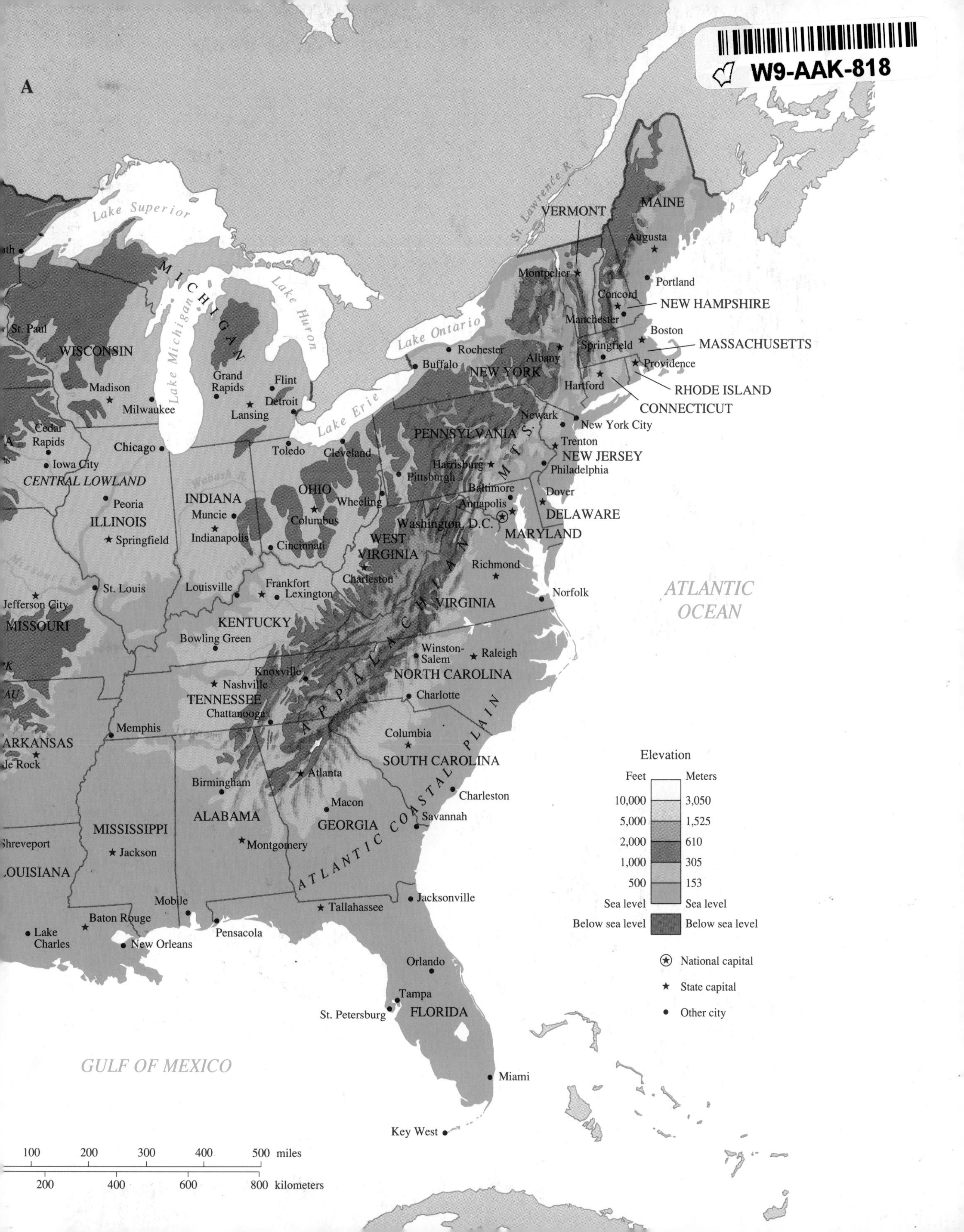
A
Lake Superior
Lake Michigan
Lake Huron
Lake Ontario
Lake Erie
St. Lawrence R.
Wabash R.
Missouri R.
Ohio
MICHIGAN
WISCONSIN
MINNESOTA
St. Paul
Madison
Milwaukee
Grand Rapids
Flint
Lansing
Detroit
Cedar Rapids
Iowa City
CENTRAL LOWLAND
Chicago
Peoria
ILLINOIS
Springfield
INDIANA
Muncie
Indianapolis
Toledo
Cleveland
OHIO
Columbus
Cincinnati
Wheeling
St. Louis
Jefferson City
MISSOURI
Louisville
Frankfort
Lexington
KENTUCKY
Bowling Green
Nashville
Knoxville
TENNESSEE
Chattanooga
Memphis
ARKANSAS
Little Rock
MISSISSIPPI
Jackson
Shreveport
LOUISIANA
Baton Rouge
Lake Charles
New Orleans
Mobile
Pensacola
Birmingham
ALABAMA
Montgomery
Atlanta
Macon
GEORGIA
Savannah
Tallahassee
Jacksonville
Orlando
Tampa
St. Petersburg
FLORIDA
Miami
Key West
GULF OF MEXICO
Columbia
SOUTH CAROLINA
Charleston
Charlotte
Winston-Salem
Raleigh
NORTH CAROLINA
Richmond
Norfolk
VIRGINIA
WEST VIRGINIA
Charleston
Washington, D.C.
Annapolis
Baltimore
MARYLAND
Dover
DELAWARE
Philadelphia
Harrisburg
Pittsburgh
PENNSYLVANIA
Trenton
NEW JERSEY
Newark
New York City
NEW YORK
Buffalo
Rochester
Albany
Hartford
CONNECTICUT
Providence
RHODE ISLAND
Springfield
Boston
MASSACHUSETTS
Manchester
Concord
NEW HAMPSHIRE
Montpelier
VERMONT
Portland
Augusta
MAINE
APPALACHIAN MTS.
ATLANTIC COASTAL PLAIN
ATLANTIC OCEAN
Elevation
Feet
Meters
10,000
3,050
5,000
1,525
2,000
610
1,000
305
500
153
Sea level
Sea level
Below sea level
Below sea level
National capital
State capital
Other city
100
200
300
400
500 miles
200
400
600
800 kilometers

Making America

A History of the United States

Making America

A History of the United States

Second Edition

Carol Berkin
Baruch College, City University of New York

Christopher L. Miller
The University of Texas—Pan American

Robert W. Cherny
San Francisco State University

James L. Gormly
Washington and Jefferson College

HOUGHTON MIFFLIN COMPANY
Boston New York

Associate Sponsoring Editor: Colleen Shanley Kyle
Senior Project Editor: Carol Newman
Senior Production/Design Coordinator: Jill Haber
Senior Manufacturing Coordinator: Florence Cadran
Marketing Manager: Sandra McGuire

Cover design: Diana Coe.

Cover photo research: Linda Sykes.

Cover image: *Building the Bridge,* 1918, painting by Claire Shuttleworth. Private Collection, Buffalo, NY.

Text photo research: Pembroke Herbert and Sandi Rygiel/ Picture Research Consultants.

Printed in the U.S.A.

Library of Congress Catalog Card Number: 98-71986

ISBN: 0-395-89485-9 (Student Edition)

1 2 3 4 5 6 7 8 9-VH-03 02 01 00 99 98

BRIEF CONTENTS

CONTENTS

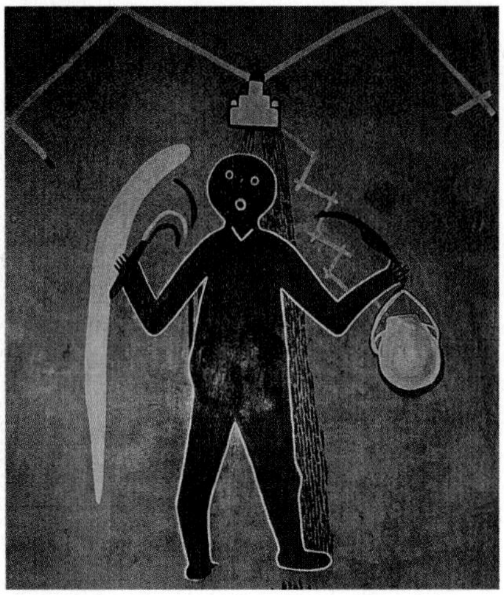

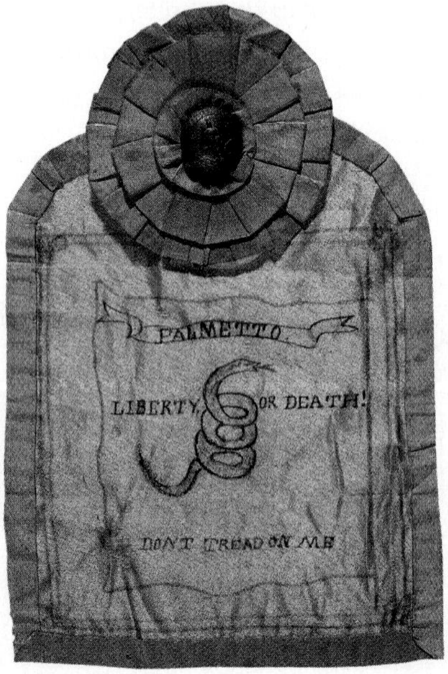
PALMETTO
LIBERTY, OR DEATH!
DON'T TREAD ON ME

DEAN C. WORCESTER ON THE PHILIPPINES
HARPER'S WEEKLY
A JOURNAL OF CIVILIZATION
NEW YORK, SATURDAY, NOVEMBER 18, 1899
U.S. COMMERCIAL EXPANSIONIST
A FAIR FIELD AND NO FAVOR!

A VOTE FOR
DAVIS
&
BRYAN
IS A VOTE
AGAINST
SPECIAL PRIVILEGE·REMEMBER
TEA·POT DOME

MAPS

**Note: Maps listed in boldface type indicate chapter-opening maps.*

FEATURES

Individual Choices

Making History

Chronologies

Figures

Tables

PREFACE

On a snowy day in January 1998, on the last day of the semester, a student approached one of the authors of *Making America*. Putting out his hand, he shook hers and then rather shyly said: "Thanks for the life preserver." Seeing she was a little puzzled, he laughed. "You know," he said, "*Making America*—the book that rescued me from drowning in the sea of history."

As the authors of *Making America*, we take considerable satisfaction in this young man's endorsement. From the beginning, our goal has been to create a different kind of textbook, one suited to the modern college classroom—with its rich cultural diversity, its mixture of native-born Americans and recent immigrants, and its significant number of serious-minded men and women whose formal skills lagged behind their interest and enthusiasm for learning. As professors in large public universities located on three of the nation's borders—the Pacific Ocean, the Atlantic, and the Rio Grande—we knew the basic elements needed in such a survey text: a historical narrative that did not demand a lot of prior knowledge about the American past; information organized sequentially, or chronologically, so that students were not confused by too many topical digressions; and a full array of integrated and supportive learning aids to help students at every level of preparedness comprehend and retain what they read.

The first edition of *Making America* was an account of the American past firmly anchored by a political chronology framing the many centuries under discussion. In it, people and places were brought to life not only through words but also with maps, paintings, and photos. We made a genuine effort to communicate with students rather than to impress them. And *Making America* presented history as a dynamic process shaped by human expectations, difficult choices, and often surprising consequences. With this focus on history as a process, *Making America* encouraged students to think historically and to develop into citizens who value the past.

Yet, as veteran teachers, we the authors of *Making America* knew that any history project, no matter how good, could be improved. Having scrawled "Revise" across the top of student papers for several decades, we decided to impose the same demands on ourselves. As we worked on this revised edition of the text, we were guided by suggestions from professors and students across the country who had used the first edition of *Making America*.

The Approach

Professors and students who have used the first edition of *Making America* will recognize immediately that we have preserved many of its central features. We have again set the nation's remarkable and complex story within an explicit political chronology, relying on a basic and familiar structure that is broad enough to accommodate generous attention to social, economic, and diplomatic aspects of our national history. We remain confident that this political framework allows us to integrate the experiences of all Americans into a meaningful and effective narrative of our nation's development. Because our own scholarly research often focuses on these very topics, we would not have been content with a framework that excluded or marginalized that history. *Making America* continues to be built on the premise that all Americans are historically active figures, playing significant roles in creating the history that we and other authors narrate.

Once again, we have infused the text with the perception of history as a dynamic process resulting from the decisions and actions of all women and men in our American past. Thus, our second edition continues the tradition of ECCO, our acronym for four fundamental aspects of the historical process: expectations, constraints, choices, and outcomes. In each chapter, *Making America* examines the variety of *expectations* people held about their futures; the *constraints* of time, place, and multiple social and economic factors that these historical figures faced; the *choices* they made, given the circumstances of their lives; and the expected and unexpected *outcomes* flowing from their decisions. In this revised edition, we have chosen to retain ECCO as an explicit device in each chapter introduction and summary but have made it implicit within the chapter narrative, allowing students to recognize the dynamic ECCO elements as providing an underlying structure and organizing principle rather than as a surface device.

Themes

This edition continues to thread five central themes through the *Making America* narrative. The first of these themes, the political development of the nation, is evident in the text's coverage of the creation and revision of the federal and local governments, the contests waged over domestic and diplomatic policies, the internal and external crises faced by the United States and its political institutions, and the history of political parties. The second theme is the diversity of a national citizenry created by immigrants. To do justice to this theme, *Making America* explores not only English and European immigration but immigrant communities from Paleolithic times to the present. The text attends to the tensions and conflicts that arise in a diverse population, but it also examines the shared values and aspirations that define the majority of ordinary, middle-class American lives.

Making America's third theme is the significance of regional economies and cultures. This regional theme is developed for society before European colonization and for the colonial settlements of the seventeenth and eighteenth centuries. It is evident in our attention to the striking social and cultural divergences that existed between the American Southwest and the Atlantic coastal regions as well as between the antebellum South and North. A fourth theme is the rise and impact of large social movements, from the Great Awakening in the 1740s to the rise of youth cultures in the post–World War II generations, prompted by changing material conditions or by new ideas challenging the status quo.

The fifth theme is the relationship of the United States to other nations. In *Making America* we explore in depth the causes and consequences of this nation's role in world conflict and diplomacy, whether in the era of colonization of the Americas, the eighteenth-century independence movement, the removal of Indian nations from the their traditional lands, the impact of the rhetoric of manifest destiny, American policies of isolationism and interventionism, or in the modern role of the United States as a dominant player in world affairs.

Learning Features

The chapters in *Making America* follow a format that provides students essential study aids for mastering the historical material. Each chapter begins with a map that sets the scene for the most significant events and developments in the narrative that follows. Accompanying the map is a chronological chart of these significant events and a time line that illustrates where these events fit in a broader time frame. On the chapter-opening page, there is a topical outline of the new material students will encounter in the chapter, along with several new and, we think, thought-provoking critical thinking questions to help students focus on the broad, overarching themes of the chapter. Then, to help students focus on the broad questions and themes, at the beginning of each major chapter section we reintroduce the critical thinking questions.

Each chapter offers an introduction in which we apply the ECCO model to the subject matter the students are about to explore. Each chapter ends with a summary, also structured in accordance with the ECCO model, plus suggestions for further reading on events, movements, or people as well as a selected bibliography at the end of the text citing the best scholarship in the field, old and new.

To ensure that students have full access to the material in each chapter, we provide a page-by-page glossary, defining terms and explaining their historically specific usage the first time they appear in the narrative. This running glossary will help students build their vocabularies and review for tests, and they reflect our concern about communicating fully with student readers without sacrificing the complexity of the history we are relating.

The illustrations in each chapter provide a visual connection to the past, and their captions analyze the subject of the painting, photograph, or artifact and comment on its significance. For this edition we have selected many new illustrations to reinforce or illustrate the themes of the narrative.

Within each chapter is an "Individual Choices" feature, which helps students understand an important point raised in the chapter. The "Individual Choices" provide intimate portraits of famous people such as President Grover Cleveland and the antislavery reformer Frederick Douglass and ordinary people such as the eighteenth-century servant James Revel and the twentieth-century farmers' advocate Milo Reno. By exploring how individuals arrived at decisions that shaped their lives, "Individual Choices" dramatize the fact that historical events are not inevitable but are the result of real people making real choices.

New to This Edition

In this new edition we have preserved what our colleagues and their students considered the best and most useful aspects of the first edition of *Making America*. We also have replaced what was less successful, revised what could be improved, and added new elements to strengthen the book—and we have achieved each of these goals without increasing the length of the text.

A new chapter places the English colonial world and the empire of which it was a part in their broad historical context. Chapter 2, "A Continent on the Move, 1400–1725," prepares students to see the origins of the Anglo-American world in the expansionist ideology of western Europe, to recognize that the colonies were part of a transatlantic community of ideas and policies, and to understand that Indians, Europeans, and the English were all critical players in the development of the seventeenth- and eighteenth-century society that became the United States.

Changes that improve the coverage of content in *Making America* are evident in every chapter. The newest contributions to scholarship in American history have been integrated throughout the text. There is, for example, more coverage of the West throughout the text, and the coverage of the Kennedy and Johnson presidencies has been revised to reflect the insights of the best new work in this field of modern politics and diplomacy. In other chapters, including those on antebellum society, important material has been recast in the preferred chronological form rather than in topical fashion.

This new edition also offers a new feature: "Making History: Using Sources from the Past." This feature encourages students to work with primary documents in order to answer important historical questions. In each "Making History" feature, the student is presented with a brief background statement entitled "The Context." This is followed by the statement of a problem, "The Historical Question." Then students are given "The Challenge" to write an essay or hold a discussion on the challenge question, drawing on knowledge and information that they gain from reading the text and extrapolating from primary sources that accompany the feature. There is no single, correct answer, of course; students will come to different conclusions just as historians do. This feature is flexible enough to provide teachers the opportunity to hone students' essay-writing skills, critical thinking abilities, and understanding of historical methods of inquiry and standards of proof. The historical issue raised in each feature is a significant one and arises from the material covered in the chapters that immediately precede it.

We the authors of *Making America* believe that this new edition will be effective in the history classroom. Please let us know what you think by sending us your views through Houghton Mifflin's American history web site, located at www.hmco.com/college/.

Study and Teaching Aids

A number of useful learning and teaching aids accompany the second edition of *Making America.* They are designed to help students get the most from the course and to provide instructors with some useful teaching tools.

@history: an interactive American history source is a multimedia teaching/learning package that combines a variety of material on a cross-platformed CD-ROM—primary sources (text and graphic), video, and audio—with activities that can be used to analyze, interpret, and discuss primary sources; to enhance collaborative learning; and to create multimedia lecture presentations. @history also has an accompanying web site, located at www.hmco.com/college/, where additional primary sources, online resources for *Making America,* and links to relevant sites can be found.

The ***two-volume Study Guide,*** written by Eli Faber of John Jay College of Criminal Justice, provides students with many review exercises and tips on how to study and take tests effectively. Each chapter includes learning objectives, an annotated outline of the chapter, and approximately twenty-five key terms, concepts, and people. The fifteen multiple-choice questions per chapter include a text-page reference and a rejoinder for all answers. Also included in each chapter are three to five essay questions with answer guidelines, one question based on analysis of a primary source, and one map exercise.

An ***On-line Study Guide*** is also available for students. Accessible through Houghton Mifflin's

@history web site (www.hmco.com/college/), it functions as a tutorial, providing rejoinders to all multiple-choice questions that explain why the student's response is or is not correct.

The ***Instructor's Resource Manual,*** prepared by Kelly Woestman of Pittsburgh State University, includes for every chapter instructional objectives that are drawn from the textbook's critical thinking questions, a chapter summary and annotated outline, and three lecture topics that include resource material and references to the text. Each chapter also includes discussion questions, answers to the critical thinking questions that follow each major heading in the text, cooperative and individual learning activities, map activities, ideas for paper topics, and a list of audiovisual resources.

A ***Test Items*** file, prepared by the late Bill Cecil-Fronsman, formerly of Washburn University, provides twenty key terms and definitions, forty to fifty multiple-choice questions, five to ten essay questions with answer guidelines, and an analytical exercise to test critical thinking skills.

A ***Computerized Test Items File*** is available for IBM PC or compatible and Macintosh computers. This computerized version of the printed Test Items file allows professors to create customized tests by editing and adding questions.

A set of over 150 full-color ***American History Map Transparencies*** is available in two-volume sets upon adoption.

A variety of ***videos***, documentaries and docudramas by major film producers, is available for use with *Making America.*

Please contact your local Houghton Mifflin representative for more information about the ancillary items or to obtain desk copies.

Acknowledgments

We the authors have benefited from the critical reading of *Making America* through two editions. We would like to thank the following instructors, who helped us with the second edition:

James Brooks, University of Maryland

Barry A. Crouch, Gallaudet University

James T. Gay, State University of West Georgia

Emily Greenwald, University of Nebraska

Perry Kaufman, Burlington County College

Janet Lindman, Rowan College

Roberta McCutcheon, University of Alaska

Samuel T. McSeveney, Vanderbilt University

Carl H. Moneyhon, University of Arkansas at Little Rock

Joseph C. Morton, Northeastern Illinois University

Alice E. Reagan, Northern Virginia Community College–Woodbridge

David V. Stroud, Kilgore College

R. Bruce Way, Tiffin University

Carol Berkin, who is responsible for Chapters 3 through 7, wishes to thank the following scholars and teachers: Mary Beth Norton, Leslie Horowitz, Kerry Candaele, Roberta McCutcheon, Tammie McDaniel, John Woltjer, and William Mendelsohn, for their helpful discussions of new scholarship and useful sources in early American history. She also acknowledges the assistance of her graduate students Peter Vellon, Angelo Angelis, Cindy Lobel, and Hilary Hallett. Finally, she thanks her two works-in-progress, Hannah Berkin-Harper and Matthew Berkin-Harper, for keeping her firmly attached to the present despite her forays into the past.

Christopher L. Miller, who is responsible for Chapters 1 and 2 and 8 through 15, is indebted to his students at the University of Texas—Pan American for providing the constant inspiration to innovate. He owes special thanks also to Associate Vice President for Academic Affairs George Avellano for buying some unexpected research and writing time, and to Vice President for Student Affairs Judy Vinson and Project Elite for providing two excellent research associates: Laurie Hirsch and Lisa Travis. George Gause, history bibliographer for the university library and curator of the Rio Grande Valley Historical Collection, provided much-needed information and rare resources. A number of colleagues have given advice concerning revisions for this edition, including Albert Hurtado, Gregory Evans Dowd, the late Bill Cecil-Fronsman, David Vassberg, and Rudolfo Rocha. He also wishes to acknowledge the contribution of Wilbur R. Jacobs, whose recent death triggered fond memories of firm but gentle mentoring. Personal thanks are due to Parrish Kelley and Ian Kelley for keeping life interesting, and to Carol Berkin for providing curative doses of good-humored sanity.

Robert W. Cherny, who is responsible for Chapters 16 through 24, wishes to thank the students in his classes, who, over the years, have provided the testing ground for much that is included in his chapters, and especially to thank his student assistants Randolf Arguelles, Marie Bolton, Katherine Davis, Beth Haigen, Cynthia Taylor, and David Winn for their work on various stages of both the first and the second editions. Among his colleagues at San Francisco State, Jerry Combs, Bill Issel, Paul Longmore, Barbara Loomis, and Jules Tygiel stand out for their helpfulness and their advice. Rebecca Marshall Cherny and Sarah Cherny have been unfailing in their encouragement, inspiration, and support.

Jim Gormly, who is responsible for Chapters 25 through 33, would like to acknowledge the support and encouragement he received from Washington and Jefferson College. He wants to gives a special thanks to Sharon Gormly, whose support, ideas, advice, and critical eye have helped to shape and refine his chapters. Finally, he would like to thank Sharon, Susan, David, Daphne, and Seth for the moments away from the project.

The editorial staff at Houghton Mifflin demonstrated creativity, patience, and a love of history as they assisted us with this edition of *Making America.* We want especially to thank Jean Woy, editor-in-chief, and Colleen Kyle, associate sponsoring editor, who guided the project to completion with unflagging enthusiasm and unfailing good judgment. The editing suggestions by Jan Fitter enhanced the clarity and precision of our prose, and Jeff Greene and Carol Newman ensured that the final production process went as smoothly as possible. Working with this talented team of editors was a privilege.

C. B. R. W. C.
C. L. M. J. L. G.

TO THE STUDENTS

To most students, the authors of a textbook are little more than names on the spine of a heavy book. We the authors of *Making America*, however, hope you'll give us a chance to be more than "Berkin et al." If you'll give us a moment, we'll introduce ourselves—and our book—to you. We also want to give you some solid suggestions about how to get the most out of this text and out of the study of American history it is designed to assist.

We—Carol Berkin, Robert Cherny, James Gormly, and Christopher Miller—have been historians, teachers, and friends for many years. Carol and Bob went to graduate school together; Jim and Chris taught at University of Texas—Pan American together. As scholars, we spend much of our time in libraries or historical archives, leafing through centuries-old letters from a wife to a husband, reading government reports on Indian policy, analyzing election returns from the 1890s, or examining newspaper editorials on the Cold War. At those moments, immersed in the past, we feel as if we have conquered time and space, traveling to eras and to places that no longer exist. This experience is part of the reason why we are historians. But we also are historians because we believe that knowing about the past is critical for anyone who hopes to understand the present and chart the future.

About six years ago, the four of us got together to talk about history and the challenges of teaching it in the 1990s. Out of this conversation came the idea for a new textbook, *Making America*. Our goals were deceptively simple: we wanted to tell the story of America from its earliest settlement to the present, to make that story complex and interesting, and to tell it in a language and format that would help students enjoy learning that history. Achieving those goals has been hard work, and with each edition of *Making America*, we hope we move closer to success.

You and other students arrived at college with a variety of skills, interests, knowledge, and experiences, not to mention a range of motivations for being there. What you and others have in common is the decision to take this American history course, in which *Making America* is the book you will be relying on to help you master that history. This textbook is organized and designed to help you do just that. Our narrative is chronological, telling the story as it happened, decade by decade or era by era. If you look at the table of contents, you can see that, with few exceptions, the chapters cover specific time periods rather than large themes. This does not mean that themes are absent; it means that we present them to you in the context of specific moments in time.

Each chapter follows the same pattern. It begins with a map of the United States on which vital information for that chapter is provided. For instance, the chapter on English settlement in the colonial era shows you the boundaries of each colony, gives you the date it was founded, and tells you what type of colony it was. The map locates for you in space what the chronological narrative locates in time. Below the map you will see a time line, which gives you the dates of important events to be covered in the chapter and a sense of where in the larger history of the nation these events fit. On the opposite page, you will see a chapter outline with focus questions, and when you turn the page, you will see a chart that lists in chronological order the significant events that we describe in the chapter. Together, the map, time line, outline, and chronology provide an overview of what you will be reading in the pages that follow.

The introduction to each chapter is a narrative preview, which sets the scene and tells you what major themes and issues you will find as you read on. You will notice that the introductions present the story in a very particular way: as a series of *expectations,* or hopes and desires held by the people of the era; of *constraints,* or limitations that they confronted as they tried to fulfill their expectations; of *choices,* or decisions that they finally made; and of *outcomes,* or consequences of the actions prompted by those choices. Our shorthand name for this approach is ECCO, an acronym formed from the first letter of each of the four elements. Expectations, constraints, choices, outcomes—ECCO—are the dynamic elements of history. ECCO is a way to remind you that what we call "the past" was "the present" to the people who lived it. They could not know what would happen as a result of their actions—and this is the excitement of the story we have to tell.

Then the chapter itself begins. It consists of sections that you can read as mini-narratives. Each of them opens with focus questions, to alert you to the central points that will be raised and examined. A summary at the end of each chapter recaps the material in the text. If you want to make sure you have focused on the important points in the chapter, you can review by reading the summary and then trying to answer the focus questions at the beginning of each section.

Because a serious examination of a history as rich and complex as our nation's requires us to introduce you to many new people, places, events, and ideas, it is easy to get lost in details or panic over what is most important to remember. You may also encounter words that are unfamiliar or words that seem to be used in a different way from the way you use them in everyday speech. Both problems can distract you from learning what happened—and why—and enjoying the story. To prevent this distraction, we have provided a running glossary on each page to define key terms and possibly unfamiliar words when you first encounter them. Each chapter also has suggestions for further reading on the subjects covered in the text, so that you can explore other viewpoints or look in depth at subjects that interest you.

Because students learn from visual as well as written sources, each chapter provides reproductions of paintings, photographs, artifacts, cartoons, and maps. These are not intended just to be decorative—to brighten up a page or add a touch of color. They are there to give faces to the people you are reading about, to show you what the environment, both natural and constructed, was like in the era under discussion, and to provide images of objects from the era that make clear their similarity to or difference from material objects in the world around you today. In the captions we identify each visual aid and suggest ways to interpret it.

For each chapter we have created a feature called "Individual Choices." In this feature we present a man or woman from the past who needed to make a choice. After all, individuals, including you, shape their history at the same time that history is shaping their lives. We believe that by reading about real people—some famous, some not—as they face an important choice and an uncertain outcome, you will better understand the era in which they lived.

A feature called "Making History" also appears throughout the text. It gives you the opportunity to work with the raw materials of history: the primary sources that help historians reconstruct the past. This feature is designed to answer, in part, the most common question students ask a history professor: "How do you know what happened or how it happened or why?" In "Making History" we pose a question to you, provide a variety of primary sources on the topic, then challenge you to offer your interpretation of the issue. "Making History" gives you a chance to be a historian, not just to read history. You will quickly see that your conclusions are not the same as those of your classmates, and these discrepancies will demonstrate why historians often disagree about issues in the past.

At the back of the textbook, you will find some additional resources. In the Appendix you will find a bibliography listing the books on which we relied in writing the chapters. You will also find reprinted several of the most important documents in American history: the Declaration of Independence, the Articles of Confederation, and the Constitution. Here too are tables that give you quick access to important data on the presidents and their cabinets. Finally, you will see the index, which will help you locate a subject quickly if you want to read about it.

In addition, the two-volume *Study Guide,* written by Eli Faber of John Jay College of Criminal Justice, provides you with many review exercises and tips on how to study and take tests effectively (ask your bookstore for a copy). There also is an *On-line Study Guide,* accessible through Houghton Mifflin's @history web site (www.hmco.com/college/). It functions as a tutorial, providing for all multiple-choice questions rejoinders that explain why your response is or is not correct. At this web site you'll also find other resources that can help you to succeed in the course.

We the authors of *Making America* hope that our textbook conveys to you our own fascination with the American past and sparks your curiosity about the nation's history. We invite you to share your feedback on the book: you can reach us through Houghton Mifflin's American history web site, which is located at www.hmco.com/college/.

ABOUT THE AUTHORS

Carol Berkin

Born in Mobile, Alabama, Carol Berkin received her undergraduate degree from Barnard College and her Ph.D. from Columbia University. Her dissertation won the Bancroft Award. She is now professor of history at Baruch College and the Graduate Center of City University of New York, where she serves as deputy chair of the Ph.D. program in history. She has written *Jonathan Sewall: Odyssey of an American Loyalist* (1974) and *First Generations: Women in Colonial America* (1996). She has edited *Women of America: A History* (with Mary Beth Norton, 1979), *Women, War and Revolution* (with Clara M. Lovett, 1980), and *Women's Voices, Women's Lives: Documents in Early American History* (with Leslie Horowitz, 1998). She was contributing editor on southern women for *The Encyclopedia of Southern Culture* and has appeared in the PBS series *Liberty! The American Revolution* and The Learning Channel series *The American Revolution.* Professor Berkin chaired the Dunning Beveridge Prize Committee for the American Historical Association, the Columbia University Seminar in Early American History, and the Taylor Prize Committee of the Southern Association of Women Historians, and she served on the program committees for both the Society for the History of the Early American Republic and the Organization of American Historians. In addition, she has been a historical consultant for the National Parks Commission and served on the Planning Committee for the U.S. Department of Education's National Assessment of Educational Progress.

Christopher L. Miller

Born and raised in Portland, Oregon, Christopher L. Miller received his undergraduate degree from Lewis and Clark College and his Ph.D. from the University of California, Santa Barbara. He is currently associate professor of history at the University of Texas—Pan American. He is the author of *Prophetic Worlds: Indians and Whites on the Columbia Plateau* (1985), and his articles and reviews have appeared in numerous scholarly journals. In addition to his scholarship in the areas of American West and American Indian history, Professor Miller has been active in projects designed to improve history teaching, including programs funded by the Meadows Foundation, the U.S. Department of Education, and other agencies.

Robert W. Cherny

Born in Marysville, Kansas, and raised in Beatrice, Nebraska, Robert W. Cherny received his B.A. from the University of Nebraska and his M.A. and Ph.D. from Columbia University. He is now professor of history at San Francisco State University. His books include *American Politics in the Gilded Age, 1868–1900* (1997), *San Francisco, 1865–1932: Politics, Power, and Urban Development* (with William Issel, 1986), *A Righteous Cause: The Life of William Jennings Bryan* (1985, 1994), and *Populism, Progressivism, and the Transformation of Nebraska Politics, 1885–1915* (1981). His articles on politics and labor in the late nineteenth and early twentieth centuries have appeared in scholarly journals, anthologies, and historical dictionaries and encyclopedias. He has been an NEH fellow, Distinguished Fulbright Lecturer at Moscow State University (Russia), and Visiting Research Scholar at the University of Melbourne (Australia). He has also served as president of the Society for Historians of the Gilded Age and Progressive Era and of the Southwest Labor Studies Association.

James L. Gormly

Born in Riverside, California, James L. Gormly received a B.A. from the University of Arizona and his M.A. and Ph.D. from the University of Connecticut. He is now professor of history and chair of the history department at Washington and Jefferson College. He has written *The Collapse of the Grand Alliance* (1970) and *From Potsdam to the Cold War* (1979). His articles and reviews have appeared in *Diplomatic History, The Journal of American History, The American Historical Review, The Historian, The History Teacher,* and *The Journal of Interdisciplinary History.*

Making America

A History of the United States

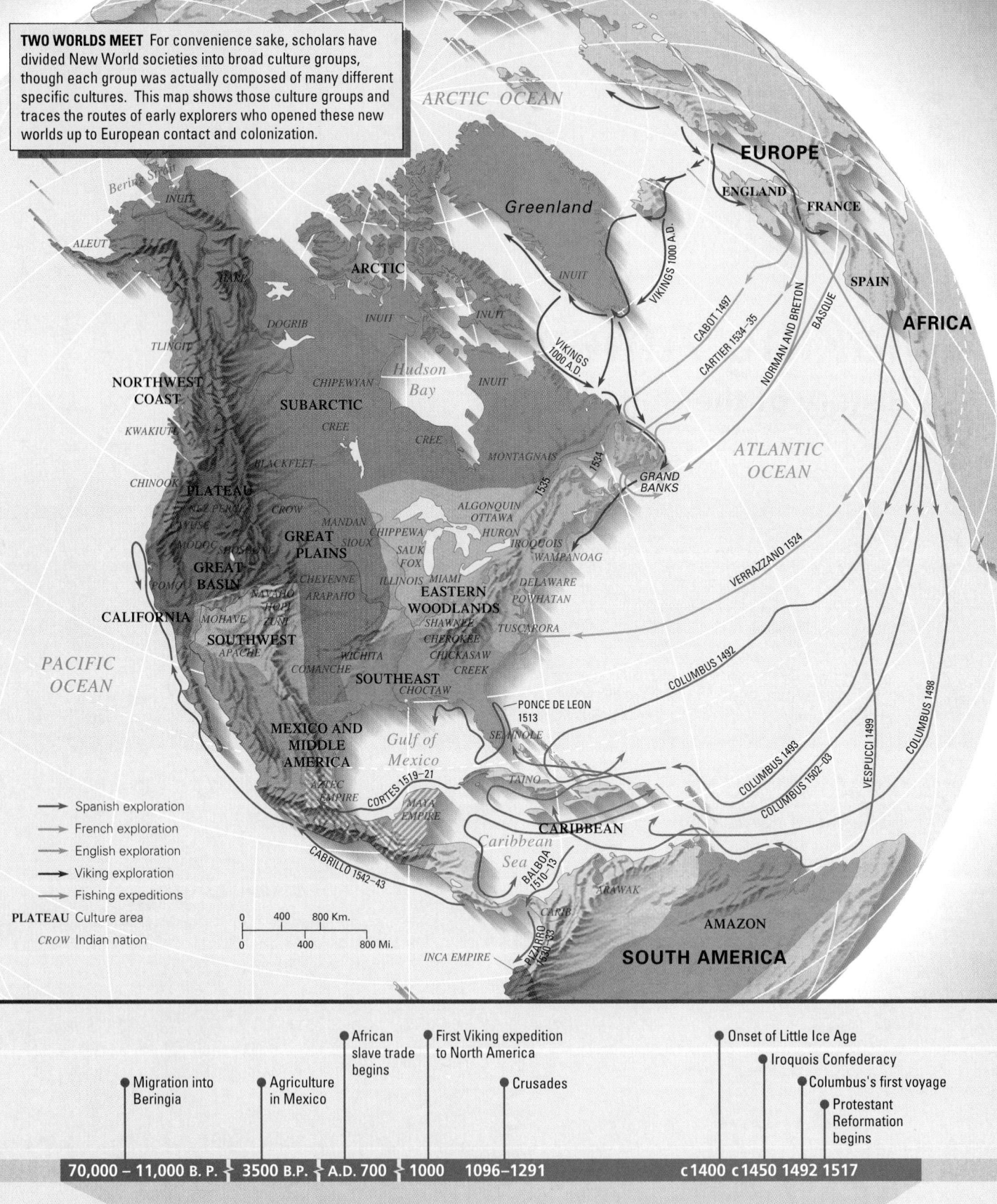

TWO WORLDS MEET For convenience sake, scholars have divided New World societies into broad culture groups, though each group was actually composed of many different specific cultures. This map shows those culture groups and traces the routes of early explorers who opened these new worlds up to European contact and colonization.

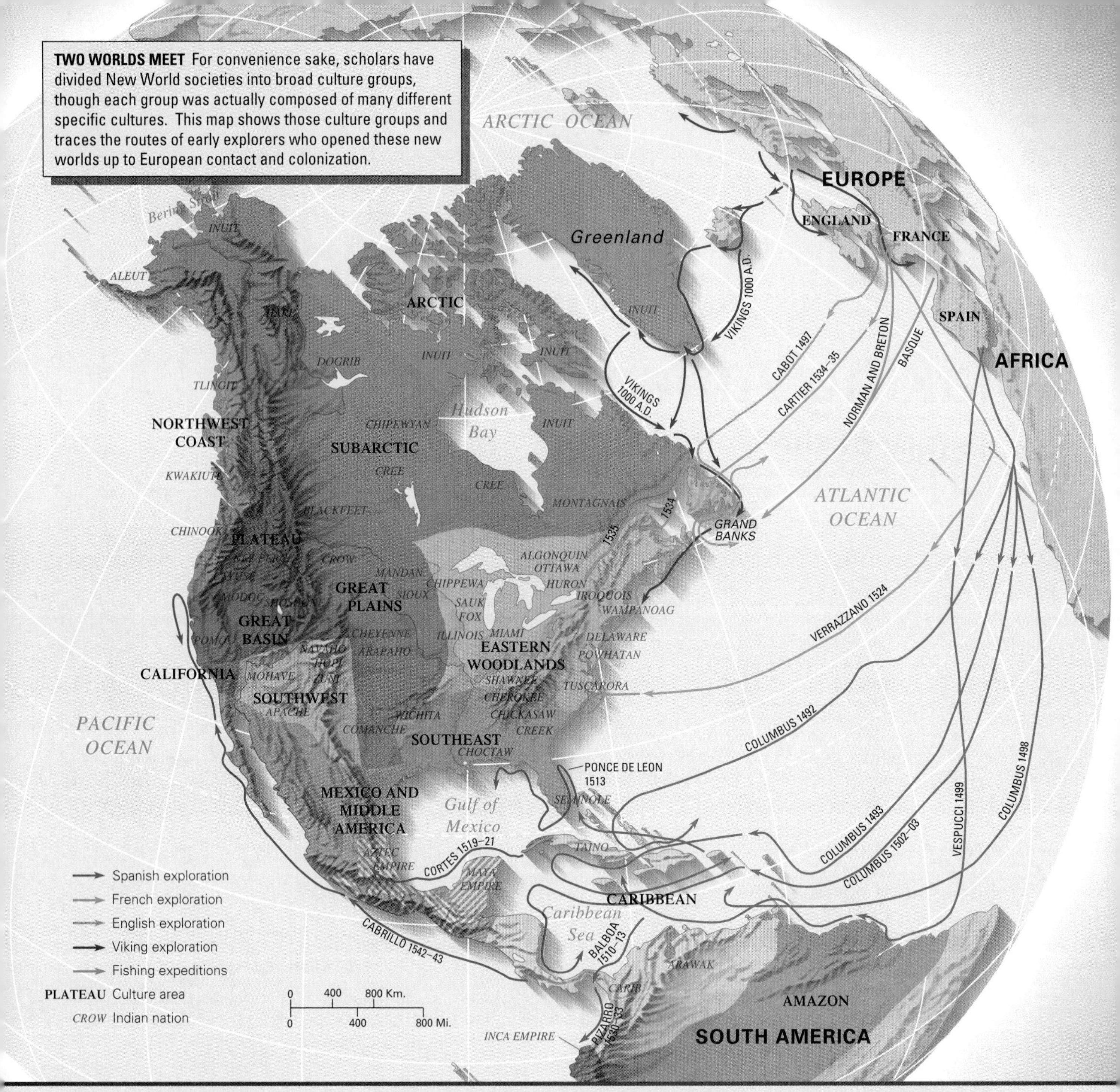

- 70,000 – 11,000 B. P.: Migration into Beringia
- 3500 B.P.: Agriculture in Mexico
- A.D. 700: African slave trade begins
- 1000: First Viking expedition to North America
- 1096–1291: Crusades
- c1400: Onset of Little Ice Age
- c1450: Iroquois Confederacy
- 1492: Columbus's first voyage
- 1517: Protestant Reformation begins

70,000 – 11,000 B.P. | 3500 B.P. | A.D. 700 | 1000 | 1100 | 1200 | 1300 | 1400 | 1500 | 1600

*Note: B.P. means before present time.

CHAPTER 1

Making a "New" World, to 1558

American Origins

- Before the arrival of Columbus, what constraints did environmental conditions impose on native cultures?
- What kinds of choices did American Indians make in response, and what were the outcomes of those choices for Indians living in various parts of the continent?

European Outreach and the Age of Exploration

- What expectations spurred Europeans to explore westward and southward around Africa?
- What geographical and political constraints stood in their way?
- How did they choose to overcome those constraints?

The Challenges of Mutual Discovery

- How did European contact affect the choices made by American Indians?
- What varied attitudes did Europeans choose to adopt in their relations with Indians and Africans?
- What were some outcomes of the Columbian Exchange?

INTRODUCTION

E xpectations
C onstraints
C hoices
O utcomes

Not many years ago, most historians would have said that the making of America began only after Christopher Columbus stumbled over the Western Hemisphere while trying to find the East Indies and Japan. But in recent decades we have learned a lot, enough to change our way of approaching American history and our understanding of how America was made.

There are four components in the process of making history—*expectations, constraints, choices,* and *outcomes* (which we call ECCO). These components do not always operate in order. They also work together as a web of causes, influences, and effects. Each ECCO component can have an impact on any other one. For example, a certain *expectation* might point to what appears to be a natural *choice.* Yet *constraints* may alter an expectation or limit the available choices to such a degree that new expectations or choices arise. A given *choice* can influence new expectations, change existing constraints, or limit or increase the variety of other choices available. All come together in *outcomes* that can, in turn, redefine other expectations, constraints, and choices. Each time any of the people connected with America's past went through the process we call ECCO, they created their own part in America's story, making this process instrumental in describing how America was made.

The first people who influenced the making of America chose to come here a very long time ago, *expecting* to find improved hunting, their primary source of food. In the ages that followed, these people made numerous *choices* in the face of natural, cultural, and economic *constraints* that gave peculiar shape to their societies and to the land they occupied. For example, between about 9,000 and 7,000 years ago, these hunters were constrained by the fact that their own population was rising quickly while that of the large game animals they depended on for food was declining. Many chose to increase their reliance on other game and on plants. The outcome for many societies was the eventual development of agriculture and city building, but other societies experienced different outcomes owing to different constraints and expectations. The overall *outcome* was a broadly diverse cultural universe in North America.

In the meantime, people in Africa, the Middle East, and Europe were making their own peculiar *choices,* giving particular historical direction to these areas as well. Two new religions from the Near East—Christianity and Islam—expanded into Europe and Africa, as did a Viking trading and military network. Muslim traders, who followed routes that the ancient Egyptians had carved into Africa, spread knowledge and goods that presented a new set of *expectations* and *choices* to Africans. One *outcome* was the rise of rich and sophisticated African kingdoms, but another was a mutual choice made by Africans and Muslims to establish a systematic slave trade.

Viking and Muslim influence in Europe led to changed *expectations* there as well. The wealth flowing through the surrounding trading world lured Europeans into increasing adventurousness. At first, their neighbors' military and diplomatic strength was a strong *constraint,* but gradually Europeans chose to test their own power, challenging Islam's control over large parts of Europe and its monopoly of the Asian and African trade. Italian merchants elbowed into the picture by forming partnerships with their Islamic neighbors, bringing new wealth and knowledge into their cities. Farther west, the Portuguese and then the Spanish swept the Muslims from their lands and began pushing farther and farther outward, expecting to get around the Muslims and their Italian trading partners. The successes they experienced led other European nations to *choose* exploration and outreach as a way of bringing new wealth and knowledge to their lands.

The *outcome* of all these expectations, constraints, and choices was a collision of Europeans, Africans, and American Indians in the Western Hemisphere. This meeting of worlds created an entirely new set of historical circumstances that transformed life on both sides of the Atlantic. Thus the story of making America must begin with the first discovery of the New World so very long before Columbus, and trace the development of the people who were already here when Columbus arrived. Then we must consider what was happening in the rest of the world, so that we might understand why others eventually came to this land. Only then will we be prepared to see how the expectations, constraints, and choices made by the people who followed Columbus to the New World had the particular outcomes we call "making America."

CHRONOLOGY

The New World

c. 70,000–10,000 B.P.	Human migration from Asia into Beringia
c. 7000 B.P.	Plant cultivation begins in North America
c. 3500 B.P.	Agriculture begins in central Mexico
c. 700	Islamic caravans to West Africa and African slave trade begins
c. 500–1000	Rise of Hopewell culture
c. 800–1700	Rise of Mississippian culture
c. 1000–1400	Vikings in North America Expansion of the Thule Inuits
1096–1291	The Crusades to the Holy Land
c. 1200	Aztecs arrive in the Valley of Mexico
c. 1400	Beginning of colder climate called the Little Ice Age
c. 1450	Hiawatha founds the Iroquois Confederacy
1492	Reconquista completed Columbus's first voyage
1500	Portuguese begin to transport and trade African slaves
1517	Protestant Reformation begins
1527–1535	Henry VIII begins English Reformation
1558	Elizabeth I becomes queen of England

American Origins

- Before the arrival of Columbus, what constraints did environmental conditions impose on native cultures?
- What kinds of choices did American Indians make in response, and what were the outcomes of those choices for Indians living in various parts of the continent?

The forces that propelled Columbus toward the **Western Hemisphere** merely echoed other forces that had sent a population to the **New World** thousands of years before. These forces resulted from countless choices that countless individuals through time made as they struggled to better their lives and those of their children. Thus the process that led to the peopling of North America and the development of a unique set of cultures began many thousands of years before Columbus and is part of the larger drama of human development.

Environment, Change, and Human History

Human culture apparently began about 4 million years ago in the east-central region of Africa. Within 1 to 2 million years, human beings were to be found throughout many parts of the **Eastern Hemisphere.** This expansion of human culture took place against a backdrop of extremely bad weather. The Quaternary era, or Great Ice Age, began about 2.5 million years ago and ended only about 10,000 years ago. During the height of the Ice Age, great sheets of ice advanced and withdrew across the world's continents, and temperatures were between fifteen and twenty degrees lower on the average than they are today.

During the last Quaternary ice advance, the Wisconsin glaciation, a sheet of ice more than 8,000 feet

B.P. Abbreviation for "before the present"; 70,000 B.P. means "70,000 years ago."

Western Hemisphere The half of the earth that includes North America, Mexico, Central America, and South America.

New World A term that Europeans used during the period of early contact and colonization to refer to the Americas, especially in the context of their discovery and colonization.

Eastern Hemisphere The half of the earth that includes Europe, Africa, Asia, and Australia.

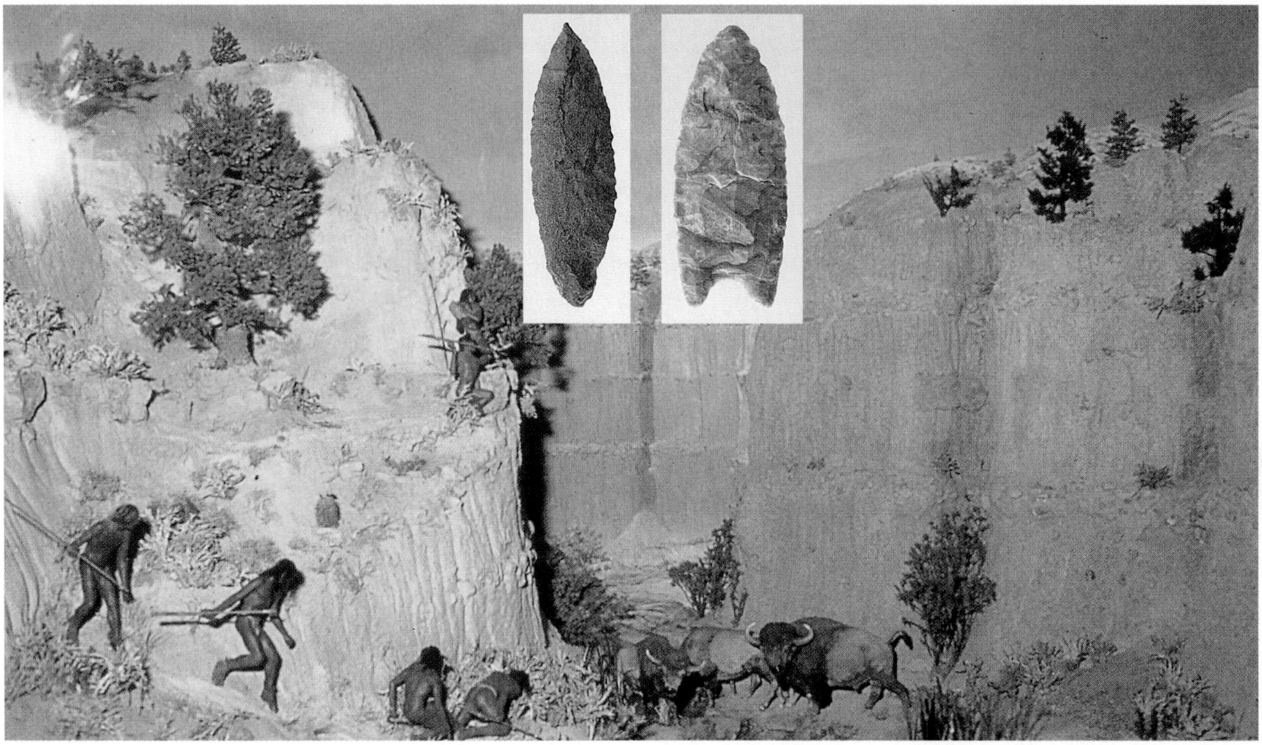

♦ Hunting large animals like the giant bison depicted here required skill, cooperative effort, and dependable tools. Two different spear points were used by Ice Age hunters in North America: fluted Clovis points east of the Rocky Mountains (right), and willow-leaf-shaped Cascade points to the west (left). Although DNA and other scientific evidence suggests that these early hunters were related genetically, the two different point shapes indicate that more than one cultural group probably crossed the Bering land bridge. *Folsom killsite: Mesa Verde National Park; Cascade and Clovis points: Great Lakes Artifact Repository.*

thick, covered the northern half of both Europe and North America. So much water was frozen into this massive glacier that sea levels dropped as much as 450 feet. Finding vast regions closed to them by the imposing ice fields, people ventured into areas exposed by the receding sea. One such region, **Beringia,** lay between present-day Siberia on the Asian continent and Alaska in North America (see Map 1.1). Now covered by the waters of the Bering Sea and Arctic Ocean, Beringia during the Ice Age was a dry, frigid grassland, low lying and thus not subject to glacier formation—a perfect grazing ground for animals such as giant bison and huge-tusked woolly mammoths, which thrived in the cold. Hosts of predators, including large wolves, saber-toothed cats, and humans, followed them into Beringia.

Scholars who have analyzed soil samples, plant remains, animal bones, and other relics now conclude that sea levels were low enough to expose Beringia about 70,000 years ago and that the area remained above sea level continually until about 10,000 years ago. Archaeological evidence yields a wide variety of dates for when people first moved southward into North America, ranging from about 40,000 to about 12,000 years ago.

Evidence based on blood DNA, differences in tooth shapes, and similarities in languages suggests that the majority of North America's original residents are descended from three separate migrating groups, each of which arrived at a different time. The first of these, the groups called Paleo-Indians, probably entered the continent between 30,000 and 40,000 years ago, and their descendants eventually

Beringia An expanse of land between present-day Siberia in Asia and Alaska in North America, now covered by water; an avenue for migration between Asia and North America in prehistoric times.

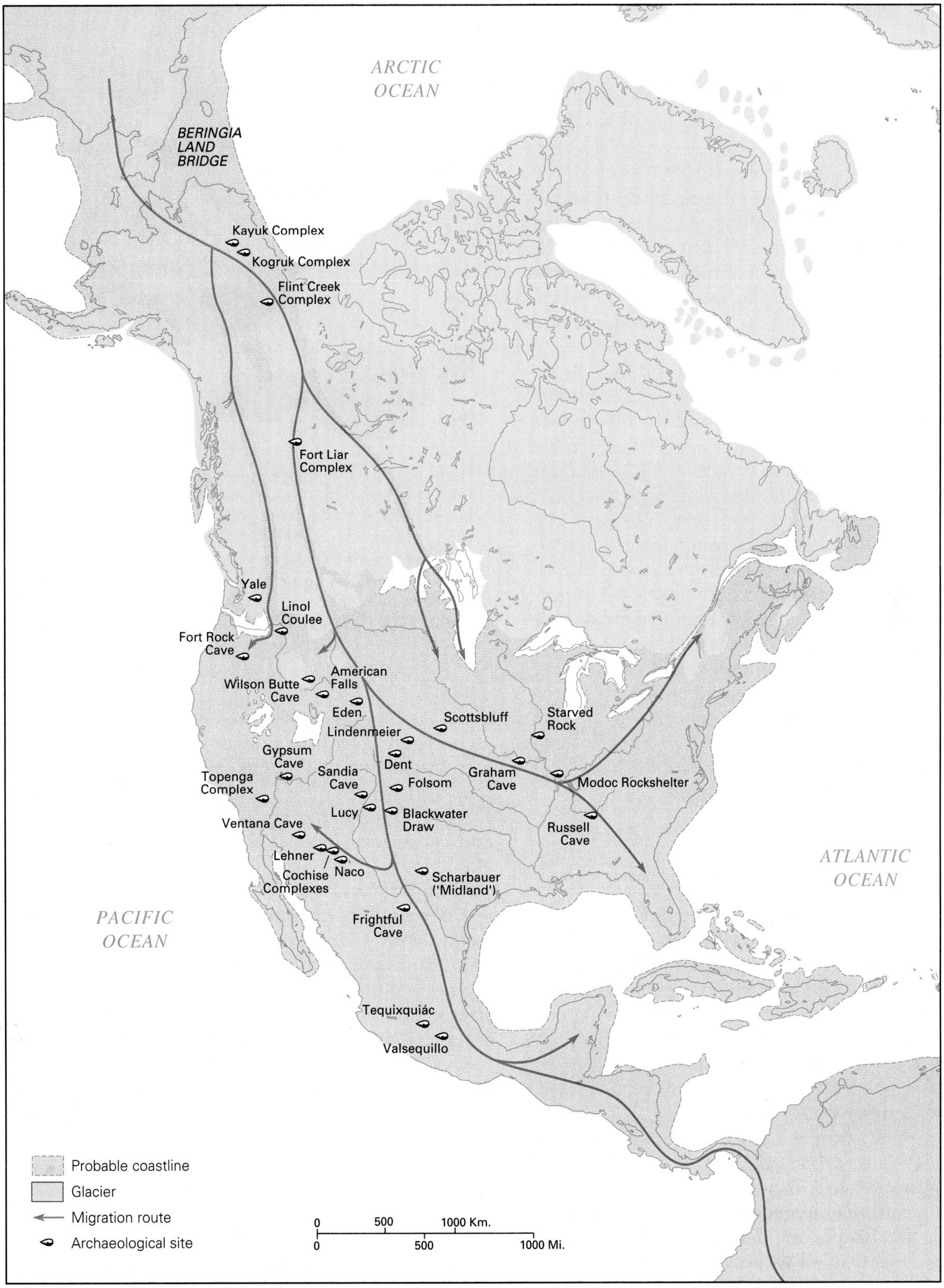

♦ **MAP 1.1 First Americans Enter the New World** Although DNA evidence indicates that all early migrants to the Western Hemisphere were genetically related, at least two cultural groups moved into North America approximately 40,000 years ago. The Old Cordilleran group, to the west of the Rocky Mountains, and the Clovis group, to the east, left records of their passing at numerous sites, the most prominent of which are labeled here.

occupied the entire area of the Western Hemisphere. The second group, collectively called the Na-Dene people, appears to have arrived very near the end of the Wisconsin era, between 10,000 and 11,000 years ago, and their descendants are concentrated in two areas: the subarctic regions of Canada and the southwestern United States. The final group, the Arctic-dwelling Inuits, or Eskimos, arrived sometime later, perhaps after the land connection between North America and the rest of the world was already gone (see Map 1.1).

Even after the Ice Age came to an end, it took between four and five thousand years for the massive glaciers to melt, and during that time the melting ice kept the climate cold and damp everywhere on the continent. But by about 9,000 years ago, the glaciers were so reduced in size that they began to lose their influence over the North American climate. The elimination of this enormous temperature-regulating system resulted in the formation of many different climates and natural environments. Most important, as temperatures warmed and the grasslands disappeared, the gigantic Ice Age creatures whose presence supplied early hunters with their primary source of meat and whose movements set the tempo and pattern for Paleo-Indian life began to die out. The hunters faced the unpleasant prospect of following the large animals into extinction if they kept trying to survive by hunting big game.

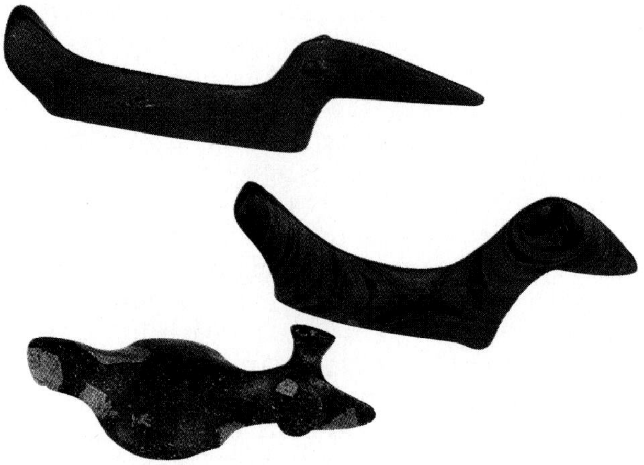

♦ Abandoning a nomadic life gave Archaic-era Indians more time to design new, more effective tools, and to create beautiful objects like these polished bird stones. Such sculptures combined both artistic and practical objectives. They were used as balance weights on spearthrowing sticks (Atlatls), and possibly for religious purposes, such as symbolizing bird spirits that would guide a spear's flight. *Ohio Historical Society.*

Seedtime for Native Cultures in North America

Over time, the changing environment forced the ancestors of the American Indians to change their ways, which marked the beginning of a host of new cultures. The first phase of the adaptation process began even as the climate change was occurring and lasted until about 3,000 years ago. **Archaeologists** call it the **Archaic phase** in Indian culture. During this period, people everywhere in North America abandoned **nomadic** big-game hunting. They began to explore new sources for food, clothing, shelter, and tools—sources that they found within newly emerging local environments.

Archaic culture emerged at different times in different places. It appears that the western part of North America was hit earliest by the changing climate. At an archaeological site in southern Oregon, a place called Fort Rock Cave, archaeologists have unearthed very early evidence of people abandoning big-game hunting and adapting to local conditions. As long as 9,600 years ago, people in this region began inventing new tools and mastering new manufacturing skills. For example, investigators found a large number of different tools for grinding seeds, a sign that these people were eating less meat and more local grass seeds, nuts, and other vegetable foods. They also found baskets, sandals, and clothing woven from grasses and reeds, indicating less dependence on animals and greater reliance on local plants. Third, investigators found small spear points and fishing and bird-hunting equipment, implying that these early Indians had stopped chasing after mammoths and had begun to hunt and fish for animals that they could find close by.

Over the next several thousand years, people throughout western North America and then all over the continent made similar adaptations, differing

Archaeologist A scholar who studies the physical remains of past societies.

Archaic phase In Native American culture, the period when people began to shift away from hunting big game and turn to agriculture and other food sources in local environments.

nomadic Having no fixed home and wandering from place to place in search of food or other resources.

only in the specific foods and types of materials they employed. In the forests that grew up to cover the eastern half of the continent, Archaic Indians developed finely polished stone tools, which they used to make functional and beautiful implements out of wood, bone, shell, and other materials. In the eastern forests and along the Pacific shore, people used large, heavy stone axes, chisels, and **adzes** to hollow out massive tree trunks, making boats from which they could harvest food from inland waterways and from the sea. During this time domesticated dogs were introduced into North America, probably by newly arriving migrants from Asia. Dogs provided companionship, protection, a domesticated food source, and hunting help, and they served as draft animals. With dogs to help carry loads on land and boats for river transportation, Archaic people were able to make the best use of their local environments by moving around to different spots during different seasons of the year. Thus they did not establish permanent towns or villages. Rather they followed an annual round of movement from camp to camp—perhaps collecting shellfish for several weeks in one spot and then moving to where wild strawberries were ripening and then on to where maturing wild onions or sunflower seeds could be harvested.

Such efficient use of local resources caused an enormous increase in two things during the Archaic period: population and spare time. Although Indian populations had grown enormously during the several millennia in which they remained primarily hunters, the precarious nature of nomadic hunting forced big-game hunters to live in small bands that could move quickly in pursuit of elusive prey. Archaic life was much more stable, and efficient manufacturing and harvesting helped prevent famine. After people began settling down, populations increased more quickly.

Being freed from the constant need to track and kill big game for meat also gave Archaic people more time for other things. One result was the continuing invention of new tools and craft skills. Another was the emergence of art. Artwork played a prominent role in elaborate burial practices that emerged everywhere in North America during this period. In central Florida, for example, bodies of the dead, along with tools and carved animal **effigies,** were sewn into weighted woven bags and then staked to the bottom of shallow ponds. Elsewhere, the bones of the dead were stripped of flesh and painted bright colors before they were buried with an assortment of art objects.

The connection between artwork and elaborate burials points to a rich religious and ceremonial life. Sculptures and pictures from the time indicate that nature lay at the heart of the Archaic religious world. Some **anthropologists** and religious scholars have speculated that these Archaic ancestors of modern Indians believed in and celebrated the animating spirits of the plants and animals that they knew so well and depended on for survival.

Although these early Indians apparently worshiped nature and adapted well to conditions around them, they also left their mark on local environments. They used fire to clear forests of unwanted scrub and to encourage the growth of berries and other plants they found valuable, while discouraging the growth of weeds. In this way they produced vegetables for themselves and also provided food for browsing animals like deer, which increased in number while other species, less useful to people, declined.

Plant Cultivation and the Rise of New Societies

A highly significant example of such environmental engineering comes from north-central Mexico, where archaeologists have found evidence that humans altered the natural growth of plants. Beginning perhaps 7,000 years ago, human intervention helped a wild strain of grass develop bigger seedpods with more nutritious seeds. Such intervention eventually transformed a fairly unproductive plant into an enormously nourishing and prolific food crop: maize.

Maize (corn), along with beans, squash, and chilies, formed the basis for an agricultural revolution in North America, allowing many people to settle in larger villages for longer periods. From its origins in central Mexico about 3,500 years ago, maize agriculture spread like wildfire, reaching settlements in New Mexico and Arizona as early as 1,000 or 2,000 years ago. From there, the plant itself and

adze An axlike tool with a broad, chisel-like curved blade, used for shaping wood.

effigy A likeness or image, usually three-dimensional.

anthropologist A scholar who studies human behavior and culture in either the past or the present.

maize Corn: the word *maize* comes from an Indian word for this plant.

♦ Cahokia was the largest city in pre-Columbian North America, occupying over six square miles and containing more than 120 earthen mounds, including several gigantic pyramids. The largest, Monk's Mound (the huge structure in the upper-right corner) was larger than the Great Pyramids of Egypt. Despite being a significant ceremonial and trading center, Cahokia probably did not have a large permanent population. *Cahokia Mounds State Historic Site/painting by L. K. Townsend.*

knowledge about how to sow its seeds and care for and harvest it spread northward and eastward.

Successful adaptation—including plant cultivation and eventually agriculture—along with population growth and the constructive use of spare time allowed some Indians in North America to build large, ornate cities. Generally these were not residential centers. Instead, most large Indian cities in North America were trading and ceremonial centers where large populations congregated from time to time. People, often from vastly different geographical and cultural settings, came to these places to trade goods and exchange knowledge and information. Large earthen mounds in various shapes—some like huge animals, others formed as pyramids or interesting geometrical patterns—are prominent features at these sites, leading archaeologists to call these trading and ceremonial centers **mound builder** societies.

The map of late Archaic America is dotted with such centers. Along the Ohio River, a complex of sites was constructed about 3,000 years ago. Archaeologists call this the Adena culture. Adena cities were centers of exchange and ceremony. Large quantities of both practical and purely decorative artifacts from all over North America have been found at Adena sites.

In Illinois and elsewhere in eastern North America, **Hopewell culture** took the place of Adena culture. Hopewell culture reached its peak between 1,500 and 1,000 years ago at Cahokia, a site near the modern city of East St. Louis, Illinois. Cahokia was more than just a trading center. It was a central clearing-house for ideas from all over the Western Hemisphere. Archaeologists have found distinctive forms of pottery, tools, and religious and artistic objects spread in concentric rings outward from Cahokia. In addition, the people at Cahokia appear to have developed both the tools and the specific knowledge required for growing corn in that region.

Despite its size and apparent influence, Cahokia probably did not have a large permanent population. Archaeologists believe that the people who came to Cahokia and to other Hopewell centers lived elsewhere, in small agricultural villages or in

mound builder Name applied to a number of Native American societies that constructed earthen mounds as monuments and building foundations.

Hopewell culture An early American Indian culture centered in the Ohio River valley; it is known for its burial mounds, tools, and pottery.

mobile hunting and gathering bands, and came to the centers to trade and to participate in ceremonial activities.

Earthen mounds shaped like flat-topped pyramids are the most distinctive feature of late Hopewell sites. Although these pyramids were constructed over ornate graves, probably those of former leaders, they also served as a base for buildings. These buildings may have served a double function—as places of worship and as administrative offices for priest-administrators who oversaw trading, planting, and invention.

About 800 years ago, Cahokia and the entire Hopewell complex fell into decline. The people who once had congregated at the Hopewell centers withdrew to their villages or bands. From time to time, however, some of them returned to the ceremonial centers, digging passages into the pyramids in order to bury important individuals.

The Complex World of Indian America

Although the broad shape of American Indian life was similar throughout North America, vast differences existed between various Indian groups, because Archaic cultures developed in direct response to local environmental conditions. Anthropologists have tried to make the extremely complicated cultural map of North America understandable by dividing the continent into a series of culture areas—regions where the similarities among native societies were greater than the differences. The chapter-opening map shows eleven such areas.

In one of these regions, the Southeast, life continued much as it had in the Adena and Hopewell cultures. Between 1,200 years ago and the time of European entry into the region in the 1700s, peoples speaking Siouan, Caddoan, and Muskogean languages formed a vibrant agricultural and urban society, which scholars have named **Mississippian culture.** Mississippian urban development, pyramid building, and political organization had ties with the earlier Adena and Hopewell cultures but were more directly influenced by contacts with adventurous traders from Mexico. At places like Natchez, fortified cities housed gigantic pyramids, and farmland radiating outward provided food for large residential populations. Unlike Adena and Hopewell sites, these were true cities, but like the earlier centers they were magnets attracting ideas, technologies, and religious notions from all parts of the Western Hemisphere.

Farther north, in the region called the Eastern Woodlands, people lived in smaller villages and combined agriculture with hunting and gathering. The **Iroquois,** for example, lived in towns numbering three thousand or more people, changing locations only as soil fertility, firewood, and game became exhausted. Each town was made up of a group of **longhouses,** structures often 60 feet or more in length. Individual family apartments ranged down both sides of a long central hallway, in the middle of which were fireplaces that served the two families living across from each other. This hallway was the center for social and political life—babies crawled, children played, men swapped hunting stories and gossip, and women cooked and cleaned in this communal space. Under the supervision of a dominant **matriarch,** the day-to-day tasks of running the household were shared out among its members.

A tradition that may go back to the time when the Iroquois lived as nomadic hunters and gatherers dictated that men and women occupy different spheres of existence. The women's world was the world of plants, healing, nurturing, and order. The men's was the world of animals, hunting, war, and disorder. By late **pre-Columbian** times, the Iroquois became strongly agricultural, and since plants were in the women's sphere, women occupied places of high social and economic status in Iroquois society. Families were matrilineal, meaning they traced their descent through the mother's line, and matrilocal, meaning a man left his home to move in with his wife's family upon marriage. Women distributed the rights to cultivate specific fields and controlled the harvest. Clan matriarchs chose the men who would sit as judges and political council members.

Variations on the Iroquois pattern were typical throughout the Northeast and in the neighboring Great Plains and the Southwest. Agricultural village

Mississippian culture An American Indian culture centered in the southern Mississippi River valley; influenced by Mexican culture, it is known for its pyramid building and its urban centers.

Iroquois Collective name for six Indian tribes that lived in present-day New York State; their cultures and languages were closely related; in Iroquois society, women were the heads of families.

longhouse A long communal dwelling, usually built of poles and bark and having a central hallway with family apartments on either side.

matriarch A woman who rules a family, clan, or tribal group.

pre-Columbian Existing in the Americas before the arrival of Columbus.

♦ Finding home sites close to the water and fertile soil in Southwestern riverbeds but safe from the frequent flash flooding that plagues the area presented a strategic problem for the Anasazi and later Pueblo people in the region. Their solution was to build compact cities on the cliffs and mesas overlooking the streams. This one, Cliff Palace at Mesa Verde, had over two hundred apartments and twenty-three ceremonial centers. *Richard Alexander Cook III.*

life was the dominant lifestyle in each region before Europeans came. In fact, migrants into the plains probably came from the east carrying seed corn from the declining Hopewell settlements. Groups like the Mandans began settling on bluffs overlooking the many streams that eventually come together to form the Missouri River. Living in substantial houses insulated against the cold winters, these people divided their time between hunting, crop raising, and trade. Over a five-hundred-year period, populations increased and agricultural settlements expanded. By 1300, such villages could be found along every stream ranging southward from North Dakota into present-day Kansas.

Just as agriculturalists in the Great Plains had strong connections to the Eastern Woodlands, Indians in the Southwest were closely tied to Mexico. As early as 3,200 years ago, corn appears to have been brought into the area. But the Southwestern Indians, unlike their contemporaries farther south, continued to engage in hunting and food gathering for a long time after experiencing the agricultural revolution. Not until about A.D. 400 did Indians in this region begin building larger and more substantial houses and limiting their migrations. The greatest change, however, came during the eighth century, when a shift in climate made the region drier and a pattern of late-summer thunderstorms created dangerous and erosive flash floods.

There seem to have been two quite different responses to this drastic change in climate. Groups whom the Navajos would later call the Anasazi (ancient alien ones) expanded their agricultural ways, cooperating to build flood-control dams and irrigation canals. This need for cooperative labor meant forming larger communities, and between about 900 and 1300 the Anasazi responded by building whole cities of multistory apartment houses along the high cliffs, safe from flooding but near their irrigated fields. In these densely populated towns Anasazi craft specialists like potters, weavers, basket makers, and tool smiths manufactured goods for the community while farmers tended fields and priests attended to the spiritual needs of the society.

Another contingent of Southwestern Indians abandoned the region, moving southward into Mexico. Here they came upon the remnants of classical city-states like Teotihuacán, which had fallen on hard times. One of several highly developed societies of central Mexico, Teotihuacán was the largest city-state in the Western Hemisphere, with a population of nearly 200,000. However, by around A.D. 600 Teotihuacán and other such societies were in decline. Over the next several hundred years, migrants from southwestern North America—so-called Chichimecs or "wild tribes"—borrowed architectural and agricultural skills from the fallen societies and built new monumental cities. Tula, the first of these, entered its heyday in about the year 1000, but within another two hundred years a civil war brought that civilization to an end.

Shortly thereafter, another Chichimec tribe rose to prominence in central Mexico. The **Aztecs** arrived in the Valley of Mexico shortly after 1200, settling on

Aztecs An Indian group living in central Mexico; the Aztecs used military force to dominate nearby tribes; their civilization was at its peak at the time of the Spanish conquest.

a small island in the middle of a brackish lake. From this unappealing center, a series of strong leaders used a combination of diplomacy and brutal warfare to establish a **tributary empire** as extensive and populated as the great empires of Europe. By the time Europeans entered Mexico in the early sixteenth century, the Aztecs may have ruled as many as 6 million people and had turned their island capital into a showplace that visitors compared favorably with the most advanced cities in Europe.

Other major changes occurred in the Southwest after 1300. During the last quarter of the thirteenth century, a long string of summer droughts and bitterly cold winters forced the Anasazi to abandon their cities. They disappeared as a people, splitting into smaller communities that eventually became the various Pueblo tribes. These small communities found their survival more certain if they engaged in both agriculture and hunting and gathering.

The arrival of an entirely new population to the region aided this adaptation. Related to the Na-Dene people, these hunter-gatherers brought new technologies, including the bow and arrow, into the Great Plains and then, splitting off from more northerly groups, they began a southward trek that eventually brought them into the Southwest. About half of them continued to be hunter-gatherers, and the rest borrowed cultivating and home-building techniques from the Pueblos. Europeans who later entered the area called the hunter-gatherers Apaches and the settled agriculturalists Navajos.

In the balance of North America, agriculture was practiced only marginally, if at all. In areas like the **Great Basin,** desert conditions made agriculture too risky, and in California, the Pacific Northwest, and the **Plateau region,** the bounty of available wild foods made it unnecessary. In these regions, hunting and gathering remained the chief occupations, and lifestyles centered around the various activities that contributed to group well-being. The Nez Perces and their neighbors living in the Plateau region, for example, moved around from season to season hunting, fishing, and gathering as different plants and animals became available. Although they occupied permanent village sites in the winter, they did not stay together in a single group all year. Rather, they formed task groups—temporary villages that came together to share the labor required to harvest a particular resource—and then went their separate ways when the task was done. These task groups brought together not only people who lived in different winter villages but often people from different tribes and even different language groups. At the peak of the salmon-fishing season, for example, large villages consisting of Nez Perces, Cayuses, Palouses, Flatheads, and members of numerous other groups formed to catch, salt, dry, and package the fish that would feed their individual villages during the coming winter.

In such groups, political authority passed among those who were best qualified to supervise particular activities. If the task group was hunting, the best and most senior hunters—almost always men—directed things. If the task group was gathering roots, then the best and most senior diggers—almost always women—directed things. Thus among Plateau people, political organization changed from season to season, and social status depended on what activities were most important to the group at a particular time.

As these examples illustrate, variations in daily life and social arrangements in pre-Columbian North America reflected variations in climate, soil conditions, food supplies, and cultural heritages from place to place across the vast continent. The only generalization we can make is that pre-Columbian Indians adopted economic strategies, social conventions, and political systems that were well suited to their ecological and historical circumstances.

It is a mistake, however, to assume pre-Columbian Americans lived in isolated tribes. Archaeological research continues to reveal complex trading patterns within and between ecological regions. In the West, for example, seed-grinding tools from the Great Basin are found at Plateau sites. **Obsidian** and other Plateau items are found in the Great Basin and beyond; varieties of shell found naturally only in the

tributary empire An empire in which subjects rule themselves but make payments, called tribute, to a higher political authority in the imperial government in return for protection and services.

Great Basin A desert region of the western United States, including most of present-day Nevada and parts of Utah, California, Idaho, Wyoming, and Oregon.

Plateau region The region of the United States and Canada bounded on the east by the Rocky Mountains, on the west by the Cascade range of mountains, on the north by the subarctic plains, and on the south by the Great Basin.

obsidian A shiny volcanic glass, often used for knives and arrowheads.

Northwest Coast region have been found in Indian villages as far away as Florida. Such findings reveal a far-reaching trading network that linked the people of North America into a single complex world of culture and experience.

European Outreach and the Age of Exploration

- What expectations spurred Europeans to explore westward and southward around Africa?
- What geographical and political constraints stood in their way?
- How did they choose to overcome those constraints?

While the Aztecs were expanding into Mexico, Europeans were feeling a similar restlessness. The **Vikings,** one group that resembled the Aztecs in many ways, extended their holdings throughout many parts of Europe and even into North America. A change in climate as well as conflict with Native Americans forced them to withdraw from their transatlantic outposts after 1300, but other Europeans began moving south and east. In the **Middle East** Christian monarchs and church leaders began a series of **Crusades** to wrest control of the **Holy Land** from the **Muslims.** As armies of Crusaders pushed their way into the region, they came into contact with many desirable things they had known only through myth and rumor—fine silks, exotic spices, and precious stones and metals. As word spread of the finery Muslims obtained through trade with Africa and the East, enterprising individuals began looking for ways to profit by supplying such luxuries to European consumers. At the same time, independent fishermen began to move into the areas of North America abandoned by the Vikings. Each of these movements led to the establishment of transatlantic ties and the creation of a new world.

Change and Restlessness in the Atlantic World

Around 800, a group of Vikings, who controlled the northern frontiers of Europe, began sweeping down along the continent's western shores. Eventually they captured the British Isles and seized a large province in western France, where they established the state of Normandy. At the same time, another group of Vikings pushed south along Europe's eastern frontier, through Russia. Eventually they extended their influence all the way to the eastern Mediterranean.

Accomplished and fearless seamen, the Vikings also sailed westward, colonizing Iceland and Greenland and eventually establishing colonies in North America. According to Viking sagas, a Viking captain named Bjarni Herjolfsson first sighted North America in 986 when he was blown off course. In about the year 1000, Viking chieftain Leif Ericson led an expedition to the new land, touching shore at Baffin Island and somewhere along the coast of Labrador. Over the next decades, several Viking colonizing expeditions established villages in North America.

The arrival of the Vikings in North America seems not to have caused a great stir on the European side of the Atlantic, but it may have influenced the balance of power among Native American groups. At the same time that the Vikings were expanding westward across the northern Atlantic, a group of Inuit hunters—the Thule people—were expanding eastward. This movement brought the Thule Inuits into contact with subarctic Indians and with the Vikings, and they seem to have played a role as trading middlemen between the two groups. Vikings in Greenland and Iceland paid tribute to their lords in Denmark and Norway in ivory from walrus tusks gained in trade with the Inuits, and archaeologists have found Viking coins and other worked-metal artifacts along with Inuit objects in sites occupied by Indians as far south as Maine. Many scholars speculate that a slight warming in the Arctic climate—the same

Vikings Late-medieval Danish, Swedish, and Norwegian groups who responded to land shortages and climatic conditions in Scandinavia by taking to the sea, establishing communities in various parts of Western Europe, Iceland, Greenland, and North America.

Middle East The region of the eastern Mediterranean, including modern Turkey, the Persian Gulf area, the Arabian Peninsula, and the Holy Land.

Crusades Military expeditions undertaken by European Christians in the eleventh through the thirteenth centuries to recover the Holy Land from the Muslims.

Holy Land The region in which the events described in the Old Testament of the Bible took place; it is sacred to Christians, Jews, and Muslims; now called Palestine, it lies in Israel, Jordan, and Syria.

Muslims People who practice the religion of Islam, a monotheistic faith that accepts Mohammed as the chief and last prophet of God.

♦ This Thule Inuit wood carving from the south coast of Baffin Island dating from the thirteenth or fourteenth century depicts a human figure in European dress, giving testimony to the transatlantic world that existed long before Columbus's journeys into the Western Hemisphere. *Canadian Museum of Civilization.*

warming trend that encouraged Viking expansion—may have encouraged the expansion of the Thule people but their role as middlemen in an early transatlantic trading system was also important to their success. The Thule Inuits seem to have guarded their trading role jealously, and this possessiveness may have been the primary reason for the Vikings' failure to expand their holdings in North America. The few accounts we have of battles between Vikings and Inuits end with a Viking retreat.

Although the Vikings maintained trading contacts with North America for another several hundred years, they began a larger retreat in the middle of the 1300s. By 1450 or so, they had withdrawn entirely from their transatlantic colonies. The most likely cause of their departure was a shift in climate. Although experts disagree about the exact timing, it appears that at some time between 1350 and 1450 a significant climatic shift called the Little Ice Age began to affect the entire world. In the Arctic and subarctic, temperatures fell, snowfall increased, and sea ice became a major hazard to navigation. This shift made it impossible for the Vikings to practice the herding, farming, and trading that supported their economy in Greenland and elsewhere, but it enhanced the Inuits' whaling and hunting activities. As the Inuits continued to thrive, both the Vikings and non-Inuit Native Americans found themselves retreating from increased cold and Inuit expansion.

Crusading, Trading, and the Rise of Nation States

While the Vikings were expanding to the south and west, an economic, religious, and political empire controlled by Muslim Arabs, Turks, and **Moors** was taking over Europe's southern and eastern frontiers (see Map 1.2). The military and political presence of the Vikings from the north and the Muslims from the south often made life unpleasant for Europeans, but it also eventually benefited the continent. Both groups helped Europeans expand their knowledge and broaden their culture. Borrowing manufacturing and transportation ideas from the invaders, Europeans were soon participating in a trading system that extended from Viking outposts in North America to Islamic trading posts in India and China. At the same time, improved farming methods increased food production so much that Europe could support an expanding population, and by about the year 1000, Europe began to experience a population explosion.

In 1096, European Christians launched the first of the Crusades to sweep the Muslims from their strongholds in the Holy Land on the eastern shore of the Mediterranean Sea. Over the next two centuries, hordes of Crusaders invaded the area, capturing key points only to be expelled by Muslim counterattacks. In the process, however, the Europeans gained knowledge, technical skill, and access to the eastern and African trade. By the time the Crusades ended in 1291, trading families centered in Italian city-states like Venice had used a combination of diplomatic skill and personal and economic daring to edge their way into the trade between Europe and the East.

Although the Crusades officially ended in 1291, the crusading spirit lived on in Europe, especially

Moors The Muslim rulers of the Iberian Peninsula in southwestern Europe, occupied by Spain and Portugal.

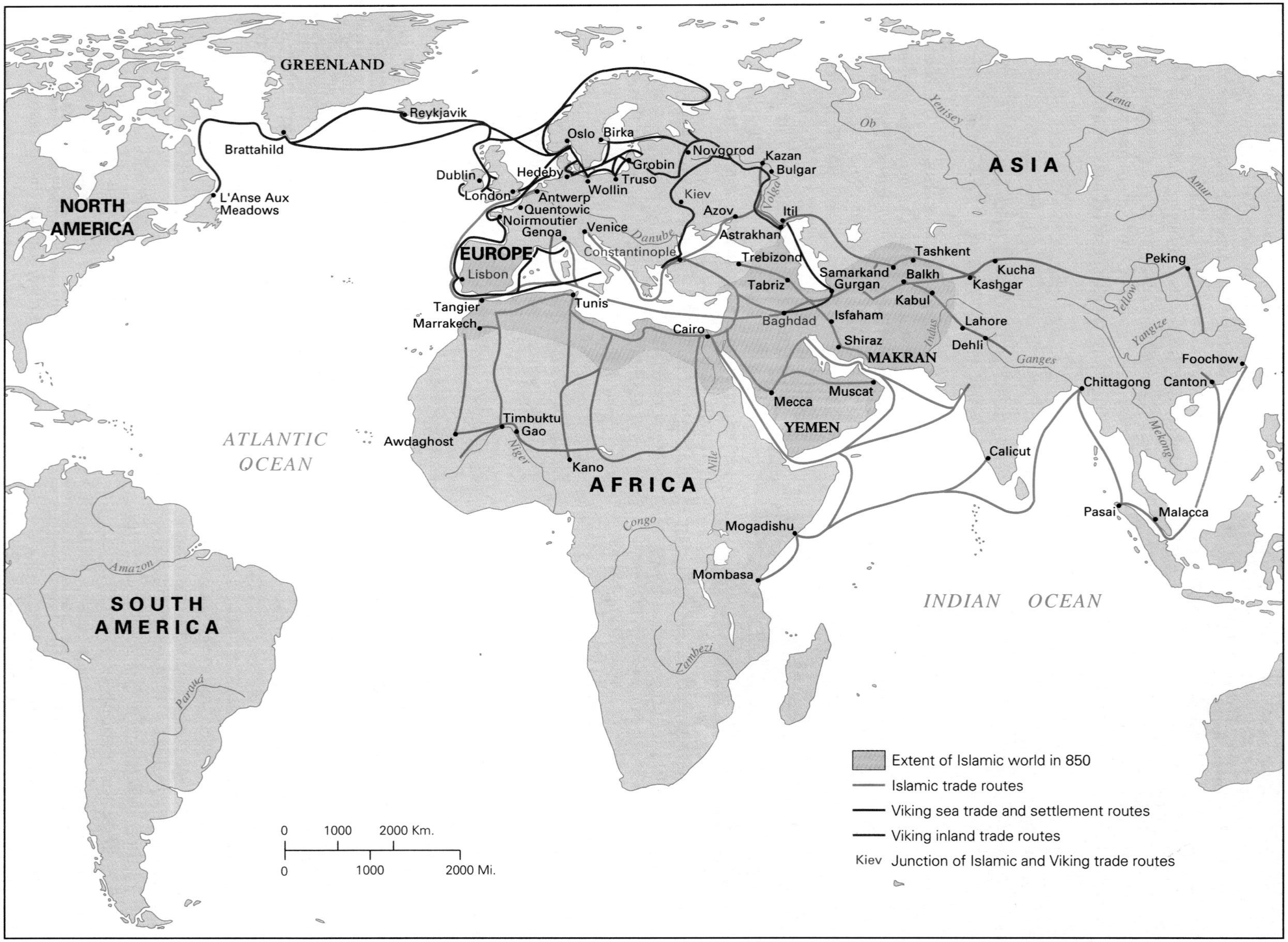

♦ **MAP 1.2 Europe and Its Neighbors, c. A.D. 1000** Europe was not isolated during Medieval times. As shown here, Viking and Islamic empires surrounded Western Europe, and their trade routes crisscrossed the region.

♦ Ferdinand and Isabella were the king of Aragon and queen of Castille—the two dominant Christian states in Spain. Their marriage in 1469 created a new nation powerful enough to drive out the Muslims and launch Spain on an expansive new course. Within a hundred years, the kingdom they created became one of the richest and most powerful nations in the world. *ARXIU MAS.*

where Muslim rule continued. The **Reconquista,** or reconquest of the Iberian Peninsula by Christian Europeans, began at about the same time as the Crusades. With the aid of English Crusaders, Portugal attained independence from Islamic rule in 1147, and by 1380, Portugal's King John I had united that country's various principalities under his rule. In Spain, unification took much longer because feuding local states found it difficult to set aside their differences. But in 1469, **Ferdinand and Isabella,** heirs to the rival thrones of Aragon and Castile, married and created a united state in Spain. Twenty-three years later, in 1492, the Spanish subdued the last Moorish stronghold on the peninsula, completing the Reconquista.

Northern European rulers attempting unification faced problems of their own. In England, France, and elsewhere, Viking populations merged with local Celtic and Teutonic peoples, creating a patchwork of petty kingdoms and principalities. Political, economic, and military rivalries among these quarrelsome groups had to be overcome if northern Europe was going to establish the sort of states that were emerging in Spain and Portugal. Consolidation finally occurred in France around 1480, when Louis XI took control of five rival provinces to create a unified kingdom. Five years later in England, Henry Tudor and the House of Lancaster defeated the rival House of York in the Wars of the Roses, ending nearly a hundred years of civil war. Tudor, as King Henry VII, cemented this victory by marrying into the rival house, wedding Elizabeth of York to finally unify the English throne.

Portuguese Exploration, Africa, and Plantation Slavery

The first of the European states to pull itself together was also the first to contest the hold of the Italian merchants and their Islamic trading partners on eastern commerce. **Henry the Navigator,** the son of Portugal's John I, had a deep, personal interest in geography, which his father encouraged. Under Prince Henry's direction, a school of navigation was established on the southwestern shore of Portugal. From there expeditions sailed west and south looking for new sources of wealth. By the 1430s, the Portuguese had discovered and taken control of the Azores, the Canaries, and Madeira, islands off the western shore of Africa. Within thirty years, Portuguese captains pushed their way to Africa itself, where they came into contact with the **Songhay Empire.**

The Songhay Empire combined the various kingdoms that flanked the Niger River into a single cultural and political entity (see Map 1.3). Before its emergence, separate kingships seem to have united networks of villages. Society was strictly divided

Reconquista The campaign undertaken by European Christians to recapture the Iberian Peninsula from the Moors.

Ferdinand and Isabella Joint rulers of Spain (r. 1469–1504); their marriage in 1469 created a united Spain from the rival kingdoms of Aragon and Castile.

Henry the Navigator Prince who founded an observatory and school of navigation and directed voyages that helped build Portugal's colonial empire.

Songhay Empire A large empire in West Africa; its capital was Timbuktu; its rulers accepted Islam in about A.D. 1000.

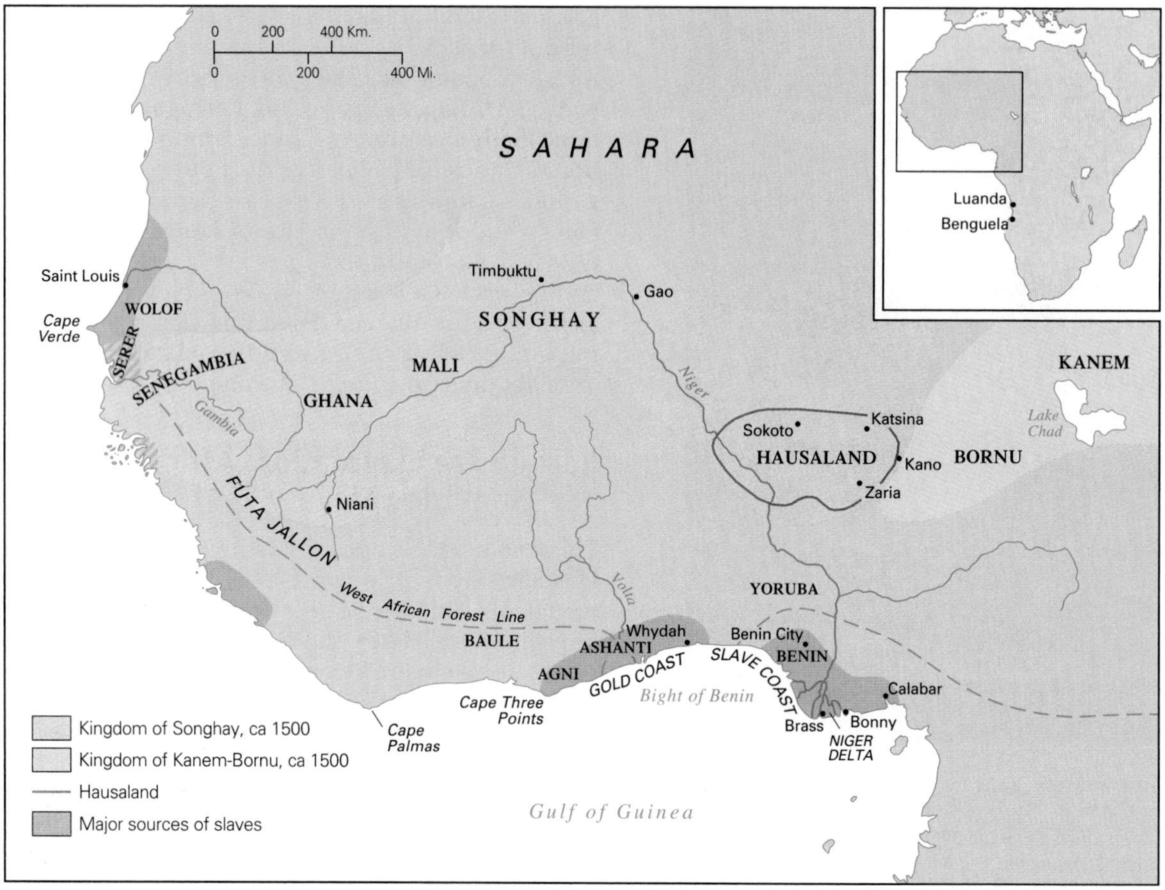

♦ **MAP 1.3 Western Africa at the Time of European Trading Contact** As shown here, the Songhay Empire straddled the main trade routes between Islamic centers north of the Sahara Desert and the rich sources for gold and slaves along the Gulf of Guinea. When Europeans began trading with these regions directly by sea, groups like the Ashanti and Benin, shown here at the heart of the Gold Coast and Slave Coast respectively, became increasingly powerful.

along class lines in these villages. At the top of the social scale was a small, elite, noble class, and at the bottom were slaves. In between were skilled manufacturers—leatherworkers, blacksmiths, and artists—who supplied goods for the nobility.

Pulled together into a single empire, these numerous village societies thrived and culture bloomed. Timbuktu, the Songhay capital, was a cosmopolitan center where African and Islamic influences met. It became a showplace. Its art, architecture, and the accomplishments of its scholars impressed all who ventured there. From Timbuktu, Songhay traders shipped valuable trade goods across the Sahara by means of caravans. The Portuguese, however, offered speedier shipment and higher profits, carrying trade goods directly to Europe by sea.

By the end of the fifteenth century, Portuguese navigators had gained control over the flow of prized items like gold, ivory, and spices out of West Africa, and Portuguese colonizers were growing sugar and other crops on the newly conquered Azores and Canary Islands. Gradually Portuguese plantation owners borrowed an institution from their former Islamic rulers and their African trading partners: slavery. From the beginning of the sixteenth century onward, the Portuguese became increasingly involved in slave trafficking, at first to their own plantations and then to Europe itself. By 1550 Portuguese ships were carrying African slaves throughout the world.

The Continued Quest for Asian Trade

Meanwhile, the Portuguese continued to venture outward. In 1487, Bartholomew Dias became the first

♦ Before the Portuguese opened the area to sea-borne trading, western Africa was connected to the Arab and European worlds by camel caravan. This gold and diamond miniature (the sculpture is only about two-and-a-half inches tall) celebrates the riches that these animals carried out of Africa. *The Metropolitan Museum of Art; gift of the Shaw Foundation, Inc. 1959.*

European to reach the **Cape of Good Hope,** at the southern tip of Africa. Ten years later, Vasco de Gama sailed around the cape and launched the Portuguese exploration of eastern Africa and the Indian Ocean.

By the end of the fifteenth century England, Spain, and France were vying with Portugal to find the shortest, cheapest, and safest sea route between Europe and Asia. Because of its early head start, Portugal remained fairly cautious in its explorations, hugging the coast around Africa before crossing the ocean to India. As latecomers, Spain and England could not afford to take such a conservative approach to exploration. Voyagers from those countries took advantage of borrowed technologies from China and the Arab world to expand their horizons. From China, Europeans acquired the magnetic compass, which allowed mariners to know roughly in what direction they were sailing even when out of sight of land. An Arab invention, the **astrolabe**—a device that allowed navigators to determine their position of latitude—also reduced the uncertainty of navigation. These inventions, together with improvements in steering mechanisms and in hull design, improved captains' control over their ships' direction, speed, and stability.

An impoverished but ambitious sailor from the Italian port city of Genoa was eager to capitalize on the new technology and knowledge. In 1484, **Christopher Columbus** approached John II of Portugal and asked him to support a risky voyage westward from Portugal, across the Atlantic, to the East Indies. When John's geographers warned that Columbus had underestimated the distance of the trip, the king refused to support the enterprise. Undaunted, Columbus peddled his idea to various European governments over the next several years but found no one willing to take the risk. Finally, in 1492, Ferdinand and Isabella's defeat of the Moors provided Columbus with an opportunity.

The Spanish monarchs had just thrown off Islamic rule and added the coastal province of Granada to their holdings. They were eager to break into overseas trading, which was dominated in the east by the Italians and their Arab partners and in the south and west by the Portuguese. Ferdinand and Isabella agreed to equip three ships, granted Columbus 10 percent of any returns from the voyage, and named him "Admiral of the Ocean Sea." In exchange, he promised them a short, safe route to the Orient. On August 3, 1492, Columbus and some ninety sailors departed on the *Niña*, *Pinta*, and *Santa Maria* for the uncharted waters of the Atlantic.

At first Columbus's little fleet enjoyed good weather and made excellent progress, but the winds died and the ships made little headway. Long after Columbus had expected to reach Asia, one of the sailors finally sighted land. Columbus's crew, which had threatened mutiny, was relieved when, on October 12, 1492, the three ships finally made landfall on a small island. Columbus thought he had reached the Indies, but he really reached the islands that we now call the **Bahamas.** Celebrating his escape from

Cape of Good Hope A point of land projecting into the ocean at the southern tip of Africa; European mariners had to sail around the cape to pass from the Atlantic to the Indian Ocean.

astrolabe An instrument that navigators used to measure the height of the sun and stars and calculate their position of latitude (that is, their distance north or south of the equator).

Christopher Columbus Italian explorer in the service of Spain who attempted to reach Asia by sailing west from Europe, thereby arriving in America in 1492.

Bahamas A group of islands in the Atlantic Ocean east of Florida and Cuba.

♦ The Kingdom of Mali, with its capital of Timbuktu, was one of the richest culturally progressive societies in the world during the fourteenth and early fifteenth centuries. This map, from the Catalan Atlas, shows the various trade routes leading into and out of Timbuktu. The figure at the center is Mausa Musa, whom the original caption describes as "the richest, the most powerful lord in all this region on account of the abundance of gold that is gathered in this land." Mali was later absorbed into the Songhay Empire and Timbuktu became a hub for the emerging sea-borne trade with Europe. *Giraudon/Art Resource, NY.*

disaster, Columbus named the place San Salvador (Holy Savior).

Over the next ten weeks, Columbus explored the mysteries of the Caribbean, making landfalls on the islands now known as Cuba and Hispaniola. He collected spices, coconuts, bits of gold, and some native captives. He called these people "Indians" because of his belief that he had reached the Indies. He described them as "a loving people without covetousness" who, he thought, would make excellent servants. Columbus then returned to Spain, carrying what he was sure was evidence that he had reached Japan and the Indies. He was welcomed home with great celebration, and his account of the trip and the goods he brought back helped gain him backing for three more voyages. Over the next several years, the Spanish gained a permanent foothold in the region that Columbus had discovered and became aware that the area was not the Indies or Japan but a world entirely new to them.

At first, the knowledge that a new world had been discovered was greeted as bad news. The purpose of westward voyages was access to the riches of Asia, not contact with some undiscovered place, and as knowledge of the New World spread, the primary goal of exploration became finding a route around or through the continent of North America. Explorers spent another four hundred years searching for this **Northwest Passage.**

England, like Spain, was jealous of Portugal's trade monopoly, and in 1497, Henry VII commissioned another Italian mariner, Giovanni Caboto, to search for a sea route to India. **John Cabot,** as the English called him, succeeded in crossing the north Atlantic, arriving in the area that Leif Ericson had colonized nearly five hundred years earlier. Shortly thereafter, another Italian, **Amerigo Vespucci,** sailing under the Spanish flag, sighted the northeastern shore of South America and sailed northward into the Caribbean in search of a passage to the East. Finally, in 1524, Giovanni da Verrazano, sailing for France, explored the Atlantic coast of North America, charting the coastline of what later became the thirteen English mainland colonies.

A New Transatlantic World

Scholars have speculated that Cabot, Verrazano, and other explorers who followed Columbus already knew what lay ahead in North America. It is certainly likely that the English and other northern Europeans had heard about the Viking settlements in Newfoundland and elsewhere. But recent research hints that Cabot had inside information from fishermen who had already made North America a regular part of their economic world.

It appears that as the Vikings withdrew from the north Atlantic, adventurous fishermen and other voyagers from England, France, and **Basque** villages in Spain and Portugal began exploring the fertile fishing grounds off the northern shores of North America. Such voyages had become so common-

Northwest Passage The rumored and hoped-for water route from Europe to Asia by way of North America that early explorers tried to find.

John Cabot Italian explorer who led the English expedition that sailed along the North American mainland in 1497.

Amerigo Vespucci Italian explorer of the South American coast; Europeans named America after him.

Basques An ethnic group that lived primarily in north-central Spain and was heavily involved in early North American fishing activities.

place after 1500 that in 1506 the king of Portugal placed a 10 percent tax on fish being imported from North America.

These voyages did more than feed the European imagination and the continent's taste for fish. It appears that these fishermen established temporary camps along the shores of North America to provide land support for their enterprise. Gradually, as the Native Americans and the fishermen came to know each other, they began to exchange goods. Europeans, even relatively poor fishermen, had many things that the Indians lacked: copper pots, knives, jewelry, woolen blankets, and hundreds of other novelties. For their part, the Indians provided firewood, food, ivory, and furs.

There is no documentary record revealing the origin of the fur trade between Europeans and such subarctic Indians as the Micmacs. However, this trade was well established before any of the formal explorations sponsored by European governments. When, in 1534, **Jacques Cartier** made the first official exploration of the Canadian coast for the French government, he was approached by party after party of Indians offering to trade furs for the goods he carried. He could only conclude that many Europeans had come before him.

Although fish continued to play an important role in transatlantic commerce, it was furs that finally drew the French ever more energetically into North American exploration and colonization. In 1542, Cartier established a small colony near present-day Quebec to take advantage of the Indians' desire to trade. But internal problems in France prevented the serious development of a fur industry for over a century.

The presence of explorers like Verrazano and Cartier and of the unknown number of anonymous fishermen and part-time traders had several effects on the native population. The Micmacs, Hurons, and other northeastern Indian groups approached the invading Europeans in friendship, eager to trade and to learn more about the strangers. In part this response was, no doubt, a sign of natural curiosity, but it also reflected some serious climatic and other changes taking place in the native world of North America.

As we have noted, the onset of the Little Ice Age had far-reaching effects. As the climate got colder, the Thule Inuits began extending their hunting territory farther south, putting pressure on hunter-gatherers in the subarctic. These groups responded by withdrawing even farther south, where they began to encroach on Algonquin and Iroquoian Indians. Meanwhile, the deteriorating climate made it more difficult for groups like the Iroquois to depend on their corn crops for food. Forced to rely more on hunting and gathering, the Iroquois had to expand their territory, and in doing so came into conflict with their neighbors.

All these changes brought at least three important outcomes. First, warfare increased among the northeastern Indians as various groups scrambled to expand their holdings. Second, as war became more common, groups grew more inclined to form formal alliances for mutual defense. One of these, the Iroquois Confederacy, created by Hiawatha around 1450 (see Individual Choices: Hiawatha), would become a major force in world diplomacy during the seventeenth and eighteenth centuries. And third, Indians found it beneficial to welcome Europeans into their midst—as trading partners bearing new tools that made survival easier under new circumstances, as allies in the evolving conflicts with neighboring Indian groups, and as powerful magicians whose **shamans** might provide explanations and cures for the hard times that had befallen the eastern Indians.

The Challenges of Mutual Discovery

- How did European contact affect the choices made by American Indians?
- What varied attitudes did Europeans choose to adopt in their relations with Indians and Africans?
- What were some outcomes of the Columbian Exchange?

Europeans approached the New World with certain ideas in mind and defined what they found there in terms that reflected what they already believed. American Indians approached Europeans in the same way. Both of these groups—as well as Africans—were thrown into a new world of understanding that challenged many of their fundamental assumptions. They also exchanged material goods that affected

Jacques Cartier Frenchman who in 1534 explored the St. Lawrence River, giving France its primary claim to territories in the New World.

shaman A person who acts as a link between the visible world and an invisible spirit world; a shaman's duties include healing, conducting religious ceremonies, and predicting the future.

INDIVIDUAL CHOICES

Confederacy over War

Hiawatha

New conditions in North America led to increasing jealousy and warfare among the five Iroquois tribes in the fifteenth and sixteenth centuries. Overcoming many constraints, Hiawatha convinced his people to form the League of the Haudenosaunee, a political, military, and religious alliance that made the Iroquois a major force in world diplomacy throughout the colonial era. The New York Public Library.

Hiawatha is an almost mythical figure, but historians have verified that the oral testimony concerning this Iroquois hero's life and the impact of his decisions on American history are rooted in fact. Probably around 1450, Hiawatha chose to rise above his own miserable condition and unify his people in pursuit of a common vision. The outcome was the Iroquois Confederacy.

Although not all of the oral accounts agree, it appears that Hiawatha was a Mohawk, born into that branch of the larger Iroquoian Indian family sometime shortly after 1400. Things were hard for all of the Iroquois at the time of his birth: climate change had made corn production less dependable, and the people were having to hunt and gather more wild foods to supplement their diet. As hunters from individual villages roamed deeper and deeper into the forests looking for food, they encountered others who, like themselves, were desperate to harvest the diminishing resources. Conflicts became common. "Everywhere there was peril and everywhere mourning," says one version of the story. "Feuds with outer nations and feuds with brother nations, feuds of sister towns and feuds of families and clans made every warrior a stealthy man who liked to kill."

Young and unmarried, Hiawatha chose to leave his village and live alone in the woods to

their physical well-being profoundly. Mutual discovery in America influenced the choices people were to make on a global scale and changed the world.

A Meeting of Minds in America

Most Europeans had a firm sense of how the world was arranged, who occupied it, and how they had come to be where they were. The existence of America, and especially the existence of American Indians, challenged that secure knowledge. In the first stages of mutual discovery in America, however, most Europeans were content to mentally reshape what they found in the New World to fit with what they expected to find. Columbus expected to find India and Indians, and he believed that was precisely what he had found. Other Europeans understood that America was a new land and the Indians were a new people, but they attempted to fit both into the cosmic map outlined in the Bible and in the science of the time. Some Europeans assumed that the inhabitants of the new land were more pure and less corrupted than Europeans. Others viewed them as poor, ignorant savages.

Columbus's initial comments about the American Indians set the tone for many of those to follow.

seek his own survival. But food was scarce, and he became a cannibal, hunting down lone travelers, killing them, and eating their flesh. One day after a successful hunt, Hiawatha was butchering a victim, but before he could begin his meal, he discovered that he had a visitor. The man, called Deganawida (Two River Currents Flowing Together), pointed out Hiawatha's sad and dishonorable state and told him of his vision to unify all the Iroquois into a great and peaceful nation. Shamed, Hiawatha vowed never to eat human flesh again and to spend his life bringing Deganawida's vision to life.

Hiawatha moved back among the Mohawks, married, and began telling the people about Deganawida's vision. Although many found his words inspiring, some, like Onondaga leader Tadadaho, opposed him. Tadadaho and his supporters finally attacked Hiawatha, killing his family and forcing him to flee once again into the woods.

Choosing not to give up, Hiawatha tried to think of some way to convince his enemies among the Iroquois to accept the idea of cooperation. He finally hit on a device: he began weaving together a belt made from wampum shell strings showing a great chain connecting the five northern Iroquois nations—Mohawk, Oneida, Onondaga, Cayuga, and Seneca. Carrying his belt, Hiawatha traveled among the five nations, telling them that they could survive only if they ceased fighting among themselves and joined together. He finally won over even Tadadaho, whose Onandaga Nation became the keeper of the council fires. Together Hiawatha, Deganawida, Tadadaho, and the other leaders of the Five Nations created a confederation government. In 1722, the Tuscarora Nation from North Carolina moved north and also joined the confederation, becoming the sixth nation in the Iroquois League. And finally, in 1754, Benjamin Franklin unsuccessfully tried to follow Hiawatha's lead by uniting the thirteen British North American colonies into a similar league that would join the Iroquois Confederacy for mutual defense against the French and their Indian allies.

Choosing to rise above his own misery—first the dishonor of becoming a cannibal and then banishment and the loss of his family—Hiawatha overcame the constraints imposed by new historical conditions and enemies like Tadadaho. Through his perseverance and oratorical skills, he finally convinced the five northern Iroquois nations to choose confederacy over war. The outcome was the emergence of a whole new Iroquois society and the dawning of a new era of Iroquois power and influence.

"They are so **ingenuous** and free with all they have," Columbus wrote, "that no one would believe it who has not seen it. Of anything that they possess, if it be asked of them, they never say no; on the contrary, they invite you to share it and show as much love as if their hearts went with it." Such writings were widely circulated in Europe and led to a perception of the Indians as noble savages, men and women free from the temptations and vanities of modern civilization.

Not all Europeans held this view of American Indians. Amerigo Vespucci shared the opinion that Indians were savage, but he found them less than noble. "They marry as many wives as they please," he explained. "The son cohabits with mother, brother with sister, male cousin with female, and any man with the first woman he meets. . . . Beyond the fact that they have no church, no religion and are not **idolaters,** what more can I say?" Much more, actually. Vespucci reported that the Indians practiced

ingenuous Lacking in sophistication; artless.
idolater A person who worships idols.

♦ Europeans had trouble understanding American Indians, sometimes casting them as noble savages and other times casting them as devils. The Brazilian Indian shown in these two works illustrates the conflicting views. In one, the feather-clad Indian is shown as a wise magus paying homage to the Christ-child; in the other, an Indian devil wears the same costume while presiding over the tortures of Hell. *"Adoration of the Magi" by Master of Viseu. Museu de Grao Vasco; "Inferno" Anonymous, Portuguese. Giraudon/Art Resource, NY.*

cannibalism and prostitution and decorated themselves in gaudy and "monstrous" ways.

Much that Vespucci and other Europeans found most objectionable about Native American peoples was the result of their trying to understand different cultures in their own terms. For example, Europeans often criticized Indian men for engaging in sport or sleeping while their women slaved in the fields. What the European observers did not understand was that what they perceived as "sport" was, in some cases, hunting necessary to the survival of the group and, in other cases, games designed as training for war or as peaceful alternatives to war. When not actively hunting or doing other activities that helped the group, men often did sleep in order to conserve energy so that those whose work was needed at that particular time would have enough food to sustain them. As for the women, their work in the fields was a source of great power—the plants and the food they produced belonged to the women and were theirs to distribute. Women worked hard, but they were working for themselves and the group, not for the men.

In some ways, the arrival of Europeans may have been easier for American Indians to understand and explain than the existence of American Indians was for the Europeans. To Indians, the world was alive, animated by a spiritual force that was both universal and intelligent. This force took on many forms—human and nonhuman. Some of these forms were visible in the everyday world of experience, some were visible only at special times, and some were never visible. Social ties based on **perceived kinship** and **reciprocal trade** linked all creatures—human and nonhuman—together into a common cosmos. These connections were chronicled in myth

perceived kinship The belief that the world is held together by mythic family connections between humans, animals, natural objects, and spiritual beings.

reciprocal trade A system of trading in which the objective is equal exchange of commodities rather than profit.

and were maintained through ritual, which often involved the exchange of ceremonial items believed to have spiritual value. Such objects included quartz and volcanic glass crystals, copper, mica, shells, and other rare and light-reflecting objects. In the pre-Columbian trading world, they passed from society to society, establishing a spiritual bond between the initial givers and the eventual receivers, even though the two groups might never meet.

Europeans and European goods slipped easily into this ceremonial trading system. The trade items—glass beads, mirrors, brass bells—that the Europeans generally offered to American Indians on first contact resembled closely the items that the Indians traditionally used to establish friendly spiritual and economic relations with strangers—mica, copper, and shells.

Europeans perceived such items as nearly worthless trinkets, of value only because they were personal property and therefore legally sacred. Native Americans perceived these objects differently. According to their beliefs, all things have spirits of their own and belong to themselves. Thus a knife, for example—whether made by an Indian stone smith or by a European metalworker—was a living being that might become exclusively associated with one person, but only by mutual agreement. This belief baffled Europeans, especially when items that they regarded as their own lifeless personal property entered into exclusive kin relationships with Indians. Such transfers of ownership, which Europeans usually defined as theft, were often the cause of ill will and violence.

Differing perceptions of land also led to misunderstanding. According to Indian belief, people cannot own land: the land is a living being—a mother—who feeds, clothes, and houses people as long as she receives proper respect. The idea of buying or selling land was unthinkable to Indians. When Europeans offered spiritually significant objects in exchange for land on which to build, farm, or hunt, Indians perceived the offer as an effort to join an already existing relationship, not to transfer ownership.

Europeans did not appear to be either superhuman or even particularly strange to the Indians. Their mode of arrival, manners, speech, and dress probably seemed odd, but no odder than the language, behavior, and appearance of traders from the Valley of Mexico or other groups active in the pre-Columbian trading world. The perceived similarity of the trade goods offered by the Europeans led Indians to accept the newcomers as simply another new group in the complex social cosmos uniting the spiritual and material worlds.

The Columbian Exchange

Even though Europeans and American Indians saw some similarities in each other, their worlds differed greatly, sometimes in ways both groups were unaware of. The natural environments of these worlds were different, and the passage of people, plants, and animals among Europe, Africa, and North America wrought profound changes in all three continents. Historians call this process the **Columbian Exchange.**

Perhaps the most tragic trade among the three continents came about as the direct and unavoidable consequence of human contact. During the period leading up to the age of exploration, many Europeans lost their lives to epidemic diseases. The Black Death of the fourteenth century, for example, wiped out over a third of Europe's population. Exposure to smallpox, measles, typhus, and other serious diseases often had devastating results, but Europeans gradually developed resistance to them. In contrast, the Indian peoples whom Columbus and other European explorers encountered lived in an environment in which contagious diseases were never a serious threat until the Europeans arrived, so they had no **acquired immunity** to the various bacteria and viruses that Europeans carried. As a result, the new diseases spread very rapidly and were much more deadly among the native peoples than they were among Europeans.

Controversy rages over the number of Indians killed by imported European diseases. Estimates of how many people lived in America north of Mexico in 1492 run from a high of 25 million to a low of 1 million. At the moment, most scholars accept a range of from 3 to 10 million. Even if the most conservative estimate is correct, the raw numbers of people who died of smallpox, typhus, measles, and other imported diseases were enormous. In areas of early and continuing association between Europeans and Indians, between 90 and 95 percent of the native population appears to have died of disease during the first century of contact. Although the percentage was probably lower in areas where contact was infrequent and where native populations

Columbian Exchange The exchange of people, plants, and animals among Europe, Africa, and North America that occurred after Columbus's arrival in the New World.

acquired immunity Resistance or partial resistance to a disease; it develops in a population over time, after exposure to harmful bacteria and viruses.

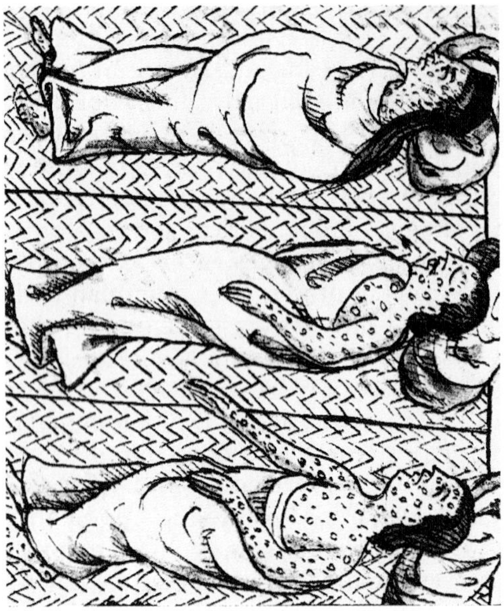

♦ European diseases killed many millions of Indians during the initial stages of contact because they had no immunity to such epidemic illnesses as influenza, measles, and plague. Smallpox was one of the deadliest of these imported diseases. This Aztec drawing illustrates smallpox's impact, from the initial appearance of skin lesions through death. Traditional Indian medical practice not only was unable to cure the disease, but physical contact between medicine men and patients actually helped to spread it. *Biblioteca Medicea Laurenziana.*

were sparse, disease took a terrible toll as it followed the lines of kinship and trade that held native North America together.

Disease, however, did not flow in only one direction—from Europe to the New World. Some diseases that originated in Africa found their way to both North America and Europe. And at least one, **syphilis,** may have originated in the Western Hemisphere and migrated eastward. This exchange of microorganisms created a peculiar pattern of contagion and immunity within the populations that converged in North America. American Indians appear to have been less devastated physically by syphilis, to which they may have possessed partial immunity. Africans were largely unaffected by various **malarial** fevers that ravaged both European and native populations. Europeans found measles to be a mildly unpleasant childhood disease, but for both Africans and Indians it was a mass killer. The march of exchanged diseases across the North American landscape and their effects on various populations provided a constant backdrop for the continent's history.

Less immediate but perhaps equally extreme ecological effects arose from the passage of plants among Europe, North America, and Africa. The introduction of plants into the New World expanded a process that had been taking place for centuries in the Old World. Trade with Asia had carried exotic plants such as bananas, sugar cane, and rice into Africa as early as 2,300 years ago. From Africa, these plants were transplanted to Iberian-claimed islands like the Canaries and eventually to America where, along with cotton, indigo, coffee, and other imports, they would become **cash crops** on European-controlled plantations. Grains like wheat, barley, and millet were readily transplanted to suitable areas in North America, as were grazing grasses and various vegetables like turnips, spinach, and cabbage.

North American plants traveled from west to east in the Columbian Exchange. Leading the way in economic importance was tobacco, a stimulant used widely in North America for ceremonial purposes and broadly adopted by Europeans and Africans as a recreational drug. Another stimulant, cocoa, also enjoyed significant popularity among Old World consumers. In addition, New World vegetables helped to revolutionize world food supplies. Remarkably easy to grow, maize thrived in Europe, the Middle East, and Africa. In addition, the white potato, tomato, manioc, squash, and beans and peas native to the Western Hemisphere were transplanted throughout the world.

Animals also moved through the Columbian Exchange. North America teemed with deer, bison, elk, moose, and uncounted species of rodents, but these animals had to be hunted rather than herded and were useless as draft animals. Europeans brought horses, pigs, cattle, oxen, sheep, goats, and domesticated fowl to America, and these Old World domesticated animals did well in their new environment.

The transplanting of European grain crops and domesticated animals reshaped the land itself in North America. Changing the contours of the land

syphilis An infectious disease usually transmitted through sexual contact; if untreated, it can lead to paralysis and death.

malarial Related to malaria, an infectious disease characterized by chills, fever, and sweating; it is often transmitted through mosquito bites.

cash crop A crop raised in large quantities for sale rather than for local or home consumption.

by clearing trees and undergrowth and by plowing and fencing changed the flow of water, the distribution of seeds, the nesting of birds, and the movement of native animals. Gradually, imported livestock pushed aside native animals, and imported plants choked out native ones. The introduction of some harmful imports was entirely accidental. Dandelions, for example, were probably introduced into the New World accidentally. But partly as the result of overgrazing by European livestock, this aggressive weed was able to force out plants with greater food value.

Probably the most important and far-reaching environmental impact of the Columbian Exchange was its overall influence on human populations. Although exchanged diseases killed many millions of Indians and lesser numbers of Africans and Europeans, the transplantation of North American plants significantly expanded food production in what had been marginal areas of Europe and Africa. At the same time, the environmental changes that Europeans wrought along the Atlantic shore of North America permitted the region to support many more people than it had sustained under Indian cultivation. The overall result in Europe and Africa was a population explosion that eventually spilled over to repopulate a devastated North America.

New Worlds in Africa and America

As the Columbian Exchange redistributed plants, animals, and populations among Europe, Africa, and North America, it permanently altered the history of both hemispheres. In North America, for example, the combination of disease, environmental transformation, and immigrant population pressure changed American Indian life and culture in profound ways.

Clearly, imported disease had the most devastating influence on the lives of Indians. Cooperative labor was required for hunting and gathering, and native groups that continued to depend on those activities faced extinction if disease caused a shortage of labor. Also, most societies in North America were **nonliterate:** elders and storytellers passed on their collective knowledge from one generation to another. Wholesale death by disease wiped out these bearers of practical, religious, and cultural knowledge. The result of this loss was confusion and disorientation among survivors. In an effort to continue, survivors banded together to share labor and lore. Members of formerly self-sustaining kinship groups joined together in composite villages or, in some cases, intertribal leagues or confederacies.

The devastation that European diseases wrought eased the way for the deeper penetration of Europeans—and the diseases they carried—into North America. Not only did the elimination of native populations make it easier for Europeans to claim the land, but the confusion and devastation brought about by the massive number of deaths pushed Indians to seek alliances with the newcomers. European tools, for example, helped make smaller work forces more productive—a true benefit, given reduced numbers—and Indians welcomed these items and their owners. Similarly, natives sought spiritual explanations and possible remedies for the hardships they faced. Many were drawn to European religion, adding features of Christianity to native beliefs and rituals in an effort to restore spiritual balance in the world. Together, economic and spiritual forces pushed the Indians into an increasingly tangled alliance with Europeans.

The Columbian Exchange also severely disrupted life in Africa. Until well into the nineteenth century, Europeans did not penetrate Africa to the extent that they penetrated the New World. European and American influences in Africa tended to be indirect and were carried inland from coastal outposts by Africans themselves.

Africa had long been a key supplier of labor throughout the world. The ancient Egyptians had imported slaves from Ethiopia and other regions south of Egypt, a practice that continued through Roman times. But it was Islamic traders who turned the enslavement of Africans into a thriving enterprise. Beginning in about A.D. 700, North African Muslims established regular caravan routes across the desert into west-central Africa, and the slaves they purchased from African traders quickly became a dominant trade item, second only to gold in overall value. Perhaps as many as 4 million people were carried across the desert and sold into slavery between A.D. 700 and the time the Portuguese redirected the trade in the sixteenth century.

European technology, wealth, and ideas helped to foster the development of aggressive centralized

nonliterate Lacking a system of reading and writing, relying instead on mnemonic (memory-assisting) devices like pictures and on storytelling.

♦ Parties of captured villagers from Africa's interior were bound together and marched to trading centers on the coast, where they were sold to Europeans or Muslims. The slave drivers were heavily influenced by outside contact. One of those shown here is wearing a Muslim-influenced turban, while the clothing of the other is more European. Note, too, he carries both a gun and a traditional African spear. *The Granger Collection.*

states along the **Gold Coast** and **Slave Coast** bordering the Gulf of Guinea on the western shore of Africa (see Map 1.3). Armed with European firearms, aggressive tribes like the Ashanti engaged in large-scale raiding deep into the Niger and Congo River regions. These raiders captured millions of prisoners, whom they herded back to the coast and sold to Portuguese, Spanish, Dutch, and other European traders to supply labor for mines and plantations in the New World.

It is difficult to determine the number of people sold in the West African slave trade from 1500 to 1800. The most recent estimates suggest that more than 9.5 million enslaved Africans arrived in the New World during this three-hundred-year period. And they were only a small portion of the total number of Africans victimized by the system. On average, between 10 and 20 percent of the blacks shipped to the Americas died on the slave ships. Adding in those who were shipped to other locations in the Eastern Hemisphere, those who were kept in slavery within Africa, and those who died during raids and on the march to the coast yields a staggering total. Africa lost a great deal in the Columbian Exchange.

A New World in Europe

The discovery of America and the Columbian Exchange also had staggering repercussions on life in Europe. New economic opportunities and new ideas demanded new kinds of political and economic organization. The discovery of the New World clearly forced a new and more modern society onto Europeans, but it also produced an air of crisis.

Europe's population was already rising when potatoes, maize, and other New World crops began to revolutionize food production. The population of Europe in 1500 was about 81 million. It grew to 100 million by 1600 and then to 120 million by 1700. This growth occurred despite nearly continuous wars and a flood of migration to the New World. Europe was literally spilling out at the seams.

With populations on the rise and overseas empires to run, European rulers and their advisers saw that centralized states appeared to offer the most promising avenue for harnessing the riches of the New World while controlling ever-increasing numbers of people at home. The sons and daughters of Europe's first generation of **absolute monarchs** chose to continue the centralization of authority begun by their parents.

As Europeans responded to social, political, and economic changes, traditional patterns of authority broke down, especially in the realm of religion. A particularly devastating blow to religious authority

Gold Coast A region of coastal West Africa in present-day Ghana, named for the large quantities of gold found in the area and brought to the coast for sale.

Slave Coast A region of coastal West Africa adjacent to the Gold Coast; the principal source of the slaves taken out of West Africa from the sixteenth to the early nineteenth century.

absolute monarch The ruler of a kingdom in which every aspect of national life—including politics, religion, the economy, and social affairs—comes under royal authority.

♦ This portrait of John Calvin by an anonymous Flemish painter captures his serious quality, even as a young man. Despite his stern appearance, Calvin emphasized devotion to God and strict self-discipline as means for creating human happiness. *Eric Lessing/Art Resource, NY.*

came from the pen of Martin Luther, a German monk. Luther preached that Christians could achieve salvation without the intercession of the Roman Catholic church. Salvation, he said, was God's gift to the faithful. In 1517, Luther presented a set of arguments, called the **Ninety-five Theses,** maintaining that only individual repentance and the grace of God could save sinners.

Luther's ideas took root among a generation of theologians who were dissatisfied with the corruption and superstition they found in the medieval Catholic church. A Frenchman, John Calvin, further undermined the church's authority. Like Luther, Calvin believed that salvation was a gift from God. But Calvin further believed that God had chosen the souls to be saved and the souls to be damned when he created the world and that no human actions—no good works, no prayers, no church intervention—could alter God's plan. Those whom God had elected to save, Calvin called **the elect.** He said that only God knew who was among the elect and who among the damned, but he urged Christians to engage in constant meditation, prayer, and scriptural study and attempt to live as though they were among the chosen. In practice, Calvinists—followers of Calvin—insisted on strict discipline and social control as keys to worldly happiness and as possible evidence of election.

Known as **Protestantism,** the doctrines of Luther, Calvin, and others who wanted to reform the Catholic church formed an ideology that appealed to a broad audience in the rapidly changing world of the sixteenth century. Ever critical of entrenched authority, the new doctrines attracted lawyers, bureaucrats, merchants, and manufacturers, whose economic and political status was on the rise thanks to expansion and the Columbian Exchange. As the **Reformation** gathered strength, members of the middling classes were most drawn to Protestant ideas, but many in the ruling classes also found aspects of the new theology attractive. In Germany, Luther's challenge to the priesthood, and by extension to the Catholic church itself, led many local princes to question the **divine right** to authority claimed by the ruler of the **Holy Roman Empire,** and they became

Ninety-five Theses A document prepared by Martin Luther in 1517 protesting certain Catholic practices that he believed were contrary to the will of God.

the elect According to Calvinism, the people chosen by God for salvation.

Protestantism From the root word *protest*, the beliefs and practices of Christians who broke with the Roman Catholic church; Protestants accepted the Bible as the only source of revelation, believed salvation to be God's gift to the faithful, and believed the faithful could have a direct, personal relationship with God.

Reformation The sixteenth-century rise of Protestantism, with the establishment of state-sponsored Protestant churches in England, the Netherlands, parts of Germany and Switzerland, and elsewhere.

divine right The idea that monarchs derive their right to rule directly from God and are accountable only to God.

Holy Roman Empire A political entity authorized by the Catholic church in 1356 unifying Central Europe under an emperor elected by four princes and three Catholic archbishops.

eager to establish a German national church. Similarly, **Henry VIII** of England, at one time a critic of Luther's ideas, found Protestantism convenient when he wanted to resist the authority of the pope and expand English national power.

Henry VIII, the son of Henry VII and Elizabeth of York, was the first undisputed heir to the English throne in several generations, and he was consumed with the desire to avoid renewed civil war by having a son who could inherit the crown. When his wife Catherine of Aragon, daughter of Ferdinand and Isabella of Spain, failed to bear a boy, Henry demanded in 1527 that Pope Clement VII grant him a divorce and permission to marry someone else. Fearful of Spanish reprisals on Catherine's behalf, Clement refused. In desperation, Henry launched an English reformation by seizing the Catholic church in England, gaining complete control of it by 1535.

Henry was probably not a staunch believer in the views aired by Luther and others. But the idea of unifying religious and civil authority under his personal control did appeal to him. In addition, the Catholic church owned extensive and valuable lands in England, estates that Henry could use to enhance his wealth and power. In his war against the pope's authority, he needed Protestant support, so he reluctantly opened the door to Protestant practices in his newly created Church of England, or Anglican church.

After Henry's death, his very young son—finally born to his third wife, Jane Seymour—ascended the throne as Edward VI. In the absence of a strong king, Protestants had virtual free rein, and the pace of reform quickened. Young King Edward, however, was a frail child and died after ruling for only six years. Mary, his oldest sister, succeeded him. Daughter of Henry's first wife, Catherine of Aragon, Mary had married Philip II of Spain and was a devout Roman Catholic. She attempted to reverse the reforming trend, cruelly suppressing Protestantism by burning several hundred leading reformers at the stake. But her brutality only drove the movement underground and made it more militant. By the time her half-sister Elizabeth, who was born and raised a Protestant, inherited the crown in 1558, the Protestant underground had become powerful and highly motivated. In fact, **Elizabeth I** spent her entire reign trying to reach a workable settlement with Protestant **dissenters** that would permit them free worship without endangering her control over church and state. Like the European-wide tension between Protestantism and Catholicism, the tension in England between dissenters and the Anglican church would significantly affect European settlement in the New World.

Henry VIII King of England (r. 1509–1547); his desire to divorce his first wife led him to break with Catholicism and establish the Church of England.

Elizabeth I Queen of England (r. 1558–1603); she succeeded the Catholic Mary I and re-established Protestantism in England; her reign was a time of domestic prosperity and cultural achievement.

dissenter A person who does not accept the doctrines of an established or national church.

SUMMARY

Expectations
Constraints
Choices
Outcomes

Making America began perhaps as long as 70,000 years ago, when the continent's first human occupants began the long process of fitting themselves to a land they would call their own. *Expecting* better conditions than they left behind in Asia, they migrated across Beringia and then overcame or adapted to *constraints* presented by the ever-changing new environment in which they found themselves. Over thousands of years, they continually made new *choices* in economic strategies, social arrangements, and politics to preserve and enhance their lives. The eventual *outcome* of these choices was a rich and flourishing world of different cultures, linked by common religious and economic bonds.

At first, the arrival of Europeans only added another society to an already cosmopolitan sphere. The Vikings came and went, as perhaps did other non-Indians. But ultimately, natural forces combined with the Atlantic crossing, and the dynamic European society that arose after the Crusades and plagues of the Middle Ages became more intrusive. The outcome presented the people in America with *constraints* that they had never dreamed of: economic crises, disease, war, and then environmental changes wrought by the Europeans who followed Columbus. These constraints soon limited the choices open to Native Americans.

In addition, influences from the New World reached out to accelerate processes that were already changing *expectations* and *constraints* in the Old World. The flow of wealth and food out of the West was increasing populations, and this growth, with the accompanying rise of powerful kings and strong nations, led to continuing conflict over newfound resources. In Africa, strong coastal states chose to raid weaker neighboring tribes, more than doubling the flow of slaves out of Africa. These *outcomes*, in turn, influenced further developments in America. As disease destroyed thousands, perhaps millions, of Indians, newcomers came pouring in. These newcomers came from very different physical environments and had distinctly foreign ideas about nature—their novel practices brought drastic changes to the face of the land. Continuing interactions among these various newcomers, and between them and the survivors of America's original people, would have a profound *outcome*: the making of America.

SUGGESTED READINGS

Brian M. Fagan. *The Great Journey : The Peopling of Ancient America* (1987).

An excellent, though thought by some an overly conservative, recounting of the peopling of North America during the last stages of the Great Ice Age.

Alfred W. Crosby. *The Columbian Exchange: Biological and Cultural Consequences of 1492* (1972).

The landmark book that brought the Columbian impact into focus for the first time. Parts of the book are technical, but the explanations are clear and exciting.

William H. McNeill. *Plagues and Peoples* (1976).

A fascinating history of disease and its impact on people throughout the period of European expansion and New World colonization.

Roland Oliver, and J. D. Fage. *A Short History of Africa* (1988).

The most concise and understandably written comprehensive history of Africa available.

Marvin B. Becker. *Civility and Society in Western Europe, 1300–1600* (1988).

A brief but comprehensive look at social conditions in Europe during the period leading up to and out of the exploration of the New World.

Peter Laslett. *The World We Have Lost Further Explored* (1983).

Updated third edition of the author's well respected characterization of British society before colonization. Highly readable and interesting.

EUROPEANS AND INDIANS IN NORTH AMERICA Although Europeans did not realize immediately that Columbus had encountered an entirely new world in 1492, they quickly came to understand the economic, political, and military potential involved in American colonization. As this map shows, exploration continued into the seventeenth century as Europeans scrambled to claim individual pieces of New World real estate.

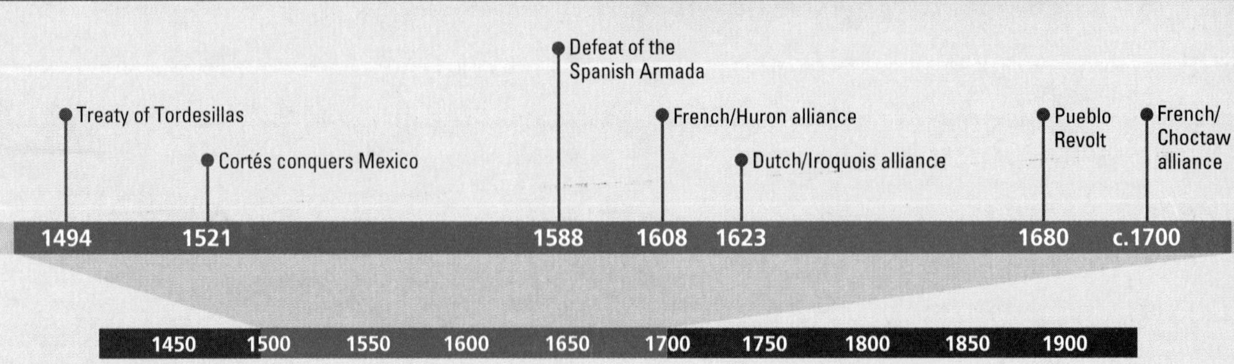

CHAPTER 2

A Continent on the Move, 1400–1725

The New Europe and the Atlantic World

- What were some economic constraints that pushed European rulers to promote exploration and colonization in North America?
- What political and religious rivalries influenced European choices regarding New World colonization?

European Empires in America

- What similarities and differences characterized the choices that Spanish, French, and Dutch officials made in starting their empires in North America?
- What constraints did the choices made by colonists themselves place on administrative policies?

Indians and the European Challenge

- What constraints did environmental changes place on Indians?
- What constraints and opportunities came with the arrival of Europeans?
- What social and political choices did Indians make in response to these changes?

Conquest and Accommodation in a Shared New World

- What constraints most affected the lives of settlers in New Mexico, Louisiana, and New Netherland?
- How did choices made by settlers and American Indians help both groups to deal with these constraints?

INTRODUCTION

Expectations
Constraints
Choices
Outcomes

The European powers that engaged in colonizing efforts in the world that Columbus had sailed into intended to impose their own political, economic, and cultural stamp on the regions they occupied. But they encountered many *constraints.* New World environments did not resemble those in the Old World, and Native Americans had their own agendas for dealing with the newcomers. As the colonizers and the colonized confronted each other and changing conditions, they found themselves making *choices* and witnessing outcomes that neither group ever expected.

As Spain's rulers moved in to capitalize on the unexpected return from their investment in Columbus's voyages, they found themselves embroiled in an emerging crisis. Portugal already claimed vast holdings to the west of Europe and feared Spanish competition, making some sort of accommodation necessary. Also, the other nation states emerging on the European continent—France, Holland, and England—were not content to watch Spain and Portugal divide the world between themselves. Stirred by *expectations* of increasing wealth and power, each of the leading European nations launched colonizing enterprises.

Spain capitalized on its lead by sending adventurous military captains on exploring tours throughout the Aztec realm they had conquered and into South America and the unknown frontiers to the north. Despite serious military setbacks, by 1700 the Spaniards controlled more New World real estate than any other power. Their empire stretched from the tip of South America up through and around the Gulf of Mexico and into the high deserts of the North American Southwest.

France was determined not to be outdone. Following up on the early trading between fishermen and Indians along the Atlantic shore, French explorers moved inland along riverways that teemed with valuable fur-bearing animals and provided a highway for carrying on commerce. Although France's early efforts at establishing large settlements in America's interior were largely unsuccessful, fur hunters continued to trace the continent's rivers. They eventually found and traveled the Mississippi River, giving France a claim to the vast midsection of North America.

Even the recently created nation of the Netherlands got into the colonizing game, establishing a fur-trading station at the mouth of the Hudson River. Radiating outward from there, Dutch fur traders and farmers began to place their own particular stamp on the land.

One *constraint* that all the European nations had to face was the large and powerful presence of Native Americans. Although they were in the midst of a serious historical crisis, Indians continued to make *choices* that influenced North American life profoundly. The Pueblo Indians drove Spain out of New Mexico altogether for a period of time. In New France and New Netherland, *choices* made by different Indian groups made the colonizing effort possible but also, at times, seriously endangered European occupation. At all times, Europeans had to be sharply aware of the *constraints* that Indian *expectations* imposed.

The *outcome* of this constant interplay among so many different European traditions, a novel physical environment, and a dynamic Indian presence was a series of new societies across the North American continent. Throughout the colonial era and beyond, these hybrid societies continued to influence historical development and color the life of the people and the nation.

CHRONOLOGY

New World Colonies and American Indians

1494 Treaty of Tordesillas

1512 Creation of the encomienda system

1517 Protestant Reformation begins

1519–1521 Cortés invades Mexico

1558 Elizabeth I becomes queen of England

1565 Spanish found St. Augustine in present-day Florida

1588 Defeat of the Spanish Armada

1598 Defeat of Ácoma pueblo by Don Juan de Oñate

1608 French/Huron alliance, completing the confederacy encompassing the Great Lakes and St. Lawrence River

1609 Henry Hudson sails up the Hudson River
Spanish found the town of Santa Fe in present-day New Mexico

1623 Beginning of Dutch/Iroquois alliance

1626 Dutch lease Manhattan Island

1634 Creation of the French West India Company

1680 Pueblo Revolt

1683 La Salle expedition down the Mississippi River to the Gulf of Mexico

c. 1700 Beginning of French/Choctaw alliance

The New Europe and the Atlantic World

- What were some economic constraints that pushed European rulers to promote exploration and colonization in North America?
- What political and religious rivalries influenced European choices regarding New World colonization?

Expansion into the New World, and the economic and political pressures that colonization created, aggravated the crisis of authority in Europe. The crisis, however, helped to promote continued and accelerated overseas enterprise. Eager to enlist political allies against Protestant dissenters, popes during this era used land grants in the New World as rewards to faithful monarchs. At the same time, Henry VIII and Elizabeth I, constantly fearful of being outflanked by Catholic adversaries, promoted the development of a powerful English navy and geographical exploration as defensive measures.

Spanish Expansion in America

Spain's entry into Atlantic exploration first created a diplomatic crisis between the Spanish and Portuguese. Portugal feared that Spain's intrusion might endanger its hard-won trading enterprises in Africa and the Atlantic islands. Spain, however, claimed the right to explore freely. In 1493, the pope settled the dispute by drawing a line approximately 300 miles west of Portugal's westernmost holdings. Spanish exploration, he declared, was to be confined to areas west of the line (that is, to the New World) and Portuguese activity to areas east of it (to Africa and India). A year later, Spain and Portugal updated the agreement in the **Treaty of Tordesillas,** which

Treaty of Tordesillas The treaty, signed by Spain and Portugal in 1494, that moved the line separating Spanish and Portuguese claims to territory in the non-Christian world, giving Spain most of the Western Hemisphere.

♦ The differences between European and American Indian styles and conceptions of warfare were often striking. This scene, from the Codex Durán, illustrates a Spanish force besieged by Aztec warriors. Note the contrast in clothing, for example. For most Indian groups, warfare was a highly spiritual affair surrounded by ceremony, often involving colorful and fanciful costumes. The European battle dress, however, bespeaks a very different conception of warfare: practical and deadly. *Archivo Fotografico.*

moved the line an additional 1,000 miles westward. Most of the Western Hemisphere fell to Spain, at least in the eyes of Roman Catholics.

With the pope's blessing, Ferdinand and Isabella in 1493 gave Columbus instructions that set the tone for Spanish colonization in America. They told him to make the conversion of the natives to Catholicism his first priority, and they assigned a team of missionaries to his crew. In addition, they authorized Columbus to establish a trading center. He would receive one-eighth of the profits, and the rest would go directly to the Spanish crown. Ferdinand and Isabella also told Columbus to continue exploring the Caribbean region for "good things, riches, and more secrets."

Although Columbus was a skillful navigator and sailor, he was not a talented businessman or a particularly gifted leader. Spanish officials and settlers could never forget that the native of Genoa was a foreigner, and they gave him grudging loyalty. As a result, not until Columbus was removed from office, and control over Spain's New World affairs fell to more aggressive and popular figures, did Ferdinand and Isabella's vision of missionary outreach along with "good things, riches, and more secrets" begin to materialize.

Hernando Cortés was one such figure. In 1519, he and an army of six hundred Spanish soldiers landed on the mainland of Mexico. Within three years Cortés and his small force had conquered the mighty Aztec Empire. There were three reasons for his decisive victory. One reason was that smallpox and other illnesses weakened the Aztecs during the two years in which Cortés maintained strained but peaceful relations with them. Another was that he and his men had body armor, combat-trained dogs, war horses, and guns, which gave them only a slight military advantage but provided a keen psychological edge: the gleaming metal breastplates, vicious dogs, massive snorting horses, and loud smoking guns impressed the Indians. Successful diplomacy was the third reason for the Spanish victory. Cortés won the support of an Indian woman whom he called Doña Marina. She served as his translator and cultural adviser, and with her help the **conquistador** gained military support from numerous tribes of Mexican Indians who resented the Aztecs' power and their continuous demand for tribute. Establishing themselves in Mexico City, the Spanish took over the Aztecs' tributary empire, quickly bringing Indian groups to the south, well into Central America, under their rule.

The Spanish crown supported many other exploratory ventures designed to bring new regions under Spain's control. In 1513 and again in 1521, Juan Ponce de León led expeditions to Florida. Following up on these voyages, Pánfilo de Narváez embarked on a colonizing mission to Florida in 1527. When his party became stranded, local Indians killed most of its members but took a few captives. One of these captives, Álvar Núñez Cabeza de Vaca, escaped with three others in 1534 (see Individual Choices: Cabeza de Vaca). The four men eventually walked all the way to Mexico, keeping detailed notes of what they saw. Cabeza de Vaca's accounts led the Spanish to send Hernando de Soto to claim the Mississippi River in 1539, and he penetrated into

Hernando Cortés Spanish soldier and explorer who conquered the Aztecs and claimed Mexico for Spain.

conquistadors Spanish soldiers who conquered Indian civilizations in the New World.

the heart of the mound builders' territory in present-day Louisiana and Mississippi. One year later, **Francisco Vásquez de Coronado** left Mexico to look for some extremely wealthy Indian towns that Cabeza de Vaca had heard about. Coronado eventually crossed what are now the states of New Mexico, Arizona, Colorado, Oklahoma, and Kansas. These explorations were but a few of the ambitious adventures undertaken by Spanish conquistadors.

All of the Spanish explorers were firmly fixed on the objectives that Ferdinand and Isabella had spelled out for Columbus during the opening years of New World exploration. Increasingly, though, the quest for "riches" outstripped the quest for souls or trade. Coronado never found Cabeza de Vaca's "cities of gold," but other Spaniards did locate enormous sources of wealth. In Bolivia, Colombia, and north-central Mexico, rich silver deposits rewarded explorers. To the south in present-day Peru, Francisco Pizarro in 1533 conquered the Inca Empire, an advanced civilization that glittered with gold. Enslaving local Indians for labor, Spanish officials everywhere in the New World quickly moved to rip precious metals out of the ground. Between 1545 and 1660, Indian and African slaves dug over 7 million pounds of silver from Spanish-controlled mines, twice the volume of silver held by all of Europe before 1492. In the process, Spain became the richest nation in Europe, perhaps in the world.

Philip, Elizabeth, and Dreams of an English Eden

Given the stormy political and religious climate that prevailed during the sixteenth century, it is not surprising that Spain's early successes in the New World stirred conflict with the other emerging states in Europe. To England, France, and other European countries, the massive flow of wealth made Spanish power a growing threat that had to be challenged. The continuing religious controversies that accompanied the Reformation (see page 29) worsened the situation. Economic, religious, and political warfare was the rule throughout the century. One of the most celebrated of these early conflicts involved Spain and England.

Tension between Spain and England had been running high ever since Henry VIII divorced his Spanish wife, Catherine of Aragon. That he quit the Catholic church to do so and began permitting Protestant reforms in England worsened the affront. Firmly wedded to the Catholic church politically and religiously, Spain was aggressive in denouncing England. For his part, Henry was concerned primarily with domestic issues and self-defense and steered away from direct confrontations with Spain or any of the other Catholic countries that continually threatened him.

During the reign of Henry's younger daughter Elizabeth, however, the continuing flow of wealth into Spain and Catholic aggression made an entirely defensive posture impossible. When Philip II of Spain, Elizabeth's brother-in-law and most fervent critic, sent an army of twenty thousand soldiers to root out Protestantism in the **Netherlands,** a few miles across the English Channel from Elizabeth's kingdom, the English queen began providing secret aid to Protestants rebelling against Spanish rule there.

Growing tensions spurred Elizabeth to strike at Philip's most valuable and vulnerable possession: his New World empire. In 1577, Elizabeth secretly authorized English **privateer** and explorer Francis Drake to attack Spanish ships in the area reserved for Spain under the Treaty of Tordesillas. Drake carried out his task with enthusiasm, raiding Spanish ships and seizing tons of gold and silver during a three-year cruise around the world.

In 1585, Elizabeth angered the Spanish king by sending an army of six thousand troops across the Channel to openly aid Dutch rebels. In the meantime, Philip was supporting various Catholic plots within England to destroy Elizabeth's authority and the Protestant state. As tensions increased, so did Drake's piracy. In 1586, Drake was at it again, not only raiding Spanish ships at sea but attacking settlements in the Caribbean. Thus by 1586, British troops were fighting the Spanish alongside Dutch rebels in the Netherlands, Spanish spies were

Francisco Vásquez de Coronado Spanish soldier and explorer who led an expedition northward from Mexico in search of fabled cities of gold, passing through present-day New Mexico, Arizona, Colorado, Oklahoma, and Kansas, giving Spain a claim to most of the American Southwest.

The Netherlands/Holland/Dutch Often used interchangeably, the first two terms refer to the low-lying area in Western Europe north of France and Belgium and across the English Channel from Great Britain; the Dutch are the inhabitants of the Netherlands.

privateer A ship captain who owned his own boat, hired his own crew, and was authorized by his government to attack and capture enemy ships.

INDIVIDUAL CHOICES

Escape and Exploration

Cabeza de Vaca

Captured by Indians along the Gulf Coast of Spanish Florida, Álvar Núñez Cabeza de Vaca was made a slave. Most of his companions were afraid to resist or run away, but Cabeza de Vaca chose freedom over safety, eventually leading a small party of men all the way back to Mexico. Courtesy of Frederick Remington Art Museum, Ogdensburg, NY.

After leaving Spain in June 1527, Álvar Núñez Cabeza de Vaca survived one disaster after another. But in November 1528 this heir to a long line of Spanish nobles found himself in a sorrier state than he ever could have imagined: he was a slave belonging to a tribe of Indians along the Gulf coast of America.

Hardship was nothing new to Núñez. Like so many others in his generation of young nobles, he had chosen a military career and, during this time of intense competition among European powers, had often been in great danger. Early in his career, he had fought in the Battle of Ravenna, in which twenty thousand men were killed, and he had earned a reputation for bravery and good sense under fire. Since that time he had established such a name for himself that he was made second-in-command of the expedition that was to colonize Florida in 1527. His future appeared bright.

But the expedition seemed cursed from the start. Arriving in the West Indies, the small fleet was hit by a hurricane, and most of the vessels were destroyed. Finally landing somewhere near Tampa Bay in May 1528, the commander, Pánfilo de Narváez, chose to divide his force, leading a small detachment overland to explore the country. The unfamiliar and rough terrain along the coast made travel difficult, and the Indians the Spaniards met were not friendly.

encouraging rebellion in England and Scotland, and British ships were raiding Spanish settlements in the New World. War loomed on the horizon.

Elizabeth was open to whatever ventures might vex her troublesome brother-in-law, especially if they promised to help her politically and economically. New World colonizing efforts promised to do both. Like the rest of Europe, sixteenth-century England experienced a population boom that put great stress on traditional economic institutions. Although Elizabeth's father had confiscated and redistributed large expanses of church-owned land during his reign, farmland was becoming extremely scarce, and members of both the traditional nobility and the **gentry**—a class that was becoming increasingly important because of its investments in manufacturing and trading ventures—wanted more space

gentry The class of English landowners ranking just below the nobility.

After a series of running battles and hair-raising escapes, the Spanish expedition was all but wiped out, the Indians enslaved the survivors.

Escape seemed impossible. The Indians held the few surviving Spaniards at sites distant from each other, eliminating any chance for them to plan a getaway. And the natives' hostility, combined with the unfamiliar terrain, promised certain death to anyone escaping alone. Most of the Spaniards settled dejectedly into life as servants. But not Núñez. He chose strategy over surrender. He later wrote, "I set to contriving how I might transfer to the forest-dwellers, who looked more propitious [agreeable]." He hit on the notion of serving as a trader, striving always "to making my traffic profitable so I could get food and good treatment." In this way, he earned a degree of freedom to travel among various tribes, and although he experienced great hardship, he was able to contact other survivors and explore for escape routes.

Núñez served as a traveling trader among the Gulf coast Indians for six years. He tried to escape, but his masters chased him down and recaptured him. He needed companions, but other survivors fearfully refused to join him. Finally, in 1534, Núñez encountered Andres Dorantes, Alonso del Castillo, and Castillo's black servant, Estevanico. For six months Núñez pleaded and planned with these three, but only when the Indians announced they were splitting up and taking their Spanish slaves in different directions did the whole company resolve to escape. "Although the season was late and the prickly pears nearly gone, we still hoped to travel a long distance on acorns which we might find in the woods," Núñez recalled.

Having made this fateful choice, Núñez and his companions were forced to see things through. For fourteen months the four Spaniards traveled from village to village, depending on the hospitality of the Indians, exchanging their skills as healers for food, clothing, and other necessities. Finally, in the early spring of 1536, the little party overtook a Spanish exploring and slave-raiding company. "They were dumbfounded at the sight of me, strangely undressed and in company with Indians," Núñez reported. "They just stood staring for a long time, not thinking to hail me or come closer to ask questions." Over the next several months, Núñez and his companions rested up and composed a memoir of their experiences, which they presented to the king himself.

The outcome of Núñez's choice to seek escape was not only his own freedom and that of his companions but a new season of territorial expansion and exploration for Spain. In the course of his travels, he visited places that no other European had ever seen, he saw things that would dazzle those who eventually followed his course, and he heard reports about treasure that prompted generations of Spaniards and others to search for gold, silver, and other riches in the deserts of the American Southwest. Núñez's stories of vast amounts of gold, silver, and precious gems located just to the north of Spain's New World frontier captured the imagination of a new generation of conquistadors and stirred enormous new interest in America's interior.

in which to expand. A relatively small island, England could acquire more territory only by conquering it or carving it out of the New World.

Thus in 1578, Elizabeth granted her friend and political supporter Sir Humphrey Gilbert permission to found a colony in America. Gilbert claimed that John Cabot's voyages under the British flag gave England a legitimate right to settle America's eastern shore. In 1583 he set out with two hundred colonists. The party arrived in the region that is now Newfoundland. But when they saw the gloomy, fog-bound shore, they quickly changed their minds and headed back to England. On the return voyage, Gilbert and his party were lost at sea.

Gilbert's vision lived on in the mind of his half-brother, **Sir Walter Raleigh,** a gallant courtier and a

Sir Walter Raleigh English courtier, soldier, and adventurer who attempted to establish the Virginia Colony.

great favorite of Queen Elizabeth. The queen gladly gave the dashing young Raleigh Gilbert's former land grant, but she specified that he colonize a huge area on the northern frontier of Spanish Florida, where the English presence was certain to irritate Philip. To repay her kindness, Raleigh promised to name the proposed colony Virginia, in honor of the unwed, and thus officially virgin, queen.

For his first settlement, Raleigh chose an island off the coast of present-day North Carolina. He advertised **Roanoke Island** as an "American Eden," assuring potential settlers that the Indians were friendly innocents and "the earth bringeth forth all things in abundance, as in the first Creation, without toile or labour."

♦ Queen Elizabeth I used her charm and intelligence to turn England into a major world power. This portrait, painted around 1588 when Elizabeth was 55 years old, shows the queen at the peak of her power, a fact depicted by the artist in the scenes visible through the windows in the background. Through the left window, we can see Elizabeth's naval fleet; through the right one, we witness the Spanish Armada sinking in the stormy Atlantic. *"Armada Portrait" of Elizabeth I. By kind permission of the Marquess of Tavistock and Trustees of the Bedford Estate.*

The Decline of Spanish Power

Despite dreams of a New World Eden, the realities of discovery and colonization were beginning to have a severe impact on life in Europe. The enormous inflow of wealth from the New World brought Spain power that no European country since the Roman Empire had enjoyed, but such rapid enrichment was a mixed blessing. Starting in Spain and radiating outward, prices began to climb as the growth of the money supply outpaced the growth of European economies. Too much money was chasing too few goods. Between 1550 and 1600, prices doubled in much of Europe, and **inflation** continued to soar for another half-century.

In addition, the social impact of the new wealth was forcing European monarchs to expand geographically and crack down domestically. As prices rose, the traditional landholding classes earned enormous profits from the sale of food and other necessities. Other groups fared less well. Artisans, laborers, and landless peasants—by far the largest class of people in Europe—found the value of their labor going down constantly. Throughout Europe, social unrest increased as formerly productive and respected citizens were reduced to poverty and begging. Overseas expansion seemed an inviting solution to the problem of an impoverished population. It was a safety valve that relieved a potentially dangerous source of domestic pressure while opening opportunities for enhancing national wealth through the development of colonies.

Sitting at the center of the new economy, Philip's Spain had the most to lose from rapid inflation and popular unrest. It also had the most to lose from New World expansion by any other European nation. Each New World claim asserted by England, France, or some other country represented the loss of a piece of treasure that Spain claimed as its own and considered necessary for its continued survival. Reeling under the pressure, Philip finally chose to undertake a desperate gamble designed to remove the Protestant threat, rid himself of Elizabeth's ongoing harassment, and demonstrate to the rest of Europe that Spain intended to exercise absolute authority over the Atlantic world. In the spring of 1585, when tensions were at their peak, Philip decided to invade England. He immediately began massing what was to be the largest marine force the world had ever witnessed.

Philip wanted to attack England in the spring or summer of 1587. But Francis Drake frustrated his plans by staging a surprise attack on the Spanish port of Cádiz, disabling part of Philip's navy. The Spanish king remained resolute, however, and by

Roanoke Island Island off North Carolina that Raleigh sought to colonize, beginning in 1585.

inflation Rising prices that occur when the supply of currency or credit grows faster than the available supply of goods and services.

the spring of 1588 he succeeded in launching an **armada** of 132 warships carrying over 3,000 cannon and an invasion force of 30,000 men. Arriving off the shores of England in July, the so-called Invincible Armada ran up against small, maneuverable British defense ships commanded by Elizabeth's pirate captains. Drake and his fleet harassed the Spanish ships, preventing them from launching a successful attack. Then a storm that blew down from the North Sea scattered the Spanish fleet, ruining Philip's expected conquest of England. Though Spanish power remained great for some time to come, the Armada disaster effectively ended Spain's near monopoly over New World colonization.

European Empires in America

- What similarities and differences characterized the choices that Spanish, French, and Dutch officials made in starting their empires in North America?
- What constraints did the choices made by colonists themselves place on administrative policies?

In the seventeenth and eighteenth centuries, Spain, France, England, and a number of other European nations vied for control of the Americas and for domination of transatlantic trade. For reasons that are explained in Chapter 3, England was somewhat delayed in its colonizing efforts, and by the time it became deeply involved in New World ventures, Spain, France, and Holland had already made major progress toward establishing empires in America. These European settlements not only affected England's colonization process profoundly, but through their interactions among themselves and with the Native Americans they also created unique societies in North America whose presence influenced the entire course of the continent's history.

The Troubled Spanish Colonial Empire

Although the destruction of the Armada in 1588 struck a terrible blow at Spain's military power and its New World monopoly, the Spanish Empire continued to grow. By the end of the seventeenth century, it stretched from New Mexico southward through Central America and much of South America into the Caribbean islands and northward again into Florida. Governing such a vast empire was difficult, and periodic efforts to reform the system usually failed. Two agencies in Spain, the House of Trade and the Council of the Indies, set Spanish colonial policy. In the colonies, Crown-appointed viceroys wielded military and political power in each of the four divisions of the empire. The Spanish colonies had local governments as well, and each town had a ***cabildo secular,*** a municipal council, as well as judges and other minor officials. The colonial administrators were appointed rather than elected, and most were envoys from Spain rather than native-born colonials.

Over the centuries, as the layers of bureaucracy developed, corruption and inefficiency developed too. The Spanish government made efforts to regulate colonial affairs, sending *visitadores* to inspect local government operations and creating new watchdog agencies. Despite these safeguards, colonial officials ignored their written instructions and failed to enforce laws.

One major source of corruption and tension stemmed from a persistent New World problem: the shortage of labor. The Spanish adapted their traditional institutions to address the demand for workers in mines and on plantations. In Spain, work was directed by **feudal** landlords, *encomenderos,* whose military service to the king entitled them to harness the labor of Spanish peasants. In New Spain, Indians took the place of the peasants in what was called the **encomienda system.** Under a law passed in 1512, administrators gave to the Spanish colonists Indian workers, who were required to labor for the Spanish for nine months each year. The *encomendero* paid a tax to the Crown for each Indian he received and agreed to teach his workers the Catholic faith, Spanish language and culture, and a "civilized" vocation.

Such workers came from among Indians who peacefully acknowledged Spanish rule. For Indians who did not, a completely different labor system prevailed. Under Spanish law, any Indian who resisted Spanish rule "had no rights save such as the conqueror might freely choose to concede to them."

armada A fleet of warships.

cabildo secular Secular municipal council that provided local government in Spain's New World empire.

feudal Relating to a system in which landowners held broad powers over peasants or tenant farmers in exchange for their loyalty and for protection from abuse by others.

encomienda system A system of bonded labor in which Indians were assigned to Spanish plantation and mine owners in exchange for the payment of a tax and an agreement to "civilize" and convert them to Catholicism.

Thus any Indian rebels who survived an uprising against Spanish authority could be put to death or enslaved.

Church leaders worried that in their desire to obtain cheap labor and avoid the tax and obligations that accompanied the encomienda system, landlords would trump up resistance by Indians as an excuse to enslave them. As a result of church pressure, the Spanish government issued a law that required the conquistadors to explain to Indians the obligations they owed to the Spanish king and to the Catholic church, and to offer to absorb them peacefully if they would acknowledge those obligations. Thereafter, all conquistadors embarking on exploration or slave-raiding trips had to take with them a priest who would certify that they had read (in Spanish, of course) a document called the **Requerimiento** to each Indian group they encountered. Indians who immediately acknowledged the king's authority were to receive the "protection" of the encomienda system. Those who did not could be enslaved.

Colonists and conquistadors often ignored even these slim protections. Conquistadors frequently stood outside an Indian village, read the Requerimiento in a whisper, and then attacked when the community made no immediate response. Some simply forged a priest's signature, anticipating that by the time the document reached administrators in faraway Madrid, no one would know the difference. Others ignored the law altogether.

As such behavior demonstrates, Spanish colonists were seldom entirely law-abiding citizens, and a degree of tension always existed between New Spain and old. Bureaucratic and church interference in the labor system was one source of tension. Taxes were another. Spanish colonists were taxed to support the huge and largely corrupt, unrepresentative, and self-serving imperial bureaucracy. But for many decades the wealth produced within this empire overshadowed all governing problems. The gold, silver, and copper mined by Indian and later by African slaves satisfied the Spanish government until the end of the seventeenth century.

The French Presence in America

If the Spanish overgoverned their New World provinces, the French may have erred in the opposite direction. Despite the long existence of the fur trade in Canada, French colonial authorities at first took little interest in it. **Samuel de Champlain,** the "father of **New France,**" established trading posts in Nova Scotia and elsewhere, founded the city of Quebec, and in 1608 formed an enduring alliance with the Huron Indians. But officials in France did little to capitalize on the achievements of Champlain and other enterprising individuals. And even when they did, they ignored the vast economic potential offered by furs.

In 1627, the king awarded a group of his favorites a charter to develop resources in New France, focusing on its minerals, forests, and fertile farmland. Little mention was made of the fur trade with the Indians. The resulting Company of One Hundred Associates failed even though the government made large grants of land available to suitable colonists. It failed for several reasons. Few French Catholics showed any interest in migrating to New France. French Protestants, who might have emigrated to avoid religious persecution, were forbidden to move to the colony. Thus the Company of One Hundred Associates did not attract enough rent-paying tenants to make the envisioned estates profitable. Equally important was the fact that the few French peasants and small farmers who did venture to the New World found life in the woods and the company of Indians preferable to, and more profitable than, a life as tenant farmers. So-called ***coureurs de bois,*** or "runners of the woods," married Indian women and lived among the tribes, returning to the French settlements only when they had enough furs to sell to make the trip worthwhile. Because of their activity, the fur trade gradually came to dominate French Canada's culture and economy.

Frustrated by the lack of profits from the Company of One Hundred Associates, the king revoked its charter in 1633 and in the following year created the **French West India Company.** This company became

Requerimiento A statement delivered in Spanish explaining the obligations of Indian people to the king of Spain and to the church and requiring their cooperation; Indians who failed to accept the statement could be killed or enslaved.

Samuel de Champlain French explorer who traced the St. Lawrence River inland to the Great Lakes, founded the city of Quebec, and formed the French alliance with the Huron Indians.

New France The colony established by France in what is now Canada and the Great Lakes region of the United States.

coureurs de bois Independent French fur traders who lived among the Indians and sold furs to the French; literally, "runners of the woods."

♦ Although this scene in Quebec was not painted until 1820, back streets like this cul de sac in the old part of the city still looked very much as they did during the heyday of the French *coereurs de bois.* So did the people. Shops, like the one on the left, sold provisions and tools—often on credit—to the outward-bound runners of the woods, binding them to bring their next load of furs back to satisfy their debt. Thus, while the French crown did little to encourage the fur business, it formed the core for Canada's woodland and urban economies. *Royal Ontario Museum © COM.*

quite profitable by ignoring the government's demands that it establish agricultural settlements and by focusing instead on the fur trade. Setting up posts in Quebec, Montreal, and some more remote locations, the French West India Company became the primary outfitter of and buyer from the coureurs de bois and made a lot of money reselling furs in Europe.

This disregard for royal authority indicates that local officials exercised considerable control over colonial affairs in New France. The governor of New France was in charge of Indian matters and military decisions. An ***intendant*** directed the judicial and commercial affairs of the colony, and a Catholic bishop supervised religious affairs. Colonists had no representative assembly, although the governor did call on colonists for their opinion and advice when he wished.

Only after 1663 did the French crown begin to intervene seriously in Canadian affairs. In that year the king revoked the French West India Company's charter and took direct control of New France, making it a royal colony in 1674. While the king continued to reap enormous profits from the fur trade, his interests ranged beyond this single source of income. In 1673, a French expedition led by Louis Joliet and Jacques Marquette set out to explore the riverways that had long been the domain of the Indians and the coureurs de bois. Leaving Green Bay on Lake Michigan, Marquette and Joliet eventually located the Fox and Wisconsin rivers and from there traced the origins of the Mississippi. Although they did not follow the great river all the way to its mouth, they speculated, correctly, that eventually they would have come out at the Gulf of Mexico.

An ambitious French nobleman, **Robert Cavelier, Sieur de La Salle,** recognized the strategic and economic promise in Joliet and Marquette's discovery. In 1683 he and a party of French coureurs de bois and Indians retraced the earlier expedition and then followed the Mississippi all the way to the Gulf of Mexico. La Salle immediately claimed the new territory for Louis XIV of France, naming it **Louisiana** in his honor. In 1698 the king sent settlers to the lower Mississippi Valley under the leadership of Pierre LeMoyne d'Iberville, who in 1699 built Louisiana's first French fort, near present-day Biloxi, Mississippi. In 1718 French authorities built the city of New Orleans to serve as the capital of the new territory.

The acquisition of Louisiana was a major accomplishment for La Salle and for France. The newly discovered riverway gave the French a rich, unexploited source of furs as well as an alternative shipping route, allowing them to avoid the cold, stormy north Atlantic. Also, if an agricultural venture could be started in the new territory, it might serve as an inexpensive source of supplies for both the fur trade in Canada and France's sugar plantations in the Caribbean. But perhaps of greatest importance was Louisiana's strategic location between Spain's

French West India Company Company of investors that became profitable by ignoring royal orders and engaging in the fur trade in Canada.

intendant A French government official who directed colonial judicial and commercial affairs.

Robert Cavelier, Sieur de La Salle French explorer who followed the Mississippi River from its origin in present-day Illinois to the Gulf of Mexico in 1683, giving France a claim to the entire riverway and adjoining territory.

Louisiana French colony south of New France; it included the entire area drained by the Mississippi River and all its tributary rivers.

claims in the Southwest and England's colonies along the eastern seaboard. Controlling this piece of real estate gave Louis a valuable bargaining chip in international diplomacy.

The Dutch Enterprise

Another source of competition to Spain's New World monopoly came from a former colony of Spain: the Netherlands. The Armada disaster tipped the scales in favor of Dutch Protestant rebels in 1588, and the newly independent nation quickly developed a thriving commercial economy. Dutch privateers outshone Queen Elizabeth's in the profitable raiding of Spanish and Portuguese treasure ships, and by the 1630s the Dutch dominated the African slave trade. In 1634, Dutch forces overcame weak Spanish and Portuguese resistance, conquering a number of islands in the Caribbean. Holland's next goal was to establish an empire on the North American mainland.

Holland's first serious claim to American territory came in 1609, when Dutch captain **Henry Hudson** explored the east coast in search for the Northwest Passage. He sailed up a large river that he hoped would lead him west to the Pacific. After realizing that he had not found the hoped-for Northwest Passage, he returned to Holland and reported to his sponsor, the Dutch East India Company, that the Hudson Valley—which he had named for himself—was "pleasant with Grasse & Flowers and Goodly Trees" and the Indians were friendly. Surely, he added, profits could be made there. Hudson's employers did not share his enthusiasm. Although the Dutch created one trading post on the river at Albany and another on Manhattan Island in 1614, the land of "Grasse & Flowers" was less attractive to them than their new Caribbean possessions.

In 1621, when the **Dutch West India Company** was formed, its charter included a provision calling for the planting of colonies on mainland America. The company's director, Peter Minuit, negotiated a lease for the entire island of Manhattan from the Manhates Indians in 1626. Minuit's main motive, however, was to safeguard Dutch claims against those of rival European traders. For three more years, the company did nothing to attract settlers, and by 1629 only three hundred colonists had spread themselves in a thin ribbon from New Amsterdam on Manhattan to Albany.

But in that year, the Dutch West India Company drew up a comprehensive business plan to maximize profits and minimize dependence on local Indians for food and other support. To encourage the agricultural development necessary to support the fur industry, the company offered huge estates called **patroonships** to any company stockholder willing and able to bring fifty colonists to **New Netherland** at his own expense. The patroons—men wealthy enough to accept the offer—would enjoy broad powers over their tenants.

As attractive as the offer may sound, few prosperous Dutchmen were interested in becoming New World pioneers. Rensselaerswyck, the estate of Kilian Van Rensselaer, was the only patroonship to develop in accordance with the company's plan. Settlers seeking land did come on their own, however.

At first, settlers from just about anywhere were welcome in New Netherland—the colony attracted an extremely diverse population including German and French Protestants, free and enslaved Africans, Catholics, Jews, and Muslims. In 1638, four hundred Swedish immigrants settled in the Delaware River valley. They established their own colony, **New Sweden,** within New Netherland, with the financial help and the political blessings of the Dutch company, which was eager to increase the population of the region. For about seventeen years, New Sweden existed peacefully and independently as a fur-trading community. By 1655, however, the Swedes had become so successful as fur traders that they earned the professional jealousy of New Netherland governor Peter Stuyvesant. To bring them under direct Dutch control, he sent a militia force larger than the colony's entire population to demand their submission. They had little choice but to agree.

Henry Hudson Dutch ship captain and explorer who sailed up the Hudson River in 1609, giving the Netherlands a claim to the area now occupied by New York.

Dutch West India Company Dutch investment company formed in 1621 to develop colonies in North America.

patroonship A huge grant of land given to any Dutchman who, at his own expense, brought fifty colonists to New Netherland; the colonists became the tenants of the estate owner.

New Netherland The name of the colony founded by the Dutch West India Company in present-day New York; its capital was New Amsterdam on Manhattan Island.

New Sweden Swedish fur-trading community established with the assistance of the Dutch on the Delaware River in 1638 and absorbed by New Netherland in 1655.

♦ Its location at the mouth of the Hudson River made the Dutch settlement of New Amsterdam a particularly important colonial trading center. Furs flowed down the river from Fort Orange (near modern Albany, New York) while guns, tools, and other trade goods traveled the other way. Both river and sea traffic were central to the city's existence as shown in the painting of the Dutch statehouse from 1679, which stood overlooking the harbor. *Prints Collection, Miriam and Ira D. Wallach Division of Art, Prints and Photography. The New York Public Library, Astor, Lenox, and Tilden Foundation.*

Indians and the European Challenge

• What constraints did environmental changes place on Indians?

• What constraints and opportunities came with the arrival of Europeans?

• What social and political choices did Indians make in response to these changes?

Native Americans did not sit idly by while the European powers carved out empires in North America. Some joined the newcomers, serving as advisers and companions. Others sought to use the Europeans as allies to accomplish their own economic, diplomatic, or military goals (see Map 2.1). Still others, overwhelmed by the onset of European diseases and shifting population pressures, withdrew into the interior. The changes in native America created both obstacles and opportunities, giving shape to the patterns of expansion and conflict that characterized the colonial world.

The Indian Frontier in New Spain

Indian assistance had been critical in Spain's successful campaigns against the Aztecs and Incas. In Mexico, for example, groups who had been forced to pay tribute to the Aztec Empire gladly allied themselves with the Spanish in what the natives perceived as an opportunity to win their independence. Their hopes were soon dashed when the Spanish simply replaced the Aztecs as the new lords of a tributary empire. Loyal partnership with the Spanish earned these people only the traditional feudal protection under the encomienda system, which was better than slavery but far from the liberation they had expected.

A similar pattern occurred wherever the Spanish went in North America. The rumors of great wealth that spread after Cabeza de Vaca's adventure pulled conquistadors northward. The Spanish repeatedly encountered new Indian populations, read the Requirimiento—in good faith or not—and placed the Indians under Spanish rule as either **serfs** or slaves.

Spanish expansion met little native resistance until 1598, when a particularly brutal conquistador named **Don Juan de Oñate** led a large expedition to the Rio Grande region of New Mexico. Many of the Pueblo people greeted Oñate with a mixture of curiosity and friendship and found themselves subjected to Spanish and Catholic authority. Some, however, resisted Oñate's efforts to force Spanish culture and religion onto them. The conquistador chose to make an example of one such community, **Ácoma pueblo.** It took Oñate's troops three days to subdue the settlement, but Spanish steel finally overcame Ácoma clubs and stone knives. When the battle was over, Oñate ordered 800 Indians executed and made slaves of the nearly 700 remaining survivors, mostly women and children. In addition,

serfs Peasants who were bound to a particular estate but unlike slaves, were not the personal property of the estate owner and received traditional feudal protections.

Don Juan de Oñate Spaniard who conquered New Mexico and claimed it for Spain in the 1590s.

Ácoma pueblo Pueblo Indian community that resisted Spanish authority in 1598 and was destroyed by the Spanish.

♦ **MAP 2.1 Indian Economies in North America** Indian economic activities helped to shape patterns of European settlement and investment in the New World. Regions that were primarily agricultural, like the Atlantic shoreline, lent themselves to European farming activities. Farther north and west, however, where hunting played a more prominent role in native life, the fur trade was a more attractive investment for European settlers.

each male survivor over the age of twenty-five had one foot chopped off to prevent his escape from slavery. Two **Hopi Indians** who had been visiting Ácoma at the time of the battle had their right hands cut off and were sent home as an example of the price of resistance.

Oñate's excesses led eventually to his removal by Spanish authorities. After his departure, some members of his company founded the town of **Santa Fe** in 1609, and others set themselves up on ranches spread throughout the region. Spanish authorities placed the Indian survivors of Oñate's savagery under joint military and religious control.

Although raids by Apaches and Navajos were common, things remained relatively peaceful in New Mexico for nearly a century. Then in 1680 the Pueblo Indians rebelled against Spanish attempts to destroy their native religion. Led by a religious prophet named Popé, the **Pueblo Revolt** left 400 Spaniards dead. The rebels captured Santa Fe and drove the surviving Spaniards from the land. The Spanish needed

Hopi Indians Indians who were related to the Comanches and Shoshones and took up residence among the Pueblo Indians as agricultural town-dwellers; their name means "peaceful ones."

Santa Fe Spanish colonial town established in 1609; eventually the capital of the province of New Mexico.

Pueblo Revolt Indian rebellion against Spanish authority in 1680 led by Popé; succeeded in driving the Spanish out of New Mexico for nearly a decade.

almost a decade to regroup sufficiently to reinvade New Mexico. In 1689 troops moved back into the region and over the next several years waged a brutal war to recapture the territory. The fighting continued off and on until the end of the century, but Spanish settlers began returning to New Mexico after the recapture of Santa Fe in 1693.

Elsewhere along the northern frontier of New Spain, the unsettled nature of Indian life and the arid and uninviting character of the land made settlement unappealing to the Spaniards. Efforts at mining, raising livestock, and missionizing in Arizona and Texas were largely unsuccessful until after 1700.

The Indian World in the Southeast

Members of Spanish exploring expeditions under would-be conquistadors like Ponce de León, de Narváez, and de Soto were the first Europeans to contact the mound builder societies and other Indian groups in the Southeast. Although their great cities impressed the Spaniards, the Cherokees, Creeks, and other agricultural groups had no gold and could not be enslaved easily. The conquistadors moved on without attempting to impose Spanish rule or the Catholic religion on these peoples. Given sufficient incentive, however, the Spanish were quick to strike at Indian independence and culture.

In Florida, for example, the need to protect Spanish ships from British and other raiders led Spain to establish garrisons like **St. Augustine,** founded in 1565 by Pedro Menéndez de Aviles. Using these military posts as staging areas, Jesuit and Franciscan missionaries ranged outward to bring Catholicism to Indians in the region. By 1600, they had established missions from the gulf coast of Florida all the way to Georgia.

Although the Spanish presence in the region was small, its impact was enormous. The Spanish introduced European diseases into the densely populated towns in the Mississippi River region. Epidemics wiped out entire Native American civilizations and forced survivors to abandon their cities and entirely modify their ways of life.

In much the same way in which climate change had affected the Indians in the Northeast, epidemic disease forced the Cherokees, Creeks, and other groups to abandon city life in favor of a village-based economy that combined agriculture, hunting, and gathering. The consequences in the Southeast were similar to those in the Northeast. Warfare became increasingly common. Groups became more inclined to join in formal alliances for mutual support. And when new Europeans arrived in the seventeenth and eighteenth centuries, Indians found it beneficial to welcome them as trading partners and allies.

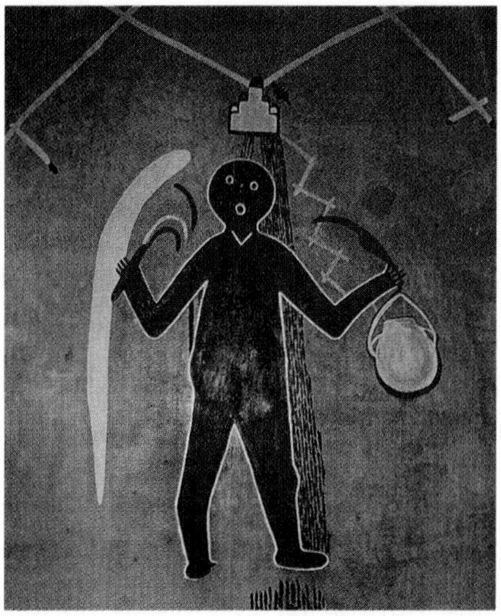

♦ Among the Pueblo Indians kachinas, like the one depicted here, were central to every aspect of life. These spiritual beings represented revered ancestors and helped to maintain contact between people and the spirit world. When the Spanish brought Christianity to the American Southwest, they expected the Pueblo people to give up their belief in such spiritual beings and began a campaign to destroy traditional religion. In 1680 the Pueblo people rose up to defend their religion, driving the Spanish out of New Mexico. *Private Collection.*

One example of this process was the **Powhatan Confederacy,** formed in the Chesapeake region in the late 1500s. Soon after 1607, pleading for peaceful relations between his people and the English at Jamestown (see page 63), Powhatan, the head chief of the confederacy, explained, "you may understand that I, having seen the death of all my people thrice, and not one living of those three generations but myself, I know the difference of peace and war better than any in my Country." For the rest of his life, Powhatan practiced careful diplomacy in an attempt to keep his people at peace among themselves and with the English.

St. Augustine First colonial city in the present-day United States; located in Florida and founded by Pedro Menéndez de Aviles for Spain in 1565.

Powhatan Confederacy Confederacy of Indians living along the shores of Chesapeake Bay in present-day Virginia led by Powhatan.

Farther west, the **Creek Confederacy,** a union of many groups who had survived the Spanish epidemics, also played a careful diplomatic game. Internally, members created an economic and social system in which each group contributed to the welfare of all and differences were settled through athletic competition—a ballgame not unlike modern lacrosse—rather than warfare. Externally, the confederacy balanced the competing demands of the Spanish and French, and later the English, taking as much advantage as possible of the competition among the European powers.

The Indian World in the Northeast

By the time Europeans had begun serious exploration and settlement of the Northeast, the economic and cultural changes among Indians that had begun between 1350 and 1450 had resulted in the creation of two massive alliance systems. On one side were the Hurons, Algonquins, Abenakis, Micmacs, Ottawas, and several smaller tribes. On the other was the Iroquois Confederacy.

The costs and benefits of sustained European contact first fell to the Hurons and their allies. The Abenakis, Micmacs, and others who lived along the northern shore of the Atlantic were the first groups drawn into trade with French and other fishermen. As the coureurs du bois pushed farther and farther into Indian territory, these were the Native American groups they met in the woods and with whom they settled and intermarried. These family ties became firm economic bonds when formal French exploration brought these groups into more direct contact with the European trading world. Seeking advantage against the Iroquois, the Hurons and their neighbors created a great wheel of alliance with France and the fur trade at its hub.

The strong alliance between these Indians and the French posed a serious threat to Iroquois plans for expansion. The arrival of the Dutch in the Albany area, however, offered the Iroquois an attractive diplomatic opportunity. In 1623, the Dutch West India Company invited representatives from the Iroquois Confederacy to a meeting at **Fort Orange,** offering them friendship and trade. The Iroquois responded enthusiastically, but in a way that the Dutch did not expect. Instead of entering peacefully into the trade, the Iroquois sought to dominate it by imposing their authority over all of the Indian groups already trading with the Dutch. They began a bloody war with the **Mohicans,** who had been the Dutch traders' main source for furs in the Hudson Valley. By 1627 the Iroquois had driven the Mohicans away from the river and had taken control over the flow of furs.

Recognizing the value of an alliance with such a powerful native force, the Dutch abandoned a long-standing policy of neutrality in Indian wars and a prohibition against the sale of guns to the natives. Throughout the 1630s, guns flowed up the Hudson and into the hands of the Mohawks and other Iroquois tribes, while furs from northern and western New York flowed down to Manhattan.

The Iroquois were so enthusiastic about this trade that they soon wiped out fur supplies in their own territory and began an even more serious push to acquire new lands. Beginning in the late 1630s, the Iroquois Confederacy entered into a long-term aggressive war against the Hurons and their allies in New France; against the Munsees, Delawares, and other groups in the Susquehanna and Delaware river valleys to the south; and even against the Iroquois-speaking Eries to the west.

Through it all, the Dutch maintained a pro-Iroquois policy, occasionally joining their allies in military campaigns. Following the massacre of a Mohican party by a joint Dutch/Mohawk force in 1643, non-Iroquois Indians living along the lower Hudson Valley finally became disgusted with Dutch policies. They raided outlying Dutch settlements and maintained a light siege on Manhattan itself. The Dutch responded with a winter campaign, staging surprise attacks against Indian settlements, burning houses and food stores, killing those who resisted, and capturing and enslaving those who did not. By the spring of 1644, Indian resistance was broken but Indian resentment was still very much alive. One survivor spoke for many when he told Dutch officials: "In the beginning of your voyages, you left your people here with their goods; we traded with them . . . and cherished them . . . we

Creek Confederacy Confederacy of Indians living in the Southeast; formed after the spread of European diseases to permit a cooperative economic and military system among survivors.

Fort Orange Dutch trading post established near present-day Albany, New York, in 1614.

Mohicans Algonkian-speaking Indians who lived along the Hudson River, were dispossessed in a war with the Iroquois Confederacy, and eventually were all but exterminated.

♦ Alfred Jacob Miller based this 1837 painting of eighteenth-century mounted buffalo hunters on interviews with Shoshoni Indians he met on a trip through the American West. It illustrates clearly the enormous impact the arrival of horses had on Plains Indian life. Note how few mounted men it took to drive vast numbers of animals over a cliff to their deaths. The meat, bones, and hides that would be taken from the butchered bison would provide food, clothing, tools, tents, and trade goods sufficient to support an entire band of Indians for some time. The arrival of the horse on the Plains in the late 1600s marked the beginning of 150 years of unprecedented wealth and power for the Indians in the region. *Alfred Jacob Miller, Walter's Art Gallery, Baltimore.*

gave them our daughters for companions, who have borne children . . . and now you villainously massacre your own blood."

The New Indian World of the Plains

Though largely unexplored and untouched by Europeans, the vast area of the Great Plains also underwent profound change during the period of initial contacts. Climate change, the pressure of shifting populations, and the introduction of novel European goods through lines of kinship and trade created an altogether new culture and economy among the Indians in this region.

Before about 1400, Indians living on the plains rarely strayed far from the riverways that form the Missouri River drainage, where they lived in villages based on agriculture, hunting, and gathering (see pages 11–12). The climate change that affected their neighbors to the east had a similar effect on them: growing seasons became shorter, and the need to hunt became greater. But this climatic force that undermined their existing way of life provided an attractive alternative as well: buffalo.

The **buffalo,** or American bison, is particularly well adapted to survival in cold climates. Unlike European cattle, which often starve when snow buries the grasses on which they graze, buffalo use their hooves to dig out the grass they need, and their efficient metabolism extracts nutrients from even poor-quality food. Although buffalo were always a presence on the plains, the cold weather during the Little Ice Age spurred a massive increase in their numbers. Between 1300 and 1800, herds numbering in the millions roamed the new environment created by the climate change.

Some groups—like the **Caddoan**-speaking Wichitas, Pawnees, and Arikaras—virtually abandoned their agricultural villages and became hunters. Others, like the Hidatsas, split into factions. Those called Hidatsas remained in their villages, and those called Crows went off to the grasslands to hunt. The Mandans and several other groups chose to remain in their villages and established a thriving trade with hunters like the Arikaras, who provided fresh

buffalo The American bison, a large member of the ox family, native to North America and the staple of the Plains Indian economy between the fifteenth and mid-nineteenth centuries.

Caddoan A family of languages spoken by the Wichitas, Pawnees, Arikaras, and other Plains Indians.

meat and other buffalo products in exchange for the vegetables and tobacco the village people continued to produce.

The increase in buffalo not only provided an attractive resource for the Indians already on the Great Plains but also drew new groups to the area. As the climate farther north became unbearably severe, the **Blackfeet** and other Indians swept down from the subarctic northeast to hunt on the plains. Other Algonkian-speaking Indians, such as the Gros Ventres, Cheyennes, and Arapahos, soon followed.

At the time that the buffalo was attracting people to the plains, pressures elsewhere were pushing them in that direction. As the climate change affected the Northeast and groups like the Hurons and Iroquois expanded their territories, many other groups chose to flee rather than fight or be absorbed by the warring confederacies. These pressures became even more severe as the coureurs du bois carried the fur trade ever farther westward and Indians like the Ojibwas began invading new lands looking for pelts. Experiencing such pressure, groups like the **Lakotas** abandoned village life, moving into the plains to hunt but maintaining trading relations with their **Dakota** neighbors in Minnesota, who continued to farm and harvest wild rice and other crops.

The buffalo also began to play an important role on the southern plains. There, groups like the Apaches, Comanches, and Kiowas specialized in hunting the ever-increasing herds and then exchanging part of their take for village-based products from their neighbors and kinsmen the Navajos, Hopis, and Pueblos.

Although buffalo hunting was attractive to many of the groups displaced by climate change and population pressure, at first the life of a hunter was extremely difficult. Lacking any draft animals larger than dogs, early plains hunters had to travel light and on foot. That changed and a mature buffalo-hunting culture came into being after the Pueblo Revolt in New Mexico in 1680.

One unintentional outcome of the Pueblo Revolt was the liberation of thousands of Spanish horses. The Pueblos had little use for these animals, but their trading partners, the Kiowas and Comanches, quickly put the animals to use. Horses could move much larger loads than dogs and could survive on a diet of grass rather than taking a share of the meat. In less than a generation, horses became a mainstay of the buffalo-hunting culture in the southern plains. And from there, horses spread quickly to other hunting people.

Northern plains dwellers like the Shoshones quickly began acquiring horses from their southwestern kinsmen and trading partners. Following a northward path along the eastern flank of the Rocky Mountains, horses were passed from one group to another in the complex trading system that had come into existence in the plains region. Well adapted to grasslands, virtually free from natural predators or diseases, and highly prized and thus well protected by their new human owners, horses greatly increased in number. By 1730, virtually all of the plains hunting peoples had some horses and were clamoring for more.

The continual demand for horses and the need for space in which to hunt created a new dynamic on the Great Plains and set a new economy into motion (see Map 2.2). After the Spanish reconquest of New Mexico, Indians could obtain horses only through warfare and trade, and both increased significantly. Surprise raids to steal horses from neighboring Indian groups and European settlements brought both honor and wealth to those who were successful. As groups raided back and forth, human captives also became valuable prizes, both as replacements for individuals lost in the fighting and as items of trade. In exchange for horses, human captives might be sold as slaves to the Spanish. Thus horse trading and slave trading became linked.

Conquest and Accommodation in a Shared New World

- What constraints most affected the lives of settlers in New Mexico, Louisiana, and New Netherland?
- How did choices made by settlers and American Indians help both groups to deal with these constraints?

Old World cultures, Native American historical dynamics, and New World environmental conditions combined to create dynamic new societies in European pioneer settlements. Despite the regulatory efforts of Spanish bureaucrats, French royal officials,

Blackfeet Algonkian-speaking Indians from the Canadian subarctic who moved onto the Great Plains in the sixteenth century.

Lakotas/Dakotas Collectively the Sioux Nation; Lakotas are the western branch, living mostly on the Great Plains, and Dakotas are the eastern branch, living mostly in the prairie and lakes region of the Upper Midwest.

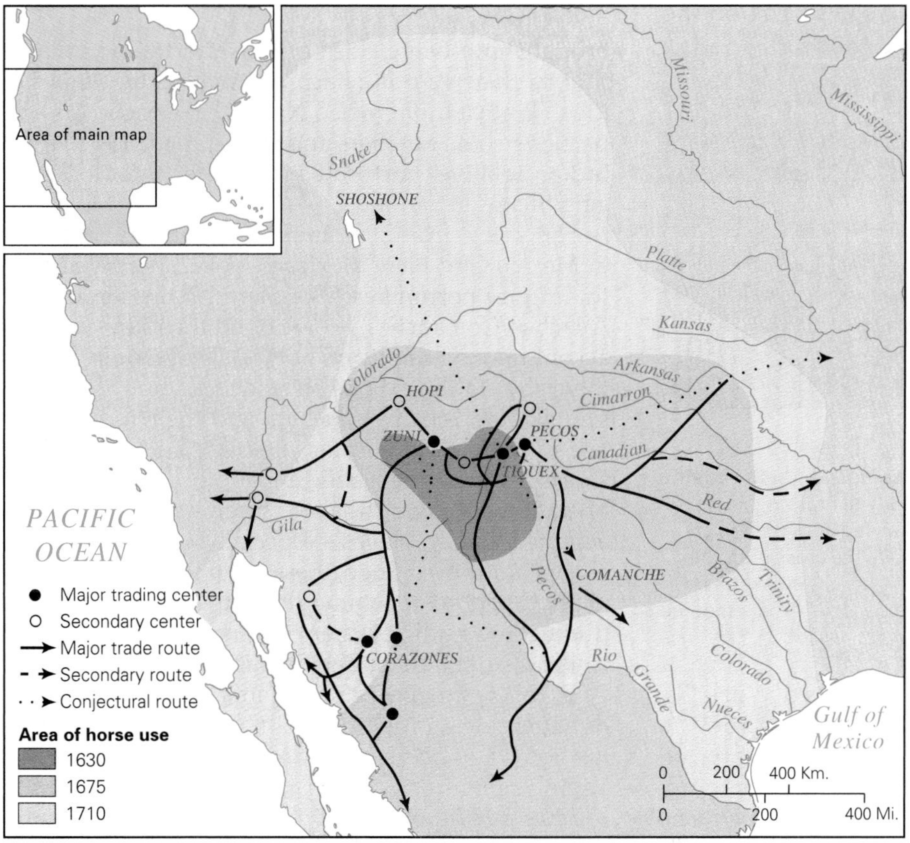

♦ **MAP 2.2 Intergroup Trading on the Southern Plains** Located on New Spain's northern frontier and Louisiana's western frontier, the southern plains became a hotbed of cultural and economic interchange among Indian groups and between them and Europeans. As this map shows, trade routes that had existed before Europeans entered the region acquired added importance in distributing the novel technologies and ideas that the newcomers brought with them. The most important of these was horses, which followed these trade routes and became the single most important feature in Plains Indian life.

and Dutch company executives, life in the colonies developed in its own peculiar ways. Entire regions in what would become the United States assumed cultural contours that would shape all future developments in each.

New Spain's Northern Frontiers

Easy to see in the course of daily life along the Spanish frontier in New Mexico were the formality of Spain's highly organized imperial structure and the disorderliness that one might expect to find in a place so distant and different from the rest of the empire. In a tradition traceable to prehistoric times, Spanish notions of civil order were rooted in the local community—city, town, or village—and its ruling elite. Responsibility for maintaining order belonged to the *cabildo secular,* the secular town council composed of members of the elite or their appointees. In all of its colonies in the New World, Spain established towns and immediately turned authority over to a ruling cabildo. In Mexico, Peru, and elsewhere this practice was appropriate and usually successful, but in the high desert of New Mexico it was at odds with environmental and cultural conditions.

After suppression of the Pueblo Revolt, Spaniards began drifting back into New Mexico, although economic conditions there were not particularly inviting. Unlike areas to the south, New Mexico offered no rich deposits of gold or silver, and the climate would not support large-scale agriculture. With neither mines nor plantations to support the encomienda system, the basic underpinnings of the

♦ San Esteban Rey, a Catholic church built at Pueblo de Ácoma in about 1642, stands as a monument to the mixing of cultures in colonial New Mexico. The building's adobe construction, rising towers, and curving corners reflect traditional Pueblo architecture, while the crosses on the top identify its European purpose. Churches like this provided an anchor for the multicultural society that emerged in the region. *Lee Marmon.*

traditional ruling order never emerged. Even so, the Spanish colonial bureaucracy followed conventional imperial procedures and made Santa Fe the official municipal center for the region after its recapture from the Indians in 1693. But there were no encomenderos to provide wealth. The sole sources of economic support for Santa Fe were the church, which was channeling money for missions into the region, and the Spanish government, which allocated both military and civic support funds. People in neither the church's nor the state's employ had to find their own way.

As in the days before the Pueblo Revolt, the most attractive economic enterprise in the region was ranching. During the period of control by the Pueblos, the small flocks of sheep abandoned by the fleeing Spanish grew dramatically. By the time the Spanish returned, sheep ranching had become a reliable way to make a living. Thus, rather than concentrating near the municipal center in Santa Fe, the population in New Mexico spread out across the land, forming two sorts of communities. South of Santa Fe, people settled on scattered ranches. Elsewhere, they gathered in small villages established along streams, and they pooled their labor to make a living from irrigated **subsistence farming.**

Like colonists elsewhere in Spain's New World empire, the New Mexico colonists were almost entirely male. Isolated on the sheep ranch or in small villages, these men sought Indian companionship and married into local populations. The marriages not only created a new hybrid population but also brought into being lines of kinship, trade, and authority that were in sharp contrast to the imperial ideal. For example, when Navajo or Apache raiding parties struck, ranchers and villagers turned to their Indian relatives for protection rather than to Spanish officials in Santa Fe.

Far away from the imperial economy centered in Mexico City, New Mexicans looked northward for trading opportunities. Southern Plains Indians—Apaches, Comanches, Kiowas, and their kin—needed a continuous supply of horses. They could obtain them by raiding Spanish ranches, but doing so brought reprisals by ranchers and their Indian relations. Trade was a safer alternative. Facing labor shortages and financially unable to take advantage of traditional Spanish labor systems, New Mexicans accepted Indian slaves—especially children—in exchange for horses. Soon, these young captives became another important commodity in the already complex trading and raiding system that prevailed among the southwestern Indians and Spanish New Mexicans.

In this frontier world, a man's social status came to depend less on his Spanish background and connections than on his ability to work effectively in the complicated world of kinship that prevailed in the Indian community. The people who eventually emerged as the elite class in New Mexico were those who perfected these skills. Under their influence, Santa Fe was transformed from a traditional mission and imperial town into a cosmopolitan frontier trading center. During the next two centuries, this multiethnic elite absorbed first French and then Anglo-American newcomers while maintaining its own social, political, and economic style.

Life in French Louisiana

France's colony in Louisiana had many of the same qualities and faced many of the same problems as Spain's North American possessions. Like most European settlements, Louisiana suffered from a critical shortage of labor, leading first to dependence on the Indians and eventually to the wholesale adoption of African slavery. Like all Europeans who settled in North America, Louisianans found themselves embroiled in a complicated Native American world that usually defied European understanding.

subsistence farming Farming that produces enough food for survival but does not produce a surplus that can be sold.

♦ The French had difficulty persuading settlers to come to the New World province of Louisiana. As a result, the region's development depended on native Indians and imported Africans for labor. Alexander de Batz's 1735 painting gives us a good idea of what the population looked like. *Peabody Museum, Harvard University.*

Uninterest was perhaps the biggest problem faced by the Louisiana colony during the seventeenth century. Despite the territory's strategic location, fertile soils, and fur-bearing animals, few Frenchmen showed any interest in settling there. In the first years of the colony's existence, the population consisted primarily of three groups: military men, who were generally members of the lower nobility; coureurs de bois from Canada looking for new and better sources of furs; and French craftsmen seeking in the New World the economic and social opportunities that were denied them in France. The men in each group had little in common with those in the other groups, and, more important, they all had no knowledge of or interest in food production.

Recognizing the problem, the French government tried everything it could think of to make the colony more attractive to French farmers, resorting to some rather odd and extreme measures. For example, in the late 1690s officials in Louisiana noted that the absence of women was one serious deterrent to attracting useful colonists and proposed that the government pay the passage of young women of good character to the colony. For several years, agents in France tried to recruit young women but attracted only twenty-four or so, who arrived in the colony in 1704. Like the noblemen and craftsmen who preceded them, these young women—refugees from orphanages and other public institutions—were ill suited for the primitive life offered by Louisiana and were entirely unprepared to work as farm labor. By 1708 even officials who had been enthusiastic about the project were advising that it be discontinued. As a result, French men, like their Spanish neighbors, married Indians and, later, African slaves, creating a hybrid **creole** population.

In the absence of an agricultural establishment, the small number of settlers in Louisiana had to depend on imported food. At first, ships from France carried provisions to the colonies, but war in Europe frequently interrupted this source. In desperation, the colonists turned to the Indians.

The **Natchez, Chickasaws,** and **Choctaws** were all well provisioned and close by. The Chickasaws refused to deal with the French, and the Natchez, divided between quarreling factions, were sometimes helpful and sometimes hostile. But the Choctaws, locked into a war with the Chickasaws and a tense relationship with the Natchez, found the prospect of an alliance with the French quite attractive.

creole In colonial times, a term referring to anyone of European or African heritage who was born in the colonies; in Louisiana, a term referring to the ethnic group that was the result of intermarriage by people of mixed languages, races, and cultures.

Natchez Indians An urban, mound-building Indian people who lived on the lower Mississippi River until they were destroyed in a war with the French in the 1720s; survivors joined the Creek Confederacy.

Chickasaw Indians An urban, mound-building Indian people who lived on the lower Mississippi River and became a society of hunters after the change in climate and introduction of disease after 1400; they were successful in resisting French aggression throughout the colonial era.

Choctaw Indians Like the Chickasaws, a mound-building people who became a society of hunters after 1400; they were steadfast allies of the French and helped them in wars against the Natchez and Chickasaws.

Over the first several decades of the eighteenth century, the Choctaws provided food and military aid to the struggling colony and helped to shape France's Indian policies and expansion plans. After disastrous flooding along the Gulf coast during the winter of 1719–1720, for example, the French chose to relocate settlements onto Natchez land rather than into Choctaw territory. When the Natchez eventually went to war with the French, the Choctaws helped their European allies destroy the tribe—the entire Natchez Nation was either killed or sent into exile. The Choctaws also assisted the French in a thirty-year-long conflict with the Chickasaws, though with less success.

Despite the Choctaw alliance, which guaranteed ample food supplies and made territorial acquisitions possible, Louisiana remained unattractive to French farmers. Although Louisiana officials advised against it, the French government finally resorted to recruiting German refugees, paupers, and criminals to people the new land. But even with these newcomers there was not enough labor to ensure survival, much less prosperity. Increasingly, settlers in Louisiana imported slaves to do necessary work. By 1732, slaves made up two-thirds of the population.

The Dutch Settlements

The existence of Rensselaerswyck and other great landed estates made it seem as though the New Netherland colony was prosperous and secure, but in actuality it was neither. Few of the wealthy stockholders in the Dutch West India Company wanted to trade their lives as successful gentleman investors for a pioneering existence on a barely tamed frontier. The economy in Holland was booming, and only the most desperate or adventurous wanted to leave. But having no one to pay their way, most could not afford to emigrate to the colony.

Desperate to draw settlers, the Dutch West India Company created an alternative to the patroonship, offering to grant a tract of land to any free man who would agree to farm it. This offer appealed to many groups in Europe who were experiencing hardship in their own countries but for one reason or another were prohibited from moving to other colonies. French Protestants, for example, were experiencing terrible persecution at home, but imperial law forbade them from going to France's New World provinces. Roman Catholics, Quakers, Jews, Muslims, and a wide variety of others chose to migrate to New Netherland. Most of the colonists settled on small farms, called *bouweries* in Dutch, and engaged in the same agricultural pursuits they had practiced in Europe. Thus New Netherland was dotted with little settlements, each having its own language, culture, and internal economy.

Farming was the dominant activity of the emigrants, but some followed the example of the French coureurs du bois and went alone or in small groups into the woods to live and trade with the Indians. Called ***bosch loopers*** (Dutch for "woods runners"), these independent traders traveled through the forests, trying to intercept Indian parties on their way to Dutch West India Company posts. They traded cheap brandy and rum for the Indians' furs, which they then sold to the company for enormous profits. Although both tribal leaders and company officials complained about the bosch loopers' illegal activities, the authorities could not control them.

In fact, the Dutch West India Company was unable to control much of anything in New Netherland. The incredible diversity of the settlers no doubt contributed to this administrative impotence. For example, Dutch law and company policy dictated that the Calvinistic **Dutch Reform Church** was to be the colony's official and only church. But instead of drawing everyone into one religion, the policy had the opposite effect. As late as 1642 there were no churches of any denomination in the entire colony. Poor leadership and unimaginative policies also contributed to the general air of disorder. Following Peter Minuet's dismissal by the company in 1631, a long line of incompetent governors ruled the colony. In the absence of any legislative assembly or other local body to help keep matters on track, one bad decision kept following another. One of these governors, William Kieft, was not only incompetent but dangerously hot tempered. He personally ordered the massacre that touched off a disastrous Indian war in 1643 and 1644. The company finally replaced Kieft in 1647 with the much more competent Peter Stuyvesant, but his authoritarian style alienated settlers who were used to doing things in their own way, and his uncompromising attitude toward the Indians kept relations with the lower Hudson River tribes unstable.

bosch loopers Independent Dutch fur traders; literally, "woods runners."

Dutch Reform Church Calvinistic Protestant established church in the Dutch Republic and the official church in New Netherland.

SUMMARY

E xpectations
C onstraints
C hoices
O utcomes

Spain's opening ventures in the Americas were wildly successful, making the Iberian kingdom the envy of the world. With *expectations* of cashing in on similar finds, other European nations began to contest Spain's monopoly on American colonization, creating an outward explosion of exploring energy. Although slow to consolidate an imperial presence in North America, England was the first to confront the Spanish in force, wounding them severely. France and the Netherlands took advantage of the situation to begin building their own American empires.

For Native Americans the entry of Europeans into their realms combined with other forces to create an air of crisis. Presented with a series of new *constraints,* Indians created altogether new societies and sought new ways to solve their problems. This often involved difficult *choices,* perhaps allying with the newcomers, resisting them, or fleeing. As different groups exercised different options, the *outcome* was a historically dynamic world of interaction involving all the societies that were coming together in North America

This dynamic interaction yielded interesting fruit. In New Spain, New France, Louisiana, New Netherland, and throughout the Great Plains, new societies emerged. These were truly cosmopolitan societies, bearing cultural traits and material goods taken from throughout the world. As we will see in Chapter 3, societies on the Atlantic coast, too, were evolving as English colonists interacted with the land and its many occupants. The *outcome* of such interchange, over the centuries, was the emergence of a multicultural, multiethnic, and extraordinarily rich culture—an essential element in the making of America.

SUGGESTED READINGS

Charles R. Boxer, *The Dutch Seaborne Empire, 1600–1800* (1965).

A comprehensive overview of Dutch colonial activities and the trading economy that evolved in the Netherlands following its independence from Spain.

W. J. Eccles, *France in America* (rev. ed., 1990)

A newly revised version of the classic work on France's activities in the New World; inclusive and readable.

Daniel K. Richter and James H. Merrell, *Beyond the Covenant Chain: The Iroquois and Their Neighbors in Indian North America* (1987).

Two leading ethnohistorians collaborated to write this excellent study of the changing Indian world of the Northeast during the colonial era.

David Weber, *The Spanish Frontier in North America* (1992).

A broad synthesis of the history of New Spain by the foremost scholar in the field.

Richard White, *The Middle Ground: Indians, Empires, and Republics in the Great Lakes Region, 1650–1815* (1991).

Although it covers material far beyond the chronological scope of this chapter, students interested in the relations between Indians and Europeans in the colonial era will find this book extraordinarily rich.

THE COLONIES AND THEIR MAJOR CITIES The creation of the English mainland colonies spanned almost 150 years, from the first settlement at Jamestown, Virginia in 1607 to the founding of the last colony of Georgia in 1732. This map indicates the year each colony was founded, the type of charter governing it, and the date in which eight of these colonies came directly under royal control. The map also locates the major colonial cities in each region.

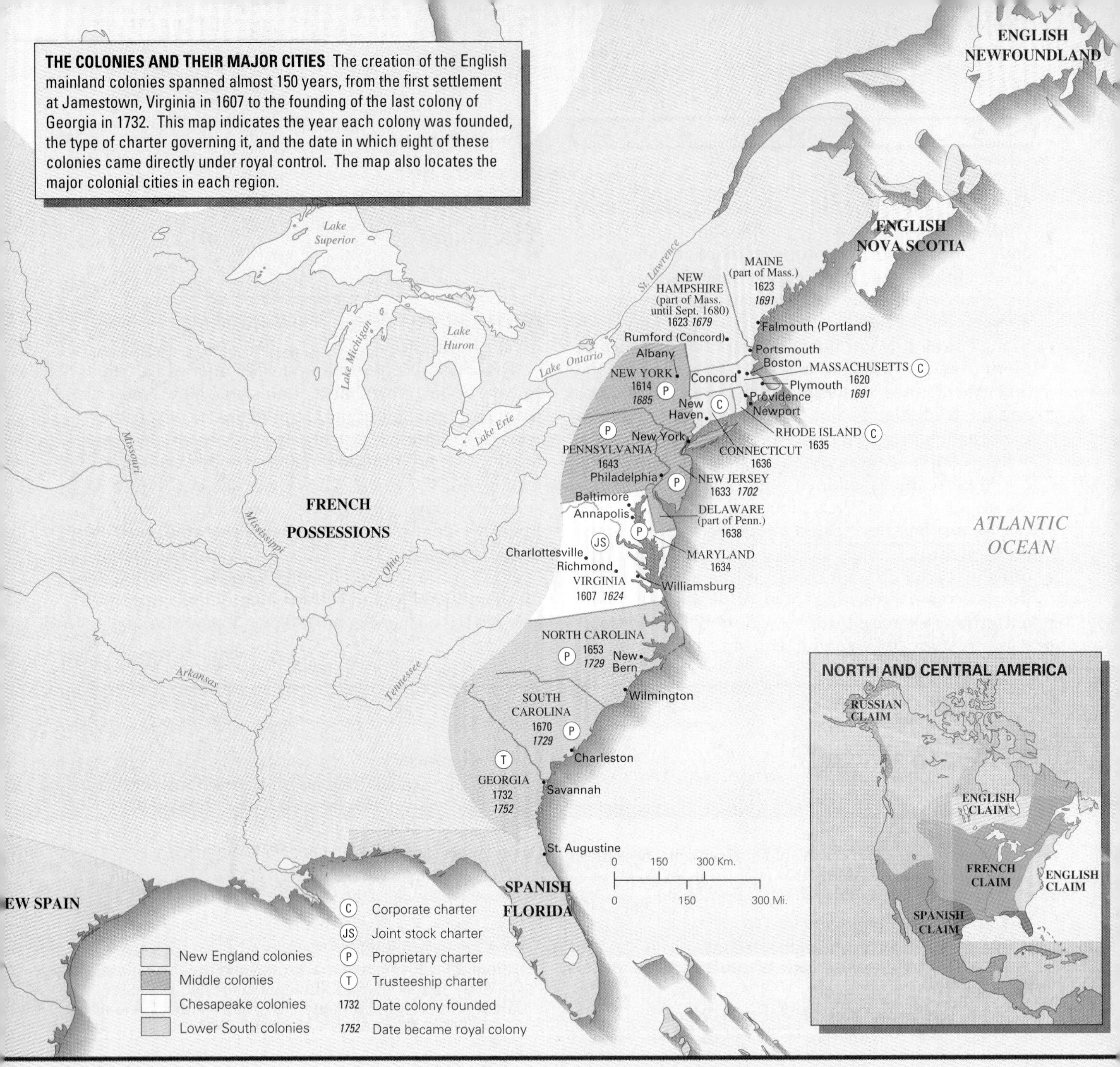

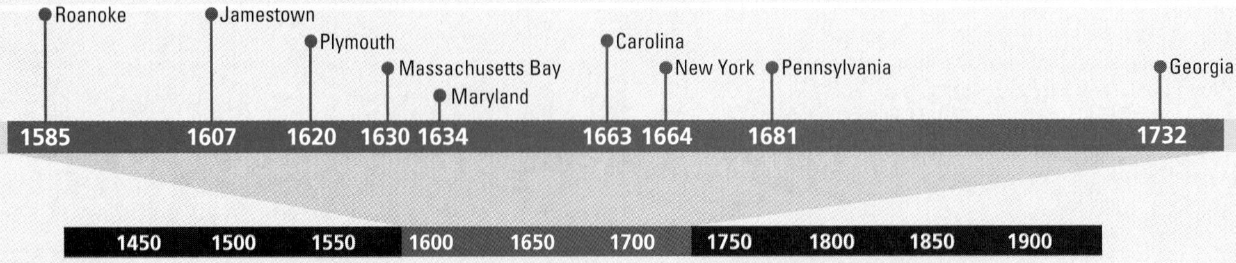

CHAPTER 3

Founding the English Mainland Colonies, 1585–1732

England and Colonization

- What was the outcome of the failure of the Roanoke Colony?
- What constraints in England encouraged people to migrate to America?

Settling the Chesapeake

- What expectations did the Virginia Company and the Calvert family have for their Chesapeake colonies? Did the outcomes satisfy or disappoint these founders?
- How did Chesapeake colonists choose to resolve conflicts within their communities?

New England: Colonies of Dissenters

- Why did English religious dissenters choose to settle in America?
- What kind of society did the Puritans expect to create?
- What constraints did Puritan authorities impose to discourage dissent? What was the outcome of dissenters' actions?

The Pluralism of the Middle Colonies

- Why did the Dutch and the English choose to encourage a multicultural population in New York?
- What made the expectations for Pennsylvania so distinctive?

The Colonies of the Lower South

- What type of society did the founders of Carolina expect to create? How did the outcome differ from their expectations?
- Why did philanthropists choose to create Georgia? Why did the king choose to support this project?

INTRODUCTION

Expectations
Constraints
Choices
Outcomes

Beginning in the late sixteenth century, many English men and women set out on the adventure of their lives: colonizing what, to them, was a new world. Whatever their *expectations,* the *choice* to begin life anew on the mainland of North America shaped their fates. Driving many of these men and women to emigrate were the *constraints* they faced at home—poverty, religious persecution, the terrors of civil war, or dizzying economic transformations. Others were spurred by the love of danger or dreams of sudden fame and fortune. Still others were pursuing the promise of land, even if they first had to work as the servants of other colonists for several years. Only one group of colonists—arriving as slaves from Africa, often by way of the Caribbean—had no *choice* at all.

The *constraints* and dangers awaiting the colonists proved fatal to many. Some did not survive the ocean voyage. Others died of diseases they had never encountered in their homeland. And many died in the recurrent brutal warfare that raged between Indians and Europeans and among rival European settlements. But circumstances in England and in Europe continued to prompt new groups of immigrants to the English colonies. By the end of the seventeenth century, there were twelve colonies, and in 1732 the last of these original colonies, Georgia, was established. These thirteen original colonies clustered in regions known as the Chesapeake, New England, the Middle Colonies, and the Lower South. Although each colony had its own individual history, the colonies of a region usually shared a common economy and labor system, or the same religious heritage, or a special feature such as ethnic pluralism. Whether they were established by groups of investors, by wealthy proprietors, by conquest, or by the division of one colony into two or more, every colony grew through experimentation, adjustment, cooperation, and conflict.

Seventeenth-century colonists and their leaders were faced with a seemingly endless series of critical *choices*—including where to settle, how to organize their communities, and how to sustain themselves. Through trial and error, they began to *choose* the crops they would grow, the labor force they would employ, the rules governing who would be welcome within their society. Although the colonists often *expected* to re-create family patterns and social institutions they had left behind, most colonies were fragile communities. The earliest settlers lacked important resources to achieve their goals, including the skills to survive in a new environment. In many areas the colonists lacked churches, schools, courts, and other familiar and essential institutions of their English and European cultures. And because the American Indians opposed their efforts to push farther inland or to clear and cultivate lands that the native populations had long claimed, deadly conflict was often the *outcome.*

No matter how wide the Atlantic Ocean seemed, events in England affected the lives of all colonists. Formal government policy and English law, in particular, often cut across regional boundaries and individual colonial borders, placing *constraints* on colonial behavior and reshaping colonial *expectations.* Nevertheless, by the eighteenth century, both England and its colonists knew that the American settlements were no longer outposts but permanent communities.

England and Colonization

- What was the outcome of the failure of the Roanoke Colony?
- What constraints in England encouraged people to migrate to America?

On a typically hot and humid July day along the Atlantic coast of what we call North Carolina, two small English ships bobbed on the waters east of the barrier islands that protected the Carolina mainland. The year was 1584. Excitement spread among the men on board as the islands came into view and a party of explorers prepared to put ashore. Although the land looked peaceful and inviting after a long ocean voyage, the Englishmen who disembarked took no chances: each wore armor, and all carried heavy weapons. The men made their way carefully through a dense forest of cypress, sweet

CHRONOLOGY

Settling the Mainland Colonies

1585	English colonize Roanoke Island
1603	James I becomes king of England
1606	Creation of the Virginia Company
1607	Jamestown founded
1611	Pilgrims flee to Holland from England
1612	Tobacco cultivation begins in Virginia
1619	Virginia House of Burgesses meets
1620	Pilgrims found Plymouth Plantations
1625	Charles I becomes king of England
1630	Puritans found Massachusetts Bay Colony
1634	First English settlements in Maryland
1636	Roger Williams founds Providence
1637	Anne Hutchinson banished from Massachusetts Pequot War in New England
1642–1648	English Civil War
1649	Charles I executed Cromwell and Puritans come to power in England
1660	Restoration of English monarchy
1662	Half-Way Covenant
1663	Carolina chartered
1675	King Philip's War in New England
1676	Bacon's Rebellion in Virginia
1681	Pennsylvania chartered
1685	James II becomes king of England
1686	Dominion of New England established
1688	Glorious Revolution in England
1689	Leisler's Rebellion in New York
1691	Massachusetts becomes royal colony
1692	Salem witch trials
1732	Georgia chartered

gum, pines, and flowering dogwood that began at the edge of the sandy shoreline. Cedars towered above their heads, and the rustling forest sounds told them wild game and fowl were nearby. This lush landscape contrasted sharply with the carefully cultivated farmland of their native England. That afternoon, as the men were busy setting up tents for their first night in what, to them, was a strange new world, a canoe carrying three Indians came into view. It would be difficult to say who were more amazed by what they saw. Despite all they had read, or any sketches they had seen, the Englishmen surely found these native people exotic, dressed as they were in loinclothes, their bodies decorated with tattoos and with necklaces and bracelets of shells. The Indians, in turn, must have wondered at these strangers, encased in heavy metal and multiple layers of clothing, a foolish costume for laboring in the humid summer afternoon.

What brought this party of Englishmen to the mainland of North America? They were sent by Sir Walter Raleigh, a wealthy adventurer who financed the costly project out of his own personal fortune. Their task was to reconnoiter the area and report whether it was suitable for the next phase of Raleigh's new and ambitious project: establishing the first English colony in America.

The English left North Carolina in August. But the following year Raleigh sent a group of settlers to the same area. More than half of these volunteers were actually soldiers, many of them veterans of the recent violent conquest of Ireland. Clearly, Raleigh worried that relations between the colonists and the Indians might not remain peaceful. He was right. The first blows were struck by the English, whose haughty sense of superiority was not dampened by their dependence on the local Indian community for food. Before the year was over, however, the colonists had given up and returned to England, driven away by Indian attack. Raleigh tried again in 1587, this time sending more than a hundred colonists, most of them civilians and many of them members of families. Despite Raleigh's best intentions, the Spanish Armada's attack on England prevented him from sending supplies to the colony for three years. When English ships did at last reach the Roanoke colony, the people aboard were stunned to find nothing but abandoned ruins. Every settler had vanished without a trace. Whether the Roanoke colonists had fled from Indian hostility or been rescued from some natural danger or disaster with Indian support Raleigh never discovered. Nor would it have mattered. Raleigh's fortune was gone—wasted, as friends and enemies alike declared, on a foolish dream of glory. The English did not attempt to colonize in North America again until the seventeenth century.

Religious and Political Tensions in Seventeenth-Century England

Between 1603 and 1688, the English people lived through periods of intense religious conflict, economic upheavals and dislocations, civil war, and the removal of two kings from the throne. In the midst of these dramatic events, wealthy men found ways to finance risky colonizing ventures, members of religious sects established communities in America, and impoverished men and women decided to seek their fortunes across the ocean.

The political unrest began soon after the death of Queen Elizabeth in 1603, when first the son (James I) and then the grandson (Charles I) of the Catholic queen Mary Stuart came to the English throne. Neither James nor Charles was especially committed to Protestantism. In fact, both were thought to be secretly practicing Catholics. Their lack of commitment to Protestantism disturbed a growing number of English people who wished to see the Protestant reforms begun in the sixteenth century go further than Henry VIII or Elizabeth I had ever considered. These religious radicals campaigned to eliminate all traces of Catholic custom, church organization, rituals, or beliefs. In their words, they wished to "purify" the **Church of England.** Elizabeth's policy toward these Puritans had been simple: she allowed them to voice demands and then totally ignored them. This kind of diplomatic tolerance was not James I's strong suit. He was offended by the calls to "purify" the national religion, and he was equally offended by any opposition to his royal authority as head of the Church of England. Both James and his son, Charles I, harassed Puritans and other dissenters and actively squelched demands for religious reform. Yet Puritan opposition only grew stronger in the first half of the seventeenth century.

James I and Charles I did not welcome challenges to their political authority any more than they did to their religious leadership. They had little respect for an English political culture that set limits on the king's royal prerogative, or arbitrary decision making, by giving important powers to the legislative branch, called **Parliament.** Members of the elected house of Parliament, the House of Commons, expected to play an active role in governing the nation. But James was not shy about declaring his commitment to **absolutism,** the exercise of complete jurisdiction over the liberties and the property of his subjects. When James lectured Parliament on the subject, its political leaders were stunned—and appalled—and decided that a challenge had been hurled at the rights of English citizens everywhere.

The Stuart kings underestimated the determination of parliamentary leaders to have a commanding voice in matters of finance, religious reform, and even foreign policy. And because the House of Commons controlled how tax monies were raised and used, Parliament had a powerful weapon to hold over the king's head. Throughout James's reign, the king and Commons fought each other over matters of policy and taxation. Many in the House of Commons also supported the Puritan religious reforms, and this sharpened the conflict. When Charles I came to the throne in 1625, his solution to the problem was to dismiss Parliament and rule without any legislature at all, attempting to finance his government by his own arbitrary imposition of taxes.

In 1640, however, a rebellion in Scotland forced Charles to call Parliament back into session in order to raise an army. The reinstated legislature quickly

Church of England The Protestant church that King Henry VIII established as Engand's official church in the sixteenth century; also known as the Anglican church.

Parliament The lawmaking branch of the English government, composed of the House of Lords, representing English nobility, and the House of Commons, an elected body of untitled English citizens.

absolutism The exercise of complete and unrestricted power in government.

♦ In 1616, London was a dirty, overcrowded city of some three hundred thousand people. Severe economic depression had driven thousands of rural people into the city, where they sought day labor, begged, or survived through theft and prostitution. The sight of so many poverty-stricken people persuaded many prosperous Londoners that their nation was overpopulated. They hoped colonies in America could serve as "dumping grounds" for the poor. *Courtesy of the Trustees of the British Library.*

challenged the king. Even when Charles agreed to certain of their demands, radical members of the Commons were not satisfied. In 1642, civil war erupted, pitting those loyal to the Stuart monarchy against the political and religious dissenters represented in the Commons. In 1649, the leader of the rebels, Oliver Cromwell, completed the Puritan revolution and brought monarchy to an end by having the king executed. For almost a dozen years, the nation was a **Commonwealth,** a republic dominated by Puritans, merchants, and gentry. Cromwell headed that government until his death in 1658, but many felt he ruled with as dictatorial a style as the Stuart kings. By 1660, popular support for the Commonwealth had faded, and the Stuart family was invited to take the throne once again. Monarchy was thus restored.

For fifteen years, Charles II set the tone for this **Restoration era,** leading an extravagant, sensual life. Although the king cooperated with Parliament, his elegant lifestyle and evidence of his Catholic sympathies spread anti-Catholic fear through the nation. It grew to crisis proportions when Charles died with no legitimate children and his brother James II came to the throne. James had openly declared his Catholicism when he was Duke of York.

James's reign lasted only three years. In 1688, Parliament's anti-Catholic leadership offered the English throne to James's Protestant daughter, Mary, and her Dutch husband, Prince William of Orange. In December 1688, James fled to the safety of France with his Catholic wife and their infant son. Without a drop of blood being spilled, William and Mary began their rule, as a king and queen who understood clearly that they depended on Parliament for their crowns. Protestant England hailed the event as the **Glorious Revolution.**

Colonizers and Colonies

For almost a century, the women and men of England had lived in turbulent, sometimes violent, and often rapidly changing circumstances. Their passionate disputes over religious issues had divided them and frequently led those in power to persecute and harass those who dissented or protested. The shift from an agricultural society to a more commercial, mercantile economy had made some people fabulously wealthy but had left others in poverty or in fear of poverty. Their political struggles over the powers belonging to king and to Parliament, and their concerns over the rights and liberties of English citizens, had prompted such remarkable events as the execution of a king, a civil war, the creation of

Commonwealth The republic established after the defeat of King Charles I's royal army by Oliver Cromwell's forces during the English Civil War; the Commonwealth lasted from 1649 until the restoration of the monarchy in 1660.

Restoration era The period marking the return of monarchy to England, beginning in 1660 with King Charles II and ending with the exile of King James II in 1688.

Glorious Revolution The events in 1688 that resulted in the removal of James II from the throne of England and the crowning of the Protestant monarchs, William and Mary.

the Commonwealth, and the transfer of the throne from one monarch to another. Yet in the midst of this social turmoil, economic instability, and political conflict, England at last began to create its empire.

Surely these precarious conditions at home provided compelling motives for thousands of English men and women to seek a new life across the Atlantic. But neither the Stuart kings, Cromwell, nor individual noblemen were willing to lay out the great sums needed for colonizing North America. This critical ingredient for empire building was provided by England's merchant **entrepreneurs,** independent businessmen who had devised methods for sharing the burdens of potentially profitable but risky shipping ventures. These merchants realized they could protect themselves from losing their entire fortunes if they joined together in purchasing shares in a venture, splitting the costs so that no single individual would face ruin if the venture failed. In the early seventeenth century, **joint-stock companies,** modeled after these successful mercantile practices, took the lead in planting American colonies. Later on, the kings' political supporters and personal friends grew more willing to attempt colonial settlements, encouraged by grants of great tracts of land from the monarch that became **proprietary colonies.** The kings also gave religious or political opponents permission to found colonies, in an effort to rid the nation of such people. And eventually the rulers themselves established or took control of some colonies, making them **royal colonies.**

Once the English began to plant their colonies, they proved resourceful in overcoming many constraints, whether in the cost of settlement, in the struggles to survive in a new and alien environment, or in their troubled and often violent relationships with one another and with the Indians on whose lands they were trespassing. The outcome of over a century of colonization was impressive: by the beginning of the eighteenth century, English settlements formed a crescent, stretching from present-day Maine to South Carolina. (The last of the mainland colonies, Georgia, was not established until 1732.)

The colonists who lived in these North American settlements thought of themselves not as members of a single society but as residents of four distinct regions. The Chesapeake, or Upper South, composed of Virginia and Maryland, was the site of the first successful English foothold in North America. Soon afterward, New England was settled. The Middle Colonies—New York, New Jersey, Pennsylvania, and Delaware—already colonized by the Swedes and the Dutch—came under English control through conquest at midcentury. Below the Chesapeake, the Lower South, made up of North and South Carolina and eventually Georgia, carried the English flag to the borders of Spanish Florida. But in 1603, when King James I granted permission to two joint-stock companies to plant colonies, neither he nor anyone in England could have predicted such an outcome.

Settling the Chesapeake

In 1603, King James I granted not one but two enterprising groups of merchant investors a chance to establish colonies in North America. Although both the Plymouth Company and the London Company received royal charters to settle Virginia, these rivals did not worry about their settlements intruding on one another. In the minds of the king and his subjects, Virginia was a huge and vaguely defined region, embracing much of the Atlantic coast of North America and stretching from one ocean to the other. The Plymouth Company's colony on the rocky Maine coast was quickly destroyed by sickness and Indian attack, and its investors just as quickly lost all interest in America. The London Company, now known simply as the Virginia Company, did not send out its first shipload of settlers until December 1606. Their outpost near the Chesapeake Bay became the basis for England's first successful colony in the New World.

The Planting of Jamestown

Toward the end of April in 1607 three Virginia Company ships entered the calm, broad waters of Chesapeake Bay and made their way up a river the

entrepreneur A person who organizes and manages a business enterprise that involves risk and requires initiative.

joint-stock company A business financed through the sale of shares of stock to investors, who share both the profits and the losses from a risky venture.

proprietary colonies Colonies owned by an individual or group of individuals who determined how settlement would take place and the rules and laws under which the colonists would live.

royal colonies Colonies under the direct authority of the king or queen.

colonists named the James to a spot they dubbed **Jamestown**—both in honor of their king. Like the Englishmen who scouted Roanoke Island, these ship-weary Virginia colonists found themselves in a land of warm sun, thick forest, and fragrant air. But they soon discovered that survival in this beautiful but alien world would be a formidable challenge. These first settlers, like those who followed them across the ocean each spring, battled starvation, disease, and the local Indian populations.

These early colonists were poorly equipped for the tasks they faced. Several were gentlemen, accustomed to having servants care for them. Few of the ordinary settlers knew anything about clearing forests. Few knew what was edible and what was not. Stubbornly, they ignored the advice of the local Powhatan Indians who warned that, at certain times, the waters of the James River were dangerous to drink and could bring on disease and death. Exhausted by the trip across the ocean, disoriented by their new surroundings, and weakened by the onslaught of illnesses like typhoid and dysentery, the majority of the people who huddled in Jamestown lacked the energy to plant adequate crops or build adequate shelters even had they been willing to do so. That the colony survived at all was probably due to the efforts of a larger-than-life **mercenary** and loud-mouthed self-promoter named John Smith, whose boasts of bravery and resourcefulness fortunately proved to be true.

In 1608 Captain Smith took control of the settlement, forcing all its original survivors and all newcomers to build, plant, fish, and lay away supplies for the coming winter. Smith's rule was simple: only those who worked would eat. Despite his efforts, the death toll remained high, for disease carried off many of the settlers. But the Virginia Company approved of the strict discipline Smith had imposed. It continued to run the colony like a military outpost for many years after Smith returned to England—and to new adventures elsewhere.

Smith's legacy included an arrogant, aggressive, and sometimes self-defeating stance toward Jamestown's neighbors, Chief Powhatan and his Powhatan Indians. In 1609 the first of several wars broke out in which both sides behaved brutally. Englishmen murdered enemy women and children and decapitated their victims while Indians flayed captives alive or scalped them. There was no victory for either side. During that winter—known as "the starving time"—desperate colonists ate dogs, cats, snakes, and shoe leather in an effort to survive. An act of cannibalism was reported. By 1610, only sixty of the five hundred settlers who had made the transatlantic voyage were alive.

While each spring's survivors waited for fresh supplies and new colonists to arrive, investors at home were bemoaning their financial fate. Their yearly expenses gave them a new, more realistic understanding that colonization was a slow, costly undertaking. The company seemed caught in an investor's nightmare, pumping good money after bad in hopes of delaying a total collapse. Tobacco, a weed native to the Americas, proved to be the colony's salvation, for pipe smoking had been a steady habit in England since the midsixteenth century. At first, Virginia seemed an unlikely source of marketable tobacco since the local variety was too harsh for English tastes. But one of the colonists, a young man named John Rolfe, managed to transplant a milder strain of West Indian tobacco to the colony. This success changed Rolfe's life, earning him the respect and admiration of his neighbors. Rolfe also briefly changed English-Indian relationships in Virginia by his marriage to Powhatan's daughter, Pocahontas, who died soon afterward while visiting England.

By 1612, Virginia colonists were engaged in a mad race to plant and harvest as many acres of tobacco as possible. "Brown gold" made Rolfe and many of his neighbors wealthy, but the Virginia Company continued to groan under the weight of its expenses. Not wanting to try to sell more shares in the company, the stockholders chose instead to allow potential colonists to become investors. They did this through the **headright system,** an arrangement that gave a man a deed for 50 acres of land for every settler he brought to the colony at his own expense. In this way the Virginia Company shifted to the colonists the cost of populating and developing the colony. But the headright system also ended the company's monopoly on Virginia's primary resource: the land and its distribution. The company soon made other important concessions to the Virginia colonists. Military-style discipline was aban-

Jamestown The first permanent English settlement in mainland America, established in 1607 by the Virginia Company and named in honor of King James I.

mercenary A professional soldier, hired to serve in a foreign army.

headright system Devised by the Virginia Company, it granted a colonist 50 acres of land for each settler whom that colonist paid to transport to the colony.

♦ Baltimore was founded in 1629 and served as a shipping center for Maryland tobacco growers. By 1752, when this view was drawn, it had begun to show signs of developing into a prosperous port city. After the American Revolution, Baltimore expanded and by the 1790s boasted a population of over twenty thousand. *"Baltimore 1752," from a sketch by John Moale, Esq. Maryland Historical Society, Baltimore.*

doned. In 1618, the company created an elected, representative lawmaking body called the **House of Burgesses,** which gave the landholders—planters—of Virginia a voice in the colony's civil government.

The company showed no skill or thoughtfulness in dealing with its other problem: Indian relations. It continued John Smith's aggressive policies. By 1622, the English seemed to have the upper hand, for the colony's population had grown and tobacco had brought a measure of prosperity. With Virginia planters pressing farther inland and seizing land along local rivers, Opechancanough, Chief Powhatan's successor, decided to strike back. On what the Christian settlers called Good Friday, he mounted a deadly attack on Jamestown, killing a quarter of the colonists in a single day. As quickly as possible, the Virginia Company sent weapons to the colony. This second Anglo-Powhatan war raged for two years. Bloodshed then became less frequent, but a final peace was not reached for a decade. By that time, fewer than 500 of the Powhatan people, who had once numbered 40,000, were still alive. When news of the 1622 war reached King James, he was already investigating the Virginia Company's management of the colony. He revoked the company's charter and declared Virginia to be a royal possession.

If the king's advisers tallied up the cost in human life for the planting of this first English colony in the same manner that the company tallied up the cost in pence and pounds, they found the outcome sobering: by 1624, only 1,275 of the 8,500 settlers who had arrived since 1607 remained alive.

Maryland: A Catholic Refuge

As Virginians spread out along the riverways of their colony, searching for good land on which to plant tobacco, plans for a second southern colony, to be called Maryland, were brewing in England. The man behind this project was George Calvert, a wealthy Catholic who had just been made a nobleman by King Charles I. In addition to his new title, Lord Baltimore, Calvert was granted a royal charter to land lying east and north of Chesapeake Bay. Unlike the Virginia Company investors, Calvert had little interest in making a profit. Instead, the proprietor of this new colony wanted to create a Catholic society composed of powerful noblemen and obedient tenant farmers. In the 1630s, Calvert was a reactionary thinker with a radical plan.

George Calvert died before any colonists could be recruited for the Maryland Colony, but his oldest son, Cecilius Calvert, the second Lord Baltimore, eagerly continued the project. Few English Catholics shared his enthusiasm, however. When Calvert's first shipload of colonists sailed up Chesapeake Bay in 1634, most of the two hundred volunteers aboard were young Protestants seeking a better life. Calvert soon realized that his colony would not grow unless he adopted the headright system developed by Vir-

House of Burgesses The representative lawmaking body of Virginia, established by the Virginia Company in 1618, which first met in 1619.

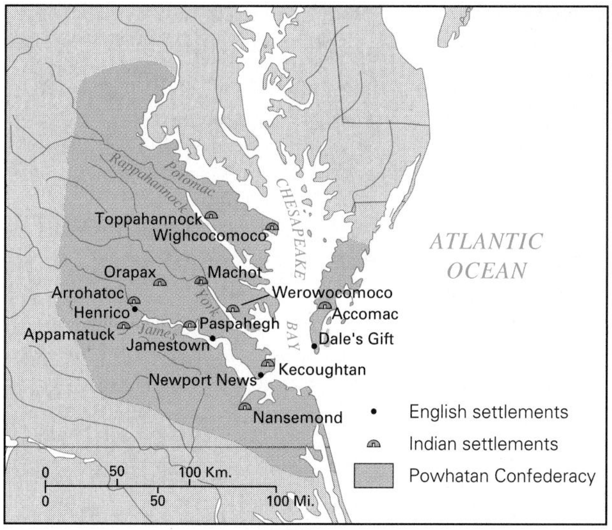

♦ **MAP 3.1 Early Chesapeake Settlement** This map shows the location of both Indian and English colonial settlements in the early seventeenth century. As the English communities grew in number and size, conflicts between the Indians of the Powhatan Confederacy and the colonists also grew, eventually leading to warfare and considerable loss of life.

ginia. Maryland quickly grew to resemble the neighboring colony. Colonists turned to tobacco growing, joining the scramble for good riverfront land and using trickery, threats, or violence to pry acres away from resisting Indians.

By midcentury, the success of tobacco as a **staple crop** for export to what the English colonists called the mother country had ensured a measure of prosperity for Virginia and Maryland. But it did not ensure peacefulness in these Chesapeake colonies. Political crises in England produced shock waves in both Virginia and Maryland, often intertwining with local tensions among colonists or between colonists and Indians (see Map 3.1).

Troubles on the Chesapeake

Despite Maryland's Protestant majority, Lord Baltimore's control of the colony ensured its Catholic colonists both political influence and security. But when Oliver Cromwell established the Commonwealth in England, Calvert realized that these Catholic settlers were in danger. To prevent the colony's Protestant population from persecuting or harassing the Catholic minority, Calvert offered equal protection to both religious groups. In 1649, he issued the innovative Toleration Act, which protected all "persons . . . professing to believe in Jesus Christ" from being "troubled [or] molested . . . in respect of his or her religion." Unfortunately, Cromwell had no intention of supporting this experiment in religious toleration. He repealed Calvert's Toleration Act, and in 1654 Parliament went further, taking Maryland away from the Calvert family and establishing a Protestant assembly in the colony. Exactly as Calvert had feared, a wave of anti-Catholic persecution swept over Maryland.

Within a year, a bloody civil war had erupted, pitting Catholic and Protestant colonists against one another. The Protestants won the Battle of the Severn, but their victory was short lived. With Cromwell's death and the restoration of the monarchy in England, Maryland was returned to the Calvert family. Hostilities between Catholic and Protestant settlers continued, however, and Protestants organized unsuccessful rebellions in 1659, in 1676, and again in 1681. Then, in the wake of the Glorious Revolution in England, Protestant Marylanders achieved victory, led by an unlikely warrior, the stooped and nearly crippled **John Coode.** In 1691, Coode's Protestant Association persuaded the Crown to make Maryland a royal colony. Many years later, in 1715, the fourth Lord Baltimore gave up Catholicism and joined the Church of England. This conversion to Anglicanism prompted the English king to return to him the colony that generations of Calverts had once expected to be a haven for Catholics.

Virginians were not deeply affected by the religious controversies in England. The colony did, however, suffer from a violent conflict between wealthy planters and ambitious newcomers that seemed to echo the social conflict of the English Civil War. Things came to a head in the 1760s when Nathaniel Bacon, an aggressive and **charismatic** Englishman, came to Virginia to seek his fortune. Bacon was a gentleman planter, tall, slender, well educated, and well mannered. But like most new arrivals to the colony, he found himself unable to acquire any of

staple crop A basic or necessary agricultural item, produced for sale or export.

John Coode Leader of a rebel army, the Protestant Association, that won control of Maryland in 1691.

charismatic Having a spiritual power or personal quality that stirs enthusiasm and devotion in large numbers of people.

♦ Nathaniel Bacon came to Virginia as a gentleman in the 1670s, but his resentment of the economic and political domination of the colony by a small group of planters transformed him into a backwoods rebel. In 1676, Bacon led an army of discontented farmers, servants, and slaves against the powerful coastal planters—and almost won. In this stained glass window, discovered and restored in the twentieth century, Bacon's social class and his commanding presence are both evident. *The Association for the Preservation of Virginia Antiquities at Bacon's Castle, Library of Virginia.*

the highly desirable coastal lands, held exclusively by the established aristocracy. Bacon resented the economic advantage these men enjoyed. It forced newcomers and poorer men to compete for land in the backcountry, where Indian resistance to white expansion and the blatantly unfair taxation policy of a colonial government dominated by the coastal elite heightened economic disadvantages.

In 1676, an outbreak of violence between Indians and backcountry planters led to heated demands for a military force along the settlement frontier. The elderly governor, William Berkeley, did not want to end his career in Virginia with a full-scale Indian war, so he refused to enlist or send any troops. When western planters demanded permission to raise an army of their own, Berkeley said no to that as well. His refusal enraged Nathaniel Bacon, and under Bacon's leadership, westerners decided to take matters into their own hands. They planned to mount a **vigilante action** against the Indians, but only after they had taught their political enemies in the colonial government a lesson. Bacon's men armed themselves and marched on Jamestown, threatening to destroy the colonial capital unless the government endorsed the Indian campaign. The frightened governor gave in. As soon as Bacon's army left the city, however, Berkeley pronounced Bacon and his men "rebells and traytors" and ordered their army to disband at once.

Bacon was not impressed. His "rebells and traytors" returned to Jamestown and made good on their earlier threats to demolish the town. As Bacon's army marched toward the capital, poor farmers, black and white servants, and craftsmen joined its ranks. Female servants and farm wives surprised many colonists by arming themselves and marching with Bacon's forces. What began as a vigilante uprising was rapidly turning into a social revolution against a privileged elite.

With Bacon's followers looting and burning Jamestown, English authorities at last recognized how serious the Virginia situation had become. The king ordered five companies of soldiers to aid the terrified governor in suppressing the revolt. These military reinforcements proved unnecessary, for Nathaniel Bacon, who had returned to searching for hostile Indians, died of exposure and dysentery on white Virginia's frontier. Without its leader, **Bacon's Rebellion** lost its momentum and his army retreated. The governor revenged himself by executing twenty-three of Bacon's lieutenants. Although members of Bacon's army continued to resist for several years, the rebellion never regained its force.

Colonial Chesapeake Life

The Chesapeake colonies were stirred by the religious and social conflicts that preoccupied English men and women in the seventeenth century, but the Chesapeake differed from the Mother Country in several significant ways. With its unusual family structure, the nature and organization of agricultural work, and the biracial work force that had come into being by the end of the century, the Chesapeake would have shocked most of the English men and women who remained at home.

vigilante action People taking the law into their own hands.

Bacon's Rebellion A revolt by backcountry farmers and planters against the colonial government of Virginia, triggered by unfair tax policies and strife with the Indians. It collapsed after the death of Nathaniel Bacon.

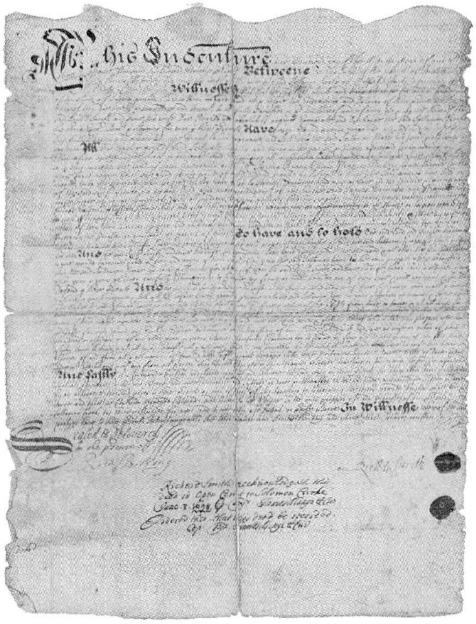

♦ Throughout much of the seventeenth century, Chesapeake tobacco planters relied on indentured or bound servants as their labor force. Mostly young, single and impoverished men from the English countryside, these immigrants signed a contract such as the one shown here, agreeing to labor four to seven years for a master in exchange for passage to America and the promise of land when their term of service was completed. *The Library of Virginia.*

Tobacco set rhythms of work and play in Maryland and Virginia that differed dramatically from those in England. Planting, tending, harvesting, and drying tobacco leaves took almost ten months of the year, beginning in late winter and ending just before Christmas. In the short period between the holiday and the beginning of a new cycle of planting, Chesapeake planters, their families, and their servants frantically tried to catch up on other, neglected farm chores. They did repairs, sewed and mended, built new cabins and sheds, cut timber and firewood. They also compressed whatever social life they had into these winter weeks, engaging—whenever possible—in hasty courtships followed by marriage.

Because tobacco quickly exhausted the soil in which it grew, planters moved frequently to new acres on their estates or to newly acquired lands farther west. With each move, they left behind drying sheds and field workers' shacks. Well into the eighteenth century, planters placed little value on permanent homes or on creating permanent social institutions such as schools. Virginians and Marylanders thus chose to sacrifice many of the familar forms of community life to the demands of their profitable crop.

Planters engaged in an endless search for a labor force large enough and cheap enough to ensure their profits. Fortunately for the seventeenth-century Virginians and Marylanders, poverty and despair were common in England. The Chesapeake held out one last, desperate choice to the thousands of landless and jobless men and women in England: **indentured servitude.** Anyone who was young, single, and marginally healthy could sign away from four to seven years of his or, less commonly, her life as a tobacco field worker in exchange for passage to America and the promise of land when the term of service ended. Planters preferred a male work force, for they shared the general European assumption that agricultural labor was a masculine activity. This preference for young male workers created an unusual population profile in Virginia and Maryland. Men outnumbered women by 3 to 1 and in some areas by as much as 6 to 1.

More than three-quarters of the white immigrants to the Chesapeake in the seventeenth century arrived as indentured servants. They spent long, backbreaking days bending and stooping down among the tobacco plants, receiving a meager food ration and often punishment by the whip. A shocking number of these young men did not survive their term of service. Disease and malnutrition took many of them. Even the most comfortable of planters was not safe from early death caused by diseases to which the English had no immunity. The mortality rate was the major cause of the **demographic disaster** that the region experienced: early death, combined with a skewed ratio of men to women, meant the white population was unable to reproduce itself except by continuing immigration.

By the end of the century, the steady supply of English workers dried up as economic conditions in England itself improved. Tobacco planters, as desperate for laborers as ever, turned increasingly to the purchase of African slaves. George Calvert's vision of a society of great landowners with permanently bound laborers working the land was going to become a reality in the Chesapeake (see pages 90–92).

indentured servitude Compulsory service for a fixed period of time, usually from four to seven years, most often agreed to in exchange for passage to the colonies. A labor contract called an indenture spelled out the terms of the agreement.

demographic disaster The outcome of a high mortality rate and skewed ratio of men to women among the colonists of the Chesapeake.

New England: Colonies of Dissenters

- Why did English religious dissenters choose to settle in America?
- What kind of society did the Puritans expect to create?
- What constraints did Puritan authorities impose to discourage dissent? What was the outcome of dissenters' actions?

While Captain John Smith was barking orders at the settlers in Jamestown, some religious dissenters in a small English village were preparing to escape King James's wrath. These residents of Scrooby Village were people of modest means, without powerful political allies or a popular cause. But they had gone one step further than the majority of Puritans, who continued to be members of the Anglican church despite their criticism of it. The Scrooby Villagers had left the church, feeling the need to separate themselves from a religious institution whose practices they believed endangered their souls. James I despised these **Separatists** and declared his intention to drive them out of England—or worse.

The Scrooby Village Separatists took James I's threat seriously. In 1611, they decided to make a pilgrimage—a religious journey—to the Protestant city of Leyden in the Netherlands. These **Pilgrims** were welcomed warmly by the Dutch, and their small community prospered. However, some Pilgrim leaders viewed this comfortable circumstance with alarm. **William Bradford** spoke for this group when he said that the pleasant life in Leyden was diminishing the Pilgrims' devotion to God. By 1620, Bradford and his supporters had packed their belongings and begun a new pilgrimage—to America.

The Plymouth Colony

A second group of Separatists from England joined the Leyden Pilgrims aboard their old, creaky ship, the *Mayflower.* On board, too, was a contingent of "strangers," outsiders to this religious sect, who sought passage to America. Crammed together in close and uncomfortable quarters, the Pilgrims and their fellow passengers weathered a nightmare of violent storms and choppy waters. After nine difficult weeks at sea, the captain brought the *Mayflower* to anchor at Cape Cod—almost a thousand miles north of its Virginia destination. The exhausted passengers fell to the ground and gave thanks. Once the thrill of standing on dry land had passed, however, many of them sank into depression. The early winter landscape was dreary and alien, and there were no welcoming colonists to greet or assist them. William Bradford's wife Dorothy may have felt this despair more powerfully than others, for she fell or jumped to her death from the ship soon after it dropped anchor (see Map 3.2).

Bradford admitted that the landscape had a "weatherbeaten face." The majority of the passengers—non-Pilgrims who expected to start a new life in a tobacco-rich colony—were already talking of a second attempt to reach Jamestown. Mutiny was in the air. To avert a crisis, Bradford negotiated an unusual contract with every man aboard the ship: Pilgrim and stranger, laborers and gentlemen, even the servants and sailors. This contract, called the **Mayflower Compact,** granted political rights to any

♦ The Bible was the most cherished book, and often the only book, in a colonist's home. To safeguard this treasure, many Pilgrims stored their Bibles in hand-carved boxes like this one belonging to William Bradford. This box, once decorated with the lion and unicorn symbol of England, was politicized during the American Revolution, when the British lion was scraped off.

Separatists English Protestants who chose to leave the Church of England because they believed it was corrupt.

Pilgrims A small group of Separatists who left England in search of religious freedom and sailed to America on the *Mayflower* in 1620.

William Bradford Pilgrim leader who organized the *Mayflower* journey and served as first governor of Plymouth Plantations.

Mayflower Compact An agreement drafted in 1620, when the Pilgrims reached Cape Cod, granting political rights to all male colonists willing to abide by the colony's laws.

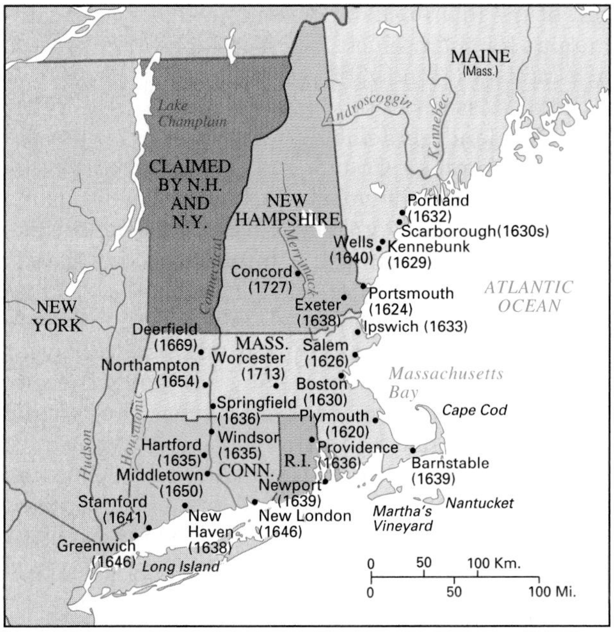

♦ **MAP 3.2 New England Settlement in the Seventeenth and Early Eighteenth Centuries** This map shows the major towns and cities of New England and their settlement dates. By the end of the seventeenth century, the region had four colonies. Colonists seeking land moved west and south toward the New York border and north toward French Canada. Those involved in trade, shipping, and crafts migrated to the seaport cities.

man willing to remain and to abide by whatever laws the new colony enacted. This was an unheard-of opportunity for the poorer men to participate in political decision making. The Mayflower Compact ended all talk of leaving, and the new colony of Plymouth Plantations began to prepare for the long winter ahead.

In Plymouth Plantations, as in Virginia, the first winter brought sickness and death. Half of the colonists did not survive. When a Patuxet Indian, **Squanto,** came upon the settlement in the spring of 1621, he found the remaining English women, men, and children huddled in flimsy shelters, trapped between a menacing forest and a dangerous ocean. Squanto understood both their confusion and their longings for home, for he had crossed the Atlantic in 1605 aboard an English trading ship and spent several years in an alien culture. He also understood what it meant to be a survivor, for the Pilgrims had settled where his own village had once stood. His entire family and tribe had been wiped out by disease carried by English traders and fishermen.

Squanto helped the colonists, teaching them how to plant corn, squash, and pumpkins. The close cooperation among Squanto, the local Wampanoag Indians and their leader Massasoit, and the Pilgrims saved the colony, and in the fall of 1621 English settlers and members of the Indian community sat down to a harvest feast of Thanksgiving.

Over the next decades, Plymouth Plantations grew at a slow, steady pace. Most colonists farmed, fished, or cut timber from the dense forests nearby. A few grew wealthy by developing a fur trade with the Indians. Unlike the Jamestown settlers, the Pilgrims preserved their friendship with the local Indians by purchasing rather than seizing the lands they cultivated. They also cemented that friendship by joining Massasoit's people in bloody warfare against competing Indian tribes. The colonists proved to be such ferocious fighters that they were known to friends and enemies alike as "Wotoroguenarge," or "Cutthroats."

Massachusetts Bay and Its Settlers

James I focused his threats on the Separatists, but his son Charles I took a hostile stance toward the Puritan reformers as well. After 1625, systematic persecution, combined with a growing economic depression in England, led many Puritans to consider the long ocean voyage to America. In 1629, led by 23-year-old lawyer and landowner **John Winthrop,** influential Puritans formed the Massachusetts Bay Company and applied for a charter to establish a new northern colony in America.

King Charles I granted the company its charter, for he was more than willing to help dissenters leave England. Advertising their colony as "a refuge for many who [God] means to save out of the general calamity," Winthrop and his colleagues had no trouble recruiting Puritans to migrate. Unlike the humbler Pilgrims or Jamestown's first disorganized settlers, the Puritans who came to Massachusetts found shelters and cleared fields waiting when they arrived in 1630, for the company had sent an advance crew ahead to ensure a smooth beginning.

Squanto A Patuxet Indian who taught the Pilgrims survival techniques in America and acted as translator for the colonists.

John Winthrop English Puritan who was one of the founders of Massachusetts Bay Colony and served as its first governor.

♦ The meeting house, or church, stood at the center of every Puritan community in colonial New England. Built in 1681, the Old Ship Meeting House of Hingham, Massachusetts, was designed to resemble the hull of an upside down ship. Although the Hingham church is simple and unadorned, the placement of the pews and their assignment to local families based on their wealth, background, and social standing, makes clear that the Puritans were not radical egalitarians like the Quakers. *Pilgrim Society, Pilgrim Hall Museum.*

Over the next decade, religious tensions and economic distress in England fueled a **Great Migration** of Puritans to the Bay Colony.

Massachusetts developed into a society of small farming villages and small seaport towns. Puritan colonists believed these close-knit settlements would help them create model Christian communities. They had no compelling reason to sacrifice communal life for the isolation of a large plantation anyway. The region's short growing season and rocky soil meant no profitable staple-crop economy could develop. In their new communities, the early Massachusetts settlers re-created the village architecture and the social life they had left behind in English regions like West Anglia. The result was a hub-and-spoke design, with houses clustered tightly near a village green or common pasture, a church beside this green, and most of the fields and farms within walking distance of the village center. This design set a natural limit on the size of any village or town because beyond a certain point—usually measured in a winter's walk to church—a farm family was considered outside the community circle. As town populations grew and farmlands along the periphery became the only available sites, villagers on the outer rim of the town usually chose to create a new community for themselves. Puritans called this process of establishing a new village "hiving off."

Like Massachusetts, New Haven and the other New England settlements that followed were societies of families. Colonists who flocked to Massachusetts during the years of Charles I's reign came primarily in family groups. Unlike the Chesapeake, where men dramatically outnumbered women, New England had a balance between the sexes that persisted throughout the seventeenth century, except in towns decimated by war with the Indians or by the loss of young men seeking new land. The cool temperature and the good drinking water made early New England an extremely healthy place for Europeans, healthier than England itself. Children survived, reached marriageable age, and produced families of their own. A couple could expect to live a long life together and raise a family of five to seven children. One outcome of this longevity was a rare phenomenon in the seventeenth-century English world: grandparents.

Both Puritans and neighboring Pilgrims spoke of the family as "a little commonwealth," the building block with which the larger society was constructed. Obedience was a priority in child rearing, in part because Puritans believed that sinfulness and disobedience were the twin results of **original sin.** Breaking a child's will was thus a necessary step toward ensuring that child's salvation. The larger society actively reinforced a parent's right to demand respect and a child's duty to obey. Massachusetts Bay Colony's Book of Laws and Liberties made criticizing a parent a crime punishable by death. The penalty was rarely administered, but its presence in the legal code shows the importance of obedience within the family.

A wife was also expected to obey her husband. Puritan ministers reinforced this ideal of a **hierarchy** or well-defined chain of command, within a family by saying, "Wives are part of the House and Family, and ought to be under a Husband's Government: they should Obey their own Husbands." At the

Great Migration The movement of Puritans from England to America in the 1630s, caused by political and religious conflict in England.

original sin In Christian doctrine, the condition of sin that all human beings share because of Adam and Eve's first disobedience to God in the Garden of Eden.

hierarchy A system in which people or things are ranked one above another.

same time, a husband was bound by obligations and a demanding code of conduct toward his wife. He must rule his household without "rigour, haughtiness, harshness, severity; but with the greatest love, gentleness, kindness, tenderness." Marriage had many practical obligations as well. Wives were expected to strive to be "notable housewives"—industrious, economical managers and skilled at several crafts. They were to spin yarn, sew, cook, bake, pickle and preserve garden and orchard crops, milk cows, butcher farm animals, cure meat, churn butter, and set cheeses. In close-knit communities, women were able to help one another by exchanging butter for eggs, assisting with a neighbor's childbirth, or helping out in times of sickness or death. Husbands were expected to labor in the fields or the shop or the countinghouse to provide for their families.

Although obligated to be both tender and loving, the husband controlled the resources of the family. This was true in all English colonies, not just in the Puritan communities of New England. Under English law, a married woman, or **feme covert,** was under the governance of her husband. She lacked the right to acquire, sell, or will property to another person. She could not sue or be sued or claim the use of any wages she earned. She could gain such legal rights only through special contracts made with her husband. Puritan communities frowned on any such arrangements. In the "little commonwealth" of the family, a man was the undisputed head of the household and thus had authority over all its economic resources. As head of the household, he also represented the family's interest in the realm of politics. No matter how wise or how wealthy a woman might become, she was denied a political voice. This was true in all English colonies.

Government in Puritan Massachusetts

The directors of the Massachusetts Bay Company expected every colonist to cooperate in creating a model Puritan society. When John Winthrop addressed his fellow passengers aboard the *Arbella* as it sailed toward New England in 1630, he spoke of the new colony as a "city upon a hill," an example to Christians everywhere. He warned those on board that "the eyes of all peoples are upon us." More importantly, he said, God was watching them. If they forgot their mission, they would be punished. Winthrop went on to describe the society he envisioned. It was not an egalitarian community. Like most of his fellow passengers, Winthrop believed that it was natural and correct for some people to be rich and some to be poor—"some high and eminent in power and dignity, others mean and in subjugation." Nor would all free male colonists have a voice in governing Massachusetts. The first government, in fact, consisted solely of Winthrop and the eleven other stockholders of the Massachusetts Bay Company who had emigrated. Later, the company permitted a representative assembly to be elected, but even then the qualifications for citizenship differed dramatically from those a settler might expect in Virginia or Maryland. This Puritan community permitted no man to have a full political voice unless he was an acknowledged church *member,* not simply a churchgoer. Church membership, or **sainthood,** was granted only after a person testified to an experience of "saving faith," a moment of intense awareness of God's power and of intense desire for salvation. Thus, in politics, religious qualifications were as important as economic ones.

Massachusetts differed from the Chesapeake colonies in other significant ways. The colony's government enforced biblical law as well as English civil and criminal law, which meant that government regulated a colonist's religious beliefs and practices, style of dress, sexual conduct, and personal behavior. For example, every colonist was required to attend church and to observe the Sabbath as Puritan custom dictated. In addition, the church joined the government in supervising business dealings, parent-child relationships, and marital life.

In the early decades of the colony, the Puritan sense of mission left little room for religious toleration. Colonial leaders saw no reason to welcome those who disagreed with their Puritan views. English America was large, they argued, and men and women of other faiths could settle elsewhere. Winthrop's government was particularly aggressive against members of a new sect called the **Quakers,** who were determined to convert Puritans to their beliefs. Quakers entering the colony could expect to be flogged, beaten, imprisoned, or branded with hot

feme covert A legal term defining a married woman as being unable to sue or be sued, own or sell property, and earn wages.

sainthood Full membership in a Puritan church.

Quakers Members of the Society of Friends, a radical Protestant sect that believes in the equality of men and women, pacifism, and the presence of a divine "inner light" in every individual.

irons. After all that, if they persisted, they were hanged.

Puritan leaders showed just as little tolerance toward members of their own community who criticized or challenged the rules of the Bay Colony. Because the government actively enforced religious rules and practices, anyone who raised serious theological doubts in public was seen not only as a **heretic** but as a political threat.

One of the alleged heretics was **Roger Williams,** a Puritan minister. Only a year after the colony was established, the Salem church invited Williams to serve as assistant minister. His electrifying sermons and his impressive knowledge of the Scriptures attracted a devoted following. But he soon attracted the attention of colonial authorities as well, for his sermons were highly critical of the Bay Colony government. From the pulpit Williams condemned the government for seizing Indian lands, calling its tactics of intimidation and warfare a "National Sinne." He also condemned laws requiring church attendance. True religious belief was a matter of personal commitment, Williams argued, and cannot be compelled. "Forced religion," he told his congregation, "stinks in God's nostrils."

When the Salem congregation decided to promote Roger Williams to minister in 1635, John Winthrop's government struck out against their most vocal critic. They banished Roger Williams from the colony. With snow thick on the ground, Williams left Salem and sought refuge with the Narragansett Indians. When spring came, many from the Salem congregation joined their minister in exile. Together, in 1636, they created a community called Providence that welcomed dissenters of all kinds, including Quakers and Jews.

Providence also attracted other Massachusetts colonists, tired of the tight controls imposed on their lives by Winthrop and his friends. John Winthrop took no steps to undermine Providence since he considered it a dumping ground for troublemakers in his own colony. In 1644, the English government granted Williams a charter for his colony, first called Providence Plantations but later renamed Rhode Island. Within their colony, Rhode Islanders firmly established the principle of the separation of church and state.

Roger Williams was not the only Puritan to challenge the Bay Colony's government and its religious precepts. In 1634, **Anne Hutchinson,** her husband William, and their several children emigrated to Massachusetts. The Hutchinsons made an impressive addition to the colonial community. He was a successful merchant. She was eloquent, witty, exceptionally well versed in the Scriptures, and clearly knowledgeable about the religious debates of the day. Like Williams, Hutchinson put little stock in the power of a minister or in any rules of behavior to assist in an individual's search for salvation. She believed that only God's grace could save a person's soul. And she declared that God made a "covenant of grace," or a promise of salvation, that did not depend on any church, minister, or worship service.

Hutchinson's opinions, aired in popular meetings at her home, disturbed the Puritan authorities. That she was a woman made her outspoken challenge even more shocking. Men like John Winthrop believed that women ought to be silent in the church and had no business criticizing male authorities, particularly ministers and **magistrates,** or government officials. A surprising number of Puritans, however, were untroubled by Hutchinson's sex. Male merchants and artisans who lacked political rights because they were not members of the sainthood welcomed her attacks on these authorities. Hutchinson also attracted Puritan saints who disliked the tight reins that colonial government held on their business, personal, and social life.

In the end, none of Hutchinson's supporters could protect her against the determined opposition of the Puritan leadership. In 1637, she was arrested and brought to trial. Although she was in the last months of a troubled pregnancy, her judges forced her to stand throughout their long, exhausting, repetitive examination. Hutchinson seemed to be winning the battle of words despite her physical discomfort, but eventually she blundered. In one of her answers, she seemed to claim that she had direct communication with God. Such a claim went far beyond the acceptable bounds of Puritan belief. Triumphantly, John

heretic A person who does not conform with an established attitude, doctrine, or principle, usually in religious matters.

Roger Williams A minister banished from Massachusetts for criticizing its religious rules and Indian policies; in 1636, he founded Providence, a community based on religious freedom and separation of church and state.

Anne Hutchinson A religious leader banished from Massachusetts in 1637 because of her criticism of the colonial government and what were judged to be her heretical religious beliefs.

magistrate A civil officer charged with the administration of the law.

Winthrop and his colleagues declared her a heretic, "unfit to our society." They banished her from Massachusetts. Even after her departure, the government seemed to worry about her influence. They encouraged rumors that she was a witch and claimed that the miscarriage she suffered shortly after the trial revealed a demonic fetus.

Many Puritans who left Massachusetts were not banished but chose to leave the colony voluntarily. For example, in 1636, Reverend Thomas Hooker and his entire Newton congregation abandoned Massachusetts and resettled in the Connecticut River valley. They sought freedom from Winthrop's domination, and the richer soils of the river valley attracted them. Other Puritan congregations followed these Newton families. By 1639, the Connecticut valley towns had drafted their own government, and in 1644, they united to create the colony of Connecticut. Other Bay colonists, searching for new or better lands, made their way north to what later became Maine and New Hampshire. New Hampshire settlers won a charter for their own colony in 1679, but Maine remained part of Massachusetts until it became a state in 1820.

Indian Suppression

Although the Puritan colonists hoped to create a godly community, they were often motivated by greed and jealousy. Between 1636 and the 1670s, New Englanders came into conflict with one another over desirable land. They also waged particularly violent warfare against the Indians of the region.

When the Connecticut valley towns sprang up, for example, Winthrop tried to assert Bay Colony authority over them. His motives were personal: he and his friends had expected to develop the valley area lands someday for their own profit. The Connecticut settlers successfully ignored both Winthrop's claims and his threats to block their independence from Massachusetts. But Connecticut colonists could not ignore the Indians of the area, who understood clearly the threat that English settlers posed to their territories and their way of life. Sassacus, leader of the **Pequots,** hoped that an armed struggle would break out between Winthrop and the new Connecticut towns, destroying them both. Instead, however, the two English rivals struck a bargain: the Connecticut valley lands would go to whoever managed to conquer the Pequots first.

By 1637, the Pequots were under attack from both Massachusetts and Connecticut armies. John Winthrop, who had managed to recruit five hundred Narragansett soldiers, decided to avoid a confrontation with the Pequot warriors. Instead, he ordered an attack on the Pequot civilian population at Mystic Village. Captain John Underhill of the Massachusetts army recorded the slaughter with obvious satisfaction: "Many [Pequots] were burnt in the fort, both men, women, and children." When the survivors tried to surrender to the Narragansetts, Puritan soldiers killed them. The brutal war did not end until all the Pequot men had been killed and the women and children sold into slavery. Connecticut claimed credit for this victory and, despite the massacre at Mystic, Massachusetts grudgingly conceded. If the Narragansett Indians believed their alliance with Winthrop provided some protection against English aggression, they were mistaken. Within five years the Puritans had assassinated the Narragansett chief, an act of insurance against problems with these Indian allies.

For almost three decades, an uneasy peace existed between colonists and Indians. But the struggle over the land continued. When war broke out again, it was two old allies—the Plymouth colonists and the Wampanoags—who took up arms against each other. By 1675, the friendship between these two groups had been eroded by Pilgrim demands for new Indian lands. Chief **Metacomet,** known to the English as King Philip, made the difficult decision to resist. When Metacomet used **guerrilla tactics** effectively, staging raids on white settlements, the colonists retaliated by burning Indian crops and villages and selling Indian captives into slavery. By the end of the year, Metacomet had forged an alliance with the Narragansetts and several small regional tribes. Metacomet's early, devastating raids on white settlements terrified the colonists, but soon the casualties grew on both sides. Atrocities were committed by everyone involved in this struggle, which the English called King Philip's War. With

Pequots An American Indian people inhabiting eastern Connecticut; when the Pequots resisted colonial expansion, the Massachusetts Bay colonists declared war on them.

Metacomet A Wampanoag chief, known to the English as King Philip, who led the Indian resistance to colonial expansion in New England in 1675.

guerrilla tactics A method of warfare in which small bands of fighters in occupied territory harass and attack their enemies, often in surprise raids; the Indians used these tactics in King Philip's War.

♦ King Philip's War was one of the bloodiest conflicts in colonial history. One out of every sixteen adult male colonists was killed, and local tribes like the Wampanoag and Narragansett were virtually exterminated. The Puritan victory at the Battle of Hadley, depicted in this nineteenth-century drawing, was a turning point in this bitter struggle. Soon afterward, the leader of the Indian uprising, Metacomet (King Philip), was trapped and killed. *"General Goffe Repulsing the Indians at Hadley." Library of Congress.*

the help of Iroquois troops sent by the governor of New York, the colonists finally defeated the Wampanoags. Metacomet was murdered, and his head was impaled on a stick.

Indian objections to colonial expansion in New England had been silenced. Indeed, few native peoples remained to offer resistance of any sort. Several tribes had been entirely wiped out in the war, or their few survivors had been sold into slavery in the Caribbean. The few who escaped enslavement or death scattered to the north and the west. The victory had cost the English dearly also. More than two thousand New England colonists lost their lives as the war spread from Plymouth to nearby settlements. And the war left a legacy of hate that prompted Indian tribes west of Massachusetts to block Puritan expansion whenever possible. The costs of New England's Indian policy prompted colonial leaders in other regions to try less aggressive tactics in dealing with local Indians. For the Wampanoags, the Narragansetts, and the Pequots, however, this decision came too late.

Change and Reaction in England and New England

Both the Pilgrim and the Puritan leaders had expected the broad expanse of the Atlantic Ocean to protect their colonists from the political turmoil and religious tensions of seventeenth-century England. Like their Chesapeake counterparts, both were wrong. From the beginning, of course, Puritan migration to New England had been prompted by Charles I's hostility to dissenters. When Oliver Cromwell and his Puritan armies challenged the Stuart king in 1642, Bay Colony settlers rejoiced. Many chose to return home to fight with Cromwell's armies. Throughout the decade, population shrank in Massachusetts.

Massachusetts faced a crisis in the post–Civil War years. The sense of mission and the religious commitment that accompanied it seemed to be declining. Few native-born colonists petitioned for full membership, or sainthood, in their local churches, perhaps because of their growing involvement with trade and commerce. And few new saints migrated to the Bay Colony after Cromwell's victory or during the Restoration era. In fact, most of the newcomers in the 1660s were not Puritans at all but Anglicans or members of other Protestant groups interested in economic opportunities. The Bay Colony leaders could not prevent them from settling, as John Winthrop had once done, for King Charles II would not allow it.

The decline in religious zeal troubled ministers and government officials alike, for it marked a sharp decline in eligible voters and officeholders. It troubled the saints, who feared their own children would never join the church and thus never become full citizens in the colony. The problem was made worse by the growing demands of prosperous non-Puritan men for an active role in the government. Some towns began to compromise, allowing men of property and good standing in the community to participate in local decision making. But the saints were not willing to formally abolish the church membership requirement. In 1662, they decided to introduce the **Half-Way Covenant,** an agreement that allowed

Half-Way Covenant An agreement that gave partial membership in Puritan churches to the children of church members even if they had not had a "saving faith" experience.

the children of church members to join the church even if they did not make a convincing declaration of their own salvation. This compromise kept political power in the hands of Puritans—for the moment.

Pressures from England could not be dealt with so easily, however. Charles II cast a doubtful eye on a colony that sometimes ignored English civil law if it conflicted with biblical demands. In 1683, Charles insisted that the Bay Colony revise its charter to weaken the influence of biblical teachings and eliminate the unusual voting requirements. The Massachusetts government said no. With that, Charles revoked the charter. Massachusetts remained in political limbo until 1685, when James II came to the throne. Then conditions worsened.

In an effort to centralize administration of his growing American empire, King James II revoked the charter of every English mainland colony and in 1686 combined several of the northern colonies into one large unit under direct royal control. This mega-colony, the **Dominion of New England,** included Massachusetts, Rhode Island, Connecticut, Plymouth Plantations, and the newly acquired colonies of New Jersey and New York. James expected the Dominion to increase the **patronage,** or political favors, he could provide to his loyal supporters—favors such as large grants of land or appointments to colonial administrative positions. He also expected to increase revenues by imposing duties and taxes on colonial goods in the vast region he now controlled.

What King James did not expect was how strongly colonists resented his Dominion and the man he chose to govern it. That man was the arrogant and greedy Sir Edmund Andros. Andros immediately offended New England Puritans by establishing the Church of England as the official religion of the new colony. Then he added insult to injury by commandeering a Puritan church in Boston for Anglican worship. Andros also alienated many non-Puritans in Massachusetts by abolishing the representative assembly there. These men had been struggling to be *included* in the assembly, not to have the assembly abolished. Andros's high-handed tactics united Massachusetts colonists who had been at odds with each other. One sign of this came when the Dominion governor imposed new taxes: saints and nonsaints alike refused to pay them.

When Boston citizens received news of the Glorious Revolution, they imprisoned Edmund Andros and shipped him back to England to stand trial as a traitor to the nation's new Protestant government. Massachusetts Puritans hoped to be rewarded for their patriotism, but they were quickly disappointed. Although William and Mary abolished the Dominion, they chose not to restore the Bay Colony charter. In 1691, Massachusetts became a royal colony, its governor appointed by the Crown. **Suffrage,** or voting rights, were granted to all free males who met the standard English **property requirement.** Church membership would never again be a criterion for citizenship in the colony.

Over the course of its sixty-year history, Massachusetts had undergone many significant changes. The Puritan ideal of small, tightly knit farming communities whose members worshiped together and shared common values and goals had been replaced for many colonists by an emerging "Yankee" ideal of trade and commerce, bustling seaport cities, diverse beliefs, and a more secular, or nonreligious, orientation to daily life. This transition increased tensions in every community, especially during the difficult years of the 1680s. Those tensions were the context for one of the most dramatic events in the region's history: the Salem witch trials.

In 1692, a group of young women and girls in Salem Village began to show signs of what seventeenth-century society diagnosed as bewitchment. They fell into violent fits, contorting their bodies and showing great emotional distress. Under questioning, they named several local women, including a West Indian slave named Tituba, as their tormentors (see Individual Choices: Tituba). The conviction that the devil had come to Massachusetts spread quickly, and the number of people accused of witchcraft grew. By summer, more than a hundred women, men, and children were crowded into local jails, awaiting trial for witchcraft. Accusations, trials, and even executions—nineteen in all—continued until the new royal governor, Sir William Phips, arrived in the colony and forbade any further arrests. Phips dismissed the court that had passed judgment based

Dominion of New England A mega-colony created in 1686 by James II; it brought Massachusetts, Connecticut, Rhode Island, Plymouth, New Jersey, and New York under the control of one royal governor; William and Mary dissolved the Dominion when they came to the throne.

patronage Jobs or favors distributed on a political basis, usually as a reward for loyalty to the government in power.

suffrage The right to vote.

property requirement The limitation of voting rights to people who own certain kinds or amounts of property.

INDIVIDUAL CHOICES

Choosing to Confess

Tituba

Although often described as an African, Tituba was probably a South American Indian. Tituba's accounts of witch craft in Massachusetts were a powerful combination of her own Indian background, African traditions learned on the Barbadian plantation, and the Puritan beliefs acquired in Reverend Parris's household. Tituba Reluctant Witch of Salem by Elaine G. Breslaw.

In 1692, rumors of witchcraft and dark magic shook the small Massachusetts community of Salem Village. A group of young women and girls complained of strange nightmares and mysterious physical ailments. Their suffering soon became visible to their neighbors, who watched anxiously as the young women fell down in violent fits, shouted out in pain, screamed obscenities, and pointed to bruises and blood that appeared suddenly on their bodies.

The local minister, Samuel Parris, chose to investigate these disturbing developments. He was especially concerned since two of the afflicted were members of his own household. Questioning his daughter, his niece, and their friends, Parris soon learned that they had delved into forbidden magic, trying to discover whom they would marry and whether they would be rich or poor. Betsy Parris and her friends also confessed that magical rituals that revealed the future had been performed right in the Parris kitchen with the help of the minister's own slave, Tituba. With that, the attention of the whole community turned to Tituba.

Although Reverend Parris beat Tituba severely, she denied any involvement in the events connected to the suffering of Parris's

on "spectral evidence," testimony by the alleged victims that they had seen the spirits of the accused tormenting them. In January 1693, Phips assembled a new court that acquitted the remaining prisoners.

The witch trials expressed the struggle between saintly Puritan farmers of Salem Village and the town's more worldly merchants: the accusers were members of the farming community; the accused were often associated with commercial activities. Nevertheless, the witch-hunts reflected the belief among people—whether farmers or merchants—that the devil and his disciples could work great harm in a community.

The Pluralism of the Middle Colonies

- Why did the Dutch and the English choose to encourage a multicultural population in New York?
- What made the expectations for Pennsylvania so distinctive?

Between the Chesapeake and New England lay the vast stretch of forest and farmland called New Netherland, a Dutch colony that was home to settlers from Holland, Sweden, Germany, and France. In the 1660s, Charles II seized the area and drove the Dutch from the Atlantic coast of North America. The daughter and her friends. A slave's claim of innocence was less persuasive, however, than accusations made by proper young Puritan girls. After Tituba was imprisoned by local authorities, she chose to confess. Her confession set in motion the witch-hunts that made Salem Village famous.

Accounts of the Salem witch-hunts usually describe Tituba as an African woman schooled in the arts of magic, but she was neither black nor a practitioner of witchcraft. Tituba was a South American Indian, probably an Arawak, whom the English kidnapped as a child and sold into slavery on the island of Barbados. She remained in the Caribbean until the widowed Samuel Parris purchased her to keep house for his family. Tituba's background was crucial in shaping her confession, for her understanding of the sources of evil was rooted in her tribal culture. Arawaks and other South American Indians always expected evil to originate outside the community, from strangers or rival tribes. Thus, in constructing a confession, Tituba told a story that seemed to her most convincing, a tale of powerful magical strangers who enlisted her, and others in the community, to aid their sinister cause. Tituba embellished her confession, however, with details that drew on the Puritan Christian images with which she had become familiar during her years as the Parris family slave. She told local authorities of night flights, in which a witch soared through the skies, and of midnight gatherings in the forest. Her Puritan listeners superimposed their own cultural explanations of evil on Tituba's. In this way, the devil came to Massachusetts.

Puritan assumptions that Indians and other "dark" races had intimate knowledge of the occult made Tituba's testimony more convincing. Thus when Tituba described a number of upstanding, often wealthy, local citizens who had chosen to join witches' covens, local authorities began to make their arrests. The outcome was a search for witches that soon spread to nearby towns and villages and fed the infamous trials that led to nineteen executions of men, women, and children.

Why did Tituba choose to confess? She had lived long enough in Puritan society to know that confession and repentance often ensured greater leniency from the authorities. Thus she probably expected to escape hanging or a lifetime of imprisonment if she admitted her guilt. This expectation proved correct, although Tituba paid a high price for her survival. Prison officials sold her to a new master in order to recover her jail fees and, when he took her away from Salem in April 1693, she was permanently separated from her own daughter.

Tituba may have had motives other than simple survival, including the desire to assert her power over a society that had enslaved her, taken her from her homeland, and separated her forever from her family. This much is certain: for a brief moment, Tituba overcame the constraints of slavery as she asserted her own culture's explanation for the trouble in her master's household.

English divided the conquered territory into three colonies: New York, New Jersey, and Pennsylvania. Although the region changed hands, it did not change its character: the middle colonies remained a multicultural, commercially oriented, and competitive society no matter whose flag flew over them (see Map 3.3).

From New Amsterdam to New York

Before 1650, Europe's two major Protestant powers had maintained a degree of cooperation, and their American colonies remained on friendly terms, assisting each other, for example, in conflicts with Indians. But a growing rivalry over the transatlantic trade and conflicting land claims in the Connecticut Valley soon eroded this neighborliness. Beginning in 1652, England and Holland fought three naval wars. After each, the Dutch lost ground, and their decline made it likely that the New Netherland settlement would be abandoned.

King Charles II of England wanted New Netherland very much, and James, Duke of York (later King James II), was eager to satisfy his brother's desires. In 1664, Charles agreed to give James control of the region lying between the Connecticut and

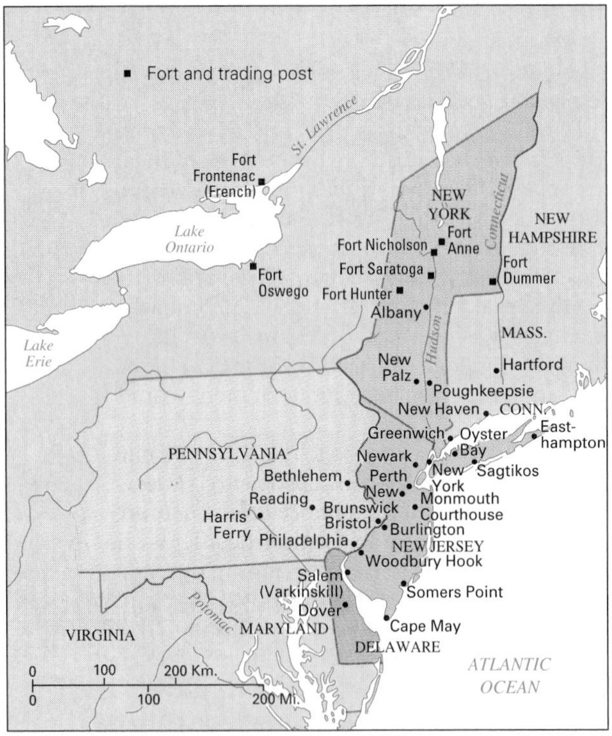

♦ **MAP 3.3 The Middle Colonies** This map shows the major towns, cities, and forts in the colonies of New York, Pennsylvania (including Delaware), and New Jersey. The prosperity of the region was based on the thriving commerce of its largest cities, Philadelphia and New York, and on the commercial production of wheat.

Delaware rivers—if James could wrest it from the Dutch. The promise and the prize amounted to a declaration of war on New Netherland.

When the duke's four armed ships arrived in New Amsterdam harbor and aimed their cannon at the town, Governor Peter Stuyvesant tried to rally the local residents to resist. They refused. Life under the English, they reasoned, would probably be no worse than life under the Dutch. Perhaps it might be better. The humiliated governor surrendered the colony, and in 1664 New Netherland became New York without a shot being fired.

James proved to be a very liberal ruler, allowing the Dutch and other European colonists to keep their lands, practice their religions, and conduct their business in their native languages. But the duke's generosity and tolerance did not extend to taxation matters. James saw his colonists much as his brother the king saw every colonist: as a source of personal revenue. James taxed New Yorkers heavily and allowed no representative assembly that might interfere with his use of those taxes. All political offices in the new colony, high or low, went to the duke's friends, creating a patronage system that impressed even King Charles.

James's colony did not develop as he hoped, however. Settlement did not expand to the north and east as he wished. He could not enlist the aid of influential New Yorkers in his expansion plans, even though he offered them the incentive of a representative assembly in 1682. By 1685, James—now king of England—had lost interest in the colony, abandoning his schemes for its growth and abolishing the representative assembly as well.

Leisler's Rebellion

Although James viewed New York as a failure, the colony actually grew rapidly during his rule. Population doubled between 1665 and 1685, reaching fifteen thousand the year the duke ascended to the English throne. These new settlers added to the cultural diversity that had always been a mark of the region. The colony became a religious refuge for French Protestants, English Quakers, and Scottish **Presbyterians.** New York's diverse community, however, did not always live in harmony. English, Dutch, and German merchants competed fiercely for control of New York City's trade and for dominance in the city's cultural life. An equally intense rivalry existed between New York City merchants and the fur traders of Albany. Only one thing united these competitors: a burning resentment of James's political control and the men he chose to enforce his will. Their anger increased when James created the Dominion of New England, merging New York with the Puritan colonies.

In 1689, news of the Glorious Revolution prompted a revolt in New York City similar to the revolt in Boston. **Jacob Leisler,** a German merchant, emerged as the leader of the uprising. Leisler took control of the entire colony, and, acting in the name of the new English monarchs, William and Mary, he not only

Presbyterians Members of a Protestant sect that eventually became the established church of Scotland but in the seventeenth century was sometimes persecuted by Scotland's rulers.

Jacob Leisler German merchant who led a revolt in New York in 1689 against royal officials representing the Dominion of New England; he was executed as a traitor when he refused to surrender control of the colony to a governor appointed by William and Mary.

removed Dominion officials but imprisoned several of his local opponents, declaring them enemies of Protestantism. He then called for city elections to oust James's remaining cronies. Leisler expected an era of home rule to follow his rebellion, but England's new monarchs had no intention of leaving a local merchant in charge of a royal colony. When William and Mary sent a new governor to New York, Leisler refused to surrender the reins of government. This time, the abrasive, headstrong merchant found few supporters, and eventually he was forced to step down. To Leisler's surprise, he was then arrested and charged with treason. Both he and his son-in-law were tried, found guilty, and executed. As befit traitors in the seventeenth century, the two rebels were hanged, disemboweled while still alive, and then beheaded. Afterward, their mutilated bodies were quartered. In death, Leisler became a hero and a martyr. Popular anger was so great that, to quiet the discontent, the new governor had to permit a representative assembly. Several of the men elected to this new legislature were ardent Leislerites, and for many years New York politics remained a battleground between Leislerites and supporters of the royal governor and the king.

♦ William Penn was about 50 years old when this chalk drawing was done. Although Pennsylvania was famous for its religious tolerance and welcoming of non-English immigrants, Penn held many views in common with New England's Puritan leaders. He believed that government should impose and enforce a moral code, because drunkenness, luxury, gambling, and cursing were not only "sins against Nature" but "sins against Government." *"William Penn" by Francis Place. The Historical Society of Pennsylvania.*

William Penn's Holy Experiment

More than most dissenting sects, Quakers had paid a high price for their strongly held convictions. Members of the Society of Friends had been jailed in England and Scotland and harassed by their neighbors throughout the empire. Quaker leaders had strong motives to create a refuge for members of their beleaguered church. In the 1670s, a group of wealthy Friends purchased New Jersey from its original proprietors and offered religious freedom and generous political rights to its current and future colonists, many of whom were Puritans. The best known of these Quaker proprietors was **William Penn,** who had abandoned a life of elegance, luxury, and self-indulgence in Restoration society and embraced the morally demanding life of the Friends.

Penn's father, Admiral Sir William Penn, was one of England's naval heroes and a political adviser to King Charles II. The senior Penn and his son had little in common except their loyalty to the king and their willingness to give him generous loans to support his extravagant lifestyle. Eventually, Charles rewarded the Penns' devotion, in 1681 granting the younger Penn a charter to a huge area west of the Delaware River. This gave Penn the opportunity to create for Quakers a refuge that fully embodied their religious principles.

Penn called his new colony Pennsylvania, meaning "Penn's Woods," in memory of his father. (The southernmost section of Penn's grant, added later by Charles II, developed independently of Penn's control and in 1776 became the state of Delaware.) Like most colonial proprietors, Penn expected to make a personal profit from his lands. But his religious beliefs ensured that he would not govern by whim. Instead, Quaker values and principles were the basis for his "holy experiment." At the heart of these religious beliefs was the conviction that the divine spirit, or "inner light," resided in every human being. Quakers thus respected all individuals. By their plain dress and their refusal to remove their hats in the presence of their social "betters," Quakers demonstrated this belief that all men and women were equal. In keeping with their egalitarian principles, Quakers also recognized no distinctions of wealth or social status in their places of worship. At the strikingly simple Quaker meeting, or worship service, any member who felt moved to speak

William Penn English Quaker who founded the colony of Pennsylvania in 1681.

♦ This sketch of a Quaker meeting highlights one of the most radical of Quaker practices: allowing women to speak in church. Most Protestant denominations, because of their reading of Saint Paul, enforced the rule of silence on women. But Quakers struck a blow at seventeenth-century gender notions by granting women an active ministerial role, a voice in church policy, and decision-making responsibilities on issues relating to the church and the family. *"The Quaker Meeting" (detail) by Egbert Van Heemskerk. The Quaker Collection, Haverford College Library.*

was welcome to participate, no matter how poor or uneducated and no matter what sex or age. Although they actively sought converts, Quakers were always tolerant of other religions.

Pennsylvania's political structure reflected this egalitarianism. All free male residents had the right to vote, and the legislature they elected had full governing powers. Unlike his patron Charles II, William Penn had no intention of interfering in his colony's lawmaking process. He honored the legislature's decisions even when they disturbed or amazed him. The political quarrels that developed in Pennsylvania's assembly actually shocked Penn, but his only action was to urge political leaders not to be "so noisy, and open, in your dissatisfactions."

Penn's land policy also reflected Quaker principles. Unlike many proprietors, he wanted no politically powerful landlords and no economically dependent tenant farmers. Instead, he actively promoted a society of independent, landowning farm families. Penn also insisted that all land be purchased fairly from the Indians, and he pursued a policy of peaceful coexistence between the two cultures. William Penn took an active role in making Pennsylvania a multicultural society, recruiting non-English settlers through pamphlets that stressed the religious and political freedoms and economic opportunities his colony offered. More than eight thousand immigrants poured into the colony in the first four years. Many did come from England, but Irish, Scottish, Welsh, French, Scandinavian, and German settlers came as well. To their English neighbors who did not speak German, newcomers from Germany such as the Mennonites and Amish were known as the "Pennsylvania Dutch" (*Deutsch,* meaning "German" would have been correct).

When William Penn died in 1717, he left behind a successful, dynamic colony. Philadelphia was already emerging as a great shipping and commercial center, rivaling the older seaports of Boston and New York City. But this success came at some cost to Penn's original vision and to his Quaker principles. The commercial orientation here, as in Puritan Massachusetts, attracted colonists who were more secular in their interests than the colony's founders. These colonists had no strong commitment to egalitarianism. For example, many newcomers saw Penn's Indian policy as a check on their ambitions and preferred to seize land from the Indians rather than purchase it. The demand for military protection from Indians by these land-hungry farmers in the western part of the colony became a major political issue and a matter of conscience for Quakers, whose religious principles included **pacifism.** Eventually many Quakers chose to resign from the colonial government rather than struggle to uphold a holy experiment that their neighbors did not support.

The Colonies of the Lower South

- What type of society did the founders of Carolina expect to create? How did the outcome differ from their expectations?
- Why did philanthropists choose to create Georgia? Why did the king choose to support this project?

William Penn was not the only Englishman to benefit from the often extravagant generosity of King Charles II. In 1663, the king surprised eight of his favorite supporters by granting them several million acres lying south of Virginia and stretching from the Atlantic to the Pacific Ocean. This gesture by Charles was both grand and calculated. France, Spain, Holland, and the Indian tribes that inhabited this area all laid claim to it, and Charles thought it would be wise to secure England's control of the region by colonizing it. The eight new colonial propri-

pacifism Opposition to war or violence of any kind.

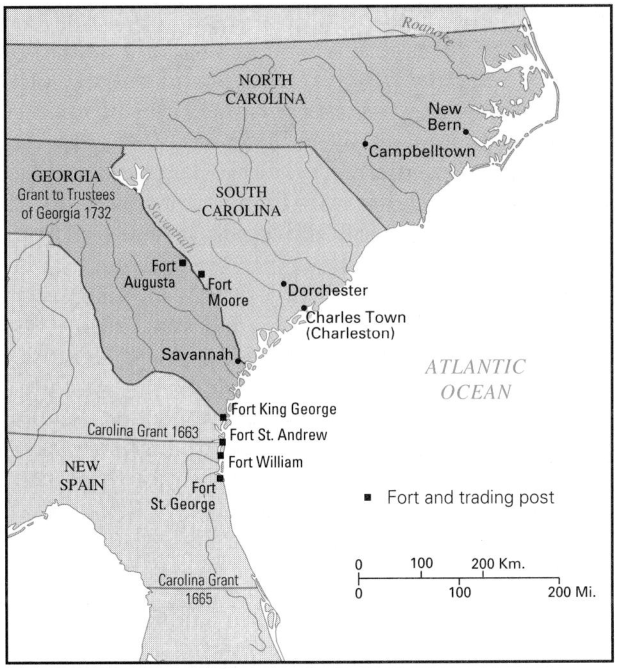

♦ **MAP 3.4 The Settlements of the Lower South** This map shows the towns and fortifications of North Carolina, South Carolina, and Georgia as well as the overlapping claims by the Spanish and the English to the territory south and west of Fort King George. The many Georgia forts reflect that colony's role as a buffer state between rice-rich South Carolina and the Spanish troops stationed in Florida.

etors named their colony Carolina to honor the king's late father, who had lost his head to the Puritan Commonwealth (and whose name in Latin was Carolus; see Map 3.4).

The Carolina Colony

The proprietors' plan for Carolina was similar to Lord Baltimore's medieval dream. The philosopher John Locke helped draw up the *Fundamental Constitution of Carolina,* an elaborate blueprint for a society of great landowners, **yeomen** (small, independent farmers), and serfs (agricultural laborers) bound to work for their landlords. Locke later became famous for his essays on freedom and human rights (see page 100)—a far cry from the social hierarchy proposed in the Carolina constitution. Like the Calverts, however, the Carolina proprietors discovered that few English people were willing to travel 3,000 miles across the ocean to become serfs. Bowing to reality, they offered the incentive of the headright system used in Virginia and Maryland decades earlier.

The early settlers in Carolina made their way to the southeastern portion of the colony, drawn there by the fine natural harbor of the port city, Charles Town (later Charleston), and the fertile lands surrounding it. Despite the dangers of the Spanish to the south in Florida and the Yamassee Indians to the Southwest, Charles Town grew rapidly, becoming the most important city in the southern colonies. These early Carolinians experimented with several moneymaking activities. Some established trade with the Indians of the region, exchanging English goods for deerskins and for Indians taken as prisoners in tribal warfare. The deerskins were shipped to England. The Indians were shipped as slaves to the Caribbean. Other colonists tapped the region's pine forests to produce naval stores—the timber, tar, resin, pitch, and turpentine that were used in building and maintaining wooden ships.

Carolinians experimented with several cash crops, including sugar cane, tobacco, silk, cotton, ginger, and olives. But none of these crops was particularly profitable. The first real success turned out to be cattle raising, a skill the settlers learned from African slaves brought into the colony by planters relocating from the West Indian sugar island of Barbados (see page 87). By the 1680s, Carolina cattlemen had begun to use their profits to begin a new enterprise: rice cultivation. In 1719, when members of the Charleston planter elite wrested control of their part of Carolina from the original proprietors, the southern part of the colony, now called South Carolina, boasted the richest English colonists on the mainland.

The northern region of Carolina developed in the shadow of its southern neighbor. Bordered by the Great Dismal Swamp to the north and by smaller swamps to the south, this isolated area did not attract many colonists. The land around Albemarle Sound was fertile enough, but the remaining coastline was cut off from the Atlantic by a chain of barrier islands that blocked access to oceangoing vessels. Despite all these constraints, some poor farm families and freed white indentured servants had drifted in from Virginia, searching for unclaimed land and a fresh start. They had modest success in Carolina, growing tobacco and producing naval stores.

In 1729, the Albemarle colonists followed the lead of their elite neighbors around Charleston and rid themselves of proprietary rule. Then these North

yeomen Independent landowners entitled to suffrage.

♦ This 1739 painting of Charles Town [later Charleston], South Carolina, shows a bustling seaport and a city with elegant homes and public buildings. Charleston was one of the four largest cities in British America by the eighteenth century, its population swelling during the summer months when wealthy Carolina rice planters and their families fled their inland homes for the healthier, cooler climate of this coastal capital. *South Carolina Historical Society.*

Carolinians went one step further: they officially separated from the rice-rich southern section of the colony. In this way, the colonists of Carolina restored to the Crown what King Charles II had once given away, for both South Carolina and North Carolina became royal colonies.

Georgia, the Last Colony

More than one hundred years after the first Jamestown colonists struggled against starvation and disease in Virginia, a new colony was established in the Lower South. In 1732, **James Oglethorpe,** a wealthy English social reformer, and several of his friends requested a charter for a colony on the Florida border. Oglethorpe's motives were philanthropic: he hoped to provide a new, moral life for many of the English men and women imprisoned for minor debts. He and his colleagues wanted no profits from the colony. King George II had other motives for granting the charter: he was anxious to create a protective buffer between the valuable rice-producing colony of South Carolina and the Spanish in Florida. The king inserted a clause in the Georgia charter requiring military service from every male settler. Thus he ensured that the poor men of Georgia would protect the rich men of South Carolina.

Oglethorpe and his colleagues added their own special restrictions on the lives of the Georgia colonists. Although their concern about the welfare of English debtors was genuine, they believed that poverty was the outcome of a weak character or, worse, of an addiction to vice. Thus they forbade a representative assembly and denied the settlers a voice in selecting political leaders and military officers. Because they were eager to reform the character of their colonists, the trustees set other rules designed to ensure that everyone worked hard and led a modest, moral life. All land grants were to be small, and no colonist could legally buy or sell property within Georgia. Slavery, the main source of labor in the southern colonies by this time, was banned, and free blacks were barred from the colony. The colonists would have to work their own fields and harvest their own crops.

Oglethorpe interviewed many imprisoned debtors, searching for members of the "deserving poor" who would benefit from Georgia. But few of these men and women met his standards. Most of the colony's settlers turned out to be South Carolinians looking for new land, and English immigrants from their society's middling ranks. These colonists did not welcome the trustees' paternalistic attitudes, and they soon challenged all the restrictive rules and regulations in the charter. They won the right to accumulate and sell land. They introduced slave labor in defiance of the trustees, and by the 1740s illegal slave auctions were a common sight in Georgia's largest town, Savannah. By 1752, Oglethorpe and his fellow trustees had lost enthusiasm for their reform project and, with relief, returned Georgia to the king.

James Oglethorpe English philanthropist who established the colony of Georgia as a refuge for debtors.

S U M M A R Y

E xpectations
C onstraints
C hoices
O utcomes

The failed Roanoke Colony was the only significant English effort to colonize mainland America in the sixteenth century. In the seventeenth century, however, political conflict, economic instability, and religious persecution prompted many English people to *choose* to plant new colonies. The political struggle between Parliament and the Stuart kings led to the English Civil War in 1642 and the establishment of a Commonwealth government that lasted until the Restoration of the Stuarts in 1660. Fear of a Catholic on the throne led to the Glorious Revolution in 1688. The *outcome* was political stability under Protestant monarchs after 1688. Also in the seventeenth century, England experienced an economic transformation from an agricultural society to an entrepreneurial, commercial society. The *outcome* was economic insecurity and poverty for many. At the same time, Puritans *chose* to demand reform of the Anglican Church, leading to persecution of these dissenters and to heightened religious tensions until the Glorious Revolution.

The Virginia Company founded Jamestown in 1607, *expecting* profits from gold and silver. But the Virginians found no precious metals. *Constrained* by illness and conflicts with the Powhatan Indians, the early colonists *chose* to cultivate tobacco. The *outcome* was concentration on staple-crop production, reliance on indentured servants as an agricultural labor force, and the creation of a coastal planter elite who ruled over a struggling frontier population. In 1634, the Calvert family established the colony of Maryland as a haven for Catholics. Maryland settlers also *chose* to grow tobacco. An unhealthy climate, a preponderance of male settlers, and high mortality *constrained* the development of a traditional family structure in the Chesapeake. Major conflicts among settlers emerged in both Chesapeake colonies. In 1676, Virginia's backcountry farmers *chose* to organize Bacon's Rebellion against the unfair policies of the governor and assembly. In Maryland, Protestants and Catholics battled for control.

Pilgrims, dissenters from the Church of England, *chose* to seek refuge from religious persecution in America. They overcame opposition to settling in New England by offering broad political rights to all adult males in the Mayflower Compact. They established peaceful relationships with the local Indians. The *outcome* was seventy-one years of stability in this small colony. Puritans founded Massachusetts with the *expectation* of creating a model Protestant society, a "city upon a hill." Bay Colony leaders *expected* colonists to obey biblical laws and restricted political participation to saints—full members of the church. The *outcome* of this experiment was not what the Puritans *expected.* Dissenters challenged the government's policies and were exiled. One of these dissenters, Roger Williams, established Rhode Island. Other colonists freely *chose* to leave to escape the severe regulation of their lives by the Bay Colony government. Some went to Rhode Island, and others created Connecticut. The Puritans ultimately lost control of Massachusetts in 1691, when King William revoked the colonial charter. One *outcome* of the tensions produced by political change and economic growth was the Salem witch-hunts.

The region between the Chesapeake and New England, originally claimed and colonized by the Dutch, was conquered by the English in 1664. Tolerant policies in the middle colonies led a diverse population to *choose* to settle in New York and New Jersey, as well as in Pennsylvania, the "holy experiment" founded by Quaker William Penn.

In the Lower South, the proprietors of Carolina *expected* to create a hierarchical society but faced the same *constraints* the Calverts of Maryland had faced: settlers did not *choose* to come to such a colony. Carolina colonists eventually developed a thriving rice economy that relied on slave labor. The *outcome* in South Carolina was that a small planter elite dominated the culture. Georgia, the last of England's mainland colonies, was founded by philanthropists who *expected* to reform "worthy debtors" languishing in English prisons. The king *expected* Georgia to serve as a buffer between South Carolina and Spanish-held Florida.

SUGGESTED READINGS

Kai T. Erikson. *Wayward Puritans: A Study in the Sociology of Deviance* (1966).

The author discovers the values and ideals of Massachusetts Puritan society by examining the behavior and ideas these Puritans condemned, including witchcraft and Quakerism.

John Demos. *A Little Commonwealth: Family Life in Plymouth Colony* (1970).

A beautifully written and very engaging portrait of family and community life in Plymouth Plantations.

Philip Barbour. *Pocahontas and Her World* (1970).

A factual account of the life of an American Indian princess celebrated in folklore.

Elaine G. Breslaw. *Tituba, Reluctant Witch of Salem: Devilish Indians and Puritan Fantasies* (1996).

The author reconstructs the life of the Caribbean-born Indian slave who was a central figure in the Salem witch trials.

THE BRITISH COLONIES IN THE EIGHTEENTH CENTURY By the 1750s the mainland colonies were a multicultural society stretching from Maine to Georgia. This map of settlement by six major immigrant groups reveals important patterns, including the concentration of English immigrants in the coastal areas and of African-Americans in the plantation South as well as settlement of the back country by the newer immigrants from Germany and Ireland.

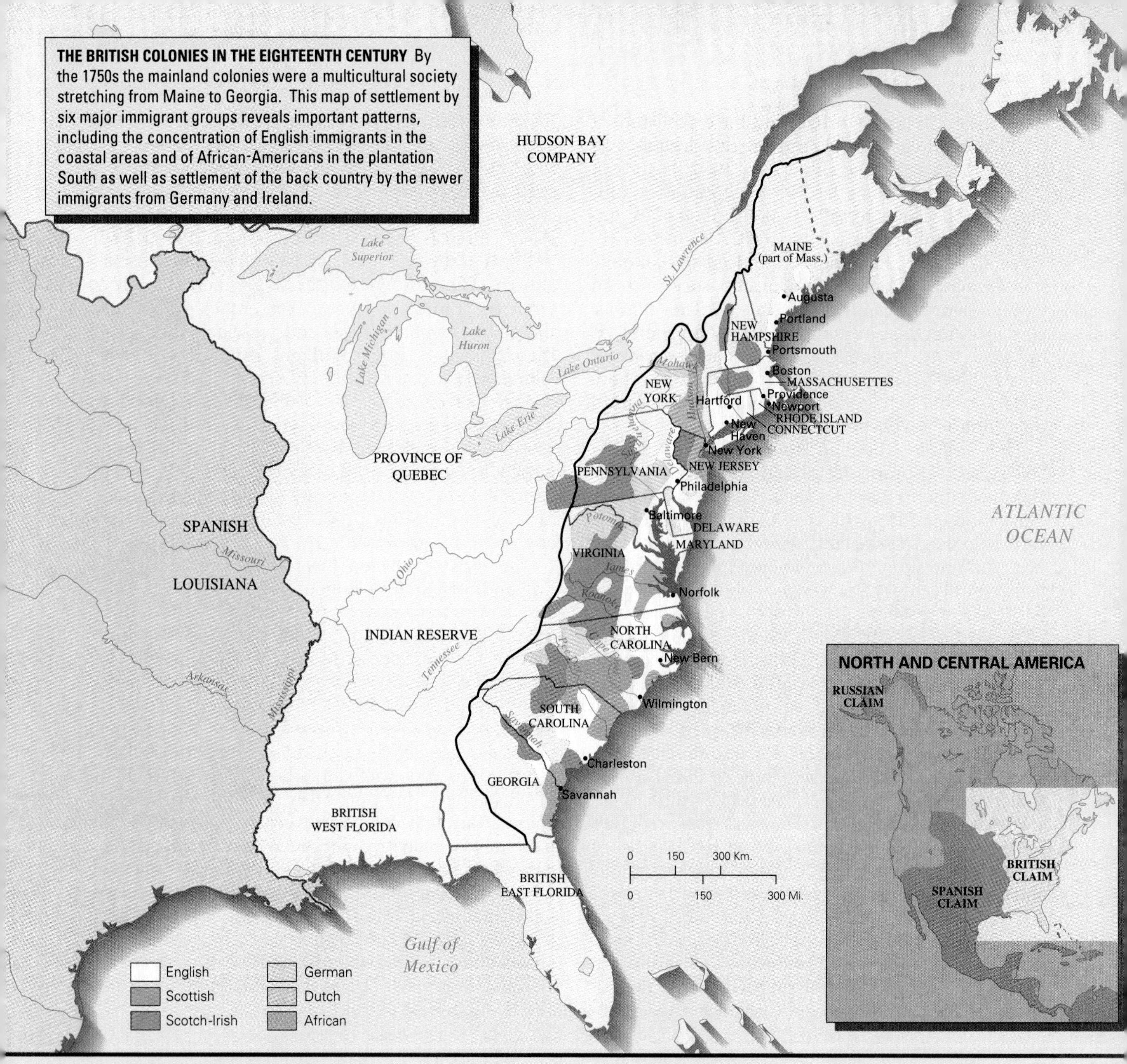

- **1690** Locke's theories
- **1711** Tuscarora War begins
- **1734** Great Awakening begins
- **1739** Stono Rebellion in South Carolina
- **1754** Great War for Empire
- **1760** King George III comes to the throne
- **1763** Treaty of Paris
- **1771** Carolina Regulators defeated

1450 1500 1550 1600 1650 1700 1750 1800 1850 1900

CHAPTER 4

The English Colonies in the Eighteenth Century, 1689–1763

The English Transatlantic Communities of Trade

- What variations in commercial activity could someone traveling from Maine to Georgia expect to find?
- In which region did new immigrants seem to have the best economic choices?

Community and Work in Colonial Society

- What changes occurred in New England society and culture and what were the outcomes of these changes?
- Why did colonists in the Chesapeake and Lower South choose to shift from indentured servants to slaves as their primary labor force? What choices and constraints did African Americans face in slavery?
- What was distinctive about life in the Middle Colonies?
- What expectations led most immigrants to the backcountry?

Reason and Religion in Colonial Society

- What political and personal expectations arose from Enlightenment philosophy?
- What were the significant outcomes of the Great Awakening?

Government and Politics in the Mainland Colonies

- What constrained a colonial governor's exercise of royal power?
- What was the outcome of the struggle for power between the colonial assemblies and the colonial governors?

North America and the Struggle for Empire

- What did Europeans and American Indians expect to gain from diplomacy and warfare in North America?
- What constraints did the imperial wars place on the American colonists?
- What outcomes of the French and Indian War affected people in North America?

INTRODUCTION

Expectations
Constraints
Choices
Outcomes

In 1748, a European traveler named Peter Kalm arrived in the colonial city of Philadelphia, one of many stops in his journey through the English colonies. Like tourists in every century, Kalm jotted down his impressions of the things he saw and the people he encountered. Unlike most travelers, however, Kalm *chose* to publish his diary. Kalm was a keen observer, and his *Travels in North America* are filled with details on how eighteenth-century Americans lived and worked.

Kalm was clearly impressed with Pennsylvania's "City of Brotherly Love," a prosperous, bustling city, whose "fine appearance" and "agreeable situation" rivaled even the most ancient towns of Europe. Kalm knew his readers might wonder how such a city had arisen "so suddenly from nothing," so he provided an explanation. The liberty Philadelphians enjoyed, he wrote, acted as a great magnet, drawing women and men from all over Europe to the colony. Pennsylvania did not need to promise instant riches or use force to persuade these immigrants to venture over "wide and stormy seas." They *chose* to leave their native lands, their property, and their families because they *expected* to be "well secured by the laws in . . . person and property, and enjoy such liberties, that a citizen of *Philadelphia* may in a manner be said to live in his house like a king." In his positive evaluation of American life, Kalm echoed another eighteenth-century commentator, the Frenchman Michel Crevecoeur, whose *Letters from an American Farmer* referred to America as a "smiling country."

Few members of the English or European elite were influenced by these glowing reports on colonial life. They continued to think of the colonies as a dumping ground for misfits and hayseeds who struggled to survive on a violent frontier. Members of the English Parliament viewed the colonists as a constant source of problems and continued to expect the worst from them. They *expected* insubordinate colonial legislatures, merchants who violated trade regulations, and a dangerously unstable political atmosphere in a society that gave common men such a great voice in government.

But Peter Kalm's positive portrait of American society stirred the hearts of many less prosperous Europeans. These people, who faced the *constraints* of poverty, religious persecution, or political oppression, marveled at the accounts of colonial liberty and opportunities. Thousands *chose* to emigrate to the English mainland colonies. Here, they discovered that American society actually had several distinct regional economies and cultures.

To the north, where land and climate *constrained* agriculture, New Englanders had created a commercially oriented, bustling society, its cities and towns filled with wealthy merchants, impoverished widows, struggling dockworkers, and ambitious shopkeepers. In the more fertile middle colonies, comfortable family farms were common, but vast estates worked by tenant farmers could be found in the Hudson Valley of New York. The cultural diversity that Crèvecoeur admired during his years in New York turned out to have many troubling aspects: social tensions, political factions, and racial conflicts. In the Chesapeake and the Lower South, a planter aristocracy dominated social and political life, and the growth of a slave labor force contradicted both Crèvecoeur's and Kalm's portraits of a land of liberty and boundless opportunity. In the backcountry of the South and along the boundaries of settlement to the north as well, life seemed to confirm the European and English elite's notion of a colonial world of struggling frontierspeople and embattled Indians.

The *outcomes* of this regionalism, including the great variation in day-to-day work patterns, in family life and structure, and in the social institutions the colonists created, produced a complex, contradictory society that even an observant visitor like Peter Kalm did not fully grasp. Yet there were significant shared influences on the lives of all American colonists, especially the *constraints* placed on them by English imperial policies and by the rivalries among the European nations for territory and control of trade. Wars between England, France, and Spain disrupted the lives of most colonists and cast a long shadow over life from Maine to Georgia.

CHRONOLOGY

From Settlements to Societies

1690–1691	John Locke publishes *Essay on Human Understanding* and *Two Treatises of Government*
1701	Yale College founded
1702	Queen Anne's War begins
1704	Pro-French Indians attack Deerfield, Massachusetts
1711	Tuscarora War begins in North Carolina
1712	New York City slave revolt
1715	Colonists defeat Creek and Yamassee Indians of Georgia
1722	Dummer's War begins in Massachusetts
1734	Great Awakening begins in New England
1739	Stono Rebellion in South Carolina
1740	King George's War begins George Whitefield begins his preaching tour
1756	Great War for Empire begins
1759	British capture Quebec
1763	Treaty of Paris ending Seven Years War Paxton Boys revolt in Pennsylvania
1771	North Carolina Regulator movement defeated

The English Transatlantic Communities of Trade

- What variations in commercial activity could someone traveling from Maine to Georgia expect to find?
- In which region did new immigrants seem to have the best economic choices?

Although the English spoke of "the colonial trade," British America did not have a single, unified economy. Instead, there were four distinctive regional economies on the mainland, concentrated along the Atlantic coastline and bordered on the west by the **subsistence society** commonly found on the edge of white settlement. To the south, the sugar islands of the Caribbean made up a fifth, unique regional economy. Each of these economies arose from environmental conditions, natural resources, English commercial policy, the labor force, and the available technological knowledge.

Regions of Commerce

The sugar-producing islands of the West Indies were the brightest jewels in the English imperial crown. Spain had first laid claim to most of these islands, but England had gobbled up many because the Spanish chose to concentrate on the gold- and silver-mining colonies of Peru and Mexico. By the eighteenth century, the English flag flew over St. Kitts, Barbados, Nevis, Montserrat, and Jamaica. On each island, English plantation owners built fabulous fortunes on the sugar and molasses that African slaves produced. While the absentee planters lived in luxury in England, black slaves lived—and died in staggering numbers—on the islands, working the cane fields and tending the fires that burned day and night under the sugar vats of the "great Boiling houses."

Few mainland colonists enjoyed the wealth of the "Sugar Interest." Still, in the Lower South, planters of South Carolina and Georgia amassed considerable fortunes of their own by growing rice in the lowlands along the Atlantic coast. By the 1730s, this American rice was feeding the people of the Mediterranean, Portugal, and Spain. By midcentury,

subsistence society A society that produces the food and supplies necessary for survival but does not produce a surplus that can be marketed.

♦ Suriname, or Dutch Guinea, was a small Dutch colony on the northeastern coast of South America. Slave labor produced the sugar cane that attracted American ships to Suriname ports. Rhode Islanders dominated this illegal trade, and some of the men in this painting, *Sea Captains Carousing in Surinam,* may have been Rhode Island colonists, eager to exchange horses, food, and their colony's tobacco for the Dutch planters' molasses. *"Sea Captains Carousing in Surinam" (detail) by Greenwood. The Saint Louis Art Museum, Museum Purchase.*

planters were making additional profits from the harvest of indigo, used to make a blue textile dye. Other Carolinians continued to profit from raising cattle. Like the sugar planters, Carolina and Georgia rice growers based their production on slave labor, but these plantation masters never became permanent **absentee landowners.**

Tobacco continued to dominate the economy of the Chesapeake, although by the eighteenth century, "brown gold" was no longer the only crop Virginians and Marylanders were willing to plant. In fact, at the turn of the century, when the price of tobacco was driven down by high taxes and competition from Mediterranean sources, many **tidewater** planters chose to diversify their crops. They began producing wheat and other grains for export. As a result, tobacco production shifted west to the area along the Potomac, the James River valley, and the **piedmont** foothills. The second major shift came in the labor force used in tobacco cultivation. By the eighteenth century, African slaves had replaced indentured servants in the fields. Planters who could afford to purchase a number of slaves enjoyed a competitive advantage over their neighbors in both the old and the new tobacco areas, because they had the necessary labor force to plant and harvest bigger crops. This large-scale production kept tobacco the number-one export of the mainland colonies.

Together, these two southern regions provided the bulk of the mainland's agricultural exports to Great Britain. The New England regional economy depended far less on Britain as a market. Except in the Connecticut River valley, where tobacco was grown, the rocky soil of their region allowed New Englanders little opportunity to engage in large-scale farming. Instead, they developed both a fishing and a lumbering industry, shipping the dried fish and timber to the West Indies. But it was shipbuilding and the ambitious **carrying trade** connected to it that dominated New England's economy. Colonists made great profits from an extensive shipping network that carried colonial exports across the Atlantic and distributed foreign goods and English manufactured products to the colonies. Some merchant-shippers such as the slave traders of Newport, Rhode Island, specialized, but most were willing to carry any cargo that promised a profit. By the eighteenth century, New England shipping made these colonists rivals of English merchants rather than useful sources of profit for the Mother Country.

Sandwiched between the South and New England, the colonies of New York, New Jersey, and Pennsylvania developed their own regional economy. The Middle Colonies combined the successes of both their neighbors, creating profits from staple-crop farming and from trade. The forests of the Pocono Mountains and of upper New York were a source of wood and wood products for the shipbuilding industry, and locally harvested flaxseed was exported to Ireland for its linen industry. The central crop, however, was wheat. Fortunately for the colonists of this area, the price of wheat rose steadily during the eighteenth century. The carrying trade was equally important in this mixed regional economy. Ships carrying cargoes of grain and flour milled in New York City across the Atlantic and into the Caribbean crossed paths with other colonial

absentee landowner An estate owner who collects profits through farming or rent but does not live on the land or help cultivate it.

tidewater Low coastal land drained by tidal streams in Maryland and Virginia

piedmont Land lying at the foot of a mountain range.

carrying trade The business of transporting goods across the Atlantic or to the Caribbean.

ships, bringing manufactured goods and luxury items from abroad through the region's two major port cities, New York and Philadelphia. By 1775, Philadelphia had become the second largest city in the British Empire.

Not everyone in Maryland grew tobacco for the market, of course, and not everyone in Massachusetts was a sailor, a lumberjack, a ship captain, or an urban shopkeeper. The market-oriented activity was concentrated in the older, coastal settlements of each region, where harbors and riverways provided the necessary transportation routes for the shipment of crops, goods, and supplies. Inland from these farms, towns, and cities, most colonies had a backcountry that was sparsely populated and farmed by European immigrants, ex-servants, or the families of younger sons from older communities. There, on what the white settlers thought of as the frontier and the Indians thought of as the invasion line, colonists struggled to produce enough for survival. They lacked the labor force to clear or to work sufficient land for a marketable crop, or they lacked the means to get that crop to market. They lacked the resources, both financial and political, to quickly solve either problem. As a result, this region was characterized by a subsistence economy that extended like a border from Maine to western Pennsylvania, to inland Carolina, along every region of the mainland colonies. But even these backcountry farms had a fragile link to the world of international trade, for settlers brought with them the farm tools and the basic household supplies that had been manufactured in England or imported through colonial ports.

The Cords of Commercial Empire

England's mainland colonists traded, both directly and indirectly, with many European nations and their colonies. Salt, wine, and spices reached colonial tables from southern Europe, and sugar, rum, molasses, and cotton came to them from the West Indies. But the deepest and broadest channels in the transatlantic trade were those that connected the mother country and the colonies. The British purchased over half of all the crops and furs and mined resources that colonists produced for market, and 90 percent of all colonial purchases came from England. Strong cords of exchange thus bound England's American colonists closely to the mother country, even if many colonists were second-, third-, or even fourth-generation Americans and others traced their roots to different nations and even different continents.

The English mainland colonies were also bound to each other, despite a deserved reputation for dispute, disagreement, and endless rivalries. New Englanders might exchange insults with Pennsylvanians, but in the shops and on the wharfs, Pennsylvania flour, Massachusetts mackerel, Carolina rice, and scores of domestic products and produce changed hands in a lively and cheerful commerce. Domestic trade was greater in volume, although lower in value, than all foreign trade in this eighteenth-century world.

Community and Work in Colonial Society

- What changes occurred in New England society and culture, and what were the outcomes of these changes?
- Why did colonists in the Chesapeake and Lower South choose to shift from indentured servants to slaves as their primary labor force? What choices and constraints did African Americans face in slavery?
- What was distinctive about life in the Middle Colonies?
- What expectations led most immigrants to the backcountry?

Visitors to eighteenth-century America saw both physical and cultural variation as they traveled from the carefully laid-out towns of New England, through the crowded seaport cities of the Middle Colonies, and into the isolated rural worlds of the plantation South. The colonists lived and worked in societies whose ways of living differed as strikingly as their economies.

The Emergence of the "Yankee"

In the early eighteenth century, New England's seaport towns and cities grew steadily in size and economic importance. With the rise of this profitable, international commerce, the Puritan culture of the village gave way to the new, more secular culture of the "Yankee." Wealthy merchants became prominent in local politics and society, and economic competition and the pursuit of wealth replaced older, communal values. Still, certain intellectual traditions did remain. New Englanders continued to create and maintain public institutions such as schools and colleges. In 1701, Yale College opened its doors in New Haven, Connecticut, giving the sons of elite New Englanders an alternative to Massachusetts' Harvard College, founded in 1636. New Englanders

♦ Beginning in 1641, New Englanders made their way to the small island of Nantucket, located off the southern coast of Cape Cod, Massachusetts. These colonists earned their livings from the sea. Nantucket fishermen sailed north as far as the banks of Newfoundland and Nova Scotia while whalers ventured out into the Atlantic in pursuit of the valuable sperm whale. Throughout the colonial period, Nantucket remained a prosperous commercial community. *"Nantucket, 1725" by Phoebe Folger, Houghton Library, Harvard University.*

supported newspapers and printing presses that kept their communities informed about local, regional, and even international events. The new Yankees probably preferred reading the political theory of English philosopher John Locke, rather than the terrifying portrait of Judgment Day the Puritans found in Michael Wigglesworth's poem *The Day of Doom.* But New Englanders in both centuries sustained a lively intellectual life.

Even in more traditional New England villages, changes were evident. Family patterns of settlement were shifting as land grew scarce in these rural communities. By the eighteenth century, many fathers no longer had enough farmland to provide adequately for all their sons. Thus many younger sons left their families and friends behind and sought their fortunes elsewhere. Some chose to go west, pushing the frontier of settlement as they searched for fertile land. Others went north, to less-developed areas like Maine. In the process, they created new towns and villages, causing the number of backcountry New England towns to grow steadily until the end of the colonial period.

Still other young men chose to abandon farming entirely and relocate to the commercial cities of the region. They may have nurtured great expectations, but their new life in the cities often disappointed them. In New England's urban centers, inequality of wealth and opportunity went hand in hand with the overall prosperity. In Boston, a growing number of poor widows and landless young men scrambled for employment and often wound up dependent on public charity. As news of the scarcity of land, urban poverty, and competition for work spread, European immigrants to the colonies decided to bypass New England and settle in the Middle Colonies or along the southern frontier.

Planter Society and Slavery

Southern society was also changing slowly but with results as dramatic as those in New England. By the end of the seventeenth century, the steady supply of cheap labor from England had begun to disappear. The English economy was improving, and young men who might once have signed on as indentured servants in Virginia or Maryland now chose to remain at home. (see Individual Choices: James Revel) Those who did immigrate preferred to indenture themselves to farmers and merchants of the Middle Colonies, where work conditions were less harsh and economic opportunities were brighter. While

♦ This eighteenth-century English handkerchief is rich with social history. It depicts the two forms of unfree labor in the colonies: slavery and indentured servitude. Working side by side, the English convict laborer—transported to the Chesapeake—and the African-American slaves hoe the tobacco field in their bare feet. The pained expression on the convict's face suggests the same remorse that James Revel reveals in his poem. *Colonial Williamsburg Foundation.*

this supply of indentured servants was declining, however, a different labor supply was beginning to increase: enslaved Africans.

Although Africans had been brought to Virginia as early as 1619, the legal differences between black workers and white workers were vague until the 1660s, when the slowly increasing numbers of African Americans elicited the different, and harsher, treatment that defined slavery in the Caribbean and South America. By midcentury, it became the custom in the Chesapeake to hold black servants for life terms, although their children were still considered free. By the 1660s, colonists turned these customs of **discrimination** into law. In 1662, Virginia took a major step toward making slavery an inherited condition by declaring that "all children born in this country shall be held bond or free according to the condition of the mother."

Slaves did not become the dominant labor force in southern agriculture for several decades, although southern planters were probably well aware of the advantages of slave labor over indentured servitude. First, a slave, bound for life, would never compete with his former master the way freed white servants did. Second, most white colonists did not believe that the English customs regulating a master's treatment of servants had to be applied to African workers. For example, Christian holidays would not need to be honored for African laborers, and the workday itself could be lengthened without any white colonists expressing concern. Why, then, were the early Chesapeake planters reluctant to import slaves as colonists in the Caribbean and South America had done? Two factors made them hesitate. Dutch control of the African slave trade kept purchasing prices high, and the disease environment of the Chesapeake cut human life short. Until the end of the seventeeth century, therefore, planters considered the financial investment in African laborers both too costly and too risky.

In the 1680s, however, the drawbacks to African slavery began to vanish. Mortality rates fell in the Chesapeake, and the English broke the Dutch monopoly on the slave trade. Fierce competition among English slavers drove prices down and at the same time ensured a steady supply of slaves. Under these conditions, Chesapeake planters moved quickly to secure slave labor. Although only 5 percent of the roughly 9.5 million Africans brought to the Americas came to the North American mainland colonies, their number in the Chesapeake rose dramatically in the eighteenth century. By 1700, 13 percent of the Chesapeake population was African or of African descent. In Virginia, where only 950 Africans lived in 1660, the black population grew to 120,000 by 1756. At the end of the colonial period, blacks made up 40 percent of Virginia's population.

Colonists who could not afford to purchase African slaves were at an economic disadvantage. Poor white Virginians and Marylanders moved west, and new immigrants to the colonies avoided the coastal and piedmont plantation society. Colonial merchants and skilled craftspeople also avoided the Chesapeake, for the planters purchased goods directly from England or used slave labor to manufacture barrels, bricks, and other products. As a result, this region saw the development of few towns or cities that could provide a dense community life. The Chesapeake remained a rural society, dominated by a slaveowning class made prosperous by the labor of African Americans who lived in slavery all their lives.

If tobacco provided a comfortable life for an eighteenth-century planter, rice provided a luxurious one. The Lower South, too, was a plantation

discrimination Treatment based on class, gender, or racial category rather than on merit; prejudice.

INDIVIDUAL CHOICES

Choosing Between Prison and Servitude

James Revel

This illustration of a young man shackled in a leg brace and handcuffs in a bare prison cell in 1728 suggests why James Revel chose to serve his sentence as an indentured servant rather than in jail. Marshalsea Prison, 18th c. print. Fotomas Index Picture Library.

James Revel was one of the thousands of young men and women who made their way to London in the seventeenth century in search of work. Although the economic depression that had swept the country was lifting by 1690, Revel still faced fierce competition for low-paying jobs. Like other desperate people before him, Revel chose to turn to crime. The unlucky young man was caught and imprisoned. English authorities offered Revel one more choice: he could sell himself and his labor for several years to a stranger in the southern colonies, or he could serve his long term in prison. He chose servitude.

Revel's dilemma was not unique, but the fact that he recorded his choice—and that this record has survived—is unique. Revel tells his story in a remarkable autobiographical poem, which he wrote after surviving his term as an indentured servant in Virginia. He describes his life of crime, his capture, and his experiences in a Chesapeake tobacco colony that was already turning away from the use of white servants to the purchase of black slaves. Whatever expectations and fears the 17-year-old boy had, noth-

society, dominated by the wealthiest mainland colonists, the rice growers of the coastal regions of Carolina and Georgia. Members of this planter elite concentrated their social life in the elegant town of Charles Town, where they moved each summer to avoid the heat, humidity, and unhealthy environment of their lowland plantations. With its beautiful townhouses, theaters, and parks, Charles Town was the single truly cosmopolitan city of the South and perhaps the most sophisticated of all mainland cities in North America.

The prosperity that these Lower South planters enjoyed, like the prosperity of the tidewater planters, was based on the forced labor of their slaves. Indeed, the Barbadian families who settled South Carolina had never relied on indentured servants because they arrived with the slaves from their Caribbean plantations. By 1708, one-half of the colonial population in Carolina was black. By 1720, Africans and African Americans outnumbered their white masters. In Georgia the colonists openly defied the trustees' ban on slavery until that ban was finally lifted.

Slave Experience and Slave Culture

Most slaves brought to the mainland colonies did not come directly from Africa. Instead, these men ing appears to have prepared him for the reality of a servant's life in America. He wrote about his arrival in Virginia:

At length a grim old man unto me came
He ask'd my trade, and likewise ask'd my Name:
I told him I a Tin-man was by trade
And not quite eighteen years of age I said.
At last to my new master's house I came,
All the town of Wicoccomoco call'd by name,
Where my European clothes were took from me,
Which never after I again could see.
A canvas shirt and trowsers that they gave,
With a hop-sack frock in which I was to slave:
No shoes nor stockings had I for to wear,
Thus dressed into the field I next must go,
Amongst tobacco plants all day to hoe,
At day break in the morn our work began,
And so held to the setting of the Sun.

Revel worked beside African slaves, whom he found more sympathetic and kind than the countryman who was his master. He describes the constraints that they shared in common:

We and the Negroes both alike did fare,
Of work and food we had an equal share;
But in a piece of ground we call our own,
The food we eat first by ourselves were sown,
Six days we slave for our master's good,
The seventh day is to produce our food.
And if we offer for to run away,
For every hour we must serve a day:
Much hardships then in deed I did endure,
No dog was ever nursed so I'm sure,
More pity the poor negroe slaves bestowed
Than my inhuman brutal master showed.

Revel was in his thirties when his term of service ended. A free man, he chose to return to England rather than remain to seek his fortune in the colonies. He clearly hoped that the outcome of his own choices in life would serve as a lesson to others:

At length my fourteen years expired quite,
Which fill'd my very soul with fine delight
To think I should no longer there remain,
But to old England once return again.
My country men take warning e'er too late,
Lest you should share my hard unhappy fate;
Altho' but little crimes you here have done,
Consider seven or fourteen year to come.

and women were re-exported to the Chesapeake or the Lower South after a short period of **seasoning** in the tropical climate of the West Indies. But all imported slaves, whether seasoned or new to the Americas, began their bondage when African slavers, armed with European weapons, captured men, women, and children and delivered them in chains to European ships anchored along the coast of West Africa. Many captives died on the long march from the interior to the coast. Others chose suicide over enslavement, leaping into the ocean waters as they were paddled by canoe to the waiting ships. Slave traders tried to prevent these suicides but were not surprised by them. The slaves, they commented, dreaded life in America more than their captors dreaded hell.

The transatlantic voyage, or **middle passage,** was a nightmare of death, disease, suicide, and sometimes mutiny. The casualties included the white officers and crews of the slave ships, who died of diseases in such

seasoning A period during which slaves from Africa were held in the West Indies for adjustment to the climate and disease environment of the American tropics.

middle passage The crowded, often deadly voyage in which indentured servants or slaves were transported across the Atlantic Ocean from Europe or Africa.

♦ This drawing shows the interior of the slave ship *Vigilante.* On board, 227 male slaves were confined to a 37- by 22-foot room, and 120 female slaves were crowded into a 14- by 19-foot room. The ceilings were less than 5 feet high. Although this is an 1822 slave ship, captured off the coast of Africa by the English navy, the conditions shown here differed little from those described in the eighteenth century by slaves and by commentators on slavery. *Courtesy, American Antiquarian Society.*

great numbers that the waters near Benin in West Africa were known as the "white man's grave." But the loss of black lives was far greater. Slave ships were breeding grounds for scurvy, yellow fever, malaria, dysentery, smallpox, measles, and typhus—each bringing painful death. When smallpox struck his slave ship, one European recorded that "we hauled up eight or ten slaves dead of a morning. The flesh and skin peeled off their wrists when taken hold of." Perhaps 18 percent of all the Africans who began the middle passage died on the ocean.

Until the 1720s, most Chesapeake slaves worked alone on a tobacco farm with the owner and his family or in small groups of two or three. This isolation made both marriage and a sustaining slave community almost impossible. Even on larger plantations, the steady influx of newly imported slaves, or "outlanders," during the first decades of the eighteenth century made it difficult for African Americans to work together to create a culture in response to their disorienting circumstances. The new arrivals had to be taught to speak English and to adapt to the demands of slavery. Slowly, however, these involuntary immigrants from different African societies, speaking different languages, practicing different religions, and surviving under the oppressive conditions of slavery, did create a sense of community, weaving together African and European traditions. The result was an African-American culture that gave meaning to, and a sense of identity within, the slave's world (see pages 351–353).

In the Lower South, slaves were concentrated on large plantations where they had limited or no contact with white society. This isolation from the dominant society allowed them an earlier opportunity to develop a creole, or native, culture. Local languages evolved that mixed a basic English vocabulary with words from a variety of African tongues. One of these languages, Gullah, spoken on the Sea Islands off the coast of Georgia and South Carolina, remained the local dialect until the end of the nineteenth century.

For many slaves, the sense of community that came with this culture was a form of resistance to the system of enslavement their white masters had created. But African Americans also developed other ways to show their hatred of slavery. The diary of Virginia planter William Byrd is filled with accounts of daily resistance: slaves who challenged orders, field hands who broke tools and staged work slowdowns, men who pretended sickness and women who claimed pregnancies, household servants who stole supplies and damaged property, and slaves of all ages who ran away to the woods for a day or two or to the slave quarters of a neighboring plantation. African Americans with families, and those who understood the odds against escape, preferred to take actions like these that undermined the slave system, rather than risk almost certain death in open rebellion.

White slave masters feared slave revolts, however, for they knew that slaves had what the Puritan minister Cotton Mather called a "fondness for freedom." Southern colonies took elaborate precautions to prevent rebellions, creating armed patrols that policed the roads and woods near the plantations. These patrols were usually efficient, and the punishment they inflicted was deadly. Even if rebels escaped immediate capture, few safe havens were available to them. Individual runaways had a hard time sustaining their freedom, but dozens of rebels from one plantation were usually doomed once whites on neighboring plantations were alerted. Despite these odds, slaves continued to seek their liberty, often timing their revolts to coincide with epi-

♦ Enslaved Africans living on the sea islands off the Georgia and South Carolina coast had little contact with white colonists. Although they learned English, they were able to retain many language patterns from their homeland, developing a dialect known as Gullah, which their descendents still speak today. In 1995, the American Bible Society published the gospel of Luke in this sea-island dialect. *Courtesy of the Penn Center, History and Culture Department, St. Helena Island, SC.*

demics or imperial wars that distracted the white community.

The most famous slave revolt of the eighteenth century, the **Stono Rebellion,** took place in the midst of a yellow fever epidemic in Charleston just as news of war between England and Spain reached the colony of South Carolina. Early on a Sunday morning in September 1739, about twenty slaves gathered at the Stono River, south of Charleston. They seized guns and gunpowder, killed several planter families and storekeepers, and then headed south. Rather than traveling quietly through the woods, the rebels marched boldly in open view, beating drums to invite slaves on nearby plantations to join them in their flight to Spanish Florida.

Other slaves answered the call, and the Stono rebels' ranks grew to almost one hundred. But in Charleston, planters were gathering to put an end to the rebellion. By late Sunday afternoon white militias had caught up with and surrounded the escaping slaves. The Stono rebels stood and fought, and many died attacking the white militiamen. Those captured were executed. Those who escaped into the countryside were hunted down.

The Stono Rebellion terrified white South Carolinians, who hurried to make the colony's already harsh slave codes even more brutal. The government increased the slave patrols in both size and frequency. It also raised the bounties or rewards offered for the capture of runaways to make sure fleeing slaves taken alive and unharmed, or brought in dead and scalped, were worth hunting down.

The Urban Culture of the Middle Colonies

The small family farms of Pennsylvania, with their profitable wheat crops, earned the colony its reputation as the "best poor man's country." Tenant farmers and hired laborers were not unknown in eastern Pennsylvania, but the colony boasted more comfortable or middling-class farm families than neighboring New York. In New York, great landed estates along the Hudson River controlled much of the colony's good farmland, and one outcome was a series of eighteenth-century land riots led by New England **squatters** and Dutch, German, and Scottish tenant farmers.

What made the Middle Colonies distinctive was not these bitter disputes over land or the sight of prosperous farms and comfortable farmhouses. The region's distinguishing feature was the dynamic urban life of its two major cities, New York and Philadelphia. Although only 3 percent of the colonial population lived in the eighteenth-century cities, they were a magnet for young men and women, widows, free African Americans and slaves, and some of the immigrant population pouring into the colonies from Europe. By 1770, Philadelphia's 40,000 residents made it the second largest city in the British Empire. In the same year, 25,000 people crowded onto the tip of New York's Manhattan Island.

Stono Rebellion Slave rebellion in South Carolina in 1739; it prompted the colony to pass harsher laws governing the movement of slaves and the capture of runaways.

squatter A person who settles on unoccupied land without legal claim, often in the hope of establishing ownership simply by his or her presence.

♦ Coopers, who made the large barrels seen in this illustration as well as other wooden containers, were essential to colonial commerce. In New England and the middle colonies, free white men dominated this craft, but in the Lower South, slaves made the barrels that carried rice and indigo to English markets. *Courtesy, American Antiquarian Society.*

New York residents shared their cramped living space with chickens and livestock and their streets with roving packs of dogs and pigs. On the narrow cobblestone or gravel streets, pedestrians jostled one another and struggled to avoid being run down by carts, carriages, men on horseback, or cattle being driven to slaughter. Although colonial cities were usually thought to be cleaner than European cities, with better sewerage and drainage systems, garbage and excrement left to rot on the streets provided a feast for flies and for scavenging animals, including free-roaming pigs.

City residents faced more serious problems than runaway carts and snarling dogs. From ships docked at Philadelphia or New York rats emerged carrying plague and sailors carrying venereal diseases. These and other communicable diseases spread rapidly in overcrowded areas. Fires also raced through these cities of wooden houses, wharfs, and shops. And crime—especially robbery and assault—was no stranger in the urban environment, where taverns, brothels, and gambling houses were common.

These eighteenth-century cities offered a wide range of occupations and experiences that attracted many a farmer's daughter or son but sometimes overwhelmed a new arrival from the countryside. One farmboy wrote to his father of the "Noise and confusion and Disturbance. I must confess, the jolts of Waggons, the Ratlings of Coaches, the crying of meat for the Market, the [hollering]of negroes and the ten thousand junggles and Noises, that continually Surround us in every Part almost of the Town, confuse my Thinking."

Young men who could endure the noise and confusion sought work as **apprentices** in scores of artisan trades ranging from the luxury crafts of silver and goldsmithing or cabinet making, to the elite trades of shipbuilding, blacksmithing, or butchering, to the more modest occupations of ropemaking, baking, barbering, or shoemaking. The poorest might find work on the docks or as servants, or they might go to sea. Young women had fewer choices because few trades were open to them. Some might become dressmakers or **milliners,** but domestic service or prostitution were more likely choices. In the Middle Colony cities, as in Boston, widowed farm wives came seeking jobs as nurses, laundresses, teachers, or seamstresses. A widow or an unmarried woman who had a little money could open a shop or set up a tavern or a boarding house.

New York City had the highest concentration of African Americans in the northern colonies. The city attracted many free African-American men and women. Only perhaps 5 percent of all mainland colony African Americans were free, and those **manumitted** by their plantation masters frequently chose to remain in the South, although they faced legal and social harassment including special taxes and severe punishment for striking a white person even in self-defense. Others, though, made their way to the cities of New England and the Middle Colonies, eking out a living as laborers and servants or sailors. In addition, although slave labor was not common in New England or on the family farms of the Middle Colonies, slaves were used on New York's docks and wharfs as manual laborers.

Racial tension was thus a part of urban life, and white New Yorkers showed the same fear of slave rebellions as Carolina or Virginia planters. In 1712, two dozen slaves set buildings afire in New York. Firemen kept the flames from spreading, however, and armed New Yorkers cut off any hope of escape for the slaves. Faced with capture, several of the

apprentice A person bound by legal agreement to work for an employer for a specific length of time in exchange for instruction in a trade, craft, or business.

milliner A maker or designer of hats.

manumit To free from slavery or bondage; emancipate.

♦ Few women worked in the skilled trades or crafts, although widows and daughters might manage a shop after a husband or father died. The mantua maker shown here was considered an artisan and could command a good price for her skill at making fancy gowns and other elaborately sewn clothing. *Courtesy, American Antiquarian Society.*

African Americans committed suicide. Those who were taken alive suffered horrible punishment. According to the colonial governor, Robert Hunter, "some were burnt, others were hanged, one broke on the wheel, and one hung alive in chains in the town." Twenty-nine years later, the mere rumor of a conspiracy by African Americans to commit arson was enough to move white residents to violence. Despite the lack of any evidence to support the charge, 101 of the city's black residents were arrested—18 of them were hanged and 18 burned alive.

Life in the Backcountry

Thomas Malthus, a well-known English economist and careful student of population, believed the eighteenth-century population explosion in the English mainland colonies was "without parallel in history" (see chapter-opening map). The colonial white population climbed from 225,000 in 1688 to over 2.5 million in 1775, and the number of African Americans reached 500,000 in the same year. Natural increase accounted for much of this growth, for over half of the colonists were under age 16 in 1775. But hundreds of thousands of white immigrants arrived during the eighteenth century, risking hunger, thirst, dampness, fear, and death on the transatlantic voyage to start life over in America. The majority of these immigrants found their way to the backcountry of the colonies.

The migration west, whether by native-born or immigrant white colonists, shifted the population center of mainland society. Newcomers from Europe and Britain, as well as descendants of Puritan settlers and the younger sons of the tidewater Chesapeake, all saw their best opportunities in the sparsely settled regions of western New York, northern New England, western Pennsylvania, Virginia's Shenandoah Valley, or the Carolina backcountry. Many of these settlers were squatters who cleared a few acres and laid claim by their presence to a promising piece of land.

The flow of settlers west was part of the American landscape throughout the century, but it became a flood after 1760. A seemingly endless train of carts, sledges, and wagons moved along Indian paths to the west, and the rivers were crowded with rafts and canoes carrying families, farm tools, and livestock. Many of these new immigrants traveled south from Pennsylvania along a wagon road that ran 800 miles from Philadelphia to Virginia, North Carolina, and Augusta, Georgia. Others chose to remain in the Middle Colonies. New York's population rose 39 percent between 1760 and 1776, and in 1769, on the day the land office opened at Fort Pitt (Pittsburgh), over twenty-seven hundred applicants showed up to register for land.

By 1760, perhaps 700,000 new colonists had made their homes in the mainland colonies. In the early part of the century, the largest immigrant groups were the **Scots-Irish.** Later, German settlers dominated. But travelers on the wagon roads might be Italians, Swiss, Irish, Welsh, or European Jews. Most striking, the number of British immigrants swelled after 1760, causing anger and alarm within the British government. The flood of young English men and women out of the country prompted government officials to consider passing laws curbing

Scots-Irish Protestant Scottish settlers in British-occupied northern Ireland, many of whom migrated to the colonies in the eighteenth century.

♦ When backcountry settlers failed to get the military protection they felt they deserved, they sometimes resorted to vigilante action. After a series of Indian raids in 1763, the Paxton Boys took revenge by attacking a peaceful Conestoga Indian village. This drawing shows the Paxton Boys murdering several Conestogas who had taken refuge in the Lancaster jail. Eventually, Benjamin Franklin negotiated a truce with these western colonists. *Courtesy, American Antiquarian Society.*

emigration. What prompted this transatlantic population shift? It was not always desperation or oppression. Many of those who arrived brought savings enough to finance their new life in the colonies. Some became indentured servants or **redemptioners** only to preserve those savings. While unemployment, poverty, the oppression of landlords, and crop failures *pushed* men and women out of Europe or Britain, it is also true that the availability of cheap land, a greater likelihood of religious freedom, and the chance to pursue a craft successfully *pulled* others toward the colonies.

Backcountry settlers were likely to face two enemies: Indians and the established political powers of their own colony. Often the clashes with the colonial government were about Indian policy. Eighteenth-century colonial legislatures and governors preferred diplomacy to military action, but western settlers wanted a more aggressive program to push Indians out of the way. Even when bloodshed occurred between settlers and Indians, the colonists of the coastal communities were reluctant to spend tax money to provide protection along the settlement line. In the end, bitter western settlers frequently took matters into their own hands. Bacon's Rebellion was the best example of this kind of vigilante action in the seventeenth century. The revolt by Pennsylvania's **Paxton Boys** was the most dramatic eighteenth-century episode.

More than most colonies, Pennsylvania's Quaker-dominated government encouraged settlers to find peaceful ways to coexist with local tribes. But the eighteenth-century Scots-Irish settlers did not share the Quaker commitment to pacifism. They demanded protection against Indian raids on isolated homesteads and small frontier towns. In 1763, frustrated settlers from Paxton, Pennsylvania, attacked a village of peaceful Conestoga Indians. Although the murder of these Indians solved nothing and could not be justified, hundreds of western colonists supported this vigilante group known as the Paxton Boys. The group marched on Philadelphia, the capital city of Pennsylvania, to press their demands for an aggressive Indian policy. With Philadelphia residents fearing their city would be attacked and looted, the popular printer and political leader Benjamin Franklin met the Paxton Boys on the outskirts of the city and negotiated a truce. The outcome was a dramatic shift in Pennsylvania Indian policy, illustrated by an offical bounty for Indian scalps.

Vigilante action, however, was not always connected to Indian conflicts. In South Carolina, trouble arose because coastal planters refused to provide basic government services to the backcountry. Settlers in western South Carolina paid their taxes, but their counties had no courts, so they had to travel long distances to register land sales or deeds or bring lawsuits for debt. The government provided no sheriffs either, and outlaws preyed on these communities. Because the coastal planters refused to admit any backcountry representatives to the colonial legislature, settlers could do little but petition and demand relief. In the 1760s, they took matters into their own hands, choosing to "regulate" back-

redemptioner An emigrant from Europe who completed payment for the voyage to America by a short period of servitude.

Paxton Boys Settlers from Paxton, Pennsylvania, who massacred Conestoga Indians in 1763 and then marched on Philadelphia to demand that the colonial government provide better defense against the Indians.

country affairs themselves through vigilante action. These **Regulators** pursued and punished backcountry outlaws, dispensing justice without the aid of courts or judges.

In North Carolina, a similar power struggle led to a brief civil war. Here, a Regulator movement was organized against legal "outlaws," a collection of corrupt local officials in the backcountry appointed because of their political connections to the colony's slaveholding elite. These officials awarded contracts for building roads and bridges to friends; charged exorbitant fees to register deeds, surveys, or even the sale of cattle; and set high poll taxes on voters. The North Carolina Regulators wanted these men removed, but the legislature ignored all their demands. The outcome was a taxpayers' rebellion. When tax collection stopped, the governor acted, raising a militia of twelve hundred men to march on the backcountry rebels. The showdown took place in 1771 near the Alamance River, where the governor's army easily defeated the two thousand poorly armed regulators. Six of the movement's leaders were then hanged. The brief east-west war ended in North Carolina, but the bitterness remained. During the Revolutionary War, when most of North Carolina's coastal elite cast their lot for independence, the farmers of the backcountry cast theirs with England.

Reason and Religion in Colonial Society

- What political and personal expectations arose from Enlightenment philosophy?
- What were the significant outcomes of the Great Awakening?

Trade routes tied the eighteenth-century colonial world to parent societies across the Atlantic. The bonds of language and custom tied the immigrant communities in America to their homelands too. In addition to these economic and cultural ties, the flow of ideas and religious beliefs helped sustain a transatlantic community.

The Impact of the Enlightenment

At the end of the seventeenth century, a new intellectual movement arose in Europe: the **Enlightenment.** Enlightenment thinkers argued that reason, or rational thinking, rather than divine revelation, tradition, intuition, or established authority, was the true path to reliable knowledge and to human progress. A group of brilliant French thinkers called **philosophes,** including Voltaire, Rousseau, Diderot, Buffon, and Montesquieu, were the central figures of the Enlightenment. These philosophers, political theorists, and scientists disagreed about many issues but embraced the belief that nature could provide for all human wants and that human nature was basically good rather than flawed by original sin. Humans, they insisted, were rational and capable of making progress toward a perfect society if they studied nature, unlocked its secrets, and carefully nurtured the best human qualities in their children. This belief in progress became a central Enlightenment theme.

The Enlightenment was the handiwork of a small, intensely intellectual elite in Europe, and only the colonial elite had access to the books and essays that these philosophers produced. Elite colonists were drawn to two aspects of Enlightenment thought: its new religious philosophy of **deism** and the political theory of the **social contract.**

Deism appealed to colonists such as the Philadelphia scientist, writer, and political leader Benjamin Franklin and Virginia planters George Washington and Thomas Jefferson, men who were intensely interested in science and the scientific method. Deists believed that the universe operates according to logical, natural laws, without divine intervention. They thus denied the existence of any miracles after the Creation and rejected the value of prayer in this rational universe.

The most widely accepted Enlightenment ideas in the colonies were those of the English political

Regulators Frontier settlers in the Carolinas who protested the lack or abuse of government services in their area; the North Carolina Regulators were suppressed by government militia in 1771.

Enlightenment An eighteenth-century intellectual movement that emphasized the pursuit of knowledge through reason and refused to accept ideas on the basis of religious belief or tradition alone.

philosophe Any of the popular French intellectuals or social philosophers of the Enlightenment, such as Diderot, Rousseau, or Voltaire.

deism The belief that God created the universe in such a way that no divine intervention was necessary for its continued operation.

social contract An agreement among members of an organized society, or between the government and the governed, that defines and limits the rights and duties of each.

theorist John Locke, who published his *Essay Concerning Human Understanding* in 1690 and *Two Treatises of Government* in 1691. In his political essays, Locke argued that human beings have certain natural rights that they can not alienate (give away) and that no one can take away from them. Those rights include the right to own themselves and their own labor and the right to own that part of nature on which they have labored productively—that is, property. However, in exchange for the government's protection of their natural rights to life, liberty, and property, people make a social contract to live under a rule of law and give up absolute freedom. According to Locke, the government created by the social contract receives its political power from the consent of those it governs, and it cannot claim a divine right to rule. In Locke's scheme, the people express their will, or their demands and interests, through a representative assembly, and the government is obligated to protect and respect the natural rights of its citizens and serve their interests. If the government fails to do this, Locke said, the people have a right, even a duty, to rebel. Locke's theory was especially convincing because it meshed with political developments in England from the Civil War to the Glorious Revolution that were familiar to the colonists.

Religion and Religious Institutions

Deism attracted little attention among ordinary colonists, but many eighteenth-century Americans were impressed by the growing religious diversity of their society. The waves of immigration had greatly increased the number of Protestant sects in the colonies, and colonists began to see religious toleration as a practical matter. The commitment to religious toleration did not come at an even pace, of course, and it did not extend to everyone. No colony allowed Catholics to vote or hold elective office, and even Maryland did not permit Catholics to worship openly until Catholics in the city of Baltimore broke the law and founded a church in 1763. Connecticut granted freedom of worship to "sober dissenters" such as Anglicans, Quakers, and Baptists as early as 1708, but in 1750 its legislature declared it a felony to deny the **Trinity.** Colonists did not mean the separation of church and state when they spoke of religious toleration. The tradition of an **established church,** supported by taxes from all members of a community regardless of where they worshiped, went unchallenged in the southern colonies, where Anglicanism was established, and in Massachusetts and Connecticut, where **Congregationalism** was established.

As the diversity in churches was growing, the number of colonists who did not regularly attend any church at all was growing too. Some colonists were more preoccupied with secular concerns, such as their place in the economic community, than with spiritual ones. Others were losing their devotion to churches where sermons were more intellectual than impassioned and the worship service was more formal than inspiring.

Into this moment stepped a group of **charismatic** preachers, men who denounced the obsession with profit and wealth they saw around them, condemned the sinfulness and depravity of all people, warned of the terrible punishments of eternal hell fires, and praised the saving grace of Jesus Christ. In a society divided by regional disputes and economic competition, these preachers held out a promise of social harmony based on the surrender of individual pride and a renewed love and fear of God. In voices filled with "Thunder and Lightning," they called for a revival of basic Calvinist belief.

The Great Awakening

The religious revival of the eighteenth century was based as much on a new approach to preaching as on the message itself. This new-style preaching first appeared in New Jersey and Pennsylvania in the 1720s, when two itinerant preachers—Theodore Frelinghuysen and William Tennant, Jr.—began denouncing the local churches for lack of devotion to God and for "cold" preaching. Tennant established what he called a "log college" to train fiery preachers who could spread a Christian revival throughout the colonies.

Trinity In Christian doctrine, the belief that three divine persons—Father, Son, and Holy Spirit—are united in one God.

established church The official church of a nation or colony, usually supported by tax revenues.

Congregationalism A form of Protestant church government in which each local congregation is independent and self-governing; in the colonies, the Puritans were Congregationalists.

charismatic Having a spiritual power or personal quality that stirs enthusiasm and devotion in large numbers of people.

♦ The Congregationalist minister, Jonathan Edwards, mesmerized church-goers of Northampton, Massachusetts with his sermons on the eternal punishments facing those who failed to seek and find salvation. His dire warnings, coupled with his urgent call for repentence, helped usher in the religious revival known as the Great Awakening. *Yale University Art Gallery, Bequest of Eugene Philips Edwards.*

In New England, the scholarly, brooding Congregationalist minister **Jonathan Edwards** introduced the revival from his pulpit in Northampton, Massachusetts, in 1734. Like Frelinghuysen and Tennant, Edwards condemned the lukewarm preaching of local ministers and then turned to the task of saving lost souls. He roused terror in his listeners with his vivid descriptions of human helplessness, God's displeasure, and the eternal agony of hell. In his most powerful sermon, "Sinners in the Hands of an Angry God," Edwards compared mortals to spiders, dangling by a fragile thread over the deadly fires of hell. The revival, or **Great Awakening,** sparked by men like Edwards and Tennant spread rapidly throughout the colonies, carried from town to town by wandering ministers sometimes called "Awakeners." These preachers stirred entire communities to renewed religious devotion.

The success of all these evangelists paled before the impact of the greatest Awakener, **George Whitefield.** Whitefield was actually not a Calvinist at all but an Anglican minister who was sympathetic to a new movement within his church called **Methodism.** In 1740, Whitefield came to the colonies to preach, on a tour that took him from Charleston to Maine. Everywhere the young preacher went, crowds gathered to hear him. Often the audience grew so large that the church could not hold everyone, and Whitefield finished his service in a nearby field or open space. His impact was electric. "Hearing him preach gave me a heart wound," wrote one colonist, and even America's most committed deist, Benjamin Franklin, confessed that Whitefield's sermons moved him. Whitefield himself recorded his effect on a crowd: "A wonderful power was in the room and with one accord they began to cry out and weep most bitterly for the space of half an hour." As the sermon progressed, the audience response became more intense: "Some of the people were as pale as death; others were wringing their hands; others lying on the ground; others sinking into the arms of their friends; and most lifting their eyes to heaven, and crying to God for mercy."

The Great Awakening did not go unchallenged. Some ministers had gladly turned over their pulpits to "Awakeners." But others, angered by the criticisms of their preaching and suggestions that they had not achieved true salvation, launched a counterattack against the revivalists and their "beastly brayings." Members of the colonial elite were roused to political action against a movement that constantly condemned worldly amusements such as dancing, gambling, drinking, theater, and elegant clothing. In Connecticut, for example, the assembly passed a law banning itinerant ministers from preaching outside their own parishes.

Bitter fights within congregations and **denominations** developed. "Old Light" Congregationalists up-

Jonathan Edwards Congregationalist minister whose sermons threatening sinners with damnation helped begin the Great Awakening.

Great Awakening Series of religious revivals, characterized by fiery preaching, that swept over the American colonies during the second quarter of the eighteenth century.

George Whitefield English evangelist in the Great Awakening who drew huge crowds during his preaching tours through the colonies.

Methodism Protestant church movement founded in England in the 1730s; Methodists stressed the importance of repentance and faith and the availability of salvation to all believers.

denomination A group of religious congregations that accept the same doctrines and are united under a single name.

held the established service, "New Lights" chose revivalism, and "Old Side" Presbyterians battled "New Sides" over preaching styles and the content of the worship service. Congregations split, and the minority groups hurriedly formed new churches. Many awakened believers left their own denominations entirely, joining the Baptists or the Methodists. Antirevivalists also left their strife-ridden churches and became Anglicans. These religious conflicts became intertwined with other, secular issues. Colonists who had long-standing disagreements over Indian policy or economic issues lined up on opposite sides of the Awakening. Class tensions influenced religious loyalties, as poor colonists expressed their hostility to their rich neighbors through the religious vocabulary that condemned luxury, dancing, and gambling.

Thus, rather than fulfilling its promise of social harmony, the Great Awakening increased strife and tension among colonists. Yet it had positive effects as well. For example, the Awakening spurred the growth of higher education. During the complicated theological arguments between Old Lights and Awakeners, the revivalists came to see the value of theological training. They founded new colleges, including Rutgers, Brown, Princeton, and Dartmouth, to prepare their clergy just as the Old Lights relied on Harvard and Yale to train theirs. One of the most important effects of the Great Awakening was also one of the least expected. The resistance to authority, the activism involved in creating new institutions, the participation in debate and argument—these experiences reinforced a sense that protest and resistance were acceptable, not just in religious matters but in the realm of politics as well.

Government and Politics in the Mainland Colonies

- What constrained a colonial governor's exercise of royal power?
- What was the outcome of the struggle for power between the colonial assemblies and the colonial governors?

The English mainland colonies were part of a large and complex empire, and the English government had many agencies that set or enforced imperial policy for them. Parliament passed laws regulating colonial affairs, the royal navy and army determined colonial defense, and English diplomats decided which foreign nations were friends and which were foes. But from the beginning, most proprietors, joint-stock companies, and kings had also found it convenient to create local governments within their colonies to handle day-to-day affairs. Virginia's House of Burgesses was the first locally elected legislative body in the colonies, but by 1700 all the mainland colonies boasted a representative assembly generally made up of the wealthiest men in the community.

In the first half of the eighteenth century, the British government decided to restructure its colonial administration, hoping to make it more efficient. Despite this reorganization, the government did not rigorously enforce many of the laws and regulations pertaining to the colonies. Even so, colonists often objected to the constraints imperial law placed on them and challenged the role of the king or the proprietors in shaping local political decisions. This resistance led to a long and steady struggle for power between colonial governors and colonial assemblies. Over the first half of the century, the colonists did wrest important powers from the governors. But the British government remained adamant that ultimate power, or **sovereignty,** rested in the hands of king and Parliament.

Imperial Institutions and Policies

In 1696, the British government's first step in reorganizing its colonial administration was to establish a board of trade, formally known as the Lords Commissioners of Trade and Plantations. The board's sixteen members were drawn from the King's Privy Council, or cabinet, and from a pool of civil servants who claimed some expertise in colonial affairs. On paper, the board had responsibility for most aspects of colonial administration, but in practice, its authority was far from absolute. In most matters, it was simply an advisory board, expected to observe, gather information, evaluate **policy,** and make recommendations to the many existing and entrenched offices and agencies. Despite the reorganization, authority thus remained divided. The treasury board, for example, continued to supervise all colonial financial affairs, and its customs office collected all trade revenues. The admiralty board, not the board of trade, had the authority to enforce trade regulations.

sovereignty The ultimate political power in a nation or a state.

policy A course of action adopted and pursued by a government or ruler.

The potential for conflict among all these departments, commissions, and agencies was great. But British indifference to colonial affairs helped to preserve harmony. Parliament set the tone for colonial administration in the eighteenth century with a policy of **salutary neglect.** Salutary, or healthy, neglect meant the relaxed enforcement of most regulations as long as the colonies remained loyal in military and economic matters. As long as colonial raw materials continued to flow into British hands and the colonists continued to rely on British manufactured goods, salutary neglect suited the expectations of the king, Parliament, and most government officials.

Salutary neglect did not mean that the colonists were free to do exactly as they pleased. Even in local, or domestic, matters the colonial governments could not operate as freely as many of them desired. The most intense political conflicts before the 1760s centered on the colonial assemblies' power to govern local affairs as they chose.

♦ This elegant residence was built for Virginia's Governor Alexander Spotswood in the early eighteenth century. Spotswood and his successors hoped that the Governor's Place would symbolize the majesty and power they represented as agents of the Crown. *Colonial Williamsburg Foundation.*

Local Colonial Government

The eighteenth-century mainland colonies remained a mixture of royal, proprietary, and **corporate colonies,** although the majority were held directly by the king. Whatever the form of ownership, however, the colonies were strikingly similar in the structure and operation of their governments. Each colony had a governor appointed by the king or the proprietor or, in Connecticut and Rhode Island (the two corporate colonies), elected to executive office. Each had a council, usually appointed by the governor, though sometimes elected by the assembly, which served as an advisory body to the governor. And each had an elected representative assembly with lawmaking and taxing powers.

The governor was the linchpin of local government because he represented imperial authority and imperial interests in the local setting. In theory, his powers were impressive. He alone could call the assembly into session, and he had the power to dismiss it. He also could veto any act passed by the assembly. He had the sole power to appoint and dismiss judges, justices of the peace, and all government officials. He could grant pardons and reprieves. The governor made all land grants, oversaw all aspects of colonial trade, and conducted diplomatic negotiations with the Indians. Because he was commander in chief of the military and naval forces of the colony, he decided what action, if any, to take in conflicts between colonists and Indians. Armed with such extensive powers, the man who sat in the English colonial governor's seat ought to have been respected—or at least obeyed.

A closer look, however, reveals that the governor was not so powerful after all. First, in many cases he was not free to exercise his own judgment because he was bound by a set of instructions written by the board of trade. Though highly detailed and specific, these instructions often bore little relation to the realities the governor encountered in his colony. Instead, they limited his ability to improvise and compromise and were a burden rather than an aid to many a frustrated governor.

Second, the governor's own skills and experience were often limited. Few men in the prime of their careers wanted to be sent 3,000 miles from England to the provinces. Thus governorships went

salutary neglect The British policy of relaxed enforcement of most colonial regulations as long as the mainland colonies remained a loyal and profitable segment of the British trade economy.

corporate colony A self-governing colony, not directly under the control of proprietors or the Crown.

to **bureaucrats** nearing the end of sometimes unimpressive careers or to younger men who were new to the rough-and-tumble games of politics. Many colonial governors were honorable and competent, but enough of them were fools, scoundrels, or eccentrics to give the office a poor reputation.

Finally, most governors served brief terms, sometimes too brief for them to learn which local issues were critical or to discover who their friends and enemies in the colonial government were. For many, the goal was simply to survive the ordeal. They were willing to surrender much of their authority to the local assembly in exchange for a calm, uneventful, and, they hoped, profitable term in office.

Even the most ignorant or incompetent governor might have managed to dominate colonial politics if he had the grease that oiled eighteenth-century political wheels: patronage. The kings of England had learned that political loyalty could be bought on the floor of Parliament with royal favors. By midcentury, over half of the members of Parliament held Crown offices or had received government contracts. Unfortunately for the colonial governor, he had few favors to hand out. The king could also bribe voters or intimidate them to ensure the election of his supporters to Parliament, but the governor did not have this option either. The number of eligible voters in most colonies was far too great for a governor's resources.

The greatest restraint on the governor's authority was not his rigid instructions, his inexperience, or his lack of patronage, but the fact that the assembly paid his salary. England expected the colonists to foot the bill for local government, including compensation for the governor. Governors who challenged the assembly too strongly or too often found that a sudden, unaccountable budget crisis was going to delay or diminish their salaries. Those who bent to assembly wishes could expect bonuses in the form of cash or grants of land.

While the governors learned that their great powers were less than they seemed, the assemblies in every colony learned how to broaden their own power. They fought for and won more freedom from the governor's supervision and influence, gaining the right to elect their own speaker of the assembly, make their own procedural rules, and settle contested elections. They also increased their power over taxation and the use of revenues or, in eighteenth-century parlance, their **power of the purse.**

In their pursuit of power, these local political leaders had several advantages besides the governor's weaknesses. They came from a small social and economic elite who were regularly elected to office for both practical and social reasons. First, they could satisfy the high property qualifications set for most officeholding. Second, they could afford to accept an office that cost more to win and to hold than its modest salary could cover. Third, a habit of **deference**—respect for the opinions and decisions of the more educated and wealthy families in a community—won them office. Although as many as 50 to 80 percent of adult free white males in a colony could vote, few were considered appropriate to hold office. Generations of fathers and sons from elite families thus dominated political offices. These men knew each other well, and although they fought among themselves for positions and for power, they could effectively unite against outsiders like a governor. Finally, their long careers in the legislature helped them hone the political and administrative abilities and skills at **oratory** that they needed in their battles with the governor.

Conflicting Views of the Assemblies

The king and Parliament gave local assemblies the authority to raise taxes, pay government salaries, direct the care of the poor, and see to the upkeep of bridges and roads. To the colonists, this division of authority indicated an acceptance of a two-tiered system of government: (1) a central government that created and executed imperial policy and (2) a set of local governments that managed colonial domestic affairs. If these levels of government were not equal in their power and scope, at least—in the minds of the colonists—they were equally legitimate. On both points, however, the British disagreed. They did not acknowledge a multilevel system. They saw a single vast empire ruled by one government consisting of king and Parliament. The colonial governments may have acquired the power to establish temporary operating procedures and to pass laws, but British lead-

bureaucrat A government official, usually nonelected, who is rigidly devoted to the details of administrative procedure.

power of the purse The political power enjoyed by the branch of government that controls taxation and the use of tax monies.

deference Yielding to the judgment or wishes of another person, usually seen as a social superior.

oratory Persuasive and eloquent speech.

ers did not believe they had acquired a share of the British government's sovereign power. As the governor of Pennsylvania put it in 1726, the assembly's actions and decisions should in "no ways interfere . . . with the Legal Prerogative of the Crown or the true Legislative Power of the Mother State." "True Legislative Power" belonged with Parliament, and most British political leaders considered the assemblies to be little more than **ad hoc** bodies, specially created to meet immediate needs and act like surrogates or deputies for those with real authority.

North America and the Struggle for Empire

- What did the Europeans and American Indians expect to gain from diplomacy and warfare in North America?
- What constraints did the imperial wars place on the American colonists?
- What outcomes of the French and Indian War affected people in North America?

During the seventeenth century, most of the violence and warfare in colonial America arose from struggles between Indians and colonists over land or from struggles among colonists over political power and the use of revenues and resources. By 1690, however, the most persistent dangers to colonial peace and safety came from the fierce rivalries among the French, Spanish, and the English. Between 1688 and 1763, these European powers waged five bloody and costly wars (see Table 4.1). Most of these wars were motivated by politics at home. Colonial ambitions spurred the last and most decisive of them. No matter where these worldwide wars began, or what their immediate cause, colonists were usually drawn into them.

France, England, and Spain had the same basic motives for empire building in the Americas: they sought access to profitable natural resources, and they wanted the increased prestige that an empire guaranteed. Their success was uneven. Spain surpassed its rivals in the search for wealth-producing natural resources, for neither the French fur trade nor the tobacco and rice production of the English colonies could match the wealth generated by gold, silver, and copper mining in Spanish America. In the Caribbean, all three nations managed to enjoy profits from sugar production. Only England was able to develop a valuable market for its manufactured goods in its colonies. The financial drain of governing and protecting colonies troubled each of these nations, yet they remained willing to go to war to protect or expand their empires (see Map 4.1).

When imperial wars included fighting in America, English colonists were expected to fight without the assistance of British troops. Often the enemy the colonists faced was neither French nor Spanish but Indian, because Indian tribes formed alliances with Europeans to advance their own interests. These wars left their mark on every generation of colonists, for periods of peace were short and the shadow of war hung over colonial society until Britain's major triumph in 1763.

Indian Alliances and Rivalries

From the earliest days of European mainland settlement, many Indian tribes had formed alliances with colonists to assist the newcomers, protect their own safety and advance their own interests, or defeat local rivals. The long alliance between Wampanoags and Pilgrims, for example, had ensured the survival of the struggling Plymouth Plantations and helped the tribe fend off attacks by enemy tribes. Although this alliance eventually unraveled, leading to the terrible destruction of King Philip's War, other seventeenth-century alignments remained intact. The Huron-dominated confederacy and the French continued to find the profits from the fur trade a powerful economic bond (see Map 4.2). The Hurons, like many eastern Indians, were also linked to their European ally by a growing dependence on European manufactured goods and weapons. The Iroquois Confederacy had a similar relationship with the English, who fully appreciated the strategic importance of Indian allies living south of the Great Lakes, along routes crucial to the fur trade. Intertribal competition over hunting grounds and longstanding animosities contributed to the strength of these alliances, for the Hurons and the Iroquoian Mohawks were bitter rivals.

In the South, the **Creek Confederacy** and the English found an alliance mutually beneficial. Colonists and Creeks established a trade in deerskins and in captive Indians, whom Creek war parties sold as

ad hoc Created for, or concerned with, one specific purpose.

Creek Confederacy A confederacy of the Creeks and smaller tribes living in the Southeast.

TABLE 4.1 Imperial and Colonial Wars

Name	Date	Participants	Treaty
In colonies: King William's War *In Europe:* War of the League of Augsburg	1688–1697	In *Europe:* France vs. England, Holland, Sweden, and Spain In *North America:* Colonists and their Iroquois allies vs. French and their Indian allies *Area:* New England and Northern New York	Treaty of Ryswick (1697) *Results* Port Royal in Acadia (Nova Scotia) is returned to France French is still a presence in North America
In colonies: Queen Anne's War *In Europe:* War of the Spanish Succession	1702–1713	In *Europe:* England, Holland, and Austria vs. France and Spain In *North America:* English colonists vs. French and Spanish powers in North and South and their Indian allies	Treaty of Utrecht (1713) *Results* France renounces plans to unite with Spain under one crown England gains Caribbean Islands, St. Kitts, Gibraltar, and Minorca English flag flies over Nova Scotia, New Foundland, and Hudson Bay War takes a financial toll on the colonies
War of Jenkins Ear	1739–1740	In *Europe:* England vs. Spain In *North America:* English colonists clash with Spanish in interior regions (Georgia, South Carolina, Virginia)	None—Conflict expands into King George's War
In colonies: King George's War *In Europe:* War of the Austrian Succession	1740–1748	In *Europe:* Austria and England vs. Prussia, France, and Spain In *North America:* English colonists in New England vs. French and their Indian allies	Treaty of Aix-la-Chapelle *Results* England returns Louisbourg to French in exchange for Madras (in India)
In colonies: French and Indian War *In Europe:* Seven Years War	1756–1763	In *Europe:* England and Prussia vs. France and Austria In *North America:* English colonists vs. French and their Indian allies *Area:* Global war; in colonies, all regions	Treaty of Paris *Results* French Empire shrivels France's presence in North America is greatly reduced France loses trading posts in Africa and exits India Britain takes Florida from Spain and Canada from France France gives up Louisiana to Spain as compensation for Florida British government is deeply in debt The borders of Britain's North American colonies are secured

slaves to the South Carolina planters. This alliance grew firmer in the eighteenth century when Creek military forces joined the English in an attack on Spanish Florida and Creek patrols captured runaway slaves for rice planters. The Creeks, along with the Yamassees of Georgia, also helped the English defeat the Tuscaroras in 1711. But this alliance broke down as land-hungry colonists invaded Creek lands. In 1715, southern colonists made war on both the Creeks and the Yamassees. The defeated Creeks fled west, and the Yamassees went south to align themselves with the Spanish in Florida.

English relationships with the Indians were never as solid as French, largely because of English

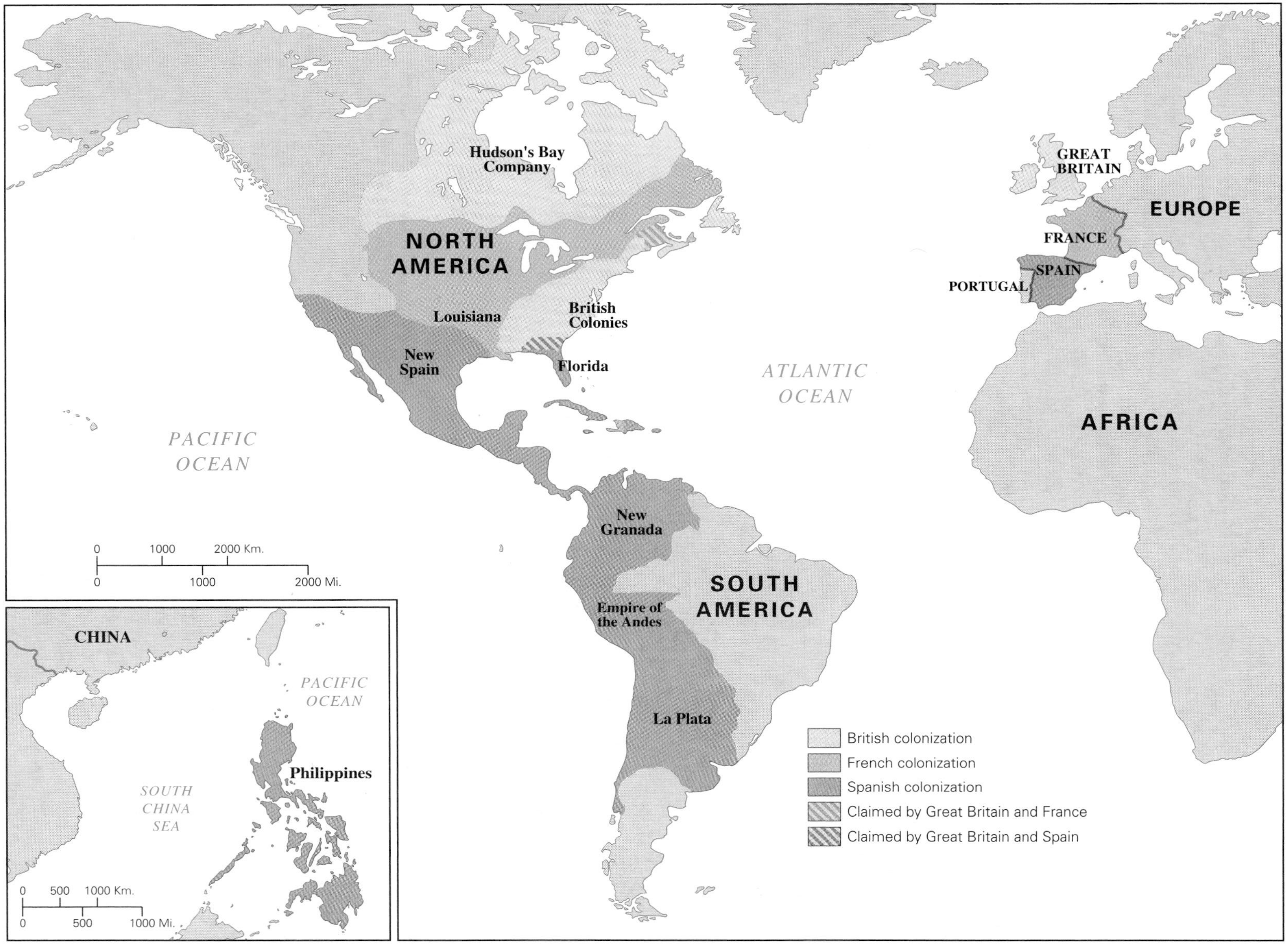

♦ **MAP 4.1 The European Empires in Eighteenth-Century America** This map shows the colonization of the Americas and the Philippines by three rival powers. It is clear from the map why British colonists felt vulnerable to attack by England's archenemies, France and Spain, until English victory in the Great War for Empire in 1763.

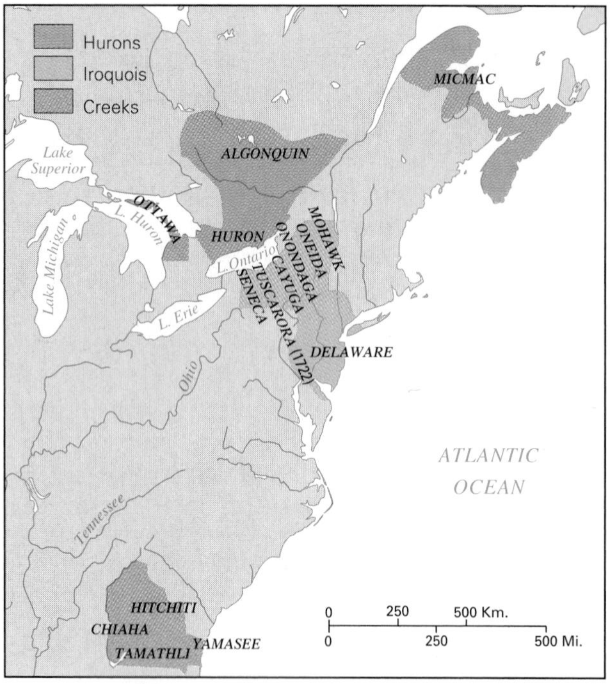

♦ **MAP 4.2 The Indian Confederacies** This map shows the three major Indian military and political coalitions—the Huron, Iroquois, and Creek confederacies. Unlike the squabbling English mainland colonies, these Indian tribes understood the value of military unity in the face of threats to their land and their safety and the importance of diplomatic unity in negotiating with their European allies.

colonists' demand for land in Indian territories. When imperial rivalries led to warfare, southern tribes often took up arms against the English, not in support of the French or the Spanish but to recover or protect their own lands. In the North, the English could not automatically count on their Iroquois allies for military support. At critical moments, the Iroquois pursued an independent strategy of neutrality until they perceived some concrete economic or territorial advantages in fighting with the English.

An Age of Imperial Warfare

In 1689, shortly after William and Mary took the throne, war broke out in Europe. This war pitted France, which had risen to fill the power vacuum left by the decline of Spain, against England, Holland, Sweden, and Spain, which had formed a temporary alliance to block French expansionism. In Europe the war was known as the War of the League of Augsburg, but colonists called it King William's War. In America, the enemy's stronghold was north and northwest of the British colonies, and thus New England and northern New York bore the brunt of the conflict. Despite the dangers, especially to the border settlements, Britain sent no troops to protect the exposed colonies. Colonial armies and their Iroquois allies were to defend British interests in America. The French government expected the same of its colonists, but the raw militiamen who made up colonial forces, many of them poor or unemployed, were ill suited for battle.

The war in America was both long and vicious, marked by massacres and atrocities. Following the French slaughter of surrendering men, women, and children at Fort Loyal (Portland), Maine, the governments of Massachusetts, Plymouth, Connecticut, and New York made a rare attempt at cooperation. They pledged to combine their resources in order to invade Canada. In the end, however, few made good on their promises of men or money, and colonial attacks on Montreal and Quebec both failed.

For several years after the failure at Quebec, the war degenerated into a chilling series of frontier raids, particularly in Maine, New Hampshire, and northern New York. In 1696, the French began a major offensive, but the threat of further destruction was cut short when European diplomats negotiated the Treaty of Ryswick in 1697. Peace returned to the colonies, but the legacy of war was apparent throughout New England and northern New York. At least 650 colonists had died in battle, in raids, or in captivity. The death toll for the Iroquois Confederacy was higher—between 600 and 1300. The lessons of the war were equally apparent. First, colonists paid a high price for their disunity and lack of cooperation. Second, no New Englander could ever feel secure until the French had been driven out of Canada. Third, the colonists could not drive the French away without the aid of the English army and navy.

The peace established at Ryswick did not last long. In 1702, the French king's scheme to unite Spain and France under a single ruler led the new English queen to declare war once again. In this eleven-year struggle, known as the War of the Spanish Succession in Europe and as Queen Anne's War in the colonies, England, Holland, and Austria fought against France and Spain. In America, this meant that the English colonists faced enemies to their south as well as on their northern borders.

Once again, England expected the colonists to wage their own war. Much of the military energy in the South was directed at crushing Indian opposition. In this, the colonists enjoyed some success. The most brutal fighting in this region came in the final years of the war as part of a secondary struggle between land-hungry North Carolinians and enraged Tuscarora Indians. Between 1711 and 1713, casualties in this Tuscarora War were staggering. Some 150 settlers were killed in the opening hours of the war, and in the following months news of atrocities on both sides spread. Stakes were run through the bodies of women, children were murdered, and Indian captives were roasted alive. South Carolina and Virginia sent arms and supplies to aid the North Carolina colonists, and the Creek and Yamassee Indians fought beside the white settlers against the Tuscaroras. When this war within a war ended in 1713, more than a thousand Tuscaroras were dead and nearly four hundred had been sold into slavery. The survivors took refuge in the land of the Iroquois.

The war in the North began on the New England frontier. In February 1704, Indian allies of the French attacked the town of Deerfield, Massachusetts, killing many of its residents and taking others into captivity. Massachusetts tried to strike back, but an expedition against French fortifications at Port Royal, Nova Scotia, retreated homeward without attacking.

As the war dragged on, colonists called repeatedly for the assistance of British troops to defend their borders. Early in 1709, the board of trade promised both a fleet and an army to mount the much-needed offensive against Canada. Neither arrived. Disappointed New Englanders raised an army of nearly thirty-five hundred men and moved against Port Royal once again. This time they did not retreat. In October 1710, the colonists triumphantly took control of Port Royal and with it all of Nova Scotia.

In 1713, the Treaty of Utrecht ended the eleven-year war. The results were mixed. France was far from defeated but renounced all plans to join France and Spain under one crown. England gained the Caribbean Island of St. Kitts, and the islands of Gibraltar and Minorca, off the European coast. More importantly for the New Englanders, the English flag now flew over Nova Scotia, Newfoundland, and Hudson Bay. Maine settlers could expect relief from enemy raids. New England fishermen could fish the banks of Newfoundland more safely. And colonial fur traders could profit from Hudson Bay's resources. Still, this war had cost New Englanders dearly. The high death toll combined with the deaths in King William's War was staggering: nearly one of every four soldiers in uniform had died. The financial cost was equally high. Four-fifths of Massachusetts' revenues in 1704–1705 went for military expenses. Homeowners in Boston saw their taxes rise 42 percent between 1700 and 1713. The city's streets were filled with beggars and its homes with widows. In Connecticut and Massachusetts, colonists spoke bitterly of the Mother Country's failure to protect them.

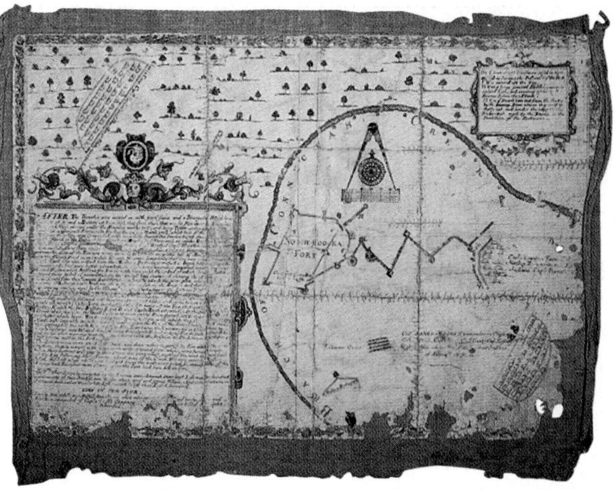

♦ Imperial wars between England and her rivals often drew the colonists and neighboring Indian tribes into conflict. Between 1711 and 1713, land-hungry North Carolinians, joined by South Carolina and Virginia militias and by Creek and Yamassee troops, turned Queen Anne's War into a brutal and successful war on the nearby Tuscarora Indians. *South Carolina Historical Society.*

For a generation following the Utrecht treaty, Europeans kept the peace. In America, however, violence continued along the line of settlement, as the colonists tried to weaken Indian support for the Spanish and French or assert their claims to Indian lands. In Massachusetts, colonists battled the French-allied Abenakis from 1722 to 1726 in what came to be called Dummer's War. In the South, colonists made war against their former allies, the Yamassees in 1715. The short but ferociously fought Yamassee War left four hundred of South Carolina's five thousand colonists dead in the first twelve months of fighting, a higher death rate than white Massachusetts had sustained in King Philip's War. Although the Yamassees fled to Florida in 1716, Carolina's backcountry was not secure. Yamassees, Creeks, and runaway slaves continued to launch raids against settlements there for many years.

By the end of the 1730s, anti-Spanish sentiment flared again in Britain, prompted by sea captain Robert Jenkins's claim that a Spanish official had lopped off his ear (which he freely displayed, carrying it around for seven years). By October 1739, Europeans were at war again. In the ensuing War of Jenkins Ear, the colonies did not come under direct attack. In 1740, however, hostilities between Spain and England were absorbed into a larger war in which Prussia, Spain, and France battled Austria and England. This war, known in the colonies as King George's War, again meant enemy attacks on both the northern and southern colonies. New Englanders, riding the crest of the religious revival, known as the Great Awakening, viewed the war as a Protestant crusade against Catholicism, a holy war designed to rid the continent of religious enemies. When a New England force captured the French stronghold of Louisbourg on Cape Breton Island in 1745, they exalted at their victory. They were crushed, however, when England returned Louisbourg to France in the Treaty of Aix-la-Chapelle, which ended the war.

In both Queen Anne's War and King George's War, the colonists relied on volunteer armies rather than militiamen. Hatred of the Catholic French spurred some of these volunteers, but cash bounties for enlistment and the promise of plunder spurred many others. Such rewards paled, however, once these soldiers reached the battlefields, where the screams of the wounded and dying, the mangled bodies of friends and neighbors, and the sound of cannon or of muskets overwhelmed participants on both sides. Death off the battlefield was common too, for disease swept through the army camps, killing more soldiers than battle. Yet veterans of these wars, and their civilian supporters, generally thought of the colonial armies as excellent military forces—forces that could defeat Indian enemies and capture important French forts without any aid from British regulars.

The Great War for Empire

Despite the pride colonists took in the defense of their communities, many remained angry and bewildered by the mother country's military neglect. From their perspective, they were being dragged into European wars that did not concern them. Then in 1756, colonial westward expansion triggered a great war for empire, referred to in Europe as the Seven Years War and in the colonies as the French and Indian War.

The problem began in the 1740s, as the neutral zone between the French colonial empire and the British mainland settlements began to shrink. As thousands of new immigrants poured into the English colonies, the colonists pressed farther westward, toward the Ohio Valley. Virginia land speculators began to woo the Indians of the region with trading agreements. The English colonial interest in the valley alarmed the French and threatened to interfere with their own plans for the region. They hoped to unite their mainland empire, connecting Canada and Louisiana with a chain of forts, trading posts, and missions across the Ohio Valley.

The growing military presence of the French troubled Virginia's governor, Robert Dinwiddie, who urged the British government to take notice of the potential crisis developing thousands of miles away from London. In 1754, Britain approved Dinwiddie's plan to send an expedition to assess French strength and warn the French to abandon a new fort on French Creek. Dinwiddie chose an inexperienced Virginia planter and colonial militia officer, Major George Washington, to lead the expedition. When Washington conveyed the warning, the French commander responded with insulting sarcasm. Tensions escalated rapidly. Dinwiddie later sent Major Washington to challenge the French at Fort Duquesne, near present-day Pittsburgh, but the French forced him to surrender.

Fearing another war, colonial political leaders decided to act decisively—and to attempt cooperation. In June 1754, seven colonies sent representatives to Albany, New York, to organize a united defense. Unfortunately this effort at cooperation failed. When the **Albany Plan of Union** was presented to the colonial assemblies, none was willing to approve it. Instead, American colonists looked to Britain to act. This time, Britain did. Parliament sent Major General Edward Braddock, a battle-hardened veteran, to drive the French out of Fort Duquesne. Braddock's humiliating failure was only the first of many for the English in America.

English and French forces engaged each other in battle four times before war was officially declared in 1756. Soon, every major European power was involved and the fighting spread rapidly across Europe, the Philippines, Africa, India, the Caribbean, and North America. In America, France's Indian allies joined the war more readily than England's. Iro-

Albany Plan of Union A proposal that the colonies form a union with a representative government and an army; Benjamin Franklin drafted it in 1754, but the colonies never adopted it.

♦ Louisbourg was an imposing fortress capital on Nova Scotia, almost six hundred miles northeast of Boston. In May of 1745, during King George's War, Massachusetts merchant William Pepperrell led four thousand New England volunteers in a successful campaign to seize Louisbourg from the French. The New Englanders hailed their victory as a Protestant triumph over Catholicism and were stunned when Britain returned the city to the enemy at war's end. *Yale University Art Gallery, Mable Brady Garven Collection.*

quois tribes opted for neutrality, waiting until 1759 to throw in their lot with the English. Although Mohawks were willing to fight as mercenaries in New York and Iroquois in western Pennsylvania were willing to suppress Delaware attacks on English colonists there, some members of the Iroquois Confederacy, including the Senecas, fought with the French in 1757 and 1758. The British made repeated efforts to win a commitment of troops from the Iroquois tribes, offering gifts and more favorable trade terms in exchange for military support. But the Iroquois strategy reflected French domination of the fighting in America during the early years of the war. A British defeat seemed likely. In the South, the Cherokees played the French and English against each other whenever possible in an effort to win better trading prices from each. About 250 Cherokee warriors did sign up to fight with the Virginia militia in 1757, but as mercenaries rather than allies. Although negotiations dragged on between the English agents and the Cherokee chiefs, skirmishes between the Indians and backcountry settlers kept tensions high. By 1760, a full-scale war between colonists and Cherokees had erupted in the southern colonies. Although the Cherokee Rebellion of 1759–1761 ended in Indian defeat, the war drained off many of the southern colonial resources that might have been used against the French.

French inroads into English territories continued throughout the opening years of the war. By the end of 1757, western and central New York were in French hands, Albany was threatened, and western New England was in jeopardy. In the winter of 1756, as news of defeats and of atrocities continued to pour in, the English government turned over the direction of the war to the ardent imperialist William Pitt. More than willing to take drastic steps, Pitt committed the British treasury to the largest war expenditures the nation had ever known and then put together the largest military force that North America had ever seen, combining 25,000 colonial troops with 24,000 British regular army soldiers. The fortunes of war soon reversed. In July 1758, Louisbourg was once again in English hands. By the end of 1759, the upper Ohio Valley had been taken from the French. And in August of that year, General James Wolfe took the war to the heart of French Canada: the fortress city of Quebec.

With his piercing eyes and his long red hair, Wolfe looked the part of the military hero he was. Only 31 years old, he had already seen eighteen years of military service. Still, even he was daunted by the difficult task ahead of him. Quebec, heavily manned and well armed, sat on top of steep cliffs rising high above the St. Lawrence River. Inside, the formidable French general Louis-Joseph Montcalm was in command. The only possible approach was from the west of the city, across the Plains of Abraham. The problem was how to get to the plain itself.

Wolfe was uncharacteristically hesitant until he discovered a blockaded roadway running to the top of the 175-foot cliff. On the evening of September 12, forty-five hundred British soldiers climbed this diagonal path to the top. When the thoroughly surprised Montcalm saw a double line of scarlet uniforms forming on the plain, he gathered a force of more than four thousand and marched out to meet the British. The French fired several rounds, but Wolfe ordered his men to hold their fire until the enemy was within 60 yards. Then the redcoats fired, and the French turned and ran. Among the British wounded was General James Wolfe, shot through the chest. Hearing that the French were in retreat, the dying general murmured, "Now, God be

♦ For most Americans, the English victory in the Battle of Quebec was the most dramatic event of the Seven Years War. When Benjamin West painted "The Death of General Wolfe," he acknowledged the role Indian allies had played on both sides of this imperial struggle by adding an Indian observer to the scene. *National Gallery of Canada, Ottawa.*

praised, I will die in peace." Among the French casualties was Louis-Joseph, Marquis de Montcalm, who died the following day from internal injuries caused by a musket ball to his midsection.

Five days after the Battle of the Plains of Abraham, Quebec formally surrendered. In 1760, the city of Montreal also fell to the British. With that, the French governor surrendered the whole of New France to his enemies, and the war in North America was over. The fighting in this most global of eighteenth-century wars continued elsewhere until 1763. Spain entered the struggle as a French ally in 1761, but English victories in India, the Caribbean, and the Pacific squelched any hopes the French had. The **Treaty of Paris** established the supremacy of the British Empire.

The Outcomes of the Great War for Empire

The war had redrawn the map of the world. The French Empire had shriveled, with nothing remaining of New France but two tiny islands between Nova Scotia and Newfoundland. Six thousand Acadians, French colonists of Nova Scotia, were refugees of the war, deported from their homes by the English because their loyalty was suspect. These Acadians, who relocated to France or made the exhausting trek to French-speaking Louisiana, were living reminders of the French Empire's eclipse. The only other remnants of the French Empire in the Western Hemisphere were the sugar islands of Guadeloupe, Martinique, and St. Domingue, left to France because England's sugar interest wanted no further competition in the British market. Across the ocean, France lost trading posts in Africa, and on the other side of the world, the French presence in India vanished.

The 1763 peace treaty dismantled the French Empire but did not destroy France itself. Although the nation's treasury was empty, its borders were intact. France's alliance with Spain held firm, cemented by the experience of defeat. Britain was victorious, but victory did not mean Britain had escaped unharmed. The British government was deeply in debt and faced new problems associated with managing and protecting its greatly enlarged empire.

In the mainland colonies, people lit bonfires and staged parades to celebrate Britain's victory and the safety of their own borders. But the tension of being both members of a colonial society and citizens of a great empire could not be easily dismissed. The war left scars, including memories of the British military's arrogance toward provincial soldiers and lingering resentment over the quartering of British soldiers at colonial expense. The colonists were aware that the British had grounds for resentment also, particularly the profitable trade Americans had carried on with the enemy even in the midst of the war. Suspicion and resentment, a growing sense of difference, a tug of loyalties between the local community and the larger empire—these were the unexpected outcomes of a glorious victory.

Treaty of Paris Treaty that ended the French and Indian War in 1763; it gave all of French Canada and Spanish Florida to Britain.

SUMMARY

Expectations
Constraints
Choices
Outcomes

Each of the colonial regions developed its own unique culture and society. Each region was directly connected to Britain by a well-established pattern of trade, but trade also connected them to one another. The colonies were often at odds with each other, yet they sometimes *chose* to unite against common enemies.

The social and cultural diversity among the colonies developed within a common imperial structure. In many regions, society changed significantly in the eighteenth century. In New England, the *outcome* of increased commercial activity and a royal government was a shift from a "Puritan" culture to a more secular "Yankee" culture. In the South, the planter elite continued to focus on the production of staple crops, but planters *chose* to shift from a labor force of indentured servants to a labor force of African slaves. By midcentury, these enslaved Africans had begun to develop their own community life and their own African-American culture. The Middle Colonies developed a lively urban culture, but most people who immigrated to British North America after 1700 *chose* to settle in the backcountry. Here opportunity was greater, although conflict with Native Americans was a common *constraint*.

Intellectual life in the eighteenth century changed dramatically as Enlightenment ideas encouraged the *expectation* of progress through reliance on reason. Colonial elites *chose* to adopt John Locke's theory of natural rights as well as a skepticism about religious dogmas. The Great Awakening revealed a second, and opposing intellectual current. Revivalist George Whitefield and other evangelical ministers carried the religious revival throughout the colonies. "Awakeners" *expected* to challenge all authority except the individual spirit, and many colonists *chose* to embrace the same beliefs.

A similar challenge to authority spread to politics and imperial relations. England *chose* a policy of salutary neglect in governing the colonies, yet colonial assemblies felt *constrained* by royal officials and *chose* to assert their own claim to power against appointed governors and other British officials. Strains in the relationship between colonial assemblies and imperial officers ran deep.

In the eighteenth century, intense rivalry among England, France, and Spain led to five major wars between 1688 and 1763. Colonists were *expected* to defend their own borders in most of these wars. In the French and Indian War, however, the British *chose* to play an active role in driving the French out of mainland America. British victory in 1763 altered the colonial map of North America and changed power relations in the European world.

SUGGESTED READINGS

Richard Hofstadter. *America at 1750: A Social Portrait* (1971).

This highly accessible work includes chapters on indentured servitude, the slave trade, the middle-class world of the colonies, the Great Awakening, and population growth and immigration patterns.

Bernard Bailyn. *Voyagers to the West: A Passage in the Peopling of America on the Eve of the Revolution* (1986).

Bailyn won a Pulitzer Prize for this survey of the character of, and motives for, emigration from the British Isles to America during the eighteenth century.

Ian Kenneth Steele. *"Betrayals," Fort William Henry and the Massacre* (1980).

Dramatized in James Fenimore Cooper's popular novel *The Last of the Mohicans,* this horrific attack on the garrison of a New York frontier outpost, after its surrender, was carried out by Indian allies of the French. Steele finds the roots of the massacre in radically different European and Indian concepts of warfare and victory.

Thomas A. Lewis. *For King and Country: The Maturing of George Washington, 1748–1760* (1993).

This look at the early career of George Washington follows him as a colonial soldier of the Crown, a Virginia planter, and a young man of ambition.

KEY EVENTS IN THE PREREVOLUTIONARY ERA In the 1760s and 1770s, American colonists organized political opposition to British policies and cooperated in economic protest against new taxes. They also participated in crowd demonstrations that led to acts of violence. This map indicates the major events leading to the declaration of American independence.

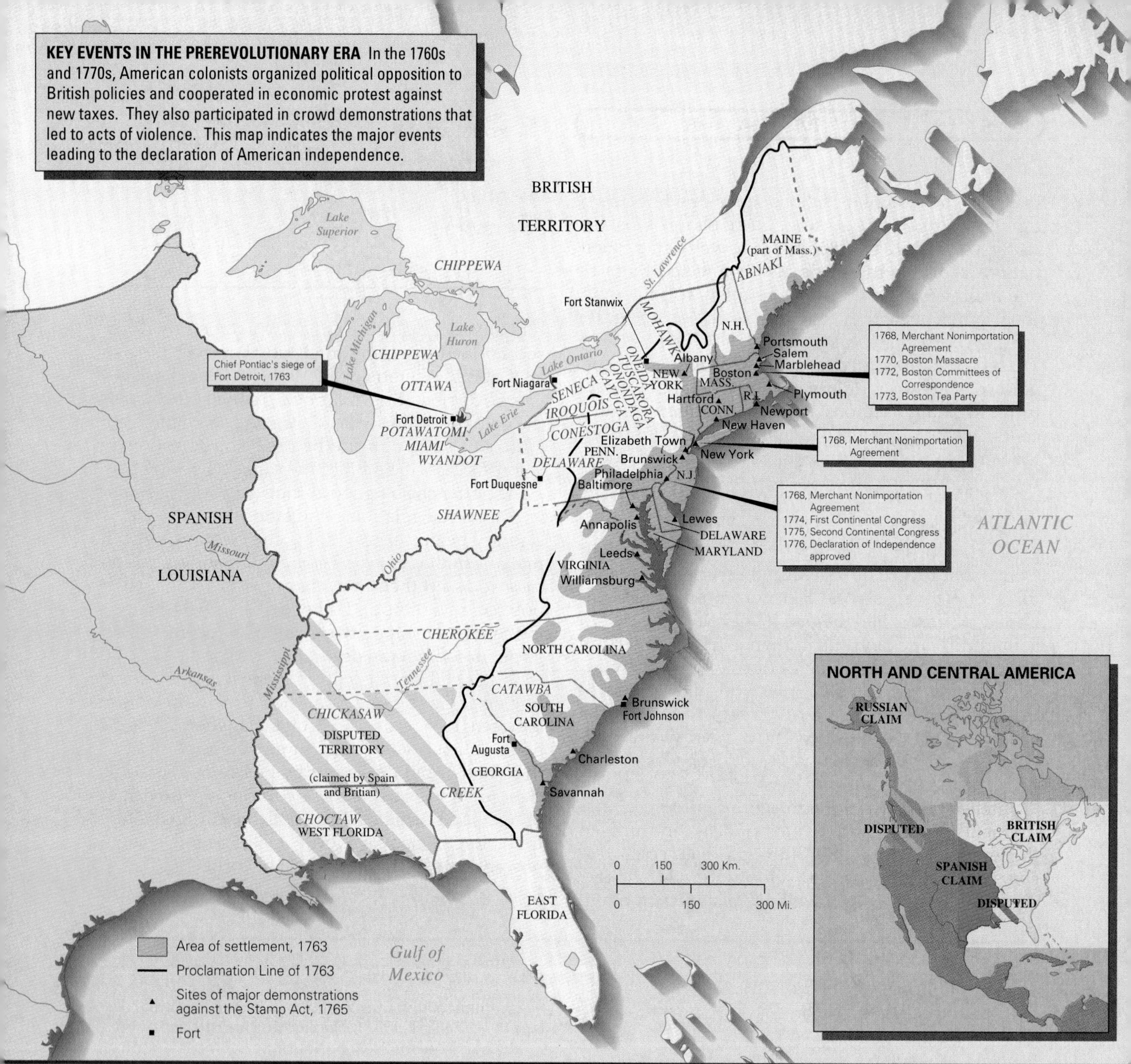

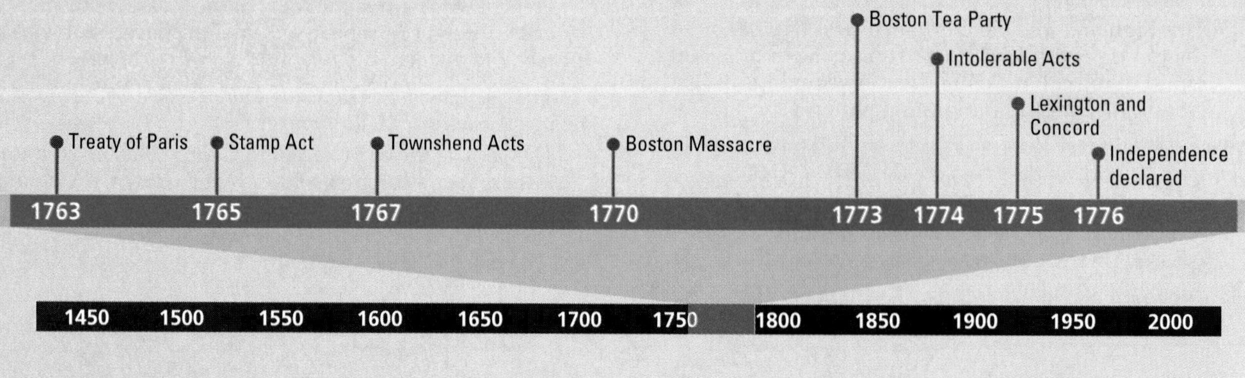

CHAPTER 5

Deciding Where Loyalties Lie, 1763–1776

Victory's New Problems

- Why did George Grenville expect the colonists to accept part of the burden of financing the British Empire in 1764?
- Why were the colonists alarmed by Grenville's choice to impose a stamp tax in 1765?
- How did the colonists choose to protest against taxation by Parliament?

Asserting American Rights

- Why did Charles Townshend expect his revenue-raising measures to be successful?
- What forms of resistance did the colonists choose to force the repeal of Townshend's measures?
- What were the outcomes of colonial resistance?

The Crisis Renewed

- What British choices led Americans to see a plot against their rights and liberties?
- What constraints did the king place on Massachusetts to crush resistance there?
- How did the Continental Congress choose to respond?

The Decision for Independence

- Could the Revolutionary War have been avoided?
- What choices on both sides might have kept compromise alive?
- What different expectations and constraints influenced some colonial groups to become loyalists and others to become patriots?

INTRODUCTION

The British victory over France in 1763 raised *expectations* in England and in the colonies for an era of economic growth, westward settlement, and a spirit of cooperation between Mother Country and colonies that would continue "for Ages to come." Perhaps no expectation of harmony and good will ever suffered such crushing blows as this one, however. Less than two years after the Treaty of Paris ended the war, England's mainland colonists had risen in protest against the *constraints* placed on them by British Indian policy and British trade regulations. In the thirteen strife-filled years that followed, the colonists and the British government discovered fundamental political differences existed between them. They found that they did not agree over the meaning of representative government or the proper division of power between Parliament and the local elected assemblies. They realized that they did not agree on what the empire's best interests were either. Although English officials thought that curtailing westward settlement would prevent costly Indian wars, American colonists believed westward settlement would provide economic opportunity for loyal citizens. The British government and the colonists also disagreed on what obligations the colonists shared with men and women in England. The British insisted that the Americans ought to help pay the costs of maintaining the empire, but the colonists believed that this was the duty of those who remained in the Mother Country. By the 1770s, Americans who had once toasted the king and the empire drank instead to liberty and to resistance to tyrants. By 1775, a new *choice* faced the colonists: loyalty or rebellion.

E xpectations
C onstraints
C hoices
O utcomes

The American Revolution was the *outcome* of the troubled years between 1763 and 1775. However, the colonists who *chose* to protest taxation by the British government in 1765 and 1767, or oppose the creation of courts without jury trials, or resent the presence of troops in their towns in peacetime did not know they were laying the groundwork for a revolution. We can look back on their expectations, constraints, and choices and see that the likely outcome was a break with England. But the people who made that revolution did not know it was coming, nor did they plan it.

Events between 1763 and 1776 forced the colonists to *choose* between two versions of patriotism—loyalty to the king or loyalty to colonial independence—and between two visions of the future—as members of a great and powerful empire or as citizens of a struggling new nation. These events also forced Indians and African American slaves to *choose* an alliance with England or with the rebels. The war that resulted set neighbor against neighbor, father against son, wife against husband, and slave against master. For thousands, the outcome of this crisis of loyalty was exile from home and family. For others, it meant death or injury on the battlefield, widowhood, or life as an orphan. In 1776, however, the *outcome* was unclear.

Victory's New Problems

- Why did George Grenville expect the colonists to accept part of the burden of financing the British Empire in 1764?
- Why were the colonists alarmed by Grenville's choice to impose a stamp tax in 1765?
- How did the colonists choose to protest against taxation by Parliament?

In the midst of the French and Indian War King George II died in his bed. Loyal subjects mourned the old king and in 1760 crowned his young grandson **George III.** At 22, the new monarch was hardworking but highly self-critical, and he was already showing the symptoms of an illness that produced **delusions** and severe depression. Although he was inexperienced in matters of state, George III meant

George III King of England (r. 1760–1820); his government's policies produced colonial discontent that led to the American Revolution in 1776.

delusion A false belief strongly held in spite of evidence to the contrary.

CHRONOLOGY

Loyalty or Rebellion?

1763	Treaty of Paris ends French and Indian War Pontiac's Rebellion Proclamation Line
1764	Sugar Act
1765	Stamp Act Sons of Liberty organized Stamp Act Congress Nonimportation of British goods
1766	Repeal of the Stamp Act Declaratory Act
1767	Townshend Acts John Dickinson's *Letters from a Farmer in Pennsylvania*
1768	Nonimportation of British goods Massachusetts circular letter
1770	Boston Massacre Repeal of the Townshend Acts
1772	Burning of the *Gaspée*
1773	Tea Act Boston Tea Party
1774	Intolerable Acts First Continental Congress The Continental Association Declaration of Rights and Grievances Suffolk Resolves
1775	Battles of Lexington and Concord Second Continental Congress Olive Branch Petition Declaration of the Causes and Necessity of Taking Up Arms
1776	Tom Paine's *Common Sense* Declaration of Independence

to rule—even if he had to deal with politicians, whom he distrusted, and engage in politics, which he disliked.

George III had hoped to work with and be guided by his old tutor and adviser, the earl of Bute, whom he appointed **prime minister.** But the earl was so widely disliked that the king had to replace him with **George Grenville.** It fell to Grenville, therefore, to handle the two most pressing postwar tasks: negotiating England's victory treaty with France and its allies and designing Britain's peacetime policies.

Grenville's diplomats met with little resistance at the negotiating table. France was defeated, and it was up to the British government to decide what the spoils of war would be. England could take possession of a French Caribbean sugar island or the French mainland territory of Canada, a vast region stretching north and northwest of the English colonies. English sugar planters raised loud objections to the first option, for another sugar island would mean new competitors in the profitable English sugar markets. There was strong support, however, for adding Canada (see Map 5.1). Doing so would ensure the safety of the mainland colonies, whose people were increasingly important as consumers of English-made goods. With Canada, too, would come the rich fishing banks off the Newfoundland coast and the fertile lands of the Ohio Valley. Such arguments in favor of Canada carried the day. By the end of 1763, George III could look with pride on an empire that had grown in physical size, on a nation that dominated the markets of Europe, and on a navy that ruled the seas.

Unfortunately, victory also brought new problems. Above all, the new English glory did not come cheaply. To win the war, William Pitt had spent vast sums of money, leaving the new king with an enor-

prime minister The chief minister of a ruler or a nation, usually responsible for setting government policy.

George Grenville British prime minister who sought to tighten British controls over the colonies and impose taxes to raise revenues.

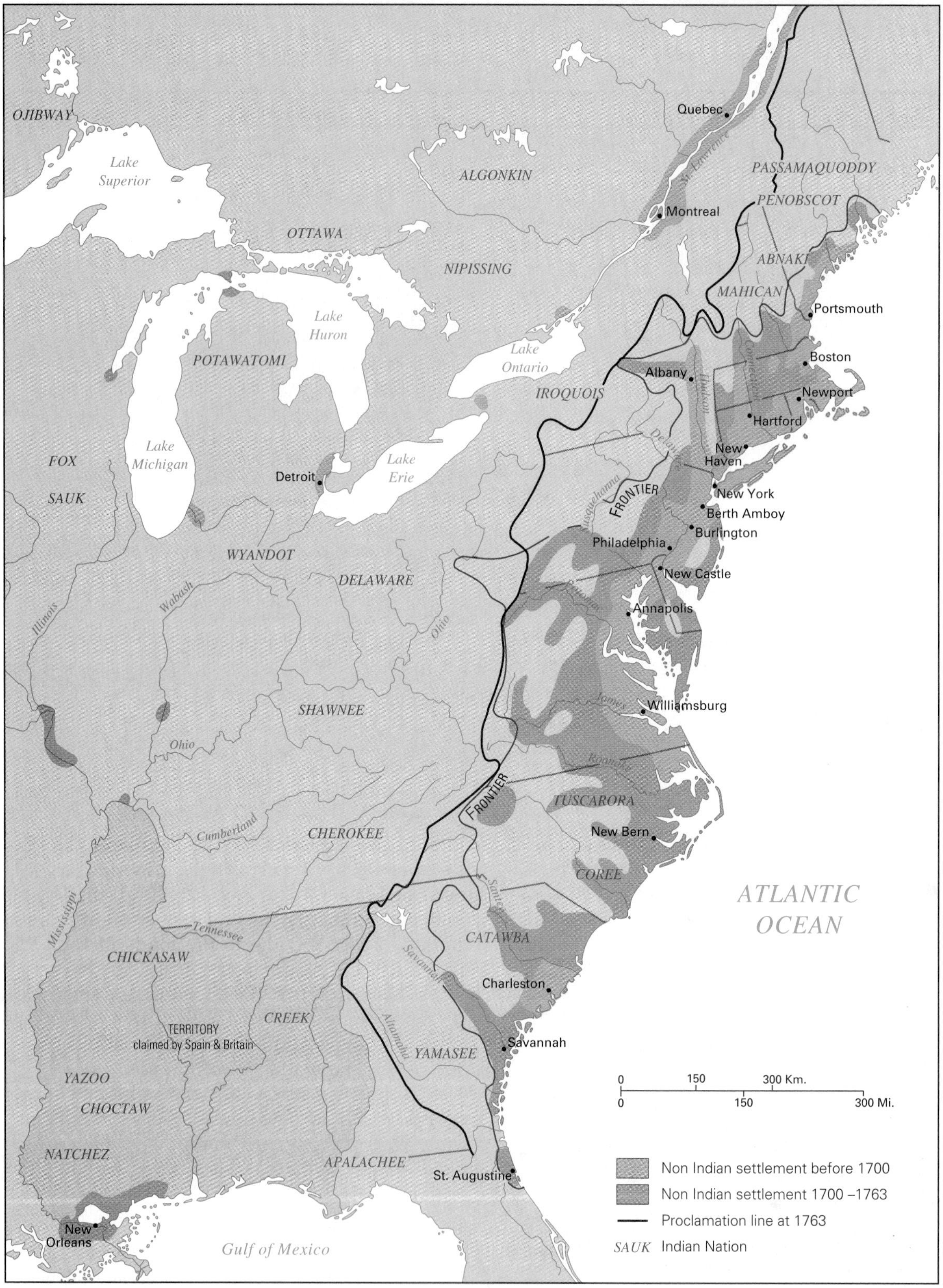

♦ **MAP 5.1 The Proclamation Line of 1763** This map shows European settlement east of the Appalachian Mountains and the numerous Indian tribes with territorial claims to the lands between the Appalachians and the Mississippi River. The Proclamation Line, which roughly follows the mountain range, was the British government's effort to temporarily halt colonial westward expansion and thus to prevent bloodshed between settlers and Indians. This British policy was deeply resented by land-hungry colonists.

mous war debt. English taxpayers, who had groaned under the wartime burden, now demanded tax relief, not tax increases. The new Canadian territory posed serious governance problems because the Indians were unwilling to pledge their allegiance to the English king and the French Canadians were unwilling to abandon their traditions, laws, or religious institutions despite the change in government.

Dealing with Indian and French Canadian Resistance

Both the Canadian tribes and Spain's former Indian allies along the southeastern borders of the English colonies saw the threat to their interests in Britain's recent victory. For decades, Indian diplomats had protected their lands by playing European rivals against each other. However, the new and decisive shift in the balance of power among the European nations endangered Indian interests. The Creeks and Cherokees of the Southeast felt the effects even before the war ended. As the beleaguered Spanish withdrew military support from the tribes, English settlers from the southern colonies poured into Indian territory. The Cherokees mounted full-scale resistance along the Virginia and Carolina western settlement line, but the British crushed this rebellion. They then forced Cherokee leaders to sign treaties that opened their lands to both English settlement and English military bases.

A similar invasion of Indian territory began in the Ohio Valley and the Great Lakes region in 1763. White settlers flooded the interior where Delawares and Mingoes made their homes. The British added insult to injury by raising the price of the goods they traded with these tribes. Highly dependent by now on European weapons, tools, clothing, and liquor, the tribes resented the added cost for essential supplies. In response, the region's Indians created an intertribal alliance known as the **Covenant Chain.** The Covenant Chain brought together Senecas, Ojibwas, Potowatomis, Hurons, Ottawas, Delawares, Shawnees, and Mingoes, all of whom stood ready to resist colonial settlers, British trading policy, and the terms of military occupation of frontier forts.

By the spring of 1763, Ottawa chief **Pontiac,** driving force behind the alliance, had begun a siege of Fort Detroit. Throughout the summer and early fall, alliance members attacked other frontier forts. Casualties were high, but the English held their ground. In late October, Pontiac ended his siege, and by winter the alliance had conceded failure. Member tribes acknowledged British control of the Ohio Valley.

♦ European governments traditionally struck commemorative medals to celebrate historic events or individual heroics. The British and French adapted the use of medals for the colonial setting, presenting them as gifts to Indian leaders to encourage an alliance or to reward acts of loyalty. This medal, produced in 1764, celebrates the virtues of English-Indian military cooperation. On it, an Englishman and Indian shake hands and share a peace pipe beneath the message "Happy While United." *Massachusetts Historical Society.*

The British realized that such costly victories would not ensure permanent peace in the west. As long as the "middle ground" between Indian and colonial populations continued to shrink, Indians would mount resistance. And as long as Indians resisted what Creeks bluntly called "people greedily grasping after the lands of red people," settlers would demand expensive military protection as they pushed westward. If the army did not respond, settlers were willing to take action on their own. When the Paxton Boys of western Pennsylvania avenged an Indian raid by murdering a village of innocent Conestogas (see page 98), the dangers of this type of vigilante action became painfully clear. Violence would lead to violence—unless Grenville

Covenant Chain An alliance of Indian tribes established to resist colonial settlement in the Ohio Valley and Great Lakes region and to opppose British trading policies.

Pontiac Ottawa chief who led the unsuccessful resistance against British policy in 1763.

could keep Indians and settlers at arm's length. Grenville's solution was a proclamation, issued in 1763, temporarily banning all colonial settlement west of the Appalachian Mountains.

Grenville's **Proclamation Line of 1763** outraged colonists (see Map 5.1). With the Indian enemy reeling from defeat, settlers argued, this was the perfect moment to cross the mountains and stake claims to the land. Most colonists ignored Grenville's policy. Over the next decade, areas like Kentucky began to fill with eager homesteaders, creating a wedge that divided northern and southern Indian tribes from one another and increased Indians' anxiety about their own futures. Border conflicts like the 1774 Lord Dunmore's War, between Virginians and Mingoes and Shawnees, continued to erupt despite British policy or peacekeeping efforts.

Spurred by their long tradition of anti-Catholic sentiment, American colonists also objected to Grenville's policy toward French-speaking, Catholic Canadians. George III's advisers preferred to win these Canadians over rather than strong-arm them. Thus, to balance the French Canadians' loss of their fishing and fur-trading industries, Grenville promised them the right to preserve their religious and cultural life. Britain's colonists considered this concession to the losers in the war scandalous.

Demanding More from the Colonists

Colonists were not the only ones growing discontent. In London, the king, his ministers, and many members of Parliament were impatient with colonial behavior and attitudes. Hadn't the colonists benefited more than anyone from the French defeat, asked George Grenville. And hadn't they contributed less than anyone to securing that victory? Such questions revealed the subtle but important rewriting of the motives and goals of the French and Indian War. Although Britain had waged the war to win dominance in European affairs, not to benefit the colonies, Grenville now declared that the war had been fought to protect the colonists and to expand their opportunities for settlement.

This new interpretation fit well with the government's increasing doubts about colonial commitments to the empire's trade interests. It seemed clear to Grenville that something had gone wrong in the economic relationship between England the colonies. Colonial cities like Boston, Philadelphia, and New York had grown, yet their growth did not make England as rich as **mercantile theory** said it should. One reason was that in every colony locally produced goods competed with English-made goods. A more important reason, however, was illegal trade. Colonists seized economic opportunity wherever they found it—even in trade with England's rivals. In fact, to English amazement, colonials had continued to trade with the French Caribbean islands throughout the French and Indian War. In peacetime, colonists avoided paying **import duties** on foreign goods by bribing customs officials or landing cargoes where no customs officers were stationed.

George Grenville was often mocked for having a bookkeeper's mentality, but few laughed at what the prime minister discovered when he examined the imperial trade books. By the 1760s, the Crown had collected less than £2,000 in revenue from colonial trade with other nations while the cost of collecting these duties was over £7,000 a year. Discoveries like this fueled British suspicions that the colonies were underregulated and undergoverned as well as ungrateful and uncooperative. When the strong doubts about colonial loyalty met up with the reality of the British government debts and soaring expenses, something drastic could be expected to follow. And it did. In 1764, Grenville proposed reforms of colonial policy that Parliament greeted with approval. Colonists greeted those reforms with shock and alarm.

Separately, each of Grenville's measures addressed a loophole in the proper relationship between Mother Country and colonies. For example, a **Currency Act** outlawed the printing of paper money in the colonies. In part, this was done to ensure the colonial market for English manufacturers. Although the colonists had to pay for imported English products with hard currency (gold and silver), they could use paper money to pay for locally produced goods. With paper money banned, local manufacturers would be driven out of business.

Proclamation Line of 1763 Boundary that Britain established to ban white settlement west of the Appalachian Mountains; it was intended to reduce conflict between Indians and colonists.

mercantile theory The theory that a nation should amass wealth by exporting more than it imports; colonies are valuable in a mercantile system as a source of raw materials and as a market for manufactured goods.

import duty A tax on imported goods.

Currency Act British law (1764) banning the printing of paper money in the American colonies.

Grenville believed the major loopholes were related to illegal international trade. The Americans were getting away with smuggling foreign goods. In fact, so many officers accepted bribes that smuggling had become an acceptable, even respectable, form of commerce. To change this, Grenville had to reform the **customs service.** His first step was to increase the powers of the customs officers, allowing them to use blanket warrants, called writs of assistance, to search ships and warehouses for smuggled goods.

Grenville's next step was to reform the import regulations. In the 1764 American Revenue Act, known popularly as the **Sugar Act,** Grenville demonstrated his practical bent. He conceded that trying to halt the importation of French sugar or molasses was a waste of time and resources. Instead, he resolved to make a profit for the Crown from this trade. He lowered the import tax on the foreign sugar but raised the stakes for attempted smuggling. Until 1764, a colonist accused of smuggling was tried before a jury of his neighbors in a **civil court.** He expected, and usually got, a favorable verdict from his peers. Grenville now declared that anyone caught smuggling would be tried in a juryless **vice-admiralty court,** where a conviction was likely. Once smuggling became too costly and too risky, Grenville reasoned, American shippers would declare their cargoes of French molasses and pay the Crown for the privileges of importing them.

The Colonial Response

Grenville's reforms were spectacularly ill timed as far as Americans were concerned. The colonial economy was suffering from a postwar **depression,** brought on in part by the loss of the British army as a steady market for American supplies and of British soldiers as steady customers who paid in hard currency rather than paper money. The effects of this postwar depression could be seen in colonial cities, where unemployment was high among artisans, dockworkers, and sailors. Colonial merchants found themselves caught in a credit squeeze—unable to pay their debts to British merchants because they were owed so much money by colonial customers with no cash to pay for their purchases. Financially troubled Americans could not be expected to cheer a currency act that shut off a source of money or a Sugar Act that established a new get-tough policy on foreign trade. In the eyes of many colonists, the English government was turning into a greater menace than the French army had ever been.

Some colonists, however, saw these hard times and the need to tighten their belts as a welcome brake on their society's **materialism.** These Americans believed that a love of luxuries weakened people's spirit, sapped their independence, and led to moral decay. They felt this moral decay was epidemic in Britain, where extravagance and corruption infected society and tainted the nation's political leaders. After 1763, these colonists appealed to their neighbors to embrace simplicity and sacrifice. They urged prosperous women, for example, to abandon fashion, with its "gaudy, butterfly, vain, fantastick and expensive Dresses bought from Europe," and put on the "decent plain Dresses made in their own Country." Convinced that the eighteenth-century **consumer revolution** in the colonies had eroded virtue, these colonists called for a **boycott** of all goods manufactured in England.

Other views and other proposals for action soon filled the pages of colonial newspapers. Running through the discussions was recognition that Grenville's reforms had raised profound issues of liberty and the rights of citizens and of the relationship between Parliament and the colonial governments—issues that needed to be resolved. The degree to which Parliament had, or ought to have, power over colonial economic and political life required serious, public pondering. Years later, with the benefit of hindsight, Massachusetts lawyer and

customs service A government agency authorized to collect taxes on foreign goods entering a country.

Sugar Act British law (1764) that taxed sugar and other colonial imports to pay for some of Britain's expenses in protecting the colonies.

civil court Any court that hears cases regarding the rights of private citizens.

vice-admiralty court Nonjury British court in which a judge heard cases involving shipping.

depression A period of drastic economic decline, characterized by decreasing business activity, falling prices, and unemployment.

materialism Great or excessive interest in worldly matters, especially in acquiring goods.

consumer revolution The significant rise in the colonial market for manufactured goods, particularly luxury items, which occurred in the eighteenth century.

boycott An organized protest in which people refuse to buy goods from a nation or group of people whose actions they object to.

revolutionary John Adams commented on the importance of the Sugar Act in starting America down the road to independence. "I know not why we should blush to confess," wrote Adams, "that molasses was an essential ingredient in American independence. Many great events have proceeded from much smaller causes." But in 1764, Americans were far from agreement over the issue of parliamentary and local political powers. They were not even certain how to respond to the Sugar Act.

The Stamp Act

Did Grenville stop to consider the possibility of "great events" arising from his postwar policies? Probably not. He was hardly a stranger to protest and anger, for he had often heard British citizens grumble about taxes and assert their rights against the government. As he saw it, his duty was to fill the treasury, reduce the nation's staggering debt, arm its troops, and keep the royal navy afloat. The duty of loyal British citizens, he believed, was to obey the laws of their sovereign government. Grenville had no doubt that the measures he and Parliament had taken to regulate the colonies and their revenue-producing trade were constitutional. Some colonists, however, had doubts. Thus the next piece of colonial legislation Grenville proposed was designed not only to raise revenue but to settle the principle of parliamentary sovereignty.

The **Stamp Act** of 1765 was to be the first **direct tax** ever laid on the colonies by Parliament, raising funds by taxing many vital goods and services. There was nothing startling or novel about the revenue-collecting *method* Grenville proposed to use. It raised money by requiring the use of government "stamped paper" on certain goods or as part of the cost for certain services. A stamp tax was simple and efficient, and several colonial legislatures had adopted this method themselves. What was startling, however, was that Parliament would consider imposing such a tax on the colonists. A direct tax threatened the traditional relationship between the colonial assemblies and Parliament. Up until 1765, Parliament had passed many acts regulating colonial trade. Sometimes these regulations on imports generated revenue for the Crown, and the colonists accepted them as a form of **external taxation.** But colonists expected direct taxation only from their local assemblies. If Grenville's Stamp Act became law, it would mark a radical change in the distribution of political power and a powerful assertion of Parliament's sovereignty. This, of course, was exactly what Grenville intended.

Most members of Parliament saw the Stamp Act as an efficient and modest redistribution of the burdens of the empire—and a constitutional one. Colonists were certainly not being asked to shoulder the entire burden, since the estimated £160,000 in revenue from the stamped paper would cover only one-fifth of the cost of maintaining a British army in North America. Under these circumstances, Parliament saw no reason to deny Grenville's proposed tax.

The Stamp Act passed in February 1765 and was set to go into effect in November. The nine-month delay gave Grenville time to print the stamped paper, arrange for its shipment across the Atlantic, and appoint agents to receive and distribute the stamps in each colony. News of the tax, however, crossed the ocean rapidly and was greeted with outrage and anger. Opposition was widespread among the colonists because virtually every free man and woman was affected by a tax that required stamps on all legal documents, on newspapers and pamphlets, and even on playing cards and dice. Grenville was reaching into the pockets of the rich, who would need stamped paper to draw up wills and property deeds and to bring suit in court. And he was emptying the pockets of the poor, who would feel the pinch when dealing a hand of cards in a tavern or buying a printed **broadside** filled with advertising. Other segments of the colonial society would also feel the sting of the new tax. Unless colonial merchants and ship captains used stamped clearances for all shipments, the royal navy could seize their cargoes. Lawyers feared the loss of clients if they had to add the cost of the stamps to their fees. With the stamp tax Grenville united northern merchants and southern planters, rural women and urban workingmen, and he riled the most articulate and argumentative of all Americans: their lawyers and newspaper publishers.

Stamp Act British law (1765) that levied direct taxes on a large variety of items, including newspapers, playing cards, and legal documents.

direct tax A tax imposed to raise revenues rather than to regulate trade.

external taxation Revenue raised that is incidental to the main goal of regulating trade with other nations.

broadside An advertisement, public notice, or other publication printed on one side of a large sheet of paper.

St—p! ſt—p! ſt—p! No:

Tueſday-Morning, December 17, 1765.

THE True-born Sons of Liberty, are deſired to meet under LIBERTY-TREE, at XII o'Clock, THIS DAY, to hear the the public Reſignation, under Oath, of ANDREW OLIVER, Eſq; Diſtributor of Stamps for the Province of the *Maſſachuſetts-Bay.*

A Reſignation? YES.

♦ The Sons of Liberty first appeared in Boston, but this organization that united elite and working class protesters spread quickly to other American cities. In the 1765 broadside above, the Boston Sons call a meeting to demand the resignation of local stamp collector, Andrew Oliver. Ten years later, New York's pro-British editor, James Rivington, used the illustration above while reporting that a New Brunswick mob had hung him in effigy. The New York Sons promptly made good on the threat to Rivington, attacking his office, destroying his press, and forcing his paper to close. *Mr. Rivington: Library of Congress; Sons of Liberty Broadside: Massachusetts Historical Society.*

The Popular Response

Many colonists were determined to resist the new legislation. Massachusetts, where the new customs regulations threatened the colony's smuggling activities and where power struggles between Crown officers and assembly members were already common, led the way. During the summer of 1765, a group of Bostonians formed a secret resistance organization called the **Sons of Liberty.** Spearheading the Sons was the irrepressible **Samuel Adams,** a Harvard-educated member of a prominent Massachusetts family who preferred the company of local working men and women to the conversation of the elite. More at home in the dockside taverns than in the comfortable parlors of his relatives, Adams was a quick-witted, dynamic champion of working-class causes. He had a genius for writing propaganda and for mobilizing popular sentiment on political and community issues. Most members of the Sons of Liberty were artisans and shopkeepers, and the group's main support came from men of the city's laboring classes, who had been hard hit by the postwar depression and would suffer from the stamp tax. These colonists had few voices in the legislature and little influence with Crown officials. They compensated by using public demonstrations and protests to make their opinions known.

The Sons of Liberty had been created to oppose *British* policies, but with class divisions widening in Boston, these crowds sometimes added protests against local issues and local elites. Prosperous Bostonians saw the potential danger in the mobilization of such crowds. For these elites, crowd protest was a double-edged sword, a useful weapon that could be deadly in the wrong hands.

By August 1765, Sons of Liberty organizations had sprung up in other cities and towns across the colonies. Demonstrations and protests escalated, and once again Boston led the way. On August

Sons of Liberty A secret organization first formed in Boston to oppose the Stamp Act.

Samuel Adams Massachusetts revolutionary leader and propagandist who organized opposition to British policies after 1764.

14, shoemaker **Ebenezer McIntosh** led a crowd to protest the appointment of the colony's stamp agent, wealthy merchant Andrew Oliver. Until recently, McIntosh had led one of two major workers' organizations in town, a **fraternal** group of artisans, apprentices, and day laborers known to the city's disapproving elite as the South End "gang." But on this August day, city gentlemen disguised themselves as workingmen and joined McIntosh's gang members as they paraded through the city streets, carrying an effigy of Oliver. The crowd destroyed the stamp agent's dockside warehouse and later broke all the windows in his home. The message was clear—and Oliver understood it well. The following day Andrew Oliver resigned as stamp agent. Boston Sons of Liberty celebrated by declaring the tree on which they hanged Oliver's effigy the "liberty tree."

Oliver's resignation did not end the protest. Customs officers and other Crown officials living in Boston were harassed and threatened. The chief target of abuse, however, was the haughty merchant **Thomas Hutchinson,** hated by many of the ambitious younger political leaders because he monopolized appointive offices in the colony's government and by the workingmen because of his obvious disdain for ordinary people. Late one August evening, a large crowd surrounded Hutchinson's elegant brick mansion. Warned of the impending attack, Hutchinson and his family had wisely fled, escaping just before rocks began to shatter the parlor windows. By dawn, the house was in ruins, and Hutchinson's furniture, clothing, and personal library had been trashed.

Thomas Hutchinson was a political target of those who opposed the Stamp Act. But because he represented the privilege and power of the few and the well placed, he was also a social target of the working people in the crowd. The destruction of his home led many of Boston's elite to withdraw their support from popular protests of any kind. Perhaps, they reasoned, the tensions between rich and poor were more dangerous than any parliamentary reform.

The campaign against the stamp agents spread like a brushfire across the colonies. In Connecticut, the merchant Jared Ingersoll resigned after a crowd held him captive for three hours. Agents in Rhode Island, Maryland, and New York were also threatened and harassed. The angry crowds and the threats of violence caused most who had accepted a commission as stamp agent to change their minds. When the stamps reached colonial ports in November, only the young and conservative colony of Georgia could produce anyone willing to distribute them.

Colonial governors responded by refusing to allow any colonial ships to leave port. They hoped the disruption of trade would force local merchants to use their influence to end the resistance. Their strategy backfired. Violence increased as hundreds of unemployed sailors took to the streets, terrorizing customs officers and any colonists suspected of supporting the king's taxation policy.

Political Debate

While the Sons of Liberty and their supporters demonstrated in the streets, most colonial political leaders were proceeding with caution. Virginia lawyer and planter **Patrick Henry** briefly stirred the passions of his colleagues in the House of Burgesses when he suggested that the Stamp Act was evidence of the king's tyranny. Not everyone agreed with him that the measure was so serious. Many did agree, however, that the heart of the matter was not stamped paper but parliamentary sovereignty versus the rights of colonial citizens. "No taxation without representation"—the principle that citizens cannot be taxed by a government unless they are represented in it—was a fundamental assumption of free white Englishmen on both sides of the Atlantic. The crucial question was, Did the House of Commons represent the colonists even though no colonist sat in the House and none voted for its members? If the answer was no, then the Stamp Act violated the colonists' most basic "rights of Englishmen."

Stating the issue in this way led to other concerns. Could colonial political leaders oppose a single law such as the Stamp Act without completely denying the authority of the government that was responsi-

Ebenezer McIntosh Boston shoemaker whose workingman's organization, the South End "gang," became the core membership of the city's Sons of Liberty in 1765.

fraternal Being a body of people associated to pursue common interests.

Thomas Hutchinson Boston merchant and judge who served as lieutenant governor and later governor of Massachusetts; Stamp Act protesters destroyed his home in 1765.

Patrick Henry Member of the Virginia House of Burgesses and American revolutionary leader noted for his oratorical skills.

ble for its passage? Massachusetts lawyer **James Otis** pondered this question when he sat down to write his *Rights of the British Colonists Asserted and Proved.* Any opposition to the Stamp Act, he decided, was ultimately a challenge to parliamentary authority over the colonies. Such a challenge, Otis reluctantly concluded, would surely lead to colonial rebellion and a declaration of colonial independence. He, for one, was not prepared to become a rebel.

The logic of his own argument disturbed Otis and prompted him to propose a compromise: the colonists should be given representation in the House of Commons. Few political leaders took this suggestion seriously. Even if Parliament agreed, a small contingent of colonists could be easily ignored in its decision making. Most colonial leaders thought it best to declare that American rights and liberties were under attack and to issue warnings that the assemblies would oppose any further threats to colonial rights. They carefully avoided, however, any treasonous statements or threats of rebellion. In the most popular pamphlet of 1765, Pennsylvania lawyer Daniel Dulaney captured this combination of criticism and caution. His *Considerations on the Propriety of Imposing Taxes on the British Colonies* reaffirmed the dependence of the colonies on Great Britain. But it also reminded Parliament that Americans knew the difference between dependence and slavery.

Colonial assemblymen knew that a final question hung in the air. If Parliament asserted its right to govern the colonies directly, what powers would remain to them as members of the colonial legislatures? In the end, the majority agreed that a firm stand had to be taken. After much debate, most assemblies, led by Patrick Henry's own House of Burgesses, issued statements condemning the Stamp Act and demanding its repeal. Massachusetts reinforced this unusual show of unity among the colonies when its assembly issued a call for an intercolonial meeting of delegates to discuss the Stamp Act crisis. The call to meet was greeted with enthusiasm.

Grenville's policies appeared to be bringing about what had once seemed impossible: united political action. Until the Stamp Act, competition among the colonial governments was far more common than cooperation. Yet in the fall of 1765 delegates from nine colonies met in New York "to consider a general and unified, dutiful, loyal and humble Representation [**petition**]" to the king and Parliament. The petitions this historic **Stamp Act Congress** ultimately produced were far bolder than the delegates first intended. They were powerful, tightly argued statements that conceded parliamentary authority over the colonies but denied Parliament's right to impose a direct tax on them. "No taxes," the Congress said, "ever have been, or can be Constitutionally imposed" on the colonies "but by their respective Legislatures." Clearly Americans expected this tradition to be honored.

Repeal of the Stamp Act

Neither the protest in the streets nor the arguments of the Stamp Act Congress moved the king or Parliament to repeal the stamp tax. But economic pressure did. English manufacturers relied heavily on their colonial markets and were certain to be hurt by any interruption in the flow and sale of goods to America. Thus the most powerful weapon in the colonial arsenal was a refusal to purchase English goods. On Halloween night, just one day before the stamp tax officially went into effect, two hundred New York merchants announced that they would not import any new British goods. Local artisans and laborers rallied to support this boycott. A mixture of patriotism and self-interest motivated both these groups. The merchants saw the possibility of emptying warehouses bulging with unsold goods because of the postwar depression. Unemployed and underemployed artisans and laborers saw the chance to sell their own products if the supply of cheaper English-made goods dried up. The same combination of interests existed in other colonial cities and thus the **nonimportation** movement spread quickly. By the end of November, several colonial assemblies had publicly endorsed the nonimportation agreements signed by local merchants. There was popular support as well. In many cities and towns, women publicly announced their commitment to nonimporta-

James Otis Boston lawyer and assembly leader who argued that the writs of assistance violated colonists' rights and who called for colonial representation in Parliament.

petition A formal written request to a superior authority.

Stamp Act Congress A meeting of colonial delegates in New York in 1765 that issued a declaration of rights and grievances to the British government.

nonimportation Colonial policy of refusing to import British goods, undertaken to protest the Stamp Act and later the Townshend Acts.

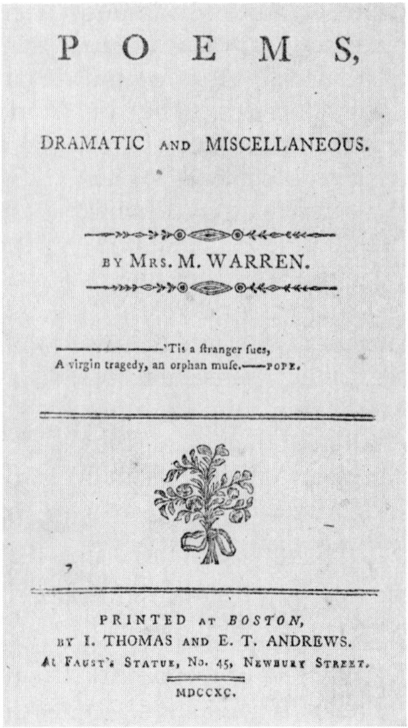

P O E M S,

DRAMATIC AND MISCELLANEOUS.

BY MRS. M. WARREN.

———'Tis a ſtranger ſues,
A virgin tragedy, an orphan muſe.—POPE.

PRINTED AT BOSTON,
BY I. THOMAS AND E. T. ANDREWS.
At FAUST'S STATUE, No. 45, NEWBURY STREET.
MDCCXC.

♦ Massachusetts playwright, poet, and historian Mercy Otis Warren penned some of the most popular and effective propaganda for the American cause. In her plays, she portrayed pro-British officeholders as greedy, power hungry traitors, while she praised Boston radicals as noble heroes. The collection of poems shown here includes an appeal to American women to show their patriotism by supporting the boycott of British imported goods. *Mercy Otis Warren: "Mercy Otis Warren" by John Singleton Copley. Courtesy of Museum of Fine Arts, Boston, bequest of Winslow Warren; Book of poems: Chicago Historical Society.*

tion and vowed to spend long hours spinning their own cloth rather than purchase it ready-made from England.

English exporters complained bitterly of the damage done to their businesses and pressured Parliament to take colonial protest seriously. Talk of repeal grew bolder and louder in the halls of Parliament. The Grenville government reluctantly conceded that enforcement of the Stamp Act had failed miserably. Even in colonies where royal officials dared to distribute the stamped paper, Americans refused to purchase it. Colonists simply ignored the hated law and continued to sue their neighbors, sell their land, publish their newspapers, and buy their playing cards as if the stamped paper and the Stamp Act did not exist.

By winter's end, Grenville was no longer prime minister, although his departure owed more to English politics than to the furor across the Atlantic. For the king's new prime minister, Lord Rockingham, the critical issue was not whether to repeal the Stamp Act but how to do so without appearing to cave in to colonial pressure. After much debate and political maneuvering, the government came up with a satisfactory solution. It repealed the Stamp Act but at the same time passed a **Declaratory Act,** which asserted Parliament's absolute right to pass legislation for and raise taxes from the North American colonies.

Colonists celebrated the repeal with public outpourings of loyalty to England that were as impressive as their public protests had been. There were

Declaratory Act British law (1766) that asserted Parliament's right to make laws for and impose taxes on the American colonies.

cannon salutes, bonfires, parades, speeches, and public toasts to the king and Rockingham. In Boston, Sons of Liberty built a pyramid and covered its three sides with political poetry. In Anne Arundel County, Maryland, colonists erected a "liberty pillar" and buried "Discord" beneath it. And, in a spectacular but poorly executed gesture, the Liberty Boys of Plymouth, Massachusetts, tried to move Plymouth Rock to the center of town. When the famous rock on which the Pilgrims were said to have landed split in two, half of it was carried to Liberty Pole Square, where it remained until 1834.

Asserting American Rights

- Why did Charles Townshend expect his colonial revenue-raising measures to be successful?
- What forms of resistance did the colonists choose to force the repeal of Townshend's measures?
- What were the outcomes of colonial resistance?

The Declaratory Act firmly asserted that Parliament had "the sole and exclusive right" to tax the colonists. This was a clear rejection of the colonial assemblies' claim to power, yet the colonists greeted it with little emotion. Those who commented on it dismissed it as a face-saving device. To a degree, they were correct. But the Declaratory Act expressed the views of powerful men in Parliament, and within a year they put it to the test.

By the summer of 1766, Rockingham had been replaced by a man George III admired greatly: William Pitt. The aging Pitt was now too preoccupied with his failing health to exercise the control over the government he had exercised during the French and Indian War. A young playboy named **Charles Townshend,** serving as **chancellor of the exchequer,** rushed in to fill the leadership void. Townshend wasted little time putting together a new package of taxes on the colonies.

The Townshend Acts and Colonial Protest

During the Stamp Act crisis, Benjamin Franklin had assured Parliament that, although American colonists opposed direct taxes, they conceded the British government's right to any revenue generated from the regulation of colonial trade. In 1767, Townshend used this alleged distinction between direct and indirect revenue raising to propose new regulations on a mixture of necessities and luxuries that Americans imported. These items, however, were *not* the products of foreign nations. Instead, the **Townshend Acts** of 1767 set import taxes on products made in Britain.

The Townshend Acts taxed glass, paper, paint, and lead products made in England, all part of the luxury trade. The acts also placed a 3-penny tax on tea, the most popular drink among colonists everywhere. To ensure that the revenue would be collected, Townshend continued the reforms of the customs service that Grenville had begun, expanding its scope and powers. He ordered new customs boards established in the colonies and created additional vice-admiralty courts in the major port cities of Boston, Charleston, and Philadelphia to try any cases of smuggling or tax evasion that might occur. In case Americans tried to harass customs officials, as they had so effectively done during the stamp tax protests, Townshend ordered British troops transferred from the western regions to the major colonial port cities. He knew this troop relocation would anger the colonists, but he was relying on the presence of uniformed soldiers—known as "redcoats" because of their scarlet jackets—to keep the peace. To help finance this military occupation of the key cities, Townshend invoked the 1766 **Quartering Act,** which required colonists to provide room and board, "candles, firing, bedding, cooking utensils, salt and vinegar" and a ration of beer, cider, or rum to any troops stationed in their midst.

Clearly, Townshend was taking every precaution to avoid the embarrassment Grenville had suffered in the Stamp Act disaster. But he made a serious error in believing that colonists would meekly agree to pay import duties on British-made goods. When news of the new regulations reached the colonies,

Charles Townshend Leader of the British government from 1766 to 1770; imposed the Townshend Acts on the colonies in 1767.

chancellor of the exchequer Head of the British government department in charge of taxation; the exchequer is similar to the U.S. Treasury Department.

Townshend Acts British laws (1767) requiring colonists to pay duties on goods such as glass, lead, paint, and tea that were manufactured in England and sold in the colonies.

Quartering Act British law (1766) requiring the colonial governments to provide barracks and supplies to British troops.

the response was immediate, determined, and well-organized resistance.

If the newspapers reflected popular sentiment accurately, the colonists were united in their opposition to the Townshend Acts and to the Mother Country's repressive enforcement policies. Some were incensed that the government was once again trampling on the principle of "no taxation without representation." In Boston, Samuel Adams voiced his outrage: "Is it possible to form an idea of Slavery, more compleat, more miserable, more disgraceful than that of a people, where justice is administer'd, government exercis'd, and a **standing army** maintain'd at the expense of the people, and yet without the least dependence upon them?" Others worried more about the economic burden of the new taxes and the quartering of the troops than about political rights. Boston lawyer Josiah Quincy, Jr., asked readers of the *Boston Gazette:* "Is not the bread taken out of the children's mouths and given unto the Dogs?"

John Dickinson, a well-respected Pennsylvania landowner and lawyer, laid out the basic American position on imperial relations in his pamphlet *Letters from a Farmer in Pennsylvania* (1767). Direct taxation without representation violated the colonists' rights as English citizens, Dickinson declared. But by imposing any tax that did not regulate *foreign* trade, Parliament also violated those rights. Dickinson also considered, and rejected, the British claim that Americans were represented in the House of Commons. According to the British argument, colonists enjoyed **virtual representation** because the House of Commons represented the interests of all citizens in the empire who were not members of the nobility, whether those citizens participated directly in elections to the House or not. Like most Americans, Dickinson discounted virtual representation. What Englishmen were entitled to, he wrote, was **actual representation** by men they had elected to government to protect their interests. For qualified voters in the colonies, who enjoyed actual representation in their local assemblies, virtual representation was nothing more than a weak excuse for exclusion and exploitation. As one American quipped: "Our *privileges* are all *virtual,* our sufferings are *real.*"

While political theorists set out the American position in newspaper essays and pamphlets, protest leaders organized popular resistance. Samuel Adams set in motion a massive boycott of British goods to begin on January 1, 1768. Just as before, some welcomed the chance a boycott provided to "mow down luxury and high living." But simple economics also contributed forcefully to support for the boycott. Boston artisans remained enthusiastic about any action that stopped the flow of inexpensive English-made goods to America. Small-scale merchants were also eager to see nonimportation enforced. They had little access to British credit or goods under normal circumstances, and the boycott would eliminate the advantages enjoyed by the merchant elite who did. Merchants and shippers who made their living smuggling goods from the West Indies supported the boycott because it cut out the competing English-made products. The large-scale merchants who had led the 1765 boycott were not enthusiastic, however. By 1767, their warehouses no longer were overflowing with unsold English stock, and the boycott might cut off their livelihood. Many of these elite merchants delayed signing the agreements. Others did not sign at all.

The strongest voices raised against the boycott, and against resistance to the Townshend Acts in general, were the voices of colonists holding Crown-appointed government offices. These fortunate few—including judges and customs men—shared their neighbors' sensitivity to abuse or exploitation by the Crown. But they had sworn to uphold and carry out the programs and policies of the British government. And their salaries came from England. Because their careers and their identities were closely tied to the power and authority of the Crown, they were inclined to see British policymakers as well intentioned and acceptance of British policy as a patriotic duty.

Jonathan Sewall, the king's attorney general in Massachusetts, was perhaps typical of these royal officeholders. Sewall had deep roots in his colonial community, for his family went back many generations and included lawyers, judges, merchants, and assemblymen. His closest friend was **John Adams,** cousin of Samuel Adams, and the wealthy

standing army A permanent army maintained in both peacetime and wartime.

virtual representation The idea that all citizens who were not members of the nobility were represented by the House of Commons regardless of whether they had participated directly in the election of House members.

actual representation Representation by delegates directly elected to speak for voters' interests in Parliament or a colonial assembly.

John Adams Massachusetts lawyer and revolutionary; he later became the second president of the United States.

Boston merchant and smuggler **John Hancock** would soon become his brother-in-law. Yet Sewall became a staunch public defender of Crown policy. In his newspaper articles he urged his neighbors to ignore the call to resistance, and he questioned the motives of the leading activists, suggesting that greed, thwarted ambition, and envy rather than high-minded principles motivated the rabble-rousers. But, despite their prestige and their positions of authority, Crown officers like Sewall were not able to prevent the boycott or slow the spread of resistance.

Just as the Sons of Liberty and the Stamp Act demonstrations brought common men into the political arena, the 1678 boycott brought politics into the lives of women. When in 1765 the inexpensive, factory-made cloth produced in England had been placed high on the list of boycotted goods, an old, neglected, and tedious domestic skill became both a real and a symbolic element in the American protest strategy. In 1768, many women responded to the challenge. Taking a bold political stance, women, including wealthy mothers and daughters, formed groups called the Daughters of Liberty and staged large public **spinning bees** to show support for the boycott. Wearing cloth spun at home became a mark of honor and a political statement. As one male observer noted, "The ladies . . . while they vie with each other in skill and industry in their profitable employment, may vie with the men in contributing to the preservation and prosperity of their country and equally share in the honor of it." Through the boycott, politics had entered the domestic circle.

The British Humiliated

Townshend faced sustained defiance of British authority in almost every colony, but Massachusetts provided the greatest embarrassment for the Crown. Massachusetts governor Francis Bernard began losing control of local political affairs in February 1768 when the colony's assembly circulated a letter to other colonial legislatures, calling for collective protest against the Townshend Acts. Bernard's superiors ordered him to take a firm, uncompromising stand on this **circular letter,** and he dutifully but doubtfully ordered the assembly back into session to **rescind** it. Although the assembly unexpectedly did as it was told, that fall a newly elected, more radical assembly reissued the appeal for an intercolonial petition for repeal. Bernard had little choice but to dissolve this new assembly, thus temporarily suspending representative government in Massachusetts.

Bernard's ability to ensure law and order eroded rapidly. Throughout 1768 enforcers of the boycott roamed the streets of Boston, intimidating pro-British merchants and harassing anyone wearing British-made clothing. Boston mobs openly threatened customs officials, and the Sons of Liberty protected smuggling operations. Despite the increased number of customs officers policing the docks and wharves, illegal importation of both foreign goods and the English goods named in the Townshend Acts was thriving. One of the town's most notorious smugglers, the flamboyant John Hancock, grew more popular with his neighbors each time he broke the customs laws and unloaded his illegal cargoes of French and Spanish wines or West Indian molasses. In June 1768, customs officers seized Hancock's vessel, the *Liberty,* because it carried **contraband.** In response, protesters beat up senior customs men, and mobs visited the homes of other royal officials. The unhappy Governor Bernard sent an urgent plea for help to the British government.

In October 1768, four thousand troops arrived in Boston. The Crown clearly believed that the presence of one soldier for every four citizens would be enough to restore order quickly. John Adams marveled at what he considered British thickheadedness. The presence of so many young soldiers, far from home and surrounded by a hostile community, was certain to worsen the situation. Military occupation of Boston, Adams warned, made more violence inevitable.

Adams was right. With time on their hands, the soldiers passed the hours courting any local women who would speak to them and pestering those who would not. They angered local dockworkers by moonlighting in the shipyards when off duty and taking jobs away from colonists by accepting lower

John Hancock Wealthy Boston merchant and well-known smuggler; he later became president of the First Continental Congress and was the first signer of the Declaration of Independence.

spinning bee A meeting of women to compete or work together in spinning thread or yarn.

circular letter A public letter distributed to a large number of people.

rescind To repeal or invalidate a measure—in this case, the Massachusetts circular letter.

contraband Goods prohibited by law from being imported or exported.

♦ Paul Revere's engraving of the Boston Massacre appeared in newspapers the day after the confrontation between redcoats and Boston citizens. Despite the fact that Captain Preston and most of his soldiers were acquitted of wrongdoing, Revere's striking image of innocent civilians and murderous soldiers remained fixed in the popular mind. It reinforced suspicion that the British were plotting to deprive Americans of their rights and liberties. *"Boston Massacre" by Paul Revere. Library of Congress.*

pay. For their part, civilians taunted the sentries, insulted the soldiers, and refused the military any sign of hospitality. News of street-corner fights and tavern brawls inflamed feelings on both sides. Samuel Adams and his friends did their best to fan the flames of hatred, publishing daily accounts of both real and imaginary confrontations in which soldiers threatened the honor or endangered the safety of innocent townspeople.

The military occupation dragged on through 1769 and early 1770. On March 5, the major confrontation most people expected occurred. An angry crowd began throwing snowballs—undoubtedly laced with bricks and rocks—at British sentries guarding the customs house. The redcoats, under strict orders not to fire on civilians, issued a frantic call for help in withdrawing to safety. When Captain Thomas Preston and his men arrived to rescue the sentries, the growing crowd immediately enveloped them. How, and under whose orders, Preston's soldiers began to fire is unknown, but they killed five men and wounded eight other colonists. Four of the five victims were white laborers. The fifth, Crispus Attucks, was a free black sailor.

Massachusetts protest leaders' account of what they called the **Boston Massacre** appeared in colonial newspapers everywhere and included a dramatic anti-British illustration engraved by silversmith **Paul Revere.** A jury of colonists later cleared Preston and all but two of his men of the charges against them. But nothing that was said at their trial—no sworn testimony, no lawyer's arguments—could erase the image of British brutality against British subjects.

Even before the bloodshed of March 5, Edmund Burke, a member of Parliament known for his sympathy to the colonial cause, had warned the House of Commons that the relationship between Mother Country and colonies was both desperate and tragic. "The Americans," Burke said, "have made a discovery, or think they have made one, that we mean to oppress them; we have made a discovery, or think we have made one, that they intend to rise in rebellion. We do not know how to advance; they do not know how to retreat." Burke captured well the growing American conviction of a conspiracy or plot by Parliament to deprive the colonists of their rights and liberties. He also captured the British government's growing sense that a rebellion was being hatched. But the government was ready to act to ease the crisis and make a truce possible. A new minister, **Frederick Lord North,** was given the reins of government, and on the very day Captain Preston's men fired on the crowd at Boston, Lord North repealed the Townshend Acts and allowed the hated Quartering Act to expire. Yet if Lord North acknowledged the wisdom of repealing the Townshend Acts, he, like Rockingham, wanted to give no ground on the question of parliamentary control of the colonies. For this reason, North kept the tax on tea—to preserve a principle rather than fill the king's treasury.

Boston Massacre Incident in Boston on March 5, 1770, in which British troops fired on a crowd, killing five colonists.

Paul Revere Boston silversmith and engraver whose engraving of the Boston Massacre was widely reproduced; he later participated in the Boston Tea Party and helped warn the countryside of the British army's approach before the Battle of Lexington.

Frederick Lord North British prime minister, beginning in 1770, who imposed the Tea Act and the Intolerable Acts; he was prime minister throughout the American Revolution.

Success Weakens Colonial Unity

Repeal of the Townshend Acts allowed the colonists to return to the ordinary routine of their lives. But it was not true that all tensions had vanished. Troubling ones remained—and they were largely among the colonists themselves.

The economic boycott begun in 1768 exposed and deepened the growing divisions between the merchant elite and the coalition of smaller merchants, artisans, and laborers. During the years of nonimportation, many of the wealthy merchants had secretly imported and sold British goods whenever possible. When repeal came in 1770, the demand for locally manufactured goods was still low, and artisans and laborers still faced poor economic prospects. These groups were reluctant to abandon the boycott even after repeal. But few merchants, large or small, would agree to continue it.

Many elite colonists gladly abandoned the radical **activism** they had shown in the 1760s in favor of social **conservatism.** Their fear of British tyranny dimmed, but their fear of the lower classes' demand for political power grew. Artisans and laborers did indeed continue to press for broader participation in local politics and for more representative political machinery. The tyranny that some of them opposed was close to home. "Many of the poorer People," observed one supporter of expanded political participation, "deeply felt the Aristocratic Power, or rather the intolerable Tyranny of the great and opulent." The new political language in which these common men justified their demands made their social superiors uneasy. Their own impassioned appeals to rights and liberties were returning to haunt some of the colonial elite.

The Crisis Renewed

- What British choices led Americans to see a plot against their rights and liberties?
- What constraints did the king place on Massachusetts to crush resistance there?
- How did the Continental Congress choose to respond?

Lord North's government took care not to disturb the calm created by the repeal of the Townshend Acts. Between 1770 and 1773, North proposed no new taxes on the colonists and made no major changes in colonial policy. American political leaders took equal care not to make any open challenges to British authority. Both sides recognized that their political truce had its limits. It did not extend to smugglers and customs men, who continued to lock horns, nor did it erase the distrust colonists and the British government felt for each other.

Disturbing the Peace of the Early 1770s

Despite the repeal of the Townshend duties, the British effort to crack down on American smuggling continued. New England merchants whose fortunes were built on trade with the Caribbean resented the sight of customs officers at the docks and customs ships patrolling the coastline (see Map 5.2). Rhode Island merchants were especially angry and frustrated by the determined—and highly effective—customs operation in their colony. They took their revenge one June day in 1772 when the customs patrol boat, the *Gaspée,* ran aground as it chased an American vessel. That evening a band of colonists boarded the *Gaspée,* taunted the stranded customs men, and then set fire to their boat.

Rhode Islanders called the burning of the *Gaspée* an act of political resistance. The English called it an act of vandalism and appointed a royal commission to investigate. To their amazement, no witnesses came forward, and no evidence could be gathered to support any arrests. The British found the conspiracy of silence among the Rhode Islanders appalling.

Many American political leaders found the royal commission appalling. They were convinced that the British government had intended to bring its suspects to England for trial and thus deprive them of a jury of their peers. They read this as further evidence of the plot to destroy American liberty, and they decided to keep in close contact in order to monitor British moves. Following the Virginia assembly's lead, five colonies organized a communications network called the **committees of correspondence,** instructing each committee to circulate careful accounts of any questionable royal activities in its colony. These committees of correspondence were also a good mechanism for coordinating protest or resistance should the need arise. Thus the

activism The assertive use of militant action, such as demonstrations and the creation of protest organizations, usually for political ends.

conservatism The desire to maintain the existing or traditional order.

committees of correspondence Groups formed throughout the American colonies in 1772 to quickly circulate news of British activities on the mainland.

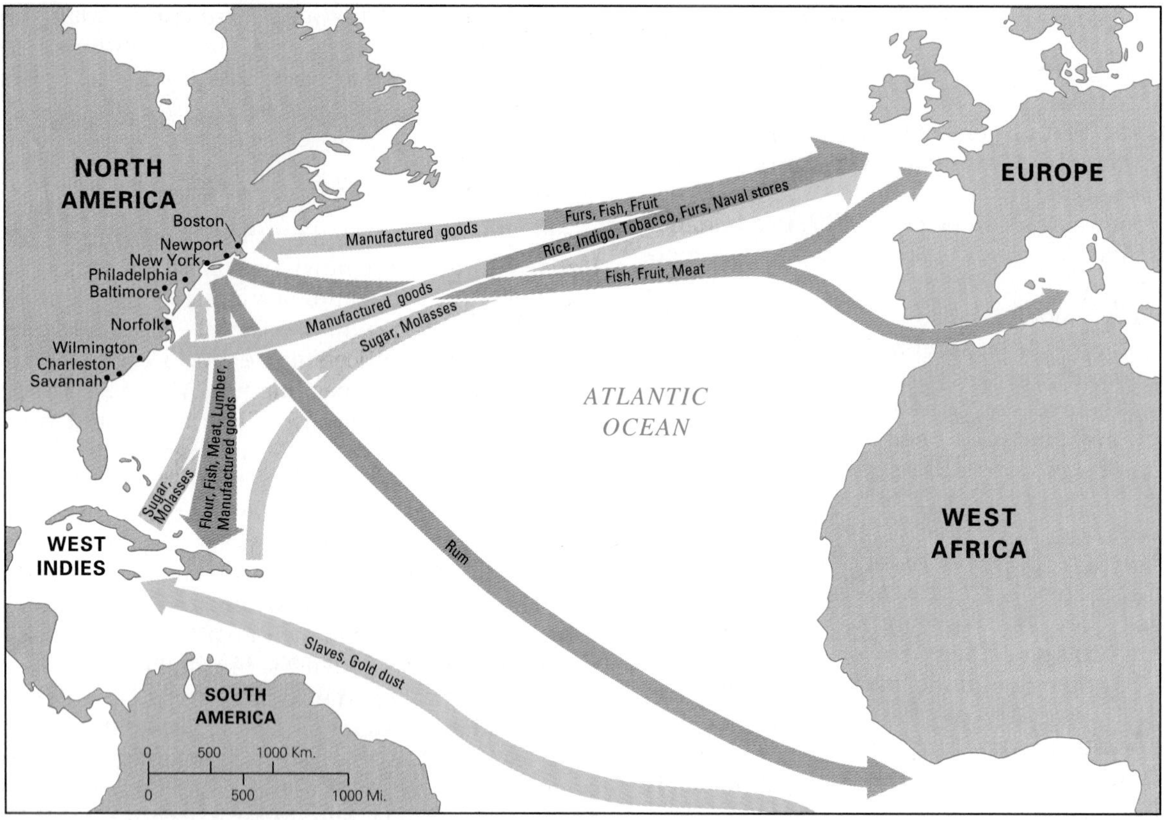

♦ **MAP 5.2 Colonial Transatlantic Trade in the 1770s** This map shows the major trade routes between the British mainland colonies, West Africa, the Caribbean, and Europe and the most important export and import cargoes carried along these routes. The central role Northern seaport cities played in carrying colonial agricultural products across the Atlantic and bringing British manufactured goods into the colonies is clear. Note also the role the Northern colonies played in the slave trade.

colonists put in place their first permanent machinery of protest.

The Tea Act and the Tea Party

During the early 1770s, colonial activists worked to keep the political consciousness of the 1760s alive. They commemorated American victories over British policy and observed the anniversary of the Boston Massacre with solemn speeches and sermons. The New York Sons of Liberty celebrated their founding day with dinners, endless toasts, and rituals that linked the Sons with a tradition of English **radicalism.** Without major British provocation, however, a revival of mass action was unlikely.

In 1773, Parliament provided that provocation. This time the government was not setting new colonial policy. It was trying to save a major commercial enterprise, the East India Tea Company. Tea was the most popular nonalcoholic drink in British culture, so the East India Company ought to have shown a steady profit. But in America boycotts and smuggled Dutch tea had hurt sales badly. The company was also suffering from mismanagement. In 1773, with its warehouses bursting with unsold tea, the East India Company came to Parliament, expecting to be rescued.

The company directors asked for permission to ship the tea directly from their India warehouses to the colonies. This arrangement would bypass the merchants in England who acted as middle men, cut

radicalism The belief that fundamental or revolutionary changes are needed in current customs or institutions.

♦ In this 1775 drawing of the Boston Tea Party, bare-chested Americans, their hair pulled back Indian-fashion, pour tea into the harbor. The British lion appears as the figurehead of the tea ship, in case the true object of the protest was in doubt. The artist also added a large crowd of colonists content to watch rather than do anything to prevent this destruction of private property. *Library of Congress.*

shipping costs, and allow the company to lower the price of its tea in America. Even with the 3-penny tax on tea that remained from the Townshend era, English tea would be cheaper than the Dutch tea smuggled into the colonies. Lord North also realized that by paying the tea tax, Americans who purchased the cheaper English tea would be confirming Parliament's right to tax the colonies. Parliament made the company's arrangement legal through passage of the **Tea Act.**

Colonists read the Tea Act as an insult, a challenge, another chilling sign of a conspiracy against their well-being and their liberty. First, they resented the concession made to the East India Company, because the government had altered its colonial trade policy to suit the needs of a special interest. Second, they feared that the East India Company would raise its prices dramatically once all foreign teas were driven off the market. And they were concerned that if other companies marketing products in the colonies followed the East India Company's example, prices for scores of products would soar. These objections, however, paled beside the colonists' recognition that the Tea Act was a chance to confirm Parliament's right to tax them. The tea that Americans drank might be cheap, but the price of conceding the legitimacy of the tea tax was high.

Colonists mobilized their resistance in 1773 with the skill acquired from a decade of experience. In several cities, crowds met the ships carrying the East India tea and prevented the unloading of their cargoes. They used the threat of violence to persuade ship captains to return to England with the tea still on board. As long as both the captains and the local royal officials gave in to these pressures, no serious confrontation occurred. But in Massachusetts, the most famous victim of mob violence, Thomas Hutchinson, was serving as governor, and he was not willing to give in. A stalemate resulted: colonists refused to allow crews to unload the tea, but Hutchinson refused to allow the tea ships to leave Boston harbor without unloading. Boston activists broke the stalemate on December 16, 1773, when some sixty men, thinly disguised as Mohawk Indians, boarded the tea ships. Working calmly and methodically, they dumped 342 chests of tea, worth almost £10,000, into the waters of Boston harbor.

The Intolerable Acts

The **Boston Tea Party** delighted colonists everywhere. The Crown, however, failed to see the humor in this deliberate destruction of valuable private property. The tea had barely settled into the harbor mud before Parliament retaliated. The king and his minister meant to make an example of everyone in Boston, the source of so much trouble and embarrassment over the past decade. Americans on the scene in England warned friends and family back home of the growing rage against the colonies. Arthur Lee, serving in London as Massachusetts' colonial agent, drew a gloomy picture of the dangers ahead in a letter to his brother. "The storm, you

Tea Act British law (1773) that lowered the price of British tea but kept the tax on tea sold to the colonies.

Boston Tea Party Protest against the Tea Act staged by Boston citizens in 1773; protesters boarded ships carrying British tea and dumped the tea into Boston harbor.

♦ Cartoons, distributed as broadsides, were a common form of political propaganda. In "The Bostonians in Distress," British political reformers demonstrate their sympathy for the Massachusetts colonists, suffering from the effects of the Boston Port Act. In this cartoon, the presence of British naval power, cannon, and soldiers cannot prevent humble American fishermen from aiding starving Boston patriots, who have been imprisoned in a cage hung from a Liberty Tree. *John Carter Brown Library.*

see, runs high," he wrote, "and it will require great prudence, wisdom and resolution, to save our liberties from shipwreck."

The four acts that Parliament passed in 1774 to discipline Massachusetts were as harsh and uncompromising as Arthur Lee predicted. The colonists called them the **Intolerable Acts.** The Port Act declared the port of Boston closed to all trade until the citizens compensated the East India Tea Company fully for its losses. The Massachusetts Government Act transferred much of the power of the colony's assembly to the royal governor, including the right to appoint judges, sheriffs, and members of the colonial legislature's upper house. The colony's **town meetings,** which had served as forums for anti-British sentiment and protests, also came under the governor's direct control. A third measure, the Justice Act, allowed royal officials charged with **capital crimes** to stand trial in London rather than before local juries. And a new Quartering Act gave military commanders the authority to quarter troops in private homes. To see that these laws were enforced, the king named General Thomas Gage, commander of the British troops in North America, as the acting governor of Massachusetts.

At the same time that Parliament passed these punitive measures, the British government issued a comprehensive plan for the government of Canada. The timing of the **Quebec Act** may have been a coincidence, but its provisions infuriated Americans. The Quebec Act granted the French in Canada the right to worship as Catholics, retain their language, and keep many of their legal practices—all marks of a tolerance that the Crown had refused to show its English colonists. The Quebec Act also expanded the borders of Canada into the Ohio Valley at the expense of the English-speaking colonies' claim to western land. The endorsement of Catholicism and the blow to western expansion seemed to connect the Quebec Act to the attack on American liberty that Parliament had launched with the Intolerable Acts.

The king expected the harsh punishment of Massachusetts to isolate that colony from its neighbors. But the Americans resisted this divide-and-conquer strategy. In every colony newspaper essays and editorials urged readers to see Boston's plight as their own. "This horrid attack upon the town of Boston," said the South Carolina *Gazette,* "we consider not as an attempt upon that town singly, but upon the whole Continent." George Washington, by now an influential Virginia planter and militia officer, declared that "the cause of Boston now is and ever will be the cause of America." Indeed the Intolerable Acts produced a wave of sympathy for the beleaguered Bostonians, and relief efforts sprang up across the colonies. The residents of Surry County, Virginia, declared they had gathered "upwards of 150 barrels of Indian corn and wheat . . . for the benefit of those firm and intrepid sons of Liberty." Throughout the year, much-needed supplies found their way to Boston despite British efforts to isolate the city.

Intolerable Acts The name colonists gave to four laws passed by Parliament in 1774 to punish Boston for the destruction of the tea.

town meeting An assembly of townspeople who meet to discuss political matters and vote; the characteristic form of local government in New England.

capital crime An offense that is punishable by death.

Quebec Act British law (1774) designed to reform the government of the former French colony of Canada; several of its provisions angered English colonists.

Colonists did not stop at sympathy for the victims of the Intolerable Acts. In pamphlets and political essays, they placed these acts into the larger context of systematic oppression by the Mother Country. Political writers referred to the British government as the "enemy," conspiring to deprive Americans of their liberty, and urged colonists to defend themselves against the "power and cunning of our adversaries."

This unity of sentiments, however, was more fragile than it appeared. In the cities, bitter divisions quickly developed, and artisans struggled with merchants to control the mass meetings that would make strategy choices. Samuel Adams and the radical artisans and workers of Boston suggested what might be at stake in this struggle between elites and ordinary citizens when they formed a "solemn league and covenant" to lead a third intercolonial boycott of British goods. As most Bostonians knew, the words *solemn league* referred to a pact between the Scottish Presbyterians and English Puritans who had overthrown royal government in the 1640s and beheaded a king. Adams and his allies had made their choice: armed rebellion. Yet even in crisis-torn Boston, not everyone wanted matters to go that far.

Creating a National Forum: The First Continental Congress

On September 5, 1774, delegates from every colony but Georgia gathered in Philadelphia for a continental congress. Few of the delegates or the people they represented thought of themselves as revolutionaries. "We want no revolution," a North Carolina delegate bluntly stated. Yet in the eyes of their British rulers, he and other colonists were treading dangerously close to treason. After all, neither the king nor Parliament had authorized the congress to which colonial assemblies and self-appointed committees had sent representatives. And that congress was intent on resisting acts of Parliament and defying the king. English men and women had been hanged as traitors for far less serious betrayals of the English government.

Some of the most articulate political leaders in the colonies attended this First Continental Congress. Conservative delegates like Joseph Galloway of Pennsylvania hoped to slow the pace of colonial resistance by substituting petitions to Parliament for the total boycott proposed by Samuel Adams. Their radical opponents—including Samuel Adams and his cousin John, Patrick Henry, and delegates from the artisan community of Philadelphia—demanded the boycott and more. Most of the delegates were desperately searching for a third choice: a way to express their grievances and demand that injustices be corrected without further eroding their relationship with England. The mounting crisis in Massachusetts, however, diminished the chances of a moderate solution.

Rumors spread that the royal navy was planning to bombard Boston and that General Gage was preparing to invade the countryside. Thousands of Massachusetts militiamen had begun mustering in Cambridge. The growing conflict drove many delegates into the radical camp. In this atmosphere of dread and anxiety, the Continental Congress approved the **Continental Association,** a boycott of all English goods to begin on December 1, 1774. The Congress also passed strong resolutions demanding the repeal of the Intolerable Acts.

The Congress had chosen radical tactics, but many delegates were torn between loyalties to two governments and their conflicting claims to power. Parliament insisted on an unconditional right to make laws for and regulate the colonies. The colonial assemblies claimed that they alone had the right to tax the colonists. **Thomas Jefferson,** a young Virginia planter and intellectual, tried to find a way out of this dilemma by separating loyalty to the king from resistance to Parliament. He argued that the colonists owed allegiance to the nation's king, not to Parliament, and that each colony did indeed have the right to legislate for itself. Not everyone agreed.

If no compromise could be reached, the delegates—and Americans everywhere—would have to choose where their strongest loyalties lay. Pennsylvania's Joseph Galloway, another wealthy landowner and lawyer, believed that he had worked out the necessary compromise. In his **Plan of Union,** Galloway proposed a drastic restructuring of imperial relations. The plan called for a Grand Council, elected by each colonial legislature, that would share with

Continental Association A boycott of all English goods approved by the First Continental Congress in 1774.

Thomas Jefferson Virginia planter and intellectual, delegate to the First and Second Continental Congresses, and author of the Declaration of Independence; he later became the third president of the United States.

Plan of Union Joseph Galloway's plan to restructure relations between the colonists and Britain to give the colonies a greater say about local laws.

Parliament the right to originate laws for the colonies. The Grand Council and Parliament would have the power to veto or disallow each other's decisions if necessary. A governor-general, appointed by the Crown, would oversee the Council and preserve imperial interests.

After much discussion and debate, Congress rejected Galloway's compromise by the narrowest of margins. Then it was John Adams's turn to propose a solution. Under his skillful urging and direction, the Congress adopted the **Declaration of Rights and Grievances.** The Declaration politely but firmly established the colonial standard for acceptable legislation by Parliament. Colonists, said the Declaration, would consent to acts meant to regulate "our external commerce." But they absolutely denied the legitimacy, or lawfulness, of an "idea of taxation, internal or external, for raising a revenue on the subjects of America, without their consent."

The delegates knew that the force behind the Declaration came neither from the logic of its argument nor from the genius of its political reasoning. Whatever force it carried came from the unspoken but nevertheless real threat of rebellion that would occur if the colonists' demands were not met. To make this threat clearer, Congress endorsed a set of resolutions rushed to Philadelphia from Suffolk County, Massachusetts. These **Suffolk Resolves** called on the residents of that county to arm themselves and prepare to resist British military action. Congressional support for these resolves sent a clear message that American leaders were willing to choose rebellion if politics failed.

The delegates adjourned and headed home, bringing news of the Congress's decisions with them to their families and their communities. There was nothing to do now but wait for the Crown's response. When it came, it was electric. "Blows must decide," declared King George III, "whether they are to be subject to this country or independent."

♦ British troops came to Concord in April 1775 to destroy the cache of arms and ammunition stored there. In this painting, soldiers carry out the mission while their commanding officers keep watch for the local militia. They found the Minutemen at the North Bridge, where, in a three-minute exchange of fire, five men were killed. For New Englanders, the Revolutionary War had begun. *"A View of the Town of Concord," 1775. Attributed to Ralph Earle. Concord Museum, Concord, MA.*

The Decision for Independence

- Could the Revolutionary War have been avoided?
- What choices on both sides might have kept compromise alive?
- What different expectations and constraints influenced some colonial groups to become loyalists and others to become patriots?

Americans were anxious while they waited for the king and Parliament to respond to the Declaration of Rights and Grievances, but they were not idle. In most colonies, a transfer of political power was occurring, as Americans withdrew their support for and obedience to royal governments and recognized the authority of anti-British, **patriot** governments. The king might expect blows to decide the issue of colonial autonomy, but independent local governments were becoming a reality before any shots were fired.

Taking Charge and Enforcing Policies

Imperial control broke down as communities in each colony refused to obey royal laws or acknowledge the authority of royal officers. For example,

Declaration of Rights and Grievances A resolution, passed by the First Continental Congress in 1774, that denied Parliament's right to tax the colonies without their consent.

Suffolk Resolves Resolutions adopted in 1774 by Boston and other towns in Suffolk County, Massachusetts, calling on local citizens to take up arms against the British.

patriot An American colonist who opposed British rule and fought for independence.

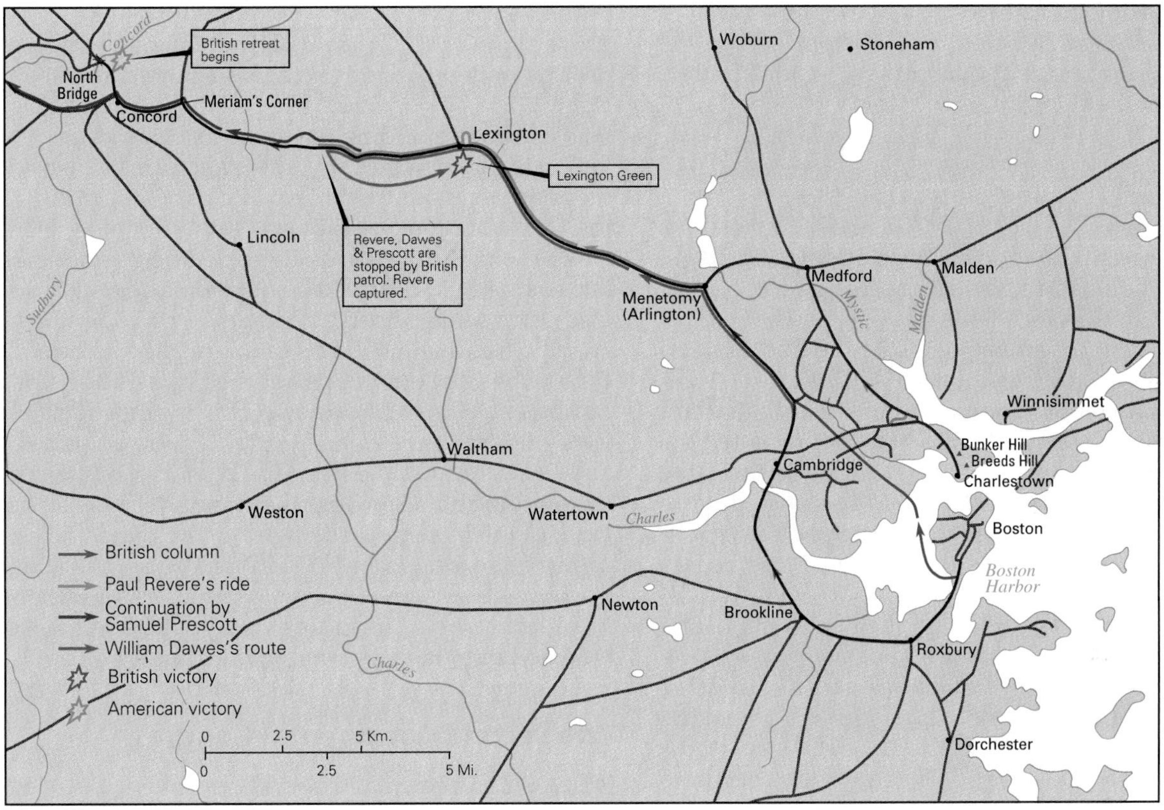

♦ **MAP 5.3 The First Battles in the War for Independence, 1775** This map shows the British march to Concord and the routes taken by the three Americans who alerted the countryside of the enemy's approach. Although Paul Revere was captured by the British and did not complete his ride, he is the best remembered and most celebrated of the nightriders who spread the alarm.

when General Thomas Gage, the acting governor of Massachusetts, refused to convene the Massachusetts assembly, its members met anyway. Their first order of business was to prepare for military resistance to Gage and his army. While the redcoats occupied Boston, the rebellious assembly openly ordered the colonists to stockpile military supplies near the town of Concord (see Map 5.3).

The transition from royal to patriot political control was peaceful in communities where anti-British sentiment was strong. Where it was weak, or where the community was divided, radicals used persuasion, pressure, and open intimidation to advance the patriot cause. These radicals became increasingly impatient with dissent, disagreement, or even indecision among their neighbors. They insisted that people choose sides and declare loyalties.

In most colonial cities and towns patriot committees arose to enforce compliance with the boycott of British goods. These committees publicly exposed those who did not obey the Continental Association, publishing violators' names in local newspapers and calling on the community to shun them. These tactics were effective against merchants who wanted to break the boycott and consumers willing to purchase English goods if they could find them. When public shaming did not work, most committees were ready to use threats of physical violence and to make good on them.

Colonists suspected of sympathizing with the British were brought before committees and made to swear oaths of support for the patriot cause. Such political pressure often gave way to violence. In Connecticut, a group of patriots hauled a 70-year-old Anglican man from his bed, dragged him naked into the winter night, and beat him brutally because his loyalty to the Church of England made him suspect. In New England, many pro-British citizens, or

loyalists, came to fear for their lives. In the wake of the Intolerable Acts, hundreds of them fled to the city of Boston, hoping General Gage could protect them from their neighbors.

The Shot Heard Round the World

The American situation was frustrating, but King George continued to believe that resistance in most colonies would fade if the Massachusetts radicals were crushed. In January 1775, he ordered General Gage to arrest the most notorious leaders of rebellion in that colony: Samuel Adams and John Hancock. Although storms on the Atlantic prevented the king's orders from reaching Gage until April, the general had independently decided it was time to take action. Gage planned to dispatch a force of redcoats to Concord with orders to seize the rapidly growing stockpile of weapons.

The patriots, of course, had their spies in Boston. Reports of the arrest orders and of suspicious troop preparations reached the militias gathered outside the occupied city. The only question was when and where Gage would attack. The Americans devised a warning system: as soon as Gage's troops began to move out of Boston, spies would use lanterns to signal from the bell tower of the North Church. On April 18, 1775, riders waiting outside Boston saw one lantern, then another, flash from the bell tower. Within moments, silversmith Paul Revere and his fellow messengers rode off to give news of the British army's approach to the militia and the people living in the countryside.

Around sunrise on April 19, an advance guard of a few hundred redcoats reached the town of Lexington. In the pale light, they saw about seventy colonial militamen waiting on the village green. As the badly outnumbered colonists began to disperse, eager and nervous redcoats broke ranks and rushed forward, sending up a triumphant cheer. No order came to fire, but in the confusion shots rang out. Eight Americans were killed, most of them shot in the back as they ran for safety. Nine more were wounded. Later Americans who told the story of the skirmish at Lexington would insist that the first musket fired there sounded a "shot heard round the world."

The British troops marched from Lexington to Concord. Surprised to find the town nearly deserted, they began a methodical search for weapons. All they uncovered were five hundred musket balls, which they dumped into a nearby pond. They then burned the town's liberty tree. Ignoring this act of provocation, the Concord **Minutemen,** in hiding nearby, waited patiently. When the moment seemed right, they swooped down on the unsuspecting British troops guarding the town's North Bridge.

The sudden attack by the Americans shocked the redcoats, who fled in a panic back toward Boston. The Minutemen followed, gathering more men along the path of pursuit. Together, these American farmers, artisans, servants, and shopkeepers terrorized the young British soldiers, firing on them at will from behind barns, stone walls, and trees. When the shaken troops reached the British encampment across the Charles River from Boston, 73 of their comrades were dead, 174 were wounded, and 26 were missing. The day after the **Battles of Lexington and Concord,** thousands of New England militiamen poured in from the surrounding countryside, dug trenches, and laid siege to Boston. As far as they and thousands of other Americans were concerned—including the loyalist refugees crowded into the city—war had begun.

The Second Continental Congress

When the Continental Congress reconvened in May 1775, it began at once to ready the colonies for war. This Second Continental Congress authorized the printing of American paper money for the purchase of supplies and appointed a committee to oversee foreign relations. It approved the creation of a Continental Army and chose George Washington, the Virginia veteran of the French and Indian War, to serve as its commander.

The Congress was clearly ready to defend Americans' rights and protect their liberties. But was it ready to declare a complete break with England? Some delegates still hoped to find a peaceful solution to the crisis, despite the bloodshed at Lexington and Concord. This sentiment led the Congress to

loyalist An American colonist who remained loyal to the king during the Revolution.

Minutemen Nickname first given to the Concord militia because of their speed at assembling and then applied generally to colonial militia at the time of the Revolution.

Battles of Lexington and Concord Two confrontations in April 1775 between British soldiers and patriot minutemen—the first recognized battles of the Revolution.

draft the **Olive Branch Petition,** which offered the king a choice: the colonists would end their armed resistance if the king would withdraw the British military and revoke the Intolerable Acts. Many delegates must have doubted the king's willingness to make such concessions, for the very next day the Congress issued a public statement in defense of the war preparations. This *Declaration of the Causes and Necessity of Taking Up Arms* boldly accused the British government of tyranny. It stopped short, however, of declaring colonial independence.

Across the Atlantic, British leaders struggled to find some negotiating points despite the king's refusal to bend. Almost two months before the battles at Lexington and Concord, Lord North had drafted a set of Conciliatory Propositions for Parliament and the American Continental Congress to consider. North's proposals gave no ground on Parliament's right to tax the colonies, but they did offer to suspend taxation if Americans would raise the money for their own military defense. Members of Parliament who were sympathetic toward the Americans also pressed for compromise. They insisted that it made better sense to keep the colonies as a market for English goods than to lose them in a battle over raising revenue.

Cooler heads, however, did not prevail. Americans rejected Lord North's proposals in July 1775. The king, unmoved by the logic of compromise, rejected the Olive Branch Petition. George III then persuaded Parliament to pass an **American Prohibitory Act** instructing the royal navy to seize American ships engaged in any form of trade, "as if the same were the ships . . . of open enemies." For all intents and purposes, King George III declared war on his colonies before the colonies declared war on their king.

The Impact of *Common Sense*

Although war was a fact, few American voices were calling for a complete political and emotional break with Britain. Even the most ardent patriots continued to justify their actions as upholding the British constitution. They were rebelling, they said, to preserve the rights guaranteed English citizens, not to establish an independent nation. Their drastic actions were necessary because a corrupt Parliament and corrupt ministers were trampling on those rights.

Although in 1764 Patrick Henry had dramatically warned the king to remember that tyrants were often deposed, few colonists had yet traced the source of their oppression to George III himself. If any American political leaders believed the king was as corrupt as his advisers and his Parliament, they did not make this view public. Then, in January 1776, Thomas Paine, an Englishman who had emigrated to America a few years earlier, published a pamphlet he called ***Common Sense.*** Paine's pamphlet broke the silence about King George III.

Tom Paine was a corsetmaker by trade but a political radical by temperament. As soon as he settled in Philadelphia, he became a wholehearted and vocal supporter of the colonial protest to defend colonial rights, but he preferred American political independence. In *Common Sense,* Paine spoke directly to ordinary citizens, not to their political leaders. Like the preachers of the Great Awakening, he rejected the formal language of the elite, adopting instead a plain, urgent, and emotional vocabulary and writing style designed to reach a mass audience.

Common Sense was unique in its content as well as its style. Paine made no excuses for his revolutionary zeal. He expressed no admiration for the British constitution or reverence for the British political system. Instead, he attacked the **sanctity** of the monarchy head-on. He challenged the idea of a hereditary ruler, questioned the value of monarchy as an institution, and criticized the personal character of the men who ruled as kings. The common man, Paine insisted, had the ability to be his own king and was surely more deserving of that position than most of the men who had worn crowns. Paine put it bluntly and sarcastically: "Of more worth is one honest man to society, and in the sight of God, than all the crowned ruffians that ever lived." He dismissed George III as nothing more than a "Royal Brute," and he urged Americans to establish their own republic.

Common Sense sold 120,000 copies in its first three months in print. Paine's defiance of traditional

Olive Branch Petition Resolution, adopted after the Battles of Lexington and Concord by the Second Continental Congress in 1775, that offered to end armed resistance if the king would withdraw his troops and repeal the Intolerable Acts.

American Prohibitory Act British law (1775) that authorized the royal navy to seize all American ships engaged in trade; it amounted to a declaration of war.

Common Sense Revolutionary pamphlet written by Thomas Paine and published in 1776; it attacked George III and argued against the monarchial form of government.

sanctity The quality of being sacred or inviolable.

authority and open criticism of the men who wielded it helped many of his readers, both male and female, discard the last shreds of loyalty to the king and to the empire. The impact of Paine's words could be seen in the taverns and coffee houses, where ordinary farmers, artisans, shopkeepers, and laborers took up his call for independence and the creation of a republic. Political leaders acknowledged Paine's importance, although some begrudged the popular admiration lavished on this poorly educated artisan. The Harvard-trained John Adams reluctantly admitted that *Common Sense* was a "tolerable summary of the arguments I have been repeating again and again in Congress for nine months." But Adams's social snobbery led him to criticize Paine's language and his flamboyant writing style, suitable, Adams insisted, only "for an emigrant from new Gate [an English prison] or one chiefly associated with such company." Unshaken by such criticism, Tom Paine was content to see his message move so many into the revolutionary camp.

♦ In 1776, patriots everywhere celebrated independence by destroying local symbols of royal authority. New Yorkers, however, combined the practical with the symbolic, tearing down an imposing statue of King George III that had stood near the tip of Manhattan since 1770 and recycling its lead to make ammunition for the revolutionary army. *"Pulling Down the Statue of George III" by William Walcott. Private Collection.*

Declaring Independence

The Second Continental Congress, lagging far behind popular sentiment, inched its way toward a formal declaration of independence. But even John Adams, who had fumed at its snail's pace, took heart when the Congress opened American trade to all nations except Great Britain in early April 1776 and instructed the colonies to create official state governments. Then, on June 7, Adams's close ally in the struggle to have independence declared, Virginia lawyer Richard Henry Lee, rose on the floor of the Congress and offered this straightforward motion: "That these United Colonies are, and of right ought to be, free and independent States, that they are absolved from all allegiance to the British Crown, and that all political connection between them and the State of Great Britain is, and ought to be, totally dissolved."

Lee's resolution was no more than a statement of reality, yet the Congress chose to postpose its final vote until July. The delay would give members time to win over the few faint-hearted delegates from the Middle Colonies. It also would allow the committee appointed to draft a formal declaration of independence time to complete its work.

Congress had chosen an all-star group to draft the declaration, including John Adams, Connecticut's Roger Sherman, Benjamin Franklin, and New York landowner Robert Livingston. But these men delegated the task of writing the document to the fifth and youngest member of the committee, Thomas Jefferson. They chose well. The 32-year-old Virginian was not a social radical like Samuel Adams and Tom Paine. He was not an experienced politician like John Adams and Benjamin Franklin. And he lacked the reputation of fellow Virginians George Washington and Richard Henry Lee. But he had his strengths, and the committee members recognized them. Jefferson could draw on a deep and broad knowledge of political theory and philosophy. He had read the works of Enlightenment philosophers, classical theorists, and the writers of the seventeenth-century English revolutionary tradition. And though shy and somewhat halting in his speech, Thomas Jefferson was a master of written prose.

Jefferson began the **Declaration of Independence** with a defense of revolution based on "self-evident" truths about humanity's "unalienable rights"—rights

Declaration of Independence A formal statement, adopted by the Second Continental Congress in 1776, that listed justifications for rebellion and declared the American colonies' independence from Britain.

that included life, liberty, and the pursuit of property (wealth). Jefferson argued that these rights were natural rather than historical. In other words, they came from the "Creator" rather than developing out of human law, government, or tradition. Thus they were broader and more sacred than the specific "rights of Englishmen." With this philosophical groundwork in place, Jefferson moved on to list the grievances that demanded that America end its relationship with Britain. He focused on the king's abuse of power rather than on the oppressive legislation passed by Parliament. All government rested on the consent of the governed, Jefferson asserted, and the people had the right to overthrow any government that tyrannized rather than protected them, that threatened rather than respected their unalienable rights.

Declaring Loyalties

Delegates to the Second Continental Congress approved the Declaration of Independence on July 2, 1776, and made their approval public on July 4 (the text of the Declaration is reprinted in the Documents appendix at the back of this book). As John Adams was fond of saying, "The die was cast," and Americans had to weigh loyalty to king against loyalty to a new nation. For Americans of every region, religion, social class, and race, this decision weighed heavily. In the face of such a critical choice, many wavered. Throughout the war that followed the Declaration, a surprising number of colonists clung to neutrality, hoping that the war could be resolved without their having to participate or choose sides.

Those who did commit themselves based their decision on deeply held beliefs and personal considerations as well as fears (see Individual Choices: Esther Quincy Sewall). Many loyalists believed that tradition, commitment, and common sense argued for acknowledging parliamentary supremacy and the king's right to rule. These colonists had a deep respect for the structure of the British government, with its balance among royalty, aristocracy, and the common people and its ability to preserve the rights of each group. In their judgment, the advantages of remaining within the protective circle of the most powerful nation in Europe seemed too obvious to debate. The likelihood of swift and bloody defeat at the hands of the British army and navy seemed too obvious to risk. Many of the men who articulated the loyalist position were members of the colonial elite. They frankly admitted their fears that a revolution would unleash the "madness of the multitude." The tyranny of the mob, they argued, was far more damaging than the tyranny of which the king was accused.

Not all colonists who chose loyalism feared the mob or revered the principles on which the British political system was based. For many, the deciding issues were economic. Holders of royal offices and merchants who depended on trade with British manufacturers found loyalty a compelling alternative. The loyalist ranks were also filled with colonists from the "multitude." Many small farmers and tenant farmers gave their support to the Crown when their political and economic foes—the great planters of the South or the New York manor lords—became patriots. The choice of which side to back often hinged, therefore, on local struggles and economic conflicts rather than on imperial issues.

For some of the perhaps 150,000 active loyalists, loyalism was a matter of personal character as much as conscious self-interest. Reluctance to break a solemn oath of allegiance to the king, anxiety over breaking ties with the past, fear of the chaos and violence that were a real part of revolution—any and all of these feelings could motivate a colonist to remain loyal rather than rebel.

For African Americans, the rallying call of liberty was familiar long before the Revolution began. Decades of slave resistance and rebellion demonstrated that black colonists did not need the impassioned language of a Patrick Henry or a Samuel Adams to remind them of the value of freedom. Instead, many slaves viewed the Revolution as they viewed epidemics and imperial warfare: as a potential opportunity to gain their own liberty. In the same way, free blacks saw the Revolution as a possible opportunity to win civil rights they had been denied before 1776.

African Americans pointed out the inconsistencies of the radical position even before the Declaration of Independence. In 1773, a group of enslaved blacks in Boston petitioned the governor and the assembly for their freedom, "in behalf of all those, who . . . are held in a state of SLAVERY, within the bowels of a FREE country." There were white colonists who appreciated the injustice of a white slaveholding community in crisis over threats to its liberty. In 1774, while John Adams debated the threat of political slavery for colonial Englishmen in the First Continental Congress, his wife Abigail observed: "It always appeared a most iniquitous [sinful] scheme to me—to fight ourselves for what we are daily robbing and plundering from those who have as good a right to freedom as we have." Tom

INDIVIDUAL CHOICES

Choosing Loyalty

Esther Quincy Sewall

This is the home Esther Sewall chose to leave in 1775 when she accompanied her loyalist husband, Jonathan, to England on the eve of the Revolutionary War. Faced with an uncertain life abroad, she nevertheless chose to stay with her husband rather than remain in Boston and enjoy the safety and certainty her friends and family provided. Harvard University Archives.

On November 13, 1790, Esther Quincy Sewall took up her pen to answer a letter from her brother-in-law, the famous patroit John Hancock. Hancock had written, pleading with Esther Sewall to return to her family and friends in their native city, Boston. "I wish it was in my power to accept of your kind invitation," Esther wrote from the isolated loyalist settlement in New Brunswick, Canada; "however this is a pleasure I must post pone for a future day."

Esther Quincy Sewall's exile from her beloved Massachusetts was voluntary. Unlike her husband, Jonathan Sewall, she had not been named a political enemy of the newly independent state. Yet despite the encouragement of her sisters and brothers, she chose to continue her exile. For Esther Quincy Sewall the choice was a matter of personal loyalties and commitments as strong as the political ones that shaped her husband's life.

Esther Quincy first met Jonathan Sewall at a boating party in 1759. He was struck by her beauty and her good humor and placed her immediately in "the rank of the Agreeables." She was, he observed, a woman of "unaffected Modesty," with good judgment, delicate manners, and "real Good sense." Their courtship began at once, but the couple did not marry until 1764, when Jonathan's legal career was better

Paine agreed. Writing as "Humanus" in a Philadelphia newspaper, Paine urged white patriots to abolish slavery and give freed blacks western land grants.

Other patriots worried that slaves would seek their freedom by supporting the British in the war. The royal governor of Virginia was ready to make an offer of freedom to the colony's slaves. In 1775, Governor Dunmore expressed his intention to "arm all my own Negroes and receive all others that will come to me whom I shall declare free." Rumors of this plan threw terror into neighboring Maryland planters, who demanded that their governor issue arms and ammunition to protect against slave insurrection. Throughout the South, white communities braced themselves for a black struggle for freedom that would emerge in the midst of the colonial struggle for independence.

When Dunmore did offer freedom to "all indentured Servants, negroes or others . . . able and willing to bear Arms" who escaped their masters," he was more interested in disrupting the slave-based plantation economy of his American enemies than in African American rights. Yet slaves responded, established. Esther's family and friends approved the match, for although Jonathan was from a poor branch of a distinguished family, his talent and ambition led them to predict a good future for the couple. Their predictions were correct. By the eve of the Revolution, Jonathan Sewall held several highly prized positions in the colony's royal government, and Esther lived in quiet elegance with her husband and two sons in their Cambridge home.

The escalating conflicts of 1775 put a sudden end to the life the Sewalls knew. Jonathan Sewall was among the first loyalists to leave America for England in 1775. Esther said goodbye to her patriot relatives and went with him. As the war dragged on, the Sewalls' finances grew strained. They moved from rooming house to rooming house, finally settling in the port city of Bristol.

Exile and the American victory made Jonathan Sewall bitter and psychologically distant. Esther Sewall bore the brunt of his despair. He vented his anger and frustration on his wife, sarcastically wishing her "tyed to the Tail of the Comet of 1668." Esther did not hide her homesickness, and this provoked her husband's anger. He railed against the "deviltry and matrimony" that had ruined his life—and insisted that Esther return to America and leave him in peace.

Despite his accusations and insults, Esther Sewall never considered leaving her physically ailing and depressed husband. She accompanied him to Canada in 1787, joining a small community of loyalist exiles in Nova Scotia. As Sewall's condition deteriorated, Esther became his constant companion and nurse. On September 25, 1796, she began a three-day vigil by his bedside, remaining with him until he died on September 27. Having done her duty as a wife, Esther Sewall felt free to choose her own future. After twenty-one years of exile, she packed her few belongings and went home. Whatever her private regrets or satisfactions, she never recorded a word of regret at the choice of loyalties that shaped her life.

crossing into British lines in great enough numbers to create an "Ethiopian Regiment" of soldiers. These black loyalists wore a banner across their uniforms that read "Liberty to Slaves." Only six hundred to two thousand slaves managed to escape their masters in 1775–1776, but in the southern campaigns of the long war that followed, thousands of black men, women, and children made their way to the British lines. Once in uniform, black soldiers were usually assigned to work in road construction and other manual labor tasks rather than participate in combat. Perhaps as many as fifty thousand slaves gained their freedom during the war, as a result of either British policy or the disruptions that made escape possible.

Indians' responses to news of the war were far from uniform. At first, many considered the Revolution a family quarrel that should be avoided. The revolutionaries would have been satisfied to see Indians adopt this policy of neutrality. They knew they were unlikely to win Indian support given the legacy of border warfare and the actions of land-hungry settlers. As early as 1775, the Second Continental Congress issued a proclamation warning

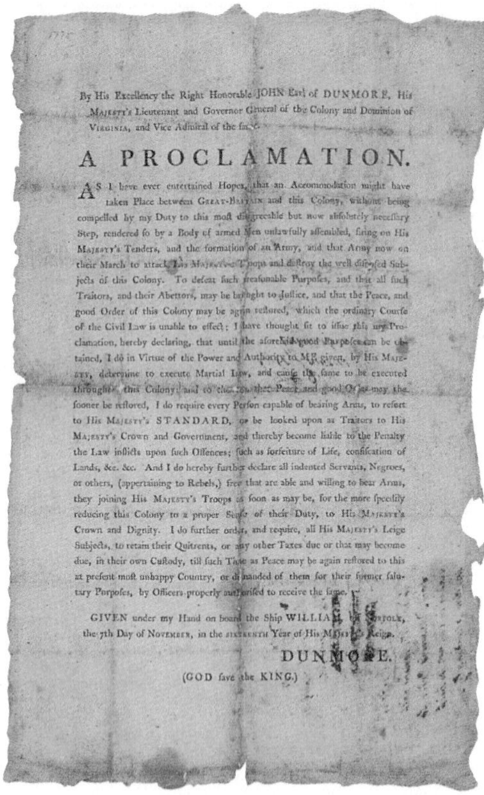

By His Excellency the Right Honorable JOHN Earl of DUNMORE, His MAJESTY's Lieutenant and Governor General of the Colony and Dominion of VIRGINIA, and Vice Admiral of the same.

A PROCLAMATION.

AS I have ever entertained Hopes, that an Accommodation might have taken Place between GREAT-BRITAIN and this Colony, without being compelled by my Duty to this most disagreeable but now absolutely necessary Step, rendered so by a Body of armed Men unlawfully assembled, firing on His MAJESTY's Tenders, and the formation of an Army, and that Army now on their March to attack His MAJESTY's Troops and destroy the well disposed Subjects of this Colony. To defeat such treasonable Purposes, and that all such Traitors, and their Abettors, may be brought to Justice, and that the Peace, and good Order of this Colony may be again restored, which the ordinary Course of the Civil Law is unable to effect; I have thought fit to issue this my Proclamation, hereby declaring, that until the aforesaid good Purposes can be obtained, I do in Virtue of the Power and Authority to ME given, by His MAJESTY, determine to execute Martial Law, and cause the same to be executed throughout this Colony: and to the end that Peace and good Order may the sooner be restored, I do require every Person capable of bearing Arms, to resort to His MAJESTY's STANDARD, or be looked upon as Traitors to His MAJESTY's Crown and Government, and thereby become liable to the Penalty the Law inflicts upon such Offences; such as forfeiture of Life, confiscation of Lands, &c. &c. And I do hereby further declare all indented Servants, Negroes, or others, (appertaining to Rebels,) free that are able and willing to bear Arms, they joining His MAJESTY's Troops as soon as may be, for the more speedily reducing this Colony to a proper Sense of their Duty, to His MAJESTY's Crown and Dignity. I do further order, and require, all His MAJESTY's Leige Subjects, to retain their Quitrents, or any other Taxes due or that may become due, in their own Custody, till such Time as Peace may be again restored to this at present most unhappy Country, or demanded of them for their former salutary Purposes, by Officers properly authorised to receive the same.

GIVEN under my Hand on board the Ship WILLIAM, off NORFOLK, the 7th Day of NOVEMBER, in the SIXTEENTH Year of His MAJESTY's Reign.

DUNMORE.

(GOD save the KING.)

♦ In November, 1775, Virginia's royal Governor, Lord Dunmore, enraged and frightened patriots by issuing this proclamation, which offered freedom to "all indentured Servants, Negroes, or others" who would help Britain squelch the impending rebellion. Thousands of enslaved men, women, and children eventually made their way to freedom behind British lines, choosing loyalism as their route to liberty. *Special Collections, University of Virginia Alderman Library.*

Indians to remain neutral. But the British, recognizing their advantage, made strong efforts to win Indian support. Indian leaders proceeded cautiously, however. When a British negotiator boasted to Flying Crow that British victory was inevitable, the Seneca chief was unimpressed. "If you are so strong, Brother, and they but as a weak Boy, why ask our assistance." The chief was unwilling to commit his tribe based on issues that divided Crown and colonists but meant little to the welfare of his own people. "You say they are all mad, foolish, wicked, and deceitful—I say you are so and they are wise for you want us to destroy ourselves in your War and they advise us to live in Peace."

The British continued to press for Indian participation in the war, and many Indian tribes and confederations eventually decided that the Crown would better serve their interests and respect their rights than would the colonists. First, the colonists were much less likely than the British to be able to provide a steady supply of the manufactured goods and weapons the Indians relied on in the eighteenth century. Second, colonial territorial ambitions threatened the Indians along the southern and northwestern frontiers. Third, an alliance with the British offered some possibility of recouping land and trading benefits lost in the past. No uniformity emerged, however. Among the Iroquois, for example, conflicting choices of loyalties led pro-British Senecas to burn the crops and houses of Oneidas who had joined forces with the patriots. Among the Potowatomis, similar divisions occurred. Intertribal rivalries and Indians' concerns about the safety of their own villages often determined alignments. In the southern backcountry, fierce fighting between Indians and revolutionaries seemed a continuation of the century's many border wars. But even there, alignments could shift. Although the Cherokees began the war as British allies, a split developed, producing an internal civil war similar to the one among the Iroquois tribes.

Fewer than half of the colonists threw in their lot with the revolutionaries. Among those who did were people whose economic interests made independence seem worth the risk, including artisans and urban laborers, merchants who traded outside the British Empire, large and small farmers, and many members of the southern planter elite. Colonists affected by the Great Awakening and by its message of egalitarianism often chose the patriot side. Americans with a conscious, articulated radical vision of society—the Tom Paines and Samuel Adamses—supported the Revolution and its promise of a republic. Many who became revolutionaries shared the hope for a better life under a government that encouraged its citizens to be virtuous and to live in simplicity.

As Americans—English, European, Indian, and African American—armed themselves or fled from the violence and bloodshed they saw coming, they realized that the conflict wore two faces: this was a war for independence, but it was also a civil war. In the South, it pitted slave against master, Cherokee against Cherokee, and frontier farmer against tidewater planter. In New England, it set neighbor against neighbor, forcing scores of loyalist families to flee. In some instances, children were set against parents, and wives refused to support the cause their husbands had chosen. Whatever the outcome of the struggle ahead, Americans knew that it would come at great cost.

SUMMARY

Expectations
Constraints
Choices
Outcomes

The British victory over France and Spain in the Great War for Empire made Britain the most powerful European nation. The *outcome* produced new problems, however. The British had to govern the French population in Canada and maintain security against Indians on the colonial frontier. They had to pay an enormous war debt while maintaining a strong and well-equipped army and navy to keep the empire they had won. Given these *constraints,* the English government *chose* to impose revenue-raising measures on the colonies. The *outcome* was growing tension between Mother Country and colonies.

The Sugar Act of 1764 tightened customs collections, the Stamp Act of 1765 placed a direct tax on legal documents, and the Townshend Acts of 1767 set import taxes on English products such as paint and tea. In response to these *constraints,* the colonists *chose* protest, including crowd actions directed by the Sons of Liberty and boycotts of English goods. Crowds attacked royal officials, and in Boston five civilians died in the Boston Massacre, a clash with British troops. American colonists saw Parliament's revenue-raising acts as an abuse of power, and political debate began to focus on colonial rights and the possibility that the British government was threatening to curtail American liberties.

Protest led to the repeal of the acts, but political activists *chose* to prepare themselves for a quick and united response to any new crises by creating organizations like the committees of correspondence. In 1773, the British passed the Tea Act, *expecting* little American opposition. The *outcome* was immediate protest, and in Boston a group of activists dumped thousands of pounds' worth of tea into the harbor.

Moving to punish the colonists, the English closed the port of Boston to all trade. This and other Intolerable Acts infuriated colonists, who took united action in support of Massachusetts. A new colonial forum, the First Continental Congress, met in 1774 to debate the colonies' relationship to England and to issue united protests. A Declaration of Rights and Grievances was sent to the king. The king *chose* to reject the colonists' appeal for compromise. Instead he declared that "blows must decide."

After British troops and militiamen fought at Lexington and Concord, a Second Continental Congress began to prepare for war. Tom Paine's pamphlet *Common Sense* pushed many reluctant colonists into the revolutionary camp. In July 1776, Congress issued the Declaration of Independence, drafted by Thomas Jefferson, defending the colonists' right to resist the destruction of their liberty by a tyrannical king. In 1776, Americans faced the difficult task of *choosing* sides: loyalty to the Crown or revolution. Not only white colonists but African Americans and Indians had to decide whether to offer support to one side or the other or try to remain neutral in the midst of revolution. The *outcome* was both a war for colonial independence and a civil war that divided families and communities across America.

SUGGESTED READINGS

Howard Fast. *Citizen Tom Paine* (1943).

This novel traces Tom Paine's life from his early English roots to his radical politics during the Revolutionary War.

David Hackett Fischer. *Paul Revere's Ride* (1994).

This lively account details the circumstances and background of the efforts to rouse the countryside in response to the march of British troops toward Lexington.

Edward Countryman. *The American Revolution* (1985).

An excellent narrative of the causes and consequences of the Revolutionary War.

Colin G. Calloway. *The American Revolution in Indian Country: Crisis and Diversity in Native American Communities* (1995).

A well-written account of the variety of Indian experiences during the American revolutionary era.

"Liberty!" PBS series on the American Revolution.

Using the actual words of revolutionaries, loyalists, and British political leaders, this six-hour series follows events from the Stamp Act to the Constitution.

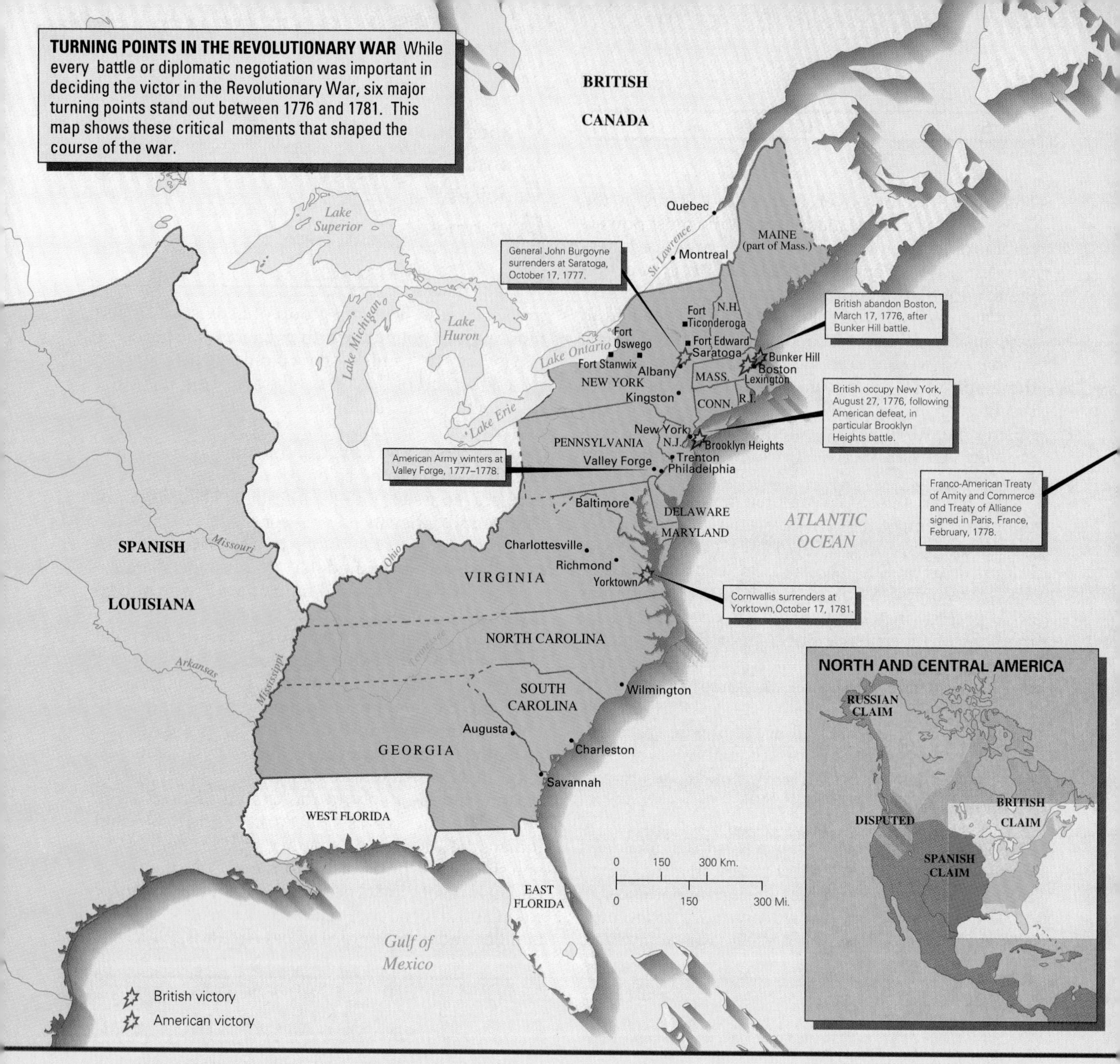

TURNING POINTS IN THE REVOLUTIONARY WAR While every battle or diplomatic negotiation was important in deciding the victor in the Revolutionary War, six major turning points stand out between 1776 and 1781. This map shows these critical moments that shaped the course of the war.

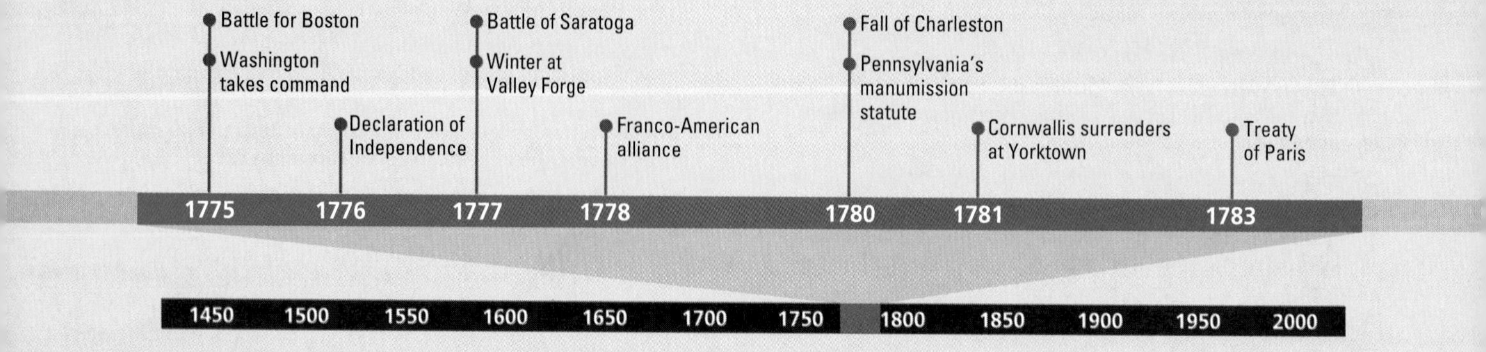

CHAPTER 6

Recreating America: Independence and a New Nation, 1775–1783

The First Two Years of War

- What expectations shaped the British and American strategies in the early years of the war?
- What choices and constraints kept the British from achieving the quick victory many expected?

Influences from off the Battlefield

- Why did the French choose to assist the Americans secretly in the early years of the war?
- Why did they choose to enter the war after Saratoga?

From Stalemate to Victory

- What choices led to General Cornwallis's surrender at Yorktown?
- What were the most important outcomes of the peace treaty negotiations?

Republican Expectations in a New Nation

- How did the Revolution affect Americans' expectations regarding individual rights, social equality, and the role of women in American society?
- What choices were open to African Americans during and after the Revolution?
- What choices were open to the loyalists?

INTRODUCTION

Expectations
Constraints
Choices
Outcomes

What began in April 1775 as a skirmish at Concord's North Bridge grew into an international war costing millions of dollars and thousands of lives. While Great Britain *expected* victory over the colonial rebels, the Americans hardly dared *expect* anything at all. Even the commander in chief of the Continental Army, General George Washington, frequently expressed his doubts that independence could be won on the battlefield.

Washington understood the *contraints* and dangers the rebels faced better than most Americans. To crush the colonial rebellion, Great Britain *chose* to commit vast human and material resources. Indeed, between 1775 and 1781, the English government deployed more than fifty thousand British soldiers and marines and hired thirty thousand German mercenaries to join them in North America. The well-trained and harshly disciplined British ground troops were assisted and supplied by the most powerful navy in the world, and they carried the flag of the richest imperial power of Europe. Many Indian tribes, including most of the Iroquois, *chose* to fight as allies of the British, and the Crown could *expect* thousands of white and black loyalists to fight beside them also.

The American war effort, in contrast, labored under a variety of *constraints.* The Continental Congress had a nearly empty treasury, and the country's resources did not include the foundries or factories needed to produce arms, ammunition, or other military supplies. The army administration was inefficient, the population was wary of professional soldiers, and the state governments were unwilling to raise tax monies to contribute to the Congress's war chest. Through most of the war, therefore, American officers and enlisted men could *expect* to be underpaid or not paid at all, to go into battle poorly equipped, often half starved, and frequently dressed in rags. Unlike the British redcoats, these Americans had little military skill or formal military training. Except for the soldiers of Washington's Continental Army, few American enlisted men were exposed to or mastered the disciplined field and marching maneuvers of the professional eighteenth-century soldier. Most American enlisted men were *expected* to take orders from officers no better trained than they were. Although some officers were skilled veterans and others proved to have a feel for military strategy and tactics, many were just rash young men dreaming of glory. Finally, enlistments and terms of service in the Continental regiments, in state militia units, and in the local black and white guerrilla bands shifted with the seasons and with the rebellion's progress. Thus when General Washington and his fellow commanders *chose* a strategy, waged a campaign, or led troops into battle, they did not know how many soldiers would be marching with them.

Britain's advantage was great but not absolute. To fight the war, the British had to transport arms, provisions, and men across thousands of miles of ocean. They risked delays, disasters, and destruction of supplies on the open seas. They found it difficult to keep their armies supplied once they reached American soil and difficult to maneuver them on unfamiliar terrain. The Americans were fighting on familiar terrain, and geography gave them an additional advantage: their vast, rural society could not be easily conquered even if major colonial cities were taken or an entire region was occupied. Centuries-old European rivalries also worked to the advantage of the Americans and gave them valuable allies. Holland, France, and Spain all *expected* to benefit from England's distress and *chose* to lend money and provide much-needed supplies to the rebellion. When France and Spain *chose* to recognize American independence formally, the consequences were immediate and dramatic. The war expanded into an international, global struggle, and the support of the French navy transformed General Washington's military strategy. After the victory at Yorktown, even the most patriotic Americans realized that their independence was the *outcome* of international politics as much as military heroism or popular commitment to the Revolution.

Although the *outcome* of the war was often in doubt, its impact on American men and women was not. No matter what eighteenth-century Americans felt about the war, no matter which side they supported, or what role they played, they shared the experience of extraordinary events and the need to make extraordinary *choices* when the war disrupted the flow of their ordinary lives. In this most personal and immediate sense, the *outcome* was revolutionary.

CHRONOLOGY

Rebellion and Independence

1775	Battle for Boston George Washington assumes command of the Continental Army
1776	Declaration of Independence British campaigns in the South and mid-Atlantic region George Mason's Declaration of Rights
1777	Burgoyne's New York campaign Battle of Saratoga Winter at Valley Forge
1778	Franco-American alliance
1779	British begin second southern campaign
1780	Fall of Charleston Treason of Benedict Arnold Pennsylvania enacts manumission statute
1781	Cornwallis surrenders at Yorktown Loyalists evacuate the United States Articles of Confederation adopted
1782	British Parliament votes to end war
1783	Treaty of Paris signed

The First Two Years of War

- What expectations shaped the British and American strategies in the early years of the war?
- What choices and constraints kept the British from achieving the quick victory many expected?

In 1775, **Thomas Gage,** the British general who was military governor of Massachusetts and commander of His Majesty's army of occupation there, surely wished he were anywhere but Boston. The town was unsophisticated by British standards, many of its inhabitants were unfriendly, and its taverns and lodging houses bulged at the seams with complaining loyalist refugees from the countryside. Gage's army was restless, and his officers were bored. The American encampments outside the city were growing daily, filling with local farmers and artisans after the bloodshed of Lexington and Concord. These thousands of colonial **militiamen** gathering on the hills surrounding Boston were clearly the military enemy. Yet in 1775 they were still citizens of the British Empire not foreign invaders or foes. Gage, like his American opponents, was caught up in the dilemmas of an undeclared war.

The Battle for Boston

With proper artillery, well placed on the hills surrounding the city, the Americans could have done serious damage to Gage's army of occupation. The problem was that the rebels had no cannon to train on their enemy. A remedy to this situation emerged when a young Philadelphia soldier named **Benedict Arnold** joined forces with Vermont's Ethan Allen and his band of **Green Mountain Boys.** Arnold and Allen succeeded in seizing Fort Ticonderoga in New York in May 1775. With great difficulty, rebels transported the fort's cannon across hundreds of miles to Boston. By the time the artillery reached the city, however, a bloody battle between Gage and the American militia had already taken place.

In early June, Gage had issued a proclamation declaring all armed colonists traitors, but he offered **amnesty** to any rebel who surrendered to British

Thomas Gage British general who was military governor of Massachusetts and commander of the army of occupation in 1775.

militiamen Soldiers who are not members of a regular army but are ordinary citizens ready to be called out in case of an emergency.

Benedict Arnold Pharmacist-turned-military leader, whose acts of daring and bravery made him an American hero and a favorite of George Washington until, in 1780, he committed treason against the Revolution.

Green Mountain Boys Vermont militiamen led by Ethan Allen; together, they and Benedict Arnold captured Fort Ticonderoga in May 1775.

amnesty A general pardon granted by a government, especially for political offenses.

♦ American artist John Trumball painted *The Battle of Bunker Hill* in 1786, over a decade after the bloody encounter between redcoats and American militiamen. Trumball was a student of the famous American painter Benjamin West, who had won his reputation celebrating the English victories of the French and Indian War. Trumball and other American students of West built their reputations by celebrating American victories in the artistic style that West taught them. *"The Death of General Warren at Bunker Hill" by John Trumball, Yale University Art Gallery. Trumball Collection.*

authorities. When the militiamen ignored the general's offer, Gage decided a show of force was necessary. On June 17, 1775, under cover of cannon fire from a British battleship in Boston harbor, Gage's fellow officer, **William Howe** led a force of twenty-four hundred soldiers against rebel-held Breed's Hill. Despite the heat and humidity of the day, General Howe ordered his men to advance in full dress uniform, weighed down with wool jackets and heavy knapsacks. Howe also insisted on making a "proper" frontal attack on the Americans. From the top of the hill, Captain William Prescott's militiamen immediately opened fire on the unprotected redcoats. The result was a near massacre. The tables turned, however, when the Americans ran out of ammunition. Most of Prescott's men fled in confusion, and the British soldiers bayoneted the few who remained to defend their position.

Even battle-worn veterans were shocked at the carnage of the day. The British suffered more casualties that June morning than they would in any other battle of the war. The Americans, who retreated to the safety of Cambridge, learned a costly lesson on the importance of an effective supply line of arms and ammunition to their fighting men. Little was gained by either side. That the battle was misnamed the **Battle of Bunker Hill** captured perfectly the confusion and the absurdity of the encounter.

Congress Creates an Army

While militiamen and redcoats turned the Boston area into a war zone, the Continental Congress took its first steps toward recruiting and supplying an army. The "regular" army that took shape was not really a national force. It was a collection of small

William Howe British general in command at the Battle of Bunker Hill; three years later, he became commander-in-chief of British forces in America.

Battle of Bunker Hill British assault on American troops on Breed's Hill near Boston in June 1775; the British won the battle but suffered heavy losses.

state armies whose recruits preserved their identities as Marylanders or Pennsylvanians and so on. These soldiers chose most of their own officers, although they allowed the Continental Congress to appoint officers over the rank of colonel. The Continental Congress continued to rely on the state militias to play an active role in any fighting that occurred within their boundaries.

Congress chose the veteran of the French and Indian War, **George Washington,** to command the Continental forces. Before leaving his Virginia plantation, Washington pondered the enormity of the task before him. Nothing he saw when he reached Massachusetts on July 3, 1775, made him more optimistic. A carnival atmosphere seemed to prevail inside the militiamen's camps. Soldiers fired their muskets at random, often using their weapons to start fires or to shoot at geese flying overhead. In the confusion, they sometimes accidentally wounded or killed themselves and others. Washington wrote in amazement to a friend that "Seldom a day passes but some persons are shot by their friends."

The camps resembled pigsties. The stench from open latrines was terrible, and rotting animal carcasses, strewn everywhere, added to the aroma. The men were dirty and infected with lice, and most soldiers were constantly scratching, trying to relieve an itch that left them covered with scabs and raw, peeling skin. General Washington was disturbed but not surprised by what he saw. He knew that the men in these camps were country boys, away from home for the first time in their lives. The chaos they created resulted from a combination of fear, excitement, boredom, inexperience, and plain homesickness, all brewing freely under poor leadership. Despite his sympathy for these young men, Washington acted quickly to reorganize the militia units, replace incompetent officers, and tighten discipline within the camps.

The British meanwhile laid plans for the evacuation of Boston, spurred in part by the knowledge that Arnold's wagon train of cannon was nearing Massachusetts. In March 1776 a fleet arrived to carry Thomas Gage, his officers, the British army, and almost a thousand loyalist refugees north to the safety of Halifax, Nova Scotia. There, Gage gladly turned over command of His Majesty's war to the Howe brothers—General William Howe, commander of the Breed's Hill attack, and **Richard Howe,** an admiral in the royal navy. With the help of military strategists and the vast resources of the Crown, the Howes were expected to bring the rebellion to a speedy end and restore order to the colonies.

The British Strategy in 1776

General Howe's invasion and occupation strategy was simple: locate areas with high concentrations of loyalists and mobilize them to win back the allegiance of their undecided and even rebellious neighbors. Howe and his advisers correctly identified two centers of loyalist strength. The first—New York, New Jersey, Pennsylvania—had a legacy of social and economic conflicts, such as the revolt of the Paxton Boys, that caused many of the region's prosperous families to fear that **anarchy,** civil violence, and persecution would follow if independence was won. A second stronghold was the frontier regions of the Carolinas. There, decades of bitter struggle between the coastal planters and the backcountry farmers led to the Regulator movement (see page 99) and to intense loyalist sentiment among the embattled westerners.

There were flaws in General Howe's strategy, however. First, although many people in these two regions were loyal, their numbers were never as great as the British expected. Second, Britain's own troops undermined the effort to win back the affections of neutral and anti-British populations. Everywhere they went, British and **Hessian troops** left behind a trail of destruction and memories of abuse. One American soldier recorded the sight in Pennsylvania and New Jersey of "cattle killed and lying about the fields and pastures . . . household furniture hacked and broken into pieces . . . wells filled up and . . . farmers' tools destroyed." Such treatment helped drive undecided Americans into the revolutionary camp.

Howe launched his military assault against the Carolinas and the mid-Atlantic region in 1776. The campaign in the South went badly. In North Carolina, loyalists did turn out to fight for the Crown, but Howe's officers could not deliver the strong

George Washington Commander-in-chief of the Continental Army; he led the Americans to victory in the Revolutionary War and later became the first president of the United States.

Richard Howe British admiral who commanded British naval forces in America; General William Howe was his brother.

anarchy The complete absence of any political authority; lawlessness.

Hessian troops German soldiers from the state of Hesse; Great Britain hired them to fight for the British in the American Revolution.

troop support needed to ensure loyalist victories. When the badly armed and outnumbered Carolina loyalists met the rebel militia on February 27 in the **Battle of Moore's Creek,** they were decisively defeated. After this loss, the king's army moved southward, virtually abandoning its North Carolina allies. Bitter and disappointed, these loyalists had to fend for themselves.

By June 1776, the British were ready to avenge the North Carolina failures with an attack on South Carolina. They arrived at Charleston with an impressive fleet of fifty ships and three thousand men, more than enough to take this elegant city. But incompetence combined with sheer bad luck when General Henry Clinton relied on poor **reconnaissance** reports and misjudged the tide in the harbor. Planning to wade ashore, his soldiers found themselves stranded on small islands surrounded by tidal waters. Meanwhile, the Americans enjoyed a stroke of remarkably good fortune. Working frantically to defend the harbor, they constructed a flimsy fort out of local palmetto wood. To the surprise of both sides, cannon balls fired by British ships sank harmlessly into the absorbent, pulpy palmetto wood. The fort—and the city of Charleston—remained standing.

Embarrassed and frustrated by their foolish errors and unexpected defeats in both Carolinas, the British command abruptly ended its southern campaign. General Clinton, a gloomy man under the best of circumstances, sailed north, eager to escape the scene of his humiliation. The South Carolina loyalists, however, could not escape British failures. They had been denounced, mobbed, imprisoned, and sometimes tortured since 1775. Their situation grew worse when the British withdrew.

Escape from New York

While Clinton was failing in the Carolinas, the Howe brothers were preparing a massive invasion of the mid-Atlantic region. In July 1776, Admiral Howe and General Howe sailed into New York harbor with the largest **expeditionary** force of the eighteenth century. With thirty-thousand men, one-third of them Hessian mercenaries, this British army was larger than the peacetime population of New York City.

The expected assault on New York did not begin at once, for the Howes did not relish a military victory. Unlike most British officers, the brothers were genuinely fond of Americans, and they hoped to be agents of compromise and negotiation rather than of destruction. Perhaps, they reasoned, a spectacular show of force and a thorough humiliation of rebel commander George Washington would be enough to bring the Americans to their senses and to end the rebellion.

General Washington had anticipated the Howes' plan to occupy New York and had rushed his army south from Massachusetts in April. He had few illusions, however, that his twenty-three thousand men, many of them sick and most of them inexperienced at war, could repel the invading British forces. In the middle of his defense preparations, Washington received a copy of the newly approved Declaration of Independence. He immediately ordered his brigades to line up on the parade grounds so that he could read Thomas Jefferson's stirring words aloud to them. He was gratified to hear the men cheer the Declaration. But would they fight, he wondered, and if they would not, what would the consequences be?

For a month, the Howes made no move on the city. Finally, in the early morning of August 22, 1776, the British began their advance, moving toward the Brooklyn neck of Long Island (see Map 6.1). Washington's troops quickly broke. Cut off from one another, confused by the sound and sight of the attack, almost all the American troops surrendered or ran. A single Maryland regiment made a heroic stand against the landing forces but was destroyed by the oncoming British. Washington, at the scene himself, might have been captured had the Howes pressed the rout. But they withdrew, content that they had made the American commander look foolish.

Washington worried little about the Howes' motives. Instead, he took advantage of the moment and slipped away with his men to the temporary safety of Manhattan Island. On September 15, the British attacked him there, and once again the farm boys-turned-soldiers fled in confusion. Angry and frustrated, Washington threw his hat to the ground and shouted, "Are these the men with whom I am to defend America!"

Washington's army retreated steadily toward the north to escape the narrow trap of Manhattan Is-

Battle of Moore's Creek Battle at which patriots defeated loyalists near Wilmington, North Carolina, in February 1776.

reconnaissance Exploration of an area to gather military information.

expeditionary Designed and transported for military operations abroad.

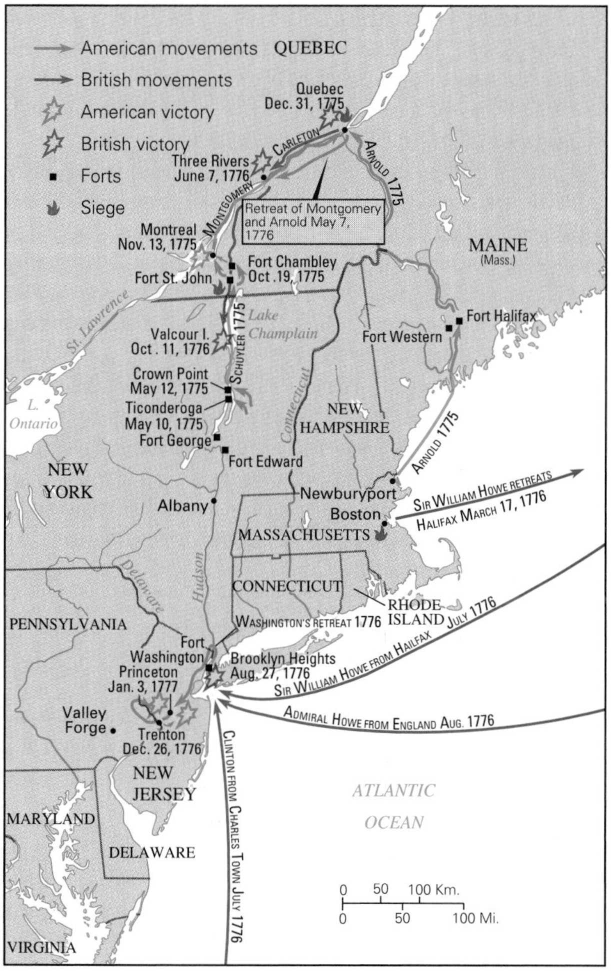

♦ **MAP 6.1 The War in the North, 1775–1777** The American attempt to capture Canada and General George Washington's effort to save New York from British occupation were failures, but Washington did manage to stage successful raids in New Jersey before retreating to safety in the winter of 1777. This map details the movements of both British and American troops during the Northern Campaign, and it indicates the victories and defeats for both armies.

land. The British were in hot pursuit. In a skirmish at Harlem Heights, the American commander was relieved to see his men stand their ground and win their first combat victory. Washington was even more relieved by the strange failure of the British to press their advantage, for despite the Harlem Heights success, his own army was still in retreat toward Westchester. The British had only to follow and deliver a crushing blow, but they did not. It was October 12 before they engaged Washington again, at White Plains, but he was able to retreat safely.

The British were the biggest problem Washington faced that fall, but they were not the only one. Intrigues and plots seemed to swirl against the commander-in-chief, instigated by other American generals jealous of his popularity with the public and with his soldiers. Such rivalries were legendary among British officers in the eighteenth century, and Washington was rapidly discovering their impact. That summer, he had uncovered—and squelched—a plot to assassinate him. Now, he barely escaped capture because of the actions of an eccentric military genius, **Charles Lee,** serving under his command. Driven by envy and ambition, General Lee put the lives of thousands of soldiers at risk by stubbornly refusing to send reinforcements from the Hudson River forts under his command to protect Washington's retreat. Despite Lee's **insubordination,** Washington did escape the Howes, crossing the Hudson River to New Jersey and marching his army west, across the Delaware River into Pennsylvania (see Map 6.1).

Winter Quarters and Winter Victories

Following European customs, General Howe established winter quarters for his troops before the cold set in. Redcoats and Hessians made their camps in the New York area and in Rhode Island that December, expecting Washington to make camp somewhere as well. But Washington, safe for the moment in Pennsylvania, was too restless to settle in just yet. Enlistment terms in his army would soon be up and without some encouraging military success, the general expected few of his soldiers would sign on for a second tour of duty. Thus Washington looked eagerly for a good target to attack—and found one. Across the Delaware, on the Jersey side, two or three thousand Hessians troops held a garrison near the town of Trenton.

On Christmas night, in the midst of a howling storm, General Washington led twenty-four hundred of his men back across the river. Although the soldiers faced a grueling 9-mile march through a blizzard of hail, snow, rain, and ice, the hostile weather worked

Charles Lee Revolutionary general who on several occasions tried to undermine Washington's authority and military strategy; he was eventually dismissed from service.

insubordination Disobedience to authority.

♦ John Trumbull's famous "Washington Before the Battle of Trenton," depicts the elegant, confident military leader who became the undisputed hero of the Revolution. In truth, however, when Washington led his tired, hungry men across the icy waters of the Delaware on Christmas Day in 1776, he was more despairing than confident. Repeatedly defeated and driven back by the British in the battles of New York, Washington's surprise attack on Trenton was a desperate attempt to score a victory before his army's terms of enlistment were up. His success, at Trenton and Princeton, restored the morale of both the General and his army. *Metropolitan Museum of Art.*

to Washington's ultimate advantage. The Hessians, never expecting anyone to venture out on such a night, drank heavily before falling into their beds. When the Americans caught them by surprise the following morning, the dazed and confused Hessians quickly surrendered. Washington did not lose a single man in the **Battle of Trenton,** and he had nine hundred prisoners and many badly needed supplies, including six German cannon, to show for his daring raid. Washington took full advantage of the moment, making a rousing appeal to his men to re-enlist. About half of the soldiers agreed to remain (see Map 6.1).

Trenton was a much-needed victory, but Washington enjoyed his next success even more. In early January he again crossed into New Jersey from the safety of Pennsylvania and made his way toward the British garrison at Princeton. On the way, his advance guard ran into two British regiments. As both sides lined up for battle, Washington rode back and forth in front of his men, shouting encouragement and urging them to stand firm. His behavior was reckless, for it put him squarely in the line of fire, but it was also effective. When the British turned in retreat, Washington rashly rode after them, clearly delighted to be in pursuit for once in the war.

The Trenton and Princeton victories raised the morale of the Continental Army as it settled at last into its winter quarters near Morristown, New Jersey. They stirred popular support also. Americans everywhere referred to the two winter raids as a "nine-day wonder." Of course, the revolutionary forces had done little to stop the Howes, who could be expected to march on Philadelphia when warm weather revived the war again. And try what he may—polite requests, reasoned arguments, angry demands—Washington could not get from Congress the assistance or support that he needed to sustain a solid army. His requests for supplies during the winter months at Morristown were met by "permission" from the Congress in Philadelphia to **commandeer** from residents nearby whatever he needed. Washington refused. English highhandedness and cruelty had turned many people of the area into staunch supporters of the Revolution, and Washington did not mean to alienate them by seizing their livestock, food, or weapons.

Burgoyne's New York Campaign

In July 1777 General William Howe sailed with fifteen thousand men up the Chesapeake Bay toward Philadelphia. The Continental Congress had already fled the city, anticipating that Washington and his troops could not prevent its occupation. Although the Americans made two efforts to block Howe, first at Brandywine Creek and then at Germantown, the British faced no real threat to their occupation of the capital. The problems they did face in 1777 came not from Washington but from the poor judgment of one of their own generals.

While General Howe was settling in at Philadelphia, startling developments were unfolding in northern New York. **John Burgoyne** had persuaded

Battle of Trenton Battle on December 26, 1776, when Washington led his troops across the Delaware River and captured a Hessian garrison wintering in New Jersey.

commandeer To seize for military use.

John Burgoyne British general forced to surrender his entire army at Saratoga in October 1777.

♦ As Burgoyne's army moved south, Catherine Van Rensselaer rushed from Albany to rescue the furnishings of her country estate in Saratoga. Although panicked refugees fled past her, Van Rensselaer refused to turn back. She not only saved her furniture but set fire to her wheat fields to prevent the enemy from harvesting the grain. Such acts of sabotage were frequently carried out by patriot and loyalist women. *Los Angeles County Museum of Art; bicentennial gift of Mr. and Mrs. J. M. Schaaf, Mr. and Mrs. Charles C. Shoemaker, and Mr. and Mrs. Julian Ganz, Jr.*

the British government to support an elaborate effort to sever New England from the rest of the American colonies: General Burgoyne would move his army southward from Montreal, while a second army of redcoats and Iroquois, commanded by Colonel Barry St. Leger, would veer east across the Mohawk Valley from Fort Oswego. At the same time, William Howe would send a third force north from New York City. The three armies would rendezvous at Albany, effectively isolating New England and, it was assumed, giving the British a perfect opportunity to crush the rebellion.

The plan was daring and—on paper—seemed to have every chance of success. In reality, however, it had serious flaws. First, neither Burgoyne nor the British officials in England had any knowledge of the American terrain that had to be covered. Second, they badly misjudged Indian support and loyalty. Third, General Howe, no longer in New York City, was told nothing of his own crucial role in the plan.

Blissfully unaware of these problems, Burgoyne led his army from Montreal in high spirits in June 1777 (see Map 6.2). The troops floated down Lake Champlain in canoes and flat-bottom boats and easily retook Fort Ticonderoga. From Ticonderoga, the invading army continued to march toward Albany. From this point on, however, things began to go badly for Burgoyne.

In true eighteenth-century British style, "Gentleman Johnny" Burgoyne chose to travel well rather than lightly. The thirty wagons moving slowly behind the general contained more than the 138 pieces of artillery for the campaign. They also contained Burgoyne's mistress, her personal wardrobe and his, and a generous supply of champagne. The extra baggage might have been only a minor inconvenience across mild terrain, but after Ticonderoga, the wagons had to make their way through swamps and forest, across gullies and ravines. Movement slowed to a snail's pace.

The Americans took full advantage of Burgoyne's circumstances. Ethan Allen and his Green Mountain Boys harassed the British as they entered Allen's home region of Vermont. To protect his column, Burgoyne paused to confront Allen head-on. But the bloody battle that followed near Bennington only slowed his army's advance even more. When Burgoyne finally reached Albany in mid-September, he was disturbed to discover neither St. Leger nor Howe waiting there.

Like Burgoyne, St. Leger had enjoyed early successes on his eastward march to Albany. But he had counted on the support of all the tribes within the Iroquois Confederation, when in fact some Iroquois were fighting with the Americans. St. Leger faced resistance that grew bloodier and more exhausting the closer he got to the rendezvous point. When he learned that Benedict Arnold and an army of a thousand Americans were on their way to challenge him, St. Leger decided to abandon all commitments to the Burgoyne plan and take his tired men to the safety of Fort Niagara.

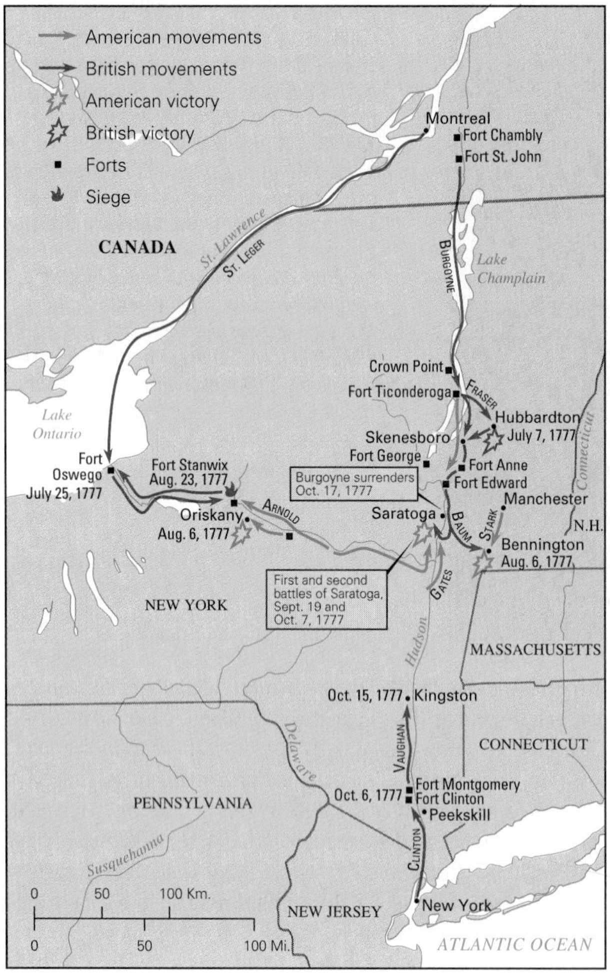

♦ **MAP 6.2 The Burgoyne Campaign, 1777** The defeat of General John Burgoyne and his army at Saratoga was a major turning point in the war. It led to the recognition of American independence by France and later by Spain and to a military alliance with both these European powers. This map shows American and British troop movement and the locations and dates of the Saratoga battles leading to the British surrender.

St. Leger's battle fatigue and William Howe's apparent ignorance of his role in this military operation left Burgoyne stranded in the heart of New York. By mid-September 1777, his supplies dwindling, he had little choice left but to break through the American lines and retreat northward to the safety of Canada—or surrender. On September 19, Burgoyne attacked American forces under the command of **Horatio Gates** at Saratoga, hoping to open a path of retreat for his army. "Granny" Gates, as the elderly general was affectionately called, lacked daring or cunning, but he needed neither to drive back the exhausted, dispirited British soldiers. Burgoyne tried again on October 7, and again Gates and his men held their ground. On October 17, 1777, General John Burgoyne surrendered.

News that a major British army had been defeated spread quickly on both sides of the Atlantic. It was a powerful boost to American confidence and an equally powerful blow to British self-esteem. The most important consequence of this military victory, however, was its positive impact on American diplomatic efforts abroad. Even before formally declaring independence, Congress had sent diplomats to the royal courts of Spain and France and to the government of Holland, to ask for supplies, loans, and military support. American pleas had met with some success, but after the stunning victory at Saratoga, hopes ran high that France might openly acknowledge the independence of the United States and join the war against Britain.

Winter Quarters in 1777

For General Washington, news of the upset at Saratoga was a mixed blessing. Diplomacy might yield a military alliance with France, but no one knew when. In the meantime, influential American leaders were caught up in the popular but unreasonable conviction that the war was practically at an end. John Adams, who never wore a uniform, had once toasted a "short and Violent war." After Burgoyne's defeat, many Americans believed that Adams's wish was coming true. Washington believed differently. From his winter quarters at Valley Forge, Pennsylvania, the commander-in-chief sent urgent requests for more money to support his Continental Army. But Congress, short on funds as usual and suddenly overcome by optimism, ignored the general. The result was the long and dreadful winter at **Valley Forge.**

Valley Forge was 20 miles from Philadelphia, where General Howe and his army were comfortably housed for the winter. Throughout December 1777, Washington's men labored to build the huts

Horatio Gates Elderly general from Virginia who led the American troops to victory in the Battle of Saratoga.

Valley Forge Winter encampment of Washington's army in Pennsylvania in 1777–1778, where soldiers were poorly supplied and suffered from cold and hunger.

♦ "Washington and LaFayette at Winter Quarters," shows the commander and his friend, the young aristocrat from France, sharing a moment of conversation while soldiers huddle together around a fire at Valley Forge. While British officers enjoyed the social life of Philadelphia, General Washington, his officers, and his men suffered from inadequate food, supplies, firewood, and shelter in their winter encampment, a situation due, in part, to the corruption and greed of military suppliers and the incompetence of the quartermaster corp. *Stock Montage.*

and cabins they needed. While two officers were assigned to share quarters, a dozen enlisted men were expected to crowd into a 14-by-16-foot hut. Rations were a problem from the start. Technically, each man was entitled to raw or cured meat, yet most soldiers at Valley Forge lived entirely on a diet of fire cakes, made of flour and water baked in the coals or over the fire on a stick. Blankets were scarce, coats were rare, and firewood was precious. An army doctor named Waldo summed up conditions when he wrote: "Poor food—hard lodgings—cold weather—fatigue—nasty clothes—nasty cookery—vomit half my time—smoked out of my senses—the devil's in it—I can't endure it."

Dr. Waldo, however, did endure it. So did the soldiers he tended to daily, men like the barefoot, half-naked, dirty young man who cried out in despair, "I am sick, my feet lame, my legs are sore, my body covered with this tormenting itch." While civilians mastered the steps of the latest dance craze, "the Burgoyne surrender," soldiers at Valley Forge traded the remains of their uniforms and sometimes their muskets for the momentary warmth and sense of well-being provided by liquor.

The enlisted men who survived the winter at Valley Forge shared a common background and social profile. Men from the rich and comfortable classes entered the military as officers, but these enlisted soldiers were unmarried farm boys, farm laborers, servants, apprentices, artisans, and even former slaves. Although some of the Continental soldiers left behind, or brought with them, wives and children, most of them had few dependents and few hopes of economic advancement. They were exactly the sort of person most Americans believed ought to fight the war. Poverty, however, had not driven them into Washington's army. There were other, easier choices than soldiering. They could have secured more money, better food, and greater comfort if they had taken up begging or lived off local charity. Even if they preferred a military life, they could have enlisted for a brief stint as a substitute for a wealthier man in his local militia unit, for which they would have been well paid. They might have gone into privateering. Instead, they chose to enlist in George Washington's Continental Army—and they intended to see the war to its conclusion. The contrast between their own patriotism and the apparent indifference of the civilian population made many of these soldiers bitter. Private Joseph Plumb Martin summed up their feelings when he said "a kind and holy Providence" had done more to help the army while it was at Valley Forge "than did the country in whose service we were wearing away our lives by piecemeal."

What these soldiers needed, besides new clothes, good food, and hot baths, was professional military training. And that is exactly what they got, beginning in the spring of 1778, when an unlikely Prussian volunteer arrived at Valley Forge. **Baron Friedrich von Steuben** was almost 50 years old, dignified, elegantly dressed, with a dazzling gold and diamond medal always displayed on his chest. Like most foreign volunteers, many of whom plagued

Baron Friedrich von Steuben Prussian military officer who served as Washington's drillmaster at Valley Forge.

Washington more than they helped him, the baron claimed to be an aristocrat, to have vast military experience, and to have held high rank in a European army. In truth, he had purchased his title only a short time before fleeing his homeland in bankruptcy, and he had only been a captain in the Prussian army. A penniless refugee, von Steuben hoped to receive a military pension for his service in the American army. He had not, however, exaggerated his talent as a military drillmaster.

All spring, the baron could be seen drilling Washington's troops, alternately shouting in rage and applauding with delight. He expected instant obedience from the soldiers, set high standards, and criticized freely. But he also gave lavish praise when it was due and revealed a genuine affection and respect for the men. Washington appreciated the arrival of only a few of the foreign volunteers—especially the young, modest, polite Frenchman, the **Marquis de LaFayette,** an aristocrat deeply committed to the ideal of liberty. But General Washington considered von Steuben a most unexpected and invaluable surprise.

In the spring of 1778 Washington received news that the British government had recalled General William Howe and replaced him with **Sir Henry Clinton,** who immediately laid plans to abandon Philadelphia and return to New York. News also reached Washington that France had formally recognized the independence of the United States. He immediately declared a day of thanks, ordering cannon to be fired in honor of the new alliance. That day, the officers feasted with their commander, and Washington issued brandy to each enlisted man at Valley Forge.

Influences from off the Battlefield

- Why did the French choose to assist the Americans secretly in the early years of the war?
- Why did they choose to enter the war after Saratoga?

Like most wars, the Revolutionary War was not confined to the battlefields. At the time that Congress appointed Washington commander-in-chief, it also appointed diplomats to negotiate support for the Revolution in Europe. America needed money, supplies, safe harbors for its ships, and, if at all possible, formal recognition of its independence and the open military assistance that would allow. On the home front, Congress also needed citizens' cooperation and support for the government's policies. Britain had similar diplomatic and domestic concerns off the battlefields. The English government worked to prevent any formal alliances between European powers and the American rebels and struggled to sustain support for the war among its own citizens. General Burgoyne's defeat spurred a shift in popular support for the war in both England and America, in part because French recognition of American independence turned the Revolution into an international war.

The Long Road to Formal Recognition

In 1776, England had many enemies and rivals in Europe, each happy to see George III expend his resources and military personnel in an effort to quell a colonial rebellion. Although these nations expected the American Revolution to fail, they were more than eager to keep the conflict going as long as possible. Thus, soon after independence was declared, an American entrepreneur, Arthur Lee, sailed to France. There, Lee joined forces with an adventurer and writer, Caron de Beaumarchais, and, together with King Louis XVI's chief minister, the Comte de Vergennes, devised a scheme for siphoning weapons and funds from France to the revolutionaries. They created a private commercial firm, headed by Beaumarchais and funded entirely by the French government. The firm provided loans and weapons that came directly from French government arsenals. France also agreed to open ports to American privateers and to provide French ships and seamen for raids on British commercial shipping.

In December 1776, Congress sent the printer-politician-scientist **Benjamin Franklin** to Paris in hopes of winning formal recognition of American independence. The charming and witty Franklin was the toast of Paris, adored by aristocrats and common people alike, but even he could not persuade the king to support the Revolution openly. Burgoyne's surrender changed everything. After Saratoga, the British government began scrambling

Marquis de Lafayette Young French aristocrat who served on Washington's staff during the Revolution.

Sir Henry Clinton General who replaced William Howe as commander of the British forces in America in 1778 after the British surrender at Saratoga.

Benjamin Franklin American writer, inventor, scientist, and diplomat who negotiated a French alliance with the United States in 1778 and later helped negotiate the treaty ending the Revolutionary War.

to end a war that had turned embarrassing, and the French government began scrambling to reassess its diplomatic position. Vergennes suspected that the English would quickly send a peace commission to America after Burgoyne's defeat. If the American Congress agreed to a compromise ending the rebellion, France could gain nothing more. But if the French kept the war alive by giving Americans reason to hope for total victory, perhaps they could recoup some of the territory and prestige lost to England in the Seven Years War. This meant, of course, recognizing the United States and entering a war with Britain. Vergennes knew a choice had to be made—but he was not yet certain what to do.

Meanwhile, the English government was indeed preparing a new peace offer for Congress. At the heart of the British offer were two promises that George III considered to be great concessions. First, Parliament would renounce all intentions of ever taxing the colonies again. Second, the Intolerable Acts, the Tea Act, and any other objectionable legislation passed since 1763 would be repealed. Many members of Parliament thought these promises were long overdue. They had been vocal critics of their government's policies in the 1760s and 1770s and had refused to support the war. After Burgoyne's defeat, popular support for compromise also increased in England. The Americans, however, were unimpressed by the offers. For Congress, a voluntary return to colonial status was now unthinkable.

Benjamin Franklin knew that Congress would reject the king's offer. But he was too shrewd to relieve the Comte de Vergennes's fear that a compromise was in the works. Franklin warned that France must act quickly and decisively or accept the consequences. His gamble worked, and in 1778 France and the United States signed a treaty linking French and American fates tightly together, for neither country could make a separate peace with Great Britain. By 1779, Spain had also formally acknowledged the United States, and in 1780 the Netherlands did so too. George III had little choice but to declare war against these European nations.

The Revolution had grown into an international struggle that taxed British resources and made it impossible for Britain to concentrate all its military might and naval power in America. With ships diverted to the Caribbean and to the European coast, Britain could no longer blockade American ports as effectively as before or transport troops to the American mainland as quickly. Above all, the entrance of the French into the war opened new strategic possibilities for General Washington and his army. If the Americans could count on the cooperation of the French fleet, a British army could be trapped on American soil, cut off by French ships from supplies, reinforcements, and any chance of escape.

War and the American Public

News of the alliance with France helped release an orgy of spending and purchasing by American civilians. The conditions were ripe for this in 1778. With the value of government-issued paper money dropping steadily, spending made more sense than saving. And with profits soaring from the sale of supplies to the army, many Americans had more money to spend than ever before. Also, not all of the credit that diplomats had negotiated with European allies went toward military supplies. Some of it was available for the purchase of manufactured goods. But despite these conditions, civilians were wary of spending freely, because of the prospect of a long and unsuccessful war and the suspicion that they thought buying would raise about their patriotism. These fears vanished with the French treaty. The combination of optimism, **cheap money,** and the availability of foreign goods led to a wartime spending spree.

Many of the goods that were imported into America in the next few years were actually British-made. American consumers apparently saw no contradiction between their strong patriotism and the purchase of enemy products. A **black market**—a network for the sale of illegally imported English goods—grew rapidly, and profits from it soared. Abandoning the commitment to "virtuous simplicity" that had led them to dress in homespun, Americans stampeded to purchase tea and other imported luxuries.

Both the government and the military succumbed to this spirit of self-indulgence. Corruption and **graft** grew common, as both high- and low-ranking officials sold government supplies for their own profit or charged the army excessive rates for goods and services. Cheating the government and the army was a game civilians could play, too.

cheap money Paper money that is readily available but has declined in value.

black market The illegal business of buying and selling goods that are banned or restricted.

graft Unscrupulous use of one's position for profit or advantage.

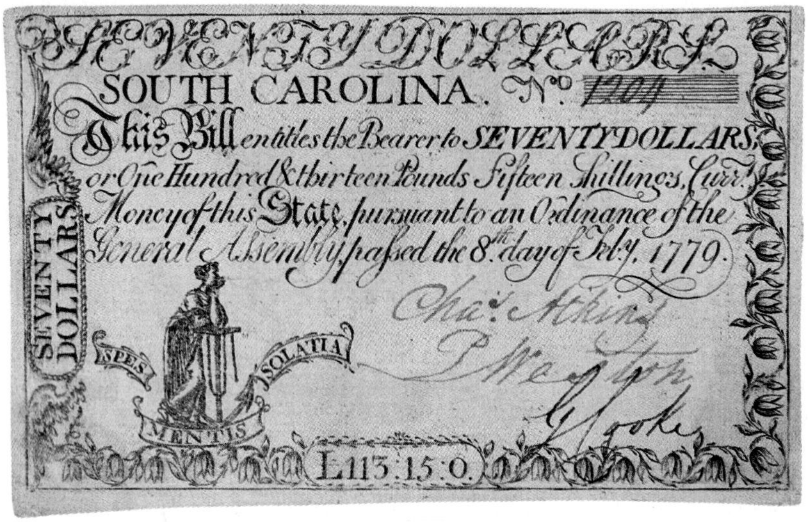

♦ Every state issued paper money to finance its part in the Revolution. Because this currency had little solid backing, it lost value almost immediately. By the time these South Carolina notes were printed, their real value was only 10 percent of their face value. One outcome of such drastic drops in the value of money was that even inelegant dressers like patriot Samuel Adams had to pay $2,000 for a new hat and suit. *Eric P. Newman Numismatic Education Society.*

Wagoners carting pickled meat to military encampments drained the brine from the barrels to lighten their load so they could carry more. The results were spoiled meat, soldiers suffering from food poisoning—and a greater profit for the cartmen. Soldiers became accustomed to defective weapons, defective shoes, and defective ammunition, but many of them joined the profit game by selling off their army-issued supplies to any available buyers. Recruiters pocketed the bounties given to them to attract enlistees. Officers accepted bribes from enlisted men seeking discharges.

Popular optimism and the spending frenzy unleashed by the French treaty contrasted sharply with the financial realities facing Congress. Bluntly put, the government was broke. By 1778, both Congress and the states had exhausted their meager sources of hard currency. The government met the crisis by printing more paper money. The result was rampant inflation. The value of the **Continental,** as the congressional paper money was called, dropped steadily with each passing day.

Military enlistments fell as the governments' inability to pay the soldiers became known. Both the state militias and the Continental Army resorted to impressment, or forced military service, to fill their ranks. Men forced to serve, however, were men more likely to mutiny or to desert. Officers found themselves caught between the demands of discipline and of compassion for their unpaid and involuntary soldiers. Some chose to execute any deserters or mutineers under their command. Some whipped them. And some pardoned them. Congress acknowledged the justice of the soldiers' complaints by giving them pay raises in the form of certificates that could be redeemed—after the war.

From Stalemate to Victory

- What choices led to General Cornwallis's surrender at Yorktown?
- What were the most important outcomes of the peace treaty negotiations?

The entrance of France into the war did not immediately alter the strategies of British or American military leaders. English generals in the North displayed caution after Burgoyne's surrender, and Washington waited impatiently for signs that the French fleet would come to his aid. The result was a stalemate. The active war shifted to the South, where in late 1778 the British waged a second major campaign.

The War Stalls in the North

Sir Henry Clinton, the new commander of the British army in North America, knew that the French fleet could easily blockade the Delaware River, which was the main supply line to occupied Philadelphia. Thus the cautious Clinton laid immediate plans to abandon Philadelphia for the safety of New

Continental Paper money issued by the Continental Congress to finance the Revolution; its value declined steadily because it was not backed by gold or silver.

York. By the time warm weather set in, his army was on the march, heading east through New Jersey, en route to New York.

Clinton's army, burdened by a long train of slow-moving supply wagons, made an irresistible target for Washington. The general put the troublesome Charles Lee in charge of the attack, hoping that the self-centered officer would redeem himself. Unfortunately, Washington underestimated Lee's potential for outrageous behavior. Lee led his men to the designated attack point at Monmouth, New Jersey, but signaled them to retreat as soon as the enemy began to return fire. Washington arrived at Monmouth in time to be stunned by the sight of American troops in flight with British troops closing in.

Washington rallied the retreating Americans, calling on them to re-form their lines and stand their ground. Trained by von Steuben, the men responded well. To the astonishment of the advancing British and to the chagrin of Charles Lee, the Americans moved forward with precision and speed, driving the redcoats back. The **Battle of Monmouth** was not the decisive victory Washington had dreamed of, but it was a fine recovery from what first appeared to be certain defeat. As for Lee, Washington saw to it that he was discharged from the army.

Monmouth was only the first of several missed opportunities that summer of 1778. In August, the French and Americans launched their first joint effort, sending a combined land and naval attack against the British base at Newport, Rhode Island. At the last minute, however, French admiral D'Estaing decided that the casualty rate would be too high, abruptly gathered up his own men, and sailed to safety on the open seas. The French flight left the American troops to retreat as best they could.

Throughout the fall and winter of 1778 the main part of the Continental Army remained inactive, and General Washington's frustration with the French navy grew steadily as the weeks passed. News coming from the western front did little to improve Washington's bleak mood. In Kentucky and western Virginia, deadly Indian attacks had decimated many American settlements. The driving force behind these attacks was a remarkable British official named Harry Hamilton, who had won the nickname "Hair Buyer" because of the bounties he paid for American scalps. In October, Hamilton led Indian troops from the Great Lakes tribes into the Illinois-Indiana region and captured the fort at Vincennes. The American counterattack was organized by a stocky young frontiersman, **George Rogers Clark,** whose own enthusiasm for scalping earned him the nickname "Long-Knife." To Washington's relief, Clark and his volunteer forces managed to drive the British from Vincennes. They also reported some success in containing the damage done by Indian raids in the Northwest.

♦ Mohawk chief Thayendanegea (Joseph Brant) believed that Iroquois lands would be lost if the Americans were victorious. He urged an Iroquois alliance with the British, fought for the British, and directed a series of deadly raids against settlements in Pennsylvania and New York. After the war—as Brant had feared—his people were forced to relocate to Canada. *"Joseph Brant" by Wilhelm von Moll Berczy c. 1800. National Gallery of Canada, Ottawa.*

Britain's Indian allies remained a serious threat in most frontier regions, however, especially when tribes could rely on loyalist support. General John Sullivan learned just how effective this combination could be when his regular army expedition to upstate New York was badly defeated by Indian and loyalist forces led by Mohawk chief **Thayendanegea.** The humiliated Sullivan took revenge by burning

Battle of Monmouth New Jersey battle in June 1778 in which Charles Lee squandered a decisive American advantage.

George Rogers Clark Virginian who led Virginia troops to successes against the British and Indians in the Ohio Territory in 1778.

Thayendanegea Mohawk chief known to the Americans as Joseph Brant; his combined force of loyalists and Indians defeated John Sullivan's expedition to upstate New York in 1779.

forty Indian villages, an act of violence and cruelty that deeply embarrassed General Washington.

Spring and summer of 1779 passed and still Washington waited for the French navy's cooperation. Fall brought the general the worst possible news: Admiral D'Estaing and his fleet had sailed for the West Indies under orders to protect valuable French possessions in the Caribbean and, if possible, to seize English possessions there. News of D'Estaing's departure spurred a new wave of discipline problems among Washington's idle troops. Mutinies and desertions increased. From his winter headquarters in Morristown Heights, New Jersey, Washington wrote to von Steuben: "The prospect, my dear Baron, is gloomy, and the storm thickens." The real storm, however, was raging not in New Jersey but in the Carolinas.

The Second Carolinas Campaign

Since the fall of 1778, the British had been siphoning off New York–based troops for a new invasion of the South. The campaign began in earnest with the capture of Savannah, Georgia (see Map 6.3). Then, in the winter of 1779, General Henry Clinton sailed for Charleston, South Carolina, eager to avenge his embarrassing retreat in the 1776 campaign. Five thousand Continental soldiers hurried to join the South Carolina militia in defense of the city. From the "Citadel," a fortification spanning the northern neck of the city's peninsula, these American forces bombarded the British with all they could find, firing projectiles made of glass, broken shovels, hatchets, and pickaxes. From aboard their ships, the British answered with a steady stream of mortar shells. On May 12, 1780, after months of deadly bombardment and high casualties on both sides, the Citadel fell. Satisfied, General Clinton returned to New York.

Clinton left the southern campaign in the hands of **Charles Cornwallis,** an ambitious and able general who set out with more than eight thousand men to conquer the rest of South Carolina. Cornwallis and his regular army were joined by loyalist troops who were as eager to take their revenge on their enemies as Clinton had been. Since the British had abandoned the South in 1776, small, roving bands of loyalist guerrillas had kept resistance to the Revolution alive. After the British victory at Charleston, the guerrillas increased their attacks, and a bloody civil war of ambush, arson, and brutality on both sides resulted. By the summer of 1780, fortunes had reversed: the revolutionaries were now the resistance, and the loyalists were in control.

The revolutionary resistance produced legendary guerrilla leaders, including **Francis Marion,** known as the "Swamp Fox." Marion organized black and white recruits into raiding bands that steadily harassed Cornwallis's army and effectively cut British lines of communication between Charleston and the interior of South Carolina. While Marion did his best to trouble the British, Thomas Sumter's guerrillas and other resistance forces focused their energies on the loyalists.

When guerrillas and loyalists met head-on in battle, they honored few of the rules of war. In October 1780, for example, in the **Battle of King's Mountain,** revolutionaries surrounded loyalist troops and picked them off one by one. As this bitter civil war continued, marauding bands terrorized civilians and plundered their farms. Often the worst damage was done by outlaws posing as soldiers.

The regular American army, under the command of the Saratoga hero, "Granny" Gates, had little success against Cornwallis. In August 1780, Gates and his men suffered a crushing defeat at Camden, South Carolina. That fall, Washington wisely replaced Gates with a younger, more energetic officer from Rhode Island, **Nathanael Greene.**

The fourteen hundred Continental soldiers Greene found when he arrived in South Carolina were tired, hungry, and poorly clothed. They were also, Greene discovered, "without discipline and so addicted to plundering that the utmost exertions of the officers cannot restrain them." Greene's first steps were to ease the strains caused by civil war, raids, and plundering by offering pardons to loyalists and proposing alliances with local Indian tribes. In the end, Greene managed to win all but the Creeks away from the British.

Greene's military strategy was to wear the British out from chasing his small army across the South.

Charles Cornwallis British general who was second-in-command to Henry Clinton; his surrender at Yorktown in 1781 brought the Revolutionary War to a close.

Francis Marion South Carolina leader of guerrilla forces during the Revolutionary War; known as the "Swamp Fox," he harassed British forces during the second southern campaign.

Battle of King's Mountain Battle fought in October 1780 on the border between the Carolinas; revolutionary troops defeated loyalists.

Nathanael Greene American general who took command of the Carolinas campaign in 1780.

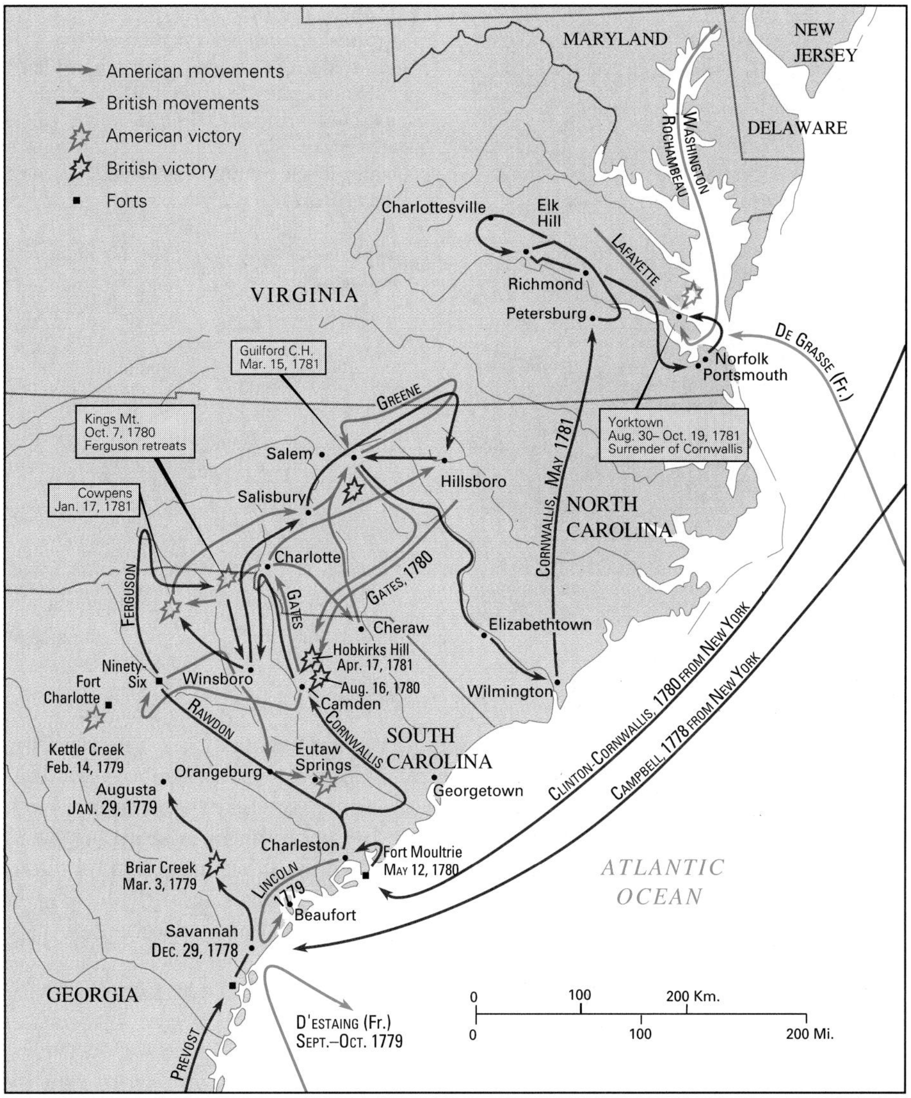

♦ **MAP 6.3 The Second Southern Campaign, 1778–1781** This map of the second attempt by Britain to crush the rebellion in the South shows the many battles waged in the Lower South before Cornwallis's encampment at Yorktown and his surrender there. This decisive southern campaign involved all the military resources of the combatants, including British, Loyalist, French, and American ground forces and British and French naval fleets.

Toward this end, he sent Virginian Daniel Morgan and six hundred men to western South Carolina, where they led Cornwallis lieutenant Banastre Tarleton in hectic pursuit across rough countryside. By the time Tarleton's men cornered the Americans on an open meadow called the Cowpens, the British soldiers were tired and frustrated. When the outnumbered Americans chose to stand their ground and fight instead of surrendering, the weary redcoats panicked and fled. Afterward, Morgan and his soldiers rejoined the main American force under General Greene.

Annoyed by this turn of events, Cornwallis decided to take the offensive. This time, Greene led the British on a long, exhausting chase. In March 1781, the two armies finally met at Guilford Courthouse, North Carolina. Although the Americans lost the battle and withdrew, British losses were so great

♦ In this painting patriots stand their ground against cavalrymen led by Lieutenant Banastre Tarleton in a 1781 skirmish near Cowpens. As the painting shows, black as well as white Americans supported the revolutionary cause in the South. *"Tarleton's Cavalrymen After the Battle of Cowpens" 1781 by William Ranney. Collection of the State of South Carolina/photo by Hunter Clarkson, Alt Lee, Inc.*

that Cornwallis had to rethink the southern campaign. The revolutionaries' strength in the Carolinas and the growing weakness of loyalist sentiment made the price for conquering the Lower South more than he was willing to pay. Disgusted, Cornwallis ordered his army northward to Virginia. Perhaps, he mused, he would have better luck there.

Treason and Triumph

In the fall of 1780, the popular general Benedict Arnold defected to the British. Arnold's treason saddened General Washington and struck a blow to American morale. Early in the war, Washington had befriended Arnold and assisted his career. He appointed Arnold commandant at Philadelphia and stood by the young officer even after he was convicted of embezzling military funds. Washington's support ensured leniency for Arnold. Arnold repaid his many kindnesses by plotting treason. He persuaded Washington to assign him command of the fort at **West Point,** New York, which he meant to turn over to the British—and with it, control of the Hudson River. At the last minute, the treason was discovered and West Point remained secure. But the name Benedict Arnold became permanently associated with betrayal.

In May 1781, Washington's gloomy wait for French action suddenly ended when a war council with the French at last materialized. Meeting with the French general, the Comte de Rochambeau, Washington pressed for an attack on British-occupied New York. Rochambeau, however, had made up his mind to move against Cornwallis in Virginia. Since he had already ordered Admiral de Grasse and his fleet to the Chesapeake, Washington had little choice but to concur.

On July 6, 1781, a French army joined Washington's Continental forces just north of Manhattan for the long march to Virginia. The French soldiers, elegant in their sparkling uniforms, were openly amazed and impressed by their bedraggled allies. "It is incredible," wrote one French officer, "that soldiers composed of whites and blacks, almost naked, unpaid, and rather poorly fed, can march so well and stand fire so steadfastly."

Within a few months, General Cornwallis would be forced to admire the American army's stamina too. In July, however, the British commander was unaware that a combined army was marching toward him. His first clue that trouble lay ahead came when a force of regular soldiers, led by Baron von Steuben and the Marquis de Lafayette, appeared in

West Point Site of a fort above the Hudson River north of New York City.

♦ John Trumbull celebrated the surrender of Cornwallis at Yorktown in this painting. However, neither Cornwallis nor Washington actually participated in the surrender ceremonies. The British commander claimed illness and sent his general of the guards as his deputy. Washington, always sensitive to status as well as to protocol, promptly appointed an officer of equal rank, General Benjamin Lincoln, to serve as his deputy. *"Surrender of Lord Cornwallis" by John Trumbull. Yale University Art Gallery. Trumbull Collection.*

Virginia. Soon afterward, Cornwallis moved his army to the peninsula port of **Yorktown** to prepare for more serious battles ahead. The choice of Yorktown was one he would heartily regret.

By September 1781, the French and American troops coming from New York had joined forces with von Steuben and LaFayette's men. Admiral de Grasse's navy of 27 ships, 74 cannon, and an additional 3,000 French soldiers was in place in Chesapeake Bay. General Clinton, still in New York, had been devastatingly slow to realize what the enemy intended. In desperation, he now sent a naval squadron from New York to rescue the trapped Cornwallis. He could do little more, since most of the British fleet was in the Caribbean.

Admiral de Grasse had no trouble fending off Clinton's rescue squad. Then he turned his naval guns on the redcoats at Yorktown. From his position on land, Washington also directed a steady barrage of artillery fire against the British, producing a deafening roar both day and night. The noise dazed the redcoats and prevented them from sleeping. On October 17, 1781, Lord Cornwallis admitted the hopelessness of his situation and surrendered.

Despite the stunning turn of events at Yorktown, fighting continued in some areas. Loyalists and patriots continued to make war on each other in the South for another year. Bloody warfare against the Indians also meant more deaths along the frontier. The British occupation of Charleston, Savannah, and New York continued. But after Yorktown the British gave up all hope of military victory against their former colonies. On March 4, 1782, Parliament voted to cease "the further prosecution of offensive war on the Continent of North America, for the purpose of reducing the Colonies to obedience by force." The war for independence had been won.

Yorktown Port town in Virginia on the York River near Chesapeake Bay; its location on a peninsula allowed American and French forces to trap the British there and compel General Cornwallis to surrender.

Winning Diplomatic Independence

What Washington and his French and Spanish allies had won, American diplomats had to preserve. Three men represented the United States at the peace talks in Paris: Benjamin Franklin, John Adams, and John Jay. At first glance, this was an odd trio. The elderly Franklin, witty and sophisticated, had spent most of the war years in Paris, where he earned a deserved reputation as an admirer of French women and French wines. Adams, competitive, self-absorbed, and socially inept, did not hide his distaste for Franklin's flamboyance. Neither man found much comfort in the presence of the prudish, aristocratic John Jay of New York. Yet they proved to be a highly effective combination. Franklin brought a crafty skill and a love of strategy to the team as well as a useful knowledge of French politics. Adams provided the backbone, for in the face of any odds he was stubborn, determined, fiercely patriotic, and a watchdog of American interests. Jay was calm, deliberate, and though not as aggressive as his New England colleague, he matched Adams in patriotism and integrity.

European political leaders expected the Americans to fare badly against the more experienced British and French diplomats. But Franklin, Jay, and Adams were far from naive. They were all veterans of wartime negotiations with European governments, having pursued loans, supplies, and military support. And they understood what was at stake at the peace table. They knew that their chief ally, France, had its own agenda and that England still wavered on the degree of independence America had actually won at Yorktown.

Despite firm orders from Congress to rely on France at every phase of the negotiations, the American diplomats quickly put their own agenda on the table. They issued a direct challenge to Britain: you must formally recognize American independence as a precondition to any negotiations at all. The British commissioner reluctantly agreed. Additional negotiations continued for more than a year, with all sides debating, arguing, and compromising until the terms of a treaty were finally set.

In the **Treaty of Paris** of 1783 the Americans emerged with two clear victories. First, the boundaries of the new nation were extensive, although the British did not give up Canada as the Americans had hoped. Second, the treaty granted the United States unlimited access to the fisheries off Newfoundland, a particular concern of New Englander John Adams. It was difficult to measure the degree of success on other issues, however, since the terms for carrying out the agreements were so vague. For example, Britain ceded the Northwest to the United States. But the treaty said nothing about approval of this transfer of power by the Indians of the region. Neither did it set a timetable for British evacuation of the forts in the territory. This lack of clarity would cause problems for the Americans, but in other cases, the vague language worked to American advantage. The treaty contained only the most general promise that the American government would not interfere with collection of the large prewar debts southern planters owed to British merchants. The promise to urge the states to return confiscated property to loyalists was equally vague.

The peacemakers were aware of the treaty's shortcomings and its lack of clarity on key issues. But this was the price for avoiding stalemate and dangerous confrontation on controversial issues. Franklin, Adams, and Jay knew the consequences might be serious, but for the moment they preferred to celebrate rather than to worry.

Republican Expectations in a New Nation

- How did the Revolution affect Americans' expectations regarding individual rights, social equality, and the role of women in American society?
- What choices were open to African Americans during and after the Revolution?
- What choices were open to the loyalists?

As an old man, John Adams reminisced about the American Revolution with his family and friends. Although he spoke of the war as a remarkable military event, Adams insisted that the Revolution was more than battlefield victories and defeats. The Revolution took place, Adams said, "in the hearts and the minds of the people." What he meant was that changes in American social values and political ideas were as critical as artillery, swords, and battlefield strategies in creating the new nation. "The people" were, of course, far more diverse than Adams was ever willing to admit. And they often differed

Treaty of Paris Treaty that ended the Revolutionary War in 1783 and acknowleged American independence.

in their "hearts and minds." Race, region, social class, gender, religion, even the national origin of immigrants—all played a part in creating diverse interests and diverse interpretations of the Revolution. Adams was correct, however, that significant changes took place in American thought and behavior during the war and the years immediately after. Many of these changes reflected a growing identification of the new American nation as a **republic** that ensured not only representative government but also the protection of individual rights, an educated citizenry, and an expanded **suffrage.**

The Protection of Individual Rights

By the time Thomas Jefferson wrote the Declaration of Independence, many Americans insisted that a legitimate government must protect such fundamental individual rights as life, liberty, property, and, as Jefferson put it, "the pursuit of happiness." The belief that Britain had failed to respect or protect individual rights had been critical in justifying the Revolution. Thus, whatever form Americans chose for their new, independent government, they were certain to demand the protection of these fundamental rights.

This emphasis on individual rights had many social consequences. For example, it opened the door to a reform of government-supported religious codes and policies. In the seventeenth century, individual dissenters such as Roger Williams and Anne Hutchinson had voiced the demand for the separation of church and state. After the Great Awakening, the same demands were made by organized dissenter communities such as the Baptists, who protested the privileges that established churches enjoyed in most colonies. Full commitment to the principle of freedom of conscience came slowly, however. In 1776, Virginia approved George Mason's Declaration of Rights, which ensured state residents the right to "the free exercise of religion." Yet Virginia continued to use tax monies to support the Anglican church. Even with the strong support of Thomas Jefferson, dissenters' demands were not fully met until 1786, when the Statute of Religious Freedom guaranteed an end to tax-supported churches and complete freedom of conscience, even for atheists. Other southern states followed Virginia's lead, ending tax support for their Anglican churches.

New Englanders proved more resistant to **disestablishment.** Many wished to continue government support of the Congregational church. Others wished to keep the principle of an established church alive. As a compromise, communities were sometimes allowed to decide which local church received their tax money, although each town was required to designate some church as the established church. New England did not separate church and state entirely until the nineteenth century.

The protection of other rights—freedom of speech, of assembly, and of the press, and the right to a trial by jury—were written into the new constitutions of several states.

Protection of Property Rights

Members of the revolutionary generation who had a political voice were especially vocal about the importance of private property and protection of a citizen's right to own property. In the decade before the Revolution, much of the protest against British policy had focused on this issue. For free, white, property-holding men—and for those servants, tenant farmers, or apprentices who hoped to join their ranks someday—life, liberty, and happiness were interwoven with the right of ownership.

The property rights of some infringed on the freedoms of others, however. Claims made on western lands by white Americans often meant the denial of Indian rights to that land. Masters' rights included a claim to the time and labor of their servants or apprentices. In the white community, a man's property rights usually included the restriction of his wife's right to own or sell land, slaves, and even her own personal possessions. And the institution of slavery transformed human beings into the private property of others.

All free white males had the right to property, but not all of them were able to acquire it. When the Revolution began, at least one-fifth of the American people lived in poverty or depended on public charity. The uneven distribution of wealth among white colonists was obvious on the streets of colonial Boston, in the rise in **almshouses** in Philadelphia, and in the growth of voluntary relief organizations

republic A nation in which supreme power resides in the citizens, who elect representatives to govern them.

suffrage The right to vote.

disestablishment Depriving a church of official government support.

almshouse A public shelter for the poor.

that aided the homeless and the hungry in other cities and towns. For some, taking advantage of opportunities to acquire property was difficult even when those opportunities arose. Washington's Continental soldiers, for example, were promised western lands as delayed payment for their military service. But when they mustered out of the army in 1783, most of them were penniless, jobless, and sometimes homeless. They had little choice but to sell the land warrant certificates they received, trading their future as property owners to ensure their immediate survival.

Legal Reforms

Although economic inequality actually grew in the decades after the Revolution, several legal reforms were spurred by a commitment to the republican belief in social equality. The targets of this legal reform included laws of **primogeniture** and **entail.** In Britain, these inheritance laws had led to the creation of a landed aristocracy. The actual threat they posed was small in America, for few planters ever adopted them. But the principle they represented remained important to republican spokesmen like Thomas Jefferson who pressed successfully for their abolition in Virginia and North Carolina.

The passion for social equality—in appearance if not in fact—affected customs as well as laws. To downplay their elite status as landowners, revolutionaries stopped the practice of adding "Esquire" (abbreviated "Esq.") after their names. George Washington, Esq., became plain George Washington.

Even unintentional elitist behavior could have embarrassing consequences. When General George Washington and the officers who served with him in the Revolutionary War organized the Society of the Cincinnati in 1783, they were motivated by the desire to sustain wartime friendships. The society's rules, however, brought protest from many Americans, for membership was hereditary, passing from officer fathers to their eldest sons. Warnings that a military aristocracy was being formed and that it posed a threat to republican government drove Washington and his comrades to revise the offending society bylaws.

In some states, the principle of social equality had concrete political consequences. Pennsylvania and Georgia eliminated all property qualifications for voting among free white males. Other states lowered their property requirements for voters but refused to go as far as universal white manhood suffrage. They feared that the outcome of such a sweeping reform was unpredictable. Even women might demand a political voice.

Women in the New Republic

The war did not erase differences of class, race, region, or age for either men or women. Thus its impact was not uniform for all American women. Yet some experiences, and the memories of them, were probably shared by the majority of white and even many black women. They would remember the war years as a time of constant shortages, anxiety, harassment, and unfamiliar and difficult responsibilities. Men going off to war left women to manage the farm or the shop, to cope with the critical shortages of food and supplies, and to survive on meager budgets in inflationary times. Many, like the woman who pleaded with her soldier husband to "pray come home," may have feared they would fail in these new circumstances. After the war, however, many remembered with satisfaction how well they had adapted to new roles. They expressed their sense of accomplishment in letters to husbands that no longer spoke of "your farm" and "your crop" but of "our farm" and even "my crop."

Many women found they enjoyed the sudden independence from men and from the domestic hierarchy that men ruled in peacetime. Even women in difficult circumstances experienced this new sense of freedom. Grace Galloway, wife of loyalist exile Joseph Galloway of Pennsylvania, remained in America during the war in an effort to preserve her husband's property. Shunned by her patriot neighbors, reduced from wealth to painful poverty, Grace Galloway nevertheless confided to her diary that "Ye liberty of doing as I please Makes even Poverty more agreable than any time I eve spent since I married."

If Galloway experienced new self-confidence and liberty during wartime, not all women were so fortunate. For the victims of rape and physical attack by soldiers on either side, the war meant more traditional experiences of vulnerability. American soldiers sang songs of flirtation and of their hopes for kisses from admiring young women, but occupying

primogeniture The legal right of the eldest son to inherit the entire estate of his father.

entail A legal limitation that prevents property from being divided, sold, or given away.

armies, guerrilla bands, and outlaws posing as soldiers left trails of abuse, particularly in New Jersey, along the frontier, and in the Carolinas.

For women, just as for men, the war meant adapting traditional behavior and skills to new circumstances. Women who followed the eighteenth-century custom of joining husbands or fathers in army camps took up the familiar domestic chores of cooking, cleaning, laundering, and providing nursing care. On some occasions, however, they crossed gender boundaries dramatically. Women like **Mary Ludwig** and Margaret Corbin carried water and ammunition to their soldier husbands and took up the men's guns when they fell wounded. After the war, a number of these "Molly Pitchers" applied to the government for pensions, citing evidence of wounds they had received in battle.

Both loyalist and patriot women served as spies or saboteurs or risked their lives by sheltering soldiers or hiding weapons in their basements. Sometimes they made the choice to burn their own crops or destroy their homes to prevent the enemy from using them. These were conscious acts of patriotism rather than wifely duties. The same was true of the small number of women who chose to disguise themselves as men, enlist in the military, and fight until they were wounded, killed, or discovered (see Individual Choices: Deborah Sampson). Their actions erased rather than stretched the traditional lines dividing male and female experiences.

In the postwar years, members of America's elite discussed women's role in the family and in a republican society. They articulated a new ideal for women, based on a more positive evaluation of women's "nature" and suggested a more active role for women in sustaining a republican society. **Republican womanhood,** as this set of new ideas was called, stressed the importance of women as educators of the next generation of republican patriots.

Republican womanhood had roots in economic and social changes that began before the Revolution, including the growth of a prosperous urban class that could purchase many household necessities. No longer needing to make cloth or candles or butter, prosperous urban wives and mothers had time to devote to raising children. Republican womanhood probably had little immediate impact in the lives of free ordinary women, who remained unable to purchase essential goods or to pay others to do household chores, or in the lives of African-American or Indian women. Many of the assumptions of republican womanhood—particularly those about women's intellectual and moral potential—came from the writings of European and English philosophers, social critics, and reformers. Yet the Revolution did give Republican womanhood particular American qualities. The republican woman was expected to possess an independence of mind and an ability to survive in times of crisis and disaster. Her active role in the education of the next generation was defined as a public, political contribution, not simply a private, family role. Republican

♦ The wealthy Connecticut matron, Mary Floyd Tallmadge, shown here with three-year-old Maria, and infant son Henry in 1790, would have childrearing responsibilities unknown to most seventeenth-century mothers. Educators and political leaders of the new republic called for a major change in family roles, urging elite women like Tallmadge, rather than their husbands, to oversee the moral education of their sons as well as their daughters. This innovation led to the growth of formal education for women. *"Mrs. Benjamin Tallmadge and Children Henry and Maria" by Ralph Earl, 1790. The Litchfield Historical Society.*

Mary Ludwig Wife of a soldier at Fort Monmouth; one of many women known popularly as "Molly Pitchers" because they carried water to cool down the cannons their husbands fired in battle.

republican womanhood A role for women that stressed the importance of instructing children in republican virtues such as patriotism and honor.

INDIVIDUAL CHOICES

Choosing to Fight

Deborah Sampson

Whether attracted by adventure, the promise of a pension, or the bounty soldiers received upon enlistment, Deborah Sampson decided to disguise herself as a man and enlist in the continental army in 1781. She served for over two years before officers discovered she was female and discharged her. This portrait, drawn by Joseph Stone Framingham in 1797, depicts Sampson in female dress, but surrounds her with the military emblems befitting a veteran of the revolution. Rhode Island Historical Society.

Deborah Sampson was born in 1760 in a small village near Plymouth, Massachusetts. Her father was a descendant of two of the original Pilgrim settlers, and her mother could trace her family roots back to Pilgrim governor William Bradford. Despite this rich heritage, the Sampsons were a poor, struggling farm family. When Deborah was a small child, her father abandoned his wife and six children. Mrs. Sampson had little choice but to bind out some of her children, including Deborah, as servants in neighbors' homes.

While the protest against Britain grew stronger and the Revolutionary War began, Deborah Sampson grew into a tall, healthy young woman. But she was not a free woman until the fall of 1779, when her term as an indentured domestic servant ended. Within a year, Deborah Sampson made the most important choice of her life: to be a soldier in the Continental Army. Without a word to anyone, she vanished from the community. With a change of clothes and a change of name, she became Robert Shurtleff, private in the Continental Army's Massachusetts line.

As a woman, Sampson might have played a role in the struggle for independence by serving as a courier or a spy. Or she might have chosen to join thousands of other women in the army camp, where they performed valuable services as cooks, laundresses, and nurses. Or she might have chosen to assist the war effort by knitting

thinkers promoted the notion of women as civic participants. What they did not do, however, was suggest direct political participation for female Americans.

Although American republicanism expected mothers to instill patriotism in their children, it also expected communities to provide formal education for future citizens. Arguing that a citizen could not be both "ignorant and free," several states allotted tax money for public elementary schools. Some went even further. By 1789, for example, Massachusetts required every town to provide free public education to its children. After the Revolution, *children* meant girls as well as boys.

This new emphasis on female education was at the heart of educational reform in the young re-socks or making uniforms for the poorly clad men in General Washington's army. Why did Deborah Sampson choose the life of a soldier?

Perhaps like many male farm hands and city workers, she saw military service as a risky but rare opportunity for economic mobility. With no dowry and no inheritance, she had little hope of marrying or becoming mistress of her own home. As a soldier, however, she could expect to receive an enlistment bonus, a pension, and, by 1782, a promise of land when the war ended. These tangible benefits prompted thousands of poor, single young men to sign on for military service.

Perhaps Deborah Sampson chose to trade her petticoats and bonnets for a soldier's uniform because of the adventure and excitement army life offered. Eager to see new places and have new experiences, she refused to be constrained by her gender.

Perhaps patriotism stirred her as it did other volunteers over the seven years of war. Later, the man who wrote down the story of her military career emphasized her desire to play a direct role in the defense of her country. She had chosen a place on the battlefield, he said, because she believed in liberty and wished to be present at the birth of her nation. That choice was possible for Robert Shurtleff, not for Deborah Sampson.

Whatever her motives, Sampson performed honorably in battle. As Private Robert Shurtleff, she was wounded when a musket ball lodged in her leg. Amazingly, she managed to hide her identity as a woman despite the injury. The truth was discovered, however, when she was hospitalized with a fever while stationed in Philadelphia. The authorities insisted that she be dismissed at once, but they did not prosecute her for her deception. On October 25, 1783, she was given an honorable discharge—and Robert Shurtleff disappeared forever.

Deborah Sampson returned to Massachusetts in November 1783. In April 1784, she married a farmer named Benjamin Gannett and began a family. As a wife and mother, Deborah Sampson Gannett was constrained by custom and law from an active life in the public sphere. In 1802, however, she made a second, equally daring choice to cross the boundaries her society believed separated the sexes. She began to give public lectures on her military career. The tales she told the crowds who flocked to hear and see her were full of exaggerated claims of bravery, skill, and battlefield experiences. But dressed in her uniform once again, and performing a precision drill in front of her audience that would make Baron von Steuben proud, Deborah Sampson demonstrated the unexpected impact of the revolution on an ordinary American's life.

public. Before the Revolution, the education of daughters was haphazard at best. Colleges and the preparatory schools that trained young men for college were closed to female students. A woman got what formal knowledge she could by reading her father's or her brother's books. Some women, most notably Anne Hutchinson and the Massachusetts revolutionary propagandist Mercy Otis Warren, were lucky enough to receive a fine education from the men in their family. But most women had to be content to learn domestic skills rather than geography, philosophy, or history. After the Revolution, however, educational reformers insisted that mothers must be well versed in history and even political theory if they were to teach the essential principles of citizenship.

♦ Black loyalists who settled in Nova Scotia faced serious racial discrimination and open hostility from white refugees. This woodcutter may have been among the African-American loyalists who chose to relocate to Sierra Leone in the 1790s. *"A Rare View of a Black Woodcutter at Work in Shelburne, Nova Scotia," 1788 by William Booth. National Archives Canada, Ottawa (C-40162).*

Judith Sargent Murray and Benjamin Rush were the foremost republican advocates of female education. Murray boldly challenged old notions of women's limited intellectual capacity. Provide women with the same education as men, she argued, and they will display the same ability to reason and to think. Others agreed. By the 1780s, private academies had opened to educate the daughters of wealthy American families. These privileged young women enjoyed the rare opportunity to study mathematics, history, and geography. Although their curriculum was often as rigorous as the curriculum in a boys' preparatory school, the addition of courses in fancy needlework reminded the girls that their futures lay in marriage and motherhood.

The War's Impact on Slaves and Slavery

The protection of liberty and the fear of enslavement were major themes of the Revolution. Yet the denial of liberty was a central reality in the lives of most African Americans. As the movement for independence developed, slaves' political and military loyalties reflected their best guess about their chance for freedom. Ironically, the desire for freedom set many of them *against* the Revolution. Of the fifty thousand or so slaves who won their freedom in the war, half did so by escaping to the British army. Only about five thousand African-American men joined the Continental Army once Congress opened enlistment to them in 1776. Black soldiers were generally better treated by the British than by the revolutionaries. In both armies, however, African-American troops received lower pay than white soldiers and were often assigned to the most dangerous duties.

With American victory in 1781, African-American loyalist soldiers faced a difficult decision: to remain in America and risk re-enslavement or to evacuate along with the British army. Many stayed, prompting a group of angry owners to complain that there was "reason to believe that a great number of slaves which were taken by the British army are now passing in this country as free men." The British transported those who chose to leave to Canada, to England, to British Florida, to the Caribbean, or to Africa. Three thousand former slaves from New York City settled initially in Nova Scotia, but the racism of their white loyalist neighbors led more than one thousand of these veterans to emigrate a second time. Led by an African-born former slave named Thomas Peters, they sailed to Sierra Leone, in West Africa, where they established a free black colony.

Slaves found other routes to freedom besides military service during the war. They escaped from farms and plantations to the cities, where they passed as free people. Or they fled to the frontier, where they joined sympathetic Indian tribes. Women and children, in particular, took advantage of wartime disruptions to flee their master's control.

The long war affected the lives of those who remained in slavery. Control and discipline broke

Judith Sargent Murray Massachusetts advocate of educational opportunities for women; her essays on women's rights and abilities were influential in the early republic.

♦ As a child, Phillis Wheatley was brought from Africa and was sold to a Boston couple who came to recognize and encourage her literary talent. Wheatley's patriotic poetry won approval from George Washington and praise from many revolutionary leaders. She died free but in poverty in the 1780s. *Library of Congress.*

down when the southern campaigns dragged on, distracting slaveowners and disrupting work routines. Slave masters complained loudly and bitterly that their slaves "all do now what they please every where" or "pay no attention to the orders of the overseer." These exaggerated complaints point to real but temporary opportunities for slaves to alter the conditions under which they worked and lived.

In the northern states, the revolutionaries' demand for liberty undermined black slavery. Loyalists taunted patriots, asking, "how is it that we hear the loudest yelps for liberty among the drivers of negroes?" The question made the contradiction between revolutionary ideals and American reality painfully clear. Not all slaveowners, however, needed to be shamed by others into grappling with the hypocrisy of their position. In the 1760s and 1770s, influential political leaders such as James Otis, Thomas Paine, and Benjamin Rush campaigned against the continuation of slavery. In Boston, **Phillis Wheatley,** a young African-born slave whose master recognized and encouraged her literary talents, called on the revolutionaries to acknowledge the universality of the wish for freedom. "In every human breast," Wheatley wrote, "God had implanted a Principle, which we call love of freedom; it is impatient of Oppression, and pants for Deliverance . . . . I will assert, that the same Principles live in us." George Washington was among those who admired Wheatley's talents and respected her demands for black freedom, and he publicly acknowledged her as an American poet.

Free black Americans joined with white reformers to mobilize antislavery campaigns in Pennsylvania, Massachusetts, Rhode Island, and Connecticut. In Boston and Philadelphia, slaves petitioned on their own behalf to be "liberated from a state of Bondage, and made Freemen of this Community." There were few slaves in these states, and the regional economy did not depend on unfree labor. Thus it was easier there to acknowledge the truth in the slave's cry: "We have no property! . . . we have no children! . . . we have no city! . . . we have no country!"

Manumission increased during the 1770s, especially in the North. In 1780, Pennsylvania became the first state to pass an emancipation statute, making manumission a public policy rather than a private matter of conscience. Pennsylvania lawmakers, however, compromised on a gradual rather than an immediate end to slavery. Only slaves born after the law was enacted were eligible, and they could not expect to receive their freedom until they had served a twenty-eight-year term of indenture. By 1804, all northern states except Delaware had committed themselves to a slow end to slavery.

Slavery was far more deeply embedded in the South, as a labor system and as a system that regulated race relations. In the Lower South, white Americans ignored the debate over slavery and took immediate steps to replace missing slaves and to restore tight control over work and life on their plantations. Manumission did occur in the Upper South. Free black communities appeared in both Maryland and Virginia after the Revolutionary War, and planters openly debated the morality of slavery in a republic and the practical benefits of slave labor. They did not all reach the same conclusions. George Washington freed all his slaves at his death, but Patrick Henry, who had often stirred the souls of his fellow Virginia legislators with his spirited defense of American liberty, justified his decision to continue slavery with blunt honesty. Freeing his slaves, he said, would be inconvenient (see Figure 6.1).

Phillis Wheatley African-born poet who became the first widely recognized black writer in America.

manumission The legal act of freeing a slave.

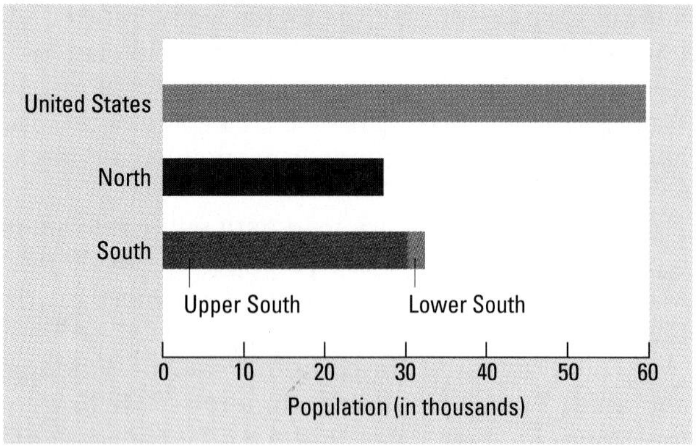

♦ **FIGURE 6.1 Free Black Population, 1790** This graph shows the number of free African Americans in the United States in 1790 as well as their regional distribution. These almost 60,000 free people were less than 10 percent of the African-American population of the nation. Although 40 percent of northern blacks were members of this free community, only about 5.5 percent of the Upper South African Americans and less than 2 percent of the Lower South lived outside the bounds of slavery.

The Fate of the Loyalists

Before independence was declared, white Americans loyal to the Crown experienced the isolation and disapproval of their communities. Some faced the physical danger of **tarring and feathering,** imprisonment, or beatings. Still others saw their property destroyed. After 1775, loyalists flocked to the safety of British-occupied cities, crowding first into Boston and later into New York City and Philadelphia. When the British left an area, the loyalists evacuated with them. More than a thousand Massachusetts loyalists boarded British ships when Boston was abandoned in 1776, and fifteen thousand more sailed out of New York harbor when the war ended. Altogether, as many as a hundred thousand men, women, and children left their American homes to take up new lives in England, Canada, and the West Indies.

Wealth often determined a loyalist's destination. Rich and influential men like Thomas Hutchinson of Massachusetts took refuge in England during the war. But life in England was so expensive that it quickly ate up their resources and drove them into debt. Accustomed to comfort, many of these exiles passed their days in seedy boarding houses in the small cities outside London. They lost more than servants and fine clothes, however. In a society dominated by aristocrats and royalty, loyalist men who had enjoyed status and prestige in America suddenly found themselves socially insignificant, with no work and little money. Loyalists in England grew more desperately homesick each day.

When the war ended, most of the loyalists in England departed for Nova Scotia, New Brunswick, or the Caribbean. Many of these exiles were specifically forbidden to return the the United States by the new state governments. Others refused to go back to America because they equated the new republican society with **mob rule.** Those who were willing to adjust to the new American nation returned slowly. Less prosperous loyalists, especially those who served in the loyalist battalions during the war, went to Canada after 1781. The separation from family and friends, as much as the bleak climate of Canada, at first caused depression and despair in some exiles. One woman who had bravely endured the warfare and its deprivations broke down and cried when she landed at Nova Scotia. Like the revolutionaries, these men and women had chosen their political loyalty based on a mixture of principle and self-interest. Unlike the revolutionaries, they had chosen the losing side. They lived with the consequences for the rest of their lives.

Canada became the refuge of another group of loyalists: members of the Indian tribes that had supported the Crown. The British ceded much of the Iroquois land to the United States in the Treaty of Paris, and American hostility toward "enemy savages" made peaceful coexistence seem impossible. Thus, in the 1780s, Mohawks, Onondagas, Tuscaroras, Senecas, Oneidas, and Cayugas along with Delawares, Tutelos, and Nanticokes created new, often multiethnic settlements on the banks of the Grand River in Ontario. These new communities marked an end to the dislocation and suffering many of these refugees had experienced during the Revolution, when steady warfare depleted Indian resources and made thousands dependent on the British for food, clothing, and military supplies. A majority of those who settled in Canada had already spent years in makeshift encampments near Fort Niagara after American armies destroyed their farms, homes, and villages.

tarring and feathering Covering a person with hot tar and then rolling that person in feathers; the victim could die from the burns.

mob rule Government by people using violence to enforce their will.

SUMMARY

E xpectations
C onstraints
C hoices
O utcomes

When the colonies *chose* independence and war with Great Britain, both sides had *expectations* that proved incorrect. The British outnumbered and outgunned the Americans and *expected* a short war. The Americans *expected* the British to abandon a war fought so far from home. The war, however, dragged on for seven years.

The British *chose* initially to invade New York and the southern colonies, *expecting* to find strong loyalist support in both regions. But *constrained* by the difficulty of waging war in unfamiliar territory and baffled by Washington's hit-and-run tactics, the British suffered several early defeats and were not able to deliver a crushing blow.

The most dramatic turning point in the war came in 1777 when British general John Burgoyne *chose* to try to isolate New England from the rest of the rebelling colonies—and failed. He was forced to surrender at Saratoga, New York. The *outcome* of this American victory was an alliance between France and the United States and the expansion of the war into an international conflict. When the British again *chose* to invade the South in 1778, their campaign ended in disaster. French and American forces together defeated General Cornwallis at Yorktown, Virginia, in October 1781. Fighting continued for a time, but in March 1782, the British Parliament *chose* to end the conflict. The war for American independence had been won. The Treaty of Paris was negotiated in 1783. Despite several diplomatic *constraints*, the Americans won important concessions.

Independence from British rule was not the only *outcome* of the war. Victory led to transformations in American society. Individual rights were strengthened for free white men. A republican spirit changed the outlook, if not the condition, of those whose rights were *constrained* by habit, custom, and law. Many white women, for example, developed a new sense of the importance of their domestic role as "republican mothers" in the new nation. Black Americans also made some gains. Fifty thousand slaves won their freedom during the war, thousands by serving in the Continental Army. Some northerners moved to outlaw slavery, but southern slaveholders *chose* to preserve the institution despite intense debate. Loyalists, having made their political *choices*, had to live with the consequences of defeat. For most, the *outcome* was exile from their homeland.

SUGGESTED READINGS

Joseph Plumb Martin. *Ordinary Courage: The Revolutionary War Adventures of Joseph Plumb Martin*, ed. James Kirby Martin (1993).

The military experiences of a Massachusetts soldier who served with the Continental Army during the American Revolution.

William Nelson. *The American Tory* (1961).

An account of those who chose to align themselves with the British during the war.

Wallace Sterne Randall. *Benedict Arnold: Patriot and Traitor* (1990).

The author tries to make sense of a man who might have been remembered as a great hero of the Revolution but whose name is synonymous in American history with *traitor.*

Revolution

This feature-length film starring Al Pacino is available in most well-stocked video stores. Although it is a romance, the film captures some of the mood and spirit of the revolutionary era.

A Revolution in Women's Education

The Context

In 1787, the Young Ladies Academy of Philadelphia opened its door to the daughters of America's revolutionary generation, offering a rigorous course of study that included literature, composition, sciences, arithmetic, oratory, and rhetoric. In the three decades that followed, similar schools appeared across the United States, in major cities like New York City, Boston, and New Haven, and in smaller towns like Medford, Massachusetts, Litchfield, Connecticut, and Warrenton, North Carolina. The result, many believed, was a revolution in female education. (For further information on the context, see pages 168–172.

The Historical Question

Modern historians have traced the rapid growth of educational institutions for women in the young republic. The significance of this "rise of the female academy" is debated, however. Did this educational trend reflect a change in ideas about women's intellectual capacities? Did it arise from or lead to a major shift in women's roles in American society?

The Challenge

Using the sources provided, along with other information you have read, write an essay or hold a discussion on the following question. Cite evidence in the sources to support your conclusions. **What new ideas about women's intellectual abilities and their role in society may have found expression in the growth of women's educational institutions?**

The Sources

1 In 1635, John Winthrop, the Puritan governor of Massachusetts, recorded in his journal this judgment on the illness suffered by a woman:

Mr. Hopkins . . . came to Boston and brought his wife with him . . . who was fallen into a sad infirmity, the loss of her understanding and reason, which had been growing upon her . . . by occasion of her giving herself wholly to reading and writing . . . if she had attended to her household affairs, and such things as belong to women, and not . . . meddle[d] in such things as are proper for men, whose minds are stronger . . . she [would have] kept her wits.

2 This colonial advertisement, appearing in the *Virginia Gazette* in 1772, describes a curriculum the school mistress believed appropriate for female students. It reads:

E. Armston . . . continues the Schools at Point Pleasant, Norfolk Borough, where [there] is a large and convenient House proper to accommodate young Ladies as Boarders; at which School is taught Petit Point in Flowers, Fruit, Landscapes, and Sculpture, Nuns Work, Embroidery in Silk, Gold, Silver, Pearls, or embossed, Shading of all Kinds, in the various Works in Vogue, Dresden Point Work, Lace, Catgut in different Modes, Muslin after the Newest Taste, and most elegant Pattern, Waxwork in Figure, Fruit, or Flowers, Shell ditto, or grotesque, Painting in Water Colours and Mezzotints . . . Specimens of the Subscriber's Work may be seen at her House, as also of her Scholars; having taught several

Years in Norfolk, and elsewhere to general Satisfaction. She flatters herself that those Gentlemen and Ladies who have hitherto employed her will grant her their further indulgence, as no endeavors shall be wanted to complete what is above mentioned, with a strict attention to the Behavior of those Ladies entrusted to her Care.

3 Wealthy Philadelphia matron Esther De-Berdt Reed helped organize women's voluntary associations to raise funds and supplies for the American army during the Revolution. In "The Sentiments of an American Woman," printed in 1780, Reed discusses female patriotism. She says:

On the commencement of actual war, the Women of America manifested a firm resolution to contribute as much as could depend on them, to the deliverance of this country. Animated by the purest patriotism . . . they aspire to render themselves more really useful; and this sentiment is universal from the north to the south of the Thirteen United States . . . if the weakness of our [women's] Constitution, if opinion and manners did not forbid us to march to glory by the same paths as the Men, we should at least equal and sometimes surpass them in our love for the public good. I glory in all that which my sex has done great and commendable . . . Who knows if persons disposed to censure, and sometimes too severely with regard to us, may not disapprove . . . we are at least certain, that he cannot be a good citizen who will not applaud our efforts for the relief of the armies which defend our lives, our possessions, our liberty.

4 Like other advocates of female advancement, poet Susanna Haswell Rowson argued that nurture, not nature or divine dictates, created women's moral and intellectual inferiority to men. In "The Virtues of an Educated Wife," she wrote:

When the Creator formed this world in common,
His last, best work, his master-piece, was woman.
Taken from the side of man, and next his heart,
Of all his virtues she partakes a part;
And from that source, poor woman got a share
Of vice and folly, mingled here and there.
But would you treat us, scorning custom's rules,
As reasonable beings, not as fools,
And from our earliest youth, would condescend
To form our minds, strengthen, correct, amend:
Teach us to scorn those fools, whose only joys,
Are placed in trifling idleness and noice.
Teach us to prize the power of intellect;
And whilst inspiring love, to keep respect;
You'd meet the sweet reward of all your care;
Find in us friends, your purest joys to share.

5 In July 1787, Dr. Benjamin Rush, one of Philadelphia's leading intellectuals and social reformers, addressed the entering class of the Young Ladies Academy of Philadelphia. Rush said:

I know that the elevation of the female mind, by means of moral, physical, and religious truth, is considered by some men as unfriendly to the domestic character of a woman. But this is the prejudice of little minds and springs from the same spirit which opposes the general diffusion of knowledge among the citizens of our republic. If men believe that ignorance is favorable to the government of the female sex, they are certainly deceived, for a weak and ignorant woman will always be governed with the greatest difficulty . . . It will be in your power, LADIES, to correct the mistakes and practices of our sex upon these subjects by demonstrating that the female temper can only be governed by reason and that the cultivation of reason in women is alike friendly to the order of nature and to private as well as public happiness.

THE FEDERALIST AND ANTIFEDERALIST STRUGGLE OVER THE CONSTITUTION The battle over ratification of the Constitution was fiercely fought throughout 1787 and 1788. This map shows the areas of strong antifederalism, the areas of Federalist strength, and the scattered pockets where opinion was evenly divided. The map also provides the final ratification vote for each state. Note that Rhode Island did not ratify the Constitution until after the new government went into effect.

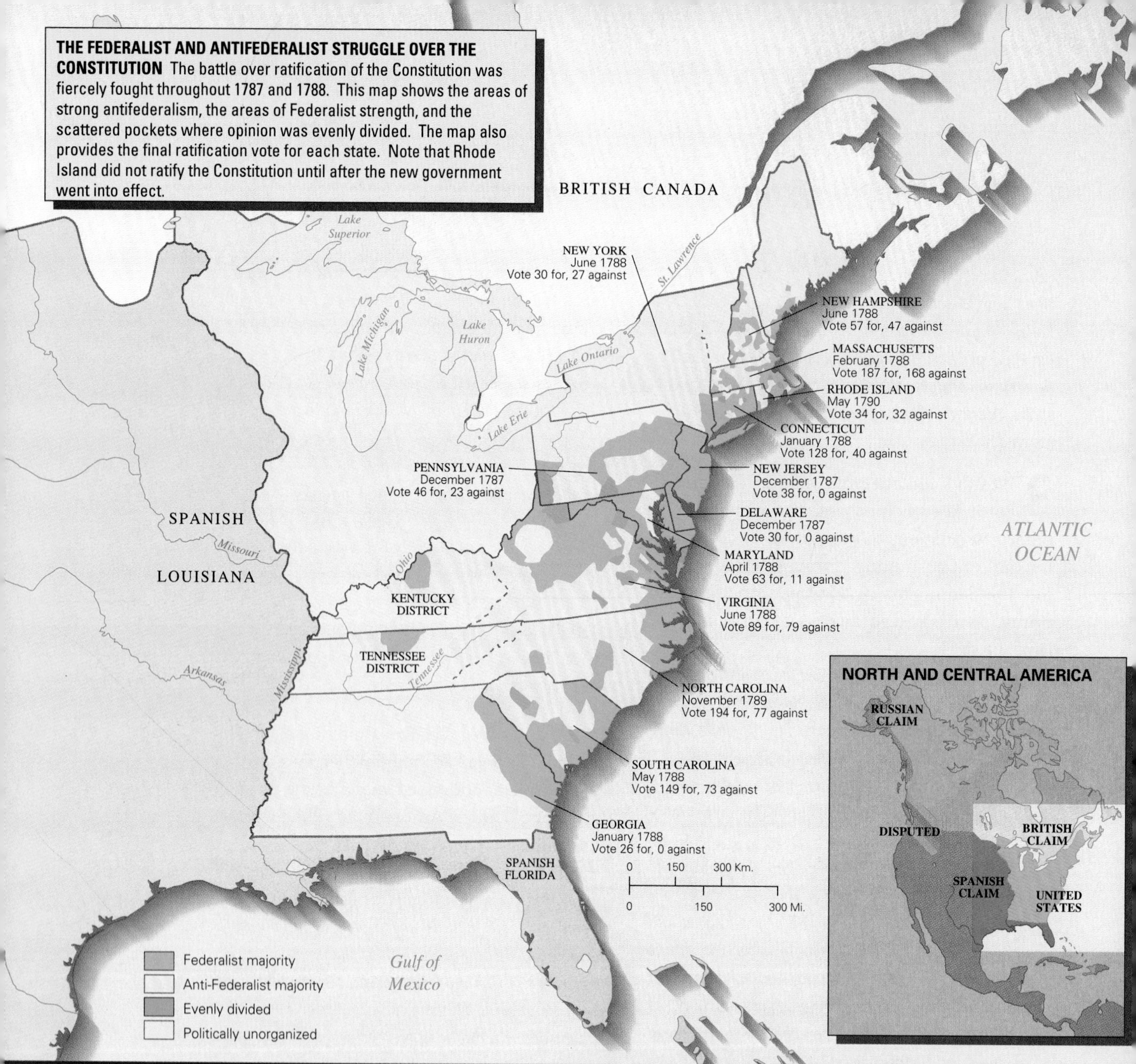

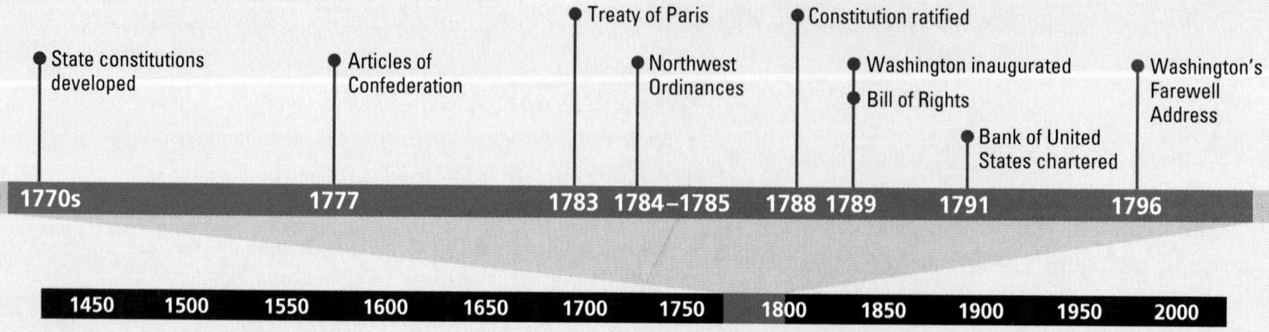

CHAPTER 7

Competing Visions of the Virtuous Republic, 1770–1796

What Kind of a Republic?

- How did Americans choose to define a good citizen of a republic?
- How did colonial experiences influence the outcome of state constitution writing?
- What constraints did the Articles of Confederation place on the central government?

Challenges to the Confederation

- What constraints undermined the Confederation, and what was the outcome?
- What was the outcome of Shays' Rebellion for national politics?
- What gains did nationalists expect from a stronger central government?

Creating a New Government

- What major compromises did the framers choose to make in writing the new constitution?
- What positive outcome did James Madison see in his "checks and balances" system?

Resolving the Conflict of Vision

- What arguments did Antifederalists choose to make against the Constitution? What arguments did Federalists use to support it?
- What was the outcome of the ratification process?

Competing Visions Re-emerge

- How did Alexander Hamilton's expectations for the new nation differ from Thomas Jefferson's? What were the outcomes of this conflict of vision?
- How did the French Revolution affect the diplomatic choices made during George Washington's presidency?

INTRODUCTION

E xpectations
C onstraints
C hoices
O utcomes

"The mere independence of America," Tom Paine declared, did not constitute a true revolution. If the leaders of the new nation *chose* to model their government after "the corrupt system of the English Government," Paine said, he would have no part in it. Most free, white Americans also rejected the notion of an American monarchy. Like the author of *Common Sense*, they *expected* to live in a republic. A republic, however, could take many forms, and Americans who enjoyed a political voice disagreed on what form was best for the new nation. As a consequence, the transition from independence to nationhood generated heated debate.

Like all momentous *outcomes*, American independence resolved one set of critical questions only to raise new ones. How should power be divided between local and national governments? How should laws be made, and by whom? Who should be empowered to administer those laws? American constitution writers on the state and national levels also had to *choose* the best way to protect the unalienable individual rights that free white Americans believed they possessed.

These critical political *choices* had to be made within the context of serious postwar *constraints*. After the Revolution, the nation struggled with economic depression, unpaid war debts, and vanishing credit. States competed with one another over trade and territory. The national government had diplomatic problems with foreign nations and Indians, particularly over control of the West. Disputes among Americans, especially large land proprietors and frontier settlers, sometimes erupted into violence. Americans' *choices* in dealing with these problems influenced the type of governments they created. In turn, the ability of a government to solve these problems often determined people's commitment to it.

The first national government was established by the Articles of Confederation. This government guided Americans through the last years of the war and the peace negotiations and organized the northwest territories for settlement. The Confederation government did not survive the decade of postwar adjustment, however. Instead, leading political figures *chose* to design a new government. The *outcome* was the U.S. Constitution, fashioned from compromises between the interests of small states and large ones and between southern and northern regional interests. The Constitution greatly strengthened and expanded the central government's role in the regulation of interstate and foreign trade and provided the central government with powers that the Confederation lacked, including the right to levy taxes and to amend the national constitution itself without the unanimous consent of the states.

The creation of a new federal government was controversial, and in most states political struggles over ratification of the Constitution were intense. Opponents of the Constitution were known as Antifederalists. They said it rejected many of the basic ideals of the Revolution, especially the commitment to local representative government and the guarantee of protection from the dangers of centralized authority. Antifederalists believed the new government would be dominated by the wealthiest citizens. Supporters of the constitution called themselves Federalists. They argued that the new government would save America from economic disaster, international scorn, and domestic unrest. Leading patriots of the 1760s and 1770s could be found on both sides of this debate, but the Federalists carried the day.

The framers of the Constitution knew that the list of unresolved problems remained long. Tensions between northern and southern states were growing. The nation was seriously divided over foreign policy and the *choice* between allies and enemies in Europe. And many Americans continued to believe that strong local governments rather than an active central government offered the best protection of their liberties. Nevertheless, when President George Washington said his farewells to public life in 1796, most Americans *expected* their young nation to survive.

CHRONOLOGY

From Revolution to Nationhood

1770s	State constitutions developed
1776	New Jersey constitution gives property-holding women the right to vote
1777	Congress adopts Articles of Confederation Slavery abolished in Pennsylvania
1781	States ratify Articles of Confederation Cornwallis surrenders at Yorktown
1784–1785	First two Northwest Ordinances
1786	Annapolis conference
1786–1787	Shays' Rebellion in Massachusetts
1787	Constitutional Convention
1787	Third Northwest Ordinance
1787–1788	States ratify the Constitution
1789	First congressional elections George Washington inaugurated as first president Judiciary Act of 1789 French Revolution begins
1791	First Bank of the United States chartered Bill of Rights added to the Constitution Alexander Hamilton's *Report on Manufactures*
1792	Washington re-elected
1793	Genêt affair Jefferson resigns as secretary of state
1794	Whiskey Rebellion in Pennsylvania Battle of Fallen Timbers
1795	Congress approves Jay's Treaty Treaty of San Lorenzo
1796	Washington's Farewell Address

What Kind of a Republic?

- How did Americans choose to define a good citizen of a republic?
- How did colonial experiences influence the outcome of state constitution writing?
- What constraints did the Articles of Confederation place on the central government?

If asked, most free white men in late-eighteenth-century America could define the basic elements of a republican form of government. First and most important, the people, rather than a king or queen, held the sovereign, or ultimate, political power. Second, the people elected those who governed them. Third, the government's main function was to represent the people's interests and protect the people's individual rights. In the opinion of most Americans, these principles made a **republic** the best form of government, although they knew that it was also the most fragile. What type of citizen was needed for a republic to survive? When Americans debated this question, both sides used the same vocabulary but meant very different things.

Competing Notions of Republicanism

Tom Paine spoke for many when he declared that republicanism was a moral code of behavior as well as a system of government. No representative government, no matter how well designed, could endure without virtuous citizens who led lives of simplicity and industry and were willing to make sacrifices in the best interests of the community. If citizens became selfish or corrupt, a republic would succumb to tyranny.

Americans who linked virtue and republicanism drew on several intellectual and political sources to

> **republic** A political system in which the supreme power lies in a body of citizens who are entitled to elect representatives responsible to them.

support their argument. Many of the Revolution's leaders had studied the history of the ancient European world. They particularly admired the **Roman Republic** as it was portrayed in the books they read. Roman citizens—described as hardworking, simple, and patriotic—seemed to them to be much like eighteenth-century Americans. English history also influenced this view of republicanism. In pamphlets and political tracts, England's seventeenth-century revolutionaries had issued impassioned warnings against the dangers of luxury and **decadent** living among men in power.

This belief that a republic depended on individual virtue was widespread but not universally held in eighteenth-century America. A second language of republicanism was spoken by those who believed that independent individuals, left free to pursue their own self-interest, were best suited to sustain a republic. The advocates of individual self-interest took their arguments from such economists and philosophers as **Adam Smith.** They insisted that a government that did not interfere with individuals' pursuit of wealth and success would win all citizens' enduring loyalty.

Any discussion of the proper republican citizen exposed other, often serious divisions. For example, backcountry farmers often denied the possibility that "moneyed men"—bankers, land speculators, and wealthy planters or merchants—could be true republicans. Wealthy Americans, in turn, voiced concern that backcountry settlers were nothing more than "villains . . . runaway debtors [and] criminals" who would trample on the rights of others and destroy government by law. When backcountry men and women spoke of a republic, they described a nation of small, self-regulating communities left free to make laws and follow customs that local people supported. Urban elites, however, often envisioned a strong central government producing uniform rules and procedures by which men could pursue their individual self-interest.

The State Constitutions

The writers of state constitutions were the first to grapple with definitions of citizenship and to debate how widespread political participation should be. Should women be allowed to vote? Could landless men, servants, or apprentices enjoy a political voice? John Adams feared that any discussion of voting rights, or **suffrage,** would raise the specter of a dangerous democracy. Once the question was posed, he said, "there will be no end of it . . . women will demand a vote, lads from twelve to twenty-one will think their rights are not enough attended to, and every man who has not a **farthing** will demand an equal voice with any other in all acts of state."

English political tradition supported Adams's conviction that political rights were not universal. Under English law, "rights" were, in fact, particular *privileges* that a group enjoyed because of special social circumstances—including age, sex, wealth, or family ties. In their first constitutions, several states decided to extend these privileges to all free white men, a group that still met special circumstances of race and sex.

The state constitutions reflected the variey of opinion on this matter of democracy within a republic. At one end of the spectrum was Pennsylvania, whose constitution abolished all property qualifications and granted the vote to all white males in the state. At the other end was Maryland, whose constitution continued to link the ownership of property to voting. To hold office, a Marylander had to meet even higher standards of wealth than the voters.

Constitution makers were also divided over how much power popularly elected representatives should have in the new governments. Again, Pennsylvania produced the most democratic answer to this question. Pennsylvania's constitution concentrated all power to make and to administer law in a one-house, or **unicameral,** elected assembly. The farmers and artisans who helped draft this state constitution eliminated both the executive office and the upper house of the legislature, remembering that these had been strongholds for the wealthy in colonial times. Pennsylvania also required annual elections of all legislators to ensure that the assembly remained responsive to the people's will. Maryland, in contrast, divided powers among a governor, or executive branch, and a **bicameral** legislature

Roman Republic A republic in ancient Rome that lasted from 500 B.C. to 44 B.C., when it was replaced by the Roman Empire.

decadent Being in a state of moral decay.

Adam Smith Scottish economist (1723–1790) and advocate of the principles of free trade.

suffrage The right to vote.

farthing An old British coin worth one-fourth of a penny and thus a term used to denote something of very little value.

unicameral Consisting of a single legislative house.

bicameral Consisting of two legislative houses.

♦ The men who drafted the New Jersey constitution took care to include a property qualification for voting but forgot to specify the sex of an eligible voter. Thus women who owned property had the right to vote from 1776 to 1807, when the "error" was corrected. New Jersey did not choose to grant women the vote again for over a century. *The Bettmann Archive, Inc.*

whose upper house required higher property qualifications for its members than did the lower house, or assembly. In this manner, political leaders in Maryland ensured to their elite citizens a voice in lawmaking.

Pennsylvania and Maryland represent the two ends of the democratic spectrum. The remaining states fell between these poles. The constitutions of New Hampshire, North Carolina, and Georgia followed the democratic tendencies of Pennsylvania. New York, South Carolina, and Virginia chose Maryland's more conservative or traditional approach. New Jersey and Delaware took the middle ground, with at least one surprising result. New Jersey's first constitution, written in 1776, gave the vote to "all free inhabitants" who met modest property qualifications. This requirement denied the vote to propertyless men but granted voting rights to property-holding women. A writer in the New York *Spectator* in 1797 snidely remarked that New Jersey women "intermeddl[ing] in political affairs" made that state's politics as strange as those of the "emperor of Java [who] never employs any but women in his embassies." Nevertheless, for thirty-one years, New Jersey women regularly exercised their right to elect the men who governed them. Then in 1807, state lawmakers took away that right, arguing that "the weaker sex" was too easily manipulated by political candidates to be allowed to vote.

A state's particular history often determined the type of constitution it produced. For example, coastal elites and lowland gentry had dominated the colonial governments of New Hampshire, South Carolina, Virginia, and North Carolina. These states sought to correct this injustice by ensuring representation to small farming districts in interior and frontier regions. The memory of high-handed colonial governors and elitist upper houses in the legislature led Massachusetts lawmakers to severely limit the powers of their first state government. The constitutions in all of these states reflected the strong political voice that nonelites had acquired during the Revolution.

Beginning in the 1780s, however, many states revised their constitutions. Most expanded the powers of the government but created safeguards they believed would prevent abuse. The 1780 Massachusetts constitution was the model for many of these revisions. Massachusetts political leaders built in a system of "checks and balances" among the legislative, judicial, and executive branches to ensure that no branch of the government could grow too powerful or overstep its assigned duties. Over the opposition of many farmers and ordinary citizens, these newer state constitutions also curbed the democratic extension of voting and officeholding privileges. Thus wealth returned as a qualification to govern, although the revised constitutions did not allow the wealthy to tamper with the basic individual rights of citizens. In seven states, these individual rights were safeguarded by a **bill of rights** guaranteeing freedom of speech, religion, and the press as well as the right to assemble and to petition the government.

The Articles of Confederation

After independence was declared, political leaders recognized that some form of national government was needed. Popular sentiment, however, ran against a powerful central government. Instead, as John Adams later recalled, Americans wanted "a Confederacy of States, each of which must have a separate government."

bill of rights A formal statement of essential rights and liberties under law.

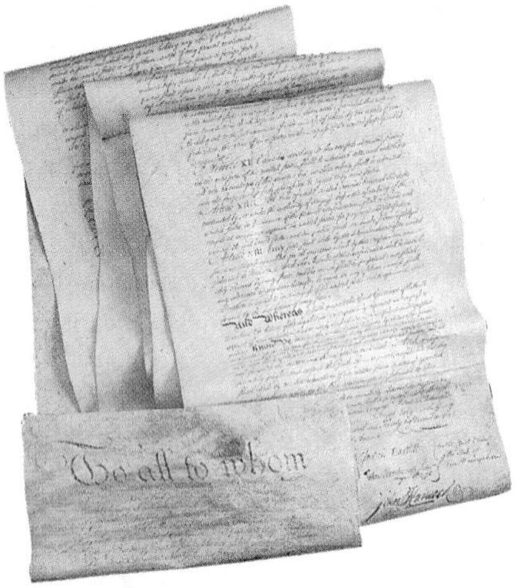

♦ The Articles of Confederation was debated for almost as many years as it was in effect. Proposed in 1775, it was not ratified until 1781. Eight years later, the Constitution replaced it. Eighteenth-century citizens hotly debated the virtues and shortcomings of the Articles, and historians have continued to disagree over the merits of this blueprint for a first American government. *The National Archives of the United States published by Harry N. Abrams, Inc. Photograph by Jonathan Wallen.*

Pennsylvania's **John Dickinson** was assigned to draft the new government's constitution. After submitting his blueprint for a strong national government to the Continental Congress, Dickinson watched in wonder and dismay as his colleagues transformed his plan, called **Articles of Confederation,** into a government that preserved the rights and privileges of the states.

Members of the Continental Congress, itself a unicameral legislature, agreed that the new government would be a unicameral legislature. The Articles made no provision for an executive branch and none for a separate **judiciary.** Democrats like Tom Paine and Samuel Adams praised this concentration of lawmaking, administrative, and judicial powers in the hands of an elected assembly. Conservatives like John Adams condemned the new government as "too democratical," lacking "any equilibrium" among the social classes.

Both Tom Paine and John Adams were eager to see a government that could protect the nation from tyranny. Paine, however, feared tyranny from above, from a power-grasping executive or an elitist upper house. Adams feared tyranny from below, from a majority of ordinary citizens who could exercise their will. Tyranny of any sort seemed unlikely from the proposed Confederation government because its powers were so limited. It had no authority to tax or to regulate trade or commerce. These powers were reserved to the state governments. Many Americans believed that such powers should be kept with local governments whose actions could be closely monitored. Thus the Confederation had to rely on the states to finance its operations, although it had no legal right to compel states to provide funds and no practical means of forcing them to contribute.

Dickinson's colleagues agreed that the state legislatures, not the voters themselves, would choose representatives to the Confederation Congress. But argument arose over whether the states should have equal representation or **proportional representation** based on population. Dickinson argued steadfastly for a one-state, one-vote rule. Fellow Pennsylvanian Benjamin Franklin insisted that large states such as his own deserved more influence in the new government. This time, Dickinson's argument carried the day, and the Articles established that each state, large or small, was entitled to a single vote when the Confederation roll was called. The same jealous protection of state power also shaped the amendment process spelled out in the Articles of Confederation. Any amendment required the unanimous consent of the states.

Arguments over financial issues were as fierce as those over representation and sovereignty. How was each state's share of the federal operating budget to be determined? Dickinson reasoned that a state's contribution should be based on its population, including inhabitants of every age, sex, and legal condition (free or unfree). This proposal brought southern political leaders to their feet in protest. Because their states had large, dependent slave populations, the burden of tax assessment would fall

John Dickinson Philadelphia lawyer and revolutionary pamphleteer who drafted the Articles of Confederation.

Articles of Confederation The first constitution of the United States; it created a central government with limited powers and was replaced by the Constitution in 1788.

judiciary A system of courts of law for the administration of justice.

proportional representation Representation in the legislature based on the population of each state.

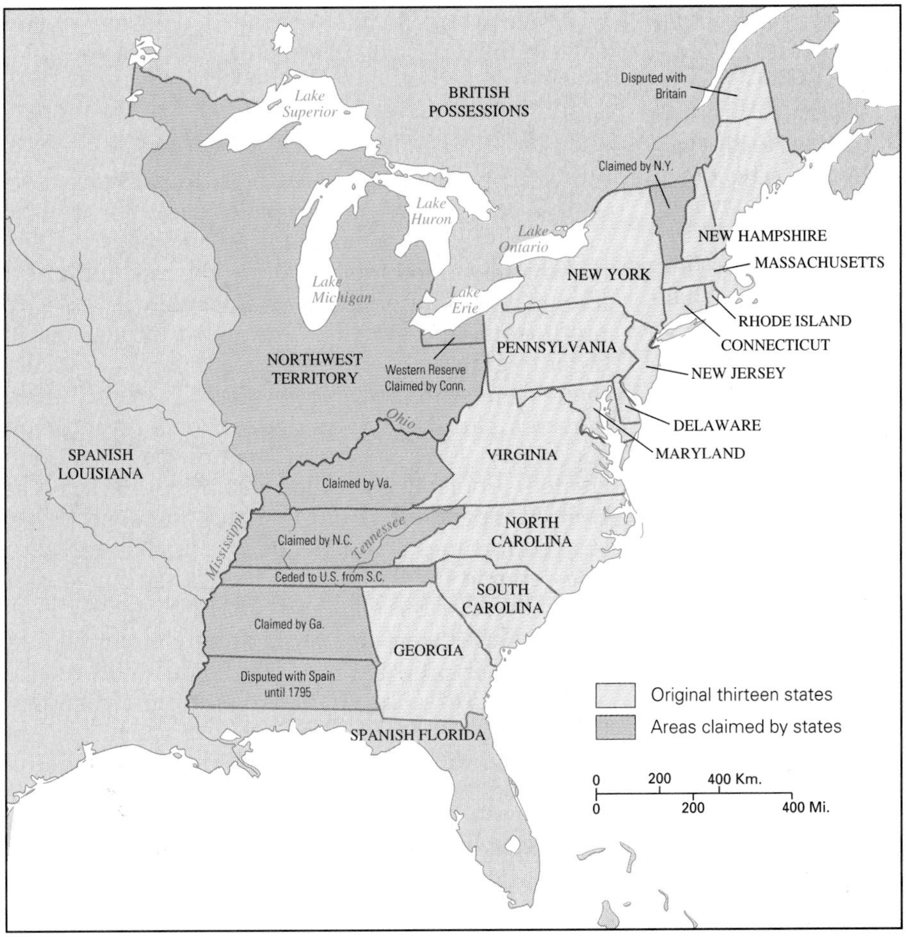

♦ **MAP 7.1 Western Land Claims After American Independence** This map indicates the claims made by several of the thirteen original states to land west of the Appalachian Mountains and in the New England region. The states based their claims on the colonial charters that governed them before independence. Until this land was ceded to the federal government, new states could not be created here as they were in the Northwest Territory.

heavily on slave masters and other free white men. They wanted slaves to be considered not as people but as property. Southerners lost this debate, although the Continental Congress carefully avoided any final decision on the larger question of whether slaves were property or people.

When Congress finally submitted the Articles to the states for their approval, the fate of the western territories proved to be the major stumbling block to **ratification.** In his draft of the Articles, Dickinson had designated the Northwest Territory as a national domain. During the debates in the Continental Congress, however, Virginia, Pennsylvania, Massachusetts, and other states with sea-to-sea clauses in their colonial charters reasserted their competing claims to this vast region bounded by the Ohio River, the Great Lakes, and the Mississippi River (see Map 7.1).

Protest immediately arose from New Jersey, Maryland, and other states whose colonial charters defined their boundaries and thus deprived them of any claim to the western territory. Most of them reluctantly ratified the Articles of Confederation, but Maryland delegates dug in their heels, insisting that citizens of any state ought to have the right to

ratification To give approval to a proposal.

pioneer the northwestern territories. Maryland's ultimatum—no national domain, no ratification—threatened to delay the establishment of the Confederation indefinitely. To break the stalemate, Virginia, which claimed the lion's share of the Northwest, agreed to cede all claims to Congress. The other states with claims followed suit. In 1777, Maryland became the thirteenth and final state to ratify the Confederation government. Establishing this first national government had taken three and a half years. (The text of the Articles of Confederation is reprinted in the Documents appendix at the back of this book.)

Challenges to the Confederation

- What constraints undermined the Confederation, and what was the outcome?
- What was the outcome of Shays' Rebellion for national politics?
- What gains did nationalists expect from a stronger central government?

The members of the first Confederation Congress had barely taken their seats in 1781 when Lord Cornwallis surrendered at Yorktown and peace negotiations began in Paris. Even the most optimistic of the Confederation leaders could see that the postwar problems of the new nation were more daunting than negotiations with French or British diplomats. The physical, psychological, and economic damage caused by the long and brutal home-front war was extensive. In New Jersey and Pennsylvania, communities bore the scars of rape and looting by the British occupying armies. In the South, where civil war had raged, a steady stream of refugees filled the cities. In Charleston, "women and children . . . in the open air round a fire without blanket or any Cloathing but what they had on" were a common sight. In many communities, livestock had vanished, and crops had been seized or ruined. In New England, a natural disaster magnified problems created by the war: insects wiped out wheat crops, worsening food shortages and the local economic depression.

After the war, economic depression spread rapidly throughout the states. Four years after the American victory, Thomas Jefferson wrote enthusiastically from France that a visit to Europe would make Americans "adore [their] country, its climate, its equality, liberty, laws, people and manners." America's unemployed sailors, debt-ridden farmers, widowed women, and orphaned children would have found it difficult to share his enthusiasm.

Depression and Financial Crisis

Financial problems plagued wealthy Americans as well as poor farmers and unpaid Revolutionary War veterans. Many merchants feared ruin because they had overextended their credit in the race to import foreign goods after the war. **Speculators** eager to profit from land sales had borrowed too heavily in order to grab up confiscated loyalist lands or secure their claims in the Northwest Territory. Greed played a part in the risks these merchants and land speculators took, but the success of the Revolution created problems for other wealthy Americans as well. Independence from England damaged or destroyed fortunes that depended on English markets. The demand for staple crops like rice dropped dramatically after the war, and by 1786 the New England fisheries were operating at only about 80 percent of their prewar level. The English showed no eagerness to ease the plight of their former colonists. British orders-in-council of 1783 banned the sale of American farm products in the West Indies and limited the rights of American vessels to carry goods to and from Caribbean ports. These restrictions hit New England shipbuilding so hard that whole communities were impoverished.

The Confederation government did not create these economic problems, but it had grave difficulty trying to solve them. In fact, the postwar depression aggravated the Confederation's own most pressing problem—debt. To finance the war, the Continental Congress had printed more than $240 million in paper money backed by "good faith" rather than by the hard currency of gold and silver. As doubts grew that the government could ever **redeem** these Continentals for hard currency, their value fell rapidly. A new phrase, "not worth a continental," indicated popular attitudes about the government as well as its finances. Congress was also embarrassed by the substantial debts to foreign nations it could not repay.

speculator A person who buys and sells land or some other commodity in the hope of making a profit.

redeem To pay a specified sum in return for something; in this case, to make good on paper money issued by the government by exchanging it for hard currency, silver or gold.

Since Congress could not raise taxes, it decided to appoint the leading financial wizard of the era, Philadelphia shipper and merchant **Robert Morris,** to direct a fundraising campaign. Realizing that he could not rely on the generosity of the state governments, for many were struggling with financial problems of their own, Morris pressed the states to allow the Confederation to impose federal **tariffs** on imported goods.

In 1782, 1783, and again in 1784, Congress requested approval for a duty of 5 percent on imported goods, payable in hard currency rather than paper money. Revenues from this tariff would be used to repay foreign loans and thus re-establish American credit abroad. Virginia and Rhode Island said no. Disgusted by this lack of cooperation, Morris handed in his resignation in January 1783. To add insult to injury, some states adopted Morris's fundraising strategy and passed their own tariffs on British goods. The failure of the tariff strategy prompted one critic of the Confederation government to comment: "Thirteen wheels require a steady and powerful regulation to keep them in good order." Until Congress could act without the unanimous consent of all states, nothing could "prevent the machine from becoming useless."

The Northwest Ordinances

Having lost the tariff battle, the Confederation looked to the sale of western lands in the Northwest Territory to provide needed income. Here at least Congress had the authority to act, for it was empowered to set policy for the settlement and governance of all national territories. In 1784, 1785, and 1787, national land policy took shape in three **Northwest Ordinances.** These regulations had political significance beyond their role in raising money for the government: they guaranteed that the men and women who moved west would not be colonial dependents of the original states.

The 1784 ordinance established that five new states would be carved out of the region, each with a status equal to that of the older, original states. Progress toward statehood was linked to population growth. In the earliest stages of settlement, each territory would have an appointed governor. As soon as the number of eligible voters increased, they would elect a representative assembly, and the territory would begin to govern itself. In the final step, the territory's voters would draft a state constitution and elect representatives to the Confederation

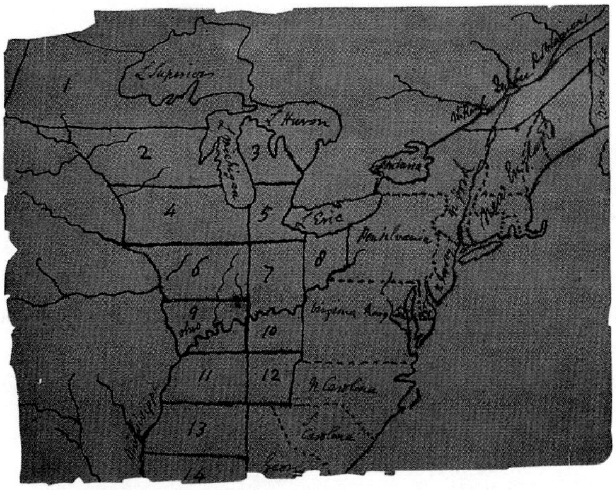

♦ Thomas Jefferson dreamed of creating fourteen new states out of the nation's western territories, suggesting names like "Metropotamia" and "Pelisipia" to evoke the glory of republican Rome. Congress chose instead to carve out five territories. Under the terms of the Northwest Ordinances, they eventually became the states of Ohio, Illinois, Indiana, Michigan, and Wisconsin. *William L. Clements Library, University of Michigan.*

Congress. Ohio, Indiana, Illinois, Michigan, and Wisconsin each followed this path to full statehood (see Map 7.2 and the table "Admission of States into the Union" in the Tables appendix at the back of the book).

The ordinance of 1785 spelled out the terms for sale of the land. Mapmakers divided the region into five distinct districts and subdivided each district into townships. Each township, covering 6 square miles, was broken down in a gridlike pattern of thirty-six 640-acre plots. Congress intended to auction these plots off to individual settlers rather than to land speculators. The original selling price of $1 per acre in hard currency proved too high for the average farm family, however. So, to boost lagging sales, Congress lowered the price and lifted the ban on sales to speculators.

Robert Morris Pennsylvania merchant and financial expert who advised the Continental Congress during the Revolution and served as a fundraiser for the Confederation government.

tariff A tax on imported or exported goods.

Northwest Ordinances Three laws (1784, 1785, 1787) that dealt with the sale of public lands in the Northwest Territory and established a plan for the admission of new states to the Union.

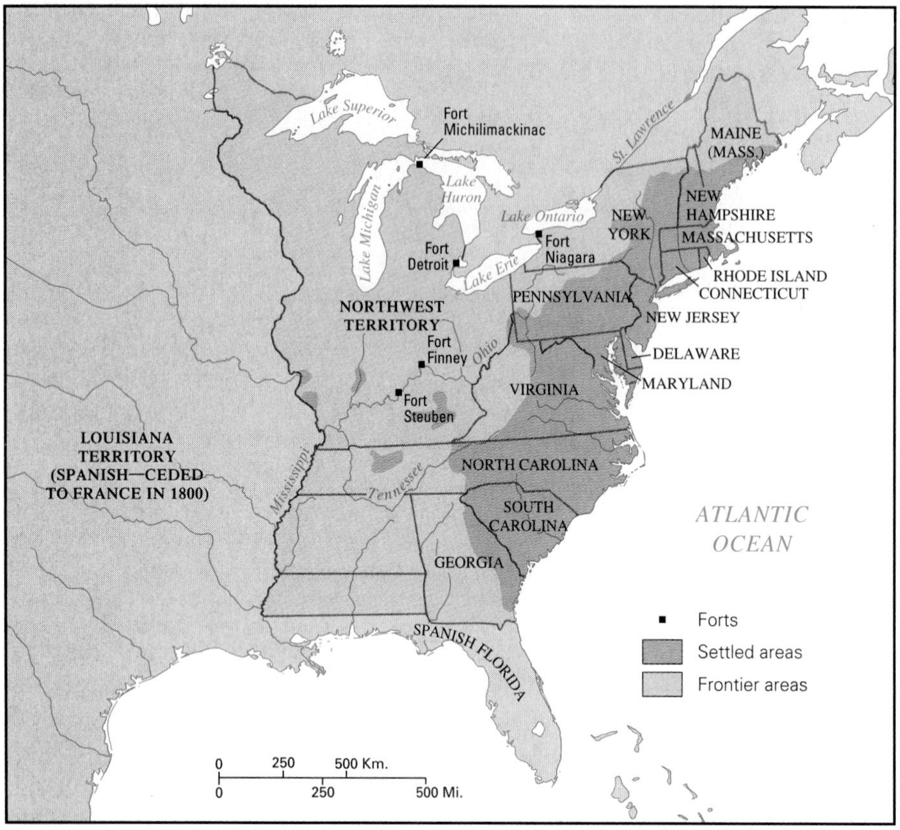

♦ **MAP 7.2 The United States in 1787** This map shows the extent of American westward settlement in 1787 and the limits placed on that settlement by French and Spanish claims west of the Mississippi and in Florida. Plans for the creation of three to five states in the Northwest Territory were approved by Congress in 1787, ensuring that the settlers in this region would enjoy the same political rights as the citizens of the original thirteen states.

The ordinance of 1787 clarified the population base needed for each step to statehood, ensuring that any territory with sixty thousand white males could apply for admission as a state. Thomas Jefferson, who drafted this ordinance, took care to protect the liberties of the settlers with a bill of rights and to ban slavery north of the Ohio River. Jefferson's ordinance trampled on the rights of American Indians, however, for their claims to the land were ignored in favor of white settlement.

Diplomatic Problems

The Confederation Congress did not solve its financial woes through the sale of western lands, but the encouragement that the ordinances gave to western settlement did have other consequences. It roused both the British and the Indians of the region into active opposition. Although the British had agreed in the Treaty of Paris (1783), to evacuate their western forts, they refused to carry out their promise as long as the Americans failed to repay their war debts or allow loyalists to recover confiscated property.

The British supported Indian resistance to American settlement in the Ohio Valley, providing a steady supply of weapons to the Shawnees, Miamis, Delawares, and other tribes that rejected the Confederation's claim to the valley lands. The American government based those claims on two treaties. Congress argued that the 1784 **Treaty of Fort Stanwix,** made with the remnants of the Iroquois

Treaty of Fort Stanwix Treaty signed in 1784 that opened all Iroquois lands to white settlement.

Confederacy, opened all Iroquois lands to white settlement and that the **Hopewell Treaties** of 1785, signed by Choctaw, Chickasaw and Cherokee chiefs, granted Americans settlement rights in the Southwest. The Shawnees and their allies were unpersuaded. By what right, they asked, did those tribes speak for them? Throughout the 1780s, both sides resorted to warfare rather than negotiation.

The Confederation preferred diplomacy to armed conflict when dealing with European powers. Congress sent John Adams to Great Britain, but not even this stubborn New Englander could wring any concessions from the British. The American bargaining position was weak. Trade with France and Holland had not developed as rapidly after independence as some patriots had predicted. American merchants remained economically dependent on England as a source of manufactured goods, and American shippers continued to follow old trading routes that led to British colonies in the Caribbean. England would do nothing to diminish this profitable dependency.

The Confederation had problems with allies as well as with enemies. Spain, for example, watched with growing alarm as American settlers poured into the land east of the Mississippi. Almost fifty thousand Americans had already moved into what would become Kentucky and Tennessee, and thousands more were eager to farm the rich, river-fed lands of the region. Worried that its hold on the land west of the Mississippi River might be challenged, Spain took steps to slow the flow of Americans into the area. The Spanish government, which controlled access to the Mississippi River and to the port of New Orleans, banned all American traffic on the river. The Confederation appointed **John Jay,** fresh from his success as a Paris peace commissioner, to negotiate with Spain on this and other issues, but Jay could make no headway.

The Confederation had no better luck in dealing with the **Barbary pirates**. For many years, the rulers of Algiers, Tunisia, Tripoli, and Morocco had taken advantage of their location along the Barbary Coast of North Africa to attack European vessels engaged in Mediterranean trade. Most European nations kept this piracy under control by paying blackmail or by providing an armed escort for their merchant ships. The Barbary pirates showed no mercy to American ships, which were no longer protected by the British bribes or the British navy. In 1785 a New England ship was captured, its cargo seized, the crew stripped and sold into slavery. Protest from northern shippers was intense, but the Confederation Congress had no navy and no authority to create one. Congress did raise some protection money but not enough to buy safe passage on the Mediterranean.

A Farmer's Revolt

From the "Wild Yankees" of Pennsylvania's Susquehanna Valley to the "Liberty-Men" of Maine, eighteenth-century backcountry settlers organized to resist speculators' claims on the land and to demand that political power remain with local communities rather than state governments. After the Revolution, these agrarian activists used the language of republicanism to defend their protests and justify the occasional violence that erupted in their areas. "We fought for land & liberty, & it is hard if we can't enjoy either," wrote one **squatter** in response to a land speculator's claim to his farm. "Who can have a better right to the land than we who have fought for it, subdued it & made it valuable." Farmers suffering from the postwar economic depression protested rents, land prices, heavy taxes, debts, high judicial fees, and the failure of central governments to provide protection from Indian attacks and frontier bandits. These backcountry settlers often made members of the political and economic elite uneasy. When farmers in western Massachusetts began an organized protest in 1786, this uneasiness reached crisis proportions.

The farmers of western Massachusetts were among the hardest hit by the postwar depression and the rising inflation that accompanied it. Many were deeply in debt to creditors who held mortgages on their farms and lands. In the 1780s, these farmers looked to the state government for temporary relief, hoping that it would pass **stay laws** that

Hopewell Treaties Treaties signed in 1785 in which the Choctaws, Chickasaws, and Cherokees granted Americans settlement rights in the Southwest.

John Jay New York lawyer and diplomat who negotiated with Great Britain and Spain on behalf of the Confederation; he later became the first chief justice of the Supreme Court and negotiated the Jay Treaty with England.

Barbary pirates Pirates along the Barbary Coast of North Africa who attacked European and American vessels engaged in Mediterranean trade.

squatter A person who settles on unoccupied land to which he or she has no legal claim.

stay laws Laws suspending the right of creditors to foreclose on debtors; they were designed to keep indebted farmers from losing their land.

♦ In 1786, western Massachusetts farmers began an agrarian revolt against high taxes and mortgage foreclosures that soon spread to other New England states. Most of the leaders of the uprising, known as Shays' Rebellion, were veteran officers of the American Revolution; many had participated in the protest and resistance that preceded the war itself. The government of Massachusetts crushed the rebellion, jailing leaders like Shattucks and driving Shays to seek asylum in Vermont. News of the uprising prompted elite political leaders like George Washington and Alexander Hamilton to press for a more powerful central government, able to ensure "law and order" throughout the nation. *National Portrait Gallery, Washington, D.C.*

would suspend creditors' right to foreclose on, or seize, lands and farm equipment. The Massachusetts assembly responded sympathetically and thus aroused the anger of merchants and other creditors who were themselves deeply in debt to foreign manufacturers. The upper house of the state legislature, with its more elite members, was sympathetic to the creditors and blocked the passage of stay laws. The Massachusetts government then dismayed the farmers by raising taxes.

In 1786, hundreds of farmers turned to armed resistance. They believed they were protecting their rights and their communities as true republicans must do, but their creditors viewed their actions quite differently. To them, the farmers appeared to be dangerous rebels, threatening the state with "anarchy, confusion, and total ruin." They accused **Daniel Shays,** a 39-year-old veteran of Bunker Hill, of leading the revolt.

In 1786, farmers known as Shays' rebels closed several courts and freed a number of their fellow farmers from debtors' prison. Their actions struck a chord among desperate farmers in other New England states, and the rebellion began to spread. Fear that a widespread uprising was beginning spurred the Massachusetts government to action. It ordered a military force of six hundred men led by General William Sheperd to march to Springfield, where more than a thousand farmers, most armed with pitchforks rather than guns, had gathered to close the local courthouse. Sheperd waited until the farmers were within range and let loose a cannon barrage that killed four and set the remaining men to flight. Then, on February 4, 1787, a government force of some four thousand surprised the remaining "rebels" in the village of Petersham. Although Daniel Shays managed to escape, the farmers' revolt was over.

Shays' Rebellion revealed the temper of the times. When the government did not respond to their needs, the farmers chose to act as they had been encouraged to act in the prerevolutionary years. They organized and they protested—and when government did not respond, they took up arms against what they considered to be injustice. Across the country, many Americans sympathized with these farmers. But many did not. Abigail Adams, whose husband John had been labeled an irresponsible troublemaker by loyalist opponents only a decade earlier, turned this language against the leaders of the farmers' revolt. She condemned them as "ignorant, restless, desperadoes, without conscience or principles," who were persuading a "deluded multitude to follow their standards."

The revolt raised fears of slave rebellions and pitched battles between debtors and creditors, haves and have-nots. Above all, it raised doubts among influential political figures about the ability of either state governments or the Confederation to preserve the rule of law. To men like George Wash-

Daniel Shays Revolutionary War veteran considered the leader of the farmers' uprising in western Massachusetts called Shays' Rebellion.

ington, once again a planter and private citizen, Shays' Rebellion was a national tragedy, not for its participants but for the reputation of the United States. When the farmers' protest began, Washington wrote to authorities in Massachusetts, urging them to act fairly but decisively. "If they have real grievances," he said, the government should acknowledge them. But if not, authorities should "employ the force of government against them at once. . . . To be more exposed to the eyes of the world, and more contemptible than we already are, is hardly possible."

The Revolt of the "Better Sort"

The Articles of Confederation embodied one element of the republican ideal: a limited central government that directed diplomacy and coordinated the military defense of the nation but left the major tasks of governing to local, representative governments. Such a government, however, had its costs and consequences. The burden of national survival fell to the states because the Confederation lacked the power to solve serious problems. By 1786, members of the nation's elite, or the "better sort," believed those problems had reached crisis proportions. Washington predicted "the worst consequences from a half-starved, limping government, always moving upon crutches and tottering at every step." For him and those like him who thought of themselves as **nationalists**, the solution was clear. "I do not conceive we can long exist as a nation," Washington remarked, "without having lodged somewhere a power which will pervade the whole Union in as energetic a manner as the authority of the State government extends over the several states." Here was a different form of republican government to consider.

Support for a stronger national government grew in the key states of Virginia, Massachusetts, and New York. Men of wealth and political experience urged a reform agenda that included giving the central government taxing powers, an easier amendment process, and some legal means to enforce national government policies that a state might oppose. They wanted a government able to establish stable diplomatic and trade relations with foreign countries. They also wanted a national government strong enough to preserve their property and their peace of mind.

The first signs of an active nationalist strategy came in 1786, when a group of influential Virginians called for a forum on interstate trade restrictions, such as the imposition of import taxes on goods carried from one state to market in a neighboring state. Acknowledging this growing problem, the Confederation Congress approved a meeting of state delegates at Annapolis, Maryland. The meeting organizers also meant to test the waters on a broader issue: support for revising the nation's constitution.

Only a third of the states participated in the Annapolis conference. The nationalists were convinced, however, that the move for government revision had strong support. They asked Congress to call a convention in Philadelphia so that political leaders could continue to discuss interstate problems and other aspects of government reform. Some members of Congress were reluctant, but news of Shays' Rebellion tipped the balance in favor of the convention.

Creating a New Government

- What major compromises did the framers choose to make in writing the new constitution?
- What positive outcome did James Madison see in his "checks and balances" system?

Late in May 1787, George Washington called the convention to order in Philadelphia. Before him sat delegates from twelve of the thirteen states, closeted behind curtained windows and locked doors in the heat and humidity of a Philadelphia summer because they wished to speak frankly about the nation's political and economic problems without fear that foreign governments would use that information to their advantage. Only Rhode Island refused to participate, accusing the convention of masquerading as a discussion of interstate trade in order to drastically revise the national government. The accusation by "Rogue's Island," as critics called the smallest state, was correct. The fifty-five prominent and prosperous men did expect to make significant changes in the structure of the government. Here was another reason to keep the deliberations secret.

Most of the men gathered in that room were lawyers, merchants, or planters—Americans of social

nationalists Americans who preferred a strong central government rather than the limited government of the Articles of Confederation.

♦ In 1867, Thomas Pritchard Rossiter painted his "Signing of the Constitution of the United States," honoring a group of statesmen that included James Madison, Alexander Hamilton, and George Washington, who presided over the constitutional convention. Thomas Jefferson, absent because of his duties as ambassador to France, referred to the fifty-five delegates who crafted the constitution as a gathering of "demigods." *Signing of the Constitution of the United States" by Thomas Pritchard Rossiter, 1867. Fraunces Tavern Museum.*

standing though not necessarily intellectual achievement. When the absent Thomas Jefferson referred to the convention members as "demigods," he was probably thinking of the likes of Benjamin Franklin, whose sparkling wit and crafty political style set him apart from his colleagues despite his advanced age (he was 81), or of the articulate, brilliant **Alexander Hamilton** of New York, reputed to be a financial mastermind equal to the Confederation's adviser Robert Morris, or of **James Madison** (Hamilton's only intellectual equal in the room), the prim Virginia planter who turned out to be the chief architect of a new constitution. Several notable men were absent. Jefferson, author of the Declaration of Independence, was abroad, serving as ambassador to France. John Adams, driving force behind the influential Massachusetts constitution of 1780, was in London, serving as ambassador to England. And the two great propagandists of the Revolution, Samuel Adams and Thomas Paine, were also absent, for both opposed any revision of the Articles of Confederation.

Revise or Replace?

Most of the delegates were nationalists, but they did not necessarily agree on how best to proceed. Should they revise the Articles or abandon them? For five days the convention discussed this question. Then Virginia planter and lawyer Edmund Randolph rose to present a plan that effectively amended the Articles of Confederation out of existence.

Although Randolph introduced the **Virginia Plan** on the convention floor, James Madison was its guiding spirit. The 36-year-old Madison was no dashing figure. He was small, frail, charmless, and a hypochondriac. But he was highly respected as a scholar of philosophy and history and as a student of political theory, and his long service as a member of the Virginia legislature and in Congress gave him a practical understanding of politics and government. At the convention, Madison brought all his knowledge to bear on this question: what was the best form of government for a strong republic? He concluded, as John Adams had done early in the 1780s, that the fear of tyranny should not rule out a powerful na-

Alexander Hamilton New York lawyer, political theorist, and economic strategist who wrote many of the influential *Federalist Papers* essays in support of the ratification of the Constitution; he served as the first secretary of the treasury.

James Madison Virginia planter and political theorist known as the "father of the Constitution"; he became the fourth president of the United States.

Virginia Plan A proposal for a federal government introduced by a Virginia delegate to the Constitutional Convention; it gave states representation in a bicameral legislature in proportion to their population.

♦ James Madison described himself as "feeble" and "sickly" and suffered all his life from dizzy spells and stomach disorders. But this small, shy Virginia planter and lawyer won the respect of his colleagues as a brilliant political theorist during the drafting of the Constitution, and later as a genius for organizing the machinery of party politics. *Library of Congress.*

tional government. The dangerous abuse of power could be avoided if internal checks and balances were built into the republican structure.

Madison's Virginia Plan embodied this conviction. It called for a government with three distinct branches—legislative, executive, and judicial—to replace the Confederation's Congress, which was performing all three functions. By dividing power in this way, Madison intended to ensure that no individual or group of men could wield too much authority, especially for self-interested reasons. Madison's plan also gave Congress the power to **veto** laws passed by the state legislatures and the right to intervene directly if a state acted to interrupt "the harmony of the United States."

The notion of a strong government able, as Madison put it, "to control the governed" but "obliged to control itself" was strongly endorsed by the delegates. But they were in sharp disagreement over many specific issues in the Virginia Plan. The greatest controversy swirled around representation in the legislative branch—Congress—a controversy familiar to those who had helped draft the Articles of Confederation. Madison proposed a bicameral legislature with membership in each house based on proportional representation. Large states supported the plan, for representation based on population worked to their advantage. Small states objected heatedly, calling for equal representation for each state. Small states argued that proportional representation would leave them helpless against a federal government dominated by the large ones. Small-state delegates threw their support behind a second proposal, the **New Jersey Plan,** which also called for three branches of government and gave Congress the power to tax and to control national commerce. This plan, however, preserved an equal voice and vote for every state within a unicameral, or one-house, legislature.

Debate over the two plans dragged on through the steamy days of a June heat wave. Tempers flared, and at times the deadlock seemed hopeless. Threats to walk out of the convention came from both sides. A compromise was needed to prevent distrust and hostility from destroying the convention. The delegates from Connecticut, led by Roger Sherman, came up with a compromise. Connecticut's **Great Compromise** took sensible advantage of the opportunities of a two-house legislature, proposing proportional representation in the lower house (the House of Representatives) and equal representation in the upper house (the Senate).

The Great Compromise resolved the first major controversy at the convention but opened the door to the next one. The delegates had to decide how the representatives to each house were to be elected. A compromise also settled this issue. State legislatures were given the right to select senators, and the eligible voters of each state were given the right to directly elect their state's representatives to the lower house. This formula allowed the delegates to acknowledge the sovereignty of the state governments but also to accommodate the republican commitment to popular elections in a representative government.

veto The power or right of one branch of government to cancel the decisions of another branch.

New Jersey Plan A proposal for a federal government submitted by the New Jersey delegation to the Constitutional Convention; it gave all states equal representation in a unicameral legislature.

Great Compromise A proposal for a bicameral legislature with one house providing equal representation to all states and the other providing proportional representation.

The delegates faced one last stumbling block over representation: which Americans were to be counted to determine a state's population? This issue had been divisive when the Articles of Confederation were drafted. Once again southern delegates argued that slaves, who composed as much as one-third and sometimes more of each plantation state's residents, should not be included in the population count that decided a state's share of taxes but should be included in the population count that decided the number of seats a state would have in the House of Representatives. Northern delegates protested, declaring that slaves should be considered property in both instances. If slaves were considered property, the North would dominate the lower house.

A compromise that defied reason but made brilliant political sense settled this question. The **Three-Fifths Compromise** established that three-fifths of the slave population would be included in a state's critical headcount. A clause was then added that permitted the slave trade to continue for a twenty-year period. Some southern leaders, especially in South Carolina, wanted this extension badly because they had lost many slaves during the Revolution. But not all slaveowners supported this clause. Virginia's George Mason spoke passionately of the harm slavery did to his region. It not only prevented white immigration to the South, Mason said, but infected the moral character of the slave master. "Every master of slaves," Mason argued, "is born a petty tyrant." Slaveowners "bring the judgment of heaven upon a country," particularly one intended as a republic.

Drafting an Acceptable Document

The Three-Fifths Compromise ended weeks of debate over representation. No other issue arose to provoke such controversy, and the delegates proceeded calmly to implement the principle of checks and balances. For example, the president, or executive, was named commander-in-chief of the armed forces and given primary responsibility for foreign affairs. To balance these **executive powers,** Congress was given the right to declare war and to raise an army. Congress received the critical "power of the purse," but this power to tax and to spend the revenues raised by taxation was checked in part by the president's power to veto congressional legislation. As yet another balance, Congress could override a presidential veto by the vote of a two-thirds majority. Following the same logic of checks and balances, the delegates agreed to give the president the authority to name judges to the federal courts, but the Senate had to approve all such appointments.

Occasionally, as in the system for electing the president, the convention chose awkward or cumbersome procedures. For example, many delegates opposed direct, popular election of the president, agreeing with the elitist sentiments of George Mason, who said this "would be as unnatural . . . as it would [be] to refer a trial of colours to a blind man." But other delegates objected that the election of the president by state legislators would be too great a concentration of power. As a compromise, the delegates created the **Electoral College,** a group of special electors to be chosen by the states to vote for presidential candidates. Each state would be entitled to a number of electors equal to the number of its senators and representatives sitting in Congress, but no one serving in Congress at the time of a presidential election would be eligible to be an elector. If two presidential candidates received the same number of Electoral College votes, or if no candidate received a majority of the Electoral College votes, the House of Representatives would chose the new president. This complex procedure honored the **discretion** of the state governments but limited the power of individuals already holding office.

Thus the summer of conflict and compromise ended with a new plan for a national government. Would the delegates be willing to put their names to the document they had created in secrecy and by overreaching their authority? Benjamin Franklin fervently hoped so. Though sick and bedridden, Franklin had friends help him onto the convention floor, where he pleaded for unanimous support for the new government. When a weary George Washington at last declared the meetings adjourned on September 17, 1787, only three delegates left without signing the new American constitution.

Three-Fifths Compromise An agreement to count three-fifths of a state's slave population for purposes of determining a state's representation in the House of Representatives.

executive powers Powers given to the president by the Constitution.

Electoral College A body of electors chosen by the states to elect the president and vice president; each state gets a number of electors equal to the number of its senators and representatives in Congress.

discretion The power or right to act according to one's own judgment.

Resolving the Conflict of Vision

- What arguments did Antifederalists choose to make against the Constitution? What arguments did Federalists use to support it?
- What was the outcome of the ratification process?

The framers of the Constitution called for special state **ratifying conventions** to discuss and then vote on the proposed change of government. They argued that these conventions would give citizens a more direct role in this important political decision. But the ratifying procedure also gave the framers two advantages. First, it allowed them to bypass the state legislatures, which stood to lose power under the new government and were thus likely to oppose it. Second, it allowed them to nominate their supporters and campaign for their election to the ratifying conventions. The framers added to their advantage by declaring that the approval of only nine states was necessary to establish the Constitution. Perhaps reluctantly, the Confederation Congress agreed to all these terms and procedures. By the end of September 1787, Congress had passed the proposed Constitution on to the states, triggering the next debate over America's political future.

The Ratification Controversy

As Alexander Hamilton boasted: "The new Constitution has in favor of its success . . . [the] very great weight of influence of the persons who framed it." Hamilton was correct. Men of wealth, political experience, and frequently great persuasive powers put their skills to the task of achieving ratification. But what Hamilton did not mention was that many revolutionary heroes and political leaders opposed the Constitution with equal intensity—most notably Patrick Henry, Samuel Adams, and George Clinton, the popular governor of New York. Boston's most effective revolutionary propagandist, **Mercy Otis Warren,** immediately took up her pen against the Constitution and even canvassed her neighbors to stand firm against what she called an attack on republican values. Thus the leadership on both sides of the issue was drawn from the political elite of the revolutionary generation.

The pro-Constitution forces won an early and important victory by confusing the language of the debate. They abandoned the label "nationalists," which drew attention to their belief in a strong central government, and chose to call themselves **Federalists**, a name originally associated with a system of strong state governments and limited national government. This shrewd tactic cheated opponents of the Constitution out of their rightful name. The pro-Constitution forces then dubbed their opponents **Antifederalists.** This label implied that their adversaries were negative thinkers, pessimists, and a group lacking a program of its own.

Although the philosophical debate over the best form of government for a republic was an important one, voters considered other, practical factors in choosing a Federalist or Antifederalist position. Voters in states with a stable or recovering economy were likely to oppose the Constitution because the Confederation system gave their states greater independent powers. Those in small, geographically or economically disadvantaged states were likely to favor a strong central government that could protect them from their competitive neighbors. Thus the small states of Delaware and Connecticut ratified the Constitution quickly, but in New York and Virginia ratification was hotly contested.

To some degree, Federalist and Antifederalist divisions matched the divisions between the relatively urban, market-oriented communities of the Atlantic coast and the frontier or rural communities of the inland areas. For example, the backcountry of North and South Carolina and the less economically developed areas of Virginia saw little benefit in a stronger central government, especially one that might tax them. But coastal centers of trade and overseas commerce such as Boston, New York City, and Charleston were eager to see an aggessive and effective national policy regarding foreign and interstate trade. In these urban centers, artisans, shopkeepers, and even laborers joined forces with wealthy merchants and shippers to support the Constitution as they had once joined them to make the Revolution. No generalization can explain every political choice, of course. No economic or social

ratifying convention A meeting of delegates in each state to determine whether that state would ratify the Constitution.

Mercy Otis Warren Writer and historian known for her influential anti-British plays and essays during the prerevolutionary era; an active opponent of the Constitution.

Federalists Supporters of ratification of the Constitution; they believed in a strong central government.

Antifederalists Opponents of ratification of the Constitution; they believed a strong central government was a threat to American liberties and rights.

group was unified under the Federalist or the Antifederalist banner. On the whole, however, it can be said that the Federalists were better organized, had more resources at their disposal, and campaigned more effectively than the Antifederalists.

In the public debates, the political differences between the Federalists and Antifederalists were sharply defined. Antifederalists rejected the claim that the nation was in a "critical period," facing economic and political collapse. As one New Yorker put it: "I deny that we are in immediate danger of anarchy and commotions. Nothing but the passions of wicked and ambitious men will put us in the least danger. . . . The country is in profound peace . . . and the lives, the liberty and property of individuals is protected." Nevertheless, the Federalists were successful in portraying the moment as a crisis or turning point for the young republic—and in insisting that their plan for recovery was better than no plan at all.

The Antifederalists struck hard against the dangerous elitism they saw in the Constitution. They portrayed the Federalists as a privileged, sophisticated minority, ready and able to tyrannize the people if their powerful national government were ratified. Be careful, one Massachusetts man warned, because "These lawyers, and men of learning, and moneyed men, that talk so finely and gloss over matters so smoothly, to make us poor illiterate people swallow down the pill, expect to get into Congress themselves." And New York Antifederalist Melancton Smith predicted that the proposed new government would lead inevitably to rule by a wealthy, unrepresentative minority. Smith argued with simple eloquence that members of a House of Representatives who had so much power ought to "resemble those they represent . . . and be disposed to seek their true interests." But this was impossible, Smith reasoned, when the representative body was so small and the political ambitions and financial resources of the elite were so great. The Virginia revolutionary leader Richard Henry Lee was flabbergasted that his generation would even consider ratification of the Constitution. "'Tis really astonishing," he wrote to a New York opponent in the summer of 1788, "that the same people, who have just emerged from a long and cruel war in defence of liberty, should agree to fix an elective **despotism** upon themselves and posterity."

The Antifederalists' most convincing evidence of elitism and its potential for tyranny was that the Constitution lacked a bill of rights. Unlike many of the state constitutions, the proposed new national Constitution contained no written guarantees of the people's right to assemble or to worship as they saw fit, and it gave no assurances of a trial by jury or the right to bear arms. Antifederalists put the question to both voters and delegates: what did this glaring omission tell Americans about the framers' respect for republican ideals? The only conclusion, Antifederalists argued, was that the Constitution was a threat to republican principles of representative government, a vehicle for elite rule, and a document unconcerned with the protection of the people's individual liberties. Its supporters, Antifederalists warned, were crying "wolf" over economic and social problems in order to seize power.

The Federalist strategy was indeed to portray America in crisis. They pointed to the stagnation of the American economy, to the potential for revolt and social anarchy, and to the contempt that other nations were showing toward the young republic. They also argued that the Constitution fulfilled and could preserve the republican ideals of the Revolution far better than could the Articles of Confederation. Their cause was put forward most convincingly by Alexander Hamilton, James Madison, and John Jay, who entered the newspaper wars over ratification in the key state of New York. Together, they produced a series of essays known today as the ***Federalist Papers.*** Although these 85 essays were all signed "Publius," Hamilton wrote 51 of them, Madison 29, and Jay 5. Their common theme was the link between American prosperity and a strong central government.

The Federalist Victory

Practical politics rather than political theory seemed to influence the outcome of many of the ratifying conventions. Delaware, New Jersey, Georgia, and Connecticut—all small states—quickly approved the Constitution. In Pennsylvania, Antifederalists in the rural western regions lost control of the convention to the Federalists and thus that state endorsed the Constitution. In the remaining states, including Massachusetts, Virginia, and New York, the two sides were more evenly matched.

despotism Rule by, or as if by, a tyrant.

Federalist Papers Essays written by Alexander Hamilton, John Jay, and James Madison in support of the Constitution.

♦ The unknown artist of *The Federal Procession in New York, 1788* captured the jubilant mood of Americans as they celebrated their new Constitution with parades, bonfires, and banquets. As the "Ship of State" float indicates, New Yorkers were particularly eager to acknowledge the role of their own Alexander Hamilton in launching the new government. *Library of Congress.*

Antifederalists were in the majority in the Massachusetts convention, where most of the delegates were small farmers from the western counties and more than twenty of them had participated in Shays' Rebellion. The Federalists' strategy was to make political deals with key delegates, winning over Antifederalists such as Samuel Adams and John Hancock, for example, with promises to demand the addition of a bill of rights to the Constitution. Class divisions, however, turned out to be critical during the convention balloting. Men of high social and economic status voted 107 to 34 for ratification. The less wealthy delegates were more divided, voting against the Constitution by a ratio of two to one. At the final count, a 12-vote margin gave the Federalists a narrow victory in Massachusetts.

After Massachusetts ratified, the fight shifted to New Hampshire. Here, too, Federalists won by a small majority. Rhode Island, true to its history of opposition to strong central authority, rejected the Constitution decisively. But Maryland and South Carolina ratified it, and the tide in favor of the new government influenced the next critical vote: that of Virginia. There, Antifederalist leaders Lee, Henry, and James Monroe focused on the absence of a bill of rights in the proposed Constitution. Edmund Randolph, James Madison, and George Washington himself, the chair of the Constitutional Convention, directed the Federalist counterattack. In the end, the presence of Washington proved irresistible because Virginians knew that this war hero and admired colleague was certain to be the first president of the United States if the Constitution went into effect. When the vote was taken on June 25, 1788, Virginia became the tenth state to ratify the new government.

New York's battle was equally intense. Acknowledging that the absence of a bill of rights was a major political error, Federalist leaders Jay and Hamilton made a public pledge to support its inclusion. By then, however, ten states had already ratified the Constitution and the new government was a **fait accompli.** Realizing this, on July 26, 1788, a majority of New York delegates voted yes on ratification.

President George Washington

The election of senators and congress members was almost complete by February 4, 1789, when presidential electors met to choose the nation's first president. Although George Washington did not seek the position, he knew the nation expected him to be its first president. The general was among the very few in the revolutionary generation to have a national reputation. He was hailed as the hero of the Revolution, and he looked and acted the part of the dignified, virtuous patriot. Washington became president by a unanimous vote of the Electoral College. For regional balance, New Englander John Adams was chosen vice president.

In April 1789, as Washington made his way to his inauguration in New York City, the temporary national capital, Americans thronged to greet him with parades, bell ringing, cannon fire, and sharply dressed military escorts. Near Trenton, New Jersey, the scene of his first victory in the Revolutionary War, he passed through a triumphal arch 20 feet high, supported by thirteen pillars, and inscribed in gold with the date of the Battle of Trenton. As his barge took him across the Hudson River, private boats sailed alongside, their passengers singing songs composed in his honor. Thousands of supporters gathered to see him take the oath of office. Yet Washington and his closest advisers knew the future was uncharted and uncertain. "We are in a wilderness," Madison observed, "without a single footstep to guide us."

fait accompli An accomplished deed or fact that cannot be reversed or undone.

♦ In 1789, engraver Amos Doolittle commemorated a landmark event in the history of the young republic: Washington taking the oath of office as the first president of the United States. Although Doolittle captured the stately architecture of New York City's Federal Hall and the gathering of dignitaries on its balcony, his engraving fails to give any hint of the huge crowds that witnessed the historic moment. Washington's cheering supporters filled the streets and shouted from the rooftops of nearby buildings, just as crowds had saluted the president at every point along his route from Mt. Vernon to New York City. The Bible Washington used at the swearing in ceremony, shown here also, was borrowed from a local Masonic lodge. *Painting: "Federal Hall" by Amos Doolittle, 1789. Henry Francis du Pont Winterthur Museum; Bible: Charles Phillips.*

Washington agreed. The new president understood that he symbolized a national experiment in government and that friends and critics of the United States would be watching his behavior in office carefully. Since he was the first to hold the presidency, his every action had the potential to become a ritual and to set a precedent for those who followed. "Few . . . can realize," he wrote, "the difficult and delicate part which a man in my situation has to act. . . . I walk on untrodden ground."

Washington proceeded with caution and deliberation. He labored carefully over each of his selections to the almost one thousand federal offices waiting to be filled. He took particular care in choosing the men to head four executive departments created with approval from Congress. Naming his **protégé** Alexander Hamilton to the Treasury Department was probably Washington's easiest decision. He asked the Massachusetts military strategist Henry Knox to head the War Department and fellow Virginian Edmund Randolph to serve as attorney general. Washington chose another Virginian, Thomas Jefferson, to be secretary of state. Over time, the president established a pattern of meeting with this **cabinet** of advisers on a regular basis to discuss policy matters. Together, they made major decisions and, as Washington expected, expressed serious disagreements that exposed him to differing viewpoints on policy.

Competing Visions Re-emerge

- How did Alexander Hamilton's expectations for the new nation differ from Thomas Jefferson's? What were the outcomes of this conflict of vision?
- How did the French Revolution affect the diplomatic choices made during George Washington's presidency?

A remarkable but, as it turned out, short-lived spirit of unity marked the early days of Washington's administration. Federalists had sought and won the

protégé Someone whose welfare or career is promoted by an influential person.

cabinet A body of officials appointed by the president to run the executive departments of the govenment and to act as the president's advisers.

overwhelming majority of seats in the new Congress and this success enabled them to work quickly and efficiently on matters they felt had priority. But the unity was fragile. By 1792, sectional divisions were deepening, and as the government debated foreign policy and domestic affairs, two distinct groups, voicing serious differences of opinion, began to form. Alexander Hamilton's vision for America guided one group. At the heart of the other was the vision of Thomas Jefferson.

Unity's Achievements

In addition to creating the four executive departments that became the cabinet, the First Congress passed the **Judiciary Act of 1789.** This act established a Supreme Court, thirteen district courts, and three circuit courts. It also empowered the Supreme Court to review the decisions of state courts and to nullify any state laws that violated either the Constitution or any treaty made by the federal government. President Washington chose John Jay to serve as first chief justice of the Supreme Court.

The First Congress also managed to break the stalemate on the tariff issue. Southern leaders had opposed a tariff because a tax on imported goods added to the cost of the consumer goods that southern agriculturalists had to purchase. Northeastern leaders had favored tariff legislation because a tax on imported goods worked to the benefit of their region's merchants and manufacturers. During Washington's first term, southerner James Madison took the lead in conducting the delicate negotiations over tariffs. The result was an import tax on items such as rum, cocoa, and coffee.

Madison also prodded Congress to draft the promised **Bill of Rights.** Although more than two hundred suggestions were submitted to Congress, Madison honed them down to twelve. On December 15, 1791, ten of these were added to the Constitution as the Bill of Rights. Eight of these original constitutional amendments spelled out the government's commitment to protect individual **civil liberties.** They guaranteed that the government could not limit free speech, interfere with religious worship, deny U.S. citizens the right to keep or bear arms, force the quartering of troops in private homes, or allow homes to be searched without proper search warrants. They stated clearly that the government could not force persons accused of crimes to testify against themselves, nor could citizens be denied the right of trial by jury. The government also could not deprive a citizen of life, liberty, or property without "due process of law" or impose excessive bail or administer "cruel and unusual punishments." The Ninth Amendment made clear that the inclusion of these protections and rights did not mean that others were excluded. The Tenth Amendment stated that any powers not given to the federal government or denied to the states belonged solely to the states or the people.

Condensed into these ten amendments was a rich history of struggle for individual rights in the face of abusive power. It was a history that recalled the experiences of colonists protesting the illegal search and seizure of cargoes in Boston harbor, the British government's insistence on quartering troops in New York homes, and the religious persecution of men and women who dissented from established churches both in England and in the colonies.

Hamilton's and Jefferson's Differences

Alexander Hamilton was consumed by a bold dream: to transform agricultural America into a manufacturing society that rivaled Great Britain. His blueprint for achieving this called for tariffs designed to protect developing American industry rather than simply raise revenue. It also called for **subsidies,** or government financial support, for new enterprises and incentives to support new industries. It relied on strong economic and diplomatic ties with the mercantile interests of England. Hamilton's vision had great appeal in the Northeast but few advocates in the southern states. Indeed, his ambitious development program seemed to confirm Patrick Henry's worst fears: that the new government would produce "a system which I have ever dreaded—subserviency of Southern to Northern Interests."

Judiciary Act of 1789 Law establishing the Supreme Court and the lower federal courts; it gave the Supreme Court the right to review state laws and state court decisions to determine their constitutionality.

Bill of Rights The first ten amendments to the U.S. Constitution, added in 1791 to protect certain basic rights of American citizens.

civil liberties Fundamental individual rights such as freedom of speech and religion, protected by law against interference by the government.

subsidy Financial assistance that a government grants to an enterprise considered to be in the public interest.

♦ Author of many of *The Federalist Papers* essays and first Secretary of the Treasury, Alexander Hamilton was admired for his intellectual brilliance and his political vision even by bitter political opponents. Hamilton was a true American success story: an illegitimate son of a Barbadoes gentleman, he immigrated to the mainland as a teenager where he enjoyed a meteoric career. Hamilton served as Washington's aide-de-camp, became a leader of the New York bar, and entered New York's social elite by his marriage into the Schuyler family. In 1803, a political enemy, Aaron Burr, killed Hamilton in a duel. *"Alexander Hamilton" by Charles Wilson Peale. Courtesy Independence National Historical Park Collection.*

Virginia planters Thomas Jefferson and James Madison offered a different vision of the new nation: a prosperous, agrarian society. Instead of government tariffs designed to encourage American manufacturing, they advocated a national policy of **free trade** to keep consumer prices low. The agrarian vision did not entirely rule out commerce and industry in the United States. As long as commercial society remained "a handmaiden to agriculture," Jefferson saw no danger that citizens would be exploited or be lured into the love of luxury that destroyed republics. In the same fashion, Hamilton was content to see agriculture thrive as long as it did not drain away the scarce resources of the national government or stand in the way of commercial growth. Hamilton and men of similiar vision around him spoke of themselves as true **Federalists.** Those who agreed with Jefferson and Madison spoke of themselves as **Republicans.**

The emergence of two political camps was certain to trouble even the men who played a role in creating them. The revolutionary generation believed that **factions,** or parties, were responsible for the deterioration of English politics. John Adams seemed to speak for all these political leaders when he declared: "a division of the republic into two great parties . . . is to be dreaded as the greatest political evil." Yet as President Washington was quick to see, **sectionalism** fueled the growth of just such a division.

Hamilton's Economic Plan

As secretary of the treasury, Alexander Hamilton was expected to seek solutions to the nation's **fiscal** problems, particularly the foreign and domestic debts hanging over America's head. His proposals were the source of much of the conflict that divided Congress in the early 1790s.

In January 1790 Hamilton submitted a *Report on Public Credit* to the Congress. In it, he argued that the public debt fell into three categories, each requiring attention: (1) foreign debt, owed primarily to France; (2) state debts, incurred by the individual states to finance their war efforts; and (3) a national debt in the form of government securities (the notorious paper Continentals) that had been issued to help finance the war. To establish credit, Hamilton said, and thus to be able to borrow money and attract investors in American enterprises, the nation had to find a way to make good on each of these debts.

Hamilton proposed that the federal government assume responsibility for the repayment of all three categories of debt. He insisted that the Continentals be redeemed for the amount showed on the certificate, regardless of what their current value might be. And he proposed that *current* holders of Conti-

free trade Trade between nations without protective tariffs.

Federalists Political group formed during Washington's first administration and led by Alexander Hamilton; they favored commercial growth and an active government role in fostering that growth.

Republicans Political group formed during Washington's first administration and led by Thomas Jefferson and James Madison; they favored limited government involvement and the continued dominance of agriculture in the national economy.

faction A political group with shared opinions or interests that members advocate.

sectionalism Excessive regard for local or regional interests.

fiscal Relating to government finances.

nentals should receive that payment regardless of how or when they had acquired them. These recommendations, and the political vision for economic growth they revealed, raised furious debate within Congress.

Before Hamilton's *Report on Public Credit,* James Madison had been the voice of unity in Congress. Now, Madison leaped to his feet to protest the treasury secretary's plan. The government's debt, both financial and moral, Madison argued, was not to the current creditors holding the Continentals but to the *original* holders. Many of the original holders were ordinary citizens and Continental soldiers who had sold these certificates to speculators at a tremendous loss during the postwar depression. The state treasuries of New York, Pennsylvania, and Maryland were three of the largest speculators, buying up great quantities of these bonds when they were disgracefully cheap. If Hamilton's plan were adopted, these speculators, rather than the nation's true patriots, would reap enormous profits.

Madison's emotional opposition to Hamilton's debt program came from a deep distrust of certain ways of attaining wealth. Although enslaved men and women performed the work done on Madison's plantation, the Virginia planter believed that wealth acquired by productive labor was moral but wealth gained by the manipulation of money was corrupt. Hamilton simply sidestepped the moral issue by explaining the difficulty of identifying and locating the original holders of the Continentals. Whatever the ethical merits of Madison's argument, Hamilton said, his solution was impractical. Congress supported Hamilton, but the vote revealed the growing rift between regions.

Madison was far from silenced, however. He led the opposition to Hamilton's proposal that the federal government assume, or take over, the states' debts. Here, Hamilton's motives were quite transparent: as a fierce nationalist, he wished to concentrate both political and economic power in the federal government at the expense of the states. He knew that creditors, who included America's wealthiest citizens, would take a particular interest in the welfare and success of any government that owed them money. By concentrating the debt in the federal government, Hamilton intended to give America's elite a stake in America's success. Hamilton also knew that a sizable debt provided a compelling reason for raising revenue. By assuming the state debts, the federal government could increase its financial resources and at the same time decrease the state governments' justification for new taxes.

Congress saw the obvious **inequities** of the plan. Members from states like Maryland and Virginia quickly pointed out that their governments had paid all their war debts during the 1780s. If the national government assumed state debts and raised taxes to repay them, citizens of Maryland and Virginia would be taxed for the failure of Massachusetts or New York to pay off their debts. Although the Senate approved the assumption of state debts, members of the House strongly objected and deferred a decision. Hamilton, realizing he faced defeat, moved to break the deadlock with a behind-the-scenes compromise with Madison and his ally Jefferson. Hamilton was confident he had something valuable to bargain away: the location of the national capital.

In 1789, the new government had made New York its temporary home until Congress could settle on a permanent site. The choice turned out to be politically delicate because of regional jealousy and competition. Hamilton was willing to put the capital right in Jefferson's backyard in exchange for the Virginian's support on assumption. The bargain clearly appealed to southern regional pride, but Madison and Jefferson had deeper motives for agreeing to it. Like many good Republicans, they believed it was important to monitor the deliberations of a powerful government. But in an age of slow land travel and slower communication it was difficult to keep watch from a distance. New Englanders also knew that "watching" meant the chance to influence the government. "The climate of the Potomac," one New Englander quipped, would prove unhealthy, if not deadly, to "northern constitutions." Nevertheless, by trading away the capital, Hamilton ensured the success of his assumption plan.

The year 1791 began with another proposal from the secretary of the treasury. This time, Hamilton outlined a plan for chartering a national bank. The bank, modeled on the Bank of England, would serve as fiscal agent for the federal government, although it would not be an exclusively public institution. Instead, the bank would be funded by both the government and private sources in a partnership that fit nicely with Hamilton's plan to tie national prosperity to the interests of private wealth.

Once again, James Madison led the opposition. He argued that the government had neither the

inequities Unfair circumstances or proceedings.

express right nor the **implied power** to create a national institution such as the bank. The majority of Congress did not agree, but Madison's argument that the bank was unconstitutional did cause President Washington to hesitate over signing the congresssional bill into law. As usual, Washington decided to consult advisers on the matter. He asked both Secretary of State Jefferson and the Treasury head Hamilton to set down their views.

Like Madison, Jefferson was a **strict constructionist** in his interpretation of the Constitution. On February 15, 1791, he wrote of the dangers of interpreting the government's powers broadly. "To take a single step beyond the boundaries . . . specifically drawn around the powers of Congress," he warned, "is to take possession of a boundless field of power." A **broad constructionist,** Hamilton saw no such danger in the bank. He based his argument on Article 1, Section 8, of the Constitution, which granted Congress the right to "make all Laws which shall be necessary and proper" to exercise its legitimate powers. As he put it on February 23: "The powers contained in a constitution . . . ought to be construed liberally in advancement of the public good." And, because it seemed obvious that "a bank has a natural relation to the power of collecting taxes," Hamilton believed there could be no reasonable constitutional argument against it. Hamilton's argument persuaded the president, and the bank was chartered on February 25, 1791. By July 4, 1791, stock in the newly established Bank of the United States was offered for sale.

Hamilton's assumption strategy and the creation of a bank were just preliminaries to the ambitious economic development program that he put forward in 1792 in his *Report on Manufactures.* His call for policies suited to an aggressively industrializing nation—including protective tariffs and government incentives and subsidies—was too extreme to win much support in Congress. Still, the Bank of the United States, which provided much-needed working **capital** for new commercial and manufacturing enterprises, and the establishment of sound national credit, which attracted foreign capital to the new nation, had gone far toward moving the economy in the direction of Hamilton's vision.

Foreign Affairs and Deepening Divisions

In 1789, just as George Washington became the first president of the United States, the **French Revolution** began. And in the years in which Hamilton was advancing his economic programs, that revolution stirred new controversy within American politics.

The first signs of serious resistance to the French monarchy came when **Louis XVI,** king of France, asked for new taxes. Reformers within the French parliament, or Estates General, refused, choosing instead to reduce the king's power and create a constitutional monarchy. Outside the halls of government, crowds took to the streets in the name of broad social reform. On July 14, 1789, Parisian radicals stormed the Bastille prison, a symbol of royal oppression, tearing down its walls and liberating its political prisoners.

The crowds filling the Paris streets owed some of their political rhetoric and ideals to the American Revolution. The Marquis de Lafayette acknowledged this debt when he sent his old friend President Washington the key to the Bastille. Like most Americans in these early days of the French Revolution, Washington was pleased to be identified with this new struggle for the "rights of man." Briefly, enthusiasm for the French Revolution united Hamilton's Federalists and Jefferson's Republicans.

By 1793, however, American public opinion began to divide sharply on the French Revolution. Popular support faded when the revolution's most radical party, the Jacobins, imprisoned and then executed the king and his wife. Many shocked Americans denounced the revolution completely when the Jacobins, in their **Reign of Terror** against any who

implied power Power that is not specifically granted to the government by the Constitution but can be viewed as necessary to carry out the governing duties that are listed in the Constitution.

strict constructionist A person who believes the government has only those powers specifically named in the Constitution.

broad constructionist A person who believes the government can exercise any implied powers that are in keeping with the spirit of the Constitution.

capital Money needed to start a commercial enterprise.

French Revolution Political rebellion against the French monarchy and aristocratic privileges; it began in 1789 and ended in 1799.

Louis XVI The ruling monarch (r. 1774–1792) when the French Revolution began; he and his wife, Marie Antoinette, were executed in 1793 by the leaders of this revolution.

Reign of Terror The period from 1793 to 1794 in the French Revolution, during which thousands of people were executed as enemies of the state.

opposed their policies, began marching moderate French reformers as well as members of the nobility to the guillotine to be beheaded.

Soon after eliminating their revolutionary opponents, the Jacobin government launched a campaign to bring "liberty, equality, and brotherhood" to the peoples of Europe. This campaign to spread the revolution led France into war with England, Spain, Austria, and **Prussia.** At the very least, France expected the Americans to honor the terms of the treaty of 1778, which bound the United States to protect French possessions in the West Indies from enemy attack. The enemy most likely to strike was England, a fact that suddenly made a second war between England and the United States a possibility.

American opinion on a second war with England was contradictory and complex. George Blake, a Boston lawyer and political figure, reminded his fellow citizens, "The [French] cause is half our own, and does not our policy and our honor urge us to most forcibly cherish it?" But others who continued to support the French Revolution, including Thomas Jefferson, did not want the United States to become embroiled in a European war. Many who condemned the French Revolution nevertheless were eager to use any excuse to attack the British, who still were occupying forts in the Northwest and restricting American trade in the Caribbean. Political leaders who, like Alexander Hamilton, were working toward better relations with England, were appalled not only by the French assault on other nations but also by the prospect of American involvement in it. While Americans struggled with these contradictory views, the French decided to mobilize American support directly.

In 1793, the new French republic sent a diplomatic minister to the United States. When Citizen **Edmund Genêt** arrived in Charleston, he wasted no time on formal matters such as presenting his credentials as an official representative from France to either the president or the secretary of state. He immediately launched into a campaign to recruit Americans to the war effort. By all accounts, Genêt was charming, affable, and, in the words of one observer, so humorous that he could "laugh us into the war." President Washington, however, was not amused. Genêt's total disregard for formal procedures infuriated Washington, who was undecided about whether to officially recognize the French minister. Genêt's bold attempts to provoke incidents between the United States and Spain stunned Hamilton. Even Thomas Jefferson grew uncomfortable when the Frenchman used the port of Philadelphia to transform a captured British ship into a French privateer!

On April 22, 1793, Washington decided to act. Publicly, the president issued a proclamation that declared American **neutrality** without actually using the term. While allowing Washington to avoid a formal **repudiation** of America's treaty with France, the proclamation made clear that the United States would give no military support to the French. Privately, Washington asked the French government to recall Genêt.

The Genêt affair had domestic as well as diplomatic repercussions. For the first time, George Washington came under public attack. A Republican newspaper whose editor was employed by Jefferson in the State Department questioned the president's integrity in refusing to honor the Franco-American treaty. Washington was furious with this assault on his character. Federalist newspapers struck back, insisting that Jefferson and his followers had actively encouraged the outrageous behavior of Genêt, and Federalists issued resolutions condemning Genêt. By the end of 1793, Jefferson had resigned from Washington's government, more convinced than ever that Hamilton and his supporters posed a serious threat to the survival of the American republic.

More Domestic Disturbances

Hamilton's Federalists agreed that the republic was in danger—from Jefferson's Republicans. By Washington's second term (he was re-elected in 1792), both political groups were trying to rouse popular sentiment for their programs and policies and against those of their opponents. Just as in the pre-revolutionary years, these appeals to popular opinion broadened participation in the debate over the

Prussia A northern European state that became the basis for the German Empire in the late nineteenth century.

Edmund Genêt Diplomat whom the French revolutionary government sent to the United States to bring the United States into France's war with Britain and Spain.

neutrality The policy of treating both sides in a conflict in the same way and thus favoring neither.

repudiation The act of rejecting the validity or authority of something.

♦ In 1794, western Pennsylvania grain farmers rose up in armed opposition to the federal government's new tax on whisky. For these rebels, distilling their crop into a non-perishable and easily transported liquor was the only way to insure a yearly profit. At Hamilton's urging, President Washington led an army of over twelve thousand young soldiers like the one pictured here to crush this Whiskey Rebellion. *Henry Francis du Pont Winterthur Museum.*

future of the nation. Ordinary citizens did not always wait until their political leaders solicited their views, however. In the wake of the French Revolution and British interference in the West and on the seas, organizations rose up to make demands on the government. The most troubling of these to President Washington were the **Democratic-Republican societies.**

Between 1793 and 1794, thirty-five Democratic-Republican societies were created. Made up primarily of craftsmen and men of the "lower orders," these pro-French political groups also had their share of professional men, merchants, and planters. In Philadelphia, for example, noted scientist and inventor David Rittenhouse and Alexander Dallas, secretary to the governor of Pennsylvania, were society members. In Kentucky, which had separated from Virginia in 1792, local elites organized their own society, separate from the one run by western farmers. No matter what the background of the membership, these societies shared a common agenda: to serve as a platform for expressing the public's will. They insisted that political officeholders were "the agents of the people," not their leaders, and thus should act as the people wished.

In 1794, many western farmers believed the government was not responding to the needs of its citizens. Kentucky settlers worried about the navigation of the Mississippi, while Pennsylvania and Carolina farmers resented a new federal excise tax on whiskey. Although the Democratic-Republican societies denied an active role in spurring a new farmers' revolt against the government, a belief that the government ought to respond to its citizens' demands did seem to motivate Pennsylvania, Carolina, and Kentucky farmers to tar and feather excise men, burn the barns of tax supporters, and intimidate other government officials in their counties. The most determined and organized resistance seemed to come from Pennsylvania, where, in July 1794, a crowd ransacked and burned the home of the federal excise inspector and then threatened to march on Pittsburgh if the tax on whiskey were not repealed.

President Washington, haunted by the memory of Shays' Rebellion and worried that the radical spirit of the French Revolution was spreading throughout America, determined to firmly crush this **Whiskey Rebellion.** Calling up fifteen thousand militiamen, the president marched to do battle with a few hundred citizens armed with rifles and pitchforks. In the face of such an overwhelming military force, the whiskey rebels abruptly dispersed.

Washington publicly laid the blame for the western insurrection on the Democratic-Republican societies. Federalists in Congress rushed to propose a resolution condemning those groups. Fisher Ames, the ardent Federalist from Massachusetts, delivered an impassioned condemnation of the societies, accusing them of spreading "jealousies, suspicions, and accusations" against the government. They had, Ames declared, "arrogantly pretended sometimes to be the people and sometimes the [people's] guardians, the champions of the people." Instead, he said, they represented no one but themselves.

Democratic-Republican societies Political organizations formed in 1793 and 1794 to demand greater responsiveness by the state and federal governments to the needs of the citizens.

Whiskey Rebellion A protest by grain farmers against the 1794 federal tax on whiskey; militia forces led by President Washington quelled this Pennsylvania uprising.

The Jeffersonians, generally believed to be sympathetic to the societies, knew it would be politically damaging to defend them in the aftermath of the Whiskey Rebellion. Instead, they worked to see a more moderate expression of disapproval emerge from Congress.

By 1796, the Democratic-Republican organizations had vanished from the American political scene. The president's public condemnation and Congress's criticism undoubtedly damaged them. But improvements on the western borders also diminished the farmers' interest in protest organizations. In October 1795, Carolina planter Thomas Pinckney won the concession from Spain that Jay had been unable to win in earlier negotiations: free navigation of the Mississippi River. Pinckney's **Treaty of San Lorenzo** not only gave western farmers an outlet to ocean trade through the port of New Orleans but also ensured that Indian attacks would not be launched from Spanish-held territories.

Jay's Treaty

During Washington's second administration, the diplomatic crisis continued to worsen. England resented America's claim to neutrality, believing it helped France. The British, therefore, ignored American claims that "free ships made free goods" and began to seize American vessels trading with the French Caribbean islands. These seizures prompted new calls for war with Great Britain.

Anti-British emotion ran even higher when the governor of Canada actively encouraged Indian resistance to American settlers in the Northwest. Washington and the general public considered Indian relations dismal enough without Lord Dorchester's meddling, especially since efforts to crush the Miamis of Ohio had recently ended in two embarrassing American defeats. In February 1794, as General Anthony Wayne headed west for a third attempt against the Miamis, Dorchester's fiery remarks were particularly disturbing.

Jefferson's departure meant that there was little anti-British sentiment in the cabinet. But it remained strong in the Congress, where the House of Representatives considered restricting trade with England. Outside the government, war hysteria showed itself as mobs attacked English seamen and tarred and feathered Americans expressing pro-British views. What would Washington do?

Early in 1794, the president sent Chief Justice John Jay to England as his special **envoy.** Jay's mission was to produce a compromise that would prevent war between the two nations. Jay, however, was pessimistic. Britain wanted to avoid war with the United States, but what would British diplomats concede to his weak nation?

Jay's negotiations resolved some old, nagging issues. In the treaty that emerged, Britain agreed to evacuate the western forts but did not agree to end support for Indian resistance to American western settlement. Britain also granted some small trade favors to America in the West Indies. The United States agreed to see that all prewar debts owed to British merchants were at last paid. In the end, however, Jay gave up more than he gained: he abandoned America's demand for freedom of the seas and conceded the British navy's right to remove French property from any neutral ship.

Jay's Treaty did little to enhance John Jay's reputation or popularity. After reading it, fellow New Yorker Robert R. Livingston said bluntly: "Mr. Jay has sacrificed the essential interests of this country." In Congress, judgments on the treaty were openly **partisan.** Federalists credited Jay's Treaty with preserving the peace, but Republicans condemned it as an embarrassment and a betrayal of France. Worried that the angry debate over ratification would fan popular outrage, the president banned public discussion of the treaty. Republican congressmen, however, leaked accounts to the press. Once again, the president came under attack, and Kentucky settlers threatened rebellion, warning Washington that if he signed Jay's Treaty, "western America is gone forever—lost to the Union." The treaty finally squeaked through the Senate in the spring of 1795 with only two southern senators supporting ratification. The House debate on appropriations for the treaty, chaired by Pennsylvania's Frederick Muhlenberg, was equally bitter and prolonged

Treaty of San Lorenzo Treaty between the United States and Spain negotiated in 1795 by Thomas Pinckney; Spain granted the United States the right to navigate the Mississippi River and use the port of New Orleans as an outlet to the seas.

envoy A government representative who is sent on a special diplomatic mission.

Jay's Treaty Controversial treaty between the United States and England negotiated in 1794 by John Jay to ensure American neutrality.

partisan Taking a strong position on an issue out of loyalty to a particular political group or leader.

INDIVIDUAL CHOICES

Choosing Conscience over Career

Frederick Muhlenberg

Frederick Muhlenberg began his political career as a staunch Federalist, but in Congress his sympathies seemed to shift toward the Jeffersonian faction. Thus, when the House began to debate the Jay Treaty, neither party was certain of Muhlenberg's loyalty. His choice would determine the fate of the treaty.

Nothing revealed the deepening divisions within the new American government as clearly as the debate over Jay's Treaty. Hamilton's economic programs had sparked the formation of factions in the new republic, and years of disagreement over the nation's foreign policy further divided the nation's political leader into two camps. By 1795, when the bitter struggle over ratification and funding for Jay's Treaty began in Congress, both the Republicans and the Federalists called on the men in office to demonstrate their party loyalty.

Frederick Augustus Conrad Muhlenberg certainly understood these expectations. In 1795, Muhlenberg was no stranger to state or national politics. Although he began his public life as a Lutheran minister, he chose to enter the world of politics in 1775 when his home state of Pennsylvania sent him to the Continental Congress. Later, Muhlenberg was called on to preside over Pennsylvania's constitutional ratifying convention. He was an active supporter of the new national government, despite the fact that Antifederalist sentiment was strong in his state. When he went to Congress in 1789, Federalists rewarded him for his efforts in the Consti-

(see Individual Choices: Frederick Muhlenberg). In the end, however, Congress endorsed Jay's handiwork. Despite the criticism, Jay knew he had accomplished his mission, for American neutrality in the European war continued.

Jay's negotiations with England damaged the prestige and authority of Washington's administration. The president did far better, however, in military and diplomatic affairs in the West. In August 1794, Anthony Wayne's army defeated the northwestern Indians at the **Battle of Fallen Timbers.** Wayne then lived up to his reputation as "Mad Anthony" by rampaging through enemy villages, destroying all that he could. These terror tactics helped produce the **Treaty of Greenville** in August 1795. By

Battle of Fallen Timbers Battle in August 1794 in which Kentucky riflemen defeated Indians of several tribes, helping to end Indian resistance in the Northwest.

Treaty of Greenville Treaty in 1795 by which the United States paid northwestern Indians about $10,000 to cede land that later became the state of Ohio.

tution's behalf by making him the first Speaker of the House. Two years later, however, Republican criticism of Hamilton and his programs seemed to have influenced Muhlenberg. He was, Federalists noted with concern, only a "lukewarm" supporter of the administration. Yet when Muhlenberg chose to run for governor of Pennsylvania in 1793, he campaigned as a Federalist. When he lost the election to a Jeffersonian, he returned to the House of Representatives, where he again confounded both factions by cooperating sometimes with one and sometimes with the other. His apparent growing sympathy for the Jeffersonians led House Republicans to back him for Speaker of the House when he returned for the third session of Congress. Thus, when the tense debate over Jay's Treaty moved from the Senate to the House, each party had good reason to believe it could expect Muhlenberg's support.

The Senate had ratified the treaty, but the House of Representatives had the power to grant or deny the funds needed to implement it. Convening as a committee of the whole, the entire House began its long, torturous debate over appropriations. Frederick Muhlenberg was chosen to chair these sessions. Thus, while men on each side of the issue delivered impassioned speeches, Muhlenberg maintained an impartial silence. When the roll call on the treaty was finally taken, the outcome was every politician's nightmare: the House was deadlocked, with 49 yeas and 49 nays.

All eyes now turned to the chair to cast the deciding vote. Frederick Muhlenberg shifted uneasily in his seat, and paused for what seemed to the men gathered in the room to be an eternity. Then he chose to vote as his conscience dictated. Perhaps Muhlenberg was influenced by the nightmare image of continuing frontier bloodshed if the treaty failed, an image offered by the gaunt, ailing Massachusetts Federalist Fisher Ames in what John Adams called the most moving and dramatic speech ever to be heard in Congress. Or perhaps Muhlenberg was moved by Jonathan Dayton's call to his fellow representatives to "sacrifice every resentment, every prejudice, and every personal consideration to love of country," and endorse John Jay's handiwork. Perhaps the fact that leading Republicans such as James Madison and Pennsylvania's Albert Gallatin had reluctantly voted "aye" in the Senate led Muhlenberg to his own decision. Whatever his motivation, Frederick Muhlenberg gave the Federalists their much-desired victory.

Afterward, Federalists spoke of Muhlenberg's bravery in voting his conscience. But Republicans, especially in Pennsylvania, chose to call him a traitor. Soon after the vote, Muhlenberg's own brother-in-law, an ardent Republican, drew a knife and stabbed him! Pennsylvania's other Republicans contented themselves with political assassination: they made sure that, in the next election, Frederick Muhlenberg did not win a seat in the House.

this treaty, the Indians ceded most of the land that later became the state of Ohio. These victories, combined with the terms of Pinckney's Treaty of San Lorenzo, won praise for the troubled president.

Washington's Farewell

The bitter political fight over Jay's Treaty, combined with the steady and nagging criticism of his policies in the press and the hardening of party lines between Federalists and Republicans, helped George Washington make an important decision: he would not seek a third term as president. Instead, in 1796 he would return to his beloved Virginia home, Mount Vernon, and resume the life of a gentleman planter.

When Washington retired, he left behind a nation very different from the one whose independence he had helped win and whose survival he had helped secure. The postwar economic depression was over, and the war raging in Europe had produced a steadily rising demand for American foodstuffs. More fundamentally, in the fifteen years since the

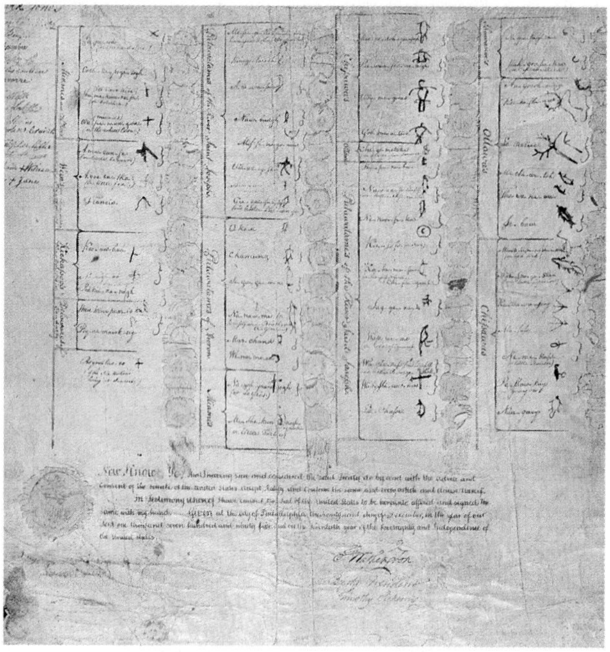

♦ Independence sparked renewed westward migration by land hungry Americans. The federal government took steps to legitimate these incursions into Indian homelands by persuading selected chiefs and warriors of the Northwest to cede all rights to vast tracts of this Ohio Valley land. The document above provides a sample of the eleven hundred signatures obtained in the Greenville Treaty of 1795, a treaty that ceded almost two-thirds of present day Ohio and portions of Indiana. Many tribes protested such treaties on the grounds that the signers were not legitimate spokesmen for their people. *Library of Congress.*

Revolution, the U.S. economy had moved decisively in the direction that Alexander Hamilton had envisioned. The values and expectations of a **market economy**—with its stress on maximizing profit and the pursuit of individual economic interests—had captured the imagination and shaped the actions of many white Americans. Hamilton's policies as secretary of the treasury had both reflected and advanced a growing interest in the expansion of trade, the growth of markets, and the development of American manufacturing and industry. In its political life, the republic had been reorganized and the relationships between the states and the central government redefined. The new Constitution granted greater diplomatic and commercial powers to the federal government but protected individual citizens through the Bill of Rights. America's political leader, committed to the belief that factions were dangerous to the survival of the republic, had nevertheless created and begun to work within an evolving party system.

In his **Farewell Address** to the public, Washington expressed his thoughts on many of these changes. Although Jefferson had thought the president was a Federalist partisan, Washington spoke with feeling against parties in a republic, urging the nation to return to nonpartisan cooperation. Washington also warned America and its new leaders not to "interweave our destiny with any part of Europe" or "entangle our peace and prosperity in the toils of European ambition." An honorable country must "observe good faith and justice toward all nations," said the aging Virginian, but not let any alliance develop that draws the nation into a foreign war. The final ingredient in Washington's formula for America's success and its "permanent felicity" was the continuing virtue of its people.

market economy An economy in which production of goods is geared to sale or profit.

Farewell Address Speech that George Washington made at the end of his second term as president; in it, he called for nonpartisan cooperation in the federal government and warned against involvement in foreign affairs.

SUMMARY

E xpectations
C onstraints
C hoices
O utcomes

After fighting for and winning independence, Americans faced the challenge of creating a new nation out of thirteen distinct states. *Constrained* by enormous debt and still surrounded by real and potential enemies, the new nation's ability to survive seemed doubtful to many Americans and foreigners.

One cause for concern was the states' jealous protection of their individuality. During the Revolution and immediately after, the states drafted their own constitutions, some *choosing* democratic forms of government while others *chose* to keep less democratic features such as high property qualifications for voting. A second *constraint* on state cooperation was the Articles of Confederation government, in which state representatives were guaranteed the power to withhold important powers from the national governing body. The *outcome* of working within this weak central government was continuing financial crises and debt, for individual states could not be forced to commit themselves to financial support of the Confederation.

The Confederation *chose* the sale of western lands, made legal through the Northwest Ordinances, as one solution to its financial problems. However, the *outcome* was conflict with the British, Indians, and Spanish who claimed parts of the West. Farmers, too, felt the *constraints* of economic depression and indebtedness, and Massachusetts farmers rose in revolt during Shays' Rebellion. The continuing national crisis convinced many of the nation's elite that critical *choices* had to be made about revising the system of government.

In the summer of 1787 a group of experienced political leaders met in Philadelphia to do just that. The Constitution of the United States was the *outcome* of their deliberations. It was a document of compromise, steering a middle course between a central government that was too powerful and one that was too weak. The Constitution was ratified by the states in 1788 after a vigorous battle between Federalists and Antifederalists, and George Washington was elected the nation's first president.

The new government settled some major concerns, but differences in political opinion emerged, especially between Alexander Hamilton's Federalist followers and Thomas Jefferson's Republicans. These factions *chose* different positions on economic and foreign policy. Federalists wanted an industrial nation and opposed U.S. military support to France in its war with England after the French Revolution of 1789. Republicans expected the United States to remain agrarian and for the most part supported the French in their revolution and its aftermath. The *outcome* was deepening divisions between these two political groups. The United States, however, did manage to remain neutral when France and Britain went to war.

By the end of Washington's second term, the United States had expanded its borders, negotiated with Spain for access to the Mississippi River, and established a national bank at the center of an economic system that brought economic growth. It had survived new domestic unrest and the development of political parties, largely reflecting sectional divisions. The departing Washington warned that Americans should continue to cooperate and not allow competing visions of American society to harm them.

SUGGESTED READINGS

Lyman Butterfield, et al., eds. *The Book of Abigail and John: Selected Letters of the Adams Family, 1762–1784* (1975).

The editors of the Adams Papers have collected part of the extensive correspondence between John and Abigail Adams during the critical decades of the independence movement.

Richard B. Morris. *Witness at the Creation* (1985).

A distinguished scholar re-creates the drama of the Constitutional Convention by focusing on the personalities and motives of the framers.

Thomas P. Slaughter. *The Whiskey Rebellion* (1986).

This is a vivid account of the major challenge to the Washington government.

Gary Wills. *Cincinnatus: George Washington and the Enlightenment* (1984).

This is a beautifully written intellectual biography of America's first president and his times.

AMERICAN EXPANSION AND INDIAN LAND CESSIONS, TO 1800
Growth was a dominant characteristic of the United States during the late 1700s. As this map shows, population was becoming increasingly dense and pushing westward. At the same time, Indians were forced to withdraw, ceding large expanses of land, often under threat of violence.

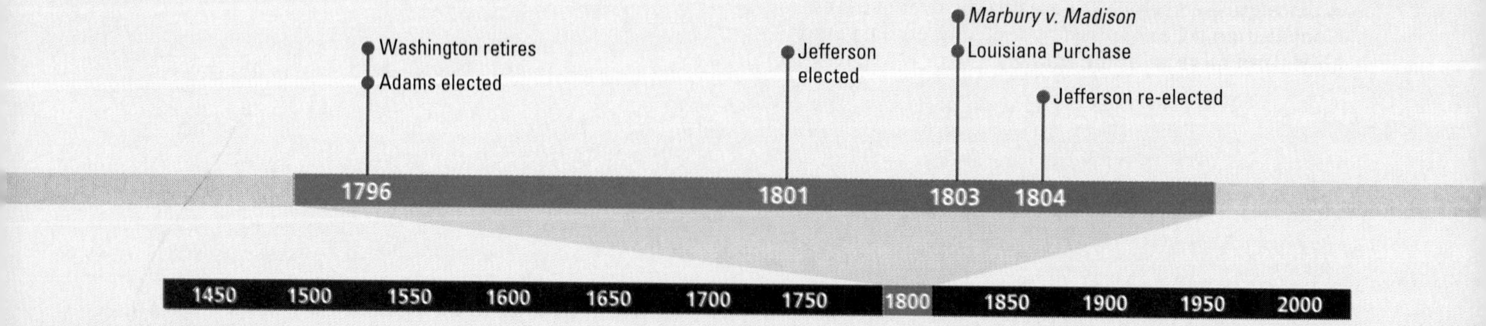

CHAPTER 8

The Early Republic, 1796–1804

Conflict in the Adams Administration

- What did Federalists expect to accomplish by waging a limited war against France in 1798?
- How did Republicans respond to the constraints that Federalists imposed during the Quasi-War?

The "Revolution of 1800"

- Before the Federalists left office, what constraints did they try to impose on the incoming Republican president?
- What did Thomas Jefferson mean when he said that "Every difference of opinion is not a difference of principles"?
- How did Republicans choose to deal with Federalist constraints and Jefferson's political agenda?

Republicanism in Action

- What were Jefferson's expectations for American development?
- What policies did he choose to meet those expectations?

Challenge and Uncertainty in Jefferson's America

- How did the expectations of most Americans change during Jefferson's presidency?
- What were Jeffersonians' expectations concerning Native Americans and African Americans? What constraints faced each group during the Jeffersonian era?

INTRODUCTION

Expectations
Constraints
Choices
Outcomes

The end of George Washington's second presidential term came at a critical time in the nation's political development. Despite the general's personal dislike for partisan politics, the wounds inflicted during the debate over the Constitution not only had not healed but appeared to have worsened. Quarreling factions seemed poised to tear the nation apart.

Many Federalists had *expected* a national government more moderate than the government that Washington, his cabinet, and Congress had created. Even James Madison, the inventor of American federalism and author of the Constitution, sided with critics over issues like the national debt, the Bank of the United States, and the Whiskey Rebellion. Disputes over the proper role of the United States in international affairs also fueled conflict and forced *choices.* The nation had to pick its way through a complicated diplomatic maze of conflicting *constraints* imposed by continuing war between France and England. Republicans favored France, but Federalists regarded France as excessively democratic. Federalists supported England, which Republicans regarded as a natural enemy of the United States.

In domestic politics, Americans seemed to have conflicting expectations. Federalists *expected* disaster if they lost political control and intended to retain it at any cost. *Constrained* by increasing Republican pressure and international crisis, they *chose* to pursue a vigorous policy designed to preserve the order they had worked so hard to instill. If necessary, they were willing to destroy democracy before allowing disorder to run rampant, and they turned to the courts in an effort to destroy political opposition. On the international front, Federalists encouraged policies that pushed France to the brink of war with the United States. For their part, Republicans *expected* that if Federalists maintained power, the nation would soon become a satellite for Great Britain. *Constrained* by Federalist aggression, they *chose* to oppose centralized power, organizing into a political opposition faction and seeking support from state governments.

The *outcome* of Federalist efforts to maintain power at any cost was the alienation of many Americans, who believed they heard echoes of George III's policies in the Federalist program. In 1800, the majority of voters *chose* to remove Federalists from office, turning government over to the Virginia radical who had written the Declaration of Independence: Thomas Jefferson. But enough people remained faithful to the Federalist position to maintain that faction's existence and ensure that it acted as a continuing *constraint* on Republican political activity.

Given the chance to craft their own policies, Republicans made political *choices* about national expansion, economic policies, and diplomacy. Jefferson claimed that he distrusted and disapproved of federal power, but he used his authority as president to pursue his policy goals. Although no constitutional provision permitted it, Jefferson asserted a federal privilege to purchase Louisiana Territory, thereby doubling the nation's geographical size.

Some called the *outcome* of Jefferson's presidency a political revolution, for the entire direction of national development seemed to change. Purchasing Louisiana, eliminating internal taxes, and speaking loudly about the virtues of farming told Americans that the days of eastern-oriented mercantilism were at an end and the nation's future was tied to the West. Most Americans saw significant improvement in their *expectations,* and the nation became increasingly optimistic. Some, however, saw little or no improvement in their daily lives.

CHRONOLOGY

Partisan Tension and Jeffersonian Optimism

1796 George Washington's Farewell Address
First contested presidential election: John Adams elected president, Thomas Jefferson vice president

1797 XYZ affair

1798 Alien and Sedition Acts
Kentucky and Virginia Resolutions

1799 Fries's Rebellion
Napoleon seizes control in France
Convention of Mortefontaine

1800 Jefferson and Aaron Burr tie in the Electoral College
Spain gives Louisiana back to France

1801 Jefferson elected president in the House of Representatives, Burr vice president
Judiciary Act of 1801
John Marshall becomes chief justice
War begins between American navy ships and the Barbary pirates
Outdoor revival meeting at Cane Ridge, Kentucky

1802 Congress repeals all internal taxes
Congress repeals Judiciary Act of 1801
French invade Santo Domingo

1803 Marbury v. Madison
Impeachment of justices John Pickering and Samuel Chase
Louisiana Purchase

1804 Twelfth Amendment ratified
Jefferson re-elected

1804–1806 Lewis and Clark's expedition

1806–1807 Zebulon Pike's expedition

1816 African Methodist Episcopal church formed in Philadelphia

Conflict in the Adams Administration

- What did Federalists expect to accomplish by waging a limited war against France in 1798?
- How did Republicans respond to the constraints that Federalists imposed during the Quasi-War?

Retiring president George Washington spoke for many in 1796 when he warned of "the baneful effects of the spirit of party" in his Farewell Address. Men like Washington believed in the ideal of republican citizenship, of sacrificing personal interest for the good of the republic. To such men, all political ideas that did not correspond with their vision of the republic's welfare were dangerous, even traitorous. Strong Federalists like Hamilton were sure that the Republican faction growing up around Jefferson constituted such a danger and wanted desperately to destroy it. For their part, Republicans were equally sure that Federalists were motivated by no higher motives than personal interest. And having spent several years organizing for a confrontation, Republicans were eager to unseat the politicians responsible for suppressing the Whiskey Rebellion and for tying the United States diplomatically to England. As the two groups prepared to face off, however, new factional lines opened.

The Split Election of 1796

As the broadly accepted leader of the opposition to Hamilton and his policies, Thomas Jefferson was the Republicans' logical choice to represent them in the presidential election in 1796. Most people at the time were not surprised that Republicans chose **Aaron Burr,** a brilliant young New York attorney and member of the Senate, to balance the ticket. Though many years apart in age and from vastly different backgrounds, both Jefferson and Burr were

Aaron Burr New York lawyer and vice-presidential candidate in 1796; he became Thomas Jefferson's vice president in 1801 after the House of Representatives broke a deadlock in the Electoral College.

veterans of the revolutionary struggles in 1776 and outspoken champions of democracy.

Despite his democratic trappings, Burr had been born to greatness—his grandfather was the famous evangelical minister Jonathan Edwards (see page 101). But young Burr wanted to make a life on his own and decided to study law rather than follow the family tradition of entering the ministry. During the Revolutionary War, Burr accepted a commission in the Continental Army, where he found common cause with the radical democrats who had formed the Sons of Liberty (see page 123). By 1784, the young attorney had used his political connections and backing from the Sons of Liberty to win a place in the New York state assembly. In 1791, the New York Sons of Liberty, now calling themselves the Society of St. Tammany, maneuvered Burr's nomination and election to the U.S. Senate.

Meanwhile, Jefferson had returned from Paris in 1789 to join Washington's cabinet as secretary of state. He was deeply disturbed to find that the once-unified revolutionary forces he knew from 1776 had divided into what he called "a republican side" and a "kingly one," and he complained that "a preference of kingly over republican government was evidently the favorite sentiment." This gave him common cause with Aaron Burr and his associates in the Society of St. Tammany, who were equally dismayed.

The apparent unity among Republicans contrasted sharply with divisions in the Federalist faction. The clear opinion leader and policymaker among the Federalists was Hamilton, but the secretary of the treasury's illegitimate birth and antidemocratic policies made him much too controversial to seek elective office.

Although Hamilton was not considered for the presidency, he tried to play an important role in determining who would be. The most serious among the Federalist contenders were **Thomas Pinckney** of South Carolina and John Adams, George Washington's vice president and one of the architects of the Revolution in Massachusetts.

Pinckney, the younger son of a prestigious South Carolina planter, had been a prominent military figure during the Revolution and became governor of South Carolina during the late 1780s. His negotiation of the treaty with Spain that opened the Mississippi River to American commerce won Pinckney the unreserved admiration of both southerners and westerners (see page 189). A devout Federalist, Pinckney won Hamilton's support, both because he was less associated with radical causes than was Adams and because Hamilton felt he could exercise more influence over the mild-mannered South Carolinian than he could over the stiff-necked Yankee.

Most Federalists, however, aligned behind the old warhorse from Massachusetts. A descendant of New England **Calvinists,** Adams was a man of strong principles, fighting for what he believed was right despite anyone's contrary opinion. He was quick-tempered and had little patience with those who practiced insincere politics. Despite his reputation for distrusting the popular will, he remained Thomas Jefferson's close friend, and both he and his wife Abigail maintained a spirited correspondence with the red-haired Virginian during his stay in Paris. Like Washington, Adams was seen by many old revolutionaries as above politics, as a **statesman** whose conscience would help the new nation avoid the pitfalls of factionalism.

Hamilton's scheming nearly lost the election for the Federalists. The treasury secretary was counting on a peculiarity in the election process. According to Article II, Section 1, of the Constitution, each member of the Electoral College could vote for two candidates. The highest vote getter became president, and the runner-up became vice president. Hamilton urged Pinckney supporters to withhold votes from Adams so that Pinckney would win more votes than the former vice president. But Hamilton underestimated Pinckney's unpopularity in the North, Adams's unacceptability among southerners, and Jefferson's growing popularity among northern dissidents. Nor did the treasury secretary expect Adams supporters to learn of the plot, but they did and withheld votes from Pinckney to make up for the votes being withheld from Adams.

Because of the squabbling within the Federalist faction, Jefferson received the votes of disgruntled Federalist electors as well as electors within Republican ranks. He thus ended up with more votes than Pinckney—and only three fewer votes than Adams. So the nation emerged from the first truly contested presidential election with a split administration: the president and vice president belonged to different factions and held opposing political philosophies.

Thomas Pinckney South Carolina politician and diplomat who was an unsuccessful Federalist candidate for president in 1796.

Calvinists Protestant followers of John Calvin, whose theology emphasizes the absolute power of God, human sinfulness, and people's inability to effect salvation.

statesman A political leader who acts out of concern for the public good and not out of self-interest.

♦ This miniature portrait of John Adams painted by John Trumbull in 1792 shows the stable (some said stodgy) statesman that Americans turned to after George Washington chose to step down as president. *"John Adams" by John Trumbull, 1792. Yale University Art Gallery, Trumbull Collection.*

Never known for charm, subtlety, or willingness to compromise, Adams was ill suited to lead a deeply divided nation. Although he disavowed any monarchist sentiments in his inaugural address, the new president's aloofness did little to put Republicans' fears to rest, and he made few **conciliatory** gestures. In fact, from Washington's cabinet he retained Oliver Wolcott, James McHenry, and Timothy Pickering, all of whom were Hamilton men through and through. This move thoroughly angered Republicans, who had hoped Hamilton's influence would wane now that he had retired from government service to practice law. And then Adams withheld an expected diplomatic appointment from James Madison. Clearly the factions were still alive and well and locked in conflict. This disunity enticed interested parties both at home and abroad to try to undermine Adams's authority and influence.

XYZ: The Power of Patriotism

One group seeking to take advantage of the divisions in the United States was the revolutionary government in France. American minister James Monroe sympathized with the French cause, but the pro-British impact of Jay's Treaty and the antirevolutionary rhetoric adopted by Federalists led the French to suspect American sincerity. During the election of 1796, France sought to influence American voting by actively favoring the Republican candidates, threatening to close diplomatic relations if the vocally pro-British Federalists won. True to its word, the revolutionary government of France broke off relations with the United States as soon as Adams was elected.

In 1797 Adams angrily responded, calling home the sympathetic Monroe and replacing him with devout Federalist **Charles Cotesworth Pinckney**, the older brother of Hamilton's favored candidate for the presidency. The French refused to acknowledge Pinckney as ambassador and began seizing American ships. Faced with what was fast becoming a diplomatic crisis, and possibly a military one as well, Adams wisely chose to pursue two courses simultaneously. Asserting that the United States would not be "humiliated under a colonial spirit of fear and a sense of inferiority," he pressed Congress to build up America's military defenses. At the same time, he dispatched John Marshall and Elbridge Gerry to join Pinckney in Paris, where they were to arrange a peaceful settlement of the two nations' differences.

Still playing a complicated diplomatic game, French foreign minister **Charles Maurice de Talleyrand-Périgord** declined to receive Pinckney and the peace delegation. As weeks passed, three businessmen residing in Paris suggested a solution to the stalemate. If the American peace commission was willing to pay a bribe to key members of the French government and guarantee an American loan of several million dollars to France, the three businessmen would be able to get them a hearing. Offended at such treatment, Pinckney broke off diplomatic relations. Reporting the affair to President Adams, Pinckney refused to name the three businessmen, calling them only "X," "Y," and "Z."

conciliatory Striving to overcome distrust or to regain someone's good will.

Charles Cotesworth Pinckney Federalist politician and brother of Thomas Pinckney; he was sent on a diplomatic mission to Paris in 1796 during a period of unfriendly relations between France and the United States.

Charles Maurice de Talleyrand-Périgord French foreign minister appointed by the revolutionary government in 1797; he later aided Napoleon Bonaparte's overthrow of that government and served as his foreign minister.

♦ Americans saw the XYZ affair as proof of European corruption standing in sharp contrast to American virtue. In this 1798 engraving by Charles Williams, a maidenly America is flattered to distraction by courtly Europeans while members of the French Directory prepare to plunder her wealth. *Lilly Library*

Americans' response to the **XYZ affair** was overwhelming. To a new nation seeking international respect, France's diplomatic slight seemed a slap in the face. In Philadelphia, people paraded in the streets to protest French arrogance. The crowds chanted Pinckney's reported response: "No, no, not a sixpence!" The American people rallied around the president, supporting his vow to end diplomatic relations with France until the U.S. envoy was "received, respected and honored as a representative of a great, free, powerful and independent nation."

The wave of patriotism that grew out of the XYZ affair overcame the spirit of division that had plagued the Adams administration, giving the president a virtually unified Congress and country. In the heat of the moment, Adams pressed for increased military forces, and in short order Congress created the Department of the Navy and appropriated money to start building a fleet of warships. At the same time, Congress authorized privateering against French ships. Congress also created a standing army of twenty thousand troops and ordered that the militia be expanded to thirty thousand men. Washington added his prestige to the effort by coming out of retirement to lead the new army, with Hamilton as his second-in-command. Although running sea battles between French and American ships resulted in the sinking or capture of many vessels on both sides, Congress shied away from actually declaring war, which led to the conflict being labeled the **Quasi-War.**

Despite the military buildup and actual combat, Adams continually pressed for a peaceful solution. He opposed Hamilton's supporters, who persisted in trying to turn the Quasi-War into a real war by getting Congress to issue a formal declaration. Genuine patriotism and moral outrage no doubt contributed to the Federalists' desire for an all-out war with France, but the continuing demand for an aggressive policy was more political than diplomatic in nature.

To Hamilton and his followers, the Reign of Terror in France (see page 202) was proof positive of the evils that occur when power falls to the common people. Hamilton and his supporters would have done nearly anything to help crush the French revolutionary state. In addition, because Jefferson and his Republican faction had been openly sympathetic to the French Revolution and to France's experiment in democracy, Hamilton believed that a full-scale war, with its attending patriotic fervor, might help to undermine those who he feared would loose a Reign of Terror in the United States if they ever gained power. Blaming political factionalism and Jeffersonians' sympathy toward France for the country's precarious position, Hamilton and his partisans urged the hyper-patriotic Congress to silence criticism and destroy organized opposition once and for all.

The War at Home

Congressional Federalists perceived two primary sources of support for Jefferson's faction. One source was **naturalized** American citizens. The revolutionary promises of "life, liberty, and the pursuit of happiness" had drawn many immigrants to the United States. Disappointed by Hamilton's approach to government and economics, they were also drawn to Jefferson's political rhetoric—

XYZ affair A diplomatic incident in which American envoys to France were told that the United States would have to loan France money and bribe government officials as a condition for negotiation.

Quasi-War Diplomatic crisis triggered by the XYZ affair; fighting occurred between the United States and France, but neither side issued a formal declaration of war.

naturalized Granted full citizenship (after having been born in a foreign country).

especially his stress on equal opportunity and his attacks on entrenched elites. The other source of support for Jefferson was a partisan Republican press, which vied with its Federalist counterpart in spewing forth biased news and criticism.

In 1798, Federalists in Congress passed three acts designed to counter the influence of immigrants. The Naturalization Act extended the residency requirement for citizenship from five to fourteen years. The **Alien Act** authorized the president to deport any foreigner he judged "dangerous to the peace and safety of the United States." The Alien Enemies Act permitted the president to imprison or banish any foreigner he considered dangerous during a national emergency. The Naturalization Act was designed to prevent recent immigrants from supporting the Republican cause by barring them from the political process. The other two acts served as a constant reminder that the president or his agents could arbitrarily imprison or deport any resident alien who stepped out of line.

Later in 1798, congressional Federalists passed the **Sedition Act** to silence the Jeffersonian press. In addition to outlawing conspiracies to block the enforcement of federal laws, the Sedition Act outlawed the publication or utterance of any criticism of the government or its officials that might be regarded as "false, scandalous and malicious" or that would bring the government or its officials "into contempt or disrepute." In the words of one Federalist newspaper, "it is patriotism to write in favour of our government, it is **sedition** to write against it." Federalists brandished the law against all kinds of criticism directed toward either the government or the president, including perfectly innocent political editorials. Not surprisingly, most of the defendants in the fifteen cases brought by federal authorities under the Sedition Act were prominent Republican newspaper editors.

One case involved a Republican journalist named James Thompson Callender, a notorious English radical who had been drawn to America by its revolutionary promise. In the United States, he wielded his pen in support of Jefferson and became widely disliked by the Federalists he attacked in print. In 1798, Callender wrote a pamphlet called *The Prospect Before Us,* in which he attacked Adams, federalism, and especially the French situation. He sent advance copies to Jefferson, who wrote a letter back saying, "Such papers cannot fail to produce the best effect." The vice president, however, refused to sign the letter, stating that he believed Federalist postal officials were screening his mail. "Indeed," he concluded, "a period is now approaching during which I shall discontinue writing letters as much as possible, knowing that every snare will be used to get hold of what may be perverted in the eyes of the public." Jefferson managed to avoid such snares, but Callender was less fortunate. The journalist was arrested and tried before the strongly Federalist judge Samuel Chase, who fined the pamphleteer $200, sentenced him to nine months in jail, and ordered him to post a bond of $1,200 to ensure his continued compliance with the Sedition Act.

Republicans asserted that the Alien and Sedition Acts violated the Bill of Rights, but Congress and the federal judiciary, controlled as they were by Adams loyalists, paid no attention. Dissidents like Jefferson and Madison, with good reason to fear Federalist "snares," had little choice but to take their political case to the state governments, which they did in the fall of 1798. Madison submitted a resolution to the Virginia legislature, and Jefferson submitted one in Kentucky.

Although differing in detail, the **Virginia and Kentucky Resolutions** both argued that the national government was simply a compact created by the individual states and maintained for their common interest. Federal power thus depended on the good will of the states, which could declare inappropriate federal laws null and void. In the Virginia Resolution, Madison asserted that the states could overrule any federal action with which a majority of states disagreed. Jefferson went further in the Kentucky Resolution, arguing that each individual state had the "natural right" to interpose its own authority to protect the rights of its citizens.

The Virginia and Kentucky Resolutions passed in their respective state legislatures, but no other states followed suit. Even within Kentucky and Virginia,

Alien Act Law passed by Congress in 1798 authorizing the president to order out of the United States any alien regarded as dangerous to the public peace or safety.

Sedition Act Law passed by Congress in 1798 outlawing any criticism of the U.S. government that might bring the government into disrepute; the law was enforced mainly against Republicans.

sedition Conduct or language inciting rebellion against the authority of a state.

Virginia and Kentucky Resolutions Statements that the Virginia and Kentucky legislatures issued in 1798 in response to the Alien and Sedition Acts; they asserted the right of states to overrule the federal government.

great disagreement arose over how far state authority should extend. Nevertheless, this response to the Federalists' use of federal power brought the disputed relationship between federal law and **states' rights** into national prominence. This relationship is still a major bone of contention.

Another bone of contention was the methods used to finance the Quasi-War with France and the impact these methods had on various groups of Americans. Consistent with Hamilton's views on finance, tariffs and **excises** were to be the primary source of revenue, and they had the greatest impact on people who needed manufactured or imported items but had little hard cash. In addition, Federalists imposed a tax on land, hitting cash-poor farmers especially hard. In 1799, farmers in Northampton County, Pennsylvania, refused to pay the tax and began harassing tax collectors. Several tax resisters were arrested, but an auctioneer named John Fries raised an armed force to break them out of jail. Later, federal troops sent by Adams to suppress what Federalists characterized as Fries's Rebellion arrested Fries and two of his associates. Charged with treason, the three were tried in federal court, found guilty, and condemned to death.

Settlement with France

The Federalists' seeming overreaction to French provocation and domestic protest alienated increasing numbers of Americans. Very soon after the XYZ affair, a small but effective peace movement began to develop. Its aim was to end the Quasi-War with France and to undermine growing Federalist strength. Only three months after Pinckney's confrontation in Paris, George Logan, a Pennsylvania Quaker and Republican, secretly departed for France, where he sought to open the way for a peaceful solution to the diplomatic crisis (see Individual Choices: George Logan). Although, or perhaps because, his mission was disavowed by Adams's government, Logan gained quick admission to see Foreign Minister Talleyrand, who greeted him respectfully and told him that France would gladly receive an American peace **overture.** When Logan returned to America, Adams ignored his cabinet's advice and met with him. Soon thereafter, without consulting his cabinet, Adams instructed the American minister to the Netherlands, William Vans Murray, to lead a delegation to Paris.

Hamilton and his supporters were furious, but the president remained firm, widening the fissure that had opened between Adams and Hamilton during the election in 1796. Adams responded angrily to his Federalist critics. He fired Pickering, Wolcott, and McHenry, Hamilton's primary supporters in his cabinet. In addition, he granted a presidential pardon to the Pennsylvanians who had been condemned after Fries's Rebellion.

Adams's diplomatic appeal to France was well timed. When Murray and his delegation arrived in Paris in November 1799, they found that whatever belligerence still existed toward the United States had been swept away. On November 9, 1799, **Napoleon Bonaparte** had overthrown the government that was responsible for the XYZ affair. Napoleon was more interested in establishing an empire in Europe than in continuing an indecisive conflict with the United States. After some negotiation, Murray and Napoleon drew up and signed the Convention of Mortefontaine, which ended the Quasi-War.

The "Revolution of 1800"

- Before the Federalists left office, what constraints did they try to impose on the incoming Republican president?
- What did Thomas Jefferson mean when he said that "Every difference of opinion is not a difference of principles"?
- How did Republicans choose to deal with Federalist constraints and Jefferson's political agenda?

According to the partisan press, the political situation in 1800 was as simple as the contrast between the personalities of the major presidential candidates. The Republican press characterized Adams as a monarchist and a **spendthrift.** Republican writers

states' rights The political position in favor of limiting federal power to allow the greatest possible self-government by the individual states.

excise A tax on the production, sale, or consumption of a commodity or on the use of a service within a country.

overture An act or proposal designed to initiate a relationship; the first step in negotiating a peace treaty.

Napoleon Bonaparte General who took control of the French government at the end of France's revolutionary period; he eventually proclaimed himself emperor of France and conquered much of the continent of Europe.

spendthrift A person who spends money recklessly or wastefully.

charged that Adams's efforts to expand the powers of the federal government were really attempts to rob citizens of freedom and turn the United States back into a colony of England. In contrast, the Republican press characterized Jefferson as a man of the people, someone who would respond to the appeals of southern and western agricultural groups who felt ignored or abused by northeastern Federalists and their constituents. Farmers in both the South and the West echoed the desire for local **autonomy** voiced in Jefferson's Kentucky Resolution, repeatedly asserting that they wanted freedom from outside interference more than they wanted economic or political stability.

According to Federalist newspapers, however, Vice President Jefferson was a dangerous radical and an atheist, a man who shared French tastes for radical politics, dandyism, and immorality. In the eyes of the Federalists, Adams was a man whose policies and steady-handed administration would bring stability and prosperity, qualities that appealed to manufacturers and merchants in New England, as well as to Calvinists and other supporters of a conservative social and political order.

The Lesser of Republican Evils

As the Federalists approached the election of 1800, the split between the Adams and Hamilton wings of the Federalist faction widened. Disgusted by the president's pacifism and angered by his lack of loyalty to Federalist ideology, the Hamilton wing sought to place a stalwart Federalist in the vice-presidential slot, advancing the candidacy of Charles Cotesworth Pinckney, hero of the XYZ affair.

Having gotten Pinckney that far, Hamilton tried to maneuver the 1800 election as he had the election of 1796. But this time he chose not to leave things quite so much to chance. As the election campaign progressed, the former treasury secretary engaged in direct lobbying and wrote a pamphlet in which he questioned Adams's suitability for the presidency. His essay was so inflammatory that it no doubt would have landed him in jail under the Sedition Act had he been a Republican.

Hamilton's methods backfired. Federalists cast one more vote for Adams than for Pinckney. And Hamilton's scheming and his faction's consistent promanufacturing stance so alienated southern Federalists that many chose to support Jefferson. With Jefferson pulling in the southern vote and his running mate—Burr again—pulling in the craftsmen and small-farm vote in New York, the Republicans

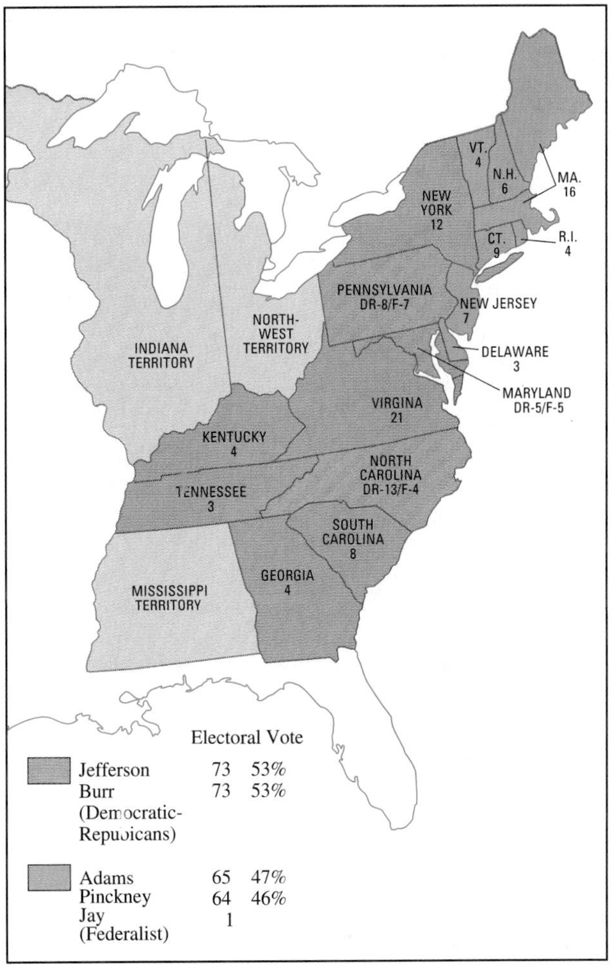

♦ **Map 8.1 Election of 1800** The political partnership between Thomas Jefferson and Aaron Burr allowed the Republicans to unseat Federalist John Adams in the election of 1800. As this map shows, only New England voted as a bloc for the Federalist while Burr's political home, New York, went entirely to Jefferson.

outscored the Federalists by sixteen votes in the Electoral College, but that did not settle the election. Burr and Jefferson had won the same number of electoral votes (see Map 8.1). The tie threw the election into the House of Representatives, which was still stocked with hard-line Federalists elected during the Quasi-War hysteria in 1798.

Undoubtedly many Federalists in the House wished they could overturn the election of 1800 altogether, but the Constitution specifically barred them from doing so. Instead, they faced the task of

autonomy Self-government or the right of self-determination.

INDIVIDUAL CHOICES

Choosing Peace

George Logan

The United States was caught up in a wave of patriotism when the French slighted President Adams's ambassadors in the X, Y, Z affair. Federalists promoted war, but George Logan chose to resist emotionalism and Federalist pressure by going to France to iron out the two nations' difficulties, thus ending the threat of war. "George Logan" by Gilbert Stuart. The Historical Society of Pennsylvania.

The very idea of the United States fighting a war presented a serious personal dilemma for George Logan. He was a loyal American with deep roots in the nation's history—his grandfather James Logan had been one of the first generation of pioneers in Pennsylvania. Like many descendants of Pennsylvania's first families, George was a Quaker and was morally opposed to war. His father, a conscientious objector during the Revolutionary War, had sent him to study medicine in Scotland and Paris while the war continued. Returning to the United States in 1780, George learned that his family was dead and much of the considerable Logan estate had been destroyed.

Some of the family's landholdings had survived, but, Logan noted, his primary inheritance consisted of "piles of utterly depreciated paper currency." He turned to farming to support himself and then, in 1785, to politics, winning a seat in the Pennsylvania assembly. Ever a critic of Federalist economic and diplomatic strategies, he followed his friend Thomas Jefferson as the Republican faction became an opposition party. His became a prominent voice for Republican principles in the Pennsylvania legislature.

By 1798, Logan seemed well on his way to recovering the fortune and prominence that war had robbed him of. But then President John

choosing between two men most of them viewed as dangerous radicals bent on destroying the Federalists' hard work—and perhaps even the republic itself. Their **ambivalence** was plain: in ballot after ballot over six grueling days early in 1801, neither Jefferson nor Burr could win a clear majority of House votes. Burr could have ended the deadlock at any time by withdrawing, but he sat silent, lending some support to Hamilton's description of him as a man whose "public principles have no other spring or aim than his own aggrandizement."

In addition to exhaustion and frustration, two things combined to break the deadlock. First, Hamilton convinced several Federalists that even though Jefferson's rhetoric was dangerous, the Virginian was a gentleman of property and integrity while Burr was "the most dangerous man of the community." Second, Virginia and Pennsylvania mobilized their mili-

ambivalence Mixed feelings or uncertainty.

Adams's peace delegation to France was rebuffed, and as news of the XYZ affair spread, war again seemed inevitable. Recalling his father's frustration as the colonies were drawn into war in 1776, Logan made a fateful choice: he would risk his property, his reputation, even his life, to prevent another war.

Quietly Logan began selling off some of his land, accumulating cash to support a private peace effort. He then went to his friend Jefferson, who gave him letters of introduction to important people in France. Federalist agents learned of Logan's aims and put him under surveillance, but they could not prevent him from sailing for Hamburg, Germany, during the summer of 1798. There he met with Lafayette, who used his influence to get Logan into France and arrange an audience with French foreign minister Talleyrand.

Locked into a war with England, the last thing Talleyrand wanted was to alienate the only other revolutionary and democratic nation in the world. Meeting with Talleyrand and other French officials in early August, Logan capitalized on this fact. He told them that most Americans supported democracy in France but warned that French seizure of American ships and especially the XYZ affair were undermining that support. If the French released the American sailors they were holding and ended the embargo placed on American ships, he assured them, American popular support would turn back to France and force the Federalist government to end the Quasi-War.

Returning from Paris, Logan received a warm welcome from his fellow Republicans and, surprisingly, from President Adams, who ignored his party's advice and immediately sought peace with France. Within a year, William Vans Murray and Napoleon solidified the peace Logan had negotiated. Thus Logan succeeded. Choosing to risk all for peace, he overcame official constraints and averted a war.

Outraged Federalists in Congress responded by passing the "Logan Act," which imposed a fine of $5,000 and a three-year prison term on any American citizen who conducted a private diplomatic mission to a foreign government. Passed after Logan's meetings with Talleyrand, the Logan Act could not be used to punish the courageous Quaker from Pennsylvania for his interference in 1798. In fact, Logan emerged from the whole affair with his reputation and position firmer than ever. He joined the U.S. Senate in 1801, where he remained a Republican force until he retired in 1807.

Logan's principles were to be tested yet again, however. In part because of his success in winning peace between the United States and France, relations with Great Britain began to deteriorate. By 1810 war with England was looming large. Again, Logan risked all for peace. He sailed to England in an effort to get that nation to recognize American neutrality, but this time he failed. Returning to the United States, he might have been prosecuted under the Logan Act, but no charges were brought against him. He retired to his farm in Philadelphia, his name immortalized only in the federal law designed to punish the moral integrity he personified so well.

tias, intent on preventing a "legislative usurpation" of the popular will. As Delaware senator James Bayard described the situation, Federalists had to admit "that we must risk the Constitution and a Civil War or take Mr. Jefferson." Finally, on the thirty-sixth ballot, Jefferson emerged with a clear majority.

Federalists and Republicans agreed about very little, but the threat of civil war frightened both factions equally. Not long after Jefferson's election, both parties aligned briefly to pass the **Twelfth Amendment** to the Constitution, which requires separate balloting in the Electoral College for president and vice president, thereby preventing deadlocks like the one that nearly wrecked the nation in 1800. The new electoral procedure led to new sorts of political intrigues, but the manipulation that Hamilton

Twelfth Amendment Constitutional amendment, ratified in 1804, that provides for separate balloting in the Electoral College for president and vice president.

attempted was no longer possible after the Twelfth Amendment was ratified in 1804.

Federalist Defenses and Loyal Opposition

The Federalists outmaneuvered themselves in the election of 1800 but were not about to leave office without erecting some defenses for the federal structure they had created. The Federalist-controlled judiciary, which had proved its clout during the controversy over the Alien and Sedition Acts, appeared to offer the strongest bulwark against radical tampering with the Constitution. Thus during their last days in office, the Federalist **lame ducks** in Congress passed the **Judiciary Act of 1801**, which created sixteen new federal judgeships, six additional circuit courts, and a massive structure of federal marshals and clerks. President Adams then rushed to fill all these positions with loyal Federalists, signing appointments right up to midnight on his last day in office. The appointments came in such large numbers and so late in the day that **John Marshall**, Adams's secretary of state, was unable to deliver all the appointment letters before his own term ran out. But Marshall did deliver one letter promptly: the one addressed to himself, making him chief justice of the Supreme Court.

♦ This portrait of the young John Marshall, painted in 1801 as he assumed the Chief Justiceship, conveys the vibrancy and willful resolve that would make him the nation's primary legal authority for the next thirty years. *"Chief Justice John Marshall" by Ferret de Saint Memin 1801. Duke University Archives.*

Considering the ill will evident in the Alien and Sedition Acts and the electioneering in 1800, Jefferson's inaugural address was oddly conciliatory. "We are all Republicans; we are all Federalists," Jefferson said, seeming to abandon partisan politics and align himself with those who had recently labeled him a "brandy-soaked defamer of churches" and a "contemptible hypocrite." In his mind, all Americans shared the same fundamental principles—the principles of 1776. But even Jefferson considered the election of 1800 a revolution—"as real a revolution in the principles of our government as that of 1776 was in its form."

Jefferson was right in many respects about the revolutionary nature of the election of 1800. Although his inaugural address preached kinship between Federalists and Republicans, the new president repeatedly criticized his opponents for their lack of faith in democracy and the American people. He vowed to restore the republic—"the world's best hope"—envisioned by revolutionaries twenty-five years before. But unlike the Federalists, Jefferson was unalterably opposed to sedition acts or other government restraints directed against those who opposed his political position. "If there be any among us who would wish to dissolve this Union or to change its republican form," he said, "let them stand undisturbed as monuments of the safety with which error of opinion may be tolerated, where reason is left free to combat it."

In keeping with Jefferson's philosophical commitment to free speech, the Republican Congress let the Sedition Act and the Alien Acts expire in 1801

lame duck An officeholder who has failed to win, or is ineligible for, re-election but whose term in office has not yet ended.

Judiciary Act of 1801 Law that the Federalist Congress passed to increase the number of federal courts and judicial positions; President Adams rushed to fill these positions with Federalists before his term ended.

John Marshall Virginia lawyer and politician whom President Adams made chief justice of the Supreme Court; his legal decisions helped shape the role of the Supreme Court in American government.

and 1802 and did not seek to replace them. Congress also repealed the Naturalization Act, replacing its fourteen-year probationary interval with a five-year naturalization period.

As a result of Jefferson's reconciliatory address, the nation began to share the president's view that "Every difference of opinion is not a difference of principles." Even extreme Federalists like Fisher Ames came to understand that "party is an association of honest men for honest purposes, and when the State falls into bad hands, is the only efficient defense; a champion who never flinches, a watchman who never sleeps." Ames went on to describe how a loyal **opposition party** should behave. "We are not to revile or abuse magistrates, or lie even for good cause," he said. "We must act as good citizens, using only truth, and argument, and zeal to impress them." With parties such as these, a system of loyal opposition could become a permanent part of a republican government without risk to security or freedom. Thus the election of 1800 launched what would become the two-party political tradition in the United States.

Confident in Americans' ability to reason, Jefferson outlined a plan for a "wise and frugal government" that would seek "Equal and exact justice to all men of whatever state or persuasion, religious or political." He would, he said, support state governments "in all their rights" but would not tear down the federal structure or fail to pay its debts.

Madison Versus the Midnight Appointments

Aware of the purpose behind the Judiciary Act of 1801 and Adams's midnight appointments, Republicans sought to reverse Federalist control of the justice system. In January 1802, Republicans in Congress moved to repeal the Judiciary Act of 1801, arguing that the new circuit courts were outrageously expensive and unnecessary. Federalists countered that if Congress repealed the act, it would in effect be terminating judges for reasons other than the "high crimes and misdemeanors" mentioned in the Constitution, thereby violating the separation of powers. Congress proceeded anyway, replacing the Judiciary Act of 1801 with the Judiciary Act of 1802, and awaited the response of the Federalist courts.

The **constitutionality** of the new Judiciary Act was never tested, but the power of the judicial branch to interpret and enforce federal law did become a major issue during the following year. On taking office, Jefferson's secretary of state James Madison held back the appointment letters that John Marshall had been unable to deliver before the expiration of his term. One jilted appointee was William Marbury, who was to have been justice of the peace for the newly created District of Columbia. Marbury, with the support of his party, filed suit in the Supreme Court, claiming Section 13 of the Judiciary Act of 1789 gave the Court the power to issue an order demanding that Madison deliver Marbury's appointment letter.

Marbury v. Madison was Chief Justice Marshall's first major case, and in it he proved his political as well as his judicial ingenuity. Marshall was certain that the Judiciary Act of 1789 required Madison to deliver the appointment letter, but the chief justice was keenly aware that if he ordered Madison to deliver it and Madison refused, the Court did not have the power to enforce the order. In such a direct confrontation between the executive and judicial branches, Marshall was sure to lose. Rather than risking a serious blow to the dignity of the Supreme Court, Marshall ruled in 1803 that the Constitution contained no provision for the Supreme Court to issue such orders as the Judiciary Act of 1789 required and that therefore the law was unconstitutional.

With this ruling, Marshall deftly placed the political shoe on the other foot. Jefferson and Madison accepted Marshall's decision because it meant they did not have to place Adams's handpicked men in powerful judicial positions. But it also meant that the authors of the Virginia and Kentucky Resolutions had to acknowledge that in at least some cases the Supreme Court had the right to determine the constitutionality of federal laws. Although this **precedent** for **judicial review** did not immediately invalidate

opposition party A political party opposed to the party or government in power.

constitutionality Agreement with the principles or provisions of the Constitution.

Marbury v. Madison Supreme Court decision (1803) declaring part of the Judiciary Act of 1789 unconstitutional, establishing an important precedent in favor of judicial review.

precedent An event or decision that may be used as an example in similar cases later on.

judicial review The power of the Supreme Court to review the constitutionality of laws passed by Congress and by the states.

the principles set forth in Jefferson's and Madison's earlier **manifestos,** it established the principle that federal courts, rather than states, could decide the constitutionality of acts of Congress.

The War on the Courts

Marshall's decision in *Marbury v. Madison* gave the Republicans the power to withhold undelivered letters of appointment from the Adams administration, but it gave them no power to control the behavior of judges whose appointments were already official. Thus, in the aftermath of the *Marbury* decision, Republican radicals in Congress decided to wage war on particularly partisan Federalist judges.

John Pickering of New Hampshire was an easy target. An alcoholic who suffered from mental illness, he was known to rave incoherently both on and off the bench, usually about the evils of Jefferson and republicanism. No one, not even staunch Federalists, doubted that the besotted man was incompetent, but it was far from certain that he had committed the "high crimes and misdemeanors," for which he was **impeached.** Whether he had or not, the Senate found him guilty and removed him from office.

Emboldened by that easy victory and armed with a powerful precedent, radical Republicans took on what was expected to be the first in a series of more challenging opponents, Supreme Court justice Samuel Chase. A signer of the Declaration of Independence and a die-hard Federalist, Chase was notorious for making partisan decisions—like the conviction of Republican journalist James Callender under the Sedition Act and condemning John Fries to death—and for using the federal bench as an anti-Republican soapbox. Many felt that with the radical Republican vice president Aaron Burr presiding over the impeachment proceedings, the Senate would easily convict Chase, opening the way to remove any fiercely anti-Republican judge. Burr, however, surprised everyone by conducting the trial with enormous decorum and impartiality, giving Chase every opportunity to defend himself. In the end, both Federalists and many Republicans voted to dismiss the charges, returning Chase to his position on the Supreme Court. The Republican radicals' failure to impeach Chase reinforced Jefferson's authority in calling for conciliation. The radicals now had little choice but to accept Jefferson's leadership or bolt the party.

Republicanism in Action

- What were Jefferson's expectations for American development?
- What policies did he choose to meet those expectations?

When Jefferson assumed office, he ushered a new spirit into national politics and the presidency. He was the first president to preside in the new national capital, the still largely uncompleted Washington City. A combination of circumstances and personal preferences moved him to lead a much simpler life than his predecessors in office had led. He refused, for example, to ride in a carriage, choosing to go by horseback through Washington's muddy and rutted streets. He continued to give parties as he had done in Paris, but he sat his guests at a round table so that no one could be seen as more important than anyone else. He abandoned the fashion of wearing a wig, letting his red hair stand out, and he sometimes entertained wearing frayed slippers and work clothes.

Despite this show of simplicity and his conciliatory inaugural address, Jefferson was a hardworking politician and administrator who sought to turn the nation around with all possible speed. He quickly launched a program to renovate the American economy and give the United States a place in the international community. Along the way, he captured Americans' affection and their political loyalty.

Jefferson's Vision for America

Jefferson had a strong, positive vision for the nation, and the party made every effort to put his policies into effect. He embraced a specific notion of proper political, economic, and social behavior. The greatest dangers to a republic, he believed, were high population density and the social evils it generated, and the concentration of money in the hands of a few. Accordingly, Jefferson wanted to steer America away from the large-scale, publicly supported industry of Hamilton's vision and toward an economy founded on yeoman farmers—men who owned

manifesto A written statement publicly declaring the views of its author.

impeach To formally charge a public official with criminal conduct in office; once Congress has impeached a federal official, the official is then tried in the Senate on the stated charges.

♦ Suffering a life-long sensitivity to cold as well as a dislike for formality, Thomas Jefferson usually chose to dress practically, in fairly plain clothes that kept him warm. This 1822 portrait by Thomas Sully captures the former president in his customary greatcoat, unadorned suit, and well-worn boots. *"Thomas Jefferson" by Thomas Sully, West Point Museum, United States Military Academy, West Point, N.Y.*

their own land, produced their own food, and were beholden to no one. Such men, Jefferson believed, could make political decisions based solely on pure reason and good sense.

But Jefferson was not naive. He knew Americans would continue to demand the comforts and luxuries found in industrial societies. His solution was simple. In America's vast lands, he said, a nation of farmers could produce so much food that "its surplus [could] go to nourish the now perishing births of Europe, who in return would manufacture and send us in exchange our clothes and other comforts." Overpopulation and **urbanization**—the twin causes of corruption in Europe—would not occur in America, for here, Jefferson said, "the immense extent of uncultivated and fertile lands enables every one who will labor, to marry young, and to raise a family of any size. Our food, then, may increase geometrically with our laborers, and our births, however multiplied, become effective."

Making such a system work would require a radical change in economic policy. The government would have to let businesses make their own decisions and succeed or fail in a marketplace free of government interference. In an economy with absolutely free trade and an open marketplace, the iron law of **supply and demand** would determine the cost of goods and services. This view of the economy was a direct assault on mercantilist notions of governments controlling prices and restricting trade to benefit the nation-state.

Jefferson believed that free trade in a truly open international economy would benefit the United States because there was a shortage of raw materials and foodstuffs in war-torn and overcrowded Europe but an oversupply of manufactured items. If the European nations could be convinced to drop trade restrictions and let the marketplace decide the value of goods, the iron law of supply and demand would ensure profits for American producers and shippers.

Responsibility for planning and implementing this economic policy fell to Treasury Secretary **Albert Gallatin.** Gallatin's first effort as secretary of the treasury was to try to settle the nation's debts. His goal was to make the United States entirely debt free by 1817. With Jefferson's approval, Gallatin implemented a radical course of budget cutting, going so far as to close several American embassies overseas to save money. At home, Gallatin and Jefferson pared administrative costs by reducing staff and putting an end to the fancy receptions and other social events that President Adams had so enjoyed. The administration cut the military by half, reducing the army from four thousand to twenty-five hundred men and the navy from twenty-five ships to a mere seven.

In selecting the sorts of cuts he did, Gallatin subtly weakened the central government's economic presence, putting more responsibilities onto

urbanization The growth of cities in a nation or region and the shifting of the population from rural to urban areas.

supply and demand The two factors that determine price in an economy based on private property: (1) how much of a commodity is available (supply) and (2) how badly people want it (demand).

Albert Gallatin Treasury secretary in Jefferson's administration; he favored limited government and reduced the federal debt by cutting spending.

♦ Jefferson's efforts to stop Barbary pirate extortion nearly ended in tragedy when the pirate fleet captured the American frigate *Philadelphia* (center), which they might have turned to their own use. A young naval officer named Stephen Decater turned the tide when he sailed the smaller *Intrepid* (left) past the defenses in Tripoli harbor and burned the *Philadelphia* at her moorings. *Courtesy of the Mariners Museum, Newport News, Virginia.*

the states, where his and Jefferson's philosophy said they belonged. In addition, Gallatin's plan called for a significant change in how the government raised money. In 1802, the Republican Congress repealed all internal taxes, leaving customs duties and the sale of western lands as the sole sources of federal revenue. With this one sweeping gesture, Gallatin struck a major blow for Jefferson's economic vision by tying the nation's financial future to westward expansion and foreign trade.

The success of the economic policy that Gallatin and Jefferson were trying to implement depended to a large extent on Jefferson's skillful handling of foreign affairs. During Jefferson's presidency, two foreign issues loomed large. One was the need to maintain and enhance navigation on North America's inland waterways. The other was the need to ensure unrestricted trade and free navigation of the open seas. Scheming by France and Spain posed a major challenge to the first of these, and pirates threatened the other.

War in the Mediterranean

During Jefferson's first term, a challenge to free trade came from pirates who patrolled the northern coast of Africa from Tangier to Tripoli, controlling access to the Mediterranean Sea. Ever since gaining independence, the United States had been paying the Barbary pirates not to attack American ships (see page 189). By 1800, fully a fifth of the federal budget was earmarked for this purpose, a cost Gallatin wished to see eliminated as he tried to balance the nation's books. To Jefferson, principle was as important as financial considerations. "Peace is our passion," he announced. But noting that "tribute or war is the usual alternative of these Barbary pirates," Jefferson decided on war. Asserting presidential privilege as commander-in-chief, he dispatched navy ships to the Mediterranean in 1801.

The war that followed was far from successful from anyone's point of view. After some indecisive engagements between the American fleet and the pirates, Jefferson's navy suffered a major defeat with the capture of its prize warship, the *Philadelphia,* and its entire crew. A bold but unsuccessful attempt to assault Tripoli by land across the Libyan desert led only to a threat to kill the crew of the *Philadelphia* and other hostages. The war dragged along until 1805, when the United States finally negotiated peace terms, agreeing to pay $60,000 for the release of the hostages, and the pirates promised to halt pirate raids on American shipping.

Crisis in America's Interior

The threat to inland navigation within North America came as the result of a deal between France and Spain. As settlers continued to pour into the region between the Appalachian Mountains and the Mississippi River, the commercial importance of the Mississippi and the rivers flowing into it increased. Whoever controlled the mouth of the Mississippi—the place where it flows past New Orleans and into the Gulf of Mexico—would have the power to make or break the economy of the interior.

In accordance with Pinckney's treaty of 1795 (see page 214), Spain had granted American farmers the right to ship cargoes down the Mississippi without paying tolls, and Spain had given American merchants permission to transship goods from New Orleans to Atlantic ports without paying export duties. In 1800, however, Napoleon had traded some of France's holdings in southern Europe to Spain in exchange for Spain's land in North America. Because the United States had no agreement with France concerning navigation on the Mississippi, the deal between Spain and France threatened to scuttle American commerce on the river, especially if the aggressive Napoleon decided to extend his vision of conquest into the New World. Such fears took on substance when, preparatory to the transfer of the land to France, Spanish officials suspended free trade in New Orleans.

Jefferson responded on two fronts. Backing away from his usual anti-British position, he announced, "The day France takes possession of New Orleans we must marry ourselves to the British fleet and nation," and he dispatched James Monroe to Europe to talk with the British about a military alliance. He also had Monroe instruct the American minister to France, Robert Livingston, that he could spend as much as $2 million to try to purchase New Orleans and as much adjacent real estate as possible.

Napoleon may have been considering the creation of a Caribbean empire when he acquired Louisiana from Spain. Rich with sugar, the island of **Santo Domingo** was strategically well placed to serve as a hub for French exploitation of the North American interior. France and Spain had shared ownership of the island until a slave army under the leadership of a former slave named **François Dominique Toussaint L'Ouverture** liberated the French half in 1791 and the Spanish half ten years later. With backing from the French, Toussaint made himself president of the unified nation, but in 1802 Napoleon betrayed him by sending an invasion force to reclaim Santo Domingo, raising fears among Americans that the French army's next destination would be New Orleans.

The French army was able to defeat and capture Toussaint, but was not able to leave Santo Domingo. The rebels' military skills combined with yellow fever, malaria, and other tropical diseases to destroy the French force. By this time Napoleon, intent now on extending his holdings in Europe, was seeking to raise money to finance a continental war. Thus, by the time James Monroe and Robert Livingston entered into negotiations with the French, Napoleon had instructed Foreign Minister Talleyrand to offer the whole of Louisiana to the Americans for $15 million.

♦ With backing from the French, François Dominique Toussaint L'Ouverture (center) led his fellow slaves in a revolt against their French and Spanish masters, driving the Europeans from the West Indian island of Santo Domingo in 1791. Emperor Napoleon Bonaparte double-crossed L'Ouverture in 1802, sending a French army to seize the island. Although L'Ouverture was captured, his army defeated the French, creating the republic of Haiti in 1804. *"Toussaint L'Ouverture" by William Edouard Scott. Amistad Research Center, New Orleans, AFAC Collection.*

The Louisiana Purchase

Although Livingston and Monroe had been authorized to spend only $2 million, they jumped at the

Santo Domingo Caribbean island (now called Hispaniola) shared by the modern nations of Haiti and the Dominican Republic.

François Dominique Toussaint L'Ouverture Black revolutionary who liberated the island of Santo Domingo, only to see it reinvaded by the French in 1802.

A gull for the People
Two Millions!
The PRAIRIE DOG sickened at the sting of the HORNET
or a Diplomatic Puppet exhibiting his Deceptions!

♦ Although Jefferson's aggressive geographical expansion policies were popular with most Americans during his first administration, not everyone agreed. This political cartoon illustrates his critics' perspective. Napoleon, styled as a hornet, stings prairie dog Jefferson, forcing him to cough up "Two Millions" in gold coins (the price offered to the French to pressure Spain into selling Florida to the United States) while his "diplomatic puppet"displays two secret bills Jefferson had submitted asking Congress to authorize the purchase. *Library of Congress.*

deal, hoping that President Jefferson would approve. The president not only approved but was overjoyed. The deal offered three important benefits for Jefferson and the nation. It removed one European power—France—from the continent and saved Jefferson from having to ally the United States with Britain. It secured the Mississippi River for shipments of American agricultural products to industrial Europe. And it doubled of the size of the United States, opening uncharted new expanses for settlement by yeoman farmers.

The **Louisiana Purchase** was immensely popular among most Americans but raised significant constitutional issues that helped to keep party divisions alive. The framers of the Constitution had made no provision for the acquisition of new territories by the United States. Opponents of the Louisiana Purchase—mostly northeastern Federalists who feared the dilution of their political and economic power—asserted that the nation was prohibited from extending westward beyond its then-current boundaries without specific constitutional authorization. Ignoring the constitutional issue, Jefferson submitted the purchase to Congress for ratification in November 1803, winning an overwhelming majority. He later defended this action, stating that "Strict observance to the written laws is doubtless one of the high duties of a good citizen, but it is not the highest. The laws of necessity, of self-preservation, of saving our country when in danger, are of a higher obligation."

Even before the Louisiana Purchase, "laws of necessity" had led Jefferson to assert presidential power in an unusual way. Although Spanish, French, and American fur traders, outlaws, and soldiers of fortune had crisscrossed Louisiana over the years, little systematic exploration had been done. When rumors of the land transfer between France and Spain began circulating, Jefferson started preparations to send his private secretary, **Meriwether Lewis,** and a small party into the territory to take a look at the land (see Map 8.2). In a series of confidential letters, Jefferson informed Lewis and his co-commander, Indian fighter **William Clark,** that they were to pretend that scientific research was their sole mission, and the president issued them false papers to that effect. Their primary mission, however, was to note the numbers of French, Spanish, and other agents in the area, along with the numbers and condition of the Indians, and to chart major wa-

Louisiana Purchase The U.S. purchase of Louisiana from France for $15 million in 1803; the Louisiana Territory extended from the Mississippi River to the Rocky Mountains.

Meriwether Lewis Jefferson aide who was sent to explore the Louisiana Territory in 1803; he later served as its governor.

William Clark Soldier and explorer who joined Meriwether Lewis on the expedition to explore the Louisiana Territory; he was responsible for mapmaking.

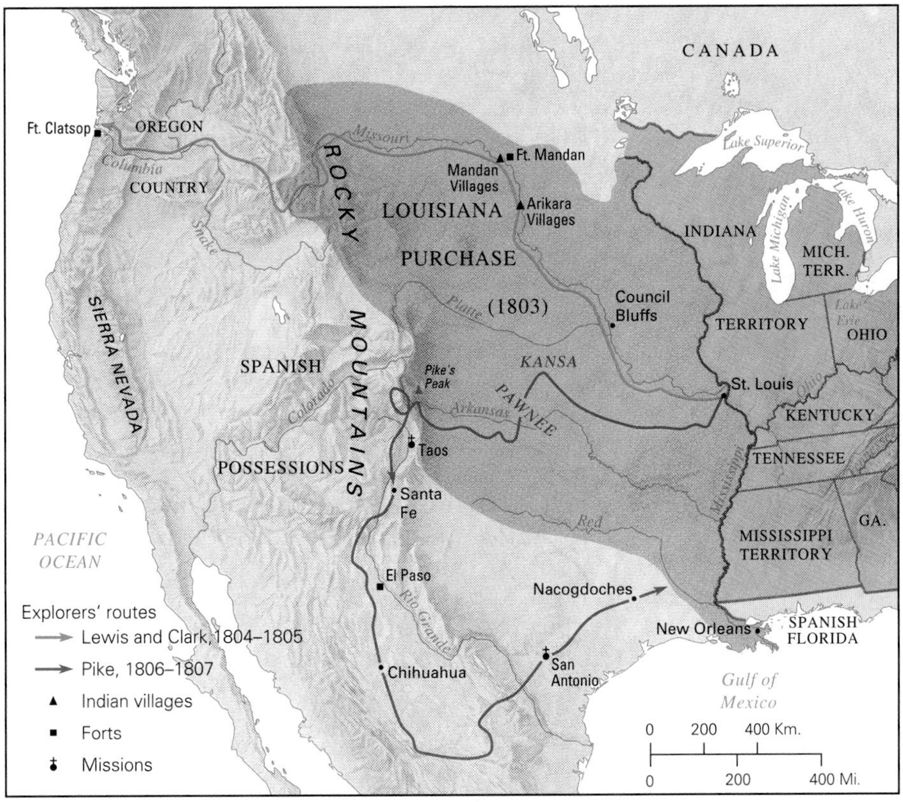

♦ **Map 8.2 Louisiana Purchase and the Lewis and Clark Expedition** As this map shows, President Jefferson added an enormous tract of land to the United States when he purchased Louisiana from France in 1803. The president was eager to learn as much as possible about the new territory and sent two exploration teams into the West. In addition to collecting information, Lewis and Clark's and Pike's expeditions sought to commit Indian groups along their paths to alliances with the United States and to undermine French, Spanish, and British relations with the Indians, even in those areas that were not officially part of the United States.

terways and other important strategic sites. They were also to open the way for direct dealings between the Indians and the United States, undermining the Indians' relations with the Spanish and French whenever possible. Early in 1803, months before Congress authorized the Louisiana Purchase, the president sought and received a secret congressional **appropriation** granting the funds necessary to finance the mission.

The expedition set out by boat in the spring of 1804. Pushing its way up the Missouri River, the party arrived among the **Mandan** Indians in present-day North Dakota in the late fall. By that time heavy snow blocked the passes through the mountains to the west, and the expedition stayed among the Mandans through the winter. This forced pause may have ensured the expedition's success. The Mandans were a settled agricultural group who had been farming along the upper Missouri for over a thousand years. Unlike many of their neighbors, they had resisted the temptation to abandon their villages for mounted buffalo hunting when horses had arrived on the northern plains after 1700. Their villages, which offered food and shelter for the wandering hunting tribes, soon became hubs in the evolving Plains trading and raiding system (see pages 50, 536–537). By wintering with the Mandans, the expedition came into contact with many of the Indian and European groups that participated in the

appropriation Public funds set aside for a specific purpose.

Mandans A Siouan-speaking Native American group that lived in permanent villages and practiced agriculture in the Red River valley in present-day North Dakota; they hosted the Lewis and Clark expedition during the winter of 1804.

♦ This Mandan Indian buffalo robe illustrates some of the military information Lewis and Clark acquired on their expedition. It depicts the continuing military struggle between the Mandans and the various Sioux nations. Lewis and Clark played on such intergroup rivalries, offering to provide arms and other supplies to groups like the Mandans in exchange for their diplomatic and military alliance with the United States. *Peabody Museum, Harvard University. Photograph by Hillel Burger.*

complicated economy of the West. Lewis and Clark acted on Jefferson's secret instructions by learning all they could from the Mandans and their visitors about the fur trade, the nature of military alliances, and the tribes that lived farther west.

One particularly important contact Lewis and Clark made during the Mandan winter was with a French trapper named Charbono and his Shoshone wife **Sacajawea.** Between the two of them, Sacajawea and Charbono spoke most of the languages understood by the Indians in the Far West, and both possessed vast knowledge about the geography and the various peoples in the area. With their help, Lewis and Clark were able to make contact with the Shoshones, who aided them in crossing the Rocky Mountains. From there, the expedition passed from Indian group to Indian group along a chain of friendship. The Nez Perce Indians, for example, were allied to the Shoshones and accepted the party hospitably. The Nez Perces then sent word down the Columbia River that these men were allies, ensuring their safe and speedy passage. Following this chain of Indian hospitality, the expedition finally reached the Pacific Ocean in November 1805.

After wintering near the mouth of the Columbia River, the party retraced its steps back through the Indian alliance system, finally arriving back in the United States in the fall of 1806. In addition to a wealth of curios and volumes of new information about lands never systematically explored before, Lewis and Clark also brought news of friendly Indians who had accepted the party as allies and promised to join in friendship with the new American republic. It appeared that the United States had gained recognition as a player in the vast and complicated world of economics and diplomacy that existed in the Great Plains and Rocky Mountain West.

But while many Native American groups genuinely welcomed Lewis and Clark, others remained dubious about the newcomers. On the return trip, part of the expedition had ventured off its original outward course to explore new territory and had encountered a party of Blackfoot Indians. Allied closely with trading interests in Canada and involved in sporadic war with the Shoshones, the Blackfeet were not at all friendly, seeing the Americans as a dangerous unsettling factor in Plains diplomacy. The Indians attacked the expedition, but the Americans were able to fight them off long enough to make a strategic retreat.

Europeans in the interior were also fearful of American disruption and competiton. In 1806, Lieutenant Zebulon M. Pike set out on a venture to explore the territory between the Missouri and Red rivers south of Lewis and Clark's route. The Pawnee and Kansa Indians in the region received Pike with great reserve, pointing out that the Spanish had recently sent an army through their territory demanding Indian allegiance. Undaunted, Pike continued his journey by following the trail left by the Spanish force, eventually arriving in what is now Colorado (see Map 8.2). From there, he pushed southward in search of the Red River but blundered into New Mexico, where he and his party were captured by a Spanish army detachment. After three months in Spanish hands, Pike and his men were finally escorted back to the United States and set free with a warning to stay out of Spanish lands and Spanish affairs.

Sacajawea Shoshone woman who served as guide and interpreter on the Lewis and Clark expedition.

Challenge and Uncertainty in Jefferson's America

• How did the expectations of most Americans change during Jefferson's presidency?

• What were Jeffersonians' expectations concerning Native Americans and African Americans? What constraints faced each group during the Jeffersonian era?

Jefferson's policies not only put the nation on a new road politically and economically but brought a new spirit into the land. The Virginian's commitment to opportunity and progress, to openness and frugality, offered a stark contrast in approach and style to the policies of his predecessors. The congressional elections of 1802 and the presidential election of 1804 proved Jefferson's popularity and the strong appeal of the Republican party. Nevertheless, some disturbing social and intellectual undercurrents began to surface during his second term. National expansion strained conventional social institutions as white farmers, entrepreneurs, and adventurers seized the opportunities that Republican economic and expansion policies offered. Adding to the strain was the fact that the Jeffersonian spirit was more of a promise than a commitment and Jefferson's vision for the republic excluded some people.

The Heritage of Partisan Politics

The popularity of Jefferson's party was abundantly clear in 1804. Jefferson had won an extremely narrow victory in 1800, and his Republican party had won significant but less-than-overwhelming majorities in Congress. The congressional elections of 1802, however, had virtually eclipsed Federalist power, and Federalists faced the presidential election of 1804 with dread. Former president John Adams commented that "the power of the Administration rests upon the support of a much stronger majority of the people throughout the Union than the former administrations ever possessed since the first establishment of the Constitution."

Despite an abiding faith in the emerging two-party system, Federalist leader Fisher Ames withdrew from public life, followed by John Jay and other prominent leaders. Some traditional Federalists, however, continued to fight. The party tapped former vice-presidential candidate Charles Cotesworth Pinckney to head the 1804 presidential ticket. For the vice presidency, the Federalists chose Rufus King, a defender of the notion of loyal opposition and the two-party system.

Considering the apparent success of Jefferson's policies during his first administration, Federalists had trouble identifying issues on which to build a viable campaign. Hoping to capitalize on **anti-expansionist** fears in New England and sentiments favoring states' rights in the South, the Federalists focused their campaign on Jefferson's acquisition of Louisiana. In a direct appeal to Yankee frugality, Federalists charged that Jefferson had paid too much for the new territory and was attempting to use the region to build a unified antimercantile political faction. Pinckney focused on Jefferson's use of presidential, hence federal, power to acquire the new territory, in contradiction of the president's own Kentucky Resolution.

Jefferson just needed to point to his record in office. Although some Republicans felt that the president had departed from his principles by purchasing Louisiana and in some other matters, they could not question his overall success in accomplishing Republican goals. During his first administration, Jefferson had eliminated internal taxes, encouraged westward migration, eliminated the hated Alien and Sedition Acts, and fostered hope in the hearts of many disaffected Americans.

He also had proved that he was no threat to national commerce or to individual affluence. Under Alexander Hamilton's influence, America's international earnings from commercial activities had doubled during the 1790s, but despite Federalist fears, the same growth rate continued during Jefferson's tenure in office. In the process, those who engaged in international trade amassed enormous fortunes. Such economic growth permitted Jefferson to maintain a favorable **balance of payments** throughout his first administration, a feat unachieved by his predecessors. And with Gallatin's help, Jefferson had proved his fiscal responsibility by building up a multi-million-dollar treasury surplus without borrowing money or enacting new taxes.

The enormous scope of Jefferson's successes and the limited scope of his opponent's platform helped

anti-expansionist Opposed to the policy of expanding a country by acquiring new territory.

balance of payments The difference between of a nation's total payments to foreign countries and its total receipts from abroad.

swing the election of 1804 firmly over to the Republicans. Jefferson won 162 electoral votes to Pinckney's 14, carrying every state except Connecticut and Delaware.

Westward Expansion and Social Stress

One source of political concern, especially among old-line Federalists, was the startling growth of the West and its emergence as a powerful political force likely to overwhelm northeastern dominance in government. A baby boom had followed the Revolution, and by 1810 a massive population of young adults grabbed at Jefferson's frontier vision. As new territories opened in the West, people streamed into the region at a rate that alarmed many. The population of Ohio, for example, grew from 45,000 in 1800 to 231,000 in 1810, and similar rates of growth occurred in the new states of Tennessee and Kentucky and in territories from Louisiana north to Michigan and west to Missouri. Business interests in the East were alarmed because they saw westward expansion drawing off population, which in time would drive up the price of labor and reduce profits. Authorities in the West, meanwhile, found the increase frightening as they tried to deal with the practical matters of maintaining governments, economies, and peaceful relations among the new settlers and between the settlers and neighboring Indians.

Most of the people who moved west hoped to achieve the agrarian self-sufficiency that Jefferson advocated, but life in the West was far from what Jefferson had hoped it would be. Inexpensive, reliable transportation was impossible in the vast, rugged interior, and Jefferson's notion of breadbasket America trading with industrial Europe was doomed without it. No navigable streams ran eastward from America's interior, across the Appalachians, to the Atlantic, and the ridges of those mountains made road building extremely difficult.

Only two reliable routes existed for transporting produce from the interior to shipping centers in the East. The Ohio-Mississippi-Missouri drainage system provided a reliable watercourse, and huge cargoes flowed along its stream. Shipping goods on the Mississippi, however, was a dangerous and expensive operation. Because of the river's strong current, loads could be shipped only one way—downstream. Rafts were built for the purpose and then were broken up and sold for lumber in New Orleans. Shippers had to return home by foot on the **Natchez Trace**. On both legs of the journey, travelers risked attack by river pirates, Indians, and sickness. Moreover, it was virtually impossible for shippers to take manufactured goods back with them because of the condition of the roads and the distances involved.

The other river route—the St. Lawrence River, flowing east from the Great Lakes to the northern Atlantic—presented similar problems. Transporting goods upstream against the current was impossible. Another drawback was that the river crossed British territory.

As a result of geographical isolation and the rapid pace of settlement, the economy in the West became highly localized. Settlers arriving with neither food nor seed bought surplus crops produced by established farmers. The little capital that was generated in this way supported the development of local industries in the hundreds of farming villages. Enterprising craftsmen ranging from **coopers** to wheelwrights produced hand-manufactured items on demand.

As long as people kept moving into an area, local economies boomed. But when new arrivals stopped coming in, the market for surplus crops and local manufactures collapsed, and the economy went bust. Swinging from boom to bust and back again became a way of life in newly settled areas.

Along with economic instability, social instability was also common. The odd mixture of ethnic, religious, and national groups that made their way to western villages did little to bring cohesiveness to community life. Most of the population consisted of young men; there were few women or older people to encourage stable behavior.

The expansion of the American West also had an unsettling effect on communities in the East. During the eighteenth century, older people maintained authority by controlling the distribution of land to their children. With only so much worthwhile land to go around, sons and daughters lived with and worked for their parents until their elders saw fit to deed property over to them. As a result, children living in the East generally did not become independent—that is, they did not become church members, marry, or operate their own farms or businesses—until they were in their thirties. Economic opportunities available on the frontier, however, lessened young peo-

Natchez Trace A road connecting Natchez, Mississippi, with Nashville, Tennessee; it was commercially and strategically important in the late eighteenth and early nineteenth centuries.

cooper A person who makes or repairs wooden barrels.

♦ The Mississippi River drainage system was the only reliable transportation route for Americans moving into the West during the early 1800s. Farmers moved produce to market on keelboats like the one depicted in this painting by Karl Bodmer. The problem with this mode of transport was that the current on the giant river made upstream travel impossible during much of the year, so boats like this one were often sold for lumber after they reached New Orleans. *"Ohio-Mississippi River Keelboat" by Karl Bodmer, 1832. Maximilian-Bodmer Collection, Joslyn Art Museum.*

ple's need to rely on their parents for support and lowered the age at which they began to break away.

During the early part of the nineteenth century, the age at which children attained independence fell steadily. By the 1820s, children were joining churches in their teens and marrying in their early-to-mid twenties. Breathing the new air of independence, intrepid young people moved out of their parents' homes, migrating westward to find land and new opportunities.

The Religious Response to Social Change

The changes taking place in the young republic stirred conflicting religious currents. One was **rationalism** in religious thought. The other was a new **evangelicalism.**

Many members of the revolutionary generation—including radicals like Jefferson, Franklin, and Paine—embraced the French Enlightenment notion of **deism.** They viewed God as a vague "first cause," a watchmaker of sorts, whose universe was a perfectly crafted machine that had been left to run itself according to rational laws. Religion had to be plain, reasonable, and verifiable in order to be acceptable to such rationalists. Jefferson, for example, edited his own version of the Bible, keeping only the moral principles and the solid historical facts and discarding anything supernatural. Thomas Paine went even further, rejecting Christianity altogether as irrational, the "strangest religion ever set up," because "it committed a murder upon Jesus in order to redeem mankind from the sin of eating an apple."

Rationalism also began to permeate mainstream religion. During the revolutionary period, some New England Congregationalists began to question the doctrine of **predestination,** emphasizing the individual's role in salvation and especially the significance of the use of reason in that pursuit. Like Jefferson, these rationalist reformers rejected much of the mystery in Christian faith, including the ideas of the **Trinity** and Christ's divinity. **Unitarianism,** as this rationalist form of Christian worship came to be called, grew by leaps and bounds during the Revolution and finally came into its own while Jefferson was president. Unitarians even captured control of Harvard College, formerly the educational heart of orthodox Puritan America.

Unitarianism and other forms of rational thought held great appeal for a young generation on the

rationalism The theory that the exercise of reason, rather than the acceptance of authority or spiritual revelation, is the only valid basis for belief and the best source of spiritual truth.

evangelicalism Protestant movements that stress the importance of personal conversion and salvation by faith.

deism The belief that God created the universe in such a way that no divine intervention was necessary for its continued operation.

predestination The doctrine that God has predetermined everything that happens, including the final salvation or damnation of each person.

Trinity The Christian belief that God consists of three divine persons: Father, Son, and Holy Spirit.

Unitarianism A religion that denies the Trinity, teaching that God exists only in one person; it also stresses individual freedom of belief and the free use of reason in religion.

♦ Evangelical denominations gained ever wider followings during the early nineteenth century as the uncertainties accompanying rapid expansion took their toll on national self-confidence. Mass baptisms like this one painted by Russian tourist Pavel Svinin celebrated the emotional moment of conversion and the individual's rebirth as a Christian. *"A Philadelphia Anabaptist Immersion During a Storm" by Pavel Svinin. The Metropolitan Museum of Art, Rogers Fund, 1942. (42.95.20)*

move, especially people in fast-growing port cities like Boston. In a nation where young people were carving out economic lives for themselves in the worlds of commerce and manufacturing, the notion that they were powerless to effect their own salvation seemed increasingly ridiculous. Rationalism gave young people a vehicle by which to empower themselves spiritually, just as they were empowering themselves economically, socially, and politically.

While deism and Unitarianism were gaining strong footholds in eastern cities, disorder, insecurity, and missionizing activities were helping to foster a very different kind of religious response in the West. Although Methodists, Baptists, Presbyterians, and evangelical Congregationalists disagreed on many specific principles, they all emphasized the spirited preaching that could bring about the emotional moment of conversion—that moment of realization that one is damned and can be saved only by the grace of God. Each of these denominations concentrated on training a new, young ministry and sending it to preach in every corner of the nation. In this way, another religious awakening swept across America, beginning in Cane Ridge, Kentucky, in 1801 and spreading throughout the South and West.

The new evangelicalism stressed the individual's role in salvation but at the same time emphasized the importance of Christian community. Looking back to the first generation of Puritans in America, the new evangelicals breathed new life into the old Puritan notion of God's plan for the universe and the leading role that Americans were to play in its unfolding. As early-nineteenth-century Presbyterian divine Lyman Beecher put it, "It was the opinion of [Jonathan] Edwards that the millennium would commence in America. When I first encountered this opinion, I thought it Chimerical [imaginary]: but all providential signs of the times lend corroboration to it."

Early-nineteenth-century evangelicals formed official synods, councils, and conventions as well as hundreds of voluntary associations designed to carry out God's plan for America. These organizations helped to counterbalance the forces of extreme individualism and social disorder by providing ideological underpinnings for the expansive behavior of westerners and a sense of mission to ease the insecurities produced by venturing into the unknown. They also provided an institutional framework that brought some stability to communities in which traditional controls were lacking. These attractive features helped evangelicalism to sweep across the West. During the early nineteenth century it overtook rationalism as the dominant religious persuasion in that region.

The Problem of Race in Jefferson's Republic

Jefferson's policies enabled many Americans to benefit from the nation's development, but they certainly did not help everyone. Neither Indians nor

Benjamin Bannaker's
PENNSYLVANIA, DELAWARE, MARY-
LAND, AND VIRGINIA
ALMANAC,
FOR THE
YEAR of our LORD 1795;
Being the Third after Leap-Year.
BANNAKER.
PHILADELPHIA:
Printed for WILLIAM GIBBONS, Cherry Street

♦ A celebrated mathematician, engineer, and surveyor, Benjamin Bannaker was one of a handful of African Americans who attained celebrity in Jefferson's America. This almanac, published in 1795, demonstrated Bannaker's scientific knowledge and was one of the reasons for his being selected as part of the team that designed the new capitol city in Washington, D.C. Despite this evidence, Jefferson refused to acknowledge Bannaker's intellectual accomplishments. *Courtesy, American Antiquarian Society.*

blacks had much of a role in Jefferson's America, and each group was subject to different forms of unequal treatment during the Jeffersonian era.

A slaveholder himself, Jefferson held strong views about the role blacks were to play in American society. In his *Notes on the State of Virginia* (1781) Jefferson asserted that blacks were "inferior to whites in the endowments both of body and mind." When presented with direct evidence of superior black intellectual accomplishments, Jefferson refused to accept that they had the same mental and physical abilities as whites. Even the attainments of black mathematician, astronomer, and engineer **Benjamin Banneker** could not change Jefferson's mind. Writing to Banneker after receiving an advance copy of an almanac prepared by the black scholar, Jefferson stated, "No body wishes more than I do to see such proofs as you exhibit, that nature has given to our black brethren, talents equal to those of the other colors of men." However, he refused to acknowledge that Banneker's work provided such proofs, claiming that it was evidence of the man's "moral eminence" rather than intellectual equality.

Throughout the Jeffersonian era, the great majority of blacks in America were slaves, and most of them lived in the southern states. But from the 1790s onward, the number of free blacks increased steadily. Emancipation did not bring equality, however, even in northern states. Many states did not permit free blacks to testify in court, vote, or exercise other fundamental freedoms accorded to whites. Public schools often refused admission to black children. Even churches were often closed to blacks who wished to worship.

Free blacks began to respond to systematic exclusion and to express their cultural and social identity by forming their own institutions. In Philadelphia, tension between white and free black Methodists led former slave Richard Allen to form the Bethel Church for Negro Methodists in 1793. Two years later, Allen became the first black deacon ordained in America. Ongoing tension with the white Methodist hierarchy, however, eventually led Allen to secede from the church and form his own **African Methodist Episcopal church** (Bethel) in 1816. Similar controversies in New York led black divine James Varick to found an African Methodist Episcopal church (Zion) in that city in 1821.

The African Methodist Episcopal (AME) church grew rapidly. Within a few decades, membership in AME churches exceeded twelve thousand. Besides providing places of worship and centers for cultural and social activities, AME churches joined with black Presbyterians, Baptists, and members of other denominations to provide schools and other necessary services withheld by whites. Bishop Allen's organization, for example, launched the first black magazine in America and eventually founded its own college, Wilburforce University.

Benjamin Banneker African American mathematician and astronomer who published an almanac that calculated the movements of stars and planets.

African Methodist Episcopal church African American branch of Methodism established in Philadelphia in 1816 and in New York in 1821.

Jefferson thought differently of Indians than he did of African Americans. He considered them to be "savages" but was not convinced that they were biologically inferior to Europeans: "they are formed in mind as well as in body, on the same module with the '*Homo Sapiens Europaeus*,'" he said. Jefferson attributed the differences between Indians and Europeans to what he termed the Indians' cultural retardation. He compared Indian culture to the culture of northern Europeans during the Roman Empire, arguing that small populations, harsh economic conditions, and lack of a written language had kept the Indians in a condition of "barbarism." Jefferson was confident that if whites lifted Indians out of their uncivilized state and put them on an equal footing with Europeans, Indian populations would grow, Indians' physical condition would improve, and Indians would be able to participate in the yeoman republic on an equal footing with whites.

Jefferson's Indian policy reflected this attitude. Jefferson created a series of government-owned trading posts at which Indians were offered goods at cheap prices. He believed that Indians who were exposed to white manufactures would come to agree that white culture was superior and would make the rational decision to adopt that culture wholesale. Until the process of **acculturation** was complete, however, Jefferson believed the Indians, like children, should be protected from those who would take advantage of them or lead them astray. Also like children, the Indians were not to be trusted to exercise the rights and responsibilities of citizenship. Thus Indian rights were not protected by the Constitution but were subject to the whims of the Senate, which drafted and ratified Indian treaties, and of the army, which enforced those treaties.

The chief problem for Jeffersonian Indian policy was not the Indians' supposed cultural retardation but their rapid modernization. Among groups like the Cherokees and Creeks, members of a rising new elite—often the offspring of European fathers and Indian mothers—led their people toward greater prosperity and diplomatic independence. Alexander McGillivray of the Creeks, for example, deftly played American, French, and Spanish interests off against each other while building a strong economic base founded on both communally and privately owned plantations. In similar fashion, the rising Cherokee elite in 1794 established a centralized government that began pushing the Cherokees into a new era of wealth and power.

Indians in other parts of the country adopted different strategies for coping with the changes that affected their lives. Among the Iroquois, for example, a religious prophet named **Handsome Lake** began preaching a new creed designed to help his people absorb what was best about European culture while preserving what was best about their own. The prophet recommended that Seneca children be sent to the schools of the whites to learn their ways, and he approved of using European farming techniques, tools, and houses. He counseled his people to abandon witchcraft, except for healing, and to enjoy the blessings of marriage and family. His strongest condemnation was heaped on alcohol, which he said had been given to the white man to ease his labors but was never intended for Indians and must be avoided. He also advocated the preservation of tribal ceremonies and ritual clothing, saying that these things would help the people retain their identity.

Although Jefferson might have greeted such acculturation with enthusiasm, the Indians' white neighbors generally did not. From their self-serving perspective, Native Americans were occupying lands that by right belonged to individual states and by extension to westward-looking pioneers. States like Georgia contended that Indians within their borders were an internal affair that was no concern of the federal government. Jefferson probably agreed in principle, but he insisted that federal authority over Indian affairs was essential for maintaining peace and ensuring the Indians' and the nation's future welfare.

Envisioning all-out war between the states and the Indians—war that his reduced government could do little about—Jefferson advanced what he thought would be an alternative to Indian extinction. Having acquired Louisiana, Jefferson suggested the creation of large reserves to which Indians currently residing within states could move, taking themselves out of state jurisdictions and removing themselves from the corrupting influence of the "baser elements" of white society. Although he did not advocate the use of force to move Indians west of the Mississippi, he made every effort to convince them to relocate. This idea of segregating Native Americans from other Americans formed the basis for Indian policy for the rest of the century.

acculturation Changes in the culture of a group or an individual as a result of contact with a different culture.

Handsome Lake Seneca Indian religious prophet who taught that Indians should adopt the best features of white culture, reject its worst features, and hold on to native ceremonial and religious traditions.

SUMMARY

Expectations
Constraints
Choices
Outcomes

Americans faced a difficult *choice* in 1796: to continue in a Federalist direction with John Adams or to move into new and uncharted regions of democracy with Thomas Jefferson. Factionalism and voter indecision led to Adams's election as president and Jefferson's as vice president. The split *outcome* frightened Federalists, and they used every excuse to make war on their political opponents. Diplomatically, they let relations with France sour to the point that the two nations were at war in all but name. At home, they used measures like the Alien and Sedition Acts to try to silence opponents, and they imposed tariffs and taxes that were hateful to many. Seeing in these *constraints* specters of what they had rebelled against in the Revolution, in 1800 the American people *chose* to give Jefferson and the Republican faction a chance.

Although Jefferson would call the election "the revolution of 1800," even hard-line Federalists like Hamilton were sure that the general direction in government would not change. Just to be safe, however, Federalists stacked the court system so that Republicans would face insurmountable *constraints* if they tried to change government too much. At the same time, they organized themselves into a true political party, an ever-present watchdog on the activities of their rivals.

Jefferson's inaugural address in 1801 seemed to announce an end to partisan warfare, but both Madison and radicals in Congress attempted to restrict Federalist power in the court system. The Republican program, however, was not entirely negative. Jefferson looked toward a future in which most Americans could own enough land to produce life's necessities for themselves and would be beholden to no one and thus free to vote as their consciences and rationality dictated. To attain this end, Jefferson ordered massive reductions in the size of government, the elimination of internal federal taxes, and rapid westward expansion, including the purchase of the vast territory called Louisiana. For some the *outcome* was a spirit of excitement and optimism, but not everyone shared such *expectations*. Many were unsure and fearful of the new order's novelty and of the stresses of rapid expansion as social change disrupted lives and communities.

Jefferson clearly wanted most Americans to share in the bounty of an expanded nation, but not all were free to share equally. For American Indians, the very success of Jefferson's expansion policy meant contraction of the lands where they could live and *constraints* on their freedom of action. African Americans also found that the equality that Jefferson promised to others was not intended for them.

SUGGESTED READINGS

Stephen E. Ambrose. *Undaunted Courage: Meriwether Lewis, Thomas Jefferson, and the Opening of the American West* (1996).

A critically acclaimed and highly readable narrative exploring the relationship between Jefferson and Lewis and their efforts to acquire and explore Louisiana.

Alexander DeConde. *This Affair of Louisiana* (1976).

An excellent account by one of America's premier diplomatic historians.

Joseph J. Ellis. *American Sphinx: The Character of Thomas Jefferson* (1996)

Winner of the National Book Award, this new biography focuses on Jefferson's personality seeking to expose his inner character; highly readable.

Richard Hofstadter. *The Idea of a Party System* (1969).

The classic account of the rise of legitimate opposition in the American party system.

Gary B. Nash. *Forging Freedom: The Formation of Philadelphia's Black Community, 1720–1840* (1990).

A brilliant and exciting exploration of how African Americans in early Philadelphia created their own urban community.

James Ronda. *Lewis and Clark Among the Indians* (1984).

A bold retelling of the expedition's story, showcasing the Indian role in both Lewis and Clark's and the nation's successful expansion into Louisiana.

Restraining Federal Power

The Context

The Alien and Sedition Acts raised serious questions about Congress's right to pass laws affecting free speech and free assembly. They also raised questions about who had the right to determine whether acts of Congress violated the Constitution. Kentucky and Virginia passed legislative resolutions, written by Thomas Jefferson and James Madison respectively, laying out two approaches to this issue. Other states responded, outlining their views on this fundamental problem in the checks and balances system and the separation of powers. (For further information on the context, see pages 217–218.)

The Historical Question

Historians continue to debate the constitutional issues relating to the Alien and Sedition Acts. Now, as then, the question hinges on interpreting exactly what the Constitution really means in various of its articles. Madison and Jefferson each offered slightly different opinions, and others challenged their interpretations. What were the most appropriate avenues for questioning the constitutionality of the acts? What legitimate recourse could individuals have pursued? What responsibilities did various branches of government have to protect individual rights from potential violation? What, really, did the Constitution say?

The Challenge

Using the sources provided, the Constitution (printed as an appendix at the end of this book), and other information you have read, write an essay or hold a discussion on the following question. Cite evidence in the sources to support your conclusions.

If you were an interested and impartial citizen living in the United States in 1798, which of the arguments presented here would you find most convincing? Why?

The Sources

1 Thomas Jefferson was sure that the Sedition Act was unconstitutional, but there was no clear mechanism for challenging a federal law. In the first Kentucky Resolution, written in October 1798, Jefferson came to the following conclusion:

. . . *the government created by this compact [the Constitution] was not made the exclusive or final judge of the extent of the powers delegated to itself; since that would have made its discretion, and not the Constitution, the measure of its powers; but that as in all other cases of compact among parties having no common Judge,* each party has an equal right to judge for itself, as well of infractions as of the mode and measure of redress. . . .

. . . *"the powers not delegated to the United States by the Constitution, nor prohibited by it to the States, are reserved to the States respectively or to the people;" and that no power over the freedom of religion, freedom of speech, or freedom of the press being delegated to the United States by the Constitution, nor prohibited by it to the States, all lawful powers respecting the same did of right remain, and were reserved to the States, or to the people. . . . therefore [the Sedition Act], which does abridge the freedom of the press, is not law, but is altogether void and of no effect.*

2 James Madison was particularly concerned that with Federalists in control of all three branches of the national government , the separation of powers he had built into the Constitution had broken down. Some other check seemed to be necessary in the "checks and balances" system. Madison said:

. . . the [Alien Act] exercises a power nowhere delegated to the Federal Government, and which, by uniting legislative and judicial powers to those of [the] executive, subverts the general principles of free government, . . .

. . . the good people of this commonwealth, having ever felt and continuing to feel the most sincere affection for their brethren of the other states, the truest anxiety for establishing and perpetuating the union of all and the most scrupulous fidelity to that Constitution . . . doth solemnly appeal to the like dispositions of the other states, in confidence that they will concur with this Commonwealth in declaring, as it does hereby declare, that the acts aforesaid are unconstitutional; and that the necessary and proper measures will be taken by each for co-operating with this state, in maintaining unimpaired the authorities, rights, and liberties reserved to the states respectively, or to the people.

3 No other state joined Kentucky and Virginia in challenging the constitutionality of the Alien and Sedition Acts. Several, in fact, issued proclamations criticizing the Resolutions. The Rhode Island legislature had this to say:

"The judicial power shall extend to all cases arising under the laws of the United States,"—vests in the Federal Courts, exclusively, and in the Supreme Court of the United States, ultimately, the authority of deciding on the constitutionality of any act or law of the Congress of the United States.

That for any state legislature to assume that authority would be—

1st. Blending together legislative and judicial powers;

2d. Hazarding an interruption of the peace of the states by civil discord, in case of a diversity of opinions among the state legislatures; each state having, in that case, no resort, for vindicating its own opinions, but the strength of its own arm;

3d. Submitting most important questions of law to less competent tribunals; and

4th. An infraction of the Constitution of the United States, expressed in plain terms.

4 Timothy Pickering, Adams's secretary of state and a stalwart Federalist, denied that the acts were in any way unreasonable. He wrote:

The Sedition Act has . . . been shamefully misrepresented as an attack upon the freedom of speech and of the press. But we find, on the contrary, that it prescribes a punishment only for those pests of society and disturbers of order and tranquillity "who write, print, utter, or publish any false, scandalous, and malicious writings against the government of the United States, or either house of the Congress of the United States, or the President, with intent to defame, or bring them into contempt or disrepute, or to excite against them the hatred of the good people of the United States; or to stir up sedition, or to abet the hostile designs of any foreign nation."

What honest man can justly be alarmed at such a law, or can wish unlimited permission to be given for the publication of malicious falsehoods, and with intentions the most base.

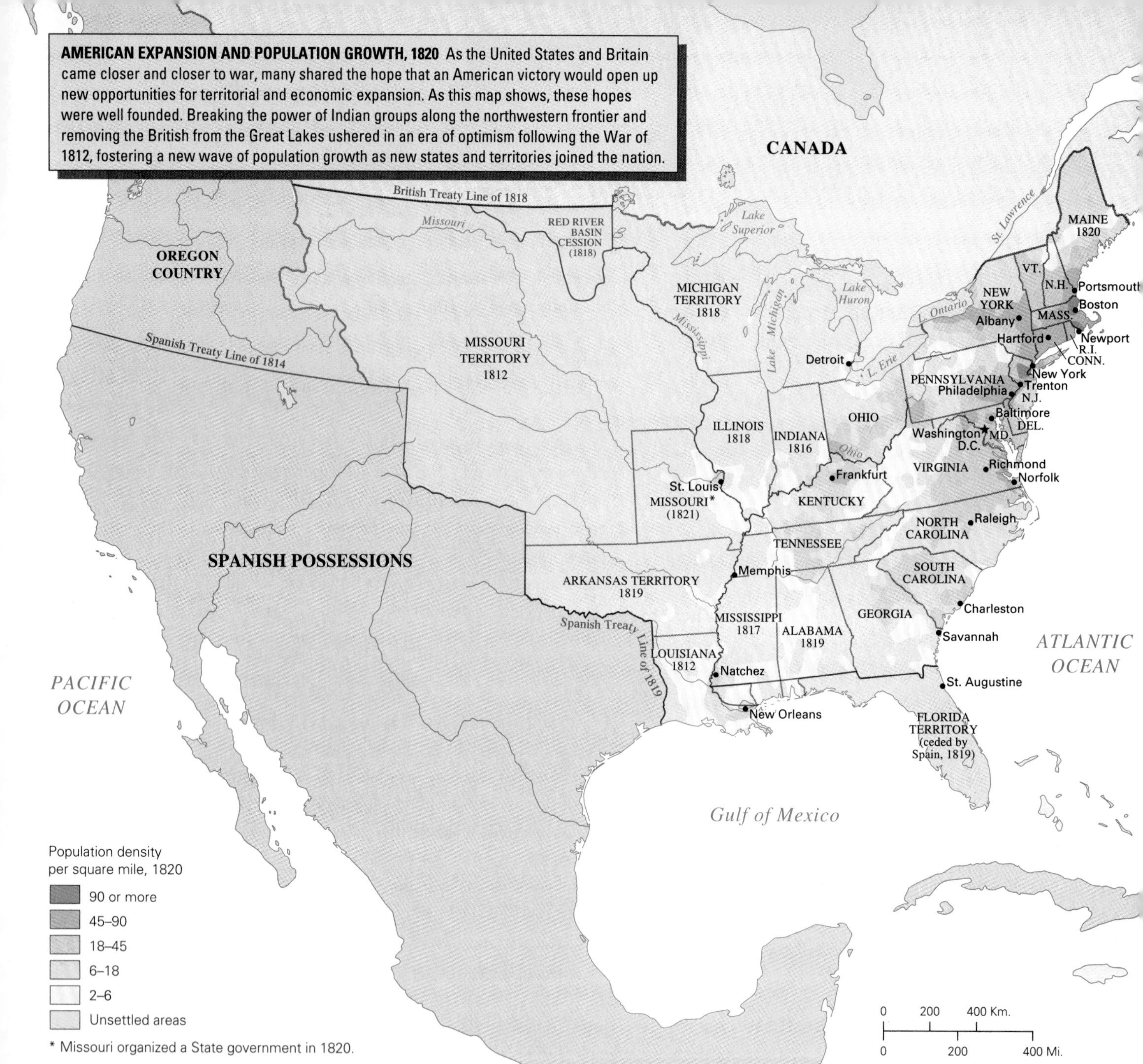

AMERICAN EXPANSION AND POPULATION GROWTH, 1820 As the United States and Britain came closer and closer to war, many shared the hope that an American victory would open up new opportunities for territorial and economic expansion. As this map shows, these hopes were well founded. Breaking the power of Indian groups along the northwestern frontier and removing the British from the Great Lakes ushered in an era of optimism following the War of 1812, fostering a new wave of population growth as new states and territories joined the nation.

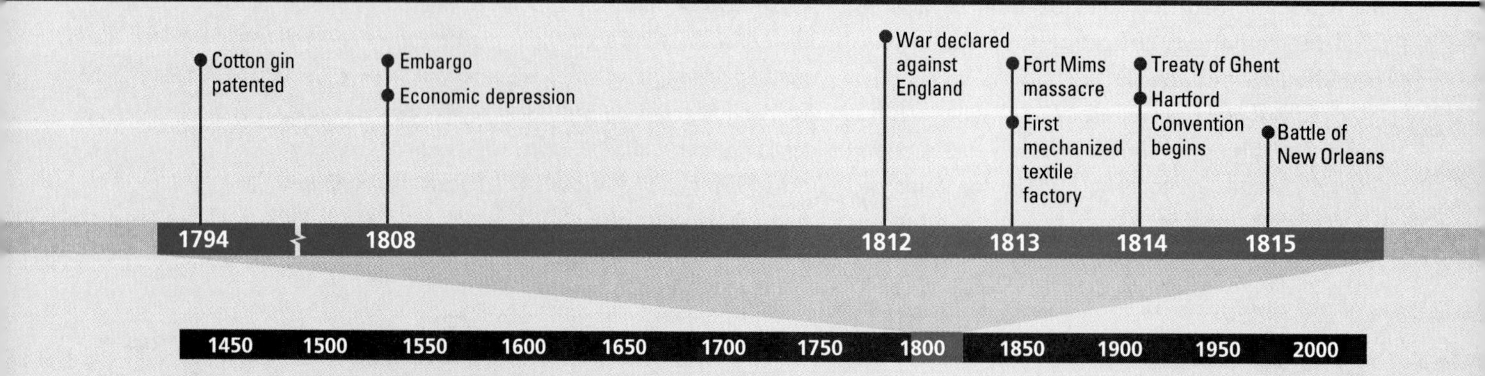

CHAPTER 9

Increasing Conflict and War, 1805–1815

Troubling Currents in Jefferson's America

- How did changes in the relations of the regions of the United States with Europe and with one another constrain Jefferson's political and economic expectations?

Crises in the Nation

- What constraints arose from Jefferson's economic and Indian policies?
- How did the expectations of frontier politicians like William Henry Harrison help to bring the nation to war in 1812?

The Nation at War

- What geographic and economic factors constrained Americans in their war effort against Great Britain and Britain's Indian allies?
- Why were American military choices successful or not successful?

Peace and the Rise of New Expectations

- How did events during the War of 1812 help to foster new expectations for Americans after peace arrived?

INTRODUCTION

E xpectations
C onstraints
C hoices
O utcomes

Jefferson's first term in office can only be described as an unqualified success. Federalists like Hamilton had *expected* political and financial collapse when the red-headed radical assumed the presidency, but they were wrong. The president's supporters had *expected* a revolution in the spirit of government and were not disappointed. A two-party system seemed to have replaced the snarl of warring political factions, and the hard feelings of the past apparently were forgiven and forgotten. The *outcome* was a new sense of stability and unity in the nation's politics. And the *outcome* of Jefferson's and Gallatin's careful financial management was an economy that was riding high. A new spirit was alive in the land, and Americans were growing ever more confident that their future would be glorious.

But Jefferson's greatest accomplishments resulted from continuing crises in world affairs—crises that became powerful *constraints* during his second administration. His successful acquisition of Louisiana, for example, came as the result of tension between England, France, and Spain. The rebounding economy was also a product of international problems rather than of Jefferson's choices. Although Jefferson's and Gallatin's cost cutting certainly helped to save money, it was Europeans' involvement in nearly constant war among themselves that allowed Americans to make money. National security and economic prosperity depended on Jefferson's ability to keep the United States a neutral player on the world stage, a role that became harder and harder to sustain in his second term.

Increasing *constraints* on American trade forced Jefferson, and then his successor James Madison, to make hard choices. Believing that Europe needed American food and raw materials more than the United States needed European manufactures, Republicans *chose* to close down trade with Europe. The *outcome* was economic depression in the United States and diplomatic crisis worldwide. Adding to the problem were widening cracks in Jefferson's party support. Many Republicans were less than pleased with the president's *choice* to use executive power in accomplishing goals like the Louisiana Purchase. They believed that such action pointed to a retreat from the antifederalism Jefferson had declared so clearly in the Kentucky Resolution. Federalists too were displeased, especially those in the Northeast. It seemed to them that Jefferson had *chosen* to serve southern and western interests to the exclusion of theirs.

The expectations and choices of others played havoc with Jefferson's hopes for a peaceful and prosperous nation. French and English policymakers *chose* not to respect American neutrality. *Expecting* to advance their own political visions, American politicians of various stripes *chose* to oppose the president. In the West, whites seeking land for expansion *expected* that war against the Indians and the British would best serve their ends, and Indians increasingly *chose* to stop retreating.

The *outcome* was war. Underfinanced, unprepared, and deeply divided internally, the United States faced off against a unified English and Indian force. The Americans suffered defeat after defeat during the war's opening years, and political infighting and economic crisis were dividing the nation even further. But then, a series of improbable American victories crippled English efforts. In England, voters tired after a generation of warfare demanded peace, and the Crown was forced to comply.

The war ended with nothing officially changed. The Treaty of Ghent simply restored relations between England and the United States to what they had been before hostilities had broken out. But in reality, much had changed. Americans emerged from the conflict with a new sense of pride and national purpose, a growing range of economic *choices*, and a new set of expectations about the future.

CHRONOLOGY

Domestic Expansion and International Crisis

1794 Eli Whitney patents the cotton gin

1803 Louisiana Purchase
Renewal of war between France and Britain
Britain steps up impressment

1804 Duel between Alexander Hamilton and Aaron Burr
Jefferson re-elected

1805 Beginning of Shawnee religious revival
Battles of Trafalgar and Austerlitz

1806 Napoleon issues Berlin Decree

1807 Burr conspiracy trial
Founding of Prophetstown
Chesapeake affair

1808 Embargo goes into effect
Economic depression begins
James Madison elected president

1809 Non-Intercourse Act
Fort Wayne Treaty
Chouteau brothers form the Missouri Fur Company

1810 Macon's Bill No. 2
Formation of the War Hawks

1811 United States breaks trade relations with Britain
John Jacob Astor builds Astoria at the mouth of the Columbia River
Battle of Tippecanoe and destruction of Prophetstown

1812 United States declares war against England
United States invades Canada
James Madison re-elected

1813 Fort Mims massacre
Battle of Put-in-Bay
Embargo of 1813
First mechanized textile factory, Waltham, Massachusetts
Battle of the Thames

1814 Battle of Horseshoe Bend
Napoleon defeated
British capture and burn Washington, D.C.
Battle of Plattsburgh
Treaty of Ghent

1815 Battle of New Orleans
Treaty of Fort Jackson
Portage des Sioux treaties

1819 Treaty of Edwardsville

1825 Prairie du Chien treaties

Troubling Currents in Jefferson's America

• How did changes in the relations of the regions of the United States with Europe and with one another constrain Jefferson's political and economic expectations?

Jefferson's successes, culminating in his victory in the 1804 election, seemed to prove that the Republicans had absolute control over the nation's political reins. But factions that would challenge Jefferson's control were forming. A small but vocal coalition of disgruntled Federalists threatened to **secede** from the Union. Even within his own party, voices were raised against Jefferson, threatening his political control. And diplomatic problems joined these domestic ones to trouble Jefferson's second administration.

Emerging Factions in American Politics

The Federalists' failure in the election of 1804 nearly spelled the troubled party's demise. With the West

secede To withdraw formally from membership in a political union.

and the South firmly in Jefferson's camp, disgruntled New England Federalists found their once-dominant voice being drowned out by those who shared Jefferson's rather than Hamilton's view of America's future. Proclaiming that "The people of the East cannot reconcile their habits, views, and interests with those of the South and West," Federalist leader Timothy Pickering advocated the formation of a northern confederacy and withdrawal from the Union, and he brought together a tight political coalition called the **Essex Junto** to carry out this scheme.

Regional fissures began to open inside Jefferson's party as well. Throughout Jefferson's first administration, some within his party, especially those from the South, criticized the president for turning his back on republican principles by expanding federal power and interfering with states' rights. One of Jefferson's most vocal critics was his cousin **John Randolph** of Roanoke. A moody man equally famous for his nasty temper as for his Virginia charm, Randolph considered himself the last true Republican, and he strode the floor of Congress with a whip in hand, opposing any legislation that violated his principles.

The tension between the two Virginia Republicans came to a head in 1804 over the **Yazoo affair,** a scandal stemming from a crooked land deal that had taken place in Georgia in 1795. Jefferson advocated federal compensation for speculators who had lost money when outraged voters forced the Georgia legislature to overturn the fraudulent sale. Randolph claimed that would violate Republican principles and plain morality, and he used his power in Congress to block Jefferson's efforts.

In 1806 Jefferson again irritated Randolph by approaching Congress for a $2 million appropriation to be used to win French influence in convincing Spain to sell Florida to the United States. Randolph bristled, both at Jefferson's expansionism and, more particularly, at what he regarded as open bribery. Saying, "I found I might co-operate or be an honest man," Randolph chose honesty. He split with Jefferson, forming a third party, the **Tertium Quid**, and fracturing the Republican united political front.

A second fissure in the party opened over controversial vice president Aaron Burr's political scheming. Scandal had eroded Burr's political and personal fortunes since his nearly successful bid to snatch the presidency from Jefferson in 1800. Jefferson snubbed him throughout his first four years in office and then dropped him from the ticket in 1804. But Burr's political failures constituted an opportunity for the Essex Junto: Pickering offered to help Burr become governor of New York if Burr would deliver the state to the northern confederacy and support secession. Burr agreed, but mainstream New York Federalists were furious, especially Alexander Hamilton. During the **gubernatorial** election, Hamilton was quoted by the press as saying that Burr was "a dangerous man, and one who ought not to be trusted with the reins of government." Burr lost the election in a landslide, killing the Junto's scheme and pushing himself into an even greater personal and political crisis.

Never willing to accept defeat gracefully and convinced that Hamilton was the sole source for his political misfortune, Burr demanded that Hamilton retract his statements. Hamilton refused, and Burr challenged him to a duel. Although Hamilton was a man of great courage, proven repeatedly on the battlefield during the Revolution, he hated physical violence, especially dueling. Still, he accepted Burr's challenge, swearing that he would not shoot at his rival, thinking perhaps that Burr would be shamed into changing his mind. But Burr could not be shamed. An excellent shot, the vice president put a bullet directly through Hamilton's liver, wounding him gravely. After thirty-six hours of horrible suffering, Hamilton died in July 1804.

Rather than enjoying honor and a political resurrection, Burr found himself indicted for murder and fled. While in hiding, he made contact with James Wilkinson, a Revolutionary War commander who had become something of a soldier of fortune. The two men hatched a plot, though no one knows exactly what it consisted of. Wilkinson told Spanish of-

Essex Junto Group of Federalists in Essex County, Massachusetts, who called for New England and New York to secede from the United States during Jefferson's second term.

John Randolph Virginia Republican politician who was a cousin of Thomas Jefferson; he believed in limited government and several of Jefferson's policies.

Yazoo affair Corrupt deal in which the Georgia legislature sold a huge tract of public land to speculators for a low price; the sale was overturned by a new legislature a year later.

Tertium Quid Republican faction formed by John Randolph in protest against Jefferson's plan for acquiring Florida from Spain.

gubernatorial Of or relating to a governor.

ficials that he and Burr intended to establish an independent republic in the Mississippi Valley, thus weakening U.S. claims along the Spanish frontier. Burr, however, informed the British that they intended to carve a republic out of Spanish territory in what is now Texas, New Mexico, and California. Whatever they had in mind, when Burr emerged from hiding and resumed his role as vice president and chair of the Senate, he arranged for Wilkinson to be appointed governor of the Louisiana Territory.

Finally turned out of office in 1805, Burr ventured west, sailing down the Mississippi to recruit associates. Rumors that Burr and Wilkinson intended to seize Louisiana soon surfaced. Federal authorities became interested late in 1806 and jumped into the case when they received a letter from Wilkinson in December. Pretending innocence, Wilkinson warned of a "deep, dark, wicked, and wide-spread conspiracy" against the United States and implicated Burr. Learning that Wilkinson had turned him in, Burr tried to reach Spanish Florida but was captured early in 1807 and put on trial for treason.

Burr's trial was a circus, an open arena for Jefferson and his critics to air their views on such touchy subjects as presidential power, westward expansion, and national loyalty. Chief Justice John Marshall, no friend of Jefferson, presided over the hearing and made it clear that he believed Burr was the victim, not the perpetrator, of a conspiracy. In fact, Marshall went so far as to attend a dinner party thrown by Burr's defense lawyer at which Burr was also a guest.

Jefferson, however, made it clear that he believed Burr was guilty, and the president was determined to have him prosecuted to the full extent of the law. Using the powers of his office, Jefferson offered pardons to conspirators who would testify against Burr, and he released documents that would make his former vice president look guilty. He also refused to honor a **subpoena** issued by Marshall requiring the president to appear in court and produce papers that Marshall wanted to see in evidence. In this instance, Jefferson embarrassed the chief justice by recalling that Marshall had supported George Washington's assertion of presidential privilege when he refused to present key papers to Congress relating to Jay's Treaty (see page 205). Marshall backed down, and neither Jefferson nor his executive papers appeared in court. But Marshall struck back in his own way.

The chief justice informed the jury that the Constitution defined treason as "levying war against the United States or adhering to their enemies" and that two witnesses had to produce direct evidence of Burr having done these things before a guilty verdict could be reached. Because Burr had not waged war, and because neither Spain nor Britain was an enemy of the United States at that time, the jury acquitted the former vice president, to the glee of Jefferson's critics and to the president's deep chagrin.

The Problem of American Neutrality

Internal tensions in American politics were matched by growing stress in the nation's diplomatic and economic relations. Owing to its lack of heavy manufacturing and to Jefferson's economic policies, the United States depended on Europe for manufactured items in exchange for American agricultural produce. As long as England and France were at war, as they were almost constantly after the French Revolution in 1789, the resulting instability opened up enormous opportunities for Americans. Europeans—with their fleets engaged in naval battles, their people locked in combat, and their lands crisscrossed by marching armies—needed American ships, American labor, and American food supplies. Although tensions might arise, as in the Quasi-War with France, if all the contending parties in Europe agreed to the diplomatic principle of neutrality, and if the United States could stay neutral, American prosperity seemed assured.

Shortly after Jefferson had assumed the presidency in 1801, however, affairs in Europe settled down, and opportunities for American **profiteering** from foreign wars dried up. The Treaty of Amiens (1802), which suspended the fighting between France and England, cut severely into American trade. Although crop failures in Europe and the West Indies prevented the bottom from falling out of America's foreign markets, the value of American exports fell from $93 million to $72 million during the first year of the peace and bottomed out at $56 million during the treaty's second year. But the war did not remain stalled. Having lost his chance to extend his empire into North America (see page 228), French emperor Napoleon Bonaparte

subpoena A writ, or order, requiring appearance in court to give testimony.

profiteering Making excessive profits on goods in short supply.

chose to pursue more aggressive campaigning in Europe: a mere two weeks after selling Louisiana to Jefferson, he launched a new military offensive that eventually embroiled all of Europe.

Americans immediately grasped at the new opportunities opened to them. Following the renewal of war in Europe in 1803, the total value of American exports rose by over 65 percent. A significant proportion of the increase came from the shipment of foreign goods to foreign markets by way of neutral American ports. So-called **re-exports** rose in value from $14 million in 1803 to $60 million in 1807. The rise in re-exports helped prompt a rapid growth in earnings for American shipping. In 1790, net income from shipping amounted to a mere $5.9 million. By 1800, the amount had increased to $26.2 million. Then, as a result of Americans seizing opportunities opened by the European war, the volume surged to $42.1 million by 1807.

Prospects seemed bright for America's economic and diplomatic future and for Jefferson's dream of agricultural America feeding overcrowded, war-torn Europe. But politicians in both England and France cared about military victory, not about American prosperity. Their decisions, especially those relating to neutral shipping, disrupted American trade and forced Jefferson to further violate his republican principles.

Impressment and American Pride

Impressment threatened American neutrality and trade after the European war heated up in 1803. British law empowered the king's warships to press any British citizen into military service. This ancient recruiting method helped make up for the shortage of seamen resulting from the exceedingly cruel conditions and low pay in His Majesty's navy. England, strapped for mariners by renewed warfare, pursued a vigorous policy of reclaiming British sailors, even if they were on neutral American ships and, more provocatively, even if they had become naturalized citizens of the United States. It is estimated that the British abducted as many as eight thousand sailors from American ships between 1803 and 1812. The loss of so many seamen hurt American shippers economically, but it wounded American pride even more. Like the XYZ affair, impressment seemed to be a direct denial of the United States' status as a legitimate nation.

Pressure on American neutrality increased after 1805, when the British won a decisive naval victory at Trafalgar and the French an equally decisive land victory at Austerlitz. A military deadlock followed, with Britain supreme at sea and France in control on the continent of Europe. Stuck in a stalemate, both sides used whatever nonmilitary forces were available to them in an effort to turn the balance in their favor. Thus the war changed from one of military campaigning to one of diplomatic and economic maneuvering.

Napoleon made the first move in this newly altered war. Seeking to close off foreign supplies to England, the French emperor issued the **Berlin Decree** in November 1806. This order barred ships that had anchored at British harbors from entering ports controlled by France. It also declared that all British-made items found on neutral ships would be subject to confiscation by French authorities. The British Parliament responded to the Berlin Decree by issuing a series of orders in council that virtually blockaded Europe but permitted neutral ships to sail to European ports if they first called at a British port to pay a transit tax. It was thus impossible for a neutral ship to follow the laws of either nation without violating the laws of the other. All this European blustering, however, had little immediate effect on the American economy. From the issuance of the Berlin Decree to the end of 1807, American exports and shipping rose more than they had risen during any similar period.

Toward Economic War

As the stalemate continued, both England and France waited impatiently for an opportunity to strike and bring the war to a quick end. Seeking to break France's dependence on America as a source for food and other supplies, Napoleon sought an alliance with Russia, and in the spring of 1807 his diplomatic mission succeeded. Having acquired an alternative source for grain and other foodstuffs,

re-exports Products shipped to a neutral nation during wartime and then reshipped to their final destination under a neutral flag.

impressment Procedure permitted under British maritime law that authorized commanders of warships to force English civilian sailors into military service.

Berlin Decree Napoleon's order declaring the British Isles under blockade and authorizing the confiscation of British goods from any ship found carrying them.

♦ The impressment of sailors into the British navy from American ships was one of the more prominent causes of the War of 1812. This 1790 engraving shows an American sailor being seized at gunpoint while those who might try to assist him are elbowed aside. *Library of Congress.*

Napoleon immediately began enforcing the Berlin Decree, hoping to starve England into submission. The British countered by stepping up enforcement of their European blockade, and while they were at it, they aggressively pursued impressment to strengthen the royal navy.

The escalation in both France's and Britain's economic war efforts quickly led to confrontation with Americans and a diplomatic crisis. A pivotal event occurred in June 1807. The British **frigate** *Leopard*, patrolling the American shoreline, confronted the American warship *Chesapeake*. Even though both ships were inside American territorial waters, the *Leopard* ordered the American ship to halt and hand over any British sailors on board. When the *Chesapeake*'s captain refused, the *Leopard* fired several **broadsides,** crippling the American vessel, injuring eighteen sailors, and killing three. The British then boarded the *Chesapeake* and dragged off four men, three of whom were naturalized citizens of the United States. Americans were outraged.

Americans were not the only ones outraged by British aggression. Shortly after the *Chesapeake* affair, word arrived in the United States that Napoleon had responded to more aggressive British enforcement by declaring a virtual economic war against neutrals. In the **Milan Decree,** he vowed to seize any neutral ship that so much as carried licenses to trade with England. What was worse, the Milan Decree stated that ships that had been boarded—even against their crews' will—by British authorities would be subject to immediate French capture.

Many Americans viewed the escalating French and English sanctions as insulting treachery that cried out for an American response. The *Washington Federalist* newspaper observed, "We have never,

frigate A very fast warship, rigged with square sails and usually carrying thirty guns on its gun deck.

broadside The simultaneous discharge of all the guns on one side of a warship.

Milan Decree Napoleon's order authorizing the capture of any neutral vessels sailing from British ports or submitting to British searches.

♦ The embargo that took effect in 1808 was designed to force the British and French to respect American neutrality, but many Americans saw it as an attack on legitimate trading. In this cartoon, the embargo, in the shape of a giant snapping turtle, walks over a trading license to grab a merchant, preventing him from trading with a British ship in the harbor. *The New-York Historical Society.*

on any occasion, witnessed . . . such a thirst for revenge." If Congress had been in session, the legislature surely would have called for war, but Jefferson stayed calm. War with England or France or, worse still, with both would bring Jefferson's whole political program to a crashing halt. He had insisted on inexpensive government, lobbied for American neutrality, and hoped for renewed prosperity through continuing trade with Europe. War would destroy all those things. It appeared that doing nothing, however, was going to be impossible.

Believing that Europeans were far more dependent on American goods and ships than Americans were on European money and manufactures, Jefferson chose to violate one of his cardinal principles. The U.S. government would interfere in the economy to force Europeans to recognize American neutral rights. In December 1807, the president issued an **embargo**—an absolute ban—on all American trade with Europe. It went into effect at the beginning of 1808.

Crises in the Nation

- What constraints arose from Jefferson's economic and Indian policies?
- How did the expectations of frontier politicians like William Henry Harrison help to bring the nation to war in 1812?

Whether because of European aggression or Jefferson's reaction to it, the unfolding events were now strangling American trade and with it America's internal economic development. In addition, it is easy to forget how weak the nation's hold was on vast regions in the American interior. European countries still had legitimate claims on much of North America, and the Indians who continued to occupy most of the continent had enough military power to destroy the United States if properly motivated and mobilized (see Map 9.1). While impressment, blockade, and embargo paralyzed America's Atlantic frontier, a combination of European and Indian hostility along the western frontier added to the air of national emergency. The resulting series of domestic crises played havoc with Jefferson's vision of a peaceful, prosperous nation.

The Depression of 1808

Although Jefferson felt justified in suspending free trade to protect neutral rights, the result was the worst economic depression since the founding of the British colonies in North America. Critics like John Randolph pronounced Jefferson's solution worse than the problem—like trying "to cure corns by cutting off the toes."

Although Jefferson's "damn-bargo," as critics called it, was only halfheartedly enforced, re-exports, domestic exports, and imports slumped disastrously. Taken together, all American exports fell from $109 million to $22 million, and net earnings from shipping fell by almost 50 percent. During 1808, earnings

embargo A government order that bans trade with another nation or group of nations.

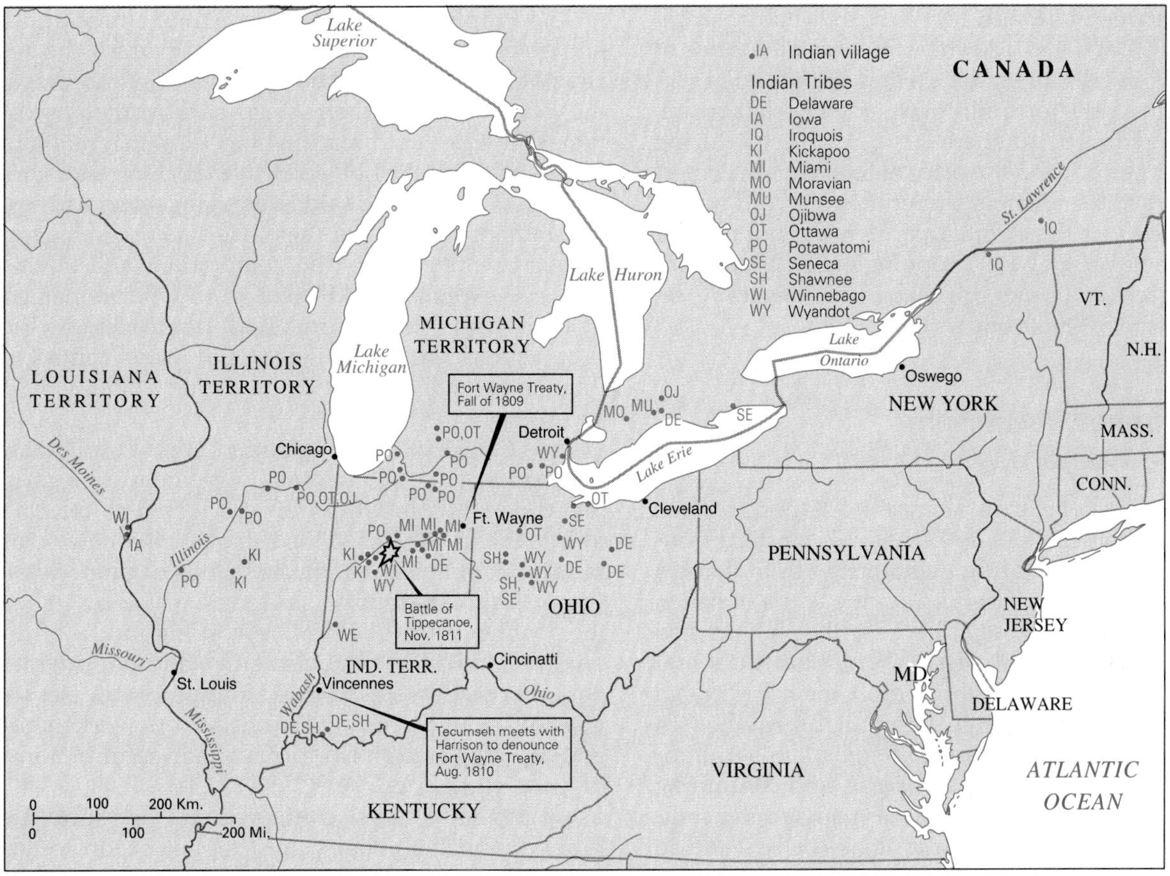

♦ **Map 9.1 Indian Territory, c. 1812** Frontier leaders like William Henry Harrison were very worried about unified Indian resistance in the years leading up to the War of 1812, and this map shows why. Strong Indian groups, some of which were allied with Tecumseh, formed a nearly solid frontier line on the nation's western borders. Harrison's efforts and the War of 1812 virtually destroyed this constraint on American expansion.

from legitimate business enterprise in America declined to less than a quarter of their value in 1807.

The depression shattered economic and social life in many eastern towns. It has been estimated that thirty thousand sailors were thrown out of work and that as many as a hundred thousand people employed in support industries were laid off. In New York City alone, 120 businesses went bankrupt, and the combination of unemployment and business failure led to the imprisonment of twelve hundred New Yorkers for debt in 1808. New England, where the economy had become almost entirely dependent on foreign trade, was hit harder still. There, Federalists began spelling the hated word *embargo* backward—"o-grab-me"—to indicate what Jefferson's policy was doing to their economic fortunes. In light of Jefferson's policies and the collapsing economy, the extremism expressed by the Essex Junto three years earlier began to sound reasonable. The Federalists enjoyed a comeback, not in spite of but because of their rhetoric calling for disobedience to federal law and the possibility of secession.

New Englanders screamed loudest about the impact of the embargo, but southerners and westerners were just as seriously affected by it. The economy of the South had depended on the export of staple crops like tobacco since colonial times and was rapidly turning to cotton. Embargo meant near-death to all legitimate trade. In response to the loss of foreign markets, tobacco prices fell from $6.75 per hundredweight to $3.25, and cotton from 21 to 13 cents per pound. In the West, wholesale prices for agricultural products spiraled downward also. Overall, the prices of farm products were 16 percent lower between 1807 and 1811 than they had been between 1791 and 1801. At the same time, the price of virtually every consumer item went up. For example, the price of building materials—hardware, glass, and milled lumber—rose 11 percent during the same period, and the price of textiles rose 20 percent. In fact, the only consumer item that did not go up in price was the one item farmers did not need to buy: food. Faced with dropping incomes and increasing costs, farmers probably felt the trade restrictions more profoundly than others.

The Prophet, Tecumseh, and the Western War Hawks

As the crisis developed along the Atlantic frontier, evolving problems along the nation's western frontier gathered momentum. Relations with Indians in the West had been peaceful since the Battle of Fallen Timbers in 1794, but only because the Indians had been crushed into submission. The Shawnees and other groups had been thrown off their traditional homelands in Ohio by the Treaty of Greenville (see page 206) and forced to move to new lands in Indiana. There, food shortages, disease, and continuing encroachment by settlers caused many young Indians to lose faith in their traditional beliefs and in themselves as human beings. A growing number turned to alcohol to escape feelings of helplessness and hopelessness.

In the midst of the crisis, one disheartened, diseased alcoholic rose above his sickness to lead the Indians into a brief new era of hope. A young Shawnee named Lalawathika seemed destined to play an influential role in Indian affairs. One of a set of triplets born to an influential family, he was confident of his special nature and was given to bragging (his name meant "Noise-Maker"). But his prospects had declined along with those of his people, leading him to hopelessness, to alcoholism, and finally, in 1805, to critical illness. Lalawathika claimed that he remembered dying and meeting the Master of Life, who showed him the way to lead his people out of degradation, telling him to return to the world of the living so he could tell the Indians what they must do to recover their dignity. He then awoke, cured of his illness. Launching a full-fledged religious and cultural revival designed to teach the ways revealed to him by the Master of Life, he adopted the name Tenskwatawa ("The Way"). Whites called him "the Prophet."

The Prophet preached a message of ethnic pride, nonviolence, and passive resistance. Blaming the decline of his people on their adoption of white ways, the Prophet taught them to go back to their traditional lifestyle—to discard whites' clothing, religion, and especially alcohol—and live as their ancestors had lived. Whites, he said, were dangerous witches, and Indians must avoid them. He also urged his followers to unify against the temptations and threats of white exploiters and hold on to what remained of their lands. If they followed his teachings, the Prophet insisted, the Indians would regain control of their lives and their lands, and the whites would vanish from their world.

In spite of white opposition, the Prophet attempted to create a religious settlement on former Shawnee lands in Ohio but was forced to relocate to Indiana in 1807. Here he established a new community, Prophetstown, on the banks of Tippecanoe Creek. This community was to serve as a center for the Prophet's activities and as a living model of revitalized Indian life. Liquor, guns, and other white paraphernalia were banned from the new settlement. The residents of Prophetstown worked together, using traditional forms of agriculture, hunting, and gathering.

As white settlers continued to pressure the Prophet and his people, the Prophet began to advocate more forceful solutions to the Indians' problems. In a speech to an intertribal council in April 1807, he for the first time suggested that warriors unite to resist white expansion. Although he did not urge his followers to attack the whites, he made it clear that the Master of Life would defend him and his followers if war was pressed on them.

While the Prophet continued to stress spiritual means for stopping white aggression, his brother **Tecumseh** advocated a more political course of action. Seven years older than the Prophet, Tecumseh had always inclined more toward politics and warfare. Known as a brave fighter and a persuasive political orator, Tecumseh traveled throughout the western frontier, working out political and military

The Prophet Shawnee religious visionary who called for a return to Indian traditions and founded the community of Prophetstown on Tippecanoe Creek in Indiana.

Tecumseh Shawnee leader and brother of the Prophet; he tried to establish an Indian confederacy along the frontier as a barrier to white expansion.

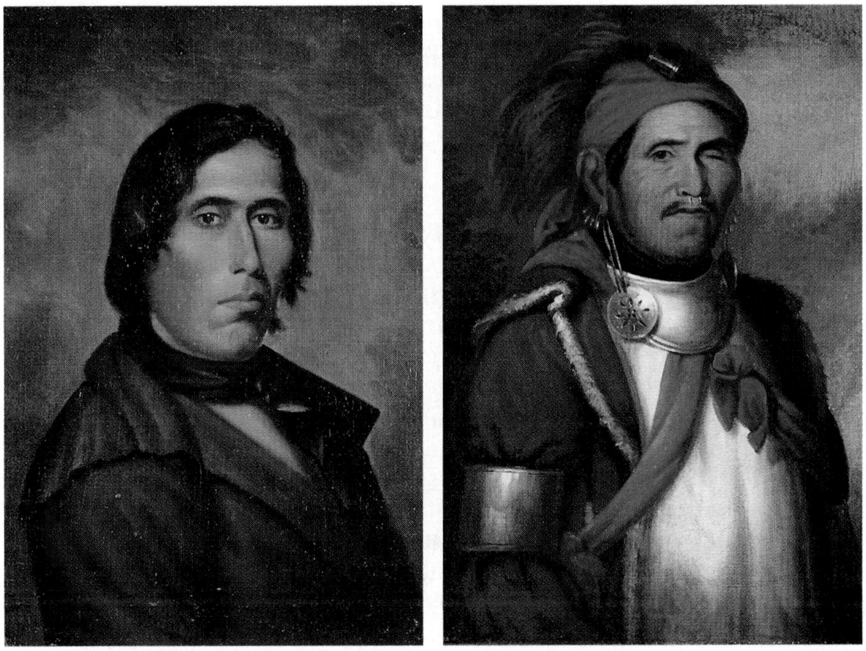

♦ Although they were half-brothers and shared a common vision concerning the future for American Indians, Tecumseh (*left*) and the Prophet (*right*) had very different personal styles. The portrait of Tecumseh shows a determined man whose dress conveys a comfortable acquaintanceship with European ways of doing things. The Prophet, on the other hand, appears much more traditional, in keeping with his teaching that white ways were a form of evil witchcraft. *"Tecumseh." Field Museum of Natural History FMNH Neg # A993851; "The Prophet, Tenskwatawa" by Henry Inmen after Charles Bird King. National Portrait Gallery, Smithsonian/Art Resource, NY.*

alliances designed to put a stop to white expansion once and for all. Although he did not want to start a war against white settlers, Tecumseh exhorted Indians to defend every inch of land that remained to them. In 1807, he warned Governor Thomas Kirker of Ohio that they would do so with their lives.

Tecumseh's plan could have brought about the end foreseen by his brother. Faced by a unified defensive line of Indians stretching along the American frontier from Canada to the Gulf of Mexico, the United States probably would have found it virtually impossible to expand any farther. Whether or not the American eagle would have vanished, it certainly would have been declawed, and the Indian confederacy would have become a dominant force in America's future.

The brilliance of Tecumseh's reasoning and his success at organizing Indian groups caused a great deal of confusion among whites. Various white officials were convinced that the Shawnee leader was a spy either for the French or for the British and was attempting to destabilize diplomacy in the continuing European chess match of wartime statecraft.

Wrong though this suspicion was, identifying Tecumseh as a British spy served the purposes of some Americans. Indiana governor **William Henry Harrison,** for example, had good reason to link Tecumseh and the British. The son of Declaration of Independence signer Benjamin Harrison, William had built a military career and then a political career as an advocate for uncontrolled westward expansion. A decoration for valor at the Battle of Fallen Timbers helped catapult Harrison into the position

William Henry Harrison Indiana governor who led efforts to obtain Indian lands in the Great Lakes region; he later became the ninth president of the United States.

of secretary for the Northwest Territory in 1798 and then governor of Indiana Territory in 1801. Harrison and men like him believed it was the United States' right to control all of North America and anything standing in the way deserved to be brushed aside by whatever means were available. Britain and the Indians were thus linked in their thinking. Both were seen as obstacles to national destiny—and to the personal ambitions of frontier politicians.

Harrison and his associates prayed for the outbreak of war with the United States on one side and the British and Indians on the other. Such a war would provide an excuse for attacking the Indians along the frontier to break up their emerging confederation and dispossess them of their land. In addition, a war would justify invading and seizing Canada, fulfilling what many considered a natural but frustrated goal of the American Revolution. At the same time, taking Canada from the British would open rich timber, fur, and agricultural lands for American settlement. More important, it would secure American control of the Great Lakes and St. Lawrence River—the primary shipping route for agricultural produce from upper New York, northern Ohio, and the newly opening areas of the Old Northwest.

Frontiersmen, like other Americans, blamed Britain for the economic depression that began in 1808. And they believed, rightly or wrongly, that eliminating British interference would restore the boom economy that had drawn so many to farmland at the edge of American settlement. Thus westerners banded together to raise their voices in favor of American patriotism and war against Britain, adding to Jefferson's political and diplomatic woes.

Choosing War

Despite the escalating crisis in the country, Jefferson remained popular and powerful, but like Washington, he chose to step down from the presidency after serving two terms. When he chose not to run for reelection in 1808, he made it clear to party officials that he favored James Madison to replace him. Although Madison and Jefferson had much in common and were long-time friends, they seemed very different from each other. Unlike the tall, outgoing, red-headed Jefferson, Madison was short, dark, and introverted. Few could say they knew him well, but those who did found him captivating: a man of few words but of piercing intellect and unflinching conviction. If Madison had a fatal flaw, it was his thoughtfulness. Those of lesser intelligence thought the quiet Virginian indecisive. Where Jefferson tended to act on impulse, Madison approached matters of state as he approached matters of political philosophy—with caution, patience, and reason.

Riding his reputation as a brilliant political thinker and his status as Jefferson's chosen successor, Madison easily defeated his Federalist opponent, Charles Cotesworth Pinckney. But the one-sided results disguised deep political divisions in the nation at large. Federalist criticism of Jefferson's policies, especially of the embargo, was finding a growing audience as the depression deepened, and in the congressional election in 1808 the Republicans lost twenty-four seats to Federalists.

Internal dissent also weakened the Republican party. Dissatisfied with Jefferson's policies, both southern and northeastern party members had contested Madison's succession. The Tertium Quid had challenged Jefferson's authority in the **party caucus** and tried to secure the nomination for the stately and conservative **James Monroe**, but Jefferson managed to hold the party's southern wing in line. However, northeasterners, stinging under the pressure of the embargo, had bucked the decision of the party caucus and nominated their own presidential candidate: New Yorker George Clinton, who was already the vice-presidential candidate nominated by the party's mainstream. Although Clinton polled only six electoral votes for the presidency, his nomination was a sign of growing divisions over the problems that the United States faced in 1808.

During Madison's first two years in office, his wavering policies seemed to confirm critics' doubts about his abilities as a diplomat and problem solver. Although the Republicans regained fourteen of the seats they had lost in the House in 1808 and picked up two additional Senate seats in the congressional elections in 1810, the majority of new Republicans in Congress belonged to dissident factions within the party. Sixty-three mainstream Republican congressmen lost their seats to Republicans who did not sup-

party caucus A meeting of members of a political party to decide on questions of policy or leadership or to register preferences for candidates running for office.

James Monroe Republican politician from Virginia who served in diplomatic posts under Thomas Jefferson; he later became the fifth president of the United States.

port Madison or his commitment to a conciliatory policy toward the British. The new members of Congress were mostly young southerners and westerners whose farmer constituents were being ravaged by the agricultural depression. In the months to come, their increasingly strident demand for aggressive action against England earned them the nickname **War Hawks**.

With the nation reeling from the economic impact of the embargo, Congress revoked it and replaced it with the **Non-Intercourse Act** early in 1809. The new law forbade trade with England and France only and gave the president the power to reopen trade if either of the combatants lifted its restrictions against American shipping. Even though this act was much less restrictive than the embargo, American merchants were relieved when it expired in the spring of 1810. At that point, Congress passed an even more liberal boycott, **Macon's Bill No. 2**. According to this new law, merchants could trade with the combatants if they wanted to take the risk, but if either France or England lifted its blockade, the United States would stop trading with the other.

Hoping to cut England off from needed outside supplies, Napoleon responded to Macon's Bill in August by sending a letter to the American government promising to suspend French restrictions on American shipping. In secret, however, the French emperor issued an order to continue seizing American ships. Despite Napoleon's devious intentions, Madison sought to use the French peace overture as a lever: he instructed the American mission in London to tell the British that France was dropping its restrictions and that Macon's Bill would force the president to close down trade with Britain unless England did the same. Sure that Napoleon was lying, the British refused, backing the president into a diplomatic corner. In February 1811, the provisions of Macon's Bill forced Madison to close trading with Britain for its failure to remove economic sanctions, stepping up tensions all around.

Later in the year, events in the West finally brought the diplomatic crisis to a head. The underlying origin of the problem was an agreement, the Fort Wayne Treaty, signed in the fall of 1809 between the United States and representatives of the Miamis, Potawatomis, and Delawares. In return for an outright bribe of $5,200 and individual **annuities** ranging from $250 to $500, the leaders of these three tribes sold over 3 million acres of Indian land in Indiana and Illinois—land already occupied by many other Indian groups.

In August 1810, Tecumseh and a delegation met with Governor William Henry Harrison in Vincennes, Indiana, to denounce the Fort Wayne Treaty. Harrison insisted that the agreement was legitimate. Speaking for those whose lands had been sold out from under them, Tecumseh said, "They want to save that piece of land, we do not wish you to take it. . . . I want the present boundary line to continue. Should you cross it, I assure you it will be productive of bad consequences." Having reached a complete stalemate, both Harrison and Tecumseh withdrew.

The Vincennes meeting convinced the Indians that they must prepare for a white attack. The Prophet increasingly preached the Master of Life's commitment to support the faithful in a battle against the whites. Tecumseh traveled up and down the American frontier, enlisting additional allies into his growing Indian confederacy.

Harrison grew more and more anxious to attack the Indians before they could unite fully. He got his chance in the fall of 1811. An isolated Potawatomi raid on a settler village in Illinois provided an excuse to mount a punitive assault on Prophetstown, even though Indians there had had nothing to do with the raid.

When Harrison's force of more than one thousand arrived and made camp near Tippecanoe Creek, the Prophet chose to ignore his older brother's advice to avoid confrontation and loosed a force of restless young Indians from Prophetstown on the governor's army. Prepared for the assault, white soldiers drove the attackers into the woods. The rout mocked the Prophet's assurance that the Master of Life would make the Indians victorious. Disheartened, most of the warriors from Prophetstown deserted the settlement, leaving it helpless against Harrison's reprisals.

War Hawks Members of Congress from the West and South who campaigned for war with Britain in the hopes of stimulating the economy and annexing new territory.

Non-Intercourse Act Law passed by Congress in 1809 reopening trade with all nations except France and Britain and authorizing the president to reopen trade with them if they lifted restrictions on American shipping.

Macon's Bill No. 2 Law passed by Congress in 1810 that offered exclusive trading rights to France or Britain, whichever recognized American neutral rights first.

annuity An allowance or income paid annually.

♦ In this romantic characterization of the Battle of Tippecanoe, a dashing William Henry Harrison prepares to ride into the thick of the fighting while his officers try to convince him to remain in safety. Such images fixed Harrison as a national hero in the American mind. Nearly thirty years later, Harrison was still remembered as "Old Tippecanoe" when he ran for president. *Collection of David J. and Janice L. Frent.*

In the so-called **Battle of Tippecanoe**, the army of enraged frontiersmen burned the village—and with it the Prophet's vision.

Tecumseh was away trying to win southwestern Indians over to his cause when Harrison's men burned Prophetstown. When he learned that hope for a peaceful settlement had gone up in smoke, he began gathering an army of Indian allies to make good on his word to defend Indian territory. Having succeeded in setting the Indian frontier ablaze, Harrison immediately called on the federal government for military support, claiming to be the victim of Indian and British aggression.

Headlining Harrison's call for assistance, a Kentucky newspaper proclaimed, "the war on the Wabash is purely BRITISH, the SCALPING KNIFE and TOMAHAWK of British savages, is now, again devastating our frontiers." Together with the breakdown of Congress's attempts at economic coercion and with confrontations between English and American ships, the outbreak of violence on the frontier was finally enough to push Madison into action. Still hoping for some sort of peaceful resolution, the president chose his words carefully when he told Congress, "We behold . . . on the side of Great Britain, a state of war against the United States; and on the side of the United States, a state of peace toward Britain."

John C. Calhoun, acting chairman of the House Foreign Relations Committee, issued a more forceful report stating, "The mad ambition, the lust of power, and the commercial avarice of Great Britain have left to neutral nations an alternative only between the base surrender of their rights, and a manly vindication of them." Having thrown down the gauntlet, Calhoun shortly thereafter introduced a war bill in Congress.

When the vote was finally cast in 1812, the war bill passed by a vote of 79 to 49 in the House and 19 to 13 in the Senate. Although they seemed to have the most to lose from continued indecisive policies, representatives from the heavily Federalist regions that depended the most on overseas trade—Massachusetts, Connecticut, and New York, for example—voted against war, while strongly Republican western and southern representatives voted in favor.

The Nation at War

- What geographic and economic factors constrained Americans in their war effort against Great Britain and Britain's Indian allies?
- Why were American military choices successful or not successful?

Although it must have seemed to many that the outbreak of war was inevitable, the nation was woefully unprepared when the breach with England finally came. With virtually no army or navy, the United States was taking a terrible risk in engaging what was fast becoming the most awesome military power in the world. Not surprisingly, defeat and humiliation were the main fruits of American efforts as the two nations faced off.

Battle of Tippecanoe Battle near Prophetstown in 1811, where American forces led by William Henry Harrison defeated the followers of the Shawnee Prophet and destroyed the town.

John C. Calhoun Congressman from South Carolina who was a leader of the War Hawks; he later became an advocate of states' rights.

♦ Naval victories like the sinking of the H.M.S. *Guerrièr* by the U.S.S. *Constitution*, shown here in an 1812 painting by Michael Felice Corne, were the only things keeping American morale alive during the disastrous first year of the War of 1812. *"Constitution & Guerrière" by Michael Felice Corne. The New Haven Colony Historical Society.*

The Fighting Begins

Despite years of agitation, the war's actual arrival caught the United States terribly unprepared. Republican cost cutting had virtually disbanded the military during Jefferson's first term in office. Renewed fighting with pirates in the Mediterranean and building tensions in the Atlantic had forced Republicans to increase military spending, but the navy still had fewer than twenty vessels and the army could field fewer than seven thousand men in 1812. And for all its war fever, Congress balked at appropriating new funds even after war had been declared. Thus the first ventures in the war went forward with only halfhearted financial support.

In line with what the War Hawks wanted, the first military campaign was a three-pronged drive toward Canada and against the Indians (see Map 9.2). One force, commanded by Harrison, was successful in raiding undefended Indian villages but was unable to make any gains against British troops. Farther east, a force led by Major General Stephen Van Rensselaer was defeated by a small British and Indian army. Meanwhile, the third force, commanded by Henry Dearborn, lunged at Montreal but nervously withdrew back into U.S. territory after an inconclusive battle against the British.

American sailors fared much better during the war's opening days. Leading the war effort at sea were three frigates: the *Constitution* (popularly known as **Old Ironsides**), the *President*, and the *United States*. In mid-August, the *Constitution* outmaneuvered and eventually sank what the British described as "one of our stoutest frigates," H.M.S. *Guerrière*. The *United States*, under the command of Stephen Decatur, enjoyed a victory against the British frigate H.M.S. *Macedonian*. Enduring thirty broadsides fired by the *Macedonian*, Decatur's gunners splintered the British ship with seventy broadsides of their own. Though no stranger to the horrors of war, Decatur was shocked by what he found when he boarded the crippled vessel: "fragments of the dead scattered in every direction, the decks slippery with blood, and one continuous agonizing yell of the unhappy wounded." American privateers also enjoyed naval success. During the first six months of the war, privateering vessels captured 450 British merchant ships valued in the millions.

American naval victories were all that kept the nation's morale alive in 1812. Former treasury secretary Albert Gallatin summarized the nation's military efforts: "The series of misfortunes," he wrote to Jefferson, "exceeds all anticipations made even by those who had least confidence in our inexperienced officers and undisciplined men." The land war had been, as another politician would recall, a "miscarriage, without even the heroism of disaster."

Old Ironsides Nickname of the U.S.S. *Constitution*, the 44-gun American frigate whose victory over the *Guerrière* bolstered sagging national morale during the War of 1812.

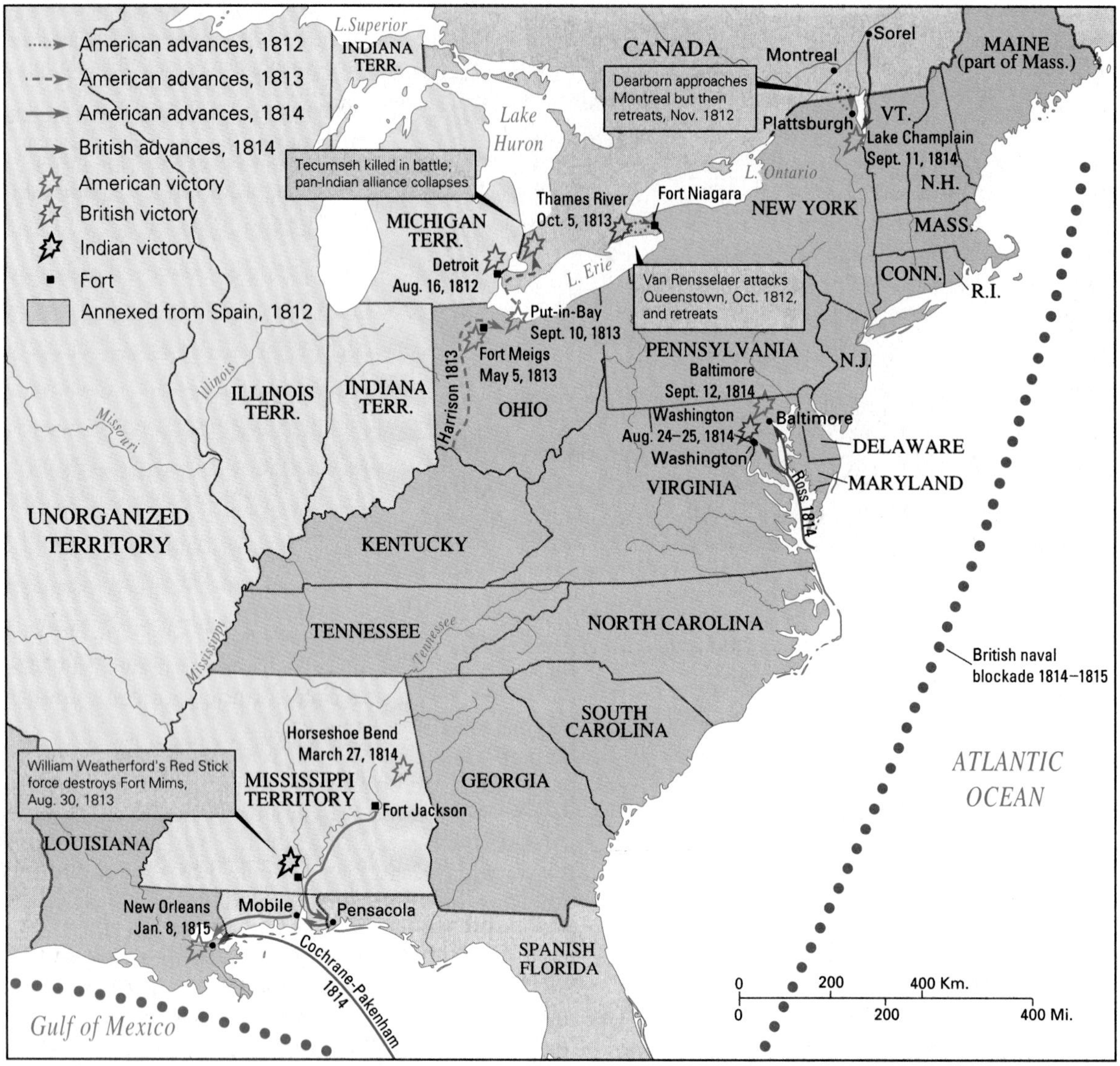

♦ **Map 9.2 The War of 1812** The heaviest action during the first two years of the War of 1812 lay along the U.S./Canadian border. In 1814, the British sought to knock the United States out of the war by staging three offensives: one along the northern frontier at Plattsburg, New York; one into the Chesapeake; and a third directed at the Mississippi River at New Orleans. All three offensives failed.

Vowing to reverse the situation, Congress increased the size of the army to fifty-seven thousand men and offered a $16 bonus to encourage enlistments.

Thus, in 1812, Madison stood for re-election at a time when the nation's military fate appeared uncertain and his own leadership seemed shaky. Although the majority of his party's congressional caucus supported him for re-election, nearly a third of the Republican congressmen—mostly those from New York and New England—rallied around New Yorker DeWitt Clinton, nephew and political ally of Madison's former challenger George Clinton. Like his uncle, DeWitt Clinton was a Republican who favored Federalist economic policies and agreed with New England Federalists that the war was unnecessary. Most Federalists supported Clinton, and the party did not field a candidate of its own.

When the campaign was over, the outcome was nearly the same as the outcome of the congressional vote on the war bill earlier in the year. New York

♦ Solid alliances with Indians who were disaffected by Jefferson's aggressive expansionism gave the British the edge in the opening years of the War of 1812. Here a British commander bids farewell to his Indian allies after playing a key role in the capture of Fort McKay at Prairie du Chien. *"Captain W. Andrew Bulger Saying Farewell at Fort McKay" by Peter Rindisbacher. Amon Carter Museum of Western Art.*

and New England rallied behind Clinton. The South and West continued to support Madison, the Republicans, and war. Madison won but was in no position to gloat. His share of electoral votes had fallen from 72 percent in 1808 to 58.9 percent, barely enough to win. At the same time, Republican party strength in the House dropped by over 13 percent, in the Senate by about 8 percent.

When military campaigning resumed in the spring of 1813, it appeared that the U.S. Army would fare as badly as it had fared in the embarrassing fall just past. The problem on the Canadian front was that the British controlled the Great Lakes and could depend on an uninterrupted supply line. In contrast, American forces and their supplies moved along undeveloped roads and were easy targets for Indian and British attackers. As soon as the spring thaw made sailing on the Great Lakes possible, the Americans moved to destroy Britain's advantage. On Lake Ontario they met frustration, as Americans, British, and Indians launched raids and counterraids that accomplished little. But on Lake Erie, the Americans met with some success.

Oliver Hazard Perry, a young naval tactician, had been given command of a small fleet assigned to clear Lake Erie of British ships. After months of playing hide-and-seek among the shore islands, British and American ships met in battle at Put-in-Bay in September 1813. Two hours of cannon fire left Perry's **flagship,** the *Lawrence,* nearly destroyed, and 80 percent of the crew lay dead or wounded. Perry refused to surrender. He slipped off his damaged vessel and took command of another ship standing nearby. What remained of his command then sailed back into the heart of the British force and after three hours of close combat subdued and captured six British ships. Perry immediately sent a note to William Henry Harrison stating, "We have met the enemy and they are ours."

Harrison's land campaign was not going nearly so well. In the spring of 1813, British general Henry Procter and Tecumseh, with a joint force of nine hundred British soldiers and twelve hundred Indians, laid siege to Harrison's command camped at Fort Meigs on the Maumee Rapids in Ohio. An army of twelve hundred Kentucky militiamen finally arrived and drove the enemy off, but they were so dis-

Oliver Hazard Perry American naval officer who led the fleet that defeated the British in the Battle of Put-in-Bay during the War of 1812.

flagship The ship that carries the fleet commander and bears the commander's flag.

organized that they lost nearly half of their number in pursuing the British and Indian force. Harrison was shocked, proclaiming the Kentuckians' "excessive ardour scarcely less fatal than cowardice."

Procter and Tecumseh continued to harass American forces through the summer of 1813. Then, with winter approaching, the British and Indians withdrew to Canada. Harrison, who had been busy raising additional troops, decided to pursue. His army caught up with the English and Indian force at the Thames River, about 50 miles east of Detroit, on October 5. A piercing cavalry charge caught the British unaware, and they soon surrendered. The Indians held out longer. But when word spread that Tecumseh had been killed, they melted into the woods, leaving the body of their fallen leader to be torn apart by the victorious Americans.

Another war front also opened during 1813. Although the Creek Confederacy as a whole wished to remain neutral, one faction had allied with Tecumseh in 1812. When war broke out, members of this faction, calling themselves the Red Sticks, violated tradition by raiding settlements in what are now Alabama and Mississippi without confederacy approval. Finally, in the summer of 1813 Red Stick leader William Weatherford led a force against Fort Mims, killing all but about thirty of the more than three hundred whites, Indians, and blacks there (see Individual Choices: William Weatherford).

The so-called Fort Mims massacre enraged whites in the Southeast. In Tennessee, twenty-five hundred militiamen rallied around **Andrew Jackson,** a young brawler and Indian fighter. Already called "Old Hickory" because of his toughness, Jackson promised that "the blood of our women & children shall not call for vengeance in vain." In the course of that summer and fall, the Red Stick Creeks suffered a series of staggering defeats and withdrew into hiding.

While these battles raged on land, the British shut down American forces at sea. Embarrassed by the success of Old Ironsides and the other American frigates, the British admiralty ordered that "the naval force of the enemy should be quickly and completely disposed of" and sent sufficient ships to do the job. The American naval fleet and **merchant marine** found themselves bottled up in port by the world's strongest navy.

The Politics of War

The war had wound down for the winter by the time Congress reconvened in December 1813, but things were not looking good, and the senators and representatives were anxious. Republican representative William Murfree spoke for many when he said, "The result of the last campaign disappointed the expectations of every one." President Madison tried to be optimistic. Recalling the victories during the year, he said, "The war, with its **vicissitudes,** is illustrating the capacity and destiny of the United States to be a great, a flourishing, and a powerful nation."

Madison's optimism seemed justified later in December when the British offered to open direct peace negotiations with the Americans. The president quickly instructed John Quincy Adams, James A. Bayard, Henry Clay, Jonathan Russell, and Albert Gallatin to form a peace commission. But until the commission's work was done, Madison and Congress still had to worry about the practical issues of troops and money, both of which were in critically short supply.

Despite increases in army pay and the payment of bonuses to new recruits, enlistments were falling off in 1813. Congressional Republicans responded by increasing the bonuses, including grants of 160 acres of land in the western territories for all new recruits. Congress also authorized the president to extend the term of enlistment for men already in service. By 1814, Congress had increased the size of the army to more than sixty-two thousand men but had not figured out how to pay for all the changes.

Presenting the federal budget for 1814, Treasury Secretary William Jones announced that the government's income would be approximately $16 million but its expenses would amount to over $45 million. Traditional enemies of internal taxes and public debt, the Republicans faced a dilemma. Shortly after convening, members of Congress had passed a set of new taxes and could not imagine explaining another increase to their constituents. So congressional Republicans decided to borrow instead, authorizing a $35 million deficit.

Adding to the money problem was the fact that to this point in the war, the United States had permit-

Andrew Jackson General who defeated the Creeks at Horseshoe Bend in 1814 and the British at New Orleans in 1815; he later became the seventh president of the United States.

merchant marine A nation's commercial ships.

vicissitudes Sudden or unexpected changes encountered during the course of life.

ted neutral nations to trade freely in American ports, carrying American exports to England and Canada and English goods into eastern ports. As a result of this flourishing trade, American currency was flooding out of the United States at an alarming rate, weakening the nation's economy. At the same time, American food was rolling directly into British military commissaries, strengthening the enemy's ability and will to fight.

In a secret message to Congress, the president proposed an absolute embargo on all American ships and goods—neither was to leave port—and a complete ban on imports that were customarily produced in Great Britain. Federalists, especially those from New England, screamed. They called the proposal "an engine of tyranny, an engine of oppression," no different, they said, from the Intolerable Acts imposed on American colonies by Britain in 1774 (see page 134). But congressional Republicans, following advice in a party newspaper that "the duty of the friends of the embargo was to act, not to speak," refused to enter into debate. They passed the embargo a mere eight days after Madison submitted it.

The **Embargo of 1813** was the most far-reaching trade restriction bill the American Congress ever passed. It confined all trading ships to port, and even fishing vessels could put to sea only if their masters posted sizable **bonds.** Government officials charged with enforcing the new law had unprecedented **discretionary powers.** The impact was far-reaching: the embargo virtually shut down the New England and New York economies, and it severely crippled the economy of nearly every other state.

New British Offensives

While Congress debated matters of finance and trade restrictions, events in Europe were changing the entire character of the war. On March 31, 1814, the British and their allies took Paris, forcing Napoleon to abdicate his throne. Few in America mourned the French emperor's fall. Jefferson wrote, "I rejoice . . . in the downfall of Bonaparte. This scourge of the world has occasioned the deaths of at least ten millions of human beings." Napoleon's defeat, however, left the United States as Great Britain's sole military target. Republican Joseph Nicholson expressed a common lament when he said, "We should have to fight hereafter not for 'free Trade and sailors rights,' not for the Conquest of the Canadas, but for our national Existence."

As Nicholson feared, a virtual flood of combat-hardened British veterans began arriving in North America after Napoleon's fall, and the survival of the United States as an independent nation was indeed at issue. By September 1814, British troop strength in Canada had risen to thirty thousand men. From this position of strength, the British prepared a chain of three offensives to bring the war to a quick end.

Although fighting raged sporadically all along the Canadian frontier, the main thrust of the British offensive in the North was against eastern New York. Sir George Prevost, governor-general of Canada, massed ten thousand troops for an invasion of the United States through Plattsburgh, New York. The British force arrived just north of Plattsburgh on September 6, pausing there to await support from the British fleet that controlled Lake Champlain. However, a small American fleet under the command of Lieutenant Thomas Macdonough outmaneuvered the imposing British fleet and forced it to surrender on September 11.

In the meantime, Prevost had begun his attack against the defenders at Plattsburgh, but when he learned that the British lake fleet was defeated and in flames, he lost his nerve and ordered his men to retreat. Prevost and his forces managed to withdraw 8 miles before the surprised Americans realized what had happened. The New Yorkers gave chase and turned the retreat into a rout.

While Prevost's offensive was under way in the North, the British opened a second front farther south. In August 1814, twenty British warships and several troop transports sailed up Chesapeake Bay toward Washington, D.C. The British landed a force outside Washington at midday on August 24. Three lines of Maryland militiamen, numbering perhaps seven thousand in all, managed to hold off the experienced British regulars until most of the civilians in the capital, including the president, had been evacuated. Even so, much of value was lost in this humiliating blow to American pride. The British sacked the city, looting many buildings, including the White House, and then torched most of the struc-

Embargo of 1813 An absolute embargo on all American trade and British imports.

bond A sum of money paid as bail or security.

discretionary powers Powers to be used at one's own discretion or judgment.

INDIVIDUAL CHOICES

Choice in Civil War

William Weatherford

Tecumseh's effort to unite all Indians into a single political military alliance split the Creek Confederacy into two warring factions. At first, William Weatherford tried to mediate between the two, but he encountered serious constraints and finally chose to lead the "red stick" faction into war against the United States. Tennessee State Library & Archives

William Weatherford had the potential to be the most powerful man in the Creek Nation. Like his maternal uncle Alexander McGillivray, Weatherford was part white and part Indian. But the Creeks are matrilineal, tracing family roots back only through the mother's line, so he was fully Creek in the tribe's eyes. Creek tradition also marked him to inherit McGillivray's position as the dominant chief in the confederacy. But by 1800, historical pressures on the Creeks had eroded traditional ways of doing things, and Weatherford's position was far from secure. In 1812, he found himself facing a difficult choice: he had to choose sides, for the Creek Nation was split by civil war.

The Creek Nation was a confederacy of Indian groups that spoke a variety of languages, had different customs, and practiced quite different economies. Over time, these groups had aligned themselves into two large organizations: the Lower Towns—villages in the low-lying southern part of Creek territory in modern-day Georgia and Alabama—and the Upper Towns—villages in the more mountainous and heavily wooded northern part of the region. Geographical and cultural diversity helped to hold the Creek Confederacy together: the many different resources controlled by different Creek member villages led them to depend on each other.

By the end of the eighteenth century, the mutually dependent economy that had kept the Creek towns aligned was giving way to greater dependence on the Europeans. In the Upper Towns, where Weatherford was born, the fur trade distracted hunters from providing meat and other necessities to the confederacy. In the Lower Towns, the lure of growing cotton and tobacco for sale to the whites distracted the people from providing corn. In many villages, essential commodities had to be purchased outside the confederacy.

The economic separation between the two areas became a source of major conflict after 1808, when President Jefferson's embargo triggered a depression. Suddenly, Creeks in the Upper Towns had no market for their furs. Blaming whites for their dependency on the fur trade, and the fur trade for their dire economic situation, many in the Upper Towns found the Shawnee Prophet's message of turning away from white ways appealing. More appealing still was Tecumseh's suggestion of empowerment through joint action. Not surprisingly, then, when Tecumseh visited the Creeks in 1811, he was well received in the Upper Towns, and many chose to follow Tecumseh's red war stick.

It appears that Weatherford was leery of Tecumseh, but the response by the Lower Towns to Tecumseh's visit forced Weatherford's hand. Allied by common economic interests with southern white planters, Creeks in the Lower Towns feared that rumors of an alliance between Creeks in the Upper Towns and the Shawnees might ruin their economy further and, more important, close off avenues of improvement through political cooperation with their white neighbors. Creeks in the Lower Towns began putting enormous pressure on the Upper Towns to turn away from Tecumseh's message. Weatherford and other responsible leaders tried to keep the peace, but when war broke out between the Americans and the British in 1812, that became hard to do. In February 1813, rogue bands of Red Sticks went on forays against settlements, aiming to punish whites for attacks or rumored attacks on Indians.

Bent on preventing war with the Americans, the Creeks in the Lower Towns sent an armed party against the Upper Towns to put an end to Red Stick violence. That only worsened the situation. Determined to defend themselves, the Upper Towns sent a party under Red Stick leader Peter McQueen to the Spanish post at Pensacola to buy guns and ammunition. Though not yet committed to the Red Stick position, Weatherford accompanied this party, possibly hoping to prevent further outbreaks. A combined force of white militiamen and Creeks from the Lower Towns stumbled on them at midday on July 27, attacking them while they ate lunch. Most of McQueen's party was able to escape, but the bodies of the twenty men who were killed in the surprise attack were brutally defiled. For Weatherford, that was the last straw. An honorable peace no longer seemed possible, and he chose war.

A little over a month later, Weatherford led about seven hundred Red Sticks on a raid against Fort Mims, a post jointly occupied by Creeks from the Lower Towns and by white militiamen with their families. Weatherford and his force launched their assault as the lunch bell rang at noon on August 30. Within moments they swept into the surprised post, and a general melee began. When the fighting stopped, between three hundred and five hundred people lay dead, and the fort was in flames. Major Joseph P. Kennedy, who arrived at the fort ten days after the battle, reported, "Indians, negroes, white men, women, and children lay in one promiscuous ruin."

Though he preferred peace and was no convert to the teachings of Tecumseh and the Prophet, Weatherford had seen his choices narrow as differing interests among the Creeks pulled the confederacy apart. Pushed finally into making a choice, his decision forever altered the Creek Nation's future. After the massacre at Fort Mims, there was no going back: the destiny of the Creeks depended on the outcome of Tecumseh's plan and British military success.

tures, including the Capitol. With little left to destroy, the British abandoned the ruins of Washington on August 25, marching through Alexandria toward the key port city of Baltimore.

At Baltimore, the British navy had to knock out Fort McHenry and take the harbor before the army could take the city. On September 12, British ships armed with heavy **mortars** and rockets attacked the fort. During a twenty-five-hour bombardment, the British fired more than fifteen hundred rounds at the American post. Despite the pounding, when the sun rose on September 14, the American flag continued to wave over Fort McHenry. The sight moved a young Georgetown volunteer named **Francis Scott Key,** who had watched the shelling as a prisoner aboard one of the British ships, to record the event in a poem that was later set to music and became the national anthem of the United States. Having failed to reduce the fort, the British were forced to withdraw, leaving Baltimore undisturbed.

On yet another front, the British pressed an offensive against the Gulf coast designed to take pressure off Canada and close transportation on the Mississippi River. The defense of the Gulf coast fell to Andrew Jackson and his Tennesseans. Having spent the winter raising troops and collecting supplies, in March 1814 Jackson and his army of four thousand militiamen and Cherokee volunteers resumed their mission to punish the Red Stick Creeks. Learning that the Red Sticks had established a camp on the peninsula formed by the **Horseshoe Bend** of the Tallapoosa River, Jackson led his men on a forced march to do battle. On March 27, Jackson's force massacred nearly eight hundred Indians, destroying Red Stick opposition and severely crippling Indian resistance in the South.

After the massacre at Horseshoe Bend, Jackson moved his army toward the Mississippi. Arriving in New Orleans on December 1, he found the city ill prepared to defend itself. The local militia, consisting mostly of French and Spanish residents, would not obey American officers, and local banks and businesses refused to support government efforts. Ever a man of action, Jackson permitted no opposition or apathy. "Those who are not for us are against us, and will be dealt with accordingly," he proclaimed, and through the example of his own energy and enthusiasm he transformed the community. Soon volunteers flooded to the general's assistance. Free blacks in the city formed a regular army corps, and Jackson created a special unit of black refugees from Santo Domingo under the command of Colonel Jean Baptiste Savary. White citizens protested Jackson's arming runaway slaves, but he ignored their objections. "Legitimate citizens" protested too when Jackson accepted a company of river pirates under the command of **Jean Laffite.** "Hellish Banditti," Jackson himself called them, but the pirate commander and the general hit it off so well that Laffite became Jackson's constant companion and unofficial assistant during the campaign.

Having pulled his ragtag force together, Jackson settled in to wait for the British attack. On the morning of January 7, 1815, it came. The British force, commanded by General Edward Pakenham, emerged from the fog at dawn, directly in front of Jackson's defenses. Waiting patiently behind hastily constructed barricades, Jackson's men began firing cannon, rifle, and musket as the British moved within range. According to one British veteran, it was "the most murderous fire I have ever beheld before or since." Pakenham tried to keep his men from running but was cut in half by a cannon ball.

The British lost more than two thousand men in the **Battle of New Orleans.** The victorious Americans lost only seventy. This was by far the most successful battle fought by American forces during the War of 1812. But, ironically, when it took place, the war was already officially over.

The War's Strange Conclusion

While the British had been closing in on Washington in the summer of 1814, treaty negotiations designed to end the war were beginning in Ghent, Belgium.

mortar A portable, muzzle-loading cannon.

Francis Scott Key Author of "The Star-Spangled Banner," which chronicles the British bombardment of Fort McHenry in 1814; Key's poem, set to music, became the official U.S. national anthem in 1916.

Horseshoe Bend Site of a battle in 1814 in which Tennessee militia massacred Creek Indians in Alabama, ending Red Stick resistance to white westward expansion.

Jean Laffite Leader of a band of pirates in southeast Louisiana; he offered to fight for the Americans at New Orleans in return for the pardon of his men.

Battle of New Orleans Battle in the War of 1812 in which American troops commanded by Andrew Jackson decimated the British force attempting to seize New Orleans.

♦ The nearly miraculous American victory in the Battle of New Orleans—fought two weeks after the Americans and British had signed a peace treaty—helped launch a new era in American nationalism. And, as this illustration from a popular magazine shows, it made Andrew Jackson, shown waving his hat to encourage his troops, a national hero of greater than human proportions. *Library of Congress.*

Madison's peace commission found the British delegation "arrogant, overbearing, and offensive." The British were confident that their three-pronged attack against the United States would soon knock the Americans out of the war. In no hurry to end the war by diplomacy, the British negotiators refused to discuss substantive issues, insisting that impressment and the formation of a permanent Indian frontier between Canada and the United States were non-negotiable.

At that point, however, domestic politics in England began to play a deciding role. After nearly a generation at arms, the English people were tired of war, and especially tired of paying for it. As one British official put it, "Economy & relief from taxation are not merely the War Cry of Opposition, but they are the real objects to which public attention is turned." The failures at Plattsburgh and Baltimore made it appear that at best the war would drag on at least another year, at an estimated cost to Britain of an additional $44 million. Moreover, continuation of the American war was interfering with Britain's European diplomacy. Trying to arrive at a peace settlement for Europe at the Congress of Vienna, a British official commented, "We do not think the Continental Powers will continue in good humour with our Blockade of the whole Coast of America." Speaking for the military, the duke of Wellington reviewed British military successes and failures in the American war and concluded, "You have no right . . . to demand any **concession** . . . from America."

In the end, the **Treaty of Ghent,** completed on December 24, 1814, simply restored diplomatic relations between England and the United States to what they had been prior to the outbreak of war. The treaty said nothing about impressment, blockades, or neutral trading rights. Neither military action nor diplomatic finagling netted Canada for the War Hawks. And the treaty did nothing about the supposed conspiracies between Indians and British agents, for they had never existed. Although Americans called the War of 1812 a victory, they actually

concession Something given up during negotiations.

Treaty of Ghent Treaty ending the War of 1812, signed in Belgium in 1814; it restored peace but was silent on the issues over which the United States and Britain had clashed.

won none of the things that Madison's war statement had declared the nation was fighting for.

Peace and the Rise of New Expectations

• How did events during the War of 1812 help to foster new expectations for Americans after peace arrived?

Despite repeated military disasters, loss of life, and diplomatic failure, the war had a number of positive effects on the United States. Just to have survived a war against the British—a nation that had emerged after a generation at arms as the most powerful military force in the world—was enough to build national confidence, but to have scored major victories like those at Plattsburgh and especially at New Orleans was truly worth boasting about. Americans emerged from the conflict with a new sense of national pride and purpose. And many side effects from the fighting itself gave Americans new hopes and plans.

New Expectations in the Northeastern Economy

Although trading interests in the Northeast suffered following Jefferson's embargo and were nearly ruined by the war and Madison's embargo, a new avenue of economic expansion opened in New England. Cut off from European manufactured goods, Americans started to make more textiles and other items for themselves.

Samuel Slater, an English immigrant who had been employed in manufacturing in Britain, introduced the use of machines for spinning cotton thread to the United States in 1790. His mill was financially successful, but few others tried to copy his enterprise. Even with shipping expenses, tariffs, and other added costs, buying machine-made British cloth was still more practical than investing large sums at high risk to build competing factories in the United States. And after 1800, Jefferson's economic policies discouraged such investment. But the embargo changed all that. After it went into effect, British fabrics became increasingly unavailable and prices soared. Slater and his partners moved quickly to expand their spinning operations to fill the void. And now his inventiveness was widely copied.

Another entrepreneur, Francis Cabot Lowell, chose to go even farther than Slater. Left in the lurch economically by the embargo, Lowell ventured to England in 1810. While there, he engaged in wholesale industrial espionage, observing British textile-manufacturing practices and machinery and making detailed notes and sketches of what he saw. Returning to the United States just before war broke out in 1812, Lowell joined with fellow New Englanders Nathan Appleton and Patrick Tracy Jackson to form the Boston Manufacturing Company. In 1813, the company used the plans Lowell had smuggled back to the United States to build a factory in Waltham, Massachusetts. The new facility included spinning machines, power looms, and all the equipment necessary to **mechanize** every stage in the production of finished cloth, bringing the entire process under one roof. Like Slater's innovations, Lowell's too were copied quickly by economically desperate New Englanders.

The spread of textile manufacturing during the embargo and war eras was astonishing. Prior to 1808, only fifteen cotton mills of the sort Slater had introduced had been built in the entire country. But between the passage of the embargo and the end of 1809, eighty-seven additional mills had sprung up, mostly in New England. And when war came, the pace increased, especially when Lowell's idea of a mechanized textile factory proved to be highly efficient and profitable. The number of people employed in industry increased from four thousand in 1809 to perhaps as many as a hundred thousand in 1816. In the years to come, factories in New England and elsewhere supplied more and more of the country's consumer goods, changing economic roles and hopes for many Americans.

A Revolution in the Southern Economy

In the years before the War of 1812, the southern economy had been sluggish, and the future of the region's single-crop agricultural system was doubtful. Tobacco, the mainstay of the South's economy, was no longer the glorious profit maker it had been during the colonial period. Sea Island cotton, rice, sugar, and other products continued to find markets, but they grew in limited areas and could not

mechanize To substitute machinery for human labor.

♦ During the War of 1812, interruption in American trade with Great Britain led to a shortage of manufactured goods. In villages all over New England, small mills like this one, built in 1814, began springing up to fill the void. A good mill site—one with dependable water power and a rock solid foundation—often attracted many factories, turning what had once been a small rural village into a manufacturing city. *"Globe Village" by Francis Alexander, 1822. Jacob Edwards Library, Southbridge, MA. Photo by Clive Russ.*

expand much farther. However, the technological and economic changes that came in the war's wake pumped new energy into the South's economy. In only a few decades, an entirely new South was going to emerge.

Southern planters had been growing cotton since colonial times, although the demand for it and profits from its sale were small. The mechanization of the British textile industry in the late eighteenth century brought dramatic changes. The production of cotton cloth rapidly increased, and the need for raw cotton fiber grew.

Large areas of the South were suitable for growing short-staple, or short-fiber, cotton, but the time and labor required to pick the sticky seeds from the compact **cotton bolls** made the crop unprofitable. **Eli Whitney**, a 1792 graduate of Yale College, found a solution to the problem and gave a shot in the arm to the South's stagnating economy. In 1793, Whitney was a guest at a plantation in Georgia. There he learned about the difficulty of removing the seeds from short-staple cotton. In a matter of weeks, Whitney designed a machine that quickly combed out the seeds without damaging the fibers and did not require an army of skilled operators. He obtained a **patent** for the cotton gin (short for "cotton engine") in 1794 and set up a factory in New Haven, Connecticut, to manufacture the machine. Whitney's engine, though revolutionary in its impact, was a relatively simple mechanism, and despite his patent, other manufacturers and individual planters stole the design and built their own cotton gins.

cotton boll The pod of the cotton plant; it contains the plant's seeds surrounded by the fluffy fiber that is spun into thread.

Eli Whitney American inventor and manufacturer; his invention of the cotton gin revolutionized the cotton industry.

patent A government grant that gives the creator of an invention the sole right to produce, use, or sell that invention for a set period of time.

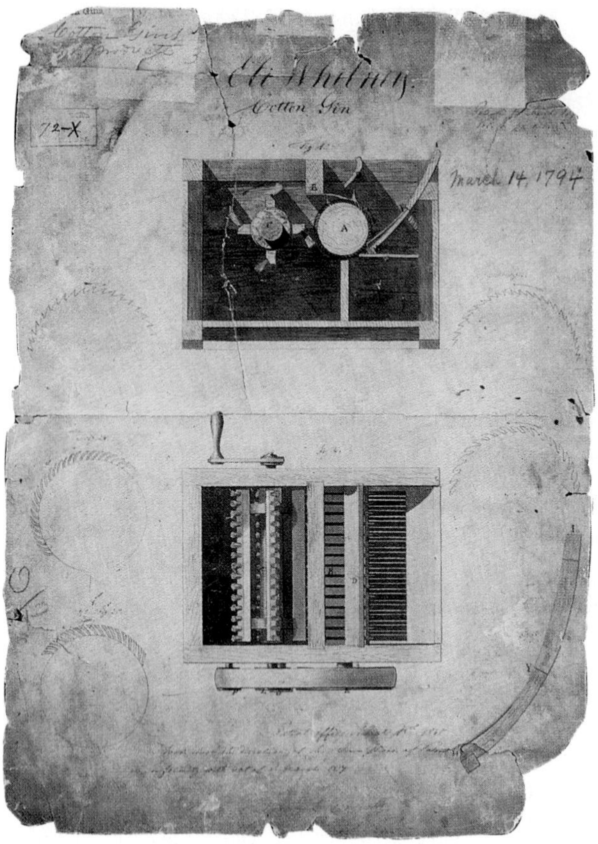

♦ The simple mechanism shown in this 1794 patent drawing by Eli Whitney revolutionized the world's economy in the early nineteenth century. The cotton gin allowed most of the American South to profit by growing cotton, which in turn helped to spur greater investment in mechanized textile manufacturing throughout the world. So many people violated Whitney's patent that the inventor never made a cent from this revolutionary tool. *National Archives.*

The outcome of Whitney's inventiveness was the rapid spread of short-staple cotton throughout inland South Carolina and Georgia. Then, just as it seemed that the southern economy was about to bloom, embargo and war closed down exports to England. Although some cotton growers were able to shift sales from England to the rising new factories in New England, a true explosion of growth in cotton raising had to await war's end.

With the arrival of peace and the departure of the British naval blockade, cotton growing began to spread at a staggering rate. The massacre of the Red Stick Creeks removed the final major threat of Indian resistance in the South, and southerners rushed into frontier areas, spreading cotton agriculture into Alabama and Mississippi and then into Arkansas, northern Louisiana, and east Texas. From 1815 onward, the South's annual cotton crop grew by leaps and bounds. By 1840, annual exports reached nearly a million and a half bales, and increasing volumes were consumed within the United States by the mushrooming textile factories in the Northeast. In fact, the swelling flow of cotton from the South helped spur the development of industrialization in the North, and northern demand in turn encouraged southern suppliers to plant more cotton. This dynamic interaction between North and South pushed the economies of both regions forward but propelled them in different directions. Although both remained predominantly rural, the North moved toward mechanization and urbanization, and the South depended more and more on the labor of people rather than on the power of machines. These transformations and their impact on American life are discussed in Chapter 11.

New Opportunities in the West

Cotton growers were not the only people who saw new opportunities in the West after the war. As the economy began to recover and then to race following 1815, many rushed to the frontier to seek their fortunes.

One of the most important outcomes of the War of 1812 was the change wrought in the relations between the United States and the various Indian nations. When Harrison's soldiers burned Prophetstown and later killed Tecumseh, they wiped out all hopes for a pan-Indian confederacy. In addition, the civil war among the Creeks, followed by Jackson's victories against the Red Stick faction, removed all meaningful resistance to westward expansion in the South. Many Indian groups continued to wield great power, but accommodationist leaders like those who formed the Cherokee government and acculturationist philosophies like that of Handsome Lake (see page 236) suggested that cooperation with federal authorities was the best course.

Collaboration between the United States and Native Americans helped to prevent renewed warfare, but at enormous cost to the Indians. Within a year of the Battle of Horseshoe Bend, Jackson forced the Creeks to sign the Treaty of Fort Jackson, which confiscated over 20 million acres of land from the Creek Confederacy. A similar but more gradual assault on Indian landholding began in the Northwest in 1815. In a council meeting at Portage des Sioux in Illinois

♦ Following the War of 1812 and the death of Tecumseh, aggressive American expansionists put great pressure on Indians living on the east side of the Mississippi River to move farther west. Artist James Otto Lewis was present at the 1825 Prairie du Chien treaty meetings, where various Sauk and Fox, Menominee, Iowa, Winnebago, Ojibwa, and Sioux bands gave up much of their land. He was present the following year at similar talks at Fond du Lac, where he painted these three Chippewa (Ojibwa) women. *"Chippeway Squaws at the Treaty of Fond du Lac" by James Otto Lewis, 1826. Chicago Historical Society.*

Territory, the United States signed peace accords with the various tribes that had joined the British during the war. Both sides agreed that their earlier hostilities would be "forgiven and forgotten" and that all the agreeing parties would live in "perpetual peace and friendship." The northwestern Indians, however, possessed some 2 million acres of prime real estate between the Illinois and Mississippi rivers—land that the United States government had already given away as enlistment bonuses to white war volunteers. Moving the Indians off that land as quickly as possible thus became a matter of national priority.

Over the next several years, government agents used every tactic they could think of to coerce groups like the Kickapoos into ceding their lands. Finally, in 1819, the Kickapoo Nation signed the Treaty of Edwardsville, turning over most of the land the United States had demanded.

Having secured this enormous tract, government agents then turned their attention to the vast holdings of tribes like the Sauk, Fox, Chippewas, and Dakotas in western Illinois, Wisconsin, and Michigan. As they had done with the Kickapoos, American negotiators used bribery, threat, and manipulation of local tensions to pursue their goal, eventually winning an enormous cession of land in the Prairie du Chien treaties of 1825.

With these lands opened and the Indian situation apparently resolved, pioneers came flooding into the West in astounding numbers. The population of Ohio had already soared from 45,000 in 1800 to 231,000 in 1810, but it more than doubled again by 1820, reaching 581,000. Indiana, Illinois, Missouri, and Michigan experienced similar growth.

Most of those who flooded into the newly opened West were farmers, but subsistence agriculture was not the only economic opportunity that drew entrepreneurs into the region. Big business, too, had great expectations for finding new wealth in the West.

One of the designs behind the Lewis and Clark and the Zebulon Pike expeditions had been to gain entry for the United States into the burgeoning economy in North America's interior (see pages 228–230). Although the economy was complex, with many commodities being traded, and was little understood by most Americans, one facet was well known and very desirable to entrepreneurs: the brown gold of beaver, mink, and other animal furs.

Even before the War of 1812, individual fur traders had tried to break the monopoly that the English and Canadians held over the trade along the northern frontier and the monopoly of the Spanish and French farther south. One particularly visionary businessman had already put a plan in motion to create a continent-wide trading network before the war. John Jacob Astor, a German immigrant who arrived in the United States in 1783, announced that he intended to establish "a range of Posts or Trading houses" along the route that Lewis and Clark had followed from St. Louis to the Pacific (see Map 8.2).

The key to Astor's vision of a fur empire was a post at the place where the Columbia River flows into the Pacific Ocean. His employees began building it in March 1811. Astor planned to collect furs at this post and ship them directly to Asia, where neither the rival English Hudson's Bay Company nor the Canadian North West Company could trade directly because of British law. In Asia, the furs would be exchanged for tea, spices, silks, and other popular trade items. The outbreak of war in 1812 dashed Astor's immediate hopes: the British seized his Pacific post, forcing Astor and his partners to sell their far western operation to the North West Company. Despite this setback, Astor continued to expand his domain in the western fur business and the Asia trade, becoming a leading figure in world commerce. When he died in 1848, John Jacob Astor was the richest man in the United States.

Another visionary entrepreneur sought a similar fortune in the Southwest. Auguste Chouteau was French by birth, but like many frontiersmen, he changed nationalities as frequently as the land changed owners. Chouteau had helped to found the town of St. Louis and had been instrumental in establishing that city as the capital for a fur-trading empire. Through a complex tapestry of intermarriage, he and his brother Pierre created a massive kinship network that included important French, Spanish, and Indian connections. With kinship ensuring cooperative trading partners, the Chouteau brothers were able to extend their reach deep into the Missouri region and establish trade between St. Louis and the Spanish far western trading capital at Santa Fe (see pages 46 and 52). As Americans began to penetrate the area, the Chouteau brothers took the change in stride, inviting William Clark of the Lewis and Clark expedition and fur entrepreneur Andrew Henry to join forces with them in founding the Missouri Fur Company in 1809.

As with Astor's enterprise, the war disrupted the activities of the Missouri Fur Company, but when the war was over, business went on with increasing vigor. Pierre Chouteau and his various American partners pushed continually farther into the West, using their strategy of forming traditional Indian trading partnerships, often rooted in intermarriage, to expand business. Chouteau also used his kin partnerships and capital from the fur trade to branch into other businesses. He was a cofounder of the Bank of Missouri and served as its president for a number of years. He also operated flour mills and distilleries and speculated in real estate. Members of his extended family later helped to found Kansas City, pioneer mining in Colorado, and finance railroad building in the Dakotas.

The joint efforts of individual farmers and business tycoons like Astor and the Chouteaus opened the West and proved to the satisfaction of many that great fortunes and good lives could be had on the frontier. Though the promise was always greater than the reality, the allure of the West was unmistakable. And after the War of 1812, the nation's aspirations became more and more firmly tied to that region's growth and development.

SUMMARY

E xpectations
C onstraints
C hoices
O utcomes

After Jefferson's triumphal first four years in office, factional disputes at home and diplomatic problems began to *constrain* the Republicans. Although the Federalists were in full retreat, many within Jefferson's own party *chose* to oppose some of his policies. When Jefferson stepped down in 1808, tapping James Madison as his successor, Republicans in both the Northeast and the South bucked the president, supporting James Monroe and George Clinton, respectively.

To a large extent, the Republicans' problems were the *outcome* of external stresses. On the Atlantic frontier, the United States tried to remain neutral in the wars that engulfed Europe. On the western frontier, the Prophet and Tecumseh were successfully unifying dispossessed Indians into a single nation devoted to stopping U.S. expansion. Jefferson *chose* to use federal and executive power to meet these *con-*

straints and settle disputes, and his enemies rose in protest.

Things went from bad to worse when Jefferson's use of economic sanctions gave rise to the worst depression since the beginnings of English colonization. The embargo strangled the economy in port cities, and the downward spiral in agricultural prices threatened to bankrupt many in the West and South.

The combination of economic and diplomatic *constraints* brought aggressive politicians to power in 1808 and 1810. Men like William Henry Harrison *expected* that war with England would permit the United States to finally prove independence—forcing freedom of the seas, eliminating Indian hostility, and justifying the conquest of the rest of North America. Despite Madison's continuing peace efforts, southern and western interests finally pushed the nation into the *choice* for war with England.

Although there were some glimmering moments of glory for the Americans, the war was mostly disastrous. But after generations *constrained* by fighting one enemy or another, the English people *chose* to demand peace. When their final offensive in America failed to bring immediate victory in 1814, the British *chose* to negotiate. Finally, on Christmas Eve, the two nations signed the Treaty of Ghent, ending the war. From a diplomatic point of view, it was as though the war had never happened: everything was simply restored to what it had been before 1812.

Nevertheless, in the United States the economic and political *outcomes* of the war created strong feelings of national pride and confidence, and new *expectations* arose for great things to come. In the Northeast, the *constraints* of war provoked entrepreneurs to explore new industries, creating the first stage of an industrial revolution in the country. In the South, the economy was revolutionized by the cotton gin and the growing demand for fiber being made by English and then American manufacturers. In the West, the defeat of Indian resistance combined with new economic opportunities to start a wave of westward migration. The clouds that had begun gathering a decade before were lifting, and Americans were ready for a springtime of good feelings.

SUGGESTED READINGS

Gregory E. Dowd. *A Spirited Resistance: The North American Indian Struggle for Unity, 1745–1815* (1992).

Hailed by many as one of the best new works on Native American history, this well-written study covers the efforts by Indians to unite in defense of their lands and heritages, culminating in the struggles during the War of 1812.

R. David Edmunds. *The Shawnee Prophet* (1983); *Tecumseh and the Quest for Indian Leadership* (1984).

Each of these biographies is a masterpiece, but taken together they present the most complete recounting of the lives and accomplishments of these two fascinating Shawnee brothers and their historical world.

William F. Fowler, Jr. *Jack Tars and Commodores* (1984).

A look at one of the more interesting aspects of the War of 1812: the sea battles and the men who fought them.

Donald Hickey. *The War of 1812: A Forgotten Conflict* (1989).

Arguably the best single-volume history of the war, encyclopedic in content, but so colorfully written that it will hold anyone's attention.

Drew McCoy. *The Last of the Fathers: James Madison and the Republican Legacy* (1989).

Hailed by most critics as the best treatment yet written on Madison and his role in making the early republic.

Robert A. Rutland. *Madison's Alternatives: The Jeffersonian Republicans and the Coming of War, 1805–1812* (1975).

An interesting review of the events leading up to the outbreak of war in 1812 and the various alternatives Jefferson and Madison had to choose from in facing the evolving diplomatic and political crises.

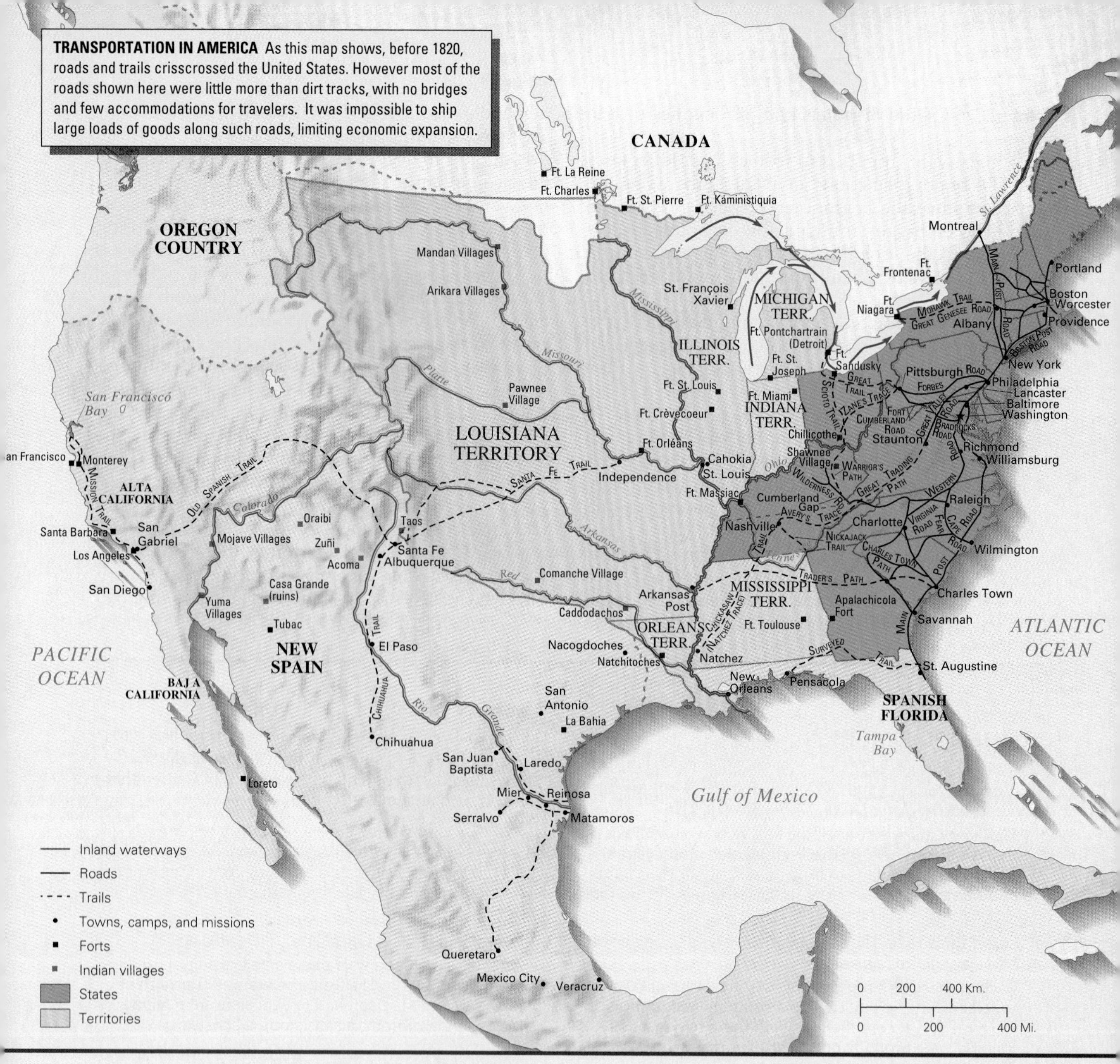

TRANSPORTATION IN AMERICA As this map shows, before 1820, roads and trails crisscrossed the United States. However most of the roads shown here were little more than dirt tracks, with no bridges and few accommodations for travelers. It was impossible to ship large loads of goods along such roads, limiting economic expansion.

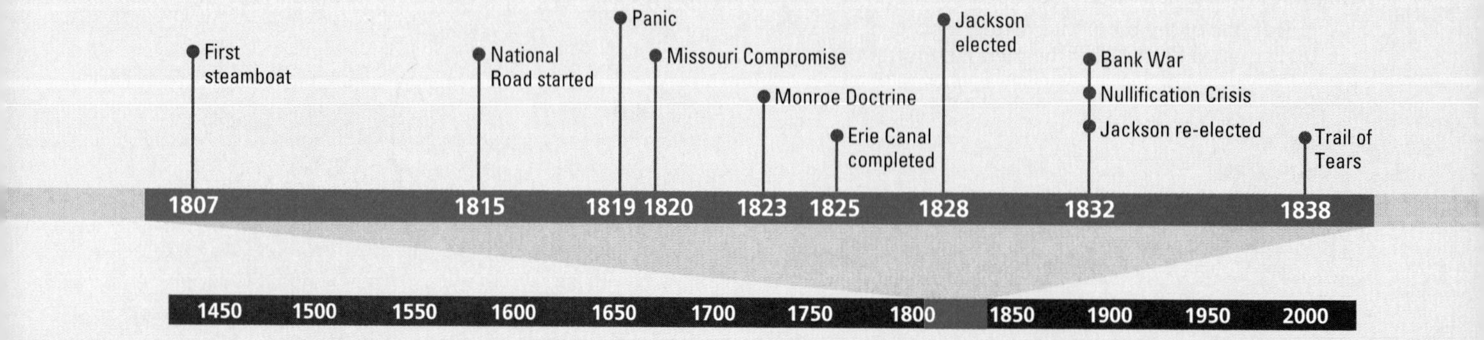

CHAPTER 10

The Rise of a New Nation, 1815–1836

An "Era of Good Feelings"

- What new expectations did Americans have as they emerged from the War of 1812?
- What economic constraints did they seek to overcome, and how did they choose to overcome them?
- How did new expectations influence choices in foreign affairs?

Dynamic Growth and Political Consequences

- How did the expectation of prosperity and economic growth help lead to economic panic in 1819?
- How did growth and panic contribute to choices that led to sectional conflict and political contention?

The "New Man" in Politics

- What factors helped change Americans' political expectations during the mid-1820s?
- How did the election of Andrew Jackson in 1828 reflect those new expectations?

The Reign of King Andrew

- Analyze the choices Jackson made in his Indian policy.
- What constraints faced by each region of the country influenced the national divisions reflected in the nullification crisis and the Bank War?

INTRODUCTION

E xpectations
C onstraints
C hoices
O utcomes

The United States emerged from the War of 1812 with new confidence. The seasoned veterans in the British army "attest the prowess of our troops," one Protestant preacher declared at war's end, "and the world is astonished at the facility with which our naval heroes have conquered, when they met upon terms of equality, those who have conquered all other nations." Many believed that the United States had finally become a nation to contend with, and nationalism emerged as the dominant force in domestic and international affairs. For some, loyalty to their states or regions remained paramount, but many began to think of themselves as Americans for the first time.

Confident *expectations* for national development led to *choices* that greatly influenced the country's future. Both James Madison and his successor James Monroe strongly favored a coherent national economy, and each president worked to shape one. Strong nationalists like Henry Clay and John C. Calhoun proposed and piloted through Congress bills designed to expand transportation systems, strengthen the nation's currency, and encourage economic development. At the same time, other nationalists like diplomat John Quincy Adams and soldier Andrew Jackson were at work expanding the nation itself, pushing the country's borders farther into the continent.

Expanding economic opportunities, too, created optimistic *expectations*, and many Americans *chose* to invest in transportation systems and in new, specialized forms of manufacturing and agriculture. Initial *constraints* were brushed aside as a confident generation developed new technologies, new systems of engineering, and organizational innovations. New York and other states leaped to accept the federal invitation to develop transportation and communication systems, and the entire country began to feel the pressure to modernize. But an integrated "American System" of economics was not possible until fundamental changes were made in federal law. And even then, varying customs and lifestyles in the North, West, and South had to be made more compatible. For the moment, the optimistic *expectations* of most Americans produced a spirit of cooperation—an "Era of Good Feelings"—that pervaded the nation's politics. But paradoxically, regional economic specialization—with its accompanying *outcome* of distinct sectional cultures and political interests—was pulling the nation apart even as technology and economic interdependence was drawing it closer together.

Politics, too, underwent profound change in the new nation that emerged from the War of 1812. The old generation of Revolutionary War statesmen was dying out and being replaced by a new, young, and restless generation of politicians. This new generation called out for freer access to government, even for men who owned no property. Like a knight on a tall charger, General Andrew Jackson became their champion. Sweeping from the backwoods of Tennessee and into the White House, the frontier Democrat brought a new kind of politics onto the national scene. Assuming greater presidential powers than even Jefferson could have imagined, Jackson placed his own personal stamp on the era and on the nation.

CHRONOLOGY

New Optimism and a New Democracy

1807 Robert Fulton tests the *Clermont*

1814 Treaty of Ghent

1814–1815 Hartford Convention

1815 Government funding for the Cumberland Road
Stephen Decatur defeats the Barbary pirates

1816 Tariff of 1816
First successful steamboat run from Pittsburgh to New Orleans
James Monroe elected president

1817 Second Bank of the United States opens for business
Rush-Bagot Agreement
Construction of the Erie Canal begins
Congress suspends installment payments on public land purchases

1818 Convention of 1818
Andrew Jackson invades Spanish Florida

1819 *Dartmouth College v. Woodward*
McCulloch v. Maryland
Adams-Onís Treaty
Missouri Territory applies for statehood
Panic of 1819

1820 Monroe re-elected
Missouri Compromise
Northeastern congressmen propose protective tariffs and reduction of public land prices

1823 Monroe Doctrine

1824 *Gibbons v. Ogden*
Western congressmen join northeastern congressmen to pass increased protective tariffs
Jackson wins electoral plurality and popular majority in the presidential election

1824–1828 Suffrage reform triples the number of voters

1825 House of Representatives elects John Quincy Adams president
Prairie du Chien treaties

1826 Disappearance of William Morgan and beginning of the Antimasons

1827 Ratification of Cherokee constitution
Federal removal of the Winnebagos

1828 Tariff of Abominations
Publication of *The South Carolina Exposition and Protest*
First issue of the *Cherokee Phoenix*
Jackson elected president

1830 Webster-Hayne debate

1831 Federal removal of Sauks and Choctaws
Cherokee Nation v. Georgia

1832 *Worcester v. Georgia*
Bank War
Nullification crisis
Black Hawk War
Seminole War begins
Jackson re-elected

1836–1838 Federal removal of Creeks, Chickasaws, and Cherokees

An "Era of Good Feelings"

- What new expectations did Americans have as they emerged from the War of 1812?
- What economic constraints did they seek to overcome, and how did they choose to overcome them?
- How did new expectations influence choices in foreign affairs?

James Madison had been the butt of jokes and the cause of dissension within his own party during the War of 1812, but he emerged from the war a national hero with considerable political clout. The nationalism that arose after the war seemed to bring political dissension to a close. Commenting on the decline of partisan politics, a Federalist newspaper in Boston proclaimed the dawn of what it called an "**Era of Good Feelings.**"

Not only did the conflicts between Republicans and Federalists appear to be over, but Madison appeared to have gained the upper hand in the internal affairs of his own party. Although his fellow Republicans may have considered his wartime policies indecisive, after the war Madison immediately seized the political initiative to inaugurate vigorous new diplomatic and domestic programs. His successor, James Monroe, then picked up the beat, pressing on with a new nationalistic Republican agenda.

The "American System" and New Economic Direction

The nation was much more unified politically as the war ended in 1815 than it had been for years. The war's outcome and the growth that began to take place immediately following the peace settlement had largely silenced Madison's critics within the Republican party. And the Federalists could do little but go along. During the waning days of the war, extreme Federalists had so embarrassed the party that they were at a severe political disadvantage.

The Essex Junto was primarily responsible for the Federalists' embarrassment. As the war had dragged on from defeat to defeat, and as Republicans had continued to borrow money and pass rigid trade restrictions, the Junto grew in strength. From mid-December 1814 until January 5, 1815, New England Federalists met in Hartford, Connecticut. At the Hartford Convention, party members finally went public with their threat to secede. If Madison did not repeal the Embargo of 1813 and submit constitutional amendments that restricted the presidency to one term, required a two-thirds congressional vote to admit new states, and abolished the Three-Fifths Compromise, New England was ready to leave the Union. News of the Treaty of Ghent and Battle of New Orleans, however, caused many to view the Federalists' efforts as either foolish or treasonous. Riding a postwar wave of patriotism, Madison and the Republicans were able to drive their political opponents into retreat. Federalists managed to hold on in hard-core areas of New England until the 1820s, but the party as a whole was on a steepening decline.

From this new position of political strength, Madison chose in December 1815 to launch an aggressive new domestic policy. In an address to Congress, he challenged the senators and representatives to correct the economic ills that had caused depression and helped propel the nation into war. He also encouraged the states to invest in the nation's future by sponsoring transportation systems and making other internal improvements. Former critics like DeWitt Clinton, Henry Clay, and John C. Calhoun quickly rallied behind the president and his nationalistic economic and political agenda.

Clay took the lead. He had come to Congress as one of the War Hawks in 1810 and quickly became the dominant voice among the younger representatives. Born in Virginia in 1777, Clay had moved at the age of 20 to the wilds of Kentucky to practice law and carve out a career in politics. He was fantastically successful, becoming Speaker of the Kentucky state assembly when he was only 30 years old and winning a seat in the House of Representatives four years later. He became Speaker of the House during the prewar crisis. Now aligning himself firmly with the new economic agenda, Clay became its champion, calling it the **American System.** As enunciated by Madison and carried out by Monroe, Clay, Calhoun, and other Republican nationalists, the American System depended on three necessary developments.

First, Republicans conceded that a national bank was essential to the country's continued economic growth. True, Republicans had attacked Alexander

Era of Good Feelings The period from 1816 to 1823, when the decline of the Federalist party and the end of the War of 1812 gave rise to a time of political cooperation.

American System An economic plan sponsored by nationalists in Congress; it was intended to spur U.S. economic growth and the domestic production of goods previously bought from foreign manufacturers.

Hamilton's Bank of the United States, claiming that it gave the central government too much power over the economy, and they had refused to recharter it in 1811. But during the war, bankers, merchants, and foreign shippers had chosen not to accept the paper currency issued by local and state banks. The postwar call for a unified national economy prompted Republicans to press again for a national currency and for a national bank to regulate its circulation. In 1816, the overwhelmingly Republican Congress voted to charter the Second Bank of the United States for a twenty-year period. The Second Bank had many of the same powers and responsibilities as Hamilton's bank. Congress provided $7 million of its $35 million in opening capital and appointed one-fifth of its board of directors. The Second Bank opened for business in Philadelphia on January 1, 1817.

Second, the war had shown that improvements in communication and transportation were needed for the nation to reach its economic potential. Access to reliable transportation by means of the Great Lakes and the Ohio and Mississippi rivers had been one of the principal planks in the War Hawk platform in 1812, and poor lines of supply and communication had spelled disaster for American military efforts during the war itself. Announcing that they would "bind the republic together with a perfect system of roads and canals," Republicans in Congress put forward a series of proposals designed to improve transportation.

Third, Republicans advocated **protective tariffs** to help the fledgling industries that had hatched during the war grow to maturity. Incubated by the embargoes, American cotton-spinning plants had mushroomed between 1808 and 1815. But with the return of open trade at war's end, British merchants dumped accumulated inventories of cotton and woolen cloth below cost to hamper further American development. Although some New England voices protested tariffs as unfair government interference, many northeasterners supported protection. Most southerners and westerners, however, remained leery of its impact on consumer prices. Still, shouting with nationalistic fervor about American economic independence, westerners like Clay and southerners like Calhoun were able to raise enough support to pass Madison's proposed **Tariff of 1816,** opening the way for continued tariff legislation in the years to come.

Taken together, the various components of the American System were designed to create a national **market economy.** In the colonial period and increasingly thereafter, local market economies grew up around the trading and manufacturing centers of the Northeast. Individuals in these areas produced single items for cash sale and used the cash they earned to purchase goods produced by others. Specialization was the natural outcome. Farmers, for example, chose to grow only one or two crops and sell the whole harvest for cash, which they used to buy various items they had once grown or made for themselves.

What Clay, Calhoun, and other advocates of the American System were sponsoring was interdependence on a much larger scale. They envisioned a time when whole regions would specialize in producing commodities for which geography, climate, and the temperament of the people made a region most suitable. Agricultural regions in the West, for example, would produce food for the industrializing Northeast and the fiber-producing South. The North would depend on the South for efficiently produced cotton, and both South and West would depend on the Northeast for manufactured goods. Improved transportation systems would make this flow of goods possible, and a strong national currency would ensure orderly trade between states. Advocates of the American System were confident that the balance eventually established among regions would free the nation as a whole from economic dependence on manufacturing centers in Europe.

The popularity of Madison's programs was apparent in the outcome of the 1816 elections. His handpicked successor, fellow Virginian James Monroe, won by a decisive electoral majority: 184 votes to Federalist Rufus King's 34. Congressional Republicans enjoyed a similar sweep, winning more than three-fourths of the seats in the House of Representatives and the Senate. Presented with such a powerful mandate and the political clout necessary to carry it out, Republicans immediately set about expanding Madison's agenda for the nation.

protective tariff Tax on imported goods intended to make them more expensive than similar domestic goods, thus protecting the market for goods produced at home.

Tariff of 1816 First protective tariff in U.S. history; its purpose was to protect America's fledgling textile industry.

market economy An economic system based on the buying and selling of goods and services, in which the forces of supply and demand are allowed to set prices.

The Transportation Problem

If the new national economy was going to succeed, vast improvement had to be made in transportation systems. The control of the Mississippi River, the Great Lakes, and other inland waterways had been the cause of repeated diplomatic conflicts before the War of 1812. Although the Mississippi and the Great Lakes were now more or less under U.S. control, river networks did not feed all the areas of the country that needed development, and river traffic could not flow upstream. Roads offered one alternative to transportation by water, but travel along existing roads was uncomfortable, undependable, and expensive. Without some coordination—of the sort that only the federal government could provide—neither roads nor rivers could be made to tie together the national economy.

In the years before the War of 1812, travel on the nation's roads was a wearying experience. People who could afford transportation by stagecoach were crammed into an open wagon bouncing behind four horses on muddy, rutted, winding roads. Stagecoaches crept along at 4 miles per hour—when weather, equipment, and **blue laws** permitted them to move at all. And the enjoyment of such dubious luxury did not come cheaply: tolls for each mile of travel equaled the cost of a pint of good whiskey.

Recognizing the need for more and better roads, entrepreneurs sought to profit by building private **turnpikes** between heavily traveled points. In 1791, for example, a private company opened a 66-mile-long road between Philadelphia and Lancaster, Pennsylvania, hoping to make money on tolls. Between that time and the outbreak of war in 1812, private companies invested millions of dollars to construct several thousand miles of turnpike.

Despite such grand private efforts, it was clear to many after the war that only the large-scale resources available to state and federal governments could make a practical difference in the transportation picture. Immediately after the war, Calhoun introduced legislation in Congress to finance a national transportation program. Congress approved, but Madison vetoed the bill, stating that the Constitution did not authorize federal spending on projects designed to benefit the states. Instead, Madison recommended that the states either pass a constitutional amendment that would specifically authorize federal involvement, or carry out the task of building roads themselves.

Despite this setback, Clay and Calhoun continued their efforts and finally won Madison's support later in 1815. They did so by convincing the president that a government-funded national road between Cumberland, Maryland, and Wheeling, Virginia, was a military and postal necessity and therefore the initial federal expenditure of $30,000 for the **Cumberland Road** was permissible under the Constitution.

While people and light loads might move efficiently along the proposed National Road, water transportation remained the most economical way to ship bulky freight. Unfortunately, with few exceptions, navigable rivers and lakes did not link up to form usable transportation networks. Holland and other European countries had solved this problem by digging canals to expand the areas served by waterways. Before the War of 1812, some Americans had considered this solution, but enormous costs and engineering problems had limited canal construction to less than 100 miles. After the war, however, the entry of the state and federal governments into transportation development opened the way to an era of canal building.

New York State was most successful at canal development. New York City merchants and the state's rural farmers were demanding expanded markets. In 1817, the state started work on a canal that would run more than 350 miles from Lake Erie at Buffalo to the Hudson River at Albany. Aided by Governor DeWitt Clinton's unswerving support and the gentle terrain in western New York, engineers planned the **Erie Canal.** Three thousand workers dug the huge ditch and built the **locks,** dams, and **aqueducts** that would transport barges carrying freight and passengers across the state.

blue laws Local legislation designed to enforce Christian morality by forbidding certain activities, including traveling, on Sunday.

turnpike A road on which tolls are collected at gates set up along the way; private companies hoping to make a profit from the tolls built the first turnpikes.

Cumberland Road A national highway built with federal funds; it eventually stretched from Cumberland, Maryland, to Vandalia, Illinois, and beyond.

Erie Canal A 350-mile canal stretching from Buffalo to Albany; it revolutionized shipping in New York State.

lock A section of canal with gates at each end, used to raise or lower boats from one level to another by admitting or releasing water; locks allow canals to compensate for changes in terrain.

aqueduct An elevated structure raising a canal to bridge rivers, canyons, or other obstructions.

♦ Before the transportation revolution, traveling was highly risky and uncomfortable. This painting by Russian traveler Pavel Svinin shows a rather stylish stagecoach, but its well-dressed passengers are clearly being jostled. Note how the man in the front seat is bracing himself, while the man behind him loses his hat under the wheels. *"Travel by Stagecoach Near Trenton, NJ" by Pavel Svinin. The Metropolitan Museum of Art, Rogers Fund, 1942, (42.95.11)*

Canals were really little more than extensions of the natural river courses, and fighting the current of the great rivers that they fed into remained a problem. Pushed along by current and manpower, a barge could make the trip south on the Ohio and Mississippi from Pittsburgh to New Orleans in about a month. Returning north, against the current, took more than four months, if a boat could make the trip at all. As a result, most shippers barged their freight downriver, sold the barges for lumber in New Orleans, and walked back home along the **Natchez Trace,** a well-used path that eventually became another national road.

In 1807, Robert Fulton wedded steam technology borrowed from England with his own boat design to prove that steam-powered shipping was practical. Steam-driven water-wheels pushed his 160-ton ship, *Clermont,* upstream from New York City to Albany in an incredibly quick thirty-two hours. Unfortunately, the design of the *Clermont* was not well suited to most of America's waterways. Heavy and narrow beamed, Fulton's ship needed deep water and large amounts of fuel to carry a limited **payload.** Only after the War of 1812 did engineers design broader-beamed, lighter vessels that could carry heavy loads along the shallow western rivers that the canal systems were making accessible.

The leading pioneer in the postwar revolution in technology was Henry M. Shreve, a career boat pilot and captain who began experimenting with new designs immediately after the War of 1812 ended. Shreve borrowed the hull design of the shallow-draft, broad-beamed keelboats that had been sailing up and down inland streams for generations. He added two lightweight high-compression steam engines, each one driving an independent side wheel. He also added an upper deck for passengers, thereby creating the now-familiar multilayered wedding-cake look of Mississippi steamboats. Funded by merchants in Wheeling, Virginia—soon to be the western terminus for the Cumberland Road—Shreve successfully piloted one of his newly designed boats upriver, from Wheeling to Pittsburgh. Then, in 1816, he made the first successful run south, all the way to New Orleans.

Legal Anchors for New Business Enterprise

Before massive changes could take place in American transportation and business, some thorny legal issues needed to be resolved. The American System required economic cooperation between citizens in different states. This requirement made questions of authority over finance and interstate commerce increasingly important. In three landmark legal cases,

Natchez Trace A road connecting Natchez, Mississippi, with Nashville, Tennessee; it evolved from a series of Indian trails.

payload The part of a cargo that generates revenue, as opposed to the part needed to fire the boiler or supply the crew.

John Marshall resolved such questions, extending the authority of the federal government and clearing the way for the expansion of interstate trade.

If businesses were going to build and operate large interstate enterprises, they had to have confidence in the sanctity of legal contracts. In the case of *Dartmouth College v. Woodward* (1819), the Supreme Court made contracts secure. The case involved a charter given to Dartmouth College in 1769 by King George III of England, specifying that the board of trustees for the college would be self-perpetuating. In 1816, to gain control over the college, the New Hampshire state legislature passed a bill that would have allowed the state's governor to appoint board members. Members of the board brought suit, claiming that the college's charter was a legal contract and that the legislature had no right to abridge it. In his ruling, Chief Justice John Marshall agreed, noting that the Constitution protected the sanctity of contracts and that state legislatures could not interfere with them. From that point on, legal contracts came directly under the authority of the Constitution and were seen as safe from interference.

In another landmark case heard in the same year, Marshall established the superiority of the federal government over state authorities in matters of finance, securing the powers of the new Bank of the United States. The case of *McCulloch v. Maryland* (1819) involved a clerk in the bank's Baltimore branch who refused to put state **revenue stamps** on federal bank notes as required by Maryland law. McCulloch (the clerk) was indicted by the state but appealed to federal authorities. Marshall ruled that the states could not impose taxes on federal institutions and that McCulloch was right in refusing to comply with Maryland's revenue law. Rejecting Maryland's argument that the federal government was simply a creation of the several states and was therefore subject to state control or taxation, Marshall wrote, "The Constitution and the laws made in pursuance thereof are supreme: that *they control the constitution and laws of the respective states,* and cannot be controlled by them."

Marshall's third landmark case, *Gibbons v. Ogden* (1824), again demonstrated the supremacy of federal authority. This case involved an 1808 charter given to steamboat pioneer Robert Fulton and Robert Livingston by the New York state legislature, granting them exclusive rights to run steamboats on rivers in that state. Fulton and Livingston had granted licenses to various operators, including Aaron Ogden, who ran a steamboat service between New York and New Jersey. Another individual, Thomas Gibbons, was also running a steamboat service in the same area, but he was operating under license from the federal government. When a conflict between the two competing companies ended up in court, Marshall ruled in favor of Gibbons, arguing that the monopoly New York had granted conflicted with federal authority and was therefore invalid. In cases of interstate commerce, Marshall ruled, Congress's authority "is complete in itself" and the states could not challenge it.

Those three cases helped ease the way for the development of new business ventures. With contracts secure from state and local meddling, the sanctity of federal financial offices secure, and the superiority of Congress in interstate commerce established, businesses had the security they needed to expand into new areas and attempt to turn Clay's dream of a national market economy into a reality.

James Monroe and the Nationalist Agenda

Leadership for the transition into a new era fell to a seeming unlikely figure. Most characterized James Monroe as stolid and uncreative—citing his preference for revolutionary-era clothing (revealed in John Vanderlyn's portrait)—but he was a highly motivated and skillful administrator. Consistent with the image of an era of good feeling, the new president was less a politician than a statesman. He had served primarily as a diplomat during the contentious period that preceded the War of 1812, and as president he turned his diplomatic skills to the task of calming political disputes. He was the first president since Washington to take a national goodwill tour, during which he persistently urged various political factions to merge their interests for the benefit of the nation at large.

Monroe's cabinet was well chosen to carry out the task of smoothing political rivalries while flexing nationalistic muscles. He selected John Quincy Adams, son and heir of Yankee Federalist John Adams, as secretary of state because of his diplomatic skill and to win political support in New England. Monroe tapped southern nationalist John C. Calhoun for secretary of war and balanced his appointment with that of southern states'-rights advocate William C. Crawford as secretary of the treasury. With his team

revenue stamps Stickers affixed to taxed items by government officials indicating that the tax has been paid.

♦ This portrait of James Monroe, painted as he entered the White House in 1816 by artist John Vanderlyn, captures the president's conservative bearing. His clothing, for example, is much more typical of the revolutionary years than the nineteenth century. His conservatism endeared him to many who were tired of political strife. *"James Monroe" by John Vanderlyn. National Portrait Gallery, Smithsonian Institution/Art Resource, NY.*

assembled, Monroe launched the nation on a course designed to increase its control over the North American continent and improve its position in world affairs.

Only a few months after the war with Britain ended, Madison launched an aggressive diplomatic policy, setting the tone for the years to come. Taking advantage of U.S. involvement in the War of 1812, Barbary pirates (see page 226) had resumed their raiding activity against American shipping. In June 1815, Madison ordered a military force back to the Mediterranean to put an end to those raids. Naval hero Stephen Decatur returned to the region with a fleet of ten warships. Capturing two Algerian pirate vessels and then training his guns on the port of Algiers itself, Decatur threatened to level the city if the pirates did not promise to stop raiding American shipping. The Algerians and the rest of the Barbary pirates signed treaties ending the practice of exacting **tribute.** They also released all American hostages and agreed to pay compensation for past seizures of American ships. Celebrating the victory, Decatur gave voice to a militant new American nationalism, proclaiming, "Our Country! In her intercourse with foreign nations may she always be in the right; but our country, right or wrong."

As though in direct response to Decatur's pronouncement, Monroe maintained Madison's firm stand as he attempted to resolve important issues not settled by earlier administrations. Secretary of State Adams began negotiating for strict and straightforward treaties outlining America's economic and territorial rights.

The first matter Adams addressed was loose ends from the Treaty of Ghent (1814). One thorny problem had been the **demilitarization** of the Great Lakes boundary between the United States and British Canada. In the 1817 Rush-Bagot Agreement, both nations agreed to cut back their Great Lakes fleets to only a few vessels. A year later, the two nations drew up the Convention of 1818. The British agreed to honor American fishing rights in the Atlantic, to recognize a boundary between the Louisiana Territory and Canada at the 49th parallel, and to occupy the Oregon Territory jointly with the United States.

With these northern border issues settled, Adams set his sights on defining the nation's southern and southwestern frontiers. Conditions in Spanish Florida were extremely unsettled. Pirates, runaway slaves, and displaced Indians used Florida as a base for launching raids against American settlements and shipping. By December 1817, matters in the Florida border region seemed critical. Reflecting on the situation there, General Andrew Jackson wrote the president advocating the invasion of Spanish Florida. "This can be done without implicating the government," Jackson confided. "Let it be signified to me through any channel . . . that the possession of the Floridas would be desirable to the United States, and in sixty days it will be accomplished."

A short time later, Secretary of War Calhoun ordered Jackson to lead a military expedition into southern Georgia. Jackson's assignment was simply to patrol the border to keep raiders from crossing

tribute A payment of money or other valuables that one group makes to another as the price of security.

demilitarization The removal of military forces from a region and the restoration of civilian control.

into the United States, but Jackson claimed that he received secret authorization from Monroe to invade Spanish Florida. In either case, while Adams conducted talks with Spanish minister Don Luis de Onís, Jackson crossed into Spanish territory, brutally destroyed peaceful Seminole villages, and drove the Indians into the swamps. Not content with that, he invaded the Spanish capital at Pensacola on May 24, 1818, forcing the governor and his retinue to flee to Cuba. The zealous general then capped his already reckless venture by arresting two British citizens, charging them with conspiring with the Indians, and summarily executing them on June 19.

Spain and Britain vigorously protested Jackson's actions, and Secretary of War Calhoun and others recommended that the general be severely disciplined. Adams, however, saw an opportunity to settle the Florida border issue. He announced that Jackson's raid was an act of self-defense that would be repeated unless Spain could police the area adequately. Fully aware that Spain could not guarantee American security, Adams knew that the Spanish would either have to give up Florida or stand by and watch the United States take it by force. Understanding his country's precarious position, Onís chose to cede Florida in the Adams-Onís Treaty of 1819. The United States got all of Florida in exchange for releasing Spain from $5 million in damage claims resulting from pirate and Indian raids. In addition, Spain gave up any claims it had to the Oregon Territory, and the United States disavowed any claims to Texas.

Spain's inability to police its New World territories led to a more general diplomatic problem. As the result of Spain's weakness, many of its colonies in Latin America had rebelled and established themselves as independent republics. Fearful of the anticolonial example being set in the Western Hemisphere, Austria, France, Prussia, Russia, and other traditional European powers seemed poised to help Spain reclaim its overseas empire.

Neither England, which had developed a thriving trade with the new Latin American republics, nor the United States felt that Europe should be allowed to intervene in the affairs of the Western Hemisphere. Many people in the United States hoped the new Latin American republics would follow in American footsteps, moving toward greater democracy, and encouraged their continued independence. Others favored an independent Latin America as a fertile ground for American expansion. Still others, including perhaps Monroe and Adams, saw political advantage in promoting a strong American position in the patriotic atmosphere that followed the War of 1812.

In 1823, British Foreign Minister George Canning proposed that the United States and England form an alliance to end European meddling in Latin America. Most members of Monroe's cabinet supported the notion of allied action, but Adams protested that America would be reduced to a "cock-boat in the wake of the British man-of-war." Instead, he suggested a **unilateral** statement to the effect that "the American continents by the free and independent condition which they have assumed, and maintain, are henceforth not to be considered as subject for future colonization by any European power."

Monroe remained undecided. He trusted Adams's judgment but did not share the secretary of state's confidence in the nation's ability to fight off European colonization without British help. Monroe nevertheless conceded the nationalistic necessity for the United States to "take a bolder attitude . . . in favor of liberty." The president's indecision finally vanished in November 1823 when he learned that the alliance designed to restore Spain's colonies was faltering. With the immediate threat removed, Monroe rejected Canning's offer and in his annual message in December announced that the United States would regard any effort by European countries "to extend their system to any portion of this hemisphere as dangerous to our peace and safety." He went on to define any attempt at European intervention in the affairs of the Western Hemisphere as a virtual act of war against the United States.

The **Monroe Doctrine,** as this statement was later called, was exactly the proud assertion of principle "in favor of liberty" that Monroe had hoped for. It immediately won the support of the American people. The Monroe Doctrine, like Decatur's "Our country . . . right or wrong" speech, seemed to announce the arrival of the United States on the international scene. Both Europeans and Latin Americans, however, thought it was a meaningless statement. Despite proud assertions, the policy depended on the British navy and on Britain's informal commitment to New World autonomy.

unilateral Undertaken or issued by only one side and thus not involving an agreement made with others.

Monroe Doctrine President Monroe's 1823 statement declaring the Americas closed to further European colonization and discouraging European interference in the affairs of the Western Hemisphere.

Dynamic Growth and Political Consequences

- How did the expectation of prosperity and economic growth help lead to economic panic in 1819?
- How did growth and panic contribute to choices that led to sectional conflict and political contention?

During the **Napoleonic wars,** massive armies had drained Europe's manpower, laid waste to crops, and tied up ships, making European nations dependent on America. After those wars ended in 1815, Europeans continued to need American food and manufactures as they rebuilt a peacetime economy. Encouraged by a ready European market and expanding credit offered by the Second Bank of the United States and by various state banks, budding southern planters, northern manufacturers, and western and southwestern farmers embarked on a frenzy of speculation. They rushed to borrow against what they were sure was a golden future to buy equipment, land, and slaves.

Although all shared the same sense of optimism, entrepreneurs in the North, West, and South had different ideas about what the best course was for the American economy. As the American System drew the regions together into increasing mutual dependency, the tensions among them began to swell. As long as economic conditions remained good, there was little reason for conflict, but when the speculative boom collapsed, sectional tensions increased dramatically.

The Panic of 1819

Earlier changes in federal land policy had helped to begin inflating the speculative balloon. In 1800 and again in 1804 Congress had passed bills lowering the minimum number of acres of federal land an individual could purchase and the minimum price. After 1804 the minimum purchase became 160 acres and the minimum price was $1.64. The bill also permitted farmers to pay the government in **installments.** For most Americans, the minimum investment of $262.40 was still out of reach, but the installment option encouraged many to take the risk and buy farms they could barely afford.

Land speculators complicated the problem. Taking advantage of the new land prices, they too jumped into the game, buying land on credit. Unlike farmers, however, speculators never intended to put the land into production. They hoped to subdivide and sell it to people who could not afford to buy 160-acre lots directly from the government. To make sales, speculators too extended credit, thereby pyramiding the already teetering tower of debt.

Banks—both relatively unsupervised state banks and the Second Bank of the United States—then added to the problem. Farmers who bought land on credit seldom had enough cash to purchase farm equipment, seed, materials for housing, and the other things necessary to put the land to productive use. So the banks extended liberal credit on top of the credit already extended by the government and by land developers, many of whom were already in debt to the banks. Farmers thus had acreage and tools, but they also had an enormous debt.

Two developments in the international economy combined to undermine the nation's tower of debt. The economic optimism that fed the speculative frenzy rested on profitable markets. But as the 1810s drew to a close and recovery began in Europe, this demand began to drop. Compounding the problem was the recent independence of many of Europe's Latin American colonies, depriving the Europeans of the gold and silver that had driven international economics since the discovery of America. Europe became less and less dependent on American goods and, at the same time, less and less able to afford them. Thus the bottom began to fall out of the international market that had fueled speculation in the United States.

Congress noted the beginning of the collapse late in 1817 and tried to head off disaster by tightening credit. The government stopped installment payments on new land purchases and demanded that any new land purchased be paid for in hard currency. The Second Bank of the United States followed suit in 1818, demanding immediate repayment of loans in either gold or silver. State banks then followed and were joined by land speculators. Instead of curing the problem, however, tightening credit and recalling loans drove the economy over the edge. The speculative balloon burst, and the tower of debt to which it was tied collapsed. This was the **Panic of 1819.**

Napoleonic wars Wars in Europe waged by or against Napoleon Bonaparte between 1803 and 1815.

installment Partial payment of a debt to be made at regular intervals until the entire debt is repaid.

Panic of 1819 A financial panic that began when the Second Bank of the United States tightened credit and recalled government loans.

♦ Notes like these, issued by state and local banks, insurance companies, and even individual merchants, helped feed the speculating frenzy after the War of 1812. Wild speculation created a roller-coaster economy that collapsed in the Panic of 1819. *Eric P. Newman. Numismatic Education Society.*

Six years of economic depression followed the panic. As prices declined, individual farmers and manufacturers, unable to repay loans for land and equipment, faced **repossession** and imprisonment for debt. In Cincinnati and other agricultural cities, bankruptcy sales were a daily occurrence. In New England and the West, factories closed, idling both owners and workers. In New York and other manufacturing and trading cities, the ranks of the unemployed grew steadily. The number of paupers in New York nearly doubled between 1819 and 1820, and in Boston thirty-five hundred people were imprisoned for debt. Shaken by the enormity of the problem, John C. Calhoun observed in 1820, "There has been within these two years an immense revolution of fortunes in every part of the Union; enormous numbers of persons utterly ruined; multitudes in deep distress."

Economic Woes and Political Sectionalism

Despite Monroe's efforts to merge southern, northern, and nationalist interests during the Era of Good Feelings, the Panic of 1819 drove a wedge between the nation's geographical sections. The depression touched each of the major regions differently, calling for conflicting solutions. For the next several years, the halls of Congress rang with debates rooted in each section's particular economic needs.

The issue that pitted section against section more violently than any other during these years was protective tariffs. Before 1816, Congress enacted tariffs designed to produce tax revenue. Protecting American commerce was a coincidental byproduct. The goal of President Madison's Tariff of 1816, however, was protection, and its success at protecting the fledgling textile industry and raising revenue placed tariff legislation high on Congress's list of economic tools.

As the Panic of 1819 spread economic devastation throughout the country, tariffs seemed to be the one proven method for handling emergencies. Beginning in Pennsylvania and spreading through the Middle Atlantic states into southern New England and then into Ohio and Kentucky, industries centering on coal, iron, and textiles began clamoring for protection.

Farmers were split on the issue. Small farmers favored a free market that would keep the price of the manufactures that they had to buy as low as possible. In contrast, the increasing number of commercial farmers—those who had chosen to follow Henry Clay's ideas and were specializing to produce cash crops of raw wool, hemp, and wheat—joined industrialists, factory managers, and industrial workers in supporting protection against the foreign dumping of such products.

Southern commercial farmers, however, did not join with their western counterparts in favoring protection. After supporting the protective Tariff of 1816, John C. Calhoun and other southerners became firm opponents of tariffs. Their dislike of protection reflected a complex economic reality. Specialization in cotton growing had slowed the development of industry in the South, and Britain, not the United States, was the South's main supplier of manufactured goods and its primary market for raw cotton. Protective tariffs raised the price of the former and might cause Britain to enact its own tariff on cotton imports from the South. If that happened,

repossession The reclaiming of land or goods by the seller or lender after the purchaser fails to pay installments due.

southerners would pay more for manufactures but receive less profit from cotton.

In 1820, northern congressmen proposed a major increase in the tariff rates that had been set in 1816. Small farmers in the West and cotton growers in the South combined to defeat the measure. Northerners then wooed congressmen from the West, where small farmers were begging for relief from high land prices and debt. The northerners supported one bill that lowered the minimum price of public land to $1.25 per acre and another that allowed farmers who had bought land before 1820 to pay off their debt at the reduced price. The bill also extended the time over which those who were on the installment plan could make payments. Then in 1822, northerners backed a bill authorizing increased federal spending on the Cumberland Road, a vital interest to westerners. Such blandishments finally had the desired outcome. In 1824, western congressmen joined with northern manufacturing interests to pass a greatly increased tariff.

The northern effort to woo western congressmen illustrates an important political reality of the years following 1800. Of the six western states admitted to the Union after 1800, three—Ohio, Indiana, and Illinois—were predominantly farming states, split between commercial and nonspecialized farming. The other three—Louisiana, Mississippi, and Alabama—teetered between subsistence farming and cotton growing. As long as northern commercial interests could pull support from Ohio, Indiana, and Illinois, the balance of power remained relatively even. But new expansion in either North or South had the potential to throw political dominance one way or the other. As all three regions fought to implement specific solutions to the nation's economic woes, the regional balance of power in Congress became a matter of crucial importance.

The Missouri Compromise

The delicate balance in Congress began to wobble when Missouri Territory applied for statehood in 1819. The political crisis came when New York congressman James Tallmadge, Jr., proposed to amend the conditions under which Congress would accept Missouri's application for statehood. He suggested that no new slaves be taken into Missouri and that those already in the territory be emancipated gradually. It is uncertain whether moral or political concerns motivated Tallmadge, but his amendment generated a moral and political debate that lasted for two years and nearly led to national collapse.

The political issue in the Missouri controversy was straightforward. If Missouri was admitted as a slave state, its economy would resemble the economies of the southern states, and its congressional **bloc** would undoubtedly support the southern position on tariffs and other key issues. But if Missouri was admitted as a free state, its economy would resemble the economies of states in the Old Northwest, and its congressmen would be susceptible to northern political deal making.

Both sides in the debate about Missouri were deeply entrenched, but in 1820 Henry Clay suggested a compromise. Late in 1819, Maine had separated from Massachusetts and applied for admission to the United States as a separate state. The **Missouri Compromise** proposed by Clay was to admit Missouri as a slave state and Maine as a free state. Clay also proposed that after the admission of Missouri, slavery be banned forever in the rest of the Louisiana Territory above 36°30′ north latitude, the line that formed Missouri's southern border (see Map 10.1). With this provision, Congress approved the Missouri Compromise, and the issue of slavery in the territories quieted down for a while.

But conflict flared again in 1821, when Missouri submitted its state constitution for congressional approval. The sticking point was a provision prohibiting free blacks from entering the new state. Ample precedents for such a law existed even in northern states, but critics held that it was unconstitutional. Free blacks were full citizens in New York State, for example, so critics claimed that Missouri's constitutional ban denied black citizens of New York the Constitution's protection of "all privileges and immunities of citizens in the several States."

When this new issue threatened to shatter the Missouri Compromise, Clay suggested a solution. He proposed that the Missouri constitution should never be construed to mean that U.S. citizens could be denied privileges and immunities. Missouri, in turn, would agree to pass no laws that would infringe on the rights of any citizen. Although this

bloc A group of people united for common action.

Missouri Compromise Law proposed by Henry Clay in 1820 admitting Missouri to the Union as a slave state and Maine as a free state and banning slavery in the Louisiana Territory north of latitude 36°30′.

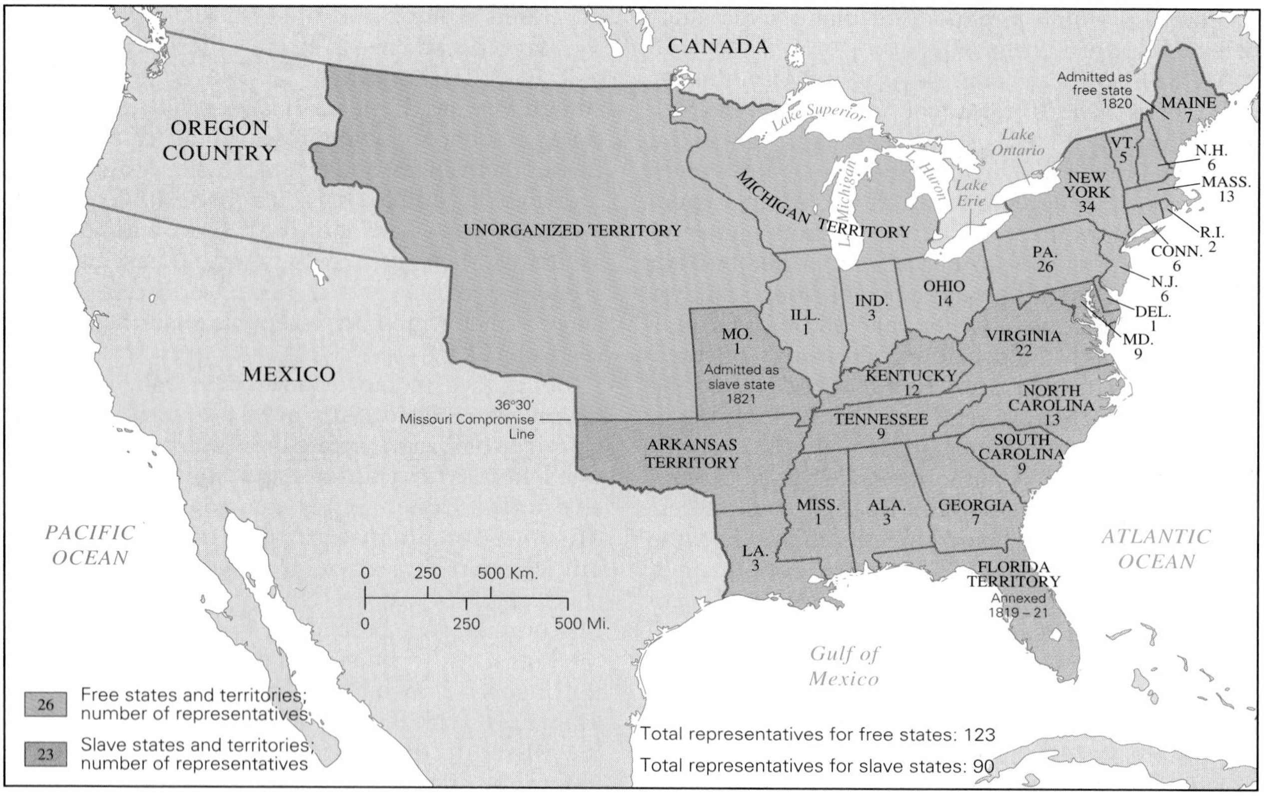

♦ **MAP 10.1 Missouri Compromise and Representative Strength** The Missouri Compromise fixed the boundary between free and slave territories at 36°30′. This map shows the result both in geographical and political terms. While each section emerged from the Compromise with the same number of Senators (24), the balance in the House of Representatives and Electoral College tilted toward the North.

resolution had no legal and little logical value, it confused the issue enough that Clay was able to push through the acceptance of Missouri's constitution, ending the crisis.

New Politics and the End of Good Feelings

The Missouri crisis was more than a simple debate over economic interests and congressional balances. Although economic issues had caused the conflict, slavery—its expansion and, for a few, its very existence—had become part of a struggle between sections for national power. For former Federalists like Rufus King, the crisis offered an opportunity to use the slavery issue to woo northerners and westerners away from the traditionally southern-centered Republican coalition. Thus DeWitt Clinton and other northeastern dissidents joined with former Federalists to criticize their party's southern leadership and challenge Monroe's dominance. Wise to this political "party trick," Jefferson observed that "King is ready to risk the union for any chance of restoring his party to power and wriggling himself to the head of it."

Conducted in the midst of the Missouri crisis, the presidential election of 1820 went as smoothly as could be. Monroe faced no meaningful political opposition. The people's faith in Jefferson's party and his handpicked successors remained firm. As the nation approached the election of 1824, however, it became clear that the depression following the Panic of 1819 and the Missouri crisis had broken Republican unity and destroyed the public's confidence in the party's ability to solve domestic problems.

Approaching the end of his second term, Monroe knew that no more gentleman Republicans from Virginia were in line to carry the presidential torch. Although he probably favored John Quincy Adams as his successor, the president carefully avoided naming him as the party's **standard-bearer,** leaving that task to the Republican congressional caucus. If Monroe was hoping that the party would nominate Adams, he was disappointed when the southern-dominated party caucus named Georgia states'-rights advocate William Crawford as its candidate. Certainly nationalists were disappointed, and prominent nationalists Clay and Adams each immediately defied party discipline by deciding to run against Crawford without the approval of the caucus. Encouraged by the apparent death of the caucus system for nominating presidential candidates, the Tennessee state legislature chose to name its own candidate, Andrew Jackson.

The election that followed brought home how deeply divided the nation had become. Northern regional political leaders rallied behind Adams, southern sectionalists supported Crawford, and northwestern commercial farmers and other supporters of the American System lined up behind Clay. But a good portion of the American people—many of them independent yeoman farmers, traditional craftsmen, and immigrants—defied their political leaders by supporting the hero of New Orleans: Jackson.

The source of Jackson's political popularity is something of a mystery because the Tennessean remained almost entirely silent during the campaign. But his posture as a man of action—a doer rather than a talker—and the fact that he was a political outsider certainly played key roles. For whatever combination of reasons, once the ballots were cast, it became apparent that this groundswell of popular enthusiasm was a potent political force. Though a political **dark horse,** Jackson won the popular election with 153,544 votes to Adams's 108,740, Clay's 47,136, and Crawford's 46,618 (see Map 10.2). The electoral vote, however, was much closer. Jackson had 99 electoral votes to Adams's 84, Crawford's 41, and Clay's 37, but he did not have enough to win the election. Jackson's opponents had a combined total of 162 of the 261 electoral votes cast. Thus Jackson won a **plurality** of electors but did not have the "majority of the whole number of electors" required by the Constitution. The Constitution specifies that in such cases, a list of the top three vote getters be passed to the House of Representatives for a final decision.

By the time the House had convened to settle the election, Crawford, the third-highest vote getter, had suffered a disabling stroke, so the list of candidates had only two names: John Quincy Adams and Andrew Jackson. Because Clay had finished fourth, he was not in contention in the **runoff election.** As

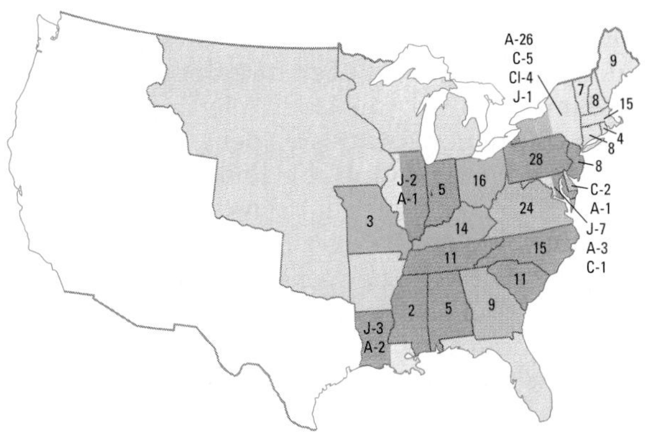

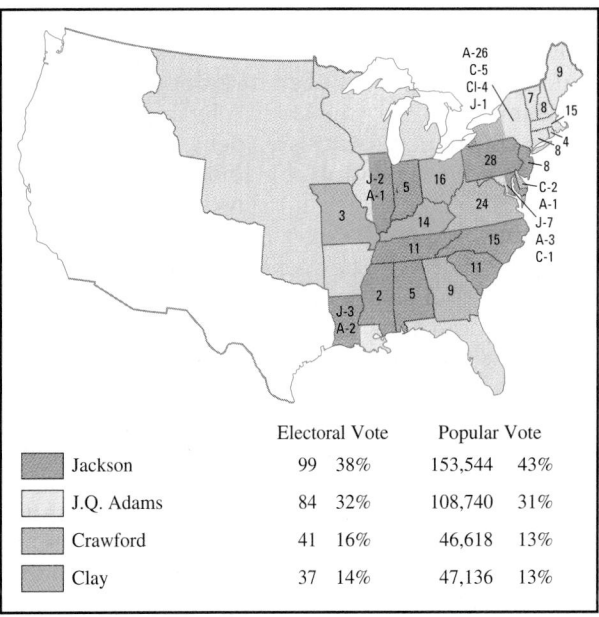

	Electoral Vote		Popular Vote	
Jackson	99	38%	153,544	43%
J.Q. Adams	84	32%	108,740	31%
Crawford	41	16%	46,618	13%
Clay	37	14%	47,136	13%

♦ **MAP 10.2 Election of 1824** This map showing the 1824 presidential election illustrates how divided the nation had become politically. William Crawford, the official Republican Party nominee, placed third in the Electoral College. The two most successful candidates, Andrew Jackson and John Quincy Adams, represented no political party. Speaker of the House Henry Clay, who finished fourth, played a key role in the outcome. Under his leadership, the House elected Adams.

Speaker of the House, however, he was in a particularly good position to influence the outcome. Both Jackson backers and Adams backers approached him for support. Seeing himself as the leading spokesman for western and nationalistic interests, Clay viewed Jackson as a rival rather than as a kindred spirit. Having locked horns with Adams over several issues during Monroe's presidency, Clay had no great love for the New Englander either.

standard-bearer The recognized leader of a movement, organization, or political party.

dark horse A political candidate who has little organized support and is not expected to win.

plurality In an election with three or more candidates, the number of votes received by the winner when the winner receives less than half of the total number of votes cast.

runoff election A final election held to determine a winner after an earlier election has eliminated the weakest candidates.

Still, Adams's and Clay's views on tariffs, manufacturing, foreign affairs, and other key issues were quite compatible. Clay therefore threw his support to Adams, who won the House election and in 1825 became the nation's sixth president.

Clay and Adams were able to resolve their differences and foster some unity in the threatened Republican party. But Jackson and his supporters were not easily soothed. They considered Clay a betrayer of western and southern interests. Their suspicions turned to outright accusations when Adams assumed the presidency and named Clay his secretary of state—the position that had been the springboard to the presidency for every past Republican who held it. Jacksonians railed at Adams, proclaiming his election a "corrupt bargain," and they called Clay the "Judas of the West." In anger and disgust, Jackson supporters withdrew from the party of Jefferson, bringing an end to the one-party system that had emerged under the so-called **Virginia Dynasty** and dealing the knockout blow to the Era of Good Feelings.

The "New Man" in Politics

- What factors helped change Americans' political expectations during the mid-1820s?
- How did the election of Andrew Jackson in 1828 reflect those new expectations?

Since Washington's day the presidency had been considered an office for gentlemen and statesmen. The first several presidents avoided partisan politics whenever possible and tried to maintain an air of polite dignity while in office. And voters were generally pleased with that orderly approach. But with the massive social changes taking place after the War of 1812, the conduct of national politics changed drastically. New voters from new professions with radically varying political and economic views began making demands. Many felt isolated from a political system that permitted the presidency to pass from one propertied gentleman to another. Clearly, changing times called for political change, and the American people began to press for it in no uncertain terms.

Adams's Troubled Administration

John Quincy Adams may have been the best-prepared man ever to assume the office of president. The son of revolutionary giant and former president John Adams, John Quincy had been born and raised in the midst of America's most powerful political circles. By the time of his controversial election in 1825, Adams had been a foreign diplomat, a U.S. senator, a Harvard professor, and an exceptionally effective secretary of state. Despite his impressive résumé, however, Adams was singularly lacking in the personal warmth and political skill that might have made him a successful chief executive.

Rigidly idealistic, the new president believed himself to be above partisan politics and refused to use political favors to curry support. As a result, Adams had no effective means of rallying those who might have supported him or of pressuring his opponents. Because of the lukewarm support from his friends and the constant sniping of his enemies, Adams's administration was a deeply troubled one.

Adams's policy commitments did nothing to boost his popularity. The new president promised to increase tariffs to protect American manufacturing and raise revenues to pay for "the improvement of agriculture, commerce, and manufactures." He also wanted the Second Bank of the United States to stabilize the economy while providing ample loans to finance new manufacturing ventures. And he advocated federal spending to improve "the elegant arts" and advance "literature and the progress of the sciences, ornamental and profound." High sounding though Adams's objectives were, Thomas Jefferson spoke for many when he observed that such policies would establish "a single and splendid government of an aristocracy . . . riding and ruling over the plundered ploughman and beggared yeomanry." Jefferson's criticism seemed particularly apt in the economic turmoil that followed the Panic of 1819. Moreover, the increase in federal power implied by Adams's policies frightened southerners, and this fear, combined with their traditional dislike of tariffs, virtually unified opposition to Adams in the South.

Led by John C. Calhoun, Adams's opponents tried to manipulate tariff legislation to broaden support for their cause. Calhoun proposed that northeasterners who had supported Jackson in 1824 should move to raise tariffs to an unprecedented level in an effort to woo manufacturing interests to their side. Meanwhile, Jackson supporters in the West and South could increase their hold on their

Virginia Dynasty Term applied to the U.S. presidents from Virginia in the period between 1801 and 1825: Jefferson, Madison, and Monroe.

constituents by opposing the increases. Sure that the bills would never pass, the anti-Adams faction put together a hodgepodge of tariff legislation called the **Tariff of Abominations.** But Calhoun and his fellow conspirators had not counted on the growing strength of manufacturing interests. When the tariff package came to the floor in May 1828, key northeastern congressmen engineered its passage. Although this outcome was not what Calhoun had expected, it served his ends by establishing tariff rates that were unpopular with almost every segment of the population, and the blame could be placed at the president's doorstep.

Democratic Styles and Political Structure

Compounding Adams's problems were his demeanor and outlook, which seemed more suited to a man of his father's generation than to his own. The enormous economic and demographic changes that occurred during the first decades of the nineteenth century created a new political climate, one in which Adams's archrival Andrew Jackson felt much more at ease than did the stiff Yankee who occupied the White House.

One of the most profound changes in the American political scene was an explosion in the number of voters. Throughout the early years of the republic's history, voting rights were limited to white men who held real estate. Because this group included a wide proportion of men in the land-rich nation, the fact of limited suffrage raised little controversy. But as economic conditions elevated new, unpropertied men to important roles in middle-class professions, a movement in favor of suffrage reform emerged. In 1800, only three of the sixteen states—Kentucky, Vermont, and New Hampshire—had no qualifications for voting, and Georgia, North Carolina, and Pennsylvania permitted taxpayers to vote even if they did not own real property. By 1830, only five of the twenty-four states continued to demand property qualifications, nine required tax payment only, and ten made no property demands at all. As a result, the raw number of voters grew enormously and rapidly. In the election of 1824, 356,038 people cast votes for the presidency. Four years later, more than three times that number of men voted.

Complementing the impact of the expanding **electorate** were significant changes in the structure of politics itself. Key among them was the method for selecting members of the Electoral College (see page 194). Gradually, state after state adopted the popular election of electors until by 1828 state legislatures in only two states continued to name electors. At the same time, more and more government jobs that had traditionally been appointive became elective. Thus more voters would vote to fill more offices and could affect the political process in new, profound ways. In addition, states increasingly dropped property qualifications for officeholding as well as voting, opening new opportunities to break the gentlemanly monopoly on political power.

Political opportunists were not slow to take advantage of the new situation. Men like New Yorker **Martin Van Buren** quickly came to the fore, organizing political factions into tightly disciplined local and statewide units. A long-time opponent of Governor DeWitt Clinton's faction in New York, Van Buren molded disaffected Republicans into the so-called Bucktail faction. In 1820, the Bucktails leveled charges of political corruption and aristocratic ambitions at the Clintonians and garnered enough popular support to sweep Clinton out of office. Although the Clintonians regained power by leveling similar charges at Van Buren in 1824, the Bucktails and their political strategy were clearly on the rise, thanks to a combination of political patronage—the ability of the party in power to distribute government jobs—**influence peddling,** and fiery speeches to draw qualified voters into the political process.

Although they were finally allowed to participate in politics, the new voters sensed that their participation was not having the impact it should. They resented the "corrupt bargain" that had denied the presidency to the people's choice—Andrew Jackson—in the election of 1824. Voters in upstate New York and elsewhere pointed at organizations like the **Masons,** claiming that they used secret signs

Tariff of Abominations Tariff package designed to win support for anti-Adams forces in Congress; its passage in 1828 discredited Adams but set off sectional tension over tariff issues.

electorate The portion of the population that possesses the right to vote.

Martin Van Buren New York politician known for his skillful handling of party politics; he helped found the Democratic party and later became eighth president of the United States.

influence peddling Using one's influence with people in authority to obtain favors or preferential treatment for someone else, usually in return for payment.

Masons An international fraternal organization with many socially and politically prominent members, including a number of U.S. presidents.

♦ As suffrage requirements loosened, politicians began canvassing for votes among common people. This painting by George Caleb Bingham captures the spirit of the new politics, showing an office seeker drumming up support from people on the street. *"Canvassing for a Vote," 1852 by George Caleb Bingham. The Nelson Gallery-Atkins Museum of Art, Kansas City, Missouri (purchase: Nelson Trust) 52-9.*

and rituals to ensure the election of their own members, maintain the supremacy of political parties, and thwart the popular will. In the fall of 1826, a bricklayer and Mason named William Morgan decided to publish some of the Masons' lesser secrets. Morgan was promptly arrested—charged with owing a debt of $2.69—and jailed. What happened after that remains a mystery. Some unknown person paid Morgan's debt, and he was released. But as he emerged from jail, he was seized, bound and gagged, and dragged into a carriage that whisked him out of town (Canandaigua, New York). He was never seen again.

Morgan's disappearance caused a popular outcry, and political outsiders demanded a complete investigation. No clues turned up, and it became apparent to many that the Masons were using their political clout to suppress the facts. Within a year, opportunistic young politicians, including New Yorkers Thurlow Weed and William Seward and Pennsylvanian Thaddeus Stevens, had harnessed this democratic unrest and formed a new political organization: the **Antimasonic party.** Based exclusively on the alienation felt by small craftsmen, farmers, and others, the Antimasons had no platform beyond their disapproval of political business as usual. The Antimasonic party was, in effect, a political party whose sole cause was to oppose political parties.

What was happening in New York was typical of party and antiparty developments throughout the country. As the party of Jefferson dissolved, a rash of political factions broke out across the nation. This was precisely the sort of politics that Adams disdained, but it suited a man like Jackson perfectly. So, while Antimasons pointed accusing fingers at both Clinton and Van Buren, Van Buren was busy forging with the hero of New Orleans an alliance that would fundamentally alter American politics.

The Rise of King Andrew

Within two years of Adams's election, Van Buren had brought together into a new political party northern outsiders like himself, dissident southern Republicans like John C. Calhoun, and western spokesmen like **Thomas Hart Benton** of Missouri and John H. Eaton of Tennessee. Calling itself the

Antimasonic party Political party formed in 1827 to capitalize on popular anxiety about the influence of the Masons; it opposed politics as usual without offering any particular substitute.

Thomas Hart Benton U.S. senator from Missouri and legislative leader of the Democrats; he was a champion of President Jackson and a supporter of westward expansion.

Democratic-Republicans—**Democrats** for short—this party railed against the neofederalism of Clay's and Adams's National Republican platform. The Democrats called for a return to Jeffersonian simplicity, states' rights, and democratic principles. Behind the scenes, however, they employed the tight organizational discipline and manipulative techniques that Van Buren had used to such good effect against the Clintonians in New York. Lining up behind the recently defeated popular hero Andrew Jackson, the new party appealed to both opportunistic political outsiders and democratically inclined new voters. In the congressional elections of 1826, Van Buren's coalition drew the unqualified support of both groups, unseating enough National Republicans to gain a twenty-five-seat majority in the House of Representatives and an eight-seat advantage in the Senate.

Aligning behind Andrew Jackson was perhaps as important to the Democrats' success as their ideological appeal and tight political organization. In many ways, Jackson was a perfect reflection of the new voters. Like many of them, he was born in a log cabin on the nation's western frontier. His family faced more than its share of hardships. Andrew's father died two weeks before the birth of his son, and Andrew lost his two brothers and his mother during the Revolutionary War. In the waning days of the Revolution, at the age of 13, Jackson joined a mounted militia company and was captured by the British. His captors beat their young prisoner and then let him go, a humiliation he would never forgive.

At the end of the war, Jackson set out to make his own way in the world. Like many of his contemporaries, he chose the legal profession as the route to rapid social and economic advancement. In 1788, he was appointed **public prosecutor** for the district that later split off from North Carolina to become Tennessee. Driven by an indomitable will and a wealth of native talent, Jackson became the first U.S. congressman from the state of Tennessee and eventually was elected to the Senate. He also was a judge on the Tennessee Supreme Court.

Along the way, Jackson's exploits established his solid reputation as a heroic and natural leader. Even before the War of 1812, his toughness had earned him the nickname "Old Hickory" (see page 258). Also, in the popular view, it was Jackson's brashness, not Adams's diplomatic skill, that finally won Spanish Florida for the United States.

Jackson's popular image as a rough-hewn man of the people was untarnished by his political alliance with business interests, his activities as a land speculator, and his large and growing personal fortune and stock of slaves. In the eyes of frontiersmen, small farmers, and to some extent urban workingmen, he remained a common man like them. Having started with nothing, Jackson seemed to have drawn from a combination of will, natural ability, and divine favor to become a man of substance without becoming a snob.

♦ These campaign medals from 1828 show the options presented to voters in the election of that year. The stodgy and statesmanlike Adams appears on the right, and the flamboyant Jackson appears on the left. *Collection of David J. and Janet L. Frent.*

Caricature and image making rather than substantive issues dominated the election campaign of 1828. Jackson forces accused Adams of being cold, aristocratic, and corrupt. They charged him with diverting public funds to buy personal luxuries, providing the Russian tsar with a young American mistress to win his diplomatic support, and bowing to speculators and **special interests** in defining his tariff and land policies. Adams supporters charged Jackson with being a dueler, an insubordinate military adventurer, and an uncouth backwoodsman whose disregard for propriety had led him to live with a woman before she divorced her first husband.

Democrats Political party that brought Andrew Jackson into office; it harked back to Jeffersonian principles of limited government and drew its support from farmers, craftsmen, and small businessmen.

public prosecutor A lawyer appointed by the government to prosecute criminal actions on behalf of the state.

special interest A person or organization that seeks to benefit by influencing legislators to support particular policies.

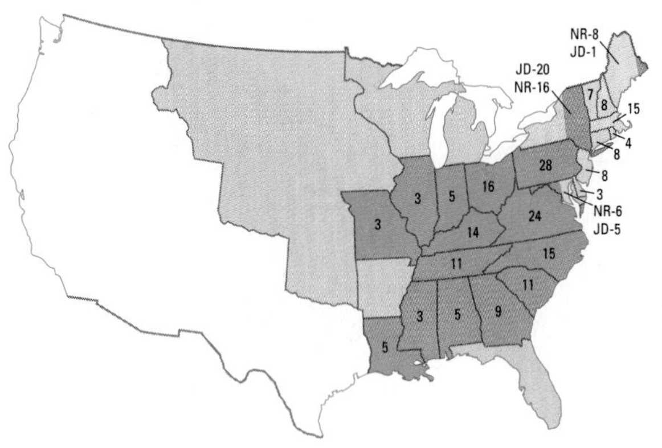

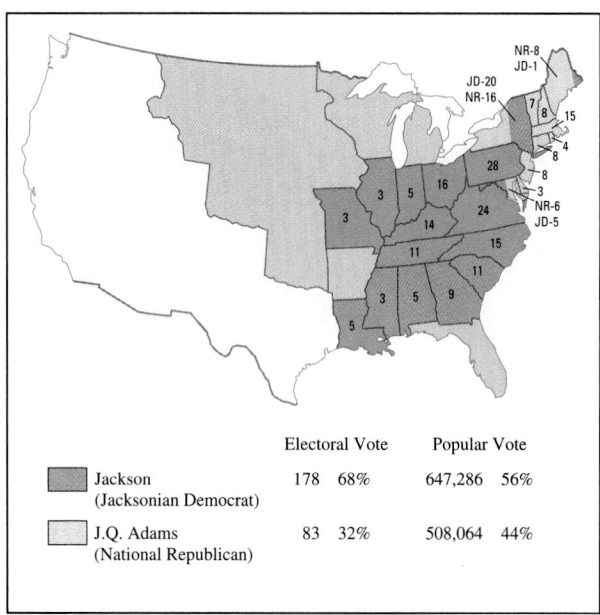

	Electoral Vote		Popular Vote	
Jackson (Jacksonian Democrat)	178	68%	647,286	56%
J.Q. Adams (National Republican)	83	32%	508,064	44%

♦ **MAP 10.3 Election of 1828** This map shows how the political coalition between Andrew Jackson and Martin Van Buren turned the tables in the election of 1828. Jackson's Democratic Party won every region except Adams's native New England.

The characterization of Adams as cold was accurate, but charges of corruption were entirely untrue, though Adams's refusal to respond led many to believe them true. The charges against Jackson were all too true, but voters saw them as irrelevant. Rather than damaging Jackson's image, such talk made him appear romantic and daring, all the more like what the new voters wished they could be. When all was said and done, the Tennessean polled over a hundred thousand more popular votes than did the New Englander and won the vast majority of states, taking every one in the South and West (see Map 10.3).

As if in response to his supporters' desires and his opponents' fears, Jackson swept into the White House on a groundswell of unruly popular enthusiasm. Ten thousand visitors crammed into the capital to witness Jackson's inauguration on March 4, 1829. Showing his usual disdain for tradition, Jackson took the oath of office and then pushed through the crowd and mounted his horse, galloping off toward the White House followed by a throng of excited onlookers. When they arrived, the mob flowed behind him into the presidential mansion, where they climbed over furniture, broke glassware, and generally frolicked. The new president was finally forced to flee the near-riot by climbing out a back window. A new spirit was alive in the nation's politics.

Launching Jacksonian Politics

The first president in over a quarter of a century who did not belong to the party of his predecessor, Jackson had courted public support with the implied promise that he would run the nation for the benefit of the people against the manipulations of the privileged. He had pulled together a coalition of supporters from all three sections of the nation, but the task of keeping together the coalition—or the Union itself, for that matter—was not easy in a time of increasing sectional tension.

Because no new party had come to power since Jefferson's election in 1800, Jackson faced a novel problem: over the previous twenty-eight years Republicans had used patronage to give government jobs to some ten thousand **civil servants**—people whose loyalty Jackson could not trust and many of whose abilities were questionable. One of his supporters' complaints about politics as usual was the tendency of political insiders to protect their jobs and their friends' jobs at any cost and to appoint party loyalists to government positions regardless of their qualifications. Jackson declared that he would introduce regular rotation in office for federal officials. Appointments in his administration, he promised, would last only four years. After then, civil servants would have to return to "making a living as other people do."

Like many of Jackson's policies, this rotation system was designed to accomplish more than a single goal. First, getting rid of entrenched bureaucrats and replacing them with supposedly honest, public-minded men appealed to the people who had elected Jackson. He solidified this support when he denied that only professional civil servants had the expertise to carry out public responsibilities. Such duties, Jackson insisted, were "so plain and simple that men of intelligence may readily qualify themselves for their performance." Second, rotation in office opened up many federal jobs. The Jacksonian adage became "To the victor belong the **spoils**," and the Democrats made every effort to advance their party's hold on power by distributing government jobs to loyal party members.

civil servants Nonelected government workers; at the time, they were usually appointed by officeholders.

spoils Jobs and other rewards for political support.

Patronage appointments extended to the highest levels in government. Jackson selected cabinet members not for their experience but for their political loyalty and value in satisfying the various factions that formed his coalition. This approach caused no real harm because the president abandoned his predecessors' practice of regularly seeking his cabinet members' advice on major issues. Jackson called virtually no cabinet meetings and seldom asked for his cabinet's opinion. Instead, he surrounded himself with an informal network of friends and advisers. This so-called **Kitchen Cabinet** worked closely with the president on matters of both national policy and party management.

Throughout his administration, Jackson conducted himself in a manner very unlike that of any of his predecessors. He was known to rage, pout, and storm at suspected disloyalty or those who simply disagreed with him. Earlier presidents had at least pretended to believe in the equal distribution of power among the three branches of government. Jackson acted on his belief that the executive should be supreme because the president was the only member of the government elected by all the people and was their advocate in the face of entrenched interests, whether in banks, factories, or the halls of Congress.

In dealing with his administration's crises, Jackson was not above threatening military action to get his way, and he made it clear that he would stand in opposition to both private and congressional opponents. Reflecting his generally testy relationship with the legislative branch, he vetoed twelve bills in the course of his administration, three more than all his predecessors combined. Such arrogant assertions of executive power led Jackson's opponents in and out of Congress to call the new president "King Andrew."

♦ Andrew Jackson always styled himself as a friend of the Indians, but this satirical drawing captures his attitude that they were as unimportant as dolls. The engraving shown in the upper right corner depicts his approach to Indian resistance: Liberty with her foot on the neck of a conquered enemy. *William L. Clements Library, University of Michigan, Ann Arbor.*

The Reign of King Andrew

- Analyze the choices Jackson made in his Indian policy.
- What constraints faced by each region of the country influenced the national divisions reflected in the nullification crisis and the Bank War?

Jackson had promised the voters "retrenchment and reform." He gave them retrenchment, but reform was more difficult to arrange. Jackson tried to implement reform in four broad areas: (1) Indian affairs, (2) internal improvements and public land policy, (3) the collection of revenue and enforcement of federal law, and (4) the nation's banking and financial system. The steps that Jackson took appealed to some of his supporters but strongly alienated others. Thus, as Jackson tried to follow through on his promise to reform the nation, he nearly tore the nation apart.

Jackson and the Indians

At the end of the War of 1812, the powerful Cherokees, Choctaws, Seminoles, Creeks, and Chickasaws—the so-called **Five Civilized Tribes**—numbered nearly seventy-five thousand people and

Kitchen Cabinet President Jackson's informal advisers, who helped him shape both national and Democratic party policy.

Five Civilized Tribes Term used by whites to describe the Cherokee, Choctaw, Seminole, Creek, and Chickasaw Indians, many of whom were planters and merchants.

occupied large holdings within the states of Georgia, North and South Carolina, Alabama, Mississippi, and Tennessee. These Indians had made significant strides toward becoming acculturated to European ways as Jefferson had envisioned. Nevertheless, they were seen as an obstruction to westward migration, especially by grasping planters on the make who saw great potential profits from growing cotton on Indian land. A similar situation prevailed in the Northwest. Though neither as numerous nor as Europeanized as the Civilized Tribes, groups like the Peorias, Kaskaskias, Kickapoos, Sauks, Foxes, and Winnebagos were living settled and stable lives along the northern frontier.

Throughout the 1820s, the federal government plied tribes along the frontier with money and the promise of escape from white pressure, offers that proved attractive to many desperate Indians. The outcome was terrible factionalism within Indian societies as some lobbied to sell out and move west while others fought to keep their lands. Playing on this factionalism, **federal Indian agents** were able to extract land cessions that consolidated the eastern tribes onto smaller and smaller holdings. One such transaction, the 1825 Treaty of Indian Springs, involved fraud and manipulation so obnoxious that President Adams overturned the ratified treaty and insisted on a new one.

Adams's protective attitude did not extend to all Indians, however. The Prairie du Chien treaties (see page 267) called for the gradual removal of the northwestern tribes to the west side of the Mississippi. Drawn by the presence of gold and rich soil, impatient white miners and farmers moved onto the treaty lands even before the Indians left. In 1827, the Winnebagos, under Red Bird, resisted this invasion by raiding mining settlements in what was still legally Indian territory. White miners called for federal troops to join their own militia companies in putting an end to Winnebago resistance. Despite the illegality of the miners' actions, the Adams administration complied, driving Red Bird and his people out of the disputed region.

Adams at least paid lip service to honest dealings with the Indians and the sanctity of treaties. Jackson opposed both. In 1817, he had told President Monroe, "I have long viewed treaties with the Indians an absurdity not to be reconciled to the principles of our government." "The Indians are subjects of the United States," he went on, "inhabiting its territory and acknowledging its sovereignty, then is it not absurd for the sovereign to negotiate by treaty with the subject?" As president, Jackson advocated removing all the eastern Indians to the west side of the Mississippi (see Map 10.4). Following Jackson's direction, Congress passed the **Indian Removal Act** in 1830, appropriating the funds necessary to purchase all of the lands held by Indian tribes east of the Mississippi River and to pay for their resettlement in the West. More important, it gave the president the power to force the tribes to relocate.

It did not take Jackson long to begin implementing his new authority. Like the Winnebagos, the Sauk and Fox Indians also resisted violations of the Prairie du Chien treaties. When white farmers penetrated the territory of Sauk leader **Black Hawk** dur-

♦ German Prince Maximilian von Wied-Neuwied was very vocal in opposing the Indian Removal Act of 1830. Sure that removal would destroy all trace of Indian culture, Maximilian commissioned Karl Bodmer to paint as many pictures as he could of native people before they and their culture became extinct. This painting shows two Choctaw Indians he met at Natchez. *"Choctaws at Natchez" by Karl Bodmer, 1833. Maximilian-Bodmer Collection, Joslyn Art Museum.*

federal Indian agents Government officials who were responsible for negotiating treaties with Native American groups; at this time they were employed by the War Department.

Indian Removal Act Law passed by Congress in 1830 providing for the removal of all Indian tribes east of the Mississippi and the purchase of western lands for their resettlement.

Black Hawk Sauk leader who brought his people back to their homeland in Illinois; he was captured in 1832 when U.S. troops massacred his followers.

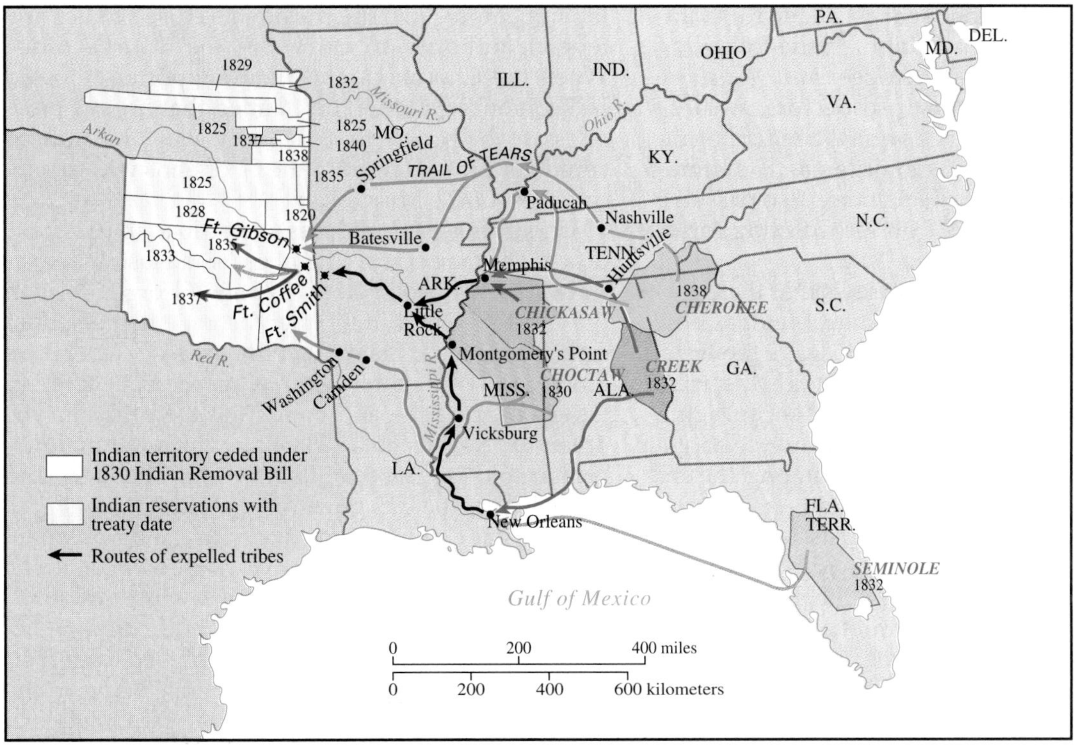

♦ **MAP 10.4 Indian Removal** The outcome of Andrew Jackson's Indian policy appears clearly on this map. Between 1830 and 1835, all of the Civilized Tribes except Osceola's faction of Seminoles were forced to relocate west of the Mississippi River. Thousands died in the process.

ing the summer of 1831, the Jackson administration authorized federal troops to forcibly move the entire band of more than a thousand Indian men, women, and children across the Mississippi. During the following spring, however, Black Hawk and his people recrossed the river and began farming on their old lands. Harassed by Illinois militia units, members of Black Hawk's band valiantly clung to their territory until troops marched in from Illinois and Missouri. Federal and state military forces massacred the Sauk band, killing more than three hundred people and capturing Black Hawk.

At the same time, whites were exerting similar pressure on the southern tribes. The case of the Cherokees provides an excellent illustration of the new, more aggressive attitude toward Indian policy. Having allied with Jackson against the Creeks in 1813, the Cherokees emerged from the War of 1812 with their lands pretty well intact, and a rising generation of progressive leaders pushed strongly for the tribe to embrace white culture and become members of the new American nation. In the early 1820s, the Cherokees created a formal government with a bicameral legislature, a court system, and a professional, salaried civil service. In 1827, the tribe drafted and ratified a written constitution modeled on the Constitution of the United States. In the following year the tribe began publication of its own newspaper, the *Cherokee Phoenix*, printed in English and in the Cherokee alphabet devised earlier in the decade by tribal member **George Guess (Sequoyah).**

Rather than winning the acceptance of their white neighbors, however, those innovations led to even greater friction. From the frontiersmen's point of view, Indians were supposed to be dying out, disappearing into history, not founding new governments and competing successfully for economic

George Guess (Sequoyah) Cherokee silversmith and trader who created an alphabet that made it possible to transcribe the Cherokee language according to the sounds of its syllables.

power. Thus in 1828, the Georgia legislature **annulled** the Cherokee constitution. In the following year, gold was found on Cherokee land. As more than three thousand greedy prospectors violated tribal territory, the state of Georgia extended its authority over the Cherokees and ordered all communal tribal lands seized. The legislature also passed a law prohibiting Cherokees from prospecting for or mining gold on their own land.

That was the first in a series of laws that the Georgia legislature passed to make life as difficult as possible for the Cherokees to get them to leave the state. When Christian missionaries living with the tribe began protesting the state's actions and encouraging the Cherokees to seek federal assistance, Georgia passed a law that required teachers among the Indians to obtain licenses from the state—a law expressly designed to eliminate the missionaries' influence. When two missionaries, Samuel Austin Worcester and Elizar Butler, refused to apply for the licenses, a company of Georgia militia invaded their mission in the heart of Cherokee country, arrested the missionaries, and marched them off to jail.

Two notable lawsuits came out of the combined efforts of the missionaries and Cherokees to get justice. In the first case, ***Cherokee Nation v. Georgia*** (1831), the Cherokees claimed that Georgia's action in extending authority over them and enforcing state law within Cherokee territory was illegal because they were a sovereign nation in a treaty relationship with the United States. The U.S. Supreme Court refused to hear this case. Speaking for the Court, Chief Justice John Marshall stated that the Cherokee Nation was neither a foreign nor a domestic state but was a "domestic dependent nation" and as such had no standing in federal court.

As American citizens, however, Worcester and Butler did have legitimate standing in federal law, and in 1832 Marshall was able to render a decision in the case of ***Worcester v. Georgia.*** In this case, the Court ruled that the Cherokee Nation was a distinct political community recognized by federal authority and that Georgia did not have legitimate power to pass laws regulating Indian behavior or to invade Indian land. He thus declared all the laws Georgia passed to harass the Cherokees null and void and ordered Georgia to release Worcester and Butler from jail (see Individual Choices: Samuel Austin Worcester).

Although the Cherokees had grounds for celebration, their joy was short lived. When Jackson heard the outcome of *Worcester v. Georgia,* he reportedly fumed, "John Marshall has made his decision, now let him enforce it." The president refused to use any federal authority to carry out the Court's order. When the Cherokees and their supporters pressed Jackson on the matter, he claimed that he was powerless to help and that the only way the Indians could get protection from the Georgians was to relocate west of the Mississippi.

Under this sort of pressure, tribal unity broke down. The majority of Cherokees stood fast with their stalwart leader John Ross, fighting Georgia through the court system. But another faction emerged advocating relocation. Playing on the division, federal Indian agents named the dissenters as the true representatives of the tribe and convinced them to sign the **Treaty of New Echota** (1835), in which the minority faction sold the last 8 million acres of Cherokee land in the East to the U.S. government for $5 million.

A similar combination of pressure, manipulation, and outright fraud led to the dispossession of all the other Civilized Tribes. During the winter of 1831–1832, the Choctaws in Mississippi and Alabama became the first tribe to be forcibly removed from their lands to a designated Indian Territory between the Red and Arkansas rivers in what is now Oklahoma. They were joined by the Creeks in 1836 and by the Chickasaws in 1837. John Ross and the other anti-treaty Cherokee leaders continued to fight in court and to lobby in Congress, but in 1838 federal troops rounded up the entire Cherokee tribe, nearly twenty thousand people, and force-marched them to Indian Territory. Like all of the Indian groups that were forcibly removed from their native lands, the Cherokees suffered terribly. In the course of the long trek, which is known as the **Trail of Tears** (see Map 10.4),

annul To declare a law or contract invalid.

Cherokee Nation v. Georgia Supreme Court case (1831) concerning Georgia's annulment of all Cherokee laws; Chief Justice John Marshall ruled that Indian tribes did not have the right to appeal to the Supreme Court.

Worcester v. Georgia Supreme Court case (1832) concerning the arrest of two missionaries to the Cherokees in Georgia; the Court found that Georgia had no right to rule in Cherokee territory.

Treaty of New Echota Treaty in 1835 by which a minority faction gave all Cherokee lands east of the Mississippi to the U.S. government in return for $5 million and land in Indian Territory.

Trail of Tears Forced march of the Cherokee people from Georgia to Indian Territory in the winter of 1838, during which thousands of Cherokees died.

nearly a fourth of the twenty thousand Cherokees who started the march died of disease, exhaustion, or heartbreak.

The only one of the Civilized Tribes to abandon legal defenses and adopt a policy of military resistance was the Seminoles. Like the other tribes, the Seminoles were deeply divided. Some chose peaceful relocation. Others advocated rebellion. After the conciliatory faction signed the Treaty of Payne's Landing in 1832, a group led by **Osceola** broke with the tribe, declaring war on the protreaty group and on the United States. After years of guerrilla swamp fighting, Osceola was finally captured in 1837, but the antitreaty faction fought on. The war continued until 1842, when the United States withdrew its troops, having lost fifteen hundred men during the ten-year conflict. Eventually, even the majority of Osceola's followers agreed to move west, though a small faction of the Seminoles remained in Florida's swamps, justly proud that they were neither conquered nor dispossessed by the United States.

Jackson and the West

Jackson's Indian policy enhanced his popularity in the ever-expanding West, but two other issues important to westerners proved troublesome for Old Hickory. One, the continuing clamor for federally funded internal improvements, threatened Jackson's notions of small and frugal government. The other, demands for more liberal public land policies, endangered government revenues and Jackson's relationship with supporters outside the West.

Although Jackson was a westerner, his views on federal spending for roads, canals, and other internal improvements seemed based more on politics than on ideology or regional interest. For example, when Congress passed a bill calling for federal money to build a road in Kentucky—from Maysville, on the Ohio border, to Lexington—Jackson vetoed it. He claimed that it would benefit only one state and was therefore unconstitutional. But three practical political issues influenced his decision. First, party loyalists in places like Pennsylvania and New York where Jackson hoped to gain support opposed federal aid to western states. Second, Lexington was the hub of Henry Clay's political district, and by denying aid that would benefit that city, Jackson was putting his western competitor in political hot water. Finally, Jackson's former congressional district centered on Nashville—already the terminus of a national road and therefore a legitimate recipient of federal funds. Thus Jackson could lavish money on his hometown while seeming to stand by strict constitutional limitations on federal power.

Disposing of the **public domain** was the other persistent problem Jackson faced. By the time he came to power, land policy had become a major factor in sectional politics. Although the price of $1.25 per acre for public land established in the wake of the Panic of 1819 was a significant improvement over the former price, it was still too high for many hopeful farmers. Abandoning his predecessors' notion that public land sales should profit the government, Jackson took the position that small farmers should be able to buy federal land for no more than it cost the government to **survey** the land and process the sale.

Jackson thus directed Congress that "public lands shall cease as soon as practicable to be a source of revenue," and western Jacksonians like Senator Thomas Hart Benton of Missouri responded immediately. In 1830, Benton proposed that the price of government land be dropped gradually from $1.25 to just 25 cents an acre and that any lands not sold at that price simply be given away. He also suggested that squatters—anyone who was currently settled illegally on public land—be given the first chance to buy the tract they were squatting on when the government offered it for sale.

Such measures pleased Jackson's western supporters but frightened easterners and southerners. His supporters in the East and South feared that migration would drain population and give the West an even bigger say in the nation's economic and political future. In addition, southerners were concerned that Congress would replace revenues lost from the sale of public land by raising tariffs, threatening the South's economic relationship with Europe. Northerners were afraid that the drain on population as people moved west would drive up the price of labor, increasing the cost of production and lowering profits. The result was nearly three years of debate in Congress. A frustrated Henry Clay, desperate to save any scrap of his economic plans for the nation, suggested that the distribution of public

Osceola Seminole leader in Florida who opposed removal of his people to the West and led resistance to U.S. troops; he was captured by treachery while bearing a flag of truce.

public domain Land owned and controlled by the federal government.

survey To determine the area and boundaries of land through measurement and mathematical calculation.

INDIVIDUAL CHOICES

Choosing Justice or Union

Samuel Austin Worcester

Samuel Austin Worcester chose to help the Cherokee Indians when Georgia passed a series of discriminatory laws. This aid led to Worcester's imprisonment. He took his case all the way to the Supreme Court, and the court sided with him. But he chose to back away from his position when it became clear that civil war would be the result of defending Cherokee rights. From "Cherokee Messenger" by Althea Bass, University of Oklahoma Press.

During the waning days of 1830, two very different groups met in Georgia to discuss the impact of the Indian Removal Act. One, the Georgia state legislature, was flush with victory: when enforced, the new federal law would sweep the Cherokees out of western Georgia, freeing up the tribe's rich lands. The other was a group of missionaries. At its head was the frail-looking and scholarly heir to seven generations of New England ministers, Reverend Samuel A. Worcester, who, with his associates, vowed to resist Cherokee removal.

Announcing their vow in the *Cherokee Phoenix*, Worcester stated that Andrew Jackson's Indian policy had moral as well as political implications "inasmuch as it involves the maintenance or violation of the faith of our country." Moreover, the American Board of Commissioners for Foreign Missions had declared in 1810 that it would bring about the Christian conversion of the entire world within a single generation, and removing the Cherokees would delay their conversion and imperil the board's agenda.

For their part, the Georgia state legislators had spent years attempting to drive the Cherokees out of the state, and they regarded missionary support for the Indians as an irritation. Now, with victory nearly at hand, the legislators wanted to cut off missionary assistance. They passed a new law ordering the missionar-

land be turned over to the states. Congress, relieved to have the matter taken out of its hands, passed Clay's bill in 1833. But Jackson vetoed it, taking another slap at Clay and affirming that the distribution of the public domain was a federal matter.

The Nullification Crisis

Southern concerns about rising tariffs during the debate over western lands reflected the South's abiding political and economic posture during the Jackson administration. For years, southerners had complained that tariffs discriminated against them. From their point of view, they were paying at least as much in tariffs as the North and West but were not getting anything like the same protection for the price of the things they had to sell.

This matter had come to a head in 1829 when John Quincy Adams's rebellious Congress passed the Tariff of Abominations. The new tariffs roused ies to sign a loyalty oath to the state promising to comply with Georgia law. If they signed the oath, Georgia could legally order them to stop helping the Indians. If they did not sign the oath, they would be imprisoned.

The new law became effective on March 1, 1831, and shortly thereafter Worcester and his colleagues were arrested. Because Worcester was the federal postmaster for the community of New Echota, a Georgia judge released him. But on May 15, Worcester received notice from Georgia governor George R. Gilmer that politicians had pulled strings in Washington to have his postmaster's commission suspended. The governor told Worcester that he had ten days to sign the oath, leave the state, or face arrest. Writing back to the governor, Worcester asserted that he did not believe the state of Georgia had the authority to enforce its will within the Cherokee Nation. Even if it did, he said, he was answerable to a Higher Law.

On July 7, Worcester was arrested again. He posted a bond and regained his freedom, but threats of further harassment forced him to move to neighboring Tennessee, leaving his ailing wife and baby at the mission in New Echota. On August 14, his baby daughter died, and when he rushed home to be with his family, he was arrested. When the court learned why he had returned to Georgia, he was released but was forced to return to exile in Tennessee.

Worcester thus lived like a fugitive, separated from his family and subject to legal harassment, until his case finally came to trial on September 16. The facts were clear. Worcester's own letter to the governor had declared his guilt, and the jury quickly made it official. Samuel Worcester and ten other missionaries were sentenced to four years at hard labor in the Georgia state penitentiary.

After refusing to hear the case of *Cherokee Nation v. Georgia*, Chief Justice John Marshall informed Cherokee tribal lawyers that he was eager for them to bring a stronger case. Worcester's case filled the bill, and the Cherokee Nation and the American Board jointly appealed Worcester's conviction before the Supreme Court. The Court agreed to hear the case, and in a landmark decision ordered Worcester and his codefendants released, declaring all the laws passed to harass the Cherokees null and void.

Technically, Worcester should have been a free man, but President Jackson refused to acknowledge Marshall's decision and would not order Georgia to release him. The American Board's attorneys had to return to Marshall and ask for a federal court order instructing Jackson to force Worcester's release. In the meantime, however, the Bank War and the nullification crisis had hit the nation with full force, threatening the fabric of the Union itself. Hoping to avoid yet another blow, newly elected Georgia governor Wilson Lumpkin told Worcester and his associates that he would grant them a pardon if they chose not to press their case. The American Board instructed the missionaries to accept the pardon and end the legal struggle. Given the constraints surrounding them, their decision to follow the board's instruction is understandable, but there is truth to the charge leveled by historian William G. McLoughlin that Worcester and the American Board chose to "sacrifice the Cherokees to save the Union."

loud protest from states like South Carolina, where soil exhaustion and declining prices for agricultural produce were putting strong economic pressure on men who were deeply invested in land and slaves. Calhoun, who took office as Jackson's vice president in 1829, led the protest.

Calhoun had turned away from Clay's nationalist program to support strictly southern interests and states' rights as the economy turned sour in 1819. In 1828, he wrote a pamphlet called *The South Carolina Exposition and Protest.* The South Carolina legislature published it anonymously. In this work Calhoun argued that, like the Maysville Road (which Jackson had vetoed), tariffs benefited only one part of the country rather than the nation at large and should be considered unconstitutional. More important, Calhoun asserted that the states merely agreed to create an agent to carry out their mutual will when they ratified the Constitution. Neither the executive, the legislative, nor the judicial branch, nor all three

♦ Throughout the West, people without money simply camped on publicly owned land. This painting by George Caleb Bingham captures one such family as they pause outside their log cabin. Western politicians like Thomas Hart Benton argued that such "squatters" had a legitimate right to claim the land they settled and fought for legislation protecting squatters' rights. *"The Squatters" by Bingham 1850. Courtesy of Museum of Fine Arts, Boston.*

branches together, Calhoun claimed, could determine the national government's legitimate power. Only the sovereign states could do so.

Getting down to his main point, Calhoun asserted that the Tariff of Abominations could not be imposed on states that believed it to be unjust. A state that believed any federal law was unconstitutional, Calhoun said, had the right to call a popular convention to consider the matter. If the state convention decided against the law, the law would not be binding within the state. In other words, a state had the right to nullify a federal law, and so this idea came to be called **nullification.**

Calhoun's sentiments reflected notions being expressed throughout the nation. And as Calhoun's pamphlet circulated to wider and wider audiences, nationalists like Clay and Jackson got more and more anxious about the potential threat to federal power. The test came in 1830, when Senator Robert Y. Hayne of South Carolina and Senator **Daniel Webster** of Massachusetts entered into a debate over Calhoun's ideas. Hayne supported Calhoun completely, while Webster appealed to nationalism in one of the most stirring orations ever delivered in the Senate. Asserting that the Constitution was "the people's Constitution" and was not something to be toyed with by petty local politicians, Webster concluded by proclaiming, "Liberty and Union, now and for ever, one and inseparable!"

Many have maintained that Hayne's speech was better argued than Webster's, but the only thing that really mattered was how the president and the nation viewed the debate. Jackson soon made his position clear. At a political banquet, he offered the toast, "Our Federal Union—It must be preserved," indicating that he would brook no nullification arguments. Calhoun, who was sitting near the president, then rose and countered Jackson's toast with one of his own: "The Union—next to our liberty most dear. May we always remember that it can only be preserved by distributing evenly the benefits and burthens of the Union."

For Jackson, who valued loyalty above all else, his vice president's action was inexcusable. Still, two years passed before the crisis finally came.

In 1832 nullification advocates in South Carolina called for a special session of the state legislature to consider the matter of state versus federal power. The convention met in November and voted overwhelmingly to nullify the tariff. The legislature also elected Hayne, nullification's most prominent spokesman, as governor and named Calhoun as his replacement in the Senate. The vice president, who realized that he would not be Jackson's running mate in the coming election, finally admitted writing the *Exposition and Protest* and resigned from the vice presidency to lead the pronullification forces from the Senate floor.

Jackson quickly proved true to his toast of two years before. Bristling that nullification violated the Constitution and was "destructive of the great object for which it was formed," Jackson immediately reinforced federal forts in South Carolina and sent warships to enforce the tariff's collection. He also asked Congress to pass a "force bill" giving him the power to invade the rebellious state if doing so proved necessary to enforce federal law. In hopes of placating southerners and winning popular support in the upcoming election, Congress passed a lowered tariff, but it also voted to give Jackson the power he asked for.

South Carolina nullifiers immediately called a new convention, which withdrew its nullification of the previous tariff but passed a resolution nullifying the force bill. Because Jackson no longer needed the

nullification Refusal by a state to recognize or enforce a federal law within its boundaries.

Daniel Webster Massachusetts senator and lawyer who was known for his forceful speeches and considered nullification a threat to the Union.

♦ This 1832 political cartoon shows Andrew Jackson engaged in a cut-throat game of bragg (an early form of poker) against his political enemies. Across from the president, Anti-Mason William Wirt grins confidently at the frowning John Calhoun, who hides "Nullification" and "Anti-Tariff" cards under the table. Although Jackson appears to be losing the poker game, he won the election handily, despite his enemies trying to stack the political deck against him. *The Library Company of Philadelphia.*

force bill to enforce federal law and collect the new tariff, he chose to ignore this action. Thus there was no real resolution to the problem, and the gash over federal versus states' rights remained unhealed. It continued to fester until it was finally cauterized by Civil War.

Jackson and the Bank

Another major crisis also related to federal power. In this case, however, the president stood on the side of those in favor of limiting the power of the national government. The Second Bank of the United States, chartered in 1816, was an essential part of Henry Clay's American System. In addition to serving as the depository for federal funds, the Second Bank issued national currency, which could be exchanged directly for gold, and served as a national clearing-house for notes issued by state and local banks. In that capacity, the Second Bank could regulate currency values and credit rates and help control the activities of state banks by refusing to honor their notes if they lacked sufficient gold to back them. The Second Bank could also police state and local banks by calling in loans and refusing credit—actions that had helped bring on the Panic of 1819 and had made the Second Bank very unpopular.

In 1823, **Nicholas Biddle** became president of the Second Bank. An able administrator and talented economist, Biddle enforced firm and consistent policies that restored some confidence in the bank and its functions. But many Americans still were not ready to accept the notion of an all-powerful central banking authority. Opponents of the Second Bank tended to be Democrats and supporters of Jackson, who opposed the bank himself.

Opposition came from several quarters. The vast majority of opponents were Americans who did not understand the function of the Second Bank, viewing it as just another instrument for helping the rich get richer. These critics tended instinctively to support the use of hard currency called **specie,** coins minted from gold and silver. Other critics, including many state bankers, opposed the Second Bank because they felt that Biddle's controls were too strict and they were not receiving their fair share of federal revenues. Speculators and debtors also opposed the bank. When they gambled correctly, they could benefit from the sort of economic instability the bank was designed to prevent.

Looking for any device to try to shake Jackson's popularity, Webster and Clay decided the Second Bank would make the perfect weapon. Although its twenty-year charter was not due for renewal until 1836, Jackson's enemies in Congress proposed to renew the charter on the eve of the 1832 presidential election. Clay and Webster hoped that Biddle's leadership had established the bank as a necessary part of the nation's economy, even in critics' minds, and that Democratic party discipline would break down if the president tried to prevent the early renewal of the charter.

Nicholas Biddle President of the Second Bank of the United States; he struggled to keep the bank functioning when President Jackson tried to destroy it.

specie Coins minted from precious metals.

♦ Published in 1833, this political cartoon entitled "The Diplomatic Hercules (Andrew Jackson) Attacking the Political Hydra (The Second Bank of the United States)" illustrates why the Bank War enhanced rather than hurt Jackson at the polls. Many voters saw the bank as a monster that used its tentacles of complicated financial policy to choke common people while enriching the speculators and merchants who supported it. *New-York Historical Society.*

Jackson's opponents were partially right—Congress passed the renewal bill, and Jackson vetoed it—but the envisioned rift between Jackson and congressional Democrats did not open. The president stole the day by delivering a powerful veto message geared to appeal to the mass of Americans on whose support his party's congressmen depended. Jackson denounced the Second Bank as an example of vested privilege and monopoly power that served the interests of "the few at the expense of the many" and injured "humbler members of society—the farmers, the mechanics, and laborers—who have neither the time nor the means of securing like favors to themselves." And Jackson went even further, asserting that foreign interests, many of which were seen as enemies to American rights, had used the bank to accumulate large blocks of American securities.

Although the charter was not renewed, the Second Bank could operate for four more years on the basis of its unexpired charter. Jackson, however, wanted to kill the Second Bank immediately, to "deprive the conspirators of the aid which they expect from its money and power." The strategy Jackson chose was to withdraw federal funds and redeposit the money in state banks. According to the laws authorizing the Second Bank, only the secretary of the treasury was permitted to make withdrawals. Therefore Jackson ordered Treasury Secretary Louis McLane to withdraw the federal funds. When he refused Jackson's order, the president fired and replaced him with William J. Duane, who also refused to carry out Jackson's order. Jackson quickly fired him too and appointed Kitchen Cabinet member Roger B. Taney to head the Treasury Department.

Instead of transferring federal funds directly from the Second Bank to state banks, Taney simply kept paying the government's bills with money from the federal accounts while placing all new deposits in so-called **pet banks**—state banks whose directors had agreed to support Jackson's dismantling of the Second Bank.

Bank president Biddle was not going to give up without a fight. Powerless to stop Taney's withdrawal of federal funds, Biddle sought to replace dwindling assets by calling in loans owed by state banks and by raising interest rates. In this way, the banker believed, he not only would head off the Second Bank's collapse but would trigger a business panic that might force the government to reverse its course. "Nothing but the evidence of suffering . . . will produce any effect," Biddle said as he pushed the nation toward economic instability.

Biddle was correct that there would be "evidence of suffering." But the full effect of the **Bank War** would not be felt until after the reign of "King Andrew" had ended. As the end of Jackson's first term approached in 1832, the nation's economy, like its politics, was unruly and divided but vigorous as it evolved to reflect a nation in profound transformation.

pet banks State banks into which Andrew Jackson ordered federal deposits to be placed to help deplete the funds of the Second Bank of the United States.

Bank War The political conflict that occurred when Andrew Jackson tried to destroy the Second Bank of the United States, which he thought represented special interests at the expense of the common man.

SUMMARY

Expectations
Constraints
Choices
Outcomes

With the end of the War of 1812, President Madison and the Republicans *chose* to promote a strong agenda for the nation, in line with the new *expectations* of an excited American populace. Madison joined with former critics like Henry Clay and John C. Calhoun to push for a national market economy, sponsoring federal legislation for a national bank, controlled currency, and tariff protection for American industry. In addition, Madison gave free rein to nationalists like Stephen Decatur, John Quincy Adams, and Andrew Jackson, who succeeded in extending the nation's military reputation and expanding its sphere of influence.

While the nation moved forward in accomplishing its diplomatic goals, the Republicans' economic agenda was being *constrained* by the lack of a coherent transportation and communication system. *Expecting* quick and enormous profits, New York *chose* to respond by building the Erie Canal, the first successful link between the increasingly urban and manufacturing East and the rural, agricultural West. Convinced finally that transportation improvements were necessary for national defense and for carrying out the work of the government, Madison and his successors joined with state officials to begin the process of building a truly national system of roads and canals.

But what had begun as an age of optimism closed in a tangle of conflict and ill will. Optimistic *expectations* were partially responsible. A much-hoped-for prosperity was *constrained* by shrinking markets, with the *outcome* of economic panic in 1819 and a collapse in the speculative economy. Economic hard times, in turn, triggered increased competition among the nation's geographical sections, as leaders *chose* to wrestle for control over federal power in an effort to rid particular areas of economic despair. Supporters of the American System tried to craft a solution, but their compromise did not entirely satisfy anyone. And in the sea of contention that swelled around the Missouri Compromise, the Era of Good Feelings collapsed.

Meanwhile, distressed by what seemed an elite conspiracy to run American affairs, newly politicized voters *chose* to sweep the gentlemanly John Quincy Adams out of office and replace him with the more exciting and presumably more democratic Andrew Jackson. Backed by a political machine composed of northern, western, and southern interests, Jackson had to juggle each region's financial, tariff, and Indian policy demands while trying to hold his political alliance and the nation together. The *outcome* was a series of regional crises—the Bank War, nullification, and Indian removal—that alienated each region and together constituted a crisis of national proportions.

SUGGESTED READINGS

George Dangerfield. *The Era of Good Feelings* (New York, 1952).

An older book, but so well written and informative that it deserves its status as a classic. All students will enjoy this grand overview.

Angie Debo. *And Still the Waters Run: The Betrayal of the Five Civilized Tribes* (1940; reprint, 1972).

A classic work by one of America's most talented and sensitive historical writers, a truly engaging history of this tragic sequence of events.

Michael Paul Rogin. *Fathers and Children: Andrew Jackson and the Subjugation of the American Indian* (1975).

A controversial and enjoyable psychoanalysis of Andrew Jackson focusing on his Indian policy, but giving an interesting view of his entire personality.

Charles G. Sellers. *The Market Revolution: Jacksonian America, 1815–1846* (1991).

A far-reaching reassessment of economics and politics during this period focusing on the rise of the market economy and the responses, both positive and negative, that led to the rise of Jacksonian democracy.

John William Ward. *Andrew Jackson: Symbol for an Age* (1955).

More a study of American culture during the age of Jackson than a biography of the man himself, Ward seeks to explain Old Hickory's status as a living myth during his own time and a continuing monument in American history.

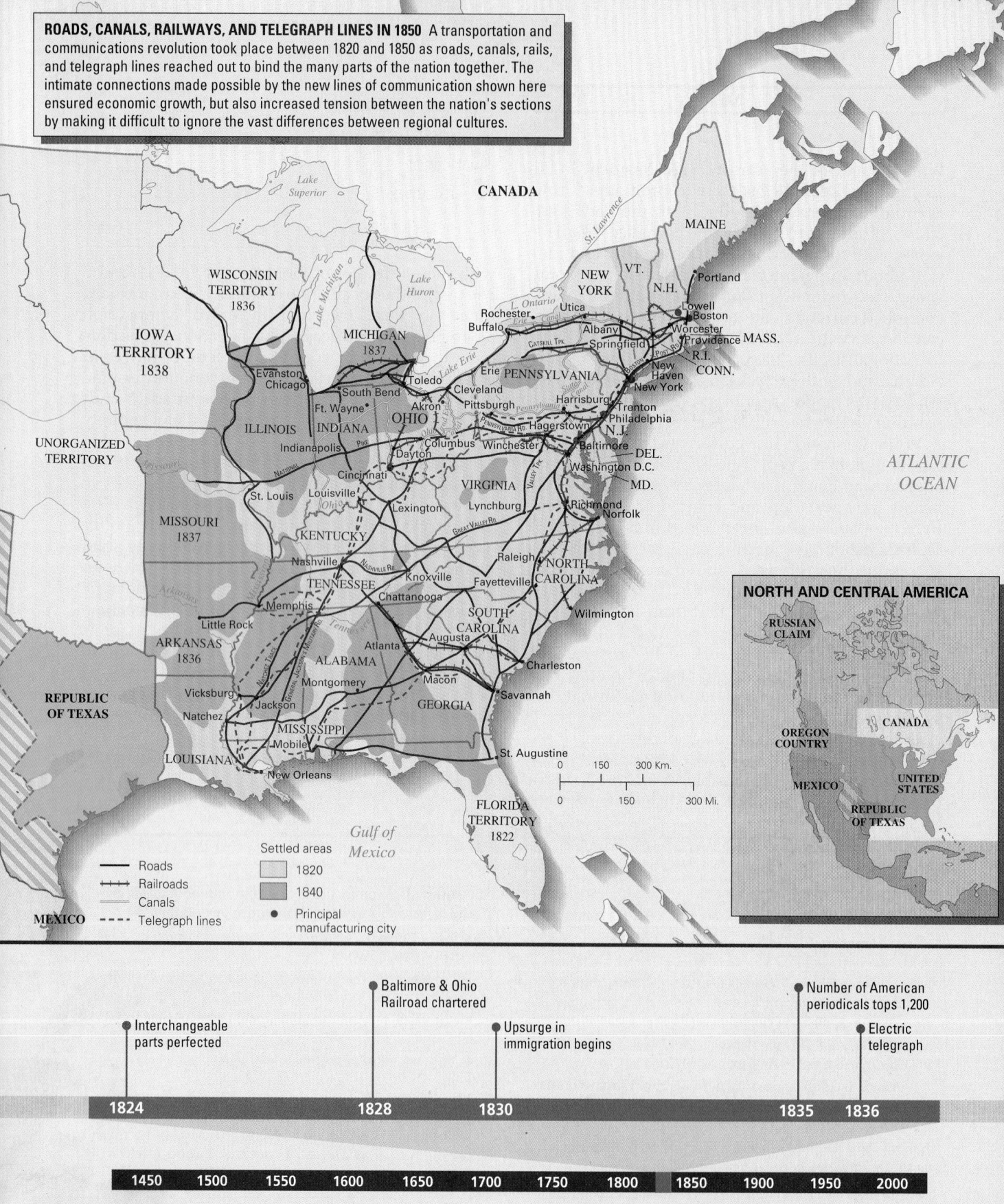

ROADS, CANALS, RAILWAYS, AND TELEGRAPH LINES IN 1850 A transportation and communications revolution took place between 1820 and 1850 as roads, canals, rails, and telegraph lines reached out to bind the many parts of the nation together. The intimate connections made possible by the new lines of communication shown here ensured economic growth, but also increased tension between the nation's sections by making it difficult to ignore the vast differences between regional cultures.

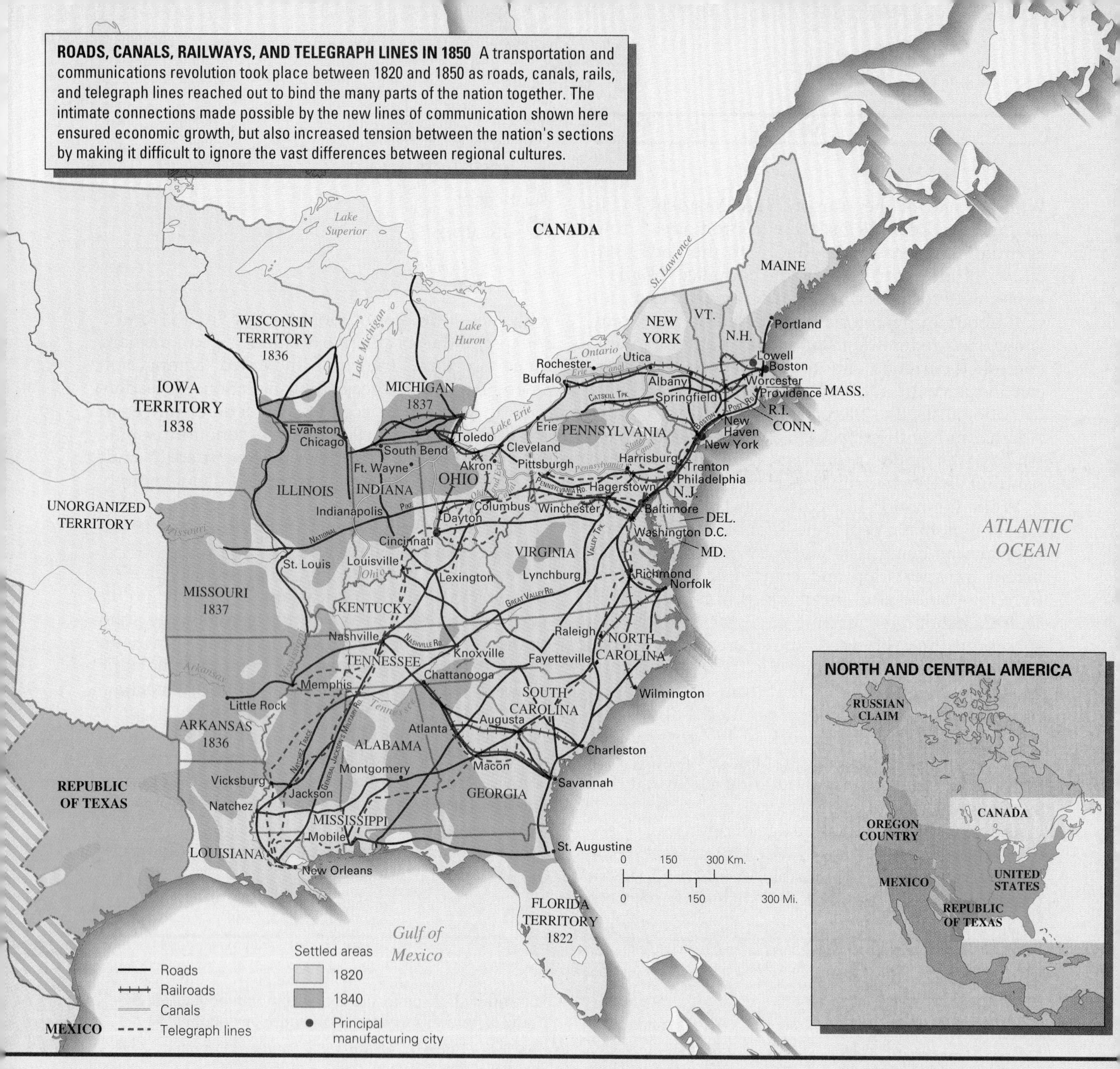

- **1824** Interchangeable parts perfected
- **1828** Baltimore & Ohio Railroad chartered
- **1830** Upsurge in immigration begins
- **1835** Number of American periodicals tops 1,200
- **1836** Electric telegraph

1450 1500 1550 1600 1650 1700 1750 1800 1850 1900 1950 2000

CHAPTER 11

The Great Transformation, 1828–1840

The Transportation Revolution

- How did newly emerging networks of transportation and communication change the expectations of Americans in the North, West, and South?

The Manufacturing Boom

- How did new manufacturing techniques following the adoption of interchangeable parts change the nature of work?
- How did the developing factory system affect the expectations of artisans and elite and middle-class Americans?

The New Cotton Empire in the South

- How did the expectations of southerners—black and white—change after 1820?
- How did white southerners choose to respond, and what new constraints resulted for slaves, free blacks, and poor whites?

INTRODUCTION

E xpectations
C onstraints
C hoices
O utcomes

During the twelve years that Andrew Jackson (1829–1837) and then his fellow Democrat Martin Van Buren (1837–1841) occupied the White House, the United States embarked on the first steps toward a new era in the nation's history. In large part the fruit of efforts by visionaries like Henry Clay and John C. Calhoun, a national market economy began to emerge, changing nearly every aspect of life for the American people.

Serious *constraints* stood in the way of national growth and economic expansion. One of the most serious of these was the problem of American geography: seemingly impassable mountains stood between the manufacturing centers of the Northeast and the sprawling open lands of the new West, making difficult the movement of people or goods either way between these regions. But individuals, states, and the federal government made the *choice* to confront this problem by extending the pioneering roads and canals that had been started after the War of 1812. The *outcome* was a network of transportation and communications systems that enabled the country to make its first struggling steps toward a full-scale industrial revolution.

At the same time that transportation routes were being extended, the economy in the northeastern section of the country was undergoing profound change. With the practical harnessing of interchangeable parts by John H. Hall in 1824, the nation rushed into new techniques for manufacturing durable goods like guns, clocks, and machinery. Soon these joined textiles as factory-produced items, and their cost, reliability, and availability improved significantly. At the same time, however, the new techniques for manufacturing consumer goods created an avalanche of unexpected *outcomes.* No longer were skilled workers required to make complicated machines, and the value of labor declined along with the range of *choices* open to workers. Factory owners and their wives isolated themselves in a genteel world of high finance and high fashion, leaving the day-to-day operation of their factories to a newly emerging class of clerks and managers. These men and women, in turn, had to make *choices* about how to cope in the soulless world of strangers that industrializing cities were becoming.

The American South, too, was undergoing transformation during this era. With the renewal of trading with Britain's cotton-hungry industries and the rise of American textile manufacturing, southerners had great *expectations* for enormous prosperity, and they were not disappointed. Despite the economic setback caused by the Panic of 1819, southerners chose to expand cotton growing to every region that would support it. With the astounding growth of cotton plantations came equal growth in the institution of slavery. These two intimately related institutions created a political and social economy in the South that would shape every soul in the region and influence the entire nation.

Each step in this great transformation generated waves of change, altering *expectations,* removing old *constraints* and then imposing new ones, and forcing a whole generation to make *choices* the like of which no previous generation of Americans had encountered. One long-term *outcome* of the choices these people made was that the foundation for a modern America was set firmly in place.

CHRONOLOGY

The Dawn of Modernization

1824 John H. Hall perfects interchangeable parts for gun manufacturing

1830 Steam locomotive Tom Thumb beaten in a race by a stagecoach horse

1830–1840 10-year immigration figure for the United States exceeds 500,000

1833 Ohio Canal completed

1834 Main Line Canal from Philadelphia to Pittsburgh completed

1835 Number of periodicals published in the United States exceeds 1,250, with a combined circulation of 90 million

1836 Samuel F. B. Morse invents the electric telegraph
Bronson Alcott's *Conversations with Children on the Gospels*

1838 National Road completed to Vandalia, Illinois

The Transportation Revolution

• How did newly emerging networks of transportation and communication change the expectations of Americans in the North, West, and South?

To pull together the sort of integrated national market economy that leaders like Henry Clay envisioned, Americans had to find ways to overcome the vast distances and difficult terrain that separated the various regions of the country. Directly after the War of 1812, presidents Madison and Monroe joined with visionary congressmen and inventive entrepreneurs in establishing new transportation routes and technologies, but much more was called for to effect the great transformation. What the country needed were intersecting networks of transportation and communications that could channel the produce of the West and South into the industrializing North, and the manufactures of the North into the markets of the South and West.

Extending the Nation's Roads

Under the leadership of aggressive expansionist congressmen like Henry Clay and John C. Calhoun, both government and private enterprise embarked on road-building projects after the War of 1812. Between 1815 and 1820, the so-called National Road snaked its way across the Cumberland Gap in the Appalachian Mountains and extended its reach from the Atlantic shore to the Ohio River at Wheeling, Virginia. Then, in 1822, a political deal between northeastern congressmen and their western colleagues extended funding and further extended the road (see page 283). By 1838 this state-of-the art highway—with its evenly graded surface, gravel pavement, and stone bridges—had been pushed all the way to Vandalia, Illinois. Within a few more years, it reached St. Louis, the great jumping-off point for the Far West.

At the same time that the Cumberland Road was being extended, a series of other roads were beginning to merge into a transportation network. The Natchez Trace, on which Mississippi rivermen had long hiked back home after delivering barges of cargo to New Orleans, also enjoyed federal patronage, as did the so-called Military Road connecting Nashville more directly to New Orleans. The Nashville Road, in turn, connected Nashville to Knoxville, where a traveler could pick up the Great Valley Road to Lynchburg, Virginia, and from there the Valley Turnpike, which connected with the Cumberland Road. Or one could keep going north from Nashville through Lexington, Kentucky, and on to Columbus, Ohio, joining the Cumberland Road there.

Eventually towns from Portland, Maine, to St. Augustine, Florida, and from Natchez, Mississippi, to New Haven, Connecticut were linked by intersecting highways (see chapter-opening map). Increasing numbers of people used these new roads to head west looking for new opportunities. Farmers, craftsmen, fur hunters, and others already settled in the West used them too, moving small loads of goods to

♦ Networks of improved roads made travel much easier in the 1820s and 1830s than it had been earlier in the century, but led to a new complication: traffic jams. This picture of the Fairview Inn in 1829 illustrates the problem, as riders, wagons, and herds of animals all crowd for space on this road outside Baltimore. *"The Fairview Inn, 1829" by Thomas Coke Ruckle. Maryland Historical Society.*

the nearby towns and small cities that always sprang up along the new transportation routes.

These new and improved roads helped to alleviate the transportation problems faced by the growing nation, but they hardly solved them. Well suited to carrying light traffic, the roads eased the lot of travelers but did little to advance commerce. Some small manufactured goods could be hauled from east to west along the new roads, and western products like livestock on the hoof and relatively lightweight items like whiskey could move the other way. But heavy and bulky products were still difficult and expensive to move. At a minimum, hauling a ton of freight along the nation's roads cost 15 cents a mile. At that rate, the cost of shipping a ton of oats from Buffalo to New York City amounted to twelve times the value of the cargo.

A Network of Canals

In addition to linking small farms with neighboring villages, the new roads linked rural America to an ever-expanding network of waterways that made relatively inexpensive long-distance hauling of freight possible. Completed in 1825, the Erie Canal revolutionized shipping (see page 276). The cost of shipping a ton of oats from Buffalo to Albany fell from $100 to $15, and the transit time dropped from twenty days to just eight. All of New York State celebrated, especially when Governor Clinton announced in 1826 that the canal had already generated three-quarters of a million dollars in profits. Businessmen in New York City were particularly happy. During the early nineteenth century, the flood of goods from America's interior allowed New York City to eclipse Boston, Philadelphia, and Baltimore, making it the most important commercial center in the nation.

The spectacular success of the Erie Canal prompted businessmen, farmers, and politicians throughout the country to promote canal building. State governments offered exclusive charters to canal-building companies, giving them direct financial grants, guaranteeing their credit, and easing their way in every possible manner. The result was an explosion in canal building that lasted through the 1830s (see chapter-opening map).

Pennsylvania's experiences were typical. Jealous of New York's success, Pennsylvania projected a massive system of canals, roads, and natural waterways, advertised as a "Golden Link to the West" and designed to make Pennsylvania the commercial center of the Western Hemisphere. Pennsylvanians threw themselves into canal building and related internal improvements with enthusiasm. Central to their plan was the **Main Line Canal** to connect the Delaware and Schuylkill rivers at Philadelphia with the Ohio River at Pittsburgh. The problem was that a mountain range more than 2,000 feet high separated the two cities. The Main Line Canal would have needed locks five times as great as the locks used on the Erie Canal—an engineering feat beyond the abilities of even the best designers in the country. Engineering veterans of the New York effort fi-

Main Line Canal Ambitious canal-building enterprise by the state of Pennsylvania to connect the Delaware River at Philadelphia with the Ohio River at Pittsburgh.

♦ The Allegheny Portage Railroad was an engineering marvel for its time. This painting by Karl Bodmer illustrates how it worked. Railcars were submerged in the canal at the base of the incline. A barge was floated over the car, which then lifted it out of the water. Railcar and barge were then hauled up the incline. Four inclines later they were hauled across the mountain's peak and then lowered down another five inclines and into the water on the opposite side. *"View of Mauch Chunk, Pennsylvania with Railroad" by Karl Bodmer, 1832. Maximilian-Bodmer Collection, Joslyn Art Museum.*

nally resorted to **portage.** They designed a portage railroad over the Allegheny Mountains.

Completed in 1834, in its heyday the **Allegheny Portage Railroad** permitted passengers and cargo to make the trip across the mountains on land but without leaving the canal boats they had boarded in Philadelphia or Pittsburgh. The Main Line Canal approached the mountains from the east and from the west. On each side of the mountains, canal boats were floated onto submerged railcars. The railcars were attached to a cable, and steam power pulled them up a series of inclined planes. The process was somewhat similar to the initial climb of a roller coaster—but it was not followed by an exciting downhill ride.

At the top of one incline, horses and later locomotives towed the railcars over level ground to the next incline. After being pulled up five steep inclines, the railcars—still carrying the canal boats with their passengers and cargo—began the descent to the canal at the other side of the mountains. The cable system carefully lowered the railcars down five inclines, and the boats were placed in the canal to continue the trip by water to Philadelphia or Pittsburgh.

The portage railroad was an engineering marvel. As one Philadelphia newspaper commented after the first successful trip, the canal boat "rested on top of the mountain at Blairs Gap like Noah's Ark on Ararat, and descended next morning into the valley of the Mississippi and sailed for St. Louis!" Experiencing the dizzying ride, British novelist Charles Dickens commented, "Occasionally the rails are laid upon the extreme verge of a giddy precipice; and looking from the carriage window, the traveller gazes sheer down without a stone or a scrap of fence between, into the mountain depths below."

Exciting as the Allegheny Portage Railroad was, both as a means of transportation and as an engineering feat, it was expensive to build and was only one of several massive projects necessary to complete Pennsylvania's "Golden Link." Engineers designed and built tunnels, aqueducts, and enormous locks, all at outrageous cost. By the time the Main Line system was completed, a family intent on migrating to the West could travel at a good speed and in relative comfort all the way from Philadelphia to Pittsburgh, but the tolls alone cost as much as 6 acres of prime farmland. In the long run, the Main Line Canal was a dismal financial failure, never earning investors one cent of profit although enough goods flowed along the channel to make Philadelphia an important commercial center for a while.

Despite Pennsylvania's bad experience, nearly every state in the North and West undertook some canal building between 1820 and 1840. States and

portage The carrying of boats or supplies overland between two waterways.

Allegheny Portage Railroad A rail line that carried canal boats over the Allegheny Mountains as part of the Main Line Canal system.

private individuals invested more than $100 million on nearly 3,500 miles of canals during the heyday of canal building. One of the most important examples was Ohio's canal system. Seeking to complete a circuit of inland waterways, Ohio began building a canal connecting Cleveland on Lake Erie to Portsmouth on the Ohio River. After the **Ohio Canal** was completed in 1833, it became possible for a merchant in New York to ship manufactured goods up the Hudson River to Albany, along the Erie Canal to Buffalo, along the shore of Lake Erie to Cleveland, on the Ohio Canal to Portsmouth, then down the Ohio and Mississippi rivers all the way to New Orleans without the cargo ever leaving the water. With the development of steamboats after Robert Fulton's and Henry Shreve's successful experiments (see page 277), meat, grain, ore, and other western products could move just as easily the other way.

But this new mobility did not come cheaply. Canals like those in Ohio and neighboring Indiana cost as much as $20,000 to $30,000 a mile to build, and financing was always a problem. Hoping for large profits, entrepreneurs like John Jacob Astor (see page 268) invested heavily in canal building. Between the mid-1820s and 1836, careful investors could make from 15 to 20 percent interest by loaning money to canal developers, but by the 1840s most canal companies faced bankruptcy, as did the states that had helped finance them. Canal building catapulted Pennsylvania into a debt of $34 million by 1842, and the state was forced to suspend payments for three years, enacting new and extremely harsh tax codes to refinance its loans. Maryland, Virginia, Ohio, Illinois, and virtually every other state that got caught up in the canal boom shared the same fate.

Steam Power

Steam power took canal building's impact on inland transportation a revolutionary step further. After Shreve's pioneer voyage in 1816, the cost of shipping a ton of goods down American rivers fell annually. By 1840, the price had declined from an average of $1\frac{1}{4}$ cents a mile to less than half a cent, and the cost of upstream transport fell even more dramatically, from over 10 cents a mile to about half a cent. In addition, steamboats could carry bulky and heavy objects that could not be hauled upstream for any price by any other means. The impact of steam technology on the economies of the South and West was staggering. The presence of dependable transportation on the Mississippi drew cotton cultivation farther into the nation's interior, western farmers flooded into the Ohio Valley, and fur trappers and traders pressed up the Missouri River.

Steam technology also had applications in areas without navigable rivers. Towns lacking water routes to the interior began losing revenue from inland trade to canal towns like New York and Philadelphia. Predictably, entrepreneurs in places like Boston and Baltimore looked for other ways to move cargo. Again, European technology suggested a solution: the steam railroad.

Demands from Baltimore merchants spurred Maryland to take the lead in developing this new transportation technology. In 1828, the state chartered the **Baltimore and Ohio Railroad (B & O).** Although the venture appeared to be highly risky, based as it was on new technology, the B & O soon demonstrated its potential when inventor Peter Cooper's steam locomotive Tom Thumb sped 13 miles along B & O track. Steam railroading, however, did not seem destined to succeed. Claiming that his little engine could outrun any horse in the country, Cooper was disgraced when a stagecoach horse beat the Tom Thumb in a race held in August 1830. The B & O abandoned steam power, replacing it with coaches pulled along the rails by horses.

Despite the B & O's failure, South Carolina chose to invest in steam technology and chartered a 136-mile rail line from Charleston to Hamburg. Here, the first full-size American-built locomotive pulled cars—until the engine exploded, taking much of the train and many of its passengers with it. Rather than giving up on the idea of steam power, however, the Charleston and Hamburg Railroad began putting "buffer" cars filled with cotton bales between the engine and the passenger and freight cars, to protect passengers and cargoes from boiler explosions. Massachusetts followed this practice as well as it tried to compete with New York and the Erie Canal by building a railroad from Boston through Worcester and on to Albany.

Although rail transport enjoyed some success during this early period, it could not rival water-based transportation systems. By 1850 individual compa-

Ohio Canal A canal connecting Cleveland to Portsmouth, completing a network of waterways linking the Hudson River, Great Lakes, and Mississippi River system.

Baltimore and Ohio Railroad First steam railroad commissioned in the United States; it resorted to using horse-drawn cars after a stagecoach horse beat its pioneer locomotive in a race.

♦ Though painted many years after the event, this picture captures the excitement of the historic race between the steam-powered Tom Thumb and a stagecoach horse that took place in the summer of 1830. The horse won, leading the Baltimore and Ohio Railroad to scrap steam power, hitching horses to their cars rather than locomotives. *"The Race of the Tom Thumb" by Herbert D. Stitt. The Chessie System, B&O Railroad Museum Archives.*

nies had laid approximately 9,000 miles of track, but not in any coherent network. There was little or no standardization of track size, and the distance between tracks varied from company to company. As a result, cargoes had to be unloaded from the cars of one company's trains at line's end, lugged to the railhead of another line, and reloaded onto the other company's cars. There were other problems too. Boiler explosions, fires, and derailments were common because pressure regulators, spark-arresters, and brakes were inadequate. Also, entrenched interest groups—especially investors who hoped to profit from canals, roads, and steam shipping—used their power in state legislatures to limit the extension of railroads. Because of these obstacles, railroads did not become a major factor in American life until a combination of technological, financial, and political changes occurred in the 1850s.

Information Revolution

Migrants, adventurers, and goods were not the only cargoes carried by the new transportation systems. Information was another important payload.

Distance impaired not only American commerce but also the conduct of the republic itself. Since the nation's founding, American leaders had expressed the fear that the sheer size of the continent would make true federal democracy impractical. During the 1790s, for example, it took a week for news to travel from Virginia to New York City and three weeks for a letter to get from Cincinnati to the Atlantic coast. Voting returns, economic data, and other information crucial to running a republic seemed to take an impossibly long time to get out, and the problem promised to get worse as the nation grew. This difficulty led Thomas Jefferson and others to speculate that the continent would become a series of allied republics, each small enough to operate efficiently given the slow speed of communication. The transportation revolution, however, made quite a difference in how quickly news got around.

After the Erie Canal opened, letters posted in Buffalo could reach New York City within six days and might get to New Orleans within two weeks. The improved flow of information caused an explosion in the number of newspapers and magazines published in the country. In 1790, the 92 newspapers being published in America had a total **circulation** of around 4 million. As the nation expanded, as economics and social life became more complicated, Americans felt growing pressure to keep up with news at home and in the nation's new territories. The revolution in transportation helped them do so. With the transport of printed matter made speedier and cheaper, by 1835 the number of periodicals had risen to 1,258 and circulation had surpassed 90 million.

The explosion in the volume and speed of communications was enhanced by a true revolution in information technology that was in its starting phases. In the mid-1830s, Samuel F. B. Morse, painter, sculptor, and president of the New York School of Design, became interested in experiments

circulation The number of copies of a publication sold or distributed.

in chemistry and electricity. The object of his curiosity was the **electric telegraph,** the world's first form of electronic communication, which he perfected in 1836. Simple in design, Morse's transmitter consisted of a key that closed an electrical circuit, thereby sending a pulse along a connected wire. How long the key was pressed determined the length of the pulse. Morse developed a code consisting of dots (short pulses) and dashes (longer pulses) that formed letters of the alphabet. With this device a skilled operator could quickly key out long messages and send them at nearly the speed of light. Over the next several years, Morse worked on improvements to extend the distance that the impulses would travel along the wires. Finally, in 1843, Congress agreed to finance an experimental telegraph line from Washington, D.C., to Baltimore. Morse sent his first message on the experimental line on May 24, 1844. His message, "What hath God wrought!" was a fitting opening line for the telecommunications revolution.

The Manufacturing Boom

- How did new manufacturing techniques following the adoption of interchangeable parts change the nature of work?
- How did the developing factory system affect the expectations of artisans and elite and middle-class Americans?

During the opening years of the nineteenth century, manufacturing in America was largely a home-based affair. Before the 1820s, American households produced most of the manufactured items they used. For example, more than 60 percent of the clothing that Americans wore was spun from raw fibers and sewn by women in their own homes. Some householders even crafted sophisticated items—furniture, clocks, and tools—but skilled artisans usually made such products. These craftsmen, too, usually worked in their homes, assisted by family members and an extended family of **artisan** employees: **apprentices** and **journeymen.**

Beginning with the cotton-spinning plants that sprang up during the War of 1812, textile manufacturing led the way in pushing production in a radical new direction (see page 265). From 1820 onward, manufacturing increasingly moved out of the home and into factories, and cities began to grow up around the factories. The intimate ties between manufacturers and workers were severed, and both found themselves surrounded by strangers in the new urban environments. "In most large cities there may be said to be two nations, understanding as little of one another, having as little intercourse, as if they lived in different lands," said Unitarian minister William Ellery Channing in 1841. "This estrangement of men from men, of class from class, is one of the saddest features of a great city."

The "American System" of Manufacturing

The transition from home manufacturing to factory production did not take place overnight, and the two processes often overlapped. Pioneer manufacturers like Samuel Slater relied on home workers to carry out major steps in the production of textiles. Using what was called the **putting-out system,** cotton spinners supplied machine-produced thread to individual households, where families carried out tasks like weaving on their own looms during their spare time. Such activities provided much-needed cash to farm families, enabled less productive family members (like the elderly or children) to contribute, and gave entire families worthwhile things to do during lulls in the farming calendar.

But innovations in manufacturing soon began displacing such home crafting. With good reason, the factory designs pioneered by Henry Cabot Lowell and his various partners were widely copied during the 1820s and 1830s. Spinning and weaving on machines located in one building significantly cut both the time and the cost of manufacturing. Quality control became easier because the tools of the trade, owned by the manufacturer rather than by

electric telegraph Device invented by Samuel F. B. Morse in 1836 that transmits coded messages along a wire over long distances; the first electronic communications device.

artisan A person whose primary employment is the specialized production of hand-manufactured items; a craftsperson.

apprentice A person who is bonded to a craftsman, providing labor in exchange for learning the skills associated with the craft.

journeyman A person who has finished an apprenticeship in a trade or craft and is a qualified worker in the employ of another.

putting-out system Manufacturing system through which machine-made components, like thread, were distributed to individual families who used them to craft finished goods..

♦ Women who worked in the new textile factories complained about the noise, tedium, and dangers. This engraving, from the *Memoir of Samuel Slater* (1836), shows the conditions under which they worked. *Museum of American Textile History.*

the worker, were standardized and employees were under constant supervision. As a result, the putting-out system for turning thread into cloth went into serious decline, falling off by as much as 90 percent in some areas of New England. Even home production of clothes for family use slid into decline. The reasons were that machine-made cloth was cheap and readily available and more and more women were working in factories and were not at home making things for their families. Throughout the 1830s and 1840s, ready-made clothing—often cut, machine-sewn, and finished by semiskilled workers in factory settings—became standard wearing apparel.

A major technological revolution helped to push factory production into other areas of manufacturing as well during these years. In traditional manufacturing, individual artisans crafted each item one at a time, from the smallest part to the final product. A clockmaker, for example, either cast or carved individually by hand all the gears, levers, and wheels. As a result, the innards of a clock worked together only in the clock for which they had been made. If that clock ever needed repair, new parts had to be custom-made for it. The lack of **interchangeable parts** made manufacturing extremely slow and repairs difficult, and it limited employment in the manufacturing trades to highly skilled professionals.

While serving as ambassador to France, Thomas Jefferson had encountered the idea of standardizing parts, so that a wheel from any given clock could be used in any other similar clock. Eli Whitney, inventor of the cotton gin (see page 265), was the first American to propose the large-scale use of interchangeable parts—in a gun-manufacturing scheme in 1798. Whitney's efforts failed because he lacked money and precision machine tools, but early in the nineteenth century the idea was successfully put into practice.

Much of the credit for the successful use of interchangeable parts in manufacturing goes to John H. Hall, at one time a partner of Whitney. Bringing together the necessary skill, financing, and tools at the federal armory in Harpers Ferry, Virginia, in 1824, Hall proved that manufacturing guns from interchangeable parts was practical. From Harpers Ferry this "American system of manufacturing," as it was called, spread to the Springfield Armory in Massachusetts and out to private gun manufacturers like Simeon North and Samuel Colt. Within twenty years, a wide range of products—padlocks, sewing machines, clocks, and farm implements—was being made from interchangeable parts.

Like mechanized spinning and weaving, the use of interchangeable parts speeded up the manufacture of important products and improved their dependability. The new technology also made repairing guns and other standardized mechanisms easy and relatively cheap. Like the textile mills, factories assembling interchangeable parts slashed production costs. They made it possible to hire relatively unskilled workers to do what had once required highly trained and talented artisans—and do it more efficiently (see Individual Choices: Chauncey Jerome).

interchangeable parts Parts that are identical and can be substituted for each other.

INDIVIDUAL CHOICES

Choosing the Modern Way

Chauncey Jerome

Clockmaker Chauncey Jerome became one of the most successful businessmen in America when he chose to abandon tradition by manufacturing clocks out of standardized interchangeable parts. He launched a revolution in the clock industry and forever changed how Americans would think about time. But when he chose to join up with American showman and huckster P. T. Barnum in a stock scheme, the outcome was poverty and dishonor. Collection of Col. Leland Martin, Ret.

No one who knew Chauncey Jerome as a boy would ever have thought he would amount to much. The son of a very poor blacksmith in rural Connecticut, Jerome was able to attend school for only three years before being pressed into working for his father making house nails. His father died when Chauncey was only 11 and his mother could not afford to support him, so Chauncey went on the road working as a casual farm laborer. He finally bonded himself as an apprentice to a house carpenter when he was 15.

House building was a seasonal industry in early-nineteenth-century Connecticut, and Jerome found the idle winters boring. He gained permission from his master to take on woodcrafting jobs when they were not building homes. He soon found that he had considerable skill at making wooden parts for clocks and became a regular putting-out worker for local clockmakers. After the end of his apprenticeship contract and military service in the War of 1812, Jerome sought employment with famed Plymouth, Connecticut clockmaker, Eli Terry. He began designing and building the wooden cases that housed Terry's clockworks and learned the art of building timepieces. Then, in 1817, Jerome set up a small clock making shop of his own, buying clockworks from Terry and assembling finished timepieces himself.

For the next four years Chauncey had a difficult time making ends meet. He was skilled at assembling reliable instruments, but building good clocks required a lot of time and money, and as a newly married small businessman he had little of either. He met this constraint by leasing space in a local mill, using its water wheel to power a circular saw that allowed him to make large numbers of identically crafted clock cases. By buying wood, veneers, and other materials in bulk, he could make large numbers of clock cases, fit them with movements purchased from Terry, and sell the resulting clocks more cheaply than his competitors.

With the capital he generated in this way, he formed a partnership with his brother and another man in 1824 to build brass clock movements. Borrowing ideas from Terry and other manufacturers, he laid out a manufacturing plant of unusual efficiency. "I will venture to say, that I can pick out three men who will take the brass . . . cut the teeth, and make all of the wheels for five hundred clocks in one day." As efficient as his production line was, his movements were somewhat bigger than those of his competitors like Seth Thomas. This forced Jerome to design a new type of clock case, which he began manufacturing with the same efficiency as he did clock movements. Jerome's company was soon manufacturing ten thousand of what he called his "brass looking-glass clocks" a year. No one, he later observed, had ever before been able to manufacture more than two thousand eight-day movement clocks in a year. "This proves and shows what can be done by system," he proclaimed. Selling at the comparatively modest price of $20 apiece, Jerome's clocks began appearing in the genteel and especially the middle-class homes that began springing up throughout the Northeast.

Jerome's business continued to improve annually through 1836, but the economic panic of 1837 threatened to destroy everything he had accomplished. Finding himself in Richmond, Virginia, on business in the fall of 1837, he went to bed and lay awake worrying about finances. "I am sure that I had lost . . . more than one hundred thousand dollars, and felt very much discouraged," he recalled. On a table in his room there was an old, inexpensive wooden one-day movement clock ticking away the time. "That minute I was looking at the wood clock on the table and it came into my mind instantly that there could be a cheap one-day brass clock that would take the place of the wood clock. . . . The idea had always been that a brass clock must be an eight day, and all one day should be of wood, and the plan of a brass one day had never been thought of."

Jerome returned to Connecticut and immediately set about designing a one-day brass clock movement. Early in 1838 his company went into production. The quality was so good that competitors counterfeited Jerome's labels so they could pass off their work as his. But more important, by using modern manufacturing techniques, he could produce a reliable timepiece that sold for well under $10. Now, not only could the genteel and the middle classes afford to own clocks, nearly anyone could. Between 1838 and 1841, while most businesses in the country were losing money, Jerome's company paid off its debts and managed to clear a profit of $35,000.

Thus choosing to abandon traditional materials and manufacturing techniques revolutionized life for Chauncey Jerome and for the nation. His one-day clock forever changed the way Americans think about time. As more people came to own clocks, the more regimented their lives became and the more deeply they found themselves enmeshed in the new market economy.

Even Jerome was affected in an unexpected way. In 1850, while he was away on business, his partners entered into a merger with a clock company managed by famous showman P. T. Barnum. According to Jerome's account, Barnum misrepresented the value of the inventory he had in clocks and lied outright about the debt his company owed. By the time Jerome was able to figure out the problem, his company had gone bankrupt. By 1855 Jerome had lost everything.

Jerome's choices had revolutionized time but did not have the outcome he had expected. In a book published in 1860, Jerome complained bitterly about the dehumanizing impact of the new economy and society that his earlier choices had helped to create.

New Workplaces and New Workers

Factory production, especially after the successful use of interchangeable parts, allowed employers to hire unskilled and inexperienced workers. With machines now producing standardized parts for complex mechanisms like clocks, the worker's job was reduced to simply assembling premade components. The centuries-old **guild** organization for artisans—preserved in the hierarchical system of apprentices, journeymen, and master craftsmen—rapidly fell away as extensive training in the manufacturing arts became irrelevant. In the new labor system, a journeyman gunsmith with years of experience was likely to find himself working on equal terms alongside a teenager or a new immigrant with no craft experience at all.

In the beginning, owners found they had to use various means to attract workers into the new factories. Some entrepreneurs developed **company towns.** In New England they resembled traditional New England villages. Families recruited from the economically depressed countryside were installed in neat row houses, each with its own small vegetable garden. The company employed each family member. Women worked on the production line. Men ran heavy machinery and worked as **millwrights,** carpenters, or haulers, or as day laborers dredging out the **millraces.** Children did light work in the factories and tended gardens at home.

Lowell's company had developed another system at its factories in Waltham and Lowell. Hard-pressed to find enough families to leave traditional employment and come to work in the factories, Lowell recruited unmarried farm girls. The company built dormitories to house working women, offering cash wages and reasonable prices for room and board, as well as cultural events and educational opportunities. Because most of the girls saw factory work as a transitional stage between girlhood and marriage, Lowell assured them and their families that the company would strictly control the moral atmosphere in the dorms so that the girls' reputations would remain spotless.

Not everyone was convinced that factory work, even under strict supervision, was appropriate for young women. "Few of them ever marry," Boston journalist Orestes A. Brownson incorrectly observed. "Fewer still ever return to their native places with reputations unimpaired. 'She has worked in a factory' is almost enough to damn to infamy the most worthy and virtuous girl." Others, however, like Reverend Henry A. Mills, commented that "This system . . . is of great and important effect in driving unworthy persons from our city, and in preserving the high character of our operatives." Even the operatives themselves defended the system. In a letter to the editor, one young woman attacked Brownson personally. "And now, if Mr. Brownson is a *man* . . . let him come among us: let him make himself as well acquainted with us as our pastors and superintendents are; . . . he would not see worthy and virtuous girls consigned to infamy, because they work in a factory."

In New York, Philadelphia, and other cities, immigrant slums offered enterprising manufacturers an alternative source of labor. Neighbors could be given responsibility for one part of the manufacturing process. In the shoe industry, for example, one family would make soles, another would make heels, and so forth. This type of operation was not as efficient as the large shoe factories in eastern Massachusetts and elsewhere, but it did offer the manufacturer some advantages. The money that urban manufacturers saved by not building factories and by paying rock-bottom wages to desperate slum-dwellers made it possible for them to compete successfully in the open market.

The combination of machine production and a growing pool of labor proved economically devastating to the working class. No longer was the employer a master craftsman or a **paternalistic** entrepreneur who felt some responsibility to look out for his workers' domestic needs. Factory owners were obligated to investors, bankers, and others and had to squeeze the greatest possible profit out of the manufacturing process. They kept wages low, regardless of the workers' cost of living. As the swelling supply of labor allowed employers to offer lower and lower wages, increasing numbers of working people faced poverty and squalor.

guild An association of craftspeople with the same skills who join together to protect their mutual interests.

company town A town built and owned by a single company; its residents depend on the company not only for jobs but for stores, schools, and housing.

millwright A person who designs, builds, or repairs mills or mill machinery.

millrace The channel for the fast-moving stream of water that drives a mill wheel.

paternalistic Treating social dependents as a father treats his children, providing for their needs without allowing them rights or responsibilities.

For example, between 1820 and 1830, slightly more than 151,000 people immigrated to the United States. In the decade that followed, that number increased to nearly 600,000, and between 1840 and 1850, well over a million and a half people moved to the United States from abroad (see Map 11.1). This enormous increase in immigration changed not only the demographic but also the cultural and economic face of the nation. The flood of immigrants collected in the port and manufacturing cities of the Northeast, where they joined Americans fleeing economic depression in the countryside after the economic panics of 1819 (see page 281) and 1837 (see page 358). Adding to the resulting brew were former master craftsmen, journeymen, and apprentices who no longer had a secure place in the changing economy. Together, though seldom cooperatively, these groups helped to form a new social class in America.

Nearly half of all the immigrants who flooded into the United States between 1820 and 1860 came from Ireland—a nation beset with poverty, political strife, and, after a devastating blight began killing the potato crop in 1841, starvation. For centuries the Irish had lived as a conquered people, subject to the British, so it is not surprising that few of these immigrants had marketable skills or more money than the voyage to America cost. They arrived penniless, many of them speaking not English but Gaelic, and most had little or no chance of finding employment.

Similar conditions beset many members of the second most numerous immigrant group: the Germans. Radical economic change and political upheaval in Germany were putting both peasants and skilled craftsmen to flight. Like Irish peasants, German farmers arrived in America destitute and devoid of opportunities. Trained German craftsmen had a better chance of finding employment, but the changeover from handicraft to industrial production—the very change that in many cases drove them from Germany—was also taking place in America. Adding to the difficulties of these German-speakers was their lack of fluency in English.

Not only were the new immigrants poor and often unskilled, but also most were culturally different from native-born Americans. Religion was their most noted cultural distinction: the majority were Roman Catholics. Their Catholicism separated them from most Americans, who claimed to be Protestant whether they worshiped actively or not. It also made them suspect in the minds of people steeped in anti-Catholic sentiments handed down from earlier generations of Presbyterian, Congregationalist, Quaker, and other immigrants who had fled religious persecution at Catholic hands. In religion, then, as well as in language, dress, and eating and drinking habits, the new immigrants were very different from the sorts of people whose culture had come to dominate American society.

Poverty, cultural distinctiveness, and the desire to live among people who understood their ways and spoke their language brought new immigrants to neighborhoods where their fellow countrymen and countrywomen had already found places to live. In New York, Philadelphia, and other cities, ethnic neighborhoods came into being. Here, people with the same culture and religion built churches, stores, pubs or beer halls, and other familiar institutions that helped them cope with the shock of transplantation from Europe and gave them a chance to adapt gradually to life in the United States. Because the new immigrants were poor, housing in their neighborhoods was often substandard, and living conditions were crowded, uncomfortable, and unsanitary. They started fraternal organizations and clubs to overcome the loneliness, isolation, and powerlessness they were experiencing.

Desperate for work and eager to make their own way in their new country, the new immigrants were willing to do nearly anything to earn money. Lacking the money to buy farms and lacking the skills to enter professional trades, they were the perfect work force for the newly evolving industrial economy. As the flow of immigrants increased, the traditional labor shortage in America was replaced by a **labor glut,** and the social and economic status of all workers declined accordingly.

Living Conditions in Blue-Collar America

Working conditions for **blue-collar workers** in factories reflected the labor supply, the amount of capital available to the manufacturing company, and the personal philosophy of the factory owner. Girls at Lowell's factories described an environment of familiar paternalism. Factory managers and boardinghouse keepers supervised every aspect of their lives in much the same manner that authoritarian fathers saw to the details of life on traditional New England

labor glut Oversupply of labor in relation to the number of jobs available.

blue-collar workers Workers who wear work clothes, such as coveralls and jeans, on the job; their work is likely to involve manual labor.

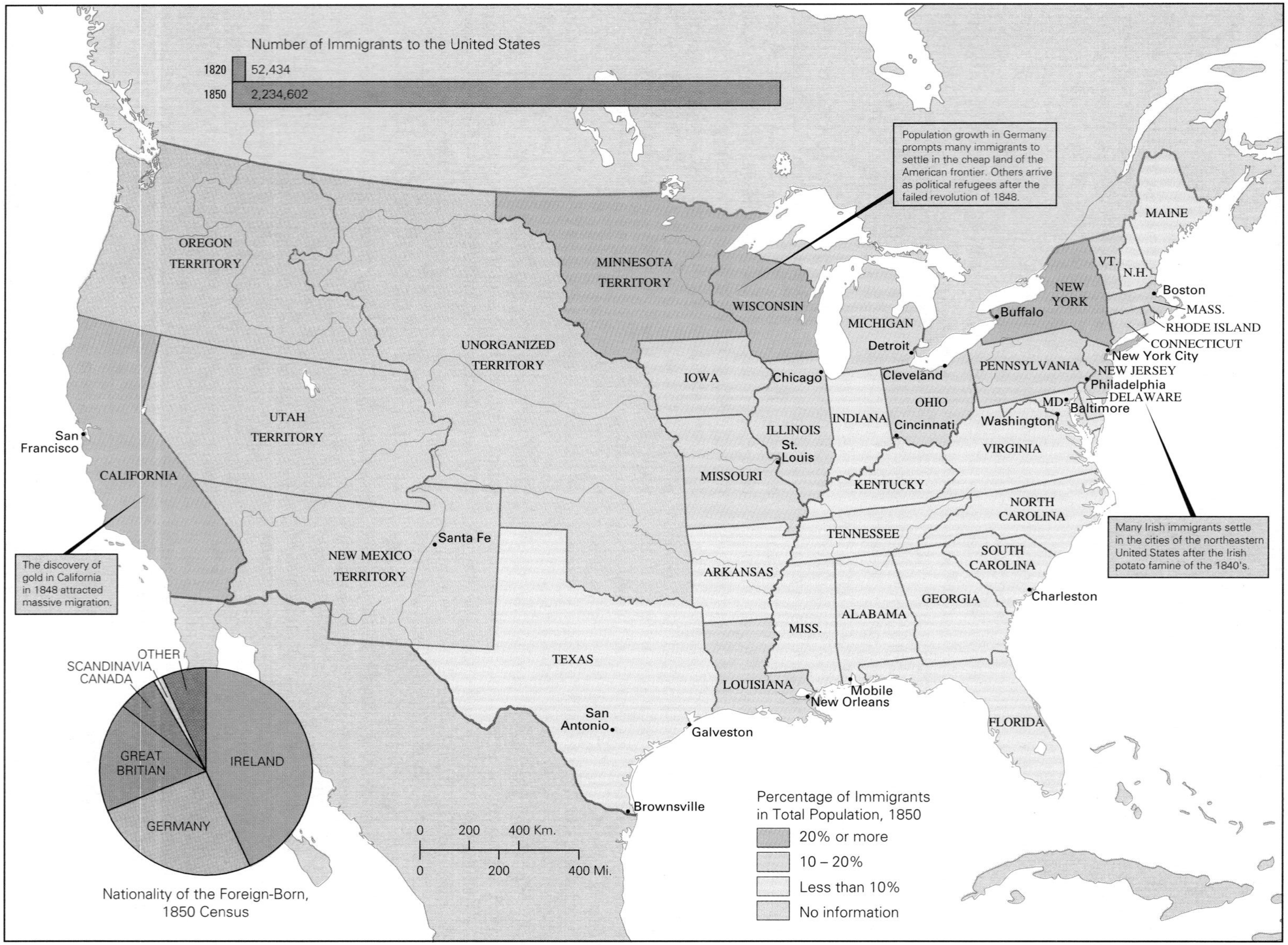

♦ **MAP 11.1 Origin and Settlement of Immigrants, 1820–1850** Immigration was one of the most important economic, political, and social factors in American life during the antebellum period. As this map shows, with the exception of Louisiana, immigration was confined almost exclusively to areas where slavery was not permitted. This gave the North, Northwest, and California a different cultural flavor than the rest of the country, and also affected the political balance between those areas and the South.

♦ Working-class neighborhoods like the infamous Five Points District in New York, shown in this anonymous 1829 picture, were filthy, unhealthy, and crime-ridden. Reformers sought to help by changing workers' habits and morals, but seldom addressed their economic plight. *"Five Points District," artist unknown, c.1829. Courtesy of Mr. and Mrs. Screven Lorillard, photo by Josh Nefsky.*

farms. As for the work itself, one mill girl commented that it was "not half so hard as . . . attending the dairy, washing, cleaning house, and cooking." What bothered factory workers most was the repetitiousness of the work and the resulting boredom. One of Lowell's employees described the tedium. "The time is often apt to drag heavily till the dinner hour arrives," she reported. "Perhaps some part of the work becomes deranged and stops; the constant friction causes a belt of leather to burst into a flame; a stranger visits the room, and scans the features and dress of its inmates inquiringly; and there is little else to break the monotony."

That mill girl went on to note that daydreaming provided relief from the boredom and the ear-shattering noise of the machinery. But daydreaming in front of fast-moving equipment could have disastrous consequences for what a New Jersey magazine called "the human portion of the machine." Inattentive factory workers were likely to lose fingers, hands, or whole arms to whirring, pounding, slashing mechanisms. Not a few lost their lives. Some owners tried to make the workplace safe, but investors discouraged many from buying safety devices. Samuel Slater, for example, complained bitterly to his investors after a child was chewed up in a factory machine. "You call for yarn," he declared, "but think little about the means by which it is to be made."

The paternalism of Slater and Lowell became rare as factory owners withdrew from overseeing day-to-day operations and turned away from experiments like Slater's manufacturing villages and Lowell's dormitories. The influx of laborers from the depressed countryside and of foreign immigrants wiped out both decent wages and the sorts of incentives the early manufacturing pioneers had employed. Not only did wages fall but also laborers were usually expected to provide their own housing, food, and entertainment.

Hulking **tenements** darkened what had been empty blocks and areas of small homes. Factory workers, journeymen, and day laborers crammed into boxlike rooms. Large houses formerly occupied by domestic manufacturers and their apprentices were broken up into tiny apartments by profit-hungry speculators who rented them to desperate laborers. Cellars and attics became living spaces like the rest of the building. In cities like New York, laborers lived 50 to a house in some working-class areas. As population densities reached 150 people an acre in such neighborhoods, sewage disposal, drinking water, and trash removal became difficult to provide. Life in such conditions was grossly unpleasant and extremely unhealthy.

Making matters worse, families with too little living space to start with had to make room in their homes for their work. Investigating living and working conditions, the New York *Tribune* sent a reporter to visit fifty cellar apartments in 1845. He found conditions deplorable. "The floor is made of

tenement An urban apartment house, usually with minimal facilities for sanitation, safety, and comfort.

rough plank laid loosely down, and the ceiling is not quite so high as a tall man," he reported. "The walls are dark and damp and," he went on, "the miserable room is lighted only by a shallow sash partly projecting above the surface of the ground and by the light that struggles from the steep and rotting stairs." In this dark and tiny space, he observed, "often lives the man and his work bench, the wife, and five or six children of all ages; and perhaps a palsied grandfather and grandmother and often both. . . . Here they work, here they cook, they eat, they sleep, they pray."

Social Life for a Genteel Class

The factory system not only altered life for the working class but also changed the daily lives of those who owned and operated manufacturing businesses. In earlier years, when journeymen and apprentices had lived with master craftsmen, they were in effect members of a craftsman's extended family. The master craftsman/owner exercised great authority over his workers but felt obligated to care for them almost as a parent would have done. Such working arrangements blurred the distinction between employee and employer. Crammed together in the same household, owner and workers shared the same general lifestyle, kept the same hours, ate the same food, and enjoyed the same leisure activities. The factory system ended this relationship. The movement of workers out of the owners' homes permitted members of the emerging elite class to develop a **genteel** lifestyle that set them off from the army of factory workers.

Freed from the need to house workers and conduct business at home, genteel families aimed at the complete separation of their private and public lives. Men in the manufacturing elite class spent their leisure time in new activities. Instead of drinking, eating, and playing with their employees, business owners began to socialize with each other in private clubs and in church and civic organizations. Instead of attending the popular theater, elite patrons began endowing opera companies and other highbrow forms of entertainment.

The lives of the factory owners' wives also changed. The mistress of a traditional manufacturing household had been responsible for important tasks in the operation of the business. Genteel women, in contrast, were expected to leave business dealings to men. They became enfolded in what is called a **cult of domesticity**—a strong commitment to home and family. Ensconced in private houses set apart from the new centers of production and marketing, genteel women found themselves with time on their hands. To give themselves something to do, they sought areas of activity that would provide focus and a sense of accomplishment without imperiling their genteel status by involving them in what was now perceived as the crass, masculine world of commerce. Many found outlets for their creative energies in fancy needlework, reading, and art appreciation societies. But some wished for more challenging activities. Sarah Huntington Smith, for example, a member of Connecticut's genteel elite, spoke for many when she complained in 1833, "To make and receive visits, exchange friendly salutations, attend to one's wardrobe, cultivate a garden, read good and entertaining books, and even attend religious meetings for one's own enjoyment; all this does not satisfy me."

One activity that consumed genteel women was motherhood. Magazines and advice manuals, which began appearing during the 1820s and 1830s, advised that children needed to be nurtured rather than punished, guided rather than directed. Influential author and teacher Bronson Alcott helped to convince an entire generation of the need for a gentle and supporting hand. Alcott denied the concept of **infant depravity** that had so affected Puritan parents during the colonial era and led them to break their children's will, often through harsh measures (see page 70). Instead, he stated emphatically that "The child must be treated as a free, self-guiding, self-controlling being."

Alcott was equally emphatic that child rearing was the mother's responsibility. As his wife, Abigail, wrote of family management in Alcott's household, "Mr. A aids me in general principles, though nobody can aid me in the detail." And, according to Alcott, women should feel especially blessed for having such an opportunity. "Good mothers, spiritually minded mothers, are very happy, when they find a child is going to be given them," he wrote in

genteel The manner and style associated with elite classes, usually characterized by elegance, grace, and politeness.

cult of domesticity The belief that women's proper role lies in domestic pursuits.

infant depravity The idea that children are naturally sinful because they share in the original sin of the human race but have not learned the discipline to control their evil instincts.

1836. Only thankless mothers "think of the care and trouble these will give them."

Books like Alcott's *Conversations with Children on the Gospels* (1836–1837) flooded forth during these years and appealed greatly to isolated and underemployed women. Many adopted the advertised culture of domesticity completely. Turning inward, these women centered their lives on their homes and children. In doing so, they believed they were performing an important duty for God and country and fulfilling their most, perhaps their only, natural calling.

Other genteel women agreed with the general tone of the domestic message but widened the woman's supposedly natural sphere outward, beyond the nursery, to encompass the whole world. They banded together with other women to get out into the world in order to reform it. "I want to be where every arrangement will have unreserved and constant reference to eternity," Sarah Huntington Smith explained. Smith herself chose to become a missionary. Other genteel women during the 1830s and 1840s involved themselves in a variety of reform movements, such as those against alcohol abuse or founding Sunday schools, that let them use their nurturing and purifying talents to improve what appeared to be a chaotic and immoral society.

Life and Culture Among the New Middle Class

Large-scale manufacturing not only changed industrial work but also introduced demands for a new class of skilled managerial and clerical employees. Under the old system of manufacturing, the master craftsman or his wife had managed the company's accounts, hired journeymen and apprentices, purchased raw materials, and seen to the delivery of finished products. The size of the new factories made such direct contact between owners, workers, and products impossible. To fill the void, a new class of professionals came into being. In these days before the invention of the typewriter, firms like Lowell's Boston Manufacturing Company employed teams of young men as clerks. These clerks kept accounts, wrote orders, and drafted correspondence, all in longhand using **quill pens.** As elite owners like Lowell and his partners became wrapped up in building new factories, pursuing investors, and entering new markets, both clerical and manufacturing employees were increasingly supervised by professional managers. These men had either risen through the ranks of the company or had been master craftsmen or entrepreneurs whose own businesses had been overwhelmed by the breakneck speed of industrialization.

The new class of clerks, bookkeepers, and managers, like their employers, sought associations among their own class. These **white-collar workers** and their dependents had many of the same prejudices and ideals as the elite class. They read the same advice magazines, often attended the same churches, and sometimes belonged to the same civic and reform societies. Nevertheless, the lives of these two classes were different in many respects.

One distinguishing characteristic of the new middle class was its relative youth. These young people, many of them the sons and daughters of rural farmers, had flocked to newly emerging cities in pursuit of formal education. They stayed to seek employment away from the economic instability and **provincialism** of the farm. The experience of Elizabeth Yale Hancock, a country girl from upstate New York, was not unusual.

After attending public school in Champlain, Elizabeth transferred to the Plattsburgh Academy. She studied there full time for two terms before taking a job teaching at a public school while continuing classes at the academy part time. She then went to the Female Seminary in Buffalo, where she enrolled in college-level classes. While pursuing her studies, she worked as a resident tutor in the family of a returned missionary. Finally graduating from the seminary, Elizabeth took a job as a full-time teacher at a select school and began applying for jobs as a foreign missionary.

Men too attended school when and where they could get financial support and then settled down where they could find employment and the company of others like themselves. And, as Elizabeth Hancock's experience indicates, women joined men in moving into new professions. While middle-class men found employment as clerks, bookkeepers, and managers, middle-class women parlayed their formal education and their gender's perceived gift for nurturing children into work as teachers. It became

quill pen A pen made from the shaft of a feather; the end of the quill is sharpened with a knife and then dipped in ink.

white-collar workers Workers able to wear white shirts on the job because they do no grubby manual labor.

provincialism The limited and narrow perspective thought to be characteristic of people in rural areas.

♦ A flood of new publications carried the message about the sentimental ideal for middle-class family life to an ever-widening audience. Articles proclaimed the domestic ideal, but pictures were worth a thousand words. This cover illustration from one of the thousands of pamphlets issued by the American Tract Society depicts the idealized family doing what all such families increasingly were being expected to do, going as a group to church on Sunday. *American Tract Society Archives.*

acceptable for women to work as teachers for several years before marriage, and many avoided marriage altogether to pursue their hard-won careers. Elizabeth Hancock's career was unusual but not unique. Elizabeth succeeded in becoming an unmarried teacher in the employ of America's largest missionary organization.

Middle-class men and women tended to put off marriage as long as possible while they established themselves socially and economically. They also tended to have fewer children than their parents had had. In the new urban middle-class setting, children were an economic liability rather than an asset. Parents felt compelled to send their children to school so that they could take their place on the career ladder chosen by their parents. Thus children made no economic contribution to the family. Late marriage and various forms of birth control kept middle-class families small.

A lack of traditional ties affected the lives of both married and unmarried middle-class people. Many unmarried men and women seeking their fortunes in town boarded in private homes or rooming houses. They sometimes exchanged labor as domestics, hired hands, or tutors for some or all of their keep. After marriage, middle-class men and women emulated the close-knit isolation of the elite. Middle-class city life cut people off from the comforting sociability of farm families and the church-centered communities that shaped and directed rural life. Accordingly, these young people looked to each other for both companionship and guidance.

Like the elite class, this new group sought bonds in **voluntary associations.** Students in colleges and universities formed a variety of discussion groups, preprofessional clubs, and benevolent societies. Groups like the Odd Fellows and the Masons brought people out of school together for companionship. Such organizations helped enforce traditional values through rigid membership standards stressing moral character, upright behavior, and, above all, order.

The *Odd Fellows' Manual* summarized the philosophy of these organizations well. "In the transaction of our business we pursue strict parliamentary rules, that our members may be qualified for any public stations to which they may be called by their fellow-citizens," the manual asserts. "And when business has been performed, we indulge in social intercourse, and even in cheerful and innocent hilarity and amusement. But all in strict order and decorum, goodfellowship and prudence are constantly to be kept in view." In such clubs, people could discuss the latest books or world affairs with others of similar education and lifestyle, but always in the spirit of self-improvement, never in the form of a debate. As the *Odd Fellows' Manual* went on to say, "Exercise yourself in the discussions of your Lodge not for the purpose of mere debate, contention, or 'love of opposition,' but to improve yourself in suitably expressing your sentiments." Young people also created and joined professional and trade groups. These associations served a social function, but they also became forums for training novices and for setting standards for professional methods and modes of conduct.

Members of the new middle class also used their organizing skills to press for reforms. The rank and file of organizations such as the American Tract Society, American Bible Society, and American

voluntary association An organization or club through which individuals engage in voluntary service, usually associated with charity or reform.

♦ The plight of the handicapped became one of the new obsessions for reformers during the 1830s. One of the leading educational reformers of the day, Samuel Gridley Howe, took the blind, deaf, and mute Laura Dewey Bridgman under his care when she was seven years old. After ten years of schooling, she had learned to read using a raised letter system Howe devised, and to communicate her ideas both in writing and using sign language. She was introduced to James K. Polk in 1846, who described her as "the most remarkable person." *"Laura Dewey Bridgman" by Auguste Edouart, 1843. National Portrait Gallery, Smithsonian Institution, Washington, D.C./Art Resource, NY.*

Board of Commissioners for Foreign Missions—each a multi-million-dollar reforming enterprise—was formed primarily by young middle-class men and women.

The New Cotton Empire in the South

- Why did the expectations of southerners—black and white—change after 1820?
- How did white southerners choose to respond, and what new constraints resulted for slaves, free blacks, and poor whites?

While increasing multitudes collected into industrializing towns in the North, the South exploded outward seeking new lands to grow the glamour crop of the century: cotton. In 1820, cotton was being grown heavily in parts of Virginia, South Carolina, and Georgia. Within a matter of decades, the cotton empire had expanded to include most of Alabama, Mississippi, and Louisiana and extensive portions of east Texas, Kentucky, Tennessee, Arkansas, and central Missouri. The new dependence on a single crop changed the outlook and experiences not just of large planters but also of the slaves, free blacks, and poor whites whose labor made cotton king.

A New Birth for the Slavery System

Before the emergence of King Cotton, when the South's agricultural system was foundering, many southerners were already questioning the use of slaves. In 1782 Virginia made it legal for individual masters to free their slaves, and many did so. In 1784 Thomas Jefferson proposed a land ordinance that would have prohibited slavery in all of the nation's territories after 1800. But the act was not passed. Some southern leaders advocated abolishing slavery and transporting freed blacks to Africa. But the booming southern economy after the War of 1812 required more labor than ever before. As a result, black slavery expanded as never before.

Viewed side by side, a map showing cotton production and one showing slave population would appear nearly identical (see Map 11.2). In the 1820s, when cotton production was most heavily concentrated in South Carolina and Georgia, the greatest density of slaves occurred in the same area. During the 1840s, as cotton growing spread to the West, so too did slavery. By 1860, both cotton growing and slavery would appear on the map as a continuous belt stretching from the Carolinas through Georgia and Alabama and on to the Mississippi River.

Although cotton planting led to the expansion of slavery during the early nineteenth century, slaves did much more in the American South than just pick cotton. A survey of large and medium-size plantations between 1797 and 1865 shows that 58 percent of the men and 69 percent of the women were employed primarily as **field hands.** Of the rest, only 2 percent of slave men and 17 percent of slave women were employed as **house slaves.** The remaining 14 percent of slave women were employed in nonfield occupations like sewing, weaving, and food processing. Seventeen percent of slave men were em-

field hands People who do agricultural work such as planting, weeding, and harvesting.

house slaves People who did domestic work such as cleaning and cooking.

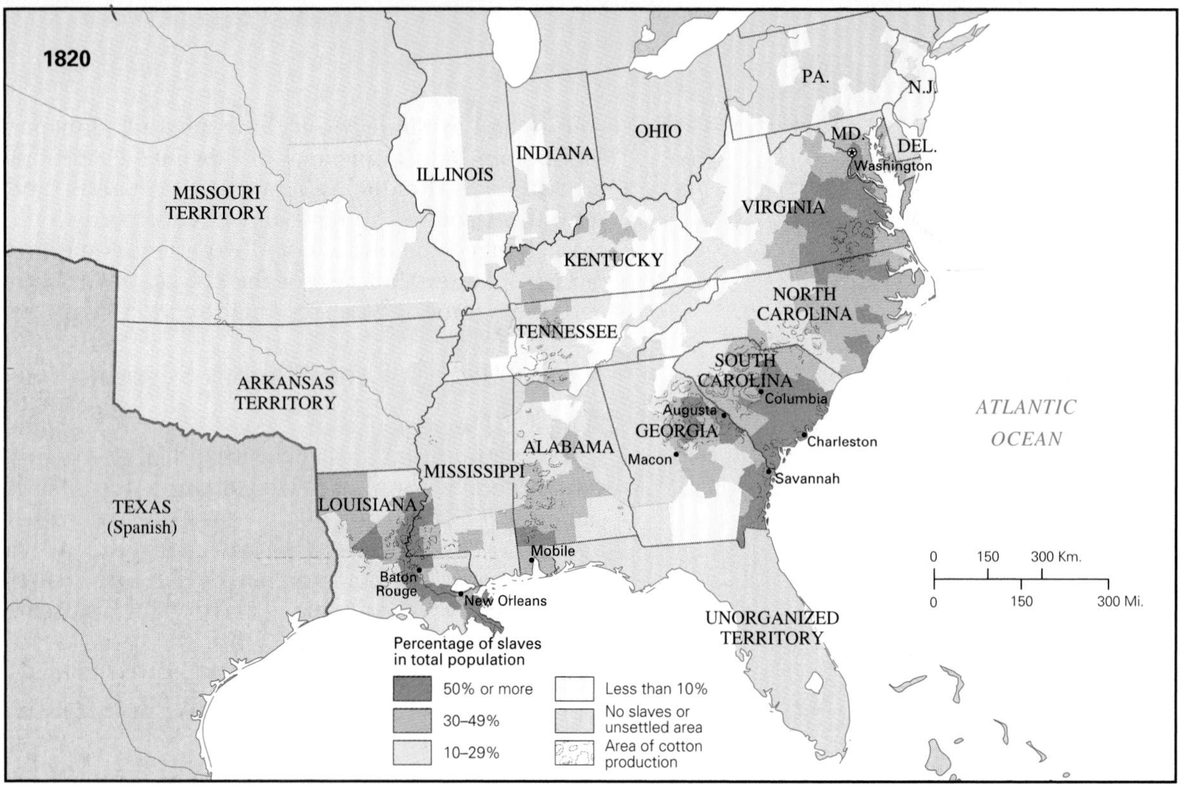

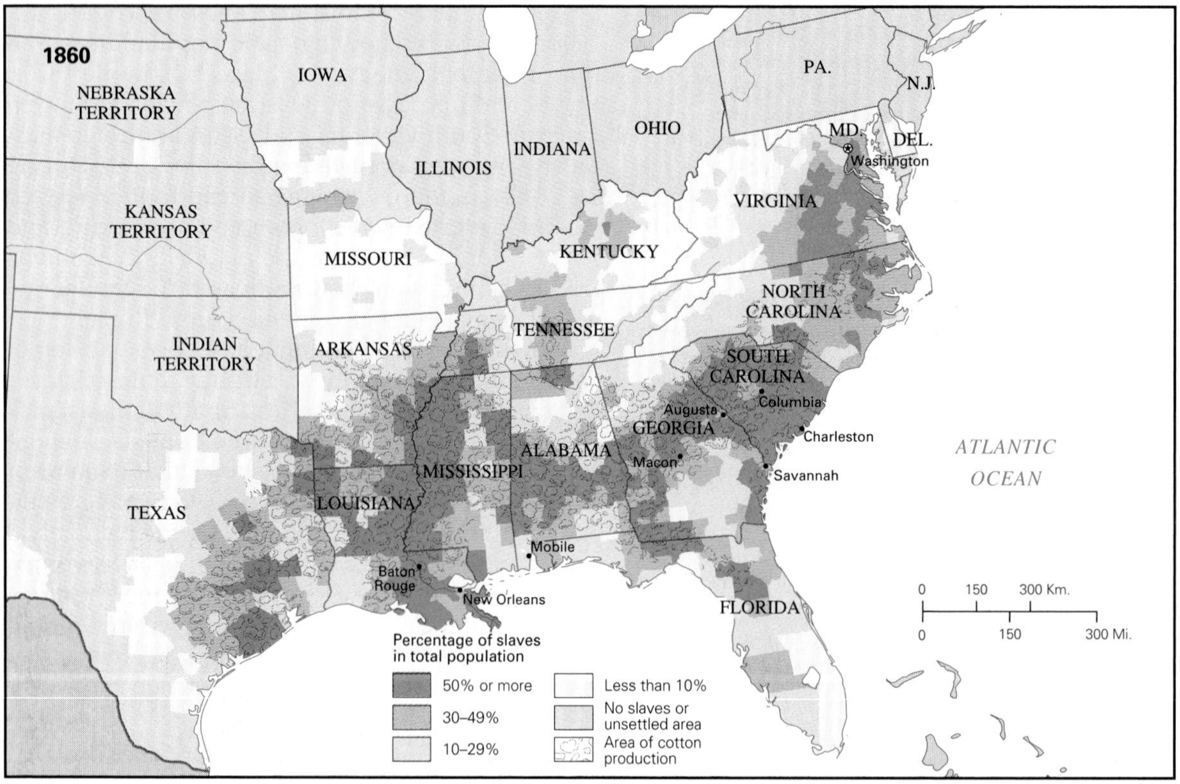

♦ **MAP 11.2 Cotton Agriculture and Slave Population** Between 1820 and 1860, the expansion of cotton agriculture and the extension of slavery went hand-in-hand. As these maps show, cotton production was an isolated activity in 1820, and slavery remained isolated as well. By 1860, both had extended westward.

ployed in nonfield activities like driving wagons, piloting riverboats, and herding cattle.

Most male slaves who were not employed as field hands—nearly a quarter of the total number on plantations—were managers and craftsmen. This percentage was much higher in cities, where slave artisans were often allowed to hire themselves out on the open job market in return for handing part of their earnings over to their owners. In Charleston, Norfolk, Richmond, and Savannah, slave artisans formed guilds. Feeling threatened by their solidarity, white craftsmen appealed to state legislatures and city councils for restrictions on slave employment in skilled crafts. Such appeals, and the need for more and more field hands, led to a decline in the number of slave artisans during the 1840s and 1850s. Nevertheless, they remained a significant proportion of the slave population.

The owners of cotton plantations made an excellent living from the labor of their slaves. Although they often complained of debt and poor markets, it appears that large-scale planters could expect an annual **return on capital** of between 8 and 10 percent—the equivalent of what the most successful northern industrialists were making. Agricultural profits in non-cotton-producing areas were significantly lower, but even there slavery netted white landowners major profits. Outside the **Cotton Belt,** former growers of tobacco, rice, and sugar went into the business of breeding and selling slaves. The enormous demand for workers in the heart of the Cotton Belt created a profitable interstate trade in slaves and enriched slaveowners throughout the South. Thus even planters who did not grow cotton came to have a significant investment in its cultivation and in the labor system that made cotton king.

Slaves were a major capital investment for the great plantation owner and for the struggling farmer alike. At the height of the slave trade, a healthy male field hand in his mid-twenties sold for an average of $1,800, a skilled craftsman for $2,500. Younger and older men or those in less than perfect health sold for less, but even a male child too young to work in the fields or a man in his fifties would cost a would-be owner anywhere from $250 to $500. The price for female slaves was more highly variable and depended on what they were to be used for. A female field hand might not accomplish quite as much in a day as a healthy male of the same age and thus cost proportionately less. A woman skilled at weaving or some other desirable craft might sell for as much as or more than a craftsman. And a particularly beautiful young woman might bring as much as $5,000 at auction. Such women generally became the mistresses of the men who could afford to buy them. The South's peculiar sex code was said to justify this practice. As one southerner put it, "I do not hesitate to say that the intercourse which takes place with enslaved females is less depraving in its effects [on white men] than when it is carried on with females of their own caste."

Living Conditions for Southern Slaves

Slaveowners' enormous economic investment in their human property played a significant role in the treatment slaves received. Damaging or, worse, killing a healthy slave resulted in a large financial loss. Slaveholders, however, had to keep production and efficiency levels high to make any income at all. This need led to the writing of increasingly harsh **slave codes** during the late eighteenth and early nineteenth centuries, giving slaveowners virtual life-and-death control over their human property. A delicate balance between power and profit shaped planters' policies toward slaves and set the tone for slave life. Like important machines in northern factories, slaves received the minimum maintenance required to keep them in proper working order.

Housing for slaves was seldom more than adequate. Generally, slaves lived in one-room log cabins with dirt floors and a fireplace or stove. The cabins were usually about 16-by-18-feet square. Mindful of the need to maintain control and keep slaves productive, slaveowners seldom crowded people into slave quarters. As one slaveowner explained, "In no case should two families be allowed to occupy the same house. The crowding [of] a number into one house is unhealthy. It breeds contention; is destructive of delicacy of feeling, and it promotes immorality between the sexes." Though not all planters shared this view, census figures suggest that the average slave cabin housed five or six people.

Though not cramming 50 to a house, as some slums did in New York, slave quarters were not particularly comfortable. The cabins had windows but

return on capital The yield on money that has been invested in an enterprise or product.

Cotton Belt The region in the southeastern United States in which cotton is grown (see Map 11.2).

slave codes Laws that established the status of slaves, denying them basic rights and classifying them as the property of slaveowners.

♦ This early photograph, taken on a South Carolina plantation before the Civil War, freezes slave life in time, giving us a view of what slave cabins looked like, how they were arranged, how slaves dressed, and how they spent what little leisure time they had. *Collection of William Gladstone.*

generally only wooden shutters and no glass. The windows let in flies in summer and cold in winter, but closing the shutters shut out the light. When the shutters were closed against flies and cold, the most reliable source of light was an open fireplace or stove, which was also used for heat and cooking. Various accounts of slave life note that the need for light and a cooking fire prompted slaves to build fires even at the hottest time of year. Ever-present fires increased the danger of cabins burning down, especially because chimneys were generally made of sticks held together with dried mud. As one slave commented, "Many the time we have to get up at midnight and push the chimney away from the house to keep the house from burning up."

Furnishings in slave houses were usually fairly crude. Bedding generally consisted of straw pallets stacked on the floor or occasionally mounted on rough bedsteads. Other furnishings were equally simple—rough-hewn wooden chairs or benches and plank tables.

Clothing was very basic. One Georgia planter outlined the usual yearly clothing allotment for slaves: "The proper and usual quantity of clothes for plantation hands is two suits of cotton for spring and summer, and two suits of woolen for winter; four pair of shoes and three hats." These articles could be provided most cheaply if the planter could afford to assign some slaves the task of manufacturing cloth. On many plantations, slave women spun, wove, and sewed cotton fabric called osnaburg. This material was durable but rough and uncomfortable to wear. As one slave complained, the material was "like needles when it was new." Women generally wore simple dresses or skirts and blouses made from the scratchy osnaburg. Children often went naked in the summer and were fitted with long, loose-hanging osnaburg shirts during the colder months.

It appears that the slave diet, like slave clothing and housing, was sufficient to maintain health but not particularly pleasing. One slave noted that there was "plenty to eat sich [sic] as it was," but in summer flies were all over the food. Her master, she said, would laugh about that, saying the addition of flies "made us fat." Despite justified complaints, the fact is that the average slave diet was rich by comparison with the diet of many other Americans and many people in the rest of the world at the time. Slaves in the American South ate significantly more meat than their contemporaries in the urban North or in Germany and Italy. In addition to meat, slaves consumed milk and corn, potatoes, peas and beans, molasses, and fish. Generally the planter provided this variety of food, but owners also occasionally permitted slaves to hunt and fish and to collect wild roots, berries, and vegetables. Theft also added to the quantity and variety of foods available in the slave quarters.

Although the diet provided to slaves kept them alive and functioning, the southern diet in general lacked important nutrients, and diet-related diseases plagued slave communities. These problems, however, were probably no more common among slaves than among their owners, who also lived on corn and pork. The diseases and other afflictions that befell slaves more frequently than they affected southern whites included hernia, pneumonia, and lockjaw (tetanus, usually resulting from a deep wound). Each, in its way, was the product of slaves' working and living conditions. Because of the lack of proper sanitation, slaves also suffered from dysentery and cholera more severely than did southern whites. These diseases were natural to poverty—a condition that also afflicted northern workers, who died by the thousands when cholera epidemics struck manufacturing cities during the early nineteenth century.

With the possible exception of sexual exploitation, no area of slave existence has generated more controversy than that of violence. The image of sadistic white men beating slaves permeates the dark side of the southern myth. Such behavior, however, though not unknown, was far from typical. Slaves were money, and damaging slaves was expensive behavior that most slaveowners could not afford. Still, given the need to keep up production and efficiency, slaveowners were not shy about using measured force. One southern plantation owner disciplined his overseer in 1854, pointing out that "when he [the overseer] flogs, he puts it on in two Large doses. I think moderate Flogings the best."

That slaveowner went on to record what he thought were appropriate punishments: "I always punish according to the crime, if it is a Large one I give him a genteel floging with a strop, about 75 Lashes I think is a good whipping." Noting the practical limitations even to this "genteel" form of discipline, he went on to observe, "When picking cotton I never put on more than 20 stripes and verry [sic] frequently not more than 10 or 15." Not all plantation owners were gentle or even practical when it came to discipline. The historical record is filled with accounts of slaveowners who were willing to take a financial loss by beating slaves until they became useless or even until they died.

The discussion of slavery to this point has centered on the experience of people living on relatively large plantations in the Cotton Belt. Although most slaves lived under such circumstances, a very large minority of slaves lived on small farms in communities of between five and ten slaves. It appears that slaves on such farms were usually not much better off than slaves on large plantations. Economic life for southern farmers was always difficult. They lived a hand-to-mouth existence, often short of food, clothing, and housing. Small farmers saw slaves as vehicles for social and economic advancement—and they were willing to starve, overwork, or sell their slaves if doing so meant economic betterment for their own families. When all was going well, slaves might be treated like members of the farmer's family—much as apprentices might be considered members of a northern craftsman's family. But when conditions were not going well, slaves were the first victims.

Life Among Common Southern Whites

Federal census figures for the early nineteenth century reveal that fully two-thirds of free southern families owned no slaves, and among the minority who did, half owned fewer than five. A small number of these families owned stores, craft shops, and other urban businesses in Charleston, New Orleans, Atlanta, and other southern cities. Some were attorneys, teachers, doctors, and other professionals. The great majority, however, were proud small farmers who either owned, leased, or simply squatted on the land they farmed.

Often tarred with the label "poor white trash" by their planter neighbors, and described as shiftless, idle backcountry rabble, these yeomen were often productive stockraisers and farmers. They concentrated on growing and producing what they needed to live, but all aspired to produce small surpluses of grains, meat products, and other commodities that they could sell either to neighboring plantations or to merchants for export. Many of these small farmers tried to grow cotton in an effort to raise cash, though they generally could not do so on a large scale. Whatever cash they raised they usually spent on necessary manufactures, as well as on land and slaves—the signs of social and economic status.

These small farmers had a troubled relationship with white planters. On the one hand, many yeoman farmers wanted to join the ranks of the great planters, hoping they could transform their small holdings into cotton empires. On the other hand, they resented the aristocracy and envied the planters' exalted status and power. They also feared the expansion of large plantations, which often forced small holders to abandon their hard-won farms and slaves.

Although they seldom rebelled openly against their social superiors, common white people did complain about their second-class status and often used the power of the ballot box to make their dissatisfactions known. For despite the enormous power of the plantation elite, they were greatly

♦ Despite the popular image that antebellum planters lived lives of idle luxury in great mansions, most actually lived in modest homes and worked alongside their employees and slaves, as this 1838 painting by an anonymous artist shows. *"Ye Southern Planter" 1838. Dr. Richard Saloom.*

outnumbered by the lesser class of whites, who had the power to wreck the entire social and economic structure if they became sufficiently disgruntled. Thus the ***noblesse oblige*** practiced by aristocrats toward poorer whites was as much a practical as a romantic affectation.

Free Blacks in the South

A group entirely absent from the myth of the South was the population of free African Americans. Some communities of free blacks could trace their origins back to earliest colonial times, when Africans, like Europeans, served limited terms of indenture. The majority, however, had been freed recently because of diminishing plantation profits during the late 1700s. Most of these people lived not much differently from slaves, working for white employers as day laborers.

Some opportunities were available for a handful of free blacks who had desirable skills. In the Upper South—Delaware, Maryland, and Virginia—master carpenters, coopers, painters, brick masons, blacksmiths, boatmen, bakers, and barbers hired young black boys as apprentices. Those who could stick out their apprenticeship might make an independent living. The situation was different for black girls. They had few opportunities as skilled laborers. Some became seamstresses and washers, others became cooks, and a few grew up to run small groceries, taverns, and restaurants. Folk healing, **midwifery,** and prostitution also led to economic independence for some black women.

It is worth noting that perhaps as many as 10 percent of free black heads of households were slaveowners, though this statistic may be somewhat misleading. Many free black men were forced to buy their wives and children in order to reunite families and often were prevented by restrictive slave codes from legally freeing them. Still, a good many people of African descent owned plantations and gangs of slave laborers, though these possessions seldom granted black masters entry into local elite circles.

In fact, mounting restrictions on free blacks during the first half of the nineteenth century limited their freedom of movement, their economic freedom, and the protection they could expect to receive by law. In the town of Petersburg, Virginia, for example, when a free black woman named Esther Fells irritated her white neighbor, he took it upon himself to whip her for disturbing his peace. The sheriff did not arrest the assailant but instead took Mrs. Fells into custody, and the court ordered that she be given fifteen more lashes for "being insolent to a white person." Skin color left free blacks open to abuses and forced them to be extremely careful in their dealings with their white neighbors—yeoman farmers, white businessmen, and plantation aristocrats alike.

noblesse oblige The belief that members of the elite are obliged to treat others charitably, especially those of lower status than themselves.

midwifery The practice of assisting women in childbirth

♦ Most African Americans living in the antebellum South were plantation slaves, but some held skilled jobs in southern cities. For example, in Richmond, Virginia, free blacks had a virtual guild monopoly on barbering, a profession that at the time was the social equivalent of being a physician today. *Valentine Museum, Richmond, Virginia.*

A New Planter Aristocracy

Few images have persisted in American history longer than that of courtly southern planters in the years before the Civil War. Throughout the nineteenth and much of the twentieth century, songs and stories immortalized the myth of a southern aristocracy of enormous wealth and polished manners upholding a culture of romantic **chivalry.** Charming though this image is, it is not accurate.

Statistics from the **antebellum** South suggest that the great planters of popular myth were few and far between. Of the third of all southerners who owned slaves, large-scale planters were a tiny minority. By far the largest class of slaveholders—nearly three-quarters of the total—was the "farmer" class, people who owned between 80 and 160 acres of land and fewer than ten slaves. Next on the social ladder came a "gentry" class—about 15 percent of the slaveholding population—people who owned up to 800 acres and between ten and twenty slaves. The rest, about 12 percent of slaveholders, were true planters, possessing more than 800 acres and more than twenty slaves. Of course, as these figures indicate, members of the planter class, though few in number, controlled the biggest share of productive land and labor. As a result, their economic, political, and social importance was far out of proportion to the size of their population.

Even among the handful of true southern planters, the aristocratic manners and trappings of the idealized plantation were unusual. The rapidly rising cotton economy brought a new sort of man to the forefront. These new aristocrats were generally not related to the old colonial plantation gentry. Most had begun their careers as land speculators, financiers, and rough-and-tumble yeoman farmers. They had parlayed ruthlessness, good luck, and dealings in the burgeoning cotton market into large landholdings and armies of slaves. For diversion they enjoyed hunting and horseracing. As one slave recalled, "My master's habits were such as were common enough among the dissipated planters of the neighborhood; and one of their frequent practices was to assemble on Saturday or Sunday . . . and gamble, run horses, or fight game-cocks, discuss politics, and drink whisky and brandy and water all day long."

The wives of these planters bore little resemblance to their counterparts in popular fiction. Far from being frail, helpless creatures, southern plantation mistresses carried a heavy burden of responsibility. A planter's wife was responsible for all domestic matters. She supervised large staffs of slaves, organized and ran schools for the children on the plantation, looked out for the health of everyone on the plantation, and managed all plantation operations in the absence of her husband. "The busiest women I ever saw," one southerner recalled of plantation mistresses. A former slave remarked of his mistress, "She was with all the slave women every time a baby was born. Or, when a plague of misery hit the folks she knew what to do and what kind of medicine to chase off the aches and pains."

chivalry The code of honor among medieval knights, central to the concept of *noblesse oblige* among southern planters.

antebellum The decades before the Civil War, the period from 1815 to 1860; *antebellum* means "before the war."

♦ These two images show the tightrope walked by southern women. As August Köllner's 1845 painting (*left*) shows, a southern woman was expected to be a loving and subservient wife to her plantation husband, but, as the 1836 drawing by August Herview (*right*) shows, she was also expected to be a harsh mistress toward her black servants. *"Virginia Planter's Family" watercolor by A. Köllner, 1845. Library of Congress; "Clear Starching in Louisiana" drawing by August Herview, 1846. Library of Congress.*

All those duties were complicated by a sex code that relegated southern women to a peculiar position in the plantation hierarchy—between white men and black slaves. On the one hand, southern white women were expected to exercise absolute authority over their slaves. On the other, they were to be absolutely obedient to white men. "He is master of the house," said plantation mistress Mary Boykin Chesnut about her husband. "To hear [him] is to obey." This contradiction put great pressure on southern women, adding severe anxiety to their other burdens. "All the comfort of my life depends upon his being in a good humor," Chesnut remarked, concluding, "There is no slave . . . like a wife."

This is not to say that the image of grand plantations and aristocratic living is entirely false. The enormous profits earned from cotton in the 1840s and 1850s permitted some planters—or, more often, the children of successful cotton capitalists—to build elegant mansions and to affect the lifestyle that they associated with a noble past. Voracious readers of romantic literature, planters assumed what they imagined were the ways of medieval knights, adopting courtly manners and the nobleman's paternalistic obligation to look out for the welfare of their social inferiors, both black and white. Women decked out in the latest gowns flocked to formal balls and weekend parties. Young men were sent to academies where they could learn the twin aristocratic virtues of militarism and honor. Young women attended private "seminaries" where they were taught, in the words of one southern seminary mistress, "principles calculated to render them useful and rational companions." Courtship became highly ritualized, an imitation of imagined medieval court manners.

Practical concerns, however, always threatened to crack this romantic veneer. Aristocratic parents were leery of having their children marry down on the social ladder, a prejudice they sought to instill firmly in the younger generation. Both young men and young women sought to maintain or improve their social and economic position through marriage. "As to my having any sweethearts that is not thought of," one young southern woman complained. "Money is too much preferred, for us poor Girls to be much caressed."

Thus even the most privileged among southerners found themselves constrained by the transformed political economy of the cotton empire. Locked into arranged marriages of convenience, southern women bore the twin burdens of corseted idealization and plantation management while their husbands spent their passions in the slave quarters. As for the men, they found themselves using the military training they received as part of their education to maintain strict round-the-clock patrols to ensure that neither slaves, free blacks, nor disgruntled common whites would rise up against their authority. Increasingly, the extension of slavery and the stratification of society limited the freedoms of both whites and blacks, and the South came to resemble a police state.

SUMMARY

Expectations
Constraints
Choices
Outcomes

Although seemingly the most old-fashioned region of the country, the South that emerged during the years leading up to 1840 was a profoundly different place than it had been before. As an industrial revolution overturned the economies in Great Britain and the American Northeast, *expectations* for southerners changed radically. Although they clothed their new society in romanticized medieval garb, they were creating an altogether new kind of economy and society. The efficient production of cotton by the newly reorganized South was an essential aspect of the emerging national market economy and a powerful force in a great transformation.

Change in the North was more obvious. As factories replaced craft shops and cities replaced towns, the entire fabric of northern society seemed to come unraveled. The new economy and new technology created wonderful new *expectations* but also imposed serious *constraints*. A new social structure replaced the traditional order as unskilled and semiskilled workers, a new class of clerks, and the genteel elite made *choices* concerning their lives. As in the South, the *outcome* was a great transformation in the lives of everyone in the region.

And tying these two regions together was a new network of roads, waterways, and communications systems that accelerated the process of change. After 1840 it was possible to ship goods from any one section of the country to any other, and people in all sections were learning more about conditions in far distant parts of the growing country. Often this new information raised *expectations* of prosperity, but it also made more and more people aware of the enormity of the transformation taking place and the glaring differences between the nation's various regions. The twin *outcomes* would be greater integration in the national economy and increasing tension as mutually dependent participants in the new marketplace struggled with change and with each other.

SUGGESTED READINGS

Ira Berlin. *Slaves Without Masters* (New York, 1975).

A masterful study of a forgotten population: free African Americans in the Old South. Lively and informative.

Bill Cecil-Fronsman. *Common Whites: Class and Culture In Antebellum North Carolina* (1992).

A pioneering effort to describe the culture, lifestyle, and political economy shared by the antebellum South's majority population: nonslaveholding whites. Though confined in geographical scope, the study is suggestive of conditions that may have prevailed throughout the region.

Nancy M Cott. *The Bonds of Womanhood: "Woman's Sphere" in New England, 1780–1835* (1977).

A classic work on the ties that held the woman's world together, but collectively bound them into a secondary position in American life.

Thomas Dublin. *Women at Work: The Transformation of Work and Community in Lowell, Massachusetts, 1826–1860* (1979).

An interesting look at the way in which the nature of work changed and the sorts of changes that were brought to one manufacturing community.

Benita Eisler, ed. *The Lowell Offering: Writings by New England Mill Women, 1840–1845* (1977).

First-hand accounts of factory life and changing social conditions written by the young women who worked at Lowell's various factories.

Elizabeth Fox-Genovese. *Within the Plantation Household* (Chapel Hill, 1988).

A look at the lives of black and white women in the antebellum South. This study is quite long, but is well written and very informative.

Margaret Mitchell. *Gone With the Wind* (New York, 1936).

Arguably the most influential book in conveying a stereotyped vision of antebellum southern life. The film version, directed by Victor Fleming in 1939, was even more influential.

Mary P. Ryan. *Cradle of the Middle Class: The Family in Oneida County, New York, 1790–1865* (1981).

A marvelous synthesis of materials focusing on the emergence of a new social and economic class in the midst of change from a traditional to a modern society.

George Rogers Taylor. *The Transportation Revolution, 1815–1860* (New York, 1951).

The only comprehensive treatment of changes in transportation during the antebellum period and their economic impact. Nicely written.

Prescribing Middle Class Expectations

The Context

Chapter 11 discusses, in part, the emergence of a new economic and social class in the United States: the middle class. Being a new class and living under new circumstances, these people had to figure out new rules for appropriate behavior, proper appearance, and desirable relationships. Those rules then had to be communicated. What emerged was a flood of what historians call "prescriptive literature," writing that prescribes certain modes of behavior, dress, and social conduct. Through mass publishing syndicates like the American Tract Society, literature prescribing middle-class cultural values spread to every class in America. (For further information on the context, see pages 319–321.)

The Historical Question

Few historians would dispute that a major cultural shift took place during the forty-five years that separated the War of 1812 and the Civil War, but many questions remain concerning the causes for this shift, the exact nature of it, and the media by which it spread. Examining prescriptive literature from the period is one way to approach those questions. What did the prescriptive literature have to say about class roles, gender roles, and roles for different age groups? How does advice given to one such group help to inform us about desirable roles for the other groups? What expectations were being formed about people's behavior, dress, and social relations?

The Challenge

Using the sources provided, along with other information you have read, write an essay or hold a discussion on the following question. Cite evidence in the sources to support your conclusions. **What roles and responsibilities were being prescribed for middle-class men, women, and children during the early nineteenth century? How do these roles reflect new economic and social realities during the period?**

The Sources

1 Prescriptive literature for young women took many forms—ranging from parables to sentimental poetry. Catherine Beecher was inclined to write manifestoes. In *The Duty of American Women to Their Country* (1845), she says:

Women, then, are to be educated for teachers, and sent to the destitute children of this nation by hundreds and by thousands. This is the way in which a profession *is to be created for women—a profession as honourable and as lucrative for her as the legal, medical, and theological are for men. . . .*

And who else, in such an emergency as this, can so appropriately be invoked to aid? It is woman who is the natural and appropriate guardian of childhood. It is woman who has those tender sympathies which can most readily feel for the wants and sufferings of the young. . . . It is woman, too, who has that conscientiousness and religious devotion which, in any worthy cause, are the surest pledges of success.

Every woman has various duties pressing upon her attention. It is right for her, it is her duty, to cultivate her own mind by reading and study, not merely for her own gratification or credit, but with the great end in view of employing her knowledge and energies for the good of others. It is right, and a duty for a woman to attend to domestic affairs; but, except in cases of emergency, it is not right to devote all her time to this alone. It is a duty for her to attend to religious efforts and ordinances; but it is not right for her to give all her time to these alone. . . .

2 Prescriptive literature for men usually avoided the sentimental and took on an air of friendly conversation. T. S. Arthur's *Advice to Young Men on Their Duties and Conduct in Life* (1853) was one such advice manual. Arthur wrote:

. . . It is no light task which a man takes upon himself—that of sustaining, by his single efforts, a whole family. . . . You have an education that enables you to take a respectable position in society; you have a groundwork of good principles; habits of industry; in fact, all that a young man need ask for in order that he may rise in the world; and for these you are indebted to your father. To give you such advantages, cost him labor, self-denial, and much anxious thought. Many times has he been pressed down with worldly difficulties. . . . He has seen his last dollar, it may be, leave his hand, without knowing certainly where the next was to come from. But still, his love for his children has urged him on. . . .

. . . you should make it a point of duty always to go with your sisters into company, and to be their companion, if possible, on all public occasions. By so doing, you can prevent the introduction of men whose principles are bad; or, if such introductions are forced upon them in spite of you, can throw in a timely word of caution. . . . The great thing is to guard, by every means in your power, these innocent ones from the polluting presence of a bad man. You cannot tell how soon he may win the affections of the most innocent, confiding, and loving of them all, and draw her off from virtue. And even if his designs be honorable . . . he cannot make her happy, for happy no pure-minded woman ever has been, or ever can be made by a corrupt, evil-minded, and selfish man.

. . . But not only should you seek to guard them from the danger just alluded to,—your affection for them should lead you to enter into their pleasures as far as in your power to do so; to give interest and variety to the home circle; to afford them, at all times, the assistance of your judgment in matters of trivial as well as grave importance.

3 Probably more prescriptive words were written to and about children than about any other subject during the antebellum period. An anonymous pamphlet issued by the American Tract Society said this:

Be careful in the formation of intimate friendships. Attach yourself to those chiefly who are diligent, thoughtful, and amiable. Behave always in the most respectful manner to your teachers, and to all that occasionally visit you. Avoid the extremes of bashfulness and bold presumption; frankness and modesty form a happy union. In diet be moderate; in apparel neat; among your companions, cheerful and kind. . . . Never tell a lie, nor conceal the truth when it is your duty to make it known; at the same time remember that a tale-bearer in a school is an odious character.

4 Not all prescriptive material was written. Then, as now, pictures were an extremely useful medium for influencing people's behavior. On page 320 there is a cover illustration from an early-nineteenth-century tract entitled "On the Lord's Day." In it the artist is making a number of powerful statements about how families should look.

POPULATION GROWTH AND CHANGING SUFFRAGE QUALIFICATIONS Two of the most important changes that accompanied the great transformation in American society were population growth and the extension of political suffrage. As this map shows, population density was going up in virtually every part of the country. At the same time, most states were easing their requirements for voter qualifications. These two forces together changed the face of American politics as the number of people participating in the political system expanded explosively.

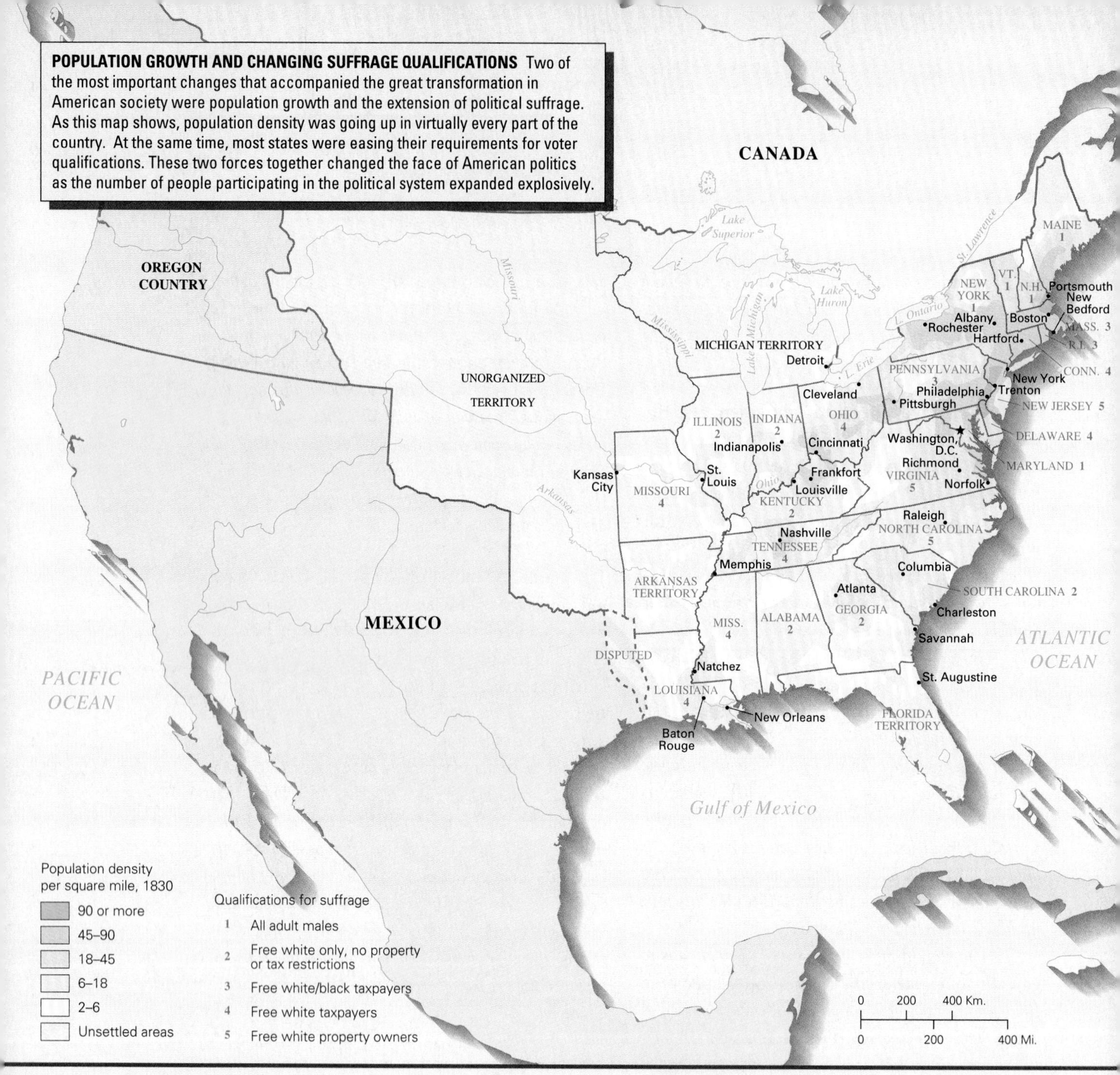

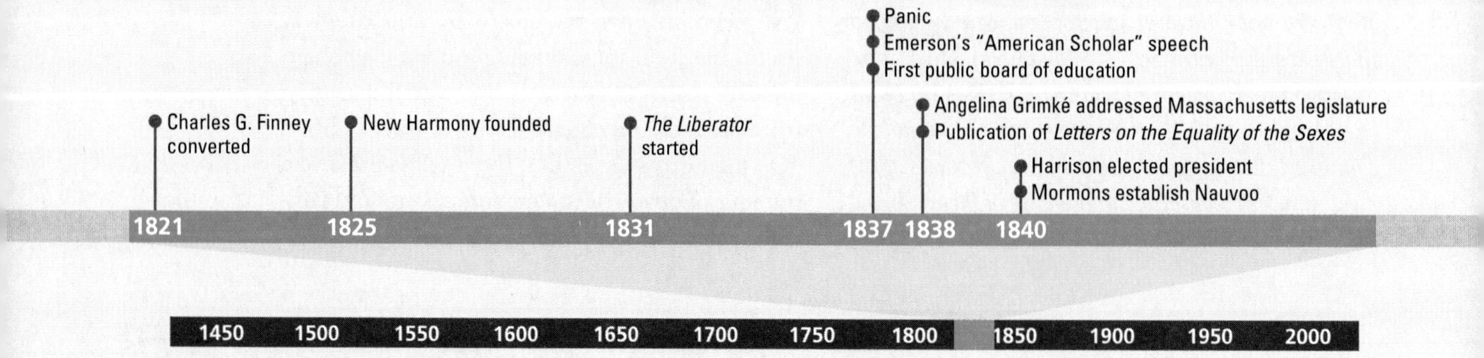

CHAPTER 12

Responses to the Great Transformation, 1828–1840

Reactions to Changing Conditions

- What choices did Americans make in dealing with the stresses created by rapid change during the Jacksonian era?
- What was the cultural outcome?

Toward an American Culture

- How did the choices made in American arts and letters reflect the spirit of change during the Jacksonian era?
- What were some other cultural outcomes of the stresses of rapid change during the era?

The Whig Alternative to Jacksonian Democracy

- What expectations did Jackson's opponents have when they built their coalition to oppose the Democrats?
- Was the outcome what they expected? Why or why not?

INTRODUCTION

E xpectations
C onstraints
C hoices
O utcomes

The great transformation in American economics and society created vast new opportunities for people during the antebellum period, instilling new and exciting *expectations.* But new *constraints* arose as quickly as new hopes. A man could, like Chauncey Jerome, amass a fortune one day and find a place among the genteel elite, only to lose it the next and find himself among the mass of hourly wage workers. Some entrepreneurs experienced this cycle many times during their careers. Others experienced no mobility at all; they were stuck either as underpaid urban workers or, worse yet, as slaves.

Different groups of Americans reacted differently to this precarious situation, as their *choices* attest. Some found relief in a new evangelical faith that empowered them to rule their own souls while forging them into close-knit congregations. Others responded more violently, attacking those they believed were responsible for the *constraints* in their lives. Some banded together in tightly organized societies bent on removing from the world sinfulness, drunkenness, ignorance, and a thousand other evils. Others chose to escape the world altogether, isolating themselves in communes devoted to anything from socialism to celibacy to free love. The *outcome* was a peculiar mixture of emerging societies that often were at odds with each other, frequently adding to the tensions that had driven them to make particular *choices.*

At the same time, various American cultures were coming into being. The elite and the middle class could choose to sip tea and read romantic poems or the novels of Nathaniel Hawthorne and James Fenimore Cooper. But the economic and social constraints that working-class people faced led them to choose cheap whiskey and rowdy theater performances or athletic competitions. Slaves faced even more serious *constraints, choosing* to stave off the worst effects of their condition by crafting a creative African-American culture. The *outcome* of these various *choices* was the foundation for the rich culture the United States enjoys today.

In politics, too, change was in the air. Old-line nationalists like Henry Clay and Daniel Webster chafed under Andrew Jackson's personal political style. Southerners like John C. Calhoun found Jackson's forcefulness discomforting and a dangerous threat to states' rights. And many Americans, like those who flocked to the Antimasonic movement, were skeptical of politics in general and of Jackson's politics in particular. Seeking to end the reign of "King Andrew," these disaffected groups invited reforming evangelicals to join them in a new coalition to unplug the Jacksonian political machine. In 1840, the Whig party used every political trick it could think of to woo voters away from the Democrats. The Whigs won that election, and one *outcome* was a new kind of politics that forever changed the way Americans conducted their public business.

Reactions to Changing Conditions

- What choices did Americans make in dealing with the stresses created by rapid change during the Jacksonian era?
- What was the cultural outcome?

In the grasping, competitive conditions that were emerging in the dynamic new America, an individual's status, reputation, and welfare seemed to depend exclusively on his or her economic position. Looking back on sixty years in the clock business, Chauncey Jerome (see page 312) observed bitterly in 1860, "One of the most trying things for me now, is to see how I am looked upon by the community since I lost my property. I never was any better when I owned it than I am now, and never behaved any better. . . . But how different is the feeling towards you, when your neighbors can make nothing more out of you, politically or pecuniarily. . . . It makes no difference what, or how much you have done for them heretofore, you are passed by without notice now. . . . It is all money and business, business and money which make the man now-a-days; success is everything." The combination of rapid

CHRONOLOGY

Modernization and Rising Stress

1806	Journeyman shoemakers' strike in New York City
1821	Charles G. Finney experiences a religious conversion
1823	James Fenimore Cooper's *The Pioneers*
1825	Thomas Cole begins Hudson River school of painting Robert Owen establishes community at New Harmony, Indiana
1826	Shakers have eighteen communities in the United States
1828	Weavers protest and riot in New York City Andrew Jackson elected president
1829	Grand jury in Rochester, New York, declares alcohol the most prominent cause of crime
1830	Joseph Smith, Jr., publishes the Book of Mormon
1831	Nat Turner's Rebellion William Lloyd Garrison begins publishing *The Liberator*
1832	Jackson re-elected
1834	Riot in Charlestown, Massachusetts, leads to the destruction of a Catholic convent George Bancroft publishes volume one of his American history
1835	Five Points riot in New York City
1836	Congress passes the gag rule Martin Van Buren elected president
1837	Horace Mann heads the first public board of education Panic of 1837 Ralph Waldo Emerson's "American Scholar" speech
1838	Emerson articulates transcendentalism Angelina Grimké addresses the Massachusetts state legislature on the evils of slavery
1840	Log-cabin campaign William Henry Harrison elected president Mormons build Nauvoo, Illinois
1841	Brook Farm established
1842	*Commonwealth v. Hunt*
1843	Dorothea Dix advocates state-funded asylums for the insane

geographical expansion and new opportunities in business produced a highly precarious social world for all Americans. Desperate for some stability, many pushed for various reforms to bring the fast-spinning world under control.

A Second Great Awakening

Popular religion was a major counterbalance to the tendencies that shocked Chauncey Jerome and his contemporaries. Beginning in the 1790s, the Protestant establishment had to respond to the social, political, and economic forces that were producing broad-reaching change throughout America. Both theologians and popular preachers sought to create a new Protestant creed that would maintain the notion of Christian community in an atmosphere of increasing individualism and competition.

Mirroring tendencies in the political and economic realms, Protestant thinking during the opening decades of the nineteenth century emphasized the role of the individual. Traditional Puritanism was rooted in a belief in predestination—the idea that no human actions can alter God's divine plan and that individuals can do nothing to win salvation. Preachers like Jonathan Edwards and George Whitefield had strayed from this doctrine somewhat during the Great Awakening of the 1740s in emphasizing the emotional nature of the conversion experience (see page 101). Many Protestant theologians, however, continued to share the conviction that salvation was a gift from God that individuals could do nothing to earn.

Timothy Dwight, Jonathan Edwards's grandson, took the first step toward liberalizing this position in the 1790s, when he began to accept the idea that the individual might have a role in salvation. But it fell to his students at Yale College, especially Nathaniel Taylor, to create a new theology that was entirely consistent with the new secular creed of individualism. According to this new doctrine, God offers salvation to all who seek it, and it is the individual's responsibility to initiate the necessary relationship with God. Thus the individual has "free will" to choose or not choose salvation.

Taylor's ideas struck a responsive chord in a restless and expanding America. Hundreds of ordained ministers, licensed preachers, and **lay exhorters** carried the message of a democratic God. Unlike Calvinist Puritanism, which characterized women as the weaker sex, the new evangelicalism stressed women's spiritual equality with—and even spiritual superiority to—men. Not surprisingly, young women generally were the first to respond to the new message. The most highly effective preachers of the day took advantage of this appeal, turning women into agents spreading the word to their husbands, brothers, and children. One of the most effective at employing this tactic was Charles Grandison Finney.

A former schoolteacher and lawyer, Finney experienced a soul-shattering religious conversion in 1821 at the age of 29. Declaring that "the Lord Jesus Christ" had retained him "to plead his cause," Finney performed on the pulpit as a spirited attorney might argue a case in court. A religious revival "is not a miracle, or dependent on a miracle in any sense," Finney announced, to the shock of conservative Calvinists. Arguing for souls was like moving a judge to make the right decision in a lawsuit—the result of effective persuasion.

Seating those most likely to be converted on a special "anxious bench," Finney focused his whole attention on them as a lawyer might try to move a jury. The result was likely to be dramatic. Many of the targeted people fainted, experienced bodily spasms, or cried out in hysteria. Such dramatic presentations and results brought Finney enormous publicity, which he and an army of imitators used to gain access to communities all over the West and Northeast. The result was a nearly continuous season of religious revival. The **Second Great Awakening** spread from rural community to rural community like a wildfire until, in the late 1830s, Finney carried the fire into Boston and New York.

Revival meetings were remarkable affairs. Usually beginning on a Thursday and continuing until the following Tuesday, they drew together huge crowds who listened to spirited preaching in the evenings and engaged in religious study, conversation, and wrenching soul searching during the daylight hours. At one such meeting, between ten and twenty-five thousand people listened to forty different preachers. As one witness proclaimed, there were "loud ejaculations of prayer . . . some struck with terror . . . others, trembling weeping and crying out . . . fainting and swooning away."

The new revivals led to the breakdown of traditional church organizations and the creation of various Christian denominations. **Evangelical sects** like the Presbyterians, Baptists, and Methodists split between those who supported the new theology and those who clung to more traditional notions. Splits also occurred for reasons that now seem petty but at the time represented serious questions of commitment. One Baptist congregation, for example, split over the hypothetical question of whether it would be a sin to lie to marauding Indians in order to protect hidden family members. Those who said lying to protect one's family was no sin formed a separate congregation of so-called Lying Baptists. Those who said lying was sinful under any circumstances created a church of Truth-Telling Baptists.

In the face of such fragmentation, all denominations voiced concern that state support of any one church would give that denomination an artificial advantage in the continuing competition for souls. Oddly, those most fervent in their Christian beliefs joined deists and other Enlightenment-influenced

lay exhorter A church member who preaches but is not an ordained minister.

Second Great Awakening Series of religious revivals that began around 1800 and were characterized by revival meetings.

revival meeting A meeting for the purpose of reawakening religious faith, often characterized by impassioned preaching and emotional public testimony by converted sinners.

evangelical sects Protestant groups that emphasized the sole authority of the Bible and the necessity of actively striving to convert others.

♦ Marking his triumphant arrival in New York City, evangelist Charles G. Finney had this massive tabernacle built to his own specifications. Here he held the same sort of revival meetings he had been leading in rural tents and village churches for years before arriving in the city. *Oberlin College Archives*

thinkers in arguing steadfastly for the continued and even more stringent separation of church and state. This, in turn, added to the spirit of competition, for individual congregations were forced to rely on the voluntary contributions of new converts to keep their churches alive.

Even though religious conversion had become an individual matter and competition for contributions a genuine concern, revivalists did not ignore the notion of community. At revival meetings, for example, when individuals were overcome by the power of the spirit, others, already awakened, immediately began "surrounding them with melodious songs, or fervent prayers for their happy resurrection, in the love of Christ." In fact, preachers like Finney put great emphasis on creating a single Christian community to stand in opposition to sin. One of Finney's converts proclaimed deep impatience with "Old Church Hipocrites who think more of their particular denomination than Christ Church." Finney himself wrote that during his revivals "Christians of every denomination generally seemed to make common cause, and went to work with a will, to pull sinners out of the fire." As one Finney convert wrote to his sister during a revival, "We are either marching toward heaven or towards hell. How is it with you?"

"I know this is all algebra to those who have never felt it," Finney said. "But to those who have experienced the agony of wrestling, prevailing prayer, for the conversion of a soul, you may depend on it, that soul . . . appears as dear as a child is to the mother who brought it forth with pain." This intimate connection forged bonds of mutual responsibility, giving a generation of isolated individuals something to rally around, a common starting point for joint action. According to the new theology, it was the convert's duty to carry the message of available salvation to the multitudes still in darkness. This requirement formed the core for an activist ideology by which new congregations, missionary societies, and a thousand other benevolent groups rose up to lead America and the world in the continuing battle against sin.

Free and Slave Labor Protests

While the new forms of religion appealed to many northern workers and southern slaves, others in both groups blamed their miseries not on sin but on their exploitation by others. In view of their working and living conditions, it is not surprising that some manufacturing workers and slave laborers protested their situations. In both cases, the most skilled and well educated took the lead in making their dissatisfaction with the new modes of production known to factory owners and masters.

The first organized labor strike in America took place in 1806, when a group of journeyman shoemakers stopped work to protest the hiring of unskilled workers to perform, for a low wage, some tasks that higher-paid journeymen and apprentices

♦ Shoemakers, like those shown in this early nineteenth-century daguerrotype, were among the first skilled craftspeople to organize into unions in order to bargain collectively with employers. They lost their first contest in a New York court, but eventually won a case in Massachusetts that provided the precedent for unionization among skilled workers. *Library of Congress.*

had been doing. The strike failed (a New York court intervened and declared the shoemakers' actions illegal), but it set the precedent for labor actions for the next half-century.

The source of the dispute in the New York shoemakers' strike continued to be a cause of labor unrest. Journeymen reacted to the mechanization that threatened their jobs and their social position. In addition, they bemoaned the decline in craftsmanship and their loss of power to set hours, conditions, and wages for the work they performed. Industrialization was costing journeymen their status as independent contractors and forcing some to become wage laborers.

Instead of attacking or even criticizing industrialization, however, journeymen simply asked for what they believed was their fair piece of the pie: decent wages and working conditions and some role in decision making—all of which they had traditionally had. Throughout the industrializing cities of the Northeast and the smaller manufacturing centers of the West, journeymen banded together in **trade unions:** assemblies of skilled workers grouped by specific occupation. During the 1830s, trade unions in one town joined with trade unions in other towns to form the beginnings of a national trade union movement. In this way, house carpenters, shoemakers, handloom weavers, printers, and comb makers established national unions through which they attempted to enforce uniform wage standards in their industries. In 1834, journeymen's organizations from a number of industries joined to form the **National Trades' Union,** the first labor organization in the nation's history to represent many different crafts.

The trade union movement, however, accomplished little during the antebellum period. Factory owners, bankers, and others who had a vested interest in keeping labor cheap and, in their view, making it more efficient used every device available to prevent unions from gaining the upper hand. Employers countered the national trade unions by forming associations to resist union activity. They also used the courts to keep unions from disrupting business. A series of local court decisions upheld employers and threatened labor's right to organize.

Despite such efforts, a number of strikes affected American industries during the 1830s. In 1834, women working in the textile mills in Lowell, Massachusetts, closed production down in response to a 25 percent reduction in their wages. And they proved their organizational skills and economic clout again two years later when they struck over an increase in boarding-house rates. Such demonstrations of power by workers frightened manufacturers, and gradually over the next two decades, employers replaced native-born women in the factories with immigrants, who were less likely to organize successfully and, more important, less likely to win approval from sympathetic judges or consumers.

Still, workers won some small victories in the battle to organize labor. A significant breakthrough finally came in 1842. The Massachusetts Supreme Court decided in the case of *Commonwealth v. Hunt* that Boston's journeymen bootmakers were within

trade union A labor organization whose members work in a specific trade or craft.

National Trades' Union The first national association of trade unions in the United States; it was formed in 1834.

their rights to organize "in such manner as best to subserve their own interests" and to call strikes. By that time, however, the Panic of 1837 (see page 358) had so undermined labor's ability to withstand the rigors of strikes and court cases that legal protection became somewhat meaningless.

Not all labor protests were as peaceful as the shoemakers' strike. In 1828, for example, immigrant weavers protested the low wages paid by Alexander Knox, New York City's leading textile employer. Storming Knox's home to demand higher pay, the weavers invaded and vandalized the house and beat Knox's son and a cordon of police guards. The rioters then marched to the garret and basement homes of weavers who had not joined the protest and destroyed their looms.

Not all the riots that occurred in American cities during these years were directly related to working conditions, but they were certainly signs of workers' desperation. Notable were ethnic riots that shook New York, Philadelphia, and Boston during the late 1820s and 1830s. In 1834, for example, rumors began circulating in Boston that innocent girls were being held captive and tortured in a Catholic convent in nearby Charlestown. A Protestant mob stormed the building, leaving it a heap of smoldering ashes. A year later, in New York's notoriously overcrowded and lawless Five Points district, roving gangs of native-born Protestant and immigrant Irish Catholic men battled in the streets. The ethnic tension evident in these and other riots was the direct result of declining economic power and terrible living conditions. Native-born journeymen blamed immigrants for lowered wages and loss of status. Immigrants simmered with hatred at being treated like dirt by their native-born colleagues.

Despite poverty, violence, and poor living conditions, working people in America during the early nineteenth century did little beyond drinking and fighting among themselves to protest their fate. Why were American workers so unresponsive? One reason may be that as poor as conditions were in American manufacturing cities, they were better than conditions in Ireland, Germany, and other places that workers had left. Another reason is that workers did not see themselves staying in the city or staying poor. As one English observer commented in 1842, women in America's factories were willing to endure boring twelve-hour workdays because "none of them consider it as their permanent condition; all look forward to its termination in a few years at the farthest," and men expected to "accumulate enough to go off to the West, and buy an estate at $11\frac{1}{4}$ dollar an acre, or set up in some small way of business at home."

Most slaves, too, restricted themselves to passive resentment rather than open protest in the face of dismal living and working conditions. Unlike workers in the North, who at least had some legal protections and civil rights, slaves had nothing but their own wits to protect them against a society that classed them as disposable personal property (see pages 323–325). Slaves were skilled at the use of **passive resistance.** Clever strategies for getting extra food, clothing, and other supplies were passed on from generation to generation. Slaves developed various techniques for manipulating their masters and undermining their authority. Slaves often stole food, not because they were hungry but because its unexplainable disappearance flustered their masters. Farm animals also disappeared mysteriously, tools broke in puzzling ways, people fell ill from unknown diseases, and workers got lost on the way to fields—all these events were subtle signs of slaves' discontent. Slaves also used flattery and misdirection—for example, to convince whites that slave-initiated improvements were really the master's idea.

The importance of passive resistance was evident in the tales slaves told among themselves and the songs they sang. Perhaps the best-known example is the stories of Br'er—that is, Brother—Rabbit, a physically weak but clever character who uses deceit to get what he wants. In one particularly revealing tale, Br'er Rabbit is caught by Br'er Fox. Unable to start a fire to cook the helpless rabbit, Fox threatens Rabbit with all sorts of horrible tortures. Rabbit replies that Br'er Fox can do anything he wants to do as long as he does not throw him into the nearby briar patch. Seizing on Rabbit's apparent fear, Fox unties Br'er Rabbit and pitches him deep into the middle of the briar patch, expecting to see the rabbit struggle and die amid the thorns. Br'er Rabbit, however, scampers away through the briars, calling back over his shoulder that he was born and bred in a briar patch and laughing at how he tricked Br'er Fox into doing exactly what he wanted him to do. Such stories taught slaves how to deal cleverly with powerful adversaries, and every day they used the lessons they learned.

Not all slave resistance was passive. Perhaps the most common form of active resistance was running

passive resistance Resistance by nonviolent methods.

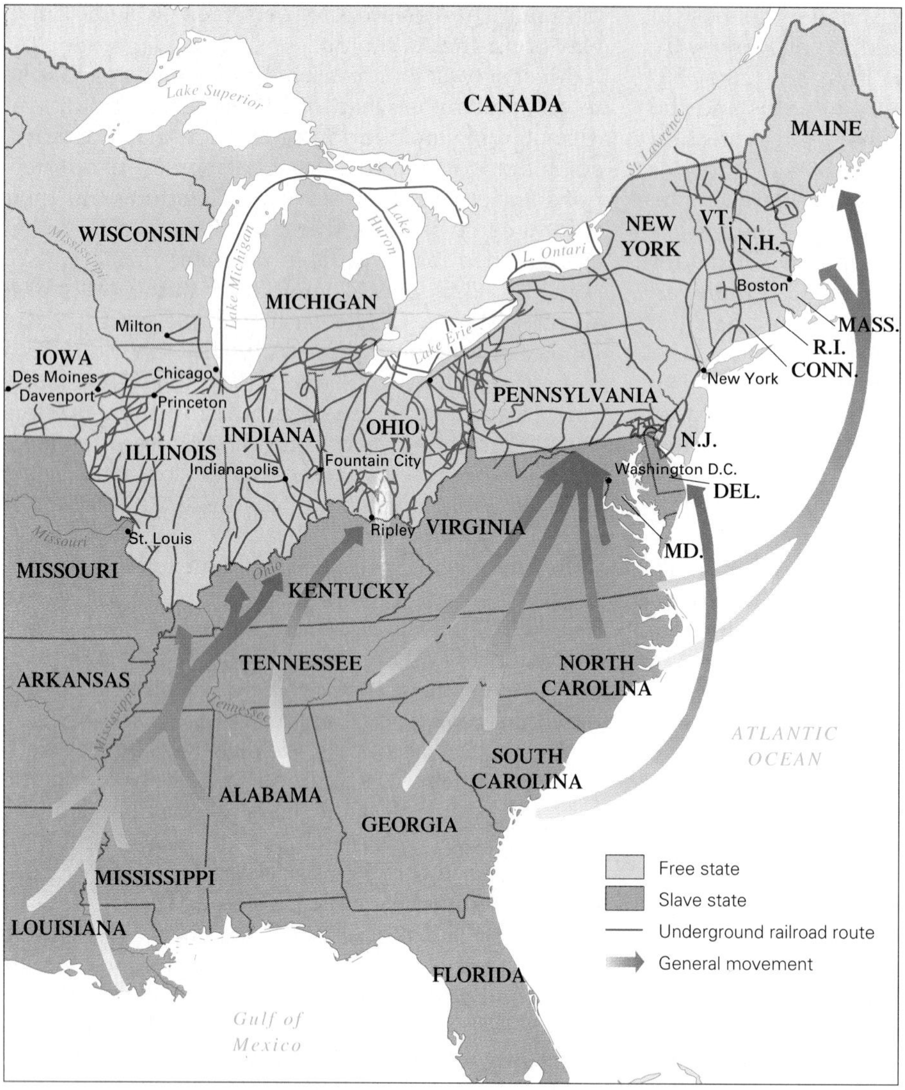

♦ **MAP 12.1 Escaping from Slavery** Running away was one of the most prominent forms of slave resistance during the antebellum period. Success often depended on help from African Americans who had already gained their freedom and from sympathetic whites. Beginning in the 1820s an informal and secret network called the Underground Railway provided escape routes for slaves who were daring enough to risk all for freedom. The routes shown here are based on documentary evidence, but the network's secrecy makes it impossible to know if they are drawn entirely accurately.

away (see Map 12.1). The number of slaves who escaped may never be known. Probably an average of about a thousand made their way to freedom each year. Most of them lived in **border states,** where freedom lay perhaps only a few miles away from the slave quarters. Large numbers also escaped from Texas and other states where the nearby Mexican border or the Indian frontier promised protection and relative freedom.

Of all the slaves who ran away during the reign of King Cotton, fully a third were artisans, wagoners, boat pilots, and other specially skilled and

border states The slave states of Delaware, Maryland, Virginia, Kentucky, and Missouri, which shared a border with states in which slavery was illegal.

privileged slaves, and more than 80 percent were men between the ages of 16 and 35. None of these figures should be particularly surprising. Young men were not likely to be burdened with family responsibilities and had the physical strength to resist capture. Artisans, almost all of whom were men, had viable economic options in the free world and the relative liberty to move around without constant supervision.

But even those with privileges found running away a dangerous thing to do. One former slave, a high-ranking manager while in bondage, recalled, "No man who has never been placed in such a situation can comprehend the thousand obstacles thrown in the way of the flying slave. Every white man's hand is raised against him—the patrollers are watching for him—the hounds are ready to follow on his track."

Runaway slaves left few documents explaining why they were willing to face such dangers. Besides the undeniable appeal of freedom, some more immediate things seem to have prompted them to take the risk. Frederick Douglass, who later became a famous abolitionist leader, was a skilled craftsman who ran away because he finally grew tired of turning his wages over to his master. Most contemporary observers thought that fear of punishment for some crime was the most common motivation for running away. Some slaves, however, reported that they ran not because they had done something that merited punishment but to keep themselves from doing something of the sort. "They didn't do something and run," one former slave reported. "They run before they did it, 'cause they knew that if they struck a white man there wasn't going to be a nigger. In them days they run to keep from doing something." Yet another strong motivation for running was to keep families together or to reunite, if only for a short time. Advertisements for runaway slaves often contained such comments as "He is no doubt trying to reach his wife."

The most active and most frightening form of slave resistance was open and armed revolt. Despite slaveholders' best efforts, slaves planned an unknown number of rebellions during the antebellum period, and many of them were actually carried out.

Nat Turner, a black preacher, carried out the most serious and violent of the antebellum slave revolts. After years of planning and organization, in 1831 Turner led a force of about seventy slaves in a predawn raid against the slaveholding households in Southampton County, Virginia. It took four days for white forces to stop the assault. During that time, the slaves slaughtered and mutilated fifty-five white men, women, and children. Angry, frightened whites finally captured and executed Turner and sixteen of his followers.

♦ No pictures of famed slave revolt leader Nat Turner are known to exist, but this nineteenth-century painting illustrates how one artist imagined the appearance of Turner and his fellow conspirators. White southerners lived in terror of scenes such as this and passed severe laws designed to prevent African Americans from ever having such meetings.

Whites were not slow to see the connection between Turner's relative freedom of motion as an educated preacher and his leadership in the uprising. In the wake of Turner's Rebellion, southern courts and legislatures clapped stricter controls on the freedoms granted to slaves and to free blacks. In most areas, free blacks were denied the right to own guns, buy liquor, hold public assemblies, testify in court, and vote. Slaves were forbidden to own any private property, to attend unsupervised worship services, and to learn reading and writing. Also, codes that prevented slaves from being unsupervised in towns virtually eliminated slaves as independent urban craftsmen after 1840.

Fear of slave revolts reached paranoid levels in the South, especially in areas where slaves greatly outnumbered whites. After reading about and seeing a play depicting a slave insurrection, Mary Boykin Chesnut gave expression to the fear that plagued whites in the slave South: "What a thrill of terror ran through me as those yellow and black brutes came jumping over the parapets! Their faces were like so many of the same sort at home.... How long would they resist the seductive and irresistible call: 'Rise, kill, and be free!'"

Outnumbered whites felt justified in passing strong restrictions and using harsh methods to enforce them. In many areas of the South, white citizens formed local **vigilance committees.** These armed men rode through the countryside to overawe slaves and dissuade them from attempting to escape or rebel. Local authorities pressed court clerks, ship captains, and other officials to limit the freedom of blacks. White critics of slavery—who had been numerous, vocal, and well respected before the birth of King Cotton—were harassed, prosecuted, and sometimes beaten into silence.

♦ After seeing the conditions under which the mentally ill lived in antebellum Massachusetts, Dorothea Dix, shown in this early photograph, campaigned for special asylums where they could receive special care and treatment. *Boston Athenaeum.*

Middle-Class and Moral Reform

Witnessing the squalor and violence in working-class districts and the deteriorating condition for slaves led many genteel and middle-class Americans to push for reforms. The missionary activism that accompanied the Second Great Awakening dovetailed with this reformist inclination. The Christian **benevolence** movement gave rise to hundreds of voluntary societies ranging from maternal associations designed to improve child rearing to political lobby groups aiming to outlaw alcohol, Sunday mail delivery, and other perceived evils. These organizations provided genteel and middle-class men and women with a purpose and an outlet missing from their lives. Such activism drew them together in common causes and led to deep friendships and a shared sense of commitment—antidotes to the alienation and loneliness common in the competitive world of the early nineteenth century.

As traditional family and village life broke down in the new America, voluntary societies pressed for public intervention to address social problems. The new theology reinforced the reforming impulse by emphasizing that even the most depraved might be saved if proper means were applied. This idea had immediate application in the realm of crime and punishment. Reformers characterized criminals not as evil but as lost and in need of divine guidance. In Auburn, New York, an experimental prison system put prisoners to work during the day, condemned them to absolute silence during mealtimes, and locked them away in solitary confinement at night. Reformers believed that this combination of hard work, discipline, and solitude would put criminals on the path to productive lives and spiritual renewal.

Mental illness underwent a similar change in definition. Rather than viewing the mentally ill as hopeless cases suffering an innate spiritual flaw, reformers now spoke of them as lost souls in need of help. **Dorothea Dix,** a young, compassionate, and reform-minded teacher, learned firsthand about the plight of the mentally ill when she was called to teach a Sunday school class in a Boston-area prison. Advocating publicly funded asylums for the insane, she told the Massachusetts state legislature in 1843: "I tell what I have seen . . . Insane persons confined within the Commonwealth, in cages, closets, cellars, stalls, pens! Chained, naked, beaten with rods, and lashed into obedience!" For the balance of the cen-

vigilance committees Groups of armed private citizens who use the threat of mob violence to enforce their own interpretation of the law.

benevolence Acts of kindness.

Dorothea Dix Philanthropist, reformer, and educator who was a pioneer in the movement for specialized treatment of the mentally ill.

tury, Dix toured the country pleading the cause of the mentally ill, succeeding in winning both private and public support for mental health systems.

A hundred other targets for reform joined prisons and asylums on the agenda of middle-class Christian activists. Embracing their Puritan ancestors' strict observance of the Sabbath, newly awakened Christians insisted on stopping Sunday mail delivery and demanded that canals be closed on Sundays. Others joined Bible and tract societies that distributed Christian literature, or they founded Sunday schools or opened domestic missions designed to win either the **irreligious** or the wrongly religious (as Roman Catholics were perceived to be) to the new covenant of the Second Great Awakening.

Many white-collar reformers acted in earnest and were genuinely interested in forging a new social welfare system. A number of their programs, however, seemed more like social control than social reform, because they tried to force people to conform to a middle-class standard of behavior. Viewing ethnic behavior as a useless and inferior holdover from an impoverished European peasant experience, reformers believed that immigrants should willingly discard their traditional customs and beliefs and learn American ways. Immigrants who chose to cling to familiar ways were suspected of disloyalty. This aspect of benevolent reform was particularly prominent in two important movements: public education and **temperance.**

Some communities, like Puritan Boston, had always emphasized compulsory education for children. Before the War of 1812, however, most Americans believed that education was the family's responsibility and did not require children to attend school. Many people depended on the apprenticeship system rather than on schools to provide the rudiments of reading, writing, and figuring. But as the complexity of economic, political, and cultural life increased during the opening decades of the nineteenth century, **Horace Mann** and others came out in favor of formal schooling.

Mann, like his contemporary Charles Finney, was trained as a lawyer. But Mann believed that ignorance, not sin, lay at the heart of the nation's problems. Mann, a Bostonian, became the nation's leading advocate of publicly funded education freely accessible to children of all social classes. "If we do not prepare children to become good citizens," Mann proclaimed, "if we do not enrich their minds with knowledge, then our republic must go down to destruction, as others have gone before it." Democracy could continue only where there was equality, and, Mann believed, public education was "a great equalizer of the conditions of men—the balance wheel of the social machinery."

Mann and Massachusetts took the lead in formalizing schooling in 1837, when the state founded the country's first public board of education, with Mann at its head. Seizing control of Massachusetts's educational establishment, Mann immediately extended the school year to a minimum of six months, organized a state teachers' association, and increased teachers' salaries. Gradually the state board changed the curriculum in Massachusetts schools to emphasize "practical" education, replacing classical learning and ministerial training with courses like arithmetic, practical geography, and physical science.

Education reformers were interested in more than "knowledge." Mann and others were equally concerned that new immigrants and the children of the urban poor be trained in Protestant values and middle-class habits. Thus the books used in public schools emphasized qualities like promptness, persistence, discipline, and obedience to authority. In Philadelphia and other cities where Roman Catholic immigrants settled in great and concentrated numbers, Catholic parents resisted the cultural pressure applied on their children by Protestant-dominated public school boards. They supported the establishment of **parochial schools**—a development that worsened the tension between native-born Protestants and immigrant Catholics.

Adding to tension between the evangelicals and those they sought to reform was the crusade against alcohol. Drinking alcohol had always been common in America. Unhealthy drinking water, the absence of affordable alternatives like coffee and tea, and the desire for an escape from difficult and uncomfortable surroundings had turned the United States into what one historian has described as "the alcoholic republic." Before the early nineteenth century, however, the consumption of alcohol was not broadly perceived as a significant social problem.

irreligious Hostile or indifferent to religion.

temperance Moderation in the consumption of alcoholic drinks.

Horace Mann Educator who called for publicly funded education for all children and was head of the first public board of education in the United States.

parochial school A school supported by a church parish; in the United States, the term usually refers to a Catholic school.

Two factors contributed to a new perception. One was the increasing visibility of drinking and its consequence, drunkenness, as populations became more concentrated in manufacturing and trading cities. In Rochester, New York, for example, a town that went through the throes of modernization in the late 1820s, the number of drinking establishments multiplied rapidly as the population grew. By the mid-1830s, there were nearly a hundred drinking establishments in Rochester. Anyone with a few cents could get a glass of whiskey at grocery stores, at either of two candy stores, at barbershops, at private houses, or even at small businesses—all within a few steps of wherever a person might be.

The other factor contributing to a new view of alcohol was the changing tastes of genteel and middle-class people living comfortably in their private neighborhoods. As better drinking water became available to them, and as coffee and tea became affordable to them, they reduced their consumption of alcohol and disapproved of those who did not do the same. In 1829, the county grand jury sitting in Rochester charged that strong drink was "the cause of almost all of the crime and almost all of the misery that flesh is heir to." The middle-class point of view was that drinking made self-control impossible and endangered both morality and industry. Thus behavior that had been acceptable in the late eighteenth century was judged to be a social problem in the nineteenth.

Like most of the reform movements, the temperance movement began in churches touched by the Second Great Awakening; it then spread outward. Drunkenness earned special condemnation from reawakened Protestants, who believed that people were responsible not only for their sins but also for their own salvation. A person whose reason was besotted by alcohol simply could not rise to the demand. Christian reformers, therefore, believed that temperance was necessary not only to preserve the nation but also to save people's souls.

The religious appeal of temperance was enhanced by a powerful economic appeal. Factory owners and managers recognized that workers who drank often and heavily, on or off the job, threatened the quantity and quality of production. Owners and supervisors alike rallied around the temperance movement as a way of policing the undisciplined behavior of their employees both in and out of the factory. By promoting temperance, these reformers believed they could not only increase production but also clean up the worst aspects of city life and turn the raucous lower classes into clean-living, self-controlled, peaceful workers.

The Rise of Abolitionism

Another reform movement that had profound influence in early-nineteenth-century America was **abolitionism.** In the decades following the War of 1812, the Christian excitement that vibrated in the North and the sectional politics that shook the nation brought increasing attention to the plight of slaves.

Although some people had always had doubts about the morality of slavery, there was little organized opposition to it before the American Revolution. During the Revolution, many Americans saw the contradiction between asserting the "unalienable rights" of "life, liberty, and the pursuit of happiness" and holding slaves (see page 173). By the end of the Revolution, only Georgia and South Carolina continued to allow the importation of slaves, and Massachusetts and Pennsylvania specifically prohibited slavery altogether. Even the plantation states showed increasing flexibility in dealing with slavery, as some elite southerners began to doubt the practicality if not the morality of the institution. After Virginia authorized owners to free their slaves in 1782, Delaware and Maryland soon did likewise. By the mid-1780s, most states, including those in the South, had active antislavery societies. In 1807, when Congress voted to outlaw the importation of slaves, little was said in defense of the institution of slavery. But by 1815, the morality of slavery had begun to emerge as a national issue.

Public feeling about slavery during these years is reflected in the rise of the **American Colonization Society,** founded in 1817. Economic pragmatism and humanitarian concern for slaves' well-being were not the only reasons for participation in the Colonization Society. Some members expressed the belief that blacks were not equal to whites and that the two races could not live together. They attacked the institution of slavery because it meant continued contacts between blacks and whites. In line with this preju-

abolitionism A reform movement favoring the immediate freeing of all slaves.

American Colonization Society Organization established in 1817 to send free blacks from the United States to Africa; it used government money to buy land in Africa and founded the colony of Liberia.

dice, the organization advocated that if slaveowners wished to emancipate their slaves or if funds could be raised to purchase their freedom, the freed slaves should immediately be shipped to Africa. Others noted that because many slaves had embraced Christianity, they might be agents in the extension of enthusiastic religious conversion. Theologian Samuel Hopkins, who believed slavery to be a sin, pointed out that God had allowed it "so that blacks could embrace the gospel in the New World and then bear the glad tidings back to Africa."

Although the American Colonization Society began in the South, its policies were particularly popular in the Northeast and West. In eastern cities, workers fearful for their jobs lived in dread of either enslaved or free blacks flooding in, lowering wages, and destroying job security. In western states like Indiana and Illinois, farmers feared that competition could arise from a slaveholding aristocracy. In both regions, white supremacists argued that the extension of slavery beyond the Mississippi River and north of the **Mason-Dixon Line** would eventually lead to blacks mixing with the white population, a possibility they found extremely distasteful.

Most preachers active in the Second Great Awakening supported the idea of colonization, but a few individuals advocated more radical reforms. The most vocal leader among the antislavery forces during the early nineteenth century was **William Lloyd Garrison.** A Christian reformer from Massachusetts, Garrison in the late 1820s concentrated all his energies in the antislavery cause. In 1831, he founded the nation's first prominent abolitionist newspaper, *The Liberator.* In it he advocated immediate emancipation for blacks and no compensation for slaveholders, whom he considered beneath contempt. In the following year, Garrison founded the New England Anti-Slavery Society and then, in 1833, branched out to found the national American Anti-Slavery Society.

At first, Garrison had few followers. Some Christian reformers joined his cause, but the majority held back. For the same reasons that they supported colonization, most northern whites detested the notion of immediate emancipation, and radical abolitionists at this early date were almost universally ignored or, worse, attacked when they sought to win followers. Throughout the 1830s, riots often accompanied abolitionist rallies, and angry mobs stormed stages and pulpits to silence abolitionist speakers. Still, support for the movement gradually grew (see Individual Choices: Angelina Grimké). In 1836, petitions flooded into Congress demanding an end to the slave trade in Washington, D.C. Not ready to engage in an action quite so controversial, Congress passed a **gag rule** that automatically tabled any petition to Congress that addressed the abolition of slavery. The rule remained in effect for nearly a decade.

Toward an American Culture

- How did the choices made in American arts and letters reflect the spirit of change during the Jacksonian era?
- What were some other cultural outcomes of the stresses of rapid change during the era?

During the first decades of the nineteenth century, profound changes took place in the relationship between the individual and society. While some found solace in evangelical and reform communities, both frontiersmen and city-dwellers became increasingly self-reliant, giving rise to a widely shared commitment to individualism. The changing economic, social, and political systems that came to maturity in the Jacksonian era, as well as the character of the popular president himself, helped to fix this individualistic creed as a dominant force in an evolving American culture.

Traditional community ties based on close-knit, long-time social and family relationships could not survive in communities where migrating opportunity seekers came and went. Nor could such ties thrive in the growing trading and manufacturing centers where throngs of strangers massed to seek a better living. Instead, as visiting French nobleman **Alexis de Tocqueville** observed, Americans seemed to be "animated by the most selfish cupidity [greed]." Indeed, a new world of opportunity seemed open to those with the talent, desire, and

Mason-Dixon Line The boundary between Pennsylvania and Maryland; it marked the northern division between free and slave states before the Civil War.

William Lloyd Garrison Abolitionist leader who founded and published *The Liberator,* an antislavery newspaper.

gag rule A rule that limits or prevents debate on an issue.

Alexis de Toqueville French traveler and historian who toured the United States in 1831 and wrote *Democracy in America,* a classic study of American institutions and the American character.

INDIVIDUAL CHOICES

Choosing to Speak Out

Angelina Grimké

Born in the South to a prominent slaveholding family, Angelina Grimké moved to the North to distance herself from an institution she hated. When she discovered that northerners were no more sympathetic about the plight of slaves than southerners and would not give abolition a free hearing, she chose to do something about it. She toured the Northeast, speaking at first to groups of women and then to large mixed audiences. She capped her tour by becoming the first woman to address the Massachusetts state legislature. Her courage won new respect both for abolitionists and for women. Library of Congress.

On March 22, 1838, Boston newspapers reported an unprecedented historical event. On the day before, a young woman had become the first of her gender to address a committee of the legislature of the state of Massachusetts. The young woman was Angelina Emily Grimké, and her speech was a ringing condemnation of slavery.

Many thought it odd that a woman barely out of her twenties would stand before the legislature to speak on any subject, but to speak so boldly on a topic so controversial was odder still. And more than just odd, to speak out against slavery, even in Boston, was dangerous. And that was precisely why Angelina Grimké made the choice to do it.

Angelina was born in 1808, the thirteenth child of Judge John Faucheraud Grimké and his wife Mary Smith Grimké. Both of her parents were descendents of old South Carolina aristocratic families and members in good standing of the state's social and political elite. But Angelina was never comfortable in this environment of carefree gentility. Raised mostly by her older sister Sarah, young Angelina was extremely serious minded. When presented for confirmation in her parents' Episcopal faith, she refused, saying, "If, with my feelings and views as they now are, I should go through that form, it would be acting a lie. I cannot do it."

Sarah, too, was uncomfortable with plantation life and Episcopalian ritual and while on a trip to Philadelphia became attracted to Quakerism. She brought this new faith home. But being a Quaker in antebellum South Carolina was anything but easy—the congregation in Charleston consisted of but two old men. Sarah finally chose to leave her family and move to Pennsylvania, where she could practice her faith. Angelina too eventually converted to the Quaker faith and finally, in 1829, chose to follow her sister to Philadelphia.

One of the things that drew Sarah and Angelina to Quakerism was its rejection of slavery. Though raised in a slaveholding family, several of the Grimké children opposed the institution. Their brother Thomas, for example, was one of the key organizers of the American Colonization Society. Most of their Quaker friends, too, supported colonization and the society's gradual approach, but this was not acceptable to Angelina. Just before leaving South Carolina, she wrote about slavery in her diary: "May it not be laid down as an axiom, that the system must be radically wrong which can only be supported by transgressing the laws of God."

Angelina was at first disappointed and then angered by northern indifference to the slavery issue. Even in Quaker circles, conservative leaders sought to maintain peace in congregations by prohibiting the discussion of slavery. And non-Quakers were outright hostile to those who vocally attacked the institution. In 1834, riots broke out in New York and Philadelphia when abolitionist speakers tried to give public addresses. Finally, in the late summer of 1835, after a year of repeated outbreaks, William Lloyd Garrison published an appeal in *The Liberator* calling for the citizens of Boston to stop mob violence and give abolitionist speakers a fair hearing. His courage in standing up to the mobs was like a personal call for Angelina. Although she tried to resist the temptation, she felt compelled to write a letter to Garrison praising his stand.

"The ground upon which you stand is holy ground," she wrote, "never—never surrender it. If you surrender it, the hope of the slave is extinguished." Garrison was so moved by the letter that he immediately published it, casting a spotlight on the young South Carolina woman who had written it. "I had some idea it might be published," Angelina wrote in her diary, "but did not feel at liberty to say it must not be." Friends, family members, even her sister Sarah begged Angelina to withdraw the letter, but she refused. "I cannot describe the anguish of my soul," she wrote. "Nevertheless I could not blame the publication of the letter, nor would I have recalled it if I could."

As to the danger, she had written to Garrison, "If persecution is the means which God has ordained for the accomplishment of this great end, EMANCIPATION; then . . . I feel as if I could say, LET IT COME; for it is my deep, solemn deliberate conviction, that this is a cause worth dying for."

From that point on, there was no turning back. In 1836 she wrote an *Appeal to the Christian Women of the South,* calling for them to stand up and put an end to the institution of slavery. In the following year she addressed an *Appeal to the Women of the Nominally Free States.* Then she accepted an invitation from the American Anti-Slavery Society to begin a lecture tour, speaking at first only to groups of women but eventually to large mixed audiences. The acclaim she won finally led to her appearance at the State House in Boston, where the committee not only listened to her arguments but invited her back for an additional session. "The chairman," she reported, "was in tears almost the whole time that I was speaking."

Angelina's choice and the wide acceptance she gained through her eloquence made it easier from then on for abolitionist speakers to win the hearing Garrison had begged for. And the precedent she set, first in speaking to large audiences of men and women together and then in addressing the Massachusetts legislature, proved to women that they could and should publicly proclaim their ideas, even on dangerous subjects.

good luck to pursue it. As Tocqueville also observed, "The government of democracy brings the notion of political rights to the level of the humblest citizens, just as the dissemination of wealth brings the notion of property within the reach of all the members of society."

Romanticism and Genteel Culture

Underlying the new mood in American thought and culture was a philosophical attitude sweeping across the Atlantic. **Romanticism,** the European philosophers' rebellion against Enlightenment rationalism (see page 99), stressed the heart over the mind, the wild over the controlled, the mystical over the rational. The United States, with its millions of acres of wilderness, teeming populations of wild animals, and colorful frontier myths, was the perfect setting for romanticism to flower.

Uniting individualism and romanticism, many of the era's leading intellectuals chose to emphasize the positive aspects of life in the United States, celebrating it in forms of religious, literary, and artistic expression. In the process, they launched new forms of thought and presentation that won broad recognition among the genteel and middle classes.

Romanticism and individualism had their earliest and perhaps greatest impact in the religious realm, although they touched nearly every aspect of American life during the nineteenth century. Reeling under the shock of social change that was affecting every aspect of life, many young people sought a religious anchor to bring them some stability. A large number gave themselves over to the emotionally charged preaching of Charles G. Finney and other figures of the Second Great Awakening, but others wanted a more thoughtful religious experience. These people found a voice in a New Englander: **Ralph Waldo Emerson.**

The son of a Unitarian minister, Emerson chose to follow a clerical life, attending Boston Latin School and Harvard College. After a brief period of running a school for young women, he completed his divinity degree and by 1829 had become pastor of the prestigious Second Unitarian Church in Boston. He was soon struck by tragedy, however. His young wife, Ellen Louisa, died in 1831 after only two years of marriage, throwing Emerson into a religious crisis. Looking for new inspiration, he traveled to Europe and there met the famous Romantic poets William Wordsworth and Thomas Carlyle, who influenced Emerson to seek truth in nature and spirit rather than in rationality and order. Emerson combined this Romantic influence with his already strong Unitarian leaning, creating a new philosophy and religion: **transcendentalism.** Recovered from his grief, he returned to the United States to begin a new career as an essayist and lecturer, spreading the transcendentalist message.

"Historical Christianity has fallen into the error that corrupts all attempts to communicate religion," Emerson told the students at the Harvard Divinity School in 1838. "It has dwelt, it dwells, with noxious exaggeration about the person of Jesus. Men have come to speak of revelation as somewhat long ago given and done, as if God were dead." Emerson, however, believed that God was far from dead. "The world is not the product of manifold power," Emerson taught, "but of one will, of one mind; and that one mind is everywhere active, in each ray of the star, in each wavelet of the pool." This being the case, Emerson went on, "The prayers and even the dogmas of our church, are . . . wholly insulated from anything now extant in the life and business of the people." Only through direct contact with the **transcendent** power in the universe could men and women know the truth. "It cannot be received at second hand," Emerson insisted, but only through the independent working of the liberated mind.

Although Emerson emphasized **nonconformity** and dissent in his writings, his ideas were in tune with the cultural and economic currents of his day. In celebrating the individual, Emerson validated the surging individualism of Jacksonian America. In addition, because each person had to find his or her own path to knowledge, Emerson could celebrate many of the disturbing aspects of modernizing

romanticism Artistic and intellectual movement characterized by interest in nature, emphasis on emotion and imagination over rationality, and rebellion against social conventions.

Ralph Waldo Emerson Philosopher, writer, and poet whose essays and poems made him a central figure in the transcendentalist movement and an important figure in the development of literary expression in America.

transcendentalism A philosophical and literary movement asserting the existence of God within human beings and in nature and the belief that intuition is the highest source of knowledge.

transcendent Lying beyond the normal range of experience.

nonconformity Refusal to accept or conform to the beliefs and practices of the majority.

♦ Devastated by the death of his young wife, Ralph Waldo Emerson abandoned a successful career as a minister to seek answers for his grief. While visiting England he came in contact with the Romantic movement and crafted a new faith that would be called transcendentalism. This early portrait by an unknown artist captures Emerson as a young man, filled with the hope and enthusiasm of his calling. *"Ralph Waldo Emerson" artist unknown. The Metropolitan Museum of Art, Bequest of Chester Dale, 1962 (64.97.4).*

America as potentially liberating forces. Rather than condemning the "selfish cupidity" that Tocqueville said characterized Jacksonian America, Emerson stated that money represented the "prose of life" and was, "in its effects and laws, as beautiful as roses." Little wonder, then, that Emerson's ideas found a fairly wide following among young people of means in the Northeast.

Emerson not only set the tone for American religious inquiry but also suggested a bold new direction for American literature. In 1837, he issued a declaration of literary independence from European models in an address at Harvard University entitled "The American Scholar." Young American writers responded enthusiastically. During the twenty years following this speech, Henry David Thoreau, Walt Whitman, Henry Wadsworth Longfellow, and other writers and poets spread the transcendentalist message, emphasizing the uniqueness of the individual and the role of literature as a vehicle for self-discovery. "I celebrate myself, and sing myself," Whitman wrote. They also carried the Romantic message, celebrating the primitive and the common. Longfellow wrote of the legendary Indian chief Hiawatha and sang the praise of the village blacksmith. In "I Hear America Singing," Whitman conveyed the poetry present in the everyday speech of mechanics, carpenters, and other common folk.

Perhaps the most radical of the transcendentalists was Emerson's good friend and frequent house guest **Henry David Thoreau.** Emerson and his other followers made the case for self-reliance, but Thoreau embodied it, camping on the shore of Walden Pond near Concord, Massachusetts, where he did his best to live independent of the rapidly modernizing market economy. "I went to the woods because I wished to live deliberately," Thoreau wrote, "and not, when I came to die, discover that I had not lived."

Like Thoreau, a number of women were also seeking meaning through their writing. Sarah Moore Grimké, elder sister of abolitionist Angelina Grimké, published a well-received essay on women's rights called *Letters on the Equality of the Sexes and the Condition of Women* in 1838. Margaret Fuller picked up on the same theme in her *Woman in the Nineteenth Century* (1845), after demonstrating her own equality by editing the highly influential transcendentalist magazine *The Dial* as well as serving as chief literary critic for the *New York Tribune.*

But the most popular women writers of the day were those who were most successful at communicating the sentimentalized role for the new genteel woman. Lydia Sigourney was one of the first American women to carve out an independent living as a writer. Her first book, *Moral Pieces, in Prose and Verse,* was published in 1815, and by 1830 she was a regular contributor to over thirty popular magazines. Like many critics, Edgar Allan Poe dismissed her work as shallow and sentimental, but he actively solicited her writing for his own magazine,

Henry David Thoreau Writer and naturalist and friend of Ralph Waldo Emerson; his best-known work is *Walden* (1854).

♦ This 1827 painting by Thomas Cole, capturing a scene from James Fenimore Cooper's *Last of the Mohicans,* illustrates the romantic mood current during the early nineteenth century. In line with artistic romanticism, nature dwarfs all else. Even a large Indian camp seems insignificant in size, lost in an exaggerated image of the mountains in the Hudson River region of New York. *"Last of the Mohicans" by Thomas Cole. New York State Historical Association, Cooperstown.*

the *Southern Literary Messenger.* In 1833 she published two bestsellers, *How to be Happy* and *Letters to Young Ladies,* both of which emphasized Christian activism and the domestic ideal. Catharine Beecher was another woman writer who enjoyed enormous popularity for her practical advice guides aimed at making women more effective homemakers.

Three other authors joined Sigourney and Beecher in pushing American literature in sentimental and Romantic directions. James Fenimore Cooper, Herman Melville, and Nathaniel Hawthorne each helped to popularize American themes and scenes in their writing. Even before Emerson's "American Scholar," Cooper had launched a new sort of American novel and American hero. In *The Pioneers* (1823), Cooper introduced Natty Bumppo, also called Hawkeye, a frontiersman whose honesty, independent-mindedness, and skill as a marksman represented the rough-hewn virtues so beloved by Romantics and popularly associated with the American frontier. Altogether, Cooper wrote five novels featuring the plucky Bumppo, and they all sold well.

Like Cooper, Herman Melville emphasized primitive scenes and noble savages in his adventure novels. Beginning with *Typee* (1846) and *Omoo* (1847), Melville's semi-autobiographical accounts of an American seaman among the natives of the South Pacific became overnight bestsellers. Melville followed these with his most famous novel, *Moby-Dick,* published in 1851, an **allegorical** tale of a good man turned bad by his obsession for revenge against a whale he believes to be evil. Both literary critics and the public hated *Moby-Dick.* Their negative response led to Melville's virtual withdrawal from fiction writing.

allegorical Like an allegory, a story in which characters and events stand for abstract ideas and suggest a deep, symbolic meaning.

Nathaniel Hawthorne had more success than Melville in exploring the contest between good and evil. In *Twice-Told Tales* (1837), Hawthorne presented readers with a collection of moral allegories stressing the evils of pride, selfishness, and secret guilt. He brought these themes to fruition in his novel *The Scarlet Letter* (1850), in which adulteress Hester Prynne overcomes shame to gain redemption and her secret lover, Puritan minister Arthur Dimmesdale, is destroyed by his hidden sins.

George Bancroft did for American history what novelists like Cooper did for American literature. A prominent Jacksonian, Bancroft set out to capture in writing the unique nature of the American experience. His history of the United States from the first settlement of the continent through the American Revolution eventually filled ten volumes, published between 1834 and 1874. From Bancroft's perspective, Jacksonian democracy was the perfect form for human government and was the product of the complex history of the American nation. Focusing on strong leaders who carried out the work of liberty's providence, Bancroft made clear that the middle-class qualities of individualism, self-sufficiency, and a passionate love of liberty were the essence of American history and of the American genius. Bancroft's history became the definitive work of its kind, influencing generations of American students and scholars in their interpretations of the nation's past.

The drive to celebrate American scenes and the young nation's uniqueness also influenced the visual arts during this period. **Neoclassicism** had dominated the art scene during the late eighteenth century and first decades of the nineteenth. Influenced by Enlightenment rationalism, neoclassical artists brought to their painting and sculpture the simple, logical lines found in Greek and Roman art. They often used classical imagery in their portrayals of contemporary figures and events. Horatio Greenough's statue of George Washington, for example, presented the nation's first president wrapped in a toga and looking like the Greek god Zeus.

After 1825, however, classical scenes were gradually being replaced by American ones. Thomas Cole, a British immigrant painter who arrived in the United States in 1818, was the dominant force in this movement. Cole studied art in Philadelphia but became disenchanted with the neoclassical training he was receiving and began traveling into the American interior. He fell in love with the landscapes he saw in the Hudson River valley, and he painted exaggeratedly beautiful renderings of these locales. The refreshing naturalness and Americanness of Cole's landscapes attracted a large following, and other artists took up the style. This group of landscapists is known as the **Hudson River school,** after the area where most of its members painted.

Another movement in American art that reflected the temper of the time is exemplified by the paintings of George Caleb Bingham. Bingham was born in Virginia and educated for a time in Pennsylvania before he went west to Missouri. There, he painted realistic pictures of common people engaged in everyday activities. The flatboatmen, marketplace-dwellers, and electioneering politicians in Bingham's paintings were artistic testimony to the emerging democratic style of America in the Jacksonian period (see photos on pages 288 and 298).

Culture Among Workers and Slaves

Most genteel people in the antebellum era would have denied that working people, whether the wage-earning immigrants in northern cities or slaves in the South, had a culture. But each of these groups crafted viable cultures that suited their living and working conditions and were distinct from the genteel culture of their owners or supervisors.

Wretched living conditions and dispiriting poverty encouraged working-class people in northern cities to choose social and cultural outlets that were very different from those of upper- and middle-class Americans. Offering temporary relief from unpleasant conditions, drinking was the social distraction of choice among working people. Whiskey and gin were cheap and available during the 1820s and 1830s as western farmers used the new roads and canals to ship distilled spirits to urban markets. In the 1830s, consumers could purchase a gallon of whiskey for 25 cents.

Even activities that did not center on drinking tended to involve it. While genteel and middle-class people remained in their private homes reading Sigourney or Hawthorne, working people attended

neoclassicism A revival in architecture and art in the eighteenth and nineteenth centuries inspired by Greek and Roman models and characterized by order, symmetry, and simplicity of style.

Hudson River school The first native school of landscape painting in the United States (1825–1875); it attracted artists rebelling against the neoclassical tradition.

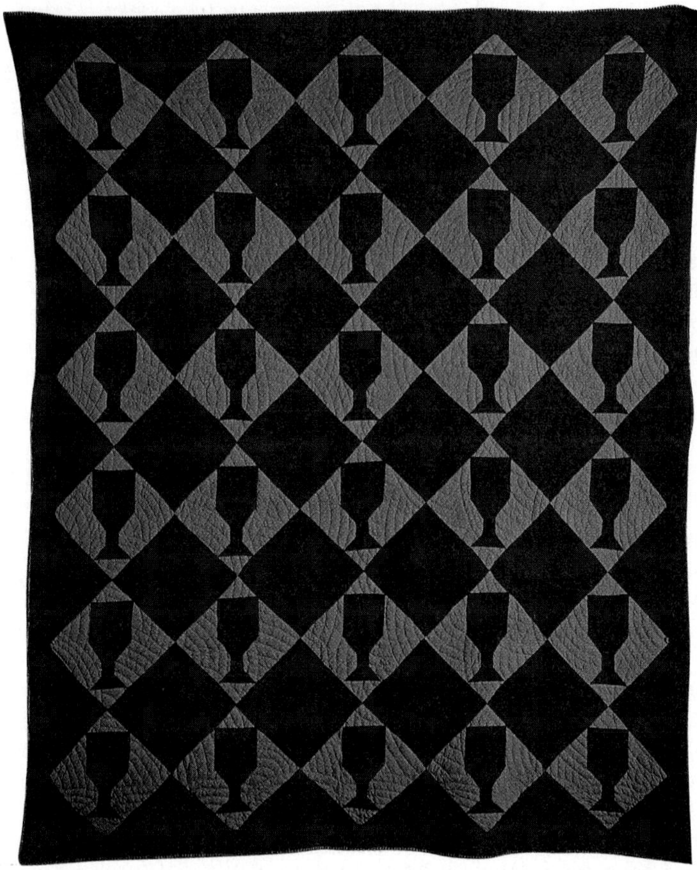

♦ Slaves were often gifted craft workers, blending African traditions with European and American ones. These two artifacts were both crafted by slaves before the Civil War. The reed basket suggests the survival of African crafting techniques, while the quilt adopts European design motifs and methods. *Museum of the Confederacy; The American Museum in Britain. Photo Courtesy of the Museum of the Confederacy.*

popular theaters that put on entertainments designed to appeal specifically to them. **Minstrel shows** featured fast-paced music and raucous comedy. Plays, such as Benjamin Baker's *A Glance at New York in 1848,* depicted caricatures of working-class "Bowery B'hoys" and "G'hals" and of the well-off Broadway "pumpkins" they poked fun at. To put the audience in the proper mood, theater owners sold cheap drinks in the lobby or in basement pubs. Alcohol was usually also sold at sporting events that drew large working-class audiences—bare-knuckle boxing contests, for instance, where the fighting was seldom confined to the boxing ring.

Stinging from their low status in the urbanizing and industrializing society, angry about living in hovels, and freed from inhibitions by hours of drinking, otherwise rational workingmen often pummeled one another to let off steam. And in working-class neighborhoods, where police forces were small, fistfights often turned into brawls and then into the riots described earlier, pitting Protestants against Catholics, immigrants against the native-born, and whites against blacks.

Working-class women experienced the same dull but dangerous working conditions and dismal living circumstances as working-class men, but their lives were even harder. Single women were particularly bad off. They were paid significantly less than men but had to pay as much and sometimes more for living quarters, food, and clothing. Marriage could reduce a woman's personal expenses—but at a cost. While men congregated in the barbershop or candy store drinking and socializing during their leisure hours, married women were stuck in tiny apartments caring for children and doing household chores. Adding insult to injury, social convention banned women from many activities that provided their husbands, boyfriends, and sons some relief.

Like their northern counterparts, slaves fashioned for themselves a rich culture that helped them

minstrel show A variety show in which white actors made up as blacks presented jokes, songs, dances, and comic skits.

survive and maintain their humanity under inhumane conditions. The degree to which African practices endured in America is remarkable, for slaves seldom came to southern plantations directly from Africa. That many African practices were passed on from one generation to another demonstrates the strength of slave families, religion, and folklore. What evolved was a truly unique African-American culture.

Traces of African heritage were visible in slaves' clothing, entertainment, and folkways. Often the plain garments that masters provided were upgraded with colorful head scarves and other decorations similar to those worn in Africa. Hairstyles often resembled those characteristic of African tribes. Music, dancing, and other forms of public entertainment and celebration also showed strong African roots. Musical instruments were copies of traditional ones, modified only by the use of New World materials. Other links to Africa abounded. Healers among the slaves used African ceremonies, Christian rituals, and both imported and native herbs to effect cures. Taken together, these survivals and adaptations of African traditions provided a strong base on which blacks erected a solid African-American culture.

Strong family ties helped to make possible this cultural continuity. Slave families endured despite family ties made fragile by their highly precarious life. Husbands and wives could be sold to different owners or be separated at the whim of a master, and children could be taken away from their parents. Families that remained intact, however, remained stable. When families did suffer separation, the **extended family** of grandparents, uncles, aunts, and other relatives offered emotional support and helped maintain some sense of continuity.

Despite the extended-family structure, which had probably been common in Africa, relationships within slave families closely resembled relationships among white families. As in southern white families, black women, when not laboring at the assigned tasks of plantation work, generally performed domestic work and tended children while the men hunted, fished, did carpentry, and performed other "manly" tasks. Children were likely to help out by tending family gardens and doing other light work until they were old enough to join their parents in the fields or learn skilled trades.

Slaves' religion also resembled the religion of southern whites, but religion, like family structure, was another means for preserving unique African-American traits. White churches virtually ignored the religious needs of slaves before the mid-eighteenth century. During the Great Awakening (see page 101), however, many white evangelicals turned their attention to the spiritual life of slaves. "Your Negroes may be ignorant and stupid as to divine Things," evangelical Samuel Davies told slaveowners, "not for Want of Capacity, but for Want of Instruction; not through their Perverseness, but through your Negligence." In the face of slaveowners' negligence, evangelical Presbyterians, Baptists, and Methodists took it upon themselves to carry the Christian message to slaves.

The Christianity that slaves practiced resembled the religion practiced by southern whites but also differed from it in many ways. Slave preachers untrained in white theology often equated Christian and African religious figures, creating unique African-American religious symbols. Ceremonies too combined African practices like group dancing with Christian prayer. The joining of African musical forms with Christian lyrics gave rise to a new form of Christian music: the **spiritual.** Masters often encouraged such worship, thinking that the Christian emphasis on obedience and meekness would make slaves better and more peaceful servants. Some, however, discouraged religion among their slaves, fearing that large congregations of slaves might be moved to rebellion. Thus some religious slaves had to meet in secret to practice their own particular form of Christianity.

Radical Attempts to Regain Community

To many of all classes, society seemed to be spinning out of control as modernization rearranged basic lifestyles during the antebellum period. Some religious groups and social thinkers tried to ward off the excesses of Jacksonian individualism by forming communities that experimented with various living arrangements and ideological commitments. They hoped to strike a new balance between self-sufficiency and community support. **Brook Farm,** a

extended family A family group consisting of various close relatives as well as the parents and children.

spiritual A religious folksong originated by African Americans, often expressing a longing for deliverance from the constraints and hardships of their lives.

Brook Farm An experimental farm based on cooperative living; established in 1841, it first attracted transcendentalists and then serious farmers before fire destroyed it in 1845.

commune near Boston founded in 1841 by transcendentalist George Ripley, was such a community.

Born and raised an avid evangelical, Ripley brought to transcendentalism the zeal that he had once felt for Calvinism. Like his friend and associate Henry David Thoreau, Ripley was not satisfied simply to contemplate transcendentalist principles. He said that his goal in establishing Brook Farm was to "prepare a society of liberal, intelligent and cultivated persons, whose relations with each other would permit a more wholesome and simple life than can be led amidst the pressure of our competitive institutions." The enterprise was set up as a joint-stock company: its twenty-four shares of stock sold for $500 a share. Each member was expected to work on the farm in an attempt to make the group self-sufficient.

During the commune's opening years, few people actually lived at the site full time, though Nathaniel Hawthorne lived there for six months. Most of the members and the intellectuals who, like Ralph Waldo Emerson, dropped in from time to time, had outside sources of income. This changed somewhat in 1844 when Ripley adopted a new constitution based on the **socialist** ideas of Frenchman Charles Fourier. **Fourierism** emphasized community self-sufficiency, the equal sharing of earnings among members of the community, and the distribution of tasks and status to prevent boredom and elitism. With this new disciplined ideology in place, Brook Farm began to appeal to serious artisans and farmers, but a disastrous fire in 1845 cut the experiment short.

Brook Farm was not the only Fourierist community founded during this period. Nearly a hundred such organizations sprang up from Massachusetts to Michigan. None was as visible as Brook Farm or populated by such talented members, and each ended in failure.

The same fate befell utopian experiments by Robert Owen. Owen, a wealthy Welsh industrialist, had come to believe that the solution to poverty in modern society was to collect the unemployed into self-contained and self-supporting villages. In 1825, he purchased a tract of land on the Wabash River in Indiana from a failed agricultural commune called **New Harmony.** At New Harmony, Owen tried to realize his scheme by opening a textile factory in which ownership was held communally and decisions were made by group consensus. Even though the community instituted innovations like an eight-hour workday, cultural activities for workers, and the nation's first school offering equal education to boys and girls, New Harmony did not succeed. Owen and his son, Robert Dale Owen, were outspoken critics of organized religion and joined their close associate Frances (Fanny) Wright in advocating birth control, women's rights, and other untraditional causes. These activities made the Owens unpopular with more traditional Americans, and when their mill experienced economic hardship in 1827, they were forced to close the community.

Other communal experiments were grounded in various religious beliefs. The **Oneida Community,** established in central New York in 1848, for example, reflected the notions of its founder, John Humphrey Noyes. Though educated in theology at Andover and Yale, Noyes could find no church willing to ordain him, because of his strange beliefs: that Christ had already returned to earth and commanded his followers to escape sin through faith in God, communal living, and group marriage. Unlike Brook Farm and New Harmony, the Oneida Community was very successful financially, establishing thriving logging, farming, and manufacturing businesses. It was finally dissolved as the result of local pressures directed at the "free love" practiced by its members.

Economically successful communes operated by the **Shakers,** an offshoot of the Quakers, avoided the Oneida Community's problems by banning sex altogether. By 1826 there were eighteen Shaker communities in eight states. Throughout the Jacksonian era

socialist Practicing socialism, the public ownership of manufacturing, farming, and other forms of production so that they benefit society rather than create individual profit.

Fourierism Social system advanced by Charles Fourier, who argued that people were capable of living in perfect harmony under the right conditions, which included communal life and republican government.

New Harmony Utopian community that Robert Owen established in Indiana in 1825; economic problems and discord among members led to its failure two years later.

Oneida Community A religious community established in central New York in 1848; its members shared property, practiced group marriage, and reared children under communal care.

Shakers A mid-eighteenth-century offshoot of the Quakers; Shakers practiced communal living and strict celibacy.

♦ On one of his western tours, artist Karl Bodmer paused to paint this view of New Harmony, Welsh philanthropist Robert Owen's experimental utopian community in Indiana. Like many similar communities, this peaceful commune was destroyed by a combination of internal dissention and pressure from suspicious and often jealous outsiders. *"View of New Harmony" by Karl Bodmer, 1833. Maximilian-Bodmer Collection, Joslyn Art Museum.*

and after, the Shakers established communal farms and grew to a population of nearly six thousand. The Shaker communities succeeded by pursuing farming activities and the manufacture and sale of furniture and handcrafts admired for their design and workmanship. But rules of celibacy spelled their end. Shaker survival depended totally on the conversion of outsiders, and celibacy surely put off some potential converts. After 1860, the Shaker movement slowly ground to a halt, dying out completely in the first half of the twentieth century.

Most successful at joining the religious fervor of the Second Great Awakening with the inclination to communalism was a peculiarly American movement founded by **Joseph Smith, Jr.**, a New York farmer. Smith's story is surrounded by a haze of religious enthusiasm and myth, but he claimed to have made a great discovery sometime during 1827. He reported that an angel named Moroni had confronted him and led him to a set of golden plates inscribed in a strange hieroglyphic language. Smith and a series of secretaries worked for nearly two years to translate the writing on the plates. The result of their effort was the Book of Mormon, printed and available for purchase in 1830.

Although the Book of Mormon greatly resembled the books of the Old Testament and purported to be a truly ancient document, it captured many of the themes that most appealed to Americans during the restless Jacksonian era. In line with Romantic literature, the Book of Mormon appealed to a mythic past. In adventure passages that rival Cooper's, Smith's testament traces the history of America back to the migrations of several Old World groups during biblical times. According to the Book of Mormon, one group, the Lamanites, sank into barbarity and became the forefathers of the American Indians. Another group, the Nephites, tried to return the

Joseph Smith, Jr. Founder of the Church of Jesus Christ of Latter-Day Saints, also known as the Mormon church, its members called Mormons; he transcribed the Book of Mormon and led his congregation westward from New York to Illinois. He was later murdered by an anti-Mormon mob.

Lamanites to the true religion but was unsuccessful and nearly destroyed by the Lamanites. Finally, according to Smith's account, there were only two Nephites left: Mormon and his son Moroni. In the year 384, they buried the golden plates chronicling America's hidden past and its place in God's unfolding plan for the universe. Moroni, in the form of an angel, waited for a true spiritual descendant to whom he might reveal the plates and their truths. Smith proclaimed that he was that descendant.

In 1830, Smith founded the Church of Jesus Christ of Latter-Day Saints—also called the Mormon church, after the prophet Mormon. Announcing that he had experienced a revelation that called for him to establish a community "on the borders by the Lamanites," Smith led his congregation as a unit out of New York in 1831 to settle in the northeastern Ohio village of Kirtland. There the people known as Mormons thrived for a while, stressing notions of community, faith, and hard work. The Mormons tended to be clannish, however, keeping to themselves and excluding others, making outsiders suspicious of them despite their laudable principles. In addition, non-Mormons were jealous of the tight discipline and industriousness that made the Mormon community more prosperous than most surrounding farms and villages.

In the aftermath of the Panic of 1837, economic pressure, internal dissension, and religious persecution convinced Smith to lead his followers farther west into Missouri. There too the Mormons faced serious resentment from frontiersmen. Smith then decided to lead his congregation to the Illinois frontier, founding the city of Nauvoo in 1840. Continuing conversions to the new faith brought a flood of Mormons to Smith's Zion in Illinois, and in 1844, Nauvoo, with a population of fifteen thousand Mormons, dwarfed every other Illinois city.

The Whig Alternative to Jacksonian Democracy

- What expectations did Jackson's opponents have when they built their coalition to oppose the Democrats?
- Was the outcome what they expected? Why or why not?

The rapidly changing character of the nation also had an impact in political circles. Although Andrew Jackson was quite possibly the most popular president since George Washington, not all Americans agreed with his philosophy, policies, or political style. As the Bank War illustrates (see page 300), men like Henry Clay and Daniel Webster, who inherited the crumbling structure of Jefferson's Republican party, continually opposed Jackson in and out of Congress but seemed unable to overcome sectional differences enough to challenge Jackson's enormous national power. Gradually, however, anger over Jackson's policies and anxiety about change allowed dissidents to combine into a new national party.

The End of the Old Party Structure

Eighteen thirty-two was a landmark year in the nation's political history. In the course of that single year, the Seminoles declared war on the United States, Jackson declared war on the Second Bank, South Carolina declared war on the binding power of the Constitution, and the Cherokees waged a continuing struggle in and out of court to hold on to their lands. The presidential election that year reflected the air of political crisis.

Henry Clay had started the Bank War for the purpose of creating a political cause to rally Jackson's opponents. The problem was that Jackson's enemies were deeply divided among themselves. Clay opposed Jackson because the president refused to support the American System (see page 274) and used every tool at his disposal to attack Clay's economic policies. Southern politicians like Calhoun, however, feared and hated Clay's nationalistic policies as much as they did Jackson's assertions of federal power. And political outsiders like the Antimasons distrusted all political organizations. These divisions were clear in the 1832 election.

The Antimasons (see page 288) kicked off the anti-Jackson campaign in September 1831 when they held a national nominating convention in Baltimore. Thurlow Weed's skillful political manipulation had pulled in a wide range of people who were disgusted with what Jefferson had called "political party tricks," and the convention drew a national constituency. Using all his charm and influence, Weed cajoled the convention into nominating William Wirt, a respected lawyer from Maryland, as its presidential candidate.

Weed and Wirt fully expected that when the Republicans met in convention later in the year, they would rubber-stamp the Antimasonic nomination and present a united front against Jackson. But the Republicans, fearful of the Antimasons' odd combination of **machine politics** and antiparty philosophy, nominated Clay as their standard-bearer. The party then issued a formal **platform,** a ringing document supporting Clay's economic ideas and attacking Jackson's use of the spoils system.

Even having two anti-Jackson parties in the running did not satisfy some. Distrustful of the Antimasons and hating Clay's nationalist philosophy, southerners in both parties refused to support any of the candidates. They finally backed nullification advocate John Floyd of Virginia.

Lack of unity spelled disaster for Jackson's opponents. Wirt and Floyd received votes that might have gone to Clay. But even if Clay had gotten those votes, Jackson's popularity and the political machinery that he and Van Buren controlled would have given the victory to Jackson. The president was re-elected with a total of 219 electoral votes to Clay's 49, Wirt's 7, and Floyd's 11. Jackson's party lost five seats in the Senate but gained six in the House of Representatives. Despite unsettling changes in the land and continuing political chaos, the people still wanted the hero of New Orleans as their leader.

♦ Calling themselves Whigs after the English political party that opposed royal authority, Henry Clay, John C. Calhoun, and Daniel Webster joined forces to oppose what they characterized as Andrew Jackson's kingly use of power. This lithograph from 1834 depicting Jackson in royal dress stepping on the Constitution expresses their view quite vividly. *Tennessee Historical Society.*

The New Political Coalition

If one lesson emerged clearly from the election of 1832, it was that Jackson's opponents needed to pull together if they expected to challenge the growing power of King Andrew. Imitating political organizations in Great Britain, Clay and his associates began calling Jackson supporters Tories—supporters of the king—and calling themselves Whigs. The antimonarchial label stuck, and the new party formed in 1834 was called the **Whig party.**

The Whigs eventually absorbed all the major factions that opposed Jackson. At the heart of the party were Clay supporters: advocates of strong government and the American System in economics. The nullifiers in the South, however, quickly came around. Late in 1832, Clay and Calhoun had found themselves on the same side in opposing Jackson's appointment of Van Buren as American minister to England. Joining forces, the two led the Senate in rejecting Van Buren's appointment. This successful campaign, combined with Calhoun's growing awareness that Jackson was perhaps more dangerous to his constituents' interests than was Clay, led the southerner and his associates back into Clay's camp.

As the congressional elections of 1834 approached, the Antimasons also joined the Whig coalition. Disgusted by Jackson's use of patronage and back-alley politics—not to mention the fact that the president was a Mason—they overcame their distrust of Clay's party philosophy. A final major group to rally with the Whigs was the collection of Christian reformers whose campaigns to eliminate alcohol, violations of the Sabbath, and dozens of

machine politics The aggressive use of influence, favors, and tradeoffs by a political organization, or "machine," to mobilize support among its followers.

platform A formal statement of the principles, policies, and promises on which a political party bases its appeal to the public.

Whig party Political party that came into being in 1834 as an anti-Jackson coalition and that charged "King Andrew" with executive tyranny.

other perceived evils had become increasingly political during the opening years of the 1830s. Evangelicals disapproved of Jackson's personal lifestyle, his views on slavery, his Indian policy, and his refusal to involve government in their moral causes. The orderly and sober society that Clay and the Whigs envisioned appealed to such people.

The congressional elections proved the new Whig coalition's ability to unseat Jacksonian Democrats. In their first electoral contest, the Whigs won nearly 40 percent of the seats in the House of Representatives and more than 48 percent in the Senate.

Van Buren in the White House

Jackson had seemed to be a tower of strength when he was first elected to the presidency in 1828, but he was aging and ill by the end of his second term. Nearly 70 years old and plagued by various ailments, Old Hickory decided to follow Washington's example and not run for a third term. Instead, Jackson used all the power and patronage at his command to ensure that Martin Van Buren would win the presidential nomination at the Democratic party's convention.

Meanwhile, Clay and his Whig associates were hatching a plot to deny the election to the Democrat. Instead of holding a convention and thrashing out a platform, the Whigs let each region's party organization nominate its own candidates. As a result, four **favorite sons** ran on the Whig ticket. Daniel Webster of Massachusetts represented the Northeast. Hugh Lawson White, a Tennessean and former Jackson supporter, and South Carolina nullifier W. P. Mangum each claimed to represent the South and Southwest. William Henry Harrison, former governor of Indiana Territory and victor at the Battle of Tippecanoe in 1811 (see page 254), represented the Northwest. Whig leaders, especially experienced political manipulator Thurlow Weed, hoped the large number of candidates would confuse voters and throw the election into the House of Representatives, where skillful political management might unseat the Democrats.

Weed was partially right, but he underestimated the Democrats' hold on the minds of the voters. Van Buren captured 765,483 popular votes—more than Jackson had won in the previous election. But his performance in the Electoral College was significantly weaker than Jackson's had been. Van Buren squeaked by with a winning margin of less than 1 percent, but it was a victory, and the presidential election did not go to the House of Representatives. House Democrats lost thirty-seven seats to Whigs. In the Senate, however, Democrats increased their majority to more than 62 percent. Even with that slight edge, Van Buren could expect trouble getting Democratic policies through Congress.

Van Buren was undoubtedly a political genius, but he was not the charismatic character Jackson had been, and people never really warmed to him. His reputation suffered a blow just weeks after he took office, when the economy collapsed.

The Panic of 1837 was a direct outcome of the Bank War and Jackson's money policies, but it was Van Buren who shouldered the blame. The crisis had begun with Nicholas Biddle's manipulation of credit and interest rates in an effort to discredit Jackson and have the Second Bank rechartered in spite of the president's veto (see page 300). Jackson had added to the problem by removing paper money and credit from the economy in an effort to win support from hard-money advocates. Arguing that he wanted to end "the monopoly of the public lands in the hands of speculators and capitalists," Jackson had issued the **Specie Circular** on August 15, 1836. From that day forward, the Circular ordered, payment for public land had to be made in specie.

The contraction in credit and currency had the same impact in 1837 as in 1819: the national economy collapsed. By May 1837, New York banks were no longer accepting any paper currency, and soon all banks had adopted the policy of accepting specie only. Unable to pay back or collect loans, buy raw materials, or conduct any other sort of commerce, hundreds of businesses, plantations, farms, factories, canals, and other enterprises were thrown into bankruptcy by the end of the year. More than a third of the population was thrown out of work, and people who were fortunate enough to keep their jobs found their pay reduced by as much as 50 percent. Fledgling industries and labor organizations were cast into disarray, and the nation sank into both an economic and an emotional depression.

As credit continued to collapse through 1838 and 1839, President Van Buren tried to address the prob-

favorite son A candidate nominated for office by delegates from his or her own region or state.

Specie Circular Order issued by President Jackson in 1836 stating that the federal government would accept only specie—gold and silver—as payment for public land.

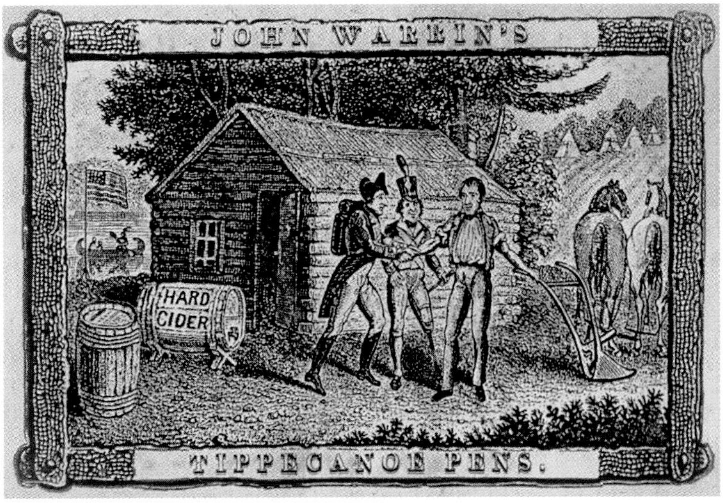

♦ The presidential election in 1840 was a contest between images more than a contest between men. The Whig pull-card (left) shows Van Buren sipping champagne and grinning, but when the tab is pulled, he drinks some of Harrison's plain hard cider and grimaces. On the right, an advertising card shows the imaginary Harrison outside a log cabin with a huge barrel of hard cider in front. *(left) Smithsonian Institution; (right) Collection of David J. and Janet L. Frent.*

lems but only made them worse. His first mistake was to extend Jackson's hard-money policy, which caused the economy to contract further. Then, in an effort to keep the government solvent, Van Buren cut federal spending to the bone, shrinking the money supply even more. Then, to replace the stabilizing influence lost when the Second Bank was destroyed, he created a national treasury system endowed with many of the powers formerly wielded by the bank. But he did not deposit federal specie in state and regional banks, which would have circulated it into the regional economies. Instead, he established regional treasury offices that would accept only hard money as payment for federal lands and other obligations and from which federal expenses and debts were to be paid. The result was to suck hard currency out of local banks and local economies. The treasury system, which Congress finally approved on the eve of the presidential election in 1840, became the last nail in the political coffin of Martin Van Buren.

Log-Cabin and Hard-Cider Campaign of 1840

The Whigs had learned their lesson in the election of 1836: only a unified party could possibly destroy the political machine built by Jackson and Van Buren. As the nation sank into depression, the Whigs lined up behind a single candidate for the 1840 election, determined to use whatever means were necessary to destroy the Democrats' grip on the voters.

Once again, Henry Clay hoped to be the party's nominee, but Thurlow Weed convinced the party that William Henry Harrison would have a better chance in the election. Weed chose Harrison because of his distinguished military record and because the general, who had been a political lion thirty years earlier (see page 251), had been out of the public eye for a long time and had few enemies left. For Harrison's running mate, the party chose **John Tyler,** a Virginia senator who had bolted from Jackson's Democratic party during the Bank War. Weed clearly hoped that the Virginian would draw votes from the planter South while Harrison drew support from the West and North.

Although the economy was in bad shape, the Whig campaign avoided addressing any serious issues. Instead, the Whigs launched a smear campaign against Van Buren. He was in fact the son of a

John Tyler Virginia senator who left the Democratic party after conflicts with Andrew Jackson; he was elected vice president in 1840 and became president when Harrison died.

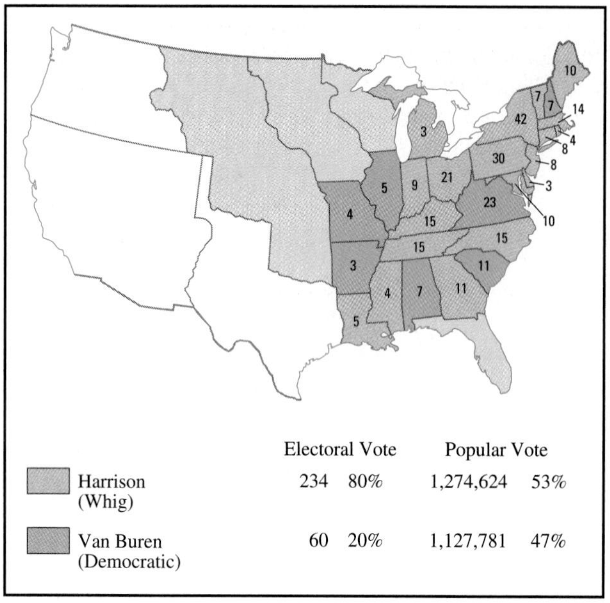

♦ **MAP 12.2 Election of 1840** Although the difference in popular votes between William Henry Harrison and Martin Van Buren was small in the election of 1840, Harrison won a landslide victory in the Electoral College. This map shows why. After floundering through several elections, the Whig party was finally able to organize a national coalition, giving it solid victories in all of the most populous regions of the country. Only the far west, which was still sparsely settled, voted as a bloc for Van Buren.

tavernkeeper, but the Whig press portrayed him as an aristocrat whose expensive tastes in clothes, food, and furniture were signs of dangerous excess during an economic depression. Harrison, in contrast, actually had been born into the Virginia aristocracy, but the Whigs played on the Romantic themes so popular among their genteel and middle-class constituents by characterizing him as a simple frontiersman who had risen to greatness through his own efforts. Whig claims were so extravagant that the Democratic press soon satirized Harrison in political cartoons showing a rustic hick rocking on the porch of a log cabin and swilling hard cider. The satire backfired. Whig newspapers and speechmakers seized on the image and sold Harrison, the longtime political insider, as a simple man of the people who truly lived in a log cabin. At campaign rallies, Whigs passed out cider to voters.

Van Buren had little with which to retaliate. Harrison had a fairly clean and certainly a distinguished political and military career behind him. Tyler too was well respected. And Van Buren had simply not done a good job of addressing the nation's pressing economic needs. Voters, from former Antimasons to Christian reformers, cried out for change, and Van Buren could not offer them one. The combination of political dissatisfaction and hype brought the biggest voter turnout to that time in American history: nearly twice as many voters came to the polls in 1840 as had done so in 1836.

Although Harrison won only 53 percent of the popular vote, he claimed nearly 80 percent of the electoral votes and swept out of his log cabin and into the White House (see Map 12.2).

SUMMARY

Expectations
Constraints
Choices
Outcomes

William Henry Harrison inherited an excitingly dynamic and deeply troubled country from outgoing president Martin Van Buren. Economic *constraints* triggered by Andrew Jackson's unwise choice in issuing the Specie Circular were worsened by Van Buren's in revamping the treasury system, and both were compounded by Nicholas Biddle's malevolence. The new party system that emerged promised great excitement and political sport but not much in the way of solutions. Still, Americans must have had great *expectations* from the new politics: nearly twice as many men made the *choice* to vote in the 1840 election as had done so in any other presidential contest.

This outcome came on top of a number of other *choices* Americans made in response to the many unsettling changes that had been taking place as part of the great transformation. Different economic classes responded by creating their own cultures and by choosing specific strategies for dealing with anxiety. Some chose violent protest, some passive resistance. Some looked to heaven for solutions and others to earthly utopias. And out of this complex swirl of new *expectations* and *constraints*, something entirely new and unexpected emerged. The *outcome* was a new America, on its way to being socially, politically, intellectually, and culturally modern.

In the election of 1840, a man who had become a national figure by fighting against Indian sovereignty and for westward expansion swept a new sentiment into national politics. Increasingly Americans shared the *expectation* that the West would provide the solutions to the problems raised by the great transformation. In the short term, the *outcome* was an exciting race by Americans toward the Pacific. But new *constraints* pared down available *choices*, propelling the nation toward a sectional crisis.

SUGGESTED READINGS

Eugene D. Genovese. *From Rebellion to Revolution: Afro-American Slave Revolts in the Making of the Modern World* (1979).

Although it focuses somewhat narrowly on confrontation, as opposed to more subtle forms of resistance, this study traces the emergence of African American political organization from its roots in antebellum slave revolts.

Karen Haltunen. *Confidence Men and Painted Women: A Study of Middle-Class Culture in America, 1830–1870* (1982).

A wonderfully well researched study of an emerging class defining and shaping itself in the evolving world of early-nineteenth-century urban space.

Edward Pessen. *Most Uncommon Jacksonians: The Radical Leaders of the Early Labor Movement* (1967).

A look at early labor movements and reform by one of America's leading radical scholars.

Anthony F.C. Wallace. *Rockdale: The Growth of an American Village in the Early Industrial Revolution* (1978).

A noted anthropologist's reconstruction of a mill town and the various class, occupational, and gender cultures that developed there during its transition from a traditional village to a mill town.

Ronald G. Walters. *American Reformers, 1815–1860* (1978).

The best overview of the reform movements and key personalities who guided them during this difficult period in American history.

Sean Wilentz. *Chants Democratic: New York City and the Rise of the American Working Class, 1788–1850* (1984).

An insightful view of working-class culture and politics in the dynamic setting of Erie Canal era New York City.

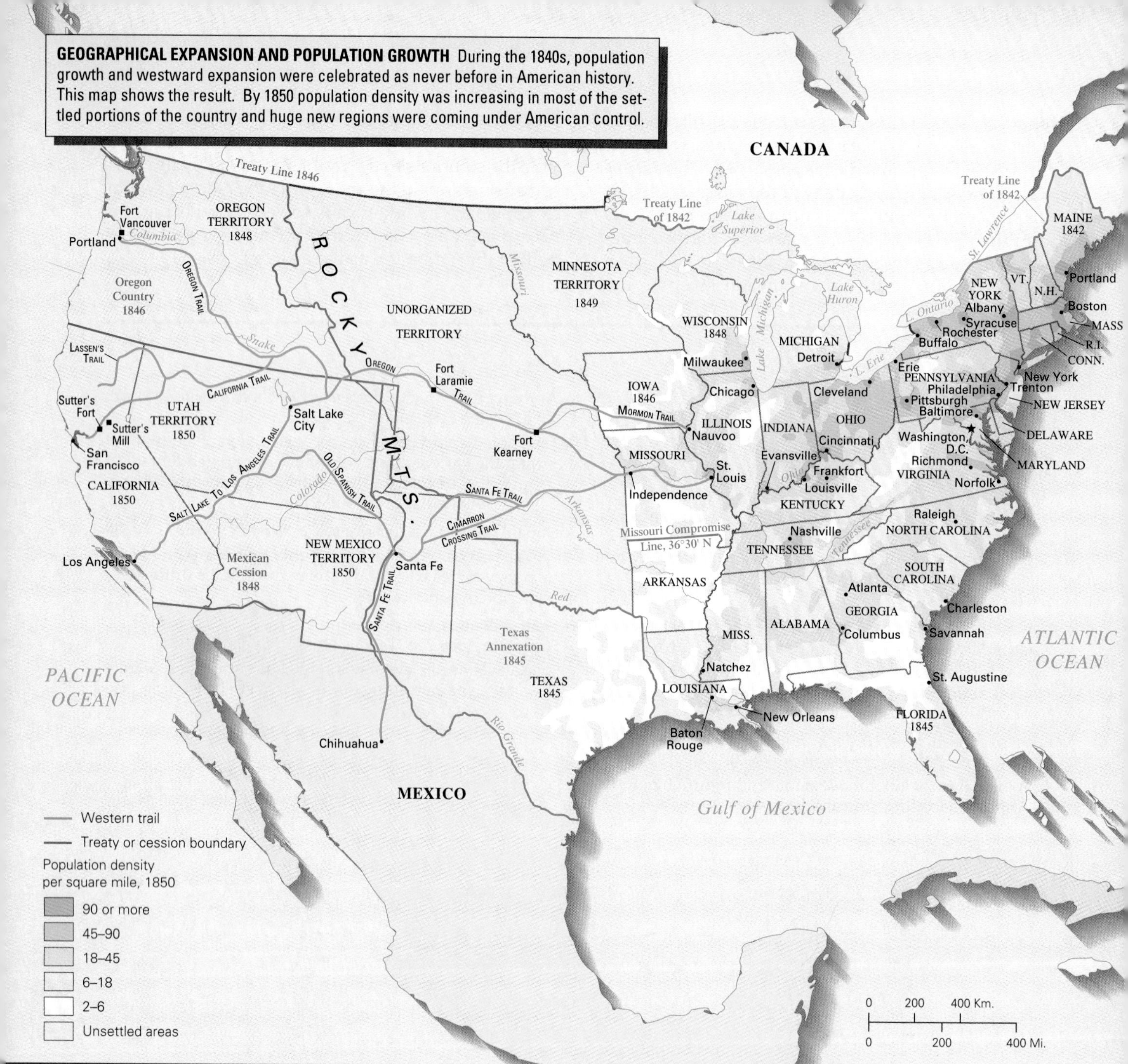

GEOGRAPHICAL EXPANSION AND POPULATION GROWTH During the 1840s, population growth and westward expansion were celebrated as never before in American history. This map shows the result. By 1850 population density was increasing in most of the settled portions of the country and huge new regions were coming under American control.

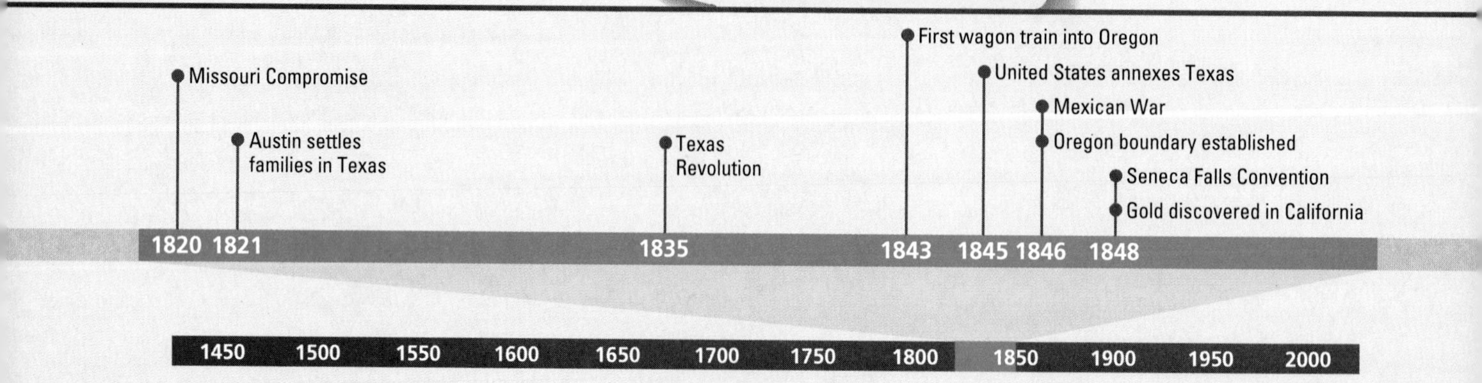

CHAPTER 13

Westward Expansion and Manifest Destiny, 1841–1849

The Explosion Westward

- What expectations pulled Americans westward between 1820 and 1848?

The Social Fabric in the West

- In what ways did constraints in the West force people to adapt? What were the cultural outcomes?

The Triumph of "Manifest Destiny"

- What expectations contributed to the concept of manifest destiny?
- Did choices by American settlers in Oregon and Texas reflect those expectations? Why or why not?

Expansion and Sectional Crisis

- How did expansionist and economic expectations shape Americans' positions on slavery in the 1840s?

INTRODUCTION

E xpectations
C onstraints
C hoices
O utcomes

The election of William Henry Harrison to the presidency in 1840 was but one milestone in a progressive westward tilt in the nation's political and cultural focus. As transportation systems extended the American frontier, and as industrialization generated new capital, adventurous speculators *chose* to invest in the newly opened West. Americans looking for economic opportunities, places to transplant particular religious or political beliefs, or simply adventure quickly followed those entrepreneurs. They *expected* to find a wide open land of opportunity.

But men and women moving into the West faced many *constraints.* The land itself was often not what they expected. Water was frequently in short supply, and wild animals were a constant threat to crops and livestock. In addition, most of the land in the West was already claimed, either by Indians or by the Spanish, British, and other Europeans. What the United States considered its "right" of ownership did not go unchallenged.

Environmental and cultural *constraints* forced most pioneers to adapt. The *outcome* was the creation of new societies. Mormon farmers in the deserts of Utah, for example, had to learn to cooperate with each other in building irrigation systems. Pioneers in the Southwest had to learn about the Spanish language and culture.

While western pioneers were changing and being changed by the lands to which they migrated, expansion itself was bringing great pressure to bear on the nation's political and economic institutions. Most people in the East began to entertain the *expectation* that the United States would soon encompass all of North America, but there was significant disagreement about what sorts of institutions should be planted in the new territories. Southerners viewed manifest destiny as a campaign to spread cotton agriculture. Northerners were equally convinced that a diversified entrepreneurial economy was the wave of the future. And each region had very specific notions about tariffs, taxes, money supply, and the role of the federal government in controlling or nurturing local arrangements.

Each section made the *choice* to push for its own vision of manifest destiny, but each met the *constraints* of political opposition from the other and from western environmental, cultural, and political realities. The United States fought a war with Mexico over westward expansion and then faced a national crisis over what to do with newly acquired territories. The *outcome* was a political dispute that rocked the halls of Congress and moved some to call for outright civil disobedience, perhaps even revolution.

At the core of the debate lay the issue of slavery. Although its moral implications disturbed only a handful of Americans, slavery, more than any other institution, symbolized the cultural, economic, and political differences between northerners and southerners. Independent farmers and businessmen—people who often were at risk of financial failure—feared the *constraint* of competition from wealthy southern planters. Workers felt the same way: they wondered how they could compete successfully against slave laborers. While more and more people in the North and Old Northwest *chose* to raise their voices against the expansion of slavery, southerners, for whom slavery meant the difference between large-scale profits and devastating financial losses, worked all the harder to ensure their freedom to take slaves anywhere they chose.

As the debate over slavery and expansion broadened, another group of Americans chafed under discrimination. Holding the *expectation* that they would bring morality and order to a sinful world, evangelical women had *chosen* to participate in a wide variety of reform movements, including abolitionism. With few exceptions, however, men inside and outside these movements refused to give them the political and economic voice they believed they needed to carry out their mission. Increasing frustration was the *outcome,* but some women *chose* to act, holding a national convention to protest their treatment.

CHRONOLOGY

Expansion and Crisis

1820	Missouri Compromise
1821	Stephen F. Austin settles Americans in Texas William Becknell opens the Santa Fe Trail
1831	Nez Perce and Flathead delegation asks whites to live among them
1834	Mexican government begins seizure of California mission lands
1835	Texas Revolution begins
1836	Rebellion in California against Mexican rule
1838	Senate rejects annexation of Texas Armed confrontation between Maine and New Brunswick
1839	John Sutter founds New Helvetia
1840	Split between moderates and radicals in the American Anti-Slavery Society
1841	John Tyler becomes president Congress passes pre-emption bill
1842	Elijah White named federal Indian agent for Oregon
1843	First wagon train into Oregon Oregon adopts First Organic Laws
1844	James K. Polk elected president Murder of Joseph Smith
1845	United States annexes Texas John L. O'Sullivan articulates "manifest destiny"
1846	Mexican War begins Oregon boundary established; United States and Britain end joint occupation
1847	Whitman Massacre Mormons arrive in Utah California declares itself a republic
1848	Gold discovered in California Treaty of Guadalupe Hidalgo Women's Rights Convention at Seneca Falls Zachary Taylor elected president
1855	Indians in the Pacific Northwest settled on reservations

The Explosion Westward

• What expectations pulled Americans westward between 1820 and 1848?

Ever since the Louisiana Purchase (see page 228), Americans had been moving west. This outward thrust unsettled the nation politically and economically. Western pioneers seldom sought to create new and different lifestyles for themselves, but the physical and cultural environments in the West shaped their society in peculiar ways. Thus cultures that contrasted sharply with those in the industrializing North and the plantation South emerged in the new West.

The Complicated Worlds of the West

Two views of the West, tied to Americans' earlier explorations there, dominated the popular imagination in the 1840s. One, traceable to Zebulon Pike's expedition in 1806–1807 (see page 230), envisioned the West as a "great American desert" unsuitable for habitation by any but the hardiest and most primitive Indians. The other, traceable to the Lewis and

Clark expedition, imagined a verdant region rich in resources. Common to both was the notion that the West, whether desert or paradise, was largely unoccupied: a virgin land free for the taking.

Realities in the **Far West** were much more complex than the myths suggested. Indeed, vast areas of the region had extremely dry and fragile ecologies largely unsuitable for the sort of economic exploitation nineteenth-century Americans desired. At the other extreme, some regions were so wet that their rain forests were virtually impassable by horses or vehicles without a huge investment of backbreaking labor to clear the way. And all over the West, in areas large and small, a thousand local ecologies stood between the two extremes. But nowhere was there virgin land.

For thousands of years, various Indian groups had extracted a rich living from the many different environments in the Far West. Through the twin strategies of moving from place to place and intergroup trading, Indians had taken advantage of the West's diversity, receiving what each ecological zone had to offer. This flexible approach to the complicated and often fragile ecology of the Far West provided an excellent living and did minimal damage to natural resources. As surely as Europeans did, Indians managed and exploited available resources. If the land appeared to expansionists in the United States to be unoccupied, it was only because they would not, or could not, recognize a system of land use with which they were unfamiliar.

With the arrival of Spanish, French, Russian, and other Europeans, the already complex world of intergroup relations in the West became even more complicated. Indians on the Great Plains used the mobility provided by European horses to expand not just their hunting range but also their trading range. Goods from the plains made their way regularly to Spanish settlements in New Mexico, and replacement horses, guns, and other European goods flooded northward in return (see page 50). This was the world into which early western entrepreneurs like John Jacob Astor and Auguste Chouteau had entered earlier in the century (see pages 267–268). No unexploited land or great American desert could have supported their monumental visions of an inland empire providing rare furs to genteel cosumers in Europe and in the eastern states. What both men did was to tap into an already complicated trading world, and both became extremely wealthy and influential as a result.

The image of the solitary trapper braving a hostile environment and even more hostile Indians is the stuff of American adventure novels and movies. Although characters like Christopher ("Kit") Carson and Jeremiah ("Crow Killer") Johnson really did exist and experienced many hair-raising adventures, these men were merely advance agents for an **extractive industry** geared to the efficient removal of animal pelts.

♦ In the rough-and-tumble world of the Missouri fur trade, men earned respect through ability and toughness alone. Jim Beckwourth, a former slave from Virginia, had both, and was widely recognized as one of the era's leading mountain men. *Courtesy, Colorado Historical Society.*

What drew men like Carson and Johnson into the Far West in the 1830s and 1840s was an innovation in the fur business instigated by a former Astor employee and one-time partner of Chouteau, William Henry Ashley. Taking advantage of the presence of large numbers of underemployed young men seeking fortune and adventure in the West, Ashley broke

Far West In North America, the lands west of the Mississippi River.

extractive industry An industry, such as fur trapping, logging, and mining, that removes natural resources from the environment.

♦ This painting by Alfred Jacob Miller captures the color and spirit of the annual fur rendezvous and shows the wide variety of colorful people the event brought together—not only Indians and mountain men, but sightseeing English lords like William Drummond Steward (shown here on his white horse). *Joslyn Art Museum, Omaha, Nebraska. Gift of the Enron Foundation.*

the long tradition of depending exclusively on Indian labor for collecting furs. In 1825, he set up the highly successful **rendezvous system** for collecting pelts. Under this arrangement, individual trappers—white adventurers like Carson and Johnson, free blacks like James Beckwourth, and a large number of Indians—combed the upper Missouri, trapping, curing, and packing furs. Each hunter carved out his own territory in the western Rocky Mountains and enforced his claim through a combination of mutual respect and violence. Once each year Ashley conducted a fur rendezvous in the mountains, where the trappers brought their furs and exchanged them for goods. Pioneer missionary Pierre Jean de Smet called these gatherings "great events" and "one of the most picturesque features of early frontier life in the Far West."

Ashley's, Chouteau's, and Astor's strategies for extracting wealth from the Far West were successful and made these men extremely rich and important. But the success of their complex business inadvertently led to its decline. The expansion in international commerce flowing out of the fur trade helped open the way for the importing of vast amounts of silk from Asia. Soon silk hats became a fashion rage among genteel consumers in both America and Europe, displacing the beaver hats that had consumed most American furs. In addition, the efficiency with which these gigantic organizations extracted fur from the western wilderness virtually wiped out beaver populations in the Rocky Mountains. Through the 1830s and 1840s, the beaver business slowed to a near standstill.

Many beaver hunters stayed in the West, however, becoming founding members of new communities. As early as 1840, fur trapper Robert ("Doc") Newell reportedly told his companion Joe Meek, "Come, we are all done with this life in the mountains—done with wading in Beaver-dams, and freezing or starving alternately—done with Indian trading and Indian fighting. The fur trade is dead in the Rocky Mountains, and it is no place for us now, if ever it was." The two men then headed to the Willamette Valley in Oregon to become settlers. The great captains in the fur industry came to similar conclusions, founding banks, operating mills, speculating in real estate, and financing canals and rail systems.

Often the first people to join the former fur trappers in settling the West were not rugged yeoman

rendezvous system A system in which trappers gathered furs independently in their own territories and met traders once a year to exchange the furs for goods.

farmers but highly organized and well-financed land speculators and developers. From the earliest days of the republic, federal public land policy favored those who could afford large purchases and pay in cash. Liberalization of the land laws during the first half of the nineteenth century put smaller tracts—for less money and on credit terms—within reach of more citizens, but speculators continued to play a role in land distribution by offering often even smaller tracts and more liberal credit. This was particularly true as states granted **rights-of-way,** first to canal companies and then, increasingly, to railroad developers as a way of financing internal improvements. Land along transportation routes was especially valuable, and developers could often turn an outright grant into enormous profits.

A third group of expectant fortune hunters headed into the Far West, lured by the same vision that had drawn the Spanish to the American Southwest: the discovery of gold. Since colonial times, Americans had persistently hunted precious metals, usually without much success. The promise of gold continued to draw people westward, however, onto Winnebago lands in 1827 and into Cherokee territory in 1829 (see pages 292–294). Most of these fortune hunters did not discover gold, but many of them stayed to establish trading businesses, banks, and farms. Others moved on, still seeking their fortunes. But eventually they too, for the most part, settled down to become shopkeepers, farmers, and entrepreneurs.

The Attraction of the West

Distinct waves of Americans pushed westward into the areas opened by gold seekers, trappers, and land speculators. All of these migrants were responding to promises of relatively cheap and exceptionally fertile land in America's interior. But different groups were reacting to very different conditions in the East, and those differences gave shape to their migration and to the settlements they eventually created.

The underlying cause for westward migration, as for the colonial migration that preceded it, was the hope of economic opportunity. The promise of cheap land was especially enticing after the panics of 1819 and 1837. "To make money was their chief object," one young pioneer woman in Texas commented; "all things else were subsidiary to it." Many settlers went to the Southwest to improve their fortunes by taking advantage of rising cotton prices. They hoped to become prosperous as inland planters.

Although the promise of economic opportunity pulled most people westward, many had ideological reasons for choosing to move where they did. Migrants from New England were established Yankees. Two sources of land pressure combined to uproot these descendants of the colonial Puritans. First, the long-established New England tradition of dividing family holdings equally among adult children had created a significant shortage of workable farms in the region. Second, innovations in spinning and weaving made large-scale wool processing economical, creating a new demand for this fiber. Starting after 1824 a sheep-raising craze swept New England, especially in the Connecticut River valley. Sheep required little labor but a lot of land, and people who had the capital to amass large herds soon began buying out their less fortunate neighbors. Between 1825 and 1840 sheep displaced people throughout much of the New England countryside.

Thus young people in New England faced a choice between moving into cities or moving west and trying to establish New England–style farming in new areas. Many chose the former, but a significant number opted to migrate westward. Seeking an environment friendly to their moral and religious outlook, these sons and daughters of the Puritans chose to move into areas like upper New York, Michigan, and Oregon, where Protestant missionaries were establishing little New Englands in the wilderness. One missionary organization announced "a Plymouth Colony in Oregon" as its model for western settlements.

The image of the independent frontier farmer fleeing the restrictions of civilized life and hewing out a living with an ax, a hoe, and single-minded self-sufficiency is a persistent myth in American history. Although a few antisocial sorts moved to the frontier to escape the ringing of a neighbor's ax, most people went west as part of a larger community.

Most of the migrants to Texas in the 1820s and 1830s came in large groups under the direction of men like **Stephen F. Austin** and Martin de Leon.

right-of-way The right to build highways, railroads, and other facilities that cut across land belonging to another party, such as the government.

Stephen F. Austin American colonizer in Texas and leading voice in the Texas Revolution.

♦ Shown here with his trusty dog and gun, Stephen F. Austin leans against a tree and considers the vast domain granted to him by the Spanish government. Austin was not only one of the leading landowners in Texas, but was also a leader of the Texas Revolution. *"Stephen Austin" by Brand. Archives division, Texas State Library.*

The Spanish government in Mexico gave these **empresarios** land grants and the right to assess fees in exchange for encouraging settlement in Spain's northern New World colonies. Austin's father, Moses Austin, was the first Anglo-American empresario. On January 17, 1821, Spanish authorities gave him permission to settle three hundred American families within a 200,000-acre tract between the Brazos and Colorado rivers, but they stipulated that all of the families had to be Roman Catholic or willing to convert to Catholicism.

The elder Austin died of pneumonia before he could act on his license, but his son quickly seized the opportunity by having his father's grant transferred to himself. In the aftermath of the Panic of 1819, Austin's ability to offer families large plots of land for a filing fee of only $12\frac{1}{2}$ cents an acre meant that he had no trouble finding willing settlers. "I am convinced," he exclaimed, "that I could take on fifteen hundred families as easily as three hundred if permitted to do so." He led his first overland party from Louisiana into Texas in the winter of 1821. When Mexico became independent of Spain later in the same year, Austin convinced the Mexican government to extend his license, and he continued as the region's leading empresario.

Migrants to Texas generally traveled in small-to-medium-size parties. Some of them ventured overland, and others traveled by boat. One settler, Jared E. Groce, transported an entire plantation from Georgia to Texas—fifty wagons full of personal belongings and more than a hundred slaves—but that was unusual. More typical was the experience of a young woman named Rabb. She traveled in a family group of seven adults and eight children, who found and settled with other relatives when they arrived in Texas. Even single pioneers did not remain independent on the Texas frontier very long. One young man who ventured west alone reported the need for group effort and protection. "Those of us who have no families of our own, reside with some of the families in the settlement," he commented. "We remain here notwithstanding the scarcity of provisions, to assist in protecting the settlement."

Migration to Oregon also involved group effort but followed a different pattern. The first permanent agricultural settlements in the Pacific Northwest were begun by missionaries carrying the Second Great Awakening's message of Christianity and Americanism to the Indians, who welcomed and in some cases had even invited them. In line with the notion of a "Plymouth Colony in Oregon," these missionaries encouraged mass migration to the new territory. "Who will come & possess the land, who?" Henry H. Spalding wrote from his mission station in Oregon, requesting that farmers, mechanics, and additional missionaries rush westward immediately. Missionaries all over the Northwest repeated his call, and it echoed in the religious and secular newspapers and magazines that enjoyed wide circulation during the 1830s and 1840s. Coming on the heels of the Panic of 1837, these calls appealed strongly to people eager for economic opportunity in familiar cultural surroundings. Thus, when the Methodist church issued a call for a "great reinforcement" for

empresario In the Spanish colonies, a person who organized and led a group of settlers in exchange for land grants and the right to assess fees.

♦ The men and women who crossed the continent following the Oregon Trail left behind many artifacts as evidence of their passing. The dress had been resewn and lined with a flour sack, evidence of how precious it was to its owner. The diary is one of many left behind by overland travelers, who recorded the often tedious events of the daily trek. *Henry Groskinsky.*

its mission in Oregon, it received a flood of applications, and three separate reinforcements arrived in Oregon by ship in 1840. But not until 1843 did large-scale immigration begin.

In the spring of 1843 and every spring thereafter for decades, families from all over the East gathered in Missouri to start the overland trek. "Probably there were sixty-five or seventy, or possibly more than that, wagons in our train, and hundreds of loose cattle and horses," one young woman pioneer reported, and that was just one of the wagon trains on the trail that summer. "We were not allowed to travel across the plains in any haphazard manner," she continued. "No family or individual was permitted to go off alone from the company."

Although trail life was novel for most of the Oregon-bound emigrants, the division in domestic labor remained much as it was at home. "Everybody was supposed to rise at daylight, and while the women were preparing breakfast, the men rounded up the cattle, took down the tents, yoked the oxen to the wagons and made everything ready for an immediate start after the morning meal was finished."

Even social customs remained the same. "Life on the plains was a primitive edition of life in town or village," the same pioneer woman remarked. "We were expected to visit our neighbors when we paused for rest. If we did not, we were designated as 'high-toned' or 'stuck-up.' . . . Human nature is the same the world over. Bickerings and jealousies arose just as they would have done in a settlement of the same size."

And so life went on during the six months it took to cross the more than 2,000 miles separating the settled part of the nation and the **Oregon Country.** Once in Oregon, families arriving in the wagon trains tended to settle in rings around the already-existing missions, which soon became the hubs for New England–style villages in the Pacific Northwest.

Oregon Country The region to the north of Spanish California extending from the crest of the Rocky Mountains to the Pacific Coast.

♦ With two wives and several children to help share the burden of work, this Mormon settler was in a good position to do well, even in the harsh conditions that prevailed in the near-desert environment of Utah. Sensitive to disapproval from more traditional Christians, families like this tended to associate exclusively with other Mormons and pressured outsiders to leave as quickly as possible. *Denver Public Library.*

Another migration pattern led toward the **Great Basin.** Despite their growth in numbers and prosperity, Joseph Smith's community of Mormons in Nauvoo, Illinois, continued to be victims of religious and economic persecution. On June 27, 1844, Joseph Smith was murdered by a mob in neighboring Carthage, Illinois. The remaining church leaders concluded that the Mormons would never be safe until they moved far from mainstream American civilization. **Brigham Young,** Smith's successor, decided to move his people beyond the Rocky Mountains in search of a safe refuge and led sixteen hundred Mormons out of Nauvoo. After establishing a base camp in Iowa, Young put together a contingent of 146 young men and women and set out for the Far West, laying out roads, building bridges, and planting crops so that the main body of the church could follow in comfort and safety. On July 24, 1847, Young's party finally pushed into the valley of the **Great Salt Lake.** Young immediately assigned some followers to begin an irrigation project and sent others on to California to buy livestock. The rest of the congregation soon arrived, and within a matter of weeks the Mormon community had become a thriving settlement of nearly two thousand.

Despite their differences, pioneers shared one fundamental problem: hard cash was always in short supply. Frontier farmers in every region of the West lived on a shoestring, barely making ends meet when conditions were good and falling into debt when weather or other hazards interrupted farming. Still, those who were lucky and exercised careful management were able to carve out excellent livings. Strongly centralized authority and a deeply felt sense of community helped the Mormons, for example, to overcome even bad luck and deficient skills. Many in other communities, however, had their land repossessed for debts or had to sell out for enough cash to pay off creditors. Pulling up stakes again, they often moved to new lands exhausted of furs and opened to settlement by merchant-adventurers and Indian agents.

Many pioneers had no legal claim to their lands. People bankrupted by unscrupulous speculators or by their own bad luck or poor management often settled wherever they could find land that seemed unoccupied. Thousands of squatters living on unsold federal lands were a problem for the national government when the time came to sell off the public domain. Always with an eye to winning votes, western politicians frequently advocated bills guaranteeing "squatter rights" as Thomas Hart Benton had done in 1830 (see page 295). Western congressmen finally maneuvered the passage of a **pre-emption bill** in 1841, giving squatters the right to

Great Basin A desert region of the western United States including most of Nevada and parts of Utah, California, Idaho, Wyoming, and Oregon.

Brigham Young Mormon leader who took over in 1844 after Joseph Smith's death and guided the Mormons from Illinois to Utah, where they established a permanent home for the church.

Great Salt Lake A shallow, salty lake in the Great Basin near which the Mormons established a permanent settlement in 1847.

pre-emption bill A temporary law that gave squatters the right to buy land they had settled on before it was offered for sale at public auction.

settle on unsurveyed federal land. Of course, this right did not guarantee that they would have the money to buy the land once it came up for sale or that they would make profitable use of it while they were squatting there. Thus shoestring farming and debt continued to challenge frontier farmers.

The Social Fabric in the West

- In what ways did constraints in the West force people to adapt? What were the cultural outcomes?

Although migrants to places like Texas, Oregon, and Utah headed for and found strange new lands, most had no intention of carving out a new social order in the West. Rather they intended to re-create the society they were leaving behind. The physical and cultural environments into which they moved, however, forced change on them. The West, after all, was not an unpopulated place, and pioneers had to accommodate themselves to the geography and people they found there. Thus the different origins and eventual destinations of various migrants resulted in some significant differences in the culture and society of the Far West. There was not one frontier but a patchwork of frontier areas.

The New Cotton Country

Migrants to cotton country in the Southwest brought a particular lifestyle with them. Often starting out as landless herders, migrating families carved out claims beyond the **frontier line** and survived on a mixture of raised and gathered food until they could put the land into agricultural production. The Indians who preceded them in the Mississippi Valley unintentionally simplified life for these families, for the Indians had already cleared large expanses of land for agriculture. Removal of the Indians to the Far West and the continuing devastation of Indian populations by disease meant that southern frontiersmen could plant corn and cotton quickly and reap early profits with minimal labor.

Although some areas were cleared and extremely fertile, others were swampy, rocky, and unproductive. In this less desirable region, settlers were allowed to survey their own claims. The result was odd-shaped farms, differences in the quality of land owned by neighboring farmers, and the re-creation of the southern class system in the new lands. Those fortunate enough to get profitable lands might become great planters; those less fortunate had to settle for lesser prosperity and lower status.

During the pioneer phase of southern frontier life, all the members of migrating families devoted most of their time to the various tasks necessary to keep the family alive. Even their social and recreational life tended to center on practical tasks. House building, planting, and harvesting were often done in cooperation with neighbors. On such occasions those gathered consumed plenty of food and homemade whiskey, and at day's end music and dancing often lasted long into the night. Women gathered together separately for large-scale projects like group quilting, talking for hours as they worked and forging strong supportive networks. Another community event for southwestern settlers was the periodic religious revival, which brought people from miles around to revival meetings that might last for days (see page 336). Here they could make new acquaintances, court sweethearts, and discuss the common failings in their souls and on their farms.

Westering Yankees

For migrants to areas like Michigan and Oregon, the overall frontier experience differed in many respects from that of the southwesterners. In the Old Northwest, Indians had also cleared the land for planting, easing the task for incoming farmers. As arriving whites pushed out the Winnebagos and others, pioneers snatched up the Indians' deserted farms. In the Old Northwest, professional surveyors had already carved the land into neat rectangular lots before it was sold. These surveys generally included provision for a township, where settlers quickly established villages like those left behind in New England, in which they re-created the social institutions they already knew and respected. Law courts, churches, and schools were likely to be the first institutions brought into being in northwestern towns. Their presence and the similarity between farming practices required in this region to conditions in New England helped to prevent the sort of social distinctions that developed so quickly along the southern frontier. That is not to say that all

frontier line The outer limit of agricultural settlement bordering on areas still under Indian control or unoccupied.

northern frontiersmen fared equally, but class differences among them were not so vast or so obvious as between members of the slaveholding elite and their poorer neighbors.

Conditions in the Oregon Country resembled those farther east in most respects, but some significant differences did exist. Most important, the Indians in the Oregon Country had never practiced agriculture—their environment was so rich in fish, meat, and wild vegetables that farming was unnecessary—and they still occupied their traditional homelands and outnumbered whites significantly. Although both of these facts might have had a profound impact on life in Oregon, early pioneers were bothered by neither. Large open prairies flanking the Columbia, Willamette, and other rivers provided fertile farmland. And the Indians helped rather than hindered the pioneers.

Much like the Indians in colonial New England, groups like the Nez Perces, Cayuses, and Kalapuyas made whites welcome. In fact, in 1831, the Nez Perces, who had hosted Lewis and Clark in 1805 (see page 230), and the Flatheads issued an appeal for whites to come live among them, spurring the rush of missionaries who opened the Oregon Country for American settlement. Although occasional tensions arose between white settlers and Indians, no serious conflict took place until the winter of 1847, when a combination of disease, white population pressure, and factionalism within the tribe led a group of Cayuse Indians to kill missionaries Marcus and Narcissa Whitman. The Whitman Massacre triggered the Cayuse War and led to a concerted effort by white Americans in the Oregon Country to remove Indians. In 1855, territorial governor and federal Indian agent Isaac I. Stevens concluded a series of treaties with all the northwestern tribes, settling them on reservations.

Like their southwestern counterparts, pioneers in both the Old and the Pacific Northwest cooperated in house building, annual planting and harvesting, and other big jobs, but a more sober air prevailed at these gatherings among the descendants of New England Puritans. Religious life was also more solemn. Religious revivals swept through Yankee settlements during the 1830s and 1840s, but the revival meetings tended to be held in churches at the center of communities rather than in outlying campgrounds. As a result, they were usually briefer and less emotional than their counterparts in the Southwest and strongly reinforced the Yankee notion of village solidarity.

The Hispanic Southwest

In physical and cultural environment, California differed greatly from the Pacific Northwest, and frontier life in California was in many ways unique. One major reason for the difference was that Spain had colonized California and the Spanish had left a lasting cultural imprint.

Systematic Spanish exploration into what is now the state of California did not begin until 1769. Prompted in part by Russian expansion into Spanish-claimed territory, Gaspar de Portolá, the governor of Spanish California, led an expedition northward from Baja California and established garrisons at San Diego and Monterey. **Junípero Serra,** a Franciscan monk, accompanied Portolá's expedition and established a mission, San Diego de Alcalá, near the present city of San Diego. Eventually Serra and his successors established twenty-one missions, each placed one day's travel from the next, extending from San Diego to the town of Sonoma, north of San Francisco.

The mission system provided a framework for Spanish settlement in California. Established in terrain that resembled the hills of Spain, the missions were soon surrounded by groves, vineyards, and lush farms. Labor for these efforts was provided by California Indians, whom the missionaries often forced into the missions, where they became virtual slaves. Although the death rate from disease and harsh treatment among the mission Indians was terrible, their labor turned California's coastal plain into a vast and productive garden.

The Franciscans continued to control the most fertile and valuable lands in California until after Mexico won independence from Spain. Between 1834 and 1840, however, the Mexican government seized the mission lands in California and sold them off to private citizens living in the region. An elite class of Spanish-speaking Californians snatched up the rich lands. Taking advantage of continuing turmoil in the Mexican government and the distance between California's fertile coast and Mexico City, these landholding **Californios** amassed a great

Junípero Serra Spanish missionary who went to California in 1769; he and his successors established near the California coast a chain of missions that depended on Indian labor.

Californios Spanish colonists in California in the eighteenth and nineteenth centuries.

♦ Using Indian labor, Franciscan missionaries transformed the dry California coastal plain into a blooming garden and built beautiful missions in which to celebrate their religion. This early nineteenth-century painting by Oriana Day shows the Carmel Mission at the peak of its prosperity. *"Mission San Carlos Borromeo de Carmelo" by Oriana Day, oil on canvas 20" x 30". The Fine Art Museum of San Francisco. Gift of Mrs. Eleanor Martin.*

degree of political and economic power. Never numbering more than about a thousand people, this Hispanic elite class eventually owned some 15 million acres of California's richest land. In 1836, the Californios and non-Hispanic newcomers together rebelled against Mexico to place Californio Juan Bautista Alvarado in the governorship of California. The landholding elite never ended California's official relationship with Mexico but nevertheless ran the region's government.

At first, the Californios welcomed outsiders as neighbors and trading partners. Ships from the United States called at California ports regularly, picking up cargoes of beef **tallow,** cow hides, and other commodities to be shipped around the world, and settlers who promised to open new lands and business opportunities were given generous grants and assistance. **John Sutter,** for example, a Swiss immigrant, received an outright grant of land in the Sacramento Valley, where in 1839 he established a colony called New Helvetia and built Sutter's Fort. This settlement drew trappers, traders, Indians, and other settlers like a magnet, opening new economic opportunities for the Californios as well as for the newcomers.

In New Helvetia, San Francisco, and other northern centers in California, a cosmopolitan society of many languages and cultures emerged. People of many races and classes could be found strolling the lanes in and around Sutter's Fort. Farther south, however, in the heartland of Spanish California, the Hispanic landholding elite resented intrusions by lower-class Mexicans and other newcomers. Thus, although new pioneers had been instrumental in elevating him to power, Governor Alvarado worried constantly about their designs and motivations and had a number of American and British citizens arrested on the suspicion that they were plotting to overthrow his government.

A similar but more harmonious pattern of interracial cooperation existed in other Spanish North

tallow Hard fat obtained from the bodies of cattle and other animals and used to make candles and soap.

John Sutter Swiss immigrant who founded a colony in California; in 1848 the discovery of gold on his property attracted hordes of miners who seized his land, leaving him financially ruined.

American provinces. In 1821, trader William Becknell began selling and trading goods along the Santa Fe Trail from St. Louis to New Mexico. By 1824, the business had become so profitable that people from all over the frontier moved in to create a permanent Santa Fe trade. As had taken place in St. Louis, an elite class emerged in Santa Fe from the intermingled fortunes and intermarriages among Indian, European, and American populations, and a strong kinship system developed. Thus, based on kinship, the Hispanic leaders of New Mexico, unlike those of California, consistently worked across cultural lines, whether to fight off Texan aggression or eventually to lobby for **annexation** to the United States.

Intercultural cooperation also characterized the early history of Texas settlement. Spanish and Mexican officials aided the empresarios, hoping the aggressive Americans would form a frontier line between southern Plains Indians, such as the Comanches and Apaches, and prosperous silver-mining communities south of the Nueces River. Tensions rose, however, as population increased. Despite the best efforts of the Mexican government to encourage Hispanics to settle in Texas, fully four-fifths of the thirty-five hundred land titles perfected by the empresarios went to non-Hispanics, most of whom were impoverished frontiersmen from the southern United States.

In Texas, economic desperation combined with cultural insensitivity and misunderstanding to create the sort of tensions that were rare in New Mexico. As a result of the relative lack of harmony and the enormous stretches of land that separated ethnic groups in Texas, **Texians**—non-Hispanic settlers—tended to cling to their own ways, and **Tejanos**—migrants from Mexico—did the same.

The Mormon Community

Physical and cultural conditions in the Great Basin led to a completely different social and cultural order in that area. Utah is a high desert plateau where water is scarce and survival depends on careful management. The tightly knit community of Mormons was perfectly suited to that place, and their social order responded well to the hostile environment.

Mormons followed the principle that "Land belongs to the Lord, and his Saints are to use so much as they can work profitably." The church measured off plots of various sizes, up to 40 acres, and assigned them to settlers on the basis of need. Thus a man with several wives, a large number of children, and enough wealth to hire help might receive a grant of 40 acres, but a man with one wife, few children, and little capital might receive only 10. The size of a land grant determined the extent to which the recipient was obligated to support community efforts. When the church ordered the construction of irrigation systems or other public works, a man who had been granted 40 acres had to provide four times the amount of labor as one who had been granted 10 acres. Like settlers elsewhere, the Mormons in Utah joined in community work parties, but cooperation among them was more rigidly controlled and formal. As on other frontiers, when the system worked it was because it was well suited to natural conditions.

Mormons had their own peculiar religious and social culture, and because of their bad experiences in Missouri and Illinois, they were unaccepting of strangers. The General Authorities of the church made every effort to keep Utah an exclusively Mormon society, welcoming all who would embrace the new religion and its practices but making it difficult for non-Mormons to stay in the region. The one exception was the American Indian population. Because Indians occupied a central place in Mormon sacred literature, the Mormons practiced an accepting and gentle Indian policy. Like other missionaries, Mormons insisted that Indians convert to their religion and lifestyle, but the Mormon hierarchy used its enormous power in Utah to prevent private violence against Indians whenever possible.

The Triumph of "Manifest Destiny"

- What expectations contributed to the concept of manifest destiny?
- Did choices by American settlers in Oregon and Texas reflect those expectations? Why or why not?

Economic opportunity was the primary reason for westward movement before the Civil War erupted in 1861, but cultural and religious concerns also pushed people west, following migrants they knew

annexation The incorporation of a territory into an existing political unit such as a neighboring country.

Texians Non-Hispanic settlers in Texas in the nineteenth century.

Tejanos Mexican settlers in Texas in the nineteenth century.

personally or people whose religious views and cultural values resembled their own. Political ideology, too, promoted westward expansion. The idea that proved most influential in pushing people westward was not new, but it received a name only in 1845: **manifest destiny.**

The Rise of Manifest Destiny

To some extent, manifest destiny was as old as the Puritan idea of a "Wilderness Zion." Like John Winthrop and his associates, many early-nineteenth-century Americans believed they had a mission to go into new lands. During the antebellum period, romantic nationalism, land hunger, and Second Great Awakening evangelicalism shaped this sense of divine mission into a new and powerful commitment to westward expansion.

The American Board of Commissioners for Foreign Missions noted in its annual report for 1827, "The tide of emigration is rolling westward so rapidly, that it must speedily surmount every barrier, till it reaches every habitable part of this continent." The power of this force led many to conclude that the westward movement was not just an economic process but was part of a divine plan for North America and the world.

The earliest and most aggressive proponents of this new commitment to expansion were Christian missionary organizations. Their many magazines, newsletters, and reports were the first to give it formal voice. Politicians, however, were not far behind in picking up the message. Democratic warhorse and expansion advocate Thomas Hart Benton of Missouri quickly adopted the tone and content of the missionary rhetoric in his speeches promoting liberal land policies, territorial acquisition, and overseas expansion. In 1825, for example, Benton argued in favor of American colonization of the Pacific coast for two reasons: it would bring "great and wonderful benefits" not only to the Indians but also to the Chinese and Japanese; and it would allow "science, liberal principles in government, and true religion [to] cast their lights across the intervening sea." Not until 1845 did Democratic journalist John L. O'Sullivan coin the expression "manifest destiny" in his now-famous statement that it was "the fulfillment of our manifest destiny to overspread the continent allotted by Providence for the free development of our yearly multiplying millions." But by then manifest destiny was already an old idea that had had a profound impact on cultural and political life in America.

Expansion to the North and West

One major complication standing in the way of the nation's perceived manifest destiny was the fact that Spain, Britain, Russia, and other countries already owned large parts of the continent. The continued presence of the British, for example, proved to be a constant source of irritation. During the War of 1812, the War Hawks had advocated conquering Canada and pushing the British from the continent altogether (see page 252). Although events thwarted this ambition, pressure remained to acquire as much territory as possible from the British, legally or through other means.

One confrontation flared in 1838, when Canadians began logging and building a railroad through an area claimed by the state of Maine. The United States and Britain had been disputing Maine's boundaries since the Treaty of Paris in 1783. Growing impatient, Canadian loggers moved into the disputed region during the winter of 1838–1839 and began cutting trees. American lumberjacks resolved to drive them away, and fighting soon broke out. The Canadian province of New Brunswick and the state of Maine then mobilized their militias, the American Congress nervously called up fifty thousand men in case of war, and President Van Buren ordered in **Winfield Scott.** Once on the scene, General Scott was able to calm tempers and arrange a truce, but tension continued to run high.

Another source of dispute between the United States and Great Britain was the **Oregon Question**—a complex diplomatic knot with many threads and a long history. The vast Oregon tract had been claimed at one time or another by Spain, Russia, France, England, and the United States (see Map 13.1). By the

manifest destiny Term first used in the 1840s to describe the inevitability of the continued westward expansion of the United States.

Winfield Scott Virginia soldier and statesman who led troops in the War of 1812 and the war with Mexico; he was still serving as a general at the start of the Civil War.

Oregon Question The question of the national ownership of the Pacific Northwest; the United States and England renegotiated the boundary in 1846, establishing it at 49° north latitude.

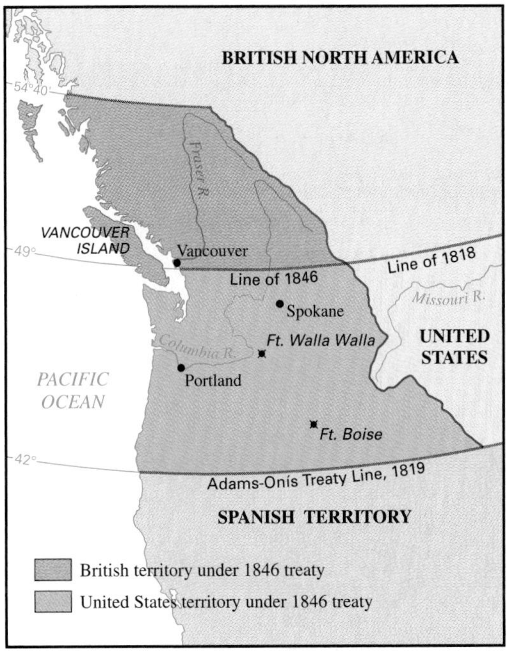

♦ **MAP 13.1 Oregon Territory** This map shows the changing boundaries and shifting possession of the Oregon country. As a result of Polk's aggressive stance and economic pressures, Britain ceded all land south of the 49th parallel to the United States in 1846.

1820s, only England and the United States continued to contest for its ownership. At the close of the War of 1812, the two countries had been unable to settle their claims and had agreed to joint occupation of Oregon for ten years. They extended this arrangement indefinitely in 1827, with the **proviso** that either country could end it with one year's notice.

Oregon's status as neither British nor American was a problem even before wagon trains of Americans began pouring into the region. In 1841, wealthy American pioneer Ewing Young died without leaving a will. Because the Oregon Country had no laws, there were no guidelines on who was entitled to inherit his property. Finally, Methodist missionary officials created a **probate court** and instructed it to follow the statutes of the state of New York. At the same time, the missionaries appointed a committee to frame a constitution and draft a basic code of laws. Opposition from the British put an end to this early effort at self-rule, but the movement continued.

Two years later, Americans in Oregon began agitating again, this time supposedly because of wolves preying on their livestock. Settlers in the Willamette Valley held a series of "Wolf Meetings" in 1843 to discuss joint protection and resolved to create a civil government. They called a constitutional convention for May 2. Although the British tried to prevent the convention, the assembly passed the **First Organic Laws** of Oregon on July 5, 1843, making Oregon an independent republic in all but name. Independence, however, was not the settlers' long-term goal. The document's preamble, announcing that the code of laws would continue in force "until such time as the United States of America extend their jurisdiction over us," was a clear plea for annexation.

Revolution in Texas

Questions about the nation's southwestern borders were quite different from questions in the Northeast and Pacific Northwest. Unlike the situation in northern Maine and the Oregon Country, the matter of ownership in the Southwest was fairly clear. The area including present-day Texas, New Mexico, Arizona, California, Nevada, and portions of Colorado, Oklahoma, Kansas, and Wyoming belonged to Spain prior to Mexico's successful revolution in 1821, and after that revolution common precedent dictated that it belonged to Mexico. But owning this vast region and controlling it were two different matters. The distance and rough terrain separating the capital in Mexico City from the northern provinces made governing the region difficult. Moreover, large areas of Texas and New Mexico were home to strong and independent Indian groups like the Comanches, who made the extension of both settlement and law difficult.

Although the Spanish and then the Mexican government had invited Anglo-Americans to settle in the Southwest, these pioneers generally ignored Mexican customs, including their pledge to practice Roman Catholicism, and often ignored Mexican law.

proviso A clause making a qualification, condition, or restriction in a document.

probate court A court that establishes the validity of wills and administers the estates of people who have died.

First Organic Laws A constitution adopted by American settlers in the Oregon Country on July 5, 1843, establishing a government independent from Great Britain and requesting annexation by the United States.

This was particularly the case after 1829, when Mexico abolished slavery in all its territories. Bad feelings grew over the years, but the distant and politically unstable Mexican government could do little to enforce laws and customs. In addition, despite the friction between cultures in Texas, many Tejanos were disturbed by the corruption and political instability in Mexico City and were as eager as their Texian counterparts to participate in the United States' thriving cotton market.

Assuming responsibility for forging a peaceful settlement to the problems between settlers in Texas and the Mexican government, Stephen F. Austin went to Mexico City in 1833. While Austin was there, **Antonio López de Santa Anna** seized power after a series of revolutions and disputed elections. A former supporter of federalism and a key figure in the adoption of a republican constitution in 1824, Santa Anna had come to the conclusion that Mexico was not ready for democracy. Upon assuming power, he suspended the constitution, dismissed congress, and set himself up as the self-declared "Napoleon of the West."

Austin met with Santa Anna and presented several petitions advocating reforms and greater self-government in Texas to the Mexican president. Believing that Santa Anna agreed with his ideas, Austin departed for home, only to be arrested and dragged back to Mexico City in chains on charges of advocating revolution in Texas. The empresario was finally released and cleared of all charges in 1835, but Santa Anna had made clear that he intended to exert his authority over Texians and Tejanos. Upon arriving back in Texas, Austin declared that "War is our only recourse." At a banquet given in his honor early in September, Austin asserted to the mixed Tejano and Texian audience, "The constitutional rights and the security and peace of Texas—they ought to be maintained; and jeopardized as they now are, they demand a general consultation of the people." He was immediately made chairman of a committee to call for a convention of delegates from all over Texas. Members of the group that convened followed Austin's terminology, referring to themselves as the "Consultation."

Mexican officials, viewing the unrest in Texas as rebellion against their authority, issued arrest warrants for all the Texas troublemakers they could identify and deployed troops to San Antonio. Austin's committee immediately sent out word for Texans to arm themselves. The first battle in the **Texas Revolution** came quickly thereafter when the little town of Gonzales refused to surrender a cannon to Mexican officials on September 29, 1835 (see Map 13.2).

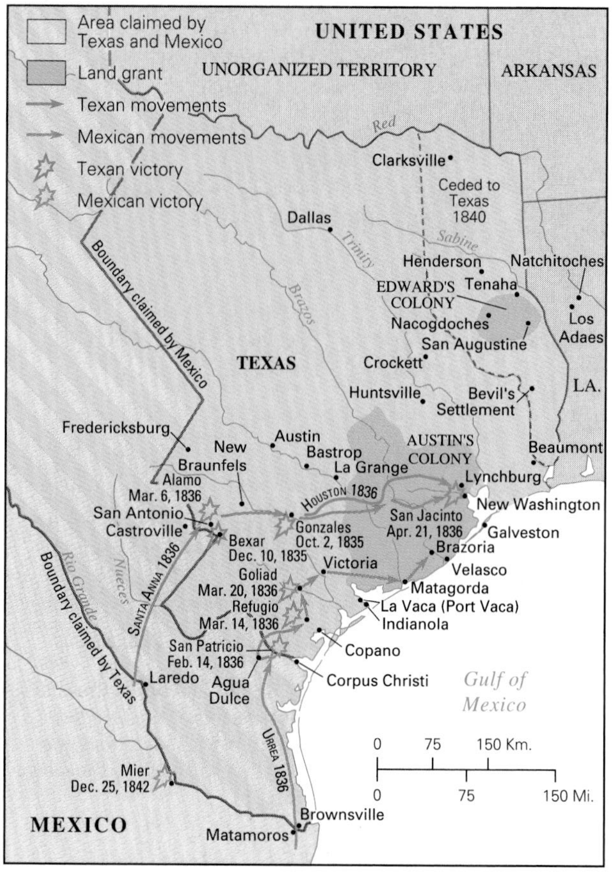

♦ **MAP 13.2 Texas Revolution** This map shows troop movements and the major battles in the Texas Revolution, as well as the conflicting boundary claims made by Texans and the Mexican government. The Battle of San Jacinto and the Treaty of Velasco ended the war, but the conflicting land claims continued when Mexico repudiated the treaty.

After the battle in Gonzales and several other small encounters, the Texas Consultation formed itself into a provisional government in November 1835 and adopted the Mexican federalist constitution of 1824, recently suspended by Santa Anna, as

Antonio López de Santa Anna Mexican general who was president of Mexico when he led an attack on the Alamo in 1836.

Texas Revolution A revolt by American colonists in Texas against Mexican rule; it began in 1835 and ended with the establishment of the Republic of Texas in 1836.

♦ Greatly outnumbered, Texas forces held off a siege at the Alamo by the Mexican army under Antonio López de Santa Anna, but the old mission's walls eventually were breached and the Texans were overcome in hand-to-hand fighting. This painting is an artist's conception of the last moments of the battle, before the remaining Texans were finally defeated. *"Fall of the Alamo" by Robert Onderdonk.*

its legal foundation. But the Consultation shied away from declaring independence from Mexico. Soon after the convention broke up, a force of Texans under Colonel Edward Burleson attacked San Antonio, moving into the city on December 5. After three days of house-to-house fighting, the Mexican force retreated into the **Alamo** but finally surrendered because it lacked provisions.

Angered by the rebels' success, Santa Anna personally led the Mexican army into Texas and headed straight for San Antonio, arriving on February 23, 1836. Knowing that Santa Anna was on his way, Texas commander William Travis had moved his troops into the Alamo, which the Mexican army immediately surrounded. On March 6 Santa Anna ordered an all-out assault on the Alamo. Storming the walls, the Mexican army sustained staggering casualties but in the end was able to capture the former mission. Most of the post's defenders were killed in the assault, and Santa Anna executed those who survived the battle, including former American congressman and frontier celebrity Davy Crockett.

While Santa Anna was busy in San Antonio, Texas rebels elsewhere were occupied with consolidating the revolution. On March 2, a convention met at Washington-on-the-Brazos and issued a declaration of independence. The convention also pieced together a constitution, based largely on the Constitution of the United States, and ratified it on March 16. On the following day, David G. Burnet was elected president of the new republic, and Lorenzo de Zavala, one of the many Tejanos who had joined the rebellion, was elected vice president (see Individual Choices: Lorenzo de Zavala). **Sam Houston** had earlier been named commander of the army.

Alamo A fortified Franciscan mission at San Antonio; rebellious Texas colonists were besieged and wiped out there by Santa Anna's forces in 1836.

Sam Houston American general and politician who fought in the struggle for Texas's independence from Mexico and became president of the Republic of Texas.

INDIVIDUAL CHOICES

Choosing Texas and Independence

Lorenzo de Zavala

Lorenzo de Zavala fought against tyranny in his native Mexico. When the government he helped establish after a successful revolution against Spain refused to create a democracy, de Zavala moved to Texas. In 1835 he chose to join the Texas Revolution against Mexico and was elected vice president of the Republic of Texas. "Lorenzo de Zavala" by C. E. Proctor, Archives Division, Texas State Library. Photo by Eric Beggs.

Although Lorenzo de Zavala was a physician by training, his heart persistently pulled him into politics. An ardent liberal and federalist, he was elected to the Merida city council in his native Yucatán, in southern Mexico, when he was only 23 years old. Then in 1814 he was elected a delegate to the Spanish parliament, though he never assumed his seat. The young liberal was imprisoned by Spain's King Ferdinand VII for antimonarchial sentiments. Gaining his release in 1817, de Zavala returned to Yucatán.

De Zavala chafed at Spanish rule, and as revolutionary movements broke out in all parts of Mexico in 1820, he again entered politics, winning election as the secretary of the Yucatán assembly. From this position, he assisted the Mexican independence movement. Shortly after it succeeded in 1821, he was elected to the Mexican constituent congress, serving there and in the national senate until 1827, when he was made governor of the province of Mexico.

By 1829, de Zavala was having doubts about how things were going in Mexico. The independent government had proved far from stable, and the ruling authorities seemed just as reactionary as the Spaniards. The liberals' demand to allocate farmland to peasants, for example, was continually refused by the government. Seeking some way to help the peasants, de Zavala resigned his governorship and secured

Despite the loss at the Alamo, Texans continued to underestimate Santa Anna's strength and his resolve to put down the rebellion. Although Houston personally ordered James Fannin to evacuate the town of Goliad, the Texans remained. On March 18 a large Mexican detachment under General Jose Urrea captured the town and Fannin's entire force. Over the next several days, Urrea swept through the area, capturing all the rebel detachments he could find and bringing them as prisoners to Goliad. Finally, on Palm Sunday (March 27) in 1836, Urrea ordered all able-bodied prisoners to be marched out of town, where their guards shot and killed them. According to Mexican sources, the 445 men were executed at Santa Anna's personal order.

Vengeance came on April 21 after Santa Anna had ordered his personal detachment of the Mexican Army to pause at the San Jacinto River. Arriving in an empresario grant to settle five hundred poor Mexican families in Texas.

For the next several years, de Zavala traveled and wrote a history of the revolutionary movement in Mexico, which he published in 1831. Then, finding himself in Paris, de Zavala accepted a post as Mexico's ambassador to France in 1833, returning to public service and politics. In 1834, Antonio López de Santa Anna pushed his way into power, suspending the constitution, dissolving the national congress, and assuming dictatorial control. Watching events unfold from his post in Paris, de Zavala became increasingly disaffected by Santa Anna. In 1835 he resigned as ambassador and sailed for Texas, where, he believed, he might join with others to oppose Santa Anna and restore the constitution. When Stephen F. Austin called for a "general consultation of the people" in the fall of 1835, de Zavala sought and won a seat.

Like many settlers in Texas—whether they were originally from the United States, Europe, or Mexico—de Zavala wanted reform but not necessarily independence. Thus he agreed with the Consultation's decision in November 1835 to form a provisional government using the Mexican constitution of 1824—a document he had helped write—as a legal foundation. But when Santa Anna declared all members of the Consultation traitors and ordered troops into Texas, de Zavala gave up hope of a peaceful settlement. On March 2, 1836, he chose to join his colleagues in signing a declaration of independence and then threw himself into the task of writing a constitution for Texas. The resulting document was an interesting hybrid: a mixture of de Zavala's and James Madison's views concerning liberal federalism.

The Texas Consultation ratified the new constitution on March 16, 1836. Then, in recognition of de Zavala's strong political voice and the significant role he had played in helping to launch the revolution, the Consultation unanimously elected him vice president of the Republic of Texas.

The revolution and the establishment of the Texas Republic represented a victory of views that de Zavala and many Mexican-born Texans had held for a lifetime. Throughout his political career, de Zavala had fought for reform in Mexico, helping to win independence from Spain and pushing for liberal federalism. His expectations had been dashed by the harsh constraints imposed by self-interested political factions, which had created such instability that Santa Anna had been able to bully his way to the top and suspend liberal government. For de Zavala and many others, the choice was clear: if Mexico could not be reformed, they would throw their lot in with a new state where their views might become reality. The Republic of Texas became the seat for their dreams.

the vicinity undetected, Houston's force of just over nine hundred formed up quietly and attacked. Shouting "Remember the Alamo" and "Remember Goliad," the Texans stormed the unsuspecting Mexican camp. In just eighteen minutes, 630 Mexican soldiers lay dead. Disguised in a private's uniform, Santa Anna attempted to escape but was captured and brought to Houston. In exchange for his release, in May 1836 the Mexican president signed the **Treaty of Velasco.** In the treaty, Santa Anna officially recognized Texas independence and agreed to withdraw his troops from the new republic. He also

Treaty of Velasco Treaty that Santa Anna signed in May 1836 after his capture at the San Jacinto River; it granted recognition to the Republic of Texas but was later rejected by the Mexican congress.

acknowledged that the Rio Grande was to be the border between Texas and Mexico. Santa Anna then returned to Mexico and was immediately deposed as president. The new government repudiated the treaty with Texas, but was in no immediate position to do anything about it.

As in Oregon, many leaders in Texas hoped their actions would lead to annexation by the United States. In 1838, Houston, by then president of the Republic of Texas, invited the United States to annex Texas. John Quincy Adams, elected to Congress after his loss in the presidential election of 1828, **filibustered** in the House of Representatives for three weeks against the acquisition of such a big block of potentially slave territory—all of Texas lay below the Missouri Compromise line (see pages 283–284). Seeking to avoid national controversy, the Senate refused to ratify an annexation treaty. Political currents in the nation, however, worked to keep Texas in the public eye despite the Senate's efforts.

The Politics of Manifest Destiny

Although Adams was typical of one wing of the Whig coalition, he certainly did not speak for the majority of Whigs on the topic of national expansion. The party of manufacturing, revivalism, and social reform inclined naturally toward the blending of political, economic, and religious evangelicalism that was manifest destiny. William Henry Harrison himself, the united party's first national candidate, was a colorful figure in American westward expansion. He had been a prominent War Hawk and Indian fighter in the years leading up to the War of 1812 (see pages 251–253), and his political campaign in 1840 celebrated the simple pleasures and virtues of frontier life, appealing to a westering population. When Harrison died soon after taking office in 1841, his vice president, John Tyler, picked up the torch of American expansionism.

Tyler was a less typical Whig than even Adams. A Virginian and a states'-rights advocate, he had been a staunch Democrat until the nullification crisis, when he bolted the party in protest against Jackson's strong assertion of federal power (see pages 296–299). As president, Tyler seemed still to be more Democrat than Whig. Although he had objected to Jackson's use of presidential power, like Old Hickory, Tyler as president was unyielding where political principles were concerned. He vetoed high protective tariffs, internal improvement bills that he perceived as unnecessary, and attempts to revive the Second Bank of the United States. In fact, during Tyler's administration, Whigs accomplished only two moderate goals: they eliminated Van Buren's hated treasury system (see pages 358–359), and they passed a slightly higher tariff. Tyler's refusal to promote Whig economic policies led to a general crisis in government in 1843, when his entire cabinet resigned over his veto of a bank bill.

Tyler did share his party's desire for expansion, however. He assigned his secretary of state, Daniel Webster, to negotiate a treaty with Britain to settle the Maine matter once and for all. The resulting **Webster-Ashburton Treaty** (1842) gave more than half of the disputed territory to the United States and finally established the nation's northeastern border with Canada. Tyler also adopted an aggressive stance on the Oregon Question by appointing a federal Indian agent for the region in 1842—an act of doubtful legality in view of the mutual occupation agreement between the United States and Great Britain. His appointee, former missionary Elijah White, was one of the organizers of the Wolf Meetings and helped draft the First Organic Laws. Historians have speculated that Tyler also encouraged Marcus Whitman to help guide a large party of immigrants into Oregon in 1843 as a way of enhancing the U.S. claim to the region.

Tyler also pushed a forceful policy toward Texas and the Southwest. In 1842, Sam Houston repeated his invitation for the United States to annex Texas, only to be rebuffed by Secretary of State Webster, a New Englander who shared Adams's views. When Webster resigned with the other cabinet officers in 1843, however, Tyler replaced him with fellow Virginian Abel P. Upshur, who immediately reopened the matter of Texas annexation.

Negotiations between Houston's representatives and Tyler's secretary of state—Upshur at first, then, after Upshur's death, John C. Calhoun—led to a treaty of annexation on April 11, 1844. In line with the repudiated Treaty of Velasco, the annexation document named the Rio Grande as the southern

filibuster To use obstructionist tactics, especially prolonged speechmaking, in order to delay legislative action.

Webster-Ashburton Treaty Treaty that in 1842 established the present border between Canada and northeastern Maine.

♦ This campaign banner celebrating the candidacy of James K. Polk and George M. Dallas on the Democratic ticket carries a subtle message conveying the party's platform. Surrounding Polk's picture are twenty-five stars, one for each state in the Union. Outside the corner box, a twenty-sixth star stands for Texas, which Polk promised to annex. *Collection of David J. and Janet L. Frent.*

boundary of Texas. Annexation remained a major arguing point between proslavery and antislavery forces, and the treaty failed ratification in the Senate. The issue of Texas annexation then joined the Oregon Question as a major campaign issue in the presidential election of 1844.

As the Whigs and the Democrats geared up for a national election, it became clear that expansion would be the key issue. This put the two leading political figures of the day, Democrat Martin Van Buren and Whig Henry Clay, in an uncomfortable position. Van Buren was on record as opposing the extension of slavery and was therefore against the annexation of Texas. Clay, the architect of the American System (see page 274), was opposed to any form of uncontrolled expansion, especially if it meant fanning sectional tensions, and he too opposed immediate annexation of Texas. Approaching the election, both issued statements to the effect that they would agree to annexation only if Mexico agreed.

Despite Clay's somewhat ambiguous stance on expansion and the fact that Tyler had done much to advance the cause of manifest destiny, President Tyler's constant refusal to support the larger Whig political agenda led the party to nominate Clay. Van Buren was not so lucky. The strong southern wing of the Democratic party was so put off by Van Buren's position on slavery that it blocked him, securing the nomination of Tennessee congressman **James K. Polk.**

The Democrats based their platform on the issues surrounding Oregon and Texas. The Democrats implied that the regions rightfully belonged to the United States, stating "that the re-occupation of Oregon and the re-annexation of Texas at the earliest practicable period are great American measures." Polk vowed to stand up to the British by claiming the entire Oregon Country up to 54°40′ north latitude and to defend the territorial claims of Texas. The Democrats played up both regions to appeal to the manifest destiny sentiments of both northerners and southerners. For his part, Clay continued to waffle on expansionism, emphasizing economic policies instead.

The temper of the people is evident in the election's outcome. Clay was a national figure, well respected and regarded as one of the nation's leading

James K. Polk Tennessee congressman who was a leader of the Democratic party and the dark-horse winner of the presidential campaign in 1844.

statesmen. Polk was a dark horse barely known outside Tennessee. Even so, Polk polled forty thousand more popular votes than Clay and garnered sixty-five more electoral votes, sliding into the presidency with a narrow margin of victory.

Continuing in his role as a rogue Whig, outgoing president Tyler accomplished one of the Democrats' platform goals before Polk had a chance to assume office. In a special message to Congress in December 1844, Tyler proposed a **joint resolution** annexing Texas. Tyler agreed to accept the Texans' claim for a southern border along the Rio Grande. But in the case of conflict, he said, Texas would have to accept any boundaries that might be negotiated between the United States and Mexico. Many congressmen who had opposed annexation could not ignore the clear mandate given to manifest destiny in the presidential election, and the bill to annex Texas passed in February 1845, just as Tyler prepared to turn the White House over to his Democratic successor.

Whigs pretended that the incoming president was politically inexperienced, asking, "Who is James K. Polk?" In reality, Polk was a very experienced politician. Often called "Young Hickory" because of his political resemblance to Andrew Jackson, Polk had entered politics in Tennessee as a very young man, serving fourteen years in Congress and two years as governor of the state. Like Jackson, Polk was tenacious, choosing to grapple with tough political problems until he had defeated them. He supported Jacksonian political notions, disavowing protective tariffs and national banks while embracing expansionism.

Holding to the position he had taken prior to the election, Polk asked Congress to end the joint occupation of Oregon in his annual message for 1845. Referring to the largely forgotten Monroe Doctrine (see page 280), the president insisted that no nation other than the United States should be permitted to occupy any part of North America and urged Congress to sue for exclusive control over the Oregon Country even if doing so meant war.

Neither the United States nor Britain intended to go to war over Oregon. The only issue was where the border would be. Recalling the rhetoric that had gotten him elected, Polk insisted on 54°40′. The British lobbied for the Columbia River as the boundary, but their position softened quickly. The fur trade along the Columbia was in rapid decline and had become unprofitable by the early 1840s. As a result, in the spring of 1846, the British foreign secretary offered Polk a compromise boundary at the 49th parallel. The Senate recommended that Polk accept the offer, and a treaty settling the Oregon issue was ratified on June 15, 1846. Sectional politics, however, delayed the admission of Oregon as a territory for a few years.

Expansion and Sectional Crisis

- How did expansionist and economic expectations shape Americans' positions on slavery in the 1840s?

At the heart of the significant political controversy that accompanied expansion lay slavery. Although only a few radicals totally opposed slavery, many people in the North and West strongly opposed its expansion. For them this was less a moral than an economic issue. The expansion of slavery meant open economic competition with slaves or slaveholders for jobs and profits. Southerners, in contrast, demanded that slavery be allowed to expand as far as economic opportunity permitted. And, not surprisingly, southerners believed the nation's manifest destiny was to expand into areas where cotton would grow and slavery would be most profitable. Given these strong economic motives, the congressional gag rule passed in 1836 (see page 345) could not prevent the debate over expansion from turning into a debate over slavery.

The Texas Crisis and Sectional Conflict

Any action that President Polk took on Texas would have been controversial and would have promoted a political crisis, but action of some sort could not be avoided. In setting the Rio Grande as the southern boundary of Texas, Tyler and Calhoun had offended the Mexican government. The position of the Mexican government was that Texas was still a province of Mexico, not an independent republic, but if annexation was in the cards, the southern boundary should be the Nueces River, not the Rio Grande. When Congress adopted the joint resolution annexing Texas and establishing the Rio Grande as its southern border, Mexico's popular press linked the event with an uprising in New Mexico in 1837 and

joint resolution A special resolution adopted by both houses of Congress and subject to approval by the president; if approved, it has the force of law.

continued restlessness in California, raising fears of an American conspiracy against Mexican sovereignty. The press demanded that Mexico sever diplomatic relations with the United States. The government did so immediately and threatened war. For his part, Polk blustered that not only should Texas belong to the Union but the entire Southwest should be annexed.

Polk sought his objectives peacefully but prepared to use force in case Mexico rejected his overtures. Late in 1845, the president dispatched John Slidell to Mexico City to negotiate the boundary dispute, and he authorized Slidell to purchase New Mexico and California if possible. He also dispatched American troops to Louisiana, ready to strike if Mexico resisted Slidell's offers. And he notified the American consul in California, Thomas O. Larkin, that the Pacific fleet had orders to seize California ports if war broke out with Mexico. If American citizens in the region then wished to rebel against Mexico, the president said, the United States would support them and invite them to join the Union.

Nervous but bristling over what seemed to be preparations for war, and rightfully upset that Polk had disregarded the break in diplomatic relations by sending an emissary, the Mexican government refused to receive Slidell. In January 1846 Slidell sent word to the president that his mission was a failure. Receiving that report, Polk ordered **Zachary Taylor** to lead troops into the disputed area between the Nueces River and the Rio Grande. Shortly thereafter, an American military exploration party led by **John C. Frémont** violated Mexican territory by crossing the mountains into California's Salinas Valley.

By April, the Mexican government had had enough. On April 22, Mexico proclaimed that its territory had been violated by the United States and declared war. Two days later, Mexican troops engaged a detachment of Taylor's army at Matamoros on the Rio Grande, killing eleven and capturing the rest. Polk had already drafted a war declaration, claiming that "the cup of forbearance had been exhausted." When news reached Washington of Taylor's battle at Matamoros, he immediately redrafted his war message, proclaiming that Mexico "has invaded our territory, and shed American blood upon American soil." He went on to say that a war with Mexico would be short and decisive and predicted that victory would bring not only Texas but also California and New Mexico into the Union. Although the nation was far from united on the issue, Congress agreed to declare war on May 13, 1846 (see Map 13.3).

The outbreak of war disturbed many Americans. In New England, for example, protest ran high. Transcendentalist Henry David Thoreau was an outspoken critic and chose to be jailed rather than pay taxes that would support the war. "All men recognize the right of revolution," Thoreau wrote. "When a sixth of the population of a nation which has undertaken to be the refuge of liberty are slaves, and a whole country is unjustly overrun and conquered by a foreign army, and subjected to military law, I think that it is not too soon for honest men to rebel and revolutionize."

Despite Thoreau's resounding call for revolution, American expansionism was never the issue in most protests. The only question was what sort of expansion was acceptable. Protesters saw what Thoreau also saw quite clearly: the connection between the war with Mexico and slavery.

The annexation of Texas brought slavery to the attention of the American people like nothing before and made the connection between American expansion and American slavery crystal clear. To southerners, the broad stretch of land lying south of 36°30′ (the Missouri Compromise line) represented both economic and political power. The adoption of proslavery constitutions in newly acquired territories would ensure the immigration of friendly voters and the installation of congenial governments, which would strengthen the South's economic and political interests in Congress. Northerners understood the political and economic implications but saw something much more alarming in the southern expansion movement. Since the Missouri Compromise (1820), some northerners had come to believe that a slaveholding **oligarchy** controlled life and politics in the South. Abolitionists warned that this "Slave Power" sought to expand its reach until it controlled every aspect of American life. Many viewed Congress's adoption of the gag rule in 1836

Zachary Taylor American general whose defeat of Santa Anna at Buena Vista in 1847 made him a national hero and the Whig choice for president in 1848.

John C. Frémont Explorer, soldier, and politician who explored and mapped much of the American West and Northwest; he later ran unsuccessfully for president.

oligarchy A small group of people or families who hold power.

♦ **MAP 13.3 The Southwest and the Mexican War** When the United States acquired Texas, it inherited the Texans' boundary disputes with Mexico. This map shows the outcome: war with Mexico in 1846 and the acquisition of the disputed territories in Texas as well as most of Arizona, New Mexico, and California through the Treaty of Guadalupe Hidalgo.

and the drive to annex Texas as evidence of the Slave Power's influence. Thus debates over Texas pitted two regions of the country against each other in what champions of both sides saw as mortal combat.

The contenders joined battle in earnest over appropriations for the war effort. In August 1846, David Wilmot, a Democratic representative from Pennsylvania, proposed an amendment to a military appropriations bill specifying that "neither slavery nor involuntary servitude shall ever exist" in any territory gained in the Mexican War. The **Wilmot Proviso** passed in the House of Representatives but failed in the Senate, where equal state representation gave the South a stronger position. At Polk's request, Wilmot refused to propose his proviso when the House reconsidered the war appropriations bill, but Van Buren Democrats defied Polk by attaching the amendment again, and the House approved it once more. Again the Senate rejected the amended bill. In opposing the amendment, John C. Calhoun (re-elected to the Senate after serving as Tyler's secretary of state) argued that any territory acquired in the war would belong to all the American people, and that for Congress to forbid any citizen from taking slaves into the area would violate the constitutional protection of life, liberty, and

Wilmot Proviso Amendment to an appropriations bill in 1846 proposing that any territory acquired from Mexico be closed to slavery; it was defeated in the Senate.

property. The House finally decided in April to appropriate money for the war without stipulating whether or not slavery would be permitted.

War with Mexico

While all this political infighting was going on in Washington, D.C., a real war was going on in the Southwest. In California, American settlers, fearing reprisals by Mexican authorities, rallied in open rebellion in the Sacramento Valley. The rebels captured the town of Sonoma in June 1846 and declared themselves independent. They crafted a flag depicting a grizzly bear and announced the birth of the Republic of California, also called the Bear Flag Republic. Rushing to Sonoma, Frémont's force joined the Bear Flag rebels and began to march south toward Monterey. The little army arrived on July 19, only to find that the Pacific fleet had already acted on Polk's orders and seized the city. The Mexican forces were in full flight southward.

To round out the greater southwestern strategy, Polk ordered Colonel Stephen Kearney to invade New Mexico on May 15. After leading his men across 800 miles of desert to Santa Fe, Kearny found a less-than-hostile enemy force facing him. Members of the interracial upper class of Santa Fe had already expressed interest in joining the United States. Given the opportunity, they surrendered without firing a shot.

Within a short time, all of the New Mexico region and California were securely in the hands of U.S. forces. Zachary Taylor in Texas, however, faced more serious opposition. Marching across the Rio Grande, Taylor headed for the Mexican city of Monterrey, which he attacked in September 1846. He managed to capture the city, but only at the cost of agreeing to let the enemy garrison pass unmolested through his lines. From Monterrey, Taylor planned to turn southward toward Mexico City and lead the main attack against the Mexican capital, but politics intervened.

At the outbreak of the war, President Polk had named Winfield Scott as the commander of the Rio Grande campaign, even though Scott was a powerful Whig. Polk, however, soon became worried that Scott might use military success as a springboard to challenge him for the presidency, and he withdrew Scott's appointment. After Taylor's successful siege at Monterrey, however, Polk's new general suddenly seemed a greater political threat than Scott. In addition, the fact that Taylor had allowed the Mexican garrison to escape convinced the president that Taylor was not aggressive enough to win the war quickly. Thus Polk turned back to Scott. He ordered Scott to gather an army at the port of Tampico, on the Gulf of Mexico, drawing men from Taylor's and other forces, and then sail down to Vera Cruz (see Map 13.3). From there the army was to move inland to take Mexico City, forcing the Mexicans to sue for peace.

♦ Slaves look on in obvious interest as men gathered at the post office devour the latest news from the front in the war with Mexico. One newspaperman in Baltimore reported "The news from the army on the Rio Grande has caused more general excitement in this city than has before taken place, perhaps during the present generation." *"War News from Mexico" by Richard Cator Woodville, 1848, the Manogian Foundation © 1996 Board of Trustees, National Gallery of Art, Washington, D.C.*

Polk complicated the military situation by plotting with deposed Mexican president Santa Anna, who had been exiled to Cuba after his defeat at San Jacinto. Santa Anna promised that he would end the war and settle the border dispute in Polk's favor if Polk would help him return to Mexico. The American president agreed, and Santa Anna sneaked back into Mexico, where he soon resumed the presidency. To Polk's dismay, however, Santa Anna also took command of the Mexican army and vowed to resist

♦ An American private, Samuel E. Chamberlain, made this drawing of the Battle of Buena Vista. Present at the battle, Chamberlain watched as Mexican forces overran an artillery emplacement. The Americans eventually turned the tide and the battle came out a draw. Even so, troops under Santa Anna were forced to retreat into the Mexican interior, spoiling the general's hope for a quick and easy victory against the invading Americans. *"Battle of Buena Vista" by Samuel Chamberlain, 1847. San Jacinto Museum of History Association.*

American territorial expansion into the disputed territory. Thus, while Scott and Taylor were realigning the American forces, Mexico's most able general resumed command and chose to strike.

Planning to crush Taylor's remaining force and then wheel around to attack Scott, Santa Anna and his numerically superior army encountered Taylor at Buena Vista in February 1847. Tired and dispirited from forced marching across the desert, the Mexican army was in no shape to fight, but Santa Anna ordered an attack anyway. Although the **Battle of Buena Vista** was a draw, Taylor's fresher troops stalled Santa Anna's force, and the worn-out Mexicans withdrew into the interior of Mexico.

The Battle of Buena Vista short-circuited Santa Anna's strategy, permitting Scott's forces to capture Vera Cruz on March 9. His eyes firmly on a quick victory, Scott moved relentlessly toward Mexico City. An ambush at Cerro Gordo designed to halt the Americans' progress turned into a disaster for the Mexicans. Scott's forces captured three thousand Mexican troops, most of Santa Anna's equipment and provisions, and even the president's personal effects. By May 15, however, Scott had run into trouble. Many of his troops were serving under twelve-month enlistments, which had just expired. Feeling they had no obligation to stay, nearly a third of his army went home, leaving the general powerless to proceed.

Finally, after three months of waiting, Scott received supplies and reinforcements and resumed his march on Mexico City. After a crushing assault, Scott and his force routed the Mexican defenders and captured the city on September 13, 1847. In all, his army had covered 260 miles without losing a battle.

With all of Texas, New Mexico, and California in American hands, the direction of treaty talks should have been fairly predictable. Scott's enormous success, however, caused Santa Anna's government to collapse, leaving no one to negotiate with American peace commissioner Nicholas Trist. After a month

Battle of Buena Vista Battle in February 1847 during which U.S. troops led by Zachary Taylor forced Santa Anna's forces to withdraw into the interior of Mexico.

had passed with no settlement, Polk concluded that Trist was not pressing hard enough and removed him as peace commissioner. But by the time Polk's orders arrived, the Mexican government had elected a new president and on November 11 had told Trist that Mexico was ready to begin negotiations. When Trist received Polk's removal order, he ignored it and pressed on with negotiations. Finally, on February 2, 1848, Trist and the Mexican delegation signed the **Treaty of Guadalupe Hidalgo,** granting the United States all the territory between the Nueces River and the Rio Grande and all the territory between there and the Pacific. In exchange, Trist agreed that the United States would pay Mexico $15 million, and he committed the United States to paying all claims made by Texans for damages resulting from the war.

Polk was very angry when he heard the terms of the treaty. Although the United States had obtained everything it had gone to war for, Polk felt that Scott's sweeping victory at Mexico City should have netted the United States more territory for less money. Political realities in Washington, however, prevented Polk from trying to get a more aggressive treaty ratified by the Senate. Although the president had strong support for his own position in favor of annexing all of Mexico, many antislavery voices loudly protested the bringing of so much land south of the Missouri Compromise line into the Union. Others opposed the annexation of Mexico because they feared that the largely Roman Catholic population might be a threat to Protestant institutions in the United States. Still others, many of whom had opposed the war, had moral objections to taking any territory by force. Perhaps more convincing than these arguments, however, was the fact that the war had cost a lot of money and congressmen were unwilling to allocate more if peace was within reach. Thus Polk submitted the treaty Trist had negotiated, and the Senate approved it by a vote of 38 to 14.

The Anti-Slavery Crusade and Women's Rights

Being opposed to the expansion of slavery was not the same as opposing the institution of slavery, but although antislavery sentiments were not widespread among the American people during the 1840s, as the debates over the Mexican War indicate, abolitionist voices were getting louder. Despite strong and sometimes violent opposition, the abolition movement had continued to grow, especially among the privileged and educated classes in the Northeast. Throughout the 1830s, evangelicals increasingly stressed the sinful nature of slavery and broke away from the **gradualism** of the American Colonization Society (see page 344). Driven by their vision of an American **millennium,** men and women steeped in evangelical zeal joined with William Lloyd Garrison and Angelina Grimké in urging the immediate, uncompensated liberation of slaves.

Garrison, however, consistently alienated his followers. Calling the Constitution "a covenant with death and an agreement with hell," Garrison burned a copy of it, telling his followers, "so perish all compromises with tyranny," and he urged them to have no dealings with a government that permitted so great an evil as slavery. Citing the reluctance of most organized churches to condemn slavery outright, Garrison urged his followers to break with them as well. He also alienated many of his white, evangelical supporters by associating with and supporting free black advocates of abolition.

During the 1830s, even moderates within the abolition movement had celebrated **Frederick Douglass, Sojourner Truth,** and other black abolitionists, welcoming them as members of the American Anti-Slavery Society. But in the late 1830s and 1840s, more insistent black voices began to frighten white abolitionists. Black abolitionist David Walker cried, "The whites want slaves, and want us for their slaves, but some of them will curse the day they ever saw us." Walker advocated that blacks "kill or be killed." Another black spokesman, Henry Highland Garnet, proclaimed, "Strike for your lives and

Treaty of Guadalupe Hidalgo Treaty (1848) in which Mexico gave up Texas above the Rio Grande and ceded New Mexico and California to the United States in return for $15 million.

gradualism The belief that slavery in the United States should be abolished gradually, by methods such as placing territorial limits on slavery or settling free blacks in Africa.

millennium A thousand-year period of justice, peace, and prosperity, predicted in the Bible.

Frederick Douglass Abolitionist and journalist who escaped from slavery in 1838 and became an influential lecturer in the North and abroad.

Sojourner Truth Abolitionist and feminist who was freed from slavery in 1827 and became a leading preacher against slavery and for the rights of women.

♦ Although she initially disapproved of her sister Angelina's vocal activism in the abolitionist cause, Sarah Grimké eventually also became a vocal activist, but in the movement for woman's rights. In 1838 she published *Letters on the Equality of the Sexes and the Condition of Woman,* a stinging indictment of women's inequality in antebellum America. Her writings provided one of the foundations for the Seneca Falls Convention in 1848. *Library of Congress.*

liberties. Now is the day and hour. Let every slave in the land do this and the days of slavery are numbered. Rather die freemen than live to be slaves."

Many of Garrison's followers found his ties to impatient black reformers frightening and his rejection of both church and state unacceptable. In 1840, moderates in the American Anti-Slavery Society withdrew from Garrison's organization to found the American and Foreign Anti-Slavery Society.

Another of Garrison's attitudes was also eroding support for him among more conservative reformers: his persistent insistence that women should play a key role in the abolition effort. Having assumed the burden of eliminating sin from the world (see page 319), many evangelical women rallied around Garrison and the antislavery cause. Their growing prominence in the movement led Garrison to insist that they play a more equal role. In 1840 he proposed that a woman be elected to the executive committee of the American Anti-Slavery Society. And later that year women were members of Garrison's delegation to the first World's Anti-Slavery Convention in London. British antislavery advocates, however, like their American counterparts, considered the presence of women inappropriate and refused to seat them. Garrison's group walked out in protest. Increasingly in the 1840s, slights like that made women in the abolition movement feel there was a similarity between their condition and that of the slaves they were seeking to free.

Angelina Grimké was one of the first to make a public proclamation of the frustration women were feeling (see pages 346–347). In her speech before the Massachusetts state assembly in 1838 she had asked "Are we aliens, because we are women? Are we bereft of citizenship because we are mothers, wives and daughters of a mighty people? Have women *no* country—*no* interests staked in public weal—no liabilities in the common peril—no partnership in a nation's guilt and shame?" In that same year, her sister Sarah went further, writing a powerful indictment against the treatment of women in America and a call for equality. In *Letters on the Equality of the Sexes and the Condition of Woman,* Sarah proclaimed, "the page of history teems with woman's wrongs . . . and it is wet with woman's tears." Women must, she said, "arise in all the majesty of moral power . . . and plant themselves, side by side, on the platform of human rights, with man, to whom they were designed to be companions, equals and helpers in every good word and work."

Like Sarah Grimké, many women began backing away from the male-dominated abolitionist cause and began advancing their own cause. In 1848, two women who had been excluded from the World's Anti-Slavery Convention, **Lucretia Mott** and **Elizabeth Cady Stanton,** called women to a convention

Lucretia Mott Quaker minister who founded the Philadelphia Female Anti-Slavery Society (1833) and co-organized the Seneca Falls Women's Rights Convention in 1848.

Elizabeth Cady Stanton Pioneering woman-suffrage leader, co-organizer of the first Women's Rights Convention, held in Seneca Falls, New York, in 1848.

at Seneca Falls, New York, to discuss their common problems. At Seneca Falls, they presented the Declaration of Sentiments based on the Declaration of Independence, citing "the history of repeated injuries and usurpations on the part of man toward woman, having in direct object the establishment of an absolute tyranny over her." The convention adopted eleven resolutions relating to equality under the law, rights to control property, and other prominent issues. A twelfth resolution, calling for the right to vote, failed to receive unanimous endorsement.

Issues in the Election of 1848

Despite the best efforts of conservative American churchmen, statesmen, and politicians to keep the slavery controversy at arm's length, public performances like those of the Grimké sisters continued to elevate public awareness. In 1840, abolitionism finally moved out of the purely moral and religious sphere into the political arena with the formation of the **Liberty party.**

Specifically disavowing Garrison's radical aims, Liberty party leaders like presidential candidate James G. Birney argued that slavery would eventually die on its own if it could be confined geographically. In addition, the Liberty party called for the abolition of slavery in Washington, D.C., and in all the territories where it already existed. Even this moderate message proved unpopular: in 1840 Birney garnered only about 7,000 out of the nearly 2.5 million votes cast. But in 1844, when he again ran on the Liberty party ticket, he won 62,000 popular votes. Clearly a moderate antislavery position was becoming more acceptable.

The presidential election in 1848 came along at the peak of national tension. Sectional differences were reaching crisis proportions, and various groups within the population were clearly alienated by the way things were going. Rather than offering solutions, however, both major parties continued to practice the politics of avoidance.

Suffering ill health, Polk chose not to run for a second term, leaving the Democrats scrambling for a candidate. They chose Lewis Cass of Michigan—a long-time moderate on slavery issues—as their presidential candidate and balanced the ticket with General William Butler of Kentucky. The Whigs hoped to ride a wave of nationalism following the Mexican War by running military hero Zachary Taylor, a Louisianan and a slaveholder, for president and moderate New Yorker Millard Fillmore for vice president.

During the election campaign, Cass tried to avoid offending anyone by advocating the abandonment of any set policy or arbitrary limits on slavery in the territories. Instead, he advanced a policy of **popular sovereignty,** which would permit the territories to choose for themselves whether or not to admit slavery. Taylor refused to go even that far, echoing Calhoun's opinion that Congress did not have the authority to control slavery in the territories.

A third party cut to the heart of the issues at hand. A number of northern Democrats who had supported the Wilmot Proviso felt that Cass's and the Democratic party's position on slavery was too weak-kneed. Casting about for alternatives, they joined with a number of northern Whigs who could not support the slaveholding Taylor and with members of the former Liberty party to promote the candidacy of antislavery advocate Martin Van Buren. Adopting the slogan "Free soil, free speech, free labor, and free men," this northern antislavery coalition dubbed itself the **Free-Soil party.** Even more than the Liberty party before it, the Free-Soil party avoided taking a radical stand on the issue of slavery itself but was firm about excluding slavery from the territories.

The two major parties split more than 2.5 million votes almost evenly—Taylor polled 1,360,000 to Cass's 1,220,000 and won the presidency with 163 electoral votes to Cass's 127. The Free-Soilers, however, made a stronger showing than their predecessors had made. When the votes were counted, Van Buren had won almost 300,000, nearly 10 percent of the total votes cast, but no electoral votes. Congress remained split between Whigs and Democrats, though many northern Whigs were leaning in a Free-Soil direction. Sectional issues had not yet fragmented the political system, but large cracks were showing.

These fissures widened almost immediately when a new issue, even more powerful than mani-

Liberty party The first antislavery political party; it was formed in Albany, New York, in 1840.

popular sovereignty The doctrine that the people of a territory had the right to determine whether slavery would exist within their territory.

Free-Soil party A political party that opposed the extension of slavery into any of the territories newly acquired from Mexico.

♦ Sure that they would find a fortune in gold, Forty-Niners often had photographs taken of themselves with their riches even before they left home. This example shows a Minnesota schoolteacher named George W. Northrop as he expected to look after striking it rich. Unfortunately, Northrop died, killed by Indians, before reaching California. *Minnesota Historical Society.*

fest destiny, came to the fore. During the winter of 1847–1848, California land baron John Sutter had ordered workers to dig a ditch near his flour mill. In the course of digging, workmen found flakes and then chunks of gold. Despite Sutter's efforts to suppress the news, word soon reached San Francisco that gold had been discovered at New Helvetia. By mid-May 1848, men were rushing into the Sacramento Valley from all over California and Oregon to prospect for gold. By September, news reached the East that the light work of panning for gold in California could yield $50 a day, two months' wages for an average northern workingman. In 1849, more than a hundred thousand **forty-niners** took up residence in California.

The combination of massive wealth and a massive new American population in California once again raised the twin issues of expansion and slavery. Like Texas, much of California lay south of the Missouri Compromise line and was thus open for slavery. But northerners, already fearful of a wealthy and well-organized conspiracy of slaveowners, were not about to turn the richest source of gold yet discovered over to the Slave Power. Thus, although the discovery of gold in California seemed to announce God's approval of American expansionism and manifest destiny, it drove an enormous wedge into an already cracking political system. Soon the problem of expansion and slavery would have to be resolved.

forty-niners Prospectors who streamed into California in 1849, after the discovery of gold at New Helvetia in 1848.

SUMMARY

E xpectations
C onstraints
C hoices
O utcomes

During the first half of the nineteenth century the westward movement of Americans steadily gained momentum. Some successful entrepreneurs like William Henry Ashley made enormous profits from their *choice* to move west, initially as heads of fur-trading empires. Land speculators and gold seekers, too, helped open areas to settlement. Such pioneers were usually followed by distinct waves of migrants who *chose* to go west, *expecting* land and opportunity.

In Texas, Oregon, California, Utah, and elsewhere in the West communities sprang up like weeds. One *outcome* was the development of a variety of cultures and economies, which evolved from the interplay of old habits, new ideals, and environmental *constraints,* including the presence of those with prior claims to the land.

Conflicting *expectations* about the country's manifest destiny promoted an air of crisis in the nation at large. Northerners wanted a West that would be free for diversified economic development. Southerners wanted to sow every suitable acre with cotton. And people from each region *chose* to try to use expansion to add to their power in Congress, hoping to further their economic and political demands—tariff, tax, and internal improvement measures that would favor their region, for example.

In the course of the debate, one issue—slavery—began to eclipse all others in symbolizing the differing demands made by North and South. For northerners, the idea of going to war to win Oregon was acceptable because the Missouri Compromise prohibited slavery there, but the idea of going to war to acquire Texas, which won independence from Mexico in 1836, was quite another matter. The possibility of two, or perhaps as many as ten, new southern senators and an unknown number of new southern representatives filled northerners with dread. Nevertheless, the nation *chose* to fight a war with Mexico in 1846–1848, and won, gaining California and vast territories in the Southwest. The discovery of gold in California in 1848 made that region a new bone of contention in the sectional debate.

Meanwhile, voices challenging slavery's moral implications gained a wider audience, although radical abolitionists like William Lloyd Garrison still labored for acceptance. Part of what made Garrison's message so hard for many to accept was his insistence on an equal role for women in the task of eliminating evil from the world. But severely discriminatory conditions *constrained* the many women who participated in abolition and other reform movements. One *outcome* was the Seneca Falls conference in 1848, where politically active women called for greater equality with men.

SUGGESTED READINGS

Ray Allen Billington. *America's Frontier Heritage* (1966).

A broad overview of America's western experience from a Turnerian point of view.

Thomas R. Hietala. *Manifest Design* (1985).

An interesting and well-written interpretation of the Mexican-American War and the events leading up to it.

Patricia Nelson Limerick. *The Legacy of Conquest* (1988).

Considered by many to be the Bible of the New Western History, this wonderfully written interpretation of events in the West challenges many assumptions and stereotypes.

Donald W. Meinig. *Imperial Texas* (1969).

A fascinating look at Texas history by a leading historical geographer.

Christopher L. Miller. *Prophetic Worlds* (1985).

Critics have called this a seductive reinterpretation of the history of Indians and whites in the Oregon Country.

Paul Rodman. *California Gold* (1947; reprint 1965).

A classic, but still the best account of the Gold Rush and its impact on life in California.

Wallace E. Stegner. *The Gathering of Zion* (1964).

A masterfully written history of the Mormon Trail by one of the West's leading literary figures.

John David Unruh. *The Plains Across* (1979).

Arguably the best one-volume account of the overland passage to Oregon. The many pages melt as the author captures the reader in the adventure of the Oregon trail.

THE COMPROMISE OF 1850 The acquisition of Texas and California brought a showdown between North and South over representation in the national government. As this map shows, the Compromise of 1850 permitted Texas and California to be admitted to the Union without seriously undermining the balance of power in the Senate. In the House of Representatives, however, the balance favored the North.

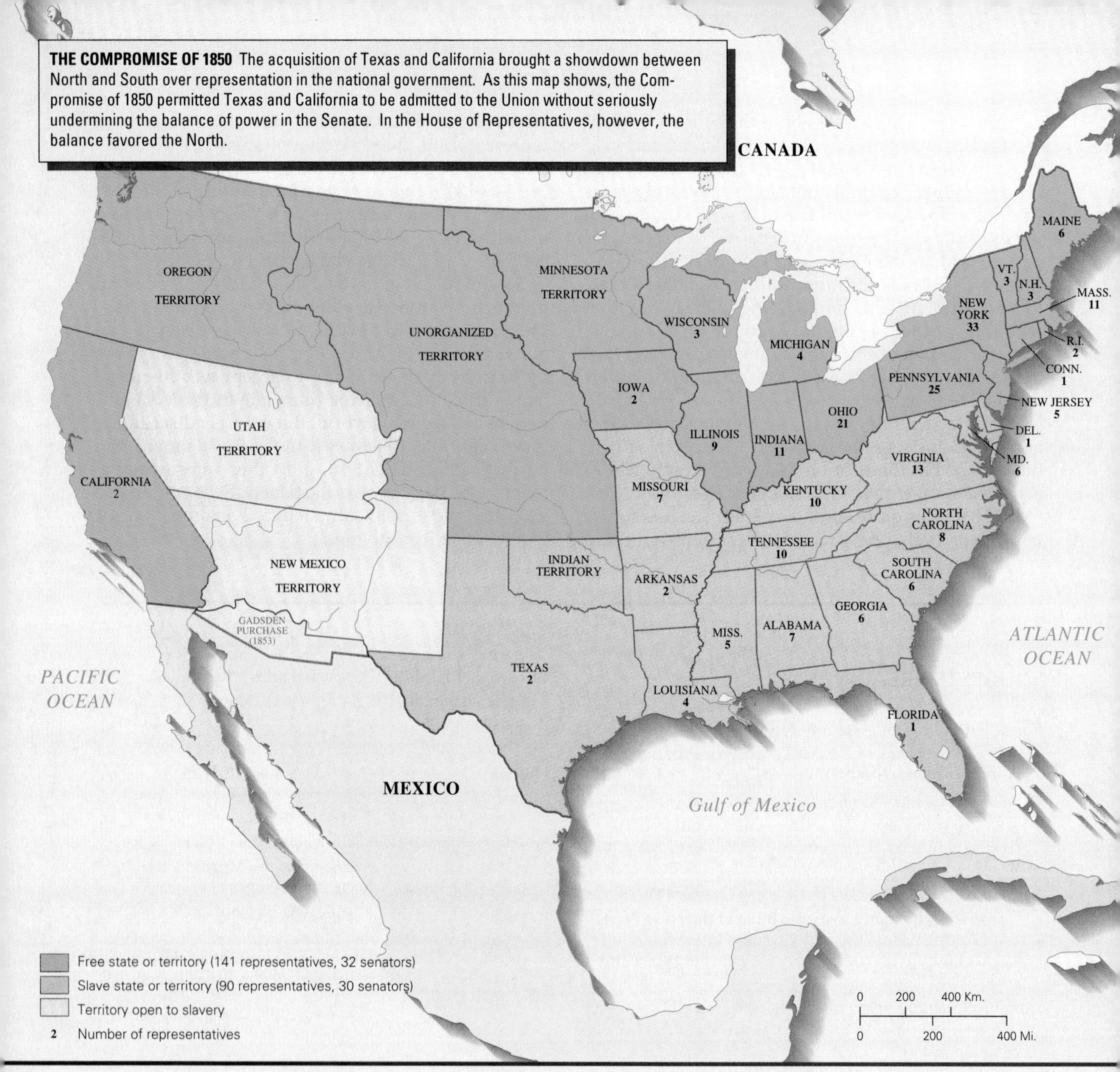

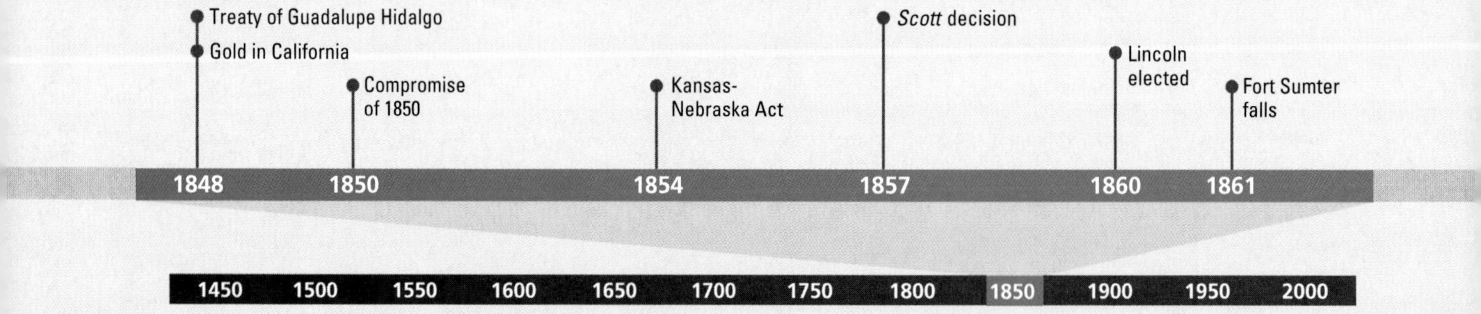

CHAPTER 14

Sectional Conflict and Shattered Union, 1850–1860

New Political Choices

- What considerations shaped the political choices that average Americans made during the 1850s?
- What was the outcome for the political party system?

Toward a House Divided

- How did various groups react to the Kansas-Nebraska Act, and what expectations led to those reactions?

The Divided Nation

- What did northerners and southerners expect to happen as a result of the presidential election in 1860?
- Why did they expect those outcomes?

The Nation Dissolved

- What choices were available to Abraham Lincoln and Jefferson Davis in March 1861?
- What political factors constrained their choices?

INTRODUCTION

E xpectations
C onstraints
C hoices
O utcomes

The United States entered a period of major growth and transition during the 1850s. The nation had increased in size, and wealth and population grew dramatically as technology and industry continued their rapid advance. After the successful military adventure against Mexico, many Americans *expected* their nation's wealth and vitality to fuel continued growth and development, opening the way to great opportunities in a proud and expansive society. Most Americans believed that the nation simply needed to chart a correct course to claim its manifest destiny.

But implementing a course of action to achieve national destiny meant *choosing* particular goals and specific methods. Despite the appearance of unity, sharp disagreement *constrained* Americans seeking the correct national course. Most people agreed, for example, that railroad development was good, but not everyone agreed on where the rail lines should run, how development should be funded, or what should be carried on the rails. Technological advances and industrial development brought new *constraints,* altering the nation's social structure and adding to disagreement. As factories sprang up, displacing native-born artisans with unskilled immigrant laborers, the harsh realities of industrial development brought massive social disruption. Disruption also occurred as the expansion of commercial cotton growing pushed slave labor farther and farther into the American continent, renewing and amplifying political, economic, and ethical disagreements over slavery.

These problems quickly became political agendas as voters searched for leaders and parties that would address the new issues and direct the nation's progress. Old-line northeastern and southern political interests continued to clash over traditional matters like tariffs and currency control, but rising immigration and westward migration brought new voters and new interests into play, particularly regarding the expansion of slavery. Also, as the nation's social complexion continued to change, various reformers tried to restore order and virtue, creating political blocs to fight for moral reform. All of these voter groups had extremely diverse *expectations* about the correct course for the nation, the role government should play, and the values that should guide these *choices.*

As individuals joined in new voting affiliations, one *outcome* was significant change in the nation's political environment, first at the local and state levels and eventually at the national level. Both Whigs and Democrats attempted to direct and exploit the events of the 1850s. But both faced new *constraints,* including internal strife, for the commonality that had held each party together disappeared as the nation's social, economic, and political climate changed. The total number of voters grew significantly, but—more important—so did the diversity of the electorate. Building a coalition strong enough to win a national election became increasingly difficult as regional, ethnic, and social distinctions influenced voters.

In this fragmented climate, the expansion of slavery into the territories became the dominant political issue and the largest single factor facing both Whigs and Democrats. In a changing society rife with the problems of expansion, immigration, industrialization, and urbanization, political leaders *chose* either to seek compromise or try to ignore the slavery question. In reality, they could do neither. Through all the debates, political platforms, and confrontations, two societies—North and South—attempted to control and direct the course of national destiny.

As the nation's leaders wrestled with a host of new issues amid political fragmentation, the confrontation between those two societies peaked. Although many people wanted peace and favored reconciliation, the political structure their *choices* had created thwarted that desire. The new political coalitions of the 1850s more accurately reflected the new social and economic environment. But *constrained* by the regional interests that had given birth to them, these coalitions proved incapable of compromise. Ultimately, both sides *chose* to reject compromise, and the outcome was the end of Union and the beginning of America's most destructive and deadly war.

CHRONOLOGY

Toward a Shattered Union

1848	Zachary Taylor elected president Immigration to the United States exceeds 100,000 for the first time
1850	Southern rights convention called Compromise of 1850
1852	First railroad line completed to Chicago Harriet Beecher Stowe's *Uncle Tom's Cabin* Franklin Pierce elected president Collapse of the Whig party American party emerges
1853	Gadsden Purchase
1854	Formation of the Republican party Kansas-Nebraska Act Ostend Manifesto
1855	Sack of Lawrence, Kansas Pottawatomie Massacre
1856	James Buchanan elected president
1857	*Dred Scott* decision Proslavery Lecompton constitution adopted in Kansas Hinton Rowan Helper's *Impending Crisis of the South*
1858	Lincoln-Douglas debates Minnesota admitted to the Union
1859	Oregon admitted to the Union John Brown's raid on Harpers Ferry
1860	Abraham Lincoln elected president Critenden compromise fails
1861	Formation of the Confederate States of America Shelling of Fort Sumter

New Political Choices

- What considerations shaped the political choices that average Americans made during the 1850s?
- What was the outcome for the political party system?

The presidential election in 1848 had celebrated American expansion and nationalism, but events in the newly acquired territories were pushing the nation toward crisis. The flow of Americans into California and the promise of gold flooding back out seemed to demand federal attention, so newly elected president Zachary Taylor ordered Californians to draw up a state constitution and apply for statehood. A constitutional convention in Sacramento promptly did so but fueled the flames of sectional conflict by producing a document that barred slavery in the state. Putting the national interest foremost, Taylor recommended that California be admitted as a free state and that Utah and New Mexico be organized as territories without reference to slavery.

Taylor's proposal frightened and angered southerners, for most of the region lay south of the Missouri Compromise line, and southerners had assumed that it would be open to slavery. They contended that Taylor's move would unbalance sectional representation in the Senate, a realistic concern (see the chapter-opening map). John C. Calhoun stated, "I trust we shall persist in our resistance until restoration of all our rights, or disunion, one or the other, is the consequence." Southerners agreed, calling a southern rights convention in June 1850 to discuss withdrawing from the Union.

The Politics of Compromise

Henry Clay, who had successfully crafted the Missouri Compromise (see page 283), believed that any successful agreement would have to address all sides of the issue. He proposed a complex **omnibus** bill—a series of separate proposals—to the Senate on January 20, 1850. California would enter the Union

omnibus Including or covering many things.

♦ This painting shows Henry Clay attempting to convince his fellow senators to support his omnibus compromise bill in 1850. Clay failed, but Illinois senator Stephen Douglas was able to get the compromise passed by breaking up the complicated bill, calling for a vote on each separate provision. *Library of Congress.*

as a free state, but the slavery question would be left to popular sovereignty—the vote of the people—in all other territories acquired through the Treaty of Guadalupe Hidalgo (see page 389). The bill also directed Texas to back down on a continuing border dispute with New Mexico in exchange for federal assumption of Texas's public debt. Clay then called for an end to the slave trade in Washington, D.C., to appease abolitionists and for a new, more effective **fugitive slave law** to ensure southern support.

Written to satisfy all sectional interests, the omnibus bill pleased no one, and Congress debated it for seven months. Despite appeals to reason by Clay and Daniel Webster, Congress remained hopelessly deadlocked. President Taylor further complicated negotiations by threatening to veto any measure that deviated from Clay's proposals. Finally, in July 1850, the proposals were defeated. The 73-year-old Clay left the capital tired and dispirited, but **Stephen A. Douglas** of Illinois revived the compromise by proposing each component of Clay's omnibus package as a separate bill. Using practical economic arguments and backroom political arm twisting, he steered each bill forward and pushed a final compromise toward completion. President Taylor died on July 9. His more moderate successor, Vice President **Millard Fillmore,** influenced northern Whig support for the bills. Finally, in September, Congress passed the **Compromise of 1850.**

The Compromise of 1850 did little to relieve underlying regional differences. That slaveowners

fugitive slave law Law providing for the return of escaped slaves to their owners.

Stephen A. Douglas Illinois senator who tried to reconcile northern and southern differences over slavery through the Compromise of 1850 and the Kansas-Nebraska Act.

Millard Fillmore Vice President who succeeded Zachary Taylor when he died in office and who tried to occupy a middle ground on slavery.

Compromise of 1850 Plan intended to reconcile North and South on the issue of slavery; it recognized the principle of popular sovereignty and included a strong fugitive slave law.

could pursue runaway slaves into northern states and return them into bondage brought slavery too close to home for many northerners. Southerners too found no reason to celebrate. They had lost the balance of power in the Senate and gained no positive protection for slavery, either in the territories or at home. Still, the compromise created a brief respite from the slavery-extension question, freeing Whigs and Democrats to begin planning for the upcoming presidential election of 1852.

Superficially the Whigs seemed well organized and surprisingly unified. They passed over Millard Fillmore in favor of General Winfield Scott, veteran of both the War of 1812 and the Mexican War. The Democrats remained divided through forty-nine ballots, unable to decide between Lewis Cass of Michigan, Stephen A. Douglas of Illinois, and **James Buchanan** of Pennsylvania. They finally settled on the virtually unknown **Franklin Pierce** of New Hampshire, who pledged to live by and uphold the Compromise of 1850 and keep slavery out of politics. This promise was enough to win Martin Van Buren back to the Democrats, and he brought many Free-Soilers back with him. Many others, though, abandoned Van Buren and joined with "conscience" Whigs, who opposed slavery (unlike "cotton" Whigs, who favored it).

Scott was a national figure and a distinguished military hero, but Pierce gathered 254 electoral votes to Scott's 42. This one-sided victory, however, revealed more about the disarray in the Whig party than it did about Pierce's popularity or Democratic strength. Splits between "cotton" and "conscience" groups splintered Whig unity. Regional tension escalated as Free-Soil rhetoric clashed with calls for extending slavery. Confrontations between Catholics and Protestants and between native-born and immigrant caused bitter animosity. In the North, where immigration, industrialization, and antislavery sentiment were most prevalent and economic friction was most pronounced, massive numbers of voters, believing the Whigs incapable of addressing current problems, deserted the party. The election of 1852 marked not only the end of the Whig party but also the beginning of a major political realignment, which finally gelled in the election of 1860.

A Changing Political Economy

During the 1850s industrial growth accelerated, further altering the nation's economic structure. By 1860 less than half of all northern workers made a living from agriculture as northern industry increasingly specialized in processing agricultural products grown in other regions. Steam began to replace water as the primary power source, and factories were no longer limited to locations along rivers and streams. The use of interchangeable parts became more sophisticated and intricate. In 1851, Isaac Singer devised an assembly line using this technology and began mass-producing sewing machines, fostering a boom in ready-made clothing. As industry expanded, the North became more reliant on the West and South for raw materials and for the food consumed by those working in northeastern factories.

Railroad development stimulated economic and industrial growth. Between 1850 and 1860, the number of miles of railroad track in the United States increased from 9,000 to more than 30,000. The vast majority of these lines linked the Northeast with the Midwest, carrying produce to eastern markets and eastern manufactures to western consumers. In 1852, the Michigan Southern Railroad completed the first line into Chicago from the East, and by 1855 that city had become a major transportation hub linking regions farther west with the eastern seaboard.

Developing this transportation system was difficult. A lack of bridges over major rivers, particularly over the Ohio, impeded rail traffic. Because there still was no standard **rail gauge**—at least twelve different measurements were used—cargo frequently had to be carted from one rail line to another. Despite these problems, railroads quickly became an integral part of the expanding American economy. Western farmers, who had previously shipped their products downriver to New Orleans on slow and undependable barges and boats (see page 277) now sent them much more rapidly by rail to the eastern industrial centers. The availability of reliable transportation induced farmers to cultivate more land, and enterprising individuals started up related businesses such as warehouses and **grain elevators,**

James Buchanan Pennsylvania senator who was elected president in 1856 after gaining the Democratic nomination as a compromise candidate.

Franklin Pierce New Hampshire lawyer and Democratic politician nominated as a compromise candidate and elected president in 1852.

rail gauge The distance between train tracks.

grain elevator A building equipped with mechanical lifting devices and used for storing grain.

AN EXPRESS FREIGHT SHIPMENT OF 30 COACHES, APRIL 15, 1868
BY ABBOT, DOWNING & CO., CONCORD, N.H. TO WELLS, FARGO CO., OMAHA, NEB.

♦ The expansion of railroads facilitated transportation in a number of ways. Not only could western farmers get their produce to market and buy bulky manufactured goods delivered by train, but other modes of transportation were made easier. This illustration shows thirty stagecoaches built by a New Hampshire firm being hauled in a single load to the Wells Fargo Company in Omaha, Nebraska who, in turn, used them to haul passengers and small freight to places the trains did not go. *New Hampshire Historical Society, Concord.*

simplifying storage and loading along railroad lines. Mining boomed, particularly the iron industry, for the railroads not only transported ore but also became a major consumer.

Because of the economic benefits from increased transportation, government actively supported railroad development and expansion. Building a railroad required huge sums of money. In populous areas, where passenger and freight traffic was heavy, the promise of a quick and profitable return on investment allowed railroads to raise sufficient capital by selling company stock. In sparsely settled regions, however, where investment returns were much slower, state and local governments loaned money directly to rail companies, financed them indirectly by purchasing stock, or extended state tax exemptions. The most crucial aid to railroads, however, was federal land grants.

The federal government, which owned vast amounts of unsettled territory, gave land to developers who then leased or sold plots of ground along the proposed route to finance construction. In 1850, one such federal proposal made by Illinois senator Stephen A. Douglas resulted in a 2.6-million-acre land grant to Illinois, Mississippi, and Alabama for a railroad between Chicago and Mobile. Congress also invested heavily in plans for a transcontinental railroad, and on March 4, 1853, appropriated $150,000 for a survey of potential routes across the continent.

While Americans were enjoying the rail boom, Europe was suffering from massive crop failures and war and was hungering for agricultural products. During the 1850s, the price of grain rose sharply in world markets. Railroads allowed western farmers to ship directly to eastern seaports and on to Europe. Meanwhile, technological advances in farming equipment allowed American farmers, facing a constant labor shortage, to harvest enough grain to meet world demand.

The steel plow devised in 1837 by **John Deere** allowed farmers to cultivate more acres with greater

John Deere American industrialist who pioneered the manufacture of steel plows especially suited for working prairie soil.

♦ Cyrus McCormick's mechanical reaper, shown here in an 1846 advertisement from *The Cultivator* magazine, was one of the technological wonders of its time, permitting a single farmer to harvest as much grain as fourteen field hands could using conventional tools. *State Historical Society of Wisconsin.*

ease. The mechanical reaper invented in 1841 by **Cyrus McCormick** could harvest more crops than fourteen field hands. Railroads distributed these new, heavy pieces of equipment at a reasonable cost. The combination of greater production potential and speedy transportation prompted westerners to increase farm size and concentrate on cash crops. The outcome of these developments was a vast increase in the economic and political power of the West.

Western grain markets provided the foodstuffs for American industrialization, and Europe provided much of the labor. Factories employed unskilled workers for the most part, and immigrants made up the majority of that labor pool as food shortages, poverty, and political upheaval drove millions from Europe, especially from Ireland and Germany (see page 315). Total immigration to the United States exceeded 100,000 for the first time in 1848, and in 1851, 221,000 people migrated to the United States just from Ireland. In 1852, the number of German immigrants reached 145,000. Many of these newcomers, particularly the Irish, were not trained in skilled crafts and wound up settling in the industrial urban centers of the Northeast, where they could find work in the factories.

This combination of changes set the stage for political crisis. Liberalized suffrage rules transformed naturalized immigrants into voters, and both parties courted them, adding their interests to the political pot. Meanwhile, a mechanized textile industry hungry for southern fiber lent vitality to the continued growth of the cotton kingdom and the slave labor system that gave it life. Northern political leaders visualized an industrial nation based on free labor, but that view ran counter to the southern elite's ideals of **agrarian capitalism** based on slavery. In the West, most continued to believe in the Jeffersonian ideal of an agrarian nation of small and medium-size farms and could not accept either industrial or cotton capitalism as positive developments.

What emerged were competing regional versions of what constituted national destiny and progress. As one clear-sighted northern minister pointed out in 1852, the debate was not about whether there

Cyrus McCormick Virginia inventor and manufacturer who developed and mass-produced the McCormick reaper, a machine that harvested grain.

agrarian capitalism A system of agriculture based on the efficient, specialized production of crops intended to generate profits rather than subsistence.

should be progress but about "different kinds and methods of progress." Differing visions of national destiny were about to cause the breakdown of the existing party system.

Slavery seemed to loom behind every issue and debate. But another, and immediately more important issue loomed behind slavery. Most Americans, even southerners, had no personal investment in slavery during the 1850s. The two-thirds of southerners who owned no slaves tolerated the institution but were largely independent from it. Most of them had only fleeting contact with the great plantations and the peculiar labor system operating on them. Northerners, too, were largely indifferent. Men like young Illinois state congressman **Abraham Lincoln** believed the institution was unfair but were not inclined to do anything about it. What mattered to people like these was not slavery as such but autonomy—control over local affairs and over their own lives.

The slavery question challenged notions of autonomy in both North and South. In their widely disseminated rhetoric, abolitionists expanded the specter of the Slave Power conspiracy (see page 385), especially in the aftermath of the Compromise of 1850. Growing numbers perceived this conspiracy as intent on imposing southern ways onto all parts of the country and installing southern elites or their sympathizers in positions of power in every section of the nation. Whether they were farmers in western states like Indiana or Illinois or artisans in Pennsylvania or New York, common people were jealous of their own local institutions and would resist a southern takeover. Nor would common people in the South accept interference from outsiders. But in the face of an antisouthern crusade by northern radicals, how long could small remote farmers in the South hold out? Even as late as 1860, North Carolina leader C. B. Harrison pointed out that to "unite the *masses* of any Southern State . . . against the Union & in favor [of] slavery" required instilling a fear of northern dominance.

Decline of the Whigs

The matter of local autonomy had particular significance in the Northeast. As industrialization accelerated and immigration increased, so did the dislocation of artisans and the overcrowding in the cities that had begun to be problems earlier in the century. During the 1850s many unemployed artisans were forced to accept factory work at a time when the flood of immigrants was driving wages down. For such men, politics came to seem less a game designed to win national glory and more a device for protecting hard-won rights. They wanted a political party that would address their most pressing problems: loss of status, income, and jobs.

The Whig party had been their voice in politics during the party's glory days but was losing support quickly. During the elections in 1848, the Whigs had tried to win Catholic and immigrant voters away from the Democrats, but the strategy backfired. Not only did the Whigs not win over large numbers of immigrants, but they alienated two groups of supporters. One group was artisans, who saw immigrants as the main source of their economic and social woes. The other was Protestant evangelicals, to whom Roman Catholic Irish and German immigrants symbolized all that was wrong in the world and threatening to the American republic. Unable to agree on national policies to deal with the changing economic, social, and political issues that confronted Americans, Whig leaders could do little to address voters' immediate concerns. Increasing numbers left the Whig party to form state and local coalitions more in tune with voters' hopes and fears over matters of autonomy. Between 1852 and 1856, the Whig party dissolved, leaving different local political organizations pointing to different threats to local authority.

The first of these locally oriented groups to move into the national political arena was the anti-Catholic, anti-immigrant **Know-Nothings.** This loosely knit political organization traced its origins back to secret **nativist** societies that had come into existence during the ethnic tension and rioting in Philadelphia, Boston, and New York in the 1830s (see page 339). These secret fraternal organizations at first dabbled in politics by endorsing candidates who shared their view that immigration was the pri-

Abraham Lincoln Illinois lawyer and politician who argued against popular sovereignty in debates with Stephen Douglas in 1858; he lost the senatorial election to Douglas but was elected president in 1860.

Know-Nothings Members of anti-Catholic, anti-immigrant organizations who eventually formed the American party on a national level.

nativist Favoring native-born inhabitants of a country over immigrants.

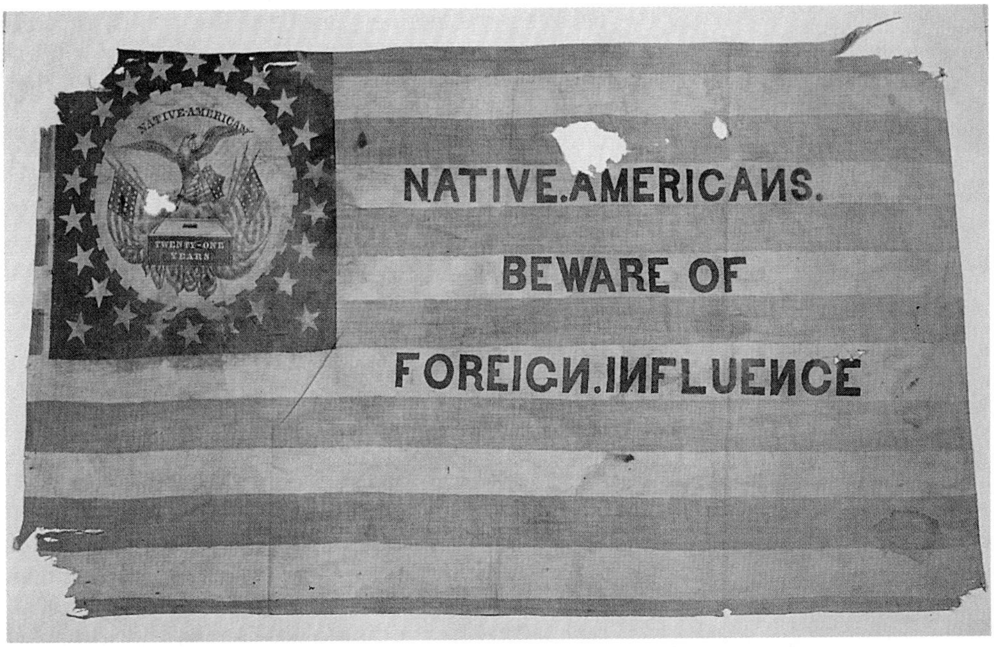

♦ Convinced that slavery and other sectional issues were blinding Americans to the true dangers stemming from uncontrolled immigration and foreign influence, the Know-Nothing party ran Millard Fillmore for president in 1856. Banners like this one warned Americans and solicited their votes. Fillmore succeeded in getting 21 percent of the popular vote. *Milwaukee County Historical Society.*

mary evil facing the nation. Remaining underground, these groups told their members to say "I know nothing" if they were questioned about the organization or its political intrigues, hence the name Know-Nothings. After the election of 1852, the societies began coming out into the open, nominating and voting for their own candidates. A national coalition of Know-Nothing groups, finally calling itself the American party, expressed fear of the Catholic church's political influence. Know-Nothings charged that immigrants were part of a Catholic plot to overthrow democracy in the United States and to impose an elite of priests and bishops onto every community in the country. Seeking to counter this perceived threat to local controls, Know-Nothings contended that "Americans must rule America," and they adopted a platform advocating a twenty-one-year naturalization period, a ban against naturalized citizens holding public office, and the use of the Protestant Bible in the public schools.

Know-Nothings from different regions disagreed about many things, but they all agreed that the Whig and Democratic parties were corrupt and that the only hope for the nation lay in scrapping traditional politics and starting anew. Like the Antimasonic movement in the 1820s, in which many Know-Nothing leaders got their start in politics (see page 288), the Know-Nothing party expressed antiparty sentiments, alleging wholesale voter fraud and government corruption by both major parties. As Ohio governor and future president Rutherford B. Hayes noted, the people were expressing a "general disgust with the powers that be." Party leaders contended that unscrupulous individuals had gained control of Whig and Democratic organizations and that party conventions and caucuses were removing local voters from the candidate selection process. The platforms and publications of the Know-Nothing party consistently noted the "corrupt nature" of politics and called for "restriction of executive patronage" and "reformation" of the "National Legislature."

Various antislavery coalitions also vied for local political support. The Compromise of 1850 momentarily eased regional fears, but sectional tensions still smoldered beneath the surface, dooming all

♦ Harriet Beecher Stowe's novel *Uncle Tom's Cabin* captivated northeastern reading audiences with its depiction of the evils of southern slavery. This early illustrated edition sported a cover drawing of a runaway slave mother crossing ice floes to escape her mounted pursuers. *From the collection of Edith Hariton/Antique Textile Resource, Bethesda.*

Whig attempts to formulate national policy. The embers of sectionalism flamed anew in 1852 with the publication of *Uncle Tom's Cabin* by **Harriet Beecher Stowe.** Stowe portrayed the darkest inhumanities of southern slavery in the first American novel to include African Americans as central characters. Published first in serial form in the *National Era,* an abolitionist newspaper, *Uncle Tom's Cabin* was reissued in book form and sold three hundred thousand copies in its first year. Adapted for the stage, it became one of the most popular plays of the period. The book stirred public opinion and breathed new life into antislavery sentiments, leading Free-Soilers and "conscience" Whigs to renew their efforts to limit or end slavery. When they saw that the Whig party was incapable of addressing the slavery question in any effective way, they began to look for other political options.

Many evangelical reformers—another major segment of the Whig's northern constituency—believed the nation was beset by a host of evils that were threatening its existence. Progress without Christian principles and individual morality, they thought, had led to the fall of the Roman and all previous empires and posed a great danger for the United States—the "Empire of Liberty." Evangelicals viewed slavery, alcohol, Catholicism, religious heresy, and corrupt government as threats to the nation's moral fiber. In their efforts to create moral government and to direct national destiny, these reformers advocated social reform through both religious and political action.

Both antislavery and evangelical Whigs bitterly opposed provisions in the Compromise of 1850 that allowed slave catchers to follow runaway slaves into the North, arrest them, and return them to bondage—such invasion of local autonomy was unacceptable. Throughout the 1850s, some northerners sought to help slaves escape from the South. Known as the **Underground Railroad,** a network of northerners provided hiding places and aid for runaway slaves. Frederick Douglass was skeptical about how effective this network was, but he and a number of other former slaves, particularly Harriet Tubman and Sojourner Truth, attempted to persuade people to support slaves in their attempts to gain freedom. Tubman made frequent excursions into the South and may have brought back more than three hundred individuals. She and others also delivered lectures on their life in slavery to white audiences across the North, increasing northern awareness of the plight of the slaves and stirring hostility toward the fugitive slave provisions of the Compromise of 1850 (see Individual Choices: Harriet Tubman).

Temperance forces (see page 343) also made great gains during the early part of the decade. Thirteen states enacted laws prohibiting the manufacture and sale of liquor. Overall, however, progress seemed slow, and reformers became impatient with Whig tactics. Temperance advocates and other reformers had much in common with the Know-Nothings and with antislavery forces, for immigrants reputedly drank more heavily than native-born Americans,

Harriet Beecher Stowe American novelist and abolitionist whose novel *Uncle Tom's Cabin* fanned antislavery sentiment in the North.

Underground Railroad The secret network of northerners who helped fugitive slaves escape to Canada or to safe areas in free states.

and Catholics supposedly supported the Democrats and slavery. When the Whigs seemed unable to address the pressing moral and religious issues that the crusaders believed were wrecking their cities and their nation, the crusaders deserted the Whig party for local and state-level coalitions designed to combat "Rum, Romanism, and Slavery."

While the Whig party was collapsing under the pressure from changing social and economic issues of the 1850s, the Democratic party and Franklin Pierce, its representative in the White House, were not immune to the pressures of a changing electorate. Pierce, at 48 the youngest president the nation had ever had, was considered a "doughface": a northern Democrat with southern sympathies. He was part of the Young America movement within the Democratic party in the late 1840s. While attempting to ignore the slavery issue, the Young Americans advocated romantic and aggressive nationalism, manifest destiny, and support of republican revolutions anywhere.

Increasing Tension Under Pierce

In line with the Young America agenda, Pierce emphasized expansion, but he could not avoid the slavery issue, no matter how he tried. Choosing a route for a transcontinental railroad became the keystone in his program for the nation. Southerners hungered for room to grow economically and politically. They knew that a railroad based in the South not only would allow direct commerce with California but also would open new areas for settlement and allow the spread of cotton agriculture, which had been confined to those areas where rivers could provide bulk transportation. Eventually the new territories would become states, increasing the South's national political power.

That model of development was totally unacceptable to several groups: to northern evangelicals, who viewed slavery as a moral blight on the nation; to Free-Soil advocates, who believed the spread of slavery would degrade white workers; and to northern manufacturers, who wanted to maintain dominance in Congress to ensure continued economic protection. Nevertheless, in May 1853, only two months after assuming office, Pierce inflamed antislavery forces by sending James Gadsden, a southern railroad developer, to Mexico to purchase a strip of land lying below the southern border of the territories of Arizona and New Mexico. Any rail line built westward from a southern city would have to cross that land as it proceeded from Texas to California, and Pierce and his southern supporters wanted to make sure that it was part of the United States. The **Gadsden Purchase,** ratified by Congress on June 29, 1853, added 29,640 square miles of land to the United States for a cost of $10 million. It also finalized the southwestern border of the United States.

Rather than enhancing Pierce's reputation as a nationalist, the Gadsden Purchase fed the perception that he was a southern sympathizer aiding in the extension of slavery. It also led to a more serious sectional crisis. The Gadsden Purchase prompted advocates of a southern route for the transcontinental railroad, led by Secretary of War **Jefferson Davis,** to push for government sponsorship of the project. They found themselves blocked, however, by Illinois senator Stephen A. Douglas.

A consummate politician who spent most of his adult life in public office, Douglas was short in stature but hugely ambitious. A compelling orator and fierce debater, he became known as the "Little Giant." Arguing that the nation "must have Rail Roads and Telegraphs from the Atlantic to the Pacific, through our own territory," Douglas began supporting western expansion and a transcontinental railroad in the 1840s. The "vast wilderness fifteen hundred miles in breadth, filled with hostile savages, and cutting off direct communication" with the newly acquired Pacific territories, he insisted, had to be civilized and settled.

Douglas wanted a national railroad that would pass through Chicago and the Midwest, enhancing that region's economic and political strength and furthering his own career. He also had a financial interest in the Chicago route. Using his position as chairman of the Senate's Committee on Territories, Douglas blocked Davis's effort to build a transcontinental railroad through the South. Douglas favored a northern route that would make his constituent city, Chicago, the pivot for a northern coast-to-coast rail system. Because this northern transcontinental

Gadsden Purchase A strip of land in present-day Arizona and New Mexico that the United States bought from Mexico in 1853 to secure a southern route for a transcontinental railroad.

Jefferson Davis Secretary of War under Franklin Pierce; he later became president of the Confederacy.

INDIVIDUAL CHOICES

To Free Others

Harriet Tubman

Fearful of being torn from her family in Maryland and sold to a cotton plantation in the Deep South, Harriet Tubman chose to run away from slavery. Seeking to reunite her family, she returned to the South to help them escape. Despite personal danger to herself, she chose to continue her efforts, finally conducting as many as three hundred slaves along the Underground Railroad to freedom. She is seen here (on the left) with some of the slaves that she helped free. Sophia Smith Collection.

Resisting slavery seemed second nature to Harriet Tubman. Born a slave on a Maryland plantation in 1820, she quickly developed a fiery spirit and was not shy about protesting bad treatment. One such incident so angered the plantation overseer that he hit her over the head with a lead weight, inflicting a permanent brain injury that caused her to suddenly lose consciousness several times a day for the rest of her life. To overcome this disability, she worked on building herself up physically, becoming an uncommonly strong woman. It was said that she could single-handedly haul a boat fully loaded with stones, a feat deemed impossible for all but the strongest men.

Although Tubman dreamed about freedom after learning of Nat Turner's Rebellion in 1831, her disability and fear of being caught prevented her from acting. But in 1849, all that changed when the owner of her plantation died. Rumors began circulating that the man's estate was going to be liquidated and that the slaves were to be sold "down the river" to cotton plantations in the Deep South. The thought of being taken so far away from any avenue to freedom forced Tubman to choose.

Leaving the plantation, she slowly made her way northward by land, stopping at places she had heard about where free blacks or sympathetic whites would provide food and shelter. After a harrowing flight, she finally arrived in Philadelphia. She was free but was not content with winning freedom just for herself. Tubman

route would have to pass through territory that had not yet been organized, Douglas introduced a bill on January 4, 1854, that called for incorporating the entire area into a new territory that would be called Nebraska.

Douglas knew that he would need both northern and southern support to get his bill through Congress, so he tried to structure the legislation in such a way that it would alienate neither section. Fearful that the bill would generate yet another debate over slavery, Douglas sought to silence possible opposition by proposing that the matter be left to popular sovereignty within the territory itself—let the voters decide. Noting that the proposed territory was had left a large family behind in Maryland and would not be happy until she had won their freedom as well.

Soon after arriving in Pennsylvania, Tubman met William Still, a black clerk for the Pennsylvania Anti-Slavery Society. Still had worked since 1847 as a "conductor" on the Underground Railroad. Every so often, he and others like him made their way secretly into the South, contacted slaves who wanted to escape, and led them northward, stopping at prearranged "stations"—homes and businesses owned by free blacks or white abolitionists—for food and shelter. With the passage of the Fugitive Slave Act in 1850, Tubman decided that the only way she could win freedom for her family was to become a conductor herself. She chose to risk her freedom—even her life—to bring her parents, her brother and his family, and her own two children out of slavery.

It took Tubman several trips into the slave South to accomplish her aim of reuniting her family. In the course of her adventure, what began as a commitment to her immediate kin became a mission to her entire people. In all, Tubman made nineteen trips to the South between 1850 and the outbreak of civil war in 1861, and it was said that she was personally responsible for conducting three hundred slaves to freedom. In between trips she, like Frederick Douglass, Sojourner Truth, and other escaped slaves, told her story to northern audiences, seeking support for her efforts to free individual slaves and for the larger effort to free all slaves. Her activities as a speaker and as an underground agent brought her acclaim and notoriety. John Brown consulted her while planning his raid on Harpers Ferry, and authorities in the South acknowledged her impact by posting a $40,000 reward for her capture.

Tubman continued her activities after war broke out in 1861. Like other black women who either had been born into or had won freedom, she again volunteered to go into the South with Union forces to serve as a nurse and cook and to help evacuate slaves from areas won by federal troops. She also continued speaking out in the interest of her people. To beat the South, she admonished, President Lincoln must set the slaves free.

above the Missouri Compromise line, southerners pointed out that Congress might prohibit popular sovereignty from functioning. Douglas responded that the Compromise of 1850 repudiated the 1820 Missouri Compromise, but he finally supported an amendment to his original bill. The amendment divided the territory in half—Nebraska in the north and Kansas in the south (see Map 14.1). Assuming that popular sovereignty would lead to slavery in Kansas and a system of free labor in Nebraska, Douglas calculated that the existing balance between slave and free states would be maintained in the Senate and that both northerners and southerners would support the bill.

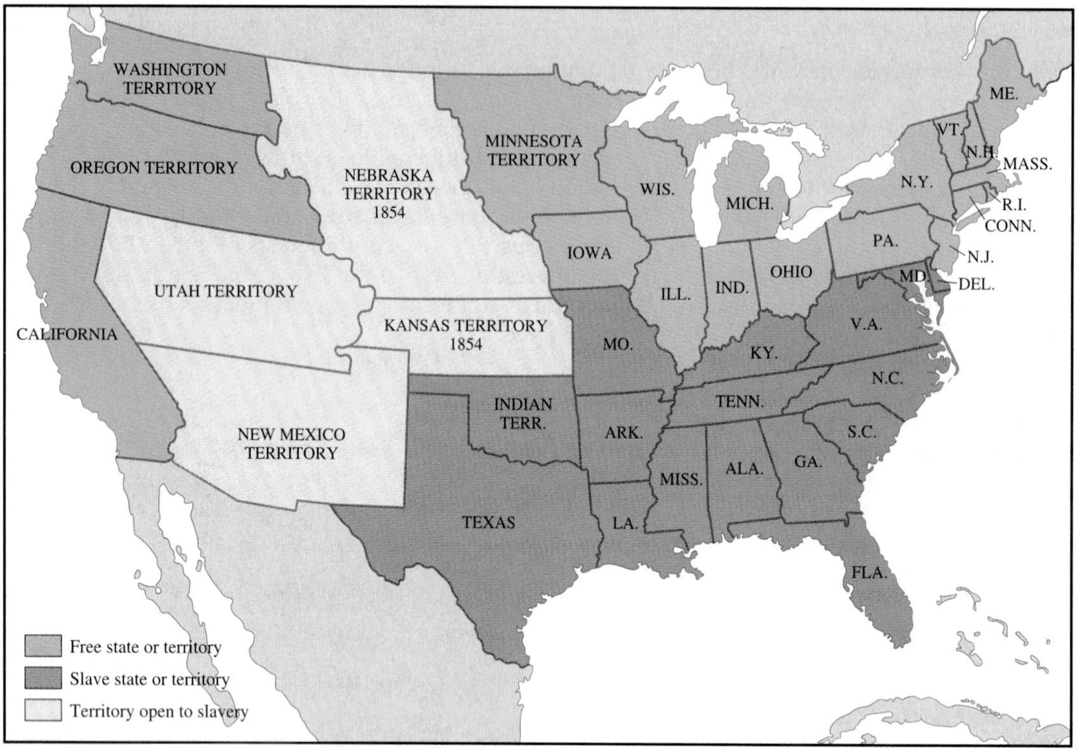

♦ **MAP 14.1 The Kansas-Nebraska Act** This map shows Stephen Douglas's proposed compromise to the dilemma of organizing the vast territory separating the settled part of the United States from California and Oregon. His solution, designed to win profitable rail connections for his home district in Illinois, stirred a political crisis by repealing the Missouri Compromise and replacing it with popular sovereignty.

Toward a House Divided

• How did various groups react to the Kansas-Nebraska Act, and what expectations led to those reactions?

The Kansas-Nebraska bill outraged many northern Democrats, "conscience" Whigs, and free-soil advocates. All of them feared that without the Missouri Compromise limitations, slavery would spread throughout the territories. Once again slavery threatened national political stability. In the North, opponents of the bill formed local coalitions to challenge its passage. On January 24, 1854, a group of Democrats including Salmon P. Chase, Gerrit Smith, Joshua Giddings, and **Charles Sumner** published "The Appeal of the Independent Democrats in Congress, to the People of the United States." They called the bill an "atrocious plot" to make Nebraska a "dreary region of despotism, inhabited by masters and slaves." On February 28, opponents of the Kansas-Nebraska bill met in Ripon, Wisconsin, and recommended the formation of a new political party. Similar meetings took place in several northern states as opposition to the bill grew. What emerged was the **Republican party.**

A Shattered Compromise

Despite this strong opposition, Douglas and Pierce rallied support in Congress. On May 26, 1854, after gaining approval in the House of Representatives, the bill passed the Senate, and Pierce soon signed

Charles Sumner Massachusetts senator who was brutally beaten by a southern congressman in 1856 after delivering a speech attacking the South.

Republican party Political party that arose in the 1850s and opposed the extension of slavery into the western territories.

the **Kansas-Nebraska Act** into law. Passage of the Kansas-Nebraska Act crystallized northern antislavery sentiment. To protest, many northerners threatened **noncompliance** with the fugitive slave law of 1850. As Senator William Seward of New York stated, "We will engage in competition for the virgin soil of Kansas, and God give the victory to the side which is stronger in numbers as it is in right."

Antislavery forces, however, remained divided into at least three major groups. The Free-Soil contingent opposed any extension of slavery but did not necessarily favor abolishing the institution. The other two groups—Garrisonians and evangelicals—wanted immediate abolition but disagreed on many particulars. William Lloyd Garrison and his followers believed that slavery was the primary evil facing the nation, and they embraced anyone who held that position. Evangelicals agreed that slavery was evil, but they believed it was just one of several threats facing the nation. All three groups constantly agitated against slavery and what they perceived as southern control of national politics. They weakened the Democratic party's strength in the North but could not bring themselves to align behind a single opposition party.

Talk of southern expansion also threatened Democratic unity. Many southerners believed that the expansion of slavery was necessary to prevent northern domination. Unless the number of slave states remained at least equal to the number of free states, they contended—or unless the South became a separate nation—the southern way of life was at risk. Increased northern wealth and continued conflict over the expansion of slavery convinced many southern Democrats that northern manufacturing and commercial power threatened to reduce the South to a "colony" controlled by northern bankers and industrialists.

Some southern nationalists attempted to expand slavery by mounting private expeditions into the Caribbean and Central America to take over new territories. Although all these expeditions were the work of a few power-hungry individuals, many northerners believed them to be part of the Slave Power conspiracy. President Pierce perhaps unintentionally aggravated this sentiment. He publicly opposed an expedition into Cuba in 1854. But, like several presidents before him, he hoped to purchase the island. The Spanish, however, were unwilling to negotiate. In October 1854, three of Pierce's European ministers, including future president James Buchanan, met in Ostend, Belgium, and secretly drafted a statement outlining conditions that might justify taking Cuba by force. When the so-called **Ostend Manifesto** became public in 1855, many northerners feared that Pierce and the Democratic party secretly approved of adventurism to expand slavery. These perceptions stirred antislavery anxieties and fueled the growth of the newly formed anti-Democrat coalitions.

Bleeding Kansas

Meanwhile, political friction was bringing Kansas Territory to a low boil. In April 1854, abolitionist Eli Thayer of Worcester, Massachusetts, organized the New England Emigrant Aid Society to encourage antislavery supporters to move to Kansas. They reasoned that flooding a region subject to popular sovereignty with right-minded emigrants could effectively "save" the region from slavery. This group eventually sent two thousand settlers to Kansas, founding Lawrence and other communities. Northern ministers collected funds to purchase rifles and ammunition for these settlers. With similar designs, proslavery southerners, particularly those in Missouri, also encouraged settlement of the territory. Like their northern counterparts, these southerners came armed and ready to fight for their cause.

President Pierce appointed governors in both Kansas and Nebraska and instructed them to organize elections for territorial legislatures. As proslavery and abolitionist settlers vied for control of Kansas, the region became a testing ground for popular sovereignty. When the vote came on March 30, 1855, a large contingent of armed slavery supporters from Missouri—so-called border ruffians—crossed into Kansas and cast ballots for proslavery candidates. According to later Senate investigations, 60 percent of the votes cast were illegal. These unlawful ballots gave proslavery supporters a large majority in the Kansas legislature. They promptly expelled all antislavery legislators and enacted the Kansas Code—a group of laws meant to drive all antislavery forces out of the territory. Antislavery

Kansas-Nebraska Act Law passed by Congress in 1854 that allowed residents of Kansas and Nebraska territories to decide whether to allow slavery.

noncompliance Failure or refusal to obey a law or request.

Ostend Manifesto Declaration by American foreign ministers in 1854 that if Spain refused to sell Cuba, the United States might be justified in taking it by force.

♦ This drawing by Felix O. C. Darley shows a stream of "border ruffians" crossing the border out of Missouri into Kansas. Armed with long rifles and Bowie knives, such proslavery advocates used political manipulation and violent terrorism to make Kansas a slave state. *"Border Ruffians Invading Kansas" by Felix O. C. Darley. Yale University Art Gallery.*

advocates refused to acknowledge the validity of the election or the laws. They organized their own free-state government and drew up an alternative constitution, which they submitted to the voters.

Bloodshed soon followed. Congress had not recognized either the proslavery or the antislavery government. In the absence of instructions from President Pierce, federal troops made no move to prevent violence. Attempting to bring the conflict to conclusion, one proslavery territorial judge, Samuel LeCompte, charged a jury to indict members of the free-state government for treason and sent a **posse** of about eight hundred proslavery men armed with rifles and five cannon to Lawrence. There they "arrested" the antislavery forces and sacked the town, burning buildings and plundering shops and homes. With that, civil war erupted in Kansas.

Hearing news of the "Sack of Lawrence," **John Brown,** an antislavery zealot, vowed to "fight fire with fire." He reasoned that at least five antislavery supporters had been killed since the conflict began, so with his four sons and three others he abducted five proslavery men living along the Pottawatomie River south of Lawrence and murdered them. It turned out that they had nothing to do with the siege of Lawrence. The Pottawatomie Massacre triggered a series of episodes in which more than two hundred men were killed. Much of the violence was the work of border ruffians and zealots like Brown, but to many people in both North and South the events symbolized the "righteousness" of their cause.

The Kansas issue also led to violence in Congress. During the debates over the admission of the ter-

posse A group of people usually summoned by a sheriff to aid in law enforcement.

John Brown Abolitionist who fought proslavery settlers in Kansas in 1855; he was hanged after seizing the U.S. arsenal at Harpers Ferry in 1859 as part of an effort to liberate southern slaves.

ritory, Charles Sumner, a senator from Massachusetts, delivered an abusive and threatening speech, entitled "The Crime Against Kansas," against the proslavery elements in Congress. In particular, he made several insulting remarks about South Carolina and its 60-year-old senator Andrew Butler. Butler, he contended, was a "Don Quixote" who had "chosen a mistress" and "made his vows" to "the harlot, slavery." Butler was out of town, but three days after the speech, Representative Preston Brooks, Butler's nephew, accosted Sumner, accused him of libel, and beat him unconscious with a cane to avenge his uncle's honor. Sumner was badly hurt and needed almost three years to recover. Though **censured** by the House of Representatives, Brooks was overwhelmingly re-elected by his home district and openly praised for his actions—he received canes as gifts from admirers all over the South. Northerners were appalled.

As the presidential election of 1856 approached, the Pierce administration's actions, southern expansionism, and the Kansas-Nebraska controversy accelerated Republican growth. Immigration also remained a major issue, but the Know-Nothings, despite their success at the local and state levels, split over slavery at their initial national convention in 1855. Disagreement over a **plank** dealing with the Kansas-Nebraska Act caused most northerners to bolt from the convention. Some formed an antislavery group called the Know-Somethings, but many joined Republican coalitions.

In 1856, the remaining Know-Nothings reconvened and nominated former president Millard Fillmore as the American party's standard-bearer. John C. Frémont, a moderate abolitionist who had achieved fame as the liberator of California, got the Republican nomination. The few remaining Whigs endorsed Fillmore at their convention, while some former Know-Nothings met separately and endorsed Frémont. The Democrats rejected both Pierce and Douglas and nominated James Buchanan from Pennsylvania, believing him less controversial to the Free-Soil Democrats whom Van Buren had brought back to the party. They selected John C. Breckinridge of Kentucky as Buchanan's running mate to balance the ticket between North and South.

Amid the clutter of disintegrating parties and new factions, the election became a contest for political viability rather than a national referendum on slavery. Buchanan received 45 percent of the popular vote and 163 electoral votes. Frémont finished second with 33 percent of the popular vote and 114 electoral votes. Fillmore received 21 percent of the popular vote but only 8 electoral votes. Frémont's surprisingly narrow margin of defeat demonstrated the appeal of the newly formed Republican coalition to northern voters. The Know-Nothings, fragmented over slavery, disappeared and never again attempted a national organization.

Bringing Slavery Home to the North

On March 4, 1857, James Buchanan became president of the United States. The 65-year-old Pennsylvanian had begun his political career in Congress in 1821 and owed much of his success to southern support. His election came at a time when the nation needed strong leadership, but Buchanan seemed unable to provide it. During the campaign, he had emphasized national unity, but he proved incapable of achieving compromise. His prosouthern tendencies and the events that occurred during his presidency only strengthened northern radicalism. **Regionalism** colored all political issues, and every debate became a contest between competing social, political, and economic ideologies.

Two days after Buchanan assumed office, the Supreme Court issued a ruling that sent shock waves through the already troubled nation and divided Democratic party. **Dred Scott,** a slave and manservant owned by John Emerson, resided in Missouri, a slave state. But Emerson, an army surgeon, had lived for two years in Illinois, where slavery was illegal, and had served in Wisconsin Territory, where the Missouri Compromise banned the practice. Scott's attorney argued that living in Illinois and Wisconsin had made Scott a free man. When Missouri courts rejected this argument, Scott, with the help of abolitionist lawyers, appealed to the Supreme Court.

In a 7-to-2 decision, the Court ruled against Scott. Chief Justice Roger B. Taney, formerly a member of

censure To issue an official rebuke, as by a legislature to one of its members.

plank One of the articles of a political platform.

regionalism Loyalty to the interests of a particular region of the country.

Dred Scott Slave who sued for his liberty in the Missouri courts, arguing that four years on free soil had made him free; the Supreme Court's 1857 ruling against him negated the Missouri Compromise.

♦ In attempting to win his freedom, Dred Scott unintentionally set a legal process in motion that would deny Congress's right to control the extension of slavery. This 1858 painting captures Scott's resolution and strength of character. *"Dred Scott" by Louis Schultze 1881. Missouri Historical Society.*

Andrew Jackson's Kitchen Cabinet and a stalwart Democrat, argued that in the eyes of the law slaves were not people but property, could not be citizens of the United States, and had no right to petition the Court. Taney then ignited a political powder keg by stating that Congress had no constitutional authority to limit slavery in a federal territory, thus totally negating the Missouri Compromise.

Antislavery forces and northern evangelical leaders responded immediately, calling the *Dred Scott* decision a mockery of justice and a crime against a "higher law." Some radical abolitionists, harking back to the Hartford Convention's threat of **secession** (see page 274), argued that the North should separate from the Union. Others advocated impeaching the Supreme Court. Already incensed by events in Kansas, antislavery leaders contended that the next move of the Slave Power conspiracy would be to get the Supreme Court to strike down antislavery laws in northern states.

While debates raged over the *Dred Scott* decision, the Kansas issue simmered. The fact that very few slaveholders actually moved into the territory did nothing to deter proslavery leaders, who met in Lecompton, Kansas, in June 1857 to draft a state constitution favoring slavery. When the **Lecompton constitution** was submitted for voters' approval, antislavery forces protested by refusing to vote, so it was easily ratified. But when the constitution was submitted to Congress for approval, northern Democrats joined Republicans in denouncing it. Stephen Douglas denied that the vote represented the will of the people and called it a fraud because more than two thousand nonresidents had voted illegally.

With the Buchanan administration joining southerners in support of admitting Kansas to the Union as a slave state, the statehood bill passed in the Senate but not in the House of Representatives. Congress then returned the Lecompton constitution to Kansas for another vote. This time Free-Soilers participated in the election and defeated the proposed constitution. Kansas remained a territory.

The Kansas controversy proved a hard pill for Douglas to swallow. He believed in popular sovereignty but could not support the fraudulent election that brought the Lecompton constitution to Congress for approval. And the *Dred Scott* decision had virtually nullified his pet solution because the ruling prevented citizens of a territory from legally prohibiting the importing of slavery. Still entertaining political ambitions, Douglas sought a solution that might win him both northern and southern support in a run for the presidency in 1860. His immediate goal, however, was re-election to the Senate.

To run against Douglas for the Senate in 1858, Illinois Republicans selected a small-town lawyer and moderate antislavery man: Abraham Lincoln. Born on the Kentucky frontier in 1809, Lincoln had accompanied his family from one failed farm to another, picking up schooling in Indiana and Illinois as opportunities arose. As a young man he worked odd jobs—farm worker, ferryman, flatboatman, sur-

secession Withdrawal from the United States.

Lecompton constitution State constitution written for Kansas in 1857 at a convention dominated by proslavery forces; it would have allowed slavery, but Kansas voters rejected it.

veyor, and store clerk—and was a member of the Illinois militia that massacred Black Hawk's people in 1832 (see page 293). Two years after the war, Lincoln was elected to the Illinois legislature and began a serious study of law. He was admitted to the Illinois state bar in 1836. A strong Whig, Lincoln followed Henry Clay's economic philosophy and steered a middle course between the "cotton" and "conscience" wings of the Whig party. Lincoln acknowledged that slavery was evil but contended that it was the predictable consequence of black racial inferiority. The only way to get rid of the evil, he believed, was to prevent the expansion of slavery into the territories and make arrangements to separate the two races forever. In the absence of expansion, he expected, the institution would die out on its own in the South.

In the contest with Douglas, Lincoln was decidedly the underdog and sought to improve his chances by challenging the senator to a series of debates about slavery and its expansion. Douglas agreed to seven debates in various parts of the state. During the debate at Freeport, Lincoln asked Douglas to explain how the people of a territory could exclude slavery in light of the Dred Scott ruling. Douglas's reply became known as the **Freeport Doctrine.** Slavery, he said, needed the protection of "local police regulations." In any territory, citizens "opposed to slavery" could "elect representatives" who would "by unfriendly legislation" prevent the introduction of slavery "into their midst." Lincoln did not win Douglas's Senate seat, but the Little Giant's prominence drew national attention to the Illinois race, and Lincoln won recognition as an up-and-coming Republican and an opponent of slavery.

Radical Responses to Abolitionism and Slavery

Southerners reacted with fear to the threat of limitations on the extension of slavery. Because intensive agriculture depleted the soil in the South, expansion seemed necessary for economic survival as well as for political reasons. Many southerners agreed with Lincoln that confining slavery sentenced it to death. Even though Republican leaders maintained that they had no intention of outlawing slavery where it already existed, their commitment against expansion appeared to doom the southern way of life.

Southern apologists defended their system against northern charges that it was immoral and evil. Charles C. Jones and other southern evangelical leaders offered a religious defense of slavery. Jones argued that whites had a moral responsibility to care for blacks and instruct them in the Christian faith. Those who claimed that the Bible condoned slavery pointed out that the Israelites practiced slavery and Jesus walked among slaves but never mentioned freedom. The apostle Paul, they argued, even commanded slaves to obey their masters.

Many southerners, like some of their Republican opponents, were less interested in the slave than in how slavery affected white society and white labor. When the Republicans argued that slavery defiled labor, southern apologists countered that slavery was a "mudsill," or foundation, supporting democracy. Southerners contended that whites in the South enjoyed a greater degree of freedom than northern whites because slaves did all the demeaning and mind-numbing work in the South, freeing whites to explore philosophy and art.

Influenced by the sociological writings of Thomas Malthus and Karl Marx, southern lawyer George Fitzhugh argued that both North and South relied on a subjugated work force: southerners on **chattel slavery** and northerners on **wage slavery.** Fitzhugh argued that poor northern whites—underpaid and trapped in debt, living in tenements and slums—were a "mudsill" as surely as blacks were in the South. The difference between wage slaves and slaves in the South, Fitzhugh concluded, was that northerners accepted no responsibility for housing and feeding their work force. Chattel slavery, he said, subjugated blacks, but it also cared for them and was more humane than wage slavery, which, he claimed, chained white workers in poverty and squalor.

These ideas infuriated northerners as much as antislavery arguments angered southerners, for they challenged cultural and social values. Northern radicals increasingly called for the violent overthrow of

Freeport Doctrine Stephen Douglas's belief, stated at Freeport, Illinois, that a territory could exclude slavery by writing local laws or regulations that made slavery impossible to enforce.

chattel slavery The bondage of people who are considered to be the movable personal property of their owners.

wage slavery The bondage of workers who, though legally free, are underpaid, trapped in debt, and living in extreme poverty.

♦ Seeing himself as an avenging angel, John Brown, shown here in an 1856 photograph, used the same terrorist tactics employed by border ruffians in Kansas. A year after this picture was taken, Brown attempted to set off civil war by raiding the federal armory at Harpers Ferry, Virginia. He was hanged for treason in 1859. *Boston Athenaeum.*

slavery, and Kansas radical John Brown moved to oblige them. In 1857 Brown came to the East, where he convinced several prominent antislavery leaders to finance a daring plan to raise an army of slaves in an all-out insurrection against their masters. Brown and twenty-one followers, including four free blacks, attacked the federal arsenal at **Harpers Ferry,** Virginia, on October 16, 1859, attempting to seize weapons.

The arsenal proved an easy target, but Brown's force could not convince any slaves to join the uprising. Local citizens surrounded the arsenal, firing on Brown and his followers until federal troops commanded by Colonel **Robert E. Lee** arrived. On October 18, Lee's forces battered down the barricaded entrance and arrested Brown. He was tried, convicted of treason, and hanged on December 2, 1859.

John Brown's raid on Harpers Ferry captured the imagination of radical abolitionists, and it terrified southerners. Republican leaders denounced it, but other northerners proclaimed Brown a martyr. Church bells tolled in many northern cities on the day of his execution, and radical evangelicals offered eulogies to Brown's cause and his actions. In New England, Ralph Waldo Emerson proclaimed Brown "That new saint." Brown's raid, his martyrdom, and the perception that the Republicans had secretly sponsored his actions caused many moderate southerners to seriously consider secession. The Alabama, Mississippi, and Florida state legislatures resolved that a Republican victory in the upcoming presidential election would provide sufficient justification for such action.

Southern dismay grew with the publication of *The Impending Crisis of the South* (1857), a book by **Hinton Rowan Helper,** a southern racist, who argued that slavery degraded white southern workers, kept them poor, and enabled slaveowners to profit at their expense. Armed with statistics, Helper claimed that abolishing slavery would improve economic conditions in the South and allow the region's "plain folk" to share in its prosperity. Republican New York newspaper editor Horace Greeley distributed the book, and by the end of 1859, sympathetic northerners were purchasing more than five hundred copies a day. Endorsement of the book by several prominent Republicans further strained southern loyalty to the Union as the election of 1860 approached.

The Divided Nation

- What did northerners and southerners expect to happen as a result of the presidential election in 1860?
- Why did they expect those outcomes?

The Republicans were a new phenomenon on the American political scene: a purely regional political

Harpers Ferry Town in present-day West Virginia and site of the U.S. arsenal that John Brown briefly seized in 1859.

Robert E. Lee A Virginian with a distinguished career in the U.S. Army who resigned to assume command of the Confederate army in Virginia when the Civil War began.

Hinton Rowan Helper Southern author who in *The Impending Crisis of the South* (1857) attacked slavery not because it exploited slaves but because it was ruining small white farmers.

party. Rather than making any attempt to forge a national coalition, the party drew its strength and ideas almost entirely from the North. The Republican platform—"free Soil, Free Labor, and Free Men"—stressed the defilement of white labor by slavery and contended that the Slave Power conspiracy was eroding the rights of free whites. By taking up a cry against "Rum, Romanism, and Slavery," the Republicans drew former Know-Nothings and temperance advocates into their ranks. The Democrats hoped to maintain a national coalition, but as the nation approached a new presidential election, their hopes began to fade.

The Dominance of Regionalism

During the Buchanan administration, Democrats found it increasingly difficult to achieve national party unity. Northern Democrats, under Republican pressure in their own states, realized that any commitment to the southern Democratic demand for extending or protecting slavery would cost them votes at home. In April 1860 the party convened in Charleston, South Carolina. Each side was ready to do battle for its political life.

The fight began over the party platform. Northern supporters of Stephen A. Douglas championed a popular sovereignty position. Southern radicals demanded a plank calling for the legal protection of slavery in the territories. After heated debates, neither side would compromise. When the delegates finally voted, the Douglas forces carried the day. Disgusted delegates from eight southern states walked out of the convention. Shocked, the remaining delegates adjourned the convention and reconvened in Baltimore in June.

Most southern delegates boycotted the Baltimore proceedings, and Douglas easily won the presidential nomination. Moderate southerner Herschel V. Johnson of Georgia was his running mate. The party's final platform supported popular sovereignty and emphasized allegiance to the Union, hoping to attract moderate voters from both North and South.

The southern Democratic contingent met one week later in Baltimore and nominated vice president John C. Breckinridge of Kentucky as its presidential candidate and Joseph Lane of Oregon as his running mate. The southern Democrats' platform vowed support for the Union but called for federal protection of the right to own slaves in the territories and for the preservation of slavery where it already existed.

In May 1860, a group of former Whigs and Know-Nothings along with some disaffected Democrats convened in Baltimore and formed the **Constitutional Union party.** They nominated John Bell, a wealthy slaveholder from Tennessee, for president and Edward Everett of Massachusetts, a former northern Whig leader, as his running mate. Hoping to resurrect the politics of compromise, the party resolved to take no stand on the sectional controversy and pledged to uphold the Constitution and the Union and to enforce the laws of the nation.

The front runner for the Republican nomination appeared to be William Seward of New York. A former Whig and long-time New York politician, Seward had actively opposed any extension of slavery during the early 1850s but had switched to the popular sovereignty position of Stephen Douglas during the Kansas controversy. He had also supported the Harpers Ferry raid but later repudiated John Brown.

Several other Republican favorites—Salmon P. Chase of Ohio, Simon Cameron of Pennsylvania, and Edward Bates of Missouri—appeared to have a chance for nomination, but Illinois favorite son Abraham Lincoln emerged as the major contender. Many delegates considered Seward too radical; and he and his campaign manager, Thurlow Weed (see page 358), had earned the distrust of many prominent Republicans for their political wheeling and dealing. Lincoln, in contrast, had a reputation for integrity and had not seriously alienated any of the Republican factions. Lincoln polled 102 votes on the first ballot taken and won the nomination on the third ballot.

The Election of 1860

The 1860 presidential campaign began as two separate contests. Lincoln and Douglas competed for northern votes, and Breckinridge and Bell vied for the South. The Republicans were not even on

Constitutional Union party Political party that organized on the eve of the Civil War with no platform other than preservation of the Constitution, the Union, and the law.

♦ Although there were four prominent candidates for the presidency in 1860, Abraham Lincoln and Stephen Douglas dominated the race in the North and West. These campaign pins show the adversaries from Illinois as they looked during the election: Douglas looking tired but determined, and Lincoln beardless and intense. *Museum of American Political Life.*

the ballot in the **Deep South,** and they scarcely campaigned at all in the five border states where slavery was legal. Breckinridge and the southern Democrats expected no support in the North. Douglas proclaimed himself the only national candidate but received most of his support from northerners who feared the consequences of a Republican victory. Bell and the Constitutional Unionists attempted to campaign in both regions but attracted mostly southern voters who wanted to avoid the crisis of disunion.

Slavery and sectionalism were the critical issues, but the Republicans also used revelations of Democratic fraud and corruption as a campaign issue. In June 1860, a House investigation revealed information about graft, bribery, and shady dealings in the Buchanan administration. Republicans linked these charges to the Slave Power conspiracy. The slaveholding elite, they contended, not only had attempted to subvert liberty but had used fraudulent means to keep the Democratic party of Buchanan—and Douglas—in power. "Honest Abe Lincoln," the man of the people, would lead the fight against the forces of slavery and corruption. This argument drew in many northern voters, including a lot of former Know-Nothings.

Sensing that Lincoln would win the North, Douglas launched a last-ditch effort to win the election and hold the Union together by pushing his campaign into the South. Douglas and his forces tried unsuccessfully to form a coalition between moderate Democrats and Constitutional Unionists. Already in poor health, Douglas all but exhausted himself trying to prevent disunion, and his failed efforts probably contributed to his death a year later.

As the election drew near, the likelihood of a Republican victory deeply alarmed southerners. Rumors of slave uprisings incited by Yankee strangers led to hysteria. Reports of violence, arson, and rape in faraway places such as Texas filled southern newspapers. Although no hard evidence supported these rumors, they contributed to the climate of gloom spreading over the South. Even moderate southerners started to believe that the Republicans intended to crush their way of life and to enslave southern whites economically while freeing southern blacks. Republican actions in the North reinforced that impression. Some Republicans in New York, for example, pressed for a state constitutional amendment that would grant voting rights to African Americans. The pro-Democratic *New York Herald* contended that the election of Lincoln would bring "hundreds of thousands" of slaves north to compete with whites for jobs, resulting in "African amalgamation with the fair daughters of the Anglo-Saxon, Celtic, and Teutonic races."

To improve the party's image, national Republican leaders forged a platform that contained no planks ordering an end to slavery in areas where it already existed, but they did oppose its extension. The Republican platform called for higher tariffs (to appeal to northern industrialists) and for internal improvements and public lands legislation (to appeal to westerners). Particularly in the Midwest, party leaders worked hard to portray themselves as "the white man's party" rather than as "black Re-

Deep South The region of the South farthest from the North; usually said to comprise the states of Alabama, Florida, Georgia, Louisiana, Mississippi, and South Carolina.

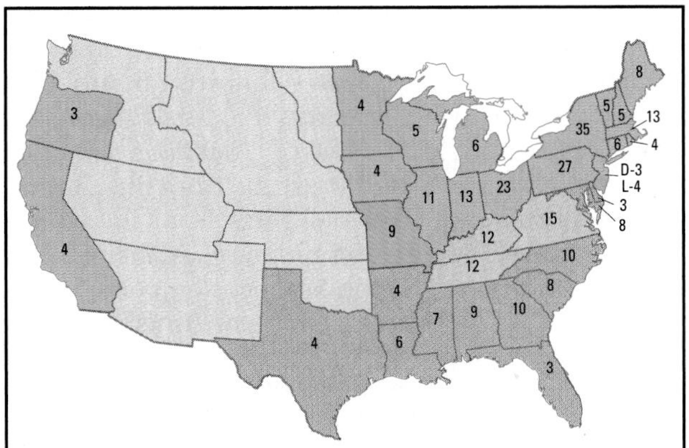

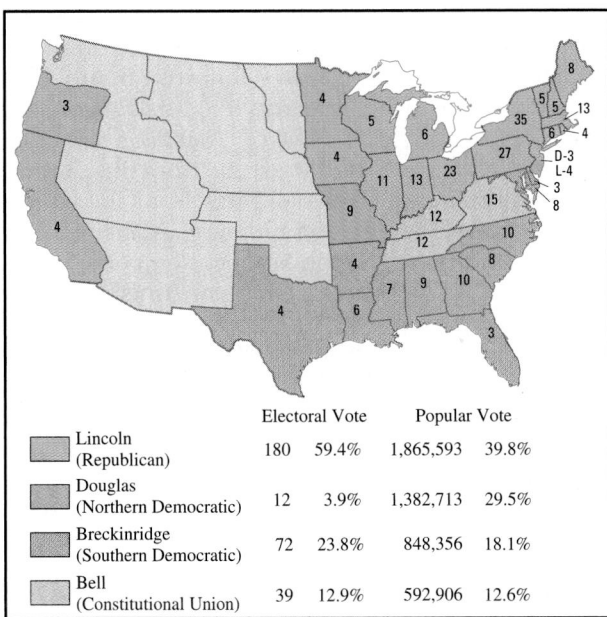

	Electoral Vote		Popular Vote	
Lincoln (Republican)	180	59.4%	1,865,593	39.8%
Douglas (Northern Democratic)	12	3.9%	1,382,713	29.5%
Breckinridge (Southern Democratic)	72	23.8%	848,356	18.1%
Bell (Constitutional Union)	39	12.9%	592,906	12.6%

♦ **MAP 14.2 Election of 1860** The election of 1860 confirmed the worst fears expressed by concerned Union supporters during the 1850s: changes in the nation's population made it possible for one section to dominate national politics. As this map shows, the Republican and southern Democratic parties virtually split the nation, and the Republicans were able to seize the presidency.

publicans," as their opponents contemptuously called them. In line with the position Lincoln had taken in his 1858 debates with Douglas, Republicans argued that excluding slavery meant excluding blacks from competition with whites. These tactics alienated a few abolitionists but appealed to many northerners and westerners.

On November 6, 1860, Abraham Lincoln was elected president of the United States with 180 electoral votes—a clear majority—but only 40 percent of the popular vote. Lincoln carried all the northern states, California, and Oregon (see Map 14.2). Douglas finished second with 29 percent of the popular vote but only 12 electoral votes. He won only Missouri. Bell won in Virginia, Kentucky, and Tennessee. Breckinridge, as expected, carried the Deep South but won only 72 electoral votes and 18 percent of the popular vote nationwide. For the first time in American history, a purely regional party held the presidency. The Republicans, who had made no effort to win votes in the South, also swept congressional races in the North and had a large majority in Congress for the upcoming term.

The First Wave of Secession

After the Republican victory, southern sentiment for secession snowballed, especially in the Deep South. The Republicans were a "party founded on a single sentiment," stated the *Richmond Examiner*: "hatred of African slavery." The *New Orleans Delta* agreed, calling the Republicans "essentially a revolutionary party." But this party now controlled the national government. To a growing number of southerners, the Republican victory was proof that secession was the only alternative to political domination.

Most Republicans did not believe that the South would actually leave the Union. Calls for secession had been heard in the South for a decade. Seward had ridiculed threats of secession as an attempt "to terrify or alarm" the northern people. Lincoln himself believed that the "people of the South" had "too much sense" to launch an "attempt to ruin the government." During the campaign, he had promised "no interference by the government, with slaves or slavery within the states." He urged moderation but came to believe that southerners would perceive anything he said as an additional threat.

In a last-ditch attempt at compromise, **John J. Crittenden,** senator from Kentucky, introduced several proposals in the Senate on December 18, 1860. He suggested extending the Missouri Compromise line westward across the continent, forbidding slavery to the north of the line, and protecting slavery to the south. Crittenden's plan also upheld the interstate trade in slaves and called for compensation to slaveowners who were unable to recover fugitive slaves from northern states. These proposals, Crittenden believed, could become permanent constitutional amendments incapable of being repealed even by future amendments.

Although Crittenden's plan seemed to favor the South, it had some appeal in the North, especially among businessmen who feared that secession would cause a major depression. Thurlow Weed, Seward's political adviser, seemed ready to listen to such a compromise, but Lincoln wrote to Weed saying that he was "inflexible on the territorial question." The extension of the Missouri Compromise

John J. Crittenden Kentucky senator who made an unsuccessful attempt to prevent the Civil War by proposing a series of constitutional amendments protecting slavery south of the Missouri Compromise line.

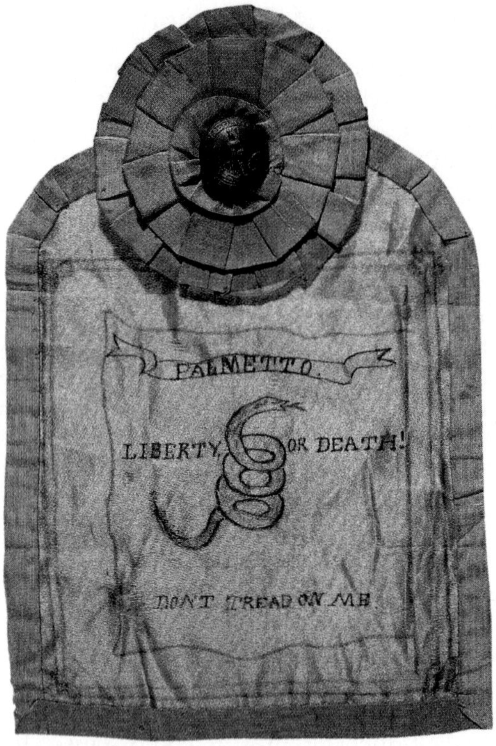

♦ This cockade, which someone would have worn on a hat or sleeve, depicts a coiled snake with the legend "Don't Tread On Me." This was a popular symbol during the American Revolution, which southerners dusted off in support of their claim that they were a colonized people fighting a foreign tyranny. *Chicago Historical Society.*

line, Lincoln warned, would "lose us everything we gained by the election." He let senators and congressmen know that he wanted no "compromise in regard to the extension of slavery." The Senate defeated Crittenden's proposals by a vote of 25 to 23. The Kentuckian then proposed putting the measure to a vote of the people, but Congress rejected that idea as well.

Meanwhile, on December 20, 1860, delegates in South Carolina met to consider seceding from the Union. South Carolina had long been a hotbed of resistance to federal authority (see pages 298–300), and state officials determined to take action before the newly elected Republican administration came to power. The convention, complete with bands, fireworks, and rallies, had a carnival-like atmosphere. Amid the general jubilation South Carolina delegates voted 169 to 0 to dissolve their ties with the United States. Nullifying the Constitution and seceding from the Union, they proclaimed, were the sovereign rights of a state. Just as the radicals hoped, other southern states followed South Carolina's lead. During January 1861, delegates convened in Mississippi, Florida, Alabama, Georgia, and Louisiana and voted to secede from the Union.

On February 4, 1861, delegates from the six seceding states met in Montgomery, Alabama, and formed the provisional government of a new political entity: the **Confederate States of America,** or the Confederacy, as it was commonly known. Shortly afterward, despite nationalist pleas from Sam Houston, former president of Texas, Texans voted to leave the Union and join the Confederacy. The Confederate congress drafted a constitution, and the six Confederate states ratified it on March 11, 1861.

The Confederate constitution created a government modeled on the government of the United States—but with a few notable differences. It emphasized the "sovereign and independent character" of the states and guaranteed the protection of slavery in any new territories acquired, though it forbade the importation of slaves. The Confederate constitution allowed tariffs for the purpose of raising government revenue but in a rather vague clause prohibited protective tariffs. It prohibited government funding of internal improvements and limited the president and vice president to a single six-year term. The legislature was exactly like that of the United States—a Senate and a House of Representatives. A cabinet composed of six executive department heads rounded out the government. The Confederate congress declared that the U.S. Constitution, excluding provisions in conflict with the Confederate constitution, would remain in force in the Confederacy.

Responses to Disunion

Even as late as March 1861, not all southerners favored secession. John Bell and Stephen Douglas together had received more than 50 percent of southern votes in 1860, winning support from southerners who desired compromise and had only limited stakes

Confederate States of America Political entity formed by the seceding states of South Carolina, Georgia, Florida, Alabama, Mississippi, and Louisiana in February 1861; Texas, Virginia, Arkansas, Tennessee, and North Carolina joined later.

in upholding slavery. These "plain folk" joined together with some large planters, who stood to suffer economic loss from disunion, in calls for moderation and compromise. The border states, which were less invested in cotton and had numerous ties with the North, were not strongly inclined toward secession. In February, Virginia had called for a peace conference. It met in Washington in an effort to forestall hostilities, but, like Crittenden's efforts, this attempt also failed to hold the Union together.

The division in southern sentiments was a major stumbling block to the election of a Confederate president. Many moderate delegates to the constitutional convention refused to support radical secessionists, believing them to be as responsible as the Republicans for the crisis. The convention remained deadlocked until two prosecession Virginia legislators sent word that they would support Mississippi moderate Jefferson Davis as a compromise candidate.

Davis appeared to be the ideal choice. Austere and dignified, he had not sought the job but seemed extremely capable of handling it. A West Point graduate, he served during the Mexican War, was elected to the Senate soon afterward, then left the Senate in 1851 to run unsuccessfully for governor in Mississippi. After serving as secretary of war under Franklin Pierce, he returned to the Senate in 1857 but resigned immediately after Lincoln's victory in 1860.

Although Davis had long championed southern interests and owned many slaves, he was no romantic, fire-eating secessionist. Before 1860 he had been a strong **Unionist,** arguing only that the South be allowed to maintain its own economy, culture, and institutions, including slavery. He had supported the Compromise of 1850. When he had fought for a southern route for a transcontinental railroad as secretary of war, he believed that it would benefit the South economically, but he also felt it would tie the nation more firmly together. Like many of his contemporaries, however, Davis had become increasingly alarmed by the prospect of declining southern political power.

The initial northward tilt in the Senate created by California's admission in 1850 had been aggravated in 1858 by admitting Minnesota and by Oregon's statehood in 1859. To moderates like Davis, the presidential election of 1860 was simply a forceful demonstration of a fact already in evidence: unless the South took a strong stand against outside interference, the region would no longer be able to control its own internal affairs, and the institution of slavery itself would be threatened. Southerners, Davis believed, needed to act in concert to convince northerners to either leave the South alone or face the region's withdrawal from the nation. "To rally the men of the North, who would preserve the government as our fathers found it," Davis proclaimed, "we . . . should offer no doubtful or divided front."

Elected president of the Confederate States of America unanimously on February 9, 1861, Davis addressed the cheering crowds in Montgomery a

♦ This card depicts Jefferson Davis, the first and only president of the Confederate States of America. Southerners showed their support for the Confederacy by displaying cards like this one in their windows or other prominent places. *Collection of David J. and Janice L. Frent.*

Unionist Loyal to the United States of America.

week later and set forth the Confederate position: "The time for compromise has now passed," he said. "The South is determined to maintain her position, and make all who oppose her smell Southern powder and feel Southern steel." In his inaugural address several days later, he stressed a desire for peace but reiterated that the "courage and patriotism of the Confederate States" would be "found equal to any measure of defense which honor and security may require."

Northern Democrats and Republicans alike watched developments in the South with dismay. President Buchanan (Lincoln had not yet been sworn in) argued that secession had no constitutional validity and that any state leaving the Union did so unlawfully. He confused the issue, however, by stating his belief that the federal government had no constitutional power to "coerce a State" to remain in the Union. Buchanan accepted no responsibility for the situation and did little to alleviate the tension. He blamed the crisis on "incessant and violent agitation on the slavery question." He chided northern states for disregarding fugitive slave laws, and he called for a constitutional amendment protecting slavery. Such statements only strengthened Republican resolve.

During the four months between the election and Lincoln's inauguration, the Republicans could do nothing about secession, for the reins of government remained in the hands of Democrats. They did discuss it, however. Lincoln wrote, "My opinion is that no state can, in any way, lawfully get out of the Union, without the consent of the others." He wrote to Alexander H. Stephens, who would soon become vice president of the Confederacy, trying to reassure him that "a republican administration" would not "directly or indirectly, interfere with their slaves, or with them, about their slaves," but he refused to consider any compromise on the extension of slavery.

Black abolitionist Frederick Douglass summed up Lincoln's dilemma concerning slavery, secession, and war. "Much as I value the current apparent hostility to Slavery," Douglas stated, "I plainly see that it is less the outgrowth of high and moral conviction against Slavery, as such, than because of the trouble its friends have brought upon the country." The South had divided the nation by seceding, and as Douglass indicated, many northerners were much more concerned about the breakup of the nation and potential hostilities between the North and South than they ever had been about slavery. Lincoln, who was dedicated to maintaining the Union, faced a crisis that many feared would inevitably lead to armed conflict.

Lincoln first had to unite his party. In an attempt to appease all the Republican factions, he chose his cabinet with great care. His vice president, the moderate Hannibal Hamlin of Maine, had supported Lincoln but was also a friend of William Seward and had been chosen to balance the ticket factionally. Lincoln continued this balancing act by appointing to his cabinet his four main rivals for party control. Seward received the job of secretary of state. Moderate Edward Bates of Missouri became attorney general. Although many Republicans considered Simon Cameron of Pennsylvania to be "destitute of honor and integrity," Lincoln, in the interest of appeasing Cameron's supporters and maintaining party unity, reluctantly named him secretary of war. Salmon P. Chase of Ohio, a long-time politician and sometime radical on the slavery question, became secretary of the treasury. Despite Lincoln's evenhandedness, his political balancing act was not easy to maintain. Chase and Seward, for instance, had a long history of political infighting and hated each other. That Lincoln would appoint Chase to any position so angered Seward that he threatened to resign. Lincoln finally persuaded him to remain.

The Nation Dissolved

- What choices were available to Abraham Lincoln and Jefferson Davis in March 1861?
- What political factors constrained their choices?

Abraham Lincoln was inaugurated on March 4, 1861. In his inaugural address he repeated themes that he had been stressing since the election: no interference with slavery in states where it existed, no extension of slavery into the territories, and no tolerance of secession. "The Union," he contended, was "perpetual." The Constitution, according to its Preamble, had been written to form a "more perfect union," and no state could withdraw. Lincoln believed that the nation remained unbroken, and he pledged to see "that the laws of the Union be faithfully executed in all the States." This policy, he continued, necessitated "no bloodshed or violence, and there shall be none, unless it is forced upon the national authority. The power confided in me will be used to hold, occupy, and possess the property and places belonging to the government, and to collect the duties and imposts." If war came, he argued, it would be over secession, not slavery, for the federal government had a duty to maintain the Union by any means, including force.

Lincoln, Sumter, and War

Lincoln's first presidential address drew mixed reactions. Most Republicans found it firm and reasonable without being conciliatory and applauded its tone. Union advocates in both North and South thought the speech held promise for the future. Even former rival Stephen Douglas stated, "I am with him." Moderate southerners commended Lincoln's "temperance and conservatism" and believed the speech was all "any reasonable Southern man" could have expected. Confederates and their sympathizers, however, branded the speech a "Declaration of War." Lincoln had hoped the address would foster a climate of reconciliation, show his commitment to maintaining the Union, and demonstrate his determination to find a peaceful solution, for he desperately needed time to organize the new government and formulate a plan of action. But such luxuries were not forthcoming.

Even before Lincoln assumed office, South Carolina officials had ordered the state militia to seize two federal forts—Fort Moultrie and Castle Pinckney—and the federal arsenal at Charleston. In response, Major Robert Anderson had moved all federal troops from Charleston to **Fort Sumter,** an island stronghold in Charleston harbor. The Confederate congress determined that "immediate steps be taken to obtain possession" of forts still under U.S. control and demanded that President Buchanan remove all federal troops from the sovereign territory of the Confederacy. Despite his sympathy for the southern cause, Buchanan had announced that Fort Sumter would be defended "against all hostile attacks, from whatever quarter." On January 3, 1861, a Charleston harbor **battery** fired on a supply ship, the *Star of the West,* as it attempted to reach the fort. Buchanan denounced the action but did nothing. Lincoln, powerless to act, stated that the federal government "should hold the forts, or retake them."

Immediately after taking office, Lincoln received a report from Fort Sumter saying that supplies were running low. The new president faced a major decision. Under great pressure from northern public opinion to do something without starting a war, he responded cleverly, informing South Carolina governor Francis Pickens of his peaceful intention to send unarmed boats carrying food and supplies to the besieged fort. Lincoln thus placed the Confederacy in the no-win position of either accepting the resupply of federal forts and losing face or firing on the unarmed supply ships and starting a war. From Lincoln's perspective, the plan could not fail. If no shots were fired, he would achieve his stated objective by holding the federal post. But if armed conflict evolved, he could blame the Confederates for starting it and could act freely to punish the aggressors.

Confederate officials, after studying the situation, determined not to allow Sumter to be resupplied. President Davis ordered the Confederate commander at Charleston, General P. G. T. Beauregard, to demand the evacuation of Sumter and if the federals refused, to "proceed, in such a manner as you may determine, to reduce it." On April 12, with supply ships on the way, Beauregard demanded that Anderson surrender. When Anderson refused, shore batteries opened fire on the island fortress. After a thirty-four-hour artillery battle, Anderson surrendered. Neither side had inflicted casualties on the other, but civil war had officially begun.

Across the North, newspapers and the public rallied behind the Union cause, contrasting the president's resolute but restrained policy with the violent aggression of the Confederates. In New York, where southern sympathizers had once vehemently criticized abolitionist actions, a million people attended a Union rally. Even northern Democrats rallied behind the Republican president, hearkening to Stephen Douglas's statement that "There can be no neutrals in this war, only patriots—or traitors." Spurred by the public outcry and confident of support, Lincoln called for seventy-five thousand militiamen to be mobilized "to maintain the honor, the integrity, and the existence of our National Union, and the perpetuity of popular government." Northern states responded immediately and enthusiastically. Across the Upper South and the border regions, however, the call to arms meant that a decision had to be made: whether to continue in the Union or join the Confederacy.

Fort Sumter Fort at the mouth of the harbor of Charleston, South Carolina; it was the scene of the opening engagement of the Civil War in April 1861.

battery An army artillery unit, usually supplied with heavy guns.

♦ In this vivid engraving, South Carolina shore batteries under the command of P. G. T. Beauregard shell Fort Sumter, the last federal stronghold in Charleston Harbor, on the night of April 12, 1861. Curious and excited civilians look on from their rooftops, never suspecting the horrors that would be the outcome of this rash action. *Library of Congress.*

Choosing Sides in Virginia

The task of convincing **unaligned** states to join the Confederacy fell to its new president, Jefferson Davis. The need for southern unity in the face of what he saw as northern aggression pushed Davis to employ a combination of political finesse and force to create a solid southern alignment. He selected his cabinet with this in mind, choosing one cabinet member from each state except his own Mississippi and appointing men of varying degrees of radicalism. The fledgling Confederacy sorely needed the support of the Upper South, and Davis was determined to get it.

Seven slaveholding states had by now seceded, but eight remained in the Union. These states were critical, for they contained more than half of the entire southern population (two-thirds of its white population), possessed most of the South's industrial capacity, produced most of its food, and raised more than half of its horses. In addition, many experienced and able military leaders lived in these states. If the Confederacy was to have any chance of survival, the human and physical resources of the Upper South were essential.

After Lincoln's call to mobilize the militia, Virginia began a second wave of secession. Governor John Letcher refused to honor Lincoln's demand for troops, and on May 23 voters in Virginia overwhelmingly ratified an ordinance of secession. By then Letcher and the convention had offered **Richmond** as a site for the new nation's capital. The Confederate congress accepted the offer in order to strengthen ties with Virginia and because facilities in Montgomery were less than adequate.

Not all Virginians were flattered by becoming the seat for the Confederacy. Residents of the western

unaligned Not allied with either side in a conflict.

Richmond Port city on the James River in Virginia; it was already the state capital and became the capital of the Confederacy.

portion of the state had strong Union ties and long-standing political differences with their neighbors east of the Allegheny Mountains. Forty-six counties called mass Unionist meetings to protest the state's secession, and in a June convention at Wheeling, they elected their own governor, Francis H. Pierpoint, and drew up a constitution. The new constitution was ratified in an election open only to voters willing to take an oath of allegiance to the Union. Eastern Virginians considered the entire process illegal, but the West Virginia legislature finally convened in May 1862 and requested admission to the United States.

For many individuals in the Upper South, the decision to support the Confederacy was not an easy one. No one typified this dilemma more than Virginian Robert E. Lee. Lee—the son of Revolutionary War hero Henry ("Light Horse Harry") Lee—had strong ties to the Union. A West Point graduate and career officer in the U.S. Army, he had a distinguished record in the Mexican War and as superintendent of West Point. General Winfield Scott, commander of the Union forces, called Lee "the best soldier I ever saw in the field." Recognizing his military skill, Lincoln offered Lee field command of the Union armies, but the Virginian refused, deciding that he should serve his native state instead. Lee agonized over the decision but told a friend, "I cannot raise my hand against my birthplace, my home, my children." He resigned his U.S. Army commission and accepted command of Virginia's defenses in April 1861. When he informed Scott, a personal friend and fellow Virginian, of his decision, Scott replied, "You have made the greatest mistake of your life, but I feared it would be so." Though also a southerner by birth, Scott chose to remain loyal to the Union.

A Second Wave of Secession

Influenced by the Virginia convention and by Lee's decision, three other states joined the Confederacy. Arkansas had voted against secession in March, hoping that bloodshed might be averted, but when Lincoln called for militia units, Governor Henry M. Rector answered, "None will be furnished. The demand is only adding insult to injury." The state then called a second convention and on May 6 seceded from the Union. North Carolinians had also hoped for compromise, but moderates turned secessionist when Secretary of War Simon Cameron **requisitioned** "two regiments of militia for immediate service" against the Confederacy. Governor John W. Ellis replied, "I regard the levy of troops made by this administration for the purpose of subjugating the states of the South [to be] in violation of the Constitution and a gross usurpation of power." North Carolina seceded on May 20.

Tennessee, the eleventh and final state to join the Confederacy, was the home of many moderates, including John Bell, the Constitutional Union candidate in 1860. Eastern residents favored the Union, and those in the west favored the Confederacy. The state's voters at first rejected disunion overwhelmingly, but after the fighting began, Governor Isham C. Harris and the state legislature initiated military ties with the Confederacy, forcing another vote on the issue. Western voters carried the election, approving the agreement and seceding from the Union on June 8. East Tennesseans, who remained loyal Unionists, tried to divide the state much as West Virginians had done, but Davis ordered Confederate troops to occupy the region, thwarting the effort.

Trouble in the Border States

Four slave states remained in the Union, and the start of hostilities brought political and military confrontation in three of the four. Delaware quietly stayed in the Union. Voters there had given Breckinridge a plurality in 1860, but the majority of voters disapproved of secession, and few of the state's citizens owned slaves. Maryland, Missouri, and Kentucky, however, each contained large, vocal secessionist minorities and appeared poised to bolt to the Confederacy.

Maryland was particularly vital to the Union, for it enclosed Washington, D.C., on the three sides not bordered by Virginia. If Maryland had seceded, the Union might have been forced to move its capital. Maryland voters overwhelmingly supported Breckinridge in 1860, and southern sympathizers controlled the legislature. But Governor Thomas Hicks, a Unionist, refused to call a special legislative session to consider secession.

On April 6, a Massachusetts regiment responding to Lincoln's call for troops passed through Baltimore on the way to the capital. A mob confronted the soldiers, and rioters attacked the rear companies with bricks, bottles, and pistols. The soldiers returned fire. When the violence subsided, twelve Baltimore residents and four soldiers lay dead, and

requisition To demand for military use.

♦ Like the citizens in western Virginia, people in eastern Tennessee remained faithful to the Union. Men like those shown here swore allegiance to the United States flag and tried to split the state in two—one rebel and the other loyal—but Confederate troops put a stop to their efforts. *Library of Congress.*

dozens more were wounded. Secessionists reacted violently, destroying railroad bridges to keep additional northern troops out of the state. In effect, Washington, D.C., was cut off from the North.

Lincoln and General Scott ordered the military occupation of Baltimore and declared **martial law.** The state legislature finally met and voted to remain neutral. Lincoln then had the army arrest suspected southern sympathizers and hold them without formal hearings or charges. When the legislature met again and appeared to be planning secession, Lincoln ordered the army to surround Frederick, the legislative seat—just as Davis had ordered the Confederacy to occupy eastern Tennessee. With southern sympathizers suppressed, new state elections were held. The new legislature, overwhelmingly Unionist, voted against secession.

Kentucky had important economic ties to the South but was strongly nationalistic. Like Kentuckians Henry Clay and John Crittenden, most in the state favored compromise. The governor refused to honor Lincoln's call for troops, but the state legislature voted to remain neutral. Both North and South honored that neutrality. Kentucky's own militia, however, split into two factions, and the state became a bloody battleground where even members of the same family fought against one another.

In Missouri, Governor Claiborne F. Jackson, a former proslavery border ruffian, pushed for secession, arguing that Missourians were bound together "in one brotherhood with the States of the South." When Unionists frustrated the secession movement, Jackson's forces seized the federal arsenal at Liberty and wrote to Jefferson Davis requesting artillery to support an assault on the arsenal at St. Louis. Union sympathizers, however, fielded their own forces and fought Jackson at every turn. Rioting broke out in St. Louis as civilians clashed with soldiers, and mob violence marred the nights. Jackson's secessionist movement sent representatives to the Confederate congress in Richmond, but Union forces maintained nominal control of the state and drove prosouthern leaders into exile.

martial law Temporary rule by military authorities, imposed on a civilian population in time of war or when civil authority has broken down.

S U M M A R Y

E xpectations
C onstraints
C hoices
O utcomes

As social and economic change heightened Americans' expectations during the 1850s, individuals made a variety of *choices*, creating a new political environment. New political allegiances changed party composition and platforms. As the Compromise of 1850 failed to alleviate regional tension, and debates over slavery dominated the political agenda, the Whig party, *constrained* by fragmentation among its members, disintegrated. Two completely new groups—the American and Republican parties—competed to replace the Whigs. A series of events—including the Kansas-Nebraska Act and the *Dred Scott* decision—intensified regional polarization, and radicals on both sides fanned the flames of sectional rivalry.

The new regional political coalitions of the 1850s more accurately reflected the changed composition of the electorate, but the *constraints* imposed by regional interests left them with far less ability to achieve compromise than their more nationally oriented predecessors. Even the Democratic party could not hold together, splitting into northern and southern wings. By 1859, the young Republican party, committed to *constraining* slavery, seemed poised to gain control of the federal government. Southerners *expected* that the loss of political power would doom their way of life, and neither side felt it could afford to back down.

With the election of Abraham Lincoln in 1860, six southern states *chose* to withdraw from the Union. Last-minute efforts at compromise, like the Crittenden proposal, failed, and on April 12, 1861, five weeks after Lincoln's inauguration, Confederate forces fired on federal troops at Fort Sumter in Charleston Harbor.

Lincoln believed that secession was illegal, his constituency *expected* action, but his *choices* were limited by the varied ideologies of his supporters. Similarly, Jefferson Davis and the newly created Confederacy faced problems resulting from disagreement about secession.

Lincoln's call to arms forced wavering states to *choose* sides. Internal division in Virginia, Tennessee, Maryland, Kentucky, and Missouri caused a painful *choice* that frequently brought further violence and military action. A second wave of secession and conflict over the border states solidified the physical lines between the two competing societies. The stakes were set, the division was complete, but few realized how devastating the *outcome* would be. The nation faced the bloodiest war in its history.

SUGGESTED READINGS

Don E. Fehrenbacker. *Prelude to Greatness* (1962).

A well-written and interesting account of Lincoln's early career.

Don E. Fehrenbacher. *Slavery, Law, and Politics: The Dred Scott Case in Historical Perspective* (1981).

An excellent interpretive account of this landmark antebellum legal decision, placing it firmly into historical context.

William E. Gienapp, et al. *Essays in American Antebellum Politics, 1840–1860* (1982).

A collection of essays by the rising generation of new political scholars. Exciting and challenging reading.

Michael F. Holt. *The Political Crisis of the 1850s* (1978).

Arguably the best single-volume discussion of the political problems besetting the nation during this critical decade.

Stephen B. Oates. *To Purge This Land with Blood* (1984).

The best biography to date on John Brown, focusing on his role in the emerging sectional crisis during the 1850s.

David Potter. *The Impending Crisis, 1848–1861* (1976).

An extremely long and detailed work but beautifully written and informative.

James Rawley. *Race and Politics: "Bleeding Kansas" and the Coming of the Civil War* (1969).

An interesting look at the conflicts in Kansas, centering around racial attitudes in the West. Insightful and captivating reading.

Harriet Beecher Stowe. *Uncle Tom's Cabin* (1852; reprint, 1982).

This edition includes notes and chronology by noted social historian Kathryn Kish Sklar, making it especially informative. See also the one-hour film version produced by the Program for Culture at Play, available on videocassette from Films for the Humanities.

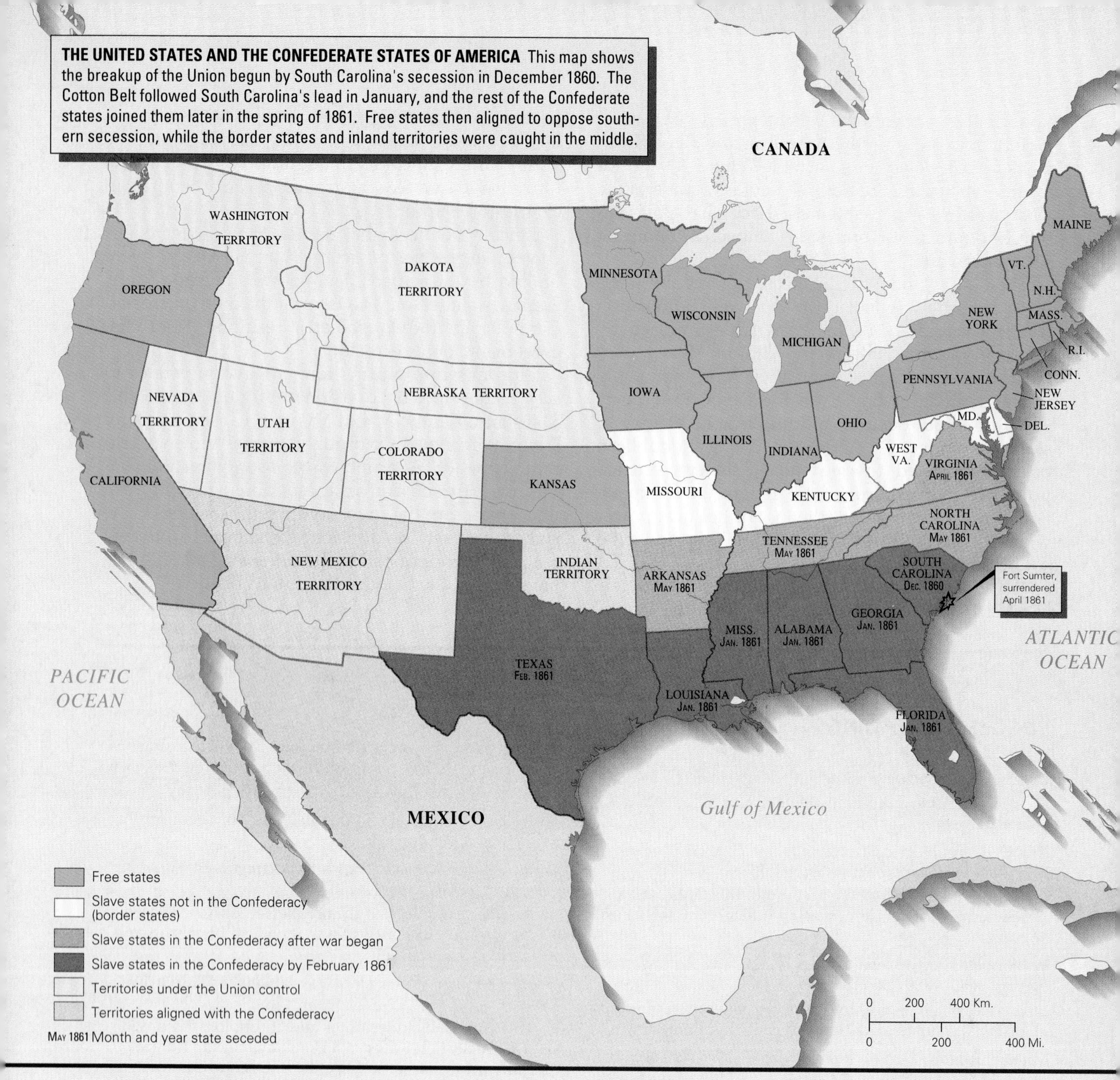

THE UNITED STATES AND THE CONFEDERATE STATES OF AMERICA This map shows the breakup of the Union begun by South Carolina's secession in December 1860. The Cotton Belt followed South Carolina's lead in January, and the rest of the Confederate states joined them later in the spring of 1861. Free states then aligned to oppose southern secession, while the border states and inland territories were caught in the middle.

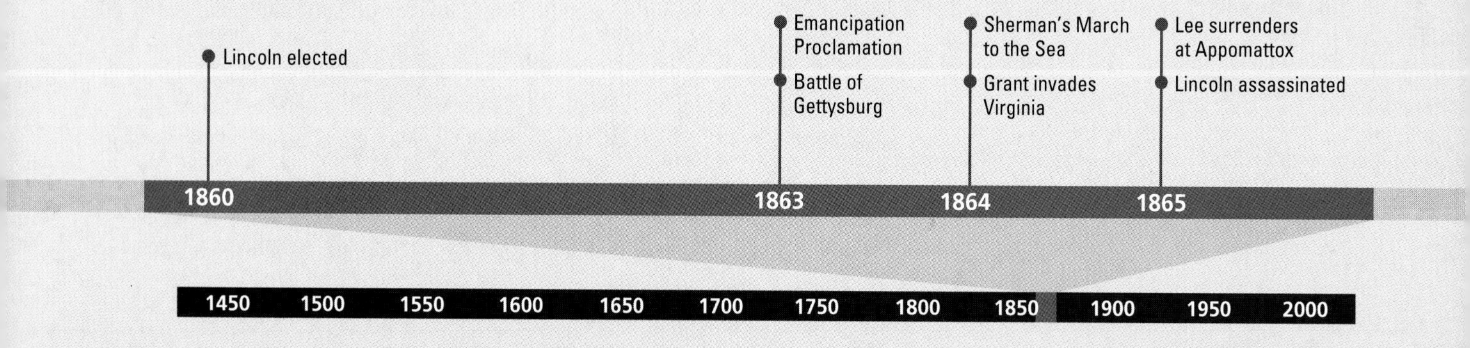

CHAPTER 15

A Violent Choice: Civil War, 1861–1865

The Politics of War

- What constraints did Abraham Lincoln and Jefferson Davis face as they led their respective nations into war?
- How did they choose to deal with those constraints?

From Bull Run to Antietam

- How did military action during the opening years of the war affect the expectations of people in the North and South?
- How did Lincoln's choice to issue the Emancipation Proclamation affect expectations about the war's outcome? Why?

The Human Dimensions of War

- How did constraints created by the war affect society during the course of the fighting?
- What choices did individuals and governments make to meet those constraints?

Waging Total War

- What expectations contributed to the Union choice to wage total war after 1863?
- Did the outcome justify the choice? Why or why not?

INTRODUCTION

E xpectations
C onstraints
C hoices
O utcomes

The election of 1860 polarized the nation. Southerners feared becoming a colony of the North and *chose* to secede from the United States. In the North, the Republicans *chose* not to yield any of their newly gained power, for they *expected* that compromise would threaten their economic and moral commitments. Each side contended that its point of view represented the proper course for the nation. In the face of such political *constraints,* the *outcome* was war.

Union president Abraham Lincoln and Confederate president Jefferson Davis faced serious political, economic, and military *constraints* as they mobilized for the conflict. Lincoln felt *constrained* by a rapidly aging army, a tiny navy, and a sluggish economy, yet even that was more than Davis had to work with. In addition, both Lincoln and Davis had to contend with political disagreements and demands. These *constraints* combined to shape each president's *expectations* and *choices.* Davis *chose* to pursue a defensive strategy, *expecting* that the North would tire of war and simply let the South leave the Union. Lincoln, blessed with superior manpower, manufacturing capability, and natural resources, *chose* to use the military to squeeze the South economically, *expecting* that the Confederacy would soon sue for peace. When a series of disastrous losses early in the war and political pressure from radicals in the Republican party combined to upset Lincoln's plan, he *chose* a more aggressive approach. The Union's refusal to weaken and leave the South in peace forced Davis to *choose* a more aggressive course also.

The economy in the North actually grew as industry moved into high gear to supply the troops. The Union army kept Confederates from disrupting northern production, and the Union navy kept international commerce flowing. Some of the new affluence was illusionary, because the federal government *chose* to finance the war effort with unbacked currency and bonds. Workers worried about the job competition that they would face if the slaves were freed. Workers also resented that they could be drafted for military service but rich men could buy their way out. Riots broke out in northern cities over both issues, and many people began to doubt Lincoln's abilities—both as a war leader and as a politician.

Meanwhile, the South was economically devastated. *Expecting* sales of cotton overseas to keep money flowing in for the war effort, southerners were disappointed when Britain stopped buying cotton and remained neutral. *Constrained* by dwindling resources, the South *chose* to issue a fortune in paper currency. Southerners also had to face the terrible reality of invading troops marching across their land and the fighting of pitched battles where corn, beans, and cotton once grew. The *outcome* was economic chaos. Southern people—black as well as white, loyal as well as rebel—starved.

In the fall of 1862, expecting to achieve his own political survival as well as an end to the suffering, Lincoln boldly *chose* to change the direction of the war by announcing the Emancipation Proclamation. Knowing that the South would not sue for peace after that development, Lincoln pressed his generals to deal a death blow to southern resistance. In the summer of 1864, Ulysses S. Grant and William Tecumseh Sherman gave him his wish, *choosing* military strategies that took a terrible human toll. While Sherman slashed his way through the Deep South, Grant sacrificed tens of thousands of men's lives to contain the Confederate forces under Robert E. Lee. The *outcome,* on April 9, 1865, was Lee's surrender. The war was essentially over.

Lincoln then began planning how to bring the defeated South back into the Union. But the man who had led the nation through the war did not survive to pursue his plans for peace. Lincoln was shot in the head by an actor sympathetic to the South. The president died, leaving the nation in mourning, uncertain what the final *outcome* would be.

CHRONOLOGY

War Between the States

1861 Lincoln takes office and runs the Union by executive authority until July
Fort Sumter falls
Battle of Bull Run
McClellan organizes the Union army
Union naval blockade begins

1862 Grant's victories in the Mississippi Valley
U.S. Navy captures New Orleans
Battle of Shiloh
Peninsular Campaign
Battle of Antietam
African Americans permitted in Union army

1863 Emancipation Proclamation takes effect
Union enacts conscription
Battle of Chancellorsville and death of Stonewall Jackson
Union victories at Gettysburg and Vicksburg
Draft riots in New York City

1864 Grant invades Virginia
Sherman captures Atlanta
Lincoln re-elected
Jefferson Davis proposes emancipation of black troops
Sherman's March to the Sea

1865 Sherman's march through the Carolinas
Lee abandons Petersburg and Richmond
Lee surrenders at Appomattox
Lincoln proposes a gentle reconstruction policy
Lincoln is assassinated

The Politics of War

- What constraints did Abraham Lincoln and Jefferson Davis face as they led their respective nations into war?
- How did they choose to deal with those constraints?

Running the war posed complex problems for both Abraham Lincoln and Jefferson Davis. At the outset, neither side had the experience, soldiers, or supplies to wage an effective war. Foreign diplomacy and international trade were vital to both sides. The Union needed to convince the world that this was an internal conflict, while the Confederacy tried to convince the world that it was a war between legitimate nations. The distinction was important. International law permits neutral nations to trade, negotiate, and communicate with nations engaged in a war. Such nations are known as belligerents. International law forbids neutral nations from having any dealings with groups in **rebellion** against a legally constituted government.

Perhaps the biggest challenge confronting both Davis and Lincoln, however, was internal politics. Lincoln had to contend not only with northern Democrats and with **Copperheads**—northerners who sympathized with the South—but also with divisions in his own party. Not all Republicans agreed with the president's war aims. Davis also faced internal political problems. The Confederate constitution guaranteed a great deal of autonomy to the Confederate states, and each state had a different opinion about war strategy and national objectives.

Union Policies and Objectives

Abraham Lincoln took the oath of office in March 1861, but Congress did not convene until July. This delay placed Lincoln in an awkward position. Article I, Section 8, of the U.S. Constitution gave Congress, not the president, the power "To declare war"

rebellion Open, armed, and organized resistance to a legally constituted government.

Copperheads Derogatory term (the name of a poisonous snake) applied to northerners who supported the South during the Civil War.

♦ Though most Americans entered the Civil War hesitantly, some, like these two Union cavalrymen (left) and this Confederate volunteer (right), were armed and eager to fight. Such enthusiasm usually did not last. The Confederate man shown here died in the first battle of the war at Bull Run. For those who lived longer, the days and weeks of boredom punctuated by brief but heated battles caused enormous anxiety that eroded their fighting spirit. *(left) Courtesy Richard F. Carlile Collection from* Echoes of Glory, Arms and Equipment of the Union *© 1991, Time-Life Books, Inc.; (right) Courtesy Bill Turner Collection from* Echoes of Glory, Arms and Equipment of the Confederacy *© 1991, Time-Life Books, Inc. Photo High Impact/Larry Sherer.*

and "To provide for calling forth the militia to execute the laws of the Union, suppress insurrection [that is, rebellion], and repel invasions." The secession of the southern states and the immediate threat to federal authority at Fort Sumter, however, required a response, and Lincoln was not the sort of man who would hesitate to make one.

Lincoln had spent his entire life dealing with difficult situations. Moving from farm to farm as a boy, he had seen to his own early education, and when he was called to political office after the Black Hawk War (see pages 292–293), he rose to the occasion by studying law. Lincoln believed that the South had risen in rebellion against the federal Union and, according to his reading of the Constitution, that the president had not only the authority but also the responsibility to bring the rebelling states to heel.

In effect, Lincoln ruled by executive proclamation for three months, assuming, as he thought he must, both the power and the responsibility for ending the challenge to national unity. In so doing, he set precedents that vastly expanded the wartime powers of the presidency. Thus, despite the fact that Congress was not in session, Lincoln called for seventy-five thousand militiamen from the states to put down the rebellion. And, ignoring specific constitutional provisions, he suspended the civil rights of citizens in Maryland when it appeared likely that they would join the Confederacy (see page 424). Also, feeling pressured to control southern sympathizers throughout the North, in April 1861 Lincoln suspended the constitutional right of **habeas corpus**—the right of a prisoner to be brought before a court and charged with a crime or else be released. Freed from the constraint of habeas corpus, the military could imprison, without trial, anyone suspected of treason or any other antigovernment activity.

Having assumed nearly absolute authority, Lincoln faced the need to rebuild an army in disarray. When hostilities broke out, the Union had only sixteen thousand men in uniform, and nearly one-third of the officers resigned to support the Confederacy. What military leadership remained was aged: seven of the eight heads of army bureaus had been in the service since the War of 1812, and General in Chief Winfield Scott was 74 years old. Only two Union officers had ever commanded a brigade, and both were in their seventies. Weapons were old, and supplies were low. On May 3, Lincoln again exceeded his constitutional authority by calling for regular army recruits to meet the crisis. "Whether strictly legal or not," he asserted, such actions were based on "a popular demand, and a public necessity," and he expected "that Congress would readily ratify them."

Lincoln then ordered the U.S. Navy to stop all incoming supplies to the states in rebellion. The naval blockade became an integral part of Union strategy. In 1861, the Union navy had as few resources as the Union army, but the leadership in the Navy Department quickly turned that situation around. Navy Secretary Gideon Welles, whom Lincoln called "Father Neptune," was an able administrator and a valuable member of the cabinet. He had the brilliant help of Assistant Secretary Gustavus V. Fox. Starting with almost nothing, these two purchased ships and built an effective navy that could both blockade the South and support land forces. By the end of 1861, the Union navy had 260 warships on the seas and a hundred more under construction.

The aged Winfield Scott drafted the initial Union military strategy. He advised that the blockade of southern ports be combined with a strong Union thrust down the Mississippi River, the primary artery in the South's transportation system. This strategy would break the southern economy and split the Confederacy into two isolated parts. Like many northerners, Scott believed that economic pressure would bring southern moderates forward to negotiate a settlement and perhaps return to the Union. However, this passive, diplomacy-oriented strategy did not appeal to war-fevered northerners who hungered for complete victory over those "arrogant southerners." The northern press ridiculed what it called the **anaconda plan,** sneering that Scott intended to "squeeze the South to military death."

The president convened Congress and addressed a special session on July 4, 1861, explaining his actions and outlining his plans. He reiterated that he had no constitutional authority to abolish slavery and no intention of doing so. Rebellion, not slavery, had caused the crisis, he said, and the seceding states must be brought back into the Union, regardless of the cost. "Our popular government has been called an experiment," he argued, and the point to be settled now was "its successful maintenance against a formidable internal attempt to overthrow it." On July 22 and 25, 1861, both houses of Congress passed resolutions validating Lincoln's actions.

This seemingly unified front lasted only a short time. Viewing vengeance as the correct objective, **Radical Republicans** pressured Congress to create an investigative committee to oversee the conduct of the war. Radical leader **Thaddeus Stevens** of Pennsylvania growled, "If their whole country must be laid waste, and made a desert, in order to save this union, so let it be." Stevens and the Radicals pressed for and passed a series of confiscation acts that inflicted severe penalties against individuals in rebellion. Treason was punishable by death, and anyone aiding the Confederacy was to be punished with imprisonment, confiscation of property, and the emancipation of slaves. All persons living in the eleven seceding states, whether loyal to the Union or not, were declared enemies of the Union and subject to the provisions of the law.

The Radicals splintered any consensus Lincoln might have achieved in his own party, and northern Democrats railed against his accumulation of

habeas corpus The right of a detained person to be brought before a court to determine whether he or she is being held legally or should be released.

anaconda plan Winfield Scott's plan (named after a snake that smothers prey in its coils) to blockade southern ports and take control of the Mississippi River, thus splitting the Confederacy, cutting off southern trade, and causing an economic collapse.

Radical Republicans Republican faction that tried to limit presidential power and enhance congressional authority during the Civil War, and that opposed moderation toward the South or any toleration of slavery.

Thaddeus Stevens Pennsylvania congressman who was a leader of the Radical Republicans.

♦ Though many northerners thought it was too passive, General Winfield Scott's Anaconda Plan was actually a very well conceived strategy. As this 1861 lithograph shows, Scott called for a naval blockade of the South and seizure of the Mississippi River, shutting down transportation routes to ruin the region's economy. Though Scott resigned in disgrace following the Battle of Bull Run, his plan continued to shape Union military efforts throughout the war. *Library of Congress.*

power. To keep an unruly Congress from undermining his efforts, Lincoln shaped early Union strategy to appease all factions and used military appointments to smooth political feathers. He had to perform a skillful political juggling act in order to prosecute the war, and he faced stiff opposition to his ideas about how the Confederates should be treated when the war ended. His attitudes frequently enraged radical abolitionists, but Lincoln maintained his calm in the face of their criticism and merely reinforced his intentions. "What I do about slavery and the colored race," he stated in 1862, "I do because it helps to save the Union; and what I forbear, I forbear because I do not believe it would help to save the Union." Such words, however, did not mend the ongoing divisiveness that hindered his efforts to run the war.

Nevertheless, Lincoln had far greater physical and human resources at his command than did the Confederates (see Table 15.1). The Union was home to more than twice as many people as the Confederacy, had vastly superior manufacturing and transportation systems, and enjoyed almost a monopoly in banking and foreign exchange. Lincoln also had a well-established government structure and formal diplomatic relations with other nations of the world. Still, these advantages could not help the war effort unless properly harnessed.

Confederate Policies and Objectives

At the start of the war, the Confederacy had no army, no navy, no war supplies, no government structure, no foreign alliances, and a political situation as ragged as the Union's. Each Confederate state had its own ideas about the best way to conduct the war. After the attack on Fort Sumter, amassing supplies, troops, ships, and war materials was the main task for Davis and his cabinet. Politics, however, influenced southern choices about where to field armies and who would direct them, how to run a war without offending state leaders, and how to pursue foreign diplomacy.

The Union naval blockade posed an immediate problem. The Confederacy had no navy and no capacity to build naval ships. Nevertheless, it had a secretary of the navy: the extremely resourceful Stephen Mallory. Under Mallory's direction, southern coastal defenders converted river steamboats, tugboats, and **revenue cutters** into harbor patrol gunboats, and they developed and placed explosive mines at the entrance to southern harbors and rivers. Commander James D. Bulloch traveled to England and purchased boats from the British. On one occasion, he bought a fast merchant ship, loaded it with Enfield rifles, gunpowder, ammunition, and cannon, maneuvered through the Union blockade at Savannah, and then armed and equipped the vessel to ram Union blockaders. Commander Raphael Semmes, in command of the C.S.S.

revenue cutter A small, lightly armed boat used by government customs agents to look for merchant ships violating customs laws.

TABLE 15.1 Comparison of Union and Confederate Resources

	Union (23 States)	Confederacy (11 States)
Total population	20,700,000	9,105,000[a]
Manufacturing establishments	110,000	18,000
Manufacturing workers	1,300,000	110,000
Miles of railroad	21,973	9,283
Troop strength (est.)	2,100,000	850,000

Source: Data from *Battles and Leaders of the Civil War* (1884–1888; reprinted ed., 1956).
[a]Includes 3,654,000 blacks, most of them slaves and not available for military duty.

Sumter, captured or burned eighteen Union ships during the first months of the war. Despite the gallant efforts of these men, however, the Confederates could not match the northern capacity to build and outfit ships. As the war progressed, the Union blockade became more and more effective.

Confederates pinned their main hope of winning the war on the army. Fighting for honor was praiseworthy behavior in the South, and southerners strongly believed they could "lick the Yankees" despite their disadvantage in manpower and resources. Southern boys rushed to enlist to fight the northern "popinjays," expecting a quick and glorious victory. Thousands volunteered before the Confederate war department was even organized. By the time Lincoln issued his call for seventy-five thousand militiamen, the Confederates already had sixty thousand men in uniform.

Despite this rush of fighting men, the South faced major handicaps. Even with the addition of the four Upper South states, the South built only 4 percent of all locomotives and only 3 percent of all firearms manufactured in the United States in 1860. The North produced almost all of the country's cloth, **pig iron,** boots, and shoes. Early in the war, the South could produce enough food but lacked the means to transport it where it was needed. Quartermaster General Abraham Myers drew the mammoth task of producing and delivering tents, shoes, uniforms, blankets, horses, and wagons. All were in short supply.

The miracle worker in charge of supplying southern troops with weapons and ammunition was Josiah Gorgas, who became chief of **ordnance** in April 1861. Gorgas purchased arms from Europe while his ordnance officers bought or stole copper pots and tubing to make **percussion caps,** bronze church bells to make cannon, and lead weights to make bullets. He built factories and foundries to manufacture small arms. But despite all his skill, he could not supply all of the Confederate troops. When the Confederate congress authorized the enlistment of four hundred thousand additional volunteers in 1861, the war department had to turn more than half of the enlistees away because it lacked equipment for them.

Internal politics also plagued the Davis administration. Despite the shortage of arms, state governors hoarded weapons seized from federal arsenals for their own state militias and then criticized Confederate strategies, particularly the actions of the war department. Although the South had many more qualified officers at the beginning of the war than did the North, powerful state politicians with little military experience—such as Henry A. Wise of Virginia and Robert A. Toombs of Georgia—received appointments as generals. That practice may have made good political sense, but it did not make good military sense.

pig iron Crude iron, direct from a blast furnace, that is cast into rectangular molds called pigs in preparation for conversion into steel, cast iron, or wrought iron.

ordnance Weapons, ammunition, and other military equipment.

percussion cap A thin metal cap containing gunpowder, needed to fire the guns used in the Civil War.

Davis himself contributed to the political problems by constantly interfering with the war department, squabbling with some of his generals, and remaining at odds with state politicians and many Confederate congressmen. By 1863, one Confederate representative wrote, "We as Congressmen have forborne and tried to harmonize with the President. His friends have tried to get him to change his policy, give up bad generals, and surrender his favorites in the army—neither they nor the pressure of public opinion have any effect."

Going into the conflict, Davis favored waging a defensive war. He felt that by counterattacking and yielding territory when necessary to buy time, the Confederacy could prolong the war and make it so costly that the Union would finally give up. Although defensive strategies ran counter to southern notions of pride and honor, each state's leaders demanded that their state's borders be protected, ignoring that such a strategy would spread troops so thin that no state would be safe. In any case, most southerners preferred an aggressive policy. As one southern editor put it, the "idea of waiting for blows, instead of inflicting them is altogether unsuited to the genius of our people."

The Diplomatic Front

Perhaps the biggest challenge facing the Confederacy was gaining international recognition and foreign aid—weapons and other manufactured goods, gold, and ships. The primary focus of Confederate foreign policy was Great Britain. For years, the South had been exporting large amounts of cotton to Britain, and many southerners felt that formal recognition of the Confederate States of America as an independent nation would immediately follow secession and the organization of a government. Political, diplomatic, and economic realities doomed them to disappointment. After all, the United States, divided as it was, was still an important player in international affairs, and the British were not going to risk offending such an emerging industrial power without good cause. Also many English voters were morally opposed to slavery and would have objected to an open alliance with the slaveholding Confederacy. Thus, while the British allowed southern agents to purchase ships and goods, they crafted a careful policy. On May 13, 1861, Queen Victoria proclaimed official neutrality but granted **belligerent status** to the South. This meant that Britain recognized the Confederates not as rebels but as responsible leaders in a legitimate war for independence. But it also meant that they did not recognize the Confederate States of America as yet ready to enter the international community.

The British pronouncement set the tone for other European responses and was much less than southerners had hoped for. It was also a major blow to the North, however, for Britain did not accept Lincoln's position that the conflict was rebellion against duly authorized government. Lincoln could do little but accept British neutrality, for to provoke Britain might lead to full recognition of the Confederacy or to calls for arbitration of the conflict. At the same time, he cautiously continued efforts to stop all incoming aid to the Confederacy. Despite his best intentions, an incident at sea nearly scuttled British-American relations.

In November 1861 James Murray Mason, the newly appointed Confederate emissary to London, and John Slidell, the Confederate minister to France, were traveling to their posts aboard the *Trent,* a British merchant ship bound for London. After the *Trent* left Havana, the U.S. warship *San Jacinto,* under the command of Captain Charles Wilkes, stopped the British ship. Wilkes had Mason, Slidell, and their staffs removed from the *Trent* and taken to Boston for confinement at Fort Warren.

Northerners celebrated the action and praised Wilkes, but the British were not pleased. They viewed the *Trent* affair as aggression against a neutral government, a violation of international law, and an affront to their national honor. President Lincoln, Secretary of State William Seward, and U.S. Ambassador to England Charles Francis Adams (son of President John Quincy Adams) calmed the British by arguing that Wilkes had acted without orders. They ordered the release of the prisoners, and they apologized to the British, handling the incident so adroitly that the public outcry was largely forgotten when Mason and Slidell arrived in London.

The Union's First Attack

Confident that the Union could bring the war to a quick end, General Irvin McDowell moved his troops into Virginia to campaign against Confeder-

belligerent status Recognition that a participant in a conflict is a nation engaged in warfare rather than a rebel against a legally constituted government; full diplomatic recognition is one possible outcome.

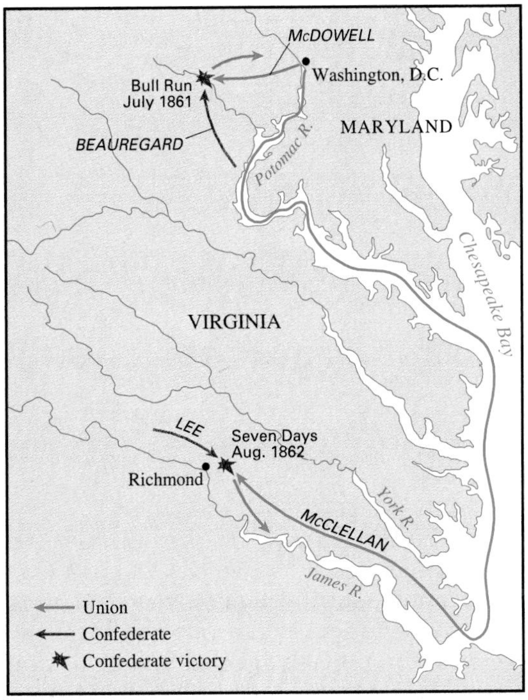

♦ **MAP 15.1 Union Offensives into Virginia, 1861–1862**
This map shows two failed Union attempts to invade Virginia: the Battle of Bull Run (July 1861) and the Peninsular Campaign (August 1862). Confederate victories embarrassed the richer and more populous Union.

ate troops led by General P. G. T. Beauregard (see Map 15.1 and Table 15.2). McDowell's troops, though high-spirited, were poorly trained and undisciplined. They ambled along as though they were on a country outing. Their dawdling allowed Beauregard enough time to position his troops in defense of a vital rail center near Manassas Junction along a creek called **Bull Run.**

McDowell attacked on Sunday, July 21, and maintained the offensive most of the day. He seemed poised to overrun the Confederates until southern reinforcements under **Thomas J. Jackson** took a position on a hill and, fighting furiously, stalled the Union advance. As one Confederate woman observed, the sky was "darkened by cannon smoke," and "the roar of guns seemed never to cease." General Jackson's stand at Bull Run earned him the nickname "Stonewall," and under intense cannon fire, Union troops panicked and began fleeing into a throng of northern spectators who had come to watch the battle from what they thought would be a safe distance. Thoroughly humiliated before a hometown crowd, Union soldiers retreated pell-mell toward Washington. Jefferson Davis immediately ordered the invasion of the Union capital, but the Confederates were also in disarray and made no attempt to pursue the fleeing Union forces.

This battle profoundly affected both sides. In the South, the victory stirred confidence that the war would be short and victory complete. Northerners, disillusioned and embarrassed, pledged that no similar retreats would occur. Under fire for the loss and hoping to improve both the management of military affairs and the competence of the troops, Lincoln replaced General Scott with **George B. McClellan,** who was to create the **Army of the Potomac** to defend the capital from Confederate attack and spearhead any offensives into Virginia. Lincoln also replaced Secretary of War Cameron with Edward Stanton, a politician and lawyer from Pennsylvania.

General McClellan's strengths were in organization and discipline and in inspiring his troops. All were sorely needed. Before Bull Run, Union officers had lounged around Washington, and raw recruits in army camps received no training. Under McClellan, months of training turned the 185,000-man army into a well-drilled and efficient unit. Calls to attack Richmond began anew, but McClellan, seemingly in no hurry for battle, continued to drill the troops and remained in the capital. An ambitious, self-assured man, McClellan had been the darling of the Radical Republicans, who had supported his promotion because they wanted to see more action. Now his stubborn inactivity cost him their support as Lincoln pressed the reluctant general to do something.

The new year began with Lincoln taking a much more aggressive stance. On January 27, 1862, he

Bull Run A creek in Virginia not far from Washington, D.C., where Confederate soldiers forced federal troops to retreat in the first major battle of the Civil War, fought in July 1861.

Thomas J. Jackson Confederate general nicknamed "Stonewall"; he commanded troops at both battles of Bull Run and was mortally wounded by his own troops at Chancellorsville in 1863.

George B. McClellan U.S. general who replaced Winfield Scott as general in chief of Union forces; a skillful organizer but slow and indecisive as a field commander.

Army of the Potomac Army created to guard the U.S. capital after the Battle of Bull Run in 1861; it became the main Union army in the East.

TABLE 15.2 Battle of Bull Run, July 22, 1861

	Union Army	Confederate Army
Commanders	Irvin McDowell	P. G. T. Beauregard
Troop strength	17,676	18,053
Losses		
Killed	460	387
Wounded	1,124	1,582
Captured, missing	1,312	13
Total losses	2,896	1,982

Source: Data from *Battles and Leaders of the Civil War* (1884–1888; reprinted ed., 1956).

called for a broad offensive, but his general in chief ignored the order and delayed for nearly two months. Completely frustrated, Lincoln removed McClellan as general in chief on March 11 but left him in command of the Army of the Potomac. Even so, Union forces in the East mounted no major offensives. And when combat did take place, the Confederates, though almost always outnumbered, were usually victorious.

From Bull Run to Antietam

- How did military action during the opening years of the war affect the expectations of people in the North and South?
- How did Lincoln's choice to issue the Emancipation Proclamation affect expectations about the war's outcome? Why?

Reorganizing the military and forming the Army of the Potomac did not accomplish Lincoln's and the nation's goal of toppling the Confederacy quickly and bringing the rebellious South back into the Union. In the second year of the war, frustration followed frustration as Confederate forces continued to outwit and outfight numerically superior and better-equipped federal troops. After Bull Run it was clear that the war would be neither short nor glorious. Military, political, and diplomatic strategies became increasingly entangled as both North and South struggled for the major victories that would end the war.

The War in the West

While the war in the East slid into inactivity, events in the West seemed almost as futile for the Union forces. In the border state of Missouri, the conflict rapidly degenerated into guerrilla warfare. Confederate William Quantrill's Raiders matched atrocities committed by Unionist guerrilla units called Jayhawkers. Union officials seemed unable to stop the ambushes, arson, theft, and murder, and Missouri remained a lawless battleground throughout the war.

Both the United States and the Confederacy coveted the western territories nearly as much as they did the border states. In 1861 Confederate Henry Hopkins Sibley led an expedition in an attempt to gain control of New Mexico and Arizona. Bearing authority directly from Jefferson Davis, Sibley recruited thirty-seven hundred Texans and marched into New Mexico. He defeated a Union force at Valverde, but his losses were high. Needing provisions to continue the operation, he sent units to raid abandoned Union storehouses at Albuquerque and Santa Fe, but withdrawing federal troops had burned whatever supplies they could not carry. The small Confederate force at Santa Fe encountered a much larger federal force and won a miraculous victory, but the effort left the Confederates destitute of supplies. Under constant attack, the starving Confederate detachment evaded Union troops and retreated back into Texas.

As the war intensified, leaders on both sides were forced to concentrate on regional defenses and focus on potential confrontations with enemy armies. Union officers pulled most of their troops back into the areas of concentrated fighting, leaving vast areas of the sparsely settled West with no military protection. In 1862, the Santee Sioux took advantage of the situation by attacking and killing more than eight hundred settlers in the Minnesota River valley. An army of fourteen hundred volunteers finally put

♦ A successful planter following the "Trail of Tears," Stand Watie allied with the Confederacy in 1861, raising a volunteer regiment called the Cherokee Mounted Rifles. By war's end, Watie had risen to the rank of brigadier general in the Confederate army and was the last field officer to surrender after the fall of Richmond. *Special Collections, John Vaughan Library, Northeastern State University, Tahlequah, OK.*

down the uprising, but the lack of federal troops in frontier regions created severe anxiety in western communities.

Confederate leaders sought alliances with several Indian tribes at the onset of war, particularly tribes in the newly settled Indian Territory south of Kansas. Many of the residents there had endured the Trail of Tears (see pages 294–295) and had no particular love for the Union. Arkansas, Louisiana, and Texas were all vulnerable to Union attack, and if these Indian tribes aligned with the Confederacy, they not only could supply troops but also could form a buffer between Union forces in Kansas and the thinly spread Confederate defenses west of the Mississippi River.

Governor Edward Clark of Texas optimistically informed Davis that at least twenty thousand Indians could be recruited. Davis appointed General Albert Pike, an Arkansas lawyer who had represented the Creeks in court, as special commissioner for the Indian Territory in March 1861. Pike negotiated with several tribes and on October 7 signed a treaty with **John Ross,** chief of the Cherokee Nation. The treaty, which applied to some members of the Cherokee, Choctaw, Creek, Chickasaw, and Seminole tribes, granted the Indians more nearly equal status—at least on paper—than any previous federal treaty had granted, and it guaranteed that they would fight only to defend their own territory. One Cherokee leader, Stand Watie, became a Confederate general and distinguished himself in battle, leading his Confederate troops in guerrilla warfare against Union forces.

Despite Watie's success, Confederate Indian troops never provided the kind of assistance hoped for. Although they served, they disliked army discipline and became disgusted when promised supplies failed to materialize. Many Indian troops defected when ordered to attack other Indians for no better reason than that they had chosen to support the wrong side in what was largely a war between whites.

Still, several battles, such as the 1862 Battle of Pea Ridge in Arkansas, pitted Indian troops on each side against each other. The divisions between Indian groups allied with the North and with the South often reflected long-standing tribal animosities and traditional rivalries. Free to prey on each other, they often burned Indian homes and villages as they raided enemy locations.

With all the destruction, and despite the considerable bravery displayed by Indian participants on both sides, the war brought little benefit to the tribes involved.

Struggle for the Mississippi

While McClellan stalled in the East, one Union general finally had some success in the western theater of the war. Following the strategy outlined in General Scott's anaconda plan, **Ulysses S. Grant** moved against southern strongholds in the Mississippi Valley in 1862. On February 6, he took Fort Henry along the Tennessee River and ten days later captured Fort Donelson on the Cumberland River near Nashville, Tennessee (see Map 15.2). Grant's army

John Ross Cherokee leader who had reluctantly directed the forced removal of the Cherokees from Georgia to Oklahoma Territory in the 1830s.

Ulysses S. Grant U.S. general who became commander in chief of the Union army in 1864 after the Vicksburg campaign; he later became president of the United States.

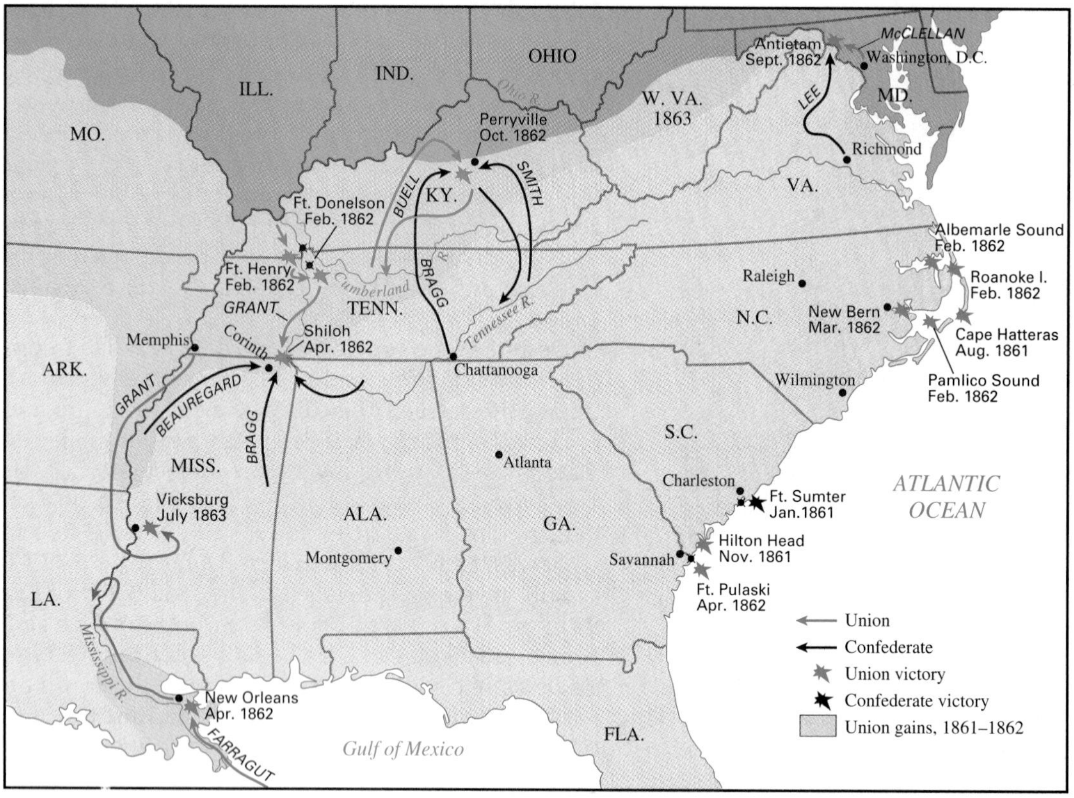

♦ **MAP 15.2 The Anaconda Plan and the Battle of Antietam** This map illustrates the anaconda plan at work. The Union navy closed southern harbors while Grant's troops worked to seal the northern end of the Mississippi River. The map also shows the Battle of Antietam (September 1862), in which Confederate troops under Robert E. Lee were finally defeated by a Union army under General George McClellan.

suffered some casualties but took more than fifteen thousand prisoners of war. As Union forces approached Nashville, the Confederates evacuated and retreated to Corinth, Mississippi. In this one short stroke, Grant successfully penetrated Confederate western defenses and brought Kentucky and most of Tennessee under federal control.

At Corinth, Confederate general Albert Sidney Johnston finally reorganized the retreating southern troops while Grant was waiting for reinforcements. Early on April 6, to Grant's surprise, Johnston attacked at Pittsburg Landing, Tennessee, near a small country meetinghouse called Shiloh Church (see Table 15.3). Some Union forces under General **William Tecumseh Sherman** were driven back, but the Confederate attack soon lost momentum as Union defenses stiffened. The **Battle of Shiloh** raged until midafternoon. When Johnston was mortally wounded, General Beauregard took command and by day's end believed the enemy defeated. But Union reinforcements arrived during the night, and the next morning Grant counterattacked, pushing the Confederates back to Corinth.

What stunned northerners and southerners alike about Shiloh was that losses on both sides were staggering—by far the heaviest to date in the war. The Battle of Shiloh made the reality of war apparent to everyone but made a particularly strong impression on the common soldier. After Shiloh, one Confederate wrote: "Death in every awful form, if it really be death, is a pleasant sight in comparison to

William Tecumseh Sherman U.S. general who captured Atlanta in 1864 and led a destructive march to the Atlantic coast.

Battle of Shiloh Battle in Tennessee in April 1862 that ended with an unpursued Confederate withdrawal; both sides suffered heavy casualties for the first time, and neither side gained ground.

TABLE 15.3 Battle of Shiloh, April 6–7, 1862

	Union Army	Confederate Army
Commanders	William Tecumseh Sherman Ulysses S. Grant	Albert Sidney Johnston (killed) P. G. T. Beauregard
Troop strength	75,000	44,000
Losses		
Killed	1,754	1,723
Wounded	8,408	8,012
Captured, missing	2,885	959
Total losses	13,047	10,694

Source: Data from *Battles and Leaders of the Civil War* (1884–1888; reprinted ed., 1956).

the fearfully and mortally wounded." Few people foresaw that the number of casualties at Shiloh was but a taste of the carnage to come.

Farther south, Admiral David G. Farragut led a fleet of U.S. Navy gunboats against New Orleans, the commercial and banking center of the South, and on April 25 forced the city's surrender. Farragut then sailed up the Mississippi, hoping to take the well-fortified city of **Vicksburg,** Mississippi. He scored several victories until he reached Port Hudson, Louisiana, where the combination of Confederate defenses and shallow water forced him to halt. Meanwhile, on June 6, Union gunboats destroyed a Confederate fleet at Memphis, Tennessee, and brought the upper Mississippi under Union control. Vicksburg remained the only major obstacle to Union control over the entire river (see Map 15.2).

Realizing the seriousness of the situation in the West, the Confederates regrouped and invaded Kentucky. That campaign ended in a stand-off after Union forces under General William S. Rosecrans stopped Confederate general Braxton Bragg's force on December 31 at Stone's River and did not pursue when the Confederates retreated. Back in Mississippi, Grant launched two unsuccessful attacks against Vicksburg in December, but then Union efforts stalled. Nevertheless, northern forces had wrenched control of the upper and lower ends of the river away from the Confederacy.

Lee's Aggressive Defense of Virginia

The anaconda plan was well on its way to cutting the Confederacy in two, but the general public in the North thought that the path to real victory led to Richmond, capital of the Confederacy. Thus, to maintain public support for the war, Lincoln needed victories over the Confederates in the East, and campaigns there were given higher priority than campaigns in the West.

Confederate leaders realized that Richmond would be an important prize for the North, and they took dramatic steps to keep their capital city out of enemy hands. Defending Richmond was the South's primary goal: more supplies and men were assigned to campaigns in Virginia than to defending Confederate borders elsewhere.

A naval battle occurring early in 1862 cleared the way for a Union offensive that Lincoln hoped would lead directly to the fall of Richmond. Hoping to clear Virginia's coastline of Union blockaders and protect their capitol from amphibious invasion, Confederate naval architects had redesigned a captured Union ship named the *Merrimac.* They encased the entire ship in iron plates and renamed it the *Virginia.* Operating out of the safe harbor of Norfolk, the Confederate ironclad ship forayed against Union blockaders, sinking several in a single day. In response, the Union navy built the *Monitor,* a low-decked ironclad vessel with a revolving gun turret. In March the *Virginia* and the *Monitor* shelled each other for five hours. Both were badly damaged but still afloat when the *Virginia* withdrew, making its way back to Norfolk, never to leave harbor again.

Vicksburg Confederate-held city on the Mississippi River that surrendered on July 4, 1863, after a siege by Grant's forces.

♦ Desperate to break the grip of the Union anaconda, the Confederate navy captured the U.S.S. *Merrimac* and converted it into the ironclad C.S.S. *Virginia*. Virtually immune to any weapon carried by Union frigates, the *Virginia* dominated the sealanes out of Norfolk. Eager to launch an invasion up the Chesapeake, Union officials commissioned their own ironclad, the U.S.S. *Monitor,* and sent it into battle against the *Virginia*. After five hours of repeated ramming and artillery pounding, the *Virginia* was so badly damaged that it retreated to Norfolk and never saw action again. *"Engagement Between Monitor and Merrimac" by J.G. Tanner. National Gallery of Art, Gift of Edgar William and Bernice Chrysler Garbisch.*

With the *Virginia* out of service, McClellan devised precisely the amphibious assault that Virginians had been fearing. Expecting to surprise the Confederates by attacking Richmond from the south, he transported the entire Army of the Potomac by ship to Fort Monroe, Virginia. After coming ashore at the fort, the army marched up the peninsula between the York and James rivers (see Map 15.1). In typical fashion, McClellan proceeded cautiously. The outnumbered Confederate forces took advantage of his indecision and twice slipped away, retreating toward Richmond while McClellan followed. On May 31, General Joseph E. Johnston, commander of the Confederate Army of Northern Virginia, attacked at Seven Pines, hoping to surprise his opponent and overcome the odds. Johnston was severely wounded, forcing Jefferson Davis to find a replacement.

Robert E. Lee was probably the best general the Confederacy had. Prior to the encounter at Seven Pines, Lee had advised Davis and helped organize the defense of the Atlantic coast. Daring, bold, and tactically aggressive, he enjoyed combat, pushed his troops to the maximum, and was well liked by those serving under him. Lee had an uncanny ability to read the character of his opponents, predict their maneuvers, and exploit their mistakes. He was well suited to leadership, and on June 2, 1862, Davis named him commander of the Army of Northern Virginia.

As McClellan continued to work his way toward Richmond, Confederate stalwart Stonewall Jackson staged a brilliant diversionary thrust up the Shenandoah Valley toward Washington. Jackson, who had grown up in the region, seemed to be everywhere at once. In thirty days, he and his men (who became known as the "foot cavalry") marched 350 miles, defeated three Union armies in five battles, captured and sent back to Richmond a fortune in provisions and equipment, inflicted twice as many casualties as they received, and confused and immobilized Union forces in the region.

Meanwhile, Union forces were marking time near Richmond while McClellan waited for reinforcements. Following Jackson's campaign, Lee launched a series of attacks to drive McClellan away from the Confederate capital. In a move that became typical of his generalship, Lee split his forces and attacked from all sides over a seven-day period in August, forcing McClellan into a defensive position. The **Peninsular Campaign** was over. The self-promoting Union general had been beaten in part by his own indecisiveness.

Fed up with McClellan, Lincoln gave command of the Army of the Potomac to General John Pope,

Peninsular Campaign McClellan's attempt in the spring and summer of 1862 to capture Richmond by advancing up the peninsula between the James and York rivers; Confederate forces under Lee drove his troops back.

but Pope's command was brief. Union forces encountered Lee's army again at the Manassas rail line on August 30. The Confederates pretended to retreat, and when Pope followed, Lee soundly defeated Lincoln's new general in the **Second Battle of Bull Run.** Thoroughly disappointed with Pope's performance, and not knowing whom else to turn to, Lincoln once again named McClellan commander of the Army of the Potomac.

Lee's Invasion of Maryland

Feeling confident after the second victory at Bull Run, Lee devised a bold offensive against Maryland. His plan had three objectives. First, he wanted to move the fighting out of war-torn Virginia so that farmers could harvest food. Second, he hoped that he might attract volunteers from among the many slaveowners and southern sympathizers in Maryland to beef up his undermanned army. Third, he believed that a strong thrust against Union forces might gain diplomatic recognition for the Confederacy from Europe. In the process, he hoped to win enough territory to force the Union to sue for peace. On September 4, Lee crossed the Potomac into Maryland, formulating an intricate offensive by dividing his army into three separate attack wings. But someone was careless—Union soldiers found a copy of Lee's detailed instructions wrapped around some cigars at an abandoned Confederate campsite.

If McClellan had acted swiftly on this intelligence, he could have crushed Lee's army piece by piece, but for some unknown reason he waited sixteen hours before advancing. By then Lee had learned of the missing orders and planned an immediate withdrawal. After bitter fighting at Fox's Gap, Lee reunited some of his forces at Sharpsburg, Maryland, around **Antietam Creek** (see Map 15.2). There, on September 17, the Army of the Potomac and the Army of Northern Virginia engaged in the bloodiest single-day battle of the Civil War.

The casualties in this one battle were more than double those suffered in the War of 1812 and the Mexican War combined. "The air was full of the hiss of bullets and the hurtle of grapeshot," one Union soldier said, and "the whole landscape turned red." The bitter fighting exhausted both armies. After a day of rest, Lee retreated across the Potomac. Stonewall Jackson, covering Lee's retreat, soundly thrashed a force that McClellan sent in pursuit. But for the first time, General Lee experienced defeat.

Although Lee's offensive had been thwarted, Lincoln was in no way pleased with the performance of his army and its leadership. He felt that McClellan could have destroyed Lee's force if he had attacked earlier or, failing that, that McClellan should have pursued the fleeing Confederate army with all haste. He fired McClellan again, this time for good, and placed Ambrose E. Burnside in command of the Army of the Potomac.

Burnside moved the Army of the Potomac to the east bank of the Rappahannock River overlooking **Fredericksburg,** Virginia (see Map 15.3), where he

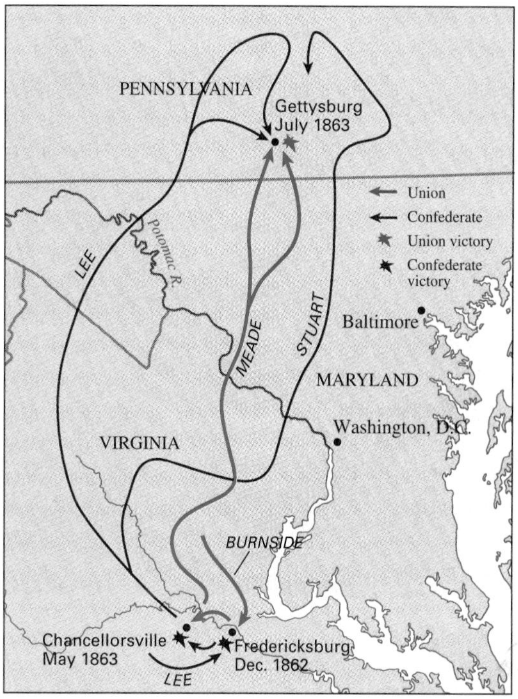

♦ **MAP 15.3 Fredericksburg, Chancellorsville, and Gettysburg** This map shows the campaigns that took place during the winter of 1862 and spring of 1863, culminating in the Battle of Gettysburg (July 1863). General Meade's victory at Gettysburg may have been the critical turning point in the war.

Second Battle of Bull Run Union defeat near Bull Run in August 1862; Union troops led by John Pope were outmaneuvered by Lee.

Antietam Creek Site of a battle that occurred in September 1862 when Lee's forces invaded Maryland; both sides suffered heavy losses, and Lee retreated into Virginia.

Fredericksburg Site in Virginia of a Union defeat in December 1862, which demonstrated the incompetence of the new Union commander, Ambrose E. Burnside.

♦ Many soldiers entered the Civil War expecting excitement and colorful pageantry, but the realities of war were harsh and ugly. This photograph by Union cameraman Andrew J. Russell shows a line of southern soldiers who were killed while defending a position at Fredericksburg. Even after Union soldiers had breached the wall, the Confederates fought on using their rifles as clubs until they were all mowed down. Scenes like this became so common that veterans reported that they became numb to the shock of death. *Library of Congress.*

delayed for almost three weeks. Lee used the time to fortify the heights west of the city with men and artillery. On December 13, in one of the worst mistakes of the war, Burnside ordered a day-long frontal assault. The results were devastating. Federal troops, mowed down from the heights, suffered tremendous casualties, and once again the Army of the Potomac retreated back to Washington.

Diplomacy and the Politics of Emancipation

The first full year of the war ended with mixed results for both sides. Union forces in the West had scored major victories, breaking down Confederate defenses and taking Memphis and New Orleans. But the failure of the Army of the Potomac under three different generals and the brilliant maneuvers by Lee and Jackson seemed to outweigh the Union's success in the West. Lee's victories, however, carried heavy casualties, and the South's ability to supply and **deploy** troops was rapidly diminishing. A long, drawn-out conflict favored the Union unless Jefferson Davis could secure help for the Confederacy from abroad.

The Confederacy still expected British aid. The British challenged the Union blockade from time to time, and attempts by federal ships to enforce it strained relations between the United States and Great Britain. But nothing seemed to shake Britain's commitment to neutrality. To a large extent, this result was due to the efforts of Charles Francis Adams, Lincoln's ambassador in London, who demonstrated his diplomatic skill repeatedly during the war. Also, Britain possessed a surplus of cotton and did not need southern supplies, limiting the South's ability to use economic pressure to exact its diplomatic goals.

Davis and the Confederacy sought any type of foreign recognition that might lead to international pressure on the North to negotiate a peace with

deploy To position troops in readiness for combat.

an independent Confederacy. Then if the North refused to engage in such negotiations, foreign nations might assist the southern military effort. In 1862, following early Confederate military success, Britain considered such action. Lord John Russell, the British foreign minister, and Lord Palmerston, the prime minister, suggested "an arrangement on the basis of separation" and planned to offer mediation as a forerunner to "recognition of the independence of the Confederates." If Britain had led, Spain and France would probably have followed. But the plan never matured, in part because of Lee's failure at Antietam. Even so, the threat of foreign recognition of the Confederacy added to Lincoln's frustration as he tried to turn the tide of war.

Radical Republicans were also frustrated. No aspect of the war was going as they had expected. They had hoped that the Union army would defeat the South in short order. Instead the war effort was dragging on. More important from the Radicals' point of view, nothing was being done about slavery. They pressed Lincoln to take a stand against slavery, and they pushed Congress for legislation to prohibit slavery in federal territories.

Politically astute as always, Lincoln acted to appease the Radical Republicans, foster popular support in the North for the war effort, and increase favorable sentiment for the Union cause abroad. During the summer of 1862, he drafted a proclamation freeing the slaves in the Confederacy and submitted it to his cabinet. Cabinet members advised that he postpone announcing the policy until after the Union had achieved a military victory. In August, **Horace Greeley,** founder of the *New York Tribune,* called for the immediate emancipation of all slaves. But Lincoln reiterated that his objective was "to save the Union," not "to save or destroy slavery." On September 22, however, five days after the Battle of Antietam, Lincoln unveiled the **Emancipation Proclamation,** which abolished slavery in the states "in rebellion" and would go into effect on January 1, 1863.

Although the Emancipation Proclamation was a major step toward ending slavery, it actually freed no slaves. The proclamation applied only to slavery in areas controlled by the Confederacy, not in any area controlled by the Union. Some found this exception troubling, labeling the proclamation an empty fraud, but the president's reasoning was sound. He could not afford to alienate the four slave states that had remained in the Union, nor could he commit any manpower to enforce emancipation in the areas that had been captured from the Confederacy. Lincoln made emancipation entirely conditional on a Union military victory, a gambit designed to force critics of the war, whether in the United States or Great Britain, to rally behind his cause.

Whether or not it was successful as a humanitarian action, issuing the Emancipation Proclamation when he did and in the form he did was a profoundly successful political step. Although a handful of northern Democrats and a few Union military leaders called it an "absurd proclamation of a political coward," more joined Frederick Douglass in proclaiming, "We shout for joy that we live to record this righteous decree." Meanwhile, some in Britain pointed to the paradox of the proclamation: it declared an end to slavery in areas where Lincoln could not enforce it, but it had no effect on slavery in areas under Lincoln's control. Most, however, applauded the document and rallied against recognition of the Confederacy.

Lincoln's new general in chief, Henry Halleck, understood the underlying significance of the proclamation. He explained to Grant that the "character of the war has very much changed within the last year. There is now no possible hope of reconciliation." The war was now about slavery as well as secession, and the Emancipation Proclamation committed the Union to conquering the enemy. As Lincoln told one member of his cabinet, the war would now be "one of subjugation."

The Human Dimensions of War

- How did constraints created by the war affect society during the course of the fighting?
- What choices did individuals and governments make to meet those constraints?

The Civil War imposed tremendous stress on American society. As the men marched off to battle, women faced the task of caring for families and property alone. As casualties increased, the number of voluntary enlistments decreased, and both sides searched for ways to find replacements for dead and wounded

Horace Greeley Journalist and politician who helped found the Republican party; his newspaper the *New York Tribune* was known for its antislavery stance.

Emancipation Proclamation Lincoln's order abolishing slavery in states "in rebellion" but not in border territories still loyal to the Union, as of January 1, 1863.

soldiers. The armies consumed vast amounts of manufactured and agricultural products—constantly demanding not only weapons and ammunition but also food, clothing, and hardware. Government spending was enormous, hard currency was scarce, and inflation soared as both governments printed paper money to pay their debts. Industrial capability, transportation facilities, and agricultural production often dictated when, where, and how well armies fought. Society in both North and South changed to meet an array of hardships as individuals facing unfamiliar choices attempted to carry on their lives in the midst of the war's devastation.

Instituting the Draft

By the end of 1862, heavy casualties, massive desertion, and declining enlistments had depleted both armies. Although the North had a much larger population pool than the South to draw from, its enlistments sagged with its military fortunes during 1862. More than a hundred thousand Union soldiers were absent without official leave. Most volunteers had enlisted in 1861 for limited terms, which would soon expire, and the Lincoln administration faced a potential crisis. State drafts netted few replacements because the Democrats, who made tremendous political gains at the state level in 1862, openly criticized Republican policies and at times refused to cooperate. In March 1863, Congress passed the **Conscription Act,** trying to bypass state officials and ensure enough manpower to continue the war. The law declared all single men between the ages of 20 and 45, and married men between 20 and 35, eligible to be drafted. Government agents collected names in a house-to-house survey, and draftees were selected by a lottery.

The conscription law offered a way to avoid military service to drafted men who could "provide," or hire, an "acceptable substitute" or pay a $300 fee to purchase exemption. The burden of service thus fell on farmers and urban workers—a large proportion of whom were immigrants—who were already suffering from the economic burden of high taxation and inflation caused by the war. Added to that was workers' fear that multitudes of former slaves freed by the Emancipation Proclamation would pour into the already crowded job market, further lowering the value of labor. Together, conscription and emancipation created among the urban poor a sense of alienation, which exploded in the summer of 1863.

♦ Angered by the fact that rich men were virtually exempt from the draft, frightened by the prospect of job competition from freed southern slaves, and frustrated by the lack of resolution on the battlefield, working men took to the streets in New York City during the summer of 1863 to protest against the war. Well-dressed men, African Americans, and leading war advocates were the main targets of mob violence during five days of uncontrolled rioting. Many homes, businesses, and the Colored Orphan Asylum were burned and an unknown number of people were killed and injured. *Library of Congress.*

The trouble started on July 13 in New York City. Armed demonstrators protesting unfair draft laws engaged in a spree of violence, venting their frustration at the troubles plaguing working people. During five days of rioting, white working men beat many African Americans and lynched six. The Colored Orphan Asylum and several homes owned by

Conscription Act Law passed by Congress in 1863 that established a draft but allowed wealthy people to escape it by hiring a substitute or paying the government a $300 fee.

blacks were burned. Mobs ransacked businesses owned by blacks and by people who employed blacks. Irish men and women and members of other groups that seemed to threaten job security also felt the fury as mobs attacked the churches, businesses, and homes of immigrants.

The rioters also expressed their frustration against Republican spokesmen and officials. They let Republican journalist Horace Greeley **hang in effigy** and sacked the homes of other prominent Republicans and abolitionists. Protesting draft exemptions for the rich, rioters also set upon well-dressed strangers on the streets.

After five days of chaos, federal troops put down the riot. Fearful of future violence, the city council of New York City voted to pay the $300 exemption fee for all poor draftees who chose not to serve in the army.

The Confederacy also instituted a draft after the first wave of enlistments dried up. Conscription in the South, as in the North, met with considerable resentment and resistance. Believing that plantations were necessary to the war effort and that slaves would not work unless directly overseen by masters, in 1862 Confederate officials passed the **Twenty Negro Law,** which exempted from military service planters owning twenty or more slaves. Like the exemptions in the North, the southern policy fostered the feeling that the poor were going off to fight while the rich stayed safely at home. The law was modified in 1863, requiring exempted planters to pay $500, and in 1864, the number of slaves required to earn an exemption was lowered to fifteen. Nevertheless, resentment continued to smolder.

Confederate conscription laws also ran afoul of states'-rights advocates, who feared that too much power was centered in Richmond. Southerners developed several forms of passive resistance to the draft laws. Thousands of draftees simply never showed up, and local officials, jealously guarding their political autonomy, made little effort to enforce the draft.

Wartime Economy in the North and South

Although riots, disorder, and social disruption plagued northern cities, the economy and industry of the Union actually grew stronger as the war progressed. In his 1864 message to Congress, Abraham Lincoln stated that the war had not depleted northern resources. The region, he said, had more men and more supplies than when the war began, and its natural resources were inexhaustible.

Although the president exaggerated a bit, the statement contained some truth. Northern industry and population did grow during the Civil War. Operating in cooperation with government, manufacturing experienced a boom. Manufacturers of war supplies benefited from government contracts. Textiles and shoemaking boomed as new labor-saving devices improved efficiency and increased production. Congress stimulated economic growth by means of railroad subsidies and land grants to support a transcontinental railroad, higher tariffs to aid manufacturing, and land grants that states could use to finance higher education. Food shortages were never as bad in the North as they were in the South. In 1862 Congress passed the **Homestead Act** to make land available to more farmers. The law granted 160 acres of the public domain in the West to any citizen who had lived on, and improved, the land for five years.

Of course, the economic picture was not entirely positive. The Union found itself resorting to financial tricks to keep the economy afloat. Facing a cash-flow emergency in 1862, Congress passed the Legal Tender Act, authorizing Treasury secretary Samuel Chase to issue $431 million in paper money, known as **greenbacks** because of their color. But the greenbacks were backed not by specie but only by the government's commitment to redeem them. Financial support also came through selling bonds. In the fall of 1862, Philadelphia banker Jay Cooke started a bond drive. More than $2 billion worth of government bonds were sold, and most of them were paid for in greenbacks. These emergency measures helped the Union survive the financial pressures created by the war, but the combination of bond

hang in effigy To hang a crude likeness or dummy—an effigy—representing a hated or despised person.

Twenty Negro Law Confederate law that exempted planters owning twenty or more slaves from the draft on the grounds that overseeing farming done by slaves was necessary to the war effort.

Homestead Act Law passed by Congress in 1862 that promised ownership of 160 acres of public land to any citizen who had lived on and cultivated the land for five years.

greenbacks Paper money issued by the Union; it was not backed with gold.

issues and paper money not backed by gold or silver set up a highly unstable situation that came back to haunt the Republicans after the war.

The South, an agrarian society, began the war without an industrial base and in desperate need of outside help if it was to have any chance of winning. In addition to lacking transportation, raw materials, and machines, the South lacked managers and skilled industrial workers. The Confederate government intervened more directly in the economy than did its Union counterpart, offering generous loans to new or existing companies that would produce war materials and agree to sell at least two-thirds of their production to the government. Josiah Gorgas started government-owned production plants in Alabama, Georgia, and South Carolina. These innovative programs, however, could not compensate for inadequate industrialization.

The supply of money was also a severe problem in the South. Like the North, the South tried to ease cash-flow problems by printing paper money, eventually issuing more than $1 billion in unbacked currency. The outcome was runaway inflation. By the time the war ended, southerners were paying more than $400 for a barrel of flour and $10 a pound for bacon.

Southern industrial shortcomings severely handicapped the army. During Lee's Maryland campaign, many Confederate soldiers were barefoot because shoes were in such short supply. Ordnance was always in demand. Northern plants could produce more than five thousand muskets a day; Confederate production never exceeded three hundred. The most serious shortage, however, was food. Although the South was an agricultural region, most of its productive farmland was devoted to commercial agriculture. Corn and rice were the primary food products, but supplies were continually reduced by military campaigns and Union occupation of growing areas. Southern cattle, though abundant, were range stock, grown for hides and tallow rather than for food, and hog production suffered from the same disruptions as vegetable growing. Hunger became part of daily life for the Confederate armies. Before the war ended, many Union soldiers referred to their opponents as "scarecrows."

Civilians in the South suffered from the same shortages as the army. Because of prewar shipping patterns, the few rail lines that the Confederacy had ran north and south. Distribution of goods became almost impossible as invading Union forces cut rail lines and disrupted production. The flow of cattle, horses, and food from the West diminished when Union forces gained control of the Mississippi. Imported goods had to evade the Union naval blockade. Some blockade runners made it through, but their number decreased as the war continued. The fall of New Orleans, the South's major export-import center, was devastating to the southern economy. Cities faced major food shortages, newspapers were printed on wallpaper, clothes were made from curtains, and pins were made from dry thorns. Southern society, cut off from the outside world, consumed its existing resources and found no way to obtain more.

Women in Two Nations at War

Because the South had fewer men than the North to send to war, a larger proportion of southern families were left in the care of women. Some women worked farms, herded livestock, and supported their families. Others found themselves homeless, living in complete poverty, as the ravages of war destroyed the countryside. One woman wrote to the Confederacy's secretary of war, pleading that he "discharge" her husband so that "he might do his children some good" rather than leaving them "to suffer." Some tried to persuade their husbands to desert, to come home to family and safety. One woman shouted to her husband, who was being drafted for the second time, "Desert again, Jake." The vast majority, however, fully supported the war effort despite the hardships at home and at the front.

Women became responsible for much of the South's agricultural and industrial production, overseeing the raising of crops, working in factories, managing estates, and running businesses. As one southern soldier wrote, women bore "the greatest burden of this horrid war." Indeed, the burden of a woman was great—working the fields, running the household, and waiting for news from loved ones at the front or for the news that she was now a widow or childless.

Women in the North served in much the same capacity as their southern counterparts. They maintained families and homes alone, working to provide income and raise children. Although they did not face the shortages and ravages of battle that made life so hard for southern women, they did work in factories, run family businesses, teach school, and supply soldiers. Many served in managerial capacities or as writers and civil servants.

Even before the war ended, northern women were going south to educate former slaves and help them find a place in American society. Women assumed new roles that helped prepare them to become more involved in social and political life after the war.

Women from both South and North actively participated in the war itself. Many women on both sides served as scouts, **couriers,** and spies, and more than four hundred disguised themselves as men and served as active soldiers until they were discovered. General William S. Rosecrans expressed dismay when one of his sergeants was delivered of "a bouncing baby boy," which was, the general complained, "in violation of all military regulations." Army camps frequently included officers' wives, female camp employees, camp followers, and women who came to help in whatever way they could. One black woman served the 33rd U.S. Colored Troops for four years and three months without pay. She taught the men to read and write and bound up their wounds.

Free Blacks, Slaves, and War

The changes the Civil War brought for African Americans, both free and slave, were radical and not always for the better. At first, many free blacks attempted to enlist in the Union army but were turned away. In 1861, General Benjamin F. Butler began using runaway slaves, called contrabands, as laborers. Several other northern commanders quickly adopted the practice. As the number of contrabands increased, however, the Union grappled with problems of housing and feeding them.

In the summer of 1862 Congress authorized the acceptance of "persons of African descent" into the armed forces, but enlistment remained low. After the Emancipation Proclamation, Union officials actively recruited former slaves, raising troops from among the freedmen and forming them into regiments known as the U.S. Colored Troops. Some northern state governments sought free blacks to fill state draft quotas. Agents offered generous bonuses to those who signed up. By the end of the war, about 180,000 African Americans had enlisted in northern armies.

Army officials discriminated against African-American soldiers in a variety of ways. Units were segregated, and until 1865, blacks were paid less than whites. All black regiments had white commanders, for the government refused to allow blacks to lead blacks. Only one hundred were commissioned as officers, and no black soldier ever received a commission higher than major.

At first, African-American regiments were used as laborers or kept in the rear rather than being allowed to fight. But several black regiments, when finally allowed into battle, performed so well that they won grudging respect. These men fought in 449 battles in every theater of the war and had a casualty rate 35 percent higher than white soldiers. Still, acceptance by white troops was slow, and discrimination was the rule, not the exception.

As the war progressed, the number of African Americans in the Union army increased dramatically. By 1865, almost two-thirds of Union troops in the Mississippi Valley were black. Some southerners violently resented the Union's use of these troops, and black soldiers suffered atrocities because some Confederate leaders refused to take black prisoners. At Fort Pillow, Tennessee, for example, Confederate soldiers massacred more than a hundred black soldiers who were trying to surrender.

About sixty-eight thousand black Union soldiers were killed or wounded in battle, and twenty-one were awarded the Congressional Medal of Honor. Probably no unit acquitted itself better in the field than the **54th Massachusetts.** On July 18, 1863, it led a frontal assault on Confederate defenses at Charleston harbor. Despite sustaining heavy casualties, the black troops gained the parapet and held it for nearly an hour before being forced to retreat. Their conduct in battle had a large impact on changing attitudes toward black soldiers and emancipation. Lincoln, in his defense of emancipation, said, "there will be some black men who can remember that, with silent tongue, and clenched teeth, and steady eye, and well-poised bayonets, they have helped mankind on to this great consummation; while, I fear, there will be some white ones, unable to forget, that with malignant heart, and deceitful speech, they strove to hinder it."

The war effort in the South relied heavily on the slave population, mostly as producers of food and as military laborers. Slaves constituted more than

courier A messenger carrying official information, sometimes secretly.

54th Massachusetts Regiment of black troops from Massachusetts commanded by Robert Gould Shaw; it led an assault on Fort Wagner at Charleston harbor.

♦ The 54th Massachusetts Regiment was an all black volunteer unit raised, in part, by Frederick Douglass. This Currier & Ives print shows the daring charge that took the parapet of Fort Wagner, South Carolina. Such bravery won grudging respect for African-American soldiers during the war. *Collection of William Gladstone.*

half of the work force in armament plants and military hospitals. Dependent as they were on slave labor, southerners treated their slaves worse after Lincoln issued the Emancipation Proclamation, fearing that slave revolts were a very real possibility.

Life and Death at the Front

Many volunteers on both sides in the Civil War had romantic notions about military service. Most were disappointed. Life as a common soldier was anything but glorious (see Individual Choices: Private Lyons Wakeman). Letters and diaries written by soldiers most frequently tell of long periods of boredom in overcrowded camps punctuated by furious spells of dangerous action, with long marches carrying 50- to 60-pound packs in between.

Though life in camp was tedious, it could be nearly as dangerous as time spent on the battlefield. Problems with supplying safe drinking water and disposing of waste constantly plagued military leaders faced with providing basic services for large numbers of people, often on short notice. Diseases like dysentery and typhoid fever frequently swept through unsanitary camps. And in the overcrowded conditions that often prevailed, smallpox, pneumonia, and malarial fevers passed rapidly from person to person. At times, as many as a quarter of the uninjured people in camps were disabled by one or another of these diseases.

Lacking in resources, organization, and expertise, the South did little to upgrade camp conditions. In the North, however, women drew on the organizational skills they had gained as antebellum reformers and created voluntary organizations to address the problem. Mental health advocate and reformer Dorothea Dix (see page 342) was one of these crusaders. In June 1861, President Lincoln responded to their concerns by creating the **United States Sanitary Commission,** a government agency responsible for advising the military on public health issues and investigating sanitary problems. "The Sanitary," as it was called, put hundreds of nurses into the field,

United States Sanitary Commission Government commission established by Abraham Lincoln to improve public health conditions in military camps and hospitals.

♦ In this photograph, taken outside an army hospital in Fredericksburg, Virginia, one of the many women who served as nurses during the Civil War sits with some of her wounded charges. Despite the efforts of women like her, medical facilities and treatment for the wounded were woefully inadequate—most of those who were not killed outright by the primitive surgical practices of the day either died from their wounds or from secondary infections. *Library of Congress.*

providing much-needed relief for overburdened military doctors. Even with this official organization in place, many women continued to labor as volunteer nurses in the camps and in hospitals behind the lines.

Nurses on both sides—most were women—showed bravery and devotion. Often working under fire at the front and with almost no medical supplies, these volunteers nursed sick and wounded soldiers, watched as they died not only from their wounds but also from infection and disease, and offered as much comfort and help as they could. **Clara Barton,** a famous northern nurse known as the "Angel of the Battlefield," called the soldiers her "boys" and in later years recalled "Speaking to and feeding with my own hands each soldier" as she attempted to nurse them back to health. Unlike Barton, most nurses labored in relative obscurity. Hospitals were unsanitary, overflowing, and underfunded. One northern nurse noted that "the cost actually dealt out" for food at the hospital where she labored was a mere "eight cents per day" per man.

The problem of dealing with the wounded was unprecedented. To a large extent, this was because of technological innovations that had taken place during the antebellum period. New rifled muskets had many times the range of the old smooth-bore weapons used during earlier wars—the effective range of the Springfield rifle used by many Union soldiers was 400 yards, and a stray bullet could still kill a man at 1,000 yards. Waterproof cartridges, perfected by gunsmith Samuel Colt, made these weapons much less prone to misfire and much easier to reload. And at closer range, the revolver, also perfected by Colt, could fire six shots without any reloading. Rifled artillery also added to the casualty count, as did exploding artillery shells, which sent deadly shrapnel ripping through lines of men.

Many surgeons at the front lines could do little more than amputate limbs to save lives. Hospitals, understaffed and lacking supplies and medicines, frequently became breeding grounds for disease. The war exacted a tremendous emotional toll on everyone, even on those who escaped physical injury. As one veteran put it, soldiers had seen "so many new forms of death" and "so many frightful and novel kinds of mutilation."

Conditions were even worse in prison camps. Throughout much of the war, an agreement provided for prisoner exchanges, but that did not prevent overcrowding and unsanitary conditions. And as the war dragged on, the exchange system stopped working effectively. In part this was because of the enormity of the task: moving and accounting for the large numbers of prisoners presented a serious organizational problem. Another contributing factor, though, was the refusal by Confederate officials to exchange African-American prisoners of war—those who were not slaughtered like the men at Fort Pillow were enslaved. Also, late in the war, Union commanders suspended all prisoner exchanges in hopes of depriving the South of much-needed replacement soldiers.

Clara Barton Organizer of a volunteer service to aid sick and wounded Civil War soldiers; she later founded the American branch of the Red Cross.

INDIVIDUAL CHOICES

Choosing to Volunteer

Private Lyons Wakeman

Different individuals had different motives for volunteering to serve in the Union Army during the Civil War. Like many, Lyons Wakeman's choice was partially economic—a signing bonus and regular army pay were attractive. But the desire for adventure was also an attractive feature. Wakeman overcame serious constraints to win adventure and economic independence, only to die before the war's end. Collection of Jackson K. Doane/Photo by Robert Burke.

Although protest against the Civil War was not uncommon and draft riots broke out in many areas, a large number of people chose to serve. Patriotism was the chief motivation of some. Hatred of slavery pushed others into Union uniforms. Not a few had economic motives. Times were hard in many areas of the North in the years leading into the war, and a signing bonus and promise of free meals had strong appeal. And some just hankered for adventure. For Lyons Wakeman, the choice to volunteer was influenced mostly by economic need and a daring, venturesome spirit.

Born in 1843 near Binghamton, New York, Wakeman was one of nine children in a farm family struggling for survival after the devastating Panic of 1837. Little is known about Wakeman's childhood except that educational opportunities were limited and Wakeman learned to read and write only passably well. Economic opportunities were scarce in Binghamton, so in 1862 Wakeman deserted farm and family. Writing back to report of being "tired of staying in that neighborhood," Wakeman took work as a canal boatman, expecting a life of adventure and perhaps a decent living.

Shortly after moving away from home, Wakeman caught "enlistment fever." Accepting a cash bounty, Wakeman signed up for a three-year hitch in the army and wrote back home that there was a possibility of getting an addi-

The most notorious of the Civil War prison camps was **Andersonville** in northern Georgia, where thousands of Union captives languished in an open stockade with only a small creek for water and virtually no sanitary facilities. Without enough food to feed its own armies and civilian population, the Confederacy could allocate little food for its overcrowded prison camps. Designed to house 10,000 men, Andersonville held more than 33,000 prisoners during the summer of 1864. As many as 100 men died of disease and malnutrition within its walls each day, and estimates put the death toll at that one

Andersonville Confederate prisoner-of-war camp in northern Georgia where some fourteen thousand Union prisoners died of disease and malnutrition.

tional $800 for extending that enlistment if the war lasted and the newly inducted private survived. Death wasn't a major concern. "I don't fear the rebel bullets, nor I don't fear the cannon," Wakeman asserted in a letter home. "If it is God's will for me to be killed here, it is my will to die."

As the war dragged on, however, Wakeman began to wonder about the decision to join up. In a letter from the front, Wakeman reported, "It would make your hair stand out to be where I have been. How would you like to be in the front rank and have the rear rank load and fire their guns over your shoulder? I have been there myself." Wakeman also got homesick, writing to ask for care packages—"a box of applies and a bottle of cider" on one occasion and "a pair of knit gloves" on another. Wakeman also asked for stamps, so the flow of letters might continue.

Being away made the old farm in Binghamton seem less like a prison and more like a haven. Wakeman's letters nagged constantly for news of mundane things such as how much grain was harvested, how many hogs were slaughtered, and every detail about the new barn that was raised. Wakeman even began talking about buying a farm, though the private acknowledged, "I think I shall have to stay my three years in the Army."

Wakeman never got the chance to return to the farm in Binghamton. The New York Volunteers were assigned to the Red River expedition, an amphibious campaign to take Shreveport, Louisiana, in 1864. Wakeman was one of some twenty-seven thousand Union soldiers who marched 200 miles in just ten days. At Pleasant Hill, 60 miles south of Shreveport, Wakeman's company fought a two-day engagement against Confederate forces. Writing from the front, Wakeman described the action: "There was heavy cannonading all day and a sharp firing of infantry . . . the next day I had to face the enemy bullets with my regiment. I was under fire about four hours and lay on the field of battle all night. There were three wounded in my company and one killed." Though not among the wounded, Wakeman did not survive the campaign. The private arrived back in New Orleans with violent diarrhea and after nearly a month of hospitalization died, one of some two hundred thousand Union soldiers who fell to disease rather than bullets.

Like so many others who chose to volunteer—whether for patriotic, idealistic, or economic reasons—Wakeman was buried in a simple grave far from home. A small stone in the Chalmette National Cemetery in New Orleans says simply, "Lyons Wakeman—N.Y." Among the many things that might have been carved there was the one thing that made Wakeman different from all the men who volunteered and makes Wakeman's choice so worthy of note: Lyons Wakeman—born Rosetta Wakeman—was a woman.

prison at nearly 14,000 over the course of the war. In the North, a camp at Elmira, New York, had a similar record for atrocity. Major General Carl Schurz, who fought for the Union at Chancellorsville, Gettysburg, and Chattanooga, summed up the agonies that faced the Civil War soldier: "There are people who speak lightly of war as a mere heroic sport. They would hardly find it in their hearts to do so, had they ever witnessed scenes like these, and thought of the untold miseries connected with them that were spread all over the land."

Even death itself came to be redefined as 8 percent of the white male population in the United States between the ages of 13 and 43 died in such a short time and in such horrible ways. People at the front reported being numbed by the horror. "I pass over the putrifying bodies of the dead . . . and feel as . . . unconcerned as though they were two hundred pigs," one army surgeon reported. Nor was distance any insulation from the horrors of death. The new art of photography brought graphic images of the carnage directly into the nation's parlors. "Death does not seem half so terrible as it did long ago," one Texas woman reported. "We have grown used to it."

Waging Total War

- What expectations contributed to the Union choice to wage total war after 1863?
- Did the outcome justify the choice? Why or why not?

As northerners anticipated the presidential election of 1864, Lincoln faced severe challenges on several fronts. The losses to Lee and Jackson in Virginia and the failure to catch Lee at Antietam had eroded public support. Many northerners resented the war, conscription, and abolitionism. Others feared Lincoln's powerful central government.

Northern Democrats advocated a peace platform and turned to George B. McClellan, Lincoln's ousted general, as a potential presidential candidate. Lincoln also faced a challenge from within his own party. Radical Republicans, who felt he was too soft on the South and unfit to run the war, began planning a campaign to win power. They championed the candidacy of John C. Frémont (see page 411), who had become an ardent advocate of the complete abolition of slavery.

Lincoln's Generals and Southern Successes

The surest way for Lincoln to stop his opponents was through military success. Lincoln had replaced McClellan with Burnside, but the results had been disastrous. Lincoln tried again, demoting Burnside and elevating General Joseph Hooker. Despite Hooker's reputation for bravery in battle—his nickname was "Fighting Joe"—Lee soundly defeated his forces at **Chancellorsville** in May 1863 (see Map 15.3 and Table 15.4). After Hooker had maneuvered Lee into a corner, Stonewall Jackson unleashed a vicious attack, and Fighting Joe simply "lost his nerve," according to one of his subordinates. Hooker resigned, and Lincoln replaced him with General George E. Meade.

Chancellorsville was a devastating loss for the North, but it was perhaps more devastating for the Confederates. They lost Stonewall Jackson. After he led the charge that unnerved Hooker, Jackson's own men mistakenly shot him as he rode back toward his camp in the darkness. Doctors amputated Jackson's arm in an attempt to save his life. "He has lost his left arm," said Lee, "but I have lost my right." Eight days later, Jackson died of pneumonia.

In the West too, Union forces seemed mired during the first half of 1863. General Rosecrans was bogged down in a costly and unsuccessful campaign to take the vital rail center at Chattanooga,

♦ This engraving captures the last meeting between two Confederate military giants, Robert E. Lee (left) and Thomas J. "Stonewall" Jackson, as they conversed before the Battle of Chancellorsville. Jackson's force defeated a Union army under General Joseph "Fighting Joe" Hooker, but Confederate troops mistook his returning soldiers for Union cavalry and fired on them, wounding Jackson. Doctors amputated his arm in an effort to save his life, but he soon died. *"Lee's Last Meeting with Jackson" (Chancellorsville) by E.B.D. Julio. Museum of the Confederacy.*

Chancellorsville Site in Virginia where in May 1863 Confederate troops led by Lee defeated a much larger Union force.

TABLE 15.4 Battle of Chancellorsville, May 1–4, 1863

	Union Army	Confederate Army
Commanders	Joseph Hooker	Robert E. Lee
Troop strength	75,000	50,000
Losses		
Killed	1,606	1,665
Wounded	9,762	9,081
Captured, missing	5,919	2,018
Total losses	17,287	12,764

Source: Data from *Battles and Leaders of the Civil War* (1884–1888; reprinted ed., 1956).

Tennessee. Grant had settled in for a long siege at Vicksburg (see Map 15.2). Nowhere did there seem to be a prospect for the dramatic victory Lincoln needed.

Democrats advocated peace while Radicals pushed for a tougher stance against southerners and immediate military results. More and more northerners, distressed and frustrated with the war, were saying openly that Lincoln was not the man to lead the nation.

The summer of 1863, however, turned out to be a major turning point in the war. Facing superior northern resources and rising inflation, Confederate leaders met in Richmond to consider their options. Davis and his cabinet considered sending troops into Tennessee or to relieve Vicksburg, but Lee advocated another major invasion of the North. Such a maneuver, he believed, would allow the Confederates to gather supplies and could encourage the northern peace movement, revitalize the prospects of foreign recognition, and perhaps capture the Union capital. Confederate leaders agreed and approved Lee's plan.

Lee began his advance north on the day that Meade took charge of northern defenses (see Map 15.3). Confederates met only weak opposition as they crossed the Potomac River and marched into Union territory. In Maryland and Pennsylvania they seized livestock, supplies, food, clothing, and shoes. Then, on June 30, a Confederate brigade searching for shoes encountered a Union cavalry unit west of **Gettysburg,** Pennsylvania. Meade, who had been trailing Lee's army as it marched north from Chancellorsville, moved his forces into Gettysburg. On the following day, the two armies began a furious three-day battle.

After an early setback, Meade took up an almost impregnable defensive position on the hills along Cemetery Ridge. The Confederates hammered both ends of the Union line but could gain no ground. On the third day, Lee ordered a major assault on the middle of the Union position. Eleven brigades, more than thirteen thousand men, led by fresh troops under Major General George E. Pickett, tried to cross open ground and take the steep hills held by Meade while Major J. E. B. ("Jeb") Stuart's cavalry attacked from the east. Lee made few strategic mistakes during the war, but Pickett's charge was foolhardy. Meade's forces drove off the attack. The whole field was "dotted with our soldiers," wrote one Confederate officer. Lee met his retreating troops with the words "It's all my fault, my fault." Losses on both sides were high (see Table 15.5), but Confederate casualties exceeded twenty-eight thousand men, more than half of Lee's army. Lee retreated, his invasion of the North a failure.

On the heels of this major victory for the North came news from Mississippi that Vicksburg had fallen to Grant's siege on July 3. Sherman had been beating back Confederate forces in central Mississippi, and Union guns had been shelling the city continuously for nearly seven weeks, driving residents

Gettysburg Site in Pennsylvania where in July 1863 Union forces under General George Meade defeated Lee's Confederate forces, turning back Lee's invasion of the North.

TABLE 15.5 Battle of Gettysburg, July 1–3, 1863

	Union Army	Confederate Army
Commanders	George E. Meade	Robert E. Lee
Troop strength	75,000	50,000
Losses		
Killed	3,155	3,903
Wounded	14,529	18,735
Captured, missing	5,365	5,425
Total losses	23,049	28,063

Source: Data from *Battles and Leaders of the Civil War* (1884–1888; reprinted ed., 1956).

into caves and shelters. But it was starvation and disease that finally subdued the defenders. Then on July 9, **Port Hudson,** the last Confederate garrison on the Mississippi River—whose defenders had been existing on a diet of mules and rats—surrendered after receiving news of Vicksburg's fate. The Mississippi River was totally under Union control. The "Father of Waters," said Lincoln, "again goes unvexed to the sea."

The losses at Gettysburg and Vicksburg devastated the Confederates. Cut off from almost any hope of foreign intervention and low on food, munitions, uniforms, shoes, and weapons, they embarked on a new phase of the war. No longer able to pursue victory, they attempted to forestall the impending defeat.

For the moment, however, despite jubilation over the recent victories, Lincoln and the North remained frustrated. Northern newspapers proclaiming Gettysburg to be the last gasp of the South had anticipated an immediate southern surrender, but Meade, like McClellan, acted with extreme caution and failed to pursue Lee and his retreating troops. Back in Washington, Lincoln waited for word of Lee's capture, believing it would signal the end of the rebellion. When he learned of Lee's escape, the president said in disbelief, "Our Army held the war in the hollow of their hand and they would not close it."

Disappointment in Tennessee also soon marred the celebration over Gettysburg and Vicksburg. Rosecrans had taken Chattanooga. But on September 18, Bragg's forces attacked Rosecrans at Chickamauga Creek. The Union forces scurried in retreat to take refuge back in Chattanooga. Bragg followed and laid siege from the heights of Missionary Ridge and Lookout Mountain, overlooking the city.

With Lee and his army intact and Rosecrans pinned down in Tennessee, the war, which had appeared to be so nearly over, was, in Lincoln's words, "prolonged indefinitely." Lincoln needed a general with killer instincts.

Grant, Sherman, and the Invention of Total War

Among the available choices, Grant had shown the kind of persistence and boldness Lincoln thought necessary. Lincoln placed him in charge of all Union forces in the West on October 13. Grant immediately replaced Rosecrans with a more intrepid and decisive general, George H. Thomas. Sherman's troops joined Thomas under Grant's command on November 14. This united force rid the mountains above Chattanooga of Confederate strongholds and drove Bragg's forces out of south Tennessee. Confederate forces also withdrew from Knoxville in December, leaving the state under Union control. Delighted with Grant's successes, Lincoln promoted him again on March 10, 1864, this time to general in chief. Grant

Port Hudson Confederate garrison that surrendered to Union forces in July 1863, thus giving the Union unrestricted control of the Mississippi River.

♦ Disliked by most of his fellow officers because of his course behavior and binge drinking, Ulysses S. Grant had the right combination of daring, unconventionality, and ruthlessness to wear down Robert E. Lee's forces in Virginia and finally defeat the Confederate Army. *National Archives.*

immediately left his command in the West to prepare an all-out attack on Lee and Virginia. He authorized Sherman to pursue a campaign into Georgia.

In Grant and Sherman Lincoln had found what he needed. On the surface, neither seemed a likely candidate for a major role in the Union army. Both were West Point graduates but left the army after the Mexican War to seek their fortunes. Neither had succeeded in civilian life: Grant was a binge drinker who accomplished little, and Sherman had failed as a banker and a lawyer. Both were "political generals," owing their Civil War commissions to the influence of friends or relatives. Despite their checkered pasts, these two men invented a new type of warfare that eventually brought the South to its knees. Grant and Sherman were willing to wage **total war**—warfare conducted not only against the government and armed forces of the Confederacy but also against the civilian population. Their goal was to destroy the South's will to continue the struggle.

Preparing for the new sort of war he was about to begin waging, Grant suspended prisoner-of-war exchanges. Realizing that the Confederates needed soldiers badly, he understood that one outcome of this policy would be slow death by starvation for Union prisoners. Cruel though his policy was, Grant reasoned that victory was his primary goal and that suffering and death were unavoidable in war. Throughout the remainder of the war, this single-mindedness pushed Grant to make decisions that cost tens of thousands of lives on both sides but led to Union victory.

On May 4, Grant and Meade moved into Virginia, toward Richmond and Robert E. Lee. The next day, Union and Confederate armies collided in a tangle of woods called **The Wilderness** near Chancellorsville (see Map 15.4). Two days of bloody fighting followed, broken by a night during which hundreds of the wounded burned to death in brushfires that raged between the two lines. Grant decided to skirt Lee's troops and head for Richmond, but Lee anticipated the maneuver and blocked Grant's route at Spotsylvania. Twelve days of fighting ensued. Grant again attempted to move around Lee, and again Lee anticipated him. On June 1, the two armies met at **Cold Harbor,** Virginia. Grant ordered a series of frontal attacks against the entrenched Confederates. Lee's veteran troops waited patiently in perhaps the best position they had ever defended, while Union soldiers expecting to die marched toward them. The assault failed amid unspeakable slaughter.

One southerner described Grant's assaults as "inexplicable and incredible butchery." The wounded were left to die between the lines while the living fell back exhausted into their trenches. Many of the young federal attackers at Cold Harbor had pinned

total war War waged with little regard for the welfare of troops on either side or for enemy civilians; the objective is to destroy both the human and the economic resources of the enemy.

The Wilderness Densely wooded region of Virginia that was the site in May 1864 of a devastating but inconclusive battle between Union forces under Grant and Confederates under Lee.

Cold Harbor Area of Virginia, about 10 miles from Richmond, where Grant made an unsuccessful attempt to drive his forces through Lee's center.

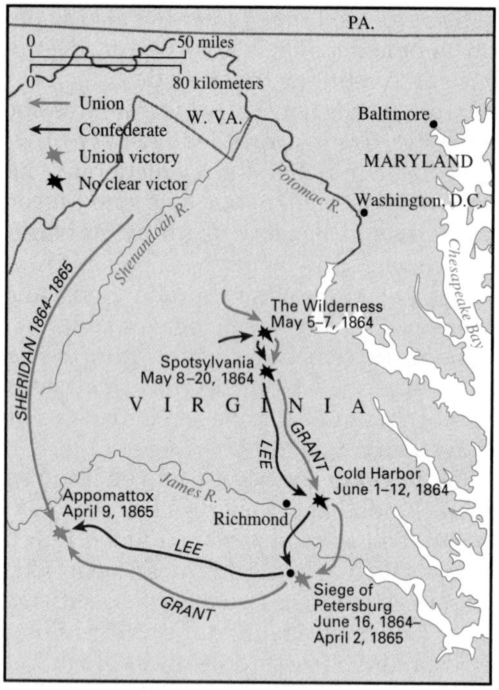

♦ **MAP 15.4 Grant's Campaign Against Lee** This map shows the series of battles in which Grant's army suffered staggering casualties. Union forces finally drove Lee into retreat, forcing him into a defensive position in Petersburg. Lee finally made a daring attempt to escape in April 1865 but was headed off by General Philip Sheridan's Union forces.

their names on their shirts in the hope that their shattered bodies might be identified after the battle. Casualties on both sides at Spotsylvania and Cold Harbor were staggering, but Union losses were unimaginably horrible. As one Confederate officer put it, "We have met a man, this time, who either does not know when he is whipped, or who cares not if he loses his whole army." During the three campaigns, Grant lost a total of sixty thousand troops, more than Lee's entire army. On June 3, in a single day of frontal assaults at Cold Harbor, twelve thousand Union soldiers fell in piles before the Confederate lines. Said Lee, "this is not war, this is murder." But Grant's seeming wantonness was calculated, for the Confederates lost more than twenty-five thousand troops. And Grant knew, as did Lee, that the Union could afford the losses but the Confederacy could not.

After Cold Harbor, Grant guessed that Lee would expect him to try to assault nearby Richmond next. Instead, he again attempted to sidle southward around the Confederate army. This time he headed south of Richmond for Petersburg to try to take the vital rail center and cut off the southern capital.

However, Lee rapidly shifted the **vanguard** of his troops, beat back Grant's advance, and occupied Petersburg. Grant bitterly regretted this failure, feeling that he could have ended the war. Instead, the campaign settled into a ten-month siege that neither side wanted. Lee and the Confederates could ill afford a siege that ate up supplies and munitions. And elections were rapidly approaching in the Union.

The Election of 1864 and Sherman's March to the Sea

Lincoln was under fire from two directions. On May 31, 1864, Radical Republicans met in Cleveland and officially nominated John C. Frémont as their presidential candidate. Lincoln's wing of the party, which began calling itself the Union party, held its nominating convention in June and renominated Lincoln. To attract Democrats who still favored fighting for a clear victory, Union party delegates dumped Vice President Hannibal Hamlin and chose **Andrew Johnson,** a southern Democrat, as Lincoln's running mate.

In August, the Democratic National Convention met at Chicago. The Democrats allied many Copperheads with other northerners who were so upset by the heavy casualties that they felt the war needed to be stopped even at the cost of allowing slavery to continue. The Democrats selected McClellan as their presidential candidate and included a peace plank in their platform. Thus Lincoln sat squarely in the middle between one group that castigated him for pursuing the war and another group that rebuked him for failing to punish the South vigorously enough.

Confederate president Jefferson Davis did not face an election in 1864, but he too had plenty of political problems. As deprivation and military losses mounted, some factions began to resist the war effort. The Confederate congress called for a new draft from the states, but several refused to comply. Gov-

vanguard The foremost position in any army advancing into battle.

Andrew Johnson Tennessee senator who became Lincoln's running mate in 1864 and who succeeded to the presidency after Lincoln was killed.

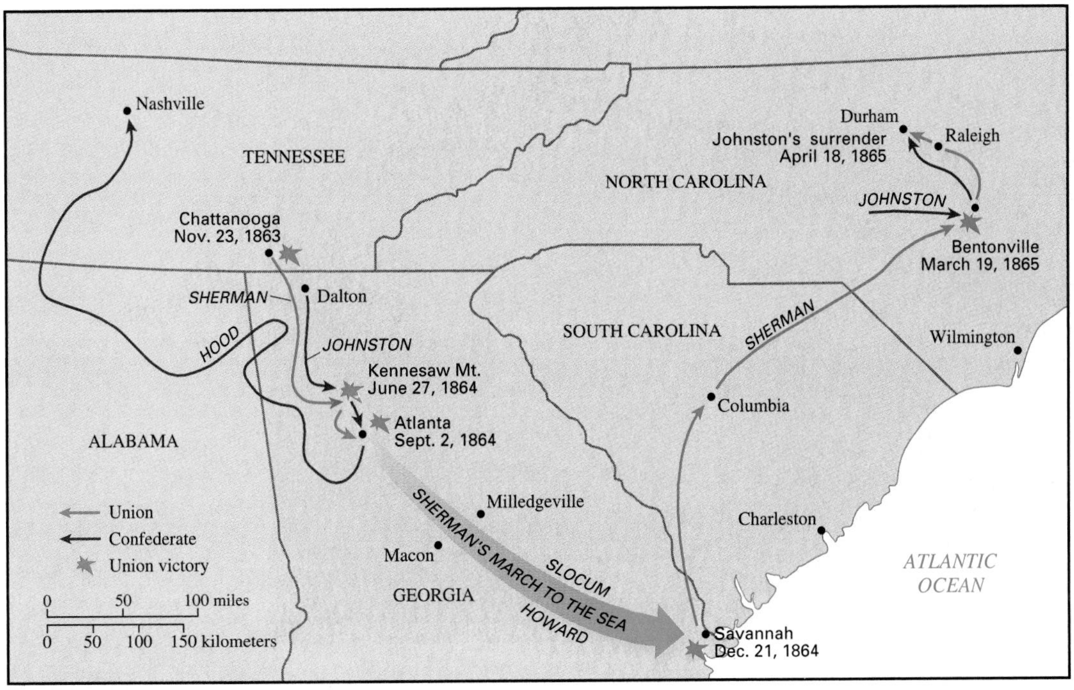

♦ **MAP 15.5 Sherman's Campaign in the South** This map shows how William Tecumseh Sherman's troops slashed through the South, destroying both civilian and military targets and reducing the South's will to continue the war.

ernors in Georgia, North Carolina, and South Carolina, who controlled their state's militia, kept troops at home and defied Davis to enforce conscription. Like Lincoln, Davis was under growing pressure to end the war.

Eager to solve their problems, Lincoln and Davis had conversations about negotiating a settlement. Lincoln stated his terms: reunion, abolition, and amnesty for Confederates. Davis replied that "amnesty" applied to criminals and said that the South had "committed no crime." He contended that "independence" or "extermination" was the only possible outcome of the war for the South, even if it meant enduring the sight of "every Southern plantation sacked and every Southern city in flames." The words proved prophetic.

Grant had instructed Sherman "to get into the interior of the enemy's country as far as you can, inflicting all the damage you can against their war resources." Sherman responded with a vengeance. Slowly and skillfully his army advanced southward from Tennessee toward Atlanta, one of the South's few remaining industrial centers, against Confederate armies under the command of General Joseph E. Johnston (see Map 15.5). Only Johnston's skillful retreats kept Sherman from annihilating his army. President Davis then replaced Johnston with John Bell Hood, who vowed to take the offensive. Hood attacked, but Sherman inflicted such serious casualties that Hood had to retreat to Atlanta.

For days Sherman shelled Atlanta and wrought havoc in the surrounding countryside. When a last-ditch southern attack failed, Hood evacuated the city on September 1. The victorious Union troops moved in and occupied Atlanta on the following day. Sherman's victory caused tremendous despair among Confederates and gave great momentum to Lincoln's re-election campaign.

Also boosting Lincoln's re-election efforts was General Philip Sheridan's campaign in the Shenandoah Valley, an important source of food for Lee's army. Adopting the same sort of devastating tactics that Sherman used so successfully, Sheridan's men lived off the land and destroyed both military and civilian supplies whenever possible. Accepting high casualties, Sheridan drove Confederate forces from the region in October, laying waste to much of Lee's food supply in the process.

♦ Determined to "make Georgia howl," William Tecumseh Sherman and his band of "bummers" slashed their way through the South during the winter of 1864, destroying military and civilian property along the way. This painting shows Sherman astride a white horse looking on while his men rip up a rail line and burn bridges and homes. *Collection of David H. Sherman.*

These victories proved the decisive factor in the election of 1864. Sherman's and Sheridan's successes defused McClellan's argument that Lincoln was not competent to direct the Union's military fortunes and quelled much antiwar sentiment in the North. Equally undermined, the Radical Republican platform and the Frémont candidacy disappeared before election day. As late as August, Lincoln had been expecting to lose the election in November, but the victory in Atlanta gave him some hope. When the votes were counted, Lincoln learned that he defeated McClellan by half a million popular votes but had won in the Electoral College by a margin of 212 to 21.

The southern peace movement had viewed a Democratic victory as the last chance to reach a settlement. Without it, all hope of negotiation appeared lost. Amid the bleak prospects, animosity toward Jefferson Davis increased in the South. But Lee's forces still remained in Petersburg, as did Hood's in Georgia. Southern hopes were dimmed but not extinguished.

Sherman soon grew bored with the occupation of Atlanta and posed a bold plan to Grant. He wanted to ignore Hood, leave the battered Confederates loose at his rear, go on the offensive, and "cut a swath through to the sea." "I can make Georgia howl," he promised. Despite some misgivings, Grant agreed and convinced Lincoln.

A week after the election, Sherman began preparing for his 300-mile **March to the Sea** (see Map 15.5) His intentions were clear. "We are not only fighting hostile armies, but a hostile people," he stated. By devastating the countryside and destroying the South's ability to conduct war, he intended to break down southerners' will to resist. "We cannot change the hearts of those people of the South," he concluded, but we can "make them so sick of war that generations would pass away before they would again appeal to it." With that, he burned most of Atlanta and then set out on his march to Savannah, on the coast. His troops plundered and looted farms

March to the Sea Sherman's march through Georgia from Atlanta to Savannah from November 16 to December 20, 1864, during which Union soldiers carried out orders to destroy everything in their path.

and towns on the way, foraging for food and supplies and destroying everything in their path.

While Sherman headed toward Savannah, Confederate general Hood turned north and attacked General George Thomas's Union forces at Franklin, Tennessee, on November 30. Hood lost convincingly in a bloody battle. The Confederate Army of Tennessee fragmented, and all opposition to Sherman's march dissolved. Sherman entered Savannah unopposed on December 20.

The March to the Sea completed, Sherman turned north. In South Carolina, the first state to secede and fire shots, Sherman's band of "bummers" took special delight in ravaging the countryside. When they reached Columbia, flames engulfed the city. Whether Sherman's men or retreating Confederates started the blaze was not clear, but African-American regiments in Sherman's command helped put out the fires after Sherman occupied the South Carolina capital on February 17, 1865.

With the capital in flames, Confederate forces abandoned their posts in South Carolina, moving north to join with Joseph E. Johnston's army in an effort to stop Sherman from crossing North Carolina and joining Grant in Virginia. Union forces quickly moved into abandoned southern strongholds, including Charleston, where Major Robert Anderson, who had commanded Fort Sumter in April 1861, returned to raise the Union flag over the fort that he had surrendered four years earlier.

The Fall of Lee and Lincoln

Sherman's marches were the centerpiece of a Union strategy that was a brutal variation of Winfield Scott's anaconda plan. In concert with Sherman's efforts, other Union armies attacked various southern strongholds. Admiral Farragut had already closed the port of Mobile, Alabama, and Union forces successfully closed the ports of Fort Fisher and Wilmington, North Carolina. The primary target, however, was Lee. Grant maintained the siege at Petersburg while Sherman moved north, laying waste to the Carolinas on his way to join Grant in defeating Lee and ending the war.

Lincoln had already taken steps to bring southerners back into the Union. In December 1863, he had issued a Proclamation of Amnesty and Reconstruction offering pardons to any Confederates who would take a loyalty oath. After his re-election, Lincoln began to plan for the Confederacy's eventual surrender, and he pushed for a constitutional ban on slavery, which passed on January 31, 1865.

Davis too had been flirting with the idea of ending slavery, though his motives were different from Lincoln's. On November 7, 1864, Davis advocated offering slaves emancipation in exchange for military service. Lee supported Davis's plan as the only method for averting defeat, but the proposal was voted down in the Confederate congress. By March 1865, however, desperation had set in. Lee had contacted Lincoln to request peace negotiations, but Lincoln demanded unconditional surrender before any negotiations could occur. Pressed against the wall, almost out of supplies and troops, the Confederate congress passed an act paving the way for slaves to become soldiers. The legislation did not state that freedom would accompany military service, but Davis told his war department that no one should be asked to fight as a slave—military conscription would bring freedom.

Hoping to head off immediate disaster and keep the Confederacy alive, Lee made a surprising move. Advising Davis to evacuate Richmond, Lee abandoned his stronghold in Petersburg and moved west as rapidly as possible, toward Lynchburg (see Map 15.4). From Lynchburg Lee hoped to use surviving rail lines to move his troops south to join with Johnston's force in North Carolina.

Suffering none of his predecessors' indecisiveness, Grant ordered an immediate assault as Lee's forces retreated from Petersburg. Lee had little ammunition, almost no food, and only thirty-five thousand men. As they retreated westward, under constant pressure from harassing attacks, hundreds of southern soldiers collapsed from hunger and exhaustion. By April 9, Union forces had surrounded Lee's broken army. Saying, "There is nothing left for me to do but go and see General Grant, and I would rather die a thousand deaths," Lee sent a note offering surrender.

The two generals met at a private home in the little village of Appomattox Courthouse, Virginia. Grant offered generous terms, allowing Confederate officers and men to go home "so long as they observe their paroles and the laws in force where they reside." This guaranteed them immunity from prosecution for treason and became the model for surrender. Grant sent the starving Confederates rations and allowed them to keep their horses.

On the following day, Lincoln addressed a crowd outside the White House about his hopes and plans for rebuilding the nation. He talked about the need

♦ The nation's mood shifted from celebration to shock when it learned that President Lincoln had fallen to an assassin's bullet. His funeral provided an occasion for the entire country to mourn, not only his death but also the deaths of the hundreds of thousands of Americans who had fallen in the Civil War. In Chicago, a huge arch was erected at the lakefront, the starting point from which Lincoln's coffin was paraded through the city led by a military honor guard and thirty-six schoolgirls dressed all in white, each representing one of the thirty-six now reunited states.

for flexibility in pulling the nation back together after the long and bitter conflict. Three days later, after an exhausting day in conference with his cabinet and with General Grant, Lincoln chose to relax by attending a play at Ford's Theater in Washington. At about ten o'clock, **John Wilkes Booth,** an actor and a southern sympathizer, entered the president's box and shot him behind the ear. Meanwhile, one of Booth's accomplices entered the home of Secretary of State Seward, who was bedridden as a result of a carriage accident, and stabbed him several times before being driven out by Seward's son and a male nurse. Another accomplice was supposed to assassinate Vice President Johnson but apparently lost his nerve. He was arrested while sitting drunk in the bar at the hotel where Johnson was staying. Although the conspiracy had failed, one of its main objectives succeeded: Lincoln died of his wound on the following morning.

Even though Lincoln was dead and Lee had fallen, the war continued. Joseph E. Johnston, whose forces succeeded in preventing Sherman from joining Grant, did not surrender until April 18. And although most of his forces had been defeated, Jefferson Davis remained in hiding and called for guerrilla warfare and continued resistance. But one by one, the Confederate officers surrendered to their Union opponents. On May 10, Davis and the Confederate postmaster general were captured near Irwinville, Georgia, and placed in prison. Andrew Johnson, who had assumed the presidency upon Lincoln's death, issued a statement to the American people that armed rebellion against legitimate authority could be considered "virtually at an end." The last Confederate general to lay down his arms was Cherokee leader Stand Watie, who surrendered on June 23, 1865.

The price of victory was high for both the winner and the loser. More than 350,000 Union soldiers were killed in action. No exact figures exist for the Confederacy, but southern casualties probably equaled or exceeded those of the Union. The war wrecked the economy of the South, for most of the fighting occurred there. Union military campaigns wiped out most southern rail lines, destroyed the South's manufacturing capacity, and severely reduced agricultural productivity in the South. Both sides had faced rising inflation during the war, but the Confederacy's actions to supply troops and keep the war effort going had bled the South of most of its resources and money. Secession had been defeated, but reunion remained a distant and difficult objective.

John Wilkes Booth Actor and southern sympathizer who on April 14, 1865, five days after Lee's surrender, fatally shot President Lincoln at Ford's Theater in Washington.

SUMMARY

Expectations
Constraints
Choices
Outcomes

Both the Union and the Confederacy entered the war in 1861 with glowing *expectations.* Jefferson Davis *chose* to pursue a defensive strategy, certain that northerners would soon tire of war and let the South withdraw from the Union. Abraham Lincoln *chose* to use the superior human, economic, and natural resources of the North to strangle the South into submission. But many *constraints* frustrated both leaders during the first year of the war.

For Lincoln, the greatest *constraint* seemed to be military leadership. Beginning with the first Battle of Bull Run, Union forces seemed unable to win any major battles despite their numerical superiority. Although Union forces under Ulysses S. Grant's command scored victories in the Mississippi Valley, the federals seemed stalemated. Robert E. Lee and Thomas ("Stonewall") Jackson seemed able to defeat any Union general that Lincoln sent to oppose them.

The war's nature and direction changed after the fall of 1862, however. Lee *chose* to invade Maryland and was defeated at Antietam, but despite this crushing loss, Union generals still failed to capture Lee or to subdue Confederate forces in Virginia. *Constrained* by military blundering, political attacks, and popular unrest, Lincoln *chose* to issue the Emancipation Proclamation, *expecting* that it would undermine southern efforts and unify northern ones. After the proclamation, there could be no *choice* for either side but total victory or total defeat.

After further reversals in the spring of 1863, Union forces turned the tide in the war by defeating Lee's army at Gettysburg, with enormous casualties on both sides, and taking Vicksburg after a long siege to gain full control of the Mississippi. With an election drawing near, Lincoln spurred his generals to deal the death blow to the Confederacy, and two in particular rose to the occasion. During the summer of 1864, William Tecumseh Sherman wreaked havoc, making Georgia "howl." And Grant, in a wanton display of disregard for human life, drove Lee into a defensive corner. In November, buoyed by Sherman's victories in Georgia, Lincoln was reelected.

In the spring of 1865, Lee made a desperate *choice* in a final effort to keep the Confederacy alive, racing to unify the last surviving remnants of the once-proud southern army. But Grant closed a net of steel around Lee's troops, forcing surrender. With the war over, Lincoln *chose* to promote a gentle policy for reunion. But his assassination ended his effort, leaving a southern Democrat—Andrew Johnson—as president and a nation reeling in shock. In North and South, in April 1865, the *outcome* of the Civil War was uncertainty about what would follow the four years of suffering and sacrifice.

SUGGESTED READINGS

Annie Heloise Abel. *The Slaveholding Indians,* 3 vols. (1919–1925; reprint, 1992–1993).

This long-ignored classic work focuses on Indians as slaveholders, participants in the Civil War, and subjects of Reconstruction. Its three volumes have recently been updated by historians Theda Purdue and Michael Green. Each volume can stand on its own and will reward the patient reader.

Bruce Catton. *This Hallowed Ground: The Story of the Union Side of the Civil War* (1956).

Catton is probably the best in the huge company of popular writers on the Civil War. This is his most comprehensive single-volume work. More detailed but still very interesting titles by Catton include *Glory Road: The Bloody Route from Fredericksburg to Gettysburg* (1952), *Mr. Lincoln's Army* (1962), *A Stillness at Appomattox* (1953), and *Grant Moves South* (1960).

Paul D. Escott. *After Secession: Jefferson Davis and the Failure of Confederate Nationalism* (1978).

An excellent overview of internal political problems in the Confederacy by a leading Civil War historian.

Alvin M. Josephy. *The Civil War in the American West* (1991).

A former editor for *American Heritage,* Josephy writes an interesting and readable story about this little-known chapter in Civil War history.

William Marvel. *The* Alabama *& the* Kearsarge: *The Sailor's Civil War* (1996).

Military and social historians have compared this new study favorably with *The Life of Billy Yank* (1952) and *The Life of Johnny Reb* (1943), Bell Irvin Willey's classic studies of life for the common soldier, calling it an insightful narrative of the Civil War experience for the common sailor.

James McPherson. *Battle Cry of Freedom: The Civil War Era* (1988).

Hailed by many as the best single-volume history of the Civil War era; comprehensive and very well written.

Emory M. Thomas. *The Confederate Nation* (1979).

A classic history of the Confederacy by an excellent southern historian.

Garry Wills. *Lincoln at Gettysburg: The Words That Remade America* (1992).

A prize-winning look at Lincoln's rhetoric and the ways in which his speeches, especially his Gettysburg Address, recast American ideas about equality, freedom, and democracy. Exquisitely written by a master biographer.

Gettysburg (the movie)

Ronald Maxwell directed this four-hour epic detailing one of the Civil War's most famous battles. Based on Michael Shaara's Pulitzer Prize–winning novel *The Killer Angels*, this ambitious film seeks to capture not only the historical events but also the atmosphere and personalities of the era.

The Choice for Emancipation

The Context

When Abraham Lincoln became president in 1861, he swore to the nation that he had no intention of interfering with the institution of slavery. But the pressure of war and of politics made that promise difficult to keep. By March 1862 the president was asking Congress to pass a bill committing federal funds to compensate slaveholders for the value of their human property in the event that the war brought the institution down. Over the next several months he discussed various approaches to the thorny problem with members of his cabinet, but publicly he resisted any suggestion of a unilateral presidential order emancipating slaves. Finally, on September 22, 1862, he made an official announcement that shook the nation. The southern states had one hundred days to put down their weapons or he would use his powers as commander in chief of the U. S. Army and Navy to free every slave in every region of the country that was, at the appointed time, still at war with the United States. This announcement was the Emancipation Proclamation. (For further information on the context, see page 443.)

The Historical Question

During the years following the Civil War, Republicans heralded the Emancipation Proclamation as the ultimate expression of their party's commitment to American principles and their party's culture hero, Abraham Lincoln's, commitment to liberty. But many questions surround Lincoln's choice to issue the proclamation. If this was a long-standing commitment, why did he wait so long? Why did he choose to free only some slaves and not all slaves? Was there another agenda beyond a commitment to freedom?

The Challenge

Using the sources provided, along with other information you have read, write an essay or hold a discussion on the following question. Cite evidence in the sources to support your conclusions. **What were Abraham Lincoln's purposes for issuing the Emancipation Proclamation when and in the form that he did?**

The Sources

1 In his first inaugural address, Abraham Lincoln swore that he would not threaten the institution of slavery where it existed. He even denied that he had the legal right to do so. Here is what he said:

I do but quote from one of those speeches when I declare that "I have no purpose, directly or indirectly, to interfere with the institution of slavery in the States where it exists. I believe I have no lawful right to do so, and I have no inclination to do so. . . ."

I now reiterate these sentiments; and, in doing so, I only press upon the public attention the most conclusive evidence of which the case is susceptible, that the property, peace and security of no section are to be in any wise endangered by the now incoming administration.

2 On August 19, 1862 the *New York Tribune* published an open letter to President Lincoln claiming that 20 million people in the

United States were "sorely disappointed and deeply pained by the policy you seem to be pursuing with regard to the slaves of rebels." Lincoln replied:

My paramount object in this struggle is *to save the Union, and is* not *either to save or destroy Slavery. If I could save the Union without freeing* any *slave, I would do it; and if I could save it by freeing* all *the slaves, I would do it; and if I could do it by freeing some and leaving others alone, I would also do that. What I do about Slavery and the colored race, I do because I believe it helps to save this Union; and what I forbear, I forbear because I* do not *believe it would help save the Union. I shall do* less *whenever I shall believe what I am doing hurts the cause, and I shall do* more *whenever I shall believe doing more will help the cause. I shall try to correct errors when shown to be errors; and I shall adopt new views so fast as they shall appear to be true views. I have here stated my purpose according to my view of* official *duty.*

3 Less than of a month later Lincoln received a delegation representing Christian interests in Chicago, who echoed the *Tribune's* earlier complaint. Lincoln explained:

What good would a proclamation of emancipation from me do, especially as we are now situated? I do not want to issue a document that the whole world will see must necessarily be inoperative. . . .Would my word free the slaves, when I cannot even enforce the Constitution in the rebel states? Is there a single court, or magistrate, or individual that would be influenced by it there? And what reason is there to think it would have any greater effect upon the slaves than the late law of Congress, which I approved, and which offers protection and freedom to the slaves of rebel masters who come within our lines? Yet I cannot learn that that law has caused a single slave to come over to us . . . .

I admit that slavery is the root of the rebellion, . . . I will also concede that emancipation would help us in Europe, and convince them that we are incited by something more than ambition. I grant, further, that it would help somewhat at the North, though not so much, I fear, as you and those you represent imagine. . . .

4 Four days after Lincoln told the Chicago delegation that an emancipation proclamation would be futile, the Union won a major victory at Antietam. Five days after that, Lincoln issued the preliminary draft of the Emancipation Proclamation, giving the southern states one hundred days to stop the war. When the South refused to surrender, Lincoln made the following statement:

Now, therefore, I, Abraham Lincoln, President of the United States, by virtue of the power in me vested as Commander-in-Chief of the Army and Navy of the United States, in time of actual armed rebellion against the authority and government of the United States, and as a fit and necessary war measure for suppressing said rebellion, so, on this first day of January, in the year of our Lord one thousand eight hundred and sixty-three, and in accordance with my purpose to do so, publicly proclaimed for the full period of one hundred days from the day first above mentioned, order and designate [the following] as the States and parts of States wherein the people thereof, respectively, are this day in rebellion against the United States. . . .

And by virtue of the power, and for the purpose aforesaid, I do order and declare that all persons held as slaves within said designated States, and parts of States, are, and hence-forward shall be free. . . .

And upon this act, sincerely believed to be an act of justice, warranted by the Constitution, upon military necessity, I invoke the considerate judgment of mankind, and the gracious favor of Almighty God.

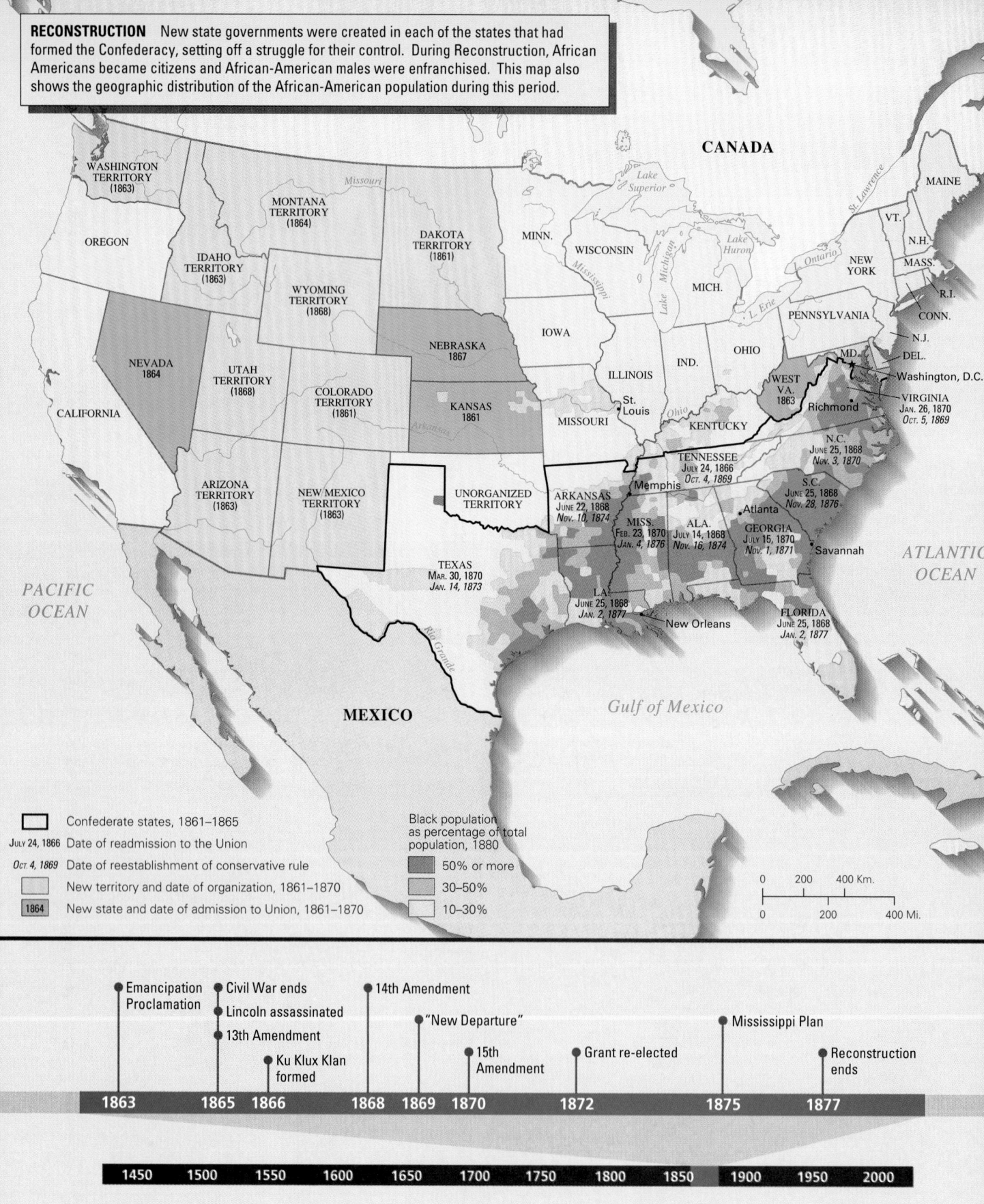

RECONSTRUCTION New state governments were created in each of the states that had formed the Confederacy, setting off a struggle for their control. During Reconstruction, African Americans became citizens and African-American males were enfranchised. This map also shows the geographic distribution of the African-American population during this period.

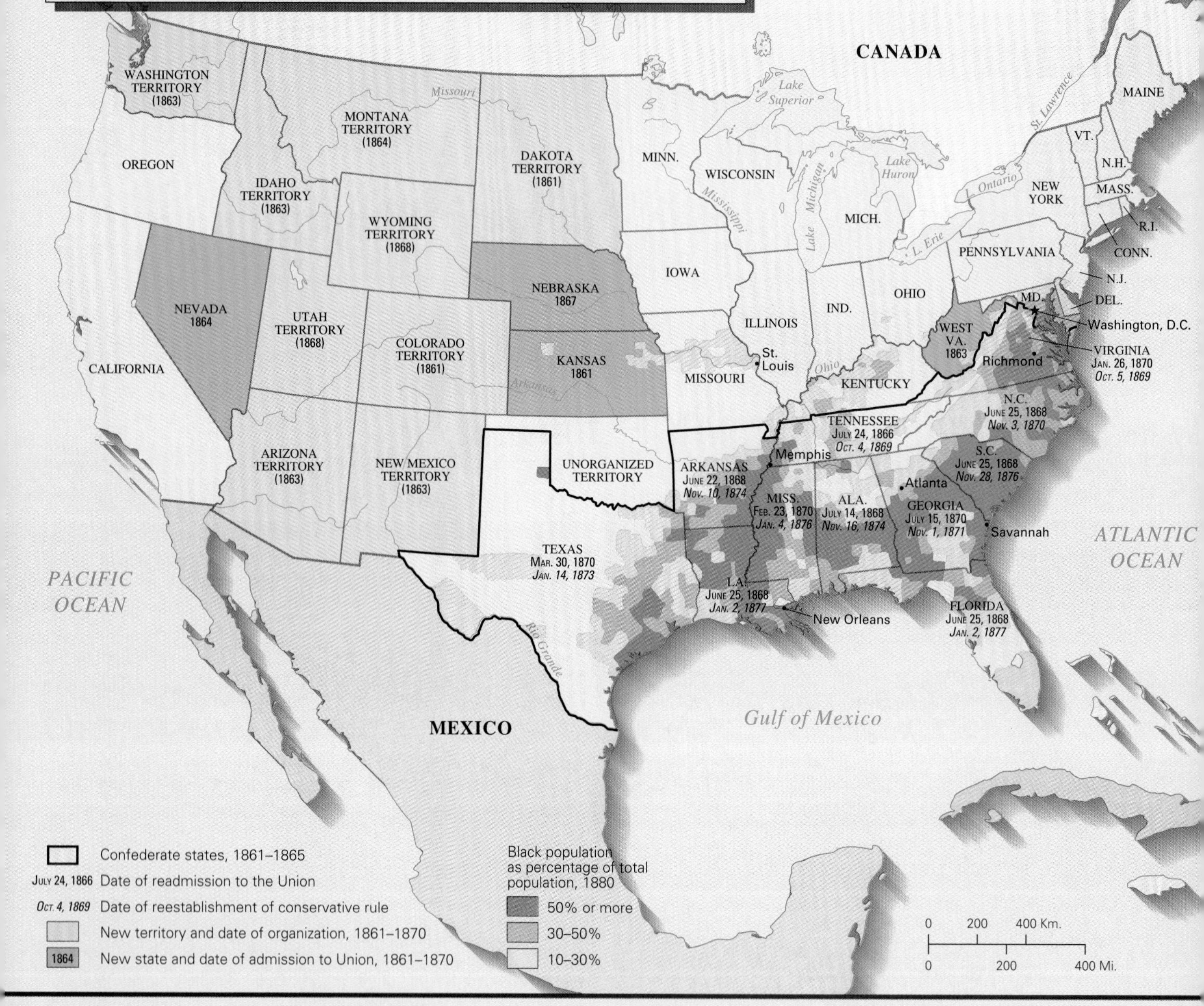

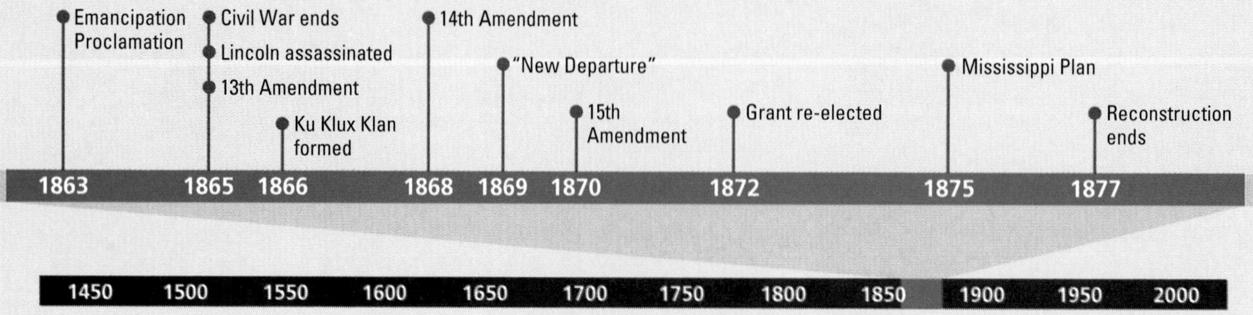

CHAPTER 16

Reconstruction: High Hopes and Broken Dreams, 1865–1877

Presidential Reconstruction

- What did President Lincoln and President Johnson expect to accomplish through their Reconstruction plans?
- At first, how did white southerners choose to respond to Lincoln's and Johnson's efforts at reconstruction—that is, what was the initial outcome of the presidents' choices?

Freedom and the Legacy of Slavery

- What expectations did freed people hold for freedom? What choices did they make based on those expectations?
- What expectations did southern whites hold at the end of the Civil War? What initial choices did they make to define the legal status of the freed people?

Congressional Reconstruction

- What did Republicans in Congress expect to accomplish by taking control of Reconstruction? What choices did they make to accomplish those goals?
- How did the Fourteenth and Fifteenth Amendments transform the nature of the federal Union?

Black Reconstruction

- Who made up the Republican party in the South during Reconstruction? Why did each major group choose to be Republican?
- What important choices did Republican state administrations make during Reconstruction? How effective were their actions?

The End of Reconstruction

- What was the Mississippi Plan, and how was it related to the end of Reconstruction?
- What were the final outcomes of Reconstruction?

INTRODUCTION

Expectations
Constraints
Choices
Outcomes

In this textbook the authors have stressed four components in the process of making history—*expectations, constraints, choices,* and *outcomes* (which we call ECCO). These components do not always operate in order, but they work together as a web of causes, influences, and effects. Each ECCO component can have an impact on any other one. For example, a certain *expectation* might point to what appears to be a natural *choice.* Yet *constraints* may alter an *expectation* or limit the available *choices* to such a degree that new *expectations* or *choices* arise. A given *choice* can influence new *expectations,* change existing *constraints,* or limit or increase the variety of other *choices* available. All come together in *outcomes* that can, in turn, redefine other *expectations, constraints,* and *choices.* Each time any of the people connected with America's past went through the process we call ECCO, they created their own part in America's story. It was this process that is instrumental in describing how America was made, and it is this process that we will use to describe Reconstruction and much of the history of the United States in the nineteenth and twentieth centuries.

When the last Confederate military resistance collapsed in 1865, ending the bloody Civil War, some 2.6 million men had served in the Union or Confederate armies since 1861, equal to almost 40 percent of all the men aged 15 to 40 in the United States in 1860. More than a half-million died—more deaths than in any other American war. Women also made important contributions to the war effort as civilians, and more than a hundred—perhaps several hundred—women disguised themselves and fought as soldiers, mostly for the Union. By 1865, the war had touched the lives of nearly every person living in the nation.

Except for Gettysburg, the major battles in the Civil War occurred in the South or the border states. Toward the end of the war, Union armies swept across the South, leaving devastation behind them: burned and shelled buildings, ravaged fields, twisted railroad tracks. This destruction, and the collapse of the region's financial system, posed significant *constraints* on economic revival in the South.

More devastating for many white southerners than the property damage and destruction was the emancipation of 4 million slaves. In 1861, fearful *expectations* about the future of slavery under Republicans had caused the South to *choose* secession. With the *outcome* of the war, fears became reality. The end of slavery forced southerners—of both races—to reconsider most of their *expectations* and to make a series of *choices* that created new patterns of social, economic, and political relations between the races.

The years between 1865 and 1877 marked Reconstruction. Although the period was a time of physical rebuilding throughout the South, the term *Reconstruction* refers primarily to the rebuilding of the federal Union and to the political, economic, and social changes that came to the South as a result of defeat in war and the end of slavery. Reconstruction involved *choices* in response to some of the most momentous questions in American history. How was the defeated South to be treated? What was to be the future of the 4 million former slaves? Were key decisions to be made in Washington by the federal government or in state capitols and county courthouses throughout the South? Which branch of the government was to establish policies?

As the dominant Republicans turned their attention from waging war to reconstructing the Union, they wrote into law and the Constitution new definitions of the very nature of the Union itself. They also made *choices* about the terms on which the South might rejoin the Union and about the rights of the former slaves. They also permanently changed the definition of American citizenship.

These changes conflicted with the *expectations* of most white southerners, some of whom *chose* to resist. *Choices* over the future of the South and the status of the former slaves also produced conflict between the president and Congress. A temporary *outcome* of this conflict was an increase in the power of Congress and a reduction in that of the president. A lasting *outcome* of these *choices* was a significant increase in the power of the federal government and new *constraints* on local and state governments.

The *outcome* of these government actions was some social change. In the end, however, the *outcome* of Reconstruction failed to fulfill most African Americans' *expectations* for freedom and equality.

CHRONOLOGY

Reconstruction

1863	Emancipation Proclamation The Ten-Percent Plan
1864	Abraham Lincoln re-elected
1865	Freedmen's Bureau created Civil War ends Lincoln assassinated Andrew Johnson becomes president Thirteenth Amendment (abolishing slavery) ratified
1866	Ku Klux Klan formed Congress begins to assert control over Reconstruction Civil Rights Act of 1866 Riots by whites in Memphis and New Orleans
1867	Military Reconstruction Act Command of the Army Act Tenure of Office Act
1868	Impeachment of President Johnson Fourteenth Amendment (defining citizenship) ratified Ulysses S. Grant elected president
1869–1870	Victories of "New Departure" Democrats in some southern states
1870	Fifteenth Amendment (guaranteeing voting rights) ratified
1870–1871	Ku Klux Klan Acts
1872	Grant re-elected
1875	Civil Rights Act of 1875 Mississippi Plan ends Reconstruction in Mississippi
1876	Disputed presidential election: Hayes vs. Tilden
1877	Compromise of 1877 Rutherford B. Hayes becomes president End of Reconstruction

Presidential Reconstruction

- What did President Lincoln and President Johnson expect to accomplish through their Reconstruction plans?
- At first, how did white southerners choose to respond to Lincoln's and Johnson's efforts at reconstruction—that is, what was the initial outcome of the presidents' choices?

On New Year's Day 1863, President Abraham Lincoln signed the Emancipation Proclamation. More than four years earlier, he had insisted that "this government cannot endure permanently half slave and half free. . . . It will become all one thing, or all the other." With the Emancipation Proclamation, Lincoln began the process by which the nation became all free. At the time, however, the Proclamation did not affect any slave, because it abolished slavery only in territory under Confederate control, where there was no way to enforce it. But every advance of a Union army after January 1, 1863, brought the reality of **emancipation** to the Confederacy.

Republican War Aims

For Lincoln and the Republican party, freedom for the slaves became a central concern in part because **abolitionists** were an influential element within the Republican party. Though the Republican party promised only to prohibit slavery in the territories during their 1860 electoral campaign, some Republican congressional leaders not only favored abolition

emancipation Release from bondage; freedom.

abolitionist Someone who condemned slavery as morally wrong and believed that it should be abolished.

♦ This engraving celebrating the Emancipation Proclamation first appeared in 1863. While it places a white Union soldier in the center, it also portrays the important role of African-American troops and emphasizes the importance of education and literacy. *The Library Company of Philadelphia.*

of slavery everywhere in the Union but also argued that emancipation would be meaningless unless the government guaranteed the civil and political rights of the former slaves. They were joined by abolitionists throughout the North—notably Frederick Douglass, an escaped slave who had become one of the most important leaders of the abolition movement. Thus this group of Republicans developed a further objective: citizenship for the former slaves and the equality of all citizens before the law. At the time, these were extreme views on abolition and equal rights, and the people who held them were called **Radical Republicans** or simply Radicals.

Thaddeus Stevens, perhaps the leading Radical in the House of Representatives, had made a successful career as a Pennsylvania iron manufacturer before he won election to the House in 1858. Born with a clubfoot, he always seemed to identify with those outside the social mainstream. He became a compelling spokesman for abolition and an uncompromising advocate of equal rights for African Americans. A masterful parliamentarian, he was known for his honesty and his sarcasm.

Charles Sumner of Massachusetts, a prominent Radical in the Senate, had argued for **racial integration** of Massachusetts schools in 1849 and won election to the U.S. Senate in 1851. Immediately establishing himself as the Senate's foremost champion of abolition, he became a martyr to the cause after a severe beating he suffered in 1856 because of an antislavery speech. After emancipation, Sumner, like Stevens, fought for full political and civil rights for the freed people.

Stevens, Sumner, and other Radicals demanded a drastic restructuring not only of the South's political system but also of its economy. They had opposed slavery not only on moral grounds but also because they believed free labor was more productive and inventive. Free labor, they argued, had contributed centrally to the dynamism of the North's economy and was crucial to democracy itself. "The middling classes who own the soil, and work it with their own hands," Stevens once proclaimed, "are the main support of every free government." Thus, the Radicals concluded, for the South to be fully democratic, it had to elevate free labor to a position of honor.

Not all Republicans accepted the proposals of the Radicals. All Republicans had objected to slavery, but not all Republicans had been abolitionists—some wanted only to ban slavery from the western territories. Similarly, not all Republicans wanted to extend full citizenship rights to the former slaves. Some favored rapid restoration of the South to the Union so that the federal government could concentrate on stimulating the nation's economy and developing the West. Republicans who did not immediately endorse severe punishment for the South or citizenship for the freed people are usually referred to as **moderates.**

Radical Republicans A group within the Republican party that advocated citizenship for former slaves and believed the South should be forced to meet congressional goals for reform.

racial integration Equal participation by people of different racial groups in a society or organization; the absence of race-based barriers on race to full and equal participation.

moderates Those whose views are midway between two more extreme positions; in this case, Republicans who favored some reforms but not all the Radicals' proposals.

♦ Radical Republicans initially hoped that Andrew Johnson would be their ally. Instead he proved to be unsympathetic to most Radical goals. His self-righteous and uncompromising personality led to conflict that eventually produced an unsuccessful effort to remove him from office in 1868. *Library of Congress.*

Lincoln's Approach to Reconstruction: "With Malice Toward None"

After the Emancipation Proclamation, President Lincoln and the congressional Radicals agreed that the abolition of slavery had to be a condition for the return of the South to the Union. However, major differences soon appeared over other terms for reunion and the roles of the president and Congress in establishing those terms. In his second inaugural address, a month before his death, Lincoln defined the task facing the nation:

> *With malice toward none; with charity for all; with firmness in the right, as God gives us to see the right, let us strive on to finish the work we are in: to bind up the nation's wounds; to care for him who shall have borne the battle, and for his widow and orphan, to do all which may achieve and cherish a just and lasting peace among ourselves, and with all nations.*

Lincoln had already begun to rebuild the Union on the basis of these principles. He hoped to hasten the end of the war by making it easy for southerners to renounce the Confederacy and to accept emancipation. He also wanted to create new state governments with a broad base of support. When Union armies occupied portions of southern states, he appointed temporary **military governors** for those regions and tried to restore civil government as quickly as possible.

Drawing on the president's constitutional power to issue pardons (Article II, Section 2), Lincoln issued a Proclamation of **Amnesty** and Reconstruction (also known as the "Ten-Percent Plan") in December 1863. In it, he offered a full pardon and restoration of all rights to those who swore their loyalty to the Union and accepted the abolition of slavery. Only high-ranking Confederate leaders were not eligible. When those who took the oath in a state amounted to 10 percent of the number of votes cast by that state in the 1860 presidential election, the pardoned voters were to write a new state constitution that abolished slavery and then elect state officials to take over from the military governor.

Many congressional Republicans thought that Congress should have a greater role in restoring the southern states to the Union. Two leading Radicals, Benjamin F. Wade and Henry W. Davis, introduced a bill to require 50 percent of all white males in a state to swear loyalty to the Union before the formation of a new civil government. The bill also guaranteed some black rights. Most Republicans voted in favor when Congress passed the Wade-Davis bill in July 1864. Lincoln, however, killed it with a **pocket veto,** fearing it would seriously slow the restoration of civil government and perhaps lengthen the war itself.

Under Lincoln's Ten-Percent Plan, new state governments were established in Arkansas, Louisiana, and Tennessee during 1864 and early 1865.

military governor Officer appointed to govern a region occupied by an army, as a substitute for civilian rule.

amnesty A general pardon granted by a government, especially for political offenses.

pocket veto Special type of presidential veto; if Congress approves a bill, sends it to the president, then adjourns within ten days, and if the president takes no action on the bill, it is "pocketed" or vetoed.

In Louisiana, the new government denied voting rights to men who were one-quarter or more black, and it maintained restrictions on plantation laborers. Radicals complained loudly, but Lincoln urged patience, suggesting the reconstructed government in Louisiana was "as the egg to the fowl, and we shall sooner have the fowl by hatching the egg than by smashing it." Events in Louisiana and elsewhere convinced Radicals that freed people were unlikely to receive equitable treatment from state governments formed under the Ten-Percent Plan. Such experiences pushed moderates toward accepting the Radicals' position that only **suffrage** could protect the freedmen in their rights and that only federal action could secure suffrage for blacks.

Abolishing Slavery Forever: The Thirteenth Amendment

Amid such questions about the rights of freed people, congressional Republicans prepared the final destruction of slavery. The Emancipation Proclamation had been a wartime measure, justified in part by military necessity. Early in 1865, state legislatures or conventions had abolished slavery in West Virginia, Maryland, Missouri, and the reconstructed state of Tennessee. Slavery was still legal in Delaware and Kentucky, however, and old, prewar state laws—which might or might not be valid—still permitted slavery in the states that had made up the Confederacy. Opponents of slavery feared that, if the legality of slavery were to be determined state by state, its ultimate status might remain uncertain. To destroy slavery forever, Congress in January 1865 approved the **Thirteenth Amendment,** which read simply: "Neither slavery nor involuntary servitude, except as a punishment for crime whereof the party shall have been duly convicted, shall exist within the United States, or any place subject to their jurisdiction."

The Constitution requires any amendment to be ratified by three-fourths of the states—then 27 of 36. By December 1865, only 19 of the 25 Union states had ratified the amendment. The measure passed, however, when eight of the reconstructed southern states did so. In the end, therefore, the abolition of slavery hinged on action by reconstructed state governments in the South.

Andrew Johnson and Reconstruction

After the assassination of Lincoln in mid-April 1865, Vice President Andrew Johnson became president. He had little formal education and in his early life struggled continually against poverty. As a young man in Tennessee, he worked as a tailor then turned to politics. A Democrat, he relied on his oratorical skills to win several terms in the Tennessee legislature. He was elected to Congress then served as governor before winning election to the U.S. Senate in 1857. His political support came especially from small-scale farmers and working people. The state's elite of plantation owners usually opposed him. Johnson, in turn, resented their wealth and power and blamed them for **secession** and the Civil War.

When secession came, Johnson was the only southern senator who rejected the Confederacy. Early in the war, Union forces captured Nashville, capital of Tennessee, and Lincoln appointed Johnson military governor. Johnson dealt harshly with Tennessee secessionists, especially wealthy planters. Radical Republicans thought that his severe treatment of former Confederates was what the South needed. Johnson was elected vice president in 1864, receiving the nomination for vice president in part because Lincoln wanted to appeal to Democrats and to Unionists in border states.

When Johnson succeeded to the presidency, Radicals hoped he would join in their plans for transforming the South. Johnson, however, soon made clear that he held a strong commitment to **states' rights** and opposed the Radicals' concept of a powerful federal government able to impose policies on the states. "White men alone must manage the South," Johnson told one visitor, although he recommended limited political roles for the freedmen. Johnson's support for emancipation stemmed in part from his desire to punish the wealthy planters. Self-righteous and uncompromising, Johnson saw the major task of Reconstruction as empowering the region's white middle class and keeping the planters from regaining power.

suffrage The right to vote.

Thirteenth Amendment Constitutional amendment, ratified in 1865, that abolished slavery in the United States and its territories.

secession The withdrawal of eleven southern states from the United States in 1860–1861, giving rise to the Civil War.

states' rights A political position favoring the limitation of the federal government's power and the greatest possible self-government by the individual states.

In practice, Johnson's approach to Reconstruction differed little from Lincoln's. Like Lincoln, he relied on the president's constitutional power to grant pardons. His desire for a quick restoration of the southern states to the Union apparently overcame his bitterness toward the southern elite, and he granted amnesty to most former Confederates who pledged loyalty to the Union and support for emancipation. In one of his last actions as president, he granted full pardon and amnesty to all southern rebels, although, by then (1868) the **Fourteenth Amendment** prevented him from restoring their right to hold office.

Johnson appointed provisional governors for the southern states not already reconstructed. He instructed them to call constitutional conventions of delegates elected by pardoned voters. Some provisional governors, however, appointed former Confederates to state and local offices, outraging those who expected Reconstruction to bring to power loyal Unionists committed to a new southern society.

The Southern Response: Minimal Compliance

Johnson expected the state constitutional conventions to abolish slavery within each state, ratify the Thirteenth Amendment, renounce secession, and **repudiate** the state's war debts. The states were then to hold elections and resume their place in the Union. State conventions during the summer of 1865 usually complied with these provisions, though some did so grudgingly. Johnson had required no action on the rights of the freed people, and all the states rejected black suffrage.

By April 1866, all the southern states had fulfilled Johnson's requirements for rejoining the Union and had elected legislators, governors, and members of Congress. Unionists scored a few victories, but former Confederates won many positions. Johnson had hoped for the emergence of new political leaders in the South, and the election of planters and former Confederate officials troubled him.

Most white southerners, however, viewed Johnson as their protector, standing between them and the Radicals. His support for states' rights and his opposition to federal determination of voting rights led white southerners to expect that they would shape the transition from slavery to freedom—that they, and not Congress, would define the status of the former slaves.

Freedom and the Legacy of Slavery

- What expectations did freed people hold for freedom? What choices did they make based on those expectations?
- What expectations did southern whites hold at the end of the Civil War? What initial choices did they make to define the legal status of the freed people?

As state conventions wrote new constitutions and as politicians argued in Washington, African Americans throughout the South set about creating new, free lives for themselves. Before the Civil War, all slaves and most free blacks in the South had led lives tightly constrained by law and custom. They were permitted few social organizations of their own, separate from those of the white South. Confronting enormous changes in almost every aspect of their lives, they experimented with the choices that their new freedom offered. From this ferment of freedom came new, black social institutions that provided the basis for southern African-American communities. Eric Foner, in his comprehensive study *Reconstruction* (1988), described the central theme of the black response to emancipation as "a desire for independence from white control, for **autonomy** both as individuals and as members of a community." The prospect of autonomy affected every aspect of life—family, churches, schools, newspapers, and a host of other social institutions. At the same time, the economic life of the South was shattered by the war and transformed by emancipation, and white southerners also faced drastic economic and social change.

Defining the Meaning of Freedom

At the most basic level, freedom was not something that Lincoln or the Union armies gave to enslaved blacks. It came, instead, every time an individual slave stopped working for a master and claimed the right to be free. Thus freedom did not come to all slaves at the same time or in the same way. For some, freedom came before the Emancipation

Fourteenth Amendment Constitutional amendment ratified in 1868 defining American citizenship and placing restrictions on former Confederates.

repudiate To refuse to acknowledge or pay.

autonomy Self-government or the right of self-determination.

♦ Before Emancipation, slaves typically made their own simple and rough clothing or they received the cast-off clothing of their owners and overseers. With Emancipation, those freed people who had an income could afford to dress more fashionably. The Harry Stephens family probably put on their best clothes for a visit to the photographer G. Gable in 1866. *Gilman Paper Company, New York.*

Proclamation, when they walked away from their owners, crossed into Union-held territory, and asserted their freedom. Toward the end of the war, as civil authority broke down throughout much of the South, many slaves declared their freedom and left their former masters. Some left for good, but many remained near where they had been born, though with a new understanding of their relationship to their former master. For the slaves in Kentucky, however, freedom did not come until ratification of the Thirteenth Amendment.

Across the South, the approach of Yankee troops set off a joyous celebration—called a Jubilee—among those who knew that their enslavement was ending. One Virginia woman remembered that "Such rejoicing and shouting you never heard in your life." A man recalled that, with the appearance of the Union soldiers, "We was all walking on golden clouds. Hallelujah!" For generations afterward, freed people from Texas and their descendants across the nation celebrated "Juneteenth Day"—June 19, the day in 1865 when African Americans in Texas learned of their freedom. Once the celebrating was over, however, the freed people faced difficult choices: what to do now, how best to use one's freedom.

The freed people expressed their new freedom in many ways. Some chose new names to symbolize their new identity and new beginnings. Many changed their style of dress, discarding the cheap clothing provided to slaves. Some acquired guns. A significant benefit of freedom was the ability to travel without a pass and without being checked by the patrols that had enforced the **pass system.** Many freed people took advantage of this new opportunity. Some felt they had to leave the site of their enslavement to experience full freedom. As one woman said, "if I stay here I'll never know I'm free." Most did not move, however, and among those who did, most traveled only short distances and usually for well-defined reasons: to find work or land to farm, to seek family members separated from them by slavery, or to return to homes that war had forced them to leave.

The towns and cities of the South also attracted freed people. The presence of Union troops and officials seemed to offer protection from the random violence against freed people that occurred in many rural areas, and the Freedmen's Bureau (see below) promised assistance with necessities and with finding work. The cities and towns also offered a few black churches, schools (which had usually operated secretly before the war), and other social institutions begun by free blacks before the war. Then, too, many African Americans came to towns and cities looking for work. Cities and towns had little housing for the influx of former slaves, however, and most crowded into black neighborhoods of hastily built shanties. Sanitation was poor and disease a common scourge. In just two weeks in September 1866, for example, more than a hundred people died of cholera in Vicksburg, Mississippi. Such conditions improved only very slowly.

pass system Laws that forbade slaves from traveling without written authorization from their owners.

Creating Communities

During Reconstruction, African Americans created their own communities with their own social institutions. Freed people hoped to strengthen family ties. Some families were reunited after years of separation caused by the sale of children away from parents or husband away from wife. Some people spent years searching for lost family members.

The new freedom to conduct religious services without white supervision was centrally important. Churches quickly became the most prominent social organizations in African-American communities. Churches were, in fact, among the very first social institutions that African Americans fully controlled. Black ministers advised and helped to educate congregation members as they adjusted to the changes that freedom brought. Ministers emerged as important leaders within developing African-American communities, and many of them provided political leadership.

Throughout the cities and towns of the South, African Americans—especially ministers and church members—worked to establish schools. Setting up a school, said one, was "the first proof" of independence. Many of the new schools were not just for children but also for adults who had been barred from learning by state laws prohibiting education for slaves. The desire to learn was widespread and intense. One freedman in Georgia wrote to a friend: "The Lord has sent books and teachers. We must not hesitate a moment, but go on and learn all we can."

Before the war, free public education had been rudimentary where it existed in the South, and wholly absent in many places. When African Americans began to set up schools, therefore, they faced a severe shortage of teachers, books, and schoolrooms—everything but students. As abolitionists and northern reformers tried to assist the transition from slavery to freedom, many of them focused especially on education.

In March 1865, Congress created the **Freedmen's Bureau,** an agency run by the War Department to assist the freed people in their transition to freedom. Among many other activities, it played an especially important role in helping to organize the new schools. Freedmen's Aid Societies sprang up in most northern cities and, along with northern churches, collected funds and supplies to assist the freed people. At first, many teachers—mostly white women, often from New England and often acting on religious impulses—came from the North. Soon northern aid societies and church organizations, together with the Freedmen's Bureau, established schools to train black teachers. Some of those schools evolved into black colleges. By 1870, the Freedmen's Bureau supervised more than 4,000 schools, with more than 9,000 teachers and 247,000 students. Still, in 1870, the schools had room for only one black child in ten of school age.

♦ Churches were the first institutions in America to be completely controlled by African Americans, and ministers were highly influential figures in the African-American communities that emerged during Reconstruction. This photograph shows the Reverend John Qualls at the pulpit of his church in New Orleans in the 1880s. *Historic New Orleans Collection.*

In addition to churches and schools, other African-American social institutions included **fraternal orders** and **benevolent societies.** *L'Union,* the first black newspaper in the South, appeared in 1862 in

Freedmen's Bureau Agency established in 1865 to aid former slaves in their transition to freedom, especially by administering relief and sponsoring education.

fraternal order An organization of men, often with a ceremonial initiation, which typically provided rudimentary life insurance; many fraternal orders also had auxiliaries for the female relatives of members.

benevolent society Group of people associated for some charitable purpose.

♦ During Reconstruction, the freed people gave a high priority to the establishment of schools, often with the assistance of the Freedmen's Bureau and northern missionary societies. This photograph of a newly established school was taken around 1870, showing both the barefoot students and the teacher. *Library of Congress.*

New Orleans, which was then occupied by Union troops. By 1866, the South had ten black newspapers led by the New Orleans *Tribune,* and black newspapers came to play important roles in emerging African-American communities.

In politics, African Americans' first objective was recognition of their equal rights as citizens. Frederick Douglass insisted that "Slavery is not abolished until the black man has the ballot." Political conventions of African Americans in 1865 attracted hundreds of delegates, including many ministers, skilled craftsmen, and former soldiers. In calling for equality and voting rights, these conventions pointed to black contributions in the American Revolution and the Civil War as evidence of patriotism and devotion. They also appealed to the nation's republican traditions, especially the Declaration of Independence and its dictum that "all men are created equal."

Land and Labor

Former slaveowners reacted to emancipation in a variety of ways. Some tried to keep their slaves from learning of their freedom. A few, like Mary Chesnut (a member of the plantation aristocracy from South Carolina), actually welcomed an end to slavery. Few provided any compensation (whether money, supplies, or land) to assist their former slaves in the transition to freedom. One freedman later recalled, "I do know some of dem old slave owners to be nice enough to start der slaves off in freedom wid somethin' to live on . . . but dey wasn't in droves, I tell you."

Many freed people began their new lives with virtually nothing, and many looked to the Union troops for assistance. When General Sherman led his army through Georgia in the closing months of the war, thousands of African-American men, women, and children left their plantations, claimed their freedom, and followed the Yankee troops. Their leaders told Sherman that what they wanted more than anything else was to "reap the fruit of our own labor." In January 1865, Sherman responded by issuing Special Field Order No. 15, setting aside the Sea Islands and land along the South Carolina coast for freed families. Each family, he specified, was to receive 40 acres and the loan of an army mule. By June, the area had filled with some forty thousand freed people settled on 400,000 acres of "Sherman land."

Sherman's action encouraged many African Americans to expect that the federal government would order a redistribution of land throughout the South. "Forty acres and a mule" became a rallying cry. Land, Thaddeus Stevens proclaimed, was the only thing that would give the freed people control of their own labor. "If we do not furnish them with homesteads," Stevens once said, "we had better left them in bondage."

At the end of the war, the Freedmen's Bureau controlled more than 850,000 acres of land abandoned by former owners or confiscated from leading Confederates. In July 1865, General Oliver O. Howard, head of the Bureau, directed Bureau agents to begin to divide this land into 40-acre plots to be given to freed people. However, when President Johnson issued pardons to the former owners of the confiscated land, he ordered Howard to halt **land redistribution** and to reclaim land already given to freed people and return it to its former owners. Johnson's order displaced tens of thousands of African Americans who had already taken their 40 acres. They and others who had hoped for land felt disappointed and betrayed. One recalled years later that they had expected "a heap from freedom dey didn't git."

The congressional act that created the Freedmen's Bureau also authorized it to assist white refugees, and, in a few states, white recipients of aid outnumbered the freed people. In addition to wartime destruction of buildings, livestock, and fields, illiteracy had always been widespread among poor whites and small-scale white farmers. Furthermore, many white Unionists—most often to be found in the hilly country away from the coasts and river valleys—had suffered vicious persecution at the hands of their fellow southerners. The vast majority of southern whites had never owned slaves, and some of them had opposed secession, but the outcome of the war meant that some lost their livelihood and many feared that they would now have to compete with the freed people for desirable farmland or wage labor. Just as nearly all freed people faced the need to earn a livelihood but had no land, tools, livestock, or even seeds, so too many southern whites lacked the means to resume or begin farming on their own. Because of the devastation of the southern economy, those with large landholdings often lacked the cash to hire farm workers to work for wages.

Sharecropping slowly emerged across much of the South as an alternative both to land redistribution and to wage labor on the plantations. **Sharecropping** derived directly from the central realities of southern agriculture. A great deal of land was in large holdings, but the landowners had no one to work it. A large number of families, both black and white, wanted to raise their own crops with their own labor but had no land, no supplies, and no money. The entire region was short of **capital.** Under sharecropping, an individual—usually a family head—signed a contract with a landowner to rent land as a home and farm. The tenant—the sharecropper—was typically to pay, as rent, a share of the harvest. The share might be half or even two-thirds of the year's crop if the landlord provided not only the land but also mules, tools, seed, and fertilizer. If the landlord provided only the land, the share was usually a quarter or a third. Many landowners preferred sharecropping because it encouraged tenants to be productive, to get as much value as possible from their shares of the crop.

♦ Sharecropping gave African Americans more control over their labor than did labor contracts. But sharecropping also contributed to the South's dependence on one-crop agriculture and helped to perpetuate widespread rural poverty. Notice that the child standing on the right is holding her kitten, probably to be certain it is included in this family photograph. *Library of Congress.*

Southern farmers—whether black or white, sharecroppers or owners of small plots—often found themselves in debt to a local merchant who had advanced supplies on credit. In return for credit at the store, the merchant typically required a lien (a legal claim) on the growing crop. Many landlords ran stores for their tenants and required the tenants to patronize those stores. All too often, the share paid as rent and the debt owed the store exceeded the value of the entire harvest. Many rental contracts

land redistribution The division of land held by large landowners into small plots that are turned over to people without property.

sharecropping Agricultural system in which tenant farmers give landlords a share of the crops, rather than cash, as rent.

capital Money needed to start a commercial enterprise.

and **crop liens** included provisions that automatically renewed them if all debts were not paid off at the end of a year. Thus, in spite of their efforts to achieve greater control over their lives and labor, many southern farm families, black and white alike, felt trapped by sharecropping and debt.

Until the 1890s, the act of casting a ballot on election day was an open process, and any observer could see how an individual was voting. Thus the power of the landlord and merchant often extended to politics. When a landlord or merchant advocated a particular candidate, the unspoken message was often an implicit threat to cut off credit at the store or to evict a farmer from his plot if he did not vote as directed. Such forms of economic coercion had the potential to undercut voting rights.

The White South: Confronting Change

The slow spread of sharecropping through much of the South, among white tenant farmers as well as black, was just one of many ways in which the end of slavery transformed the lives of white southerners. For some white southerners, the changes were nearly as profound as for the freed people. With Confederate money worthless, savings vanished. Some found their homes and other buildings destroyed. Thousands sold their landholdings and left the South.

Before the war, few white southerners had owned slaves, and even fewer had owned large numbers. Distrust or even hostility had always existed between the few privileged planter families and the whites who farmed small plots and had either a few slaves or none. Some regions populated by small-scale farmers had resisted secession, and some of them welcomed the Union victory and supported the Republicans during Reconstruction. Some southerners also welcomed the prospect of the economic transformation that northern capital might bring.

Most white southerners, however, shared what one North Carolinian described in 1866 as "the bitterest hatred toward the North." Even those with no attachment to slavery could join in detesting the Yankees who had so profoundly changed their lives. For many white southerners, the "lost cause" of the Confederacy came to symbolize their defense of their prewar lives, not southerners' attempt to break up the nation to protect slavery. Southern whites were unprepared for the extent of change facing them. Many apparently expected that prewar patterns would be restored, except for slavery. The early response of white southerners to emancipation reflects such an expectation that things might put back much as they had been before the war.

As civil governments created under presidential Reconstruction began to function in late 1865 and 1866, state legislatures passed **black codes** defining the new legal status of African Americans. Black codes varied from state to state, but every state placed significant restraints on the freedom of black people. Various black codes required African Americans to have an annual employment contract, limited them to agricultural work except with court permission, restricted them from moving about the countryside without permission, forbade them to own guns or carry weapons, restricted their ownership of land, and provided for forced labor by those found guilty of **vagrancy**—which usually meant anyone without a job. Some codes originated in prewar restrictions placed on both slaves and free blacks. Some reflected efforts to ensure that farm workers would be on hand at crucial times in the annual cycle of planting, cultivating, and harvesting. Taken together, however, the black codes represented an effort by white southerners to define a legally subordinate place for African Americans.

While white southern lawmakers were creating the black codes, some white southerners were using violence to coerce freed people into accepting a subordinate status within the new southern society. Clara Barton, who had organized women to serve as nurses for the Union army, visited the South from 1866 to 1870 and observed "a condition of lawlessness toward the blacks" and "a disposition . . . to injure or kill them on slight or no provocation." Most southern whites seem to have tolerated this kind of treatment.

Violence and terror became closely associated with the **Ku Klux Klan,** a secret organization

crop lien A legal claim to a farmer's crops, similar to a mortgage, based on the use of crops as collateral for extension of credit by a merchant.

black codes Laws passed by the southern states after the Civil War to limit the freedom of African Americans and force them to return to agricultural labor.

vagrancy The legal condition of having no fixed place of residence or means of support; in the South following the Civil War, vagrancy charges were often made against any freed person without a work contract.

Ku Klux Klan A secret society organized in the South after the Civil War to resurrect white supremacy by means of violence and intimidation.

♦ In this picture, the artist has portrayed a group of bizarrely dressed Klansmen contemplating the murder of a white Republican. *Library of Congress.*

formed in 1866 and led by a former Confederate general, Nathan Bedford Forrest. Most Klan members were small-scale farmers and workers, but the leaders were often prominent citizens—planters, merchants, lawyers, and ministers. As one Freedmen's Bureau agent said, "the most respectable citizens are engaged in it." Klan groups existed throughout the South, but there was little central control. Their major goal, however, was everywhere the same: to restore **white supremacy** and to destroy the Republican party. Other, similar organizations also formed and adopted terrorist tactics.

In the Klan's bizarre ritual, members were called ghouls. Officers included cyclops, night-hawks, and grand dragons, and the national leader was called the grand wizard. Klan members covered their faces with hoods, wore white robes, and rode horses draped in white. So attired, they set out to intimidate Republicans, typically targeting leading black Republicans and their Radical white allies. Klan members also attacked less politically prominent people, often whipping African Americans accused of not showing deference to whites. Nightriders burned black churches and schools. Using violence and threats, the Klan devastated Republican organizations in many communities.

In 1866, two events dramatized for the nation the violence that some white southerners routinely inflicted on African Americans. In early May, in Memphis, Tennessee, black veterans of the Union army came to the assistance of a black man being arrested by white police, setting off a three-day riot in which whites, including police, indiscriminately attacked African Americans. Forty-five blacks and three whites died. In late July, in New Orleans, some forty people died, most of them African Americans, in an altercation between police and a largely black pro-suffrage group. General Philip Sheridan, the military commander of the district, called it "an absolute massacre by the police." Memphis and New Orleans were unusual only in the number involved and the number killed. Local authorities seemed uninterested in stopping such violence, and federal troops were often not available where they were needed.

Congressional Reconstruction

- What did Republicans in Congress expect to accomplish by taking control of Reconstruction? What choices did they make to accomplish those goals?
- How did the Fourteenth and Fifteenth Amendments transform the nature of the federal Union?

The black codes, violence against freed people, and the failure of southern authorities to stem the violence turned opinion in Washington, and in the North more generally, against President Johnson's approach to Reconstruction. By early 1866, increasing numbers of moderate Republicans accepted the Radicals' arguments that the freed people required greater federal protection. As President Johnson proved unable to attract a popular following in the North, Republicans in Congress moved to establish their control over Reconstruction.

Challenging Presidential Reconstruction

In December 1865, the Thirty-ninth Congress (elected in 1864) met for the first time. In both houses of Congress, Republicans outnumbered Democrats by more than three to one. The president's annual message proclaimed Reconstruction complete and the Union restored, but few Republicans agreed. Radical Republicans, especially, had been angered by Johnson's lack of support for black suffrage. To accomplish black suffrage, they needed

white supremacy The racist belief that whites are inherently superior to all other races and are therefore entitled to rule over them.

both to assert congressional power over Reconstruction and to move decisions on suffrage from the state to the federal level. By then, most Republicans were committed to creating a southern economy based on free labor and to defining and protecting basic rights for the freed people. Most also agreed that Congress had the right to withhold representation from the South until state governments there met these conditions.

On the first day of the Thirty-ninth Congress, the newly elected congressmen from the South—including many former Confederates—were excluded. Republicans set up a Joint Committee on Reconstruction to evaluate the qualifications of the excluded southerners under Article II, Section 5, of the Constitution and to determine whether the southern states were entitled to representation. Some members of the committee hoped to launch a full investigation of Reconstruction and the president's policy. While the committee worked, the former Confederate states were to have no representation in Congress.

At the same time, Republicans in Congress moved to assist the freed people. As was the case with the establishment of the Joint Committee, old divisions between moderates and Radicals seemed forgotten as a largely unified Republican party approved a bill to extend the life of the Freedmen's Bureau and give it more authority to combat racial discrimination. When Johnson vetoed it, Congress passed a slightly revised version. Similar Republican unity marked the passage of a civil rights bill, a far-reaching measure that extended citizenship to African Americans and defined some rights of all citizens. Johnson vetoed both the civil rights bill and the revised Freedmen's Bureau bill, but Congress passed them over his veto. With creation of the Joint Committee on Reconstruction and passage of the Civil Rights and Freedmen's Bureau Acts, Congress took control over Reconstruction.

The Civil Rights Act of 1866

The Civil Rights Act of 1866, prompted by the black codes, defined all persons born in the United States (except Indians not taxed) as citizens. It also listed certain rights of all citizens, including the right to testify in court, own property, make contracts, bring lawsuits, and enjoy "full and equal benefit of all laws and proceedings for the security of person and property." It authorized federal officials to bring suit against violations of civil rights and specified that suits arising under it were to be tried in or appealed to federal courts rather than state courts.

The Civil Rights Act of 1866 was the first effort to define in law some of the rights of American citizenship. It placed significant restrictions on state actions on the ground that the rights of national citizenship took precedence over the powers of state governments. By expanding the power of the federal government in unprecedented ways, the law not only challenged traditional concepts of states' rights but did so on behalf of African Americans.

Much of the debate in Congress focused on the immediate situation of the freed people. Some supporters saw the measure as a way to secure the freed people's basic rights, rather than as something that redefined federal-state relations, and hoped it would encourage freed people to stay in the South. For other Republicans, however, the bill carried broader implications, because it empowered the federal government to force states to abide by the principle of equality before the law. Senator Lot Morrill of Maine described it as "absolutely revolutionary" but added, "Are we not in the midst of a revolution?"

When President Johnson vetoed the civil rights bill, he argued, in the language of the traditional Democrat that he was, that it violated states' rights. By defending states' rights and taking aim at the Radicals, Johnson may have hoped to generate enough political support to elect a more conservative Congress in 1866 and to elect him to the presidency in his own right in 1868. He probably expected the veto to appeal to antiblack sentiments among voters in both North and South and to turn them against the Radicals. Instead, the veto led most Republicans in Congress to give up all hope of cooperation with him. In April 1866, when Congress passed the Civil Rights Act over Johnson's veto, it was the first time that Congress had overridden a veto of major legislation.

Defining Citizenship: The Fourteenth Amendment

Leading Republicans worried that the Civil Rights Act could be amended or repealed by a later Congress or declared unconstitutional by the Supreme Court. They concluded that only another constitutional amendment could permanently safeguard the freed people's rights as citizens.

The Fourteenth Amendment began as a proposal made by the Radicals within the Joint Committee on Reconstruction who wanted a constitutional guarantee of equality before the law. But the final wording—the longest of any amendment—resulted from many compromises within the Republican party. Section 1 of the amendment defined American citizenship in much the same way as the Civil Rights Act of 1866, then specified that

> *No State shall make or enforce any law which shall abridge the privileges or immunities of citizens of the United States; nor shall any State deprive any person of life, liberty, or property, without due process of law; nor deny to any person within its jurisdiction the equal protection of the laws.*

The Constitution and Bill of Rights had prohibited federal interference with basic civil rights. The Fourteenth Amendment extended this protection against action by state governments. The amendment was vague on some points, however. For example, it penalized states that did not **enfranchise** African Americans—by reducing their congressional and electoral representation in proportion to the number of adult males disfranchised—but it did not specifically guarantee to African Americans the right to vote.

Some provisions of the amendment stemmed from Republicans' fears that a restored South, in alliance with northern Democrats, might try to undo the outcome of the war. One section barred from public office anyone who had sworn to uphold the federal Constitution and then "engaged in insurrection or rebellion against the same." Only a two-thirds vote of both houses of Congress could counteract this provision. (In 1872, Congress passed a blanket measure pardoning nearly all former Confederates.) The amendment also prohibited either federal or state governments from assuming any of the Confederate debt or from paying any claim arising from emancipation.

Not everyone approved of the compromise. Sumner condemned the provision that permitted a state to deny suffrage to male citizens if it accepted a penalty in congressional representation. Stevens wanted not just to bar former Confederates from holding office but to disfranchise them as well. Woman-suffrage advocates, led by **Susan B. Anthony** and Elizabeth Cady Stanton, protested that the amendment, for the first time, introduced the word *male* into the Constitution in connection with voting rights.

Despite such concerns, Congress approved the Fourteenth Amendment by a straight party vote in June 1866 and sent it to the states for ratification. Johnson opposed that action, arguing that Congress should not propose constitutional amendments until the representatives of all the southern states had taken their seats. Tennessee ratified the amendment promptly, became the first reconstructed state government to be recognized by Congress, and was therefore exempted from most later Reconstruction legislation.

Although Congress adjourned in the summer of 1866, the nation's attention remained fixed on the issues of Reconstruction. In May and July, the bloody riots in Memphis and New Orleans turned more northerners and moderates against Johnson's Reconstruction policies. Some interpreted the congressional elections that fall as a referendum on Reconstruction and specifically on the Fourteenth Amendment, pitting Johnson against the Radicals. Johnson undertook a speaking tour—dubbed a "Swing Around the Circle"—to promote his views, but his reckless tirades alienated many who heard him. Republicans swept the 1866 elections, outnumbering Democrats 143 to 49 in the new House of Representatives, and 42 to 11 in the Senate. Lyman Trumbull, senator from Illinois, voiced the view of most congressional Republicans: Congress should now "hurl from power the disloyal element" in the South.

Radicals in Control: Impeachment of the President

As Congress—and the Radicals—took charge of Reconstruction, it became clear that the Fourteenth Amendment was falling short of ratification. Rejection by ten states could prevent ratification. By March 1867, the amendment had been rejected by twelve states—Delaware, Kentucky, and all the Confederate states except Tennessee. Those Republicans who had expected the Fourteenth Amendment to be the final federal Reconstruction measure now became more receptive to other proposals that the Radicals put forth.

The Military Reconstruction Act of 1867, passed on March 2 over Johnson's veto, divided the Confederate states (except Tennessee) into five military districts. Each district was governed by a military commander authorized by Congress to use military force to protect life and property. The ten states

enfranchise To grant the right to vote to a person or group of people.

Susan B. Anthony Feminist and reformer who worked to secure the vote for women and to protect the economic rights of married women.

were to hold constitutional conventions, and all adult male citizens were to vote, except former Confederates barred from office under the proposed Fourteenth Amendment. The constitutional conventions were to create new state governments that permitted black suffrage, and the new governments were to ratify the Fourteenth Amendment. Then, perhaps, Congress might recognize those state governments as being valid. While waiting for congressional recognition, they were to be considered provisional.

On the same day, March 2, Congress limited some of Johnson's constitutional powers. The Command of the Army Act specified that the president could issue military orders only through the general of the army, then Ulysses S. Grant, who was thought to be sympathetic to Congress. It also specified that the general of the army could not be removed or sent outside Washington without Senate permission. Congress thereby blocked Johnson from direct communication with military commanders in the South. The Tenure of Office Act specified that officials appointed with the Senate's consent were to remain in office until the Senate approved a successor. This measure was intended to prevent Johnson from replacing federal officials who opposed his policies. Both measures, Johnson understood, were invasions of presidential authority.

Early in 1867, some Radicals had begun to consider impeaching President Johnson. The Constitution, in Article I, Sections 2 and 3, gives the House of Representatives exclusive power to **impeach** the president—that is, to bring charges of misconduct. The Senate has exclusive power to hold trial on those charges, with the chief justice of the Supreme Court presiding. If found guilty by a two-thirds vote of the Senate, the president is removed from office.

In January 1867, the House Judiciary Committee began to investigate charges against Johnson but failed to find convincing evidence of misconduct. Johnson, however, confronted Congress over the Tenure of Office Act by removing Edwin Stanton, a Lincoln appointee and a Radical, from his cabinet post as secretary of war. This action provided Johnson's opponents with something resembling a violation of law by the president. After an effort to secure impeachment through the House Judiciary Committee failed, the Joint Committee on Reconstruction, led by Thaddeus Stevens, took over and developed charges against Johnson. On February 24, 1868, the House adopted eleven articles, or charges, nearly all dealing with the Stanton affair. The actual reasons the Radicals wanted Johnson removed were clear to all: they disagreed with his actions and disliked him personally.

To convict Johnson and remove him from the presidency required a two-thirds vote of the Senate. Johnson's defense attorneys argued that Johnson had dismissed Stanton only to test the constitutionality of the Tenure in Office Act and that he had done nothing to warrant impeachment. The Radicals' case was weak, but they urged senators to base their vote on whether they wished Johnson to remain as president. Some moderate Republicans, however, questioned the wisdom of removing Johnson, because they feared the **precedent** it might set. The vote, on May 16 and 26, 1868, was 35 in favor of conviction and 19 against, one vote short of the required two-thirds. By this narrow margin, the nation maintained the principle that Congress should not remove the president from office simply because they disagreed with or disliked each other.

Political Terrorism and the Election of 1868

The Radicals' failure to unseat Johnson left him with less than a year remaining in office. As the election approached, the Republicans nominated Ulysses S. Grant for president. A war hero, popular throughout the North, Grant seemed the right person to end the conflict between the White House and Congress. During the war, he had fully supported Lincoln and Congress in implementing emancipation. By 1868, he had committed himself to the congressional view of Reconstruction. The Democrats nominated Horatio Seymour, a former governor of New York, and focused most of their campaign against Reconstruction.

In the South, the campaign stirred up fierce activity by the Ku Klux Klan and similar groups. **Terrorists** assassinated an Arkansas congressman, three members of the South Carolina legislature, and several delegates to state constitutional conventions. Throughout the South, mobs attacked Republican

impeach To charge a public official with improper, usually criminal, conduct. Only the House of Representatives may impeach a president; if it does, the Senate must determine whether the president should be removed from office.

precedent An event or decision that may be used later as an example in similar cases.

terrorists Those who use threats and violence to achieve ideological or political goals.

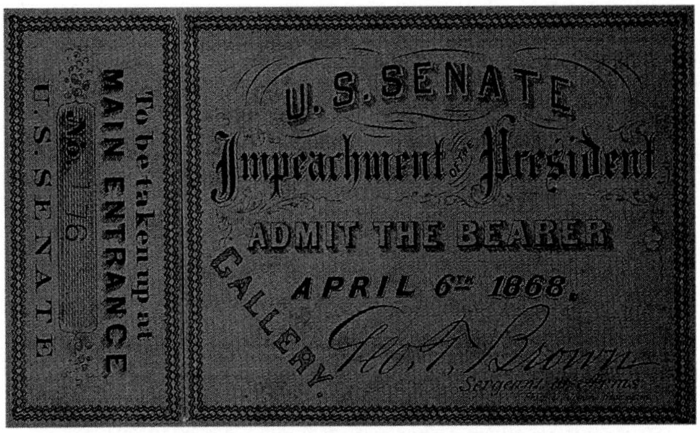

♦ Tickets such as these were in high demand, for they permitted the holder to watch the historic proceedings as the Radical leaders presented their evidence to justify removing Andrew Johnson from the presidency. *Collection of David J. and Janice L. Frent.*

newspaper offices and campaign meetings, and sometimes they attacked any black person they could find. Such coercion had its intended effect. For example, during the campaign, as many as two hundred blacks were killed in St. Landry Parish, Louisiana, where the Republicans had more than a thousand-vote majority among registered voters. On election day, not a single Republican vote was recorded from the parish.

Despite such violence, by election day many Americans may have been anticipating a calmer political future. In June 1868, Congress readmitted seven southern states that met the requirements of congressional Reconstruction. In July, the secretary of state declared the Fourteenth Amendment ratified. In August, Thaddeus Stevens died. In November, Grant easily won the presidency, carrying twenty-six of the thirty-four states and 53 percent of the vote.

Voting Rights and Civil Rights

Grant's election confirmed that Reconstruction was not likely to be overturned. Radical Republicans now addressed voting rights for all African Americans, whether in the North or the South. In 1867, Republicans in Congress had removed racial barriers to voting in the District of Columbia and in the territories, but elsewhere the states still defined voting rights. Congress had required southern states to enfranchise black males as the price of readmission to the Union, but only seven northern states had taken that step by 1869. States that had enfranchised African Americans could change their suffrage laws at any time and, once again, disfranchise black voters.

To extend to African Americans in the North the same suffrage rights that African Americans exercised in the South, and to guarantee their voting rights everywhere, Congress approved the **Fifteenth Amendment** in February 1869. Widely considered to be the final step in Reconstruction, the amendment prohibited either the federal government or any state from restricting the right to vote because of a person's "race, color, or previous condition of servitude." Like the Fourteenth Amendment, the Fifteenth marked a compromise between moderate and Radical Republicans. Some African-American leaders had argued for language guaranteeing voting rights to all male citizens, because language that prohibited some grounds for limitation might imply the legitimacy of other grounds. Similarly, some Radicals tried, unsuccessfully, to add "nativity [place of birth], property, education, or religious beliefs" to the prohibited grounds. Democrats in both North and South condemned the Fifteenth Amendment, even in its restricted form, as a "revolutionary" change in the rights of states to define voting rights.

Susan B. Anthony and other advocates of woman suffrage opposed the amendment for a different reason: it ignored restrictions based on sex. Before emancipation, supporters of woman suffrage had been among the staunchest opponents of slavery. Now, many woman-suffrage advocates urged that the vote be extended to women and black men at the same time. The break between the women's movement and the black movement was patched over somewhat once black suffrage was accomplished, but the wounds never completely healed (see Individual Choices: Frederick Douglass).

Despite such opposition, within thirteen months the proposed amendment received the approval of enough states to take effect. Success came in part because Republicans who might otherwise have been reluctant to impose black suffrage in the North recognized that the future success of their party required black suffrage in the South.

The Fifteenth Amendment did nothing to reduce the violence—especially at election time—that had become almost routine in the South after 1865. When

Fifteenth Amendment Constitutional amendment, ratified in 1870, that prohibited states from denying the right to vote because of a person's race or because a person had been a slave.

INDIVIDUAL CHOICES

Choosing Race over Gender

Frederick Douglass

Frederick Douglass was probably the most prominent African American in the nation from before the Civil War until his death in 1895. This photo was probably taken at about the time he faced a difficult choice over woman suffrage. Library of Congress.

In the fall of 1868, Frederick Douglass faced a difficult choice. He had been asked to address a woman-suffrage meeting. Should he accept? A number of considerations complicated his decision.

Douglass was then the most prominent African American in the nation. Born into slavery in 1818, he had escaped to the North at the age of 20. In the North, he soon became active in the movement to abolish slavery. His powerful intellect, eloquent oratory, and persuasive writings quickly took him to the forefront of that movement and made him internationally famous.

Douglass admired the important abolition activities of women. When the Seneca Falls Convention on women's rights met in 1848, Douglass was there. When the resolution on woman suffrage provoked strong discussion, Douglass was the only male present to speak in favor.

For nearly twenty years, the cause of women's rights and the cause of black rights marched together. Elizabeth Cady Stanton and Susan B. Anthony, two of the most forceful leaders of the women's movement, also provided strong support to the movement against slavery and, at first, to the movement for black rights.

Once black male suffrage came under discussion, however, this long-standing alliance began to fracture. In 1866, the Fourteenth Amendment for the first time introduced the word *male* into the Constitution in the context

Klan activity escalated in the elections of 1870, southern Republicans began to look to Washington for support. In 1870 and 1871, Congress adopted several Enforcement Acts—often called the Ku Klux Klan Acts—to enforce the rights specified in the Fourteenth and Fifteenth Amendments. These laws for the first time made certain crimes committed against individuals punishable under federal law.

Despite a limited budget and many obstacles, the prosecution of Klansmen began in 1871. Hundreds were indicted in North Carolina, and many were convicted. In Mississippi, federal officials indicted nearly seven hundred. In South Carolina, President Grant declared martial law and sent federal troops to occupy the region. Hundreds of arrests followed, and as many as two thousand Klansmen fled the of voting rights. Stanton and Anthony both protested vigorously. When one veteran abolitionist declared it to be "the Negro's hour" and called for black male suffrage, Anthony responded that she "would sooner cut off my right hand than ask the ballot for the black man and not for woman." Stanton went further, implying that women were more deserving of the vote than African Americans.

Douglass and other black leaders argued that a constitutional guarantee of the suffrage was essential for black Americans to recognize their political equality and to be able to protect themselves politically. He also knew that Republican members of Congress and of state legislatures throughout the North seemed willing to extend the franchise to African-American males. He knew that they did so partly from a sense of justice. At the same time, he understood that the Republican party needed the votes of southern African Americans to remain in power, and that some Republican officials hoped that the freedmen would be less likely to move North if they had the permanent protection of their political rights that came from the Constitution.

No similar political logic could be invoked in favor of woman suffrage. Further, Republican officeholders seemed more supportive of black suffrage than did voters. The voters of Kansas, in 1867, voted on removing both *white* and *male* from their state constitution's requirements for voting. Both proposals failed in that stronghold of Republicanism, and woman suffrage drew slightly less support than black male suffrage.

So when invited to speak to the 1868 woman-suffrage meeting, Douglass declined. In doing so, he first invoked his long-standing expectation for the approval of woman suffrage, declaring it to be as "sacred" as that of males. He continued:

> *It does not however follow that I can come to Washington or go elsewhere to deliver lectures on this special subject. I am now devoting myself to a cause [if] not more sacred, certainly more urgent, because it is one of life and death to the long enslaved people of this country, and this is: negro suffrage. While the negro is mobbed, beaten, stabbed, hanged, burnt and is the target of all that is malignant in the North and all that is murderous in the South, his claims may be preferred by me without exposing in any wise myself to the imputation of narrowness or meanness towards the cause of woman.*

Douglass was not alone in the stand he took. The Fifteenth Amendment provoked a split in the women's movement, as Anthony and Stanton adamantly refused to support it and other women reluctantly accepted the same logic as Douglass.

Had Douglass behaved differently, the political realities of the time made it highly unlikely he could have persuaded enough Republican leaders to achieve woman suffrage at the same time as black suffrage. Had he opposed the Fifteenth Amendment because it excluded women, he probably could not have defeated it. But if he had opposed it, he might have forfeited some of his own high standing in the Republican party and thus his future opportunities to work both on behalf of African Americans and on behalf of women's rights. Douglass himself did not waver in his commitment to woman suffrage, calling for an amendment to enfranchise women as soon as the Fifteenth Amendment was ratified.

state. By 1872, federal intervention had broken the strength of the Klan.

Congress passed one final Reconstruction measure, largely because of the persistence of Charles Sumner, who introduced a bill prohibiting **discrimination** in 1870 and in each subsequent session of Congress until his death in 1874. Passed after Sumner's death, the **Civil Rights Act of 1875** prohibited

discrimination Denial of equal treatment based on prejudice or bias.

Civil Rights Act of 1875 Law passed by Congress in 1875 prohibiting racial discrimination in selection of juries and in transportation and other businesses open to the general public.

♦ This lithograph celebrates approval of the Fifteenth Amendment in 1870. That amendment eliminated race, color, or previous condition of servitude as barriers to voting. Frederick Douglass, the most prominent black abolitionist, is depicted at top center. *Library of Congress.*

racial discrimination in the selection of juries and in public transportation and **public accommodations.** Provisions prohibiting **segregated** schools, churches, and cemeteries were deleted as too controversial—in both North and South.

Black Reconstruction

- Who made up the Republican party in the South during Reconstruction? Why did each major group chose to be Republican?
- What important choices did Republican state administrations make during Reconstruction? How effective were their actions?

Congressional Reconstruction set the stage for new developments at the state and local levels throughout the South, as newly enfranchised black men organized for political action. African Americans never completely controlled any state government, but they did form a large and important element in the governments of several states. The period when African Americans participated prominently in state and local politics, and sometimes took the lead in pushing through new laws, is usually called **Black Reconstruction.** It began with efforts by African Americans to take part in politics as early as 1865 and lasted for more than a decade. Some African Americans continued to hold elective office in the South long after 1877, but they could do little to bring about significant political change.

The Republican Party in the South

Not surprisingly, nearly all blacks who took an active part in politics did so as Republicans. Throughout Reconstruction, African Americans formed a large majority of those who supported the Republican party in the South. Nearly all black Republicans were new to politics, and they often braved considerable personal danger by participating in a political party that many white southerners saw as a tool of the conquering Yankees. In the South, the Republican party also included some southern whites along with a smaller number of transplanted northerners—both black and white.

Suffrage made politics a centrally important activity for African-American communities. The state constitutional conventions that met in 1868 included 265 black delegates. In Louisiana and South Carolina, half or more of the delegates were black, and blacks made up 40 percent in Florida and 20 percent

public accommodations Hotels, bars and restaurants, theaters, and other places set up to do business with anyone who can pay the price of admission.

segregated Characterized by the separation of a race or class from the rest of society, such as the separation of blacks from whites in most southern school systems.

Black Reconstruction The period of Reconstruction when African Americans took an active role in state and local government.

♦ This lithograph from 1883 depicts prominent African-American men, several of whom had leading roles in Black Reconstruction. *Library of Congress.*

in Arkansas, North Carolina, and Texas. With suffrage established, southern Republicans (black and white) began to elect African Americans to public office. Between 1869 and 1877, fourteen black men served in the national House of Representatives, six of them from South Carolina, three from Alabama, and one each from Florida, Georgia, Louisiana, Mississippi, and North Carolina. Mississippi sent two African Americans to the U.S. Senate: Hiram R. Revels and Blanche K. Bruce.

Across the South, the state-level offices that black men were most likely to hold were lieutenant governor and secretary of state—typically the least consequential offices in state government. Six blacks served as lieutenant governors, and one of them, P. B. S. Pinchback, succeeded to the governorship of Louisiana for forty-three days. More than six hundred black men served in southern state legislatures during Reconstruction, three-quarters of them in just four states: South Carolina, Mississippi, Louisiana, and Alabama. Only in South Carolina did blacks ever have a majority in the state legislature. Elsewhere they formed part of a Republican majority but rarely held key legislative positions. Only in South Carolina and Mississippi did legislatures elect black Speakers.

Although politically inexperienced, most of the African Americans who held office during Reconstruction had some education. Many had been free before the war—of eighteen who served in statewide offices, all but three are known to have been born free. P. B. S. Pinchback, for example, was educated in Ohio and served in the army as a captain before entering politics in Louisiana. Most black politicians first achieved prominence through army service or work in the Freedmen's Bureau, the new schools, or the religious and civic organizations of black communities.

Even in states with large black populations, southern Republicans achieved power only by securing at least some support from whites. Two groups of white Republicans are usually remembered by the names fastened on them by their political opponents: "carpetbaggers" and "scalawags." Both groups included idealists who hoped to create a new southern society, but both also included some opportunists who hoped to exploit the unstable politics of the day.

Southern Democrats used the term **carpetbagger** to suggest that northerners who came to the South after the war were a pack of second-rate opportunists, with their belongings packed in a cheap bag made of carpet material (see illustration of a carpet bag). In fact, most northerners who came south were well-educated men and women from middle-class backgrounds. Most of the men had served in the Union army and moved South soon afterward, before blacks could vote. Some were lawyers, businessmen, or newspaper editors, and some left behind prominent roles in northern communities. As investors in agricultural land, teachers in the new schools, or agents of the Freedmen's Bureau, most hoped to transform the South by creating new institutions based on northern models, especially free labor and free public schools. Although few in number compared to southerners, in state constitutional conventions and state legislatures, transplanted northerners took leading roles in government and chaired key committees. Transplanted northerners

carpetbagger Derogatory southern term for the northerners who came to the South after the Civil War to take part in Reconstruction.

♦ Bags made of carpeting, like this one, were inexpensive sacks used to pack things for traveling. Southern opponents of Reconstruction fastened the label "carpetbaggers" on northerners who came south to participate in Reconstruction, suggesting that they were cheap opportunists. *Collection of Antique Textile Resource, Nancy Gerwin.*

also emerged as prominent advocates of economic modernization.

Southern Democrats reserved their greatest contempt for those they called **scalawags,** slang for someone completely unscrupulous and worthless. Scalawags were white southerners who aligned themselves with the Republican party. They included many southern Unionists, who had opposed secession in 1860–1861, and others who thought alliance with the Republicans of the North offered the best hope for economic recovery. Scalawags also included some merchants, artisans, and professionals who favored a modernized South. Others were small-scale farmers, who had traditionally opposed the political leadership of the plantation owners. For them, Reconstruction promised an end to political domination by the plantation counties. Despite differences, freedmen, carpetbaggers, and scalawags used the Republican party to inject new ideas into the South. Throughout the South, Republicans tried to modernize state and local government and make southern states more like those in the North. They repealed laws such as those providing imprisonment for debt or public whippings (both eliminated throughout the North decades earlier) and established or expanded schools, hospitals, orphanages, and penitentiaries.

Creating an Educational System and Fighting Discrimination

Free public education was perhaps the most permanent legacy of Black Reconstruction. Reconstruction constitutions throughout the South required tax-supported public schools. Implementation, however, was expensive and proceeded slowly. By the mid-1870s, only half of southern children attended public schools.

In creating public school systems, the Reconstruction state governments faced a central question: would white and black children attend the same schools? Many blacks favored racially integrated schools. Southern white leaders, however, including many southern white Republicans, warned that integration would destroy the fledgling public school system by driving whites away. Only Florida, Louisiana, and South Carolina specified that schools not be segregated. However, no state enforced school integration, although some New Orleans public schools were racially mixed for several years. Similarly, most southern states set up separate black public colleges and universities, although South Carolina experimented, briefly and unsuccessfully, with integrating its university.

On balance, most blacks probably agreed with Frederick Douglass's newspaper that separate schools were "infinitely superior" to no public education. Some found other reasons to accept segregated schools: separate black schools gave a larger role to black parents, and they hired black teachers, who were beginning to graduate from the new black colleges.

Funding for the new schools was rarely adequate. They were funded largely through **property taxes,** and property-tax revenues declined during the 1870s as property values fell. Creating and operating two educational systems, one white and one black, was expensive. The division of limited funds posed an additional problem, and black schools almost always received less support per student than white schools. Despite their accomplishments, the segregated schools institutionalized discrimination.

scalawag Derogatory southern term for white southerners who aligned themselves with the Republican party.

property taxes Taxes paid by property owners according to the value of their property; often used in the United States to provide funding for local government and services.

♦ The Hampton Normal and Agricultural Institute was founded in 1868 with financial assistance from the Freedmen's Bureau and the American Missionary Association. Its purpose was to provide education for African Americans to prepare males for jobs in agriculture or industry, and to prepare women as homemakers. As a normal school, it also trained teachers. One of Hampton's most prominent graduates was Booker T. Washington, who attended shortly after this picture was taken around 1870. *Archival and Museum Collection, Hampton University.*

Reconstruction state governments also moved toward protection of equal rights in areas other than education. The federal occupation forces had canceled the black codes, and Congress had followed up with the Civil Rights Acts of 1866 and 1875. As Republicans gained control in the South, they often wrote into the new state constitutions prohibitions against discrimination and protections for civil rights. Some Reconstruction state governments enacted laws guaranteeing **equal access** to public transportation and public accommodations, but elsewhere efforts to pass equal access laws foundered on the opposition of southern white Republicans (scalawags). Like southern Democrats, scalawags often favored separate facilities for blacks. Such conflicts pointed up the internal divisions within the southern Republican party. Even when equal access laws were passed, they often were not enforced.

Railroad Development and Corruption

Republicans everywhere, not just in the South, sought to use the power of government to encourage economic growth and development. Efforts to promote economic development, in the North and South alike, often focused on encouraging railroad construction. In the South, some Reconstruction governments granted state lands to railroads, or lent them money, or committed the state's credit to **underwrite** bonds for construction. Sometimes they promoted railroads without adequate planning and without finding out whether companies were financially sound. Such efforts to promote railroad construction sometimes failed, as companies squandered their funds without building rail lines. During the 1870s, only 7,000 miles of new track were laid in the South, compared to 45,000 miles in the North—

equal access The right of any group to use a public facility, such as streetcars, as freely as all other groups in the society.

underwrite To assume financial responsibility for; in this case, to guarantee the purchase of bonds so that a project can go forward.

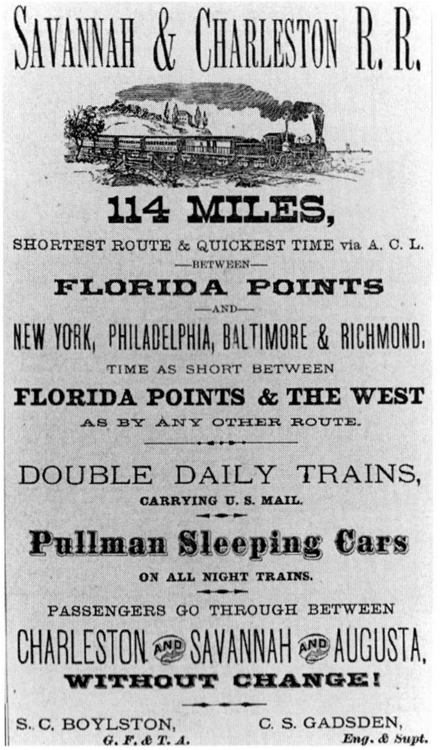

♦ During Reconstruction, state governments throughout the South tried to attract northern investments, especially for railroad construction, for they understood that economic development was crucial for creating greater economic opportunities. This advertisement appeared in Charleston in 1878. *South Carolina Historical Society.*

though that level of construction in the South was, in fact, a considerable accomplishment given the state of the postwar southern economy.

Railroad companies occasionally tried to secure favorable treatment by bribing public officials, and all too many officeholders—in the North, South, and West—accepted their offers. Given the reality of bribes in some places and the widespread favoritism that public officials nearly everywhere showed to railroads, revelations and allegations of corruption became staples in political campaigning from New York City to Mississippi to California.

Conditions in the South were especially ripe for political corruption, as government responsibilities expanded rapidly and created opportunities for the ambitious and unscrupulous. Reconstruction governments included many men—white and black—who had only modest holdings of their own and aspired to better things. One South Carolina legislator bluntly described his attitude toward electing a U.S. senator: "I was pretty hard up, and I did not care who the candidate was if I got two hundred dollars." Corruption was usually nonpartisan, but it often seemed especially prominent among Republicans because they held the most important offices. One Louisiana Republican claimed that "Corruption is the fashion," and charges of corruption became the fashion everywhere too as ambitious politicians sought to discredit their opponents. Still, in the midst of one of the most corrupt periods in the nation's history, some Reconstruction Republicans maintained reputations for honesty.

The End of Reconstruction

- What was the Mississippi Plan, and how was it related to the end of Reconstruction?
- What were the final outcomes of Reconstruction?

Most white southerners resisted the new social order that the conquering Yankees imposed on them. They created the black codes to maintain white supremacy and restore elements of a bound labor system. They used terrorism against the advocates of black rights. But instead of producing the results they hoped for, such resistance led Congress to pass still more severe terms for Reconstruction. This backlash drove some southern opponents of Reconstruction to rethink their strategy.

The "New Departure"

By 1869, some leading southern Democrats had abandoned their last-ditch resistance to change and had chosen instead to accept key Reconstruction measures and African-American suffrage. At the same time, they also tried to secure restoration of political rights for former Confederates. Behind this **New Departure** for southern Democrats lay the belief that continued resistance would cause more regional turmoil and would prolong federal intervention in state politics.

Sometimes southern Democrats supported conservative Republicans for state and local offices instead of members of their own party, hoping to defuse concern in Washington and dilute Radical influence in state government. This strategy was tried

New Departure A policy of cooperation with key Reconstruction measures that leading southern Democrats adopted in the hope of winning compromises favorable to their party.

first in Virginia, the last southern state to hold an election under its new constitution. There William Mahone, a former Confederate general, railroad promoter, and leading Democrat, forged a broad political coalition that accepted black suffrage. In 1869, Mahone's organization elected as governor a northern-born banker and moderate Republican. In this way, Mahone got state support for his railroad plans, and Virginia successfully avoided Radical Republican rule.

Similar **coalitions** of Democrats and moderate Republicans won in Tennessee in 1869 and in Missouri in 1870. Elsewhere leading Democrats also endorsed the New Departure, accepted black suffrage, and attacked Republicans more for raising taxes and increasing state spending than for their racial policies. Whenever possible they added charges of corruption. Such campaigns brought a positive response from many taxpayers, because southern tax rates had risen dramatically to support the new educational systems, subsidies for railroads, and other new programs. In 1870, Democrats won the governorship in Alabama and Georgia. For Georgia, that meant the effective end of Reconstruction.

The victories of so-called **Redeemers** and New Departure Democrats in 1869–1870 coincided with terrorist activity aimed at Republicans. The worst single incident occurred in 1872. A group of armed freedmen fortified the town of Colfax, Louisiana, to hold off Democrats suspected of planning to seize the county government. After a three-week siege, well-armed whites overcame the black defenders and killed 280 African Americans. Leading Democrats rarely endorsed such bloodshed, but they reaped political advantages from it.

The 1872 Election

The New Departure movement, at its peak in 1872, coincided with a division within the Republican party in the North. The Liberal Republican movement grew out several elements within the Republican party. Some were concerned that the Radicals had gone too far, especially with the Enforcement Acts, and had endangered federalism. Others opposed the protective tariff or favored civil service reform. All were appalled by the growing evidence of corruption in politics. Liberal Republicans soon found allies among Democrats by arguing against further Reconstruction measures.

Horace Greeley, editor of the New York *Tribune*, won the Liberal nomination for president. An ardent opponent of slavery before the Civil War, Greeley had given strong support to the Fourteenth and Fifteenth Amendments. But he had sometimes taken puzzling positions, including a willingness to let the South secede in 1860–1861. His unkempt appearance and whining voice conveyed little of a presidential image. One political observer described him as "honest, but . . . so conceited, fussy, and foolish that he damages every cause he wants to support."

Greeley had long ripped the Democrats in his newspaper columns. Even so, the Democrats made him their nominee in an effort to unite the forces opposing the re-election of Grant. Many voters saw the Democrats' action as pure opportunism, and Greeley alienated many northern Democrats by his preference for prohibiting the sale of alcohol. Grant won convincingly, carrying 56 percent of the vote and winning every northern state and ten of the sixteen southern and border states (see Map 16.1).

Redemption by Terror: The "Mississippi Plan"

As southern whites increasingly abandoned the Republicans in favor of New Departure Democrats, Black Reconstruction came to an end in several states. African Americans, however, maintained their Republican loyalties. The South polarized mostly along racial lines, and the elections of 1874 proved disastrous for Republicans. That year, Democrats won more than two-thirds of the South's seats in the House of Representatives and "redeemed" Alabama, Arkansas, and Texas.

Republican candidates in 1874 lost all across the North partly because of scandals within the Grant administration and partly because a major economic **depression** began in 1873, producing high unemployment. Before the 1874 elections, the House of Representatives included 194 Republicans and 92 Democrats. After the 1874 elections, Democrats outnumbered Republicans in the House by 169 to 109. Southern Republicans could no longer look to Congress for assistance, for the Democratic majority in

coalition An alliance, especially a temporary one of different people or groups.

Redeemers Southern Democrats who hoped to bring the Democratic party back into power and to suppress Black Reconstruction.

depression A period of drastic decline in a national or international economy, characterized by decreasing business activity, falling prices, and unemployment.

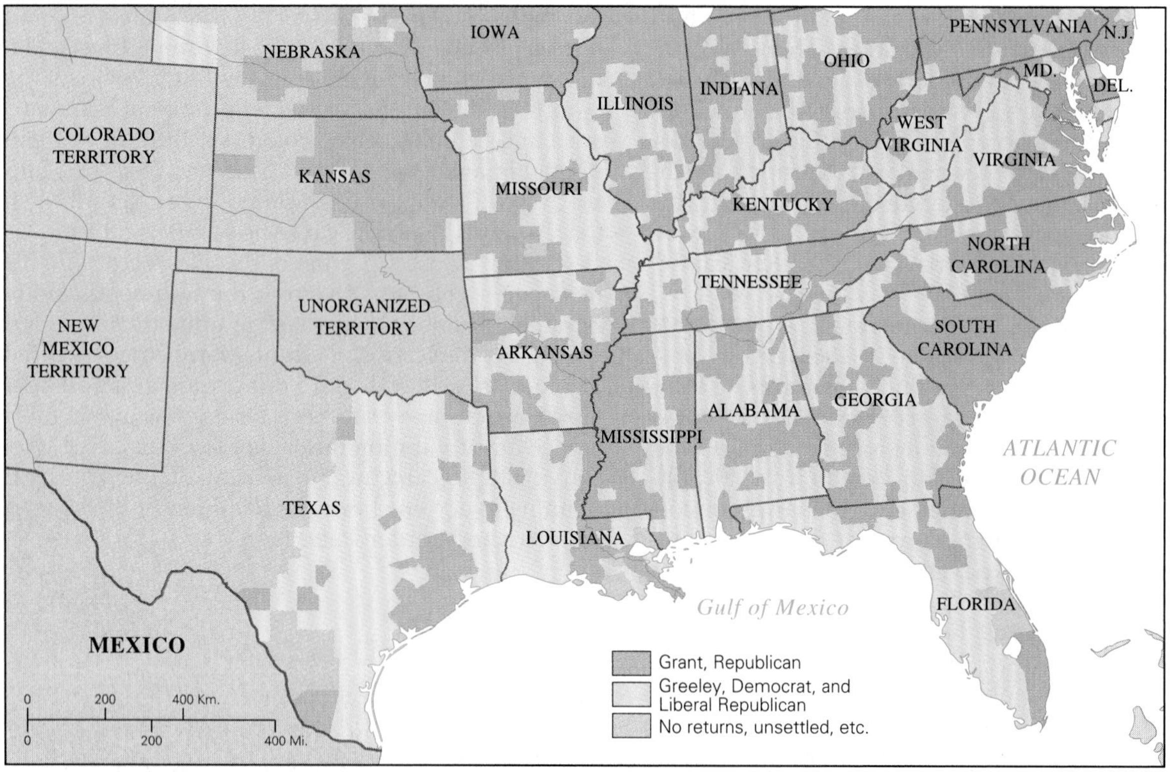

♦ **Map 16.1. Popular Vote for President in the South, 1872** This map shows which candidate carried each county in the southeastern United States in 1872. Looking at both this map and the chapter-opening map, you can see the relation between Republican voting and African-American population in some areas, as well as where the southern Republican party drew strong support from white voters.

the House of Representatives could now block legislation even though Republicans still controlled the Senate.

As had been the case before, terrorism against black Republicans and their remaining white allies also played a role in some victories by Democrats in 1874. The Klan had worn disguises and ridden at night, but in many places Democrats now openly formed rifle companies, put on red-flannel shirts (the most common article of clothing among southern males), and marched and drilled in public. In some areas, armed whites prevented African Americans from voting.

During 1875 in Mississippi, political violence reached such an extreme that the use of terror to overthrow Reconstruction became known as the **Mississippi Plan.** Democratic rifle clubs operated freely, breaking up Republican meetings and attacking Republican leaders in broad daylight. One black Mississippian described the election campaign of 1875 as "the most violent time we have ever seen." When Mississippi's carpetbagger governor, Adelbert Ames, requested federal help, President Grant hesitated, fearful that the southern Reconstruction governments had become so discredited that further federal military intervention might endanger the election prospects of Republican candidates in the Midwest.

The Democrats swept the Mississippi elections, winning four-fifths of the state legislature. When the legislature convened, it impeached and removed from office Alexander Davis, the black Republican lieutenant governor, on grounds no more serious than those brought against Andrew Johnson. The legislature then brought similar impeachment

Mississippi Plan The use of threats, violence, and lynching by Mississippi Democrats in 1875 to intimidate Republicans and bring the Democratic party to power.

charges against Governor Ames, who resigned and left the state. Ames had foreseen the result during the campaign when he wrote, "a revolution has taken place—by force of arms."

The Compromise of 1877

In 1876, on the centennial of American independence, the nation stumbled through a deeply troubled—and potentially dangerous—presidential election. As revelations of corruption grew in both North and South, the issue of reform took center stage. The Democratic party nominated Samuel J. Tilden, governor of New York, as its presidential candidate. A wealthy lawyer and businessman, Tilden had earned a reputation for reform by fighting political corruption in New York City. The Republicans also selected a reform candidate, **Rutherford B. Hayes,** a Civil War general and governor of Ohio. Hayes's unblemished reputation proved to be his greatest asset. Not well known outside Ohio, he was a candidate nobody could object to.

First election reports indicated a victory for Tilden (see Map 16.2). Most politicians assumed that Tilden would carry the border states and the South. He also secured majorities in crucial northern states, including New York, New Jersey, and Indiana. Tilden received 51 percent of the popular vote to 48 percent for Hayes. But in South Carolina, Florida, and Louisiana, the Republican party still controlled the counting and reporting of ballots. Charging **voting fraud** by Democrats in those states, Republican election boards rejected enough ballots so that the official count gave Hayes majorities in those three states and thus a one-vote margin of victory in the Electoral College.

Democrats cried fraud, and Democratic officials in all three states submitted their own versions of the vote count. Some Democrats vowed to see Tilden inaugurated by force if necessary, and some Democratic newspapers ran headlines that read "Tilden or War."

For the first time, Congress had to face the problem of disputed electoral votes that could decide the outcome of an election. To resolve the challenges, Congress created a fifteen-member commission: five senators, five representatives, and five Supreme Court justices. By party, the commission consisted of eight Republicans and seven Democrats. Initially, the balance was seven to seven with one independent from the Supreme Court, but he withdrew and a Republican replaced him.

Democrats and Republicans braced themselves for a potentially violent confrontation. However, as commission hearings droned on through January and into February 1877, a series of informal discussions took place across Washington among leading Republicans and Democrats. The result was often called the **Compromise of 1877.** Southern Democrats demanded **home rule,** by which they meant an end to federal intervention in southern politics. They also called for federal subsidies for railroad construction and waterways in the South. And they wanted one of their own as postmaster general, because that office held the key to most federal patronage. In return, southern Democrats were willing to abandon Tilden's claim to the White House if the commission ruled for Hayes.

Although the Compromise of 1877 was never set down in one place or agreed to by all parties, most of its conditions were met. By a straight party vote, the commission confirmed the election of Hayes. Soon after his peaceful inauguration, he ordered the last of the federal troops withdrawn from occupation duties in the South. The Radical era of a powerful federal government pledged to protect "equality before the law" for all citizens was over. The last three Republican state governments fell in 1877, completing the "Redemption" of the South. The Democrats, the self-described party of white supremacy, held sway in every southern state capital. One Radical journal bitterly concluded that African Americans had been forced "to relinquish the artificial right to vote for the natural right to live." In parts of the South thereafter, election fraud and violence became routine. One Mississippi judge acknowledged in 1890 that "since 1875 . . . we have been preserving the ascendancy of the white people by . . . stuffing ballot boxes, committing perjury and here and there in the state carrying the elections by fraud and violence."

Rutherford B. Hayes Ohio governor and former Union general who won the Republican nomination in 1876 and became president of the United States in 1877.

voting fraud Altering election results by illegal measures to bring about the victory of a particular candidate.

Compromise of 1877 Resolution of the disputed presidential election of 1876; it gave the presidency to the Republicans and made concessions to southern Democrats.

home rule Self-government; in this case, an end to federal intervention in the South.

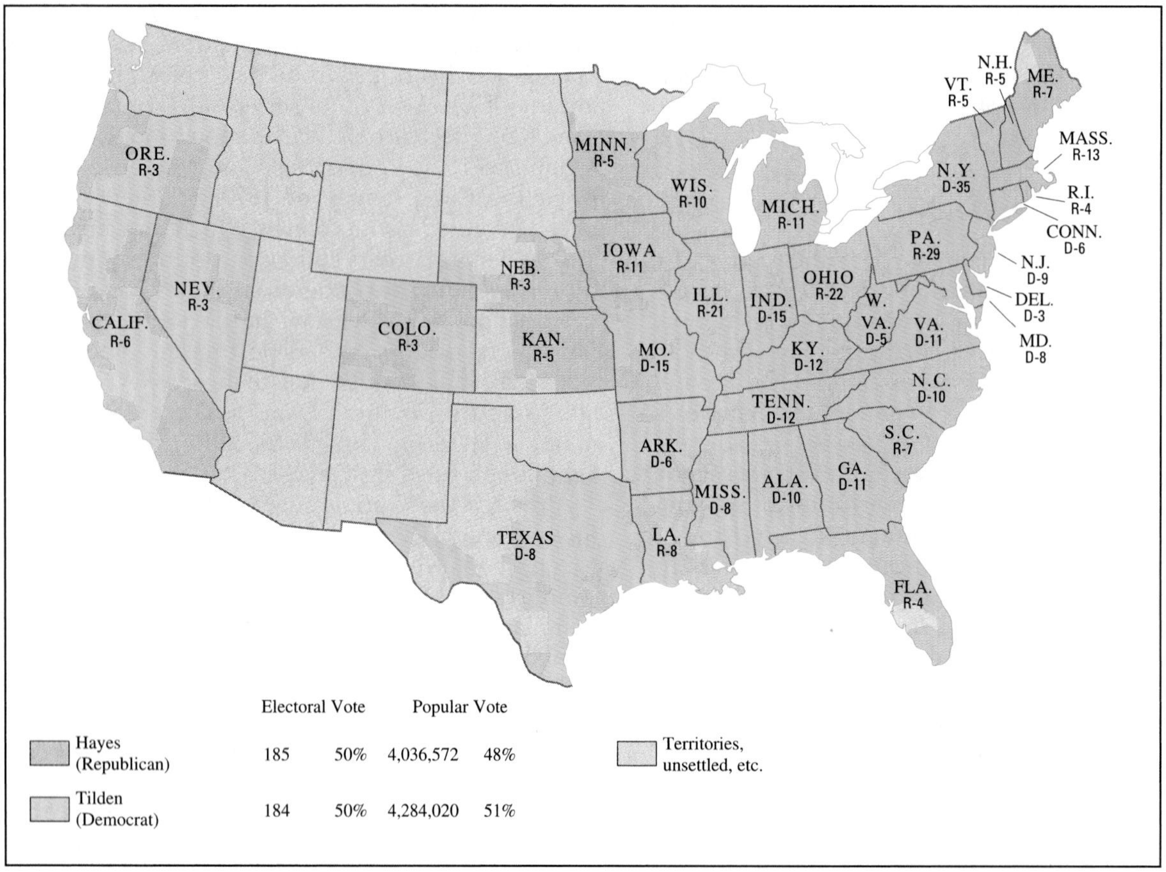

♦ **Map 16.2 Election of 1876** The end of Black Reconstruction in most of the South combined with Democratic gains in the North to give a popular majority to Samuel Tilden, the Democratic candidate. The electoral vote was disputed, however, and was ultimately resolved in favor of Rutherford B. Hayes, the Republican.

The Compromise of 1877 marked the end of Reconstruction. The war was more than ten years in the past, and the passions it had stirred had cooled. A major depression in the mid-1870s, unemployment and labor disputes, the growth of industry, the emergence of big business, and the economic development of the West (see Chapters 17 and 18) focused public attention, and the attention of Congress, on economic issues. In 1875, when Grant refused to use federal troops to protect black rights, he declared that "the whole public are tired out with these . . . outbreaks in the South." He was quoted widely and with approval throughout the North.

By then, southern Democrats had mounted a campaign to persuade northerners—on paltry evidence—that carpetbaggers and scalawags were corrupt and self-serving, manipulating black voters to keep themselves in power; that all African-American officeholders were ignorant and illiterate and could not participate in politics without guidance by whites; and that southern Democrats wanted only to establish honest self-government. The truth of the situation seemed to make little difference. Northern Democrats had always opposed Reconstruction and readily adopted the southern Democrats' version of reality.

Such one-sided portrayals found growing acceptance among other northerners too, for many people in the North had shown their own racial bias when they resisted black suffrage and kept their public schools segregated. Some Republicans, to be certain, kept the faith of their abolitionist and Radical forebears and hoped the federal government might again protect black rights. The majority of the Republican party, however, condemned violations of black rights but showed little interest in taking action to prevent such outrages.

After Reconstruction

Southern Democrats read the events of 1877 as their permit to establish new systems of politics and race relations. Most Redeemers set out to reduce taxes, to dismantle Reconstruction legislation and agencies, to take political influence away from black citizens, and eventually to reshape the South's legal system to establish African Americans as subordinate and to restrict the rights of laborers. They also began the process of turning the South into a one-party region, a situation that reached its fullest development around 1900 and persisted until the 1950s and in some areas later.

Although voting and officeholding by African Americans did not cease with Redemption, the political context changed profoundly once they lost federal enforcement of their rights. The threat of violence from nightriders and the potential for economic retaliation by landlords and merchants sharply reduced independent action by African Americans. Black political leaders increasingly recognized that efforts to mobilize black voters posed dangers to both candidates and voters, and they concluded that their political survival depended on favors from influential white Republicans or even from Democratic leaders. The public schools survived, segregated and underfunded, but important both as a symbol and as a real opportunity to learn. Many Reconstruction-era laws remained on the books, and blacks in many places continued to be admitted to theaters, bars and restaurants, and hotels and to receive equal seating on streetcars and railroads.

Not until the 1890s did black disfranchisement and thoroughgoing racial segregation become widely embedded in southern law (see pages 584–585). For a time, from the mid-1870s to the late 1890s, the South lived an uneasy compromise: African Americans had certain constitutional rights, but white supremacy had been established by force of arms, and blacks exercised their rights at the sufferance of the dominant whites. Such a compromise bore the seeds of future conflict.

For generations after 1877, Reconstruction was held up as a failure. Although far from accurate, the southern version of Reconstruction—that conniving carpetbaggers and scalawags had manipulated ignorant freedmen—appealed to the racial bias of many white Americans in the North and South alike, and it gained widespread acceptance among popular novelists, journalists, and historians. William A. Dunning, for example, fully endorsed that interpretation in his history of Reconstruction, published in 1907. Thomas Dixon's popular novel *The Clansman* (1905) inspired the highly influential film *The Birth of a Nation* (1915). Historically inaccurate and luridly racist, the book and the movie portrayed Ku Klux Klan members as heroes who rescued the white South, and especially white southern women, from domination and debauchery at the hands of depraved freedmen and carpetbaggers.

Against this pattern stood some of the first black historians, notably George Washington Williams, a Union army veteran whose two-volume history of African Americans appeared in 1882. *Black Reconstruction in America,* by **W. E. B. Du Bois,** appeared in 1935. Both presented fully the role that African Americans played in the biracial southern Republican party of the Reconstruction era. Both pointed to the accomplishments of the Reconstruction state governments and tried to rescue the reputations of black leaders from the abuse that had been heaped on them. Not until the civil rights movement of the 1950s and 1960s, however, did large numbers of American historians begin to reconsider their interpretation of Reconstruction.

Historians today recognize that Reconstruction was not the failure that had earlier been claimed. The creation of public schools was but the most important of the changes in southern life produced by the Reconstruction state governments. At a federal level, the Fourteenth and Fifteenth Amendments eventually provided the constitutional leverage to restore the principle of equality before the law that so concerned the Radicals. Historians also recognize that Reconstruction collapsed partly because of internal flaws, partly because of divisions within the national Republican party, and partly because of the political terrorism unleashed in the South and the refusal of the North to commit the force required to protect the constitutional rights of African Americans.

W.E.B. Du Bois Prominent African-American sociologist and historian and civil rights activist of the early 20th century.

SUMMARY

Expectations
Constraints
Choices
Outcomes

At the end of the Civil War, the nation held conflicting *expectations* and faced difficult *choices* regarding the future of the defeated South and the future of the freed people. Committed to an end to slavery, President Lincoln nevertheless *chose* a lenient approach to restoring states to the Union, partly to persuade southerners to accept emancipation and abandon the Confederacy. When Johnson became president, he continued Lincoln's approach.

The end of slavery brought new *expectations* for all African Americans, whether they had been slaves or not. Taking advantage of the new *choices* that freedom opened, they tried to create independent lives for themselves, and they developed social institutions that helped to define black communities. Few were able to acquire land of their own—a significant *constraint* on their economic *choices*—and most became either wage laborers or sharecroppers. White southerners also experienced economic dislocation, and some also became sharecroppers. Most white southerners also expected to keep African Americans in a subordinate role through black codes and violence.

In reaction against the black codes and violence, Congress *chose* to wrest control over Reconstruction from President Johnson and passed the Civil Rights Act of 1866, the Fourteenth Amendment, and the Reconstruction Acts of 1867. An attempt to remove Johnson from the presidency was unsuccessful. Additional federal Reconstruction measures included the Fifteenth Amendment, laws directed against the Ku Klux Klan, and the Civil Rights Act of 1875. One *outcome* of these measures was to strengthen the federal government at the expense of the states.

Enfranchised freedmen, white and black northerners who now moved to the South, and some southern whites created a southern Republican party that governed most southern states for a time. The most lasting contribution of these state governments was the creation of public school systems. Like government officials elsewhere in the nation, however, some southerners fell prey to corruption.

In the late 1860s, many southern Democrats chose a "New Departure": they grudgingly accepted some features of Reconstruction and sought to recapture control of state governments. The 1876 presidential election was very close and hotly disputed, but key Republicans and Democrats in both North and South *chose* to compromise. The Compromise of 1877 permitted Hayes to take office and brought Reconstruction to an end. Without further federal protection for their civil rights and political activities, African Americans faced severe *constraints* in exercising those rights fully. Terrorism, violence, and even death became the lot of African Americans who chose to challenge their subordinate social role. Thus the *outcome* of Reconstruction in the South was white supremacy in politics and government, the economy, and social relations.

SUGGESTED READINGS

David Donald. *Charles Sumner and the Rights of Man* (1970).

A good account not just of this important Radical leader but of important Reconstruction issues.

W. E. B. Du Bois. *Black Reconstruction in America: An Essay Toward a History of the Part Which Black Folk Played in the Attempt to Reconstruct Democracy in America, 1860–1880* (1935; reprint, 1969).

Written more than a half-century ago, Du Bois's book is still useful for both information and insights.

Eric Foner. *Reconstruction: America's Unfinished Revolution, 1863–1877* (1988).

The most thorough of recent treatments, incorporating insights from many historians who have written on the subject during the past forty years. Also available in a condensed version.

Leon F. Litwack. *Been in the Storm So Long: The Aftermath of Slavery* (1979).

An account that focuses especially on the experience of the freed people.

William S. McFeely. *Frederick Douglass* (1991).

A highly readable biography of the most prominent black political leader of the nineteenth century.

C. Vann Woodward. *Reunion and Reaction: The Compromise of 1877 and the End of Reconstruction,* rev. ed. (1956).

The classic account of the Compromise of 1877.

INDUSTRIALIZATION, 1865–1900 After the Civil War, manufacturing expanded significantly, especially in the Northeast. This map indicates major types of manufacturing as of 1900 and the location of natural resources that contributed to industrialization. Some of these natural resources were not exploited until after 1900.

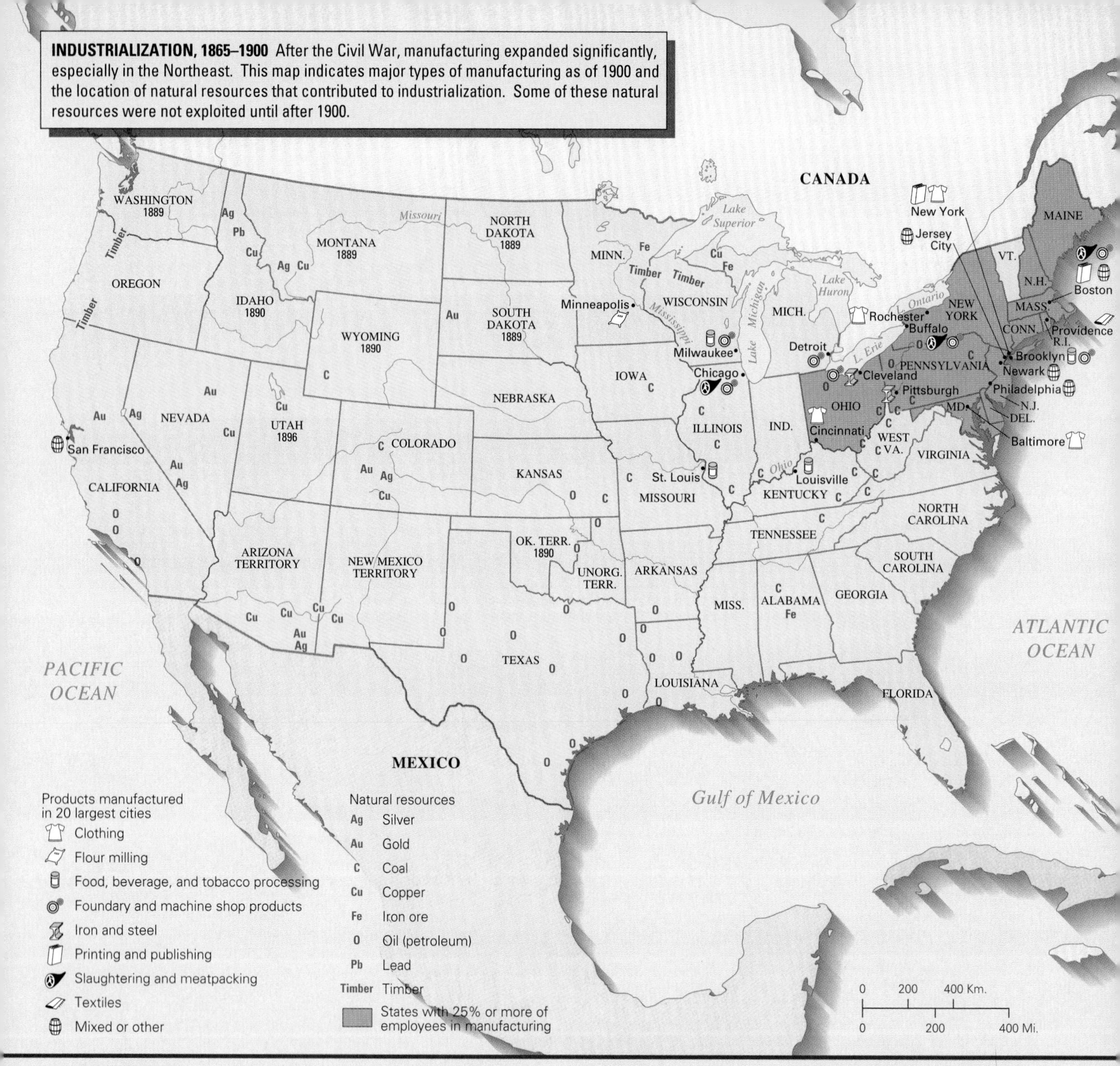

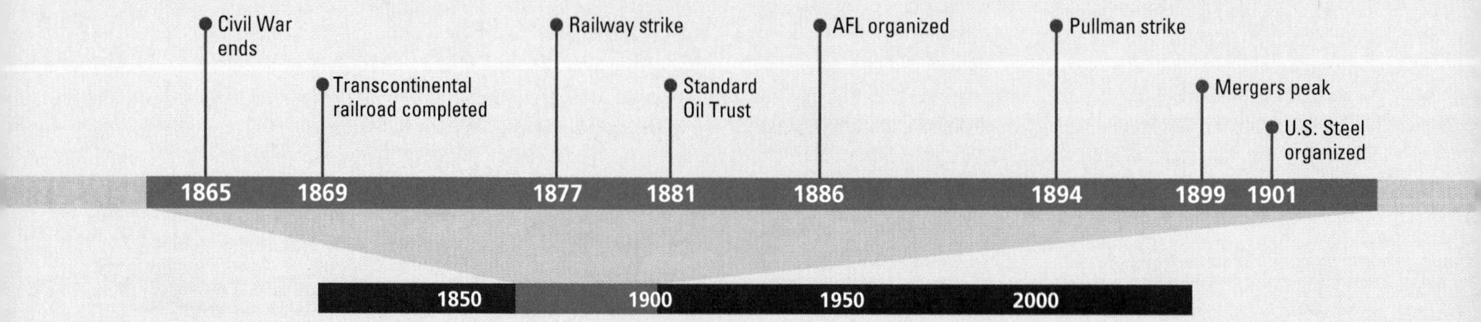

CHAPTER 17

Survival of the Fittest: Entrepreneurs and Workers in Industrial America, 1865–1900

Foundation for Industrialization

- After the Civil War, what conditions may have led Americans to expect economic growth?
- How did federal policymakers choose to encourage economic growth in the late nineteenth century?

Railroads and Economic Growth

- After the Civil War, what constraints did railroad entrepreneurs and investment bankers face?
- What choices did they make to overcome those constraints?
- What was the result for the nation's transportation system?

Entrepreneurs and Industrial Transformation

- How did technology and prevailing business practices define entrepreneurs' expectations in the late nineteenth century?
- How did Carnegie and Morgan choose to deal with competition?
- How did choices by Carnegie, Rockefeller, Edison, and Morgan change the nature of American business?

Workers in Industrial America

- How did the expectations about economic mobility portrayed by Horatio Alger compare with the realities of workers' lives in the late nineteenth century?
- How did industrialization transform the nature of work and expectations about work?

The Varieties of Labor Organization and Action, 1865–1900

- How did the expectations of American workers who joined craft unions compare with those who chose organizations like the Knights of Labor?
- How successful were the various types of labor organizations in the late nineteenth century? What choices made some more successful than others?

The Nation Transformed

- How did Americans respond to the transformation of the economy?

INTRODUCTION

E xpectations
C onstraints
C hoices
O utcomes

In January 1901, 65-year-old Andrew Carnegie used a blunt pencil to write several lines on a sheet of paper. He handed the paper to his business associate, Charles Schwab, who delivered it to J. P. Morgan. Morgan glanced at it and murmured, "I accept this price." Thereby did Carnegie sell his steel company—the nation's largest—for $480 million. Thereby did Morgan—the nation's most prominent banker—acquire the central element for his plan to create the United States Steel Corporation, the first corporation in the world to be capitalized at more than a billion dollars.

Carnegie had come a long way since his poverty-stricken parents had brought him to America as immigrants from Scotland. Morgan had started with much more, but he too had moved far in his lifetime. Both men, nevertheless, carried out one of the most extraordinary sales in American history in a manner that simple country shopkeepers would have recognized. Such behavior was increasingly rare in the complex and fast-changing business world.

By the time Morgan accepted Carnegie's scribbled offer, the economy of the United States had been dramatically and profoundly transformed from what it was during the Civil War, when both men had entered business. Back then, more than half of all American workers toiled in agriculture. And anyone contemplating the prospects for manufacturing would have noted many potential *constraints:* a poorly developed transportation system, limited amounts of capital, an unsophisticated system for mobilizing capital, and a potential shortage of workers. Some, however, would have pointed to the great potential evident in America's vast natural resources and skilled workers.

A generation later, much of that potential had been realized, and the United States stood as a major industrial power. The changes in the nation's economy far exceeded the wildest *expectations* of Americans living in 1865. Many *expected* continued economic growth, but few could have imagined that steel production could increase a thousand times by 1900, or that railroads could operate nearly six times as many miles of track, or that farms could triple their harvests. Few too could have *expected* the torrent of inventions that transformed many people's lives—adding machines, telephones, electric lights, electric streetcars, electric sewing machines, automobiles, motion pictures. By the 1890s, rapid and far-reaching change had become an ingrained part of Americans' *expectations.*

These economic changes were the result of *choices* made by many individuals—where to seek work, where to invest, whether to expand production, how to react to a business competitor, whom to trust. Among the many *choices* Americans made, however, two stand out: competition and cooperation.

As the industrial economy took off, many entrepreneurs found themselves in a love-hate relationship with competition. Carnegie loved it, expressing the *expectation* that it "insures the survival of the fittest" and "insures the future progress of the race" by producing the highest quality, largest quantity, and lowest prices. Morgan, in contrast, saw competition as the single most unpredictable factor in the economy and as a serious *constraint* on economic progress. Carnegie's zeal for competition was, in fact, unusual. Although many entrepreneurs paid lip service to the idea of the "survival of the fittest," most resembled Morgan more than Carnegie: they loved competition in the abstract but preferred to find alternatives to it in the reality of their own business *choices.*

Americans also found themselves making *choices* regarding cooperation. Individualism was deeply entrenched in the American psyche, yet the increasing complexity of the economy presented repeated opportunities for cooperation. Entrepreneurs sometimes *chose* to cooperate by dividing a market rather than competing in it. Wage earners sometimes *chose* to join with other workers in standing up to their employer and demanding better wages or working conditions. In the process, some workers found themselves not just cooperating in a union but even questioning capitalism, the economic system that paid their wages. The *outcome* of these many *choices* was the industrialization of the nation and the transformation of the economy.

CHRONOLOGY

The Growth of Industry

1850s Development of Bessemer and Kelly steel-making processes

1861 Protective tariff

1862 Homestead Act
Land-Grant College Act
Pacific Railroad Act

1865 Civil War ends

1866 National Labor Union organized

1869 First transcontinental railroad completed
Knights of Labor founded

1870 Standard Oil incorporated
Patent Office registers the first trademark

1872 Montgomery Ward opens its mail-order business

1873–1878 Depression

1875 Andrew Carnegie opens nation's largest steel plant

1876 Invention of the telephone

1877 Great Strike
Reconstruction ends

1879 Invention of the light bulb
Henry George's *Progress and Poverty*

1880s Railroad expansion and consolidation

1881 Standard Oil Trust organized
United Brotherhood of Carpenters and Joiners organized

1882–1885 Recession

1886 Last major railroad coverts to the standard gauge
First Sears, Roebuck and Co. catalogue
Peak membership in Knights of Labor
Haymarket Square bombing
American Federation of Labor founded

1887 American Sugar Refining Company formed

1890–1891 Recession

1892 Homestead strike

1893–1897 Depression

1893 World's Columbian Exposition opens

1894 Pullman strike

1901 United States Steel organized

1902 International Harvester organized

Foundation for Industrialization

• After the Civil War, what conditions may have led Americans to expect economic growth?

• How did federal policymakers choose to encourage economic growth in the late nineteenth century?

By 1865, conditions in the United States were ripe for rapid industrialization. A wealth of natural resources, a capable work force, an agricultural base that produced enough food for a large urban population, and favorable government policies laid the foundation.

Resources, Skills, and Capital

At the end of the Civil War, **entrepreneurs** could draw on vast and virtually untapped natural resources. Americans had long since plowed the fertile farmland of the Midwest (where corn and wheat dominated) and the South (where cotton was king).

entrepreneur A person who organizes and manages a business enterprise, especially one that involves an element of risk.

♦ In the popular imagination of most Americans in the late nineteenth century, the West was a vast and unpopulated storehouse of riches—fertile agricultural land, timber waiting to be cut, minerals there for the taking. Such attitudes were encouraged by popular prints such as this lithograph by Currier and Ives, entitled "Westward the Course of Empires Takes Its Way" (1868), depicting ambitious pioneers moving west. In such imaginative depictions, there was rarely any indication that, in fact, the West was already home to many American Indians and Mexican-Americans. *Museum of the City of New York.*

At the end of the war, they had just begun to farm the rich soils of Minnesota, Nebraska, Kansas, Iowa, and the Dakotas, as well as the productive valleys of California. Through the central part of the nation stretched vast grasslands that received too little rain for farming but were well suited for grazing. The Pacific Northwest, the western Great Lakes region, and the South all held extensive forests untouched by the lumberman's saw.

The nation was also rich in mineral resources. Before the Civil War, the iron industry had become centered in Pennsylvania as a result of easy access to iron ore and coal. Pennsylvania was also the site of early efforts to tap underground pools of crude oil. The California gold rush, beginning in 1848, had drawn many people west, and some of them had found great riches. Reserves of other minerals lay unused and, in most cases, undiscovered at the end of the war, including iron ore in Michigan, Minnesota, and Alabama; coal throughout the Ohio Valley and in Wyoming and Colorado; oil in the Midwest, Oklahoma, Texas, Louisiana, southern California, and Alaska; gold or silver in Nevada, Colorado, and Alaska; and copper in Michigan, Montana, Utah, and Arizona. Many of these natural resources were far from population centers, and their use awaited adequate transportation facilities. Exploitation of some of these resources also required new technologies.

Like natural resources, the work force and the skills and experience of workers were important for economic growth. In the 1790s and early nineteenth century, New Englanders had developed manufacturing systems based on **interchangeable parts** (first used for manufacturing guns and clocks) and factories for producing cotton cloth. These accomplishments gave them a reputation for "Yankee ingenuity"—a talent for devising new tools and inventive methods. Such skills and problem-solving abilities,

interchangeable parts Parts that are identical and can be substituted for each other.

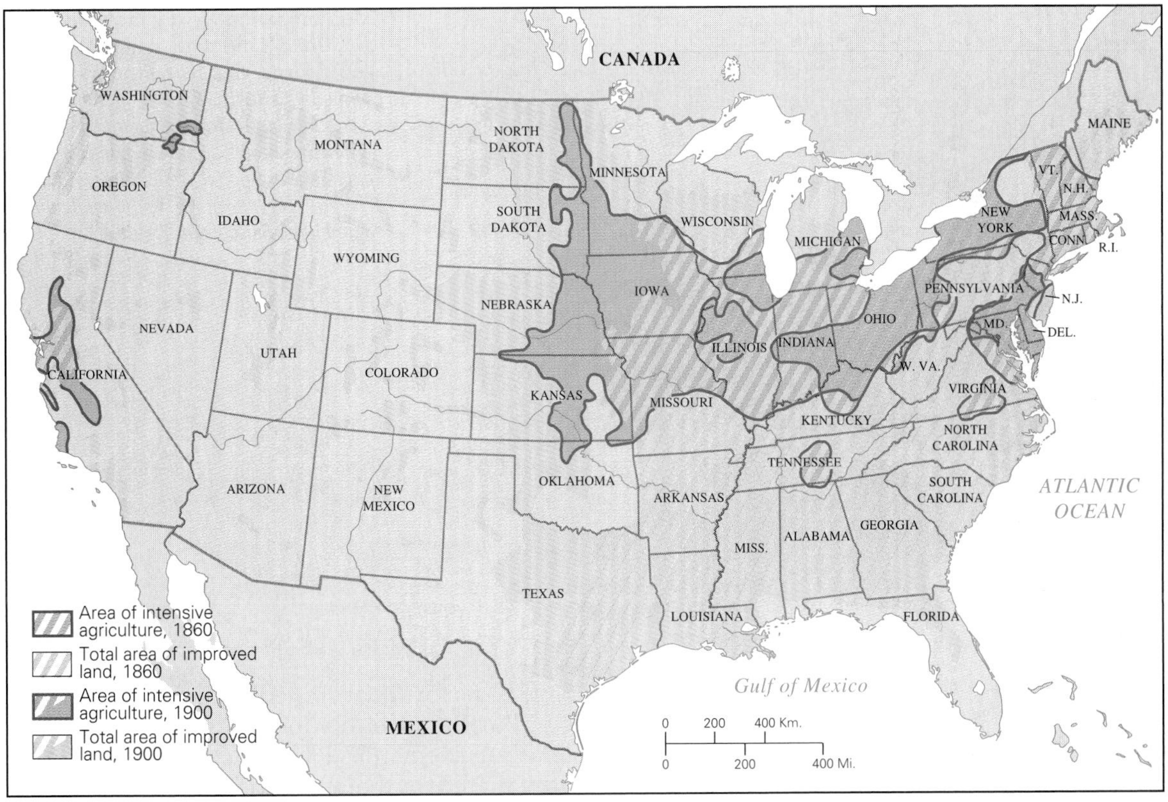

♦ **MAP 17.1 Expansion of Agriculture, 1860–1900** The amount of improved farmland more than doubled during these forty years. This map shows how agricultural expansion came in two ways—first, western lands were brought under cultivation; second, in other areas, especially the Midwest, land was cultivated much more intensely than before.

however, were not limited to New England. They were, in fact, essential to the emergence of large-scale manufacturing nearly everywhere, because most early factories relied on skilled **artisans** to direct less-skilled workers in assembling products.

Another crucial element for industrialization was capital and institutions that could mobilize capital. These too had developed before the Civil War. During the years before the war, capital became centered in the seaport cities of the Northeast—Boston, New York, and Philadelphia, especially—where prosperous merchants had invested their profits in banks and factories. Banks were important instruments for mobilizing capital. Before the Civil War, some bankers had begun to specialize in arranging financing for large-scale enterprises, and some of them had opened permanent branch offices in Britain to tap sources of capital there. **Stock exchanges** had also developed long before the Civil War as important institutions for raising capital for new ventures.

The Transformation of Agriculture

The expanding economy of the nineteenth century rested on a productive agricultural base. Improved transportation—canals early in the nineteenth century and railroads later—speeded the expansion of agriculture by making it possible to move large amounts of agricultural produce over long distances. Up to 1865, farmers had developed 407 million acres. During the next thirty-five years, this acreage more than doubled, to 841 million acres. Map 17.1 indicates where this expansion occurred.

artisan A skilled worker, whether self-employed or working for wages.

stock exchange A place where people buy and sell stocks (shares in the ownership of companies); stockholders may participate in election of the company's directors and share in the company's profits.

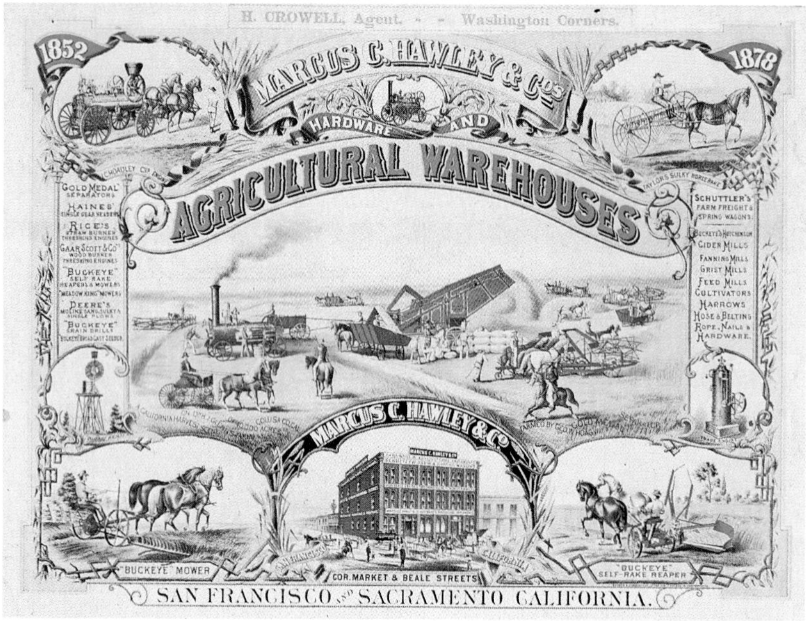

♦ Mechanization greatly increased the amount of land that an individual could farm. This 1878 lithograph depicts a California crew setting a world's record for the amount of wheat harvested in a single day. *Department of Special Collections, F. Hal Higgins Library of Agricultural Technology, University of California, Davis.*

The federal government contributed to the rapid settlement of Kansas, Nebraska, the Dakotas, and Minnesota through the **Homestead Act of 1862,** a leading example of the Republican party's commitment to using federal landholdings to speed economic development. Under this act, any person could receive free as much as 160 acres (a quarter of a square mile) of government land by building a house, living on the land for five years, and farming it. Between 1862 and 1890, 48 million acres passed from government ownership to private hands in this way. Other federally owned land could be purchased for as little as $1.25 per acre, and much more was purchased than was acquired free under the Homestead Act.

Production of leading commercial crops increased more rapidly than the overall expansion of farming. The total number of acres in farmland doubled from 1866 to 1900, but the number of acres planted in corn, wheat, and cotton more than tripled. New farming methods pushed up the harvests even more—corn by 264 percent, wheat by 252 percent, and cotton by 383 percent. Through these years, farm output increased more than twice as much as the population did.

As production of major crops rose, prices for them fell. Corn sold for 66 cents per bushel in 1866 then fell steadily to its lowest point, 21 cents, in 1896. Wheat prices fell too, from $2.06 per bushel in 1866 to a low of 49 cents in 1894. Cotton prices followed the same trend, from 9.7 cents per pound in 1876, to 8.39 cents in 1885, to 4.6 cents in 1894.

Several factors contributed to the decline in farm prices, but the most obvious was that supply rose faster than demand. Production increased more rapidly than both the population (which largely determined the demand within the nation) and the demand from other countries. According to economic theory, oversupply causes prices to fall, and falling prices lead producers to reduce their output. When American farmers received less for their crops, however, they raised more in an effort to maintain the same level of income. To increase their harvests, they bought fertilizers and new, elaborate machinery. Between 1870 and 1890, the amount of fertilizer consumed in the nation more than quadrupled.

New machinery especially affected the production of grain crops, greatly increasing the amount of land one person could farm. A single farmer with a hand-held scythe and cradle, for example, could harvest 2 acres of wheat in a day. Using the McCormick reaper (first produced in 1849), a single farmer and a team of horses could harvest 2 acres in an hour. For other crops too, a person with modern machinery could farm two or three times as much land as a farmer fifty years before.

Homestead Act of 1862 Law passed by Congress in 1862 that promised ownership of 160 acres of public land to any citizen who lived on and cultivated the land for five years.

The growth of agriculture affected other parts of the economy. The expansion of farming stimulated the farm equipment industry and, in turn, the iron and steel industry. The large volume of agricultural exports—cotton, tobacco, wheat, meat—spurred oceanic shipping and shipbuilding, and increased shipbuilding also increased demand for iron and steel. Railroads played a crucial role in the expansion and commercialization of agriculture by carrying farm products to distant markets and transporting fertilizer and machinery from factories (usually in distant cities) to farming regions.

The Impact of War and New Government Policies

At the end of the Civil War, many conditions were ripe for the emergence of a manufacturing economy. At the time, nearly three times as many Americans worked in agriculture as in manufacturing. Most manufacturing was small in scale and served people nearby—a shop with a few workers who made barrels or a shop with a half-dozen employees who built farm wagons. The war encouraged some entrepreneurs to deliver military supplies to distant parts of the nation, and some of them now sought to develop similar business patterns in peacetime. At the end of the war too, some people found themselves looking for places to invest their wartime profits. In the short run, by diverting labor and capital into war production, the Civil War may have slowed an expansion of manufacturing already under way. Still, the war brought important changes in the experience and expectations of some entrepreneurs. At the same time, new government policies encouraged a more rapid rate of economic growth in general, and the more rapid development of manufacturing in particular.

When Republicans took command of the federal government in 1861, the South seceded in reaction to the new administration's opposition to slavery, and secession produced the Civil War. While the Republicans made war against the Confederacy, abolished slavery, and undertook Reconstruction, they also made policy choices intended to stimulate economic growth. First came a new **protective tariff,** passed in 1861. The tariff increased the price of imports to equal or exceed the price of American-made goods in order to protect American-made products from foreign competition. Republicans expected the tariff to stimulate investment in manufacturing.

New federal land policies also stimulated economic growth. At the beginning of the Civil War, the federal government claimed more than a billion acres of land as federal property—the **public domain**—more than half of the land area of the nation. The Republicans chose to use this land to encourage economic development in a variety of ways, including free land for farmers, beginning with the Homestead Act (1862). Recognizing the key role of higher education in economic growth, the **Land-Grant College Act** (1862) gave federal land to each state (excluding those that had seceded) for the state to sell or otherwise use to raise the funds to establish a public university, which was required to provide education in engineering and agriculture and to train military officers. Also in 1862, Congress approved a land grant for the first transcontinental railroad, and more land grants to railroads followed.

Railroads and Economic Growth

- After the Civil War, what constraints did railroad entrepreneurs and investment bankers face?
- What choices did they make to overcome those constraints?
- What was the result for the nation's transportation system?

To many Americans of the late nineteenth century, nothing symbolized change so effectively as a locomotive—a huge, powerful, noisy, rapidly moving machine. Railroads set much of the pace for economic expansion after the Civil War. Growth of the rail network stimulated industries that supplied materials for railroad construction and operation—especially steel and coal—and industries that needed railroads to connect them to the emerging national economy. Railroad companies also came to symbolize "big business"—huge corporations with a life and personality of their own—and some Americans began to fear their power.

protective tariff A tax placed on imported goods for the purpose of raising the price of imports as high as or higher than the prices of the same item produced within the nation.

public domain All land owned by the federal government.

Land-Grant College Act Law passed by Congress in 1862 that gave states land to use to raise money to establish public universities that were to offer courses in engineering and agriculture and to train military officers.

♦ In his novel *The Octopus* (1901), Frank Norris described not just the physical power of the railroad, but also its economic and political prowess: "The galloping terror of steam and steel, with its single eye, cyclopean, red, shooting from horizon to horizon, symbol of a vast power, huge and terrible; the leviathan with tentacles of steel, to oppose which meant to be ground to instant destruction beneath the clashing wheels." This Currier and Ives lithograph from 1863, entitled "The Lightning Express Trains," captures some of that sense of power. *Museum of the City of New York.*

Railroad Expansion

At the end of the Civil War, the lack of a national rail network posed a significant constraint on economic development. Railroad companies operated on tracks of varying **gauges,** which made the transfer of railcars from one line to another impossible. Thus freight had to be moved by hand or wagon from the cars of one line to those of another. Few bridges crossed major rivers. Until 1869, no railroad connected the eastern half of the country to the booming Pacific coast region. Every route between the Atlantic and Pacific coasts required more than a month and posed serious discomfort and often outright danger: a sea voyage around the storm-tossed tip of South America; or a boat trip to Central America, then transit over mountains and through malaria-infested jungles to the Pacific, and then another boat trip up the Pacific coast; or a seemingly endless overland journey by train, riverboat, and stagecoach.

By the 1880s, all the elements were finally in place for a national rail network. The first transcontinental rail line was completed in 1869, connecting California to Omaha, Nebraska, and ultimately to eastern cities. Within the next fifteen years, three more rail lines linked the Pacific coast to the eastern half of the nation, and a fourth was completed in 1893. Between 1865 and 1890, railroads grew from 35,000 miles of track to 167,000 miles (see Map 17.2). By the mid-1880s, most major rivers had been bridged. Companies had replaced many iron rails with steel ones, allowing them to haul heavier loads. New inventions increased the speed, carrying capacity, and efficiency of trains. In 1886, the last major lines converted to a standard gauge, making it possible to transfer railcars from one line to another simply by throwing a switch. This rail network encouraged entrepreneurs to think in terms of a national economic system in which raw materials and finished products might move easily from one region to another.

gauge The distance between the rails making up the tracks.

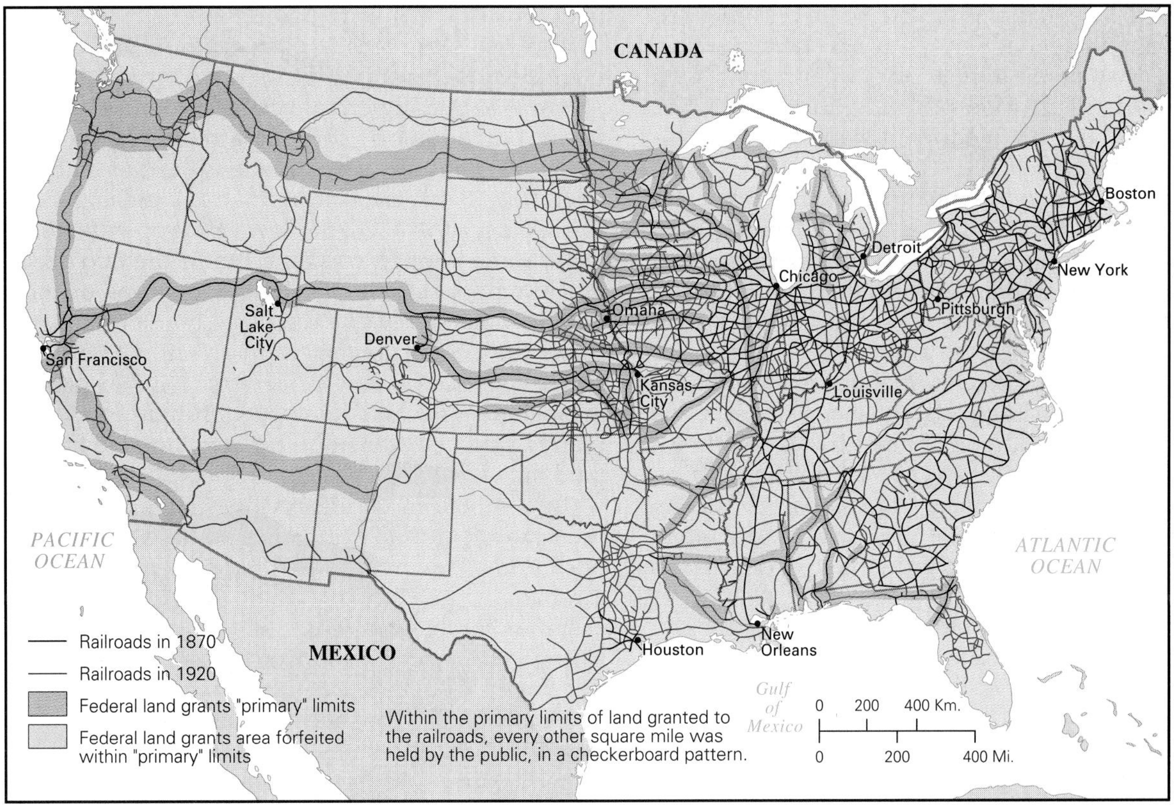

♦ **MAP 17.2 Railroad Expansion and Railroad Land Grants** Post–Civil War railroad expansion produced the transportation base for an industrial economy. In the West, federal land grants encouraged railroad construction. Within a grant, railroads received every other square mile. Land could be forfeited if construction did not meet the terms of the grant legislation.

Railroads, especially in the West, expanded with generous assistance from government. The first transcontinental rail line had benefited from the **Pacific Railway Act of 1862.** Congress had provided the Union Pacific and Central Pacific companies not only with sizable loans but also with 10 square miles of the public domain for every mile of track laid—an amount that was doubled in a subsequent act in 1864. By 1871, Congress had authorized some seventy railroad land grants, involving 128 million acres—more than one-tenth of the entire public domain, an area approximately equal to Colorado and Wyoming together. Most railroads sold their land to raise capital for railroad operations. By encouraging farmers, companies, or organizations to develop the land, railroad companies tried to build up the economies along their tracks and thereby to extend the demand for them to haul supplies to new settlers and carry their products (wheat, cattle, lumber, ore) to market.

Railroads: Model for Big Business

The expansion of railroads created the potential for a nationwide market, stimulated the economic development of the West, and created a demand for iron, steel, locomotives, and similar products. Railroad companies also provided an organizational model for newly developing industrial enterprises.

Pacific Railway Act Law passed by Congress in 1862 that gave loans and land to the Central Pacific and Union Pacific railroad companies to subsidize construction of a railroad between Omaha and the Pacific coast.

Because of their large size, they often encountered problems of scale that few companies had faced before but that other industrial entrepreneurs soon had to address. Not surprisingly, businesses that came along later often adopted solutions that railroads first developed.

Railroad companies required a much higher degree of coordination and long-range planning than most businesses up to that time. Earlier companies typically operated at a single location, but railroads functioned over long distances. They had to keep up numerous maintenance and repair facilities and maintain many stations to receive and discharge both freight and passengers. Financial transactions carried on over hundreds of miles by scores of employees required a centralized accounting office. One result was development of a company bureaucracy of clerks, accountants, managers, and agents. Railroads became training grounds for administrators, some of whom later entered other industries. Indeed, the experience of the railroads helped to define the meaning of business administration when it began to be taught in colleges in the early twentieth century.

Railroads required far more capital than most manufacturing concerns. In 1875, the largest steel furnaces in the world cost $741,000; at the same time, the Pennsylvania Railroad was capitalized at $400 million. Even railroads that received government subsidies required a large amount of private capital—and Congress gave out the last federal land grant in 1871. Private capital and support from state and local governments underwrote the enormous railroad expansion of the 1880s. The railroads' huge appetite for capital made them the first American businesses to seek investors on a nationwide and international scale. Those who invested their money could choose to buy either stocks or **bonds.** Sales of railroad stocks provided the major activity for the New York Stock Exchange through the second half of the nineteenth century.

Railroads faced higher **fixed costs** than most previous companies. These costs included commitments to bondholders and the cost of maintaining and protecting far-flung equipment and property. To pay their fixed costs and keep profits high, railroad companies tried to operate at full capacity whenever possible. Doing so, however, sometimes proved difficult. Where two or more lines competed for the same traffic, one might choose to cut rates in an effort to lure business from the other. But if the other company responded with cuts in its rates, neither stood to gain significantly more business, and both took in less income. Competition between railroad companies sometimes became so intense that no line could show a profit.

Some railroad operators chose to defuse such intense competition by forming a **pool.** The most famous was the Iowa Pool, made up of the railroads operating between Chicago and Omaha, across Iowa. Formed in 1870, the Iowa Pool operated until 1874. Some pooling continued until the mid-1880s, but few pools lasted that long. Often one or more pool members tired of a restricted market share and broke the pool arrangement in an effort to expand, thereby starting a new price war. When a pooling arrangement became known, it brought loud complaints from customers, who concluded that they paid higher rates because of the pool.

To compete more effectively, railroads adjusted their rates to attract companies that did a great deal of shipping. Favored customers sometimes received a **rebate.** Large shipments sent over long distances cost the railroad companies less per mile than small shipments sent over short distances, so companies developed different rate structures for long hauls and short hauls. Thus the largest shippers, with the power to secure rebates and low rates, could ship more cheaply than small businesses and farmers. Railroad companies explained the differences in rates in terms of differences in costs, but small shippers who paid high prices saw themselves as victims of rate discrimination.

Railroads viewed state and federal governments as sources of valuable subsidies. At the same time, they constantly guarded against efforts by their customers to use government to restrict or regulate their enterprises—by outlawing rate discrimination, for example. Companies sometimes campaigned openly to secure the election of friendly representatives and senators and to defeat unfriendly candidates. They maintained well-organized operations

bond A certificate of debt issued by a government or corporation guaranteeing payment of the original investment plus interest by a specified future date.

fixed costs Costs that a company must pay even if it closes down all its operations—for example, interest on loans, dividends on bonds, and property taxes.

pool An agreement among businesses in the same industry to divide up the market and charge equal prices instead of competing.

rebate The refund of part of the amount given in payment for something.

to **lobby** public officials in Washington, D.C., and in state capitals. Most railroad companies issued free passes to many public officials—a practice that reformers attacked as a form of bribery. Some railroads won reputations as the most influential political power in entire states—the Southern Pacific in California, for example, or the Santa Fe in Kansas.

Stories of railroad officials bribing politicians became commonplace after the Civil War. The Crédit Mobilier scandal (see page 610) touched some of the most influential members of Congress in the 1870s. A decade later, Collis P. Huntington of the Southern Pacific candidly explained his expectations regarding public officials: "If you have to pay money to have the right thing done, it is only just and fair to do it." For Huntington, "the right thing" meant favorable treatment for his company.

Investment Bankers and "Morganization"

The railroad expansion of the 1880s involved the laying of 75,000 miles of new track, but some of the new lines earned little profit. Some ran through sparsely populated areas of the West. Others were in eastern areas already served by railways. In the 1880s, however, a few ambitious, talented, and occasionally unscrupulous railway executives maneuvered to produce great regional railway systems. The Santa Fe and the Southern Pacific, for example, came to dominate the Southwest, and the Great Northern and the Northern Pacific held sway in the Northwest. The Pennsylvania and the New York Central controlled much of the shipping in the Northeast. By consolidating major lines within a region under a single management, railway executives expected to create more efficient systems with less duplication, fewer price wars, and more dependable profits.

To raise the enormous amounts of capital necessary for construction and consolidation, railroad executives turned increasingly to **investment banks.** Among investment bankers, **John Pierpont Morgan** emerged as the most prominent by the late 1880s. Born in Connecticut in 1837, he was the son of Junius Morgan, a successful merchant who turned to investment banking. After schooling in Switzerland and Germany, young Morgan began working in his father's bank in London. In 1857, he moved to New York, where his father had arranged a banking position for him. There he gradually emerged as a major banking figure.

Morgan's background and his growing stature in banking gave him access to capital within the United States and in London and Paris. His investors wanted to put their money where it would be safe and would give them a reliable **return.** Morgan therefore tried to bring the unstable aspects of railroads under control, especially the cutthroat rate competition that often resulted when several companies served one market. Financially ailing railroad companies that turned to Morgan for help in raising capital found that he insisted on reorganization to simplify corporate structures and to combine small lines into larger, centrally controlled systems. He often insisted that he or one of his partners be seated on the board of directors, to guard against risky decisions in the future. After a time, some began to refer to this process as "Morganization." "Morganized" lines included some of the largest in the country. A few other investment bankers followed similar patterns.

By the early 1900s, railroad entrepreneurs and investment bankers had assembled twelve large railroad systems that together controlled more than half of the nation's track mileage and twenty other railroad systems that operated most of the rest. These large systems, in turn, were often interlocked with each other, creating half a dozen massive networks, each affiliated with one of the leading New York banking houses.

Chicago: Railroad Metropolis

The financing of railroads was centered in New York, but Chicago experienced the most dramatic transformation as a consequence of railroad construction. Between 1850 and 1900, railroads transformed Chicago from a town of 30,000 residents to the nation's second largest city, with 1.7 million people. Thanks in part to the tireless efforts of local

lobby To try to influence the thinking of public officials for or against a specific cause.

investment bank A bank that provides capital to new or expanding companies by buying their securities and reselling them to investors.

John Pierpont Morgan American banker and industrialist who used investments in railroads and steel to turn his family fortune into a colossal financial empire.

return The yield on money that has been invested in an enterprise or product.

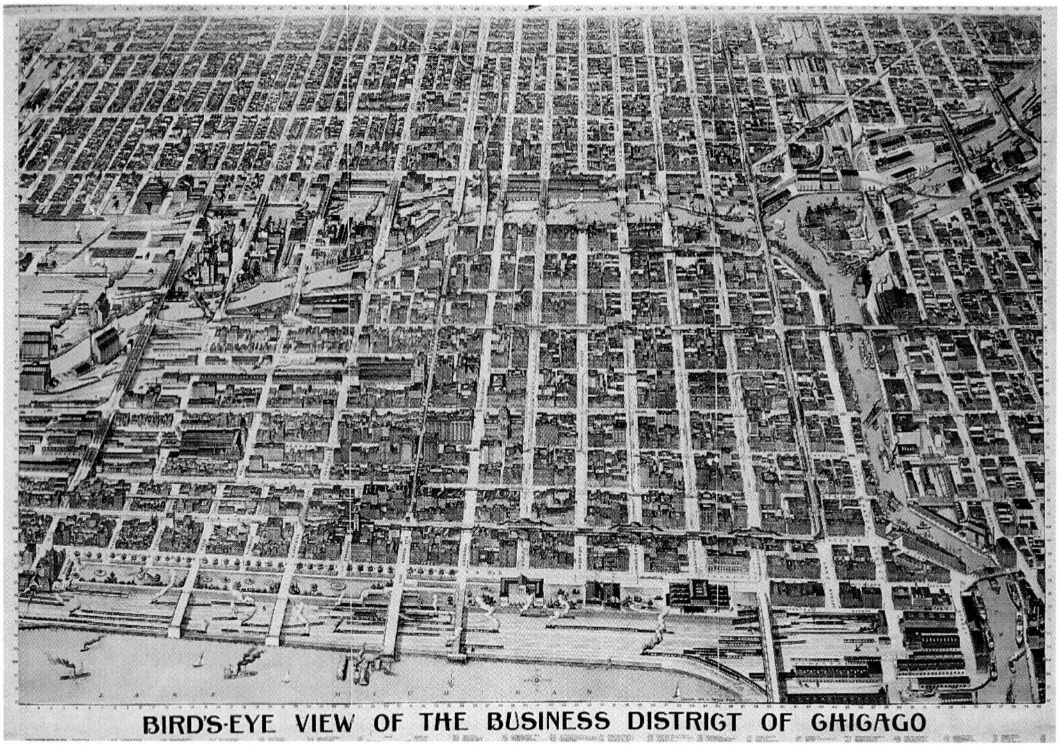
BIRD'S-EYE VIEW OF THE BUSINESS DISTRICT OF CHICAGO

♦ In this lithograph, the railroad metropolis is depicted from a spot high over Lake Michigan, looking south toward the financial and commercial center of the city. The many railroad tracks and plumes of smoke were important symbols of progress and prosperity. *Chicago Historical Society.*

promoters and in part to its geographic location, Chicago emerged as the rail center not just of the Midwest but of much of the nation. By 1880, more than twenty railroad lines connected Chicago with all parts of the United States and much of Canada. The boom in railroad construction during the 1880s only reinforced the city's prominence. Entrepreneurs in manufacturing and commerce soon developed new enterprises based on Chicago's unrivaled location at the hub of a great transportation network.

Chicago's rail connections made it the logical center for the new business of mail-order sales, and the two pioneers in that field—Montgomery Ward and Sears, Roebuck and Co.—began business there. Central location and rail connections also made it a manufacturing center. By the 1880s, Chicago's factories produced more farm equipment than the factories of any other city, and its iron and steel production rivaled that of Pittsburgh. Other leading Chicago industries produced railway cars and equipment, metal products, a wide variety of machinery, and clothing. In the 1880s, the city claimed title as the world's largest grain market.

Location and rail lines made Chicago the largest center for meatpacking. Livestock from across the Midwest and from as far as south Texas was unloaded in Chicago's Union Stockyards—over 400 acres of railroad sidings, chutes, and pens filled with cattle, hogs, and sheep. Huge slaughterhouses flanking the stockyards received a steady stream of live animals and disgorged an equally steady stream of canned and fresh meat. The development in the 1870s of refrigeration for railroad cars and ships permitted fresh meat to be sent throughout the nation and to Europe.

Chicago's rapid growth and rising economic significance gave it an aura of energy and vitality that impressed nearly all visitors. Louis Sullivan, later a leading architect, remembered his first impressions of the city in 1873: "An intoxicating rawness; a sense of big things to be done. . . . 'Biggest in the world' was the braggart phrase on every tongue." A French visitor called Chicago "the boldest" and "most American" of the cities of the United States. The poet Carl Sandburg celebrated Chicago in his poem by that name in 1914:

Hog Butcher for the World,
Tool Maker, Stacker of Wheat,
Player with Railroads and the Nation's Freight
Handler;
Stormy, husky, brawling,
City of the Big Shoulders:

Entrepreneurs and Industrial Transformation

- How did technology and prevailing business practices define entrepreneurs' expectations in the late nineteenth century?
- How did Carnegie and Morgan choose to deal with competition?
- How did choices by Carnegie, Rockefeller, Edison, and Morgan change the nature of American business?

Despite the emergence of large railroad corporations, during the late nineteenth century most American businesses remained relatively small. Even much of American manufacturing took place in a single shop run by the owner, who produced one item or service for local sale. Larger manufacturing enterprises had appeared in the 1820s and 1830s—New England textile mills are the leading example—but they often made only one product in only one location with the owner as boss. Entrepreneurs in the late nineteenth century challenged these patterns, creating large and complex enterprises with huge factories scattered through several states.

In a book published in 1889, the economist David A. Wells remarked on the "wholly unprecedented" size of recent new businesses, the "rapidity" with which they emerged, and their tendency to be "far more complex than what has been familiar." Such giant enterprises, he noted, "are regarded to some extent as evils." But, he added, "they are necessary, as there is apparently no other way in which the work of production and distribution . . . can be prosecuted." American business was changing profoundly—in size, function, and structure. By 1905, major American business enterprises resembled those of today more than those of 1865.

Andrew Carnegie and the Age of Steel

The new economy rode on a network of steel rails, propelled by locomotives made of steel. Steel plows broke the tough sod of the western prairies. Skyscrapers, which first appeared in Chicago, relied on steel frames as they boldly shaped urban skylines. Steel, a relative latecomer to the industrial revolution, defined the age. Made by combining carbon and molten iron and then burning out impurities, steel has greater strength, resilience, and durability than iron. This superior metal was difficult and expensive to make until the 1850s, when Henry Bessemer in England and William Kelly in Kentucky independently discovered ways to make steel in large quantities at a reasonable cost. Even so, the first Bessemer or Kelly process plants did not begin production in the United States until 1864. In that year, the entire nation produced only 10,000 tons of steel.

In 1875, just south of Pittsburgh, Pennsylvania, **Andrew Carnegie** opened the nation's largest steel plant. From then until 1901, Carnegie held central place in the steel industry. Born in Scotland in 1835, Carnegie and his penniless parents came to the United States in 1848. Young Andrew worked first in a textile mill then became a messenger in a telegraph office and soon a telegraph operator. His great skill at the telegraph key won him a position as personal telegrapher for a high official of the Pennsylvania Railroad. Carnegie rose rapidly within that company and became a superintendent (a high management position) at the age of 25. At the end of the Civil War, he left railroading to devote full attention to the iron and steel industry, in which he had already invested money. He quickly applied to his iron companies the management lessons he had learned with the railroad.

Carnegie's basic rule was "Cut the prices; scoop the market; run the mills full." An aggressive competitor, he took every opportunity to cut costs so that he might show a profit while charging less than his rivals did. He occasionally participated in pools with other steel-making companies, but he usually chose to undersell competitors rather than cooperate with them. In 1864, steel rails sold for $126 per ton; by 1875, Carnegie was selling them for $69 per

Andrew Carnegie Scottish-born industrialist who made a fortune in steel and believed the rich had a duty to act for the public benefit.

♦ Andrew Carnegie, as depicted by an unknown painter around 1901, when he sold his steel holdings to J.P. Morgan and transformed himself from a fiercely competitive entrepreneur into a generous philanthropist. *National Portrait Gallery.*

ton. Driven by improved technology and Carnegie's competitiveness, steel prices continued to fall, reaching $29 in 1885 and less than $20 in the late 1890s. By then, the nation produced nearly 10 million tons of steel each year.

Carnegie's company was larger and more complex than any manufacturing enterprise in pre–Civil War America. In its own day, however, it was by no means unique. Other companies operated plants that were as complex, and several challenged it in size. By 1900, three steel plants each employed between 8,000 and 10,000 workers, and seventy other factories employed more than 2,000 wage earners, producing everything from watches to locomotives, from cotton cloth to processed meat.

During the late nineteenth century, drawing in part on railroads' innovations in managing large-scale operations, entrepreneurs transformed the organizational structure of manufacturing. They often joined a range of operations formerly conducted by separate businesses—acquisition of raw materials, processing, distribution of finished goods—into one company, achieving **vertical integration.** Companies usually developed vertical integration to ensure steady operations and to gain a competitive advantage. Control over the sources and transportation of raw materials, for example, guaranteed a reliable flow of crucial supplies at predictable prices. Such control may also have denied materials to a competitor.

Steel plants stood at one end of a long chain of operations that Carnegie owned or controlled: iron ore mines in Michigan and Wisconsin, a fleet of ships that transported iron ore across the Great Lakes, hundreds of miles of railway lines, tens of thousands of acres of coal lands, ovens to produce coke (coal treated to burn at high temperatures), and plants for turning iron ore into bars of crude iron. Carnegie Steel was vertically integrated from the point where the raw materials came out of the ground through the production of steel rails and beams.

Standard Oil: Model for Monopoly

As Carnegie provided a model for other steel companies and for heavy industry in general, **John D. Rockefeller** revolutionized the petroleum industry. Rockefeller was born in upper New York State in 1839 and educated in Cleveland, Ohio. After working as a bookkeeper and clerk, he became a partner in a grain and livestock business in 1859 and earned large profits during the Civil War.

At that time, Cleveland was the center for refining oil from northwestern Pennsylvania, then the nation's main source for crude oil. The major product of oil refining was kerosene, used primarily for home lighting. Rockefeller, in 1863, chose to invest his wartime profits in a **refinery.** After the war, he

vertical integration The bringing together of a wide range of business activities—such as acquiring raw materials, manufacturing, and marketing and selling finished products—into a single organization.

John D. Rockefeller American industrialist who amassed great wealth through the Standard Oil Company and donated much of his fortune to promote learning and research.

refinery An industrial plant that transforms raw materials into finished products, especially by removing impurities; a petroleum refinery processes crude oil to produce a variety of products for use by consumers.

bought control of more refineries and incorporated them as Standard Oil in 1870.

The refining business was relatively easy to enter and highly competitive. Aggressive competition became a distinctive Standard Oil characteristic. Recognizing that state-of-the-art technology could bring a competitive advantage, Rockefeller recruited technical experts to make Standard the most efficient refiner. He secured reduced rates or rebates from the railroads by offering a heavy volume of traffic on a predictable basis. He usually sought to persuade his competitors to join the **cartel** he was creating. Failing in that, he tried to drive them out of business.

By 1881, following a strategy of **horizontal integration,** Rockefeller and his associates controlled some forty oil refineries, accounting for about 90 percent of the nation's refining capacity. The outcome of Rockefeller's strategy of taking over the companies of his competitors was a **monopoly:** Rockefeller's company, Standard Oil, had nearly exclusive control over the refining of oil in the United States. Between 1879 and 1881, Rockefeller centralized decision making among all his companies by creating the Standard Oil Trust. The **trust** was a new organizational form designed to get around state laws that prohibited one company from owning stock in another. To create the Standard Oil Trust, Rockefeller and others who held shares in the individual companies exchanged their stock for trust certificates issued by Standard Oil. Standard Oil thus controlled all the individual companies, though technically it did not own them. Eventually, new laws in New Jersey made it legal for corporations chartered in New Jersey to own stock in other companies. So Rockefeller set up Standard Oil of New Jersey as a **holding company** for all the companies in the trust.

Standard Oil then consolidated its operations by closing more than half of its refineries and building several larger plants that incorporated the newest technology. These and other innovations reduced the cost of producing petroleum products by more than two-thirds, leading to a decline in the price of fuel and lighting products by more than half from 1866 to 1890. In the 1880s, Standard moved to vertical integration by gaining control of existing oil fields, building its own transportation facilities (including pipelines and oceangoing tanker ships), and creating its own marketing operations (see Figure 17.1). Standard also took a leading role in the world market, producing nearly all American petroleum products sold in Asia, Africa, and Latin America during the 1880s. By the early 1890s, Standard Oil had achieved virtually complete vertical and horizontal integration of the American petroleum industry—a near-monopoly over an entire industry.

Rockefeller retired from active participation in business in the mid-1890s. The "Rockefeller interests" (companies dominated by Rockefeller or his managers), however, became even more powerful. They included the National City Bank of New York (an investment bank second only to the House of Morgan), railroads, mining, real estate, steel plants, steamship lines, and other industries. Standard's petroleum monopoly proved to be short-lived, however, because of the discovery of new oil fields in Texas and elsewhere. New companies emerged, tapping those fields, and quickly followed the path of vertical integration.

Technology and Economic Change

By the late nineteenth century, most American entrepreneurs had joined Rockefeller in viewing technology as an important competitive device. Railroads wanted more powerful locomotives, larger freight cars, and stronger rails, so they could carry more freight at a lower cost. Steel companies demanded larger and more efficient furnaces to make more steel more cheaply. Ordinary citizens as well as famous entrepreneurs seemed infatuated with technology. One invention followed another: a machine that made ice in 1865, the vacuum cleaner in 1869, the telephone in 1876, the phonograph in 1878, the electric light bulb in 1879, an electric welding machine in 1886, and the first American-made gasoline-engine automobile in 1895, to name only a few.

cartel A group of independent business organizations that cooperate to control the production, pricing, and marketing of goods by group members; similar to a pool.

horizontal integration The bringing together of a series of related business activities performing similar functions—such as oil refining—into a single organization.

monopoly Exclusive control by one group of the means of producing or selling a product.

trust A legal device to get around state laws that prohibited a company chartered in one state from operating in another state; first used by John D. Rockefeller to consolidate Standard Oil.

holding company A company that exists to own other companies, usually through holding a controlling interest in their stocks.

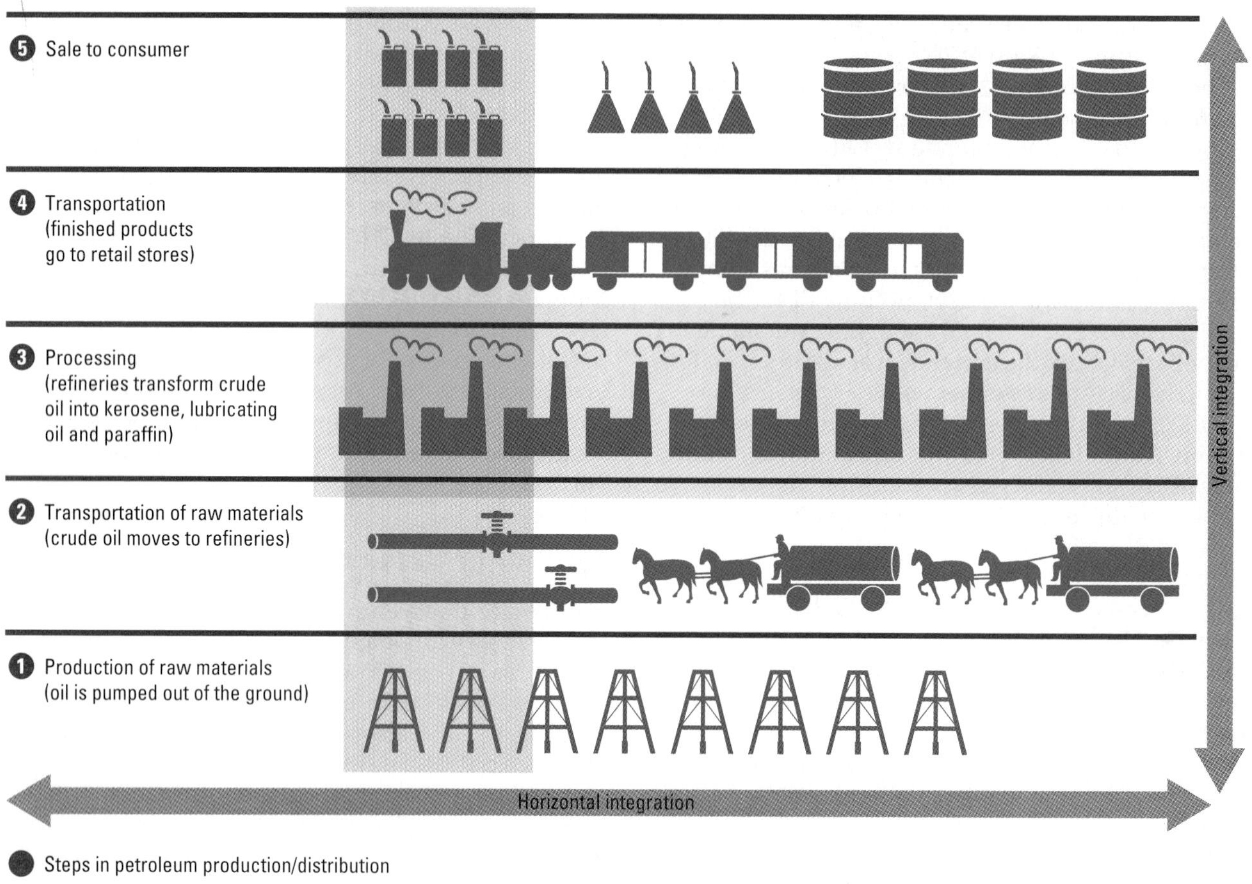

♦ **FIGURE 17.1 Vertical and Horizontal Integration of the Petroleum Industry** This diagram represents the petroleum industry before Standard Oil achieved its dominance. The symbols represent different specialized companies, each engaged in a different step in the production of kerosene. Rockefeller entered the industry by investing in a refinery, and first expanded *horizontally* by absorbing several other refineries (indicated by the blue band). His Standard Oil Company then practiced *vertical integration* by acquiring oil leases, oil wells, pipelines, advantageous contracts with railroads, and eventually even retail stores (an example of vertical integration is indicated by the green band). For a time, Standard Oil controlled nearly 90 percent of the industry.

By 1900, many Americans had come to expect a steady flow of new and astounding creations.

Many new inventions relied on electricity, and in the field of electricity one person stood out: **Thomas A. Edison.** Born in 1847, he became a telegraph operator as a teenager. He began to experiment with electrical devices and in 1869 secured the first of his thousand-plus **patents.**

In 1876, Edison set up the first modern research laboratory, where he and his staff could work. The new facility he opened in 1887 quickly became the world leader in research and development, especially for the use of electricity. Edison promised "a minor invention every ten days and a big thing every six months," and he backed up his words with results. Sometimes building on the work of others, Edison's laboratories invented or significantly improved electrical lighting, electrical motors, the storage battery, the electric locomotive, the phonograph, the mimeograph, and many other products. Such research and development by Edison's laboratories and by others soon translated into production

Thomas A. Edison American inventor, especially of electrical devices, among them the microphone (1877), the phonograph (1878), and the light bulb (1879).

patent A government grant that gives the creator of an invention the sole right to produce, use, or sell that invention for a set period of time.

♦ This photograph from 1893 shows Thomas A. Edison in his laboratory, the world's leading research facility when it opened in 1876. By creating research teams, the Edison laboratories could pursue several projects at once. They developed a dzzling stream of new products, most based on electrical power. *Library of Congress.*

and sales. Nationwide, sales of electrical equipment were insignificant in 1870 but reached nearly $2 million ten years later and nearly $22 million in 1890.

The sale of light bulbs and other new electrical devices depended on the availability of electricity. Generating and distribution systems had to be constructed, and wires for carrying electrical current had to be installed along city streets and in homes. Early developers of electrical devices and electrical distribution systems realized quickly that they needed major financial assistance, and investment bankers played an important role. General Electric, for example, came about through a series of **mergers** arranged by the banking firm of J. P. Morgan.

Selling to the Nation

Large, vertically integrated manufacturers of consumer goods often produced goods that differed little from each other and that cost virtually the same to produce. Such companies sometimes chose not to compete on the basis of price but instead to use advertising to differentiate their products.

Most advertising in the mid-nineteenth century promoted **patent medicines** and books. By 1890, however, large-scale advertising also featured packaged foods, clothing, soap, and petroleum products. Advertisements in newspapers and magazines became larger and more complex. In some cases—notably cigarettes—advertising actually created demand and expanded the market for the product. After the federal Patent Office registered the first **trademark** in 1870, companies rushed to develop logos that, they expected, would distinguish their product from its nearly identical rivals.

Advertising popularized new ways of selling goods to customers. Up until this time, most people expected to purchase the goods they needed (for example, hardware or cotton cloth) in small specialty stores, or directly from artisans who made goods on order (shoes, clothes, furniture), or in general stores, or from door-to-door peddlers. In urban areas after the Civil War, **department stores** appeared and flourished, offering a wide range of choices in ready-made products—clothing, household furnishings, shoes, and much more. They relied heavily on newspaper advertising to attract customers, especially women, from throughout the city and its suburbs. The variety presented by department stores paled, however, when compared to the vast array of goods available through the new mail-order catalogues. Led by Montgomery Ward (which issued its first catalogue in 1872) and Sears, Roebuck and Co. (1886)—both based in Chicago—mail-order houses aimed at rural America. They offered a wider range of choices than most rural-dwellers had ever before seen—everything from clothing to farm equipment—most illustrated with attractive line drawings. Department stores and mail-order houses were possible because manufacturers now produced all sorts of ready-made goods. Mail-order houses depended on railroads to deliver their catalogues and products across great distances.

merger The union of two or more organizations.

patent medicine A medical preparation that is advertised by brand name and can be bought without a physician's prescription.

trademark A name or symbol that identifies a product and is officially registered and legally restricted for use by the owner or manufacturer.

department store A new type of retail establishment developed in cities in the late nineteenth century; it featured a wide variety of merchandise organized in separate departments.

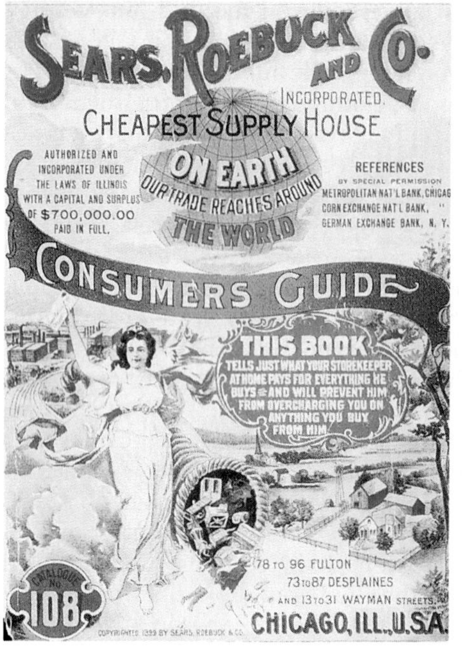

♦ Mail-order companies led by Montgomery Ward and Sears, Roebuck and Co. both based in Chicago, issued advertising catalogs that brought the most remote farm family into contact with the latest fashions and the most recent developments in equipment. The cover for this 1899 catalog depicts a giant cornucopia, the traditional symbol of abundance, filled with consumer goods. *Sears, Roebuck and Co.*

Economic Concentration and the Merger Movement

Carnegie, Rockefeller, and a few others helped to redefine the expectations of other entrepreneurs and provided models for their activities. In a number of industries, large, complex companies—vertically integrated, sometimes horizontally integrated, often employing extensive advertising—appeared relatively suddenly in the 1880s. At first they were concentrated in consumer-goods industries.

James B. Duke, for example, used efficient machinery, extensive advertising, and vertical integration to become the largest manufacturer of cigarettes. In 1890, he merged with his four largest competitors to create the American Tobacco Company, which dominated the cigarette industry.

Gustavus Swift in the early 1880s began to ship fresh meat from his slaughterhouse in Chicago to markets in the East using his own refrigerated railcars. He eventually added refrigerated storage plants in each city, along with a sales and delivery staff. Other meatpacking companies followed Swift's lead. By 1890, half a dozen firms, all vertically integrated, dominated meatpacking. Such a market, where a small number of firms dominated an industry, is called an **oligopoly** and was more typical than monopolies like Standard Oil or the similarly structured American Sugar Refining Company, created in 1887, which controlled three-quarters of the nation's sugar-refining capacity in the early 1890s.

Some of the new manufacturing companies in the 1870s and early 1880s did not sell stock or use investment bankers to raise capital. Standard Oil and Carnegie Steel, two of the largest of the new companies, never "went public"—that is, they never sold stocks on a stock exchange as a means of raising capital. Rockefeller chose to expand either through mergers or by making purchases paid for from the profits of the business itself. Similarly, Carnegie expanded by adding partners or by investing profits.

Rockefeller and Carnegie concentrated ownership and control in their own hands. The same held true for many others among the new industrial companies until late in the nineteenth century. In 1896, for example, the New York Stock Exchange sold stock in only twenty manufacturing concerns. At the turn of the century, however, a second phase of vertical and horizontal integration created the need for more capital, and investment bankers began to turn their attention from railroads to the reorganization of heavy industry.

In the late 1890s, J. P. Morgan began combining separate steel-related companies to create a vertically integrated operation that might challenge Carnegie's dominance. Carnegie had never carried vertical integration to the point of making final steel products such as wire, barrels, or tubes. By vertically integrating to include companies making finished products, Morgan threatened to close off a significant part of Carnegie's market. Faced with the prospect of building his own plants for finished products, Carnegie seemed at first to relish the prospect of no-holds-barred competition with Morgan. When Morgan offered to buy him out, however, he agreed, allowing Morgan in 1901 to create United States Steel, the nation's first corporation capitalized at over a billion dollars.

In 1902, competition between the two largest companies making agricultural implements became intense, even threatening the markets for the new United States Steel Corporation. Morgan intervened.

oligopoly A market or industry dominated by a few firms.

Using his access to capital as a lever and promising that profits would be higher and more predictable through consolidation, Morgan merged the two largest and three smaller harvester firms into International Harvester in 1902, creating a company that dominated 85 percent of the market for harvesting machines.

United States Steel and International Harvester were just two of the many new combinations in manufacturing and mining created in a relatively short time at the turn of the century. Between 1898 and 1902, the nation witnessed an astonishing number of mergers. The high point came in 1899, with 1,208 mergers involving $2.3 billion in capital. This merger movement resulted partly from economic weaknesses revealed by a depression that had begun in 1893 and lasted for four years (see page 623). Railroads were hit especially hard. Several large lines declared bankruptcy and had to be reorganized. At the end of the depression, the threat of vicious competition among manufacturing companies prompted reorganization there too.

As had been true with railroad reorganization, an investment banker usually sought two primary objectives in reorganizing an industry: to make the industry stable, so that investments would yield predictable **dividends;** and to make the industry efficient and productive, so that dividends would be high. Toward that end, investment bankers not only created new combinations but also placed their representatives on the boards of directors of the new companies, to guarantee that the companies would continue to meet those objectives. By 1912, the three leading New York banking firms together occupied 341 directorships in 112 major companies. Investment bankers argued that benefits from their activities extended far beyond the dividends that shareholders received. One of Morgan's associates claimed in 1901 that, as a result of Morganization, "production would become more regular, labor would be more steadily employed at better wages, and panics caused by over-production would become a thing of the past."

In fact, the new industrial combinations failed to produce long-term economic stability. Throughout the nineteenth and early twentieth centuries, the economy alternated between periods of **expansion,** characterized by growth, low levels of unemployment, and widespread prosperity, and periods of **contraction,** characterized by low productivity, high unemployment, and "hard times."

Though the years after the Civil War were generally ones of economic growth, a severe depression occurred from 1873 to 1878, and there were short **recessions** in the 1880s and early 1890s and another severe depression from 1893 to 1897. A period of general expansion after the late 1890s was interrupted by brief but frequent downturns in 1903, 1907–1908, 1910–1911, and 1913–1914.

Morgan's hopes for stability through centralized control failed to be realized, but his activities and those of his contemporaries created many of the characteristics of modern business. Many industries were oligopolistic, dominated by a few vertically integrated companies. **Product differentiation** through advertising had begun. The stock market had moved beyond the sale of railroad **securities** to play an important role in raising capital for industry.

Gradually, too, with the passing of the first generation of industrial empire builders, ownership grew apart from management. Many new business executives were simply hired managers. Ownership rested with hundreds or thousands of stockholders, all of whom wanted a reliable return on their investment though the vast majority of them remained uninvolved with business operations. The huge size of the new companies also meant that most managers rarely saw or talked with most of their employees, especially those not involved in management or accounting. Careful **cost analysis,** the desire for efficiency, and the need to pay regular dividends led many companies to treat most of their employees as expenses to be increased or cut as necessary, with little regard to the impact on people.

dividend A share of profits received by a stockholder.

expansion In the economic cycle, a time when the economy is growing as indicated by increased production of goods and services, and, usually, by low rates of unemployment.

contraction In the economic cycle, a time when the economy has ceased to grow, characterized by decreased production of goods and services and often by high rates of unemployment.

recession A period of economic contraction of relatively short duration, as compared to a depression, which is a period of economic contraction of longer duration.

product differentiation The use of advertising to distinguish one product from similar products.

securities Stocks and/or bonds.

cost analysis Detailed study of the cost of operations, intended to make them more efficient through careful planning.

Workers in Industrial America

- How did the expectations about economic mobility portrayed by Horatio Alger compare with the realities of workers' lives in the late nineteenth century?
- How did industrialization transform the nature of work and expectations about work?

The rapid expansion of railroads, mining, and manufacturing created a demand for labor to lay the rails, dig out the ore, tend the furnaces, operate the refineries, and carry out a thousand other tasks. America's new workers—men, women, and children from many ethnic groups—came from across the nation and around the world. Despite the lure of a rags-to-riches triumph like that of Andrew Carnegie, very few rose from the shop floor to the manager's office.

Labor and Mobility

Horatio Alger emerged as one of the most prominent popular novelists in the nation after the success of his first novel, *Ragged Dick* (1868). He eventually produced 108 more books with total sales of nearly a hundred million copies. Aimed at young people, his books repeated one refrain: a poor but hardworking youth, through some unusual opportunity—saving a child from danger, for example—attracts the attention of a wealthy and powerful person and thereby achieves success, wealth, and happiness. Alger's stories often emphasized the element of luck, but his name became a symbol of the expectation that in America anyone who worked hard and saved carefully could succeed.

The reality of life in industrial America bore little resemblance to Alger's tales. In the new industrial economy, nearly all successful business leaders came from middle-class or upper-class families. Few workers moved more than a step or so up the economic scale. An unskilled laborer might become a semiskilled worker, or a skilled worker might become a foreman, but few wage earners moved into the middle class. If they did, it was usually as the owner of a small and often struggling business.

In industrial America, the treatment received by labor differed little from the treatment of the raw materials that went into production. During efforts to cut costs, workers' wages were always a tempting target for savings. During boom periods, companies advertised for labor and ran their operations at full capacity. When the demand for manufactured goods fell, companies reduced production or even closed down. At such times, they expected to lay off workers, cut wages, or reduce hours. Unemployed workers had little to fall back on but their savings or the earnings of other family members. Some churches and private charity organizations gave out food, but state and federal governments provided no unemployment benefits. Families that failed to find work might go hungry or even become homeless. In a depression, jobs of any sort were scarce, and competition for them was intense.

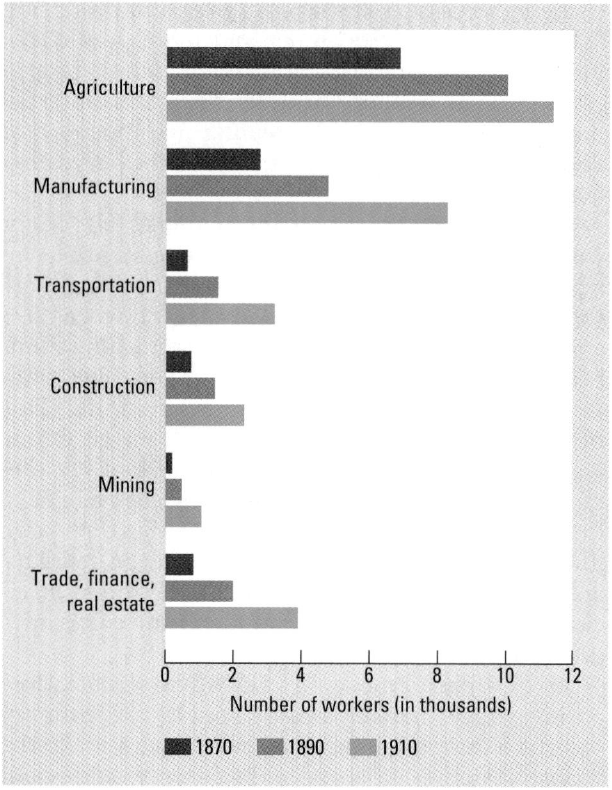

♦ **FIGURE 17.2 Industrial Distribution of the Work Force, 1870, 1890, 1910**

Workers for Industry

After the Civil War, the labor force more than doubled. The largest increases occurred in industries undergoing the greatest changes (see Figure 17.2). Agriculture continued to employ the largest share of

Horatio Alger American writer of rags-to-riches stories about impoverished boys who become wealthy through hard work, virtue, and luck.

♦ The McCormick plant in Chicago (left) produced farm equipment, and the Richmond, Virginia, factory (right) employed women to make cigars. In both factories, individual machines drew their power from a central source through a system of belts and shafts, and workers toiled under the watchful eye of the foreman, who could usually adjust the speed of the belts and shafts to speed up the machines of the individual workers. *(left) McCormack factory: State Historical Society of Wisconsin; (right) Valentine Museum.*

the labor force, ranging downward from more than half in 1870 to two-fifths in 1900, but the proportional growth of workers engaged in agriculture was the smallest of all major categories of workers.

Some of the workers for the rapidly expanding economy came from within the nation, especially from rural areas. Throughout rural parts of New England and the Middle Atlantic states especially, large numbers of people found it increasingly difficult to make a living through agriculture and moved to urban or industrial areas. In New England, some farms—usually small and unproductive—were abandoned when their owners chose to take a job in a nearby factory town or to move west.

The expanding economy, however, needed more workers than the nation itself could supply. As a result, the years from the Civil War to World War I (1865–1914) witnessed the largest influx of immigrants in American history: more than 26 million people, equivalent to three-quarters of the nation's entire population in 1865. By 1910, immigrants and their children made up more than 35 percent of the total population.

Large-scale immigration contributed many adult males to the work force—especially in mining, manufacturing, and transportation. But the expanding economy also pulled women and children into the ranks of industrial wage earners. The 1910 census revealed that nearly 2 million children (under the age of 16) worked for wages, many in mining, manufacturing, and agriculture. Others worked as newsboys, bootblacks, or domestic servants. Many children were employed in the textile industry, especially in the South. Mostly girls, they worked 70-hour weeks for between 10 and 20 cents a day.

Children worked in tobacco and cotton fields in the South, operated sewing machines in New York, assisted glass blowers in West Virginia factories, and sorted vegetables in Delaware canneries. Other children worked at home, alongside their parents who brought home **piecework.** Most working children turned over all their wages to their parents.

Most of the women who found employment outside the home were unmarried. Between 1890 and 1910, nearly half of all single women worked for wages, along with a third of widowed or divorced women. Among married women, only 5 or 10 percent did so. Black women were employed at much higher rates in all categories.

A report of the Illinois Bureau of Labor Statistics for 1884 explained that some children and mothers worked for wages because of the "meager earnings of many heads of families." A study in 1875 showed

piecework Work paid for according to the number of items turned out, rather than by the hour.

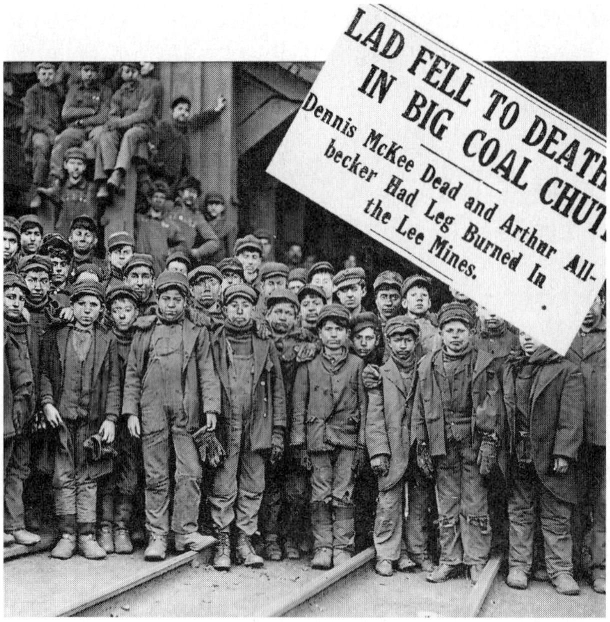
LAD FELL TO DEATH
IN BIG COAL CHUTE
Dennis McKee Dead and Arthur All-
becker Had Leg Burned In
the Lee Mines.

♦ The coal mines of Pennsylvania employed more than ten thousand boys under the age of 16. Known as "breaker boys," they sorted coal. Such work was dangerous and sometimes fatal, as attested by this 1911 headline. *Library of Congress.*

that the average male factory worker in Lawrence, Massachusetts, earned $500 per year. The study also showed that the average family in Lawrence required a minimum annual income of $600 to provide sufficient food, clothing, and shelter. In such circumstances, a family could not make ends meet without two or more incomes.

By 1900, some occupations were filled mainly by women. Females—adults and children—made up more than 70 percent of the workers in clothing factories, knitting mills, and other textile factories. Women also dominated certain types of office work. By 1900, women made up more than 70 percent of the nation's secretaries and typists and 80 percent of telephone operators. However, as women moved into office work, displacing men, wage levels fell along with the likelihood of promotion from clerical worker to managerial status. For women, office work usually paid less than factory work but was considered safer and of higher status. Women and children workers almost always earned less than their male counterparts. In most industries, work was separated by age and gender, and the jobs requiring the most skill and commanding the best pay were reserved for adult males. Even when men and women did the same work, there was usually a pay differential (see Figure 17.3), which was sometimes explained by the argument that a man had to support a family but a woman worked to supplement the income of her husband or father.

Not all women worked as wage earners. Some took in laundry in their own homes, did sewing for neighbors, or rented a room to a boarder. In one eastern factory town in 1912, 90 percent of the families where the husband was the only wage earner took in one or more boarders.

The Transformation of Work

Most adult industrial workers had been born into a rural society, either in the United States or in another part of the world. They found industrial work quite different from work they had done in the past. Farm families might work from sunrise to sunset, but they worked at their own speed. They could take a break when they felt the need and could control the pace of their work to avoid exhaustion. Self-employed blacksmiths, carpenters, dressmakers, and other skilled workers also controlled the speed and intensity of their work, although, like the farmer, they might work from sunrise to sunset.

By the late nineteenth century, the workday in most industries averaged ten or twelve hours, six days a week. People from rural settings expected to work long hours, but they found that industrial work controlled them, rather than the other way around. The speed of the machines set the pace of the work, and machine speeds were often centrally controlled. If managers ordered a **speedup,** workers worked faster but rarely received an increase in pay.

Ten- or twelve-hour days at a constant, rapid pace drained the workers. A woman textile worker in 1882 said, "I get so exhausted that I can scarcely drag myself home when night comes." Steel mills operated twenty-four hours a day. Beginning in the 1890s, most went from eight-hour shifts to twelve. During times of high demand for steel, most companies required seven-day workweeks. A 27-year-old steelworker in 1910 was blunt: "It's simply a killing pace in the steel works." The pace sometimes proved, literally, to be killing, as exhausted workers were injured or killed in industrial accidents.

Some factory managers saw dependence on skilled workers as a constraint on their control of

speedup Any effort to make employees produce more goods in the same time or for the same pay.

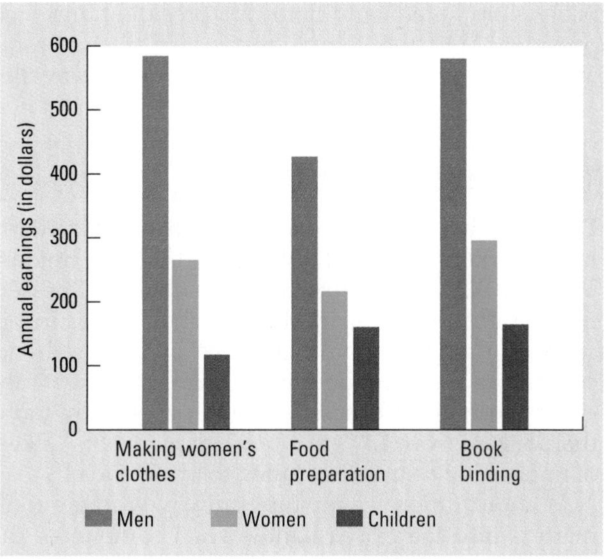

♦ **FIGURE 17.3 Average Annual Earnings for Men, Women, and Children, in Selected Industries, 1890**

production, for skilled workers often understood a plant's operations better than any manager did. The most skilled workers often set the pace of work around them, earned more than other workers, and were difficult to replace. Industrial engineer Frederick W. Taylor built a national reputation on his ability to take a complex operation, requiring a high level of skill, and break it down into its component parts. Taylor redesigned work so that relatively unskilled workers, who earned low wages, required little training, and were easily replaced, could do it. Once tasks were simplified in this way, **efficiency experts** conducted time-and-motion studies to determine the ideal speed at which each task should be performed. Such "de-skilling" was intended to increase managers' control over the process of work.

The Varieties of Labor Organization and Action, 1865–1900

- How did the expectations of American workers who joined craft unions compare with those who chose organizations like the Knights of Labor?
- How successful were the various types of labor organizations in the late nineteenth century? What choices made some more successful than others?

Just as the entrepreneurs of the late nineteenth century faced choices between competition and cooperation, so too did members of their work force. As the industrial economy grew, some workers reacted to the far-reaching changes in the nature of work by choosing to cooperate with other workers in efforts to maintain or regain control over their working conditions. In doing so, they experimented with a variety of organizations. Some organizations limited their membership to skilled workers, but others tried to unite wage earners regardless of their level of skill. Some labor organizations sought political reform, hoping to use the power of government to assist workers, but others avoided politics. Still others sought **radical** solutions to the problems workers faced, proposing alternatives to capitalism itself. European immigrants sometimes contributed to the diversity of organizations by bringing union experience or a commitment to **socialism.**

Strikes erupted on an unprecedented scale. Faced with striking workers, some entrepreneurs called for government, both state and federal, to protect property and maintain order—and to assist in suppressing the strikes.

Craft Unionism—and Its Limits

Skilled workers in many fields outside manufacturing often remained indispensable. In construction, only an experienced carpenter could build stairs or hang doors properly. In publishing, only a skilled typesetter could transform handwritten copy into lines of lead type. Such workers took pride in the quality of their work and knew that their skill was crucial to their employer's success. One union leader was referring to such workers when he said, "the manager's brains are under the workman's cap."

Skilled workers formed the first unions, called **craft unions** or trade unions because membership was limited to skilled workers in a particular craft

efficiency expert Consultant who studies industrial workplaces to determine how to minimize wasted motion and perform tasks in the shortest amount of time.

radical Advocating fundamental or revolutionary changes in current practices or institutions.

socialism An economic theory opposed to capitalism; nineteenth century socialists favored the ownership of the means of production either by the state or by workers directly, instead of ownership by private individuals or companies.

craft union Labor union that organizes skilled workers engaged in a specific craft or trade; also called a trade union.

or trade. Before the Civil War, workers in most American cities created local trade unions in attempts to regulate the quality of work, wages, hours, and working conditions for their craft. Local unions eventually formed national trade organizations—twenty-six of them by 1873, thirty-nine by 1880. They sometimes called themselves brotherhoods—for example, the United Brotherhood of Carpenters and Joiners, formed in 1881—and they drew on their craft traditions to forge bonds of unity.

The skills that defined craft unions' membership also provided the basis for their success. Skills that sometimes took years to develop made craftworkers valuable to their employers and also made them difficult to replace. Such unions often limited their membership not just to workers with particular skills but to white males with those skills. If most craftworkers within a city belonged to the local union, a strike could badly disrupt or shut down the affected businesses. The strike, therefore, was a powerful weapon in the effort of skilled workers to define working conditions.

A strike most often succeeded in times of prosperity, when the employer wanted to continue operating and was best able financially to make concessions to workers. When the economy experienced a serious downturn and employers sharply reduced work hours or laid off workers, craft unions usually disintegrated because they could not use the strike effectively. Only after the 1880s did local and national unions develop strategies that permitted them to survive depressions.

The craft union tradition served some skilled workers well but by the late nineteenth century was of little help to most industrial workers. Unskilled or semiskilled workers—the majority of employees in many emerging industries—lacked the skills that gave the craft unions bargaining power. Without such skills, they could be replaced easily if they chose to strike. The most effective unions, therefore, were groups of skilled workers—sometimes called the "aristocracy of labor."

Shortly after the Civil War, in 1866, craft unionists representing a variety of local and national organizations joined with reformers to create the **National Labor Union (NLU).** The NLU also included representatives of women's organizations and, after vigorous debate, decided to encourage the organization of black workers. The most important of the NLU objectives was to establish eight hours as the proper length for a day's work. In 1870, the NLU divided itself into a labor organization and a political party. In 1872, the political party, the National Labor Reform party, nominated candidates for president and vice president, but the campaign was so unsuccessful and divisive that neither the NLU nor the party met again.

The Great Strike of 1877

Despite such efforts to form labor organizations, most workers remained outside the budding unions. Then, in 1877, for the first time, the nation witnessed the implications of widespread labor strife. In response to a depression that began in 1873, railroad companies reduced operating costs by repeatedly cutting wages. Railroad workers' pay fell by more than a third from 1873 to 1877. Union leaders talked of organizing a strike but failed to bring one off.

Without union leadership, railway workers took matters into their own hands when companies announced additional pay cuts. On July 16, 1877, a group of firemen and brakemen on the Baltimore & Ohio Railroad stopped work in Maryland. The next day, nearby in West Virginia, a group of railway workers refused to work until the company restored their wages. Some members of the local community supported the strikers. The governor of West Virginia sent in the state militia, but the strikers still prevented the trains from running. The governor then requested federal troops, and President Rutherford B. Hayes sent them.

Federal troops restored service on the Baltimore & Ohio, but the strike spread to other lines. Strikers shut down trains in Pittsburgh. When the local **militia** refused to act against the strikers, the governor of Pennsylvania sent militia units from Philadelphia. The troops killed twenty-six people. Strikers and their sympathizers then attacked the militia, forced the troops to retreat, and burned and looted railroad property throughout Pittsburgh.

Strikes and demonstrations of support for strikers erupted across Pennsylvania and New York and throughout the Midwest. Everywhere, the strikers drew support from other members of their local

National Labor Union Federation organized at Baltimore in 1866; it lasted only six years but helped push through a law limiting government employees to an eight-hour workday.

militia A military force consisting of civilians who agree to be mobilized into service in times of emergency; organized by state governments during the nineteenth century, but now superseded by the National Guard.

♦ This engraving depicts striking railroad workers in Martinsburg, West Virginia, as they stopped a freight train on July 17, 1877, in the opening days of the great railway strike of that year. Engravings such as this, showing strikers to be heavily armed, may or may not have been accurate depictions of events. But the photography of that day could rarely capture live action, and the technology of the day could not reproduce photographs in newspapers, so the public's understanding of events such as the 1877 strike were formed through artists' depictions. *Library of Congress.*

communities. In various places, coal miners, factory workers, owners of small businesses, farmers, black workers, and women demonstrated their support. In St. Louis, local unions declared a **general strike** to secure the eight-hour workday and to end child labor. State militia, federal troops, and local police eventually broke up the strikes, but not before hundreds had lost their lives. By the strikes' end, railroad companies had suffered property damage worth $10 million, half of it in Pittsburgh.

The **Great Strike of 1877** revealed widespread dislike for the new railroad companies and significant community support for strikers. However, the strike worried many other Americans. Some considered the use of troops only a temporary expedient and, like President Hayes, hoped for "education of the strikers," "judicious control of the capitalists," and some way to "remove the distress which afflicts laborers." Others saw in the strike a forecast of future labor unrest, and they called for better means to enforce law and order.

The Knights of Labor

The Great Strike suggested that working people could unite across lines of occupation, race, and gender. No organization drew on that potential, however, until the early 1880s, when the **Knights of Labor** emerged as an alternative to craft unions.

The Noble and Holy Order of the Knights of Labor grew out of an organization of Philadelphia garment workers. Founded in 1869, the Knights proclaimed that labor was "the only creator of values or capital" and opened their ranks to all they defined as part of "the producing class"—those who, by their labor, produced value. All Knights were required to have worked for wages at some time, but the organization specifically excluded only professional gamblers, stockbrokers, lawyers, bankers, and liquor dealers.

The Knights accepted African Americans as members, and some sixty thousand joined by 1886. After one organizer formed an all-woman local organization in 1881, the Knights officially opened their ranks to women and enrolled about fifty thousand by 1886. A few women and African Americans held leadership positions at local and regional levels, and the Knights briefly appointed a woman as a national organizer. The Knights helped to provide both women and African Americans with experience in labor organizing—including the first

general strike A strike by members of all unions in a particular region.

Great Strike of 1877 A series of strikes in American cities triggered by railroad wage cuts; the strikes showed widespread support for the demands of workers.

Knights of Labor Labor organization founded in 1869; membership, open to all workers, peaked in 1886.

INDIVIDUAL CHOICES

Choosing to Serve Labor

Mother Jones

Mary Harris Jones, known as Mother Jones, faced many difficult choices in her long career as a union organizer, sometimes involving threats to her personal safety. This picture is from a protest march in 1910, when she was nearly 70 years old. Archives of Labor & Union Affairs, Wayne State University.

In 1891, a white-haired woman more than 60 years old stepped down from a train in an Appalachian mining town. A man anxiously asked her name, and she told him. Thirty years later, she still recalled his response: "The superintendent [manager for the coal-mining company] told me that if you came down here he would blow out your brains. He said he didn't want to see you 'round these parts." The threat had no effect, for she had long since chosen her life's direction. "You tell the superintendent that I am not coming to see him anyway. I am coming to see the miners." For almost fifty years, Mary Harris Jones chose "to see the miners" and to bring them the message of unionism in the face of hostility and threats from mining companies and the local officials who often did the companies' bidding.

According to her own account, Mary Harris was born in Ireland in 1830 and came to the United States as a child, with her father. As a young woman, she taught school and worked as a dressmaker or seamstress, then married George Jones, an iron molder and union activist. Her expectations as a wife and mother were shattered, however, when she lost her entire family—her husband and their four children—in a yellow-fever epidemic in 1867.

On her own, she opened a dressmaking shop in Chicago. Her clients included those she

endeavors of the legendary Mary Harris ("Mother") Jones (see Individual Choices: Mother Jones).

Terence V. Powderly, a machinist, led the Knights from 1879 to 1893. Under his leadership, they chose organization, education, and cooperation as their chief objectives. Powderly generally opposed strikes. A lost strike, he argued, often destroyed the local organization and thereby delayed the more important tasks of education and cooperation. The Knights favored political action to accomplish a range of labor reforms, including health and safety laws for workers, the eight-hour workday, prohibition of child labor, equal pay for equal work regardless of gender, and the graduated income tax. They later endorsed

Terence V. Powderly Leader of the Knights of Labor who called for cooperative production instead of a wage system.

called "the aristocrats of Chicago," and she witnessed "the luxury and extravagance of their lives." The contrast between the opulent expectations of her wealthy clients and the tightly constrained lives of the poor left her deeply disturbed.

"Often while sewing for the lords and barons who lived in magnificent houses on the Lake Shore Drive," she recalled in her autobiography, "I would look out of the plate glass windows and see the poor, shivering wretches, jobless and hungry, walking along the frozen lake front. The contrast of their condition with that of the tropical comfort of the people for whom I sewed was painful to me."

In 1871, her shop burned in the great fire that swept much of the city. Thereafter, she chose to give much of her time to helping workers, first through the Knights of Labor. In 1882, she first took part in a strike by coal miners.

As the Knights of Labor began to disintegrate after 1886, some of its trade assemblies (organizations limited to workers in one trade) chose to affiliate with the American Federation of Labor (AFL). In 1890, one received an AFL charter as the United Mine Workers of America (UMW), but it remained an industrial union that admitted both white and black members. Until her death, in 1930, Mother Jones fought for the UMW. She became a familiar figure throughout the sooty valleys of Appalachia, where miners' families lived in wretched, company-owned shacks, their lives closely constrained by the power of the mining companies, the sometimes brutal company guards, and the often compliant local officials.

Jones's white hair, grandmotherly appearance, and deep loyalty to those she called "her boys" earned her the nickname "Mother." Others called her the "miners' angel." One county attorney, however, labeled her "the most dangerous woman in the country" in recognition of her ability to inspire men and women to oppose the mining companies. Her admirers recounted stories of her bravery in the face of danger. One insisted that "she wasn't afraid of the devil."

Mother Jones's talents lay in public speaking and in organizing demonstrations to capture public attention and sympathy. In one strike in 1900, she organized miners' wives to protest against strikebreakers by pounding on pots and pans and frightening the mules that pulled the mine carts. In 1903, she took up the cause of the children who worked in textile mills. By organizing a march of mill children to the home of President Theodore Roosevelt, she captured headlines with her living, walking display of the children's deformities and injuries caused by mill work.

Mother Jones made an unusual choice in her decision to spend the second half of her life as a labor organizer and agitator. But she apparently held traditional expectations about the role of women in society, arguing that their place was in the home. She seems to have seen her own work as an extension of her role as mother. Deprived of her own family, she sought to nurture and protect a much lager family of workers.

government ownership of the telephone, telegraph, and railroad systems. In 1878, 1880, and 1882, Powderly won election as mayor of Scranton, Pennsylvania, as the candidate of a labor party.

The Knights' endorsement of cooperation was related to the labor theory of value. A major objective of the Knights was "to secure to the workers the full enjoyment of the wealth they create." Toward that end, they committed themselves in their first national meeting in 1878 to create a system of producers' and consumers' **cooperatives,** which they hoped would "tend to supersede the wage-system." They established some 135 cooperatives by the mid-1880s, but few lasted very long. Some folded because of lack of

cooperative A business enterprise in which workers and consumers share in ownership and take part in management.

capital, some because of opposition from businesses with which they competed, some because of poor organization.

By the 1880s, the Knights of Labor was the largest labor organization in the country. Members numbered 9,000 in 1879 and 703,000 in 1886. This meteoric growth suggested that many working people were seeking ways to respond to the emerging corporate behemoths or to regain some control over their own working lives. Although the Knights opposed striking, a large part of the increase in membership in 1885–1886 came because local Knights organizers played major roles in helping to organize and win strikes against prominent railroads in 1884 and 1885—strikes that had started when workers refused to accept changes in their wages and working conditions. Thus, although many members seem to have joined in order to unite against their employer, the national leadership played down such conflicts in the interests of long-term economic and political change.

1886: Turning Point for Labor?

The Great Strike of 1877 and the rise of the Knights of Labor were signs of a sense of common purpose among large numbers of working people. After 1886, however, labor organizations often found themselves on the defensive and were divided between those trying to adjust to the new realities of industrial capitalism and those seeking to change it.

On May 1, 1886, some eighty thousand Chicagoans marched through the streets in support of an eight-hour workday, a cause that united a wide variety of unions and radical groups. Three days later, Chicago police killed several strikers at the McCormick Harvester Works. Hoping to build on the unity demonstrated by the May Day parade, a group of Chicago **anarchists** called a protest meeting for the next day at Haymarket Square. When police tried to break up the rally, someone threw a bomb into the police ranks. The police opened fire on the crowd, and some of the protesters fired back. Eight policemen eventually died, along with an unknown number of demonstrators. About a hundred people, including sixty policemen, suffered injuries.

The Haymarket bombing sparked public anxiety and antiunion feelings. Employers who had opposed unions before now tried to discredit them by playing on fears of radical-inspired terrorism. Some people who supported what they saw as legitimate union goals now shrank back in horror. In Chicago, amid public furor over the violence, eight leading anarchists stood trial for inciting the bombing and, on flimsy evidence, were convicted. Four were hanged, one committed suicide, and three remained in jail until a sympathetic governor, John Peter Altgeld, released them in 1893.

Uniting the Craft Unions: The American Federation of Labor

Two weeks after the Haymarket bombing, trade union leaders met in Philadelphia to discuss the inroads that the Knights of Labor had made among their members. They proposed an agreement between the trade unions and the Knights: trade unions would recruit skilled workers, and the Knights would limit themselves to unskilled workers. When the Knights turned down this plan, the trade unions formed the **American Federation of Labor (AFL)** to coordinate their struggles with the Knights for the loyalty of skilled workers. Membership in the AFL was to be limited to national trade unions. The combined membership of the thirteen founding unions amounted only to 140,000.

Samuel Gompers became the AFL's first president. Born in London in 1850 to Dutch Jewish parents, he learned the cigarmaker's trade before coming to the United States in 1863. He joined the Cigarmakers' Union in 1864 and became its president in 1877. Except for one year in the 1890s, Gompers continued as president of the AFL from 1886 until his death in 1924. A socialist in his youth, Gompers moved to a more conservative stance as AFL president, opposing labor involvement with radicalism or politics. Instead, he and other AFL leaders came to favor what Gompers called "pure and simple" unionism, focusing on higher wages, shorter hours, and improved working conditions for members of their own unions. Although most AFL unions did not challenge capitalism, they did use

anarchist A person who believes that all forms of government are oppressive and should be abolished.

American Federation of Labor National organization of trade unions founded in 1886; it used strikes and boycotts to improve the lot of craftworkers.

Samuel Gompers First president of the American Federation of Labor; he argued to divorce labor organizing from politics and stressed practical demands involving wages and hours.

the strike to achieve their more limited goals, and they sometimes engaged in long and bitter struggles with their employers.

After the 1880s, the AFL suffered little competition from the Knights of Labor. The decline of the Knights came swiftly: 703,000 members in 1886, 260,000 in 1888, 100,000 in 1890. The failure of several strikes involving the Knights in the late 1880s cost them many supporters. The Knights themselves contributed to their decline by expelling units that were affiliated with both the Knights and an AFL union. In addition, those units of the Knights that were organized along craft lines often found that they had more in common with the new and very practical AFL than with the more visionary Powderly. The most prominent of these was probably the United Mine Workers of America (UMWA), chartered by the AFL in 1890. Though changing from the Knights to the AFL, the UMWA continued some central principles of the Knights, including the organization of African Americans as well as whites and a commitment to organizing all the workers in their industry rather than just the most skilled workers. Others who abandoned the Knights probably held unrealistic expectations about achieving a "cooperative commonwealth."

Labor on the Defensive: Homestead and Pullman

In the late 1880s and 1890s, even highly skilled workers often found that their craft unions could not withstand the power of the new industrial companies. A major demonstration of this came in 1892 in Homestead, Pennsylvania, at Carnegie's giant steel plant, a stronghold of the Amalgamated Association of Iron, Steel, and Tin Workers, the largest AFL union. One of Carnegie's partners, Henry Clay Frick, managed the **Homestead steel plant.** The Amalgamated Association had a contract with Carnegie Steel covering the plant. When Frick proposed major cuts in wages, the union refused. Frick then locked union members out of the plant and prepared to bring in replacements.

Frick hired as guards three hundred agents of the Pinkerton detective agency. They came by riverboat, but ten thousand strikers and community supporters resisted when they tried to land. Shots rang out. In the ensuing gun battle, seven Pinkertons and nine strikers were killed and sixty people injured. The Pinkertons surrendered, leaving the strikers in control. Soon after, however, the governor of Pennsylvania sent in the state militia to wrest control from the strikers and protect the strikebreakers. The militia did its job. The Amalgamated Association never recovered. This crushing defeat of the largest craft union in the nation seemed a vivid lesson that no union could stand up to the new industrial companies, especially when those companies could call on the government for assistance.

A similar fate befell the most ambitious organizing drive of the 1890s. In 1893, under the leadership of **Eugene V. Debs,** railway workers launched the American Railway Union (ARU). Born in Indiana in 1855, Debs had served as an officer of the locomotive firemen's union. Railway workers had organized separate craft unions for engineers, firemen, switchmen, and conductors, but Debs hoped to bring all railway workers together into one union. Instead of using skill as the qualification for membership, he proposed employment in the railway industry as the basis for membership, thereby creating an **industrial union.** Success came quickly. Within a year, the ARU claimed 150,000 members and was the largest single union in the nation.

The twenty-four railway companies whose lines entered Chicago had formed the General Managers Association (GMA) as a way of addressing their common problems, and they now took alarm at the rise of the ARU. They found an opportunity to challenge the new union in 1894, when workers at the Pullman Palace Car Company (a manufacturer of luxury railway cars) asked the ARU to support a strike of Pullman workers by boycotting **Pullman cars**—disconnecting them from every train and proceeding without them. When the ARU agreed, it found itself on a collision course with the GMA. The managers threatened to fire any worker who observed the boycott, but their real purpose—as expressed by the GMA chairman—was to eliminate the ARU and "to wipe him [Debs] out."

Homestead steel plant Carnegie steel plant in Pennsylvania where state troops in 1892 put down a strike after a violent clash between striking workers and Pinkerton detectives.

Eugene V. Debs American Railway Union leader who was jailed after the Pullman strike; he became a socialist and later ran for president.

industrial union Labor union that organizes all workers in an industry, skilled or unskilled, without categorizing them by occupation.

Pullman car A railroad car with private compartments and berths for sleeping.

♦ This photograph shows officials reading to the American Railway Union strikers from the court injunction that ordered them back to work, ending the Pullman strike. Though photographers rarely captured live action in the early 1890s and took very very few pictures of Pullman strikers, the strikers in this picture are in sharp contrast to those in the engraving of the striking railway workers in 1877. *Chicago Historical Society.*

Within a short time, all 150,000 ARU members walked out on strike in support of members who were fired for refusing to handle Pullman cars. Rail traffic in and out of Chicago came to a halt, affecting railways from the Pacific coast to New York State. The General Managers Association, however, found an ally in U.S. Attorney General Richard Olney, a former railroad lawyer. Olney obtained an **injunction** against the strikers by arguing that the strike prevented delivery of the mail. He also argued that it violated the Sherman Anti-Trust Act (see page 616). Olney convinced President **Grover Cleveland** to use thousands of **U.S. marshals** and federal troops to protect trains operated by strikebreakers. Mobs lashed out at railroad property, especially in Chicago, burning trains and buildings. ARU leaders condemned the violence, but a dozen people died before it ended. Union leaders, including Debs, were jailed, and the ARU was destroyed.

The depression that began in 1893 further weakened the unions. In 1894, Gompers acknowledged that nearly all AFL affiliates "had their resources greatly diminished and their efforts largely crippled" through lost strikes and unemployment. Nevertheless, the AFL hung on. By 1897, the organization claimed fifty-eight national unions as affiliates with a combined membership of nearly 270,000. By then, many working people had demonstrated both their discontent with their place in the new economic order and their hope that united, cooperative action might improve matters.

The Nation Transformed

• How did Americans respond to the transformation of the economy?

By 1901, Americans could be excused if they seemed anxious about the economic changes of the previous thirty years or uncertain about the outcomes of their many individual choices. While some Americans wandered through great **expositions** that celebrated the economic transformation, others argued over the most effective ways to achieve and maintain progress.

Celebrating the New Age

In 1893, when the World's Columbian Exposition opened in Chicago, Hamlin Garland, a writer living there, wrote to his parents in South Dakota, "Sell the

injunction A court order requiring a person or group to do or refrain from doing something; courts often used injunctions to force strikers to return to work.

Grover Cleveland New York politician and advocate of clean government who was president of the United States from 1885 through 1889 and again from 1893 through 1897.

U.S. marshal A federal law-enforcement officer.

exposition A large public exhibition, often of cultural and industrial developments.

♦ This drawing of the administration building for Chicago's Columbian Exposition emphasizes the planners' dramatic use of classical architecture, which they combined with modern electrical lighting. Because its buildings were all white, the exposition was called the "White City."*Culver Pictures.*

cook stove if necessary and come. . . . You must see this fair." Between 1876 and 1915, Americans repeatedly held great expositions, beginning with one in Philadelphia in 1876 that commemorated the centennial of independence and concluding with one in San Francisco in 1915 that celebrated the opening of the Panama Canal (see page 656). Others, on various pretexts, took place in Atlanta, Buffalo, Omaha, Portland (Oregon), San Diego, and St. Louis. The most impressive and influential was the Columbian Exposition in Chicago, marking the four-hundredth anniversary of Columbus's voyage to the New World.

These expositions typically featured vast exhibition halls where companies displayed their latest technological marvels, artists exhibited their creations, and farmers presented their most impressive produce. In other halls, states and foreign nations showed their accomplishments. The exhibits nearly always expressed the conviction that technology and industry would inevitably improve the lives of all. Behind the gleaming machines in the imitation marble palaces, however, lurked troubling questions that never appeared in the exhibits glorifying "Progress." Were democratic institutions compatible with tendencies toward concentration of power and control in industry and finance? What should be the working conditions of those whose labor created such technological marvels?

Survival of the Fittest?

The concentration of power and wealth during the late nineteenth century generated extensive comment and concern. The most prominent statement on the subject was known as **social Darwinism,** reflecting its roots in Charles Darwin's work on evolution. Darwin had concluded that those creatures that survive in competition against other creatures and against an often inhospitable environment are those that adapted best to their surroundings, and that such adaptation leads to the evolution of different species, each uniquely suited to a particular ecological niche.

Herbert Spencer in England and William Graham Sumner in the United States, both philosophers, put their own interpretation on Darwin's reasoning and applied it to the human situation, producing social Darwinism (a philosophical perspective that bore little relation to Darwin's original work). Social Darwinists contended that competition among people produced "progress" through "survival of the fittest" and that competition provided the best possible route for improving humankind and advancing civilization. Further, they argued that efforts to ease the harsh impact of competition only protected the unfit and thereby worked to the long-term disadvantage of all. Some concluded that powerful entrepreneurs constituted "the fittest" and benefited all humankind by their accomplishments.

Andrew Carnegie enthusiastically embraced Spencer's arguments and endorsed individualism and self-reliance as the cornerstones of progress. "Civilization took its start from that day that the capable, industrious workman said to his incompetent and lazy fellow, 'If thou dost not sow, thou shalt not reap,'" Carnegie wrote. When applied to

social Darwinism A philosophical argument, inspired by Charles Darwin's theory of evolution, that proclaimed that competition in human society produced "the survival of the fittest" and therefore benefited the society; social Darwinists therefore opposed efforts to regulate competitive practices.

government, this notion became a form of **laissez faire,** the belief that the economy functions best when the government leaves it strictly on its own.

Carnegie, though, was inconsistent, also preaching what he called the **Gospel of Wealth:** the idea that the wealthy should return their riches to the community from which they came by creating "the ladders upon which the aspiring can rise"—parks, art museums, educational institutions. The person who dies rich, Carnegie proclaimed, "dies disgraced." Carnegie did not die disgraced. He spent his final eighteen years giving away his fortune: 3,000 public library buildings and 4,100 church organs all across the nation, gifts to universities, Carnegie Hall in New York City, and several foundations. (One humorist, though, poked fun at Carnegie's libraries by suggesting that they would serve the community better if they contained a kitchen and beds so that the poor might eat and sleep in them.)

Like Carnegie, John D. Rockefeller spent much of his retirement disbursing his fortune—to the University of Chicago and other universities, the Baptist church, and the Rockefeller Foundation. Carnegie and Rockefeller were unusual because of the amount of their wealth and the emphasis they placed on the obligation of the wealthy toward the community, but they were not the only nineteenth-century industrialists and financiers who practiced **philanthropy**—even as some of them also built ostentatious mansions, threw extravagant parties, and otherwise flaunted their wealth. Duke University, Stanford University, Vanderbilt University, the Morgan Library in New York City, and the Huntington Library in southern California all carry the names of men who amassed fortunes in the new, industrial economy and used their fortunes to promote learning and research.

Although many Americans subscribed to the vision of social Darwinism propounded by Spencer and Sumner, many others did not. Entrepreneurs themselves often welcomed some forms of government intervention in the economy—from railroad land grants to the protective tariff to suppression of strikes—although most agreed with the social Darwinists that government should not assist the poor and destitute.

Furthermore, many Americans disagreed with the social Darwinists' equation of laissez faire with progress. Henry George, a San Francisco journalist, pointed out in *Progress and Poverty* (1879) that "amid the greatest accumulations of wealth, men die of starvation," and he concluded that "material progress does not merely fail to relieve poverty—it actually produces it." Lester Frank Ward, a sociologist, posed a carefully reasoned refutation of social Darwinism, suggesting that biological competition produced bare survival, not civilization. Civilization, he argued, represented "a triumph of mind" that derived not from "ceaseless and aimless competition" but from rationality and cooperation.

Robber Barons?

Americans disagreed over the deeds of the powerful industrialists and financiers. Some accepted them as benefactors of the nation. Others agreed with E. L. Godkin, a journalist who in 1869 compared one railroad magnate, Cornelius Vanderbilt, to a medieval robber baron—a feudal lord who robbed travelers passing through his domain. Those who have called the wealthy industrialists and bankers **robber barons** point out that they were unscrupulous, greedy, exploitative, and antisocial. Looking only at the deeds or misdeeds of individual entrepreneurs, however, hides more about the economy than it reveals. Understanding these men and the larger economic changes of the era requires more than an examination of individual behavior, whether despicable or praiseworthy.

Thomas C. Cochran, a historian, looked at the broad cultural context that affected not just prominent entrepreneurs but also most Americans. He identified three broadly shared "cultural themes" as central for understanding the period: (1) a belief that the economy operated according to self-correcting principles, especially the law of supply and demand; (2) the ideas of social Darwinism; and (3) an assumption that people were motivated primarily by a desire for material gain. These themes shed light not only on the actions of the entrepreneurs of the late nineteenth century but also on the reception they received from other Americans.

laissez faire The principle that the government should not interfere in the workings of the economy.

Gospel of Wealth Andrew Carnegie's idea that all possessors of great wealth have an obligation to spend their money on good works, to help people to help themselves.

philanthropist A person who donates money or services to benefit humanity.

robber baron Disapproving term applied to the financial giants of the late nineteenth century, especially those who flaunted their wealth.

SUMMARY

Expectations
Constraints
Choices
Outcomes

After 1865, large-scale manufacturing developed quite quickly in the United States, built on a foundation of abundant natural resources, a pool of skilled workers, expanding harvests, and favorable government policies. The *outcome* was the transformation of the U.S. economy.

Entrepreneurs made *choices* that improved and extended railway lines, eliminating *constraints* of distance and natural barriers and creating a national transportation network. Manufacturers and merchants developed new *expectations* based on a national market for raw materials and finished goods. Railroads were the first businesses to grapple with many problems related to size, and they made *choices* that other businesses imitated. Investment bankers, notably J. P. Morgan, led in combining separate rail companies into larger and more profitable systems.

Andrew Carnegie and John D. Rockefeller were the best known of many entrepreneurs whose *choices* produced manufacturing operations of unprecedented size and complexity. By 1900, *choices* spurred by competition had produced oligopoly and vertical integration in many industries. Technology and advertising emerged as important competitive devices. At the turn of the century, investment bankers led a wave of mergers in a number of industries.

Workers *chose* to migrate to expanding industrial centers from rural areas either in the United States or in another country. The new work force included not only adult males but also women and children. Industrial workers had little control over the pace or hours of their work and often faced unpleasant or dangerous working conditions.

Expecting that cooperation might improve their lot, some workers *chose* to form labor organizations to fight the *constraints* of low wages, long hours, and poor conditions. Espousing cooperatives and reform, the Knights of Labor *chose* to open their membership to the unskilled, to African Americans, and to women—groups usually not admitted to craft unions. The Knights died out after 1890. The American Federation of Labor was formed by craft unions. The AFL *chose* to reject radicalism and instead to work within capitalism to improve wages, hours, and conditions for its members. Major strikes between 1877 and 1894 revealed both the depth of workers' discontent and the strength of their organizations. By the mid-1890s, however, labor organizations were on the defensive.

Great expositions celebrated manufacturing and new technologies. Social Darwinists acclaimed unrestricted competition for producing progress and survival of the fittest. Others criticized the negative aspects of the era's economy. Some simply condemned the great entrepreneurs as robber barons, but more complex treatments analyze such figures within the cultural context of their own time.

SUGGESTED READINGS

David Brody. *Steelworkers in America: The Nonunion Era* (1960).

The lives of steelworkers and the nature of their work.

Melvyn Dubofsky. *Industrialism and the American Worker, 1865–1920,* 3d ed. (1996).

A brief introduction to the topic, organized chronologically.

Mary Harris "Mother" Jones. *The Autobiography of Mother Jones,* ed. Mary Field Parton (1925; reprint, 1980).

A self-portrait, not always precise regarding facts and dates but fascinating for its account of one woman's activism.

Naomi Lamoreaux. *The Great Merger Movement in American Business, 1895–1904* (1985).

An impressive study of the merger movement using detailed case histories of particular industries.

David Montgomery. *The Fall of the House of Labor: The Workplace, the State, and American Labor Activism, 1865–1925* (1987).

A look at the workplace and at workers' responses to it.

Glenn Porter. *The Rise of Big Business, 1860–1910,* 2d ed. (1992).

A brief introduction, surveying the role of the railroads, vertical and horizontal integration, and the merger movement.

THE WEST, 1865–1902 This map identifies various parts of the West. As you can see, the West had very few cities, and those tended to be located on the edges of the region.

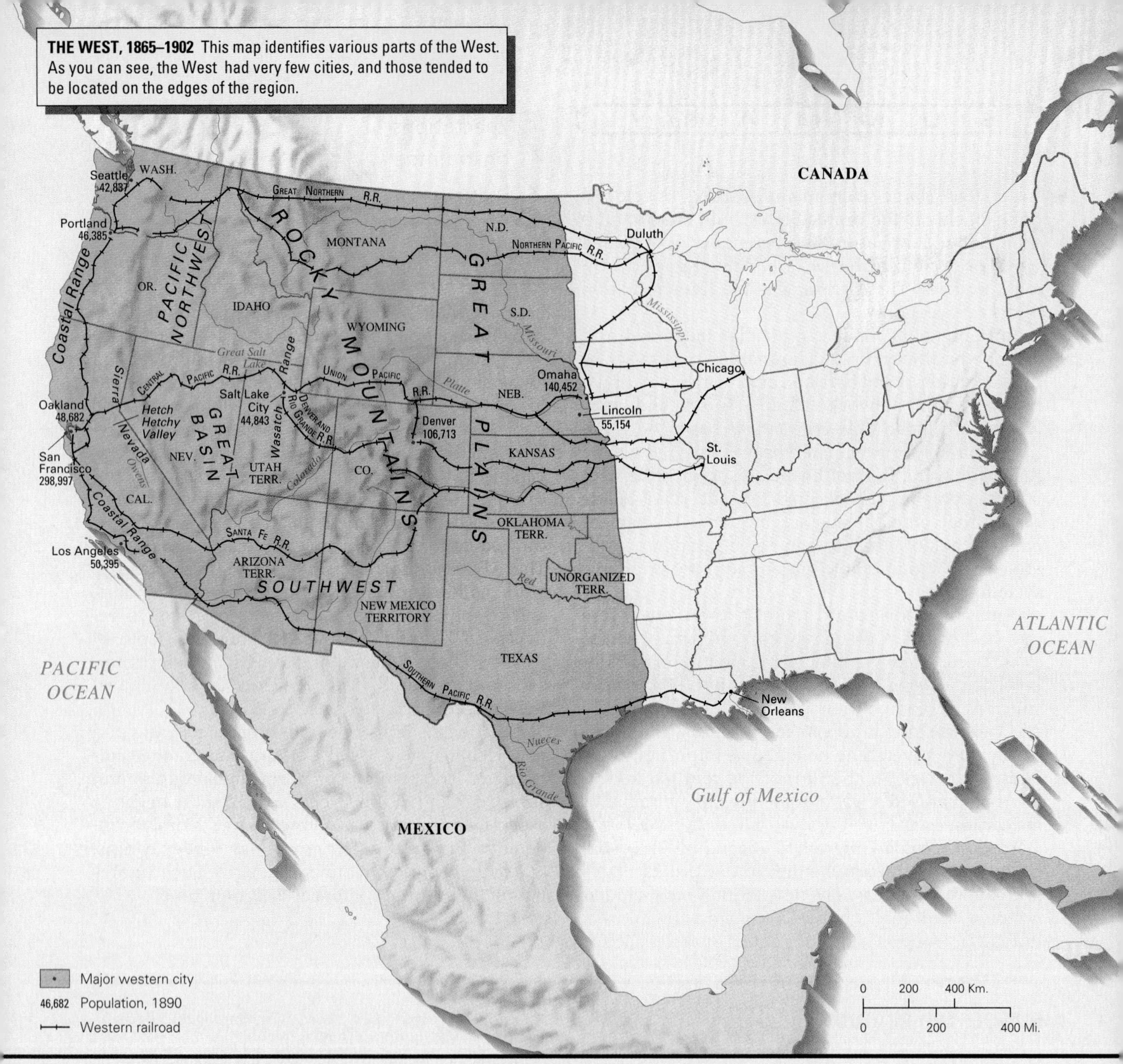

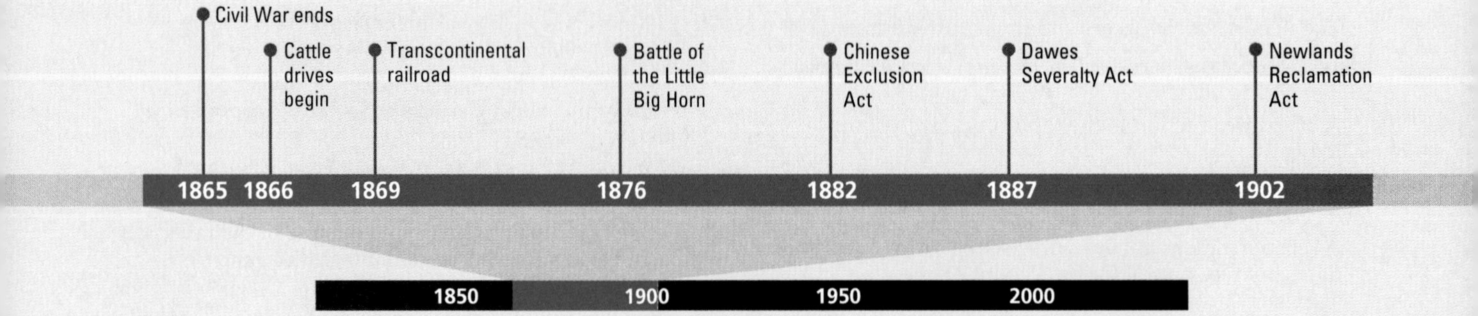

CHAPTER 18

Conflict and Change in the West, 1865–1902

War for the West

- What did federal policymakers after the Civil War hope to accomplish in their choices regarding American Indians?
- How did western Indians choose to respond?
- What different expectations probably lay behind both sets of choices? How were the expectations of the western Indians different from those of federal policymakers?

Mormons, Cowboys, and Sodbusters: The Transformation of the West, Part I

- What constraints did Mormons, the range-cattle industry, and farmers face in the West? What choices did each make in response to those constraints?
- How successful was each group in its efforts to begin new economic activities in the West—that is, what was the outcome of the choices that each group made?

Railroads, Mining, Agribusiness, Logging, and Finance: The Transformation of the West, Part II

- What constraints confronted western entrepreneurs engaged in mining, agriculture, or logging?
- What choices did those entrepreneurs make to develop their industries?
- How did economic development in the West during the late nineteenth century compare with that taking place in the eastern United States at the same time (see Chapter 17)?

Ethnicity and Race in the West

- Compare the experiences of American Indians, Mexican Americans, and Chinese Americans between the end of the Civil War (1865) and about 1900.
- What constraints did each group face? What choices did members of the group make?

The West in American Thought

- How does the myth of the West compare with the reality?

INTRODUCTION

E xpectations
C onstraints
C hoices
O utcomes

While Andrew Carnegie and John D. Rockefeller were building industrial empires in the East, the U.S. Army was eliminating the last armed Indian resistance in the West, where entrepreneurs had already begun their own empire building. Americans have shown a long-lasting interest in the West of the late nineteenth century. Popular fiction and drama have glorified the West as a land where rugged individualism held sway and pioneers overcame great odds. The reality of western life was somewhat different.

At the close of the Civil War, many Americans looked to the West with high *expectations.* For years before the war, the issue of slavery had *constrained* federal action to develop the West. The secession of the southern states removed that *constraint*, and the Republicans who took charge in Washington in 1861 moved quickly to use federal power to open the West to economic development and white settlement, through measures such as the Pacific Railroad Act and the Homestead Act, both passed in 1862.

As Americans faced west, they held some contradictory *expectations.* On the one hand, prior experience suggested the steady westward extension of family farms. It had taken American farmers more than a half-century to fill the area between the Appalachian Mountains and the Mississippi River and might take as long to extend cultivation to the Rocky Mountains. In 1827, in fact, a cabinet officer had predicted that the nation would take five hundred years to fill up the West. On the other hand, travelers to the West had described it as an area of vast deserts, forbidding mountains, and well-armed, mounted American Indian warriors. Such potential *constraints* as these suggested that parts of the West might never be developed like the eastern half of the nation.

In most of the West, rainfall was markedly less than in the eastern United States, where sufficient water was simply taken for granted. In the West, the scarcity of water *constrained* development and presented a new set of *choices*. What sort of development was appropriate in a region with little rain? How could western water be harnessed to support development? Who would control the water, and who would benefit from it?

Similarly, the ethnic and racial composition of the West differed significantly from patterns in the East and South. At the end of the Civil War, the northeastern and north-central United States was almost entirely of European descent. The South was a biracial society—white and black. Some American Indians lived east of the Mississippi, but larger numbers had been pushed westward and were sharing parts of the West with tribal groups that claimed it as their ancestral homeland. The Southwest was home to significant numbers of people who spoke Spanish, who were often of mixed white and American Indian ancestry, and whose families had lived in the region long before the arrival of the first Yankees. By the time of the Civil War, the Pacific coast had attracted immigrants from Asia, especially China, who had *chosen* to cross the Pacific, going east in the *expectation* of making their fortune in America, much as European immigrants crossed the Atlantic going west. In the late nineteenth century, these concentrations of ethnic groups marked the West as a distinctive place.

As individual Americans made *choices* that shaped the development of the West—from seeking free land under the Homestead Act to speculating in mining stock to deciding how to deal with environmental *constraints*—federal officials also faced important *choices.* The basic *choice* to use the public domain to speed economic development had already been made by 1862. But a related *choice* remained—what to do about the American Indians who occupied much of the land. Given the *choices* and *constraints* facing Americans in the West, the *outcome* of efforts to develop the land was sometimes quite different from previous experience and from the *expectations* of those involved. Overall, though, the *outcome* was that during this period the western half of the United States underwent immense change.

CHRONOLOGY

Conflict and Change in the West

1700s Horse culture spreads throughout the Great Plains

1847 First Mormon settlements near Great Salt Lake

1848 Treaty of Guadalupe Hidalgo
California gold rush begins

1851 Fort Laramie treaties

1862 Homestead Act
Pacific Railroad Act
Land-Grant College Act

1865 Civil War ends

1866–1880 Cattle drives north from Texas

1867–1868 Treaties establish major western reservations

1868–1869 Army's winter campaign against southern Plains Indians

1869 First transcontinental railroad completed

Early 1870s Cattle raising begins on northern plains

1870s Destruction of buffalo herds
Silver-mining boom in Nevada
Standard Oil incorporated

1870s–1880s Extension of farming to the Great Plains

1871–1885 Anti-Chinese riots across the West

1874 American Indian resistance ends on southern plains
Patent issued for barbed wire

1876 Spring and summer campaign on northern plains
Indian victory in Battle of Little Big Horn

1877 Army subdues last major Indian resistance on northern plains
Surrender and death of Crazy Horse
Chief Joseph and the Nez Perce flee
Workingmen's party of California attacks Chinese
Reconstruction ends

1881 Surrender of Sitting Bull

1882 Chinese Exclusion Act

1883 Northern Pacific Railroad completed to Portland

1884 Federal court prohibits hydraulic mining

1886 Surrender of Geronimo
Yick Wo v. Hopkins
AFL founded

1886–1887 Severe winter damages northern cattle business

1887 Dawes Severalty Act

Late 1880s Reduced rainfall

1890 Sitting Bull killed
Conflict at Wounded Knee Creek

1892 Sierra Club formed

1893 Great Northern Railway completed
Frederick Jackson Turner presents his frontier thesis

War for the West

- What did federal policymakers after the Civil War hope to accomplish in their choices regarding American Indians?
- How did western Indians choose to respond?
- What different expectations probably lay behind both sets of choices? How were the expectations of the western Indians different from those of federal policymakers?

When Congress chose to use the public domain—western land—to encourage economic development, most white Americans considered the West to be largely vacant. In fact, American Indians lived throughout most of the West, and their understanding of their relationship to the land differed greatly from that of most white Americans. The most tragic outcome of the development of the West was certainly the experience of the American Indians who lived there.

The Plains Indians

By the time white Americans began to move west, the acquisition of horses and, to a lesser extent, guns had already transformed the lives of many American Indians. This transformation occurred most dramatically among the tribes living on or near the **Great Plains**—the vast, relatively flat, and treeless region that stretches from north to south across the center of the nation and that was then home to huge herds of buffalo. The introduction of the horse to the Great Plains took place slowly, primarily from Spanish settlements in what is now New Mexico. In 1680, the **Pueblo Indians** of that region revolted against the Spanish, briefly drove them out, and took their herds of horses. The Pueblos traded horses to surrounding tribes, thus introducing substantial numbers of them to the plains for the first time. Even so, horses did not reach the northern plains in large numbers until the eighteenth century. At the same time, the expanding white settlements along the Atlantic coast pushed all tribes westward, toward the Great Plains. By the mid-eighteenth century, French and English traders to the northeast of the plains had begun to provide guns to the Indians in return for furs. Thus guns entered the plains from the East and Northeast, and horses entered from the Southwest. Together they transformed the culture of many of the Plains tribes.

Two different ways of life were evident among the Indians of the plains: **sedentary** farming and nomadic buffalo hunting. The farmers lived most of the year in large, permanent villages. Among this group were the Pawnees, Arikaras, and Wichitas (who spoke languages of the Caddoan family) and the Hidatsas, Mandans, Omahas, Otos, Osages, and others (who spoke Siouan languages). On the northern plains, their large, dome-shaped houses were typically made of logs and covered with dirt. In southern areas, their houses were often covered with grass. These Indians farmed the fertile river valleys, harvesting corn, squash, pumpkins, beans, sunflowers, and tobacco. They gathered wild fruit and vegetables and hunted and fished near their villages. Men were responsible for hunting, fishing, and cultivating tobacco. Women were responsible for the other farming and for food preparation. Before the arrival of horses, twice a year entire villages went—on foot—on extended hunting trips for buffalo—once in the early summer after the crops were planted, then again in the fall after the harvest. During these hunts, the people lived in **tipis,** cone-shaped tents of buffalo hide that were easy to move. The acquisition of horses changed the culture of these Indians only slightly.

In contrast, the horse revolutionized the way of life of another group of Plains Indians. A hunter on a swift horse could kill twice as many buffalo as one on foot. By increasing the killing capacity of the hunters, the horse substantially increased the number of people the plains could support. At the same time, the horse increased mobility, permitting a band to follow the buffalo herds as they moved across the plains. The buffalo provided most essentials: food (meat), clothing and shelter (made from hides), implements (made from bones and horns), and even fuel for fires (dried dung). Some groups completely abandoned farming and became nomadic, living in tipis year round and following the

Great Plains High grassland of western North America, stretching from roughly the 98th meridian to the Rocky Mountains; it is generally level, treeless, and fairly dry.

Pueblo Indians Hopis, Zunis, and other village Indians of the Southwest who lived in multilevel stone or adobe apartment houses; they were primarily farmers.

sedentary Living in fixed villages and engaging in extensive farming, as opposed to moving from camp to camp throughout the year.

tipi Conical tent made from buffalo hide and used as a portable dwelling by Indians on the Great Plains.

♦ In the 1830s, George Catlin painted this buffalo hunt in what is now Montana. The acquisition of horses greatly increased the Indians' ability to kill buffalo. The Cheyenne, for extreme example, abandoned farming and staked their livelihood entirely on hunting. *"Buffalo Chase, Mouth of the Yellowstone" by George Catlin. National Museum of American Art, Washington, DC/Art Resource, NY.*

buffalo herds. The **Cheyennes,** for example, made this transition within one generation after 1770, when a neighboring tribe destroyed their permanent village. By the early nineteenth century, the **horse culture** existed throughout the Great Plains. The largest groups practicing it included—from north to south—the Blackfeet, Crows, **Lakotas,** Cheyennes, Arapahos, Kiowas, and Comanches.

The Lakotas were the largest of all the groups. They were the westernmost members of a large group of American Indian peoples often called *Sioux,* which means "enemy" and which may stem from their custom of considering all those who were not members of their confederacy to be their enemies. The eastern Sioux were called Dakotas or Nakotas. All the Lakotas shared a common language. Membership in the Lakota confederacy was not limited to those speaking a particular language, however, as the northern Cheyennes had generally come to be considered members of the Lakota confederacy by the mid-nineteenth century.

Whether nomadic buffalo hunters or sedentary farming people, Indians living on the Great Plains and in other areas of North America understood the land very differently from white settlers. From the time of the first European migrants to America, most white Americans had considered land to be a commodity to be bought, sold, and owned by individuals. According to Indian tradition, however, land was to be used but not individually owned. Horses, weapons, tipis, and clothing were all individually owned, but not the land. Among farming peoples, a tribal leader assigned farmland among the female heads of each family on the basis of family size.

Before the arrival of horses, status among young men derived from raiding a neighboring tribe to seize agricultural produce, capture a member of that tribe as a slave, or seek revenge for a similar raid. With the development of the horse culture, wealth was measured in horses. After the arrival of horses, raids were staged primarily to steal horses, seek revenge, or both. A young man acquired status through demonstrations of daring and bravery in raids. Signs of success were the number of horses captured, the number of opponents defeated in battle, and success in returning home uninjured. An individual won special glory by counting coup—that is, by touching an enemy, either with one's hand or with a stick. (*Coup* is a French word meaning "stroke" or "blow.")

Historians and anthropologists once thought that conflict between and among Plains tribes was largely related to stealing horses and seeking honor by counting coup. More recent scholars have pointed out that there were serious contests for hunting territory—for example, between the Lakotas and the Crows. These conflicts over territory often developed as tribes were pushed to the west as tribes to their east were also pushed west by expanding European settlements along the Atlantic coast. The Lakotas and Cheyennes, for example, once lived just to the east of the northern plains but were pushed onto the plains as the tribes to their east came under pressure.

Cheyennes Indian people who became nomadic buffalo hunters after migrating to the Great Plains in the eighteenth century.

horse culture The nomadic way of life of those American Indians, mostly on the Great Plains, for whom the horse brought significant changes in their ability to hunt and travel.

Lakotas Indian people who lived on the northern Great Plains; hostile tribes called them Sioux, which means "enemy."

Among most of the Plains Indians, individual ownership of goods was not a pressing goal. A person achieved high social standing not by accumulating possessions but by sharing. Francis La Flesche, son of an Omaha leader, learned from his father that "the persecution of the poor, the sneer at their poverty is a wrong for which no punishment is too severe." His mother reinforced the lesson: "When you see a boy barefooted and lame, take off your moccasins and give them to him. When you see a boy hungry, bring him to your home and give him food."

The Plains Wars

In 1851, Congress approved a new Indian policy intended to provide each tribe with a definite territory "of limited extent and well-defined boundaries," within which the tribe was to live. The government was to supply those needs the tribes could not meet themselves from the lands they were assigned. Federal officials at first planned large reservations taking up much of the Great Plains. At a great conference held at Fort Laramie, they signed treaties that guaranteed extensive territory to the northern Plains tribes.

Before the 1851 policy, federal policymakers had considered the region west of Arkansas, Missouri, Iowa, and Minnesota and east of the Rocky Mountains to be a permanent Indian country. But farmers bound for Oregon and gold seekers on their way to California soon carved trails across the central plains, and many people soon began to talk of a railroad to connect the Pacific coast to the East. The policy initiated in 1851 was designed in part to open the central plains as a route to the Pacific.

Far more easterners thronged westward than federal officials had anticipated, and there were frequent conflicts along the trail routes. Then thousands of prospectors poured into Colorado after discovery of gold there in 1858. Withdrawal of many federal troops with the outbreak of the Civil War in 1861 may have encouraged some Plains Indians to believe they could expel the invaders. A series of Cheyenne and Lakota raids in 1864 brought demands for reprisals. Late in November, at Sand Creek in Colorado, a territorial militia unit massacred a band of Cheyennes who had no involvement in the raids. Soon after, the discovery of gold in Montana prompted construction of forts to protect a road, the **Bozeman Trail,** through Lakota territory. Cheyennes joined with Lakotas under the leadership of **Red Cloud** to organize a sustained war against the road.

In April 1868, many members of the northern Plains tribes met at Fort Laramie and agreed to a Great Sioux Reservation in what is now the western half of South Dakota. They believed that they would retain "unceded lands" for hunting in the Powder River country—present-day northeastern Wyoming and southeastern Montana. In return, the army abandoned its posts along the Bozeman Trail, a victory for the Lakotas and Cheyennes who, led by Red Cloud, had fought a two-year battle over construction of the posts.

The creation of the new reservation was part of a larger plan. With the end of the Civil War in 1865, railroad construction crews prepared to build westward. Federal policymakers now tried to stop further hostilities by creating a few great reservations in the West. One was to be for northern Plains tribes, north of the new state of Nebraska. Another was to be for southern Plains tribes, south of Kansas. The third was to be for the tribes of the mountains and the Southwest and was to be located somewhere in the Southwest. The remainder of the West was to be cleared of all but a few small reservations, thereby opening it for development—railroad building, mining, and farming. Indians on the reservations were to receive food and shelter and were to be taught how to farm and raise cattle.

The Fort Laramie Treaty of 1868 was one of several negotiated in 1867 and 1868 in fulfillment of the new policy. In 1867, a conference at Medicine Lodge Creek had produced treaties by which the major southern Plains tribes accepted reservations in what is now western Oklahoma (see Map 18.1). In May 1868, the Crows agreed to a reservation in Montana. In June 1868, the Navajos accepted a large reservation in the Southwest. By mid-1868, federal officials thought their new reservation policy had made a promising start. Given the highly fluid structure of authority among the Plains Indians, however, many of them denied that those who signed the treaties could obligate those who did not.

At the time some federal officials were negotiating these treaties, other federal officials were permitting and even encouraging white buffalo hunters to kill the buffalo—for sport, for meat, for the profit

Bozeman Trail Trail that ran from Fort Laramie, Wyoming, to the gold fields of Montana.

Red Cloud Lakota chief who led a successful fight to prevent the United States from keeping forts along the Bozeman Trail.

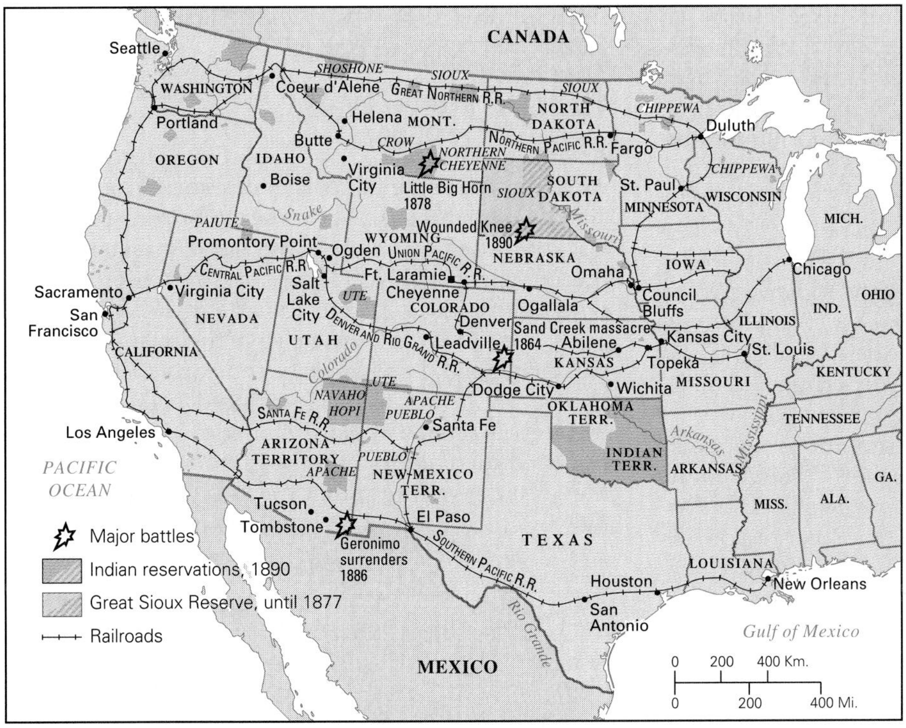

♦ **MAP 18.1 Indian Reservations** This map indicates the location of most western Indian reservations in 1890, as well as the Great Sioux Reservation before it was broken up and severely reduced in size. Note how the development of a few large reservations on the northern Plains and others on the southern Plains opened the central Plains for railroad construction and agricultural development.

to be made from the hides. Given the importance of the buffalo in the lives of the Plains Indians, their way of life was doomed once the slaughter began.

Slaughter of the buffalo proceeded rapidly once **tanneries** in the East began to buy buffalo hides. In the mid-1870s, more than 10 million buffalo were killed and stripped of their hides, which sold for a dollar or more. Nearly all the carcasses were left to rot. The southern herd was wiped out by 1878, the northern herd by 1883. Only two thousand animals survived, the remnant of a species whose numbers had once seemed as vast as the stars.

Some members of the southern Plains tribes who refused to accept the terms of the Medicine Lodge Creek treaties continued to live in their traditional territory. They resisted efforts to move them onto the reservations and occasionally attacked stagecoach stations, ranches, travelers, and military units. General William Tecumseh Sherman, who during the Civil War had devastated a wide swath of Georgia and South Carolina, now planned military strategy on the plains. After a group of southern Cheyennes inflicted heavy losses on an army unit, Sherman decreed that all Indians not on reservations "are hostile and will remain so till killed off."

Sherman's comment was the usual reaction of a conventional military force to guerrilla warfare: concentrate the friendly population in defined areas (reservations in this case) and then open fire on anyone outside those areas. In the winter of 1868–1869, the army launched a southern Plains campaign under the command of General Philip Sheridan, another Union army veteran, who directed his men to "destroy their villages and ponies, to kill and hang all warriors, and bring back all women and children." The brutal campaign that followed convinced most southern Plains tribes to abandon further resistance.

tannery An establishment where skins and hides are made into leather.

In the early 1870s, sizable buffalo herds still remained west and south of Indian Territory, in the Red River region of Texas. The Medicine Lodge Creek treaties permitted hunting in the region as long as buffalo were there. When white buffalo hunters began operations in that area in 1874, young men from the Kiowa, Comanche, and southern Cheyenne tribes attacked them. Sheridan launched another war of **attrition,** destroying tipis, food, and animals. When winter came, the cold and hungry Indians surrendered to avoid starvation. Tribal war leaders were imprisoned in Florida, far from their families. Given free rein, buffalo hunters quickly exterminated all remaining buffalo from the southern plains.

Hunting grounds outside reservations were also a cause of conflict on the northern plains. Many Lakotas and some northern Cheyennes lived on unceded hunting lands in the Powder River region, led by **Crazy Horse** and Sitting Bull. As the Northern Pacific Railroad prepared to lay track in southern Montana, uncertainty over the boundaries of the unceded lands raised the prospect of strife. Soon after, federal authorities determined to force all Indians onto the reservation, producing a conflict sometimes called the **Great Sioux War.**

Military operations in the Powder River region began in the spring of 1876. Sheridan ordered troops to enter the area from three directions and then to converge on the Indians. One part of the operation went dreadfully wrong when Lieutenant Colonel George A. Custer, without waiting for the other units, sent his Seventh Cavalry against an Indian camp that his scouts had located. The encampment, on the **Little Big Horn River,** proved to be one of the largest ever on the northern plains, combining several bands of Lakotas and Cheyennes led by Crazy Horse and Sitting Bull (see Individual Choices: Sitting Bull). Custer unwisely divided his force, and nearly three hundred men, including Custer, met their deaths.

In the winter of 1876–1877, U.S. soldiers launched another campaign of attrition on the northern plains. Troops defeated some Indian bands. Hunger and cold drove most others to surrender. Crazy Horse and his band held out until spring and surrendered only when told that they could live in the Powder River region. A few months later, Crazy Horse was killed when he resisted being put into an army jail. Sitting Bull and his band escaped to Canada and remained there until 1881, when he finally surrendered. The government cut up the Great Sioux Reservation into several smaller units and took away the Powder River region, the Black Hills (which the Lakota considered sacred), and other lands.

The Last Indian Wars

After the Great Sioux War, no Indian group had the capacity for sustained resistance. Small groups occasionally left their reservations but were promptly tracked down by troops. One notable instance was the effort by the Nez Perce, led by **Chief Joseph,** who attempted to flee to Canada in 1877 when the army tried to force them to leave their reservation in western Idaho. Between July and early October they eluded the army as they traveled east and north through Montana toward Canada. More than two hundred died along the way. Joseph surrendered on the specific condition that the Nez Perce be permitted to return to their previous home. His surrender speech is often quoted to illustrate the hopelessness of further resistance:

> *Our chiefs are killed. . . . The old men are dead. . . . It is cold and we have no blankets. The little children are freezing to death. . . . My heart is sick and sad. From where the sun now stands, I will fight no more forever!*

Federal officials sent the Nez Perce to Indian Territory, where, in an unfamiliar climate, many soon died of disease.

The last sizable group to refuse to live on a reservation was Geronimo's band of Chiricahua Apaches, who long managed to elude the army in the mountains of the Southwest. They finally gave up in 1886, and the men were sent to prison in Florida.

attrition A gradual decrease in number or strength caused by constant stress.

Crazy Horse Lakota leader who resisted white encroachment in the Black Hills and fought at the Little Big Horn River in 1876; he was killed by U.S. soldiers in 1877.

Great Sioux War War between the tribes that took part in the Battle of Little Big Horn and the U.S. Army; it ended in 1881 with the surrender of Sitting Bull.

Little Big Horn River River in Montana where in 1876 Lieutenant Colonel George Custer attacked a large Indian encampment; Custer and most of his force died in the battle.

Chief Joseph Nez Perce chief who led his people in an attempt to escape to Canada in 1877; after a grueling journey they were forced to surrender and were exiled to Indian Territory.

♦ This painting by Yellow Nose, a Ute, was done in 1891. It depicts the Ghost Dance, a religion that promised to restore the buffalo and banish the whites. The dancers' shirts were thought to make them immune to harm. The cult began in Nevada in the 1880s and gained support throughout the West until the Wounded Knee massacre. *Smithsonian Institution.*

The last major armed confrontation between the army and the Indians came late in 1890, on the Pine Ridge Reservation in South Dakota. There, some Lakotas had taken up a new religion, the **Ghost Dance,** that promised to return the land to the Indians, restore the buffalo, and sweep away the whites. Fearing an uprising, federal authorities ordered the Lakotas to stop their dance ritual. Concerned that Sitting Bull might encourage defiance, federal authorities ordered his arrest. Sitting Bull was killed in the ensuing scuffle. A small band of Lakotas, led by Big Foot, tried to flee but was captured by the Seventh Cavalry and taken to a site near **Wounded Knee Creek.** One Indian refused to surrender his gun, and shots were fired by both Indians and soldiers. The soldiers had vastly greater fire power, however, and as many as 250 Indians died, as did 25 soldiers.

The events at Wounded Knee marked the symbolic end of armed conflict on the Great Plains. In fact, the end of the horse culture was written long before, even before the Battle of Little Big Horn. Once the federal government chose to encourage rapid economic development in the West, displacement of the Indians was probably inevitable. From the beginning, the struggle was a mismatch, for the Indians faced overwhelming odds. The desperate nature of their resistance suggests that they understood that they were facing the loss not only of hunting grounds but also of their culture and even their lives.

Mormons, Cowboys, and Sodbusters: The Transformation of the West, Part I

- What constraints did Mormons, the range-cattle industry, and farmers face in the West? What choices did each make in response to those constraints?
- How successful was each group in its efforts to begin new economic activities in the West—that is, what was the outcome of the choices that each group made?

Long before the last battles between the army and the Indians, the economic development of the West was well under way. At the end of the Civil War, the West constituted more than half of the nation's land area. Its subsequent transformation reflected limitations imposed by the western environment, constraints determined by vast distances and at first by poor transportation, and the cultural values of the people seeking to live in that region. Thus decisions made by the Mormons who established themselves in the Great Basin differed significantly from those of ranchers and farmers on the Great Plains.

Zion in the Great Basin

By the end of the Civil War, development of the Great Basin region (between the Rocky Mountains and the Sierra Nevada) was already well advanced as a result of the efforts of the **Mormons.** The Mormons were controversial because of their religious beliefs, which included **polygamy.** Hounded out of one eastern state after another, Mormons settled in 1847 near the Great Salt Lake, in what was then northern Mexico. Led by Brigham Young, they

Ghost Dance Indian religion centered on a ritual dance; it promised the coming of an Indian messiah who would banish the whites, bring back the buffalo, and restore the land to the Indians.

Wounded Knee Creek Site of a conflict in 1890 between Lakota Indians and U.S. troops attempting to suppress the Ghost Dance religion; it was the last major encounter between Indians and the army.

Mormons Members of the Church of Jesus Christ of Latter-Day Saints, founded in New York in 1830.

polygamy The practice of having more than one wife at a time.

INDIVIDUAL CHOICES

Choosing to Defend His Homeland

Sitting Bull

After Sitting Bull returned to the United States from Canada in 1881, he became a favorite subject for many photographers. This photo dates to the mid-1880s, when he was about fifty years old. Denver Public Library.

The U.S. Army had high expectations for the great conference of tribes from throughout the northern plains at Fort Laramie in 1868. Federal officials had two major purposes: to end attacks along the Bozeman Trail, which ran through eastern Wyoming, and to secure agreement by the northern Plains Indians to live on a reservation well to the north of the major transportation routes that ran through the new state of Nebraska. At the conference, the army agreed to close the Bozeman Trail and to abandon the forts along it, if the Lakotas and their allies agreed to live on a Great Sioux Reservation—the entire western half of what is now South Dakota.

Many of the Lakota leaders were willing to consider the army's proposal. Their battles against the forts along the Bozeman Trail had included both great victories and serious losses. Red Cloud, leader of many of those struggles, was the most prominent of those who agreed to live on the reservation. Most of those who signed the treaty, however, probably had little idea of what they approved.

Sitting Bull chose not to accept any of the treaty's provisions. Instead, he continued to follow the buffalo herd and to defend the territories that his people, the Hunkpapa Lakotas, had wrested from their enemies, the Crows, against anyone—Indian or white—who invaded those regions. At the same time, he necessarily chose

planned to build a great Mormon state, which they called Deseret, in a region so remote that no one would interfere with them. The Great Basin region, however, was soon incorporated into the United States by the Treaty of Guadalupe Hidalgo (1848), which ended the Mexican War. It became Utah Territory in 1850, with boundaries much smaller than those Young had envisioned for Deseret.

Nevertheless, in the remoteness of the Great Basin—isolated by mountains and deserts from the rest of the nation—the Mormons created their **Zion,**

Zion A heavenly abode, hence a community based on religious precepts.

to fight against efforts by the U.S. Army to force the Hunkpapas to live on a reservation and to abandon their traditional way of life. Sitting Bull soon emerged as one of the most significant leaders of opposition to the treaty and to reservation life.

In 1868, Sitting Bull was in his mid-30s and had earned a reputation for fearlessness in battles with the enemies of the Hunkpapas, especially the Crows. He had counted his first coup at the age of 14, when he killed a Crow in a raid and earned the name Tatanka-Iotanka, Sitting Bull, a tribute to his fighting endurance. By 1857, when Sitting Bull was probably 26 years old, the Hunkpapas named him one of the tribal war chiefs in recognition of his many victories in battles with the Crows and other Indian enemies of the Lakotas. He also came to be considered a holy man, whose visions were messages from Wakantanka, the Great Mystery. To his people, Sitting Bull embodied the Lakota virtues of bravery, fortitude, generosity, and wisdom.

Sitting Bull was joined in his rejection of the Fort Laramie Treaty by perhaps a third of all the Lakotas, especially members of the Hunkpapas. The Oglala Lakotas divided, many following Red Cloud to the reservation and some following Crazy Horse to the west of the reservation to live on the "unceded lands" of northwestern Wyoming. In 1869, a group of Sitting Bull's supporters arranged a gathering of Lakotas and Cheyennes at which Sitting Bull was named to an unprecedented position: war chief of the entire Lakota Nation. Given the fluidity of leadership among the Lakotas, the reservation Lakotas did not accept this action, nor did all those who refused to observe the treaty. But it was a signal honor.

Over the next decade, Sitting Bull exercised greater leadership among the various Lakota tribes than any previous leader had. On June 6, 1876, many of the nonreservation Lakotas and Cheyennes had gathered into a very large village where the Hunkpapas held a Sun Dance, the most important religious observance among the Plains Indians. Sitting Bull sacrificed a hundred small bits of flesh from his arms to Wakantanka and then danced and sought a vision. His vision was of soldiers falling upside down into the Lakota and Cheyenne village. His vision was fulfilled when, on June 25, Lieutenant Colonel George A. Custer divided his troops and personally led just over two hundred of them in an attack on a village of Lakotas and Cheyennes that included somewhere between eight hundred and eighteen hundred warriors.

The defeat of Custer was certainly the greatest victory by the Plains Indians in all their battles with the U.S. Army, but it provoked a strong counterattack. As the army attacked and attacked again, Sitting Bull and his followers lost their tipis and their provisions. Finally they fled to Canada and remained there for several years. Soon, however, the last buffalo disappeared from the plains, ending the Hunkpapas' traditional way of life more effectively than the army had been able to accomplish. Eventually they were persuaded to return and to live on a reservation. After his return, Sitting Bull spent a few years touring with William F. ("Buffalo Bill") Cody's Wild West show, then retired to live in a log cabin on the reservation. There he died at the hands of Indian policemen, some from his own Hunkpapa tribe, in 1890.

organizing themselves into a **theocracy,** a society in which church officials governed every aspect of life. Church authority extended to politics, as a church-sponsored political party dominated elections for local and territorial officials. Although streams flowed from the nearby Wasatch mountain range, meager rainfall and poor soil made farming difficult. Young decreed communal ownership of both land and streams. Ignoring eastern laws that limited property owners from removing water from streams running through their properties, Young devised a system for creating farms and irrigation projects

theocracy A state governed by religious authority.

based on the right to divert water for irrigation. The communal ownership of land ended after 1869, when the Homestead Act of 1862 was extended to the territory, but the new definitions for water diversion remained.

With development firmly controlled by the church, the settlement thrived and established satellite communities. By the time of the Civil War, more than twenty thousand Mormons were living in Utah Territory. As the region became more populated, the church established a consumers' cooperative known as the Zion's Cooperative Mercantile Institute, or ZCMI. In addition to selling a variety of goods, the cooperative manufactured some products, including sugar made from sugar beets. Such cooperative enterprises mirrored practices within the 20 to 40 percent of families that practiced polygamy. Church officials urged some of the women in such households to take up home industries (such as silk production) or outside professional employment (such as teaching).

Mormons eventually came under strong federal pressure to renounce polygamy. Efforts to make Utah a state were blocked again and again because of that issue, as Republican leaders branded polygamy as sinful. Behind opposition to polygamy was concern over the potential political power of the Mormon church. In 1890, to clear the way for statehood, church leaders dissolved their political party, encouraged Mormons to divide themselves among the national political parties, and disavowed polygamy. Utah became a state in 1896.

Cattle Kingdom on the Plains

As the Mormons were building their centralized and cooperative society in the Great Basin, a more individualistic enterprise was emerging on the western Great Plains. There, cattle came to dominate the economy.

The expanding cities of the eastern United States were hungry for meat. At the same time, many cattle were wandering the ranges of south Texas. Cattle had first been brought into south Texas—then part of New Spain (Mexico)—in the eighteenth century. Climate encouraged the growth of the herds, and Mexican ranchers developed an open-range system of cattle raising. The cattle grazed on the unfenced plains, and vaqueros (cowboys) herded the half-wild longhorns from horseback. Many practices that developed in south Texas were subsequently transferred to the range-cattle industry, including **roundups.**

Between 1836, when Texas separated from Mexico, and the Civil War, few changes occurred in south Texas. Texans occasionally drove their cattle to distant markets, but cattle drives ended during the Civil War, when Union forces effectively cut Texas off from the rest of the Confederacy. At the end of the war, 5 million cattle ranged across Texas. At the slaughterhouses of Chicago, cattle brought ten times or more than their price in Texas.

To get cattle from south Texas to markets in the Midwest, Texans revived the cattle drive. They herded cattle north through Texas and Indian Territory (now Oklahoma) to the railroads being built westward (see Map 18.2). Half a dozen cowboys, a cook, and a foreman (the trail boss) could drive one or two thousand cattle. Not all the animals survived the drive, but enough did to yield a good profit. Between 1866 and 1880, some 4 million cattle walked north from Texas.

As railroad construction pushed westward, it created a series of cattle towns—notably Abilene and Dodge City, Kansas. Later drives followed more westerly routes. In cattle towns, the trail boss sold his herd and paid off his cowboys, most of whom quickly headed for the cattle town's saloons, brothels, and gambling houses. There eastern journalists and writers of **dime novels** discovered and embroidered the exploits of town marshals like **James B. ("Wild Bill") Hickock** and **Wyatt Earp,** giving them national reputations—deserved or not—as gunfighters on the side of the law. The popular press credited such "town-tamers" with heroic exploits. In fact, the most important changes in any cattle town came when middle-class residents—especially women—increased in number, organized churches and schools, and determined to create

roundup A spring event in which cowboys gathered together the cattle, castrated most male calves, and branded newborn calves, using a hot iron to burn the owner's unique design on their hide.

dime novel A cheaply produced novel of the mid-to-late nineteenth century, often featuring the dramatized exploits of western gunfighters.

James B. Hickock Western gambler and gunfighter who for a time was the town marshal (law enforcement officer) in Abilene, Kansas; in 1876, he was shot in the back and killed while playing poker in Deadwood, Dakota Territory.

Wyatt Earp American frontier marshal and gunfighter involved in 1881 in a controversial shootout at the O.K. Corral in Tombstone, Arizona, in which several men were killed.

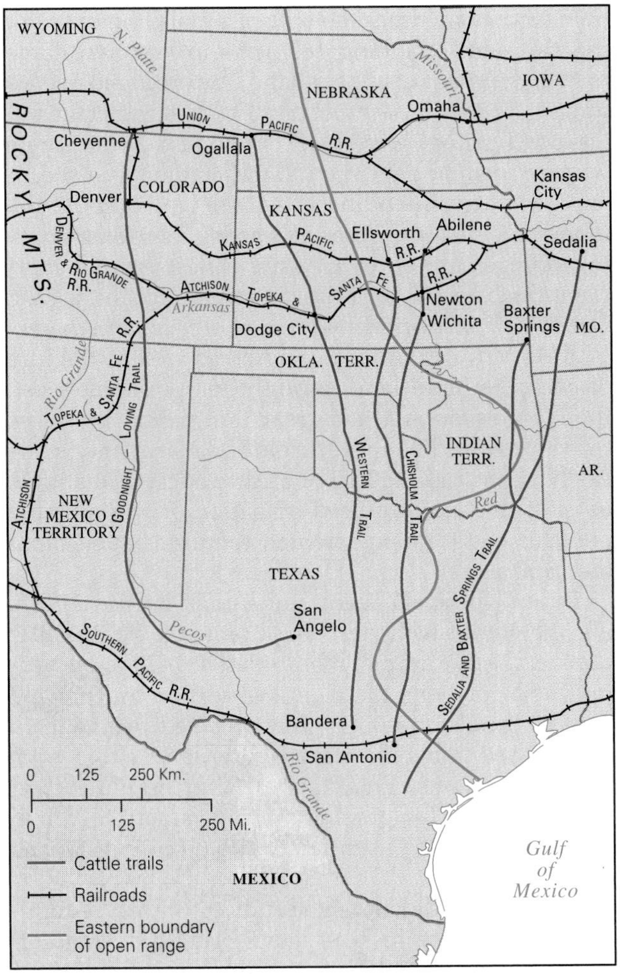

♦ **MAP 18.2 Western Cattle Trails and Railroads, 1865–1890** The demand for beef in northeastern cities encouraged Texans to drive cattle north to the railroads, which carried the cattle to eastern slaughterhouses. As railroad construction moved west, cattle trails did, too, creating a series of "cattle towns" where the trails met the tracks.

law-abiding communities like the ones they had left behind back east.

Although most Texas cattle were eventually loaded on trains to go east for slaughtering, some continued north to northern ranges where cattlemen had virtually free access to vast lands still in the public domain. One result of these "long drives," as they were called, was an extension of open-range cattle raising from Texas into the northern Great Plains. Beginning in the early 1870s, cattle raising on the northern plains attracted attention in the East as newspapers and business journals reported large profits. From the East, England, and elsewhere came investors eager to make a fortune. Some brought in new breeds of cattle, which they bred with the longhorn stock from Texas, producing hardy range cattle that yielded more meat.

In the early 1880s so many cattle ranches began operation that beef prices began to fall. The severe winter of 1886–1887 broke the boom. Uncounted thousands of cattle froze or starved to death on the northern plains. Many investors went bankrupt. Cattle raising then became more of a business and lost much of its romantic aura. Surviving ranchers fenced their ranges and made certain that they could feed their cattle during the winter.

Another important change, both on the northern plains and in the Southwest, was the rise of sheep raising. By 1900, Montana had more sheep than any other state, and the western states accounted for more than half of the sheep raised in the nation.

As the cattle industry expanded, so did the romanticizing of the cowboy. Popular fiction after the 1870s and motion pictures beginning in the 1920s created the image of the cowboy as a brave, white, and clean-cut hero, who spent most of his time defeating villains and rescuing fair-haired white women from danger. Most real cowboys were young and unschooled. Many were African American or of Mexican descent, and others were former Confederate soldiers. On a cattle drive, they worked long hours (as many as twenty a day), faced serious danger if a herd stampeded, slept on the ground, and lived on biscuits and beans. Between drives, when working on a cattle ranch, most found conditions little better, for they earned about a dollar a day and spent much of their working time in the saddle with no human companionship. Some joined unions, notably the Knights of Labor.

Plowing the Plains

Removal of the Indians and buffalo from most of the Great Plains facilitated the construction of railroads and the extension of the cattle industry. When farmers entered this region, however, they encountered an environment significantly different from that to the east. Nevertheless, many at first tried to use eastern farming methods. Some adapted successfully, but others failed and left.

After the Civil War, the land most easily available for establishing new farms stretched from what is now the northern boundary of North Dakota and Minnesota southward through the current state of Oklahoma. Mapmakers in the early nineteenth century had labeled this region the Great American Desert. It was not a desert, however, and some parts

♦ At some time in the 1870s, these cowboys put on good clothes and sat for a photographer's portrait before a painted background. They probably worked together and were friends. Most cowboys were young African Americans, Mexican Americans, or poor southern whites. *Collection of William Gladstone.*

of it were very fertile. But west of the so-called line of **aridity**—roughly the 98th or 100th **meridian**—sparse rainfall was a serious constraint on farming (see Map 18.3). Farmers who used their usual farming practices ran the risk not only of failing but also of severely damaging an **ecosystem** that was unexpectedly fragile.

When the vast region was opened for development by the Kansas-Nebraska Act (1854), the first settlers stuck to eastern areas, where the terrain and climate were similar to those they knew. After the Civil War, farmers pressed steadily westward, spurred by the promise of free land under the Homestead Act or lured by railroad advertising that promised fertile and productive land at little cost.

Those who tried to acquire this farmland were as diverse as the nation itself. Thousands of African Americans left the South, seeking farms of their own. Immigrants from Europe—especially Scandinavia, Germany, **Bohemia,** and Russia—flooded in, attracted by railroad advertising in their lands. Most homesteaders, however, were families who moved from areas a short distance to the east, where farmland had become too expensive for them to buy.

Single women, some of whom came west as schoolteachers, could and did claim 160 acres of their own land. Sometimes the wife of a male homesteader did the same, claiming 160 acres in her own name next to the claim of her husband. According to one estimate, by 1886, one-third of all homestead claims in Dakota Territory were held by women. Some single women seem to have seen homesteading as a speculative venture, intending to sell the land and use the money for such purposes as starting a business, paying college tuition, or creating a nest egg for marriage. Such efforts were almost impossible to the east, due in part to the prohibitive cost of farmland there.

Although the Homestead Act, as well as the lure of cheap railroad land, brought many people west, the Homestead Act had clear limits. The 160 acres that it provided were sufficient for a farm only in areas lying east of the line of aridity. West of that line, most of the land required irrigation or was suitable only for cattle raising (which required much more than 160 acres).

Federal officials were sometimes lax in enforcing the Homestead Act's requirements. Some cattle ranchers, for example, manipulated the law by having their cowboys file claims and then transfer the land to the rancher after they received title to it. In other cases, ranchers claimed the land along both sides of streams, knowing that surrounding land was worthless for grazing without access to water, and thus could be used without having to establish ownership.

Those who did comply with the law's requirements for building a house and farming the land often faced an unfamiliar environment. Unlike many farming areas to the east, on the plains there were few trees. The new plains settlers, therefore, had to find substitutes for the construction material and fuel that eastern pioneers had obtained without cost from the trees on their land.

At first, many families carved homes out of the land itself. Some tunneled into the side of a low hill or embankment to make a cavelike dugout. Others

aridity Dryness; lack of enough rainfall to support trees or woody plants.

meridian Any of the imaginary lines representing degrees of longitude that pass through the North and South Poles and encircle the earth.

ecosystem A community of animals, plants, and bacteria, considered together with the environment in which they are found.

Bohemia A region of Central Europe now part of the Czech Republic.

♦ Omer M. Kem (standing, slicing ripe watermelon) posed for the photographer with his children and his aged father outside his sod house in Custer County, Nebraska, in 1886. Such houses were made of sod cut into blocks and laid like bricks to make walls. Four years later, Kem was elected to the U.S. House of Representatives as a Populist, representing the grievances of western farmers. The photographer, Solomon Butcher, compiled a valuable collection of pictures illustrating the nature of life on what one historian termed "the sod-house frontier." *Nebraska State Historical Society.*

cut the tough prairie **sod** into blocks from which they fashioned a one- or two-room house. Many combined dugout and sod construction. "Soddies" became common throughout the plains but seldom made satisfactory dwellings. Forty years later, women still told their grandchildren of their horror when snakes dropped from the ceiling or slithered out of the walls. For fuel to use in cooking or heating, women sometimes burned dry cow dung or dry sunflower stalks. Sod houses were usually so dark inside that sewing, washing clothes, and many other household tasks were done outside whenever the weather permitted.

Plains families looked to technology to meet many of their needs. Barbed wire, first patented in 1874, provided a cheap and easy alternative to wooden fences. The barbs effectively kept ranchers' cattle off farmland. Ranchers eventually used it too, to keep their herds from straying. Much of the plains had abundant **ground water,** but it was deeper than in the East. Windmills pumped water from great depths. Because the sod was so tough, special plows were developed to make the first cut through it. These plows were so expensive that most farmers hired a specialist (a "sodbuster") to break their sod.

The most serious problem for pioneers on the Great Plains was a much-reduced level of rainfall compared with eastern farming areas. During the late 1870s and well into the 1880s, when the central plains were farmed for the first time, the area received unusually heavy rainfall, and one university professor naively suggested that "Rainfall follows the plow." He thought that farming changed the environment sufficiently to increase rainfall. The error of that theory became clear after the late 1880s, when rainfall fell below normal and crop failures drove many homesteaders off the plains. By one estimate, half of the population of western Kansas left between 1888 and 1892. Only after farmers learned better techniques of **dry farming,** secured improved strains of wheat (some brought by **Russian-German** immigrants), and began to practice irrigation did agriculture become viable. Even so, farming practices in some western areas failed to protect soil that had formerly been covered by natural vegetation. This exposed soil became subject to severe wind erosion in years of low rainfall.

sod Grass-covered topsoil held together by the matted roots of the grass, creating a tough surface several inches thick.

ground water Water beneath the earth's surface, often between soil and rock, that supplies wells and springs.

dry farming Farming that makes maximum use of available moisture by using techniques such as planting drought-resistant crops and harrowing after a rainfall.

Russian-Germans Immigrants from Russia of German descent, often from farming colonies established in the Ukraine in the eighteenth century.

Railroads, Mining, Agribusiness, Logging, and Finance: The Transformation of the West, Part II

- What constraints confronted western entrepreneurs engaged in mining, agriculture, or logging?
- What choices did those entrepreneurs make to develop their industries?
- How did economic development in the West during the late nineteenth century compare with that taking place in the eastern United States at the same time (see Chapter 17)?

At the end of the Civil War, most of the West was sparsely populated. (Many parts of it remain so at the end of the twentieth century.) From 1865 onward, the West of the lone cowboy and solitary prospector was also a region in which most people lived in cities. In a region of great distances, relatively few people, and widely scattered population centers, effective transportation was a necessity for economic development. Just as western cattle raisers required rail connections to send their cattle east to market, so too did western miners and farmers need railroads to carry the products of their labor to markets in the East or in San Francisco, the burgeoning metropolis of western America. Given the scarcity of water in much of the West, by 1900 many westerners had concluded that an adequate supply of water was as important for economic development as was their network of steel rails.

Western Railroads

In the eastern United States railroad construction usually meant connecting already established population centers. For eastern railroads moving through areas with developed economies and connecting major cities, there was no shortage of freight to be hauled to and from the many towns along the line. At the end of the Civil War, however, such situations existed almost nowhere in the West.

Most western railroads were built first to connect the Pacific coast to the eastern half of the country. Only slowly did they begin to find business along their routes. Railroad promoters understood that building a transcontinental line was very expensive and that such a line stood little immediate chance of carrying enough freight to justify the cost of construction. Thus they turned to the federal government for assistance with the cost of construction. The Pacific Railroad Act of 1862 provided loans and also 10 square miles (later increased to 20) of the public domain for every mile of track laid. Federal lawmakers promoted railroad construction to tie California and Nevada, with their rich deposits of gold and silver, to the Union and to stimulate the rapid economic development of other parts of the West.

The recipients of federal support for the first transcontinental railroad were two companies: the Union Pacific, which began laying tracks westward from Omaha, Nebraska, and the Central Pacific, which began building eastward from Sacramento, California. Construction began slowly, partly because crucial supplies—rails and locomotives—had to be brought to each starting point from the eastern United States, either by ship around South America to California or by riverboat to Omaha. Both lines also experienced labor shortages. The Union Pacific solved its labor shortages only after the end of the Civil War, when former soldiers and construction workers flooded west. Many were Irish immigrants. The Central Pacific found the solution to its labor shortage earlier, by recruiting Chinese immigrants.

The Central Pacific laid only 18 miles of track during 1863, and the Union Pacific laid no track at all until mid-1864. The sheer cliffs and rocky ravines of the Sierra Nevada range slowed construction of the Central Pacific. Chinese laborers sometimes dangled from ropes to create a roadbed by chiseling away the solid rock face of a mountain. Because the companies earned their subsidies by laying track, however, construction became a race in which each company tried to build faster than the other. By 1868, Central Pacific construction crews totaled six thousand workers, Union Pacific crews five thousand. In 1869, with the Sierra far behind, the Central Pacific boasted of laying 10 miles of track in a single day.

The tracks of the two companies finally met at **Promontory Summit,** north of the Great Salt Lake (see Map 17.2), on May 10, 1869, joined by spikes made of precious metals, including two golden spikes from California. Other lines followed during the next twenty years, bringing most of the West into the national market system.

Westerners greeted the arrival of the railroads in their communities with joyful celebrations, but some soon wondered if they had traded isolation for dependence on a greedy monopoly. The Southern

Promontory Summit Site in northwest Utah where in 1868 the Central Pacific and Union Pacific railroads were linked, completing the first transcontinental railroad in the United States.

♦ Only a few of the photographs of the construction of the first transcontinental railroad show the Chinese laborers who were responsible for some of the most dangerous construction on the Central Pacific route through the Sierra Nevada. This photograph was taken, apparently by a photographer for the Union Pacific, when the two lines joined near Promontory Summit, in Utah Territory. *Denver Public Library.*

Pacific, successor to the Central Pacific, became known as the "Octopus" because of its efforts to establish a monopoly over transportation throughout California. It had a reputation for charging the most that a customer could afford. Not all western railroads acquired such bad reputations. James J. Hill of the Great Northern, for example, was called the "Empire Builder," for his efforts to build up the economy and prosperity of the region alongside his rails. Whether "Octopus" or "Empire Builder," railroads provided the crucial transportation network for the economic development of the West. One major result was the rapid expansion of western mining, agriculture, and lumbering.

Western Mining

During the forty years following the California gold rush (which began in 1848), prospectors discovered gold or silver throughout much of the mountain West (see the map on page 498). Any such discovery brought a rush of fortune seekers to the area, and a boomtown sprang up almost overnight. Stores that sold picks and shovels, clothing, and groceries quickly appeared, along with boarding houses, saloons, gambling halls, and brothels. Once the valuable ore gave out, such a town was often abandoned and became a ghost town. Discoveries of precious metals and other valuable minerals in the mountainous regions of the West inevitably prompted the construction of rail lines to the sites of discovery, and the rail lines in turn permitted rapid exploitation of the mineral resources by bringing in supplies and heavy equipment.

Many of the first miners found gold by **placer mining.** The only equipment they needed was a pan, and even a frying pan would do. Miners "panning" for gold simply washed gravel that they hoped contained gold. Any gold sank to the bottom of the pan as the lighter gravel was washed away by the water.

After the early gold seekers had taken the most easily accessible ore, elaborate mining equipment became necessary. Gold-mining companies especially in California developed **hydraulic** systems that used great amounts of water under high pressure to demolish entire mountainsides. The most elaborate hydraulic mining operation, in California, used sixteen giant water cannon to bombard hillsides with 40 million gallons of water a day—about the same amount of water that was used daily by the entire city of Baltimore. Hydraulic mining wreaked havoc on the environment downstream, filling rivers with sediment and causing serious flooding. It ended only when a federal court ruled in 1884 that it inevitably damaged the property of others.

In most parts of the West, the exhaustion of surface deposits led to the construction of shafts and tunnels deep underground, as miners followed veins of ore. In Butte, Montana, for example, a gold discovery in 1864 led to additional discoveries of copper,

placer mining Washing minerals from placers—deposits of sand or gravel that contain eroded particles of gold and other valuable minerals.

hydraulic Making use of water under pressure.

silver, and zinc in what has been called the richest hill on earth. Mine shafts there eventually reached depths of a mile and required 3,000 miles of underground rail lines.

Such operations required machinery to move men and equipment thousands of feet into the earth and to keep the tunnels cool and dry. By the mid-1870s, the silver mines in Nevada boasted the most advanced mining equipment in the world. There, temperatures soared to 120 degrees in shafts more than 2,200 feet deep. Mighty air pumps circulated air from the surface to the depths, and ice was used to reduce temperatures. Massive water pumps kept the shafts dry. Powerful drills speeded the job of removing the ore, and enormous ore-crushing machines operated day and night on the surface.

The mining industry changed rapidly. Solitary prospectors panning for gold in mountain streams gave way to large mining companies whose operations were financed by banks in San Francisco and eastern cities. Mining companies became vertically integrated, operating not only mines but also ore-crushing mills, railroads, and companies that supplied fuel and water for mining. Western miners organized too, forming strong unions. Beginning in Butte and spreading throughout the major mining regions of the West, miners' unions helped to secure wages five to ten times higher than wages paid to miners in Britain or Germany.

The Birth of Western Agribusiness

Throughout the northeastern part of the nation, the family farm was the typical agricultural unit. In the South after the Civil War, family-operated farms, whether run by owners or by sharecroppers, also became typical. There were always some very large farming operations in the East and South, but they tended to be the exception. In California and other parts of the West, agriculture sometimes developed on a different scale, involving huge areas, the intensive use of heavy equipment, and wage labor. Today agriculture on such a large scale is known as **agribusiness.**

Wheat was the first major crop for which farming could be entirely mechanized, and wheat was in heavy demand both in the United States and abroad. In 1880, in the Red River valley of what is now North Dakota and in the San Joaquin valley in central California, wheat farms were as large as 100 square miles. Such farming businesses required major capital investments in land, equipment, and livestock. One Dakota farm required 150 workers during spring planting and 250 or more at harvest time. By the late 1880s, some California wheat growers were using huge steam-powered tractors and steam-powered **combines.**

Most of the huge Dakota wheat farms were broken into smaller units by the 1890s, but in some parts of California agriculture flourished on a scale largely unknown in other parts of the country. One California company, Miller and Lux, held more than a million acres, scattered through three states. In California, wheat raising declined in significance by 1900, but large-scale agriculture employing many seasonal laborers had become established for a variety of other crops. Fruit raising spread rapidly as California growers began to take advantage of the refrigerator car and refrigerator ship. Fresh fruit from California was being sold in London by 1892.

For fruit and similar crops, growers required a large work force at harvest time to pick the crops quickly so that they could get to distant markets while still fresh. At first, growers relied on Chinese immigrants to fill such seasonal labor needs. After the Exclusion Act of 1882 (discussed later in the chapter), the number of Chinese began to fall, and growers turned to other immigrant groups—Japanese, Sikhs from India, and eventually Mexicans.

Logging in the Pacific Northwest

The coastal areas of the Pacific Northwest (see the chapter-opening map and Map 18.3) are very different from the rest of the West. There, rainfall is so heavy that the region supports one of the few rain forests outside the tropics. Heavy winter rains and cool, damp, summer fogs nurture thick stands of evergreens, especially tall Douglas firs and giant redwoods.

The growth of California cities and towns from the 1850s onward required lumber, and it came first from the coastal redwoods of central and northern California. When the most easily available stands of timber there had been cut, attention shifted north to Oregon and Washington. Seattle developed as a lumber town from the late 1850s onward, as compa-

agribusiness Farming that is a large-scale business operation using heavy farm machinery and involving processing and distribution as well as the growing of crops.

combine A large harvesting machine that combines the cutting and threshing of grain.

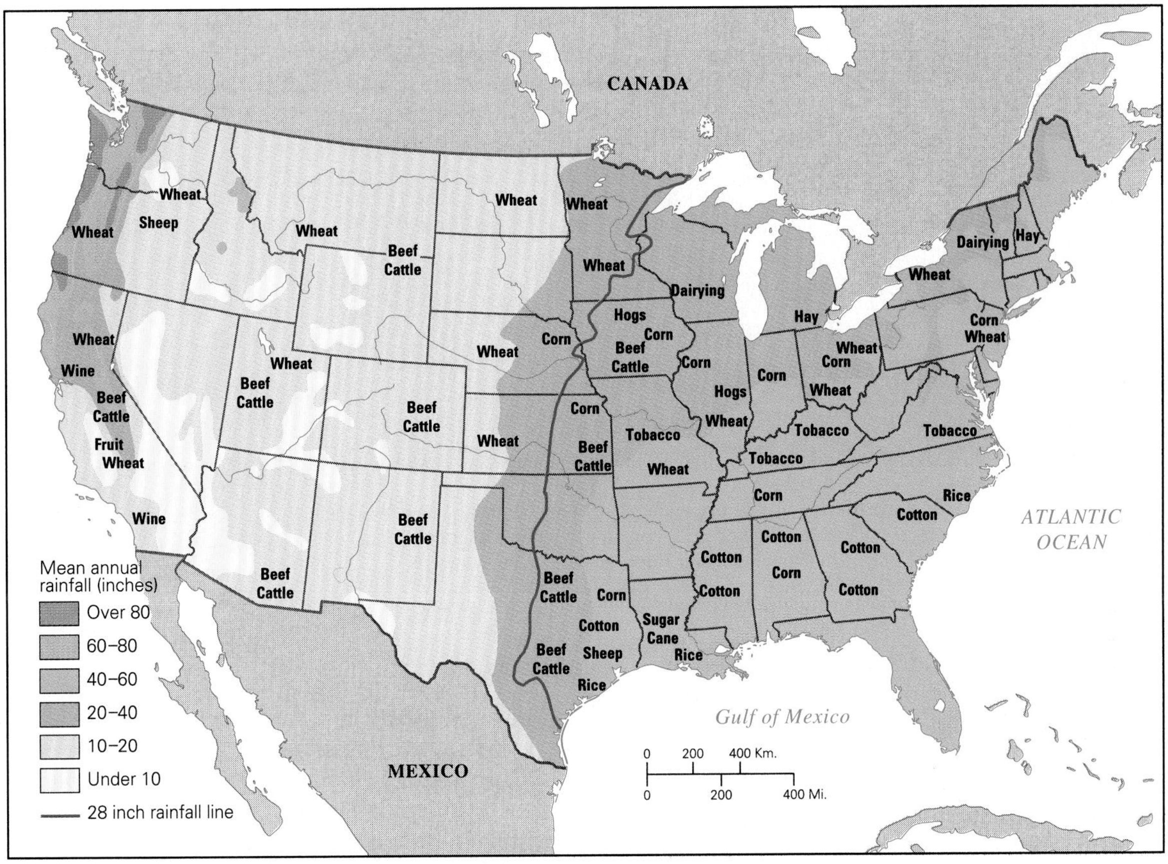

♦ **MAP 18.3 Rainfall and Agriculture, c. 1890** The agricultural produce of any given area depended upon the type of soil, the terrain, and the rainfall. Most of the western half of the nation received relatively little rainfall compared to the eastern half, and crops such as corn and cotton could not be raised in the West without irrigation.

nies in San Francisco helped to finance an industry geared to providing lumber for San Francisco and other California cities. By the late nineteenth century, some companies had become vertically integrated (see page 512), owning **lumber mills** along the northwest coast, a fleet of schooners that hauled rough lumber down the coast to California, and lumber yards in the San Francisco Bay area. In 1883, the Northern Pacific Railroad reached Portland, Oregon, and was extended to the Puget Sound area a few years later. The Great Northern completed its line to Seattle in 1893. Both railroads actively promoted the development of the lumber industry by offering cheap rates for logs to be shipped east. Lumber production in Oregon and Washington boomed, leaving behind treeless hillsides subject to severe soil erosion during heavy winter rains. Westerners committed to rapid economic development seldom gave a second thought to ecological damage, for the long-term cost of such practices was not immediately apparent.

Western Metropolis: San Francisco

Lumber companies, the Miller and Lux land company, several major mining companies, and the Southern Pacific Railroad all located their headquarters in San Francisco. Between the end of the Civil War and 1900, that city emerged as the metropolis of the West and was long unchallenged as the commercial, financial, and manufacturing center for the entire region west of the Rockies.

lumber mill A factory or place where logs are sawed into boards.

♦ San Francisco rapidly emerged as the metropolis of the western United States. This 1905 photograph shows a San Francisco policeman talking to a young girl at one of the city's busiest intersections. Note the cable car on the right. *San Francisco Maritime National Historic Park, Muhrman Collection AZZ.16.824N.*

From 1864 to 1875, the Bank of California, led by William Ralston, determined the course of development in San Francisco and the West. Like many western entrepreneurs, Ralston saw himself as one who brought civilization into the wilderness, and he expected to profit from his efforts. He once argued that "what is for the good of the masses will in the end be of equal benefit to the bankers." Seeking to build a diversified economy in California, Ralston channeled profits from Nevada's silver mines into railroad and steamboat lines and factories that made a wide range of products, from furniture to sugar to woolen goods. Ralston was not alone in his endeavors. By the 1880s, San Francisco was also home to foundries that produced locomotives, the world's most advanced mining equipment, agricultural implements for large-scale farming, and ships.

James Bryce, an English visitor, could write in the 1880s that "California, more than any other part of the Union, is a country by itself, and San Francisco a capital." The city, he explained, "dwarfs" other western cities and is "more powerful over them than is any Eastern city over its neighbourhood." This power of San Francisco over so much of the West came in part because it was home to many of the most prominent western corporations and in part from its status as the western center for finance capitalism, the Pacific coast counterpart of Wall Street. By 1900, however, a few other western cities—Denver, Salt Lake City, Seattle, Portland, and especially Los Angeles—had begun to challenge the economic dominance of San Francisco.

Water Wars

From the first efforts at western economic development, water was a central concern. Prospectors in the California gold rush needed water to separate worthless gravel from gold. On the Great Plains, a cattle rancher staked out grazing land by establishing control over a stream. Lack of water posed a major constraint on the growth of western cities. Throughout much of the West, would-be farmers learned that irrigation was vital to their success, and as early as 1899, irrigated land in the eleven westernmost states produced $84 million in crops.

Throughout much of the West, water was scarce, and competition for water sometimes led to conflict. Such disputes occasionally turned violent, but courtroom battles were more typical. Henry Miller, of Miller and Lux, once grumbled that he had spent $25 million in legal fees, mostly to protect his **water rights.** One of the most important legal decisions, *Lux v. Haggin* (1886), involved two of the largest landowners in the West: Charles Lux, of Miller and Lux, and James Ben Ali Haggin, head of the Kern County [California] Land and Water Company. When Haggin built a dam that prevented water from reaching land owned by Miller and Lux, Lux went to court. The final decision of the court was that both had some right to the water.

water rights The right to draw water from a particular source, such as a lake, an irrigation canal, or a river.

Cities also battled for access to water. Beginning in 1901, San Francisco sought federal permission to put a dam across the Hetch Hetchy Valley, on federal land adjacent to Yosemite National Park in the Sierra Nevada, in order to create a reservoir. Opposition came primarily from the **Sierra Club,** formed in 1892 in an effort to preserve Sierra Nevada wilderness in its natural state. Congressional approval did not come until 1913, and the enormous construction project took another twenty-one years to complete. Los Angeles resolved its water problems in a similar way, by diverting the water of the Owens River to its use—even though Owens Valley residents tried to dynamite the **aqueduct** in resistance.

Although individual entrepreneurs and companies undertook significant irrigation projects in the late nineteenth century, the magnitude of the efforts needed to provide enough water led many westerners to look increasingly for federal assistance, just as they had sought federal assistance to encourage railroad development. "When Uncle Sam puts his hand to a task, we know it will be done," wrote one irrigation proponent. "When he waves his hand toward the desert and says, 'Let there be water!' we know that the stream will obey his commands."

The National Irrigation Association, created in 1899, organized lobbying efforts, and Francis Newlands, member of Congress from Nevada, introduced legislation. The **Reclamation Act of 1902** promised federal construction of irrigation facilities. The Reclamation Service, established by the law, eventually became a major power in the West as it sought to move the region's water to areas where it could be used for irrigation. Reclamation projects sometimes drew criticism, however, for disproportionately benefiting large landowners.

Ethnicity and Race in the West

- Compare the experiences of American Indians, Mexican Americans, and Chinese Americans between the end of the Civil War (1865) and about 1900.
- What constraints did each group face? What choices did members of the group make?

In its ethnic and racial composition, the West has always differed significantly from the rest of the nation. In 1900, the western half of the nation included more than 80 percent of all American Indians, Chinese Americans or Japanese Americans, and Mexican Americans (see Figure 18.1). The northeastern quarter of the nation remained predominantly white until as late as World War I, and the South was largely a biracial society of whites and African Americans. The West has long had greater racial diversity.

Immigrants to the Golden Mountain

Between 1854 and 1882, some three hundred thousand Chinese immigrants entered the United States. Most came from southern China, which in the 1840s and 1850s suffered from political instability and economic distress so acute as to produce **famine.** The California gold rush attracted large numbers of Chinese, just as it attracted fortune seekers from many other parts of the world. Among the early Chinese immigrants, California became known as "Land of the Golden Mountain."

Many Chinese worked in mining in the mid-nineteenth century, accounting for a third of all miners in California in 1860 and more than half in 1870. They also formed a major part of construction labor in the West, especially for railroad building. Many hundreds, perhaps a thousand, perished just in the construction of the Central Pacific. Chinese immigrants also worked as agricultural laborers and farmers, especially in California, throughout the late nineteenth century. Some of them made important contributions to crop development, especially fruit growing.

In San Francisco and elsewhere in the West on a smaller scale, they established **Chinatowns**—relatively autonomous and largely self-contained Chinese communities. In San Francisco's Chinatown, immigrants formed kinship organizations and district associations (whose members had come from the same part of China) to assist and protect each other. A confederation of such associations, the Chinese Consolidated Benevolent Association (often

Sierra Club Environmental organization dedicated to preserving and expanding the world's parks, wildlife, and wilderness areas.

aqueduct A pipe or channel designed to transport water from a remote source, usually by gravity.

Reclamation Act Law passed by Congress in 1902 that provided for publicly funded irrigation of western lands and created the Reclamation Service to oversee the process.

famine A serious and widespread shortage of food.

Chinatown A section of a city that is inhabited chiefly by Chinese people.

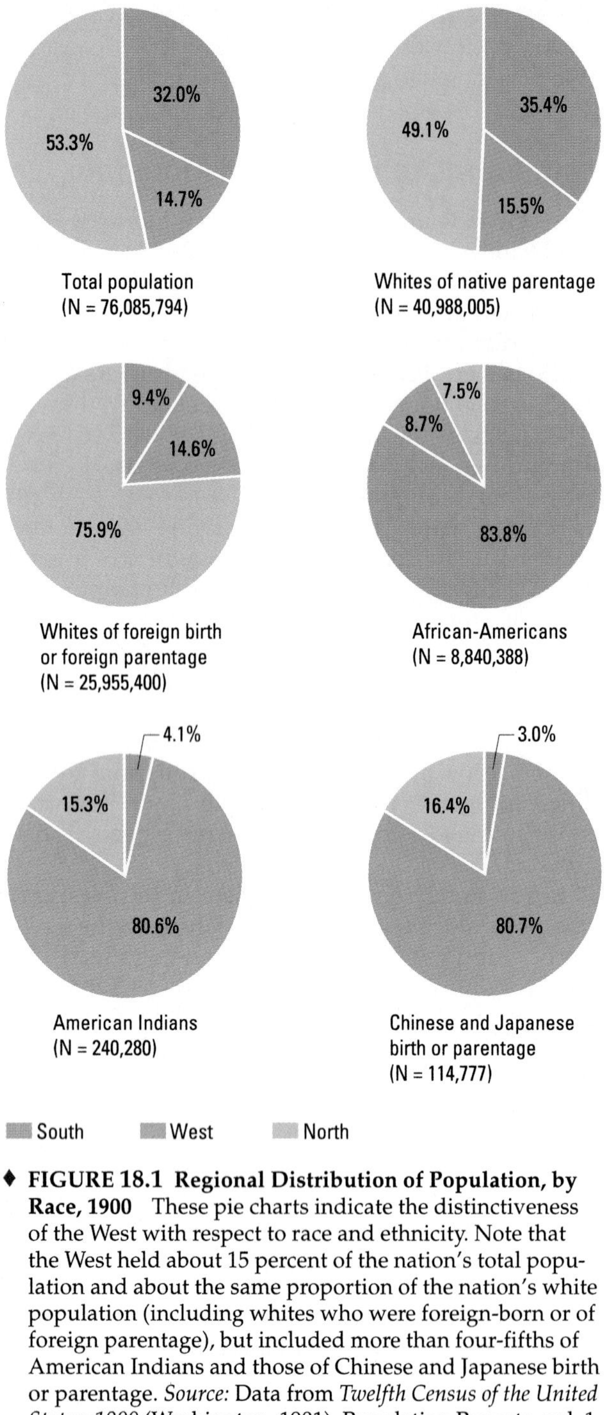

♦ **FIGURE 18.1 Regional Distribution of Population, by Race, 1900** These pie charts indicate the distinctiveness of the West with respect to race and ethnicity. Note that the West held about 15 percent of the nation's total population and about the same proportion of the nation's white population (including whites who were foreign-born or of foreign parentage), but included more than four-fifths of American Indians and those of Chinese and Japanese birth or parentage. *Source:* Data from *Twelfth Census of the United States: 1900* (Washington, 1901), Population Reports, vol. 1, p. 483, Table 9.

called the "Six Companies"), eventually exercised great power over the social and economic life of Chinatown and of Chinese communities in other parts of the West. Such communities were largely male, partly because immigration officials prevented most Chinese women from entering the country, apparently to prevent an American-born generation. As was true in many largely male communities, gambling and prostitution flourished, giving Chinatowns reputations as centers for vice.

Almost from the beginning, Chinese immigrants encountered discrimination and violence. In 1854, the California Supreme Court prohibited Chinese (as well as Indians and African Americans) from testifying in court against a white person. A state tax on foreign-born miners was often evaded by white foreigners but posed a significant burden on Chinese (and also Latino) gold seekers. When the depression of the 1870s set in, white workers in the West began to blame the Chinese for driving down wages and causing unemployment. In fact, different economic factors were depressing wage levels and employment, but anti-Chinese riots occurred in Los Angeles in 1871 and in San Francisco in 1877. In 1885, anti-Chinese riots swept through much of the West, and a mob of white miners burned the Chinatown in Rock Springs, Wyoming, and killed twenty-eight Chinese, mostly mine workers. This anti-Chinese violence prompted many Chinese to retreat to the large Chinatowns, especially the one in San Francisco.

In these riots, the message was usually the same: "The Chinese Must Go." This slogan first gained popularity in San Francisco in 1877 as part of the appeal of the Workingmen's party of California, a political organization that blamed unemployment and low wages on the Chinese and on the capitalists who hired them. In 1882, Congress responded to repeated pressures from unions, especially Pacific coast unions, by passing the **Chinese Exclusion Act,** prohibiting entry to all Chinese people except teachers, students, merchants, tourists, and officials. The law also specified that Asian immigrants were not eligible to become naturalized citizens.

In some parts of the West, the Chinese were subjected to varieties of segregation similar to those imposed on blacks in the South, including residential and occupational segregation imposed by local custom rather than law. In 1871, the San Francisco school board barred Chinese students from that city's public schools, and the ban lasted until 1885,

Chinese Exclusion Act Law passed by Congress in 1882 that prohibited Chinese laborers from entering the United States; it was extended in 1892 and again in 1902.

♦ This public letter writer in San Francisco represents an institution that Chinese immigrants brought with them to America. By the 1880s, the Chinatowns of large western cities had become places of refuge that provided immigrants with some degree of safety from anti-Chinese agitation. *California Historical Society, San Francisco E.N. Sewell FN-01003.*

when the parents of **Mamie Tape** convinced the courts to order the city to provide education for their daughter. The city then opened a segregated Chinese school. Segregated schools for Chinese American children were also set up in a few other places. In most, school segregation began to break down around the time of World War I.

Where there were large concentrations of Chinese immigrants, merchants often took the lead in establishing a strong economic base. Organizations based on kinship, region, or occupation were sometimes successful in fighting anti-Chinese legislation. When San Francisco passed a city law restricting Chinese laundry owners, they brought a court challenge. In the case of *Yick Wo v. Hopkins* (1886), the U.S. Supreme Court for the first time declared a licensing law unconstitutional because local authorities had used it to discriminate on the basis of race.

When other immigrants began to arrive from Asia, they too concentrated in the West. Significant numbers of Japanese immigrants began coming to the United States after 1890. From 1891 through 1907, nearly 150,000 arrived. After 1907, immigration of Japanese laborers stopped because of an agreement between the United States and Japan. Whites in the West, especially organized labor, had come to view Japanese immigrants in much the same way as they had earlier viewed immigrants from China.

Forced Assimilation

As the headlines about the Great Sioux War, the Nez Perce, and Geronimo faded from the nation's newspapers, many Americans began to describe American Indians as a "vanishing race." For too long, American Indians also tended to vanish from history books after the last armed conflicts of the late nineteenth century. But Indian people did not vanish. With the end of armed conflict, the relation between American Indians and the rest of the nation entered a new phase, one that is most appropriate to consider in the larger context of racial relations.

Long before the end of armed conflict, federal policymakers had begun to develop plans to **assimilate** Indians into white society. After 1871, federal policy shifted from treating Indian tribes as sovereign dependent nations, with which federal officials negotiated treaties, to viewing them as wards of the federal government. Leading scholars of the day, notably Lewis Henry Morgan of the Smithsonian Institution, viewed the acquisition of culture as an evolutionary process. Rather than seeing each culture as unique, they analyzed all peoples as being at one of three major stages of cultural development: savagery, barbarism (those who practiced agriculture and made pottery), and civilization (those with a written language). All peoples, they thought, were evolving toward "higher" cultural types. Most white Americans probably agreed that western Europeans and their descendants throughout the world had reached the highest level of cultural development.

Public support for a change in federal policy grew in response to speaking tours by American Indians and white reformers and to the publication of several exposés, notably Helen Hunt Jackson's *A Century of Dishonor* (1881). Soon federal policymakers accepted reformers' arguments for speeding up the evolutionary process for the Indians so that they would be more like their white contemporaries.

Mamie Tape Chinese girl in San Francisco whose parents sued the city in 1885 to end the exclusion of Chinese students from the public schools.

assimilate To absorb immigrants or members of a culturally distinct group into the prevailing culture.

Apparently no reformers or federal policymakers understood that American Indians had complex cultures that were very different from—but not inferior to—the culture of Americans of European descent.

Education was an important element in the "civilizing" of the Indians. Federal officials worked with churches and philanthropic organizations to establish schools at some distance from the reservations, and many Indian children were sent to them to live and study. The teachers' goal was to educate their students to become a part of white society, and they tried to accomplish that by prohibiting the students from speaking their language, practicing their religion, or otherwise following their own cultural patterns. Other educational programs aimed to train adult Indian men to be farmers or mechanics. Federal Indian Affairs officials also tried to prohibit some religious observances, notably the Sun Dance of the Plains tribes and the Snake Dance and kachina ceremony of the Hopis in the Southwest.

The **Dawes Severalty Act** (1887) was an important tool in the attempt at rapid assimilation. Its objective was to make the Indians into self-sufficient, property-conscious, profit-oriented, individual farmers—model citizens of nineteenth-century white America. The law committed the government to a policy of severalty—that is, individual ownership of land. It divided the reservations into individual family farms of 160 acres each. Once the reservation lands were divided up and each family had received its allotment, any surplus was to be sold by the government, and the proceeds from the land sales were to be used for financing Indian education projects. This policy therefore found support among both those who hoped that education would permit Indians to assimilate and those who coveted Indian lands.

Individual landownership and acquisitiveness, however, were at odds with traditional Indian views that the land was for the use of all and that sharing was a major obligation. Some Indian leaders urged Congress not to pass the Dawes Act. D. W. Bushyhead, leader of the Cherokee Nation, joined with delegates from the Cherokee, Creek, and Choctaw nations in a petition to Congress. "Our people have not asked for or authorized this," they stressed, and they explained, "Our own laws regulate a system of land tenure suited to our condition."

Despite such protests, Congress approved the Dawes Act. The result bore out the warning of Senator Henry Teller of Colorado, who had called the proposed legislation "a bill to despoil the Indians of their land." Once allotments to Indian families had been made, about 70 percent of the land area of the reservations remained, and much of it was sold outright. In the end, the Dawes Act did not end the reservation system, nor did it reduce the Indians' dependence on the federal government. It did separate the Indians from some of their land, often the areas that were most valuable.

♦ Susan La Flesche was the first Indian woman to graduate from medical college. Her sister, Susette, was a prominent crusader for Indian rights and her brother, Francis, was a leading ethnologist. Well-educated, they chose to live in and mediate between two societies—the Omaha and the dominant whites. *Nebraska State Historical Society.*

Indians responded to their situation in various ways. Some tried to cooperate with the assimilation programs. Susan La Flesche, for example, daughter of an Omaha leader, graduated from medical college in 1889 at the head of her class. But she disappointed her teachers who wanted her to abandon Indian culture completely when she set up her medical practice near the Omaha reservation, treated both white and Omaha patients, took part in tribal affairs, and managed her land allotment and that of her sister and father. However, Dr. La Flesche also participated in the local white community by taking an active part in the **temperance movement** and sometimes preaching in the local Presbyterian church.

Dawes Severalty Act Law passed by Congress in 1887 that broke up reservations to create individual farms (holding land in severalty) rather than maintaining common ownership of the land; surplus lands were sold and the proceeds used to fund Indian education.

temperance movement A movement advocating the avoidance of alcoholic drinks.

Dr. La Flesche was unusual in her ability to move between two cultures. Some Indians tried to cling to the old ways, hiding their children to keep them out of school and secretly practicing traditional religious ceremonies. Although most Indian people's cultural patterns did change, it was often not in the way that federal officials anticipated. In Oklahoma, where many groups with different traditional cultures were in close proximity, people began to borrow cultural practices from other groups. In some places, Indians became an important element in the wage-earning work force near their reservations, sometimes against the wishes of reservation officials. In the late nineteenth century, the **peyote cult,** based on the hallucinogenic properties of the peyote cactus, emerged as an alternative religion. It evolved into the Native American Church by combining elements of traditional Indian culture, elements of Christianity, and peyote use. Some Indians also took solace in alcohol.

Mexican Americans in the Southwest

The United States annexed Texas in 1845 and three years later acquired vast territories from Mexico at the end of the Mexican War. Living in those territories were many people who spoke Spanish, most of them **mestizos**—people of mixed Spanish and Indian ancestry. The treaties by which the United States acquired those territories specified that Mexican citizens living there automatically became American citizens.

Throughout the Southwest during the late nineteenth century, many Mexican Americans lost their land as the region began to attract large numbers of **Anglos**—English-speaking whites. The Treaty of Guadalupe Hidalgo, which ended the war with Mexico, guaranteed Mexican Americans' landholdings, but the vagueness of Spanish and Mexican land grants opened the door to legal challenges. In some instances, Mexican Americans were cheated out of their land through outright fraud. In California and Texas, many found themselves landless laborers in areas that their forebears had once dominated.

In California, some **Californios**—Spanish-speaking people born in California—had welcomed the break with Mexico. A number were elected to office during the early years of California statehood. Romualdo Pacheco, for example, won election as state treasurer and lieutenant governor and succeeded to the governorship for the last year of his term. The California gold rush, beginning in 1848, attracted fortune seekers from around the world, including Mexico and other parts of Latin America, especially Chile. Most, however, came from the eastern United States and Europe. In northern California, a hundred thousand gold seekers inundated the few thousand Mexican Americans. By the 1880s, the English-speaking majority had pushed them aside. Latinos (people from throughout Latin America) who came to California as gold seekers were often driven from the mines by racist harassment and a special tax on foreign miners.

By the 1870s, many of the **pueblos** (towns created under Mexican or Spanish rules) had become **barrios**—some rural, some in the midst of cities—centered on a Catholic church. In some ways, the barrios resembled the neighborhoods of European immigrants in the eastern United States at the same time. Both had mutual benefit societies, political associations, and newspapers published in the language of the community, and both often centered on a church. There was an important difference, however. Neighborhoods of European immigrants consisted of people who had come to a new land where they anticipated making some changes in their own lives in order to adjust. The residents of the barrios, in contrast, lived in regions that had been home to Mexicans for generations but now found themselves surrounded by English-speaking Americans who hired them for cheap wages, sometimes sneered at their culture, and urged them to assimilate.

In Texas, as in California, some of the **Tejanos** (Spanish-speaking people born in Texas) had welcomed the break with Mexico. Lorenzo de Zavala served briefly as the first vice president of the Texas Republic. Like the Californios, many Tejanos lost their lands through fraud or coercion. Juan Seguin, a Tejano who helped to lead the revolt against Mexico, described them as victims of "dark intrigues against the native families, whose only crime was that they

peyote cult A religion that included ceremonial use of the peyote cactus, native to Mexico and the southwestern United States, which can produce a hallucinogenic effect in those who eat it.

mestizo A person of mixed Spanish and Indian ancestry.

Anglo A term applied in the Southwest to English-speaking whites.

Californios Spanish-speaking people born in California.

pueblo Town created under Mexican or Spanish rules.

barrio A Spanish-speaking community, especially of poor laborers.

Tejanos Spanish-speaking people born in Texas.

♦ In the late nineteenth and early twentieth centuries, Mexican Americans became a major part of the work force for constructing and maintaining railroads in the Southwest. This crew of Mexican-American linemen was working in south Texas when this photograph was taken in 1910. They may have been employed by a railroad to put up and maintain its communication lines or by a telegraph or telephone company. *Texas State Library and Archives Commission.*

owned large tracts of land and desirable property." By 1900 much of the land in south Texas had passed out of the hands of Tejano families—sometimes legally, sometimes fraudulently—but the new, Anglo ranchowners usually maintained the social patterns characteristic of Tejano ranchers.

A large section of Texas—between the Nueces River and Rio Grande and west to El Paso—remained culturally Mexican, home both to Tejanos and to two-thirds of all Mexican immigrants who came to the United States before 1900. Most people living there spoke Spanish. In the 1890s, one journalist described the area as "an overlapping of Mexico into the United States." In 1859–1860, 1873–1875, and 1877, south Texas witnessed violent conflict as some Mexican Americans challenged the political and economic power of Anglo newcomers. In social relations and in politics, all but a few wealthy Tejanos came to be subordinate to the Anglos who dominated the regional economy and the professions.

In New Mexico Territory, **Hispanos** (Spanish-speaking New Mexicans) were clearly the majority of the population and the voters throughout the nineteenth century. They consistently composed a majority in the territorial legislature and were frequently elected as territorial delegate to Congress (the only position elected by the entire territory). Republicans usually prevailed in territorial politics, their party led by wealthy Hispanos and Anglos who began to arrive in significant numbers after the entrance of the first railroad in 1879. Although Hispanos were the majority and could dominate elections, many who had small landholdings lost their land in ways similar to patterns in California and Texas—except that some who enriched themselves in New Mexico were wealthy Hispanos.

From 1856 to 1910 throughout the Southwest, the Latino population grew more slowly than the Anglo population. After 1910, however, that situation reversed itself as political and social upheavals in Mexico prompted massive migration to the United States. Probably a million people—equivalent to one-tenth of the entire population of Mexico—arrived over the next twenty years. More than half stayed in Texas, but significant numbers settled in southern California and throughout other parts of the Southwest where Latino communities already existed. Inevitably, this new stream of immigrants changed some of the patterns of ethnic relations that had characterized the region since the mid-nineteenth century.

The West in American Thought

• How does the myth of the West compare with the reality?

The West has long fascinated Americans, and the "winning of the West" has become a national myth—a myth that has sometimes obscured or distorted the actual facts. Since at least the 1890s, many Americans have thought of the West in terms of the frontier, an imaginary line marking the westward advance of mining, cattle raising, farming, commerce, and the social patterns associated with them. According to this way of thinking, to the east of the frontier line lay established society, and to the west of it lay the wild, untamed West. Often this view was closely

Hispanos Spanish-speaking New Mexicans.

related to evolutionary notions of civilization like those put forth by Lewis Henry Morgan and the social Darwinists. For those who thought about the West in this way, the frontier represented the dividing point between barbarism and civilization.

The West as Utopia and Myth

During the nineteenth and much of the twentieth century, the West seemed a potential **utopia** to some of those who thought of the frontier as a line dividing emptiness from civilization. Generations of Americans dreamed of a better life on "new land" in the West, though many never ventured forth. What was the origin of this utopian view of the West? In the popular mind of the late nineteenth century, the West was vacant, waiting to be formed. There, it seemed, nothing was predetermined. A person could make a fresh start. The Mormons had done so, moving west, creating a theocratic state, and for a long time living in isolation from the rest of American society. And other people who dreamed of creating communities based on new social values also looked to the West, especially to California.

The West appealed as well to Americans who sought to fulfill the American dream of improving their social and economic standing. The presence of free or cheap land, the ability to start over, the idea of creating a place of one's own, all were part of the West's attraction—even for those who never acted on their dream. Some of those who tried to fulfill their dream did not succeed, but enough did to provide some justification for the image of the West as a land of promise.

The West achieved mythical status as popular novels, movies, and eventually television used it as the setting for stories that spoke to Americans' anxieties as well as their hopes. The "winning of the West," as depicted in popular novels, art, and movies, usually begins with the grandeur of wide grassy plains, towering craggy mountains, and vast silent deserts. In most versions, the western Indians face a tragic destiny. They are usually portrayed as a proud, noble people whose demise clears the way for the transformation of the vacated land by bold men and women of European descent. The starring roles in this drama are played by white pioneers—miners, ranchers, cowboys, farmers, railroad builders—who struggle to overcome both natural and human obstacles. These pioneers personify rugged individualism—the virtues of self-reliance and independence—as they triumph through hard work and personal integrity. Many of the human obstacles are villainous characters: brutal gunmen, greedy speculators, vicious cattle rustlers, unscrupulous moneylenders, selfish railroad barons. Some are only doubters, too skeptical of the promise of the West to be willing to risk all in the struggle to succeed.

♦ Popular fiction and Hollywood movies have contributed much to the creation of the "winning of the West" myth, which depicted much of the West as empty wilderness waiting for the transforming hand of bold white settlers. This myth either ignored or minimized previous inhabitants of the West. *Collection of David J. and Janice L. Frent.*

The novelist **Willa Cather** presents a sophisticated—and woman-centered—version of many elements in this story in *O Pioneers!* (1913) and *My Ántonia* (1918). The major character in *O Pioneers!* is Alexandra Bergson, daughter of Swedish immigrant homesteaders on the Great Plains. When her father dies, Alexandra struggles with the land, the climate, and the skepticism of her brothers to create a lush and productive farm.

My Ántonia presents Ántonia Shimerda, daughter of Czech immigrants, who survives run-ins with a land speculator, grain buyer, and moneylender, only to become pregnant outside marriage by a railroad conductor. Dishonored, Ántonia regains the respect of the community through her hard work. She builds a thriving farm, marries, raises a large family, and becomes "a rich mine of life, like the founders

utopia An ideally perfect place.

Willa Cather Early-twentieth-century writer whose novels chronicle the lives of immigrants and others on the American frontier.

of early races." *My Ántonia* explicitly presents another aspect of the myth. Jim Burden, the narrator of the story, grows up on the frontier with Ántonia but becomes a prosperous New York lawyer whose own marriage is childless. Ántonia, symbolizing western fecundity, is thus contrasted with eastern sterility.

The Frontier and the West

Starting in the 1870s, accounts of the winning of the West suggested to many Americans the existence of an America more attractive than the steel mills and urban slums of their own day, a place where people were more virtuous than the barons of industry and corrupt city politicians, where individual success was possible without labor strife or racial and ethnic discord. The myth has evolved and continues to exert a hold on Americans' imagination. From at least the 1920s onward, the cowboy has been the most prominent embodiment of the myth. The mythical cowboy is a brave and resourceful loner, riding across the West and dispelling trouble from his path and from the lives of others. He rarely does the actual work of a cowboy.

In the 1920s, this image seemed to have special appeal to Americans dissatisfied with the routine of their lives and work. In the 1950s, some found the cowboy symbolic of the American role in the Cold War, as the nation strode across the globe, rescuing grateful nations from the threat of Communist domination. In a more recent incarnation, the "urban cowboy," wearing cowboy boots and mastering mechanical bucking broncos, kicks aside the restraints of society.

Like all myths, the myth of the winning of the West contains elements of truth but also ignores some truths. The myth usually treats Indians as victims of progress. It rarely considers their fate after they meet defeat at the hands of the cavalry. Instead, they obligingly disappear from the scene. The myth rarely tempers its celebration of rugged individualism by acknowledging the fundamental role of government at every stage in the transformation of the West: dispossessing the Indians, subsidizing railroad construction, using the public domain to underwrite economic development, suppressing unions among miners, and rerouting rivers to bring their precious water to both farmland and cities. The myth often overlooks the role of ethnic and racial minorities—from African-American and Tejano cowboys to Chinese railroad construction crews—and it especially overlooks the extent to which these people were exploited as sources of cheap labor. Women typically appear only in the role of helpless victim or noble helpmate. Finally, the myth generally ignores the extent to which the economic development of the West in fact replicated economic conditions in the East, including monopolistic, vertically integrated corporations and labor unions. If such influences appear in the myth, they are usually as obstacles that the hardy pioneers overcame.

In 1893, **Frederick Jackson Turner,** a young historian, presented an essay called "The Significance of the Frontier in American History." In that essay, he challenged the prevailing idea among American historians that answers to questions about the nature of American institutions and values were to be found by studying the European societies to which white Americans traced their ancestry. Turner focused instead on the frontier as a uniquely defining factor, long absent from the European experience but characteristic of North America from the time of Jamestown to his own day, when the development of the West had finally progressed to the point where there was no longer a frontier line. Turner argued that "American social development has been continually beginning over again on the frontier" and that these experiences constituted "the forces dominating American character." The western frontier, he claimed, was the region of maximum opportunity and widest equality, where individualism and democracy most flourished.

Turner's view of the West and the importance of the frontier dominated the thinking of historians for many years. Today, however, historians focus on many elements missing from Turner's analysis: the importance of cultural conflicts among different groups of people; the experiences of American Indians, the original inhabitants of the West, and of the Spanish-speaking mestizo peoples of the Southwest, and of Asian Americans; gender issues and the experiences of women; the natural environment and ecological issues, especially those involving water; the growth and development of western cities; and the ways in which the western economy resembles and differs from the economy of the East. If frontier individualism and mobility have been important elements in the American experience, as Turner suggested, so too have been these other elements in western history.

Frederick Jackson Turner American historian who argued that the receding frontier and cheap land were dominant factors in creating American democracy and shaping national character.

SUMMARY

E xpectations
C onstraints
C hoices
O utcomes

The West changed greatly during the thirty or forty years following the Civil War. Federal policymakers held *expectations* for the rapid development of the region, and they often *chose* to use the public domain to accomplish that purpose. American Indians, especially those of the Great Plains, were seen as posing *constraints* on development, but most were defeated by the army by 1877.

Patterns of development varied in different parts of the West. In the Great Basin, Mormons created a theocracy and *chose* new approaches to irrigation to meet *constraints* posed by scarce water. A cattle kingdom emerged on the western Great Plains, as railroad construction made it possible to carry cattle east for slaughter and processing. As farming moved west, lack of rainfall *constrained* farmers' *expectations,* leading to the *choice* of new crops and improved farming methods.

Throughout the West, change was driven by *choices* made in the face of *constraints*. Railroad construction overcame *constraints* posed by vast distances, making possible most other forms of economic development. As western mining became highly mechanized, control shifted to large mining companies able to secure the necessary capital. In California, especially, landowners made *choices* that led to the development of western agriculture into a large-scale commercial undertaking. The coniferous forests of the Pacific Northwest attracted lumbering companies. By the 1870s, many entrepreneurs had made *choices* that, taken together, made San Francisco the center of much of the western economy. Water posed a significant *constraint* on economic development in many parts of the West, prompting *choices* to reroute water sources.

Immigrants from Asia, American Indians, and Latino peoples all formed substantial parts of the western population but had significantly different *expectations* and experiences. White westerners *chose* to use politics and, sometimes, terrorism to exclude and segregate Asian immigrants. Federal policy toward American Indians proceeded from the *expectation* that they could and should be rapidly assimilated and lose their separate cultural identities, but such policies largely failed. Latinos—descendants of those living in the Southwest before it became part of the United States and those who came later from Mexico or elsewhere in Latin America—had their lives and culture *constrained* by Anglo newcomers.

The *outcome* of the many *choices* made in the late nineteenth century was explosive economic development and population change. Americans have viewed the West both as a utopia and as the source of a national myth. But those views overlook important realities in the nature of western development and in the people who accomplished it.

SUGGESTED READINGS

Ray Allen Billington, and Martin Ridge. *Westward Expansion: A History of the American Frontier,* 5th ed. (1982).

The most detailed treatment of the West and the frontier, largely from a Turnerian perspective.

Dee Brown. *Bury My Heart at Wounded Knee: An Indian History of the American West* (1971).

One of the first efforts to write western history from the Indians' perspective, drawing on oral histories.

Sucheng Chan. *Asian Americans: An Interpretive History* (1990).

A good introduction to the history of Asian Americans.

Juan Gómez-Quiñones. *Roots of Chicano Politics, 1600–1940* (1994).

An overview of the political history of Mexican Americans from the first Spanish settlements in the Southwest up to the eve of World War II.

Norris Hundley, Jr. *The Great Thirst: Californians and Water, 1770s–1990s* (1992).

The most recent of a number of studies surveying the role of water in the West.

Patricia Nelson Limerick. *The Legacy of Conquest: The Unbroken Past of the American West* (1987).

A major recent criticism of the Turner thesis, posing an alternative framework for viewing western history.

Robert M. Utley. *The Lance and the Shield: The Life and Times of Sitting Bull* (1993).

An exhaustively researched biography of the Lakota leader that incorporates much of the history of the northern plains from the early nineteenth century to the end of the Indian wars.

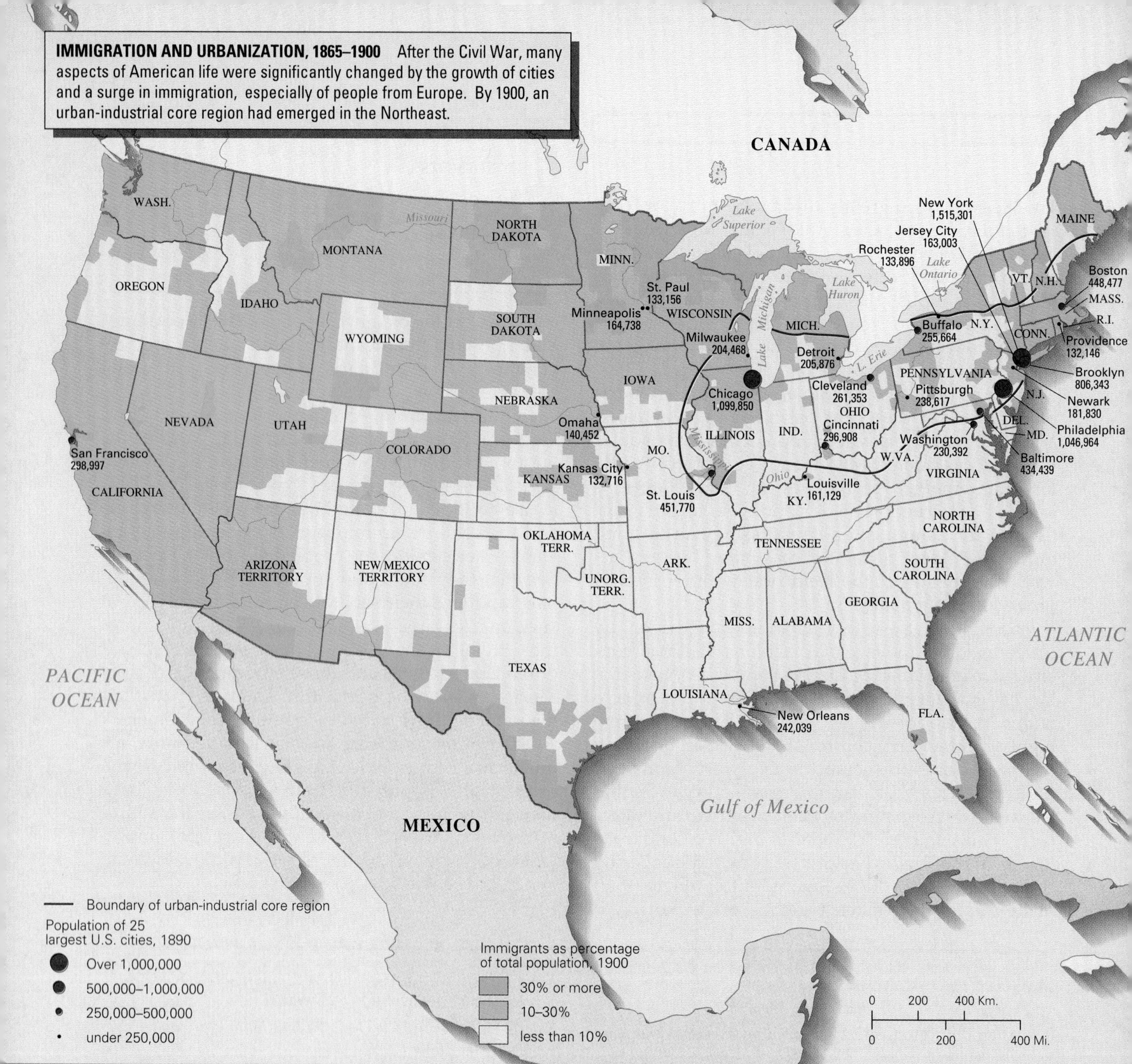

IMMIGRATION AND URBANIZATION, 1865–1900 After the Civil War, many aspects of American life were significantly changed by the growth of cities and a surge in immigration, especially of people from Europe. By 1900, an urban-industrial core region had emerged in the Northeast.

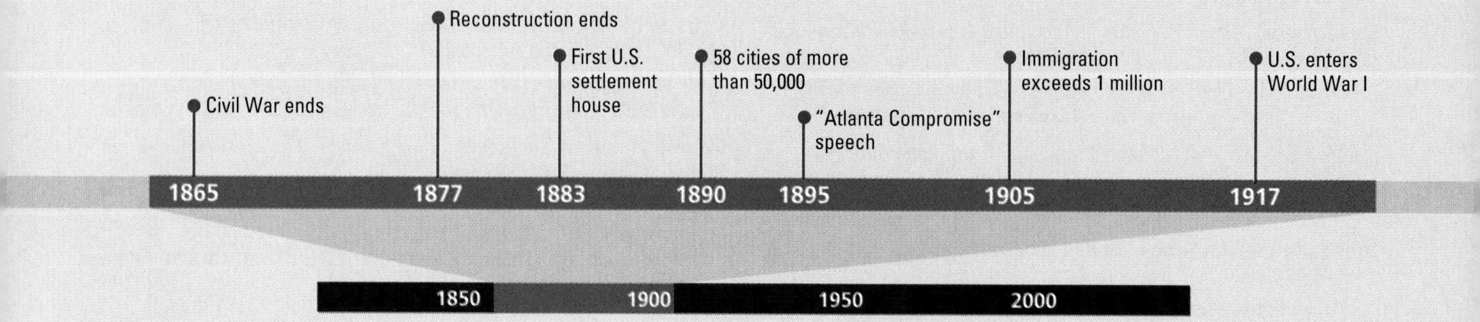

CHAPTER 19

The New Social Patterns of Gilded Age America, 1865–1900

The New Urban Environment

- What expectations led many people to move to U.S. cities during the late nineteenth and early twentieth centuries?
- What constraints did urban Americans face during those years?
- How did Americans' choices transform cities?

Poverty and the City

- What constraints and choices shaped the lives of many newcomers to the rapidly growing American cities?
- How did different groups analyze the constraints of urban poverty? What choices about assisting the poor did their analyses lead them to make?

New Americans from Europe

- What expectations prompted immigrants to leave their homelands for the United States? What constraints did they sometimes encounter?
- In what ways were immigrants' expectations and choices regarding assimilation similar to and different from those of nativists?

New South, Old Issues

- How did the economy of the South change during the late nineteenth century?
- What outcome did white southern officials seek to accomplish as they wrote new laws on race relations during the 1880s and 1890s?
- What choices did different black southerners make in response to the state of race relations in the South?

New Patterns of American Social and Cultural Life

- How did Americans' expectations and choices give rise to important social and cultural trends during the late nineteenth and early twentieth centuries?

INTRODUCTION

In 1872, two neighboring families in Hartford, Connecticut, shared dinner. As they argued over popular fiction, the two men concluded that together they could write a better novel than the novels then in vogue—and they did so. Charles Dudley Warner and Samuel L. Clemens titled their book—the first novel either of them had written—*The Gilded Age: A Tale of Today* (1873). In it, they satirized the business and politics of their day. The novel's title became the name given to the years from the 1860s through the 1890s, the Gilded Age, suggesting both the golden gleam of a gilded surface and the cheap nature of the base metal underneath. Clemens went on to fame, under the pen name Mark Twain, as author of *Huckleberry Finn* and other classics.

The previous two chapters have portrayed some aspects of late-nineteenth-century life that might justify the label "gilded." The dramatic expansion of business, the technology that typified "progress" for many people, the glittering wealth and great power of the new industrial entrepreneurs, and the rapid economic development of the West all provided the gleaming surface. The grim realities of life for most industrial workers and the plight of racial and ethnic minorities, however, lay just below that golden surface. This chapter continues to examine the *expectations, constraints, choices,* and *outcomes* of the period by looking at social and cultural changes in the late nineteenth and early twentieth centuries. New patterns of life jarred the burgeoning cities. Ethnic and racial groups related to each other in new ways. And new developments revolutionized education, gender roles, creative expression, and cultural participation.

Most of these *choices* and *outcomes* were related to the great transforming experiences of the late 1800s—industrialization, urbanization, immigration, and development of the West. Together they changed many aspects of American life, breaking down old *constraints* and creating new ones. As changes occurred, they fostered new *expectations* among many Americans about how people should live and how social groups should relate to each other. Americans' *expectations* sometimes expanded individual *choices* and opportunities and, at other times, led some groups to try to impose their values and behaviors on others.

E xpectations
C onstraints
C hoices
O utcomes

As Americans revised old expectations about social relations and forged new ones, the very pace of growth created *constraints* that sometimes forced troubling *choices.* Cities expanded so rapidly that municipal governments, sometimes unable to meet all the demands placed on them, faced difficult choices. For example, should they pave streets or build sewers? At the same time, however, the expansion of the educational system removed some *constraints* on Americans' opportunities to learn and presented many Americans with new *choices*—whether to go to college, which college to choose, what courses to take. Educational opportunities for women helped to expand career choices, including previously all-male professions such as medicine and law, and the new profession created largely by women, social work. In the South, where industrialization and urbanization lagged, some tried to develop new social and economic patterns.

The expanding industrial economy and rapidly growing cities convinced people throughout Europe to come to America. Such immigrants often made their *choice* to move with the *expectation* of acquiring free land or earning high wages. Some succeeded and turned their dreams to reality. But sometimes such hopes foundered on *constraints* posed by the difficulty of getting to areas of available land, or by unemployment and the wage cuts that came when the economy turned down.

Chapter 17 depicted how the *outcome* of *choices* by many entrepreneurs and workers was the transformation of the economy during the years between the Civil War and the early twentieth century. Chapter 18 indicated how the *outcome* of *choices* by government and individuals was the transformation of life in the West during the same time period. So, too, the *outcome* of the many *choices* by individuals and groups about where they lived, how they lived, and how they related to other groups was the transformation of many aspects of American society and culture during those years.

CHRONOLOGY

Social and Cultural Change

1865 Civil War ends
248,120 immigrants enter the United States

1868 First medical school for women

1870 25 cities have populations exceeding 50,000

1871 Great Chicago Fire
Boss Tweed indicted

1872 Samuel L. Clemens and Charles Dudley Warner name the Gilded Age

1874 Women's Christian Temperance Union founded

1876 National League (professional baseball) formed

1877 Reconstruction ends
Nicodemus, Kansas, an all-black community, founded

1879 Henry George's *Progress and Poverty*

1881 669,431 immigrants enter the United States

1883 Civil Rights cases

1885 William LeBaron Jenney designs first U.S. skyscraper
Mark Twain's *Huckleberry Finn*

1886 First U.S. settlement house opens

1887 American Protective Association founded
Florida segregates railroads

1888 First electric streetcar system

1889 Hull House opens

1890 58 cities have populations exceeding 50,000
Louis Sullivan designs Wainwright Building
Jacob Riis's *How the Other Half Lives*
Second Mississippi Plan

1892 Walt Whitman's *Leaves of Grass,* final edition

1893 Stephen Crane's *Maggie: A Girl of the Streets*

1895 Booker T. Washington delivers Atlanta Compromise

1896 South Carolina adopts white primary
Plessy v. Ferguson

1897 President Grover Cleveland vetoes immigration restriction
First steel mill in the South

1899 Scott Joplin's "Maple Leaf Rag"

1901 Frank Norris's *The Octopus*
Anarchists barred from the United States
Oil discovered in Texas, Oklahoma, and Louisiana
American League (professional baseball) formed

1902 Columbia University offers program in social work

1903 First World Series

1903—1906 Pogroms against Jews in Russia

1905 1,026,499 immigrants enter the United States

1913 President William Taft vetoes immigration restriction
Armory Show

1917 Congress requires literacy test to limit immigration, overriding President Woodrow Wilson's veto

The New Urban Environment

- What expectations led many people to move to U.S. cities during the late nineteenth and early twentieth centuries?
- What constraints did urban Americans face during those years?
- How did Americans' choices transform cities?

"The city is the nerve center of our civilization. It is also the storm center." So said Josiah Strong, a leading Protestant minister, pointing up the ambivalence with which many Americans viewed their rapidly growing cities. For recent immigrants and those whose families had lived in the United States for generations, for men and women, for industrial workers and farmers, the ever-expanding cities seemed to pose the greatest challenge to their expectations and to give them the widest range of choices.

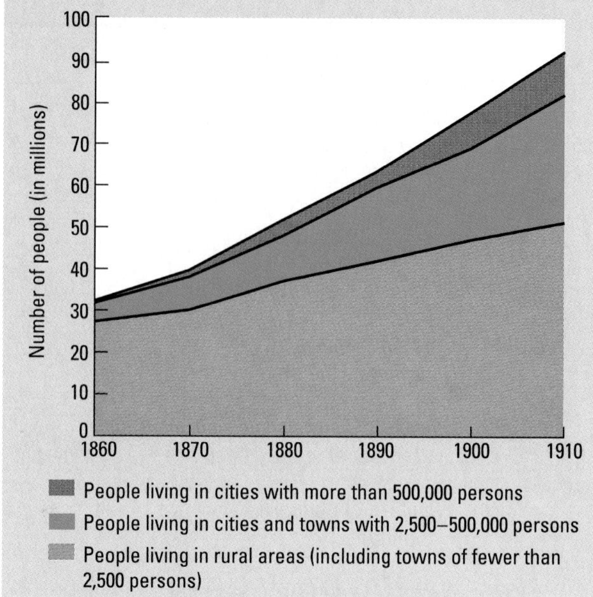

♦ **FIGURE 19.1 Urban and Rural Population of the United States, 1860–1910** Although much of the population increase between 1860 and 1910 came in urban areas, the number of people living in rural areas increased as well. Notice, too, that the largest increase was in towns and cities that had between 2,500 and 500,000 people. *Source:* U.S. Bureau of the Census, Department of Commerce, *Historical Statistics of the United States,* 2 vols. (Washington, D.C.: U.S. Government Printing Office, 1975), Series A-58, A-59, A-69, A-119.

Surging Urban Growth

What Americans saw in their cities often fascinated them. Cities boasted the technological innovations that many equated with progress. But the lure of the city stemmed from far more than telephones, streetcars, and technological gadgetry. Reverend Samuel Lane Loomis in 1887 listed the many choices to be found in cities: "The churches and the schools, the theatres and concerts, the lectures, fairs, exhibitions, and galleries . . . and the mighty streams of human beings that forever flow up and down the thoroughfares."

Not every urban vista was so appealing, however. Some visitors were shocked and repulsed by what they saw in American cities. A British traveler in 1898 described Pittsburgh as "a most chaotic city": "A cloud of smoke hangs over it by day. The glow of scores of furnaces light the river banks by night. . . . All nations are jumbled up here, the poor living in tenement dens or wooden shanties thrown up or dumped down with very little reference to roads." Guillermo Prieto, visiting San Francisco in 1877, was struck by the contrast of luxurious wealth and desperate poverty: "Behind the palaces run filthy alleys, or rather nasty dungheaps without sidewalks or illumination, whose loiterers smell of the gallows."

The odd mixture of fascination and repulsion Americans felt toward cities stemmed in part from the rapidity of urban growth. Cities with more than 50,000 people grew almost twice as fast as rural areas (see Figure 19.1). The nation had twenty-five cities of that size in 1870, with a total population of 5 million. By 1890, fifty-eight cities had reached that size and held nearly 12 million people. Most of these cities were in the Northeast and near the Great Lakes.

Where did all these city-dwellers come from so suddenly? Urban growth came largely through migration from rural areas in the United States and Europe, where millions of families and individuals faced decisions about their futures. The mechanization of farm work (see pages 503–505) meant that agriculture required fewer workers per acre than ever before. Rural birth rates remained high, however, and rural death rates were lower than in the cities. America's farmlands, then, contributed significantly to the growth of the cities, but even more of the new urban residents came from outside the United States, especially from Europe.

Growth of manufacturing went hand in hand with urban expansion. By the late nineteenth century, the nation had developed a **manufacturing belt.** This region, which included nearly all the largest cities as well as the bulk of the nation's manufacturing and finance, may be thought of as constituting the nation's industrial "core" (see the chapter-opening map). Some of the cities in this region—Boston, New York, Baltimore, Buffalo, and St. Louis, for example—had long been among the busiest ports in the nation. Now manufacturing flourished and came to be nearly as important as trade. In other cases, cities developed as industrial centers from their beginnings. Some cities became known for a particular product: iron and steel in Pittsburgh, clothing in New York City, textiles in Lowell, Massachusetts, meatpacking in Chicago, flour milling in Minneapolis. A few cities, especially New York, also stood out as major centers for finance.

New Cities of Skyscrapers and Streetcars

As the urban population swelled and the urban economy grew more complex, technological advances permitted cities to expand upward and outward. In the early 1800s, most cities measured only a few miles across, and most residents could get around on foot. Historians call such places a "**walking city.**" Buildings were low (three stories was unusual) and usually not designed for a specific economic function. Small factories existed here and there among warehouses and commercial offices near the docks. By the late nineteenth century, new technologies for building and transportation removed many previous limits on growth.

Until the 1880s, construction techniques restricted building height because the lower walls carried the structure's full weight. The higher a building, the thicker its lower walls had to be. William LeBaron Jenney usually receives credit for designing the first skyscraper—ten stories high—built in Chicago in 1885. Chicago architects took the lead in designing even taller buildings. Such ventures were possible because of new construction technology, that allowed a metal frame to carry the weight of the walls. Jenney's first skyscraper used an iron frame, but architects quickly turned to steel because of its greater strength. Other technological advances permitted the new tall buildings to be equipped with passenger elevators, a necessity for buildings of such height. Economical and efficient, tall buildings created unique city skylines.

Among the Chicago architects who developed the skyscraper, **Louis Sullivan** stands out. He recognized the skyscraper as the architectural form of the future and introduced a new way of thinking about height. In the nine-story Wainwright Building (St. Louis, 1890), Sullivan chose to emphasize height, to create what he called a "proud and soaring thing." He also designed an exterior that largely reflected the interior function, thus keeping to his rule that "form follows function." Frank Lloyd Wright, perhaps the greatest American architect of the twentieth century, described the Wainwright Building

♦ Louis Sullivan designed the Wainwright Building (1890) with the intention of creating a new way of thinking about height and about the relationship between form and function. The building was widely acclaimed and often imitated. *Missouri Historical Society/Emil Boehl.*

manufacturing belt A region that includes most of a nation's factories; in the late nineteenth century, the U.S. manufacturing belt also included most of the nation's large cities and railroad lines and much of its mining.

walking city Term that urban historians use to describe cities before changes in urban transportation permitted cities to expand beyond the distance that a person could cover on foot.

Louis Sullivan American architect of the late nineteenth century whose designs reflected his theory that the outward form of a building should express its function.

♦ This photograph, from about 1900, shows Wabash Avenue in downtown Chicago, where the elevated trains thundered between recently built multistory commercial buildings, some of which, in the distance, may have been among the nation's first skyscrapers. Elevated trains and streetcars greatly increased the size of cities and the use of steel frames permitted city buildings to rise to heights that were previously impractical. *From* Birth of a Century, *Kea Publishing Services, Ltd.*

as signifying the birth of "the 'skyscraper' as a new thing under the sun."

Just as steel-frame buildings allowed cities to grow upward, so new forms of transportation allowed cities to expand outward. In the 1850s, horses pulled the first streetcars over iron rails laid in city streets. Some cities also had elevated rail lines powered by steam locomotives, but the smoke and soot from the coal they burned made them unpopular in urban areas. By the 1870s and 1880s, some cities boasted streetcar lines powered by an underground moving cable. It was electricity, however, that transformed urban transit. Frank Sprague, a protégé of Thomas Edison, designed a streetcar driven by an electric motor that drew its power from an overhead wire. Sprague's system was first installed in Richmond, Virginia, in 1888. Electric streetcars quickly replaced horse cars and cable cars in most cities. By 1902, 97 percent of the nation's streetcars operated on electricity. In the early 1900s, some large cities, choked with traffic, moved their electrical streetcars above or below street level, thereby creating **elevated trains** and subways. New construction technologies also launched bridges spanning rivers and bays that had once posed serious constraints on urban growth. And where bridges went, streetcars followed.

By the early 1900s, elaborate networks of streetcar lines crisscrossed most large cities, connecting neighborhoods to downtown. Some carried middle-class women wearing white gloves and stylish hats to downtown department stores. Skilled workers rode others to and from their jobs. Other lines carried typists and corporate executives to and from banks and offices.

As streetcar lines pushed outward from the city's center, the old walking city expanded by annexing suburban areas that grew up along the spreading transportation lines. In 1860, Chicago occupied 17 square miles. By 1890 it took in 178 square miles. During the same years, Boston grew from 5 square miles to 39, and St. Louis from 14 square miles to 61.

As horse-drawn streetcars had expanded the city beyond distances that residents could easily cover on foot, new railroad lines began to bring outlying villages within commuting distance of urban centers. Wealthier urban residents who could afford the passenger fare could choose to escape the disorder of the city at the end of the workday. As early as 1873, nearly a hundred suburban communities sent between five and six thousand commuters into Chicago each day, and by 1890 seventy thousand suburbanites were pouring in daily. At about the same time, commuter lines brought more than a

elevated train A train that runs on a steel framework above a street and leaves the street itself free for other traffic.

hundred thousand workers daily into New York City just from its northern suburbs.

The New Urban Geography

The new technologies that transformed urban construction and transportation interacted with the growth of manufacturing, commerce, and finance to change the geography of American cities. As the largest cities grew, areas within them became increasingly specialized by economic function.

Early manufacturing in port cities was often scattered among warehouses near the waterfront. Clothing factories, for example, sometimes began in buildings formerly used by sailmakers or as warehouses. Other types of manufacturing required specially designed facilities. Iron and steel making, meatpacking, shipbuilding, and oil refining had to be established on the outskirts of a city. There, open land was plentiful and relatively cheap, and the city center suffered less from the noise, smoke, and odor of heavy industry.

Many manufacturing workers could not afford to ride the new streetcars, so they often had no choice but to live within walking distance of their work. Construction of industrial plants outside cities, therefore, usually meant working-class residential neighborhoods nearby. Some companies established planned communities: a manufacturing plant surrounded by multifamily houses, stores, and even parks and schools. Such company towns were sometimes well intended, but few earned good reputations among their residents. Workers whose employer was also their landlord and storekeeper usually resented the ever-present authority of the company—and the lack of alternatives to the rents and prices it charged.

At the same time that heavy manufacturing moved to the outskirts of the cities, areas in the city centers tended to become more specialized. By 1900 or so, the center of a large city usually had developed distinct districts. A district of light manufacturing might include clothing and printing. Next to, or overlapping with, light manufacturing was often a **wholesale** trade district with warehouses and offices of wholesalers. **Retail** shopping districts, anchored by department stores, emerged in a central location, where streetcar and railroad lines could bring middle-class and upper-class shoppers from outlying areas. In the largest cities, banks, insurance companies, and headquarters of large corporations clustered near one another to form a financial district. A hotel and entertainment district often lay close to the financial and retail blocks. These areas together made up a **central business district.**

Just as specialized downtown areas emerged according to economic function, so too did residential areas develop according to economic status. New suburbs ranged outward from the city center in order of wealth. Those who could afford to travel the farthest could also afford the most expensive homes. Those too poor to ride the new transportation lines lived in apartments or small houses in the center of the city or clustered around industrial plants. Much of the burgeoning urban middle class lived between the two extremes, far enough from the central business district that many residents rode streetcars downtown to work or shop.

Building an Urban Infrastructure

During the rapid urban growth after the Civil War, local governments did little to regulate expansion or construction practices in the public interest. Cities grew with only minimal planning. Individual landowners, developers, and builders made most choices about land use and construction. Everywhere, builders and owners hoped to achieve a high return on their investment by producing the most space for the least cost. Such profit calculations rarely left room for such amenities as varied designs or open space. Most of the great urban parks that exist today, including Central Park in New York City, Prospect Park in Brooklyn, and Golden Gate Park in San Francisco, were all established on the remote outskirts of their cities, before the surrounding areas were developed.

Given the rapid and largely unplanned nature of most urban growth, utilities and services provided by city government—fire and police protection, schools, sewage disposal, street maintenance, water supply—rarely kept pace with the growth of new neighborhoods. As a result, city residents sometimes faced contaminated drinking water, inadequate disposal for sewage and garbage, and—as

wholesale Engaged in the sale of goods in large quantities, usually for resale by a retailer.

retail Engaged in the sale of goods in small quantities directly to consumers.

central business district The part of a city that includes most of its commercial, financial, and manufacturing establishments.

a consequence—epidemic disease. Throughout the Gilded Age, officials in most cities played catch-up when it came to their **infrastructure,** but significant progress appeared by 1900.

Private companies, operating under **franchises** from the city, typically supplied such city utilities and services as gas, electricity, telephone service, public transit, and sometimes water. Entrepreneurs eagerly competed with each other for such franchises, sometimes bribing city officials to secure one. As a result, new residential areas sometimes had gas and electric lines before houses, and streetcars long before paved streets.

The quality and quantity of the water supply varied greatly from city to city. To enlarge its water supply, New York City spent $24 million over seven years to construct what was then the largest aqueduct in the world, carrying 300 million gallons of water a day. Baltimore and Boston also built huge water projects. Water quality, though, remained a problem. As more and more city officials understood that germs caused many diseases, cities introduced filtration and **chlorination** of their water to eliminate disease-carrying organisms. Even so, by the early twentieth century, only 6 percent of urban residents received filtered water.

City residents faced major obstacles in disposing of sewage, cleaning streets (especially given the ever-present horse), and removing garbage. Even when cities built sewer lines, they usually emptied the untreated sewage into some nearby body of water. No city larger than 150,000 people had a sewage treatment plant as late as 1900. One sanitary expert in 1877 called Boston harbor "one vast cesspool, a threat to all the towns it washed." The mayor of Cleveland in 1881 considered the Cuyahoga River "an open sewer through the center of the city." In most cities, few streets were paved. The rest became mud holes in the rain, threw up clouds of dust in dry weather, and froze into deep ruts in the winter. Chicagoans in 1890 could boast of 2,048 miles of streets, but only 629 miles of them were paved, often with wooden blocks. Chicago was not unusual in its choice of paving materials or in the proportion of its streets with some form of paving. In the late nineteenth century, most eastern cities began using asphalt paving. Sometimes it was easier to pave streets than to maintain them: after clearing garbage from a street in the 1890s, one Chicagoan discovered pavement buried under 18 inches of trash.

Everywhere, urban growth seemed at first to outstrip the abilities of city officials and residents to provide for it. Although change came slowly, most city utilities and services improved significantly between 1870 and 1900. After New York City created the first uniformed police force in 1845, seven other cities followed by the mid-1860s, and more did so afterward. Nevertheless, urban crime mushroomed faster than the number of police. By 1871, all major cities had also switched from volunteer fire companies to paid, professional firefighters. The **Great Chicago Fire** of 1871 dramatically demonstrated that the new system was inadequate. The fire devastated 3 square miles, including much of the downtown, killed more than 250 people, and left 18,000 homeless. The Chicago fire and serious fires elsewhere spurred efforts to improve fire protection. Pressured by citizens and fire insurance companies, officials in many cities tried to create a well-trained and well-equipped staff of firefighters and, at the same time, tried to regulate construction practices to make buildings more fire-resistant. By 1900, most American cities had impressive firefighting forces, especially compared to those in other parts of the world. Chicago had more firefighters and fire engines than London, England, a city three times its size.

Poverty and the City

- What constraints and choices shaped the lives of many newcomers to the rapidly growing American cities?
- How did different groups analyze the constraints of urban poverty? What choices about assisting the poor did their analyses lead them to make?

In 1879, in *Progress and Poverty,* Henry George pointed out that the "enormous increase in productive power" had failed to eliminate poverty. He concluded that progress and poverty went hand in hand: "The 'tramp' comes with the locomotive, and almshouses and prisons are as surely the marks

infrastructure Basic facilities that a society needs to function, such as transportation systems, water and power lines, and public institutions such as schools, post offices, and prisons.

franchise Government authorization allowing a private company to provide a public service in a certain area.

chlorination The treatment of water with the chemical chlorine in order to purify and disinfect it.

Great Chicago Fire A fire that destroyed much of Chicago in 1871 and spurred national efforts to improve fire protection.

♦ Monday was laundry day throughout much of America in the late nineteenth and early twentieth centuries, and New York tenements were no exception, as is clear from this photograph taken around 1900. Because buildings were so close together, hanging the laundry became a social event as well, as neighbors hung out their windows, pinned their clothes to the line, and exchanged greetings. Note, as well, the high density of population in such an area. *Museum of the City of New York.*

of 'material progress' as are costly dwellings, rich warehouses, and magnificent churches." George was one of many at that time who focused public attention on the growing numbers of the urban poor and on the massive and expanding slums of the cities.

"How the Other Half Lives"

In 1890, **Jacob Riis** shocked many Americans with the revelations in his book *How the Other Half Lives,* which described the lives of the poorest New Yorkers. In a city of a million and a half inhabitants, Riis claimed, half a million (136,000 families) had begged for food at some time over the preceding eight years. Of them, more than half were unemployed, but only 6 percent were physically unable to work. Most of Riis's book described the appalling conditions of **tenements**—home, he claimed, to three-quarters of the city's population.

Strictly speaking, a tenement is an apartment house occupied by three or more families, but the term came also to imply housing so overcrowded and badly maintained that it was hazardous to the health and safety of its residents. Riis described the typical, cramped New York tenement of his day as

> *a brick building from four to six stories high on the street, frequently with a store on the first floor. . . . Four families occupy each floor, and a set of rooms consists of one or two dark closets, used as bedrooms, with a living room twelve feet by ten. The staircase is too often a dark well in the center of the house, and no direct through ventilation is possible, each family being separated from the other by partitions.*

Such buildings, Riis insisted, "make for evil; because they are the hotbeds of the epidemics that carry death to rich and poor alike; the nurseries of pauperism and crime that fill our jails and police courts; . . . above all, they touch the family life with deadly moral contagion." He especially deplored the impact of poverty and miserable housing conditions on children and families.

Jacob Riis Journalist whose exposure of slum conditions in New York City appalled middle-class Americans and led to calls for improvements in housing.

tenement A multifamily apartment building, often unsafe, unsanitary, and overcrowded with poor families.

♦ Living conditions in tenements, whether in New York or other cities, were usually crowded, with all family members and perhaps one or two boarders packed into two or three rooms. All available space had to be used for multiple purposes. Privacy was almost nonexistent. *Library of Congress.*

Crowded conditions in the working-class sections of large cities developed in part because so many of the poor needed to live within walking distance of their work. By dividing buildings into small rental units, landlords packed in more tenants and collected more rent. Rents were high compared to wages, so many tenants took in lodgers. Such practices produced shockingly high population densities in lower-income urban neighborhoods.

No other city was as densely populated as New York, but nearly all urban, working-class neighborhoods were crowded. Most Chicago stockyard workers, for example, lived in small rowhouses near the slaughterhouses. Many owned their own homes. In 1911, however, three-quarters of the houses were subdivided into two or more living units, and a small shanty often sat in the backyard. Nearly all the homeowners were, therefore, also landlords. Half of all the living units (including both entire houses and apartments) had four rooms, a few had five, and none had more. More than half of all families—owners and tenants alike—took in lodgers. Lodgers who worked different shifts at the stockyards sometimes took turns sleeping in the same bed.

Few agreed on the causes or cures for the widespread urban poverty. Riis divided the blame among greedy landlords, corrupt officials, and the poor themselves. Henry George, in *Progress and Poverty,* pointed to private ownership of property. The Charity Organization Society (COS), by contrast, argued for individual responsibility. With chapters in one hundred cities by 1895, COS claimed that, in most cases, individual character defects produced poverty and that assistance for such people only rewarded immorality or laziness. Assistance, COS insisted, should be given only after careful investigation and should be temporary, only until the man or woman could secure work. COS officials expected the recipients of aid to be moral, thrifty, and hardworking.

The Mixed Blessings of Machine Politics

Not everyone blamed the urban poor for their own distress and extracted promises of moral uprightness in return for help. In most cities, in the late nineteenth century, political organizations emerged that extracted promises of another kind. Politicians built loyal followings among the residents of poor neighborhoods by addressing their needs directly and personally. Instead of repentance they wanted political loyalty from the poor.

Born in a poor Irish neighborhood of New York City, George W. Plunkitt left school at the age of 11. He chose a career in politics, eventually becoming a district leader of **Tammany Hall,** which dominated

Tammany Hall A New York City political organization that dominated city and sometimes state politics.

the city's Democratic party. In 1905, newspaper reporter William Riordon published a series of conversations with Plunkitt. In one, Plunkitt described how he kept the loyalty of the voters in his neighborhood.

> *Go right down among the poor families and help them in the different ways they need help. . . . It's philanthropy, but it's politics, too—mighty good politics. . . . The poor are the most grateful people in the world, and, let me tell you, they have more friends in their neighborhoods than the rich have in theirs. If there's a family in my district in want I know it before the charitable societies, and me and my men are first on the ground. . . . The consequence is that the poor look up to George W. Plunkitt as a father, come to him in trouble—and don't forget him on election day.*

Plunkitt typified many big-city politicians across the country. Neighborhood **saloons** often served as social gathering places, especially for working-class men. Not surprisingly, would-be politicians chose to frequent neighborhood saloons—they often owned them—and tried to build a personal rapport with the voters they met there. They responded to the needs of the urban poor by providing a bucket of coal on a cold day, or a basket of food at Thanksgiving, or a job with the city. In return, they expected the people they assisted to follow their lead in politics. Political organizations based among working-class and poor voters, usually led by men of poor, immigrant parentage, emerged in nearly all large cities and experienced varying degrees of political success. Where they amassed great power, their opponents denounced the leader as a **boss** and the organization itself as a **machine.**

One of the earliest city bosses was **William Marcy Tweed,** whose name became synonymous with urban political corruption. Tweed entered New York City politics in the 1850s and became head of the Tammany Hall organization in 1863. By 1868, this organization had nearly complete control of city and state government. Tweed and his associates built public support by spending tax funds on various charities, and they gave to the poor from their own pockets—pockets often lined with public funds or bribes. Under Tweed's direction, city government launched major construction projects: new public buildings, improvements in streets, parks, sewers, and docks. Much of the construction was riddled with corruption. Between 1868 and 1871, the so-called **Tweed Ring** may have systematically plundered $200 million from the city, mostly by giving bloated construction contracts to businesses that gave a **kickback** to the Ring. In 1871, evidence of corruption led to Tweed's indictment and ultimately his conviction and imprisonment.

In every city, opponents of the machine charged corruption. Most bosses were more cautious than Tweed, but some urban political leaders accumulated sizable fortunes—sometimes through gifts or **retainers** from companies seeking franchises or city contracts, sometimes through advance knowledge of city planning. Above all, the bosses centralized political decision-making. A machine politician in Boston, for example, insisted, "There's got to be in every ward somebody that any bloke can come to—no matter what he's done—to get help." If a pushcart vender needed a permit to sell tinware, or a railroad president needed permission to build a bridge, or a saloonkeeper wanted to stay open on Sunday in violation of the law, the machine could help them all—if they showed the proper gratitude in return. Always, the machine cultivated its base of support among poor and working-class voters.

Combating Urban Poverty: The Settlement Houses

By the 1890s, in several cities, young, college-educated men and women chose to confront urban poverty differently from either the Charity Organi-

saloon A place common to middle-class and working-class neighborhoods where patrons could buy and drink alcoholic beverages and where neighborhood residents (typically only the males) could socialize.

boss Name applied to the head of urban political organizations that based their success on lower-income voters.

machine Name applied to a political organization, usually by its opponents who sought to suggest thereby that the organization was motivated solely by greed for office and spoils.

William Marcy Tweed New York City political boss who used the Tammany machine to maintain control over city and state government from the 1860s until his downfall in 1871.

Tweed Ring The political organization of William M. Tweed, accused of using bribery, kickbacks, and padded accounts to steal money from New York City.

kickback A sum of money that a contractor illegally gives "under the table" to the official who awarded the contract.

retainer A fee paid for advice or service from a professional.

INDIVIDUAL CHOICES

Choosing to Help the Poor

Jane Addams

Born to a prosperous family, Jane Addams lived a life of leisure as a young woman, until she made the choice to devote her life to serving those less privileged than she. This portrait was done in 1896 by Alice Kellogg Tyler, an artist at Hull House, the settlement house Addams established to serve the poor. Chicago Historical Society

In her autobiography, *Twenty Years at Hull House*, Jane Addams devoted a full chapter to one difficult choice she faced as a young woman. Born in 1860 in a small town in Illinois, the youngest daughter of a bank president, Addams lived a childhood filled with higher expectations and more choices than were possible for most young women of her day. Her father believed women as well as men should go to college, and his wealth freed his daughters from the economic constraints that restricted most young women even if they wanted to attend college. In 1877, Addams entered Rockford Seminary, then transforming itself into a full-fledged women's college. There she met Ellen Gates Starr, who became a close friend and later an associate at Hull House.

Like many among the first generation of college women, Addams became a feminist at Rockford. In one of her college speeches, she defined her feminism in terms of expectations and choices: "She [the feminist of her day] wishes not to be a man, nor like a man, but she claims the same right to independent thought and action." After completing her studies at the seminary, she entered the Woman's Medical College in Philadelphia in 1881, but soon her own health problems caused her to drop out.

A college graduate of independent financial means, Addams spent many of the next several

zation Societies or the political machines. These humanitarians took an environmental approach, seeking to help the poor deal with the problems they faced in housing, nutrition, and sanitation. The **settlement house** idea, first practiced in London's Toynbee Hall in 1884, involved opening in the slums a house where idealistic university graduates lived among the poor and tried to help them. The concept spread to the United States with the establishment of a settlement house in New York in 1886.

Men staffed this first settlement house. In 1889, however, several women who had graduated from Smith College opened a settlement house in New York, and Jane Addams and Ellen Gates Starr opened **Hull House,** the first settlement house in

settlement house Community center operated by resident social reformers in a slum area in order to help poor people in their own neighborhood.

Hull House Settlement house that Jane Addams and Ellen Gates Starr founded in Chicago in 1889 to improve community and civic life in the slums.

years traveling in Europe. But in her visits to art galleries, museums, and concerts she found little purpose or satisfaction, and she began to consider ways to spend her life more productively. A Spanish bullfight pushed her to make the pivotal choice:

> *We had been to see a bullfight rendered in the most magnificent Spanish style, where greatly to my surprise and horror, I found that I had seen, with comparative indifference, five bulls and many more horses killed. . . . I had not thought much about the bloodshed; but in the evening the natural and inevitable reaction came, and in deep chagrin I felt myself tried and condemned, not only by this disgusting experience, but by the entire moral situation which it revealed. It was suddenly made quite clear to me that I was lulling my conscience. . . . I had fallen into the meanest type of self-deception in making myself believe that all this was in preparation for great things to come.*

She immediately determined that the very next day she would speak to her friend and traveling companion, Ellen Gates Starr, about this compelling new desire to seek a more productive life of service. Addams not only shared the decision but also invited Starr to join her—and she did. Before returning to the United States, Addams visited Toynbee Hall in London to learn about its revolutionary approach to helping the urban poor.

Inspired by what she saw in England, Addams made the choice to commit her life to such endeavors. Upon her return to the United States, she and Starr set up Hull House in a working-class, immigrant neighborhood in Chicago. By then, Addams seems to have chosen not to marry, a choice made by about half of the first generation of college-educated women in the United States, who seem to have considered the combination of career and family impossible.

Addams lived at Hull House for the rest of her life, attracting a circle of impressive associates and making Hull House the best-known example of settlement work. Hull House offered a variety of services to the families of its neighborhood: a nursery, a kindergarten (childcare for preschool children), classes in child rearing, a playground and gymnasium. Unlike some settlement house workers, Addams chose to confront directly some of the political factors that constrained her neighborhood's efforts at self-improvement. She and other Hull House activists challenged the power of city bosses and lobbied state legislators, seeking cleaner streets, the abolition of child labor, health and safety regulations for factories, compulsory school attendance, and more. Her efforts brought her national recognition. A delegate to the convention that nominated Theodore Roosevelt for president as a Progressive in 1912, she seconded his nomination. Her opposition to war brought her the Nobel Peace Prize in 1931, four years before her death.

Chicago. For many Americans, Jane Addams became synonymous with the settlement house movement (see Individual Choices: Jane Addams). Settlement house workers provided a wide range of assistance to slum families: cooking and sewing classes, public baths, childcare facilities, instruction in English, housing for unmarried working women. Churches sponsored some houses, and others were secular. Nearly all tried to minimize class conflict because they agreed with Jane Addams that "the dependence of classes on each other is reciprocal." Some historians have suggested that settlement house workers tried to minimize the gap between urban economic classes by imparting middle-class values to the poor and by persuading the wealthy of the need to mitigate poverty, and that their efforts reflected urban, middle-class anxieties over growing extremes of wealth and poverty. Some settlement house workers, including Addams, also became forces for urban reform, promoting better education, improved public health and sanitation, and honest government.

Settlement houses spread rapidly, with some four hundred operating by 1910. By then, three-quarters of settlement workers were women, and the settlement houses became the first institutions to be created and staffed primarily by college-educated women. When universities began to offer courses of study in social work (first at Columbia, in 1902), women tended to dominate that field too. Women college graduates thus created a new, and uniquely urban, profession at a time when many other careers still remained closed to them.

Church-affiliated settlement houses often reflected the influence of the **Social Gospel,** a movement popularized by urban Protestant ministers who were concerned about the social and economic problems of the cities. One of the best known, Washington Gladden, of Columbus, Ohio, called for "Applied Christianity," by which he meant the application to business relations of Christ's injunctions to love one another and to treat others as you would have them treat you. Another minister, C. S. Sheldon, wrote *In His Steps* (1896), the story of a fictional church congregation whose members chose to live for one year in full compliance with the teachings of Jesus. The book suggested that if all Americans did the same, both unemployment and saloons would soon disappear. A similar, socially oriented approach appeared among some Catholics, especially those inspired by *Rerum Novarum,* a message from Pope Leo XIII urging greater attention to the problems of the industrial working class.

New Americans from Europe

- What expectations prompted immigrants to leave their homelands for the United States? What constraints did they sometimes encounter?
- In what ways were immigrants' expectations and choices regarding assimilation similar to and different from those of nativists?

The United States has attracted large numbers of immigrants throughout its history, but the flood of immigrants that fed the burgeoning cities and industrial labor force during the years between the Civil War and World War I represents the highest level of immigration the nation ever experienced. Most of these immigrants came from Europe, and many settled in cities. By 1910, in eighteen of the twenty-five largest cities, immigrants and their children made up more than half of the total population. In New York and Chicago, the nation's two largest cities, more than three-fourths of the people were first- or second-generation immigrants.

A Flood of Immigrants

The numbers of immigrants varied from year to year—higher in prosperous years, lower in depression years—but the trend was constantly upward. Nearly a quarter of a million arrived in 1865, two-thirds of a million in 1881, a million in 1905. In the 1870s and 1880s, most immigrants came from Great Britain, Ireland, Germany, and **Scandinavia.** After the depression of the mid-1890s, immigration rose far above any previous levels. After 1900, most immigrants came from southern and eastern Europe, especially Austria-Hungary, Italy, and Russia. Austria-Hungary and Russia contained peoples with many languages and cultures. The 3.4 million immigrants from those two empires who lived in America in 1910 included nearly a million Jews, 750,000 Poles, 353,000 Germans, 228,000 Hungarians, 222,000 Czechs, and smaller numbers of Slovaks, Slovenes, Croats, Serbs, Lithuanians, Latvians, and others (see Figure 19.2).

Immigrants left their former homes for a variety of reasons, but most chose to come to the United States because of its reputation as the "land of opportunity." They came, as one bluntly said, for "jobs" and, as another declared, "for money." Some were also attracted by the reputation of the United States for toleration of religious difference and commitment to democracy. In fact, the reasons for coming to America varied from country to country, year to year, and person to person. A few examples will illustrate some of the forces that uprooted different groups of Europeans and the settlement patterns they established in the United States.

In Ireland, a fourfold population increase between 1750 and 1850 combined with changes in agriculture to constrain possibilities for farming. Repeated failure of potato crops after 1845 produced widespread famine and starvation. For some, English oppression contributed to the choice to leave, and America's reputation for political and religious freedom attracted them. Irish immigrants, many desperately poor, arrived in their greatest numbers between 1847 and 1854, but Irish immigration con-

Social Gospel A moral reform movement of the late nineteenth century led by Protestant clergymen who drew attention to urban problems and advocated social justice for the poor.

Scandinavia The region of northern Europe consisting of Norway, Sweden, and Denmark.

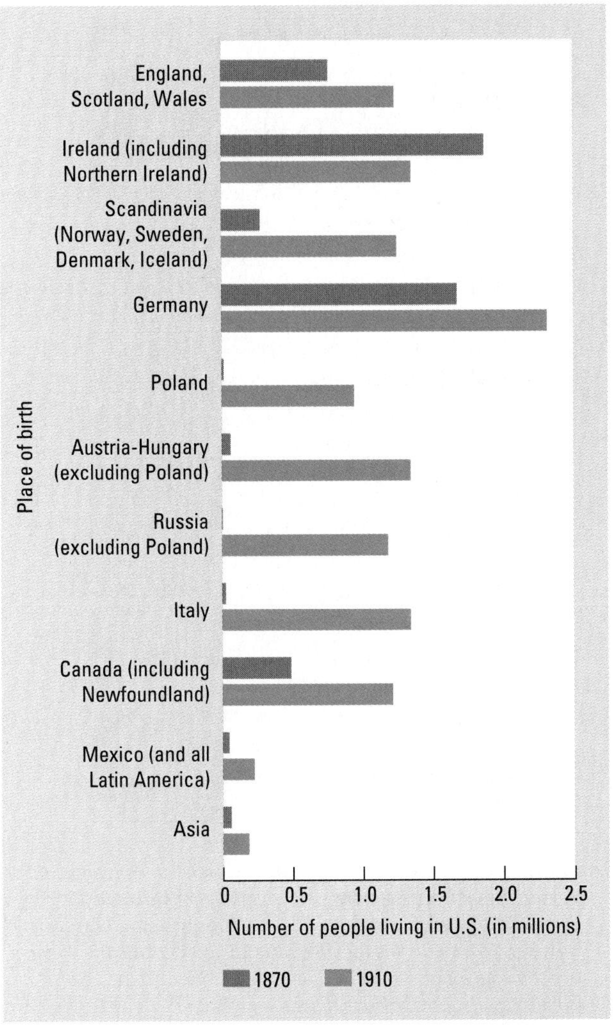

♦ **FIGURE 19.2 Place of Birth of the Foreign-Born Population, 1870 and 1910** This figure compares the number of people born in other countries who were living in the United States in 1870 and 1910. Notice the large increases from eastern and southern Europe, but also notice that in 1910 the total number of immigrants from those regions was still smaller than the total from northwestern Europe and Great Britain. *Source:* U.S. Bureau of the Census, Department of Commerce, *Historical Statistics of the United States*, 2 vols. (Washington, D.C.: U.S. Government Printing Office, 1975), Series A-58, A-59, A-69, A-119.

tinued at high levels until the 1890s. Ninety percent were Catholic. They settled at first in the cities of the Northeast, composing a quarter of the population in New York City and Boston as early as 1860. Although many Irish immigrants worked in the West, the Irish as a group remained very urban.

Throughout the late nineteenth and early twentieth centuries, Germans outnumbered all other immigrant groups in the United States, but most arrived before 1900. Rural overpopulation, changes in agriculture, and crop failures in the 1840s and 1850s all strengthened the desire to move. Religious and political persecutions affected some as well. Many German peasants chose to sell their holdings and thus arrived in the United States with some capital. Many expected to acquire farmland, and some succeeded, especially in the north-central states. Most German immigrants, however, settled in towns and cities, especially in the Midwest. Germans were of diverse religious backgrounds, including Catholics (about a third of the total), Lutherans, Calvinists, Jews, and other groups.

In many ways, Scandinavian immigration followed the German patterns. The high point of Scandinavian immigration came in the 1880s and 1890s, when it accounted for 12 percent of the immigrants to the United States—and for about a quarter of the entire population of Sweden and Norway. Scandinavian farmers were pushed from the land by **overpopulation** and changes in agriculture as well as by the hardships of farming the stony soil. Religious groups that challenged the state Lutheran church met persecution. Many Scandinavians settled in Minnesota, the Dakotas, Montana, and Nebraska, where a high proportion became farmers. Others landed in Washington State. Many Scandinavian Mormons went to Utah.

Italian immigrants illustrate a different situation. Their numbers increased slowly through the 1880s and 1890s until, between 1900 and 1915, Italians outnumbered any other single group of immigrants to the United States. Four out of five came from the overpopulated and depressed regions of southern Italy and Sicily, where many had been landless farm laborers (the *contadini*). At first, many young men worked in construction or agriculture during summers and returned to Italy during winters. Eventually some chose to stay and sent for their families to join them. Large numbers of Italians made the cities of the Northeast their home, and many found work in textile and clothing factories. In California, Italians became prominent in farming, especially in growing fruit and vegetables and grapes for winemaking.

overpopulation The growth of a population beyond the point where it can be comfortably supported by its environment.

The migration of eastern European Jews reveals still a different pattern. In the late nineteenth and early twentieth centuries, one-third of the Jews living in eastern Europe left there, and 90 percent of them came to the United States. The largest number came from Russia, accounting for nearly one-eighth of all immigrants after 1900. Overpopulation, industrialization that reduced the demand for skilled craftsmen, and legal discrimination against Jews all contributed to the choice to leave. Religious persecution, however, was the single most important reason for their migration. **Pogroms** occurred sporadically throughout these decades, notably in Russia in the early 1880s and from 1903 to 1906. Whole communities sometimes chose to emigrate, including businessmen, professionals, and intellectuals as well as workers and farmers. They became the most urban of immigrant groups, settling initially in the cities of the Northeast, especially New York, where half of all eastern European Jews in the United States resided in 1914.

Large numbers of Slavic-speaking immigrant groups began to arrive in the 1890s and after, accounting for more than a third of all European immigrants between 1900 and 1914. They emigrated primarily for economic opportunity. Poles, the largest single group, included some who were fleeing efforts by the German and Russian governments to suppress Polish nationalism. Like the Irish, Poles were nearly all Catholic. Poles settled in New York and in the cities of the Midwest. By 1910, Chicago had the largest number of Polish immigrants, and there were significant concentrations in Milwaukee, Detroit, and Buffalo as well. Most Slavic-speaking groups tended to locate in urban and industrial areas.

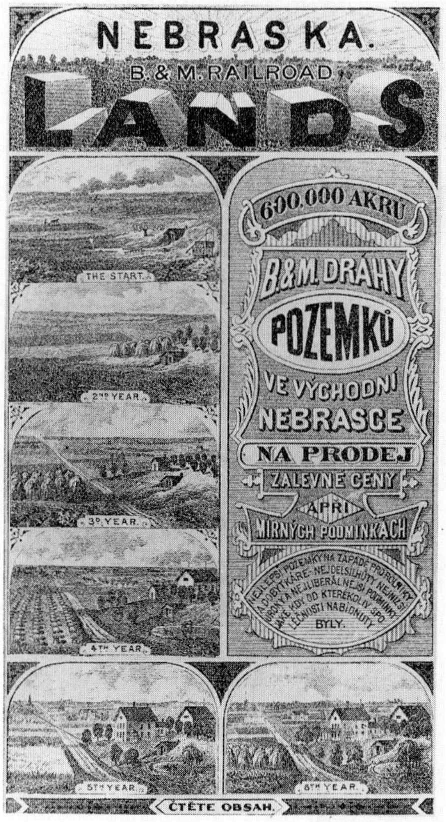

♦ Railroad companies, seeking to sell their land grants, advertised in Europe for immigrants to buy farmland in the West. This poster, issued by the Burlington and Missouri railroad, probably in the 1880s, is in Czech, but the same poster was also issued in German and Swedish. The poster's sequence of drawings shows a six-year transition from bare prairie to prosperous farm. Such advertising helped to attract many European immigrants to the north central states (see the map at the beginning of the chapter). *Nebraska State Historical Society.*

An Ethnic Patchwork

Jacob Riis, himself a Danish immigrant, provided this striking description of Manhattan in 1890:

> *A map of the city, colored to designate nationalities, would show more stripes than on the skin of a zebra, and more colors than any rainbow. The city on such a map would fall into two great halves, green for the Irish prevailing in the West Side tenement districts, and blue for the Germans on the East Side. But intermingled with these ground colors would be an odd variety of tints that would give the whole the appearance of an extraordinary crazy quilt.*

Riis then pieced in some smaller parts of the ethnic patchwork by describing neighborhoods of Italians, African Americans, Jews, Chinese, Czechs, Arabs, Finns, Greeks, and Swiss.

The chapter-opening map reveals concentrations of immigrants in the urban-industrial core region, or manufacturing belt, especially in urban areas, but distinctive immigrant communities were not limited to cities. Many of the immigrants in the north-central region became farmers, for there farmland was relatively cheap, either acquired by means of the Home-

pogrom A violent mob attack on Jewish communities, often resulting in a massacre.

stead Act or purchased from a railroad. Scandinavians, Dutch, Swiss, Czechs, and Germans were most likely to be farmers, but there were rural farming settlements of many other groups. One woman recalled that in the 1880s, when she was growing up on a farm in Nebraska, her family could attend Sunday church services in Norwegian, Danish, Swedish, French, Czech, or German. "There were, of course, American congregations also," she added.

The patterns of immigrant settlement reflect the expectations immigrants had about America, as well as the opportunities they found when they arrived. The British, Germans, Scandinavians, Czechs, and a few others came in the 1870s and 1880s, when good farmland could still be acquired relatively cheaply in the north-central states. Many of them planned to become farmers and brought enough capital to get a start in agriculture. In contrast, fewer Irish had the necessary capital, and fewer came with the expectation of becoming farmers. Some of the post-1900 immigrants, especially among Italians and Poles, came with the intention to work for a time and then return home with their earnings.

After 1890, farmland was more difficult to obtain. Newcomers at that point were more likely to find work in the rapidly expanding industrial sectors of the economy: mining, transportation, and manufacturing. Of course, there were many individual variations on these patterns. Some immigrants coming after 1890 certainly intended to become farmers and succeeded. Many who came before 1890 intended to become farmers but ended up as industrial workers.

Hyphenated America

In the nineteenth century, most **old-stock Americans** assumed that immigrants should quickly learn English, become citizens, and restructure their lives and values to resemble those of old-stock Americans. Most immigrants, however, resisted rapid assimilation. For most immigrants, assimilation took place over a lifetime or over generations. Most held fast to elements in their own culture while they were taking up a new life in America. Their sense of identity drew on two elements: where they came from and where they were now. Being conscious of their new identity as Germans in America or Italians in America, for example, immigrants often came to think of themselves as **hyphenated Americans**: German-Americans, Italian-Americans, Polish-Americans.

On arriving in America, with its strange language and unfamiliar customs, many immigrants reacted by seeking people who shared their cultural values, practiced their religion, and, especially, spoke their language. Ethnic communities emerged throughout regions with large numbers of immigrants. These communities played significant roles in newcomers' transition from the old country to America. They gave immigrants a chance to learn about their new home with the assistance of those who had come before. At the same time, they could, without apology or embarrassment, retain the values and behavior from their old country that they found most important.

Hyphenated America developed a unique blend of ethnic institutions, often unlike anything in the

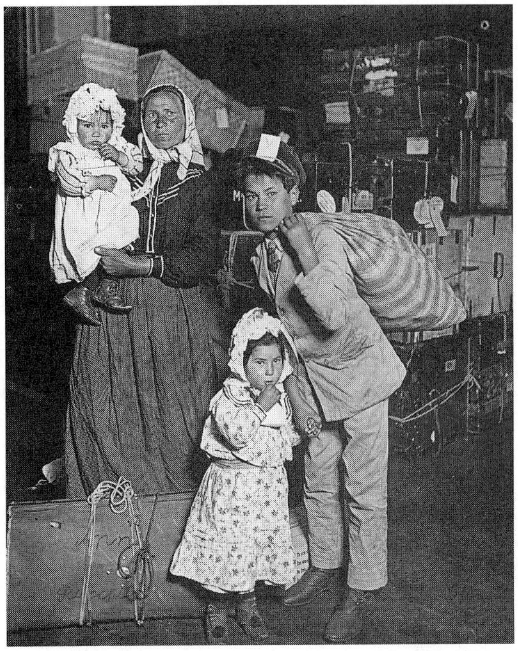

♦ The photographer Lewis Hine took this picture of a family from eastern Europe who arrived in the United States in 1905. After 1890, immigrants came ashore at Ellis Island and were processed by the Immigration Service. For millions of immigrants, Ellis Island was their portal to America. *Courtesy George Eastman House.*

old-stock Americans Term that historians use to refer to Americans descended from those present before the American Revolution; also used by the Census Bureau to describe people who were born in the United States and whose parents were born in the United States.

hyphenated Americans Americans with a sense of ethnic identity based both on their immigrant ancestry and on their participation in American culture—Irish-Americans, for example.

old country but also unlike the institutions of old-stock America. Fraternal lodges based on ethnicity sprang up and often provided not only social ties but also benefits in case of illness or death. Among these lodges were the Ancient Order of Hibernians (Irish), the Sons of Hermann (German), and the Sons of Italy. Singing societies flourished, devoted to the music of the old country. Foreign-language newspapers were vital in developing a sense of identity that connected the old country to the new, for they provided news from the old country as well as from other similar communities in the United States.

For members of nearly every group, religious institutions provided the most important building blocks of ethnic group identity. In most of Europe, a state church was officially sanctioned to perform certain functions. Membership in a religious body was voluntary in America, but religious ties often became stronger here, partly because churches and other religious organizations provided an important link among people with a similar language and cultural values. Protestant immigrant groups created new church organizations based on both theology and language. By 1900, for example, there were separate Lutheran churches speaking German, Norwegian, Swedish, Danish, Finnish, and Icelandic, and Calvinist churches conducted services in German, Dutch, and Welsh. Catholic parishes in immigrant neighborhoods often took on the ethnic characteristics of the community. Services were conducted in the language of, and special observances were transplanted from, the old country. Jewish congregations, too, often differed according to the ethnic background of their members. (Map 19.1 shows the ethnic Catholic parishes in the Chicago neighborhood where stockyard workers lived.)

Nativism

Many Americans (including some who were only a generation removed from immigrant forebears themselves) expected immigrants to lay aside their previous identities, embrace the behavior and beliefs of old-stock Americans, and blend neatly into old-stock American culture. This view of immigrants came to be identified with the image of the **melting pot** after the appearance of a play by that name in 1908. But the melting-pot metaphor rarely described the reality of immigrants' lives. Most immigrants had to change in some ways upon coming to a new land. But most did so slowly, over lifetimes, gradually adopting new patterns of thinking and behavior or modifying previous beliefs and practices.

Few old-stock Americans appreciated or even understood the long-term nature of immigrants' adjustment to their new home. Instead of seeing the ways immigrants changed, many old-stock Americans saw only immigrants' efforts to retain their own culture. They fretted over the multiplication of foreign-language newspapers and feared to go into communities where they rarely heard an English sentence. Such fears and misgivings fostered the growth of **nativism:** the view that old-stock values and social patterns were preferable to those of immigrants. Nativists argued that only their values and institutions were genuinely American, and they feared that immigrants posed a threat to those comfortable traditions.

American nativism was often linked to anti-Catholicism. Many immigrant groups included large numbers of Catholics, and many old-stock Americans came to identify the Catholic church as an immigrant church. The **American Protective Association,** founded in 1887, noisily proclaimed itself the voice of anti-Catholicism. Its members pledged not to hire Catholics, not to vote for them, and not to strike with them. They recruited Protestant immigrants and Protestant African Americans as well as old-stock white Protestants, claiming a half million members by 1894. They dominated the Republican party in parts of the Midwest, and, in a few instances, fomented mob violence against Catholics.

Jews, too, faced religious antagonism. In the 1870s, increasing numbers of organizations and businesses began to discriminate against Jews. By the early twentieth century, such discrimination intensified. Some employers refused to hire Jews. Many college fraternities and sororities and other social organizations refused to admit them, and **restrictive covenants** kept them from buying homes in certain areas.

melting pot A phrase describing the vision of American society as a place where immigrants set aside their distinctive cultural identities and are absorbed into a homogeneous culture.

nativism The view that old-stock values and social patterns were preferable to those of immigrants.

American Protective Association An anti-Catholic organization founded in Iowa in 1887 and active during the next decade.

restrictive covenant Provision in a property title designed to restrict subsequent sale or use of the property, often specifying sale only to a white Christian.

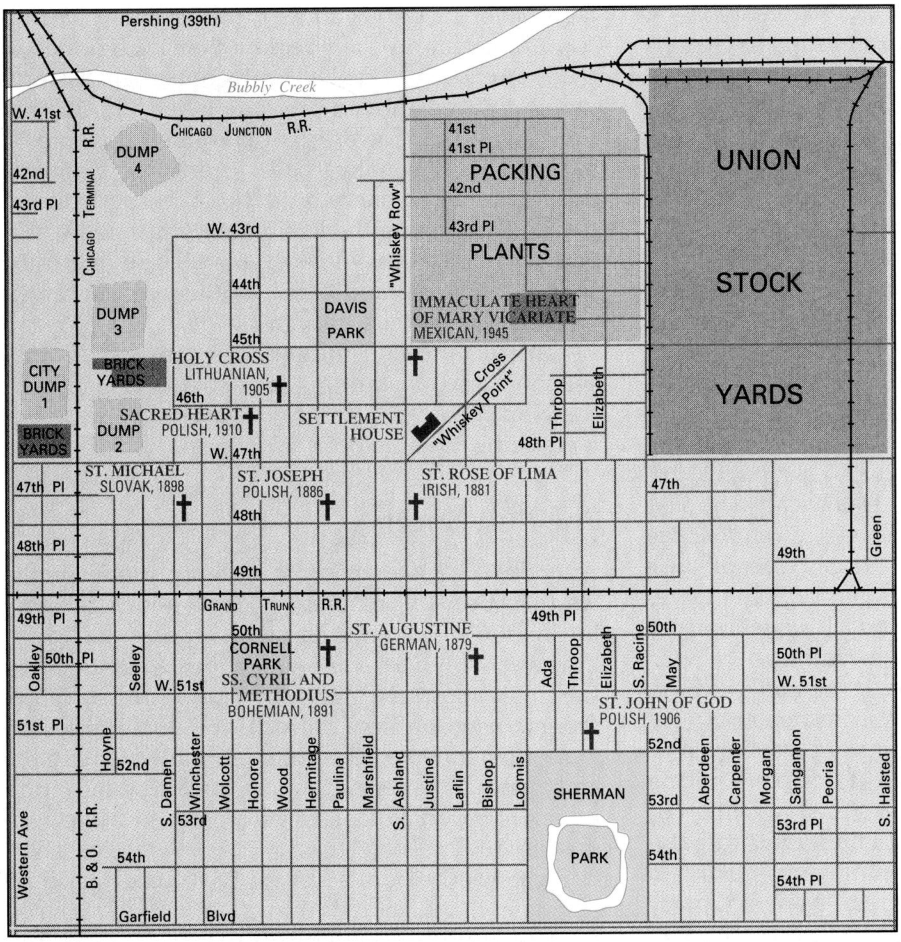

♦ **MAP 19.1 "Back of the Yards" Neighborhood** Many of the workers in Chicago's stockyards and packing plants lived in this area called "Back of the Yards." The founding dates for the neighborhood's Catholic parish churches point to the successive waves of immigrants who lived and worked there. The neighborhood also had several ethnically identifiable Protestant churches.

Labor organizations sometimes looked at unlimited immigration as a threat to jobs and wage levels—especially when economic depression brought widespread unemployment and wage reductions. Anti-Chinese sentiment among Pacific coast unions contributed to passage of the Chinese Exclusion Act in 1882 (see page 554). The depression of the 1890s may have convinced the American Federation of Labor to endorse a literacy test as a way to reduce the influx of immigrants.

The rise of labor organizations and, especially, radical political organizations also bolstered anti-immigrant sentiment. By 1900 or so, a few employers had begun to argue that unions violated American traditions of individualism and represented foreign, un-American interests. Immigrants were also sometimes associated with radicalism, especially anarchism. Newspapers claimed that "there is no such thing as an American anarchist." In 1901, Leon Czolgosz, an American-born anarchist with a foreign-sounding name, assassinated President William McKinley. Congress promptly passed a bill barring anarchists from immigrating. After 1900, Socialist party candidates received strong support from voters in some areas heavily populated with immigrants, confirming to many a link between immigrants and radicalism.

After about 1890, the shift in the sources of immigration from northwestern Europe to southern and eastern Europe—bringing large numbers of Italians, Poles, and eastern European Jews—also furthered the rise of nativism. Anti-Catholicism and anti-Semitism combined with cruel stereotypes of those from southern and eastern Europe to create a sense that these "**new immigrants**" were less desirable than "**old immigrants**" from northwestern Europe. More of the old immigrants were Protestant, and by 1900 many had managed to establish themselves as farmers, artisans, or merchants. By contrast, many of the new immigrants worked in factories or mines or as unskilled laborers.

The arrival of significant numbers of new immigrants in the late nineteenth century coincided with a wave of sentiment that glorified Anglo-Saxons (Germanic ancestors of the English) and accomplishments of the English and English Americans. Relying on social Darwinism and its argument for the survival of the fittest (see page 529), proponents of Anglo-Saxonism took alarm from statistics that showed old-stock Americans having fewer children than the new immigrants. Some voiced fears of "race suicide" in which Anglo-Saxons allowed themselves to be bred out of existence. With such anxieties feeding their prejudices, nativists became blatant racists.

By the 1890s, these religious, economic, political, and racist strains began to result in demands that the government restrict immigration from Europe. Advocates of restriction focused at first on requiring immigrants to pass a literacy test before being admitted. Opposition came from immigrants' organizations and, usually, from employers seeking a larger supply of labor. Congress passed literacy measures in 1897 and again in 1913, but both met presidential vetoes. In 1917 **President Woodrow Wilson** vetoed another effort, but Congress overrode his veto and enacted the measure into law. It had little impact. By then, most immigrants were literate in their own language, and the law did not specify English. A more sweeping restriction came in the early 1920s (see page 746).

New South, Old Issues

- How did the economy of the South change during the late nineteenth century?
- What outcome did white southern officials seek to accomplish as they wrote new laws on race relations during 1880s and 1890s?
- What choices did different black southerners make in response to the state of race relations in the South?

The term **New South** is sometimes used to refer to the South after Reconstruction. More specifically, however, it refers to efforts by some southerners, notably Henry Grady, editor of the Atlanta *Constitution,* to transform their region. Some advocates of the New South hoped their region might be economically transformed and integrated into the national economy. Toward that end, they promoted a more diverse economic base, with more manufacturing and less reliance on a few staple agricultural crops. And, during the late nineteenth century, several new industries did take root in the South. At the same time, white and black southerners continued to grapple with the legacy of slavery, Civil War, and Reconstruction. And, while urbanization and immigration were transforming social patterns in parts of the North, patterns of racial relations in the South were being redefined.

The New South

After the Civil War, the state of transportation in the South, especially railroads, posed a critical limit on the region's economic growth. During the 1880s, however, southern railroads more than doubled their miles of track. In the 1890s, J. P. Morgan led in reorganizing southern railroads into three large systems, dominated by the Southern Railway. With the emergence of better rail transportation, some entrepreneurs began to look toward creation of new industries.

Some southerners had long advocated that their cotton be manufactured into cloth in the South. Efforts to establish textile manufacturing there had been made before the Civil War, but the economic chaos of war and its aftermath slowed them. The cotton textile industry finally began to boom in the South during the 1880s. The South counted 161 textile mills in 1880 and 400 in 1900. The new mills had more modern equipment and were larger and more

new immigrants Newcomers from eastern and southern Europe who began to arrive in America in large numbers in the 1880s.

old immigrants Newcomers from Britain, Germany, Ireland, and Scandinavia, most of whom arrived in America before the 1890s.

President Woodrow Wilson Scholar and politician who established a reputation for reform and a strong progressive record as governor of New Jersey and was elected president in 1912.

New South Term that some southerners used to promote the idea that the South should become industrialized, have a more diverse agriculture, and be thoroughly integrated into the economy of the nation.

♦ Much of the new southern textile industry was based on child labor. These children were photographed by Lewis Hines in 1908. *National Archives/Lewis Hines.*

productive than the mills of New England. Some New England firms moved their operations southward rather than compete with the products of southern mills. Southern textile mills had cheaper labor costs than mills in New England, partly because they relied extensively on child labor. One official of the American Cotton Manufacturers' Association estimated that 70 percent of southern cotton-mill workers were less than 21 years of age. Another estimated that 75 percent of the cotton spinners in North Carolina were under 14. Similar patterns characterized the emergence of cigarette manufacturing as a significant new southern industry. For the most part, however, these and similar enterprises did little to transform the regional economy. Nearly all the new companies paid low wages, and some had located in the South specifically to take advantage of its large pool of cheap, unskilled, nonunion labor.

Of greater potential to transform part of the South was the iron and steel industry that emerged in northern Alabama. Dominated by the Tennessee Coal, Iron, and Railroad Company, the industry drew on coal from Tennessee and Alabama mines and iron ore from northern Alabama. By the late 1890s, Birmingham, Alabama, had become one of the world's largest producers of pig iron. In 1897, the first southern steel mill opened in Ensley, Alabama, and soon established itself as a serious rival to the mills of the North. In 1907, J. P. Morgan arranged the merger of the Tennessee Company into his United States Steel Corporation.

The turn of the century also saw the beginning of a southern oil industry near Beaumont, Texas, with the tapping of the Spindletop Pool—so productive the press labeled it "the world's greatest oil well." The center of petroleum production now shifted from the Midwest to Texas and to Oklahoma and Louisiana, where important discoveries also came in 1901. In addition to attracting attention from Standard Oil, the new discoveries prompted the growth or creation of new companies, notably Gulf and Texaco.

As the South began to develop these manufacturing and extractive industries, some southerners also tried to diversify the region's agriculture. Such efforts, however, ran up against the cotton textile and cigarette industries, both of which built factories in the South to be near their raw materials. In the end, southern agriculture changed little: owners and sharecroppers farmed small plots, obligated by their rental contracts or **crop liens** to raise cotton or tobacco. In some parts of the South, farmers became even more dependent on cotton than they had been before the Civil War. Parts of Georgia, for example,

crop lien A claim against a growing crop, typically held by a storekeeper as the price for extending credit.

produced almost 200 percent more bales of cotton in 1880 than in 1860. Fencing laws brought some long-term improvement of livestock. States adopted such laws to keep farmers from allowing their cattle and hogs to run free in unfenced, wooded areas. Fencing permitted more prosperous farmers to introduce new breeds, control breeding, and thereby improve the stock. But the law placed at a disadvantage many small-scale farmers who now had to fence their grazing areas but could not afford to buy the new breeds.

Despite repeated backing for the idea of a New South by some southern leaders, and despite growth of some new industries in the South, the late nineteenth century was also the time when the myth of the **Old South** and the so-called **Lost Cause** reached into nearly every aspect of southern life. Popular fiction and song, North and South, romanticized the pre–Civil War Old South as a place of gentility and gallantry, where "kindly" plantation owners cared for "loyal" slaves. The Lost Cause myth portrayed the Confederacy as a heroic, even noble, effort to retain the life and values of the Old South. Leading southerners—especially Democratic party leaders—promoted the Lost Cause myth, and many white southerners embraced it as justification for the dislocation and suffering that so many of them had experienced during and after the Civil War. Hundreds of statues of Confederate soldiers appeared on courthouse lawns, and gala commemorative events and organizations reflected devotion to the myth among many white southerners.

The Second Mississippi Plan and the Atlanta Compromise

Dreams of the Old South and the Lost Cause helped to fuel the politics of white supremacy that dominated the South after Reconstruction. So long as the Civil Rights Act of 1875 remained in place, African Americans were, at least in theory, protected against discrimination in public places (see pages 485–486). After the 1870s, southern state laws prohibited racial intermarriage. State or local law, or sometimes simply local custom, had produced racially separate school systems, cemeteries, hospitals, churches, and other voluntary organizations. Although African Americans shared steamboat and railroad facilities with whites, they were expected to ride only in second-class accommodations. Even so, in 1885, T. McCants Stewart, an African-American lawyer, traveled in integrated first-class railroad cars and ate in integrated restaurants all through Virginia and the Carolinas. Segregation existed throughout much of the South, but sometimes without force of law, sanctioned instead by local custom and the ever-present threat of violence against any African American who dared to challenge it. Restrictions on black political voting and officeholding were also extralegal, enforced through coercion or intimidation.

Then, in the **Civil Rights cases** (1883), the U.S. Supreme Court ruled unconstitutional the Civil Rights Act of 1875. The Court said that the "equal protection" clause of the Fourteenth Amendment applied only to states and not to individuals and companies. This meant that state governments were obligated to treat all citizens as equal before the law but private businesses did not need to offer equal access to their facilities. Given this interpretation, southern lawmakers slowly began to require businesses to practice segregation. In 1887, the Florida legislature required separate accommodations on railroad trains. Mississippi passed a similar law the next year and added separate waiting rooms. Louisiana required segregated railroad facilities in 1890, and four more states did the same in 1891. Law and social custom began to specify greater racial separation in other ways too, but patterns remained inconsistent.

Mississippi whites took a bolder step in 1890, holding a state constitutional convention to eliminate political participation by African Americans. Shrewdly, the new provisions did not mention the word *race*. Instead they specified payment of a **poll tax,** passing a literacy test, and other requirements for voting. Everyone involved understood that these measures were intended to disfranchise black voters. Men who failed the literacy test could still vote if they could explain a section of the state constitution or law to the satisfaction of a local (white)

Old South Term used in both South and North for the antebellum, or pre–Civil War South, suggesting that it was a place of gentility and gallantry.

Lost Cause Term used to refer to the Confederate struggle in the Civil War as a noble but doomed effort to preserve a way of life.

Civil Rights cases A series of cases that came before the Supreme Court in 1883, in which the Court ruled that private companies could legally discriminate against blacks.

poll tax A tax that many southern states imposed as a prerequisite to voting in order to disfranchise African Americans.

official who read it to them. The typical result was that the only illiterates who could vote were white. Most of the South followed this so-called Second Mississippi Plan (see page 492 for the first Mississippi Plan) with great interest. Except for imposing the poll tax, however, no other state moved immediately to imitate its provisions.

Then in 1895, a black educator signaled his apparent willingness to accept disfranchisement and segregation for the moment. Born into slavery in 1856, **Booker T. Washington** had worked as a janitor while studying at Hampton Institute, a school that combined preparation for elementary school teaching with vocational education in agriculture and industrial work. Before long, Washington returned to Hampton as a teacher. In 1881, the Alabama legislature authorized establishment of a black **normal school** at Tuskegee. Washington became its principal and made Tuskegee Normal and Industrial Institute into a leading black educational institution.

In 1895, Atlanta played host to the Cotton States and International Exposition, one of the many spinoffs from the Chicago Columbian Exposition. The exposition directors invited Washington to speak at the opening ceremonies. They felt he could speak successfully to the mixed crowd of southern whites, southern blacks, and northern whites who would be present. Washington did not disappoint the directors. In his speech, he seemed to accept an inferior status for blacks, at least for the present: "No race can prosper till it learns that there is as much dignity in tilling a field as in writing a poem. It is at the bottom of life we must begin, and not at the top." He also seemed to condone segregation: "In all things that are purely social, we can be as separate as the fingers, yet one as the hand in all things essential to mutual progress. . . . The wisest among my race understand that the agitation of questions of social equality is the extremest folly." He agreed that equal rights had to be earned, rather than belonging to all citizens: "It is important and right that all privileges of the law be ours, but it is vastly more important that we be prepared for the exercise of these privileges."

The speech—soon dubbed the **Atlanta Compromise**—earned great acclaim for Washington, especially among whites, at Atlanta and across the nation. His message was one that southern whites wanted to hear: a black educator urged his race to accept segregation and disfranchisement in return for interracial peace and economic opportunity. Northern whites too were receptive to the notion that the South would work out its race relations by itself. Until his death in 1915, Washington held sway as the most prominent black leader in the nation, at least among white Americans. Among African Americans, however, his message found a mixed reception. Some not only accepted but even anticipated his approach as the best that might be secured at the time. Others criticized his willingness to sacrifice black rights. Henry M. Turner, a bishop of the African Methodist Episcopal church in Atlanta,

♦ Booker T. Washington's message of racial self-help and accommodation brought him national attention and made him the most powerful African American of his day, with access to the funds of northern philanthropists and influence over Republican political patronage. When Tuskegee Institute celebrated its twenty-fifth anniversary in 1906, the president of Harvard, Charles Eliot (right), and Andrew Carnegie (second from right) dramatically symbolized Washington's access to northern cultural and philanthropic institutions. *Corbis/Bettmann.*

Booker T. Washington Former slave who became an educator and founded Tuskegee Institute, a leading black educational institution; he urged blacks to accept segregation and disfranchisement for the time being.

normal school An institution that trained schoolteachers.

Atlanta Compromise Landmark 1895 speech in which Booker T. Washington encouraged blacks to accommodate to segregation and work for economic advancement in the areas open to them.

declared that Washington "will have to live a long time to undo the harm he has done our race." Some black newspapers criticized Washington's "sycophantic attitude." Privately, Washington never accepted disfranchisement and segregation as permanent fixtures in southern life, and he quietly financed some court challenges to segregation.

Separate but Not Equal

As African Americans continued to debate the wisdom of Washington's Atlanta speech, southern lawmakers continued to redefine the legal status of African Americans. State after state followed the lead of Mississippi and disfranchised black voters. Louisiana, in 1898, added the infamous **grandfather clause,** which specified that men prevented from voting by the various changes would temporarily be permitted to enroll to vote if their fathers or grandfathers had been eligible to vote in 1867 (before the Fourteenth Amendment extended the suffrage to African Americans). The ruling reinstated whites into the electorate but kept blacks out. Although specific methods varied, each southern state set up barriers to voting and then carved holes through which only whites could pass.

A number of southern states added an additional barrier in the form of the white primary, which specified that political parties had the right to limit participation in the process by which they chose their candidates. Southern Democrats, who had long proclaimed themselves to be the "white man's party" or the party of white supremacy, quickly restricted their primaries and conventions to whites only. South Carolina took this step first, in 1896, and other states soon followed.

Southern lawmakers also began to extend segregation by law. The advocates of legally mandated segregation were given a major assist by the decision of the U.S. Supreme Court in ***Plessy v. Ferguson*** (1896), a case that involved a Louisiana law requiring segregated railroad cars. The Court ruled that "separate but equal" facilities did not violate the equal protection clause of the Fourteenth Amendment. Southern legislators soon applied that reasoning to other areas of life, requiring segregation of everything from prisons to telephone booths—and especially places open to the public like parks and restaurants. Baltimore, in 1910, first established legally segregated residential neighborhoods, and other southern cities soon did the same.

Violence directed against blacks accompanied the new laws, providing an ever-present lesson in the consequences of resistance. From 1885 to 1900, when the South was redefining relations between the races, the region witnessed more than twenty-five hundred deaths by lynching—almost one every two days. The victims were almost all African Americans. The largest numbers were in the states with the most black residents: Mississippi, Alabama, Georgia, and Louisiana. Once the new order was in place, lynching deaths declined slightly, to about eleven hundred during the years 1900 to 1915.

African Americans fought against lynching in various ways but especially by publicizing the record of brutality. One of the most prominent opponents of the horror was **Ida B. Wells.** Born in Mississippi in 1862, she attended a school set up by the Freedmen's Bureau and worked as a rural teacher from 1884 to 1891. In 1891 in Memphis, Tennessee, she helped to found, and began to write for, the black newspaper *Free Speech.* She began to attack lynching, arguing that several local victims had been targeted as a way to eliminate successful black businessmen. In response, a mob destroyed her newspaper office. She moved north and throughout the 1890s spent most of her time crusading against lynching, speaking in the North and in England, and writing a pamphlet, *A Red Record* (1895).

African Americans also sought ways to resist disfranchisement and segregation. With the violent end of Reconstruction, some began to promote an exodus from the South. Some focused their attention on **Liberia,** the nation created in western Africa before the Civil War as a home for free blacks. Interest in Liberia swept the South, but few could afford to es-

grandfather clause Provision in Louisiana law that permitted a person to vote if that person's father or grandfather had been permitted to vote in 1867; its purpose was to permit whites to vote even if they were subject to the disqualifications that were designed to prevent African Americans from voting.

Plessy v. Ferguson Case in 1896 in which the Supreme Court upheld a Louisiana law requiring segregated railroad facilities on the grounds that "separate but equal" accommodations were constitutional.

Ida B. Wells Reformer and journalist who crusaded against lynching and advocated racial justice and woman suffrage; upon marrying in 1895, she changed her name to Wells-Barnett.

Liberia A nation on the west coast of Africa founded through the efforts of the American Colonization Society and settled mainly by freed slaves between 1822 and the Civil War.

♦ During the 1890s, Ida B. Wells emerged as the leading opponent of lynching, refusing to be silenced even when threatened herself. She appealed to women especially, through the various women's organizations that developed in the late nineteenth century. *Schomburg Center for Research in Black Culture/New York Public Library/photo by Oscar B. Willis.*

tablish themselves in a new country. One shipload that left from South Carolina in 1878 met such financial difficulties as to discourage others. Senator Blanche K. Bruce of Mississippi argued against moving to Liberia, which, he felt, needed financial help to assist its modernization more than it needed "dependent, uneducated emigrants."

Other African Americans proposed leaving the South and taking advantage of homestead and railroad land in the West. A group of Kentuckians established Nicodemus, Kansas, as a black community in 1877. Well over six thousand blacks from Louisiana, Mississippi, and Texas moved north in just a few months in mid-1879, and the total may have been as high as twenty thousand. Not all who left joined the "Kansas Exodus," but Kansas probably received the largest number. The 1890s saw another swell of excitement about migration to the West and North.

In the 1880s, interest began to grow in the creation of all-black communities as places where African Americans could exercise their full political rights and enjoy full economic opportunities. Several communities were organized, most of them in the South but others scattered from Whitesboro, New Jersey, to Allensworth, California. Between 1892 and 1910, African Americans created some twenty-five all-black towns in Oklahoma. A few black leaders even hoped that Oklahoma might become an all-black state, but those hopes were never realistic.

New Patterns of American Social and Cultural Life

• How did Americans' expectations and choices give rise to important social and cultural trends during the late nineteenth and early twentieth centuries?

The decades following the Civil War brought far-reaching social change to many Americans in nearly all parts of the nation. The burgeoning cities presented new vistas of opportunity in addition to harboring foul slums. Immigrants from many lands came to the "land of opportunity" and ended up in city slums, midwestern farms, Pennsylvania coal mines, and many other places, changing the communities in which they lived even as they adjusted their own social expectations. The people of the New South—black and white—struggled to redefine their social institutions and expectations and lurched toward a society defined by a racist vision of white supremacy. (Chapter 18 explored the experiences of other social groups as well.) But the extent of social change did not stop with those groups and their experiences. At the same time, the educational system, gender roles, sexual relationships, artistic expression, and popular participation in cultural and leisure activities all took on new features.

The New Middle Class

The Gilded Age brought significant changes to the lives of middle-class Americans. In the cities, the development of giant corporations and central business districts was accompanied by the appearance of an army of accountants, lawyers, secretaries, insurance agents, and middle-level managers, who staffed corporate headquarters and professional offices. The new department stores succeeded by appealing to the growing urban middle class. Construction of streetcar lines made it possible for

♦ Sears, Roebuck and Company issued this catalog of building plans in 1911, extending its mail-order business to the developing suburbs. The cover depicts a model middle-class suburb of the period—large, square houses with spacious porches, surrounded by well-tended lawns, facing quiet, tree-lined streets. *Sears, Roebuck and Company.*

members of the middle class to live beyond walking distance of their work. Thus industrialization and urban expansion produced not only large neighborhoods of the industrial working class and enclaves of the very wealthy but also an expansion of distinctively middle-class neighborhoods and suburbs.

Single-family houses set amid wide and carefully tended lawns were common in the new middle-class neighborhoods or suburbs of the expanding cities and towns. Such developments accelerated the tendency of American urban areas to sprawl for miles and to have population densities much lower than those of expanding European cities of the same time. Acquiring land had long been a central part of the American dream, and in the nineteenth century, the single-family house became the realization of that dream for many middle-class families. To acquire that house in a suburb, outside the legal boundaries of a city but connected to the city by streetcar tracks, was especially attractive to many members of the middle class. Moving to a leafy middle-class suburb allowed them to avoid the congestion of the slums, the violence of labor conflicts, and the higher property taxes that funded city governments.

In new middle-class suburbs and middle-class areas of the cities, households often followed social patterns different from those of working-class or farm families. Middle-class families often employed a domestic servant to assist with household chores, and middle-class women were more likely to take part in social organizations outside the home. Middle-class parents rarely expected their children to contribute to the family's finances but instead usually emphasized their education—at least through high school and often beyond, for both boys and girls. Middle-class families provided the major market for an expansion of the daily press, which began to include sections designed to appeal to women—household hints, fashion advice, and news of women's organizations—and sports sections aimed largely at men. Urban middle-class households were also likely to subscribe to family magazines such as the *Ladies' Home Journal* and *Saturday Evening Post,* which included household advice, fiction, and news. Much of the new advertising of the day (see page 515) was aimed at the middle class, fostering the emergence of a "consumer culture" among middle-class women, who by 1900 were responsible for nearly all their families' shopping. Such publications, through both their articles and their advertising, also helped to extend middle-class patterns to readers across the country.

Ferment in Education

Middle-class parents' concern for their children's education combined with other factors to produce important changes in education, from kindergarten through the university. The number of kindergartens—first created outside the public schools to provide childcare for working mothers—grew from two hundred in 1880 to three thousand in 1900. In some areas, kindergartens began to be included in the public school system. Between 1870 and 1900, most northern and western states and territories established school attendance laws, requiring children between certain ages (usually 8 to 14) to attend school for a minimum number of weeks each year, typically twelve to sixteen. In the 1880s, the New York City schools began to provide textbooks to students free of charge, and the practice expanded slowly. By 1898, ten states required textbooks to be provided without charge.

Between 1870 and 1910, school enrollment among those aged 5 to 19 increased from 48 percent to 59 percent, with the largest increase at the secondary level. By 1890, high schools had extended to a fourth year (grades 9 through 12) everywhere but in the South. The high school curriculum changed significantly, adding courses in the sciences, civics, business, home economics, and skills needed by industry, such as drafting, woodworking, and the mechanical trades. The entire nation counted fewer than eight hundred high schools in 1878 but had fifty-five hundred by 1898, and the proportion of high school graduates tripled. From 1870 onward, women outnumbered men among high school graduates. The growth of high schools, however, was largely an urban phenomenon.

College enrollments also grew. The largest gains were in the new state universities created under the Land-Grant College Act of 1862. Even so, college students came disproportionately from middle-class and upper-class families and rarely from farms. The college curriculum changed greatly, from a set of courses required of all students (mostly Latin, Greek, mathematics, rhetoric, and religion), to an elective system in which students focused on a major subject and chose courses from a long list of alternatives. New subjects included economics, political science, modern languages, and laboratory sciences. Many universities also began to offer courses in engineering, business administration, and teaching for elementary and secondary schools. In 1870, the curricula in most colleges still resembled those of a century before. By 1900, curricula looked more like those of today.

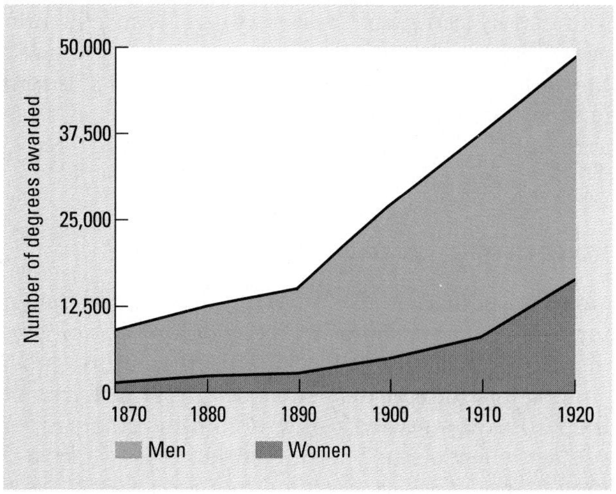

♦ **FIGURE 19.3 Number of First Degrees Awarded by Colleges and Universities, 1870–1920** This figure shows the change in the number of people receiving B.A., B.S., or other first college degrees, at ten-year intervals from 1870 to 1920. Notice that after 1890, the number of women increased more rapidly than the number of men. *Source:* U.S. Bureau of the Census, Department of Commerce, *Historical Statistics of the United States,* 2 vols. (Washington, D.C.: U.S. Government Printing Office, 1975), Series A-58, A-59, A-69, A-119.

Despite the growing female majority through the high school level, far fewer women than men marched in college graduation processions. Only one college graduate in seven was a woman in 1870, and this ratio improved only to one in four by 1900 (see Figure 19.3). In 1879, fewer than half of the nation's colleges even admitted women, although most state universities did so. Just twenty years later, four-fifths of all colleges, universities, and professional schools enrolled women.

Regardless of such gains for coeducation, some colleges remained all-male enclaves, especially prestigious private institutions such as Harvard, Princeton, and Yale. Colleges exclusively for women began to appear after the Civil War, partly because so many colleges still refused to admit women and partly in keeping with the notion that men and women should occupy "separate spheres." The first, founded in 1861, was **Vassar College,** whose faculty of eight men and twenty-two women included Maria Mitchell, a leading astronomer and the first woman member of the American Academy of Arts and Sciences.

Redefining Women's Gender Roles

Greater educational opportunities for women marked part of a change in social definitions of gender roles. Throughout the nineteenth century, most Americans defined women's social role in terms of the **cult of domesticity**—the notion that the proper place for a woman was in the home as wife and mother and that in her wife-mother role she was guardian of the family, responsible for its moral, spiritual, and physical well-being. Women might also have important roles in the church and the school. Beyond this, it was generally thought that women ought not to experience much of the world, because business and politics, with their sometimes lax moral standards, might corrupt them. The best choice, some argued, was for women to occupy a **separate sphere,** immune from such dangers. The Illinois state supreme court even ruled, in 1870, that "God designed the sexes to occupy different spheres of action." Widely advocated in the pulpits and journals of the day, the concepts of domesticity and separate spheres applied most readily to white middle-class and upper-class women in towns and cities. Farm women and working-class women (including most women of color) worked too hard and witnessed too much of the world to fit easily into the patterns of innocence and daintiness prescribed by advocates of domesticity.

Domesticity came under an increasing number of challenges in the late nineteenth century. One challenge came through education, especially at colleges. As more and more women finished college, some chose to enter the professions. Important early successes came in medicine. In 1849, Elizabeth Blackwell became the first woman to complete medical school, and she helped to open a medical school for women in 1868. By the 1880s, some twenty-five hundred women held medical degrees. About 3 percent of all physicians were women, proportionately more than in most of the twentieth century. After 1900, however, medical schools began to impose enrollment restrictions on women. Access to the legal profession proved even more difficult. Arabella Mansfield was the first woman to be admitted to the bar, in 1869, but the entire nation counted only sixty practicing women attorneys ten years later. Most law schools refused to admit women until the 1890s. Other professions also yielded very slowly to women seeking admission.

Professional careers attracted relatively few women, but many middle-class and upper-class women, especially in towns and cities, became involved in women's clubs. Women's clubs became popular among middle- and upper-class women in the late nineteenth century, claiming one hundred thousand members nationwide in the 1890s, eight hundred thousand by 1910. Ida Wells, the crusader for black civil rights who, after marrying, was known as Ida Wells-Barnett, actively promoted the development of black women's clubs. Such clubs often began within the separate women's sphere as forums in which to discuss literature or art. But they sometimes led women out of their separate sphere and to involvement with reform. (Of course, women had publicly participated in reform before, especially in the movement to abolish slavery.) In 1904, Sarah Platt Decker, president of the General Federation of Women's Clubs, bluntly proclaimed, "**Dante** is dead. He has been dead for several centuries, and I think it is time that we dropped the study of his Inferno and turned our attention to our own." Female participation swelled the ranks and produced leaders for a variety of reform organizations, especially those with some link to domesticity—temperance, opposition to prostitution, and abolition of child labor. The **Women's Christian Temperance Union,** one of the most prominent, was formed in 1874.

Women's church organizations, clubs, and reform societies all provided women experience in working together under the leadership of women, sometimes

Vassar College The first collegiate institution for women, founded in Poughkeepsie, New York, in 1861.

cult of domesticity The notion common throughout much of the nineteenth century that women's activities were ideally rooted in domestic labor and the nurture of children.

separate sphere The notion that women were meant to pursue occupations having to do with family, church, or school and not those in traditionally male fields such as business or politics, which were considered too competitive and corrupt for women.

Dante Italian poet (1265–1321), best known for his *Inferno,* about a descent into hell.

Women's Christian Temperance Union Women's organization, founded in 1874, that opposed the evils of drink and supported reforms such as woman suffrage.

seeking changes in public policy. Through them, women developed networks of working relationships. These experiences and contacts contributed to the growing effectiveness of women's efforts to establish their right to vote (see pages 605–608).

Emergence of a Gay and Lesbian Subculture

Challenges to the notions of domesticity and separate spheres came mostly from women seeking to redefine society's gender roles. But a quite different redefinition occurred at the same time, as burgeoning cities provided a setting for the development of gay and lesbian subcultures.

Homosexual behavior was illegal in all states and territories throughout the nineteenth and into the early twentieth century. At the same time, however, the variety of socially acceptable same-sex relationships was wider than it would be later. The concept of separate spheres and the tendency for schools and workplaces to be segregated by sex meant that many men and women spent much of their time with others of their own sex. In many occupations, a worker worked closely with a partner, sometimes over long periods of time. Such partners—both male or both female—could speak of each other with deep affection without violating prevailing social norms. Such same-sex relationships may or may not have involved physical contact, although kisses and hugs—and sleeping in the same bed—were common expressions of affection, especially among women. Participants in such same-sex relationships did not consider themselves to be committing what the laws called "an unnatural act," and most of them married partners of the opposite sex.

Same-sex relationships that involved genital contact, however, violated both the law and the expectations of society. In rural communities, where most people knew each other, people physically attracted to those of their own sex seem to have suppressed such tendencies or to have exercised them very discreetly. The record of convictions for **sodomy** indicates, however, that some failed to conceal their activities. A few men and somewhat more women changed their dress and behavior, passed for a member of the other sex, and married someone of their own sex.

In the late nineteenth century, in the United States and in Europe, homosexuals and lesbians recognized that the burgeoning cities permitted anonymity not possible in rural societies. They gravitated toward the largest cities and began to create distinctive **subcultures.** By the 1890s, one researcher reported that "perverts of both sexes maintained a sort of social set-up in New York City, had their places of meeting, and [the] advantage of police protection." Reports of regular meeting places for homosexuals—clubs, restaurants, steambaths, parks, streets—also came from Boston, Chicago, New Orleans, St. Louis, and San Francisco. Although most participants in these subcultures were secretive, some flaunted their sexuality. In a few places, "drag balls" featured cross-dressing, especially by men.

In the 1880s, physicians began to study members of these emerging subcultures and created medical names for them, including "homosexual," "lesbian," "invert," and "pervert." Earlier, law and religion had defined particular actions as illegal or immoral. The new definitions emphasized not the actions but instead the persons taking the action. Some theorists in the late 1800s proposed that such behavior resulted from a mental disease, but others concluded that homosexuals and lesbians were born that way.

Such medical and legal definition of *homosexuality* was accompanied by a similar definition of its opposite, *heterosexuality.* As medical and legal definitions shifted from actions to persons, the larger society also witnessed a change in the nature of same-sex relationships. Once-acceptable behavior, including expressions of deep affection between heterosexuals of the same sex, became less common as individuals tried to avoid any suggestion that they were anything but heterosexual.

New Patterns in Cultural Expression: From Realism to Ragtime

Shortly after 1900, the director of the nation's most prominent art museum, the Metropolitan Museum of New York, observed "a state of unrest all over the world" in art, literature, music, painting, and sculpture. "And," he added, "I dislike unrest." Unrest

sodomy Varieties of sexual intercourse prohibited by law.

subculture A group whose members are differentiated from the dominant culture on the basis of values or interests not typical of the dominant culture but who also share many other values and interests with the dominant culture.

meant change and Americans at that time witnessed dramatic changes in art, literature, and music—many of them directly influenced by the new urban, industrial, multiethnic society.

Leaves of Grass by **Walt Whitman,** first published in 1855 and reissued in revised and enlarged editions until his death in 1892, stands as a major work in world literature. Whitman gloried in democracy, in the scenes and rhythms of New York City, and in the faces and forms of working people. He dealt, too, with topics often considered inappropriate for public print, including intimate relationships and the human body:

Have you ever loved the body of a woman?
Have you ever loved the body of a man?

Do you not see that they are exactly the same to all in all nations and times all over the earth?

If anything is sacred the human body is sacred,
And the glory and sweat of a man is the token of manhood untainted,
And in man or woman a clean, strong, firm-fibred body, is more beautiful than the most beautiful face.

Emily Dickinson, whose poetry was first published in 1890, after her death, rejected the formal structures of most previous verse, and probed depths of anxiety and emotion:

I can wade Grief–
Whole Pools of it–
I'm used to that–
But the least push of Joy
Breaks up my feet
And I tip–drunken–

American novelists increasingly turned to a realistic—and sometimes quite critical—portrayal of life, rejecting the romantic idealism characteristic of the pre–Civil War period. The towering figure of the era was **Mark Twain** (pen name of Samuel L. Clemens), whose *Huckleberry Finn* (1885) may be read at many levels, ranging from a nostalgic account of boyhood adventures to profound social satire. In this masterpiece, Twain reproduced the everyday speech of unschooled whites and blacks, poked fun at social pretensions of the day, scorned the Old South myth, and challenged prevailing, racially biased attitudes toward African Americans. The novels of William Dean Howells and Henry James, by contrast, presented restrained, realistic portrayals of upper-class men and women. After 1890, Stephen Crane, Theodore Dreiser, and Frank Norris sharpened the critical edge of fiction. Crane's *Maggie: A Girl of the Streets* (1893) depicted how urban squalor could turn a young woman to prostitution. Norris's *The Octopus* (1901) portrayed the abusive power that a railroad could wield over people. Kate Chopin sounded feminist themes in *The Awakening* (1899), dealing with repression of a woman's desires.

As American literature moved toward realism during these years, most American painting was moving in the opposite direction. An important exception was Thomas Eakins, probably the most accomplished painter working in the United States in the 1870s and 1880s. Although he received little recognition at the time, his work is now considered a major contribution to realism. American painting changed late in the century, but largely in response to French **impressionism,** which emphasized less an exact reproduction of the world and more the artist's impression of it. Mary Cassatt was the only American—and the only woman—to rank among the leaders of impressionism, but she lived and painted mostly in France. Among artists in the United States who adopted an impressionist style, one of the most prominent was Childe Hassam, who often presented urban landscapes. Attention to the city was also characteristic of work by Robert Henri and his associates in the early 1900s. Labeled the **Ash Can School** because of their preoccupation with everyday urban life and ordinary people, they produced the artistic counterpart to critical realism in literature.

The Ash Can adherents faced a challenge, however, from artists influenced by the abstract approach then

Walt Whitman American poet whose free-verse poems were collected in *Leaves of Grass,* which celebrates the self, universal brotherhood, and the greatness of democracy.

Emily Dickinson American poet who lived her entire life as a recluse in her family home in Amherst, Massachusetts; her intense and lyrical poems were not published until after her death.

Mark Twain Pen name of Samuel Clemens, an American author who drew on his childhood along the Mississippi River to create novels such as *The Adventures of Huckleberry Finn.*

impressionism A style of painting that developed in France in the 1870s and emphasized the artist's impression of a subject.

Ash Can School New York artists of varying styles who shared a focus on urban life.

♦ In this painting of 6th Avenue at 30th Street, done in 1906, John Sloan seems to glory in the diversity and excitement of life in New York City. He was a member of the Ash Can School of painters, who often focused on ordinary life in the cities, sometimes including unpleasant subjects. *"6th Avenue at 30th St., 1907" by John Slaon/Vivian and Meyer P. Potamkin Collection.*

becoming prominent in France. In 1913, the most widely publicized art exhibit of the era permitted a half-million Americans in New York, Chicago, and Boston to view examples of this shocking new style. Known as the Armory Show, for its opening in New York's National Guard Armory, the exhibit presented some art from the previous century. But works that drew the most attention were pieces by European innovators: Pablo Picasso, Henri Matisse, Marcel Duchamp, Wassily Kandinsky, and others. Critics and newspapers alike dismissed these modernists as either insane or anarchists. One reviewer scornfully suggested that Duchamp's *Nude Descending a Staircase* be retitled "explosion in a shingle factory." The abstract, modernist style, however, soon became firmly established.

Just as with painting, many aspects of American music derived from European models. Perhaps the most influential musician at the turn of the century, however, was the African-American composer Scott Joplin. Born in Texarkana, Texas, in 1869, Joplin had formal instruction in the piano and then traveled through African-American communities from New Orleans to Chicago. As he traveled, he encountered **ragtime** and soon began to write his own. In 1899, he published "Maple Leaf Rag" and soared to fame as the best-known ragtime composer in the country. Though condemned by some at the time as vulgar, ragtime formed a major element in the development of jazz (see pages 740–742).

The Origins of Mass Entertainment

Changes in transportation (the railroads) and communication (telegraph and telephone) combined with new forms of corporate organization and increased leisure time (especially among the middle class and skilled workers) to foster new forms of entertainment. Entrepreneurs organized entertainers into traveling groups and sent them from city to city, and even to small towns, to perform.

Americans had long enjoyed traveling dramatic and musical troupes, but in the Gilded Age booking agencies managed to schedule such arts and amusements into every corner of the country. Traveling groups of actors, singers, and other performers provided the entertainment mainstay in many areas throughout the late nineteenth and early twentieth century, performing everything from Shakespeare

ragtime Music blending African rhythms and European form to create a unique style, popularized by Scott Joplin and others in the late nineteenth century.

♦ Professional baseball developed a strong popular appeal in the years after the Civil War, as most major cities acquired one or more teams. Thomas Eakins, who depicted these ballplayers at work in 1875, was the most impressive realist painter in the country at the time. *"Baseball Players Practicing" by Thomas Eakins 1875/Museum of Art, Rhode Island School of Design, Jesse Metcalf and Walter H. Kimball Funds. Photo by Cathy Carver.*

to **slapstick,** from opera to **melodrama.** In the late nineteenth century, these booking agencies helped develop the star system: each traveling company had one or two popular performers who attracted the audience and helped to make up for the inadequacies of the other players. Other traveling spectacles also took advantage of improved transportation and communication to establish regular circuits, including circuses and Wild West shows.

One of the most unusual traveling shows was the **Chautauqua,** a blend of inspirational oratory, education, and entertainment. The programs, often a week or two in length, attracted hundreds, even thousands, of people from the surrounding countryside. At the high point, thousands of towns held annual Chautauqua assemblies, and millions of people came to see and hear political figures, comedians, inspirational orators, opera, glee clubs, lectures on ancient history, string quartets, or magic-lantern shows on foreign countries. Large tents accommodated enthusiastic crowds, and electric lights permitted regular evening offerings. The programs were organized by a few companies, which scheduled bookings far in advance and arranged for performers and crews to ride from one location to the next by train.

Immediately after the Civil War, a quite different form of mass entertainment appeared: professional baseball. Teams traveled by train from city to city, and urban rivalries built loyalty among hometown fans. The formation of the National League in 1876 established a cartel, through which team owners (often drawn initially from the ranks of players) tried to monopolize the industry by excluding rival clubs from their territories and controlling the movement of players from team to team. Because African Americans were barred from the National League, separate black clubs and Negro Leagues emerged. In the 1880s and 1890s, the National League successfully warded off challenges from rival leagues and also defeated a players' union. Not until 1901 did another league—the American League—successfully organize. In 1903, the two leagues merged into a new, stronger cartel and staged the first World Series (the Boston Red Socks beat the Pittsburgh Pirates). As other professional spectator sports developed, they often adopted the patterns of organization, labor relations, and racial discrimination first established in baseball.

slapstick A boisterous form of comedy marked by chases, collisions, and crude practical jokes.

melodrama A sensational or romantic stage play with exaggerated conflicts and stereotyped characters.

Chautauqua A traveling show offering educational, religious, and recreational activities, part of a nationwide movement of adult education that began in the town of Chautauqua, New York.

SUMMARY

E xpectations
C onstraints
C hoices
O utcomes

In the Gilded Age, as industrialization transformed the economy, urbanization and immigration challenged many established social patterns. In the midst of economic and social change, Americans developed new *expectations* and faced new *choices* about their relations with each other. The *outcomes* of their many individual choices marked a major redefinition of American social and cultural life.

As rural Americans and European immigrants sought better lives in the cities, urban America changed dramatically. New technologies in transportation and communication broke down old *constraints* on individual *choices* about where to live and work. The *outcome* was a new urban geography with separate retail, wholesale, finance, and manufacturing areas and residential neighborhoods defined by economic status.

Many urban Americans struggled under the *constraints* of poverty. To gain support from the poor, urban political machines, like Tammany Hall in New York City, helped them in various ways. Social reformers established settlement houses as a different way of addressing the problems of the urban poor.

Many Europeans emigrated because of economic and political *constraints* in their homelands and their *expectations* of better opportunities in America. Immigrants often formed separate communities, usually centered around a church. The flood of immigrants, particularly from eastern and southern Europe, spawned nativist reactions among some old-stock Americans, who sought to limit immigration.

Some southerners proclaimed the creation of a New South and promoted industrialization and a more diversified agricultural base. The *outcome* was mixed—the South did acquire significant industry, but the region's poverty was little reduced. After 1890, white southerners disfranchised African Americans and extended racial segregation. Booker T. Washington emerged as the best-known African American in the nation, and he accepted such *constraints,* at least for the moment.

Urban growth brought with it a new urban middle class. Education underwent far-reaching changes, from kindergartens through universities. Challenged in part by the *expectations* of a generation of college-educated women, socially defined gender roles began to change as some women *chose* professional careers. Some also *chose* active roles in reform. Urbanization offered new *choices* to gay men and lesbians by making possible the development of urban subcultures. In response, medical specialists tried to define homosexuality and lesbianism. The new *expectations* and *choices* generated by an urban, industrial, multiethnic society contributed to critical realism in literature, new patterns in painting, and ragtime music. Urbanization and changes in transportation and communication also fostered the emergence of an entertainment industry.

SUGGESTED READINGS

Jane Addams. *Twenty Years at Hull House* (1910, reprint, 1960).

Nothing conveys the complex world of Hull House and the striking personality of Jane Addams as well as her own account.

Edward L. Ayers. *The Promise of the New South: Life After Reconstruction* (1992).

A comprehensive survey of developments in the South.

Catherine Clinton. *The Other Civil War: American Women in the Nineteenth Century* (1984).

The section on the post–Civil War period surveys the subject.

John Higham. *Strangers in the Land: Patterns of American Nativism, 1860–1925* (1965).

This classic of American history played a major role in defining the contours of American nativism and still provides an excellent introduction to the subject.

Alan M. Kraut. *The Huddled Masses: The Immigrant in American Society, 1880–1921* (1982).

A helpful introduction to immigration, especially the so-called new immigration.

Terrence J. McDonald, ed. *Plunkitt of Tammany Hall,* by William L. Riordon (1993).

McDonald provides excellent context and editing for this classic account of Tammany's relationships to voters.

Raymond A. Mohl. *The New City: Urban America in the Industrial Age, 1860–1920* (1985).

An informative, concise introduction to nearly all aspects of the growth of the cities.

New Choices for Women

The Context

The late nineteenth and early twentieth centuries saw a good deal of public attention given to the emergence of a "New Woman," the consequence in part of the emergence of a mature industrial economy and a complex, urban society. The era of "separate spheres" was rapidly passing, as women moved out from the home and into the larger society. Young women of upper- and middle-income families attended college, and some of them entered careers. Some women, mostly of middle- and upper-income levels, joined women's associations and sought political changes. Young women of working-class families entered the wage-earning work force as factory or office workers, and some of them became involved in unions. (For further information on the context, see pages 590—591.)

The Historical Question

At the time and since then, some people asked whether the breakdown of separate spheres called into question the concept of domesticity—the expectation that a woman has a special responsibility for the nurturing and protection of the family. Did the emergence of the "New Woman" significantly change expectations about women's roles in American society? Or were the older expectations of domesticity still prominent?

The Challenge

Using the sources provided, along with other information you have read, write an essay or hold a discussion on the following question. Cite evidence in the sources to support your conclusions. **Did the emergence of the "New Woman" significantly change expectations about women's roles in American society?**

The Sources

1 Mrs. Burton Harrison, writing in *Harper's Bazaar* in 1900 on "Home Life as a Profession," had this to say:

Today, when hundreds of young women of our best blood and culture in America are standing within the open doors of schools and colleges, eagerly straining their gaze out into the future, hoping to catch a glimpse of the opportunity for a "career," it seems to behoove the conservative thinkers among us to suggest to some of them the profession of home life. . . . Now, as a matter of historic fact, the cornerstone of the highest civilization has always been the home, and wifehood and motherhood the happiest estate of woman. To my mind, it is a cruel wrong to a young girl to launch her in life unadvised on these points, and imbued with the determination to independence of the other sex. . . .

Far be it from me to suggest a relapse to those dark ages of home life when a girl strummed on the piano or worked in cross-stitch tapestry. . . . On the contrary, I would have her carry back into her home her sheaves of knowledge and accomplishment, and there try to enrich and broaden the domestic sphere. . . . I do not think our homes as they are now a sufficiently satisfying exchange for the broader, more interesting channels for women's work everywhere available. But I earnestly wish they might be made so; and the question of how to accomplish this enormously important result lies largely in the palm of the girl graduate of today.

2 Rena Rietveld Verduin, an Illinois farmwife and mother with only a fifth-grade education, presented these views in 1907 in a community debate sponsored by a local club that organized cultural activities. She spoke in opposition to the proposition "Resolved that women should not enter higher education."

Through an education girls are enabled to become self-supporting and acquainted with the ways of the world. Through an education girls learn to earn a livelihood and are not so liable to throw themselves away in marriage on some worthless man. . . . When [men] discover that the girls don't have to marry—by getting an education and going into some profession—they will be more likely to behave themselves and be at some pains to make themselves worthy of the girl's acceptance. . . . Men seem to think that the women have no business on the face of the earth except to work and slave for them. . . . Girls, get an education and escape slavery.

3 Susan W. Fitzgerald prepared this argument for woman suffrage in the early twentieth century.

We are forever being told that the place of woman is in the HOME. . . .

SHE is responsible for the cleanliness of her house.

SHE is responsible for the wholesomeness of the food.

SHE is responsible for the children's health.

SHE, above all, is responsible for their morals, for their sense of truth, of honesty and decency, for what they turn out to be.

How Far Can the Mother Control These Things? . . . [The pamphlet then surveys problems of urban life—filthy streets, lack of adequate sanitation, fire hazards, and more.]

It is the MEN and NOT THE WOMEN that are really responsible for the unclean houses, unwholesome food, bad plumbing, danger of fire, risk of tuberculosis and other diseases, immoral influences of the street. In fact, MEN are responsible for the conditions under which the children live, but we hold WOMEN responsible for the results of those conditions. If we hold women responsible for the results, must we not, in simple justice, let them have something to say as to what those conditions shall be? . . . LET THEM VOTE.

Women are by nature and training, housekeepers. Let them have a hand in the city's housekeeping, even if they introduce an occasional house-cleaning.

4 Charlotte Perkins Gilman, who made her living as a writer and lecturer, was largely self-educated. This excerpt is from her article "Are Women Human Beings?" which appeared in *Harper's Weekly* in 1912.

[The] things the women want to do and be and have are not in any sense masculine. They do not belong to men. They never did. They are departments of our social life, hitherto monopolized by men. . . . we find everywhere this same pervasive error, this naïve assumption, which would be so insolent if it were not so absurd, that only men are human creatures, able and entitled to perform the work of the world; while women are only female creatures, able to do nothing whatever but continue in the same round of duties to which they have been so long restricted. . . .

Women will never cease to be females, but they will cease to be weak and ignorant and defenseless. They are becoming wiser, stronger, better able to protect themselves, one another, and their children. Courage, power, achievement are always respected. . . . [As they take] their full place in the world as members of society, as well as their partial places as mothers of it, they will gradually rear a new race of men, men with minds large enough to see in human beings something besides males and females.

REGIONAL BASES OF POLITICAL PARTIES IN THE GILDED AGE After Reconstruction ended, competition between Republicans and Democrats settled into distinct regional patterns, as revealed by this map showing the party that carried presidential elections in each state.

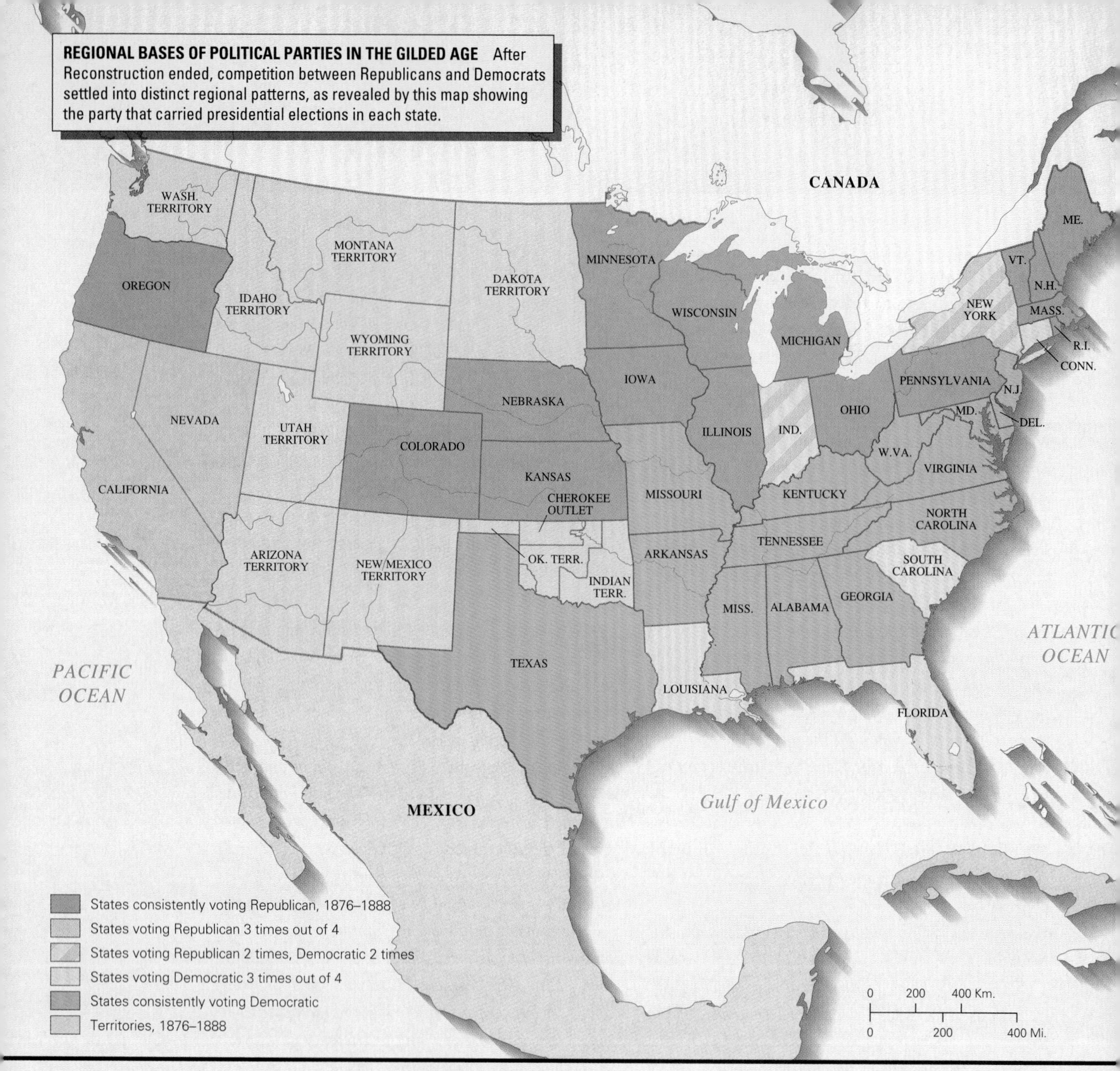

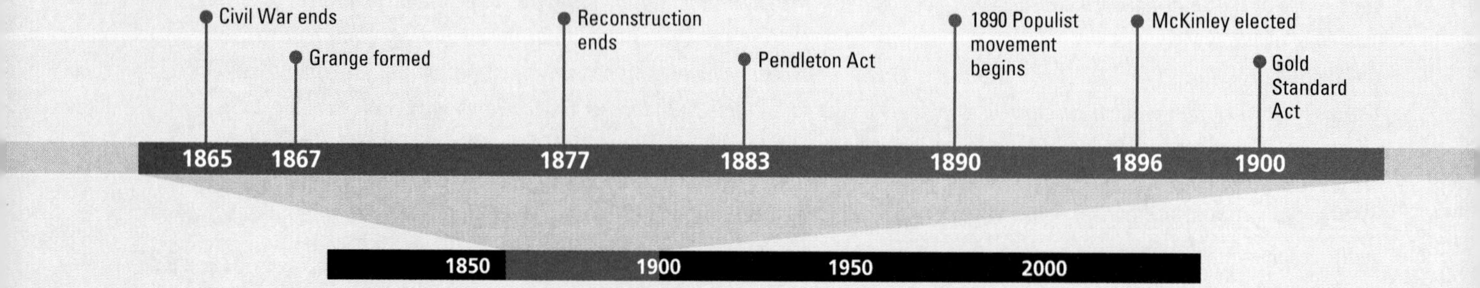

CHAPTER 20

Political Stalemate and Political Upheaval, 1868–1900

Parties, Voters, and Reformers

- During the Gilded Age, what were people's expectations about the role of political parties?
- What choices did the political parties offer voters?

Political Stalemate

- What were the sources of the political deadlock that lasted from 1874 to the 1890s?
- What major changes were enacted during that period?

Agricultural Distress and Political Upheaval

- What circumstances led some farmers to choose to form a new political party? What did they expect to accomplish?
- What was the immediate outcome of their choices?

Economic Collapse and Political Upheaval

- What choices did voters face in the 1896 presidential election?
- What were the long-term outcomes of that election?

INTRODUCTION

In July 1892, a new political party, the People's party, met in Omaha to *choose* its candidates for president and vice president. Born in protest against the economic and political events of the previous quarter-century, the new party—soon called the Populists—drafted a platform that presented its understanding of the *outcome* of industrialization: material and moral ruin, political corruption, and exploited labor. The Populists also proclaimed their *choices* for dealing with the *outcome* of industrialization. They urged immediate federal action to rescue debtors, break up monopolies, and bring railroads under government ownership. They proposed reforms to increase the power of voters to control the government. And they made clear the expected *outcome* of these changes: that "oppression, injustice, and poverty shall eventually cease in the land."

Most Americans, however, held *expectations* different from the Populists'. Consequently, most were unwilling to *choose* to create a vastly more powerful federal government, or to place severe *constraints* on the rights of property owners, or to entrust the federal government to self-proclaimed representatives of impoverished farmers and angry workers. In the end, those who gathered at Omaha failed to establish their new party as a permanent factor in American politics. The *outcome* of their efforts, however, was significant change in the nature of politics in the 1890s—and in the twentieth century as well.

Although most Americans rejected the Populists' remedies, few doubted that the *outcome* of industrialization, the economic development of the West, urbanization, and immigration had been a profound transformation of the nation's social and economic life during the years following the Civil War. During the same years, Congress and the president had grappled with complex *choices* affecting the South and Reconstruction, the future of American Indians, and the role of the federal government in developing the West. They also faced difficult *choices* regarding the nature of the federal civil service, a persistent federal budget surplus, federal tariff and monetary policies, and the relation between the federal government and the recently developed industrial corporations. However, a protracted stalemate gripped national politics from 1875 to 1896, *constraining* those who advocated political changes.

Expectations
Constraints
Choices
Outcomes

Throughout those years, men were *expected* to hold intense party loyalties—to the point that such loyalties were even seen as part of a man's gender role. (Nearly all women were *constrained* from voting throughout this period.) Despite such *expectations* for party loyalty, a few people *chose* to break with the major parties to call for changes in policies or in the nature of politics. Prominent among those demanding change were advocates of woman suffrage. But those who attracted the most attention at that time were a succession of organizations and parties that spoke out for impoverished farmers and tried, largely unsuccessfully, to forge an alliance among all the disadvantaged—rural and urban, black and white.

The Populist party was the *outcome* of a quarter-century of agrarian radicalism that began shortly after the Civil War and was fueled by the economic misfortunes of farmers. Eventually the Populists *chose* to merge with the Democrats in support of the presidential candidacy of William Jennings Bryan in 1896. In the process, the Democratic party shed its deep commitment to minimal government and embraced a more activist role for the government in the economy as a way to protect and assist farmers, workers, and small businesspeople. In 1896, voters *chose* not Bryan but William McKinley, the Republican candidate for president, thereby endorsing a more conservative approach to federal economic policy. The long-term *outcome,* however, was the transformation of the very nature of American politics.

CHRONOLOGY

Politics

1865 Civil War ends

1867 First Grange formed

1868 Ulysses S. Grant elected president

1869 National Woman Suffrage Association and American Woman Suffrage Association formed
Wyoming Territory adopts woman suffrage

1870 Utah Territory adopts woman suffrage
Standard Oil of Ohio organized

1872 Crédit Mobilier scandal
Grant reelected

1872–1874 Granger laws

1873 "Salary Grab" Act

1875 Whiskey Ring scandal

mid-1870s Grange membership peaks

1876 Secretary of War William Belknap resigns
Custer dies in battle
Disputed presidential election

1877 Rutherford B. Hayes becomes president
Reconstruction ends
Munn v. Illinois
Widespread railroad strikes

1878 Greenback party peaks
Bland-Allison Act

1879 Standard Oil trust formed

1880 James A. Garfield elected president

1881 Garfield assassinated
Chester A. Arthur becomes president

1883 Pendleton Act

1884 Grover Cleveland elected president

1885 Mark Twain's *Huckleberry Finn* published

1886 *Wabash Railway v. Illinois*
Knights of Labor reaches peak membership

1887 Congress disfranchises women in Utah Territory
Interstate Commerce Act

late 1880s Farmers' Alliances spread

1888 Benjamin Harrison elected president

1888–1892 Australian ballot adopted

1889 North Dakota, South Dakota, Montana, and Washington become states
Hull House opened

1890 Wounded Knee
National American Woman Suffrage Association formed
Idaho becomes a state
Wyoming becomes a state, the first with woman suffrage
McKinley Tariff, Sherman Anti-Trust Act, and Sherman Silver Purchase Act
Federal elections bill defeated
Populist movement begins

1892 Homestead strike
Cleveland elected president again

1893 Colorado adopts woman suffrage
Nationwide depression
Sherman Silver Purchase Act repealed

1894 Coxey's Army
Wilson-Gorman Tariff
Pullman strike

1895 J. P. Morgan stabilizes gold reserve

1896 Utah becomes a state, with woman suffrage
William Jennings Bryan's "Cross of Gold" speech
William McKinley elected president
Idaho adopts woman suffrage

1897 Dingley Tariff

1900 Gold Standard Act

Parties, Voters, and Reformers

- During the Gilded Age, what were people's expectations about the role of political parties?
- What choices did the political parties offer voters?

Political parties dominated nearly every aspect of the political process from the 1830s until the early 1900s, more so than before or since. During those years, Americans expected that politics meant party politics, and that all meaningful political choices came through the structure of parties. An understanding of politics, therefore, must begin with an analysis of political parties: what they were, what they did, what they stood for, and what choices they offered to voters.

Parties and Patronage

The two major parties—Democrats and Republicans—had similar organizations and purposes. Both nominated candidates, tried to elect them to office, and attempted to write their objectives into law.

After the 1830s, nominations for political offices came from **party conventions,** which were gatherings of delegates chosen at earlier meetings. At the most basic level, neighborhood voters gathered in party caucuses to choose one or more delegates to represent them at conventions. Conventions took place at county, state, and national levels and at the level of congressional districts and various state districts. At most conventions, the delegates listened to speech after speech glorifying their party and denouncing the opposition. They nominated candidates for elective offices or chose delegates to yet another convention. And they adopted a **platform,** a written explanation of their position on important issues and their promises for policy change. Party leaders worked out the intricate compromises that satisfied various sections of their party, sometimes in informal settings—hotel rooms thick with cigar smoke and cluttered with whiskey bottles. Such behind-the-scenes negotiations reinforced the notion of political parties as all-male institutions into which no self-respecting women would venture.

After choosing their candidates, the parties conducted their campaigns. Party organizers tried to identify all their supporters and worked to get them to vote on election day. Such party organizing was often done in places like saloons, where males congregated and women were barred. Candidates campaigned as party candidates, and campaigns were almost entirely party oriented. Nearly every newspaper identified itself with a political party. A party expected to subsidize the newspapers that gave it support and, in return, expected sympathetic treatment of its candidates and officeholders and slashing criticism of the other party. During the month or so before an election, local party organizations sponsored many activities to whip up enthusiasm among the party's supporters and to attract new or undecided voters: parades by marching clubs, free barbecues with speeches for dessert, and rallies capped by speeches that lasted for two hours or more.

Once the votes were counted, the winners immediately turned their attention to appointing people to government jobs. In the nineteenth century, government positions not filled by elections were filled through the **patronage system**—that is, newly elected presidents or governors or mayors appointed their loyal supporters to the many government jobs at their disposal, widely considered an appropriate reward for hard work during a campaign. Everyone also understood that those appointed to such jobs were expected to return part of their salaries to the party. The use of patronage for party purposes was often called the spoils system after a statement by Senator William Marcy in 1831: "to the victor belongs the spoils." Its defenders were labeled **spoilsmen.**

Party loyalists inevitably outnumbered the available patronage jobs, so competition for appointments was always fierce. When James A. Garfield became president in 1881, he was so overwhelmed with demands for jobs that he exclaimed in disgust, "My God! What is there in this place that a man should ever want to get into it?" Even after some reforms—precipitated in part by the assassination of Garfield—Secretary of the Interior L. Q. C. Lamar complained in the late 1880s that "I eat my breakfast and dinner and supper always in the company of

party convention Party meeting to nominate candidates for elective offices and to adopt a political platform.

platform A formal statement of the principles, policies, and promises on which a political party bases its appeal to voters.

patronage system System of appointment to government jobs that lets the winner in an election distribute nearly all appointive government jobs to loyal party members; also called the spoils system.

spoilsmen Defenders of the spoils system, a derogatory term for the patronage system.

Let us have peace.
Let us have a piece.
Let us have a piece.
Let us have a piece.
GOVERNMENT CAKE.
PUBLISHED BY CURRIER & IVES
125 NASSAU ST. NEW YORK.
A NICE FAMILY PARTY.

♦ This cartoon depicts government patronage as "cake" and all party leaders as greedily clamoring for a piece, despite the president's efforts to maintain peace in his party. Such frantic scrambles eventually brought reform and the introduction of the merit system for appointing people to governmental positions. *Library of Congress.*

some two or three eager and hungry applicants for office."

The government jobs most in demand involved purchasing supplies or otherwise handling government contracts. Purchasing and contracts became another form of spoils, awarded to entrepreneurs who supported the party. This system invited corruption, and the invitation was all too often accepted. In the 1890s, for example, a Post Office Department official pressured **postmasters** across the country to buy clocks from a political associate of his. Business owners competing to receive government contracts sometimes paid bribes to the officials who made the decisions. Opportunities were limited only by the imagination of the spoilsmen.

Some critics found a more fundamental defect in the system, beyond its capacity for corruption. By concentrating on patronage so much, politics ignored principles and issues and revolved instead around greed for government employment. The spoils system had many defenders, however. One Tammany loyalist explained, "You can't keep an organization together without patronage. Men ain't in politics for nothin'. They want to get somethin' out of it." This spoilsman was describing the reality that all local party activists faced: given the enormous numbers of party workers needed to identify supporters, to mobilize voters, politics required some sort of reward system.

The most persistent critics of the spoils systems were a group known as **Mugwumps** to their contemporaries. Centered in Boston and New York, these reformers were largely Republicans who enjoyed high social status. They traced many of the defects of politics to the spoils system, and they argued that eliminating patronage would drive out the machines and opportunists. Only then, they insisted, could political purity and decency be restored. Instead of basing appointments on political loyalty, the Mugwumps advocated a **merit system** based on a job seeker's ability to pass a comprehensive examination. Educated, dedicated civil servants, they believed, would stand above party politics and provide capable and honest administration.

Because the Mugwumps sometimes broke with their party, they drew the contempt of most party politicians. James G. Blaine, a leading Republican, called them "conceited, foolish . . . pretentious but not powerful." Other party politicians questioned the Mugwumps' manhood, reflecting the extent to which being a loyal party member was closely tied to men's gender role in the minds of many.

postmaster An official appointed to oversee the operations of a local post office.

Mugwumps Republicans who opposed political corruption and campaigned for reform in the 1880s and 1890s, sometimes crossing party boundaries to achieve their goals.

merit system Hiring government workers because of their abilities and their scores on competency tests instead of through patronage.

♦ Using an elephant to symbolize the Republicans and a donkey for the Democrats dates to the 1870s and the work of Thomas Nast, the most talented cartoonist of his age. At the time, Republicans often preferred an eagle or star and Democrats usually chose a rooster. *Library of Congress.*

Republicans and Democrats

Beyond the hoopla, fireworks, and interminable speeches, important differences characterized the two parties. Some of those differences appear in the ways the parties described themselves in their platforms, newspapers, speeches, and other campaign appeals.

Republicans asserted a virtual monopoly on patriotism by pointing to their defense of the Union during the Civil War and claiming that Democrats—especially southern Democrats—had proven themselves disloyal during the conflict. Trumpeting this accusation was often called "waving the bloody shirt," in reference to a Republican congressman who displayed the bloodstained shirt of a northerner beaten by white supremacists. "Every man that shot a Union soldier," Robert Ingersoll, a Republican orator, repeatedly proclaimed, "was a Democrat." Republicans exploited the Civil War legacy in other ways too. Republicans in Congress voted to provide generous federal pensions to disabled Union army veterans and to the widows and orphans of those who died. Republican party leaders carefully cultivated the **Grand Army of the Republic (GAR),** the organization of Union veterans, attending their meetings and urging them to "vote as you shot." Republican presidential candidates were almost all Union veterans, as were many state and local officials throughout the North.

Prosperity formed another persistent Republican campaign theme. Republicans pointed to the economic growth of the postwar era and boasted that it stemmed largely from their wise policies, especially the protective tariff. Many Republicans also claimed to be the party of decency and morality. Senator George Hoar of Massachusetts claimed in 1889 that all upright and virtuous citizens "commonly, and as a rule, by the natural law of their being, find their place in the Republican party." Republicans never committed themselves in favor of **prohibition,** but their national convention in 1888 pronounced itself in favor of "all wise and well-directed efforts for the promotion of temperance and morality." Republican campaigners delighted in portraying as typical

Grand Army of the Republic Organization of Union army veterans.

prohibition A legal ban on the manufacture, sale, and use of alcoholic beverages.

Democrats "the old slave-owner and slave-driver, the saloon-keeper, the ballot-box-stuffer, the Kuklux [Klan], the criminal class of the great cities, the men who cannot read or write," and they usually threw in Boss Tweed for good measure.

Where Republicans defined themselves in terms of what their party did and who they were, Democrats typically explained what they opposed. Most leading Democrats stood firm against "governmental interference" in the economy, especially the protective tariff and land grants, equating government activism with privileges for a favored few. The protective tariff, they claimed, protected manufacturers from international competition at the expense of consumers who paid higher prices. The public domain, they maintained, should provide farms for citizens, not subsidies for corporations. All in all, Democrats favored a strictly limited role for the government in the economy, a position much closer to laissez faire than that of the Republicans.

Just as the Democrats opposed government interference in the economy, so too did they oppose government interference in social relations and behavior. In the North, especially in Irish and German communities, they condemned prohibition, which they called a violation of personal liberty. And they defended Catholics against the political attacks of groups like the **American Protective Association (APA).** In the South, Democrats rejected federal enforcement of equal rights for African Americans, which they called a violation of states' rights. There, Democrats called for white supremacy and appealed to the memory of the Lost Cause.

On election day, each party tried to mobilize all its supporters and make certain that they voted. This form of political campaigning produced all-time records for voter participation. In 1876, more than 80 percent of the eligible voters cast their ballots. Turnout sometimes rose even higher (see Figure 20.1), although exact percentages were affected by poor record keeping or fraud. At the polling places, party workers distributed lists or "tickets" of their party's candidates, which voters then used as ballots. Voting was not secret until the 1890s. Before then, everyone could see which party's ballot a voter deposited in the ballot box. Such a system discouraged voters from crossing party lines.

Most voters developed strong loyalties to one party or the other, often on the basis of **ethnicity,** race, or religion. Nearly all Catholics and many Irish, German, and other immigrants supported the Democrats as the party that defended them against the American Protective Association, nativism, and prohibition. Poor voters in the disproportionately Catholic big cities usually supported the local machine, whether Democratic or Republican—but far more were Democrats. Most southern whites supported the Democrats as the party that opposed federal enforcement of black rights. The Democrats' opposition to the protective tariff attracted a few businessmen and professionals who favored more competition. The Democrats, all in all, composed a very diverse coalition, one that held together primarily because its various components could unite against government action on social or economic matters.

Outside the South, most old-stock Protestants voted Republican, as did most Scandinavian and British immigrants. Most African Americans supported the Republicans too, as the party of emancipation, as did most veterans of the abolition movement. So many Union veterans supported the Republicans that someone suggested the initials GAR stood for "generally all Republicans." Republicans always did well among the voters of New England, Pennsylvania, and much of the Midwest. In California and New Mexico Territory, many Hispanics voted Republican. For the most part, the Republicans composed the more coherent political organization, united around a set of policies that involved federal government action to encourage economic growth and to protect black rights. Democrats usually opposed such measures. As Thomas B. Reed, a leading Republican in the House of Representatives in the 1890s, put it, "The Republican party does things, the Democratic party criticizes." Neither party, however, advocated government action to regulate, restrict, or tax the newly developing industrial corporations.

Challenging the Male Bastion: Woman Suffrage

In the masculine political world of the Gilded Age, men expected one another to display strong loyalty to a political party, but they considered women—

American Protective Association An anti-Catholic organization founded in Iowa in 1887 and active during the next decade.

ethnicity Ethnicity, or ethnic background, can include a shared racial, religious, linguistic, cultural, or national heritage.

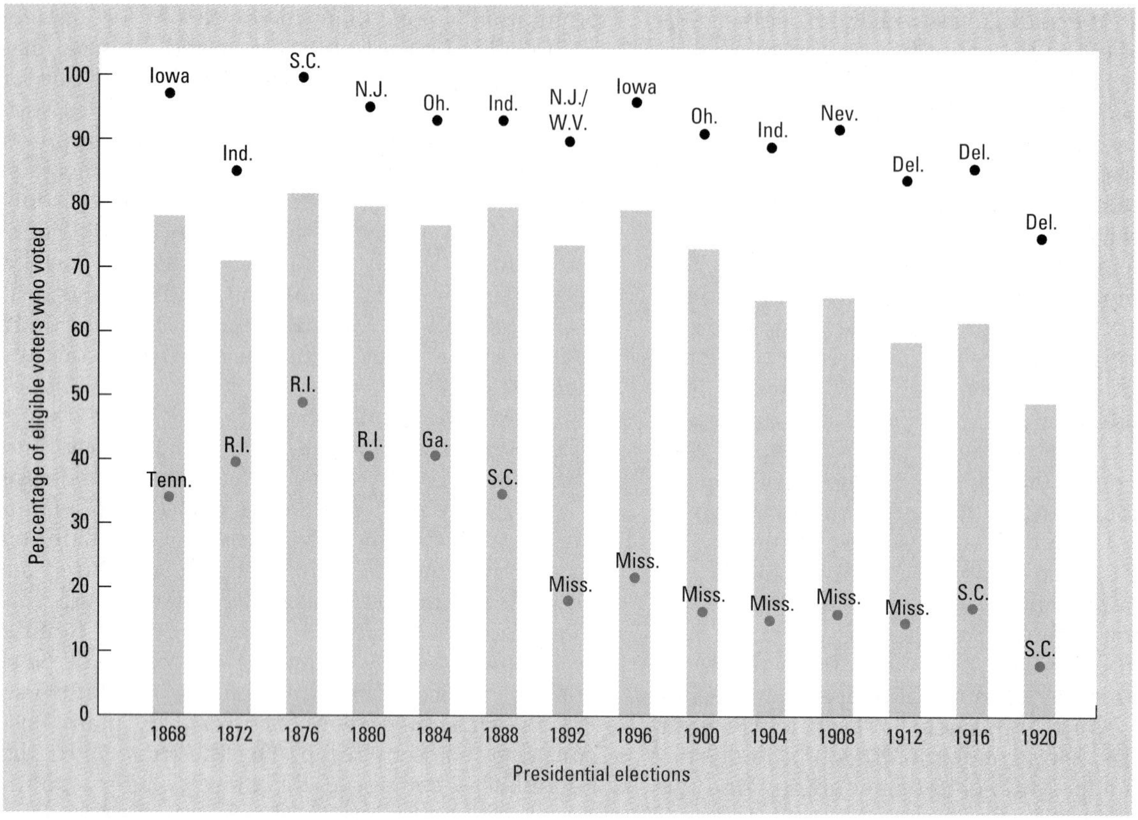

♦ **FIGURE 20.1 Voter Participation Rates for Presidential Elections, 1868–1920** This figure indicates the proportion of eligible voters who actually cast ballots. The bar represents the national average, and the two states indicate the highest and lowest rates of turnout. The average and the highs and lows all move downward after 1896. Notice the impact of the "Mississippi Plan" of 1890. *Source:* U.S. Department of Commerce, Bureau of the Census, *Historical Statistics of the United States,* 2 vols. (Washington, D.C.: U.S. Government Printing Office, 1975), pp. 1071–1072.

who could not vote—to stand outside the party system. The concepts of domesticity and separate spheres dictated that women avoid politics, especially party politics. In fact, women did involve themselves in political struggles by taking part in a variety of reform efforts, even though they could not cast a ballot on election day. In the late nineteenth century, some bold women also pushed to secure full political participation through the right to vote.

The struggle for woman suffrage was of long standing. In 1848, Elizabeth Cady Stanton and four other women had organized the world's first Women's Rights Convention, held at Seneca Falls, New York. The participants drafted a Declaration of Principles that announced, in part, "It is the duty of the women of this country to secure to themselves their sacred right to the elective franchise." Stanton became the most prominent leader in the struggle for women's rights, especially voting rights, from 1848 to her death in 1902. After 1851, Susan B. Anthony became her constant partner in these efforts. They achieved some success in convincing lawmakers to modify laws that discriminated against women, but all their labor could not change the laws that limited voting to men. During those years, women increasingly participated in public affairs: movements to abolish slavery, mobilize support for the Union, improve educational opportunities, and more.

In 1866, Stanton and Anthony unsuccessfully opposed inclusion of the word *male* in the Fourteenth Amendment (see page 473). Later, in 1869, they

♦ This sketch of women voting in Cheyenne, Wyoming Territory appeared in 1888. In 1869, Wyoming became the first state or territory to extend suffrage to women. This drawing appeared shortly before Wyoming requested statehood, a request made controversial by the issue of woman suffrage. *Library of Congress.*

formed the **National Woman Suffrage Association (NWSA),** its membership open only to women. The NWSA sought an amendment to the Constitution as the only sure route to woman suffrage. It built alliances with other reform and radical organizations and worked to improve women's status. For example, members pressed for easier divorce laws and birth control (which Stanton called "self-sovereignty") and promoted women's unions. The **American Woman Suffrage Association (AWSA),** organized by other suffrage advocates in 1869, kept a narrower focus, concentrating strictly on winning the right to vote and avoiding all issues that distracted from that goal. For twenty years, these two organizations led the suffrage cause, disagreeing not on the final goal but on the way to achieve it. They merged in 1890, under Stanton's leadership, to become the National American Woman Suffrage Association. Until the early twentieth century, however, their support came largely from middle-class women—and men—who were largely of old-stock American Protestant descent.

The first victories for suffrage came in the West. In 1869, in Wyoming Territory, the territorial legislature extended the **franchise** to women. At the time, about seven thousand men but only two thousand women lived in the territory. There was a well-organized suffrage movement among Wyoming women, and the male legislators may have been receptive to their arguments. At the same time, some of them may have hoped that woman suffrage would attract more women to Wyoming. Women exercised the suffrage without controversy in Wyoming, voting for local and territorial officials (residents of a territory could not vote for president) and also serving on juries and as public officials. In 1889, when Wyoming asked for statehood, some congressmen balked at admitting a state that permitted women to vote. Wyoming legislators, however, forthrightly stated, "We will remain out of the Union a hundred years rather than come in without the women." Congress finally voted to approve Wyoming statehood in 1890. In 1893, Colorado voters (all male) approved woman suffrage, making Colorado the first state to adopt woman suffrage through a popular vote. In addition to a well-organized campaign by Colorado women, their cause was assisted by support from the new Populist party (see below).

Utah Territory, where men and women had nearly equal numbers, adopted woman suffrage in 1870. Mormon men formed the majority of Utah's voters, but there were many Mormon women and relatively few non-Mormon women. By enfranchising women, Mormons strengthened their voting majority and may have hoped, at the same time, to silence the critics who claimed that polygamy degraded women. However, in an act aimed primarily at the Mormons, Congress outlawed polygamy in

National Woman Suffrage Association New York–based women's suffrage organization led by Elizabeth Cady Stanton and Susan B. Anthony; it accepted only women as members and worked for related issues such as unionizing female workers.

American Woman Suffrage Association Boston-based women's suffrage organization led by Lucy Stone, Julia Ward Howe, and others; it welcomed men and worked solely to win the vote for women.

franchise The right to vote; another word for suffrage.

1887 and disfranchised the women in Utah Territory at the same time. Not until Utah became a state, in 1896, did Utah women regain the vote. In neighboring Idaho, where both Mormon and Populist influences were strong, male voters approved woman suffrage in 1896.

Several states began to permit women limited voting rights, especially on matters outside party politics, such as school board elections and school bond issues. These concessions perhaps reflected the widespread assumption that women's gender roles included child rearing. By 1890, women could vote in school elections in nineteen states and on bond and tax issues in three. Despite valiant efforts by suffrage advocates, however, not one state passed a suffrage proposal between 1896 and 1910.

Structural Change and Policy Change

The Mugwumps and the advocates of woman suffrage both challenged basic features of the political system of the Gilded Age. These were only two of many different, though occasionally overlapping, groups organized to seek measures rarely addressed by the major parties: abolition of the spoils system, woman suffrage, prohibition, the secret ballot, regulation of business, an end to child labor, a monetary policy that did not disadvantage debtors, and more. Most groups pushing for political change called themselves reformers, meaning that they wanted to change the form of politics. Most reforms fall into one of two categories—structural change and policy change. *Structural change,* or *structural reform,* refers to efforts to change the structure of political decision-making. Structural issues include the way in which public officials are chosen. For example, the convention system, voting, and the selection of government employees are all matters of structure. Those seeking to eliminate the spoils system and substitute the merit system, therefore, addressed one element in the structure of politics. The eligibility to vote was another. Woman suffrage was therefore a structural change, and so was disfranchisement of African-American voters in the South. Structural issues can even involve basic constitutional matters: the Electoral College as the means for choosing the president, the method of electing members of the Senate, the nature of the president's veto power.

Policy issues, in contrast, have to do with the way the government uses its power. The debate over federal economic policy in the Gilded Age provides an array of contrasting positions. Many Democrats favored laissez faire, believing that federal interference in the economy created a privileged class. Most Republicans favored a policy of distribution, meaning that they wanted to distribute benefits to companies and individuals (land, tariff protection) to encourage economic growth. Grangers (discussed later) favored regulation: they wanted the government to enforce basic rules governing economic activity—in this case, by prohibiting pools and rebates and setting maximum rates. Greenbackers (also discussed later) wanted to use **monetary policy** to benefit debtors—or, as they would have put it, to create a monetary policy that would not benefit lenders.

Groups seeking change may find little in common with each other, or they may overlook differences to form alliances with other groups. The Mugwumps, for example, generally opposed regulation and woman suffrage. One key distinction between the National Woman Suffrage Association and the American Woman Suffrage Association was that Stanton and Anthony's NWSA often welcomed political alliances with groups like the Greenbackers who endorsed woman suffrage. The AWSA, fearing that such alliances would lose more support for suffrage than they gained, chose a narrow focus on the suffrage issue.

Some groups combined structural and policy proposals. The tiny Prohibition party, for example, wanted government to eliminate alcohol, but the Prohibitionists also favored woman suffrage because they assumed that most women voters would oppose alcohol. In this instance, they promoted a structural reform, woman suffrage, not just for its own sake but also to accomplish a policy reform, prohibition of alcohol.

One important structural change received widespread support from many political groups, and many states chose to adopt it soon after its first appearance. The **Australian ballot**—printed and distributed by the government, not by political parties, listing all candidates of all parties, and marked in a private voting booth—was adopted by the first states in the late 1880s but spread rapidly and was in

monetary policy A government plan to influence the economy by controlling interest rates or expanding or contracting the amount of money in circulation.

Australian ballot A printed ballot that is prepared by government officials, bears the names of all qualified candidates of all parties, and is distributed to voters at the polls and marked in privacy; so called because this method of voting originated in Australia.

use in most states by 1892. This reform carried important implications for political parties. No longer would it be difficult for voters to cross party lines and vote a **split ticket.** No longer would party activists see which party's ballot a voter dropped into the ballot box. The switch to the Australian ballot and the adoption of the merit system for the civil service marked the first significant efforts to limit parties' power and influence.

Political Stalemate

- What were the sources of the political deadlock that lasted from 1874 to the 1890s?
- What major changes were enacted during that period?

During the Civil War and early years of Reconstruction, the dominant Republicans had changed the very nature of the federal government. They adopted major alterations in the nature of citizenship, relations between the federal government and the states, and the relation between the federal government and the economy. Most of the economic policies established in the 1860s persisted with little change for more than a generation. The protective tariff and the policy of using the public domain to encourage rapid economic development both involved an active federal role to stimulate economic development. Thus federal economic policy during these years should not be described as pure laissez faire, even though there was little regulation, restriction, or taxation of economic activity.

A political **stalemate** made it difficult for either party to put through major changes in federal policy between 1875 and 1896. Instead, politics often revolved around scandal and spoils rather than issues of policy. The few significant new laws tended to be relatively uncontroversial, to draw support from both parties, and to have little immediate effect on the economy or society. When Republicans briefly broke the stalemate, in 1889 and 1890, by passing nearly their full party agenda, they found themselves rejected by the voters.

Formula for Stalemate

Competition between Republicans and Democrats at a national level was very close during the years 1874 to 1896. Figure 20.2 presents the popular vote and electoral vote for president during these years. Although the parties' popular vote was usually virtually identical, the electoral vote appears more decisive. But those figures are deceiving. In the elections of 1880, 1884, and 1888, New York State cast its electoral votes for the winning candidate. Had that one state voted for the other candidate, he would have won. In each of those elections, a different choice by one or two voters out of every hundred in New York would have changed the result there and for the nation.

Although most presidential elections during these decades were very close, the Republicans won all but two between 1860 and 1900. However, from the mid-1870s until 1895, the two parties had nearly equal numbers in the Senate and House of Representatives. The Democrats held a slim majority in the House in most years, and the Republicans usually held sway by a similar margin in the Senate. As a result, the Republican majority in the Senate could block any proposal by a Democratic president, and the Democratic majority in the House of Representatives could block any proposal by a Republican president.

Other factors also made significant changes in policy unlikely. The struggle between Andrew Johnson and the congressional radicals had tipped the balance of power from the presidency to the Congress, and after Johnson came a succession of presidents who did little to challenge that dominance. Both parties held attitudes toward the presidency that made it improbable that a president would seek a leadership role in policy. Outside of his responsibilities for war and diplomacy, the president was expected only to administer the laws and to point out to Congress, usually in an annual report delivered by a messenger, any problems requiring legislation. In the late nineteenth century, virtually no one expected the president to be a major policy initiator. And no president was.

The Grant Administration: Spoils and Scandals

Ulysses S. Grant's success as a general failed to prepare him for the presidency. During his two terms in office (elected in 1868 and re-elected in 1872), he rarely challenged congressional dominance of domestic policymaking. He often appointed friends

split ticket A ballot cast by an individual who has voted for candidates of more than one political party.

stalemate A deadlock; a situation in which neither side can advance.

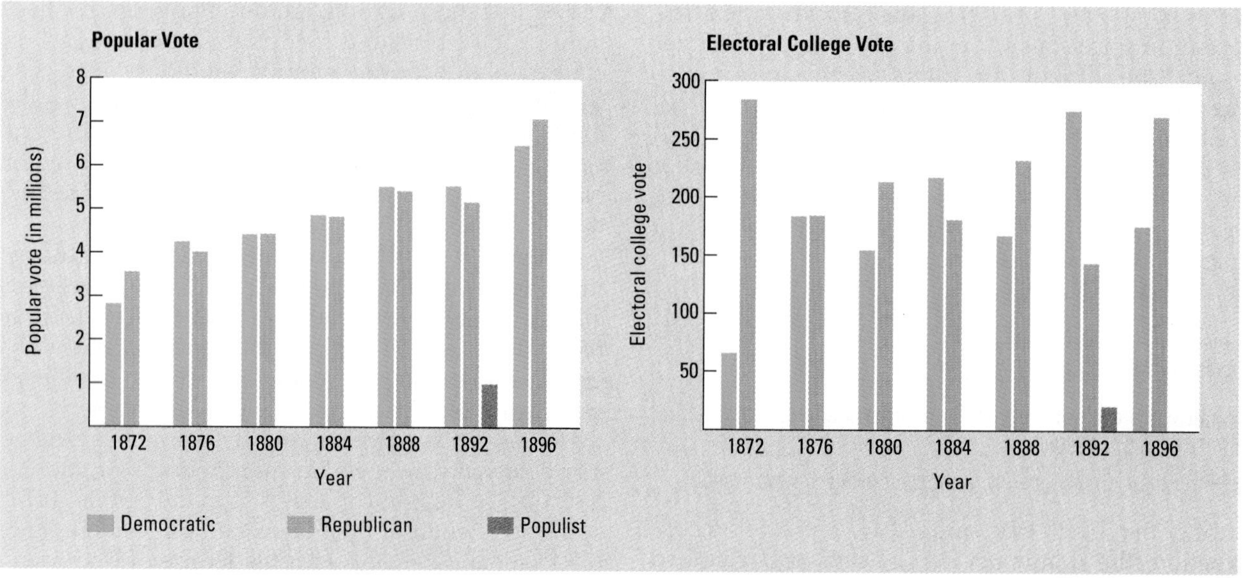

♦ **FIGURE 20.2 Popular and Electoral Vote for President, 1872–1896** *Source:* Data from Series Y 79–83, U.S. Department of Commerce, Bureau of the Census, *Historical Statistics of the United States,* 2 vols. (Washington: U.S. Government Printing Office, 1975), p. 1073.

or acquaintances to posts for which they possessed no particular qualifications. He proved unable to form a competent cabinet and faced constant turnover among his executive advisers. Many of his appointees seemed to view their positions as little more than the spoils of party victory, and Grant sometimes proved too willing to believe his appointees' denials of wrongdoing. He did choose a highly capable secretary of state, Hamilton Fish, and he eventually found in Benjamin Bristow a secretary of the treasury who vigorously combated corruption.

Congress supplied its full share of scandal. Visiting Washington in 1869, young Henry Adams (grandson of the country's second president and son of its sixth president) was surprised to hear a member of the cabinet bellow, "You can't use tact with a Congressman! A Congressman is a hog! You must take a stick and hit him on the snout!" Too many members of Congress behaved in a way that confirmed such a cynical view. In 1868, before Grant became president, several prominent congressional leaders had become stockholders in the **Crédit Mobilier,** a construction company created by the chief shareholders in the Union Pacific Railroad. The Union Pacific officers awarded to Crédit Mobilier a generous contract to build the railroad. Thus the company's chief shareholders paid themselves handsomely for constructing their own railroad. To protect this arrangement from congressional scrutiny, the company sold shares cheaply to key members of Congress. Purchasers included some leading Republicans. Revelation of these arrangements in 1872 and 1873 scandalized the nation. No sooner did that furor pass than Congress voted itself a 50 percent pay raise and made the increase two years retroactive. Only after widespread public protest did Congress repeal its "salary grab."

In 1875, Treasury Secretary Bristow took the lead in fighting widespread corruption in the collection of whiskey taxes. A **Whiskey Ring** of federal officials and distillers, centered in St. Louis, had conspired to evade payment of taxes. The 230 men indicted included several of Grant's appointees and

Crédit Mobilier Company created to build the Union Pacific Railroad; in a scandalous deal uncovered in 1872–1873, it sold shares cheaply to congressmen who approved federal subsidies for railroad construction.

Whiskey Ring Distillers and revenue officials in St. Louis who were revealed in 1875 to have defrauded the government of millions of dollars in whiskey taxes, with the collusion of federal officials.

even his private secretary. Despite the evidence, Grant could not believe his close associates were guilty. He helped his secretary avoid conviction and forced Bristow to resign. The next year, William Belknap, Grant's secretary of war, resigned shortly before he was impeached for accepting bribes in connection with an appointment to a potentially lucrative position in Indian Territory.

Hayes, Garfield, and Arthur: The Politics of Stalemate

When **Rutherford B. Hayes** became president after the contested election of 1876 (see page 493), his personal integrity and principled stand on issues helped to restore the reputation of the Republican party after the scandals of the Grant administration. Any hope he had for significant change, however, ran up against a Democratic majority in the House of Representatives and significant opposition within his own party. His harshest Republican critic was Roscoe Conkling, a flamboyant senator from New York and the boss of that state's large and hungry Republican organization. Conkling became especially hostile after Hayes refused the New Yorker's efforts to install his supporters in key federal positions.

Hayes promised to serve only one term and probably could not have secured a second nomination had he sought one. His handling of patronage alienated other Republicans in addition to Conkling, and he estranged reformers by not seeking a full-scale revision of the civil service. When the White House stopped serving alcohol, Hayes's opponents blamed Hayes's wife, Lucy Webb Hayes, the first college-educated First Lady and a committed reformer, and dubbed her "Lemonade Lucy." By mid-1880, Hayes seemed to welcome the end of his presidency.

The 1880 Republican convention saw a battle between Conkling and James G. Blaine of Maine, a spellbinding orator with a capacity for winning loyal supporters and creating bitter enemies. Blaine sought the presidential nomination. Conkling and his followers, calling themselves **Stalwarts,** tried to nominate former president Grant. Few major differences of policy separated Conkling from Blaine: Conkling showed more commitment to the spoils system and the defense of southern black voters, and Blaine took more interest in the protective tariff and economic policies encouraging industrialization and western economic development. Conkling, however, dismissed Blaine and his supporters as **Half-Breeds**—not real Republicans.

After a long deadlock, the Republicans compromised by nominating **James A. Garfield,** a congressman from Ohio. Born in a log cabin, Garfield grew up in poverty, became a minister, college president, and lawyer before the Civil War, then became the Union's youngest major general. For vice president, the convention tried to placate the Stalwarts and to secure New York's electoral votes by nominating Conkling's chief lieutenant, **Chester A. Arthur,** whom Hayes had removed as head of the New York **Customhouse.**

The Democrats nominated Winfield Scott Hancock, another former Civil War general with little political experience. Both candidates worked at avoiding matters of substance during the campaign. Garfield won the popular vote by the narrowest of margins—half a percentage point—but he won the electoral vote convincingly without carrying a single southern state, thus demonstrating that the Republicans could survive without the southern black vote.

Garfield brought to the White House a solid understanding of Congress and a tendency to study all questions carefully. Hoping to work cooperatively with both Stalwarts and Blaine supporters, he appointed Blaine as secretary of state, the most prestigious cabinet position. Discord soon appeared when Conkling demanded the right to name his supporters to key federal positions. In opposing Conkling, Garfield showed himself to be shrewder politically than any president since Lincoln. When Conkling

Rutherford B. Hayes Governor of Ohio elected president in 1876 on the Republican ticket.

Stalwarts Faction of the Republican party led by Roscoe Conkling; as the name implies, Stalwarts claimed to be the genuine Republicans.

Half-Breeds Insulting name that Republican party boss Roscoe Conkling gave to his opponents within the party, to suggest that they were not fully committed to Republican party ideals.

James A. Garfield Ohio congressman who was chosen as a compromise candidate at the 1880 Republican convention and elected twentieth president of the United States; he was shot to death four months after taking office.

Chester A. Arthur Stalwart Republican who was elected vice president in 1880 and took over the presidency on Garfield's death.

customhouse Federal office, located in port cities, that was responsible for collecting the tariff (customs) on imported goods.

acknowledged his defeat by resigning his Senate seat, Garfield scored an important victory for a stronger presidency.

On July 2, 1881, four months after taking the oath of office, Garfield was shot while walking through a Washington railroad station. His assassin, Charles Guiteau, a mentally unstable religious fanatic, called himself "a Stalwart of the Stalwarts" and claimed he had acted to save the Republican party. Two months later, Garfield died of the wound.

Vice president Chester A. Arthur became president. Long a close ally of Conkling, Arthur was probably best known, beyond his Stalwart connections, as a capable administrator and a dapper dresser. Arthur, however, proved that, as one of his former associates said, "He isn't 'Chet' Arthur any more; he's the President." In 1882, doctors diagnosed him as suffering from Bright's disease, a kidney condition that produced fatigue and depression and, eventually, death. Arthur kept the news secret from all but his family and closest friends. Overcoming both political liabilities and his own physical limitations, Arthur proved a competent president.

The Republicans had slim majorities in Congress after the 1880 election. When the Democrats recovered control over the House of Representatives in 1882, the Republicans acted quickly, before the newly elected Democrats took their seats, to enact the first major tariff revision in eight years and, in 1883, the **Pendleton Act** reforming the civil service. Both measures, however, had support from some Democrats.

Named for its sponsor, Senator George Pendleton, an Ohio Democrat, the Pendleton Act had far-reaching consequences, for it brought into being the merit system of filling federal positions. It designated certain federal positions, about 15 percent of the total, as "classified." **Classified civil service positions** were to be filled only through competitive examinations. The law also authorized the president to add positions to the classified list. When an office was first classified, the patronage appointee then holding it was protected from removal for political reasons. Presidents could therefore use the law to entrench their own appointees. When those appointees retired, however, their replacements came through the merit system. Thus the law used patronage in the short run to bring the long-term demise of the patronage system. Within twenty years, the law applied to 44 percent of federal employees. Most state and local governments eventually adopted merit systems.

Cleveland and the Democrats

In the end, Arthur proved more capable than anyone might have predicted. Given his failing health, however, he exerted little effort to win his party's nomination in 1884. Blaine—charming and quick-witted—secured the Republican nomination. The Democrats nominated Grover Cleveland, who as governor of New York had earned a reputation for integrity and political courage, particularly by attacking Tammany Hall. Many Irish voters, who made up a large component in Tammany, supported Blaine even though they were Democrats.

The campaign quickly turned nasty. Many Mugwumps disliked Blaine and revealed an old letter of his urging a cover-up of allegations that he had profited from prorailroad legislation. Blaine supporters gleefully trumpeted that Cleveland had avoided military service during the Civil War and had fathered a child outside marriage. Democrats chanted, "Blaine, Blaine, James G. Blaine! The continental liar from the state of Maine." Republicans shouted back, "Ma! Ma! Where's my pa?" The election hinged on New York, where Blaine expected to cut deeply into the usually Democratic Irish vote. A few days before the election, however, Blaine heard a preacher in New York City call the Democrats the party of "rum, Romanism [Catholicism], and rebellion." Blaine ignored this insult to his Irish Catholic supporters until newspapers blasted it the next day. By then the damage was done. Cleveland won New York by a tiny margin, and New York's electoral votes gave him the presidency.

Cleveland won with support from many who opposed the spoils system. He chose not to dismantle it but insisted on demonstrated ability in those he appointed to office. Deeply committed to minimal government and to reducing federal spending, Cleveland vetoed 414 bills—most of them granting pensions to individual Union veterans—between 1885 and 1889. This amounted to twice as many vetoes as all previous presidents put together. Cleveland provided little leadership regarding legislation but did approve several important measures produced by the Democratic House and Republican

Pendleton Act Law passed by Congress in 1883 that created the Civil Service Commission and the merit system for government hiring and jobs.

classified civil service positions Federal positions to be filled through the merit system instead of by patronage.

♦ Republicans in Denver staged this huge, torchlight parade (made even larger, perhaps, by the artist's skills) to celebrate the election of Benjamin Harrison in 1888. During the nineteenth century, political events, such as campaigns and victory celebrations, often included public meetings and parades. For the Republicans, these events almost always included a tribute to Union veterans, and, as you can see, a white-bearded veteran, in uniform, appears on horseback, next to the lead drummer. *Colorado Historical Society.*

Senate, including the Dawes Severalty Act (see page 556) and the Interstate Commerce Act.

The Interstate Commerce Act grew out of political pressure from farmers and small businesses that led several states to regulate railroads. Illinois, in 1871, created a railroad and warehouse commission to set the maximum rates companies could charge. Iowa and Wisconsin passed laws regulating railroad freight rates in 1874 (called Granger laws and discussed later in the chapter). In 1877, in *Munn v. Illinois*, the Supreme Court held that businesses with "a public interest," including warehouses and railroads, "must submit to be controlled by the public for the common good." In *Wabash Railway v. Illinois* (1886), however, the Supreme Court put severe limits on the states' power to regulate railroad rates involving interstate commerce.

In response to the *Wabash* decision as well as to continuing protests over railroad rate discrimination, Congress passed the Interstate Commerce Act in 1887, creating the **Interstate Commerce Commission (ICC),** the first federal regulatory commission. The law prohibited pools, rebates, and different rates for short and long hauls, and it required that rates be "reasonable and just." The ICC had little real power, however, until the Hepburn Act strengthened it in 1906 (see page 682).

Cleveland considered the nation's greatest problem to be the federal budget surplus. After the Civil War, the tariff usually generated more income than the country needed to pay federal expenses (see Figure 20.3). Throughout the 1880s, the surplus was often more than $100 million per year. Worried that the surplus encouraged wasteful spending, Cleveland demanded in 1887 that Congress cut tariff rates on raw materials and necessities. He hoped not only to reduce federal income but also, by reducing prices on raw materials, to encourage companies to compete with recently developed monopolies.

Cleveland's action provoked a serious division within his own party. So long as Democrats did not have responsibility for the tariff, they could criticize Republican policies without restraint. Now, however, urged to take positive action by their own party chief, they failed. Cleveland himself exerted little leadership, leaving the initiative to congressional leaders. House Democrats treated it as an exercise in party politics, creating a bill with little resemblance to Cleveland's proposal but with ample benefits for the South. Republicans in the Senate responded with amendments aimed against southern economic interests. But when Congress adjourned without voting on the bill, Cleveland's call for tariff reform came to nothing.

In the 1888 presidential election, the Democrats renominated Cleveland, but he backed off from the tariff issue and refused to campaign actively. The Republicans nominated **Benjamin Harrison,** senator

Interstate Commerce Commission Federal commission established in 1877 to oversee railroads.

Benjamin Harrison Indiana Republican senator who was elected president in 1888 on a platform of high protective tariffs and a strengthened navy.

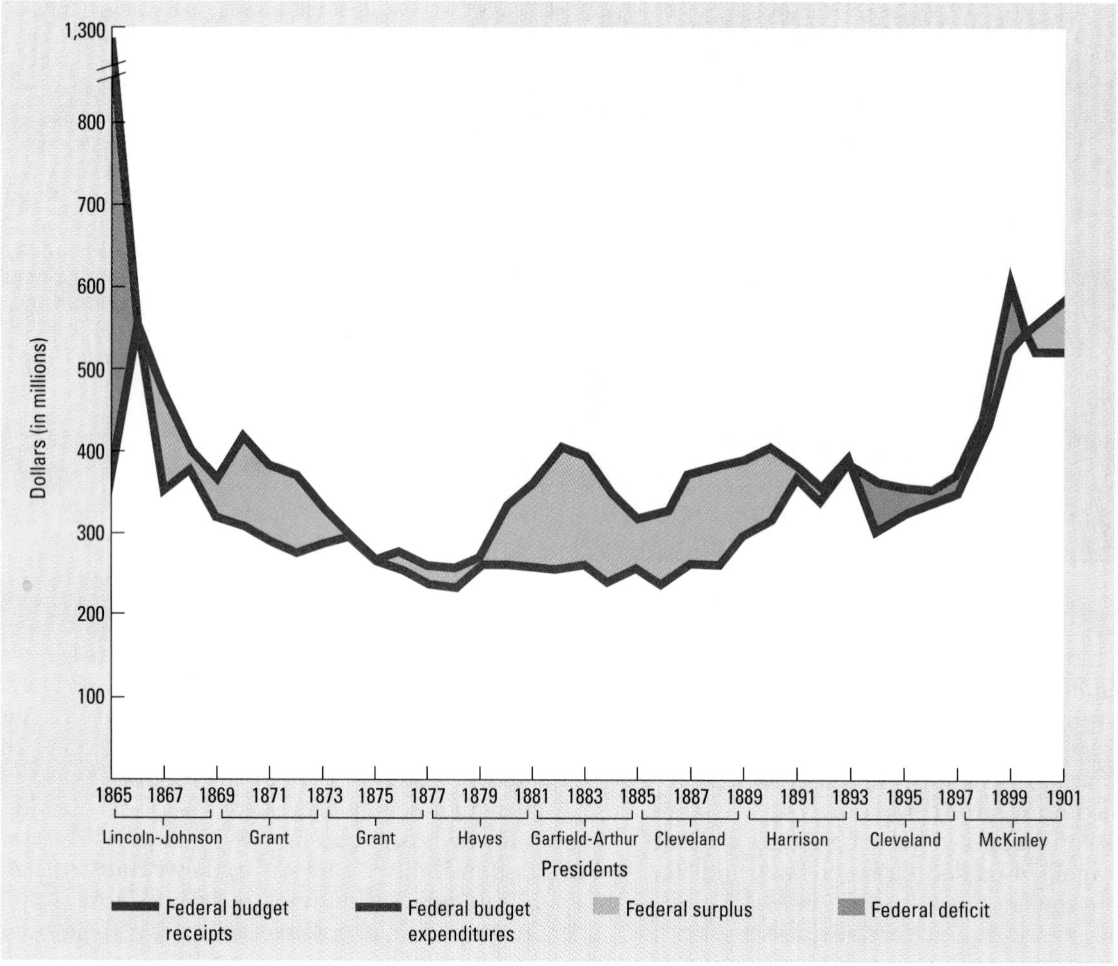

♦ **FIGURE 20.3 Federal Receipts and Expenditures, 1865–1901** The surplus usually shrank during economic downturns (the mid-1870s and mid-1890s) and grew in more prosperous periods (1880s). During the Harrison administration, however, the surplus virtually disappeared although the economy remained generally prosperous, reflecting efforts to reduce income and increase expenditures. *Source:* U.S. Department of Commerce, *Historical Statistics of the United States* (Washington, D.C.: U.S. Government Printing Office, 1975), p. 1104.

from Indiana and yet another former Civil War general. Known as thoughtful, responsible, and cautious, Harrison impressed many visitors as cool and distant. The Republicans launched a vigorous campaign focused on the virtues of the protective tariff. They raised unprecedented amounts of campaign money by systematically approaching business leaders on the tariff issue, and they used the money to print more campaign materials than ever before. Republicans also attacked Cleveland's vetoes of pensions for Union veterans, especially when speaking to audiences of Union veterans.

Harrison won in the electoral voting but received fewer popular votes than Cleveland: 47.9 percent to Cleveland's 48.7 percent. As important for the Republicans as their narrow presidential victory, however, were the majorities they secured in both House and Senate. In 1889, Republicans stood poised to create new public policies.

Harrison: Ending the Stalemate?

With Harrison in the White House and Republican majorities in both houses of Congress, the Republi-

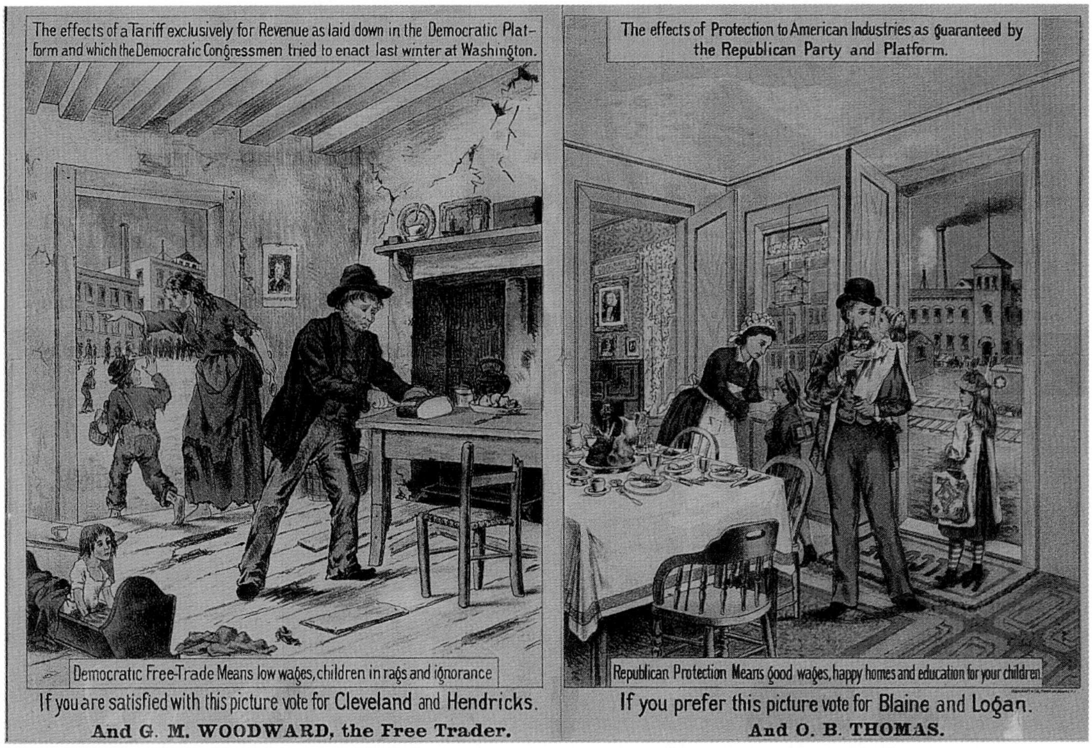
The effects of a Tariff exclusively for Revenue as laid down in the Democratic Platform and which the Democratic Congressmen tried to enact last winter at Washington.
Democratic Free-Trade Means low wages, children in rags and ignorance
If you are satisfied with this picture vote for Cleveland and Hendricks.
And G. M. WOODWARD, the Free Trader.
The effects of Protection to American Industries as guaranteed by the Republican Party and Platform.
Republican Protection Means good wages, happy homes and education for your children.
If you prefer this picture vote for Blaine and Logan.
And O. B. THOMAS.

♦ Republicans circulated this cartoon in 1884, claiming that the Democrats' proposed tariff reform would threaten wage levels and endanger little children, but Republicans' commitment to the protective tariff would protect wage levels and make families more secure. *Museum of American Political Life/photo by Steve Laschever.*

cans set out to do a lot and to do it quickly. When the fifty-first session of Congress opened in 1889, Harrison worked more closely with congressional leaders of his own party than any other president in anyone's memory had done. Democrats in the House of Representatives tried to delay action, but Speaker Thomas B. Reed—an enormous man renowned for his wit—announced new rules designed to speed up House business.

The Republicans' first major task was tariff revision. They wanted to cut the troublesome federal surplus without reducing protection. Led by William McKinley of Ohio, the **House Ways and Means Committee** drafted a tariff that moved some items to the free list (notably sugar, a major source of tariff revenue) but raised tariff rates on other items, sometimes so high as to be prohibitive. The House passed the **McKinley Tariff** in late May 1890 and sent it on to the Senate.

On July 2, the House approved the federal elections bill, nicknamed the "force bill" by its Democratic opponents. Proposed by Representative Henry Cabot Lodge of Massachusetts, the bill would have permitted federal supervision over congressional election procedures to prevent disfranchisement, fraud, or violence. The bill did not single out the South, but everyone knew that the South was its target. The measure passed the House and went to the Senate, where approval by the Republican majority seemed likely.

House Ways and Means Committee One of the most significant standing committees of the House of Representatives, responsible for initiating all taxation measures.

McKinley Tariff Tariff passed by Congress in 1890 that sought not only to protect established industries but by prohibitory duties to create new industries; it soon became extremely unpopular.

The Senate, in the meantime, was laboring over two measures named for their sponsor, Senator John Sherman of Ohio: the **Sherman Anti-Trust Act** and the Sherman Silver Purchase Act. The Anti-Trust Act, actually the work of several Republican senators close to Harrison, was potentially the most significant measure passed in 1890. Congress approved it with only a single dissenting vote, and Harrison signed it on July 2. Created in response to growing public concern about the trusts and monopolies that had developed during the 1880s (see pages 512–513), the law declared that "every contract, combination in the form of trust or otherwise, or conspiracy, in restraint of trade or commerce among the several states, or with foreign nations, is hereby declared to be illegal." Republicans thereby demonstrated their responsiveness to public concern about monopoly power, and the United States became the first industrial nation to attempt to regulate business combinations. In fact, however, the law proved difficult to interpret or enforce, and antitrust legislation had little immediate adverse impact on any companies.

The tariff and elections bills still awaited Senate approval. Harrison wanted them passed as a party package. Some Senate Republicans, however, feared that a Democratic **filibuster** against the elections bill would prevent passage of either measure. Finally a compromise emerged: if Republicans put off the elections bill until later, the Democrats would not delay the tariff bill. The deal was made. Over the strong protests of a few New England Republicans, the rest of their party sacrificed African Americans' voting rights to gain the revised tariff. (Some seventy more years passed before Congress finally acted to protect black voting rights in the South.) Harrison signed the McKinley Tariff on October 1, 1890, and the revised tariff soon produced the intended result: it reduced the surplus by cutting tariff income.

The McKinley Tariff and Sherman Anti-Trust Act were only the tip of the iceberg. In ten months the Republicans had passed what one Democrat called "a raging sea of ravenous legislation." Among the record number of new laws were a major increase in pension eligibility for disabled Union army veterans and their dependents, admission to statehood of Idaho and Wyoming, creation of territorial government in Oklahoma, and appropriations that laid the basis for a modern navy. After the long federal stalemate, Republicans hoped that they had broken the political logjam.

Agricultural Distress and Political Upheaval

- What circumstances led some farmers to choose to form a new political party? What did they expect to accomplish?
- What was the immediate outcome of their choices?

During the summer of 1890, as Republicans labored in Washington, confident that they had ended the long political deadlock, some Americans in the West and South organized to seek more radical changes in the nation's politics. Between 1890 and 1892, farmers in the Great Plains and the South, miners in the Rocky Mountains, and veterans of half a dozen reform causes joined to form a new political party, the People's party or **Populists.**

The Farmers' Complaints

During the Gilded Age, farmers became more and more dependent on the national railroad network, on fertilizer and labor-saving equipment, on grain and cotton brokers, and on sources of credit in distant cities. At the same time, some of them began to feel more and more helpless in the face of the great concentrations of economic power that seemed to be taking over their lives.

Perhaps most troubling to farmers were the prices they received for their crops. Those prices fell steadily during the years after the Civil War, as production of wheat, corn, and cotton grew much faster than the population. Some farmers, however, denied that prices were falling solely because of overproduction, pointing to the many poor, hungry, and ragged residents in the great cities. Farmers also condemned the monopolistic practices of grain and cot-

Sherman Anti-Trust Act Law passed by Congress in 1890 authorizing the federal government to prosecute any "combination" "in restraint of trade"; because of adverse court rulings, at first it was ineffective as a weapon against monopolies.

filibuster A delaying tactic, such as a long speech used by the opposing side as a way to delay legislative action.

Populists Members of the People's party, who held their first presidential nominating convention in 1892 and called for federal action to reduce the power of big business and to assist farmers and workers.

ton buyers. **Commodity markets** in distant cities determined the prices farmers received for crops. Most agricultural regions were served by only one buyer, who paid the prices set by those markets, especially in Chicago and New York. When farmers came to sell their crops, they had to accept the price that was offered. They needed cash to pay their debts, and few of them had the resources to store their crops for sale later. Farmers knew, too, that the bushel of corn that they sold for 10 or 20 cents in Kansas in October brought three or four times that amount in New York in December, and they blamed commodity brokers for their misfortunes.

Farmers had accomplished much of the post–Civil War agricultural expansion on borrowed money, and their indebtedness magnified the impact of falling prices. For example, suppose a farmer borrowed $1,000 for five years in 1881, when corn sold for 63 cents per bushel. The borrowed $1,000 would have been equivalent to 1,587 bushels of corn. In 1886, when the loan came due, corn sold for 36 cents per bushel, requiring 2,777 bushels to repay the $1,000. And this increase of nearly 50 percent was over and above the annual interest on the loan. As a result, farmers raised more and more each year just to pay their mortgages and buy necessities. Given the relation between supply and demand, the more they raised, the lower prices fell. One historian compared the farmers' plight to the character in *Alice in Wonderland* who had to run faster and faster just to stay in the same place.

The railroads also angered farmers, who relied on trains to carry their crops to market and to bring supplies in return. The railroads, farmers claimed, were greedy monopolies that charged as much as possible because small rural shippers had no choice but to pay. It sometimes cost four times as much to ship freight in the West as to ship the same amount over the same distance in the East. Farmers also protested the railroads' involvement in politics. Railroads dominated state nominating conventions and state legislatures and distributed free passes to politicians and influential members of local communities in return for favorable treatment. One North Carolina farm editor, in 1888, bemoaned the railroads' power in his state: "Do they not own the newspapers? Are not all the politicians their dependents? Has not every Judge in the State a free pass in his pocket?"

Crop prices and railroad practices were only two of the farmers' complaints. They protested, too, that local bankers charged 8, 9, or 10 percent interest—or even more—in western and southern states, compared to 6 percent or less in the Northeast. They argued that federal monetary policies contributed to falling prices and thereby compounded their debts. Southern farmers, especially, condemned the tariff for protecting manufacturers against competition from foreign imports, thereby creating artificially high prices on manufactured goods the farmers had to buy. The tariff, however, did nothing for farmers who had to sell their crops abroad and remained, therefore, at the mercy of international cotton and grain markets. Farmers complained that the giant corporations that made farm equipment and fertilizer overcharged them. Even local merchants drew farmers' reproach for charging too much. In the South, where all these problems combined with the sharecrop and crop-lien systems (see page 477–478), many farmers were so deeply in debt they saw little prospect of ever getting out.

Grangers, Greenbackers, and Silverites

After the Civil War, farmers joined organizations that they hoped would provide them some relief. Oliver H. Kelley formed the first, a lodge for farm families, in 1867. Kelley called it the Patrons of Husbandry and gave it a secret ritual modeled on the Masons. Usually known as the **Grange,** the new organization extended full participation to women as well as men. Kelley hoped that the Grange would provide a social outlet for farm families and also educate them to new methods of agriculture. It far exceeded his expectations.

The Grange grew rapidly, especially in the Midwest and the central South. In the 1870s, it became a leading proponent of cooperative buying and selling. Many local Grange organizations set up cooperative stores, and some even tried to sell their crops cooperatively. In cooperative selling, farmers tried to hold their crops back from market and to negotiate over prices rather than simply accepting the

commodity market Financial market in which brokers buy and sell agricultural products in large quantities, thus determining the prices paid to farmers for their harvests.

Grange Association of farmers that combined social activities with education about new methods of farming and cooperative economic efforts; also known as Patrons of Husbandry.

♦ This poster appeared in 1869, two years after the founding of the Grange. It depicts the farmer as a member of the producing class, laboring in the soil to produce value. It shows a military officer, railroad magnate, physician, politician, lawyer, merchant, and preacher as living off the farmer's labor. *Library of Congress.*

prices they were offered. Two state Granges began manufacturing farm machinery, and Grangers laid ambitious plans for cooperative factories producing everything from wagons to sewing machines. Some Grangers formed mutual insurance companies, and a few experimented with cooperative banks.

The Grange defined itself as nonpartisan. As Grange membership rapidly expanded in the 1870s, however, its midwestern and western members soon talked of political action. New political parties emerged in eleven states. Usually called "Granger parties," their most prominent demand was state legislation to prohibit railroad rate discrimination. Other groups, especially merchants, also sought such laws, but the role of the Grangers was so prominent that the resulting state laws, most of them dating from 1872 to 1874, were usually called **Granger laws.**

The Grange reached its zenith in the mid-1870s. Hastily organized cooperatives soon began to suffer financial problems, however, and the collapse of cooperatives often pulled down Grange organizations. Political activity brought some successes but also generated bitter disputes within the Granges. The organization lost many members, and, after the late 1870s, the surviving Granges usually avoided both cooperatives and politics.

With the decline of the Grange and its cooperatives, some farmers looked to monetary policy for relief. After the Civil War, most prices fell (a situation called **deflation**) for several reasons: increased production, more efficient techniques in agriculture and manufacturing, and the failure of the money supply to grow as rapidly as the economy. The Greenback party argued that printing more **greenbacks,** the paper money issued during the Civil War, would stabilize prices. Greenbackers were arguing for the quantity theory of money. According to this view, if the currency (money in circulation, whether of paper or precious metal) grew more rapidly than the economy, the result was inflation (rising prices), but if the currency failed to grow as rapidly as the economy, the outcome was deflation (falling prices).

Greenbackers calling for the federal government to issue more greenbacks found their most receptive audience among farmers who were in debt. In the congressional elections of 1878, the Greenback party received nearly a million votes and elected fourteen congressmen. However, the party proved unsuccessful in attracting votes nationwide. In the 1880 presidential election, the Greenback party endorsed not only inflation but also the eight-hour workday, legislation to protect workers, the abolition of child labor, regulation of transportation and communication, a **graduated income tax,** and woman suffrage. For president, they nominated James B. Weaver of Iowa, a Greenback congressman and former Union army general. Weaver got only 3.3 percent of the vote. In 1884, with a similar platform and the erratic Benjamin Butler as their presidential nominee, the Greenbackers did even worse.

Granger laws State laws establishing standard freight and passenger rates on railroads; they were passed in various states in the 1870s in response to lobbying by the Grange and other groups, including merchants.

deflation Falling prices, a situation in which the purchasing power of the dollar increases.

greenbacks Paper money, not backed up by gold, that the federal government issued during the Civil War.

graduated income tax Percentage tax that is levied on income and varies with income, so that the poor pay at a lower rate than do people who earn more money.

♦ The Grange tries to awaken the public to the approaching locomotive (a symbol of monopoly power) that is bringing consolidation (mergers), extortion (high prices), bribery, and other evils. *Culver Pictures.*

A similar monetary analysis motivated those who wanted the government to resume issuing silver dollars. Until 1873, federal law specified that federal mints would accept gold and silver in unlimited quantities and make them into coins at no charge, as the easiest way to get money into circulation. Throughout much of the nineteenth century, however, owners of silver made more money by selling it commercially than by taking it to the mint. Thus no silver dollars existed for many years. And in 1873, Congress dropped the silver dollar from the list of approved coins, following the lead of Britain and Germany, which had specified that only gold was to serve as money. Some Americans believed that adhering to this **gold standard** was essential if American businesses were to compete effectively in international markets for capital and for the sale of goods.

Soon after 1873, silver discoveries in the West drove down the commercial price of silver. The rallying cry among farmers who wanted inflation was "Free silver at 16 to 1," which meant unlimited coinage of gold and silver, with the weight of the silver in a silver dollar pegged at sixteen times the weight of the gold in a gold dollar. The proposal for **free silver** quickly found support not just among farmers but also among silver-mining interests. Members of this farming-mining coalition were soon called "silverites." In 1878, Congress passed the **Bland-Allison Act,** authorizing a limited amount of silver dollars, but the new law failed to counteract deflation. Silverites condemned it as too little, but gold supporters denounced it for diluting the gold standard. The **Sherman Silver Purchase Act** of 1890 increased the amount of silver to be coined but did not require unlimited coinage of silver. Again, both silverites and advocates of the gold standard were unhappy.

Birth of the People's Party

The Grange had demonstrated the importance of group action, but its decline after the late 1870s left a vacuum among farmers, and the Greenback party did not take its place. In the 1880s, three organizations emerged to fill the void, all called **Farmers' Alliances.** One was centered in the north-central states. Another, usually called the Southern Alliance, began in Texas and spread eastward across the South, absorbing similar local groups along its way. Because the Southern Alliance limited its membership to white farmers, a third group, the Colored Farmers' Alliance, was formed for black farmers. Like the Grange and the Knights of Labor (see page 523), the Alliances defined themselves as part of the "producing classes" and looked to cooperatives as a partial solution to their problems. Alliance stores were most common, but the Texas Alliance experimented with cooperative cotton selling, and some

gold standard A monetary system based on gold; under such a system, legal contracts typically called for the payment of all debts in gold, and paper money could be redeemed in gold at a bank.

free silver The proposal to allow the coinage of all available silver to supplement gold as currency; it was repeatedly suggested as a solution to deflation.

Bland-Allison Act Law passed by Congress in 1878 providing for federal purchase of silver to be coined into silver dollars.

Sherman Silver Purchase Act Law passed by Congress in 1890 requiring the federal government to increase its purchases of silver.

Farmers' Alliances Agricultural organizations of the 1880s and 1890s that carried forward the agrarian cause after the decline of the Grange.

midwestern local Alliances built cooperative **grain elevators.**

Local Alliance meetings featured social and educational activities. The educational program might present information on new agricultural techniques and sometimes focused on political concerns and remedies. By the late 1880s, a host of weekly newspapers across the South and West presented Alliance views. One Kansas woman described the outcome: "People commenced to think who had never thought before, and people talked who had seldom spoken. . . . Everyone was talking and everyone was thinking. . . . Thoughts and theories sprouted like weeds after a May shower."

The Alliances defined themselves as nonpartisan and expected their members to work for Alliance aims within the framework of the major parties. This was especially important in the South, where any white person who challenged the Democratic party risked being condemned as a traitor to both race and region. Although many midwestern Alliance leaders continued the Granger party tradition and some took part in the Greenback efforts of the 1880s, not until the winter of 1889–1890 did widespread farmer support materialize for independent political action in the Midwest. Corn prices had fallen so low that some farmers found it cheaper to burn their corn than to sell it and buy fuel.

As the Fifty-first Congress argued over the McKinley Tariff and the Sherman Silver Purchase Act through the hot summer of 1890, members of the Farmers' Alliance in Kansas, Nebraska, the Dakotas, Minnesota, and surrounding states formed new political parties to contest state and local elections. One leader explained that the political battle they waged was "between the insatiable greed of organized wealth and the rights of the great plain people." Organization of the new party began a decade of political change.

Soon dubbed the People's party, or Populists, the grassroots party was launched by parades of farm wagons passing down the dusty main streets of scores of country towns. The festivities ended with a picnic and rally, where speakers decried the plight of the farmer and proclaimed the sacred cause of the new party. Women took a prominent part in Populist campaigning, especially in Kansas and Nebraska. Mary Elizabeth Lease was among the most effective. A tall, red-haired woman from Kansas who had studied law while doing housework, she acquired lasting fame when newspapers quoted her as urging farmers to "Raise less corn and more hell!" Alliance newspapers throughout the region published new words to familiar songs:

I was once a tool of oppression,
And as green as a sucker could be,
And monopolies banded together
To beat a poor hayseed like me.

The railroads and old party bosses
Together did sweetly agree;
And they thought there would be little trouble
In working a hayseed like me. . . .

But now I've roused up a little
And their greed and corruption I see . . .
And the ticket we vote next November
Will be made up of hayseeds like me.

(Sung to the tune of "Save a Poor Sinner Like Me")

The Populists emphasized three elements in their platforms, speeches, and other campaign materials: **antimonopolism,** government action on behalf of farmers and workers, and increased popular control of government. Their antimonopolism drew on their own unhappy experiences with railroads, grain buyers, and the companies that manufactured farm equipment and supplies. But it derived as well from a long American tradition of opposition to concentrated economic power. Populists quoted Thomas Jefferson on the need for equal rights for all, and they compared themselves to Andrew Jackson in his fight against the Bank of the United States.

"We believe the time has come," Populists proclaimed in 1892, "when the railroad companies will either own the people or the people must own the railroads." The Populists' solution to the dangers of monopoly was government action on behalf of farmers and workers, including federal ownership of the railroads and the telegraph and telephone systems, and government alternatives to private banks. Some Populists also endorsed a scheme of the Southern Alliance called the Sub-Treasury Plan, under which crops stored in government ware-

grain elevator Storehouses for grain located near railroad tracks; such structures were equipped with mechanical lifting devices that permitted the grain to be loaded into railroad cars.

antimonopolism Opposition to monopolies—that is, to great concentrations of economic power such as trusts and giant corporations, as well as to actual monopolies.

♦ When the Populists launched their new party, one cartoonist depicted them as a hot-air balloon of political malcontents. This cartoon may have inspired Frank Baum, author of *The Wizard of Oz,* whose wizard arrived in Oz in a hot-air balloon launched from Omaha, the site of the Populists' 1892 nominating convention. *Library of Congress.*

houses might be collateral for low-interest loans to farmers. Populists also demanded inflation (through greenbacks, silver, or both) and a graduated income tax. They had some following within what remained of the Knights of Labor, and they hoped to gain broad support among urban and industrial workers. Their platform called for the eight-hour workday and prohibition of private armies like the Pinkerton agents that Henry Clay Frick used against the Homestead strikers (see page 527).

Finally, the People's party favored a series of structural changes to make government more responsive to the people, including expansion of the merit system for government employees, election of U.S. senators by the voters instead of by state legislatures, a one-term limit for the president, the secret ballot, and the **initiative** and **referendum.** Many of them also favored woman suffrage. In the South, they not only opposed disfranchisement of black voters but also posed a serious challenge to the prevailing patterns of politics by seeking to forge a political alliance of the disadvantaged of both races.

Thus the Populists wanted to use government to control, even to own, the corporate behemoths that had evolved in their lifetimes. And they wanted to increase the influence of the individual voter in political decision-making—this antiparty attitude was rooted in their distrust of the old parties.

The Elections of 1890 and 1892

The issues in the 1890 elections for members of the House of Representatives and for state and local offices varied by region. In the West, the Populists stood at the center of the campaign, lambasting both major parties for ignoring the needs of the people. In the South, Democrats held up Lodge's "force bill" as a symbol of the dangers posed by any who bolted the party of white supremacy. There, members of the Southern Alliance worked within the Democratic party to secure candidates committed to the farmers' cause. In the Northeast, Democrats attacked the McKinley Tariff for producing higher prices for consumers. In the Rocky Mountain region, nearly all candidates pledged their support for unlimited silver coinage. In parts of the Midwest, Democrats scourged Republicans for supporting prohibition and other laws unpopular with German Americans.

The new Populist party scored a number of victories, marking it as the most successful new party since the appearance of the Republicans in the 1850s. Kansas Republican senator John J. Ingalls had dismissed Populists as "a sort of turnip crusade," but so many Populists won election to the Kansas legislature that they were able to elect a Populist to replace Ingalls in the Senate. Populists in other states also elected state legislators, representatives in the House, and one other U.S. senator. All across the South, the Alliance claimed that successful Democratic candidates owed their victories to Alliance voters.

initiative Procedure allowing any group of people to propose a law by gathering signatures on a petition; the proposed law is then voted on by the electorate.

referendum Procedure whereby a bill or constitutional amendment is submitted to the voters for their approval after having been passed by a legislative body.

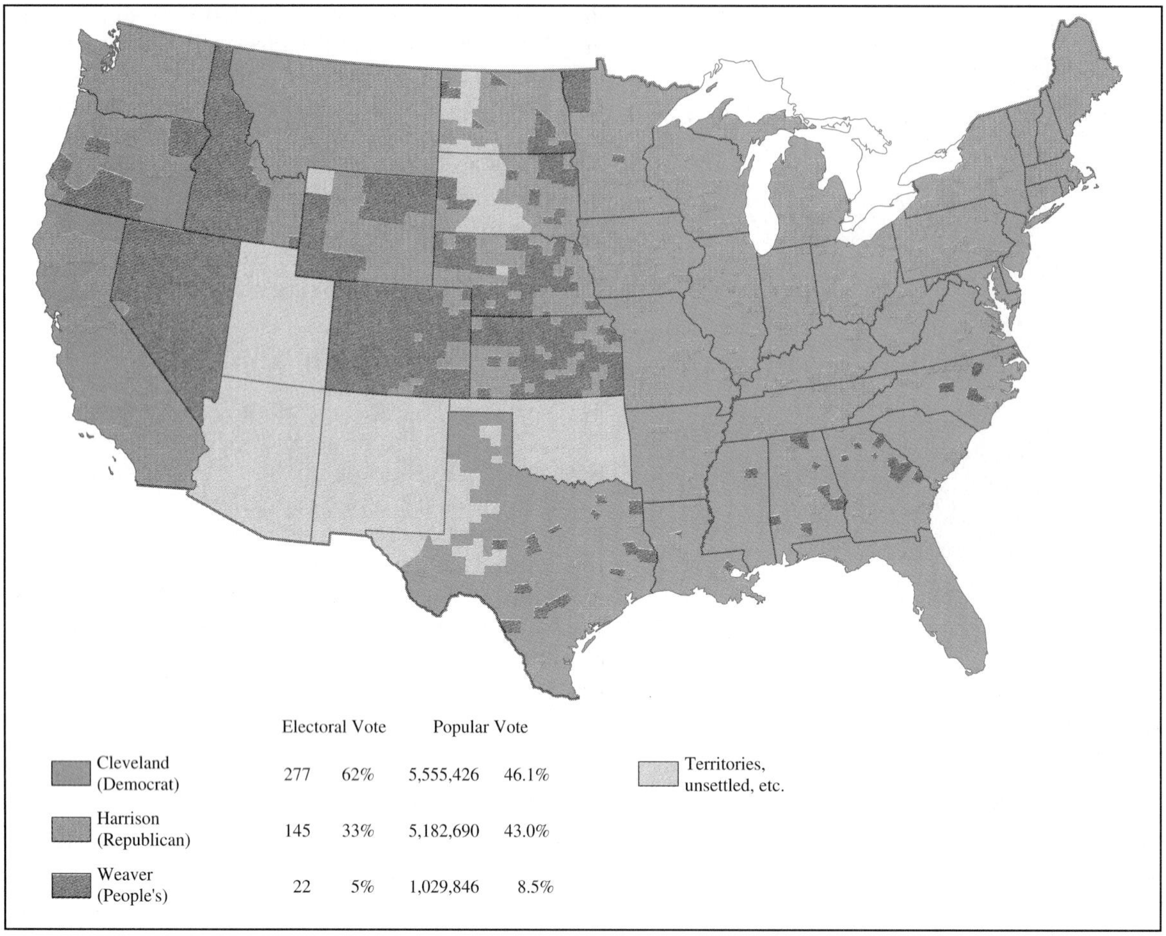

♦ **MAP 20.1 Popular Vote for Weaver, 1892** The Populist party's presidential candidate, James B. Weaver, made a strong showing in 1892. This map indicates that his support was concentrated regionally in the West and South, and that he had relatively little support in the northeastern states.

Everywhere Republicans suffered defeat, losing to Populists in the West and to Democrats in the Midwest and Northeast. In the House of Representatives, the Republicans went from 166 seats in 1889 to only 88 in 1891. Many Republican candidates for state and local offices also lost. Republican disappointment in the results of the 1890 elections bred dissension within the party, and President Benjamin Harrison proved unable to maintain even a semblance of party unity.

With the approach of the 1892 presidential election, the Republicans renominated Harrison despite a lack of enthusiasm among many party leaders. The Democrats chose Grover Cleveland as their candidate again. Farmers' Alliance activists from the South joined western Populists to form a national People's party and to nominate James Weaver, who had run for president as a Greenbacker twelve years earlier. Democrats and Populists earned the most impressive victories. Cleveland secured 46.1 percent of the popular vote, becoming the only president in American history to win two nonconsecutive terms. Harrison got 43 percent, and Weaver captured 8.5 percent. The Democrats kept control of the House of Representatives and, for the first time in twelve years, also won the Senate. Despite their weak showing nationally, Populists displayed strength in the West and South (see Map 20.1). The Democrats now found themselves where the Republicans had stood four years before: in control of the presidency and the Congress and potentially able to translate their promises into law.

Economic Collapse and Political Upheaval

- What choices did voters face in the 1896 presidential election?
- What were the long-term outcomes of that election?

After the Democrats swept to power in the 1892 elections, they suddenly faced difficult choices. Could they fulfill their campaign promises for tariff reform? Could they also halt the collapse of the national economy into a serious depression? The Democrats' failure to stabilize the economy opened the door to Republican victories in 1894 and 1896. When the Democrats in 1896 adopted some of the Populists' more moderate issues and nominated a candidate sympathetic to many Populist goals, they forced the new party to make a critical choice. Should Populists support the Democrats and risk losing their own identity as a party, or should they run their own candidate and guarantee a Republican victory?

Economic Collapse and Depression

Ten days before Cleveland took office, the Reading Railroad declared bankruptcy. A financial panic quickly set in. One business journal reported in August that "never before has there been such a sudden and striking cessation of industrial activity. . . . Mills, factories, furnaces, mines nearly everywhere shut down in large numbers." More than fifteen thousand businesses failed in 1893, more proportionately than in any year since the depression of the 1870s.

At the time, no one really understood why the economy collapsed so suddenly and so completely. In retrospect, the downturn seems to have resulted from immediate precipitating events and underlying structural weaknesses. The collapse of a major English bank led some British investors to call back some of their investments in the United States. This setback, combined with the reduction in federal revenues caused by the McKinley Tariff, resulted in a sharp decline in federal **gold reserves.** And this calamity, in turn, combined with the bankruptcy of a few large companies. As a result, the stock market crashed in May and June 1893, bringing on a depression.

The major underlying factors included the slowing of agricultural expansion and railroad construction. Railroad building drove the industrial economy in the 1880s. In the 1890s, however, some companies found they did not have sufficient traffic on their new tracks to pay their fixed costs. Several large lines declared bankruptcy, including the Erie, Northern Pacific, Santa Fe, and Union Pacific. By 1894, almost one-fifth of the nation's railroad mileage had fallen into bankruptcy, and railroad construction fell by half between 1893 and 1895.

The sharp decline in railroad construction produced a domino effect, toppling industries that supplied the railroads, especially steel. Production of steel rails fell by more than a third between 1892 and 1894, and thirty-two steel companies joined the early business failures. Banks that had invested in railroads and in steel companies collapsed along with those companies. Nearly five hundred banks failed in 1893 alone, and more than five hundred more closed by the end of 1897, equivalent to one bank out of every ten.

No agency kept careful records on unemployment, but a third or more of the wage earners in manufacturing may have been out of work. During the winter of 1893–1894, Chicago counted one hundred thousand unemployed—roughly two workers out of five. Many who kept their jobs received smaller paychecks, as employers cut wages and hours. In 1892, the average nonfarm wage earner received $482 per year. By 1894, this fell to $420.

The depression produced widespread suffering. Many of those who lost their jobs had little to fall back on except the soup dispensed by charities—if soup kitchens could be found. Newspapers told of people who chose suicide when faced with starving to death or stealing food. Susan Orcutt, a Kansas farm wife nearly nine months pregnant, saw the worst of both farm poverty and depression unemployment:

> *I take my Pen In hand to let you know that we are Starving to death It is Pretty hard to do without any thing to Eat hear in this God for saken country we would have had Plenty to Eat if the hail hadent cut our rye down and ruined our corn and Potatoes . . . My Husband went a way to find work and came home last night and told me that we would have to Starve he has bin in ten countys and did not Get no work*

Like Orcutt's husband, many men and some women left home desperate to find work, hoping to send money to their families as soon as they could. Some walked the roads, but most hopped on freight

gold reserves The stockpile of gold with which the federal government backed up the currency.

♦ In 1894, Jacob Coxey, an Ohio Populist, led his "petition in boots" on a march from Ohio to Washington, D.C., demanding that Congress provide public-works jobs to the unemployed. *Library of Congress.*

trains, riding in **boxcars.** A few found work, but most failed. Some families were never reunited.

A dramatic demonstration against unemployment began in late January 1894, when Ohio Populist Jacob S. Coxey proposed that the government hire the unemployed to build roads and repair public works and pay them with greenbacks, thereby inflating the currency. When he called on the unemployed to join him in a march on Washington to push this program, the response electrified the nation. All across the country but especially in the West, men and women tried to join the march. Given the vast distances, some western groups hijacked trains (fifty in all) and headed east pulling boxcars loaded with unemployed men. (None of the pirated trains traveled far before authorities stopped them and arrested the leaders.) Several thousand people took part in Coxey's march in some way, but most never reached Washington or reached it too late.

When Coxey and his group of several hundred did arrive in Washington, they learned that he would not be permitted to speak at the Capitol building. When he tried to do so anyway, on May 1, police arrested him and others for trespassing on the grounds of the Capitol. Mounted police with clubs dispersed the crowd. Even so, the trek of **Coxey's Army** marked the first time that so many protesters had gone to Washington and the first time that so many had urged federal officials to create jobs for the unemployed.

The Divided Democrats

When Congress met in 1893, the majority Democrats faced several demanding issues. Their platform committed them to cut the tariff, but the party disagreed over how to do that. The other thorn in their side was the Sherman Silver Purchase Act. Many business leaders opposed the Sherman legislation as the cause of the gold drain that set off the depres-

boxcar An enclosed railroad car with sliding side doors, used to transport freight.

Coxey's Army Unemployed workers led by Jacob S. Coxey who marched to Washington to demand relief measures from Congress following the depression of 1893.

sion, but many western and southern Democrats supported it as better than no silver coinage at all. On top of these issues, the depression and unemployment demanded attention. President Cleveland held to his staunch beliefs in minimal government and laissez faire. To him, it was inappropriate for the government to alleviate the suffering of the unemployed. Further, in the midst of the nation's financial crisis, Cleveland suffered a personal crisis. Doctors detected cancer in his mouth. Fearing that news of his condition might contribute to further financial panic, the president kept his surgery and recuperation secret.

Convinced that silver coinage had contributed to the economic collapse, Cleveland asked Congress to repeal the Sherman Act (see Individual Choices: Grover Cleveland). In the House of Representatives, most Republicans voted for repeal, but more than a third of the Democrats voted against their own president. In the Senate, Republicans supported Cleveland by 2 to 1, but Democrats divided almost evenly. Cleveland won, but at a disastrous political cost: he divided his party, pitting the Northeast against the West and much of the South. On other occasions, Cleveland also took positions that conservatives applauded as "principled" and "courageous" but that failed to unite the increasingly divided Democrats.

The Democrats still faced the major challenge of the tariff. After their outspoken condemnation of the McKinley Tariff, they now had to demonstrate that they kept their word. The tariff bill produced by the House Ways and Means Committee in late 1893 reduced duties, tried to balance sectional interests, and created an income tax as a means of recovering lost federal revenue. The House passed it in February 1894. In the Senate, however, Democrats held a thin majority. There some Democrats, trying to protect industries in their own states, produced so many amendments and compromises that Cleveland characterized the resulting Wilson-Gorman Tariff as "party dishonor." He refused to sign it, and it became law without his signature. (The Supreme Court soon declared the income tax unconstitutional.)

Voters recorded their disgust with the disorganized Democrats in the 1894 elections. Democrats lost everywhere but in the Deep South, giving up 113 seats. Republicans scored their biggest gain in Congress ever, adding 117. In only a few places did voters turn to the Populists, and the party lost support in some of its previous strongholds. Most voters turned decisively to the Republicans, who began to look forward eagerly to the approaching 1896 presidential election.

♦ Political buttons with pins attached to the back were patented shortly before the 1896 presidential campaign, and they were in great abundance that year. The Bryan-Sewall button pictured shows a clock at 16 minutes to 1, a reference to the Democratic party's commitment to increase the coinage of silver dollars, with a ratio of 16:1 between the weight of silver in a silver dollar to the weight of gold in a gold dollar. The McKinley campaign made a strenuous effort to reach all organized groups that might support their candidate and to appeal to their group's interest. This button celebrates support for McKinley by a wheelmen's club, that is, an organization of bicyclists. *Collection of Janice L. and David J. Frent.*

Repeal of the Sherman Act failed to stop the flow of gold from the treasury as investors responded to economic uncertainties by converting their securities to gold. The gold reserve fell dangerously low, causing some to fear that the government might be unable to meet its obligations. In desperation, in 1895 Cleveland turned to J. P. Morgan for assistance in floating a bond issue to restore the gold reserve. The hapless Cleveland came under renewed criticism, both for the price paid to Morgan and for going to Morgan—symbol of Wall Street and the trusts—in the first place.

The 1896 Election: Bryan Versus McKinley, Silver Versus Protection

When Republicans met in St. Louis to nominate a candidate for president, **William McKinley** was the leading prospect. A Union veteran who had risen to the rank of major, he won election to the House of Representatives in 1876 and built a solid reputation there, specializing in the tariff. He lost his congressional seat in 1890 but won the Ohio governorship

William McKinley Republican who defeated William Jennings Bryan in presidential elections in 1896 and 1900; he led the country into the Spanish-American War and was shot by an anarchist in 1901.

INDIVIDUAL CHOICES

Choosing Principle over Party

Grover Cleveland

President Grover Cleveland, confronted with a shattered economy, had to choose between his conservative principles and maintaining the unity of his party. Portrait Grover Cleveland by Anders Zorn. National Portrait Gallery, Smithsonian Institution/ Art Resource, NY.

Grover Cleveland took the presidential oath of office for the second time on March 4, 1893. Soon after, he faced a series of choices so difficult that he had every reason to expect intense criticism no matter what decision he made or what outcome resulted. He could not escape from making the choices, either, for he was afraid that the economic collapse that began shortly before he took office might threaten even the federal government itself.

Like many in his day, Cleveland held a traditional expectation about money. Because money must have intrinsic value, he contended, only precious metals could serve as money. In 1885, during his first term as president, he urged Congress to repeal the silver coinage act passed in 1878, on the grounds that the United States by itself could not maintain both gold and silver as money. To attempt to do so, Cleveland feared, would inevitably mean that gold would leave the country. Congress, however, refused to follow his advice in 1885.

When Cleveland's first presidency ended in 1889, the government's gold reserves stood at $197 million. When he took office again in 1893,

the next year and was re-elected by a large margin in 1893. Known as a calm and competent leader, able to manage people and affairs without making enemies, McKinley billed himself as the "Advance Agent of Prosperity." He and his campaign manager, Marcus A. Hanna, planned their preconvention strategy so well that McKinley won on the first ballot, by a 3 to 1 margin over four rivals. Hanna, a retired Ohio industrialist known as both amiable and blunt, cared for organizational details, but McKinley decided on the direction of the campaign. The Republican platform pronounced in favor of the gold standard and against silver, but McKinley preferred to focus on the tariff. When the convention voted against silver, several western Republicans walked out of the convention and out of the party.

When the Democratic convention met, silverites held the majority but were not united behind any one candidate. The platform committee chose **William Jennings Bryan** of Nebraska to close a convention debate on silver. Blessed with a commanding

William Jennings Bryan Nebraska congressman who advocated free coinage of silver, opposed imperialism, and ran for president unsuccessfully three times on the Democratic ticket.

his earlier fears seemed to be coming true, for the gold reserves had fallen to $103.5 million. This was dangerously close to the $100 million mark that Congress had earlier fixed as the point below which the nation might not be able to maintain the gold standard. The decline in gold reserves was in part the result of cuts in tariff revenues and greatly increased federal expenditures approved by the Republican Congress of 1889–1890. Another factor was widespread anxiety about the economy. Uncertain about the future, many investors chose to liquidate their holdings in return for gold. The shrinking gold reserves alarmed Cleveland.

Because so many business and financial leaders shared the expectation that money must have intrinsic value, they argued that silver coinage (authorized under the Sherman Silver Purchase Act) was dishonest because it required that silver worth only 53 cents on the open market be made into a dollar coin. The president was pressured from one side by bankers and manufacturers eager to end silver coinage and to restore the gold reserve, and from the other side by members of his own party hostile to banking interests and favorable to silver coinage. Cleveland thus faced a difficult choice. Should he do what he believed to be necessary to maintain the nation's financial integrity? Or should he compromise and thereby preserve the unity of the Democratic party and his own political popularity?

In the midst of these pressures and counterpressures, Cleveland demonstrated his courage when he underwent surgery to remove a cancer from the roof of his mouth and kept his illness secret. Seriously weakened by the surgery and uncertain that he was out of danger, Cleveland labored over a message to a special session of Congress. In his message, he made his choice clear: he asked Congress to repeal the Sherman Silver Purchase Act, knowing his action would badly divide his own party and bring on himself an avalanche of criticism.

The battle in Congress over repeal of the Sherman Silver Purchase Act was hard fought. Cleveland at times felt depressed about the prospects for success, once writing that "if I did not believe in God I should be sick at heart." But he stubbornly refused all efforts at compromise and took comfort in the knowledge that he was following his sense of integrity and duty. "I think so often of Martin Luther's 'Here I stand—God help me,'" he told a friend.

The immediate outcome was that Cleveland won in Congress, with the assistance of most Republicans and some Democrats, including some who had previously opposed him. Another outcome was that Cleveland confirmed his personal reputation for integrity, courage, and stubbornness. But the most far-reaching outcome was that the president had splintered the Democratic party and doomed any hopes he may have had for leading it.

voice, Bryan had won election to the House of Representatives in 1890 and 1892 and had achieved national attention for his eloquent defense of silver during debate on repeal of the Sherman Act.

Bryan's speech at the convention was masterful. Defining the issue as a conflict between "the producing masses" and "the idle holders of idle capital," he argued that the first priority of federal policy should be "to make the masses prosperous," rather than to benefit the rich and hope that "their prosperity will leak through on those below." His closing rang defiant: "We will answer their demand for a gold standard by saying to them: You shall not press down upon the brow of labor this crown of thorns. You shall not crucify mankind upon a cross of gold." The speech provoked an enthusiastic half-hour demonstration in support of silver and, even more so, of Bryan. Only 36 years old and not a declared candidate before his speech, Bryan won the nomination on the fifth ballot.

Populists and another splinter party, the Silver Republicans, held nominating conventions next, amid frustration that the Democrats had stolen their thunder. Given Bryan's commitment to silver, to the income tax, and to a broad range of reforms that they also favored—and given the close working relationship Bryan had developed with Populists in his home state—Populists felt compelled to give him

♦ In 1896, William Jennings Bryan (left), candidate of the Democratic, Populist, and Silver Republican parties, traveled some eighteen thousand miles in three months, speaking to about five million people. William McKinley (right), the Republican, stayed home in Canton, Ohio, greeting thousands of well-wishers. *Bryan: Nebraska State Historical Society; McKinley: Ohio Historical Society.*

their nomination too. Silver Republicans did the same. Subsequently, a group of Cleveland supporters held a convention and nominated a Gold Democratic candidate.

Bryan and McKinley both fought an all-out campaign, but they used sharply contrasting tactics. Bryan, vigorous and young, knew that his speaking voice was his greatest campaign tool. He took his case directly to the voters in four grueling train journeys through twenty-six states and more than 250 cities. Speaking to perhaps 5 million people in all, he stressed over and over that the most important issue was silver and that other reforms would follow once it was settled. He found large crowds of excited and enthusiastic supporters nearly everywhere he went.

McKinley stayed at home in Canton, Ohio, and campaigned from his front porch, but the Republican party carried the campaign to the voters for him, flooding the country with speakers, pamphlets, and campaign paraphernalia. The party also chartered trains and brought thousands of supporters to hear McKinley. Canton became accustomed to daily parades marching from the train station to McKinley's house. Many business leaders feared that Bryan and silver coinage would bring complete financial collapse, and they opposed Bryan's other proposals such as the income tax and lower tariff rates. Hanna played on such fears to secure a campaign fund more than double the size of any previous effort, and many times what the Democrats were able to raise.

McKinley won, taking 51 percent of the popular vote and 23 states with 271 electoral votes. Bryan received just under 47 percent of the vote and won 22

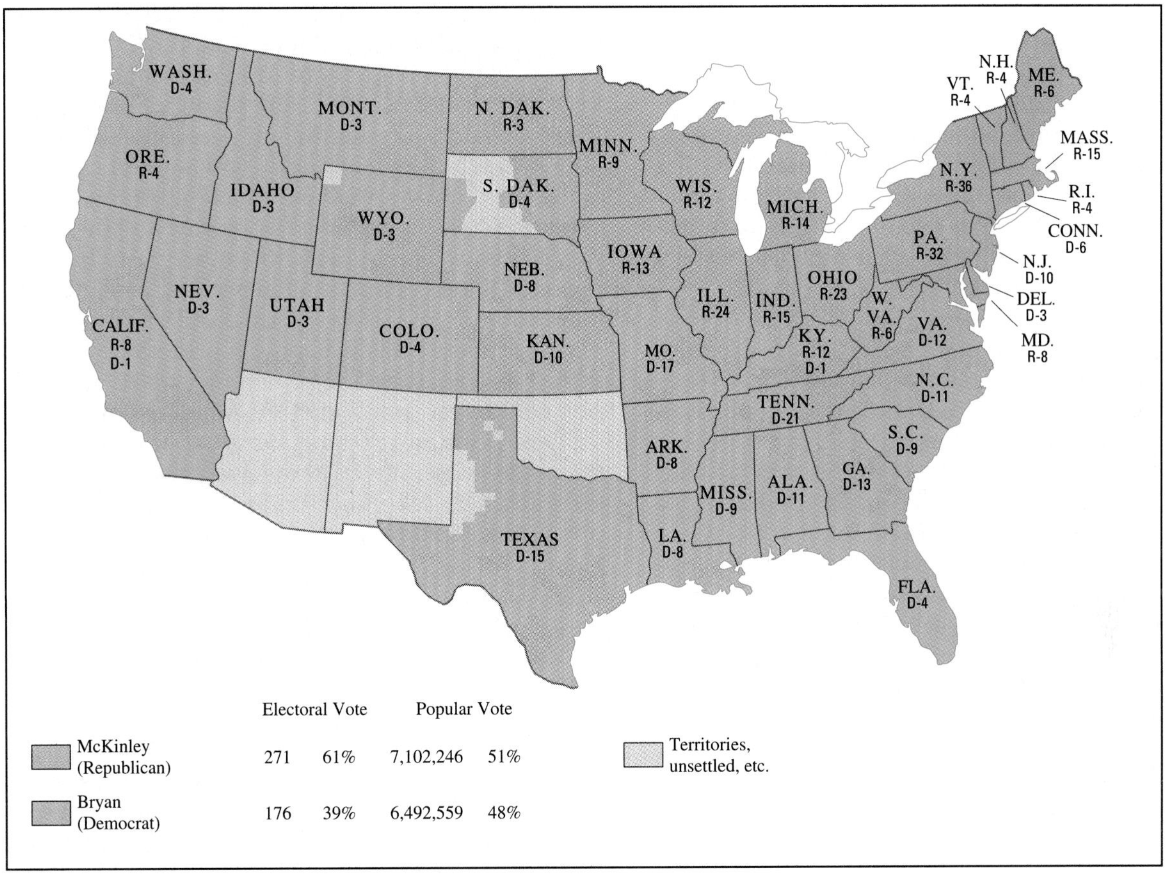

♦ **MAP 20.2 Election of 1896** Bryan could not win with just the votes of the South and West, for they had few electoral votes. Even if he won all the West, South, and border states, he still needed one or more northeastern states. McKinley won in the urban, industrial core region and the more prosperous farming areas of the Midwest.

states and 176 electoral votes. In both the popular vote and the electoral vote, McKinley scored the largest margin of victory since 1872. As Map 20.2 indicates, Bryan carried the South and nearly the entire West. McKinley's victory came in the urban, industrial Northeast (compare Map 20.2 to the map on page 562). Of the twenty largest cities in the nation, only New Orleans went for Bryan. The crucial battleground was the Midwest, and Bryan lost most of it. McKinley carried not only urban, industrial regions but also many farming areas.

Bryan's defeat spelled the end of the Populist party, as its supporters moved in different directions. Some of them moved into Bryan's Democratic party, but a few tried to hold together the tattered remnants of Populism. Others joined the Socialist party, others returned to the Republican party, and a few simply ignored politics. The Populists' influence lived on, however, especially in Bryan's wing of the Democratic party.

After 1896: The New Republican Majority

The presidential election of 1896 stands as one of the most important in American history. The campaigns of 1896 focused on economic issues, sharpened by the depression. Bryan's silver crusade appealed most to debt-ridden farmers and western miners. McKinley forged a broader appeal by emphasizing the gold standard and protective tariff as keys to economic recovery. For many urban residents—

workers and the middle class alike—silver seemed to promise higher prices, but the protective tariff meant manufacturing jobs. McKinley also won, in part, because he put a damper on his party's usual sympathy for moral reforms such as prohibition. Playing down ethnic divisions and condemning the anti-Catholic American Protective Association made it easier for McKinley to win support among immigrants, especially Germans, who approved of his stand on gold and the tariff.

McKinley's victory ushered in a generation of Republican dominance of national politics. The depression and the political campaigns of the 1890s caused some voters to re-evaluate their partisan commitments and to change parties. After 1896, no one could doubt that the Republicans were the national majority. Republicans ruled in the House of Representatives for twenty-eight of the thirty-six years after 1894, and in the Senate for thirty of those thirty-six years. Republicans won seven of the nine presidential elections between 1896 and 1932. Similar patterns of Republican dominance appeared in state and local government, especially in the manufacturing belt.

The events of the 1890s also worked significant changes in the Democratic party. As Bryan solidified his hold on the leadership of the Democratic party over the next sixteen years, he and his allies moved the party away from its commitment to minimal government and laissez faire. While retaining Democrats' traditional distrust of monopoly and opposition to government favoritism toward business, Bryan and other new Democratic leaders agreed with the Populists that the solution to the problems of economic concentration lay in a more active government that could limit monopoly power. "A private monopoly," Bryan never tired of repeating, "is indefensible and intolerable." In other ways, the Democrats changed little. They remained committed to states' rights that permitted the southern wing of the party to perpetuate white-supremacist regimes. Most northern Democrats continued to oppose nativism and moral reform.

McKinley provided strong executive leadership and worked closely with leaders of his party in Congress to develop and implement new policies. In 1897, a revised protective tariff, the **Dingley Tariff,** fulfilled Republican campaign promises. It reduced the list of imports that could enter the nation without paying the tariff, and it drove tariff rates even higher than had the 1890 McKinley Tariff. The surplus disappeared as an issue after 1892, primarily as a result of significantly larger military and naval expenditures (see page 641). In 1900, the **Gold Standard Act** wrote that Republican commitment into law.

Although the majority of American voters considered themselves Republican, many of them held their new party commitments less intensely than before. Before 1890, for most voters, ethnicity and choice of party went hand in hand. Now voters sometimes felt pulled toward one party by their economic situation and toward the other party by their ethnicity. Such voters sometimes voted a split ticket, supporting Republicans for some offices and Democrats for others. This was now much easier because of the Australian ballot. Sometimes voters resolved their conflicts by not voting. As more and more government positions became subject to the merit system, there were fewer and fewer rewards for the party workers who once labored so strenuously to mobilize voters on election day. Voter participation began to decline, dropping from 79 percent in 1896 to 65 percent in 1908 to 59 percent in 1912.

The political role of newspapers also changed. In the 1890s, technological advances in paper manufacturing and printing, together with increasing numbers of literate adults, made possible the emergence of mass circulation newspapers. Enterprising publishers, notably William Randolph Hearst and Joseph Pulitzer, transformed large urban newspapers, competing for the largest circulation through eye-catching headlines and sensational stories. As they focused on increasing their circulation and advertising, they also played down their ties to political parties. Some journalists began to develop the idea of providing balanced coverage of both parties.

American politics in 1888 looked much like American politics in 1876 or even 1844. But in the 1890s, American politics turned a corner. In the early 1900s, the continued decline of political parties and partisan loyalties among voters combined with the emergence of organized interest groups to create even more change, producing the major structural features of American politics in the twentieth century.

Dingley Tariff Tariff passed by Congress in 1897 that set a high protective tariff, averaging 57 percent.

Gold Standard Act Law passed by Congress in 1900 that made gold the monetary standard for all currency issued.

SUMMARY

E xpectations
C onstraints
C hoices
O utcomes

Americans in the late nineteenth century *expected* political parties to dominate politics. All elected public officials were nominated by party conventions and elected through efforts of party campaigners. Most civil service employees were appointed in return for party loyalty. Republicans *chose* to use government to promote rapid economic development, but Democrats argued that government is best when it governs least. Most voters divided between the major parties along the lines of ethnicity, race, and religion.

Some people rejected the *constraints* of party government and sought reform. Mugwumps argued for the merit system in the civil service, accomplished through the Pendleton Act of 1883. By the late nineteenth century, a well-organized woman suffrage movement had also emerged. Gilded Age reformers sought both structural changes and policy changes.

The closely balanced strengths of the two parties contributed to a long-term political stalemate. The presidency of Ulysses S. Grant was plagued by scandals. Presidents Rutherford B. Hayes, James A. Garfield, and Chester A. Arthur faced stormy conflict between Republican factions. As president, Grover Cleveland approved the Interstate Commerce Act. Republicans broke the *constraints* of stalemate in 1889, passing the McKinley Tariff, Sherman Anti-Trust Act, Sherman Silver Purchase Act, and other measures. But voters turned against the Republicans in 1890.

The 1890s saw important and long-lasting changes in political patterns and people's *expectations* for politics. The political upheaval began when western and southern farmers turned to political action. In the 1870s, the Grange organized cooperatives and promoted regulatory laws to resolve farmers' economic problems. In the 1880s, several groups proposed currency inflation through paper or silver money. In 1890, members of the Farmers' Alliances *chose* to launch a new political party, usually called Populists. In 1892, voters rejected the Republicans in many areas, *choosing* either the new Populist party or the Democrats.

President Grover Cleveland proved unable to meet the political challenges of a major depression that began in 1893. In 1896, the Democrats *chose* as their presidential candidate William Jennings Bryan, a critic of Cleveland and supporter of silver coinage. The Republicans *chose* William McKinley, who favored the protective tariff as most likely to end the depression. McKinley won, and important long-term *outcomes* were felt well into the twentieth century. First was the beginning of Republican dominance in national politics that lasted until 1930. And second, under Bryan's leadership, the Democratic party discarded its commitment to minimal government and instead adopted a willingness to use government against monopolies and other powerful economic interests.

SUGGESTED READINGS

James Bryce. *The American Commonwealth.* 2 vols. (1889).

A fascinating firsthand account of the politics of this period.

Robert W. Cherny. *American Politics in the Gilded Age, 1868–1900* (1997).

The most recent survey of the politics of this period.

Lewis Gould. *The Presidency of William McKinley* (1980).

A major contribution to historians' understanding of McKinley's presidency.

Suzanne Lebsock. "Women and American Politics, 1880–1920." In *Women, Politics, and Change,* ed. Louise A. Tilly and Patricia Gurin (1990).

An overview of women and politics, incorporating summaries of much of the most interesting recent research.

Henry M. Littlefield. "The Wizard of Oz: Parable on Populism." *American Quarterly* 16 (1964): 47–58.

An interesting account of populism's influence on a children's classic, but an account that has been challenged by L. Frank Baum's most recent biographer.

Robert C. McMath. Jr. *American Populism: A Social History, 1877–1898* (1993).

A brief introduction to the populist movement.

R. Hal Williams. *Years of Decision: American Politics in the 1890s* (1978).

A concise survey of national politics, strongest on congressional decision-making.

EXPANSION OF THE UNITED STATES, 1865–1917 As a result of the Spanish-American War, the United States acquired island possessions stretching half-way around the world, from Puerto Rico to the Philippines. These and other acquisitions established the United States as one of the major powers in the Pacific and East Asia, and as the dominant power in the Caribbean.

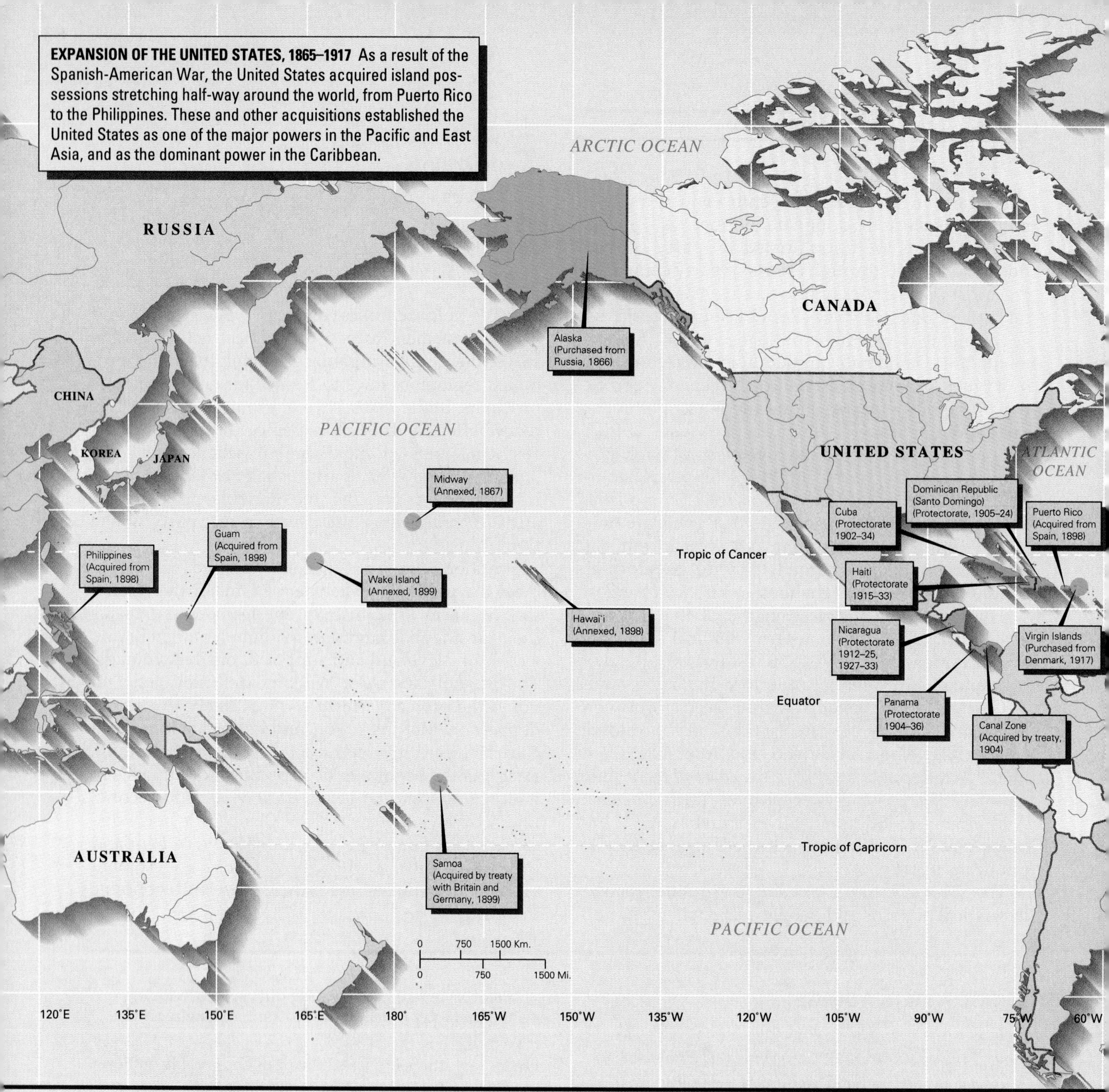

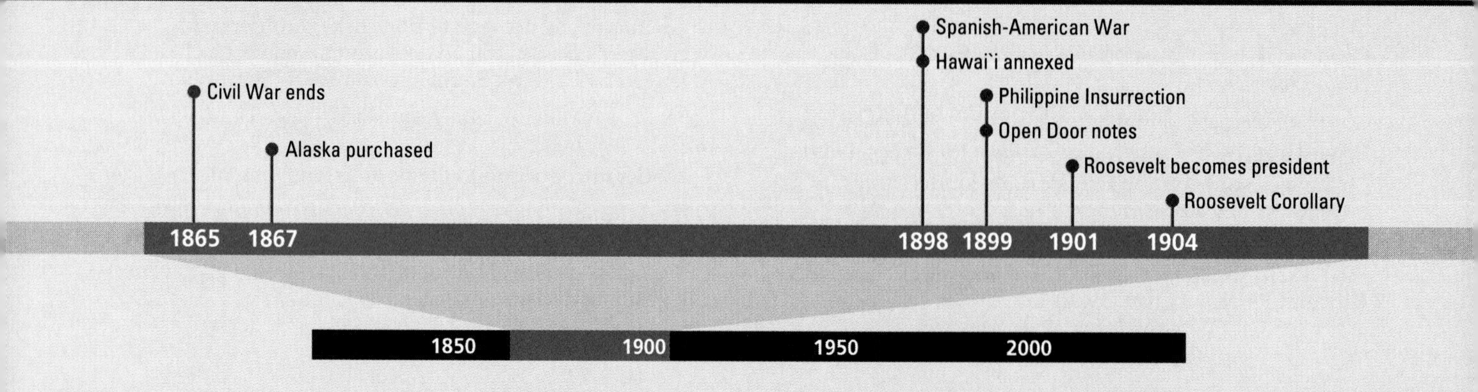

CHAPTER 21

Becoming a World Power: America and World Affairs, 1865–1913

The United States and World Affairs, 1865–1889

- How did American choices with regard to Alaska and Latin America reflect traditional expectations about world affairs?
- How did American choices with regard to eastern Asia and the Pacific reflect new conditions in world affairs?

Stepping Cautiously in World Affairs, 1889–1897

- How and why did some Americans' expectations about the U.S. role in world affairs begin to change between 1889 and 1897?
- What were the policy implications of these changes?

Striding Boldly: War and Imperialism, 1897–1901

- What were the outcomes of the war with Spain?
- What new expectations about America's role in world affairs were expressed in the debate over the acquisition of new possessions?

"Carry a Big Stick": The United States and World Affairs, 1901–1913

- What were Theodore Roosevelt's expectations about the role of the United States in world affairs?
- What choices did he make to bring about the outcomes he desired?

INTRODUCTION

In 1898, the United States went to war with Spain and quickly inflicted a stinging defeat. The *choice* to go to war climaxed a turnabout in American *expectations* regarding foreign affairs. During much of the nineteenth century, a time of far-reaching economic, social, and political change, the nation's role in world affairs was slight at best, and most Americans *expected* that their nation would stay out of foreign conflicts. George Washington had recommended that the nation "steer clear of permanent alliances with any portion of the foreign world." In 1823, President James Monroe warned the nations of Europe to stay out of the affairs of the independent nations of North and South America.

Through much of the nineteenth century, Americans had few worries about being pulled into European wars, for Europe remained relatively peaceful. The insulation imposed by the Atlantic and Pacific reinforced Americans' feeling of security, and the powerful British navy provided a protective umbrella for American commercial shipping. Thus world events posed few threats to American territory or commerce.

At the same time, as the *outcome* of treaties with European nations and war against Mexico, the nation expanded across the North American continent. "Manifest destiny"—the belief that God or Nature had destined the United States to spread its republican institutions throughout North America—fueled widespread *expectations* of continued expansion.

In the late nineteenth century, however, the United States took a place among the leading industrial nations of the world and had the potential to *choose* a powerful role in world affairs. The simultaneous emergence of two other industrial and, soon, naval giants—Germany and Japan—contributed to a growing instability in world affairs, as the British navy faced serious challenges to its domination of the seas. Japan joined the European powers in a race for empire in which much of the world seemed fair game for colonial capture. In Africa, major European nations scrambled to claim territory. In eastern Asia, they were joined by Russia and Japan. Britain and Germany sometimes seemed to look toward Latin America as another field for expansion. In eastern Asia, the Pacific, and Latin America, the United States also had long-standing interests, often derived from commerce.

E xpectations
C onstraints
C hoices
O utcomes

Toward the end of the nineteenth century, some Americans began urging the nation's policymakers to boldly *choose* not just an increased role in world affairs but a prominent one. Most presidents after the Civil War, however, were highly cautious about such a commitment. At times they seemed to take a step back for every step toward greater involvement. During the same years, a revolution in transportation and communication wiped out many *constraints* on foreign relations. American diplomatic representatives abroad had once been connected to Washington only by an occasional memorandum carried by an American ship. Now they could communicate daily by telegraph. Where sailing ships had once taken weeks to traverse the oceans, steam-powered, steel-hulled vessels could now carry many times as much cargo—or troops and military equipment—in days. Previous American representatives abroad had usually been *chosen* through the patronage system, with little or no regard for their diplomatic abilities, but the rise of the merit system in the civil service had its parallel in the diplomatic service, producing more capable representation.

Challenges to traditional *expectations* of U.S. isolationism and the dissolving of long-standing *constraints* on action presented American policymakers of the late nineteenth century with more *choices* in foreign relations than had faced their predecessors. One *outcome* of their *choices* was a foreign policy usually described as imperialism. Its foundation was the acquisition of possessions scattered halfway around the world (see chapter-opening map). But the emerging U.S. foreign policy had *outcomes* other than just colonies and the building of a navy necessary to maintain and protect them. The larger *outcome* was a redefinition of nearly every aspect of American relations with the rest of the world.

CHRONOLOGY

The United States and World Affairs, 1865–1913

1823 Monroe Doctrine

1865 Civil War ends

1867 French troops leave Mexico
Senate rejects purchase of Danish West Indies
United States purchases Alaska from Russia

1870 Senate rejects annexation of Santo Domingo

1872 Arbitration of *Alabama* claims

1877 Lewis Henry Morgan's *Ancient Society*
Reconstruction ends

1882 U.S. Navy opens Korean trade
Congress authorizes construction of a modern navy
Chinese Exclusion Act

1885 Josiah Strong's *Our Country*

1887 Outsiders force a constitution on the Hawaiian monarchy
U.S. Navy receives exclusive use of Pearl Harbor
Dawes Severalty Act

1889 First Samoa treaty

1890 Alfred Thayer Mahan's *Influence of Sea Power upon History, 1660–1783*
Significant increase in naval appropriation
McKinley Tariff

1891 Lili'uokalani becomes Hawaiian queen
President Benjamin Harrison threatens war with Chile

1893 Queen Lili'uokalani overthrown

1894 Wilson-Gorman Tariff

1895–1896 Venezuelan boundary crisis

1896 Reconcentration policy in Cuba
Insurrection in the Philippines
William McKinley elected president

1898 De Lôme letter published in the New York *Journal*
U.S. warship *Maine* explodes
Spanish-American War
United States annexes Hawai'i by joint resolution
Treaty of Paris signed

1899 Senate debates imperialism
Treaty of Paris ratified
Treaty of Berlin divides Samoa
Open Door notes
Permanent Court of Arbitration created

1899–1902 Philippine insurrection suppressed

1900 Foraker Act
McKinley re-elected
Boxer Rebellion

1901 McKinley assassinated
Theodore Roosevelt becomes president
Insular cases
Hay-Pauncefote Treaties

1902 Civil government in the Philippines
Cuba becomes a protectorate

1904 Hay–Bunau-Varilla Treaty
Panama becomes a protectorate
Roosevelt Corollary

1904–1914 Panama Canal constructed

1905 Dominican Republic becomes a protectorate
Roosevelt mediates Russo-Japanese War

1912 Nicaragua becomes a protectorate

The United States and World Affairs, 1865–1889

- How did American choices with regard to Alaska and Latin America reflect traditional expectations about world affairs?
- How did American choices with regard to eastern Asia and the Pacific reflect new conditions in world affairs?

Americans took their first steps toward a new foreign policy in the years following the Civil War, but those steps occurred largely in isolation from each other. Until the 1890s, the various components did not add up to a coherent policy. Instead, presidents and secretaries of state tended to treat particular events individually and separately from other events. Some grew out of the lingering, pre–Civil War notion of manifest destiny. Others forecast concerns that emerged clearly only in the 1890s.

Alaska, Canada, and the *Alabama* Claims

In 1866, the Russian minister to the United States hinted to Secretary of State **William H. Seward** that Tsar Alexander II might dispose of Russian holdings in North America if the price were right. Seward, one of the most capable secretaries of state in the nineteenth century, had often proclaimed his belief in America's destiny to expand across the North American continent. He made an offer, and in 1867 the two diplomats agreed on a price slightly over $7 million. The deal was done, and the land that was to become the state of Alaska was in U.S. hands. The treaty differed from earlier territory agreements in one significant way. Previous treaties had all specified that the inhabitants of the territories (except Indians) would immediately become American citizens and that the territories themselves would eventually become states. The Alaska treaty extended citizenship but carried no promise of eventual statehood. It therefore moved a half-step away from earlier patterns of territorial expansion and toward later patterns of colonial acquisition.

Some journalists derided the new purchase as a frozen, worthless wasteland and labeled the bargain "Seward's Folly." The Senate, however, greeted it with considerable enthusiasm. Charles Sumner, chairman of the **Senate Foreign Relations Committee,** looked on the purchase of Alaska as the first step toward the ultimate possession of Canada. Many others shared his hope.

Expansion by acquiring Canada was certainly on Sumner's mind as he considered a set of claims against Great Britain arising out of the Civil War. Several Confederate naval vessels, most notably the *Alabama* and its sister ship the *Florida,* had badly disrupted northern shipping. British shipyards had built the *Alabama* and the *Florida* for the Confederacy. British ports had offered refuge, repairs, and supplies to Confederate ships. The Union claimed that Britain had violated its neutrality by allowing these activities, but Britain proved unresponsive to American demands for compensation for the depredations by the Confederate cruisers. In 1869, however, as relations between Britain and Russia grew tense, the British began to fret that American shipyards might provide similar services for the Russians. Sumner argued that the damages caused by the Confederate navy included not just direct claims for shipping losses but many indirect claims as well, amounting, he insisted, to the entire cost of the last two years of the war. The total, by Sumner's calculations, was more than $2 billion—so much, he suggested, that Britain could best meet its obligation by ceding all its North American possessions, including Canada, to the United States. Grant's secretary of state, Hamilton Fish, found Sumner's claims unrealistic and convinced Grant not to support them. Instead, in the Treaty of Washington (1871), the two countries agreed to **arbitration.** The 1872 arbitration decision held Britain responsible for the direct claims and set $15.5 million as damages to be paid to the United States.

Testing the Monroe Doctrine: The United States and Latin America

After the Civil War, American diplomats turned their attention to Latin America, partly in reaction to the influence European powers had recently extended in that direction and partly because some Americans wanted the United States to exercise power in that region.

William H. Seward U.S. Secretary of State under Lincoln and Johnson, a former abolitionist who had expansionist views and arranged the purchase of Alaska from Russia.

Senate Foreign Relations Committee One of the standing, or permanent, committees of the Senate; it deals with foreign affairs, and its chairman wields considerable power.

arbitration Process by which parties to a dispute submit their case to the judgment of an impartial person or group and agree to abide by the decision of the arbiter.

♦ This painting commemorated the signing of the treaty in 1867 by which the United States purchased Alaska from Russia for $7.2 million. Secretary of State William Seward is second from the left, and the Russian ambassador is standing near the globe, with his hand over Alaska. *Collection of the Seward House, Auburn, New York.*

In late 1861, as the United States lurched into civil war, France, Spain, and Britain sent a joint force to Mexico to collect debts that Mexico could not pay. Spain and Britain soon withdrew their contingents, but French troops remained, occupying key areas despite resistance led by **Benito Juarez,** president of Mexico. Some of Juarez's conservative political opponents cooperated with the French emperor, Napoleon III, to name Archduke **Maximilian** of Austria as emperor of Mexico. Maximilian, an idealistic young man, apparently believed that the Mexican people genuinely wanted him as their leader, and he hoped to serve them well. He quickly antagonized some of his conservative supporters with talk of reform, but he failed to win support from any other quarter. Resistance became war, and Maximilian held power only because of the French army.

During these events, the United States was involved in its own civil war. The Union continued to recognize Juarez as president of Mexico but could do little else. As soon as the Civil War ended, Secretary of State Seward demanded that Napoleon withdraw his troops. At that point, the United States possessed the most experienced, and perhaps the largest, army in the world. Seward underscored his demand when fifty thousand battle-hardened troops moved to the Mexican border. Thus confronted, Napoleon III agreed to withdraw his army. The last French soldiers sailed home in early 1867, but Maximilian unwisely remained behind, where he was defeated in battle by Juarez and then executed.

In his communications with France, Seward did not refer to the **Monroe Doctrine** by name. Until then, it had been a statement with no standing in international affairs unless backed by sufficient military or naval force. However, the withdrawal of the French troops in the face of substantial American

Benito Juarez Elected president of Mexico who led resistance to the French occupation of his country in 1864–1867; the first Mexican president of Indian ancestry.

Maximilian Austrian archduke appointed by France to be emperor of Mexico in 1864; later executed by Mexican republicans.

Monroe Doctrine Announcement by President James Monroe in 1823 that the Western Hemisphere was off limits for European colonial expansion.

military force helped to create new respect in Europe for the role of the United States in Latin America.

Some Americans had long regarded the Caribbean and Central America as potential areas for expansion. One driving vision was a canal through Central America to shorten the coast-to-coast shipping route around South America. After the Civil War, both the Caribbean and the Pacific attracted attention as sites where the navy might need bases. In 1867, seeking naval bases, Secretary of State Seward negotiated treaties to buy part of the **Danish West Indies** and to secure a base site in **Santo Domingo,** but both efforts failed to win the approval of Congress.

In 1870, with Grant in the White House and Hamilton Fish as secretary of state, the dictator of Santo Domingo offered either to annex his entire country to the United States or to lease a major bay for a naval base. Over Fish's objections, urged on by Americans eager to invest in the area, Grant asked the Senate to ratify a treaty of annexation. Approval required support of two-thirds of the Senate. With Sumner leading the opposition, the treaty failed by a vote of 28 to 28. Grant nevertheless proclaimed an extension, or **corollary,** of the Monroe Doctrine, specifying that no territory in the Western Hemisphere could ever be transferred to a European power.

Rather than annexation of territory, Secretary of State Fish pressed for expansion of trade with Latin America. So did James G. Blaine, secretary of state under Garfield (1881) and Harrison (1889–1892). Blaine promoted closer relations with Latin America in part to create additional markets for American products. He believed, too, that the United States should take a more active role among Latin American nations in resolving problems that might lead to war or European intervention.

Eastern Asia and the Pacific

Americans had long taken a strong commercial interest in eastern Asia. The China trade dated to 1784, and goods from Asia and the Pacific accounted for about 8 percent of all U.S. imports after the Civil War. Exports to that area made up less than 2 percent of all exports, however, and some Americans dreamed of profits from selling to China's hundreds of millions of potential consumers. American missionaries began to preach in China in 1830. Although they counted few converts, the lectures they gave back in the United States stimulated public interest in the Asian nation.

From 1839 to 1842, the British navy humiliated Chinese naval forces in a war conducted largely in Chinese waters. The Chinese government had long placed severe restrictions on foreign trade. The war began over Chinese efforts to prevent British merchants from importing and selling **opium** in China, but the British defined the issue as the right to engage in trade without restraints. In defeat, China granted privileges to Britain and subsequently to other nations that wished to sell goods there. The first treaty between China and the United States, in 1844, included a provision granting **most-favored-nation status** to the United States, laying the basis for the American **Open Door policy.**

Japan and Korea had insulated themselves from European imperial expansion by refusing to engage in trade, thereby keeping out Western influences. In 1854, American naval forces commanded by Commodore **Matthew C. Perry** and under orders from President Millard Fillmore convinced the Japanese government to open its ports to foreign trade. A similar navy action opened Korea in 1882.

Growing trade prospects between eastern Asia and the United States fueled American interest in the Pacific. Whether in sailing ships or steamships, the American **merchant marine** needed ports in the Pacific for supplies and repairs. Interest focused especially on two groups of islands with excellent harbors, Hawai`i and Samoa. Hawai`i had attracted Christian missionaries from New England as early

Danish West Indies Island group in the West Indies, including St. Croix and St. Thomas, which the United States finally purchased from Denmark in 1917; now known as the U.S. Virgin Islands.

Santo Domingo Nation in the Caribbean that shares an island with Haiti; it became independent from Spain in 1865 and is now known as the Dominican Republic.

corollary A proposition that follows logically and naturally from an already proven point.

opium An addictive drug made from poppies.

most-favored-nation status In a treaty between nation A and nation B, a clause that means that commercial privileges extended by A to other nations automatically become available to B.

Open Door policy American position, announced in 1899–1900, that all nations should have equal access to trading and development rights in China.

Matthew C. Perry American naval commander who sailed an armed squadron into Tokyo Bay and, using diplomacy and the threat of force, persuaded the Japanese to open their ports to American trade in 1854.

merchant marine Ships engaged in commerce.

♦ Located on the Hawaiian island of Oahu, Pearl Harbor is one of the finest harbors in the Pacific. This painting was done in 1889, two years after the Hawaiian king granted use of the harbor to the United States. In return, the United States granted preferred status to Hawaiian sugar in the American market. *"Pearl Harbor from the Ocean" by Joseph Strong, 1889. Bishop Museum, Honolulu, Hawaii.*

as 1819, shortly after King Kamehameha the Great united the islands into one nation. At first concerned with preaching the Gospel and convincing the unabashed Hawaiians to wear clothes, the missionaries eventually came to exercise great influence over several Hawaiian monarchs in the early nineteenth century.

The Hawaiian Islands' location near the center of the Pacific made them an ideal place to lay in supplies of fresh food and water for ships crossing the Pacific and for whaling vessels. After 1848, ships traveling from New York around South America to San Francisco also routinely stopped in Hawai`i for supplies. As early as 1842, President John Tyler stated that the United States would not allow the islands to pass under the control of another power, but Britain and France continued to take a close interest in them.

David Kalakaua became king of Hawai`i in 1874. During his reign, relations with the United States became close. Kalakaua was the first reigning monarch ever to visit the United States, in 1874, and in 1875 he approved a treaty of reciprocity that gave Hawaiian sugar duty-free access to the United States. The outcome was a rapid expansion of the Hawaiian sugar industry as the sons and daughters of New England missionaries joined representatives of American sugar refiners in developing huge sugar plantations. Sugar soon tied the Hawaiian economy closely to the United States as nearly all Hawaiian sugar began to flow to American markets.

Despite the economic connections between Hawai`i and the United States, relations between Kalakaua and the **haole** business and planter community of Hawai`i were never comfortable, as Kalakaua tried to preserve power for **indigenous** Hawaiians. *Haoles* concluded that he paid little attention to the needs of business and the sugar plantations and that he protected corrupt officials. In 1887, the news broke that Kalakaua himself had profited from bribery related to licenses for selling opium. Leaders of the *haole* community forced a constitution on Kalakaua, reducing him to little more than a figurehead. Haoles soon dominated much of the government. Kalakaua also approved the extension of the reciprocity treaty in 1887, with an additional provision giving the U.S. Navy exclusive rights to use Pearl Harbor. (The secretary of the navy admitted at the time, though, that he had no ships to send there.) Among some members of the royal family, resentment grew over the new constitution, the Pearl Harbor provision, and the extent of *haole* control.

Samoa, in the South Pacific, drew attention not just from the United States but also from Britain and

haole Hawaiian word for persons not of native Hawaiian ancestry, especially whites.

indigenous Original to an area.

Samoa A group of volcanic and mountainous islands in the South Pacific.

Germany. When German meddling in the islands suggested an attempt at annexation, President Grover Cleveland vowed to maintain Samoan independence. All three nations dispatched warships to the vicinity in 1889, and conflict seemed likely until a typhoon scattered and damaged the ships. A conference in Berlin then produced a treaty that provided for Samoan independence under the protection of all three Western nations.

Stepping Cautiously in World Affairs, 1889–1897

- How and why did some Americans' expectations about the U.S. role in world affairs begin to change between 1889 and 1897?
- What were the policy implications of these changes?

During the administration of Benjamin Harrison (1889–1893), the earlier, tentative efforts toward redefining America's role in world affairs began to come together to form a set of objectives and commitments. One element involved a new role for the U.S. Navy and the commissioning of modern ships able to carry it out. Another involved the emergence and acceptance of new concepts of America's role in the world. Harrison seemed ready to act boldly in keeping with the new ideas, but his successor, Grover Cleveland, was more cautious.

♦ As late as 1880, the U.S. Navy specified that ship captains should only use steam power when "absolutely necessary" and otherwise should rely on sail. Alfred Thayer Mahan, pictured here, took the lead in revolutionizing American thinking about sea power. *U.S. Naval Historical Center.*

Building a Navy

At the end of the Civil War, the navy, like the army, was rapidly **demobilized.** But unlike the army, which was needed to fight Indians in the West, the navy was largely ignored. No political decision-makers thought that establishing command of the high seas was an appropriate role for the U.S. Navy, and only a few Americans appreciated the significance of the Civil War experiments with heavily armored, steam-powered ships. These attitudes fostered disastrous neglect. The navy's wooden sailing vessels deteriorated to the point that some people ridiculed them as fit only for firewood. When a coal barge accidentally ran down a navy ship, one congressman joked that the worn-out navy was too slow even to get out of the way.

Congress approved a modest program to replace the deteriorating fleet in 1882, when it authorized construction of two steam-powered cruisers—the first new ships since the Civil War. However, work at the shipyards soon became bogged down in political infighting and accusations of corruption and incompetence. Although Congress appropriated funds for four more new ships in 1883, Secretary of the Navy William C. Whitney announced in 1885 that "we have nothing which deserves to be called a navy." During Cleveland's first administration (1885–1889), Whitney prodded Congress into approving construction of several more cruisers and the first two modern battleships. Congress approved construction of a few new ships, but most decision-makers still understood the role of the navy in limited terms—protecting American coasts.

Alfred Thayer Mahan played a key role in the emergence of the modern navy. As president of the Naval War College, Captain Mahan exerted a power-

demobilize To discharge from military service.

Alfred Thayer Mahan Lecturer and writer on naval history who stressed the importance of sea power in determining political history and justified imperialism on the basis of national self-interest.

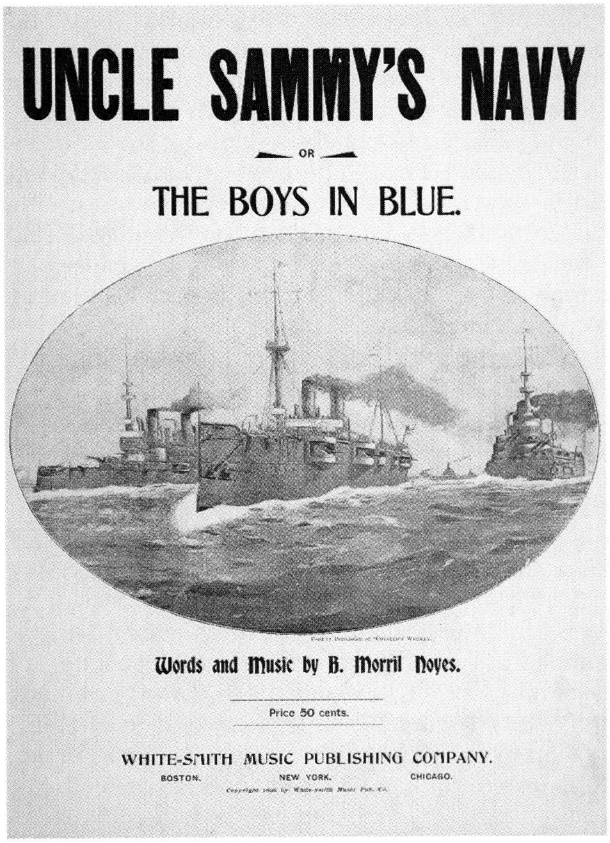

♦ The creation of a new, steel, steam-powered navy capable of navigating distant seas captured the public's imagination. This illustration of American ships under steam appeared on the cover of sheet music published in 1898, the year of the war with Spain in which the new navy figured so prominently. *John Carter Brown Library.*

ful influence, especially during the Harrison administration. In his lectures to navy officers in the War College, in several books—especially *The Influence of Sea Power upon History, 1660–1783* (1890)—and in articles in popular magazines, Mahan argued that sea power had been the determining factor in the great European power struggles from the mid-seventeenth to the early nineteenth centuries. From his study of history, he identified three elements as central to greatness on the seas: (1) production of goods for foreign trade, (2) shipping to carry on this commerce, and (3) colonies to provide both markets (usually for manufactured goods) and products (usually raw materials) to be used in the home country.

Mahan also explored the significance of geography, population, and government as they related to establishing sea power. From these studies, he drew lessons for government policy in his own day. First, Mahan urged support for a strong merchant marine. Second, he advocated a large, modern navy centered on huge, powerful battleships capable of carrying American power to distant seas. And third, he stressed a vision for empire. Extend American power beyond the national boundaries, he exhorted, in order to establish and control a canal through Central America, command the Caribbean, dominate Hawai`i and other strategic locations in the Pacific, and create naval bases at key points in the Atlantic and Pacific. His arguments were influential not just in the United States but also in Great Britain and Germany, which began large naval construction programs at about the same time as the United States.

In 1889, with Harrison in the White House and Republican majorities in both houses of Congress, Secretary of the Navy Benjamin F. Tracy urged Congress to modernize the navy and to expand it significantly: eighteen more battleships (up from two), nearly fifty more cruisers, and more smaller vessels. Tracy's ambitious proposal might have eliminated the federal budget surplus all by itself (see Figure 20.3). Congress did not give him all that he asked, but it did vote in 1890 to create a modern navy centered on battleships. When construction was under way on three new battleships equal to the best in the world, Tracy happily announced that "we shall rule [the sea] as certainly as the sun doth rise!"

A New American Mission?

Mahan's strategic arguments and Tracy's battleship launchings came as some Americans began, in Mahan's phrase, to "look outward." The appeals for change came from many sources: Protestant ministers, historians, business figures, politicians. Together they redefined the way American policymakers viewed the world and the role of the nation in world affairs. Josiah Strong, for example, offered the perspective of a Protestant minister and missionary. His book *Our Country* (1885) argued that expansion of American Protestant ideals to the world constituted a Christian duty and was practically inevitable. "The world is to be Christianized and civilized," he predicted, adding that "commerce follows the missionary."

Such beliefs were widespread in the late nineteenth century. According to Lewis Henry Morgan, whose book *Ancient Society* (1877) was long considered the authoritative work on its subject, the peoples of the world ranged themselves on a ladder of civilization in three major categories: savagery, barbarism, and civilization. The nations of western Europe and the United States represented the highest steps of "civilization," toward which all people were moving. Some policymakers—notably future president Theodore Roosevelt—implicitly accepted Morgan's analysis and used his categories in arguing that conflict was inevitable when "civilized" and "barbarian" peoples came into contact, because barbarians were inherently warlike. In such a situation, Roosevelt argued in 1899, expansion by "a great civilized power" not only extended peace but also meant "a victory for law, order, and righteousness."

"Progress" and social Darwinism (see page 529) merged with a belief in the superiority of the Anglo-Saxons—the people of England and their descendants. In the 1880s, popular books claimed that Anglo-Saxons had demonstrated a unique capacity for civilization and had a duty toward other peoples. Albert Beveridge, a Republican senator from Indiana, combined some of these ideas with American nationalism during the debate over acquisition of the Philippines in 1899 and 1900. "[God] has made us the master organizers of the world to establish system where chaos reigns," Beveridge proclaimed. Rudyard Kipling, an English poet, expressed this feeling in 1899 when he urged the United States to "take up the white man's burden," a phrase that came to describe a self-imposed obligation to go into distant lands, bring the supposed blessings of Anglo-Saxon civilization to their peoples, Christianize them, and sell them Western products.

Today historians understand Anglo-Saxonism and the "white-man's-burden" argument to represent a perspective deeply tinged with racism. Such views assumed that some people, by virtue of race, possessed superior capability for self-government and cultural accomplishment than others. Further, this thinking elevated only one cultural pattern as real civilization, dismissing other cultural patterns as inferior and ignoring their accomplishments.

♦ Queen Lili'uokalani came to the Hawaiian throne in 1891 and hoped to regain royal power that had been lost by her predecessor, King Kalakaua. Instead, in 1893, *haole* planters and businessmen overthrew the monarchy, aided by 150 U.S. marines ordered ashore by the American minister to Hawai`i. *The Lili'uokalani Trust.*

Revolution in Hawai`i

Belief in the "white man's burden" combined with new understandings of the strategic significance of the Pacific to focus the attention of American policymakers on Hawai`i when a revolution broke out there early in 1893. The most immediate causes of the revolution stemmed from changes in American tariff rates on sugar. In 1890, when the McKinley Tariff had put sugar on the free list (see page 615), all imported sugar entered the United States without paying a tariff. Previously Hawaiian sugar alone had entered duty free, but now it faced stiff competition in the American market, notably from Cuban sugar. The McKinley Tariff had also provided that sugar grown within the United States was to receive a subsidy of 2 cents per pound. Facing economic disaster, many Hawaiian planters began to talk of annexation to the United States.

In 1891, King Kalakaua died and was succeeded by his sister, **Lili'uokalani,** who hoped to restore Hawai`i to the indigenous Hawaiians and planned a new constitution returning political power to the

Lili'uokalani Last reigning queen of Hawai`i, whose desire to restore land to the Hawaiian people and perpetuate the monarchy prompted *haole* planters to depose her in 1893.

monarchy. Fearing that they might lose not only their political clout but also their economic holdings, haole entrepreneurs set out to overthrow the monarchy. On January 17, 1893, the plotters announced a provisional republican government that would seek annexation by the United States. John L. Stevens, the U.S. minister to Hawai`i, provided crucial assistance for the rebellion by ordering the landing of 150 U.S. marines. Lili'uokalani surrendered, as she put it, "to the superior force of the United States." Stevens immediately recognized the new republic, declared it a **protectorate** of the United States, and raised the American flag.

The Harrison administration, then in its closing days, **repudiated** Stevens's overzealous action, insisting he had neither authorization nor authority to establish a protectorate. At the same time, however, the administration opened negotiations with representatives of the republic. Within thirty days after Stevens brought the marines into Honolulu, Harrison sent the Senate a treaty of annexation. There it rested when Grover Cleveland became president soon after.

Cleveland was willing to consider annexing Hawai`i if the Hawaiian people requested it, but he withdrew the annexation treaty to study it further. Having earlier blocked German moves to subvert the government of Samoa, the president was upset to learn that his own nation was guilty of similar manipulation in Hawai`i. When he discovered that the revolution could not have succeeded without the marines' involvement, he asked the new officials to restore the queen. They refused, and Hawai`i became a republic, dominated by its haole business and planter community.

Crises in Latin America

Although Harrison and Cleveland acted at cross-purposes regarding Hawai`i, they moved in similar directions with regard to Latin America. Both presidents extended American involvement, and both threatened the use of force.

A rebellion in Chile in 1891 ended with victory for the rebels. Because the American minister to Chile had seemed to side against the rebels, providing protection to several high-ranking officials of the deposed government, anti-American feelings ran high. In October 1891, in Valparaiso, Chile, a mob set upon a group of American sailors on shore leave, beat them, injured several, and killed two. The Chilean government gave no sign of apologizing, so Harrison threatened "such action as may be necessary." Using language Americans considered insulting, the Chilean government insinuated that Harrison was wrong. When Harrison responded with plans for a naval war and threats to cut off diplomatic relations, Chile gave in, apologized, and promised to pay damages and to meet any other terms.

In 1895 and 1896, Grover Cleveland also took the nation to the edge of war. At issue was a long-standing boundary dispute between Venezuela and **British Guiana.** Venezuela repeatedly proposed arbitration, which Cleveland also favored, but Britain refused. Discovery of gold in the contested region intensified claims by both sides. In July 1895, Secretary of State Richard Olney demanded that Britain submit the boundary issue to arbitration. Resting his argument on the Monroe Doctrine, he bombastically proclaimed the United States to be pre-eminent throughout the Western Hemisphere. The British waited until December to respond, then rejected the notion that the Monroe Doctrine held any standing in international law and refused arbitration. Cleveland in turn asked Congress for authority to determine the boundary and enforce it. Britain faced the possibility of conflict with the United States at a time when it was becoming increasingly concerned about the rising power of Germany and when tensions were mounting between the English colony in South Africa and neighboring independent **Boer republics.** Britain agreed to arbitration.

In both instances, American presidents behaved more forcefully toward other nations than any of their predecessors had behaved in twenty years. Both times, the firm response of the United States surprised its adversary. Harrison's action toward Chile was a heavy-handed assertion of American power unlikely to encourage the closer relations

protectorate A country partially controlled by a stronger power and dependent on that power for protection from foreign threats.

repudiate To reject the validity or authority of.

British Guiana British colony in northeastern South America on the Atlantic coast whose boundary with Venezuela was long in dispute; now the independent nation of Guyana.

Boer republics Self-governing nations established by white South Africans of Dutch descent to escape British rule; Britain forcibly annexed them into its South African colony.

with Latin America envisioned by his secretary of state James G. Blaine. Seriously ill at the time of the crisis, Blaine played virtually no role in it except to urge moderation from his sickbed. Cleveland and Olney did not even consult with the Venezuelan government during the Venezuelan boundary crisis. Cleveland certainly may have hoped that standing up to Britain would help the Democrats in upcoming elections, but his major objective was to serve notice to all European imperial powers that the Western Hemisphere was strictly off-limits in the ongoing contest for colonies.

At the same time, Cleveland faced a very different situation in Cuba, and there he took a more restrained position. Cuba and Puerto Rico were all that remained of the once mighty Spanish Empire in the Americas, and Cuba had rebelled against Spain repeatedly. In the early 1890s, when the McKinley Tariff permitted Cuban sugar to enter the United States duty free, the Cuban sugar industry boomed. By 1894, the United States was receiving nearly 90 percent of Cuba's exports, primarily sugar. That year, however, the Wilson-Gorman Tariff restored a high duty on Cuban sugar, removed the tariff on Hawaiian sugar, and caused a depression in Cuba.

Fueled by economic distress, a new insurrection erupted against Spanish rule, and the advocates of *Cuba libre* ("a free Cuba") received support from sympathizers in the United States. In 1896, in an effort to combat guerrilla warfare waged by the **insurgents,** General Valeriano Weyler, the Spanish commander in Cuba, established a **reconcentration** policy. The civilian population was ordered into fortified towns or camps. Everyone who remained outside these fortified areas was assumed to be an insurgent, subject to military action. The insurgents responded by ravaging sugar and tobacco plantations, including those owned by Americans.

The U.S. government vehemently protested reconcentration, particularly after disease and starvation swept through the camps. Within two years, by one estimate, these conditions killed one of every eight Cubans. American newspapers—especially **Joseph Pulitzer**'s New York *World* and **William Randolph Hearst**'s New York *Journal*—vied with each other in portraying Spanish atrocities. Papers sent their best reporters to Cuba and exaggerated the reports to attract readers, a practice called **yellow journalism.** Sickened from the steady diet of yellow press stories, many Americans began clamoring for action to rescue the Cubans from Spanish oppression.

Cleveland reacted cautiously, intent on avoiding American involvement. He proclaimed American neutrality and warned Americans not to support the insurrection. When members of Congress began to push Cleveland to take action to secure Cuban independence, he ignored the pressures. He urged Spain to grant some concessions to the insurgents, but he doubted that the insurgents were capable of replacing Spanish rule. Just as he had opposed annexation of Hawai`i, so now Cleveland resisted the notion of intervening in Cuba—and for the same reason. He feared that intervention might lead to annexation regardless of the will of the Cuban people. Even so, by the time he left the presidency in early 1897, he had begun to warn Spain of possible American intervention.

Striding Boldly: War and Imperialism, 1897–1901

- What were the outcomes of the war with Spain?
- What new expectations about America's role in world affairs were expressed in the debate over the acquisition of new possessions?

In 1898, the United States went to war with Spain over Cuba. Far from combat, John Hay, the American ambassador to Great Britain, celebrated the conflict as "a splendid little war," and the description stuck. Some who promoted American intervention on behalf of the suffering Cubans envisioned a quick war to establish a Cuban republic. Others saw war with Spain as an opportunity to seize territory and acquire a colonial empire for the United States.

insurgents Rebels or revolutionaries.

reconcentration Spanish policy in Cuba in 1896 that ordered the civilian population into fortified camps so as to isolate and annihilate Cuban revolutionaries.

Joseph Pulitzer Hungarian-born newspaper publisher whose New York *World* printed sensational stories about Cuba that helped precipitate the Spanish-American War.

William Randolph Hearst Publisher and rival to Pulitzer whose newspaper the New York *Journal* sensationalized and distorted stories and actively promoted the war with Spain.

yellow journalism The use of sensational exposés and attention-grabbing headlines to sell newspapers.

♦ On February 15, 1898, an explosion destroyed the American warship *Maine* as it lay at anchor in the harbor at Havana, Cuba. Some two hundred sixty Americans lost their lives. Many Americans blamed the Spanish government of Cuba, although there was no evidence to suggest who was responsible. *Library of Congress.*

McKinley and War

William McKinley became president in early 1897 amid increasing demands for action regarding Cuba. Though unwilling to let Spain crush the insurgents, he moved cautiously, gradually stepping up diplomatic efforts to resolve the crisis. Late that year Spain responded by recalling General Weyler, softening the reconcentration policy, and offering the Cubans limited self-government but not independence. In February 1898, however, two events scuttled progress toward a negotiated solution.

First, Cuban insurgents stole a letter written by **Enrique Dupuy de Lôme,** the Spanish minister to the United States, and released it to the New York *Journal.* In it, de Lôme criticized President McKinley as "weak and a bidder for the admiration of the crowd." The letter also implied that the Spanish government's commitment to reform in Cuba was not serious. De Lôme's immediate resignation could not undo the damage. The letter aroused intense anti-Spanish feeling among Americans.

On February 15, a few days after publication of the de Lôme letter, an explosion ripped open the American warship ***Maine,*** anchored in Havana harbor. The *Maine* sank, with the loss of more than 260 American officers and sailors. The yellow press accused Spain of sabotage but produced no evidence. An official inquiry the next month blamed a submarine mine but could not determine whose it may have been. Regardless of how the explosion occurred, those advocating intervention had a rallying cry: "Remember the *Maine*!"

McKinley now extended his demands on Spain: an immediate end to the fighting, an end to reconcentration and measures to relieve the suffering, and **mediation** by McKinley himself. As mediator between Spain and the insurgents, he would seek to resolve their differences but would also be able to specify Cuban independence. In reply, the Spanish government promised reforms, agreed to end reconcentration, and consented to cease fighting if the insurgents asked for an **armistice**. Spain was silent, though, on mediation by McKinley and independence for Cuba. McKinley responded on April 11 by telling Congress that "the war in Cuba must stop" and asking for authority to act. Congress responded on April 19 with four resolutions: (1) declaring that

Enrique Dupuy de Lôme Spanish minister to the United States whose private letter criticizing President McKinley was stolen and printed in the New York *Journal,* increasing anti-Spanish sentiment.

Maine American warship that exploded in Havana harbor in 1898, inspiring the motto "Remember the *Maine,*" which spurred the Spanish-American War.

mediation An attempt to bring about the peaceful settlement of a dispute through the intervention of a neutral party.

armistice An agreement to halt fighting at least temporarily.

Cuba was and should be independent, (2) demanding that Spain withdraw "at once," (3) authorizing the president to use force to accomplish Spanish withdrawal, and (4) disavowing any intention to annex the island. The first three resolutions were equivalent to a declaration of war. The fourth was usually called the **Teller Amendment** for its sponsor, Senator Henry M. Teller, a Silver Republican from Colorado. In response, Spain declared war.

Nearly all Americans reacted enthusiastically to what they understood to be a war undertaken for the humanitarian purpose of bringing independence to the long-suffering Cubans. From the beginning, however, some voiced distrust of the McKinley administration's motives in battling an enfeebled colonial power. In Congress, Democrats, Silver Republicans, and Populists urged the formal recognition of the insurgents as the legitimate government of Cuba, but the McKinley administration and Republican congressional leaders defeated their efforts. The Teller Amendment also reflected a fear among legislators that McKinley might try to make Cuba an American possession rather than granting it independence.

The "Splendid Little War"

From 1895 onward, American attention had been riveted on Cuba. Thus many Americans were taken by surprise when the first engagement in the war occurred not in Cuba but in the **Philippine Islands,** on the other side of the world. A Spanish colony for more than three hundred years, the Philippines had rebelled repeatedly against Spanish rule. One such revolt had begun in 1896, shortly after the insurrection in Cuba.

Among those Americans who well understood the islands' strategic location with regard to eastern Asia was Assistant Secretary of the Navy **Theodore Roosevelt.** In late February 1898, more than six weeks before McKinley's war message to Congress, Roosevelt cabled the American naval commander in the Pacific, George Dewey, to crush the Spanish fleet at Manila Bay immediately if war broke out.

At sunrise on Sunday, May 1, Dewey carried out those orders. His squadron of four cruisers and three smaller vessels steamed into Manila Bay and quickly destroyed or captured ten Spanish cruisers and gunboats. The Spanish commander, knowing he stood no chance against superior American firepower, moved his ships away from Manila so that stray shells would not endanger civilian lives. The Spanish lost 381 men. The Americans lost one, a victim of heat prostration. An English writer described the encounter as "a military execution rather than a real contest." Dewey instantly became a national hero.

Dewey's victory at Manila focused public attention on the Pacific and immediately raised, for some, the prospect of establishing a permanent American presence in that area. This, in turn, revived interest in annexing the Hawaiian Islands as a base for supplying and protecting any future American activities in eastern Asia. The McKinley administration had negotiated a treaty of annexation with the Hawaiian government in 1897, shortly after Cleveland left the White House, but anti-imperialist sentiment in the Senate had made approval unlikely. Now, with Dewey's victory and the prospect of a permanent American base in the Philippines, McKinley revived the joint-resolution precedent by which the annexation of Texas had come about in 1844. Only a majority vote in both houses of Congress was required to adopt a joint resolution, rather than the two-thirds vote of the Senate needed to approve a treaty. Annexation of Hawai`i was accomplished on July 7, more than five years after the planters had **deposed** Queen Lili'uokalani.

Dewey's victory demonstrated that the American navy was clearly superior to the navy of Spain. In contrast, the Spanish army in Cuba outnumbered the entire American army by more than five to one. The Spanish troops, too, had years of experience fighting in Cuba. When war was declared, the American army numbered only twenty-eight thousand soldiers, but a call for volunteers brought nearly a million—five times as many as the army wanted or could take. The volunteers represented a broad cross-section of American males. Many African Americans, who were mustered into segregated units, joined up even though some black leaders voiced concern that the army might become the

Teller Amendment Resolution approved by the U.S. Senate in 1898, by which the United States promised not to annex Cuba; introduced by Senator Henry Teller of Colorado.

Philippine Islands A group of islands in the Pacific Ocean southeast of China that came under U.S. control in 1898 after the Spanish-American War.

Theodore Roosevelt American politician and writer who advocated war against Spain in 1898; McKinley's vice president in 1900, he became president in 1901 upon McKinley's assassination.

depose To dethrone or remove from power.

♦ Theodore Roosevelt's Rough Riders, on foot because there was not room aboard ship for their horses, are shown in the background of this artist's depiction of the battle for Kettle Hill, a part of the larger battle for San Juan Hill, overlooking the city of Santiago. The artist has put into the foreground members of the Ninth and Tenth Cavalry, both African-American units that also played a key role in that engagement, but one often overlooked because of the attention usually given Roosevelt and the Rough Riders. *Chicago Historical Society.*

instrument for transplanting American patterns of racial segregation to Cuba.

The army needed many weeks to train and supply those who rallied to the call. Congress declared war in late April, but not until June did the first troop transports leave for Cuba. Sent to training camps in the South, the new soldiers found chaos and confusion. Food, uniforms, and equipment arrived at one location while the men for whom they were intended stood hungry and idle at another. Uniforms were often of heavy wool, totally unsuited for the climate and season. Disease raged through some camps, killing many men. Others died from tainted food, called "embalmed beef" by the troops. Some African-American soldiers refused to comply with racial segregation, and many white southerners objected to the presence in their communities of so many uniformed and armed black men.

Once in Cuba, American forces concentrated on the port city of Santiago, where the Spanish fleet had taken refuge. Inexperienced, poorly equipped, and unfamiliar with the terrain, the Americans doggedly assaulted the fortified hills surrounding the city. Theodore Roosevelt, who had resigned as assistant secretary of the navy to organize a cavalry unit known as the **Rough Riders,** was the only one on horseback because the regiment's horses had not reached Cuba in time (see Individual Choices: Theodore Roosevelt). At Kettle Hill, he led a successful but costly charge of Rough Riders and regular army units, including parts of the Ninth and Tenth Cavalry, made up of African Americans. Driving the Spanish from the crest of Kettle Hill cleared a serious impediment to the assault on nearby, and strategically more important, San Juan Heights and San Juan Hill. Roosevelt then led his units to take a much less prominent part in the attack on those heights. Newspapers nevertheless declared Roosevelt the hero of the Battle of San Juan Hill.

Americans suffered heavy casualties during the first few days of the attack on Santiago. Nearly 10 percent of the troops were killed or wounded. Worsening the situation, the surgeon in charge of medical facilities refused assistance from trained Red Cross nurses because he thought field hospitals were not appropriate places for women. He was later overruled. Red Cross nurses, led by Clara Barton, also helped to care for injured Cuban insurgents and civilians.

Once the Americans secured control of the high ground around Santiago harbor, the Spanish fleet of four cruisers and two destroyers tried to escape from the harbor. A larger American fleet under Admiral William Sampson and Commodore Winfield Schley met them and repeated Dewey's rout at Manila.

Rough Riders The First Volunteer Cavalry, a brigade recruited for action in the Spanish-American War by Theodore Roosevelt, who served first as its lieutenant colonel, then its colonel.

INDIVIDUAL CHOICES

Choosing to Go to War

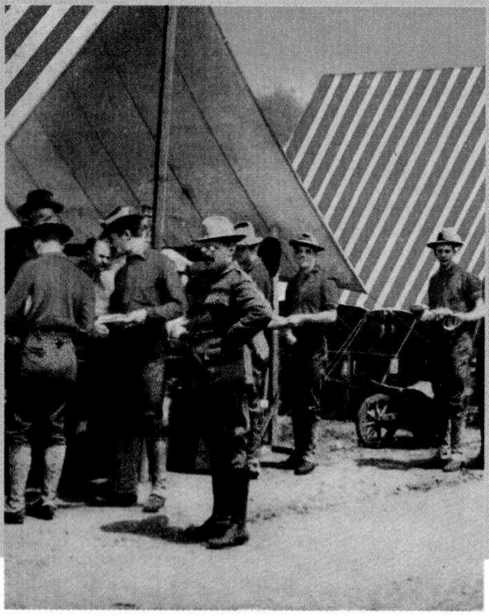

Theodore Roosevelt

Though Theodore Roosevelt prepared for his military command, in part, by cabling Brooks Brothers in New York to make him an "ordinary cavalry lieutenant-colonel's uniform in blue," this colorized photo of him outside the mess tent shows him in a less formal khaki uniform. Collection of Colonel Stuart S. Corning, Jr.

It should have been a difficult choice. Theodore Roosevelt was 39 years old, husband to an ailing wife, Edith Carow Roosevelt, and father of six children, ranging in age from 4 to 14. His refined manners pointed to his old and distinguished New York family origins, just as his thick spectacles hinted at his intellectual accomplishments. A graduate of Harvard, he had written more than a dozen books, some highly acclaimed, on history, natural history, and his own experiences as a rancher and hunter. He had also made a career for himself in Republican politics.

Family and career should have been powerful constraints against what might seem the impulsive choice to resign from a high federal office to seek wartime action in Cuba. Roosevelt, however, seems not even once to have considered them. On the contrary, he left a long trail of evidence of his expectation to fight.

In 1894, Roosevelt wrote that "At no period of the world's history has life been so full of interest, and of possibilities of excitement and enjoyment. . . . The greatest victories are yet to be won, the greatest deeds yet to be done." As early as 1895, Roosevelt wrote to the governor of New York asking to be included in whatever state militia unit might be sent to Cuba. From then on, whenever he talked about Cuba, he talked of forming a cavalry unit.

Every Spanish ship was sunk or run aground. The Spanish suffered 323 deaths, the Americans one.

Their fleet destroyed and the surrounding hills in American hands, the Spanish in Santiago still waited two weeks before surrendering. A week later American forces took over Puerto Rico. Early in the war, on June 21, an American cruiser had secured the surrender of Spanish forces on Guam without a contest. Spanish land forces in the Philippines surrendered when the first American troops arrived in mid-August. (For all locations, see Map 21.1) The "splendid little war" lasted only sixteen weeks. More than 306,000 men served in the American forces—385 of them died in battle and more than 5,000 died of disease and other causes.

The Treaty of Paris

On August 12, the United States and Spain agreed to stop fighting. The truce specified that Spain was to give up Cuba and transfer to the United States both

In the 1896 presidential campaign, Roosevelt worked hard for McKinley's election, and he worked just as hard to be appointed assistant secretary of the navy. Once appointed, he renewed his ties with Alfred Thayer Mahan, whom he had met years before. As assistant secretary of the navy, and sometimes as acting secretary, Roosevelt worked unstintingly to strengthen the navy and to prepare it for the war that he confidently expected would come. As relations with Spain worsened in early 1898, Roosevelt became a dynamo. One afternoon in February, as acting secretary, he ordered great supplies of coal and ammunition and issued contingency orders to commanders to be carried out in the event of war with Spain. The next day, when Secretary of the Navy John Long returned to the office, he thought that "the very devil seemed to possess him [Roosevelt] yesterday afternoon." But he permitted all Roosevelt's preparations to stand.

On April 11, 1898, when Congress began to debate McKinley's war message, Roosevelt threw all his great energies into securing an army appointment. Roosevelt's friends were aghast at his plans to go into the army. His friend Henry Cabot Lodge worried that Roosevelt was endangering his bright political future. A friend wrote that "I really think he is going mad . . . Roosevelt is wild to fight and hack and hew." Navy Secretary Long thought that "He has lost his head."

McKinley signed the congressional resolutions authorizing action against Cuba on April 20. Three days later, the secretary of war offered Roosevelt the command of the First U.S. Volunteer Cavalry. Roosevelt, however, declined the command in favor of his friend Leonard Wood, an experienced army officer, and instead chose the position of second-in-command. After years of fantasizing about leading men into battle, he suddenly realized that he was not prepared to organize, train, and lead a cavalry regiment. Nonetheless, the unit was known from the first as Roosevelt's Rough Riders.

Roosevelt quickly recruited an impressive mounted regiment. Some were western cowboys and rangers who fit his qualifications exactly, being "young, good shots, and good riders." Others were upper-class easterners like himself, whose riding experience came more from polo and steeplechase competition. Wood and Roosevelt turned the disparate group into a trained military unit, and by the time they arrived in Cuba, Roosevelt was in command. Far from ending his political career, his exploits in Cuba, together with his careful cultivation of the press, produced banner headlines and made his name even better known than that of Commodore Dewey. The first outcome of his choices—and his daring and his luck—came less than three months after the fighting ended when, on November 7, he was elected governor of New York. Two years later, on November 6, 1900, he was elected vice president of the United States. Less than a year later, on September 12, 1901, President William McKinley died after being shot by an assassin, and Theodore Roosevelt became the youngest person ever to become president of the United States.

Puerto Rico and one of the **Ladrone Islands.** Until a peace conference determined the final fate of the Philippines, the United States was to occupy Manila.

The only real question centered on the Philippines. Finley Peter Dunne, a popular humorist, parodied the national debate on the acquisition of the Philippines in a discussion between his fictional characters, Chicago saloonkeeper Mr. Dooley and a customer named Hennessy. Hennessy insists that McKinley should take all the islands. Dooley responds that "it's not more than two months since you learned whether they were islands or canned goods" and continues to express his own indecision: "I can't annex them because I don't know where they are. I can't let go of

Ladrone Islands Islands in the western Pacific now known as the Marianas; they include the island of Guam, which the United States acquired from Spain under the 1898 Treaty of Paris.

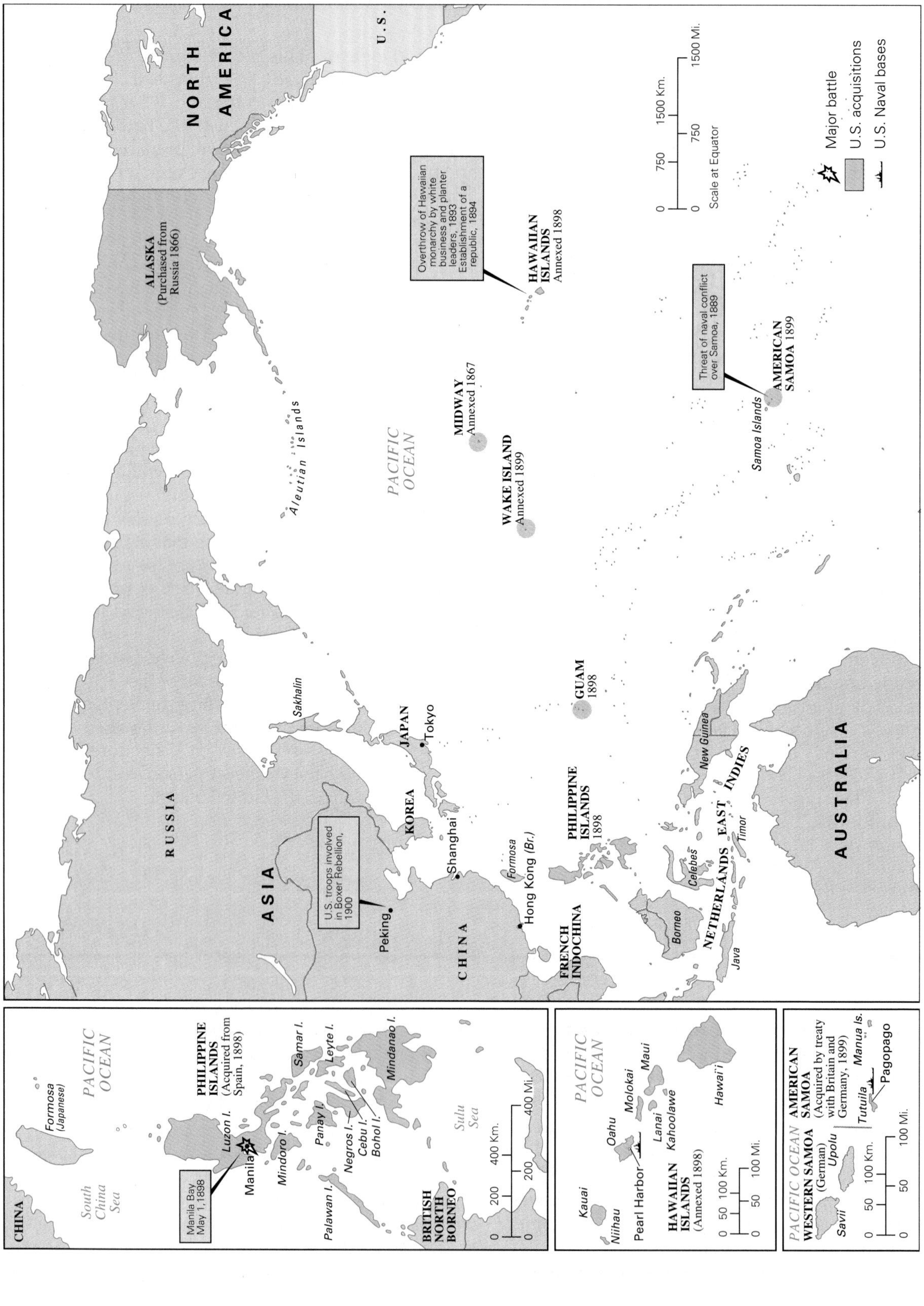

◆ **MAP 21.1 The United States and the Pacific, 1866–1900** In the 1890s, the United States became a major power in the Pacific and in eastern Asia. This map indicates major acquisitions and activities up to 1900.

them because someone else will take them if I do. . . . It would break my heart to think of giving people I've never seen or heard of back to other people I don't know. . . . I don't know what to do about the Philippines. And I'm all alone in the world. Everybody else has made up his mind."

McKinley apparently made up his mind early in favor of annexation, but in public he voiced as many doubts as Mr. Dooley. At first, he seemed inclined to request only a naval base and to leave Spain the remainder of the islands. Spanish authority collapsed everywhere on the islands by mid-August, however, as Filipino insurgents took charge. Britain, Japan, and Germany carefully watched these events. One or another seemed likely to step in if the United States withdrew. McKinley and his advisers had apparently decided by then that defending a naval base on Manila Bay would require control of the entire island group. No one seems to have seriously considered Filipino desires for independence.

McKinley was well aware of the political and strategic importance of the Philippines for establishing an American presence in eastern Asia. He invoked other reasons, however, when he explained his decision to a group of visiting Methodists. He repeatedly prayed for guidance on the Philippine question, he told them. Late one night, perhaps in answer to his prayers, he realized that "there was nothing left for us to do but to take them all, and to educate the Filipinos, and uplift and civilize and Christianize them and by God's grace do the very best we could by them, as our fellow men, for whom Christ also died." In fact, most Filipinos had been Catholics for centuries, but no one ever expressed more clearly the concept of the "white man's burden."

All through the peace conference in Paris, Spain resisted giving up the Philippines, but McKinley's representatives remained adamant. The **Treaty of Paris,** signed in December 1898, required Spain to surrender all claim to Cuba, cede Puerto Rico and the island of Guam to the United States, and sell the Philippines for $20 million. For the first time in American history, a treaty acquiring new territory failed to confer U.S. citizenship on the residents. Nor did the treaty mention future statehood. Thus these acquisitions represented a step beyond the Alaska treaty and toward a new kind of expansion. The United States now owned territories with no prospect for statehood, whose residents lacked the rights of American citizens. America had become a colonial power.

The terms of the Treaty of Paris dismayed Democrats, Populists, and some conservative Republicans. They immediately launched a public debate over acquisition of the Philippines in particular and **imperialism** in general. An active anti-imperialist movement quickly formed, including William Jennings Bryan, Grover Cleveland, Andrew Carnegie, Mark Twain, Jane Addams, and others. The treaty provisions, they argued, amounted to a denial of self-government for the newly acquired territories. For the United States to hold colonies, they claimed, threatened the very concept of democracy. "The Declaration of Independence," warned Carnegie, "will make every Filipino a thoroughly dissatisfied subject." Others worried over the perversion of American values. "God Almighty help the party that seeks to give civilization and Christianity hypodermically with 13-inch guns," prayed Senator William Morris of Illinois. Some anti-imperialists argued from a racist perspective that Filipinos were incapable of taking part in a Western-style democracy and that the United States would be corrupted by ruling over people unable to govern themselves. Union leaders, fearing Filipino migration to the United States, repeated arguments once used to demand Chinese exclusion (see page 554).

Those who defended the acquisition of the Philippines echoed McKinley's lofty pronouncements about America's solemn duty along with more mundane claims about economic benefits. Albert Beveridge, senator from Indiana after 1899, persuasively put forth the commercial benefits of expansion: "Today, we are raising more than we can consume, making more than we can use. Therefore we must find new markets for our produce." Such "new markets" were not limited to the Philippines or other new possessions. Having a major naval and military presence in the Philippines, proponents suggested, would make the United States a leading power in eastern Asia. American business could therefore anticipate continued access to the China market, then being divided among European imperialist nations and Japan. In contrast to the heated debates over the Philippines, virtually no one challenged the appropriateness of acquiring Puerto Rico.

Treaty of Paris Treaty ending the Spanish-American War, under which Spain granted independence to Cuba, ceded Puerto Rico and Guam, and sold the Philippines to the United States for $20 million.

imperialism The practice by which a nation acquires and holds colonies and other possessions, denies them self-government, and usually exploits them economically.

William Jennings Bryan, the Democratic presidential candidate in 1896, had volunteered and been appointed a colonel. He now resigned his commission, returned to politics, and urged his followers in the Senate to approve the treaty. That way, he reasoned, the United States alone could determine the future of the Philippines. Once the treaty was approved, he argued, the United States should immediately grant them independence. By a narrow margin, the Senate approved the treaty on February 6, 1899, but soon after, senators rejected a proposal for Philippine independence.

Republic or Empire? The Election of 1900

Bryan hoped to make independence for the Philippines the central issue in the 1900 presidential election. He easily won the Democrats' nomination for a second time, and the Democratic platform condemned the McKinley administration for its "imperialism." Bryan found, however, that many conservative anti-imperialists would not support his candidacy because he insisted on silver coinage and attacked big business.

The Republicans renominated McKinley. For vice president, they chose Theodore Roosevelt, "hero of San Juan Hill," who had been elected governor of New York in 1898. Roosevelt's popularity and independence frightened New York's established Republican leaders, who expected him to challenge their control of state politics. In fact, they pushed Roosevelt for the vice presidency as a means of getting him out of the statehouse. For most of its occupants, the vice presidency had been a one-way ticket to political oblivion. Roosevelt, however, eyed the presidency itself, an ambition obvious to McKinley's political adviser Mark Hanna, who warned, "There's only one life between this madman and the White House."

The McKinley re-election campaign seemed unstoppable. Republican campaigners pointed proudly to a short and highly successful war, legislation that had fulfilled party campaign promises on the tariff and the gold standard, and the return of prosperity. Bryan repeatedly attacked *imperialism.* McKinley and Roosevelt never used the term at all and instead took pride in *expansion.* Republican campaigners questioned the patriotism of anyone who proposed to pull down the flag where it had once been raised. McKinley easily won a second term with 51.7 percent of the vote, carrying not only the states that had given him his victory in 1896 but also many of the western states where populism had once flourished.

Organizing an Insular Empire

The Teller Amendment specified that the United States would not annex Cuba (see Map 21.2 for all Caribbean locations). The McKinley administration, though, consistently refused to recognize the insurgents as a legitimate government, so the U.S. Army took over the job of running the island when the Spanish left. Among other tasks, the army undertook public improvements, including sanitation projects intended to reduce disease, especially yellow fever. After two years of army rule, the McKinley administration permitted Cuban voters to hold a constitutional convention.

The convention met late in 1900 and drafted a constitution modeled on that of the United States. It did not define relations between Cuba and the United States, however. In March 1901, the McKinley administration specified, and Congress adopted, detailed provisions for Cuba to adopt before the army would withdraw, including these stipulations: (1) Cuba was not to make any agreement with a foreign power that impaired the island's independence, (2) the United States could intervene in Cuba to preserve Cuban independence and maintain law and order, and (3) Cuba was to lease facilities to the United States for naval bases and coaling stations. Cubans reluctantly accepted the conditions, added them to their constitution, and agreed to a treaty with the United States stating the same conditions. In 1902, Cuba thereby became a protectorate of the United States.

The Teller Amendment did not apply to Puerto Rico. On that island, too, the army provided a military government until 1900, when Congress approved the **Foraker Act.** That act made Puerto Ricans citizens of Puerto Rico but not citizens of the United States. It specified that Puerto Rican voters were to elect a legislature but final authority was to rest with a governor and council appointed by the president of the United States. In 1901, in the **Insular cases,** the U.S. Supreme Court issued a complex decision that, in effect, confirmed the colonial status

Foraker Act Law passed by Congress in 1900 that established civilian government in Puerto Rico; it provided for an elected legislature and a governor appointed by the U.S. president.

Insular cases Cases concerning Puerto Rico, in which the U.S. Supreme Court ruled in 1901 that people in new island territories did not automatically receive the constitutional rights of U.S. citizens.

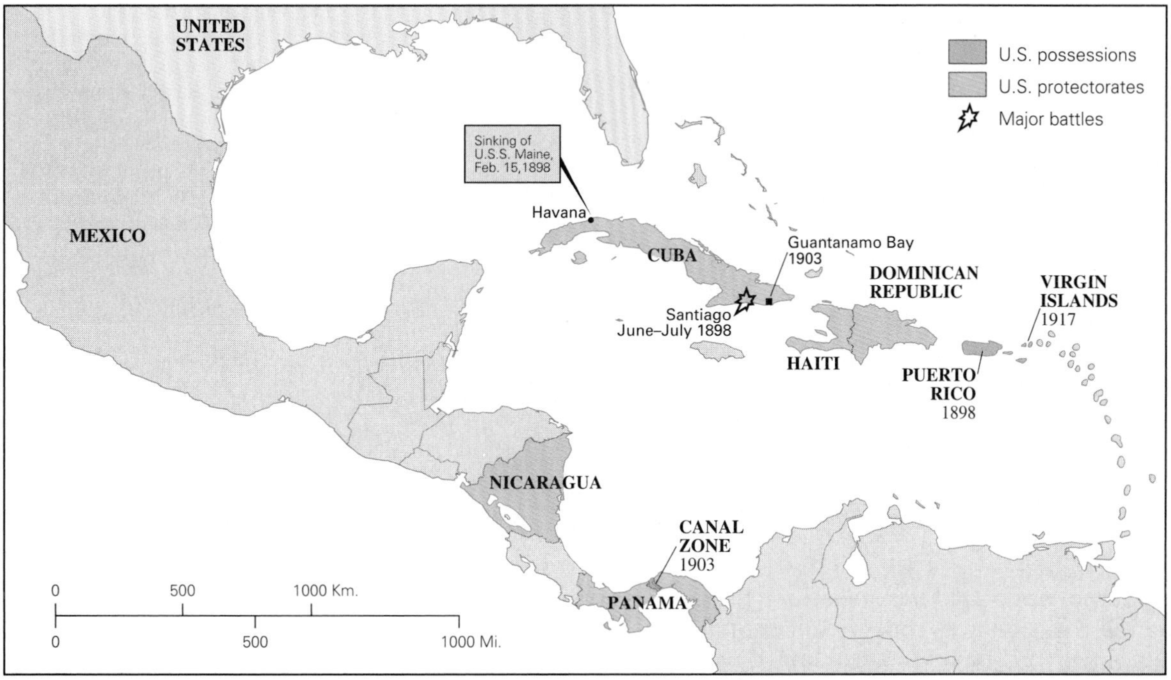

♦ **MAP 21.2 The United States and the Caribbean 1898–1917** Between 1898 and 1917, the United States expanded into the Caribbean by acquiring possessions and establishing protectorates. As a result, the United States was the dominant power in the region throughout this time period.

of Puerto Rico and, by implication, the other new possessions. The Court ruled that they were not equivalent to earlier territorial acquisitions and that their people did not possess the constitutional rights of citizens.

Establishment of a civil government in the Philippines took longer. Between Dewey's victory and the arrival of the first American soldiers three months later, a Philippine independence movement led by **Emilio Aguinaldo** had established a provisional government. Its forces controlled all the islands except Manila, which remained in Spanish hands until American troops arrived. Aguinaldo and his government had no interest in simply exchanging colonial masters. They wanted independence. When the United States decided to keep the islands, the Filipinos resisted and eventually turned to guerrilla warfare.

Quelling what American authorities called the "Philippine insurrection" required three years (1899–1902), took the lives of more than 4,200 American soldiers (more losses than in the Spanish-American War) and perhaps 20,000 guerrillas, and cost $400 million (twenty times the price of the islands). In crushing the Filipino independence movement, U.S. troops resorted to the same practice of reconcentration that the American public and Congress had so widely condemned when Spain used it in Cuba. Both sides committed atrocities during the conflict, and those by American troops confirmed the fears of anti-imperialists that a colonial policy would corrupt American values. Resistance continued into mid-1902, although American troops captured Aguinaldo in 1901.

Aguinaldo's defeat and McKinley's re-election ended any prospect for immediate Philippine independence. In 1902 Congress set up a government for the Philippines similar to that of Puerto Rico. Filipinos became citizens of the Philippine Islands, not citizens of the United States. The president of the United States appointed the governor. Filipino voters elected one house in the two-house legislature,

Emilio Aguinaldo Leader of struggles for Philippine independence, first against Spain and then against the United States.

♦ The Spanish banished Emilio Aguinaldo (on horseback) from the Philippines because of his efforts to end Spanish rule. American naval officials returned him to the islands. There he helped to establish an independent Filipino government and later led armed resistance to American authority, until he was captured in 1901. *UPI/Bettmann Archives.*

and the governor appointed the other. Both the governor and the U.S. Congress could veto laws passed by the legislature. **William Howard Taft,** governor of the islands from 1901 to 1904, tried to build local support for American control, brought about some reform in landownership, and started projects to build public schools and hospitals and to bring modern sanitation to the islands. However, when the first Philippine legislature met, in 1907, more than half of its members favored independence from the United States.

The Open Door and the Boxer Rebellion in China

Late in 1899, Britain, Germany, and the United States signed the Treaty of Berlin, which divided Samoa between Germany and the United States. The new Pacific acquisitions of the United States—Samoa, Hawai`i, the Philippines, and Guam—were all endowed with excellent harbors and sites for naval bases. Combined with the modernized navy, these acquisitions greatly strengthened American ability to protect access to commercial markets in eastern Asia and to assert American power in eastern Asia and the Pacific. The McKinley administration now began to seek a full part in the east Asian **balance of power.**

Weakened by war with Japan in 1894–1895, the Chinese government could not resist attempts by European nations to gain control over parts of its territory. By 1899, Britain, Germany, Russia, and France had all carved out **spheres of influence**—areas where they claimed special rights, usually a monopoly over trade. In keeping with the Open Door approach first adopted in the treaty of 1844, the United States claimed no such privileges in China. Now, however, American diplomats began to fear the breakup of China into separate European colonies and the consequent exclusion of American commerce.

In 1899, Secretary of State John Hay circulated a letter to Germany, Russia, Britain, France, Italy, and Japan, asking them to permit Chinese authorities to continue to collect tariff duties within their spheres of influence. Hay hoped that this measure would preserve some semblance of Chinese sovereignty. He also urged them not to discriminate against citizens of other nations engaged in commerce within their spheres. Hay was trying to prevent other nations from carving up China and, at the same time, to make American trade possible throughout China. Although some replies proved less than fully supportive, he announced in a second letter that the

William Howard Taft Governor of the Philippines from 1901 to 1904; he was elected president of the United States in 1908 and became chief justice of the Supreme Court in 1921.

balance of power In international politics, the notion that nations may restrict each other's action because of the relative equality of their naval or military forces, either individually or through alliance systems.

sphere of influence A territorial area where a foreign nation is given significant authority.

A FAIR FIELD AND NO FAVOR!
UNCLE SAM: "I'M OUT FOR COMMERCE, NOT CONQUEST!"

♦ In this 1899 cartoon celebrating the Open Door policy, Uncle Sam insists that the nations of Europe must compete fairly for China's commerce and must not seize Chinese territory. In the background, John Bull (Britain) lifts his hat in approval. *Library of Congress.*

Open Door policy was in effect. Hay's letters have usually been called the **Open Door notes.**

The next year, in 1900, a Chinese secret society took up arms to expel foreigners and foreign influence from China. Because the rebels used a clenched fist as their symbol, Westerners called them Boxers. After attacking missionaries, the Boxers laid siege to the section of Beijing, the Chinese capital, that housed foreign **legations.** Hay foresaw that the major powers, in rescuing their citizens, might use the **Boxer Rebellion** as a pretext to take full control and divide China among themselves. To block such a move, the United States took full part in a joint international military expedition—with Japan and Russia supplying the largest numbers—to rescue the Beijing hostages and to crush the Boxer Rebellion. Hay insisted, however, that American action was directed not against the Chinese government but against the rebels.

Although China did not lose territory after the Boxer Rebellion, the intervening nations required it to pay an **indemnity.** After compensating U.S. citizens for actual losses suffered during the rebellion, the United States government returned the remainder of its indemnity to China. To show its appreciation for the return of the funds, the Chinese government used the money to send Chinese students to the United States to develop good will between the two countries.

"Carry a Big Stick": The United States and World Affairs, 1901–1913

- What were Theodore Roosevelt's expectations about the role of the United States in world affairs?
- What choices did he make to bring about the outcomes he desired?

In 1901, an assassin's bullet cut down President McKinley and put Theodore Roosevelt in the White House. Roosevelt remolded the presidency, established new federal powers over the economy, and expanded America's role in world affairs. Few presidents have had so great an impact. He once expressed his fondness for what he described as a West African proverb, "Speak softly and carry a big stick; you will go far." As president, however, Roosevelt seldom spoke softly. Everything he did, it seemed, he did strenuously. Well read in history and current events, Roosevelt entered the presidency with definite ideas on the proper role for the United States in the world. He envisioned a future in which major powers would exercise international police powers. As he advised Congress in 1902, "The increasing interdependence and complexity of international political and economic relations render it incumbent on all civilized and orderly powers to in-

Open Door notes An exchange of diplomatic letters in 1899–1900 by which Secretary of State John Hay announced American support for Chinese autonomy and opposed efforts by other powers to carve China into spheres of exclusive influence.

legation A diplomatic mission in a foreign country.

Boxer Rebellion Uprising in China in 1900 directed against foreign powers who were attempting to dominate China; it was suppressed by an international army that included American participation.

indemnity Payment for damage, loss, or injury.

sist on the proper policing of the world." The United States, Roosevelt made clear, stood ready to do its share of "proper policing."

Taking Panama

While McKinley was still president, after the American victory over Spain, American diplomats pursued efforts to build, control, and protect a canal through Central America. Many people, and not just in the United States, had long shared Mahan's dream of such a passage between the Atlantic and Pacific oceans. A French company actually began construction in the late 1870s. But the task proved too great for its resources, and the builders abandoned the project.

During the Spanish-American War, the battleship *Oregon* took well over two months to steam from the west coast, around South America, to join the rest of the fleet off the coast of Cuba. A canal would have permitted the *Oregon* to reach Cuba in three weeks or less. McKinley soon pronounced an American-controlled canal "indispensable." In the Clayton-Bulwer Treaty of 1850, however, Britain and the United States had agreed that neither would exercise exclusive control over a canal. Between 1900 and 1901, Secretary of State Hay negotiated a new agreement with Britain, the **Hay-Pauncefote Treaties,** which yielded the canal project to the United States alone.

Experts identified two possible locations for a canal, Nicaragua and Panama (then part of Colombia). The Panama route was shorter, and the French canal company had completed some of the work. **Philippe Bunau-Varilla**—formerly the chief project engineer, now a major stockholder and an indefatigable lobbyist—did his utmost to sell the French company's interests to the United States. Building through Panama, however, meant overcoming formidable mountains and fever-ridden swamps. Previous studies had preferred Nicaragua. Its geography posed fewer natural obstacles, and much of the route lay through Lake Nicaragua.

In 1902, shortly before Congress was to vote on the two routes, a volcano erupted in the Caribbean. Bunau-Varilla underscored its relation to the canal by distributing to senators a Nicaraguan postage stamp showing a smoldering volcano looming over a lake. Bunau-Varilla's lobbying—and his stamps—reinforced efforts by prominent Republican senators such as Mark Hanna. The Senate approved the route through Panama if Colombia agreed to give up land for the canal. If Colombia held back, the canal would go through Nicaragua.

Negotiations with Colombia bogged down over treaty language that significantly limited Colombia's sovereignty. When the United States put on pressure, the Colombian government offered to accept the limitations on its sovereignty in return for more money. Outraged, Roosevelt called the offer "pure bandit morality." To break the impasse, Bunau-Varilla and his associates encouraged and financed a revolution in Panama. Aware of such a possibility, Roosevelt had ordered U.S. warships to the area to prevent Colombian troops from crushing the uprising. The revolution quickly succeeded, and Panama declared its independence. The United States immediately extended diplomatic recognition. Bunau-Varilla, named Panama's minister to the United States, promptly signed a treaty that gave the United States much the same arrangement earlier rejected by Colombia.

The **Hay–Bunau-Varilla Treaty** (1904) granted the United States perpetual control over a strip of Panamanian territory ten miles wide, called the Canal Zone, for a price of $10 million and annual rent of $250,000, and it made Panama the second American protectorate (see Map 21.3). The United States purchased the assets of the French company and in 1904 began construction of the canal. Roosevelt considered the Panama Canal his crowning deed in foreign affairs. "When nobody else could or would exercise efficient authority, I exercised it," he wrote in his *Autobiography* (1911). He always denied, however, that he took part in planning the revolution, although he once bluntly claimed, "I took the canal zone."

The construction proved difficult. Just over 40 miles long, the canal took ten years to build and cost nearly $400 million. Completed in 1914, just as World War I began, it was considered one of the world's great engineering feats.

Hay-Pauncefote Treaties Two separate treaties (1900 and 1901) signed by the United States and Britain, which gave the United States the exclusive right to build, control, and fortify a canal through Central America.

Philippe Bunau-Varilla Chief engineer of the French company contracted to build the Panama Canal and later minister to the United States from the new Republic of Panama.

Hay–Bunau-Varilla Treaty Treaty with Panama that granted the United States sovereignty over the Canal Zone in return for a $10 million payment plus an annual rent.

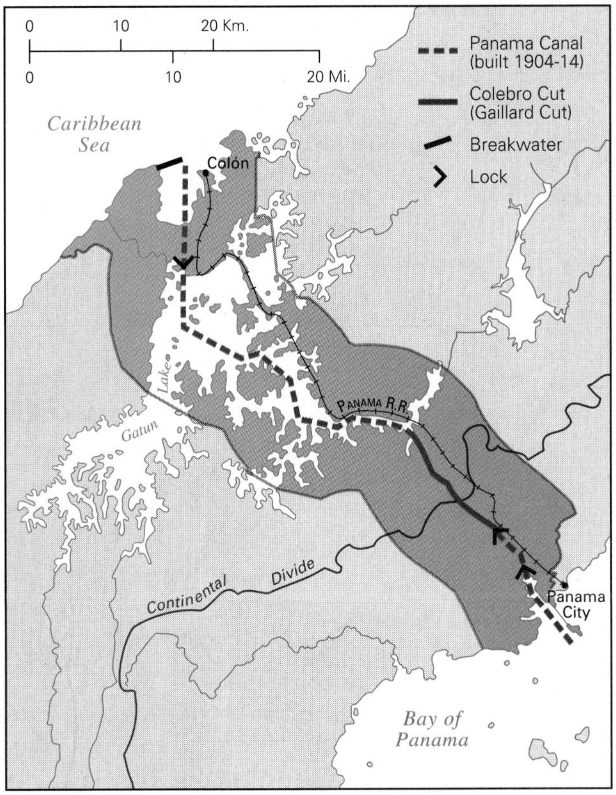

♦ **MAP 21.3 The Panama Canal** The Panama Canal could take advantage of some natural waterways. The most difficult part of the construction, however, was devising some way to move ships over the mountains near the Pacific end of the canal. This was done through a combination of cutting a route through the mountains and constructing massive locks.

Making the Caribbean an American Lake

Well before the canal was finished, American policymakers debated how best to protect it. Roosevelt determined to establish American dominance in the Caribbean and Central America, where the many islands and harbors might permit a foreign naval buildup for a strike against the canal or even the Gulf coast of the United States. Acquisition of Puerto Rico, protectorates over Cuba and Panama, and naval facilities in all three locations as well as on the Gulf coast made the United States a powerful presence in the region.

The Caribbean and the area around it contained twelve independent nations. Britain, France, Denmark, and the Netherlands held nearly all the smaller islands as well as a coastal colony. Several Caribbean nations had borrowed large amounts of money from European bankers, raising the prospect of European intervention to secure loan payments. In 1902, for example, Britain and Germany declared a blockade of Venezuela over debts owed their citizens. In 1904, when several European nations hinted that they might similarly intervene in the Dominican Republic, Roosevelt waved his "big stick." He presented to Congress what became known as the **Roosevelt Corollary** to the Monroe Doctrine, warning European nations against any intervention whatsoever in the Western Hemisphere, even if provoked by loan default or other action. If intervention by what he termed "some civilized nation" became necessary in the Caribbean and Central America in order to correct "chronic wrongdoing," Roosevelt insisted that the United States would handle it, acting as "an international police power." Roosevelt exempted Argentina, Brazil, and Chile from application of the Roosevelt Corollary. He considered them "civilized" nations and hoped they might wield a similar police power in Latin America south of the Caribbean region.

Roosevelt acted forcefully to establish his new policy. In 1905, the Dominican Republic agreed to permit the United States to collect customs and supervise government expenditures, including payment of debts. Thus the island nation became the third U.S. protectorate. The Senate initially rejected this arrangement but approved an amended version in 1907. In the meantime, Roosevelt ordered the U.S. Navy to collect Dominican customs, claiming that he could do so under his presidential powers.

Roosevelt's successors, William Howard Taft and Woodrow Wilson, continued and expanded his policy of American domination in the Caribbean region. Under Taft, the United States encouraged Americans to invest in the region. Taft hoped that diplomacy could open doors for American investments and that American investments in turn could advance foreign-policy objectives by blocking investment by other nations and by stabilizing and developing the Caribbean economies. Taft supported such **dollar diplomacy** throughout the region, especially in Nicaragua. In 1912, he sent

Roosevelt Corollary Extension of the Monroe Doctrine announced by Theodore Roosevelt in 1904, in which he proclaimed the right of the United States to police Caribbean areas.

dollar diplomacy Policy during the Taft administration of supporting U.S. commercial interests abroad for strategic purposes, especially in Latin America.

♦ Theodore Roosevelt, in his 1904 Corollary to the Monroe Doctrine, asserted that the United States was dominant in the Caribbean. Here a cartoonist capitalized on Roosevelt's boyish nature, depicting the Caribbean as Roosevelt's pond. *Culver Pictures, Inc.*

marines there to suppress a rebellion against President Adolfo Días. They remained after the turmoil settled, ostensibly to guard the American legation but actually to prop up the Días government—making Nicaragua the fourth U.S. protectorate. A treaty was drafted giving the United States responsibility for collecting customs, but the Senate rejected it. At that point, the State Department, several American banks, and Nicaragua agreed to set up a **customs receivership** through the banks.

Roosevelt and Eastern Asia

In developing American policy in eastern Asia, Roosevelt built on the Open Door notes and American participation in the international force that had suppressed the Boxer Rebellion. He found cause for both concern and optimism in the rise of Japan as a major industrial and imperial power. Alfred Thayer Mahan, his friend and naval strategist, had warned of the potential danger that Japan posed to the United States as a Pacific rival. But Roosevelt was also hopeful. He admired Japanese accomplishments and looked forward to Japan exercising the same degree of international police power in its vicinity that the United States wielded under the Roosevelt Corollary.

In 1904, Russia and Japan went to war over **Manchuria,** the northern part of China. Russia had pressured China repeatedly to grant concessions by which Manchuria slowly seemed to be turning into a Russian colony. Russia seemed also to have designs on Korea, a nominally independent kingdom. Japan saw Russia's steady expansion as a threat to its own dominance in Korea and the region and responded with force. The Japanese scored smashing naval and military victories over the Russians but had too few resources to sustain a long-term war.

Roosevelt concluded that American interests were best served by reducing Russian influence in the region so as to maintain a balance of power. Such a balance, he thought, would be most likely to preserve at least the fiction of Chinese sovereignty in Manchuria. Early in the war, he indicated some support for Japan, and, as its resources ran low, Japan asked Roosevelt to act as mediator. The president agreed, concerned by then that the Japanese victories might pose as great a danger as Russian expansion. The peace conference took place in Portsmouth, New Hampshire. The **Treaty of Portsmouth** (1905) recog-

customs receivership An agreement whereby one nation takes over the collection of customs of another nation and exercises some control over that nation's expenditures of customs receipts, thus limiting the autonomy of the nation in receivership.

Manchuria A region of northeast China that the Russians and Japanese fought to control in the late nineteenth and early twentieth centuries.

Treaty of Portsmouth Treaty in 1905 ending the Russo-Japanese War; it was negotiated at a conference in Portsmouth, New Hampshire, through Theodore Roosevelt's mediation.

♦ This souvenir bandana celebrated Theodore Roosevelt's mediation of the Russo-Japanese War, for which he received the Nobel Peace Prize in 1906. The heart-shaped ribbon around Roosevelt's portrait contains the legend, "First in War, First in Peace, First in the Hearts of His Countrymen," a tribute first applied to George Washington. That statement explains why Roosevelt's war exploits (at the top) were linked with his peace making. *Collection of Janice L. and David J. Frent.*

nized Japan's dominance in Korea and gave Japan the southern half of Sakhalin Island and Russian concessions in southern Manchuria. Russia kept its railroad in northern Manchuria. China was to have responsibility for civil authority in Manchuria. For his mediation, Roosevelt received the 1906 Nobel Peace Prize.

That same year, Roosevelt mediated another significant dispute. An order by the San Francisco school board stipulated that students of Japanese parentage were to attend the city's segregated Chinese school. The Japanese government protested what it considered a serious insult, and Japanese newspaper headlines even hinted of war. Roosevelt brought the city's school officials to Washington and convinced them to withdraw the segregation order in return for his efforts to cut off Japanese immigration. He soon carried out his part of the bargain through a so-called **gentlemen's agreement,** by which Japan agreed informally to limit the departure of laborers to the United States. In 1908, the American and Japanese governments further agreed to respect each other's territorial possessions (the Philippines and Hawai`i for the United States; Korea, Formosa, and southern Manchuria for Japan) and to honor as well "the independence and integrity of China" and the Open Door.

During the presidential administration of William Howard Taft, Roosevelt's successor, the United States extended the concept of dollar diplomacy to China. Proponents sought Chinese permission for American citizens not just to trade with China but also to invest there, especially in railroad construction. Taft and his secretary of state, Philander C. Knox, hoped that such investments could head off further Japanese expansion. The effort received Chinese government sanction, but little ever came of it, apart from alienating Japan somewhat.

The United States and the World, 1901–1913

Before the 1890s, the United States had no clear or consistent set of foreign-policy commitments or objectives. After then, its commitments were obvious to all. The Philippines, Guam, Hawai`i, Puerto Rico, eastern Samoa, and the Canal Zone were highly visible components of a new concept of America's role in world affairs.

Central to that concept was a large, modern navy, without which other commitments lacked anything more than moral force. Roosevelt was so proud of the navy that in 1907 he dispatched sixteen battleships—painted white to indicate their peaceful intent—on a fourteen-month around-the-world tour as a demonstration of American naval might. Roosevelt claimed that his primary purpose in sending the Great White Fleet "was to impress the American people." But he was clearly interested in impressing other nations too, especially Japan, and in demonstrating that the American navy was a two-ocean navy, fully capable of moving quickly from Atlantic to Pacific ports.

Another aspect of America's new role in the world revolved around American control of the Panama Canal. The need to protect the canal led the United States to establish **hegemony** in the Caribbean and Central America as a means of preventing any other

gentlemen's agreement An agreement bound only by the word of the parties; in this case, Japan agreed in 1907 to limit Japanese emigration to the United States.

hegemony The dominance of one over another.

♦ This picture was issued as a penny postcard, expressing the nation's pride in the "White Fleet." The Post Office department gave its approval to penny postcards in 1902, and the period between 1905 and 1915 is sometimes considered the "golden age" for penny postcards in the United States. The one-penny price for postage made them highly affordable, and the wide variety of subjects available made them collectable. *Collection of Picture Research Consultants and Archives.*

major power from gaining a foothold that might threaten the canal. The new American role also focused on the Pacific. Captain Mahan and other naval strategists pointed out that just as the Atlantic Ocean had been the theater of conflict among European nations in the eighteenth century, the Pacific Ocean was likely to be the theater of twentieth-century conflict. Thus considerations of commercial enterprise, such as the China trade, and naval strategy coincided and led the United States to acquire naval bases at strategic points in the central Pacific (Hawai`i), in the south Pacific (eastern Samoa), and off eastern Asia (the Philippines).

America's new vision of the world divided nations into two broad categories. On the one hand were all the "civilized" nations. On the other were those nations that Theodore Roosevelt described, at various times, as "barbarous," "impotent," or simply unable to meet their obligations. American policy toward "civilized" countries—the European powers, Japan, and the large, stable nations of Latin America—focused on efforts to find peaceful ways to realize mutual objectives, especially through arbitration. In eastern Asia, McKinley, Roosevelt, and Taft all looked to a balance of power among the contending "civilized" powers as most likely to realize the American objective of maintaining commercial access to the China market. In Europe, Roosevelt proved far more willing than any of his successors to take part in maintaining the balance of power, as he proved in 1906 by sending representatives to a conference at Algeciras, Spain, to resolve disputes over the role of the European powers in Morocco.

The conviction that arbitration was the appropriate means to settle disputes among "civilized" countries was widespread. An international conference in 1899 created a Permanent Court of Arbitration in the Netherlands. Housed in a marble "peace palace" built through a donation from Andrew Carnegie, the **Hague Court** functioned as a source of neutral arbitrators for international disputes. Both Roosevelt and Taft tried to negotiate arbitration treaties with major powers, only to find that the Senate was not willing to ratify them. Senators feared that such treaties might diminish the Senate's future role in approving agreements with other countries.

The United States and Britain repeatedly used arbitration to settle disputes between themselves, and throughout the late nineteenth and early twentieth centuries American relations with Great Britain improved steadily, primarily as a consequence of British policy choices. As Germany expanded its army and navy and increasingly challenged Britain, British policymakers sought to improve ties with the United States, the only nation besides Great Britain with a navy comparable to Germany's. During the Spanish-American War, Britain alone among the major European powers sided with the United States and encouraged its acquisition of the Philippines. In signing the Hay-Pauncefote Treaties and reducing its naval forces in the Caribbean, Britain delivered a clear signal: it not only accepted American dominance there but even depended on the good will of the United States to protect its own holdings in the region.

Hague Court Body of delegates from about fifty member nations, created in the Netherlands in 1899 for the purpose of peacefully resolving international conflicts; also known as the Permanent Court of Arbitration.

SUMMARY

Expectations
Constraints
Choices
Outcomes

From 1865 to 1889, few Americans *expected* their nation to take a major part in world affairs, at least outside North America. The United States did make *choices* to acquire Alaska and to expel the French from Mexico, and some Americans even hoped that Canada might become U.S. territory. Other American *choices* brought some involvement in the Caribbean and Central America and in eastern Asia and the Pacific.

The 1890s witnessed the development of enlarged *expectations* and daring *choices* in foreign affairs. During the administration of Benjamin Harrison, Congress approved creation of a modern navy. Although a revolution presented the United States with an opportunity to annex Hawai`i, President Grover Cleveland *chose* to reject that course. However, Cleveland boldly threatened war with Great Britain over a disputed boundary between Venezuela and British Guiana, and Britain *chose* to back down.

A revolution in Cuba led the United States into a one-sided war with Spain in 1898. The immediate *outcome* of winning the war was acquisition of an American colonial empire that included not only Cuba but also the Philippines, Guam, and Puerto Rico. Congress annexed Hawai`i in the midst of the war, and the United States acquired part of Samoa by treaty in 1899. Filipinos *chose* to resist the imposition of American authority, leading to a three-year war that cost more lives than the Spanish-American War. With the Philippines in hand and an improved navy on the seas, the United States asserted a new prominence in East Asia. It now *chose* to assert the principle of the Open Door in China, where American troops took part in suppressing the Boxer Rebellion.

President Theodore Roosevelt's *choices* played an important role in defining America's status as a world power. Roosevelt secured rights to build a U.S.-controlled canal through Panama and established Panama as an American protectorate. The Roosevelt Corollary declared outright that the United States was the dominant power in the Caribbean and Central America. In eastern Asia, however, Roosevelt *chose* to bolster the Open Door policy by maintaining a balance of power.

Roosevelt and many others believed that "civilized" nations had no need to go to war. Thus he *chose* to seek arbitration treaties with leading nations, efforts that failed because of Senate opposition. Faced with the rise of German military and naval power, Great Britain *chose* to improve its relations with the United States.

One *outcome* of America's choices in foreign affairs was the acquisition of colonies in a foreign policy usually described as imperialism. A larger *outcome* was that the United States took on the role of a world power, thereby redefining Americans' *expectations* for their nation's relations with the rest of the world.

SUGGESTED READINGS

Robert L. Beisner. *From the Old Diplomacy to the New, 1865–1900.* 2nd ed. (1986).

A concise introduction to American foreign relations in this period.

Lewis L. Gould. *The Spanish-American War and President McKinley* (1980).

The political decisions involved in war, peacemaking, and the acquisition of Spanish possessions.

Walter LaFeber. *The New Empire: An Interpretation of American Expansion, 1860–1898* (1963).

A leading treatment, the first to emphasize the notion of a commercial empire.

Lester D. Langley. *The Banana Wars: United States' Intervention in the Caribbean, 1898–1934* (1983, reprint, 1988).

A sprightly and succinct account of the role of the United States in the Caribbean and Central America.

David G. McCullough. *The Path Between the Seas: The Creation of the Panama Canal, 1870–1914* (1977).

Perhaps the most lively and engrossing coverage of this subject.

Stuart Creighton Miller. *"Benevolent Assimilation": The American Conquest of the Philippines, 1899–1903* (1982).

A thorough account.

ADOPTION OF PROGRESSIVE REFORMS BY 1915 This map shows the states that had adopted three progressive reforms during the years before 1915. Woman suffrage, long advocated, finally moved toward national adoption during these years. Prohibition was the leading example of moral reform during the period, and the initiative and referendum became popular vehicles for voter expression in some states.

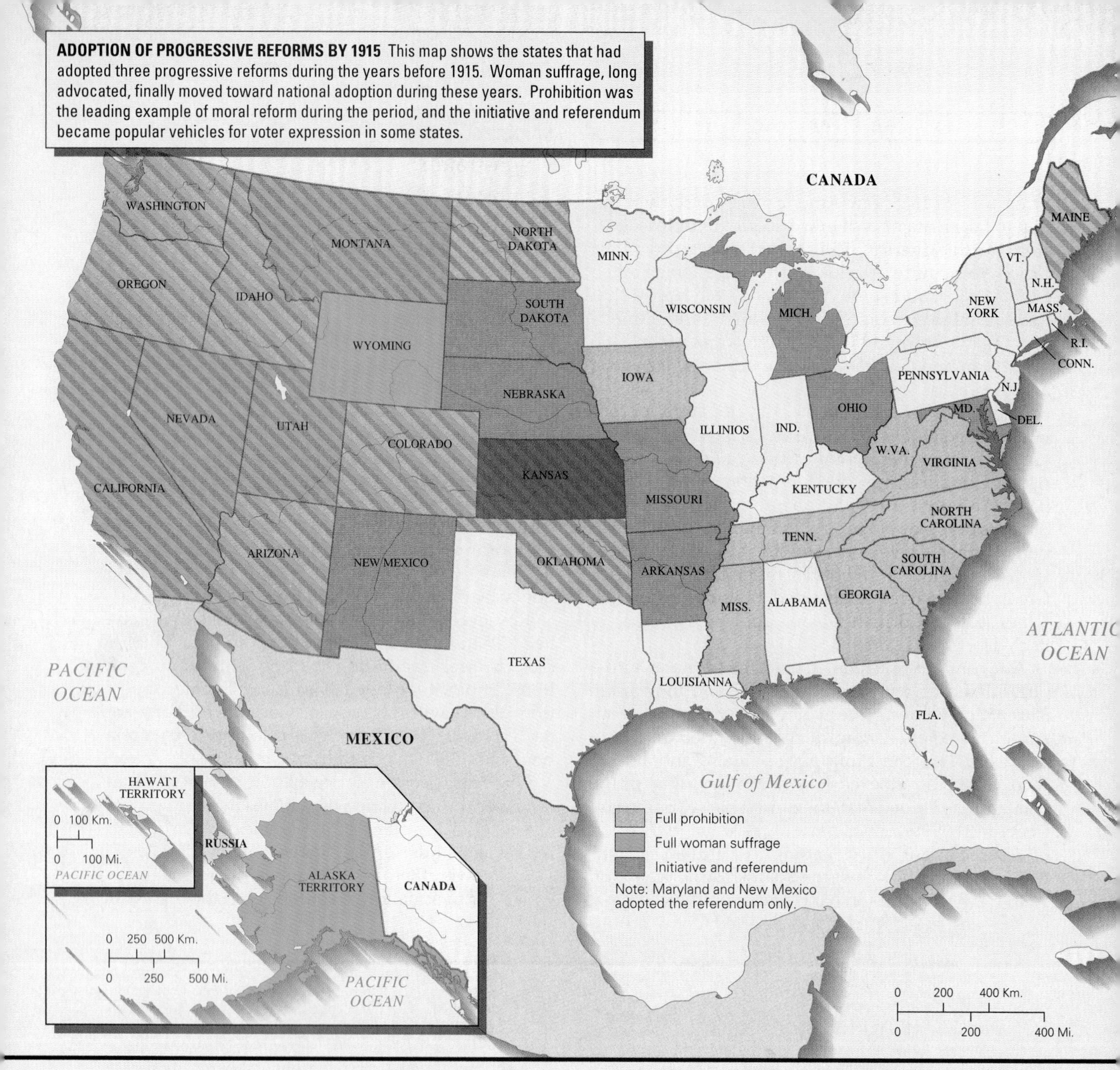

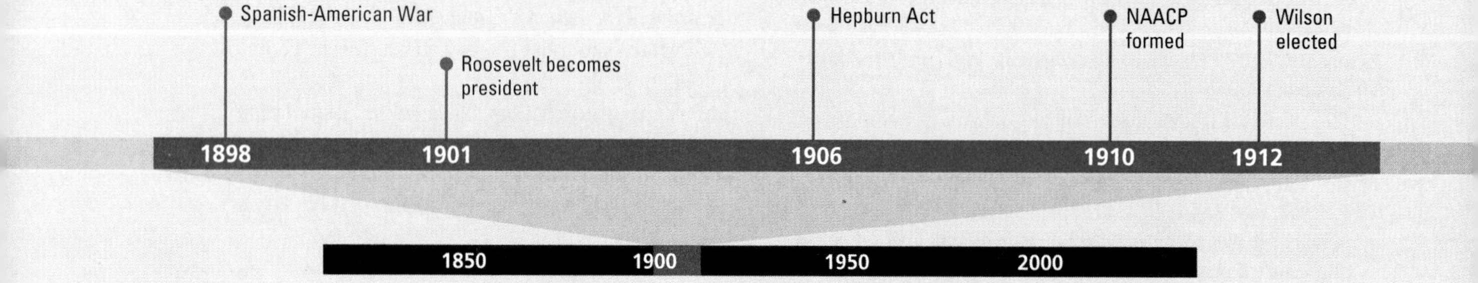

CHAPTER 22

The Progressive Era, 1900–1917

Organizing for Change

- What were some of the important changes in American politics in the early twentieth century?
- What choices by women and African Americans produced new organizations devoted to political change?

The Reform of Politics, the Politics of Reform

- How did the muckrakers and new professional groups contribute to the growth of reform?
- What were the central characteristics of reform in city and state government?
- How did the rise of interest groups reflect new expectations about politics and government?

Roosevelt, Taft, and Republican Progressivism

- What constraints did Theodore Roosevelt face, and how did he choose to deal with them?
- What were the outcomes for the role of the federal government in the economy and for the power of the presidency?

Wilson and Democratic Progressivism

- What choices confronted American voters in the presidential election of 1912?
- How did choices by Woodrow Wilson and the Democrats change the role of the federal government in the economy?

Progressivism in Perspective

- Was progressivism successful?
- What are your criteria for judging its success?
- What lasting outcomes of progressivism affect modern American politics?

INTRODUCTION

Expectations
Constraints
Choices
Outcomes

"Nothing is done in this country as it was done twenty years ago," wrote President Woodrow Wilson in 1913. He exaggerated only slightly. The late 1890s and first twenty years of the twentieth century—years historians call the Progressive era—were a time when "reform was in the air," as one small-town journalist later recalled. In 1912, Walter Weyl, a former settlement house worker, described American politics this way:

> *We are in a period of clamor, of bewilderment, of an almost tremulous unrest. We are hastily revising all our social conceptions. We are hastily testing all our political ideals.*

Weyl's description, overstated as it was, reflected the widespread popular *expectation* for change. Reform was "in the air" almost everywhere, and many different individuals and groups joined the crusade, often with quite different *expectations.* The variety of competing organizations seeking to reform politics could—and did—produce nearly as much clamor and bewilderment as Weyl described.

At the dawn of the new century, however, few Americans could have anticipated the extent of change that lay just ahead. Most probably *expected* a continuation of nineteenth-century political patterns, in which parties dominated politics and government's role in the economy was limited largely to stimulating economic development through the tariff and land policies. At the same time, however, many Americans also believed that something should be done to curb the power of the new industrial corporations and to correct the problems of the cities, and some Americans came to identify traditional political practices as a major *constraint* on reform.

Progressivism took shape through many *choices* by voters and political leaders. Most decisions were specific to a particular election or legislative proposal, but a more basic *choice* loomed behind many of them: should government play a larger role in the lives of Americans? This question lay behind debates over regulation of railroads in 1906 and regulation of banking in 1913, as well as behind proposals to prohibit alcoholic beverages and to limit working hours of women wage earners in factories. Time after time, Americans *chose* a greater role for government. Often there was such widespread agreement on the need for government intervention that the only *choices* were about the form intervention would take. As they gave government more power, Americans also sought to make it more responsive to ordinary citizens. *Constrained* by nineteenth-century patterns of political decision making, Americans put stricter limits on political parties and introduced ways for people to participate more directly in politics—such as the direct primary and the initiative and referendum. The *constraints* imposed by traditional values of private property and individualism proved more hardy. Although progressives imposed restrictions on the rights of private property, few Americans responded to calls by socialists to eliminate it. Although some reformers proposed to limit individual liberties in the name of morality, a more lasting *outcome* proved to be the breakdown of separate spheres for men and women in politics. The *outcome* of the political changes of the Progressive era, following on the heels of the political realignment of the 1890s, was a revamped pattern of politics, significantly different from that of the nineteenth century. The long-term changes in the structure and function of government wrought during these decades fundamentally altered American politics and government in the twentieth century. The Progressive era gave birth to many aspects of modern American politics.

CHRONOLOGY

Reform in the Progressive Era

1889 Hazen Pingree elected mayor of Detroit

1895 Anti-Saloon League formed
United States v. E. C. Knight
Booker T. Washington delivers Atlanta Compromise

1896 McKinley elected

1898 South Dakota adopts initiative and referendum
Spanish-American War

1900 First city commission, in Galveston, Texas
Robert M. La Follette elected governor of Wisconsin
McKinley re-elected

1901 Socialist Party of America formed
President William McKinley assassinated
Formation of U.S. Steel by J.P. Morgan
Theodore Roosevelt becomes president

1902 Muckraking journalism begins
Oregon adopts initiative and referendum
Antitrust action against Northern Securities Company
Roosevelt intervenes in coal strike
Reclamation Act

1903 Women's Trade Union League formed
W. E. B. Du Bois's *Souls of Black Folk*
Elkins Act
Expedition Act

1904 Lincoln Steffens's *The Shame of the Cities*
Ida Tarbell's *The History of the Standard Oil Company*
Roosevelt elected president

1905 Niagara Movement formed
Industrial Workers of the World organized

1906 Upton Sinclair's *The Jungle*
Hepburn Act
Pure Food and Drug Act
Meat Inspection Act

1907 Financial panic

1908 *Muller v. Oregon*
Race riot in Springfield, Illinois
First city-manager government, in Staunton, Virginia
William Howard Taft elected president

1909 Iowa passes first "red-light abatement" law
Payne-Aldrich Tariff

1910 State of Washington approves woman suffrage
National Association for the Advancement of Colored People formed
Woodrow Wilson elected governor of New Jersey
Revolt against Cannonism
Taft fires Pinchot

1911 Fire at Triangle Shirtwaist factory

1912 Progressive ("Bull Moose") party formed
Wilson elected president

1913 Sixteenth Amendment (establishing federal income tax) ratified
Seventeenth Amendment (establishing direct election of U.S. senators) ratified
Underwood Tariff
Federal Reserve Act

1914 Clayton Antitrust Act
Federal Trade Commission Act
Panama Canal completed

1915 National Birth Control League formed

1916 Louis Brandeis appointed to the Supreme Court
Montana elects Jeannette Rankin, the first woman, to Congress
Wilson re-elected

1917 United States enters World War I

Organizing for Change

- What were some of the important changes in American politics in the early twentieth century?
- What choices by women and African Americans produced new organizations devoted to political change?

During the early twentieth century, politics dramatically expanded to embrace wider-ranging concerns raised by a complex assortment of groups and individuals. In the swirl of proponents and proposals, politics more than ever before came to reflect the interaction of organized **interest groups.**

The Changing Face of Politics

As the United States entered the twentieth century, the lives of many Americans had changed in important ways. The railroad, telegraph, and telephone had transformed concepts of time and space and fostered formation of many new organizations. The executives of the new industrial corporations now thought in terms of the regional or national market for their products. Union members allied with others of their trade in distant cities. Farmers studied grain prices in Chicago and Liverpool. Physicians organized to establish nationwide standards for medical schools.

Manufacturers, farmers, merchants, carpenters, teachers, lawyers, physicians, and many others established or reorganized national associations to advance their economic or professional interests. Sometimes that meant seeking government assistance at the state or national level. As early as the 1870s, for example, associations of merchants, farmers, and oil producers had pushed for laws to regulate railroad freight rates (see pages 613, 617).

Many other forms of associative activity also developed. Some graduates emerged from the recently transformed universities (see pages 589–590) with the conviction that their knowledge and skills could help to improve society, and many formed professional associations to advance those objectives. Long-established church organizations sometimes helped to foster the emergence of new associations devoted to moral reform, especially prohibition. Some people formed groups with humanitarian goals such as ending child labor. Members of ethnic and racial groups formed societies to foster their groups' interests. Reformers organized to limit the power of the new corporations or to defeat party bosses. Overlapping with many of these new associations were the organizational activities of women, including middle-class women, new college graduates, and factory and clerical workers.

Sooner or later, many of the new associations sought changes in laws to help them reach their objectives. Increasing numbers of citizens related to politics through such organized interest groups, even as the traditional political parties found they could no longer count on the total voter loyalty typical of the Gilded Age.

Many of these new groups optimistically believed that responsible citizens, acting together, assisted by technical know-how, and sometimes drawing on the power of government, could achieve social progress—improvement of the human situation. As early as the 1890s, some had begun to call themselves "progressive citizens." By 1910, many were simply calling themselves "progressives."

Historians use the term *progressivism* to signify three related developments during the early twentieth century: (1) the emergence of new concepts of the purposes and functions of government, (2) changes in government policies and institutions, and (3) the political agitation that produced those changes. A progressive, then, was a person involved in one or more of these activities. The many individuals and groups all promoting their own visions of change made progressivism a complex political phenomenon. There was no one progressive movement. To be sure, an organized **Progressive party** emerged in 1912 and sputtered for a brief time after, but it failed to capture the allegiance of all those who called themselves progressives. Although there was no typical progressive, many aspects of progressivism reflected concerns of the urban middle class, especially urban middle-class women.

Progressivism appeared at every level of government: local, state, and federal. And progressives promoted a wide range of new government activities: regulation of business, moral revival, consumer protection, conservation of natural resources, educational improvement, tax reform, and more. In all these ways, they brought government more directly into the economy and more directly into the lives of most Americans.

interest group A coalition of people working on behalf of a particular cause, such as an item of legislation, a particular industry, or a special segment of society.

Progressive party Party formed in 1912 with Theodore Roosevelt as its candidate for president; it disintegrated when Roosevelt lost the election.

Women and Reform

Organizations formed by or dominated by women burst onto politics during the **Progressive era.** By 1900 or so, a new ideal for women had emerged from women's colleges and clubs and from discussions on national lecture circuits and in the press. The New Woman stood for self-determination rather than unthinking acceptance of roles prescribed by the cult of domesticity and separate spheres. By 1910, this attitude, sometimes called **feminism,** was accelerating the transition from the nineteenth-century women's movement for suffrage to the twentieth-century struggle for equality and individualism.

Women's increasing control over one aspect of their lives is evident in the birth rate, which fell steadily throughout the nineteenth and early twentieth centuries as couples chose (or, perhaps, women alone chose) to have fewer children. In the early nineteenth century, many women used abortion to end unwanted pregnancies, but that option became illegal after midcentury. By the end of the century, state and federal laws also banned information about contraception. As a result, women or couples seeking to prevent conception often had to rely on word of mouth or advertising for potions or devices that only hinted at their use. In 1915, a group of women formed the National Birth Control League to seek the repeal of laws that barred contraceptive information. In 1916, **Margaret Sanger,** a nurse practicing among the poor in New York City, attracted wide attention when she went to jail for informing women about birth control.

Other women also formed organizations to advance specific causes. Some, like the settlement houses, were oriented to service. The National Consumers' League (formed in 1890) and the Women's Trade Union League (1903) tried to improve the lives of working women. Such efforts received a tragic boost in 1911 when fire roared through the Triangle Shirtwaist Company's clothing factory in New York City, killing 146 workers—nearly all women—who were trapped in a building with no outside fire escapes and with exit doors locked to deter workers from taking breaks. The public outcry produced a prominent state investigation and, in 1914, a new state factory safety law.

Some states passed laws specifically to protect working women. In ***Muller v. Oregon*** (1908), the Supreme Court approved the constitutionality of one such law, limiting women's hours of work. Louis Brandeis, a lawyer working with the Consumers' Union, defended the law on the grounds that women were "in general weaker than men in muscular strength and in nervous energy" and needed special protection because of their social roles as mothers. Such arguments ran contrary to the New Woman's rejection of separate spheres and ultimately raised questions for women's drive for equality. At the time, however, the decision was widely hailed as a vital and necessary protection for women wage earners. By 1917, all but nine states had laws restricting women's working hours.

Though prominent in reform causes, most women could neither vote nor hold office. Support for suffrage grew, however, as more women recognized the

♦ Margaret Sanger is seen here in 1916, leaving court after being charged with distributing birth control information illegally. During the Progressive Era, women worked to remove legal barriers to obtaining information on preventing conception. *Smith College Collection, Smith College.*

Progressive era Period of reform in the late nineteenth and early twentieth centuries.

feminism The conviction that women are and should be the social, political, and economic equals of men.

Margaret Sanger Birth-control advocate who believed that information about birth control was essential to help women escape poverty and who disobeyed government laws against its distribution.

Muller v. Oregon Case in 1908 in which the Supreme Court upheld an Oregon law that limited the hours of employment for women.

♦ Women marched in support of suffrage in New York City in 1910. This part of the march featured women wearing academic robes to symbolize their educational accomplishments, thereby dramatizing the injustice of being denied the ballot. Other marches also demonstrated the extent of support for woman suffrage. *Schlesinger Library, Radcliffe College.*

need for political action to bring social reforms. By 1896, four western states had extended the vote to women (see page 607). No other state approved extension of the franchise until 1910, when Washington approved female suffrage. Seven more western states followed over the next five years. In 1916, **Jeannette Rankin** of Montana—born on a ranch, educated as a social worker, experienced as a suffrage campaigner—became the first woman elected to the House of Representatives. Suffrage scored few victories outside the West, however.

Convinced that only a federal constitutional amendment would gain the vote for all women, the **National American Woman Suffrage Association (NAWSA),** led by Carrie Chapman Catt and Anna Howard Shaw, developed a national organization geared to lobbying in Washington, D.C. Alice Paul advocated public demonstrations and civil disobedience, tactics she learned from suffragists in England, where she was a settlement house worker from 1907 to 1910. In 1913, Paul and her followers formed the Congressional Union to pursue their more militant strategies. Some white suffragists tried to build an interracial movement for suffrage—NAWSA, for example, condemned lynching in 1917—but most white suffragists feared that attention to other issues would weaken their position.

Despite the predominantly white and middle-class cast of its leaders, the cause of woman suffrage ignited a mass movement during the 1910s, mobilizing women of all ages and socioeconomic classes. Opponents of woman suffrage had long argued that voting would bring women into the male sphere, make them subject to the same corrupting influences as men, and thereby render them unsuitable as guardians of the moral order. But some suffrage advocates now turned the domesticity argument to their favor, claiming that women would make politics more moral and family oriented. Others, especially feminists, argued that women should vote because they deserved full equality with men.

Moral Reform

Causes other than suffrage stirred women to action during the Progressive era. Women were prominent as well in new organizations intended to bring moral reform. Moral reformers, men and women, focused especially on banning the consumption of alcohol, which the reformers called Demon Rum. The temperance movement dated to at least the 1820s, but at first most temperance advocates focused on persuading individuals to give up strong drink. By the late nineteenth century, however, they looked increasingly to government to control individual behavior by prohibiting the production, sale, or consumption of alcoholic beverages. Many saw

Jeannette Rankin Montana reformer and pacifist who in 1916 became the first woman elected to Congress; she worked to pass the woman suffrage amendment and to protect women in the workplace.

National American Woman Suffrage Association Organization formed in 1890 that united the two major women's suffrage groups of that time.

prohibition as a progressive reform and called on the government to safeguard the public interest. Few reforms could claim as many women activists as prohibition.

The drive against alcohol developed a broad base during the Progressive era. Some **old-stock** Protestant churches—notably the Methodists—termed alcohol one of the most significant obstacles to a better society. Adherents of the Social Gospel (see page 576) viewed prohibition as one of several social reforms needed to save the victims of industrialization and urbanization. Others, appealing to concepts of domesticity, emphasized the need to protect the family and home from the destructive influence of alcohol on husbands and fathers. At the same time, scientists related alcohol to certain diseases and publicized the dangerous **narcotic** and **depressive** qualities of the drug. Sociologists added studies demonstrating unmistakable links between liquor and prostitution, sexually transmitted diseases, poverty, crime, and broken families. Other evidence pointed to alcohol as contributing to industrial accidents and inefficiency on the job.

Earlier, prohibitionists had organized into either the Prohibition party or the Women's Christian Temperance Union. After its formation in 1895, however, the **Anti-Saloon League** became the model for successful interest-group politics. Proudly describing itself as "the Church in action against the saloon," it usually operated through the large old-stock Protestant denominations. The League focused much of its antagonism against the saloon, attacking it as the least defensible element in the liquor industry. Reformers viewed saloons as corrupting not only individual patrons—such as men who neglected their families—but politics as well. Saloons, where political cronies struck deals and mingled with voters, had long been identified with big-city political machines.

The League endorsed only politicians who opposed Demon Rum, regardless of their party or stand on other issues. As the prohibition cause demonstrated its growing political clout, growing numbers of politicians lined up against the saloon. At the same time, the League also promoted statewide referendums to ban alcohol. Between 1900 and 1917, voters adopted prohibition in nearly half of the states, including nearly all of the West and the South. Elsewhere, many towns and rural areas voted themselves "dry" under **local option laws.**

Opposition to prohibition came especially from immigrants—and their American-born descendants—from Ireland, Germany, and southern and eastern Europe. These groups, mostly Catholics, Lutherans, German Calvinists, and Jews, did not regard the use of alcohol as inherently sinful. For them, beer or wine was an accepted part of social life, and they opposed prohibition as an effort by old-stock Protestants to impose their moral views on others. "Personal liberty" became the slogan for these "wets." Companies that produced alcohol, especially brewers of beer, also organized in opposition to the prohibitionists and subsidized some associations, especially the German American Alliance, in an effort to build a political coalition against the "dry" crusade.

The drive against alcohol, ultimately successful at the national level (see page 744), was by no means the only target for moral reformers. Throughout the nineteenth century, many cities had tried to regulate prostitution. During the Progressive era, reformers—many of them women—tried to eliminate prostitution through state and federal legislation. Beginning in Iowa in 1909, states passed "red-light abatement" laws designed to close brothels. In 1910, Congress passed the **Mann Act,** making it illegal to take a woman across a state line for "immoral purposes." Other moral reform efforts—to ban gambling or make divorces more difficult to obtain, for example—also represented attempts to use government power to regulate individual behavior.

Racial Issues

Unlike women's issues and moral reform, racial issues during the Progressive era generally were not prominent (see pages 584–587). Despite widely

old-stock Characteristic of people whose families had been in the United States for several generations.

narcotic A drug that reduces pain and induces sleep or stupor.

depressive Tending to lower someone's spirits and to lessen activity.

Anti-Saloon League Political interest group in favor of prohibition, founded in 1893; it organized through churches and offered its endorsement to politicians who favored prohibition.

local option laws A state law that permitted an individual town or city to decide, by an election, whether to ban liquor sales.

Mann Act Law passed by Congress in 1910 designed to suppress prostitution; it made transporting a woman across state lines for immoral purposes illegal.

INDIVIDUAL CHOICES

Fighting for Equality

W. E. B. Du Bois

A brilliant young intellectual, W. E. B. Du Bois had to choose between leading the quiet life of a college professor or challenging Booker T. Washington's claim to speak on behalf of all African Americans. Schomburg Center for Research in Black Culture, New York Public Library, Astor, Lenox and Tilden Foundations.

In 1904 and 1905, William Edward Burghardt Du Bois moved toward a difficult choice. Should he, or should he not, challenge the leadership of Booker T. Washington, the "Wizard of Tuskegee," the most powerful African American in the nation? In the decade after his Atlanta Compromise address, Washington had emerged as head of a "Tuskegee Machine." His access to northern white philanthropists made him the chief channel for donations to African-American institutions. And his access to leaders of the Republican party gave him a hand in influencing many, if not most, African-American political patronage appointments in both North and South. Du Bois, by contrast, was a college professor who had few connections to funds or politics but was well known and highly respected among black intellectuals.

Born in Great Barrington, Massachusetts, an area with a very small black population, Du Bois experienced little racial hostility before leaving home. At Fisk University, in Nashville, Tennessee, however, he encountered both the constraints of racism and the African-American culture of the South. He completed his undergraduate studies at Harvard, graduated with honors, then studied in Germany and wrote a doctoral dissertation on the suppression of the African slave trade to the United States. In

expressed concerns for social justice, only a few white progressives actively opposed disfranchisement and segregation in the South. Indeed, southern white progressives often took the lead in enacting discriminatory laws. Journalist Ray Stannard Baker was one of the few white progressives to address the plight of African Americans. In his book *Following the Color Line* (1908), Baker asked: "Does democracy really include Negroes as well as white men?" For most white Americans, the answer appeared to be no.

Lynchings and violence continued as a fact of life for African Americans. Between 1900 and World War I, lynchings claimed more than eleven hundred victims, most in the South but many in the Midwest. The same years also saw several race riots in which whites attacked blacks. In 1906, Atlanta erupted into a riot as whites attacked African Americans at random, killing four, injuring many more, and destroying many homes. In 1908, in Springfield, Illinois (where Abraham Lincoln had made his home), a mob of whites lynched two black men, injured others, and destroyed black-owned businesses. In North and South alike, little effort was made to prosecute the leaders of such mobs.

1895, he became the first African American to receive a Ph.D. from Harvard.

Du Bois then taught at the college level and undertook research and scholarly writing. By the early twentieth century, however, he had chosen to do more than research and teach. In his third book, *Souls of Black Folk* (1903), he challenged Washington's accommodationist approach and insisted that African Americans should never acquiesce in the surrender of their rights. He also presented the concept of double consciousness, by which he meant that African Americans had both an African identity and an American identity and needed to be aware of both parts of their cultural heritage. He argued that the "talented tenth"—the African-American intellectual elite—had special leadership obligations. Refuting Washington's claim that African Americans should start at the bottom, Du Bois insisted instead that denial of educational opportunities for the talented tenth constrained all African Americans.

Although the book created a sensation among African-American intellectuals and some white philanthropists, Washington's first response was to invite Du Bois to Tuskegee, apparently to co-opt him into the Tuskegee Machine. Du Bois, however, held back, certain of his criticism of Washington but also concerned for the damage that Washington might be able to do to the career of a young scholar. By late 1904, however, Du Bois determined to challenge Washington directly, and early in 1905 he charged that Washington had bought and paid for much of the support he received from the black press. The next important step, in July 1905, was formation of the Niagara Movement. This body was to be the organizational vehicle for mobilizing African Americans for an assault on both white supremacy and Washington's accommodationism. Proclaiming that "persistent manly agitation is the way to liberty," the new organization chose Du Bois as its general secretary. Despite a promising beginning, the movement failed to thrive. In 1910, what was left of the Niagara Movement was transformed into the NAACP, and Du Bois became editor of its journal, *The Crisis*. At about the same time, Du Bois briefly joined the Socialist Party of America. He continued to espouse socialist ideas, and the experience of World War I moved him toward anti-imperialism and pacifism.

Du Bois's uncompromising leadership in the struggle for civil rights and his voluminous writings on both current events and black history made him probably the single most influential African-American intellectual of the twentieth century. By the end of his long life, he concluded that America would never accomplish racial equality. In 1961, he joined the Communist party and accepted citizenship in Ghana, then a socialist nation. There he died during the night of August 27, 1963, the day before one of the greatest civil rights gatherings in American history (see page 931). In announcing Du Bois's death to the huge crowd in Washington, D.C., Roy Wilkins, executive secretary of the NAACP, noted that "at the dawn of the twentieth century his was the voice calling you to gather here today in this cause."

During the Progressive era, some African Americans dared to pose alternatives to the accommodationist leadership of Booker T. Washington (see page 585). W. E. B. Du Bois, the first African American to receive a Ph.D. from Harvard, wrote some of the first scholarly studies of African Americans. He emphasized the contributions of black men and women, disproved racial stereotypes, and urged African Americans to take pride in their accomplishments. A professor at Atlanta University after 1897, Du Bois used his book *Souls of Black Folk* (1903) to criticize Washington (see Individual Choices: W. E. B. Du Bois) and to exhort African Americans to struggle for their rights "unceasingly." "The hands of none of us are clean," he argued, speaking to both whites and blacks, "if we bend not our energies to a righting of these great wrongs."

Realizing that few politicians cared about their situation, some African-American leaders organized in support of black rights. In 1905, Du Bois and others met secretly in Canada, near Niagara Falls, and drafted demands for racial equality—including civil rights and equality in job opportunities and education—and an end to segregation. The Springfield

♦ An unknown photographer captured this lynching on film and preserved all its brutality and depravity. Although there are many such photographic records of lynch mobs, local authorities nearly always claimed that they were unable to determine the identity of those responsible for the murder. *The Picture Cube.*

riot so shocked some white progressives that in 1909 they called a biracial conference to seek ways to improve race relations. In 1910, they formed a new organization, the **National Association for the Advancement of Colored People (NAACP),** destined to provide important leadership in the fight for black equality. Du Bois served as the NAACP's director of publicity and research.

Challenging Capitalism: Socialists and Wobblies

Many progressive organizations reflected middle- and upper-class concerns, such as businesslike government, prohibition, and greater reliance on experts. Not so the **Socialist Party of America (SPA),** formed in 1901. Proclaiming themselves the political arm of workers and farmers, the Socialists argued that industrial capitalism had produced "an economic slavery which renders intellectual and political tyranny inevitable." They rejected many progressive proposals as inadequate to resolve the nation's problems. Instead, they called for a cooperative commonwealth in which workers would share in the ownership and control of the means of production.

The Socialists' best-known national leader was Eugene V. Debs, leader of the Pullman strike (see page 527) and virtually the only person able to unite the many socialist factions, ranging from theoretical **Marxists** completely opposed to capitalism to municipal reformers seeking only city-owned gas, electric, water, and streetcar systems. Strong among immigrants, some of whom had become socialists in their native lands, the SPA also took in Christian Socialists (who drew their inspiration from religion rather than from Marx), farmers, and trade union activists. In addition, the party attracted support from some of the intellectuals who sought comprehensive social change, including W. E. B. Du Bois, Margaret Sanger, and Upton Sinclair.

In 1905, a group of unionists and radicals organized the Industrial Workers of the World (IWW). IWW organizers boldly proclaimed, "We have been naught, we shall be all," as they set out to organize the unskilled and semiskilled workers at the bottom of the socioeconomic ladder. They aimed their message at the multitude of people who worked in **sweatshops** in eastern cities, **migrant** farm workers who harvested western crops, southern sharecroppers, women workers, African Americans, and the "new" immigrants from southern and eastern Europe. Such workers were usually ignored by the American Federation of Labor which instead emphasized skilled workers, most of them white males.

National Association for the Advancement of Colored People Biracial civil rights organization founded in New York City in 1910; it continues to work to end discrimination in the United States.

Socialist Party of America Political party formed in 1901 and committed to socialism—that is, government ownership of most corporations.

Marxist A believer in the ideas of Karl Marx and Friedrich Engels, who opposed private ownership of property and looked to a future in which workers would control the economy.

sweatshop A shop or factory in which employees work long hours at low wages under poor conditions.

migrant Traveling from one area to another.

♦ This design appeared originally on a "stickerette," a small poster ($2\frac{1}{2}'' \times 3''$) with glue on the back. When the glue was moistened, the poster could be stuck on a fence post or inside a box car (where migratory workers often traveled). Wobblies sometimes called the stickerettes "silent agitators." *Courtesy Labor Archives and Research Center, San Francisco State University.*

IWW members, known as Wobblies, often carried little red songbooks containing new, prolabor words to well-known tunes:

Are you poor, forlorn and hungry?
Are there lots of things you lack?
Is your life made up of misery?
Then dump the bosses off your back.

(Sung to the tune of "Take It to the Lord in Prayer")

The Wobblies' objective was simple: when most workers had joined the IWW, they would call a general strike, labor would refuse to work, and capitalism would collapse.

The IWW did organize a few dramatic strikes and demonstrations and even scored a handful of significant victories. But they often met brutal suppression by local authorities and made few lasting gains for their members.

The SPA counted considerably more victories than the Wobblies. Hundreds of cities and towns—including Milwaukee, Wisconsin; Reading, Pennsylvania; and Berkeley, California—elected Socialist mayors or council members. Socialists also won election to state legislatures in several states. Districts in New York City and Milwaukee sent Socialists to the U.S. House of Representatives. Most Americans, however, had no interest in eliminating private property. And most progressive reformers looked askance at the Socialists and sometimes tried to undercut their appeal with reforms that addressed some of their concerns but stopped short of challenging capitalism.

The Reform of Politics, the Politics of Reform

- How did the muckrakers and new professional groups contribute to the growth of reform?
- What were the central characteristics of reform in city and state government?
- How did the rise of interest groups reflect new expectations about politics and government?

Progressivism emerged at all levels of government as cities elected reform-minded mayors and states swore in progressive governors. Some reformers hoped only to make government more honest and efficient. Others wanted basic changes in the structure and function of government, to make it more responsive to the needs of America's urban, industrial society. In their quest for change, reformers sometimes found themselves in conflict with the entrenched leaders of political parties and dedicated themselves to limiting the power of those parties.

Exposing Corruption: The Muckrakers

Journalists played an important role in preparing the ground for reform. By the early 1900s, magazine publishers discovered that their sales boomed when they fed the public's taste for dramatic exposés of scandal—political corruption, corporate wrongdoing, and other offenses. Those who practiced this provocative journalism acquired the name **muckrakers:** in 1906, President Theodore Roosevelt compared them to "the Man with the Muck-rake," a character in John Bunyan's classic allegory *Pilgrim's Progress.* Roosevelt intended the comparison as a rebuke, but journalists accepted the label with pride.

Though not the first to run exposés of government and business, *McClure's Magazine* led the surge in muckraking journalism that developed after 1902.

muckrakers Progressive-era journalists who wrote articles exposing corruption in city government, business, and industry.

A NAUSEATING JOB, BUT IT MUST BE DONE
(President Roosevelt takes hold of the investigating muck-rake himself in the packing-house scandal.)

♦ Upton Sinclair's novel, *The Jungle* (1906), prompted President Theodore Roosevelt to order an investigation of Sinclair's allegations about unsanitary practices. Roosevelt then used the results of that investigation to pressure Congress into approving new federal legislation to inspect meatpacking, including a stamp such as the one shown here for condemned meat. *Stamp: Chicago Historical Society; book cover: Library of Congress.*

In October 1902, *McClure's* began a series in which **Lincoln Steffens** revealed corruption in city governments. The January 1903 issue carried Steffens's installment on Minneapolis, the first article in a series by **Ida Tarbell** on Standard Oil's sordid past, and a piece by Ray Stannard Baker revealing corruption and violence in labor unions. Sales of *McClure's* boomed, and other monthlies copied the muckraking style, serving up accounts of the defects of patent medicines, fraud in the insurance industry, the horrors of child labor, and more.

Muckraking extended from periodicals like *McClure's, Collier's, Cosmopolitan,* and *American Magazine* to books. Many of the muckraking books were simply nonfiction reports on social problems. Both Steffens and Tarbell collected their articles and published them in book form (*The Shame of the Cities,* 1904; *The History of the Standard Oil Company,* 1904). The most famous muckraking book, however, was a novel: *The Jungle,* by **Upton Sinclair** (1906). In following the experiences of a fictional family of immigrants in Chicago, the novel exposed in disgusting detail the very real shortcomings of the meatpacking industry. Sinclair, a Socialist, hoped readers would recognize that the offenses he portrayed were the result of industrial capitalism. He described in chilling detail the afflictions of packinghouse workers—severed fingers, tuberculosis, blood poisoning. He shocked the nation when he wrote of men who "fell into the vats; and when they were fished out, there was never enough left of them to be worth exhibiting—sometimes they would be overlooked for days, till all but the bones of them had gone out to the world as Durham's Pure Leaf Lard!"

Sinclair's revelations horrified many Americans, and President Roosevelt appointed a commission to

Lincoln Steffens Muckraking journalist and managing editor of *McClure's Magazine,* best known for revealing political corruption in city governments.

Ida Tarbell Progressive-era journalist whose exposé revealed the ruthlessness of the Standard Oil Company.

Upton Sinclair Socialist writer and reformer whose novel *The Jungle* helped bring about government regulation of meatpacking and other industries.

investigate. Its report confirmed Sinclair's charges. Pressured by Roosevelt and the public, in 1906 Congress passed the **Pure Food and Drug Act,** which banned impure and mislabeled food and drugs, and the **Meat Inspection Act,** which required federal inspection of meatpacking, a move the industry itself welcomed to reassure nauseated consumers. Sinclair, however, was disappointed because his revelations only prodded meatpackers to reform rather than converting readers to socialism. "I aimed at the public's heart," Sinclair later complained, "and by accident I hit it in the stomach."

Reforming City Government

In the early twentieth century, muckrakers, especially Lincoln Steffens, helped to focus public concern on city government. By the time of Steffens's first article in 1902, however, advocates of reform had already won office and brought changes to some cities, and municipal reformers soon appeared in many other cities.

Municipal reformers urged honest and efficient government, and many—perhaps most—also argued that corruption and inefficiency were inevitable without major changes in the structure of city government. **City councils** usually consisted of members elected from **wards** corresponding roughly to neighborhoods. Most voters lived in middle-class and working-class wards, which therefore dominated most city councils. Reformers, however, condemned the ward system as producing city council members unable to see beyond the needs of their own neighborhoods to the problems of the city as a whole. Reformers pointed to support for political bosses and machines in poor immigrant neighborhoods and concluded, correctly, that the ward leaders' devotion to voter needs kept the machine in power despite its corruption. They argued that citywide elections, in which all city voters chose from one list of candidates, would produce city council members with broader perspectives—men with citywide business interests, for example—and would undercut the influence of ward leaders and their machines.

James Phelan of San Francisco provides an example of an early structural reformer. Son of a pioneer banker, he was equally at home in the worlds of politics, business, and the arts. Phelan attacked corruption in city government and won election as mayor in 1896. He then led in adopting a new charter that strengthened the office of mayor and required citywide election of supervisors, San Francisco's term for councilmen.

Some municipal reformers proposed more fundamental changes in the structure of city government, notably the **commission system** and the **city-manager plan.** Both reveal prominent traits of progressivism: a distrust of political parties and a desire for expertise and efficiency.

The commission system first developed in Galveston, Texas, after a hurricane and tidal wave nearly destroyed it in 1900. The governor appointed five businessmen to run the city, and they attracted widespread attention for their efficiency in administering city government in time of crisis. Within two years, more than two hundred communities had adopted a commission system. Typically all the city's voters elected the commissioners, and each commissioner then took charge of a specific city function as a way to encourage effective and efficient management. The city-manager plan—an application of the administrative structure of the corporation to city government—had simlar objectives. It featured a professional city manager (similar to a corporate executive) who was appointed by an elected city council (similar to a corporate board of directors) to handle much of municipal administration. Staunton, Virginia, tried such a system in 1908 but attracted little attention. In 1913 a serious flood led the citizens of Dayton, Ohio, to adopt a city-manager plan, and other cities then followed.

Most municipal reforms focused on changing the structure of city government to bring about honest, efficient, effective city administration, but a few reformers went beyond structural reform to advocate social reform. Hazen Pingree, a successful and socially prominent businessman, attracted national

Pure Food and Drug Act Law passed by Congress in 1906 forbidding the sale of impure and improperly labeled food and drugs.

Meat Inspection Act Law passed by Congress in 1906 requiring federal inspection of meatpacking.

city council A body of representatives elected to govern a city.

ward A division of a city or town, especially an electoral district, for administrative or representative purposes.

commission system System of city government in which all executive and legislative power is vested in a small elective board, usually composed of five members.

city-manager plan System of city government in which a small council, chosen on a nonpartisan ballot, hires a city manager who exercises full executive authority.

attention as mayor of Detroit. Elected in 1889 as an advocate of honest, efficient government, he soon began to criticize the city's gas, electric, and streetcar companies for overcharging customers and providing poor service. The depression of 1893 led him to address the needs of the unemployed with measures such as work projects and community vegetable gardens. A prosperous manufacturer, Samuel "Golden Rule" Jones, won election as mayor of Toledo, Ohio, in 1897. He boasted of running his factory in accordance with the Golden Rule—"Do unto others as you would have them do unto you"—and he brought the same standard to city government. Under his leadership, Toledo acquired free concerts, free public baths, kindergartens (childcare centers for working mothers), and the eight-hour workday for city employees. Phelan, Pingree, Jones, and a few others also advocated city ownership of utilities.

The Progressive era also saw some city governments take up **city planning.** Throughout most of the nineteenth century, urban growth had been largely unplanned, driven primarily by a market economy. In the early twentieth century, city officials began to recognize the need to establish separate zones for residential, commercial, and industrial use (first in Los Angeles in 1904 and 1908) and to develop efficient transportation systems to reduce traffic congestion. A few cities also acted to improve substandard housing. In 1907, Hartford, Connecticut, set up one of the first city planning commissions, charged with planning on a continuing basis. The emergence of city planning represents an important transition in thinking about government and the economy, for it emphasized expertise and presumed greater government control over use of private property.

Saving the Future

Just as city planning had implications for local government, the emergence of other new professions—such as public health, mental health, and social work—often led to efforts to use government to solve the problems of an urban, industrial, multiethnic society. Their fundamental objective was to use scientific and social scientific knowledge to control social forces and thereby to shape the future.

The public schools were an important arena in which professionals sought change. In the cities especially, graduates of recently established university programs for the preparation of teachers and school administrators began to seek greater control over education. Stressing the challenges of educating multiethnic urban students—many of whom did not speak English—and preparing them for life in a complex and technological society, professional educators pushed for greater centralization in school administration. They particularly wanted to reduce the role of local, usually elected, **school boards** and elected school superintendents whose only qualification tended to be the ability to win elections. Professional educators also began to rely on the recently developed intelligence tests as a way of identifying children unable to perform at average levels and to isolate them in special classes.

Advances in medical knowledge, together with efforts by the American Medical Association to raise the standards of medical colleges and to restrict access to the profession, improved the professional status of physicians. Scientific discoveries helped to transform hospitals from charities that provided minimal help for the poor into centers for dispensing the most up-to-date care to all who could afford it. New knowledge about disease and health, often developed in research universities, together with the facilities of the modernized hospitals, seemed to present an opportunity to reduce some diseases on a significant scale. Physicians helped to launch public health programs to wipe out **hookworm** in the South, **tuberculosis** in the slums, and sexually transmitted diseases. Public health emerged as a new medical field, combining the knowledge of the medical doctor with insight of the social scientist and, often, with the skills of the corporate manager.

Other emerging professional fields with important implications for public policy included mental health and social work. Mental health professionals—psychiatrists and psychologists—tried to transform **asylums** from places where the mentally ill were confined into places where they could be treated and perhaps cured. They tried, too, to ad-

city planning The practice of planning urban development by regulating land use.

school board A local board of policymakers who oversee the public schools of a city or town.

hookworm A parasite, formerly common in the South, that causes loss of strength.

tuberculosis An infectious disease that attacks the lungs, causing coughing, fever, and weight loss; it was common and often fatal in the nineteenth and early twentieth centuries.

asylum In the nineteenth and early twentieth centuries, an institution for the hospitalization or incarceration of people with mental disorders.

♦ This visiting nurse from the Henry Street settlement house is taking a shortcut between two New York tenement buildings in 1908. She has apparently gone up the stairs in one tenement, seeing families along the way, and is now crossing to the next building where she will work her way down the stairs. Programs such as visiting nurses reflect the increased influence of the professions of social work, nursing, and public health. *Photograph by Jessie Tarbox Beals/Museum of the City of New York.*

dress aspects of the larger social context that seemed to cause mental breakdown. Social workers often found themselves allied with public health and mental health professionals in their efforts to extend government control over urban health and safety codes.

Reforming State Government

As reformers launched changes in various cities and as new professionals considered ways to improve society, **Robert M. La Follette** pushed Wisconsin state government to the forefront of reform. A Republican, he entered politics soon after graduating from the University of Wisconsin. Elected to Congress in 1884, 1886, and 1888, he lost in the Democratic sweep of 1890. When he accused the leader of the state Republican organization of unethical behavior, La Follette found his political career blocked. He finally won election as governor in 1900 and by then was convinced of the need for reform.

As governor, La Follette ran into opposition from members of his own party who held sway in the state legislature. Conservatives defeated La Follette's proposals to regulate railroad rates and replace party nominating conventions with the **direct primary.** Intensely committed to his proposals, La Follette threw himself into an energetic campaign to elect a state legislature that would support reform. He earned the nickname "Fighting Bob" as he traveled the state and discussed the issues wherever a crowd gathered. Most of his favored candidates won, and La Follette built a strong political following among Wisconsin's farmers and urban wage earners. He was re-elected as governor in 1902 and 1904.

La Follette led the way to a wide range of reform legislation designed to limit both corporations and political parties. Acclaimed as a "laboratory of democracy," Wisconsin adopted the direct primary, set up a commission to regulate railroad rates, increased taxes on railroads and other corporations, enacted a merit system for hiring and promoting state employees, and limited the activities of lobbyists. In many of his efforts, La Follette drew on the expertise of faculty members at the University of Wisconsin. These reforms and reliance on experts came to be called the **Wisconsin Idea.** La Follette won election to the U.S. Senate in 1905 and served there until his death in 1925.

La Follette's success prompted imitation elsewhere. In 1901, Iowans elected Albert B. Cummins governor, and Cummins launched a campaign against railroad corporations that paralleled La Follette's. He, too, went on to the Senate. Self-proclaimed reformers won office in other states as well, but only a few matched La Follette's legislative and political success.

Progressivism came to California relatively late. Once in power, however, California progressives produced a volume of reform that rivaled the Wisconsin Idea. California reformers accused the Southern Pacific Railroad of running a powerful political machine that controlled the state by dominating the Republican party. In 1906 and 1907, a highly publicized investigation revealed widespread bribery in San Francisco government. The ensuing trials made famous one of the prosecutors, **Hiram W. Johnson.**

Robert M. La Follette Governor of Wisconsin who instituted reforms such as direct primaries, tax reform, and anticorruption measures in Wisconsin.

direct primary A primary election in which voters who identify with a specific party choose among that party's candidates.

Wisconsin Idea The program of political reforms sponsored by Robert La Follette in Wisconsin; they were designed to decrease political corruption, foster direct democracy, and regulate corporations.

Hiram W. Johnson Governor of California who promoted a broad range of reforms, including regulation of railroads and measures to benefit labor.

♦ Robert La Follette enjoyed taking his campaigns to the voters. He is shown here in 1900, campaigning for election as governor of Wisconsin. When he went to the voters, he saw his speechmaking as a process of education, and he often spent an hour or more explaining the intricacies of policy issues. *Library of Congress.*

Reform-minded Republicans persuaded Johnson to run for governor in 1910. He conducted a vigorous campaign and won.

Stubborn and principled, Johnson proved to be an uncompromising foe of corporate influence in politics. As governor, he pushed the legislature to adopt an array of reforms—regulation of railroads and public utilities, far-reaching restrictions on political parties, protections for labor, and conservation. Progressives in the legislature proposed to amend the state constitution to provide for woman suffrage, and California voters approved the measure. Johnson showed more sympathy for labor than did most progressive reformers. He appointed union 'eaders to state positions and supported a variety o measures to benefit working people, including an eight-hour workday law for women, **workers' compensation,** and restrictions on child labor. These and other improvements pushed California to the front of the reform movement. California progressives in both parties vied with each other, however, in the vehemence of their attacks on Asian immigrants and Asian Americans. In 1913, Johnson and the progressive Republicans pushed through a law that prohibited Asian immigrants from owning land in California.

Like La Follette, Johnson carved out a career in national politics after serving as governor. In 1912, he was the vice-presidential candidate of the new Progressive party. Re-elected governor in 1914, he won election to the U.S. Senate in 1916 and served there until his death in 1945.

The Decline of Parties and Rise of Interest Groups

Like California, most states moved to restrict political parties. City and state reformers charged that party bosses and their machines manipulated nominating conventions, managed public officials, and controlled law enforcement. They claimed, too, that bosses, in return for payoffs, used their influence on behalf of powerful interests, especially companies that did business with city or state government. Articles by muckrakers and a few highly publicized bribery trials convinced many voters that the reformers were correct. The mighty party organizations that had dominated politics so completely during the nineteenth century now found themselves under attack on every side.

Reforms intended to increase the power of the individual voter and to reduce the power of political party organizations sprouted nearly everywhere. State after state adopted the direct primary, and most reformers also sought to introduce or strengthen the

workers' compensation Payments that employers are required by law to award to workers injured on the job.

merit system so as to reduce the number of state positions filled through patronage. In most states, judgeships, school board seats, and educational offices were made nonpartisan.

A number of states also chose to adopt the initiative and referendum (see chapter-opening map). Adopted first in South Dakota in 1898, the initiative and referendum gained national attention after they were adopted in Oregon in 1902. Oregon reformers led by William U'Ren, a former Populist who became a progressive Republican, quickly employed the initiative to create new laws. The Oregon reformers received such national attention for their efforts that the initiative and referendum were sometimes called the **Oregon System.** Some states also adopted the **recall,** a procedure that permits voters, though the petition process, to initiate a special election to remove an elected official from office. The direct primary, initiative and referendum, and recall are known collectively as *direct democracy* because they remove intermediate steps between the voter and final political decisions.

One outcome of the switch to direct primaries and direct election of U.S. senators (discussed later in this chapter) was a new style of campaign. Candidates now appealed directly to voters rather than to party leaders and convention delegates. Whereas nineteenth-century party leaders had often insisted on informal **term limits,** voters now returned the same candidates to office again and again. Individual candidates built up their own organizations (separate from party organizations) to win renomination and re-election. As campaigns focused more on individual candidates and much less on parties, advertising supplanted the armies of party retainers who had mobilized voters in the nineteenth century. Without party efforts to get out the vote, voter turnout began to fall. The emergence of so many new channels for political participation created the illusion of a vast outpouring of public involvement in politics—even though the proportion of those exercising their right to vote steadily dropped.

New avenues of political participation opened not only through direct democracy but also through organized interest groups. As the power of political parties and party leaders faded, organized interest groups became more involved in politics as the most direct way to advance their specialized concerns. Such groups cooperated with each other when their political objectives coincided, as when merchants and farmers both favored regulation of railroad rates. At other times, they found themselves in conflict, perhaps over tariff policy. The many groups that advocated change sometimes fought among themselves over which reform goals were most important and how best to achieve those goals. More and more groups took up the tactics of the Anti-Saloon League: ignoring political parties, pressuring individual candidates to accept the group's position, and urging their members to vote only for candidates who did so. In 1904, for example, the National Association of Manufacturers (NAM) targeted and defeated two key prolabor members of Congress, one in the House and one in the Senate. The American Federation of Labor (AFL) responded in 1906 with a similar strategy and managed to elect six union members to the House of Representatives.

Organized interest groups focused greater attention on the legislative process. When Congress was in session, they retained the services of one or more full-time representatives, or **lobbyists,** in Washington. Lobbyists urged members of Congress to support their group's position on pending legislation, reminded senators and representatives of the electoral power of the group, and arranged campaign support for those who voted in keeping with the group's positions. Eventually some legislators became dependent on lobbyists for information about the attitudes of important groups of their **constituents** and even relied on lobbyists to help draft legislation. Similar patterns developed in state legislatures.

Thus, as political parties receded from the dominant position they once occupied, organized interest groups moved in. Some elected officials came to see themselves less as loyal members of a political party and more as mediators among competing interest groups. Pushed one way by the AFL and the other by the NAM, under opposing pressure from the Anti-Saloon League and liquor interests, some politicians responded by counting the number of

Oregon System Name given to the initiative and referendum, first used widely in state politics in Oregon after 1902.

recall Procedure by which voters submit a petition to hold a special election to remove an elected official from office.

term limit A limit on the number of times one person can be elected to the same political office.

lobbyist A person who tries to influence the opinions of legislators or other public officials for or against a specific cause.

constituents Voters in the home district of a member of a legislature.

voters each group could influence in their districts and voting in the way likely to cost them the fewest votes in the next election.

Roosevelt, Taft, and Republican Progressivism

- What constraints did Theodore Roosevelt face, and how did he choose to deal with them?
- What were the outcomes for the role of the federal government in the economy and for the power of the presidency?

The American public came to identify Theodore Roosevelt with progressivism more than any other single person. Elected vice president in 1900, he became president in 1901 after the assassination of President William McKinley (see Individual Choices: Theodore Roosevelt, pages 648–649). The 42-year-old Roosevelt was the youngest president in the nation's history. His buoyant optimism and energy fascinated Americans as much as his bristling mustache, pince-nez glasses, and prominent front teeth delighted cartoonists.

Roosevelt later wrote, "I cannot say that I entered the Presidency with any deliberately planned and far-reaching scheme of social betterment." In seven years, however, he changed the nation's domestic policies more than any president since Lincoln—and made himself a legend. One visitor to the United States reported that the most exciting things he had seen were "Niagara Falls and the President, . . . both great wonders of nature!"

Roosevelt: Asserting the Power of the Presidency

Roosevelt was unlike most politicians of his day. Wealthy, thanks to his inheritance and his writings, he saw politics as a duty he owed the nation rather than as an opportunity for personal advancement. He defined his political views in terms of character, morality, hard work, and patriotism rather than in the stale phrases of party rhetoric. Uncertain whether to call himself a "radical conservative" or a "conservative radical," he considered political power a tool to achieve an ethical and socially stable society. Confident in his own personal principles, Roosevelt did not hesitate to wield to the fullest the powers of the presidency. He also used the office as what he called a "bully pulpit," to gain attention for his message of character and responsibility.

♦ President Theodore Roosevelt's distinctive face attracted photographers and cartoonists, and he was often shown with a big grin. He loved fun, and a friend of his once observed that "You must always remember that the President is about six." *Brown Brothers.*

In his first message to Congress, in December 1901, Roosevelt sounded a theme that he was to repeat throughout his political career: the growth of powerful corporations was "natural," but some of them exhibited "grave evils" that the law needed to overcome. Roosevelt later explained that "when I became President, the question as to the method by which the United States Government was to control the corporations was not yet important. The absolutely vital question was whether the Government had power to control them at all." He set out to establish that power.

The chief obstacle to the exercise of power over the new corporations was the Supreme Court decision in ***United States v. E. C. Knight*** (1895), preventing the Sherman Anti-Trust Act from being used

United States v. E. C. Knight Case in 1895 in which the Supreme Court ruled that the Sherman Anti-Trust Act did not prohibit manufacturing monopolies; it seriously impaired the enforcement of antitrust laws.

against manufacturing monopolies. Roosevelt soon found an opportunity to challenge the *Knight* decision. Some of the nation's most prominent business leaders—J. P. Morgan, the Rockefeller interests, and railroad magnates James J. Hill and Edward H. Harriman—had joined forces to create the Northern Securities Company—a railroad monopoly in the Northwest. The *Knight* case involved manufacturing, but the Northern Securities Company dealt in interstate transportation. Roosevelt believed that if any industry could satisfy the Supreme Court that it fit the language of the Constitution authorizing Congress to regulate interstate commerce, the railroads could.

In February 1902, Roosevelt advised Attorney General Philander C. Knox to seek dissolution of the Northern Securities Company for violating the Sherman Act. Wall Street leaders condemned Roosevelt's action, but most other Americans responded positively. For the first time, they witnessed a serious federal challenge to the ever-increasing might of powerful corporations. In 1904, the Supreme Court agreed that the Sherman Act could be applied to the Northern Securities Company and ordered it dissolved.

Bolstered by this confirmation of federal power, Roosevelt launched additional antitrust suits and gloried in his reputation as a **trustbuster.** In all, he initiated more than forty antitrust actions, though not all were successful. He used trustbusting selectively, however. Large corporations, in Roosevelt's view, were natural, inevitable, and potentially beneficial. He thought it made more sense to regulate them than to break them up. Companies that met Roosevelt's standards of character and public service—and acknowledged the supremacy of the presidency—had no reason to fear antitrust action. Acknowledging the power of the president sometimes meant informal understandings between Roosevelt and corporate heads. For example, in 1907, in the midst of a financial panic, officials of United States Steel Corporation first secured Roosevelt's consent before taking over the Tennessee Coal and Iron Company, arguing that the takeover would stabilize the industry.

Roosevelt's willingness to take bold action did not stop at reining in the trusts. In time of crisis, he felt, the president should "do whatever the needs of the people demand, unless the Constitution or the laws explicitly forbid him to do it." A year after he took office, he asserted new presidential powers to deal with a strike by coal miners.

In June 1902, miners of **anthracite coal** in Pennsylvania went on strike, seeking higher wages, an eight-hour workday, and **union recognition.** The railroads in the coal-mining region owned the mines and refused to negotiate or even to meet with representatives of the **United Mine Workers,** led by president John Mitchell. The president of the Reading Railroad, George F. Baer, led the mining companies. When urged to negotiate with the union, Baer wrote in reply,

> *The rights and interests of the laboring men will be protected and cared for—not by the labor agitators, but by the Christian men to whom God in his infinite wisdom has given control of the property interests of this country.*

Baer's claim to God-given control failed to impress the miners, much of the public, or Roosevelt.

As cold weather approached and coal prices edged upward, public concern grew because so many people heated their homes with coal. In early October, Roosevelt called both sides to Washington, where he took the bold and unusual step of urging them to submit their differences to arbitration. The mine owners haughtily refused and insisted that the president use the army against the miners, as Cleveland had done against the Pullman strikers ten years before. Roosevelt, now angry, considered the owners "insolent" and "obstinate"—even "utterly silly."

Believing that "great crises" required "immediate and vigorous executive action," Roosevelt began preparations to use the army to take over the mines and reopen them. The threat of military intervention apparently convinced the mine owners to grudgingly accept Roosevelt's proposal for an arbitration board to recommend a solution to the dispute. The arbitrators granted the miners higher wages and a nine-hour workday but denied union recognition. No president before had ever intervened in a strike by treating a union as equal to the owners, let alone threatening to use the army on the side of labor. The coal strike settlement represented what Roosevelt

trustbuster Label applied to Theodore Roosevelt and others who sought to prosecute or dissolve business trusts.

anthracite coal Hard, clean-burning coal widely used to heat homes and businesses in the early twentieth century.

union recognition Agreement by a company that a union may represent the company's employees for the purposes of collective bargaining.

United Mine Workers Union of coal miners organized in 1890.

liked to call a **Square Deal,** an outcome in which each side received fair treatment.

The Square Deal in Action: Creating Federal Economic Regulation

Roosevelt's trustbusting and settlement of the coal strike brought him great popularity across the country. In 1903, Congress approved several measures he requested or endorsed: the Expedition Act, to speed up prosecution of antitrust suits; creation of a cabinet-level Department of Commerce and Labor, including a Bureau of Corporations to investigate corporate activities; and the **Elkins Act,** which amended the Interstate Commerce Act by setting penalties for railroads that paid rebates.

When Roosevelt sought election in 1904, he won by one of the largest margins up to that time, securing more than 56 percent of the popular vote. Conservatives had temporarily taken control of the Democratic party and hoped to attract enough support from conservatives to defeat Roosevelt. But Alton B. Parker, their drab nominee, took only 38 percent in one of the Democrats' worst showings ever. Elected in his own right, with a powerful demonstration of public approval, Roosevelt set out to implement meaningful regulation. The railroads, largest of the nation's big businesses, were his target.

He and reformers in Congress wanted to move beyond the relatively uncontroversial Elkins Act to the question of rates. In Roosevelt's year-end message to Congress in 1905, he asked the legislators to pass laws regulating railroad rates, opening financial records of railroads to government inspection, and increasing the government's power in strikes involving interstate commerce. At the same time, the attorney general initiated suits against some of the nation's largest corporations, and muckrakers (some of them friends of Roosevelt) launched exposés of railroads and attacks on Senate conservatives.

Although he had to compromise from time to time with conservative Republicans, Roosevelt accomplished most of his agenda. On June 29, 1906, Congress passed the **Hepburn Act,** allowing the Interstate Commerce Commission (ICC) to establish maximum railroad rates and extending ICC authority to other forms of transportation. The act also limited railroads' ability to issue free passes, a practice reformers had long considered bribery. The next day, on June 30, Congress approved the Pure Food and Drug Act and the Meat Inspection Act, as the aftermath to Sinclair's stomach-turning revelations. Congress also passed legislation defining employers' liability for workers injured on the job in the District of Columbia and on the interstate railroads.

Regulating Natural Resources

An outspoken proponent of strenuous outdoor activities, Roosevelt took great pride in establishing five national parks and more than fifty wildlife preserves, to save what he called "beautiful and wonderful wild creatures whose existence was threatened by greed and wantonness." Preservationists, such as John Muir of the Sierra Club, applauded creation of such parks and refuges and urged that wilderness areas be kept forever safe from developers. Setting aside parks and wildlife refuges, however, was only one element in Roosevelt's view of conservation.

Roosevelt and **Gifford Pinchot,** the president's chief adviser on natural resources, believed conservation required not only preservation of wild and beautiful lands but also careful planning of the use of federally owned resources. Trained in scientific forestry in Europe, Pinchot combined scientific and technical expertise with a managerial outlook. He and Roosevelt worked to conserve timber and grazing resources by withdrawing large tracts of federal land from public sale or use. By maintaining close federal management of these lands, they hoped to provide for the needs of the present and still leave resources for the future. While president, Roosevelt withdrew nearly 230 million acres from public sale, more than quadrupling the land under federal protection.

Roosevelt's attitude toward western water clearly reveals his definition of conservation. He strongly supported the Reclamation Act of 1902 (also known as the Newlands Act, because Nevada representative Francis Newlands introduced the legislation in

Square Deal Theodore Roosevelt's term for his efforts to deal fairly with all.

Elkins Act Law passed by Congress in 1903 that supplemented the Interstate Commerce Act of 1887 by penalizing railroads that paid rebates.

Hepburn Act Law passed by Congress in 1906 that authorized the Interstate Commerce Commission to set maximum railroad rates and extended ICC authority to other forms of transportation.

Gifford Pinchot Head of the Federal Bureau of Forestry from 1898 to 1910; he helped begin the conservation movement.

♦ In 1903, at Yosemite National Park, Theodore Roosevelt met with John Muir, a leading advocate for the preservation of wilderness. While Roosevelt made important contributions to the preservation of parks and wildlife refuges, he was more interested in the careful management of national resources, including federal lands. *Culver Pictures, Inc.*

Congress). The act set aside proceeds from the sale of federal land in sixteen western states to finance irrigation projects, and it established a commitment later expanded many times: the federal government had the responsibility for constructing western dams, canals, and other facilities that made agriculture possible in areas of slight rainfall. Thus water, perhaps the single most important resource in the arid West, was to be managed. Far from preserving the western landscape, however, federal water projects profoundly transformed it and vividly illustrate the vast difference between the preservation of wilderness that Muir advocated and the careful management of productive resources that motivated Pinchot and Roosevelt.

Taft's Troubles

Soon after Roosevelt won the election of 1904, he announced that he would not seek another term in 1908. By 1908, he may have regretted this statement, but he kept his word. He remained immensely popular, however, and virtually named his successor. The Republican national convention nominated William Howard Taft. A graduate of Yale and former federal judge, Taft had served as governor of the Philippines before joining Roosevelt's cabinet as secretary of war in 1904.

William Jennings Bryan, leader of the progressive wing of the Democratic party, faced no serious opposition and won his party's nomination for the third time. Roosevelt's popularity and his endorsement of Taft overcame a lackluster Republican campaign. Taft won just under 52 percent of the vote, and Republicans kept control of the Senate and the House. Soon after turning the reins of office over to Taft, Roosevelt set off to hunt big game in Africa.

Roosevelt had been Taft's mentor in politics, but Taft's approach was far more restrained than his predecessor's. Unlike Roosevelt, Taft hated campaigning and disliked conflict. His legalistic approach to the presidency often appeared timid when compared to Roosevelt's boldness. But Taft worked to demonstrate his support for Roosevelt's Square Deal. His attorney general initiated some ninety antitrust suits in four years, twice as many as during Roosevelt's seven years. And Taft approved several efforts to strengthen regulatory agencies, as in 1910 when Congress extended the power of the Interstate Commerce Commission to cover most communication companies.

Taft's administration also saw two constitutional amendments. Reformers had long considered an income tax to be the fairest means of raising federal revenues. With support from Taft, the **Sixteenth Amendment,** permitting a federal income tax, won ratification by enough states to take effect in 1913. By contrast, Taft took no position on the **Seventeenth Amendment,** proposed in 1912 and adopted shortly after he left office in 1913. It changed the

Sixteenth Amendment Constitutional amendment ratified in 1913 that gives the federal government the right to establish an income tax.

Seventeenth Amendment Constitutional amendment ratified in 1913 that authorizes the direct popular election of U.S. senators.

♦ This postcard depicts how President Theodore Roosevelt, in command of the Republican party, persuaded his friend William Howard Taft to run for president in 1908. Taft was not eager for that office, but Roosevelt succeeded in convincing him to seek it. With Roosevelt's strong support, Taft was elected, but he proved a disappointment to Roosevelt. *Collection of Janice L. and David J. Frent.*

method of electing U.S. senators from election by state legislatures to direct election by the voters of each state, another long-time goal of reformers, who claimed that corporate influence and even outright bribery had swayed the state legislatures.

Roosevelt had handed Taft a Republican party divided by battles over the Hepburn Act and other presidential actions. Divisions between conservatives and progressives continued, and after 1909 Taft increasingly sided with the conservatives. That year, he called a special session of Congress to reform the tariff. The resulting **Payne-Aldrich Tariff,** however, retained high rates on most imports. Though disappointed, Taft signed the bill. When Republican progressives—mostly from midwestern farm states that would have benefited from lower tariffs—protested, Taft became defensive, alienating them even more by calling it "the best bill that the Republican party ever passed."

The battle within the Republican party intensified when Republican progressives attacked the high-handed exercise of power by Joseph Cannon, Speaker of the House of Representatives since 1902. Known for his profanity and poker playing, Cannon used the Speaker's power to support conservatives and to stifle progressives. Though Taft first looked favorably on Republican progressives seeking to replace Cannon, he backed off when he realized that the progressives lacked the votes, and he made his peace with Cannon. In 1910, Nebraska representative George W. Norris led Republican progressives in a "revolt against Cannonism" that gained the support of the Democrats and permanently reduced the power of the Speaker.

A dispute over conservation further widened Republican divisions. Taft kept Gifford Pinchot as head of the Forest Service. Pinchot soon charged that Taft's secretary of the interior, Richard A. Ballinger, had weakened the conservation program and favored corporate interests by opening lands previously designated as reserves. Taft concluded, however, that Ballinger was reversing improper actions by Roosevelt's administration. Pinchot persisted and publicly aired other charges against Ballinger. Taft, who considered Pinchot "a radical and a crank," fired him early in 1910. An investigation by Congress cleared Ballinger, but the affair further estranged Taft from congressional progressives and undermined his generally strong record on conservation.

Payne-Aldrich Tariff Tariff passed by Congress in 1909; the original bill was a Republican attempt to reduce tariffs, but the final version retained high tariffs on most imports.

By 1912, when Taft faced re-election, the Republican party was in serious disarray, and he faced opposition from most progressive Republicans.

Wilson and Democratic Progressivism

- What choices confronted American voters in the presidential election of 1912?
- How did choices by Woodrow Wilson and the Democrats change the role of the federal government in the economy?

"We stand at Armaggedon," thundered former president Theodore Roosevelt in 1912, invoking the biblical prophecy of a final battle between good and evil. "And," he continued, "we battle for the Lord." He soon bolted the Republican party to run for president as the candidate of the newly formed Progressive party. The Democratic presidential candidate that year was **Woodrow Wilson,** who, like Roosevelt, claimed to be the true voice of progressivism. Roosevelt and Wilson, however, presented quite different proposals for dealing with big business and attacked each other's right to claim the title "progressive." They agreed only that William Howard Taft, the incumbent president and the Republican candidate, was not a progressive at all.

The presidential election of 1912 marks a moment when Americans actively and seriously debated their future. All three nominees were well educated and highly literate: Theodore Roosevelt graduated from Harvard in 1880, William Howard Taft from Yale in 1878, and Woodrow Wilson from Princeton in 1879. Roosevelt and Wilson were authors of respected books on American history and politics. They approached politics with a sense of destiny and purpose and talked frankly to the American people about their ideas for the future.

Debating the Future: The Election of 1912

As the hapless Taft watched the Republican party unravel, Theodore Roosevelt was traveling abroad, first hunting in Africa and then hobnobbing with European leaders. When he returned in 1910, he had already met with the indignant Pinchot and other former associates. He then undertook a speaking tour and, without criticizing Taft, proposed a broad program of reform that he labeled the **New Nationalism.** Roosevelt did not openly question Taft's re-election, but other Republican progressives began to do so. In the 1910 congressional elections, Republican candidates fared badly, plagued both by divisions within their party and by an economic downturn. For the first time since 1892, Democrats won a majority in the House of Representatives. Democrats, including Woodrow Wilson in New Jersey, also won a number of governorships.

By early 1911, many Republican progressives were looking to Robert La Follette as their candidate to wrest the Republican nomination from Taft. Roosevelt, however, found La Follette too radical and thought him irresponsible in his attacks on corporations. Roosevelt criticized Taft, sometimes in public, for failing to maintain Republican unity, for his approach to conservation, and for his antitrust policies, which seemed to ignore Roosevelt's distinctions based on behavior rather than size. A federal lawsuit against United States Steel Corporation because of its acquisition of Tennessee Coal and Iron implied that when Roosevelt had approved the deal he either had been fooled into aiding the growth of a monopoly or had done so on purpose.

In February 1912, Roosevelt announced he would oppose Taft for the Republican presidential nomination. Thirteen states had established direct primaries to select delegates to the national nominating convention, and Roosevelt enjoyed great popularity at the primary polls, winning 278 delegates to 48 for Taft and 36 for La Follette. Elsewhere, however, Taft had all the advantages of an incumbent president in control of the party machinery. At the Republican nominating convention, many states sent rival delegations, one pledged to Taft and one to Roosevelt. Taft's supporters controlled the **credentials committee** and gave most of the contested seats to delegates supporting their man. Roosevelt's delegates walked out, claiming that Taft was stealing the nomination. The remaining delegates nominated Taft on the first ballot.

Woodrow Wilson President of the United States from 1913 to 1921; a Democrat, college professor, university president, and governor of New Jersey before becoming president.

New Nationalism Program of labor and social reform that Theodore Roosevelt advocated before and during his unsuccessful bid to regain the presidency in 1912.

credentials committee Party convention committee that settles disputes arising when rival delegations from the same state demand to be seated.

♦ Political buttons continued to be ubiquitous in 1912. Roosevelt and his running mate, Hiram Johnson, the governor of California, are pictured with the Bull Moose that came to symbolize the Progressive party after Roosevelt exclaimed that he felt as fit as a bull moose. Taft, the Republican candidate, and Wilson, the Democrat, are depicted with more traditional symbols of patriotism and party. *Collection of Janice L. and David J. Frent.*

Roosevelt's angry supporters regrouped to form the Progressive party, nicknamed the **Bull Moose party** after Roosevelt's boast that he was "as fit as a bull moose." The delegates sang "Onward, Christian Soldiers" and issued a platform based on the New Nationalism, including tariff reduction, regulation of corporations, a minimum wage, an end to child labor, woman suffrage, and the initiative, referendum, and recall. Women were more prominent at the Progressive convention than at any presidential nominating session since the Populists'. They helped draft the platform—especially sections dealing with labor—and Jane Addams addressed the convention to second the nomination of Roosevelt.

When the Democratic convention opened, delegates were overjoyed, certain that the Republican split gave them their best chance at the presidency in twenty years. The nomination was hotly contested, and the convention took forty-six ballots to nominate Woodrow Wilson, the governor of New Jersey, who had earned a reputation as a progressive. Their platform attacked monopolies and called for limits on campaign contributions by corporations, a single term for the president, and major tariff reductions. Wilson labeled his program the **New Freedom.**

Much of the attention in the campaign focused on Roosevelt's and Wilson's views of big business. Roosevelt continued to maintain that the behavior of corporations was the problem, not their size. Before winning the nomination, Wilson had criticized big business but had no proposal for dealing with it. After his nomination, he met with **Louis Brandeis,** a Boston attorney and leading critic of corporate consolidation. Brandeis convinced Wilson to center his campaign on the issue of big business and to offer a solution significantly different from Roosevelt's. Roosevelt and the Progressives were promising regulation. Wilson depicted monopoly itself as the most serious problem, not the misbehavior of individual corporations. Breaking up monopolies and restoring competition, he argued, would benefit consumers because the outcome would be better products and lower prices. He also pointed to what he considered the most serious flaw in Roosevelt's proposals for regulation: as long as monopolies faced regulation, they would continually and naturally seek to control the regulator—the federal government. Only antitrust actions, Wilson argued, could protect democracy from this threat.

Taft, the Republican nominee, claimed a stronger record as a trustbuster than Roosevelt but was clearly the most conservative of the candidates. Eugene V. Debs, the Socialist candidate, rejected both regulation and antitrust actions and argued instead for government ownership of monopolies. The real

Bull Moose party Popular name given to the Progressive party in 1912 as a tribute to its presidential candidate, Theodore Roosevelt.

New Freedom Program of reforms that Woodrow Wilson advocated during his 1912 presidential campaign, including reducing tariffs, revising the monetary system, and prosecuting trusts.

Louis Brandeis Lawyer and reformer who opposed monopolies and defended individual rights; in 1916 he became the first Jewish justice on the Supreme Court.

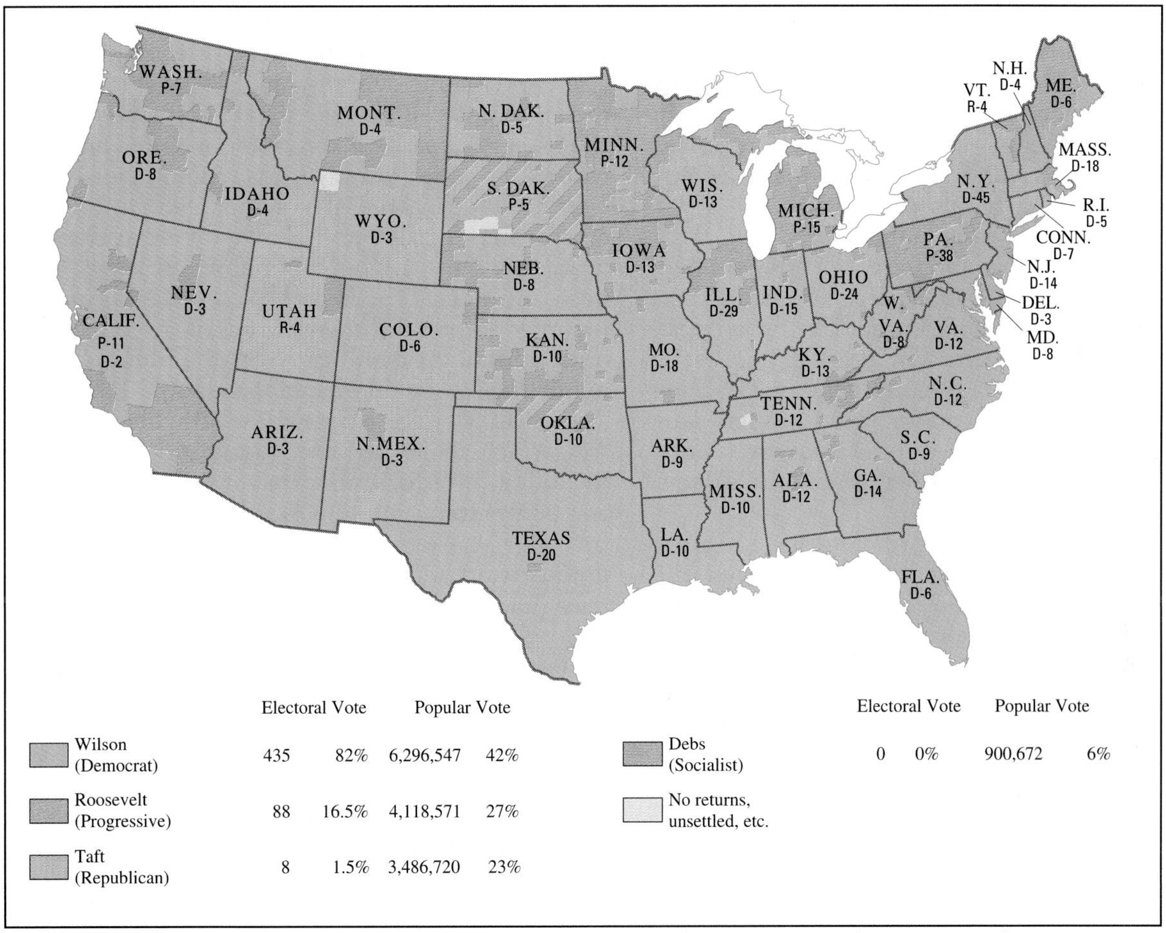

♦ **MAP 22.1 Election of 1912, by Counties** The presidential election of 1912 was complicated by the campaign of former president Theodore Roosevelt running as a Progressive. Roosevelt's campaign split the usual Republican vote without taking much away much of the usual Democratic vote. Woodrow Wilson, the Democratic candidate, carried many parts of the West and Northeast that Democratic candidates rarely won.

contest was between Roosevelt and Wilson. In the end, Wilson received most of the usual Democratic vote and won with 42 percent of the total. Democrats also won sizable majorities in both houses of Congress. Roosevelt and Taft split the traditional Republican vote, 27 percent for Roosevelt and 23 percent for Taft. Debs, with but 6 percent, did come in first in some counties and in some city precincts (see Map 22.1).

Wilson and Reform, 1913–1914

Born in Virginia in 1856, Woodrow Wilson grew up in the South during the Civil War and Reconstruction. His father, a Presbyterian minister, impressed on him lessons in morality and responsibility that remained with him his entire life. Wilson earned a Ph.D. in political science from Johns Hopkins University, and his first book, *Congressional Government,* analyzed federal lawmaking. A professor at Princeton University after 1890, he proved a popular lecturer but struck many as cold and uncomfortable when dealing with people. He became president of Princeton in 1902 and introduced educational reforms that brought him national attention.

In 1910, New Jersey Democrats needed a respectable candidate for governor. Party leaders picked Wilson because of his reputation as a conservative and a good public speaker. He won the election and, as governor, suddenly embraced reform, shocking his party's conservative leaders. In two years as governor, he led the legislature to adopt many progressive measures, including a direct primary and regulation of railroads and public utilities. His record won support from many Democratic progressives, including Bryan, when he sought the 1912 presidential nomination.

Wilson firmly believed in party government and an active role for the president in policymaking. He set out to work closely with Democrats in Congress and succeeded to such an extent that, like Roosevelt, he changed the nature of the presidency itself. Confident that a persuasive orator could change people's views, he went to the Capitol to address Congress in person, the first president since John Adams to do so.

Wilson focused first on tariff reform, tying his party's long-time opposition to the protective tariff to the argument that high tariff rates helped to create monopolies by reducing competition. Despite the opposition of many manufacturers, Congress passed the Underwood Tariff in October 1913, establishing the most significant reductions since the Civil War. To offset the subsequent federal revenue losses, the **Underwood Act** also brought into being the income tax recently authorized by the Sixteenth Amendment.

The next matter facing Wilson and the Democrats was reform of the banking system. The national banking system dated to 1863, and periodic economic problems, such as the **Panic of 1907,** had made evident the system's shortcomings. Chief among them was that it had no real center to provide direction and no way to adjust the **money supply** to the needs of the economy. In 1913, a congressional investigation also revealed the concentration of a great deal of power in the hands of the few investment bankers with vast corporate control. Conservatives, led by Carter Glass of Virginia, joined with bankers in proposing a system that would minimize regulation by the government. Progressive Democrats, especially William Jennings Bryan (now Wilson's secretary of state) and Louis Brandeis, favored strong federal control.

The debate over control ended in compromise when, in December 1913, Wilson approved the **Federal Reserve Act,** establishing twelve regional Federal Reserve Banks, which were regulated and supervised by the Federal Reserve Board, a new federal agency with members chosen by the president. The district banks were "bankers' banks," places where commercial banks kept their reserves. All national banks were required to belong to the Federal Reserve System, and state banks were invited to join. The participating banks owned all the stock in their regional Federal Reserve Bank and named two-thirds of its board of directors, and the president named the other third. In his appointments to the board, Wilson named men sympathetic to banking, choices that puzzled and outraged progressives but reassured the banking community that the "Fed" posed no threat. The Federal Reserve Act stands as the most important domestic act of the Wilson administration, for it still provides the framework for regulating the nation's banking system.

In 1914, Congress passed the **Clayton Antitrust Act,** which prohibited specified business practices, including **interlocking directorates** among large companies that could be proven to reduce competition. It also exempted farmers' organizations and unions from antitrust prosecution under the Sherman Act. The antitrust sections in the final version of the Clayton Act, however, provided little basis for breaking up big corporations. The weakening of the Clayton Act partly reflected a change of course by Wilson. Instead of breaking up big business, Wilson now moved closer to Roosevelt's position that regulation had more potential for protecting small businesses. Wilson also supported passage of the **Federal Trade Commission Act** (1914), a regulatory

Underwood Act Law passed by Congress in 1913 that substantially reduced tariffs and made up for the lost revenue by providing for a small graduated income tax.

Panic of 1907 Minor depression brought about by a stock market collapse and several bank failures; it showed the need for banking reform.

money supply The amount of money in the economy, such as cash and the contents of checking accounts.

Federal Reserve Act Law passed by Congress in 1913 establishing twelve Federal Reserve Banks to hold the cash reserves of commercial banks.

Clayton Antitrust Act Law passed by Congress in 1914 banning monopolistic business practices such as price fixing and interlocking directorates; it also exempted farmers' organizations and unions from prosecution under antitrust laws.

interlocking directorate Situation in which the same individuals sit on the boards of directors of various "competing" companies in one industry.

Federal Trade Commission Act Law passed by Congress in 1914 that outlawed unfair methods of competition in interstate commerce and created a commission appointed by the president to investigate illegal business practices.

measure designed to prevent unfair methods of business competition.

Wilson and Social Reform

Progressives generally applauded the Wilson administration for tariff reform, the Federal Reserve System, and the Clayton Act. But many progressives criticized his appointees to the Federal Trade Commission and the Federal Reserve Board for their sympathies with business and banking. Congress fulfilled a Democratic campaign promise by creating a separate cabinet-level Department of Labor, and as secretary of labor Wilson appointed William Wilson (not a relative), a union member and labor advocate. President Wilson did little more, however, to appeal to progressives who favored social reform. He considered federal action to outlaw child labor to be unconstitutional, and he questioned the need to amend the Constitution for woman suffrage.

During his first year in office, Wilson drew sharp criticism from some northern social reformers when his appointees began to institute racial segregation in several federal agencies. A southerner by birth and heritage, Wilson undoubtedly believed in segregation even though he resisted the most extreme racists in his party. At a cabinet meeting shortly after Wilson took office, the postmaster general (a southerner) proposed racial segregation of all federal employees. No cabinet member objected, and several federal agencies began to segregate African Americans. In the South, some Wilson appointees began to fire African Americans from federal jobs. Wilson was surprised at the swell of protest, not just from African Americans but also from some white progressives in the North and Midwest. He never designated a change in policy, but the process of segregating federal facilities thereafter slowed greatly.

Late in 1914, Wilson announced that he was satisfied and would seek no further reforms. In part, this choice reflected his underlying conservatism and earlier disinterest in social reform. Early in 1916, however, he reversed direction in anticipation of the coming election. Wilson had received less than half of the popular vote in 1912 and won the White House only because of the split among Republicans. He joined Democratic progressives in Congress, therefore, in pushing measures intended to secure their claim as the true voice of progressivism and to capture the loyalty of all progressive voters.

As a first step, Wilson nominated Louis Brandeis for the Supreme Court. Brandeis's reputation as a staunch progressive and critic of business aroused intense opposition from conservatives. He would be the first Jewish member of the Court, and some opposition to his confirmation carried anti-Semitic overtones. The Senate vote on the nomination was close, but he was confirmed in 1916 with support from a few progressive Republicans. Wilson followed up the Brandeis nomination with support for a number of reform measures—improved credit facilities for farmers, workers' compensation for federal employees, and a law to eliminate child labor. Under threat of a national railroad strike, in 1916 Congress also passed and Wilson signed the **Adamson Act,** securing an eight-hour workday for railroad employees.

The presidential election of 1916 was conducted against the background of the war that had been raging in Europe since 1914 (it is discussed in the next chapter). Wilson's shift toward the social reformers helped solidify his support among some progressives. His support for organized labor gave him strong backing among unionists, and labor's votes probably ensured his victory in certain states, especially California. In states where women could vote, many of them seem to have supported Wilson, probably because he backed issues of interest to women, such as outlawing child labor and keeping the nation out of war. In a very close election, Wilson won with 49 percent of the popular vote to 46 percent for Charles Evans Hughes, a moderately progressive Republican.

Progressivism in Perspective

- Was progressivism successful?
- What are your criteria for judging its success?
- What lasting outcomes of progressivism affect modern American politics?

The Progressive era began with efforts at municipal reform in the 1890s and sputtered to a close during World War I. Some politicians who called themselves progressives remained in prominent positions afterward, and progressive concepts of efficiency and expertise continued to guide government decision making. But the war, which the United States entered

Adamson Act Law passed by Congress in 1916 at the urging of the railway unions to establish an eight-hour workday on all interstate railroads.

in 1917, diverted public attention from reform, and by the end of the war political concerns had changed. By the mid-1920s, many of the major leaders of progressivism had passed from the political stage.

The changes of the Progressive era transformed American politics and government. Before the Hepburn Act and the Federal Reserve Act, the federal government's role in the national economy consisted largely of instituting land-grant subsidies and protective tariffs. After the Progressive era, the federal government became a significant and permanent player in the economy, regulating a wide range of economic activity. The income tax, first treated almost as a joke, quickly became the most significant source of federal funds, without which it is impossible to imagine the activities that the federal government has assumed during the course of the twentieth century—from vast military expenditures to social welfare to support for the arts. Since at least the 1930s, the income tax has also been seen as a potential instrument of social policy, by which the federal government can redistribute income.

The decline of political parties and emergence of political campaigns based largely on personality and advertising accelerated in the second half of the twentieth century under the impact of television and public opinion polling. Organized pressure groups have proliferated and become ever more influential. Women's participation in politics has continued to increase, especially in the last third of the twentieth century.

The assertion of presidential authority by Roosevelt and Wilson, though not echoed in the administrations of their immediate successors, reappeared in the presidency of Franklin D. Roosevelt (1933–1945). Theodore Roosevelt, Woodrow Wilson, and Franklin Roosevelt transformed Americans' expectations regarding the office of the presidency itself. Throughout the nineteenth century, Congress had dominated the making of domestic policy. During the twentieth century, Americans came to expect domestic policy to flow from forceful executive leadership in the White House.

Perhaps the most instructive legacy from progressivism is the understanding that reforms rarely fulfill all the expectations of their supporters. Some advocates of prohibition, for example, predicted that crime and poverty would diminish once alcohol was banned. Prohibition, however, helped give birth to organized crime, as suppliers of illegal liquor began to cooperate among themselves rather than engage in cutthroat competition. Those who attacked the power of political parties hoped to destroy political machines and bosses. Some such organizations proved highly resilient, however, adapting themselves to new conditions and continuing—not as before, but continuing nonetheless—with a significant role in politics. So the Progressive era taught America that even the most well-intended reforms are not cure-alls.

Finley Peter Dunne, the leading political humorist of the Progressive era, voiced a cynical view of reform when he observed that "a man that would expect to train lobsters to fly in a year is called a lunatic; but a man that thinks men can be turned into angels by an election is called a reformer and remains at large." The lesson from the sometimes disappointing outcome of progressive reforms is not to avoid change, however. Americans have tinkered with the structure and function of their government repeatedly and will continue to do so. Such changes are normal parts of American politics. As Dunne wrote, reform was like housecleaning, and he quoted this conversation between a woman who ran a boarding house and one of her lodgers:

> *"I don't know what to do," says she. "I'm worn out, and it seems impossible to keep this house clean. What is the trouble with it?"*
>
> *"Madam," says my friend Gallagher, . . . "the trouble with this house is that it is occupied entirely by human beings. If it was a vacant house, it could easily be kept clean."*

Thus, Dunne concluded about progressive reform, "The noise you hear is not the first gun of a revolution. It's only the people of the United States beating a carpet."

SUMMARY

E xpectations
C onstraints
C hoices
O utcomes

Progressivism, a phenomenon of the late nineteenth and early twentieth centuries, refers to new concepts of government, to changes in government that made those concepts reality, and to the political process by which change occurred. Those years marked a time of far-reaching political transformation, brought about through many *choices* by groups and individuals who approached politics with fresh but often quite different *expectations.* Organized interest groups became an important part of this process. Women broke through long-standing *constraints* to take a more prominent role in politics and succeeded in gaining the suffrage in several states. The Anti-Saloon League was the most successful of a number of organizations that *chose* to reshape government to enforce their moral standards. Some African Americans *chose* to fight the *constraints* of segregation and disfranchisement, looking to W. E. B. Du Bois for leadership. Socialists and the Industrial Workers of the World saw capitalism as the source of many problems, but few Americans *chose* their radical solutions.

Political reform took place at every level, from cities to states to the federal government. Muckraking journalists exposed corruption, wrongdoing, and suffering. Municipal reformers introduced modern methods of city government in a quest for efficiency and expertise. Some *chose* to use government to remedy social problems by employing the expertise of new professions such as public health and social work. Reformers also *chose* to attack the power of party bosses and machines by reducing the role of political parties through the reforms that composed direct democracy.

At the federal level, Theodore Roosevelt set the pace for progressive reform. He *chose* to challenge judicial *constraints* on federal authority over big business, and he advocated other forms of economic regulation. The *outcome* was an increase in the federal government's power within the economy. He also *chose* to regulate the use of natural resources. His successor, William Howard Taft, failed to maintain Republican party unity and eventually sided with conservatives against progressives.

In 1912, Roosevelt *chose* to form a new political party, the Progressives, making that year's presidential election a three-way contest. Roosevelt called for regulation of big business, whereas Wilson, the Democrat, favored breaking up huge corporations through antitrust action. Wilson won the election but soon *chose* regulation over antitrust actions. He presided over the creation of the Federal Reserve System to regulate banking nationwide. As the 1916 election approached, Wilson also pushed for social reforms, including restrictions on child labor, in an effort to unify all progressives behind his leadership.

Progressive reforms have had a profound impact on American politics throughout the twentieth century. In many ways, the *outcome* of the Progressive era was the origin of modern American politics.

SUGGESTED READINGS

John Whiteclay Chambers, II. *The Tyranny of Change: Americans in the Progressive Era, 1890–1920,* 2d ed. (1992).

A concise overview of American life during the Progressive era.

K. Austin Kerr. *Organized for Prohibition: A New History of the Anti-Saloon League* (1985).

A recent treatment of the organization that formed the prototype for many organized interest groups.

David Levering Lewis. *W. E. B. Du Bois: Biography of a Race, 1868–1919* (1993).

A powerful biography of Du Bois that delivers on its promise to present the "biography of a race" during the Progressive era.

Arthur S. Link. and Richard L. McCormick. *Progressivism* (1983).

A thorough survey of progressivism, including the views of historians.

Theodore Roosevelt. *An Autobiography* (1913; abridged ed. reprint, 1958).

Roosevelt's account of his actions sometimes needs to be taken with a grain of salt but nevertheless provides insight into Roosevelt the person.

Upton Sinclair. *The Jungle,* introduction by James R. Barrett (1906; reprint, 1988).

This socialist novel about workers in Chicago's packinghouses is a classic example of muckraking.

THE DOMESTIC IMPACT OF WAR World War I had a major impact on the lives of Americans. This map shows two different examples: (1) Labor shortages in industry encouraged African Americans to leave the South and move north or, in some cases, west, and (2) increased food demand encouraged more farming, especially of wheat.

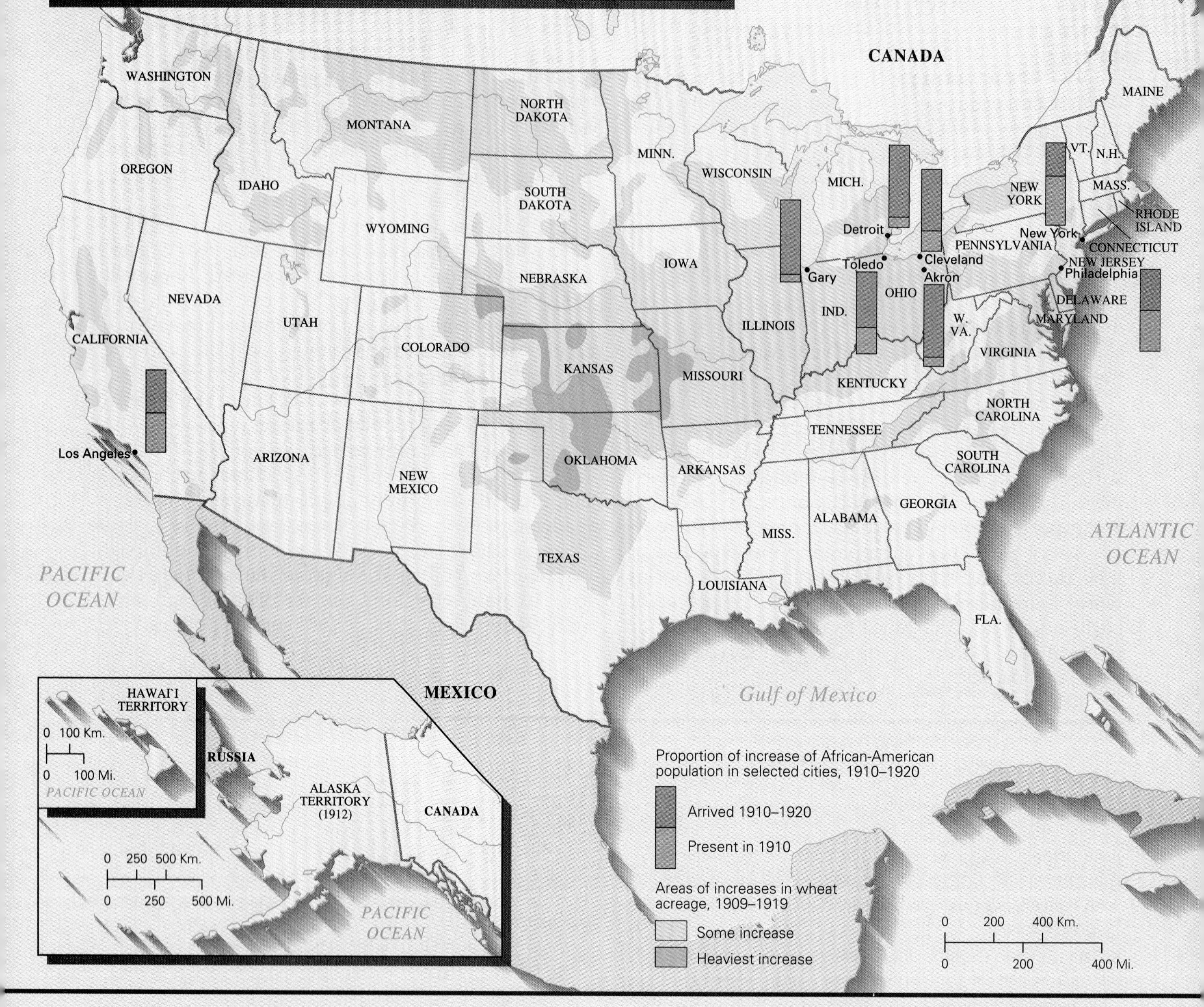

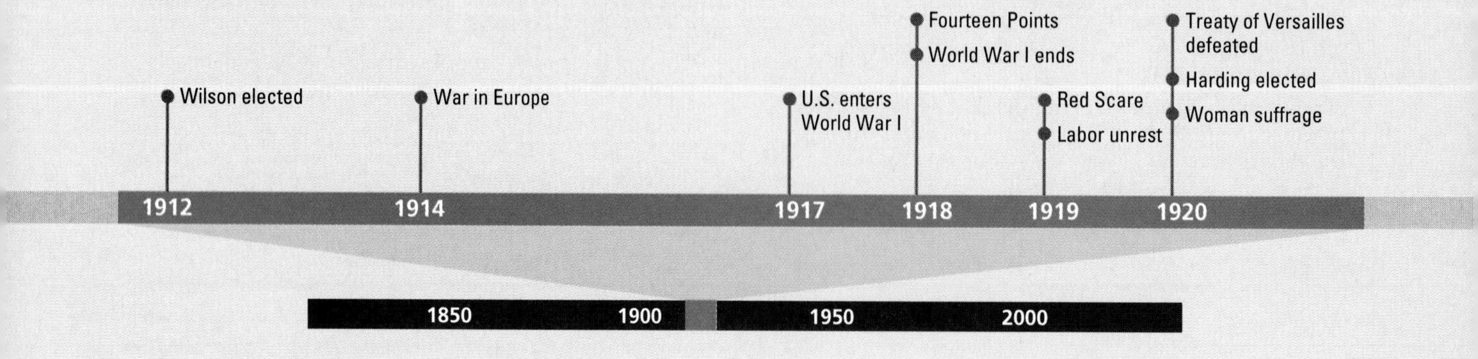

CHAPTER 23

America and the World, 1913–1920

Inherited Commitments and New Directions

- What major choices did Wilson make in dealing with other nations before the United States entered World War I?
- Which of Wilson's actions established new directions for U.S. foreign policy?

From Neutrality to War, 1914–1917

- What were Wilson's expectations regarding American neutrality?
- What constraints did he face in seeking to maintain neutrality?
- What choices did he make in an effort to do so? What was the final outcome?

The Home Front

- What choices did the federal government make in mobilizing the economy and society in support of the war?
- How did the war affect Americans (including women, African Americans, and opponents of war)?

Americans "Over There"

- What role did American ships and troops play in ending the war?
- Why did Wilson choose to keep the AEF as separate as possible from the troops of the other Allies?

Wilson and the Peace Conference

- What did Wilson expect to accomplish at the peace conference, and what constraints did he face in meeting his objectives?
- What was the outcome of his efforts?
- How did divisions within the Senate contribute to the defeat of the treaty there?

Trauma in the Wake of War

- How did Americans' expectations change as a result of the outcome of the war and the events of 1919?
- How did these new expectations affect Americans' choice in the 1920 presidential election?

INTRODUCTION

Expectations
Constraints
Choices
Outcomes

On June 28, 1914, a Serbian terrorist killed Archduke Franz Ferdinand, heir to the throne of Austria-Hungary, and his wife Sophie. They were visiting Sarajevo, in Bosnia-Herzegovina, which the Austrians had recently annexed against the wishes of the neighboring kingdom of Serbia. In response to the assassinations, Austria first consulted with its ally, Germany, then made stringent demands on Serbia. Serbia sought help from Russia, which was allied with France. Tense diplomats invoked elaborate, interlocking alliances. Huge armies began to move. By August 4, most of Europe was at war.

Earlier, in 1899, Theodore Roosevelt had probably voiced the *expectations* of many Americans when he claimed that war had become practically obsolete among what he called the world's "civilized" nations. As president, Roosevelt helped to shape Americans' *expectations* of security when he argued that the best way to preserve peace was by *choosing* to develop naval and military strength. Given the widely held *expectation* that war had become obsolete among civilized nations, many Americans were shocked, saddened, and repelled in August 1914 when the leading "civilized" nations of the world—all of which had been busily accumulating arsenals for the previous two decades—lurched into war.

When European leaders *chose* war in August 1914, the United States was already playing a major role in world affairs, in part as the result of *choices* made between 1898 and 1908. In that decade, America acquired the Philippines and the Panama Canal, came to dominate the Caribbean and Central America, and pursued an active and continuing involvement in the balance of power in eastern Asia. The three presidents of the Progressive era—Theodore Roosevelt, William Howard Taft, and Woodrow Wilson—agreed wholeheartedly that the United States should exercise a major role in world affairs. But by 1914 the United States was the only large, industrial nation that *chose* not to join in the elaborate network of treaties and understandings among the powers of Europe and Asia. During the first years of the war Woodrow Wilson *chose* to try to maintain U.S. neutrality.

When Wilson entered the White House in 1913, he *expected* to spend most of his time dealing with domestic issues. Though well read on international affairs, he brought to the White House neither significant international experience nor carefully considered foreign policies. For secretary of state he *chose* William Jennings Bryan, who also had devoted most of his political career to domestic matters and had little experience that qualified him as the nation's foreign-policy chief. Both Wilson and Bryan were devout Presbyterians, sharing a confidence that God had a plan for humankind and that all people shared a basic bond. Both hoped too—idealistically and perhaps naively—that their foreign policy *choices* might make the United States a model among nations for the peaceful settlement of international disputes. Neither man *expected* that they and the nation were soon to face difficult *choices* over a war so immense and so horrible that—no matter who was victorious—its *outcome* would be a profoundly altered world.

Inherited Commitments and New Directions

- What major choices did Wilson make in dealing with other nations before the United States entered World War I?
- Which of Wilson's actions established new directions for U.S. foreign policy?

When Woodrow Wilson entered the White House, he first fixed his foreign-policy attention on the three areas of greatest American involvement: Latin America, the Pacific, and eastern Asia. There, he tried to balance the anti-imperialist principles of his Democratic party against the **interventionist** commitments of his Republican predecessors. He marked out some new directions, but in the end he

interventionist Tending to get involved in the affairs of another nation.

CHRONOLOGY

The United States and World Affairs, 1913–1920

1912 Woodrow Wilson elected president

1913 Victoriano Huerta takes power in Mexico
Wilson denies U.S. recognition to Huerta
Secretary of State Bryan proposes cooling-off treaties

1914 U.S. Navy occupies Veracruz
War breaks out in Europe
United States declares neutrality
Stalemate on the western front
Bryan-Chamorro Treaty

1915 German U-boat sinks the *Lusitania*
United States occupies Haiti

1915–1920 Great Migration

1916 U.S. troops pursue Pancho Villa into Mexico
National Defense Act
United States purchases Virgin Islands from Denmark
Sussex pledge
United States occupies Dominican Republic
Wilson re-elected

1917 Wilson calls for "peace without victory"
American troops leave Mexico
Germany resumes submarine warfare
Overthrow of tsar of Russia
United States declares war on Germany
Committee on Public Information
War Industries Board
Selective Service Act
Espionage Act
Race riot in East St. Louis
Government crackdown on IWW
Bolsheviks seize power in Russia
Russia withdraws from the war
Bolsheviks publish secret treaties
Railroads placed under federal control

1917–1918 Union membership rises sharply
Lynchings increase

1918 Wilson presents Fourteen Points to Congress
Germans launch major offensive
National War Labor Board
Sedition Act
U.S. troops in northern Russia and Siberia
Successful Allied counteroffensive
Republican majorities in Congress
Armistice in Europe

1918–1919 Worldwide influenza epidemic
Civil war in Russia
Rampant U.S. inflation

1919 Versailles peace conference
Prohibition approved
General strike in Seattle
Urban race riots
Wilson suffers stroke
Boston police strike
Senate defeats Versailles treaty

1919–1920 Steel strike
Red Scare
Palmer raids

1920 Senate defeats Versailles treaty again
Nineteenth Amendment (woman suffrage) approved
Warren G. Harding elected president

not only accepted but actually extended most previous commitments.

Anti-Imperialism, Intervention, and Arbitration

Wilson's party had criticized many of the foreign policies of McKinley, Roosevelt, and Taft, especially imperialism. Secretary of State Bryan was a leading anti-imperialist who had faulted Roosevelt's "Big Stick" approach to foreign affairs. "The man who speaks softly does not need a big stick," Bryan said, adding that "if he yields to temptation and equips himself with one, the tone of his voice is very likely to change." Wilson shared Taft's commitment to American commercial expansion, but he criticized dollar diplomacy for using the State Department to advance the interests of particular companies.

During the Wilson administration, the Democrats' long adherence to anti-imperialism produced two measures. In 1916, Congress established a bill of rights for residents of the Philippine Islands and promised them eventual independence. Congressional Democrats could not agree on a date, though, so the law specified none. The next year, Puerto Rico became a U.S. territory, and its residents became U.S. citizens. Thus the Democrats wrote into law a limited version of the anti-imperialism they had proclaimed for more than twenty years.

Democrats had criticized Roosevelt's actions in the Caribbean, but in the end Wilson intervened more in Central America and the Caribbean than had any other administration during any comparable eight-year period. In Nicaragua, Taft had used marines to prop up the rule of President Adolfo Días. Wilson now wanted to revise a proposed treaty to give the United States even more authority within that country. Senate Democrats rejected his efforts, reminding Wilson and Bryan of their party's opposition to further protectorates. Even so, the **Bryan-Chamorro Treaty** of 1914 gave the United States significant concessions, including the right to build a canal through Nicaragua.

In Haiti, which owed a staggering debt to foreign bankers, the dictatorial president ordered many of his opponents put to death in 1915. When a mob then tore him apart, Wilson sent in American marines. A treaty followed, making Haiti a protectorate in which American forces controlled nearly all aspects of government until 1933. Wilson sent marines into the Dominican Republic in 1916, and U.S. naval officers took control there until 1924. In 1916, too, the United States agreed to buy the Virgin Islands from Denmark for $25 million.

Although Wilson made few changes in previous policies regarding the Caribbean, he enthusiastically encouraged efforts by Bryan to promote arbitration of international disputes. Roosevelt's and Taft's secretaries of state had tried to promote international arbitration, but their efforts foundered on the Senate's refusal to yield any degree of its role in foreign relations. Learning from those failures, Bryan in 1913 drafted a model arbitration treaty and obtained approval of it from the Senate Foreign Relations Committee. The State Department then distributed the proposal—called "President Wilson's Peace Proposal"—to the forty nations that maintained diplomatic relations with the United States. Negotiations produced twenty-two ratified treaties, all of which featured a cooling-off period for disputes, typically a year, during which the nations agreed not to go to war and instead to seek outside fact finding and arbitration. The arbitration treaties marked the beginning of a process by which Wilson sought to redefine international relations, substituting rational negotiations and arbitration for raw power.

Wilson and the Mexican Revolution

In Mexico, Wilson faced choices that led him into brazen power politics. **Porfirio Díaz** had ruled Mexico as a dictator for a third of a century, supported by the great landholders, the church, and the military. By the early twentieth century, discontent was brewing among nearly everyone else—peasants, workers, and intellectuals. Rebellion broke out in the south, led by **Emiliano Zapata,** and in the north, led by Pascual Orozco and **Francisco "Pancho" Villa** (see Map 23.1). Mobs took to the streets demanding that Díaz resign. He did so in 1911. Francisco Madero, a leading advocate of reform, assumed the presidency to great acclaim but proved incapable of uniting the country. Discontent rolled across Mexico as peasant armies calling for *tierra y libertad* ("land and liberty") attacked the mansions of great landowners. Conservatives feared Madero as a reformer, but Zapata and the radicals dismissed him as too timid. Conservative forces launched an uprising in Mexico City in February 1913, working with the commander of the army, General **Victoriano Huerta.** Huerta took control of the government and had Madero executed.

Most European governments quickly extended diplomatic recognition to Huerta because his government clearly held power in Mexico City, but Taft—about to hand over the presidency—left that

Bryan-Chamorro Treaty Treaty in 1914 in which Nicaragua received $3 million in return for granting the United States exclusive rights to a canal route and a naval base.

Porfirio Díaz Mexican soldier and politician who became president after a coup in 1876 and governed Mexico until 1911.

Emiliano Zapata Mexican Indian revolutionary who led a peasant revolt demanding agrarian reforms from 1910 until his death in 1919.

Francisco "Pancho" Villa Mexican bandit and revolutionary who led a raid into New Mexico in 1916, which prompted the U.S. government to send troops into Mexico in unsuccessful pursuit.

Victoriano Huerta Mexican general who overthrew the president, Francisco Madero, in 1913 and established a military dictatorship until forced to resign in 1914.

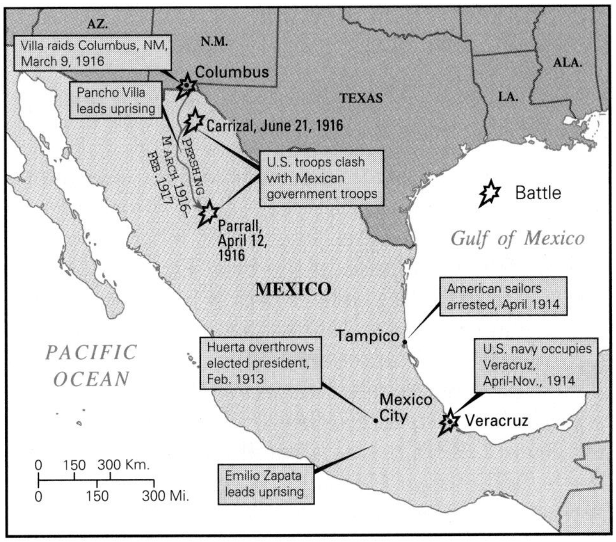

♦ **MAP 23.1 The United States and the Mexican Revolution** This map identifies the key locations for understanding relations between the United States and Mexico during 1913–1917.

matter to his successor. Thus Wilson had to take action soon after his inauguration. American companies with investments in Mexico, especially mining and oil, urged recognition because they considered Huerta likely to protect their holdings against the radicals. Wilson, however, considered Huerta a murderer and vowed "not to recognize a government of butchers."

Wilson announced that his decision came because Huerta's regime did not rest on the consent of the governed. The addition of such a moral dimension to diplomatic recognition constituted a new approach in American foreign policy. Previous American presidents had extended diplomatic recognition to all governments in power as simple acknowledgment of their existence. Labeled "missionary diplomacy," Wilson's denial of recognition implied that the United States assumed the responsibility to discriminate between pure and impure governments. Telling one visitor, "I am going to teach the South American republics to elect good men," Wilson engaged in what he called "watchful waiting," seeking an opportunity to act against Huerta. In the meantime, anti-Huerta forces in northern Mexico, led by **Venustiano Carranza,** began to make significant gains.

In April 1914, Wilson found an excuse to intervene when Mexican officials in Tampico arrested a few American sailors who had come ashore. The city's army commander immediately released them and apologized. Wilson, however, used the incident to justify ordering the U.S. Navy to occupy **Veracruz** (see Map 23.1). As the leading Mexican port, Veracruz was the major source of the Huerta government's revenue, from customs collected on imports, and the landing point for most government military supplies. The occupation cut these off. It also cost more than a hundred Mexican lives and turned many Mexicans against Wilson for violating their national sovereignty over a petty dispute. Huerta, facing the steady advance of Carranza's armies and deprived of munitions and customs revenues, fled the country in mid-July. Wilson withdrew the last American forces from Veracruz in November.

Carranza succeeded Huerta as president, and Wilson officially recognized his government. Carranza faced armed opposition, however, from Pancho Villa in northern Mexico. When Villa suffered serious defeats, he apparently decided his best hope for defeating Carranza was to incite a war between the Carranza government and the United States. Villa's men murdered several Americans in Mexico and then, in March 1916, raided across the border and killed several Americans in Columbus, New Mexico. After securing reluctant approval from Carranza, Wilson sent an expedition of nearly seven thousand men, commanded by General John Pershing, into Mexico to punish Villa. Villa deftly evaded the American troops, all the while drawing them ever deeper into Mexico.

Carranza became alarmed, protesting the size of the American expedition and the distance it had invaded. When a clash between Mexican government forces and American soldiers produced deaths on both sides, Carranza asked Wilson to withdraw the American troops. Wilson refused. Villa then doubled behind the American army and raided into Texas, killing more Americans. When Wilson sent more men into Mexico, Carranza insisted that all the American forces be withdrawn. Wilson still refused. Only in early 1917, when Wilson began to anticipate that America might soon be at war with Germany,

Venustiana Carranza Mexican revolutionary leader who helped to lead armed opposition to Victoriano Huerta and who succeeded to the presidency in 1914; his government was overthrown in 1920.

Veracruz Major port city, located in east-central Mexico on the Gulf of Mexico; in 1914, Wilson ordered the U.S. Navy to occupy the port.

♦ This dramatic cartoon suggesting that President Woodrow Wilson had erred in his intervention in Mexico appeared in the German magazine *Simplicissimus* in 1914, only a few months before Germany and the rest of Europe plunged into war themselves. *"Simplicissimus" May 11, 1914. The Bancroft Library, University of California Berkeley.*

did he order the troops to withdraw, leaving a deep reservoir of Mexican resentment and even hatred toward the United States.

From Neutrality to War, 1914–1917

- What were Wilson's expectations regarding American neutrality?
- What constraints did he face in seeking to maintain neutrality?
- What choices did he make in an effort to do so? What was the final outcome?

At first, Americans paid only passing attention to the assassinations at Sarajevo. The nations of Europe, however, began methodically—sometimes regretfully, sometimes enthusiastically—to activate their intricate alliance networks. When Europe plunged into war, Wilson and all Americans faced difficult choices.

The Great War in Europe

Europe's great powers—Britain, France, Germany, Austria-Hungary, and Russia—had avoided armed conflict with each other since 1871, when Germany had humiliated France in the brief Franco-Prussian War. During those years, however, competition for world markets and colonies encouraged nations to accumulate arms and seek allies. European diplomats had constructed two major alliance systems by 1907. The **Triple Entente** linked Britain, France, and Russia. Britain was also allied with Japan. The **Triple Alliance** of Germany, Austria-Hungary, and Italy stood in opposition.

As European nations formed their alliance networks, most European governments also encouraged their citizens to identify strongly with their nation, thereby cultivating the intense patriotism known as **nationalism.** Among the peoples of Central Europe, particularly within the ethnically diverse empires of Austria-Hungary, Russia, and Turkey, a different sort of nationalism fueled aspirations for independence among groups whose language and culture differed from those of the ruling groups, including Poles, Czechs, and other **Slavic** groups in Austria-Hungary; Poles and others in Russia; and Arabic-speaking groups in Turkey. Such ethnic antagonisms and aspirations were especially powerful in the **Balkan Peninsula,** where the Ottoman (Turkish) Empire had lost territory as various groups had succeeded in securing their independence. Some of the new Balkan

Triple Entente Informal alliance that linked France, Great Britain, and Russia in the years before World War I.

Triple Alliance Alliance that linked Germany, Italy, and Austria-Hungary in the years before World War I.

nationalism A patriotic feeling for one's nation, or a movement that favors a separate nation for an ethnic group that is part of a multiethnic state.

Slavic Relating to the Slavs, a linguistic group that includes the Poles, Czechs, Slovaks, Slovenes, Serbs, Croats, and Bosnians of central Europe, as well as Russians, Ukrainians, Belarussians, and other groups in eastern Europe.

Balkan peninsula Region of southeastern Europe; once ruled by the Ottoman Empire, it included a number of relatively new and sometimes unstable states in the early twentieth century.

states, however, were weak, attracting the attention of the neighboring Austrian and Russian empires. As Austria-Hungary sought to annex new territories, Russia tried to establish itself as the protector of other Slavic peoples.

Imperialism and nationalism spawned an unprecedented arms buildup and an increasingly professionalized military officer corps. By 1900, most European powers had instituted universal military service. Technological advances produced powerful weapons like the machine gun. Military planners quickly adapted automobiles and airplanes, too, for their own purposes. Germany had the most powerful army in Europe and, in 1898, launched a naval construction program designed to make its navy as powerful as Britain's.

Thus the events at Sarajevo occurred in the midst of an arms race between rival alliances. The assassinations themselves grew out of conflict between Austria-Hungary and Serbia. Austria-Hungary, whose empire included a number of restive Slavic ethnic groups, feared that Serbia might form the nucleus of a strong Slavic state on its south. Russia, alarmed over Austrian expansion in the Balkans, presented itself as the protector of Serbia, which, like Russia and unlike Austria, was Orthodox in religion and used the Cyrillic rather than the Latin alphabet. Called the "powder keg of Europe," the Balkans lived up to their explosive nickname in 1914.

Austria first assured itself of Germany's backing, then declared war on Serbia. In turn, Russia confirmed France's support and began to **mobilize** its army in support of Serbia. Germany declared war on Russia on August 1 and on France two days later. German strategists planned to bypass French defenses along the Franco-German border by moving through neutral Belgium (see Map 23.2). When the Belgian government refused permission for German troops to cross its territory, Germany declared war on Belgium. Britain entered the conflict in defense of Belgium on August 4. Eventually Germany and Austria-Hungary combined with Bulgaria and the Ottoman Empire to form the **Central Powers.** Italy abandoned its Triple Alliance partners and joined the Allies: Britain, France, Russia, Romania, and Japan.

At first, Secretary of State Bryan took a hopeful view of the war. "It may be," he suggested, "that the world needed one more awful object lesson to prove conclusively the fallacy of the doctrine that preparedness for war can give assurance for peace." Sir Edward Grey, Britain's foreign minister, was far less optimistic. At twilight on August 3, 1914, he mourned to a friend, "The lamps are going out all over Europe. We shall not see them lit again in our lifetime." Grey proved a more accurate prophet than Bryan.

The Germans expected to roll through Belgium, a small and militarily weak nation, and land a quick knockout blow. The Belgians, however, resisted long enough for Britain and France to position their troops to block the Germans. The opposing armies thus settled into defensive lines over the **western front**—475 miles of Belgian and French countryside, extending from the English Channel to the Alps (see Map 23.2). By the end of 1914, the opposing troops had dug elaborate networks of trenches separated from each other by a desolate **no man's land** filled with coils of barbed wire, where any movement brought a burst of machine-gun fire. As the war progressed, terrible new weapons—poison gas, aerial bombings, tanks—took many thousands of lives but failed to break the deadlock.

American Neutrality

Wilson's initial reaction to the European conflagration revealed his own deep religious beliefs. He wrote to his closest adviser, Edward House, on August 3, of his confidence that "Providence has deeper plans than we could possibly have laid for ourselves." The next day, he announced that the United States was not committed to either side and was to be accorded all neutral rights. The death of his wife, Ellen, on August 6, briefly diverted the grief-stricken Wilson from the war. Then, on August 19, he spoke to the nation, urging Americans to be "neutral in fact as well as in name . . . impartial in thought as well as in action." He hoped not only that America would remain outside the conflict but that he, head of the most powerful neutral nation, might serve as the peacemaker.

Wilson's hopes for peace proved unrealistic. Most of the warring nations wanted to gain territory, and only a decisive victory could deliver such a prize. The longer they fought, the more territory they coveted to satisfy their losses. So long as they saw a

mobilize To make ready for combat.

Central Powers In World War I, the coalition of Germany, Austria-Hungary, Bulgaria, and the Ottoman Empire.

western front The line of battle between the Allies and Germany in World War I, located in French and Belgian territory.

no man's land The field of battle between the lines of two opposing, entrenched armies.

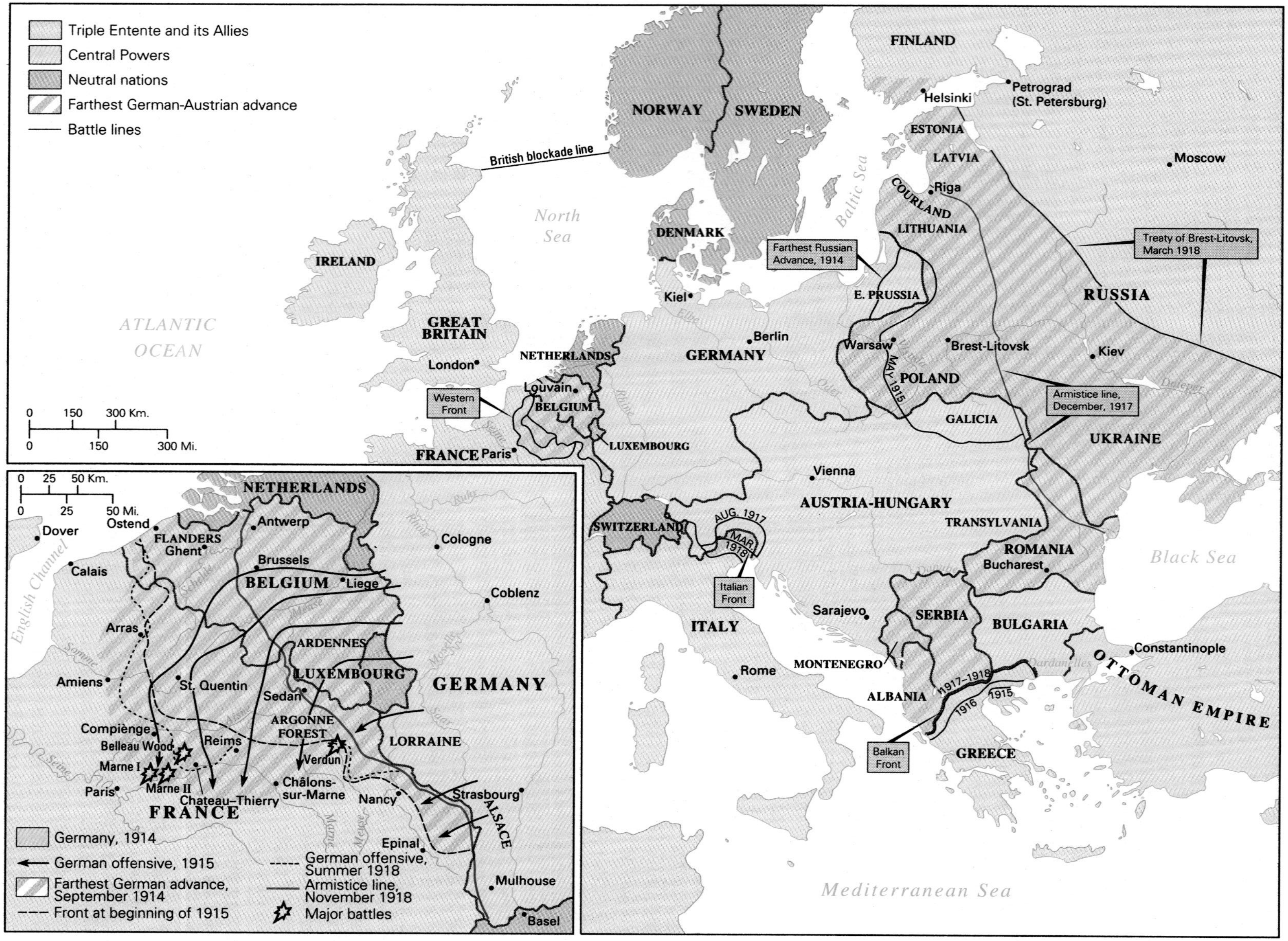

♦ **MAP 23.2 The War in Europe 1914–1918** This map identifies the members of the two great military coalitions: the Central Powers and the Allies. Notice how much territory Russia lost by the Treaty of Brest-Litovsk as compared to the armistice line (the line between the two armies when Russia sought peace).

♦ This painting, entitled "Over the Top," by John Nash, depicts British troops being sent into the no-man's land between their trenches and those of the Germans. The development of the machine gun made such efforts highly dangerous and contributed to the staggering losses of that war. The artist, one of only twelve survivors of a company of eighty sent against the enemy's trenches, recalled that "it was bitterly cold and we were easy targets in snow and daylight." *"Over the Top" by John Nash. Imperial War Museum.*

chance of winning, they had no interest in the appeals of Wilson or other would-be peacemakers.

Wilson's hope that Americans could remain impartial was also unrealistic. American socialists probably came the closest. They condemned all the warring nations for seeking imperial spoils at the expense of the workers who filled the trenches. Most Americans probably sided with the Allies. England had cultivated American friendship since at least the mid-1890s. A shared language and cultural heritage joined the upper classes in both countries, while trade and finance united many members of their business communities. Memories of French assistance during the American Revolution fueled enthusiasm for France. And the martyrdom of Belgium aroused American sympathy. Allied propagandists worked hard to generate anti-German sentiment in America, publicizing—and sometimes exaggerating—German atrocities in Belgium and portraying the war as a conflict between civilized peoples and barbarian **Huns.**

Not all Americans sympathized with the Allies. Nearly 8 million of the 97 million people in the United States had one or both parents from Germany or Austria. And, not surprisingly, many of them disputed the depictions of their cousins as bloodthirsty barbarians. Many of the five million Irish Americans disliked England for ruling their ancestral homeland and held no sympathy for the English in the war.

Neutral Rights and German U-Boats

Wilson and Bryan agreed on the need to keep American interests separate from those of either side in the European conflict, and both men believed that the United States should remain neutral. They developed different approaches for carrying out that policy, however. Bryan proved willing to sacrifice traditional neutral rights if insistence on those rights seemed likely to pull the United States into the conflict. Wilson, in contrast, stood firm on maintaining all traditional rights of neutral nations, a posture that proved favorable to the Allies. For example, Bryan initially opposed loans to **belligerent** nations as incompatible with neutrality. Wilson agreed at first, hoping to starve the war financially. But once he saw that the ban hurt the Allies more than it hurt the Central Powers, Wilson modified it to permit buying goods on credit. Eventually, he dropped the ban on loans, partly because neutrals had always been permitted to lend to belligerents and partly perhaps because the freeze endangered the stability of the American economy.

Hun Disparaging term used to describe Germans during World War I; the name came from a warlike tribe that invaded Europe in the fourth and fifth centuries.

belligerent A nation formally at war.

Traditional neutral rights included freedom of the seas: neutrals could trade with all belligerents. However, the warring European powers quickly realized that new technologies called into question traditional expectations regarding neutral rights. Wilson soon found himself in conflict with both sides over the rights of neutral ships, as both sides turned to naval warfare to break the deadlock on the western front.

Britain commanded the seas during the war's first months and began to redefine neutral rights by announcing a blockade of German ports and of neutral ports from which goods could reach Germany. Britain also expanded traditional definitions of **contraband** to include anything that might give even indirect aid to its enemy—even cotton and food. Britain also took liberties with the traditional right to "visit and search," which enabled belligerent nations to stop and search neutral ships for contraband. Insisting that large, modern ships could not be searched at sea, Britain escorted neutral ships to port, thus imposing costly delays.

Germany, in turn, declared a blockade of the British Isles, to be enforced by its submarines, called **U-boats.** Because U-boats were relatively fragile, a lightly armed merchant ship might sink one that surfaced and ordered the merchant ship to stop in the traditional manner. Consequently, submarines struck from below the surface, without the warning that traditional rules of naval warfare called for. When Britain began disguising its ships by flying the flags of neutral countries, Germany countered that neutral flags no longer guaranteed protection from U-boat attacks. Wilson had issued token protests over Britain's practices, but he now strongly denounced those of Germany. Because the outcome of Germany's assaults on neutrality was the loss of human lives, he considered them to be of a different order from Britain's, which resulted only in property loss.

On February 10, 1915, Wilson warned that the United States would hold Germany to "strict accountability" for its actions and would do whatever was necessary to "safeguard American lives and property and to secure to American citizens the full enjoyment of their acknowledged rights on the high seas." On May 7, 1915, a German U-boat torpedoed the British passenger liner ***Lusitania,*** which sank so quickly that few passengers survived—1,198 died, including 128 Americans. Americans reacted with shock and horror. When Bryan learned that the *Lusitania* carried rifle cartridges and other contraband, he urged restraint in drafting a message to Germany. Wilson, however, wrote a protest message that stopped just short of demanding an end to submarine warfare against unarmed merchant ships. When the German response was noncommittal, Wilson composed an even stronger ultimatum. Bryan feared it would lead to war, and he resigned as secretary of state rather than sign it.

Robert Lansing, Bryan's successor, was outspoken in favor of the Allies. Where Bryan had counseled restraint, Lansing urged a show of strength. As other U-boat attacks followed the sinking of the *Lusitania,* Wilson continued to protest. But he knew that most Americans opposed going to war over the issue. The sinking of the unarmed French ship *Sussex* in March 1916, injuring several Americans, led Wilson to warn Germany that if unrestricted submarine warfare did not stop, "the United States can have no choice" but to sever diplomatic relations—usually the last step before declaring war. Germany responded with the ***Sussex* pledge,** promising that U-boats would no longer strike noncombatant vessels without warning, provided the United States convinced the Allies to obey "international law." Wilson accepted the pledge but did little to persuade the British to change their tactics.

America's economic ties to the Allies grew as the war progressed. The British blockade stifled Americans' trade with the Central Powers, which fell from around $170 million in 1914 to almost nothing two years later. But trade with Britain and France more than offset this decline. American companies sent $756 million in exports to those two nations in 1914 and $2.7 billion in 1916. American companies exported $6 million worth of explosives in 1914 and $467 million in 1916. Even more significant was the transformation of the United States from a debtor to a **creditor nation.** By April 1917, American bankers had loaned more than $2 billion to the Allied governments.

contraband Goods prohibited by international law or treaty from being imported or exported.

U-boat A German submarine (in German, *Unterseeboot*).

Lusitania British passenger liner torpedoed by a German submarine in 1915; more than one thousand drowned, including 128 Americans, creating a diplomatic crisis between the United States and Germany.

***Sussex* pledge** German promise in 1916 to stop sinking merchant ships without warning if the United States compels the Allies to obey "international law."

creditor nation A nation that has more money (public and private) loaned outside the nation than the total of all loans from outsiders.

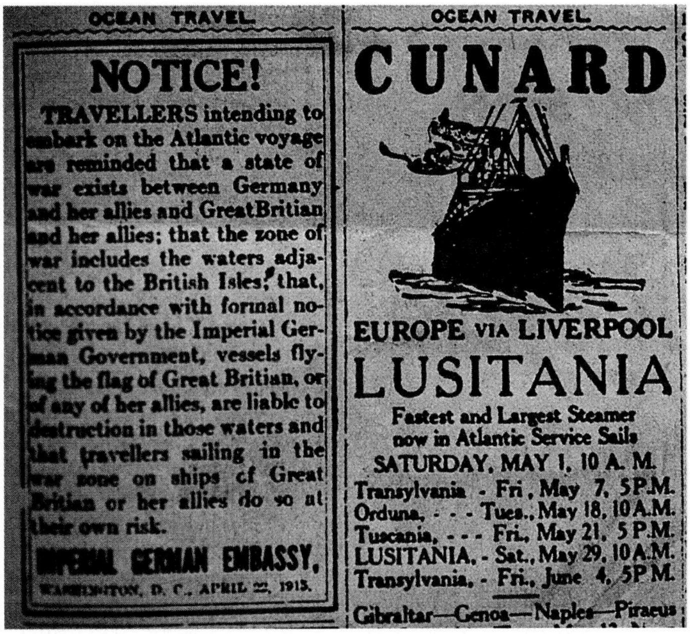

OCEAN TRAVEL

NOTICE!

TRAVELLERS intending to embark on the Atlantic voyage are reminded that a state of war exists between Germany and her allies and Great Britian and her allies; that the zone of war includes the waters adjacent to the British Isles; that, in accordance with formal notice given by the Imperial German Government, vessels flying the flag of Great Britian, or of any of her allies, are liable to destruction in those waters and that travellers sailing in the war zone on ships of Great Britian or her allies do so at their own risk.

IMPERIAL GERMAN EMBASSY,
WASHINGTON, D. C., APRIL 22, 1915.

OCEAN TRAVEL

CUNARD

EUROPE VIA LIVERPOOL

LUSITANIA

Fastest and Largest Steamer now in Atlantic Service Sails
SATURDAY, MAY 1, 10 A. M.

Transylvania - Fri., May 7, 5 P.M.
Orduna, - - - Tues., May 18, 10 A.M.
Tuscania, - - - Fri., May 21, 5 P.M.
LUSITANIA, - Sat., May 29, 10 A.M.
Transylvania, - Fri., June 4, 5 P.M.

Gibraltar—Genoa—Naples—Piraeus

♦ Though New York newspapers carried warnings from the German embassy about the dangers of trans-Atlantic travel, the passengers who boarded the *Lusitania* on May 1, 1915, probably did not imagine themselves in serious danger from submarine attack. The ship was sunk on May 7. Of the 1,959 passengers and crewmembers, 1,198 died, including 128 Americans. *Warning: Cobb Heritage Center, photo by Larry O. Nighswander/NGS; Sketch: Culver Pictures.*

Deeply convinced that the best way to keep the United States neutral was to end the war, Wilson sent Edward M. House to London and Berlin early in 1916 to sound out the British and Germans on the possibility for peace. Wilson directed that House should present proposals for peace, **disarmament,** and a league of nations to maintain peace in the future. Receiving no encouragement from either the British or the Germans, House concluded that neither side wanted a negotiated end to the war. Discouraged, Wilson yielded to the increasing numbers of Americans who sought "preparedness"—a military buildup. In the summer of 1916, Congress passed the **National Defense Act,** more than doubling the size of the army, and appropriated the largest naval expenditures in the country's peacetime history.

The Election of 1916

By promoting preparedness, Wilson took control of an issue that otherwise might have helped the Republicans in the 1916 presidential campaign. The Democrats nominated Wilson for a second term and campaigned on his progressive domestic record, his support for preparedness, and his success in keeping the nation out of war. Democrats frequently repeated their most popular campaign slogan, "He kept us out of war." Republicans nominated Charles Evans Hughes, a Supreme Court justice and former governor of New York who had a reputation as a progressive. Hughes avoided taking a clear position on preparedness and neutrality, hoping to keep support from German-American organizations upset with Wilson's harshness toward Germany and from others who pressed for maximum assistance for the Allies. As a result, he failed to present a compelling alternative to Wilson. Hughes made other errors too, as in California, where he slighted unions and Senator Hiram Johnson, both powerful forces. Wilson narrowly carried California.

disarmament The reduction or abolition of a nation's military forces or weaponry.

National Defense Act Law passed by Congress in 1916 enlarging the army, strengthening the national guard, and providing for an officers' reserve corps.

The contest was very close. Most voters still identified with the Republicans and Wilson could win only by getting support from some of them. First election reports—from eastern and midwestern states—were so strongly for Hughes that some Democrats conceded defeat. But Wilson won by uniting the always-Democratic South with the West, much of which was Republican and progressive. He also received significant backing from unions, socialists, and women in states where women could vote. In the end, Wilson received 49.4 percent of the vote to 46.2 percent for Hughes.

The Decision for War

After the election, Wilson spoke to the Senate in late January 1917 and presented his views on the best way to achieve and preserve peace. The galleries were packed and hushed as he eloquently called for a league of nations to keep peace in the future and to replace the old balance-of-power concept with "a community of power." He urged that the only lasting peace would be a "peace without victory" and a "peace among equals" in which neither side exacted gains from the other. He called for government by consent of the governed, freedom of the seas, and reductions in armaments. The speech received an enthusiastic welcome from most Democrats and progressives. Wilson admitted privately, however, that he had really aimed his speech toward "the *people* of the countries now at war" in an effort to persuade the warring governments to soften their stances. He won praise from left-wing opposition parties in France and Britain and from the Russian government, which was reeling from severe losses and eager to find any way out. The British, French, and German governments, however, had no interest in "peace without victory."

In Germany, the initiative passed to those who wanted to break the western-front stalemate by resuming unrestricted submarine warfare. Germany announced it would do so on February 1, 1917. Germany knew this move was likely to bring the United States into the war but gambled on being able to defeat the British and French before American troops could reinforce them. Wilson broke off diplomatic relations with Germany on February 3, 1917. The U-boats began immediately to take a devastating toll on shipping.

On March 1, Wilson released a decoded message from German foreign minister **Arthur Zimmermann** to the German minister in Mexico. Writing on January 16, Zimmermann had proposed that if the United States went to war with Germany, Mexico should ally itself with Germany and attack the United States. As its reward, if Germany won the war, Mexico would recover its "lost provinces" of Texas, California, and the Southwest. The British had intercepted the message and, on February 24, gave it to American representatives. Zimmermann's suggestions outraged Americans, and the public outcry lent support to Wilson's proposal to arm American merchant ships for protection against the U-boats. Not everyone agreed that arming merchant ships was the best way to protect them. A few senators, mostly progressives, blocked the measure, arguing that a safer strategy was to bar merchant ships from the war zone. Wilson then authorized merchant ships to be armed on his own.

Between February 3 and March 21, German U-boats sank six American ships, backing Wilson into a corner. The only way he could avoid war was to back down from his previous insistence on "strict accountability." He did not retreat. On April 2, 1917, Wilson spoke to a special session of Congress and asked for a declaration of war. Previously, he had concentrated on neutral rights and only occasionally had spoken of larger concerns, such as his proposal for a league of nations. Now he thought that the nation was unlikely to go to war solely to protect American commerce, and he himself was probably unwilling to seek war unless he could justify it in more noble terms. In fact, his major objective in going to war seems to have been to put the United States, and himself, in a position to demand the sort of peace he had outlined in January.

In asking for war, Wilson tried to unite Americans in a righteous, progressive crusade. He condemned German U-boat attacks as "warfare against mankind" and defined American war aims idealistically. "The world must be made safe for democracy," he pleaded. He repeated his terms from January, promising that the United States would fight for democracy, self-government, "the rights and liberties of small nations," and a league of nations to "bring peace and safety to all nations and make the world itself at last free."

Arthur Zimmermann German foreign minister who proposed in 1917 that if the United States declared war on Germany, Mexico might become a German ally and win back Texas, Arizona, and New Mexico.

Not all members of Congress agreed that war was necessary, and not all were ready to join Wilson's crusade to make the world safe for democracy. During the four days of debate that ensued, Senator George W. Norris, a progressive Republican from Nebraska, best voiced the arguments of the opposition. The nation, he claimed, was going to war "upon the command of gold" to "preserve the commercial right of American citizens to deliver munitions of war to belligerent nations." In the Senate, Norris, Robert La Follette, and four others voted no, but eighty-two senators voted for war. Jeannette Rankin of Montana, the first woman to serve in the House of Representatives, was among those who said no when the House voted 373 to 50 for war. In December, Congress also declared war against Austria-Hungary.

The Home Front

- What choices did the federal government make in mobilizing the economy and society in support of the war?
- How did the war affect Americans (including women, African Americans, and opponents of war)?

Historians call World War I the first "total war" because it was the first war to demand mobilization of an entire society and economy. The war altered nearly every aspect of the economy, as the progressive emphasis on expertise and efficiency produced unprecedented centralization of economic decision making. Mobilization extended beyond war production to the people themselves, their attitudes toward the war, and their response to the need for labor.

Mobilizing the Economy

The ability to wage war effectively depended on a fully developed industrial economy. Thus, each warring nation sought to organize nearly all activities around supplying the war machine. In the United States, shortages of military supplies, railway transportation snarls, and serious delays in military equipment deliveries led to increased federal direction over manufacturing, food and fuel production, and transportation. The American experience in this regard was not unusual and probably was less extreme than in other nations because the United States entered the war later. Even so, the extent to which the federal government exercised direct control over the U.S. economy during World War I has never been matched.

Though unprecedented, much of the government intervention was also voluntary. Business enlisted as a roughly equal partner with government and supplied its cooperation and expertise. Many prominent entrepreneurs even volunteered their full-time services for a dollar a year. Much of the wartime centralization of economic decision making came through new agencies composed of government officials, business leaders, and prominent citizens.

The **War Industries Board (WIB)** was established in 1917 to oversee production of war materials. At first, it had only limited success in mobilizing industrial productivity. Then, in early 1918, Wilson appointed Bernard Baruch, a successful Wall Street speculator, to head the board. By pleading, bargaining, and sometimes threatening, Baruch usually managed to persuade companies to do what he wanted: set and meet production quotas, allocate raw materials, develop new industries, and make the entire economy more efficient. Confrontation was sometimes necessary. Baruch once threatened steel company executives with a government takeover, but he accomplished most WIB goals without coercing corporate America. Under WIB prompting, industrial production increased by 20 percent.

Efforts to conserve fuel included the first use of **daylight saving time.** To make rail transportation more efficient, the federal government consolidated the country's railroads in 1917 and ran them as a single system for the duration of the war. The government took over the telegraph and telephone system under a similar arrangement and also set in motion a huge shipbuilding program to expand the merchant marine.

The **National War Labor Board,** created in 1918 to mediate labor disputes, endorsed **collective bargaining** and gave some support for an eight-hour workday in return for a no-strike pledge from labor. Many unions secured contracts that brought significant wage increases, and union membership

War Industries Board Board headed by Bernard Baruch that coordinated American production during World War I.

daylight saving time Setting of clocks ahead of standard time to provide more daylight at the end of the workday during late spring, summer, and early fall.

National War Labor Board Board appointed by President Wilson in 1918 to mediate labor disputes.

collective bargaining Negotiation between the representatives of organized workers and their employer to determine wages, hours, and working conditions.

♦ Once the nation went to war, all aspects of the economy were mobilized, including food. Farmers were encouraged to raise more, with the slogan "Wheat Will Win the War." Housewives were urged to conserve food, as in this poster that directly connected American food conservation to the suffering of the Allies. *Museum of the City of New York. Gift of John W. Campbell.*

♦ This poster encouraged Americans to buy Liberty bonds (that is, loan money to the government) by emphasizing the image of the vicious and brutal Hun. This was part of a larger process of demonizing the people of the Central Powers that extended to condemning the music of Beethoven and the writings of Goethe. *Collection of Robert Cherny.*

boomed from 2.7 million in 1916 to more than 4 million by 1919. Most established labor leaders fully supported the war. Samuel Gompers, president of the AFL, called it "the most wonderful crusade ever entered upon in the whole history of the world."

One crucial American contribution to the Allies was food, for the war severely disrupted much of European agriculture. Food Administrator **Herbert Hoover,** a prominent mining engineer who had skillfully directed the relief program in Belgium, promoted increased production and conservation of food, urging families to conserve food through Meatless Mondays and Wheatless Wednesdays and to plant "war gardens" to raise more of their own food. Farmers also brought large areas under cultivation for the first time. (The chapter-opening map indicates the expansion of wheat growing.) As a result, food shipments to the Allies tripled.

Some progressives urged that the Wilson administration pay for the war solely by taxing the wartime profits and earnings of corporations. That did not happen, but taxes—especially the relatively new income tax—did account for almost half of the $33 billion that the United States spent on the war between April 1917 and June 1920. The government borrowed the rest, most of it through **Liberty Loan** drives. Rallies, parades, and posters pushed all Americans to buy "Liberty bonds." Groups like the Red Cross and the YMCA urged people to donate time and energy in support of American soldiers. Wilson himself raised funds for the Red Cross by selling wool from sheep that grazed on the White House lawn—not only as replacements for gardeners drafted into the military but also as a lesson in using every possible resource to expand production.

Mobilizing Public Opinion

Not all Americans fully supported the war. Some German Americans were reluctant to see their sons sent to war against their cousins. Some Irish Americans took even less interest in saving Britain after

Herbert Hoover U.S. food administrator during World War I known for his proficient handling of relief efforts; he later served as secretary of commerce (1921–1928) and as president (1929–1933).

Liberty Loan One of a series of four bond issues floated by the U.S. Treasury Department from 1917 to 1919 to help finance World War I.

the English brutally suppressed an attempt at Irish independence in 1916. After the Socialist party voted its opposition to entering the war, Socialist candidates greatly increased their share of the vote in several cities in 1917—to 22 percent in New York City and 34 percent in Chicago—suggesting that their antiwar stance attracted many voters.

To mobilize public opinion in support of the war, Wilson in 1917 created the Committee on Public Information (CPI), headed by George Creel. Once a muckraking journalist, Creel set out to sell the war to the American people. The **Creel Committee** eventually counted 150,000 lecturers, writers, artists, actors, and scholars championing the cause and whipping up hatred of the "Huns." Social clubs, movie theaters, and churches all joined what Creel called "the world's greatest adventure in advertising." Most of those serving with the Creel Committee did so as "Four-Minute Men"—that is, they were ready to make a four-minute speech anytime and anywhere a crowd gathered—and they made 755,190 speeches in all, in 5,000 towns.

The fierce patriotism kindled by military exploits overseas and fanned by the Creel Committee sometimes sparked extreme measures against those considered "slackers" and pro-German. "Woe to the man or group of men that seeks to stand in our way in this day of high resolution," warned Wilson. "He who is not with us, absolutely and without reserve of any kind," proclaimed former president Theodore Roosevelt, "is against us, and should be treated as an alien enemy." Zealots across the country took up the cry. "Americanization" drives sought to persuade immigrants to give up their native cultures. Some states prohibited the use of foreign languages in public, and in many places officials removed German books from libraries and sometimes publicly burned them. Some communities banned the music of Bach and Beethoven, and some dropped German classes from their schools. Even words became objectionable: *sauerkraut* became "liberty cabbage," and *German measles* was renamed "liberty measles." Sometimes mobs hounded people with German names and occasionally attacked or even lynched people suspected of antiwar sentiments.

Civil Liberties in Time of War

German Americans suffered the most from the wartime hysteria, but pacifists, socialists, and other radicals also became targets for government and vigilante repression. Congress passed the **Espionage Act** in 1917 and the **Sedition Act** in 1918, prohibiting interference with the draft and outlawing criticism of the government, the armed forces, or the war effort and specifying large fines and long prison terms for violators. Officials arrested some fifteen hundred people for violating the Espionage and Sedition Acts, including Eugene V. Debs, leader of the Socialist party. One passage in the Espionage Act gave the postmaster general the power to decide what could pass through the nation's mails. By the war's end, the Post Office Department had denied mailing privileges to some four hundred periodicals, including, at least temporarily, some mainstream publications, such as *The Saturday Evening Post* and *The New York Times.*

Those who voiced dissenting opinions found they could not rely on the courts for protection. When opponents of the war challenged the Espionage Act as unconstitutional, the Supreme Court ruled that freedom of speech was never absolute. Just as no one has the right to falsely shout "Fire" in a theater and create panic, said Justice Oliver Wendell Holmes, Jr., so in time of war no one has a constitutional right to say anything that might endanger the security of the nation. The Court also upheld the Sedition Act in 1919, by a vote of 7 to 2.

Although the Industrial Workers of the World (IWW) made no public pronouncement against the war, most Wobblies probably opposed it. IWW members and leaders quickly came under relentless attack from employers, government officials, and patriotic vigilantes. In September 1917, Justice Department agents raided IWW offices nationwide and arrested the union's leaders, who were sentenced to jail terms of up to twenty-five years and to fines totaling millions of dollars. Deprived of most of its leaders and virtually bankrupted, the IWW never recovered.

Creel Committee The U.S. Committee on Public Information (1917–1919), headed by journalist and editor George Creel; it used films, posters, pamphlets, and news releases to mobilize American public opinion in favor of World War I.

Espionage Act Law passed by Congress in 1917 mandating severe penalties for anyone found guilty of interfering with the draft or encouraging disloyalty to the United States.

Sedition Act Law passed by Congress in 1918 to supplement the Espionage Act by extending the penalty to anyone deemed to have abused the government in writing.

♦ Labor shortages attracted new people into the labor market and opened up some jobs to women and members of racial minorities. In May 1918, these women worked in the Union Pacific Railroad freight yard in Cheyenne, Wyoming. Most of them seem delighted to have their picture taken in their work clothes. *Wyoming State Museum.*

A few Americans protested the abridgment of civil liberties. One group formed the Civil Liberties Bureau—forerunner of the American Civil Liberties Union, or ACLU—under the leadership of Roger Baldwin. Most Americans, however, did not object to the repression. Many others who were sympathetic to the victims kept silent.

The grounds for suppressing civil liberties were not limited to espionage and sedition. To discourage prostitution, General Pershing informed his troops that "sexual intercourse is not necessary for good health, and complete continence is wholly possible." Military officials soon went beyond such verbal recommendations and arrested any woman found within the "pure zone"—that is, anywhere within 5 miles of a military establishment. As a result, 15,520 women had been arrested and forcibly detained by the war's end. Such measures proved little more successful in keeping soldiers healthy than had Pershing's moral instruction. So, by the end of the war, the army was giving out millions of condoms as more reliable protection—and coincidentally providing the most widespread government sex education program up to that time.

Changes in the Workplace

Intense activism and remarkable productivity characterized American labor's wartime experience. Union membership almost doubled, and a significant number of women were among the surge of new cardholders. In addition, unions benefited from the encouragement that the National War Labor Board gave to collective bargaining between unions and companies as the most effective way to keep labor peace. The board also stepped in and helped to settle labor disputes through mediation. Never before had a federal agency interceded this way. Nevertheless, many workers felt that their purchasing power was not keeping pace with increases in prices.

Demands for increased production at a time when millions of men were marching off to war opened opportunities for women in many fields. Employment of women in factory, office, and retail jobs had increased before the war, and the war accelerated those trends. At the war's end, many women's wartime jobs returned to male hands, but in office work and some retail positions women continued to predominate after the war.

Most women who worked outside the home were young and single. Some middle-class women who now entered the paid labor force not only gave up their homebound roles but also rejected their parents' standards of morality and behavior. Some adopted instead the less-restricted lifestyles that had long been experienced by many wage-earning, working-class women, taking control over their income and using it to establish their autonomy from familial controls.

♦ Labor shortages and high wages drew African Americans from the South to the North. This family, including members of three generations, posed for the photographer upon their arrival in Chicago from the South, as part of the Great Migration during World War I. *Schomburg Center for Research in Black Culture, New York Public Library.*

The Great Migration and White Reactions

The war also had a great impact on African-American communities. Until the war, about 90 percent of all African Americans lived in the South, 75 percent in rural areas. By 1920, perhaps as many as a half-million had moved north in what has been called the **Great Migration.**

The largest proportional increases in the African-American population came in the industrial cities of the Midwest. Gary, Indiana, showed one of the greatest gains—1,284 percent between 1910 and 1920. Outside the Midwest, New York City, Philadelphia, and Los Angeles also attracted many blacks (see the chapter-opening map). Several factors combined to stimulate and feed this migration, but the most important were probably the brutality of southern life and the economic opportunities in the cities of the North. "Every time a lynching takes place in a community down South," T. Arnold Hill of Chicago's Urban League pointed out, "colored people will arrive in Chicago within two weeks." Economic disaster in the South provided further impetus. In 1915 and 1916, southern farmers alternately battled drought and severe rains and fought the **boll weevil** throughout.

Perhaps the most significant factor in the Great Migration was American industry's desperate need for workers at the same that European immigration declined sharply. The wartime labor needs of northern cities attracted hundreds of thousands of African Americans seeking better jobs and higher pay. A laundress or cook in the North could earn $1.50 to $2 a day plus carfare and meals, almost as much as for a week's work in the South. Many industrial jobs paid $3 a day, compared to 50 cents for picking cotton. The impact on some southern cities was striking. Jackson, Mississippi, for example, was estimated to have lost half of all working-class African Americans and between a quarter and a third of black business owners and professionals.

The war heightened racial tensions in the South because some whites resented the new options available to blacks. For example, black women who received money from their men in uniform or in

Great Migration Movement of about a half-million black people from the rural South to the urban North during World War I.

boll weevil Small beetle that infests cotton plants and damages the cotton bolls, which contain the cotton fibers.

wartime jobs sometimes found that they no longer needed farm work. Some city officials in Arkansas tried to extend the nation's "work or fight" rule to black women who refused to work in the cotton fields. Under this rule, anyone not aiding the war effort by either working or fighting could be arrested. African-American women leaving other jobs were also harassed. In Vicksburg, Mississippi, a mob tarred and feathered two black women who quit their jobs. Lynchings continued: lynch mobs killed at least thirty-eight African-Americans in 1917 and fifty-eight in 1918, most of them in the South.

Severe wartime racial conflicts erupted in several cities at the northern end of the Great Migration trail. One of America's worst race riots swept through the industrial city of East St. Louis, Illinois, on July 2, 1917. Thousands of African-American laborers, most from the South, had settled in the city during the previous two years. A least thirty-nine of them perished in the riot, and six thousand found themselves homeless. Incensed that such brutality could occur so soon after the nation's moralistic entrance into the war, W. E. B. Du Bois charged, "No land that loves to lynch 'niggers' can lead the hosts of Almighty God." He and the NAACP soon led a parade of ten thousand people through **Harlem** in a silent protest.

Americans "Over There"

- What role did American ships and troops play in ending the war?
- Why did Wilson choose to keep the AEF as separate as possible from the troops of the other Allies?

With the declaration of war, the United States needed to mobilize quickly for combat in a distant part of the world. The navy was already large and powerful after nearly three decades of shipbuilding, and the preparedness measures of mid-1916 had further strengthened U.S. sea power. The army, however, was tiny compared to the armies contesting in Europe. Millions of men and thousands of women had to be enlisted or drafted, trained, supplied, and transported to Europe.

Mobilizing for Battle

Almost immediately the navy was able to strike back successfully at the German fleet. The American and British navies' convoy technique, in which several ships traveled together under the protection of destroyers, helped to cut shipping losses in half by late 1917. By the following spring, U-boats ceased to pose a significant danger.

The army, however, was not ready for action in April 1917—the combined strength of the U.S. Army and National Guard stood at only 372,000 men. Many men volunteered but not enough. Congress therefore rushed into law the **Selective Service Act** in May, requiring men aged 21 to 30 (later extended to 18 to 45) to register with local boards to determine who was to be called to duty. Some, including members of Congress, objected that conscription (usually called "the draft") was undemocratic. The law exempted those who opposed war on religious grounds, but such **conscientious objectors** were sometimes badly treated.

Few people demonstrated against the draft, and most seemed to accept it as efficient and fair. Eventually, 24 million men registered and 2.8 million were drafted—about 72 percent of the entire army. By the end of the war, the combined army, navy, and marine corps counted 4.8 million members.

No women were drafted, but almost 13,000 joined the military, most serving in clerical capacities in the navy and marines. For the first time, women held full military rank and status. The army, however, refused to enlist women, considering it a "most radical departure." Nearly 18,000 women served in the Army Corps of Nurses, but without army rank, pay, or benefits. At least 5,000 civilian women served in various capacities in France, sometimes near the front lines. The largest number served through the Red Cross, which helped to staff hospitals and rest facilities.

Nearly 400,000 African Americans served during World War I. Almost 200,000 served overseas, nearly 30,000 on the front lines. Emmett J. Scott, an African American and former secretary to Booker T. Washington, became special assistant to the secretary of war and was responsible for ensuring the uniform application of the draft and for the morale of African Americans, military and civilian alike. Nevertheless, black soldiers were often treated as second-

Harlem A section of New York City in the northern part of Manhattan; it became one of the largest black communities in the United States.

Selective Service Act Law passed by Congress in 1917 establishing compulsory military service for men aged 21 to 30.

conscientious objector Person who refuses to bear arms or participate in military service because of religious beliefs or moral principles.

♦ About 10,000 American Indians enlisted or were drafted into the army during World War I, including John Miller (left) and Charlie Wolf, members of the Omaha tribe. In some cases, the Indians who went to war first underwent tribal ceremonies, long unpracticed, for preparing warriors for battle, and thus may have contributed to the preservation of traditional customs. Indians' participation in the war led to increased demands for full citizenship and enfranchisement for all American Indians, a step that came in 1924. *Nebraska State Historical Society.*

class citizens. They served in segregated **Jim Crow** units in the army, were limited to food service in the navy, and were excluded from the marines altogether. More than 600 African Americans earned commissions as officers, but they were trained in separate camps, and the army was reluctant to commission more than a few. White officers commanded most black troops.

"Over There"

By mid-1918, it seemed that Allied troops all along the western front had taken up a tune by the popular American composer George M. Cohan:

Over there, over there,
Send the word, send the word over there,
The Yanks are coming, the Yanks are coming,
And we won't come back 'til it's over over there.

A few Yanks—troops in the **American Expeditionary Force (AEF)**—arrived in France in June 1917, commanded by General John J. Pershing, recently returned from Mexico. Most American troops, however, were still to be drafted, supplied, trained, and transported across the Atlantic.

As the first American troops began to trickle into France, the Central Powers seemed close to victory. French offensives in April 1917 had failed, and a British summer effort in Flanders produced enormous casualties but little gain. The Italians suffered a major defeat late in the year. A Russian drive in midsummer proved disastrous, and, soon after the **Bolsheviks** took power in November 1917, Russia withdrew from the war. As German-Russian peace talks began, German troops moved from east to west. Hoping to win the war before many American troops arrived, the Germans planned a massive offensive for spring 1918.

The German offensive came in Picardy with sixty-four divisions smashing into the point where the French and British lines joined. As the Germans pushed forward, AEF units were hurried to the front to block their advance. In mid-May, an AEF officer described trench life in a letter to his sister:

> *We have to lay low all day to escape observation. . . . At nine* P.M. *we emerge and do various work all night: digging trenches, wiring, carrying ammunition, burying the dead. . . . It is scary . . . when the shelling begins, the rockets and flares all along the near horizon lighting up the weird scene, the Boche flashlights [German searchlights] simulating the aurora, the everlasting crack and roar of our own artillery . . . and the whine of the innumerable shells passing overhead, the sputtering of the machine guns, and in the midst of it all the persistent singing of a nightingale down in the ravine.*

By late May, the Germans were within 50 miles of Paris. French officials considered evacuating the capital, and all available troops were rushed to that area. AEF units fought bravely and effectively. At Chateau-Thierry and at Belleau Woods, they took

Jim Crow Name for laws or practices that discriminate against black people; probably derived from a minstrel-show character named Jim Crow.

American Expeditionary Force American army commanded by General John J. Pershing that served in Europe during World War I.

Bolsheviks Radicals, later called Communists, who seized power in Russia in November 1917.

♦ In this dramatic cartoon, Uncle Sam confidently pats General John J. Pershing on the shoulder as American troops march to the front past French troops. *Collection of Colonel Stuart S. Corning, Jr.*

8,000 casualties during a month-long battle over a single square mile of wheatfield and woods. Of 310,000 AEF troops who fought in the **Marne River** region, 67,000 were killed or wounded.

Throughout the war, Wilson held the United States apart from the Allies, referring to this country as an Associated Power, rather than one of the Allies, and trying as much as possible to keep American troops separate. This distinction stemmed partly from his distrust of Allied war aims but more from his wish to make the American contribution to victory as prominent as possible in order to maximize American influence in peacemaking.

The Allies launched a counteroffensive in July as fresh American troops continued to pour into France, topping the million mark that month. The American command insisted on having its own sector of the front, and in September Pershing successfully launched a stunning one-day offensive against the St. Mihiel **salient** (see Map 23.2). AEF forces then joined a larger Allied offensive in the Meuse-Argonne region, the last major assault of the war and one of the fiercest battles in American military history (see Individual Choices: Alvin York). By then, the German general staff was urging the German government to seek an armistice. Fighting ended at 11 A.M., November 11 (the eleventh hour of the eleventh day of the eleventh month), 1918. By then, more than 2 million American soldiers were in France, giving the Allies an advantage of about 600,000 men.

Thirty-two nations, including the United States, had entered the war against Germany or the other Central Powers. Nearly 9 million men in uniform died: Germany lost 1.8 million, Russia 1.7 million, France 1.4 million, Austria-Hungary 1.2 million, the British Empire 908,400. France lost half its men between the ages of 20 and 32. More than 20 million combatants suffered wounds, producing many permanent disabilities. American losses were small in comparison—115,000 casualties, including 48,000 killed in action. Millions of people worldwide, including civilians, died from starvation and disease, especially during a global **influenza** epidemic in 1918 and 1919 that killed 500,000 Americans.

Among the American casualties were African Americans. Some Americans, though, tried to hide the presence in Europe of African-American soldiers. Many black units were assigned to menial tasks behind the lines, although some saw action. Even so, some white Americans, including some military officers, worried that experiences in France might cause African-American soldiers to resist segregation at home. In August 1918, AEF headquarters confidentially requested that the French not prominently commend black units. The French, however, awarded the **Croix de Guerre** to several all-black units that had distinguished themselves in combat and presented awards to individual soldiers for acts

Marne River River in northeast France that was the site of pivotal fighting in World War I, including a successful French and American counterattack on German forces in July 1918.

salient Battle line that projects closest to the enemy.

influenza Contagious viral infection characterized by fever, chills, congestion, and muscular pain; an unusually deadly strain of it swept across the world in 1918 and 1919.

Croix de Guerre French military decoration for bravery in combat; in English, "the Cross of War."

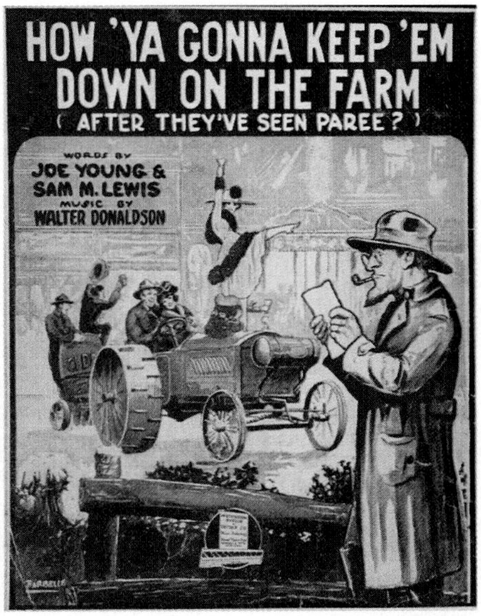

♦ A black bandleader, James Reese Europe (left) went to France as a lieutenant, commanding a machine-gun company and saw frontline action. When he and other black musicians were reassigned to present musical entertainment behind the lines, they were among the first to play jazz in France. Upon returning to the United States in 1919, he and his band recorded "How 'Ya Gonna Keep 'Em Down on the Farm After They've Seen Paree?" (right). Many groups recorded the popular song, but black musicians may have given it a different emphasis: how can black soldiers be kept "down" after they experienced less oppressive racial patterns in France? *Europe: Howard University Museum Archives, Moorland-Spingarn Research Center; sheet music: The John Hay Library, Brown University, photo by Brooke Hammerle.*

of bravery and heroism. When the Allies staged a grand victory parade down Paris's Champs Elysées, the British and French contingents included all races and ethnicities, but American commanders permitted no African-American troops to march.

Wilson and the Peace Conference

- What did Wilson expect to accomplish at the peace conference, and what constraints did he face in meeting his objectives?
- What was the outcome of his efforts?
- How did divisions within in the Senate contribute to the defeat of the treaty there?

When the war ended, Wilson hoped that the peace treaty would not contain the seeds of future wars. He hoped, too, to create an international organization to keep the peace. Most of the Allies, however, had more interest in grabbing territory and punishing Germany.

Bolshevism, the Secret Treaties, and the Fourteen Points

In March 1917, war-weary, hungry Russians had overthrown their tsar. In November, the Bolsheviks seized power from the more moderate prime minister, Alexander Kerensky. Soon renamed Communists, the Bolsheviks condemned capitalism and imperialism and sought to destroy them. **Vladimir Lenin,** the Bolshevik leader, immediately began peace negotiations with the Central Powers. Despite Germany's harsh and humiliating terms, Lenin saw no choice but to accept. By the **Treaty of Brest-Litovsk,** in March 1918, Russia surrendered vast holdings—Finland, its Baltic provinces, parts of Poland and the Ukraine—making up a third of its population, half of its industries, fertile agricultural land, and a quarter of its territory in Europe.

In December 1917, the Bolsheviks tried to demonstrate that the war was nothing more than a scramble for imperial spoils. They published secret treaties, negotiated before and during the war, by

Vladimir Lenin Leader of the Bolsheviks and of the Russian Revolution of 1917 and head of the Soviet Union until 1924.

Treaty of Brest-Litovsk Humiliating treaty with Germany that Russia signed in 1918 in order to withdraw from the war; Russia had to surrender vast territories along its western boundary.

INDIVIDUAL CHOICES

The Choice to Fight

Alvin York

Alvin York, a devout Christian, had to choose between his moral compunctions about killing and his sense of obligation to his country. This photograph was taken in 1919, the year York was promoted to sergeant and received the Congressional Medal of Honor, as well as similar awards from many of the Allies for his exploits in battle. Brown Brothers.

Long before Alvin York won the nation's admiration for his amazing demonstration of bravery and coolness under fire on October 8, 1918, he underwent a personal crisis of conscience over his choice to fight. Born in the Cumberland Mountains of Tennessee in 1887, York was raised in a backwoods community where people expected to secure food for their tables through skill with their hunting rifles. He grew up with guns, remembering that his father "threatened to muss me up right smart if I failed to bring a squirrel down with the first shot or hit a [wild] turkey in the body instead of [shooting] its head off." From his youth, red-haired Alvin York was highly proficient with both rifle and pistol.

As a young man, York was known for his drinking, carousing, recklessness, and sometimes violent behavior. He put all that behind him when he became a born-again Christian in 1915 and joined a small fundamentalist church. He took his new faith seriously, and his commitment posed difficult choices for him when the war came:

> *I loved and trusted old Uncle Sam and I have always believed he did the right thing. But I was worried clean through. I didn't want to go and kill. I believed in my Bible. And it distinctly*

which the Allies agreed to take colonies and territories from the Central Powers and to divide those spoils among themselves. These exposés strengthened Wilson in his intent to separate American war aims from those of the Allies and to impose his war objectives on the Allies.

On January 8, 1918, Wilson spoke to Congress about those war objectives. Elaborating on the goals he had first presented nearly a year before, he directly challenged the secret treaties and tried to seize the initiative in defining a basis for peace. He stressed that American war objectives derived from "the principle of justice to all peoples and nationalities, and their right to live on equal terms of liberty and safety with one another, whether they be strong or weak." Wilson presented fourteen specific objectives, soon called the **Fourteen Points.** Points one through five provided a general context for lasting peace: no secret treaties, freedom of the seas, reduc-

Fourteen Points President Wilson's program for maintaining peace after World War I, which called for arms reduction, national self-determination, and a league of nations.

said "thou shalt not kill." And yet old Uncle Sam wanted me. And he said he wanted me most awful bad. And I jest didn't know what to do. I worried and worried. I couldn't think of anything else. My thoughts just wouldn't stay a hitched.

York chose to seek exemption from the draft as a conscientious objector but was refused. Called to active duty, he made "good friends" with his new rifle and excelled at target practice. Deeply troubled about the morality of war, however, he shared his concern with his battalion commander, Major Edward Buxton, who spent long hours discussing the Bible with York and trying to convince him that a good Christian might morally choose to go to war. Buxton recognized York's sincerity, however, and offered him the choice of noncombatant duty if he decided he could not kill on the battlefield. After struggling with his religious beliefs, York finally decided not only that he could fight in good conscience but that he was doing the Lord's work in helping bring peace.

His choice made, he arrived with his unit on the front lines in France in late June 1918, took part in the attack on the St. Mihiel salient in September, and was then dispatched to the Meuse-Argonne sector. Part of a sixteen-man unit sent to take out some enemy machine guns, York—now a corporal—helped to capture a small group of Germans. Then a sudden burst of machine-gun fire killed or wounded nine members of his unit, including his sergeant. York was closest to the enemy gun. While the six surviving Americans remained with the prisoners, York coolly practiced his mountaineer marksmanship, killing fourteen or so Germans as they trained machine-gun fire in his direction and tried to determine his position. When six Germans charged him with fixed bayonets, he dropped them all with his pistol. He then captured the German lieutenant in command and had him call on his men to surrender. York shot those who resisted. Prisoners in tow, York and other members of his unit moved from position to position, using the German lieutenant to order each to surrender. Credited with killing twenty-five enemy soldiers and silencing thirty-five machine guns, York and the six other Americans marched 132 prisoners back to their stunned commanding officer. The next day, York returned to the area searching for survivors. There he knelt and prayed for the souls of the dead, including those he had killed.

Promoted to sergeant and given national attention by an article in *Saturday Evening Post,* York received the Congressional Medal of Honor, the Croix de Guerre, and similar awards from many of the other Allies. Still, the blessings of his contemporaries were not enough to settle the matter. Toward the end of his life, confined to bed, Alvin York pressed his son, a minister, for assurance that God would accept the choice he had made and the action he had taken in the Argonne forest.

Source: Adapted from David D. Lee, *Sergeant York: An American Hero* (Lexington: University Press of Kentucky, 1985), Chs. 1–3.

tion of barriers to trade, reduction of armaments, and adjustment of colonial claims based partly on the interests of colonial peoples. Points six through thirteen addressed particular situations: return of territories France had lost to Germany in 1871 and self-determination in Central Europe and the Middle East. The fourteenth point called for "a general association of nations" that could afford "mutual guarantees of political independence and territorial integrity to great and small states alike."

The major Allies reluctantly accepted Wilson's Fourteen Points as a basis for discussion but expressed little enthusiasm for them. The Germans were more interested. When they asked for an end to the fighting, they made clear that their request was based on the Fourteen Points.

The World in 1919

In December 1918, Wilson sailed for France. This was the first time that an American president in office had gone to Europe and the first time that a president had personally taken part in negotiations with other world leaders. Wilson brought along some two hundred experts on European history, culture, ethnology, and geography. In France, Italy, and

Britain, huge welcoming crowds paid homage to the great "peacemaker from America."

Delegates to the peace conference assembled amid far-reaching change. The Austro-Hungarian Empire had crumbled, producing the new nations of Poland and Czechoslovakia and the republics of Austria and Hungary. In Germany, **Kaiser Wilhelm** had **abdicated,** and a republic was being formed. In January 1919, Berlin witnessed an unsuccessful communist uprising. Amid the ruins of the Russian Empire, Finland, Estonia, Latvia, Lithuania, Ukraine, and regions in the Caucasus were asserting their independence. The Ottoman Empire was collapsing, too, as Arabs revolted with aid from Britain and France. Throughout Europe and the Middle East, national **self-determination** and government by the consent of the governed—part of Wilson's design for the postwar world—seemed to be stumbling into reality. Nor were the British and French colonial empires immune, for both faced growing independence movements among their many possessions.

In Russia, civil war raged between the Bolsheviks' Red Army and the White (anti-Communist) armies of their opponents. When the Bolsheviks left the world war, the Allies pushed Wilson to join them in intervening in Russia, ostensibly to protect war supplies from falling into German hands. In mid-1918, Wilson included American troops in Allied expeditions to northern Russia and eastern Siberia. In Siberia, his role was primarily to head off a Japanese grab of territory. American troops stayed in northern Russia until May 1919 and in eastern Siberia until early 1920. Many historians have long seen these actions as fueling Bolshevik suspicions of the Allies and Americans, but Lenin accepted the initial British and French intervention in northern Russia as necessary to block German expansion in the region and only later became opposed to it.

Wilson at Versailles

The peace conference opened on January 18, 1919, just outside Paris, at the glittering Palace of Versailles, once home to French kings. Representatives attended from all the nations that had declared war against any of the Central Powers, but major decisions were made by the Big Four: Woodrow Wilson of the United States, David Lloyd George of Britain, Georges Clemenceau of France, and Vittorio Orlando of Italy. Germany was excluded. Terms of peace were to be imposed, not negotiated. Russia, too, was absent, on the grounds that it had withdrawn from the war earlier and made a separate peace with Germany. Although Russia was barred from Versailles, the specter of bolshevism was all too present at the proceedings, affecting decisions about Eastern Europe especially.

Wilson quickly learned that the European leaders were far more interested in pursuing their own national interests than in implementing his Fourteen Points. Clemenceau, nicknamed "the Tiger," carried painful memories of Germany's humiliating defeat of France in 1871 and wanted to disable Germany so that it could never again invade his nation. Lloyd George agreed in principle with many of Wilson's proposals but came to Paris with a mandate from British voters to exact heavy **reparations** from Germany. Orlando insisted on all the territorial gains promised when Italy joined the Allies in 1915. Other war aims had been spelled out in the secret treaties, so various Allies were expecting to gain territory at the expense of Germany, Austria-Hungary, and the Ottoman Empire. In addition, the European Allies all feared the spread of bolshevism into Western Europe.

Facing the insistent and acquisitive Allies, Wilson had no choice but to compromise. He did secure the creation of a **League of Nations.** Instead of "peace without victory," however, the **Treaty of Versailles** imposed harsh victors' terms, requiring Germany to accept the blame for starting the war, to pay the Allies reparations (the exact amount to be determined later), and to surrender all its colonies, Alsace-Lorraine (which Germany had taken from France in 1871), and other European territories (see Map 23.3.) To prevent further aggression, the treaty deprived Germany of its navy and merchant marine and limited its army to one hundred thousand men. German representatives signed on June 28, 1919.

Kaiser Wilhelm II German emperor who had worked to create the great military machine and system of alliances that precipitated the outbreak of World War I.

abdicate To formally relinquish a high office.

self-determination The freedom of a given people to determine their own political status.

reparations Payments required from a defeated nation as compensation to the victors for damage or injury during a war.

League of Nations A world organization proposed by President Wilson and founded in 1920; it worked to promote peace and international cooperation.

Treaty of Versailles Treaty between Allies and Germany ending World War I, signed in 1919; it imposed harsh terms on Germany and set up the League of Nations.

♦ Wilson toured the country in support of the League of Nations, including this appearance in Boston. *Detroit Public Library, National Automotive History Collection.*

Wilson reluctantly agreed to the massive reparations but insisted that colonies taken from Germany should not go to the Allies. Called **mandates,** they were instead to be administered by one of the Allies on behalf of the League of Nations. Most mandates were intended to move toward self-government and independence. In nearly every case, however, the mandate went to the nation slated to receive the territory under the secret treaties. Wilson blocked Italy's most extreme territorial demands but gave in on others. The peace conference recognized the new nations of central Europe, thereby creating a so-called "quarantine zone" between Russian bolshevism and western Europe. But the Treaty of Versailles ignored other matters of self-determination. No one gave a hearing to people—from Ireland to Vietnam—seeking the right of self-determination in colonies held by one of the victorious Allies. Japan failed to secure a statement supporting racial equality.

In the end, Wilson compromised on nearly all of his Fourteen Points, but every compromise intensified his commitment to the League of Nations. The League, he hoped, would resolve future controversies without war and would solve problems created by the compromises he had accepted. Even so, the Allies agreed to include the **League Covenant** in the treaty only after Wilson threatened to make a separate peace with Germany. Wilson was especially pleased with Article 10 of the League Covenant—he called it the League's "heart." It specified that League members would protect each other's independence and territory against external attacks and would take joint economic and military action against aggressors.

The Senate and the Treaty

While Wilson was in Paris, opposition to his plans was taking shape at home. The Senate, controlled by Republicans since the 1918 election, had to approve any treaty. In response to the concerns of some senators, Wilson had added several provisions to the League Covenant. However, Wilson's delegation to Versailles included no senators and no prominent Republicans.

Faced with the treaty, the Senate split into three groups. **Henry Cabot Lodge,** chairman of the Senate Foreign Relations Committee, led the largest faction, called *reservationists* after the reservations, or amendments, to the treaty that Lodge developed. Chief among Lodge's misgivings was his concern that Article 10 of the League Covenant might be used to commit American troops to war without congressional approval. A smaller group, mostly Republicans, earned the name *irreconcilables* because it opposed any American involvement in European affairs. A third Senate group, mostly Democrats, supported the president and his treaty.

Wilson decided to appeal directly to the American people. In September 1919, he undertook an arduous speaking tour—9,500 miles with speeches in twenty-nine cities. Huge crowds came to hear his eloquent arguments, but the effort proved too demanding for his fragile health. He collapsed in

mandate A territory that the League of Nations authorized one of its member nations to govern, with the understanding that the region would move toward self-government.

League Covenant The constitution of the League of Nations, which was incorporated in the Versailles treaty in 1919.

Henry Cabot Lodge Massachusetts senator who led congressional opposition to the Versailles treaty and the League of Nations.

♦ **MAP 23.3 Postwar Boundary Changes in Central Europe and the Middle East** This map shows the boundary changes in Europe and the Middle East that resulted from the defeat of the four large, multiethnic empires—Austria-Hungary, Russia, Germany, and the Ottoman Empire.

Pueblo, Colorado, on September 25 and returned to Washington. Soon after, he suffered a serious stroke.

Half-paralyzed and weakened, Wilson remained in seclusion and carried on few of his duties. Lodge proposed that the Senate accept the treaty with fourteen reservations, his retort to the Fourteen Points. Some of his amendments were minor, but others took aim squarely at Article 10 by permitting Congress to block action to fulfill League commitments, especially those involving military force. Wilson refused to compromise. His refusal produced a deadlock. On November 19, 1919, the Senate defeated the treaty with the Lodge reservations by votes of 39 to 55 and 41 to 50, with the irreconcilables joining the president's supporters in opposition. Then the Senate defeated the original version of the treaty by 38 to 53, with the irreconcilables joining the reservationists in voting no. The treaty with reservations came to a vote again in March 1920. By then, some treaty supporters had concluded that the League could never be approved without Lodge's reservations, so they joined the reservationists to produce a vote of 49 to 35. Approval, however, required a two-thirds majority of those voting. Enough Wilson loyalists—following their stubborn leader's order not to compromise—joined the irreconcilables to defeat the treaty once again. The United States would not join the League of Nations.

Legacies of the Great War

Roosevelt, Wilson, and most other prewar leaders had projected the progressive mood of optimism and confidence. Wilson invoked this tradition in claiming that the United States was going to war to make the world "safe for democracy." One of his most optimistic supporters even described World War I as the "war to end war," a holy struggle to eliminate war for all time. Just as progressives defined their domestic policies in terms of progress, democracy, and social justice, so Wilson had tried to invest his foreign policy with similarly enlightened values. In doing so, however, he fostered unrealistic expectations that world politics might be transformed overnight.

Americans who believed that rational, civilized people had outgrown war found the conflict a disillusioning experience. Many became disenchanted by the contrast between Wilson's lofty idealism and the Allies' cynical opportunism at Versailles. The war to make the world "safe for democracy" turned out to be a chance for Italy to grab Austrian territory and for Japan to seize German concessions in China. In addition, the "war to end war" spun off several wars in its wake. Romania invaded Hungary in 1919, Poland invaded Russia in 1920, the Russian civil war continued until 1921, and Greece and Turkey battled until 1923.

The peace conference left unresolved many problems. Wilson's elevation of self-government and self-determination encouraged aspirations for independence throughout the colonial empires retained by the Allies. Some of the new nations of Central Europe, supposedly based on ethnic self-determination, actually included different and sometimes antagonistic ethnic groups. Above all, the war and the treaty helped to produce economic and political instability in much of Europe, making it a breeding ground for totalitarian and nationalistic movements that eventually brought another world war.

Trauma in the Wake of War

- How did Americans' expectations change as a result of the outcome of the war and the events of 1919?
- How did these new expectations affect Americans' choice in the 1920 presidential election?

Almost as soon as French church bells pealed for the armistice, the United States began to demobilize. The military immediately discharged more than 600,000 men, and by November 1919 nearly the entire force of 4 million men and women was out of uniform. Industrial demobilization occurred even more quickly, as officials canceled war contracts with no more than a month's notice. The year 1919 saw not only the return of the troops from Europe but also raging inflation, massive strikes, bloody race riots, widespread fear of radical **subversion,** violations of civil liberties, and passage of an unenforceable law to prohibit alcohol.

"HCL" and Strikes

Inflation—described in newspapers as "HCL" for "High Cost of Living"—was the most pressing single problem Americans faced after the war. Between 1913 and 1919, the average American family saw its cost of living double. Such inflation contributed to labor unrest. When the armistice ended unions'

subversion Efforts to undermine or overthrow an established government.

wartime pledge not to go on strike, organized labor made wage demands to keep up with the soaring cost of living. In 1919, however, management was ready for a fight.

Some companies determined to return labor relations to prewar patterns. They blamed wage increases won by organized labor for the rise in prices, and they traced strikes and unions in the United States to "dangerous foreign ideas" from Bolshevik Russia. In February 1919, Seattle's Central Labor Council called out all the city's unions in a five-day general strike to support striking shipyard workers. The walkout revived fears of the IWW, and Seattle's mayor inflamed such alarms by claiming the strike was a Bolshevik plot. Boston's police struck in September 1919 after the city's police commissioner fired nineteen policemen for joining an AFL union. Massachusetts governor **Calvin Coolidge** refused to negotiate and instead activated the state guard to maintain order and break the union. "There is no right to strike against the public safety by anybody, anywhere, anytime," he proclaimed. No polls measured public opinion on strikes and unions in 1919, but by midyear it was clear that conservative political leaders had joined with business figures in an effort to roll back the union gains of the war years.

The largest and most dramatic labor conflict in 1919 came against the United States Steel Corporation. Few steelworkers were represented by a union after the 1892 Homestead strike. Steel companies often hired recent immigrants, keeping the work force divided by language and culture. Many steelworkers put in twelve-hour workdays and, when they were reassigned from one shift to another, sometimes slogged through twenty-four hours in the mills without rest. Wages had not increased as fast as inflation—or as fast as company profits. In 1919, the AFL launched an ambitious unionization drive in the steel industry, and many steelworkers responded eagerly.

The men who ran the steel industry firmly refused to deal with the new organization. So the workers went on strike in late September, demanding union recognition, collective bargaining, the eight-hour workday, and higher wages. United States Steel, however, blamed the strike on radicals and effectively mobilized public opinion against the strikers. Company guards protected strikebreakers, and U.S. military forces moved into Gary, Indiana, to help round up what they called "the Red element." By January 1920, after eighteen workers had been killed and hundreds beaten, the strike was over and the unions were ousted.

Red Scare

The steel industry's charges of bolshevism to discredit strikers came at a time when many government and corporate leaders decried the dangers of bolshevism at home and abroad. In late April 1919, thirty-four bombs addressed to prominent Americans—including J. P. Morgan, John D. Rockefeller, and Supreme Court justice Oliver Wendell Holmes—were discovered in various post offices after the explosion of two others addressed to a senator and to the mayor of Seattle. In June, bombs in several cities damaged buildings and killed two people. The work of a few anarchists, the explosions set off a panic over a supposedly nationwide, radical conspiracy to overthrow the government.

With President Wilson still bedridden, Attorney General A. Mitchell Palmer organized an anti-Red campaign, hoping to enhance his own chances for the 1920 presidential nomination in the process. "Like a prairie fire," Palmer claimed, "the blaze of revolution was sweeping over every American institution." In August 1919, he appointed **J. Edgar Hoover,** a young lawyer, to head a new antiradical division in the Justice Department, the predecessor of the Federal Bureau of Investigation. In November, Palmer launched the first of what came to be called the **Palmer raids** to arrest suspected radicals. Authorities rounded up some five thousand people between November and January 1920. Although officials found only a few firearms and no explosives, the raids led to the **deportation** of several hundred aliens whose only offense was a tie to some radical organization.

In May 1919, a group of veterans formed the American Legion, which not only lobbied on behalf of veterans but also condemned radicals, endorsed the deportations, and committed itself "to foster and

Calvin Coolidge Massachusetts governor and conservative Republican who later served as vice president (1921–1923) and as president (1923–1929).

J. Edgar Hoover Official appointed to head a new antiradical division in the Justice Department in 1919; he served as head of the FBI from its official founding in 1924 until his death in 1972.

Palmer raids Government raids on individuals and organizations in 1919 and 1920 to search for political radicals and to deport foreign-born radicals.

deportation Expulsion of an undesirable alien from a country.

♦ This cartoon, entitled "Put them out and keep them out," encouraged the belief that radicalism spread by immigrants was a danger to American institutions and values. *Library of Congress.*

perpetuate a one hundred percent Americanism." The Legion signed up a million members by the end of the year. Some of its branches gained a reputation for vigilante action against suspected radicals.

State legislatures joined in with antiradical measures of their own, including **criminal syndicalism laws**—measures designed to outlaw the IWW by making advocacy of its ideology a crime. In January 1920, the assembly of the New York state legislature expelled five members elected as Socialists, solely because of their party affiliation. However, after a wide range of respected public figures denounced the assembly action as undemocratic, public opinion regarding the **Red Scare** began to shift. With the approach of May 1, the major day of celebration for socialists and communists alike, Palmer issued dramatic warnings for the public to be on guard against radical activity, including a general strike and more bombings. When nothing happened, many concluded that the radical threat might have been overstated.

As the Red Scare sputtered to an end, in May 1920 police in Massachusetts arrested **Nicola Sacco and Bartolomeo Vanzetti,** both Italian-born anarchists, and charged them with robbery and murder. Despite inconclusive evidence and the accused men's protestations of innocence, a jury found them guilty, and they were sentenced to death. While appeals delayed their execution, many Americans became convinced that the two had been convicted because of their political beliefs and Italian origins. Further, many doubted that they had received a fair trial because of the nativism and antiradicalism that infected the judge and jury. Over loud protests at home and abroad, both men were executed in 1927.

Race Riots and Lynchings

The racial tensions of the war years continued into the postwar period. Black soldiers encountered more acceptance and less discrimination in Europe than they had ever known at home. In May 1919 the NAACP journal *Crisis* expressed what the more militant returning soldiers felt:

> *We return. We return from fighting. We return fighting. Make way for Democracy! We saved it in France, and by the Great Jehovah, we will save it in the U.S.A., or know the reason why.*

Some whites in North and South greeted homecoming black troops with furious violence intended to restore the state of race relations that had prevailed before 1917. Southern mobs lynched ten returning black soldiers, some of them still in uniform. Rioters lynched more than seventy blacks in the first year after the war and burned eleven victims alive.

Rioting also struck outside the South. In July, violence reached the nation's capital, where white mobs, many of them soldiers and sailors, attacked blacks throughout the city for three days, killing several. Unprotected, the city's African Americans resorted to organizing their own, sometimes armed, defense. In Chicago in late July, war raged between white and black mobs for nearly two weeks, despite peacekeeping efforts by the militia. The rioting

criminal syndicalism laws State laws that made membership in organizations that advocated communism or anarchism subject to criminal penalties.

Red Scare Wave of anticommunism in the United States in 1919 and 1920, which included a government crackdown that focused on foreigners and labor unions.

Nicola Sacco and Bartolomeo Vanzetti Italian anarchists convicted in 1921 of the murder of a Braintree, Massachusetts, factory paymaster and theft of a $16,000 payroll; in spite of public protests on their behalf, they were electrocuted in 1927.

caused thirty-eight deaths (fifteen white, twenty-three black). More than a thousand families—nearly all black—were burned out of their homes. In Omaha, in September, a mob tried to hang the mayor when he bravely stood between them and a black prisoner accused of rape. Police saved the mayor but not the prisoner.

By the end of 1919, race riots had flared in more than two dozen places. The year saw not only rampant lynchings but also the reappearance of the Ku Klux Klan (see page 747). Attempting to capture the militant spirit African Americans displayed in these confrontations, poet **Claude McKay** wrote "If We Must Die," which so impressed Senator Henry Cabot Lodge that he inserted it into the *Congressional Record:*

If we must die, let it not be like hogs
Hunted and penned in an inglorious spot
O kinsmen! we must meet the common foe!
Though far outnumbered let us show us brave,
And for their thousand blows deal one deathblow!
What though before us lies the open grave?
Like men we'll face the murderous, cowardly pack,
Pressed to the wall, dying, but fighting back!

As W. E. B. Du Bois observed, black veterans "would never be the same again. You cannot ask them to go back to what they were before. They cannot, for they are not the same men."

The Election of 1920

Republicans confidently expected to regain the White House in the 1920 election. The Democrats had lost their congressional majorities in the 1918 elections, and the postwar confusion and disillusionment often focused on Wilson. One reporter described the stricken president as the "sacrificial whipping boy for the present bitterness."

The reaction against Wilson almost guaranteed election of any competent Republican nominee. Several candidates attracted significant support, notably former army chief of staff General Leonard Wood, Illinois governor Frank Lowden, and California senator Hiram Johnson. However, no candidate could muster a majority of the convention delegates. Harry Daugherty, campaign manager for Ohio senator **Warren G. Harding,** had foreseen such a deadlock months earlier and had predicted that it would be broken by a compromise candidate, chosen at about "eleven minutes after two o'clock on Friday morning," by about "fifteen or twenty men, bleary-eyed and perspiring profusely from the heat." And so it was. A group of party leaders, mostly senators, met late at night in a smoke-filled hotel room and picked Harding. Even some who supported him were unenthusiastic. One called him only "the best of the second-raters." For vice president, the Republicans nominated Calvin Coolidge, the Massachusetts governor who broke the Boston police strike.

The Democrats also suffered severe divisions. After forty-four ballots, they chose James Cox, the governor of Ohio, as their presidential candidate. For vice president, they nominated Wilson's assistant secretary of the navy, Franklin D. Roosevelt, a remote cousin of Theodore Roosevelt.

Usually described as good-natured and likable—and sometimes as bumbling—Harding had published a small-town newspaper in Marion, Ohio, until his wife Florence and some of his friends urged him to enter politics. He eventually won election to the Senate. Unhappy with his marriage, Harding apparently found contentment with a series of mistresses. The press knew of Harding's liaisons but, as was the usual practice, never reported them.

An uproar arose, however, over a claim by an Ohio professor that Harding's ancestry included African Americans. The story spread rapidly, and a reporter soon asked Harding, "Do you have any Negro blood?" Harding replied mildly, "How do I know, Jim? One of my ancestors may have jumped the fence." The allegation, and Harding's response to it, apparently did not hurt his cause. Most of Harding's campaign reflected his promise to "return to normalcy," and the voters responded with enthusiasm.

The election was a Republican landslide. Harding won thirty-seven of the forty-eight states and 60 percent of the popular vote—the largest popular majority up to that time. Wilson had hoped the election might be a "solemn referendum" on the League of Nations. But it proved more a response to the disappointments of the Wilson years—a war that was launched with the loftiest ideals but turned sour in the halls of Versailles, the high cost of living, the strikes and riots of 1919. Americans, it seemed, had had enough idealism and sacrifice for a while.

Claude McKay Jamaica-born poet and novelist whose 1928 novel *Home to Harlem* was the first best-seller by a black author in the United States.

Warren G. Harding Ohio politician and Republican who was elected president of the United States in 1920; his administration was marred by corruption and scandal.

SUMMARY

Expectations
Constraints
Choices
Outcomes

Woodrow Wilson took office *expecting* to focus on domestic policy, not foreign affairs. He fulfilled some Democratic party commitments to anti-imperialism but *chose* to intervene extensively in the Caribbean. He also *chose* to intervene in Mexico but was *constrained* from fully accomplishing his objectives.

When war broke out in Europe in 1914, Wilson proclaimed the United States to be neutral, and most Americans agreed. German submarine warfare and British restrictions on commerce, however, *constrained* traditional *expectations* for neutrality. Wilson secured a German pledge to refrain from unrestricted submarine warfare. He was re-elected in 1916 on the argument that "he kept us out of war." Shortly after he won re-election, however, the Germans violated their pledge, and Wilson *chose* to ask for war against Germany.

The war brought new *expectations* in nearly every aspect of the nation's economic and social life. To overcome *constraints* of inefficiency, the federal government *chose* to develop a high degree of centralized economic planning. Fearing that opposition to the war might pose a *constraint* on full mobilization, the Wilson administration *chose* to mold public opinion and to secure new laws that *constrained* some civil liberties. When the federal government *chose* to back collective bargaining, unions registered important gains. And when labor shortages threatened to *constrain* the war effort, more women and African Americans *chose* to enter the industrial work force. One *outcome* of the labor shortage was that many African Americans *chose* to move to northern and midwestern industrial cities.

Germany *chose* to launch a major offensive in early 1918, *expecting* to achieve victory before American troops could make a difference. However, the AEF was able to play a significant part in breaking the German advance. The *outcome* was that the Germans requested an armistice.

In his Fourteen Points, Wilson expressed his *expectations* for peace. *Constrained* by opposition from the Allies, Wilson *chose* to compromise at the peace conference but still *expected* that the League of Nations would be able to maintain the peace. Fearing the *constraints* that League membership might place on the United States, enough senators opposed the treaty to defeat it. The *outcome,* thus, was that the United States did not become a member of the League.

In the United States, the immediate *outcome* of the war was disillusionment and a year of high prices, costly strikes, a Red Scare, and race riots and lynchings. In 1920, the nation returned to its Republican preference when it elected Warren G. Harding, a mediocre conservative, to the White House.

SUGGESTED READINGS

Kendrick A. Clements. *The Presidency of Woodrow Wilson* (1992).

More than half of this recent account of Wilson's presidency is devoted to foreign-policy matters and the war.

Frank Freidel. *Over There: The Story of America's First Great Overseas Crusade,* rev. ed. (1990).

A vivid survey of American participation in the fighting in Europe, with many firsthand accounts.

Sinclair Lewis. *Main Street* (1920; reprint, 1961).

An absorbing novel about a woman's dissatisfaction with her life and her decision to work in Washington during the war.

Arthur S. Link. *Woodrow Wilson: Revolution, War, and Peace* (1979).

A concise introduction to Wilson's role in and thinking about foreign affairs.

Erich Maria Remarque. *All Quiet on the Western Front,* trans. A. W. Wheen (1930; reprint, 1982).

The classic and moving novel about World War I, seen through German eyes.

Barbara W. Tuchman. *The Guns of August* (1962; reprint, 1976).

A popular and engaging account of the outbreak of the war, focusing on events in Europe.

The Choice to Declare War

The Context

On April 2, 1917, President Woodrow Wilson spoke to a joint session of Congress and requested that Congress declare war on Germany in response to the German government's decision to resume unrestricted submarine warfare. Congress declared war on April 6, and for the first time the United States found itself involved in a military conflict in Europe. U. S. involvement in World War I lasted for a year and seven months, and more than forty-eight thousand Americans died on the battlefields of Europe. Once Wilson decided for war, he had to choose the way he would present this decision to Congress and to the American people. (For further information on the context, see pages 704–705.)

The Historical Question

In asking Congress to declare war on Germany, President Wilson had to choose between a narrow justification, based on American self-interest, or a broader vision of transforming international politics. Wilson chose the broad approach, but members of Congress did not necessarily agree. In calling for war, to what values did Wilson appeal? On what values did Senators Borah and Johnson base their decision to vote for war? On what values did Senators La Follette and Norris base their opposition to war?

The Challenge

Using the sources provided, along with other information you have read, write an essay or hold a discussion on the following question. Cite evidence in the sources to support your conclusions.

On what values did Wilson, Borah, La Follette, and Norris base their decisions about going to war? What evidence is there that they all drew on the same values as they came to different conclusions about war?

The Sources

1 President Woodrow Wilson, in a speech to a joint session of Congress, on April 2, 1917, asked for a declaration of war against Germany.

I am not now thinking of the loss of property involved, immense and serious as that is, but only of the wanton and wholesale destruction of the lives of non-combatants, men, women, and children, engaged in pursuits which have always, even in the darkest periods of modern history, been deemed innocent and legitimate. Property can be paid for; the lives of peaceful and innocent people cannot be. The present German submarine warfare against commerce is a warfare against mankind. . . .

We are accepting this challenge of hostile purpose because we know that in such a Government [Germany], following such methods, we can never have a friend; and that in the presence of its organized power, always lying in wait to accomplish we know not what purpose, there can be no assured security for the democratic Governments of the world. . . . We are glad, now that we see the facts with no veil of false pretense about them, to fight thus for the ultimate peace of the world and for the liberation of its peoples, the German people included: for the rights of nations great and small and the privilege of men everywhere to choose their way of life and of obedi-

ence. The world must be made safe for democracy. Its peace must be planted upon the tested foundations of political liberty. We have no selfish ends to serve. We desire no conquest, no domination.

2 Senator William E. Borah, progressive Republican from Idaho, spoke in the Senate on April 4, 1917.

There can, to my mind, be only one sufficient reason for committing this country to war, and that is the honor and security of our own people and our own Nation. . . . I join no crusade; I seek or accept no alliances; I obligate this Government to no other power. I make war alone for my countrymen and their rights, for my country and its honor.

3 Senator Robert M. La Follette, progressive Republican from Wisconsin, spoke in the Senate on April 4, 1917.

I had supposed until recently that it was the duty of Senators and Representatives in Congress to vote and act according to their convictions on all public matters that came before them. . . . Another doctrine has recently been promulgated by certain newspapers, . . . and that is the doctrine of "standing behind the President," without inquiring whether the President is right or wrong. . . . [President Wilson] says that this is a war "for the things which we have always carried nearest to our hearts—for democracy, for the right of those who submit to authority to have a voice in their own government." . . . [But] the President has not suggested that we make our support of Great Britain conditional to her granting home rule to Ireland, or Egypt, or India. . . .

Will the President and the supporters of this war bill submit it to a vote of the people before the declaration of war goes into effect? Until we are willing to do that, it illy becomes us to offer as an excuse for our entry into the war the unsupported claim that this war was forced upon the German people by their Government. . . . Who has registered the knowledge or approval of the American people of the course this Congress is called upon to take in declaring war upon Germany? Submit the question to the people, you who support it. You who support it dare not do it, for you know that by a vote of more than ten to one the American people as a body would register their declaration against it.

4 Senator George W. Norris, progressive Republican from Nebraska, spoke in the Senate on April 4, 1917.

There are a great many American citizens who feel that we owe it as a duty to humanity to take part in this war. . . . I think such people err in judgment and to a great extent have been misled as to the real history and the true facts by the almost unanimous demand of the great combination of wealth that has a direct financial interest in our participation in the war.

We are taking a step to-day that is fraught with untold danger. We are going into war upon the command of gold. . . . By our act we will make millions of our countrymen suffer, and the consequences of it may well be that millions of our brethren must shed their lifeblood, millions of broken-hearted women must weep, millions of children must suffer with cold, and millions of babes must die from hunger, and all because we want to preserve the commercial right of American citizens to deliver munitions of war to belligerent nations. . . . I feel as though we are about to put the dollar sign upon the American flag. . . .

The troubles of Europe ought to be settled by Europe. . . . [Declaring war will take] America into entanglements that will not end with this war but will live and bring their evil influence upon many generations yet unborn.

IMPROVED HIGHWAYS AND MAJOR CITIES, 1920–1930 During the 1920s, as many Americans became automobile owners, they quickly called for more and better highways. This map shows highway expansion during that decade. During the 1920s, too, the nation became increasingly urban. This map locates the largest cities.

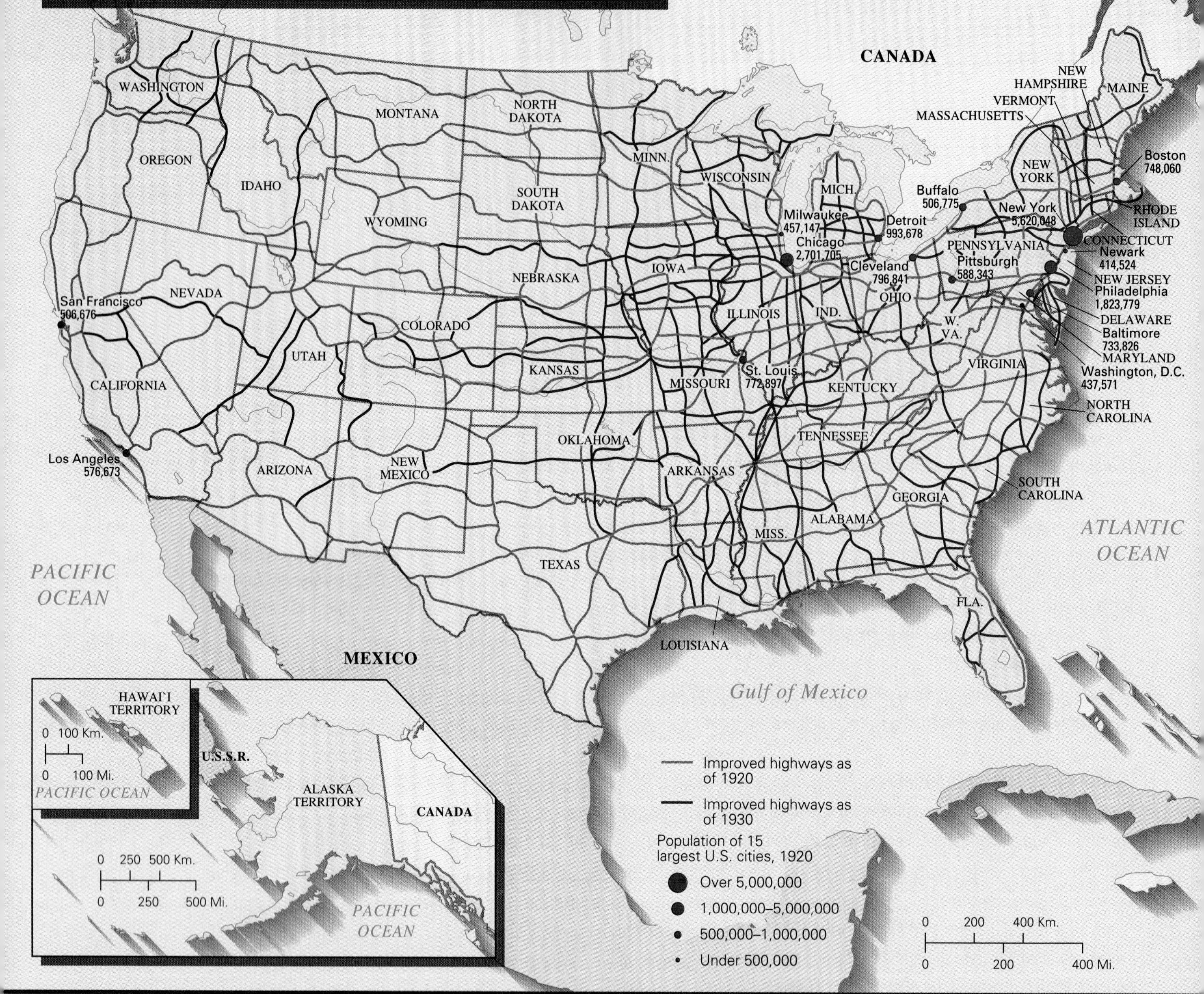

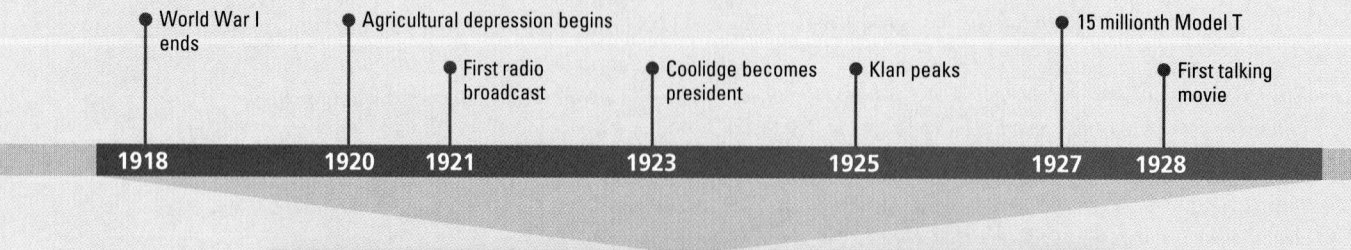

- 1918 — World War I ends
- 1920 — Agricultural depression begins
- 1921 — First radio broadcast
- 1923 — Coolidge becomes president
- 1925 — Klan peaks
- 1927 — 15 millionth Model T
- 1928 — First talking movie

1850 1900 1950 2000

CHAPTER 24

The 1920s, 1920–1928

Prosperity Decade

- What new economic choices opened for consumers during the 1920s? What new choices opened for business?
- What constraints did farmers face during this period?

The "Roaring Twenties"

- How did new expectations and choices reflect or contribute to the important social changes of the 1920s?

Traditional America Roars Back

- Why did some Americans try to restore traditional social values during the 1920s?
- How did they choose to accomplish that objective?
- What were some of the outcomes of their actions?

Race, Class, and Gender

- During the 1920s, how did constraints based on race or gender affect Americans? How did various groups respond to those constraints?
- What was the experience of working people in the 1920s?

The Politics of Prosperity

- What were the expectations of the Republican administrations of the 1920s about the proper role of the federal government in the economy?
- What policy choices resulted from those expectations?

INTRODUCTION

Expectations
Constraints
Choices
Outcomes

Called the "Jazz Age" and the "Roaring Twenties," the 1920s sometimes seems to be a swirl of conflicting images. Prohibition marked an ambitious effort to preserve the values of nineteenth-century America while "flappers" were flaunting the liberation of women from previous *constraints.* The booming stock market promised prosperity to all with money to invest even as thousands of farmers were abandoning the land because they could not survive financially. Business leaders celebrated the expansion of the economy while many wage earners in manufacturing endured the destruction of their unions and their legal protections. White-sheeted Klansmen marched as self-proclaimed defenders of Protestant American values and white supremacy as African Americans' cultural expression in art, literature, and music was flowering. The values of big business reigned supreme in politics even as the economy was lurching toward collapse.

In the 1920s, business turned as never before to focus on the consumer. Americans suddenly found themselves facing a range of consumer *choices* beyond all previous *expectations,* as they were deluged with a flood of new products within the purchasing power of most families—automobiles, radios, electric household appliances of every description, trendy fashions in clothing and household furnishings, innovative products for personal hygiene, and many others. More and more Americans began to purchase on credit as installment-plan buying swept the nation, shattering old *expectations* about paying cash and avoiding debt. By the mid-1920s, it seemed as though much of the nation had *chosen* to borrow money and go on an extended buying binge.

Not everyone shared in the *expectations* bred by the consumer culture of postwar America. The poorest farmers and wage earners were *constrained* from doing so by their economic situation. Some others *chose* not to. Disillusioned with the "war to end war" and scornful of the widespread infatuation with consumer buying, many intellectuals became alienated from American culture. They bemoaned their "botched civilization" but conceived no alternative other than complaint and despair. Dissatisfied with the *choices* that faced them in the United States, some *chose* to move to Paris—or England or elsewhere in Europe—to escape what they saw as the emptiness of American life. To them, modern America seemed a spiritual and cultural wasteland, committed to little more than consumption of standardized material goods.

Few Americans shared the gloom of such intellectuals. For most, the 1920s were a time of glittering *expectations,* when they cast aside old *constraints* and made bold new *choices.* Many revealed an unfettered optimism as they picked out a new radio, signed papers to buy a new automobile on the installment plan, and, perhaps, speculated on the stock market. For them, the immediate *outcome*—new car, new radio, new styles—seemed to fulfill the rosy *expectations* bred by advertising and the alluring consumer culture.

This optimism fed into an expansive popular culture that seemed to reflect a nationwide "age of excess." Radio and movies popularized nationwide tastes, trends, and "heroes" as never before, as entertainment became big business. Led primarily by youths of white middle-class background, many young people *chose* to flaunt behavior that defied the values of their parents' generation.

Some Americans never shared in those *outcomes,* however, and all were unprepared for the long-term *outcome* of economic collapse that lay ahead. Like the shiny new roadsters advertised in magazines, the economy roared along at high speed, fueled by easy credit and consumer spending, virtually unregulated.

CHRONOLOGY

America in the 1920s

1908 Henry Ford introduces Model T
General Motors formed

1912 Woodrow Wilson elected

1914 Universal Negro Improvement Association founded
War breaks out in Europe

1915 D. W. Griffith's Birth of a Nation
Ku Klux Klan revives

1918 World War I ends

1920 Nineteenth Amendment grants women the vote
Eighteenth Amendment (Prohibition) takes effect
Sinclair Lewis's Main Street
Warren G. Harding elected president

1920–1921 Nationwide recession
Agricultural depression begins

1921 Temporary immigration quotas
First commercial radio broadcasts
Halitosis sells Listerine
Farm Bloc formed

1922 Sinclair Lewis's Babbitt
Willa Cather's One of Ours
T. S. Eliot's The Waste Land

1923 Harding dies
Calvin Coolidge becomes president
Marcus Garvey convicted of mail fraud
Jean Toomer's Cane
American Indian Defense Association formed

1923–1927 Harding administration scandals revealed

1924 National Origins Act
Coolidge elected
First disposable handkerchiefs
Wheaties marketed as "Breakfast of Champions"
Crossword puzzle fad
Full citizenship for American Indians

1925 Scopes trial
Bruce Barton's The Man Nobody Knows
F. Scott Fitzgerald's The Great Gatsby
Ku Klux Klan claims 5 million members
Klan leader convicted of murder
One automobile for every three residents in Los Angeles
Chrysler Corporation formed

1926 Florida real-estate boom collapses
Ernest Hemingway's The Sun Also Rises
Gertrude Ederle swims the English Channel

1927 Coolidge vetoes McNary-Haugen bill
Charles Lindbergh's transatlantic flight
Duke Ellington conducts jazz at Cotton Club

1928 Coolidge vetoes McNary-Haugen again
Ford introduces the Model A

1931 Al Capone convicted and imprisoned

Prosperity Decade

- What new economic choices opened for consumers during the 1920s? What new choices opened for business?
- What constraints did farmers face during this period?

By 1920, the industrialization of America was substantially achieved—the foundations of the corporate economy were in place, controlled by large industrial corporations run by professional managers. After a difficult but short adjustment at the end of the war, the economy completed an important shift. Until then, U.S. manufacturing had been dominated by steel, heavy equipment manufacturing, and similar industries, few of which made products for sale to the average consumer. During the 1920s, though, the rise and growth of the automobile industry dramatized the new prominence of industries producing **consumer goods.** This significant change in direction carried implications for advertising, banking, and even the stock market.

The Economics of Prosperity

The end of the war in 1918 brought cancellation of orders for war supplies from ships to uniforms. At the same time, large numbers of recently discharged military and naval personnel swelled the ranks of job seekers. Such postwar conditions often bring on a recession or depression. At the end of World War I, however, there was no immediate economic collapse, thanks in part to pent-up demand. Given wartime shortages and overtime pay, many Americans had been earning more than they could spend. At the end of the war, their eagerness to spend helped to delay the postwar slump until 1920 and 1921. The **gross national product (GNP)** dropped by only 4.3 percent between 1919 and 1920, then fell by 8.6 percent between 1920 and 1921. During the war, unemployment affected only about 1 percent of the work force. The jobless rate increased to 5 percent in 1920 and 12 percent in 1921. Many of the workers who kept their jobs worked fewer hours, and some took pay cuts. In manufacturing, workers' earnings averaged $26 a week in 1920 and only $21 in 1922. One bright spot was that decreased earnings, unemployment, and declining demand halted the rampaging inflation of 1918 and 1919. In fact, consumer prices fell by 10 percent from 1920 to 1921, led by a 24 percent drop in the price of food.

The economy quickly rebounded after 1921. The GNP increased by 16 percent between 1921 and 1922, a bigger jump than during the booming war years. By 1923, unemployment had fallen to 2 percent and remained between 2 and 5 percent through 1929. By 1922, most manufacturing workers were again working full time, and their average weekly paycheck grew from $21 in 1922 to $24 in 1925 to nearly $25 in 1929 (see Figure 24.1). At the same time, prices for most manufactured goods remained stable or even went down. Declining prices for agricultural products brought lower prices for food and clothing. Thus many Americans seemed better off by 1929 than in 1920: they earned about the same and paid somewhat less for necessities.

Targeting Consumers

During the 1920s, business leaders seem to have recognized as never before that persuading Americans

♦ Advertising promised that those who used Listerine to eliminate halitosis would gain friends and even romance. *Duke University Archives.*

to consume an array of products was crucial to keeping the economy healthy. The marketing of Listerine demonstrates the rising importance of creative advertising. Listerine had been devised as a general antiseptic, but in 1921 Gerard Lambert devised a more persuasive—and profitable—approach when he plucked the obscure term *halitosis* from a medical journal. Through aggressive advertising using the word, he fostered anxieties about the impact of bad breath on popularity and made millions by selling Listerine to combat the offensive condition.

consumer goods Products such as clothing, food, automobiles, and radios, intended for purchase and use by people, as opposed to products such as steel beams, locomotives, and electrical generators, intended for purchase and use by corporations.

gross national product The total market value of all goods and services that a nation produces during a specified period; now generally referred to as gross domestic product.

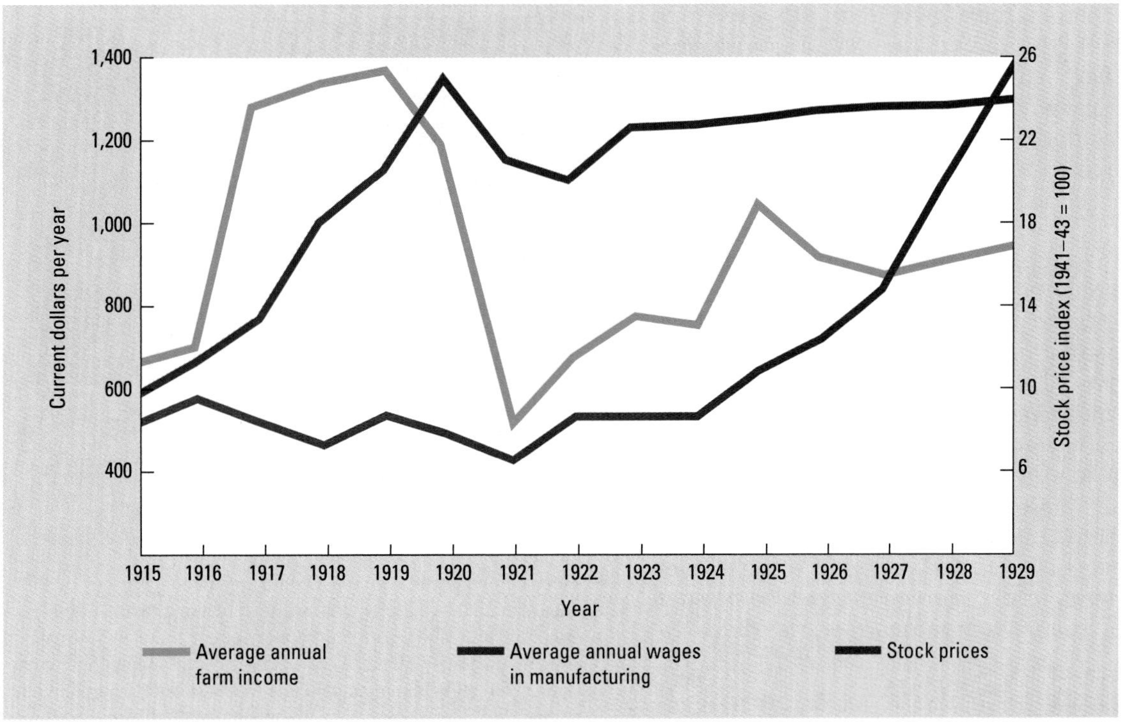

♦ **FIGURE 24.1 Economic Indicators, 1915–1929** This figure presents three measures of economic activity for the period covering World War I and the 1920s. Farm income and wages should be read on the left-hand scale; stock prices should be read on the right-hand scale. *Note:* Incomes are in current dollars, not adjusted for changes in purchasing power. *Source:* U.S. Department of Commerce, Bureau of the Census, *Historical Statistics of the United States, Colonial Times to 1970,* Bicentennial Edition, 2 vols. (Washington, D.C.: U.S. Government Printing Office, 1975), I: 483, 170; II: 1004.

Also in 1921, General Foods Company invented Betty Crocker to give its baking products a womanly, domestic image. In 1924, General Mills first advertised Wheaties as the "Breakfast of Champions," thereby tying consumption of cold cereal to the growing popularity of sports figures. Americans responded by buying those products and others with similarly creative pitches. "We grew up founding our dreams on the infinite promises of American advertising," later wrote Zelda Sayre Fitzgerald.

Changes in fashion also encouraged increased consumption and economic growth. The popularity of short hairstyles for women, for example, led to the development of hair salons and stimulated sales of the recently invented **bobby pin.** Cigarettes became more fashionable after World War I, for soldiers had found them easier to carry and smoke than pipes or cigars. Cigarette advertisers also began to target women. The American Tobacco Company advised women to "Reach for a Lucky instead of a sweet" to attain a fashionably slim figure. Style and technology combined to invent disposable products, thereby promoting regular, recurring consumer buying of throwaway items. Kotex, the first manufactured disposable sanitary napkin, appeared on the market in 1921, its production made possible by technological advances in the processing of wood cellulose fiber. In 1924, the same technology produced the first disposable handkerchiefs, later known as Kleenex tissues.

Technological advances contributed in other ways to the growth of consumer-oriented manufacturing. In 1920, about one-third of all residences had electricity. By 1929, electrical power had reached

bobby pin Small metal hair clip with ends pressed tightly together, designed for holding short or "bobbed" hair in place.

most urban homes (but fewer than 10 percent of rural homes). As the number of residences with electricity increased, advertisers stressed the time and labor that housewives could save by using electric washing machines, irons, vacuum cleaners, and toasters. Between 1919 and 1929, consumer expenditures for household appliances grew by more than 120 percent.

This increased consumption contributed to a change in people's spending habits. Before the war, most urban families saved their money until they could pay cash for most of what they needed, but in the 1920s many retailers urged buyers to "Buy now, pay later." And many consumers responded, taking home their new radio today and worrying about paying for it tomorrow. By the late 1920s, about 15 percent of all retail purchases were made through the installment plan, including most furniture, phonographs, washing machines, and refrigerators. Charge accounts in department stores also became popular, and **finance companies** grew rapidly.

The Automobile: Driving the Economy

More than any other single product, the automobile epitomized the consumer-oriented economy of the 1920s. Automobiles remained luxuries until American entrepreneurs found ways to bring prices within the budgets of most families. **Henry Ford,** a former mechanic, scored the greatest success by developing a mass-production system that drove down production costs. Other companies jostled with Ford for the patronage of American car buyers, and, by the late 1920s, about 80 percent of the world's registered vehicles were in the United States. By then, America's roadways sported nearly one automobile for every five people.

Ford built his success on the **Model T,** introduced in 1908. A Model-T Ford was the first middle-class dream come true for many Americans, and families came to love their ungraceful but reliable "Tin Lizzies" (so named because of their lightweight metal bodies). By 1927, Ford had produced more than 15 million of them, dominating the market by selling the largest possible number of cars at the lowest possible price. "Get the prices down to the buying power," Ford ordered. And his dictatorial style of management combined with technological advances and high worker productivity to bring the price of a new Model T as low as $290 by 1927. Cheap to buy, run, and maintain, the Model T made Henry Ford into a folk hero—a wealthy one. By 1925 Ford showed a daily profit of some $25,000.

"How did he ever get the money to buy a car"
Perhaps he *doesn't* make as much as you do—but he took advantage of this quick, easy, sure way to own an automobile
Ford Weekly Purchase Plan

♦ Henry Ford constantly worked to reduce car prices on his cars. He also promoted installment buying, promising in this ad that "with even the most modest income, [every family] can now afford a car of their own." This ad also encouraged impulse buying: "You live but once and the years roll by quickly. Why wait for tomorrow for things that you rightfully should enjoy today?" *Library of Congress.*

Not only streamlined production but also competition helped to keep prices low for middle-class cars. Other automobile companies challenged Ford's predominance, notably General Motors (GM), founded by William Durant in 1908, and Chrysler Corporation, created by Walter Chrysler in 1925. GM and Chrysler adopted some of Ford's techniques, but their cars also offered more comfort and style than the Model T. Ford finally ended production of the Model T in 1927 and the next year introduced the Model A, which incorporated some features promoted by his competitors.

finance company Business that makes loans to clients based on some form of collateral, like a new car, thus allowing a form of installment buying when sellers do not extend credit.

Henry Ford Inventor and manufacturer who founded the Ford Motor Company in 1903 and pioneered mass production in the auto industry.

Model T Lightweight automobile that Ford produced from 1908 to 1927 and sold at the lowest possible price on the theory that an affordable car would be more profitable than an expensive one.

♦ Ford pioneered the automobile assembly line as a way to reduce both costs and dependence on skilled workers. During the 1920s, he paid the highest wages in Detroit, but he required complete obedience from his employees, even to the point of prohibiting whistling while working. *From the Collections of Henry Ford Museum & Greenfield Village.*

Ford's company also provides an example of efforts by American businesses to reduce labor costs by improving efficiency. In the process, however, work on Ford's assembly line became a thoroughly dehumanizing experience. Ford workers were prohibited from talking, sitting, smoking, singing, or even whistling while working. As one critic put it, workers were to "put nut 14 on bolt 132, repeating, repeating, repeating until their hands shook and their legs quivered." Ford, however, paid his workers more than any of his competitors paid theirs—enough that they could afford a Model T. Auto workers thus came to enjoy some of the consumer buying previously restricted to middle- and upper-income groups.

The automobile came to symbolize not only the ability of many Americans to acquire material goods but also technology, progress, and the freedom of the open road. The industry worked to promote this heady image. One car salesman remarked in 1926, "When I sold a car, I sold it with the honest conviction that I was doing the buyer a favor in helping him to take his place in a big forward movement."

The automobile industry in the 1920s often led the way in promoting new sales techniques. Installment buying became so widespread that by 1927 two-thirds of all American automobiles were sold on credit. The largest companies kept prices low on models aimed at middle-income Americans. The Model T had emphasized no-frills reliability, but after 1928 Ford, like GM, tended to introduce new models every year. This practice enticed owners to trade in their cars to keep up with the latest fashions in design, color, and optional features. Dozens of small automakers closed when they could not compete with the low prices and yearly models offered by the Big Three. By 1929, Chrysler, Ford, and GM were making 83 percent of all cars manufactured in the country. The industry had become an **oligopoly.**

Changes in Banking and Business

Just as Henry Ford led the way in bringing automobiles within reach of most Americans, **A. P. Giannini** did the same for banking. The son of Italian immigrants, Giannini founded the Bank of Italy in 1904 as a bank for shopkeepers and workers in the Italian neighborhood of San Francisco. The greatest innovator in twentieth-century American banking, Giannini not only based his bank on dealings with ordinary people but also opened branches throughout California, near people's homes and workplaces. Until then, most banks had only one location, in the center of a city, and limited their services to businesses and substantial citizens with hefty accounts. Giannini broadened the base of banking by encouraging working people to open small checking and savings accounts and to borrow for such investments as car purchases. In the process, his bank—later renamed Bank of America—became the third largest in the nation by 1927.

Giannini's bank and Ford's auto factory survived as relics of family management in a new world of modern corporations with large bureaucracies. Ownership and control continued to grow apart as salaried managers came to run most big businesses.

Although the number of corporations increased steadily, from 345,600 in 1920 to 518,700 in 1930, a great corporate merger wave also accelerated as the 1920s progressed—309 mergers in 1922, and 1,245 in 1929. These mergers continued earlier patterns toward greater economic concentration. By 1930, 5 percent of American corporations were receiving 85 percent of all net corporate income, up from 78 percent in 1921.

oligopoly An industry or market dominated by a few firms.

A. P. Giannini Italian American who changed the banking industry by opening multiple branches and encouraging the use of banks for small accounts and loans.

Business giants like Henry Ford emerged as popular and respected figures and were widely viewed as socially responsible trustees of the public interest. In 1925, in a book entitled *The Man Nobody Knows,* Bruce Barton (later founder of a leading advertising agency) suggested that Jesus Christ could best be understood as a chief executive who "had picked up twelve men from the bottom ranks of business and forged them into an organization that conquered the world." Portraying Jesus' parables as "the most powerful advertisements of all time," Barton's book led the nonfiction bestseller lists for two years.

"Get Rich Quick"—Speculative Mania

More than ever before, the stock market captured people's imagination as a certain route to riches. Stock market speculation—buying a stock and expecting to make money by selling it at a higher price—ran rampant. Articles in popular periodicals proclaimed that everyone could participate and get rich in no time, even with a small investment. By 1929, some 4 million Americans owned stock, equivalent to about 10 percent of American households.

Just as Americans bought their cars and radios on the installment plan, some hastened to buy stock on credit, expecting to sell it at an enormous profit, pay off the debt, and be wealthy. It was possible to purchase stock listed at $100 a share with as little as $10 down and the other $90 "on margin"—that is, owed to the stockbroker. If the stock price advanced to $150, the investor could sell, pay off the broker, and gain a profit of $50 (500 percent!) on the $10 investment. Unfortunately, if the stock price fell to $50, the investor would still owe $90 to the broker. Actually, fewer than 1 percent of those who bought stocks did so on margin, and the size of the margin rarely exceeded 45 or 50 percent. A larger number of people borrowed money to buy stocks. The **easy-money policy** of the Federal Reserve Board encouraged borrowing. Buying stocks with borrowed money, however, carried the same potential for disaster as buying on margin.

Driven partly by real economic growth and partly by speculation, stock prices rose higher and higher (see Figure 24.1). Standard and Poor's index of common stock prices tripled between 1920 and 1929. As long as the market stayed **bullish** and stock prices kept going up, prosperity seemed endless.

The ease of borrowing funds, stock speculation, and the ever-rising stock prices and corporate dividends of the 1920s sometimes encouraged the creation of holding companies (see page 513)—organizations designed not to sell actual goods or services but to keep dividends flowing to investors. Samuel Insull created a vast empire of electrical utilities companies. Much of his enterprise—and others like it—consisted of holding companies, which existed solely to own the stock of another company, which often existed primarily to own the stock of yet another company, and so on. The entire structure rested on the dividends that the underlying **operating companies** produced. Those dividends enabled the holding companies to pay dividends on their bonds. Any interruption in the flow of dividends from the operating companies was likely to bring the collapse of the entire pyramid, swallowing up the investments of speculators.

Although the stock market held the nation's attention as the most popular path to instant riches, other speculative opportunities abounded. One of the most prominent was a land boom in Florida. During the early 1920s, people poured into Florida, especially Miami, attracted by the climate, the beaches, and the ease of travel from the cities of the chilly Northeast. Encouraged partly by easy-money policies, speculators large and small began to buy land—almost any land—amid predictions that its value would soar. Stories circulated of land whose value had increased 1,500 percent over ten years. Like stocks, land was bought with borrowed money, to be resold at a profit. Early in 1926, however, the population influx slowed, and the boom began to falter. It collapsed completely when a hurricane slammed into Miami in September 1926. By 1927, many speculators were facing bankruptcy.

Agriculture: Depression in the Midst of Prosperity

Prosperity never extended to agriculture. Farmers made up nearly 30 percent of the work force at the

easy-money policy Federal Reserve strategy to encourage banks to extend credit; the Fed reduces the interest rate that it charges banks and reduces the cash reserves that it requires banks to maintain.

bullish Optimistic and confident.

operating company A company that exists to sell goods or services, as opposed to a holding company that exists to own other companies, including operating companies.

end of World War I, and many of them never recovered from the postwar recession. During the war, many farmers had expanded their operations in response to government demands for more food. Between 1914 and 1920, exports of farm products had nearly quadrupled. After the war, as European farmers resumed production, the glut of agricultural goods on world markets caused prices to fall. Exports of farm products tumbled by half. Throughout the 1920s, American farmers produced more than the domestic market could absorb.

Prices fell as a consequence of this **overproduction.** When adjusted for inflation, corn and wheat prices never rebounded to their prewar levels. Even in current dollars, corn and wheat sold for about half of what they brought during the war. The average farm's net income for the years 1917 to 1920 had ranged between $1,196 and $1,395 per year (see Figure 24.1). Farm income fell to a dreadful $517 in 1921, then slowly began to rise but never reached the levels of 1917 to 1920 until World War II. Although farmers' income fell, their mortgage payments more than doubled from prewar levels, partly because of debts that farmers had incurred to expand production during the war. Tax increases, the cost of tractors and trucks—now necessities on most farms—and the growing cost of fertilizer and other essential supplies bit further into farmers' meager earnings.

Throughout the 1920s, farmers pressed the government for help. In 1921, farm organizations worked with a bipartisan group of senators and representatives to form a congressional **Farm Bloc,** which promoted legislation to assist farmers. The bloc enjoyed a substantial boost in the 1922 elections, when distraught farmers across the Midwest turned out conservatives and elected candidates who voiced sympathy for farmers' problems. Congress passed a few assistance measures in the early 1920s, but none addressed the central problems of overproduction and low prices. In the mid-1920s, proposals to tackle these two key issues invariably met presidential vetoes.

As the farm economy continued to hemorrhage, the average value of an acre of farmland, in constant dollars, fell by more than half between 1920 and 1928. The average farm was actually less valuable in 1928 than in 1912. Thousands of people left farming each year, and the proportion of farmers in the work force fell from nearly 30 percent to less than 20 percent. The 1920s was not the prosperity decade for rural America.

The "Roaring Twenties"

- How did new expectations and choices reflect or contribute to the important social changes of the 1920s?

"The world broke in two in 1922 or thereabouts," wrote novelist Willa Cather, and she indicated her distaste for much that came after. F. Scott Fitzgerald, another novelist, agreed with the date but embraced the change. He believed 1922 marked "the peak of the younger generation," who brought about an "age of miracles"—that, he admitted, became an "age of excess." For most Americans, evidence of sudden and dramatic social change was easy to see, from automobiles, radios, and movies to a new youth culture and an impressive cultural outpouring by African Americans in northern cities.

The Automobile and American Life

During the 1920s, the automobile profoundly changed American patterns of living. Highways significantly shortened the traveling time from rural areas to cities, reducing the isolation of farm life. One farm woman, when asked why her family had an automobile but no indoor plumbing, responded, "Why, you can't go to town in a bathtub." Trucks allowed farmers to take more products to market more quickly and conveniently than ever before. In the fields, tractors saved weeks' worth of time. The spread of gasoline-powered farm vehicles also reduced the need for human farm labor and so stimulated migration to urban areas.

If the automobile changed rural life, it made an even more profound impact on life in the cities. The 1920 census, for the first time, recorded more Americans living in urban areas than in rural ones. As the automobile freed suburbanites from their dependence on commuter rail lines, new suburbs mushroomed. Most of the growth was in the form of single-family houses. From 1922 through 1928, construction began on an average of 883,000 new homes each year, many of them in the new suburbs. New home construction rivaled the auto as a major driving force behind economic growth. The automobile

overproduction Production that exceeds consumer need or demand.

Farm Bloc Bipartisan group of senators and representatives formed in 1921 to promote legislation to assist farmers.

♦ This postcard from Los Angeles includes many of the features that made southern California attractive in the early twentieth century: mountains, beaches, broad highways, and semitropical greenery. It also features the new City Hall and modern high-rise office buildings.

also discouraged the use of streetcars, which steadily declined after 1923.

By the late 1920s, the automobile had also begun to demonstrate its ability to strangle urban traffic. Detroit introduced the first traffic lights in 1920. Although they spread rapidly to other large cities, traffic congestion worsened. By 1926, cars in the evening rush hour in Manhattan crawled along at less than 3 miles per hour—slower than a person could walk.

Los Angeles: Automobile Metropolis

Most of Manhattan was not designed to handle automobile traffic, but the fastest-growing major city of the early twentieth century—Los Angeles—was. The population of Los Angeles increased tenfold between 1900 and 1920, then more than doubled by 1930, reaching 2.2 million. The expansion of citrus fruit raising, major oil discoveries, and the development of the motion-picture industry laid an economic foundation for rapid population growth in southern California. Manufacturing also expanded, and between 1919 and 1930 the city moved from twenty-eighth to ninth place among American cities based on manufacturing. Lack of sufficient water threatened to limit growth until city officials bought up water rights throughout the Owens Valley and diverted most of the Owens River to Los Angeles through a 233-mile-long aqueduct, opened in 1913. Throughout the 1920s, southern California promoters attracted hundreds of thousands of people by presenting an image of perpetual summer, tall palm trees lining wide boulevards filled with automobiles, fountains gushing water into the sunshine, and broad sandy beaches.

The rapid growth of Los Angeles came at the time the automobile industry was promoting the notion of a car for every family. By 1925, Los Angeles had one automobile for every three residents, twice the national average. The **Los Angeles basin** also had an excellent streetcar system. Partly because of the streetcar system, partly because of the activities of real-estate promoters, and especially because of the automobile, urban development in the Los Angeles basin was **multinucleated,** unlike development in most cities of the nineteenth century, which had a clearly defined central business district.

Automobiles and the streetcar system made it possible for Angelenos to live farther from work than ever before. Real-estate developers promoted the ideal of the single-family home. By 1930, about 94 percent of all residences in Los Angeles were single-family homes, an unprecedented level for a major city, and Los Angeles consequently had the lowest urban population density in the nation.

Life in Los Angeles came to be organized around the automobile to an extent unknown in most other

Los Angeles Basin The area now occupied by much of the city of Los Angeles and by its suburbs; it is surrounded on three sides by mountain ranges, giving it the shape of a dish or basin.

multinucleated Having several commercial centers instead of a single central business district; this type of development is typical of twentieth-century cities designed to accommodate cars.

major cities—but in ways that set the pace for urban development everywhere. The first modern supermarket, offering "one-stop shopping," appeared in Los Angeles, and the "Miracle Mile" along Wilshire Boulevard was the nation's first large shopping district designed for the automobile. The *Los Angeles Times* put it this way in 1926: "Our forefathers in their immortal independence creed set forth 'the pursuit of happiness' as an inalienable right of mankind. And how can one pursue happiness by any swifter and surer means. . . than by the use of the automobile?"

♦ Rudolph Valentino, the leading male movie star of the 1920s, is shown outfitted as a desert sheik, a role he played in *The Sheik* and *Son of the Sheik.* He died in 1926, at age 31, from complications following removal of his appendix. *Son of the Sheik* was released to his adoring fans after his death. *Culver Pictures, Inc.*

A Homogenized Culture Searches for Heroes

As the automobile cut traveling time and as more people moved to urban areas, restrictive immigration laws were closing the door to immigrants from abroad. These factors, together with the new technologies of radio and film, began to **homogenize** the culture—that is, to make it increasingly uniform by breaking down cultural differences based on region or ethnicity.

In 1921, the first commercial radio broadcasting station opened. Within six years, 681 were operating. By 1930, 40 percent of all households had radios. By the mid-1920s, too, most towns of any size boasted at least one movie theater. Movie attendance increased rapidly, from a weekly average of 40 million people in 1922 to 80 million in 1929. The equivalent of two-thirds of the total population went to the cinema every week. As Americans all across the country tuned in to the same radio broadcast, and families in rural villages as well as urban neighborhoods laughed or wept at the same movie, radio and film did their part to homogenize American life.

Radio and film joined newspapers and magazines—the media—in creating and publicizing national trends and fashions as Americans pursued one fad after another. In 1923, the opening of the fabulous tomb of the Egyptian pharaoh Tutankhamen led to a passion for things Egyptian. Crossword puzzle books captured the attention of many Americans in 1924, and contract bridge, a card game, did the same in 1926. Such fads, in turn, created markets for new consumer goods, from Egyptian-style furniture to folding card tables to crossword dictionaries.

The media also contributed to the development of national sports heroes. In the 1920s, spectator sports became an obsession. Baseball had long been the pre-eminent national sport, and radio now began to broadcast baseball games nationwide. Boxing and college football vied with baseball for national favor and for spectators' dollars. Most Americans were familiar with the exploits of baseball greats such as Lou Gehrig, Ty Cobb, and Babe Ruth, as well as boxers like Jack Dempsey and Gene Tunney and golfers like Bobby Jones. Gertrude Ederle won national acclaim in 1926 when she became the first woman to swim the English Channel and did so two hours faster than any previous man. Fame extended even to race horses, notably Man o' War.

The rapid spread of movie theaters created a new category of fame—the movie star. Charlie Chaplin, Buster Keaton, Harold Lloyd, and others brought laughter to the screen. Tom Mix was the best known of those introducing the western as a rugged dramatic genre. Sex, too, sold movie tickets and made

homogenize To make something uniform throughout.

♦ Charles Lindbergh chose photo settings in which he was alone with his plane, thereby emphasizing the individual nature of his flights. This photo was taken before his solo flight across the Atlantic. *Culver Pictures, Inc.*

stars of Theda Bara, the **vamp,** and Clara Bow, the "It" girl, whose publicists not only said that she had "it" but also insisted that no one had to ask what "it" was. Rudolph Valentino soared to fame as a male sex symbol, with his most famous film, *The Sheik,* set in a fanciful Arabian desert.

The greatest popular hero of the 1920s, however, was neither an athlete nor an actor but a small-town airmail pilot named **Charles Lindbergh.** At the time, aviation was barely out of its infancy. The earliest regular airmail deliveries in the United States began only in 1918, and night flying did not become routine until the mid-1920s. There had been a few transatlantic flights by 1926, but the longest nonstop flight was from San Diego to New York—2,500 miles.

Lindbergh, in 1927, decided to collect the prize of $25,000 offered by a New York hotel owner to the pilot of the first successful nonstop flight between New York and Paris—3,500 miles. His plane, *The Spirit of St. Louis,* was a stripped-down, one-engine craft. In a sleepless, 33½-hour flight, Lindbergh earned both the $25,000 and the adoration of crowds on both sides of the Atlantic. In an age devoted to materialism and dominated by a corporate mentality, Lindbergh's accomplishment seemed to proclaim that old-fashioned individualism, courage, and self-reliance could still triumph over adversity.

Alienated Intellectuals

Lindbergh went to Paris to win a prize and became a living legend. Other Americans, too, went to Paris and to other European cities in the 1920s, but for a different reason. These **expatriates** left the United States to escape what they considered America's intellectual shallowness, dull materialism, and spreading uniformity. As Malcolm Crowley put it in *Exile's Return* (1934), his memoir of his life in France, "by expatriating himself, by living in Paris, Capri or the South of France, the artist can break the puritan shackles, drink, live freely, and be wholly creative." He added that Paris in the 1920s "was a great machine for stimulating the nerves and sharpening the senses."

Though **Sinclair Lewis** and H. L. Mencken did not move to Paris, they were among the leading critics of mainstream values. Lewis, in *Main Street* (1920) and *Babbitt* (1922), presented small-town, middle-class existence as not just boring but stifling. Title character George F. Babbitt was Lewis's version of a typical suburban businessman—materialistic, narrow-minded, and complacent—who speaks in clichés and buys every gadget on the market. H. L. Mencken, the influential editor of *The American Mercury,* relentlessly pilloried the "booboisie," jeered at all politicians (reformers and conservatives alike), and celebrated only those writers who shared his distaste for most of American life.

Other writers also expressed a rejection of traditional values and disillusionment with postwar society. In Willa Cather's *One of Ours* (1922), for example, the sensitive and romantic main character dies

vamp A woman who uses her sexuality to entrap and exploit men.

Charles Lindbergh American aviator who made the first solo transatlantic flight in 1927 and became an international hero.

expatriate A person who takes up long-term residence in a foreign country.

Sinclair Lewis Novelist who satirized middle-class America in works such as *Babbitt* (1922) and became the first American to win the Nobel Prize for literature.

in the war and thereby escapes the stifling emptiness of the postwar triumph of technological materialism. Others turned to seeking pleasure and excitement. Poet Edna St. Vincent Millay captured this spirit in 1920:

My candle burns at both ends;
It will not last the night;
But ah, my foes, and oh, my friends—
It gives a lovely light!

Where Millay celebrated rebellion, F. Scott Fitzgerald, in *The Great Gatsby* (1925), revealed a dark side of the hedonism of the 1920s as he portrayed the pointless lives of wealthy pleasure seekers and their careless disregard for life and values. Ernest Hemingway, in *The Sun Also Rises* (1926), depicted disillusioned and frustrated expatriates. Others extended the theme of hopelessness. In *The Waste Land* (1922), T. S. Eliot, a poet who had fled to England in 1915, presented the grim barrenness of modern life, where a search for meaning yielded "the empty chapel, only the wind's home." Some writers moved beyond despair to predict the end of Western civilization. Joseph Wood Krutch, in 1929, concluded that "ours is a lost cause," that modern civilization was so decadent that it could not rejuvenate itself and could only wait to be overthrown by barbarians, as Rome had been in its day.

♦ By the time this 1923 photo was taken, F. Scott Fitzgerald had soared to fame as author of two novels and two collections of short stories, most of them depicting the hedonistic youth culture of the Jazz Age. Zelda, a writer, too, was best known as the beautiful and tormented wife of the handsome author. *Papers of F. Scott Fitzgerald, Manuscript Division. Department of Rare Books and Special Collections, Princeton University Libraries.*

Renaissance Among African Americans

For the most part, such feelings of despair and disillusionment troubled white writers and intellectuals. They were rarely apparent in the striking outpouring of literature, music, and art by African Americans in the 1920s.

Many blacks moved to northern cities in the 1920s, continuing patterns begun earlier. Harlem emerged as a large, predominantly black neighborhood in New York City. It quickly became a symbol of the new, urban life of African Americans. The term **Harlem Renaissance,** or Negro Renaissance, refers to a literary and artistic movement in which black artists and writers insisted on the value of black culture and used African and African-American traditions to shape an abundance of literature, painting, and sculpture. Alain Locke, a leading black author, likened it to "a spiritual emancipation." Black actors, notably **Paul Robeson,** began to appear in serious theaters and earn acclaim for their abilities. Earlier black writers, notably Locke, James Weldon Johnson, and Claude McKay, encouraged and guided the novelists and poets of the Renaissance.

Among the movement's poets, Langston Hughes became the best known. His poetry rang with the voice of the people, for he sometimes used folk language to convey powerful images (see Individual Choices: Langston Hughes). Zora Neale Hurston came from a poor southern family, won a scholarship to Barnard College, and began her long writing

Harlem Renaissance Literary and artistic movement in the 1920s, centered in Harlem, in which black writers and artists described and celebrated African-American life.

Paul Robeson African-American singer and actor prominent from the early 1920s through the 1950s, when he was driven from public life by repeated accusations that he was a communist.

INDIVIDUAL CHOICES

Choosing to Live in Harlem

Langston Hughes

Langston Hughes, an acclaimed author, chose to celebrate black people in his writing and develop opportunities for other black artists to cultivate their creativity. This portrait by Winold Reiss was made in 1925, when Hughes, in his early twenties, was already a significant figure in the Harlem Renaissance. National Portrait Gallery, Smithsonian Institution/Art Resource, NY.

In the late 1940s, Langston Hughes bought a house on East 127th Street, in central Harlem. He could have afforded a house in a wealthy suburb, but he chose to live in Harlem. This decision was in line with other choices he had made throughout his writing career: he chose to write for and about African Americans.

Born in Joplin, Missouri, in 1902, Hughes lived for a time with his grandmother, Mary Langston, from whom he learned lessons in social justice. He began to write poetry in high school, briefly attended college, then chose to work and travel in Africa and Europe. He continued writing poetry, some of which won prizes from African-American journals.

By 1925, Hughes was a significant figure in the Harlem Renaissance, sometimes reading his poetry to the musical accompaniment of jazz or the blues. Some of his work presents images from black history, like "The Negro Speaks of Rivers" (1921). Other works, like "Song for a Dark Girl" (1927), vividly depict the constraints of racism:

Way Down South in Dixie
(Break the heart of me)
They hung my black young lover
To a cross roads tree.

Way Down South in Dixie
(Bruised body high in air)

career with several short stories in the 1920s. Jean Toomer's novel *Cane* (1923), dealing with African Americans in rural Georgia and Washington, D.C., has been praised as "the most impressive product of the Negro Renaissance."

The Renaissance included **jazz,** which was becoming a central element in a distinctly American music. Jazz developed in the early twentieth century, drawing from several strains in African-American music, particularly the blues and ragtime (see page 593). Created and nurtured by African-American musicians in southern cities, especially

jazz Style of music developed in America in the early twentieth century, characterized by strong, flexible rhythms and improvisation on basic melodies.

I asked the white Lord Jesus
What was the use of prayer.

Way Down South in Dixie
(Break the heart of me)
Love is a naked shadow
On a gnarled and naked tree.

Other poems look to the future with an expectation for change and for new choices, as in "I, Too" (1925):

I, too, sing America.

I am the darker brother.
They send me
To eat in the kitchen
When company comes,
But I laugh,
And eat well,
And grow strong.

Tomorrow
I'll sit at the table
When company comes.
Nobody'll dare
Say to me,
"Eat in the kitchen,"
Then.

Besides
They'll see
How beautiful I am
And be ashamed.

I, too, am America.

In the early 1930s, as the Harlem Renaissance waned and the Depression deepened, Hughes, like other American intellectuals, turned to socialism. He traveled again and began writing short stories and plays. Few theaters at that time staged works by or about African Americans, and few hired African-American actors. So Hughes used his prestige and his time to create black theater companies in Harlem, Los Angeles, and Chicago.

Hughes's writings poured forth in a near-torrential stream. By the end of his life, in 1967, he had produced ten volumes of poetry; sixty-six short stories; some twenty plays, musicals, and operas; two autobiographical volumes; more than a hundred published essays, both serious and humorous; and several novels, histories, and children's books. One outcome of his devotion to writing and his choice to focus on the African-American experience was the prominent place that he established for himself among American authors of his time. Another and perhaps more significant outcome was his role in shaping the Harlem Renaissance and encouraging the development of African-American poetry, fiction, drama, and other writing.

New Orleans, jazz had been introduced to northern and white audiences by 1917. It became so popular that the 1920s have been called the Jazz Age. Jazz influenced leading white composers, notably George Gershwin, whose *Rhapsody in Blue* (1924) brought jazz into the symphony halls. Some attacked the new sound, claiming it excited "basic human instincts" and encouraged people to abandon self-restraint, especially with regard to sex. But despite—or perhaps because of—such condemnation, the wail of the saxophone became as much a part of the 1920s as the roar of the automobile and the flicker of the movie projector.

Louis "Satchmo" Armstrong emerged as a leading jazz innovator. His trumpet playing could transform the most ordinary tune into something original and compelling. Bessie Smith, the "Empress of the Blues," was the outstanding vocalist of the decade.

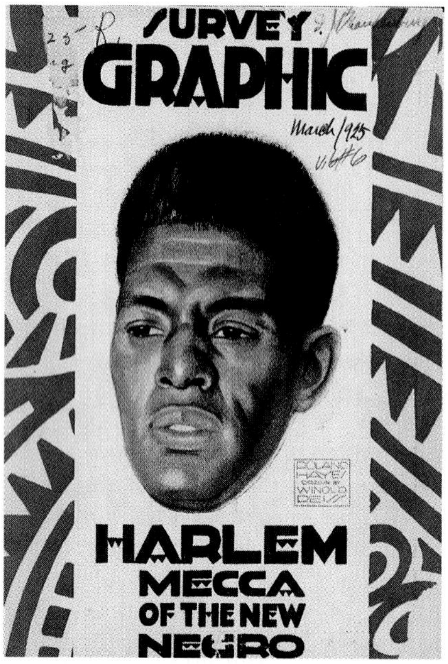

♦ This was the cover of a special issue of *Survey Graphic* in March 1925. A popular magazine of the period, *Survey Graphic* devoted the entire issue to Harlem and the emergence of a new consciousness among its African-American residents. *Survey Graphic 1925.*

♦ Louis Armstrong, born in 1900, first began to play the trumpet in New Orleans but emerged as a leading innovator in jazz after 1924, when he joined Fletcher Henderson's orchestra in New York. Some of his recordings from the 1920s are among the most original and imaginative contributions to jazz. *Frank Driggs Collection.*

The great black jazz musicians of the 1920s—Armstrong, Smith, Fletcher Henderson, Ferdinand "Jelly Roll" Morton, and others—drew white audiences into black neighborhoods to hear them. As increasing numbers of whites went "slumming" to Harlem, the area came to be associated with exotic nightlife and glittering jazz clubs, of which the Cotton Club was best known. There Edward Kennedy "Duke" Ellington came in 1927, to lead the club band until 1931, and there he began to develop the works that made him a respected twentieth-century American composer.

The fanfare of the Cotton Club seemed remote from the experience of most African Americans, but one Harlem black leader did affect black people throughout the country and beyond. **Marcus Garvey,** born in Jamaica, advocated a form of **black separatism.** His organization, the Universal Negro Improvement Association (UNIA), founded in 1914, stressed racial pride, the importance of Africa, and racial solidarity across national boundaries. After World War I, UNIA offices appeared in many black urban ghettos. Garvey supporters contended that blacks from around the world needed to help Africans overthrow colonial rule and build a strong African state, which would develop in prestige and power to become a symbol of black accomplishment. Garvey established a steamship company, the Black Star Line, which he hoped would carry American blacks to Africa, and he tried to promote other black economic enterprises. The UNIA message of racial pride and solidarity attracted wide support among blacks in the United States—especially in the cities—and also in the Caribbean and in Africa. However, black integrationist leaders, especially W. E. B. Du Bois of the NAACP, opposed Garvey's separatism and argued that the first task facing blacks was integration and equality in the United States. Garvey and Du Bois each labeled the other a traitor to his race.

Marcus Garvey Jamaican black nationalist active in America in the 1920s.

black separatism A strategy of creating separate black institutions, based on the assumption that African Americans can never achieve equality within white society.

Federal officials eventually charged Garvey with irregularities in his fundraising, and he was convicted of mail fraud in 1923. He spent two years in jail and then was deported to his native Jamaica. Garvey continued to lead UNIA in exile and the organization persisted, but most of the local offices lost members and influence.

"Flaming Youth"

Although African Americans created jazz, those who danced to it, in the popular imagination of the 1920s, were white—a male college student, clad in a swank raccoon-skin coat with a hip flask of illegal liquor in his pocket, and his female counterpart, the uninhibited **flapper** with bobbed hair and a daringly short skirt. This stereotype of "flaming youth," the title of a popular novel, reflected far-reaching changes among many white, college-age youths of middle- or upper-class background.

Although the term *adolescence* dated to 1904, it was the 1920s that saw the emergence of adolescents as a separate subculture. The prosperity of the 1920s allowed many middle-class families to send their children to college. On the eve of World War I, just over 3 percent of the population aged 18 to 24 were enrolled in college. By 1930, that proportion had more than doubled. Larger increases came among women than among men. In 1916, 30 percent of all bachelor's degrees went to women, and in 1930, women received 40 percent. On campus, students reshaped colleges into youth centers, where football games and dances assumed as much significance as examinations and term papers. The use of the term *date* to describe an unchaperoned outing by a young man and woman could be found among the working class as early as the 1890s, but by the 1920s it was in widespread use among most Americans.

For some young women—especially college students but also others from urban backgrounds—the changes of the 1920s seemed especially dramatic. Called "flappers" because of the flapping sound made by their fashionably unfastened galoshes, many young women scandalized their elders with skirts that stopped at the knee, stockings rolled below the knee, short hair often dyed black, and generous amounts of rouge and lipstick. Many observers assumed that the outrageous look reflected outrageous behavior and that suddenly young women were ignoring the insistence of their parents' generation on chastity. In fact, women's sexual activity outside marriage had begun to increase before the war, especially among working-class women and radicals. In the 1920s, such changes began to affect college and high school students, most of them from middle-class families. About half of the women who came of age during the 1920s had intercourse before marriage, a marked increase from prewar patterns.

♦ On the one hundred fiftieth anniversary of the Declaration of Independence, *Life* presented this cover parodying the famous painting, the "Spirit of '76," by depicting the "Spirit of '26"—an uninhibited flapper, a jazz saxophonist and drummer, and banners with the snappy sayings of the day. The caption reads: "One Hundred and Forty-three Years of LIBERTY and Seven Years of PROHIBITION." *Harvard College Library.*

Such changes in behavior were often linked to the automobile. It brought greater freedom to young people, for behind the wheel they had no chaperone and could go where they wanted. Sometimes they went to one of the many **speakeasies.** Before the passage of federal laws outlawing the

flapper In the 1920s, a young woman with short hair and short skirts who discarded old-fashioned standards of dress and behavior.

speakeasy A place that illegally sells liquor and sometimes offers entertainment.

manufacture and sale of alcoholic beverages (see below), few women who valued their reputation entered saloons. Mandatory prohibition, however, seemed to glamorize drinking. Men and women alike began to go to speakeasies, to drink and smoke together, and to dance to popular music derived from jazz. While some adults criticized the frivolities of the young, others emulated them, launching the first American youth culture. F. Scott Fitzgerald later called the years after 1922 "a children's party taken over by elders."

Traditional America Roars Back

- Why did some Americans try to restore traditional social values during the 1920s?
- How did they choose to accomplish that objective?
- What were some of the outcomes of their actions?

Many Americans, while embracing some new elements in the 1920s—from cars and electric appliances to movies and crossword puzzles—felt threatened by the pace of change and the upheaval in social values, which seemed centered in the cities. Nevertheless, to see the 1920s as a time of cultural warfare between rural and urban values is to oversimplify. Rural people often embraced the changes of the Roaring Twenties, and city-dwellers often gave full support to efforts to preserve traditional values. In nearly every case, efforts to stop the tide of change dated to the prewar era. Even then, some Americans sensed a threat to their way of life from immigration or from new patterns of thought and behavior. In the 1920s, however, several such movements came to fruition at the same time as Fitzgerald's "age of excess."

Prohibition

The issue of prohibition epitomized the cultural struggle to preserve white, old-stock Protestant values. Spearheaded by the Anti-Saloon League (see page 669) prohibition advocates gained strength throughout the Progressive era. They convinced Congress to pass a temporary prohibition measure in 1917, as a war measure to conserve grain. A more important victory for the "dry" forces came later that year, when Congress adopted and sent to the states the **Eighteenth Amendment,** prohibiting the manufacture, sale, or transportation of alcoholic beverages. Intense and single-minded lobbying by dry advocates persuaded three-fourths of the state legislatures to ratify the amendment in 1919, and it took effect in January 1920. In some ways, it was the last gasp of the reforming zeal that had generated much of progressivism.

Many Americans simply ignored the Eighteenth Amendment, and it grew less popular the longer it lasted. By 1926, a poll indicated that only 19 percent of Americans supported prohibition, 50 percent wanted the amendment modified, and 31 percent favored outright **repeal.** Prohibition, however, remained the law, if not the reality, from 1920 until 1933, when the Twenty-first Amendment finally did repeal it. But even after 1933, some states continued to ban alcohol within their borders.

Prohibition did reduce drinking somewhat, and it apparently produced a decline in drunkenness and in the number of deaths from alcoholism. It was never well enforced anywhere, however, partly because of the immensity of the task and partly because Congress never provided enough money for more than token federal enforcement. In 1923, a federal agent visited major cities to see how long it took to get an illegal drink: it took only 35 seconds in New Orleans, 3 minutes in Detroit, and 3 minutes and 10 seconds in New York City.

Prohibition produced unintended consequences. Whereas neighborhood saloons had often functioned as social centers for working-class and lower-middle-class men, the new speakeasies were often more glamorous, attracting an upper- and middle-class clientele, women as well as men. **Bootlegging**—production and sale of illegal beverages—flourished. Some bootleggers brewed only small amounts of beer and sold it to their neighbors. In the cities, however, the thirst for alcohol provided criminals with a fresh and lucrative source of income, part of which they used to buy influence in city politics and protection from police.

In Chicago, the gang led by **Al Capone** counted nearly a thousand members and, in 1927, took in

Eighteenth Amendment Constitutional amendment, ratified in 1919, that forbade the manufacture, sale, or transportation of alcoholic beverages.

repeal Annulment of an official act; repeal of a constitutional amendment requires a new amendment.

bootlegging Illegal production, distribution, or sale of liquor.

Al Capone Italian-born American gangster who ruthlessly ruled the Chicago underworld until he was imprisoned for tax evasion in 1931.

more than $100 million—$60 million of it from bootlegging. The scar-faced Capone realized such huge revenues in part by systematically eliminating members of competing gangs, something he accomplished through violence unprecedented in American cities. Gang warfare raged in Chicago throughout the 1920s, producing some five hundred slayings. In 1931, federal officials finally managed to convict Capone—of income-tax evasion—and send him to prison.

The blood-drenched gangs of Chicago had their counterparts elsewhere, as other gangsters—many of recent immigrant background, including Italians, Irish, Germans, and Jews—followed similar paths to wealth. Gangs also found riches in gambling, prostitution, and **racketeering.** Through racketeering they gained power in some labor unions. Some Americans regarded these developments as the result of prohibition—a policy that the federal government was unwilling either to enforce or to repeal. The gangs, killings, and corruption confirmed other Americans' long-standing distrust of cities and immigrants, and they clung to the vision of a dry America as the best hope for renewing traditional values.

Fundamentalism and the Crusade Against Evolution

Another effort to maintain traditional values came with the growth of fundamentalist Protestantism. **Fundamentalism** emerged from a conflict between Christian modernism and traditional beliefs. Religious modernists tried to reconcile their religious beliefs with modern science. Fundamentalists, however, rejected anything incompatible with a literal reading of the Scriptures and argued that every word of the Bible is the revealed word of God. The fundamentalist movement grew throughout the first quarter of the twentieth century, led by figures such as Billy Sunday, a baseball player turned evangelist.

In the early 1920s, some fundamentalists focused especially on **evolution** as contrary to the Bible. Biologists cite the theory of evolution to explain how living things have developed over millions of years, but the Bible states that God created the world and all living things in six days. Fundamentalists saw in evolution not just a challenge to the Bible's account of creation but also a challenge to religion itself.

William Jennings Bryan, the former Democratic presidential candidate and secretary of state, fixed on the evolution controversy after 1920. Until his death, he provided fundamentalists with their greatest champion. His energy, eloquence, and enormous following—especially in the rural South—guaranteed that the issue received wide attention. "It is better," Bryan wrote, "to trust in the Rock of Ages than to know the age of rocks." Bryan played a central role in the most famous of the disputes over evolution—the **Scopes trial.**

In March 1925, the Tennessee legislature passed a law making it illegal for any public school teacher to teach evolution. The **American Civil Liberties Union (ACLU)** offered to defend a teacher willing to challenge the law, and John T. Scopes, a young biology teacher in Dayton, Tennessee, accepted. Bryan volunteered to assist the local prosecutors, who faced an ACLU defense team that including the famous attorney **Clarence Darrow.** Bryan claimed that the only issue was the right of the people to regulate public education as they saw fit, but Darrow insisted he was there to prevent "bigots and ignoramuses from controlling the education of the United States."

The court proceedings were carried nationwide, live, on radio. Toward the end of the trial, in a surprising move, Darrow called Bryan to the witness stand as an authority on the Bible. Under Darrow's withering questioning, Bryan revealed that he knew little about findings in archaeology, geology, and linguistics that cast doubt on biblical accounts, and he also admitted, to the dismay of many fundamentalists, that he did not always interpret the words of the Bible literally. "Darrow never spared him," one reporter wrote, "It was masterful, but it was pitiful." Bryan died a few days later.

racketeering Commission of crimes such as extortion, loansharking, and bribery, sometimes behind the front of a seemingly legitimate business or union.

fundamentalism A religious movement emphasizing the literal truth of the Bible and opposing religious modernists who seek to reconcile the Bible with science.

evolution The central organizing theorem of the biological sciences, which holds that organisms change over generations, mainly as a result of natural selection; it includes the concept that humans evolved from nonhuman ancestors.

Scopes trial Trial in 1925 in which John Scopes, a high school biology teacher, was prosecuted for teaching evolution in violation of Tennessee law.

American Civil Liberties Union Private organization founded in 1920 that donates its services in cases involving constitutional rights.

Clarence Darrow Lawyer known for his defense of unpopular causes; he defended John Scopes.

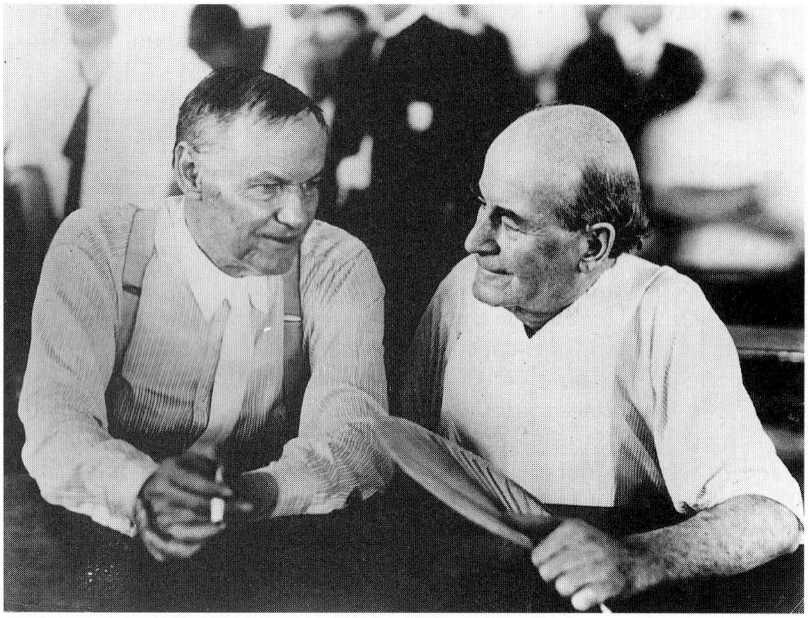

♦ William Jennings Bryan and Clarence Darrow had both spent distinguished careers battling for similar causes before they found themselves on opposite sides of the courtroom in the Scopes trial. In the hot Tennessee courtroom, they set the sartorial style by shedding their formal coats and working in their shirtsleeves. *Brown Brothers*

Scopes was found guilty, but the Tennessee Supreme Court threw out his sentence on a technicality, preventing appeal. The Tennessee law remained in force until 1968, and the last state law against teaching evolution was struck down by the U.S. Supreme Court only in 1987.

Nativism and Immigration Restriction

Prohibition and laws against teaching evolution were efforts to use government to define individual behavior and beliefs. Laws designed to restrict immigration had a similar origin, resulting in major part from nativist antagonism against immigrants, especially those from southern and eastern Europe (see pages 576–578). After a hiatus in immigration during the war, 430,000 immigrants arrived in 1920 and 805,000 in 1921, more than half from southern and eastern Europe.

Since the 1890s, some groups had urged Congress to cut off immigration, but earlier efforts met either congressional indifference or presidential vetoes. However, the disquieting presence of so many German Americans during the war with Germany, the Red Scare and fear of foreign radicalism, and the continued influx of poor immigrants at a time of growing unemployment all combined in 1921 to win greater support for restriction. The result was an emergency act to limit immigration from any country to 3 percent of the number of people from that country living in the United States at the time of the 1910 census.

The act of 1921 slowed the arrival of immigrants, but advocates of restriction considered it only a stopgap measure. In 1924, a permanent law, the **National Origins Act,** limited total immigration to 150,000 people each year. Quotas for each country were to be based on 2 percent of the number of Americans whose ancestors came from that country. While statisticians worked at determining the ancestry of all Americans, quotas were based on the 1890 census (before the largest influx of immigrants from southern and eastern Europe). In attempting to freeze the ethnic composition of the nation, the law reflected the arguments of those nativists who argued that immigrants from southern and eastern Europe made less desirable citizens than people from northern and western Europe. The law completely excluded Asians, upsetting relations with Japan, but it permitted unrestricted immigration from Canada and Latin America.

National Origins Act Law passed by Congress in 1924 establishing quotas for immigration to the United States; it limited immigration from southern and eastern Europe, permitted larger numbers of immigrants from northern and western Europe, and prohibited immigration from Asia.

Throughout the 1920s, nativism and discrimination flourished, sometimes taking violent forms. In West Frankfort, Illinois, for example, during three days in August 1920, rioting townspeople beat and stoned Italians, pulling them out of their homes and setting the houses on fire. Other discrimination was more subtle. Exclusive eastern colleges placed quotas on the number of Jews admitted each year, and some companies refused to hire Jews. In 1920, Henry Ford, in a magazine for Ford dealers, accused Jewish bankers of controlling the American economy and then broadened his attack to suggest an international Jewish conspiracy to control virtually everything from baseball to bolshevism. After Aaron Sapiro, an attorney, sued Ford for libel and challenged him to prove his claims, Ford retracted his charges and apologized in 1927.

♦ This image is from a Ku Klux Klan pamphlet published in the mid-1920s, when the Klan claimed as many as five million members nationwide. The Klan portrayed itself as defending traditional, white, Protestant America against Jews, Catholics, and African Americans. *Private collection.*

The Ku Klux Klan

Nativism, anti-Catholicism, anti-Semitism, and fear of radicalism all contributed to the spectacular growth of the Ku Klux Klan in the early 1920s. The original Klan, created during Reconstruction to intimidate former slaves, had long since died out. D. W. Griffith's hugely popular film *The Birth of a Nation,* released in 1915, glorified the old Klan and focused attention on efforts to resurrect it.

The new Klan portrayed itself as a patriotic order devoted to traditional American values, old-fashioned Protestant Christianity, and white supremacy. Attacking Catholics, Jews, immigrants, and blacks, along with bootleggers, corrupt politicians, and gamblers, the Klan fed on the insecurities of the early 1920s. Growth came slowly at first, to only five thousand members by 1920, but then a new recruiting scheme offered local organizers $4 out of every $10 initiation fee. This incentive combined with the postwar wave of nativism and antiradicalism to produce 5 million members nationwide by 1925.

The Klan was strong in the South, Midwest, West, and Southwest, and it mushroomed in towns and cities as well as in rural areas. The organization participated actively in local politics. Its leaders sometimes exerted powerful political influence in communities and in state governments, most notably in Texas, Oklahoma, Kansas, Oregon, and Indiana. In Oklahoma, the Klan led a successful impeachment campaign against a governor who tried to restrict its activities. In Oregon, the Klan claimed responsibility for a 1922 law aimed at eliminating Catholic schools, but the Supreme Court eventually ruled the law unconstitutional. Many local and state elections in 1924 divided along pro- and anti-Klan lines.

Although Klan members in 1923 hailed themselves as "the return of the Puritans in this corrupt, and jazz-mad age," extensive corruption underlay the Klan's self-righteous rhetoric. Some Klan leaders joined primarily for the profits, both legal (from recruiting) and illegal (mostly from political payoffs). Some lived personal lives in stark contrast to the morality they preached. In 1925, D. C. Stephenson, Grand Dragon of Indiana and one of the most prominent Klan leaders, was convicted of second-degree murder after the death of a woman who had accused him of raping her. When the governor refused to pardon him, Stephenson produced records proving the corruption of many Klan-endorsed officials, including the governor, a member of Congress, and the mayor of Indianapolis. Thereafter, Klan membership fell sharply amid factional disputes and further evidence of fraud and corruption.

Race, Class, and Gender

- During the 1920s, how did constraints based on race or gender affect Americans? How did various groups respond to those constraints?
- What was the experience of working people in the 1920s?

The "spiritual emancipation" that Alain Locke ascribed to the Harlem Renaissance, on the one hand, and the terror of Klan nightriders, on the other, represent the polar extremes of race relations in the 1920s. For most people of color, the realities of daily life fell somewhere in between. For working people, the 1920s represented what labor historian Irving Bernstein has termed "the lean years," when many gains from the Progressive era and World War I were lost and unions remained largely on the defensive. For women, the 1920s opened with a political victory in the form of suffrage, but the unity developed in support of that measure soon broke down.

Race Relations: North, South, and West

Discrimination against Jews, violence against Italians, and the Klan's appeal to white Protestants all point to the continuing significance of ethnicity in American life during the 1920s. Throughout the decade, racial relations remained deeply troubled at best, violent at worst.

Although the Harlem Renaissance helped to produce greater appreciation for black music and other accomplishments, racial discrimination continued to confront most African Americans, no matter where they lived. A few gained better jobs by moving north, but many found work only in low-paying service occupations. In nearly every city, social pressures and **restrictive covenants** limited access to desirable housing. Those who did succeed sometimes found themselves the targets of racial hostility, like the black physician whose home was attacked by a white mob when he moved into a white Detroit neighborhood in 1925.

Throughout the 1920s, the NAACP tried to secure a federal antilynching law, but southern legislators defeated the attempt each time, arguing against any federal interference in the police power of the states. As part of its efforts to combat lynching, the NAACP tried to educate the public by publicizing crimes against blacks. A typical handbill presents the disgraceful record:

> THE SHAME OF AMERICA. . . . *Do you know that the United States is the Only Land on Earth where human beings are* BURNED AT THE STAKE? . . . *In Four Years, 1918–1921, Twenty-Eight People Were Publicly* BURNED BY AMERICAN MOBS . . . *3,436 People Lynched 1889 to 1922.*

In the eastern United States, both North and South, race relations usually meant black-white relations. In the West, race relations were always more complex, and became even more so in the years preceding and following World War I, when Filipinos began to arrive in Hawai`i and on the West Coast, most of them working in agriculture and aboard ships. In 1920, some eight thousand workers on Hawaiian sugar plantations, most of them Japanese and Filipino, went on strike for higher wages. After six months, however, most of the strikers gave up in defeat. Sikhs from India also entered the West Coast work force, mainly as agricultural laborers.

California had long led the way among western states in passing laws discriminating against Asian Americans. Westerners, especially Californians, had also compiled a lengthy record of violence aimed at Asians (see pages 553–555). By the late 1920s, California laws forbidding Asian immigrants to own or lease land (see page 678) had been copied by other western states.

Some Asian immigrants and Asian Americans responded to discriminatory actions through court actions, but with little success. In the early 1920s, the U.S. Supreme Court affirmed that only white persons and persons of African descent could become naturalized citizens, denying persons born in Japan or India. The U.S. Supreme Court also ruled that Mississippi could require a Chinese-American schoolchild to attend the segregated school established for African Americans.

Beginnings of Change in Federal Indian Policy

Although Asian Americans made few gains in the 1920s, advocates of the rights of American Indians had more success. In the administration of President Warren G. Harding, Interior Secretary Albert Fall tried to lease parts of reservations to white developers and to extinguish the Pueblo Indians' title to sizable lands along the Rio Grande. In the face of

restrictive covenant Provision in a property title that prohibits the sale of property to specified groups of people, especially people of color.

♦ African Americans intensified their efforts to put an end to lynching. This protest parade was held in Washington, D.C., in 1922. The NAACP's efforts to secure a federal anti-lynching law, however, were repeatedly defeated by southerners in Congress. *UPI/Bettmann.*

significant opposition, Fall's proposals were either dropped or modified. The Pueblo land question led directly to the organization of the **American Indian Defense Association (AIDA),** created in 1923 by John Collier, an eastern social worker, to support the Pueblos.

Collier and the AIDA soon emerged as the leading voice calling for changes in federal Indian policy. Their goals were an end to land allotments, better health and educational services on the reservations, creation of tribal governments, and tolerance of Indian religious ceremonies and other customs. In sum, they proposed a major policy change, from assimilation to recognition of Indian cultures and values. The political pressure that the AIDA and similar groups applied, as well as political efforts by Indians themselves, secured several new laws favorable to Indians, including one in 1924 extending full citizenship to all Indians.

In 1926, Secretary of the Interior Hubert Work ordered a comprehensive study of Indian life. Completed in 1928, the report described widespread poverty and health problems among Indians, demonstrated the lack of adequate healthcare and education on the reservations, and condemned allotment as the single most important cause of Indian hardship. The efforts to support and extend Indian rights, especially the work of Collier, laid the basis for a significant shift in federal policy in the 1930s (see page 813).

Mexicans in California and the Southwest

California and the Southwest, home to Mexican and Mexican-American families since the region was part of Mexico (see pages 557–558), attracted growing numbers of Mexican immigrants in the 1920s. Many Mexicans went north, most of them to Texas and California, to escape the revolution and civil war that devastated their nation from 1910 into the 1920s. Nearly one Mexican in ten may have fled to the United States between 1910 and 1930, nearly

American Indian Defense Association Organization founded in 1923 to defend the rights of American Indians; it pushed for an end to allotment and a return to tribal government.

♦ Immigration from Mexico increased dramatically during the early twentieth century, as improvements in transportation made it easier to reach the northern border and as the Mexican Revolution produced social and economic displacement in many areas. Institutions such as Benito Juarez School, in Brownsville, Texas, helped Mexican Americans to retain their cultural traditions. *The Center for American History, University of Texas at Austin.*

seven hundred thousand of them legally and probably as many more illegally. At the same time, southern California and south Texas also experienced large increases in their Anglo populations.

Population changes in southern California and south Texas came as the agricultural economies of those regions also changed. In south Texas, some cattle ranches were converted to farms, especially for cotton but for fruit and vegetables too. By 1925, the Southwest was producing 40 percent of the nation's fruits and vegetables, crops that were highly labor-intensive. In the late 1920s, Mexicans made up 80 to 85 percent of farm laborers in southern California and south Texas. These changes in population and economy reshaped relations between Anglos and Mexicans.

In south Texas, many Anglo newcomers cared little about the accommodations worked out between ranch owners—mostly Anglos—and Mexicans in the late nineteenth century. Looking on Mexicans as what one Anglo called a "partly colored race," white newcomers tried to import elements of southern black-white relations—sharecropping, disfranchisement, and segregation. Disfranchisement was unsuccessful, but some schools and other social institutions were segregated despite Mexican opposition. Efforts organized through the League of United Latin American Citizens (LULAC) occasionally halted discrimination by businesses—but only occasionally.

In California, Mexican workers' efforts to organize and strike for better pay and working conditions often sparked violent opposition. Strikes involving thousands of workers in the early 1920s were broken quickly and brutally. Local authorities arrested and often beat strikers, and growers' armies of private guards beat or kidnapped them. Leaders found themselves subject to deportation. Nevertheless, Mexican labor had become vital to agriculture, and growers adamantly opposed any proposals to restrict immigration from Mexico. The landowners made certain that the revised immigration law of 1924 permitted unlimited immigration from the Western Hemisphere.

Labor on the Defensive

Difficulties in establishing unions among Mexican workers mirrored a larger failure of unions in the 1920s. When unions tried to recover lost purchasing power by striking in 1919 and 1920, nearly all failed. After 1921, business took advantage of the conservative political climate to challenge Progressive-era legislation benefiting workers. The Supreme Court responded by limiting workers' rights, voiding laws that eliminated child labor, and striking down minimum wages for women and children.

Many companies undertook anti-union drives. Arguing that unions were no longer necessary and had become either corrupt or radical, some employers used the term **American Plan** to describe their refusal to recognize unions as representing employees. At the same time, many companies began an approach known as **welfare capitalism.** The strategy

American Plan Term that some employers in the 1920s used to describe their policy of refusing to negotiate with unions.

welfare capitalism Program that some employers adopted to discourage unions by providing benefits such a lunchrooms, paid vacations, bonuses, and profit-sharing plans.

was to provide workers with benefit programs such as insurance, retirement pensions, cafeterias, paid vacations, and stock purchase plans. Such innovations stemmed both from genuine concern about workers' well-being and from the expectation that such improvements would increase productivity and discourage unionization.

The 1920s marked the first period of prosperity since the 1830s when union membership declined, falling from 5 million in 1920 to 3.6 million in 1929, a 28 percent decline at a time when the total work force increased by 15 percent. In addition to hostile government policies, welfare capitalism, and the American Plan, unions also suffered from lost strikes. Prohibition devastated once-strong unions of brewery workers and bartenders. Some unions suffered from internal battles. For example, the International Ladies' Garment Workers' Union lost two-thirds of its members during power struggles between Socialists and Communists.

The Communists sought influence and power within other unions, but the **American Communist party (CP)** never gained the number of supporters characteristic of the Socialist party before World War I. In 1929, the CP counted only ninety-three hundred members. Always closely tied to the leadership of the Soviet Union, the CP labored strenuously to organize workers throughout the 1920s, first by working within AFL unions and then by creating separate unions. Although CP organizers tried to organize the unskilled, people of color, women, and others outside AFL craft unions, they had little success.

Changes in Women's Lives

The attention given to the flapper in accounts of the 1920s should not conceal important changes in the nature of women's gender roles during those years. Significant changes occurred in the size and structure of the family and in politics.

Marriage among white middle-class women and men came increasingly to be valued as companionship between two partners. Although the ideal of marriage was often expressed in terms of man and woman taking equal responsibility for a relationship, the actual responsibility for the smooth functioning of the family typically fell on the woman. In the 1920s, however, many women seem to have increased their control over decisions about childbearing.

Usually in American history, prosperity brings increases in the birth rate. In the 1920s, however, changing social values together with more options for birth control resulted in fewer births. Women who came of childbearing age in the 1910s and 1920s are distinctive in three ways when compared with women of both earlier and later time periods: (1) they had fewer children on the average, (2) more of them had no children at all, and (3) far fewer had very large families (see Figure 24.2).

The declining birth rate in the 1920s reflected, in part, some degree of success for earlier efforts to secure wider availability of birth-control information and devices. More women used diaphragms rather than relying on males to use condoms. Margaret Sanger continued to carry the banner in the battle to extend birth-control information (see page 667), and she persuaded more doctors to join her efforts. As the birth-control movement gained the backing of male physicians, it became a more respectable, middle-class reform movement. By 1925, the American Medical Association, the New York Academy of Medicine, and the New York Obstetrical Society had all declared their support for birth control, and the Rockefeller Foundation began to fund medical research into contraception methods. Nevertheless, until 1936, federal law restricted public distribution of information about contraception.

Although the domestic burden of many middle-class women lightened with the introduction of labor-saving devices such as vacuum cleaners and electric irons, working-class women still spent long days struggling to economize to maintain their families. As before, these women and their children sometimes worked outside the home because the family needed additional income. The proportion of women working for wages remained quite stable during the 1920s, at about one in four. The proportion of married women working for wages increased, though, from 23 percent of the female labor force in 1920 to 29 percent in 1930.

Perhaps the most publicized event in women's lives was national woman suffrage. In June 1919, by a narrow margin, Congress proposed the **Nineteenth Amendment,** to enfranchise women over 21, and sent it to the states for ratification. After a grueling, state-by-state battle, ratification came in August 1920.

American Communist party Party organized in 1919, devoted to destroying capitalism and private property and replacing them with a system of socialism.

Nineteenth Amendment Constitutional amendment, ratified in 1920, that prohibited federal or state governments from restricting the right to vote on account of sex.

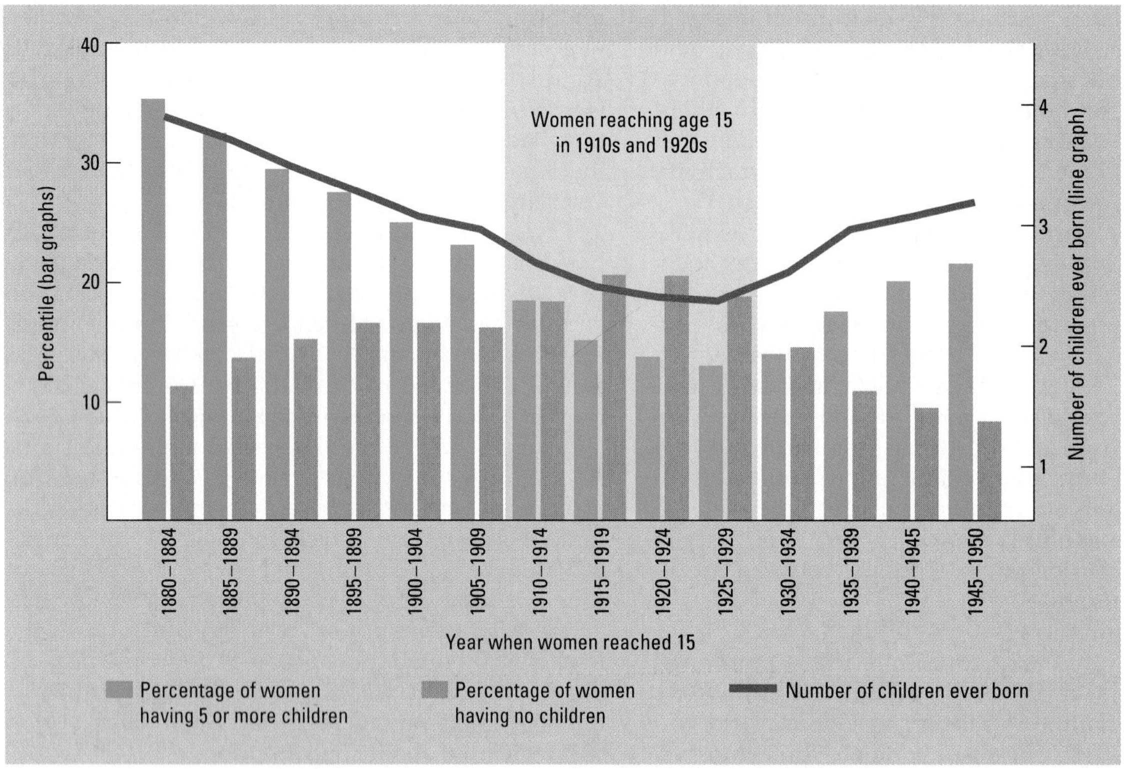

♦ **FIGURE 24.2 Changing Patterns of Childbearing Among Women** This figure depicts three different choices regarding family size: (1) the number of children born to women ever married, (2) the percentage of women having large families, and (3) and the percentage of women having no children at all. *Note:* Child-bearing ages are considered to be between 15 and 45. *Sources:* For women born in 1914 and before, Series B42–48, Percent Distribution of Ever-Married Women (Survivors of Birth Cohorts of 1835–39 to 1920–24) by Race and By Number of Children Ever Born, as Reported in Censuses of 1910, 1940, 1950, 1960, and 1970, U.S. Bureau of the Census, *Historical Statistics of the United States, Colonial Times to 1970,* Bicentennial Edition, 2 vols. (Washington, D.C.: U.S. Government Printing Office, 1975), I:53. For women born in 1916 and after, Table 270, Children Ever Born and Marital Status of Women by Age, Race, and Spanish Origin: 1980, U.S. Bureau of the Census, *1980 Census of Population: Detailed Population Characteristics: United States Summary,* (Washington, D.C.: U.S. Government Printing Office, 1984), p. 1–103.

As women began to participate in the political mainstream, the unity of the suffrage movement disintegrated in disputes over the proper role for women voters. Both major political parties welcomed women as voters and modified the structure of their national committees to provide that each state be represented by both a national committeeman and a national committeewoman. Some suffrage activists, however, joined the League of Women Voters, a nonpartisan group committed to social and political reform. The Congressional Union, led by Alice Paul (see page 668), converted itself into the National Woman's party and, after 1923, focused its efforts largely on securing an **Equal Rights Amendment** to the Constitution. The League of Women Voters disagreed, arguing that such an amendment would endanger laws that provided special rights and protections for women. In the end,

Equal Rights Amendment Proposed constitutional amendment, first advocated by the National Woman's party in 1923, to give women in the United States equal rights under the law.

woman suffrage seems not to have dramatically changed either women or politics.

Development of Gay and Lesbian Subcultures

In the 1920s, gay and lesbian subcultures became more established and, in some cities, including New York, Chicago, New Orleans, and Baltimore, relatively open. *The Captive,* a play about lesbians, opened in New York in 1926, and some movies included unmistakable references to gays or lesbians. Novels with gay and lesbian characters circulated in the late 1920s and early 1930s. By the late 1920s, some nightclub acts included material about gays and lesbians in performances intended for audiences that were largely heterosexual. In Chicago, the Society for Human Rights was organized to advocate equal treatment.

A relatively open gay and lesbian community emerged in Harlem, mostly of African Americans. Some popular blues singers referred to gay men and lesbians in songs, and some prominent figures of the Renaissance were gay or bisexual. In the early 1930s, the nation's largest gay and lesbian event was the annual Hamilton Lodge drag ball in Harlem, and at the height of its popularity, as many as seven thousand revelers and spectators of all races attended.

At the same time, however, more and more psychiatrists and psychologists were labeling homosexuality a **perversion.** Shortly before World War I, as the work of **Sigmund Freud** became well known, the view that homosexuality was physiological in origin was replaced by a different explanation. Most psychiatrists and psychologists now labeled homosexuality a sexual disorder that required a cure, though no "cure" ever proved viable. Thus Freud's theories may have been a liberating influence with regard to heterosexual relations, but they proved harmful for same-sex relations.

The new medical definitions were slow to work their way into the larger society. The navy and army, for example, continued previous practices, making little effort to prevent homosexuals from enlisting and taking disciplinary action only against behavior that clearly violated the law. However, during the 1920s, many middle-class men seemed to become increasingly anxious to assert a heterosexual gender identity.

The late 1920s and early 1930s brought increased suppression of gays and lesbians. New state laws gave police greater authority to prosecute them and ban open expressions of their identity and culture. In 1927, New York City police raided *The Captive* and other plays with gay or lesbian themes, and the New York state legislature banned all such plays. In 1929 Adam Clayton Powell, a leading Harlem minister, launched a highly publicized campaign against gays. Motion-picture studios instituted a morality code that, among its wide-ranging provisions, prohibited any depiction of homosexuality. The end of prohibition after 1933 brought increased regulation of businesses selling liquor, and local authorities used this regulatory power to close establishments that tolerated gay or lesbian customers. Thus, by the 1930s, many gays and lesbians were becoming more secretive about their sexual identities.

The Politics of Prosperity

- What were the expectations of the Republican administrations of the 1920s about the proper role of the federal government in the economy?
- What policy choices resulted from those expectations?

Sooner or later, nearly all the social and economic developments of the 1920s found their way into politics, from highway construction to prohibition, from immigration restriction to the teaching of evolution, from farm prices to lynching. After 1918, the Republicans returned to the majority role they had exercised from the mid-1890s to 1912, and they continued as the unquestioned majority party throughout the 1920s. Progressivism largely disappeared, although a few veterans of earlier struggles, led by Robert La Follette and George Norris, persisted in their vigil to limit corporate power. The Republican administrations of the 1920s, instead, shared a faith in the ability of business to establish prosperity and thereby to benefit the American people. Those in power considered government the partner of business, not its regulator.

Harding's Failed Presidency

Elected in 1920, Warren G. Harding looked presidential—handsome, gray-haired, dignified, warm,

perversion Sexual practice considered abnormal or deviant.

Sigmund Freud Austrian who played a leading role in developing the field of psychoanalysis, known for his theory that the sex drive underlies much individual behavior.

♦ In 1924, the Democrats tried to capitalize on the Republicans embarrassment over the Teapot Dome scandal. They received little response because the death of Harding brought Calvin Coolidge to the presidency, and Coolidge's personal honesty and morality were unquestioned. *Collection of David J. and Janice L. Frent.*

and outgoing—but had little intellectual depth below the charming surface. To some positions, he named the most respected leaders of his party, including Charles Evans Hughes for secretary of state, Andrew Mellon for secretary of the treasury, and Herbert Hoover for secretary of commerce. Harding, however, was most at home in smoke-filled rooms, drinking whiskey and playing poker with friends, and he gave hundreds of government jobs to his cronies and political supporters. They betrayed his trust and turned his administration into one of the most corrupt in American history. As their misdeeds began to come to light, Harding put off taking action until after a trip to Alaska. During his return, on August 2, 1923, he died when a blood vessel burst in his brain.

The full extent of corruption became clear after Harding's death. Interior Secretary Fall had accepted huge bribes from oil companies for leases on government oil reserves at Elk Hills, California, and Teapot Dome, Wyoming. Attorney General Harry Daugherty and others had accepted bribes to approve the sale of government-held property for less than its value, and Daugherty may also have been involved in protecting bootleggers. The head of the Veterans Bureau had swindled the government out of more than $200 million. In all, three cabinet members resigned, four officials went to jail, and five men committed suicide. As if the corruption were not enough, in 1927 Nan Britton published a book revealing that she had been Harding's mistress, had his child, and carried on trysts with him in the White House.

The Three-Way Election of 1924

When Harding died, Vice President Calvin Coolidge was visiting his father's farm in Vermont. Fortunately for the Republican party, the new president exemplified the honesty, virtue, and sobriety associated with rural New England. In 1924, Republicans quickly chose Coolidge as their candidate for president.

The Democratic convention, however, sank into a long and bitter deadlock. Since the Civil War, the party had had two major wings—southerners, who were mostly Protestant and committed to white supremacy; and northerners, who were often city-dwellers and of recent immigrant descent, including many Catholics. In 1924, the Klan was approaching its peak membership and exercised significant influence among many Democratic delegates from the South and Midwest. Northern Democrats that year tried to nominate **Al Smith** for president. Highly popular as governor of New York, Smith epitomized urban America. Catholic and the son of immigrants, he was everything the Klan—and most of the southern convention delegates—hated. His chief opponent for the nomination, William G. McAdoo of California, boasted progressive credentials but had done legal work for an oil company executive tainted by the Elk Hills scandal. After nine hot days of stalemate and 103 ballots, the exhausted Democrats turned to a compromise candidate, John W. Davis. Davis had served in the Wilson administration and then became a leading corporate lawyer. All in all, the convention seemed to confirm the observation of the contemporary humorist Will Rogers: "I belong to no organized political party. I am a Democrat."

Americans committed to progressivism found little attractive in either Coolidge or Davis and welcomed the independent candidacy of Senator Robert M. La Follette of Wisconsin. La Follette was

Al Smith New York governor who unsuccessfully sought the Democratic nomination for president in 1924 and was the unsuccessful Democratic candidate for president in 1928; his Catholicism and desire to repeal Prohibition were political liabilities.

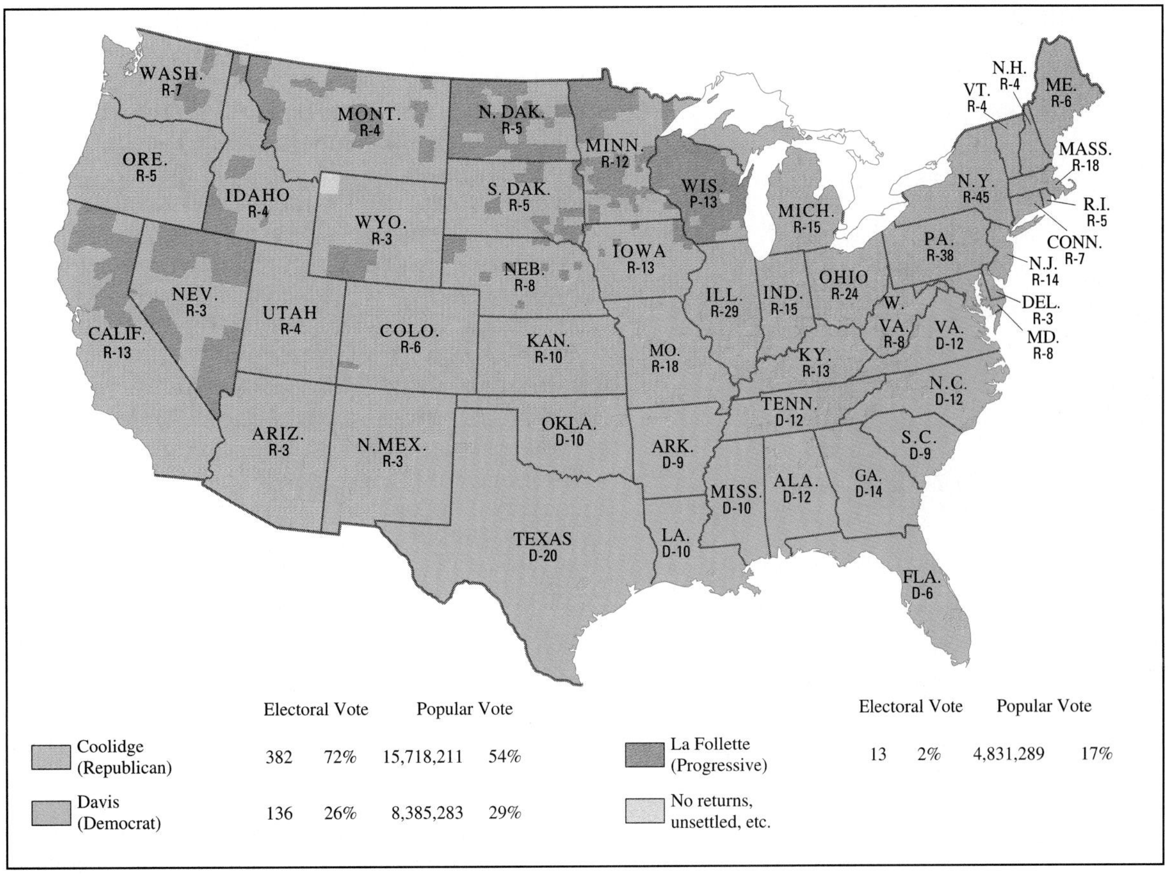

♦ **MAP 24.1 Election of 1924** The presidential election of 1924 was complicated by the campaign of Senator Robert La Follette of Wisconsin, who ran as a Progressive. As you can see, much of his support came from Republicans living in the north-central and northwestern regions where the agricultural economy was most hard hit.

nominated as a Progressive at a convention that expressed the concerns of labor, farmers, and an assortment of reformers dating back as far as the Populist party of the 1890s. The La Follette Progressives attacked big business and embraced collective bargaining, reforms of the political process, public ownership of railroads and water power resources, and a public referendum on questions of war and peace. La Follette was the first presidential candidate to be endorsed by the American Federation of Labor. The Socialist Party of America threw him its support as well.

Republican campaigners largely ignored Davis and focused on portraying La Follette as a dangerous radical. Coolidge himself claimed the key issue was "whether America will allow itself to be degraded into a communistic or socialistic state or whether it will remain American." Coolidge won with nearly 16 million votes and 54 percent of the total, as voters seemed to champion the status quo. Davis held on to most traditional Democratic voters, especially in the South, receiving 8 million votes and 29 percent. La Follette carried only his home state of Wisconsin but garnered almost 5 million votes, 17 percent, and did well both in urban working-class neighborhoods and in the rural Midwest and Northwest (see Map 24.1).

The Politics of Business

If the voters wanted Coolidge to continue as before, he did not disappoint them. Resolved to limit government and content to let problems work themselves out, Coolidge tried to reduce the significance of the presidency—and succeeded. Having once announced that "the business of America is business,"

♦ This cartoon depicts Coolidge playing the praises of big business. Big business, dressed like a flapper, responds by dancing the Charleston with wild abandon and singing a paraphrase of a popular song, "Yes Sir, He's My Baby." *Library of Congress.*

he believed that the free market and free operation of business leadership would best sustain economic prosperity for all. As president, he set out to prevent government from interfering in the operation of business.

The Coolidge administration's firm commitment to an unfettered market economy meant the executive had little sympathy for proposals to use the federal government to assist the faltering farm economy. Still, Congress tried to address the related problems of low prices for farm products and persistent agricultural surpluses with the **McNary-Haugen bill.** This measure would have created federal price supports and authorized the government to buy farm surpluses and sell them abroad at prevailing world prices. After long effort, the Farm Bloc finally pushed the bill through Congress in 1927, only to have Coolidge veto it. The same thing happened in 1928.

Andrew Mellon, an aluminum magnate and one of the wealthiest men in the nation, served as secretary of the treasury throughout the Republican administrations of the 1920s. Widely acclaimed by Republicans and business leaders as the greatest secretary of the treasury since Alexander Hamilton, Mellon secured substantial tax cuts for the wealthy and for corporations. He argued that high taxes on the very affluent stifled the economy and that tax cuts at those levels would result in economic benefits to all as a result of the "productive investments" that the wealthy would make. Herbert Hoover, secretary of commerce during the Harding and Coolidge administrations, urged Coolidge to regulate the increasingly wild use of credit, which inflated stock values and produced rampant stock market speculation, but Coolidge refused.

Coolidge cut federal spending and staffed federal agencies with people who shared his distaste for government. Unlike Harding, Coolidge found honest and competent appointees. Like Harding, he named probusiness figures to regulatory commissions and put conservative, probusiness judges in the courts. The *Wall Street Journal* described the outcome: "Never before, here or anywhere else, has a government been so completely fused with business."

McNary-Haugen bill Farm relief bill that provided for government purchase of crop surpluses during years of large output; Coolidge vetoed it in 1927 and in 1928.

SUMMARY

E xpectations
C onstraints
C hoices
O utcomes

The 1920s was a decade of prosperity: unemployment was low, GNP grew steadily, and many Americans fared well. Sophisticated advertising campaigns created bright *expectations,* and installment buying freed consumers from the old *constraints* of having to pay cash. Many consumers did *choose* to buy more and to buy on credit—stimulating manufacturing and an expansion of personal debt. Easy credit and *expectations* of continuing prosperity also helped to loosen *constraints* on speculation. Fueled by many individual *choices,* the stock market climbed higher and higher. Agriculture, however, did not share in this prosperity.

As *expectations* changed during the Roaring Twenties, Americans experienced significant social change. The automobile, radio, and movies broke down old *constraints* on travel and communication and, abetted by immigration restriction, produced, as one *outcome,* a more homogeneous culture. Many American intellectuals, however, *chose* to reject the consumer-oriented culture. During the 1920s, African Americans produced an outpouring of significant art, literature, and music. Some young people *chose* to reject traditional *constraints,* and one *outcome* was a so-called youth culture.

Not all Americans embraced change. Some *chose* instead to try to maintain or restore earlier cultural values. The *outcomes* were mixed. Prohibition was largely unsuccessful. Fundamentalism grew and prompted a campaign against the teaching of evolution. Nativism helped produce significant new restrictions on immigration. The Ku Klux Klan, committed to nativism, traditional values, and white supremacy, experienced nationwide growth until 1925, but membership declined sharply thereafter.

Discrimination and occasional violence continued to *constrain* the lives of people of color. Federal Indian policy had long stressed assimilation and allotment, but some groups *chose* to promote different policies based on respect for Indian cultural values. Immigration from Mexico greatly increased the Latino population in California and the Southwest, and some Mexicans working in agriculture tried, unsuccessfully, to organize unions. Nearly all unions faced strong opposition from employers.

Some older *expectations* and *constraints* regarding women's roles broke down as women gained the right to vote and exercised more control over the choice to have children. An identifiable gay and lesbian subculture emerged, especially in cities.

The politics of the era were marked by greater conservatism than before World War I. Warren G. Harding was a poor judge of character, and some of his appointees lived by graft and disgraced their chief. Harding and his successor, Calvin Coolidge, both *expected* government to act as a partner with business, and they made *choices* that minimized regulation and encouraged speculation. With some exceptions, progressive reform disappeared from politics, and efforts to secure federal assistance for farmers fizzled. One *outcome* was a federal government that was strongly conservative, staunchly probusiness, and absolutely unwilling to intervene in the economy.

SUGGESTED READINGS

Frederick Lewis Allen. *Only Yesterday: An Informal History of the Nineteen-Twenties* (1931; reprint, 1964).

An anecdote-filled account that brings the decade to life.

F. Scott Fitzgerald. *The Great Gatsby* (1925).

A fictional portrayal of high living and pleasure seeking among the wealthy of New York.

Nathan Irvin Huggins. *Harlem Renaissance* (1971).

A thorough and thoughtful work that places the Harlem Renaissance into the larger context of race relations in the 1920s.

William E. Leuchtenburg. *The Perils of Prosperity, 1914–1932,* rev. ed. (1993).

A comprehensive yet readable account by a leading historian.

The Smithsonian Collection of Classic Jazz. Five compact disks (1987).

An outstanding collection that reflects the development of American jazz, with annotations and biographies of performers.

Jules Tygiel. *The Great Los Angeles Swindle: Oil, Stocks, and Scandal During the Roaring Twenties* (1996).

A recent, engagingly written account of Los Angeles in the 1920s.

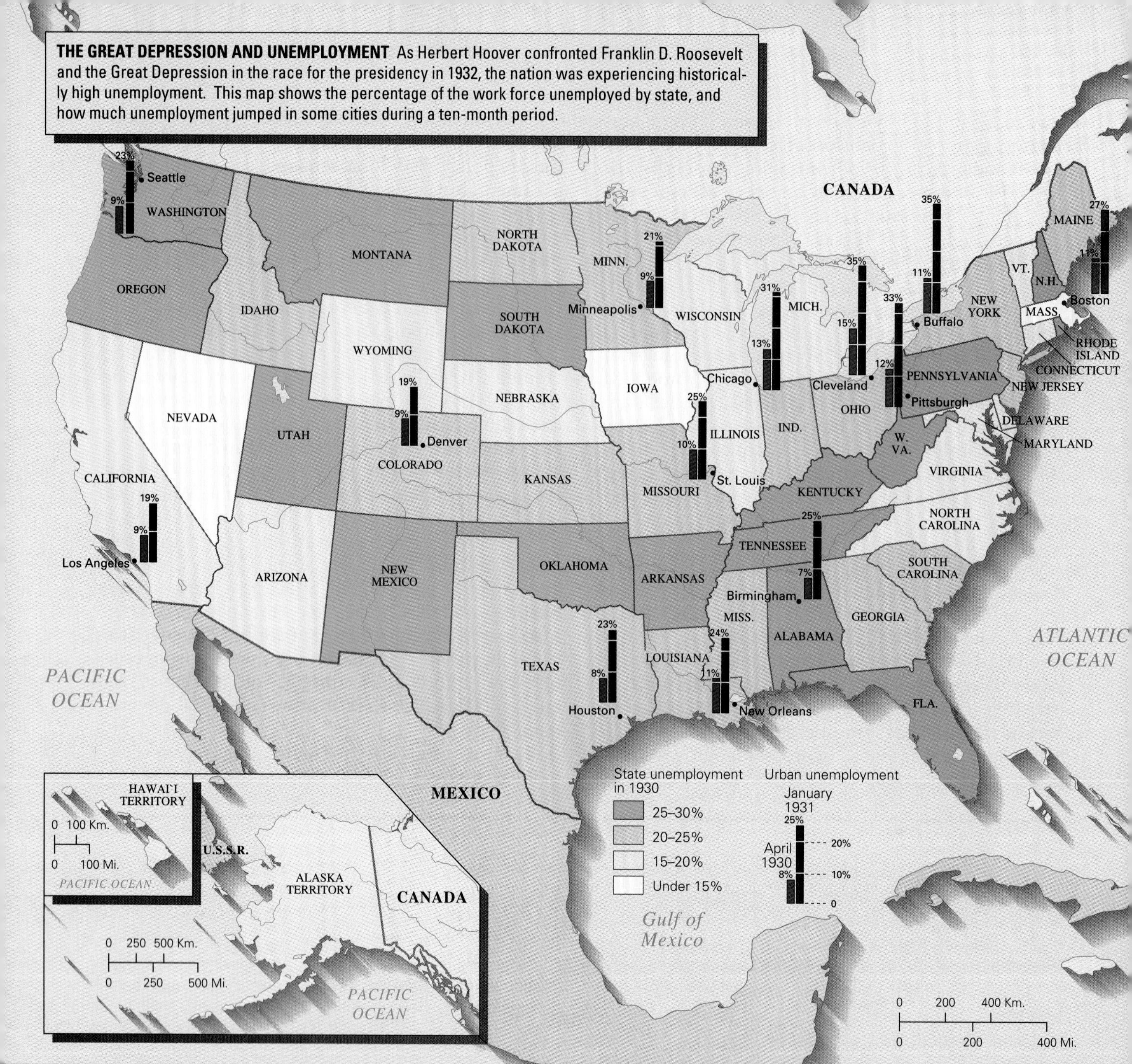

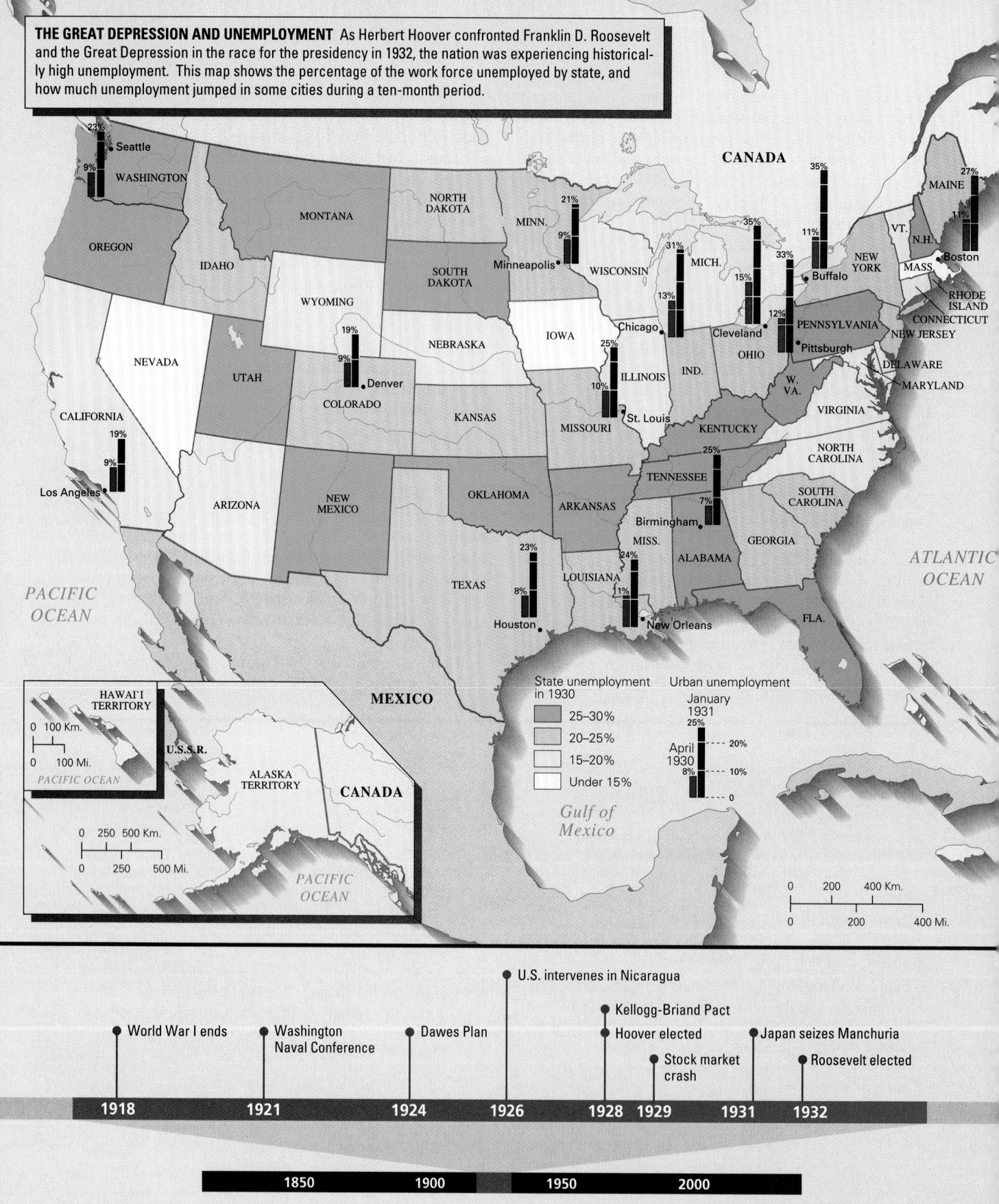

THE GREAT DEPRESSION AND UNEMPLOYMENT As Herbert Hoover confronted Franklin D. Roosevelt and the Great Depression in the race for the presidency in 1932, the nation was experiencing historically high unemployment. This map shows the percentage of the work force unemployed by state, and how much unemployment jumped in some cities during a ten-month period.

- 1918 World War I ends
- 1921 Washington Naval Conference
- 1924 Dawes Plan
- 1926 U.S. intervenes in Nicaragua
- 1928 Kellogg-Briand Pact
- 1928 Hoover elected
- 1929 Stock market crash
- 1931 Japan seizes Manchuria
- 1932 Roosevelt elected

1850 1900 1950 2000

CHAPTER 25

From Good Times to Hard Times, 1920–1932

The Diplomacy of Prosperity

- What two goals defined "independent internationalisms"?
- How did the United States' economic power enhance U.S. influence in Latin America and Europe?
- What were American expectations of the Washington meetings that focused on Japan and China? Did the outcomes match the expectations?

The Failure of Prosperity

- What expectations did Americans have in 1928 when they chose Herbert Hoover instead of Al Smith to be president?
- What major weaknesses constrained the American economy in 1929, and why were they not clearly seen?

Government and Economic Crisis

- What choices did Hoover make in dealing with the problems created by the Depression? How did his expectations about the role of government limit his choices?
- Why were the outcomes of Hoover's efforts to fight the Depression unsuccessful?
- Why did Hoover's choice to use noncoercive diplomacy produce different outcomes in Asia and Latin America?

Depression America

- Amid the social changes taking place during the Depression, what choices did Americans make that indicated the continuity of social and cultural values?
- What economic and social choices did minorities make during the Depression? What constraints did they face?
- How did women's opportunities and challenges change as an outcome of the Depression?

INTRODUCTION

E xpectations
C onstraints
C hoices
O utcomes

As the Roaring Twenties ended, the United States was reaching new levels of prosperity, fueling much of the world's economic growth. Representing the world's strongest economic power and most abundant source of capital, American business interests swept into Europe, Asia, the Middle East, and Latin America. At the same time, the United States government *chose* to avoid a direct role in world politics. In place of collective security and participation in international organizations, American policymakers from Harding to Hoover *expected* indirect and private means to promote the American interests of a stable and peaceful world.

At home, the Republican presidents of the 1920s relied less on government supervision and more on unfettered American business to build a prosperous and stable America. For Herbert Clark Hoover, often called the "Great Engineer and Humanitarian," the outlook in 1928 seemed bright. He *expected* to be elected president and to guide the continued growth of American and world prosperity through noncoercive and cooperative means. He was confident that domestic poverty would nearly disappear and international peace would prevail.

This chapter examines the failure of these *expectations,* as the Great Depression made a mockery of prosperity, leadership, and the quest for a cooperative world. Hoover faced the decline of the economy with principles and policies that he *expected* would produce continued growth. He found, however, that they only heightened disillusionment and individual hardship. Confronted with dismal realities, Hoover altered policy, but his new *choices* failed to change the course of the Depression. As individuals and society responded to the Depression, many, like Hoover, questioned their long-held values and revised their expectations, especially about the role of government. By 1932 it was obvious that the Depression had thwarted Hoover's hopes and ruined his political career. The American people *chose* change, and the *outcome* was the election of a president pledged to activism: Franklin D. Roosevelt.

The Depression also revealed the weaknesses of the *expectations* and *choices* that had governed American foreign policy throughout the 1920s. The *constraints* of economic failure dashed hopes of basing peace and international stability on economic growth and voluntary agreements. The *outcome* was an increasingly dangerous world, as nations moved to protect and promote their own economic goals at the expense of others and, in the case of Japan, of world peace.

The Diplomacy of Prosperity

- What two goals defined "independent internationalism"?
- How did the United States' economic power enhance U.S. influence in Latin America and Europe?
- What were American expectations of the Washington meetings that focused on Japan and China? Did the outcomes match the expectations?

Two realities shaped American foreign policy in the 1920s: the rejection of Woodrow Wilson's internationalism following World War I and the continuing quest for economic expansion by American business. President Warren Harding dismissed any American role in the League of Nations and refused to accept the **Treaty of Versailles** (see page 716). Anxious to restore normal relations with Germany and other defeated Central Powers, the administration and Congress simply declared the war to be over. Harding's secretary of state, Charles Evans Hughes, then quickly concluded separate peace treaties with the Central Powers. Hughes also supported efforts by American banks and corporations to expand their business activities around the world. Undamaged by the war, American firms outproduced and outtraded the rest of the world. U.S. trade amounted to 30 percent of the world's total, and American firms produced more than 70 percent

Treaty of Versailles Treaty signed at Versailles in France in 1919 that ended the war with Germany and created the League of Nations.

CHRONOLOGY

A New Era

1921–1922 Washington Naval Conference
Nine Power Pact

1921–1928 5,000 rural banks close in the Midwest and South

1922 Fordney-McCumber Tariff

1923 France occupies the Ruhr Valley

1924 Dawes Plan
U.S. forces withdraw from Dominican Republic

1926 United States intervenes in Nicaragua

1927 Peace of Titiapa
Augusto Sandino begins guerilla war in Nicaragua

1928 Kellogg-Briand Pact
Herbert Hoover elected president

1929 Agricultural Marketing Act
Stock market crash

1929–1933 4,000 U.S. banks fail
90,000 American businesses fail

1930 Rafael Trujillo seizes power in Dominican Republic
Hawley-Smoot Tariff

1931 Japan seizes Manchuria
Mexican repatriation begins
Scottsboro Nine convicted

1932 U.S. forces begin withdrawal from Nicaragua
United States announces Stimson Doctrine
Glass-Steagall Banking Act
Federal Home Loan Bank Act
Reconstruction Finance Corporation
Emergency Relief Division of Reconstruction Finance Corporation created
Milo Reno forms Farmers' Holiday Association
Bonus Army marches to Washington
Franklin D. Roosevelt elected president

1933 Unemployment reaches 25 percent
Japan withdraws from League of Nations
Drought turns Midwest into Dust Bowl

1934 U.S. forces withdraw from Haiti
Anastasio Somoza murders Sandino

1936 Somoza becomes president of Nicaragua

of the world's oil and almost 50 percent of the world's coal and steel. American bankers loaned billions of dollars to other nations, expanding the global economy.

Because neither Harding nor Coolidge had any expertise or interest in foreign affairs, they deferred making and implementing policy to their secretaries of state: Hughes and Frank Kellogg, respectively. Both were capable men interested in developing American business and influence abroad through "independent internationalism." Independent internationalism had two central thrusts: avoidance of political and international responsibilities—sometimes called **isolationism**—and expansion of economic opportunities overseas. As secretary of commerce for both Harding and Coolidge, Herbert Hoover was involved in promoting American business activities worldwide. In Asia, the Commerce and State Departments encouraged private American investments in Japan and China. In the Middle East, the United States worked hard to overcome British opposition and provide openings for American oil companies seeking drilling rights in Iran,

isolationism Sentiment widespread during the 1920s and 1930s that the United States should avoid political, diplomatic, and military entanglements with other nations.

Iraq, the Persian Gulf region, and Saudi Arabia. Successes in Asia and the Middle East were limited, but efforts to expand the American economic position in Latin America and Europe were quite successful.

The United States and Latin America

The Monroe Doctrine, direct American investments, control of the Panama Canal, and, when necessary, the use of direct armed intervention all projected U.S. influence throughout Latin America (see Map 25.1). When President Harding took office in 1921, the United States had troops stationed in Panama, Haiti, the Dominican Republic, and Nicaragua. During the presidential campaign, Harding had criticized Wilson's "bayonet rule" in Haiti and the Dominican Republic as too costly and had expressed his intention to end the American occupation of those adjoining nations. The withdrawal of American troops proceeded slowly, however, because Harding, Coolidge, and Hoover did not want anti-American governments to seize power after they left. To ensure continued American influence and local governments that could keep order, Americans maintained controls over national finances and installed American-trained national guards to act as each nation's police force. With such precautions in place, American troops left the Dominican Republic in 1924, Nicaragua in 1932, and Haiti in 1934. In the Dominican Republic and in Haiti, the United States held on to control of the customhouse and import-tax revenues until the 1940s.

When American troops withdrew from the Dominican Republic and Haiti, they left better roads, improved sanitation systems, governments favorable to the United States, and well-equipped national guards. But years of occupation had not advanced educational systems, national economies, or the standard of living for most native people. In Haiti, social divisions were made worse by American-imposed segregation and favoritism toward the minority, light-colored **mulattos** who were given charge of the economic and political structure. Nor did the United States promote the cause of democracy, favoring stability over freedom even if it meant accepting dictators like Rafael Trujillo, who seized power in the Dominican Republic in 1930 and ruled the country brutally until his death in 1961.

In Nicaragua, American forces sent by President Taft in 1916 (see page 696) left in 1925, only to be reintroduced in mid-1926 by President Coolidge to protect the Nicaraguan government after a civil war broke out. Coolidge also sent Henry L. Stimson to negotiate an agreement between the major warring groups. The **Peace of Titiapa** (1927) ended most of the fighting, leaving only followers of **Augusto Sandino** continuing the war. Sandino, a nationalist who wanted to see Nicaragua free of American influence, rejected the Peace of Titiapa. Vowing to continue the war until all American forces were out of Nicaragua, Sandino fought a guerrilla war through 1933. When the United States finally withdrew its forces from Nicaragua in 1933, it left an American-equipped and -trained national guard to maintain order. In 1934, Nicaraguan president Juan Bautista Sacasa and **Anastasio Somoza,** his nephew and commander of the Guardia Nacional, arranged a peace conference with the rebel. After a farewell dinner, Somoza ordered Sandino and his aides seized and executed. Somoza next turned against Sacasa and in 1936, using the national guard as a political weapon, ensured his own election as president. Anastasio Somoza ruled either directly or through puppet presidents until his assassination in 1956. His family remained in power until 1979, when rebels calling themselves Sandinistas—after their hero Sandino—drove the Somozas out of Nicaragua.

Elsewhere in Latin America, the 1920s saw American interventions of another sort—not military but commercial. Throughout Central America, American firms like the United Fruit Company purchased thousands of acres of land for plantations on which to grow tropical fruits, especially bananas. In Venezuela and Colombia, American oil companies, with State Department help, successfully negotiated profitable contracts for drilling rights, pushing aside European oil companies like Royal Dutch Shell and British Petroleum. U.S. investments in Latin America rose from nearly $2 billion in 1919 to over $3.5 billion in 1929.

mulatto A person of mixed black and white ancestry.

Peace of Titiapa Agreement negotiated by Henry L. Stimson in 1927 that sought to end factional fighting in Nicaragua.

Augusto Sandino Nicaraguan guerrilla leader who successfully resisted Nicaraguan and American troops in a rebellion from 1925 to 1933; murdered following a peace conference in 1934 at the orders of Anastasio Somoza.

Anastasio Somoza General who established a military dictatorship in Nicaragua in 1933, deposed his uncle to become president in 1934, and ruled the country for two decades, amassing a personal fortune and suppressing all opposition.

♦ **MAP 25.1 The United States and Latin America, 1919–1939** As this map shows, between the two world wars, the United States continued to play an active role in promoting its interests throughout Central and South America and the Caribbean. In some cases, as in Nicaragua in the 1920s, this included military intervention, but during the 1920s and the terms of Hoover and Roosevelt, political and economic pressures replaced military force as the primary means to protect U.S. interests.

♦ During the 1920s, American businesses greatly expanded their operations overseas. In Latin America, corporations such as United Fruit Company oversaw a wide-range of enterprises, from running shiplines to growing bananas. Here, recently picked bananas begin their journey from the field to American homes. *Benson Latin American Collection, University of Texas at Austin.*

Oil also played a key role in American relations with Mexico and nearly led to armed American intervention. Following the Mexican Revolution (see pages 696–698), the Mexican constitution of 1917 limited foreign ownership, and Mexico moved to **nationalize** all of its subsurface resources, including oil (see Map 25.1). The United States, supported by American businessmen, objected strongly, especially to the nationalization of oil. By 1925, American oil men and some members of the Coolidge administration were calling for military action to protect American oil interests in northern Mexico from "bolshevism." To resolve the dispute, Coolidge sent Dwight W. Morrow—a college friend—as ambassador to Mexico with instructions "to keep us out of war with Mexico." Morrow understood Mexican nationalism and pride, knew some Spanish, and clearly appreciated Mexico and its people. He cultivated a personal relationship with Mexican president Plutarco Calles, which reduced tensions and delayed Mexico's nationalization of existing oil properties until 1938.

America and the European Economy

While World War I was shattering most of Europe physically and economically, the United States was climbing to unprecedented economic heights and emerged as the world's leading creditor nation. After the war, the United States sought to expand exports and restrict imports. High tariffs inched higher throughout the 1920s. In 1922, the **Fordney-McCumber Tariff** set records in protective rates for most industrial goods imported into the United States. The effect not only limited European imports but also made it difficult for Europe to acquire the dollars needed to repay war debts to the United States. When Britain, France, and Italy asked that the United States forgive their war debts, Coolidge reportedly replied, "They hired the money, didn't they," and demanded full payment with interest.

While Harding and Coolidge sought debt repayment, Secretary of State Hughes and Secretary of Commerce Hoover worked to expand American economic interests in Europe, especially Germany. They believed that if Germany recovered economically and was able to pay its $33 billion war reparations, other European nations would recover as well and repay their war debts. With government encouragement, over $4 billion in American investments flowed into Europe, doubling the total American investment there by the end of the decade. General Motors purchased Opel, a German automobile firm. Ford built the largest automobile factory outside the United States, in England, and constructed a tractor factory in the Soviet Union.

Even with the infusion of American business capital, Germany could not keep up with its reparations burden and in 1923 failed to make its payments to France and Belgium. France responded by sending troops to occupy the **Ruhr Valley** of Germany, a key economic region, igniting an international emergency. Hughes sent Chicago banker Charles G. Dawes to Europe to negotiate a plan to restore the payments and renew progress toward economic stability. Under the **Dawes Plan,** American bankers

nationalize To convert an industry or enterprise from private to government ownership and control.

Fordney-McCumber Tariff Tariff passed by Congress in 1922 to protect domestic production from foreign competitors; it raised tariff rates to record levels and provoked foreign tariff reprisals.

Ruhr Valley Region surrounding the Ruhr River in northwestern Germany, which contained many major industrial cities and valuable coal mines.

Dawes Plan Plan for collecting World War I reparations from Germany; it scheduled annual payments and stabilized German currency.

loaned $2.5 billion to Germany for economic development, and the Germans promised to pay $2 billion in reparations to the Europeans. The Europeans, in turn, paid $2.5 billion in war debts to the United States. This circular flow of capital was the butt of jokes at the time, but the remedy worked fairly well until 1929, when the Depression ended nearly all loans and payments.

Although committed to independent internationalism, American policymakers understood that international cooperation was the only means to achieve some American goals and solve some international problems. On such matters, the United States was willing to cooperate with other nations, sign treaties, and play an active role, but only with the understanding that compliance was voluntary. Disarmament was such an issue. The destruction caused by World War I had spurred pacifism and calls for disarmament. Disarmament, advocates urged, would reduce the number of weapons and military spending, and might even allow lower taxes. In the United States support for arms cuts was widespread and vocal, as proponents pressed Harding to trim military budgets and take the initiative in world disarmament efforts. In early 1921, Senator William E. Borah of Idaho suggested an international conference to reduce the size of the world's navies. Fearing that cumbersome naval expenditures would prevent tax cuts, Secretary of the Treasury Andrew Mellon and many congressmen strongly supported the idea. In November 1921, Harding invited the major naval powers to Washington for discussions on reducing "the crushing burdens of military and naval establishments."

But pacifism and reducing military spending were not the sole factors favorable to naval disarmament. Other reasons reflected American concerns about China and Japan. Tied for first in naval strength, the United States and Britain had no desire to expand their navies. But Japan, the third-place naval power, seemed inclined to continue its naval buildup. Americans also worried about growing Japanese pressures on China that could endanger Chinese territory and the Open Door policy that allowed the United States to trade throughout the country. To deal with the Japanese, Harding and Hughes were willing to reject isolationism and host international discussions with the primary objectives to limit the size of navies and to ensure the status quo in China. If successful, the meetings could move the world closer to disarmament, limit Japanese naval expansion, and protect China.

When the naval powers assembled for the **Washington Naval Conferences,** Hughes shocked delegates with a radical proposal that called for participants to scrap nearly 2 million tons of warships, primarily battleships. He also called for a ten-year ban on naval construction and for limits to the size of navies, based on a tonnage ratio that would keep the Japanese navy behind the British and American navies. Hughes put forth a ratio of 5 to 5 to 3 for Britain, the United States, and Japan. Italy and France were allocated smaller ratios—1.67 each. "Cadillac, Cadillac, Ford," one observer quipped. Hughes's plan generated immediate favor among the American public and most of the nations attending—but not Japan. The Japanese called the ratio a national insult and demanded equality. Discussions dragged on for two months until the Japanese finally agreed—as Hughes knew they would. Having broken the Japanese diplomatic code, Hughes knew that Tokyo had instructed delegates to concede if Hughes held firm.

When the conference ended in February 1922, nine treaties were generated among the participating nations. The United States, Britain, Japan, France, and Italy agreed to build no more **capital ships** for ten years and abide by the ratio for such ships. A British observer commented that Hughes had sunk more British ships in one speech "than all the admirals of the world have sunk in . . . centuries." The powers also agreed to prohibit the use of poison gas and not attack one another's Asian possessions. The **Nine Power Pact,** concluded at the same time, affirmed support for the sovereignty and territorial boundaries of China and guaranteed equal commercial access to China—the Open Door.

Hughes rightfully considered the two meetings successful, although critics complained that the agreements included no provisions for enforcement

Washington Naval Conference International conference that in 1921–1922 produced a series of agreements to limit naval armaments and prevent conflict in the Far East and the Pacific.

capital ships Generally, a navy's largest, most heavily armed ships; at the Washington Naval Conference, ships weighing over 10,000 tons and using guns with at least an 8-inch bore were classified as capital ships.

Nine Power Pact Agreement signed in 1922 by Britain, France, Italy, Japan, the United States, China, the Netherlands, Portugal, and Belgium to recognize China and affirm the Open Door policy.

♦ In an era of isolationism, the United States hosted its first major international conference, the Washington Naval Conference, to limit the naval arms race and protect its interests in China. At the center of the conference was Secretary of State Charles Evan Hughes (pictured here), who shocked everyone by asking for major reductions in naval strength. *Brown Brothers.*

and that smaller naval ships, including submarines, were not even considered. As it turned out, the Washington Naval Conference was the only successful disarmament conference of the 1920s. Other attempts to reduce naval and land forces had mixed outcomes. After a failure in 1927 to limit the number of smaller naval vessels, Britain, the United States, and Japan established a series of ratios at the 1930 London Conference similar to those of the Washington Naval Conference—for cruisers and destroyers. That was the last positive stroke. Thereafter, competition reigned: by the mid-1930s, Japan's demands for naval equality ended British and American cooperation and spurred renewed naval construction by all three powers.

Many Americans and Europeans applauded the achievements of the Washington Naval Conference but wanted to go even further. They sought total disarmament and a repudiation of war. In 1923, Senator Borah introduced a resolution in the Senate to outlaw war. It failed but the idea remained active, and in 1927 French Foreign Minister Aristide Briand hoped to use the concept to establish a treaty of friendship with the United States. He suggested a French-American pact to formally outlaw war between France and the United States, privately hoping that such an agreement would commit the United States to aid France if attacked. Secretary of State Kellogg wanted to avoid any such commitment and deflected the proposal by suggesting a multinational statement opposing war. By expanding the number of nations involved, Kellogg removed any hint of an American commitment to aid any nation under attack. Briand was left no choice but to agree, and the Pact of Paris, or **Kellogg-Briand Pact,** was signed on August 27, 1928, by the United States and fourteen other nations, including Britain, France, Germany, Italy, and Japan. Each renounced war "as an instrument of national policy" and agreed to settle disputes by peaceful means. Eventually sixty-four nations signed the resolution expressing hope for world peace. But the pact included no enforcement provisions, and nearly every **signatory** maintained its right to defend itself and its possessions.

By the end of 1928, American independent internationalism seemed to be a success. American business investments and loans were fueling an expansive world economy and adding to American prosperity. Avoiding entangling alliances, the United States had acted to protect its Asian and Pacific interests against Japan while promoting the idealism of world disarmament and peace. In Latin America, it had moderated its interventionist image by with-

Kellogg-Briand Pact Treaty signed in 1928 by fifteen nations, including Britain, France, Germany, the United States, and Japan, renouncing war as a means of solving international disputes.

signatory One who has signed a treaty or other document.

drawing American troops in the Caribbean, not applying force in Mexico, and trying to mediate a peace among warring factions in Nicaragua. Foreign policies based on economic expansion and noncoercive diplomacy appeared to be establishing a promising era of cooperation and peace in world affairs.

The Failure of Prosperity

- What expectations did Americans have in 1928 when they chose Herbert Hoover instead of Al Smith to be president?
- What major weaknesses constrained the American economy in 1929, and why were they not clearly seen?

In August 1927, Calvin Coolidge called reporters from his vacation spot in South Dakota and told them, "I do not choose to run in 1928." Coolidge's announcement stunned the country and his party. Former Secretary of Commerce Herbert Hoover immediately declared his candidacy. He seemed the ideal candidate, representing what most believed was best about America: individual effort and honestly earned success.

A Quaker farm boy from Iowa, Hoover had grown up among thrifty, self-sufficient farmers who believed that hard work was the only way forward. Graduating from Stanford University with a degree in geology, he worked "like a dog," taking jobs in Australia and China. He formed his own mining engineering company in 1908, and by 1914 his fortune was estimated to be more than $4 million. Having reached the top in business, Hoover wanted to apply his belief in hard work and sound planning to public service. So when World War I broke out, he offered his organizational skills and energy to help provide relief to Belgium through the Committee for the Relief of Belgium. Called by some "The Great Humanitarian," Hoover traveled across wartorn Europe seeking funds and materials for Belgium. "This man is not to be stopped anywhere under any circumstance," the Germans noted on his passport. When the United States entered the war, President Wilson named him to head the U.S. Food Administration (see page 706). By war's end, Hoover was an international hero.

The 1928 Election

Receiving the Republican nomination before thousands of supporters gathered in the Stanford football stadium, Hoover sounded the theme of this candidacy: American prosperity. "We in America today are nearer to the final triumph over poverty than ever before. . . . The poorhouse is vanishing among us," he boldly announced.

The Democrats nominated Al Smith, four-time governor of New York. Like Hoover, Smith was a self-made man. But unlike his opponent, who had gone to Stanford, Smith had received his education on the streets of the Lower East Side of New York City and as part of Tammany Hall, the Democratic machine that ran the city. As a reform-minded, progressive governor, Smith had streamlined government, improved government efficiency, and supported legislation to set a minimum wage and maximum hours of work and to establish state ownership of hydroelectric plants.

Despite his progressive record, Smith had a number of liabilities that allowed Republicans to make him the main issue of the election. Opponents attacked his Catholic religion, his big-city background, his opposition to Prohibition, his Tammany connections, and even his New York accent. Anti-Catholic sentiment burned hotly in many parts of the country, often fanned by the remnants of the Klan, whose fiery crosses marked the route of Smith's campaign train in some areas. Evangelist Billy Sunday called Smith supporters "damnable whiskey politicians, bootleggers, crooks, pimps and businessmen who deal with them."

For many voters, the choice in 1928 seemed to be between a candidate who represented hard work and the pious values of small-town, old-stock, Protestant America and a candidate who represented urban upheaval, machine politics, foreigners, and Catholics.

Hoover won easily, with 58 percent of the popular vote, owing in large part to the prosperity Republicans claimed as their accomplishment. Although Smith's religion and position against Prohibition cost him support in the South, those factors helped Democrats make important gains in northern cities. In 1920 and 1924, the twelve largest cities had voted Republican, but in 1928 only one, Los Angeles, voted heavily Republican. As the nation became more urban, the strength of Democrats in cities surfaced as a potential political advantage.

The first president born west of the Mississippi River, Hoover came to the presidency with some definite ideas about how the nation and its foreign affairs should be run. More than Harding and Coolidge, he meant to be an active president, creating a "New Day" for America at home and overseas.

♦ The 1928 presidential election offered Americans a clear choice in candidates. In one corner was Al Smith, product of the streets of New York, Roman Catholic, and opposed to prohibition. Opposing him was Iowa-born Herbert Hoover, the "Great Engineer and Humanitarian," a self-made millionaire, and a proven administrator. Although he gave only seven campaign speeches, Hoover won easily. *Collection of David J. and Janice L. Frent.*

Hoover's goal was to promote economic and social growth through the concept of **associationalism**—voluntary cooperation among otherwise competing groups. The role of government, he believed, was to promote cooperation without resorting to punitive measures like antitrust laws. He warned that once government, especially the federal government, stepped in to solve society's problems directly, the people gave up their freedom and the government became the problem. Of course, Hoover recognized that problems existed and that the federal government had a responsibility to help find solutions. The key word for Hoover, though, was *help:* the government should help but not solve. In foreign affairs, he and his secretary of state, Henry L. Stimson, trod a similar path, following closely the economic and noncoercive policies that had characterized the 1920s.

Origins of the Depression

When Herbert Hoover took office, rising stock prices, shiny new cars, and rapidly expanding suburbs seemed to verify his observation about "the final triumph over poverty." But behind the rush for radios, homes, and vacuum cleaners lay several economic weaknesses. The prosperity of the 1920s depended in large part on a few major industries such as construction, automobiles, and consumer goods. Other important sectors of the economy—textiles, railroads, steel, and iron, for example—were barely making a profit, while farming and mining were suffering steady losses. Farmers watched the demand for their goods shrink and their income and property values decline to about half of their wartime highs (see Table 25.1). Throughout the Midwest and South, rural banks closed—five thousand between 1921 and 1928—adding to the crisis in agriculture. Caught in an economic squeeze of lower profits and increasing production costs, hundreds of thousands of people left farms throughout the 1920s.

But agriculture's troubles were only part of the origins of the **Great Depression.** Other important causes were the maldistribution of wealth and overproduction of goods. For the upper and middle classes and for some industrial workers, the 1920s was a decade of prosperity. Corporate profits rose 62 percent and dividends 65 percent. Wages increased nearly 11 percent while prices on many popular consumer goods fell. National income jumped from $65 billion to $83 billion, and total savings soared from $15 billion to $35 billion. By 1929, the nation had 513 families with annual incomes over $1 million, and the top fifth of the population controlled nearly 60 percent of the nation's wealth. But such statistics covered some hard realities. Seventy percent of American families earned less than what the **Brookings Institute** determined was an adequate income—$2,500 a year—and 80 percent had no savings. Most people were exhausting nearly all of their monthly income and increasingly put what they could on credit. For nearly three-fourths of the pop-

associationalism President Hoover's belief that the government could foster economic and social progress by promoting voluntary cooperation among competing groups and interests.

Great Depression The years 1929 to 1941 in the United States, during which the economy was in a severe decline and millions of people were out of work.

Brookings Institute A nonprofit, nonpartisan organization founded by Robert Brookings in 1916 that studies government, economic, and international issues.

TABLE 25.1 Drop in Agriculture Prices, 1928–1932

	1928	1929	1932
Wheat	$1.37/bushel	$1.02/bushel	.37/bushel
Cotton	.19/lb	.17/lb	.07/lb
Corn	.92/bushel	.91/bushel	.31/bushel
Beef	9.45/100lb	9.55/100lb	4.35/100lb

Source: Data from U.S. Department of Commerce, *Historical Statistics of the United States, Colonial Times to 1970,* Part 1 (Washington, D.C.: U.S. Government Printing Office, 1975), pp. 510–511, 517, 519.

ulation any change in employment, credit policy, or paycheck meant economic hard times.

Maldistribution of wealth meant there was too much money in too few hands to fuel growth through consumer spending. But there also was too much production. Responding to the growth of the 1920s, companies were producing more goods even though the public's ability to purchase was declining. Wanting to deplete their surpluses, factories cut production and laid off workers. By 1929, even the boom industries were showing signs of weakness caused by the decline in spending. Decreasing construction starts in 1926 had a rippling effect. Furniture companies expecting an unlimited market had produced far too much and were forced to cut their labor force to shave production costs. Similar stories held for other industries, especially those making consumer goods.

The laying off of workers might not have been so necessary if corporations had been willing to lower prices or able to sell their products overseas. But with two hundred major corporations controlling over half of the nation's wealth and dominating the production of most goods, there was little competitive pressure to substantially lower prices. Nor was the overseas market able to take up the surplus left by the shrinking American market. On assuming office, President Hoover tried to stimulate trade by lowering some tariffs as much as 50 percent. Most Republicans, however, wanted higher not lower tariffs.

The Stock Market Plunge

Credit contributed significantly to consumer buying, added to the vision of American prosperity, and helped to generate the boom in the stock market through margin buying (see page 734). The desire to invest in the stock market fed a speculative fervor that pushed stock prices higher and higher, until by 1929 the price of many stocks had little relationship to the dividends the stocks paid or the actual worth of the company they represented. Finally in the fall of 1929, the realities of wages, credit, inflated stock prices, and the slowing American economy collided.

When Americans awoke on the morning of Thursday, October 24, 1929, no one realized they would experience one of those days that would change their lives and their nation. It was business as usual as men and women prepared to go to work. In the Midwest, people braced themselves against a frigid, unseasonable ice and snow storm. Not being shareholders, most Americans hardly noticed the rise and fall of stock prices on Wall Street. Instead, many followed the lurid story of millionaire theater owner Alexander Pantagas, on trial for assaulting a 17-year-old dancer who had wanted to audition for his show. (He was found guilty.)

Despite the lack of public concern, the events that occurred in the New York Stock Exchange on October 24, 1929, would have profound consequences for all Americans. On that morning, later called **Black Thursday,** the bottom suddenly fell out of the stock market. Immediately, no one wanted to buy stocks and everyone clamored to sell. As buyers failed to materialize, the selling price and the value of stocks plummeted. By 11:30, the ticker tape that relayed

Black Thursday October 24, 1929, when the stock market fell dramatically in what proved to be the beginning of the Great Depression.

♦ The day the stock market crashed, the entire nation suddenly became aware of Wall Street. The collapse of the stock market historically signals the beginning of the greatest depression in American history. Despite the efforts of Hoover and Roosevelt, it was only the economic activity generated by World War II that revived the economy. *"Black Friday: Richard Whitney and the Stock Exchange," 1939 by Edward Laning. Collection of John P. Axelrod.*

stock prices across the nation ran nearly two and a half hours behind, further contributing to the sense of panic. By noon, the stock exchange was a frenzied sea of waving arms, raised fists, and screaming voices. Outside, a large crowd gathered in what one observer called "horrified" disbelief, giving off a subdued murmur. In brokerage offices across the country, there was less calm. Brokers rushed to place sell orders. No refuge was untouched by the panic: in the mid-Atlantic, aboard the passenger liner *Berengaria,* cosmetics mogul Helena Rubenstein watched stock prices fall, and when she finally sold her fifty thousand shares of Westinghouse Company, she had lost more than $1 million.

When the exchange closed for lunch, New York's financial leaders hurriedly met to deal with the panic and try to restore confidence. They were able to do so—briefly. Prices recovered somewhat. Then on Monday, October 28, they dipped, and on Black Tuesday, they plunged. This time there was no recovery. Between September and mid-November, the *New York Times* **industrials** fell from 469 to 221 (reaching 58 by mid-1932). Other stocks likewise plummeted—RCA fell from 101 to 28, Montgomery Ward from 138 to 49, Union Carbide from 138 to 59. Hundreds of brokers and speculators were ruined. By mid-November, stories circulated about New York hotel clerks asking guests whether they wanted rooms for sleeping or jumping. Still, politicians, economists, and businessmen voiced trust in the market and the economy. John D. Rockefeller said that he and his sons were confident and buying common stocks. Comedian Eddie Cantor quipped, "Sure, who else has any money left?"

Black Thursday was not responsible for the Great Depression, but it probably pushed a weakened economy into a depression. Since 1927, the overall economy had been slowing down and unemployment had been inching upward, resulting in decreasing consumption. Like much of the public, many corporations were in debt and some even had borrowed in order to invest in the market. When the market crashed, brokers and banks that had invested and lent money found their resources dwindling. They demanded payment of loans, and as people and corporations defaulted on loans, banks and lending institutions found themselves unable to cover the demands of depositors. With the failure of banks, many people in the upper and middle classes suddenly found they had little or no savings—no buffer against hard times. For those without savings, dependent on jobs and installment payments to cover debts, the crash forecast a serious economic crisis.

The stock market crash undermined economic confidence. Americans had viewed the soaring stock market as a symbol of the vigor of the economy and nation. Now, investors were wary to invest. Corporations were more ready to cut production and lay off workers. Consumers were hesitant to spend money. The impact of the stock market crash, coupled with weaknesses within the economy, resulted in the worst, longest-lasting depression in American history.

industrials Industrial stocks chosen as indicators of trends in the economy.

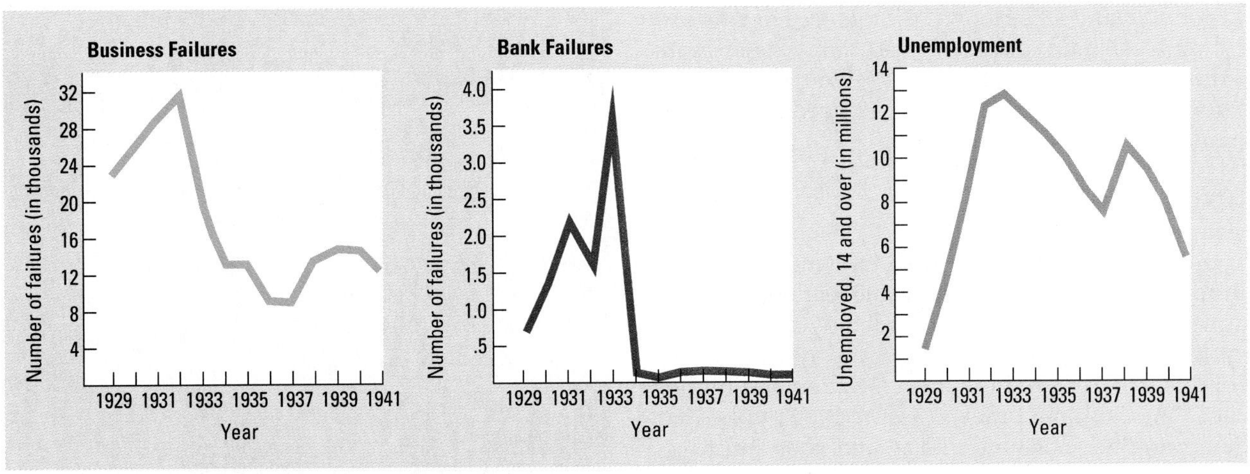

♦ **FIGURE 25.1 Charting the Economics of the Depression** Between 1929 and 1933, there was an expanding number of unemployed people seeking work, and banks and businesses closing their doors. By 1933, over 4,000 banks had failed, unemployment had reached 24.9 percent, and over 100,000 firms had closed. As the New Deal began, not only did the statistics improve, but for most Americans there was also a feeling of hope and improvement.

The effect of the stock market crash and the declining American economy had an international impact as well. The European economy had never fully recovered from the destruction of the First World War and was partly dependent on American loans and markets. Loans by American banks declined as did purchases by American corporations. To protect American business from foreign competition, in 1930 Congress passed the **Hawley-Smoot Tariff.** Though a victory for American economic nationalism, it was a catastrophe for world trade. Angered by American actions, twenty-three foreign governments raised their tariffs on American goods, further stifling world trade. By 1932, American exports had fallen to their lowest level since 1905, contributing to global depression.

By 1932, the world and American economies were in shambles. American exports had fallen to their lowest level since 1905. Stock prices were still tumbling. By mid-1932, stock in United States Steel Corporation had fallen from a precrash high of 262 to 22. General Motors stock dropped to 73, then to 8. Many companies did not survive. Between 1929 and 1933, ninety thousand businesses failed, corporate profits fell 60 percent, nine thousand banks closed (see Figure 25.1), and depositors lost $2.5 billion. As the money supply shrank, dropping by a third between 1930 and 1933, the average expenditure for goods plummeted by 45 percent. Purchases of automobiles dropped by 75 percent. At the same time, unemployment rose from 3 percent in 1929, to 9 percent in 1930, to 25 percent by 1933 (see the chapter-opening map). With the downward spiral of the economy and stock market, nearly everyone felt the effects of the Great Depression.

Government and Economic Crisis

- What choices did Hoover make in dealing with the problems created by the Depression? How did his expectations about the role of government limit his choices?
- Why were the outcomes of Hoover's efforts to fight the Depression unsuccessful?
- Why did Hoover's choice to use noncoercive diplomacy produce different outcomes in Asia and Latin America?

Within the Hoover administration, the immediate response to the plunge in stock prices was not gloom and doom but guarded optimism. Secretary of the Treasury Mellon thought the drop would strengthen the market and cleanse the economy of inflated values. He believed the government should let the

Hawley-Smoot Tariff Tariff passed by Congress in 1930 in response to the Depression, setting the highest tariff rates in U.S. history and thus undermining world trade.

economy heal itself. Hoover disagreed. He was unwilling to sit idle and let the economy deteriorate without exerting any effort to reverse the economic slide. Government, he believed, needed to play some, even if only a limited, role.

Hoover's Early Policies

As the stock market declined and the money supply shrank, Hoover called together the leaders of banking, industry, and labor. He pleaded with employers not to cut wages or production and not to lay off workers. He exhorted unions not to demand higher wages. At the same time, he assured the public that the economy was sound and would soon improve. These cooperative efforts were not successful.

When cheerleading and voluntary action failed to improve the worsening situation, public pressure grew for the federal government to take more direct action. Hoover continued to make optimistic speeches but also began to lean toward more direct government involvement. To help improve the money supply, he accepted unbalanced federal budgets to maintain government spending, and he lowered taxes and interest rates. He also convinced Congress and state and local governments to increase spending for the construction of **public works projects,** including highways, government facilities, and **Boulder Dam.** Federal, state, and local governments doubled their spending on public works, but the economy continued to worsen despite these unprecedented efforts. Increasingly, Americans blamed Hoover for their hardships. A popular jingle went

Mellon pulled the whistle
Hoover rang the bell
Wall Street gave the signal
And the country went to hell.

By the end of 1932, workers' income had dropped 40 percent and unemployment had reached an alarming 25 percent. Small industrial towns were especially hard hit. Donora, Pennsylvania, for instance, had only 277 jobs for its population of over 14,000. Many, like Donora's future baseball great, Stan Musial, left home seeking greener pastures, moving from one community to another looking for work. Most would be unsuccessful. Ed Paulson left his hometown in Montana to find work. Arriving in San Francisco, he heard of a job and at 5 A.M. dashed to the job site, only to find more than "three thousand men, carpenters, cement men, guys who knew machinery and everything else" were already there.

♦ The Great Depression produced large-scale unemployment, reaching 25 percent in 1933. This picture, titled "Unemployed," painted by Reginald Marsh effectively captured the despair of men and women seeking jobs. *"Unemployed" by Reginald Marsh, 1932. Library of Congress.*

Paulson and thousands of displaced men and women roamed the country looking for work, developing a "coyote mentality." "You were a predator," he said. "You had to be. The coyote is crafty. . . . We were coyotes in the Thirties." Private, state, and local charities, bread lines and soup kitchens, and relief agencies vainly tried to meet the needs of the millions in need. But the numbers were too overwhelming. Across the country, shantytowns, bitterly named **"Hoovervilles,"** housed the homeless.

public works projects Highways, dams, and other construction projects financed by public funds and carried out by the government.

Boulder Dam Dam on the Colorado River between Nevada and Arizona, begun during Hoover's administration and completed in 1935.

"Hooverville" Crudely built camp set up by the homeless on the fringes of a town or city during the Depression.

Farmers were among the thousands displaced. Many agricultural states like Alabama and South Dakota had unemployment rates that matched the worst of the industrial states. Agriculture had been in a depression before 1929, and the stock market crash just made things worse. Hoover responded to the agricultural crisis of the 1920s by asking Congress to create a federal Farm Board to help stabilize prices by buying agricultural products on the open market. Although conservatives attacked the plan as a leap into socialism, Congress passed the **Agricultural Marketing Act** in May 1929. The Farm Board was initially successful in supporting farm prices. The world price of wheat was 55 cents a bushel in February 1931, but because the Farm Board had bought over 257 million bushels—one-fourth of the world supply—the American price held steady at 80 cents a bushel. However, farm prices tumbled when the Farm Board ran short of funds and could no longer provide economic support. More farmers were forced into bankruptcy. About a third of all farm homesteads—60 percent in South Dakota—in 1932 were taken away from their owners by **foreclosure,** many auctioned off to the highest bidder.

Adding to their plight, farmers in the Midwest experienced searing heat and drought, and swarms of grasshoppers devoured whole fields of crops. Grasshoppers, heat, and drought laid the land bare (see Map 25.2). The region became known as the **Dust Bowl** in the 1930s, when winds whipped up clouds of dust, sometimes stretching more than 200 miles across and from 7,000 to 8,000 feet high. Dust descended on the Midwest, and winds blew more than halfway across the Atlantic what once had been topsoil. In 1938, the worst year of the disaster, over 850 million tons of topsoil were lost to erosion. Dust hung in the air and filtered into homes, covering clothing, furniture, food, everything. One reporter observed that an "uncorked jug placed on a sidewalk two hours . . . [was] found to be half filled with dust."

Declining farm prices, drought, and dust destroyed hopes, and many farmers turned to direct action. The **Farmers' Holiday Association,** led by Milo Reno, formed in 1932 in the Midwest and called on farmers to destroy their products and to resist foreclosures (see Individual Choices: Milo Reno). "When you took a man's horse and his plow away, you denied him food, you just convicted his family to starvation," recalled one farmer, who added that the "people were desperate." Angry and frequently armed, farmers used their numbers and threats of violence to ensure that foreclosed properties were sold at auction to their previous owners for a fraction of their value. One such "penny auction" returned Walter Crozier's farm in Haskins, Ohio, for a high bid of $1.90. Other farmers burned their corn, killed their livestock, and dumped milk and eggs onto the ground. Critics of the agrarian protest blamed **outside agitators,** including "international Jews, the IWW, Socialists, and Commu-

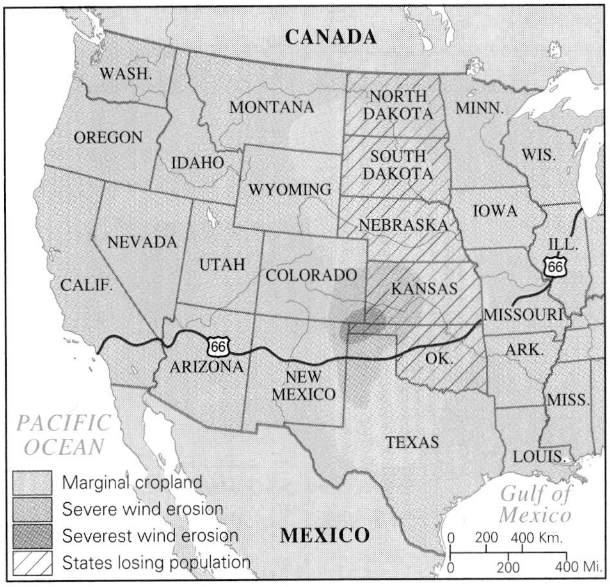

♦ **MAP 25.2 The Dust Bowl** Throughout the 1930s, sun and wind eroded millions of acres of crop land, sending tons of topsoil into the air, generating tidal waves of dust—and the Dust Bowl. This map shows the regions most affected by the Dust Bowl and loss of population, and Route 66, which many chose to travel, hoping that it would lead to a better life in California.

Agricultural Marketing Act Law passed by Congress in 1929 to stabilize farm prices; it created a Farm Board to buy crop surpluses; the price support program ended in 1931.

foreclosure Confiscation of property by a bank when mortgage payments are delinquent.

Dust Bowl Name given to the Great Plains region devastated by drought and dust storms during the 1930s.

Farmers' Holiday Association Farmers' organization led by Milo Reno of Iowa, which organized a strike in the summer of 1932 to protest the drastic decline in farm income.

outside agitator Term applied to a radical organizer who instigates protests in an area or industry where he or she does not belong.

INDIVIDUAL CHOICES

Choosing Confrontation

Milo Reno

In 1918 Milo Reno chose to become a spokesman for the farmer and organized the Farmers' Holiday Association. In 1933, he chose to reject Roosevelt's agricultural recovery program, and lost support of most farmers, who supported the president. State Historical Society of America.

Born in 1866, Milo Reno was raised in Iowa, the heartland of populism and enthusiasm for William Jennings Bryan. An ordained Disciples of Christ, Campellite minister, Reno gave up the ministry to pursue his true calling—organizing farmers for political action. He joined the Farmers' Union in 1918, dominating it until his death in 1936, and he was the driving force behind the Farmers' Holiday Association. Wearing a ten-gallon hat and flaming red necktie, Reno captured farmers' hearts with evangelical-style speeches that combined simple explanations, personalized enemies, biblical quotes, and rural wisdom.

In 1932, claiming Hoover's farm policies were driving hardworking, decent people from the land, he called for a farmers' strike. He commanded the farmers to "stay home, buy nothing, sell nothing," to force change and break "the grip of Wall Street and international bankers on government." Farmers across Iowa and neighboring states heeded his call, refusing to sell their products. In some places they erected barricades across highways to prevent farm products from reaching processors. Outside Sioux City and other midwestern towns, farmers armed with clubs and pitchforks

nists." But the protesters were homegrown and simply wanted government support for the farmer. Democrats blamed Hoover and the Farm Board for the deepening problems and promised change.

Hoover's Final Efforts

By December 1931, giving in to political pressure and a worsening economy, Hoover was moving toward more direct federal involvement. He created agencies to study unemployment and asked Congress for banking reforms, financial support for home mortgages, the creation of the **Reconstruction Finance Corporation** (1932), and higher taxes to pay for it all. In 1932, Congress responded with the **Glass-Steagall Banking Act,** which increased bank

Reconstruction Finance Corporation Organization to promote economic recovery established at Hoover's request in 1932; it provided emergency financing for banks, life insurance companies, railroads, and farm mortgage associations.

Glass-Steagall Banking Act Law passed by Congress in 1932 that expanded credit through the Federal Reserve System in order to counteract foreign withdrawals and domestic hoarding of money.

clashed with truck drivers and sheriff's deputies. By mid-August more than eighty picketers had been arrested, and fearful of further violence and arrests, Reno called a "temporary halt" to the strike.

Confrontations at the barricades gave the strike national news coverage and prompted politicians to respond to the farmers' distress. Midwestern governors listened to Farmers' Holiday spokesmen and pushed Hoover for increased support for farmers. Presidential candidate Franklin D. Roosevelt emphasized that Democrats promised farm prices "in excess of cost." Reno, like millions of other Americans, saw in Roosevelt a chance for hope, cheered his election in 1932, and waited anxiously for the New Deal to begin.

As Roosevelt assumed office, Reno and the Farmers' Holiday movement, now claiming ninety thousand members, continued to attract national attention by stopping farm foreclosures and forcing "penny auctions." Again, direct action seemed to work. Many banks and credit companies halted foreclosures, and ten states passed foreclosure "moratorium laws." But with Roosevelt in office, farmers received less public support for their activism. Many politicians and journalists linked their movement with communism, and Reno faced a hard choice. Should he continue direct action or support Roosevelt's agriculture program?

Responding to negative public opinion, Reno asked farm activists to pull back from confrontation and give Roosevelt time to implement his farm programs. Still, Reno had doubts. He disliked Henry A. Wallace as secretary of agriculture, considered Roosevelt an "enigma," and was angry when the New Deal's first agriculture program did not include cost-of-production provisions. He told a friend, "I have no faith whatever in the gestures that are being made by the administration. It is simply the same old tactic to hand the people a little measure of relief to suppress rebellion, with no intention of correcting a system that is fundamentally wrong."

In October 1933, Reno made a difficult decision. Roosevelt, he was sure, would eventually "crush all . . . independence and liberty . . . setting up a bureaucratic, autocratic, dictatorial government." So he renewed the call for a strike and stated that a third political party was the only possible solution "to clean up the stinking mess" in Washington. Most farmers, however, had begun to trust Roosevelt's promise of federal support and chose to ignore the strike calls. The spread of the federal government into agricultural affairs had halted the momentum of the farmers' protest. Increasingly out of touch with most farmers, Reno fell into periods of depression and heavy drinking until, stricken with influenza in March 1936, he checked into a sanitarium. "Tell them I'm really sick," he said. Milo Reno died on May 5, 1936.

reserves to encourage lending, and the **Federal Home Loan Bank Act,** which allowed homeowners to remortgage their homes at lower rates and payments. But it was through the Reconstruction Finance Corporation (RFC) that Hoover intended to fight the Depression, by pumping money into the economy. Using federal funds, the RFC was to provide loans to banks, **savings and loan associations,** railroads, insurance companies, and large corporations to prevent their collapse and encourage expanded operations. Hoover and his advisers believed that the money would "trickle down" to workers and the unemployed through higher wages and new jobs.

This effort by the federal government to intervene directly in the private sector and stimulate the economy was unprecedented. Conservatives called it "an experiment in socialism." Senator Burton Wheeler

Federal Home Loan Bank Act Law passed by Congress in 1932 that established twelve banks across the nation to supplement lending resources to institutions making home loans in an effort to reduce foreclosures and to stimulate the construction industry.

savings and loan association Cooperative mutual financial institutions that use funds from members to finance long-term real estate mortgages.

(Democrat from Montana) warned that RFC handouts would create a welfare state in which loans and credits eventually would be given to nearly everyone. Within five months of operation, the RFC had loaned more than $805 million, mostly to large businesses, but little relief or money seemed to be trickling down to workers. Liberal critics labeled the program "welfare for the rich" and insisted that Hoover do more for the poor and unemployed through **direct relief payments** and more public works projects.

Hoover opposed direct federal relief—the "dole"—for several basic reasons. He believed that it would be too burdensome for the federal budget and that private organizations and local government should instead distribute relief. "Where people divest themselves of local government responsibilities," he explained, "they at once lay the foundation for the destruction of their liberties." He and others also were convinced that the dole would erode the work ethic and bring about a class of idle Americans who preferred to live on relief rather than work. Still, in the spring of 1932, it was getting harder and harder for Hoover to resist congressional and public pressure to provide assistance. Finally, he agreed to create the Emergency Relief Division within the RFC, providing $300 million to lend to states for relief.

Relief grants, however, never were enough to match needs. Headed by a conservative board of directors, the RFC loaned relief money very cautiously. By the end of 1932, the RFC had spent only 10 percent of its relief fund. Further, states and cities whose budgets were already overstrained hesitated to increase their debt by borrowing more. West Virginia, for example, received a grant of more than $9 million for a seven-month period, which provided only $10 a month for each needy family.

The patience of many Americans seemed at an end by the summer of 1932. The Farmers' Holiday movement was spreading across the Midwest, and twenty thousand unemployed veterans, the Bonus Expeditionary Force, were marching toward Washington. The **Bonus Army** was coming to the capital to lobby for the Patman bill, which stipulated early payment of the veterans' bonus originally scheduled to be paid in 1945. Against the warnings of advisers, Hoover allowed the Bonus marchers to enter the District of Columbia and even ensured that tents, clothing, medicine, and food were available as the marchers set up their Hooverville across from Congress in Anacostia Flats.

Hoover respected the veterans' right to assemble and lobby, but when the Senate rejected the Patman bill, the president thought the marchers should go home. More than half left, but nearly ten thousand stayed behind at Anacostia Flats or in condemned buildings within Washington. When the police attempted to clear the buildings, nearly five thousand veterans and eight hundred police clashed. Two Bonus marchers were killed. When the police withdrew, Hoover turned to the army to evict the squatters. A force under army chief of staff General Douglas MacArthur used sabers, rifles, tear gas, and fixed bayonets to drive the veterans from the abandoned buildings. MacArthur then proceeded to Anacostia Flats, where in a one-sided fight the soldiers forced the veterans and their families from their huts and tents, which were set afire. More than one hundred veterans were injured in the melee, but rumors quickly swelled the number and added several deaths, including that of a baby who reportedly died from the tear gas. The rumors intensified the public's angry reaction. Hoover defended the eviction and stated that most of the marchers were Communists.

Whatever slim chance Hoover had for re-election died at the "Battle of Anacostia Flats." On hearing of the forced eviction of the marchers, the governor of New York, Franklin D. Roosevelt crowed, "This will elect me."

The Diplomacy of Depression

When Hoover entered the presidency, the world appeared stable and peaceful. Hoover intended to continue the foreign policies of his predecessors, using economic and noncoercive means to protect American interests and promote world prosperity.

Since the days of Theodore Roosevelt, Latin Americans had accused the United States of being a "new Rome," of creating an empire based on money rather than territory. When Hoover took office in 1929, Latin Americans were adamant in opposing the Roosevelt Corollary (see page 657) and demanding the withdrawal of American troops from Haiti and Nicaragua (see Map 25.1). Hoover promised to continue removing troops, and the made public a memorandum written by Assistant Secretary of State J. Reuben Clark that stated that the Monroe Doctrine did not give the United States the right to

direct relief payments Payments that government agencies make directly to the poor and unemployed.

Bonus Army Unemployed World War I veterans who marched to Washington in 1932 to demand early payment of a promised bonus; Congress refused and the army evicted protesters who remained.

♦ The sign in front of the "Bonus Dugout" reads, "We have come to collect the gratitude that was promised us for participating in the World War." They received neither gratitude nor the bonus. Instead, Hoover commented: "Thank God we still have a government that knows how to deal with a mob." *Library of Congress.*

intervene in Latin American affairs. Hoover let American investors and bankers know that they should not expect the government to come to their rescue when they found themselves or their investments threatened. Overall during Hoover's administration, relations between Latin America and the United States improved greatly.

Elsewhere, however, Hoover's efforts to promote prosperity and peace abroad came to little. And at home, growing numbers of Americans denounced even a cooperative role for the United States in world affairs. As the Depression became entrenched, so did isolationism. Most Americans were far more concerned about keeping their jobs and homes than about international affairs. Many, including Hoover, blamed a major part of the country's economic woes on the Europeans. Republican Senator George W. Norris of Nebraska publicly linked his state's farm foreclosures with the events spawned by the Europeans and the First World War. He urged the United States to look out for its own interests and let Europe take care of itself.

If most Americans reacted to the Depression by spurning foreign involvements, the opposite was true in Japan. Japan relied heavily on international trade for its economic growth and its food supply, and as the Depression and shrinking world trade weakened its economy, calls arose among the Japanese for their government to protect national interests. Rejecting most Western values and free trade, many nationalists advocated a Japanese sphere of influence, or empire, and looked hungrily toward Manchuria.

Situated north and west of Japanese-controlled Korea, Manchuria was rich in iron and coal, accounted for 95 percent of Japanese overseas investment, and supplied large amounts of vital foodstuffs to the island nation. More important, the Japanese maintained a military presence in Manchuria to protect Japanese interests. Conflict was increasing between the Japanese military authorities in Manchuria and the government of Jiang Jieshi (Chiang Kai-shek), which was seeking to reassert China's control there. In September 1931, fearful of growing Chinese power, a small group of young, anti-Western Japanese army officers executed a plan to establish Japanese rule over the region. Members of the Japanese Manchurian army, the Guandong, blew up a section of track of the Southern Manchurian Railroad and blamed the Chinese. Then, without informing the civilian government of Japan, the Guandong attacked Chinese forces and took control of the province (see Map 25.3).

World reaction was one of shock and eventual condemnation but little else. The League of Nations sheepishly called for peace and appointed a com-

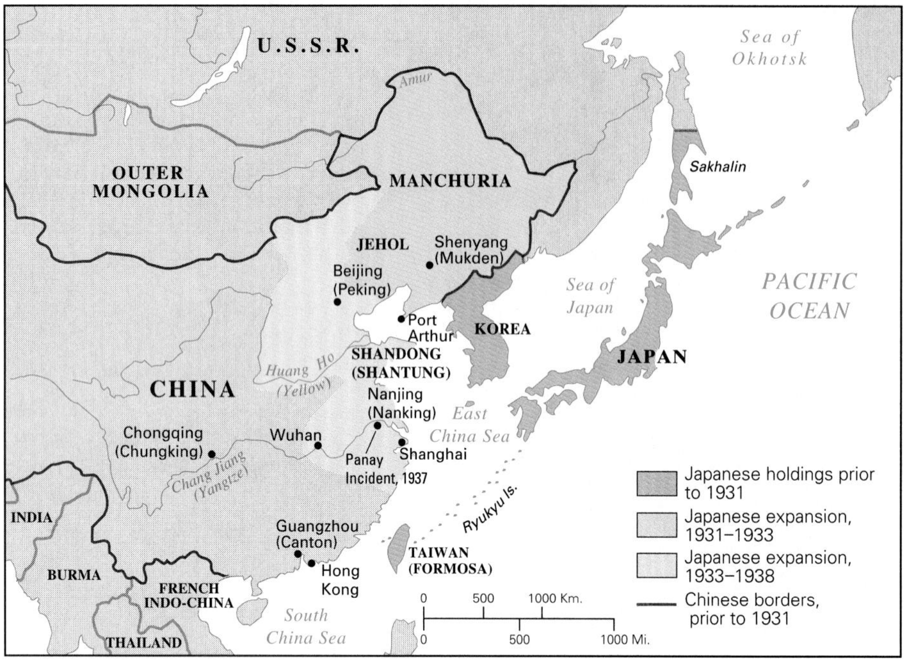

♦ **MAP 25.3 Japanese Expansion, 1931–1938** As this map indicates, in 1931 at China's expense, Japan began to expand its empire in East Asia. Although other nations condemned Japanese aggression, they took no direct action, and Japan continued to occupy more and more of China, forcing the Chinese government to move its capital to Chongqing (Chungking).

mittee to investigate the conflict. Neither the United States nor Great Britain, the two major Pacific naval powers, wanted to become involved in an Asian war. Denouncing Japan for its aggression, the United States invoked the **Stimson Doctrine,** implementing the policy of nonrecognition, which meant ignoring Japan's control over **Manchukuo,** its newly created Manchurian puppet state. In American eyes, Manchuria remained a part of China.

The Japanese had violated the Nine Power Pact, the Kellogg-Briand Pact, and principles of the League of Nations, but the ensuing barrage of spoken and written protests did nothing to deter their aggression. American humorist Will Rogers sarcastically noted that world leaders would run out of stationery penning their protests before Japan would run out of soldiers. In Japan, the successful conquest of Manchuria magnified the power of pro-imperial and anti-Western groups. In 1933, the Japanese government, dominated by militant nationalists, withdrew from the League of Nations. When Franklin Roosevelt ran for the presidency in 1932 (see below), the world was a much different place than it had been in 1928. The cheery optimism of a prosperous world at peace had been replaced with serious concerns about the global depression and the possibility of other wars.

Depression America

- Amid the social changes taking place during the Depression, what choices did Americans make that indicated the continuity of social and cultural values?
- What economic and social choices did minorities make during the Depression? What constraints did they face?
- How did women's opportunities and challenges change as an outcome of the Depression?

As Americans contemplated the presidential race in November 1932, it was not the problems in

Stimson Doctrine Declaration by the U.S. secretary of state in 1932 that the United States would not recognize Manchukuo or any other arrangement that threatened China's independence.

Manchukuo Puppet state established in Manchuria, eastern China, by Japan in 1932 and not recognized by the United States.

TABLE 25.2 Consumer Prices, 1931

Food		Other goods	
Rye Bred	$ .05 a loaf	Eastman Camera	$6.95
Apples	.25 for 4 lbs	Philco Baby Grand Radio	79.95
Bananas	.19 for 4 lbs	Sears Refrigerator	139.50
Round Steak	.28 a pound	Men's Dress Shirt	.50
Chicken Broilers	.39 a pound	DeSoto Six (Automobile)	695.00
Ground Beef	.29 for 2 lbs		
Shredded Wheat	.19 for 2 boxes		
Clorox	.16 a bottle		
Cigarettes	.27 for 2 packs		
Coffee	.69 for 2 lbs		
Butter	.59 for 2 lbs		
Sugar	1.25 for 25 lbs		
Flour	.79 for 25 lbs		
Lifebuoy Soap	.25 for 4 cakes		
Milk	.10 for a quart		

Source: Data from *Observer Reporter* (Washington, PA), July, 1931.

Manchuria that they considered. Most of their concerns were much closer to home. The Depression had touched every American, forcing changes in lifestyle, thought, and politics. Poverty was no longer reserved for those viewed as lazy or unworthy, and it was no longer relegated to remote areas and inner cities. Poverty was dragging down blue- and white-collar workers and even a few of the formerly rich. The average person on relief was a 38-year-old head-of-household male who had been an experienced worker.

Families in the Depression

Average annual income dropped 35 percent between 1929 and 1933, from $2,300 to $1,500. Although income rose after 1933, nagging fears of cuts in wages or loss of work remained. To help those facing economic insecurity, magazines and newspapers provided useful hints and "Depression recipes" that stretched budgets and included information about nutrition. According to trained home economists, a careful shopper and creative cook could feed a family of five on as little as $8 a week (see Tables 25.2 and 25.3). This was comforting news for those with that much money to spend on food a week, but for many families and for relief agencies $8 a week for food was beyond possibility. To feed his family of seven, Angelos Douvitos received **work relief** from Ann Arbor, Michigan, at 30 cents an hour and received a mere $4.20 a week. New York City provided only $2.39 a week for each family, and comedian Groucho Marx joked that things were bad when "pigeons started feeding people in Central Park." In 1931, New York hospitals reported 95 deaths from starvation.

Many people worried about basic survival, but some also feared that the Depression was causing a dangerous decline in family values and morality. They pointed to the drifters uprooted by hard times, to families deserted by fathers, and to reports of increasing abortions and premarital and deviant sexual activities. Generally, their fears were unfounded. The vast majority of Americans clung tightly to traditional family values and emphasized family unity. Church attendance rose during the Depression, and the number of divorces declined. The percentage of people getting married dropped slightly, and the nation's birth rate fell during the 1930s. But marriages

work relief A system of governmental monetary support which provided work for the unemployed, usually paid a limited wage determined by the hour or the day.

TABLE 25.3 Depression Menu, 1932

Breakfast	Lunch	Dinner
Oatmeal with milk	Macaroni and cheese	Salmon croquettes
Scrambled eggs	Cole slaw	Creamed potatoes
Toast	Corn bread	Stewed tomatoes
Milk	Baked apples	Bread
Coffee	Milk	Milk
Cost $1.72		

Source: Data from Susan F. West, "Low Cost Diets Planned According to Different Standards," *Journal of Home Economics* (February 1932): 113–118.

were only delayed, not put off entirely, and the lower birth rate resulted not from abortions or sexual practices but from economic fears and the increased availability of birth-control devices, especially condoms and diaphragms. One could even order contraceptives through the Sears, Roebuck mail-order catalogue. Although some decried an increasing abortion rate, the estimated number of abortions—based on the number of abortion-related deaths (about 9,000 a year)—remained steady throughout the Depression. Studies also indicated that sexual activity, rather than becoming more varied and promiscuous, actually decreased.

The Middle and Working Classes and Hard Times

For many of the American middle class and most of the working class, the most common fear was economic insecurity. Would the next day bring a reduction in wages, the loss of a job, or the closing of a business? Some saw their businesses go bankrupt and found new careers. Harry S Truman closed his haberdashery and turned to politics. E. Y. Harburg lost his family's hardware store, borrowed $500 from a friend, and started writing songs—striking a common plea with "Brother, Can You Spare a Dime?" Others worked for less, lost and found other jobs, or, disheartened, accepted relief.

Observers, in a study of Muncie, Indiana, noted that middle-class neighborhoods during the Depression looked much as they had in the mid-1920s. Clean, neatly kept houses stood behind green lawns, seemingly resisting the "ricocheting process of . . . change outside." But closer examination showed the growing impact of harder and harder times. Newspapers carried more pages of tax delinquencies, evictions, and foreclosures. Signs appeared in yards and in windows announcing a variety of services—household beauty parlors, kitchen bakeries, rooms for boarders. A Milwaukee wife recalled, "I did baking at home to supplement our income. I got 9 cents for a loaf of bread and 25 cents for an apple cake. . . . I cleared about $65 a month." When a state health inspector informed her of the regulations she was breaking, she responded that if he closed her bakery she would "have to go on relief." He agreed to allow her "business" as long as no neighbor complained. "I guess there were no complaints," she recalled. "I kept baking for another two and one half years."

In Muncie and across the country, "Use it up, wear it out, make it do, or do without," was a motto adopted by nearly every family. To save money, many women sewed, baked bread, and canned, reaffirming traditional female roles. A Singer sewing machine salesman commented that he was selling more and more machines to people who in the past would not have sewn. Feed sacks became a source of material. "I grew up in a small, exclusive suburb," recalled Florence Davis, who remembered her mother making a pretty new school dress out of one sack that had "a sky-blue background with gorgeous mallard ducks on it."

People dined out less and took fewer trips. Economic necessity kept families at home playing board games and cards, reading, and listening to the radio. People could fantasize about becoming a mil-

When You
BUY an AUTOMOBILE
You GIVE
3 Months' Work
to Someone
Which
Allows
Him to
BUY
OTHER PRODUCTS
BUY A CAR NOW—HELP BRING BACK PROSPERITY

♦ Recognizing the connection between sales and jobs, this ad asked readers to purchase an automobile and keep workers working so that they too could spend and stimulate the economy. Unfortunately, the number of people with enough money to spend was never enough to rekindle the economy and the Depression continued. *Private collection.*

lionaire and laugh about going broke while playing the new game Monopoly. During the 1920s, the automobile had pulled families away from their porches and backyards. They returned during the Depression. Men tended backyard grills, cooking "al fresco," and entire families tended vegetable and flower gardens. A "mania for flower gardens" and flower shows struck the middle class. Away from the house, use of the local park and library, dances, and movies provided inexpensive ways of spending time while escaping from daily problems. An estimated 65 percent of the population paid 10 cents to see a movie once a week. The official censor of Hollywood movies, **Will Hays,** ensured that films portrayed conventional, traditional values and morals and forbade profanities on the screen. In the movies and across the nation, family togetherness was praised as one positive outcome of the Depression. An Indiana newspaper editorialized, "All . . . are hoping for a quick return of prosperity . . . but in the mean time millions of Americans already have a kind of prosperity that includes strengthening the family."

Working-class Americans confronted the same challenges as did middle America but more often faced the prospect of losing a job and eviction. In Gary, Indiana, nearly the entire working class was out of a job by 1932. Approximately one-sixth of all urban families, having lost their homes, "doubled up" with relatives. Don Blincoe remembered that most households seemed like his, "where father, mother, children, aunts, uncles and grandma lived together" and pooled their earnings. Blincoe and his three brothers sold newspapers on the street and kept a penny for each paper sold.

Living with relatives, however, did not always help. Unemployed males, especially fathers, often felt shamed by their economic problems. A social worker wrote, "I used to see men cry because they didn't have a job. . . . They were belittled before the eyes of their families and they couldn't take it." John Boris, a Slavic immigrant, after working loyally for Ford Motor Company for fourteen years, was among the ninety-one thousand workers that the automaker laid off. He was devastated by the dismissal: "Last July, I was a good man," he lamented. "I ain't a man now." Boris lost his home and his dignity, but he survived by living with relatives, supported by his children. He never recovered his job at Ford or his sense of pride.

Boris, however, was fortunate to be able to stay with family members. Not all families remained stable and united. Unable to find jobs or support their families, some people took to the road. Many rode the rails—"hoboes"—hitching rides in boxcars, living in shantytowns, begging and scrounging for food and supplies along the road. "We never went through garbage cans for food," one hobo recalled. "The cans usually contained only ashes. . . . It was better to try a home . . . and ask the lady of the house for a few sandwiches." Estimates in 1932 placed the number of homeless migrants at between 1 and 2

Will Hays Organizer in 1922 of the Motion Picture Producers and Distributors of America, through which the movie industry censored itself.

♦ Dorothea Lange became one of the most famous photographers of the Depression. Her photo of a migrant mother and her children at a migrant camp in Nipomo, California captured the human tragedy of the Depression. Seeking jobs and opportunities, over 350,000 people traveled to the state, most finding few opportunities. *Library of Congress.*

million. Other statistics were more grim. Suicides increased, as did the number of people admitted to state mental hospitals and children placed in orphanages.

Included in the so-called migration of despair were thousands from rural areas, especially parts of Texas, Arkansas, and Oklahoma. Many families—like the **"Arkies" and "Okies"** characterized in John Steinbeck's novel *The Grapes of Wrath* (1939)—were forced from their farms by insects, dust, debt, and landlords. Many loaded their meager possessions on their jalopies and headed for California, with its warm climate and still-intact agricultural sector. By the end of the decade, California's population had jumped by over a million. Some migrants found jobs, but most continued to wander, looking for new opportunities.

Discrimination in the Depression

The Depression intensified the economic and social difficulties of minorities. For the majority of African Americans, who lived in the rural South and worked the fields of cotton and other crops, the Depression started in the 1920s with the decline of agricultural prices. By 1930, few were making more than $200 a year. As agricultural prices continued to shrink, black sharecroppers, farm hands, and tenant farmers either left or were forced from the farm. Nearly four hundred thousand left the South. Most headed north to urban centers like Harlem, where the black population more than doubled during the 1930s. Those who stayed behind were unemployed or worked for extremely meager wages. In some parishes of Louisiana, cotton pickers earned only 40 cents a day, some only $40 a year. Racial violence and injustice increased as whites used violence and intimidation to drive blacks from jobs and maintain social dominance.

Nowhere was racial bigotry more glaring than in the celebrated Scottsboro case. In 1931, nine black men were arrested in Alabama for raping two white prostitutes. Without any physical evidence, based on the testimony of the two women, an all-white male jury quickly found the **Scottsboro Nine** guilty. Eight were sentenced to death. Years of appeals and retrials followed, with the Supreme Court twice ordering new trials. Though never acquitted, by 1950 all nine defendants were free. Alabama dropped charges against four in 1935, four others received early paroles, and one escaped to Michigan, whose governor refused to return him to Alabama.

Generally, African Americans living in the North found that white racial attitudes there were much like those in the South. As jobs grew scarce, whites demanded and got the jobs previously held by minorities. Unemployment among urban blacks ran 20 to 50 percent higher than among urban whites. Nationally, for most of the Depression, 50 percent of the black population was out of work or on relief. In

"Arkies" and "Okies" Name applied to dispossessed farmers and sharecroppers from Arkansas and Oklahoma, both black and white, who migrated to California during the Depression.

Scottsboro Nine Nine African Americans convicted of raping two white women in a freight train in Alabama in 1931; their case became famous as an example of racism in the legal system.

♦ In one of the most controversial cases of the decade, nine African-American men, the Scottsboro Nine, shown here with one of their lawyers, were convicted of raping two white women. Eight were sentenced to death by an all-white jury, but in 1937 after a series of appeals and retrials, only five were sentenced to jail. Four of the five were paroled in 1944, the fifth man had successfully escaped to Michigan. *Brown Brothers.*

Harlem, low wages, limited relief funds, and racial tensions sparked a race riot in 1935 that cost four lives and millions of dollars in damage.

African-American women, especially in northern cities, also saw significant drops in employment even though they held mostly low-paying and low-status jobs. In Chicago, Cleveland, and Philadelphia between 1929 and 1940, the decline in employment among black women averaged 22.6 percent as white women and men competing for lower-paying jobs pushed them out of the labor force.

Like African Americans, Latinos found that the Depression aggravated Anglo hostility and made a hard life harder. Since 1914 the Latino, largely Mexican, population of the United States had grown rapidly, not only in California and the Southwest but in the Midwest as well. In 1910 only about seven hundred Latinos lived in Illinois, but as industries recruited Mexican workers, the population grew to more than four thousand, nearly half living in the Chicago area. There and elsewhere, most Mexican nationals and Mexican Americans squeezed out a meager living. They filled menial jobs, worked in the fields, and farmed small plots of land, many living on the margin even in good times. The Depression forced many into deeper poverty. In a number of **colonias** in southern California conditions were, according to an observer, "deplorable" with mothers and children going "up and down alleys, searching . . . for cast-off food."

Racial hostility intensified as Anglos demanded that Latino workers be fired to provide jobs for whites. In Tucson, Arizona, Anglos accused Mexicans of "taking the bread out of our white children's mouths." Orange County, California, offered free transportation to the border to about two thousand Mexican nationals to reduce relief notes—an option adopted by private, municipal, and state agencies. Across the country, by 1937, the lack of jobs, together with Anglo pressure and the Mexican government's encouragement, convinced more than half a million Mexicans to leave the United States. Those who remained found jobs scarce and pay pitiful. On the farms in California, an estimated 2.36 workers vied for every job, and Anglos, including those fleeing the Dust Bowl, were replacing Mexican laborers. For those finding work in the fields, the average wage was $289 a year, about a third of what the government described as a subsistence budget. As farm wages dropped and working conditions deteriorated, Mexican-American agricultural unions organized strikes. In a few cases, the unions won small pay raises, but usually the growers, supported by local authorities and public opinion, easily broke the strikes. A California deputy sheriff stated the case bluntly: "We protect our farmers here in Kern County. They are our best people. . . . They keep the county going. They put us in here and they can put us out again, so we serve them. But the Mexicans are trash. They have no standard of living. We herd them like pigs."

Asians, too, faced hardships and growing hostility. In San Francisco, nearly one-sixth of the Asian population was on relief. They received about 10 to

colonia Communities of Mexicans and Mexican Americans living in a village-like settlement; in southern California *colonias* were frequently constructed by or for citrus workers.

♦ For much of the Hispanic community in the West, the primary occupations available were agricultural pickers and packers. In the citrus industry in California, migrating from one grove to another, men usually picked the fruit while women worked in the packing sheds crating it. The Depression not only saw the repatriation of many pickers to Mexico, but increased competition from non-Hispanics. For those picking and packing, yearly family incomes averaged from $600 to $800. *California Museum of Photography.*

20 percent less than whites, because relief agencies concluded that Asians could subsist on a less expensive diet. Some, especially second-generation Japanese, hoped that by assimilating, becoming "200 percent American," they could remove economic and social barriers. The Japanese-American Citizens League was organized in 1930 and worked to overcome discrimination and to repeal anti-Asian legislation. By 1940, it had six thousand members but had made little headway. Asians remained isolated in ethnic enclaves.

Women in the Depression

While minorities saw their already low status declining, some women were discovering new opportunities. More women, especially white women, entered the work force than ever before. But employment patterns were uneven. More jobs were available at lower salaries and occupational levels. Because in many industries women received less pay than men and were considered more dependable, they were less likely to be laid off than men. But gender worked against women seeking higher-level jobs in the professions. The number of women in the professions, especially teaching, declined from 14.2 to 12.3 percent during the Depression. No matter what the job level, women workers encountered hostility and frequently sexual harassment. A Chicago meatpacker remembered, "You could get along well if you let the boss slap you on the behind and feel you up."

Public opinion polls found that most people, including women, believed that jobs should go first to men. Women, especially married women, were accused of stealing jobs from men. Many companies and local governments had a policy not to employ married women. A survey of fifteen hundred school districts found that 77 percent did not hire married women as teachers and 63 percent fired women when they married. By 1932, 2 million women were out of work. In 1933, an estimated 145,000 women were homeless, wandering across America, adding to the concerns that family and moral values were eroding.

For many rural women the Depression provided few opportunities and more challenges. Not only did rural women continue to do the housework, bear and raise children, and work in the field, but during the 1930s they had to do all of those things with less. In addition, the Depression took away a major avenue to new status: migration to the city. During the 1930s, the domestic and other service jobs that during the 1920s had drawn rural women, white and black, to the cities became scarce. Frequently, too, foreclosures and drought destroyed farm life. Rural women, symbolized by the heroic Ma Joad in *The Grapes of Wrath,* had to adapt to life on the road as more than 2.5 million farm families migrated seeking farmland and work.

Among working women who entered the work force, few found that bringing home the paycheck changed either their status or their role within the family. Husbands still maintained authority and dominance in the home. Rarely did even unemployed husbands help with household chores. One husband agreed to help with the laundry but refused to go outside and hang the wash for fear that neighbors might see him doing woman's work. Still, as wives and mothers if not as workers, women won praise as pillars of stability in a changing and perilous society. Reflecting on her own steadiness, one woman remembered, "I did what I had to do. I seem to always find a way to make things work."

Franklin D. Roosevelt

As Americans sought to adapt to the economic crisis and reacted to the spectacle of U.S. Army tanks chasing unarmed men and women on Anacostia Flats, many looked to the Democratic party for leadership and a change. Throughout the early months of 1932, **Franklin D. Roosevelt** had campaigned for the Democratic presidential nomination, saying that government needed to be concerned about the "forgotten man" who, through no fault of his own, suffered in the Depression.

Born into wealth and privilege, Roosevelt had attended elite schools popular with America's aristocracy: Groton Academy, Harvard University, and Columbia Law School. Neither academically nor athletically gifted, Roosevelt was nonetheless popular. With a recognizable name (Theodore Roosevelt was his fifth cousin), family wealth, and influential connections, he easily entered New York politics in 1910, winning a seat in the New York legislature. Tall, handsome, charming, glib, and willing to work with Tammany Hall, Roosevelt moved up the political ladder quickly. In 1920, James Cox made him his running mate, and even though Cox was defeated, Roosevelt's career continued to climb. The climb seemed suddenly over in 1921, however, when Roosevelt was stricken with polio.

♦ In the 1932 election, Roosevelt campaigned across the nation, always appearing confident and cheerful. Some said that his smile was the biggest political weapon he had—not only against Hoover but the Depression. *FPG.*

Paralyzed from the waist down, Roosevelt might have retired from politics and become a forgotten man himself. But he and his wife Eleanor (see pages 811–812) were determined to overcome his handicap. For two years, Roosevelt worked hard to advance from being a bedridden invalid to being barely mobile. He was never able to walk except with the aid of heavy steel leg braces and crutches. At the same time, Eleanor Roosevelt toiled tirelessly to keep his political career alive. Largely through her efforts, he got the opportunity to deliver the

Franklin D. Roosevelt New York governor elected president in 1932 with the promise of a "new deal for the American people."

nominating speech for Al Smith at the 1924 Democratic convention. Making his return to the political battlefield, Roosevelt ran for governor of New York in 1928. Smith lost in a Hoover landslide, but Roosevelt won.

As governor, Roosevelt too faced the Depression, but unlike Hoover, he saw nothing wrong with using government activism to deal with economic disaster. He was one of the few governors to mobilize his state's limited resources to help the unemployed and poor. Although he made little headway against the Depression, his efforts made him seem a more caring and energetic leader than Hoover. His brave struggle to overcome polio combined with his actions as governor and his cheery disposition to earn him a reputation as champion of the "forgotten man" and made him a candidate for the presidency.

The 1932 Election

Roosevelt was nominated on the fourth ballot, over Al Smith and Speaker of the House John Nance Garner of Texas. Traditionally, candidates did not attend the convention and accepted the nomination from their homes. Showing his dynamic flair, Roosevelt broke that tradition and flew to Chicago to accept the nomination. In his acceptance speech, the nominee emphasized two points: he was a man of action who promoted change, and his health was good, his paralysis in no way hindering his capacity for work. Roosevelt also established the theme for the coming campaign. Pointing to his tradition-breaking trip to the convention, he emphatically announced that he and the Democratic party had no fear of breaking "all foolish traditions." He closed by promising a "new deal for the American people." Roosevelt placed no special emphasis on the phrase **New Deal,** but the media quickly focused on it, handing him a clever, symbolic slogan for his campaign. Although the acceptance speech offered no concrete solutions to the problems plaguing the country, it stirred the desire for hope and change.

Roosevelt selected Garner as his vice-presidential nominee, a good choice that helped to heal East-West, North-South, urban-rural splits within the party. During the campaign, Roosevelt tried to avoid any commitments and policies that might offend voters or blocs among the Democrats, while promising all things to all people. He supported direct federal relief but promised to balance the budget. Hoover, who called Roosevelt a political "chameleon," emphasized their philosophical differences. He claimed that the campaign was "more than a contest between two men." It was, he said, "a contest between two philosophies of government." Few people seemed to care, and Roosevelt continued to rely on his sharpest campaign tools: his dynamic energy and contagious optimism.

The election was a huge success for the Democratic party and Roosevelt. Across the nation, people voted for Democrats for state and local officials, for Congress, and most important, for president. Roosevelt won in a landslide, burying Hoover, with 57.4 percent of the more than 39.7 million votes cast. Hoover carried only six states (see Map 25.4), and huge Democratic majorities emerged in both houses of Congress.

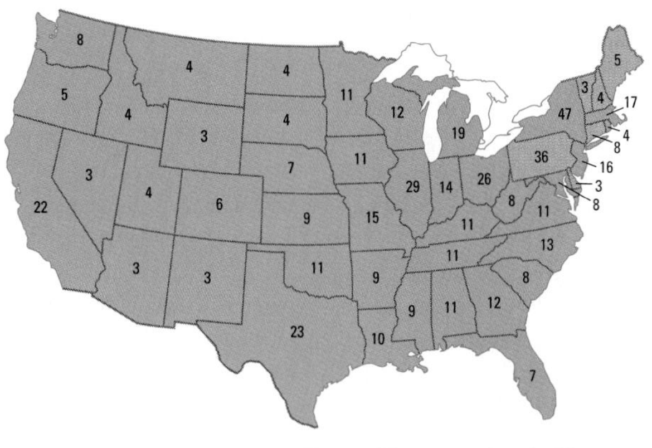

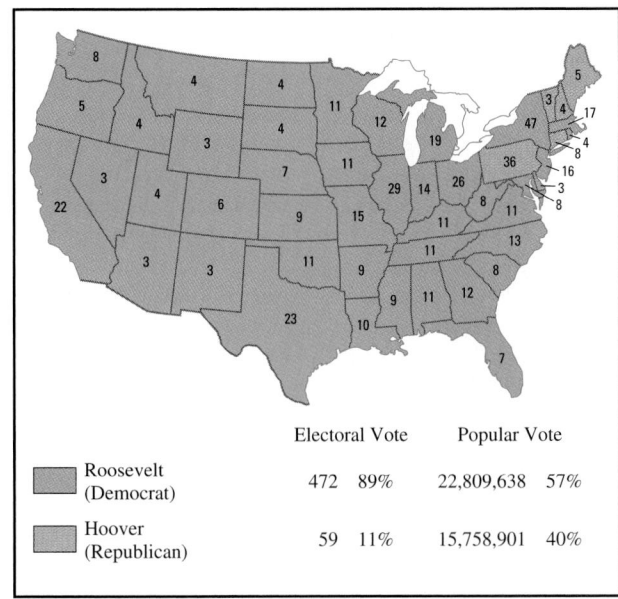

	Electoral Vote		Popular Vote	
Roosevelt (Democrat)	472	89%	22,809,638	57%
Hoover (Republican)	59	11%	15,758,901	40%

♦ **MAP 25.4 Election of 1932** In the election of 1932, Herbert Hoover faced not only Franklin D. Roosevelt but also the Great Depression. With many Americans blaming Hoover and the Republicans for the economic catastrophe and with Roosevelt promising a New Deal, the outcome was not close. Roosevelt won 42 of 48 states.

New Deal Term applied to Roosevelt's policies to attack the problems of the Depression, which included relief for poor and unemployed, efforts to stimulate economic recovery, and social security.

SUMMARY

Expectations
Constraints
Choices
Outcomes

From 1928 to 1932, the United States underwent major changes of lasting importance. A heroic figure, Hoover assumed the presidency, widely regarded as well qualified to direct the course of the nation. *Expectations* were high that further growth in the economy would enhance prosperity and the quality of American life. The onslaught of the Depression changed Hoover's and the nation's fortunes. The flaws that *constrained* the economy, largely hidden by the apparent prosperity of the 1920s, were exposed as banks and businesses closed. The economic collapse originated in part from internal weaknesses in the economy and the government's *choices* to promote easy money and to encourage speculation.

More than previous presidents, Hoover *chose* to expand the role of the federal government to meet the nation's needs in the economic crisis. He initiated a series of measures, including the Reconstruction Finance Corporation, by which the federal government tried to stimulate the economy. But Hoover's philosophy of limited government still *constrained* the effort. The *outcome* was that the economy continued to worsen, and many not only held Hoover responsible but also believed him callous to the hardships facing many Americans. By 1932, most Americans had lost their faith in Hoover, Republicans, and American business. With altered *expectations* about the role of government, voters *chose* to put their faith instead in Roosevelt and his promise of a New Deal.

The Depression affected the lives of all Americans. They had to adjust their values and lifestyles to meet the economic and psychological crisis, but industrial workers and minorities faced extra burdens of discrimination and loss of status. Although many Americans had to make difficult *choices* that disrupted their lives, the *outcome* was that society generally remained stable as most people learned to cope with the Great Depression as best they could.

The Depression also made a mockery of Hoover's *expectations* about a prosperous and peaceful world. During the 1920s, the United States had *chosen* a policy of independent internationalism that stressed voluntary cooperation among nations, while at the same time enhancing private American economic opportunities around the world. Although relations with Latin America improved under Hoover, elsewhere an *outcome* of the worldwide depression was international instability, as symbolized by Japan's invasion of Manchuria. *Constrained* by economic worries, however, more and more Americans withdrew into isolationism.

SUGGESTED READINGS

Michael A. Bernstein. *The Great Depression* (1987).

A detailed economic examination of the causes and effects of the Depression, with American manufacturing as a primary focus.

Caroline Bird. *The Invisible Scar* (1966).

An excellent study of how people responded to the impact of the Depression.

Warren I. Cohen. *Empire Without Tears: American Foreign Relations, 1921–1933* (1987).

A short but informative overview of American foreign policy during the 1920s.

Robert S. Lynd and Helen Merrell Lynd. *Middletown in Transition* (1937).

A classic sociological study of Muncie, Indiana, during the Depression.

Robert McElvaine. *The Great Depression: America, 1929–1941* (1984).

An excellent overview of the origins of and responses to the Depression.

Studs Terkel. *Hard Times: An Oral History of the Great Depression* (1970).

A classic example of how oral histories can provide the human dimension to history.

Gordon Thomas and Max Morgan-Witts. *The Day the Bubble Burst: The Social History of the Wall Street Crash of 1929* (1979).

A view of the American economy and the stock market crash as experienced by selected individuals.

Joan Hoff Wilson. *Herbert Hoover: Forgotten Progressive* (1970).

A positive evaluation of the life of Herbert Hoover that stresses his accomplishments as well as his limitations.

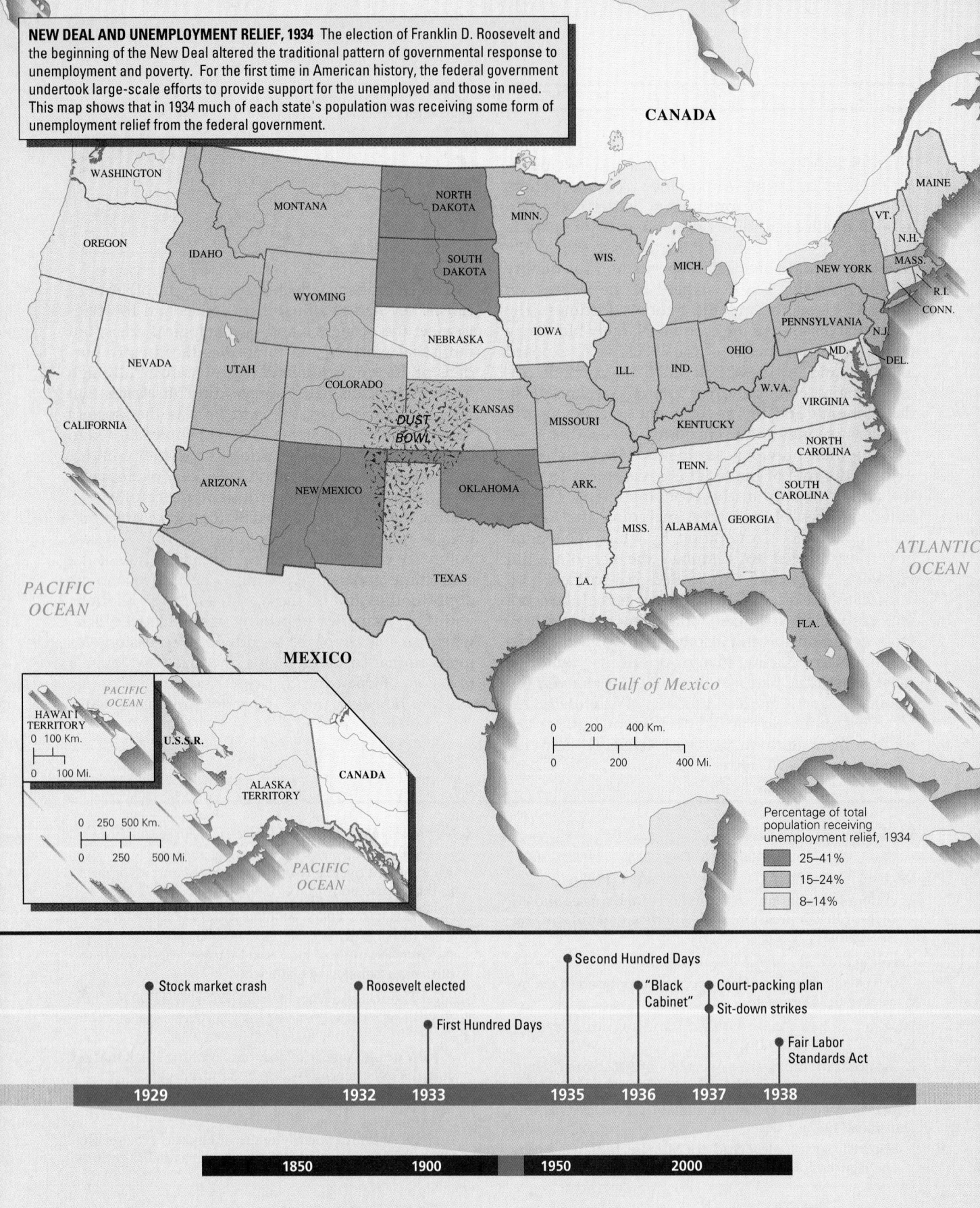

NEW DEAL AND UNEMPLOYMENT RELIEF, 1934 The election of Franklin D. Roosevelt and the beginning of the New Deal altered the traditional pattern of governmental response to unemployment and poverty. For the first time in American history, the federal government undertook large-scale efforts to provide support for the unemployed and those in need. This map shows that in 1934 much of each state's population was receiving some form of unemployment relief from the federal government.

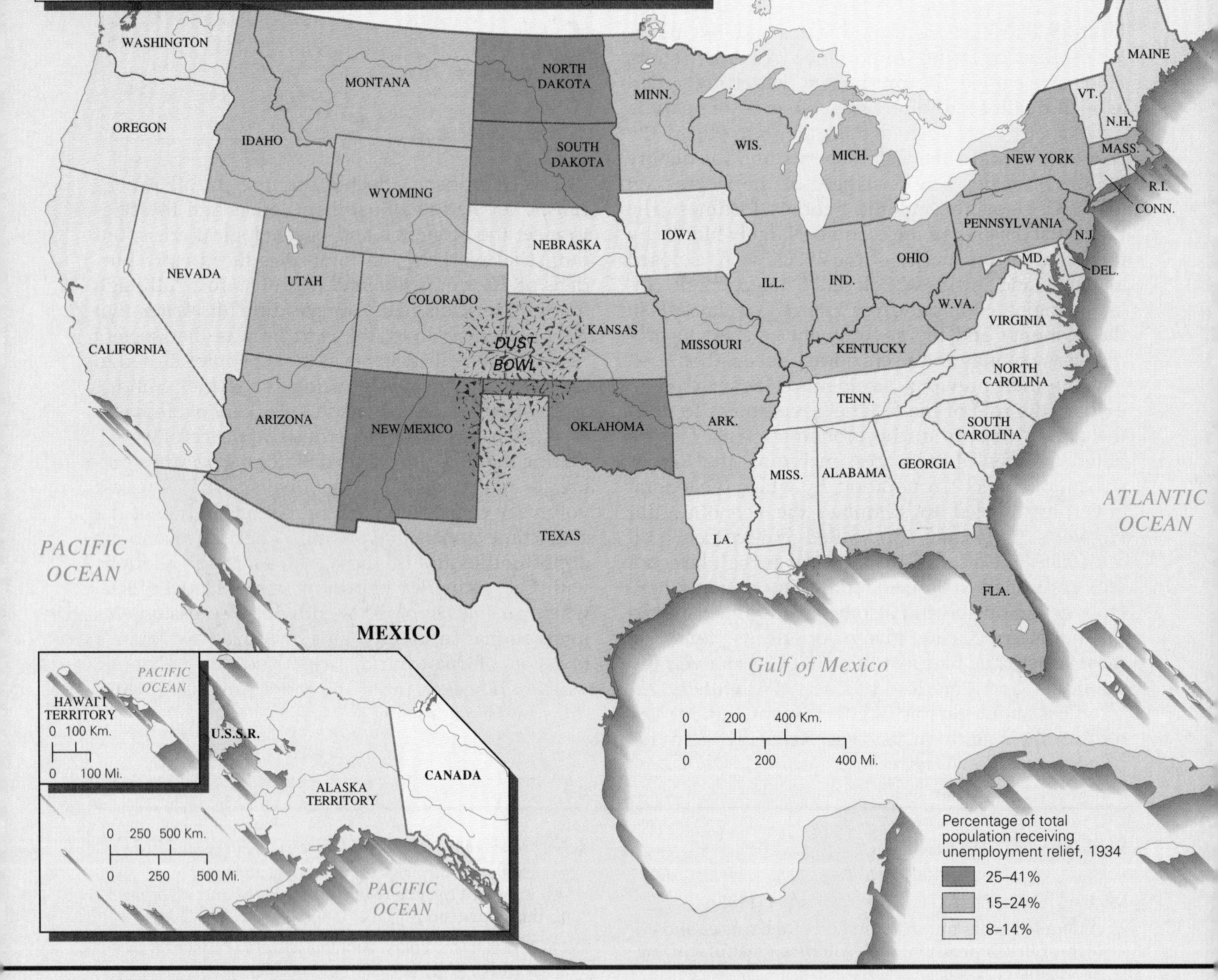

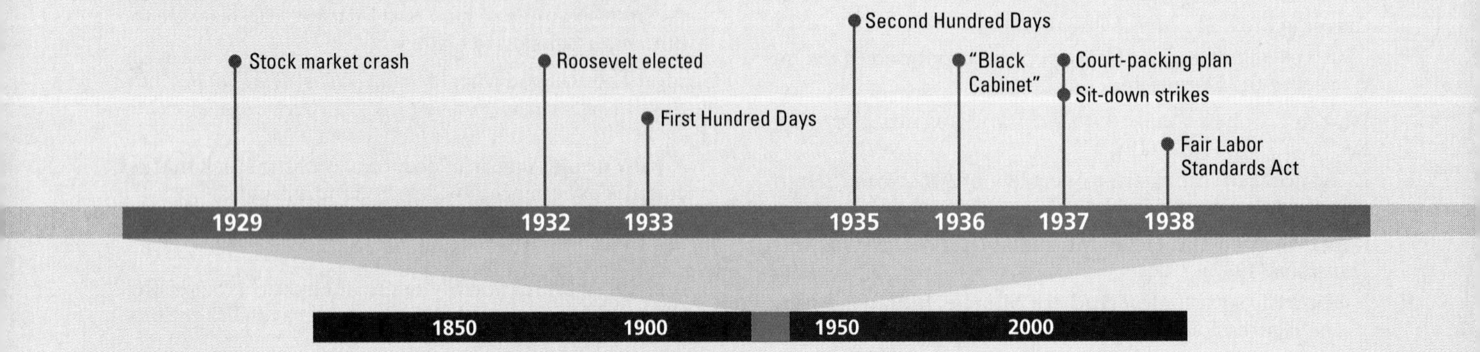

CHAPTER 26

The New Deal, 1933–1940

A New President, a New Deal

- How did public and political expectations constrain Roosevelt's choices during the First Hundred Days?
- How well did the NRA and the AAA meet the expectations of Roosevelt and his advisers?
- How did political and social constraints shape the outcome of New Deal relief efforts?

The Second Hundred Days

- What were the sources of opposition to Roosevelt's First Hundred Days?
- What methods that would be better than Roosevelt's measures did Long, Townsend, and Coughlin expect to use to combat the Depression?
- How and why did the Second Hundred Days focus more on people and reform than on national economic recovery?

The New Deal and Society

- What were some of the outcomes of the New Deal for cities across America?
- What were Roosevelt's expectations regarding civil rights? How did the New Deal affect the choices of women, African Americans, Hispanics, and American Indians?

The New Deal Winds Down

- Why did Roosevelt choose to attempt to pack the Supreme Court? What led to his failure?
- What factors constrained Roosevelt's efforts to maintain the political initiative after his re-election?
- What was the outcome of the New Deal in terms of the structure of government and Americans' expectations about government?

INTRODUCTION

Expectations
Constraints
Choices
Outcomes

Elected in 1932, Franklin D. Roosevelt dominated American history for the next thirteen years. He had few qualms about using the power of the government to combat the Depression and reform society, and the dire economic problems gave him unparalleled opportunities to reshape the federal government's relationship to the country.

Americans' *expectations* created opportunities for Roosevelt, but he faced serious *constraints* as well. Crisis or not, there were political and ideological limits on how much the president could change and how much he wanted to change. Many on the political left saw Roosevelt's election as a chance to reform society to achieve social justice for all and to restructure American capitalism to make it more humane and responsive. But Roosevelt had no intention of abandoning capitalism or restructuring American society. Eleanor Roosevelt, more socially liberal than her husband, reflected, "I'm the agitator; he's the politician." As a politician, Roosevelt knew that many conservatives, including those in the southern wing of the Democratic party, would oppose any form of government activism and expansion of federal power. Another constraint was the lack of precedent: no one knew what kinds of intervention would work on the reeling economy. Even among Roosevelt's advisers there was disagreement on the nature of programs and the extent and type of government activism.

Roosevelt's *choices* were thus shaped by public and political *expectations* and *constraints* as they intersected with the economic and social needs caused by the Depression. The *outcome* was the New Deal, a three-part barrage of legislation to bring about economic recovery, relief for victims of the Depression, and reforms to better regulate the economic sector. This *outcome* was to change the definition of liberalism and the responsibilities and power of the federal government. Roosevelt would be revered and hated, but no one could deny his impact.

In 1933, riding a wave of popular support, Roosevelt easily overcame most political *constraints* as he initiated the First Hundred Days of the New Deal. A year later the tide had changed. Inside and outside government many who had given Roosevelt a free hand in 1933 began to oppose him and his programs. Conservatives condemned economic and business controls and federal spending as excessive government. Liberals called for fewer compromises with business, increased spending, and more programs for workers, minorities, the poor, and the unemployed. With his popularity confirmed by the 1934 elections, Roosevelt *chose* to consider new approaches that placed a stronger emphasis on people than on business recovery. The *outcome* was a Second Hundred Days of legislation in 1935.

The New Deal expanded not only the functions of government but also the ranks of those voting Democratic. New Deal programs attracted women, minorities, and blue-collar workers, who *chose* to support Roosevelt and his party. The president's overwhelming victory in 1936 confirmed the party's increased strength and raised the possibility of a third hundred days that would further expand the government's social programs. However, such *expectations* quickly evaporated, *constrained* by the growing power of conservative political opposition and Roosevelt's own tactical errors. By 1938, the New Deal was sputtering to an end. It had not promoted a full economic recovery, but it had restored Americans' faith in the economic and political system. It had rescued American capitalism. It had also profoundly changed the role and function of government. The long-term *outcome* of the New Deal was the emergence of the federal government, especially the executive branch, as the most powerful and important level of government in the nation. Before the 1930s, people had looked to local, county, and state government for help. After the New Deal, people looked to Washington for assistance, and government and politics were forever changed.

CHRONOLOGY

Out of Depression

1933 Franklin D. Roosevelt becomes president
U.S. unemployment reaches 25 percent
National Bank Holiday
First fireside chat
First Hundred Days (March 9–June 16)
Civilian Conservation Corps created
Agricultural Adjustment Administration created
Tennessee Valley Authority created
Home Owners Loan Corporation (HOLC) created
National Industrial Recovery Act passed (NRA and PWA)
Twenty-first Amendment (repealing Prohibition) ratified

1934 Huey Long's Share the Wealth plan
Father Francis Coughlin forms National Union for Social Justice
Indian Reorganization Act
Securities and Exchange Commission created
American Liberty League established
Dr. Francis Townsend's movement begins

1935 Second Hundred Days
Works Progress Administration created
NRA ruled unconstitutional in Schecter case
Rural Electrification Administration formed
National Youth Administration created
National Labor Relations Board created (Wagner Act)
Social Security Act passed
Long assassinated
Congress for Industrial Organization established

1936 AAA ruled unconstitutional in Butler case
Roosevelt re-elected
"Black Cabinet" organized
Sit-down strikes begin

1937 Court-packing plan
Republic Steel strike
"Roosevelt's recession"
U.S. Unemployment climbs to 19 percent

1938 Works Progress Administration rolls double
Fair Labor Standards Act
AAA re-established
Orson Welles's broadcast of "War of the Worlds"
Republican victories in congressional elections

1939 Marian Anderson's concert at Lincoln Memorial
John Steinbeck's *The Grapes of Wrath*

1940 Richard Wright's *Native Son*

A New President, a New Deal

- How did public and political expectations constrain Roosevelt's choices during the First Hundred Days?
- How well did the NRA and the AAA meet the expectations of Roosevelt and his advisers?
- How did political and social constraints shape the outcome of New Deal relief efforts?

In the months between the presidential election of 1932 and the day Roosevelt took office, fate seemed to be playing a cruel joke on the nation. In those winter months, many more people lost homes and jobs, more banks and factories closed their doors, and more families suffered and lost hope. Still, Roosevelt's election raised optimism that the new president and his advisers were ready and able to combat the Depression. During the campaign and after, Roosevelt had surrounded himself with a number of advisers whom the press labeled the **Brain Trust.** The existence of this group convinced many that Roosevelt was working on a program to end the Depression and restore prosperity.

Brain Trust Group of specialists in law, economics, and social welfare who, as advisers to President Roosevelt, helped develop the social and economic principles of the New Deal.

♦ Franklin and Eleanor Roosevelt and their son James pose before going to the White House on Inauguration Day, March 4, 1933. With soaring unemployment, businesses and banks closing, and farmers protesting, Roosevelt told the American people they had "nothing to fear but fear itself," and began to restore people's confidence in the government and nation by promising quick action in fighting the Depression. *UPI/Bettmann Archives.*

In reality, neither Roosevelt nor his advisers had a coherent plan, and his advisers were deeply divided. One group, led by Columbia professors Rexford Tugwell and Raymond Moley, believed the concentration of American business in fewer and fewer hands was inevitable and favorable. Like Theodore Roosevelt, they applauded big business as efficient, economical, and, with the proper controls, beneficial. Their solution to the economic crisis was corporate regulation and public planning done by an energetic executive branch. Except for Tugwell, those supporting the national planning approach had little concern for the "forgotten man." Felix Frankfurter represented another faction within the Brain Trust. He disagreed about the benefits derived from the concentration of business and centralization of planning. Frankfurter distrusted big business and wanted more competition along with social programs to help those most harmed by the Depression.

Despite their differences, the Brain Trust members agreed on a number of basic ideas that shaped the New Deal. They believed the origins and dynamics of the Depression were rooted within the economy and government of the United States and required internal solutions. They also asserted the necessity of federal action to fight the Depression.

Roosevelt had no strong economic convictions and relished his advisers' debates. But in the end he made up his own mind, for reasons he rarely shared. He did what seemed expedient and discarded whatever cost too much or did not work, politically or socially.

Bank Holiday

As Roosevelt's inauguration approached, the nation faced a severe banking crisis. Unable to collect debts owed and drained by too many investments in the sinking stock market, many banks had gone out of business since the 1929 crash, leaving depositors penniless. In 1932, 1,456 banks had failed. By March 1933, the entire banking system seemed ready to collapse. The public's dwindling confidence in banks caused a growing number of **runs** on banks as depositors demanded their money. Most banks lacked sufficient funds and were forced to close their doors. By March 4, Inauguration Day, nearly all the country's banks were either closed or operating under severe restrictions. The governors of all forty-eight states had declared their state banks closed until further notice. With banks unable to operate, the economy of the United States was stiffening with paralysis. In the face of such an immediate crisis, the country waited anxiously to see how the new chief executive would respond.

On Inauguration Day, Franklin D. Roosevelt reassured the nation that he was going to take action. Millions listened to the speech on radio as the president calmly stated that Americans had "nothing to fear but fear itself" and that the American economy was sound and would revive. But, he stressed, talk alone would not revive the nation. "We must act quickly," he cautioned, telling the public that he intended to ask Congress for sweeping powers to deal with the crisis.

run A panic in which depositors fearful of bank failure demand to withdraw their money.

On March 6, Roosevelt made his first move. He announced a national **Bank Holiday** that closed all the country's banks. Three days later, as freshmen congressmen were still finding their seats in the House and Senate, the president presented Congress with a request for an emergency banking bill. Without even seeing a written version of the bill, Democrats and Republicans responded almost immediately, giving Roosevelt what he wanted in less than four hours. Drafted partly by holdover Hoover officials, the **Emergency Banking Act** allowed the Federal Reserve to examine banks and certify those that were sound. It also allowed the Federal Reserve and the Reconstruction Finance Corporation (which had outlasted Hoover) to support the nation's banks by providing funds and buying stocks of preferred banks.

On Sunday evening, March 12, in the first of his so-called **fireside chats,** Roosevelt's soothing and confident voice told Americans that they had nothing to fear and that the federal government was solving the banking crisis. Federal banking officials were going to inspect banks, he announced, and those banks determined to be sound would be allowed to reopen. Banks would be safe again. "I can assure you," he joked, "it is safer to keep your money in a reopened bank than under the mattress." More than 60 million Americans listened to the speech, and most believed in the president. When banks in the twelve Federal Reserve cities reopened on Monday, customers appeared to deposit rather than withdraw money. Within a month—before examiners could inspect many banks, nearly 75 percent of the nation's banks were operating again.

Roosevelt's quick and effective action in dealing with the banking crisis established a positive national mood. The New Deal was under way. Over the next one hundred days, the new president signed fifteen major pieces of legislation. The legislation, Roosevelt explained in another fireside chat, was moving along three paths: relief, recovery, and reform. Actual legislation almost always overlapped the three tracks.

The stock market crash, the Depression, and the banking crisis indicated that reforms were needed to prevent abuses in the banking and stock market industries. Fulfilling Roosevelt's promise during the banking crisis, in June 1933 Congress passed the Banking Act of 1933, which reorganized the banking and financial system, gave new powers and responsibilities to the Federal Reserve System, and created the **Federal Deposit Insurance Corporation (FDIC).** The FDIC provided federal insurance for accounts of less than $5,000, and within six months more than 97 percent of all commercial banks had joined the FDIC program, providing safety to millions of depositors. Reforms for the stock market came in May 1933, with the Federal Security Act, which required companies to provide information about their economic condition to stock buyers. A second reform came with the creation in June 1934 of the **Securities and Exchange Commission (SEC),** which regulated stock market activities, including the setting of margin rates. Public approval for the reforms was high: "Let the seller beware," applauded supporters.

Roosevelt also moved quickly to relieve the country of Prohibitions calling on Congress to approve a Beer and Wine Act permitting the manufacture, sale, and consumption of wine and beer with a 3.2 percent alcohol content. Congress quickly passed it on March 22. With a tax of $5 a barrel, the act provided only a small amount of revenue but greatly boosted public morale. Later that year, in December, the **Twenty-first Amendment** repealed Prohibition altogether.

Seeking Agricultural Recovery

As Roosevelt assumed office, the plight of farmers appeared near disaster. The Farmers' Holiday Association threatened to call a farmers' strike across the nation unless Congress acted to restore farm profits. Roosevelt and his advisers were ready to respond.

Bank Holiday Temporary shutdown of banks throughout the country by executive order of President Roosevelt in March 1933.

Emergency Banking Act Law passed by Congress in 1933 that permitted sound banks in the Federal Reserve System to reopen and allowed the government to supply funds to support private banks.

fireside chats Radio talks in which President Roosevelt promoted New Deal policies and reassured the nation.

Federal Deposit Insurance Corporation Agency created by the Banking Act of 1933 to insure deposits up to a fixed sum in member banks of the Federal Reserve System and state banks that chose to participate.

Securities and Exchange Commission Bipartisan agency created by Congress to license stock exchanges and supervise their activities, including the setting of margin rates.

Twenty-first Amendment Constitutional amendment ratified in 1933 that repealed the Eighteenth Amendment and thus brought Prohibition to an end.

♦ Unable to get adequate prices for their crops, farmers were destroying their crops and killing their livestock. Milo Reno's Farmers' Alliance and other farmer organizations called for swift government action to protect the family farm. Here, Wisconsin dairy farmers protest low milk prices by pouring milk onto the ground. *World Wide Photos.*

They believed that the family farm was an essential part of American life and needed to be saved. Roosevelt knew that a successful farm program would help tie the Farm Bloc to him and the Democratic party. The goal was to raise farm prices through national planning to a point of **parity,** where the profits that farmers received matched those of the profitable years before World War I. Reducing rural poverty would be a byproduct—recovery, not relief, was the goal.

New Dealers, especially Secretary of Agriculture Henry A. Wallace, were convinced that neither individual farmers nor state governments could solve agriculture's problems without direct help from the federal government. Wallace also believed that the nation's economic problems could not be solved without reducing agricultural overproduction and raising farm profits. The challenge was to convince farmers to modify farming methods and cut production. On March 12, the administration introduced the **Agricultural Adjustment Act (AAA).** It was passed three months later on May 12.

The central part of the act, the Domestic Allotment Plan, encouraged farmers to reduce production by paying them not to plant. A national planning board determined how much agricultural production needed to be reduced to raise farm prices and then allocated specific reductions to the states for wheat, cotton, field corn, rice, tobacco, hogs, and milk and milk products. State boards divided production cuts among participating farmers and compensated them for lost crops and livestock. A special tax on industrial food processors generated money for paying farmers not to plant.

Because the AAA was not approved until May, after spring sowing, thousands of acres of already planted corn, cotton, and tobacco crops had to be plowed under. Likewise, farmers had to destroy thousands of hogs and dairy cows and huge quantities of milk and milk products. The continuing drought in the Midwest made it relatively easy for ranchers and wheat and corn farmers to take land out of production, accounting for more than 90 percent of the reduction of wheat crops in 1934. But many people, especially those concerned about the hungry, shuddered at the waste, criticized the plan, and pressed for the surplus food to be made available for the needy. Others complained that the Agricultural Adjustment Act primarily benefited large-scale producers who had enough land to remove from cultivation. They also pointed out that many landlords chose to evict sharecroppers and tenant

parity The fair value of something compared to its market value.

Agricultural Adjustment Act Law passed by Congress in 1933 to reduce overproduction by paying farmers not to grow crops or raise livestock.

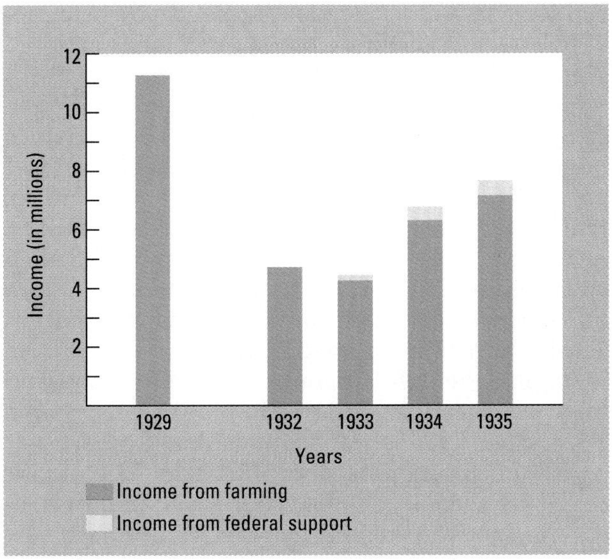

♦ **FIGURE 26.1 Farm Income, 1929–1935** Prices for farm products fell rapidly as the Depression set in (see Table 25.1), but by 1933, with support from New Deal programs like the Agricultural Adjustment Act, some farm incomes were rising. Note, however, that some of the increase was a direct result of government payments. *Source:* U.S. Department of Commerce, *Historical Statistics of the United States, Colonial Times to 1970* (2 parts) (Washington, D.C.: U.S. Government Printing Office), pp. 483–484, part 1.

farmers when selecting land to take out of production to meet AAA reduction quotas. In all, evictions and the Depression pushed more than 3 million people off the farm, leaving behind a more efficient and **highly capitalized** farm industry.

Despite the removal of large amounts of land from production, output often did not drop. Farmers took their least productive lands out of cultivation and used more scientific farming methods to grow more on fewer acres. To ensure true crop reduction, in 1934 Congress passed two additional acts that levied special taxes on cotton and tobacco farmers who exceeded their production quotas.

Because the Agricultural Adjustment Act took time to implement, in October 1933 Roosevelt initiated the **Commodity Credit Corporation** to rescue many farmers financially. Financed through the Reconstruction Finance Corporation, the Commodity Credit Corporation lent money to participating farmers based on the price of their crop. If the crop price rose higher than the amount of the loan, farmers could sell their crops, pay back the loan, and make a profit. If the crop price fell so that farmers could not repay the loan, the government took their crops. Nonpayment, however, did not prevent farmers from taking out another loan the following year. The government distributed the seized agricultural commodities to the needy through relief agencies.

By 1935, recovery in the agricultural sector was under way (see Figure 26.1). Farm prices were rising, and the purchasing power of farmers was increasing. Farmers' support for the agricultural programs remained high even as the Supreme Court in 1936 declared the Agricultural Adjustment Act unconstitutional in ***Butler v. the United States.*** The Court ruled that the federal government could not set production quotas and that the special tax on food processing was illegal.

Quickly, the Roosevelt administration pushed the Soil Conservation and Domestic Allotment Act through Congress to circumvent the Court's decision. The act allowed the **Soil Conservation Service,** established in April 1933, to pay farmers for cutting back on soil-depleting crops like cotton, tobacco, and wheat, and adopting better conservation methods. Finally, in 1938, Congress approved a second Agricultural Adjustment Act, which re-established the principle of federally set commodity quotas, acreage reductions, and parity payments.

The combination of drought and government policies took sizable amounts of land out of production, stabilized farm prices, and saved farms. From 1932 to 1939, farm income more than doubled, and the government provided over $4.5 billion in aid to farmers—more direct help than it gave to any other economic group. At first regarded by the administration as short-term measures to re-energize agriculture, the second AAA and the Commodity Credit Corporation became accepted as **entitlements** as well as solutions to farm problems. These policies

highly capitalized Requiring large amounts of wealth in the form of money and property.

Commodity Credit Corporation Government agency authorized to lend money to farmers using their crops as collateral.

Butler v. the United States Supreme Court decision (1936) declaring the Agricultural Adjustment Act invalid on the grounds that it unconstitutionally extended the powers of the federal government.

Soil Conservation Service Agency established by Congress for the prevention of soil erosion; by paying farmers to cut back on soil-depleting crops, it also reduced overproduction.

entitlements Guaranteed benefits to specific groups provided by a government agency.

contributed to stable agricultural prices, frequently higher than the world market price, for more than fifty years. Equally important, Roosevelt's farm programs significantly changed the relationship between agricultural producers and the federal government, linking the government inescapably to the farmers' future.

Seeking Industrial Recovery

With the AAA in place, Roosevelt and his advisers addressed the problem of industrial recovery but disagreed about the best means to promote industrial and business growth. The Tugwell-Moley group favored national economic planning and controls to stabilize production, prices, employment, and wages. Frankfurter's faction opposed a national plan and preferred an industry-by-industry approach. In Congress, Democratic liberals were pushing in yet another direction, calling for massive public works programs and a 30-hour workweek. Fearful of losing the initiative, Roosevelt asked Moley to mesh congressional ideas with those of the administration. The result was the **National Industrial Recovery Act (NIRA).** Introduced in Congress on May 15, 1933, it was approved a month later.

A relief as well as a recovery plan, the NIRA offered something for everyone and quickly earned widespread support from business, labor, the unemployed, and community leaders. In a two-part offensive, the **Public Works Administration (PWA)** was created and given $3.3 billion to put people to work immediately, and the **National Recovery Administration (NRA)** was created to provide programs to restart the nation's industrial engine and create permanent jobs. Both were viewed as temporary measures, to last only until the nation's economy was stronger.

Roosevelt expected business and labor leaders, consumers, and government officials to work together on planning boards to promote industrial growth. The National Recovery Administration was, Roosevelt explained in a fireside chat, a "partnership in planning, and a partnership to see that the plans are carried out." To achieve their goals, the planning boards developed "industrial codes" that set prices, production, and wages. In turn, the government suspended antitrust laws for two years. Roosevelt selected **General Hugh Johnson** to command the NRA and placed Secretary of the Interior **Harold Ickes** in charge of the Public Works Administration. Meticulous and always watchful for corruption and inefficiency, Ickes moved slowly to provide PWA jobs, exerting pressure on Johnson to implement the national recovery program.

During World War I, Johnson, nicknamed "Old Iron Pants," headed the War Industries Board, which mobilized American industries for the war effort (see page 705). Johnson now confronted the Depression, immersing himself in efforts to promote the NRA. A blue eagle was selected as the emblem of the NRA and "We Do Our Part" as its motto. From the start, movie newsreels touted the NRA, and city officials across the nation organized parades in support—in Memphis the NRA parade drew fifty thousand marchers. Nearly overnight, the blue eagle appeared everywhere as Americans promised to do their part.

Within six months, the NRA had 557 specific codes; by the end of 1934, over seven hundred industries and 2.5 million workers were covered by codes. At first, business and labor rallied behind the codes. The head of the AFL hailed Section 7a of the codes as the Magna Carta of labor because it gave workers the right to organize and bargain collectively. The codes also outlawed child labor and established minimum wages and maximum hours of work. But as the codes were written and implemented, it became clear that business elements were dominating the planning boards. They were the best-organized and best-prepared groups and usually had the support of Johnson, who believed that the NRA's goal was "to get industry back to making a profit." He usually supported business interests over the interests of consumers and workers. "Who

National Industrial Recovery Act Law passed by Congress in 1933 establishing the National Recovery Administration to supervise industry and the Public Works Administration to create jobs.

Public Works Administration Agency that the NIRA established to increase employment and to stimulate economic recovery by putting people to work to expand consumer buying power; it spent more than $4.25 million on 34,000 public works projects.

National Recovery Administration Agency that the NIRA created to draft and supervise the implementing of national industrial codes.

General Hugh Johnson Head of the National Recovery Administration; consumer and labor advocates charged him of being too favorable to business interests.

Harold Ickes Secretary of the Interior and director of the Public Works Administration; an efficient administrator who opposed racial discrimination.

♦ The National Recovery Administration was Roosevelt's main vehicle to restore industrial recovery during his First One Hundred Days. Headed by General Hugh Johnson, the NRA's goal was to mobilize management, workers, and consumers under the symbol of the Blue Eagle; establish national production codes; and get America moving again. *Collection of David J. and Janice L. Frent.*

the hell cares what your board thinks?" he yelled at one group of consumers.

By 1934, critics from all sides were attacking the NRA—soon dubbed the "National Run Around." Workers complained that too many codes instituted low wages and often ignored code-set minimum wages for blacks and women. They also complained that employers frequently violated the negotiated wage, hour, and unionization provisions of the codes. Consumers lost faith in the blue eagle as prices rose without any corresponding growth in wages or jobs. Farmers complained that NRA-generated price increases on the products they used ate up any AAA benefits they received.

Within the administration, Tugwell and others, angered by business activities and the level of **price-fixing** and profits, wanted tougher anti-price-fixing and antimonopoly provisions. Even businesses benefiting from the NRA complained about mountains of paperwork, criticized Section 7a, and feared further restrictions on their business practices. To nearly everyone's relief, on May 27, 1935, the Supreme Court declared the National Recovery Administration unconstitutional in ***Schechter Poultry Corporation v. the United States*** ("the sick chicken case"). The Court ruled that the Constitution did not permit the federal government to set national codes or wages and hours for companies that were not engaged in interstate commerce. The Public Works Administration remained in place, but with the NRA gone, Roosevelt was forced to consider other ways to rekindle the economy.

TVA and REA

Perhaps the most innovative and successful recovery program of the New Deal was the **Tennessee Valley Authority (TVA),** passed midway through Roosevelt's First Hundred Days. The Tennessee River and its **tributaries** ran through some of the most economically disadvantaged areas of the nation. The river basin offered great potential for development of vitally needed flood controls, river navigation, and hydroelectric power. At the center of the plan was harnessing the river system of the Tennessee Valley region through the construction of flood-control systems and hydroelectric dams (see Map 26.1). The project built or refurbished twenty-five dams and brought seasonal flooding more under control. Hundreds of miles of river and lakes became more navigable.

The first benefit was new jobs (relief), but the chief outcome was long-term regional planning and economic vitalization (recovery). TVA directors used the AAA and various government agencies to improve agriculture, and TVA provided inexpensive

price-fixing A government's or industry's artificial setting of commodity prices.

Schechter Poultry Corporation v. the United States Supreme Court decision (1935) declaring the NRA unconstitutional because it regulated companies not involved in interstate commerce.

Tennessee Valley Authority Independent public corporation created by Congress in 1933 and authorized to construct dams and power plants in the Tennessee Valley region.

tributary A river or stream that flows into a larger river.

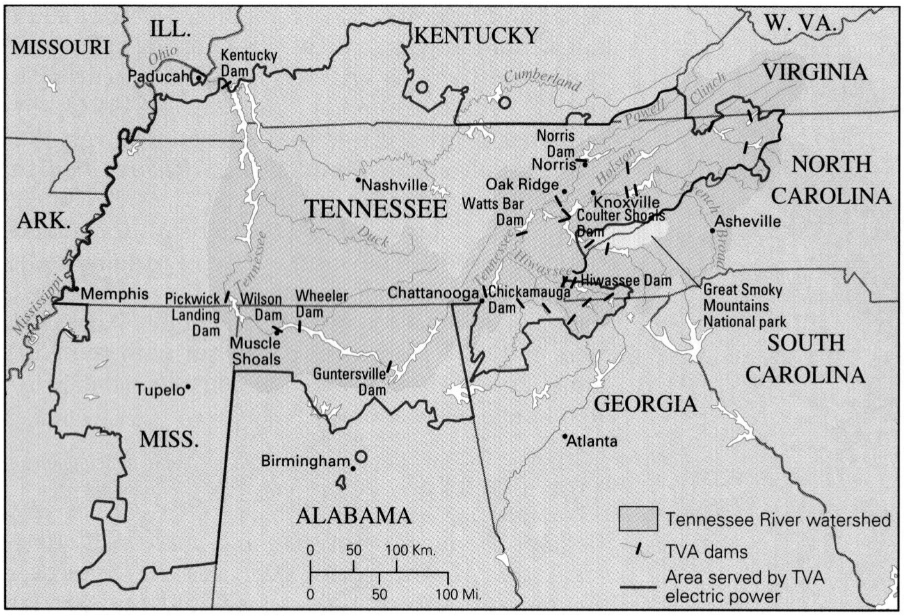

♦ **MAP 26.1 The Tennessee Valley Authority** One of the most ambitious New Deal projects was developing the Tennessee Valley by improving waterways, building hydroelectric dams, and providing electricity to the area. This map shows the various components of the TVA and the region it changed.

electricity through federally owned and operated hydroelectric systems. Only 2 percent of the homes and farms in the region had electricity in 1933. Twelve years later the number of electrified homes had reached 75 percent and, drawn by the low cost of electricity, several industries, including Monsanto Chemical and American Aluminum, had moved into the region.

Although many hailed the TVA's accomplishments, it had its critics. Reflecting local racial attitudes, the TVA accepted segregation—excluding African Americans from many jobs and paying lower wages to the few it hired. Private utility companies and conservatives called the TVA socialistic and opposed government-owned agencies operating factories and power companies. Such conservative opposition was largely responsible for Congress's failure to approve seven TVA-like projects in 1937.

The TVA's electrification program nevertheless became a precedent for a nationwide effort. Utility companies had argued that rural America was too isolated and poor to make service profitable, and in the early 1930s only about 30 percent of farms had electricity. In 1935, the Roosevelt administration created the **Rural Electrification Administration (REA)** to bring electricity to rural America, working with rural electrical cooperatives and bypassing opposition from private utilities and state power commissions. By 1945, electricity was flowing to 45 percent of rural homes and farms. By 1951, 90 percent of America's farms had electricity, generating some of the most important social and economic changes resulting from the New Deal. Running water, the ability to use a variety of household electrical appliances, and improved education, health, and sanitation helped integrate rural areas with the culture of modern, urban America.

Remembering the "Forgotten Man"

Recovery programs could not provide relief for all who needed it. Roosevelt had campaigned on the slogan of helping the "forgotten man," his metaphor for the men and women facing unemployment and

Rural Electrification Administration Government agency established in 1936 for the purpose of loaning money to rural cooperatives to produce and distribute electricity in isolated areas.

TABLE 26.1 Relief, Recovery, Reform, 1933–1938

Relief	Recovery	Reform
	1933	
Civilian Conservation Corps (CCC) Federal Emergency Relief Act (FERA) Home Owner's Loan Corporation (HOLC) Public Works Administration (PWA) Civil Works Administration (CWA)	Emergency Banking Relief Act Tennessee Valley Authority Act (TVA) Agricultural Adjustment Act (AAA) National Recovery Administration (NRA)	Beer and Wine Revenue Act Banking Act, 1933 (guaranteed deposits) Federal Securities Act Glass-Steagall Banking Act
	1934	
National Housing Act Federal Housing Administration (FHA)	Gold Reserve Act	Securities and Exchange Act Reciprocal Trade Agreements
	1935	
Frazier-Lemke Farm Bankruptcy Act Resettlement Administration National Youth Administration (NYA) Works Progress Administration (WPA) Soil Conservation and Domestic Act		National Labor Relations Act Rural Electrification Administration Social Security Act Public Utility Holding Company Act Revenue Act
	1937	
Farm Security Administration		U.S. Housing Authority
	1938	
	Second Agricultural Adjustment Act	Fair Labor Standards Act

poverty. In March 1933, unemployment was at a historic high: 25 percent of the population, nearly 12 million people. In industrial states like New York, Ohio, Pennsylvania, and Illinois unemployment pushed 33 percent. Recognizing that state and private relief sources were unable to cope with the Depression, Roosevelt accepted federal responsibility. During his First Hundred Days, he proposed and Congress enacted four major relief programs (see Table 26.1). All were seen as temporary measures, but they established a new role for the federal government (see chapter-opening map).

♦ Here, Civilian Conservation Corps workers plant seedlings to reforest a section of forest destroyed by fire. Before its demise in 1942, the CCC enrolled over 2.75 million young men. In addition to its work in conservation, the CCC also taught around thirty-five thousand men how to read and write. *UPI/Bettmann.*

The first was the **Civilian Conservation Corps (CCC),** passed on March 31, 1933. Patterned after the military, the CCC established over 2,650 army-style camps to house and provide a healthy, moral environment for unemployed, urban males aged 18 to 25. Within months the program enrolled more than 300,000 men, paying them $30 a month, $25 of which they had to send home. By 1941, enrollment was more than 2 million men. The federally clothed, housed, fed, and paid "Conservation Army" swept across the nation building, developing, and improving national park facilities, cutting out roads and **firebreaks,** erecting telephone poles, digging irrigation ditches, and planting trees. But the CCC was not for everyone. Until 1936, most of those selected were by policy white males from urban areas.

The Civilian Conservation Corps touched only a small percentage of those needing relief. To provide a wider range of relief programs, the Roosevelt administration created the **Federal Emergency Relief Administration (FERA)** in May and the Public Works Administration (PWA), mentioned above, in June 1933. The FERA, headed by **Harry Hopkins,** a former social worker and relief organizer, was funded with $500 million to give to states for their relief efforts. Hopkins and his staff soon discovered that some states did not make very good use of these grants and showed little compassion for the poor. Oregon's governor, for example, opposed payments to anyone able-bodied enough to work and thought that the feeble-minded and aged asking for aid should instead be **chloroformed** to death. Despite such obstacles, by 1935 the FERA was spending over $300 million a year on relief measures.

Although much of the FERA's funds went to states, Hopkins instituted several programs to meet particular needs. One program opened special centers to provide housing, meals, and medical care for many of the homeless roaming the nation. In the program's first year of operation, as many as 5 million people received care. Ed Paulson was one. Riding the rails, he and other hoboes were pulled off a train in Omaha and forced into trucks by deputies. "You're not going to jail," they told him. "You're going to the transient camp." There, Paulson was deloused and given a bath, a bed, and "a spread with

Civilian Conservation Corps Organization created by Congress in 1933 to hire young, unemployed men for conservation work, such as planting trees, digging irrigation ditches, and caring for national parks.

firebreak Strip of cleared or plowed land used to stop the spread of a fire.

Federal Emergency Relief Administration Created in May 1933, it provided direct grants to states and municipalities to spend on relief.

Harry Hopkins Head of several New Deal agencies, first organizing emergency relief and then public works; he remained a close adviser to Roosevelt during World War II.

chloroformed Chloroform is a chemical used as an anesthetic for surgery; used here as a verb to mean to painlessly end a person's life (euthanasia).

scrambled eggs, bacon, bread, coffee, and toast." He recalled years later, "We ate a great meal. We thought we'd gone to heaven." In other programs, more than half a million people attended literacy classes and 1 million people received free vaccinations and immunizations.

The Public Works Administration, directed by Secretary of the Interior Harold Ickes, paid 45 cents an hour for unskilled labor and $1.10 for skilled workers, regardless of race, and eventually provided over $4 billion to state and local governments for more than thirty-four thousand projects, including construction of sidewalks and roads, schools, and community buildings. As with FERA, not all PWA projects fulfilled intended relief criteria. Urban bosses used PWA and other relief money to make jobs for political supporters, and many communities often ignored their poorest neighborhoods when spending PWA funds. One Texas town on the Mexico border used PWA money to hire Mexican Americans to plant palm trees along the main street and paint Protestant churches, while making no effort to improve the town's barrio—where the workers lived—or to paint Catholic churches.

In November 1933, as high unemployment continued despite the CCC, FERA, and PWA, Roosevelt established the **Civil Works Administration (CWA)** to provide nearly 4 million immediate jobs, especially during the winter of 1933–1934. Rapidly instituted, the CWA was administered directly by the federal government. CWA workers participated in a wide variety of work programs and were paid from 30 to 50 cents an hour for unskilled labor, $1.00 to $1.20 for skilled work. Critics complained of "make-work" projects that wasted money, but overall CWA funds were well spent. The CWA built over half a million miles of roads and forty thousand schools. It paid the salaries of more than fifty thousand rural schoolteachers. Despite its success, Roosevelt ended the CWA in February 1934, when the immediate crisis was over and the PWA and FERA could fill the need for relief.

Not all relief programs were aimed at the homeless and poor. Two aided homeowners. The **Home Owner's Loan Corporation (HOLC),** created in May 1933, permitted homeowners to refinance their mortgages at lower interest rates through the federal government. Before it stopped making loans in 1936, the HOLC had refinanced 1 million homes, including 20 percent of all mortgaged urban homes. The National Housing Act, passed in June 1934, created the **Federal Housing Administration (FHA),** which still provides federally backed loans for home mortgages and repairs, providing stimulus for the purchase of single-family homes.

The Second Hundred Days

- What were the sources of opposition to Roosevelt's First Hundred Days?
- What methods that would be better than Roosevelt's measures did Long, Townsend, and Coughlin expect to use to combat the Depression?
- How and why did the Second Hundred Days focus more on people and reform than on national economic recovery?

The New Deal had begun with almost total support in Congress and among the people. By mid-1933, however, most Republicans were actively opposing New Deal legislation, objecting to relief programs, federal spending, and increased government controls over business. Conservatives fumed that Roosevelt threatened free enterprise, if not capitalism itself. They thought it bad enough when Roosevelt in April 1933 pulled the nation off the **gold standard,** which many considered the foundation of world capitalism. Then in January 1934 he nationalized gold deposits in Federal Reserve Banks and devalued the dollar to 59 cents.

To warn the country about Roosevelt and his "baloney dollars," conservatives became increasingly vocal in their attacks on the president and the New Deal. The Hearst newspaper chain instructed its editors to expose the New Deal as a "raw deal" and to warn the public that Roosevelt planned to "Soak the Successful" and lead the nation into socialism. In August 1934, a coalition of anti-Roosevelt and anti–New Deal Democrats and Republicans

Civil Works Administration Emergency unemployment relief program in 1933 and 1934; it hired 4 million jobless people for federal, state, and local work projects.

Home Owner's Loan Corporation Government agency created in 1933 that refinanced home mortgage debts for nonfarm owners and allowed homeowners to borrow money from the agency to pay taxes and make repairs.

Federal Housing Administration Agency created by the National Housing Act (1934) to insure loans made by banks and other institutions for new construction, repairs, and improvements of housing.

gold standard An internationally established value for a nation's currency based on a specific weight of gold; it meant that paper money could be exchanged for a specified amount of gold.

joined forces with many leaders of American business to form the **American Liberty League,** to mobilize political opposition to Roosevelt. By 1935, the group claimed nearly 150,000 supporters, including many Democrats. According to the American Liberty League, not only was the NRA unconstitutional, but also the AAA had resulted in "fascist control" of agriculture and relief meant the "end of democracy."

Populist Voices

For the majority of the American people, however, Roosevelt and the New Deal still spelled hope and faith in the future. In 1934 Democrats friendly to Roosevelt gained overwhelming victories, winning twenty-six of thirty-five contested Senate races and nine additional seats in the House of Representatives. The elections virtually wiped out the segment of the Republican party most opposed to the New Deal. Newly elected Democrats arrived in Washington eager to support Roosevelt, even as the president increasingly worried that economic recovery was not progressing as projected. Unemployment had been reduced, but primarily through government work programs, which still supported nearly 8 million households, or 22 percent of the population.

Encouraged by the election results and angry at business elements and conservatives for their dissent, Roosevelt was ready to switch approaches to fighting the Depression. Pushing Roosevelt toward a new approach was the unexpected grassroots criticism that the New Deal was not doing enough to help the "forgotten man." The nation seemed especially interested in the views and activities of three outspoken critics: Father Charles Coughlin, Senator Huey Long, and Dr. Francis Townsend.

At three o'clock every Sunday afternoon, **Father Charles Coughlin,** a Roman Catholic priest, used the radio to reach out to nearly 30 million Americans with a mix of anticommunism, anti-elitism, and populist political and economic arguments. Coughlin had lashed out at Hoover and anyone else who opposed relief. "God would have been condemned for giving manna in the desert because it was a dole," he told his audience. Throughout 1932 and 1933, the "radio priest" of Royal Oak, Michigan, strongly supported Roosevelt and the New Deal. But by mid-1934, he had turned his influential radio voice first against the National Recovery Administration and then against the whole New Deal and Roosevelt. In November, he formed the National Union for Social Justice, calling it the "people's lobby," to promote politicians and legislation that would help the masses. Coughlin advocated a guaranteed annual income, the redistribution of national wealth, tougher antimonopoly laws, and the nationalization of banking. Within a year his organization claimed more than 5 million members.

Coughlin was not alone in proclaiming that Roosevelt was not doing enough for the "forgotten man." In the Senate, **Huey Long** of Louisiana, another one-time supporter, hotly criticized the president. Known for his red hair and purple shirts, Long had achieved power in Louisiana by attacking big money and promising to help poor whites. As governor, he had built roads, schools, and hospitals, provided free textbooks, and imposed new taxes on oil companies and the wealthy. Developing a similar, anti-elitist plan for the nation in 1934, he broke with Roosevelt and advocated a **Share the Wealth** plan. It called for the federal government to provide every American family with an annual check for $2,000, a home, a car, a radio, and a college education for each child. The plan would be funded by having incomes over $1 million taxed at 100 percent and by inheritance laws that would make it nearly impossible to inherit more than $5 million. Crying "Soak the Rich!" Share the Wealth societies mushroomed around the nation, soon enrolling more than 4 million followers.

By 1935, Democratic leaders feared that Long was considering a run for the presidency, which, if he joined forces with Father Coughlin to form a third party, might pull several million votes away from Roosevelt. Prospects of a third party had soared in

American Liberty League Conservative organization that existed between 1934 and 1940 to oppose the New Deal.

Father Charles Coughlin Roman Catholic priest whose influential radio addresses in the 1930s at first emphasized social justice but eventually became anti-Semitic and profascist.

Huey Long Louisiana governor, then U.S. senator, who ran a powerful political machine and whose advocacy of redistribution of income was gaining him a national political following at the time of his assassination in 1935.

Share the Wealth Movement that sprang up around the nation in the 1930s urging the redistribution of wealth through government taxes or programs; its slogan was "Every man a king."

♦ In 1934, Huey Long, a fiery Populist politician from Louisiana, claimed that Roosevelt was not helping the common man enough. A dramatic and flamboyant speaker, Long proclaimed his support for the "little man" with the slogan, "Every Man a King" and the Share the Wealth program that would tax the rich and "spread the wealth among all our people." Before Long could become a real political threat to Roosevelt he was assassinated in September 1935. *Corbis-Bettman.*

1934 when **Dr. Francis Townsend,** another popular spokesman for the poor, particularly the elderly, appeared willing to join with Long and Coughlin. The elderly, ignored by work programs and frequently denied relief because they owned property, were among those most cruelly hit by the Depression. Nearly 70 himself, Dr. Townsend advocated a federal old-age pension plan that would provide every nonworking American aged 60 and over with a monthly $200 pension check. Townsend proposed a national sales tax of 2 percent on business transactions to finance the payments. Thousands of clubs formed in support of Townsend's idea, with an estimated membership of several million, including sixty members of Congress.

The growing popularity of Long, Coughlin, and Townsend reflected the frustration of a large segment of the American population, largely blue collar and lower middle class, who believed that after nearly two full years of the New Deal, government was still doing too little to help them. Long's and Townsend's programs were attractive because they would aid people, not businesses, and would push the country toward recovery by promoting consumption. It was a position similar to the one that several of Roosevelt's advisers, particularly Felix Frankfurter and Harry Hopkins, were strongly recommending.

A Shift in Focus

Responding to the growing pressures to modify the New Deal and showing his irritation with business leaders, Roosevelt announced a change in priorities in his 1935 State of the Union address: the administration would focus more on people than on business. He asked Congress to provide more work relief, to develop an old-age and unemployment insurance program, and to pass legislation regulating holding companies and utilities. During the period dubbed the Second Hundred Days, a solidly Democratic and largely liberal Congress responded with a series of acts. In April 1935, Congress allocated nearly $5 billion for relief to be divided among the CCC, PWA, FERA, and the newly created **Works Progress Administration (WPA).**

Roosevelt named Harry Hopkins to head the WPA, whose goal—more than that of the PWA—was to provide jobs as quickly as possible. The Works Progress Administration established a maximum 140-hour work month with wages based on skill level, gender, race, and geography. Wages varied from area to area and were usually higher than relief payments but lower than local wages, except for nonwhites and women, whose WPA wages generally exceeded local wages. Between 1935 and 1938, the WPA employed more than 2.1 million people a year. Most did manual labor, building roads,

Dr. Francis Townsend California public health physician who proposed the Townsend Plan in 1933, under which every retired person over 60 would be paid a $200 monthly pension to be spent within the month.

Works Progress Administration Agency established in 1935 and headed by Harry Hopkins; it hired the unemployed for construction, conservation, and arts programs.

♦ The Works Progress Administration not only built roads and buildings, but also provided employment for teachers, writers, and artists. A common theme among WPA artists and writers was the strength and dignity of common people as they faced their difficult lives. Here, a Michigan WPA artist sketches WPA workers. *National Archives.*

schools, and public buildings, but the WPA employed professional and white-collar workers as well. In Georgia, the WPA not only built but also staffed 145 new libraries. Teachers, writers, artists, actors, photographers, composers, and musicians were among other professionals who benefited. Historians conducted numerous oral interviews, wrote state and local histories and guidebooks, and produced a significant study of slavery based on their research. The WPA's Writers Project provided Jewish novelist and future Pulitzer Prize winner Saul Bellow with his first literary job—writing short biographies—and allowed African-American author Richard Wright to write his highly acclaimed novel *Native Son* (1940). Professional theater groups featuring well-known actors toured towns and cities performing Shakespearean and other plays. By 1939, an estimated 30 million people had watched WPA productions.

The art programs were designed primarily to help artists but were also conceived as a way to elevate the public's awareness of art—"Art for the Millions"—and to promote positive themes and images of American society, especially the importance of the farmer, the worker, the common man. This concept was especially evident in the federally sponsored mural project, in which government-funded artists created more than 2,500 murals and 100,000 paintings, most for public buildings. Some people objected to artists and writers receiving aid. Art was not real work, they argued, to which Hopkins responded, "Hell, they've got to eat just like other people."

The WPA also made special efforts to help women, minorities, students, and young adults. Prodded by Eleanor Roosevelt, the WPA employed between 300,000 and 400,000 women a year. Although some were hired as teachers and nurses, the majority, especially in rural areas, worked on sewing and canning projects. WPA efforts to ensure African-American employment thrived in the northeastern states but stalled in the South. The **National Youth Administration (NYA)** was an especially successful venture that provided aid for college and high school students and programs for young people not in school. In 1936, more than two hundred thousand students

National Youth Administration Program established by executive order in 1935 to provide employment for young people and to help needy high school and college students continue their education.

were receiving aid and several education-work programs had been established. **Mary McLeod Bethune,** an African-American educator, directed the NYA's Office of Minority Affairs, and through determination and constant, skillfully applied pressure, she obtained support for black schools and colleges and increased African-American enrollments in vocational and recreational programs.

More dramatic than the creation of the Works Progress Administration was passage of the **Social Security Act** of 1935. Whereas the WPA was a temporary expedient to reduce unemployment, Social Security was to be a permanent modification of the government's role in society. Only 15 percent of workers were covered by any sort of pension plan, and many of those plans no longer functioned in 1935. The primary force behind the Social Security Act was Frances Perkins, the first woman cabinet member, who accepted the position of secretary of labor with the understanding that the administration would pass some type of old-age pension system (see Individual Choices: Frances Perkins). In 1934, encouraged by the popularity of Dr. Townsend's plan, Perkins chaired the Committee on Economic Security to draft a social security bill. Passed by Congress in August 1935, the Social Security Act had three sections.

The most controversial part of the legislation created the Social Security system. Conservatives called it socialistic and insisted it would remove the incentive to work. As approved by Congress, the law provided a pension plan for retirees 65 or older. They were to receive initial payments ranging from $10 to $85 a month. The more a worker paid into the system, the larger his or her pension would be. The program was to begin in 1937 when the Federal Insurance Contribution Act (FICA) created a new tax—to be collected from workers and employers—and the first Social Security payments would be made in 1942. Not all workers were covered. Many occupations, including domestic and agricultural laborers, were exempt. Compared to Townsend's dream and many existing European systems, U.S. Social Security was limited and conservative, although it represented a major shift in the U.S. government's responsibility for the welfare of society.

A less controversial section of the Social Security Act established at the state level a federally supported system of unemployment compensation funded by a new federal tax levied on employers. Within two years, every state was part of the system, paying the jobless between $15 and $18 a week in unemployment compensation and supplying support to more than 28 million people. A third section of the law made federal funds available to states for aid to families with dependent children and the disabled. This provision aided more than 4 million impoverished female-headed families.

The National Labor Relations Act, passed in July 1935, emphasized another change in the role of government. Largely the work of Senator Robert Wagner of New York, and generally called the **Wagner Act,** it strengthened the union movement by putting the power of government behind the workers' right to organize and to bargain with employers for wages and benefits. It created the National Labor Relations Board to ensure workers' rights, to conduct elections for union representatives, and to prevent unfair labor practices like firing or **blacklisting** workers for union activities. Roosevelt's support for the Wagner Act helped clinch labor support for him and the Democrats. By 1936, union contributions to the Democratic party were among the largest.

The Wagner Act and the Social Security Act reduced the credibility of those who called Roosevelt too conservative. Similar political goals were evident in other acts of the Second Hundred Days. When considering tax reforms, Roosevelt's adviser Raymond Moley suggested that the New Dealers "steal Long's thunder" by placing higher taxes on inheritance and gifts, raising income-tax rates for the wealthy, and instituting a graduated income tax for corporations. Roosevelt agreed and asked Congress for the Revenue Act of 1935, which passed in August. Among workers and the not-so-wealthy, the law was clearly popular. The new tax structure, however, did little to redistribute wealth. In fact,

Mary McLeod Bethune African-American educator who founded Bethune College and who, as director of the Office of Minority Affairs within the National Youth Administration, was a strong and vocal advocate for equality of opportunity for African Americans during the New Deal.

Social Security Act Law passed by Congress in 1935 to create systems of unemployment, old-age, and disability insurance and provide for child welfare.

Wagner Act Law passed by Congress in 1935 that defined unfair labor practices and protected unions against coercive measures such as blacklisting.

blacklisting Practice in which businesses share information to deny employment to workers known to belong to unions.

INDIVIDUAL CHOICES

Choosing to Serve

Frances Perkins

Beginning in 1911, Frances Perkins sought to improve working conditions for the nation's men, women, and children. Perkins was the first woman cabinet member, and as Secretary of Labor, she tirelessly worked to create the Social Security system, establish a minimum wage for workers, and limit the number of hours people could be required to work. New York Historical Society.

On February 1, 1933, responding to a month-long flurry of rumors in the press and among "those in the know" that she was to be chosen secretary of labor, Frances Perkins wrote President-elect Franklin D. Roosevelt saying that she "honestly" hoped the rumors were wrong. Shortly after the letter, Mary Dewson, director of the Women's Division of the Democratic National Committee, visited Perkins to convince her to take the cabinet position if offered. Dewson, who had recommended Perkins to Roosevelt, reminded Perkins of the many years she had spent fighting to establish unemployment compensation and a minimum wage and to abolish child labor. "You want these things done," Dewson argued. "You have ideas. . . . Nobody else will do it." She told Perkins, "You owe it to the women. . . . Too many people count on what you do."

On February 22, Roosevelt asked Frances Perkins to be secretary of labor. She replied that if she accepted she would push for the abolition of child labor, the establishment of unemployment insurance, old-age pensions, and a minimum wage and a limit on maximum hours of work. Roosevelt responded that she would "have to invent the way to do these things" and that she should not "expect too much help from" him. She chose to accept the position. After some opposition from organized labor, she was easily confirmed by the Senate and became secretary of labor—"Madam Secretary," the first woman to serve in a president's cabinet.

She arrived at the position through hard work and a commitment to improving workers' lives. The daughter of a conservative middle-class family, she had been introduced to the lives of workers while taking an economics class at Mount Holyoke College. She quickly immersed herself in the spirit of the Progressive era, participating in the settlement house movement and helping to investigate working conditions as part of the New York Factory Commission that arose after the tragic fire at the Triangle Shirtwaist Company in 1911. Through her work on the commission and with the Consumers' League, she became involved in New York politics as a supporter of Al Smith. She served Governor Smith as a member of the Industrial Commission, working to improve the circumstances of workers. When Franklin D. Roosevelt replaced Smith as governor in 1929, he named her industrial commissioner, a state cabinet-level position—making her the first woman to hold such a position at the state level. Beginning in 1930, she moved to support legislation that reduced the workweek for women to 48 hours, created a minimum wage, and developed unemployment insurance. Thus, when appointed secretary of labor in 1933, she already was experienced in the politics of improving the life of the worker.

During the First Hundred Days of Roosevelt's administration, Perkins and the Department of Labor helped to create the Civilian Conservation Corps and the Federal Emergency Relief Administration. In 1934, as the chair of the newly created Committee on Economic Security, she began to draft a social security bill. In encouragement, Roosevelt told her: "You care about this thing. You believe in it. Therefore I know you will put your back to it more than anyone else, and you'll drive it through."

The Social Security Act of 1935 was the outcome of many choices, most of which involved Perkins, Harry Hopkins, and Roosevelt. It was decided, for fiscal and political reasons, to have workers pay into the system as opposed to having the government pay for it out of taxes. Perkins wanted to include medical coverage, but it had to be excluded from the social security package, in large part because of the hostile reaction of the medical profession. To convince Congress to pass a social security program, she made hundreds of public speeches and countless appearances before countless Congressional committees. With its passage on August 14, 1935, the relationship between the federal government and the people permanently changed.

Frances Perkins took pride in the passage of the Social Security Act, but she was overjoyed when the Fair Labor Standards Act became law in 1938. "A self-supporting and self-respecting democracy," she testified, "can plead no justification for the existence of child labor, no economic reason for chiseling workers' wages or stretching workers' hours." The bill was attacked by conservatives and union leaders as allowing too much government intrusion. Conservatives called it a form of socialism, while union leaders argued that collective bargaining—not the government—should gain wage and hour benefits for workers. Nevertheless, the bill became law on June 25, 1938, and more than 12 million workers felt its effect. It immediately raised the pay of 300,000 people and shortened the workday for a million more. Together, the Social Security Act and the Fair Labor Standards Act changed the economic and social values of the nation and ushered in a new relationship between the government and the people.

Frances Perkins continued to serve Roosevelt and his successor Harry S Truman as an advocate of government support of workers and their families. Retiring in 1953, she wrote, lectured, and joined the faculty at Cornell University. She died in 1965, and her tombstone reflects the fateful choice she made in 1933:

FRANCES PERKINS WILSON
1880–1965
SECRETARY OF LABOR OF U.S.A.
1933–1945

YEARS OF DUST
DUST STORM
RESETTLEMENT ADMINISTRATION
Rescues Victims
Restores Land to Proper Use

♦ The creation of the Resettlement Administration in 1935 established a means to deal with rural poverty by providing low-cost loans, equipment, and education to poor farmers, sharecroppers, and tenant farmers who had been evicted from their farms. Ben Shahn's "Years of Dust" effectively depicts a demoralized sharecropper and the Resettlement Administration's goal of rescuing victims. *Library of Congress.*

from 1933 to 1939, the wealthiest 1 percent increased their personal wealth 2.3 percent, controlling 30.6 percent of the nation's wealth. Still, Roosevelt's tax measures further angered business interests and conservatives, as did other reform acts of his Second Hundred Days, like the Banking Act and the Public Utilities Holding Company Act. Both provided more government controls and enhanced the government's ability to conduct fiscal policy—and prompted conservatives to warn against a New Deal dictatorship.

Other acts reasserted Roosevelt's support for the "forgotten man." To help small farmers, sharecroppers, and tenant farmers, the **Resettlement Administration** was established and the Farm Mortgage Moratorium Act was passed. The latter, introduced by William Lemke of North Dakota and initially opposed by Roosevelt, allowed federal courts to reduce the debts of farmers and provided a three-year **moratorium** on some farm seizures. Headed by Brain Truster Rexford Tugwell, the Resettlement Administration tried to resettle marginal farmers on better land and established a few planned communities and communal farms. Although both acts helped only a small percentage of those in need, they, along with the WPA, Social Security, and the Wagner Act, emphasized Roosevelt's concern for the common man just in time for the 1936 presidential election.

The New Deal and Society

- What were some of the outcomes of the New Deal for cities across America?
- What were Roosevelt's expectations regarding civil rights? How did the New Deal affect the choices of women, African Americans, Hispanics, and American Indians?

Just as the Depression had an impact on every segment of society, so too did the New Deal. Newly restored confidence found expression in the popular entertainment of the time. And within some segments of the population, the New Deal encouraged hope for overcoming obstacles that had long limited opportunities.

The New Deal and Urban America

As the Depression pushed many men and women into cities looking for jobs and shelter, city governments found that their resources were too few to maintain the city, much less to care for the needy. From 1929 to 1933, property values declined 18 percent in many major cities because many individuals and businesses failed to pay their property taxes. In 1933, 145 of the largest cities collected only 75 percent of the property-tax revenues they were owed. To "save" their budgets, cities cut wages and laid off policemen, firemen, teachers, and other municipal

Resettlement Administration Agency established in 1935 to resettle poor families on new farms or in new communities and to make loans enabling sharecroppers to buy their own land.

moratorium Suspension of an ongoing or planned activity.

workers. Some cities issued their own paper money to pay wages and fell further into debt. By 1934, Los Angeles was spending 78 percent of its budget on debt payments. Before Houston bankers loaned the city money, they demanded control over which positions and programs would be trimmed or eliminated. In most cities relief programs were among those targeted for elimination or reduction. "I am as much in favor of relief for the unemployables as anyone, but I am unwilling to continue this relief at the expense of bankrupting the City of Birmingham," stated the head of the city commission.

The New Deal provided new hope for cities by providing public works projects that eased the burdens of unemployment and relief. In many cities, especially in the West and South, public works projects also improved the existing **infrastructure** by constructing roads, bridges, hospitals, schools, and other public buildings. San Francisco saw the construction of the Golden Gate Bridge. Southern California, especially the Los Angeles basin, drew additional benefits from the water and cheap electrical power supplied with the completion of Boulder Dam in 1935. There were also political gains to be made from federal money and projects. "Roosevelt Is My Religion" was the 1936 campaign slogan of Mayor Edward J. Kelly, who kept Chicago solvent with federal funds. Roosevelt carried Chicago by over a half-million votes. In Pittsburgh, Democrats led by David Lawrence used federal programs and money to end Republican control of the city.

Other federal programs shaped the growth of urban areas in more subtle ways. Agencies like the HOLC and the FHA saved thousands of urban homes and supported the building of single-family units, rather than high-density multifamily structures. The outcome was to encourage suburbanization rather than the development of central metropolitan areas.

Popular Culture

Movies and radio, the most popular forms of entertainment throughout the 1930s, provided a break from the worries of Depression life. *Gone with the Wind, The Wizard of Oz,* and dozens of musicals like *Top Hat* and the *Broadway Melody* series afforded a brief escape from the gloom of the daily routine. Movies offered not only escape, however. Some also reflected the social and political changes generated by the Depression and the New Deal. The cheerful musical *Golddiggers of 1933* delighted audiences with its lavish sets and attractive, young chorus line, but it also contained social commentary. In one scene, unemployed men march across the stage while the lead singer implores,

Remember my forgotten man,
You put a rifle in his hand,
You sent him far away,
You shouted, "Hip Hooray!"
But look at him today.

Romantic comedies were also popular, but they too could look seriously at the troubles of the times. A favorite plot involved romance between people of opposite economic and social backgrounds. Delighted audiences laughed at the problems created by the couple's social differences and the meddling of their snobbish, class-conscious relatives and friends. In the end, good sense and love prevailed, honest virtues were rewarded, and different social classes found a common ground.

Gangster films remained popular but underwent a slight change. Before the New Deal, famous stars frequently played heroic but doomed gangsters. But as the New Deal became part of the American experience, those big names were increasingly cast as brave government officials who brought villains to justice. James Cagney became an FBI agent in *G-Men;* Humphrey Bogart was a crusading district attorney in *Crime School* and *Marked Woman.* Both actors had achieved fame playing tough guys, usually convicts or con men. Such character changes reflected a more positive vision of government than ever before and renewed emphasis on Hollywood's **production codes,** which stressed uplifting themes like honesty and courage.

Radio was even more popular than the movies. Nearly 90 percent of American households had at least one radio. Like movies, radio provided escape from the "De-repression," as the Depression was frequently called on the popular "Amos 'n' Andy Show." In 1932 radio introduced comedians—commonly called "gloom chasers"—like the Marx Brothers, George Burns and Gracie Allen, and Jack Benny to the American public. Singers Al Jolson and Bing Crosby also crooned their first songs over the radio in 1932. Two years later, radio fueled an amateur

infrastructure An underlying base for a system or organization; the basic facilities, services, and installations needed for the functioning of a community.

production code Standards that Hollywood film companies adopted to keep material considered immoral or indecent out of movies.

♦ Throughout the Depression, the most popular form of entertainment was the movies, providing escape from daily hardships into a prosperous world of fantasy. At twenty cents a ticket, movies attracted as many as seventy-five million people a week. In this photo, taken at a movie theatre in San Diego, children display door prizes given during the matinee. *San Diego Historical Society, Photograph Collection.*

craze with the "Original Amateur Hour." Few contestants ever became professional entertainers, but the audience loved the idea that an ordinary person could walk in off the street and, with a little luck and boldness, become a success. When amateur programs began to fade in 1937, radio turned to quiz shows that allowed the common person to show uncommon knowledge and skill. Keeping pace in popularity with comedians, amateur shows, and quiz programs were crime fighters like the Shadow, Dick Tracy, and the Lone Ranger and Tonto. Such heroes proved again and again that truth, justice, honor, and courage always prevailed.

Although both movies and radio provided hours of entertainment and escape from everyday life, radio also played a key role in providing information about world and national events. News commentators like Walter Winchell drew faithful audiences, and the president's fireside chats frequently attracted more than 20 percent of radio listeners. Equally popular was Eleanor Roosevelt's spot on the "Vanity Fair" program. Perhaps radio's biggest impact occurred when Orson Welles merged news with entertainment in his 1938 Halloween broadcast of "War of the Worlds," a science-fiction story in which Martians invade New Jersey. Welles presented the tale in such a skillful newscast style that millions of panic-stricken Americans believed earth really had been invaded.

Although movies and radio rarely criticized American politics and society, many novelists certainly did. Pushing for change, some writers stressed the immorality of capitalism and the inequities caused by racism and class differences. But few advocated an end to capitalism or the downfall of democracy. Instead they found heroes among those who refused to break under the strain of the Depression. Erskine Caldwell's *Tobacco Road* (1933), John Steinbeck's *The Grapes of Wrath* (1939), and Richard Wright's *Native Son* (1940) described "losers" whose misery was not of their own making but the fault of society. In these and similar novels, authors assailed the rich and powerful, praised the poor's noble humanitarian spirit and sense of fair play and equality, and stressed social morality and responsibility.

Although many feared that the Depression would swell the ranks of those who rejected American social, economic, and political values, the main thrust of popular culture was to affirm traditional American values. Popular themes expressed faith that the long-term effects of democracy would allow the integrity of the nation's people and leaders to emerge.

A New Deal for Minorities and Women

President Roosevelt was not alone in fostering the idea of a caring government. Perhaps even more than the president, Eleanor Roosevelt was sensitive to the needs of ordinary Americans, especially minorities and women. The first truly active First Lady, she crisscrossed the country meeting, listening to, and talking with coal miners, waitresses, farmers, housewives—a cross-section of American society. Those who missed her personal visits could read her daily newspaper column, "My Day," or write to her, as thousands did, generally describing their hardships and asking for help. Rarely able to provide any direct assistance, Eleanor Roosevelt in her replies emphasized hope and explained changes being made by the New Deal. Within the White House, she goaded her husband and New Dealers not to neglect the poor, women, and minorities.

Eleanor Roosevelt took the lead in supporting women and African Americans. She worked publicly and privately to reduce discrimination in the government and throughout the country. In 1933, she helped to convene a special White House conference on the needs of women. Together with Frances Perkins, Ellen Woodward—director of the Women's Division of the WPA—and other women in the administration, she labored to ensure that women received more than just token consideration from New Deal agencies and the Democratic party. The First Lady made herself available to women as a source of information, inspiration, and help. Mary "Molly" Dewson, head of the Women's Division of the Democratic National Committee, noted, "When I wanted help on some definite point, Mrs. Roosevelt gave [me] the opportunity to sit by the President at dinner and the matter was settled before we finished our soup." Mrs. Roosevelt also directly helped women journalists by holding news conferences just for women reporters. With Eleanor Roosevelt as role model and supporter, the New Deal provided for women in government and politics more opportunities than they had received at any previous time in American history.

For women outside politics and the professional class, the New Deal was much less beneficial. There was little effort to raise women's wages. NRA codes maintained lower wages for women as did many public works jobs funded by New Deal agencies. Waitresses and agricultural and domestic laborers were not covered by Social Security or minimum-wage requirements. Women made up about 10 percent of the WPA work force, but their jobs were in traditional female occupations—sewing was the largest program for women.

♦ President Franklin D. Roosevelt campaigned on helping the "forgotten man." As shown in this political cartoon, as First Lady, Eleanor Roosevelt did not forget women. She worked diligently to ensure that they benefited from the New Deal and had access to government and the Democratic Party. *Franklin D. Roosevelt Library.*

Eleanor Roosevelt was also determined to affirm the equality and significant contributions of African Americans. Working with black educators and administrators like Mary Bethune of the National Youth Administration, she sought to generate new opportunities for blacks. In 1939, she demonstrated her commitment to racial equality when the Daughters of the American Revolution refused to allow renowned black opera singer Marian Anderson to sing at their concert hall in Washington, D.C. In a highly visible protest, Eleanor Roosevelt resigned her membership in the DAR and helped arrange a larger, public concert on the steps of the Lincoln Memorial. Marian Anderson's performance before

♦ In 1935 Mary McLeod Bethune (front center), became the first African-American woman to hold a high-ranking government position, serving as the Head of the Office of Minority Affairs in the National Youth Administration. Here, she is shown with the Council of Negro Women, which she helped organize in 1935 to focus on the problems faced by African Americans at the national level. *New York Public Library, Schomburg Center for Research in Black Culture.*

Lincoln's statue attracted more than seventy-five thousand people.

Eleanor Roosevelt's support for equality and better treatment for African Americans was welcomed, but most black leaders perceived that the existing patterns of prejudice, discrimination, and segregation remained untouched by the New Deal. A political realist, President Roosevelt recognized the key role of white southern Democrats in Congress and the Democratic party and so retreated from promoting civil rights legislation, even an antilynching law. When black leaders complained, he admitted, "If I come out for the antilynching bill now, they will block every bill I ask Congress to pass. . . . I just can't take that risk."

Nevertheless, the New Deal and the Roosevelts brought about positive changes in favor of racial equality. Several African Americans were appointed to positions throughout the government, and in August 1936 Mary Bethune organized African Americans within the administration into a **"Black Cabinet,"** which acted as a semiofficial advisory commission on racial relations. "Let us forget the particular office each one of us holds," she said. "We must think in terms as a 'whole' for the greatest service of our people." Among the most pressing need for African Americans, the Black Cabinet concluded, was access to relief and jobs. In northern cities, black unemployment ran from 50 to 90 percent, and it was not uncommon for state and local agencies routinely to deny relief to African Americans. Fortunately, Ickes and Hopkins were proponents of racial equality and used the PWA, CWA, and WPA to provide African Americans with relief and jobs.

Not every New Deal administrator or agency was as committed to equality as Hopkins and the WPA. The Civilian Conservation Corps and the Tennessee Valley Authority openly practiced segregation and discrimination, and even within the PWA and WPA many federal administrators frequently found antiblack attitudes too great to overcome. Skilled African-American workers were almost always given unskilled, low-paying public works jobs, and the Texas state legislature especially wanted minority women to be trained only in cooking, cleaning, and sewing. Even in the best of cases, federal sup-

"Black Cabinet" African-American members of the Roosevelt administration organized by Mary McLeod Bethune into a semiofficial advisory committee on racial issues.

♦ In San Antonio, Texas, many Mexican Americans held jobs as pecan shellers and were among the worst paid in the nation—sometimes working a 54-hour week for only $3. *Benson Latin American Collection, University of Texas at Austin.*

port was not enough to help more than a small segment of the black population. Even plans to tear down slums and build low-income housing frequently underwent local revisions and resulted in segregated, middle-income housing instead. Slums merely changed address.

Still, by 1938, New Deal programs were providing nearly 30 percent of the African-American population with some federal relief, often over the opposition of local authorities. Most African Americans praised Roosevelt and promised their political support. "The WPA came along and Roosevelt came to be a god. . . . You worked, you got a paycheck, and you had some dignity." By 1934, in northern cities and wherever African Americans could vote, blacks were bolting from the Republican party of Lincoln and enlisting in the Democratic party. In the 1936 presidential election, Roosevelt received nearly 90 percent of the nation's black vote.

Latinos benefited from the New Deal in much the same way as African Americans—indirectly. In San Antonio, for instance, 30 percent of blacks and 29 percent of Mexican Americans were on relief. Agencies like the PWA and WPA not only gave jobs to Latinos but also paid wages that usually exceeded what they received in the **private sector.** The WPA paid $8.54 a week for unskilled labor, whereas Mexican Americans received an average of $6.02 or less a week from private employers. New Deal legislation also helped union organizers trying to assist Latino workers throughout the West and Southwest. There were few successful strikes, but, after strikes in 1934 and 1935, San Antonio's Mexican-American pecan shellers, led by local union activist "Red" Emma Tenayuca, finally succeeded in getting higher wages and union recognition in 1938. In the fields of central California, however, Mexican-American unions had little success in protecting the interests of farm workers, although federal relief agencies supplying food and clothing often helped strikers.

Like African Americans, most Hispanics became poorer during the 1930s but recognized in Roosevelt a compassionate president. Senator Dennis Chavez of New Mexico served as Roosevelt's adviser on Hispanic-American affairs and was able to ensure that New Deal programs did not neglect the Latino population.

Unlike most Mexican Americans and African Americans, American Indians benefited directly from the New Deal. Secretary of the Interior Ickes and Commissioner of Indian Affairs John Collier opposed existing Indian policies, which since 1887 had sought to destroy the reservation system and obliterate Indian cultures. At Collier's urging, Congress passed the **Indian Reorganization Act** in 1934. The act returned land and community control to tribal organizations, thereby reaffirming the reservation system. It provided for Indian self-rule on the reservations and prevented individual ownership of tribal lands. To improve the squalid conditions of most reservations and to provide jobs, Collier organized a CCC-type agency solely for Indians and ensured that other New Deal agencies played a part in improving Indian lands and providing jobs.

private sector Businesses run by private citizens rather than by the government.

Indian Reorganization Act Law passed by Congress in 1934 that ended Indian allotment and returned surplus land to tribal ownership; it also sought to encourage tribal self-government and improve economic conditions on reservations.

♦ John Collier worked to ensure the passage of the Indian Reorganization Act. Designed to restore tribal sovereignty under federal authority, each tribe had to ratify the act to participate. Not all tribes did; seventy-seven rejected it, including the Navajos, the nation's largest tribe. This photo shows a group of Navajos meeting with Collier to discuss government-imposed limitations on the number of sheep each Navajo could own. *Wide World Photos.*

Working with tribal leaders, Collier also took measures to protect, preserve, and encourage Indian customs, languages, religions, and folkways. Although it was a positive effort, Collier's New Deal for Indians could not reverse the problems created by years of poverty and government neglect. At best, his programs slowed the pace of a long-running economic decline and allowed American Indians to regain some control over their culture and society.

The New Deal Winds Down

- Why did Roosevelt choose to attempt to pack the Supreme Court? What led to his failure?
- What factors constrained Roosevelt's efforts to maintain the political initiative after his re-election?
- What was the outcome of the New Deal in terms of the structure of government and Americans' expectations about government?

By the presidential election year of 1936, the Second Hundred Days had effectively reasserted Roosevelt's leadership and popularity. The likelihood of a successful Republican or third-party challenge to Roosevelt was remote. Huey Long had died in 1935, the victim of an assassin's bullet. Another Louisiana populist, Gerald L. K. Smith, joined forces with Coughlin and Townsend to form a third party, the Union party, which nominated William Lemke for president, but it never posed a threat to Roosevelt. Nor did the Socialist or Communist parties mount any noticeable opposition. The Depression had caused more people to flirt with Marxism, and membership in the Communist party by 1936 had mushroomed to between fifty and sixty thousand from only seven thousand in 1930. But as in the Socialist party, many members of the Communist party left disenchanted soon after joining, and both parties were torn by constant internal disputes over whether to support Roosevelt and the New Deal.

The Republican party was hardly more of a worry to the Democrats. In a less-than-enthusiastic convention, Republicans nominated the only available candidate, **Alfred Landon.** Landon had an impressive record as governor of Kansas, having cut taxes and streamlined the administration while aligning work and relief programs in Kansas with federal New Deal agencies. He accepted most New Deal programs in principle, objecting primarily to their inefficient administration. Most Republicans, however, wanted him to attack Roosevelt and the New Deal as destroying the values of America. Reluctantly, Landon agreed, gaining support from the American Liberty League, which announced that the election presented a choice between the "clean, pure, fresh air of free America, and the foul breath of Communistic Russia."

Roosevelt followed a politically wise path, reminding voters of the New Deal's achievements and stressing his support for the "forgotten man." He attacked big business—the "economic royalists" who, he charged, wanted to rule like kings over the people. The tactics worked, and Roosevelt won in a landslide. Landon carried only two states, Maine and Vermont, an achievement that earned him a woeful eight electoral votes.

The Democratic victory in 1936, which included still more seats in Congress, demonstrated not only the personal popularity of Roosevelt but also the realignment of political forces around the concept of

Alfred Landon Kansas governor who ran unsuccessfully for president on the Republican ticket in 1936.

an activist New Deal government that could foster social and economic gains. Prior to 1930, only two major interest groups successfully influenced government: big business and the South. With Roosevelt and the New Deal a new political coalition was formed that included new groups like northern liberals and the CIO (see below) and some older groups like agricultural interests. Wooed by the Democratic party through legislation, relief policies, and symbolic actions, women, minorities, the aged, the unemployed, workers—especially organized labor—and farmers voted Democratic and expected new legislation to meet their needs. The political challenge for Roosevelt and future Democrats was to keep as many interest groups as possible within the fold. By 1936, Roosevelt had lost support from business elements, but as the 1936 election showed, his ability to keep the rest of the coalition intact more than offset that loss. Recognizing this, Roosevelt promised a government intent on seeking "social justice" and passing laws to bring it about. The political majority that Roosevelt attracted in 1932 was strengthened in 1936 and made the Democratic party the majority party for years to come.

Roosevelt's second inaugural address raised expectations that there would be a third hundred days. "I see millions of families trying to live on incomes so meager that the pall of family disaster hangs over them day by day," he announced. "I see one-third of a nation ill-housed, ill-clad, ill-nourished." The words seemed to promise new legislation aimed at helping the poor and the working class. But the third hundred days failed to materialize.

Roosevelt and the Supreme Court

Instead of promoting new social legislation, Roosevelt pitted his popularity against the Supreme Court—and lost. The president's anger at the high court had been growing since the *Schechter* case, because the Court continued to nullify New Deal legislation. It ruled in the *Butler* case (1936) that the AAA was unconstitutional and wreaked havoc with many other New Deal concepts. A quota plan for the oil industry, the Railroad Retirement Act, a New York law establishing a minimum wage for women—all were declared illegal. As 1937 began, legal challenges to the Wagner Act and the Social Security Act were on the Court's docket, and Roosevelt feared the Court was going to undo much of the Second Hundred Days' legislation. The president believed that before he could proceed with new programs, he had to protect what had already been passed. To alter the political philosophy of the Supreme Court, Roosevelt wanted to appoint six additional justices to ensure it would have a pro–New Deal majority.

Without consulting congressional leaders or even his closest advisers, in early February 1937 Roosevelt presented to Congress a plan to reorganize the Supreme Court. Claiming that the Court was overburdened and that its elderly judges could not meet the demands of their office, he asked for additional justices to help carry the judicial load. His goal was a new justice for every one over age 70 who had served more than ten years on the Court. Although changing the size of the Supreme Court was within the powers of Congress, many thought Roosevelt's action threatened the checks and balances of government as established by the Constitution. He had made a major political miscalculation with this **Court-packing plan,** and many conservative Democrats who had reservations about the New Deal welcomed the opportunity to join with Republicans and say no to Roosevelt.

Still aglow from his election victory, Roosevelt ignored the growing opposition and pressed on. To gain public support, he told political adviser Jim Farley, "All I have to do is to devise a better speech." Roosevelt's case weakened further, however, when the Court made a series of split, 5-to-4 decisions that favored the New Deal, including the Wagner Act and the Social Security system. Even Roosevelt's supporters in Congress now questioned the need to enlarge the Court. The president's position collapsed completely in May when conservative justice Willis van Devanter announced his retirement. By July, Roosevelt conceded defeat and dropped the issue, taking some solace in appointing Hugo Black, a southern New Dealer, to the Court. Before Roosevelt died in 1945, he was able to appoint eight other justices and ensure a Supreme Court that would approve of and expand the role of government.

Despite the Court's favorable decisions, Roosevelt had squandered important political assets in trying to win a hopeless cause. Having safely broken with Roosevelt on the Court issue, many Democrats—mainly from the South—found it possible, even popular, to oppose other Roosevelt initiatives. The election of 1936 had brought into being a strong

Court-packing plan Roosevelt's unsuccessful proposal in 1937 to increase the number of Supreme Court justices; it was an effort to circumvent Supreme Court hostility to the New Deal.

Democratic coalition of northerners and southerners, liberals and conservatives. The Court fight, however, had weakened that bloc and produced a new conservative grouping composed of Republicans, business interests, and southern Democrats. Consequently, a third hundred days was now impossible. The New Deal was slowing to a crawl.

Resurgence of Labor

Labor strife also dampened many Americans' enthusiasm for the New Deal. During his first administration, Roosevelt had supported unions and workers through the National Recovery Administration and passage of the Wagner Act. To raise and protect wages, the NRA had spelled out workers' rights in its industrial codes. Although the NRA itself had not always protected wages, union organizers found that proworker sections of the codes were useful in convincing workers to unionize. "President Roosevelt wants you to join the union," was a common plug that labor organizers used to recruit workers. Mostly the response was positive, and by mid-1934 unions were growing and becoming more militant.

There were over eighteen hundred strikes in 1934, involving more than 1.5 million workers. Union membership doubled that year. The rise of organized labor was especially pronounced in the mass-production industries. When the leadership of the craft-based American Federation of Labor discouraged industry-wide unionization in 1935, a minority element formed the Committee for Industrial Organizations (CIO) to continue organizing industrial unions (see page 527). Unionization drives were launched in the automobile, rubber, and electrical industries. The CIO also took an active political stance, pushing workers to support only those politicians who were friends of labor. In 1938, the CIO completed its break from the AFL and formed an independent labor organization: the **Congress of Industrial Organizations.**

In March 1936, the CIO supported workers striking against the rubber industry in Akron, Ohio, home of the three major producers of tires and rubber products: Firestone, Goodyear, and Goodrich. Wanting recognition of their union and higher wages, workers stopped work and refused to leave the factory, launching one of the first major **sit-down strikes** in the United States. With the strikers occupying the factory, the employer could not use **strikebreakers.** When the rubber industry quickly agreed to most of the strikers' demands, the benefits of sit-down strikes seemed clear to labor.

Encouraged by the Akron results, Walter Reuther and other leaders of the **United Automobile Workers (UAW)** planned a sit-down strike against General Motors. The situation for automobile workers had deteriorated steadily during the Depression. In 1928, more than 435,000 workers were employed. By 1933, only 244,000 were. Wages had dropped from an average of $33 to $20 a week. To prevent unions from organizing, the industry had formed company associations and paid thousands of dollars to agents to spy on and disrupt union activities. Chrysler alone paid $72,000 to such infiltrators in 1935.

In planning the General Motors strike, the UAW focused on plants that supplied car bodies for GM assembly lines. The sit-down strike began on November 30, 1936, when workers at the Flint, Michigan, plant took over the factory. Despite cutting off heat in 16-degree weather and trying to block deliveries of food and other supplies, GM was unable to dislodge the strikers. On January 11, 1937, company guards and city police armed with guns, clubs, and tear gas attacked the factory. The strikers fought back using fire hoses and homemade slingshots that flung 2-pound door hinges. Frustrated, the guards and police opened fire. Fourteen workers and thirty-seven police were injured, but the strikers held their ground. GM then asked Governor Frank Murphy to send in state militia units to remove the strikers, but when the liberal Democrat refused, the company settled with the UAW. The strike had lasted forty-four days. Weeks later, Chrysler gave in to sit-down strikers and also recognized the UAW.

In March, United States Steel Corporation accepted the steelworkers' union without a strike. Throughout 1937, labor staged more than forty-seven hundred strikes and won more than 80 percent of them. Union membership soared. *Time* magazine observed, "Sitting down has replaced baseball as the national pastime."

Congress of Industrial Organizations Labor organization established in 1938 by a group of powerful unions that left the AFL to unionize workers by industry rather than by trade.

sit-down strike Strike in which workers refuse to leave their place of employment until their demands are met.

strikebreakers Temporary workers hired by employers to substitute for striking workers.

United Automobile Workers Union of workers in the automobile industry; it used sit-down strikes in 1936 and 1937 to end work speed-ups and win recognition for the fledgling labor organization.

♦ In 1936 these workers from the Fisher Body Plant in Flint, Michigan used a new tactic in the United Autoworkers strike against General Motors—the sit-down strike. Workers took over the plant and held it against all attempts to reclaim it for forty-four days, until GM agreed to negotiate a settlement. In 1939 the Supreme Court declared the sit-down strike illegal. *Library of Congress.*

Not all union efforts were effective, however. In Ohio, the national guard broke through **picket lines** and shielded strikebreakers, allowing several steel mills to continue operation. In Chicago, police staunchly protected Republic Steel from strikers and, on Memorial Day 1937, attacked a rally of workers and their families. Ten of those attending the rally were killed, nearly ninety were wounded, and sixty-seven were arrested.

As strikes spread and violent incidents multiplied, unions did not fare well in public opinion. Many Americans equated strikes and labor militancy with radicalism and pointed to the seemingly large numbers of Socialists and Communists within the labor movement. Critics also blamed unions for most of the strike-related violence and considered sit-down strikes to be an illegal seizure of property. In 1939, the Supreme Court agreed, declaring sit-down strikes unconstitutional.

The End of New Deal Legislation

By 1937, Roosevelt faced a political environment increasingly hostile to New Deal legislation. Disturbed by Roosevelt's Court-packing plan and alarmed by some union activities, a growing number of moderates, including many Democrats, joined conservatives in viewing Roosevelt as too radical and antibusiness. The economy seemed steady: industrial outputs had reached their 1929 level, and unemployment had fallen to 14 percent. Thus many joined Secretary of the Treasury Henry Morganthau in arguing that the administration should reduce government activism, which he asserted was unpopular and hampering further recovery, and balance the federal budget. Roosevelt agreed. He cut government spending and closed many federal job programs. Nearly 1.5 million workers were released from the WPA alone. Unemployment rapidly soared to 19 percent, and recovery collapsed in **"Roosevelt's Recession."**

Roosevelt's liberal advisers called for more government controls and spending. The WPA promptly

picket line Procession of strikers or protesters that blocks the entrance to a place of business to prevent its operation.

"Roosevelt's Recession" Economic downturn that occurred when Roosevelt, responding to improving economic figures, cut $4 billion from the federal budget, a large part of it coming from reductions in relief funding.

rehired those dropped from the rolls, but Roosevelt's efforts to marshal liberal forces to provide new legislation failed. The political mood had changed since 1933, and a coalition of conservative forces in Congress blocked passage of most of Roosevelt's requested programs. Harry Hopkins observed that most Americans were now "bored with the poor, the unemployed, and the insecure."

In June 1938, congressional New Dealers managed to overcome conservative and union opposition and pass the **Fair Labor Standards Act.** The act established a maximum workweek of 44 hours, set a minimum wage of 25 cents an hour, and outlawed child labor (under age 16). With its minimum-wage provision, the Fair Labor Standards Act was especially beneficial to unskilled, nonunion, and minority workers. It was also the last piece of New Deal legislation (see Table 26.1). By the November 1938 congressional elections, "Roosevelt's recession" was ending, but 3.3 million people were still receiving federal aid, and the public's mood had become decidedly conservative and opposed to further New Deal–type legislation. During the elections, Roosevelt actively campaigned for liberal candidates but saw few victories. The new Congress was more Republican, conservative, and determined to oppose any of the president's "socialistic" ideas. Roosevelt recognized political reality and asked for no new domestic programs. By 1939, the economy had reached the point where it had been in 1929 and 1937, and the New Deal was over.

The New Deal's Impact

The New Deal failed to achieve full economic recovery. In 1939 millions of people were still unemployed or underemployed. What finally reduced unemployment, permitted the termination of federal relief efforts, and propelled the American economy to new levels of prosperity was the spending necessitated by another world war. Yet the New Deal changed the government and the American people. It ended the fear generated by the Depression, and it restored a sense of stability to society and the economy. The size, power, and prestige of the executive branch mushroomed. Nearly all New Deal agencies were under the control of the executive branch, enhancing the power of the presidency beyond what it had ever been.

Equally important, the New Deal altered the basic relationships between government and society and between government and the economy. Before the New Deal, the federal government barely touched the lives of most Americans, but by 1939 it had become a focal point of civic life. Institutions that Roosevelt created still regulate the nation's banking and financial systems. The economic health of agriculture continues to rely on a series of price-support and loan programs started by the New Deal. The Wagner Act remains the chief tool for oversight of labor-management relations. With Social Security, the government assumed some responsibility for the economic welfare of the elderly. Although relief agencies were eliminated over the years that followed, the belief in government responsibility for the needy remains part of the American memory and experience. The combination of the Depression and the New Deal altered expectations about government: people came to believe that they were entitled to certain things, and they looked to the federal government and the president for leadership, for legislation, and for solutions not only to the nation's problems but, increasingly, to social, local, and regional problems.

Evaluations of the New Deal are numerous and generally reflect attitudes about the proper role of government in society. Conservatives argue that the positive legacy of the New Deal is an illusion. Government intervention, they say, was the problem rather than the solution because it undermined individualism and free enterprise, creating an expensive and overbearing government. Liberals praise Roosevelt and the New Deal for effectively balancing the needs of the economy with those of society. From the liberal viewpoint, the New Deal promoted stable economic growth and contributed to the overall health of American society. More radical, leftist critics of the New Deal focus on missed opportunities and what the New Deal failed to accomplish. They point out that the same groups that held power and wealth before the New Deal were still in control afterward, and they contend that Roosevelt made little effort to combat racism or economic inequalities. Roosevelt, they argue, faced few political or social constraints and could have made more significant social and economic changes but chose not to do so.

Fair Labor Standards Act Law passed by Congress in 1938 that established a minimum wage and a maximum workweek and forbade labor by children under 16.

SUMMARY

Expectations
Constraints
Choices
Outcomes

The Great Depression brought Franklin D. Roosevelt to power amid widespread *expectations* that he would actively use the federal government to overcome the causes and effects of the Depression, restoring prosperity and stability. Although never a coherent, specific, overarching plan, the New Deal attacked the Depression on three fronts: recovery, relief, and reform.

The First Hundred Days witnessed a barrage of legislation, in which Roosevelt *chose* to deal with immediate problems of unemployment and economic collapse. In 1935, assailed by both liberals and conservatives, he *chose* to respond with a second burst of legislation—the Second Hundred Days—that focused more on social legislation and putting people to work—concerns for the "common man"—than on business-oriented recovery. The overwhelming Democratic victory in 1936 confirmed the popularity of Roosevelt and the changes brought by his New Deal and raised *expectations* for more social and economic regulatory legislation. A third hundred days, however, never materialized. The Court-packing scheme, an economic downturn, labor unrest, and growing conservatism generated more political *constraints* than New Deal forces could overcome. The *outcome* was that the New Deal wound down after 1937.

The New Deal's recovery programs failed to restore prosperity, although programs like those formed by the AAA aided the farmer and still contribute to the price stability of agriculture. Reforms of the financial and securities systems left a much more secure and stable financial industry. Relief agencies helped the unemployed and poor and reduced the sense of fear and panic in American society. In the end, the New Deal strengthened capitalism and opened new political doors to many of those frequently ignored by government and blocked from achieving the American dream. Farmers, blue-collar workers, women, and minorities, all, in varying degrees, had their own New Deal, which left each with stronger *expectations* about government's role in promoting their interests and enhancing their ability to participate in politics.

The *outcome* of the New Deal was a profound shift in the nature of government and in society's *expectations* about the federal government's role. Because of the New Deal, the economy, society, and government and politics were forever changed.

SUGGESTED READINGS

Andrew Bergman. *We're in the Money: Depression America and Its Films* (1971).

An interesting look at the movie industry and how it reflected the Great Depression.

Roger Biles. *A New Deal for the American People* (1991).

A brief interpretive overview of the New Deal that focuses on the impact of New Deal programs on people and emerging patterns of public welfare.

Julia Kirk Blackwelder. *Women of the Depression: Caste and Culture in San Antonio, 1929–1939* (1984).

A tightly focused study on Mexican-American, African-American, and Anglo women in the world of San Antonio during the Depression.

Lizabeth Cohen. *Making a New Deal: Industrial Workers in Chicago, 1919–1939* (1990).

A detailed examination of the inclusion of African-American and immigrant workers in the CIO and in New Deal politics.

William Leuchtenberg. *Franklin D. Roosevelt and the New Deal* (1983).

A comprehensive, classic account of how Roosevelt directed the nation from his 1932 election until 1941.

Harvard Sitkoff. *A New Deal for Blacks* (1978).

A review of how African Americans benefited from and were otherwise affected by the New Deal and the Roosevelts.

Susan Ware. *Holding Their Own: American Women in the 1930s* (1982).

An examination of the impact of the Depression on the lives and lifestyles of women.

THE HOME FRONT War-related production finally ended the Great Depression, but it also required many Americans to move, especially to western states where the jobs were. This map shows major war-related industries and the states that gained and lost population. For Japanese Americans, relocation did not mean new jobs, but a loss of freedom as they were assigned to one of ten relocation centers across the country.

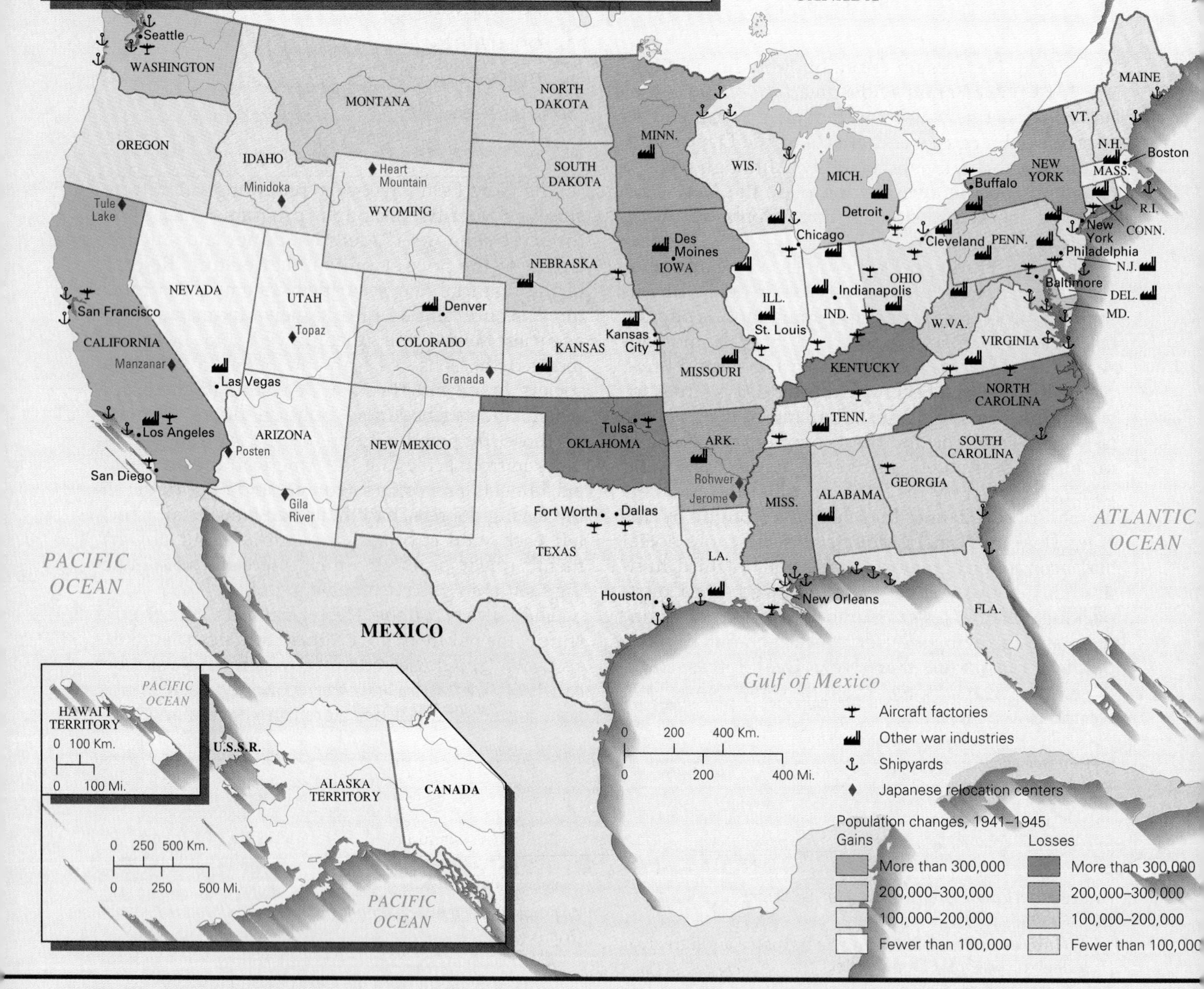

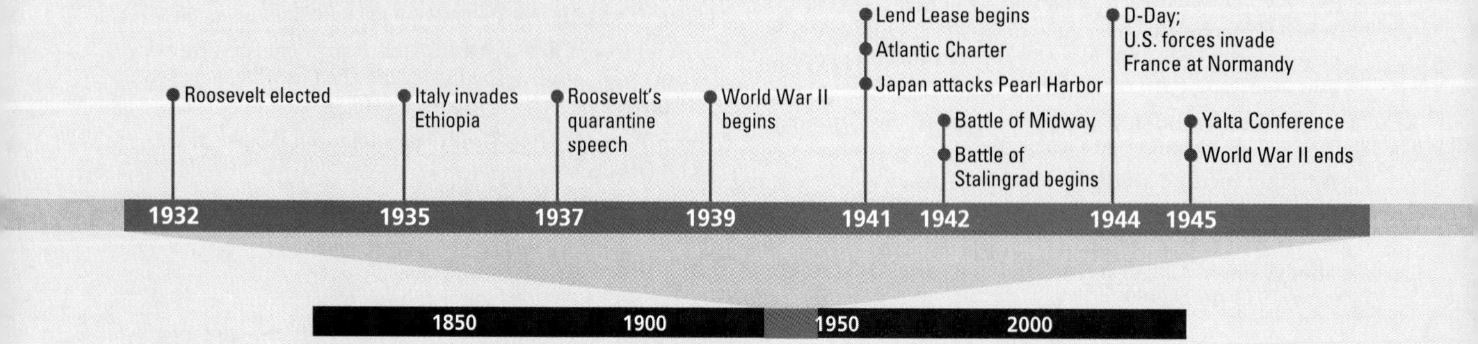

CHAPTER 27

America's Rise to World Leadership, 1933–1945

Roosevelt and Foreign Policy

- In what ways did Roosevelt's choices in dealings with Latin America reflect the ideals of the Good Neighbor policy?
- How did isolationism constrain American foreign-policy choices from 1932 to the outbreak of World War II?

The Road to War

- What constraints did Roosevelt face in trying to implement a more interventionist foreign policy?
- In reshaping American neutrality, what choices did Roosevelt make regarding Britain and Japan?

America Responds to War

- What actions did Roosevelt choose to mobilize the nation for war?
- What new social and economic choices did Americans confront as the nation became the "arsenal of democracy"?
- What new opportunities and old constraints did women and minorities encounter on the home front and in their military experiences?

Waging World War

- What choices and constraints did Roosevelt and Truman confront in shaping America's strategy for global conflict?
- What were the stresses within the Grand Alliance?
- What expectations prompted Truman and his advisers to choose to use the atomic bomb?

INTRODUCTION

E xpectations
C onstraints
C hoices
O utcomes

When Roosevelt assumed office in 1933, the cheery optimism of a prosperous world at peace that had greeted Hoover four years earlier was gone. By 1935, three nations seemed intent on changing the international system and willing to *choose* military conquest if necessary to achieve their goals. Japan, seeking an empire in Asia, had annexed Manchuria and was threatening China. In Germany, the Depression had helped Adolf Hitler and the National Socialist (Nazi) party gain political dominance amid promises of restoring Germany's military and diplomatic prowess. And in Italy, having seized power in 1922, Benito Mussolini used nationalism, imperial designs, and military power to tighten his control. Roosevelt faced the events in Asia and Europe as an internationalist and as a politician. He wanted the United States to take a more active role in world affairs, but he was *constrained* by the strong isolationist views of Congress and the public. In addition, he understood that American economic recovery was his first priority, at least in the short term.

Between 1933 and 1939, Roosevelt wrestled with two problems: how to improve U.S. economic and political positions abroad while protecting economic and political interests at home. For Roosevelt the international *outcome* was an unhappy one—generally deferring to Congress's and the public's *choices* regarding American interests. The onslaught of war, however, allowed Roosevelt to chart a path toward international activism. To help defeat Hitler, Roosevelt provided economic and military assistance to Britain. To *constrain* Japanese expansion, he used trade restrictions. Japan's *choice* to attack Pearl Harbor in December 1941 drew the United States into World War II.

The war managed to do what the New Deal had not done—restore American prosperity. An *outcome* of the United States becoming the "arsenal of democracy" was full recovery and full employment, with unparalleled cooperation among business, labor, and government. As more than 15 million Americans marched off to war, those at home faced new opportunities and *constraints.* Society became more mobile when Americans on the home front moved to take war-related jobs, especially those on the West Coast. The *outcome* for women and minorities was mixed: they experienced greater opportunities, but they also were *expected* by most to relinquish their new opportunities once the war ended.

For presidents Roosevelt and Harry S Truman, defeating the Axis Powers required not only mobilizing America's resources but also making strategic decisions that shaped the course and *outcome* of the war. Roosevelt *chose* to allocate most of the nation's resources to defeat Hitler first, agreeing to invade North Africa and Italy before invading France. In the Pacific, the victory at Midway gave the United States a naval and air advantage that allowed American forces to close the circle on Japan. By the end of May 1945, Hitler's Third Reich was in ruins, American forces were on the verge of victory over Japan, and Roosevelt had died. Truman, facing the prospect of huge casualties with an invasion of Japan, *chose* to use the atomic bomb. The *outcome* was the surrender of Japan, the beginning of a new age of atomic power, and the emergence of the United States as a superpower.

Roosevelt and Foreign Policy

- In what ways did Roosevelt's choices in dealings with Latin America reflect the ideals of the Good Neighbor policy?
- How did isolationism constrain American foreign-policy choices from 1932 to the outbreak of World War II?

Before Franklin Roosevelt ran for the presidency, he was an outspoken internationalist who supported American activism in world affairs. As a presidential candidate, he generally tried to avoid making foreign policy statements and instead concentrated on domestic issues—the New Deal and economic recovery. Yet at heart he remained an internationalist who believed that international cooperation would create a better world.

Soon after taking office, Roosevelt sent Secretary of State Cordell Hull to the London Economic Con-

CHRONOLOGY

A World at War

1933 Franklin D. Roosevelt becomes president
London Economic Conference
Gerardo Machado resigns as president of Cuba
United States recognizes Soviet Union
Hitler and Nazi party take power in Germany

1934 Fulgencio Batista assumes power in Cuba

1935 Italy invades Ethiopia
First Neutrality Act

1936 Germany reoccupies the Rhineland
Spanish Civil War begins
Second Neutrality Act

1937 Third Neutrality Act
Roosevelt's quarantine speech
Sino-Japanese War begins
Japanese aircraft sink the *Panay*

1938 Germany annexes Austria
Munich Conference

1939 Germany invades Czechoslovakia
German-Soviet Nonaggression Pact
World War II begins as Germany invades Poland
Soviets invade Poland
Neutrality Act of 1939
Soviets invade Finland

1940 Germany occupies most of Western Europe
U.S. economic sanctions against Japan
Burke-Wadsworth Act
Destroyers-for-bases agreement
Roosevelt re-elected

1941 Lend-Lease Act
Fair Employment Practices Commission created
U.S. forces occupy Greenland and Iceland
Germany invades Soviet Union
Atlantic Charter
U-boats attack U.S. warships
Manhattan Project begins
Japan attacks Pearl Harbor
United States enters World War II

1942 War Production Board created
Japanese conquer Philippines
Japanese Americans interned
Battles of Coral Sea and Midway
Congress of Racial Equality founded
U.S. troops invade North Africa

1943 U.S. forces capture Guadalcanal
Soviets defeat Germans at Stalingrad
Smith-Connally War Labor Disputes Act
Detroit race riot
U.S. and British forces invade Sicily and Italy
Tehran Conference

1944 Operation Overload
Allies reach the Rhine
G.I. Bill becomes law
U.S. forces invade the Philippines
Roosevelt re-elected
Soviet forces liberate Eastern Europe
Battle of the Bulge

1945 Yalta Conference
Roosevelt dies
Harry S Truman becomes president
Soviets capture Berlin
Germany surrenders
U.S. forces capture Iwo Jima and Okinawa
Potsdam Conference
United States drops atomic bombs on Hiroshima and Nagasaki
Japan surrenders

ference to help shore up international currencies and facilitate world trade. But while Hull worked, Roosevelt, ignoring the State Department, retreated from international economic cooperation and the global lowering of tariffs. He publicly rejected using the dollar and an international gold standard to stabilize worldwide currencies. An uninformed Hull was humiliated at Roosevelt's shift and watched as the economic conference collapsed without American support. It was not the last time that Roosevelt would conduct foreign policy without considering Hull or the State Department. Still, Hull managed some policy successes a year later when Congress and Roosevelt approved the **Reciprocal Trade Agreements Act** and the establishment of the **Import-Export Bank.** The reciprocal trade law allowed the president to lower some tariffs by as much as 50 percent if the benefiting nations gave the United States most-favored-nation trading status. The Import-Export Bank allowed the government to lend money to foreign nations for the purpose of buying American goods. Initially, neither act had much economic impact, but over time both became central parts of American economic policy.

The Good Neighbor Policy

In Latin America, Roosevelt built on the improving relations already begun by Hoover. He promised that the United States would be a "good neighbor," respecting Latin American views and interests and not interfering in Latin American affairs. His promise was soon tested in Cuba, where the actions of President Gerardo "the Butcher" Machado fed political unrest. To stabilize Cuba in the summer of 1933, Roosevelt sent special envoy Sumner Welles to encourage Machado to resign. Wells succeeded but considered the new government of Ramón Grau San Martín to be "frankly communistic" and recommended using American military force to overthrow Grau. Roosevelt rejected sending in the marines. Instead he exercised "friendly" political intervention by refusing to recognize the Grau government. Welles continued to search for a local solution and convinced **Colonel Fulgencio Batista** to overthrow Grau and form a government acceptable to the United States—which he did. The United States recognized the new government and signed a favorable trade agreement. Batista, who was the real power in Cuba, controlled the island nation until 1959.

Watching American actions in Cuba, many Latin Americans questioned the reality of Roosevelt's **Good Neighbor policy** and pressed for U.S. renunciation of all forms of foreign intervention. Though hesitant at first to renounce the principle of intervention to protect American citizens, the United States finally rejected all armed foreign intervention in 1938.

Roosevelt's commitment to nonintervention was quickly tested. In 1938 Mexico's president **Lázaro Cárdenas** nationalized foreign-owned oil properties. American oil interests quickly called for action against Mexico to protect their property and profits. Hull supported the oil companies and sent inflammatory messages to the Mexican government demanding the return of "American property." Rather than deliver the harsh dispatches, U.S. Ambassador Josephus Daniels modified them to avoid offending the Mexican government. He also recommended to Roosevelt that the United States accept nationalization and negotiate a fair settlement. "We are strong. Mexico is weak. It is always noble for the strong to be generous and generous and generous," he told the president. Roosevelt followed Daniels's advice, and in 1941 the United States and Mexico agreed on monetary compensation to American oil companies. By the end of his first administration, Roosevelt had vastly improved the United States' image and position of leadership throughout Latin America.

Roosevelt and Isolationism

While Roosevelt was improving the image of the United States in Latin America, tensions were increasing in Europe and Asia. Rejecting the demo-

Reciprocal Trade Agreements Act Law passed by Congress in 1934 authorizing the president to lower tariffs on imports from nations that gave the United States trading status equal to the most favorable terms given to other nations.

Import-Export Bank Bank established by the U.S. government to lend money to foreign nations that wished to buy American goods.

Colonel Fulgencio Batista Dictator who ruled Cuba from 1934 through 1958; his corrupt, authoritarian regime was overthrown by Fidel Castro's revolutionary movement.

Good Neighbor policy Roosevelt's Latin American policy, based on noninterference in Latin American affairs.

Lázaro Cárdenas Mexico's president from 1934 to 1940; he distributed land to peasants, instituted social reforms, and nationalized foreign-owned oil properties.

cratic system that in 1933 had brought him to power in Germany, Adolf Hitler by 1935 had ruthlessly instituted a **dictatorship,** expanded the German military, and promised to re-establish a German empire. Having seized Manchuria in 1931 (see page 777), the Japanese spoke openly of establishing a larger Japanese sphere of influence, the **Greater East Asian Co-Prosperity Sphere,** and they increased pressure on China (see Map 25.3). Resting uneasily between the Japanese and the Germans, the Soviet Union, led by Joseph Stalin, sought to improve relations with the United States, western European states, and China. Roosevelt, seeking trade possibilities and hoping to stiffen Soviet resolve in the face of possible Japanese and German expansion, also sought improved relations. The result was American recognition of the Soviet Union (USSR) in November 1933, but little else. There was no expansion of U.S.-Soviet trade or any attempt to bridge the ideological gap and the decade of distrust separating the two nations.

Within the United States, Roosevelt's decision to establish relations with the USSR prompted protests that he meant to abandon isolationism and embrace Wilsonian internationalism. By 1934, isolationists were in full cry, even repudiating U.S. entry into World War I and suggesting that the "true origins" of the war were profits and British propaganda. A congressional investigation chaired by Senator Gerald P. Nye of North Dakota alleged that America's entry into the war had been the product of arms manufacturers, bankers, and war profiteers—"the merchants of death." Novelists like Ernest Hemingway (*A Farewell to Arms,* 1929) and John Dos Passos (*Three Soldiers,* 1921) added to antiwar and isolationist sentiments with powerful stories depicting the senseless horror of war. As college students called for arms limitations and peace, a Gallup poll revealed that 67 percent of Americans believed that the nation's intervention in World War I had been wrong.

By 1935, tensions in Asia, Africa, and Europe combined with American isolationism to generate neutrality laws that many hoped would prevent American involvement in future foreign wars. In August 1935, Congress passed the **Neutrality Act of 1935** prohibiting the sale of arms and munitions to any nation at war. The law also permitted the president to warn Americans traveling on the ships of belligerent nations that they sailed at their own risk. If Roosevelt opposed the legislation, announced Senator Key Pittman of Nevada, he was "riding for a fall." Anxious to see the Second Hundred Days successfully through Congress, Roosevelt gave up his preference for discriminatory neutrality and accepted political reality. Isolationist Senator Hiram Johnson of California cheered the Neutrality Act and viewed it as the means to keep the United States "out of European controversies, European wars, and European difficulties."

Many Americans felt the 1935 Neutrality Act came just in time, for soon after it was passed the two leading **fascist** nations of Europe, Italy and Germany, sought to overturn the international status quo. On October 3, Benito Mussolini's Italian troops invaded the African nation of Ethiopia. Roosevelt immediately announced American neutrality toward the Ethiopian conflict, denying the sale of war supplies to either side. The arms embargo had little effect on Italy, whose modern army overpowered the nineteenth-century-style soldiers of Ethiopia's emperor **Haile Selassie.** Aware that Italy was buying increasing amounts of American nonwar goods, including coal and oil, Roosevelt asked Americans to apply a "moral embargo" on Italy. The request had no effect. American trade continued, as did Italian victories. On May 9, 1936, Italy formally annexed Ethiopia.

The end of the Italian-Ethiopian war did not reduce international tensions. In March, German troops violated the Treaty of Versailles by occupying the **Rhineland,** and in July, civil war broke out in Spain. Roosevelt proclaimed that the remilitarization of the Rhineland, a part of Germany, was of no concern to the United States and then left on a planned fishing trip. Most Americans agreed with the president. But public opinion was sharply divided about the conflict in Spain. Liberals and

dictatorship State or government controlled by a tyrant, or absolute ruler.

Greater East Asian Co-Prosperity Sphere Japan's plan to create and dominate an economic and defensive union in East Asia, using force if necessary.

Neutrality Act (1935) Law passed by Congress prohibiting arms shipments to nations at war and authorizing the president to warn U.S. citizens against traveling on belligerents' vessels.

fascist Advocating fascism, an oppressive, dictatorial political system that glorifies the state, nation, and race at the expense of the liberties and rights of individuals.

Haile Selassie Emperor of Ethiopia, whose country fell to Mussolini's Italian forces in 1935–1936.

Rhineland Region of western Germany along the Rhine River, which under the terms of the Versailles treaty was to remain free of troops and military fortifications.

♦ Painted by Pablo Picasso in 1937 to attack the "brutality and darkness" of war, *Guernica* commemorates the destruction of the Spanish town of Guernica, where, in one night, bombs from fascist planes killed more than 1000 people and destroyed the village. *Guernica by Pablo Picasso, 1937. ©1995 Artists Rights Society (ARS), New York/SPADEM, Paris.*

leftists supported the elected Spanish government's **Republican** forces. Conservatives and most Catholics supported the rebels led by the antidemocratic **Francisco Franco.** Even though they might support one side or the other, however, most Americans believed that the United States should avoid any active role in the Spanish Civil War and agreed when Roosevelt applied the neutrality legislation to both sides. At the same time, Congress modified the neutrality legislation to require noninvolvement in civil wars and to forbid making loans to any country at war, whether victim or aggressor.

While the United States, Britain, and France remained neutral in the Spanish Civil War, Italy and Germany actively aided Franco with planes, tanks, and infantry, taking the opportunity to test their military capability. Facing better-equipped and larger armies, the Republican forces fought bravely but were forced to surrender city after city. What little support the government received came from the Soviet Union and from individuals and leftist groups in Europe and the United States. With the fall of Madrid in March 1939, Franco defeated the last Republican forces and ended the civil war. His harsh dictatorship over Spain lasted for thirty-six years.

With the Italian conquest of Ethiopia, German remilitarization, and the war in Spain as background, both American political parties entered the 1936 elections as champions of neutrality. Roosevelt told an audience at Chautauqua, New York, that he hated war and if it came to "the choice of profits over peace, the nation will answer—must answer—'We choose peace.'" Alfred Landon and the Republicans were equally adamant that they were the real party of peace and isolationism. Roosevelt easily defeated Landon (see page 814) and with strong public support approved the **Neutrality Act of 1937.** It required warring nations to pay cash for all "nonwar" goods and to carry them away on their own ships, and it barred Americans from sailing on belligerents' ships. For Roosevelt, who disliked the inflexibility of strict neutrality, the new act provided a small victory. One section allowed him to determine

Republican In Spain, a left-wing political coalition that won national elections in 1936 but was prevented from carrying out its programs by a military rebellion and the outbreak of civil war.

Francisco Franco Spanish general whose rebel forces defeated the Republicans in the Spanish Civil War (1936–1939); he ruled as dictator of Spain until his death in 1975.

Neutrality Act of 1937 Law passed by Congress requiring warring nations to pay cash for "nonwar" goods and barring Americans from sailing on their ships.

which nations were at war and which goods were nonwar goods.

Roosevelt used that provision in late July 1937, after a Japanese invasion of northern China. Ignoring reality and disregarding protests, he refused to recognize that China and Japan were fighting a war and allowed American trade to continue with both nations. Hoping that isolationist views had softened, on October 5, Roosevelt suggested that the United States and other peace-loving nations should **quarantine** "bandit nations" that were contributing to "the epidemic of world lawlessness." The so-called quarantine speech was applauded in many foreign capitals but not in Berlin, Rome, or Tokyo, and not at home. Within the United States, it only heightened cries for isolationism while Japan continued gobbling up Chinese territory (see Map 25.3).

On December 12, 1937, Japanese aircraft strafed, bombed, and sank the American gunboat *Panay*. Two Americans died and nearly fifty others were wounded. Roosevelt was outraged and wanted to take some retaliatory action, but public opinion and Congress insisted otherwise. Within forty-eight hours of the *Panay* bombing, isolationists in the House of Representatives pushed forward a previously proposed constitutional amendment drafted by Louis Ludlow of Indiana that would require a public referendum before Congress could declare war. Public opinion polls indicated that 70 percent of Americans supported the idea. Only after Roosevelt had expended a great deal of political effort did the House vote 209 to 188 to return the amendment to committee, effectively killing it. Understanding that there was no support for any action against Japan, Roosevelt had no choice but to accept Japan's apology and payment of damages for the *Panay* attack.

"GERMANY SHALL NEVER BE ENCIRCLED."

♦ Despite Hitler's assurances about the limited territorial goals of Nazi Germany, following the invasion of Poland, most people quickly realized that his true goal was world domination. *Frank Wood Collection.*

The Road to War

- What constraints did Roosevelt face in trying to implement a more interventionist foreign policy?
- In reshaping American neutrality, what choices did Roosevelt make regarding Britain and Japan?

World peace was crumbling fast as 1938 started. The fighting in China and Spain raged on with increased intensity. From Berlin, Hitler pronounced his intentions to unify all German-speaking lands and create a new German empire, or Reich. Hitler's first step was the forced Anschluss, or merger, of Austria with Germany. Hearing only mild protests from other nations, Hitler then moved to incorporate the Sudeten region of western Czechoslovakia into the German Reich. With a respectable military force and defense treaties with France and the Soviet Union, the Czechoslovakian government was prepared to resist. However, France, the Soviet Union, and Britain wanted no confrontation with Hitler. Choosing to negotiate, Britain's prime minister, **Neville Chamberlain,** met with Hitler in Munich in late September. Hitler agreed to seek no further territory, and Chamberlain accepted Germany's annexation of the Sudetenland (see Map 27.1). France concurred. Without British and French support, the Czechs had no option but to concede the territory. Chamberlain

quarantine To isolate, in this case politically and economically.

Neville Chamberlain British prime minister who in relations with the fascist regimes of Europe before World War II pursued a policy of appeasement, granting concessions to maintain peace.

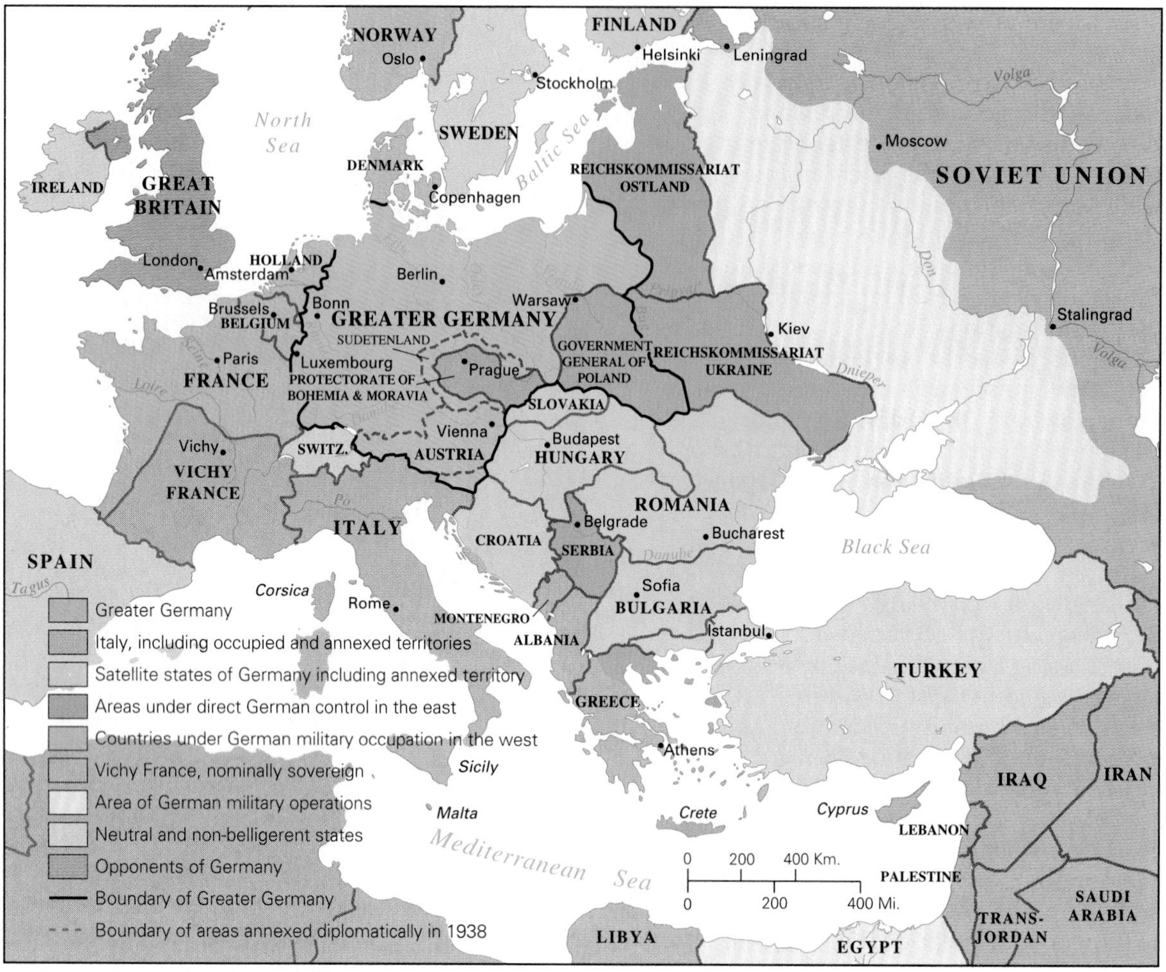

♦ **MAP 27.1 German and Italian Expansion, 1933–1942** By the end of 1942, the Axis nations of Italy and Germany, through conquest and annexation, had occupied nearly all of Europe. This map shows the political and military alignment of Europe as Germany and Italy reached the limit of their power.

returned to England smiling and promising "peace for our time." Roosevelt wired his congratulations to the prime minister.

Within Germany, Hitler stepped up the persecution of the country's nearly half a million Jews. In 1938, Hitler launched government-sponsored violence against the German-Jewish population. Synagogues and Jewish businesses and homes were looted and destroyed. Detention centers—concentration camps—at Dachau and Buchenwald soon confined more than fifty thousand Jews. Thousands of German and Austrian Jews fled to other countries. Many applied to enter the United States, but most were turned away. American anti-Semitism was strong, and the State Department, citing immigration requirements that no one be admitted to the country who would become "a public charge," routinely denied entry to German Jews whose property and assets the German government had seized. Despite thousands of applications between 1933 and 1939, the State Department implemented the immigration laws so strictly that nearly three-fourths of the 27,400-person quota for Germany and Austria went unfilled. Roosevelt regretted this rebuff of Jewish immigrants, but with little public interest in changing immigration rules, he did nothing more than offer sympathetic words to those wanting to allow more Jewish émigrés to enter America.

Convinced that Hitler was a threat to humanity, Roosevelt sounded a dire warning to Americans in his 1939 State of the Union address. "Events abroad have made it increasingly clear to the American peo-

♦ In September 1939, Germany introduced the world to a new word and type of warfare, *blitzkrieg*—lightening war. Combining the use of tanks, aircraft, and infantry, German forces quickly overran first Poland then most of Western Europe. This picture shows a German victory parade in Warsaw, Poland. *Hugo Jaeger/LIFE Magazine. ©Time Warner Inc.*

ple that the dangers within are less to be feared than dangers without," he warned. "This generation will nobly save or meanly lose the last best hope of earth." Quickly, events seemed to verify Roosevelt's prediction of danger. In 1939, Hitler ominously concluded a military alliance with Italy—the "pact of steel"—invaded and seized what remained of Czechoslovakia, and demanded that Poland turn over to Germany the **Polish Corridor,** which connected Poland to the Baltic Sea. British and French officials, unwilling to appease Hitler any longer, pledged to protect Poland. Meanwhile, unable to conclude an agreement with the British and the French, the Soviet Union had reached an agreement with Germany—the **German-Soviet Nonaggression Pact** of August 23, 1939. No longer worried about a Soviet attack, Hitler invaded Poland on September 1, 1939. Two days later, Britain and France declared war on Germany. Within a matter of days, German troops overran nearly all of Poland. On September 17, Soviet forces entered the eastern parts of Poland as secretly agreed on in the German-Soviet Nonaggression Pact (see Map 27.1). World War II had begun.

Roosevelt and American Neutrality

In the United States there was little desire to come to the aid of Poland, Britain, or France. Congressional and public isolationism remained strong. Just weeks before the invasion of Poland, 54 percent of the respondents to a *Fortune* magazine poll said they believed that no international question was important enough to involve the United States in a war. Sixty-six percent opposed the United States going to war to save France and Britain from defeat by an unnamed dictatorship. Roosevelt, however, was determined to do everything possible, short of war, to help those nations opposing Hitler.

When Germany invaded Poland, the president proclaimed neutrality but emphasized that he would not ask Americans to be neutral in their thoughts. He called Congress into special session and announced that he would enforce neutrality restrictions that prevented loans to warring nations and kept Americans out of combat zones. But he also asked that the cash-and-carry policy of the Neutrality Act of 1937 be modified to allow the sale of any goods, including arms, to any nation, provided the goods were paid for in cash and carried away in ships belonging to the purchasing country. A "peace bloc" argued that the request was a ruse to aid France and Britain and would certainly drag the United States into the war. With the rapid collapse of Poland providing the president with needed votes, however, Congress passed the **Neutrality Act of 1939** in November. Any nations could now buy weapons from the United States. But, Roosevelt calculated, with German ships denied access to American ports by the British navy, only Britain and France would be able to obtain American supplies.

To protect merchant ships approaching American ports and to aid the British navy, Roosevelt established a 300-mile neutrality zone around the Western Hemisphere, excluding Canada and other British and French possessions. With the U.S. Navy patrolling to enforce the decree, warships of the belligerent nations were forbidden in the zone. If the navy happened to sink any German submarines, Roosevelt joked to his cabinet, he would respond

Polish Corridor Strip of land in northern Poland, adjoining the city of Danzig; it gave Poland access to the Baltic Sea.

German-Soviet Nonaggression Pact Agreement in which Germany and the USSR in 1939 pledged not to fight one another and secretly arranged to divide Poland after Germany invaded it.

Neutrality Act of 1939 Law passed by Congress repealing the arms embargo and authorizing cash-and-carry exports of arms and munitions even to belligerent nations.

♦ Hitler ordered the German airforce to attack British cities in an effort to break the will of the British people. London, like the British people, suffered tremendous damage but withstood the onslaught. By the end of 1942, the small British airforce was winning the battle against Germany for the air space over Britain. *William Vandivert ©Time Warner Inc.*

like "the Japs do, 'So sorry. Never do it again.' Tomorrow we sink two."

As Roosevelt shaped American neutrality, Hitler mopped up Polish resistance and quietly readied his armies for an attack on the west in the spring. Not so secretly, the Soviets continued their expansion by invading Finland in 1939 and incorporating the Baltic republics (Latvia, Estonia, and Lithuania) into the Soviet Union. Finland surrendered, and in April 1940 Hitler unleashed his forces on Denmark and Norway, which quickly fell under Nazi domination. On May 10, the German offensive against France began with an invasion of Belgium and the Netherlands. On May 26, Belgian forces surrendered, while French and British troops began their remarkable evacuation to England from the French port of Dunkirk (see Map 27.1). That 350,000 British and French forces avoided total defeat at Dunkirk was the only bright spot in an otherwise dismal showing by Britain and France. On June 10, Mussolini entered the war on Germany's side and invaded France from the southeast. Twelve days later, France surrendered.

Germany and Italy, called the **Axis Powers,** controlled almost all of Western and Central Europe, leaving Britain to face the seemingly invincible German army and air force alone. England's new prime minister, the feisty **Winston Churchill,** pledged never to surrender until the Nazi scourge was destroyed. On August 8, 1940, the **Battle of Britain** began with the German air force bombing targets throughout England in preparation for an invasion of the island. Defending Britain was the Royal Air Force (RAF), which outfought the German Luftwaffe and denied it the air supremacy necessary for invasion. "Never has so much been done by so few for so many," Churchill declared.

Even before the fall of France, Churchill had turned to Roosevelt for aid. He needed forty or fifty destroyers and a huge number of aircraft. Roosevelt promised to help. He convinced Congress to increase the military budget, placed orders for the production of more than fifty thousand planes a year, and ordered national guard units to active federal duty. The president argued that with American support Britain could defeat the Axis without America having to enter the conflict. Even so, isolationists bitterly denounced Roosevelt for pushing the nation toward war. As both parties prepared for the 1940 presidential election, opinion polls on American foreign policy showed public confusion. Ninety percent of those asked hoped the United States would stay out of the war, but 70 percent approved giving Britain the destroyers, and 60 percent wanted to support England even if doing so led to war.

Roosevelt pressed his support for Britain. In September, he signed the **Burke-Wadsworth Act,** creating the first peacetime military draft in American history, and by executive order he exchanged

Axis Powers Coalition of nations that opposed the Allies in World War II, first consisting of just Germany and Italy and later joined by Japan.

Winston Churchill Prime minister who led Britain through World War II; he was known for his eloquent speeches and his refusal to give in to the Nazi threat.

Battle of Britain Battles between British and German planes fought over Britain from August to October 1940, during which English cities suffered heavy bombing.

Burke-Wadsworth Act Law passed by Congress in 1940 creating the first peacetime draft in American history.

fifty old, mothballed destroyers for 99-year leases over British military bases in Newfoundland, the Caribbean, and British Guiana. According to one opinion poll, 70 percent of the public supported the deal—primarily as a means to enhance American security. By the end of 1940, Roosevelt had been reelected and Congress had approved over $37 billion for military spending, more than the total cost of World War I.

In 1940, faced with a world becoming increasingly dangerous by the minute, Roosevelt took the unprecedented step of running for a third term. Republicans nominated **Wendell Willkie** of Indiana, a public utilities executive and ex-Democrat. At first, Willkie accepted the bulk of the New Deal and supported aid to Britain and increased military spending. But with Willkie trailing in the preference polls despite widespread opposition to Roosevelt's running for a third term, Republican leaders convinced Willkie to be more critical of the New Deal and to attack Roosevelt for pushing the nation toward war. Willkie's popularity surged upward. Roosevelt countered with a promise to American mothers: "Your boys are not going to be sent into any foreign wars." Although Roosevelt won easily, he received fewer votes than in 1936, and Democrats lost seats in both the Senate and the House of Representatives.

The Battle for the Atlantic

As Roosevelt knew, the destroyers-for-bases deal was only a temporary solution to Britain's growing shortage of cash. By December 1940, Churchill had asked Roosevelt for loans to pay for supplies and for help to protect merchant ships from German submarines. Roosevelt agreed, and knowing that both requests would face tough congressional and public opposition, he turned to his powers of persuasion. In his December fireside chat, he told his audience that a strong England was America's best defense against Germany. If England fell, he warned, Hitler would attack the United States next. He urged the people to make the nation the "arsenal of democracy" and to supply Britain with all the material help it needed to defeat Hitler. He then presented Congress with the lend-lease bill, which would allow the president to lend, lease, or in any way dispose of war materials to any country considered vital to American security. The request drew the expected fire from isolationists. Senator Burton K. Wheeler called it a military Agricultural Adjustment Act that would "plow under every fourth American boy." Supporters countered with "Send guns, not sons." Despite isolationist opposition, Congress easily passed the **Lend-Lease Act** on March 11, 1941, and the 60-year-old president breathed a sigh of relief.

For a while, it appeared that the lend-lease arrangement was approved too late. German submarines were destroying so much cargo and sinking so many irreplaceable ships that virtually none of the supplies that Britain needed were reaching its ports. In March 1941, Churchill warned Roosevelt that Germany's foes could not afford to lose the battle for the Atlantic. In response, Roosevelt sent part of the Pacific fleet to the Atlantic and extended the neutrality zone to include Greenland and Iceland. By the summer of 1941, U.S. Navy patrols of the neutrality zone were overlapping Hitler's Atlantic war zone. It was only a matter of time until American and German ships confronted each other.

Meanwhile, German forces plowed into Yugoslavia and Greece, heading toward the Mediterranean and North Africa. The nonaggression pact having served its purpose, Hitler planned to crush the Soviets with the largest military force ever assembled on a single front. On June 22, 1941, German forces, supported by allied Finnish, Hungarian, Italian, and Romanian armies, opened the eastern front. Few believed that the Soviet army would last more than three months, and many saw a ray of hope in the bloody fighting between the fascists and the communists. As American ambassador to Japan Joseph Grew wrote, "Let the Nazis and the Communists so weaken each other that the democracies will soon gain the upper hand or at least will be released from their dire peril." Yet despite initial crushing victories in which German soldiers surrounded Leningrad and advanced within miles of Moscow, by November 1941 it was becoming clear that the Soviets were not going to collapse. Claiming he would join even with the devil to defeat Hitler, Churchill made an ally of Stalin, and Roosevelt extended credits and lend-lease assistance to the Soviet Union.

In May, as Hitler prepared to invade Russia, the *Robin Moor* became the first American merchant

Wendell Willkie Business executive and Republican presidential candidate who lost to Roosevelt in 1940.

Lend-Lease Act Law passed by Congress in 1941 providing that any country whose security was vital to U.S. interests could receive arms and equipment by sale, transfer, or lease from the United States.

♦ From the beginning of World War II, Roosevelt was determined to help defeat the forces of fascism. Meeting with Churchill, on board a cruiser off the coast of Newfoundland in August 1941, the two leaders signed the Atlantic Charter as a prelude to the United States waging war against Germany. *FDR Library.*

ship sunk by a German submarine. With the number of American naval ships protecting convoys of merchant ships growing, the inevitable encounter between warships took place on September 4, 1941. A German U-boat fired two torpedoes at the American destroyer *Greer.* Both missed. Roosevelt immediately sought changes in the neutrality laws to allow merchant ships to be armed and sent into combat zones. Following an attack on the U.S.S. *Kearney* in October, and the sinking of the U.S.S. *Reuben James,* Congress rescinded all neutrality laws. Privately, Roosevelt explained that when he saw America at war, it would be with aid to allies and "naval and air forces only."

Even before the German attacks on the *Greer,* with the battle for the Atlantic heating up, Roosevelt and Churchill met secretly off the coast of Newfoundland (the Argentia Conference, August 9–12, 1941). They discussed strategies, supplies, and future prospects. But Roosevelt's main concern was more political than strategic. He wanted to develop a political base to support America's entry into the war by announcing principles that would draw distinctions between the open, multilateral world of the democracies and the closed, self-serving world of fascist expansion. He and Churchill produced the **Atlantic Charter,** which set forth Wilsonian goals of self-determination, freedom of trade and the seas, agreement to seek no territorial gains, and the establishment of a "permanent system of general security" in the form of a new world organization. Churchill reminded Roosevelt that Britain could not fully accept the goals of self-determination and free trade within the Commonwealth and British Empire. Roosevelt, who saw the Atlantic Charter as a domestic tool and not a blueprint for foreign policy, had no objection to the prime minister's exceptions.

Pearl Harbor

Since 1937, Japanese troops had seized more and more of coastal China while the United States did little but protest. By 1940, popular sentiment favored not only beefing up American defenses in the Pacific but also using economic pressure to slow Japanese aggression. In July 1940, Roosevelt placed some restrictions on Japanese-American trade, forbidding the sale and shipment of aviation fuel and scrap iron. Many Americans believed the action was too limited and pointed out that Japan was still allowed to buy millions of gallons of American oil and was using it to "extinguish the lamps of China."

The situation in East Asia soon worsened. The **Vichy** French government, knuckling under to German and Japanese pressure, allowed Japanese troops to enter French Indochina (see Map 27.2), and Japan signed a defense treaty with Germany and Italy. Promptly America strengthened its forces in the Philippines, tightened trade restrictions on Japan, and sent long-range bombers to the Philippines to "set the paper cities of Japan on fire" as a deterrence. Within the Japanese government of Prime Minister Fumimaro Konoye, those fearful of confrontation with the United States sought to negotiate. The subsequent discussions between Hull and Admiral Kichisaburo Nomura, Japan's ambassador to the United States, were confused and nonproductive. The lack of progress in the negotiations convinced many in the Japanese government that war was unavoidable. They believed that force would be needed to break the "circle of force" that denied Japan its interests. High on the list of interests was Japanese

Atlantic Charter Joint statement issued by Roosevelt and Churchill in 1941 to formulate American and British postwar aims of international economic and political cooperation.

Vichy City in central France that was the capital of unoccupied France from 1940 to 1942; the Vichy government continued to govern French territories and was sympathetic to the fascists.

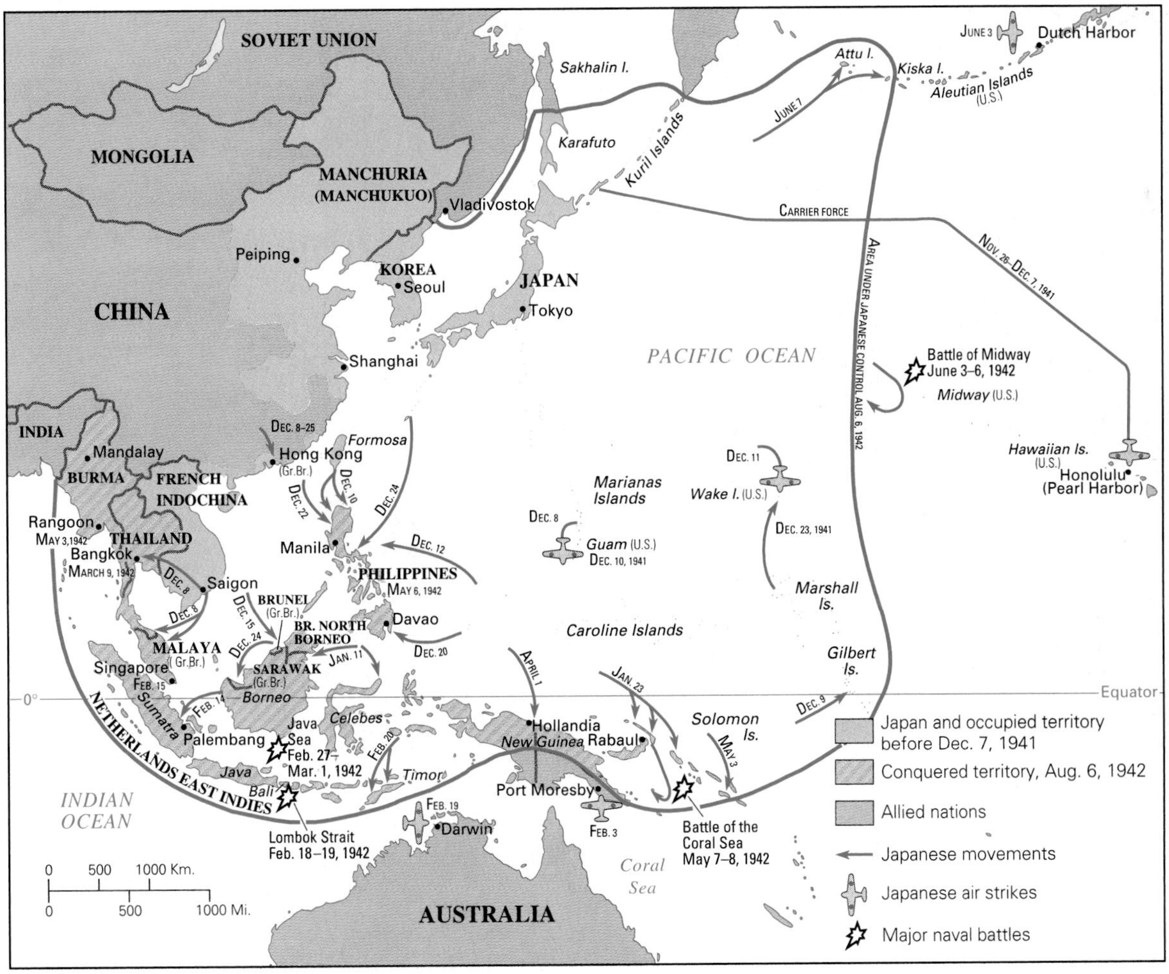

♦ **MAP 27.2 Japanese Advances, December 1941–1942** Beginning on December 7, 1941, Japanese forces began carving out a vast empire, the East Asian Co-Prosperity Sphere, by attacking American, British, Dutch, and Australian forces from Pearl Harbor to the Dutch East Indies. This map shows the course of Japanese expansion until the critical naval battles of the Coral Sea and Midway in the spring of 1942 that halted Japanese advances in the Pacific.

control over Malaya and the Dutch East Indies (Indonesia)—sources of vital raw materials, including oil. Seizing those regions, they concluded, would probably involve fighting the United States.

For Minister of War Hideki Tojo, the choice had become simple: either submit to American demands, giving up the achievements of the last ten years and accepting a world order defined by the United States, or safeguard the nation's honor and achievements by initiating a war. The only way to deter the decision for war was if the United States, which had frozen Japanese assets in July, agreed to stop its aid to China, not to expand its military presence in the Pacific, and to resume full trade with Japan. If these concessions did not occur, Tojo decided, Japan would begin military operations in the first week of December. Naval aircraft would strike the American fleet at Pearl Harbor and the army would invade the Philippines, Malaya, Singapore, and the Dutch East Indies. Negotiations remained stalled until November 26, when Hull made it clear that the United States would make no concessions and wanted Japan to withdraw from China.

On November 26, Admiral Isoroku Yamamoto dispatched part of the Japanese fleet, including six aircraft carriers, toward Hawai`i. American observers, however, focused on the activity of a larger part of the Japanese fleet, which joined troop ships

♦ Roosevelt called it "A Day of Infamy"—December 7, 1941, when Japanese planes attacked Pearl Harbor, Hawai`i, without warning and before a declaration of war. In this photo, *USS West Virginia* sinks in flames, one of eight battleships sunk or badly damaged in the attack. *National Archives.*

sailing on December 5 toward the South China Sea and the Gulf of Siam.

At 7:49 A.M. (Hawaiian time) on December 7, before Japan's declaration of war had been received in Washington, Japanese planes struck the American fleet anchored at **Pearl Harbor.** By 8:12 along Battleship Row seven battleships of the American Pacific fleet were aflame, sinking, or badly damaged. Eleven other ships had been hit, nearly two hundred American aircraft had been destroyed, and twenty-five hundred Americans had lost their lives. Fortunately, U.S. aircraft carriers were not at Pearl Harbor, and Admiral Chuichi Nagumo decided to withdraw without launching further attacks that would have targeted the important support facilities—repair shops, dry docks, and oil storage tanks. These incurred only light damages.

The attack on Pearl Harbor, however, was only a small part of Japan's strategy. Elsewhere that day, Japanese planes struck Singapore, Guam, the Philippines, and Hong Kong. Everywhere, British and American positions in the Pacific and East Asia were being overwhelmed. Roosevelt declared that the unprovoked, sneak attack on Pearl Harbor represented "a day which will live in infamy" and asked Congress for a declaration of war against Japan. Only the vote of Representative Jeannette Rankin of Montana, a pacifist, kept the December 8 declaration of war from being unanimous. Three days later, Germany and Italy declared war on the United States. Americans were angry, full of fight. In England Churchill "slept the sleep of the saved and thankful." He knew that with the economic and human resources of the United States finally committed to war, the Axis would be "ground to powder."

Pearl Harbor American naval base in Hawai`i bombed by Japanese planes on December 7, 1941, in an attack that prompted the United States to declare war on Japan.

America Responds to War

• What actions did Roosevelt choose to mobilize the nation for war?

• What new social and economic choices did Americans confront as the nation became the "arsenal of democracy"?

• What new opportunities and old constraints did women and minorities encounter on the home front and in their military experiences?

The attack on Pearl Harbor unified the nation as no other event had done. Afterward, it was almost impossible to find an isolationist. Thousands of young men rushed to enlist, especially in the navy and marines. On December 8, in New York City, twelve hundred applicants besieged the navy recruiting station, some having waited outside the doors all night. Eventually more than 16.4 million Americans would serve in the armed forces during World War II.

The shock of Japan's attack on Pearl Harbor raised fears of further attacks, especially along the Pacific coast. On the night of December 7 and throughout the next week, West Coast cities reported enemy planes overhead and practiced blackouts. Phantom Japanese planes were spotted above San Francisco and Los Angeles. In Seattle, crowds hurled rocks at an offending blue neon light that defied the blackout and then, venting both fear and rage, rioted across the city. The Rose Bowl game between Oregon State and Duke was moved from the Bowl's home in Pasadena to Duke's stadium in Durham, North Carolina. Stores everywhere removed from their shelves goods made in Japan. Alarm and anger were focused especially on Japanese Americans. Rumors circulated wildly that they intended to sabotage factories and military installations in order to pave the way for the invasion of the West Coast. Within a week, the FBI had arrested 2,541 citizens of Axis countries: 1,370 Japanese, 1,002 Germans, and 169 Italians. Attorney General Francis Biddle announced that he did not believe it would be necessary to arrest more. Biddle soon changed his mind as anti-Japanese hysteria spread.

Japanese-American Internment

The feelings against Japanese Americans were a product of long-standing racist attitudes and an immediate reaction to the war. Of the nearly 125,000 Japanese Americans in the country, about three-fourths were **Nisei,** who had been born in the United States. The rest were **Issei,** officially citizens of Japan although nearly all had lived in the United States more than eighteen years.

Fueling the hatred following the attack on Pearl Harbor were the actions of General John L. De Witt, commanding general of the Western Defense District. On December 7, he had seen Japanese planes over San Francisco where none existed, and he believed that everyone of Japanese heritage was a threat. Except for individual cases, the nation did not need to worry about Americans of Italian or German ancestry, he pronounced, but the Japanese were a different matter. "We must worry about the Japanese all the time," De Witt stated, "until he is wiped off the map." Unable to discover any acts of espionage or sabotage, California Attorney General Earl Warren nonetheless concluded that a plot existed and it was only a matter of time until "zero hour," when the enemy within would carry out its sinister plans. Echoing long-standing anti-Japanese feelings, California moved to "protect" itself. Japanese Americans were fired from state jobs and had their law and medical licenses revoked. Banks froze Japanese-American assets, stores refused service, and loyal citizens vandalized Nisei and Issei homes and businesses.

Although some doubted the reality of any threat from the Japanese-American community, few came forward to speak on its behalf or to protest the growing cry to relocate people of Japanese ancestry away from the coast. President Roosevelt was no exception. On February 19, 1942, he signed **Executive Order #9066,** which allowed the military to remove from official military areas anyone deemed a threat. When the entire West Coast was declared a military area, the eviction of the Japanese Americans from the region began. By the summer of 1942, more than 110,000 Nisei and Issei had been transported to ten **internment camps** (see chapter-opening map). When tested in court, the Executive Order was upheld by the Supreme Court in *Korematsu v. United States* (1944).

Nisei A person born in America of parents who emigrated from Japan.

Issei A Japanese immigrant to the United States.

Executive Order #9066 Order of President Roosevelt in 1942 authorizing the removal of "enemy aliens" from military areas; it was used to isolate Japanese Americans in internment camps.

internment camps Camps to which more than 110,000 Japanese Americans living in the West were moved soon after the attack on Pearl Harbor.

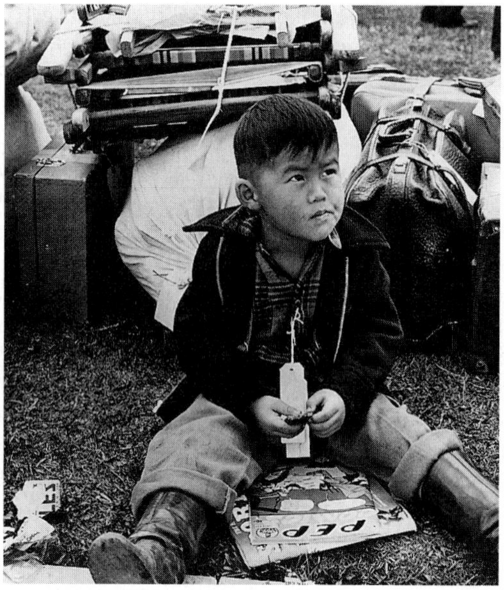

♦ In February 1942, President Roosevelt signed an order sending all Japanese Americans living on the West Coast to internment camps. This photo shows a young boy, with a chocolate bar and comic books, awaiting transportation to one of the ten camps. *FDR Library.*

The orders to relocate gave Japanese Americans almost no time to prepare. Families had to pack the few personal possessions they were allowed to take and to store or try and sell the rest of their property, including homes and businesses. Some had two weeks, others had two days, but it did not matter. Finding storage facilities was nearly impossible, and most families had to sell their possessions at ridiculously low prices. "It is difficult to describe the feeling of despair and humiliation experienced," one man recalled, "as we watched the Caucasians coming to look over all our possessions and offering such nominal amounts knowing we had no recourse but to accept." A twenty-six-room hotel was sold for $500; a pickup truck went for $25; farms sold for a fraction of what they were worth. When denied a few additional days to harvest his strawberry crop, one bitter farmer plowed it under. The FBI promptly arrested him for sabotage. Japanese-American families lost an estimated $810 million to $2 billion in property and possessions.

As if having to dispose of a lifetime of possessions almost overnight was not bad enough, the process of internment produced a feeling of helplessness and isolation. Tags with numbers were issued to every family to tie to luggage and coats—no names, only numbers. "From then on," wrote one woman, "we were known as family #10710." Going to the camp, she had lost her identity, dignity, and privacy. In camps, Nisei and Issei were surrounded by barbed wire and watched over by guards in towers mounted with machine guns pointing inward. Photographers were not allowed to take pictures of the wire or the guard towers. Families and individuals were assigned to apartments measuring 20 by 25 feet in long barracks of plywood covered with tar paper. On average, eight people were assigned to each apartment. A cot, a straw-filled mattress, and three army blankets were furnished to each person. Between rows of barracks were communal bathrooms and eating areas. Within each camp, the internees were expected to create a community complete with farms, shops, and small factories. And within a remarkably short period of time, they did. Making the desert bloom, the internees at Manzanar by 1944 were producing more than $2 million worth of agricultural products.

Some internees were able to leave the camps by working outside, supplying much-needed labor, especially farm work. By the fall of 1942, one-fifth of all males had left the camps to work. Others volunteered for military service, the other escape route from the camps. Japanese-American units served in both the Pacific and Europe. The most famous unit was the four-thousand-man 442nd Regimental Combat Team, which saw action in Italy, France, and Germany. The men of the 442nd were among the most decorated in the U.S. Army (see Individual Choices: Daniel Ken Inouye).

Aware of rabidly anti-Japanese public opinion, Roosevelt waited until after the off-year 1943 elections to allow internees who passed a loyalty review to go home. A year later, the camps were empty, each internee having been given train fare home and $25. Returning home, the Japanese Americans discovered that nearly everything they owned was gone. Stored belongings had been stolen. Land, homes, and businesses had been seized by the government for unpaid taxes. Denied even an apology from the government, Japanese Americans began to re-establish their homes and businesses. Decades later, in 1988, and after several lawsuits on behalf of victims, a semiapologetic federal government paid $20,000 in compensation to each of the surviving sixty thousand internees.

Mobilizing the Nation for War

When President Roosevelt made his first fireside chat after the attack on Pearl Harbor, "Dr. New

Deal" became "Dr. Win the War." He called on Americans to produce the goods necessary for victory. Factories were to run twenty-four hours a day, seven days a week. Gone was every trace of the antibusiness attitude that had characterized much New Deal rhetoric, and in its place was the realization that only big business could produce the vast amount of armaments and supplies needed.

Secretary of War Henry Stimson noted: "You have to let business make money out of the process or business won't work." With Americans stepping forward to enlist, many corporate executives flocked to Washington to take "dollar-a-year" jobs, contributing their business skills to help the war effort. Most stayed on their company's payroll, and few saw any conflict of interest in awarding million-dollar contracts to the corporate world they had just left. Eighty-two percent of government contracts during the war went to the nation's top hundred corporations. The coastal West saw great economic gains as many of the new military-based industries built and expanded factories there. A corridor from San Diego to Los Angeles emerged as the country's "largest urban military-industrial complex." Wrote one observer, "It was [as] if someone had tilted the country: people, money, and soldiers all spilled west." Small companies that produced nonwar goods received very little of the $240 billion paid out by the U.S. government, and during the war more than a half-million small businesses collapsed.

By 1942, one-third of all production was geared to the war, and the government was allocating millions of dollars to improve production and to build new plants in vital industries like aluminum and synthetic rubber. By the end of the war, the United States had pumped more than $320 billion into the American economy, and the final production amounts exceeded almost everyone's expectations: U.S. manufacturers had built over 300,000 aircraft, 88,140 tanks, and 86,000 warships. "Sir Launchalot," Henry J. Kaiser, had dramatically improved methods of shipbuilding—incorporating the use of many **prefabricated** sections. His shipyard in California cut the time it took to build a merchant ship from about three hundred days before the war to an average of eighty days in 1942.

As the nation's economy began to retool to become the arsenal of democracy, Roosevelt acted to provide government direction and planning. His first step in 1941 was to establish the **Office of Price Administration (OPA)** to control prices. In January 1942, in the aftermath of Pearl Harbor, Roosevelt established the War Production Board and the War Labor Board. Working together, these boards plus the OPA were to coordinate and plan production, establish the allotment of materials, and ensure harmonious labor relations. At first, these agencies were unable to create a smoothly working economy, and Congress, in the fall of 1942, passed the Stabilization Act, expanding the powers of the OPA and regulating agricultural prices. Roosevelt added a new umbrella agency—the Office of Economic Stabilization—to better coordinate prices, rents, and wages. He appointed former Supreme Court justice James F. Byrnes as its chief. Further expanding government coordination and Byrnes's powers, in May 1943 Roosevelt established the **Office of War Mobilization** with Byrnes as its director.

Armed with extensive powers and the president's trust, Byrnes, known as the "Assistant President," controlled a far-flung economic empire of policies and programs that touched every American. The Office of War Mobilization coordinated the production, procurement, transportation, and distribution of civilian and military supplies. "If you want something done, go see Jimmie Byrnes," became the watchword. Government agencies set prices, froze wages and rents, and instituted a rationing system that limited purchases of gasoline, tires, butter, sugar, cheese, meat, and other commodities. By the end of 1942, most Americans had a ration book containing an array of different-colored and -valued coupons that limited what they could buy and eat. Under rationing, most Americans were allowed 3 gallons of gasoline a week. A bomber, Roosevelt explained in 1943, required nearly 1,100 gallons of fuel to bomb Naples, the equivalent of about 375 gasoline ration tickets. Still, despite all government efforts, a strong black market thrived. The right amount of money could buy nearly any item, no matter how restricted.

By mid-1943, production was booming, jobs were plentiful, wages and family incomes were rising, and inflation was under control—held to around 8

prefabricated Manufactured in advance in standard sections that are easy to ship and assemble when needed.

Office of Price Administration Agency established by executive order in 1941 to set prices for critical wartime commodities.

Office of War Mobilization Umbrella agency headed by James Byrnes to coordinate the production, procurement, and distribution of civilian and military supplies.

INDIVIDUAL CHOICES

Fighting for Democracy

Daniel Ken Inouye

As it did for many Americans, World War II changed Daniel Inouye's expectations and life. He chose to temporarily abandon his plans to become a physician and enlist in the army. While fighting in Europe, he suffered serious wounds, which effectively ended all hope of a medical career. After the war, he chose to enter politics in order to achieve "full citizenship" for Hawaiians and Japanese Americans. He is now Hawai`i's senior senator. From the office of U.S. Senator Daniel Inouye.

On December 7, 1941, as the Japanese bombed Pearl Harbor, 17-year-old Daniel Ken Inouye rushed to a Red Cross aid station to care for the first American civilian casualties of World War II. He wanted to enlist, but Nisei were being discharged from the armed forces, and on the mainland Japanese Americans were being interned. Internment did not occur in Hawai`i, however, where other Hawaiians supported freedom for Japanese Americans, who represented 40 percent of the population. Still, Inouye knew, "No matter how hard we worked . . . there would always be those who would look at us and think—and some would say it aloud—'Dirty Jap.' "

In September 1942, the Nisei got their chance to serve. Volunteers were being accepted for the newly created 442nd Regimental Combat Team. At first turned down because of his student status and his work with the Red Cross, Inouye left school and quit the Red Cross and became the second-to-last man to be assigned to the 442nd. Training in Mississippi, he and other Nisei were told they would have to fight not only the enemy but also "prejudice and discrimination" and that the best way to deal with both foes was to be exemplary soldiers. Those who survived would "have a chance to make a world where every man is a free man and the equal of his neighbor." It was a patriotic speech, but to Inouye and other Nisei the words were prophetic.

Serving with the 442nd, Inouye experienced the carnage of battle, earning a battlefield com-

percent. Even farmers were climbing out of debt: farm income had tripled since 1939. Taxes were also up, reflecting Roosevelt's desire to fund the war through taxes. The 1942 and 1943 Revenue Acts expanded the number of taxpayers and raised rates. In 1939, 4 million Americans paid income taxes, and by the end of the war that number had surpassed 40 million. Those making $500,000 or more a year paid 88 percent in taxes. Corporate taxes averaged 40 percent, with a 90 percent tax on excess profits.

These tax changes moderately altered the basic distribution of income by reducing the holdings of the upper two-fifths of the population, but taxes paid for only about half of the cost of the war. The government borrowed the rest. The national debt jumped from $40 billion to $260 billion by 1945 (see mission as a second lieutenant. In the final days of the European war, his platoon was pinned down by German machine-gun fire from three bunkers. Not waiting for the Germans "to get us all," Inouye dashed forward. Wounded in the leg and stomach, he silenced two of the enemy positions. Then, crawling to within 10 feet of the third machine gun, he rose to throw a grenade, but a German fired first, shattering Inouye's right arm. "It dangled there," still holding the live grenade, he remembered. Throwing the grenade with his left hand, Inouye destroyed the last emplacement. For his actions, he received the nation's second highest award for valor, the Distinguished Service Cross, and spent two years recovering from his wounds and learning to live with only one arm.

Inouye returned to Hawai`i, married, completed his education—including law school—and dove into Hawaiian politics. War had changed him and other Japanese Americans: "We didn't want to go back to the plantations." Upon Hawai`i's admission to statehood in 1959, Inouye was elected by an overwhelming margin to the House of Representatives, moving to the Senate in 1962. In Congress, he was effective in getting legislation passed but kept a low, even bland, public profile.

In 1973, he served on the Senate Select Committee that investigated the Watergate cover-up (see pages 979–980). Not fooled by his quiet demeanor, a White House adviser said that Inouye's name should be pronounced " 'Ain't no way,' for no way he's going to give us anything but problems." The observation proved correct. During the televised hearings, Inouye's public approval rating rose to 84 percent—even as the lawyer representing President Nixon's chief of staff called him a "fat Jap."

In 1987, Inouye chaired the Senate's investigation of the Reagan administration's illegal arms sales to the Contra rebels in Nicaragua (see page 1003). As in the Watergate hearings, it was clear that he disliked those who abused their power. Concluding the Iran-Contra hearings, he condemned the administration's actions as a "chilling . . . disregard for the rule of law." To him, the defendants' assertions that national survival in a "dangerous world" justified going beyond the limits of the law were nothing more than "an excuse for autocracy." As a Japanese American who was raised in "respectable poverty" and felt the sting of discrimination, as a World War II veteran and a U.S. senator who had fought for democracy, Inouye was pleased to announce that, in the United States, "the people still rule."

Figure 27.1). The most publicized borrowing effort encouraged the purchase of **war bonds.** Movie stars and other celebrities asked Americans to "do their part" and buy bonds, especially Series E bonds worth $25 and $50. The public responded by purchasing more than $40 billion of individual bonds, but the majority of bonds—$95 billion—was sold to corporations and financial institutions.

The war brought an end to the Depression and created full employment. With the formation of the War Labor Board, Roosevelt sought to prevent labor

war bond Bonds sold by the government to finance the war effort.

Don't Let That Shadow Touch Them
Buy WAR BONDS

♦ Using the threat to children that fascism posed, this American war bond poster asked patriotic Americans to protect their children by buying war bonds. *National Archives.*

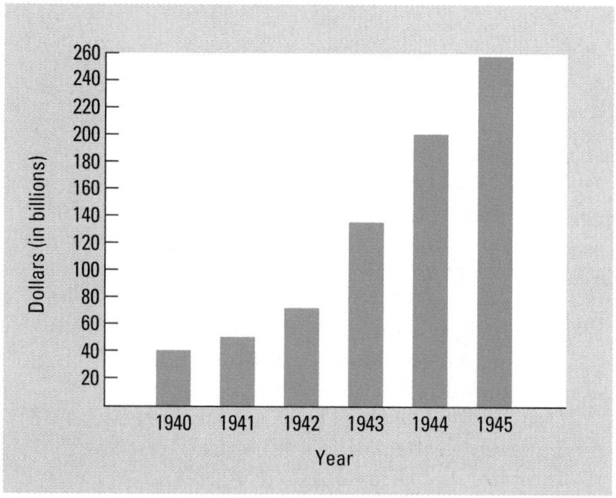

♦ **FIGURE 27.1 The Cost of War, 1940–1945** As the United States fought to defeat the Axis nations, its national debt soared. Rather than further raise taxes, the government chose to borrow about 60 percent of the cost, adding to a $259 billion national debt.

disputes while at the same time protecting the needs of the worker. The board set wages—adopting a 15 percent increase over 1941 wages—and hours, and it promoted collective bargaining. Union membership rose to 15 million in 1945, and most workers and employers accepted these government guidelines as a patriotic duty. But not every one did so. In 1943, John L. Lewis and his United Mine Workers went on strike, demanding higher wages and safer working conditions. An angry president threatened to seize the mines and jail Lewis. It was a threat that he did not want to carry out. In June, Congress passed, over Roosevelt's veto, the **Smith-Connally War Labor Disputes Act,** which gave the president the power to seize and operate any strike-bound plant or operation deemed vital for war production. Eventually, the parties in the mine strike compromised, allowing special circumstances under which wages could exceed the the 15 percent wage formula. Other strikes broke out during the war, but war production was never in jeopardy, and most workers' wages rose during the war. Higher wages, Roosevelt's veto of the Smith-Connally Act, and support for a wartime president kept labor loyal to Roosevelt as he prepared for the 1944 presidential race.

Wartime Politics

While Roosevelt was mobilizing the nation for war, Republicans and conservative Democrats moved to bury what was left of the New Deal. The congressional elections of November 1942 indicated that Roosevelt and liberal Democrats were facing hard political times. People secure in wartime jobs were no longer very concerned about social welfare programs. They griped about higher taxes, rents, and prices; about the scarcity of goods to buy, especially the limits on gasoline and meat; and about government inefficiency. And they aimed their complaints at Roosevelt and the Democrats. Early military defeats in the Pacific added to the dissatisfaction. Consequently, many Americans who had once supported the New Deal and voted Democratic either decided not to vote or voted Republican in 1942. Bolstered by Republican victories, business-oriented publications like *Fortune* and the *Wall Street Journal* sounded the attack on remaining New Deal

Smith-Connally War Labor Disputes Act Law passed by Congress in 1943 authorizing the government to seize plants in which labor disputes threatened war production; it was later used to take over the coal mines.

statism, especially social welfare programs. Congress was not far behind, axing the CCC, WPA, and NYA and slashing the budgets of several other government agencies.

To keep the social activism of the New Deal alive during the election year of 1944, Roosevelt linked national security with a social agenda. He called for a **G.I. Bill of Rights** and a commitment to achieving "freedom from want." In June, the G.I. Bill became law. It guaranteed a year's unemployment compensation for veterans while they looked for "good" jobs, provided economic support if they chose to go to school, and offered low-interest home loans.

Republicans nominated Governor Thomas Dewey of New York as their 1944 presidential candidate. Responding to the conservative tone of the nation, Roosevelt allowed party conservatives to drop the liberal Henry Wallace as vice president and selected the moderately conservative **Harry S Truman,** senator from Missouri, in Wallace's place. Roosevelt campaigned on a strong wartime economy, his record of leadership, and, by November 1944, a successful war effort. Dewey had little with which to attack Roosevelt except accusations of inefficiency and waste in the government and the claim that Roosevelt, at 62, was too old for the job. A Republican-inspired "whispering campaign" hinted that Roosevelt was close to death. Voters, however, were less concerned with Roosevelt's age than they were with Dewey's youth (42) and arrogance. Dewey could "strut sitting down," observed a critic. Roosevelt's winning totals, though not as large as in 1940, were still greater than pollsters had predicted and proved that the president could still generate widespread support.

A People at Work and War

Within sixteen days of Pearl Harbor, nearly 600,000 volunteers were in uniform. Needing still more, the government turned to the draft, or Selective Service. The more than 10 million drafted during the war were required to serve until the war was over. By 1945, the U.S. military had over 12 million people in uniform.

At home the call-up and need to manufacture the goods necessary to win the war began to change everyday life. Cotton, silk, gasoline, and items made of metal, including hair clips and safety pins, became increasingly scarce. The War Production Board established fashion rules to conserve cotton and wool. Garment makers eliminated vests and shirt cuffs and narrowed the lapels on men's suits. The amount of fabric in women's skirts was also reduced, and the two-piece bathing suit was introduced as "patriotic chic." Families collected scrap metals, paper, and rubber to be recycled for the war effort and grew **victory gardens** to support the war. When individuals complained about shortages and inconveniences, someone was bound to reply, "Don't you know there's a war on?"

For entertainment, Americans turned to comic books and cheap paperback novels, especially mysteries, and continued to watch movies in increasing numbers. The public loved movies like *Holiday Inn* (1942), with its popular song "White Christmas" sung by Bing Crosby, and *Casablanca* (1942), starring Humphrey Bogart and Ingrid Bergman.

One sure sign there was a war on was that people were moving and taking new jobs as never before. Prior to the war nearly 3.8 million Americans were unemployed, but by the end of 1942 a severe labor shortage existed. To fill gaps in the work force, employers increasingly turned to people excluded prior to the war: women and minorities. Even the Nisei were allowed to leave their relocation camps if their labor was needed. To reach new jobs, 15 million Americans relocated between 1941 and 1945. Two hundred thousand people, many from the rural South, headed for Detroit, but more went west, where defense industries beckoned. Shipbuilding and the aircraft industry sparked boomtowns that could not keep pace with the growing need for local services and facilities. San Diego, California, once a small retirement community with a quiet naval base, mushroomed into a major military and defense industrial city almost overnight. Nearly fifty-five thousand people flocked there each year of the war. Thousands of them lived in small travel trailers that they leased from the federal government for $7 a month. Mobile, Alabama; Norfolk, Virginia; Seattle, Washington; Denver, Colorado—all experienced similar rapid growth (see the chapter-opening map).

statism The concept or practice of placing economic planning and policy under government control.

G.I. Bill of Rights Law passed by Congress in 1944 to provide financial and educational benefits for American veterans after World War II; *G.I.* stands for "government issue."

Harry S Truman Democratic senator from Missouri whom Roosevelt selected in 1944 to be vice president; in 1945 Truman became president.

victory garden Small plot cultivated by a patriotic citizen during World War II to supply household food and allow farm production to be used for the war effort.

War industrial cities with expanding populations experienced massive problems providing homes, water, electricity, and sanitation. Crime flourished. Marriage, divorce, family violence, and juvenile delinquency rates soared. Twelve thousand sailors and soldiers looking for a good time gave Norfolk a reputation as a major sin city. Police estimated that from two to three thousand prostitutes worked in its alleys, taxis, clubs, and restaurants.

Contributing to the social problems of the booming cities were problems posed by many unsupervised teenagers. Juvenile crime increased dramatically during the war, much of it blamed on lockout and latchkey children whose working mothers left them unsupervised. In Mobile, authorities speculated that two thousand children a day skipped school, some going to movies but most just hanging out looking for something to do.

Particularly worrisome to authorities were those nicknamed "V-girls." Victory girls were young teens, sometimes called "khaki-wacky teens," who hung around gathering spots like bus depots and drugstores to flirt with GIs and ask for dates. Wearing "sloppy-joe" sweaters, hair ribbons, bobby sox, and saddle shoes, their young faces thick with makeup and bright red lipstick, V-girls traded sex for movies, dances, and drinks. Seventeen-year-old Elvira Taylor of Norfolk took a different approach—she became an "Allotment Annie." She simply married the soldiers, preferably pilots, and collected their monthly **allotment checks.** Eventually, two American soldiers at an English pub showing off pictures of their wives discovered they both had married Elvira. It turned out she had married six servicemen.

New Opportunities and Old Constraints in Wartime

Mobilization for war forced change. Economic and human resources had to be restructured and redirected, at least temporarily. Families had to adjust to new challenges. Minorities and women confronted new roles and accepted new responsibilities, both on the home front and in the military. Like men, many women were eager to serve in the military. But the armed forces did not employ women except as nurses. To expand women's roles, Congresswoman Edith Norse Rogers prodded Congress and the army, in March 1942, to create the Women's Auxiliary Army Corps (WAAC), which became the Women's Army Corps (WAC) a year later. The other services—with differing levels of enthusiasm—followed suit. The navy created the Women Appointed for Volunteer Emergency Service (WAVES), and the marines created the Women's Reserve. Relegated to noncombat roles, most women served as nurses and clerical workers, but there were notable exceptions. Women's Airforce Service Pilots (WASPS) tested planes, ferried planes across the United States and Canada, and trained male pilots. At the marines' flight training center at Cherry Point, North Carolina, all the flight instructors were women. By war's end, more than 350,000 women had donned uniforms, earned equal pay with men who held the same rank, and provided a new image for women.

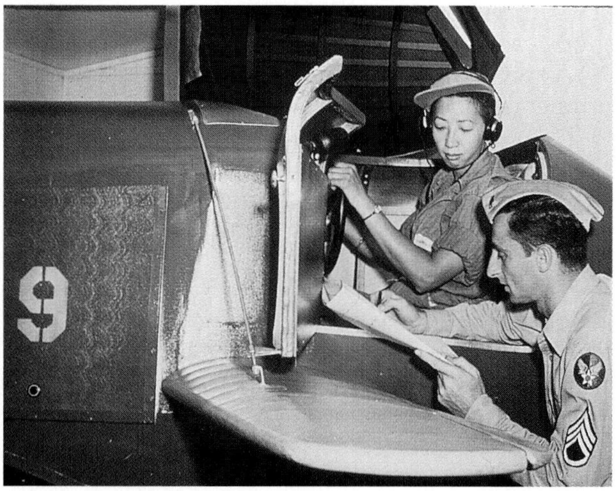

♦ More than 350,000 women served in the military during the war, including Lt. Hazel Ying Lee, a Women's Airforce Service Pilot. WASPs flew "noncombat," ferrying planes and supplies across the United States and Canada. Already an experienced pilot in China, Lt. Lee is seated here in the cockpit of a trainer. Lt. Lee died in 1943, when her plane crashed. *Texas Woman's University.*

Women serving in the military was not the only break with tradition. With more than 10 million men marching off to war, employers increasingly turned to women. Until 1943, employers did not actively recruit women, preferring to hire white males. But as the labor shortage deepened, they turned to women and minorities to work on assembly lines. The federal government applauded the move and conducted an

allotment check Check that a soldier's wife received from the government, amounting to a percentage of her husband's pay.

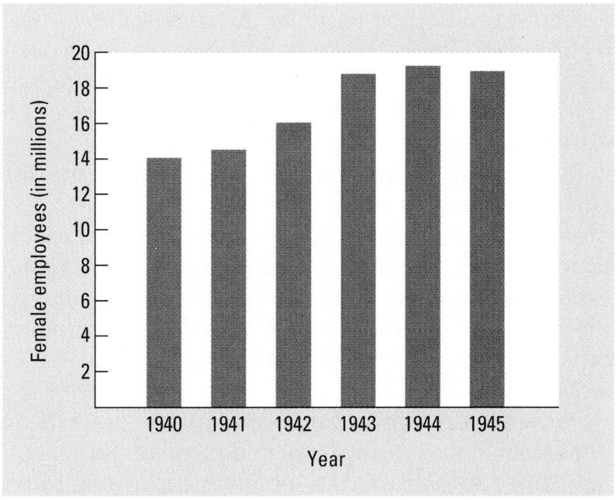

♦ **FIGURE 27.2 Women in the Work Force, 1940–1945** As men went to war, the nation turned increasingly to women to fill vital jobs. With government's encouragement, the number of women in the work force swelled from 14 million to nearly 20 million. With the war's end, however, many women left the workplace and returned to home.

emotional campaign suggesting that women could shorten the war if they left home and went to work. Rosie the Riveter became the symbol of patriotic women doing their part. As more jobs opened, women did fill them—some because of patriotism but most because they wanted both the job and the wages. Leaving home, Peggy Terry worked in a munitions plant and considered it "an absolute miracle. . . . We made the fabulous sum of $32 a week. . . . Before, we made nothing." Other women left menial jobs for better-paying positions in industry and the federal government. By 1944, 37 percent of all adult women were working, almost 19.4 million (see Figure 27.2). Of these, the majority (72.2 percent) were married and over half were 35 or older. Despite the number of women entering the work force, most women—over 66 percent—stayed home. They supported the war effort in their homes and communities, providing volunteers and energy to organizations like the Red Cross and Civil Defense.

Women working and volunteering, however, experienced some old constraints. Professional and supervisory positions were still dominated by men, and not all was rosy at work. Male workers resented and harassed women, who generally received lower wages than men, and constantly reminded them that their jobs were temporary. Employers and most men expected that when the war was over, women would happily return to their traditional roles at home. Without adequate childcare and nursery facilities, worried about abandoning traditional family roles and their families, some women found it difficult to balance family needs and work. With regret, many gave up their jobs.

With the end of the war, the government reversed itself and pronounced that patriotism lay at home with the family. By the summer of 1945, many women who had entered the work force during the war found themselves unemployed. Shipyards and aircraft plants dismissed nearly three-fourths of their women employees. In Detroit, the automobile industry executed a similar cut in women workers, from 25 to 7.5 percent. Those who managed to remain at work were frequently transferred to less attractive, poorly paying jobs. Thus, for most women, the war experience was a mixed one of new choices followed by traditional constraints.

Like the war experiences of women, those of minorities were mixed. New employment and social opportunities existed but were accompanied by increased racial and ethnic tensions and the knowledge that, when the war ended, the opportunities were likely to vanish. Initially, the war provided few opportunities for African Americans. Shipyards and other defense contractors wanted white workers. **Closed-shop agreements** between white-only AFL unions and employers even squeezed black skilled workers out of existing jobs. Sometimes when African-American workers were hired, white unions responded with job actions. North American Aviation Company spoke for the aircraft industry when, in early 1942, it announced that it would not hire blacks "regardless of their training."

The antiblack bias began to change by mid-1942 as businesses felt pressure from the worsening labor shortage—especially in the West—the growing unwillingness of African Americans to be denied the equality and rights due all Americans, and the efforts of the federal government. In California, these pressures dissolved the color line by the end of 1942. West Coast shipyards were the first to integrate. Lockheed Aircraft then broke the color barrier in August. Word soon spread to the South that blacks could find work in California, and between the spring of 1942 and 1945, more than 340,000 African Americans moved to Los Angeles. Overall, nearly

closed-shop agreement An agreement requiring workers in a business or factory to be union members; such a workplace is known as a closed shop.

400,000 African Americans abandoned the South for the West. Thousands of others went north to cities like Chicago and Detroit.

The availability of jobs for African Americans was not just the result of labor needs. It was also the product of growing pressure on government from African-American leaders. In early 1941, **A. Philip Randolph,** leader of the powerful Brotherhood of Sleeping Car Porters union, declared that without direct pressure from the black population, Roosevelt and the government would never provide legal, social, or economic justice for blacks. Randolph proposed that African Americans march en masse on Washington to demand equality in jobs and the armed forces. In June, fearing that a hundred thousand African Americans were prepared to descend on Washington, Roosevelt created the **Fair Employment Practices Commission (FEPC)** and forbade racial job discrimination by the government and by companies holding government contracts. The FEPC was not always willing or successful in promoting job equality, but by 1945, 9 percent of the work force was African American. Black wages, still only about 65 percent of the wages of white males, rose from an average of $457 to $1,976 a year.

Across the nation, blacks supported the "Double V" campaign: victory over racist Germany and victory over racism at home. The membership of the NAACP and the Urban League increased as both turned to public opinion, the courts, and Congress to attack segregation, lynching, and discrimination. In 1942, the newly formed **Congress of Racial Equality (CORE)** adopted the sit-in tactic to attempt to integrate public facilities. Successes were minor but still noteworthy. Led by James Farmer, CORE integrated some public facilities in Chicago and Washington, although it failed in the South, where many CORE workers were badly beaten.

In the North, patterns of hostility, discrimination, and violence hardened as the population of African Americans increased. Jobs at Ford and Chrysler paid $5 a day, but suitable wages hardly compensated for white hostility. When three black workers were promoted, white workers went on strike, harping, "We'd rather see Hitler and Hirohito win than work beside a nigger on the assembly line." Similar attitudes existed in Detroit's schools and stores, and real-estate and property-owner associations ensured that blacks were tightly restricted to certain residential areas. A violent confrontation occurred in 1942 when African-American families tried to move into the federally constructed Sojourner Truth housing development. Eventually, Michigan's governor had to deploy national guard soldiers to protect the families as they moved in. A Justice Department examination reported, "White Detroit seems to be a particularly hospitable climate for native fascist-type movements."

With racial hatred and violence just below the surface in Detroit, it took only a small incident to set off a major confrontation. On a hot summer Sunday, June 20, 1943, a series of small racial fights escalated rapidly into a major race riot. Federal troops arrived the morning of June 21 and restored order by noon, but not before twenty-five blacks and nine whites were dead.

The opportunities and difficulties of African Americans in uniform paralleled those of black civilians. Prior to 1940, blacks served at the lowest ranks and in the most menial jobs in a segregated army and navy. The Army Air Corps and the Marine Corps refused to accept blacks at all. Compounding the problem, most in the military openly agreed with Secretary of War Stimson when he said, "Leadership is not embedded in the Negro race." The manpower needs of war, however, changed the role of the black soldier, opening up new ranks and occupations.

In April 1942, Secretary of the Navy James Forrestal permitted blacks to be **noncommissioned officers** in the U.S. Navy, but blacks had to wait until 1944 before they could be commissioned as officers. With only a small number of African-American officers, the army in 1940 began to encourage the recruitment of black officers and promoted **Benjamin O. Davis, Sr.,** from colonel to general. By the beginning of 1942, the Army Air Corps had an all-black unit, the 99th Pursuit Squadron. Eventually six hundred African Americans were commissioned as pilots.

A. Philip Randolph African-American labor leader who organized the 1941 march on Washington that pressured Roosevelt to issue an executive order banning discrimination in defense industries.

Fair Employment Practices Commission Commission established in 1941 to halt discrimination in war production and government.

Congress of Racial Equality Civil rights organization founded in 1942 and committed to using nonviolent techniques such as sit-ins to end segregation.

noncommissioned officer Enlisted member of the armed forces who has been promoted to a rank such as corporal or sergeant, conferring leadership over others.

Benjamin O. Davis, Sr. Army officer who in 1940 became the first black general in the U.S. Army.

♦ Captain William Campbell served in the 99th Pursuit Squadron, which was commanded by General Benjamin O. Davis. During the war, about 700,000 African Americans served in segregated units in all branches of the military and faced discrimination at all levels. At one air base in Arizona, the barracks were color-coded; those for whites were painted white and those for African Americans were covered with black tar paper. *"William Ayers Campbell" by Betsy Graves Reyneau, 1994. National Portrait Gallery. Gift of the Harmon Foundation.*

Higher ranks and better jobs for a few did not disguise the fact that for most blacks, even officers, military life was often demeaning and brutal and almost always segregated. In Indiana, more than a hundred black officers were arrested for trying to integrate an officers' club. Across the country, blacks objected to the Red Cross practice of segregating the blood supply. In Salinas, Kansas, German prisoners of war could eat at any local lunch counter and go to any movie theater, but their black guards could not. One dismayed soldier wrote, "The people of Salinas would serve these enemy soldiers and turn away black American GIs. . . . If we were . . . in Germany, they would break our bones. As 'colored' men in Salinas, they only break our hearts." In truth, many black soldiers had bones broken and their lives taken on the home front. As in the civilian world, blacks in the military resisted discrimination and called on Roosevelt and the government for help. But their requests accomplished little.

Latinos, too, found new opportunities during the war while encountering continued segregation and hostility. Like other Americans, Latinos, almost invariably called "Mexicans" by their fellow soldiers, rushed to enlist as the war started. More than three hundred thousand Latinos served—the highest percentage of any ethnic community—and seventeen won the nation's highest award for valor: the Medal of Honor. Although they faced some institutional and individual prejudices in the military, Latinos, unlike African Americans and most Nisei, served in integrated units and generally faced less discrimination in the military than in civilian society.

For those remaining at home, more jobs were available, but Latinos almost always worked as common laborers and agricultural workers. In the Southwest, not until 1943 did the FEPC attempt to open semiskilled and skilled positions to Mexican Americans. Gains thus made came only with increased Anglo hostility and, on numerous occasions, with the clear understanding that the new opportunities would vanish when the war was over.

Jobs drew Mexican Americans to cities, creating a serious shortage of farm workers. After having deported Mexicans during the Depression (see page 783), the government had to ask Mexico to supply agricultural workers. Mexico agreed but insisted that the ***braceros*** (Spanish for "helping arms") receive fair wages and adequate housing, transportation, food, and medical care. In practice, whatever guarantees were promised in *bracero* contracts mattered little. Most ranchers and farmers paid low wages and provided substandard facilities. The average Mexican-American family earned about $800 a year, well below the government-established $1,130-a-year minimum standard for a family of five.

Young Mexican Americans known as ***pachucos*** expressed their rejection of Anglo culture and values by wearing flamboyant clothes such as zoot suits—a long jacket with wide lapels and padded shoulders worn over pleated trousers, pegged and cuffed at the ankle—topped off by a pancake hat

braceros Mexican nationals who worked on U.S. farms beginning in 1942 because of the labor shortage during World War II.

***pachucos*/zoot suiters** A Spanish term originally meaning bandit, pachucos became a term associated with juvenile delinquents of Mexican-American/Latino heritage; zoot suiters were those wearing the distinctive zoot suit that to many reflects racial/ethnic identity.

♦ Secure communications on the battle field are a necessity, and no communications were more secure than those provided by the code-talkers—American Indians, who spoke in their native languages. Here Henry Bake, Jr. and George H. Kork, Navahos, "talk code" in the jungle of Bougainville in the Solomon Islands. *National Archives.*

and gold chains. In the summer of 1943, tensions between Anglos and Mexican Americans were running high in Los Angeles, which had a history of discrimination in housing, jobs, and education toward its large Mexican-American population. Newspaper articles had been highlighting a Mexican crime wave and depicting **zoot suiters** as dope addicts and draft dodgers. On three successive nights, Anglo mobs, including several hundred servicemen, descended on East Los Angeles. They dragged zoot suiters out of movies, stores, and even houses, beating them and tearing apart their clothes. When the police acted, it was to arrest Mexican Americans—more than six hundred youths were taken into "preventive custody." The riot lasted a week. Afterward, the Los Angeles city council outlawed the wearing of zoot suits.

Like other disadvantaged groups, American Indians took advantage of new job opportunities and served gallantly during the war in the military. At least twenty-five thousand Indians served in the military. Among the most famous were three hundred Navajos who served as **code talkers** for the Marine Corps, using their native language as a secure means of communication. Though often called "chief," American Indians, unlike other minorities, met little discrimination in the military. Military life and wages for most compared favorably to reservation life, and Indians, like many other soldiers, found the travel and experiences of the military positive and educational. Once the war was over, the 1944 G.I. Bill provided many American Indians with their first chance to go to college.

During the war, not only the military but also civilian jobs and higher wages lured more than forty thousand American Indians away from their reservations. Mostly unskilled, these wartime workers boosted their families' average income from $400 a year in 1941 to $1,200 in 1945. Many of those who left the reservation assimilated into American culture and never returned to the old patterns of life.

Less visible in the military than women and minorities were homosexuals. Even though the military services had an official policy of not enlisting homosexuals, *Newsweek* complained that too many "inverts managed to slip through" an ineffective screening process that only asked if a person was a homosexual and looked for obvious effeminate behavior. In the military, many gays and lesbians discovered that they could manage both military and personal needs and that the military generally tolerated them as long as they were not caught in a sexual act. In a circular letter sent to military commanders, the Surgeon General's office asked that homosexual relationships be tolerated as long as they did not disrupt the unit. During the war, gays' war records were much like other soldiers'. "I was super patriotic," said one combat veteran. With the war over, most homosexuals gathered in urban areas. Some, like other soldiers who faced prejudice, were determined to fight discrimination and in 1950 founded the Mattachine Society (see page 900).

Waging World War

- What choices and constraints did Roosevelt and Truman confront in shaping America's strategy for global conflict?
- What were the stresses within the Grand Alliance?
- What expectations prompted Truman and his advisers to choose to use the atomic bomb?

In December 1941, within the United States, 4 million people were unemployed, another 7.5 million were earning less than the minimum wage of 40

code talkers Navajos serving in the U.S. Marine Corps who communicated by radio in their native language so the enemy could not understand what they were saying.

cents an hour, and ongoing economic and ethnic differences continued to divide society. To many, the outbreak of war promised a reversal of those trends, generating national unity and a sense of purpose as well as a return of prosperity. *Time* magazine commented that the attack on Pearl Harbor was "a reverse earthquake that in one terrible jerk shook everything disjointed, distorted, askew back into place."

The Japanese attack also convinced most Americans that defeating Japan should be the country's first priority. The navy too was pushing hard for a Japanese-first strategy, but, to Churchill's relief, Roosevelt still considered victory in Europe the first priority. Both leaders believed that Hitler was the most dangerous enemy.

In late April 1942, Soviet foreign minister V. M. Molotov arrived in Washington to ask for increased lend-lease supplies and the opening of a second front in Western Europe to force the withdrawal of some of the 3.3 million Germans fighting in the Soviet Union. Establishing a western front would require an Allied invasion across the English Channel separating Britain and continental Europe. Roosevelt promised more lend-lease materials and a second front sometime in 1942. Roosevelt's commitment to the European theater of operations cemented what was called the Grand Alliance of the United States, Great Britain, and the Soviet Union to defeat Hitler and to establish a lasting peace following the war.

The British vigorously opposed a cross-channel invasion. It was too risky, they warned, and there would not be enough troops or supplies available within a year. Instead, the British promoted the idea of an Allied landing in western North Africa: Operation Torch. It would be an easier, safer venture that also would help the British army fighting in western Egypt. Believing the people needed a victory, Roosevelt ignored the opposition of his **Joint Chiefs of Staff** and approved the operation. Head of the Joint Chiefs, **George C. Marshall,** selected **Dwight David Eisenhower** to command American forces in Europe and North Africa. Impressed with Eisenhower's planning and organizational ability, General Marshall chose Eisenhower over 366 more senior generals.

As planning began for the invasion of North Africa in 1942, the course of the war darkened for the Allies. German forces under General Erwin Rommel were advancing toward Egypt and the Suez Canal. A renewed German offensive was penetrating deeper into the Soviet Union. In the Atlantic, German U-boats were sinking ships at an appalling rate. In May, commanding General Douglas MacArthur fled by sea as the last American forces in the Philippines surrendered. General Patrick Hurley admitted, "We were out-shipped, out-planed, out-manned, and outgunned by the Japanese" (see Map 27.2).

Halting the Japanese Advance

Despite the commitment to the North Africa campaign, Roosevelt and military planners decided to move against the Japanese offensive in the Pacific. The first major action in the Pacific occurred on May 7, 1942, when the navy reported a victory at the **Battle of the Coral Sea** (see Map 27.3). Aware that Japan was preparing to invade Port Moresby, New Guinea, the aircraft carriers *Lexington* and *Yorktown* intercepted the invasion fleet and turned it back in an air-to-ship battle, despite the loss of the *Lexington.*

The Battle of the Coral Sea stopped the Japanese thrust toward the south, but a second part of Admiral Yamamoto's plan was to seize **Midway Island** and draw the American fleet into a major battle. The Battle of Midway (see Map 27.3) on June 4, 1942, helped change the course of the war in the Pacific. The air-to-sea battle was several hours old when thirty-seven American dive-bombers attacked the Japanese aircraft carriers as they were rearming and refueling their planes. The result was cataclysmic. Their decks cluttered with planes, fuel, and bombs, the Japanese carriers suffered staggering casualties and damage. Three sank immediately, and a fourth

Joint Chiefs of Staff Military advisory group to the president that consists of the chiefs of the army, navy, air force, and marine corps.

George C. Marshall Chief of staff of the U.S. Army during World War II; he became President Truman's secretary of state in 1947 and worked to rebuild the economy of Western Europe after the war.

Dwight David Eisenhower Supreme commander of Allied forces in Europe during World War II; he directed the D-day invasion and later became president of the United States.

Battle of the Coral Sea U.S. victory in the Pacific in May 1942; it prevented the Japanese from invading New Guinea and thus isolating Australia.

Midway Island Strategically located Pacific island that the Japanese navy tried to capture in June 1942; warned about Japanese plans by U.S. naval intelligence, American forces repulsed the attack and inflicted heavy losses on Japanese planes and carriers.

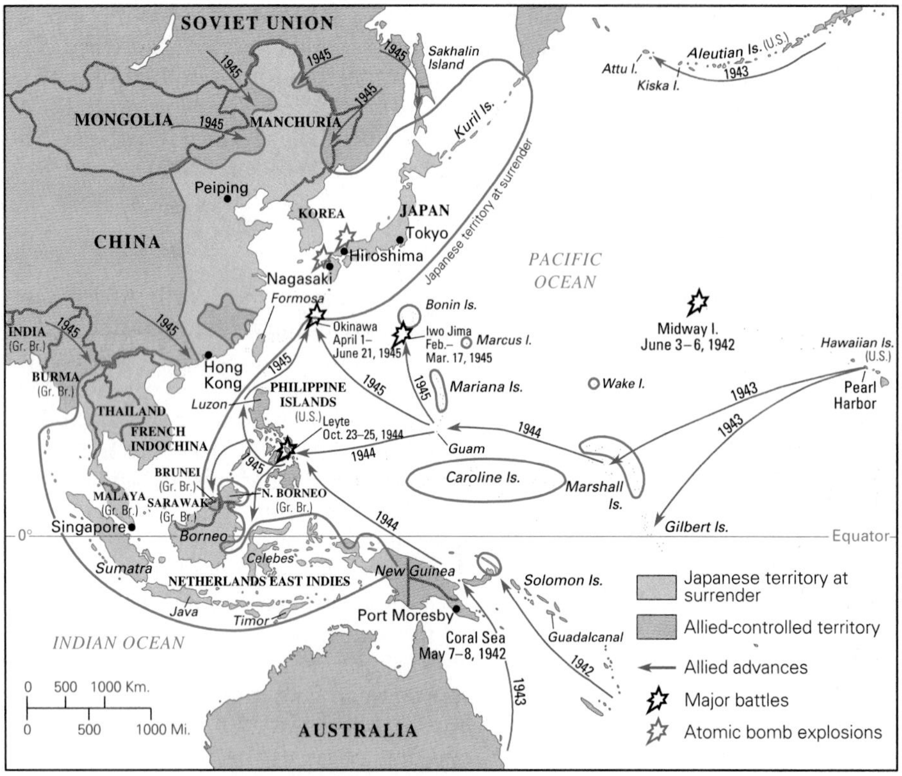

♦ **MAP 27.3 Closing the Circle on Japan, 1942–1945** Following the Battle of Midway, with the invasion of Guadalcanal (August 1942), American forces began the costly process of island hopping. This map shows the paths of the American campaign in the Pacific, closing the circle on Japan. After the Soviet Union entered the war and Hiroshima and Nagasaki were destroyed by atomic bombs, Japan surrendered on August 15, 1945.

sank later in the battle. Although the *Yorktown* too went down, the carriers and the air superiority of the Japanese had been destroyed.

After the victories at Coral Sea and Midway, the next step was to retake lost territory. General Douglas MacArthur and the army were given primary responsibility for an offensive beginning in New Guinea and advancing toward the Philippines from the south. The navy, under the direction of Admiral Chester Nimitz, was to seize selected islands and atolls in the Solomon, Marshall, Gilbert, and Mariana island groups, approaching the Philippines from the east. Eventually, both forces would join for the final attack on Japan.

On August 7, 1942, soldiers of the 1st Marine Division waded ashore on **Guadalcanal Island** in the Solomons. Japan, considering the invasion to be "the fork in the road that leads to victory for them or for us," furiously defended the island. Fierce fighting continued through November, but after heavy losses at sea and on land, Japan withdrew its last troops from Guadalcanal in early February 1943.

In the fierce fighting that characterized the war in the Pacific, both sides suffered significant losses, but Japanese casualties far surpassed American. Between Midway and Guadalcanal, the tide had turned against Japan. Japan was now on the defensive, unable to match growing American strength. The chief of Japan's naval general staff concluded after the war that the "cause of our setback . . . was our inability to increase our forces at the same speed as you did." One sign of the superiority of the industrial base of the United States was the U.S. ability between 1942 and 1945 to launch fourteen new aircraft carriers. Japan was able to launch only six.

Guadalcanal Island Pacific island secured by U.S. troops in February 1943 in the first major U.S. offensive action in the Pacific.

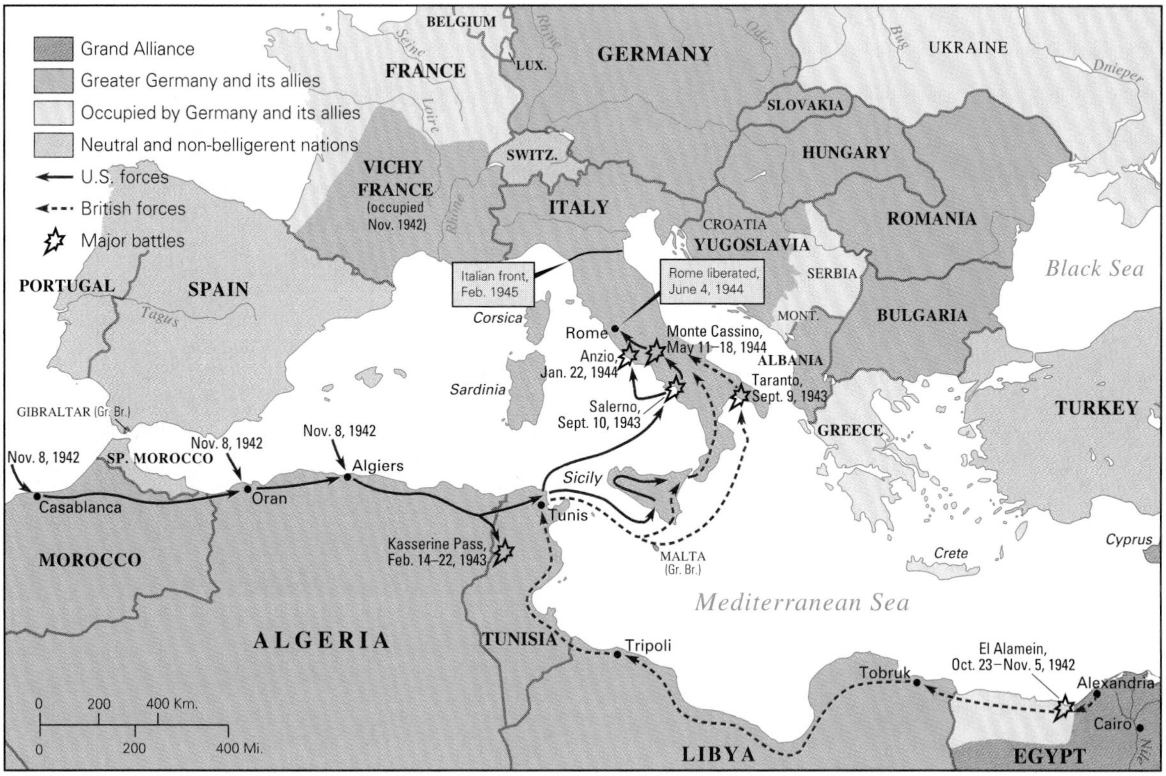

♦ **MAP 27.4 The North African and Italian Campaigns** Having rejected a cross-channel attack on Hitler's "Atlantic Wall," British and American forces in 1942 and 1943 invaded North Africa and Italy, where victory seemed more assured. This map shows the British and American advances across North Africa and the invasions of Sicily and Italy. German forces fought stubbornly in Italy, slowing Allied advances up the peninsula. By February 1945, Allied forces were still advancing toward the Po Valley.

The Tide Turns in Europe

By late 1942, as American marines sweated in the jungles of Guadalcanal, British and American forces were closing in on Rommel's Afrika Corps (see Map 27.4). After halting Rommel's advance at El Alamein, a British offensive led by General Bernard Montgomery drove the German "Desert Fox" westward out of Egypt toward Tunisia. To the west, British and American forces landed in Morocco and Algeria in Operation Torch. The inexperienced American forces weathered a sharp defeat at the Kasserine Pass and then under **George S. Patton** overcame stiff resistance to link up with Montgomery. Caught between the two Allied armies, the last German forces in North Africa surrendered on May 13, 1943.

German losses in North Africa were light compared with those in Russia, where Soviet and German forces were locked in a titanic struggle. During the summer and fall of 1942, German armies advanced steadily, but during the winter the Soviet army drove them from the oil fields of the Caucasus and trapped them at Stalingrad (see Map 27.5).

On February 2, 1943, after a three-month Soviet counteroffensive in the dead of winter, 300,000 German soldiers surrendered, their Sixth Army having lost more than 140,000 men. As German strength in Russia ebbed, Soviet strength grew. Although it was hard to see in February 1943, the tide of the war had turned in Europe. For the next two years, Soviet forces continued to grind down the German army all the way to Berlin (see Map 27.5).

George S. Patton American general who commanded troops in North Africa, Sicily, and Europe in World War II and who was known as a brilliant tactician.

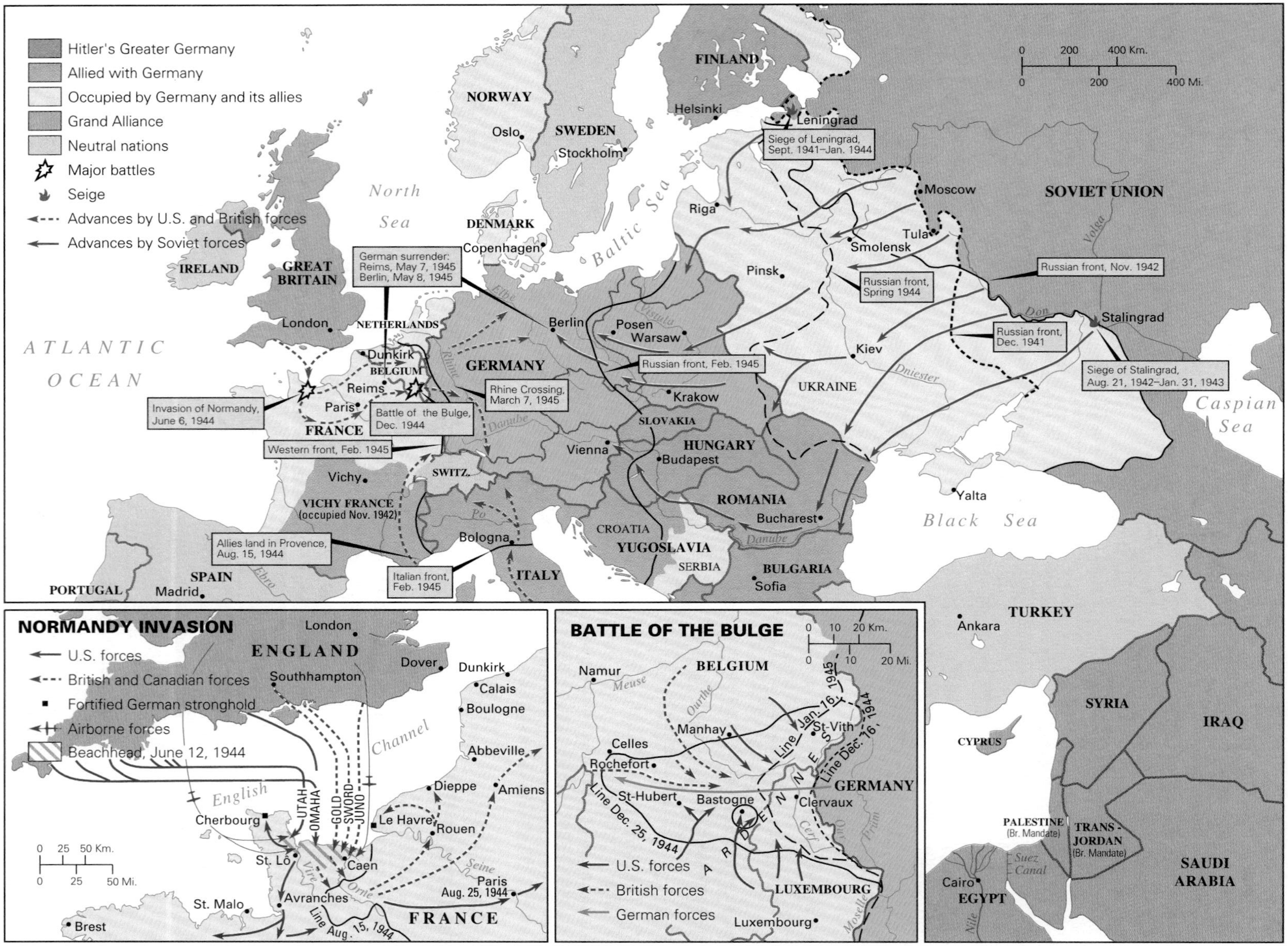

♦ **MAP 27.5 The Fall of the Third Reich** In 1943 and 1944, the war turned in favor of the Allies. On the Eastern front, Soviet forces drove German forces back toward Germany. On June 6, 1944, D-Day, British, Canadian, and American forces landed on the coast of Normandy to begin the liberation of France. This map shows the course of the Allied armies as they fought their way toward Berlin. On May 7, 1945, Germany surrendered.

In February 1943, however, Stalin knew only that the **Battle of Stalingrad** had cost the Russians dearly and that German strength was still formidable. He again demanded a second front in western Europe, and again he was disappointed. Churchill had met with Roosevelt at Casablanca (January 14–24, 1943) and once more had overcome American recommendations for a cross-channel attack. Roosevelt agreed instead to invade Sicily and Italy, targets that Churchill called the "soft underbelly of the Axis." General Albert Wedemeyer expressed the U.S. military reaction: "We lost our shirts . . . we came, we listened, and we were conquered." Stalin was told that there would be no second front in 1943. To placate him, Roosevelt and Churchill promised more supplies and pronounced the principle of "unconditional surrender," promising they would make no separate peace with Hitler.

The invasion of Sicily—Operation Husky—took place in early July, and in a month the Allies controlled the island (see Map 27.4). In response, the Italians overthrew Mussolini, installed a new government under the leadership of General Pietro Badoglio, and immediately opened negotiations with Britain and the United States to change sides. Italy surrendered unconditionally on September 8, just hours before Allied troops landed at Salerno in Operation Avalanche. Immediately thereafter, German forces assumed the defense of Italy. German troops also raided Mussolini's prison and freed him, proclaiming him ruler of Italy.

The "soft underbelly" of the Axis turned out to be far from soft. Strong German defenses halted the advance just north of Salerno. Not until late May 1944 did Allied forces finally break through the German defenses. On June 4, U.S. General Mark Clark's forces entered Rome. Two days later, the world's attention turned toward Normandy along the west coast of France. At long last, the second front demanded by Stalin was opening (see Map 27.5).

Approval for the cross-channel attack had come at the **Tehran Conference** (November 27 to December 1, 1943). Roosevelt and Churchill had met with Stalin in the Iranian capital to discuss strategy and to consider the process of establishing a postwar settlement. Roosevelt, asserting that he could handle that "old buzzard" Stalin, wanted to win Soviet support for a new world organization and obtain Soviet commitment to a declaration of war against Japan. He left Tehran pleased. Stalin had agreed to support a world organization and to enter the war against Japan once the battle with Hitler was over. Militarily, the Big Three had agreed on plans to coordinate a Soviet offensive with the Allied landings at Normandy.

The invasion of Normandy, France—**Operation Overlord**—was the grandest **amphibious assault** ever assembled: 6,483 ships, 1,500 tanks, and 200,000 men. Opposing the Allies were thousands of German troops behind the Atlantic Wall they had constructed along the coast to stop such an invasion. On D-day, June 6, 1944, American forces landed on Utah and Omaha beaches while British and Canadian forces hit Sword, Gold, and Juno beaches (see Map 27.5). At the landing sites, German resistance varied: the fiercest fighting was at Omaha Beach, where the American 1st Division suffered heavy casualties. After a week of attacks and counterattacks, the five beaches finally were linked, and British and American forces coiled to break through the German positions blocking the road to the rest of France. On July 25, American forces under General Omar Bradley pierced the stubbornly held German defensive lines at St.-Lô. Paris was liberated on August 23, and in early November, the German city of Aachen on the west side of the Rhine River fell to the Allies. From November 1944 to March 1945, American forces readied themselves to attack across the Rhine (see Map 27.5).

While the British and Americans were advancing across France, Allied bombers and fighter-bombers were doing what they had been doing since the spring of 1942: bombing German-held Europe night and day. They destroyed vital industries and transportation systems as well as German cities. In one of the worst raids, during the night of February 13–14, 1945, three flights of British and American bombers set **Dresden** aflame, creating a firestorm that killed

Battle of Stalingrad Battle for the Russian city that was besieged by the German army in 1942 and recaptured by Soviet troops in 1943.

Tehran Conference Meeting in Iran in 1943 at which Roosevelt, Churchill, and Stalin discussed the invasion of Western Europe and considered plans for a new international organization; Stalin also renewed his promise to enter the war against Japan.

Operation Overlord D-day—Allied invasion of Europe on June 6, 1944, across the English Channel to Normandy; D-day is short for "designated day."

amphibious assault A military operation in which assault troops land on shore from seaborne transports.

Dresden Industrial city in eastern Germany that was almost totally destroyed by Allied firebombing in 1945.

more than 135,000 civilians. Nearly 600,000 German civilians died in Allied air raids, and another 800,000 were injured.

Stresses Within the Grand Alliance

As Allied forces struggled to move eastward toward the Rhine, the Soviets advanced rapidly westward, pushing the last German troops from Russia by the end of June 1944. Behind Germany's retreating eastern armies, the Soviets occupied parts of Poland, Romania, Bulgaria, Hungary, and Czechoslovakia. Following the Red Army were Soviet officials and Communists from Eastern Europe who had lived in exile in the Soviet Union before and during the war. The Soviet goal was to establish in Eastern Europe new governments that would be "friendly" to the Soviet Union. A Communist Lublin government (named after the town where the government was installed) was established in Poland. In Romania and Bulgaria "popular front" governments, heavily influenced by local and returning Communist party members, took command. Only Czechoslovakia and Hungary managed to establish non-Communist-dominated governments as the German occupation collapsed.

On February 4, 1945, the Big Three met at the Black Sea resort of **Yalta** amid growing apprehension about Soviet territorial and political goals in Eastern Europe. Again confident that he could work with Stalin, Roosevelt hoped to secure a Soviet declaration of war on Japan and support for the new **United Nations.** Both were necessary to usher in peace and international stability. He also wanted the Soviets to show some willingness to modify their controls over Eastern Europe. Stalin's diplomatic goals were Western acceptance of a Soviet sphere of influence in Eastern Europe, the weakening of Germany, and the economic restoration of the Soviet Union. He also wanted a postwar international system based primarily on Big Three cooperation.

Roosevelt's and Stalin's views on Germany were nearly parallel. To prevent Germany from ever again posing a military threat to its neighbors, the American and Soviet leaders wanted to divide Germany into small, weak states. Churchill disagreed, saying that the dismemberment of Germany would be too harsh and disruptive. Unable to agree about the future of Germany, the Big Three postponed further discussions until their next meeting.

The question of which Polish government represented Poland, however, could not be put off. The Soviet Union supported the Lublin government as the only legitimate government of postwar Poland. Roosevelt and Churchill supported a London-based government-in-exile. They considered the Lublin government to be a puppet of the Soviet Union and hoped to establish a Polish government that could hold free and honest elections. Their goal matched the ideals of the Atlantic Charter but was at odds with the **geopolitics** of the Soviet Union. Stalin be-

♦ As allied armies fought their way closer to Berlin, Roosevelt, Churchill, and Stalin met at the Black Sea resort of Yalta, in February 1945, to discuss military strategy and postwar concerns. Among the most important issues were the Polish government, German reparations, and the formation of the United Nations. Two months later, Roosevelt died and Harry S Truman assumed the presidency. *National Archives.*

Yalta Site in the Crimea of the last meeting, in 1945, between Roosevelt, Churchill, and Stalin; they discussed the final defeat of the Axis Powers and the problems of postwar occupation.

United Nations International organization established in 1945 to maintain peace among nations and foster cooperation in human rights, education, health, welfare, and trade.

geopolitics Government policy based on the influence of geographic and political factors on national interests.

lieved that the London-based government would be hostile and demanded a friendly government in Poland. After considerable bitter haggling, the powers agreed on a compromise phrased in language that Admiral William Leahy, one of Roosevelt's primary advisers, ruefully noted was so vague that its meaning could be "stretched from Yalta to Washington" without breaking. Roosevelt realistically concluded that it was the best he could do for Poland at the moment. The Yalta Conference also left control over Eastern Europe firmly in Soviet hands. Even so, Roosevelt accomplished his two major goals. Stalin promised to enter the war against Japan within three months of Germany's surrender and to support the formation of the United Nations.

Roosevelt was extremely tired and seriously ill with high blood pressure and a bad heart throughout the Yalta meetings. Nevertheless, he played the diplomatic game on a par with Churchill and Stalin and consistent with his goals and resources. Believing that there could be no postwar stability and security without Soviet cooperation, Roosevelt permitted Stalin to keep what he already had or could easily take. Short of ending friendly relations with the Soviet Union, Roosevelt had no means to reduce Soviet power in Eastern Europe or to prevent the Soviets from declaring war on Japan and taking whatever they wanted in East Asia. Roosevelt hoped that his good will would encourage Stalin to respond in kind, maintaining at least a semblance of representative government in the nations of Eastern Europe and continuing to cooperate with the United States. Publicly and privately, both Stalin and Roosevelt were pleased with the results and were buoyed by the "spirit of Yalta." Only Churchill, who feared growing Soviet influence, left Yalta in a gloomy mood.

Hitler's Defeat

With his forces crumbling in the east, Hitler approved a last-ditch attempt to halt the Allied advance late in 1944. Taking advantage of bad weather that grounded Allied aircraft, German forces launched through the Ardennes Forest an attack that drove 50 miles into Belgium. If successful, the attack would have split American forces, but it was a desperate gamble that failed. Though surprised by the attack, not all American forces were pushed aside. At Bastogne, a critical crossroads, the 101st Airborne Division refused to retreat, and when invited to surrender, General A. C. McAuliffe simply told the Germans, Nuts." After ten days, the weather improved, the German offensive slowed and halted, and a relief column reached Bastogne. The **Battle of the Bulge** delayed Eisenhower's eastward assault briefly, but it cost Germany valuable reserves and equipment (see Map 27.5) and hastened the end of the war. By the end of 1944, the war was also winding down in Italy. When German armies began to surrender in April 1945, Italian partisans captured Mussolini and hanged him.

On March 7, 1945, American forces crossed the Rhine at Remagen and began to battle their way into the heart of Germany. While American and British troops moved steadily eastward, Russian soldiers began the bloody, house-to-house conquest of Berlin. On April 25, American and Soviet infantrymen shook hands at the Elbe River 60 miles south of Berlin. Inside the city, unwilling to be captured, Hitler committed suicide on April 30. His aides burned his body. On May 8, 1945, German officials surrendered. The war in Europe was over.

Although Roosevelt had worked since 1939 to ensure Hitler's defeat, he did not live to see it. On April 12, while relaxing and recovering from the strains of Yalta, he died of a massive cerebral hemorrhage at Warm Springs, Georgia. Nor did Roosevelt live to know the full horror of what came to be called the **Holocaust.** In 1941, Nazi political leaders had decided on what they called the **Final Solution**—a plan to rid German-occupied Europe of Jews. In concentration camps, Jews, along with homosexuals, Gypsies, and the mentally ill, were brutalized, starved, worked as slave labor, and systematically exterminated. At Auschwitz, Nazis used gas chambers—disguised as showers—to execute twelve thousand victims a day. By the time the camps and the remaining inmates were liberated by Allied armies in 1945, 6 million Jews had been slaughtered in the death camps, nearly two-thirds of prewar Europe's Jewish population.

Battle of the Bulge The last major Axis counteroffensive, in December 1944, against the Allied forces in Western Europe; German troops gained territory in Belgium but were eventually driven back.

Holocaust Mass murder of European Jews and other groups systematically carried out by the Nazis during World War II.

Final Solution German plan to eliminate Jews through mass executions by isolating them in concentration camps; by the end of the war, the Nazis had killed 6 million Jews.

♦ Hitler ordered the "final solution"—the extermination of Europe's Jews—soon after the United States entered the war. In this picture, German troops arrest residents of the Warsaw ghetto for deportation to concentration camps. Few would survive the camps where over six million Jews died. *YNO Institute for Jewish Research.*

Closing the Circle on Japan

Victory in Europe—**V-E Day,** May 8, 1945—touched off parades and rejoicing in the United States. But Japan still had to be defeated. Japan's defensive strategy was simple: to force the United States to invade a seemingly endless number of Pacific islands before it could launch an invasion against Japan—with each speck of land costing the Americans dearly in lives and materials. The American military, however, realized that it had to seize only the most strategic of islands. With carriers providing mobile air superiority, the Americans could bypass and isolate others.

Throughout 1943, General MacArthur advanced up the northern coast of New Guinea while the navy and marines fought their way through the Solomon Islands. By mid-1944, MacArthur was ready to fulfill his promise to return to the Philippines. At the same time, far to the northeast, the U.S. Navy and the Marines Corps were establishing footholds in the Gilbert and Marshall islands. Exemplifying the bitter fighting was "bloody Tarawa," where marines fought their way ashore on November 21, 1943. Overcoming five thousand well-entrenched Japanese troops—nearly all of whom fought to the death—American marines suffered nearly three thousand casualties. With the Gilbert and Marshall islands neutralized, Admiral Nimitz approached Guam and Saipan in the Marianas (see Map 27.3). In their effort to halt the American invasion of Saipan, the Japanese lost 243 planes and three more aircraft carriers. On Saipan itself, the Japanese defenders, including twenty-two thousand Japanese civilians, expended all their ammunition and then committed suicide rather than surrender. Marines next seized the nearby islands of Tinian (August 1) and Guam (August 11).

By July 1944, the southern and eastern approaches to the Philippines were in American hands. From airfields on Tinian, Saipan, and Guam, long-range American bombers—B-29s—began devastating raids against the homeland of Japan. In October, American forces landed on Leyte in the center of the Philippine archipelago. Again, the Japanese navy acted to halt the invasion, and with the same results. In the largest naval battle in history, the **Battle of Leyte Gulf** (October 23–25, 1944), American naval forces shattered what remained of Japanese air and sea power. On October 23, wading ashore with an escort of subordinates and at least one photographer, General MacArthur returned to the Philippines.

After the Battle of Leyte Gulf, the full brunt of the American Pacific offensive bore down on Iwo Jima and Okinawa, only 750 miles from Tokyo. To defend

V-E Day May 8, 1945, the day marking the official end of the war in Europe, following the unconditional surrender of the German armies.

Battle of Leyte Gulf Naval battle in October 1944 in which American forces near the Philippines crushed Japanese air and sea power.

the islands, Japan resorted to a new tactic: the *kamikaze*—suicide attacks by pilots in explosive-laden airplanes. The American assault on Iwo Jima began on February 19 and became the worst experience faced by U.S. marines in the war. Virtually all of the 21,000 Japanese defenders fought to the death, and American losses approached one-third of the landing force: 6,821 dead and 20,000 wounded.

On **Okinawa,** the carnage was even worse. While American forces took heavy losses along Japanese defensive lines, nine hundred Japanese planes, including three hundred flown by *kamikaze* pilots, rained terror and destruction on the American fleet. The Japanese air onslaughts continued throughout May and June but steadily weakened as Japan ran out of planes and pilots. By the end of June, Okinawa was in American hands, but at a fearful price: 12,000 Americans, 110,000 Japanese soldiers, and 160,000 Okinawan and Japanese civilians dead.

Entering the Nuclear Age

Okinawa proved a painful warning for strategists planning the invasion of Japan. Fighting for their homeland, the Japanese could be expected to resist until death. American casualties would be extremely high, perhaps as many as a million. But by the summer of 1945, the United States had an alternative to invasion: a new and untried weapon—the atomic bomb. The **A-bomb** was the product of years of British-American research and development, an undertaking known as the **Manhattan Project.** Since the beginning of the war, science had played a vital role by developing and improving the tools of combat. Among the outcomes were radar, sonar, flamethrowers, rockets, and other useful and deadly products. But the most fearsome and secret of the projects was the effort started in 1941 to construct a nuclear weapon. Between 1941 and 1945, the Manhattan engineers, led by J. Robert Oppenheimer and Edward Teller, were able to control a chain reaction involving uranium and plutonium and create the atomic bomb. By the time Germany surrendered, the Manhattan Project had cost more than $2 billion, but the bomb had been born. When it was tested at Alamogordo, New Mexico, on July 16, 1945, the results were spectacular. In the words of General Leslie Groves:

> *The effect could well be called unprecedented, magnificent, beautiful, stupendous and terrifying. . . . The whole country was lighted by a searing light. . . . Thirty seconds after the explosion came . . . the air blast . . . followed almost immediately by the strong, sustained, awesome roar which warned of doomsday and made us feel that we puny things were blasphemous to dare tamper with the forces heretofore reserved to The Almighty.*

Word of the successful test was quickly relayed to Truman, who had assumed the presidency when Roosevelt died in April. Truman was meeting with Churchill and Stalin at Potsdam.

President Truman had traveled to Potsdam with a new secretary of state, James F. Byrnes. Before leaving for Germany, they agreed not to tell Stalin any details about the atomic bomb (although both knew about a Soviet spy ring within the Manhattan Project) and to use the bomb as quickly as possible against Japan. Using the atomic bomb, Truman and Byrnes hoped, would serve two purposes. It would force Japan to surrender without an invasion, and it would impress the Soviets and, just maybe, make them more amenable to American views.

Soon after his arrival at Potsdam, Truman met privately with Stalin and received the Soviet dictator's promise to enter the war against Japan in mid-August. Later, in a major understatement, Truman informed Stalin that the United States had a new and powerful weapon to use against Japan, never mentioning that it was an atomic bomb. Stalin appeared uninterested and told Truman to go ahead and use the weapon. Then, with British prime minister **Clement Attlee,** Truman released the **Potsdam Declaration,** which called on Japan to surrender by August or face total destruction. The declaration reflected two developments: one Japan knew about; the other it was soon to learn.

Japanese officials had asked the "neutral" Soviets to ask the Americans if they would consider negotiating a Japanese surrender. Stalin, Attlee, and Truman agreed to reject the idea and insist on unconditional

Okinawa Pacific island that U.S. troops captured in the spring of 1945 after a grueling battle in which over a quarter-million soldiers and civilians were killed.

A-bomb The first nuclear weapon.

Manhattan Project A secret scientific research effort begun in 1941 to develop an atomic bomb.

Clement Attlee British prime minister who replaced Churchill following parliamentary elections in July 1945.

Potsdam Declaration The demand for Japan's unconditional surrender, made after the July 1945 Potsdam Conference.

♦ On August 6, 1945 the world entered the atomic age when the city of Hiroshima was destroyed by an atomic bomb. "We had seen the city when we went in," said the pilot of the Enola Gay, "and there was nothing to see when we came back." The city and most of its people had died. *National Archives.*

surrender. In the Potsdam Declaration, the Japanese could read the rejection of their overture, but they had no way of knowing that the utter destruction referred to in the declaration meant using the A-bomb. On July 25, Truman ordered the use of the bomb as soon after August 3 as possible, provided the Japanese did not surrender (see Making History: The Dropping of the Atomic Bomb).

On the island of Tinian, B-29s were readied to carry the two available bombs to targets in Japan (a third bomb was waiting to be assembled). A B-29 bomber named the *Enola Gay* dropped the first bomb over **Hiroshima** at 9:15 A.M. on August 6. Japan's eighth largest city, Hiroshima had a population of over 250,000 and, to that point, had not suffered heavy bombing. In the atomic blast and fireball, almost a hundred thousand Japanese were killed or terribly maimed. Another hundred thousand later died from the effects of radiation. The United States announced that unless the Japanese surrendered immediately, they could "expect a rain of ruin from the air, the like of which has never been seen on this earth."

In Tokyo, peace advocates in the Japanese government again sought to use the Soviets as an intermediary. They wanted some guarantee that Emperor Hirohito would be allowed to remain as emperor and a symbol of Japan. The Soviet response

TABLE 27.1 War Dead

Country	Dead
Soviet Union	13.5 million
China	7.4 million
Poland	6.0 million
Germany	4.6 million
Japan	1.2 million
Britain and Commonwealth	430,000
United States	220,000

was to declare war and advance into Japanese-held Manchuria on August 8, exactly three months after V-E Day. On August 9, as a high-level Japanese council considered surrender, the second atomic bomb destroyed **Nagasaki.** Nearly sixty thousand people were killed. Although some within the Japanese army argued for continuing the fight, Emperor Hirohito, watching the Red Army slice through Japanese forces and afraid of losing more cities to atomic attacks, made the final decision. Japan must "bear the unbearable," he said, and surrender. On August 14, 1945, Japan officially surrendered, and the United States agreed to leave the position of emperor intact.

World War II was over, but much of the world lay in ruin. Some 50 million people, military and civilian, had been killed (see Table 27.1). The United States was spared most of the destruction. It had suffered almost no civilian casualties, and its cities and industrial centers stood intact. In many ways, in fact, the war had been good to the United States. It had decisively ended the Depression, and although some economists predicted an immediate postwar recession, the overall economic picture was bright. Government regulation and planning for the economy that had their beginning in the New Deal took root during the war. As the war ended, only a few wanted a return to the laissez-faire-style government of the 1920s. Big government was here to stay, and at the center of big government was a powerful presidency ready to direct and guide the nation.

Hiroshima Japanese city that was the target on August 6, 1945, of the first atomic bomb.

Nagasaki City in western Japan devastated on August 9, 1945, by the second atomic bomb.

SUMMARY

E xpectations
C onstraints
C hoices
O utcomes

Franklin Roosevelt *chose* to promote better relations with Latin America and succeeded. But elsewhere the international situation grew steadily worse, and *expectations* of conflict increased. Japan had seized Manchuria in 1931 and in 1937 invaded China, and Mussolini and Hitler were seeking to expand their nations' power and territory. In the lengthening shadow of world conflict, the majority of Americans maintained isolationism. Wanting to take a more active role in world affairs, Roosevelt found himself *constrained* by isolationist sentiment—characterized by a set of neutrality acts—and by his own *choice* to fight the Depression at home first. Even as Germany invaded Poland in September 1939, the majority of Americans were still anxious to remain outside the conflict. Roosevelt, however, was determined to provide all necessary aid to those nations fighting Germany and Italy.

Roosevelt also *chose* to increase economic and diplomatic pressure on Japan to halt its conquest of China and occupation of Indochina. But the pressure only heightened the crisis, convincing many in the Japanese government that the best *choice* was to attack the United States before it grew in strength. Japan's attack on Pearl Harbor on December 7, 1941, brought a fully committed American public and government into World War II.

Mobilizing the nation for war ended the Depression and increased government intervention in the economy. Another *outcome* of the war was a range of new *choices* for women and minorities in the military and the workplace. For Japanese Americans, however, the *outcome* was the loss of freedom and property, as anti-Japanese sentiment caused the government to *choose* a policy of internment.

Fighting a two-front war—in Europe and the Pacific—American planners *chose* to give first priority to defeating Hitler. The British and American offensive to recover Europe began in North Africa and expanded to Italy in 1943 and to France in 1944. By the beginning of 1945, Allied armies were threatening Nazi Germany from the west and the east, and on May 8, 1945, Germany surrendered.

In the Pacific theater, the victory at Midway in mid-1942 checked Japan's offensive and allowed the use of aircraft carriers to begin tightening the noose around Japan. Worried about casualties if American troops had to invade Japan, and about Soviet intentions, Truman *chose* to use the atomic bomb to hasten Japan's surrender. Indeed, the *outcome* of victory in the war was that the United States became economically and militarily stronger than it had been when the war started. Many confident Americans *expected* the postwar years to begin "America's Century."

SUGGESTED READINGS

John Morton Blum. *V Was for Victory* (1976).

A good introduction to society and politics during the war.

Robert Dallek. *Franklin D. Roosevelt and American Foreign Policy, 1932–1945* (1979).

An excellent, balanced study of Franklin Roosevelt's foreign policy.

Roger Daniels. *Concentration Camps, USA* (1971).

An in-depth and compassionate look at the internment of Japanese Americans.

Sherna B. Gluck. *Rosie the Riveter Revisited: Women, the War, and Social Change* (1987).

An important work examining the changes that took place among women in society during the war.

Manfred Jonas. *Isolationism in America* (1966).

A solid examination of the varieties of isolationist attitudes in the United States, especially in the 1930s.

John Keegan. *The Second World War* (1990).

An excellent one-volume work that summarizes the military and diplomatic aspects of World War II.

Ronald Spector. *Eagle Against the Sun* (1988).

One of the best-written general accounts of the war in the Pacific.

David Wyman. *The Abandonment of the Jews* (1985).

A balanced account of the Holocaust.

The Decision to Drop the Atomic Bomb

The Context

On August 6, 1945, at 8:15 A.M. the *Enola Gay* dropped the first atomic bomb on the Japanese city of Hiroshima. More than 100,000 people died and another 100,000 were injured. Three days later the United States exploded a second atomic bomb over Nagasaki, killing about 60,000 Japanese. On August 14, Japan surrendered. Within the United States there was widespread rejoicing—the bomb had ended the war. Many also realized that the development of the atomic bomb and the decision to use it heralded a new age: the atomic era. The bomb was not just a powerful weapon but also a revolutionary development with far-ranging military, ethical, international, and scientific consequences. (For further information on the context, see pages 885–886.)

The Historical Question

Since the detonation of the atomic bomb, historians and others have asked if the choice to destroy the cities was necessary. Did military expediency necessitate dropping the bomb? What other expectations did those involved in building and deciding to use "the gadget" have? Did they consider moral and other aspects of their decision?

The Challenge

Using the sources provided, along with other information you have read, write an essay or hold a discussion on the following question. Cite evidence in the sources to support your conclusions. **What did those involved in planning the use of the atomic bomb consider, and what goals lay behind the final decision?**

The Sources

1 Secretary of War Henry L. Stimson was directly involved in planning the use of the atomic bomb. In an article for *Harper's* in 1947 he explained the military-based decision to use the new weapon. He wrote:

To extract a genuine surrender from the Emperor and his military advisers, they must be administered a tremendous shock which would carry convincing proof of our power to destroy the Empire. Such an effective shock would save many times the number of lives, both American and Japanese, than it would cost. . . . we estimated . . . that such an operation might cost over a million casualties to American forces . . . enemy casualties would be much larger than our own.

2 A committee of scientists involved in building the atomic bomb met throughout May, June, and July to consider a variety of issues with regard to the use of the bomb. In June 1945, the Franck Committee reported:

The military advantages and the saving of American lives, achieved by the sudden use of the atomic bombs against Japan, may be outweighed by the ensuing loss of confidence and wave of horror and repulsion sweeping over the rest of the world, and perhaps dividing even public opinion at home.

. . . If we consider international agreement on total prevention of nuclear warfare as the paramount objective . . . this kind of introduction of atomic weapons to the world may easily destroy all

our chances of success. Russia, and even allied countries which bear less mistrust of our ways and intentions, as well as neutral countries, will be deeply shocked. It will be very difficult to persuade the world that a nation which was capable of secretly preparing and suddenly releasing [such] a weapon . . . is to be trusted in its proclaimed desire of having such weapons abolished by international agreement.

3 Most of the planning to use the atomic bomb was delegated to a special Interim Committee approved by President Harry Truman shortly after he assumed office. It was chaired by Stimson and was composed of three scientists, representatives of the State and War Departments, and a special representative of the president. Except for Stimson, none of the committee members knew about the military plans for the invasion of Japan. Another group within the committee also considered which cities made suitable targets for atomic weapons. In May 1945, the committee reported:

We should not give the Japanese any warning. . . . we should seek to make a profound psychological impression on as many of the inhabitants as possible . . . that the most desirable target would be a vital war plant employing a large number of workers and closely surrounded by workers' houses.

Hiroshima—This is an important army depot and port . . . in the middle of an urban industrial area. It is a good . . . target and it is such a size that a large part of the city could be extensively damaged . . . adjacent hills . . . are likely to produce a focusing effect which would considerably increase the blast damage.

4 President Truman told Secretary of War Stimson to move ahead with the plans to drop the atomic bomb. On July 26, through the Potsdam Declaration, the United States demanded Japan's unconditional surrender and warned that Japan would face total destruction if surrender did not come. Recounting his thoughts on using the bomb, Truman wrote in his diary on July 18, 1945:

This weapon is to be used against Japan between now and August 10th. I have told the Sec. of War, Mr. Stimson, to use it so that military objectives and soldiers and sailors are the target and not women and children. Even if the Japs are savages, ruthless, merciless and fanatic, we as the leader of the world for the common welfare cannot drop that terrible bomb on the old capital or the new.

. . . we will issue a warning statement asking the Japs to surrender and save lives. I'm sure they will not do that, but we will have given them the chance. It is certainly a good thing for the world that Hitler's crowd or Stalin's did not discover this atomic bomb. It seems to be the most terrible thing ever discovered, but it can be made the most useful.

POSTWAR AMERICA, 1947–1953 Postwar America was characterized by a growing affluency as many Americans enjoyed the fruits of a booming economy, rising wages, and a large variety of consumer goods. But as this map indicates, amid the prosperity and growth of metropolitan areas, there was a deep-seated fear generated by the Cold War and the possibility of nuclear war.

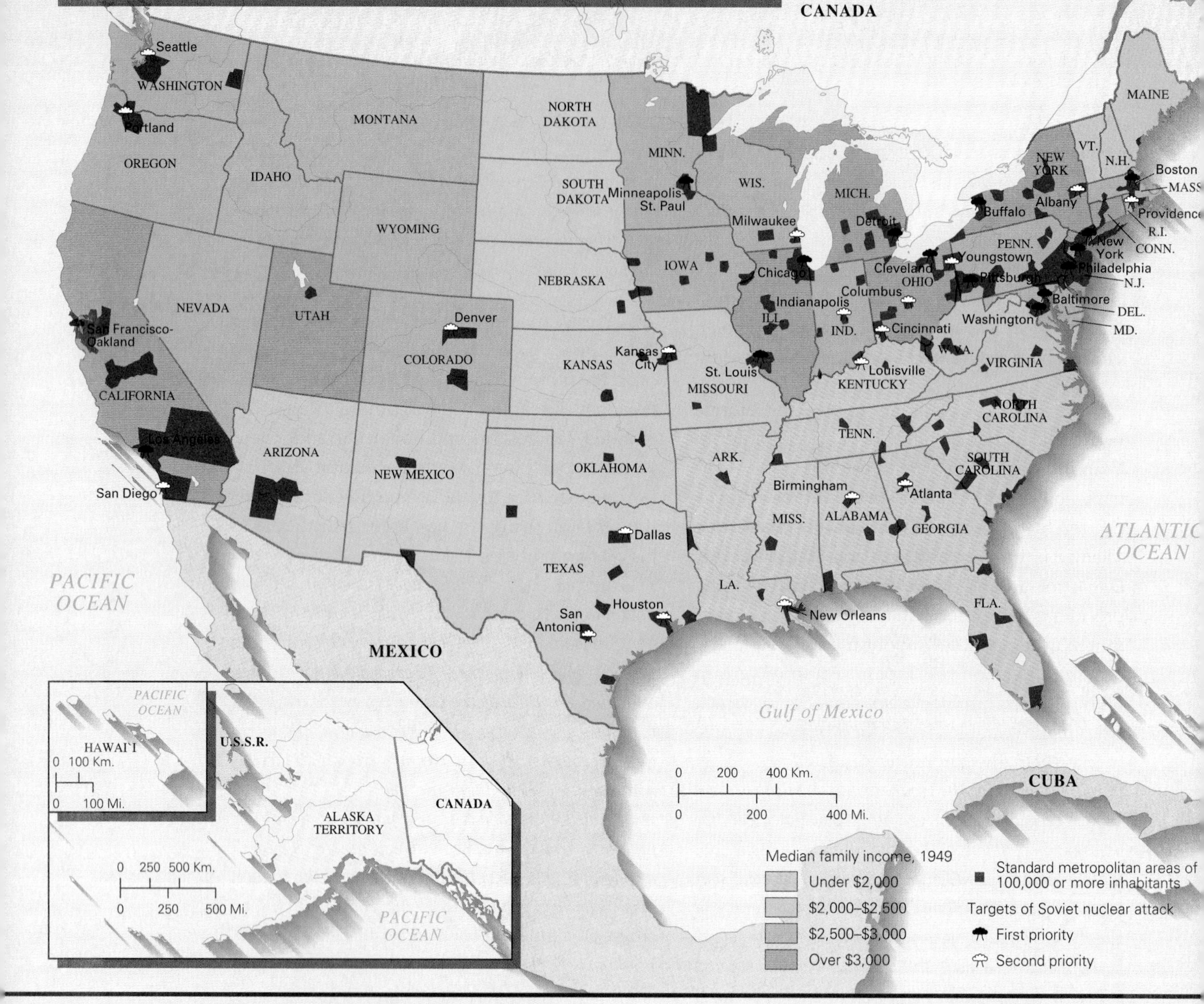

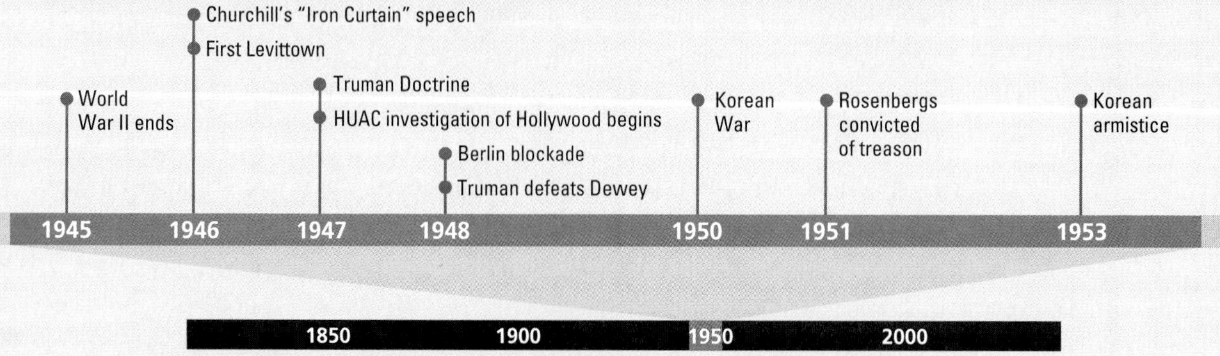

CHAPTER 28

Truman and Cold War America, 1945–1952

The Cold War Begins

- What expectations did Americans have about the postwar world and the Soviet Union?
- How was the containment theory applied to Western Europe between 1947 and 1951?
- Outside Western Europe, what choices did the Truman administration make to promote and protect American interests?

The Korean War

- As the North Koreans invaded South Korea, what choices and constraints did Truman confront when considering policy options?
- What expectations did Truman and General MacArthur have about defeating the North Koreans and unifying Korea? What was the outcome for both leaders?

Homecomings and Adjustments

- What were the social and economic expectations of most Americans as World War II ended? What were the outcomes of these for women and minorities?
- How did the developing Cold War strengthen conservative opposition to New Deal–style programs?
- What constraints did Truman face in implementing his domestic programs? How did they influence his choices?
- Why did Truman win the 1948 election? What choices did members of the New Deal coalition have in 1948, and why did most Democrats vote for Truman?

Cold War Politics

- What fears and events heightened society's fear of internal subversion, and what choices did politicians make in response to them?
- Why and how did Joseph McCarthy become so powerful by 1952?

INTRODUCTION

Expectations
Constraints
Choices
Outcomes

When World War II ended, Americans hoped for a bright future. The Great Depression was over, the war had reignited American industry, creating jobs and prosperity, and the United States stood as the world's most powerful economic and military power. Many Americans, especially returning veterans, looked forward to living the "American dream," which included owning a home, a car, and a variety of consumer products designed to make life easier. More than ever before, women and minorities shared in *expectations* for greater opportunity—trusting that the new economic and social openings created during the war would extend into the postwar era.

In world affairs, President Harry S Truman faced *choices* in shaping a new international system out of the ashes of the war. Isolationism had virtually vanished amid the wreckage of Pearl Harbor and Hiroshima, leaving the United States the greatest world power. The *Los Angeles Times* expressed the *expectations* of most Americans: the United States would lead the postwar world because it had "no other direct interest" except a lasting, just peace. Seeking this lasting peace, between 1945 and 1952 Truman tried to forge the structure of postwar world affairs, but the *outcome* was not what most expected. By the end of 1947, American and Soviet leaders had made *choices* that ended their wartime cooperation and produced a bitter rivalry—the Cold War, which polarized the world, expanded America's global role, and elevated fear of the Soviet Union and communism into a potent force in American society. When North Korea invaded South Korea, Truman committed American troops to halt Communist aggression. At home, the activities of anti-Communists like Senator Joseph McCarthy exposed a dark side of American politics and society, one less tolerant of change and liberalism.

Amid the hopes for postwar economic growth and prosperity and the fear of communist expansion, political conservatives anticipated the demise of the New Deal. They argued that the liberalism of the New Deal was no longer necessary and that society and the economy should revert to traditional norms. They sought to place *constraints* on the economic and social gains made by minorities, women, and workers. Unions, they asserted, had become too powerful and must be restrained. Women, many argued, should give up their jobs and greater independence and return full-time to the roles of wife and mother. For African Americans and other minorities, it was a familiar story: "last hired, first fired." Many were dismissed from wartime jobs with the *expectation* they would return to their customary place in American society.

Which direction would the nation *choose:* the path of the liberal New Deal or a more conservative path? Would Truman expand on New Deal progressivism? Would he provide support for minorities, workers, and women in their quests for continued opportunity? Or would he buckle under the conservative opposition that had halted Roosevelt in 1938? The *outcome* that emerged from the "politics of the possible" pleased neither ardent liberals nor staunch conservatives. It reflected what some called the "vital center" of American politics—an acceptance of, and even some expansion on, existing government activism but little political or public support for any new programs.

Despite increased prosperity and conservatism, American society began to seem less stable and unified, clouding some Americans' *expectations* for a bright future. Labor unions clashed with employers, many women and minorities found their *expectations* thwarted, and the Korean War—which most people had believed would end in a quick American victory—dragged on in stalemate. The *outcome,* by the end of Truman's second term, was widespread political dissatisfaction and a general desire for change. Conservatives like Senator Robert Taft, and even some moderates, blamed America's problems on Truman and New Deal liberalism. Both, in their opinion, followed "a policy of appeasing the Russians abroad and of fostering Communism at home."

CHRONOLOGY

From World War to Cold War

1945 Yalta Conference
President Roosevelt dies
Harry S Truman becomes president
Soviets advance across Eastern Europe
United Nations formed
Germany surrenders
Potsdam Conference
Japan surrenders

1946 Kennan's "Long Telegram"
Churchill's "Iron Curtain" speech
Iran crisis
Strikes by coal miners and railroad workers
Construction begins on first Levittown

1947 Truman Doctrine
Truman's employee loyalty program
Taft-Hartley Act
House Un-American Activities Committee begins investigation of Hollywood
Jackie Robinson joins the Brooklyn Dodgers
Marshall Plan announced
To Secure These Rights issued
Rio Pact organized

1948 Communist coup in Czechoslovakia
Western zones of Germany unified
State of Israel founded
Congress approves Marshall Plan
Berlin blockade begins
Truman defeats Dewey

1949 North Atlantic Treaty Organization created
Berlin blockade lifted
Peekskill riot
West Germany created
Soviet Union explodes atomic bomb
Communist forces win civil war in China
Alger Hiss convicted of perjury

1950 U.S. hydrogen bomb project announced
McCarthy's announcement of Communists in the State Department
NSC-68
Korean War begins
Rosenbergs arrested for conspiracy to commit espionage
Inchon landing
North Korean forces retreat from South Korea
UN forces cross into North Korea
China enters Korean War

1951 General MacArthur relieved of command
Korean War peace talks begin
Rosenbergs convicted of espionage
Dennis et al. v. United States

1953 Korean War armistice signed

The Cold War Begins

- What expectations did Americans have about the postwar world and the Soviet Union?
- How was the containment theory applied to Western Europe between 1947 and 1951?
- Outside Western Europe, what choices did the Truman administration make to promote and protect American interests?

Germany, Italy, and Japan had been defeated, and the world hoped that an enduring peace would follow. But could the cooperative relationship of the victorious Allies continue into the postwar era without a common enemy to bind them together?

Before 1941, suspicion and distrust marked the normal relationship between the United States and the Soviet Union. In 1917, when the Soviets seized power, the Wilson administration refused to recognize the new Soviet state and with other European powers intervened in the civil war between Soviet and anti-Communist forces (see page 716). The last American troops left in 1920, but Washington refused to recognize the Soviet Union until 1933. During that period, the United States and the Soviet Union remained isolated from active participation in world affairs, and there was little official contact between the two governments. Ideologically, the United States remained opposed to communism, as reflected in the Red Scare in 1919 (see page 721). Even after President Franklin D. Roosevelt established official ties with Moscow, relations remained frosty. When the Soviets signed their alliance with Nazi Germany in 1939, most Americans saw little real difference between the brutal totalitarianism of nazism and communism.

American policy toward the Soviets altered in 1941, when Hitler invaded the Soviet Union. Quickly, relations with the Soviets improved as the United States supported the Communists in their war against the Germans. Ideological and other differences were de-emphasized, and Joseph Stalin, once portrayed as ruthless, became "Uncle Joe." But even during the war, the two powers viewed each other suspiciously over issues like the timing of the second European front and the creation of pro-Soviet governments in Eastern Europe. Roosevelt believed he could work with the Soviets and was willing to accept the composition of the Soviet-sponsored regimes in Eastern Europe in exchange for Soviet cooperation in world affairs. Harry S Truman, however, had a different attitude. It was his opinion that "the Soviet Union needs us more than we need them."

When Roosevelt died on April 12, 1945, Truman faced the imposing job of finishing the war and creating the peace. Winning the war was mostly a matter of following existing policies and listening to the military planners, but formulating a new international order required new ideas and policies. Truman loved history and the idea that great individuals shaped it. Lazy men caused trouble, he wrote, and those who "worked hard had the job of rectifying their mistakes." A plaque on his desk proclaimed, "THE BUCK STOPS HERE." Truman had read history; now he hoped to shape it.

Truman and the Soviets

Truman and other American leaders identified two overlapping paths to peace: international cooperation and **deterrence** based on military strength. They concluded that the United States must continue to field a strong military force with bases in Europe, Asia, and the Middle East. But deterrence alone could not guarantee peace and a stable world. Policymakers needed to address the underlying causes of war. Examining the origins of World War II, Americans blamed the Depression for bringing men like Hitler and Mussolini to power and appeasement for allowing the tyrants' aggressive actions. An isolationist America, an ineffective League of Nations, and a weak-kneed Britain and France had allowed Mussolini, Hitler, and the Japanese military to embark on a global war that had cost millions of lives and billions of dollars. To prevent history from repeating itself, a strong world organization, a determination not to appease aggressors, and a prosperous world economy were necessary. These were the ideals of the Atlantic Charter (see page 832), and most Americans saw them as fundamental values on which to construct peace. However, if international cooperation failed, the United States should rely on its military strength to ensure global peace.

Not all nations accepted the American vision for peace and stability. Having different political and economic systems and historical experiences—two invasions from Western Europe in thirty years—the Soviets wanted to be treated as a major power, to have Germany reduced in power, and to see "friendly" governments in neighboring states, especially in Eastern Europe. When World War II ended, many Americans worried about Soviet actions in Eastern Europe. There, it seemed, the Soviets were unwilling to allow an open political and economic system, contradicting American democratic and capitalistic principles. At the Tehran and Yalta conferences (see pages 851–852), Roosevelt had generally acquiesced to Soviet influence in Eastern Europe and, in return, had received Soviet support for the creation of the United Nations (UN) and pledges of continued cooperation with the United States.

Roosevelt had presented the idea of a new world organization to Churchill during the meeting that had produced the Atlantic Charter. In the fall of 1944, the Big Four (the United States, the Soviet Union, Britain, and China) mapped out the basic organization of the United Nations at the **Dumbarton Oaks Conference.** At Yalta, Roosevelt, Stalin, and Churchill further refined their agreements, permitting a meeting in San Francisco (April 1945) to write a charter for the new world organization. The UN charter established a weak **General Assembly** com-

deterrence Measures, often including a military buildup, that a state takes to discourage attacks by other states.

Dumbarton Oaks Conference Meeting in Washington, D.C., in 1944 at which representatives of China, Britain, the Soviet Union, and the United States drew up a blueprint for the charter of the United Nations.

General Assembly Assembly of all members of the United Nations; it debates issues but neither creates nor executes policy.

♦ In July 1945, Truman met with Stalin and Churchill at Potsdam on the outskirts of Berlin. Meeting with Churchill and Stalin for the first time, Truman was surprised that the Soviet leader was shorter than he, and thought Churchill talked too much, giving him "a lot of hooey." Later, Truman wrote, "you never saw such pig-headed people as are the Russians." Here, Stalin and Truman *(left)* and advisers Byrnes and Molotov *(right)* pose for photographers. *Truman Library.*

posed of all member nations. It could discuss issues but would have no authority to create or execute policies. Decisions were to be made by a smaller, executive-type **Security Council** composed of the Big Five (the Big Four plus France) as permanent members and six other nations elected by the General Assembly for two-year terms. The Security Council would establish and implement policies and would have the power to apply economic and military pressure against aggressor nations. Each of the Big Five could veto Security Council decisions, to ensure that the council would not interfere with their national interests. The United Nations represented the concept of peace through world cooperation, but its structure clearly left the future of peace in the hands of the major powers.

In July 1945 the Senate approved the United Nations charter and American membership by a vote of 89 to 2. Truman believed that the choice of New York City as the site of the permanent UN headquarters proved that the center of Western civilization and power had shifted from Western Europe to the United States.

Truman had very limited knowledge of diplomatic and military affairs. Roosevelt had not confided in his vice president on either issue. In fact, when Truman took office, he knew nothing about the Yalta Conference or the atomic bomb. Immediately, he sought experienced advisers and advice about how to deal with the Soviets. W. Averell Harriman, ambassador to the Soviet Union, and Admiral William Leahy, one of Roosevelt's military and diplomatic advisers, pictured the Soviet advance across Eastern and Central Europe in 1945 as a threat to peace and Western civilization. Truman agreed, noting that Soviet actions in Poland and Romania violated proper behavior, the principles of the Atlantic Charter, and the Yalta agreements.

Determined to be decisive, Truman quickly confronted Soviet foreign minister V. M. Molotov and berated the Soviet Union for not fulfilling its Yalta promises to allow self-determination in Eastern Europe. At nearly the same time, the United States abruptly stopped lend-lease goods en route to the Soviet Union and Britain. Although he moderated his toughness toward the Soviets during the next few months, it was clear that Truman was less willing to consider Soviet "needs" than Roosevelt had been. In July 1945, Truman had his only face-to-face meeting with Stalin at the Potsdam Conference. As a meeting to begin shaping the postwar world, Potsdam accomplished little. The United States expressed concern about the lack of democracy in Eastern Europe but accepted Soviet promises of change in the future. Truman found Stalin tough, not unlike political bosses in American cities, and

Security Council The executive agency of the United Nations; it includes five permanent members (China, France, Russia, Britain, and the United States) and six members chosen by the General Assembly for two-year terms.

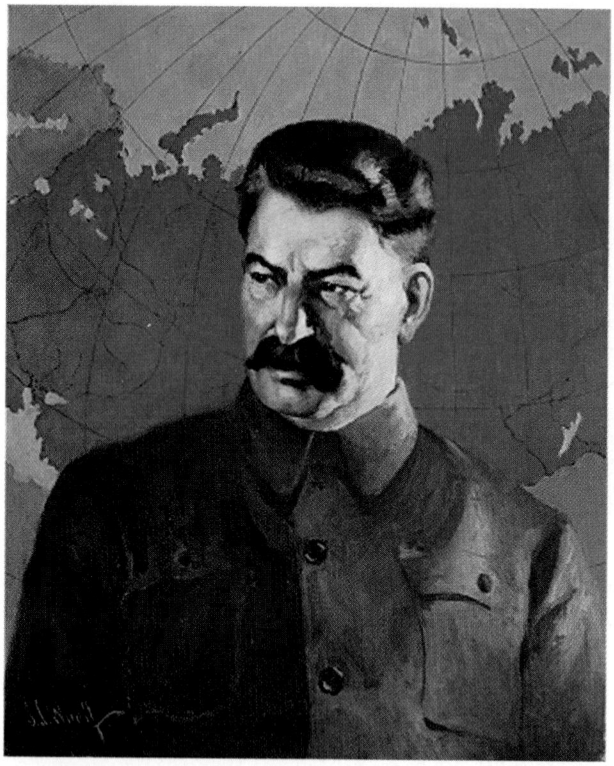

♦ Joseph Stalin controlled the Soviet Union from 1926 until his death in 1955. During World War II, the popular image of the Soviet dictator was that of "Uncle Joe." By the time the Truman Doctrine was signed in March 1947, his image had changed to resemble Hitler's. At the Potsdam conference in July 1945, Truman's first impression of Stalin was that he was "dishonest but smart as hell" and they could work together. One of Truman's closest advisers bluntly stated that Stalin was "a liar and a crook." *National Portrait Gallery, Smithsonian Institution, Gift of Muriel Woolf Hobson/Art Resource, N.Y.*

was more convinced than ever that the Soviets were a major obstacle to world stability.

By early 1946, Truman was "tired of babying the Soviets" and believed that it was time for them to prove their peaceful intentions. But the Soviets seemed uninterested in improving relations. The Soviet press warned of "capitalist encirclement" and accused the United States of poisoning Soviet-American relations. In Eastern Europe, every indication suggested that the Soviets were tightening their controls over Poland, Romania, and Hungary, by denying economic, political, and civil freedoms. On February 9, 1946, Stalin asserted that future wars were inevitable because of "present capitalist conditions." Most American observers saw his statement as proof of Soviet hostility. Secretary of the Navy James Forrestal, a long-time anti-Communist, distributed a private study that concluded the Soviets were committed to "global, violent, **proletarian** revolution." Supreme Court justice William O. Douglas called Stalin's speech "a declaration of World War III." The War Department and navy officials agreed, and the Joint Chiefs of Staff recommended a foreign policy that would support nations threatened by Soviet hostility. The State Department was less alarmed, but it too concluded that the Soviets were following an "ominous course."

Anxious to confirm Soviet intentions, the State Department asked George Frost Kennan, the **chargé d'affaires** in Moscow, to evaluate Soviet policy. He described Soviet totalitarianism as internally weak. Soviet leaders, he said, held Communist ideology secondary to remaining in power. To rule, Soviet leaders relied on fear, repression, and resistance to a foreign enemy. To stay in control, Soviet leaders needed Western capitalism to serve as that enemy, Kennan wrote. Therefore, they could not afford to reach meaningful, long-lasting agreements with the West. Kennan recommended a policy of **containment,** meeting head-on any attempted expansion of Soviet power. His eight-thousand-word report, the "Long Telegram," immediately received praise from Washington's official circles. Soon thereafter, Truman adopted a policy designed to "set will against will, force against force, idea against idea . . . until Soviet expansion is finally worn down."

Fear of Soviet expansion quickly became a bipartisan issue. Both Democrats and Republicans tried to educate the public about the Soviet threat—ending any possibility of a return to isolationism. One of the most dramatic warnings, however, came from Winston Churchill on March 5, 1946, at Westminster College in Fulton, Missouri. With President Truman sitting beside him, the former prime minister of Britain decried Soviet expansionism and stated that an **"iron curtain"** had fallen across Europe. He called

proletarian Relating to the working class, especially industrial wage laborers.

chargé d'affaires A high-ranking member of an embassy, frequently the highest-ranking career diplomat of the mission.

containment The U.S. policy of checking the expansion or influence of the Soviet Union by making strategic alliances, aiding friendly nations, and supporting weaker states in areas of conflict.

"iron curtain" Name given to the military, political, and ideological barrier established between the Soviet bloc and Western Europe after World War II.

for a "fraternal association of the English-speaking peoples" to halt the Russians. Truman thought it was a wonderfully eloquent speech and would do "nothing but good." Churchill, *Time* magazine pronounced, had spoken with the voice of a "lion."

As Churchill gave his address, it appeared that an "American lion" was needed in Iran. During World War II, the Big Three had stationed troops in Iran to ensure the safety of lend-lease materials going by that route to the Soviet Union. The troops were to be withdrawn by March 1946, but as that date neared, Soviet troops remained in northern Iran. Suddenly, on March 2, reports flashed from northern Iran that Soviet tanks were moving toward Tehran, the Iranian capital, as well as toward Iraq and Turkey. Some believed that war was imminent. Britain and the United States sent harshly worded telegrams to the Soviets and petitioned the United Nations to consider an Iranian complaint against the Soviet Union. War did not break out. Soviet tanks never got close to Tehran, Iraq, or Turkey, and Soviet forces soon evacuated Iran. The crisis was over, but it convinced many Americans that the Soviets were aggressive and would retreat only when confronted with firmness.

Throughout the rest of 1946, the United States hardened its resolve in Europe, making postwar credits and loans available on the basis of ideology and geography. Thus Britain received a $3.8 billion loan and France a $650 million loan, but the Soviet Union and Soviet-influenced Czechoslovakia received nothing. In Allied-occupied Germany, the United States promised that American troops would remain as long as necessary to protect the German people. By the end of 1946, public opinion showed concern about the possibility of Soviet aggression. *Woman's Home Companion* magazine reported that 3.6 million women believed war with Russia would come within fifteen years. The story line seemed clear: "Red fascism" had replaced Nazi fascism as a threat to civilization.

The Division of Europe

Kennan provided the form and justification for containment. Truman had to determine how to implement the policy—how to set apart and use American resources to construct a political, economic, and, if necessary, military wall around the Soviet Union. As the crisis in Iran receded, events in Europe assumed first priority. Throughout western and southern Europe, economic and social turmoil was adding to the popularity of **leftist** and Communist groups, which argued that the future of Europe rested on socialism and closer relations with the Soviet Union. In the eastern Mediterranean, Turkey was being pressured by the neighboring Soviets to permit some degree of Soviet control over the Dardanelles, the straits linking the Black Sea to the Mediterranean. Nearby, Greece was torn by a civil war between Communist-backed rebels and the British-supported conservative government (see Map 28.1).

No longer able to provide economic and military aid for Greece and Turkey, Britain in February 1947 asked the United States to assume that support. The Truman administration was eager to take on the "job of world leadership with all of its burdens and all of its glory." The central question, however, was whether he could persuade a penny-pinching Congress and the American public that a free Greece and Turkey were vital to American and world security.

Truman's secretary of state George Marshall and assistant secretary of state **Dean Acheson** explained to a select group of senators from both parties that all Communist activities were directed from Moscow and warned that Greece was on the brink of collapse. A Communist victory there, they predicted, would endanger neighboring states and eventually the entire eastern Mediterranean and Middle East. The Soviets were on the move, Acheson told the senators, and would triumph unless the United States stepped forward and stopped them. Impressed, Senator Arthur Vandenberg of Michigan suggested that to win congressional and public support, Truman needed to "scare the hell" out of the country.

The president took the advice. On March 12, 1947, he stood before Congress and set forth the **Truman Doctrine.** He offered an ideological, black-and-white view of world politics and blamed almost every threat to peace and stability on an unnamed villain: the Soviet Union. He implied a national commitment by the United States to an activist world role in supporting freedom, saying that it was

leftist Holding various liberal or radical political beliefs, often resting on sympathy with the working class and a conviction that government should provide for the basic needs of its people.

Dean Acheson Diplomat who took over as secretary of state in 1949; he helped formulate U.S. policy in Korea and advocated a firm stand against Soviet aggression in the Berlin crisis.

Truman Doctrine Anti-Communist foreign policy that Truman set forth in 1947; it called for military and economic aid to countries whose political stability was threatened by communism.

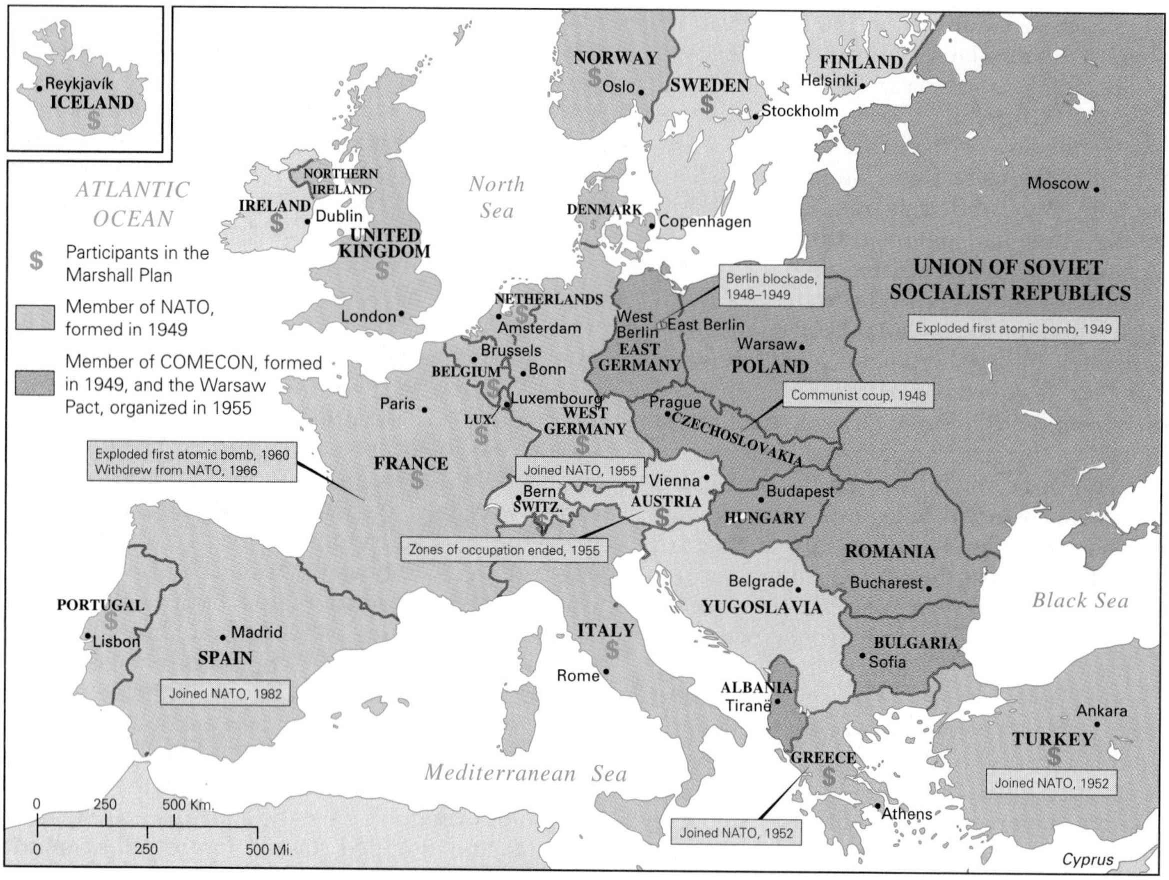

♦ **MAP 28.1 Cold War Europe** Following World War II, Europe was divided by what Winston Churchill called the "iron curtain," which divided most of the continent politically, economically, and militarily into an eastern bloc (the Warsaw Pact) led by the Soviet Union and a western bloc (NATO) supported by the United States. This postwar division of Europe lasted until the collapse of the Soviet Union in the early 1990s.

the duty of the United States "to support free people" who resisted subjugation "by armed minorities or by outside pressure," and he asked Congress for $400 million in aid for Greece and Turkey. Receiving American support, Turkey resisted Soviet pressure and retained control over the straits, and the Greek government was able to defeat the Communist rebels in 1949.

Although the Truman administration asked Congress only for $400 million in aid for Greece and Turkey, officials admitted among themselves that the request was just the beginning. "It happens that we are having a little trouble with Greece and Turkey at the present time," stated a War Department official, "but they are just one of the keys on the keyboard of this world piano."

On June 5, 1947, in a commencement address at Harvard, Secretary of State Marshall uncovered the keyboard and offered Europe a program of economic aid: the **Marshall Plan.** The United States had already loaned nearly $9 billion to Western European nations, but more was needed to ward off a possible European economic collapse. Not only had the war destroyed thousands of homes, farms, and factories, but drought and an extremely bitter winter had, by 1947, brought Europe close to social and economic chaos. Because of rapidly diminishing supplies of fuel and food, millions could not heat their homes and were existing on less than 1,200 calories a day. Feeding on the social and economic

Marshall Plan Program to foster economic recovery in Western Europe in the postwar period through massive amounts of U.S. financial aid, which began in 1948.

THE MAINTENANCE OF INTERNATIONAL STABILITY
SAM, I'LL HAVE TO HAVE HELP OR I'M GOING TO DROP THIS!!
ENGLAND

♦ In many people's views, Truman's decision to support Greece and Turkey and his announcement of the Truman Doctrine (March 1947) represented the transfer of world responsibility from Great Britain to the United States. In Truman's words, "The free peoples of the world look to us for support in maintaining their freedoms."

turmoil, Communist and Socialist parties were gaining in popularity and strength. Italian Communists represented a third of the electorate, whereas in France nearly a quarter voted Communist. European prosperity had to be restored if only to deny leftists their points of attack. And the United States was the only nation with the resources to do it. With American business more than ready to sell to Europe, American planners urged Truman to provide Europeans with credit that would both rebuild Europe and ensure a long-term market for American products.

For the Truman administration, the question was not whether to provide Western Europe with aid but whether to include the Soviets and Eastern Europeans. To allow the Soviets and their satellites to participate seemed contrary to the intent of the Truman Doctrine. Would a Congress that had just spent $400 million to keep Greece and Turkey out of Soviet hands be willing to provide millions of American dollars to the Soviet Union? But if the Soviets were excluded, the United States might seem to be encouraging the division of Europe, an image the State Department wanted to avoid. Chaired by Kennan, the State Department planning staff recommended that the United States take "a hell of a big gamble" and offer economic aid to all Europeans. Kennan believed that the Soviets' unwillingness to cooperate economically and politically with capitalists would keep them from taking part. Thus, when Marshall spoke at Harvard, he invited all Europeans to work together and write a program "designed to place Europe on its feet economically."

The gamble worked. At a June 26, 1947, meeting in Paris of potential Marshall Plan participants, Soviet foreign minister Molotov rejected a British and French written proposal for an economically integrated Europe, joint economic planning, and a requirement to purchase mostly American goods. At first the Marshall Plan looked like a "tasty mushroom," commented one Soviet official, but on closer examination it turned out to be a "poisonous toadstool." Unwilling to participate in any form of economic integration with non-Communist Europe, the Soviets and the Eastern Europeans left the conference. Molotov blasted the Marshall Plan, condemning it for violating national sovereignty, forcing the division of Europe, and allowing the reindustrialization of Germany. The Soviet Union took steps to solidify Communist influence in and control over Eastern Europe. In July 1947, Moscow announced the Molotov Plan, a move to incorporate Eastern European economies into the Soviet system. Non-Communist elements were expelled from the Hungarian government, and in September, the Soviet Union formed the Communist Information Bureau (Cominform) to ensure Soviet direction of Europe's Communist parties.

Meanwhile, attracted by the prospect of American aid, sixteen nations stayed in Paris and drafted a European recovery program. Completed on September 22, 1947, the plan called for four years of American assistance amounting to more than $20 billion. In December, Truman asked Congress for $17 billion. Without such a program, he said, the iron curtain might soon rest on the Atlantic shore. Congress gave its consent in 1948, but not until it had cut the total to $12.5 billion.

The Marshall Plan produced far-reaching consequences for countries both east and west of the iron curtain. In Germany, the United States moved to unify the western zones (see Map 28.2) into a political and economic whole and informed Western European countries that in order to receive full American aid, they had to purge Communist elements from their governments. As Congress debated Marshall Plan funding in February 1948, the Soviets

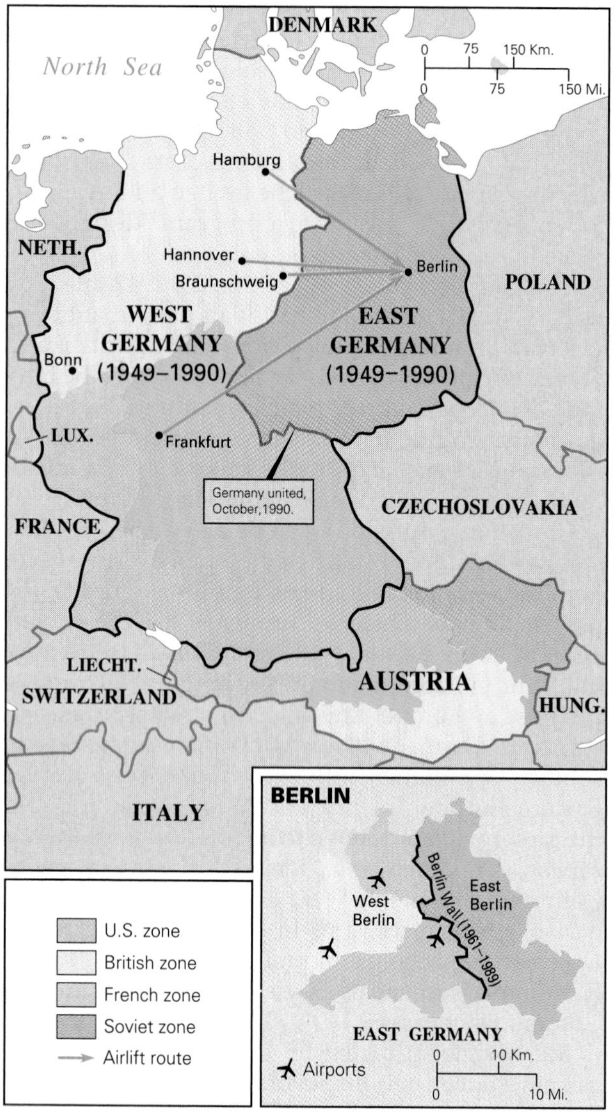

♦ **MAP 28.2 Cold War Germany** This map shows how Germany and Berlin were divided into occupation zones. Meant as temporary divisions, they became permanent, transformed by the Cold War into East and West Germany. In 1948, with the Berlin airlift, and again in 1961, with the erection of the Berlin Wall, Berlin became the flash point of the Cold War. With the end of the Cold War, the division of Germany also ended. In 1989, the Berlin Wall was torn down, and in 1990 the two Germanies were unified.

engineered a **coup** in Czechoslovakia and installed a Communist government, proving to many Americans their hostile intentions. "We are faced with exactly the same situation with which Britain and France were faced in 1938 and 1939 with Hitler," Truman announced. With "sovietization" taking place in Eastern Europe, the United States, Britain, and France moved to unify their German occupation zones into a West German state. In March 1948, the United States announced that Germany's western zones were eligible for Marshall Plan aid, were to hold elections to select delegates to a constitutional convention, and would use a standard currency. The meaning of these actions seemed clear: a West German state was being formed.

Faced with the prospect of a pro-Western, industrialized, and eventually remilitarized Germany, Stalin reacted. On June 24, the Russians blockaded all land traffic to and from Berlin, which had been divided into British-, French-, Soviet-, and U.S.-controlled zones after the war (see Map 28.2). The Russians also shut off the electricity to the city's western zones. With a population of more than 2 million, West Berlin lay isolated 120 miles inside the Soviet zone of Germany. The Soviet goal was to force the West either to abandon the creation of West Germany or to face the loss of Berlin. Americans viewed the blockade simply as further proof of Soviet hostility and were determined not to retreat. Churchill affirmed the West's stand. We want peace, he stated, "but we should by now have learned that there is no safety in yielding to dictators, whether Nazi or Communist." The prospect of war loomed.

American strategists confronted the question of how to stay in Berlin without starting a shooting war. Although some in the army recommended fighting their way across the Soviet zone to the city, Truman chose another option, one that would not violate Soviet occupied territory or any international agreements. Marshalling a massive effort of men, supplies, and aircraft, British and Americans flew supply planes to three Berlin airports on an average of one flight every three minutes. To drive home to the Soviets the depth of American resolve, Truman ordered a wing of B-29 bombers, the "atomic bombers," to Britain. These planes carried no atomic weapons, but the general impression was that their presence lessened the likelihood of Soviet aggression.

The **Berlin airlift** was a tremendous victory for the United States. The unceasing flow of aircraft and

coup Sudden overthrow of a government by a group of people, usually with military support.

Berlin airlift Response to the Soviet blockade of West Berlin in 1948, in which American and British planes made continuous flights to deliver supplies.

♦ When the Soviets blockaded the western zones of Berlin, in one of the first confrontations of the Cold War, the United States replied by staging one of the most successful logistical feats of the twentieth century, Operation Vittles, in which vital supplies were flown into the city. The airlift lasted 321 days and American planes flew more than 272,000 missions. *Walter Sanders LIFE Magazine ©Time, Inc.*

supplies testified not only to America's economic and military power but also to America's resolve to contain Soviet power and protect Europe. The crisis bore other fruit, too, sweeping away almost all congressional opposition to the Marshall Plan and the creation of West Germany and silencing those who had protested a permanent military commitment to Western Europe.

Truman followed the Berlin action with a call for an American military alliance with Western Europe. And by April 1949, negotiations to create the **North Atlantic Treaty Organization (NATO)** were completed (see Map 28.1). Finding no diplomatic gain from the blockade, the Soviets ended it in May 1949 without explanation. Two months later, Congress approved American entry into NATO. Membership in the alliance ensured that American forces would remain in the newly created West Germany and that Western Europe would be eligible for additional American economic and military aid. The Mutual Defense Assistance Act passed in 1949 provided $1.5 billion in arms and equipment for NATO member nations. By 1952, 80 percent of American assistance to Europe was military aid.

A Global Presence

American foreign policy from 1945 to 1950 focused on rebuilding Western Europe and containing Soviet power but did not ignore the rest of the world. Called one part humanitarianism and one part imperialism by a British official, U.S. foreign policy worked to expand American economic and political interests in Latin America, the Middle East, and Asia. To the south, the Truman administration rejected requests from Latin Americans for a Marshall Plan–style program. Instead, it encouraged private firms to develop the region through business and trade. To ensure that the Western Hemisphere remained under the American eagle's wing, however, the United States organized the Rio Pact of 1947. It established the concept of collective security for Latin America and created a regional organization—the **Organization of American States**—to coordinate defense, economic, and social concerns.

In the Middle East, fear of future oil shortages led the United States to promote the expansion of American petroleum interests. In Saudi Arabia, Kuwait, and Iran, the goal was to replace Britain as the major economic and political influence. At the same time, the United States became a powerful supporter of a new Jewish state. Truman's support for such a nation, to be created in **Palestine,** arose from several considerations—moral, political, and international. As early as August 1945, he had asked that at least a hundred thousand displaced European Jews be allowed to migrate to Palestine, then under British rule. Considering the Nazi terror

North Atlantic Treaty Organization Alliance formed in 1949 among most of the nations of Western Europe and North America; its mutual defense agreement was a basic element in the effort to contain communism.

Organization of American States An international organization composed of most of the nations of the Americas, including the Caribbean, which deals with the mutual concerns of its members. Cuba is not currently a member.

Palestine Region on the Mediterranean that was a British mandate after World War I; the UN partitioned the area in 1948 to allow for a Jewish state (Israel) and a Palestinian state, which was never established.

against Jews, he believed that the Jews should have their own nation—a view strongly advocated by the well-organized, pro-Jewish lobbying effort across the United States.

In May 1947, Britain announced it no longer had the resources or the desire to maintain control over Palestine. The stage was therefore set for the United Nations to divide the region into two nations: one Arab and one Jewish. When the United Nations voted to **partition** Palestine into Arab and Jewish states on May 14, 1948, Truman recognized the nation of Israel within fifteen minutes. And when war quickly broke out between Israel and the surrounding Arab states—which refused to accept partition—Truman and most Americans applauded the victories of Israeli armies.

If Americans were pleased with events in Latin America and the Middle East, Asia provided several disappointments. Under American occupation, Japan's government had been reshaped into a democratic system and placed safely within the American orbit, but success in Japan was offset by diplomatic setbacks in China and Korea. During World War II, the **Nationalist Chinese government** of Jiang Jieshi (Chiang Kai-shek) and the Chinese Communists under Mao Zedong (Mao Tse-tung) had moderated their hostility toward each other to fight the Japanese. But when the war ended, old animosities quickly resurfaced. In late 1945, General Marshall traveled to China to try to arrange a coalition government between Mao and Jiang, but the effort failed and the truce between the two forces collapsed.

By February 1946, civil war flared in China, and American supporters of Jiang were recommending that the United States increase its economic and military support for the Nationalist government. Especially vocal in promoting the cause of the Nationalists was the "China Lobby," led by *Time* and *Life* publisher Henry R. Luce, a long-time friend of Jiang. Luce and others argued that Soviet power threatened China and the rest of Asia as much as it did Europe. Truman and Marshall (he was now secretary of state) were of a different opinion. Though dreading Communist success in China, they blamed the corrupt and inefficient Nationalist government under Jiang for China's military, political, and economic turmoil, and they questioned whether Jiang could ever effectively rule the country. They were willing to continue some political, economic, and military support, but neither of them wanted to commit American power to an Asian war. Providing more aid would be like "throwing money down a rat hole," Truman told the cabinet.

Faced with an efficient and popular opponent, unable to mobilize the Chinese people and resources, and lacking increased American support, Jiang's forces steadily lost the civil war. In 1949, his army disintegrated, and the Nationalist government fled to the island of Formosa (Taiwan). Conservative Democrats and Republicans labeled the rout of Jiang as a humiliating American defeat and complained that the Truman administration was too soft on communism. To quiet critics and to protect Jiang, Truman refused to recognize the People's Republic of China on the mainland and ordered the U.S. Seventh Fleet to the waters near Taiwan.

Increasingly, Truman was feeling pressure to expand the containment policy to areas beyond Europe. The pressure intensified in late August 1949, when the Soviets detonated their own atomic bomb, shattering the American nuclear monopoly. Suddenly, it seemed to many Americans that the United States was losing the Cold War. From inside and outside the administration came calls for a more global and aggressive policy against communism. David Lilienthal, one of Truman's atomic advisers and head of the Atomic Energy Commission, in 1950 recommended building a **hydrogen bomb.** A joint Pentagon–State Department committee, headed by Paul Nitze, concluded that the Soviets were driven by "a new fanatic faith, antithetical to our own," whose objective was to dominate the world. The group speculated that the Soviets would be able to launch a nuclear attack on the United States as early as 1954. The committee's report, NSC Memorandum #68, issued by the **National Security Council (NSC),** called for global containment and a massive buildup of American military force. In fact, NSC-68 called for an almost 400 percent increase in military spending for the next fiscal year, which would have raised military expenditures to nearly $50 billion.

partition To divide a country into separate, autonomous nations.

Nationalist Chinese government The government of Jiang Jieshi, who fought the Communists for control of China in the 1940s; Jiang and his supporters were defeated and retreated to Taiwan in 1949, where they set up a separate government.

hydrogen bomb Nuclear weapon of much greater destructive power than the atomic bomb.

National Security Council Executive agency established in 1947 to coordinate the strategic policies and defense of the United States; it includes the president and four cabinet members.

Truman studied the report but worried about the impact of such large-scale military production on the manufacturing of domestic goods. A separate report concluded that the projected mobilization of industry for the Cold War would reduce automobile construction by nearly 60 percent and the production of radios and television sets might fall to zero. Truman eventually agreed to a "moderate" $12.3 billion military budget for 1950 that included building the hydrogen bomb. Supporters of NSC-68 won the final argument on June 25, 1950, when North Korean troops stormed across the **38th parallel.**

The Korean War

- As the North Koreans invaded South Korea, what choices and constraints did Truman confront when considering policy options?
- What expectations did Truman and General MacArthur have about defeating the North Koreans and unifying Korea? What was the outcome for both leaders?

When World War II ended, Soviet forces occupied Korea north of the 38th parallel, and American forces remained south of it (see Map 28.3). Like the division of Germany, the division of Korea was expected to be temporary, with the United States and the Soviet Union working to create a reunited Korean nation. American policymakers had little confidence in Korean political abilities and had projected that the Soviet-American trusteeship might last as long as twenty-five years. Most Koreans felt otherwise and quickly began pressing Soviet and American authorities for immediate independence. Internal politics and growing Soviet-American hostility quickly dashed hopes for a unified Korea. By mid-1946, with an American-supported government led by **Syngman Rhee** in the south and a Communist-backed government headed by **Kim Il-Sung** in the north, the division of Korea appeared more permanent than temporary.

In 1949, believing Korea to be of little political or strategic importance, the Soviet and American governments withdrew their forces, leaving behind two hostile regimes, each claiming to be Korea's rightful government. Both Koreas launched raids across the border. Neither side gained much ground, but within a year more than one hundred thousand Koreans had lost their lives in the conflict, and both sides had expanded their military capabilities.

Having received approval from the Soviets, on June 25, 1950, Kim Il-Sung launched a full-scale invasion of the south. Apprised of the invasion, Truman drew parallels to Manchuria, Ethiopia, and Austria in the 1930s and quickly announced that Korea was vital to American interests and needed protection from Communist aggression. Truman and most other Americans assumed that Moscow had directed the invasion, and this assumption seemed to confirm the wisdom of the NSC-68 recommendations for a global, military-backed campaign of containment.

The UN Responds to Communist Aggression

Within days, the army of South Korean was fleeing before the stronger and better-equipped North Korea forces. Immediately, the United States asked the UN Security Council to intervene. The Security Council called for a cease-fire and asked member nations to provide assistance to South Korea. To blunt the invasion, Truman ordered **General Douglas MacArthur** to commit American naval and air units south of the 38th parallel. Two days later, as North Koreans captured Seoul, the South Korean capital, the Security Council approved an international military force to defend South Korea—that is, to push the invaders back into North Korea and restore peace. General MacArthur was named commander of the United Nations forces. As a member of the Security Council, the Soviet Union could have blocked the actions with its veto, but at the time of the invasion the Russians were boycotting the council for its refusal to recognize the People's Republic of China. The Soviets returned to the Security Council in August.

Although more than 70 percent of Americans polled supported Truman's decision to intervene, there was no rush to arms as in World War II.

38th parallel Negotiated dividing line between North and South Korea; it was the focus of much of the fighting in the Korean War.

Syngman Rhee Korean politician who became president of South Korea in 1948; his dictatorial rule ended in 1960, when he was forced out of office and into exile.

Kim Il-Sung Leader of North Korea installed by the Soviets; he served as premier from 1948 to 1972, when he became president, a position he held until his death in 1994.

General Douglas MacArthur Commander of Allied forces in the Southwest Pacific during World War II and of UN forces in Korea until a conflict over strategy led Truman to dismiss him.

♦ The Korean War was one of ebb and flow, advances and retreats—the movement of troops up and down the rugged Korean peninsula. Here, American troops advance while Korean women and children march in the opposite direction hoping to avoid the destruction of war. Over 33,000 Americans lost their lives in Korea during the conflict. *Corbis-Bettman.*

National guard and reserve forces had to be called to active duty to fill the ranks, and the draft was again used to ensure a monthly quota of fifty thousand soldiers. General Lewis B. Hershey, head of the Selective Service, noted, "Everyone wants out; nobody wants in." On July 1, the first American soldiers, officially under United Nations control, arrived in Korea. Fearful that a congressional declaration of war against North Korea might expand the conflict to involve the Chinese and Russians, Truman never sought one. American troops served in Korea under United Nations resolutions and followed Truman's orders as commander in chief. For the record the war was called the "Korean Conflict," a "police action" to defeat a "bandit raid." Few in Congress objected, and with little dissent the House and Senate approved large-scale expansions of the military and its budget.

The infusion of American troops did not halt the North Korean advance, and by the end of July, North Korean forces were occupying most of South Korea. United Nations forces, including nearly 122,000 Americans and the whole South Korean army, held the southeastern corner of the peninsula—the **Pusan perimeter** (see Map 28.3)—and prepared for an offensive. On September 15, a bold maneuver turned the tide. Seventy thousand American troops landed at Inchon, near Seoul, nearly 200 miles north of the Pusan defensive perimeter. This brilliant tactical move surprised the enemy and not only threatened North Korean supply and communication lines but also could block the retreat of North Korean troops. Eleven days later, forces advancing north from Pusan joined forces driving east from Inchon. Their army collapsing, the North Koreans fled back across the 38th parallel. Seoul was liberated on September 27. United Nations forces had achieved the purpose of the police action: the South Korean government was saved, and the 38th parallel was again a real border.

Seeking to Liberate North Korea

Now, however, restoring the conditions that had prevailed before the invasion was not enough. The South Korean leadership, MacArthur, Truman, and most Americans wanted to unify the peninsula under South Korean rule. Bending under American pressure, the United Nations approved the new goal on October 7, giving MacArthur a green light to "liberate" North Korea from Communist rule.

An invasion seemed the best plan. North Korean forces were in disarray, and intelligence sources discounted the possibility of either Soviet or large-scale Chinese intervention. By mid-October, United Nations forces were moving quickly northward toward the Korean-Chinese border at the Yalu River. The Chinese threatened intervention if the invaders approached the border, and some UN units had already encountered Chinese "volunteer" troops. Nevertheless, UN commander General MacArthur was supremely confident. If Chinese forces did cross the border, he explained to Truman, they would not number more than thirty thousand and American air power would slaughter them. Less than convinced, a concerned Truman ordered MacArthur to use only South Korean forces in approaching the Yalu River. The overconfident general, however, bri-

Pusan perimeter Area near the city of Pusan in South Korea; it was the center of a beachhead held by UN forces in 1950.

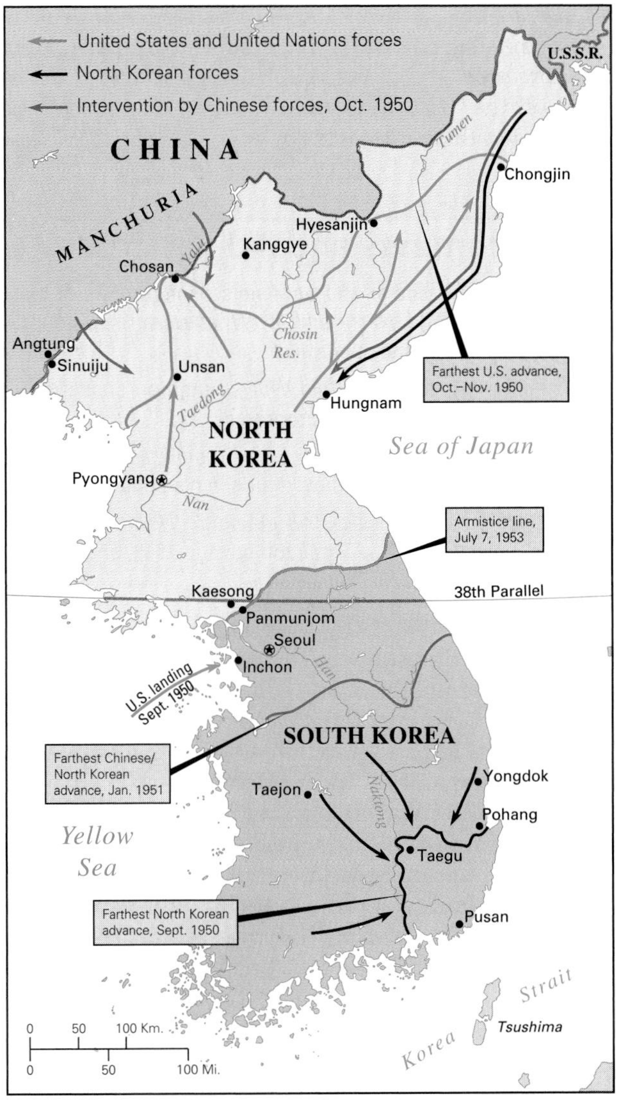

♦ **MAP 28.3 The Korean War, 1950–1953** Seeking to unify Korea, North Korean forces invaded South Korea in 1950. To protect South Korea, the United States and the United Nations intervened. After driving North Korean forces northward, Truman sought to unify Korea under South Korea. But as United Nations and South Korean forces pushed toward the Chinese border, Communist China intervened, forcing UN troops to retreat. This map shows the military thrusts and counterthrusts of the Korean War as it stalemated roughly along the 38th parallel.

dled at being restrained by his civilian commander, and on November 24, in violation of his orders, MacArthur moved American, British, and Korean forces to within a few miles of the Yalu. He also publicly promised to have victorious American soldiers home by Christmas. Two days later, nearly three hundred thousand Chinese soldiers entered the Korean Conflict.

In the most brutal fighting of the war, with their bugles blowing, the Chinese attacked in waves, hurling grenades, taking massive casualties, and encircling and nearly trapping several American and South Korean units. MacArthur had assumed that vastly superior American air and fire power would stop any Chinese invaders. He had not foreseen the arrival of hundreds of thousands of Chinese soldiers, the bitter winter weather, or night battles that severely limited the role of American aircraft. Across northern North Korea, UN forces fell back in bitter combat. The U.S. 1st Marine Division, nearly surrounded at the Chosin Reservoir, battled its way to the port of Hungnam by leap-frogging units to clear the road in front of them. During the Communist offensive, American casualties exceeded twelve thousand, but the Chinese lost more than three times as many, lending grim proof to General O. P. "Slam" Smith's statement about the "retreat" from Chosin: "Gentlemen, we are not retreating. We are merely advancing in another direction."

Within three weeks, the North Koreans and Chinese had shoved the UN forces back to the 38th parallel. During the retreat, General MacArthur asked for permission to bomb bridges on the Yalu River and Chinese bases across the border. He also urged a naval blockade of China and the possible use of Nationalist Chinese forces against the mainland. Believing such escalation could lead to World War III, Truman allowed only the Korean half of the bridges to be bombed and flatly rejected MacArthur's other suggestions. In the face of the new military reality, Truman abandoned the goal of a unified pro-Western Korea and sought a negotiated settlement to end the conflict even if it would leave two Koreas.

The decision was not popular. Americans wanted victory. Encouraged by public opinion polls and vocal Republican critics of Truman, in March and April 1951, General MacArthur publicly took exception to the limitations his commander in chief had placed on him. He put it simply: there was "no substitute for victory." Already displeased by MacArthur's arrogance, Truman used the general's direct challenge to presidential power as grounds to fire him.

Replaced by General Matthew Ridgway on April 11, 1951, MacArthur returned to the United States and received a hero's welcome, including a ticker-tape parade down New York's Fifth Avenue. Only a quarter of those asked supported the president's decision to recall the popular general. Jokes circulated about ordering a "Truman beer"—"one without a head." Across the country some called for Truman's impeachment and MacArthur's nomination for president. Congressional hearings to investigate the conduct of the war followed in June 1951, with MacArthur testifying that an expanded war could achieve victory. The administration responded by projecting fears of a nuclear world war and effectively made the case for a limited war and the need for civilian authority over the military.

In the face-off between MacArthur and Truman there was no winner. Polls showed Truman's public approval rating continuing to fall, reaching a dismal 24 percent by late 1951. At the same time, MacArthur's hopes for a presidential candidacy collapsed because most Americans feared his aggressive policies might indeed result in World War III. By the beginning of 1952, frustrated by the war, the vast majority of Americans were simply tired of it, calling it "useless" and wanting it to end.

The Korean front, meanwhile, stabilized along the 38th parallel. Four-power peace talks among the United States, South Korea, China, and North Korea began on July 10, 1951, amid sharp and ugly fighting. The negotiations did not go smoothly. For two years, the powers postured and argued about prisoners, cease-fire lines, and a multitude of lesser issues while soldiers fought and died over scraps of territory. UN casualties exceeded 125,000 during the two years of peace negotiations. When the Eisenhower administration finally concluded the cease-fire on July 26, 1953, the Korean Conflict had cost more than $20 billion and 33,000 American lives.

The "hot war" in Korea had far-reaching military and diplomatic results for the United States. The expansion of military spending envisioned by NSC-68 had proceeded rapidly after the North Korean invasion. In Europe, Truman moved forward with plans to rearm West Germany and Italy and, in the name of anticommunism, improved relations with Spain's dictator, Francisco Franco. Throughout Asia and the Pacific, a large American presence was made permanent. In 1951, the United States concluded a settlement with Japan that kept American forces in Japan and Okinawa. The Australian–New Zealand–United States (ANZUS) treaty of 1951 promised American military protection to Australia and New Zealand. At the same time, the United States was increasing its military aid and commitments to Nationalist China and French **Indochina.** The containment policy that George F. Kennan had envisioned to protect Western Europe had been expanded—formally and financially—to cover East Asia and the Pacific. Kennan objected to the growing number of commitments, but his arguments were more than offset by policymakers stressing the global struggle against the forces of communism. According to the philosophy of the day, a Communist victory anywhere threatened the national security of the United States.

Homecomings and Adjustments

- What were the social and economic expectations of most Americans as World War II ended? What were the outcomes of these for women and minorities?
- How did the developing Cold War strengthen conservative opposition to New Deal–style programs?
- What constraints did Truman face in implementing his domestic programs? How did they influence his choices?
- Why did Truman win the 1948 election? What choices did members of the New Deal coalition have in 1948, and why did most Democrats vote for Truman?

In September 1944, the War Department had announced that as soon as the war against Germany was over, demobilization would begin—the "boys" would start coming home. Germany had hardly surrendered in May 1945 when soldiers' wives across the nation organized "Bring Daddy Back" clubs and began flooding Washington with letters demanding a speedier return of their husbands. With the defeat of Japan three months later, soldiers in the Pacific sent letters and telegrams to their congressmen saying, "No boat; no vote." Despite protests from the military and the State Department, and against Truman's own better judgment, by November 1945, 1.25 million GIs were returning home each month, wanting to rediscover family, jobs, and the American way of life—the American dream. Of course, that American dream differed from person to person, but in general it centered around Franklin D. Roosevelt's 1944 Economic Bill of Rights: the right to a decent job, to sufficient food, shelter, and clothing, and to financial protection during unemployment, illness, and old age. Armed with the G.I. Bill, which provided educational benefits, low-interest home loans, and a year's unemployment compensation (see page 841), returning veterans were eager to begin civilian life.

Indochina French colony in Southeast Asia, including present-day Vietnam, Laos, and Cambodia; it began fighting for its independence in the mid-twentieth century.

♦ As World War II ended, Americans flocked to the suburbs, creating a demand for new housing—a demand matched by developers of planned communities like Levittown. In 1949, on one day alone, more than 1400 people signed contracts for their dream homes, some of which included automatic dishwashers and built-in televisions. *Joe Scherschel, LIFE Magazine ©Time Warner, Inc.*

Adjusting to Peace at Home

At first, in 1945 and 1946, not enough homes were available for the reunited families. The nation faced a massive housing shortage, especially in California and major cities. Streetcars were converted into homes in Chicago, grain silos became apartments in North Dakota, and across the country families doubled up. Of course, most desired to live in the charming "dream homes" advertised in popular magazines, and by mid-1946 William Levitt and other developers were supplying mass-produced, prefabricated houses—the suburban **tract house**—to meet the demand. Using building techniques developed during the war, Levitt boasted that he could construct a house on an existing concrete slab in sixteen minutes. Standardized, with few frills, his homes cost slightly less than $8,000, a very attractive price to many returning soldiers. The first Levittown sprang up in Hempstead, Long Island, soon to be followed by others in Pennsylvania and New Jersey.

In California and along the West Coast, Henry Kaiser built homes using the same efficient methods he had used to build ships during the war. Nowhere were tract homes more prominent than in southern California. Fostered since the 1920s by the automobile, Los Angeles's multinucleated development was different from development in eastern and midwestern cities (see pages 736–737). During and after the war, networks of roads extended out from southern California cities, which developed several economic centers, pulling businesses, homes, and industries away from the central cities. In the Los Angeles area retail sales in the downtown district fell by 50 percent from prewar totals. A rush to the suburbs exploded as residents and the many people who migrated to the region followed the roads outward. To further the process, Governor Earl Warren in 1947 allocated nearly $300 million over a ten-year period to build 105 miles of freeways in southern California—most crisscrossing the Los Angeles area. Statewide gasoline taxes and registration fees were to pay for the new roads.

At the same time, across the country, streetcar and interurban rail systems were vanishing rapidly and increasingly were being replaced by bus lines. Living and working along the old transit routes were the poor and minorities, who thus were linked by economic and social forces to the downtown industrial and business centers that were declining in all regions. The "typical" American family—white, middle-class, and Christian—lived in suburban developments, where African Americans, Jews, and other minorities were not welcome.

In 1948, the Supreme Court ruled in ***Shelly v. Kraemer*** that restrictive housing covenants written to exclude minorities could not be enforced by lower courts. But the decision did little to integrate most suburbs. Banks rarely made home loans to

tract house One of numerous houses of similar design built on a plot of land.

Shelly v. Kraemer Supreme Court ruling (1948) that barred lower courts from enforcing restrictive agreements that prevented minorities from living in certain neighborhoods; it had little impact on actual practices.

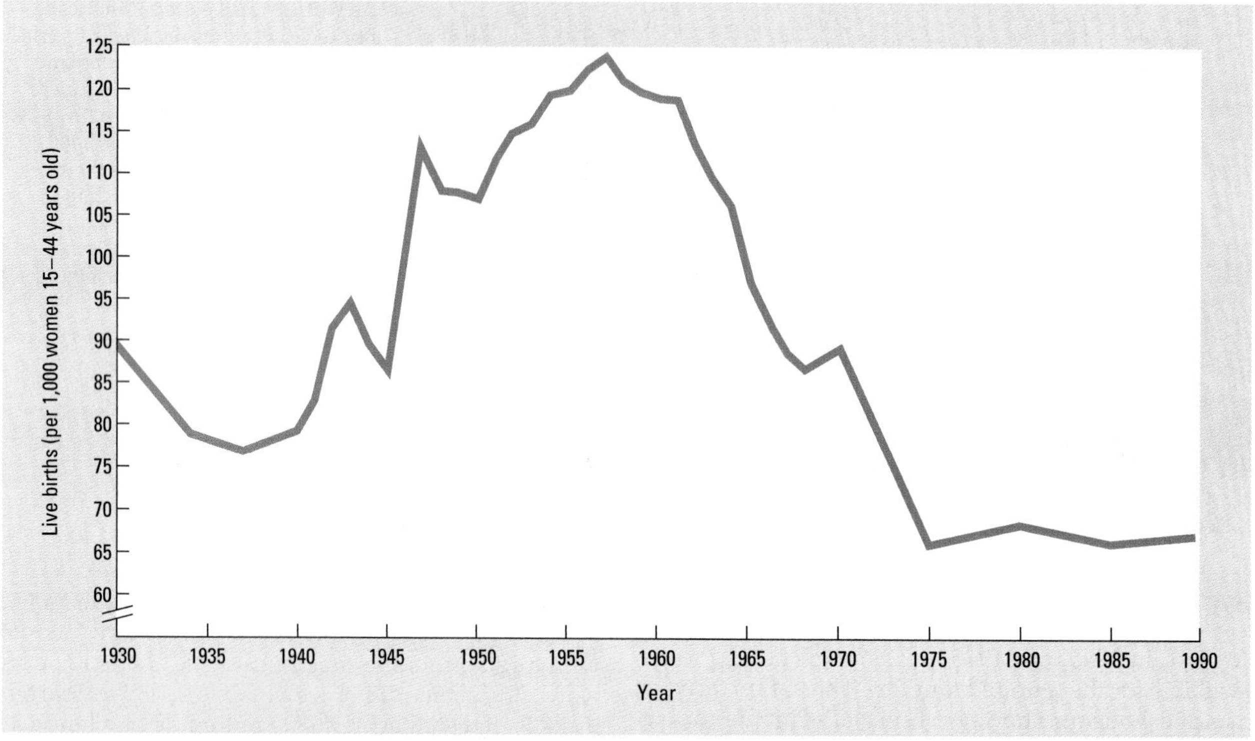

♦ **FIGURE 28.1 Birth Rate, 1930–1990** Between 1946 and 1957, rebounding from the low birth rate of the Depression, families choose to have more children. This increase is often called the "baby boom." Since the 1960s, the birth rate has slowed, and since the 1970s, it has remained fairly constant.

minorities trying to buy a house in a typical white neighborhood, and real-estate agents continued to abide by the Realtors' Code of Ethics, which called it unethical to permit the "infiltration of inharmonious elements" into a neighborhood. Across the nation, less than 5 percent of suburban neighborhoods provided nonwhites access to the American dream house. In the San Francisco Bay Area, less than 1 percent of the more than 100,000 homes built between 1945 and 1950 were sold to nonwhites.

Cozy homes were only part of the postwar dream. Veterans expected jobs, too, and they expected the workers—especially married women—who had been hired while the menfolk "fought for democracy" to relinquish their jobs. A *Fortune* poll in the fall of 1945 revealed that 57 percent of women and 63 percent of men believed that married women should not work. Psychiatrists and marriage counselors argued that men wanted their wives to be feminine and submissive, not their fellow workers. Fashion, designers, like Christian Dior in his "New Look," lengthened skirts and accented waists and breasts to emphasize femininity.

Not all women accepted the role of contented wife and homemaker. When one former GI informed his wife that she could no longer handle the finances because doing so was not "woman's work," she indignantly reminded him that she had successfully balanced the checkbook for four years and that his return had not made her suddenly stupid. Reflecting such tensions and too many hasty wartime marriages, the divorce rate jumped dramatically. Twenty-five percent of all marriages were ending in divorce in 1946, and by 1950 over a million GI marriages had broken apart.

Despite the growing divorce rate, however, marriage was more popular than ever: by 1950, two-thirds of the population was married and having children. From a Depression level of under 19 per 1,000, the birth rate rose to over 25 per 1,000 within two years of the war (see Figure 28.1). The so-called **baby boom**

baby boom Sudden increase in the birth rate that occurred in the United States after World War II and lasted until roughly 1961.

had arrived. It lasted for nearly twenty years. The baby boom did not occur merely because soldiers returned home, however. Other forces contributed as well. Fear of "male scarcity" caused by war losses encouraged some women to choose marriage earlier than before. But more important was a new attitude that viewed marriage as the ideal state for young people. Many women's magazines and marriage experts championed the idea that men should marry at around age 20 and women at age 18 or 19.

Like women, nonwhites saw "fair employment" vanish as employers favored white males once the war was over. The skilled and industrial jobs that had opened to Latinos and African Americans during the war became scarce by 1946. In 1943, more than a million African Americans were employed in the aircraft industry. By 1950, the number had shrunk to 237,000. The decline was less marked in the automobile, rubber, and shipbuilding industries, but minority job levels dropped there too as employers routinely chose to exclude nonwhites from many of the skilled and higher-paying positions.

Discrimination, denial of educational opportunities, and language barriers continued to trap a majority of Mexican Americans as common laborers. Throughout the Southwest and West, Mexican-American migration to urban areas continued to heighten the agricultural labor shortage. Mechanization made up for some of the loss, but more workers were necessary and Mexico was the logical source. In 1947, when Mexico pressed for higher wages and better working conditions for those Mexicans working in the *bracero* program (see page 845), the United States allowed American farmers to contract directly for Mexican workers and set virtually no restrictions on wages and working conditions. The result was that between 1947 and 1950 nearly twice as many undocumented Mexican workers were recruited than had worked under the *bracero* program.

Nonwhite Americans at the end of World War II still lived in a distinctly segregated world. From housing to jobs, from healthcare to education, white society continued to deny nonwhites full participation in the American dream. Still, African Americans and Latinos looked eagerly toward the postwar period. Despite ongoing discrimination, minorities had achieved social and economic gains during the war, and despite immediate postwar adjustments, more progress seemed possible. In 1945, for example, Jackie Robinson broke the color barrier in professional baseball when team owner Branch Rickey signed him to play for the Brooklyn Dodgers' farm team, the Montreal Royals. Robinson joined the Dodgers in 1947 as the first African-American player in the previously all-white major leagues and that season was voted the National League's Rookie of the Year.

♦ Jackie Robinson broke the color barrier in major league baseball in 1947, when he joined the Brooklyn Dodgers. After serving as a lieutenant in the army during the war, Robinson, an All-American in football and baseball at UCLA, played with the Kansas City Monarchs of the Negro American Baseball League until he was signed by the Dodgers in 1945. Moved from the minors to the majors in 1947, he earned "Rookie of the Year" honors and later was inducted into the Baseball Hall of Fame. *Collection of Michael Barson/Past Perfect.*

Having fought for democracy, Latino and African-American veterans insisted that democracy be practiced at home. W. E. B. Du Bois echoed their feelings, stating that the real problems facing the United States came not from Stalin and Molotov but from racists like Mississippi's Senator Theodore Bilbo and Congressman John Rankin. "Internal injustice done to one's brother," Du Bois warned, "is far more dangerous than the aggression of strangers from abroad." When the Anglos of Three Rivers, Texas, refused to bury war hero Felix Longoria in the city cemetery, Latino veterans protested to Washington. Wanting to avoid a civil rights confrontation, the Truman administration agreed to bury Longoria in Arlington National Cemetery. In 1948, Mexican-American veterans organized the G.I. Forum in Corpus Christi and with other Latino organizations protested the segregation of Latino schoolchildren. Although they won many of the court cases they filed against several school districts, including the 1948 Supreme Court ruling that Latin Americans should not be segregated, "Mexican ward schools" remained throughout the Southwest. Still, changes were taking place, and minorities hoped that President Truman would protect and extend the benefits acquired during the war.

Truman and Liberalism

When Roosevelt died, many wondered if Truman would continue the Roosevelt–New Deal approach to domestic policies. Would he work to protect the social and economic gains that labor, women, and minorities had earned during the Depression and the war? Conservatives and some of Truman's friends predicted that the new president was "going to be quite a shock to those who followed Roosevelt—that the New Deal is as good as dead . . . and that the 'Roosevelt nonsense' was over."

What would happen to the economy? The war had produced a massive transfer of resources from peacetime to wartime needs and had increased federal spending. Would the expected cuts in the federal budget and industry's switch to domestic production generate high unemployment, reduced wages and profits, and inflation—a depression or deep recession? Surprisingly, the economic conversion to a peacetime economy was smoother than expected, and by 1948 the economy was quickly growing again with little unemployment or inflation. As for the tone of the Truman administration, Truman ended that speculation in September when he presented to Congress what one Republican critic called an effort to "out–New Deal the New Deal." Truman asked Congress for a twenty-one point program to re-energize the New Deal. He wanted to continue government controls over the economy, especially on prices, and to renew the Fair Employment Practices Commission (see page 844). He recommended an expansion of Social Security coverage and benefits, an increase in the minimum wage to 65 cents an hour, and the development of additional housing programs and Tennessee Valley–style projects. Truman also advised Congress that he would soon ask for a national health system to ensure medical care for all Americans.

The expanded New Deal that Truman projected never fully developed. Republicans, conservative Democrats, business leaders, and a variety of conservative groups had successfully contained the New Deal in 1937, and as the war ended in 1945, they set their sights on squelching any further expansion of the welfare state and federal management of the economy. To promote their political views, they embarked on a campaign to persuade the American public of the dangers of "New Deal socialism" and of the benefits of a return to business-directed free enterprise. The National Association of Manufacturers spent nearly $37 million on such propaganda in one year. "Public sentiment is everything," wrote an officer of Standard Oil. "He who molds public sentiment goes deeper than he who enacts statutes or pronounces decisions."

Warning that Truman's "socialistic" program involved too much government, threatened to destroy private enterprise, and endangered existing class and social relations, conservatives flatly rejected nearly all of his proposals. Conservatives in Congress, with surprisingly little opposition from the White House, either killed or significantly modified nearly all of them. The Fair Employment Practices Commission faded away. The liberal full-employment bill was revised to eliminate any government requirement to ensure full employment.

Seeking to protect jobs and wages, workers struck in large numbers throughout 1946, feeding the conservative mood of the nation. Prices rose—25 percent during the first eighteen months after the war—as most workers' incomes fell. Lack of overtime and lower wages decreased buying power by nearly 30 percent, and labor wanted corresponding wage hikes. A government study recommended less, an 18.5 percent raise. But with an oversupply of workers, employers saw little need to offer any increased wages at all. Nearly 4.5 million workers responded by going on more than five thousand strikes. Congress and state and local governments responded to strikes and agitation with antilabor measures designed to weaken unions and end strikes. Right-to-work laws banned compulsory union membership and in some cases provided legal and police protection for workers crossing picket lines during strikes.

♦ Workers march in New York City in support of unions, the FEPC, and worldwide worker solidarity. As the war ended, business and government assumed a more hostile attitude toward organized labor—many claiming that unions were socialistic or communistic. The outcome of this attitude was laws, including the Taft-Hartley Act, that restricted union activities and contributed to a decline in union membership. *UPI/Bettmann Archives.*

Other laws restricted boycotts and secondary, **sympathy strikes** or promoted the **open shop** and company-organized workers' associations.

Even Truman squared off against the coal miners' and railroad unions. In April 1946, he faced down John L. Lewis and four hundred thousand striking United Mine Workers. Considering Lewis "a Hitler at heart, a demagogue in action, and a traitor in fact," the president seized the mines, ordered miners back to work, and applauded when a federal court fined Lewis and the union $3.5 million. "Lewis folded up on Saturday," he wrote in his diary after the miners had returned to work. "He is, as all bullies are, as yellow as a dog pound pup." When locomotive engineers struck in late May, Truman asked Congress for power to draft striking workers into the army. The railroad strike was soon settled, and the "draft strikers" bill never passed.

The strikes, soaring inflation, and divisions within Democratic ranks fit the Republican party's prescription for a 1946 election bonanza. "Had enough?" Republican candidates asked the voters. Voters responded affirmatively, filling both houses of the Eightieth Congress with anti-Truman and anti–New Deal forces. Undeterred by Republican successes during the congressional elections, a bold Truman opened 1947 by proposing a near repeat of his 1945 program. As expected, Congress ignored Truman's domestic proposals and focused on passing a tax cut and anti-union legislation.

The **Taft-Hartley Act,** passed in June 1947 over Truman's veto, was a clear victory for management over labor. It banned the closed shop, prevented industry-wide collective bargaining, and legalized state-sponsored right-to-work laws that made union organizing more difficult. Echoing Truman's actions in the coal strike, the law also empowered the president to use a court injunction to force striking workers back to work for an eighty-day cooling-off period. Privately, Truman liked the Taft-Hartley Act and had cast his veto knowing it would be overridden, because he also knew his veto would help "hold labor support in the election next year." In December, a tax cut was also passed over Truman's veto.

On civil rights, Truman was cautious but generally supportive. Responding to Soviet criticism of American segregation, Truman stated, "The top dog in a world . . . ought to clean his own house." Blacks applauded his call for the continuation of the Fair Employment Practices Commission but were disappointed at his failure to prevent its termination. African Americans and liberals, including Eleanor

sympathy strikes Strikes that workers from one union conduct in support of workers from other unions who are on strike; these secondary strikes frequently target businesses that use the goods or services of the originally targeted business.

open shop A business or factory in which workers are not required to join a union in order to obtain a job; its opposite is called a closed shop.

Taft-Hartley Act Law passed by Congress in 1947 banning closed shops, permitting employers to sue unions for broken contracts, and requiring unions to observe a cooling-off period before striking.

Roosevelt, organized a protest in Washington. Their placards demanded, "Speak, Speak, Mr. President," to prod Truman and Congress into confronting racial violence that had been rising since the war ended. Admitting that he did not know how bad conditions were for blacks, Truman agreed in December 1946 to create a committee on civil rights to examine race relations in the country. The committee was a product of Truman's belief in equality, of pressure from blacks and liberals, and of hints that many northern blacks might vote Republican.

In October 1947, the committee presented a lengthy report, *To Secure These Rights,* describing the racial inequalities in American society and calling on the government to take steps to correct the imbalance. Among its recommendations were the establishment of a permanent commission on civil rights, the enactment of antilynching laws, and the abolition of the poll tax (see page 584). The committee also called for integration of the U.S. armed forces and support for integrating housing programs and education. Truman asked Congress in February 1948 to act on the recommendations but provided no direction or legislation. Nor did the White House make any effort to fully integrate the armed forces until black labor leader A. Philip Randolph once again threatened a march on Washington. Faced with the prospect of an embarrassing mass protest only months before the 1948 election, Truman issued an executive order asking the military to integrate its forces. The navy and air force complied, but the army resisted until high casualties in the summer of 1950 in Korea forced the integration of black replacements into previously white combat units. Despite his caution, Truman had done more in the area of civil rights than any president since Lincoln, a record that ensured African-American and liberal support for his 1948 bid to be elected president in his own right.

♦ Many considered Harry S Truman's 1948 victory over Thomas E. Dewey a major political upset—nearly all of the major polls had named the Republican an easy winner. Here Truman holds up the *Chicago Tribune's* incorrect headline announcing Dewey's triumph. *UPI/Bettmann Archives.*

The 1948 Election

Republicans' hopes were high in 1948. To take on Truman they chose New York's governor **Thomas E. Dewey.** In his loss to Roosevelt in 1944, Dewey had earned a respectable 46 percent of the popular vote, and his prospects looked very good in 1948. Republican candidates had done well in congressional elections, and Truman's approval ratings remained low. The Democrats were also mired in bitter infighting over the direction of domestic policy. Many Democratic liberals and minorities were dissatisfied that Truman had not worked harder to sell his New Deal–type programs to the public and to push them through Congress. After unsuccessfully maneuvering to replace him on the ballot, these dissenters grudgingly marched into line behind Truman. At the convention, however, they managed to write a strong New Deal–style party platform that included a civil rights plank.

Many southern Democrats, after losing the fight to exclude civil rights from the party platform, walked out of the convention waving Confederate flags. Unwilling to support a Republican, they met in Birmingham and organized the States Rights Democratic party, better known as the **Dixiecrat party,** nominating South Carolina's governor

Thomas E. Dewey New York governor who twice ran unsuccessfully for president as the Republican candidate, the second time against Truman in 1948.

Dixiecrat party Party organized in 1948 by southern delegates who refused to accept the civil rights plank of the Democratic platform; they nominated Strom Thurmond of South Carolina for president.

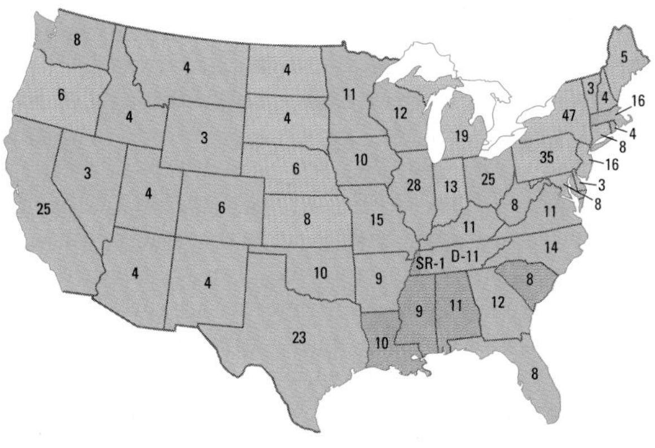

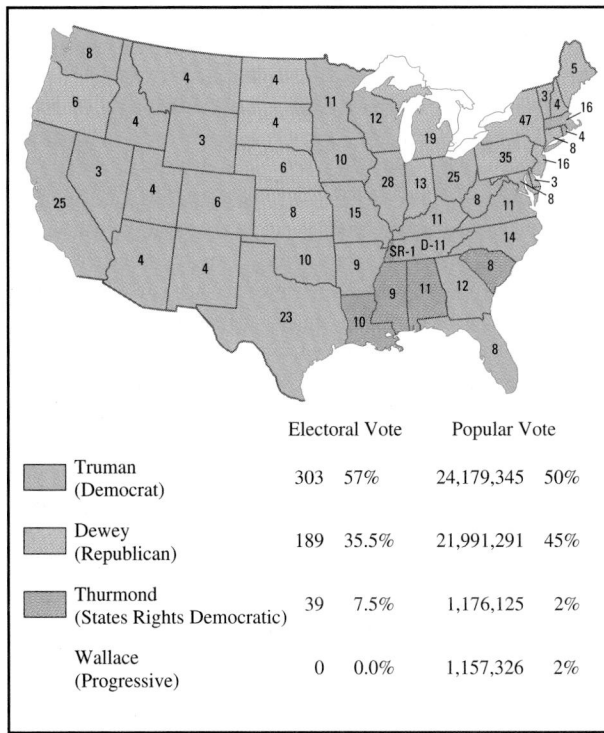

	Electoral Vote		Popular Vote	
Truman (Democrat)	303	57%	24,179,345	50%
Dewey (Republican)	189	35.5%	21,991,291	45%
Thurmond (States Rights Democratic)	39	7.5%	1,176,125	2%
Wallace (Progressive)	0	0.0%	1,157,326	2%

♦ **MAP 28.4 Election of 1948** In the 1948 presidential election, Harry S Truman confounded the polls and analysts by upsetting his Republican opponent Thomas Dewey, earning 50 percent of the popular vote and 57 percent of the electoral vote.

J. Strom Thurmond for president. Some liberals also deserted Truman and supported Henry A. Wallace, forming the Progressive party. With the Democratic party so splintered and public opinion polls showing a large Republican lead, Dewey, not known for his charm or speaking ability, conducted a low-key campaign almost devoid of debate on issues and contact with the public. In contrast, "Give Em Hell" Truman, running for his political life, crossed the nation by train, making hundreds of speeches that stressed the gains made under the progressive policies of the Democrats. He attacked the "do nothing" Eightieth Congress and its business allies. He told one audience, "Wall Street expects its money to elect a Republican administration that will listen to the gluttons of privilege first and not to the people at all." Truman also emphasized his expertise in foreign policy and his experience in standing up to Stalin.

Confounding the pollsters, Truman defeated Dewey (see Map 28.4). His margin of victory was the smallest since 1916—slightly over 2 million votes. Nevertheless, Truman's victory was a triumph for Roosevelt's New Deal coalition. Despite the Dixiecrat candidate, most southerners did not abandon the Democratic party, and Thurmond carried only four southern states. Wallace carried none, as Truman's veto of the Taft-Hartley Act and his position on civil rights kept labor, northern liberals, and minorities loyal to the party. Most of the West and Midwest voted Democratic. Black voters in Los Angeles, Chicago, and Cleveland played key roles, adding California, Illinois, and Ohio to Truman's electoral votes.

With Congress once again solidly in Democratic hands, Truman hoped that in 1949 he would be able to succeed with his domestic program, which he called the **Fair Deal.** In his inaugural address, Truman again held up the images of the New Deal. He asked for increases in Social Security, public housing, and the minimum wage, the repeal of the Taft-Hartley Act, and the creation of a national health program. He also gave civil rights and federal aid to education a place on the national agenda. Rewarding farmers for their role in his victory, Truman submitted the Brannan Plan, which included federal benefits for small farmers.

Cold War Politics

- What fears and events heightened society's worries about internal subversion, and what choices did politicians make in response to them?
- Why and how did Joseph McCarthy become so powerful by 1952?

Congress responded favorably to Truman's programs in areas already well established by the New Deal: a 65-cent minimum hourly wage, funds for low- and moderate-income housing, and increases in Social Security coverage and payments. Proposals going beyond the scope of the New Deal, however, encountered entrenched, organized opposition. Attacks on the Fair Deal revolved around a time-honored objection: so much government intrusion would move the country down a communististic path. Conservatives emphasized the "Communist" nature of a national health system and government intervention in education. Civil rights legislation was held captive by the

Fair Deal President Truman's plan for legislation on civil rights, fair employment practices, and educational appropriations.

southern wing of the Democratic party, which considered it part of a Communist conspiracy to undermine American unity. Agribusiness leaders and conservatives attacked the Brannan Plan as socialistic and class oriented. One of Truman's aides wrote that "the consuming fear of communism" fostered a widespread belief that change was subversive and that those who supported change were Communists or **fellow-travelers.**

Even before the 1948 election, responding to fears of Communists within the government—fears that Republicans exploited—Truman had moved to beef up the existing loyalty program. Nine days after his Truman Doctrine speech (March 12, 1947), the president issued Executive Order #9835, establishing the Federal Employee Loyalty Program. The order stated that, after a hearing, a federal employee could be fired if "reasonable grounds" existed for believing he or she was disloyal in belief or action. Attorney General Tom Clark provided a lengthy list of subversive organizations, and government administrators screened their employees for membership. Soon supervisors and workers also began to accuse each other of "un-American" thoughts and activities. Between 1947 and 1951, the government discharged more than three thousand federal employees because of their supposed disloyalty. In almost every case, the accused had no right to confront the accusers or to refute evidence. Few of those forced to leave government service were Communists. Fewer still were threats to American security.

The Red Scare

Truman's loyalty program, despite all the discharges, intensified hysteria about an "enemy within." And among those stepping forward to protect the nation from the insidious internal enemy, none were more vicious than the **House Un-American Activities Committee (HUAC)** and **Joseph McCarthy,** Wisconsin's Republican senator. Working with FBI director J. Edgar Hoover, HUAC announced in 1947 its intention to root out communism within the government and society. The committee targeted State Department officials, New Dealers, labor activists, entertainers, writers, educators, and individuals known to have liberal philosophies. Director Hoover proclaimed that there was one American Communist for every 1,814 loyal citizens, and Attorney General Clark warned that Communists were everywhere, "in factories, offices, butcher shops, on street corners, in private businesses," carrying "the germs of death for society."

HUAC made its first Cold War splash with its investigation of Hollywood. The committee's goals were to grab headlines, remove people with liberal, leftist viewpoints from the entertainment industry, and ensure that the mass media promoted American capitalism and traditional American values. Just as World War II had required mobilization of the film industry, committee supporters reasoned, the Cold War necessitated that movies continue to promote the "right" images. With much fanfare, HUAC called Hollywood notables to testify about Communist influence in the industry. Many of those called used the opportunity to strut their patriotism and denounce communism. Actor Ronald Reagan, president of the Screen Actors Guild, denounced Communist methods that "sucked" people into carrying out "red policy without knowing what they are doing" and testified that the Conference of Studio Unions was full of Reds.

Not all witnesses were cooperative. Some who were or had been members of the Communist party, including the "Hollywood Ten," took the Fifth Amendment and lashed out at the activities of the committee. Soon labeled "Fifth Amendment Communists," the ten were jailed for contempt of Congress and blacklisted by the industry. Eric Johnson, the president of the Motion Picture Association, announced that no one would be hired who did not cooperate with the committee. He also stated that there would be no more films like *The Grapes of Wrath* (see page 810), featuring the hardships of poor Americans or "the seamy side of American life." Moviemakers soon produced a new code—*A Screen Guide for Americans*—that demanded, "Don't Smear the Free Enterprise System"; "Don't Deify the Common Man"; "Don't Show That Poverty Is a Virtue."

Anticommunism proved to be a useful weapon for a variety of causes. Manufacturers, including tobacco giant R. J. Reynolds, conducted a multimillion-dollar ad blitz that successfully harnessed

fellow-traveler Someone who sympathizes with or supports the beliefs of the Communist party without being a member.

House Un-American Activities Committee Congressional committee, created in 1938, that investigated suspected Communists during the McCarthy era and that Richard Nixon used to advance his career.

Joseph McCarthy Senator who in 1950 began a Communist witch-hunt that lasted until his censure by the Senate in 1954.

♦ A member of the House Un-American Activities Committee, Congressman Richard M. Nixon gained a national audience by leading the investigation into the allegations that Alger Hiss, one-time New Dealer and State Department official, was a spy for the Soviet Union in the 1930s. In this picture Nixon displays the headline proclaiming Hiss's perjury conviction. The important thing, Nixon later stated, was "we got across the point that Hiss was a spy, a liar, and a Communist." *UPI/Bettmann Archives.*

patriotism and anti-Red hysteria both to defeat CIO efforts to unionize southern industry and to break existing unions throughout the country. Protecting itself from further anti-Red attacks, the CIO expelled eleven unions for having Communist leaders and members. Southerners used anticommunism to fight the civil rights movement. Neighborhoods and communities organized "watch groups" that screened books, movies, and public speakers, and questioned teachers and public officials, seeking to ban or dismiss those considered suspect. In 1949 in Peekskill, New York, "loyal" Americans attacked the concert of singer, actor, and activist Paul Robeson, turning it into a riot (see Individual Choices: Paul Robeson).

Just before the election of 1948, HUAC focused on spies within the government, bringing forth a number of informants who had once been Soviet agents and were now willing to name other Americans who allegedly had sold out the United States. The most sensational revelation came from one of the editors of *Time*, a repentant ex-Communist named Whittaker Chambers. Chambers accused **Alger Hiss,** a New Deal liberal and one-time State Department official who had been with Roosevelt at Yalta, of being a Communist. At first Hiss denied even knowing Chambers, but under questioning by HUAC members, especially Congressman Richard M. Nixon of California, Hiss admitted an acquaintance with Chambers in the 1930s but denied he was or had been a Communist. When Hiss sued Chambers for libel, Chambers escalated the charges. He stated that Hiss had passed State Department secrets to him in the 1930s, and he produced rolls of microfilm that he said Hiss had delivered to him. In a controversial and sensationalized trial, Hiss was found guilty of **perjury** (the statute of limitations on espionage had expired) and was sentenced to five years in prison.

As the nation followed the Hiss case, news of the Communist victory in China and the Soviet explosion of an atomic bomb heightened American fears. Many people believed that such Communist successes could have occurred only with help from American traitors. Congressman Harold Velde of Illinois proclaimed, "our government from the White House down has been sympathetic toward the views of Communists and fellow-travelers, with the result that it has been infiltrated by a network of spies." Congress responded in 1950 by passing, over Truman's veto, the **McCarran Internal Security Act.** The law required all Communists to register with

Alger Hiss State Department official accused in 1948 of being a Communist spy; he was convicted of perjury and sent to prison.

perjury The deliberate giving of false testimony under oath.

McCarran Internal Security Act Law passed by Congress in 1950 requiring Communists to register with the U.S. attorney general and making it a crime to conspire to establish a totalitarian government in the United States.

INDIVIDUAL CHOICES

Speaking Out

Paul Robeson

Paul Robeson was a brilliant actor, opera singer, and civil rights activist. By choosing to support communism, whose principles he thought would advance the cause of social equality, he sacrificed his career and everything else for which he had worked. National Portrait Gallery, Smithsonian Institution/Art Resource, NY.

Paul Leroy Bustill Robeson was exceptional at nearly everything he did. A scholar-athlete, he earned several varsity letters and was named an All-American in football before graduating Phi Beta Kappa from Rutgers in 1919—only its third black graduate. He attended Columbia School of Law and played professional football on weekends to cover living expenses. In 1922, Robeson took his first acting role in a play staged by the Harlem YMCA. He received his law degree the following year, but believing he could do more for African Americans as an actor than as a lawyer, he returned to the theater as an actor and concert singer. Working with playwright Eugene O'Neill, Robeson was cast as the lead in the Broadway production of O'Neill's *The Emperor Jones* and in his controversial new play about interracial marriage, *All God's Chillun Got Wings.* Critics wrote rave reviews, and Robeson was soon one of the most sought-after actors in the United States and Britain. But more than an entertainer, he was an activist—choosing to advocate equal rights, especially for blacks. "The artist must elect to fight for freedom or for slavery. I have made my choice," he explained.

In fighting for freedom, Paul Robeson walked picket lines for striking workers, demonstrated against lynchings and segregation, and refused to work on any stage that practiced segregation. In 1939, he announced he would no

the attorney general and made it a crime to conspire to establish a totalitarian government in the United States. The following year the Supreme Court upheld the **Smith Act** (passed in June 1940) in *Dennis et al. v. United States,* ruling that membership in the Communist party was equivalent to conspiring to overthrow the American government and that no specific act of treason was necessary for conviction.

Congressman Velde's observation about spies seemed proven in February 1950, when English authorities arrested British scientist Klaus Fuchs for passing technical secrets to the Soviet Union. A physicist, Fuchs had worked at Los Alamos, New

Smith Act The Alien Registration Act, passed by Congress in 1940, which made it a crime to advocate or to belong to an organization calling for the overthrow of the government by force or violence.

longer act in movies because the film industry did not allow him to show "the life or express the . . . interests, hopes, and aspirations of the struggling people from whom I come." Also in the 1930s, he spoke out loudly against fascism, entertaining Republican troops in Spain and raising money for Jewish refugees from nazism. In 1934, he visited the Soviet Union and was impressed with Soviet social equality. "I feel like a human being for the first time. . . . Here I am not a Negro but a human being." He told Soviet filmmaker Sergei Eisenstein, "Here . . . I walk in full human dignity."

Despite his activism and his support of liberal causes and the Soviet Union, Robeson's popularity continued to soar. He performed before thousands in the United States and Europe and broke racial barriers everywhere. In 1942, he became the first African American in modern American theater to be cast as Othello. During World War II, he campaigned for war bonds and toured the European theater of operations in the first integrated USO show. But not everyone was tolerant. Even as he patriotically pushed war bonds, the FBI listed his name on its Detain Communist List (DetComList).

With the onset of the Cold War, Robeson's views, especially his refusal to condemn the Soviet Union and its policies, became unacceptable to most Americans and effectively ended his artistic career. Considering him a Communist, the mayor of Peoria, Illinois, canceled his concert in 1947. And in 1949, more than a hundred fans were injured in Peekskill, New York, when an anti-Robeson, anti-Communist mob attacked those who came to hear him. The Peekskill riot was a direct outcome of his statement that blacks would not fight against the Soviet Union "on behalf of those who have oppressed us for generations." From over $100,000 in 1946, his income fell to under $6,000 by 1949.

Considering Robeson an undesirable representative of the country, the State Department took away his passport in 1950. For the next eight years, Robeson was a prisoner in the United States, until the Supreme Court upheld his right as a citizen to travel. Free again, he left for Europe. He also published his autobiography, *Here I Stand*, proclaiming that civil rights should become a mass movement, independent of whites, and urging blacks to become aware of their African heritage.

Ill, he returned from Europe in 1963 and retired in virtual seclusion. By the 1970s, however, Paul Robeson was again popular, recognized and appreciated for his great talents and—despite great personal costs—his advocacy of civil and social rights. At a Carnegie Hall celebration of his 75th birthday, Coretta King, widow of slain civil rights leader Martin Luther King, Jr. (see page 909), remarked that Robeson "had been buried alive because . . . he had tapped the . . . wells of latent militancy among blacks." Unable to attend the gala affair, Robeson sent a simple message from the lyrics of "Old Man River," a song he had sung in 1936 in the musical *Show Boat:*

> *"You can be sure that in my heart I go on singing:*
> *But I keeps laughin' instead of cryin';*
> *I must keep fightin' until I'm dyin'*
> *And Ol' Man River, he just keeps rollin' along!"*

Mexico, on the Manhattan Project (see page 855). Fuchs named an American accomplice, Harry Gold, who in turn named David Greenglass, an army sergeant at Los Alamos. Greenglass then claimed that his sister Ethel and her husband Julius Rosenberg were part of the Soviet atomic spy ring. In a controversial trial, the prosecution alleged that the information obtained and passed to the Soviets by **Ethel and Julius Rosenberg** was largely responsible for the successful Soviet atomic bomb. The Rosenbergs claimed innocence but were convicted of espionage because of the testimony of Gold and Greenglass. During the trial, J. Edgar Hoover asked that

Ethel and Julius Rosenberg Wife and husband who were arrested and tried for conspiracy to commit espionage in 1951 after being accused of passing atomic bomb information to the Soviets; they were executed in 1953.

the death penalty not be considered for Ethel Rosenberg, but both she and her husband were executed in 1953. Soviet documents indicate that Julius Rosenberg was guilty but that Ethel was probably guilty only of being loyal to him.

Joseph McCarthy and the Politics of Loyalty

Feeding on the furor over the enemy within, Senator Joseph McCarthy of Wisconsin emerged at the forefront of the anti-communist movement. He had entered the public arena as a candidate for Congress following World War II. Running for the Senate in 1946, he invented a glorious war record for himself that included the nickname "Tail-gunner Joe" and several wounds—he even walked with a fake limp—to help himself win the election. Some regarded him as among the worst senators in Washington—available to lobbyists, totally lacking moral principles, and absent most of the time. In February 1950, he was looking for an issue on which to focus in his re-election bid. After conferring with friends, he settled on the internal Communist threat as an issue "with sex appeal."

The senator tried his gambit first in Wheeling, West Virginia. He announced to a Republican women's group that the United States was losing the Cold War because of traitors within the government. He claimed to know of 205 Communists working in the State Department. The senator next told a few curious reporters that in reality he had a list of "207 bad risks" in the State Department. McCarthy kept changing the number of people on his list but continued to hammer away at security risks, traitors who he could prove existed in the State Department. But he never produced his list of names for reporters.

McCarthy's accusations were quickly examined by a Senate committee and shown to be at best inaccurate. When the chair of the committee, Democrat Millard Tydings of Maryland, pronounced McCarthy a hoax and a fraud, the Wisconsin senator countered by accusing Tydings of questionable loyalty. During Tydings's 1950 re-election campaign, McCarthy worked for his defeat, spreading false stories and pictures that supposedly showed connections to American Communists, including a faked photograph showing the Democrat talking to Earl Browder, head of the American Communist party. When Tydings lost by forty thousand votes, McCarthy's stature increased. Republicans and conservative Democrats rarely opposed him and frequently supported his wild accusations. The Senate's most powerful Republican, Robert Taft of Ohio, slapped McCarthy on the back saying, "Keep it up, Joe," and sent him the names of State Department officials who merited investigation. Taft encouraged him: "If one case doesn't work out, bring up another."

The outbreak of the Korean War and the reversals at the hands of the Chinese only increased the senator's popularity. Supported by Republican political gains in the 1950 elections, **McCarthyism** became a powerful political and social force. Politicians flocked to the anti-Communist bandwagon, making it ever more difficult for Truman to push his Fair Deal. Federal Trade Commissioner John Carson despaired that liberals "were on the run" and that reactionaries were "winning the fight."

By 1952, Truman's popularity was almost nonexistent: only 24 percent of those who were asked said they approved of his presidency. The Korean Conflict was stalemated, and Republicans were having a field day attacking "cowardly containment" and calling for victory in Korea. The Fair Deal was dead, and Truman had lost control over domestic policy. Compounding his problems, a probe of organized crime by a congressional committee chaired by Tennessee senator **Estes Kefauver** had found scandal, corruption, and links to organized crime within the government. Presidential aide Harry Vaughan and other administration appointees were accused of accepting gifts and selling their influence.

When Truman lost the opening presidential primary in New Hampshire to Kefauver, he withdrew from the race, leaving the Democrats with no clear choice for a candidate. As in 1948, Republicans looked to the November election with great anticipation. At last, they were sure, voters would elect a Republican president—someone who, in Thomas Dewey's opinion, would "save the country from going to Hades in the handbasket of paternalism-socialism-dictatorship."

McCarthyism Attacks by Joseph McCarthy on liberals and others suspected of being Communists or supporters of Communist ideology; often the attacks were based on unsupported assertions and carried out without regard for basic liberties.

Estes Kefauver Tennessee legislator who chaired a series of Senate hearings that exposed nationwide crime syndicates that had links to state and local political machines.

SUMMARY

Expectations
Constraints
Choices
Outcomes

People hoped that the end of World War II would usher in a period of international cooperation and peace. This *expectation* vanished as the world entered the Cold War, a period of armed and vigilant suspicion. To protect the country and the world from Soviet expansion, the United States *chose* to assume a primary economic, political, and military role around the globe. The *outcome* was Truman's containment policy. First applied to Western Europe, it eventually included Asia as the Cold War became a hot war in Korea. By 1952, with the "loss" of China and the stalemate in Korea, Americans turned against Truman's foreign policy. Many thought that the United States was losing the Cold War and that containment was not a strong enough policy to defeat communism and protect American interests.

At home the Cold War had its impact as well, acting as a *constraint* on the expansion of liberalism. Many moderates and conservatives alike *chose* to use the fear of communism to promote their own political, social, and economic interests. They attacked liberals, unions, and civil rights advocates as radicals, fellow-travelers, and Communists. Economic prosperity also reduced public support for further growth of the New Deal as postwar Americans turned their attention toward enjoying the "good life." Politically the *outcome* was mixed. Some existing New Deal–style programs—Social Security, a minimum wage, and farm supports—grew in scope. But initiatives like civil rights and national healthcare, which would have enlarged the federal government's domestic role, were rejected.

As Americans adjusted to postwar life, one major *outcome* was a re-emphasis on home and family. Women experienced strong social pressure to give up their wartime jobs and responsibilities and take up "domestic" life. Marriages and births rose as many Americans *chose* to move to suburbs. While jobs and homeownership multiplied for white males and white families seemed poised to achieve the American dream, minorities found that the *constraints* of discrimination ended or limited many of the economic and social gains they had made during the war. Though pushed out of the work force or into lesser jobs, and still living in a socially segregated society, many nonwhites, joined by some white women, *chose* to resist being cast in customary roles.

SUGGESTED READINGS

Barton Bernstein. *Politics and Policies of the Truman Administration* (1970).

An excellent collection of essays on the Truman administration from a generally critical point of view.

Paul Boyer. *By the Bomb's Early Light: American Thought and Culture at the Dawn of the Atomic Age* (1985).

A useful analysis of the impact of atomic energy and the atomic bomb on American society, from advertising to mock "atomic air bomb drills."

John L. Gaddis. *The United States and the Origins of the Cold War* (1972).

A comprehensive and balanced view of the origins of the Cold War.

Max Hastings. *The Korean War* (1987).

A short, well-written study of the military dimension of the Korean War.

David McCullough. *Truman* (1992).

A highly acclaimed biography of Truman.

Thomas Reeves. *The Life and Times of Joe McCarthy* (1982).

A solid but critical study of Joseph McCarthy and his role in the Red Scare.

Jules Tygiel. *Baseball's Great Experiment: Jackie Robinson and His Legacy* (1983).

Reflections on the life experiences and decisions that brought Jackie Robinson to break the color barrier in professional baseball.

Stephen J. Whitfield. *The Culture of the Cold War* (1991).

A critical account of the impact of the Cold War on the United States that argues that a cultural, social, and political consensus that equated "Americanism" with militant anticommunism dominated American life. Especially useful is the examination of the effect of the Cold War on American social values and popular culture.

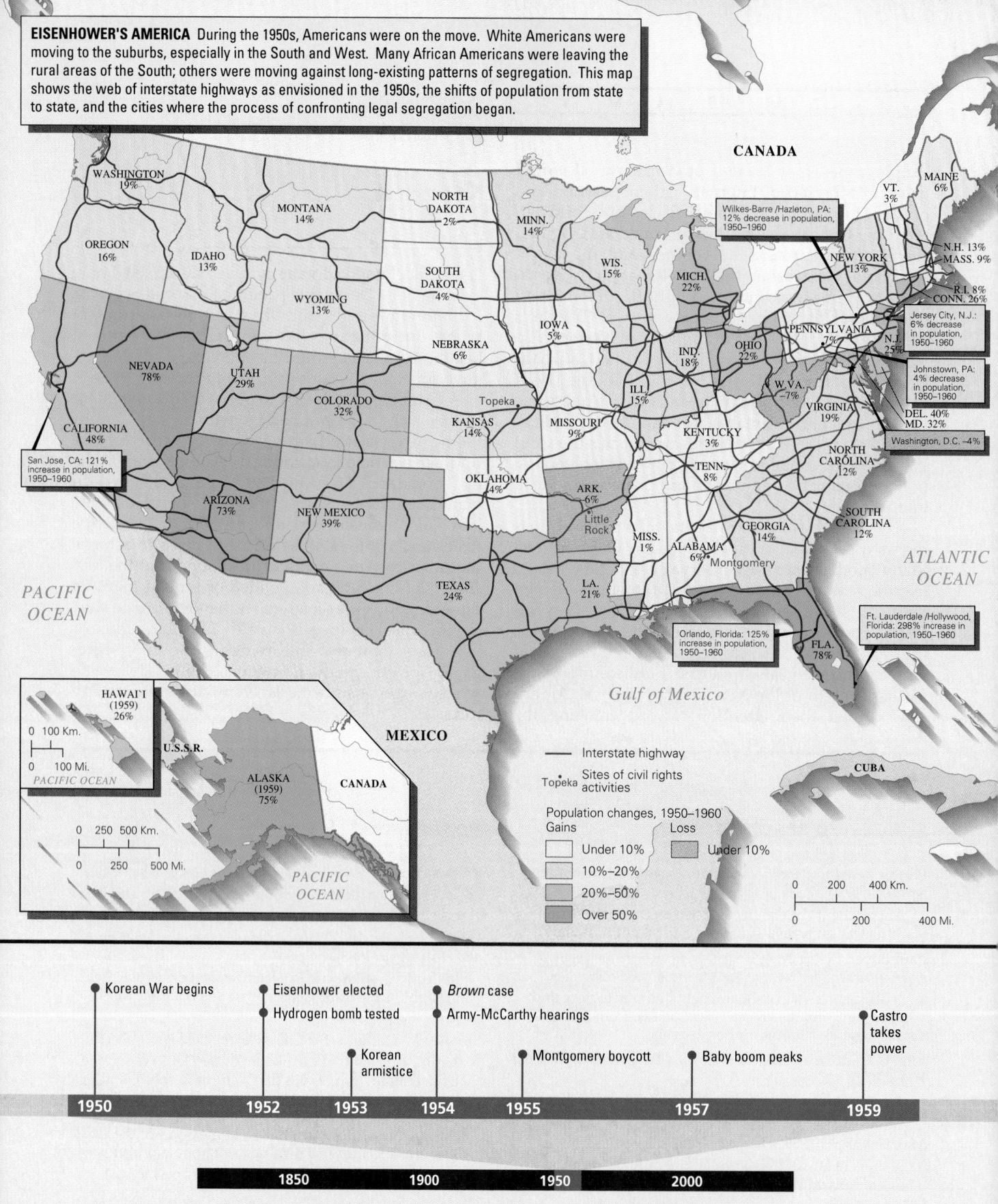

EISENHOWER'S AMERICA During the 1950s, Americans were on the move. White Americans were moving to the suburbs, especially in the South and West. Many African Americans were leaving the rural areas of the South; others were moving against long-existing patterns of segregation. This map shows the web of interstate highways as envisioned in the 1950s, the shifts of population from state to state, and the cities where the process of confronting legal segregation began.

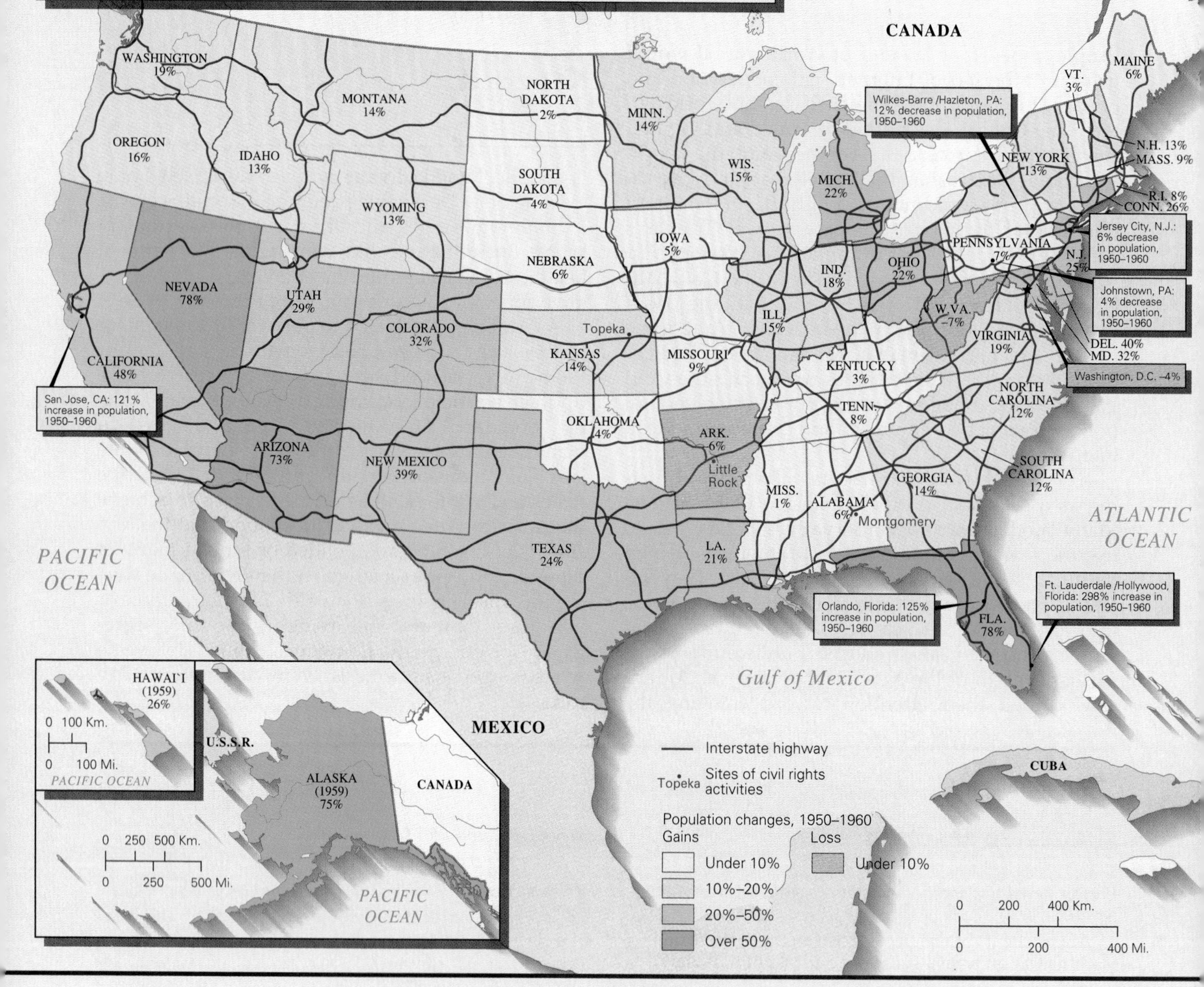

- **1950** Korean War begins
- **1952** Eisenhower elected; Hydrogen bomb tested
- **1953** Korean armistice
- **1954** *Brown* case; Army-McCarthy hearings
- **1955** Montgomery boycott
- **1957** Baby boom peaks
- **1959** Castro takes power

1850 1900 1950 2000

CHAPTER 29

Quest for Consensus, 1952–1960

The Best of Times

- What factors contributed to prosperity in the 1950s?
- What expectations led American middle-class families to embrace suburban culture? What constraints did the critics of that culture condemn?

Politics of Consensus

- What constraints did Eisenhower and other Republicans encounter in trying to roll back the New Deal?
- How did the outcome reflect what Eisenhower called the "middle path"?

Seeking Civil Rights

- How did African-American leaders choose to attack *de jure* segregation in American society during Eisenhower's administration?
- What role did the federal government play in promoting civil rights during the 1950s?
- What constraints strengthened the strategy of confrontation and litigation in shaping the civil rights movement?

Eisenhower and a Hostile World

- What constraints lay behind the New Look?
- What were the weaknesses of "massive retaliation," and how did Eisenhower choose to address them?

INTRODUCTION

Expectations
Constraints
Choices
Outcomes

In 1952, Republicans represented change. A victory by Dwight David Eisenhower ended twenty years of Democratic control of the White House. Many Republicans *expected* Eisenhower's presidency to reverse two "dangerous" trends: creeping socialism in the form of New Deal–style programs and appeasement of communism in the guise of containment. Most people *expected* Eisenhower and a Republican Congress to end the Korean War, to reduce government intervention in social and economic affairs, to expand prosperity by supporting capitalism, and to win some victories in the Cold War. But most of all, Americans *expected* to enjoy their lives to the fullest, in the strongest, most democratic, and most prosperous nation in the world.

The United States of the 1950s seemed to justify this expectation. The country was experiencing one of the longest periods of sustained economic growth in its history, one that in most people's opinion offered every citizen an opportunity to live free from the fear of economic want. This affluent America meshed with the image of a gentle, quiet president who presided over a prosperous nation composed of families that *chose* a stable, suburban life in which the husband worked and the wife raised their children.

For a large segment of the population, this America was real. But not all Americans, even those in the suburbs, led happy, stable, or fulfilling lives. Many men and women were dissatisfied with their roles as husband and father, wife and mother. Dissatisfaction also struck many American youths, who *chose* to reject the values of suburban culture, turning to the driving rhythms of rock 'n' roll and displaying antisocial behavior. At the same time, intellectual and cultural critics condemned the sameness and lack of vitality of the suburban culture. The *outcome* was an American society fragmented by social realities that fed into differing expectations.

Nor did prosperity touch all Americans. For minorities in 1950, the *constraints* against achieving the American dream appeared insurmountable. Poverty, prejudice, and segregation remained the norm. Nevertheless, some groups nurtured *expectations* of change that would open new *choices.* By mid-decade, African Americans were tearing down barriers that blocked their access to the American dream. The *outcome* was a civil rights movement that attacked existing social and legal restrictions and forced government, political parties, and society to confront long-standing contradictions in the country's democratic image.

Like the decade of the 1950s itself, President Eisenhower was more complex than commonly realized at the time. On the surface "Ike" seemed to live up to the popular joke: "What happens when you wind up an Eisenhower doll? Absolutely nothing!" But the real Eisenhower was an effective behind-the-scenes leader who recognized that a political and social consensus accepted the structure of government as shaped by the New Deal. Faced with this *constraint* on any effort to dismantle New Deal–style programs, he *chose* to modify them by cutting spending and reducing government regulations where possible.

In foreign policy, Eisenhower made similar choices. He *chose* to maintain the basic strategy of containment, placing new areas of the globe under an American nuclear umbrella. *Constrained* by his desire to balance the budget, he adopted the New Look, stressing use of atomic weapons, the air force, alliances, and covert activities as foreign policy tools. Thus, responding to political and international constraints established by the Great Depression, World War II, and the Truman years, Eisenhower shaped an *outcome* built on existing patterns of domestic and foreign policy rather than initiating new ones.

CHRONOLOGY

The Fifties

1948 Alfred Kinsey's Sexual Behavior in the Human Male

1950 Korean War begins
David Riesman's The Lonely Crowd

1951 J. D. Salinger's Catcher in the Rye
Mattachine Society formed
Allen Freed's "Moondog's Rock 'n' Roll Party"

1952 Dwight David Eisenhower elected president
Eisenhower visits Korea
United States tests hydrogen bomb

1953 Korean armistice at Panmunjom
Mohammed Mossadegh overthrown in Iran
Joseph Stalin dies
Senator McCarthy investigates USIA
Kinsey's Sexual Behavior in the Human Female
Termination policy for American Indians implemented
Earl Warren appointed chief justice of Supreme Court
Father Knows Best debuts on television
Playboy begins publication

1954 Brown v. Board of Education
St. Lawrence Seaway Act
Federal budget balanced
Army-McCarthy hearings
Jacobo Arbenz overthrown in Guatemala
Gamal Nasser assumes power in Egypt
Battle of Dienbienphu
Geneva Agreement (Vietnam)
SEATO founded

1955 Montgomery bus boycott
Salk vaccine approved for use
AFL-CIO merger
Warsaw Pact formed
McDonald's opens in California
Baghdad Pact formed
Geneva Summit
Eisenhower's Open Skies proposal

1956 Federal Highway Act
Gayle et al. v. Browser
Southern Christian Leadership Conference formed
Eisenhower re-elected
Suez crisis
Soviets invade Hungary
Allen Ginsberg's Howl
Grace Metalious's Peyton Place
Elvis Presley records "Heartbreak Hotel"

1957 Little Rock crisis
Civil Rights Act
Eisenhower Doctrine
United States joins Baghdad Pact
Soviets launch Sputnik I
Jack Kerouac's On the Road
Nevil Shute's On the Beach
Baby boom peaks at 4.3 million births

1958 Anti-U.S. demonstrations in Latin America
Berlin crisis
United States sends troops to Lebanon
National Defense Education Act
NASA established
Nuclear test moratorium

1959 Fidel Castro takes control in Cuba
CENTO formed
Alaska and Hawai`i become states
Nikita Khrushchev visits the United States
Cooper v. Aaron

1960 Soviets shoot down U-2 and capture pilot
Paris Summit

The Best of Times

- What factors contributed to prosperity in the 1950s?
- What expectations led American middle-class families to embrace suburban culture? What constraints did the critics of that culture condemn?

According to the middle-class magazine *Reader's Digest,* in 1954 the average American male stood 5 feet 9 inches tall and weighed 158 pounds. He liked brunettes, baseball, bowling, and steak and french fries. In seeking a wife, he could not decide if brains or beauty was more important, but he definitely wanted a wife who could run a home efficiently. The average female was 5 feet 4 inches tall and weighed 132 pounds. She preferred marriage to career, but she wanted to remove the word *obey* from her marriage vows. Both were enjoying life to the fullest, according to the *Digest,* and buying more of nearly everything. The economy appeared to be bursting at the seams, providing jobs, good wages, a multitude of products, and profits.

The nation's "easy street" was a product of big government, big business, and an expanding population. World War II and the Cold War had created military-industrial-governmental linkages that primed the economy through government spending. National security needs by 1955 accounted for half of the U.S. budget, equaling about 17 percent of the gross national product, and exceeded more than the total net incomes of all American corporations. The connection between government and business went beyond spending, however. Government officials and corporate managers moved back and forth in a vast network of jobs and directorships. Few saw any real conflict of interest. Frequently, cabinet positions and regulatory agencies were staffed by people from the businesses to be regulated. Secretary of Defense Charles E. Wilson, who had been the president of General Motors, voiced the common view: "What was good for our country was good for General Motors and vice versa." It was an era of "new economics," in which, according to a 1952 ad in the *New York Times,* industry's "efforts are not in the selfish interest" but "for the good of many . . . the American way."

Direct military spending was only one aspect of government involvement in the economy. Federal research and development (R&D) funds flowed into colleges and industries, producing not only new scientific and military technology but also a variety of marketable consumer goods, including polyester fabrics, Teflon, and "silly putty."

♦ In the popular culture of the 1950s, one of the most memorable events in any young person's life was the high school prom. Here, on this cover of the *Saturday Evening Post,* painted in 1957 by Norman Rockwell, is a young man in his tuxedo and a young woman in her prom dress having an after-prom milkshake at the local diner. Is that Dad behind the counter? *Courtesy of the Norman Rockwell Family Trust and Curtis Archives.*

Technological advances also increased profits and productivity. Profits doubled between 1948 and 1958, with 574 of the largest corporations making nearly 53 percent of all business income. Over the same time, worker productivity climbed 35 percent, despite an overall decline in the industrial work force. Many small companies, however, could not afford to keep up with technology and **automation.** During the 1950s, more than four thousand mergers took place as large corporations swallowed up less-well-off competitors. By 1960 only 5 percent of American corporations were generating 90 percent of corporate income. Meanwhile, the number of American multinational corporations increased as American firms constructed plants overseas, closer to growing markets and cheaper labor.

automation A process or system designed to allow equipment to function automatically; one outcome of automation is the replacement of workers with machines.

The "new economics" also witnessed a different attitude within the work force and organized labor. Following negotiations between the United Automobile Workers and General Motors in 1948, a new kind of contract became popular. In seeking these "postwar contracts," unions focused on getting better pensions, cost-of-living raises, and paid vacations for their members, giving up efforts to gain some control over the workplace and production. Salaries for industrial workers increased steadily from about $55 a week in 1950 to nearly $80 in 1960. While wages rose, inflation remained low, and unemployment—except for brief **recessions** in 1953 and 1958—hovered at around 4 percent. Despite favorable contracts, however, union membership remained stable, at about 18.5 million, even after the merger of the AFL and the CIO in 1955. As a percentage of the work force, union membership fell from 35.5 percent in 1950 to about 32 percent in 1960. Despite their shrinking percentage of the work force, unions made little effort to organize agricultural workers, the growing number of white-collar workers, or people working in the economically booming **Sunbelt.**

Not everyone benefited from the growing economy. Agricultural and minority wages remained well below the national average, and unemployment for minorities remained at about 10 percent. But for those able to reach the fruits of prosperity, life seemed good. One economist bragged that most Americans had access to a quality of life "in which not even the rich rejoiced a century ago." For many Americans, that quality of life was best experienced in the suburbs.

Suburban and Consumer Culture

People wanted to live in the suburbs, and all levels of government tried to make living there easy. Counties and cities changed **zoning laws** to ease construction of suburban housing developments and shopping centers. State and local governments helped developers spend millions to connect workplaces, schools, parks, and shopping centers with suburban homes. Along with the streets went water systems, electricity, and sewer systems. The **Federal Highway Act of 1956** provided $32 billion over thirteen years to build a national highway system that not only linked the nation together but also improved access to an expanding number of suburbs surrounding cities. Originally projected to consist of 41,000 miles of federal highway, the interstate highway system by 1980 had opened 33,796 miles of interstate highways to traffic, but the cost had nearly tripled.

The housing trend begun after the Second World War accelerated in the 1950s, so that by 1960, more than 214 million single-family homes had been built since 1945. Many of them were grouped into planned suburban communities. One such development—the first to have a garbage disposal built into each kitchen sink—was Lakewood, California, advertised as the "perfect place to raise children." Planners provided not only homes with large backyards, but also elementary schools, parks, swimming pools, and small shopping areas for each neighborhood. Unifying the neighborhoods were the high school and a major shopping center. When in 1960 "the Center" scored a major success by opening an upscale department store, the high school's band and cheerleaders highlighted the opening ceremony. For the residents of white Lakewood, it seemed that life could only get better year after year.

As Americans sought the pleasant life of suburbia, many cities deteriorated at an accelerating rate. Following the middle class and part of the working class into the suburbs, shopping centers lured stores and businesses to areas where parking was not a problem. As freeways crisscrossed cities, vast areas of land became concrete wastelands. In south and east-central Los Angeles, freeway interchanges gobbled up 10 percent of the housing space and divided neighborhoods and families.

Shrinking tax bases, eroded by the departure of homeowners, businesses, and shoppers, made it difficult for cities to afford to maintain services, buildings, and mass transportation. Growing use of automobiles damaged roads, left railroad stations largely deserted and in disrepair, and added to noise and air pollution. Programs to rebuild homes in cities rarely succeeded in meeting the needs of the poor who increasingly made up the urban core's population.

recession A decline in the economy that is less severe than a depression.

Sunbelt A region stretching from Florida in a westward arc to the state of Washington.

zoning laws Local regulations that limit particular types of buildings, such as residences, businesses, or factories, to specified sections of a city or town.

Federal Highway Act Law passed by Congress in 1956 appropriating $32 billion for the construction of interstate highways.

♦ As Americans took to their automobiles in the 1950s, a variety of businesses, especially motels and eateries, sprang up alongside highways and interstates. The drive-in and diner became fixtures of the American landscape. In this picture, a California drive-in used automation to replace waitresses. As you can see, food is being delivered to each car by a conveyer belt. *FPG.*

According to the 1960 census, across the nation suburbia was 98 percent white, and minorities were becoming majorities in many major cities, including Washington, D.C., and Atlanta.

The automobile industry benefited from and contributed to the development of both roads and suburbs. By 1960, 75 percent of all Americans had at least one car, increasing the pressure on governments and businesses to consider the needs of automobile owners. New industries arose to service the needs of automobile-borne consumers—amusement parks like Disneyland, miniature golf courses, drive-in theaters, and fast-food restaurants. The McDonald's chain, begun in San Bernardino, California, in 1955 by entrepreneur Ray Kroc, sold a standardized hamburger for 15 cents and changed the eating habits of America.

The suburban market was a result of expanding purchasing power made possible by higher wages and ready credit. Why pay cash when consumer credit was available? The Diner's Club credit card made its debut in 1950 and was soon followed by American Express and a host of other plastic cards. Credit purchases leaped from $8.4 billion in 1946 to more than $44 billion in 1958. Americans were buying not only "necessities" like washing machines, cars, and televisions but also an ever-expanding array of other products: high-fidelity record players and records, patio furniture, and toys and recreational equipment (see Table 29.1). Many of these nonessential items, and even some of the basic goods, incorporated a new dimension of marketing—**planned obsolescence,** in which a product is designed to be discarded and replaced by a newer model within a short period of time. The automobile industry was especially good at changing styles or adding gadgets to cars every few years to encourage people to trade in their old model and buy a new and better one.

To sell products, advertisers continued to use images of youth, glamour, sex appeal, and sophistication. In the forefront of the advertising onslaught was the tobacco industry, persuading people that smoking cigarettes was a stylish way to relax from the rigors of work and family. When medical reports surfaced about health risks connected to smoking, the tobacco giants intensified their advertising and stressed that new, longer, filtered cigarettes were milder and posed no health hazard. Cigarette advertising increased 400 percent between 1945 and 1960, whereas advertising in general increased "only" a little more than 250 percent.

Family Culture

Many Americans were sure that the 1950s was the best of all possible times. At the center of those feel-

planned obsolescence Practice of designing consumer goods to last or be fashionable for only a short time, guaranteeing purchase of a replacement.

TABLE 29.1 Consumer Prices, July 1955

Rye bread	$ .20 a loaf
Apples	.19 for 2 pounds
Bananas	.15 a pound
Round steak	.70 a pound
Chicken fryers	.49 a pound
Wheaties	.43 for two boxes
Clorox	.19 a bottle
Coffee	.91 a pound
Margarine (oleo)	.45 for 2 pounds
Sugar	.49 for 5 pounds
Flour	.95 for 10 pounds
Frozen orange juice	1.00 for 8, 6-ounce cans
Lifebuoy soap	.28 for 3 cakes
Milk	.23 a quart
Kodak Brownie camera	13.65
Portable, B & W 14-inch television set	120.00
Refrigerator	519.95
Oldsmobile 88 automobile	2381.62
"Scrabble" game	2.39

Source: Data from *Observer-Reporter,* Washington, PA, July 1955.

ings lay the economy, the home, the family, and the church. Religion, with an emphasis on family life, enjoyed new popularity. Church attendance rose to 59.5 percent in 1953, a historic high. Religious leaders were rated as the most important members of society, and those who used television to reach huge audiences were among the most respected and popular. Such preachers stressed positive, religious, patriotic, and anti-Communist pronouncements. In 1954, the **Reverend Norman Vincent Peale** was named one of the nation's ten most successful salesmen. In keeping with the spirit of the times, Congress added "under God" to the Pledge of Allegiance in 1954, and "In God We Trust" to the American currency in 1955. Not every church leader was pleased with being regarded as a salesman. Some theologians and philosophers like Reinhold Niebuhr and Paul Tillich worried that churches were softening their theology to attract parishioners and that Americans selected churches more on the basis of the music and activities than the religious teaching.

After the disruptions of Depression and war, family took on a renewed importance. The divorce rate slowed and the numbers of marriages and births climbed—the baby boom continued (see page 878), peaking at 403 million births in 1957. The popular image of the ideal place for women was in the home raising children. Those not eager to rush into wedded bliss were suspected of being homosexual, neurotic, emotionally immature, too involved in a career, or irresponsible. For guidance on how to raise babies and children, millions of Americans turned to Dr. Benjamin Spock's popular book *Baby and Child Care.* A mother's love and positive parental examples were seen as keys to raising healthy, well-adjusted children. Strict rules and corporal punishment were to be avoided. Equally widespread was the view that, to ensure proper sex identity among children, boys should participate in sports and outdoor activities and girls should concentrate on their appearance and domestic skills. Toy guns and doctor bags were for boys; dolls, tea sets, and nurse kits were for girls. Conforming—being part of the group—was as important for children as it was for their parents. At college, many students became

Reverend Norman Vincent Peale Minister who told his congregations that positive thinking could help them overcome all their troubles in life.

NEW WHEATIES OUTDOOR LIVING SWEEPSTAKES
WIN EVERY PRIZE IN THIS PICTURE!

♦ "No jingles to write . . . no boxtops to mail!"—just enter and win a chunk of the American dream, as the "new and improved" Wheaties offered everyone a chance to enjoy life to the fullest in the "great outdoors" by winning the products in this picture. From a 16-foot boat, to golf clubs, and charcoal brazier, what family's life would not be enriched by owning these symbols of affluent America? *Collection of Picture Research Consultants.*

part of the **silent generation,** enjoying a social life that centered around fraternities and **sock hops,** and hoping for corporate jobs and marriage after graduation. A college dean described the perfect student as one who had "an 80 or 85 average . . . and plenty of extracurricular activities." This educator had little use for the "brilliant introvert."

The home was the center of "togetherness," defined in 1954 by *McCall's* magazine and portrayed in popular television shows like *Leave It to Beaver* (1957) and *Father Knows Best* (1953). The ideal middle-class TV families were white, lived in all-white neighborhoods, and had hardworking fathers and attractive, savvy mothers who shared household chores. Their children, usually numbering between two and four, did well in school, were not overly concerned about the future, and provided the usually humorous dilemmas that Mom's common sense and sensitivity untangled. Reality, however, rarely duplicated television's images of togetherness.

Another View of Suburbia

Unlike the wives shown on television, more and more married women were working outside the home even though they had young children. Some desired careers, but the majority worked to safeguard their family's existing **standard of living.** The percentage of middle-class women who worked for wages rose from 7 percent in 1950 to 25 percent in 1960. Most held part-time jobs or sales clerk and clerical positions that paid low wages and provided few benefits (see Figure 29.1). Women represented 46 percent of the banking work force—filling most secretary, teller, and receptionist slots—but held only 15 percent of upper-level positions.

Nor were all homemakers happy with togetherness. A study of husband and wife cooperation found that of eighteen household chores, men were willing to do three—lock up at night, do yard work, and make repairs—leaving fifteen other routine tasks to the woman. Other surveys discovered that more than one-fifth of suburban wives were unhappy with their marriages and lives. Many women complained of the drudgery and boredom of housework and the lack of understanding and affection from their husbands. Women were also more sexually active than generally thought, shattering the image of loyal wife and mother. Research on women's sexuality conducted by **Alfred Kinsey** and described in his book *Sexual Behavior in the Human Female* (1953) indicated that a majority of American women had had sexual intercourse before marriage and 25 percent were having affairs while married.

Men also showed signs of being less than satisfied with the popular role of suburban Dad. In 1953, Hugh Hefner first published *Playboy,* urging men to break away from the boring middle-class, husband-father image and cater to their own pleasures. The popularity of *Playboy* and other "men's magazines" grew with the decade. Reflecting the shadier side of middle-class life in fiction, the best-selling novel *Peyton Place* (1956), by Grace Metalious, set America buzzing over the licentious escapades of the resi-

silent generation Name applied to the young people who came of age in the 1950s, because of their perceived complacency and lack of political involvement.

sock hop A party or dance at which teens took off their shoes and danced in their socks in order not to damage the floor of the school gym, where such dances were usually held.

standard of living Level of material comfort as measured by the goods, services, and luxuries currently available.

Alfred Kinsey Biologist whose studies of human sexuality attracted great attention in the 1940s and 1950s, especially for his conclusions on infidelity and homosexuality.

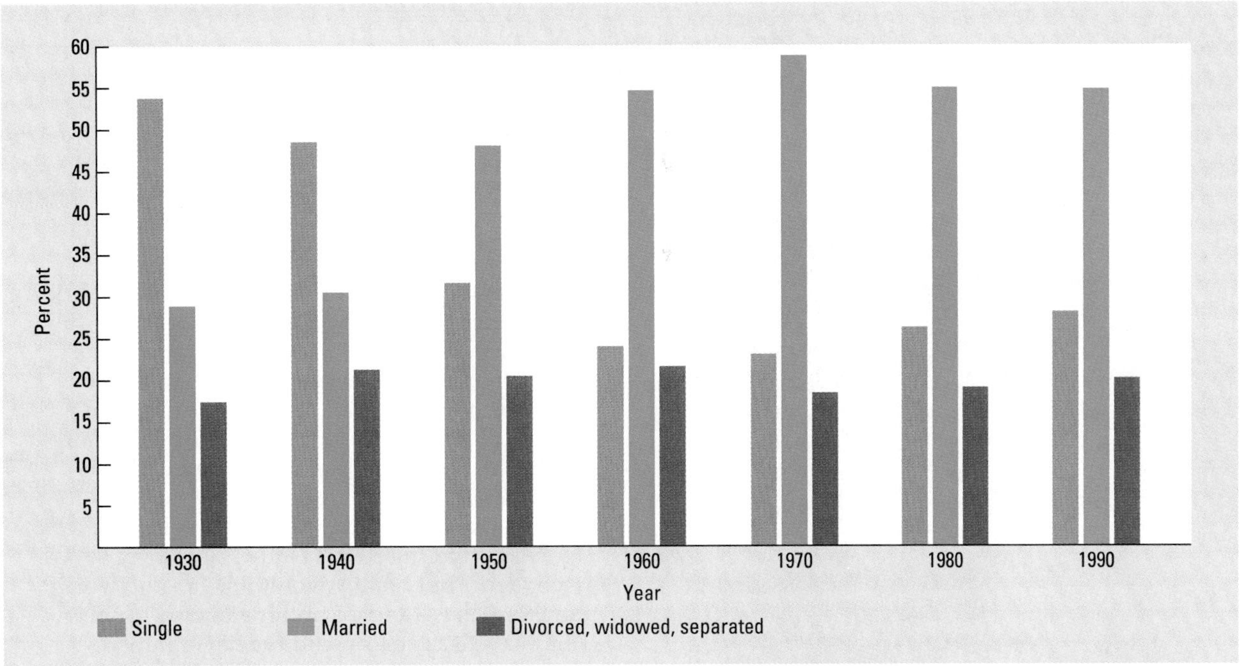

♦ **FIGURE 29.1 Marital Status of Women in the Work Force, 1930–1990** This figure shows the percentage of women in the work force from the Great Depression through 1990. While the number of women who fall into the category of divorced, widowed, and separated remained fairly constant, there was a significant shift in the number of single and married women in the work force, with the number of single women declining as the number of married women increased. *Source:* U.S. Department of Commerce, *Historical Statistics of the United States, Colonial Times to 1970,* Vol. I (Washington, D.C.: U.S. Government Printing Office, 1970), pp. 20–21, 131–132; and U.S. Department of Commerce, *Statistics of the United States, 1993* (Washington, D.C.: U.S. Government Printing Office, 1993), pp. 74, 399.

dents of a quiet town in traditionally staid New England. Hollywood kept pace with stars like **Marilyn Monroe.** Starting in 1952, the "blonde bombshell" was repeatedly cast in slightly dumb but very sexy roles in which she was usually romanced by slightly older, more worldly men.

Americans seemed to consider sex symbols in the movies and men's magazines as a minor threat to the image of family, community, and nation. Homosexuality, however, was another matter. Many people believed it threatened the moral and social fabric of society. Kinsey's 1948 study of male sexuality shocked readers by claiming that nearly 8 percent of the population lived a gay lifestyle and that homosexuality existed throughout American society. An increasingly open gay subculture that centered around gay bars in every major city seemed to support his findings.

In a postwar society that emphasized the traditional family and feared internal subversion, homosexuals represented a double threat. A Senate investigating committee concluded that because of sexual perversions and lack of moral fiber, one homosexual could "pollute a Government office." Responding to such views, the Eisenhower administration barred homosexuals from most government jobs. Taking their cue from the federal government, state and local authorities intensified their efforts to control homosexuals and, if possible, purge them from society. **Vice squads** made frequent raids on gay and lesbian

Marilyn Monroe American actress who became an icon, famous for her blonde hair, her sex appeal, and her vulnerability; she died apparently by suicide in 1962, at the age of 36.

vice squad Police unit charged with the enforcement of laws dealing with vice—that is, immoral practices such as gambling and prostitution.

INDIVIDUAL CHOICES

Rejecting Consensus

Allen Ginsberg

Allen Ginsberg was born in Paterson, New Jersey, in 1926. He graduated from Columbia University, then moved to San Francisco. Dissatisfied with his traditional job and lifestyle, he chose to stop working and start writing poetry. Eventually, he became one of the leading Beat poets and voices of his generation. Robert Kelley, LIFE magazine, ©Time Warner, Inc.

In the mid-1950s, Allen Ginsberg left New York for California. "I had passed one session of my life," he remembered, "and it was time to start all over again." In the San Francisco area, he took a job with a small market-research firm and explored poetry, but he was not personally satisfied. He sought psychotherapy, and psychiatrist Philip Hicks asked him what he would like to do. "Doctor, I don't think you're going to find this very healthy," Ginsberg responded, "but I really would like to stop working forever . . . and do nothing but write poetry and have leisure to spend the day outdoors and go to museums and see friends. And I'd like to keep living with someone—maybe even a man—and explore relationships." Hicks said, "Do it." Making his choice, Ginsberg established a long-term relationship with Peter Orlovsky, retired from work, and wrote his first long-lined poem, *Howl.*

Howl—a semi-autobiographical cry of outrage and despair against a destructive and abusive society that worships Moloch, the god of materialism and conventionality—exploded on American society in 1956:

Moloch whose mind is pure machinery!
Moloch whose blood is running money!
Moloch whose fingers are ten armies!
Moloch whose heart is a cannibal dynamo!

bars, and newspapers often listed the names, addresses, and employers of those arrested. In response to the virulent attacks, many took extra efforts to hide their homosexuality, but some organized to confront the attacks. In Los Angeles, Henry Hay formed the Mattachine Society in 1951 to fight for homosexual rights, and in San Francisco in 1955, Del Martin and Phyllis Lyon organized a similar organization for lesbians, the Daughters of Bilitis.

Also viewed as extreme were the **Beats,** or "beatniks," a group of often controversial artists, poets, and writers. Allen Ginsberg, in his poem *Howl* (1956), and Jack Kerouac, in his novel *On the Road* (1957), graphically denounced American materialism and **sexual repression** and glorified a freer,

Beats Group of American writers, poets, and artists in the 1950s, including Jack Kerouac and Allen Ginsberg, who rejected traditional middle-class values and championed nonconformity and sexual experimentation.

sexual repression Strict control that prevents the natural development or expression of the sex drive.

Moloch whose love is endless oil and stone!
Moloch whose soul is electricity and banks!

At the end of the poem, Ginsberg celebrates his victory over Moloch's control of his conventional identity.

Howl not only rejected traditional American values but immediately became a target of censorship by San Francisco authorities, who claimed that the poem was obscene and pornographic. Almost as soon as it was published, San Francisco police arrested its publisher, Lawrence Ferlinghetti, and sought to confiscate existing copies of the poem. In the obscenity trial that followed, a parade of respected poets and literary critics testified that the poem had merit, forcing the judge to declare it was not obscene. *Howl* and the furor over it promptly established a virtually unknown author as a leading Beat poet.

An opponent of social norms, Ginsberg believed it was necessary to save the nation by rejecting conventionality and calling on the people to discover their true spirits. Interviewed by the *Village Voice* newspaper in 1959, he argued that recent history was "a vast conspiracy to impose . . . a level of mechanical consciousness" on humankind and that the "suppression of contemplative individuality" was nearly complete. Fortunately, according to Ginsberg, "a few individuals, poets, have had the luck and courage . . . to glimpse something new through the crack of mass consciousness" and "have entered the world of Spirit" to battle "an America gone mad with materialism, a police-state America, a sexless and soulless America."

Ginsberg became the model for Beat writers—writing in the language of the streets about unliterary topics—and fulfilled the popular expectations of the "hipster" beatnik. As the fifties dissolved into the sixties, Ginsberg and his apartment in San Francisco's Haight-Ashbury neighborhood became a center of the counterculture. He coined the term *flower power,* while advocating spirituality and individual freedom induced by using psychedelic drugs and practicing Asian philosophies and Buddhism. Opposed to the war in Vietnam, he asked antiwar protesters to demonstrate for peace, but peacefully, arguing that flowers, bells, and chants would overcome jeers and oppression. In 1967, he organized the first "Gathering of the Tribes for a Human Be-In" in San Francisco. It was the first of hundreds of counterculture festivals.

As a poet, Ginsberg chose to write about his political and social concerns, attacking what he described as the evil forces in society. In 1973, his *The Fall of America, 1965–1971* presented Moloch in the guise of the war in Vietnam, nuclear energy, threats to the environment, and America's rampant materialism. It won a National Book Award. From the obscenity trial to prestigious literary awards, the outcome of Allen Ginsberg's choice is a literary Horatio Alger story about a "dirty" Beat poet—a hipster predicted to self-destruct—who became one of the country's best and best-known modern poets and "the biographer of his time." Alan Ginsberg died in 1997.

natural life with little social or self-restriction (see Individual Choices: Allen Ginsberg). Although some college students found the beatnik critique of "square America" meaningful, most Americans had few qualms about condemning the Beats' message and lifestyles. In an article in *Life* magazine in 1959, Paul O'Neil described beatniks as smelly, dirty people in beards and sandals, who were "sick little bums" and "hostile little females."

Most Americans could justify the suppression of beatniks and homosexuals because they appeared to reject traditional values of family and community. Other critics of American society, however, were more difficult to dismiss. Several respected writers and intellectuals claimed that the suburban and consumer culture was destructive—stifling diversity and individuality in favor of conformity. Mass-produced homes, meals, toys, fashions, and the other trappings of suburban life, they said, created a gray sameness about Americans. Sociologist David Riesman argued in *The Lonely Crowd* (1950) that postwar Americans, unlike earlier generations, were "outer-directed"—less sure of their values and morals and overly concerned about fitting into a group.

Peer pressure, Riesman suggested, had replaced individual thinking. In *The Organization Man* (1955) William H. Whyte, Jr., examined a Chicago suburb and found the same lack of individuality and independence. Both authors urged readers to resist being packaged like cake mixes and reassert their own identities.

Serious literature also highlighted a sense of alienation from the conformist society. Much of Sylvia Plath's poetry and her novel *The Bell Jar* (1963) reflect those forces, especially as they affected women torn between the demands of society and the quest for individual freedom. Similar themes were central to many contemporary novels, including Saul Bellow's *Henderson the Rain King* (1959), Sloan Wilson's *The Man in the Gray Flannel Suit* (1955), and J. D. Salinger's *Catcher in the Rye* (1951), whose hero Holden Caulfield concludes that the major features of American life are all phony. Sociologist C. Wright Mills went further and attacked the structure of American politics and prosperity. In *The Power Elite* (1956), he wrote that the United States was falling under the control of an interlocking elite of government bureaucrats and military, corporate, and labor, leaders that made real democracy in America a fiction.

♦ In 1954, Elvis Presley's first record was released and within a year a new rock'n'roll star had burst onto the music scene. Elvis's style blended rhythm and blues, country, and gospel into a unique sound that along with his body language, created an American icon. *Michael Barson Collection/Past Perfect.*

The Trouble with Kids

Any threat to suburban culture posed by beatniks and gays was largely imaginary. But juvenile delinquency was another matter. Juvenile crime and gangs, especially among the urban poor, were not new to American society, but in the 1950s many observers saw an alarming new style of delinquency among white, middle-class, suburban teens. To most parents, the violent crime associated with inner-city gangs was not as troublesome as teenage disrespect for adults and teens running amok in cars in pursuit of amusement, which often involved alcohol and sex. One study of middle-class delinquency concluded that the automobile not only allowed teens to escape adult controls but also provided "a private lounge for drinking and for petting or sex episodes." Yet the availability of the automobile was only one of many causes cited for youthful misbehavior. Others were **rock 'n' roll,** comic books, television, and lack of proper family upbringing. The film *Rebel Without a Cause,* (1955) featured three new, soon-to-be-major teen stars—James Dean, Sal Mineo, and Natalie Wood—whose rebellious characters came from atypical suburban homes. In one of these families, gender roles were reversed: audiences saw a dominating mother and a father who cooked and assumed many traditional housewifely duties. To the adult audience, the message was clear: an "improper" family environment bred juvenile delinquents.

The problem with kids also seemed wedded to rock 'n' roll. Cleveland disc jockey Alan Freed coined the term in 1951. He had noticed that white teens were buying rhythm-and-blues (R&B) records popular among African Americans, but he also knew that few white households would listen to a radio

rock 'n' roll Style of music that developed out of rhythm-and-blues in the 1950s, with a fast beat and lyrics appealing to teenagers.

program playing "black music." Freed decided to play the least sexually suggestive of the R&B records and call the music rock 'n' roll. His radio program, "Moondog's Rock 'n' Roll Party," was a smash hit. Quickly the barriers between "black music" and "white music" began to blur as white singers copied and modified R&B songs to produce **cover records.**

Cover artists like Pat Boone and Georgia Gibbs sold millions of records that avoided suggestive lyrics and were heard on hundreds of radio stations that had refused to play the original versions created by black artists. By mid-decade, African-American artists like **Chuck Berry,** Little Richard, and Ray Charles were successfully "crossing over" and being heard on "white" radio stations. At the same time, white artists, including 1956's most dynamic star, **Elvis Presley,** were making their own contributions. Beginning with "Heartbreak Hotel" in 1956, Presley recorded fourteen gold records within two years. In concerts, he drove his audiences into frenzies with sexually suggestive movements that earned him the nickname "Elvis the Pelvis."

Some sociologists argued that because of its roots in lower-class, especially African-American, society, rock 'n' roll glamorized behavior that led to crime and delinquency. Blaming rock 'n' roll for a decline in morals, if not civilization, a Catholic Youth Center newspaper asked readers to "smash" rock 'n' roll records because they promoted "a pagan concept of life." But such opponents were waging a losing battle. Rock 'n' roll continued to surge in popularity, and by the end of the decade Dick Clark's *American Bandstand,* a weekly television show featuring teens dancing to rock 'n' roll, was one of the nation's most-watched and most-accepted programs.

Politics of Consensus

- What constraints did Eisenhower and other Republicans encounter in trying to roll back the New Deal?
- How did the outcome reflect what Eisenhower called the "middle path"?

In 1952, Republicans expected finally to end the Democrats' twenty-year hold on the White House. The lingering war in Korea and the soft-on-communism label, along with revelations of government corruption and low ratings in the polls, convinced Truman to retire. Eventually, Democrats nominated Illinois governor **Adlai E. Stevenson,** who not only carried Truman's political handicaps but also added his own. Recently divorced, Stevenson was widely regarded as too intellectual and too liberal.

♦ In this picture, the triumphant Republican nominees for the White House pose with smiles and wives—Pat Nixon and Mamie Eisenhower. Seen as a statesman and not a politician during the campaign, Eisenhower worked hard to ensure his nomination over Robert Taft, and then chose Richard Nixon to balance the ticket because he was a younger man, a westerner, and a conservative. *UPI Bettmann Archives.*

Crying, "It was time for a change," Republicans selected the politically inexperienced General Dwight David Eisenhower. "Ike" appeared to be the perfect candidate. He was well known, revered as a war hero, and carried the image of an honest man thrust into public service. In truth, Eisenhower wanted to be president and, supported by moderate Republicans, skillfully outmaneuvered conservative

cover record A new version of a song already recorded by an original artist.

Chuck Berry African-American rock musician and composer whose songs chronicled teenage experiences and sentiments and who helped establish rock 'n' roll in the 1950s.

Elvis Presley Immensely popular rock 'n' roll musician from a poor white family in Mississippi; many of his songs and concert performances were considered sexually suggestive.

Adlai E. Stevenson Illinois governor who became the Democratic candidate for president in 1952 and 1956 and lost both times to Eisenhower.

Senator Robert Taft of Ohio for the nomination. Eisenhower chose Richard M. Nixon of California as his vice-presidential running mate. Nixon was young and had risen rapidly in the party because of his outspoken anticommunism and his aggressive role in the investigation of Alger Hiss (see page 885).

The Republican campaign took two paths. One concentrated on the popular image of Eisenhower. Republicans introduced "spot commercials" on television, aired in the middle of popular shows like *I Love Lucy.* Stressing Ike's honesty, integrity, and "American-ness," the ads proved to be extremely effective. Public appearances were much the same. Eisenhower crusaded for high standards and good government and posed as another George Washington. A war-weary nation applauded his promise to go to Korea "in the cause of peace." The second campaign path was taken by McCarthy, Nixon, and others who brutally attacked the Democrats' Cold War and New Deal record. Proudly boasting that there were "no Communists in the Republican Party," they called the containment policy cowardly and promised to roll back communism. They also vowed to end the liberal spending of the Democrats and dismantle the New Deal.

With a smile as powerful as Franklin Roosevelt's grin, Eisenhower buried Stevenson in popular (55 percent) and electoral (442 to 89) votes (see Map 29.1). Ike's broad political coattails ensured a Republican majority in Congress. Four years later, the 1956 presidential election was a repeat of 1952, with Eisenhower receiving 457 electoral votes and again swamping Stevenson. But in 1956, the Republican victory was Eisenhower's alone, as Democrats maintained their 1954 majorities in both houses of Congress.

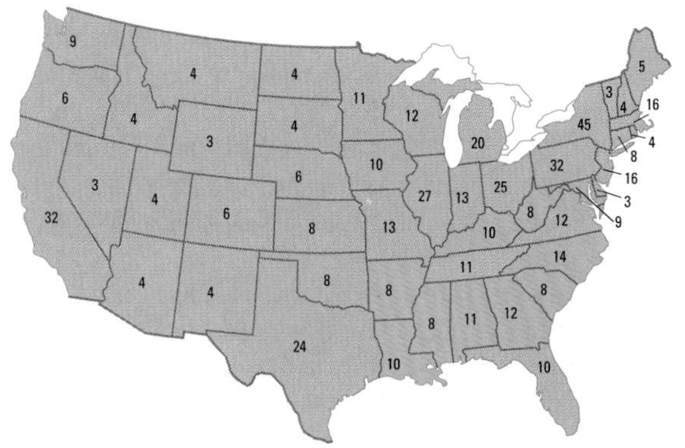

	Electoral Vote		Popular Vote	
Dwight D. Eisenhower (Republican)	442	83%	33,936,234	55%
Adlai E. Stevenson (Democrat)	89	17%	27,314,992	44%

♦ **MAP 29.1 Election of 1952** Dwight David Eisenhower and the Republicans swept into office in 1952. Leading the ticket, Eisenhower swamped his Democratic opponent Adlai Stevenson with 83 percent of the electoral vote and 55 percent of the popular vote. Republicans also won majorities in both houses of Congress. In the 1956 presidential election, Eisenhower beat Stevenson by even larger margins, but Democrats regained majority status in Congress.

The Middle Path

The presidential victory of 1952 placed in office two Eisenhowers: one public, one private. The public Eisenhower was Ike, a warm, friendly, slightly bumbling, grandfather figure. He was the personification of calm and stability in a nation seeking soothing, consensus-type solutions. He sometimes seemed almost an absentee president, often leaving the government in the hands of Congress and his cabinet while he played golf or bridge. The other Eisenhower had no intention of being an absentee president. He oversaw the formation and implementation of most policies, but he did so from behind the scenes in what has been labeled the "hidden-hand presidency." In military fashion, Eisenhower relied on his staff to provide a full discussion of any issue. We had a "good growl," he would say after especially heated cabinet talks. Willing to let subordinates receive credit and praise for policy, Eisenhower expected them to shoulder blame and responsibility as well. He was impressed by successful businesspeople, and the majority of his cabinet and other appointments came from the ranks of business. Few had political connections or any governmental administrative experience.

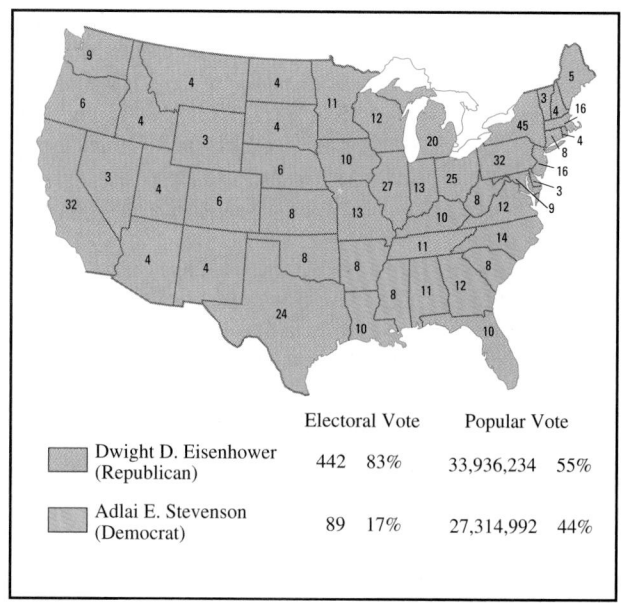

Eisenhower called himself a modern Republican and wanted to follow a "middle course" that was "conservative when it comes to money and liberal when it comes to human beings." The president's first priority was the budget, and he considered the balanced budgets of 1954 and 1960 as two of his greatest achievements. Facing Truman's projected deficits for 1952 and 1953, Eisenhower knew it was necessary to end the war in Korea and make substantial cuts in the defense budget.

Fulfilling his campaign pledge, President-elect Eisenhower flew to Korea in December 1952 for a three-day visit. After visiting the front line to get a feel for the war, he was convinced that a negotiated peace was the only solution to the conflict. The problem was how to persuade the North Koreans and Chinese that such a settlement would be in their best interests.

To prod the Communists, after his inauguration Eisenhower used the aggressive images of liberation that had been part of his election campaign. Through public and private channels, he and his secretary of state **John Foster Dulles** implied that the United States would escalate the war and use atomic weapons unless a negotiated settlement was soon reached. By July 1953, the "atomic diplomacy" had worked. A truce signed at Panmunjom ended the fighting, brought home almost all the troops, and left Korea divided by a **demilitarized zone.**

With the war in Korea over, Eisenhower was able—despite much foot dragging by the military and legislators from both parties—to significantly reduce military spending and achieve a balanced budget by 1954. In addition to balancing the budget, one of Eisenhower's major goals was to reverse the "creeping socialism" of the New Deal by cutting domestic programs, removing or reducing federal regulations, and returning power and control to local and state governance. He rejected new social programs and any effort to establish a national health system, including government intervention to provide inoculations against **polio.** He also vetoed housing projects, public works bills, and antipollution proposals as inappropriate for the federal government.

Eisenhower hoped to eliminate or drastically reduce the role of the federal government in programs involving American Indians, energy, and agriculture. He scored his most complete success in eliminating federal economic support to tribes and liquidating selected reservations. As a result, a growing number of Indians sold tribal lands. By 1960, nearly half of all American Indians had abandoned their reservations. Critics blasted Eisenhower's "termination" policy as an attack on American Indian culture and society and argued that most tribes were economically and socially worse off than they had been before Eisenhower took office.

Eisenhower also was able to reduce federal control over energy sources and return them to state and private hands. Over Democratic opposition, the government permitted private companies to own and operate atomic power plants and gave states access to offshore oil sources. Eisenhower attempted to push back the New Deal legacy of farm subsidies (see page 794), but despite minor modifications, the cost of federal subsidies continued to grow.

♦ One of Eisenhower's goals was to reduce federal spending and controls. In line with this policy, he tried to turn Indian affairs over to the states and liquidate federal services and reservations. Between 1954 and 1960, sixty-one tribes were affected. This picture shows a 4-year-old Tuscarora boy protesting state and federal policies that attacked Indian rights. *Wide World.*

Elsewhere, Eisenhower had little desire to roll back the New Deal. Reflecting on the limits of the "middle path," he told his brother that any political party that tried to "abolish social security and eliminate labor laws and farm programs" would never be heard from again. Not wanting to preside over the

John Foster Dulles Secretary of State under Eisenhower; he used the threat of nuclear war to deter Soviet aggression.

demilitarized zone An area from which military forces, operations, and installations are prohibited.

polio Acute viral infection that usually struck children and often caused partial or total paralysis; it was common in the United States until Jonas Salk announced an effective vaccine in 1954.

demise of the Republican party, Eisenhower oversaw the addition of 7 million Americans to Social Security rolls and accepted a raise in the minimum wage from 75 cents to $1 an hour. He also expanded the size of government, creating the Department of Health, Education, and Welfare—directed by Oveta Culp Hobby, who had commanded the WACs during World War II.

When Eisenhower increased government spending, his rationale was generally based on national economic and security needs. He signed into law the St. Lawrence Seaway Act (1954), which committed U.S. support for building an inland waterway to connect the Great Lakes with the Atlantic. He justified this act on the grounds that the seaway would benefit the nation by increasing trade. He approved the Federal Highway Act (1956) to meet the needs of an automobile-driven nation and to provide the military with a usable nationwide transportation network. After the Soviet Union launched the space satellites ***Sputnik I*** (1957) and *Sputnik II* (1958), Eisenhower pointed to national security needs to justify his request for spending more federal money on education.

The successful orbiting of the Soviet satellites—*Sputnik II* actually carried a dog into space—created a multilevel panic across the United States. Not only did the nation seem vulnerable to Soviet missiles, but *Sputnik* seemed to underscore basic weaknesses in the American educational system. American schools, many critics argued, stressed soft subjects and social adjustment rather than hard subjects: science, languages, mathematics. *Sputnik* spurred Eisenhower and Congress to pass the National Defense Education Act of 1958 approve grants to schools developing strong programs in those subjects. The act also provided $295 million for **National Defense Student Loans** for college students. Congress's creation in 1958 of the National Aeronautics and Space Administration (NASA) immediately made manned flight its major priority, starting Project Mercury to lift an astronaut into space.

The Problem with McCarthy

During the 1952 presidential campaign, Senator Joseph McCarthy had taken a prominent role in attacking Democrats as being soft on communism. With Ike in the White House and Republicans controlling Congress, many Republicans, including Eisenhower, hoped that McCarthy would quietly disappear. But the senator from Wisconsin enjoyed the spotlight, relished his power, and had no intention of fading from view. He continued his search for subversives, ripping through the State Department, and the **United States Information Agency (USIA).** Government workers thought to be security risks

♦ At the heart of the Red Scare was Senator Joseph McCarthy. Using inquisition-style tactics to destroy opponents and bolster his own power, McCarthy became one of the most powerful politicians in the nation by 1952. In his televised efforts to discredit the United States army, McCarthy lost the public's approval, which hastened his censorship by Congress in 1954 and his ultimate fall from power. *National Portrait Gallery, Smithsonian Institution, Gift of Ernest and Louise Frankel/Art Resource, NY.*

Sputnik I The first artificial satellite launched into space; this feat by the Soviet Union in 1957 marked the beginning of the space race. A month later, the larger *Sputnik II* was launched.

National Defense Student Loans Loans established by the U.S. government in 1958, designed to encourage the teaching and study of science and modern foreign languages.

United States Information Agency Agency established by Congress in 1953 to distribute information about U.S. culture and political policies and gain support for American international goals.

were discharged or pressured to resign, and the USIA cleaned its library shelves of questionable titles, including those by Mark Twain. Although few of the individuals McCarthy attacked were guilty of any form of disloyalty, the agitation helped to rid the government of Democratic-appointed officials and allowed their replacement with faithful Republicans.

But when McCarthy, furious at the army for drafting his aide David Schine, threatened to "expose" army favoritism toward known Communists, anti-McCarthy forces in Congress, quietly supported by Eisenhower, concluded that the time to silence the senator had come. Charging that he was trying to blackmail the U.S. Army, the Senate investigated McCarthy. The American Broadcasting Company's telecast of the 1954 **Army-McCarthy hearings** allowed more than 20 million viewers to see McCarthy's ruthless bullying firsthand. Public and congressional opposition to the senator rose, and when the army's lawyer Joseph Welch asked the brooding McCarthy, "Have you no sense of decency?" the nation burst into applause. Several months later, with Republicans evenly divided, the Senate voted 67 to 22 to censure McCarthy's "unbecoming conduct." Drinking heavily, rejected by his colleagues, and ignored by the media, McCarthy died in 1957. But for years McCarthyism, refined and tempered, remained a potent political weapon against liberal opponents.

Seeking Civil Rights

- How did African-American leaders choose to attack *de jure* segregation in American society during Eisenhower's administration?
- What role did the federal government play in promoting civil rights during the 1950s?
- What constraints strengthened the strategy of confrontation and litigation in shaping the civil rights movement?

The average American depicted by *Reader's Digest* lived in suburbia, had white skin, and belonged to the middle class. This was not the world of the nation's racial minorities, most of whom faced poverty, degradation, and segregation. Legal, or ***de jure,*** segregation existed not only in the South but also in the District of Columbia and several western and midwestern states. Discrimination and ***de facto*** segregation were nationwide realities. Politically, neither party wanted to risk its unity by championing the cause of minorities too actively. Aware of Democratic and Republican apathy, African-American leaders forged ahead on their own to attack racial inequalities in America.

Changes had occurred, but most African Americans regarded them as minor tokens, indicating no real shift in white America's racial views. By 1952 the NAACP had won cases permitting African-American law and graduate students to attend white colleges and universities, even though the separate-but-equal ruling established in 1896 by the Supreme Court in *Plessy v. Ferguson* (see page 586) remained intact. In cities like Atlanta, Birmingham, and Montgomery blacks had enrolled to vote in growing numbers and had even been hired by the police force. But throughout the country, African Americans still occupied the lowest rungs of the social ladder and worked at the most menial jobs.

The *Brown* Decision

A step toward change came in 1954 when the Supreme Court considered the case of ***Brown v. Board of Education, Topeka, Kansas.*** The *Brown* case had started four years earlier, when Oliver Brown sued to allow his daughter to attend a nearby white school rather than the black school across town. The Kansas courts had rejected his suit, pointing out that the availability of a school for African Americans fulfilled the Supreme Court's separate-but-equal ruling. The NAACP appealed. In addressing the Supreme Court, NAACP lawyer **Thurgood Marshall** argued that the concept of "separate but equal" was inherently unequal. He used statistics to show that black schools were separate and unequal in financial resources, quality and number of teachers, and physical and educational resources. He also read

Army-McCarthy hearings Congressional investigation of Senator Joseph McCarthy televised in 1954; the hearings revealed McCarthy's villainous nature and ended his popularity.

de jure According to, or brought about by, law.

de facto Existing in practice, though not officially established by law.

Brown v. Board of Education Case in 1954 in which the Supreme Court ruled that separate educational facilities for different races were inherently unequal.

Thurgood Marshall Civil rights lawyer who argued thirty-two cases before the Supreme Court and won twenty-nine; he became the first African American justice of the Supreme Court in 1967.

into the record a psychological study indicating that black children educated in a segregated environment suffered from low self-esteem. Marshall stressed that segregated educational facilities, even if physically similar, could never yield equal products.

In 1952, a divided Court was unable to make a decision, but two years later the Court heard the case again. Now sitting as chief justice was **Earl Warren,** the Republican former governor of California, regarded by most as a legal conservative. Appointed to the Court by Eisenhower in 1953, the new chief justice made the difference. Using his persuasive skill, he convinced two justices to alter their views and support a unanimous decision that decreed "separate educational facilities are inherently unequal." In 1955, in addressing how to implement the *Brown* decision, the Court gave primary responsibility to local school boards. Not expecting integration overnight, the Court wanted school districts to proceed with "all deliberate speed." The justices instructed lower federal courts to monitor progress according to this vague guideline.

Reactions to the case were predictable. African Americans and liberals hailed the decision and hoped that segregated schools would soon be an institution of the past. Southern whites loudly protested and vowed to resist integration by all possible means. Virginia passed a law closing any integrated school. Southern congressional representatives issued the **Southern Manifesto,** in which they proudly pledged to oppose the *Brown* ruling. Eisenhower, who believed the Court had erred, refused to publicly support the decision.

While both political parties carefully danced around school integration and other civil rights issues, school districts in Little Rock, Arkansas, moved forward with "all deliberate speed." Central High School was scheduled to integrate in 1957. Opposing integration were the parents of the school's students and Governor Orval Faubus, who ordered national guard troops to surround the school and prevent desegregation. When Elizabeth Eckford, one of the nine integrating students, walked toward Central High, national guardsmen blocked her path amid jeers from a hostile mob roaring, "Lynch her! Lynch her!" Spat on by the crowd, she retreated to her bus stop. Central High remained segregated.

For three weeks the national guard prevented the black students from enrolling; then on September 20 a federal judge ordered the integration of Central High School. Faubus complied and withdrew the national guard. But the crisis was not over. Segregationists remained determined to block integration and were waiting for the black students on Monday, September 23, 1957. When they discovered that the nine had slipped into the school unnoticed, the mob rushed the police lines and battered the school doors open. Inside the school, Melba Patella Beaus thought, "We were trapped. I'm going to die here, in school." Hurriedly, the students were loaded into cars and warned to duck their heads. School officials ordered the drivers to "start driving, do not stop. . . . If you hit somebody, you keep rolling, 'cause [if you stop] the kids are dead."

With the black students safely away, the crowd's rampage quieted. Integration had lasted almost three hours. The following morning angry throngs began looting and burning part of the city, and the mayor asked for federal troops. Faced with insurrection, Eisenhower, on September 24, nationalized the Arkansas National Guard and dispatched a thousand troops of the 101st Airborne Division to Little Rock. Speaking to the nation, the president emphasized that he had sent the federal troops not to integrate the schools but to uphold the law and to restore order. The distinction was lost on most white southerners, who fumed as soldiers protected the nine integrating students for the rest of the school year.

In the school year that followed (1957–1958), the city closed its high schools rather than integrate them. To prevent such actions, the Supreme Court ruled in ***Cooper v. Aaron*** (1959) that an African American's right to attend school could not "be nullified openly and directly by state legislators or state executive officials nor nullified indirectly by them by evasive schemes for segregation." Little Rock's high schools reopened, and integration slowly spread to the lower grades. But in Little Rock, as in other communities, many white students fled the integrated

Earl Warren Chief justice of the Supreme Court from 1953 to 1969, under whom the Court issued decisions protecting civil rights, the rights of criminals, and First Amendment rights.

Southern Manifesto Statement issued by one hundred southern congressmen in 1954 after the *Brown v. Board of Education* decision, pledging to oppose desegregation.

Cooper v. Aaron Supreme Court decision (1959) that barred state authorities from interfering with desegregation either directly or through strategies of evasion.

♦ As Elizabeth Eckford approached Little Rock's Central High School, the crowd began to hurl curses, yelling "Lynch her! Lynch her!" and a national guardsman blocked her entrance into the school with his rifle. Terrified, she retreated down the street away from the threatening mob. A week later, with army troops protecting her, Elizabeth Eckford finally attended—and integrated—Central High School. *Francis Miller, LIFE Magazine ©Time Warner Inc.*

public schools to attend private schools that were beyond the reach of the federal courts. With no endorsement from the White House and entrenched southern opposition, "all deliberate speed" amounted to a snail's pace. By 1965, less than 2 percent of all southern schools were integrated.

The Montgomery Bus Boycott

In Montgomery, Alabama, African Americans were also willing to confront another form of white social control: segregation on the city bus line. The confrontation began softly on December 1, 1955, when **Rosa Parks** refused to give up her seat on the bus so that a white man could sit. At 42, Mrs. Parks, a high school graduate who earned $23 a week as a seamstress, had not boarded the bus with the intention of disobeying the law, although she strongly opposed it. But that afternoon, her fatigue and humiliation were suddenly too much. She refused to move and was arrested.

Hearing of her arrest, local African-American leaders Jo Ann Robinson and Edward Nixon felt they had found the right person committed enough to contest segregation. African-American community leaders called for a boycott of the buses to begin on the day of Mrs. Parks's court appearance. Accordingly, they submitted a list of proposals to city and bus officials calling for courteous drivers, the hiring of black drivers, and a more equitable system of bus seating, although they did not insist on an end to separate seating.

On December 5, 1955, the night before the boycott was to begin, nearly four thousand people filled and surrounded Holt Street Baptist Church to hear **Martin Luther King, Jr.,** the newly selected leader of the boycott movement—now called the Montgomery Improvement Association. The 26-year-old King firmly believed that the church had a social justice mission and that violence and hatred, even when considered justified, brought only ruin. In shaping his evening's speech, he faced the problem of how to balance disobedience with peace, confrontation with civility, and rebellion with tradition. His words electrified the crowd: "We are here this evening to say to those who have mistreated us so long that we are tired of being segregated and humiliated, tired of being kicked about by the brutal feet of oppression." King asked the crowd to boycott the buses, urging his listeners to protest "courageously, and yet with dignity and Christian love," and, when confronted with violence, to "bless them that curse you."

On December 6, Rosa Parks was tried, found guilty, and fined $10, plus $4 for court costs. She appealed, and the boycott, 90 percent effective, stretched into days, weeks, and finally months. Police issued basketfuls of traffic tickets to drivers taking part in the car pools that provided transportation for the boycotters. Insurance companies canceled

Rosa Parks Black seamstress who refused to give up her seat to a white man on a bus in Montgomery, Alabama, in 1955, triggering a bus boycott that stirred the civil rights movement.

Martin Luther King, Jr. Ordained Baptist minister, brilliant orator, and civil rights leader committed to nonviolence; he led many of the important protests of the 1950s and 1960s.

♦ On December 1, 1955, Rosa Parks made a fateful choice—she refused to give up her seat to a white man on a Montgomery, Alabama bus. She was arrested and fined $14 as a result of her decision. Her courageous act of defiance ignited a grassroots effort by African Americans to eliminate discrimination, and with it Martin Luther King, Jr. emerged as a national leader for civil rights. "I had no idea history was being made," she stated later, "I was just tired of giving in." *Corbis-Bettmann.*

their automobile coverage, and acid was poured on car pool cars. On January 30, 1956, a stick of dynamite was thrown onto King's front porch, destroying it and almost injuring King's wife and a friend. King nevertheless remained calm, reminding supporters to avoid violence and maintain the boycott. Finally, as the boycott approached its first anniversary, the Supreme Court ruled in *Gayle et al. v. Browser* (1956) that the city's and bus company's policy of segregation was unconstitutional. "Praise the Lord. God has spoken from Washington, D.C.," cried one boycotter.

The Montgomery bus boycott shattered the traditional white view that African Americans accepted segregation, and it marked the beginning of a pattern of nonviolent resistance. King himself was determined to build on the energy generated by the boycott and fight segregation throughout American society. In 1956, he and other black leaders had formed a new civil rights organization, the **Southern Christian Leadership Conference (SCLC),** and across the South thousands of African Americans were ready and eager to take to the streets and use the federal courts to achieve equality.

Ike and Civil Rights

As the press covered the Montgomery boycott, from the White House came either silence or carefully selected platitudes. When asked, Eisenhower gave elusive replies: "I believe we should not stagnate. . . . I plead for understanding, for really sympathetic consideration of a problem. . . . I am for moderation, but I am for progress; that is exactly what I am for in this thing." Personally, Eisenhower believed that government, especially the executive branch, had little role in integration. Max Rabb, the president's adviser on minority affairs, thought that "Negroes were being too aggressive." On a political level, cabinet members and Eisenhower were disappointed in the low number of blacks who had voted Republican in 1952 and 1956.

Southern Christian Leadership Conference Group formed by Martin Luther King, Jr., and others after the Montgomery bus boycott; it became the backbone of the civil rights movement in the 1950s and 1960s.

But not all within the administration were so unsympathetic toward civil rights. Attorney General Herbert Brownell drafted the first civil rights legislation since Reconstruction. The Civil Rights Act of 1957 passed Congress after a year of political maneuvering, having gained the support of Democratic majority leader Lyndon B. Johnson of Texas. A moderate law, it provided for the formation of a Civil Rights Commission and opened the possibility of using federal lawsuits to ensure voter rights. The SCLC had hoped to enroll 3 million new black voters in the South but fell far short of the goal, enrolling only 160,000 between 1958 and 1960. Ella Baker, who headed the underfunded and understaffed effort, faced effective opposition from southern whites and local and state officials. In 1960, Congress passed a voting rights act that offered little help. To remove the barriers to black voting, the act mandated the use of the cumbersome and expensive judiciary system—again placing the burden of forcing change on African Americans. Critics acknowledged that Eisenhower had sent troops to Little Rock and signed two civil rights acts, but they argued that the president had provided little political or moral leadership and that such leadership was needed if the nation was to commit itself to civil rights.

Eisenhower and a Hostile World

- What constraints lay behind the New Look?
- What were the weaknesses of "massive retaliation," and how did Eisenhower choose to address them?

Eisenhower provided little leadership on civil rights because he questioned the basic role of the executive branch in promoting integration and because he felt ill at ease with the issue. But when it came to foreign affairs, he had no such misgivings. He firmly believed that foreign policy was almost exclusively the territory of the executive branch and that he was eminently qualified to conduct it. During the 1952 campaign, it appeared that he would steer the United States away from the "appeasement" of containment and toward an aggressive effort to "rollback" communism and liberate captive peoples across the globe. As the new administration took office in 1953, Soviet premier Joseph Stalin suddenly died. Many hoped that the new Soviet leadership might be willing to soften East-West confrontation, and once in office President Eisenhower quickly dismissed policies of liberation and roll-back as too provocative. Instead, he sought a modification of Truman's containment that would be less expensive and would move the nation away from confrontation while weakening the Soviet Union and ending the Cold War. The new policy was called the **New Look.**

The New Look

The New Look relied on nuclear deterrence—cheaper than conventional forces—an enhanced arsenal of nuclear weapons and delivery systems, and the threat of **"massive retaliation"** to protect American international interests. In explaining the shift to more atomic weapons, Vice President Nixon stated, "Rather than let the communists nibble us to death all over the world in little wars, we will rely . . . on massive mobile retaliation." Secretary of Defense Wilson quipped that the policy sought "more bang for the buck" (see Map 29.2). Demonstrating the country's nuclear might, the United States had exploded its first hydrogen bomb in November 1952 (the Soviets tested theirs in August 1953).

The New Look was sold to the public as more positive than Truman's defensive containment policy, but insiders recognized that it had several flaws. The central problem was where the United States should draw the massive-retaliation line. The question became, What if the enemy calls our bluff? "How do you convince the American people and the U.S. Congress to declare war?" asked one planner. The answer was to make the bluff so convincing that it would never be called. Potential aggressors had to be convinced that the United States would strike back, raining nuclear destruction not only on the attackers but also on the Soviets and Chinese, who obviously would be directing the aggression. This policy was called **brinksmanship,** because it required

New Look National security policy under Eisenhower that called for reductions in the size of the army, development of tactical nuclear weapons, and the buildup of strategic air power employing nuclear weapons.

"massive retaliation" Term that John Foster Dulles used in a 1954 speech implying that the United States was willing to use nuclear force in response to Communist aggression anywhere.

brinksmanship Practice of seeking to win disputes in international politics by creating the impression of being willing to push a highly dangerous situation to the limit.

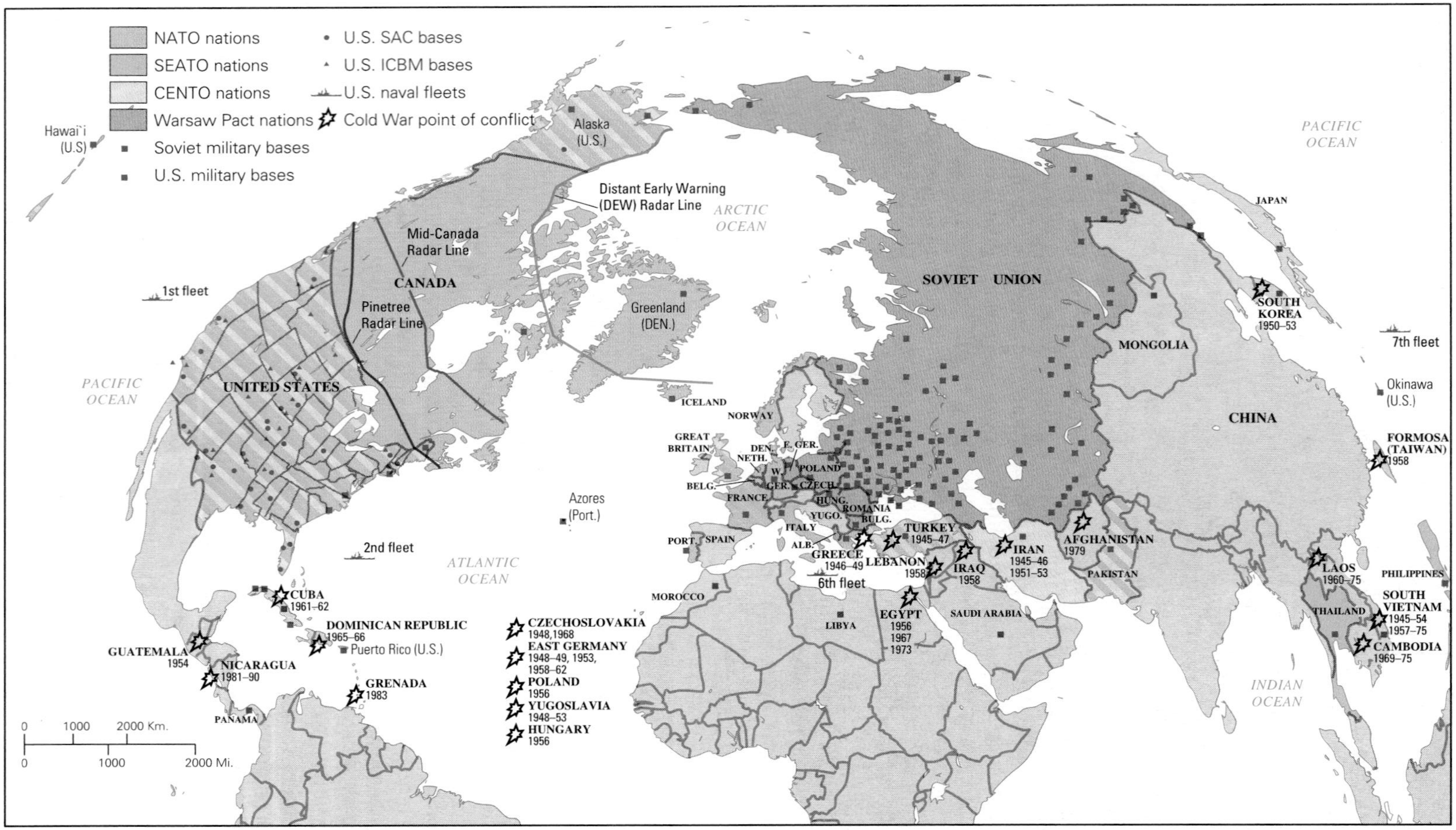

♦ **MAP 29.2 The Global Cold War** During the Cold War, the United States and the Soviet Union faced each other as enemies. The United States attempted to construct a ring of containment around the Soviet Union and its allies, while the Soviets worked to expand their influence and power. This map shows the nature of this military confrontation—the bases, alliances, and flash points of the Cold War.

♦ As the Cold War intensified and the Soviets became a nuclear power, the government began to consider methods to survive a nuclear war. One "solution" was to encourage people to build backyard bomb shelters. Pictured here is one family's atomic bomb shelter that slept six. The cost was $1250 in 1951. *Corbis-Bettman.*

the administration to take the nation to the brink of war and trust that the opposition would back down. Thus Dulles and Eisenhower indulged in dramatic speeches stressing that nuclear weapons were as usable as conventional ones. It was necessary "to remove the taboo" from using nuclear weapons, Dulles informed the press.

Almost immediately, the nuclear threats seemed to produce results. The North Koreans and Chinese chose to sign a truce agreement. Although the death of Stalin was the deciding factor, Eisenhower concluded that atomic diplomacy was paying off and reaffirmed his belief in the new approach. To further the New Look's nuclear approach, Eisenhower deployed intercontinental bombers carrying hydrogen bombs, and he dispatched **tactical nuclear weapons** to Europe.

To strengthen the rationale for "going nuclear" and make the possibility of World War III less frightening, the administration introduced efforts related to surviving a nuclear war. Public and private underground **fallout shelters**—well stocked with food, water, and medical supplies—could, it was claimed, provide safety against an attack. A 32-inch-thick slab of concrete, *U.S. News and World Report* reported, could protect people from an atomic blast "as close as 1,000 feet away." Across the nation, civil defense drills were established for factories, offices, and businesses. "Duck-and-cover" drills were held in schools. Teachers shouted "Drop!" and students immediately got into a kneeling or prone position, covered their faces, and placed their hands behind their necks.

While educators and government agencies worked to convince people that they could survive a nuclear war, movies and novels showed the horror of nuclear death and destruction. Nevil Shute realistically portrayed the extinction of humankind in his novel *On the Beach* (1957), and in *Them!* (1954) and dozens of other B movies, giant ants and other hideous creatures mutated by atomic fallout threatened the world.

Despite the emphasis placed on massive retaliation, Eisenhower recognized the limits of American power—areas under Communist control could not be liberated, and a thermonuclear war would yield no winners. Consequently, the administration sought ways to avoid a nuclear solution to international problems. Alliances and **covert operations** seemed logical alternatives. Alliances would identify areas protected by the American nuclear umbrella, and they would protect the United States from being drawn into limited, "brushfire" wars. When small conflicts broke out, the ground forces of regional allies, perhaps supported with American naval and air strength, would deal with them.

tactical nuclear weapons Low-yield, short-range nuclear weapons designed to be used on the battlefield; strategic nuclear weapons are used at long range, employing large yields, and are used against strategic targets like cities.

fallout shelter Underground shelter stocked with food and supplies that was intended to provide safety in case of atomic attack; *fallout* refers to the nuclear particles falling through the atmosphere after a nuclear attack.

covert operations Not practiced openly, something done in secret.

Mindful of existing tensions in Asia, Eisenhower concluded **bilateral** defense pacts with South Korea (1953) and Taiwan (1955) and a **multilateral** agreement, the Southeast Asia Treaty Organization (SEATO, 1954), that linked the United States, Australia, Thailand, the Philippines, Pakistan, New Zealand, France, and Britain. In the Middle East, the United States officially joined Britain, Iran, Pakistan, Turkey, and Iraq in the **Baghdad Pact** in 1957, later called the Central Treaty Organization (CENTO) when Iraq withdrew in 1959. In Europe, the United States helped to rearm West Germany and welcomed it into NATO. The Soviet bloc responded to that last move with the formation of a military alliance between Eastern European nations and the Soviet Union, the **Warsaw Pact,** in 1955.

Brinksmanship was also of little use in dealing with new Soviet and Chinese efforts to enlist the support of emerging nations. Throughout the 1950s, the European colonial empires were retreating in the face of nationalism and decolonization. In 1953, the Soviets stopped their denunciation of non-Communist nations and announced their willingness to help nonaligned nations. Trade and economic agreements followed as Moscow improved relations with nations such as India, Egypt, Guinea, and Guatemala. No longer could the United States ignore developing parts of the world or rely on its European allies to provide stability. As Dulles explained: "In the old days we used to be able to let South America go through the wringer of bad times . . . but the trouble is, now, when you put it through the wringer, it comes out red." To prevent social change from "coming out red," Eisenhower relied on economic and political pressures and on the **Central Intelligence Agency (CIA).** It seemed a never-ending task. "While we are busy rescuing Guatemala or assisting Korea and Indochina," Eisenhower observed, the Communists "make great inroads in Burma, Afghanistan, and Egypt."

Turmoil in the Middle East

In the Middle East, Arab nationalism, fired by anti-Israel and anti-Western attitudes, posed a serious threat to American interests. Iran and Egypt offered the greatest challenges. In Iran, Prime Minister Mohammed Mossadegh had nationalized British-owned oil properties and seemed likely to sell oil to the Soviets. Eisenhower considered him to be "neurotic and periodically unstable" and, along with the British, favored forcing him from power. Eisenhower gave the CIA the green light to overthrow the Iranian leader and replace him with a pro-Western government. On August 18, 1953, a mass demonstration funded and orchestrated by the CIA toppled the Mossadegh government. Quickly, millions in American money flowed into Iran to support the new government. A thankful Iranian government, headed by **Shah Mohammed Reza Pahlevi,** awarded the United States 40 percent of Iranian oil production.

Like Mohammed Mossadegh, Egyptian leader **Gamal Nasser,** an army colonel who assumed power in 1954, was attempting to develop his nation's economic resources independent of European controls and influence. At first the United States supported his government, hoping to woo him with loans, cash, arms, and an offer to help build the **Aswan Dam** on the Nile. Eventually Nasser rejected the American offers, in large part because Americans pushed an Egyptian-Israeli peace and closer ties with Britain. Nasser then looked to the Soviet Union for support. When he bought Soviet-bloc weapons, Eisenhower concluded that he was an "evil influence" in the region and canceled the Aswan Dam project (July 1956). Days later, claiming the need to finance the dam, Nasser nationalized the

bilateral Involving two parties.

multilateral Involving more than two parties.

Baghdad Pact A regional defensive alliance signed between Turkey and Iraq in 1955; Great Britain, Pakistan, and Iran soon joined; the United States supported the pact but did not officially join until mid-1957.

Warsaw Pact Alliance for mutual defense made in 1955 by the Soviet Union and the nations of Eastern Europe; it was the Soviet bloc's answer to NATO.

Central Intelligence Agency Agency established by Congress in 1947 to gather data and organize intelligence operations in foreign countries; it has also conducted more active covert operations in some countries, including fomenting rebellions and assassinations.

Shah Mohammed Reza Pahlevi Iranian ruler who received the hereditary title *shah* from his father in 1941 and with CIA support helped to oust the militant nationalist Mohammed Mossadegh in 1953.

Gamal Nasser Nationalist prime minister and president of Egypt in the late 1950s; he sought to return valuable foreign-owned resources to Egyptian control.

Aswan Dam Dam on the Nile River in Egypt, intended to provide electric power and stop seasonal flooding; construction began in 1960.

Anglo-French–owned **Suez Canal,** through which the majority of European-bound oil passed. Some within the administration suggested that Nasser be killed, but Eisenhower rejected that option. There was, he explained, no suitable replacement.

Israel, France, and Britain, however, responded with military action to regain control of the canal. On October 29, Israeli forces sliced through the Sinai Desert toward Egypt. Over the next week, French and British forces bombed Egyptian targets and seized the canal zone. Eisenhower was furious. He disliked Nasser but could not approve of armed aggression. Joined by the Soviets, Eisenhower sponsored a UN General Assembly resolution (November 2, 1956) calling for an end to the fighting, the removal of foreign troops from Egyptian soil, and the assignment of a United Nations peacekeeping force there. Faced with worldwide opposition and intense pressure from the United States—including a threat to withhold oil shipments—France, Britain, and Israel withdrew their forces. Nasser regained control of the canal and, as Eisenhower had feared, emerged as the uncontested leader of those opposing Western influence in Arab countries.

Nasser's prestige and the growth of Soviet influence in the Middle East forced the Eisenhower administration to affirm American interests in the region and to support a regional anti-Soviet alliance with the northern tier of Middle Eastern states: the Baghdad Pact/CENTO. Eisenhower also redoubled his effort to contain Nasser's **pan-Arab movement** and an expanding Soviet presence in the region. To protect Arab friends from Communist-nationalist rebellions, Eisenhower asked Congress for permission to commit American forces if requested to resist "armed attack from any country controlled by internationalism" (by *internationalism* Eisenhower meant the forces of communism). Congress agreed in March 1957, establishing the so-called **Eisenhower Doctrine** and providing $200 million in military and economic aid to improve military defenses in the nations of the Middle East.

It did not take long for Eisenhower to use his powers. When an internal revolt threatened Jordan's King Hussein in 1957, the White House announced Jordan was "vital" to American interests, moved the U.S. Sixth Fleet into the eastern Mediterranean, and supplied more than $10 million in aid. King Hussein put down the revolt, dismissed parliament and all political parties, and instituted authoritarian rule. In 1958, when Lebanon's Christian president Camile Chamoun ignored his country's constitution and ran for a second term, opposition leaders—including Muslim nationalistic, anti-West elements—rebelled. Chamoun requested American intervention, and Eisenhower committed nearly fifteen thousand troops to protect the pro-American government. The U.S. Army arrived at the Beirut airport amid hordes of tourists while U.S. Marines waded ashore in full battle gear as beachgoers watched from the sand. The American forces left in three months—after Chamoun had stepped down and, with American approval, been replaced by General Fuad Chehab. Eisenhower had demonstrated his willingness to protect American interests but had done little to resolve the problems faced by Lebanon and the rest of the Middle East.

A Protective Neighbor

During the 1952 presidential campaign, Eisenhower had charged Truman with following a "Poor Neighbor policy" toward Latin America, allowing the development of economic problems and popular uprisings that had been "skillfully exploited by the Communists." He was most concerned about Guatemala, disapproving of the reformist president, Jacobo Arbenz, who had instituted agrarian reforms by nationalizing thousands of acres of land, much of it owned by the American-based United Fruit Company. These radical actions convinced the administration to use the CIA to remove Arbenz. The CIA organized and supplied a rebel army in Honduras, led by Guatemalan Colonel Carlos Castillo Armas. Colonel Armas launched the effort to "liberate" Guatemala on June 18, 1954, and within two weeks a new, pro-American government was installed in Guatemala City. On July 8, 1954, a military **junta** named Colonel Armas president.

Suez Canal Canal running through Egypt from the Mediterranean Sea to the Red Sea; it was under French and British control until 1955, when it was nationalized by Egypt.

pan-Arab movement Attempts to politically unify the Arab nations of the Middle East; its followers advocated freedom from Western control and opposition to Israel.

Eisenhower Doctrine Policy under Eisenhower of providing military and economic aid to Arab nations in the Middle East to help defeat Communist-nationalistic rebellions.

junta Group of military officers ruling a country after seizing power.

♦ For nearly four decades, Fidel Castro has plagued American presidents and policymakers. Gaining power in a popular revolution against the dictator Batista in 1959, Castro quickly moved Cuba into the Soviet bloc. Eisenhower sought to use a CIA-trained army to overthrow Castro, but left office before the plan could be executed. Kennedy implemented the plan, but it failed miserably. *Andrew St. George/Magnum Photos.*

Eisenhower had created a pro-American government in Guatemala but had done little to reduce social and economic inequalities, blunt the cry for revolution, or foster good will toward the United States among Latin Americans. When Vice President Nixon toured Latin America in 1958, demonstrators in Lima, Peru, stoned his car, and an angry mob in Caracas, Venezuela, almost overturned it. Nixon called the demonstrators "Communist thugs." And, while Nixon toured Latin America, Fulgencio Batista, who had controlled Cuba through the 1940s and 1950s, was beset by a rebellion led by **Fidel Castro.**

The corrupt and dictatorial Batista had become an embarrassment to the United States, and many Americans believed that Castro could be a pro-American leader who would reform Cuba. By 1959, rebel forces had control of the island, but by mid-year many of Castro's economic and social reforms were endangering American investments and interests. American interests dominated Cuba's economy, controlling 40 percent of Cuba's sugar industry, 90 percent of Cuba's telephone and electric companies, 50 percent of its railroads, and 25 percent of its banking. In addition, 70 percent of Cuba's imports came from the United States. Concerned about Castro's political leanings, Washington tried to push Cuba in the right direction by applying economic pressure. In February 1960, Castro reacted to the American arm-twisting by signing an economic pact with the Soviet Union. Eisenhower seethed: Castro was a "madman . . . going wild and harming the whole American structure." In March, Eisenhower approved a CIA plan to prepare an attack against Castro. Actual implementation of the effort to overthrow the Cuban leader, however, was approved by Eisenhower's successor (see page 932).

The New Look in Asia

When Eisenhower took office, Asia was the focal point of Cold War tensions. Fighting continued in Korea, and in Indochina the Communist **Viet Minh** directed by Ho Chi Minh was fighting a "war of national liberation" against the French. Truman had supported France, and Eisenhower saw no reason to alter American policy. By 1954, the United States had dispatched more than three hundred advisers to Vietnam, was paying nearly 78 percent of war's cost, and was watching the French military position worsen. A believer in the **domino theory,** Eisenhower warned that if Indochina fell to communism, the loss "of Burma, of Thailand, of the [Malay] Peninsula, and Indonesia" would certainly follow, endangering Australia and New Zealand.

In Vietnam, the Viet Minh forces led by General Vo Nguyen Giap encircled the French fortress at Dienbienphu and launched murderous attacks on the beleaguered garrison. Asserting, "My God, we must not lose Asia," Eisenhower transferred forty bombers and detailed two hundred air force mechanics to bolster the French in Vietnam. The French—and some members of the Eisenhower administration—wanted a more direct American role, but Eisenhower believed that "no military victory is possible in that kind of theater" and rejected such

Fidel Castro Cuban revolutionary leader who overthrew the corrupt regime of dictator Fulgencio Batista in 1959 and established a communist state.

Viet Minh Vietnamese army made up of Communist and other nationalist groups, which fought from 1946 to 1954 for independence from French rule.

domino theory The idea that if one nation came under Communist control, then neighboring nations would also fall to the Communists.

options. After a fifty-five-day siege, Dienbienphu fell on May 7, 1954, and Eisenhower was left no option but to try to salvage a partial victory at an international conference in Geneva.

But there was no victory for the West at Geneva either. The **Geneva Agreement** "temporarily" partitioned Vietnam along the 17th parallel and created the neutral states of Cambodia and Laos. Within two years, the two Vietnams were to hold elections to unify the nation and neither was to enter into military alliances or allow foreign bases on its territory. American strategists called the settlement a "disaster"—half of Vietnam was lost to communism. Showing its displeasure, the United States refused to sign the agreement. Eisenhower rushed advisers and aid to the government of South Vietnam's prime minister, Ngo Dinh Diem, to ensure an anti-Communist South Vietnam. With American blessings, Diem ignored the Geneva-mandated unification elections, repressed his political opposition, and in October 1955 staged a **plebiscite** that created the Republic of Vietnam and elected him president. As will be seen in Chapters 30 and 31, the predicament of Vietnam was just beginning.

The Soviets and Cold War Politics

Eisenhower feared and opposed the spread of Communist influence. He also realized that improving American-Soviet relations would reduce the expanding arms race and limit points of conflict throughout the world. Both Eisenhower and Dulles, however, questioned the Soviets' commitment to peace and their willingness to keep agreements, and both knew that adversaries in the U.S. military and Congress and among the American public would condemn any softening of U.S. policy toward the Soviets. Still, growing Soviet nuclear capabilities and the death of Stalin in 1953 provided the need and the opportunity to reduce tensions.

Soon after Stalin's death, the new Soviet leader, Georgii Malenkov, called for "peaceful coexistence." Dulles dismissed the suggestion, but Eisenhower, with an eye on world opinion, called on the Soviets to demonstrate openly a change of policy and their willingness to cooperate with the West. Malenkov complied. He agreed to consider some form of on-site inspection to verify any approved arms reductions. Eisenhower responded by asking the Soviets in December 1953 to join him in the **Atoms for Peace plan** and to work toward universal disarmament.

Both countries by then were testing hydrogen **thermonuclear** bombs hundreds of times more powerful than atomic bombs. And world concern was growing not only about the threat of nuclear war but about the dangers of radiation from the testing. Throughout 1954, worldwide pressure grew for a summit meeting to deal with the "balance of terror." In 1955, Eisenhower agreed to a summit meeting in Geneva with the new Soviet leadership team

♦ In this cartoon, Soviet Premier Khrushchev and President Eisenhower sit atop the negotiating table, balanced precariously on the tip of a nuclear warhead. Having tested their first H-bombs in 1953, both superpowers had an impressive array of nuclear weapons aimed at each other by 1960. Some observers spoke of the MAD (mutually assured destruction) strategy that ensured that there would be no winners in a nuclear World War III. *©1959 Newsweek, Inc. All rights reserved. Reprinted by permission/Bob Engle.*

Geneva Agreement Truce signed at Geneva in 1954 by French and Viet Minh representatives, dividing Vietnam along the 17th parallel into the Communist North and the anti-Communist South.

plebiscite Special election that allows people to either approve or reject a particular proposal.

Atoms for Peace plan Eisenhower's proposal to the United Nations in 1953 that the United States and other nations cooperate to develop peaceful uses of atomic energy.

thermonuclear Relating to the fusion of atomic nuclei at high temperatures or to weapons based on fusion, like the hydrogen bomb (as distinct from weapons based on fission).

of Nikolai Bulganin and **Nikita Khrushchev,** who had replaced Malenkov. Eisenhower expected no resolution of the two major issues—disarmament and Berlin (see pages 869–871)—and instead saw the meeting as good public relations. He intended to make a bold disarmament initiative—the Open Skies proposal—that would earn broad international support. In a dramatic presentation, highlighted by a sudden thunderstorm that momentarily blacked out the conference room, Eisenhower asked the Soviets to share information about military installations and to permit aerial reconnaissance to verify the information while work began on general disarmament. Bulganin voiced official interest, but Khrushchev, speaking privately, called the proposal a "very transparent espionage device."

Eisenhower recognized that Khrushchev represented the real power in the Soviet Union and that his response meant rejection of the proposal. Thus the Geneva Summit went as expected: the Americans and Soviets agreed to disagree. Nevertheless, Eisenhower was pleased. The Open Skies proposal was popular, and the meeting had generated a "spirit of Geneva" that reduced East-West tensions without appeasing the Communist foe. Besides, he knew that the United States would soon have in service a new high-altitude jet plane, the U-2, which it was thought could safely fly above Soviet antiaircraft missiles while taking close-up photographs of Soviet territory. This was Cold War gamesmanship at its best.

The spirit of Geneva quickly vanished when Soviet forces invaded Hungary in November 1956 to put down a nationalistic, anti-Soviet revolt. Many Americans favored supporting the Hungarian freedom fighters, but facing the Suez crisis and seeing no way to send aid to the Hungarians without risking all-out war, the administration could only watch as the Soviets crushed the revolt.

After the Hungarian crisis, Soviet-American relations cooled and rivalry intensified. Seeking to gain an advantage while gathering worldwide public support, Eisenhower and Khrushchev jousted with each other over nuclear testing and disarmament. First one and then the other, with little belief in success, offered to end nuclear testing and eliminate nuclear weapons if certain provisions were met. In the spring of 1958, both sides temporarily ended nuclear testing, but when discussion on how to implement and verify a test-ban treaty failed, nuclear testing resumed.

The simmering issue of Berlin was also intensifying tensions. In November 1958, the Soviets announced they and East Germany intended to sign a treaty that would terminate the West's right to occupy West Berlin and would unify the city under East German control. For Eisenhower this was unthinkable. Supported by the British and French, he declared that the Western Allies would remain in West Berlin, and American and NATO forces made plans for the defense of the city. Faced with unflinching Western determination, Khrushchev announced a permanent delay in the treaty and suggested that he and Eisenhower exchange visits and hold a summit meeting. During Khrushchev's twelve-day tour of the United States in September 1959, the Soviet leader and Eisenhower announced that they would attend a summit in Paris in May and that Eisenhower would later visit the Soviet Union.

Neither event fully materialized. On May 1, 1960, the Soviets shot down an American U-2 spy plane over the Soviet Union and captured its pilot, Major Francis Gary Powers. At first, the United States feebly denied the purpose of the flight, saying the U-2 was a weather plane that had strayed from its Turkish flight plan. Khrushchev then showed pictures of the plane's wreckage and presented Major Powers, clearly proving the American spy mission. In Paris, Eisenhower took full responsibility but refused to apologize for such flights, which he contended were necessary to prevent a "nuclear Pearl Harbor." Khrushchev withdrew from the summit, and Eisenhower canceled his trip to the Soviet Union. The Cold War thaw was over.

Eisenhower returned home a hero, having stood up to the Soviets. But public support was temporary. The loss of the U-2, Soviet advances in missile technology and nuclear weaponry, and a Communist Cuba only 90 miles from Florida provided the Democrats with strong reasons to claim that the Republicans and Eisenhower had been deficient in meeting Soviet threats. In 1960, turning the Republicans' tactics of 1952 against them, Democrats cheerfully accused their opponents of endangering the United States by being too soft on communism.

Nikita Khrushchev Soviet premier who denounced Stalin in 1956 and improved the Soviet Union's image abroad; he was deposed in 1964 for his failure to improve the country's economy.

SUMMARY

E xpectations
C onstraints
C hoices
O utcomes

"Had enough?" Republicans asked voters in 1952, offering the choice of a new vision of domestic and foreign policy. Americans answered by electing Eisenhower. With Ike in the White House, the 1950s spawned popular, if flawed, images of America that reflected the *expectations* of many whose lives centered on affluent suburbs and a growing consumer culture. The images were partially true. Many white, middle-class Americans fulfilled their *expectations* by moving to the suburbs and living the American dream. But many other Americans faced *constraints* that kept them from achieving the dream; prosperity and stability did not extend to all Americans.

Economic realities, social prejudice, and dissatisfaction *constrained* many Americans and led to *choices* contradicting the popular imagery. More married women *chose* to enter the work force. Many men and women behaved contrary to the supposed norms of family and suburban culture, and teens and young adults turned to forms of expression that seemed to reject or criticize established norms and values. The *outcome,* even in affluent suburbia, was that society and culture were less stable than they appeared. And while Eisenhower spoke about a social and political consensus, African Americans *chose* to reshape the nation's social and political agenda. The *outcome* was that racial equality became an issue that neither society nor government could ignore.

Though promising change, Eisenhower in practice *chose* foreign and domestic policies that continued the basic patterns established by Roosevelt and Truman. Republican beliefs, pervasive anticommunism, and budget concerns allowed reductions in some domestic programs, but public acceptance of existing federal responsibilities *constrained* any large-scale dismantling of the New Deal. The New Look relied on new tactics, but Cold War foreign policies did not change significantly. Using alliances, military force, and covert activities, Eisenhower continued containment and expanded American influence in southern Asia and the Middle East. Meanwhile, relations with the Soviet Union deteriorated with the launching of *Sputnik,* another Berlin crisis, Castro's victory in Cuba, and the U-2 incident.

SUGGESTED READINGS

Stephen E. Ambrose. *Eisenhower: The President* (1984).

A generally positive and well-balanced biography of Eisenhower as president by one of the most respected historians of the Eisenhower period.

Robert F. Burk. *The Eisenhower Administration and Black Civil Rights* (1984).

An insightful examination of federal policy and the civil rights movement.

Robert A. Devine. *Eisenhower and the Cold War* (1981).

A solid and brief account of Eisenhower's foreign policy, especially toward the Soviet Union.

John Patrick Diggins. *The Proud Decades: America in War and Peace, 1941–1960* (1988).

A short, well-written, and well-researched examination of the postwar period.

David J. Garrow. *Bearing the Cross* (1986).

An in-depth description of the development of the civil rights movement and the role of Martin Luther King, Jr.

David Halberstam. *The Fifties* (1993).

A positive interpretive view of the 1950s by a well-known journalist and author, especially recommended for its description of famous and not-so-famous people.

Eugenia Kaledin. *Mothers and More: American Women in the 1950s* (1984).

A thoughtful look at the role of American women in society during the 1950s.

Douglas T. Miller, and Marion Novak. *The Fifties: The Way We Really Were* (1977).

An interesting, useful, and often quoted description of American society during the 1950s.

THE STRUGGLE FOR CIVIL RIGHTS, 1960–1968 In the mid-1950s, African Americans chose to confront the system of prejudice and segregation that existed across the United States. This map shows the national scope of the civil rights movement from 1960 to 1968.

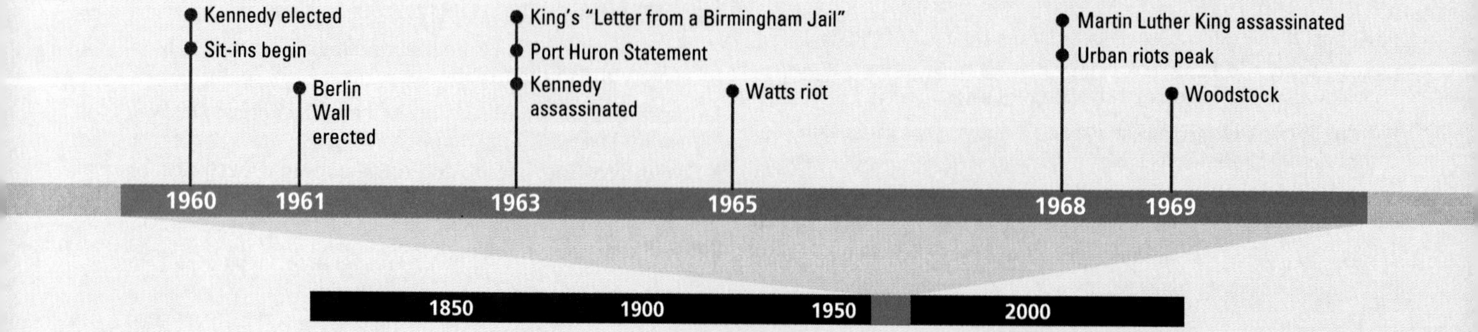

CHAPTER 30

Great Promises, Bitter Disappointments, 1960–1968

Kennedy and the New Frontier

- What images did John Kennedy and his advisers project, and how did those images compare with political reality?
- How did Kennedy's civil rights choices differ from Eisenhower's?
- How did civil rights activists choose to confront those resistng integration in the South?

Flexible Response

- What expectations shaped Kennedy's choices in foreign policy?
- What were some of the outcomes of Kennedy's concerns and interests in the Third World?

Beyond the New Frontier

- How did Lyndon Johnson's Great Society program expand on the New Deal?
- How did Johnson choose to attack the constraints that African Americans and other minorities were facing?

New Agendas

- What constraints influenced the civil rights movement in the mid-1960s? What was the outcome?
- What changes did the youth movement seek? How justified were young people's criticisms of traditional American society?

INTRODUCTION

Expectations
Constraints
Choices
Outcomes

In the election campaign of 1960, Democratic candidate John F. Kennedy symbolized a new level of youth and vigor in government that raised *expectations.* He represented a more interventionist government in both foreign and domestic affairs. Seeing himself as more of a foreign-policy president than a domestic one, Kennedy promised to overcome the "missile gap" and regain ground lost to communism. To defeat the global threat of communism, Kennedy *chose* "flexible response" over massive retaliation, and he loosened military budget *constraints,* funding both an arms race and a space race with the Soviet Union. He placed new emphasis on developing regions of the world, especially Latin America and South Vietnam. Yet, despite Kennedy's self-confidence and efforts, the *outcome* was not a safer and less-divided world. The erection of the Berlin Wall, the Cuban missile crisis, and events in Vietnam heightened Cold War tensions.

While promising a return to the policies of the New Deal, with government providing a better society for all Americans, Kennedy energized the nation, raising *expectations* especially among the poor and minorities that he would press for solutions to end poverty and discrimination. But Kennedy faced political *constraints* in the form of conservatives in Congress who objected to an expansion of liberal programs and civil rights legislation. Faced with Republican and southern Democratic opposition, Kennedy *chose* to delay civil rights legislation and not to press forward with aid to education and healthcare. The *outcome* was a domestic record of legislation that expanded on existing programs but did not chart new paths of social policy.

Building on Kennedy's legacy, Lyndon Johnson *chose* to create the largest expansion of New Deal–style legislation since the Depression. Johnson's Great Society program waged war on poverty and discrimination, promoted education, and created a national system of healthcare for the aged and poor. But Johnson also faced *constraints.* Conservatives, after their defeat in the 1964 election, were able to strengthen their opposition to the Great Society, and some moderates and even a few liberals also voiced objections to many of the programs. An expanding war in Vietnam also *constrained* Johnson's domestic program.

By 1968, growing social and political turmoil was undermining liberal policies. The optimistic *expectations* Kennedy had inspired were declining amid the apparent divisions and excesses of American society. Within the civil rights movement, Black Power leaders *chose* confrontation over compromise. Urban riots and violence drove wedges between African-American leaders and some white supporters. The emergence of a youth-centered counterculture that rejected traditional social and moral values and stressed personal freedoms also worked to fragment American society. The *outcome* was a decade that began with great optimism but ended with diminished *expectations.* By 1968, few Americans believed that the federal government could ensure a positive future.

Kennedy and the New Frontier

- What images did John Kennedy and his advisers project, and how did those images compare with political reality?
- How did Kennedy's civil rights choices differ from Eisenhower's?
- How did civil rights activists choose to confront those resisting integration in the South?

The last years of the 1950s were not kind to the Republican party. The Cold War seemed to be going badly as the Soviets downed an American spy plane over the Soviet Union, launched *Sputnik* into space, and supported Fidel Castro in Cuba. Domestically, there seemed little or no direction from the White House or from Republicans in Congress to deal with the problems of the country: civil rights, a weak economy that in 1960 tumbled into another recession, and a national debt that had soared to $488 billion by 1960. Democratic victories in the congressional elections of 1958 signaled that Democrats were again the majority party. Vice President Richard Nixon speculated that to win the presidential election, a Republican "would have to

CHRONOLOGY

New Frontiers

1960 Sit-ins begin
SNCC formed
Boynton v. Virginia
John F. Kennedy elected president

1961 Peace Corps formed
Alliance for Progress
Bay of Pigs invasion
Freedom rides begin
Vienna summit
Berlin Wall erected

1962 *Baker v. Carr*
Harrington's *The Other America*
SDS's Port Huron Statement
Engle v. Vitale
James Meredith enrolls at the University of Mississippi
Cuban missile crisis

1963 *Gideon v. Wainright*
Equal Pay Act
Martin Luther King's "Letter from a Birmingham Jail"
Limited Test Ban Treaty
March on Washington
Diem assassinated
Kennedy assassinated; Lyndon Baines Johnson becomes president
16,000 advisers in Vietnam

1964 War on Poverty begins
Escobedo v. Illinois
Freedom Summer in Mississippi
Civil Rights Act
Office of Economic Opportunity created
Berkeley Free Speech movement
Johnson elected president

1965 Malcolm X assassinated
Selma march
Elementary and Secondary Education Act
Griswold v. Connecticut
Medicaid and Medicare
Voting Rights Act
Immigration Act

1966 Black Panther party formed
Stokely Carmichael announces Black Power
Miranda v. Arizona
Model Cities Act

1967 Urban riots in one hundred twenty-seven cities

1968 Kerner Commission Report
Martin Luther King, Jr., assassinated
Open Housing Law

get practically all Republican votes, more than half of the independents and, in addition, the votes of 5 to 6 million Democrats."

On the Democratic side stood **John Fitzgerald Kennedy,** a youthful, vigorous senator from Massachusetts who had run a successful primary campaign—beating Hubert Humphrey and **Lyndon Baines Johnson**—and gained a first-ballot nomination. A Harvard graduate, Kennedy came from a wealthy, Catholic Massachusetts family. Some worried about his young age (43) and lack of experience. Others worried about his religion—no Catholic had ever been elected president. To lessen these possible liabilities, Kennedy had astutely added the politically savvy Senate majority leader Lyndon Johnson of Texas to the ticket, called for a new generation of leadership, and emphasized that those who were making religion an issue were bigots. Drawing on the legacy of Franklin Roosevelt, he challenged the nation to enter a **New Frontier,** to improve the overall quality of life of all Americans, and to re-energize

John Fitzgerald Kennedy Massachusetts senator who was elected president in 1960; he projected a spirit of youth and activism; he was assassinated in 1963.

Lyndon Baines Johnson Senate majority leader from Texas who became vice president in 1961 and then president in 1963, when Kennedy was assassinated.

New Frontier Program for social and educational reform that Kennedy put forward; Congress resisted much of it.

♦ The 1960 presidential race was the closest in recent history, with many people believing that the outcome hinged on the public's perception of the candidates during their nationally televised debates. The majority of viewers believed that Kennedy won the debates and looked more in control and presidential than Nixon. Kennedy won the election by fewer than 120,000 votes. *UPI/Bettmann Archives.*

American foreign policy to stand fast against the Communist threat.

Facing Kennedy was Eisenhower's vice president, Richard M. Nixon. Trying to distance himself from the image of Eisenhower's elderly leadership, Nixon promised a forceful, energetic presidency and emphasized his executive experience and history of anticommunism. He, too, promised to improve the quality of life, support civil rights, and defeat international communism. Several political commentators called the candidates "two peas in a pod" and speculated that the election would probably hinge on appearances more than on issues.

Trailing in the opinion polls and hoping to give his campaign a boost, Nixon agreed to televised debates with Kennedy. He was proud of his debating skills and thought he could adapt them successfully to radio and television. Kennedy seized the opportunity, recognizing that the candidate who appeared most calm and knowledgeable—more "presidential"—would "win" each debate. Before the camera's eye, in the war of images, Kennedy appeared fresh and confident, while Nixon, having been ill, appeared tired and haggard. He looked at Kennedy and not at the camera whenever answering questions—a good debating technique but a disastrous television tactic. Worst of all, Nixon seemed to sweat. In contrast, Kennedy faced the television camera while speaking, looking relaxed and in control. The differences in appearance were critical. Unable to see Nixon, the radio audience believed he won the debates, but to the 70 million television viewers the winner was the self-assured and sweat-free Kennedy.

The televised debates helped Kennedy, but victory depended on his ability to hold the Democratic coalition together, maintaining southern Democratic support while wooing African-American and liberal voters. The Texan Johnson used his political clout to keep the South largely loyal even as Kennedy blasted the lack of Republican leadership on civil rights. Martin Luther King, Jr., had been arrested for civil rights activities in Atlanta, and in a grand gesture, Kennedy telephoned Coretta Scott King to express his concern about her husband's jailing. Kennedy's brother Robert used his influence to get King freed, convincing even the staunchest Protestant black ministers, including Martin Luther King, Sr., to overlook Kennedy's religion and endorse him.

Every vote was critical. When the ballots were counted, Kennedy scored the narrowest of victories. Nixon carried more states, 25 to 21, but Kennedy had a narrow margin over Nixon in popular votes and won the electoral count, 303 to 219. (Independent southern candidate Harry Byrd earned 15 electoral votes.) Despite voting irregularities in Chicago, Illinois, and Texas, Nixon did not contest the election (see Map 30.1).

The New Frontier

The weather in Washington was frigid when Kennedy gave his inaugural address, but his speech fired the imagination of the nation. Speaking in idealistic terms, avoiding any mention of specific programs, he promised to march against "the common enemies of man: tyranny, poverty, disease, and war itself." He asked all Americans to participate, exhorting them to "ask not what your country can do for you; ask what you can do for your country."

Despite his call for public involvement, Kennedy believed that most national problems were "technical" and "administrative" and that solutions would come from experts, so there was little need for any groundswell of popular support. Kennedy's staff and cabinet, dubbed by a journalist "the best and the brightest," reflected the images of expertise and activism. Rhodes scholars and Harvard professors were prominent, including historian Arthur Schlesinger, Jr., economist John Kenneth Galbraith (both personal advisers), and Dean Rusk (secretary of state). Ford Motor Company president Robert McNamara was tapped for secretary of defense. In a controversial move, Kennedy gave the position of attorney general to his younger brother Robert. John Kennedy praised his choices as men with "know-how," experienced in solving problems. Not everyone, however, was convinced. Referring to the lack of political background among appointees, Speaker of the House Sam Rayburn remarked that he would "feel a whole lot better . . . if just one of them had run for sheriff once."

Rayburn had noted a critical point. Kennedy and his staff wanted to be activists, leading the nation along new paths of liberalism, but they would not be able to convince Congress to move along that path. Democrats dominated Congress, but since 1937 a powerful coalition of conservative, southern Democrats had voted with Republicans to prevent any notable expansion of the New Deal. Knowing it would be "very difficult" to pass controversial legislation, Kennedy decided to focus on legislation within the "vital center"—neither overly liberal nor conservative—that would improve the economy

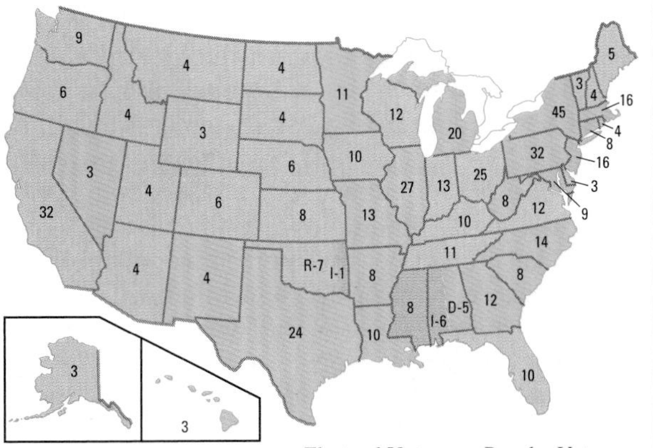

	Electoral Vote		Popular Vote	
Kennedy (Democrat)	303	56.5%	34,226,731	50%
Nixon (Republican)	219	40.75%	34,108,157	50%
Byrd (Independent)	15	2.75%	501,643	0%

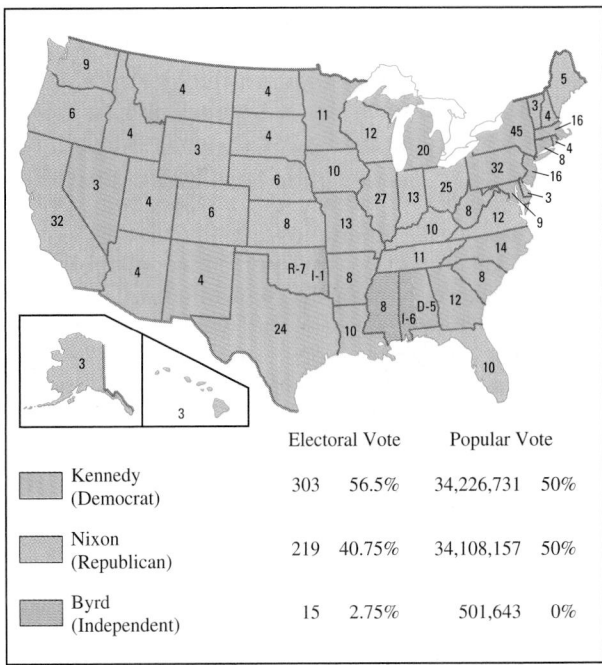

♦ **MAP 30.1 Election of 1960** Although Richard Nixon won in more states than John F. Kennedy, in the closest presidential election in the twentieth century, Kennedy defeated his Republican opponent by a slim 84 electoral votes and fewer than nineteen thousand popular votes.

and the services provided under existing New Deal–style programs.

Like Truman, Kennedy asked Congress for a wide range of domestic programs, but he received only a modest, Eisenhower-like result. By 1963, Congress had approved small increases in Social Security coverage and benefits and in the minimum wage (to $1.25 an hour), an extension of unemployment insurance, a housing and **urban renewal** bill, and manpower and aid-to-depressed-areas bills. Bills for national health coverage, education, and civil rights remained bottled up in Congress.

Kennedy had better luck in spurring economic recovery. He turned to the **"new economics"** advocated by Walter Heller, his chairman of the Council

urban renewal Effort to revitalize rundown city centers by providing federal funding for the construction of apartment houses, office buildings, and public facilities.

"new economics" Planning and shaping the national economy through the use of tax policies and federal spending.

of Economic Advisers, and called for more government spending and cuts in business and income taxes. With little opposition, in the face of a seemingly more aggressive Soviet Union, Congress raised the defense budget by almost 20 percent ($6 billion) and funded an expensive space program, providing direct stimulation that helped lift the economy out of the recession. As unemployment fell by 2 percent from a 1960 high of nearly 7 percent, a new problem, inflation, arose. Hoping to stem inflation, Kennedy established informal price and wage guidelines for businesses and labor unions.

Most accepted the president's formulas, but in early 1962 United States Steel Corporation and a few other steel makers raised their prices above Kennedy's ceiling. He denounced United States Steel for not acting in the public interest and threatened to reduce its government contracts. Facing an angry president and being undersold by other steel companies, United States Steel lowered prices. As 1962 ended, the White House boasted that the economy was strong and manageable. Among the public and within many corporations and federal agencies, "new economics" gave rise to a belief that the economy was one of those technological problems that the best and brightest could manage. Heller wrote that there was a growing belief that "modern economics can . . . deliver the goods" and that economists "can meet a crisis and help carry an expansion."

Civil Rights and the Kennedys

Even as the economy improved, many liberals questioned Kennedy's moral and executive leadership in promoting civil rights. In his first two years in office, Kennedy moved cautiously. He appointed several blacks to high office and to district courts, including Thurgood Marshall to the U.S. Circuit Court, but civil rights advocates were far from satisfied. They noted that several of his judicial appointments went to recognized segregationists, including Harold Cox of Mississippi, who once, in court, had referred to African Americans as "chimpanzees." They also noted that despite his campaign pledge to do so immediately, Kennedy did not lift his pen to ban segregation in federal housing until November 1962. In response, Kennedy argued that opposition from Republicans and conservative Democrats made greater success unlikely and that nothing was to be gained by "raising hell" too early. But civil rights was not a movement that could be managed; it was a grassroots movement with its own dynamics.

♦ As Kennedy took office, the sit-in movement was spreading across the South as students from colleges and universities sought to integrate places of public accommodation. In this picture, whites harass students from Tougaloo College as they "sit-in" at a Woolworth lunch counter in Jackson, Mississippi. *State Historical Society of Wisconsin.*

Civil rights leaders remained resolved to confront segregation and, if necessary, to force government action. Even as Kennedy assumed office, a new wave of black activism was striking at segregation in the South in the form of **sit-ins** and boycotts. The sit-ins began when four freshmen at North Carolina Agricultural and Technical College in Greensboro, North Carolina, decided to integrate the public lunch counter at the local F. W. Woolworth store. On February 1, 1960, they entered the store, sat down at the counter, and ordered a meal. A black waitress told them she could not serve them, but still they sat and waited for service until the store closed. They were not served, but no one tried to remove or arrest them. The next day twenty A&T students sat at the lunch counter demanding service. By the end of the week, similar sit-ins had spread throughout the South.

The sit-ins remained largely a student movement supported by the more established civil rights groups, especially the Congress of Racial Equality (CORE) and King's Southern Christian Leadership Conference (SCLC) (see pages 844 and 910). At a

sit-in The act of occupying a segregated establishment to protest racial discrimination.

conference in Raleigh in April 1961, SCLC official Ella Baker laid the foundation for a new civil rights organization built around those in the sit-in movement—the **Student Nonviolent Coordinating Committee** (**SNCC,** pronounced "snick"). Although its statement of purpose emphasized **nonviolence,** SNCC members were more militant than civil rights activists generally had been. As one activist stated, "We do not intend to wait placidly for those rights which are already legally and morally ours." SNCC workers quickly spread across the South, emphasizing community solidarity and action and incorporating the music of freedom as a vital part of protest. Music aroused the spirit, instilled courage, and created "a circle of trust." A spiritual, rewritten for the movement—"We Shall Overcome"—became an anthem.

Soon more than seventy thousand people had protested for integrated public facilities in more than 140 cities, including some outside the South, in Nevada, Illinois, and Ohio. Many of those participating in demonstrations were, like Alice Walker, young college students (see Individual Choices: Alice Walker). In some cities, including Greensboro, equal service was achieved with a minimum of resistance. But elsewhere, particularly in the Deep South, whites resisted violently to protect segregation. Thousands of participants in sit-ins were beaten, blasted with high-pressure fire hoses, and jailed.

Sharing headlines with those "sitting-in" were the **freedom riders.** Before Kennedy took office, the Supreme Court had ruled in *Boynton v. Virginia* (1960) that all interstate buses, trains, and terminals be desegregated. CORE's James Farmer planned a series of "freedom rides" to force integration on southern bus lines and stations. Farmer knew that riders would meet with opposition and probably violence, creating a crisis and putting pressure on the executive branch to uphold the Court's decision. The first buses of freedom riders left Washington, D.C., in May 1961, headed toward Alabama and Mississippi. The freedom riders expected trouble. In Anniston, Alabama, a mob of angry whites attacked the buses, smashing their windows and setting them on fire and severely beating several freedom riders. The savagery continued at Birmingham, where one freedom rider needed fifty-three stitches to close his head wound. When asked why no police were at the station to protect the riders, Birmingham's public safety commissioner Eugene "Bull" Connor explained that it was a holiday—Mother's Day.

♦ Anniston, Alabama was the end of the line for this bus of freedom riders. As riders got off the bus, they were pelted by stones and savagely beaten by a white mob. The bus was fire-bombed and its tires slashed. A second bus continued on to Montgomery. *UPI/Bettmann Archives.*

As Farmer had predicted, the violence forced the federal government to respond. At first, the Kennedy administration asked Farmer to stop the rides at least for a "cooling-off" period. Kennedy was facing a summit meeting with Soviet premier Nikita Khrushchev and did not want civil unrest to cloud foreign-policy issues. Farmer refused, noting that African Americans had been cooling off for 150 years. U.S. Attorney General Robert Kennedy then arranged state and local protection for the riders through Alabama and placed federal agents on the buses. It did little good. When the buses arrived in Montgomery, the police and national guard escorts vanished, and a large mob attacked the riders. The attack left many freedom riders injured, including

Student Nonviolent Coordinating Committee Organization formed to give young blacks a greater voice in the civil rights movement; it initiated black voter registration drives and freedom rides but in 1966 changed philosophy and advocated black nationalism and separatism.

nonviolence The rejection of violence in favor of peaceful tactics as a means of gaining political objectives.

freedom riders Civil rights protesters who rode buses throughout the South in 1961 to press for integration in bus terminals and who helped to pressure governments to enforce the *Boynton v. Virginia* decision.

INDIVIDUAL CHOICES

Choosing Activism

Alice Walker

The first African-American woman to receive the Pulitzer Prize for literature, Alice Walker chose to merge her life with her art. She has stressed the dignity and survival of the oppressed, and, moving beyond civil rights and feminism, she has chosen to advocate freedom, justice, and dignity for humans and nonhumans alike. George Steinmetz.

In 1961, at age 17, Alice Malsenior Walker enrolled at Spelman College in Atlanta. Born in Eatonton, Georgia, in 1944, the youngest of eight children, she was the daughter of sharecroppers who earned only $300 a year. Despite their poverty, the Walkers instilled in their children a strength of character based on proud dignity and hope based on ability. To emphasize human dignity and to promote a society based on abilities, Alice Walker chose to become an activist, making justice and equality a central theme in her life and writings. Encouraged by historians Howard Zinn and Staughton Lynd, she and other Spelman students took to the streets of Atlanta on weekends, demonstrating for an end to segregation and for black equality. We were "young and burst with fear and determination to change our world," she recalled.

Dissatisfied with Spelman's conservatism and the dismissal of Zinn for his radical views and civil rights activities, she transferred to the largely white, liberal, all-women Sarah Lawrence College, in New York. She majored in English, continued her civil rights activism—participating in King's March on Washington—and traveled to Africa to discover her spiritual self. She returned in the fall of 1964, pregnant and suicidal. Recovering from an abortion, she

federal agent John Seigenthaler, who was beaten unconscious when he rushed to help a female rider. After an hour of terror, the police finally arrived and restored order.

Furious, the attorney general deputized local federal officials as marshals and ordered them to escort the freedom riders to the state line, where Mississippi forces would take over. Battered and bloodied, the riders continued to the state capital, Jackson. There they were peacefully arrested for violating Mississippi's recently passed **public order laws.** The jails quickly filled as more freedom riders arrived and were arrested—328 by the end of the summer. The freedom rides ended in September 1961 when the Interstate Commerce Commission declared it would uphold the Supreme Court decision prohibiting segregation. Faced with direct federal

public order laws Laws passed by many southern communities to discourage civil rights protests; they allowed the police to arrest anyone suspected of intending to disrupt public order.

wrote her first volume of poetry, *Once* (published in 1968). Like nearly all her writings, the poems reflected her life and her understanding of the African-American experience.

Graduating in 1965, she moved to Mississippi, the "heart of the civil rights movement," and merged her activism with writing, winning the *American Scholar*'s essay contest for her personal account of the civil rights movement in Mississippi. She also married Melvyn Leventhal, a Jewish civil rights lawyer—challenging Mississippi's laws against interracial marriage. "Love, politics, work—it was a mighty coming together," she explained. In Mississippi she registered African-American voters and taught black history and writing. In 1969, Walker published her first novel, *The Third Life of Grange Copeland.*

She "escaped" Mississippi for the East Coast, teaching, lecturing, working as a contributing editor for *Ms.* magazine, and writing—winning critics' praise and national awards. Drawing on her experiences, she extended her themes beyond civil rights and focused on the plight of African-American women, who were considered inferior by most male civil rights and radical activists. Her "womanist" views—a term she used to describe black feminism—drew attention and condemnation, as women became central characters in her writings. In *You Can't Keep a Good Woman Down* (1981), she asserted that African-American women were among the nation's "greatest heroes," oppressed beyond recognition not only by whites but also by black men. Comments about her views on race and women increased with the publication of her third and most praised novel, *The Color Purple* (1982). Although a bestseller that won her the first Pulitzer Prize given to an African-American woman, Walker received bitter criticism for her portrayal of African Americans in the novel. Many people objected to her characters using what she called black folk language and her depiction of black men who abused and brutalized women. In a positive review, one critic noted that her works could be followed "as an ongoing narrative of an African-American woman's emergence from the voiceless obscurity of poverty and racial and sexual victimization to become a reshaper of culture and tradition."

In her actions and more recent works, *The Temple of My Familiar* (1989) and *Living by the Word* (1988), Walker's range of activism and efforts to reshape culture and tradition have extended beyond African Americans to encompass world issues, environmental and nuclear destruction, and oppressed people around the globe. She champions change that will be brought about by "alternative Americans," people of all colors who recognize where they came from, who they are, and where they can go. About American history, she wrote that there have been "ancestors we have been encouraged to avoid, not to praise, not to know. This alone tells us much. In the America we are building, they laid many a foundation. In the America that will be, they will have an honored place."

involvement, most state and local authorities desegregated bus and train terminals.

Hoping to steer the activism away from freedom rides and sit-ins, the Kennedy administration argued that efforts should be focused on voter registration drives. There followed the Voter Education Project, a cooperative movement among the major civil rights organizations, which with federal protection would provide the right to vote to many who had been denied since the days of Reconstruction. The results of this effort, which ended in 1964, seemed impressive: black voters in the South increased from 29.4 to 43.1 percent of blacks eligible to vote. But most of the success came in urban areas, where white opposition was less pronounced than in rural areas. In addition, many of those involved in voter registration were brutally attacked and jailed. The reality was that the federal government provided minimal protection and preferred to work through the court system. The Justice Department was not, one official commented, a national police force.

In some instances, Robert Kennedy hoped to prevent racial violence by a show of federal force, as in

♦ On August 28, 1963, one-quarter of a million people gathered in Washington, D.C. to support racial equality. Martin Luther King, Jr. electrified the crowd by saying "I have a dream that my four little children will one day live . . . where they will not be judged by the color of their skin but the content of their character." *Francis Miller, LIFE Magazine ©Time Warner Inc.*

the case of **James Meredith,** who integrated the University of Mississippi in 1962. The attorney general sent a hundred federal marshals to guard Meredith, who transferred to the university from a black college. The tactic did not work. Thousands of white students and nonstudents attacked Meredith and the marshals. Two people were killed and 166 marshals were wounded before five thousand army troops arrived and restored order. Protected by federal forces, Meredith finished the year. In May 1963, the University of Mississippi had its first African-American graduate.

In 1963, Martin Luther King, Jr., and the SCLC focused their attention on overturning segregation in Birmingham, Alabama. Organizers planned a series of protest marches demanding the integration of Birmingham's businesses. King expected a violent white reaction to force federal intervention and raise national support. On Good Friday in 1963, he led the first march and along with others was quickly arrested. From his cell, he wrote a nineteen-page "letter" defending his confrontational tactics and aimed at those who denounced his activism in favor of patience. The "Letter from a Birmingham Jail" called for immediate and continuous, peaceful civil disobedience. Freedom was "never given voluntarily by the oppressor," King asserted, but "must be demanded by the oppressed." Smuggled out of jail and read aloud in churches and printed in newspapers across the nation, the letter rallied support for King's efforts in Birmingham.

On May 3, young and old alike filled the streets of Birmingham and confronted "Bull" Connor's police, who attacked the marchers with nightsticks, attack dogs, and high-pressure fire hoses. Television caught it all, including the arrest of more than thirteen hundred battered and bruised children. Connor's brutality not only horrified much of the American public but caused many Birmingham blacks to reject the tactic of nonviolence. The following day, many African Americans fought the police with stones and clubs. Fearing more violence, King and Birmingham's business element met on May 10, 1963, and white business owners agreed to hire black salespeople. Neither the agreement nor King's pleading, however, halted the violence, and two days later President Kennedy ordered three thousand troops to Birmingham to maintain order and to uphold the integration agreement. "The sound of the explosion in Birmingham," King observed, "reached all the way to Washington."

Indeed, Birmingham had helped Kennedy conclude that the time had come to fulfill his campaign promise to make civil rights a priority. In June 1963, he announced that America could not be truly free "until all its citizens were free" and that he would

James Meredith Black student admitted to the University of Mississippi under federal court order in 1962 amid rioting by racist mobs.

send Congress civil rights legislation that would mandate integration in places of public accommodation.

To pressure Congress to act on the bill, King and other civil rights leaders organized a **March on Washington.** The August 28 march was the largest crowd to assemble in American history, with upward of 250,000 people. King capped the day with an address that electrified the throng. He promised to continue the struggle until justice flowed "like a mighty stream," and he warned about a "whirlwind of revolt" if black rights were denied. "I have a dream," he offered, "that even Mississippi could become an oasis of freedom and justice" and that "all of God's children, black men and white men, Jews and Gentiles, Protestants and Catholics, will be able to join hands and sing . . . 'Free at last! Free at last! Thank God almighty, we are free at last!'"

In the South, however, bigotry and violence continued. In Birmingham, within weeks of King's "I Have a Dream" speech, a church bombing killed four young girls attending Sunday School, and black leaders vowed to continue their fight for Dr. King's dream.

Flexible Response

- What expectations shaped Kennedy's choices in foreign policy?
- What were some of the outcomes of Kennedy's concerns and interests in the Third World?

If Kennedy was slow to bring federal power to bear on civil rights, he, like Eisenhower, had no reluctance to use executive power to conduct foreign policy. He favored foreign over domestic policy. In his inauguration address, he dropped most of the material on domestic policy and concentrated on foreign policy, generating the powerful lines: "We shall pay any price, bear any burden, meet any hardship, support any friend, oppose any foe to assure the survival and success of liberty." Advised by his close circle of "action intellectuals," Kennedy was willing to take immediate risks to meet whatever challenges the United States faced, from the arms race, to the space race, to winning the allegiance of Third World countries.

To back up his foreign policies, Kennedy asked for, and received, a 20 percent increase in military spending, surpassing all previous peacetime military budgets. Quickly, the Pentagon began a buildup of both nuclear and conventional forces. Space exploration also received new priority and a substantial increase in its budget. When the Soviets hurled the first human being, cosmonaut Yuri Gagarin, into space, Kennedy challenged them to "race to the moon." In July 1969, after spending nearly $33 billion, Neil Armstrong won the race and became the first human to step forth on the surface of the moon.

But the country's Cold War challenges were not limited to racing against Soviet arms development and space exploration. An equally important confrontation was occurring in the developing regions of the globe. There, key problems remained—economic inequalities, nationalism, and revolution. Kennedy meant to combat those with a multifaceted **flexible response,** which included economic and military strategies. The economic strategies involved increasing direct government aid and private investment to "friendly" nations, especially less-developed nations. The latter also benefited from the personal involvement of American volunteers participating in the **Peace Corps.** Beginning in March 1961 more than ten thousand idealistic young Americans enrolled for two years in the Peace Corps. To help win the "hearts and minds" of what Kennedy called "the rising peoples" around the world, they went to developing nations to teach in schools and construct homes, build roads, and make other improvements.

To promote pro-American governments and destabilize or remove procommunist governments, Kennedy also relied on military operations by special units, such as the Green Berets, trained to deal with insurgency and live off the countryside while gaining the people's trust. These forces would work with friendly government forces or behind enemy lines to help defeat anti-American foes and provide stability. The CIA continued its varied roles, but with increased emphasis on covert operations.

March on Washington Meeting of more than a quarter of a million civil rights supporters in Washington, D.C., in 1963, at which Martin Luther King, Jr., delivered his "I Have a Dream" speech.

flexible response Kennedy's strategy of considering a variety of military and nonmilitary options when facing foreign-policy issues.

Peace Corps Program that Kennedy established in 1961 to send young American volunteers to assist less-developed nations at the grassroots level.

Confronting the Soviets

Kennedy saw Latin America as an opportunity to develop the Western Hemisphere economically, socially, and politically and introduced in 1961 the **Alliance for Progress,** a foreign-aid package, consisting of more than $20 billion in aid to show that "liberty and progress walk hand in hand." In return, Latin American governments were to introduce land and tax reforms and commit themselves to improving education and their people's overall standard of living. Action fell short of promises. The United States granted far less than proposed, and Latin American governments implemented few reforms and frequently squandered the aid, much of which ended up in the pockets of government officials. Throughout the 1960s in Latin America, the gap between rich and poor widened, and the number of military dictatorships increased.

The Alliance for Progress was only one part of Kennedy's Latin American strategy—there was also the problem of Castro. Determined to remove the Cuban dictator, Kennedy decided to implement the Eisenhower administration's covert plan to topple the Cuban leader. In March 1960, the Central Intelligence Agency had begun training Cuban exiles and mercenaries for an invasion of Cuba, which included plans to assassinate Castro.

The invasion of Cuba began on April 17, 1961. More than fourteen hundred Cuban exiles landed at the Bahia de Conchinos, the **Bay of Pigs.** However, the predicted uprisings in support of the invaders did not occur, and within three days Castro's forces had captured or killed most of them. Kennedy took responsibility for the fiasco but indicated no regrets for his aggressive policy and the violation of Cuban territory, vowing to continue the "relentless struggle" against Castro and communism. Responding to Kennedy's orders to disrupt Cuba, CIA operatives raided the island, destroyed factories and agricultural crops, and on about thirty occasions tried to assassinate Castro.

The Bay of Pigs disappointment did not deter Kennedy's willingness to use covert and special operations. The CIA directed raids against China and North Vietnam and maintained a "secret" army of Hmong tribesmen and an air force (Air America) in supposedly neutral Laos. In the newly independent Congo (the Democratic Republic of the Congo), the CIA and special military forces played a shadowy role in removing the pro-Soviet regime of Patrice Lumumba and bringing to power the anti-Communist government of Joseph Kasavubu.

After the Bay of Pigs disaster, in early June 1961, Kennedy met with Soviet leader Nikita Khrushchev in Vienna. Both men were eager to show their toughness. After the first private meeting, Kennedy was shaken and angry and thought Khrushchev had bullied him. Worse, he believed his response had been feeble. Consequently, in following meetings, Kennedy stood his ground more firmly and stressed the determination of the United Staes to fulfill its international commitments. The issue of Berlin was especially worrisome because Khrushchev was threatening to sign a peace treaty with East Germany that would give it control of the city and force the Western Allies out of West Berlin. The Cold War was about to get warmer.

Returning home, Kennedy asked for large increases in military spending, tripled the draft, and called fifty-one thousand reservists to active duty. Meanwhile, Khrushchev, in military uniform, reaffirmed Moscow's commitment to wars of national liberation, and he renewed atmospheric nuclear weapons testing. He also reaffirmed his commitment to East Germany and his determination to force the West from Berlin. Kennedy responded by beginning American nuclear testing and voicing his strong support for West Berlin. Some within the administration advocated the use of force if the East Germans or the Soviets interfered with West Berlin. With both sides posturing, many feared that Berlin might lead to armed confrontation.

In August, the tension finally broke. The Soviets and East Germans suddenly erected a wall between West and East Berlin to choke off the flow of refugees fleeing East Germany and Eastern Europe. Although the Berlin Wall challenged Western ideals of freedom, it did not directly threaten the West's presence in West Berlin.

Far more serious than the Berlin crisis was the possibility of nuclear confrontation over Cuba in October 1962. On October 14, an American U-2 spy plane flying over the island discovered that medium-range nuclear missile sites were being built there. Launched from Cuba, such missiles would

Alliance for Progress Program that Kennedy proposed in 1961, through which the United States was to provide aid for social and economic programs in Latin American countries.

Bay of Pigs Site of an invasion of Cuba in 1961 by Cuban exiles and mercenaries sponsored by the CIA; the invasion was crushed within three days and embarrassed the United States.

♦ Soviet leader Nikita Khrushchev met with John Kennedy at the Vienna Summit in June 1961. After their first meetings, Kennedy, who had been warned that Khrushchev's style ranged from "cherubic to choleric," was convinced that the Soviet leader had bested him, and that he had appeared to be a man "with no guts." Following the Vienna summit, Kennedy was determined to be tougher with the Soviets. "If Khrushchev wants to rub my nose in the dirt, it's all over," Kennedy stated after their meeting. *Wide World Photos.*

drastically reduce the time the United States had to launch a counterattack on the Soviet Union. Kennedy promptly decided on a showdown with the Soviets and organized a small crisis staff.

Negotiations were out of the question until the missiles were removed or destroyed. The military offered a series of recommendations ranging from a military invasion to a "surgical" air strike to destroy the missiles. All were rejected as too dangerous, possibly inviting a Soviet attack on West Berlin or on American nuclear missile sites in Turkey. President Kennedy, supported by his brother, the attorney general, decided to impose a naval blockade around Cuba until Khrushchev met the U.S. demand to remove the missiles. On Monday, October 22, Kennedy went on television and radio to inform the public of the missiles and his decision to quarantine Cuba. As 180 American warships got into position to stop Soviet ships carrying supplies for the missiles, army units converged on Florida. The **Strategic Air Command (SAC)** kept a fleet of nuclear-bomb-carrying B-52s in the air at all times. On Wednesday, confrontation and perhaps war seemed imminent as two Soviet freighters and a Russian submarine approached the quarantine line. Robert Kennedy recalled, "We were on the edge of a precipice with no way off." Voices around the world echoed his anxiety.

The Soviet vessels, however, stopped short of the blockade. Khrushchev had decided not to test Kennedy's will. After a series of diplomatic maneuvers, the two sides reached an agreement on October 27. The United States would not invade Cuba and would remove American missiles from Turkey, and the Soviets would remove their missiles. At nearly the same time as the terms of an agreement were being sent to Moscow, Castro sent his own message calling for a nuclear strike against the United States if Cuba was invaded. Khrushchev regarded the suggestion as madness. "We are not struggling against imperialism in order to die," he replied.

Castro was furious at Khrushchev—calling him a bastard. General Curtis LaMay, commander of SAC, was furious at Kennedy—calling the agreement "the greatest defeat in our history." But most of the world breathed a collective sigh of relief. Kennedy basked in what many viewed as a victory, but he recognized how near the world had come to nuclear war and concluded that it was time to improve Soviet-American relations. A "hot line" telephone link was established between Moscow and Washington to allow direct talks in case of another East-West crisis.

In a major foreign-policy speech in June 1963, Kennedy suggested an end to the Cold War and offered that the United States, as a first step toward improving relations, would halt its nuclear testing.

Strategic Air Command U.S. Air Force agency formed in 1946 to control America's long-range nuclear strike force.

By July, American-Soviet negotiations produced the **Limited Test Ban Treaty,** which forbade those who signed to conduct nuclear tests in the atmosphere, in space, and under the seas. Underground testing, with its verification problems, was still allowed. By October 1963, one hundred nations had signed the treaty, although the two newest atomic powers, France and China, refused to participate and continued to test in the atmosphere.

Vietnam

South Vietnam represented one of the most challenging issues Kennedy faced. Like Eisenhower, Kennedy saw it as a place where the United States could stem communism and develop a stable, democratic nation. But by 1961, President **Ngo Dinh Diem** was losing control of his nation. South Vietnamese Communist rebels, the **Viet Cong,** controlled a large portion of the countryside, having battled Diem's troops—the Army of the Republic of Vietnam (ARVN)—to a standstill. Military advisers argued that the use of American troops was necessary to turn the tide. Kennedy was more cautious. "The troops will march in, the bands will play," he said privately, "the crowds will cheer; and in four days everyone will have forgotten. Then we will be told we have to send in more troops. It's like taking a drink. The effect wears off and you have to take another." The South Vietnamese forces would have to continue to do the fighting, but the president agreed to send more "advisers." By November 1963, the United States had sent $185 million in military aid and had committed sixteen thousand advisers to Vietnam—compared with only a few hundred in 1961.

The Viet Cong was only part of the problem. Diem's administration was unpopular and out of touch with the majority of South Vietnamese. A Roman Catholic who was no believer in republican forms of government or a democratic society, Diem ruled through a handpicked, largely Catholic bureaucracy. Everywhere there appeared political opposition to his rule, from Buddhists, crime bosses, political reformers, and his own military. With American support and direction, Diem cracked down on his opponents. Reformers, rival officers, and protesting Buddhists were jailed, tortured, and killed. Protesting Diem's rule, on June 10, 1963, a Buddhist monk set himself on fire. Other **self-immolations** followed. To the shock of many Americans, Diem's sister-in-law, Madame Nhu referred to the protests as "Buddhist barbecues" and "the barbecue show."

♦ In 1963 Buddhist monks protested the harsh regime of South Vietnamese President Ngo Dinh Diem. Some, like this young priest, committed ritual suicide by fire. Demonstrations like these helped to convince the Kennedy administration that the Diem government was too unstable and needed to be replaced. In November 1963 the army overthrew and murdered Diem. *UPI/Bettmann Archives.*

Diem and his inner circle became liabilities to Kennedy and his advisers, and the administration secretly informed several Vietnamese generals that it would approve of a change of government. The army acted on November 1, killing Diem and creating a new military government. The change of government, however, brought neither political stability nor improvement in the ARVN's capacity to fight the Viet Cong.

Death in Dallas

With his civil rights and tax cut legislation in limbo in Congress, a growing military commitment to

Limited Test Ban Treaty Treaty signed by the United States, the Soviet Union, and nearly one hundred other nations in 1963, banning nuclear weapons tests in the atmosphere, in outer space, or under water.

Ngo Dinh Diem Catholic who became president of South Vietnam in 1954; he jailed and tortured his opponents and was assassinated in a coup in 1963.

Viet Cong South Vietnamese Communist rebels in South Vietnam.

self-immolation Suicide by fire as an act of sacrifice to a cause.

Vietnam, and a sluggish economy, Kennedy in late 1963 watched his popularity rating drop below 60 percent. He decided to visit Texas in November to try to heal divisions within the Texas Democratic party. He was assassinated there on November 22, 1963. The police quickly captured the reputed assassin, Lee Harvey Oswald. The next day a local nightclub owner and gambler, Jack Ruby, shot Oswald to death in the basement of the police station.

Many wondered whether Kennedy's assassination was the work of Oswald alone or part of a larger conspiracy. To dispel rumors, the government hastily formed a commission headed reluctantly by Chief Justice Earl Warren to investigate the assassination and determine if others were involved. The commission hurriedly examined most, but not all, of the available evidence and announced that Oswald was a psychologically disturbed individual who had acted alone and that no other gunmen were involved nor was there any conspiracy. Most Americans willingly accepted the findings.

Kennedy's assassination traumatized the nation. Many people canonized the fallen president as a brilliant, innovative chief executive who combined vitality, youth, and good looks with forceful leadership and good judgment. Lyndon B. Johnson, sworn in as president as he flew back to Washington on the plane carrying Kennedy's body, did not appear to be cut from the same cloth. Kennedy had attended the best eastern schools, enjoyed the cultural and social life associated with wealth, and liked to surround himself with intellectuals. Johnson, a product of public schools and a state college of education, distrusted intellectuals. Raised in the hill country of Texas, his passion was politics. By 1960, his congressional experiences were unrivaled: he had served from 1937 to 1948 in the House of Representatives and from 1949 to 1961 in the Senate, where he had become Senate majority leader. Johnson knew how to wield political power and get things done in Washington.

Beyond the New Frontier

- How did Lyndon Johnson's Great Society program expand on the New Deal?
- How did Johnson choose to attack the constraints that African Americans and other minorities were facing?

Johnson had entered politics as a New Dealer and had kept his belief that government should actively help those whom Roosevelt had called the "forgotten man." For Johnson that meant those with few or no economic or social opportunities—minorities and the poor. He wanted to build a better society, "where progress is the servant of the neediest." Recognizing the political opening generated by the assassination, Johnson immediately committed himself to Kennedy's agenda, intending to expand on it and make it his own. Five days after Kennedy's death, Johnson asked Congress for "no memorial oration or eulogy" other than the passage of Kennedy's civil rights bill. At the same time, Johnson worked on several politicians, and in February 1964 Kennedy's tax cut was approved. The civil rights bill moved more slowly, especially in the Senate, where it faced a stubborn southern **filibuster.** Johnson traded political favors for Republican backing to silence the fifty-seven-day filibuster, and the **Civil Rights Act of 1964** became law on July 2. The law made it illegal to discriminate for reasons of race, religion, or gender in places and businesses that served the public. Putting force behind the law, Congress established a federal Fair Employment Practices Committee (FEPC) and empowered the executive branch to withhold federal funds from institutions that violated the act.

Johnson had passed two major pieces of New Frontier legislation, but he intended to have a domestic program as ambitious as his political passion. He declared a **War on Poverty** in 1964 and in the next year announced his program to achieve a **Great Society.** His Great Society programs would attack racial injustice and poverty. In 1962, Michael Harrington had alerted the public to wide-scale poverty in America with his book *The Other America.* Harrington's study projected that one-fifth of the population, 35 million people, were living in poverty. A government study established the poverty line at $3,130 for an urban household of four, $1,925 for a

filibuster An obstructionist tactic of prolonged speechmaking used in the legislature to prevent a vote or bill from being considered.

Civil Rights Act of 1964 Law passed by Congress to bar segregation in public facilities and forbid employers to discriminate on the basis of race, religion, sex, or national origin.

War on Poverty Lyndon Johnson's program to help Americans escape poverty through education, job training, and community development.

Great Society Social program that Johnson announced in 1965; it included the War on Poverty, protection of civil rights, and funding for education.

♦ Johnson wanted to be remembered for his domestic programs, especially his effort to reduce poverty. During his presidency, Congress passed a variety of new programs, including Medicaid and Head Start, that targeted the 35 million Americans living below the poverty line. *Richard Wallmeyer/LBJ Library.*

rural family. Those figures indicated that nearly 34.6 million Americans were living in poverty, almost 40 percent of them (15.6 million) under the age of 18.

The War on Poverty was to be fought on two fronts: expanding opportunities and improving the social environment. Johnson believed that state and local governments were unable or politically unwilling to take the action necessary to break the cycle of poverty. Thus he projected a huge expansion of federal responsibility, funds, and power in the area of social welfare. Special efforts would be made to provide education and job training, especially for the young. "Our chief weapons will be better schools . . . better training, and better job opportunities to help more Americans, especially young Americans, to escape from squalor and misery," he declared.

The Manpower and Development Training Act, Job Corps, Head Start, and the Work Incentive Program all aimed at providing new educational and economic opportunities for the disadvantaged. In 1964, the Job Corps enrolled unemployed teens and young adults (16 to 21) needing job skills, while Volunteers in Service to America (VISTA) served as a Peace Corps for the United States, sending young, service-minded, mostly middle-class men and women to work in regions of poverty. In 1965, Head Start reached out to prekindergarten children to provide disadvantaged preschoolers an opportunity to gain important thinking and social skills. The Office of Economic Opportunity (OEO) was created in 1964 to coordinate much of the War on Poverty.

Conservative Response

Johnson's Great Society offered a tempting political target to the Republicans and **Barry Goldwater,** their presidential nominee in 1964. Senator Goldwater of Arizona had risen on a wave of conservative and ultraconservative ideology, the **New Right,** that was cresting through the Republican party. Intellectually led by William F. Buckley and the *National Review,* the New Right decried many of the political and social changes taking place in society. According to these conservatives, traditional American values of localism, self-help, and individualism were being destroyed by a New Deal–style, national welfare state. Democrats were not the only targets of conservatives. The Supreme Court, they argued, had violated its constitutional role and actively promoted liberal political and social causes. Some went so far as to demand the impeachment of Chief Justice Earl Warren.

From the mid-1950s through the 1960s, the Supreme Court under Warren handed down one decision after another that angered conservatives. To them, the Court seemed to be forcing the liberal agenda of individual rights, social justice, and equality down society's throat. The Court not only had promoted civil rights but also had expanded the rights of individuals, often at the expense of state authority. In *Yates v. United States* (1957), the Court's

Barry Goldwater Conservative Republican senator from Arizona who ran unsuccessfully for president in 1964.

New Right Conservative movement that opposed the political and social reforms of the 1960s, demanding less government intervention in the economy and a return to traditional values.

decision released fourteen officials of the American Communist party who had been imprisoned for publicly advocating the overthrow of the American government. The Court decided that verbal statements, unless accompanied by actions, did not constitute a crime. In *Gideon v. Wainright* (1963), *Escobedo v. Illinois* (1964), and *Miranda v. Arizona* (1966), the Court declared that all defendants have a right to an attorney, even if the state has to provide one, and that anyone who is arrested has to be informed of the right to remain silent and to have an attorney present during questioning (the Miranda warning).

The New Right argued that those and other decisions tipped the scale of justice too much in favor of the criminal at the expense of society. Conservatives believed that the Warren Court's actions also threatened traditional values by allowing the publication and distribution of sexually explicit materials (in *Jacobvellis v. Ohio,* 1963) and by forbidding prayers (*Engel v. Vitale,* 1962) and the reading of the Bible (*Abington v. Schempp,* 1963) in public schools. Disturbing to many, including a minority on the Court, was the 1964 *Griswold v. Connecticut* decision, which overturned Connecticut's laws forbidding the sale of contraceptives, arguing that individuals have a right to privacy that the state cannot abridge. Much less controversial was the *Baker v. Carr* ruling in 1962, which established the goal of making congressional districts "as nearly as practicable" equal in population—"one person, one vote."

Shaping the Great Society

In the opinion of the New Right, Johnson's Great Society programs and the Warren Court's judicial activism fit the same mold. Both advocated social legislation and values that rewarded not hardworking, solid American families but people whom the conservatives characterized as lazy and immoral. Plainspoken and direct, Goldwater offered most conservatives a chance to reassert their brand of traditional values and patriotic ideals. He had voted against the 1964 Civil Rights Act and, ten years earlier, against censuring Senator Joseph McCarthy (see page 906). He opposed "Big Government" and New Deal–style programs. On the world stage, Goldwater promised a more intense anti-Communist crusade. Johnson promised not to Americanize the war in Vietnam. "American boys," Johnson swore, would not "do the fighting for Asian boys." Goldwater, however, appeared willing to commit American troops in Vietnam and even to use nuclear weapons against Communist nations, including Cuba and North Vietnam.

In the war of slogans and television spots, Johnson's ads scored more points. One memorable Goldwater slogan, "In your heart you know he's right," was modified by Democrats who added, "Yeah, far right!" and, "In your guts you know he's nuts." Another Johnson ad suggested that a trigger-happy Goldwater would lead the nation into a nuclear holocaust. In a lopsided election, American voters supported liberalism over conservatism and containment (see page 866) over incinerating the Communists. Goldwater did well in the Deep South but received less than 10 percent of the electoral vote and only 38.4 percent of the popular vote.

More than forty new Democratic legislators followed Johnson to Washington, D.C., swelling the Democratic majority in the House of Representatives. Having crushed the conservatives, Johnson pushed forward legislation to enact his Great Society. Between 1965 and 1968, more than sixty programs were put in place. Most sought to provide better economic and social opportunities by removing barriers thrown up by health, education, region, and race.

One of Johnson's Great Society goals was to further equality for African Americans. Within months of his re-election, he signed an executive order that, like the old Fair Employment Practices Commission (see page 844), required that government contractors must practice nondiscrimination in hiring and on the job. He also appointed the first African American to the cabinet, Secretary of Housing and Urban Development Robert Weaver; the first African-American woman to the federal courts, Judge Constance Baker Motley; and the first African American to the Supreme Court, Justice Thurgood Marshall. Blacks applauded the president's actions but realized that large pockets of active opposition to civil rights remained—especially in Alabama and Mississippi. To keep up the pressure, Martin Luther King, Jr., explained, African Americans would peacefully press for change and would be physically attacked, and Americans, "in the name of decency," would demand federal intervention and "remedial legislation." The goal was to expand black voting in the South.

For nearly one hundred years, most southern whites had viewed voting as an activity for whites only and, through their control of the ballot, had maintained their political power and a segregated society. By mid-1964, SNCC, led by Bob Moses,

♦ The summer of 1964 was called "Freedom Summer," as hundreds of civil rights volunteers—many of them college students—converged on Alabama and Mississippi to conduct voter registration drives, often facing violent opposition. Many were beaten, some were jailed, and some lost their lives, but as Anne Moody wrote in her autobiography, *Coming of Age in Mississippi*, "threats did not stop them." *Art and Artifacts Division, Schomburg Center for Research in Black Culture, the New York Public Library, Astor, Lenox, and Tilden Foundations.*

had organized a **Freedom Summer** in Mississippi. Whites and blacks opened "Freedom Schools" to teach literacy and black history, stress black pride and achievements, and help residents register to vote. In Mississippi, as in several other southern states, a voter literacy test required that all questions be answered to the satisfaction of a white registrar. Thus a question calling for "a reasonable interpretation" of a section of the state constitution could be used to block blacks from registering.

In the face of white hostility, the work of Freedom Summer was dangerous. "You talk about fear," one Freedom Summer organizer told recruits. "It's like the heat down there, it's continually oppressive. You think they're rational. But, you know, you suddenly realize, they want to kill you." Indeed, in Mississippi from June through August of 1964, there were more than thirty-five shooting incidents, and thirty buildings, many of them churches, were bombed. Hundreds were beaten and arrested, and six Freedom Summer workers were murdered. But the crusade drew national support and registered nearly sixty thousand new African-American voters.

Keeping up the pressure, King announced that a voter registration drive was to take place in Selma, Alabama, where only 2.1 percent of eligible black voters were registered. Selma was chosen because its white community vehemently opposed integration. Selma sheriff Jim Clark, who wore mirrored sunglasses and a helmet and carried a swagger stick, had a short temper. As expected, the police confronted protesters, arresting nearly two thousand. King then called for a **freedom march** from Selma to Montgomery. On March 7, 1965, as scores of reporters watched, hundreds of freedom marchers faced fifty Alabama state troopers and Clark's forces at Pettus Bridge. After ordering the marchers to halt and firing tear gas, Clark's men chased them down, wielding whips and clubs. Television coverage of the onslaught stirred nationwide condemnation of Clark's tactics and support for King and the marchers. When staunch segregationist Governor George Wallace told President Johnson that he could not provide protection for the marchers, Johnson ordered the national guard, two army battalions, and 250 federal marshals to escort them. When the march began on March 21, it had about 3,200 marchers. When it arrived in Montgomery it had more than 25,000.

Johnson used the violence in Selma to pressure Congress to pass the **Voting Rights Act,** which he signed into law in August 1965. It banned a variety of methods that states had been using to deny blacks the right to vote, including Mississippi's literacy test, and had immediate effect. Across the South, the percentage of African Americans registered to

Freedom Summer Effort by civil rights groups in Mississippi in the summer of 1964 to register black voters and cultivate black pride.

freedom march Civil rights march from Selma to Montgomery, Alabama, in March 1965; the violent treatment of protesters by local authorities helped stir national opinion in favor of the civil rights movement.

Voting Rights Act Law passed by Congress in 1965 that suspended literacy and other voter tests and authorized federal supervision of registration in places where tests had been used.

♦ The fifty-mile Freedom March from Selma to Montgomery, Alabama caught the attention of a world-wide audience as blacks and whites marched in solidarity through jeers, threats, and violence by those opposing racial change. In this picture Reverend Martin Luther King, Jr., and Coretta Scott King (center) join with children and others in singing freedom songs as they finish the march. *Matt Herron.*

vote rose about 30 percent by 1968 (see Map 30.2). In Mississippi, it went from 7 to 67 percent, and in Selma, more than 60 percent of qualified African Americans voted in 1968, stopping Sheriff Clark's bid for re-election.

But civil rights legislation was only one of many facets of the Great Society. The Appalachian Regional Development Act (1965), Public Works and Development Act (1965), and Model Cities Act (1966) focused on developing economic growth in cities and long-depressed regional areas. An omnibus housing bill (1965) provided $8 billion for constructing low- and middle-income housing and supplementing low-income rent programs. In a related move, a cabinet-level Department of Housing and Urban Development was created. Mass-transit laws (1964 and 1966) provided needed funds for the nation's bus and rail systems, and consumer protection legislation established new and higher standards for product safety and truth in advertising. First Lady "Ladybird" Johnson's beautification program turned national attention to the environment, and the National Wildlife Preservation Act (1964) and the Clean Water Restoration Act (1966) were among the first conservation projects since Theodore Roosevelt's administration. Immigration laws also underwent major modification. The Immigration Return Act of 1965 dropped the racial and ethnic discrimination that had been established in the 1920s by setting a uniform yearly limit on immigration from any one nation.

At the top of Johnson's priorities, however, were health and education. Above all, he wanted those two "coonskins on the wall." The Elementary and Secondary Education Act (1965) was the first general educational funding act by the federal government. It granted more than a billion dollars to public and parochial schools for textbooks, library materials, and special education programs. Poor and rural school districts were supposed to receive the highest percentage of federal support. But, as with many Great Society programs, implementation fell short of intention, and much of the money went to affluent suburban school districts. Johnson's biggest "coonskin" was the Medical Care Act (1965) which established **Medicaid** and **Medicare** to help pay health-care costs for the elderly and those on welfare. In 1966, Democrats were calling the Eighty-ninth Congress, the "Congress of accomplished hopes."

Despite the flood of legislation, by 1966 many Great Society programs were diminishing in popularity. Antipoverty reformers and black leaders

Medicaid Program of health insurance for the poor; established in 1965, it provides states with funding to buy healthcare for people on welfare.

Medicare Program of health insurance for the elderly and disabled; established in 1965, it provides government payment for healthcare supplied by private doctors and hospitals.

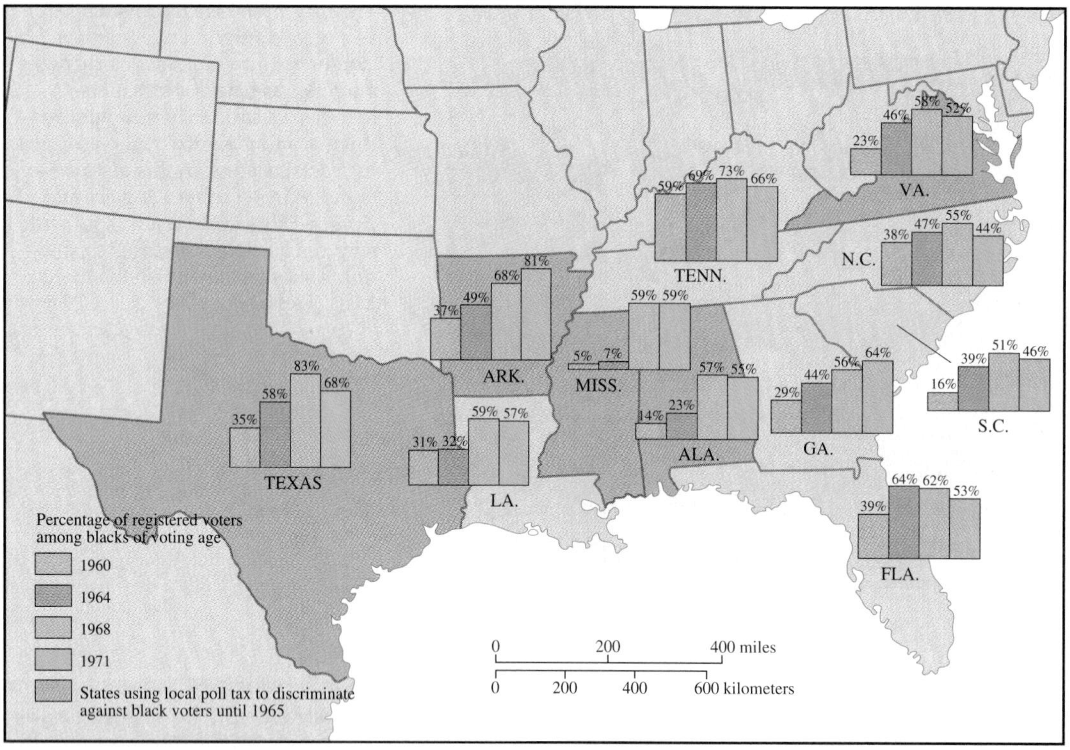

♦ **MAP 30.2 African Americans and the Southern Vote, 1960–1971** An important part of the civil rights movement was to re-establish the African-American vote that had been stripped away in the South following Reconstruction. Between 1960 and 1971, with the outlawing of the poll tax and other voter restrictions, African-American voter participation rose significantly across the South.

asked for more funds—a domestic Marshall Plan—but the dollars never came. An expanding American war in Vietnam, white backlash to urban riots, and partisan politics forced reductions in the budget of the War on Poverty and changed the administration's priorities. By 1968, the spirit of reform was gone, and Republicans and conservatives attacked the concept of the Great Society and called for a scaling back of government programs. Political scientist Theodore Lowi, in *The End of Liberalism* (1969), argued that liberal social and economic ideology was "outmoded" and that Johnson's programs were "sincere humanitarianism gone cockeyed."

Yet despite its critics, Johnson's Great Society made lasting and controversial changes in the social and political landscape. Environmental reforms, Medicare, rapid transit, urban development, and aid to education improved life for a broad range of Americans, including the middle class. The goals of the Civil Rights and Voting Rights Acts still shape social and political action and debate. The War on Poverty produced no victory, but by 1968 there was an almost 10 percent decrease in the number of people living below the poverty line and a one-third drop in the infant mortality rate. African-American unemployment fell nearly 42 percent, and average family income rose 53 percent. Johnson tackled America's social ills—racism, poverty, urban blight, education, healthcare, the environment. He cured none, but he widened the functions of the federal government more than any president since Franklin D. Roosevelt.

New Agendas

- What constraints influenced the civil rights movement in the mid-1960s? What was the outcome?
- What changes did the youth movement seek? How justified were young people's criticisms of traditional American society?

By the end of 1965, legislation had ended *de jure* segregation and voting restrictions. Equality, however, depended on more than laws. Neither the Civil

♦ In 1965 the nonviolence associated with Martin Luther King, Jr., gave way to violence in the streets of Los Angeles. The Watts riot was the first of many summer race riots that swept across the nation from 1965 to 1968. "Burn Baby Burn" quickly became a rallying cry for many urban African Americans as they protested against economic and social inequality. Thirty-four people died in the Watts riot before police and national guardsmen restored order. *Co Rentmeester, LIFE Magazine ©Time Warner Inc.*

Rights Act nor the Voting Rights Act guaranteed justice, removed oppressive poverty, provided jobs, or ensured a higher standard of living. *De facto* discrimination and prejudice remained, and African-American frustrations—born of raised expectations thwarted by poverty, prejudice, and violence—soon changed the nature of civil rights protest and ignited northern cities. Johnson had called attention to the paradox of American cities. They were "the most impressive examples of man's skill . . . as well as the worst examples of degradation and cruelty and misery." For many minorities, the latter seemed especially true.

During the 1960s more than a million mostly poor and unskilled African Americans left the South each year. Most sought a better life in northern and western cities but arrived at a time when, throughout the country, unskilled jobs were declining. The outcome of their migration was soaring urban black unemployment and increased demands on social services programs that were too meager and, often, too mean-spirited to provide adequate support. In New York City, a protester's sign spelled out the reality of civil rights for northern blacks: "I'd eat at your lunch counter—if only I had a job." Poverty and false hopes led to increases in violence and crime. At the same time, as writer James Baldwin observed, the police were seen as "the force of the white world," moving through black neighborhoods "like occupying soldiers in a bitterly hostile country." By the mid-1960s, the nation's cities were primed for racial violence. Minor race riots occurred in Harlem and Rochester, New York, during the summer of 1964, but it was the 1965 **Watts riot** that shook the nation.

New Voices

In Los Angeles, African Americans earned more per capita and owned more homes than African Americans in any other American city. But despite this upward mobility and a sizable expansion of the black middle class, many blacks in Los Angeles were poor and relied on public assistance programs. Despite their growing numbers, black Angelenos held little political power until 1963, when an African-American grassroots movement, supported by white liberals, managed to elect three black city officials. This success, however, only intensified the internal political struggle with the mayor, Sam Yorty, who was determined to maintain his control over the city.

Within Los Angeles, most African Americans lived in a 50-square-mile area called Watts. To most outside observers, Watts did not look like a ghetto. It was a community of well-maintained single-family homes and duplexes. But looks were deceptive. With a population exceeding 250,000, Watts had a population density more than four times higher per block than the rest of the city. Schools were overcrowded, and

Watts riot Race riots in a predominantly black neighborhood of Los Angeles in August 1965; it resulted in over $40 million in damages and took the lives of twenty-eight blacks and six whites.

male unemployment hovered at 34 percent. Almost two-thirds of the residents were on public assistance, and Mayor Yorty was channeling antipoverty funds to his supporters, largely at the expense of African-American neighborhoods. Patrolling Watts was the nearly all-white L.A. police force, which had a reputation for racism and brutality.

In this climate, Officer Lee Minikus stopped Marquette Frye for drunk driving on August 11, 1965. What started as a simple arrest became a scuffle, and word quickly spread through Watts that the police were attacking innocent people. Soon many residents were venting their frustration and anger by looting and setting fire to cars and stores. Thirty-six hours later, Los Angeles authorities called for the California National Guard. It took sixteen thousand poorly equipped guardsmen, police, and sheriff's deputies to calm the storm. The costs of the Watts riot were high: 34 dead, including 28 African Americans, more than 900 injured, and over $40 million in property destroyed.

The Watts riot shattered the complacency of many northern whites who had been supporting civil rights in the South while ignoring the plight of people living in the inner cities. In Los Angeles, the messages of the riot were varied. In general, African Americans were optimistic after the riot—believing that whites would at last pay attention to the needs of the black community—and they waited for the antipoverty programs they believed would be coming. Whites and Latinos were angry and afraid. They voiced stronger support for Mayor Yorty and the police, and one-third voiced the need to buy a gun for protection. Nationally, within the ranks of African Americans there was growing dissension over goals and tactics. In 1964, Martin Luther King, Jr., had received the Nobel Peace Prize, but in 1965, when he spoke to the people of Watts after the rioting, he discovered they had little use for his "dreams." He was shouted down and jeered. "Hell, we don't need no damn dreams," one skeptic remarked. "We want jobs." Watts was only the beginning. More deadly urban riots followed, and a new, militant approach to racial and economic injustices erupted: the **Black Power movement.**

The new voices of Black Power called on blacks to seek power through solidarity, independence, and, if necessary, violence. African Americans needed to use the same means as whites, argued one veteran of the battle to integrate Mississippi: "If he pose with a smile, meet him with a smile, and if he pose with a gun, meet him with a gun." Many in SNCC and CORE agreed. By the winter of 1965, SNCC leader Bob Moses had had too much of clubs, dogs, threats, and jails. Emotionally spent, he resigned, changed his name, and moved north. **Stokely Carmichael,** the new SNCC leader, exalted Black Power: "I'm not going to beg the white man for anything I deserve," he announced in 1966. "I'm going to take it." SNCC and CORE quickly changed from biracial, nonviolent organizations to Black Power resistance movements that stressed black nationalism. The insistence on independence from white allies and the violent rhetoric widened the gap between moderates and radicals. Radicals called King "Dr. Chickenwing," and moderate leaders argued that Black Power was morally wrong and harmed the movement by driving away needed allies.

The cry of "Black Power!" had established roots in inner cities across the nation. Among those receptive to a more militant approach were the **Black Muslims** (the Nation of Islam), founded by Elijah Muhammad in the 1930s. The Black Muslim movement attracted mostly young males and demanded adherence to a strict moral code that prohibited the use of drugs and alcohol. Black Muslims preached black superiority and independence from an evil white world. By the early 1960s, there were nearly a hundred thousand Black Muslims, but most whites were concerned with only one: **Malcolm X.**

A life of hard drugs, pimping, and burglary landed Malcolm Little in prison by the age of 20. Behind bars, his intellectual abilities blossomed. He devoured the prison library, took correspondence courses, and converted to the Nation of Islam—becoming Malcolm X. On his release in 1952, he quickly became one of the Black Muslims' most powerful and respected leaders. A mesmerizing

Black Power movement Movement beginning in 1966 that rejected the nonviolent, coalition-building approach of traditional civil rights groups and advocated black control of black organizations.

Stokely Carmichael Civil rights activist who led SNCC and coined the term "black power" to describe the need for blacks to use militant tactics to force whites to accept political change.

Black Muslims Popular name for the Nation of Islam, an African-American religious group founded by Elijah Muhammad, which professed Islamic religious beliefs and emphasized black separatism.

Malcolm X Black activist who advocated black separatism as a member of the Nation of Islam; in 1963 he converted to orthodox Islam and two years later was assassinated.

♦ Dropping his "slave name," Malcolm Little took the name Malcolm X—the letter "X" representing the stolen identities of African slaves. A member of the Black Muslims, he became one of the most recognized and controversial African-American nationalist leaders. He was assassinated in 1963 by members of the Nation of Islam after forming a rival organization. *Wide World Photos.*

speaker, he proclaimed the ideals of black nationalism and separatism. He rejected integration with a white society that, he said, emasculated blacks by denying them power and personal identity. "Our enemy is the white man!" he roared. But in 1964, he re-evaluated his policy. Though still a black nationalist, he admitted that to achieve their goals Black Muslims needed to cooperate with other civil rights groups and with some whites. He broke with Elijah Muhammad, and the defection cost him his life. On February 21, 1965, three Black Muslims assassinated him in Harlem. After his death, Malcolm X's *Autobiography* (1965), chronicling his personal triumph over white oppression, became a revered guide for many blacks.

Malcolm X represented only one model for urban blacks. Others advocated direct action, including violence, against white power. Huey P. Newton and Bobby Seale organized the **Black Panthers** in Oakland, California, in 1966. Although they pursued community action, like developing school lunch programs, they were more noticeable for being well armed and willing to use their weapons. FBI director J. Edgar Hoover called the Black Panthers "the most dangerous . . . of all extremist groups."

The militant black nationalism and calls for self-defense by a new wave of black leaders appeared to fuel a growing number of race riots that shook more than three hundred cities between 1965 and 1968. The summer of 1967 marked the worst year with more than seventy-five major riots. The deadliest occurred in Detroit. With its mayor strongly supporting civil rights and closely working with civil rights organizations, Detroit appeared to be a stable city. It received more than $200 million in federal grants for urban renewal, job training, and schools. Yet, as in Watts, tensions simmered beneath the surface. There were too few jobs, urban renewal projects and a new highway system were breaking apart black neighborhoods, and the police were widely seen as racist. When in July the police raided an after-hours bar, the black neighborhoods exploded. In the five days it took the army to quell the riot, thirty-four people died, seven thousand were arrested, and millions of dollars' worth of property was destroyed.

Responding to the Detroit and other riots, Johnson created a special commission chaired by Governor Otto Kerner of Illinois to investigate their causes. The commission report, issued in March 1968, put the primary blame on the racist attitudes of white America. The study described two Americas, one white and one black, and concluded: "Pervasive discrimination and segregation in employment, education, and housing have resulted in the continuing exclusion of great numbers of Negroes from the benefits of economic progress."

Just a month later, a new wave of riots spread across the United States following the assassination of Martin Luther King, Jr., by a white racist. King had worked hard to regain his leadership of the civil rights movement after the Watts riot and the emergence of Black Power. Shifting from legal rights to economic rights, he had become a champion of the

Black Panthers Black revolutionary party founded in 1966; it accepted violence as a means of social change; many of its leaders were killed in confrontations with police or sent to prison.

black urban **underclass,** criticizing the capitalistic system that relegated millions of people to poverty. Still an advocate of nonviolence, King called for mass demonstrations to compel economic and social justice. He was in Memphis supporting striking black sanitation workers when, on April 4, 1968, he was gunned down by James Earl Ray. Spontaneously, African Americans took to the streets in 168 cities, including Washington, D.C. As American cities burned and cries of "Burn, Baby, Burn," and "Black Power!" emerged from the smoke, a white backlash occurred. Many Americans, fearful of Black Power advocates and increasing urban violence, backed away from supporting civil rights. Republican politicians were especially vocal. Governor of California Ronald Reagan argued the "riff-raff" theory of urban problems: "mad dogs" and "lawbreakers" were the sole cause of the trouble. Most Americans applauded as police cracked down on the Black Panther party, arresting or killing its members. As the 1968 political campaign began, law and order replaced the Great Society as the main issue.

The Challenge of Youth

Nearly as alarming to many Americans as the changes reshaping African-American attitudes were the changes taking place among the nation's youth. The first wave of baby boomers (see page 878) were now young adults, and they were going to college in record numbers. In 1965, more than 40 percent of the nation's high school graduates were attending college, a leap of 13 percent from 1955 and of nearly 30 percent since World War II. Graduate and professional schools were churning out record numbers of advanced degrees. Although the majority of young adults remained quite traditional, an expanding number as the decade progressed advocated alternative values. The transformation was especially noticeable on college campuses.

Many students began to question the role of the university and the goal of education. Particularly at huge institutions like the University of California at Berkeley and at Los Angeles and the University of Michigan, students complained that humanism and concern for individuals were missing from education. Education seemed sterile, more like an assembly line producing a standardized product than an effort to create an independent, thinking individual. Paul Goodman, in *Growing Up Absurd* (1960), argued that schools destroyed natural creativity and replaced it with a highly structured system that stressed order and conformity. Education was designed to meet the needs of administrators and teachers, not students, he charged. Reflecting Goodman's view, many students demanded freedom of expression and a new, more flexible attitude from college administrators and faculty.

Campus activists denounced course requirements and restrictions on dress, behavior, and living arrangements. By the end of the decade, many colleges and schools had relaxed or eliminated dress codes. Long hair was accepted for males, and casual clothes like faded blue jeans and shorts were common dress for both sexes on most college campuses. Colleges also lifted dorm curfews and other residence requirements. Some dorms became coed. Academic departments reduced the number of required courses. By the beginning of the 1970s, many colleges and even some high schools had introduced programs in nontraditional fields such as African-American, Native American, and women's studies.

Setting their sights beyond the campus community, some student activists urged that the campus should be a haven for free thought and a marshaling ground for efforts to change society significantly. At the University of Michigan in 1960, Tom Hayden and Al Haber organized **Students for a Democratic Society (SDS).** SDS members insisted that Americans recognize that their affluent nation was also a land of poverty and want and that business and government chose to ignore social inequalities. In 1962, SDS issued its **Port Huron Statement,** which maintained, "The search for truly democratic alternatives to the present, and a commitment to social experimentation with them, is a worthy and fulfilling human enterprise, one which moves us and, we hope, others today." Hayden argued that the country should allocate its resources according to social need and strive to build "an environment for people to live in with dignity and creativeness."

underclass The lowest economic class; the term carries the implication that members of this class are so disadvantaged by poverty that they have little or no chance to move up economically.

Students for a Democratic Society Left-wing student organization founded in 1960 to criticize American materialism and call for social justice.

Port Huron Statement A 1962 critique of the Cold War and American materialism and complacency by Students for a Democratic Society; it called for "participatory democracy" and for universities to be centers of freedom of speech and activism.

SEPTEMBER 1967
PRICE $1
Esquire
COLLEGE ISSUE
If you think the war in Vietnam is hell, you ought to see what's happening on campus, baby.

♦ "We're in a time that's divorced from the past," wrote author Norman Mailer, and from Berkeley to Harvard Yard, college campuses were becoming battle grounds of the social, cultural, and political changes that were sweeping the nation. Whether participating in the counterculture or Freedom Summer, or opposing the war in Vietnam or college restrictions, in the 1960s it appeared that America's youth demanded new values and attitudes. *Michael Barson Collection/Past Perfect.*

SDS and other activist groups believed the campus should be a base for social criticism and activism. College authorities generally disagreed, setting the stage for further campus confrontations. One of the earliest struggles occurred at Berkeley in 1964. Led by Mario Savio, activists protested when the administration tried to prevent a campus plaza from being used to recruit supporters and solicit funds for various social and political causes. Fresh from the Freedom Summer, Savio demanded freedom of speech and political activism on campus. Claiming that the university was not fulfilling its moral obligation to provide an open forum for education and free thought, Savio asked students and faculty to disrupt the university's activities: to jam the gears, to bring the machine to its knees. More than six thousand students responded, seizing campus sites, including the administration building, boycotting classes, and yelling and chanting what many consider vulgar four-letter words. Savio and two other organizers were arrested, expelled, tried for inciting a riot, and sentenced to four months in jail—but the campus remained open to freedom of expression, including political literature.

The Berkeley Free Speech movement encouraged other campus organizers to assert their right to address social and political issues. Student activists in growing numbers focused their attention on civil rights, the environment, and social and sexual norms. By the late 1960s, though, their loudest protests opposed American foreign policy, the **military-industrial complex,** and the war in Vietnam. Opposition to the war in Vietnam and the draft expanded the number of student activists and increased pressure on the Johnson administration to modify its policies (see pages 957–958).

The youth movement's discontent with social and cultural norms also found expression in what was called the **counterculture.** Many young people spurned the traditional moral and social values of their parents and the 1950s. "Don't trust anyone over 30" was the motto of the young generation. Counterculture thinking rejected conformity and glorified freedom of the spirit and self-knowledge. A large number of teens and young adults began to accuse American society of being "plastic" in its materialism and disregard for change, and they sought ways to express their dissatisfaction.

Music was one of the most prominent forms of defiance. Some musicians, like Bob Dylan and Joan Baez, challenged society with protest and antiwar songs rooted in folk music and aimed at specific problems. For the majority, however, rock 'n' roll, which took a variety of forms, remained dominant. Performers like the **Beatles,** an English group that exploded on the American music scene in 1964, were among the most popular, sharing the stage

military-industrial complex Term first used by Eisenhower to describe the connections among government, the military, and the arms industry; in the 1960s radicals used it to refer to all those in power who benefited from U.S. militarism.

counterculture A culture with values or lifestyles in opposition to those of the established culture.

Beatles English rock group known for the intelligence of its lyrics; the group gained international fame in 1962 and disbanded in 1970.

with other British imports such as the Rolling Stones and the Animals, whose behavior and songs depicted a life of pleasure and lack of social restraints. Other musicians, like the Grateful Dead and Jimi Hendrix, turned rock 'n' roll into a new form of music, psychedelic **acid rock,** which acclaimed an unrestrained drug culture.

The message of much music of the 1960s was that drugs offered another way to be free of the older generation's values. For many in the 1960s generation, marijuana, or "pot," was the primary means to get "stoned" or "high." Marijuana advocates claimed that it was nonaddictive and that, unlike the nation's traditional drug—alcohol—it reduced aggression and heightened perception. Thus, they argued, marijuana reinforced the counterculture's ideals of peace, serenity, and self-awareness. A more dangerous and unpredictable drug also became popular with some members of the counterculture: LSD, lysergic acid diethylamide, or "acid," a hallucinogenic drug that alters perception. Harvard psychology professor **Timothy Leary** argued that by "tripping" on LSD people could "turn on, tune in, and drop out" of the rat race that was American society. Although most youths did not use drugs, drugs offered some within the counterculture and the nation a new experience that many believed was liberating. Drugs also proved to be destructive and deadly, contributing to the deaths of several counterculture figures, including musicians Jimi Hendrix, Jim Morrison, and Janis Joplin.

Another realm of traditional American values the counterculture overturned was sex. Some young people appalled their parents and society by questioning and rejecting the values that placed restrictions on sexual activities. Sex was a form of human expression, they argued, and if it felt good, why stifle it? New openness about sexuality and relaxation of the stigma on extramarital sex turned out to be a significant legacy of the 1960s. But the philosophy of **free love** also had a negative side as increased sexual activity contributed to a rapid rise in cases of sexually transmitted diseases. The notion of free love also exposed women to increased sexual assault as some men assumed that all "liberated" women desired sexual relations.

Perhaps the most colorful and best-known advocates of the counterculture and its ideals were the **hippies.** Seeking a life of peace, love, and self-awareness—governed by the law of "what feels good" instead of by the rules of traditional behavior—hippies tried to distance themselves from traditional society. They flocked in large numbers to northern California, congregating especially in the Haight-Ashbury neighborhood of San Francisco, where they frequently carried drug abuse and free love to excess. Elsewhere, some hippie groups abandoned the "old-fashioned" nuclear family and lived together as extended families on communes. Hippies expressed their nonconformity in their appearance, favoring long unkempt hair and ratty blue jeans or long flowered dresses. Although the number of hippie dropouts was small, their style of dress and grooming greatly influenced young Americans.

The influence of the counterculture peaked, at least in one sense, in the summer of 1969, when an army of teens and young adults converged on Woodstock, New York, for the largest free rock concert in history. For three days, through summer rains and deepening mud, more than four hundred thousand came together in a temporary open-air community, where many of the most popular rock 'n' roll bands performed day and night. Touted as three days of peace and love, sex, drugs, and rock 'n' roll, **Woodstock** symbolized the power of counterculture values to promote cooperation and happiness.

The spirit of Woodstock was fleeting. For most people, at home and on campus, the communal ideal was impractical, if not unworkable. Nor did the vast majority of young people who took up some counterculture notions completely reject their parents' society. Most stayed in school and continued to participate in the society they were criticizing. To be sure, the counterculture had a lasting impact on American society—on dress, sexual attitudes, music, and even personal values—but it did not reshape America in its image.

acid rock Rock music having a driving, repetitive beat, solo improvisation, and lyrics that suggest psychedelic drug experiences.

Timothy Leary Harvard professor and counterculture figure who advocated the expansion of consciousness through the use of drugs such as LSD.

free love Popular belief among members of the counterculture in the 1960s that sexual activity should be unconstrained.

hippies Members of the counterculture in the 1960s who rejected the competitiveness and materialism of American society and searched for peace, love, and individual autonomy.

Woodstock Free rock concert in Woodstock, New York, in August 1969; it attracted four hundred thousand people and is remembered as the classic expression of the 1960s counterculture.

SUMMARY

E xpectations
C onstraints
C hoices
O utcomes

The *outcome* of Kennedy's election was a wave of renewed optimism and liberalism. His call for a more responsible society and government was at the heart of his New Frontier and of Johnson's Great Society as well. Kennedy raised *expectations,* but it was Johnson's Great Society that greatly expanded the role of government in social affairs. Heightened *expectations* were clearly visible among the African Americans who looked to Kennedy, and later to Johnson, for legislation to end segregation and discrimination. As Kennedy took office, African-American leaders launched a series of sit-ins and freedom marches designed to keep the pressure on American society and the government. In 1963, Kennedy responded by introducing a civil rights bill; it was finally passed in 1964, after his assassination.

In foreign policy, Kennedy *chose* to expand the international struggle against communism. Confrontations over Berlin and Cuba, a heightened arms race, and an expanded commitment to Vietnam were *outcomes* accepted as part of the United States' global role and passed intact to Johnson.

As president, Johnson expanded on the slain president's New Frontier. The 1964 Civil Rights Act, the 1965 Voting Rights Act, and Great Society legislation were designed to wage war on poverty and discrimination while providing federal aid to education and creating a national system of health insurance for the poor and elderly. But by 1968, the growing societal and political divisions *constrained* liberalism. Despite legal and political gains, many African-American activists *chose* more militant demands for social and economic equality. The nation's youth, too, seemed unwilling to accept the traditional values of society and demanded change. Disturbed by the turmoil, conservatives and many moderate Americans opposed government programs that appeared to favor the poor and minorities at their expense. The *outcome* was that a decade that had begun with great promise produced, for many, disappointment and disillusionment.

SUGGESTED READINGS

Terry H. Anderson. *The Movement and the Sixties* (1995).

The social and cultural currents of the 1960s are skillfully woven into an overall picture of American society.

Irving Bernstein. *Promises Kept: John F. Kennedy's New Frontier* (1991).

A brief and balanced account of Kennedy's presidency that presents a favorable report of the accomplishments and legacy of the New Frontier.

Michael Beschloss. *The Crisis Years: Kennedy and Khrushchev, 1960–1963* (1991).

A strong narrative account of the Cold War during the Kennedy administration and the personal duel between the leaders of the two superpowers.

Clayborne Carson. *In Struggle: SNCC and the Black Awakening of the 1960s* (1981).

A useful study that uses the development of SNCC to examine the changing patterns of the civil rights movement and the emergence of black nationalism.

Doris Kearns. *Lyndon Johnson and the American Dream* (1977).

An effective study of how Johnson's background and values shaped his career and the Great Society.

William L. Van Deburg. *New Day in Babylon: The Black Power Movement and American Culture, 1965–1975* (1992).

A well-written study of the varieties of the Black Power movement and the development of an American consciousness.

Tom Wolfe. *The Electric Kool-Aid Acid Test* (1968).

A classic account of the dimensions of the counterculture.

Easy Rider (1969) and *The Graduate* (1967).

Two period films that critique traditional social and cultural norms and provide a glimpse of the "values" of the 1960s.

The Debate over Black Power

The Context

By 1965, the civil rights movement had made significant changes in American society. Segregation was illegal under the 1964 Civil Rights Act. Yet many African Americans still were denied equality, were mired in poverty, and felt powerless. The outcome was increasing anger among many African Americans, who replaced the philosophy of nonviolence and passive resistance with aggressive self-defense and a philosophy of "Black Power." Used initially by Paul Robeson following the Little Rock crisis (1957), the phrase burst onto front pages on June 16, 1966, when Stokely Carmichael renewed the call for Black Power. Quickly, its advocates seemed to drown out calls for "Freedom Now." A white marcher recalled that the "thundering" demands for Black Power seemed to him "chilling . . . frightening." (For further information on the context, see pages 941–944.)

The Historical Question

The phrase "Black Power" grabbed headlines. To many white Americans, it seemed threatening. To many African Americans, it signaled the need to understand the race issue and its solution in a different way and to make new choices. There was no standard definition of the term. What was Black Power? Was it a call for revolution and racial separation, a pronouncement of racial pride, a cry of desperation?

The Challenge

Using the sources provided, along with other information you have read, write an essay or hold a discussion on the following question. Cite evidence in the sources to support your conclusions. **What meanings did people give to the concept of "Black Power"? What historical and social experiences shaped these meanings?**

The Sources

1 After Stokely Carmichael called for Black Power, he wrote an essay in *The Massachusetts Review,* in which he sought to explain the origins and concerns of the Black Power movement. He said:

Negroes are defined by two forces, their blackness and their powerlessness. There have been traditionally two communities in America. The White community, which controlled and defined the forms that all institutions within the society would take, and the Negro community which has been excluded from participation in power decisions that shaped the society . . .

In recent years the answer . . . has been . . . something called "integration." According to the advocates of integration, social justice will be accomplished by "integrating the Negro into the . . . society from which he has been traditionally excluded." . . .

This concept . . . had to be based on the assumption that there was nothing of value in the Negro community . . . so the thing to do was to siphon off the "acceptable" Negroes into the surrounding middle-class white community. . . . Now, black people must look . . . to issues of collective power.

. . . The political and social rights of Negroes have been and always will be negotiable and expendable the moment they conflict with the interests of our "allies." If we do not learn from history, we are doomed to repeat it, and that is precisely the lesson of Reconstruction. . . . "

. . . To the extent that we are dependent on . . . other groups, we are vulnerable to their influence and domination.

2 Bayard Rustin, long-time civil rights advocate and a past official of CORE, opposed Carmichael's nationalism and separatism. But, as he explained in *Commentary* (1965), African Americans still faced many constraints. He wrote:

The very decade which has witnessed the decline of legal Jim Crow has also seen the rise of de facto *segregation. . . . More Negroes are unemployed today than in 1954. . . . More Negroes attend* de facto *segregated schools today than when the Supreme Court handed down its famous decision. . . .*

. . . Last summer's riots were not race riots; they were outbursts of class aggression in a society where class and color definitions are converging disastrously. . . .

We need allies. The future of the Negro struggle depends on whether the contradictions of this society can be resolved by a coalition of progressive forces which become the effective *political majority.*

3 In 1966, Lerone Bennett, Jr., the senior editor of *Ebony*, explained the underlying problems facing black Americans and American society. He wrote:

There is no Negro problem in America. . . .

The problem of race . . . is a white problem . . . white America created, invented the race problem . . . racism is a mask for a much deeper problem involving not the victims of racism but the perpetrators. . . .

It is fashionable . . . to think of racism as a vast impersonal system for which no one is responsible. . . . Racism did not fall from the sky; it was not secreted by insects. No: racism in America was made by man, neighborhood by neighborhood, law by law, restrictive covenant by restrictive covenant, deed by deed.

4 In 1967, President Lyndon Johnson created a commission chaired by Governor Otto Kerner to investigate the causes of racial strife that had swept across America and to recommend possible solutions. In March 1968, the final report provided a bleak image of race relations in the United States.

The events of the summer of 1967 are in large part the culmination of 300 years of racial prejudice. . . . Our nation is moving toward two societies, one black, one white—-separate and unequal. . . . Discrimination and segregation have long permeated much of American life; they now threaten the future of every American. . . . This deepening racial division is not inevitable. The movement apart can be reversed. . . .

Violence and destruction must be ended—-in the streets of the ghetto and in the lives of people. . . . What white Americans have never fully understood—-and what the Negro can never forget—-is that white society is deeply implicated in the ghetto. White institutions created it, white institutions maintain it, and white society condones it.

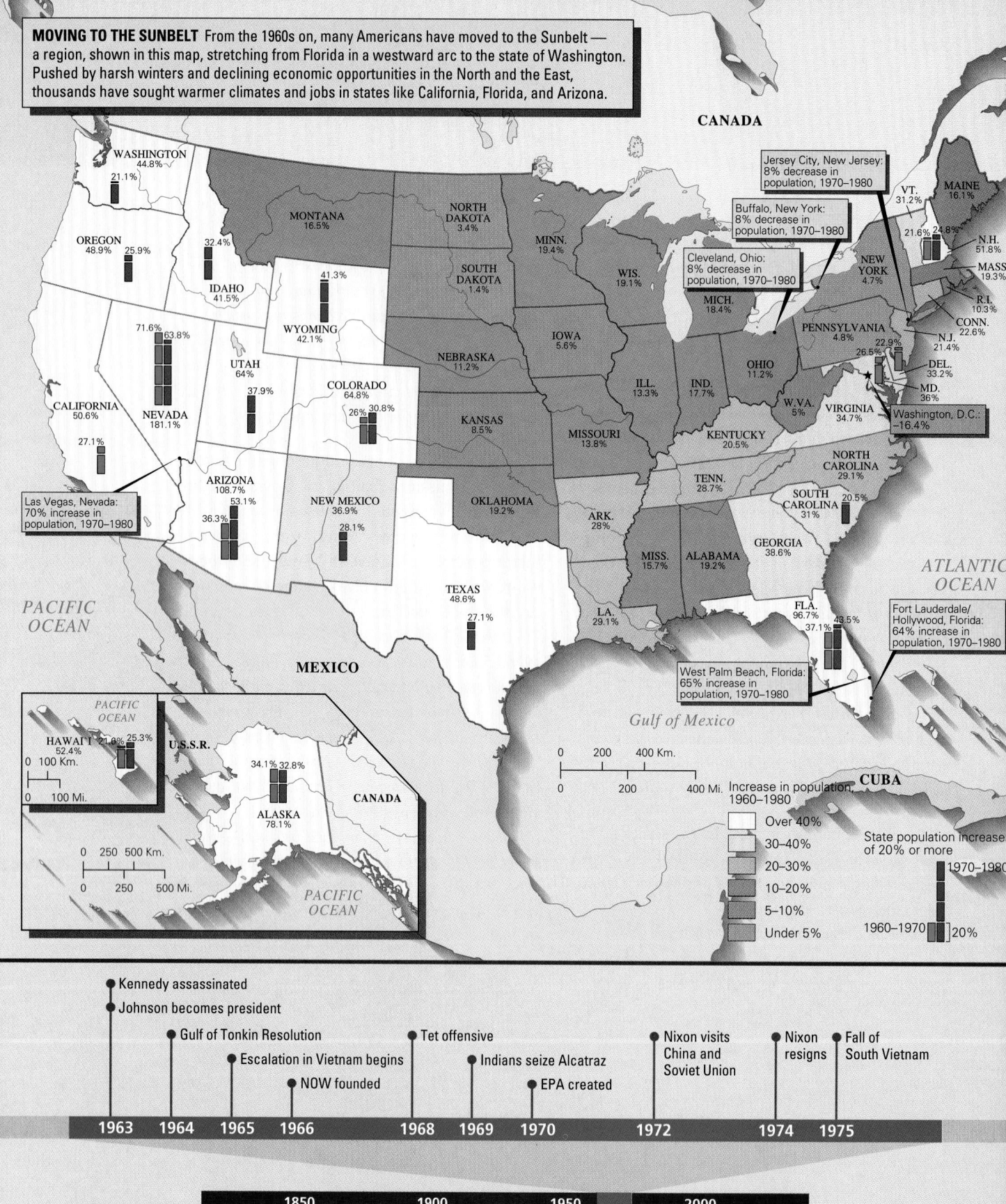

MOVING TO THE SUNBELT From the 1960s on, many Americans have moved to the Sunbelt — a region, shown in this map, stretching from Florida in a westward arc to the state of Washington. Pushed by harsh winters and declining economic opportunities in the North and the East, thousands have sought warmer climates and jobs in states like California, Florida, and Arizona.

- **1963** Kennedy assassinated; Johnson becomes president
- **1964** Gulf of Tonkin Resolution
- **1965** Escalation in Vietnam begins
- **1966** NOW founded
- **1968** Tet offensive
- **1969** Indians seize Alcatraz
- **1970** EPA created
- **1972** Nixon visits China and Soviet Union
- **1974** Nixon resigns
- **1975** Fall of South Vietnam

1850 1900 1950 2000

CHAPTER 31

America Under Stress, 1963–1975

Johnson and the World

- What expectations led Lyndon Johnson to choose the policy of escalating America's role in Vietnam?
- What were the political, social, and military outcomes of his decision?

Expanding the American Dream

- What constraints did women, Latinos, and American Indians face in American society, and how did they organize to promote change?

Nixon and the Balance of Power

- How did Richard Nixon plan to achieve an "honorable" peace in Vietnam?
- How did Nixon's choices in shaping Cold War policies differ from those favored by earlier administrations?

Nixon and Politics

- How did Nixon's choices in dealing with the economy and environment reflect his pragmatic conservatism?
- Why did Nixon achieve such a huge success in the 1972 election? What expectations and constraints led to Watergate?

INTRODUCTION

Expectations
Constraints
Choices
Outcomes

The 1960s began with a wave of optimism and confidence in the ability of the national government to improve society and promote American interests abroad. In 1963, those *expectations,* combined with Kennedy's assassination and Johnson's political skill, provided the new president an opportunity to create his Great Society. In foreign affairs, Johnson had less ambitious expectations. He seemed content to continue Kennedy's policies as he understood them, especially in Vietnam, where he was determined that the United States not be beaten by the Communists of a "two-bit" nation like North Vietnam. Unsophisticated about foreign policy, Johnson was not going to appear weak in any context.

But an array of *constraints* blocked the dramatic expansion of the American military role that many regarded as necessary to defeat the Communists. Sudden major escalation would be expensive, could weaken support for Johnson's domestic program, and might drive the Chinese and the Soviets to increase their support of North Vietnam. To the president, the best *choice* seemed a carefully controlled, gradual escalation of American force, which would convince the North Vietnamese that the cost of the war was too high. The administration *expected* the North Vietnamese would then abandon their efforts to conquer South Vietnam, and an American-supported South Vietnam would win the war.

The strategy failed miserably. North Vietnam *chose* to meet escalation with escalation, until many Americans turned against both the war and Johnson. In 1968, watching opposition to the war mount, Johnson *chose* to break the momentum of escalation and started peace negotiations with North Vietnam. Unexpectedly, he also announced his withdrawal from the presidential campaign. The 1968 Democratic convention symbolized the *outcome* of Johnson's presidency—a divided nation and an end to liberal optimism.

Republicans rallied behind Richard Nixon, who, they said, would provide the leadership necessary to restore national unity and global prestige and reassert the traditions and values that had made the nation strong. Nixon's call for unity played on the uneasy *expectations* of a society that was fragmented by the Vietnam War, urban and campus unrest, and demands from an array of social groups seeking political, economic, and social changes. After the mid-1960s, the African-American civil rights movement competed with active feminist, Latino, and American Indian groups for government and public recognition, but conservative and most moderate Americans declined to support their calls for change.

Despite their claims of wanting to bring the nation together, Nixon and Republicans *chose* to inflame social divisions to ensure their victories in 1968 and in 1972. They *expected* to construct a solid political base around a Silent Majority, composed largely of middle-class, white Americans living in suburbs, the South, and the West, who supported the war, opposed antiwar protesters and "hippies," and rejected justifications for urban riots and campus demonstrations. Promising a new, pragmatic conservatism that accepted legitimate government activism, Nixon's first administration achieved generally successful *outcomes.* Nixon improved relations with the Soviet Union and People's Republic of China and withdrew American forces from Vietnam. Domestically, his policy *choices* showed surprising flexibility, expanding some Great Society programs and using Keynesian policies to confront inflation and a sluggish economy.

Despite his successes, Nixon was not satisfied. He wanted his political enemies destroyed, and this desire contributed to the illegal activities surrounding the Watergate break-in. Watergate's *outcomes* included not only the unprecedented resignation of a president but a nationwide wave of disillusionment with politics and government.

CHRONOLOGY

From Camelot to Watergate

1960 Kennedy elected president

1962 Ceasar Chavez forms National Farm Workers Association

1963 Report of the Presidential Commission on the Status of Women
Betty Friedan's The Feminine Mystique
La Raza Unida formed in Texas
John F. Kennedy assassinated
Lyndon B. Johnson becomes president

1964 Civil Rights Act
Gulf of Tonkin Resolution
Johnson elected president

1965 U.S. air strikes against North Vietnam begin
American combat troops arrive in South Vietnam
Anti-Vietnam "teach-ins" begin
Dominican Republic intervention
National Farm Workers Association begins strike
Voting Rights Act

1966 National Organization for Women founded

1967 Antiwar march on Washington

1968 Tet offensive
My Lai massacre
Johnson withdraws from presidential race
Peace talks begin in Paris
Robert Kennedy assassinated
Mexican-American student walkouts
American Indian Movement founded
Richard Nixon elected president

1969 Secret bombing of Cambodia
Vine Deloria, Jr.'s, Custer Died for Your Sins
Warren Burger appointed to Supreme Court as chief justice
Nixon Doctrine
Anti-Vietnam march on Washington
First American troop withdrawals from Vietnam
Alexander v. Holmes
American Indians occupy Alcatraz

1970 U.S. troops invade Cambodia
Kent State and Jackson State killings
Earth Day observed
Harry Blackmun appointed to Supreme Court
Strike-for-Equality Parade
Environmental Protection Agency created
Clean Air and Clean Water Acts

1971 Nixon enacts price and wage controls
New York Times publishes Pentagon Papers
Swann v. Charlotte-Mecklenburg
William Rehnquist and Lewis Powell appointed to Supreme Court

1972 Nixon visits China and Soviet Union
Bombing of North Vietnam resumes
Watergate break-in
Revenue Sharing Act
Nixon re-elected
SALT I treaty

1973 Vietnam peace settlement
"Second battle of Wounded Knee"
Watergate hearings
Salvador Allende overthrown in Chile
War Powers Act

1974 Nixon resigns
Gerald Ford becomes president

1975 South Vietnam government falls to North Vietnamese

Johnson and the World

- What expectations led Lyndon Johnson to choose the policy of escalating of America's role in Vietnam?
- What were the political, social, and military outcomes of his decision?

Suddenly thrust into the presidency by Kennedy's assassination, Lyndon Baines Johnson moved quickly to breathe life into Kennedy's domestic program and to launch the more extensive Great Society. Johnson was comfortable dealing with domestic issues and politics. In foreign policy, however, he relied more heavily on his advisers—the "wise men," as he called them. In examining foreign affairs, both Johnson and his advisers agreed that there were two regions of special concern, Latin America and Vietnam. In both areas, Johnson was determined there would be no further erosion of American power.

Toward Latin America, Johnson revised the focus of Kennedy's Alliance for Progress policy (see page 932). Stability became more important than reform. Assistant Secretary of State Thomas Mann told Latin American leaders that political, social, and economic reforms were no longer a central requirement for American aid and support. This new perspective, labeled the **Mann Doctrine,** resulted in increases in the amounts of American military equipment and advisers that the United States provided to regimes trying to suppress the disruptive opposition they labeled "Communist." The new policy led to direct military intervention in the Dominican Republic in 1965. There, supporters of deposed, democratically elected president Juan Bosch rebelled against a repressive, pro-American regime. Johnson and his advisers decided that the pro-Bosch coalition was dominated by Communists, asserted the right to protect the Dominican people from an "international conspiracy," and sent in twenty-two thousand American troops to restore order. The troops left the island in mid-1966, after monitoring national elections that elected Joaquin Balaguer, a conservative, pro-American candidate, as president. Johnson claimed to have saved a free nation from communism, but many Latin Americans saw only an example of Yankee arrogance and intrusive power.

Americanization of the Vietnam War

By the winter of 1963 and 1964, the Viet Cong, supported by men and supplies from North Vietnam, appeared to be winning the war in Vietnam. With the ineffective South Vietnamese army teetering on the verge of collapse, many American advisers saw little hope for improvement. Captain Edwin Shank, a military adviser who flew combat missions in South Vietnam, found South Vietnamese soldiers to be "stupid, ignorant . . . [and] a menace." He believed that the war could be won only by American forces.

Within the circle of Johnson's military and civilian advisers there was general agreement that to stabilize Vietnam and turn the tide of battle would require a larger American combat role. Johnson concurred. The United States must not lose. "I am not going to be the President who saw Southeast Asia go the way China went," he asserted. But in 1964 he had Goldwater and Congress to worry about. To expand the American combat role in Vietnam during an election year was not politically wise, so Johnson decided to try to delay escalation. But planning and increased covert raids on North Vietnam began immediately.

Meanwhile, the administration began generating public support for a larger American role in defending South Vietnam. Encouraged by the White House and the **Pentagon,** throughout the spring and summer of 1964, newspapers and magazines printed articles and stories stressing the Communist threat to South Vietnam, Southeast Asia, and the Pacific. Fixed on the domino theory (see page 916), the White House awaited a chance to ask Congress for permission to use whatever force would be necessary to defend South Vietnam.

The chance came in August 1964 off the coast of North Vietnam. On August 1, North Vietnamese torpedo boats skirmished with the American destroyer *Maddox* in the Gulf of Tonkin (see Map 31.1). On August 4, experiencing rough seas and poor visibility, radar operators on the *Maddox* and another destroyer, the *C. Turner Joy,* concluded that the patrol boats were making another attack. Confusion followed. Both ships fired wildly at targets shown only on radar screens. Within hours, officers on both ships reported that the radar blips had not been

Mann Doctrine U.S. policy outlined by Thomas Mann during the Johnson administration, calling for stability in Latin America rather than economic and political reform.

Pentagon U.S. military establishment, so named because its central offices are located in a five-sided building in Arlington, Virginia, called the Pentagon.

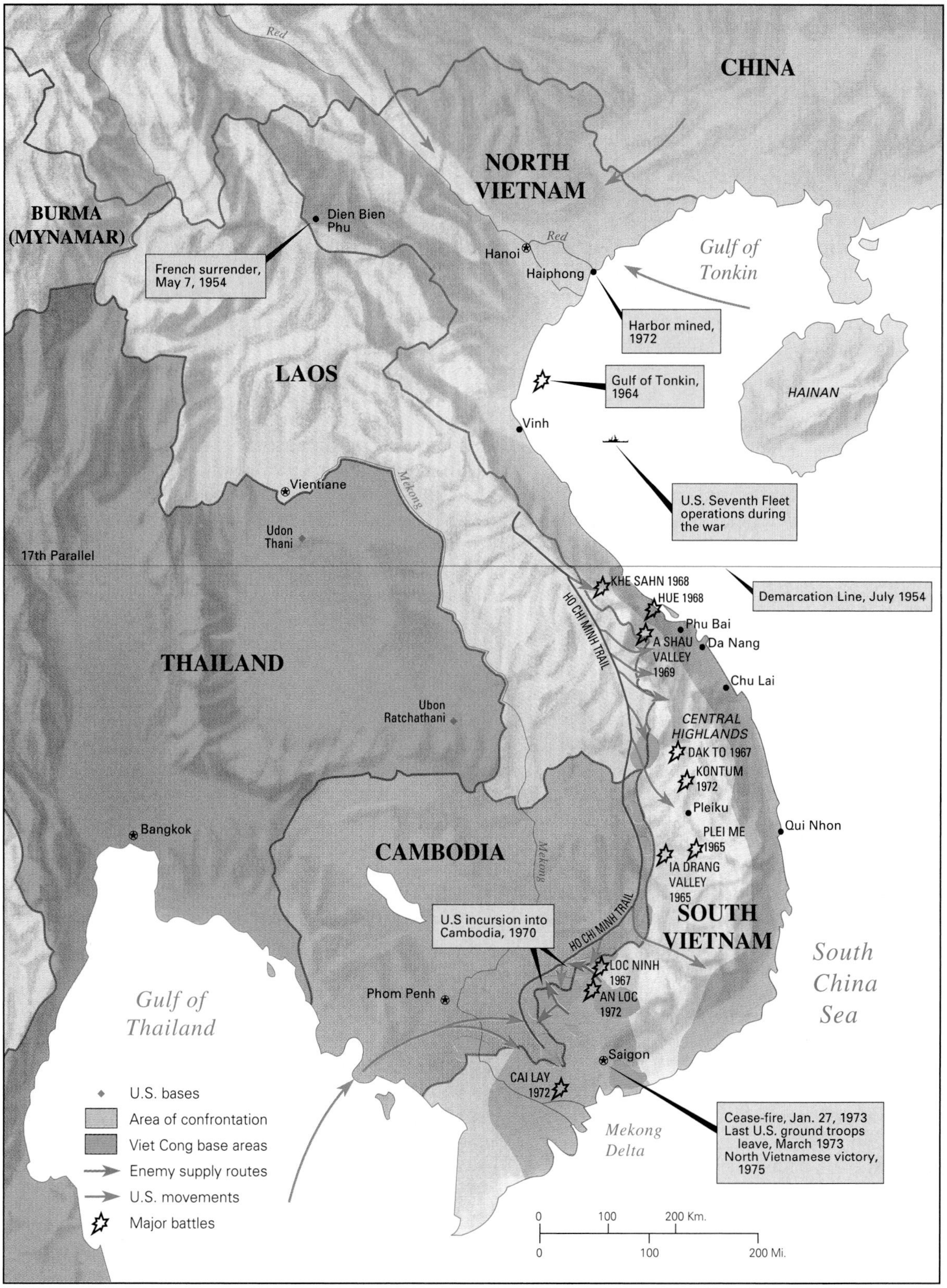

♦ **MAP 31.1 The Vietnam War, 1954–1975** Following the French defeat at Dienbienphu, the United States became increasingly committed to defending South Vietnam. This map shows some of the major battle sites of the Vietnam War from 1954 to the fall of Saigon and the defeat of the South Vietnamese government in 1975.

attacking vessels. Hearing the corrected reports, Johnson joked that the sailors had probably been shooting at whales. Still, he implemented his reactive policy and told the nation that Communist attacks against "peaceful villages" in South Vietnam had been "joined by open aggression on the high seas against the United States of America." On August 7, Congress approved the **Gulf of Tonkin Resolution,** allowing the United States "to take all necessary measures to repel" attacks against American forces and "to prevent further aggression." It was, in Johnson's terms, "like Grandma's nightgown, it covered everything." Public opinion polls showed strong support for the president, and only two senators opposed the resolution: Wayne Morse of Oregon and Ernest Gruening of Alaska.

The Gulf of Tonkin Resolution gave Johnson the freedom to take whatever measures he wanted in Vietnam, but he remained cautious. Reports from the field concluded that the Viet Cong were continuing to win the battle for land and the South Vietnamese government remained unstable and unpopular. Nearly all of Johnson's advisers agreed that two moves were needed to win the war: committing American combat troops and bombing North Vietnam. To do nothing, Secretary of Defense Robert McNamara warned, was the "worst course of action" and would "lead only to a disastrous defeat."

The Joint Chiefs of Staff, McNamara, and the National Security Council believed that the North Vietnamese would withdraw support from the Viet Cong rather than watch their nation's economic base go up in smoke. Without support from the North, they reasoned, the Viet Cong could be defeated by the American-equipped and -advised South Vietnamese army (ARVN). The need for large numbers of American ground forces would consequently be limited. Johnson listened to his "wise men" and approved and committed ground troops to protect U.S. air bases. On February 7, 1965, a Viet Cong attack on the American base at Pleiku killed eight Americans and provided a hoped-for provocation for unleashing the air assault.

Operation Rolling Thunder began on March 2. On March 8, the 3rd Marine Division arrived to take up positions around the American base at Danang. By July, American planes were flying more than nine hundred missions a week and a hundred thousand American ground forces had reached Vietnam. Near their bases, American infantry and armored units patrolled aggressively, searching out the enemy. Johnson's strategy soon showed its flaws. As the United States escalated the war, so too did the enemy, which committed units of the North Vietnamese army (NVA) to the fighting in South Vietnam. The U.S. commanding general in Vietnam, **William Westmoreland,** and others insisted that victory required taking the offensive, which necessitated even more American soldiers. Reluctantly, Johnson gave the green light. Vietnam had become an American war.

Westmoreland's plan was to use overwhelming numbers and firepower to destroy the enemy. The first major American offensive was a large-scale sweep of the Ia Drang Valley in November 1965. Ten miles from the Cambodian border, the Ia Drang Valley contained no villages and was a long-time sanctuary for Communist forces. The goal was to airlift in units of the Air Cavalry and search out and destroy the enemy.

The initial landing went without incident, but soon the Americans came under fierce attack from North Vietnamese troops. One soldier recalled that his "assault line [that] had started out erect went down to . . . a low crawl." The battle raged for three days with air and artillery supporting the outnumbered Americans. "There was very vicious fighting," North Vietnamese commander Nguyen Huu noted. The "soldiers fought valiantly. They had no choice, you were dead if not." Both sides claimed victory and drew different lessons from the engagement. Examining the losses, 305 Americans versus 3,561 Vietnamese, American officials concluded that the strategy of search and destroy worked—the enemy would be ground down. *Time* magazine named Westmoreland "Man of the Year" for 1965. Hanoi concluded that its "peasant army" had withstood America's best firepower and had fought U.S. troops to a draw. The North Vietnamese were confident: the costs would be great, but they would wear down the Americans. Both sides, believing victory was possible, committed more troops and prepared for a lengthy war.

Throughout 1966 and 1967, both sides continued to escalate. The Viet Cong and North Vietnamese suffered heavy loses of men and supplies, but their determination and ability to continue the struggle were unbroken. American aircraft rained bombs on

Gulf of Tonkin Resolution Resolution passed by Congress in 1964 authorizing the president to take any measures necessary to repel attacks against U.S. forces in Vietnam.

William Westmoreland Commander of all American troops in Vietnam from 1964 to 1968.

♦ Unlike previous American wars, Vietnam was a war without fixed front lines. At the isolated outpost of Khe Sanh, fewer than six thousand American Marines fought to hold back thirty to forty thousand North Vietnamese regulars for seventy-seven days, killing or wounding more than ten thousand of the enemy. Within weeks after the siege, the United States withdrew from the area. *Robert Ellison/ Black Star.*

North Vietnam and supply routes south, especially the **Ho Chi Minh Trail,** but arms and provisions still moved. In the fall of 1967, General Westmoreland informed Washington that the enemy was "largely confined to the periphery of South Vietnam" and that half of the enemy's forces were no longer capable of combat. At the same time, he asked for more soldiers, and the American presence increased to 542,000.

Unknown to Westmoreland, North Vietnamese leaders were planning an immense campaign aimed at capturing South Vietnamese cities during Tet, the Vietnamese new year holiday. In January 1968, the Viet Cong struck forty-one cities throughout South Vietnam, including the capital, Saigon. In some of the bloodiest fighting of the war, American and South Vietnamese forces recaptured the lost cities and villages. It took twenty-four days to oust the Viet Cong from the old imperial city of Hue, leaving the city in ruins and costing more than 10,000 civilian, 5,000 Communist, 384 South Vietnamese, and 216 American lives (see Map 31.1).

The **Tet offensive** was a military defeat for North Vietnam and the Viet Cong. It provoked no popular uprising against the South Vietnamese government, the Communists held no cities or provincial capitals, and they suffered staggering losses. More than forty thousand Viet Cong were killed. Tet was, nevertheless, a "victory" for the North Vietnamese, for it seriously weakened American support for the war. Amid official pronouncements of "victory just around the corner," Tet destroyed the Johnson administration's credibility and intensified a growing antiwar movement.

The Antiwar Movement

Throughout 1964, support for an American role in Vietnam was widespread. Most Americans accepted the domino theory and claims that horrible reprisals against non-Communists would follow a Communist victory. Those opposing the war were of little concern to the White House, which dismissed them as leftists or pacifists. A year later, little had changed, except the largely college-based opposition to the war was more outspoken. The University of Michigan held the first Vietnam "teach-in" to mobilize opposition to American policy on March 24, 1965. In April, Students for a Democratic Society (SDS) organized a protest march of about fifteen thousand in front of the White House.

Those opposing the war fell into two major types that rarely agreed on anything other than that the war should be ended. Pacifists and radical liberals on the political left opposed the war for moral and ideological reasons. Others, as the American military commitment grew and the military draft claimed more young men, opposed the war for more pragmatic reasons: the draft, the loss of lives and money, and the inability of the United States to either defeat the enemy or create a stable, democratic South Vietnam. In 1966, high school students hardly mentioned Vietnam or the draft as a problem facing their lives. Three years later, 75 percent of those polled listed both as major worries. By 1967, the possibility of being sent to Vietnam was becoming a concern of many college students. A University of Michigan student complained that if he was drafted and spent two years in the army, he would lose more than $16,000 in income. "I know I sound

Ho Chi Minh Trail Main infiltration route for North Vietnamese soldiers and supplies into South Vietnam; it ran through Laos and Cambodia.

Tet offensive Viet Cong and North Vietnamese offensive against South Vietnamese cities in January 1968; a military defeat for North Vietnam, it nevertheless undermined U.S. support for the war.

♦ In foreign affairs, Johnson relied heavily on his advisers—"wise men." In 1963 and 1964, his Vietnam advisers recommended committing American forces to stabilize South Vietnam and defeat the Viet Cong and North Vietnamese. In 1968, many of his civilian advisers told the president that victory in South Vietnam could not be obtained by military means and that the United States should look for a negotiated settlement. Here, the president is listening to General William Westmoreland as Secretary of Defense Clark Clifford speaks with Secretary of State Dean Rusk (on right). *Wide World Photos.*

selfish," he explained, "but . . . I paid $10,000 to get this education." Yet college students and graduates were not the most likely to be drafted. Far more often, those who were drafted and sent to Vietnam were poorly educated, low-income whites and minorities.

Nevertheless, it was America's middle class, especially college students, who swelled the antiwar movement and participated in a "Stop-the-Draft Week" in October 1967. That week, more than ten thousand demonstrators blocked the entrance of an induction center in Oakland, California, while over two hundred thousand people staged a massive protest march in Washington against "Lyndon's War."

Until 1967, Johnson displayed little concern about the antiwar movement. Media coverage continued to be positive, emphasizing American successes and clinging to the domino theory. Public opinion polls found that the nation stood behind Johnson's efforts to save South Vietnam. But as antiwar numbers increased in 1967, Johnson responded with **Operation Chaos,** in which federal agents infiltrated, spied on, and tried to discredit antiwar groups.

The Tet offensive broadened and intensified antiwar sentiments. The highly respected CBS news anchor Walter Cronkite had supported the war, but Tet changed his mind. Unable to reconcile the administration's claims of impending victory with the fierce Communist offensive, he went on a personal fact-finding tour of Vietnam. On his return, Cronkite announced that there would be no victory in Vietnam and that the United States should make peace. "If I have lost Walter Cronkite, then it's over. I have lost Mr. Average Citizen," Johnson lamented.

Johnson's circle of advisers also began to oppose the war. Secretary of War Robert McNamara left the administration over its war policy, while Secretary of State Dean Rusk and new secretary of defense Clark Clifford argued that victory was impossible. Clifford concluded that after four years of "enormous casualties" and "massive destruction from our bombing" there was no lessening of "the will of the enemy." Thus, following Tet, when Westmoreland called for more troops, most of Johnson's "wise men" urged sending fewer troops and seeking instead a diplomatic end to the war.

The 1968 Presidential Campaign

As Johnson prepared for the 1968 presidential race, rumors circulated that two hundred thousand more Americans were being sent to Vietnam. In New Hampshire, benefiting from such rumors, Minnesota senator **Eugene McCarthy** was running a presidential primary campaign based largely on opposition to the Vietnam War. At the heart of his New Hampshire campaign were hundreds of student volunteers who, deciding to "go clean for Gene," knocked on thousands of doors and distributed bales of flyers and pamphlets touting their candidate and condemning the war.

Operation Chaos FBI operation ordered by President Johnson that infiltrated the antiwar movement in the United States in the hope of discrediting it.

Eugene McCarthy Senator who opposed the Vietnam War and made an unsuccessful bid for the 1968 Democratic nomination for president.

♦ As a spoof on Dickens's *A Christmas Carol,* this cartoon shows Johnson being visited by the ghosts of Vietnam—past, present, and future. More than 46,000 Americans died in Vietnam. *Library of Congress.*

Expecting no real challenge to his renomination, Johnson had not entered the March 18 New Hampshire primary. But with the furor over Tet strengthening McCarthy's antiwar candidacy, Johnson's political advisers quickly organized a **write-in campaign** for the president. Johnson won, but by only 6 percent of the votes cast. Political commentators promptly called McCarthy the real winner. Adding to Johnson's political worries, New York senator **Robert Kennedy** also proclaimed his candidacy and opposition to the war in Vietnam. The war became a critical issue in the campaign and a major liability to Johnson.

On March 31, 1968, a haggard-looking president delivered a major televised speech announcing changes in his Vietnam policy. The United States was going to seek a political settlement through negotiations with the Viet Cong and North Vietnamese. The escalation of the ground war was over, and the South Vietnamese would take a larger role in the war. The bombing of northern North Vietnam was going to end, and a complete halt of the air war would follow the start of negotiations. At the end of his speech, Johnson calmly made this announcement: "I have concluded that I should not permit the presidency to become involved in the partisan divisions that are developing in this political year. . . . Accordingly, I shall not seek, and I will not accept, the nomination of my party for another term as president." Listeners were shocked. Lyndon B. Johnson had thrown in the towel. Although he later claimed that his fear of having a heart attack while in office was the primary reason for his decision not to run, nearly everyone agreed that the Vietnam War had ended Johnson's political career and undermined his Great Society.

Negotiations with North Vietnam began in Paris in May and proceeded nowhere. Still, Johnson halted the bombing of North Vietnam in October and hoped that opposition to the war would decline. Instead, antiwar opponents redoubled their efforts, keeping the war a critical issue within the Democratic party. There were now three Democratic candidates. McCarthy campaigned against the war and the "imperial presidency." Kennedy opposed the war but not executive and federal power, and he called on the government to better meet the needs of the poor and minorities. Vice President **Hubert H. Humphrey,** running in the shadow of Johnson, stood behind the president's foreign and domestic programs. Humphrey relied on party regulars and White House clout, rather than the primaries, to gain the nomination. He knew that there were enough nonprimary delegates to the national convention for him to gain the nomination without entering a primary and that most of those delegates supported him.

By June, Kennedy was winning the primary race, drawing heavily from minorities and urban Democratic voters. In the critical California primary, Kennedy gained a narrow victory over McCarthy, 46 to 41 percent, but the victory was all too short. As the winner left his election headquarters, he was shot in the head by Sirhan Sirhan, a Jordanian immigrant. Kennedy died the next day.

Kennedy's assassination stunned the nation. It also ensured Humphrey's nomination. McCarthy

write-in campaign An attempt to elect a candidate in which voters are urged to write the name of an unregistered candidate directly on the ballot.

Robert Kennedy Attorney general during the presidency of his brother John F. Kennedy; he was elected to the Senate in 1964 and was campaigning for the presidency when he was assassinated in 1968.

Hubert H. Humphrey Vice president under Lyndon Johnson; he won the Democratic nomination for president in 1968 but lost the election to Richard Nixon.

♦ Violence erupted during the 1968 Democratic National Convention in Chicago. Using nightsticks, police attacked antiwar and anti-establishment protesters that surrounded the convention hotel. The violent confrontations in Chicago did little to quell similar protests, unify the Democratic party, or help Hubert Humphrey's chances for election. *Wide World Photos.*

continued his campaign but was unable to generate much support among party regulars. By the time of the national convention in Chicago in August, Humphrey had enough pledged votes to guarantee his nomination. Nevertheless, the convention was dramatic. Inside and outside the convention center, antiwar and anti-establishment groups demonstrated for McCarthy, peace in Vietnam, and social justice. In the streets of Chicago, radical factions within the Students for a Democratic Society promised physical confrontation. So-called **Yippies** (the Youth International Party) led by Abbie Hoffman and Jerry Rubin threatened to contaminate the water supply with drugs. Chicago mayor Richard Daley was determined to maintain order. Inside the convention, delegates argued and screamed support for their positions. Outside, protesters threw eggs, bottles, rocks, and balloons filled with water, ink, and urine at the police, who responded with tear gas and nightsticks. On August 28, the police went berserk before television cameras, viciously and indiscriminately attacking protesters and bystanders alike. The violence in Chicago's streets overshadowed Humphrey's nomination and acceptance speech—and much of his campaign.

Many Americans were disgusted by the chaos in Chicago and saw it as typical of the general disruption that was plaguing the nation. **George Wallace,** the Democratic governor of Alabama, appealed to this sentiment when he left the Democratic party and ran for president as the American Independent party's candidate. The conservative Wallace opposed federal civil rights legislation and took a dim view of antiwar protesters and welfare recipients. He aimed his campaign at southern whites, blue-collar workers, and low-income white Americans, all of whom deplored the "loss" of traditional American values and society. On the campaign trail, Wallace called for victory in Vietnam and took special glee in attacking the counterculture and the "rich-kid" war protesters, who avoided serving in Vietnam while the sons of working-class Americans died there. Two months before the election, Wallace commanded 21 percent of the vote, according to national opinion polls. "On November 5," he confidently predicted, "they're going to find out there are a lot of rednecks in this country."

Republican candidate Richard Nixon easily won his party's nomination at an orderly convention. He also intended to tap the general dissatisfaction but without the hostility of the Wallace campaign. He and **Spiro Agnew,** his vice-presidential running mate, focused the Republican campaign on the need

Yippies Counterculture group that inflamed the protests that disrupted the Democratic National Convention in Chicago in 1968.

George Wallace Conservative Alabama governor who opposed desegregation in the 1960s and ran unsuccessfully for the presidency in 1968 and 1972.

Spiro Agnew Vice president under Richard Nixon; he resigned in 1973 amid charges of illegal financial dealings during his governorship of Maryland.

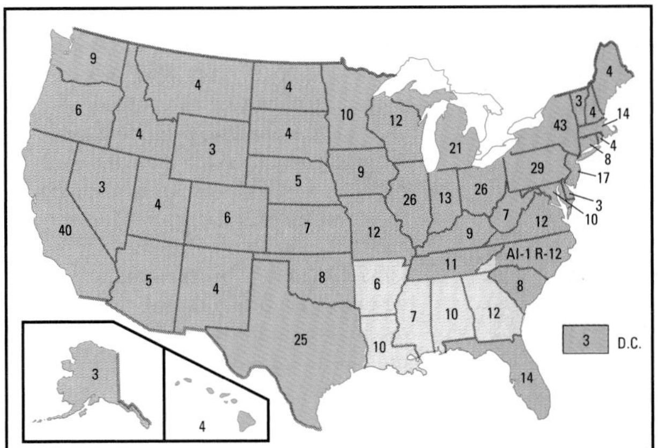

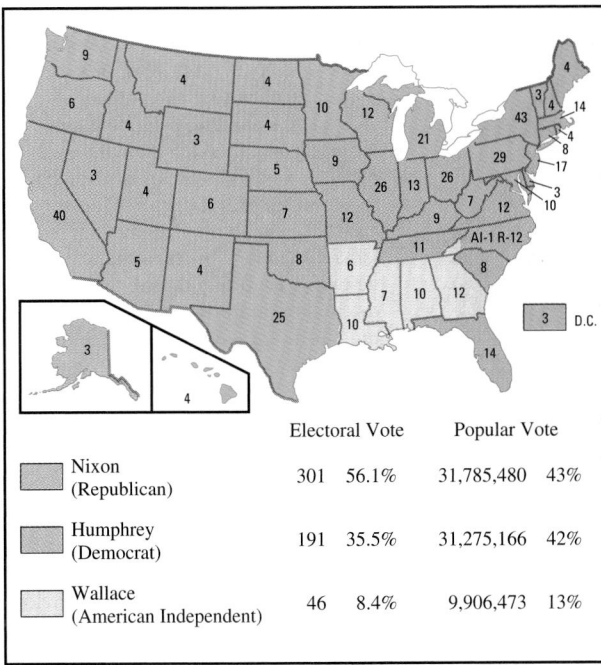

	Electoral Vote		Popular Vote	
Nixon (Republican)	301	56.1%	31,785,480	43%
Humphrey (Democrat)	191	35.5%	31,275,166	42%
Wallace (American Independent)	46	8.4%	9,906,473	13%

♦ **MAP 31.2 Election of 1968** In winning the 1968 election against Hubert Humphrey, Richard Nixon received fewer popular votes than he did in 1960, when he won more than 34 million votes. But in the all-important electoral vote, Nixon easily defeated his Democratic rival. As they did in the 1960 election, some southerners opted for a third choice, unwilling to vote for a Republican or a liberal Democrat. The third choice was George Wallace.

for effective international leadership and law and order at home, while denouncing pot, pornography, protesters, and permissiveness. Nixon announced that he would "end the war and win the peace in Vietnam" but refused to comment further. Nixon won with a comfortable margin in the Electoral College, although he received only 43.4 percent of the popular vote (see Map 31.2). Conservatives were pleased. Together, Nixon and Wallace attracted almost 57 percent of the vote, which conservatives said indicated wide public support for an end to liberal social programs and a return to traditional values.

Expanding the American Dream

- What constraints did women, Latinos, and American Indians face in American society, and how did they organize to promote change?

Part of Nixon's appeal in 1968, and again in 1972, was that he and his supporters projected a government that would enact legislation to meet the needs of the so-called **Silent Majority**—white, middle-class America—rather than to promote social experimentation and cater to minorities. The explosion of the civil rights movement during the 1960s had not only spread African-American activism to all parts of the nation but also fostered the growth of other groups demanding equal rights and access to the American dream. Joining the counterculture and antiwar and youth movements were women's rights, Mexican-American, and American-Indian movements. To some Americans, the "sudden" emergence of these trends signaled a fragmentation of American society that needed to be controlled.

The Women's Rights Movement

For women, the 1950s had been a paradox. Although many women achieved fulfillment at home from raising children and running the household, a growing number were less satisfied with their lives and work opportunities. As the 1960s began, more women were entering the work force, having fewer children, and getting divorced. Many women complained that gender stereotyping denied them access to profitable career jobs, a position affirmed by the Kennedy administration's 1963 report of the Presidential Commission on the Status of Women, which showed in stark statistics that women constituted a social and economic underclass. Compared to white men, women worked for less pay (on average 40 percent that of a man), were more likely to be fired or laid off, and had little success in reaching top career positions. Nor was it just in the workplace that women faced discrimination. Throughout the country divorce, credit, and property laws generally favored men, and in three southern states, women were not allowed to serve on juries.

To some women, the role of housewife itself symbolized oppression. **Betty Friedan** was one who concluded the chores of the housewife amounted to a form of servitude that prevented women from

Silent Majority Name given to the majority of Americans who supported the government and did not protest or riot; a typical member of the Silent Majority was believed to be white, middle class, average in income and education, and moderately conservative in values and attitudes.

Betty Friedan Feminist who wrote *The Feminine Mystique* in 1963 and helped found the National Organization for Women in 1966.

♦ In 1972, Title IX of the Education Amendments required gender equality in school and college sports, dramatically changing the nature of women's athletics by igniting a women's sports boom. In this 1967 picture, the first woman to attempt the running of the Boston Marathon—a previously all male event—is attacked by a race official and was prevented from finishing the race. Today, the Boston marathon celebrates both men and women marathon runners. *Corbis-Bettman.*

achieving their full potential. As a young woman, she had dropped out of a psychology doctoral program to get married, bear children, and keep a suburban home. In her 1963 bestseller, *The Feminine Mystique,* she pondered the question of why she and, according to several studies, thousands of other women were not satisfied. After reviewing the responsibilities of the housewife (making beds, grocery shopping, driving children everywhere, preparing meals and snacks, and pleasing her husband), she asked: "Is this all?" She concluded it was not enough. Women needed to overcome the "feminine mystique" that promised them fulfillment through the domestic arts. She called on women to set their own goals and seek careers outside the home. Her book, combined with the presidential report, provided new perspectives for women and contributed to a renewed women's movement. Also producing more activism was the passage of the 1964 Civil Rights Act, with the inclusion of **Title VII.** The original version of the civil rights bill excluded sex as a form of discrimination, but Representative Martha Griffiths (Democrat from Michigan) joined with conservative Democrat Howard Smith of Virginia to add the word *sex* to the act—she to strengthen the bill, he thinking the addition would kill it. As finally approved, Title VII prohibited discrimination on the basis of race, religion, creed, national origins, or sex.

However, the Equal Employment Opportunity Commission (EEOC), established to support the law, and the Johnson administration showed little interest in dealing with gender discrimination, so proponents organized to promote women's interests and to press the government to enforce Title VII. Many were experienced civil rights activists. In "the black movement," one woman civil rights worker wrote, "I had been fighting for someone else's oppression and now there was a way I could fight for my own freedom and I was going to be much stronger than I ever was." The most prominent woman's organization to emerge was the **National Organization for Women (NOW),** formed in 1966. With Betty Friedan as president, NOW launched an aggressive campaign to draw attention to sex discrimination, particularly in the workplace, and to redress those wrongs. It sued EEOC for not upholding the law and thirteen hundred corporations for gender discrimination. It demanded an equal rights amendment to the Constitution and pushed for easier access to birth-control devices and the right to have an abortion. NOW's membership grew rapidly, from about 300 in 1966 to 175,000 in 1968. NOW's 1970 "Strike-for-Equality Parade" demonstrated the growing mass appeal of the women's movement when fifty thousand supporters marched down New York City's Fifth Avenue.

But the movement was larger than NOW's membership and interested in more than NOW's largely economic and political agenda. Some women looked

Title VII Provision of the Civil Rights Act of 1964 that guarantees women legal protection against discrimination.

National Organization for Women Women's rights organization founded in 1966 to improve educational, employment, and political opportunities for women and to fight for equal pay for equal work.

beyond institutional changes and focused on the structure of society itself and on culture. Women attended meetings devoted to **consciousness raising** and other grassroots gatherings to promote women's issues. Calls arose for new social and sexual values. Some sought a complete redefinition of the traditional institutions of family and marriage. The "Redstocking Manifesto of 1969" reflected one of the most radical views: "We identify the agents of our oppression as men." "We are exploited as sex objects, breeders, domestic servants and cheap labor." Radical feminist Ti-Grace Atkinson defined marriage as "slavery" and "legalized rape."

The majority of women rejected Atkinson's view but approved the increased focus on women's issues. Others, while supporting equal opportunities and rights, rejected the label "feminist" and what they believed was the movement's bias toward career and working women. Still, despite the internal differences, a general feminist critique of American society succeeded in convincing many Americans that women should pursue goals and aspirations beyond the traditional roles of wife, mother, and homemaker.

The Emergence of Chicano Power

In the 1960s, Mexican Americans also organized to assert their social and political rights. As the 1960s began, despite postwar efforts by organizations like the League of Latin American Citizens and the G.I. Forum (see page 880), Mexican Americans were largely an invisible minority (see Map 31.3). Outside the Southwest, few Americans were aware of or concerned with their place in American society. Prevailing stereotypes portrayed them as docile, if not lazy, and ridiculed them as poorly educated, unskilled people who spoke English badly. Statistically, Mexican Americans were near society's lowest levels of income and education.

The New Frontier and the Great Society revived hopes, and Latino organizations began to pressure American society to recognize the needs of the Latino population. In 1963, the Mexican-American majority in Crystal City, Texas, stunned the region by toppling the established Anglo political machine and electing an all Mexican-American slate to the city council. Many Mexican Americans viewed the Crystal City vote as a revolutionary act, the beginning of the end of political and social segregation. Across south Texas, Mexican Americans banded together to form El Partido Raza Unida (the United People party) to spread the political "revolution" throughout Texas. The passage of the 1965 Voting Rights Act and Johnson's War on Poverty added more impetus. In Colorado in 1965, Rodolfo "Corky" Gonzales formed the Crusade for Justice to work for social justice for Mexican Americans, to integrate Colorado's schools, and to foster pride in Mexican heritage. In New Mexico, Reies Lopez Tijerina demanded that Mexican Americans enjoy the rights, including land grants, promised under the Treaty of Guadalupe Hidalgo (which ended the Mexican-American War in 1848) and formed the Alianza Federal de Mercedes (the Federal Alliance of Land Grants).

Throughout the Southwest, the activism of Mexican Americans frightened supporters of the status quo. Texas governor Dolph Briscoe typified conservative sentiment when he denounced the La Raza Unida movement, saying the "Communist" La Raza Unida aimed to create a "little Cuba" in south Texas.

Briscoe was wrong. The Mexican-American movement was a local one, born of poverty and oppressive segregation. Reflecting the grassroots character of the movement was the important role that youths played. Many Mexican-American teens and young adults adopted the term ***Chicano*** to stress their unwillingness to accept the dictates of Anglo society and to distinguish themselves from **accommodationist,** often middle-class Mexican Americans. Although many Mexican Americans disapproved, the term *Chicano* was soon applied to Mexican Americans who promoted their heritage and rights. In schools, Chicanos demanded better teachers, support systems, integration, and Mexican-American (Latino) studies programs. During the 1967–1968 academic year, Raul Ruiz mobilized Mexican-American students in Los Angeles: "If you are a student you should be angry! You should demand! You should protest! You should organize for a better education! This is your right!" He called for students to walk out of class and picket schools that did not meet demands. Others fought similar battles.

consciousness raising Achieving greater awareness of the nature of a political or social issue through group therapy or group interaction.

Chicano Term that many Mexican Americans adopted during the late 1960s to signify their ethnic identity; it was associated with the promotion of Mexican-American heritage and rights.

accommodationist Compromising with or adapting to the viewpoint of the opposition.

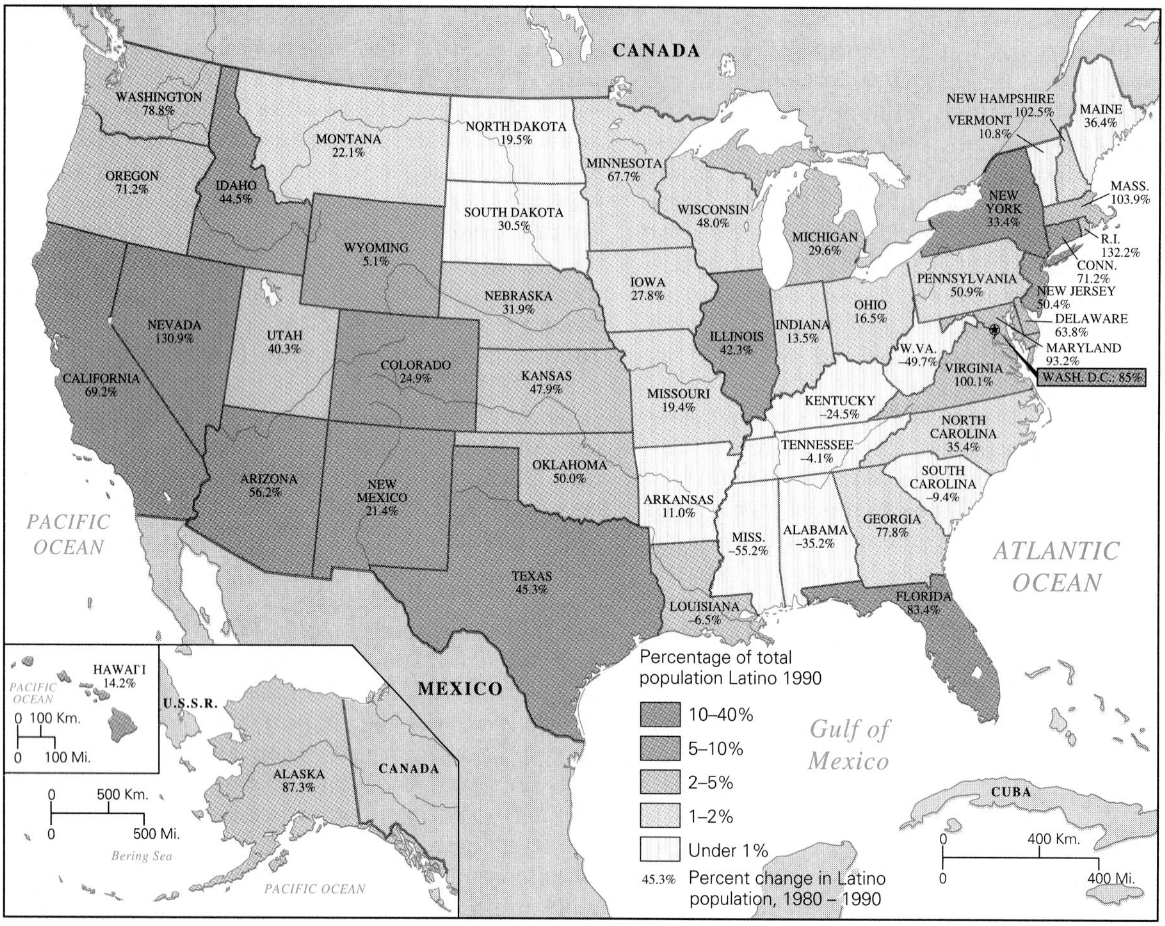

♦ **MAP 31.3 Changing Latino Population** At one time, the great majority of Latinos were Mexican Americans located in the Southwest. In the 1990s, Latinos resided in nearly every major city and included Cubans, Puerto Ricans, and others from throughout the Caribbean and Central and South America. Growing rapidly, the Latino population was projected to become the largest minority in the country by the year 2000, perhaps 12 percent of the total population.

In the small south Texas towns of Edcouch and Elsa, where the average education level for Mexican Americans was 3.5 years of schooling, Mexican-American students walked out of the high school in November 1968. They demanded dignity, respect, and an end to "blatant discrimination," including corporal punishment—paddling—for speaking Spanish on school grounds outside of Spanish class. The school board blamed "outside agitators" and suspended more than 150 students. But, like other districts, including Los Angeles, Edcouch and Elsa implemented Mexican-American studies and bilingual programs, hired more Mexican-American teachers and counselors, and adopted programs to meet the special needs of migrant farm worker children who moved from one school to another during picking season. In New York and Chicago, school districts were implementing changes to reflect demands of Puerto Rican students as well. By the 1970s, calls for bilingual education had become an important educational reform focus for the Latino community.

Schools were not the only targets of increased Latino activism. The Great Society provided opportunities for community-oriented activism within Latino communities. In San Jose, California, moderate Mexican Americans revived a Festival of the Roses to highlight Mexican culture and the community. In New York, the Puerto Rican Forum served as a coordinator for numerous organizations created to

♦ Cesar Chavez organized the first successful farm workers union in America in 1961, the United Farm Workers Association. Choosing to confront opponents by using the non-violent tactics of the Civil Rights movement, Chavez sought to give power and dignity to Mexican-American workers. *Bob Fitch/Black Star.*

combat the socioeconomic problems of the community. As in the African-American civil rights movement, divisions existed: many young Latino leaders adopted a nationalistic and militant position. Los Angeles witnessed the birth of the Brown Berets in 1967, and the Puerto Rican Young Lords mobilized Latino populations in Chicago and New York. Each group rejected assimilation into the Anglo world. "We're not in the melting pot. . . . Chicanos don't melt," stated one Brown Beret.

As their population grew, Mexican Americans and other Latinos sought more political power and community control. In Los Angeles, where the Latino population climbed from less than 10 percent in 1960 to more than 33 percent by 1990, the combination of better organization, redistricting, and the 1975 Voting Rights Act—which protected and expanded the voting rights of Latinos, Indians, and Asian Americans, and required bilingual ballots—produced increased political representation at the state and city levels. Both the Democratic and Republican parties reached out to Hispanic leaders, wooing the growing Latino vote. By 1987, Latinos were serving as mayors in sixty-seven cities, and Los Angeles elected its first Mexican American in twenty years to the city council. In 1981, Henry Cisneros was elected mayor of San Antonio and Federico Peña mayor of Denver. Both joined President Bill Clinton's cabinet in 1993.

Latino workers also continued to organize to gain respect and better working conditions. Drawing from a traditional base of worker organizations, Mexican-American workers formed unions to promote their interests. In Texas and throughout the Southwest, Mexican-American women sought to unionize the garment industry, especially along the border with Mexico. In 1972, Mexican-American workers in El Paso struck Farah Incorporated and, after a two-year struggle and boycott, gained recognition for their union. Also attracting attention were attempts by **Cesar Chavez** and others to unionize agricultural workers.

During the 1960s, nearly one-third of all Mexican Americans worked at **stoop labor** in the fields—picking perishable crops—and were deprived of education and decent housing, wages, and healthcare. Trapped at the bottom of the occupational ladder, not covered by minimum-wage or labor laws, unskilled and uneducated farm laborers were ignored by society and all levels of government. Addressing these problems, Chavez created the **National Farm Workers Association (NFWA)** in 1962. When Chavez called a strike against the grape growers of central California in 1965, NFWA had seventeen hundred members. He demanded a wage of $1.40 an hour and asked the public to buy only union-picked grapes. The boycott and strike continued for five years until most of the major growers accepted unionization and agreed to improve wages and working conditions. In 1975, California passed a law requiring growers to recognize and bargain with farm worker unions. Chavez emerged as a national figure promoting "La Causa" not only for farm workers but for all Latinos and other minorities. The "whole fight, if you're poor, and if you're

Cesar Chavez Labor organizer who founded the National Farm Workers Association; he believed in nonviolence and used marches, boycotts, and fasts to bring moral and economic pressure to bear on growers.

stoop labor Field labor that involves constant bending, usually to pick fruits and vegetables.

National Farm Workers Association Migrant workers' union organized by Cesar Chavez in 1962.

INDIVIDUAL CHOICES

La Causa

Jessie Lopez de la Cruz

Having worked in the fields picking crops for nearly forty years, in 1962 Jessie Lopez de la Cruz made a choice that changed her life and the lives of many farm workers. She became a union organizer, the first and one of the few women organizers whose role was to recruit workers in the fields. In her efforts to achieve a better life and dignity for farm workers, she also focused on the status of Latinas and became a forceful leader in efforts to improve the quality of life for women and children. AP/Wide World Photos.

Jessie Lopez de la Cruz had always been a farm worker. As a child in the 1920s, she worked alongside her family in the fields of central California, picking prunes off the ground for $4 a ton. By the time she was in her teens, she was pulling 100-pound bags of picked cotton behind her 95-pound frame, lifting them, and dumping them in a bin for weighing. Married in her teens, she at first accepted the traditional role of wife in a Mexican family—"the women couldn't do anything" without permission, she observed later. But gradually she expanded her role and freedoms, including learning how to drive a car.

Economic necessity required entire families to work in the fields, and for Jessie de la Cruz, as wife and mother, life continued in the fields. "We always went where . . . the women and the men were going to work because if it were just the men . . . we wouldn't earn enough to support a family." Infant children did not alter the pattern. "I started taking Ray with me," she recalled, "when he wasn't a year old yet. I'd carry one of those wash tubs and put it under a vine and sit him in it. . . . I would move the tub . . . as we worked." Work in the fields, especially with a short-handled hoe, was exhausting, but like most picker wives, she knew that her workday did not end in the fields. Returning home, she was expected to keep the house, cook, and care for the children.

In 1962, Jessie Lopez de la Cruz made a choice that not only changed her life but also

a minority group," Chavez argued, "is economic power."

Jessie Lopez de la Cruz was among those inspired by Chavez. Working most of her life as a migrant in the fields, she became the first woman organizer for the NFWA, seeking to improve the economic and social conditions among Latinos—and Latinas (see Individual Choices: Jessie Lopez de la Cruz). Despite many economic and political success stories, however, the majority of Latinos have not achieved social or economic equality. There have been some economic gains—the number of Latino households making $50,000 grew 234 percent between 1972 and 1984. But the Mexican-American population as a whole remains one of the poorest minorities in the United States (see Table 31.1). "Often the father helped to change the lives of many others. Cesar Chavez had just started the National Farm Workers Association and was recruiting members. He shocked many men when he argued that women should participate fully in union activities. Jessie agreed. Women worked in the fields as well as men, and in many cases their working conditions were worse than those of men. Sexual harassment was common, and bathrooms were always a problem. Frequently there were none. This forced women to wait as long as ten hours, until they could go home and have privacy. Jessie Lopez de la Cruz and her husband joined the union. Chavez's organization, however, was more than just a union interested in getting better pay and working conditions for farm workers. It was also a movement, "La Causa," that stressed pride and dignity, political and self awareness, and demanded respect and equality for all Latinos, not just men.

"Women can no longer be taken for granted—that we're just not going to stay home and do the cooking and cleaning," Jessie Lopez de la Cruz told other women farm workers. "It's way past the time when our husbands could say 'You stay home! . . . You have to do as I say'." She convinced other women to attend union meetings and express their concerns. Quickly, she rose from the rank and file to become the first woman organizer in the fields. In her activities, she merged union messages with feminist language—providing one of the bases of the Chicana movement. She urged others to break old patterns: "You know we're not back in the 20s. We can stand up! We can talk back . . . we want a share of the money . . . [made] of our sweat and our work."

Like all organizers, she faced opposition from the growers, who frequently attacked union organizers and those picketing the fields during strikes. During a strike in Kern County, growers sprayed picketers with pesticides. She also faced opposition from male farm workers. Men, she stated, "gave us the most trouble. . . . They were for the union, but they were not taking orders from women." Still, she and others continued their efforts. Eventually, some growers agreed to sign contracts, and some men agreed to be led by women.

Jessie Lopez de la Cruz's union activities and support for La Causa made her aware of larger issues that affected families and women. She worked for the inclusion of Latina women on school and community service boards. She pressured school boards to consider the needs of Latino children, especially those of migrant farm workers. She fought for bilingual education and social services for poor families, including access to food stamps for farm workers. Because of her emergence as a spokesperson for women and the poor, Jessie Lopez de la Cruz was selected to be a member of the California Commission on Women.

But despite some successful outcomes, the expectations of Latina women—living within a traditional machismo culture and being poor—remain largely unchanged. Chicano historian Rodolfo Acuña argues that although the "Chicana" represents half of the Chicano population, she remains part of a nearly "invisible" minority.

works two jobs and the mother one," recounted one researcher, "and they just can't make ends meet." Lack of economic success also impacts on education. Lacking job prospects, Latino children have scant incentive to stay in high school. The Hispanic dropout rate was 45 percent nationwide in 1990, exceeding rates for blacks and whites. Nowhere is this fact more obvious than among agricultural workers.

American-Indian Activism

American Indians, too, began to assert their rights with new vigor in the 1960s. The 1950s had been oppressive years for Indians. Federal policies encouraged more than thirty-five thousand of them to leave their reservations and move to urban areas, where the government believed they could find jobs

TABLE 31.1 Whites, African Americans, and Latinos, 1992

	Whites	African Americans	Latinos
Average income	$30,513	$18,676	$22,330
Female-headed households	11.4%	47.8%	19.1%
High school education	80.5%	66.7%	51.3%
College	22.5%	11.5%	9.7%
Unemployment	6.9%	12.4%	10.0%
Below poverty	12.1%	31.9%	28.1%

Source: Congressional Quarterly Researcher, October 30, 1992, p. 936.

and enjoy a higher standard of living. But few urban Indians found anything except discrimination, poverty, and disease (see Map 31.4).

By the 1960s, Indians on and off reservations were organizing and calling for changes in white attitudes and for new federal and state policies. Increasingly militant Indian leaders demanded the protection and restoration of their ancient burial grounds, along with fishing and timber rights. Museums were asked to return for proper burial the remains and bones of dead Indians on display. The National Indian Youth Council called for "Red Power," for Indians to use all means possible to resist further loss of Indian lands, rights, and traditions. Vine Deloria, Jr.'s, *Custer Died for Your Sins* (1969) informed readers that Indians had a culture and society of their own and asked "only to be freed of cultural oppression." "The white does not understand the Indian," Deloria wrote, "and the Indian does not wish to understand the white." The central issue was not assimilation, he and other American Indian leaders explained, but self-determination, especially in the control of reservations. Indians wanted economic prosperity and opportunity but on terms that would ensure their continued tribal and cultural existence.

In the 1960s, Kennedy and Johnson provided some change, ending the policies to reduce reservations and advocating self-rule and cultural pluralism for American Indians. Nixon continued the process by placing Indians in top-level positions within the Bureau of Indian Affairs and expanding federal programs. In 1974, Congress passed the **Indian Self-Determination and Education Assistance Act,** which gave tribes control and operation of many federal programs on their reservations. On the issue of lost lands, American Indians pressed their claims, with little prospect of success. Still, some Indian victories occurred. The Alaska Native Land Claims Act (1971) returned 40 million acres to Eskimos and other native peoples. In 1980, the Passamaquoddy and Penobscot tribes in Maine were compensated with 300,000 acres and the establishment of a $27 million trust fund for more than 12.5 million acres they claimed had been stolen. Also in 1980, the Supreme Court decided that the federal government owed in excess of $106 million to the Lakotas for the Black Hills of South Dakota, taken from them in the 1870s.

Indian leaders applauded these efforts but lamented the slow pace of change and insisted that the Bureau of Indian Affairs and federal authorities still controlled too much of reservation life. In the 1980s, the Reagan administration prompted more protest when it slashed more than one-third from federal assistance programs for Indians and suggested that the tribes look to the private sector to recoup losses from federal sources. Indian activist Deloria called Rea-

Indian Self-Determination and Educational Assistance Act Law passed by Congress in 1974 giving Indian tribes control over federal programs carried out on their reservations and increasing their control of reservation schools.

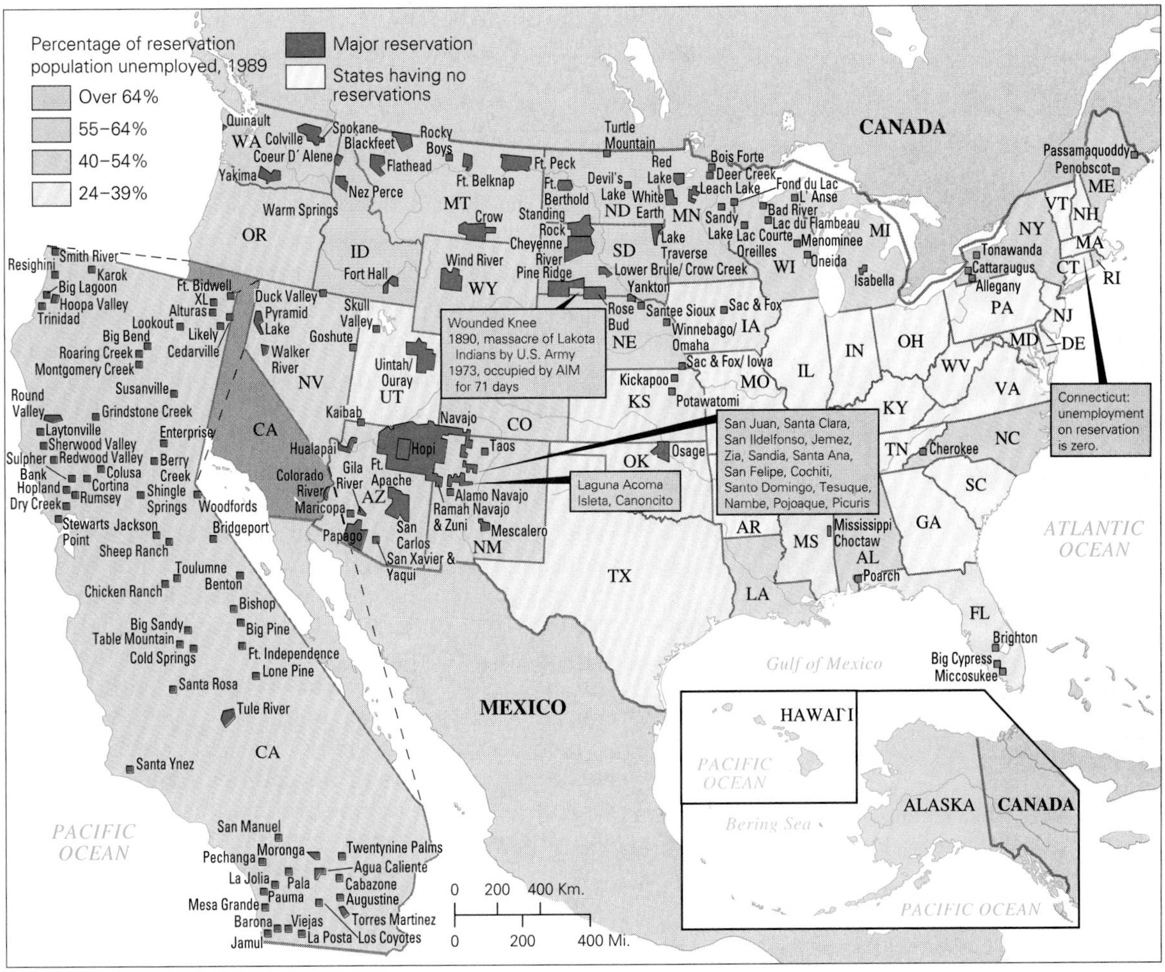

♦ **MAP 31.4 American Indian Reservations** In the seventeenth century, American Indians roamed over an estimated 1.9 billion acres, but by 1990 that area had shrunk to about 46 million acres spread across the United States. This area constitutes the federal reservation system. Composing about 1 percent of the population, American Indians are among the most impoverished people in society, facing a life expectancy of about twenty fewer years than the average non-Indian American. This map shows the location of most of the federal Indian reservations and highlights the high unemployment found on nearly every reservation. (*Note:* California is enlarged to show the many small reservations located there.)

gan's "gospel of reliance on the private sector . . . absurd when applied to reservations, where the only private enterprise has been the non-Indian trader."

American Indians also protested federal and state regulations that restrict gambling on reservations. By 1990, many tribes, like many states, were operating "high-stakes" bingo games and Las Vegas–style casinos, turning to gambling as a source of revenue and jobs. The Supreme Court opened the door to reservation gambling in 1982 and 1987 by ruling that a state that allowed bingo and other forms of gambling must also allow reservations within the state to run their own games. Despite court decisions and new legislation, the issues surrounding tribal sovereignty and federal and state controls remain complex and unclear, and state and federal courts increasingly decide issues of jurisdiction on a case-by-case basis.

Although some American Indian leaders turned to Washington and the courts to assert Indian rights,

♦ In 1973, two hundred Sioux organized by the American Indian Movement (AIM) took over Wounded Knee, South Dakota, the site of the 1890 massacre, holding out for seventy-one days against state and federal authorities. The confrontation ended after one protester was killed and the government agreed to examine the treaty rights of the Oglala Sioux. In this picture, AIM leader Russell Means receives a blessing and symbolic red paint during the siege. *Dirck Halstead, TIME Magazine.*

others took more direct action. In 1968, the Chippewas organized the **American Indian Movement (AIM)** to dramatize police brutality toward Indians in Minneapolis and to demand social justice for urban Indians. In 1969, a group of San Francisco Indian activists seized **Alcatraz Island,** offering to buy the federally owned island for $24 in beads and cloth, the amount that Dutch settlers supposedly paid in 1626 for Manhattan Island. They held Alcatraz until 1971, when federal authorities, without bloodshed, retook control. Two years later, AIM leaders Russell Means and Dennis Banks organized the armed occupation of Wounded Knee, South Dakota, the site of the 1890 massacre of the Lakotas by the army (see page 541 and Map 31.4). AIM controlled the town for seventy-one days before surrendering to federal authorities. Although the "second battle of Wounded Knee" failed to change federal policy, it did publicize Indian grievances and problems.

Nixon and the Balance of Power

- How did Richard Nixon plan to achieve an "honorable" peace in Vietnam?
- How did Nixon's choices in shaping Cold War policies differ from those favored by earlier administrations?

During the 1968 presidential campaign, Nixon had promised to work for national unity by promoting minority rights and a new style of conservatism that accepted the basic role of government in domestic affairs. He presented himself as a pragmatic and statesmanlike politician who could balance liberal and conservative views and chart a middle course. Although he worked hard to shed his negative image, like the nickname "Tricky Dick," Nixon remained reclusive, inarticulate, and vindictive. He spent an inordinate amount of effort focusing on "enemies"—those who disagreed with him, especially the press. In managing the government, Nixon distrusted the federal bureaucracy, Congress, and even members of his cabinet. He relied almost exclusively on a few personal advisers. For domestic affairs, he leaned on "the Germans"—H. R. "Bob" Haldeman and John Ehrlichman, neither of whom had ever held a major political office. For international affairs, he relied on himself and Harvard professor **Henry Kissinger,** his national security adviser.

Like Kennedy, Nixon believed his strength rested in foreign affairs. Nixon and Kissinger wanted to restructure Cold War policies, to break free of the constraints imposed by ideology and morality. They sought new policies based on "realistic" geopolitical values that stressed a combination of strength and flexibility in an ever-changing international balance

American Indian Movement Militant Indian movement organized to demand social justice for urban Indians.

Alcatraz Island Rocky island in San Francisco Bay that was occupied in 1969 by Native American activists who demanded that it be made available as a cultural center.

Henry Kissinger German-born American diplomat who was President Nixon's national security adviser and secretary of state; he helped negotiate the cease-fire in Vietnam.

♦ Together Richard Nixon and Secretary of State Henry Kissinger (shown here) sought to refocus American foreign policy by ending the war in Vietnam and improving relations with the Soviet Union and the People's Republic of China. *John Dominis, LIFE Magazine ©Time Warner.*

of power. The Soviet Union was their number-one agenda item. Nixon believed that America's military advantage over the Soviets was rapidly narrowing. Because there was little chance of persuading Congress to support the efforts needed for the United States to regain clear military superiority, Nixon concluded that it was necessary to improve relations with the Communist **superpower.** He and Kissinger recognized that the expanding Soviet-Chinese split, which had developed in the 1960s, offered the most promising diplomatic possibilities for changing the balance of Cold War power. Vietnam, however, was the most immediate problem.

Vietnamization

Vietnam dominated and shaped nearly all other issues: the budget, public and congressional opinion, foreign policy, and domestic stability. Nixon needed a solution to Vietnam before moving ahead on other fronts. Knowing the war could not be won, he emphasized "an honorable peace." Nixon dismissed calls for immediate removal of American troops, a "bug out." Not only would such a policy be politically unpopular among the Silent Majority, but it would, Nixon believed, create a global collapse of confidence in American foreign policy. "A nation cannot remain great, if it betrays its allies and lets down its friends," Nixon explained. The central problem was to find a means to protect South Vietnam, encourage the North Vietnamese to negotiate, and allow the gradual withdrawal of American forces. Nixon's solution was **Vietnamization,** reducing the American role while enhancing South Vietnam's military capability. Nixon believed that with a change in the "color of bodies" and with American soldiers coming home, large-scale opposition to the war would soon fade away. "I'm not going to end up like LBJ," he informed his advisers.

Vietnamization began in the spring of 1969, when Nixon announced that twenty-five thousand American soldiers were coming home and that the South Vietnamese were assuming a larger role in the fighting. At the same time, he pressured the news media to alter their coverage of the war. ABC's news director instructed his staff to reduce coverage of the fighting and emphasize "themes and stories under the general heading: We are on our way out of Vietnam." By the end of the year, the press was more favorable and American forces in Vietnam had declined by over 110,000 (see Figure 31.1). Expanding on the theme of limiting American involvement, the

superpower Term applied to the United States and the Soviet Union during the Cold War because both nations were powerful and heavily armed and dominated their allies in international politics.

Vietnamization The U.S. policy of scaling back American involvement in Vietnam and helping Vietnamese forces fight their own war.

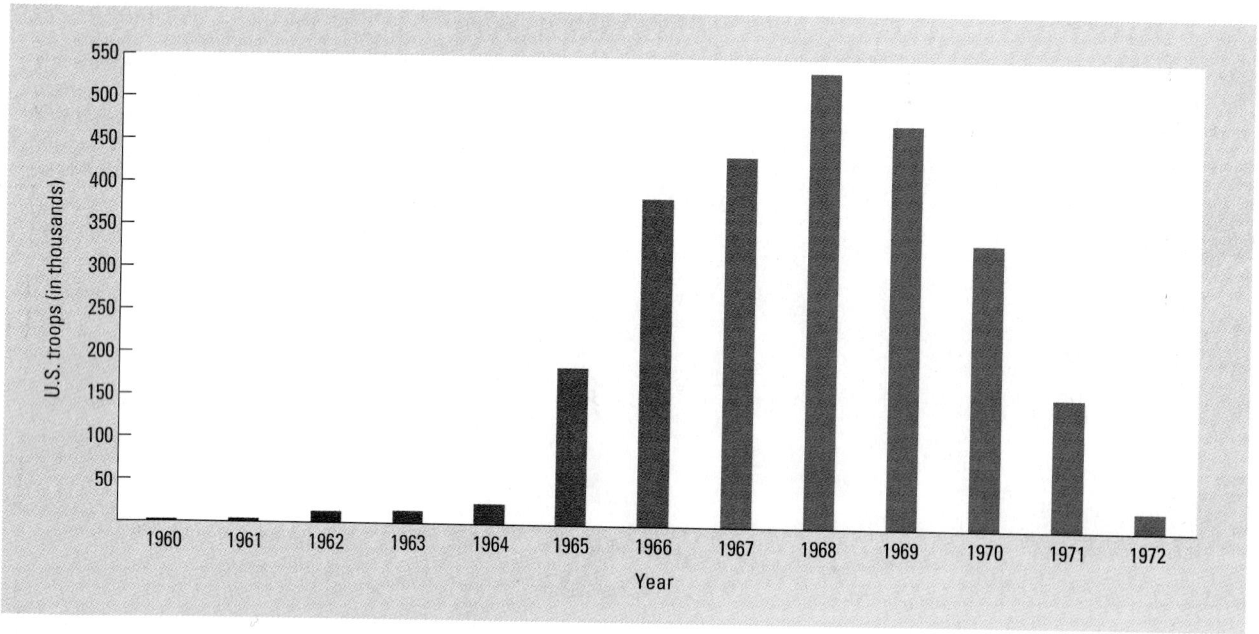

♦ **FIGURE 31.1 Troop Levels by Year** For America, the Vietnam War went through two major phases: Americanization from 1960 to 1968 and Vietnamization from 1969 to 1972.

president issued the **Nixon Doctrine**: countries warding off communism would have to shoulder most of the military burden, with the United States providing political and economic support and limited naval and air support.

Vietnamization, however, was only part of Nixon's strategy. The other element in the "peace plan" was to increase the economic, diplomatic, and military pressure on North Vietnam to end the war. This, Nixon hoped, would be done in two ways: by getting the Soviets and Chinese to reduce their support for North Vietnam and by increasing the bombing of enemy bases, including those in Cambodia and Laos. In March 1969, Nixon ordered the heavy bombardment of Communist sanctuaries inside Cambodia. To keep the operation a secret, the administration falsified air force records and denied all rumors and stories about any such strikes. The intense assault was part of a "madman strategy" that Nixon designed to convince the North Vietnamese to negotiate. Nixon said he wanted Hanoi "to believe that I've reached the point where I might do anything to stop the war." "We'll just slip the word," Nixon told his advisers, "that 'for God's sake, you know Nixon. . . . We can't restrain him when he's angry—and he has his hand on the nuclear button.'"

The strategy did not work. The North Vietnamese appeared unconcerned about Nixon's "madness," the increased bombing, or decreasing support from China and the Soviet Union. They still believed that victory was only a matter of patiently waiting until America was unwilling to continue the war. Consequently, talks between Kissinger and the North Vietnamese in Paris produced only bitter feelings. Nor did American opposition to the war fade away. In November 1969, more than 250,000 antiwar protesters calling for an end to the conflict paraded past the White House. Adding fuel to the antiwar cause, news of American atrocities at **My Lai** came to light in 1970. In March 1968, Lieutenant William Calley's platoon had "wasted" the small village, killing more than three hundred men, women, and children. The massacre seemed to many to offer incontestable proof that the Vietnam War was immoral and was unraveling the moral fiber of American soldiers—resulting in drug abuse, dementia,

Nixon Doctrine Nixon's policy of requiring countries threatened by communism to shoulder most of the military burden, with the United States offering mainly political and economic support.

My Lai Site of a massacre of three hundred fifty South Vietnamese villagers by U.S. infantrymen in 1968, an event that added to antiwar sentiment in the United States.

♦ On the morning of March 16, 1968, American soldiers entered the hamlet of My Lai and massacred more than three hundred women, children, and old men. The army successfully covered up the massacre until November 1969. Later Lt. William Calley was found guilty of mass murder and court martialed. An official evaluation by an army commander commented that some of the units "were little better than organized bands of thugs, with the officers eager participants in the body-count game." *Ron Haeberle, LIFE Magazine © Time Warner, Inc.*

and mindless slaughter. Some observers even worried that the army would disintegrate from within. The unauthorized release in 1971 of the **Pentagon Papers,** a collection of official documents gathered by former Defense Department researcher Daniel Ellsberg, further increased pubic disillusion. The documents showed that since the 1950s the government had not told the American pubic the truth about Vietnam.

Despite such setbacks, Nixon refused to change course. In 1970, he ordered American troops to cross the border into Cambodia and destroy North Vietnamese and Viet Cong headquarters and supply areas. Had the United States not invaded Cambodia, he told the public, the United States would seem "like a pitiful, helpless giant," and the free world would be threatened everywhere.

The invasion involved nearly eighty thousand American and South Vietnamese troops and destroyed large amounts of supplies. But it failed to stop the flow of supplies from North Vietnam, and it generated loud protests across the United States, especially on college campuses. At Kent State University on May 4, 1970, the Ohio National Guard fired on protesters, killing four and wounding eleven. At Jackson State University in Mississippi, police killed two students during another demonstration. Outraged students responded by shutting down more than a hundred campuses as thousands of antiwar demonstrators again marched through Washington. An angry Senate repealed the Gulf of Tonkin Resolution and forbade the further use of American troops in Laos or Cambodia.

Despite the furor over the Cambodian invasion, American soldiers were returning home, and the antiwar movement was finally ebbing, as Nixon had predicted. Nevertheless, by the end of 1971, Kissinger and Nixon were frustrated. Despite their public claims to the contrary, they knew Vietnamization was not progressing well, and there was no sign of a settlement in Paris. In March 1972, when Communist forces drove toward Saigon, a livid Nixon responded with force. "I'm going to show the bastards," he told Kissinger. "Unless they deal with us I'm going to bomb the hell out of them." He ordered massive bombing raids against North Vietnam and Communist forces in South Vietnam. By mid-June 1972, American air power had stalled the

Pentagon Papers Classified government documents detailing the policy decisions that led to U.S. involvement in Vietnam, leaked to the *New York Times* in 1971 by former Defense Department aide Daniel Ellsberg.

♦ On May 4, 1970, Ohio National Guard troops opened fire on a crowd of Kent State students protesting the American incursion into Cambodia, killing four of them. Here, a student screams in horror as she hovers over the body of one of the dead students. In outrage, campuses throughout the nation closed and students flocked to Washington to protest the war. *John Filo.*

offensive and enabled ARVN forces to regroup and drive back the North Vietnamese. With their cities under almost continuous air attacks, the North Vietnamese became more flexible in negotiations. By October, with both sides offering some concessions, a peace settlement was ready. "Peace is at hand," Kissinger announced—just in time for the 1972 presidential election.

South Vietnamese president Nguyan Van Thieu, however, rejected the plan. Reluctantly, Nixon supported Thieu and ordered the Christmas bombing of Hanoi and North Vietnam. One goal was to put additional pressure on Hanoi. Another was to convince Thieu that the United States would use its air power to protect South Vietnam. After eleven days, the bombing stopped and Washington advised Thieu that if he did not accept the next peace settlement, the United States would leave him to fend for himself. Thieu thereupon accepted a peace settlement that did not differ significantly from the one offered in October. Nixon and Kissinger proclaimed peace with honor, and Kissinger shared the 1973 Nobel Peace Prize with his North Vietnamese counterpart.

The peace settlement imposed a cease-fire, required the removal of the twenty-four thousand remaining American troops but not North Vietnamese troops, and promised the return of American prisoners of war. The peace terms permitted the United States to complete its military and political withdrawal, but the pact did little to ensure the continued existence of Thieu's government or South Vietnam. The cease-fire, everyone expected, would be temporary. When Haldeman asked Kissinger how long the South Vietnamese government could last, Kissinger answered, "If they're lucky, than can hold out for a year and a half."

As expected, the cease-fire soon collapsed. North Vietnam continued to funnel men and supplies to the south, but substantial American air and naval support for South Vietnam never arrived. Neither Congress nor the public was eager to help Thieu's government. Instead, Congress cut aid to South Vietnam and in November 1973 passed the **War Powers Act.** The law requires the president to inform Congress within forty-eight hours of the deployment of troops overseas and to withdraw those troops within sixty days if Congress fails to authorize the action. In March 1975, North Vietnam began its final campaign to unify the country. A month later, North Vietnamese troops entered Saigon as a few remaining Americans and some South Vietnamese were evacuated by helicopter—some from the roof of the American embassy. The Vietnam War ended as it had started, with Vietnamese fighting Vietnamese (see Table 31.2).

Modifying the Cold War

Ending the Vietnam War was a political and diplomatic necessity for Nixon and Kissinger, essential to their goal of redefining the Cold War. In his first inaugural address, Nixon urged that an "era of confrontation" give way to an "era of negotiation." To this end, he pursued **détente,** a policy that reduced tensions with the two Communist superpowers. China, with which the United States had had virtually no diplomatic contact since the end of the Chinese civil war in 1949, was the key to the Nixon-Kissinger strategy. The Soviets and Chinese had already engaged in several bloody clashes along

War Powers Act Law passed by Congress in 1973 to prevent the president from involving the United States in war without authorization by Congress.

détente Relaxing of tensions between the superpowers in the early 1970s, which led to increased diplomatic, commercial, and cultural contact.

TABLE 31.2 The Vietnam Generation, 1964–1975

	Men	Women
Total in military service	8,700,000	250,000
Served in Vietnam	2,700,000	6,431
Killed in Vietnam	46,000	9
Wounded	300,635*	
Missing in action	2,330	—
Draft resisters (estimate)	570,000	—
Accused	210,000	—
Convicted	8,750	—

Source: Department of Defense and Veterans Administration.
*Combined men and women

their common border, and the Chinese feared a border war. Believing that better relations with the United States would help deter Soviet aggression, the Chinese were ready to open diplomatic discussions with Nixon.

Nixon believed that American friendship with the Chinese would encourage the Soviets to improve their relations with the United States and lead to détente. Sending a signal to China, Nixon lowered restrictions on trade, and in April 1971 the Chinese responded by inviting an American Ping-Pong team to tour China. A few months later, Kissinger secretly flew to Beijing to meet with Premier Zhou Enlai. The result would, as Kissinger phrased it, "send a shock wave around the world": Nixon was going to China. In February 1972, Nixon arrived in Beijing and met with Communist party chairman Mao Zedong and Zhou. Suddenly the "Red Chinese" were no longer the enemy but "hard-working, intelligent . . . and practical" friends. The Cold War was thawing a little in the East.

Nixon's China policy, as hoped, contributed to improved relations with the Soviet Union. Kissinger followed his secret visit to China with one to Moscow, where he discussed improving relations with President **Leonid Brezhnev.** Nixon flew to Moscow in May 1972 and told Brezhnev, "I know that my reputation is one of being a very hard-line, Cold War–oriented, anti-Communist," but he now believed, he said, that the two nations should "live together and work together." Needing to reduce military spending, develop the Soviet domestic economy, and increase American trade, Brezhnev agreed. The meeting was a success. Brezhnev obtained increased trade with the West, including shipments of American grain, and the superpowers announced the **Strategic Arms Limitation agreement (SALT I),** which restricted antimissile sites and established a maximum number of **intercontinental ballistic missiles (ICBMs)** and submarine-launched missiles (SLBMs) for each side. It seemed as if détente had arrived and Nixon was reshaping world affairs.

But not all that Nixon and Kissinger did in foreign affairs differed from traditional Cold War policy. In Latin America, Nixon followed closely in Johnson's footsteps, working to isolate Cuba and prevent any additional Communist-style leaders from gaining power. Borrowing from Eisenhower's foreign policy, he used covert operations to disrupt the democratically elected socialist-Marxist government of **Salvador Allende** in Chile. For three years

Leonid Brezhnev President of the Soviet Union from 1977 until his death in 1982; he worked to foster détente with the United States during the Nixon era.

Strategic Arms Limitation agreement Agreement between the United States and the Soviet Union in 1972 to limit offensive nuclear weapons and the antiballistic missile systems that offered protection against them.

intercontinental ballistic missiles Missiles that can travel from one continent to another.

Salvadore Allende Chilean president who was considered the first democratically elected Marxist to head a government; he was killed in a coup in 1973.

♦ In efforts to redirect the Cold War, Nixon became the first president to visit China, meeting with Mao Zedung and Zhou Enlai in 1972. With regard to Chinese–Soviet relations, Nixon confided to Zhou that if Moscow marched either East or West, he was ready to "turn like a cobra on the Russians." Nixon's visit to China began the process of normalizing relations with the People's Republic of China that was finalized under Carter. *John Dominis, LIFE Magazine ©Time Warner, Inc.*

the CIA squeezed the Chilean economy "until it screamed," producing food riots, numerous strikes, and massive inflation. Finally, in September 1973, Chilean armed forces bombed and stormed the presidential palace, killing Allende. Kissinger denied any direct American role in the coup and quickly recognized the repressive military government of General Augusto Pinochet, who promptly reinstated a free market economy.

Nixon and Politics

- How did Nixon's choices in dealing with the economy and environment reflect his pragmatic conservatism?
- Why did Nixon achieve such a huge success in the 1972 election? What expectations and constraints led to Watergate?

In his foreign policy, Nixon followed new paths in dealing with the Chinese and Soviets that did not reflect traditional Republican views. This was also true in many of his domestic programs. Nixon believed that Republicans needed to be more pragmatic. They needed to emphasize a conservatism that did not automatically reject social responsibility and executive activism.

Pragmatic Conservatism

Nixon called for a style of conservatism, a **New Federalism,** that embraced the uses of federal power while eliminating useless government machinery and making programs more responsive to state and local governments. His **Revenue Sharing Act** reflected the new approach. The government would continue to raise revenue through its broad tax base, but it would release more of the money to state and local governments and reduce federal controls and restrictions on how they spent it. Some Republicans disliked the plan because it did not reduce federal spending, but in October 1972 the act passed Congress. Before the program was ended in 1986, state and local governments had received more than $83 billion in revenue sharing funds, reversing the flow of responsibility and political power for the first time since the Great Depression.

Nixon also wanted to redirect the flow of money and responsibility in the welfare system. Unlike many staunch conservatives, he was not opposed to welfare, but he and his adviser on the issue, Daniel Patrick Moynihan, believed the existing welfare system robbed people of their self-esteem, contributed to the breakup of nuclear families, and punished people for working. However, conservatives and liberals alike attacked his proposal for welfare reform—the Family Assistance Plan— and it was defeated in the Senate in 1969 and 1971. Despite that defeat, Nixon did not abandon what he saw as the political need for federal social responsibility. Without fanfare, his administration increased welfare support and approved legislation that enhanced the regulatory powers of the federal government. Food stamps became more accessible, the elderly and handicapped received direct federal support, and

New Federalism Nixon's policy of increasing the power of state and local governments and trimming waste from existing social programs.

Revenue Sharing Act Law passed by Congress in 1972 to distribute large amounts of federal tax revenues to state and local governments to use as they desired.

Social Security, Medicare, and Medicaid payments were increased. In October 1969, Nixon established a new approach to affirmative action with the "Philadelphia Plan," which required construction unions in that city working under government contracts to hire black apprentices. The following year, the plan was expanded to a national program involving all government hiring and contracting, setting aside jobs for minorities. Nixon also supported subsidized housing for low- and middle-income families, expanded the Job Corps, and oversaw the formation of the Occupational Safety and Health Administration.

Nixon believed that the Republican party could not afford to ignore social needs and public concerns in the name of conservatism. The environmental issue was a case in point. When Nixon took office in 1969, the environment was not a major concern. Few Americans thought about ecology. Almost overnight, however, the environment became a serious public issue. The ever-present Los Angeles smog, an oil slick off Santa Barbara, California, the declaration that Lake Erie was ecologically dead, and growing mountains of garbage everywhere provided graphic reminders of the ecological dangers facing the nation. Less than 6 percent of the world's population, environmentalists complained, Americans consumed 40 percent of the globe's resources and created 50 percent of the world's trash. During the second celebration of Earth Day, in April 1970, nearly every community in the nation and more than ten thousand schools and two thousand colleges hosted some type of Earth Day activities, emphasizing a national call for government action to improve environmental quality.

Nixon was not an environmentalist, but he recognized a new national agenda topic. Seizing the opportunity, two days after Earth Day 1970, he proposed the creation of the **Environmental Protection Agency (EPA).** Congress joined in, approving five major environmental acts before the year was finished, including the Clean Air Act and the Water Quality Improvement Act. Both acts directed the EPA, which was rapidly growing into the third largest government agency, to establish standards on the amount of pollutants that business and industry could discharge. Conservatives complained that the standards placed too great a burden on business, and liberals objected that the guidelines did not go far enough to protect the environment. But few denied that Nixon had moved quickly to expand government regulations in an area in which most people agreed a need existed.

Nixon also proved flexible in economic matters. When he took office, he faced a budget deficit of nearly $25 billion and a climbing rate of inflation. Nixon cut spending, increased interest rates, and balanced the budget in 1969. But economic recovery failed to follow, and inflation rose as economic growth slowed—giving rise to a new phenomenon, **stagflation.** By 1971, the economy was in its first recession since 1958. Unemployment and bankruptcies increased, but inflation still climbed, approaching 5.3 percent. Fearing that the economy would erode his support, Nixon radically shifted his approach. In April 1971, he asked for increased federal spending to boost recovery and for wage and price controls to stall advancing inflation. Conservatives were shocked and complained bitterly at the betrayal of their values. The public and the economy responded positively, however, as inflation and unemployment declined. At the end of ninety days, Nixon replaced the wage and price freeze with recommended guidelines. Freed from federal restrictions, wages and prices began to climb again.

Nixon's battle with inflation was a losing one, in part because of economic events over which he had no control. A global drought pushed up farm prices, while Arab nations raised oil prices and limited oil sales in response to the devaluation of the American dollar and continued U.S. support for Israel. After the October 1973 Arab-Israeli Yom Kippur War, Arab nations instituted an oil boycott of the United States that, before it was over in 1974, nearly doubled gasoline prices and forced many Americans to wait in long lines to gas up their cars. Increases in food and oil prices pushed the 1974 inflation rate over 10 percent. That same year, 85 percent of those asked said not only that the economy was the nation's most pressing problem but also that they expected it to get worse.

Law and Order and Southern Politics

During the 1968 campaign, Nixon had presented himself as the law-and-order candidate who would use the resources and power of government to

Environmental Protection Agency Agency created in 1970 to consolidate all major government programs controlling pollution and other programs to protect the environment.

stagflation Persistent inflation combined with stagnant consumer demand and relatively high unemployment.

combat crime. But once in office, the administration seemed more interested in using the law-and-order theme for political purposes than in attacking street crime. An aide to Attorney General **John Mitchell,** Kevin Phillips, argued in *The Emerging Republican Majority* (1969) that the future of the Republican party rested on the support of people living in suburbs, working-class neighborhoods, the South, and the **Sunbelt.** In those areas, Phillips asserted, there was little sympathy for student activists, antiwar protesters, welfare recipients, or civil rights advocates. Zealously, Vice President Spiro Agnew denounced antiwar protesters for aiding the enemy and undermining the nation's social and patriotic values, and he challenged the Silent Majority to reassert traditional values and restore stability to America. In many areas, blue-collar and middle-class America responded. Fearing integration and experiencing a slowing of economic gains, more and more of suburban America voted Republican. In southern California, residents of Lakewood felt threatened by a seeming "invasion" of blacks and Latinos, who used "their" parks and swimming pools, encroaching on what had once been a model, modern, and upwardly mobile suburb (see page 895).

As part of an ongoing "southern strategy"—an attempt to lock up the once solidly Democratic South for Republicans—the Nixon administration opposed busing to achieve school integration. In response to a 1969 request from Mississippi to postpone court-ordered integration of several school systems, Attorney General John Mitchell petitioned the Supreme Court for a delay. At the same time, the administration lobbied Congress for a revision of the 1965 Voting Rights Act that would have weakened southern compliance. Neither effort was successful. In October 1969, the Supreme Court unanimously decreed in *Alexander v. Holmes* that it was "the obligation of every school district to terminate dual school systems at once." The White House suffered another loss in 1971, when the Court reaffirmed the use of busing to achieve integration in a North Carolina case, *Swann v. Charlotte-Mecklenburg.* The Nixon administration criticized the decisions but agreed to "carry out the law." By 1973, most African-American children in the South were attending integrated public schools. Even though Nixon was unable to slow the process of integration, he won increasing political support among white southerners.

A second part of Nixon's southern strategy was to alter the composition of the Supreme Court. He wanted a more conservative Court that would more narrowly interpret the Constitution and move away from the social interventionism of the Warren Court. His first opportunity came in 1969 when Chief Justice Earl Warren retired. To take Warren's place, Nixon nominated Warren Burger, a respected, conservative federal judge, who was easily confirmed by the Senate. The resignation of Liberal justice Abe Fortas soon after gave Nixon a second chance to alter the Court.

For political reasons, Nixon wanted to appoint a southerner and nominated Clement Haynesworth of South Carolina. Haynesworth's history of antilabor and anti–civil rights statements and decisions raised predictable trouble in the Senate. Democrats and several Republicans joined forces to deny his confirmation. The rejection incensed Nixon, who was determined to force a southerner down the Senate's throat. His second choice was worse than the first. Not only was G. Harrold Carswell of Florida opposed to civil rights and labor, but his ratings as a lawyer and judge were below average. Carswell too failed confirmation. On his third try, Nixon stopped looking for a southerner and selected Harry Blackmun, a conservative from Minnesota. Blackmun was confirmed easily. In 1971, Nixon appointed two more justices, Lewis Powell of Virginia and William Rehnquist of Arizona, creating a more conservative Supreme Court.

An Embattled President

By the end of Nixon's first term, Republicans had every reason to gloat. Nearly 60 percent of those asked in national opinion polls said they approved of Nixon's record. The efforts on behalf of southern whites had ensured growing support in what had once been the "solid Democratic South." The law-and-order campaign appealed to Middle America, and protesters and activists were losing strength. The economy, though still a worry, seemed under control: unemployment was dropping and inflation held in check. Diplomatically, Nixon had scored major successes: the opening of relations with China,

John Mitchell Nixon's attorney general, who eventually served four years of prison time for his part in the Watergate scandal.

Sunbelt Region of the United States that extends from Washington, D.C., to Florida and from Texas to California and the Pacific coast; during the 1960s, its population grew dramatically because of its climate and economic opportunities.

♦ As the Watergate investigation uncovered a host of "dirty tricks" and other unethical and illegal activities by the Nixon Administration, cartoonist Edward Sorell drew the "Watergate Shootout," showing Nixon, Mitchell, and others involved in the Watergate scandal as a band of mobsters holding off the police. *"Watergate Shootout" by Edward Sorell. Collection of Byron Dobell.*

détente with the Soviets, the reduction of American forces in Vietnam, and the possibility of a peace agreement in Paris.

The 1972 campaign was marked by a confident Republican party, the continued disarray of the Democratic party, and a new group of first-time voters. Passage in 1971 of the Twenty-sixth Amendment lowered the voting age to 18 and provided a ray of hope for embattled liberal Democrats, who hoped the new voters would cast their votes for **George McGovern.**

Senator McGovern of South Dakota gained the presidential nomination after several bruising primaries and a divided nominating convention. Many Democrats believed he was too liberal and refused to support him. George Wallace—confined to a wheelchair following an assassination attempt that left him paralyzed—again bolted the party to run as a third-party candidate on the American Independent ticket.

Despite almost certain victory, Nixon was plagued by a siege mentality. He was convinced that he was surrounded by enemies: Democrats, social activists, liberals, most of the press, and even some members of his own staff and party. Repeatedly, he spoke about "screwing" his domestic enemies before they got him. He kept an "enemies list," used illegal wiretaps and infiltration to spy on suspect organizations and people, and instructed the FBI, the Internal Revenue Service, and other government organizations to intimidate and punish his opponents.

Throughout the 1972 campaign, Nixon and his campaign staff were obsessed with humiliating the Democrats. To achieve this objective, Nixon's staff and the **Committee to Re-elect the President (CREEP),** directed by John Mitchell, were willing to step outside the normal bounds of election behavior. They turned to a Special Investigations Unit, known informally as the "Plumbers," to disrupt the Democrats. The Plumbers had used illegal surveillance and even burglary to investigate sources of suspected leaks of sensitive materials such as the *Pentagon Papers.* And under former FBI agent G. Gordon Liddy and former CIA operative E. Howard Hunt, the Plumbers conducted "dirty tricks" operations against the Democrats. Seeking inside information on the opposition, CREEP approved a burglary of

George McGovern South Dakota senator who opposed the Vietnam War and was the unsucessful Democratic candidate for president in 1972.

Committee to Re-elect the President Nixon's campaign committee in 1972, which enlisted G. Gordon Liddy and others to spy on the Democrats and break into the offices of the Democratic National Committee.

Democratic National Committee headquarters in the **Watergate** building to copy documents and tap phones.

On June 17, 1972, a Watergate security guard detected the burglars and notified the police, who arrested five men carrying "bugging" equipment. Officials soon determined that they worked for Hunt and Liddy. CREEP and the White House immediately denied any connection to the burglars and worked to contain the investigation of the break-in. As Nixon "categorically" denied that anyone in the White House was involved, Mitchell and White House staffers destroyed documents indicating the opposite, and they arranged payments to those arrested in return for their silence. The White House encouraged the FBI to limit its investigation. The furor passed, and the Watergate break-in had little apparent effect on the public or the election. In November, Nixon buried McGovern in an avalanche of electoral votes, winning every state except Massachusetts.

Nixon began his second term claiming a clear mandate for his policies. From the outside it appeared that the Nixon administration had a clear field to promote its agenda. But within the White House, concern simmered with the approaching trial of the Watergate burglars. Within a few days of their arrest on June 17, 1972, Nixon had approved efforts to hide any connection between the White House and the burglars. "I want you all to stonewall it," he told John Mitchell. "Cover it up."

But as the trial approached, the cover-up began to unravel. Before being sentenced for the break-in, James McCord, who led the burglary team, informed Judge John J. Sirica that key Republicans were involved in planning the operation and that the burglars had been paid to keep quiet. *Washington Post* reporters Bob Woodward and Carl Bernstein, investigating the suspicious payments, found a path leading to the White House, John Mitchell, and CREEP. Amid growing publicity and suspicions of White House involvement, the Senate convened a special committee to investigate the break-in, chaired by a Democrat, Senator Sam Ervin, Jr., of North Carolina. One of those called before Sirica's court and Ervin's committee was White House staffer John Dean, who testified that top White House officials, including Nixon, were involved in the cover-up. By May 1973, Nixon had fired Dean, and Haldeman and Ehrlichman had resigned.

Adding to Nixon's troubles were accusations he had improperly taken tax deductions and that Vice President Agnew was guilty of income-tax evasion and influence peddling. "I am not a crook," Nixon announced, as both denied any wrongdoing. Nevertheless, Nixon agreed that he had made errors in his income-tax deductions and that he owed the government an additional half-million dollars. Agnew, certain to be convicted, pleaded no contest to the charges against him and resigned. In October 1973, Nixon named Representative Gerald R. Ford of Michigan to be vice president.

As Ford assumed office, the cover-up was disintegrating rapidly. The revelation that Nixon had secretly recorded meetings in the Oval Office, including those with John Dean, had raised demands for the release of the tapes. Responding to public pressure, Nixon appointed Archibald Cox as special Justice Department prosecutor to investigate Watergate, promising full cooperation. But when Cox demanded the Oval Office tapes, Nixon ordered him fired. Following the October 20, 1973, **"Saturday Night Massacre,"** Nixon's popularity shrank to 30 percent, and calls for his resignation or impeachment intensified.

In March 1974, the grand jury investigating the Watergate break-in indicted Mitchell, Haldeman, and Ehrlichman and named Nixon as an "unindicted co-conspirator." Under tremendous pressure, Nixon released to the House Judiciary Committee transcripts of selected tapes. The outcome was devastating. Not only did the transcripts contradict some official testimony, but Nixon's profane language, callousness, and apparent lack of moral values shocked many Americans. By the end of July, the House Judiciary Committee had charged Nixon with three impeachable crimes: obstructing justice, abuse of power, and denying subpoenas. Nixon's remaining support evaporated, and once-loyal Republicans told him that he could either resign or face impeachment. Nixon resigned on August 9, 1974, making Gerald Ford an unelected president. Eventually, twenty-nine people connected to the White House were convicted of crimes related to Watergate and the 1972 campaign.

Watergate Apartment-office complex in Washington, D.C.; it housed the headquarters of the Democratic National Committee, and its name became a synonym for the scandal over the Nixon administration's involvement in a break-in there and the president's part in the cover-up that followed.

"Saturday Night Massacre" Events on October 20, 1973, when Nixon ordered the firing of Watergate special prosecutor Archibald Cox and ended up firing those who refused to carry out his order.

SUMMARY

Expectations
Constraints
Choices
Outcomes

President Johnson *chose* to continue Kennedy's commitment to save South Vietnam from communism. The *outcome*, through a series of planned escalations, was an Americanized war in Vietnam. The *expectation* that American superiority would defeat Ho Chi Minh's Communists proved disastrous for the nation. Vietnam cost Johnson his presidency and compounded the divisions in American society.

But more than the debate over the war divided the nation. By 1968, the country was aflame with riots in urban centers, and an increasing number of groups were seeking better social, economic, and political *choices*. Those advocating social reforms, however, faced a resurgence of conservatism. As president, Nixon escaped the quagmire of Vietnam by implementing Vietnamization. He also wanted to restructure international relations by working to improve relations with the Soviet Union and China. At home, Nixon *chose* an uneven course, switching between maintaining government activism and reducing the power of government. Though opposed to government intervention, he created the Environmental Protection Agency. Politically, he sought a broader base for the Republican party by pursuing a southern strategy that diminished federal support for civil rights. Despite Nixon's domestic and foreign policy successes, however, his desire to crush his enemies led to the Watergate scandal and his downfall. Facing impeachment, the president resigned. The *outcome* of the Johnson years and the Watergate scandal was a nation with lowered expectations of politics and government and a feeling of drift, disillusionment, and disunity.

SUGGESTED READINGS

Stephen Ambrose. *Nixon: The Triumph of a Politician, 1962–1972* (1989).

An excellent examination of Nixon and his politics—the second volume of Ambrose's three-volume biography.

Philip Caputo. *Rumor of War* (1986).

The author's account of his own changing perspectives on the war in Vietnam. Caputo served as a young marine officer in Vietnam and later covered the final days in Saigon as a journalist. His views frequently reflected those of the American public.

Vine Deloria, Jr. *Behind the Trail of Broken Treaties* (1974).

An examination of U.S. government policies toward Native Americans by a leading Indian activist.

Alice Echols. *Daring to Be Bad* (1989).

An insightful and interesting account of the radical dimension of the women's movement.

Stanley Kutler. *The Wars of Watergate* (1990) and *Abuse of Power: The New Nixon Tapes* (1997).

The former work details the events surrounding the Watergate break-in and the hearings that led to Nixon's resignation. The latter provides transcripts of selected Nixon tapes.

Kim McQuaid. *The Anxious Years: America in the Vietnam-Watergate Era* (1989).

A brief, solid overview of the 1960s.

Robert Roberts. *Where the Dominoes Fell* (1990).

A brief, well-written history of America's role in Vietnam.

INCREASE IN INCOME, 1980–1989 Personal income rose more rapidly in the 1980s than in any other decade, increasing almost 85 percent. As this map indicates, these increases were not uniform. Some regions and states did better than others. Because the rate of inflation was approximately 70 percent during this period, the net gain in income was much less than this map appears to show. The graph to the right shows the increase in income with the 70 percent inflation rate both factored in and not factored in.

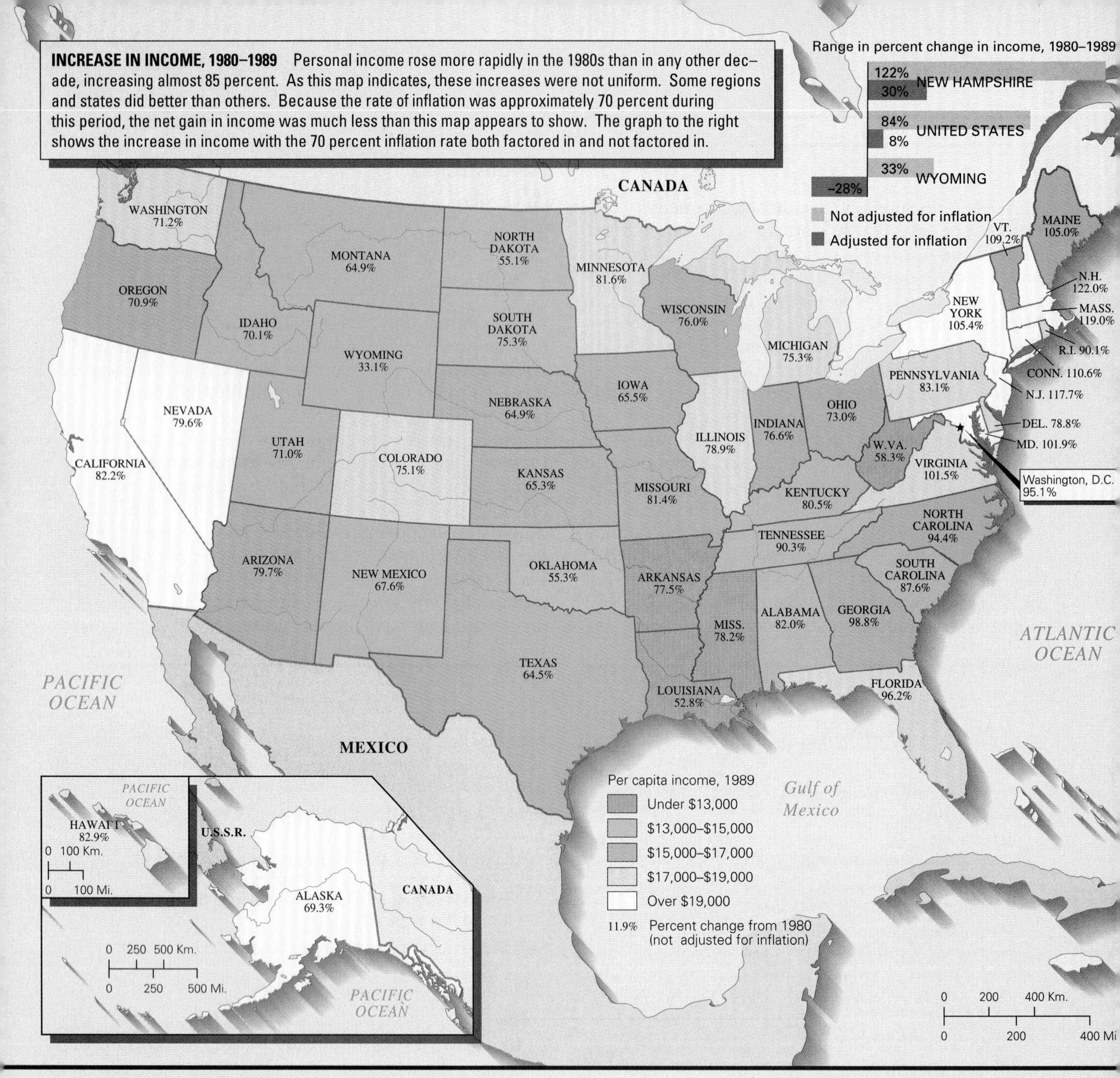

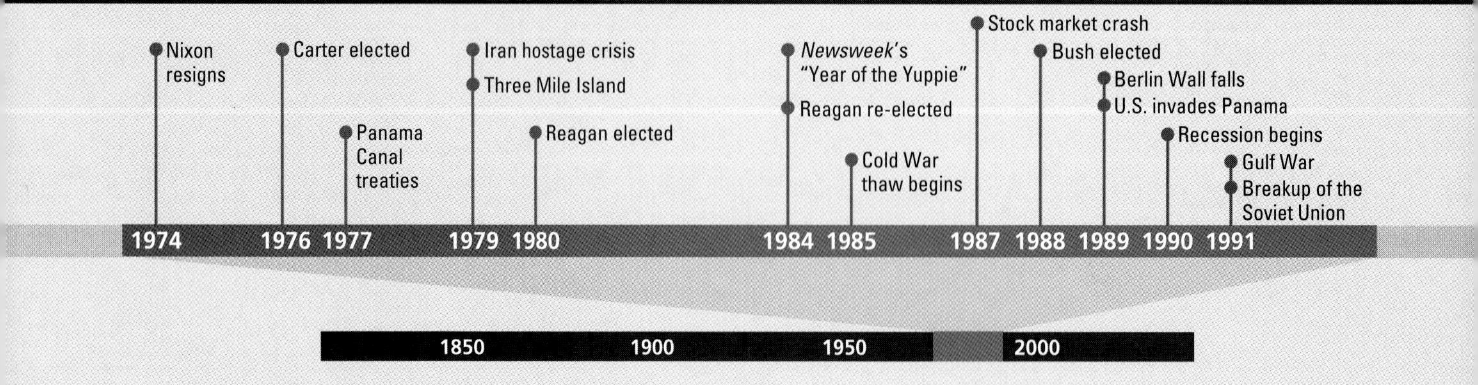

CHAPTER 32

Facing Limits, 1974–1991

Politics of Uncertainty

- What domestic problems did Gerald Ford and Jimmy Carter face? What were the political and economic outcomes of the choices they made?
- What expectations and constraints did Carter face as a Washington outsider?

Carter's Foreign Policy

- What new directions in foreign policy did Carter take? What were the outcomes of those changes?
- What constraints did Carter face in implementing a policy stressing human rights?

Enter Ronald Reagan—Stage Right

- What expectations influenced Americans who chose to vote for Reagan?
- What is "Reaganomics," and what were the outcomes of Reagan's economic policies for the economy and society?

Asserting World Power

- How did the Reagan administration's expectations about American foreign policy differ from Carter's? How did those views shape the outcomes of the Reagan administration's policies?

In Reagan's Shadow

- What new foreign-policy choices did the United States face as a result of the collapse of the Soviet Union?
- How did the outcome of Reagan's domestic policies shape expectations and outcomes for the Bush administration?

INTRODUCTION

Expectations
Constraints
Choices
Outcomes

Gerald Ford assumed the presidency after the resignation of Richard Nixon. The first unelected president, Ford faced an expanding set of policy *constraints* without Nixon's vision or toughness. The economy continued to flounder, and many of Nixon's foreign-policy initiatives, especially regarding détente, were being questioned by his own party. Also, there was the *constraint* of political cynicism generated by Vietnam and Watergate and fueled by the belief that Ford was merely an interim president. The *outcome* was a presidency with few political or foreign-policy "victories." Nevertheless, the Republican party nominated Ford for the presidency in 1976.

As the nation celebrated its two-hundredth birthday and television showed 30-second clips of proud moments in American history, few Americans *expected* the immediate future to match the success of the past. Limits seemed to loom everywhere. The sluggish economy responded to neither liberal nor conservative policy *expectations.* The liberalism that had attacked racism and poverty was out of vogue, challenged by more conservative *choices.* The Silent Majority awakened by Nixon seemed to set the tone of the nation, rejecting the idea that a more active government can solve problems and favoring a stronger emphasis on more traditional social values and less government involvement in economic and social affairs. Even James Earl Carter, the Democratic candidate for the presidency in 1976, based a large part of his political message on personal and moral *choices,* and argued that the U.S. government could not solve every problem. He urged Americans to sacrifice to overcome problems at home and abroad. As president, however, Carter failed to provide an effective domestic or foreign policy, and many Americans thought that the main *constraint* on improving the nation was not the limited capabilities Carter warned about but his own policies and a federal government that stifled individual *choices.*

Opposing Carter, the 1980 Republican candidate for president, Ronald Reagan, won popular approval by promoting the *expectation* of a renewed America, powerful and prosperous. He attacked liberal economic and social policies and re-emphasized a Cold War–style foreign policy that would "stand tall" against the Soviet "evil empire." During his administration, the economy seemed vitalized, and government was redirected away from costly social programs. Many Americans felt that business had been freed of many needless government controls, traditional social and family values had been properly reasserted, and the Cold War had been all but won.

Not everyone agreed that Reagan's *choices* produced a favorable *outcome,* however. Critics argued that he placed too much emphasis on wealth and too little on the needs of minority groups, the less well off, and the poor. Others pointed to a massive national debt and a growing trade deficit as serious economic problems. Despite Reagan's personal popularity, as the Reagan administration ended, more and more Americans were uncertain about the *outcome* of Reagan's economic and social policies.

Running in the shadow of Reagan in 1988, Vice President George Bush seized the Republican presidential nomination in a nation that seemed dissatisfied but unable to pinpoint what was wrong and how to fix it. Responding to the lack of consensus in the polls, Bush offered a "kinder, gentler nation" that would show more concern for minorities, the poor, education, and the environment. Easily defeating Michael Dukakis, the Democratic candidate, Bush assumed the presidency but had little desire to implement domestic policy changes. Instead, he *chose* to focus on foreign policy. Taking office as the Soviet Union shattered, he charted foreign policy in a new international setting: the United States was the only superpower. Bush cautiously supported democratic change in the Soviet Union and Eastern Europe and *chose* to commit American military force in Panama and Kuwait. The *outcome* was that Bush's foreign policy, unlike his domestic policies, generated widespread praise.

CHRONOLOGY

New Directions, New Limits

1974 Richard Nixon resigns
Gerald Ford becomes president and pardons Nixon
Brezhnev-Ford summit at Vladivostok

1975 Fall of South Vietnam
Helsinki Summit

1976 Jimmy Carter elected president

1977 Department of Energy created
Panama Canal treaties
SALT I treaty expires

1978 Camp David Accords
Revolution in Iran topples the shah

1979 Ayatollah Khomeini assumes power in Iran
United States recognizes People's Republic of China
Nuclear accident at Three Mile Island, Pennsylvania
Egyptian-Israeli peace treaty signed in Washington, D.C.
SALT II treaty signed in Vienna
Chrysler bailout
Hostages seized in Iran
Soviet Union invades Afghanistan

1980 Carter applies sanctions against Soviet Union
SALT II treaty withdrawn from Senate
Carter Doctrine
Iran-Iraq War begins
Ronald Reagan elected president

1981 Iran releases American hostages
Economic Recovery Tax Act

1982 United States sends marines to Beirut

1983 Congress funds Strategic Defense Initiative
Marine barracks in Beirut destroyed
United States invades Grenada

1984 Charles Murray's *Losing Ground*
Withdrawal of U.S. forces from Lebanon
Boland Amendment
Reagan re-elected
Newsweek's "Year of the Yuppie"

1985 Gramm-Rudman-Hollings Act
Mikhail Gorbachev assumes power in Soviet Union
Secret arms sales to Iran in exchange for U.S. hostages
Gorbachev-Reagan summit in Geneva

1986 U.S. bombing raid on Libya
Gorbachev-Reagan summit in Iceland

1987 Iran-Contra hearings
Stock market crash
Intermediate Nuclear Force Treaty

1988 George Bush elected president

1989 Chinese government represses democracy movement in Tiananmen Square
Berlin Wall pulled down
United States invades Panama
Gorbachev-Bush summit on Malta

1990 Recession begins
Free elections in Nicaragua
Clean Air Act
Iraq invades Kuwait
Americans with Disabilities Act

1991 Breakup of the Soviet Union
Gorbachev resigns
Gulf War

Politics of Uncertainty

• What domestic problems did Gerald Ford and Jimmy Carter face? What were the political and economic outcomes of the choices they made?

• What expectations and constraints did Carter face as a Washington outsider?

Having been appointed vice president to replace Spiro Agnew (see page 960), Gerald Ford became president in 1974 when Richard Nixon resigned. He brought a very different personality to the White House: Nixon was innovative, suspicious, and arrogant. Ford was humble, trustworthy, and personally conservative—an administrator, not an innovator. Responding to the consequences of Watergate, he sought to establish cordial relations with Congress and to restore the people's faith in government. Taking into account Ford's personality and a general desire to move beyond Watergate, many political observers believed that he would enjoy a political honeymoon with Congress. That expectation faded rapidly.

An Interim Presidency

Soon after taking office in 1974, Ford pardoned Nixon for any crimes the former president might have committed. The pardon was unpopular, unleashing public and congressional protests, and ended any idea of a political honeymoon. Democrats opposed Ford's efforts to deal with the problems of inflation, recession, and the federal deficit. He wanted to cut business taxes and federal spending and to raise interest rates. Democrats instead introduced legislation to create jobs and to increase spending for social and educational programs. Ford vetoed the bills and conducted a public opinion campaign to mobilize support for his program. The result was a political stalemate. In two years, Ford successfully blocked thirty-seven bills but never generated enough public support to advance his own programs.

Ford fared only slightly better in his foreign policies. With little knowledge about foreign affairs, he relied heavily on Henry Kissinger, who by then held the key positions of national security adviser and secretary of state. With Kissinger on board, Ford continued Nixon's policies, including Vietnamization, arms limitation, and détente. Trying to maintain the thaw in the Cold War, in November 1974 Ford traveled to Vladivostok, in Siberia, where he and Soviet premier Leonid Brezhnev made progress on strategic arms limits and generally improved Soviet-American relations. In August 1975, Ford met with Brezhnev and leaders from thirty-three other nations in Helsinki, Finland, and agreed that the United States would officially recognize the boundaries of Europe established after World War II. In return, Brezhnev and the Eastern-bloc leaders agreed to respect certain **human rights** within their countries. Critics, however, including presidential hopeful Ronald Reagan, asserted that the Helsinki agreements did nothing to reduce human rights violations and made too many concessions to the Soviets. Under fire, Ford promptly backed away from the policy of détente and adopted a more traditional Cold War attitude.

Ford's efforts to maintain economic and military support for South Vietnam (see page 974) also met with congressional opposition. When North Vietnamese forces seized Saigon in April 1975, Ford blamed Congress for the Communist victory. Most Americans, however, were happy that the conflict was no longer an American war. On a more positive note, Kissinger successfully worked to improve relations between Israel and Egypt. After a UN cease-fire in the Yom Kippur War, Kissinger had flown from one capital to another negotiating the removal of Israeli forces from Arab territory. His shuttle diplomacy paid off in September 1975, when Israel and Egypt signed an agreement whereby Israeli troops withdrew from some occupied areas and Egypt resigned from the anti-Israeli Arab coalition.

The Bicentennial Election and Jimmy Carter

After two years in office, against the background of the bicentennial celebration of American independence, Ford sought election in his own right. To gain the Republican nomination, he had to overcome a stiff challenge from California governor Ronald Reagan who was supported by many conservative Republicans. Ford's Democratic opponent, **Jimmy Carter,** had little political experience, aside from being governor of Georgia, and no national exposure.

human rights Basic rights and freedoms to which all human beings are entitled, such as the right to life and liberty, to freedom of thought and expression, and to equality before the law.

Jimmy Carter Georgia governor elected president on the Democratic ticket in 1976; he fostered concern for human issues in foreign policy and called for energy conservation in the United States.

♦ Although a Southerner, in the 1976 election African-American voters provided Jimmy Carter with the crucial margin for victory. Here the President and the First Lady worship with African-American leaders, including Coretta Scott King and Andrew Young (center). *Jimmy Carter Presidential Library.*

Carter's background should have made him an underdog against President Ford, but people were fed up with politics and politicians. Carter presented himself as a political outsider who, armed with common sense and honesty, would heal the wounds of Watergate and Vietnam. Thus "Jimmy who?" took a commanding lead in public opinion polls, which found that voters liked Ford but considered him ineffective. In a lackluster campaign, the candidates were vague on issues but expansive on smiles and photo sessions. Ford managed to close the gap between himself and Carter, but on election day, with less than 54 percent of the eligible voters bothering to cast ballots, Carter received 297 electoral votes to Ford's 240.

Brimming with enthusiasm, Carter arrived in the nation's capital in January 1977 stressing that he was free of political debts and untouched by Washington politics and the lures of special interests. He pledged honesty, simplicity, and hard work. His message to the people was without frills. "We must simply do our best," he stated, to generate a "new spirit . . . of individual sacrifice for the common good." Portraying himself as the people's president, Carter delivered Roosevelt-style fireside chats on radio and television and held "phone-ins" that gave people a chance to talk with their president. The public welcomed Carter's open, informal presidency and his pledge of honesty.

But not everyone was charmed. Could outsiders like Carter and those who now surrounded and advised him play the insiders' game of political give-and-take? Would they have the expertise and muscle to control Democratic politicians and attract Republicans? The answer seemed clear when Democratic congressional leaders flew into a rage over Carter's first budget, which axed eighteen pet projects that would have provided jobs and revenue for home districts. Angry Democrats joined with gleeful Republicans to attack the budget, forcing Carter to restore many of the cuts. Democratic representative Dan Rostenkowski of Illinois observed, "I don't see this Congress rolling over and playing dead. . . . Carter is going to set up his priorities and we are going to set up ours. We'll see where we go from there." By mid-1977, most of Carter's proposals were buried in Congress, and some Democrats and political observers were complaining about a lack of presidential wisdom, leadership, and inspiration.

Domestic Priorities

Carter faced two major domestic problems: a sluggish economy and high energy costs owing to dependence on foreign sources of oil. He concluded that the economy could not improve until the United States stopped consuming more energy than it produced—the nation was importing about 60 percent of its oil. Solving the **energy crisis** was the

energy crisis Vulnerability to dwindling oil supplies, wasteful energy consumption, and potential embargoes by oil-producing countries.

"moral equivalent of war," Carter told the American people, and the only road to economic recovery. To reduce energy consumption, he asked Americans to wear sweaters, use public transportation, and lower their thermostats. He offered Congress 113 energy proposals, including the creation of a cabinet-level Department of Energy, support for research and development of fuels other than oil, and special regulations and taxes to prevent the energy industry from reaping excess profits.

Lobbyists for automobile, oil, gas, and other industries immediately steered Congress away from conservation, regulation, and taxes and toward increased oil production. With new fields along Alaska's North Slope supplying large quantities of oil, many found it easy to dismiss Carter's recommendations. Congress passed only fragments of his plan—creating the Department of Energy in 1977, approving some incentives for conservation, and deregulating the natural-gas industry. After a 1978 revolution in Iran pushed up oil prices, Congress went further and by 1980 had approved funds for **alternative fuels** (including nuclear energy) and an excess-profits tax on the oil and gas industry. Still, Congress made no real effort to develop a comprehensive plan to achieve energy independence.

Many argued that nuclear power was the energy of the future. Claiming that it was cheap and environmentally safe, advocates called for new and larger plants that could produce all the energy the nation needed. Opponents argued that nuclear energy was expensive and potentially dangerous. Their fears came to life on March 28, 1979, when a serious accident at a nuclear power plant at **Three Mile Island** in central Pennsylvania released a cloud of radioactive gas and nearly caused a **meltdown.** It took two weeks to shut down the reactor, and more than a hundred thousand people were evacuated from the surrounding area. After the accident, more than thirty energy companies canceled nuclear building projects, and the government enacted stronger regulations. Nuclear power had become a less likely energy source, and the nation remained largely dependent on natural gas, oil, and coal.

Carter's economic policies offered little innovation and fared even worse than his energy programs. To stimulate the economy, he asked for tax reforms, the deregulation of transportation industries (trucking, railroads, and airlines), and passage of his energy program. To curb inflation, he tried to use tighter credit and higher interest rates, and he asked business and workers to hold the line on wages and prices. But to the disappointment of many Democrats, he rejected any further role by the government. There would be no wage and price controls, federally funded jobs, or increases in the minimum wage. By 1980, the country was losing the fight against inflation, which stood at 14 percent—the highest rate since 1947. With unemployment also high, at nearly 7.6 percent, Carter admitted he had not provided enough leadership but also blamed the public's unwillingness to sacrifice for a large part of the nation's woes.

The stagflation troubling the American economy was largely the product of a changing world economy over which U.S. presidents had little control. The booming economies of West Germany, Japan, Korea, and Taiwan cut into American markets—reducing American profits and prosperity. The **Organization of Petroleum Exporting Countries (OPEC)** gained strength after the Yom Kippur War of 1973 and continued to push up the price of petroleum products for the rest of the decade. Higher fuel costs not only added to inflation and unemployment but also threatened the nation's industrial base, which depended on inexpensive fuels. In the new global economy, many American industries were unable to match the production costs or retail prices of their foreign competitors or the quality of the goods produced overseas. Japanese goods, once the joke of international commerce, were gobbling up the electronics industry and cutting deeply into the American automobile market. South Korea and Taiwan were taking huge bites out of the American textile and clothing markets. Many of the nation's primary industries (iron and steel, rubber, automobiles and their parts, clothing, coal), especially those located in the Great Lakes region, were forced to cut back production, lay off workers, and close plants. In 1979, only a government-backed loan kept the

alternative fuels Sources of energy other than coal, oil, and natural gas, such as solar, geothermal, hydroelectric, and nuclear energy.

Three Mile Island Site of a nuclear power plant near Harrisburg, Pennsylvania; an accident at the plant in 1979 led to a partial meltdown and the release of radioactive gases.

meltdown Severe overheating of a nuclear reactor core, resulting in the melting of the core and the escape of life-threatening radiation.

Organization of Petroleum Exporting Countries Organization created in 1960 by eleven oil-producing nations in Africa, the Middle East, Latin America, and Asia to coordinate the price and level of production of their oil.

Chrysler Corporation from bankruptcy. Chrysler managed to recover, but from the Great Lakes to the Northeast, other industries failed or moved overseas or to the South and West, where production costs—primarily for labor and heating—were lower and governments were willing to provide economic incentives to attract industry. During the 1970s, from New York to Wisconsin, over what once had been the vibrant industrial center of the United States, spread what many termed the **Rust Belt.** Philadelphia from 1969 to 1981, for example, lost 42 percent of its factory jobs and 14 percent of its population, and its crime rate jumped by nearly 200 percent. By the mid-1980s some areas had regained some of their prosperity having modified their economic base to match the service and informational sectors of the economy (see pages 1018–1019).

Carter's Foreign Policy

- What new directions in foreign policy did Carter take? What were the outcomes of those changes?
- What constraints did Carter face in implementing a policy stressing human rights?

Carter's foreign policy was as controversial as his domestic policy. Saying that American foreign policy was preoccupied by an "inordinate fear of communism" and Cold War strategies, the president advocated more attention to the economic and social problems of the so-called **Third World,** including abuses or lack of human rights. **Cyrus Vance,** Carter's secretary of state, recognized Cold War concerns but was eager to pursue policies that focused on human issues and economic development. **Zbigniew Brzezinski,** Carter's national security adviser and an uncompromising Cold Warrior, put Europe first and looked for chances to "stick it to the Russians." Concerned about the Third World only in its Cold War context, he worried that an emphasis on human rights might weaken regimes that were pro-American but abusive. Carter expected policy clashes between Vance and Brzezinski but believed he could bridge the differences between them.

A Good Neighbor and Human Rights

Latin America seemed to Carter and Vance the best place to sound a new tone in American policy and move away from the Cold War perspective that had colored U.S. relations in the region. Carter wanted the United States to abandon its "paternalism" and instead fashion policies that considered each Latin American nation's internal priorities. He believed that Panama and the Panama Canal presented an excellent opportunity to chart a new course for U.S. policy in Latin America.

The Panama Canal Zone lay like an affluent foreign-occupied island within Panama. To Panamanians it was a daily reminder of the inequalities between themselves and the United States. When Carter took office, negotiations to turn control of the canal over to Panama had been stalled for years. Carter assigned them a high priority. Within a year, two treaties were written laying the groundwork for transferring ownership and control of the canal to Panama by 1999 and guaranteeing its neutrality.

Carter was pleased, but the American public was not. Nearly 80 percent of those asked opposed giving up the canal—it was American built and run and should remain that way, they said. Ronald Reagan labeled the agreement outright appeasement, and conservative Republican senator Jesse Helms of North Carolina promised to kill it in the Senate. He failed (by a single vote), but only after an amendment gave the United States the responsibility to intervene if the canal was ever threatened by an outside force.

Carter also hoped to promote human rights throughout Latin America, although conservatives warned that letting human rights drive policy might undermine pro-American but abusive governments, especially in Nicaragua and El Salvador. Nevertheless, in early 1979, Carter halted all direct military and economic aid to corrupt Nicaraguan dictator Anastasio Somoza, and the **Sandinista Liberation Front,** a largely Marxist-led organization, was able to

Rust Belt Industrialized Middle Atlantic and Great Lakes region containing old factories that are barely profitable or that have closed.

Third World Underdeveloped or developing countries of Latin America, Africa, and Asia.

Cyrus Vance Carter's secretary of state who wanted the United States to defend human rights and promote economic development in the Third World.

Zbigniew Brzezinski Carter's national security adviser who favored confronting the Soviet Union with firmness.

Sandinista Liberation Front Leftist guerrilla movement that overthrew Anastasio Somoza in Nicaragua in 1979 and established a revolutionary government under Daniel Ortega.

♦ One of President Carter's greatest triumphs was the signing of the 1978 peace accords between President Anwar Sadat of Egypt *(left)* and Prime Minister Menachem Begin of Israel *(right)*. The agreement followed days of personal diplomacy by Carter at the Camp David presidential retreat. Both Sadat and Begin received the Nobel Peace Prize for their efforts. *Jimmy Carter Presidential Library.*

force him from office. Hoping to encourage the Sandinistas, led by Daniel Ortega, to adopt moderate reforms, Carter provided $75 million in aid. Instead, the new government became more **autocratic** and established closer ties with the Soviet Union. These actions, in the opinion of many Americans, clearly placed Nicaragua within the Soviet bloc. In neighboring El Salvador, Carter provided aid to the newly created government of José Napoleón Duarte, which faced threats from both the left and the right.

Carter's policies in Central America drew opposition from both liberals and conservatives. Conservatives argued that Carter's human rights policy had allowed a Communist "takeover" of Nicaragua, and they wanted the government to support the **Contras,** who were fighting the Sandinistas in the jungles of Nicaragua. Liberals objected to Carter's backing away from the human rights issue and ending aid to the Ortega government. By 1980, Carter's Latin American policy, like his domestic policy, seemed in shambles, pleasing few and angering many.

The Camp David Accords

Carter credited the Panama Canal treaty to his ability to take a new approach to an old issue. He believed that such a tactic would also move Israel and its Arab neighbors toward a peace settlement (see Map 32.1). To this end, Carter invited Egypt's president Anwar Sadat and Israel's prime minister Menachem Begin for talks at the presidential retreat at Camp David in Maryland. Surprisingly both accepted.

Meeting in September 1978, Sadat and Begin did not get along well, and Carter shuttled between the two leaders, smoothing relations and stressing his personal commitment to both nations. Personally friendly with Sadat, he frequently exchanged harsh words with Begin. But he carefully negotiated agreements by which Egypt would recognize Israel's right to exist and Israel would return the Israeli-occupied Sinai Peninsula to Egypt. It took several months to finalize the **Camp David Accords,** but in a ceremony at the White House on March 26, 1979, acting like a proud midwife, Carter watched Begin and Sadat sign the first peace treaty between an Arab state and Israel. Although the treaty was a major diplomatic achievement for Carter, Arab leaders and most of the Arab world condemned it.

The Collapse of Détente

On other fronts, Carter tried to build on diplomatic efforts made by Nixon and Kissinger. Working with China's new leader, Deng Xiaoping, Carter fully resumed normal diplomatic relations with the People's Republic of China in January 1979. He also hoped to move forward with arms limitations. Despite chilly relations and difficult discussions, the two superpowers agreed to place some limits on long-range missiles, bombers, and nuclear warheads. Carter and Brezhnev signed the second strategic arms limitation treaty **(SALT II)** during their Vienna summit in June 1979. The agreement encountered widespread oppo-

autocratic Having unlimited power or authority; despotic.

Contras Nicaraguan rebels, many of them former followers of Somoza, fighting to overthrow the Sandinista government.

Camp David Accords Treaty, signed at Camp David in 1978, in which Israel agreed to return territory captured from Egypt and Egypt agreed to recognize Israel as a nation.

SALT II treaty Agreement between the United States and the Soviet Union in 1979 to limit the number of strategic nuclear missiles in each country; Congress never approved the treaty.

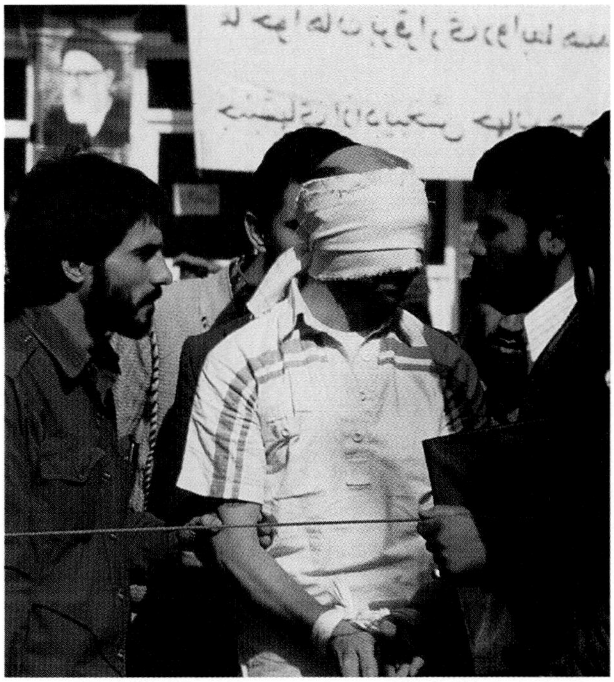

♦ In November 1979, Iranians seized the American Embassy in Teheran and took seventy-one people hostage. Blindfolded and handcuffed, the hostages were paraded through the streets as crowds jeered. Held more than a year, the hostages were released as Ronald Reagan was being sworn in as president. *Alain Mingam/Gamma Liaison.*

sition, including Ronald Reagan, who stated that it opened "a window of vulnerability." After the Soviet invasion of Afghanistan in early 1980, Carter asked the Senate to defer ratification and withdrew the treaty from consideration.

A Muslim country bordering the southern part of the Soviet Union, Afghanistan had a pro-Soviet government but a large number of anti-Soviet elements. The pro-Soviet leadership seemed to be losing control and feared that Afghan **Islamic fundamentalists** might stir unrest among Muslims in the southern republics of the Soviet Union itself. Claiming that the Afghan government had asked for help, Brezhnev sent in eighty thousand Soviet troops and occupied Afghanistan. Calling the invasion the "gravest threat to peace since 1945," Carter in 1980 reinstated registration for the draft for all 18-year-old males, imposed **economic sanctions** on the Soviet Union, boycotted the 1980 Olympic Games (held in Moscow), and increased support to the **mujahedeen,** the Afghan resistance fighters. He also announced the **Carter Doctrine**: any nation that attempted to take control of the **Persian Gulf** (see Map 32.1) would "be repelled by any means necessary, including the use of force."

The Iranian Revolution

Brezhnev's decision to intervene in Afghanistan and Carter's announcement of the Carter Doctrine were responses to more than just events in Afghanistan. Both leaders were also reacting to the 1978 revolution in Iran, which toppled the pro-American ruler, Shah Reza Pahlavi in early 1979, and established Islamic fundamentalism as a more powerful force in Middle East politics. The United States lost a military ally when the shah lost power in Iran—an ally that could be counted on to defend the Persian Gulf. The shah had received billions of dollars in American weapons and aid, but his regime had become increasingly repressive. Among those opposing him were Iran's intensely religious Shiite Muslims, led by **Ayatollah Ruhollah Khomeini.** Opposed to Western ideas and values, as well as to the shah, the Shiites and the Iranian military in February 1979 formed an alliance that forced the shah from power. Ayatollah Khomeini then created an Islamic revolutionary government, repressive and fundamentalist, which attacked the United States as the main source of evil in the world.

Carter ended economic and military aid to Iran, ordered Americans home, and reduced the embassy

Islamic fundamentalists Muslims calling for the replacement of Western secular values and attitudes with traditional Islamic values and an orthodox Muslim state.

economic sanctions Trade restrictions that one nation or several nations acting together impose on a country that has violated international law.

mujahedeen Afghan resistance group supplied with arms by the United States; it fought the Soviets after the invasion of Afghanistan in 1979.

Carter Doctrine Carter's announced policy that the United States would use force to repel any nation that attempted to take control of the Persian Gulf.

Persian Gulf Arm of the Arabian Sea and location of the ports of several major oil-producing Arab countries; its security is crucial to the flow of oil to the world.

Ayatollah Ruhollah Khomeini Religious leader of Iran's Shiite Muslims; the Shiites toppled the shah 1979, and the ayatollah established a new constitution giving himself supreme powers (*ayatollah* is a political/religious title).

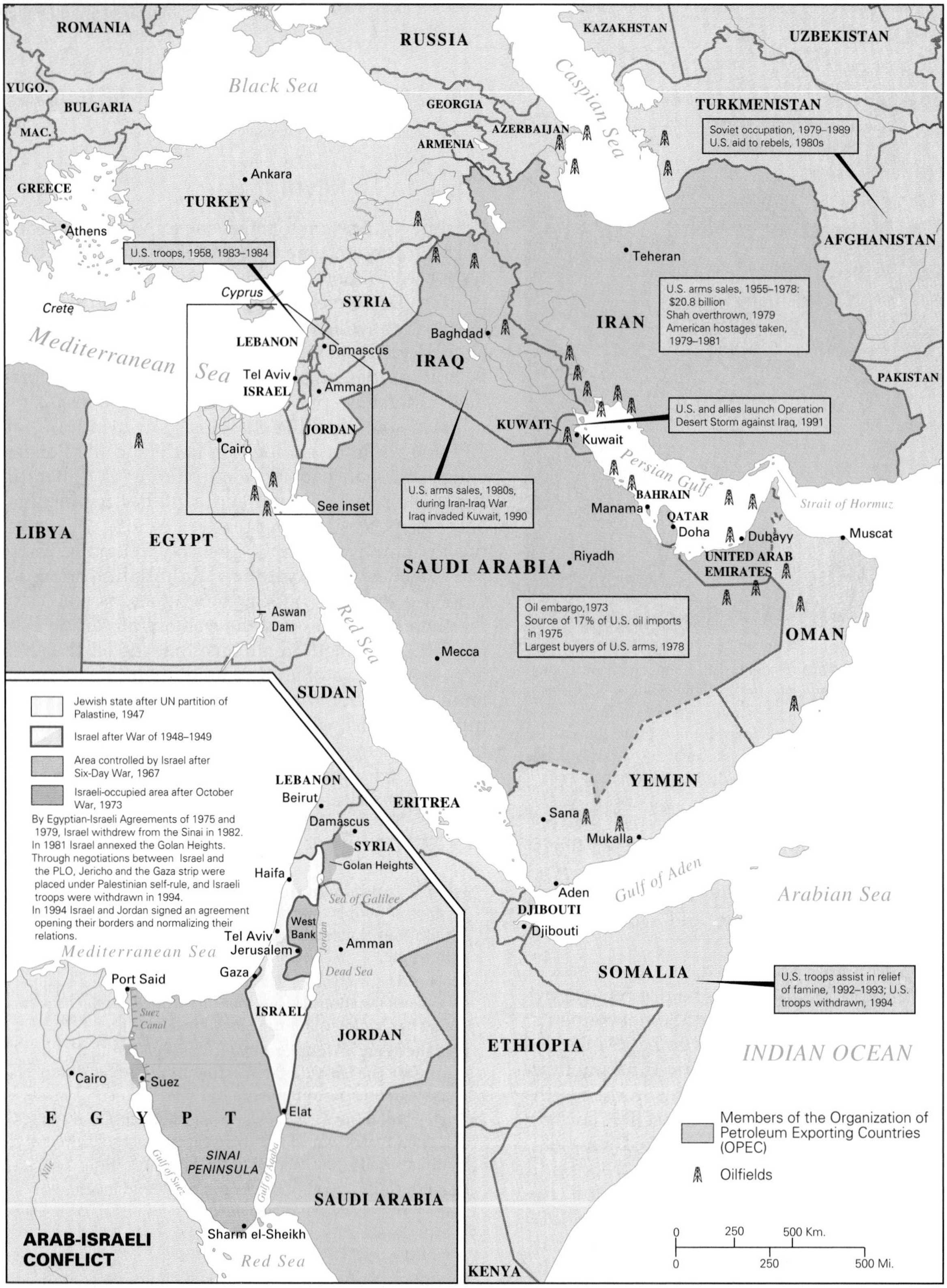

♦ **MAP 32.1 The Middle East** Since 1946, the United States has tried to balance strong support for Israel with its need for oil from the Arab states. To support U.S. interests in this volatile region, the United States has funneled in large amounts of financial and military aid and used overt and covert force to shape regional governments. Agreements signed in Washington in 1993 and 1994 between Israel and the Palestine Liberation Organization and between Israel and the kingdom of Jordan reduced tensions in the region.

staff in Tehran. On October 22, the exiled shah, who was dying, entered a New York hospital to receive cancer treatments, amid warnings of Iranian reprisals. On November 4 an angry mob stormed the American embassy in Tehran and took the remaining staff hostage. Sixty-six Americans were paraded through the streets and subjected to numerous abuses as the Iranians demanded the return of the shah for trial. The press quickly dubbed the crisis "America Held Hostage," and television accounts flooded American homes.

Carter weighed the conflicting options identified by his advisers. Brzezinski wanted to use military force to free the hostages. Vance argued for negotiation, hoping that Iranian moderates would find a way to free the hostages. Carter sided with Vance and was able to negotiate freedom for thirteen hostages, mostly women and African Americans. As further discussions failed, American frustration and anger grew, and Carter's popularity ratings fell to near 30 percent. It was time to "lance the boil," concluded Brzezinski, and in April 1980, Carter ordered a military rescue mission. The operation was a disaster. When the American forces lost vital equipment, including three helicopters, in a violent dust storm, Carter scrapped the mission.

Diplomatic efforts through the Canadians and the Algerians eventually resulted in an agreement in late 1980 to release the hostages. By that time the shah had died of cancer, and Iran was at war against Iraq and needed assets that Carter had frozen. On January 20, 1981, the hostages reached freedom, ending 444 days of captivity. On the same day, Ronald Reagan took office as president.

♦ A former movie star and host of television shows, Ronald Reagan used television and radio very effectively to outline his visions of American domestic and foreign policies. Because of his communication style, he was called "the great communicator." *UPI/Bettmann Archives.*

Enter Ronald Reagan—Stage Right

- What expectations influenced Americans who chose to vote for Reagan?
- What is "Reaganomics," and what were the outcomes of Reagan's economic policies for the economy and society?

According to Republicans in 1980, Carter's failure to free the hostages was typical of his administration's ineptness. Inflation had reached 12.4 percent, and unemployment was near 8 percent. Confident of victory in 1980, Republicans claimed that Carter was incapable of maintaining either American honor abroad or prosperity at home. Ronald Reagan, Republicans claimed, offered voters a clear alternative to Carter and the Democrats.

Reagan, a movie actor turned conservative politician, began his Hollywood career in 1937. Never a major star, he was a skilled actor who moved easily to the medium of television. Hosting television shows in the mid-1950s, Reagan frequently spoke about the successes of business and the dangers of too much government. Impressed in 1964 with Reagan's popular appeal and his speeches for Barry Goldwater (see page 936), conservative Republicans supported his quest to become governor of California in 1970. Reagan presented himself as a nonpolitician, won the election, and quickly emerged as one of the nation's most popular conservatives. After failing to unseat Ford for the Republican presidential nomination in 1976, Reagan became the Republican candidate four years later.

In his campaign for the presidency, Reagan argued that the federal government was too large and powerful, restricting individual rights and free enterprise. He promised to reduce the role of government and lower taxes, freeing American ingenuity and competitiveness. Across the country taxes had become a hot issue. In 1978, Californians had led a tax revolt by passing **Proposition 13,** which placed a limit on property taxes.

Reagan was an effective campaigner who communicated confidence and a sense of humor. "A recession," he quipped, "is when your neighbor loses his job. A depression is when you lose yours. A recovery is when Jimmy Carter loses his." Reagan presented himself as the "citizen politician, speaking out for the ideas, values, and common sense of everyday Americans." His conservative agenda called for more power for the individual and less power for the federal government. A vote for Reagan, his supporters claimed, would restore American pride, power, and traditions.

Reagan's message was welcome news not only to those who routinely voted Republican but also to many living in the Sunbelt (see the opening map in Chapter 31). By 1980, the region's population exceeded that of the industrial North and East. Politically, the Sunbelt exhibited conservative populism that opposed the power of the federal government. White southerners equated "liberal" government with altering traditional racial norms, and a **"sagebrush rebellion"** in the western Sunbelt opposed federal control and regulation of land and natural resources. Many westerners argued that that federal environmental and land-use regulations blocked growth and economic development in the West. Throughout the Sunbelt, Reagan found enthusiastic voters ready to reject liberal, activist government. Further contributing to Republican totals were voters mobilized by the **New Right,** as well as younger voters attracted by the economic goals and social stability Republicans promised. Except for the size of Reagan's majority and how many Republicans his **political coattails** would carry into office, the outcome of the election of 1980 was never in doubt.

When the voting ended, Reagan had 51 percent of the popular vote and an impressive 91 percent of the electoral count—489 to 49. Republicans held their majority in the Senate and substantially narrowed the Democratic majority in the House of Representatives. Many political observers believed the election of 1980 was the beginning of a new conservative era.

The Moral Majority and the New Right

Reagan's campaign pulled vital support from the New Right. A loosely knit alliance that combined political and social conservatives, the New Right opposed the social and cultural changes spawned during the 1960s and 1970s. Charles Murray's *Losing Ground* (1984) argued that Johnson's Great Society had caused people to lose their will to work and had encouraged destructive behavior. The New Right declared that liberal views threatened "to destroy everything that is good and moral here in America." The nation's schools, the New Right charged, had retreated from teaching positive work ethics and moral habits and needed to return to the basics: reading, writing, arithmetic, and traditional values. Those values included the conviction that abortion, pornography, and homosexuality must be restricted. To mobilize support, the New Right pioneered the effective political use of **direct mail** aimed at specific segments of the population.

Highly visible among New Right groups were evangelical Christian sects, many of whose ministers were **televangelists**—preachers who used radio and television to spread the gospel of the "religious Right." Receiving donations that exceeded a billion dollars a year, they did not hesitate to mix religion and politics. Jerry Falwell's **Moral Majority** promoted Reagan and New Right ideas on more than five hundred television and radio stations. Reaching millions of Americans, Falwell called on his listeners to wage political war against politicians whose views on the Bible, homosexuality, prayer in

Proposition 13 Measure adopted by referendum in California in 1978 cutting local property taxes by more than 50 percent.

Sagebrush rebellion A 1980s political movement in western states opposing federal regulations over the land and natural resources and seeking their return to state control.

New Right Conservative movement opposing the political and social reforms that developed in the late 1960s and demanding less government intervention in the economy and a return to traditional values; it was a major political force by the 1980s.

political coattails Term referring to the ability of a presidential candidate to attract voters to other office seekers from the same political party.

direct mail Advertising or promotional matter mailed directly to potential customers or audiences chosen because they are likely to respond favorably.

televangelist Protestant evangelist minister who conducts televised worship services; many such ministers used their broadcasts as a forum for promoting conservative values.

Moral Majority Right-wing religious organization led by televangelist Jerry Falwell; it had an active political lobby in the 1980s promoting issues such as opposition to abortion and to the Equal Rights Amendment.

♦ In the 1970s and into the 1990s, the "electronic church" developed an audience of over 100 million viewers. With fancy, high-tech showmanship, televangelists like Jerry Falwell pictured here, damned liberalism, feminism, sex education, homosexuality, and the teaching of evolution, while demanding a return to traditional Christian values and prayer in school. Praising the power of the modern, media pulpit, Falwell stated, "You can explain the issues. . . . And you can endorse candidates, right there in church on Sunday morning." *Steve McCurry/Magnum Photos.*

school, abortion, and communism were too liberal. Although many of the television evangelists were sincere in their goals and ministries, some were susceptible to the lure of wealth and power that accompanied the medium. Sex scandals, financial excesses, and abuses of personal power weakened the electronic ministry's impact on society and politics by the 1990s. Still, the New Right continued to effectively mobilize support and raise money for conservative causes.

Reaganism

Reagan brought to the White House two distinct advantages lacked by Nixon, Ford, and Carter: he had a clear and simple vision of the type of America he wanted and an unusual ability to convey that image to the American public. Called the "Great Communicator" by the press, Reagan expertly presented images and visions, but he did not create the policies to bring them about. Secretary of the Treasury Donald Regan once commented, "The President's mind is not cluttered with facts." A hands-off president, Reagan delegated authority to the cabinet and executive staff while he set the grand agenda. His lieutenants assumed the blame when policies failed or could not overcome opposition.

Reagan rode to the presidency on a wide domestic platform promising not just prosperity and less government but also morality, tapping the New Right's political strength on issues of family and gender. In office, however, he virtually ignored the New Right's social agenda and concentrated on security matters and the economic crisis of inflation, high interest rates, and unemployment.

The administration's plan to restore the economy was deceptively simple: suppress the cost of social programs, increase military spending, and reduce taxes and government restrictions. "If we can do that the rest will take care of itself," Reagan's chief of staff James A. Baker III argued.

Much of the administration's formula for cutting inflation and restoring economic vitality rested with the monetary policies of the Federal Reserve System and **supply-side economics.** To combat inflation, the Federal Reserve kept interest rates high, bringing about a substantial increase in foreign investments in the United States and a decline in American products sold overseas. While the Fed squeezed inflation, Reagan intended to stimulate growth by cutting personal and business taxes. Supply-side economists believed that lowering taxes would spur business growth and the creation of new jobs. Budget Director David Stockman fashioned a tax package that reduced income and corporate taxes. The 1981 **Economic Recovery Tax Act** cut income and most business taxes by an average of 25 percent—upper income levels received the largest tax reduction. Stockman's budget raised military spending and slashed federal spending on social programs. Conservative Democrats in the House joined with Republicans to cut $25 billion from social programs, including food stamps, **Aid to Families with Dependent Children,** and jobs and housing programs. Reagan also ended Nixon's federal revenue-sharing programs (see page 976) and reduced the amount of federal money paid to the states for Medicare and

supply-side economics Theory that reducing taxes on the wealthy and increasing the money available for investment will stimulate the economy and eventually benefit everyone.

Economic Recovery Tax Act Law passed by Congress in 1981 that cut income taxes by 25 percent across the board and further reduced taxes on the wealthy.

Aid to Families with Dependent Children A program created by the Social Security Act of 1935; it provided states with matching federal funds and became one of the states' main welfare programs.

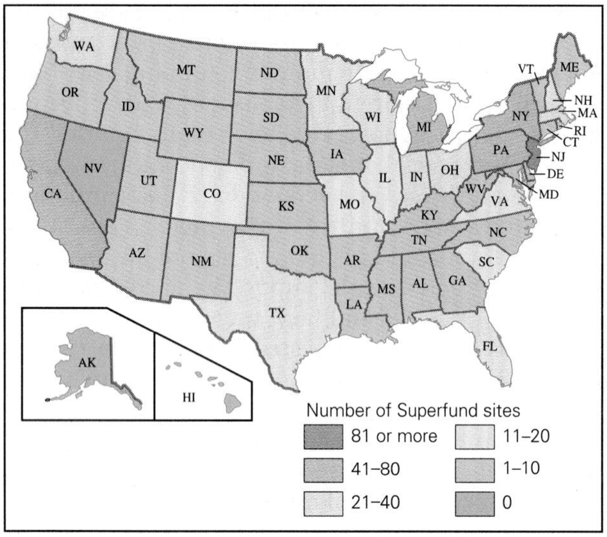

♦ **MAP 32.2 Superfund Cleanup Sites** Americans generate trash—more than $3\frac{1}{2}$ pounds for every person, every day. In addition, the United States produces nearly 300 tons of hazardous waste every year, and about 8 out of 10 Americans live near one of more than twenty-two thousand toxic waste sites. In the 1980s, Congress provided funds—Superfunds—for the cleanup of some of the worst and most health-threatening sites. This map shows that hazardous waste sites exist in nearly every state, as well as the location of the major Superfund sites.

Medicaid programs. Stockman later admitted, however, that "none of us really understand what's going on" and that the tax act was really a "Trojan Horse" to help the rich.

Cutting taxes and domestic spending was only part of the Reagan agenda for economic growth. Another aim of **Reaganomics** was deregulation—freeing businesses and corporations from restrictive regulation. Appointees to regulatory agencies were selected because of their support for deregulation and for business. Among the areas affected by deregulation were banking, transportation, and communications, but its impact was most visible in the area of environmental regulation. Secretary of the Interior James Watt sought to open federally controlled land, coastal waters, and wetlands to mining, lumber, oil, and gas companies—a policy strongly advocated by many in the West. The Environmental Protection Agency, under Anne Gorsuch Burford, weakened enforcement of federal guidelines for reducing air and water pollution and the cleanup of toxic waste sites (see Map 32.2).

Reagan's economic policies were not immediately effective. Action by the Federal Reserve reduced inflation from 14 percent in 1980 to 4 percent by 1982, but economic growth failed to materialize. Unemployment rose to over 10 percent, and small businesses and farms faced bankruptcy in increasing numbers. Also troubling was a soaring **trade deficit,** the amount by which the value of imports exceeds the value of exports. It skyrocketed from a surplus in 1980 to a deficit of $111 billion in 1984. Also growing at an alarming rate was the federal deficit, pushed by declining tax revenues and increases in military spending. Reagan called for patience, saying that his economic programs eventually would work.

The Power of Money

Suddenly in 1983, the recession ended. With inflation at 4 percent and unemployment dropping to 7.5 percent, praise was widespread for Reaganonics and for the administration's support for a positive business culture that emphasized individualism, success, and profits. Although some argued that the new business culture was based on greed, others claimed that it resulted from the creation of new business opportunities, especially in the communications and electronics fields—for example, technological developments like miniaturization, satellite transmission, the videocassette recorder (VCR), and personal computers. Businesspeople like Bill Gates, who helped develop the personal computer industry, were harnessing these new opportunities (see Individual Choices: Bill Gates).

The culture of success filled newspapers, magazines, television, and movies, publicizing people who were making money and achieving larger-than-life success. Financier Donald Trump proclaimed himself king of the "megadeal" and commanded national attention for both his business ventures and his social life. His ghost-written books, *Trump: The Art of the Deal* (1987) and *Trump: Surviving at the Top* (1990), glorified him as the master of manipulating the economic system for personal gain. It was a lifestyle sought by many young Americans. In 1974, only 46 percent of college freshmen and high school seniors had listed being "financially successful" as

Reaganomics Economic beliefs and policies of the Reagan administration, including the belief that tax cuts for the wealthy and deregulation of industry will benefit the economy.

trade deficit Amount by which the value of imports exceeds the value of exports.

the first priority in their lives. Twelve years later, in 1986, 73 percent of college freshmen put being "very well off financially," and 63 percent of high school seniors listed making "lots of money," as their first priorities. Income-conscious college graduates hoping to become highly paid, aggressive professionals eagerly applied to law, business, and other postgraduate schools. *Newsweek* declared 1984 the "Year of the **Yuppie**"—the young, upwardly mobile, urban professional, who was on the leading edge of the new economic vitality.

The economic gains being made by Gates and others were, in many cases, a product of new technology and ideas, but Reagan's tax cuts and other economic policies helped. Those with money made more. "Buy high, sell higher," *Fortune* magazine proclaimed, as the wealthiest 1 percent of Americans saw their slice of the economic pie grow from 8.1 to 15 percent. Symbolizing the connection between opportunity and government were those taking advantage of government deregulation in financial and investment industries. Riding the crest of a speculative boom, barons of buyouts and **junk bonds** amassed vast fortunes, and huge business conglomerates gobbled up smaller companies. Deregulation freed **savings and loan associations (S&Ls)** from having to lend money only for single-family homes. Many S&L operators jumped quickly into speculative and risky ventures such as office buildings, shopping malls, and junk bonds. Because the federal government, through the Federal Savings and Loan Insurance Corporation (FSLIC), covered any losses, these were no-lose deals. "Heads I win, tails FSLIC loses," became the slogan of many S&L directors, who quickly made themselves wealthy by brokering their depositors' money into multi-million-dollar investment deals.

Many Americans recoiled at the Reagan boom and its "money culture." Social critics like author Tom Wolfe complained that a "Me Generation" was succumbing to apathy , self-indulgence, and materialism. They noted that smaller appropriations and higher qualifications had reduced welfare rolls but the number of people living in poverty had increased. The growing numbers of homeless people, they argued, were the real legacy of Reagan's economic policies. Some economists pointed out that serious weaknesses in the economy still existed—specifically, the **federal deficit,** the trade deficit, the increased spending on **entitlements,** and the lack of new industrial jobs. Others noted that the national "recovery" was selective. The West Coast was doing well, but the Rust Belt was still rusting, and the wages of many American workers had actually declined. The Reagan boom, they asserted, rested on a weak foundation of shaky credit and fast profits and was not creating economic growth or an increase in buying power and wages.

On "Black Monday," October 19, 1987, economists' warning took on new weight. The stock market dropped 508 points, losing 22 percent of its value in the largest one-day decline in American history and bringing to mind images of the 1929 stock market crash and the Great Depression (see pages 768–771). The Reagan administration was shaken, but the Federal Reserve quickly acted to lower interest rates and pump money into the economy. The Fed's action stopped the panic selling, and the stock market turned slowly upward again.

With real estate values also slipping in 1987, S&Ls that had made unwise investments started losing vast sums of money, and the S&L system began to collapse. Lincoln Savings and Loan in California lost more than $2.6 billion of its depositors' money, and its president, Charles Keating, was convicted of fraud. He was not the only S&L president to bend and break the law. The S&L industry was in ruins, and the federal government was responsible for providing more than $500 billion to cover the losses. By the late 1980s, the financial boom was fading, along with the reputations of many who had fallen victim to the greed factor. Typical was Donald Trump, whose credit-based empire was crumbling—he had to sell his airline and most of his real estate to pay creditors.

Reputations were also declining in the Reagan administration. Secretary of the Interior James Watt and Attorney General Edwin Meese had received money and favors in return for using their influence with government agencies to help some businesses

Yuppie Young urban resident with a high-paying professional job and a materialistic lifestyle.

junk bond Corporate bond having a high yield and high risk.

savings and loan associations Financial institutions originally founded to provide home mortgage loans; deregulation during the Reagan era allowed them to speculate in risky ventures and led to many S&L failures.

federal deficit The total amount of debt owed by the national government.

entitlements Government programs that provide benefits to a particular group, such as the elderly, the disabled, and poor families.

INDIVIDUAL CHOICES

Leading the Computer Revolution

Bill Gates

In 1974, Bill Gates made an eventful choice. Along with a friend from high school, Paul Allen, the Harvard sophomore decided to create an operating system for a new development in the computer world: the personal computer (PC). The system worked, and Gates left Harvard and formed the Microsoft Company, creating MSDOS and software packages for what soon became the personal computer revolution. Twelve years later, his systems dominated the computer world, and he became the country's youngest billionaire. UPI/Bettmann Archives.

In December 1974, Bill Gates, a sophomore at Harvard, and his high school friend Paul Allen claimed that they could write a computer program for a new personal computer, the Altair 8080, which came unassembled and cost $397. Neither Gates nor Allen had seen the Altair computer or the microchip that made it run, but they were positive that the advent of personal computing was the beginning of a new era in information processing. "We realized that the revolution" had started, Gates recalled, and "there was no question of where life would focus." Gates and Allen chose to be a part of the revolution.

Having read only sketchy information about the Altair 8080, Gates and Allen invaded the Harvard computer lab and worked day and night for eight weeks. Ignoring his classes and sometimes sleeping at the keyboard, Gates modified the computer language BASIC to fit the Altair. He and Allen had no idea if the program would work. "If we had read the book wrong . . . we were hosed," Allen recalled. He then flew to New Mexico to demonstrate the program. Fortunately, it worked, and Gates and Allen were on the cutting edge of the computer revolution. Allen stayed to work for the computer company in New Mexico. Gates finished his academic year at Harvard. Then, over the objections of his parents, he chose to drop out of Harvard at 19 and join Allen. He and Allen formed Microsoft, a company to write software

gain lucrative contracts and avoid government regulations. Both resigned their positions. They were not alone. More than a hundred members of the Reagan administration were found guilty of unethical and illegal behavior. Reagan was untouched by the scandals, and his popularity remained high. Some called him the "Teflon President," because no criticism seemed to stick to him.

Reagan's Second Term

Throughout the presidential campaign of 1984, Republicans credited Reagan's leadership and policies for renewed prosperity and restored military superiority. Using the theme "Morning in America," Reagan's re-election campaign projected a new day of economic expansion, morality, and national for personal computers. Microsoft's success made Gates, at age 31, the youngest billionaire in America.

In 1980, their expectations rising, Gates and Allen agreed to design an operating system to run the software for IBM's entry into the personal computing field. IBM was already a giant in large business and institutional computers, and it was expected that IBM's personal computers would greatly expand the popularity and uses of personal computers. In 1980, every computer company wanted to capture and keep users by having a unique operating system to run software. IBM wanted Microsoft to formulate a new, exclusive system. Gates and Allen began by buying and then modifying an existing system—QDOS, the "quick and dirty operating system." Within a year, working in great secrecy, they created Microsoft DOS (MSDOS).

IBM's personal computers became the industry's leader and were soon being cloned by other companies. Gates wanted to offer MSDOS to those other companies. IBM at first was reluctant to share "their" system but finally agreed, and both IBM and the competing companies benefited from the decision. By the 1990s, only two major operating systems still existed for personal computers—Apple and MSDOS, and Microsoft was writing systems for both companies.

Impressed with Apple's MacIntosh system of graphic interfaces, Gates decided to develop a similar operating system for IBM-type machines. The result was Windows. Apple fought back but lost a copyright infringement lawsuit. In 1990, Microsoft introduced a much-improved version of Windows, which quickly overcame competing systems. "We bet the company on Windows," Gates recalled, and it "paid off immensely." Microsoft had become the industry giant and Gates the country's richest man.

By the mid-1990s, the Windows operating system dominated the market, operating on about 80 percent of the world's PCs and shaping the development of software. The dominance of Windows was forcing other companies to fit their programs to Microsoft's system or risk being frozen out of the market. As Microsoft's control over the software and systems market expanded, more and more critics accused Gates of monopolistic and unfair business practices. One cause of outrage was Microsoft's packaging of its Internet access system with its Windows system. Competitors claimed this practice—called bundling—made competition virtually impossible. In December 1997, a federal judge agreed and ordered Microsoft to stop it. The possibility that Microsoft would acquire a monopoly in accessing the Internet, the judge stated, was "simply too great to tolerate." Few expected the government's antitrust decisions to do much to keep Microsoft from continuing to develop—and profit from—the information revolution. As one competitor stated, Gates remained a combination of "Albert Einstein, John McEnroe, and General Patton."

power "standing tall" against communism. Reagan avoided specific issues while announcing that big-government liberalism was dead.

Democrats, meanwhile, could not unite on either a standard-bearer or the best approach to challenge Reagan. Former vice president Walter Mondale of Minnesota campaigned as a traditional Democrat. He was challenged by Senator Gary Hart of Colorado—who called for a "new generation of leadership"—and Reverend Jesse Jackson, charismatic African-American leader and eloquent spokesman for minorities and the poor. After a primary season that did more to divide than unite the Democrats, Mondale won the nomination. He selected Representative Geraldine Ferraro of New York to be his vice-presidential running mate. Many people applauded Mondale for selecting a woman, but others complained that Ferraro was not the best-qualified woman for the position. Mondale called for the revitalizing of social programs but could not energize the Democrats.

President Reagan won an overwhelming victory, taking 59 percent of the popular vote and carrying every state except Mondale's Minnesota. A postelection analysis showed that all that remained of the once-powerful Democratic voting coalition were the poor, African Americans, and Hispanics. A majority of organized labor, women, Catholics, white southerners, farmers, and the middle and upper classes all had voted for Reagan's Republican vision of "Morning in America."

A growing cloud, however, hung over Reagan's American morning: the soaring budget deficit. During his first administration, the annual deficit had gone from $73.8 billion to more than $200 billion. Although controlling and reducing the deficit had bipartisan support, how to do it remained a very partisan issue. Most Democrats took the view that cuts in military spending were necessary. They argued that a large part of the deficit came from military spending, which had risen from $164 billion in 1980 to $228 billion in 1985. Republicans, in response, blamed uncontrolled and wasteful social programs.

In late 1985, a coalition of Republicans and Democrats passed the Gramm-Rudman-Hollings Act, which established a maximum debt level and ordered across-the-board cuts if the budget failed to match the level set. The plan never worked effectively—both Congress and the White House found ways to circumvent and modify the law. By 1989, federal expenditures had climbed to $1,065 billion a year, and the national debt stood at nearly $3 trillion, requiring an annual interest payment of $200 million. The United States had become the world's largest debtor nation. If the debt had been spread evenly across the country, every American would have owed about $5,000. With the deficit seemingly out of control, many advocated a constitutional amendment to require a balanced budget.

Asserting World Power

- How did the Reagan administration's expectations about American foreign policy differ from Carter's? How did those views shape the outcomes of the Reagan administration's policies?

Reagan's victories in 1980 and 1984 resulted not only from his views on domestic issues but also from public support for his views on the role of the United States in world affairs. Throughout the 1980 presidential campaign, the Republicans had hammered at Carter's ineffective foreign policy and at slipping American prestige in the world. To reestablish the United States as the pre-eminent world leader, Reagan believed it was necessary to overcome what he termed the "Vietnam syndrome": an unwillingness to use force to defend U.S. interests. As president, Reagan promised no lack of resolve and a strong military to support American interests.

Reagan was interested in providing the context and imagery of foreign policy but had little interest in dealing with its specifics. He left them to his foreign-policy staff, especially CIA director William Casey and Secretary of State George Shultz, a close and loyal friend.

Cold War Renewed

At the center of Reagan's view of the world was his hostility toward the Soviet Union. He told a gathering of evangelical Protestants that the Soviet Union was an "evil empire" and the "focus of evil in the modern world" and that it would "commit any crime . . . lie . . . cheat," to achieve world conquest. America's grand role, Reagan believed, was to defend global freedom against communism. Large increases in the military budget were necessary, he argued, to back up the nation's diplomacy and to close the "window of vulnerability" that Carter had opened by allowing the Soviets to pull ahead in the arms race.

With almost no dissent, Congress funded Reagan's military budget, which expanded the number of nuclear weapons, increased the size of the navy, and provided more tanks and helicopters for the army. It also increased funds for research and development, especially for technologically advanced weapons like Stealth aircraft and a controversial system of defense against Soviet missiles: the **Strategic Defense Initiative (SDI).** "Star Wars," as SDI was dubbed, was at the top of Reagan's military priorities.

According to some sources, physicist Edward Teller, who had spoken to Reagan about developing a defense system that would use X-ray lasers to blast incoming Soviet missiles, had planted the idea for

Strategic Defense Initiative Research program to create an effective laser-based defense against nuclear missile attack.

♦ In March 1993, Reagan introduced the Strategic Defense Initiative (SDI) as a part of his military strategy. Based on the idea that incoming missiles could be destroyed before they struck the United States, SDI called for the development of super lasers and killer satellites. Because much of the technology was still conceptual, many saw Reagan's ideas as more science fiction than reality. In this cartoon, the science fiction image is highlighted by "Beam me up Scotty"—a trademark phrase from the television series *Star Trek. Bob Englehart,* The Hartford Courant.

SDI. Having starred in a 1950s science fiction movie that had depicted such a weapon, Reagan was immediately smitten by the idea. In March 1983, he asked Congress to fund the building of a defense system that would use lasers to make nuclear weapons "obsolete." Between 1983 and 1989, Congress provided more than $17 billion for Star Wars research amid complaints that the concept was conceptually and technologically flawed. Critics pointed out that even if the system could work and was 95 percent effective, the 5 percent of Soviet warheads that would hit the United States would still destroy the nation, if not civilization.

Reagan's military spending added more than $100 billion a year to the federal budget. By 1985 a million dollars was being spent on weapons every minute. With billions of dollars available, government and defense industry officials padded their expense accounts and exchanged bribes and kickbacks. They falsified test results and inflated costs artificially. Billion-dollar cost overruns became commonplace. Critics loudly opposed the military shopping spree, but their complaints had little effect on Congress or the public, which seemed ready to accept the U.S. role as global sheriff and the costs it required.

The Middle East

Stretching from North Africa to Afghanistan, the Middle East presented the Reagan administration with a complex series of problems that, except for Afghanistan, resisted being explained as Communist aggression. In Afghanistan, the CIA continued to supply the mujahedeen, whom Reagan called "freedom fighters," with arms to use against Soviet and Afghan government forces. Elsewhere in the Middle East, problems involving Arab nationalism, Arab-Israeli disputes, and terrorism could not so readily be understood in a Cold War context.

♦ Like Eisenhower twenty years before, President Reagan in 1983 committed American troops to Beirut, Lebanon as part of a peace-keeping operation. This intervention, however, was not successful. In October, terrorists blew up the Marine's barracks, killing 240 soldiers. "Too few to fight and too many to die," said one Congressional critic, as four months later Reagan withdrew the remaining American forces from the war-torn nation. *UPI/ Bettmann Archives.*

As Reagan assumed office, Yassir Arafat's **Palestine Liberation Organization (PLO),** committed to securing the creation of a separate state for Palestinians displaced by Israel's formation in 1948 (see page 872), had increased its raids against Israel. Other shadowy militant Islamic groups had begun a campaign of terrorism against Israel and its Western supporters. Throughout the Mediterranean region, terrorists kidnapped Americans and Europeans, hijacked planes and ships, and attacked airports and other public places. Reagan linked the terrorists to Communist organizations, the PLO, and various Arab nations and threatened reprisals. With American encouragement, Israel invaded neighboring southern Lebanon in 1982 to suppress the PLO and to halt terrorist attacks. As Israeli forces drove north and approached the capital city of Beirut, all semblance of internal stability in Lebanon collapsed, and a smoldering civil war between Christians and Muslims raged anew.

As part of an international peacekeeping effort, the United States in 1982 sent nearly two thousand marines to Beirut, where the Americans quickly became a target for Muslim terrorists. In April 1983, terrorists attacked the American embassy in Beirut and killed sixty-three people. In October, a suicide driver rammed a truck filled with explosives into the marine barracks at the Beirut airport, killing 241 marines. Reagan denounced the terrorist attack, defended the marines' presence in Beirut, and quietly made plans for their removal. In January 1984, the United States withdrew its forces from Lebanon, leaving Israel in control of southern Lebanon, Syrian forces occupying much of central Lebanon, and a civil war still raging.

Solutions were also elusive in the Persian Gulf region. Iran and Iraq had gone to war in 1980, making the Persian Gulf part of the battlefield. The **Iran-Iraq War** created two problems for American foreign policy: how to protect vital shipments of oil and how to ensure that neither Iran nor Iraq emerged from the war with the power to dominate the region. Secretly using third parties, the Reagan administration provided money and weapons to both sides, and late in the war American warships escorted all oil tankers in the gulf. By the time the Iraq-Iran War ended in 1988, it had cost more than 2 million lives, and American intelligence concluded that neither Iran nor Iraq could immediately threaten other countries in the region. To counterbalance potential aggression by Iran or Iraq, the United States stepped up supplies of military hardware to Saudi Arabia and buried stores of military supplies in the Saudi desert in case of future need.

Palestine Liberation Organization Political and military organization of Palestinians, originally dedicated to opposing the state of Israel through terrorism and other means.

Iran-Iraq War War that broke out between Iraq and Iran in 1980 over control of a disputed waterway and ended in 1988 with more than 2 million dead.

Farther west, in North Africa, Reagan faced off against **Moamar Qaddafi,** the vehemently anti-American ruler of Libya. Reagan denounced Qaddafi as the "mad dog of the Middle East" and called Libya a "rogue" nation that actively supported the PLO and terrorist groups. When American intelligence tied Qaddafi to the April 1986 terrorist bombing of a disco popular among American troops in West Berlin, which killed an American soldier, Reagan ordered a reprisal raid. American navy and air force planes bombed several targets in Libya, including Qaddafi's quarters, killing his adopted daughter. The United States, bragged one official, had shown Qaddafi "that we could get people close to him."

Central America and the Caribbean

It was hard to fit Middle Eastern problems into a Cold War context, but things seemed more black and white in Central America and the Caribbean (see Map 32.3). There, Reagan thought, any hint of Communist influence justified American action. In the southern Caribbean, Reagan focused on the tiny island of **Grenada,** where a Marxist government had ruled since independence from Britain in 1979.

In October 1983, the radical New Jewel movement took control of Grenada. The new government and the construction of a large airport runway by Cuban "advisers" suggested a potential threat to American interests and to about five hundred Americans attending medical school on the island. On October 25, Reagan ordered American forces to invade Grenada and remove the "brutal gang of thugs" that ruled. More than two thousand American soldiers quickly overcame minimal opposition, brought home the American students, and installed a pro-American government on the island. The administration basked in the light of public approval. Though small in scale, the Grenada operation implied that the "Vietnam syndrome" no longer restricted American foreign policy.

Determined to uphold his campaign pledge to defeat communism in Central America, Reagan provided billions in monetary and military support for the El Salvadoran government and the Contra "freedom fighters" in Nicaragua. Although the public and Congress strongly supported Reagan's invasion of Grenada, his efforts in Central America stirred considerable opposition. Some critics were disturbed by reports of human rights violations by "death squads" linked to the Salvadoran military. Many feared that Central America would become another Vietnam, with American troops following the aid and advisers already being sent. When the press uncovered large-scale American covert aid to the Contras, including the CIA's mining of Nicaraguan harbors in 1984, Congress passed legislation drafted by Representative Edward Boland of Massachusetts that allowed only humanitarian aid to the Contras. Reagan and CIA director Casey strongly opposed the **Boland Amendment** (1984) and found ways to work around it.

In the fall of 1985, the White House devised a plan to arm the Contras without Congress's knowledge and at the same time to gain the release of some American hostages held in Lebanon. Despite the Carter imposed U.S. trade embargo with Iran, national security advisers Robert McFarlane and John Poindexter arranged for the secret sale of arms to Iran. In return, Iran agreed to use its influence with terrorist groups in Lebanon to free American hostages. The cash that Iran paid for the arms was to be routed to the Contras, allowing them to purchase supplies and weapons.

When the press broke word of the so-called arms-for-hostages deal fourteen months later, a special White House commission, led by former Texas senator John Tower, and a congressional committee, the Iran Contra hearings, began separate investigations in 1987. Both discovered that members of the CIA and the National Security Council (NSC) had acted independently, without the knowledge or approval of Congress, and had lied to Congress to keep their operation secret. McFarlane, Poindexter, and NSC aide Oliver North were found guilty of violating a variety of federal laws and were sentenced to prison terms. Neither investigation uncovered proof that President Reagan knew of the operation, but it was clear that some of his closest aides were deeply involved. The scandal damaged his image and that of his presidency.

Moamar Qaddafi Political leader who seized power in a military coup in 1969 and imposed socialist policies and Islamic orthodoxy on Libya.

Grenada Country in the West Indies that achieved independence from Britain in 1974 and was invaded briefly by U.S. forces in 1983.

Boland Amendment Motion, approved by Congress in 1984, that barred the CIA from using funds to give direct or indirect aid to the Nicaraguan Contras.

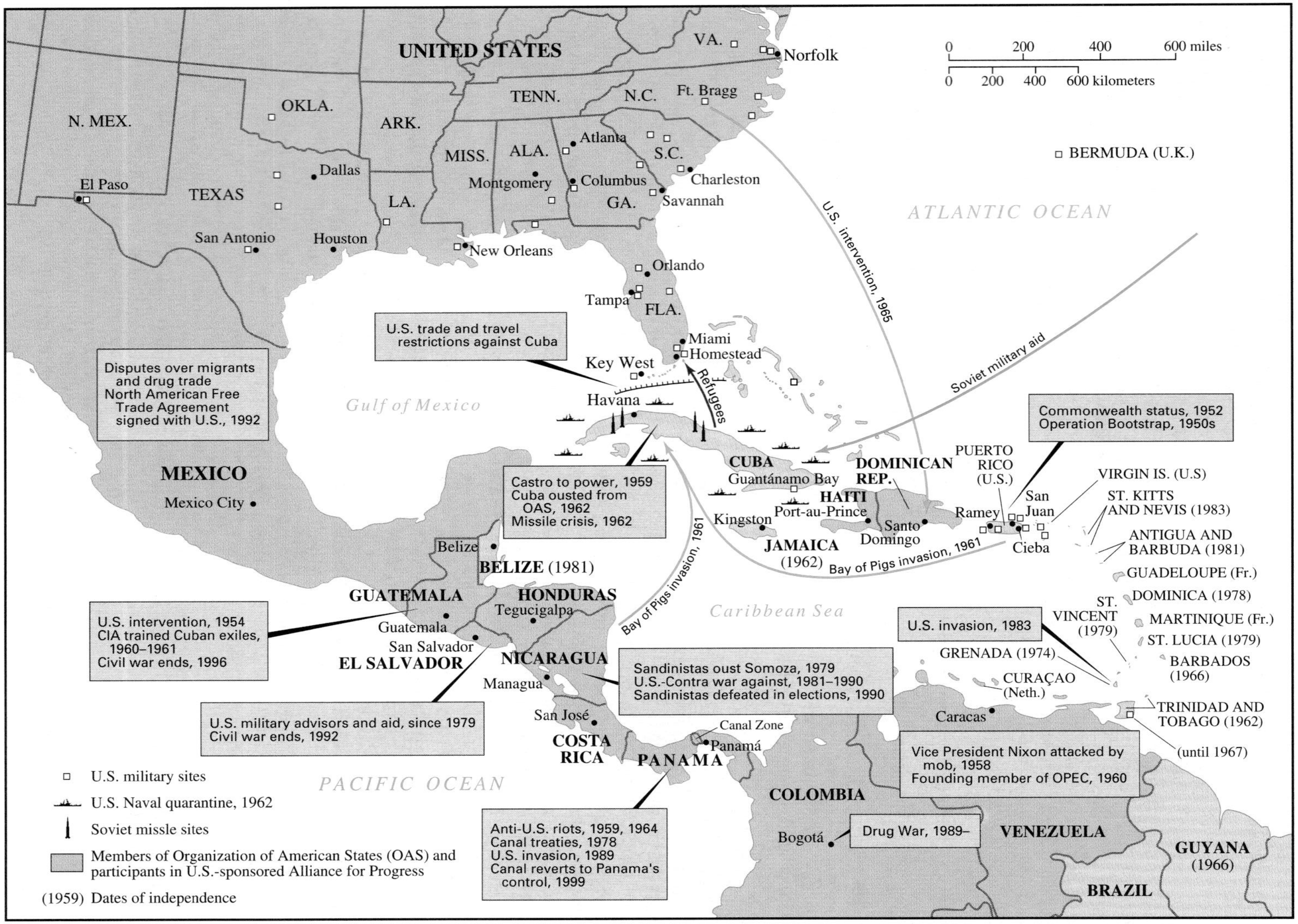

♦ **MAP 32.3 The United States and Central America and the Caribbean** Geographical nearness, important economic ties, security needs, and the drug trade continue to make Central America and the Caribbean a critical region for American interests. This map shows some of the American economic, military, and political actions taken in the region since the end of World War II.

♦ After declaring the Soviet Union an "evil empire" responsible for nearly all the world's problems, President Reagan reversed course in 1988 and opened productive discussions with Soviet reformer Mikail Gorbachev. The outcome was an intermediate-range nuclear-forces treaty that helped to end the Cold War as well as to reduce the overall number of nuclear missiles. Here, the two superpower leaders pose in front of the St. Basil cathedral in Moscow. *UPI/Bettmann Archives.*

Reagan and Gorbachev

Reagan made no attempt to improve relations with the Soviet superpower during his first term. But suddenly, early in his second term, he called, without warning, for the resumption of arms limitation talks. Then when Soviet leader Konstantin Chernenko died in March 1985, he invited Chernenko's successor, **Mikhail S. Gorbachev,** to the United States.

Gorbachev was different from previous Soviet leaders—younger and committed to change. He was determined to breathe new life into the Soviet economy, which was stagnating under the weight of military spending and government inefficiency and corruption. He also wanted to institute reforms that would provide more political and civil rights to the Soviet people. British prime minister Margaret Thatcher called him "charming" and someone with whom the West could work to improve East-West relations.

Gorbachev declined Reagan's invitation but agreed to a summit meeting in Geneva in November 1985. The two leaders at first jousted with each other. Reagan condemned the Soviets for human rights abuses, their involvement in Afghanistan, and their aid to Communist factions fighting in Angola and Ethiopia. Gorbachev attacked the proposed development of SDI. But when Gorbachev showed an interest in Hollywood, his relationship with Reagan improved. The two leaders left Geneva with a growing fondness for each other.

Shortly after the summit, Gorbachev announced two new policies: **perestroika** and **glasnost.** Reagan and Gorbachev met again in October 1986 in Reykjavik, Iceland, and the Soviet leader shocked American participants by suggesting a 50 percent reduction of strategic weapons over a five-year period and, less surprisingly, the nondeployment of SDI for ten years. Without consulting his advisers, Reagan responded that the two powers should eliminate all strategic missiles within ten years but allow the development of SDI. The summit ended without an agreement, but Soviet-American negotiations on arms limitations continued with new optimism. By December 1987, negotiators had agreed to eliminate Soviet and American intermediate-range missiles from Europe. Reagan and Gorbachev signed the **Intermediate Nuclear Force Treaty** during a December summit meeting in Washington.

Mikhail S. Gorbachev Soviet leader who came to power in 1985; he introduced political and economic reforms and then found himself presiding over the breakup of the Soviet Union.

perestroika Restructuring of the Soviet economy and bureaucracy that began in the mid-1980s.

glasnost Official policy of the Soviet government under Gorbachev emphasizing freedom of thought and candid discussion of social problems.

Intermediate Nuclear Force Treaty Treaty (1987) that provided for the destruction of all U.S. and Soviet medium-range nuclear missiles and for verification with on-site inspections.

Throughout 1988, Soviet-American relations continued to improve. Gorbachev withdrew Soviet forces from Afghanistan, the Senate approved the Intermediate Nuclear Force Treaty, and Reagan visited Moscow. To many, it seemed as if the Cold War was over and a new era of international relations was unfolding.

In Reagan's Shadow

- What new foreign-policy choices did the United States face as a result of the collapse of the Soviet Union?
- How did the outcome of Reagan's domestic policies shape expectations and outcomes for the Bush administration?

"It's not been a great year," the president's wife said about 1987. Despite the apparent thaw in the Cold War, for the first time in the Reagan administration, a combination of events had dented the image of Reagan and Republican leadership. The stock market collapse in October and the Iran-Contra revelations created the impression that the administration was not in control of events or of itself and that the president had little grasp of what was happening. Suddenly, the popularity ratings of the "Teflon President" were lower than usual. Republicans, however, were not overly concerned and expected the conservative Reagan agenda to continue to attract voters, defeat Democrats, and strengthen the nation.

Bush Assumes Office

As Republicans readied for the 1988 election, they passed the torch of Reaganism to Vice President **George Bush.** Bush had devoted many years to public service and had held several important posts under presidents Nixon and Ford: ambassador to the United Nations, chairman of the Republican National Committee, ambassador to China, and director of the Central Intelligence Agency. Bush, however, was not Reagan, and some Republicans wondered if he would promote the New Right's domestic agenda. To reassure conservatives, Bush surprised the nation by selecting as his running mate a young, conservative, and virtually unknown Indiana senator, J. Danforth Quayle.

Several Democratic contenders were eager to confront Bush, whose popularity seemed a faint shadow of Reagan's. Repeat candidates Gary Hart and Jesse Jackson and first-timers Governor Michael Dukakis of Massachusetts and Delaware senator Joseph R. Biden seemed the strongest contenders. Eventually, Dukakis pulled ahead and at the Democratic National Convention was the only viable candidate.

The 1988 campaign was dull. Both candidates lacked flair and were unable to energize the voters. Dukakis ignored most social and international issues and focused on his personal integrity and success in revitalizing the economy of Massachusetts. Bush fought to overcome the so-called wimp factor—suggestions by Democrats and some Republicans that he was not a strong leader. Proclaiming his patriotism and pointing to his years of experience, Bush promised to fight drugs and crime, to take a special interest in education and the environment, and not to raise taxes. "Read my lips, no new taxes," he said. To motivate voters, both sides relied on television and **negative campaigning,** which aimed at discrediting the opponent rather than addressing issues and policies. Republican ads were more effective than those of the Democrats and put Dukakis on the defensive, forcing him to answer charges made in the ads.

Benefiting also from falling unemployment and inflation and improved relations with the Soviet Union, Bush won election easily, with 79.2 percent of the electoral vote and 54 percent of the popular vote. He thus became the first sitting vice president to be elected president since Martin Van Buren in 1836. Although Bush trounced Dukakis, the victory was not as sweet as Bush hoped it would be. Democrats controlled the House and the Senate.

Bush and a New International Order

Bush's own preferences and international events dictated that foreign affairs would consume most of his attention. The world was changing rapidly, and Bush considered the management of international relations to be one of his strengths. Unlike Reagan, he focused on specific policies. The immediate problem that he and Secretary of State James A. Baker III faced was how to respond to the unexpected and rapid collapse of communism in Eastern Europe and the Soviet Union.

George Bush Politician and diplomat who was vice president under Ronald Reagan and was later elected thirty-sixth president of the United States.

negative campaigning Presenting a political opponent as weak, dishonest, or untrustworthy instead of addressing basic political issues.

♦ In 1988 and again in 1992, the Republican ticket of George Bush and Dan Quayle emphasized traditional American values as a cure for the social problems facing the nation. In this picture from the 1988 campaign, Bush reflects the image of a hard-working, all-American family man. © *Cynthia Johnson*/Time Magazine.

Political and economic changes were tearing apart the Communist world from Nicaragua to China. Within the Soviet Union, Mikhail Gorbachev's policies of glasnost and perestroika were producing political and religious freedom, reducing censorship and repression, and starting the privatization of business and the development of a capitalist-style economy. Soviet armed forces were being withdrawn from Afghanistan and Eastern Europe (see Map 32.4).

The Bush administration cautiously voiced support for Gorbachev's efforts, and in December 1989 Bush met with Gorbachev on the island of Malta in the Mediterranean Sea. Gorbachev declared that the Cold War was over. Bush more prudently stated that they were working toward "a lasting peace." Later, Gorbachev visited Washington and signed agreements to improve trade and reduce chemical weapons and the size of conventional and nuclear arsenals. He was cheered in the United States and around the world, but at home his popularity fell as the Soviet economy continued its downward spiral. Attacked by people wanting more reform and by hard-line Communists who feared any reform, Gorbachev asked the United States, Japan, and Western Europe to provide economic support to prevent "chaos and civil wars" in the Soviet Union.

Unable to slow the rush toward reform, the hardliners on August 19, 1991, attempted a coup. They confined Gorbachev and his family in his vacation home along the Black Sea and outlawed all political parties. In Moscow, **Boris Yeltsin,** leader of the Russian Republic, declared the coup illegal and called on the Russian people to resist. More than 150,000 Muscovites surrounded the Russian parliament building to defend Yeltsin and reformist government. Faced with popular opposition in Moscow and other cities, the coup collapsed within seventy-two hours. Released from captivity, Gorbachev announced that he was again in control of the Soviet Union, but he was commanding a sinking ship.

By 1992, there was no Soviet Union to command. All that remained was a weak federation, the **Commonwealth of Independent States.** Power rested not with Gorbachev, who soon retired from office, but with the independent republics and especially with Yeltsin, the president of the Russian Republic.

The collapse of the Soviet Union in 1991 both simplified and complicated U.S. foreign and military policies. The threat of war with the Soviet Union was gone, but the new relationship between the United States and the former Soviet Union was yet to be determined. Bush recognized the independent republics and Yeltsin as the spokesman for the Russian Republic and the Commonwealth. In June 1992, Yeltsin visited Washington to ask for American and Western economic support. He also announced that Russia was ready to eliminate nearly all of its land-

Boris Yeltsin Russian parliamentary leader who was elected president of the new Russian Republic in 1991 and provided increased democratic and economic reforms.

Commonwealth of Independent States Weak federation of the former Soviet republics; it replaced the Soviet Union in 1992 and soon gave way to total independence of the member countries.

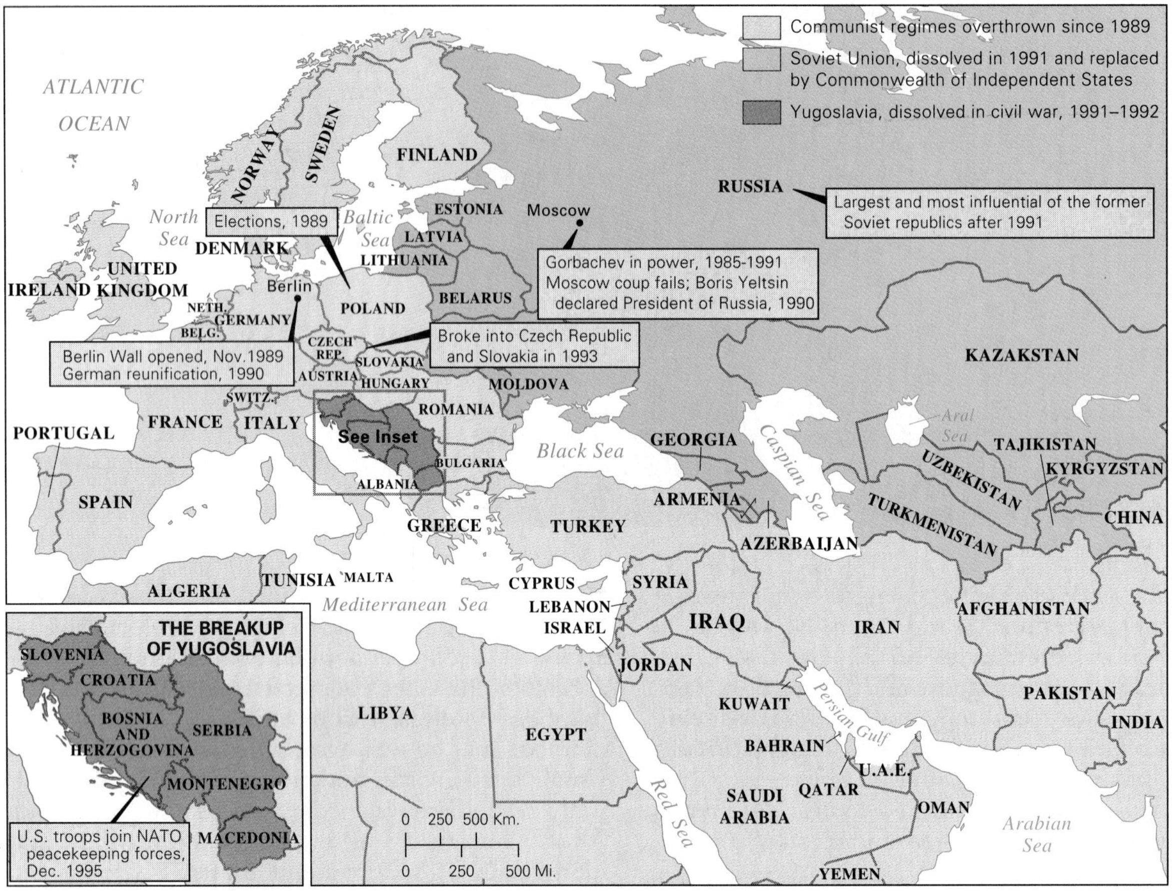

♦ **MAP 32.4 The Fall of Communism** As the Soviet Union collapsed and lost its control over the countries of Eastern Europe, the map of Eastern Europe and Central Asia changed. The Soviet Union disappeared into history, replaced by fifteen new national units. In Eastern Europe, West and East Germany merged, Czechoslovakia divided into two nations, and Yugoslavia broke into five feuding states.

based strategic missiles but could not speak for the other republics. Bush applauded the arms reduction proposal, promised increased economic support, and hoped that Yeltsin could bring some stability to what had once been the Soviet Union. Yeltsin, however, could barely provide stability for the Russian Republic.

Even before the Soviet Union collapsed, communism was in retreat throughout Eastern Europe. In December 1988, Gorbachev had announced that the Soviet Union would no longer intervene to prevent political opposition in Eastern Europe. Within a year, Poland had a new constitution, a free market economy, and a non-Communist government. In 1989, workers in Berlin tore down the **Berlin Wall.** As the wall crumbled, so too did the Communist governments of East Germany, Hungary, Bulgaria, Czechoslovakia, and Romania. By the end of 1990, a unified Germany existed, and the Baltic states—Latvia, Estonia, and Lithuania—had declared their independence from the Soviet Union.

The Bush administration hoped the changes would generate free market economies and stable and democratic governments. In some nations there was peaceful movement toward both. In others there was increased regional and ethnic conflict. Yugoslavia broke apart in 1991, and its major ethnic

Berlin Wall Wall that the Communist East German government built in 1961 to divide East and West Berlin; it was torn down in 1989 as the Cold War ended.

♦ As Communism collapsed in Eastern Europe, Chinese dissidents in May 1989 flooded Tiananmen Square in support of the prodemocracy movement. In June, the Chinese government used its power to crush the demonstrators and the movement. *Corbis-Bettmann.*

groups began a series of brutal and bloody conflicts in an effort to carve out individual republics and autonomous regions. By 1994 more than a hundred thousand people had died, many of them in **Bosnia.** The breeze of democracy was not limited to Eastern Europe. In the People's Republic of China, in Central America, and in South Africa similar movements were taking place.

In China in 1989, university students and other prodemocracy protesters took to the streets in Beijing and other cities, demanding political, economic, and civil freedoms. They filled the massive expanse of Tiananmen Square in Beijing and erected a "Goddess of Liberty" statue that looked like the Statue of Liberty. Rather than relinquishing power, however, on June 4, 1989, China's leaders resorted to force. Police and army forces brutally cleared the square and arrested many leaders of the democracy movement. Thousands were killed or injured. President Bush condemned the violent repression but resisted demands for sanctions against China. He argued that harsh action toward China would further isolate its leadership and make it even more brutal.

Although Bush's policy toward China stirred criticism, his policies toward South Africa and Central America drew praise for supporting democratic change. In South Africa the goal was to end **apartheid** and encourage the all-white South African government to share political power with black South Africans. In 1988, after South African president P. W. Botha brutally repressed anti-apartheid demonstrations, Congress, over Reagan's veto, had instituted economic sanctions. As president, Bush supported the sanctions and applauded the willingness of South Africa's new president, F. W. de Klerk, to work with **Nelson Mandela** and other black Africans to end apartheid. In 1993, Mandela and de Klerk were awarded the Nobel Peace Prize, and in April 1994 South Africa held its first multiracial free elections, electing Mandela president.

In Central America, Bush broke with Reagan's policies by willingly reducing aid to the Contras and encouraging negotiations that would end the brutal fighting in Nicaragua and El Salvador (see Map 32.3). His actions contributed to the acceptance of the **Contadora Plan,** a formula for peace in Nicaragua negotiated by a coalition of Central American nations. The Contras agreed to halt their military operations, and the Ortega government initiated political

Bosnia A region of the former Yugoslavia; its major city is Sarajevo.

apartheid Official policy of racial segregation in South Africa; its outcome was political, legal, and economic discrimination against blacks and other people of color.

Nelson Mandela South Africa's most prominent black nationalist leader; sentenced to life in prison in 1964 for conspiracy to overthrow the government, he was released in 1990 and became president of South Africa in 1994.

Contadora Plan Pact signed by the presidents of five Central American nations in 1987, calling for a cease-fire in conflicts in the region and for democratic reforms.

◆ In Operation Desert Storm, regarded by many as Bush's most successful action as president, United Nations forces led by the United States successfully pushed back the Iraqi army and liberated Kuwait. In this picture, U.S. Marines and their "humvees" prepare for action in Saudi Arabia, along the Kuwait border. *Bill Gentile/SIPA.*

and civil reforms and held free elections. In the February 1990 Nicaraguan elections, opposition candidate Violeta de Chamorro defeated Daniel Ortega. In El Salvador, American-supported peace negotiations also ended civil war. Antigovernment rebels agreed to a cease-fire and to participate in future elections. Bush proudly boasted that American efforts in both El Salvador and Nicaragua helped to produce more democratic governments.

Protecting American Interests Abroad

By mid-1991, almost everyone agreed that the Cold War was over. The Soviet Union and Soviet communism had collapsed, and the United States stood alone as the sole superpower. Liberals and many moderate Democrats called for a "peace dividend," money taken from the military budget and reallocated for social programs. But Bush resisted any reductions in America's global responsibilities and any sizable cuts in the military budget. The world was still a dangerous place, he warned, and needed the military and economic strength of the United States. The civil war in what had been Yugoslavia, Third World nations mired in poverty, ongoing tensions in the Middle East, and the daily flow of illegal drugs into the United States, all demanded a strong, activist U.S. foreign policy.

During his presidential campaign, Bush had made drugs a key issue and promised a crackdown on the flow of cocaine into the United States. In December 1989, he ordered American troops into Panama, in Operation Just Cause, to arrest Panamanian dictator Manuel Noriega on drug-related charges. Once praised by Reagan and Bush, Noriega had been implicated in the torture and murder of his political enemies, and the shipment of drugs from Colombia through Panama to the United States.

Seventy-two hours after the invasion began, American forces were in charge of the country, and Noriega was in American hands. American casualties were light (only twenty-three lost their lives), but more than three thousand Panamanians, almost all civilians, died. A Miami court later found Noriega guilty of drug-related offenses and sentenced him to prison in 1992. Panama, however, remained a major route in the smuggling of drugs into the United States.

In the fall of 1990, President Bush faced a more serious threat—from Saddam Hussein, the authoritarian ruler of Iraq. Saddam had claimed that the oil-rich sheikdom of Kuwait was waging economic war against Iraq (see Map 32.5), and, believing the United States would not intervene, Saddam had invaded and quickly overrun Kuwait in early August 1990. Kuwait was a friendly supplier of oil to the United States, Japan, and Europe. And for years Iraq had been receiving economic and military aid from the United States as a counterweight against neighboring Iran.

Many worried that Saddam intended to dominate the Persian Gulf and thus gain control over the flow of more than 40 percent of the world's supply

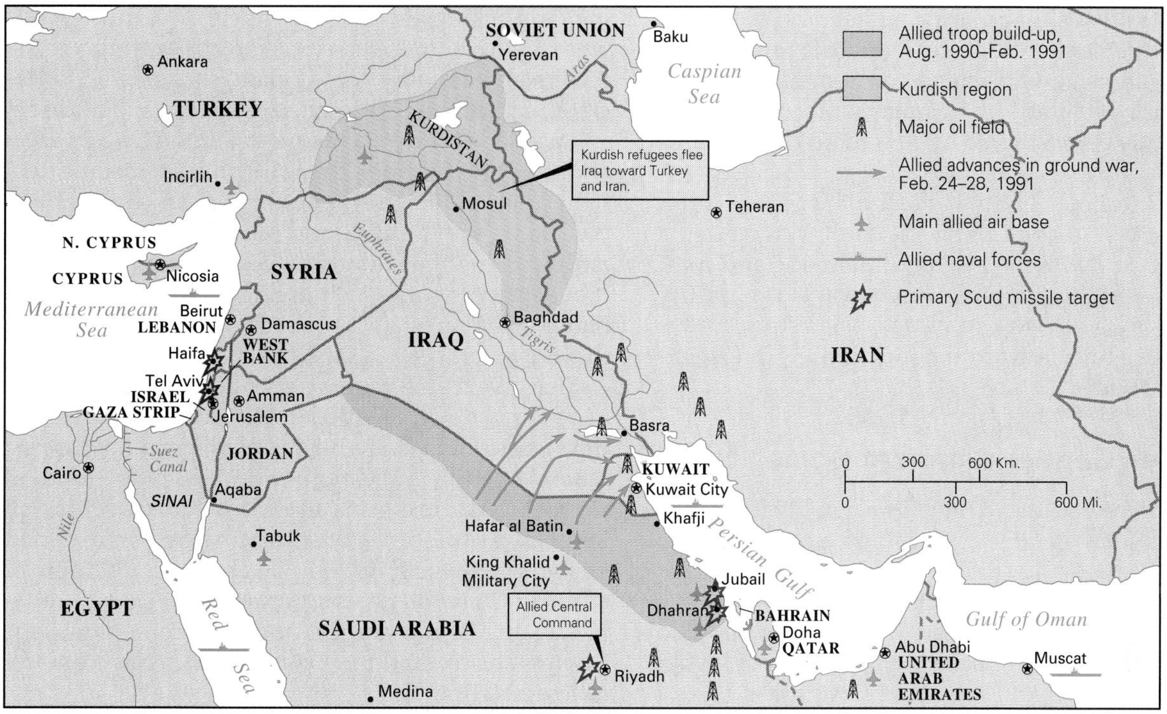

♦ **MAP 32.5 The Gulf War** On August 2, 1990, Iraq invaded Kuwait, threatening Saudi Arabia and the Persian Gulf region. In response, the United States and other nations formed an international coalition to restore Kuwait's independence. In January 1991, the coalition forces of Operation Desert Storm began to attack the forces of Saddam Hussein. The outcome was the destruction of most of the Iraqi army and Kuwait's liberation, but Saddam Hussein maintained control of Iraq.

of oil. Within hours of the invasion, Bush warned, "This will not stand," and he organized a United Nations response. A multinational force of more than 700,000, including 500,000 Americans, went to Saudi Arabia in Operation Desert Shield to protect Saudi borders and oil sources and to pressure Iraq to withdraw from Kuwait. Nearly 80 percent of the American public supported protecting Saudi Arabia, but many believed that the use of economic and diplomatic sanctions was the best way to force Iraq to leave Kuwait. Bush thought otherwise. He worked with other coalition nations to set a deadline for Iraqi withdrawal. If by January 15, 1991, Iraq still occupied Kuwait, the allies would use force.

Eighteen hours after the deadline expired, with Iraq making no move to withdraw, aircraft of the UN coalition began devastating attacks on Iraqi positions in Kuwait and on Iraq itself. American public support immediately rallied behind the **Gulf War.** After nearly forty days of air attacks United Nations ground forces prepared to push Saddam Hussein's forces out of Kuwait. Saddam had promised that the ground war would be the "mother of all battles," but General Norman Schwarzkopf, coalition force commander, was confident of victory. He ridiculed the Iraqi leader's military ability: Saddam is "neither a strategist, nor is he schooled in the operational arts, nor is he a tactician, nor is he a general, nor is he a soldier. Other than that he is a great military man."

The ground offensive, called Operation Desert Storm, started the night of February 23. Within a hundred hours, coalition forces liberated Kuwait, where thousands of demoralized Iraqi soldiers, many of whom had gone without food and water for days, surrendered to advancing coalition forces. Estimates of Iraqi losses ranged from 70,000 to 115,000 killed. The United States lost fewer than 150. It was the "mother of all victories," quipped many Americans as

Gulf War War in the Persian Gulf region in 1991, triggered by Iraq's invasion of Kuwait; a U.S.-led coalition defeated Iraqi forces and freed Kuwait.

President Bush's popularity momentarily soared above 90 percent. Some, less euphoric, speculated that the offensive had ended too soon and should have continued until all, or nearly all, of the Iraqi army had been destroyed and Saddam ousted from power.

By the summer of 1991, the United States could claim victory in two wars, the Gulf War and the Cold War, and was clearly the diplomatic and military leader of the world. Riding a wave of popularity and foreign-policy successes, the White House looked hopefully toward the forthcoming presidential campaign.

A Kinder, Gentler Nation at Home?

Bush had entered the White House in 1989 promising a "kinder, gentler nation," an administration concerned about the nation's social problems. But the Bush administration made no move to improve America's society or economy. The goal was not "to remake society" but to manage the presidency, avoid "stupid mistakes," and "see that government doesn't get in the way." More government and more money were not always the best solutions to the country's ills, Bush frequently reminded his listeners. It was a message like Reagan's, but Bush was not an effective communicator—he liked talking to people over the phone rather than face to face. Without Reagan's stage presence, Bush seemed to lack vision.

By the end of his first year in office, Bush and his advisers were confident they were managing well. They pointed to successful legislation that protected disabled Americans against discrimination (the Americans with Disabilities Act, 1990) and reduced smokestack and auto emissions and acid rain (the Clean Air Act, 1990). Bush also noted that under his administration the minimum wage had risen from $3.35 to $4.25 an hour and more funding had been provided for the Head Start program. Only two problem areas seemed to exist: the economy and his broken pledge on taxes.

In mid-1990, in part because of oil-price increases caused by Iraq's invasion of Kuwait, the nation entered into a recession. The recession, plus the growing federal deficit, had convinced Bush to work with Congress to raise taxes, despite his "no new taxes" pledge. Bush believed that by 1992 the recession would be over, the national debt would be reduced, and voters would happily re-elect him. The recession, however, continued into 1992.

For several reasons, the recession lasted longer than Bush expected. The world economy was slowing, and one result was that fewer American goods were being sold overseas. A restructuring of the American economy forced many businesses to declare bankruptcy or downsize, releasing both blue-collar and white-collar workers. Between July 1990 and July 1993, more than 1.9 million people lost their jobs, and 63 percent of American corporations cut their staffs. IBM and General Motors were among those that faced huge losses and dismissed thousands of workers. "I don't see the United States regaining a substantial percentage of the jobs lost for five to ten years," said one chief executive.

Sharply rising federal spending and the ever-increasing deficit helped to lengthen and deepen the recession. Despite Bush's pledges to hold down federal spending and reduce the deficit, the budget skyrocketed during his term, reaching $1.5 trillion in 1992. At the same time, family income dropped below 1980 levels, to $37,300 from a 1980 high of $38,900. Consumers—caught between rising unemployment, falling wages, and inflation—saw their savings shrink, and their confidence in the economy followed suit.

Bush did little to respond to the economic slide. Apart from saying that the American economy would rebound, he relied on raising interest rates and reducing trade barriers to allow foreign trade to expand. Negotiations went forward to establish a North American free trading zone with Mexico and Canada and to eliminate Japanese barriers to American trade, but these negotiations had little impact on the economy. As the recession wore on, Democrats called for tax cuts on the middle class, for increased and extended unemployment benefits, and for other social programs. Bush responded with the veto. When House majority leader Richard Gephardt was asked to define Bush's domestic program, he icily commented that it was "the veto pen." Congressional Democrats replied by blocking Bush's attempts to reduce **capital gains taxes.** The result was political gridlock. As 1992 began, Bush faced his lowest approval rating ever in public opinion polls—around 40 percent. Political observers noted, and Republicans lamented, that Bush, unlike Reagan, seemed unable to project the image of an effective leader who had a vision of where the nation or the world should be going.

capital gains tax Tax on profits resulting from the sale of assets such as securities and real estate.

SUMMARY

Expectations
Constraints
Choices
Outcomes

The years between Nixon's resignation and Reagan's retirement were ones of changing *expectations.* During the presidencies of Ford and Carter, the nation seemed beset by *constraints* that limited its domestic prosperity and international status. The policy *choices* that Ford and Carter made neither recaptured the people's faith in the nation nor established national goals. In his foreign policy, Carter chose to de-emphasize Cold War relationships and give more attention to human rights and Third World problems. The *outcome,* many believed, was a weakening of America's world position.

Reagan rejected Carter's notion that Americans should sacrifice to overcome the limits facing the nation. He argued that the only *constraint* on American greatness was government's excessive regulation and interference in society. He promised to reassert American power and renew the offensive in the Cold War. As president, Reagan *chose* a conservative program to restore the nation's values, honor, and international prestige. He fulfilled many conservative *expectations* by reducing support for some social programs, easing and eliminating some government regulations, and exerting American power around the world—altering the structure of Soviet-American relations. Supporters claimed that the *outcome* of Reagan's *choices* was a prosperous nation that faced few *constraints.* They applauded Reagan's assessment that his administration had *chosen* to "change a nation, and instead . . . changed a world."

Bush inherited the *expectations* that the Reagan administration had generated. But unlike Reagan he could not project an image of strong and visionary leadership. Finding fewer *constraints* and more opportunities in the conduct of foreign policy, Bush directed most of his attention to world affairs. As the Soviet Union and communism in Eastern Europe collapsed, Bush gained public approval for his foreign policies, also demonstrating American strength and resolve in Panama and the Persian Gulf. His foreign-policy successes, however, only highlighted his weakness in domestic policy as the nation found itself mired in a nagging recession that sapped the public's confidence in Republican leadership and the economy.

SUGGESTED READINGS

Bryan Burroughs and John Helyar. *Barbarians at the Gate: The Fall of RJR Nabisco* (1990).

A novel-like account (also a made-for-television movie) of hostile takeovers, leveraged buyouts, and the politics of greed that revolved around the Nabisco company.

Lou Cannon. *President Reagan: The Role of a Lifetime* (1992).

The most complete and detailed account of the Reagan presidency from a generally positive perspective.

Michael Duffy and Don Goodgame. *Marching in Place: The Status Quo Presidency of George Bush* (1992).

An insightful but critical analysis of the Bush presidency.

John L. Gaddis. *The United States and the End of the Cold War* (1992).

An excellent narrative of events in the Soviet Union and the United States that led to the end of the Cold War, as well as a useful analysis of the problems facing the United States in the post–Cold War world.

Burton Kaufman. *The Presidency of James Earl Carter, Jr.* (1993).

A well-balanced account and analysis of Carter's presidency and the changing political values of the 1970s.

Michael Schaller. *Reckoning with Reagan* (1992).

A brief but scholarly analysis of the Reagan administration and the society and values that supported the Reagan revolution.

Micah L. Sifry and Christopher Cerf, eds. *The Gulf War Reader* (1991).

A collection of essays and documents that provide both insight and an excellent overview of the Gulf War.

Tom Wolfe. *Bonfire of the Vanities* (1987).

A bestselling novel (also a movie) about the inside world of financial deals and the quest for power and wealth.

Wall Street (1988).

A movie that provides another example of financial wheeling and dealing and Yuppies in search of wealth and power.

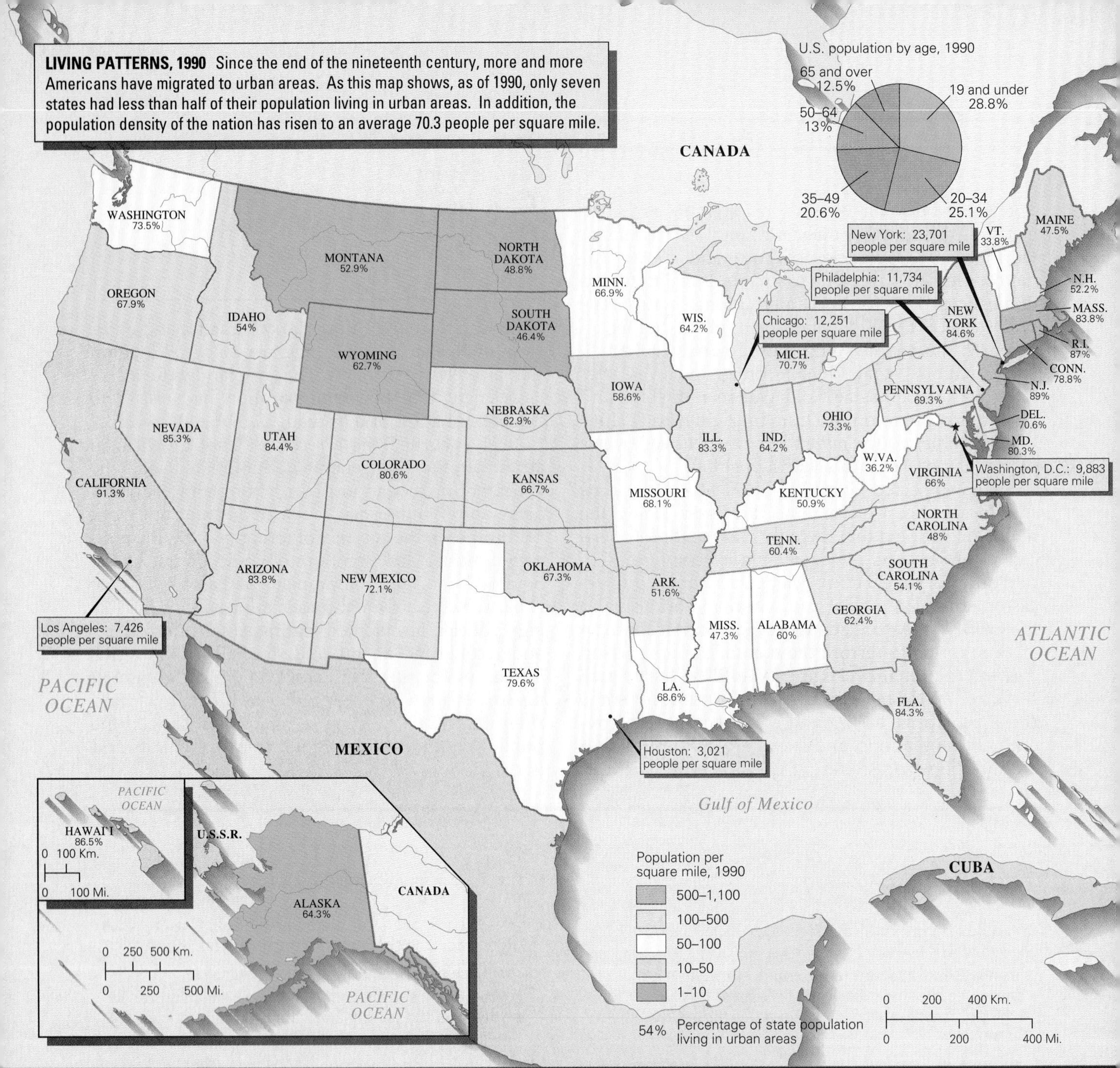

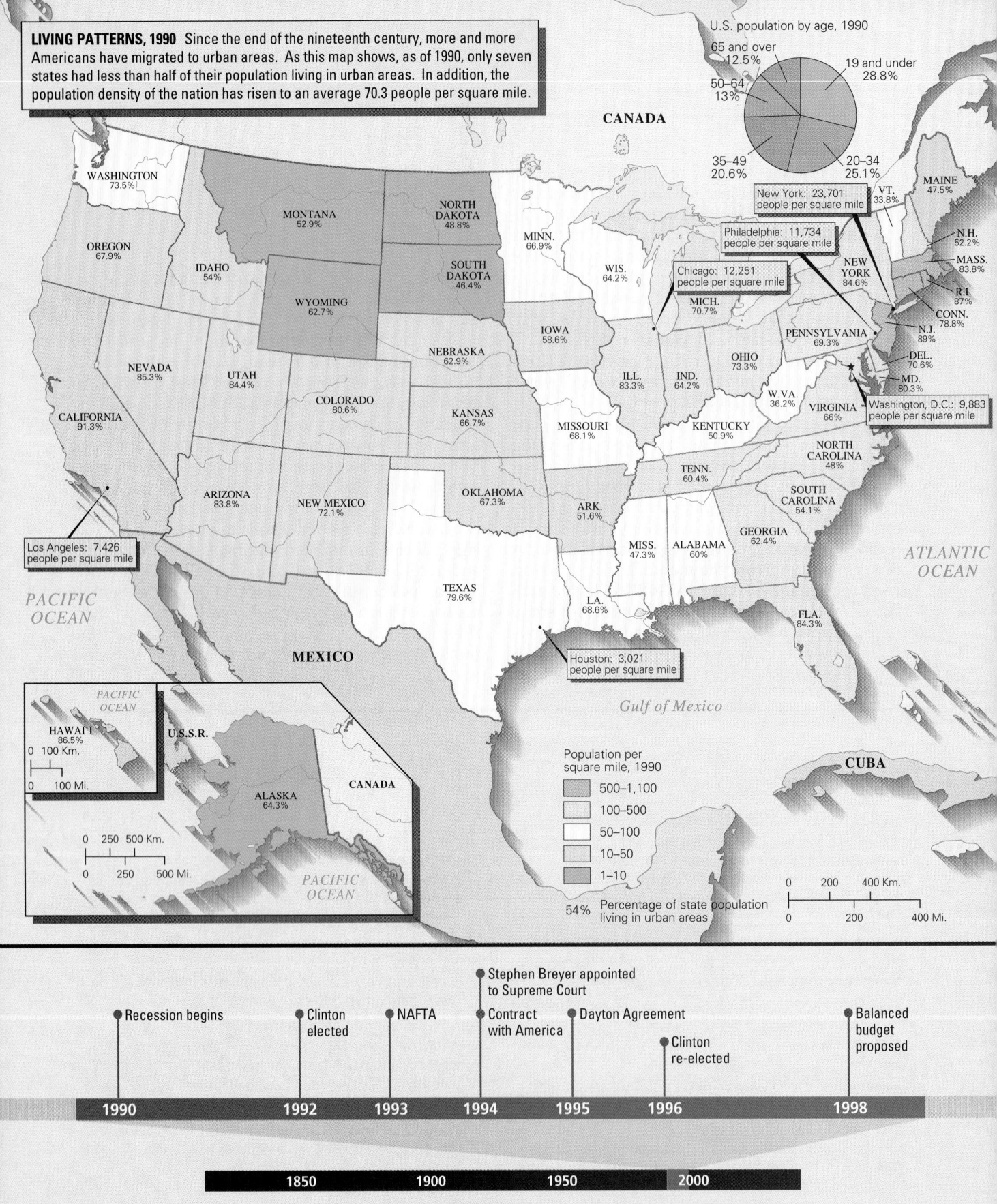

LIVING PATTERNS, 1990 Since the end of the nineteenth century, more and more Americans have migrated to urban areas. As this map shows, as of 1990, only seven states had less than half of their population living in urban areas. In addition, the population density of the nation has risen to an average 70.3 people per square mile.

- 1990 — Recession begins
- 1992 — Clinton elected
- 1993 — NAFTA
- 1994 — Stephen Breyer appointed to Supreme Court
- 1994 — Contract with America
- 1995 — Dayton Agreement
- 1996 — Clinton re-elected
- 1998 — Balanced budget proposed

1850 1900 1950 2000

CHAPTER 33

Making New Choices, 1986–1998

A Divided Society

- What changes were taking place in the American economy during the 1980s and 1990s, and how did they affect people's expectations?

The Politics of Morality

- What expectations surrounded the introduction of issues of morality and values into American politics?

Calls for Change

- Given the outcomes occurring during the Clinton presidency, what policy issues seemed most important to Americans in the mid-to-late 1990s?

INTRODUCTION

Before the election of 1992, many people *expected* the central issue of the campaign and perhaps of the 1990s to be the social and cultural divisions within American society. Instead, the election seemed more about the economy. Since the mid-1970s, the growth of the American economy had slowed, and by the mid-1980s, many families were experiencing the *outcome*. There was a widening inequality of wealth, and for the middle and lower classes the *expectation* of an improved economic future seemed at best uncertain. The percentage of Americans in poverty grew as government trimmed support for social programs. The *outcome* of the changing economy and decreased social services was most visible in the nation's urban areas, where unemployment, violence, and drugs expanded explosively. The arrival of new immigrants from Asia and Latin America only compounded social and economic tensions.

The economic changes also added to the social tensions generated between liberal and conservative values. On the liberal side were women, homosexuals, racial and ethnic minorities, and others who demanded a larger slice of the American economic and political pie and major changes in American values and attitudes. Liberals saw government as a prime force for reshaping American society, both economically and culturally. They supported the Equal Rights Amendment, affirmative action, and bans on antigay legislation as a means to ensure the federal government's role in combating job and legal discrimination.

On the other side were conservatives, led by the New Right. They argued that the policies supported by liberals were destroying the basic value system of the nation, resulting in crime, violence, other forms of immoral behavior, and the breakdown of family life. Many of the social problems of American society, they argued, would be solved by a return to traditional two-parent family values. A conservative backlash, supported by the Supreme Court, attacked liberal causes such as forced integration, affirmative action, and abortion on demand. As the nation prepared for the 1992 presidential election, conservatives predicted a clash between liberal and conservative values, a cultural and social war for the soul of the nation.

Expectations
Constraints
Choices
Outcomes

Early in 1992, many *expected* that foreign-policy successes would ensure Bush's re-election. But that *expectation* faded quickly when it became obvious that the public was most interested in economic and domestic issues. Bush's opponents—the Democratic governor of Arkansas, Bill Clinton, and an independent businessman from Texas, H. Ross Perot—had no foreign-policy expertise or any real experience in setting national policy. But the *outcome* of the campaign was a victory for Clinton, who promised to support social needs while making the *choices* necessary to control the federal budget and reduce the national debt.

Clinton's efforts to enact major domestic legislation ran into major *constraints*. Faced with strong opposition, he had to abandon his proposed healthcare plan and modify his goals for other social issues. In 1994 the *constraints* on Clinton's policies increased as Republicans gained control of Congress. Politically, Clinton proved adept at moving across the political center from liberalism toward conservatism, establishing himself as a centrist while making many of his Republican opponents seem too far to the political right. He also proved successful in foreign policy, improving the nation's trade relationships and helping to bring stability, peace, and democracy to Bosnia and Haiti. As Americans headed into the polls in the 1996 election, the United States was at peace and the economy was prospering. It was an unbeatable combination, and Clinton easily defeated Robert Dole and H. Ross Perot. Republicans still controlled Congress, but as Clinton's second administration began, both parties stated that they were willing to work with each other. Most people, however, *expected* that the spirit of cooperation would be short-lived and that each party would continue to try to reshape the political and social agenda to match its preferences.

CHRONOLOGY

New Expectations, New Directions

1969	Stonewall Riot
1972	Equal Rights Amendment begins ratification process
1973	Roe v. Wade
1974	Busing confrontation in Boston
1976	Hyde Amendment restricts federally funded abortions
1978	Regents of the University of California v. Bakke
1980	Ronald Reagan elected president
1981	Beginning of AIDS epidemic in the United States Sandra Day O'Connor appointed to Supreme Court
1982	Equal Rights Amendment fails to win ratification
1986	William Rehnquist appointed chief justice of the Supreme Court Antonin Scalia appointed to the Supreme Court
1987	Anthony Kennedy appointed to the Supreme Court
1988	George Bush elected president
1990	Recession begins Iraq invades Kuwait David Souter appointed to the Supreme Court
1991	Breakup of the Soviet Union Persian Gulf War Clarence Thomas appointed to Supreme Court
1992	Riots in south-central Los Angeles U.S. troops sent to Somalia Bill Clinton elected president Planned Parenthood of Southeastern Pennsylvania v. Casey
1993	North American Free Trade Agreement passed Clinton introduces national health package Ruth Bader Ginsburg appointed to Supreme Court
1994	Withdrawal of U.S. troops from Somalia Nelson Mandela elected president of South Africa Stephen Breyer appointed to Supreme Court Violence Against Women Act "Contract with America"
1995	Bombing of Oklahoma federal building Dayton Agreement
1996	Welfare reform passed Clinton re-elected
1997	Madeleine Albright confirmed as Secretary of State Reno v. ACLU
1998	Clinton proposes balanced budget

A Divided Society

• What changes were taking place in the American economy during the 1980s and 1990s, and how did they affect people's expectations?

When Ronald Reagan retired from the presidency in 1989, economics, social outlook, and cultural politics divided Americans. People worried about their economic future. As the economy slowed, maintaining standards of living became more difficult, and those entering the work force worried that they would not be able to achieve their parents' level of affluence. Growing economic fears intensified social and cultural divisions.

The Slowing Economy

The period from the end of World War II to the 1970s was the longest period of consistent economic growth in the history of the United States. Despite occasional recessions and setbacks, the **gross national product** and **productivity** rose at a rate slightly higher than 2$\frac{1}{2}$ percent. In personal terms, it meant that wages increased as did the American standard of living. Homeownership seemed in reach for nearly every American who held a steady job. Levels of poverty declined as the economy expanded and as government intervened with social programs to aid the poor.

By the 1970s, the American economy was still growing but at a slower rate—slightly over 1 percent. The causes of the slowdown were varied, and most were beyond the direct control of the people and the government (see pages 977 and 987–989). By the 1980s, some were arguing that the basic activity of the American economy was shifting from industrial production to the providing of information and services, often by means of computer-based technology (see Firgure 33.1). Although the information sector employed fewer people than the industrial sector, its advocates pointed to a ripple effect that provided jobs and opportunities to a wide range of people such as engineers, clerks, teachers, and accountants—"knowledge workers," as some called them.

The end of the Cold War and the shift toward a service economy had significant economic and social impact for many areas of the country. Regions that depended on industry, especially military-related industries, saw the closing or moving of plants, loss of jobs, and an economic crunch. The Rust Belt continued to decline (see page 989). In western Pennsylvania, the steel and coal industries cut back production and closed plants. Lakewood, California—the community that had seen great economic success in the three decades after World War II (see page 895)—faced economic and social changes by the mid-1980s. Jobs were no longer plentiful as defense-related industries cut workers and staff. Service-related jobs did not fill the void, either in wages or in benefits. As the economic vitality of the community declined, the largest department store in Lakewood's central mall closed, and discount stores like Kmart and Wal-Mart took its place. It seemed to many in the town that their community had been transformed almost overnight from a middle-class, optimistic community into a lower-class one. Fear and anger replaced optimism. A local min-

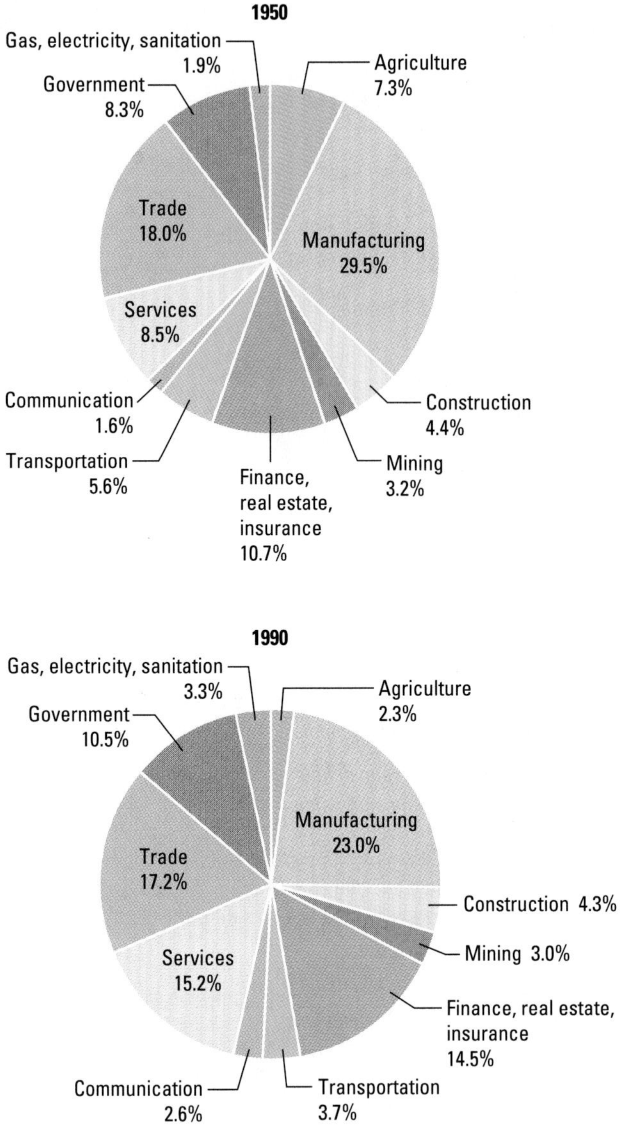

♦ **FIGURE 33.1 Main Sectors of U.S. Economy** A comparison of the 1950 and 1990 graphs shows that many of the economic sectors that deal with the production and marketing of goods, such as manufacturing, agriculture, transportation, and trade, have declined, while those sectors that mainly provide services have increased, especially government, services, and finance.

gross national product The total market value of all the goods and services produced by a nation during a specified period.

productivity The rate at which goods or services are produced, especially output per unit of labor.

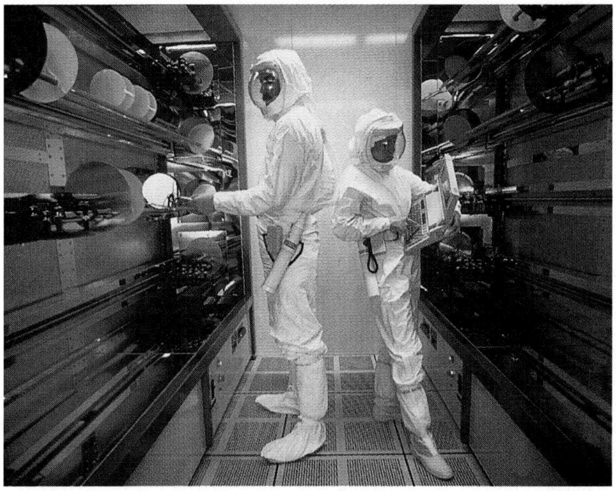

♦ Computer technology has significantly altered how Americans communicate and gain information and has stimulated the new "informational economy." Computer and semiconductor facilities, like those located in the Silicon Valley in California, compete to produce the newest computer hardware and software, further pushing the boundaries of the "informational age." Here, workers operate in the sterile environment of a clean room in a California semiconductor plant. *Paul Chesley—Photographers/Aspen.*

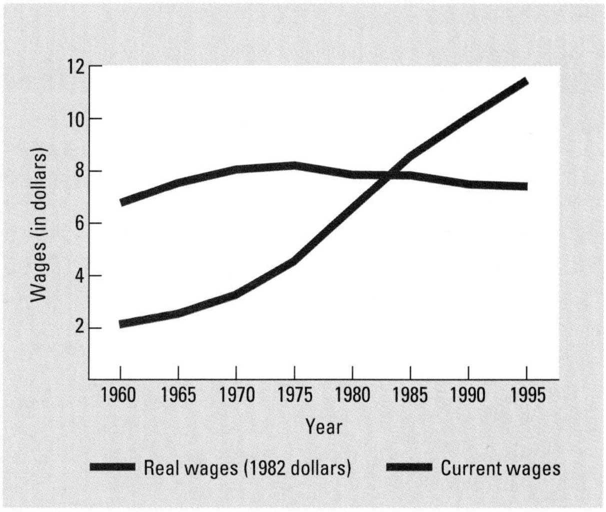

♦ **FIGURE 33.2 Real Versus Current Wages** Reflecting the growing economic uneasiness many Americans began to feel in the mid-1980s, purchasing power generated by wages began to decline, even though wages themselves continued to climb. In 1990 the average wage of $11.44 an hour was worth only $7.40, based on the amount of goods that a dollar in 1982 could buy. In contrast, in 1975 the average wage of $3.23 bought $8.12 in goods. Between 1960 and 1990, real wages remained fairly constant, fluctuating only about $1.30.

ister observed that the combination of economic decline, growth in minority residents, and the expanding permissiveness of society had generated a "feeling of being encroached upon . . . overwhelmed." Politically, Lakewood shifted from moderate and generally Democrat to conservative and Republican.

Unlike Lakewood, regions and communities connected to the increasingly high-tech information sectors flourished. Silicon Valley in northern California in the 1980s was a shining example of new growth and business spirit. It was the center for much of the microprocessing industry, with more than seventeen hundred firms involved in the information sector, and it boasted of the greatest concentration of new wealth in the nation. But Silicon Valley had a two-level economy—highly trained and frequently transient professionals at the top and low-paid service and assembly plant workers at the bottom. By the 1990s, with a slowing economy, increased competition from Asian companies, and a general recession, Silicon Valley also felt the impact of downsizing, unemployment, and relocating.

As wages failed to grow, more families found it useful, if not necessary, for both adults to work (see Figure 33.2 and Table 33.1). From the 1970s into the 1990s, most of the new wealth went to those at the top of the economy, while poverty increased, reaching 15 percent by 1993. The new "knowledge-based economy" rewarded those with technological skills and higher levels of education. The number of lawyers and doctors grew nearly 50 percent, and the Master of Business Administration (MBA) became a "hot" degree. Changes in production techniques required fewer workers, while mergers reduced the number of businesses. Not only did the number of full-time industrial jobs decline but, as the 1980s ended, so too did middle-class and professional positions. Young Americans felt the economic squeeze especially acutely. Throughout the 1980s and into the 1990s, workers younger than 25 saw their incomes fall nearly 19 percent. Downsizing, expanding costs, and rising taxes created anxieties about the future and sharpened gender, racial, and ethnic divisions.

The Face of Poverty

For those at the bottom of America's economic ladder, the slowing and restructuring of the economy deepened existing problems. The number of people in poverty climbed about 23 percent starting in the mid-1970s. By 1994, the income of 15 percent of the

TABLE 33.1 Consumer Prices, January 1998

Rye bread	$	1.59 a loaf
Apples		1.29 a pound
Bananas		0.49 a pound
Round steak		3.49 a pound
Chicken fryers		1.29 a pound
Wheaties		2.29 a box
Clorox		1.15 a bottle
Coffee		3.69 for 13 ounces
Margarine (oleo)		0.69 a pound
Sugar		2.09 for 5 pounds
Flour		1.69 for 5 pounds
Frozen orange juice		1.00 for 12 ounces
Dial soap		2.09 for 3 cakes
Milk		0.69 a quart
Kodak disposable camera	9.96	
19-inch color television set	199.99	
Refrigerator	599.99	
Oldsmobile 88 automobile	20,273.00	
"Scrabble" game	9.86	

Source: Data from *Observer-Reporter*, Washington, PA, January 1998.

population was below the official poverty line, set at $14,335 a year for a family of four. For minorities the economic facts were worse. African Americans represented 30 percent and Latinos 26 percent of those living in poverty. Also noticeable among the statistics of impoverished Americans were the number of households headed by women and the number of single mothers. In the early 1990s an estimated 31.1 percent of women who were heads of households lived in poverty. The figure for African Americans was another 10 percent higher.

Contributing to what some have described as the "feminization of poverty" was the continuing gap between men's income and women's income. In 1992, women working full-time earned on average 76 cents for every dollar earned by men. Also contributing to the impoverishment of women were new trends in divorce settlements, which reduced the amount of economic support that former husbands provided. Awards of alimony became less frequent, child support payments, when ordered, were likely to be too small to be of much help, and the enforcement of child support orders was lax. In 1990, for example, more than a fourth of spouses, mostly men, who owed child support paid nothing.

The Urban Crisis

Poverty was most noticeable in urban areas, where competition for diminishing goods and services contributed to rising social tension and violence. Through the 1980s, businesses and industries continued to leave the inner cities, taking many well-paying, full-time jobs with them and leaving behind low-paying service and part-time jobs. Those who could—including many middle-class African Americans, Latinos, and other minorities—moved to more affluent and safer suburban, integrated neighborhoods. More and more urban areas came to be peopled by what some have called the underclass, mostly nonwhite unemployed or underemployed people with little education and very little hope of escaping poverty through legal means. Fewer inner-city Latinos and African Americans graduated from high school. Dropout rates soared—among African Americans to more than 50 percent. The safety net of social services was also shrinking. Cities faced more social needs but received less tax revenue and less funding from the state and federal governments for social agencies and programs. Federal support for low-income housing fell from more than $32 billion to less than $10 billion between 1978 and 1990, while the purchasing power of benefits from Aid to Families with Dependent Children declined 42 percent.

Every American city seemed to have increasing numbers of homeless people, whose presence overwhelmed private and public efforts to provide housing, food, and basic services. By 1987, there were at least half a million homeless. They were a cross-section of the nation's poor: 46 percent single men, 36 percent families with children, 14 percent single women, 4 percent unaccompanied children. Fifty-one percent were African American, 35 percent white. An estimated 40 percent suffered from serious mental illness.

For some urban youths, one way to escape poverty and a feeling of isolation and vulnerability was to join a gang and turn to crime, especially selling drugs. In 1980, only ten cities had serious gang problems. By 1990, the number of cities with gang-related problems was 125 and growing. The lack of jobs and community programs and the expansion of the drug trade, especially in **crack cocaine,** were major factors. One expert on gangs noted that "gangs don't have membership drives" and that "kids drift toward gangs . . . where there are no [other] programs." Turning to the streets for recreation, identity, and jobs, children under the age of 10 could earn hundreds of dollars a day standing lookout, and older dealers, from 10 upward, could make thousands of dollars a day selling drugs.

Frustrated by shrinking resources, police and community groups became less and less effective against the growing crime and violence. The police complained about legal restrictions on their activities, supported gun-control measures, and joined with the public to press for harsher penalties for people involved in crime, especially the drug trade. Responding to public concerns, federal authorities by 1987 were spending nearly $15 billion a year to reduce the flow of drugs into the United States and to identify and arrest not only drug dealers but also users. Many companies, government agencies, and even schools instituted compulsory or voluntary drug testing to detect drug use. As the 1990s began, official figures showed some progress. The total amount of drug use was down—especially casual use by the middle class. But official figures also indicated that the availability of illegal drugs stayed fairly constant and that use by children was increasing.

Violence was also a graphic part of inner-city life. As violence increased and buildings deteriorated, sections of many major cities and many inner-city schools took on the appearance of war zones. By 1991, a fourth of all urban school districts had installed metal detectors to try to prevent students from bringing weapons to school. Outside and inside schools, in disputes over drug deals, over turf, even over clothing, gang-related murders mushroomed. While nationally the incidents of violent crime dropped, in the inner-city they remained high. Much of the crime was drug or gang related, but not all. Particularly worrisome was random violence—violence occurring for no particular reason—that many argued was a logical result of economic and social frustration, lack of meaningful activities, and readily available guns. By 1990, the leading cause of death for black males under the age of 35 was murder.

In April 1992, the most violent expression of racial and economic frustration exploded in south-central Los Angeles. The immediate cause of the riot was the acquittal of three white Los Angeles policemen accused of excessive violence (one policeman was found guilty) during the arrest of **Rodney King,** an African American, a year earlier. Caught on videotape by an eyewitness, four policemen had clubbed, kicked, and beaten King after he had seemingly been subdued. For many African Americans the policemen's actions were simply further proof of white and especially police racism. When an all-white jury returned the verdict, a five-day riot began, resulting in more than 16,000 arrests, the destruction of 4,000 businesses, 60 deaths and 2,300 injuries, and between $750 million and $1 billion in property damage. Like the Watts riot in 1965 (see page 941), this riot stemmed from a variety of political, social, and economic causes. But unlike Watts, this time the burning and looting were not random, localized, or just between whites and blacks.

Since 1970, the city of Los Angeles (LA), like much of California and other regions of the nation, had undergone a series of changes. Once a predominately black neighborhood, south-central LA had become a multiracial area with a significant Latino population and a growing population of Asians, especially Koreans, who operated family-owned small

crack cocaine Highly potent form of cocaine that is smoked through a glass pipe and is extremely addictive.

Rodney King African American whose beating by Los Angeles police officers was captured on videotape; the acquittal of the officers in 1992 triggered rioting in which sixty people were killed.

♦ The April 1992 rioting in Los Angeles that followed the acquittal of four policemen for the beating of motorist Rodney King lasted three days and destroyed much of South Central Los Angeles. Fifty-one people were killed and property damage exceeded $750 million. Many stores were looted before being set afire, especially in what was called "Koreatown." *Scott Weersing/Enterprise/Gamma Liaison.*

retail stores. As in other cities, tensions among the ethnic groups heightened as they competed with each other for jobs, housing, scarce public resources, and political influence. Many businesses had moved out of the once industrial core of south-central LA. Nearly seventy-five thousand well-paying jobs had disappeared, and only some of them were replaced by minimum-wage and part-time jobs. Black unemployment hovered around 50 percent. At the same time, federal, state, and local support declined, intensifying ethic competition.

Following the King decision, many African Americans and Latinos took to the streets. After setting fires and looting businesses in south-central LA, rioters quickly spread throughout the city. City, state, and federal forces fought to contain the rampage, but some areas, such as "Koreatown," were "sacrificed" by Los Angeles authorities who chose to protect more affluent sections of the city. "By Wednesday evening," one Korean recalled, "we knew the mobs would soon reach Koreatown. Desperate calls . . . to city authorities were not answered . . . no one provided us with police protection." Several Latinos and African Americans explained their attacks by claiming that Korean landlords and shopowners discriminated against and exploited them. One rioter stated "we hate" the Koreans, "everyone does." The outbursts were multiethnic and reflected trends arising from new waves of immigration to the United States following the passage of the 1965 Immigration Act (see page 939).

New Immigrants

As American society became less tolerant and government less supportive of social programs, a new wave of immigrants from Asia, Latin America, and the Caribbean arrived. The 1965 Immigration Act had ended the national quota system for immigration, allowing non-Europeans to legally enter the United States in sizable numbers. To the surprise of U.S. policymakers, the nation's Asian population had quickly grown. In 1960, Asians represented half of 1 percent of the population. By 1990, the figure had grown to 3 percent, and Asians were nearly half of all immigrants coming to America. Most came as families and tended to cluster in ethnic communities in major urban areas, especially in Hawai`i and the Pacific coast region. Some were highly educated, had marketable skills, and found economic success as engineers, medical professionals, and owners of small businesses. Chang-Lin Tien experienced such a success. Born in China, he became a professor of mechanical engineering and eventually chancellor of the University of California at Berkeley in 1990.

The success of so many Asian Americans—they are among the nation's most prosperous and best-educated minority—has caused them to be considered a "model minority." But this stereotype ignores many variables, including levels of education, dates of arrival, and ethnicity. Although immigrants from India and Japan have higher high school graduation rates than whites, those from China, the Philippines,

♦ Latinos, Asians, and people from the Caribbean comprise the majority of immigrants arriving in the United States today. Critics of immigration worry that these groups will not assimilate easily and want to limit further immigration. Supporters argue that assimilation is taking place and point to increased rates of nationalization and citizenship. Here, a Vietnamese family participates in the all-American sport of baseball (T-Ball). *Bob Daemmrich.*

and Indochina have lower ones. Many immigrants from Vietnam, Laos, and Cambodia arrived with few possessions, little education, and few skills. Mired in poverty, they frequently had difficulty assimilating into American society and faced racial hostility. Along the Gulf coast, whites fearing economic competition attacked Vietnamese shrimpers.

Many Asian Americans believe that a number of universities, under pressure from whites and from non-Asian minority groups, established quotas to limit the admission of Asians to professional and graduate programs. The consequence of growing numbers and anti-Asian prejudice convinced many to become more active in local, state, and national politics and to adopt the term *Asian American* to stress inclusiveness rather than ethnic diversity. Still, as one Asian American commented, "no one can claim to know what Asian-American ethnicity is or what it will become." Despite Asians' success and assimilation into American society, concluded one Asian-American activist, "there is a stereotype that Asians are foreigners even though they've been here for many generations."

Immigrants from Latin America, the Caribbean, and Mexico faced more negative stereotypes as they entered the country. A 1991 Gallup poll found that 64 percent of Americans favored limits on immigration and 69 percent believed that there were too many Latinos in the country. Another public opinion poll indicated that old stereotypes of Latinos as "lazy" and "unpatriotic" were still held by the non-Latino population. Prejudice and the lack of unskilled jobs keep Latino immigrants at the bottom of the economic and social ladder. "There is a growing schism between poor Latinos, on the one hand, and middle-class Latinos on the other," noted one Latino leader. Despite families working two and three jobs, he concluded, "the ladder isn't there" for newer immigrants and other poor Latinos.

Adding to the overall rate of poverty and hostility faced by Latinos is the issue of illegal immigration, primarily from Mexico. In 1986, trying to stem the flow of illegal immigrants into the United States, the **Immigration Reform and Control Act** outlawed the hiring of illegal aliens and strengthened controls to prevent illegal entry into the United States. The act also offered amnesty to illegal aliens who could provide documented proof that they had been in the United States before January 1, 1982. The law, however, did little to reduce the number of Mexicans and other Latin Americans trying to enter the United States, most of them seeking work.

The Politics of Morality

- What expectations surrounded the introduction of issues of morality and values into American politics?

Poverty, race, and new faces in American society were just part of the mixture leading to a divided society. After leaving office, C. Everett Koop, Reagan's Surgeon General, remarked that when he looked back, "the things I banged my head against were all

Immigration Reform and Control Act Law passed by Congress in 1986 that prohibits the hiring of illegal aliens; it offered amnesty and legal residence to any who could prove they had entered the country before January 1, 1982.

poverty." For Koop and others the key to the nation's problems lay in correcting poverty. Many disagreed. While liberals continued to espouse government activism as a means to promote social equality and cultural pluralism, conservatives argued that America had become a nation of interest groups clamoring for rights and power and that a sense of national identity and purpose was rapidly fading. They charged that liberal programs and attitudes had made victims of middle-class Americans, who worked hard, saved their money, and believed in strong, traditional family values.

Changing Values

Many accepted that there had been a moral breakdown in American society. They argued that the sources of the breakdown were changes born in the 1960s, such as the women's movement, the counterculture, and the **sexual revolution.** These movements, they claimed, had undermined the values of work and family by stressing personal fulfillment and advocating "fun, display, and pleasure."

The sexual revolution began with the youth movement of the 1960s (see pages 944–946). By 1970 more than half of those surveyed said they approved of premarital sex and cohabitation outside marriage. Though still the norm, marriage had lost some of its importance. Many people chose to remain single well into their twenties. Children, when they arrived, were fewer in number than they had been in earlier decades. As couples limited their families to an average of two children, the United States reached zero population growth during the 1970s.

By the 1970s, divorce rates were being pushed upward by changes in attitudes as both men and women became less willing to stay in an unsatisfactory marriage. As attitudes toward marriage and divorce changed, divorce laws also changed. **No-fault divorce** allowed spouses to dissolve their marriage because of so-called irreconcilable differences. By the end of the 1980s and continuing into the 1990s, half of all those who married eventually divorced. Responding to the high rate of divorce and studies that indicated that divorce had a long-lasting harmful effect on children, many religious institutions and a growing number of communities started to emphasize, or require, premarital counseling as a condition of a sanctioned marriage.

Divorce, the women's movement, and the sexual revolution also interacted with economic factors to affect the structure of American families. No longer was the American family the image of the typical 1950s family—white, suburban, mother as housewife. Instead, there were increasing numbers of single-parent families and families in which both spouses worked. Television reflected the changing views of American society by changing the images of the family and relationships. By the 1970s, there were few television shows showing families similar to Beaver Cleaver's family (see page 898). The majority of shows that dealt with families and family-type relationships provided different images. Some nonwhite families appeared, and many of the situation comedies featured groups of single and divorced people living and working in an urban environment. A week of television in 1997 featured several programs about white and African-American "traditional" households (with and without children)—*Cosby, Mad About You, In the House, The Simpsons*—and several single-parent households—*The Gregory Hines Show* and *Grace Under Fire.* But there were also many programs that featured divorced and never-been-married singles and revolved around work and lifestyles—*Seinfeld, Friends,* and *Ellen.* The title character in *Ellen* revealed in one episode that she is lesbian.

Keeping pace with these social changes, industry and advertising agencies found new and more explicit ways to use sexuality in their products and ads. Commercials were increasingly targeted at groups with specific age, gender, ethnic, and income-level characteristics, marital status, and lifestyles.

By the 1980s, sexual content had become standard fare in movies and on television. In 1987 it was estimated that more than sixty-five thousand sexual references were broadcast each year on prime-time television programs. During the day, sex and sex-related issues became more daring and numerous on the soaps, and talk-show hosts probed their guests for intimate details about their sex lives. Violence, too, became standard. A 1997 study indicated that 44 percent of all network programming had violent content, 73 percent of which went unpunished. Sexual and violent content appeared in combination in primetime network programming and on cable and satellite television, which boasted of even more explicit adult programming. One study

sexual revolution Dramatic change in attitudes toward sex; it began in the 1960s as more and more Americans considered premarital sex acceptable.

no-fault divorce Divorce granted without the need to establish wrongdoing by either party.

found that on the premier cable channels, 85 percent of the programming had violent content. An expanding market in sexually explicit materials was found in magazines and books, on the Internet, in X-rated films, and in clothing and sexual aids. Responding to what were termed excesses, many called for censorship and ways to limit the amount of sex and violence seen by children. By the 1990s, records, movies, and television all offered rating systems indicating the level of sex and violence in their content. Still, demands for censorship increased, including efforts to ban sexually offensive materials from the Internet, which the Supreme Court ruled unconstitutional in 1997 in the *Reno v. ACLU* decision.

Women and Changing Values

Related to the sexual revolution's effects on American society were demands by women for more personal and economic choices. As the women's movement continued into the 1980s and 1990s, it began, like other social movements, to divide and encounter more opposition. At the center of the divisions and at the heart of the opposition were differences about the meaning and importance of the sexual revolution, home, family, and children.

For many women, especially upper-middle-class women, Betty Friedan's *The Feminine Mystique* (1963) opened the door to a new self-awareness (see page 962). By the 1970s a "second wave of feminism" was fighting for both equality of opportunity and equality before the law. Unprecedented numbers of women were working and angered by the gap between their abilities and their earnings and by the treatment they received on the job. By the mid-1970s, the movement was successful in promoting the belief that women should have equal pay, opportunities, and responsibilities. Coeducational colleges and universities were barred from discriminating against women by Title IX of the Higher Education Act of 1972. Among its provisions, the act required equality in hiring and, for many colleges and high schools, further development of women's sports programs. During the 1980s, more women successfully entered politics and the professions, and the gap between men's and women's salaries narrowed. Women received more bachelor's degrees than did men. The movement also emphasized the need for changes within the culture of gender throughout American society. Included were calls for women's rights over their own bodies (especially abortion rights) and their own behavior.

Many states responded to the changing social values and to pressure from women's groups. They modified laws to reduce or eliminate gender discrimination within the law and the marketplace. Some states liberalized their abortion laws to allow women to seek legal abortions. In 1967, the National Organization for Women (NOW) and other women's groups had called for an **Equal Rights Amendment (ERA)** (see page 962). In 1972, Congress drafted one and sent it to the states for ratification. Advocates argued that the ERA was needed to eliminate, at state and local levels, laws and restrictions that blocked the achievement of women's equality. They pointed out that the ERA would also transfer the responsibility for ensuring equality from individuals and state governments to the federal government. At first, ratification appeared almost certain. Thirty-three of the necessary thirty-eight states approved it by 1974, and a 1973 Gallup poll showed that nearly 78 percent of Americans supported the amendment. But opposition stiffened, and when the already extended deadline for ratification expired in 1982, the ERA remained three states short.

The failure of the Equal Rights Amendment demonstrated the growing controversy about the goals of the women's movement and the definition of feminism. Conservative forces mounted an effective "STOP-ERA" movement by making the amendment a symbol for threats to traditional family values. **Phyllis Schlafly** and other STOP-ERA leaders changed the meaning of equal rights in the minds of many Americans. Rather than openly opposing women's rights, Schlafly labeled the ERA as a means to alter the "role of the American woman as wife and mother" and to destroy the American family. The changed definition worked to alarm many who already were increasingly uneasy about the growing sexual openness of American society, the changing attitude toward family, and the debate over abortion.

In 1973, in a 5-to-2 decision, the Supreme Court in ***Roe v. Wade*** invalidated a Texas law that prevented

Equal Rights Amendment Proposed constitutional amendment giving women equal rights under the law; Congress approved it in 1972, but it failed to achieve ratification by the required thirty-eight states.

Phyllis Schlafly Leader of the movement to defeat the Equal Rights Amendment; she believed that the amendment threatened the domestic role of women.

Roe v. Wade Supreme Court ruling in 1973 that women have an unrestricted right to choose an abortion during the first three months of pregnancy.

♦ Ever since the controversial *Roe v. Wade* decision in 1973, opponents of abortion have asked the Supreme Court, lobbied Congress, and demonstrated to ban abortions. In January 1990, with President Bush's encouragement, thousands of participants in the March for Life rallied outside the White House, demanding an end to abortions. Some radical pro-life supporters have even advocated violence against and murder of those performing abortions as a moral choice in the "war" against abortion. *Reuters Bettmann.*

abortion. Justice Harry Blackmun, writing for the majority, held that "the right to privacy" gave women the freedom to choose to have an abortion during the first three months of pregnancy. The controversial ruling struck down abortion laws in forty-six states that had made it nearly impossible for women to have an abortion except in cases of rape or to save the life of the mother. As the number of legal abortions rose from about 750,000 in 1973 to nearly a million and a half by 1980, so too did opposition.

Although most public opinion polls indicated that a majority of Americans favored giving women the right to choose an abortion, Catholics, Mormons, some Orthodox Jews, and many Protestant churches worked with conservative groups to organize a "Right to Life" campaign to oppose abortion rights on moral and legal grounds. The **Right to Life movement** easily merged with the conservative critique of American society and liberalism. Responding to conservative and anti-abortion pressure, Congress in 1976 passed the Hyde Amendment, which prohibited the use of federal Medicaid funds to pay for abortions. The Supreme Court upheld this position in 1980 in *Harris v. McRae.* As President Reagan appointed Sandra Day O'Connor and other conservative justices to the Supreme Court, many people expected the Court to eventually overturn *Roe v. Wade* (see Individual Choices: Sandra Day O'Connor). But instead, in 1992, in *Planned Parenthood of Southeastern Pennsylvania v. Casey,* the Court confirmed a woman's right to have an abortion, although it did assert that in some cases the state could modify that right. The decision did little to quiet the controversy or to prevent efforts to limit or ban abortions.

The inability of Congress to ban abortion and the Court's continued support of the right to an abortion convinced some in the Right to Life movement that more direct actions were necessary. Abortion clinics' doctors, staff, and patients became targets of violence and intimidation. Between 1978 and 1994, more than half of all abortion clinics reported varied forms of violence and intimidation, and a hundred clinics were targets of arson or bombing efforts by those willing to use terrorism to halt abortion. In 1994, the federal government passed the Freedom of Access to Clinic Entrances Act, restricting the tactics of intimidation that pro-life supporters like **Operation Rescue** could use.

Sexual harassment became a national issue in 1991 when Anita Hill, a University of Oklahoma law professor, testified during televised Senate confirmation hearings that Supreme Court nominee Clarence Thomas had sexually harassed her a decade earlier when she had worked for him in the Department of Education. Thomas was confirmed despite the allegations, but the issue of sexual harassment remained prominent in public debate. One poll at the time of the hearings revealed that 42 percent of women had been sexually abused, and the National Organization for Women claimed that physical and sexual abuse of women was a cultural norm.

Right to Life movement Anti-abortion movement that favors a constitutional amendment to prohibit abortion; it grew increasingly militant during the 1980s and 1990s; also called the pro-life movement.

Operation Rescue A militant anti-abortion group that advocates intimidation and physical confrontation as a means to stop abortion.

sexual harassment Unwanted sexual advances, sexually derogatory remarks, gender-related discrimination, or the existence of a sexually hostile work environment.

Responding to growing concerns about such abuse, Congress in 1994 passed the **Violence Against Women Act.** Part of a larger anticrime bill, it provided funds and federal support for efforts to more harshly punish sexual violence and other attacks on women and to provide resources to aid victims and prevent future attacks. On the issue of sexual harassment, by 1994, the Supreme Court had provided a controversial definition in *Meritor Savings Bank v. Vinson* (1986) and in *Harris v. Forklift Systems* (1993). In those decisions the Court judged that sexual harassment not only constituted "verbal and physical conduct" but created a "hostile environment."

Still, as the struggle over abortion continued and divisions over gender issues increased, most women tended to reject the feminist label. As the "Red Stocking Manifesto of 1969" indicated (see page 963), some feminists developed a caustic critique of what they perceived as a heterosexual, male-dominated culture and society in which women were constantly victims. These views had created a backlash against the term *feminist.* By the mid-1990s, many women who were trying to balance work and family believed that feminists were too antimarriage and antifamily and out of touch with the problems facing American women. Several women's rights spokeswomen, including Betty Friedan, wrote articles and books extolling family and motherhood and criticizing radical "**gender feminists.**" By 1995, only 20 percent of women college freshmen accepted the label "feminist," and in an article titled "What Happened to the Women's Movement?" *Newsweek* had suggested the death of feminism.

Many women's leaders, however, asserted that the movement was alive and well, despite internal tensions, and that a new "wave" of more inclusive and less ideological feminism was beginning. Most women, they said, including the 78 percent who worked, wanted to "fit their new gains at work and in the public world into . . . the story of marriage and family that they . . . inherited from their mothers." They wanted to keep the gains women had made while strengthening marriage and family, reducing sexual permissiveness, and softening the impact on young children whose mothers work. A growing number within the women's movement seek to adjust the workplace to better support family needs—programs like flextime and flexplace, job sharing, and family leave. The editor of *Ms.* magazine, a flagship of the women's movement, noted that the central issues were recognizing choices and their consequences and promoting a "woman-friendly family and a family-friendly workplace."

Gay Rights: Progress and Resistance

Women were not the only group asking society to reconsider America's traditional views of gender. Homosexuals too were demanding equality. Since the 1950s, organizations like the Daughters of Bilitis and the Mattachine Society had worked quietly to promote new attitudes toward homosexuality. Nevertheless, in most states homosexual activities remained against the law, and most homosexuals remained "in the closet," unknown to society at large. Then in the late 1960s, groups promoting gay and lesbian rights and gay liberation openly confronted American society.

The spark for the movement was a police raid in June 1969 on the Stonewall Inn, a gay bar in the Greenwich Village section of New York City. Gays fought back and were soon joined by other members of the community in what has come to be called the Stonewall Riot. One outcome of the altercation was that gays and lesbians borrowed tactics from the women's and civil rights movements, formed activist groups, and demanded an end to social values and laws that discriminated against homosexuals. Because visibility was a major tool and goal of the movement, gays and lesbians demonstrated in support of their lifestyles.

Throughout the 1970s, the gay liberation movement expanded and pressured government at all levels to end restrictions against homosexuals in employment, housing, and the military. Success came slowly. Polls indicated that the majority of Americans considered homosexuality wrong. But by the mid-1970s a slight majority of Americans opposed job discrimination based on sexual orientation and seemed willing to show more toleration of gay lifestyles. Responding to gay rights pressure in 1973, the

Violence Against Women Act Law passed by Congress in 1994 that provided federal funds and support to judicial and law-enforcement agencies to prevent violence against women, to aid victims, and to punish those convicted of sexual violence and attacks on women.

gender feminists Term applied to those within the feminist movement who seek to focus on the subordination of women and on the need for radical changes in gender-related roles and traditions.

INDIVIDUAL CHOICES

Choosing an Independent Path

Sandra Day O'Connor

In September 1981, Sandra Day O'Connor became the first woman to be appointed to the Supreme Court. Appointed by President Ronald Reagan for her conservative views, she has steadily chosen her own course, defying easy categorization. The outcome has been her gravitation toward the center of judicial opinion. When asked how she would like to be remembered, she answered as "a good judge." Tom Zimberoff/Sygma.

On July 7, 1981, President Ronald Reagan announced that his choice to replace Supreme Court justice Potter Stewart was "a person for all seasons": Sandra Day O'Connor. The 102d justice appointed to the Court, she was the first woman nominated and the first confirmed.

Reagan's choice drew conflicting responses. Many within the conservative wing of the Republican party bitterly objected to O'Connor. They reminded the president that she favored abortion rights and the Equal Rights Amendment. They pointed out that he had run on a platform promising that judges appointed by the Reagan administration would "respect family values and sanctity of human life." Some liberals applauded Reagan for nominating a woman but were suspicious. After all, O'Connor believed in judicial restraint—the idea that the Court should defer to Congress, the president, and public consensus—to resolve controversial social and political questions. The nomination, however, was quickly approved by the Senate Judiciary Committee and confirmed by the Senate. On September 26, 1981, Sandra Day O'Connor became an associate justice of the Supreme Court.

The daughter of an Arizona rancher, Sandra Day attended Stanford University, receiving a B.A. in economics and in 1952 a law degree. She graduated third in her law class, behind fellow Arizonian William Rehnquist, who by 1981 was also an associate justice of the Supreme Court.

American Psychiatric Association ended its classification of homosexuality as a mental disorder. In 1984, the United States Conference of Mayors called for legal protection of homosexual rights at all levels of government.

The growing toleration of gays in the United States and the gains made by the gay liberation movement did not end legal or political discrimination or physical attacks. The Reagan administration equated homosexuality with disease and denied entry into the United States to any "self-professed homosexuals." The New Right and Moral Majority (see page 994) campaigned actively against the rights of homosexuals. Evangelical minister Jerry Falwell called on his followers to "stop gays dead in their perverted tracks." And in 1986, Pope John

In 1952 she married John O'Connor. Despite high graduating rank and a Stanford law degree, Sandra Day O'Connor had difficulty finding a job as an attorney with a private law firm. A company in Los Angeles offered her a legal secretary's position, which she declined. Unable to land a job with a private firm, she worked as a county deputy attorney in northern California while her husband finished his law degree at Stanford. After he had graduated and received his commission in the army, she resigned from her job and joined him in Frankfurt, Germany, where she worked as a civilian lawyer for the army.

In 1957 the O'Connors returned to the United States and settled in the Phoenix area. Two years later, following the birth of the first of three sons, Sandra Day O'Connor opened her own law firm with a friend. In 1960, when her second son was born, she stopped working to become a full-time mother. Doing volunteer work, she became active in Republican politics and served on a statewide committee on marriage and the family in 1965. That year, recognizing her skills as an organizer and a lawyer, the governor appointed her an assistant attorney general for Arizona. "I wanted a family and . . . I wanted to work," she recalled.

During her first five years on the Supreme Court, O'Connor most often voted with the conservative bloc but frequently issued an independent opinion. In her opinions, she chose to emphasize two recurring themes: her belief that states are equal partners with the national government within the federal system and that courts should not play an active role in shaping social and political values.

With the arrival of other justices appointed by Reagan and by George Bush, the Court in 1990 became more activist in the name of conservatism and rewrote several earlier liberal decisions. Conservatives hoped that the Court, with its conservative agenda, would move forward to reverse positions on abortion, separation of church and state, free speech, and affirmative action. As the Court became increasingly activist, Justice O'Connor's position shifted slightly away from the conservative bloc and toward the center. During the 1990–1991 session, she frequently was the swing vote in 5-to-4 decisions. One observer of the Court commented, "As O'Connor goes, so goes the Court."

By the end of the 1991–1992 session, she was regarded as a leading member of a centrist bloc, which also included justices Anthony Kennedy and David Souter. In perhaps the most controversial decision of the Court's calendar, *Planned Parenthood of Southeastern Pennsylvania v. Casey* (1992), she co-authored the majority decision, which reaffirmed the right of women to seek an abortion, while criticizing the constitutional argument in the *Roe v. Wade* decision. Writing for the majority, O'Connor explained her choice: "Some of us as individuals find abortion offensive to our most basic principles of morality, but that cannot control our decision. Our obligation is to define the liberty of all, not to mandate our own moral code."

President Clinton's appointments of Ruth Bader Ginsburg (1993) and Stephen Breyer (1994) did not significantly alter the conservative leaning of the Court or affect O'Connor's role as a centrist. She remained difficult to categorize. Court observers expect her to join the conservative majority most of the time, but they admit that her open-minded conservative approach and lack of an overarching ideology make her opinions difficult to predict. They believe that she will continue to make her choices by judging each case on its own merits.

Paul II instructed American bishops to stop supporting gay rights efforts and labeled homosexuality a "moral disorder." Although twenty-six states had by 1986 decriminalized sexual relationships between consenting adults, only seven states and about 110 communities by 1993 had prohibited social and economic discrimination against homosexuals. In the remaining forty-three, or under federal law, no legal recourse existed for those fired from their jobs because of their sexual preference.

As the 1992 presidential election neared, the majority of gays and lesbians supported the candidacy of Democrat Bill Clinton rather than that of Republican George Bush. Bush had gained some support from the gay community during his presidency because he increased funding for AIDS research and signed into law a bill calling for the study of **hate crimes,** including attacks on homosexuals. But in 1992, in response to the right wing of the Republican party, Bush backed away from gay rights. He opposed antidiscriminatory legislation for homosexuals and applauded when several speakers at the Republican National Convention attacked gays as being abnormal and immoral. In contrast, Clinton openly supported gay antidiscrimination legislation, the right of homosexuals to be in the armed forces, and more funding to fight the AIDS epidemic.

The AIDS Controversy

The antigay opposition drew momentum not only from the Reagan administration's attitude but also from a growing fear of **acquired immune deficiency syndrome (AIDS),** a disease that spread first through a portion of the gay community and was for a time regarded primarily as a "gay disease." Fear of AIDS was critical in a 1985 decision by Massachusetts voters to reject a homosexual bill of rights. Patrick Buchanan, conservative writer and Republican presidential candidate in 1992, argued that homosexuals had violated nature and that AIDS was nature's way of getting even.

AIDS was first discovered in the United States in 1981. Within ten years, more than 195,700 cases had been reported; upward of 97,000 Americans had died of the always fatal disease; and 1.5 million were estimated to be infected by HIV (human immunodeficiency virus), the virus that causes AIDS. Initially, because the majority of those with the illness were either homosexuals or intravenous drug users, official and public response to the disease was restrained. But as the number of AIDS victims grew and came to include more and more drug-free heterosexuals, research and educational efforts were expanded and received national coverage.

As public knowledge and fear of AIDS increased, controversy flared about how best to prevent the spread of the disease and soon became part of the political battle over values. Claiming to be "realists," many recommended "safe sex," emphasizing the use of condoms as a means to reduce the possibility of getting or spreading the disease. Some advocated that high schools provide teens, a high-risk population, free condoms and information about AIDS and other sexually transmitted diseases. Some programs distributed free, clean needles to intravenous drug users to help prevent the spread of AIDS through shared infected needles. Others, however, argued that providing free condoms and clean needles would encourage sexual activity and drug use. Instead, they promoted abstinence, fidelity in marriage, and antidrug efforts as the best means to prevent the spread of AIDS.

By the mid-1990s, some advances had been made in research toward controlling AIDS. Combinations of drugs seemed to have a positive effect in slowing the advance and death rate of the disease, and public support for AIDS research and for those with the disease also improved. But there remained no cure for the disease, which by 1996 had claimed more than 280,000 American lives and had infected 20 million people around the world.

Federal Intervention and the Courts

By the 1980s, many Americans who had initially supported civil rights for African Americans and other minorities, as well as for women, were rejecting calls for continuing programs to help equalize social and economic relationships. Multiculturalism and federal intervention in support of minority rights, conservatives argued, were weakening American society and undermining traditional values like merit-based achievement and freedom of action. Among the most disastrous examples of federal intervention, many conservatives held, were requirements for forced busing and **affirmative action.** Both had been largely supported and influenced by the federal court system.

Busing for integration had become a national issue in the early 1970s, when state and federal courts began to order non-Southern school districts to adopt busing to achieve more equally balanced schools. Boston experienced violent protests in 1974 following a busing order, and twenty thousand white students eventually left the school system. In the 1980s, the Reagan and Bush administrations backed away from court-ordered busing. "We aren't going to compel children who don't want to have an

hate crimes Crimes that are motivated by prejudice based on race, religion, disability, sexual orientation, or ethnicity.

acquired immune deficiency syndrome Gradual and eventually fatal breakdown of the immune system caused by the virus HIV; it is transmitted by the exchange of body fluids through means such as sex or needle sharing.

affirmative action Policy that seeks to redress past discrimination through active measures to ensure equal opportunity, especially in education and employment.

integrated education to have one," said one Reagan official in the Justice Department's division on civil rights. They also heartened conservatives by reconfiguring the federal courts. Nominating judges who they believed supported conservative goals, presidents Reagan and Bush by 1992 had appointed nearly half of all sitting federal district and appeals judges. In selecting candidates, especially to the Supreme Court, they sought individuals who rejected judicial activism—the use of judicial power to legislate liberal social values—and practiced **judicial restraint,** deferring to the views of Congress, the presidency, and the states on legislation and policy.

Most of their Supreme Court nominations faced little opposition: eight were nominated and six appointed. In 1986, five years after appointing Sandra Day O'Connor, Reagan further reshaped the Court after Chief Justice Warren Burger retired. He named Justice William Rehnquist to be chief justice and appointed conservative Antonin Scalia to the Court. Anthony M. Kennedy joined the Court in 1987, adding to the conservative majority. The conservative direction of the Court was further reinforced by President Bush's two nominations, David Souter (1990) and Clarence Thomas (1991). The Supreme Court by 1992 had restricted criminal rights, approved the reinstatement of the death penalty, and backed away from busing. In a case involving DeKalb County, Georgia, the Rehnquist Court declared in 1992 that busing should not be used to integrate schools segregated by *de facto* housing patterns.

Affirmative action was under increasing attack by the time Reagan took office. As the economy slowed, a growing number of middle-class and blue-collar whites had come to believe that affirmative action programs limited their job and educational opportunities and constituted preferential treatment for minorities. Believing himself a victim of **reverse discrimination,** Allan Bakke sued the University of California system. Bakke claimed that the School of Medicine at the University of California at Davis had accepted black students less qualified than he and had denied him admission because of his color—white. In 1978, in *Regents of the University of California v. Bakke,* the Supreme Court decided in Bakke's favor and ruled that the university should admit him to the medical school. The Court did not totally reject color and gender as considerations for hiring, but the *Bakke* decision led to a weakening of many affirmative action programs.

Under the Reagan and Bush administrations, the federal government and the Court continued the retreat by tightening affirmative action guidelines, abolishing or creating limitations on many programs—especially those seemingly based on a **racial quota system.** During the Reagan administration, racial and gender preference systems were effectively limited by the Rehnquist Court's 1989 *Croson* decision, which declared state and local government efforts to set aside jobs and contracts for minorities to be illegal. Reacting to the Court's action, the city of Atlanta and many other municipalities abolished set-aside programs. In 1997, in a heated election, California voters approved a measure forbidding any

♦ Those supporting affirmative action were overwhelmed by California voters in 1997, who voted to eliminate consideration of race or gender in state hiring and contracting, and in admission to the state's colleges and universities. *Lou Dematteis/The Image Works.*

judicial restraint Refraining from using the judiciary as a forum for implementing social change but instead deferring to Congress, the president, and the consensus of the people.

reverse discrimination Discrimination against members of a dominant group; it results from policies established to correct discrimination against members of minority groups.

racial quota system A plan that sets aside a certain number of positions to be filled by members of a designated group.

consideration of racial or gender preferences in hiring, college admissions, or contracting. In applauding California's decision, Governor Pete Wilson announced that it "began a new chapter in the journey toward a color-blind society."

Calls for Change

• Given the outcomes occurring during the Clinton presidency, what policy issues seemed most important to Americans in the mid-to-late 1990s?

In mid-1991, Republicans and conservatives believed they had established a new political alignment of conservative voters that would continue the shift away from liberalism, big government, and "special" treatment for minorities at the expense of the white middle class. President Bush was basking in the afterglow of Operation Desert Storm and the fall of communism and enjoying an 88 percent approval rate (see page 1012). Most prominent Democrats, expecting the president to win re-election easily, decided not to compete for their party's presidential nomination. This left the door open for less-well-known Democratic candidates, including 46-year-old Governor Bill Clinton of Arkansas. Better funded and organized than other Democratic hopefuls, and focusing steadily on the economy, Clinton easily won the Democratic party's nomination. Breaking with the tradition of geographically balancing the ticket, he selected Senator Albert Gore of Tennessee, another baby boomer, as his running mate.

By the time Clinton was emerging as the Democratic front runner, Republicans were beginning to feel vulnerable. A nagging recession had turned the nation's interest away from foreign-policy victories and toward concerns about the economy. Unable to "fix" the economy, President Bush watched his popularity percentage fall to about 40 percent. He was also being challenged by conservatives within the party, who claimed that he was not conservative enough. At the Republican convention, conservatives drafted a party platform that attacked permissiveness in American society, opposed abortion and alternative lifestyles, advocated less government, and stressed "traditional American values," emphasizing family and religion. "Why experiment with new antipoverty programs," asked Kate O'Beirne of the conservative Heritage Foundation, "when the most important indicator of poverty is whether there are two parents at home?" Bush won renomination, but conservatives energized the convention with speakers like Pat Buchanan, who announced a "cultural war . . . for the soul of the nation." Uneasy with the calls for a cultural war, Bush stressed his presidential experience and knowledge of world affairs. He blamed the Democratic-controlled Congress for the political gridlock that had thwarted his efforts to institute domestic change. He called Clinton a "tax and spend Democrat" and warned that the Arkansas governor's lack of experience, especially in foreign and military affairs, would ruin the country.

Clinton insisted he was a "New Democrat," one that recognized the concerns of the middle class and the need to balance the budget. During the campaign he presented an economic plan that included higher taxes for the wealthy, programs to rebuild the nation's transportation and industrial base, and a strong commitment to a national healthcare program. He also promised to cut the federal deficit and to institute major changes in the welfare program. Bush's ads attacked Clinton's character, avoidance of the draft during the Vietnam War, and lack of experience, but Clinton steadily emphasized the economy and the need for a national system of healthcare. To keep the campaign focused on core issues, James Carville, Clinton's top political strategist, tacked reminders above his desk: "Change vs. More of the Same. It's the Economy, Stupid. Don't Forget Healthcare."

The 1992 campaign also saw the emergence of a third-party candidate. **H. Ross Perot** offered to use as much as $100 million of his own money in the campaign if his supporters could get his name on the presidential ballots in all fifty states. Perot's announcement in February 1992 drew immediate support from many Americans who were disenchanted with both political parties. His message was simple: politicians had messed up the nation, and control had to be returned to the people. "It's time to take out the trash and clean up the barn," he told listeners. The deficit was the foremost problem, he said, and he promised to shrink it. By June, one opinion poll showed the feisty Texan leading with 39 percent of the voters. Then, without warning, in July he withdrew from the race. He returned in September but never regained the momentum he had had in June.

H. Ross Perot Texas billionaire who used large amounts of his own money to run as an independent candidate for president in 1992 and 1996.

♦ Even though Bush, Clinton, and Perot dressed alike in the 1992 presidential debates many observers believed Clinton emerged the strongest. Although a candidate for the presidency again in 1996, Perot was not invited to participate in the presidential debates between Clinton and Dole—a decision upheld by a federal court that concluded he did not have enough support to be a credible candidate. *Wide World Photos.*

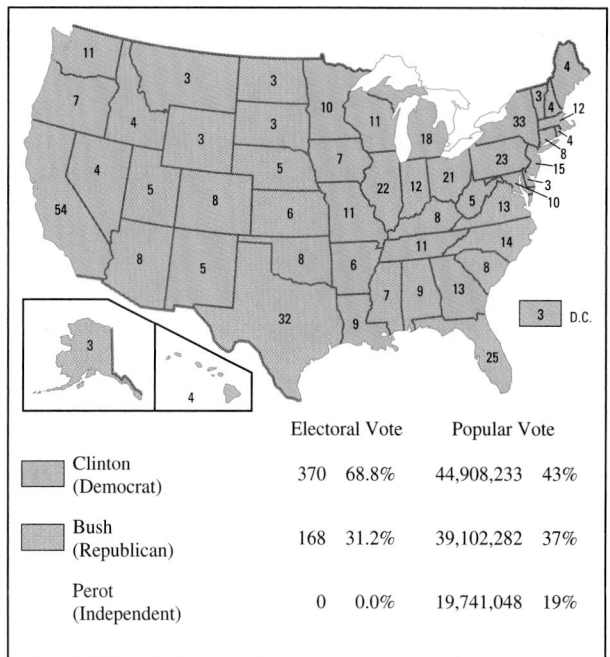

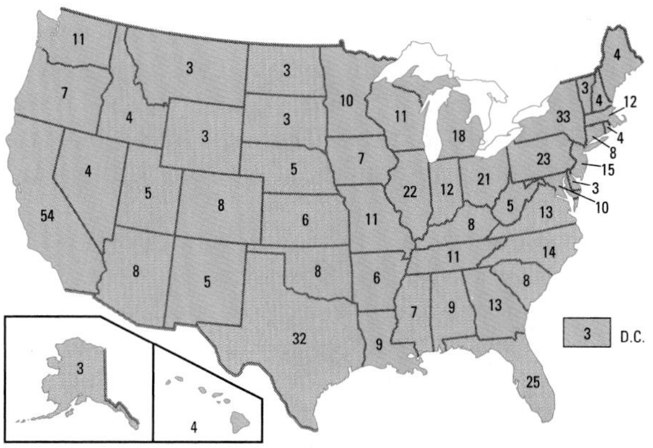

	Electoral Vote		Popular Vote	
Clinton (Democrat)	370	68.8%	44,908,233	43%
Bush (Republican)	168	31.2%	39,102,282	37%
Perot (Independent)	0	0.0%	19,741,048	19%

♦ **MAP 33.1 Election of 1992** Bill Clinton received almost 69 percent of the electoral votes—almost double the electoral votes received by George Bush. Nevertheless, Clinton received only 43 percent of the popular vote—the lowest popular vote percentage since Wilson's victory in 1912 over Theodore Roosevelt and William Taft. Third-party candidate Ross Perot drew votes from both Democrats and Republicans in equal numbers and had no impact on the electoral vote.

The campaign culminated in three televised debates among Bush, Perot, and Clinton in September and October—an estimated 88 million people watched the third debate. Both Bush and Perot gained in the public opinion polls but could not overtake the front-running Clinton, who won the election with 43 percent of the popular vote. Bush received 37.4 percent and Perot 18.9 percent. In the Electoral College, Clinton received 370 votes, 100 more than he needed to win (see Map 33.1).

Political observers wondered if Clinton's success and the success of women and minorities in elections across the nation indicated that the conservative shift in American politics that began with Reagan was at its end. Setting a liberal tone, Clinton stated that he wanted a "government that looks like America," and he appointed minorities and women to several posts in the judiciary, the cabinet, and other federal offices. Janet Reno became the first woman attorney general, and in 1993, Ruth Bader Ginsburg became the second woman on the Supreme Court. In 1997, Madeleine K. Albright became the first woman secretary of state. Clinton's most controversial appointment was his wife, Hillary Rodham Clinton, whom he named to chair the committee to draft a national healthcare plan.

Clinton, Congress, and Change

The new president was eager to begin, to make changes. "I want to get something done," he told a press conference. Despite his desire, many were unhappy with his first one hundred days. Several observers felt his administration was moving in "slow motion," with little leadership and less integrity. Republicans condemned his liberalism, especially his efforts to end discrimination against homosexuals in the military. Only months into his administration, Clinton's approval rating dropped to 36 percent. Responding to substantial opposition across the nation and in Congress and the military, Clinton retreated from recognizing homosexuals in the military and compromised. The armed forces were not to ask recruits about sexual preferences, and gays and lesbians in the service were expected to refrain from homosexual activities. The new policy failed to please either those who advocated the exclusion of gays from the military or those gay-rights activists who wanted total equality.

Clinton fared no better in creating a national health plan for the roughly 35 million people who were not covered by some form of health insurance. The healthcare task force gathered information and held hearings and sought a position between those who opposed any government-mandated system and those who sought a nationalized health insurance system operated by the government. The result was a complex plan that worked within existing insurance structures but mandated that businesses provide health insurance to their employees. The plan was difficult to understand and seemed to draw opposition from nearly everyone. Business opposed the mandated health insurance. The American Medical Association claimed the plan would give the government the right to decide the type and duration of healthcare, even limiting the choice of doctors. In general, many Americans wondered if the government could run any system cheaply and efficiently and feared rising taxes. After a year of public and congressional hearings and debate, President Clinton admitted defeat and abandoned the effort.

But not all of Clinton's legislative efforts failed. Many passed. During his first year in office his administration scored the best approval rate with Congress (86.4 percent) since Eisenhower in 1953 and Johnson in 1965. Congress passed the Family and Medical Leave Act, a gun-control act that limited the accessibility of assault weapons and required a waiting period before individuals could buy a handgun, and a major anticrime bill.

Clinton gave highest priority to the nation's economy and to improving trade. Unemployment was 7.7 percent, downsizing had cost jobs and restructured employment patterns, and in a global economy American imports exceeded exports. Continuing initiatives started by Bush, Clinton gained congressional approval of the **North American Free Trade Agreement (NAFTA)** and the General Agreement on Tariffs and Trade (GATT). Both were designed to reduce and eliminate trade barriers and to increase international trade—NAFTA for the United States, Mexico, and Canada; GATT for most of the world. Opponents claimed that both would harm the American economy by encouraging American companies to relocate their factories to nations with lower environmental, worker, and product standards. Organized labor was especially vocal about the potential loss of jobs. Because many Democrats

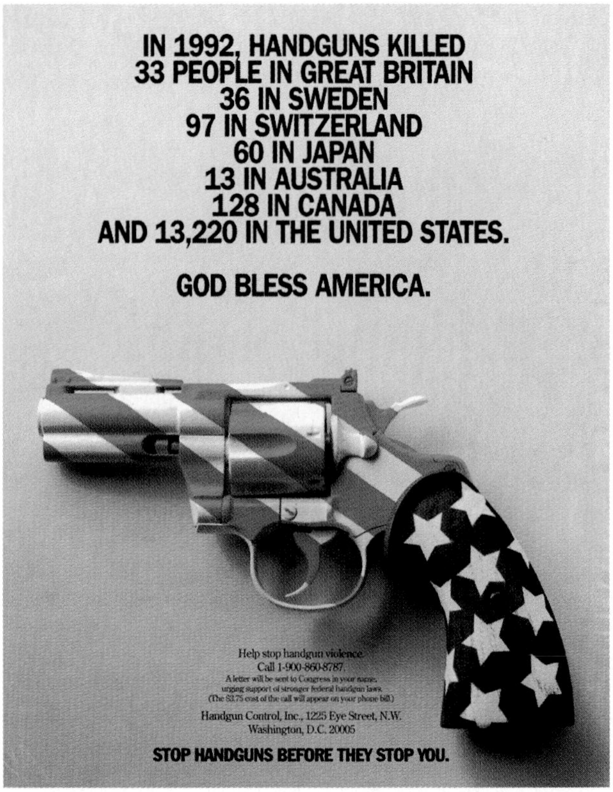

IN 1992, HANDGUNS KILLED
33 PEOPLE IN GREAT BRITAIN
36 IN SWEDEN
97 IN SWITZERLAND
60 IN JAPAN
13 IN AUSTRALIA
128 IN CANADA
AND 13,220 IN THE UNITED STATES.
GOD BLESS AMERICA.
Help stop handgun violence.
Call 1-900-860-8787.
Handgun Control, Inc., 1225 Eye Street, N.W.
Washington, D.C. 20005
STOP HANDGUNS BEFORE THEY STOP YOU.

♦ Throughout the 1980s and 1990s the issue of gun control has sharply divided the nation. This ad strongly asserts the need for controls. Opponents argue that the right to bear arms is guaranteed by the Constitution. Advocates for control won a small victory in 1993 when Congress passed the Brady Bill, which requires a five-day waiting period and background check before people can buy a handgun. *Handgun Control, Inc.*

North American Free Trade Agreement Agreement approved in 1993 that eliminated most tariffs and other trade barriers between the United States, Canada, and Mexico.

refused to support the bills, Clinton was forced to rely on Republican votes for their passage.

Clinton's plan for the budget was based on his conviction that reducing the deficit was necessary to end the recession and promote future growth. Presented in February 1993, his proposal raised taxes on the wealthiest Americans and made major spending cuts throughout the budget to reduce the deficit. It also expanded tax credits for low-income families. Republicans denounced the budget as a typical liberal Democratic "tax and spend" measure that would create a "job-killing recession" and put the nation's economy in the "gutter." Six months later, with Vice President Gore casting the tie-breaking vote in the Senate, the Clinton budget passed without the votes of any Republican senators. Over the next three years, the economy recovered, expanding at 3 percent a year, and the deficit went down. By 1996 the combined rate of inflation and unemployment was at its lowest in thirty years.

Despite Clinton's legislative and budget victories, as 1994 began, the president's popularity continued to fall. Republicans hammered away at Clinton's liberal programs and appointments and his ethics. Led by Newt Gingrich, a conservative representative from Georgia, they drafted the "**Contract with America,**" which called, in broad and general terms, for lawmakers to scale back federal spending (especially for welfare), balance the budget by 2002, promote responsive government, and support the family. Nearly all Republican aspirants to the House signed the contract, establishing a Republican agenda for the next Congress.

The 1994 congressional election appeared to repudiate liberalism, multiculturalism, and Democratic leadership. Republicans were returned to Congress in record numbers. In what some called the "revolt of angry white men," 39 percent of the electorate elected nine new Republican senators and 52 new Republican representatives, establishing a Republican majority in both houses of Congress for the first time in forty years. Conservative candidates and initiatives won voter approval at state and local levels as well. In California, voters approved a measure to deny public education and most social services to illegal immigrants. Gingrich, the new Republican Speaker of the House, said that the conservative majority was "going to change the world."

With solid Republican support in the House, Gingrich successfully pushed to enact most of the "Contract with America." Republicans passed large tax cuts, strong anticrime legislation, and increases in military spending. However, their efforts to reform welfare by ending federal entitlement programs and requiring eligible recipients to work met with two Clinton vetoes.

♦ Led by Newt Gingrich (R-Georgia), in 1994, Republican congressional candidates and Congressmen endorsed the "Contract with America" that established a series of legislative goals, including reducing taxes, regulations, and the size of government. Voters responded favorably, electing a Republican majority in the House of Representatives. Gingrich became House Majority Leader and a vocal opponent of liberal policies and President Clinton. *John Harrington/Black Star.*

Welfare reform seemed to typify the gap between liberals and conservatives. Conservatives argued that welfare programs for the poor created a class of welfare-dependent people, "welfare mothers," who

"Contract with America" Pledge taken in 1994 by some three hundred Republican candidates for the House, who promised to reduce the size and scope of the federal government and to balance the federal budget by 2002.

had little integrity and no work ethic. They cast restructuring the welfare system as a moral issue. Many agreed as more and more Americans believed that the central problem facing the nation was not the deficit or the economy but moral issues. The nation's "problems," a conservative spokesman declared, "are not material . . . [but] of spiritual and moral poverty." Liberals countered that Republican welfare programs were mean-spirited and ignored the reality of those on welfare. They argued that to replace relief with jobs required increased funding for training and educational programs and daycare for the children of working mothers. They questioned whether the private sector would be able to hire all those no longer on welfare.

In the midst of the welfare debate, in April 1995, Americans were shocked by an act of "home-grown terrorism" that seemed to symbolize the depth of division in the nation and the potential for irrational extremist responses. An advocate of radical right-wing militarism planted a bomb that destroyed the federal building in Oklahoma City. The explosion killed 168 people, 19 of them children. Although the tragedy united the nation against the dangers of extremism, it did little to lessen the differences between the Republican Congress and the Democratic White House.

♦ On April 19, 1995 a terrorist truck-bomb exploded in front of the federal building in Oklahoma City, killing 169 people. Here, a fireman carries the lifeless body of one of the nineteen children that lost their lives in a day-care center housed in the building. *Charles H. Porter IV/Sygma.*

While the welfare debate continued, Clinton and Congress squared off over social spending in the 1995–1996 budget. Clinton won a moral victory. Rather than agreeing to cuts that Republicans were demanding in return for federal operating funds, he shut down the government, sending thousands of federal employees home. By January 1996, Republicans were ready to sit down and negotiate a compromise with the White House. Endorsing a balanced budget by 2002, the two sides managed to glue together a budget. Shortly afterward, Clinton signed a slightly modified Republican welfare reform bill that phased out federal entitlements programs like Aid to Families with Dependent Children and replaced them with block grants to the states. The act also gave states the right to determine welfare eligibility and required adults to work in order to receive welfare.

Republicans argued that Clinton had adopted their positions, but the budget battle and welfare reform act had boosted the president's popularity, and he was in fact seizing the political center in an election year. A growing belief that Gingrich-style conservatives were too far to the right aided Clinton's effort. Even Republican Senate majority leader Robert Dole of Kansas echoed the sentiment when he commented on the budget battle: "It seems like the Republicans have this my-way-or-no-way attitude, and I'm tired of it."

As the 1996 presidential election approached, Clinton consolidated his hold on the center of the American political spectrum. Just as his administration had rejected the harsh, antigovernment rhetoric of conservative Republicans, it also seemed to have rejected the old, New Deal–style level of government intervention as the solution to the nation's domestic problems. Clinton's moderately interventionist policies seemed to help his standing with many Americans. His support for increased educational funding and unpaid family and medical leave and for protection of Social Security and Medicaid and Medicare, in the face of Republican opposition, gave him the initiative on the "family values" issue. One observer suggested that Clinton had effectively negated the conservative-inspired image of a liberal as someone who will "tax me and send the money to a welfare mother whose son will mug my wife at the shopping mall." And, in its place, he had fixed on Republicans the image of people "who will take the money away from my parents' Medicare and send it as tax breaks to polluters who downsize me out of work."

The election season was somewhat anticlimactic. Conservative Republicans dominated their party's convention and platform and once again tried to declare "cultural war," but their candidate, moderate Senate majority leader Bob Dole, ignored their war and concentrated on stressing his economic proposals and Clinton's ethics. The president stood accused of sexually harassing Paula Jones, a government employee when he was governor of Arkansas, and he and his wife had been involved in a failed real-estate venture for which two partners had been convicted of fraud. A number of observers questioned the legality of the Clintons' role in the **Whitewater scandal,** but the ethics issue failed to resonate with voters. Polls found that 54 percent thought Clinton was not "honest" or "trustworthy" but that such views had little impact on how they would vote.

The Dole campaign lacked energy from the start. The conservative wing of the Republican party never fully supported Dole, and more than a few Americans regarded him, at 75, as too old for the office. Perot ran again too, but with little more than a shadow of the momentum he had gained in 1992. In an election marked by low voter turnout, Clinton became the first Democratic president to be reelected since Franklin D. Roosevelt. He captured 379 electoral votes and 49 percent of the popular vote to Dole's 159 electoral votes and 41 percent (see Map 33.2). Perot managed to attract 9 percent of the vote and no electoral votes. In the bicentennial of partisan presidential elections, Clinton returned to the White House, but Republicans still kept control over Congress.

Clinton's Foreign Policy

When Clinton assumed control of foreign policy, it still was not clear what general policy would replace that of the Cold War. Americans wanted to maintain their power and influence as a superpower but were divided over what situations would warrant American intervention. Inexperienced in foreign affairs, Clinton proceeded cautiously and followed the general outline set by President Bush. In economic foreign policy, Clinton completed Bush's effort to pass the NAFTA and GATT agreements, to improve trade with China, and to encourage Japan

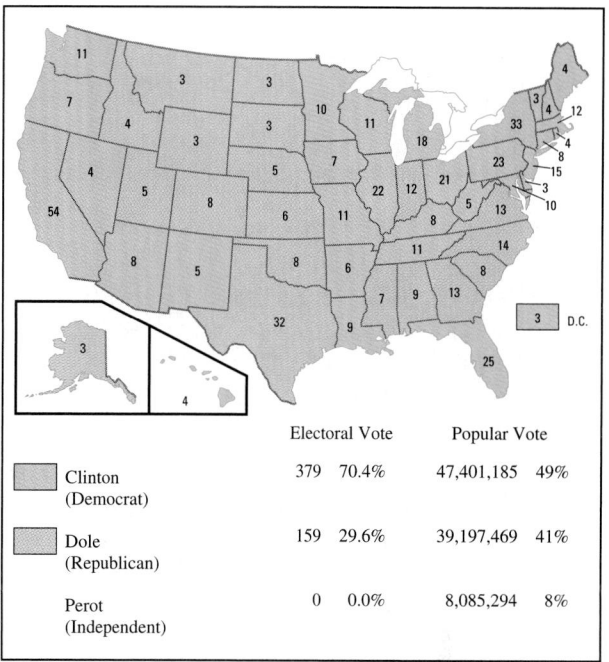

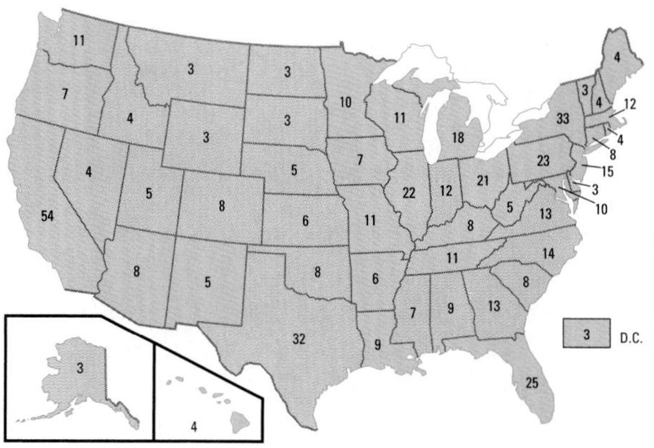

	Electoral Vote		Popular Vote	
Clinton (Democrat)	379	70.4%	47,401,185	49%
Dole (Republican)	159	29.6%	39,197,469	41%
Perot (Independent)	0	0.0%	8,085,294	8%

♦ **MAP 33.2 Election of 1996** In the 1996 election, more than 9 million fewer people voted than in 1992. Clinton gained about two and a half million votes while Republican voters remained constant. Perot voters, however, declined by over half to only 8.4 percent of the voters. Men divided their votes evenly between Clinton and Dole, but 54 percent of women voted for Clinton. Despite Clinton's victory, voters returned a Republican Congress.

to buy more American goods. Continuing earlier efforts in the Middle East, the Clinton State Department played a role in an accord establishing Palestinian self-rule in some Israeli-occupied areas and in a treaty in which Jordan and Israel pledged cooperation. Clinton also continued to support Russian leader Boris Yeltsin and to work toward agreements with former Soviet countries to destroy nuclear warheads. Efforts to promote democracy and pro-Western elements throughout Eastern Europe also continued, amid movement toward including many former members of the Warsaw Pact (see page 914) in NATO.

Clinton inherited two highly controversial commitments from the Bush administration—in Somalia, in East Africa, and in Bosnia. United States

Whitewater scandal A scandal involving a failed real-estate development in Arkansas in which President Clinton invested.

♦ In March 1998, President Clinton made a twelve-day tour of several African nations. Stating that "stereotypes" had often created distorted images and "weakened our understanding of Africa," the president promised a new American approach to Africa that stressed trade and investment and the development of stable democratic regimes. Here, Clinton meets with South African President Nelson Mandela. *Wide World Photos.*

troops had intervened in Somalia in 1992 as part of a United Nations effort to provide humanitarian aid and keep the peace between marauding factions in a civil war. But in the absence of any apparent direct U.S. interest in the country, pressure to withdraw the troops grew quickly and steadily. By April 1994, Clinton had done so, while opting to strengthen the U.S. role in finding a political settlement.

During the 1992 campaign, Clinton had chided Bush for not promoting peace in Bosnia more assertively. Once in office, he inched forward on the issue amid considerable controversy over whether UN peacekeeping and relief efforts would have any effect. As the carnage increased, however, the Clinton administration agreed to allow American forces to participate in a UN campaign to establish and protect "safe areas" for refugees of the fighting. In the fall of 1995, the United States sponsored talks between the warring elements—the Serbs, the Muslim Bosnians, and the Croats. The resulting **Dayton Agreement** partitioned the country into a Bosnian-Croat federation and Serbia, and called for UN forces, including 20,000 Americans, to police the peace. By the summer of 1996, when most American forces were withdrawn, much had been accomplished to rebuild the shattered region. Although Clinton stated that American efforts in Bosnia had been successful, in December 1997 he announced that a continued American presence in that nation was necessary to continue with the task of nation building.

A second major American intervention came in Haiti, where Clinton's policy helped restore democratic government. In 1991 a military coup had ousted the democratically elected government headed by President Jean Bertrand Aristide. When isolation and economic pressure failed to convince the ruling junta, which was brutally repressing its opponents, to restore democracy, Clinton in 1994 obtained UN support for an invasion. Under this threat, the junta opened discussions in October with a delegation led by former president Jimmy Carter. The resulting agreement allowed the junta members to leave the country and Aristide to return. Elections followed, and U.S. troops left after helping Haiti make the transition back to democracy.

Bridge to the Twenty-first Century

As Clinton began his second term, most Americans were generally pleased with society and the economy, and gave the president high approval ratings. The country was at peace and the economy was growing, providing more jobs while inflation remained low. The previous years of economic growth were broad based, helping to reduce income gaps between men and women and African Americans and whites.

In his State of the Union Address, Clinton focused on the economy's strength as he projected the first balanced budget in thirty years. The budget marked, he stated, "an end to decades of deficits that have shackled our economy, paralyzed our policies, and held our people back." He also suggested that any surplus should be set aside to ensure the future viability of social security. "Before we do anything with that surplus," he told Congress, "let's

Dayton Agreement Agreement signed in Dayton, Ohio, in November 1995 by the three rival ethnic groups in Bosnia, which pledged to end the four-year-old civil war there.

save Social Security first." In stressing what some Democrats called "smart government" not "idle government," Clinton called for increased spending on education, daycare, Medicare and Medicaid, and for medical and other scientific research. Republican critics argued that the budget was balanced through the use of "smoke and mirrors" and represented the Democratic position as a continuation of "big government." They predicted that Congress would pass few if any of the president's programs. It was politics as usual.

At the time Clinton gave his State of the Union Address, the emerging Monica Lewinsky scandal was rocking the White House and prompting some to suggest that the president should resign or be impeached. Did the president have a sexual relationship with the former White House intern? Did he ask her to lie about it under oath? Although willing to believe the accusations, most Americans did not seem to care. As the investigation and stories of a cover-up and presidential sexual misconduct continued, earning daily headline attention from the news media, Clinton's public approval rose to a record height of 79 percent. Polls suggested that a majority of the public was pleased with Clinton's performance as president and the overall state of the nation, and thought that Clinton's private life should be his own business. Still, many expected the investigation to continue for a long time.

Clinton was also receiving high marks for his tough stance toward Iraq and its stockpiling of chemical and biological weapons. Fearful of Saddam Hussein's readiness to replenish his chemical and biological weapons after the Gulf War, the United Nations required Iraq to allow United Nations' arms inspectors to inspect sites suspected of storing or producing such weapons of mass destruction. From the beginning of these forced inspections, Saddam obstructed the arms inspectors, making it difficult for them to accomplish their mission. In January 1998, Saddam flatly refused to allow inspection teams access to several suspected sites, including many presidential palaces.

As the United Nations withdrew its inspectors, the United States began to apply diplomatic pressure to force the Iraqis to allow unlimited access to suspected weapon facilities. By the end of January, military pressure was added to the diplomatic efforts. Clinton stated that the United States was willing to attack Iraq to force compliance with the United Nations' mandate to eliminate all of Iraq's biological and chemical weapons. As the United States moved military units into the Gulf region, one navy pilot was heard to say: "I don't think you can find a more powerful tool to make a statement than to park an airplane twenty miles off a guy's beach." The possibility of a United States-led attack against Iraq led to further diplomacy. The Secretary General of the United Nations, Kofi Annan, flew to Iraq in February to try to resolve the impasse. In Baghdad, Annan convinced Saddam to accept the United Nation's demand that its weapons inspectors have full access to all suspected weapons sites, thus defusing the crisis. President Clinton praised Annan's efforts, accepted the agreement, but promised to keep America's options open if Saddam Hussein violated the agreement in the future.

As Americans worried about another war with Iraq, some of the lingering questions left at the end of the Cold War and the Reagan revolution were being resolved. The American economy would remain steady and continue to drive the world's economic growth. Politics would remain centrist, revolving around the concepts of Johnson's Great Society, as they had once focused on the New Deal, and most politicians would resist expanding the social and economic responsibilities of the federal government. The Cold War was over, but the United States, as the remaining superpower, would not relinquish its role of world leadership. Americans would continue to pursue the American dream of economic and social stability but with an awareness that equal opportunity would not necessarily mean equal outcome. But as American history has shown, expectations have not always led to their expected outcomes—the making of America continues.

SUMMARY

E xpectations
C onstraints
C hoices
O utcomes

Through the 1980s and 1990s, within the context of a changing and slowing economy, social and political tensions in America increased while Democrats and Republicans attempted to establish a set of *choices* that would match the nation's need and *expectations.*

Conservatives and liberals argued heatedly about the morality of the country. From both sides of the political spectrum, activist groups promoted their points of view. Racial and ethnic minorities, gays, and women were among those insisting that government remove discriminatory laws and practices and provide more economic and social opportunities. Conservatives and many moderates argued that too many government programs were already providing special opportunities for minorities and the disadvantaged. Opposed to homosexuality, abortion, and what they considered destructive values, conservatives claimed that American society was too permissive, too preoccupied with sex and violence, and too tolerant of immorality and what they termed "alternative lifestyles." They advocated less government interference in economic and social matters and policy *choices* that stressed "traditional values."

Also widening the divisions within society was the arrival of large numbers of immigrants from Latin America and Asia. Hoping to experience the "American dream," they encountered an economy offering limited *choices,* especially for people with few skills and little education. Tension among minorities grew as competition for jobs and government assistance programs intensified amid reductions of funding for many federal programs. As the social safety net shrank and economic opportunities declined, the *outcome* was that crime, violence, and drug use became epidemic in many urban areas, and some inner cities looked more like battlegrounds than like communities. Conservatives blamed the crisis of the inner cities on the lack of values and the irresponsibility of inner-city residents. Liberals placed the blame on the lack of jobs and educational opportunities.

During the 1992 presidential election, Clinton overcame personal and political *constraints* by focusing on domestic policy. He stressed that he would support changes in American society and improve the economy. Clinton's first administration provided some images of indecisiveness and ineffective leadership but scored some legislative successes. Despite his inexperience and many people's *expectations,* his foreign policy was generally a success. Domestically, he faced more *constraints.* In 1994, Republicans gained control of Congress, and Clinton's *choices* narrowed. After facing down Republicans over the budget, he *chose* to move further to the right, adopting many aspects of Republican plans for the budget and welfare reform. Clinton's political shift, a growing economy, and foreign-policy successes ensured his re-election over Bob Dole. For some, the *outcome* of the 1996 election was a sign that the nation, while moving right of center, had rejected the dismantling of big government and drastic cutbacks in entitlements like Social Security and Medicare. Political observers also noted that the election did not necessarily mean that the public endorsed further federal efforts to improve educational and occupational opportunities or the environment. One political observer noted that "Just as the age of the New Deal is over, so is the age of the sixties. The new millennium will see not only new conflicts but new majorities."

SUGGESTED READINGS

Michael Bernstein, and David A. Adler, eds. *Understanding American Economic Decline* (1994).

A collection of essays by economists and knowledgeable observers who analyze the slowing down of the American economy and its impact.

Colin Campbell, and Bert A. Rockman, eds. *The Clinton Presidency: First Appraisals* (1995).

An informative and speculative group of wide-ranging essays that explore many aspects of Clinton's first years in office and examine broader political issues.

Congressional Quarterly's Research Reports.

A valuable monthly resource for information and views on issues facing the United States and the world.

Roger Daniels. *Coming to America* (1990).

A solid analysis of the new immigrants seeking a place in American society; especially effective on Asian immigration.

David J. Garrow. *Liberty and Sexuality: The Right to Privacy and the Making of Roe v. Wade* (1994).

An in-depth and scholarly account of the origins and impact of *Roe v. Wade* and the legal and political issues dealing with privacy, gender, and abortion.

Randy Shilts. *And the Band Played On: Politics, People and the AIDS Epidemic* (1987).

A compelling book on the AIDS epidemic and the early lack of action by society; written by a victim of AIDS.

Studs Terkel. *The Great Divide* (1988).

An interesting and informative collection of oral interviews that provide a personal glimpse of changes recently taking place in American society.

BIBLIOGRAPHY

Chapter 1 Making a "New" World, to 1558

Marvin B. Becker, *Civility and Society in Western Europe, 1300–1600* (1988); Robert F. Berkhofer, *The White Man's Indian: Images of the American Indian from Columbus to the Present* (1978); George F. Carter, *Earlier Than You Think: A Personal View of Man in America* (1980); Michael D. Coe, *Mexico* (1984); Alfred W. Crosby, Jr., *The Columbian Exchange: Biological and Cultural Consequences of 1492* (1972); Philip Curtin, *The Atlantic Slave Trade: A Census* (1969); Basil Davidson, *The African Genius: An Introduction to African Cultural and Social History* (1969); John H. Elliott, *The Old World and the New, 1492–1650* (1970); Brian M. Fagan, *Kingdoms of Gold, Kingdoms of Jade: The Americas Before Columbus* (1991); J. D. Fage, *An Introduction to the History of West Africa* (1969); Filipe Fernandez-Armesto, *Columbus* (1991); Morton Fried, *The Notion of Tribe* (1975); Stephen Greenblatt, *Marvelous Possession: The Wonder of the New World* (1991); Jack P. Greene, *The Intellectual Construction of America: Exceptionalism and Identity from 1492 to 1800* (1993); Christopher Hill, *Society and Puritanism in Pre-Revolutionary England* (1967); Alvin M. Josephy, *America in 1492: The World of the Indian Peoples Before the Arrival of Columbus* (1992); Alice B. Kehoe, *North American Indians: A Comprehensive Account.* (1992); Karen Ordahl Kupperman, ed., *America in European Consciousness, 1493–1750* (1995); Jay A. Levenson, *Circa 1492: Art in the Age of Exploration* (1991); Calvin Martin, *Keepers of the Game: Indian-Animal Relationships and the Fur Trade* (1978); William H. McNeill, *Plagues and Peoples* (1976); Wallace Notestein, *The English People on the Eve of Colonization, 1603–1630* (1954); Anthony Pagden, *European Encounters with the New World: From Renaissance to Romanticism* (1993); J. H. Parry, *The Age of Reconnaissance: Discovery, Exploration, and Settlement, 1450–1650* (1963); William Phillips, and Carla Phillips, *The Worlds of Christopher Columbus* (1992); David Beers Quinn, *North America from Earliest Discovery to First Settlements: The Norse Voyages to 1612* (1977); Ann R. Raminofsky, *Vectors of Death: The Archaeology of European Contact* (1987); A. L. Rowse, *The Elizabethans and America* (1959); Patricia Seed, *Ceremonies of Possession in Europe's Conquest of the New World, 1492–1640* (1995); Dean Snow, *The Archaeology of North America: American Indians and Their Origins* (1976); Eviatar Zerubavel, *Terra Cognita: The Mental Discovery of America* (1992).

Chapter 2 A Continent on the Move, 1400–1725

Richard Aquila, *The Iroquois Restoration: Iroquois Diplomacy on the Colonial Frontier, 1701–1754* (1997); James Axtell, *The Invasion Within; The Contest of Cultures in Colonial North America* (1985); Lynn Robison Bailey, *Indian Slave Trade in the Southwest; a Study of Slavetaking and the Traffic of Indian Captives* (1966); Jose Antonio Brandao, *Your Fyre Shall Burn No More: Iroquois Policy Towards New France and Its Native Allies to 1701* (1997); Leslie Choquette, *Frenchmen Into Peasants: Modernity and Tradition in the Peopling of French Canada* (1997); Thomas J. Condon, *New York Beginnings; the Commercial Origins of New Netherland* (1968); Charles R. Cutter, *The Protector de Indios in Colonial New Mexico, 1659–1821* (1986); Olive Patricia Dickason, *The Myth of the Savage: And the Beginnings of French Colonialism in the Americas* (1984); W. J. Eccles, *France in America* (1990); R. David Edmunds, and Joseph L. Peyser, *The Fox Wars: The Mesquakie Challenge to New France* (1993); Jack D. Forbes, *Apache, Navaho, and Spaniard* (1994); Bernardo P. Gallegos, *Literacy, Education, and Society in New Mexico, 1693–1821* (1992); Charles Gibson, *Spain in America* (1966); Robert A. Goldstein, *French-Iroquois Diplomatic and Military Relations 1609–1701* (1969); Ramon A. Gutierrez, *When Jesus Came, the Corn Mothers Went Away: Marriage, Sexuality, and Power in New Mexico, 1500–1846* (1991); Paul Horgan, *Conquistadors in North American History* (1963); Robert H. Jackson, *Indian Population Decline: The Missions of Northwestern New Spain, 1687–1840* (1994); Cornelius J. Jaenen, *Friend and Foe: Aspects of French-Amerindian Cultural Contact in the Sixteenth and Seventeenth Centuries* (1976); Elizabeth Ann Harper John, *Storms Brewed in Other Men's Worlds: The Confrontation of Indians, Spanish, and French in the Southwest, 1540–1795* (1996); Susan Lamb, *Pueblo and Mission: Cultural Roots of the Southwest* (1997); Theda Perdue, *Slavery and the Evolution of Cherokee Society, 1540–1866* (1979); Daniel Reff, *Disease, Depopulation, and Culture Change in Northwestern New Spain, 1518–1764* (1911); Oliver A. Rink, *Holland on the Hudson: An Economic and Social History of Dutch New York* (1986); Katherine A. Spielmann, ed., *Farmers, Hunters, and Colonists: Interaction Between the Southwest and the Southern Plains* (1991); John Super, *Food, Conquest, and Colonization in Sixteenth-Century Spanish America* (1988); Bruce G. Trigger, *Natives and Newcomers: Canada's "Heroic Age" Reconsidered* (1985); Marce Trudel, *The Beginnings of New France, 1524–1663* (1973); Daniel H. Usner, Jr., *Indians, Settlers, and Slaves in a Frontier Exchange Economy: The Lower Mississippi Valley Before 1783* (1992); David J. Weber, *The Spanish Frontier in North America* (1992); David J. Weber, *The Taos Trappers: The Fur Trade in the Far Southwest, 1540–1846* (1971).

Chapter 3 Founding the English Mainland Colonies, 1585–1732

James Axtell, *The Invasion Within: The Contest of Cultures in Colonial North America* (1985); Bernard Bailyn, *The New England Merchants in the Seventeenth Century* (1955); Carol Berkin, *First Generations: Women in Colonial America* (1996); Patricia Bonomi, *A Factious People* (1971); Paul Boyer and Stephen Nissenbaum, *Salem Possessed: The Social Origins of Witchcraft* (1974); Timothy Breen, *Puritans and Adventurers* (1980); Jon Butler, *Awash in a Sea of Faith* (1990); Lois Carr and David Jordan, *Maryland's Revolution of Government, 1689–1692*

(1974); David Cressy, *Coming Over: Migration and Communication Between England and New England in the Seventeenth Century* (1987); William Cronon, *Changes in the Land: Indians, Colonists, and the Ecology of New England* (1983); Andrew Delbanco, *The Puritan Ordeal* (1989); John Demos, *Entertaining Satan* (1982); Philip Gura, *A Glimpse of Sion's Glory* (1984); David Hall, *Worlds of Wonder, Days of Judgment* (1990); James Horn, *Adapting to a New World: English Society in the Seventeenth Century Chesapeake* (1994); Michael Kammen, *Colonial New York* (1975); James Lang, *Conquest and Commerce* (1975); Suzanne Lebsock, *A Share of Honor* (1984); James Lemmon, *The Best Poor Man's Country* (1972); Barry Levy, *Quakers and the American Family* (1988); H. T. Merrens, *Colonial North Carolina* (1964); Perry Miller, *Errand into the Wilderness* (1956); Edmund Morgan, *American Slavery, American Freedom* (1975); Mary Beth Norton, *Founding Mothers and Fathers: Gendered Power and the Forming of American Society* (1996); Oliver Rink, *Holland on Hudson* (1986); Frederick Siegel, *The Roots of Southern Distinctiveness* (1987); Kenneth Silverman, *The Life and Times of Cotton Mather* (1984); Harry Stout, *The New England Soul* (1986); Alan Tully, *William Penn's Legacy* (1977); Laurel Ulrich, *Goodwives: Image and Reality in the Lives of Women in Northern New England, 1650–1750* (1982); Robert Weir *Colonial South Carolina* (1983); Betty Wood, *The Origins of American Slavery: Freedom and Bondage in the English Colonies* (1997).

Chapter 4 The English Colonies in the Eighteenth Century, 1700–1763

Fred Anderson, *A People's Army: Massachusetts Soldiers and Society in the Seven Years War* (1984); Bernard Bailyn, *The Origins of American Politics* (1968); Ira Berlin and Philip Morgan, eds., *Cultivation and Culture: Labor and the Shaping of Slave Life in the Americas* (1993); Patricia Bonomi, *Under the Cope of Heaven: Religion, Society, and Politics in Colonial America* (1986); Richard Bushman, *From Puritan to Yankee* (1967); Paul Clemens, *The Atlantic Economy and Colonial Maryland's Eastern Shore: From Tobacco to Grain* (1980); Jean Friedman, *The Enclosed Garden: Women and Community in the Evangelical South* (1985); Philip Greven, *The Protestant Temperament: Patterns of Childrearing, Religious Experience, and the Self in Early America* (1977); James Henretta, *The Evolution of American Society, 1700–1815* (1982); Rhys Isaac, *The Transformation of Virginia, 1740–1790* (1982); Francis Jennings, *Empire of Fortune* (1988); Joan Jensen, *Loosening the Bonds: Mid-Atlantic Farm Women, 1750–1850* (1986); Charles Joyner, *Down by the Riverside: A South Carolina Slave Community* (1984); Susan Juster, *Disorderly Women* (1988); Michael Kammen, *Spheres of Liberty: Changing Perceptions of Liberty in American Culture* (1986); Peter Kolchin, *American Slavery, 1619–1877* (1993); Allan Kulikoff, *Tobacco and Slaves* (1986); Ned Landsman, *Scotland and Its First American Colony* (1985); Daniel Littlefield, *Rice and Slaves: Ethnicity and the Slave Trade in Colonial South Carolina* (1981); James Merrell, *The Indians' New World: Catawbas and Their Neighbors from European Contact Through the Era of Removal* (1989); Marcus Rediker, *Between the Devil and the Deep Blue Sea* (1985); Daniel Richter, *The Ordeal of the Longhouse* (1992); Sharon Salinger, *"To Serve Well and Faithfully": Labor and Indentured Servants in Pennsylvania, 1692–1800* (1987); Michael Sobel, *The World They Made Together: Black and White Values in Eighteenth Century Virginia* (1987); Laurel Ulrich, *Good Wives: Image and Reality in the Lives of Women in Northern New England, 1650–1850* (1982); Stephanie Wolf, *As Various as Their Land: The Everyday Lives of Eighteenth Century Americans* (1993).

Chapter 5 Deciding Where Loyalties Lie, 1763–1776

Bernard Bailyn, *The Ideological Origins of the American Revolution* (1967); Carol Berkin, *Jonathan Sewall: Odessey of An American Loyalist* (1974); Timothy Breen, *Tobacco Culture: The Mentality of the Great Tidewater Planters on the Eve of the Revolution* (1985); Edward Countryman, *The American Revolution* (1985); Thomas Doerflinger, *A Vigorous Spirit of Enterprise: Merchants and Economic Development in Revolutionary Philadelphia* (1986); Marc Egnal, *A Mighty Empire: The Origins of the American Revolution* (1988); Eric Foner, *Tom Paine and Revolutionary America* (1976); Paul Gilje, *The Road to Mobocracy: Popular Disorder in New York City, 1763–1834* (1987); Robert Gross, *The Minutemen and Their World* (1976); Francis Jennings, *Empire of Fortune: Crowns, Colonies and Tribes in the Seven Years War in America* (1988); Linda Kerber, *Women of the Republic: Intellect and Ideology in Revolutionary America* (1980); Pauline Maier, *American Scripture: Making the Declaration of Independence* (1997); Mary Beth Norton, *Liberty's Daughters: The Revolutionary Experience of American Women, 1750–1800* (1980); Paul Rahle, *Republics Ancient and Modern: Republicanism and the American Revolution* (1992); Steven Rosswurm, *Arms, Country, and Class: The Philadelphia Militia and the "Lower Sort" During the American Revolution* (1987); Gordon Wood, *The Radicalism of the American Revolution* (1992).

Chapter 6 Recreating America: Independence and a New Nation, 1775–1783

Bernard Bailyn, *The Ordeal of Thomas Hutchinson* (1974); Carol Berkin, *Jonathan Sewall: Odyssey of an American Loyalist* (1974); Ira Berlin and Ronald Hoffman, eds, *Slavery and Freedom in the Age of the American Revolution* (1983); Jeremy Black, *War for America* (1991); Colin Bonwick, *The American Revolution* (1991); Andrew Cayton, *The Frontier Republic* (1986); Edward Countryman, *The American Revolution* (1985); Edward Countryman, *A People in Revolution: The American Revolution and Political Society in New York, 1760–1790* (1981); Jeffrey Crow and Larry Tise, eds., *The Southern Experience in the American Revolution* (1978); John C. Dann, *The Revolution Remembered: Eyewitness Accounts of the War for Independence* (1980); James Flexner, *George Washington in the American Revolution* (1978); Jay Fliegelman, *Prodigals and Pilgrims* (1982); William Fowler and Wallace Coyle, eds., *The American Revolution: Changing Perspectives* (1979); Sylvia Frey, *Water from the Rock: Black Resistance in a Revolutionary Age* (1991); Barbara Graymont, *The Iroquois in the American Revolution* (1972); Robert Gross, *The Minutemen and Their World* (1976); Ronald Hoffman and Peter Albert, eds., *Women in the Age of the American Revolution* (1989); Michael Kammen, *A Season of Youth* (1978); Linda Kerber, *Women of the Republic: Intellect and*

Ideology in Revolutionary America (1980); Isaac Kramnick, *Republicanism and Bourgeois Radicalism: Political Ideology in Late Eighteenth Century England and America;* Duncan MacLeod, *Slavery, Race, and the American Revolution* (1974); Mary Beth Norton, *Liberty's Daughters* (1980); Mary Beth Norton, *The British-Americans* (1972); James O'Donnell, *Southern Indians in the American Revolution* (1973); Charles Royster, *A Revolutionary People at War: The Continental Army and American Character, 1775–1783* (1980); John Shy, *A People Numerous and Armed: Reflections on the Military Struggle for American Independence* (1976); James Walker, *The Black Loyalists* (1976).

Chapter 7 Competing Visions of a Virtuous Republic, 1770–1796

Joyce Appleby, *Capitalism and a New Social Order* (1984); Lance Banning, *The Jeffersonian Persuasion: The Evolution of a Party Ideology* (1978); Charles Beard, *An Economic Interpretation of the Constitution* (1913); Walker Bern, *Taking the Constitution Seriously* (1987); Richard Buel, Jr., *Securing the Revolution* (1972); Jeanne Boydston, *Home and Work: Housework, Wages and the Ideology of Labor in the Early Republic* (1990); Thomas Curry, *The First Freedom* (1986); David B. Davis, *Slavery in the Age of Revolution* (1975); Stanley Elkins and Eric McKitrick, *The Federalist Era* (1993); Joseph Ellis, *American Sphinx: The Character of Thomas Jefferson* (1997); Max Farrand, ed., *Records of the Federal Convention of 1787* (1911–1937); Richard Hofstadter, *The Idea of a Party System* (1970); Merrill Jensen, *The New Nation: A History of the United States During the Confederation, 1781–1789* (1950); Michael Kammen, *A Machine That Would Go of Itself: The Constitution and American Culture* (1986); Allan Kulikoff, *The Agrarian Origins of American Capitalism* (1992); Staughton Lynd, *Class Conflict, Slavery, and the United States Constitution* (1967); Jackson Turner Main, *The Antifederalists* (1961); Drew McCoy, *The Last of the Fathers: James Madison and the Republican Legacy* (1989); Forrest McDonald, *Novus Ordo Seclorum* (1985); William Miller, *The First Liberty: Religion and the American Republic* (1986); Edmund Morgan, *Inventing the People: The Rise of Popular Sovereignty in England and America* (1988); Thomas Pangle, *The Spirit of Modern Republicanism* (1988); Donald Robinson, *Slavery in the Structure of American Politics, 1765–1820* (1971); Barry Swartz, *George Washington: The Making of a Symbol* (1987); Steven Watts, *The Republic Reborn: War and the Making of Liberal America, 1790–1820* (1987); Gary Wills, Explaining America (1981); Gordon Wood, *The Radicalism of the American Revolution* (1992).

Chapter 8 The Early Republic, 1796–1804

Joyce Appleby, *Capitalism and the New Social Order: The Republican Vision of the 1790s* (1984): Lance Banning, *The Jeffersonian Persuasion: Evolution of a Party Ideology* (1978): Ralph Adams Brown, *The Presidency of John Adams* (1975): Andrew Burnstein, *The Inner Jefferson: Portrait of a Grieving Optimist* (1995): Robert Lowry Clinton, *Marbury v. Madison and Judicial Review* (1989); Noble E. Cunningham, *In Pursuit of Reason: The Life of Thomas Jefferson* (1987); Alexander Deconde, *The Quasi-War: Politics and Diplomacy of the Undeclared War with France, 1797–1801* (1966); Alexander DeConde, *This Affair of Louisiana* (1976); Joseph J. Ellis, *Passionate Sage: The Character and Legacy of John Adams* (1993): Richard Ellis, *The Jeffersonian Crisis: Courts and Politics in the Young Republic* (1974): David H. Fischer, *The Revolution of American Conservatism: The Federalist Party in the Era of Jeffersonian Democracy* (1965); Richard Hofstadter, *The Idea of a Party System: The Rise of Legitimate Opposition in the United States, 1780–1840* (1969); Donald Jackson, *Thomas Jefferson and the Stony Mountains: Exploring the West from Monticello* (1981); Linda Kerber, *Federalists in Dissent: Imagery and Ideology in Jeffersonian America* (1970); Richard Kohn, *Eagle and Sword: The Federalists and the Creation of the Military Establishment in America, 1783–1802* (1975); Ralph Lerner, *The Thinking Revolutionary: Principle and Practice in the New Republic* (1987); David N. Mayer, *The Constitutional Thought of Thomas Jefferson* (1994); Drew McCoy, *The Elusive Republic: Political Economy in Jeffersonian America* (1980); Forrest McDonald, *The Presidency of Thomas Jefferson* (1976); John C. Miller, *The Wolf by the Ears: Thomas Jefferson and Slavery* (1977); Gary B. Nash, *Forging Freedom: The Formation of Philadelphia's Black Community, 1720–1840* (1988); John R. Nelson, Jr., *Liberty and Property: Political Economy and Policymaking in the New Nation, 1787–1812* (1987); Bradford Perkins, *The First Rapprochment: England and the United States, 1795–1805* (1955); Malcolm Rohrbough, *The Trans-Appalachian Frontier; People, Societies, and Institutions, 1775–1850* (1978); James Ronda, *Lewis and Clark Among the Indians* (1984); Ronald Schultz, *The Republic of Labor: Philadelphia Artisans and the Politics of Class, 1720–1830* (1993); Bernard W. Sheehan, *Seeds of Extinction: Jeffersonian Philanthropy and the American Indian* (1973); Herbert E. Sloan, *Principle and Interest: Thomas Jefferson and the Problem of Debt* (1995); James Morton Smith, *Freedom's Fetters: The Alien and Sedition Laws and American Civil Liberties* (1956); Robert W. Tucker and David C. Hendrickson, *Empire of Liberty: The Statecraft of Thomas Jefferson* (1990).

Chapter 9 Increasing Conflict and War, 1805–1814

James M. Banner, *To the Hartford Convention: The Federalists and the Origins of Party Politics in Massachusetts, 1789–1815* (1970); Irving Brant, *James Madison and American Nationalism* (1968); Roger H. Brown, *The Republic in Peril: 1812* (1964); George Chapman, *Chief William McIntosh: A Man of Two Worlds* (1989); Harry L. Coles, *The War of 1812* (1965); R. David Edmunds, *The Shawnee Prophet* (1983); R. David Edmunds, *Tecumseh and the Quest for Indian Leadership* (1984); Clifford L. Egan, *Neither Peace Nor War: Franco-American Relations, 1803–1812* (1983); William F. Fowler, Jr., *Jack Tars and Commodores: The American Navy, 1783–1815* (1984); Benjamin W. Griffith, Jr., *McIntosh and Weatherford, Creek Indian Leaders* (1988); John Denis Haeger, *John Jacob Astor: Business and Finance in the Early Republic* (1991); Donald Hickey, *The War of 1812: A Forgotten Conflict* (1989); Reginald Horsman, *The Causes of the War of 1812* (1962); Reginald Horsman, *The Diplomacy of the New Republic, 1776–1815* (1986); Reginald Horsman, *The War of 1812* (1969); Ralph Ketcham, *James Madison: A Biography* (1971); Jean Gordon Lee, *Philadelphians and the China Trade, 1784–1844* (1984); Drew R. McCoy, *The Last of the Fathers: James Madison and the Republican Legacy* (1989); William G.

McLoughlin, *Cherokee Renascence in the New Republic* (1986); Bradford Perkins, *Prologue to War; England and the United States, 1805–1812* (1968); Julius W. Pratt, *Expansionists of 1812* (1925); Francis Paul Prucha, *The Sword of the Republic: The United States Army on the Frontier, 1783–1846* (1986); James P. Ronda, *Astoria and Empire* (1990); Robert A. Rutland, *Madison's Alternatives: The Jeffersonian Republicans and the Coming of War, 1805–1812* (1975); Robert Allen Rutland, *James Madison, The Founding Father* (1987); Robert Allen Rutland, *The Presidency of James Madison* (1990); J. C. A. Stagg, *Mr. Madison's War; Politics, Diplomacy, and Warfare in the Early American Republic, 1783–1830* (1983); Anthony F. C. Wallace, *Death and Rebirth of the Seneca* (1970); Steven Watts, *The Republic Reborn: War and the Making of Liberal America, 1790–1820* (1987).

Chapter 10 The Rise of a New Nation, 1815–1836

John M. Belonlavek, *"Let the Eagle Soar!" The Foreign Policy of Andrew Jackson* (1985); Lee Benson, *The Concept of Jacksonian Democracy; New York as a Test Case* (1961); Noble E. Cunningham, Jr., *The Presidency of James Monroe* (1996); George Dangerfield, *The Awakening of American Nationalism, 1815–1828* (1965); Richard Ellis, *The Union at Risk: Jacksonian Democracy, States Rights, and the Nullification Crisis* (1987); Michael Feldberg, *The Turbulent Era: Riot and Disorder in Jacksonian America* (1980); Daniel Feller, *The Public Lands in Jacksonian Politics* (1984); Ronald Formisano, *The Transformation of Political Culture: Massachusetts Parties, 1790s–1840s* (1983); Michael D. Green, *The Politics of Indian Removal: Creek Government and Society in Crisis* (1982); Bray Hammond, *Banks and Politics in America from the Revolution to the Civil War* (1957); Mary W. M. Hargreaves, *The Presidency of John Quincy Adams* (1985); Lawrence Frederick Kohl, *The Politics of Individualism: Parties and the American Character in the Jacksonian Era* (1989); Ernest May, *The Making of the Monroe Doctrine* (1975); Richard P. McCormick, *The Second American Party System: Party Formations in the Jacksonian Era* (1966); William McLoughlin, *Cherokees and Missionaries, 1789–1839* (1984); Marvin Meyers, *The Jacksonian Persuasion: Politics and Belief* (1957); Roger L. Nichols, *Black Hawk and the Warrior's Path* (1992); John Niven, *John C. Calhoun and the Price of Union: A Biography* (1988); Edward Pessen, *Jacksonian America: Society, Personality, and Politics* (1978); Francis Paul Prucha, *Broadax and Bayonet: The Role of the United States Army in the Development of the Northwest, 1815–1860* (1995); Jonathan Prude, *The Coming of Industrial Order; Town and Factory Life in Rural Massachusetts, 1810–1860* (1983); Robert V. Remini, *Henry Clay: Statesman for the Union* (1991); Robert V. Remini, *The Life of Andrew Jackson* (1988); Greg Russell, *John Quincy Adams and the Public Virtues of Diplomacy* (1995); Thomas C. Shevory, *John Marshall's Law: Interpretation, Ideology, and Interest* (1994); William Preston Vaughn, *The Antimasonic Party in the United States, 1826–1843* (1983); Anthony F. C. Wallace, *The Long, Bitter Trail: Andrew Jackson and the Indians* (1993); John William Ward, *Andrew Jackson: Symbol for an Age* (1962); Harry L. Watson, *Liberty and Power: The Politics of Jacksonian America* (1990); J. Leitch Wright, *The Only Land They Knew: The Tragic Story of the American Indians in the Old South* (1981).

Chapter 11 The Great Transformation, 1828–1840

Ira Berlin, *Slaves Without Masters: The Free Negro in the Antebellum South* (1974); Henry C. Binford, *The First Suburbs: Residential Communities on the Boston Periphery, 1815–1860* (1985); John Blassingame, *The Slave Community: Plantation Life in the Antebellum South* (1979); Menahem, Blondheim, *News Over the Wires: The Telegraph and the Flow of Public Information in America, 1844–1897* (1994); Stuart M. Blumin, *The Emergence of the Middle Class: Social Experiences in the American City, 1760–1900* (1989); James L. Crouthamel, *Bennett's New York Herald and the Rise of the Popular Press* (1989); Marcus Cunliffe, *Chattel Slavery and Wage Slavery: The Anglo-American Context, 1830–1860* (1979); William C. Davis, *A Way Through the Wilderness: The Natchez Trace and the Civilization of the Southern Frontier* (1995); Thomas Dublin, *Women at Work: The Transformation of Work and Community in Lowell, Massachusetts, 1826–1880* (1979); Clement Eaton, *The Growth of Southern Civilization, 1790–1860* (1961); Christie Anne Farnham, *The Education of the Southern Belle: Higher Education and Student Socialization in the Antebellum South* (1994); Robert W. Fogel, *Without Consent or Contract: The Rise and Fall of American Slavery* (1991); Elizabeth Fox-Genovese, *Within the Plantation Household: Black and White Women of the Old South* (1988); Karen V. Hansen, *A Very Social Time: Crafting Community in Antebellum New England* (1994); Tamara Herevan, and Maris A. Vinovskis, *Family and Population in Nineteenth-Century America* (1978); Marilynn Wood. Hill, *Their Sisters' Keepers: Prostitution in New York City, 1830–1870* (1993); Donald R. Hoke, *Ingenious Yankees: The Rise of the American System of Manufactures in the Private Sector* (1990); David J. Jeremy, *Transatlantic Industrial Revolution: The Diffusion of Textile Technology Between Britain and America, 1790–1830* (1981); Peter R. Knights, *Yankee Destinies: The Lives of Ordinary Nineteenth-Century Bostonians* (1991); Suzanne Lebsock, *Free Women of Petersburg: Status and Culture in a Southern Town, 1784–1860* (1984); Donald G. Mathews, *Religion in the Old South* (1977); Stephanie McCurry, *Masters of Small Worlds: Yeoman Households, Gender Relations, and the Political Culture of the Antebellum South Carolina Low Country* (1995); Sally McMillen, *Motherhood in the Old South: Pregnancy, Childbirth, and Infant Rearing* (1990); James Oakes, *The Ruling Race: A History of American Slaveholders* (1982); W. J. Rorabaugh, *The Craft Apprentice: From Franklin to the Machine Age in America* (1986); Kenneth A. Scherzer, *The Unbounded Community: Neighborhood Life and Social Structure in New York City, 1830–1875* (1992); Charles G. Sellers, *The Market Revolution: Jacksonian America, 1815–1846* (1991); Ronald E. Shaw, *Canals for a Nation: The Canal Era in the United States, 1790–1860* (1990); Christine Stansell, *City of Women: Sex and Class in New York, 1789–1860* (1986); Theodore Steinberg, *Nature Incorporated: Industrialization and the Waters of New England* (1991); Susan J. Tracy, *In the Master's Eye: Representations of Women, Blacks, and Poor Whites in Antebellum Southern Literature* (1995).

Chapter 12 Responses to the Great Transformation

Melvin L. Adelman, *A Sporting Time: New York City and the Rise of Modern Athletics, 1820–1870* (1986); Michael Barkun, *Crucible of the Millennium: The Burned-Over District of New York in the 1840s*

(1986); R. J. M. Blackett, *Building an Antislavery Wall: Black Americans in the Atlantic Abolitionist Movement, 1830–1860* (1983); Jeanne Boydston, *Home and Work: Housework, Wages, and the Ideology of Labor in the Early Republic* (1990); Paul S. Boyer, *Urban Masses and Moral Order in America, 1820–1920* (1978); Richard J. Carwardine, *Evangelicals and Politics in Antebellum America* (1993); Judith Wragg Chase, *Afro-American Art and Craft* (1971); Frances B. Cogan, *All-American Girl: The Ideal of Real Womanhood in Mid-Nineteenth-Century America* (1989); Janet Duitsman Cornelius, *"When I Can Read My Title Clear": Literacy, Slavery, and Religion in the Antebellum South* (1991); Lawrence A. Cremin, *American Education: The National Experience, 1783–1786* (1980); Jay P. Dolan, *The Immigrant Church: New York's Irish and German Catholics, 1815–1865* (1975); Dena J. Epstein, *Sinful Tunes and Spirituals: Black Folk Music to the Civil War* (1977); Lawrence Foster, *Religion and Sexuality: Three American Communal Experiments of the Nineteenth Century* (1981); Jenny Franchot, *Roads to Rome: The Antebellum Protestant Encounter with Catholicism* (1994); Mark Y. Hanley, *Beyond a Christian Commonwealth: The Protestant Quarrel with the American Republic, 1830–1860* (1994); Nathan O. Hatch, *The Democratization of American Christianity* (1990); T. Walter. Herbert, *Dearest Beloved: The Hawthornes and the Making of the Middle-Class Family* (1993); James Oliver Horton, *Free People of Color: Inside the African American Community* (1993); Daniel Walker Howe, *The Political Culture of the American Whigs* (1979); Paul E. Johnson, *A Shopkeepers' Millennium: Society and Revivals in Rochester, New York, 1815–1837* (1978); Carl F. Kaestle, *Pillars of the Republic: Common Schools and American Society, 1780–1860* (1983); Roger Lane, *Violent Death in the City: Suicide, Accident, and Murder in Nineteenth-Century Philadelphia* (1979); Gerda Lerner, *The Grimké Sisters from South Carolina: Pioneers for Women's Rights and Abolition* (1971); W. David Lewis, *From Newgate to Dannemora: The Rise of the Penitentiary in New York, 1796–1948* (1965); Eric Lott, *Love and Theft: Blackface Minstrels and the American Working Class* (1993); Steven Mintz, *Moralists and Modernizers: America's Pre–Civil War Reformers* (1995); Stephen B. Oates, *The Fires of Jubilee: Nat Turner's Fierce Rebellion* (1975); Lewis Perry, *Boats Against the Current: American Culture Between Revolution and Modernity, 1820–1860* (1993); Edward Pessen, *Most Uncommon Jacksonians: The Radical Leaders of the Early Labor Movement* (1967); Merrill D. Peterson, *The Great Triumvierate: Webster, Clay, and Calhoun* (1987); Charles E. Rosenberg, *The Care of Strangers: The Rise of America's Hospital System* (1987); Katherine Kish Sklar, *Catherine Beecher: A Study in American Domesticity* (1973); Richard B. Stott, *Workers in the Metropolis: Class, Ethnicity, and Youth in Antebellum New York City* (1990); Ian Tyrrell, *Sobering Up: From Temperance to Prohibition in Antebellum America, 1800–1860* (1979); Sean Wilentz, *Chants Democratic: New York City and the Rise of the American Working Class, 1788–1850* (1984); Major L. Wilson, *The Presidency of Martin Van Buren* (1984); Kenneth H. Winn, *Exiles in a Land of Liberty: Mormons in America, 1830–1846* (1989); Bryan Jay Wolf, *Romantic Re-Vision: Culture and Consciousness in Nineteenth-Century American Painting and Literature* (1982); David A. Zonderman, *Aspirations and Anxieties: New England Workers and the Mechanized Factory System, 1815–1850* (1992).

Chapter 13 Expansion, Nationalism, and Rising Tensions, 1840–1849

Paul Bergeron, *The Presidency of James K. Polk* (1987); Ray Allen Billington, *The Far Western Frontier, 1830–1860* (1956); Gene M. Brack, *Mexico Views Manifest Destiny, 1821–1846: An Essay on the Origins of the Mexican War* (1976); Newell. Bringhurst, *Brigham Young and the Expanding American Frontier* (1986); Joan E. Cashin, *A Family Venture: Men and Women on the Southern Frontier* (1991); Malcolm Clark, Jr., *Eden Seekers: The Settlement of Oregon, 1818–1862* (1981); Thomas D. Clark and John D. W. Guice, *Frontiers in Conflict: The Old Southwest, 1795–1830* (1989); William Cronon, *Nature's Metropolis: Chicago and the Great West* (1991); Coy F. Cross, II, *Go West Young Man! Horace Greeley's Vision for America* (1995); John Mack Faragher, *Women and Men on the Overland Trail* (1979); John Mack Faragher, *Sugar Creek: Life on the Illinois Prairies* (1986); Paul Wallace Gates, *The Farmer's Age: Agriculture, 1815–1860* (1960); James R. Gibson, *Otter Skins, Boston Ships, and China Goods: The Maritime Fur Trade of the Northwest Coast, 1785–1841* (1992); Richard Griswold del Castillo, *The Treaty of Guadalupe Hidalgo: A Legacy of Conflict* (1990); Neal Harlow, *California Conquered: The Annexation of a Mexican Province, 1846–1850* (1982); Thomas R. Hietala, *Manifest Design: Anxious Aggrandizement in Late Jacksonian America* (1985); Sylvia D. Hoffert, *When Hens Crow: The Woman's Rights Movement in Antebellum America* (1995); Reginald Horsman, *Race and Manifest Destiny: The Origins of American Racial Anglo-Saxonism* (1981); Julie Roy Jeffrey, *Frontier Women: The Trans-Mississippi West, 1840–1880* (1979); Theodore J. Karamanski, *Fur Trade and Exploration: Opening the Far Northwest, 1821–1852* (1983); Laurie F. Maffly-Kipp, *Religion and Society in Frontier California* (1994); Timothy M. Matovina, *Tejano Religion and Ethnicity: San Antonio, 1821–1860* (1995); Frederick Merk, *Manifest Destiny and Mission in American History; A Reinterpretation* (1963); Chaplain W. Morrison, *Democratic Politics and Sectionalism: The Wilmot Proviso* (1967); Stanley Noyes, *Los Comanches: The Horse People, 1751–1845* (1993); Norman Lois Peterson, *The Presidencies of William Henry Harrison and John Tyler* (1989); David Pletcher, *The Diplomacy of Annexation: Texas, Oregon, and the Mexican War* (1973); Catherine. Price, *The Oglala People, 1841–1879: A Political History* (1996); Karen Sánchez-Eppler, *Touching Liberty: Abolition, Feminism, and the Politics of the Body* (1993); John H. Schroeder, *Mr. Polk's War: American Opposition and Dissent, 1846–1848* (1973); Henry Nash Smith, *Virgin Land: The American West as Symbol and Myth* (1950); John E. Sunder, *The Fur Trade on the Upper Missouri, 1840–1865* (1993); David J. Weber, *The Mexican Frontier, 1821–1846: The American Southwest Under Mexico* (1982); Albert K Weinberg, *Manifest Destiny: A Study of Nationalist Expansionism in American History* (1958).

Chapter 14 Sectional Conflict and Shattered Union, 1850–1861

Tyler Anbinder, *Nativism and Slavery: The Northern Know Nothings and the Politics of the 1850s* (1992); Eugene H. Berwanger, *The Frontier Against Slavery: Western Anti-Negro Prejudice and the Slavery Extension Controversy* (1967); James D. Bilotta, *Race and the Rise of the Republican Party,*

1848–1865 (1992); Frederick J. Blue, *The Free Soilers: Third Party Politics, 1848–1854* (1973); Stanley W. Campbell, *The Slave Catchers: Enforcement of the Fugitive Slave Law, 1850–1860* (1970); William J. Cooper, *The South and the Politics of Slavery, 1828–1856* (1978); Daniel W. Crofts, *Reluctant Confederates: Upper South Unionists in the Secession Crisis* (1989); Merton L. Dillon, *Slavery Attacked: Southern Slaves and Their Allies, 1619–1865* (1991); Donald Fehrenbacher, *Slavery, Law, and Politics: The Dred Scott Case in Historical Perspective* (1981); Eric Foner, *Free Soil, Free Labor, Free Men; The Ideology of the Republican Party Before the Civil War* (1970); Lacy K. Ford, Jr., *Origins of Southern Radicalism: The South Carolina Upcountry, 1800–1860* (1988); Ronald P. Formisano, *The Birth of Mass Political Parties: Michigan, 1827–1861* (1971); George M. Fredrickson, *The Black Image in the White Mind: The Debate on Afro-American Character and Destiny, 1817–1914* (1971); William W. Freehling, *The Road to Disunion* (1990); Lawrence J. Friedman, *Gregarious Saints: Self and Community in American Abolitionism, 1830–1870* (1982); Eugene D. Genovese, *The Slaveholders' Dilemma: Freedom and Progress in Southern Conservative Thought, 1820–1860* (1992); William Gienapp, *Origins of the Republican Party, 1852–1856* (1987); Stanley Harrold, *The Abolitionists and the South, 1831–1861* (1995); Michael Holt, *The Political Crisis of the 1850s* (1970); Robert W. Johannsen, *Stephen Douglas* (1973); Paul Kleppner, *The Third Electoral System, 1853–1892: Parties, Voters, and Political Cultures* (1979); Daniel J. McInerney, *The Fortunate Heirs of Freedom: Abolition and Republican Thought* (1994); Russell B. Nye, *Fettered Freedom; Civil Liberties and the Slavery Controversy, 1830–1860* (1949); Stephen Oates, *To Purge This Land With Blood: A Biography of John Brown* (1970); James A. Rawley, *Race & Politics: "Bleeding Kansas" and the Coming of the Civil War* (1969); Richard Sewell, *Ballots for Freedom: Antislavery Politics in the United States, 1837–1865* (1976); Joel H. Silbey, *The Partisan Imperative: The Dynamics of American Politics Before the Civil War* (1984); Elbert B. Smith, *The Presidency of James Buchanan* (1975); Mitchell Snay, *Gospel of Disunion: Religion and Separatism in the Antebellum South* (1993); Mark W. Summers, *The Plundering Generation: Corruption and the Crisis of the Union, 1849–1861* (1987); John L. Thomas, *The Liberator, William Lloyd Garrison, a Biography* (1963); Larry E. Tise, *Proslavery: A History of the Defense of Slavery in America, 1701–1840* (1987); Wendy Hamand Venet, *Neither Ballots Nor Bullets: Women Abolitionists and the Civil War* (1991); Ronald G. Walters, *The Antislavery Appeal: American Abolitionism After 1830* (1977); James A. Ward, *Railroads and the Character of America, 1820–1887* (1986); Ralph Wooster, *The Secession Conventions of the South* (1962); Bertram. Wyatt-Brown, *Yankee Saints and Southern Sinners* (1985); David. Zarefsky, *Lincoln, Douglas, and Slavery: In the Crucible of Public Debate* (1990).

Chapter 15 A Violent Choice, 1861–1865

David W. Blight, *Frederick Douglass' Civil War: Keeping Faith in Jubilee* (1989); Gabor S. Boritt, *Lincoln and the Economics of the American Dream* (1978); Dudley Taylor Cornish, *The Sable Arm: Negro Troops in the Union Army, 1861–1865* (1966); David P. Crook, *The North, The South, and the Powers, 1861–1865* (1974); Richard N. Current, *Lincoln's Loyalists: Union Soldiers from the Confederacy* (1992); Leonard P. Curry, *Blueprint for Modern America: Non-Military Legislation of the First Civil War Congress* (1968); William C. Davis, *Jefferson Davis: The Man and His Hour* (1991); David Herbert Donald, *Why the North Won the Civil War* (1960); David Herbert Donald, *Lincoln* (1995); Robert F. Durden, *The Gray and the Black: The Confederate Debate on Emancipation* (1972); Clement Eaton, *A History of the Southern Confederacy* (1954); Paul D. Escott, *After Secession: Jefferson Davis and the Failure of Confederate Nationalism* (1978); Byron Farwell, *Stonewall: A Biography of General Thomas J. Jackson* (1992); Michael Fellman, *Citizen Sherman: A Life of William Tecumseh Sherman* (1995); James W. Geary, *We Need Men: The Northern Draft in the Civil War* (1991); Joseph T. Glatthaar, *Forged in Battle: The Civil War Alliance, Black Soldiers and White Officers* (1990); Randall C. Jimerson, *The Private Civil War: Popular Thought During the Sectional Conflict* (1988); Robert W. Johannsen, *Lincoln, The South, and Slavery: The Political Dimension* (1991); Archer Jones, *Civil War Command and Strategy: The Process of Victory and Defeat* (1992); Alvin M. Josephy, Jr., *The Civil War in the American West* (1991); Gerald F. Linderman, *Embattled Courage: The Experience of Combat in the American Civil War* (1989); Ella Lonn, *Desertion During the Civil War* (1928); Mary Elizabeth Massey, *Refugee Life in the Confederacy* (1964); James M. McPherson, *Abraham Lincoln and the Second American Revolution* (1990); James M. McPherson, *The Negro's Civil War: How American Negroes Felt and Acted* (1965); James M. McPherson, *Why the Confederacy Lost* (1992); James H. Moorhead, *American Apocalypse: Yankee Protestants and the Civil War, 1860–1869* (1978); Mark E. Neely, Jr., *The Fate of Liberty: Abraham Lincoln and Civil Liberties* (1991); Mark E. Neely, Jr., *The Last Best Hope of Earth: Abraham Lincoln and the Promise of America* (1993); Alan T. Nolan, *Lee Considered: General Robert E. Lee and Civil War History* (1991); Frank L. Owsley, *State Rights in the Confederacy* (1925); George C. Rable, *Civil Wars: Women and the Crisis of Southern Nationalism* (1989); James L. Roark, *Masters Without Slaves: Southern Planters in the Civil War and Reconstruction* (1977); Charles Royster, *The Destructive War: William Tecumseh Sherman, Stonewall Jackson, and the Americans* (1991); Joel Silbey, *A Respectable Minority: The Democratic Party in the Civil War Era* (1977); Emory M. Thomas, *The Confederacy as a Revolutionary Experience* (1971); Emory M. Thomas, *The Confederate Nation, 1861–1865* (1979); Emory M. Thomas, *Robert E. Lee: A Biography* (1995); Robert M. Utley, *Frontiersmen in Blue: The United States Army and the Indian, 1848–1865* (1981); Garry Wills, *Lincoln at Gettysburg: The Words That Remade America* (1992); Steven E. Woodworth, *Jefferson Davis and His Generals: The American Civil War in the West* (1990); Agatha Young, *Women and the Crisis: Women of the North in the Civil War* (1959).

Chapter 16 Reconstruction: High Hopes and Broken Dreams, 1865–1877

Herman Belz, *Emancipation and Equal Rights: Politics and Constitutionalism in the Civil War Era* (1978); Michael Les Benedict, *The Impeachment and Trial of Andrew Johnson* (1973); Albert E. Castel, *The Presidency of Andrew Johnson* (1979); LaWanda C. Cox, *Freedom, Racism, and Reconstruction* (1997); Laura F. Edwards, *Gendered Strife and Confusion: The Political*

Culture of Reconstruction (1997); John Hope Franklin, *Reconstruction: After the Civil War* (1961); John Hope Franklin and Alfred A. Moss, Jr., *From Slavery to Freedom: A History of Negro Americans,* 6th ed. (1988); Herbert G. Gutman, *The Black Family in Slavery and Freedom* (1976); William C. Harris, *With Charity for All: Lincoln and the Restoration of the Union* (1997); Harold M. Hyman and William M. Wiecek, *Equal Justice Under Law: Constitutional Development, 1835–1875* (1982); Jacqueline Jones, *Labor of Love, Labor of Sorrow: Black Women, Work and the Family, from Slavery to the Present* (1985); William S. McFeely, *Grant: A Biography* (1981); Martin E. Mantell, *Johnson, Grant, and the Politics of Reconstruction* (1973); Eric L. McKitrick, *Andrew Johnson and Reconstruction* (1960; reprint, 1988); James M. McPherson, *Ordeal by Fire: Reconstruction* (1982); David Montgomery, *Beyond Equality: Labor and the Radical Republicans, 1862–1872* (1967); Michael Perman, *Emancipation and Reconstruction, 1862–1879* (1987); Keith I. Polakoff, *The Politics of Inertia: The Election of 1876 and the End of Reconstruction* (1973); Roger L. Ransom and Richard Sutch, *One Kind of Freedom: The Economic Consequences of Emancipation* (1977); John David Smith, *Black Voices from Reconstruction, 1865–1877* (1996); Hans Louis Trefousse, *Andrew Johnson: A Biography* (1989); Hans Louis Trefousse, *Impeachment of a President: Andrew Johnson, the Blacks, and Reconstruction* (1975); Allen W. Trelease, *White Terror: The Ku Klux Klan Conspiracy and Southern Reconstruction* (1971, reprint 1995); Vernon Lane Wharton, *The Negro in Mississippi: 1865–1890* (1965; reprint, 1974); Forrest G. Wood, *The Era of Reconstruction, 1863–1877* (1975); C. Vann Woodward, *Reunion and Reaction: The Compromise of 1877 and the End of Reconstruction,* rev. ed. (1956); C. Vann Woodward, *Origins of the New South, 1877–1913* (1951).

Chapter 17 Survival of the Fittest: Entrepreneurs and Workers in Industrial America, 1865–1900

Ralph Andreano, ed., *The Economic Impact of the Civil War,* rev. ed. (1967); Paul Avrich, *The Haymarket Tragedy* (1984); Robert V. Bruce, *1877: Year of Violence* (1959); David F. Burg, *Chicago's White City of 1893* (1976); Vincent P. Carosso, *The Morgans: Private International Bankers, 1854–1913* (1987); Alfred D. Chandler, Jr., with Takashi Hikino, *Scale and Scope: The Dynamics of Industrial Capitalism* (1990); Alfred D. Chandler, Jr., *The Essential Alfred Chandler: Essays Toward a Historical Theory of Big Business,* ed. by Thomas K. McCraw (1988); Alfred D. Chandler, ed., *The Railroads: The Nation's First Big Business* (1965); Thomas C. Cochran, *American Business in the Twentieth Century* (1972); Thomas C. Cochran and William Miller, *The Age of Enterprise: A Social History of Industrial America,* rev. ed. (1961); Carl N. Degler, *In Search of Human Nature: The Decline and Revival of Darwinism in American Social Thought* (1991); Melvyn Dubofsky, *Industrialism and the American Worker, 1865–1920,* 3rd ed. (1996); Leon Fink, *Workingmen's Democracy: The Knights of Labor and American Politics* (1983); Robert Fogel, *Railroads and American Economic Growth* (1965); John A. Garraty, *The New Commonwealth, 1877–1890* (1968); Peter George, *The Emergence of Industrial America: Strategic Factors in American Economic Growth Since 1870* (1982); Louis M. Hacker, *The World of Andrew Carnegie: 1865–1901* (1968); Robert L. Heilbroner, *The Economic Transformation of America* (1977); Matthew Josephson, *The Robber Barons: The Great American Capitalists, 1861–1901* (1934; reprint, 1962); Alice Kessler-Harris, *Out to Work: A History of Wage-Earning Women in the United States* (1982); Edward Chase Kirkland, *Industry Comes of Age: Business, Labor, and Public Policy, 1860–1897* (1961); Harold C. Livesay, *Andrew Carnegie and the Rise of Big Business* (1975); David Montgomery, *Workers' Control in America* (1979); Daniel Nelson, *Managers and Workers: Origins of the New Factory System in the United States, 1880–1920* (1975); Allan Nevins, *Study in Power: John D. Rockefeller, Industrialist and Philanthropist,* 2 vols. (1953); Robert Rydell, *All the World's a Fair: Visions of Empire at American International Expositions, 1876–1916* (1984); Nick Salvatore, *Eugene V. Debs: Citizen and Socialist* (1982); Fred A. Shannon, *The Farmer's Last Frontier: Agriculture, 1860–1897* (1945); Stephan Thernstrom, *Poverty and Progress: Social Mobility in a Nineteenth Century City* (1964); Harold G. Vatter, *The Drive to Industrial Maturity: The U.S. Economy, 1860–1914* (1975).

Chapter 18 Conflict and Change in the West, 1865–1902

Albert Camarillo, *Chicanos in a Changing Society: From Mexican Pueblos to American Barrios in Santa Barbara and Southern California, 1848–1930* (1979); Sucheng Chan, *Asian Californians* (1991); Sarah Deutsch, *No Separate Refuge: Culture, Class, and Gender on an Anglo-Hispanic Frontier in the American Southwest, 1880–1940* (1987); Everett Dick, *The Sod-House Frontier, 1854–1890* (1954); Robert R. Dykstra, *The Cattle Towns* (1968); Juan Gómez-Quiñones, *Roots of Chicano Politics, 1600–1940* (1994); Wesley S. Griswold, *A Work of Giants: Building the First Transcontinental Railroad* (1962); Richard Griswold del Castillo, *The Los Angeles Barrio, 1850–1890* (1979); Frederick E. Hoxie, *A Final Promise: The Campaign to Assimilate the Indians, 1880–1920* (1984); William Issel and Robert W. Cherny, *San Francisco, 1865–1932: Politics, Power, and Urban Development* (1986); William L. Kahrl, *Water and Power: The Conflict over Los Angeles' Water Supply in the Owens Valley* (1982); Clyde A. Milner II, ed., *A New Significance: Re-envisioning the History of the American West* (1996); Douglas Monroy, *Thrown Among Strangers: The Making of Mexican Culture in Frontier California* (1990); Sandra L. Myres, *Westering Women and the Frontier Experience, 1800–1915* (1982); Victor G. Nee and Brett de Barry Nee, *Longtime Californ': A Documentary History of an American Chinatown* (1972, 1973; reprint, 1986); Donald Pisani, *From the Family Farm to Agribusiness: The Irrigation Crusade in California and the West, 1850–1934* (1984); Leonard Pitt, *The Decline of the Californios: A Social History of the Spanish-Speaking Californians, 1846–1890* (1971); Earl Pomeroy, *The Pacific Slope: A History of California, Oregon, Washington, Idaho, Utah, and Nevada* (1965); Francis Prucha, *The Churches and the Indian Schools, 1888–1912* (1979); Francis Prucha, *American Indian Policy in Crisis: Christian Reformers and the Indian, 1865–1900* (1975); Glenda Riley, *The Female Frontier: A Comparative View of Women on the Prairie and the Plains* (1988); Robert C. Ritchie and Paul Andrew Hutton, eds., *Frontier and Region* (1997); Joseph G. Rosa, *Age of the Gunfighter* (1995); Fred A. Shannon, *The Farmer's Last Frontier: Agriculture, 1860–1897* (1945); Ronald Takaki, *Strangers from the Different Shore* (1989);

Quintard Taylor, *In Search of the Racial Frontier: African Americans in the American West, 1528–1900* (1998); Robert M. Utley, *The Indian Frontier of the American West, 1846–1890* (1984); Robert M. Utley, *The Lance and the Shield: The Life and Times of Sitting Bull* (1993); Walter Prescott Webb, *The Great Plains* (1931); Donald Worster, *Rivers of Empire: Water, Aridity, and the Growth of the American West* (1985).

Chapter 19 The New Social Patterns of Gilded Age America, 1865–1900

Edward L. Ayers, *The Promise of the New South: Life After Reconstruction* (1992); Karen J. Blair, *The Clubwoman as Feminist: True Womanhood Redefined, 1868–1914* (1980); John E. Bodnar, *The Transplanted: A History of Immigrants in Urban America* (1985); Ruth Bordin, *Frances Willard: A Biography* (1986); George Chauncy, *Gay New York* (1994); Lawrence Arthur Cremin, *American Education: The Metropolitan Experience, 1876–1980* (1988); Thomas J. Curran, *Xenophobia and Immigration, 1820–1930* (1975); Roger Daniels, *Not Like Us: Immigrants and Minorities in America, 1890–1924* (1997); Allen F. Davis, *American Heroine: The Life and Legend of Jane Addams* (1973); John D'Emilio and Estelle B. Freedman, *Intimate Matters: A History of Sexuality in America* (1988); Peter Gammond, *Scott Joplin and the Ragtime Era* (1975); John A. Garraty, *The New Commonwealth, 1877–1890* (1968); William H. Gerdts, *American Impressionism* (1984); Lynn D. Gordon, *Gender and Higher Education in the Progressive Era* (1990); David F. Greenberg, *The Construction of Homosexuality* (1988); David C. Hammack, *Power and Society: Greater New York at the Turn of the Century* (1982); Louis R. Harlan, *Booker T. Washington: The Making of a Black Leader, 1856–1901* (1972); Kenneth T. Jackson, *Crabgrass Frontier: The Suburbanization of the United States* (1985); Jonathan Ned Katz, ed., *Gay American History:* Lesbians and Gay Men in the U.S.A.: A Documentary History, rev. ed. (1992); A. T. Lane, *Solidarity of Survival? American Labor and European Immigrants: 1830–1924* (1987); Lawrence W. Levine, *Highbrow/Lowbrow: The Emergence of Cultural Hierarchy in America* (1988); Eric H. Monkkonen, *America Becomes Urban: The Development of U.S. Cities and Towns, 1780–1980* (1988); Regina Markell Morantz-Sanchez, *Sympathy and Science: Women Physicians in American Medicine* (1985); H. Wayne Morgan, ed., *Victorian Culture in America, 1865–1914* (1973); Bernard B. Perlman *Painters of the Ashcan School: The Immortal Eight* (1979); Steven Riess, *Sport in Industrial America, 1850–1920* (1995); Lewis O. Saum, *The Popular Mood of America, 1860–1890* (1990); Thomas J. Schlereth, *Victorian America: Transformations in Everyday Life, 1876–1915* (1991); Robert A. Slayton, *Back of the Yards: The Making of a Local Democracy* (1986); Louise L. Stevenson, *The Victorian Homefront: American Thought and Culture, 1860–1880* (1991); Jon C. Teaford, *The Unheralded Triumph: City Government in America, 1870–1900* (1984); David Ward, *Cities and Immigrants: A Geography of Change in Nineteenth Century America* (1971); Ida B. Wells-Barnett, *Crusade for Justice: The Autobiography of Ida B. Wells*, edited by Alfreda M. Duster (1970); Mark Wyman, *Round-trip to America: The Immigrants Return to Europe, 1880–1930* (1993).

Chapter 20 Political Stalemate and Political Upheaval, 1868–1900

Walter Dean Burnham, *Critical Elections and the Mainsprings of American Politics* (1970); Paolo E. Coletta, *William Jennings Bryan*, 3 vols. (1964–1969); Carl N. Degler, *The Age of the Economic Revolution, 1876–1900*, 2d ed. (1977); Justus D. Doenecke, *The Presidencies of James A. Garfield and Chester A. Arthur* (1981); Eleanor Flexner, *Century of Struggle: The Woman's Rights Movement in the United States*, rev. ed., 1996; Milton Friedman and Anna Jacobson Schwartz, *A Monetary History of the United States, 1867–1960* (1963); John A. Garraty, *The New Commonwealth, 1877–1890* (1968); Paul W. Glad, *McKinley, Bryan, and the People* (1964, rpt. 1991); Lewis L. Gould, *The Presidency of William McKinley* (1980); Samuel P. Hays, "Political Parties and the Community-Society Continuum," in W. N. Chambers and W. D. Burnham, eds., *The American Party Systems: Stages of Political Development*, 2d ed. (1975); John D. Hicks, *The Populist Revolt: A History of the Farmers' Alliance and the People's Party* (1931); Charles Hoffman, *The Depression of the Nineties: An Economic History* (1970); Ari Hoogenboom, *Outlawing the Spoils: A History of the Civil Service Reform Movement* (1961); Ari Hoogenboom, *Rutherford B. Hayes: Warrior and President* (1995); Stanley L. Jones, *The Presidential Election of 1896* (1964); Michael Kazin, *The Populist Persuasion: An American History* (1995); Paul Kleppner, *The Third Electoral System, 1853–1892: Parties, Voters, and Political Cultures* (1979); Suzanne M. Marilley, *Woman Suffrage and the Origins of Liberal Feminism in the United States, 1820–1920* (1996); Richard L. McCormick, *The Party Period and Public Policy: American Politics from the Age of Jackson to the Progressive Era* (1986); Robert C. McMath, Jr., *American Populism: A Social History, 1877–1898* (1993); Horace Samuel Merrill, *Bourbon Leader: Grover Cleveland and the Democratic Party* (1957); H. Wayne Morgan, *William McKinley and His America* (1963); Nell Irvin Painter, *Standing at Armageddon: The United States, 1877–1919* (1987); Norman Pollack, ed., *The Populist Mind* (1967); Carlos A. Schwantes, *Coxey's Army: An American Odyssey* (1985); Theda Skocpol, *Protecting Soldiers and Mothers: The Politics of Social Provision in the United States* (1992); Homer E. Socolofsky and Allan B. Spetter, *The Presidency of Benjamin Harrison* (1987); Xi Wang, *The Trial of Democracy: Black Suffrage and Northern Republicans, 1860–1910* (1997); Richard E. Welch, Jr., *The Presidencies of Grover Cleveland* (1988); R. Hal Williams, *Years of Decision: American Politics in the 1890s* (1978).

Chapter 21 Becoming a World Power: America and World Affairs, 1865–1913

Robert L. Beisner, *Twelve Against Empire: The Anti-Imperialists, 1898–1900* (1968); Richard H. Collin, *Theodore Roosevelt: Culture, Diplomacy, and Expansion* (1985); John M. Dobson, *Reticent Expansionism: The Foreign Policy of William McKinley* (1988); Justus D. Doenecke, *The Presidencies of James A. Garfield and Chester A. Arthur* (1981); Willard B. Gatewood, *Black Americans and the White Man's Burden, 1898–1903* (1975); Lewis L. Gould, *The Presidency of Theodore Roosevelt* (1991); Lewis L. Gould, *The Presidency of William McKinley* (1980); David Healy, *U.S. Expansionism: The Imperialist Urge in the 1890s* (1970); Ari Hoogenboom, *The Presidency of Rutherford B. Hayes* (1988); Jerry Israel, *Progressivism and the Open Door: America and China,*

1905–1921 (1971); Paul M. Kennedy, *The Samoan Tangle: A Study in Anglo-German–American Relations, 1878–1900* (1974); Walter LaFeber, *Inevitable Revolutions: The United States in Central America,* rev. ed. (1993); Gerald F. Linderman, *The Mirror of War: American Society and the Spanish-American War* (1974); T. J. McCormick, *China Market: America's Quest for Informal Empire* (1967); Alfred Thayer Mahan, *The Influence of Seapower upon History, 1660–1783* (1890, rpt., 1957); C. Roland Marchand, *The American Peace Movement and Social Reform, 1898–1918* (1972); Ernest R. May, *American Imperialism: A Speculative Essay* (1968); Ernest R. May, *Imperial Democracy: The Emergence of America as a Great Power* (1961, rpt. 1973); H. Wayne Morgan, *America's Road to Empire: The War with Spain and Overseas Expansion* (1965); H. Wayne Morgan, ed., *The Gilded Age,* rev. ed. (1970); H. Wayne Morgan, *William McKinley and His America,* (1963); Thomas J. Osborne, *"Empire Can Wait": American Opposition to Hawaiian Annexation, 1893–1898* (1981); Thomas G. Paterson and Stephen G. Rabe, eds., *Imperial Surge: The United States Abroad, the 1890s–Early 1900s* (1992); Bradford Perkins, *The Great Rapprochement: England and the United States, 1895–1914* (1968); Dexter Perkins, *A History of the Monroe Doctrine* (1963); Milton Plesur, *America's Outward Thrust: Approaches to Foreign Affairs, 1865–1900* (1971); Julius W. Pratt, *Expanionists of 1898* (1936); Emily S. Rosenberg, *Spreading the American Dream: American Economic and Cultural Expansion, 1890–1945* (1982); Homer E. Socolofsky and Allan B. Spetter, *The Presidency of Benjamin Harrison* (1987); E. Berkeley Tompkins, *Anti-Imperialism in the United States: The Great Debate, 1890–1920* (1970); Richard E. Welch, Jr., *The Presidencies of Grover Cleveland* (1988); Richard E. Welch, Jr., *Response to Imperialism: The United States and the Philippine-American War, 1899–1902* (1979); William Appleman Williams, *The Roots of the Modern American Empire* (1969); Marilyn Blatt Young, *The Rhetoric of Empire: American China Policy, 1895–1901* (1968).

Chapter 22 The Progressive Era, 1900–1917

Paula Baker, The Domestication of Politics: Women and American Political Society, 1780–1920." *American Historical Review* 89 (1984): 620–647; Jack S. Blocker, Jr., *Retreat from Reform: The Prohibition Movement in the United States, 1890–1913* (1976); John Morton Blum, *The Republican Roosevelt,* 2d ed. (1977); Ruth Bordin, *Women and Temperance: The Quest for Power and Liberty, 1873–1900* (1980); H. W. Brands, *T.R.: The Last Romantic* (1997); Elisabeth Clemens, *The People's Lobby: Organizational Innovation and the Rise of Interest Group Politics in the United States, 1890–1925* (1997); Kendrick A. Clements, *The Presidency of Woodrow Wilson* (1992); Steven J. Diner, *A Very Different Age: Americans of the Progressive Era* (1998); Ellen DuBois, *Harriot Stanton Blatch and the Winning of Woman Suffrage* (1997); Louis Filler, *Appointment at Armageddon: Muckraking and Progressivism in the American Tradition,* ref. edn. (1996); Noralee Frankel and Nancy S. Dye, eds., *Gender, Class, Race, and Reform in the Progressive Era* (1991); Linda Gordon, *Woman's Body, Woman's Right: Birth Control in America,* rev. ed. (1990); Lewis L. Gould, *The Presidency of Theodore Roosevelt* (1991); Lewis L. Gould, *Reform and Regulation: American Politics from Roosevelt to Wilson,* 3rd ed. (1996); Louis R. Harlan, *Booker T. Washington: The Wizard of Tuskegee, 1901–1915* (1983); Samuel P. Hays, *Conservation and the Gospel of Efficiency* (1959); Samuel P. Hays, *American Political History as Social Analysis* (1980); Ari and Olive Hoogenboom, *A History of the ICC: From Panacea to Palliative* (1976); Arthur S. Link, *Woodrow Wilson,* 5 vols. (1947–1965); Richard Coke Lower, *A Bloc of One: The Political Career of Hiram W. Johnson* (1993); Richard L. McCormick, *The Party Period and Public Policy: American Politics from the Age of Jackson to the Progressive Era* (1986); Michael E. McGerr, *The Decline of Popular Politics: The American North, 1865–1928* (1986); Manning Marable, *W. E. B. Du Bois: Black Radical Democrat* (1986); Sally M. Miller, *Victor Berger and the Promise of Constructive Socialism, 1910–1920* (1973); Daniel Rodgers, "In Search of Progressivism." *Reviews in American History* 10 (Dec. 1982): 113–132; Nick Salvatore, *Eugene V. Debs: Citizen and Socialist* (1982); Stanley K. Schultz, *Constructing Urban Culture: American Cities and City Planning, 1880–1920* (1989); Melvin I. Urofsky, *Louis D. Brandeis and the Progressive Tradition* (1981); Robert H. Wiebe, *The Search for Order, 1877–1920* (1967); William H. Wilson, *The City Beautiful Movement* (1989).

Chapter 23 America and the World, 1913–1920

Lloyd E. Ambrosius, *Woodrow Wilson and the American Diplomatic Tradition: The Treaty Fight in Perspective* (1987); Arthur E. Barbeau and Florette Henri, *The Unknown Soldiers: Black American Troops in World War I* (1974); W. J. Breen, *Uncle Sam at Home: Civilian Mobilization, Wartime Federalism, and the Council of National Defense, 1917–1919* (1984); David Brody, *Labor in Crisis: The Steel Strike of 1919* (1965); John Whiteclay Chambers II, *To Raise an Army: The Draft Comes to Modern America* (1987); Kendrick A. Clements, *William Jennings Bryan: Missionary Isolationist* (1982); Edward M. Coffman, *The War to End All Wars: The American Military Experience in World War I* (1986); Jean Conner, *The National War Labor Board* (1983); John Milton Cooper, Jr., *The Vanity of Power: American Isolationism and World War I* (1969); Patrick Devlin, *Too Proud to Fight: Woodrow Wilson's Neutrality* (1974); Robert H. Ferrell, *Woodrow Wilson and World War I, 1917–1921* (1985); Mark T. Gilderhus, *Diplomacy and Revolution: U.S.-Mexican Relations Under Wilson and Carranza* (1977); Maurine Weiner Greenwald, *War and Work: The Impact of World War I on Women Workers in the United States* (1980); Edward Haley, *Revolution and Intervention: The Diplomacy of Taft and Wilson in Mexico, 1910–1917* (1970); Ellis Hawley, *The Great War and the Search for a Modern Order,* 2nd ed. (1997); D. Clayton James and Anne Sharp Wells, *America and the Great War, 1914–1920* (1998); Robert Johnson, *The Peace Progressives and American Foreign Relations* (1995); David M. Kennedy, *Over Here: The First World War and American Society* (1980); Thomas J. Knock, *To End All Wars: Woodrow Wilson and the Creation of the League of Nations* (1992); David D. Lee, *Sergeant York: An American Hero* (1985); C. Roland Marchand, *The American Peace Movement and Social Reform, 1898–1918* (1972); Ernest R. May, *The World War and American Isolation, 1914–1917* (1959); Arno J. Mayer, *Politics and Diplomacy of Peacemaking: Containment and Counterrevolution at Versailles, 1918–1919* (1967); Joseph A. McCartin, *Labor's Great War: The Struggle for Industrial Democracy and the Origins of Modern American Labor Relations, 1912–1921* (1997); Paul L. Murphy, *World War I and the Origin of Civil Liberties in the United States* (1979); Robert K. Murray,

Red Scare: A Study in National Hysteria, 1919–1920 (1955, rpt. 1964); Ruth Rosen, *The Lost Sisterhood: Prostitution in America, 1900–1918* (1982); Francis Russell, *A City in Terror, 1919: The Boston Police Strike* (1975); William M. Tuttle, *Race Riot: Chicago in the Red Summer of 1919* (1970); Stephen Vaughn, *Holding Fast the Inner Lines: Democracy, Nationalism, and the Committee on Public Information* (1980); James Weinstein, *The Decline of Socialism in America; 1912–1925* (1967, rpt. 1984); William C. Widenor, *Henry Cabot Lodge and the Search for an American Foreign Policy* (1980).

Chapter 24 The 1920s, 1920–1928

Carl Abbott, *Urban America in the Modern Age* (1987); William J. Barber, *From New Era to New Deal: Herbert Hoover, the Economists, and American Economic Policy, 1921–1933* (1985); Elliott Barkan, *And Still They Come: Immigrants and American Society, 1920 to the 1990s* (1996); Daniel H. Borus, ed., *These United States: Portraits of America from the 1920s* (1992); David Burner, *The Politics of Provincialism: The Democratic Party in Transition, 1919–1932* (1968); Paul A. Carter, *The Twenties in America,* 2d ed. (1987); E. David Cronon, *Black Moses: The Story of Marcus Garvey and the Universal Negro Improvement Association,* 2d ed. (1969); Lyle W. Dorset, *Billy Sunday and the Redemption of Urban America* (1991); Martin Bauml Duberman, *Paul Robeson: A Biography* (1989); Martin Bauml Duberman, Martha Vicinus, and George Chauney, Jr., eds., *Hidden From History: Reclaiming the Gay and Lesbian Past* (1989); Lynn Dumenil, *The Modern Temper: American Culture and Society in the 1920s* (1995); Richard Wrightman Fox and T. J. Jackson Lears, eds., *The Culture of Consumption: Critical Essays in American History, 1880–1980* (1983); Linda Gordon, *Woman's Body, Woman's Right: Birth Control in America,* rev. ed. (1990); Edward Jablonski, *Gershwin* (1987); Kenneth T. Jackson, *The Ku Klux Klan in the City, 1915–1930* (1967); Harvey Klehr and John Earl Haynes, *The American Communist Movement: Storming Heaven Itself* (1992); Peter Iverson, *"We Are Still Here": American Indians in the Twentieth Century* (1998); David L. Lewis, *When Harlem Was in Vogue* (1981); Robert S. Lynd and Helen M. Lynd, *Middletown* (1929); Roland Marchand, *Advertising the American Dream: Making Way for Modernity, 1920–1940* (1985); Gerald D. Nash, *A. P. Giannini and the Bank of America* (1992); Arnold Rampersad, *The Life of Langston Hughes,* 2 vols. (1986, 1988); Arthur M. Schlesinger, Jr., *The Crisis of the Old Order, 1919–1933* (1957); Arnold Shaw, *The Jazz Age: Popular Music in the 1920's* (1987); Robert Sobel, *The Great Bull Market: Wall Street in the 1920s* (1968); Ferenc Szasz, *The Divided Mind of Protestant America, 1880–1930* (1982); Jerry R. Tompkins, *D-Days at Dayton* (1965); Eugene R. Trani and David L. Wilson, *The Presidency of Warren G. Harding* (1977); Bernard A. Weisberger, *The Dream Maker: William C. Durant, Founder of General Motors* (1979); Robert H. Zieger, *American Workers, American Unions, 1920–1985* (1986).

Chapter 25 From Good Times to Hard Times, 1920–1932

Francisco Balderrama and Raymond Rodriguez, *Decade of Betrayal: Mexican Repatriation in the 1930s* (1995); Julia Kirk Blackwelder, *Women of the Depression: Caste and Culture in San Antonio, 1929–1939* (1984); David Burner, *Herbert Hoover: The Public Life* (1978); Dan T. Carter, *Scottsboro* (1969); Roger Daniels, *The Bonus March* (1971); Charles DeBenedetti, *Origins of the Modern American Peace Movement, 1915–1929* (1978); Paula Elder, *Governor Alfred E. Smith: The Politician as Reformer* (1983); Ethan Ellis, *Republican Foreign Policy, 1921–1933* (1968); Milton Friedman and Anna Schwartz, *The Great Contraction, 1929–1933* (1965); John Kenneth Galbraith, *The Great Crash, 1929* (1961); Cheryl L. Greenberg, *"Or Does It Explode?" Black Harlem in the Great Depression* (1991); David Hamilton, *From New Day to New Deal: American Farm Policy from Hoover to Roosevelt, 1928–1933* (1991); Lois Rita Helmbold, "Beyond the Family Economy: Black and White Working-Class Women During the Great Depression," *Feminist Studies,* 13 (Fall 1987); A. Iriye, *After Imperialism: The Search for New Order in the Far East, 1921–1931* (1965); Donald L. Lisio, *Hoover, Blacks, and Lily-Whites* (1985); Neil Macaulay, *The Sandino Affair* (1985); William Mullins, *The Depression and the Urban West Coast, 1929–1933* (1991); James S. Olson, *Herbert Hoover and the Reconstruction Finance Corporation, 1931–1933* (1977); Richard Pells, *Radical Visions and American Dreams: Culture and Social Thought in the Depression Years* (1973); Emily Rosenberg, *Spreading the American Dream* (1982); Louis Schraf, *To Work and to Wed: Female Employment and the Great Depression* (1980); Vicki Ruiz, *Cannery Women, Cannery Lives: Mexican Women, Unionization and the California Food Processing Industry, 1930–1950* (1987); John Shover, *Cornbelt Rebellion: The Farmers' Holiday Association* (1965); Bernard Sternsher, ed., *Hitting Home: The Great Depression in Town and Country* (1989); Peter Timim: *Did Monetary Forces Cause the Great Depression?* (1976); Susan Ware, *Holding Their Own: American Women in the Thirties* (1982); Joan Hoff Wilson, *American Business and Foreign Policy, 1920–1933* (1968); Donald Worster, *Dust Bowl: The Southern Plains in the 1930s* (1979).

Chapter 26 The New Deal, 1933–1940

Anthony Badger, *The New Deal: The Depression Years, 1933–1940* (1989); Ann Banks, ed., *First Person America* (1980); William J. Barber, *Designs Within Disorder: Franklin D. Roosevelt, the Economists, and the Shaping of American Economic Policy* (1996); John Barnard, *Walter Reuther and the Rise of the Auto Workers* (1983); Edward D. Berkowitz, *America's Welfare State: From Roosevelt to Reagan* (1991); Irving Bernstein, *A Caring Society: The New Deal, The Worker, and the Great Depression* (1985); Gary D. Best, *Pride, Prejudice, and Politics: Roosevelt Versus Recovery, 1933–1938* (1990); Roger Biles, *A New Deal for the American People* (1991); Julia Kirk Blackwelder, *No Hiring: The Feminization of Work in the United States, 1900–1995* (1997); Alan Brinkley, *Voices of the Protest: Huey Long, Father Coughlin, and the Great Depression* (1982); William U. Chandler, *The Myth of the TVA: Conservation and Development in the Tennessee Valley, 1933–1983* (1984); Kenneth S. Davis, *FDR: Into the Storm, 1937–1940: A History* (1993); Kenneth S. Davis, *FDR: The New Deal Years, 1933–1937* (1986); Sidney Fine, *Sit-Down: The General Motors Strike of 1936–1937* (1969); Colin Gordon, *New Deals: Business, Labor, and Politics in America* (1994); Peter Iverson, *"We Are Still Here:" American Indians in the Twentieth Century* (1998); James Gregory, *American Exodus: The Dust Bowl Migration and the Okie*

Culture in California (1989); Lawrence C. Kelley, *The Assault on Assimilation: John Collier and the Origins of Indian Policy Reform* (1983); Roy Lubove, *The Struggle for Social Security* (1968); Robert S. McElvaine, ed., *Down and Out in the Great Depression: Letters from the Forgotten Man* (1983); Patrick J. Maney, *The Roosevelt Presence: A Biography of Franklin Delano Roosevelt* (1992); George McJimsey, *Harry Hopkins* (1987); Jerre Mangione, *The Dream and the Deal: The Federal Writers' Project, 1935–1943* (1972); David Milton, *The Politics of U.S. Labor: From the Great Depression to the New Deal* (1980); James T. Patterson, *Congressional Conservatism and the New Deal* (1967); Kenneth Philip, *John Collier's Crusade for Indian Reform, 1920–1945* (1977); David Plotke, *Building a Democratic Political Order: Reshaping American Liberalism in the 1930s and 1940s* (1996); Theodore Saloutos, *The American Farmer and the New Deal* (1982); Lois Schraf, *Eleanor Roosevelt: First Lady of American Liberalism* (1987); Harvard Sitkoff, ed., *Fifty Years Later: The New Deal Evaluated* (1985); Catherine Stock, *Main Street in Crisis: The Great Depression and the Old Middle Class on the Northern Plains* (1992); Patricia Sullivan, *Days of Hope: Race and Democracy in the New Deal Era* (1996); Devra Weber, *Dark Sweat, White Gold: California Farm Workers, Cotton, and the New Deal* (1994); Nancy J. Weiss, *Farewell to the Party of Lincoln: Black Politics in the Age of FDR* (1983).

Chapter 27 America's Rise to World Leadership, 1933–1945

Stephen E. Ambrose, *D-Day, June 6, 1944* (1994); Allen Berube, *Coming Out Under Fire: The History of Gay Men and Women in World War II* (1990); Dorothy Borg and Shumpei Okamoto, eds., *Pearl Harbor as History* (1973); David Brinkley, *Washington Goes to War* (1988); Dominic J. Capeci, Jr., *Race Relations in Wartime Detroit: The Sojourner Truth Housing Controversy of 1942* (1984); Wayne Cole, *Roosevelt and the Isolationists* (1983); John Costello, *Virtue Under Fire: How World War II Changed Our Social and Sexual Attitudes* (1985); Lyn Crost, *Honor by Fire: Japanese Americans at War in Europe and the Pacific* (1994); Thomas Doherty, *Projections of War: Hollywood, American Culture, and World War II* (1993); Lewis A. Erenberg and Susan Hirsch, eds., *The War in American Culture: Society and Consciousness During World War II* (1996); Henry L. Feingold, *The Politics of Rescue: The Roosevelt Administration and the Holocaust, 1938–1945* (1970); Irwin F. Gellman, *The Good Neighbor Diplomacy: United States Policies in Latin America, 1933–1945* (1979); Susan Hartmann, *The Homefront and Beyond: American Women in the 1940s* (1982); Waldo H. Heinrichs, Jr., *Threshold of War* (1988); Akira Iriye, *Power and Culture: The Japanese-American War, 1941–1945* (1981); Nelson Lichtenstein, *Labor's War at Home: The CIO in World War II* (1983); Gerald D. Nash, *The American West Transformed: The Impact of the Second World War* (1985); Judy B. Litoff, *We're in This War Too: World War II Letters of American Women in Uniform* (1994); Neil R. McMillen, ed., *Remaking Dixie: The Impact of World War II on the American South* (1997); Verne W. Newton, ed., *FDR and the Holocaust* (1995); William O'Neill, *A Democracy at War: America's Fight at Home and Abroad in World War II* (1993); Richard Polenberg, *War and Society: The United States, 1941–1945* (1972); Richard Rhodes, *The Making of the Atomic Bomb* (1987); Ronald Schaffer, *Wings of Judgment: American Bombing in World War II* (1985); Martin Sherman, *A World Destroyed* (1975); Michael Sherry, *In the Shadow of War: The United States Since the 1930s* (1995); John R. Skates, *The Invasion of Japan: Alternative to the Bomb* (1994); Gaddis Smith, *American Diplomacy During the Second World War* (1965); Mark Stoler, "A Half Century of Conflict: Interpretations of World War II Diplomacy," *Diplomatic History* 18 (Summer 1994): 375–403; Susan C. Taylor, *Jewel of the Desert: Japanese American Internment at Topaz* (1994); Studs Terkel, *The Good War: An Oral History of World War Two* (1984); Jonathan Utley, *Going to War with Japan* (1985); Harold G. Vetter, *The U.S. Economy in World War II* (1985); Allen E. Winkler, *Home Front U.S.A.: America During World War II* (1986); David S. Wyman, *The Abandonment of the Jews* (1984); Neil A. Wynn, *The Afro-American and the Second World War* (1975).

Chapter 28 Truman and Cold War America, 1945–1952

Jack S. Ballard, *The Shock of Peace: Military and Economic Demobilization after World War II* (1983); William C. Berman, *The Politics of Civil Rights in the Truman Administration* (1970); Dorothy Borg and Waldo Heinrichs, eds., *Uncertain Years: Chinese-American Relations, 1947–1950* (1980); Paul Boyer, *By the Bomb's Early Light: American Thought and Culture at the Dawn of the Atomic Age* (1985); Kevin Boyle, *The UAW and the Heyday of American Liberalism* (1995); Richard M. Dalfiume, *Desegregation of the U.S. Armed Forces* (1969); Robert J. Donovan, *The Tumultuous Years: the Presidency of Harry S Truman, 1949–1953* (1982); Robert Griffith, *The Politics of Fear: Joseph R. McCarthy and the Senate* (1987); John L. Gaddis, *Strategies of Containment* (1982); John L. Gaddis, *We Now Know: Rethinking Cold War History* (1997); Herbert J. Gans, *The Levittowners* (1967); William S. Graebner, *The Age of Doubt: American Thought and Culture in the 1940s* (1991); John Halliday and Bruce Cummings, *Korea: The Unknown War* (1987); Alonzo Hamby, *Man of the People: A Life of Harry S Truman* (1995); Susan Hartman, *Truman and the 80th Congress* (1971); Gregory Herken, *The Winning Weapon* (1981); Michael Hogan, *The Marshall Plan* (1987); Kenneth T. Jackson, *Crabgrass Frontiers: the Suburbanization of the United States* (1985); Landon Y. Jones, *Great Expectations: America and the Baby Boom Generation* (1980); Burton Kaufman, *The Arab Middle East and the United States: Inter-Arab Rivalry and Superpower Diplomacy* (1996); Donald Katz, *Home Fires: An Intimate Portrait of One Middle-Class Family in Postwar America* (1992); Barbara Kelly, *Expanding the American Dream: Building and Rebuilding Levittown* (1993); Melvyn Leffler, *A Preponderance of Power* (1991); George Lipsitz, *A Rainbow at Midnight: Labor and Culture in the 1940s* (1994); Allen J. Matusow, *Farm Policies and Politics in the Truman Years* (1967); Elaine Tyler May, *Homeward Bound: American Families in the Cold War Era* (1988); William O'Neil, *American High: The Years of Confidence 1945–1960* (1986); David M. Oshinsky, *A Conspiracy So Immense: The World of Joseph McCarthy* (1983); Thomas G. Paterson, *On Every Front: The Making and Unmaking of the Cold War* (1992); James T. Patterson, *Grand Expectations: The United States, 1945–1974* (1996); Arnold Rampersad, *Jackie Robinson* (1997); Gary W. Reichard, *Politics as Usual* (1988); Michael Schaller, *The American Occupation of Japan: The Origins of the Cold War in Asia* (1985); Ellen W. Schrenker, *The Age of McCarthyism* (1994); Athan Theoharis and John S. Cox, *The Boss: J. Edgar Hoover and the Great American Inquisition* (1988).

Chapter 29 Quest for Consensus, 1952–1960

Charles C. Alexander, *Holding the Line* (1985); H. W. Brands, Jr., *Cold Warriors* (1988); Wini Breines, *Young, White, and Miserable: Growing Up Female in the Fifties* (1992); Taylor Branch, *Parting the Water: America in the King Years, 1954–1963* (1988); Larry W. Burt, *Tribalism in Crisis: Federal Indian Policy, 1953–1961* (1982); Willard W. Cochrane and Mary E. Ryan, *American Farm Policy, 1948–1973* (1976); John D'Emilio, and Estelle B. Freedman, *Intimate Matters: A History of Sexuality in America* (1988); Robert A. Devine, *Blowing in the Wind: The Nuclear Test Ban Debate* (1978); Robert A. Devine, *The Sputnik Challenge* (1993); Saki Dockrill, *Eisenhower's New Look National Security Policy, 1953–1961* (1996); Barbara Ehrenreich, *Hearts of Men* (1983); Robert Fishamn, *Bourgeois Utopias* (1987); Donald I. Fixico, *Termination and Relocation: Federal Indian Policy, 1945–1970* (1986); Lloyd Gardner, *Approaching Vietnam* (1988); William Graebner, *Coming of Age in Buffalo* (1990); Fred I. Greenstein, *The Hidden-Hand Presidency* (1982); Richard G. Hewlett and Jack M. Hall, *Atoms for Peace and War* (1989); Alice Kessler-Harris, *Out to Work: A History of Wage-Earning Women in the United States* (1982); Nicholas Lemann, *The Promised Land* (1991); George Lipsitz, *Time Passages: Collective Memory and American Popular Culture* (1991); Victory Marchetti and John D. Marks, *The CIA and the Cult of Intelligence* (1974); Karal Ann Marling, *As Seen on TV: The Visual Culture of Everyday Life in the 1950s* (1994); Waldo Martin, Jr., *Brown v. Board of Education: A Brief History with Documents* (1998); Martin E. Marty, *Modern American Religion, Vol. 3: Under God, Indivisible, 1941–1960* (1996); Joan Meyerowitz, ed., *Not June Cleaver: Women and Gender in Postwar America* (1994); Richard H. Pells, *The Liberal Mind in a Conservative Age* (1983); William Pickett, *Dwight David Eisenhower and American Power* (1995); Stephen G. Rabe, *Eisenhower and Latin America* (1988); Mark H. Rose, *Interstate* (1979); John W. Sloan, *Eisenhower and the Management of Prosperity* (1991); Jane Smith, *Patenting the Sun: Polio and the Salk Vaccine* (1990); John C. Teaford, *The Twentieth Century City* (1993); Mark V. Tushnet, *Making Civil Rights Law: Thurgood Marshall and the Supreme Court, 1936–1961* (1995); John Tytell, *Naked Angels: The Lives and Literature of the Beat Generation* (1976); Alan Winkler, *Life Under A Cloud: American Anxiety About the Atom* (1993).

Chapter 30 Great Promises, Bitter Disappointments, 1960–1968

Jervis Anderson, *Bayard Rustin: Troubles I've Seen* (1997); Terry Anderson, *The Movement and the Sixties* (1995); Alexander Bloom, ed., *'Takin' It to the Streets: A Sixties Reader* (1995); Vaughn Bornet, *The Presidency of Lyndon B. Johnson* (1983); David Burner, *John F. Kennedy and a New Generation* (1988); Eric Burner, *And Gently He Shall Lead Them: Robert Parris Moses and Civil Rights in Mississippi* (1994); David Chalmers, *And the Crooked Places Made Straight: The Struggle for Social Change in the 1960s* (1991); Claude Andrew Clegg III, *An Original Man: The Life and Times of Elijah Muhammad* (1997); David Farber, *The Age of Great Dreams: America in the 1960s* (1994); Alexander Fursendo and Timothy Naftali, *"One Hell of a Gamble": Khrushchev, Castro, and Kennedy, 1958–1964* (1998); David Garrow, *Protest at Selma: Martin Luther King and the Voting Rights Act of 1965* (1978); Paula Giddings and Cornel West, *Regarding Malcolm X* (1994); James Giglio, *The Presidency of John F. Kennedy* (1991); Hugh Davis Graham, *The Civil Rights Era: Origins and Development of National Policy, 1960–1972* (1990); Richard D. Mahoney, *JFK: Ordeal in Africa* (1983); Allen Matusow, *The Unraveling of America: A History of Liberalism in the 1960s* (1984); James Miller, *"Democracy Is in the Streets"—From Port Huron to the Siege at Chicago* (1987); Charles Murray, *Losing Ground: American Social Policy, 1950–1980* (1984); Thomas Paterson, *Confronting Castro: The United States and the Triumph of the Cuban Revolution* (1994); Thomas Paterson, ed., *Kennedy's Quest for Victory: American Foreign Policy, 1961–1963* (1989); Thomas C. Reeves, *President Kennedy: Profile of Power* (1994); Theodore Roszak, *The Making of the Counterculture* (1969); Thomas Schoenbaum, *Waging Peace and War: Dean Rusk in the Truman, Kennedy, and Johnson Years* (1988); Bernard Schwartz, *Super Chief: Earl Warren and His Supreme Court* (1983); John E. Schwartz, *America's Hidden Success: A Reassessment of Twenty Years of Public Policy* (1983); Jay Stevens, *Storming Heaven: LSD and the American Dream* (1987); Barbara L. Tischler, ed., *Sights on the Sixties* (1992); Irwin Unger, *The Movement: A History of the American New Left, 1959–1972* (1974); Melvin Urofsky, *The Continuity of Change: The Supreme Court and Individual Liberties, 1953–1986* (1991); Robert Weisbrot, *Freedom Bound: A History of America's Civil Rights Movement* (1991).

Chapter 31 America Under Stress, 1960–1975

Rodolfo F. Acuna, *Community Under Seige: A Chronicle of Chicanos East of the Los Angeles River, 1945–1975* (1984); Stephen Ambrose, *Nixon: The Triumph of the Politician, 1962–1972* (1990); Larry Berman, *Lyndon Johnson's War* (1989); Robert Buzzanco, *Masters of War: Military Dissent and Politics in Vietnam* (1996); H. W. Brand, *The Wages of Globalism: Lyndon Johnson and the Limits of American Power* (1995); Larry Cable, *Unholy Grail* (1991); Peter Caroll, *It Seemed Like Nothing Happened* (1982); Vine Deloria, Jr., *Custer Died for Your Sins* (1969); Robert Devine, *The Johnson Years, Volumes 1–3* (1981, 1987, 1994); Juan Gomez-Quinones, *Chicano Politics: Reality and Promise, 1940–1990* (1990); Richard Griswold de Castillo and Richard A. Garcia, *Cesar Chavez: A Triumph of Spirit* (1995); H. R. Haldeman, *The Haldeman Diaries: Inside the Nixon White House* (1994); Seymour Hersh, *The Price of Power: Kissinger in the Nixon White House* (1983); Troy R. Johnson, *The Occupation of Alcatraz Island: Indian Self-Determination and the Rise of American Activism* (1996); Blanche Linden-Ward and Carol Hurd Green, *American Women in the 1960s* (1993); Kim McQuaid, *The Anxious Years: America in the Vietnam and Watergate Era* (1989); Marguerite V. Marin, *Social Protest in an Urban Barrio: A Study of the Chicano Movement, 1966–1974* (1991); George D. Moss, *Vietnam: An American Ordeal* (1994); Carlos Munoz, Jr., *Youth, Identity, Power: The Chicano Movement* (1989); Armando Navarro, *Mexican American Youth Organization: Avant-Garde of the Chicano Movement in Texas* (1995); Richard Nixon, *RN: The Memoirs of Richard Nixon* (1978); James S. Olson and Randy Roberts, *My Lai: A Brief History with Documents* (1998);

Herbert Parmet, *The World and Richard Nixon* (1990); Vicki L. Ruiz, *From Out of the Shadows: Mexican Women in 20th Century America* (1997); Kirkpatrick Sales, *The Green Revolution: The American Environmental Movement, 1962–1992* (1996); Deborah Shapely, *Promise and Power: The Life and Times of Robert McNamara* (1993); Neil Sheehan, *A Bright Shining Lie: John Paul Vann and America in Vietnam* (1988); Melvin Small, *Johnson, Nixon, and the Doves* (1988); Ronald Spector, *After Tet: The Bloodiest Year in Vietnam* (1992); Steven J. Spiegel, *The Other Arab-Israeli Conflict: Making America's Middle East Policy from Truman to Reagan* (1985); Bob Woodward and Carl Bernstein, *All the President's Men* (1974); Daniel Yergin, *The Prize* (1991).

Chapter 32 Facing Limits, 1974–1991

William Berman, *America's Right Turn: From Nixon to Bush* (1994); John A. Booth and Thomas W. Walker, *Understanding Central America* (1989); Peter G. Bourne, *Jimmy Carter: A Comprehensive Biography from Plains to Post-Presidency* (1997); Paul Boyer, ed., *Reagan as President* (1990); Connie Bruck, *The Predator's Ball: The Junk Bond Raiders and the Man Who Staked Them* (1988); Dan Carter, *From George Wallace to Newt Gingrich: Race in the Conservative Counterrevolution, 1963–1994* (1996); Michael Duffy and Daniel Goodgame, *Marching in Place: The Status Quo Presidency of George Bush* (1992); Paul Dukes, *The Last Great Game* (1989); John Dumbrell, *American Foreign Policy: Carter to Clinton* (1997); Carol Felsenthal, *The Sweetheart of the Silent Majority* (1981); Lawrence Freedman and Efraim Karsh, *The Gulf Conflict, 1990–1992* (1993); Raymond Gartoff, *The Great Transition: American Soviet Relations and the End of the Cold War* (1994); John R. Greene, *The Presidency of Gerald R. Ford* (1995); William E. Griffth, ed., *Central and Eastern Europe: The Opening Curtain* (1989); Samuel P. Hays, *Beauty, Health, and Permanence: Environmental Politics in the United States, 1955–1985* (1987); Michael J. Hogan, *The Panama Canal in American Politics* (1986); Haynes Johnson, *Sleepwalking Through History: America in the Reagan Years* (1991); Charles O. Jones, *The Trusteeship Presidency: Jimmy Carter and the United States Congress* (1988); Harold H. Koh, *The National Security Constitution* (1990); Walter LaFeber, *The Panama Canal* (1989); Robert S. Leiken, ed., *Central America: Anatomy of Conflict* (1984); Robert C. Liberman and Robert Wuthnow, eds., *The New Christian Right* (1983); Theodore Lowi, *The End of the Republican Era* (1995); Donald Mabry, ed., *The Latin American Narcotics Trade* (1992); David Mervin, *George Bush and the Guardianship Presidency* (1996); John Palmer and Elizabeth Sawmill, eds., *The Reagan Record* (1984); William B. Quandt, *Camp David* (1986); T. S. Reid, *The Chip* (1985); Herbert D. Rosenbaum and Alexi Ugrinsky, eds. *The Presidency and Domestic Policies of Jimmy Carter* (1993); Robert Scheer, *With Enough Shovels* (1982); Peter Scott and Jonathan Marshall, *Cocaine Politics: Drugs, Armies, and the CIA in Central America* (1991); Laurence H. Shoup, *The Carter Presidency and Beyond* (1980); Allan P. Sindler, *Bakke, DeFunis, and the Minority Admissions* (1978); Philip Slater, *Earthwalk* (1974); Gaddis Smith, *Morality, Reason, and Power* (1986); James B. Stewart, *Den of Thieves* (1991); Strobe Talbot, *Deadly Gambits* (1984); John Kenneth White, *The New Politics of Old Values* (1988); Clyde Wilcox, *Onward Christian Soldiers: The Religious Right in American Politics* (1996); John Woodridge, *The Evangelicals* (1975).

Chapter 33 Making New Choices, 1986–1998

Dan Balz and Ronald Brownstein, *Storming the Gates: Protest Politics and the Republican Revival* (1996); Frank Bean and Marta Tienda, *The Hispanic Population of the United States* (1988); David Bender and Bruno Leane, *Abortion: Opposing Viewpoints* (1997); Susan K. Cahn, *Coming on Strong: Gender and Sexuality in 20th-Century Sport* (1994); Ruth Colker, *Abortion and Dialogue: Pro-Choice, Pro-Life, and American Law* (1992); Donald T. Crithlow, ed., *The Politics of Abortion and Birth Control in Historical Perspective* (1996); W. Avon Drake and Robert D. Holsworth, *Affirmative Action and the Stalled Quest for Black Progress* (1996); Leslie W. Dunbar, ed., *Minority Report: What Has Happened to Blacks, Hispanics, American Indians, and Other Minorities in the Eighties* (1984); Barbara Ehrenreich, *The Worst Years of Our Lives* (1990); Herbert Gans, *The War Against the Poor: The Underclass and Anti-Poverty Policy* (1995); Nathan Glazer, ed., *Clamor at the Gates: The New American Immigration* (1986); James D. Hunter, *Culture Wars: The Struggle to Define America* (1991); Michael Katz, *The Undeserving Poor: From the War on Poverty to the War on Welfare* (1989); Jonathan Kozol, *Rachael and Her Children: Homeless Families in America* (1988); Elliot Liebow, *Tell Them Who I Am: The Lives of Homeless Women* (1993); John Longone, *AIDS: The Facts* (1988); Manhattan Institute and Pacific Research Institute, *Strangers at Our Gate: Immigration in the 1990s* (1994); David Maraniss, *First In His Class: A Biography of Bill Clinton* (1995); Robert Morris, *Partners in Power: The Clintons and Their America* (1996); Michael Nelson, ed., *The Elections of 1992* (1993); Gary Orfield and Susan Eaton, *Dismantling Desegregation: The Quiet Reversal of Brown v. Board of Education* (1996); Juan Perea, ed., *Immigrants Out! The New Nativism and the Anti-Immigrant Impulse in the United States* (1997); Robert Reich, *The Work of Nations: Preparing Ourselves for Twenty-First Century Capitalism* (1991); Stanley Renshon, *High Hopes: The Clinton Presidency and the Politics of Ambitions* (1996); Farley Reynolds and Walter R. Allen, *The Color Line and the Quality of Life in America* (1987); Lillian Rubin, *Families on the Fault Line: America's Working Class Speaks About the Family, the Economy, Race, and Ethnicity* (1994); Hilda Scott, *Working Your Way to the Bottom: The Feminization of Poverty*, (1985); William Serrin, *Homestead: The Glory and Tragedy of an American Steel Town* (1992); Ruth Sildel, *Women and Children Last* (1986); James Simon, *The Center Holds: The Power Struggle Inside the Rehnquist Court* (1995); Christina Hoff Sommers, *Who Stole Feminism? How Women Have Betrayed Women* (1994); Lawrence Tribe, *Clash of Absolutes* (1992); Melvin Urofsky, *A Conflict of Rights: The Supreme Court and Affirmative Action* (1991); William Wei, *The Asian American Movement* (1993); William J. Wilson, *The Truly Disadvantaged* (1987).

Declaration of Independence in Congress, July 4, 1776

When, in the course of human events, it becomes necessary for one people to dissolve the political bonds which have connected them with another, and to assume, among the powers of the earth, the separate and equal station to which the laws of nature and of nature's God entitle them, a decent respect to the opinions of mankind requires that they should declare the causes which impel them to the separation.

We hold these truths to be self-evident: That all men are created equal; that they are endowed by their Creator with certain unalienable rights; that among these are life, liberty, and the pursuit of happiness; that, to secure these rights, governments are instituted among men, deriving their just powers from the consent of the governed; that whenever any form of government becomes destructive of these ends, it is the right of the people to alter or to abolish it, and to institute new government, laying its foundation on such principles, and organizing its powers in such form, as to them shall seem most likely to effect their safety and happiness. Prudence, indeed, will dictate that governments long established should not be changed for light and transient causes; and accordingly all experience hath shown that mankind are more disposed to suffer, while evils are sufferable, than to right themselves by abolishing the forms to which they are accustomed. But when a long train of abuses and usurpations, pursuing invariably the same object, evinces a design to reduce them under absolute despotism, it is their right, it is their duty, to throw off such government, and to provide new guards for their future security. Such has been the patient sufferance of these colonies; and such is now the necessity which constrains them to alter their former systems of government. The history of the present King of Great Britain is a history of repeated injuries and usurpations, all having in direct object the establishment of an absolute tyranny over these states. To prove this, let facts be submitted to a candid world.

He has refused his assent to laws, the most wholesome and necessary for the public good.

He has forbidden his governors to pass laws of immediate and pressing importance, unless suspended in their operation till his assent should be obtained; and, when so suspended, he has utterly neglected to attend to them.

He has refused to pass other laws for the accommodation of large districts of people, unless those people would relinquish the right of representation in the legislature, a right inestimable to them, and formidable to tyrants only.

He has called together legislative bodies at places unusual, uncomfortable, and distant from the depository of their public records, for the sole purpose of fatiguing them into compliance with his measures.

He has dissolved representative houses repeatedly, for opposing, with manly firmness, his invasions on the rights of the people.

He has refused for a long time, after such dissolutions, to cause others to be elected; whereby the legislative powers, incapable of annihilation, have returned to the people at large for their exercise; the state remaining, in the mean time, exposed to all the dangers of invasions from without and convulsions within.

He has endeavored to prevent the population of these states; for that purpose obstructing the laws for naturalization of foreigners; refusing to pass others to encourage their migration hither, and raising the conditions of new appropriations of lands.

He has obstructed the administration of justice, by refusing his assent to laws for establishing judiciary powers.

He has made judges dependent on his will alone, for the tenure of their offices, and the amount and payment of their salaries.

He has erected a multitude of new offices, and sent hither swarms of officers to harass our people and eat out their substance.

He has kept among us, in times of peace, standing armies, without the consent of our legislatures.

He has affected to render the military independent of, and superior to, the civil power.

He has combined with others to subject us to a jurisdiction foreign to our constitution, and unacknowledged by our laws, giving his assent to their acts of pretended legislation:

For quartering large bodies of armed troops among us;

For protecting them, by a mock trial, from punishment for any murders which they should commit on the inhabitants of these states;

For cutting off our trade with all parts of the world;

For imposing taxes on us without our consent;

For depriving us, in many cases, of the benefits of trial by jury;

For transporting us beyond seas, to be tried for pretended offenses;

For abolishing the free system of English laws in a neighboring province, establishing therein an arbitrary government, and enlarging its boundaries, so as to render it at once an example and fit instrument for introducing the same absolute rule into these colonies;

For taking away our charters, abolishing our most valuable laws, and altering fundamentally the forms of our governments;

For suspending our own legislatures, and declaring themselves invested with power to legislate for us in all cases whatsoever.

He has abdicated government here, by declaring us out of his protection and waging war against us.

He has plundered our seas, ravaged our coasts, burned our towns, and destroyed the lives of our people.

He is at this time transporting large armies of foreign mercenaries to complete the works of death, desolation, and tyranny already begun with circumstances of cruelty and perfidy scarcely paralleled in the most barbarous ages, and totally unworthy the head of a civilized nation.

He has constrained our fellow-citizens, taken captive on the high seas, to bear arms against their country, to become the executioners of their friends and brethren, or to fall themselves by their hands.

He has excited domestic insurrection among us, and has endeavored to bring on the inhabitants of our frontiers the merciless Indian savages, whose known rule of warfare is an undistinguished destruction of all ages, sexes, and conditions.

In every stage of these oppressions we have petitioned for redress in the most humble terms; our repeated petitions have been answered only by repeated injury. A prince, whose character is thus marked by every act which may define a tyrant, is unfit to be the ruler of a free people.

Nor have we been wanting in our attentions to our British brethren. We have warned them, from time to time, of attempts by their legislature to extend an unwarrantable jurisdiction over us. We have reminded them of the circumstances of our emigration and settlement here. We have appealed to their native justice and magnanimity; and we have conjured them, by the ties of our common kindred, to disavow these usurpations, which would inevitably interrupt our connections and correspondence. They, too, have been deaf to the voice of justice and of consanguinity. We must, therefore, acquiesce in the necessity which denounces our separation, and hold them, as we hold the rest of mankind, enemies in war, in peace friends.

We, therefore, the representatives of the United States of America, in General Congress assembled, appealing to the Supreme Judge of the world for the rectitude of our intentions, do, in the name and by the authority of the good people of these colonies, solemnly publish and declare, that these United Colonies are, and of right ought to be, FREE AND INDEPENDENT STATES; that they are absolved from all allegiance to the British crown, and that all political connection between them and the state of Great Britain is, and ought to be, totally dissolved; and that, as free and independent states, they have full power to levy war, conclude peace, contract alliances, establish commerce, and do all other acts and things which independent states may of right do. And for the support of this declaration, with a firm reliance on the protection of Divine Providence, we mutually pledge to each other our lives, our fortunes, and our sacred honor.

JOHN HANCOCK
and fifty-five others

Articles of Confederation

Whereas the Delegates of the United States of America in Congress assembled did on the fifteenth day of November in the Year of our Lord One Thousand Seven Hundred and Seventy seven, and in the Second Year of the Independence of America agree to certain articles of Confederation and perpetual Union between the States of Newhampshire, Massachusetts-bay, Rhodeisland and Providence Plantations, Connecticut, New York, New Jersey, Pennsylvania, Delaware, Maryland, Virginia, North-Carolina, South-Carolina and Georgia in the Words following, viz. "Articles of Confederation and perpetual Union between the states of New-hampshire, Massachusetts-bay, Rhodeisland and Providence Plantations, Connecticut, New-York, New-Jersey, Pennsylvania, Delaware, Maryland, Virginia, North-Carolina, South-Carolina and Georgia.

Article I The Stile of this confederacy shall be "The United States of America."

Article II Each state retains its sovereignty, freedom and independence, and every Power, Jurisdiction and right, which is not by this confederation expressly delegated to the United States, in Congress assembled.

Article III The said states hereby severally enter into a firm league of friendship with each other, for their common defence, the security of their Liberties, and their mutual and general welfare, binding themselves to assist each other, against all force offered to, or attacks made upon them, or any of them, on account of religion, sovereignty, trade, or any other pretence whatever.

Article IV The better to secure and perpetuate mutual friendship and intercourse among the people of the different states in this union, the free inhabitants of each of these states, paupers, vagabonds and fugitives from Justice excepted, shall be entitled to all privileges and immunities of free citizens in the several states; and the people of each state shall have free ingress and regress to and from any other state, and shall enjoy therein all the privileges of trade and commerce, subject to the same duties, impositions and restrictions as the inhabitants thereof respectively, provided that such restriction shall not extend so far as to prevent the removal of property imported into any state, to any other state of which the Owner is an inhabitant; provided also that no imposition, duties or restriction shall be laid by any state, on the property of the united states, or either of them.

If any Person guilty of, or charged with treason, felony, or other high misdemeanor in any state, shall flee from Justice, and be found in any of the united states, he shall upon demand of the Governor or executive power, of the state from which he fled, be delivered up and removed to the state having jurisdiction of his offence.

Full faith and credit shall be given in each of these states to the records, acts and judicial proceedings of the courts and magistrates of every other state.

Article V For the more convenient management of the general interests of the united states, delegates shall be annually appointed in such manner as the legislature of each state shall direct, to meet in Congress on the first Monday in November, in every year, with a power reserved to each state, to recal its delegates, or any of them, at any time within the year, and to send others in their stead, for the remainder of the Year.

No state shall be represented in Congress by less than two, nor by more than seven Members; and no person shall be capable of being a delegate for more than three years in any term of six years; nor shall any person, being a delegate, be capable of holding any office under the united states, for which he, or another for his benefit receives any salary, fees or emolument of any kind.

Each state shall maintain its own delegates in a meeting of the states, and while they act as members of the committee of the states.

In determining questions in the united states, in Congress assembled, each state shall have one vote.

Freedom of speech and debate in Congress shall not be impeached or questioned in any Court, or place out of Congress, and the members of congress shall be protected in their persons from arrests and imprisonments, during the time of their going to and from, and attendance on congress, except for treason, felony, or breach of the peace.

Article VI No state without the Consent of the united states in congress assembled, shall send any embassy to, or receive any embassy from, or enter into any conference, agreement, or alliance or treaty with any King, prince or state; nor shall any person holding any office of profit or trust under the united states, or any of them, accept of any present, emolument, office or title of any kind whatever from any king, prince or foreign state; nor shall the united states in congress assembled, or any of them, grant any title of nobility.

No two or more states shall enter into any treaty, confederation or alliance whatever between them, without the consent of the united states in congress assembled, specifying accurately the purposes for which the same is to be entered into, and how long it shall continue.

No state shall lay any imposts or duties, which may interfere with any stipulations in treaties, entered into by the united states in congress assembled, with any king, prince or state, in pursuance of any treaties already proposed by congress, to the courts of France and Spain.

No vessels of war shall be kept up in time of peace by any state, except such number only, as shall be deemed necessary by the united states in congress assembled, for the defence of such state, or its trade; nor shall any body of forces be kept up by any state, in time of peace, except such number only, as in the judgment of the united states, in congress assembled, shall be deemed requisite to garrison the forts necessary for the defence of such state; but every state shall always keep up a well regulated and disciplined militia, sufficiently armed and accoutred, and shall provide and constantly have ready for use, in public stores, a due number of field pieces and tents, and a proper quantity of arms, ammunition and camp equipage.

No state shall engage in any war without the consent of the united states in congress assembled, unless such state be actually invaded by enemies, or shall have received certain advice of a resolution being formed by some nation of Indians to invade such state, and the danger is so imminent as not to admit of a delay, till the united states in congress assembled can be consulted: nor shall any state grant commissions to any ships or vessels of war, nor letters of marque or reprisal, except it be after a declaration of war by the united states in congress assembled, and then only against the kingdom or state and the subjects thereof, against which war has been so declared, and under such regulations as shall be established by the united states in congress assembled, unless such state be infested by pirates, in which case vessels of war may be fitted out for that occasion, and kept so long as the danger shall continue, or until the united states in congress assembled shall determine otherwise.

Article VII When land-forces are raised by any state for the common defence, all officers of or under the rank of colonel, shall be appointed by the legislature of each state respectively by whom such forces shall be raised, or in such manner as such state shall direct, and all vacancies shall be filled up by the state which first made the appointment.

Article VIII All charges of war, and all other expences that shall be incurred for the common defence or general welfare, and allowed by the united states in congress assembled, shall be defrayed out of a common treasury, which shall be supplied by the several states, in proportion to the value of all land within each state, granted to or surveyed for any Person, as such land and the buildings and improvements thereon shall be estimated according to such mode as the united states in congress assembled, shall from time to time direct and appoint. The taxes for paying that proportion shall be laid and levied by the authority and direction of the legislatures of the several states within the time agreed upon by the united states in congress assembled.

Article IX The united states in congress assembled, shall have the sole and exclusive right and power of determining on peace and war, except in the cases mentioned in the sixth article—of sending and receiving ambassadors—entering into treaties and alliances, provided that no treaty of commerce shall be made whereby the legislative power of the respective states shall be restrained from imposing such imposts and duties on foreigners, as their own people are subjected to, or from prohibiting the exportation or importation of any species of goods or commodities whatsoever—of establishing rules for deciding in all cases, what captures on land or water shall be legal, and in what manner prizes taken by land or naval forces in the service of the united states shall be divided or appropriated.—of granting letters of marque and reprisal in times of peace—appointing courts for the trial of piracies and felonies committed on the high seas and establishing courts for receiving and determining finally appeals in all cases of captures, provided that no member of congress shall be appointed a judge of any of the said courts.

The united states in congress assembled shall also be the last resort on appeal in all disputes and differences now subsisting or that herafter may arise between two or more states concerning boundary, jurisdiction or any other cause whatever; which authority shall always be exercised in the manner following. Whenever the legislative or executive authority or lawful agent of any state in controversy with another shall present a petition to congress, stating the matter in question and praying for a hearing, notice thereof shall be given by order of congress to the legislative or executive authority of the other state in controversy, and a day assigned for the appearance of the parties by their lawful agents, who shall then be directed to appoint by joint consent, commissioners or judges to constitute a court for hearing and determining the matter in question: but if they cannot agree, congress shall name three persons out of each of the united states, and from the list of such persons each party shall alternately strike out one, the petitioners beginning, until the number shall be reduced to thirteen; and from that number not less than seven, nor more than nine names as congress shall direct, shall in the presence of congress be drawn out by lot, and the persons whose names shall be so drawn or any five of them, shall be commissioners or judges, to hear and finally determine the controversy, so always as a major part of the judges who shall hear the cause shall agree in the determination: and if either party shall neglect to attend at the day appointed, without shewing reasons, which congress shall judge sufficient, or being present shall refuse to strike, the congress shall proceed to nominate three persons out of each state, and the secretary of congress shall strike in behalf of such party absent or refusing; and the judgment and sentence of the court to be appointed, in the manner before prescribed, shall be final and conclusive; and if any of the parties shall refuse to submit to the authority of such court, or to appear to defend their claim or cause, the court shall nevertheless proceed to pronounce sentence, or judgment, which shall in like manner be final and decisive, the judgment or sentence and other proceedings being in either case transmitted to congress, and lodged among the acts of congress for the security of the parties concerned: provided that every commissioner, before he sits in judgment, shall take an oath to be administered by one of the judges of the supreme or superior court of the state, where the cause shall be tried, "well and truly to hear and determine the matter in question, according to the best of his judgment, without favour, affection or hope of reward:" provided also that no state shall be deprived of territory for the benefit of the united states.

All controversies concerning the private right of soil claimed under different grants of two or more states, whose jurisdictions as they may respect such lands, and the states which passed such grants are adjusted, the said grants or either of them being at the same time claimed to have originated antecedent to such settlement of jurisdiction, shall on the petition of either party to the congress of the united states, be finally determined as near as may be in the same manner as is before prescribed for deciding disputes respecting territorial jurisdiction between different states.

The united states in congress assembled shall also have the sole and exclusive right and power of regulating the alloy and value of coin struck by their own authority, or by that of the respective states—fixing the standard of weights and measures throughout the united states.—regulating the trade and managing all affairs with the Indians, not members of any of the states, provided that the legislative right of any state within its own limits be not infringed or violated—establishing and regulating post-offices from one state to another, throughout all the united states, and exacting such postage on the papers passing thro' the same as may be requisite to defray the expences of the said office—appointing all officers of the land forces, in the service of the united states, excepting regimental officers.—appointing all the officers of the naval forces, and commissioning all officers whatever in the service of the united states—making rules for the government and regulation of the said land and naval forces, and directing their operations.

The united states in congress assembled shall have authority to appoint a committee, to sit in the recess of congress, to be denominated "A Committee of the States," and to consist of one delegate from each state; and to appoint such other committees and civil officers as may be necessary for managing the general affairs of the united states under their direction—to appoint one of their number to preside, provided that no person be allowed to serve in the office of president more than one year in any term of three years; to ascertain the necessary sums of Money to be raised for the service of the united states, and to appropriate and apply the same for defraying the public expences—to borrow money, or emit bills on the credit of the united states, transmitting every half year to the respective states an account of the sums of money so borrowed or emitted,—to build and equip a navy—to agree upon the number of land forces, and to make requisitions from each state for its quota, in proportion to the number of white inhabitants in such state; which requisition shall be binding, and thereupon the legislature of each state shall appoint the regimental officers, raise the men and cloath, arm and equip them in a soldier like manner, at the expence of the united states, and the officers and men so cloathed, armed and equipped shall march to the place appointed, and within the time agreed on by the united states in congress assembled: But if the united states in congress assembled shall, on consideration of circumstances judge proper that any state should not raise men, or should raise a smaller number than its quota, and that any other state should raise a greater number of men than the quota thereof, such extra number shall be raised, officered, cloathed, armed and equipped in the same manner as the quota of such state, unless the legislature of such state shall judge that such extra number cannot be safely spared out of the same, in which case they shall raise, officer, cloath, arm and equip as many of such extra number as they judge can be safely spared. And the officers and men so cloathed, armed and equipped, shall march to the place appointed, and within the time agreed on by the united states in congress assembled.

The united states in congress assembled shall never engage in a war, nor grant letters of marque and reprisal in time of peace, nor enter into any treaties or alliances, nor coin money, nor regulate the value thereof, nor ascertain the sums and expences necessary for the defence and welfare of the united states, or any of them, nor emit bills, nor borrow money on the credit of the united states, nor appropriate money, nor agree upon the number of vessels of war, to be built or purchased, or the number of land or sea forces to be raised, nor appoint a commander in chief of the army or navy, unless nine states assent to the same: nor shall a question on any other point, except for adjourning from day to day be determined, unless by the votes of a majority of the united states in congress assembled.

The congress of the united states shall have power to adjourn to any time within the year, and to any place within the united states, so that no period of adjournment be for a longer duration than the space of six Months, and shall publish the Journal of their proceedings monthly, except such parts thereof relating to treaties, alliances or military operations as in their judgment require secresy; and the yeas and nays of the delegates of each state on any question shall be entered on the Journal, when it is desired by any delegate; and the delegates of a state, or any of them, at his or their request shall be furnished with a transcript of the said Journal, except such parts as are above excepted, to lay before the legislatures of the several states.

Article X The committee of the states, or any nine of them, shall be authorised to execute, in the recess of congress, such of the powers of congress as the united states in congress assembled, by the consent of nine states, shall from time to time think expedient to vest them with; provided that no power be delegated to the said committee, for the exercise of which, by the articles of confederation, the voice of nine states in the congress of the united states assembled is requisite.

Article XI Canada acceding to this confederation, and joining in the measures of the united states, shall be admitted into, and entitled to all the advantages of this union: but no other colony shall be admitted into the same, unless such admission be agreed to by nine states.

Article XII All bills of credit emitted, monies borrowed and debts contracted by, or under the authority of congress, before the assembling of the united states, in pursuance of the present confederation, shall be deemed and considered as a charge against the united states, for payment and satisfaction whereof the said united states, and the public faith are hereby solemnly pledged.

Article XIII Every state shall abide by the determinations of the united states in congress assembled, on all questions which by this confederation are submitted to them. And the Articles of this confederation shall be inviolably observed by every state, and the union shall be perpetual; nor shall any alteration at any time hereafter be made in any of them; unless such alteration be agreed to in a congress of the united states, and be afterwards confirmed by the legislatures of every state.

AND WHEREAS it hath pleased the Great Governor of the World to incline the hearts of the legislatures we respectively represent in congress, to approve of, and to authorize us to ratify the said articles of confederation and perpetual union. Know Ye that we the undersigned delegates, by virtue of the power and authority to us given for that purpose, do by these presents, in the name and in behalf of our respective constituents, fully and entirely ratify and confirm each and every of the said articles of confederation and perpetual union, and all and singular the matters and things therein contained: And we do further solemnly plight and engage the faith of our respective constitutents, that they shall abide by the determinations of the united states in congress assembled, on all questions, which by the said confederation are submitted to them. And that the articles thereof shall be inviolably observed by the states we respectively represent, and that the union shall be perpetual. In Witness whereof we have hereunto set our hands in Congress. Done at Philadelphia in the state of Pennsylvania the ninth Day of July in the Year of our Lord one Thousand seven Hundred and Seventy-eight, and in the third year of the independence of America.

Constitution of the United States of America and Amendments*

Preamble

We the people of the United States, in order to form a more perfect union, establish justice, insure domestic tranquillity, provide for the common defense, promote the general welfare, and secure the blessings of liberty to ourselves and our posterity, do ordain and establish this Constitution for the United States of America.

Article I

Section 1 All legislative powers herein granted shall be vested in a Congress of the United States, which shall consist of a Senate and a House of Representatives.

Section 2 The House of Representatives shall be composed of members chosen every second year by the people of the several States, and the electors in each State shall have the qualifications requisite for electors of the most numerous branch of the State Legislature.

No person shall be a Representative who shall not have attained to the age of twenty-five years, and been seven years a citizen of the United States, and who shall not, when elected, be an inhabitant of that State in which he shall be chosen.

Representatives and direct taxes shall be apportioned among the several States which may be included within this Union, according to their respective numbers, *which shall be determined by adding to the whole number of free persons, including those bound to service for a term of years and excluding Indians not taxed, three-fifths of all other persons.* The actual enumeration shall be made within three years after the first meeting of the Congress of the United States, and within every

* Passages no longer in effect are printed in italic type.

subsequent term of ten years, in such manner as they shall by law direct. The number of Representatives shall not exceed one for every thirty thousand, but each State shall have at least one Representative; *and until such enumeration shall be made, the State of New Hampshire shall be entitled to choose three, Massachusetts eight, Rhode Island and Providence Plantations one, Connecticut five, New York six, New Jersey four, Pennsylvania eight, Delaware one, Maryland six, Virginia ten, North Carolina five, South Carolina five, and Georgia three.*

When vacancies happen in the representation from any State, the Executive authority thereof shall issue writs of election to fill such vacancies.

The House of Representatives shall choose their Speaker and other officers; and shall have the sole power of impeachment.

Section 3 The Senate of the United States shall be composed of two Senators from each State, *chosen by the legislature thereof,* for six years; and each Senator shall have one vote.

Immediately after they shall be assembled in consequence of the first election, they shall be divided as equally as may be into three classes. The seats of the Senators of the first class shall be vacated at the expiration of the second year, of the second class at the expiration of the fourth year, and of the third class at the expiration of the sixth year, so that one-third may be chosen every second year; *and if vacancies happen by resignation or otherwise, during the recess of the legislature of any State, the Executive thereof may make temporary appointments until the next meeting of the legislature, which shall then fill such vacancies.*

No person shall be a Senator who shall not have attained to the age of thirty years, and been nine years a citizen of the United States, and who shall not, when elected, be an inhabitant of that State for which he shall be chosen.

The Vice-President of the United States shall be President of the Senate, but shall have no vote, unless they be equally divided.

The Senate shall choose their other officers, and also a President *pro tempore,* in the absence of the Vice-President, or when he shall exercise the office of President of the United States.

The Senate shall have the sole power to try all impeachments. When sitting for that purpose, they shall be on oath or affirmation. When the President of the United States is tried, the Chief Justice shall preside: and no person shall be convicted with-out the concurrence of two-thirds of the members present.

Judgment in cases of impeachment shall not extend further than to removal from the office, and disqualification to hold and enjoy any office of honor, trust or profit under the United States: but the party convicted shall nevertheless be liable and subject to indictment, trial, judgment and punishment, according to law.

Section 4 The times, places and manner of holding elections for Senators and Representatives shall be prescribed in each State by the legislature thereof; but the Congress may at any time by law make or alter such regulations, except as to the places of choosing Senators.

The Congress shall assemble at least once in every year, and such meeting *shall be on the first Monday in December, unless they shall by law appoint a different day.*

Section 5 Each house shall be the judge of the elections, returns and qualifications of its own members, and a majority of each shall constitute a quorum to do business; but a smaller number may adjourn from day to day, and may be authorized to compel the attendance of absent members, in such manner, and under such penalties, as each house may provide.

Each house may determine the rules of its proceedings, punish its members for disorderly behavior, and with the concurrence of two-thirds, expel a member.

Each house shall keep a journal of its proceedings, and from time to time publish the same, excepting such parts as may in their judgment require secrecy; and the yeas and nays of the members of either house on any question shall, at the desire of one-fifth of those present, be entered on the journal.

Neither house, during the session of Congress, shall, without the consent of the other, adjourn for more than three days, nor to any other place than that in which the two houses shall be sitting.

Section 6 The Senators and Representatives shall receive a compensation for their services, to be ascertained by law and paid out of the treasury of the United States. They shall in all cases except treason, felony and breach of the peace, be privileged from arrest during their attendance at the session of their respective houses, and in going to and returning from the same; and for any speech or debate in either house, they shall not be questioned in any other place.

No Senator or Representative shall, during the time for which he was elected, be appointed to any civil office under the authority of the United States, which shall have been created, or the emoluments whereof shall have been increased, during such time; and no person holding any office under the United States shall be a member of either house during his continuance in office.

Section 7 All bills for raising revenue shall originate in the House of Representatives; but the Senate may propose or concur with amendments as on other bills.

Every bill which shall have passed the House of Representatives and the Senate, shall, before it become a law, be presented to the President of the United States; if he approve he shall sign it, but if not he shall return it with objections to that house in which it originated, who shall enter the objections at large on their journal, and proceed to reconsider it. If after such reconsideration two-thirds of that house shall agree to pass the bill, it shall be sent, together with the objections, to the other house, by which it shall likewise be reconsidered, and, if approved by two-thirds of that house, it shall become a law. But in all such cases the votes of both houses shall be determined by yeas and nays, and the names of the persons voting for and against the bill shall be entered on the journal of each house respectively. If any bill shall not be returned by the President within ten days (Sundays excepted) after it shall have been presented to him, the same shall be a law, in like manner as if he had signed it, unless the Congress by their adjournment prevent its return, in which case it shall not be a law.

Every order, resolution, or vote to which the concurrence of the Senate and House of Representatives may be necessary (except on a question of adjournment) shall be presented to the President of the United States; and before the same shall take effect, shall be approved by him, or being disapproved by him, shall be repassed by two-thirds of the Senate and House of Representatives, according to the rules and limitations prescribed in the case of a bill.

Section 8 The Congress shall have power

To lay and collect taxes, duties, imposts, and excises, to pay the debts and provide for the common defense and general welfare of the United States; but all duties, imposts and excises shall be uniform throughout the United States;

To borrow money on the credit of the United States;

To regulate commerce with foreign nations, and among the several States, and with the Indian tribes;

To establish an uniform rule of naturalization, and uniform laws on the subject of bankruptcies throughout the United States;

To coin money, regulate the value thereof, and of foreign coin, and fix the standard of weights and measures;

To provide for the punishment of counterfeiting the securities and current coin of the United States;

To establish post offices and post roads;

To promote the progress of science and useful arts by securing for limited times to authors and inventors the exclusive right to their respective writings and discoveries;

To constitute tribunals inferior to the Supreme Court;

To define and punish piracies and felonies committed on the high seas and offenses against the law of nations;

To declare war, grant letters of marque and reprisal, and make rules concerning captures on land and water;

To raise and support armies, but no appropriation of money to that use shall be for a longer term than two years;

To provide and maintain a navy;

To make rules for the government and regulation of the land and naval forces;

To provide for calling forth the militia to execute the laws of the Union, suppress insurrections, and repel invasions;

To provide for organizing, arming, and disciplining the militia, and for governing such part of them as may be employed in the service of the United States, reserving to the States respectively the appointment of the officers, and the authority of training the militia according to the discipline prescribed by Congress;

To exercise exclusive legislation in all cases whatsoever, over such district (not exceeding ten miles square) as may, by cession of particular States, and the acceptance of Congress, become the seat of government of the United States, and to exercise like authority over all places purchased by the consent of the legislature of the State, in which the same shall be, for erection of forts, magazines, arsenals, dockyards, and other needful buildings; — and

To make all laws which shall be necessary and proper for carrying into execution the foregoing powers, and all other powers vested by this Constitution in the government of the United States, or in any department or officer thereof.

Section 9 The migration or importation of such persons as any of the States now existing shall think proper to admit shall not be prohibited by the Congress prior to the year 1808; but a tax or duty may be imposed on such importation, not exceeding $10 for each person.

The privilege of the writ of habeas corpus shall not be suspended, unless when in cases of rebellion or invasion the public safety may require it.

No bill of attainder or ex post facto law shall be passed.

No capitation, or other direct, tax shall be laid, unless in proportion to the census or enumeration herein before directed to be taken.

No tax or duty shall be laid on articles exported from any State.

No preference shall be given by any regulation of commerce or revenue to the ports of one State over those of another; nor shall vessels bound to, or from, one State, be obliged to enter, clear, or pay duties in another.

No money shall be drawn from the treasury, but in consequence of appropriations made by law; and a regular statemer[illegible]d account of the receipts and expenditures of a[illegible]ic money shall be published from time to time[illegible]

No title [illegible]ty shall be granted by the United States: and [illegible] on holding any office of profit or trust unde[illegible] shall, without the consent of the Congress, a[illegible]f any present, emolument, office, or title, of any k[illegible]d whatever, from any king, prince, or foreign state.

Section 10 No State shall enter into any treaty, alliance, or confederation; grant letters of marque and reprisal; coin money; emit bills of credit; make anything but gold and silver coin a tender in payment of debts; pass any bill of attainder, ex post facto law, or law impairing the obligation of contracts, or grant any title of nobility.

No State shall, without the consent of Congress, lay any imposts or duties on imports or exports, except what may be absolutely necessary for executing its inspection laws: and the net produce of all duties and imposts, laid by any State on imports or exports, shall be for the use of the treasury of the United States; and all such laws shall be subject to the revision and control of the Congress.

No State shall, without the consent of Congress, lay any duty of tonnage, keep troops or ships of war in time of peace, enter into any agreement or compact with another State, or with a foreign power, or engage in war, unle[illegible]ually invaded, or in such imminent danger as w[illegible]dmit of delay.

Article II

Section 1 [illegible]cutive power shall be vested in a President o[illegible]nited States of America. He shall hold his offi[illegible]ring the term of four years, and, together with the Vice-President, chosen for the same term, be elected as follows:

Each State shall appoint, in such manner as the legislature thereof may direct, a number of electors, equal to the whole number of Senators and Representatives to which the State may be entitled in the Congress; but no Senator or Representative, or person holding an office of trust or [illegible]rofit under the United States, shall be appointed an [illegible]tor.

The electors shall meet in their respective States, and vote by ballot for two persons, of whom one at least shall not be an inhabitant of the same State with themselves. And they shall make a list of all the persons voted for, and of the number of votes for each; which list they shall sign and certify, and transmit sealed to the seat of government of the United States, directed to the President of the Senate. The President of the Senate shall, in the presence of the Senate and House of Representatives, open all the certificates, and the votes shall then be counted. The person having the greatest number of votes shall be the President, if such number be a majority of the whole number of electors appointed; and if there be more than one who have such majority, and have an equal number of votes, then the House of Representatives shall immediately choose by ballot one of them for President; and if no person have a majority, then from the five highest on the list said house shall in like manner choose the President. But in choosing the President the votes shall be taken by States, the representation from each State having one vote; a quorum for this purpose shall consist of a member or members from two-thirds of the States, and a majority of all the States shall be necessary to a choice. In every case, after the choice of the President, the person having the greatest number of votes of the electors shall be the Vice-President. But if there should remain two or more who have equal votes, the Senate shall choose from them by ballot the Vice-President.

The Congress may determine the time of choosing the electors and the day on which they shall give their votes; which day shall be the same throughout the United States.

No person except a natural-born citizen, *or a citizen of the United States at the time of the adoption of this Constitution,* shall be eligible to the office of President; neither shall any person be eligible to that office who shall not have attained to the age of thirty-five years, and been fourteen years a resident within the United States.

In cases of the removal of the President from office or of his death, resignation, or inability to discharge the powers and duties of the said office, the same shall devolve on the Vice-President, and the Congress may by law provide for the case of removal, death, resignation, or inability, both of the President and Vice-President, declaring what officer shall then act as President, and such officer shall act accordingly, until the disability be removed, or a President shall be elected.

The President shall, at stated times, receive for his services a compensation, which shall neither be increased nor diminished during the period for which he shall have been elected, and he shall not receive within that period any other emolument from the United States, or any of them.

Before he enter on the execution of his office, he shall take the following oath or affirmation:—"I do solemnly swear (or affirm) that I will faithfully execute the office of the President of the United States, and will to the best of my ability preserve, protect and defend the Constitution of the United States."

Section 2 The President shall be commander in chief of the army and navy of the United States, and of the militia of the several States, when called into the actual service of the United States; he may require the opinion, in writing, of the principal officer in each of the executive departments, upon any subject relating to the duties of their respective offices, and he shall have power to grant reprieves and pardons for offenses against the United States, except in cases of impeachment.

He shall have power, by and with the advice and consent of the Senate, to make treaties, provided two-thirds of the Senators present concur; and he shall nominate, and by and with the advice and consent of the Senate, shall appoint ambassadors, other public ministers and consuls, judges of the Supreme Court, and all other officers of the United States, whose appointments are not herein otherwise provided for, and which shall be established by law: but Congress may by law vest the appointment of such inferior officers, as they think proper, in the President alone, in the courts of law, or in the heads of departments.

The President shall have power to fill up all vacancies that may happen during the recess of the Senate, by granting commissions which shall expire at the end of their next session.

Section 3 He shall from time to time give to the Congress information of the state of the Union, and recommend to their consideration such measures as he shall judge necessary and expedient; he may, on extraordinary occasions, convene both houses, or either of them, and in case of disagreement between them, with respect to the time of adjournment, he may adjourn them to such time as he shall think proper; he shall receive ambassadors and other public ministers; he shall take care that the laws be faithfully executed, and shall commission all the officers of the United States.

Section 4 The President, Vice-President and all civil officers of the United States shall be removed from office on impeachment for, and on conviction of, treason, bribery, or other high crimes and misdemeanors.

Article III

Section 1 The judicial power of the United States shall be vested in one Supreme Court, and in such inferior courts as the Congress may from time to time ordain and establish. The judges, both of the Supreme and inferior courts, shall hold their offices during good behavior, and shall, at stated times, receive for their services a compensation which shall not be diminished during their continuance in office.

Section 2 The judicial power shall extend to all cases, in law and equity, arising under this Constitution, the laws of the United States, and treaties made, or which shall be made, under their authority;—to all cases affecting ambassadors, other public ministers and consuls;—to all cases of admiralty and maritime jurisdiction;—to controversies to which the United States shall be a party;—to controversies between two or more States;—*between a State and citizens of another State;*—between citizens of different States;—between citizens of the same State claiming lands under grants of different States, and between a State, or the citizens thereof, and foreign states, citizens or subjects.

In all cases affecting ambassadors, other public ministers and consuls, and those in which a State shall be party, the Supreme Court shall have original jurisdiction. In all the other cases before mentioned, the Supreme Court shall have appellate jurisdiction, both as to law and fact, with such exceptions, and under such regulations, as the Congress shall make.

The trial of all crimes, except in cases of impeachment, shall be by jury; and such trial shall be held in the State where said crimes shall have been committed; but when not committed within any State, the trial shall be at such place or places as the Congress may by law have directed.

Section 3 Treason against the United States shall consist only in levying war against them, or in adhering to their enemies, giving them aid and comfort. No person shall be convicted of treason unless on the testimony of two witnesses to the same overt act, or on confession in open court.

The Congress shall have power to declare the punishment of treason, but no attainder of treason shall work corruption of blood, or forfeiture except during the life of the person attainted.

Article IV

Section 1 Full faith and credit shall be given in each State to the public acts, records, and judicial proceedings of every other State. And the Congress may by general laws prescribe the manner in which such acts, records, and proceedings shall be proved, and the effect thereof.

Section 2 The citizens of each State shall be entitled to all privileges and immunities of citizens in the several States.

A person charged in any State with treason, felony, or other crime, who shall flee from justice, and be found in another State, shall on demand of the executive authority of the State from which he fled, be delivered up, to be removed to the State having jurisdiction of the crime.

No person held to service or labor in one State, under the laws thereof, escaping into another, shall, in consequence of any law or regulation therein, be discharged from such service or labor, but shall be delivered up on claim of the party to whom such service or labor may be due.

Section 3 New States may be admitted by the Congress into this Union; but no new State shall be formed or erected within the jurisdiction of any other State; nor any State be formed by the junction of two or more States, or parts of States, without the consent of the legislatures of the States concerned as well as of the Congress.

The Congress shall have power to dispose of and make all needful rules and regulations respecting the territory or other property belonging to the United States; and nothing in this Constitution shall be so construed as to prejudice any claims of the United States, or of any particular State.

Section 4 The United States shall guarantee to every State in this Union a republican form of government, and shall protect each of them against invasion; and on application of the legislature, or of the executive (when the legislature cannot be convened), against domestic violence.

Article V

The Congress, whenever two-thirds of both houses shall deem it necessary, shall propose amendments to this Constitution, or, on the application of the legislatures of two-thirds of the several States, shall call a convention for proposing amendments, which, in either case, shall be valid to all intents and purposes, as part of this Constitution, when ratified by the legislatures of three-fourths of the several States, or by conventions in three-fourths thereof, as the one or the other mode of ratification may be proposed by the Congress; provided *that no amendments which may be made prior to the year one thousand eight hundred and eight shall in any manner affect the first and fourth clauses in the ninth section of the first article;* and that no State, without its consent, shall be deprived of its equal suffrage in the Senate.

Article VI

All debts contracted and engagements entered into, before the adoption of this Constitution, shall be as valid against the United States under this Constitution, as under the Confederation.

This Constitution, and the laws of the United States which shall be made in pursuance thereof; and all treaties made, or which shall be made, under the authority of the United States, shall be the supreme law of the land; and the judges in every State shall be bound thereby, anything in the Constitution or laws of any State to the contrary notwithstanding.

The Senators and Representatives before mentioned, and the members of the several State legislatures, and all executive and judicial officers, both of the United States and of the several States, shall be bound by oath or affirmation to support this Constitution; but no religious test shall ever be required as a qualification to any office or public trust under the United States.

Article VII

The ratification of the conventions of nine States shall be sufficient for the establishment of this Constitution between the States so ratifying the same.

Done in Convention by the unanimous consent of the States present, the seventeenth day of September in the year of our Lord one thousand seven hundred and eighty-seven and of the Independence of the United States of America the twelfth. In witness whereof we have hereunto subscribed our names.

GEORGE WASHINGTON
and thirty-seven others

Amendments to the Constitution*

Amendment I

Congress shall make no law respecting an establishment of religion, or prohibiting the free exercise thereof; or abridging the freedom of speech, or of the press; or the right of the people peaceably to assemble, and to petition the government for a redress of grievances.

Amendment II

A well-regulated militia being necessary to the security of a free State, the right of the people to keep and bear arms shall not be infringed.

Amendment III

No soldier shall, in time of peace, be quartered in any house without the consent of the owner, nor in time of war, but in a manner to be prescribed by law.

Amendment IV

The right of the people to be secure in their persons, houses, papers, and effects, against unreasonable searches and seizures, shall not be violated, and no warrants shall issue but upon probable cause, supported by oath or affirmation, and particularly describ-

* The first ten Amendments (the Bill of Rights) were adopted in 1791.

ing the place to be searched, and the persons or things to be seized.

Amendment V

No person shall be held to answer for a capital, or otherwise infamous crime, unless on a presentment or indictment of a grand jury, except in cases arising in the land or naval forces, or in the militia, when in actual service in time of war or public danger; nor shall any person be subject for the same offense to be twice put in jeopardy of life or limb; nor shall be compelled in any criminal case to be a witness against himself, nor be deprived of life, liberty, or property, without due process of law; nor shall private property be taken for public use without just compensation.

Amendment VI

In all criminal prosecutions, the accused shall enjoy the right to a speedy and public trial, by an impartial jury of the State and district wherein the crime shall have been committed, which district shall have been previously ascertained by law, and to be informed of the nature and cause of the accusation; to be confronted with the witnesses against him; to have compulsory process for obtaining witnesses in his favor, and to have the assistance of counsel for his defense.

Amendment VII

In suits at common law, where the value in controversy shall exceed twenty dollars, the right of trial by jury shall be preserved, and no fact tried by a jury shall be otherwise reexamined in any court of the United States, than according to the rules of the common law.

Amendment VIII

Excessive bail shall not be required, nor excessive fines imposed, nor cruel and unusual punishments inflicted.

Amendment IX

The enumeration in the Constitution, of certain rights, shall not be construed to deny or disparage others retained by the people.

Amendment X

The powers not delegated to the United States by the Constitution, nor prohibited by it to the States, are reserved to the States respectively, or to the people.

Amendment XI

[Adopted 1798]

The judicial power of the United States shall not be construed to extend to any suit in law or equity, commenced or prosecuted against one of the United States by citizens of another State, or by citizens or subjects of any foreign state.

Amendment XII

[Adopted 1804]

The electors shall meet in their respective States, and vote by ballot for President and Vice-President, one of whom, at least, shall not be an inhabitant of the same State with themselves; they shall name in their ballots the person voted for as President, and in distinct ballots the person voted for as Vice-President, and they shall make distinct lists of all persons voted for as President, and of all persons voted for as Vice-President, and of the number of votes for each, which lists they shall sign and certify, and transmit sealed to the seat of government of the United States, directed to the President of the Senate;—the President of the Senate shall, in the presence of the Senate and House of Representatives, open all the certificates and the votes shall then be counted;—the person having the greatest number of votes for President shall be the President, if such number be a majority of the whole number of electors appointed; and if no person have such majority, then from the persons having the highest numbers not exceeding three on the list of those voted for as President, the House of Representatives shall choose immediately, by ballot, the President. But in choosing the President, the votes shall be taken by States, the representation from each State having one vote; a quorum for this purpose shall consist of a member or members from two-thirds of the States, and a majority of all the States shall be necessary to a choice. And if the House of Representatives shall not choose a President whenever the right of choice shall devolve upon them, before the fourth day of March next following, then the Vice-President shall act as President, as in the case of the death or other constitutional disability of the President.

The person having the greatest number of votes as Vice-President shall be the Vice-President, if such number be a majority of the whole number of electors appointed; and if no person have a majority, then from the two highest numbers on the list the Senate shall choose the Vice-President; a quorum for the purpose shall consist of two-thirds of the whole number of Senators, and a majority of the whole number shall be necessary to a choice. But no person constitutionally ineligible to the office of President shall be eligible to that of Vice-President of the United States.

Amendment XIII

[Adopted 1865]

Section 1 Neither slavery nor involuntary servitude, except as a punishment for crime whereof the party shall have been duly convicted, shall exist within the United States, or any place subject to their jurisdiction.

Section 2 Congress shall have power to enforce this article by appropriate legislation.

Amendment XIV

[Adopted 1868]

Section 1 All persons born or naturalized in the United States, and subject to the jurisdiction thereof, are citizens of the United States and of the State wherein they reside. No State shall make or enforce any law which shall abridge the privileges or immunities of citizens of the United States; nor shall any State deprive any person of life, liberty, or property, without due process of law; nor deny to any person within its jurisdiction the equal protection of the laws.

Section 2 Representatives shall be apportioned among the several States according to their respective numbers, counting the whole number of persons in each State, excluding Indians not taxed. But when the right to vote at any election for the choice of Electors for President and Vice-President of the United States, Representatives in Congress, the executive and judicial officers of a State, or the members of the legislature thereof, is denied to any of the male inhabitants of such State, being twenty-one years of age and citizens of the United States, or in any way abridged, except for participation in rebellion, or other crime, the basis of representation therein shall be reduced in the proportion which the number of such male citizens shall bear to the whole number of male citizens twenty-one years of age in such State.

Section 3 No person shall be a Senator or Representative in Congress, or Elector of President and Vice-President, or hold any office, civil or military, under the United States, or under any State, who, having previously taken an oath, as a member of Congress, or as an officer of the United States, or as a member of any State legislature, or as an executive or judicial officer of any State, to support the Constitution of the United States, shall have engaged in insurrection or rebellion against the same, or given aid or comfort to the enemies thereof. Congress may, by a vote of two-thirds of each house, remove such disability.

Section 4 The validity of the public debt of the United States, authorized by law, including debts incurred for payment of pensions and bounties for services in suppressing insurrection or rebellion, shall not be questioned. But neither the United States nor any State shall assume or pay any debt or obligation incurred in aid of insurrection or rebellion against the United States, or any claim for the loss or emancipation of any slave; but all such debts, obligations, and claims shall be held illegal and void.

Section 5 The Congress shall have power to enforce, by appropriate legislation, the provisions of this article.

Amendment XV

[Adopted 1870]

Section 1 The right of citizens of the United States to vote shall not be denied or abridged by the United States or by any State on account of race, color, or previous condition of servitude.

Section 2 The Congress shall have power to enforce this article by appropriate legislation.

Amendment XVI

[Adopted 1913]

The Congress shall have power to lay and collect taxes on incomes, from whatever source derived, without apportionment among the several States, and without regard to any census or enumeration.

Amendment XVII

[Adopted 1913]

Section 1 The Senate of the United States shall be composed of two Senators from each State, elected by the people thereof, for six years; and each Senator shall have one vote. The electors in each State shall have the qualifications requisite for electors of [voters for] the most numerous branch of the State legislatures.

Section 2 When vacancies happen in the representation of any State in the Senate, the executive authority of such State shall issue writs of election to fill such vacancies: Provided, that the Legislature of any State may empower the executive thereof to make temporary appointments until the people fill the vacancies by election as the Legislature may direct.

Section 3 This amendment shall not be so construed as to affect the election or term of any Senator chosen before it becomes valid as part of the Constitution.

Amendment XVIII

[Adopted 1919; Repealed 1933]

Section 1 After one year from the ratification of this article the manufacture, sale, or transportation of intoxicating liquors within, the importation thereof into, or the exportation thereof from the United States and all territory subject to the jurisdiction thereof, for beverage purposes, is hereby prohibited.

Section 2 The Congress and the several States shall have concurrent power to enforce this article by appropriate legislation.

Section 3 This article shall be inoperative unless it shall have been ratified as an amendment to the Constitution by the legislatures of the several States, as provided by the Constitution, within seven years from the date of the submission thereof to the States by the Congress.

Amendment XIX

[Adopted 1920]

Section 1 The right of citizens of the United States to vote shall not be denied or abridged by the United States or by any State on account of sex.

Section 2 The Congress shall have power to enforce this article by appropriate legislation.

Amendment XX

[Adopted 1933]

Section 1 The terms of the President and Vice-President shall end at noon on the 20th day of January, and the terms of Senators and Representatives at noon on the 3rd day of January, of the years in which such terms would have ended if this article had not been ratified; and the terms of their successors shall then begin.

Section 2 The Congress shall assemble at least once in every year, and such meeting shall begin at noon on the 3d day of January, unless they shall by law appoint a different day.

Section 3 If, at the time fixed for the beginning of the term of the President, the President-elect shall have died, the Vice-President-elect shall become President. If a President shall not have been chosen before the time fixed for the beginning of his term, or if the President-elect shall have failed to qualify, then the Vice-President-elect shall act as President until a President shall have qualified; and the Congress may by law provide for the case wherein neither a President-elect nor a Vice-President-elect shall have qualified, declaring who shall then act as President, or the manner in which one who is to act shall be selected, and such persons shall act accordingly until a President or Vice-President shall have qualified.

Section 4 The Congress may by law provide for the case of the death of any of the persons from whom the House of Representatives may choose a President whenever the right of choice shall have devolved upon them, and for the case of the death of any of the persons from whom the Senate may choose a Vice-President whenever the right of choice shall have devolved upon them.

Section 5 Sections 1 and 2 shall take effect on the 15th day of October following the ratification of this article.

Section 6 This article shall be inoperative unless it shall have been ratified as an amendment to the Constitution by the Legislatures of three-fourths of the several States within seven years from the date of its submission.

Amendment XXI

[Adopted 1933]

Section 1 The eighteenth article of amendment to the Constitution of the United States is hereby repealed.

Section 2 The transportation or importation into any State, Territory, or Possession of the United States for delivery or use therein of intoxicating liquors, in violation of the laws thereof, is hereby prohibited.

Section 3 This article shall be inoperative unless it shall have been ratified as an amendment to the Constitution by conventions in the several States, as provided in the Constitution, within seven years from the date of submission thereof to the States by the Congress.

Amendment XXII

[Adopted 1951]

Section 1 No person shall be elected to the office of President more than twice, and no person who has held the office of President, or acted as President, for more than two years of a term to which some other person was elected President shall be elected to the office of President more than once. But this article shall not apply to any person holding the office of President when this article was proposed by the Congress, and shall not prevent any person who may be holding the office of President, or acting as Presi[illegible]nt, during the term within which this article becor[illegible]erative from holding the office of President or [illegible]s President during the remainder of such term.

Section 2 This article shall be ir[illegible]e unless it shall have been ratified as an ame[illegible] to the Constitution by the legislatures of three[illegible]s of the several States within seven years from [illegible]ite of its submission to the States by the Congress.

Amendment XXIII

[Adopted 1961]

Section 1 The District constituting the seat of Government of the United States shall appoint in such manner as the Congress may direct:

A number of electors of President and Vice-President equal to the whole number of Senators and Representatives in Congress to which the District would be entitled if it were a State, but in no event more t[illegible]n the least populous State; they shall be in addition t[illegible]hose appointed by the States, but they shall be considered for the purposes of the election of President and Vice-President, to be electors appointed by a State; and they shall meet in the District and perform such duties as provided by the twelfth article of amendment.

Section 2 The Congress shall have the power to enforce this article by appropriate legislation.

Amendment XXIV

[Adopted 1964]

Section 1 The right of citizens of the United States to vote in any primary or other election for President or Vice-President, for electors for President or Vice-President, or for Senator or Representative in Congress, shall not be denied or abridged by the United States or any State by reason of failure to pay any poll tax or other tax.

Section 2 The Congress shall have the power to enforce this article by appropriate legislation.

Amendment XXV

[Adopted 1967]

Section 1 In case of the removal of the President from office or of his death or resignation, the Vice-President shall become President.

Section 2 Whenever there is a vacancy in the office of the Vice-President, the President shall nominate a Vice-President who shall take office upon confirmation by a majority vote of both Houses of Congress.

Section 3 Whenever the President transmits to the President pro tempore of the Senate and the Speaker of the House of Representatives his written declaration that he is unable to discharge the powers and duties of his office, and until he transmits to them a written declaration to the contrary, such powers and duties shall be discharged by the Vice-President as Acting President.

Section 4 Whenever the Vice-President and a majority of either the principal officers of the executive departments or of such other body as Congress may by law provide, transmit to the President pro tempore of the Senate and the Speaker of the House of Representatives their written declaration that the President is unable to discharge the powers and duties of his office, the Vice-President shall immediately assume the powers and duties of the office as Acting President.

Thereafter, when the President transmits to the President pro tempore of the Senate and the Speaker of the House of Representatives his written declaration that no inability exists, he shall resume the powers and duties of his office unless the Vice-President and a majority of either the principal officers of the executive department[s] or of such other body as Congress may by law provide, transmit within four days to the President pro tempore of the Senate and the Speaker of the House of Representatives their written declaration that the President is unable to discharge the powers and duties of his office. Thereupon Congress shall decide the issue, assembling within forty-eight hours for that purpose if not in session. If the Congress, within twenty-one days after receipt of the latter written declaration, or, if Congress is not in session, within twenty-one days after Congress is required to assemble, determines by two-thirds vote of both Houses that the President is unable to discharge the powers and duties of his office, the Vice-President shall continue to discharge the same as Acting President; otherwise, the President shall resume the powers and duties of his office.

Amendment XXVI

[Adopted 1971]

Section 1 The right of citizens of the United States, who are eighteen years of age or older, to vote shall not be denied or abridged by the United States or by any State on account of age.

Section 2 The Congress shall have power to enforce this article by appropriate legislation.

Amendment XXVII

[Adopted 1992]

No law, varying the compensation for the services of the Senators and Representatives, shall take effect, until an election of Representatives shall have intervened.

Territorial Expansion of the United States

Territory	Date Acquired	Square Miles	How Acquired
Original states and territories	1783	888,685	Treaty with Great Britain
Louisiana Purchase	1803	827,192	Purchase from France
Florida	1819	72,003	Treaty with Spain
Texas	1845	390,143	Annexation of independent nation
Oregon	1846	285,580	Treaty with Great Britain
Mexican Cession	1848	529,017	Conquest from Mexico
Gadsden Purchase	1853	29,640	Purchase from Mexico
Alaska	1867	589,757	Purchase from Russia
Hawai`i	1898	6,450	Annexation of independent nation
The Philippines	1899	115,600	Conquest from Spain (granted independence in 1946)
Puerto Rico	1899	3,435	Conquest from Spain
Guam	1899	212	Conquest from Spain
American Samoa	1900	76	Treaty with Germany and Great Britain
Panama Canal Zone	1904	553	Treaty with Panama (returned to Panama by treaty in 1978)
Corn Islands	1914	4	Treaty with Nicaragua (returned to Nicaragua by treaty in 1971)
Virgin Islands	1917	133	Purchase from Denmark
Pacific Islands Trust (Micronesia)	1947	8,489	Trusteeship under United Nations (some granted independence)
All others (Midway, Wake, and other islands)		42	

Admission of States into the Union

State		Date of Admission	State		Date of Admission
1.	Delaware	December 7, 1787	26.	Michigan	January 26, 1837
2.	Pennsylvania	December 12, 1787	27.	Florida	March 3, 1845
3.	New Jersey	December 18, 1787	28.	Texas	December 29, 1845
4.	Georgia	January 2, 1788	29.	Iowa	December 28, 1846
5.	Connecticut	January 9, 1788	30.	Wisconsin	May 29, 1848
6.	Massachusetts	February 6, 1788	31.	California	September 9, 1850
7.	Maryland	April 28, 1788	32.	Minnesota	May 11, 1858
8.	South Carolina	May 23, 1788	33.	Oregon	February 14, 1859
9.	New Hampshire	June 21, 1788	34.	Kansas	January 29, 1861
10.	Virginia	June 25, 1788	35.	West Virginia	June 20, 1863
11.	New York	July 26, 1788	36.	Nevada	October 31, 1864
12.	North Carolina	November 21, 1789	37.	Nebraska	March 1, 1867
13.	Rhode Island	May 29, 1790	38.	Colorado	August 1, 1876
14.	Vermont	March 4, 1791	39.	North Dakota	November 2, 1889
15.	Kentucky	June 1, 1792	40.	South Dakota	November 2, 1889
16.	Tennessee	June 1, 1796	41.	Montana	November 8, 1889
17.	Ohio	March 1, 1803	42.	Washington	November 11, 1889
18.	Louisiana	April 30, 1812	43.	Idaho	July 3, 1890
19.	Indiana	December 11, 1816	44.	Wyoming	July 10, 1890
20.	Mississippi	December 10, 1817	45.	Utah	January 4, 1896
21.	Illinois	December 3, 1818	46.	Oklahoma	November 16, 1907
22.	Alabama	December 14, 1819	47.	New Mexico	January 6, 1912
23.	Maine	March 15, 1820	48.	Arizona	February 14, 1912
24.	Missouri	August 10, 1821	49.	Alaska	January 3, 1959
25.	Arkansas	June 15, 1836	50.	Hawai`i	August 21, 1959

Presidential Elections

Year	Number of States	Candidates	Parties	Popular Vote	% of Popular Vote	Elec-toral Vote	% Voter Partici-pation[a]
1789	11	**George Washington**	No party designations			69	
		John Adams				34	
		Other candidates				35	
1792	15	**George Washington**	No party designations			132	
		John Adams				77	
		George Clinton				50	
		Other candidates				5	
1796	16	**John Adams**	Federalist			71	
		Thomas Jefferson	Democratic-Republican			68	
		Thomas Pinckney	Federalist			59	
		Aaron Burr	Democratic-Republican			30	
		Other candidates				48	
1800	16	**Thomas Jefferson**	Democratic-Republican			73	
		Aaron Burr	Democratic-Republican			73	
		John Adams	Federalist			65	
		Charles C. Pinckney	Federalist			64	
		John Jay	Federalist			1	
1804	17	**Thomas Jefferson**	Democratic-Republican			162	
		Charles C. Pinckney	Federalist			14	
1808	17	**James Madison**	Democratic-Republican			122	
		Charles C. Pinckney	Federalist			47	
		George Clinton	Democratic-Republican			6	
1812	18	**James Madison**	Democratic-Republican			128	
		DeWitt Clinton	Federalist			89	
1816	19	**James Monroe**	Democratic-Republican			183	
		Rufus King	Federalist			34	
1820	24	**James Monroe**	Democratic-Republican			231	
		John Quincy Adams	Independent-Republican			1	
1824	24	**John Quincy Adams**	Democratic-Republican	108,740	30.5	84	26.9
		Andrew Jackson	Democratic-Republican	153,544	43.1	99	

Presidential Elections, *Continued*

Year	Number of States	Candidates	Parties	Popular Vote	% of Popular Vote	Electoral Vote	% Voter Participation[a]
		Henry Clay	Democratic-Republican	47,136	13.2	37	
		William H. Crawford	Democratic-Republican	46,618	13.1	41	
1828	24	**Andrew Jackson**	Democratic	647,286	56.0	178	57.6
		John Quincy Adams	National Republican	508,064	44.0	83	
1832	24	**Andrew Jackson**	Democratic	688,242	54.5	219	55.4
		Henry Clay	National Republican	473,462	37.5	49	
		William Wirt	Anti-Masonic	101,051	8.0	7	
		John Floyd	Democratic			11	
1836	26	**Martin Van Buren**	Democratic	765,483	50.9	170	57.8
		William H. Harrison	Whig			73	
		Hugh L. White	Whig			26	
		Daniel Webster	Whig	739,795	49.1	14	
		W. P. Mangum	Whig			11	
1840	26	**William H. Harrison**	Whig	1,274,624	53.1	234	80.2
		Martin Van Buren	Democratic	1,127,781	46.9	60	
1844	26	**James K. Polk**	Democratic	1,338,464	49.6	170	78.9
		Henry Clay	Whig	1,300,097	48.1	105	
		James G. Birney	Liberty	62,300	2.3		
1848	30	**Zachary Taylor**	Whig	1,360,967	47.4	163	72.7
		Lewis Cass	Democratic	1,222,342	42.5	127	
		Martin Van Buren	Free Soil	291,263	10.1		
1852	31	**Franklin Pierce**	Democratic	1,601,117	50.9	254	69.6
		Winfield Scott	Whig	1,385,453	44.1	42	
		John P. Hale	Free Soil	155,825	5.0		
1856	31	**James Buchanan**	Democratic	1,832,955	45.3	174	78.9
		John C. Frémont	Republican	1,339,932	33.1	114	
		Millard Fillmore	American	871,731	21.6	8	
1860	33	**Abraham Lincoln**	Republican	1,865,593	39.8	180	81.2
		Stephen A. Douglas	Democratic	1,382,713	29.5	12	
		John C. Breckinridge	Democratic	848,356	18.1	72	
		John Bell	Constitutional Union	592,906	12.6	39	
1864	36	**Abraham Lincoln**	Republican	2,206,938	55.0	212	73.8
		George B. McClellan	Democratic	1,803,787	45.0	21	
1868	37	**Ulysses S. Grant**	Republican	3,013,421	52.7	214	78.1
		Horatio Seymour	Democratic	2,706,829	47.3	80	
1872	37	**Ulysses S. Grant**	Republican	3,596,745	55.6	286	71.3
		Horace Greeley	Democratic	2,843,446	43.9	[b]	
1876	38	**Rutherford B. Hayes**	Republican	4,036,572	48.0	185	81.8

Presidential Elections, *Continued*

Year	Number of States	Candidates	Parties	Popular Vote	% of Popular Vote	Electoral Vote	% Voter Participation[a]
		Samuel J. Tilden	Democratic	4,284,020	51.0	184	
1880	38	**James A. Garfield**	Republican	4,453,295	48.5	214	79.4
		Winfield S. Hancock	Democratic	4,414,082	48.1	155	
		James B. Weaver	Greenback-Labor	308,578	3.4		
1884	38	**Grover Cleveland**	Democratic	4,879,507	48.5	219	77.5
		James G. Blaine	Republican	4,850,293	48.2	182	
		Benjamin F. Butler	Greenback-Labor	175,370	1.8		
		John P. St. John	Prohibition	150,369	1.5		
1888	38	**Benjamin Harrison**	Republican	5,477,129	47.9	233	79.3
		Grover Cleveland	Democratic	5,537,857	48.6	168	
		Clinton B. Fisk	Prohibition	249,506	2.2		
		Anson J. Streeter	Union Labor	146,935	1.3		
1892	44	**Grover Cleveland**	Democratic	5,555,426	46.1	277	74.7
		Benjamin Harrison	Republican	5,182,690	43.0	145	
		James B. Weaver	People's	1,029,846	8.5	22	
		John Bidwell	Prohibition	264,133	2.2		
1896	45	**William McKinley**	Republican	7,102,246	51.1	271	79.3
		William J. Bryan	Democratic	6,492,559	47.7	176	
1900	45	**William McKinley**	Republican	7,218,491	51.7	292	73.2
		William J. Bryan	Democratic; Populist	6,356,734	45.5	155	
		John C. Wooley	Prohibition	208,914	1.5		
1904	45	**Theodore Roosevelt**	Republican	7,628,461	57.4	336	65.2
		Alton B. Parker	Democratic	5,084,223	37.6	140	
		Eugene V. Debs	Socialist	402,283	3.0		
		Silas C. Swallow	Prohibition	258,536	1.9		
1908	46	**William H. Taft**	Republican	7,675,320	51.6	321	65.4
		William J. Bryan	Democratic	6,412,294	43.1	162	
		Eugene V. Debs	Socialist	420,793	2.8		
		Eugene W. Chafin	Prohibition	253,840	1.7		
1912	48	**Woodrow Wilson**	Democratic	6,296,547	41.9	435	58.8
		Theodore Roosevelt	Progressive	4,118,571	27.4	88	
		William H. Taft	Republican	3,486,720	23.2	8	
		Eugene V. Debs	Socialist	900,672	6.0		
		Eugene W. Chafin	Prohibition	206,275	1.4		
1916	48	**Woodrow Wilson**	Democratic	9,127,695	49.4	277	61.6
		Charles E. Hughes	Republican	8,533,507	46.2	254	
		A. L. Benson	Socialist	585,113	3.2		
		J. Frank Hanly	Prohibition	220,506	1.2		
1920	48	**Warren G. Harding**	Republican	16,143,407	60.4	404	49.2
		James M. Cox	Democratic	9,130,328	34.2	127	

Presidential Elections, *Continued*

Year	Number of States	Candidates	Parties	Popular Vote	% of Popular Vote	Electoral Vote	% Voter Participation[a]
		Eugene V. Debs	Socialist	919,799	3.4		
		P. P. Christensen	Farmer-Labor	265,411	1.0		
1924	48	**Calvin Coolidge**	Republican	15,718,211	54.0	382	48.9
		John W. Davis	Democratic	8,385,283	28.8	136	
		Robert M. La Follette	Progressive	4,831,289	16.6	13	
1928	48	**Herbert C. Hoover**	Republican	21,391,993	58.2	444	56.9
		Alfred E. Smith	Democratic	15,016,169	40.9	87	
1932	48	**Franklin D. Roosevelt**	Democratic	22,809,638	57.4	472	56.9
		Herbert C. Hoover	Republican	15,758,901	39.7	59	
		Norman Thomas	Socialist	881,951	2.2		
1936	48	**Franklin D. Roosevelt**	Democratic	27,752,869	60.8	523	61.0
		Alfred M. Landon	Republican	16,674,665	36.5	8	
		William Lemke	Union	882,479	1.9		
1940	48	**Franklin D. Roosevelt**	Democratic	27,307,819	54.8	449	62.5
		Wendell L. Wilkie	Republican	22,321,018	44.8	82	
1944	48	**Franklin D. Roosevelt**	Democratic	25,606,585	53.5	432	55.9
		Thomas E. Dewey	Republican	22,014,745	46.0	99	
1948	48	**Harry S Truman**	Democratic	24,179,345	49.6	303	53.0
		Thomas E. Dewey	Republican	21,991,291	45.1	189	
		J. Strom Thurmond	States' Rights	1,176,125	2.4	39	
		Henry A. Wallace	Progressive	1,157,326	2.4		
1952	48	**Dwight D. Eisenhower**	Republican	33,936,234	55.1	442	63.3
		Adlai E. Stevenson	Democratic	27,314,992	44.4	89	
1956	48	**Dwight D. Eisenhower**	Republican	35,590,472	57.6	457	60.6
		Adlai E. Stevenson	Democratic	26,022,752	42.1	73	
1960	50	**John F. Kennedy**	Democratic	34,226,731	49.7	303	62.8
		Richard M. Nixon	Republican	34,108,157	49.5	219	
1964	50	**Lyndon B. Johnson**	Democratic	43,129,566	61.1	486	61.7
		Barry M. Goldwater	Republican	27,178,188	38.5	52	
1968	50	**Richard M. Nixon**	Republican	31,785,480	43.4	301	60.6
		Hubert H. Humphrey	Democratic	31,275,166	42.7	191	
		George C. Wallace	American Independent	9,906,473	13.5	46	
1972	50	**Richard M. Nixon**	Republican	47,169,911	60.7	520	55.2
		George S. McGovern	Democratic	29,170,383	37.5	17	
		John G. Schmitz	American	1,099,482	1.4		
1976	50	**Jimmy Carter**	Democratic	40,830,763	50.1	297	53.5
		Gerald R. Ford	Republican	39,147,793	48.0	240	
1980	50	**Ronald Reagan**	Republican	43,899,248	50.8	489	52.6
		Jimmy Carter	Democratic	35,481,432	41.0	49	
		John B. Anderson	Independent	5,719,437	6.6	0	
		Ed Clark	Libertarian	920,859	1.1	0	

Presidential Elections, *Continued*

Year	Number of States	Candidates	Parties	Popular Vote	% of Popular Vote	Electoral Vote	% Voter Participation[a]
1984	50	**Ronald Reagan**	Republican	54,455,075	58.8	525	53.1
		Walter Mondale	Democratic	37,577,185	40.6	13	
1988	50	**George Bush**	Republican	48,901,046	53.4	426	50.2
		Michael Dukakis	Democratic	41,809,030	45.6	111[c]	
1992	50	**Bill Clinton**	Democratic	44,908,233	43.0	370	55.0
		George Bush	Republican	39,102,282	37.4	168	
		Ross Perot	Independent	19,741,048	18.9	0	
1996	50	**Bill Clinton**	Democratic	47,401,054	49.2	379	49.0
		Robert Dole	Republican	39,197,350	40.7	159	
		Ross Perot	Independent	8,085,285	8.4	0	
		Ralph Nader	Green	684,871	0.7	0	

Candidates receiving less than 1 percent of the popular vote have been omitted. Thus the percentage of popular vote given for any election year may not total 100 percent.

Before the passage of the Twelfth Amendment in 1804, the Electoral College voted for two presidential candidates; the runner-up became vice president.

Before 1824, most presidential electors were chosen by state legislatures, not by popular vote.

[a]Percent of voting-age population casting ballots.

[b]Greeley died shortly after the election; the electors supporting him then divided their votes among minor candidates.

[c]One elector from West Virginia cast her Electoral College presidential ballot for Lloyd Bentsen, the Democratic party's vice-presidential candidate.

Presidents, Vice Presidents, and Cabinet Members

The Washington Administration

President	George Washington	1789–1797
Vice President	John Adams	1789–1797
Secretary of State	Thomas Jefferson	1789–1793
	Edmund Randolph	1794–1795
	Timothy Pickering	1795–1797
Secretary of Treasury	Alexander Hamilton	1789–1795
	Oliver Wolcott	1795–1797
Secretary of War	Henry Knox	1789–1794
	Timothy Pickering	1795–1796
	James McHenry	1796–1797
Attorney General	Edmund Randolph	1789–1793
	William Bradford	1794–1795
	Charles Lee	1795–1797
Postmaster General	Samuel Osgood	1789–1791
	Timothy Pickering	1791–1794
	Joseph Habersham	1795–1797

The John Adams Administration

President	John Adams	1797–1801
Vice President	Thomas Jefferson	1797–1801
Secretary of State	Timothy Pickering	1797–1800
	John Marshall	1800–1801
Secretary of Treasury	Oliver Wolcott	1797–1800
	Samuel Dexter	1800–1801
Secretary of War	James McHenry	1797–1800
	Samuel Dexter	1800–1801
Attorney General	Charles Lee	1797–1801
Postmaster General	Joseph Habersham	1797–1801
Secretary of Navy	Benjamin Stoddert	1798–1801

The Jefferson Administration

President	Thomas Jefferson	1801–1809
Vice President	Aaron Burr	1801–1805
	George Clinton	1805–1809
Secretary of State	James Madison	1801–1809
Secretary of Treasury	Samuel Dexter	1801
	Albert Gallatin	1801–1809
Secretary of War	Henry Dearborn	1801–1809
Attorney General	Levi Lincoln	1801–1805
	Robert Smith	1805
	John Breckinridge	1805–1806
	Caesar Rodney	1807–1809
Postmaster General	Joseph Habersham	1801
	Gideon Granger	1801–1809
Secretary of Navy	Robert Smith	1801–1809

The Madison Administration

President	James Madison	1809–1817
Vice President	George Clinton	1809–1813
	Elbridge Gerry	1813–1817
Secretary of State	Robert Smith	1809–1811
	James Monroe	1811–1817
Secretary of Treasury	Albert Gallatin	1809–1813
	George Campbell	1814
	Alexander Dallas	1814–1816
	William Crawford	1816–1817
Secretary of War	William Eustis	1809–1812
	John Armstrong	1813–1814
	James Monroe	1814–1815
	William Crawford	1815–1817
Attorney General	Caesar Rodney	1809–1811
	William Pinkney	1811–1814
	Richard Rush	1814–1817
Postmaster General	Gideon Granger	1809–1814
	Return Meigs	1814–1817
Secretary of Navy	Paul Hamilton	1809–1813
	William Jones	1813–1814
	Benjamin Crowninshield	1814–1817

The Monroe Administration

President	James Monroe	1817–1825
Vice President	Daniel Tompkins	1817–1825
Secretary of State	John Quincy Adams	1817–1825
Secretary of Treasury	William Crawford	1817–1825
Secretary of War	George Graham	1817
	John C. Calhoun	1817–1825
Attorney General	Richard Rush	1817
	William Wirt	1817–1825
Postmaster General	Return Meigs	1817–1823
	John McLean	1823–1825
Secretary of Navy	Benjamin Crowninshield	1817–1818
	Smith Thompson	1818–1823
	Samuel Southard	1823–1825

The John Quincy Adams Administration

President	John Quincy Adams	1825–1829
Vice President	John C. Calhoun	1825–1829

Presidents, Vice Presidents, and Cabinet Members, *Continued*

Secretary of State	Henry Clay	1825–1829
Secretary of Treasury	Richard Rush	1825–1829
Secretary of War	James Barbour	1825–1828
	Peter Porter	1828–1829
Attorney General	William Wirt	1825–1829
Postmaster General	John McLean	1825–1829
Secretary of Navy	Samuel Southard	1825–1829

The Jackson Administration

President	Andrew Jackson	1829–1837
Vice President	John C. Calhoun	1829–1833
	Martin Van Buren	1833–1837
Secretary of State	Martin Van Buren	1829–1831
	Edward Livingston	1831–1833
	Louis McLane	1833–1834
	John Forsyth	1834–1837
Secretary of Treasury	Samuel Ingham	1829–1831
	Louis McLane	1831–1833
	William Duane	1833
	Roger B. Taney	1833–1834
	Levi Woodbury	1834–1837
Secretary of War	John H. Eaton	1829–1831
	Lewis Cass	1831–1837
	Benjamin Butler	1837
Attorney General	John M. Berrien	1829–1831
	Roger B. Taney	1831–1833
	Benjamin Butler	1833–1837
Postmaster General	William Barry	1829–1835
	Amos Kendall	1835–1837
Secretary of Navy	John Branch	1829–1831
	Levi Woodbury	1831–1834
	Mahlon Dickerson	1834–1837

The Van Buren Administration

President	Martin Van Buren	1837–1841
Vice President	Richard M. Johnson	1837–1841
Secretary of State	John Forsyth	1837–1841
Secretary of Treasury	Levi Woodbury	1837–1841
Secretary of War	Joel Poinsett	1837–1841
Attorney General	Benjamin Butler	1837–1838
	Felix Grundy	1838–1840
	Henry D. Gilpin	1840–1841
Postmaster General	Amos Kendall	1837–1840
	John M. Niles	1840–1841
Secretary of Navy	Mahlon Dickerson	1837–1838
	James Paulding	1838–1841

The William Harrison Administration

President	William H. Harrison	1841
Vice President	John Tyler	1841
Secretary of State	Daniel Webster	1841
Secretary of Treasury	Thomas Ewing	1841
Secretary of War	John Bell	1841
Attorney General	John J. Crittenden	1841
Postmaster General	Francis Granger	1841
Secretary of Navy	George Badger	1841

The Tyler Administration

President	John Tyler	1841–1845
Vice President	None	
Secretary of State	Daniel Webster	1841–1843
	Hugh S. Legaré	1843
	Abel P. Upshur	1843–1844
	John C. Calhoun	1844–1845
Secretary of Treasury	Thomas Ewing	1841
	Walter Forward	1841–1843
	John C. Spencer	1843–1844
	George Bibb	1844–1845
Secretary of Treasury	John Bell	1841
	John C. Spencer	1841–1843
	James M. Porter	1843–1844
	William Wilkins	1844–1845
Attorney General	John J. Crittenden	1841
	Hugh S. Legaré	1841–1843
	John Nelson	1843–1845
Postmaster General	Francis Granger	1841
	Charles Wickliffe	1841
Secretary of Navy	George Badger	1841
	Abel P. Upshur	1841
	David Henshaw	1843–1844
	Thomas Gilmer	1844
	John Y. Mason	1844–1845

The Polk Administration

President	James K. Polk	1845–1849
Vice President	George M. Dallas	1845–1849
Secretary of State	James Buchanan	1845–1849
Secretary of Treasury	Robert J. Walker	1845–1849
Secretary of War	William L. Marcy	1845–1849
Attorney General	John Y. Mason	1845–1846
	Nathan Clifford	1846–1848
	Isaac Toucey	1848–1849

Presidents, Vice Presidents, and Cabinet Members, *Continued*

Postmaster General	Cave Johnson	1845–1849
Secretary of Navy	George Bancroft	1845–1846
	John Y. Mason	1846–1849

The Taylor Administration

President	Zachary Taylor	1849–1850
Vice President	Millard Fillmore	1849–1850
Secretary of State	John M. Clayton	1849–1850
Secretary of Treasury	William Meredith	1849–1850
Secretary of War	George Crawford	1849–1850
Attorney General	Reverdy Johnson	1849–1850
Postmaster General	Jacob Collamer	1849–1850
Secretary of Navy	William Preston	1849–1850
Secretary of Interior	Thomas Ewing	1849–1850

The Fillmore Administration

President	Millard Fillmore	1850–1853
Vice President	None	
Secretary of State	Daniel Webster	1850–1852
	Edward Everett	1852–1853
Secretary of Treasury	Thomas Corwin	1850–1853
Secretary of War	Charles Conrad	1850–1853
Attorney General	John J. Crittenden	1850–1853
Postmaster General	Nathan Hall	1850–1852
	Sam D. Hubbard	1852–1853
Secretary of Navy	William A. Graham	1850–1852
	John P. Kennedy	1852–1853
Secretary of Interior	Thomas McKennan	1850
	Alexander Stuart	1850–1853

The Pierce Administration

President	Franklin Pierce	1853–1857
Vice President	William R. King	1853–1857
Secretary of State	William L. Marcy	1853–1857
Secretary of Treasury	James Guthrie	1853–1857
Secretary of War	Jefferson Davis	1853–1857
Attorney General	Caleb Cushing	1853–1857
Postmaster General	James Campbell	1853–1857
Secretary of Navy	James C. Dobbin	1853–1857
Secretary of Interior	Robert McClelland	1853–1857

The Buchanan Administration

President	James Buchanan	1857–1861
Vice President	John C. Breckinridge	1857–1861
Secretary of State	Lewis Cass	1857–1860
	Jeremiah S. Black	1860–1861
Secretary of Treasury	Howell Cobb	1857–1860
	Philip Thomas	1860–1861
	John A. Dix	1861
Secretary of War	John B. Floyd	1857–1861
	Joseph Holt	1861
Attorney General	Jeremiah S. Black	1857–1860
	Edwin M. Stanton	1860–1861
Postmaster General	Aaron V. Brown	1857–1859
	Joseph Holt	1859–1861
	Horatio King	1861
Secretary of Navy	Isaac Toucey	1857–1861
Secretary of Interior	Jacob Thompson	1857–1861

The Lincoln Administration

President	Abraham Lincoln	1861–1865
Vice President	Hannibal Hamlin	1861–1865
	Andrew Johnson	1865
Secretary of State	William H. Seward	1861–1865
Secretary of Treasury	Samuel P. Chase	1861–1864
	William P. Fessenden	1864–1865
	Hugh McCulloch	1865
Secretary of War	Simon Cameron	1861–1862
	Edwin M. Stanton	1862–1865
Attorney General	Edward Bates	1861–1864
	James Speed	1864–1865
Postmaster General	Horatio King	1861
	Montgomery Blair	1861–1864
	William Dennison	1864–1865
Secretary of Navy	Gideon Welles	1861–1865
Secretary of Interior	Caleb B. Smith	1861–1863
	John P. Usher	1863–1865

The Andrew Johnson Administration

President	Andrew Johnson	1865–1869
Vice President	None	
Secretary of State	William H. Seward	1865–1869
Secretary of Treasury	Hugh McCulloch	1865–1869
Secretary of War	Edwin M. Stanton	1865–1867
	Ulysses S. Grant	1867–1868

Presidents, Vice Presidents, and Cabinet Members, *Continued*

	Lorenzo Thomas	1868
	John M. Schofield	1868–1869
Attorney General	James Speed	1865–1866
	Henry Stanbery	1866–1868
	William M. Evarts	1868–1869
Postmaster General	William Dennison	1865–1866
	Alexander Randall	1866–1869
Secretary of Navy	Gideon Welles	1865–1869
Secretary of Interior	John P. Usher	1865
	James Harlan	1865–1866
	Orville H. Browning	1866–1869

The Grant Administration

President	Ulysses S. Grant	1869–1877
Vice President	Schuyler Colfax	1869–1873
	Henry Wilson	1873–1877
Secretary of State	Elihu B. Washburne	1869
	Hamilton Fish	1869–1877
Secretary of Treasury	George S. Boutwell	1869–1873
	William Richardson	1873–1874
	Benjamin Bristow	1874–1876
	Lot M. Morrill	1876–1877
Secretary of War	John A. Rawlins	1869
	William T. Sherman	1869
	William W. Belknap	1869–1876
	Alphonso Taft	1876
	James D. Cameron	1876–1877
Attorney General	Ebenezer Hoar	1869–1870
	Amos T. Ackerman	1870–1871
	G. H. Williams	1871–1875
	Edwards Pierrepont	1875–1876
	Alphonso Taft	1876–1877
Postmaster General	John A. J. Creswell	1869–1874
	James W. Marshall	1874
	Marshall Jewell	1874–1876
	James N. Tyner	1876–1877
Secretary of Navy	Adolph E. Borie	1869
	George M. Robeson	1869–1877
Secretary of Interior	Jacob D. Cox	1869–1870
	Columbus Delano	1870–1875
	Zachariah Chandler	1875–1877

The Hayes Administration

President	Rutherford B. Hayes	1877–1881
Vice President	William A. Wheeler	1877–1881
Secretary of State	William B. Evarts	1877–1881
Secretary of Treasury	John Sherman	1877–1881
Secretary of War	George W. McCrary	1877–1879
	Alex Ramsey	1879–1881
Attorney General	Charles Devens	1877–1881
Postmaster General	David M. Key	1877–1880
	Horace Maynard	1880–1881
Secretary of Navy	Richard W. Thompson	1877–1880
	Nathan Goff, Jr.	1881
Secretary of Interior	Carl Schurz	1877–1881

The Garfield Administration

President	James A. Garfield	1881
Vice President	Chester A. Arthur	1881
Secretary of State	James G. Blaine	1881
Secretary of Treasury	William Windom	1881
Secretary of War	Robert T. Lincoln	1881
Attorney General	Wayne MacVeagh	1881
Postmaster General	Thomas L. James	1881
Secretary of Navy	William H. Hunt	1881
Secretary of Interior	Samuel J. Kirkwood	1881

The Arthur Administration

President	Chester A. Arthur	1881–1885
Vice President	None	
Secretary of State	F. T. Frelinghuysen	1881–1885
Secretary of Treasury	Charles J. Folger	1881–1884
	Walter Q. Gresham	1884
	Hugh McCulloch	1884–1885
Secretary of War	Robert T. Lincoln	1881–1885
Attorney General	Benjamin H. Brewster	1881–1885
Postmaster General	Timothy O. Howe	1881–1883
	Walter Q. Gresham	1883–1884
	Frank Hatton	1884–1885
Secretary of Navy	William H. Hunt	1881–1882
	William E. Chandler	1882–1885
Secretary of Interior	Samuel J. Kirkwood	1881–1882
	Henry M. Teller	1882–1885

The Cleveland Administration

President	Grover Cleveland	1885–1889
Vice President	Thomas A. Hendricks	1885–1889
Secretary of State	Thomas F. Bayard	1885–1889

Presidents, Vice Presidents, and Cabinet Members, *Continued*

Secretary of Treasury	Daniel Manning	1885–1887
	Charles S. Fairchild	1887–1889
Secretary of War	William C. Endicott	1885–1889
Attorney General	Augustus H. Garland	1885–1889
Postmaster General	William F. Vilas	1885–1888
	Don M. Dickinson	1888–1889
Secretary of Navy	William C. Whitney	1885–1889
Secretary of Interior	Lucius G. C. Lamar	1885–1888
	William F. Vilas	1888–1889
Secretary of Agriculture	Norman J. Colman	1889

The Benjamin Harrison Administration

President	Benjamin Harrison	1889–1893
Vice President	Levi P. Morton	1889–1893
Secretary of State	James G. Blaine	1889–1892
	John W. Foster	1892–1893
Secretary of Treasury	William Windom	1889–1891
	Charles Foster	1891–1893
Secretary of War	Redfield Proctor	1889–1891
	Stephen B. Elkins	1891–1893
Attorney General	William H. H. Miller	1889–1891
Postmaster General	John Wanamaker	1889–1893
Secretary of Navy	Benjamin F. Tracy	1889–1893
Secretary of Interior	John W. Noble	1889–1893
Secretary of Agriculture	Jeremiah M. Rusk	1889–1893

The Cleveland Administration

President	Grover Cleveland	1893–1897
Vice President	Adlai E. Stevenson	1893–1897
Secretary of State	Walter Q. Gresham	1893–1895
	Richard Olney	1895–1897
Secretary of Treasury	John G. Carlisle	1893–1897
Secretary of War	Daniel S. Lamont	1893–1897
Attorney General	Richard Olney	1893–1895
	James Harmon	1895–1897
Postmaster General	Wilson S. Bissell	1893–1895
	William L. Wilson	1895–1897
Secretary of Navy	Hilary A. Herbert	1893–1897
Secretary of Interior	Hoke Smith	1893–1896
	David R. Francis	1896–1897
Secretary of Agriculture	Julius S. Morton	1893–1897

The McKinley Administration

President	William McKinley	1897–1901
Vice President	Garret A. Hobart	1897–1901
	Theodore Roosevelt	1901
Secretary of State	John Sherman	1897–1898
	William R. Day	1898
	John Hay	1898–1901
Secretary of Treasury	Lyman J. Gage	1897–1901
Secretary of War	Russell A. Alger	1897–1899
	Elihu Root	1899–1901
Attorney General	Joseph McKenna	1897–1898
	John W. Griggs	1898–1901
	Philander C. Knox	1901
Postmaster General	James A. Gary	1897–1898
	Charles E. Smith	1898–1901
Secretary of Navy	John D. Long	1897–1901
Secretary of Interior	Cornelius N. Bliss	1897–1899
	Ethan A. Hitchcock	1899–1901
Secretary of Agriculture	James Wilson	1897–1901

The Theodore Roosevelt Administration

President	Theodore Roosevelt	1901–1909
Vice President	Charles Fairbanks	1905–1909
Secretary of State	John Hay	1901–1905
	Elihu Root	1905–1909
	Robert Bacon	1909
Secretary of Treasury	Lyman J. Gage	1901–1902
	Leslie M. Shaw	1902–1907
	George B. Cortelyou	1907–1909
Secretary of War	Elihu Root	1901–1904
	William H. Taft	1904–1908
	Luke E. Wright	1908–1909
Attorney General	Philander C. Knox	1901–1904
	William H. Moody	1904–1906
	Charles J. Bonaparte	1906–1909
Postmaster General	Charles E. Smith	1901–1902
	Henry C. Payne	1902–1904
	Robert J. Wynne	1904–1905
	George B. Cortelyou	1905–1907
	George von L. Meyer	1907–1909
Secretary of Navy	John D. Long	1901–1902
	William H. Moody	1902–1904
	Paul Morton	1904–1905
	Charles J. Bonaparte	1905–1906
	Victor H. Metcalf	1906–1908
	Truman H. Newberry	1908–1909

Presidents, Vice Presidents, and Cabinet Members, *Continued*

Secretary of Interior	Ethan A. Hitchcock	1901–1907
	James R. Garfield	1907–1909
Secretary of Agriculture	James Wilson	1901–1909
Secretary of Labor and Commerce	George B. Cortelyou	1903–1904
	Victor H. Metcalf	1904–1906
	Oscar S. Straus	1906–1909
	Charles Nagel	1909

The Taft Administration

President	William H. Taft	1909–1913
Vice President	James S. Sherman	1909–1913
Secretary of State	Philander C. Knox	1909–1913
Secretary of Treasury	Franklin MacVeagh	1909–1913
Secretary of War	Jacob M. Dickinson	1909–1911
	Henry L. Stimson	1911–1913
Attorney General	George W. Wickersham	1909–1913
Postmaster General	Frank H. Hitchcock	1909–1913
Secretary of Navy	George von L. Meyer	1909–1913
Secretary of Interior	Richard A. Ballinger	1909–1911
	Walter L. Fisher	1911–1913
Secretary of Agriculture	James Wilson	1909–1913
Secretary of Labor and Commerce	Charles Nagel	1909–1913

The Wilson Administration

President	Woodrow Wilson	1913–1921
Vice President	Thomas R. Marshall	1913–1921
Secretary of State	William J. Bryan	1913–1915
	Robert Lansing	1915–1920
	Bainbridge Colby	1920–1921
Secretary of Treasury	William G. McAdoo	1913–1918
	Carter Glass	1918–1920
	David F. Houston	1920–1921
Secretary of War	Lindley M. Garrison	1913–1916
	Newton D. Baker	1916–1921
Attorney General	James C. McReynolds	1913–1914
	Thomas W. Gregory	1914–1919
	A. Mitchell Palmer	1919–1921
Postmaster General	Albert S. Burleson	1913–1921
Secretary of Navy	Josephus Daniels	1913–1921
Secretary of Interior	Franklin K. Lane	1913–1920
	John B. Payne	1920–1921
Secretary of Agriculture	David F. Houston	1913–1920
	Edwin T. Meredith	1920–1921
Secretary of Commerce	William C. Redfield	1913–1919
	Joshua W. Alexander	1919–1921
Secretary of Labor	William B. Wilson	1913–1921

The Harding Administration

President	Warren G. Harding	1921–1923
Vice President	Calvin Coolidge	1921–1923
Secretary of State	Charles E. Hughes	1921–1923
Secretary of Treasury	Andrew Mellon	1921–1923
Secretary of War	John W. Weeks	1921–1923
Attorney General	Harry M. Daugherty	1921–1923
Postmaster General	Will H. Hays	1921–1922
	Hubert Work	1922–1923
	Harry S. New	1923
Secretary of Navy	Edwin Denby	1921–1923
Secretary of Interior	Albert B. Fall	1921–1923
	Hubert Work	1923
Secretary of Agriculture	Henry C. Wallace	1921–1923
Secretary of Commerce	Herbert C. Hoover	1921–1923
Secretary of Labor	James J. Davis	1921–1923

The Coolidge Administration

President	Calvin Coolidge	1923–1929
Vice President	Charles G. Dawes	1925–1929
Secretary of State	Charles E. Hughes	1923–1925
	Frank B. Kellogg	1925–1929
Secretary of Treasury	Andrew Mellon	1923–1929
Secretary of War	John W. Weeks	1923–1925
	Dwight F. Davis	1925–1929
Attorney General	Henry M. Daugherty	1923–1924
	Harlan F. Stone	1924–1925
	John G. Sargent	1925–1929
Postmaster General	Harry S. New	1923–1929
Secretary of Navy	Edwin Derby	1923–1924
	Curtis D. Wilbur	1924–1929
Secretary of Interior	Hubert Work	1923–1928
	Roy O. West	1928–1929
Secretary of Agriculture	Henry C. Wallace	1923–1924
	Howard M. Gore	1924–1925
	William M. Jardine	1925–1929

Presidents, Vice Presidents, and Cabinet Members, *Continued*

Secretary of Commerce	Herbert C. Hoover	1923–1928
	William F. Whiting	1928–1929
Secretary of Labor	James J. Davis	1923–1929

The Hoover Administration

President	Herbert C. Hoover	1929–1933
Vice President	Charles Curtis	1929–1933
Secretary of State	Henry L. Stimson	1929–1933
Secretary of Treasury	Andrew Mellon	1929–1932
	Ogden L. Mills	1932–1933
Secretary of War	James W. Good	1929
	Patrick J. Hurley	1929–1933
Attorney General	William D. Mitchell	1929–1933
Postmaster General	Walter F. Brown	1929–1933
Secretary of Navy	Charles F. Adams	1929–1933
Secretary of Interior	Ray L. Wilbur	1929–1933
Secretary of Agriculture	Arthur M. Hyde	1929–1933
Secretary of Commerce	Robert P. Lamont	1929–1932
	Roy D. Chapin	1932–1933
Secretary of Labor	James J. Davis	1929–1930
	William N. Doak	1930–1933

The Franklin D. Roosevelt Administration

President	Franklin D. Roosevelt	1933–1945
Vice President	John Nance Garner	1933–1941
	Henry A. Wallace	1941–1945
	Harry S Truman	1945
Secretary of State	Cordell Hull	1933–1944
	Edward R. Stettinius, Jr.	1944–1945
Secretary of Treasury	William H. Woodin	1933–1934
	Henry Morgenthau, Jr.	1934–1945
Secretary of War	George H. Dern	1933–1936
	Henry A. Woodring	1936–1940
	Henry L. Stimson	1940–1945
Attorney General	Homer S. Cummings	1933–1939
	Frank Murphy	1939–1940
	Robert H. Jackson	1940–1941
	Francis Biddle	1941–1945
Postmaster General	James A. Farley	1933–1940
	Frank C. Walker	1940–1945
Secretary of Navy	Claude A. Swanson	1933–1940
	Charles Edison	1940
	Frank Knox	1940–1944
	James V. Forrestal	1944–1945
Secretary of Interior	Harold L. Ickes	1933–1945
Secretary of Agriculture	Henry A. Wallace	1933–1940
	Claude R. Wickard	1940–1945
Secretary of Commerce	Daniel C. Roper	1933–1939
	Harry L. Hopkins	1939–1940
	Jesse Jones	1940–1945
	Henry A. Wallace	1945
Secretary of Labor	Frances Perkins	1933–1945

The Truman Administration

President	Harry S Truman	1945–1953
Vice President	Alben W. Barkley	1949–1953
Secretary of State	Edward R. Stettinius, Jr.	1945
	James F. Byrnes	1945–1947
	George C. Marshall	1947–1949
	Dean G. Acheson	1949–1953
Secretary of Treasury	Fred M. Vinson	1945–1946
	John W. Snyder	1946–1953
Secretary of War	Robert P. Patterson	1945–1947
	Kenneth C. Royall	1947
Attorney General	Tom C. Clark	1945–1949
	J. Howard McGrath	1949–1952
	James P. McGranery	1952–1953
Postmaster General	Frank C. Walker	1945
	Robert E. Hannegan	1945–1947
	Jesse M. Donaldson	1947–1953
Secretary of Navy	James V. Forrestal	1945–1947
Secretary of Interior	Harold L. Ickes	1945–1946
	Julius A. Krug	1946–1949
	Oscar L. Chapman	1949–1953
Secretary of Agriculture	Clinton P. Anderson	1945–1948
	Charles F. Brannan	1948–1953
Secretary of Commerce	Henry A. Wallace	1945–1946
	W. Averell Harriman	1946–1948
	Charles W. Sawyer	1948–1953
Secretary of Labor	Lewis B. Schwellenbach	1945–1948
	Maurice J. Tobin	1948–1953
Secretary of Defense	James V. Forrestal	1947–1949
	Louis A. Johnson	1949–1950
	George C. Marshall	1950–1951
	Robert A. Lovett	1951–1953

The Eisenhower Administration

President	Dwight D. Eisenhower	1953–1961
Vice President	Richard M. Nixon	1953–1961
Secretary of State	John Foster Dulles	1953–1959
	Christian A. Herter	1959–1961

Presidents, Vice Presidents, and Cabinet Members, *Continued*

Secretary of Treasury	George M. Humphrey	1953–1957
	Robert B. Anderson	1957–1961
Attorney General	Herbert Brownell, Jr.	1953–1958
	William P. Rogers	1958–1961
Postmaster General	Arthur E. Summerfield	1953–1961
Secretary of Interior	Douglas McKay	1953–1956
	Fred A. Seaton	1956–1961
Secretary of Agriculture	Ezra T. Benson	1953–1961
Secretary of Commerce	Sinclair Weeks	1953–1958
	Lewis L. Strauss	1958–1959
	Frederick H. Mueller	1959–1961
Secretary of Labor	Martin P. Durkin	1953
	James P. Mitchell	1953–1961
Secretary of Defense	Charles E. Wilson	1953–1957
	Neil H. McElroy	1957–1959
	Thomas S. Gates, Jr.	1959–1961
Secretary of Health, Education, and Welfare	Oveta Culp Hobby	1953–1955
	Marion B. Folsom	1955–1958
	Arthur S. Flemming	1958–1961

The Kennedy Administration

President	John F. Kennedy	1961–1963
Vice President	Lyndon B. Johnson	1961–1963
Secretary of State	Dean Rusk	1961–1963
Secretary of Treasury	C. Douglas Dillon	1961–1963
Attorney General	Robert F. Kennedy	1961–1963
Postmaster General	J. Edward Day	1961–1963
	John A. Gronouski	1963
Secretary of Interior	Stewart L. Udall	1961–1963
Secretary of Agriculture	Orville L. Freeman	1961–1963
Secretary of Commerce	Luther H. Hodges	1961–1963
Secretary of Labor	Arthur J. Goldberg	1961–1962
	W. Willard Wirtz	1962–1963
Secretary of Defense	Robert S. McNamara	1961–1963
Secretary of Health, Education, and Welfare	Abraham A. Ribicoff	1961–1962
	Anthony J. Celebrezze	1962–1963

The Lyndon Johnson Administration

President	Lyndon B. Johnson	1963–1969
Vice President	Hubert H. Humphrey	1965–1969
Secretary of State	Dean Rusk	1963–1969
Secretary of Treasury	C. Douglas Dillon	1963–1965
	Henry H. Fowler	1965–1969
Attorney General	Robert F. Kennedy	1963–1964
	Nicholas Katzenbach	1965–1966
	Ramsey Clark	1967–1969
Postmaster General	John A. Gronouski	1963–1965
	Lawrence F. O'Brien	1965–1968
	Marvin Watson	1968–1969
Secretary of Interior	Stewart L. Udall	1963–1969
Secretary of Agriculture	Orville L. Freeman	1963–1969
Secretary of Commerce	Luther H. Hodges	1963–1964
	John T. Connor	1964–1967
	Alexander B. Trowbridge	1967–1968
	Cyrus R. Smith	1968–1969
Secretary of Labor	W. Willard Wirtz	1963–1969
Secretary of Defense	Robert S. McNamara	1963–1968
	Clark Clifford	1968–1969
Secretary of Health, Education, and Welfare	Anthony J. Celebrezze	1963–1965
	John W. Gardner	1965–1968
	Wilbur J. Cohen	1968–1969
Secretary of Housing and Urban Development	Robert C. Weaver	1966–1969
	Robert C. Wood	1969
Secretary of Transportation	Alan S. Boyd	1967–1969

The Nixon Administration

President	Richard M. Nixon	1969–1974
Vice President	Spiro T. Agnew	1969–1973
	Gerald R. Ford	1973–1974
Secretary of State	William P. Rogers	1969–1973
	Henry A. Kissinger	1973–1974
Secretary of Treasury	David M. Kennedy	1969–1970
	John B. Connally	1971–1972
	George P. Shultz	1972–1974
	William E. Simon	1974
Attorney General	John N. Mitchell	1969–1972
	Richard G. Kleindienst	1972–1973
	Elliot L. Richardson	1973
	William B. Saxbe	1973–1974
Postmaster General	Winton M. Blount	1969–1971
Secretary of Interior	Walter J. Hickel	1969–1970
	Rogers Morton	1971–1974
Secretary of Agriculture	Clifford M. Hardin	1969–1971
	Earl L. Butz	1971–1974

Presidents, Vice Presidents, and Cabinet Members, *Continued*

Secretary of Commerce	Maurice H. Stans	1969–1972
	Peter G. Peterson	1972–1973
	Frederick B. Dent	1973–1974
Secretary of Labor	George P. Shultz	1969–1970
	James D. Hodgson	1970–1973
	Peter J. Brennan	1973–1974
Secretary of Defense	Melvin R. Laird	1969–1973
	Elliot L. Richardson	1973
	James R. Schlesinger	1973–1974
Secretary of Health, Education, and Welfare	Robert H. Finch	1969–1970
	Elliot L. Richardson	1970–1973
	Casper W. Weinberger	1973–1974
Secretary of Housing and Urban Development	George Romney	1969–1973
	James T. Lynn	1973–1974
Secretary of Transportation	John A. Volpe	1969–1973
	Claude S. Brinegar	1973–1974

The Ford Administration

President	Gerald R. Ford	1974–1977
Vice President	Nelson A. Rockefeller	1974–1977
Secretary of State	Henry A. Kissinger	1974–1977
Secretary of Treasury	William E. Simon	1974–1977
Attorney General	William Saxbe	1974–1975
	Edward Levi	1975–1977
Secretary of Interior	Rogers Morton	1974–1975
	Stanley K. Hathaway	1975
	Thomas Kleppe	1975–1977
Secretary of Agriculture	Earl L. Butz	1974–1976
	John A. Knebel	1976–1977
Secretary of Commerce	Frederick B. Dent	1974–1975
	Rogers Morton	1975–1976
	Elliot L. Richardson	1976–1977
Secretary of Labor	Peter J. Brennan	1974–1975
	John T. Dunlop	1975–1976
	W. J. Usery	1976–1977
Secretary of Defense	James R. Schlesinger	1974–1975
	Donald Rumsfeld	1975–1977
Secretary of Health, Education, and Welfare	Casper Weinberger	1974–1975
	Forrest D. Mathews	1975–1977
Secretary of Housing and Urban Development	James T. Lynn	1974–1975
	Carla A. Hills	1975–1977
Secretary of Transportation	Claude Brinegar	1974–1975
	William T. Coleman	1975–1977

The Carter Administration

President	Jimmy Carter	1977–1981
Vice President	Walter F. Mondale	1977–1981
Secretary of State	Cyrus R. Vance	1977–1980
	Edmund Muskie	1980–1981
Secretary of Treasury	W. Michael Blumenthal	1977–1979
	G. William Miller	1979–1981
Attorney General	Griffin Bell	1977–1979
	Benjamin R. Civiletti	1979–1981
Secretary of Interior	Cecil D. Andrus	1977–1981
Secretary of Agriculture	Robert Bergland	1977–1981
Secretary of Commerce	Juanita M. Kreps	1977–1979
	Philip M. Klutznick	1979–1981
Secretary of Labor	F. Ray Marshall	1977–1981
Secretary of Defense	Harold Brown	1977–1981
Secretary of Health, Education, and Welfare	Joseph A. Califano	1977–1979
	Patricia R. Harris	1979
Secretary of Health and Human Services	Patricia R. Harris	1979–1981
Secretary of Education	Shirley M. Hufstedler	1979–1981
Secretary of Housing and Urban Development	Patricia R. Harris	1977–1979
	Moon Landrieu	1979–1981
Secretary of Transportation	Brock Adams	1977–1979
	Neil E. Goldschmidt	1979–1981
Secretary of Energy	James R. Schlesinger	1977–1979
	Charles W. Duncan	1979–1981

The Reagan Administration

President	Ronald Reagan	1981–1989
Vice President	George Bush	1981–1989
Secretary of State	Alexander M. Haig	1981–1982
	George P. Shultz	1982–1989
Secretary of Treasury	Donald Regan	1981–1985
	James A. Baker III	1985–1988
	Nicholas F. Brady	1988–1989
Attorney General	William F. Smith	1981–1985
	Edwin A. Meese III	1985–1988
	Richard L. Thornburgh	1988–1989
Secretary of Interior	James G. Watt	1981–1983
	William P. Clark, Jr.	1983–1985
	Donald P. Hodel	1985–1989

Presidents, Vice Presidents, and Cabinet Members, *Continued*

Secretary of Agriculture	John Block	1981–1986
	Richard E. Lyng	1986–1989
Secretary of Commerce	Malcolm Baldridge	1981–1987
	C. William Verity, Jr.	1987–1989
Secretary of Labor	Raymond J. Donovan	1981–1985
	William E. Brock	1985–1987
	Ann Dore McLaughlin	1987–1989
Secretary of Defense	Casper Weinberger	1981–1987
	Frank C. Carlucci	1987–1989
Secretary of Health and Human Services	Richard S. Schweiker	1981–1983
	Margaret Heckler	1983–1985
	Otis R. Bowen	1985–1989
Secretary of Education	Terrel H. Bell	1981–1984
	William J. Bennett	1985–1988
	Lauro F. Cavazos	1988–1989
Secretary of Housing and Urban Development	Samuel R. Pierce, Jr.	1981–1989
Secretary of Transportation	Drew Lewis	1981–1982
	Elizabeth Hanford Dole	1983–1987
	James H. Burnley IV	1987–1989
Secretary of Energy	James B. Edwards	1981–1982
	Donald P. Hodel	1982–1985
	John S. Herrington	1985–1989

The Bush Administration

President	George Bush	1989–1993
Vice President	Dan Quayle	1989–1993
Secretary of State	James A. Baker III	1989–1992
	Lawrence Eagleburger	1992–1993
Secretary of Treasury	Nicholas F. Brady	1989–1993
Attorney General	Richard L. Thornburgh	1989–1992
	William P. Barr	1992–1993
Secretary of Interior	Manuel Lujan, Jr.	1989–1993
Secretary of Agriculture	Clayton K. Yeutter	1989–1991
	Edward Madigan	1991–1993
Secretary of Commerce	Robert A. Mosbacher	1989–1992
	Barbara Hackman Franklin	1992–1993
Secretary of Labor	Elizabeth Hanford Dole	1989–1991
	Lynn Martin	1991–1993
Secretary of Defense	Richard B. Cheney	1989–1993
Secretary of Health and Human Services	Louis W. Sullivan	1989–1993
Secretary of Education	Lauro F. Cavazos	1989–1991
	Lamar Alexander	1991–1993
Secretary of Housing and Urban Development	Jack F. Kemp	1989–1993
Secretary of Transportation	Samuel K. Skinner	1989–1992
	Andrew H. Card	1992–1993
Secretary of Energy	James D. Watkins	1989–1993
Secretary of Veterans Affairs	Edward J. Derwinski	1989–1993

The Clinton Administration

President	Bill Clinton	1993–
Vice President	Albert Gore	1993–
Secretary of State	Warren M. Christopher	1993–1997
	Madeleine K. Albright	1997–
Secretary of Treasury	Lloyd Bentsen	1993–1995
	Robert E. Rubin	1995–
Attorney General	Janet Reno	1993–
Secretary of the Interior	Bruce Babbitt	1993–
Secretary of Agriculture	Mike Espy	1993–1995
	Daniel R. Glickman	1995–
Secretary of Commerce	Ronald H. Brown	1993–1996
	Mickey Kantor	1996–1997
	William Daley	1997–
Secretary of Labor	Robert M. Reich	1993–1997
	Alexis M. Herman	1997–
Secretary of Defense	Les Aspin	1993–1994
	William J. Perry	1994–1997
	William S. Cohen	1997–
Secretary of Health and Human Services	Donna E. Shalala	1993–
Secretary of Education	Richard W. Riley	1993–
Secretary of Housing and Urban Development	Henry G. Cisneros	1993–1996
	Andrew Cuomo	1997–
Secretary of Transportation	Federico F. Peña	1993–1997
	Rodney E. Slater	1997–
Secretary of Energy	Hazel O'Leary	1993–1997
	Federico F. Peña	1997–1998
Secretary of Veterans Affairs	Jesse Brown	1993–

CREDITS

Page 293: *Map 10.4:* "Removal of Native Americans from the South, 1820–1840" from American History Atlas by Martin Gilbert. Copyright © Routledge Limited. Used with permission.

Page 340: *Map 12.1:* From Raymond Bial, *The Underground Railroad.* Copyright © 1995 by Houghton Mifflin Company. Reprinted by permission.

Page 377: *Map 13.1:* From Norton's *A People and A Nation,* 5/e, vol. 1. Copyright © 1998 by Houghton Mifflin Company. Reprinted by permission.

Page 408: *Map 14.1:* From Norton's *A People and A Nation,* 5/e, vol. 1. Copyright © 1998 by Houghton Mifflin Company. Reprinted by permission.

Page 435: *Map 15.1:* From Norton's *A People and A Nation,* 5/e, vol. 1. Copyright © 1998 by Houghton Mifflin Company. Reprinted by permission.

Page 438: *Map 15.2:* From Norton's *A People and A Nation,* 5/e, vol. 1. Copyright © 1998 by Houghton Mifflin Company. Reprinted by permission.

Page 441: *Map 15.3:* From Norton's *A People and A Nation,* 5/e, vol. 1. Copyright © 1998 by Houghton Mifflin Company. Reprinted by permission.

Page 456: *Map 15.4:* From Norton's *A People And A Nation,* 5/e, vol. 1. Copyright © 1998 by Houghton Mifflin Company. Reprinted by permission.

Page 457: *Map 15.5:* From Norton's *A People and A Nation,* 5/e, vol. 1. Copyright © 1998 by Houghton Mifflin Company. Reprinted by permission.

Page 511: Excerpt from "Chicago" in *Chicago Poems* by Carl Sandburg. Copyright © 1916 by Holt, Rinehart and Winston, Inc. and renewed 1944 by Carl Sandburg. Reprinted by permission of Harcourt Brace and Company.

Page 592: From *The Complete Poems of Emily Dickinson,* edited by Thomas H. Johnson, Copyright © 1976. Reprinted by permission of Little, Brown and Company.

Page 622: *Map 20.1* From Bailey's *The American Pageant,* 11/e. Copyright © 1998 by Houghton Mifflin Company. Reprinted with permission.

Page 714–715: Reprinted from David D. Lee, *Sergeant York: An American Hero.* Copyright © 1985 by The University Press of Kentucky, by permission of the publishers.

Page 722: Reprinted by permission by the Archives of Claude McKay by Carl Cowl, Administrator. From *Selected Poems of Claude McKay* by Claude McKay. Copyright © Harcourt Brace, 1979.

Page 725: From Burke, ed. *The Diary Letters of Hiram Johnson,* VI: Garland Publishing, Inc., 1983. Reprinted by permission of the publisher.

Page 739: "First Fig," by Edna St.Vincent Millay. From *Collected Poems,* HarperCollins. Copyright © 1922, 1950 by Edna St.Vincent Millay.

Page 740: From *Collected Poems* by Langston Hughes. Copyright © 1994 by the Estate of Langston Hughes. Reprinted by permission of Alfred A. Knopf, Inc.

Page 741: From *Collected Poems* by Langston Hughes. Copyright © 1994 by the estate of Langston Hughes. Reprinted by permission of Alfred A. Knopf, Inc.

Page 900: Selection from "Howl," from *Collected Poems 1947–1980,* by Allen Ginsberg. Copyright © 1955 by Allen Ginsberg. Reprinted by permission of HarperCollins Publishers, Inc.

Page 940*: Map 30.2: Voter Mobilization and the Politics of Race* by Harold W. Stanley. Praeger Publishers, an imprint of Greenwood Publishing Group, Westport, CT, 1987. Copyright © 1987 by Harold W. Stanley. Reproduced with permission of Greenwood Publishing Group, Inc. Westport, CT.

Page 1004: *Map 32.3:* From Norton's *A People and a Nation,* 5/e, vol. 2. Copyright © 1998 by Houghton Mifflin Company. Reprinted by permission.

Page 1011: *Map 32.5:* From Bailey's *The American Pageant,* 11/e. Copyright © 1998 by Houghton Mifflin Company. Reprinted with permission.

Page 1037: *Map 33.2:* From Norton's *A People and a Nation,* 5/e, vol. 2. Copyright © 1998 by Houghton Mifflin Company. Reprinted by permission.

INDEX